American Constitutional Law

American Constitutional Law
by Louis Fisher
is available in two formats:

SINGLE VOLUME HARDCOVER EDITION
American Constitutional Law

TWO VOLUME PAPERBACK EDITION

VOLUME 1
Constitutional Structures
Separated Powers and Federalism

VOLUME 2
Constitutional Rights
Civil Rights and Civil Liberties

American Constitutional Law

Fourth Edition

Louis Fisher

CAROLINA ACADEMIC PRESS
Durham, North Carolina

ISBN 0-89089-214-8
LCCN 2001088780

CAROLINA ACADEMIC PRESS
700 Kent Street
Durham, North Carolina 27701
Telephone (919) 489-7486
Fax (919) 493-5668
e-mail cap@cap-press.com

Printed in the United States of America

To the
New School for Social Research

Summary of Contents

Contents

About the Author

LOUIS FISHER received his B.S. from the College of William and Mary and his Ph.D. from the New School for Social Research. After teaching political science at Queens College, he joined the Congressional Research Service of the Library of Congress in 1970, where he is Senior Specialist in Separation of Powers. He has testified before congressional committees on such issues as Congress and the Constitution, executive lobbying, executive privilege, impoundment of funds, legislative vetoes, the item veto, the pocket veto, presidential reorganization authority, recess appointments, executive spending discretion, the congressional budget process, the Balanced Budget Amendment, biennial budgeting, covert spending, and CIA whistleblowing. During 1987 he served as Research Director for the House Iran-Contra Committee.

His books include *President and Congress* (1972), *Presidential Spending Power* (1975), *The Constitution between Friends* (1978), *The Politics of Shared Power* (4th ed., 1998), *Constitutional Conflicts between Congress and the President* (4th ed., 1997), *Constitutional Dialogues* (1988), *Political Dynamics of Constitutional Law* (with Neal Devins, 3d ed., 2001), the four-volume *Encyclopedia of the American Presidency* (with Leonard W. Levy, 1994), *Presidential War Power* (1995), and *Congressional Abdication on War and Spending* (2000).

His articles have appeared in the following law journals and law periodicals: *Administrative Law Journal of American University, Administrative Law Review, American Journal of International Law, American Journal of Tax Policy, Buffalo Law Review, California Law Review, Case Western Reserve Law Review, Catholic University Law Review, Constitution, Constitutional Commentary, Cornell Journal of Law & Public Policy, Cumberland Law Review, The Federal Lawyer, George Mason University Law Review, George Washington Law Review, Georgetown Law Journal, Georgia Law Review, Harvard Journal on Legislation, Journal of Law & Politics, Journal of Legal Education, Journal of Public Law, Judges' Journal, Law and Contemporary Problems, Law and Politics Book Review, Law and Social Inquiry, Legal Studies Forum, Legal Times, National Law Journal, North Carolina Law Review, Pepperdine Law Review, Public Interest Law Review, Saint Louis University Law Journal, Saint Louis University Public Law Review, SMU Law Review, Suffolk University Law Review, Texas Law Review, U.C. Davis Journal of International Law & Policy, University of Pennsylvania Law Review, Virginia Law Review, Washington University Law Quarterly,* and *William & Mary Bill of Rights Journal.*

His articles have been published in a number of journals of political science and public administration: *Administrative Science Quarterly, Annals, Canadian Parliamentary Review, Congress & the Presidency, Congressional Studies, Corruption and Reform, Government Information Quarterly, Journal of American Studies, Journal of Political Science, Journal of Politics, Political Science Quarterly, Political Science Reviewer, Presidential Studies Quarterly, Public Administration Review, Public Budgeting & Finance, Public Manager, Review of Politics, State Legislatures,* and *Western Political Quarterly.* His articles appear frequently in encyclopedias, magazines, newspapers, and edited books.

Dr. Fisher has been active with CEELI (Central and East European Law Initiative) of the American Bar Association. He traveled twice to Bulgaria, twice to Albania, and to Hungary to lend assistance to constitution writers. In addition to these trips abroad, he participated in CEELI conferences in Washington, D.C., involving delegations from Lithuania, Romania, and

Russia, and has served on CEELI "working groups" on Armenia and Belarus. He traveled to Russia in 1992 as part of a CRS delegation to assist on questions of separation of powers and federalism and to Ukraine in 1993 to participate in an election law conference.

Dr. Fisher's specialities include constitutional law, war powers, budget policy, executive-legislative relations, and judicial-congressional relations. He is the author of more than 250 articles in law reviews, political science journals, encyclopedias, books, magazines, and newspapers. He has been invited to speak in Albania, Australia, Bulgaria, Canada, the Czech Republic, England, Germany, Greece, Israel, Macedonia, Malaysia, Mexico, the Netherlands, Oman, the Philippines, Romania, Russia, Slovenia, Taiwan, Ukraine, and United Arab Emirates.

Acknowledgments

This book, in gestation for years, has many contributors and abettors. Morton Rosenberg of the Congressional Research Service lent a guiding hand, giving encouragement when I needed it and offering importunings I sometimes ignored. I needed both signals. In reviewing the manuscript and selections for readings, he was my major source of counsel and enlightenment. Other friends and colleagues who offered important advice and comments include Phillip J. Cooper, Neal Devins, Roger Garcia, Jerry Goldman, Nancy Kassop, Jacob Landynski, Leonard W. Levy, Robert Meltz, Ronald Moe, Christopher Pyle, Harold Relyea, William Ross, Jay Shampansky, Charles Tiefer, and Stephen Wasby.

For the third and fourth editions, David Gray Adler relied on extensive classsroom experience and a creative, analytical mind to read the chapters and give me the benefit of his insights. I very much value the care and thoughtfulness of his review.

I would also like to thank the following professionals for their reviews of the first and second editions: Glen Abernathy, William Blomquist, Mark Branden, John Brigham, Susan Burgess, Murray Dry, Thomas Eimerman, James Foster, Mark Gibney, Barbara Graham, Mary Harada, Thomas Hensley, Liane Kosaki, Albert Matheny, Roger McDonald, Chris Perry, Steven Puro, Jeremy Rabkin, Peter Renstrom, Gordon Silverstein, Jerry L. Simich, and Paul Weber. Their critiques were on the mark and much appreciated.

Many of the themes included in this book were first presented at conferences sponsored by the American Enterprise Institute, the American Political Science Association, the Army War College, Barnard College, Case Western Reserve Law School, the Center for National Security Law, Claremont Institute, Columbia University, Cumberland Law School, Dickinson College, George Mason University, Harvard University, Idaho State University, John Jay College, Kennesaw College, the National War College, Northwestern University, Princeton University, State University of New York, Southern Methodist University, Suffolk University Law School, Syracuse University Law School, U.C. Davis Law School, the University of Cincinnati, the University of Dallas, the University of Delaware, the U.S. District Court for the Northern District of California, Wake Forest University, Wayne State University, the Law School at Melbourne University in Australia, the National Autonomous University of Mexico in Mexico City, the Philippine Bar Association in Manila, the Hebrew University in Jerusalem, and law schools in Athens, Greece; Sofia, Bulgaria; Tirana, Albania; Ljubljana, Slovenia; Skopje, Macedonia; Cluj and Sibiu, Romania; and Muscat, Oman.

This is my fourteenth book since graduating from the New School for Social Research in 1967. I had received a bachelor's degree in chemistry, completed some graduate work in physical chemistry, and did technical writing for a few years before taking undergraduate classes in the social sciences at the New School. In 1963, after a conference with Joseph Greenbaum, Dean of the Graduate Faculty of Political and Social Science at the New School, I was accepted into the graduate program. As I walked down the hall, exhilarated by my new venture, he stuck his head out of his office and shouted: "Don't take any more chemistry." I haven't. Grateful for four stimulating years of graduate work at an institution that urges interdisciplinary research, I am happy to dedicate this book to the New School.

The author gratefully acknowledges permission from the following sources to use their copyrighted materials:

Reading on pages 30–32 from Walter F. Murphy, "Who Shall Interpret?," 48 Review of Politics 401 (1986).

Reading on pages 51–53 from William W. Van Alstyne, "A Critical Guide to *Marbury* v. *Madison*," 1969 Duke L. J. 1.

Reading on pages 64–65 from "Constitutional Interpretation: An Interview with Justice Lewis Powell," Kenyon College Alumni Bulletin (Summer 1979), pp. 14–18.

Reading on pages 71–73 from 27 South Texas Law Review 433–66 (1986).

Reading on pages 117–18 from Alexander M. Bickel, "Foreword: The Passive Virtues," 75 Harv. L. Rev. 40 (1961).

Reading on pages 118–19 from Gerald Gunther, "The Subtle Vices of the "Passive Virtues' — A Comment on Principle and Expediency in Judicial Review," 64 Colum. L. Rev. 1 (1964).

Reading on pages 152–53 from David Lauter, "The Fine Art of Creating a Certiorari Petition," The National Law Journal, December 10, 1984.

Reading on pages 159–60 from Frank M. Coffin, *The Ways of a Judge: Reflections from the Federal Appellate Bench* (Boston: Houghton Mifflin, 1980).

Reading on pages 165–66 from William O. Douglas, "The Dissent: A Safeguard of Democracy," 32 J. Amer. Judicature Soc. 104 (1948).

Reading on pages 166–67 from Robert H. Jackson, *The Supreme Court in the American System of Government* (Cambridge, Mass.: Harvard University Press, 1955).

Reading on pages 235–37 from Louis Fisher, "Judicial Misjudgments About the Lawmaking Process: The Legislative Veto Case," 45 Pub. Adm. Rev. 705 (Special Issue, November 1985).

Reading on pages 303–04 from Erwin N. Griswold, "Secrets Not Worth Keeping," Washington Post, February 15, 1989.

Reading on page 763–64 from Lewis Powell, Jr., "Death Penalty? Society Has Ruled," Legal Times, August 15, 1988.

Political cartoon on page 1120 from Tom Toles and the Buffalo News.

Reading on pages 1185–86 from Association of the Bar of the City of New York, "Jurisdiction-Stripping Proposals in Congress: The Threat to Judicial Constitutional Review" (December 1981).

Reading on pages 1193–94 from David E. Rosenbaum, "Prayer in Many Schoolrooms Continues Despite '62 Ruling," The New York Times, March 11, 1984.

Introduction

To accommodate the leading cases on constitutional law, textbooks concentrate on court decisions and overlook the political, historical, and social framework in which these decisions are handed down. Constitutional law is thus reduced to the judicial exercise of divining the meaning of textual provisions. The larger process, including judicial as well as nonjudicial actors, is ignored. The consequence, as noted recently by a law professor, is the absence of a "comprehensive course on constitutional law in any meaningful sense in American law schools."[1]

The political process must be understood because it establishes the boundaries for judicial activity and influences the substance of specific decisions, if not immediately then within a few years. This book keeps legal issues in a broad political context. Cases should not be torn from their environment. A purely legalistic approach to constitutional law misses the constant, creative interplay between the judiciary and the political branches. The Supreme Court is not the exclusive source of constitutional law. It is not the sole or even dominant agency in deciding constitutional questions. The Constitution is interpreted initially by a private citizen, legislator, or executive official. Someone from the private or public sector decides that an action violates the Constitution; political pressures build in ways to reshape fundamental constitutional doctrines.

Books on constitutional law usually focus exclusively on Supreme Court decisions and stress its doctrines, as though lower courts and elected officials are unimportant. Other studies describe constitutional decision making as lacking in legal principle, based on low-level political haggling by various actors. I see an open and vigorous system struggling to produce principled constitutional law. Principles are important. Constitutional interpretations are not supposed to be idiosyncratic events or the result of a political free-for-all. If they were, our devotion to the rule of law would be either absurd or a matter of whimsy.

It is traditional to focus on constitutional rather than statutory interpretation, and yet the boundaries between these categories are unclear. Issues of constitutional dimension usually form a backdrop to "statutory" questions. Preoccupation with the Supreme Court as the principal or final arbiter of constitutional questions fosters a misleading impression. A dominant business of the Court is statutory construction, and through that function it interacts with other branches of government in a process that refines the meaning of the Constitution.

This study treats the Supreme Court and lower courts as one branch of a political system with a difficult but necessary task to perform. They often share with the legislature and the executive the responsibility for defining political values, resolving political conflict, and protecting the political process. Through commentary and reading selections, I try to bridge the artificial gap in the literature that separates law from politics. Lord Radcliffe advised that "we cannot learn law by learning law." Law must be "a part of history, a part of economics and sociology, a part of ethics and a philosophy of life. It is not strong enough in itself to be a philosophy in itself."[2]

A Note on Citations. The introductory essays to each chapter contain many citations to court cases, public laws, congressional reports, and floor debates. The number of these citations may seem confusing and even overwhelming. I want to encourage the reader to consult these documents and develop a richer appreciation of the complex process that shapes constitutional law. Repeated citations to federal statutes help underscore the ongoing role of Con-

---

1. W. Michael Reisman, "International Incidents: Introduction to a New Genre in the Study of International Law," 10 Yale J. Int'l L. 1, 8 n.13 (1984).
2. Lord Radcliffe, The Law & Its Compass 92–93 (1960).

gress and the executive branch in constitutional interpretation. To permit deeper exploration of certain issues, either for a term paper or scholarly research, footnotes contain leads to supplementary cases. Bibliographies are provided for each chapter. The appendices include a glossary of legal terms and a primer on researching the law.

If the coverage is too detailed, the instructor may always advise students to skip some of the material. Another option is to ask the student to understand two or three departures from a general doctrine, such as the famous *Miranda* warning developed by the Warren Court but whittled away by the Burger and Rehnquist Courts. Even if a student is initially stunned by the complexity of constitutional law, it is better to be aware of the delicate shadings that exist than to believe that the Court paints with bold, permanent strokes.

At various points in the chapters, I give examples where state courts, refusing to follow the lead of the Supreme Court, conferred greater constitutional rights than available at the federal level. These are examples only. They could have been multiplied many times over. No one should assume that rulings from the Supreme Court represent the last word on constitutional law, even for lower courts.

Compared to other texts, this book offers much more in the way of citations to earlier decisions. I do this for several reasons. The citations allow the reader to research areas in greater depth. They also highlight the process of trial and error used by the Court to clarify constitutional principles. Concentration on contemporary cases would obscure the Court's record of veering down side roads, backtracking, and reversing direction. Focusing on landmark cases prevents the reader from understanding the *development* of constitutional law: the dizzying exceptions to "settled" doctrines, the laborious manner in which the Court struggles to fix the meaning of the Constitution, the twists and turns, the detours and dead ends. Describing major cases without these tangled patterns would presume an orderly and static system that mocks the dynamic, fitful, creative, and consensus-building process that exists. No one branch of government prevails. The process is polyarchal, not hierarchical. The latter, perhaps attractive for architectural structures, is inconsistent with our aspiration for self-government.

In all court cases and other documents included as readings, footnotes have been deleted. For the introductory essays, reference works are abbreviated as follows:

Comp. Gen.	Decisions of the Comptroller General.
Elliot	Jonathan Elliot, ed., The Debates in the Several State Conventions, on the Adoption of the Federal Constitution (5 vols., Washington, D.C., 1836–1845).
Farrand	Max Farrand, ed., The Records of the Federal Convention of 1787 (4 vols., New Haven: Yale University Press, 1937).
Fisher	Constitutional Conflicts between Congress and the President (4th ed. 1997).
Landmark Briefs	Landmark Briefs and Arguments of the Supreme Court of the United States: Constitutional Law. Gerald Gunther and Gerhard Casper, eds. University Publications of America.
O.L.C.	Office of Legal Counsel Opinions, U.S. Department of Justice.
Op. Att'y Gen.	Opinions of the Attorney General.
Richardson	James D. Richardson, ed., A Compilation of the Messages and Papers of the Presidents (20 vols., New York: Bureau of National Literature, 1897–1925).
Wkly Comp. Pres. Doc.	Weekly Compilation of Presidential Documents, published each week by the Government Printing Office since 1965.

American Constitutional Law

1

Constitutional Politics

For those who teach and study constitutional law, the relationship between the judiciary and politics remains an awkward issue. Technical details of a decision have a way of driving out the political events that generate a case and influence its disposition. To infuse law with dignity, majesty, and perhaps a touch of mystery, it is tempting to separate the courts from the rest of government and make unrealistic claims of judicial independence. Similarly, studies exaggerate the extent to which the Supreme Court supplies the "last word" on constitutional law. The elected branches and the general public necessarily share in that complex, sensitive task.

Legal scholars who explored the law-politics relationship early in the twentieth century were discouraged by traditional leaders of the legal profession. To speak the truth, or even search for it, threatened judicial symbols and concepts of long standing. In 1914, when legal philosopher Morris Raphael Cohen began describing how judges make law, his colleagues warned of dire consequences. The deans of major law schools advised him that his findings, although unquestionably correct, might invite even greater recourse to "judicial legislation."

Undeterred by these warnings, Cohen had "an abiding conviction that to recognize the truth and adjust oneself to it is in the end the easiest and most advisable course." He denied that the law is a "closed, independent system having nothing to do with economic, political, social, or philosophical science." If courts were in fact constantly making and remaking the law, it became "of the utmost social importance that the law should be made in accordance with the best available information, which it is the object of science to supply." Morris R. Cohen, Law and the Social Order 380–81 n.86 (1933).

Mechanical Jurisprudence

For more than a century, the legal profession claimed that judges "found" the law rather than made it. This doctrine of mechanical jurisprudence, joined with the supposed nonpolitical nature of the judiciary, provided convenient reasons for separating courts from the rest of government. A perceptive essay by political scientist C. Herman Pritchett noted that the disciplines of law and political science drifted apart for semantic, philosophical, and practical reasons: "Law is a prestigious symbol, whereas politics tends to be a dirty word. Law is stability; politics is chaos. Law is impersonal; politics is personal. Law is given; politics is free choice. Law is reason; politics is prejudice and self-interest. Law is justice; politics is who gets there first with the most." Joel B. Grossman and Joseph Tanenhaus, eds., Frontiers of Judicial Research 31 (1969). With options drawn in that manner, no wonder courts look attractive. A famous example of mechanical jurisdiction is the claim by Justice Roberts that when an act of Congress "is appropriately challenged in the courts as not conforming to the constitutional mandate the judicial branch of the Government has only one duty,—to lay the article of the Constitution which is invoked beside the statute which is challenged and to decide whether the latter squares with the former." United States v. Butler, 297 U.S. 1, 62 (1936).

Chief Justice Warren believed that law could be distinguished from politics. Progress in politics "could be made and most often was made by compromising and taking half a loaf where a whole loaf could not be obtained." He insisted that the "opposite is true so far as the judicial process was concerned." Through the judicial process, "and particularly in the Supreme Court, the basic ingredient of decision is principle, and it should not be compromised and parceled out a little in one case, a little more in another, until eventually someone receives the full benefit." The Memoirs of Earl Warren 6 (1977).

Yet the piecemeal approach applies quite well to the judicial process. The Supreme Court prefers to avoid general rules that exceed the necessities of a particular case. Especially in the realm of constitutional law, it recognizes the "embarrassment" that may result from formulating rules or deciding questions "beyond the necessities of the immediate issue." Euclid v. Ambler Co., 272 U.S. 365, 397 (1926). Compromise, expediency, and ad hoc action are no strangers to a multimember court that gropes incrementally toward a consensus and decision. The desegregation case, *Brown* v. *Board of Education* (1954), was preceded by two decades of halting progress toward the eventual abandonment of the "separate but equal" doctrine enunciated in 1896. After he left the Court, Potter Stewart reflected on the decision to exclude from the courtroom evidence that had been illegally obtained: "Looking back, the exclusionary rule seems a bit jerry-built — like a roller coaster track constructed while the roller coaster sped along. Each new piece of track was attached hastily and imperfectly to the one before it, just in time to prevent the roller coaster from crashing, but without an opportunity to measure the curves and dips preceding it or to contemplate the twists and turns that inevitably lay ahead." 83 Colum. L. Rev. 1365, 1366 (1983).

The desegregation case of 1954 plunged the Court into a political maelstrom that pitted blacks against whites, the North against the South, and states righters against advocates of national power. Justice Jackson, viewing the briefs as sociology rather than law, was reluctant to rule segregation as unconstitutional. When he finally decided to join the majority, the case still seemed to him basically a question of politics: "I don't know how to justify the abolition of segregation as a judicial act. Our problem is to make a judicial decision out of a political conclusion...." Bernard Schwartz, Super Chief 89 (1983).

A. LITIGATION AS A POLITICAL PROCESS

Especially in the twentieth century, the cases decided by federal courts embody issues that are of vital importance to individual citizens, corporations and trade unions, and the elected branches of government. The Court moved from narrow nineteenth-century questions of private law (estates, trusts, admiralty, real property, contracts, and commercial law) to contemporary issues of public law (federal regulation, criminal law, individual liberties, equal protection, and federal taxation). The period after World War II is generally considered a high-water mark in judicial policymaking. Decisions with nationwide impact affected desegregation in 1954, reapportionment and school prayers in 1962, criminal justice in the 1960s, and abortion from 1973 onward.

Although members of Congress criticize "judicial activism," they do their part to encourage judicial policymaking. Congress passes statutes that give standing to litigants, provide fees for attorneys, and establish separate agencies (such as the Legal Services Corporation) to initiate suits on broad public issues. Instead of merely resolving private disputes between private individuals, courts develop and articulate public values on major social, economic, and political questions. Increasingly, their decisions are prospective rather than retrospective. Judges actively participate in negotiating a resolution and maintain their involvement after issuing an initial decree. Courts do more than resolve private disputes between litigants according to the principles of law. "As a result, courts are inevitably cast in an affirmative, political — activist, if you must — role, a role that contrasts with the passive umpireship we are taught to expect." Abram Chayes, "Public Law Litigation and the

Judicial Capacity for Making Social Policy

[There is a] growing recognition that there are elements of overstatement in the case against judicial review. The courts are more democratically accountable, through a variety of formal and informal mechanisms, than they have been accused of being. Equally important, the other branches are in many ways less democratically accountable than they in turn were said to be by those who emphasized the special disabilities under which judges labor....

As the debate over the democratic character of judicial review wanes, there is another set of issues in the offing. It relates not to legitimacy but to capacity, not to whether the courts *should* perform certain tasks but to whether they *can* perform them competently.

Of course, legitimacy and capacity are re-lated. A court wholly without capacity may forfeit its claim to legitimacy. A court wholly without legitimacy will soon suffer from diminished capacity....

[Judicial capacity is limited by five factors: (1) adjudication is so focused by the particular litigants that other alternatives and remedies are overlooked; (2) the piecemeal nature of adjudication leads to incremental decision-making that pushes to the side related issues; (3) judges must await the capricious timing of litigants; (4) fact-finding in adjudication is ill-adapted to the ascertainment of social facts and results in reduced understanding and abstract rulings; and (5) adjudication makes no provision for policy review and little for future consequences.]

SOURCE: Donald L. Horowitz, The Courts and Social Policy 18, 34–56 (1977).

Burger Court," 96 Harv. L. Rev. 4, 4 (1982). This activist role has been criticized by those who believe that federal judges lack both the legitimacy and the capacity to decide questions of broad social policy (see box).

Justices of the Supreme Court sometimes encourage the belief that a gulf separates law from politics. Chief Justice John Marshall insisted that "Questions in their nature political...can never be made in this court." Marbury v. Madison, 5 U.S. 137, 170 (1803). In that very same decision, however, he established a precedent of far-reaching political importance: the right of the judiciary to review and overturn the actions of Congress and the executive. As noted by one scholar, Marshall "more closely associated the art of judging with the positive qualities of impartiality and disinterestedness, and yet he had made his office a vehicle for the expression of his views about the proper foundations of American government." G. Edward White, The American Judicial Tradition 35 (1976).

During his days as law school professor, Felix Frankfurter referred to constitutional law as "applied politics." Archibald MacLeish and E. F. Prichard, eds., Law and Politics 6 (1962). "The simple truth of the matter," he said, "is that decisions of the Court denying or sanctioning the exercise of federal power, as in the first child labor case, largely involve a judgment about practical matters, and not at all any esoteric knowledge of the Constitution." Id. at 12. He regarded courts as "less than ever technical expounders of technical provisions of the Constitution. They are arbiters of the economic and social life of vast regions and at times of the whole country." Felix Frankfurter and James M. Landis, The Business of the Supreme Court 173 (1928).

Once on the bench, however, Frankfurter did his part to perpetuate the law-politics dichotomy. Refusing to take a reapportionment case in 1946, he said it was "hostile to a democratic system to involve the judiciary in the politics of the people." Colegrove v. Green, 328 U.S. 549, 553–54 (1946). In *Baker* v. *Carr* (1962) the Supreme Court liberated itself from this narrow holding and has demonstrated throughout its history an awareness of the political system in which it operates daily. Writing in 1921, Justice Cardozo dismissed the

---

Cardozo on Judicial Process

I do not doubt the grandeur of the conception which lifts [judges] into the realm of pure reason, above and beyond the sweep of perturbing and deflecting forces. None the less, if there is anything of reality in my analysis of the judicial process, they do not stand aloof on these chill and distant heights; and we shall not help the cause of truth by acting and speaking as if they do. The great tides and currents which engulf the rest of men do not turn aside in their course and pass the judges by. We like to figure to ourselves the processes of justice as coldly objective and impersonal. The law, conceived of as a real existence, dwelling apart and alone, speaks, through the voices of priests and ministers, the words which they have no choice except to utter. That is an ideal of objective truth toward which every system of jurisprudence tends. It is an ideal of which great publicists and judges have spoken as of something possible to attain.... It has a lofty sound; it is well and finely said; but it can never be more than partly true. [John] Marshall's own career is a conspicuous illustration of the fact that the ideal is beyond the reach of human faculties to attain. He gave to the constitution of the United States the impress of his own mind; and the form of our constitutional law is what it is, because he moulded it while it was still plastic and malleable in the fire of his own intense convictions.

SOURCE: Benjamin N. Cardozo, The Nature of the Judicial Process 168–70 (1921)

---

idea that judges "stand aloof" from the "great tides and currents" that engulf the rest of mankind (see box).

Although the Supreme Court is an independent branch, it is not isolated. It is buffeted by the same social winds that press upon the executive and legislative branches, even if it does not respond in precisely the same way. It does not, and should not, operate in a vacuum.

From the late nineteenth century to the 1930s, the courts struck down a number of federal and state efforts to ameliorate industrial conditions. Laws that established maximum hours or minimum wages were declared an unconstitutional interference with the "liberty of contract." Lawyers from the corporate sector helped translate the philosophy of laissez-faire into legal terms and constitutional doctrine. These judicial rulings were so spiced with conservative business values that Justice Holmes protested that cases were "decided upon an economic theory which a large part of the country does not entertain." He chided his brethren: "The Fourteenth Amendment does not enact Mr. Herbert Spencer's Social Statics." Lochner v. New York, 198 U.S. 45, 75 (1905). When it was evident that the country would no longer tolerate interference by the courts, the judiciary retreated. After retiring from the Court, Justice Roberts explained the expansion of national power over economic conditions: "Looking back, it is difficult to see how the Court could have resisted the popular urge for uniform standards throughout the country—for what in effect was a unified economy." Owen J. Roberts, The Court and the Constitution 61 (1951).

In 1927 the Supreme Court upheld Virginia's compulsory sterilization law. Buck v. Bell, 274 U.S. 200. The decision appeared in the midst of the eugenics movement, which sanctioned efforts to prevent reproduction of the "unfit." In the hands of reformers and progressives, eugenics became a respected argument for opposing miscegenation and excluding "lower stock" immigrants coming from the Mediterranean countries, Eastern Europe, and Russia. After odious efforts in Nazi Germany to conduct biological experiments on and exterminate millions of Jews, Poles, gypsies, and other groups to produce a "master race," the eugenics movement had run its course.

To associate litigation with social forces is not meant to demean the courts or reduce adjudication to just another form of politics. Judges make policy, but not in the same manner as legislators and executives. Unlike the elected branches, the judiciary is not expected to satisfy the needs of the majority. Although judges have an opportunity to engage in their own form of lobbying, they are not supposed to publicly debate a pending issue or participate in ex parte meetings that are open to only one party — privileges routinely exercised by legislators and administrators. Most lobbying of the executive and legislative branches is open and direct; lobbying the judiciary is filtered through legal briefs, professional meetings, and law review articles.

The executive and legislative branches have elaborate mechanisms for handling public relations, self-promotion, and contacts with the press. For the most part, judges release their opinions and remain silent. If executive officials and legislators are criticized in the press, they can respond in kind. Judges, with rare exceptions, take their lumps without retaliation.

The operations of the political branches can resemble those of the courts. Although responsive to majoritarian pressures, Congress and the President are also sensitive to minority rights. Since the days of President Franklin D. Roosevelt, executive orders and congressional statutes have advanced the cause of civil rights. The political branches are more at liberty to engage in ad hoc actions, but they usually follow general principles and precedents of their own and feel an obligation to present a reasoned explanation for their decisions.

B. LOBBYING THE COURTS

Private organizations accept litigation as part of the political process. They may conclude that their interests will be better served through court action than through the legislative and executive branches. Many of the major labor-management struggles were fought out in the courts, with unions and employers hiring counsel to represent their interests. In 1963 Justice Brennan called litigation "a form of political expression." Groups unable to achieve their objectives through the electoral process often turn to the judiciary: "under the conditions of modern government, litigation may well be the sole practicable avenue open to a minority to petition for redress of grievances." NAACP v. Button, 371 U.S. 415, 429–30 (1963). For groups such as the National Association for the Advancement of Colored People (NAACP) and the American Civil Liberties Union (ACLU), litigation is not merely a technique for resolving private differences. It is a form of political action. In re Primus, 436 U.S. 412, 428 (1978). In an article in 1969, Justice Thurgood Marshall explained the importance of individual and group efforts to pressure courts and the elected branches (see box on next page).

The use of litigation in the 1940s and 1950s to shape social policy led to broader public participation and produced fundamental changes in the amicus curiae (friend of the court) brief. Originally, such briefs permitted third parties, without any direct interest in the case, to bring certain facts to the attention of the court to avoid judicial error. Over the years it lost this innocent quality and became an instrument used by private groups to advance their cause. The amicus curiae brief moved "from neutrality to partisanship, from friendship to advocacy." Samuel Krislov, "The Amicus Curiae Brief: From Friendship to Advocacy," 72 Yale L. J. 694 (1963). The briefs are now regularly used as part of the interest group struggle in the courts. The number of amicus briefs increased so rapidly that the Supreme Court adopted a rule in November 1949 to discourage their filing. With the exception of government units, all parties must consent to the filing of an amicus brief. If a party objects, the applicant must request the Court's permission to file.

The political nature of litigation is underscored by many familiar examples. Through dozens of court actions, the Jehovah's Witnesses secured such rights as the refusal to salute or pledge allegiance to the American flag, the right to solicit from house to house, and the right to preach in the streets without a license. Those objectives were not available from legislatures responsive to majoritarian pressures. The NAACP created a Legal Defense and Educational Fund to pursue rights denied blacks by Congress and state legislatures. A series of victories in

Thurgood Marshall on Group Pressures

In last year's address, Justice Clark spoke to you of one of the most basic institutions for the attainment of justice—the courts. I speak to you tonight of another "institution" essential to the attainment of justice, an institution perhaps even more basic. No matter how solemn and profound the declarations of principle contained in our charter of government, no matter how dedicated and independent our judiciary, true justice can only be obtained through the actions of committed individuals, individuals acting both independently and through organized groups.

...As we move into the future, the role formerly filled for the most part by individuals will have to be filled to an increasingly large degree by organized group practice....

My message can be aptly illustrated by the history of the Civil War amendments, a history in which I was in recent years fortunate enough to have played a small part. That history demonstrates that mere declarations of rights have not been sufficient to secure justice. It further illustrates that true progress can only be made by organized effort. The rights guaranteed by our Constitution are not self-enforcing; they can be made meaningful only by legislative or judicial action. As we shall see, legislation does not pass itself and the courts cannot act in the absence of a controversy. Organized, committed effort is necessary to promote legislation and institute legal action on any significant scale.

SOURCE: Thurgood Marshall, "Group Action in the Pursuit of Justice," 44 N.Y.U. L. Rev. 661, 662–63 (1969).

---

the courts established basic rights for blacks in voting, housing, education, and jury service. The National Consumers' League channeled its resources into litigation and won important protections for factory workers. The American Liberty League, organized by conservative businessmen, turned to litigation in an effort to prevent the enactment of economic regulation by Congress.

When the Reagan administration appeared to make an inadequate commitment to environmental protection, private organizations responded with more lawsuits. A senior staff attorney for the Natural Resources Defense Council protested in 1981 that the administration was "massively disobeying these laws because they don't like them. In this context, the only mechanism we have for enforcement is the courts." National Journal, Dec. 19, 1981, at 2233. Labeling this activity "legal" rather than "political" would surprise these attorneys.

Through the publication of articles, books, and commission reports, authors hope to influence a future court decision. Reliance on this body of literature has been of deep concern to many legislators who fear that the judiciary indiscriminately considers "unknown, unrecognized and nonauthoritative text books, law review articles, and other writings of propaganda artists and lobbyists." 103 Cong. Rec. 16160 (1957). The author of this statement, Congressman Wright Patman, complained that the Supreme Court had turned increasingly for guidance to private publications and studies promoted by the administration. The research was designed, he said, not to study an issue objectively but to advance the particular views of private interests trying, through the medium of publication, to influence the judiciary's disposition of public-policy questions. Experts have pointed out that the members of these study committees and commissions are aware that lawyers will cite the reports in their briefs "and that the real impact of this might very well be in the decisions made by courts and administrative agencies." Id. at 16167 (Prof. Louis B. Schwartz).

The practice of citing professional journals goes back at least to Justice Brandeis in the 1920s. Other Justices, like Cardozo and Stone, adopted this technique as a way of keeping law current with changes in American society. Brandeis's opinions introduced a new meaning to the word *authority*. He believed that an opinion "derives its authority, just as law derives

---

Duties of Solicitor General

The following-described matters are assigned to, and shall be conducted, handled, or supervised by, the Solicitor General, in consultation with each agency or official concerned:

(a) Conducting, or assigning and supervising, all Supreme Court cases, including appeals, petitions for and in opposition to certiorari, briefs and arguments, and...settlement thereof.

(b) Determining whether, and to what extent, appeals will be taken by the Government to all appellate courts (including petitions for rehearing *en banc* and petitions to such courts for the issuance of extraordinary writs) and...advising on the approval of settlements of cases in which he

had determined that an appeal would be taken.

(c) Determining whether a brief *amicus curiae* will be filed by the Government, or whether the Government will intervene, in any appellate court.

(d) Assisting the Attorney General, the Deputy Attorney General and the Associate Attorney General in the development of broad Department program policy.

· · ·

The Solicitor General may in consultation with each agency or official concerned, authorize intervention by the Government in cases involving the constitutionality of acts of Congress.

SOURCE: 28 C.F.R. §§0.20–0.21 (1999)

---

its existence, from all the facts of life. The judge is free to draw upon these facts wherever he can find them, if only they are helpful." Chester A. Newland, 48 Geo. L. J. 105, 140 (1959).

C. THE EXECUTIVE IN COURT

The Judiciary Act of 1789 established an Attorney General to prosecute and conduct all suits in the Supreme Court concerning the government. He represented Congress as well as the President. Despite some ambiguity in the original statute as to whether the Attorney General was an executive officer in the same sense as the heads of the State, Treasury, and War Departments, the first Attorney General (Edmund Randolph) attended Cabinet meetings and was identified early on as an administrative official.

Unlike the heads of the executive departments, who received full-time salaries, the Attorney General received a nominal sum and was expected to maintain a private practice to supplement his income. Randolph complained that he was "a sort of mongrel between the State and the U.S.; called an officer of some rank under the latter, and yet thrust out to get a livelihood in the former, — perhaps in a petty mayor's or county court." Leonard D. White, The Federalists 164–65 (1948). The staff of the Attorney General was so small that outside counsel had to be hired to conduct the government's business in court. Partly to do away with this expense, in 1870 Congress established a Justice Department and created the office of Solicitor General to assist the Attorney General. To the Solicitor General fell the primary responsibility of representing the federal government in court.

The Solicitor General

Contemporary duties of the Solicitor General are broad-ranging. After consulting agency officials, the Solicitor General conducts (or assigns and supervises) Supreme Court cases, including appeals, petitions regarding certiorari, and the preparation of briefs and arguments; authorizes or declines to authorize appeals by the federal government to appellate courts; authorizes the filing of amicus briefs by the government in all appellate courts; and may authorize intervention by the government in cases involving the constitutionality of acts of Congress (see box). The Supreme Court recognizes the Solicitor General's "traditional role in conducting and controlling all Supreme Court litigation on behalf of the United States and its agencies." FEC v. NRA Political Victory Fund, 513 U.S. 88, 93 (1994).

The cases that flow through the office of Solicitor General raise complex and specialized issues, but, as a former Solicitor General remarked, the incumbent "must try to discover the social tensions, the reverberations of strife and passion, the political issues, the clashes of interest that are dressed up in technical legal forms." Simon E. Soboleff, 41 A.B.A.J. 229, 279 (1955). To discharge that responsibility, the Solicitor General juggles several conflicting assignments. As the federal government's lawyer, the Solicitor General is an advocate but is also positioned to play a somewhat detached role. By entering only at the appellate level, the Solicitor General does not begin with the same emotional attachment as do the original parties in district court (including agency attorneys). The Solicitor General must also decide, out of a multitude of cases requested by the agencies, which ones deserve the attention of the Supreme Court.

Because of the frequency of appearances before the Supreme Court, the Solicitor General has been characterized as the Court's "ninth-and-a-half" member and serves many functions for the Court:

> The Supreme Court's frequent invitation to the Solicitor General to participate as amicus in constitutional cases is one indication of his useful role. The Solicitor General and his staff have unparalleled experience in constitutional litigation. Their access to and knowledge of the government apparatus not only enable them to inform the Court of factors unknown to private parties, but also to proffer statutory grounds for a decision avoiding the constitutional issues raised. The Solicitor General may indicate the relationship of the case to others pending on the docket, or the particular infirmities or strengths of the case for resolving constitutional or statutory issues. Knowing the Justices' proclivities, the Solicitor General may be able to offer a compromise solution that can gain a majority vote of the Court. The Supreme Court, lacking an extensive staff of its own, often benefits from the Solicitor General's impartial and sophisticated analysis of such constitutional cases. 78 Yale L. J. 1442, 1480 (1969).

The long-term and "impartial" objectives of the Solicitor General compete with, and are sometimes subordinated to, the particular and immediate needs of the President. This relationship is especially common in the field of national security. In arguing cases involving the discharge of federal employees, exclusion and deportation of aliens, and actions against conscientious objectors, Solicitors General in the past have shown little sympathy for fundamental notions of due process. Kathryn Mickle Werdeger, "The Solicitor General and Administrative Due Process," 36 G.W. L. Rev. 481 (1968).

Attorneys General and Solicitors General are legal officers, operating as members of the bar and officers of the court. However, they are also executive officials responsible to the President. As underscored by the actions against Japanese-Americans during World War II, Justice Department attorneys at times swallow their doubts and defend government actions that seem to them not merely unwise but unconstitutional. Under these conditions, constitutional issues are subordinated to the task of behaving as the "President's lawyers." Peter H. Irons, Justice at War 350–61 (1982). Rex Lee, Solicitor General during the Reagan administration, said that one of his duties was "to represent his client, the president of the United States. One of the ways to implement the president's policies is through positions taken in court. When I have that opportunity, I'm going to take it." 69 A.B.A.J. 734, 736 (1983). But if a Solicitor General becomes too partisan, there is risk of losing the trust and confidence of the Supreme Court.

There is often friction between the Justice Department and the White House. For example, during the Carter presidency, Attorney General Bell complained about White House interfer-

Justice Jackson on Public Opinion

The judge who would resolve uncertainties of interpretation by conscious deference to public opinion will find new pitfalls in his path. Is there any more reliable test of prevalence of a public opinion or will than the election returns? That certainly is its legal manifestation, and I see no reason to believe that judges have better understanding of it than those the public has elected to represent them. To the extent that public opinion of the hour is admitted to the process of constitutional interpretation, the basis for judicial review of legislative action disappears. If interpretation is not to be a mere following of election returns but a legal process, the utmost deference that courts can consciously pay to political trends is a strong, but rebuttable, presumption in favor of the constitutionality of action by the political branches.

Exclude as far as humanly possible the pressures of group opinion, but let us not deceive ourselves: long-sustained public opinion does influence the process of constitutional interpretation. Each new member of the ever-changing personnel of our courts brings to his task the assumptions and accustomed thought of a later period. The practical play of the forces of politics is such that judicial power has often delayed but never permanently defeated the persistent will of a substantial majority. Judicial review in practice therefore has proved less an obstacle to majority rule than the followers of Mr. Jefferson feared and less a guaranty of the *status quo* than the followers of Mr. Hamilton hoped.

SOURCE: Vital Speeches, No. 24, Vol. XIX, at 761 (October 1, 1953).

ence in litigation that involved questions of church-state separation, affirmative action, and civil rights. Vice President Mondale, his aide Bert Carp, domestic adviser Stuart Eizenstat, and other White House officials treated many of these matters as broad policy questions rather than technical legal issues. In one case, after the Justice Department had taken a position on a church-state question, President Carter responded to political considerations and personally intervened to overrule the decision. Griffin B. Bell, Taking Care of the Law 24–25 (1982).

The Tide of Public Opinion

Efforts to subordinate constitutional principles to political tactics can backfire against the President. Faced with a nationwide strike in 1952, President Truman decided to attack the steel companies and work informally with the labor unions rather than invoke the Taft-Hartley Act, which he had vetoed. When that strategy failed, he seized the steel mills and claimed that he could act "for whatever is for the best of the country." Public Papers of the Presidents, 1952, at 273. Realizing that his definition of presidential authority had shocked the country because it raised questions about his power to seize even the press and the radio, he hastily explained that his powers were derived from the Constitution and that individual rights were protected. Id. at 301.

In district court, however, the Justice Department told Judge Pine that the courts had no power to constrain the President. Presidential power could be curbed only by the ballot box or impeachment. This audacious and ill-advised presentation may have provoked the judiciary to act boldly to reject a sweeping and dangerous theory of inherent executive authority (see reading on Steel Seizure Case). The political climate invited a rebuff to presidential power. As Chief Justice Rehnquist noted in 1987, the Steel Seizure Case was "one of those celebrated constitutional issues where what might be called the tide of public opinion suddenly began to run against the government, for a number of reasons, and that this tide of public opinion had a considerable influence on the Court." William H. Rehnquist, The Supreme Court 95 (1987). Justice Robert Jackson spoke perceptively about the impact of public opinion (see box).

Control Over Litigation

The Justice Department has made a concerted effort to retain exclusive control over agency litigation policy. Loss of authority to the agencies can produce an incoherent and ineffective strategy in court. Some of the legal setbacks of the New Deal can be traced to the splintering of litigating authority in the Roosevelt administration. The Justice Department had to compete with autonomous efforts by the Interior Department and other agencies. Peter H. Irons, The New Deal Lawyers (1982).

The tremendous growth of litigation since the 1930s has made decentralization inevitable. Congress has given several agencies independent litigating authority and the Justice Department regularly enters into special agreements called Memoranda of Understanding (MOUs), which allow agencies to litigate certain types of cases at the district and appellate levels. In 1994 the Supreme Court held that the Federal Election Commission did not have general statutory authority to appeal its cases to the Supreme Court. Like other agencies, it must receive the Solicitor General's authorization. (The FEC does have statutory authority to seek appeal from the Supreme Court in the specific area of presidential election funds.) FEC v. NRA Political Victory Fund, 513 U.S. 88 (1994).

Steel Seizure Case of 1952:
Oral Argument Before the District Court

On April 24, 1952, in oral argument before U.S. District Judge David A. Pine, Assistant Attorney General Holmes Baldridge presented the government's case in defense of the seizure of steel companies by Secretary of Commerce Charles Sawyer. Judge Pine's decision, declaring the seizure illegal, was later affirmed by the Supreme Court. The following excerpt of the oral argument comes from House Document No. 534 (Part I), 82d Cong., 2d Sess. (1952), pp. 362–63, 371–73.

Mr. Baldridge: Our position is that there is no power in the Courts to restrain the President and, as I say, Secretary Sawyer is the alter ego of the President and not subject to injunctive order of the Court.

The Court: If the President directs Mr. Sawyer to take you into custody, right now, and have you executed in the morning you say there is no power by which the Court may intervene even by habeas corpus?

Mr. Baldridge: If there are statutes protecting me I would have a remedy.

The Court: What statute would protect you?

Mr. Baldridge: I do not recall any at the moment.

The Court: But on the question of the deprivation of your rights you have the Fifth Amendment; that is what protects you.

I would like an answer to that — what about that?

Mr. Baldridge: Well, as I was going to point out in a little while —

The Court (interposing): I will give you a chance to think about that overnight and you may answer me tomorrow....

The Court: Now, Mr. Attorney General, it is getting near the time when we shall have to stop. I wonder if you would give me such assistance as you can before we stop so that I can think about your viewpoint overnight, as to your power, or as to your client's power.

As I understand it, you do not assert any statutory power.

Mr. Baldridge: That is correct.

The Court: And you do not assert any express constitutional power.

Mr. Baldridge: Well, your Honor, we base the President's power on Sections 1, 2 and 3 of Article II of the Constitution, and whatever inherent, implied or residual powers may flow therefrom.

We do not propose to get into a discussion of semantics with counsel for plaintiffs. We say that when an emergency situation in this country arises that is of such importance to the entire welfare of the country that something has to be done about it and has to be done now, and there is no statutory provision for handling the matter, that it is the duty of the Executive to step in and protect the national security and the national interests. We say that Article II of the Constitution, which provides that the Executive power of the Government shall reside in the President, that he shall faithfully execute the laws of the office and he shall be Commander-in-Chief of the Army and of the Navy and that he shall take care that the laws be faithfully executed, are sufficient to permit him to meet any national emergency that might arise, be it peace time, technical war time, or actual war time.

The Court: So you contend the Executive has unlimited power in time of an emergency?

Mr. Baldridge: He has the power to take such action as is necessary to meet the emergency.

The Court: If the emergency is great, it is unlimited, is it?

Mr. Baldridge: I suppose if you carry it to its logical conclusion, that is true. But I do want to point out that there are two limitations on the Executive power. One is the ballot box and the other is impeachment.

The Court: Then, as I understand it, you claim that in time of emergency the Executive has this great power.

Mr. Baldridge: That is correct.

The Court: And that the Executive determines the emergencies and the Courts cannot even review whether it is an emergency.

Mr. Baldridge: That is correct.

D. CONGRESSIONAL DUTIES

During the nineteenth century it was not unusual for members of Congress to maintain a flourishing business in the federal courts. Daniel Webster is the most prominent example of a Congressman with a dual career as lawyer and legislator. While serving in Congress as a Representative and a Senator, he delivered forceful arguments in major cases before the Supreme Court, which at that time was located in a chamber beneath the Senate. Congressmen supplemented their incomes by "duck[ing] into the lower chamber, so to speak, for a lucrative hour or two. After all, should not those who made laws help interpret them?" Maurice G. Baxter, Daniel Webster & the Supreme Court 31 (1966).

Although Congress depends on the Justice Department to protect its interests, members of Congress may intervene on an individual basis. In *Myers v. United States* (1926), which involved the President's power to remove executive officials, the Supreme Court invited Senator George Wharton Pepper to serve as amicus curiae. His oral argument and an extract of his brief, together with those of the appellant and the Solicitor General, are printed immediately before the Court's opinion. 272 U.S. 52, 65–88 (1926).

During the impoundment disputes of the Nixon administration, members of Congress submitted an amicus brief on behalf of the plaintiff suing the administration. State Highway Commission of Missouri v. Volpe, 479 F.2d 1099 n.1 (8th Cir. 1973). In the abortion case eventually decided by the Supreme Court in 1980, the district court permitted Senator James L. Buckley, Senator Jesse A. Helms, and Congressman Henry J. Hyde to intervene as defendants. Harris v. McRae, 448 U.S. 297, 303 (1980). The Ninth Circuit invited both the House and the Senate to submit briefs concerning a legislative veto used by Congress in deportation cases. When the case reached the Supreme Court, both Houses of Congress intervened to protect their interests and fully participated before the Court during oral argument. INS v. Chadha, 462 U.S. 919 (1983). The attorneys for Congress defended the legislative veto, but in a separate brief nine members of the House of Representatives urged the Supreme Court to declare the legislative veto unconstitutional.

Legislative precedents in the House and the Senate do not permit the Speaker or the Chair to rule on questions of constitutionality. Points of order, raising the issue of unconstitutional provisions, are referred to the full chamber for decision. In the Senate, a member may raise a point of order that a bill or an amendment is legislation that changes the Constitution. If there

Standing for Members

The item veto case was relatively easy for the Court to sidestep. To the extent that there was injury to Congress, it was self-administered. If surrendering some of its spending power to the President was repugnant, members of Congress had plenty of ways to recover the power: repeal the statute, add subsequent restrictions to the President's power, or write bills and committee reports in such a way that the President had fewer opportunities to cancel an item.

The item veto case was particularly weak for Congress. As the Court noted at the end of *Raines* v. *Byrd* (1997), Congress had not authorized Senator Byrd and his colleagues to bring the suit. In fact, both Houses of Congress had filed briefs opposing their action.

On other constitutional disputes, the President causes the injury and Congress has few or no institutional remedies. One example is the *Kennedy* pocket veto case. Because President Nixon did not return the vetoed bill to Congress, legislators had no options other than to pass the bill again and remain in session to prevent a pocket veto. Another dispute that might be litigated is the war power. Suppose Congress prohibited the President from engaging in a particular military action and the President vetoed the bill. If Congress lacked the two-thirds majority needed in each chamber to override the veto, could members bring the issue to the Court, having exhausted all legislative remedies? Without a judicial check, a President could initiate and continue a war so long as he retained a one-third plus one minority in either chamber to prevent the override. Would a court tackle that constitutional issue?

---

is substantial doubt within Congress concerning the constitutionality of a provision, legislators can place within the bill a procedure authorizing expedited review by the courts. Examples include the Federal Election Campaign Act amendments of 1974. 86 Stat. 1285, § 315. Two years later the Supreme Court declared the contested provision unconstitutional. Buckley v. Valeo, 424 U.S. 1 (1976). A similar procedure was placed in the Gramm-Rudman-Hollings Act of 1985. 99 Stat. 1098, § 274 (1985). The provision in question was struck down a year later. Bowsher v. Synar, 478 U.S. 714 (1986).

Standing for Members

A striking development over the past decade is the frequency with which members of Congress take issues directly to the courts for resolution. Senator Edward M. Kennedy was successful at both the district court and appellate court levels in challenging Nixon's attempt to use the pocket veto during brief recesses of the House and Senate. Kennedy v. Sampson, 364 F.Supp. 1075 (D.D.C. 1973); Kennedy v. Sampson, 511 F.2d 430 (D.C. Cir. 1974). As a result of those lower court decisions, the Ford administration announced that it would use the pocket veto only during the final adjournment at the end of a Congress. 121 Cong. Rec. 41884 (1975); 122 Cong. Rec. 11202 (1976). Senator Kennedy was successful because his prerogative to vote (to override a presidential veto) had been denied by the pocket veto.

Other members of Congress have been unsuccessful when they have tried to achieve political goals from the courts that are available through the regular legislative process. In such cases the members have been told by the courts that (1) they lack standing to sue, (2) the issue is not ripe for adjudication, or (3) the matter is a "political question" to be decided by Congress and the President. Legislators must overcome the standing hurdles (faced by any litigant) by showing that (1) they have suffered injury, (2) the interests are within the zone protected by the statute or constitutional provision, (3) the injury is caused by the challenged action, and (4) the injury can be redressed by a favorable court decision. Legislators face an additional obstacle. If they suffer from an injury that can be redressed by colleagues acting through the

POLITICAL DYNAMICS OF CONSTITUTIONAL LAW

```
                    ┌─────────────────────────────┐
                    │  Popular movements          │
                    │  Private organizations      │
                    │  Amicus briefs              │
                    │  Legal publications         │
                    │  International pressures     │
                    └─────────────────────────────┘

┌──────────────────────────┐   ┌──────────────┐   ┌──────────────────────────┐
│ Members of Congress      │   │              │   │ President                │
│ Congressional committees │←→ │Federal courts│   │ Attorney General         │
│ Senate and House legal   │   │              │   │ Solicitor General        │
│ counsel                  │   └──────────────┘   │ Executive agencies       │
└──────────────────────────┘                      │ Independent commissions  │
                                                   └──────────────────────────┘

                    ┌─────────────────────────────┐
                    │  State courts               │
                    │  Governors                  │
                    │  State legislatures         │
                    │  Public pressures           │
                    └─────────────────────────────┘
```

regular legislative process, a court will instruct the lawmakers to use the institutional powers available to them.

Throughout these cases, there is a general wariness on the part of judges that the controversy is really not between Congress and the executive. Rather, it is one group of legislators pitted against another. Federal judges may suspect that members of Congress turn to the courts because they have been unable to attract sufficient votes from colleagues to pass a bill. When judges believe that legislators have failed to make use of remedies available within Congress, they have been denied standing to resolve the issue in court. It was partly on that basis that the Supreme Court in 1997 denied standing to some members of Congress who had challenged the constitutionality of the Line Item Veto Act of 1996. RAINES v. BYRD, 521 U.S. 811 (1997). There may be other disputes that members of Congress could legitimately bring to court (see box on previous page).

In recent decades, members of Congress have become concerned about the refusal of the Justice Department to defend the constitutionality of certain statutory provisions. Sometimes the Department took this position after deciding that a statute infringed on presidential power or was so patently unconstitutional that it could not be defended, as in the bill of attainder case in 1946. United States v. Lovett, 328 U.S. 303 (1946). Because of statutory language, the Attorney General must now report to Congress whenever the Justice Department does not intend to defend the constitutionality of a law passed by Congress. These reports specify the statutory provision and contain a detailed explanation by the Department for calling the provision unconstitutional.

Congress has always been able to hire private counsel to defend itself, as it did in the civil action brought against it by Congressman Adam Clayton Powell in the 1960s. Yet there was no established procedure for Congress to defend its statutes when the Justice Department chose not to do so. The institutional interests of Congress, as noted by the Senate Committee on Governmental Affairs in 1977, made it "inappropriate as a matter of principle and of the constitutional separation of powers for the legislative branch to rely upon and entrust the defense of its vital constitutional powers to the advocate for the executive branch, the Attorney General." S. Rept. No. 170, 95th Cong., 1st Sess. 11. The committee recalled that in two cases involving the power of Congress to investigate, the Justice Department withdrew its representation of Congress just as the litigation reached the Supreme Court, after having represented Congress in the district and appellate courts. Id. at 12.

As part of the Ethics in Government Act of 1978, the Senate established an Office of Senate Legal Counsel. The Senate Legal Counsel and the Deputy Legal Counsel are appointed by the President pro tempore of the Senate from among recommendations submitted by the majority and minority leaders of the Senate. The principal duty of the Counsel is to defend the Senate or a committee, subcommittee, member, officer, or employee of the Senate when directed by two-thirds of the members of the Joint Leadership Group or by the adoption of a Senate resolution. Individual Senators may initiate suits on their own. In the House of Representatives, the Office of General Counsel handles litigation that involves members, House officers, and staff.

Raines v. Byrd

521 U.S. 811 (1997)

The Line Item Veto Act of 1996 provided that any member of Congress may bring a lawsuit to challenge the constitutionality of the statute. Senator Robert C. Byrd and five other legislators sued under this provision, a district judge held that the statute violated the Constitution, and the matter was brought directly to the Supreme Court.

CHIEF JUSTICE REHNQUIST delivered the opinion of the Court.

The District Court for the District of Columbia declared the Line Item Veto Act unconstitutional. On this direct appeal, we hold that appellees lack standing to bring this suit, and therefore direct that the judgment of the District Court be vacated and the complaint dismissed....

II

Under Article III, § 2 of the Constitution, the federal courts have jurisdiction over this dispute between appellants and appellees only if it is a "case" or "controversy." This is a "bedrock requirement." ... As we said in *Simon v. Eastern Ky. Welfare Rights Organization,* 426 U.S. 26, 37 (1976), "No principle is more fundamental to the judiciary's proper role in our system of government than the constitutional limitation of federal-court jurisdiction to actual cases or controversies."

...In the light of this overriding and time-honored concern about keeping the judiciary's power within its proper constitutional sphere, we must put aside the natural urge to proceed directly to the merits of this important dispute and to "settle" it for the sake of convenience and efficiency. Instead, we must carefully inquire as to whether appellees have met their burden of establishing that their claimed injury is personal, particularized, concrete, and otherwise judicially cognizable.

III

We have never had occasion to rule on the question of legislative standing presented here. In *Powell v. McCormack,* 395 U.S. 486, 496, 512–514 (1969), we held that a Member of Congress' constitutional challenge to his exclusion from the House of Representatives (and his consequent loss of salary) presented an Article III case or controversy. But *Powell* does not help appellees. First, appellees have not been singled out for specially unfavorable treatment as opposed to other Members of their respective bodies. Their claim is that the Act causes a type of institutional injury (the dimunition of legislative power), which necessarily damages all Members of Congress and both Houses of Congress equally.... Second, appellees do not claim that they have been deprived of something to which they *personally* are entitled—such as their seats as Members of Congress after their constituents had elected *them*. Rather, appellees' claim of standing is based on a loss of political power, not loss of any private right, which would make the injury more concrete. Unlike the injury claimed by Congressman Adam Clayton Powell, the injury claimed by the Members of Congress here is not claimed in any private capacity but solely because they are Members of Congress....If one of the Members were to retire tomorrow, he would no longer have a claim; the claim would be possessed by his successor instead. The claimed injury thus runs (in a sense) with the Member's seat, a seat which the Member holds (it may quite arguably be said) as trustee for his constituents, not as a prerogative of personal power....

[The Court also distinguishes the item veto suit from an earlier case, Coleman v. Miller, 307 U.S. 433 (1939), in which the Court had upheld standing for state legislators who had claimed an institutional injury. But in this state case, twenty of Kansas' forty state senators voted not to ratify the proposed Child Labor Amendment to the Federal Constitution. With the vote deadlocked 20 to 20, the amendment ordinarily would not have been ratified. However, the state's lieutenant governor, the presiding officer of the state senate, cast a deciding vote in favor of the amendment and it was deemed ratified. The twenty senators who had voted against the amendment, joined by a 21st senator and three state house members, filed an action to prevent ratification by the state. Senator Byrd and his colleagues could not argue that their votes on the Line Item Veto Act had not been given full effect. As the Court noted: "They simply lost that vote."]

There would be nothing irrational about a system which granted standing in these cases; some European constitutional courts operate under one or another variant of such a regime [allowing legislators to take constitutional questions to the courts]....But it is obviously not the regime that has obtained under our Constitution to date. Our regime contemplates a more restricted role for Article III courts....

IV

In sum, appellees have alleged no injury to themselves as individuals (contra *Powell*), the institutional injury they allege is wholly abstract and widely dispersed (contra *Coleman*), and their attempt to litigate this dispute at this time and in

this form is contrary to historical experience. We attach some importance to the fact that appellees have not been authorized to represent their respective Houses of Congress in this action, and indeed both Houses actively oppose their suit....We also note that our conclusion neither deprives Members of Congress of an adequate remedy (since they may repeal the Act or exempt appropriations bills from its reach), nor forecloses the Act from constitutional challenge (by someone who suffers judicially cognizable injury as a result of the Act)....

JUSTICE SOUTER, concurring in the judgment, with whom JUSTICE GINSBURG joins, concurring.

. . .

JUSTICE STEVENS, dissenting.

The Line Item Veto Act purports to establish a procedure for the creation of laws that are truncated versions of bills that have been passed by the Congress and presented to the President for signature. If the procedure were valid, it would deny every Senator and every Representative any opportunity to vote for or against the truncated measure that survives the exercise of the President's cancellation authority. Because the opportunity to cast such votes is a right guaranteed by the text of the Constitution, I think it clear that the persons who are deprived of that right by the Act have standing to challenge its constitutionality. Moreover, because the impairment of that constitutional right has an immediate impact on their official powers, in my judgment they need not wait until after the President has exercised his cancellation authority to bring suit. Finally, the same reason that the respondents have standing provides a sufficient basis for concluding that the statute is unconstitutional.

. . .

Assuming for the moment that this procedure is constitutionally permissible, and that the President will from time to time exercise the power to cancel portions of a just-enacted-law, it follows that the statute deprives every Senator and every Representative of the right to vote for or against measure that may become law. The appellees cast their challenge to the constitutionality of the Act in a slightly different way. Their complaint asserted that the Act "alter[s] the legal and practical effect of all votes they may cast on bills containing such separately vetoable items" and "divest[s] the[m] of their constitutional role in the repeal of legislation." Complaint ¶ 14. These two claimed injuries are at best the same as the injury on which I rest my analysis....

JUSTICE BREYER, dissenting.

. . .

I concede that there would be no case or controversy here were the dispute before us not truly adversary, or were it not concrete and focused. But the interests that the parties assert are genuine and opposing, and the parties are therefore truly adverse.... Moreover, as JUSTICE STEVENS points out, the harm that the plaintiffs suffer (on their view of the law) consists in part of the systematic abandonment of laws for which a majority voted, in part of the creation of other laws in violation of procedural rights which (they say) the Consti-

tution provides them, and in part of the consequent and immediate impediment to their ability to do the job that the Constitution requires them to do....

In sum, I do not believe that the Court can find this case nonjusticiable without overruling *Coleman*. Since it does not do so, I need not decide whether the systematic nature, seriousness, and immediacy of the harm would make this dispute constitutionally justiciable even in *Coleman*'s absence. Rather, I can and would find this case justiciable on *Coleman*'s authority. I add that because the majority has decided that this dispute is not now justiciable and has expressed no view on the merits of the appeal, I shall not discuss the merits either, but reserve them for future argument.

E. JUDGE AS LAWMAKER

From the common law of England to the decisions of American courts, judge-made law has been a fact of life. Lawmaking by legislature was a late development in our history, and one that judges opposed because of its blunt and imprecise quality. It is disingenuous to pretend that judges "find" the law rather than "make" it. Jeremiah Smith, who taught law at Harvard after a career on the New Hampshire Supreme Court, was refreshingly candid on this point. When asked "Do judges make law?" he responded: "'Course they do. Made some myself." Paul A. Freund, The Supreme Court of the United States 28 (1961). Throughout its history the federal judiciary has been accused of engaging in "judicial legislation." Few statutes or constitutional provisions are clear in meaning. Judicial interpretation, broadly exercised, becomes a substitute for legislation. Because judges fill in the "interstices" of law, Holmes said he recognized "without hesitation that judges do and must legislate." Southern Pacific Co. v. Jensen, 244 U.S. 205, 221 (1917).

There have been periods when judicial lawmaking became so flagrant and arbitrary that it provoked biting criticism. For example, at the end of the nineteenth century, after legislative attempts to regulate the economy were frustrated by Supreme Court decisions, certain members of the Court condemned what they regarded as a judicial assumption of power. When the Court in 1890 decided that the judiciary, not the legislature, was the final arbiter in regulating railroad fares, freight rates, and other charges on the public, Justice Bradley's dissent considered this an arrogation of authority the Court had no right to make. Chicago, Milwaukee & St. Paul R.R. Co. v. Minnesota, 134 U.S. 418, 462–63 (1890). In the Income Tax Case of 1895, Justice White's dissent accused his brethren of amending the Constitution by judicial fiat. For more than a century the federal government and constitutional scholars had confined the definition of direct tax to capitation and land taxes. The Court decided to add a third category: the income tax. White said that the Constitution should have been amended directly rather than by the judiciary. Pollock v. Farmers' Home & Trust Col, 157 U.S. 429, 639 (1895). It took a constitutional amendment—the Sixteenth—to override the Court.

Dissenting in a 1904 case, Justice Harlan charged that the court "entrenches upon the domain of the legislative department.... It has made, not declared, law." Schick v. United States, 195 U.S. 65, 99 (1904). In an antitrust decision in 1911 he assailed the Court for converting the formula of the Sherman Act from restraint of trade to "rule of reason." Borrowing language from an earlier decision, he charged that the Court had read into the Act *"by way of judicial legislation an exception that is not placed there by the lawmaking branch of the Government,* and this is to be done upon the theory that the impolicy of such legislation is so clear that it cannot be supposed Congress intended the natural import of the language it used. This *we cannot and ought not to do....*" By mere interpretation, he said, the Court had modified an act of Congress and deprived it of its force in combating monopoly practices. The most ominous part of the decision for Harlan was "the usurpation by the judicial branch of the Government of the functions of the legislative department." Standard Oil v. United States, 221 U.S. 1, 88, 99, 103 (1911).

Contemporary Issues

Although the Supreme Court no longer substitutes its judgment for what Congress considers necessary in economic legislation, or at least not to the degree that the judiciary interfered up to the 1930s, courts still play an active legislative role by interpreting such general concepts as "equal protection" and "due process." Other opportunities are available for judicial legislation. For example, in 1966 the Supreme Court interpreted a congressional statute, passed in 1865, to prohibit not merely obscene materials but those in which the publisher "pandered" (deliberately appealed to the customer's erotic interests). In his dissent, Justice Harlan said he feared that what the Court "has done today is in effect to write a new statute, but without the sharply focused definitions and standards necessary in such a sensitive area. Casting such a dubious gloss over a straightforward 101-year-old statute... is for me an astonishing piece of judicial improvisation." Ginzburg v. United States, 383 U.S. 463, 494–95 (1966).

The abortion decisions in 1973 represent for many scholars a spectacular example of judicial legislation. Writing for the majority, Justice Blackmun declared that during the first trimester of pregnancy a physician, after consulting with the woman, is free to perform an abortion without interference by the state. During the second trimester, the state may regulate and even prevent abortion except where it is necessary to preserve the life or health of the mother. The state's interest expands during the third trimester. Roe v. Wade, 410 U.S. 113, 162–63 (1973); Doe v. Bolton, 410 U.S. 179, 195, 199 (1973). In one of the two dissents, Justice Rehnquist said that the Court's "conscious weighing of competing factors... is far more appropriate to a legislative judgment than to a judicial one." Roe v. Wade, 410 U.S. at 173. After almost two decades of criticism, in 1992 the Court abandoned its trimester analysis. Planned Parenthood v. Casey, 505 U.S. 833 (1992).

If the weighing of competing factors constitutes an act of lawmaking, the courts do little else. Questions of federalism and the commerce power turn on the competing interests of the federal government and the states. The courts regularly balance the government's national security interests against the rights of individual freedom. The needs of law enforcement collide with the rights to privacy. A judge's decision to close a trial conflicts with the right of the press and the public to attend. The power of Congress to investigate the executive branch must be weighed against the President's privilege to withhold information.

In addition to this level of involvement, federal judges act on issues that are within the jurisdiction of Congress and could have been addressed through the regular legislative process. Justice Powell noted that much of the expanded role of the Warren Court "was a reaction to the sluggishness of the legislative branch in addressing urgent needs for reform." 62 A.B.A.J. 1454, 1455 (1976). There are other pressures on judges to legislate. If one section or provision of a statute is unconstitutional, courts may decide to "sever" that portion while retaining the balance of the statute. Such decisions require courts to judge whether the altered statute, as redesigned by the judiciary, is consistent with legislative objectives. Judicial rewriting can provoke comments from colleagues that the majority opinion erred by "simply deleting the crucial statutory language and using the words that remain as the raw materials for a new statute of his own making." Regan v. Time, Inc., 468 U.S. 641, 673 (1984). Justice Harlan once complained that the Court, in the name of interpreting the will of Congress, had resorted to "judicial surgery" to remove an offending section, so transforming the statute that the Court performed "a lobotomy." Welsh v. United States, 398 U.S. 333, 351 (1970).

If a statute is unconstitutional because it excludes a legitimate party or group, the courts may prefer to include the party rather than declare the entire statute invalid, even if the effect is to rewrite the law. Still more controversial is judicial rewriting that creates an additional charge on the public purse. If legislators dislike the judiciary's handiwork, they can rewrite the statute along constitutional lines. Until they do, the judicially amended statute continues in force. Ruth Bader Ginsburg, 28 Cleveland State L. Rev. 301 (1979).

F. JUDGE AS ADMINISTRATOR

Judicial lawmaking is a venerable and long-debated topic. A more contemporary issue, linked to the public-law litigation explosion, concerns judges who actually *administer* a political system to protect legal rights. Attorney General William French Smith offered this criticism in 1981:

> ...federal courts have attempted to restructure entire school systems in desegregation cases—and to maintain continuing review over basic administrative decisions. They have asserted similar control over entire prison systems and public housing projects. They have restructured the employment criteria to be used by American business and government—even to the extent of mandating numerical results based upon race or gender. No area seems immune from judicial administration. At least one federal judge even attempted to administer a local sewer system. 21 Judges' Journal 4, 7 (Winter 1982).

Involvement in administrative affairs is not a totally new phenomenon for the courts. Nineteenth-century judges reviewed dismissals of federal employees, ordered administrators to carry out "ministerial" (nondiscretionary) duties, and decided questions about the liability of federal officials subjected to lawsuits. With the rise of federal regulatory commissions toward the end of the nineteenth century and the early decades of the twentieth, federal courts became involved in reviewing agency rulemaking and adjudication.

The Administrative Procedure Act (APA) of 1946 provides that any person suffering legal wrong because of agency action is entitled to judicial review. The reviewing court "shall decide all relevant questions of law, interpret constitutional and statutory provisions, and determine the meaning or applicability of the terms of any agency action." Courts shall hold unlawful and set aside agency actions found to be arbitrary, capricious, an abuse of discretion, or contrary to law; contrary to constitutional right, power, privilege, or immunity; or unsupported by substantial evidence in cases subject to formal rulemaking. Although courts often defer to agency expertise and grant a presumption of regularity in favor of the federal government, judges may also require agencies to take a "hard look" at the decisions entrusted to their jurisdiction and insist on adequate documentation to support the agency's determinations.

School Desegregation

The breadth of judicial administration is reflected in the efforts of District Judge W. Arthur Garrity, Jr., to desegregate the Boston school system. In 1975 he placed South Boston High School in temporary receivership under a supervisor appointed by him. His ruling came after more than a decade of racial discrimination by the local school board. Barry Stuart Roberts, 12 N.E. L. Rev. 55 (1976). Another federal judge, seeking to promote school desegregation in

Wilmington, Delaware, "set a tax rate for the school district, ordered state payments to the district, required new training programs for teachers and administrators, mandated specific curricular offerings, ordered the reassignment of staff and called for the development of an "appropriate human relations program'...." Terry W. Hartle, 41 Pub. Adm. Rev. 595, 599 (1981). Because of opposition from citizens and elected officials, judges gradually withdrew their involvement in school desegregation.

Prisons and Mental Institutions

District Judge Frank M. Johnson, Jr., was deeply involved for more than a decade in administering certain institutions in Alabama. "The history of Alabama," he explained, "is replete with instances of state officials who could have chosen one of any number of courses to alleviate unconstitutional conditions but who chose instead to do nothing but punt the problem to the courts." Steven Brill, New York Magazine, April 26, 1976, at 38. Because of the failure of state officials to correct shocking deficiencies in state prisons, mental hospitals, and institutions for the retarded, Johnson repeatedly found violations of the Eighth and Fourteenth Amendments. He graphically described the conditions: "the evidence reflected that one resident was scalded to death when a fellow resident hosed water from one of the bath facilities on him; another died as a result of the insertion of a running water hose into his rectum by a working resident who was cleaning him; one died when soapy water was forced into his mouth; another died of a self-administered overdose of inadequately stored drugs; and authorities restrained another resident in a straightjacket for *nine years* to prevent him from sucking his hands and fingers." Frank M. Johnson, "The Constitution and the Federal District Judge," 54 Tex. L. Rev. 903 (1976).

Rather than devise specific steps to improve conditions, Johnson at first directed the state to design its own plan for upgrading the system to meet constitutional standards. After two deadlines passed without acceptable progress, Johnson intervened to define the minimal constitutional standards. The story suggests a solitary judge pitted against the state, but other parties intervened in the suit, including the Justice Department, the American Psychological Association, the American Orthopsychiatric Association, and the American Civil Liberties Union. Wyatt v. Stickney, 334 F.Supp. 1341 (M.D. Ala. 1971). Johnson was able to forge an effective alliance of state officials and private citizens to bring pressure on the legislature and the governor. A case of "judicial activism"? It is difficult to make that claim when the attorney for the state of Alabama admitted in open court that every prisoner in the state system was subjected to cruel and inhuman treatment within the meaning of the Eighth Amendment. Pugh v. Locke, 406 F.Supp. 318, 322, 329 & n.13 (M.D. Ala. 1976).

G. INDEPENDENT STATE ACTION

By interpreting their own constitutions and statutes, states can reach constitutional decisions that are markedly different from U.S. Supreme Court rulings. The federal Constitution provides only a minimum, or a floor, for the protection of individual rights and liberties. As noted by the U.S. Supreme Court, each state has the "sovereign right to adopt in its own Constitution individual liberties more expansive than those conferred by the Federal Constitution." PruneYard Shopping Center v. Robins, 447 U.S. 74, 81 (1980). When states want to express these independent views, they must make clear that their rulings depend exclusively on the constitution and laws of the state. If state courts base their decisions on "bona fide separate, adequate and independent grounds," the U.S. Supreme Court will not undertake a review. Michigan v. Long, 463 U.S. 1032 (1983). Under these circumstances, the "final word" on state constitutional law rests with the states, not the U.S. Supreme Court (see box on next page).

Many of the so-called innovations by the U.S. Supreme Court were established first at the

A State Court Analyzes "Plain View"

In 1980 the Supreme Court of Washington held that a university police officer had exceeded his authority in seizing incriminating evidence in a student's room. The officer stopped the student who was carrying a bottle of gin and appeared to be under age. The student asked permission to return to his dormitory room to retrieve his identification card and the officer followed. From an open doorway the officer noticed what appeared to be marijuana seeds and a pipe. He entered the room, confirmed that the seeds were marijuana, and concluded that the pipe smelled of marijuana. The Supreme Court of Washington held that the evidence had been obtained illegally and could not be admitted at the trial. State v. Chrisman, 619 P.2d 971 (Wash. 1980).

The U.S. Supreme Court reversed the state court decision, holding that the plain-view doctrine permits a law enforcement officer to seize incriminating evidence or contraband "when it is discovered in a place where the officer has a right to be." Washington v. Chrisman, 455 U.S. 1, 6 (1982). The case was returned to the state court for "further proceedings not inconsistent with this opinion."

In fact, on this next go-round the Supreme Court of Washington refused to accept the plain-view analysis offered by the U.S. Supreme Court. Whereas its 1980 decision cited several federal decisions, this time the Supreme Court of Washington based its reasoning "solely and exclusively on the constitution and laws of the state of Washington." It concluded that it was right the first time and excluded the evidence. State v. Chrisman, 676 P.2d 419 (Wash. 1984).

state level. Thus, in 1914 the Court ruled that papers illegally seized by federal officers had to be excluded in federal court as evidence (the exclusionary rule). Some states had already adopted that policy. When the Court applied the exclusionary rule to all of the states in 1961, it acknowledged that states were moving increasingly in that direction anyway. Even now, the exclusionary rule leaves plenty of room for independent state action. Evidence admissible in federal court is not necessarily admissible in state court. In 1984, when the Supreme Court held that evidence resulting from a defective search warrant can be admitted if police believe they are acting in "good faith," this relaxed standard was later rejected by a number of state courts (see box on page 815).

State independence is also strengthened by more explicit language in their constitutions. Although the Supreme Court has accepted the use of public funds for sectarian schools to pay for such expenses as transportation and textbooks, many state courts have denied this type of assistance because of highly restrictive language in their constitutions that prohibits the appropriation of public funds for any religious worship or instruction (see box on page 661).

Similarly, state constitutions are often far more explicit in protecting the rights of speech, assembly, and privacy. By interpreting this language, state courts can issue rulings that depart dramatically from U.S. Supreme Court doctrines. Independent constitutional interpretations by the states can satisfy the values we place on diversity, pluralism, and a distrust of centralized government.

By participating in ballot initiatives in state elections, citizens regularly offer judgments on sensitive and controversial constitutional issues. In the state of Washington, voters in 1997 rejected a measure to legalize the medical use of marijuana, rejected a law requiring trigger locks on handguns and safety courses for owners, and rejected a proposal that barred job discrimination based on sexual orientation. Voters in Houston, Texas, rejected a measure to repeal affirmative action. Citizens in Orange County, California, supported a local school board's decision to drop bilingual education. The New York Times, November 11, 1997, at A28. In 1998, voters in California supported Proposition 227, which is designed to abolish bilingual education after no more than a year of intensive immersion in English. In a ballot initiative in

2000, California voters limited marriage to the union between man and woman, thereby excluding gay couples.

H. WHO HAS THE "LAST WORD"?

The notion that the Constitution is somehow equivalent to Supreme Court decisions is a curious product of the twentieth century. One searches previous periods in vain for evidence that the judiciary wields a monopoly on constitutional law. Nevertheless, students in undergraduate, graduate, and law schools are taught that the Court announces the "last word" on what the Constitution means. In 1992 Chief Justice Rehnquist wrote: "We rightly think of our courts as the final voice in the interpretation of our Constitution, and therefore tend to think of constitutional law in terms of cases decided by the courts." William H. Rehnquist, Grand Inquests 278 (1992). Law courses concentrate almost exclusively on caselaw, rather than exploring the complex (and far more interesting) process that involves the three branches of the national government, the states, and the general public.

This book develops the theme of coordinate construction—the opportunity for all three branches to interpret and shape the Constitution. That process is heavily influenced by pressures brought to bear by the public and organized interest groups, as well as by leadership and initiatives from state governments. The courts are an important element, but not the only one, in maintaining a constitutional order. Throughout this book there are many examples that explain the dynamic, open process of constitutional interpretation, which is constantly shaped by a combination of judicial and nonjudicial forces. If private organizations find the courts unreceptive to their arguments, they will turn to executive and legislative bodies, either at the federal or the state level.

In the early decades of our Republic, constitutional analysis was by necessity dominated by Congress and the President. The Supreme Court had handed down few decision on constitutional law, giving practically no guidance for the many complex constitutional issues that perplexed legislators and executive officials. In 1789, Congress had to decide whether the President possessed an implied power to remove executive officials. Some members of Congress suggested that the issue might be better handled by the courts. James Madison disagreed, seeing no need to defer to the judiciary. There was no reason why Congress should not "expound the Constitution, so far as it relates to the division of power between the President and the Senate." 1 Annals of Cong. 439. It was just as important to Congress "that the Constitution should be preserved entire. It is our duty, so far as it depends upon us, to take care that the powers of the Constitution be preserved entire to every department of Government." Id.

The constitutionality of the Sedition Act of 1798 was never determined by the courts. Instead, it was decided by the people in the national elections of 1800, which drove the Federalist party out of office and into oblivion. President Jefferson called the Sedition Act a "nullity" and pardoned every person prosecuted under it (see box on next page). He believed that prosecution for seditious libel could be done only by the states, not the federal government. Later, Congress pronounced the statute "unconstitutional, null, and void," and appropriated funds to reimburse those who had been subjected to fines (see reading). The Supreme Court later acknowledged that the Sedition Act was struck down not by a court of law but by "the court of history." New York Times Co. v. Sullivan, 376 U.S. 254, 276 (1964).

President Jackson, who inherited some of the Jeffersonian distrust toward the judiciary, disagreed sharply with John Marshall on both personal and policy grounds. Every public officer, he said in 1832, took an oath to support the Constitution "as he understands it, and not as it is understood by others." The opinion of judges "has no more authority over Congress than the opinion of Congress has over the judges, and on that point the President is independent

Jefferson and the Sedition Act

...I discharged every person under punishment or prosecution under the sedition law, because I considered, and now consider, that law to be a nullity, as absolute and as palpable as if Congress had ordered us to fall down and worship a golden image; and that it was as much my duty to arrest its execution in every stage, as it would have been to have rescued from the fiery furnace those who should have been cast into it for refusing to worship the image. It was accordingly done in every instance, without asking what the offenders had done, or against whom they had offended, but whether the pains they were suffering were inflicted under the pretended sedition law. (Jefferson to Mrs. John Adams, July 22, 1804).

You seem to think it devolved on the judges to decide on the validity of the sedition law. But nothing in the Constitution has given them a right to decide for the Executive, more than to the Executive to decide for them. Both magistrates are equally independent in the sphere of action assigned to them. The judges, believing the law constitutional, had a right to pass a sentence of fine and imprisonment; because the power was placed in their hands by the Constitution. But the executive, believing the law to be unconstitutional, were bound to remit the execution of it; because that power has been confided to them by the Constitution. That instrument meant that its co-ordinate branches should be checks on each other. But the opinion which gives to the judges the right to decide what laws are constitutional, and what not, not only for themselves in their own sphere of action, but for the legislature and executive also, in their spheres, would make the judiciary a despotic branch.... (Jefferson to Mrs. Adams, September 11, 1804).

of both" (reading by Jackson). However, Jackson appreciated the value of judicial independence. He saw the courts as natural allies in his fight against the Nullifiers, who wanted to release the states from judgments of federal courts. Richard P. Longaker, 71 Pol. Sci. Q. 341, 358–61 (1956). Jackson's theory of the President's independent duty to interpret the Constitution provoked a sharp debate in the Senate (see reading).

In 1857, the Supreme Court held that Dred Scott (and all other black slaves and their descendants) was not a citizen of the United States or of Missouri. Chief Justice Taney refused to allow contemporary social beliefs to change the meaning of the constitution by making blacks citizens. Taney also ruled that Congress was without power to prevent the spread of slavery to the territories in the West. Dred Scott v. Sandford, 16 How. 393 (1857). During debates in a Senate race a year later, Abraham Lincoln repudiated the larger policy questions decided by the Court (see reading). In his first inaugural address, Lincoln acknowledged that Supreme Court rulings are binding on the parties to a suit and are "entitled to very high respect and consideration in all parallel cases by all other departments of the government" At the same time, he said that "if the policy of the Government upon vital questions affecting the whole people is to be irrevocably fixed by decisions of the Supreme Court, the instant they are made in ordinary litigation between parties in personal actions the people will have ceased to be their own rulers, having to that extent practically resigned their Government into the hands of that eminent tribunal."

These exchanges and volleys between the Court and the political system continue in our time. For example, during the 1970s and early 1980s, it appeared that courts were sympathetic to the arguments of those who were pro-choice on the issue of abortion. Consequently, the pro-choice community concentrated on litigation while the pro-life group appealed to the legislatures, the President, and governors. By the end of the 1980s, as a result of appointments by Presidents Nixon, Ford, Reagan, and Bush, the Supreme Court indicated that it would give less protection to the interests sought by the pro-choice organizations. Consequently, they now turned to Congress for support. On June 27, 1991, the National Abortion Rights Action League (NARAL) sent a "Supreme Court Alert" to its membership, calling attention to the abortion restrictions being enacted in the states and through regulations issued by the Bush administration. NARAL, which had relied on the courts in the past, now stated: "Clearly Congress is our Court of Last Resort. All hopes of protecting our constitutional right to choose depends upon our elected representatives in Congress reponding to the will of the American people." The American Civil Liberties Union, which had also depended heavily on litigation, sounded a similar theme: "Congress is increasingly asked to look at these [constitutional] issues because there is nobody else. It is now the court of last resort." W. John Moore, "In Whose Court?," National Journal, Oct. 5, 1991, at 2400. The question "who shall interpret" the Constitution is explored in the final reading by Walter F. Murphy.

Congress Responds to the Sedition Act

The Federalists passed the Alien and Sedition Acts of 1798 to silence domestic opponents of governmental policy. Thomas Jefferson regarded the Sedition Act as unconstitutional, although federal judges did not find it so. After his election as President in 1800, he used his executive authority to discharge whoever had been punished or prosecuted under the Sedition Act. In 1840 Congress passed a private bill to reimburse the heirs of Matthew Lyon, who had been prosecuted under the Sedition Act (6 Stat. 802, c. 45). The committee report accompanying the bill stated that the Sedition Act was "unconstitutional, null, and void" (H. Rept. No. 86, 26th Cong., 1st Sess.).

That in the month of October, 1798, the late Matthew Lyon, the father of the petitioners, at the circuit court held at Rutland, in the State of Vermont, was indicted and found guilty of having printed and published what was alleged to be a libel against Mr. John Adams, the then President of the United States. The alleged libel was in the following words, to wit: "As to the Executive, when I shall see the effects of that power bent on the promotion of the comfort, the happiness, and accommodation of the people, that Executive shall have my zealous and uniform support. But whenever I shall, on the part of our Executive, see every consideration of public welfare swallowed up in a continual grasp for power, in an unbounded thirst for ridiculous pomp, foolish adulation, and selfish avarice—when I shall behold men of real merit daily turned out of office for no other cause than independency of sentiment—when I shall see men of firmness, merit, years, abilities, and experience, discarded in their applications for office, for fear they possess that independence, and men of meanness preferred for the ease with which they can take up and advocate opinions, the consequence of which they know but little of—when I shall see the sacred name of religion employed as a State engine to make mankind hate and persecute each other, I shall not be their humble advocate!" The second count in the indictment, on which the said Matthew Lyon was convicted, charged him with printing and publishing a seditious writing or libel,

entitled "Copy of a letter from an American diplomatic character in France (Mr. Joel Barlow) to a member of Congress in Philadelphia," which was in the following words, to wit: "The misunderstanding between the two Governments has become extremely alarming; confidence is completely destroyed; mistrusts, jealousies, and a disposition to a wrong attribution of motives, are so apparent as to require the utmost caution in every word and action that are to come from your Executive—I mean if your object is to avoid hostilities. Had this truth been understood with you before the recall of Monroe—before the coming and second coming of Pinckney; had it guided the pens that wrote the bullying speech of your President, and stupid answer of your Senate, at the opening of Congress in November last, I should probably have had no occasion to address you this letter. But when we found him borrowing the language of Edmund Burke, and telling the world that, although he should succeed in treating with the French, there was no dependence to be placed in any of their engagements; that their religion and morality were at an end, and they had turned pirates and plunderers, and that it would be necessary to be perpetually armed against them, though you are at peace; we wondered that the answer of both Houses had not been an order to send him to the mad-house. Instead of this, the Senate have echoed the speech with more servility than ever George the Third experienced from either House of Parliament."

The court deemed both the publications above recited libellous, under the 2d section of the act commonly called the sedition law, passed the 4th July, 1798; which section is as follows, viz: *"And be it further enacted.* That if any person shall write, print, utter, or publish, or shall cause or procure to be written, printed, uttered, or published, or shall knowingly and wilfully assist or aid in writing, printing, uttering, or publishing, any false, scandalous, and malicious writing or writings, against the Government of the United States, or either House of the Congress of the United States, or of the President of the United States, with an intent to defame the said Government, or either House of the said Congress, or the President, or to bring them, or either of them, into contempt or disrepute, or to excite against them, or either or any of them, the hatred of the good people of the United States, &c., then such person, being thereof convicted before any court of the United States having jurisdiction thereof, shall be punished by a fine not exceeding two thousand dollars, and by imprisonment not exceeding two years."

Upon this indictment Matthew Lyon was convicted, and sentenced by the court to be imprisoned for four months; to pay a fine of one thousand dollars, and the costs of the prosecution, taxed at sixty dollars and ninety-six cents; and to stand committed until the fine and costs were paid: which were paid, as appears by the exemplification of the record of the said trial and proceedings, now in the archives of this House.

The committee are of opinion that the law above recited was unconstitutional, null, and void, passed under a mistaken exercise of undelegated power, and that the mistake ought to be corrected by returning the fine so obtained, with interest thereon, to the legal representatives of Matthew Lyon.

The committee do not deem it necessary to discuss at length the character of that law, or to assign all the reasons, however demonstrative, that have induced the conviction of its unconstitutionality. No question connected with the liberty of the press ever excited a more universal and intense interest—ever received so acute, able, long-continued, and elaborate investigation—was ever more generally understood, or so conclusively settled by the concurring opinions of all parties, after the heated political contests of the day had passed away. All that now remains to be done by the representatives of a people who condemned this act of their agents as unauthorized, and transcending their grant of power, to place beyond question, doubt, or cavil, that mandate of the constitution prohibiting Congress from abridging the liberty of the press, and to discharge an honest, just, moral, and honorable obligation, is to refund from the Treasury the fine thus illegally and wrongfully obtained from one of their citizens: for which purpose the committee herewith report a bill.

Jackson's Veto of the Bank Bill

President Andrew Jackson received a bill in 1832 to renew the Bank of the United States. Although the bill had been passed by Congress, and the constitutionality of the Bank had been upheld by the Supreme Court in *McCulloch* v. *Maryland* (1819), Jackson exercised his veto. His veto message of July 10, 1832, explains the independence of the President in determining constitutional questions notwithstanding the judgments reached by the legislative and judicial branches.

To the Senate:

The bill "to modify and continue" the act entitled "An act to incorporate the subscribers to the Bank of the United States" was presented to me on the 4th July instant. Having considered it with that solemn regard to the principles of the Constitution which the day was calculated to inspire,

SOURCE: The full veto message appears in 3 Messages and Papers of the Presidents 1139–43 (Richardson ed.)

and come to the conclusion that it ought not to become a law, I herewith return it to the Senate, in which it originated, with my objections.

A bank of the United States is in many respects convenient for the Government and useful to the people. Entertaining this opinion, and deeply impressed with the belief that some of the powers and privileges possessed by the existing bank are unauthorized by the Constitution, subversive of the rights of the States, and dangerous to the liberties of the people, I felt it my duty at an early period of my Administration to call the attention of Congress to the practicability of organizing an institution combining all its advantages and obviating these objections. I sincerely regret that in the act before me I can perceive none of those modifications of the bank charter which are necessary, in my opinion, to make it compatible with justice, with sound policy, or with the Constitution of our country.

[Jackson states his objections that various features of the bill grant monopoly and exclusive privileges to the rich at the expense of the poor. He also regarded the Bank as injurious to the states.]

It is maintained by the advocates of the bank that its constitutionality in all its features ought to be considered as settled by precedent and by the decision of the Supreme Court. To this conclusion I can not assent. Mere precedent is a dangerous source of authority, and should not be regarded as deciding questions of constitutional power except where the acquiescence of the people and the States can be considered as well settled. So far from this being the case on this subject, an argument against the bank might be based on precedent. One Congress, in 1791, decided in favor of a bank; another, in 1811, decided against it. One Congress, in 1815, decided against a bank; another, in 1816, decided in its favor. Prior to the present Congress, therefore, the precedents drawn from that source were equal. If we resort to the States, the expressions of legislative, judicial, and

executive opinions against the bank have been probably to those in its favor as 4 to 1. There is nothing in precedent, therefore, which, if its authority were admitted, ought to weigh in favor of the act before me.

If the opinion of the Supreme Court covered the whole ground of this act, it ought not to control the coordinate authorities of this Government. The Congress, the Executive, and the Court, must each for itself be guided by its own opinion of the Constitution. Each public officer who takes an oath to support the Constitution swears that he will support it as he understands it, and not as it is understood by others. It is as much the duty of the House of Representatives, of the Senate, and of the President to decide upon the constitutionality of any bill or resolution which may be presented to them for passage or approval as it is of the supreme judges when it may be brought before them for judicial decision. The opinion of the judges has no more authority over Congress than the opinion of Congress has over the judges, and on that point the President is independent of both. The authority of the Supreme Court must not, therefore, be permitted to control the Congress or the Executive when acting in their legislative capacities, but to have only such influence as the force of their reasoning may deserve.

. . .

The Senate Debates Jackson's Veto Message

President Jackson's veto of the Bank of the United States reached the Senate on July 10, 1832. Before sustaining the veto, the Senate engaged in a major debate on the substantive reasons given by Jackson in opposing the Bank. Several Senators also concentrated on the legitimacy of the veto itself. Did the President have the power to veto a proposal that had been previously passed by Congress, signed by a President (Madison), and upheld by the Supreme Court (in *McCulloch* v. *Maryland*)? Senator Daniel Webster argued that Jackson had no such right. Senator Hugh Lawson White strongly defended Jackson's action.

[*Senator Webster:*] Does the President, then, reject the authority of all precedent, except what is suitable to his own purposes to use? And does he use, without stint or measure, all precedents which may augment his own power, or gratify his wishes? But if the President thinks lightly of the

authority of Congress, in construing the constitution, he thinks still more lightly of the authority of the Supreme Court. He asserts a right of individual judgment on constitutional questions, which is totally inconsistent with any proper administration of the Government, or any regular execution of the laws. Social disorder, entire uncertainty in regard to individual rights and individual duties, the cessation of legal authority, confusion, the dissolution of free Government—all

SOURCE: *Congressional Debates*, 22nd Cong. 1st Sess. 1231–44 (1832).

these are the inevitable consequences of the principles adopted by the message, whenever they shall be carried to their full extent. Hitherto it has been thought that the final decision of constitutional questions belonged to the supreme judicial tribunal. The very nature of free Government, it has been supposed, enjoins this: and our constitution, moreover, has been understood so to provide, clearly and expressly. It is true that each branch of the Legislature has an undoubted right, in the exercise of its functions, to consider the constitutionality of a law proposed to be passed. This is naturally a part of its duty, and neither branch can be compelled to pass any law, or do any other act, which it deems to be beyond the reach of its constitutional power. The President has the same right when a bill is presented for his approval; for he is, doubtless, bound to consider, in all cases, whether such bill be compatible with the constitution, and whether he can approve it consistently with his oath of office. But when a law has been passed by Congress, and approved by the President, it is now no longer in the power, either of the same President, or his successors, to say whether the law is constitutional or not. He is not at liberty to disregard it: he is not at liberty to feel or to affect "constitutional scruples," and to sit in judgment himself on the validity of a statute of the Government, and to nullify it if he so chooses. After a law has passed through all the requisite forms: after it has received the requisite legislative sanction and the Executive approval, the question of its constitutionality then becomes a judicial question, and a judicial question alone. In the courts, that question may be raised, argued, and adjudged; it can be adjudged nowhere else.

· · ·

[*Senator White:*] The honorable Senator argues that the constitution has constituted the Supreme Court a tribunal to decide great constitutional questions, such as this, and that, when they have done so, the question is put at rest, and every other department of the Government must acquiesce. This doctrine I deny. The constitution vests "the judicial power in a Supreme Court, and

in such inferior courts as Congress may from time to time ordain and establish." Whenever a suit is commenced and prosecuted in the courts of the United States, of which they have jurisdiction, and such suit is decided by the Supreme Court, as that is the court of the last resort, its decision is final and conclusive between the parties. But as an authority, it does not bind either the Congress or the President of the United States. If either of these coordinate departments is afterwards called upon to perform an official act, and conscientiously believe the performance of that act will be a violation of the constitution, they are not bound to perform it, but, on the contrary, are as much at liberty to decline acting, as if no such decision had been made. In examining the extent of their constitutional power, the opinion of so enlightened a tribunal as our Supreme Court has been, and I hope ever will be, will always be entitled to great weight; and, without doubt, either Congress or the President would always be disposed, in a doubtful case, to think its decisions correct; but I hope neither will ever view them as authority binding upon them. They ought to examine the extent of their constitutional powers for themselves; and when they have had access to all sources of information within their reach, and given to every thing its due weight, if they are satisfied the constitution has not given a power to do the act required, I insist they ought to refrain from doing it.

... Each coordinate department, within its appropriate sphere of action, must judge of its own powers, when called upon to do its official duties; and if either blindly follows the others, without forming an opinion for itself, an essential check against the exercise of unconstitutional power is destroyed. A mistake by Congress in passing an act, inconsistent with the constitution, followed by a like mistake by the Supreme Court, in deciding such act to be constitutional, might be attended with the most fatal consequences. Let each department judge for itself, and we are safe. If different interpretations are put upon the constitution by the different departments, the people is the tribunal to settle the dispute....

Lincoln's Critique of *Dred Scott*

On July 17, 1858, at Springfield, Illinois, Abraham Lincoln responded to the Supreme Court's decision in *Dred Scott* v. *Sandford* (1857). At the same time, he rejected the defense of that decision by his opponent for the U.S. Senate, Stephen A. Douglas. Lincoln carefully

identified the portion of the decision he regarded as legally binding. He considered major parts of the decision a nullity, to be left to political resolution outside the courts.

Does Judge Douglas, when he says that several of the past years of his life have been devoted to the question of "popular sovereignty," and that all the remainder of his life shall be devoted to it, does he mean to say that he has been devoting his life to securing to the people of the territories the right to exclude slavery from the territories? If he means so to say, he means to deceive; because he and every one knows that the decision of the Supreme Court, which he approves and makes especial ground of attack upon me for disapproving, forbids the people of a territory to exclude slavery. This covers the whole ground, from the settlement of a territory till it reaches the degree of maturity entitling it to form a State Constitution. So far as all that ground is concerned, the Judge is not sustaining popular sovereignty, but absolutely opposing it....

Now, as to the Dred Scott decision; for upon that he makes his last point at me. He boldly takes ground in favor of that decision.

This is one-half the onslaught, and one-third of the entire plan of the campaign. I am opposed to that decision in a certain sense, but not in the sense which he puts on it. I say that in so far as it decided in favor of Dred Scott's master and against Dred Scott and his family, I do not propose to disturb or resist the decision.

I never have proposed to do any such thing. I think, that in respect for judicial authority, my humble history would not suffer in a comparison with that of Judge Douglas. He would have the citizen conform his vote to that decision; the Member of Congress, his; the President, his use of the veto power. He would make it a rule of political action for the people and all the departments of the government. I would not. By resisting it as a political rule, I disturb no right of property, create no disorder, excite no mobs.

. . .

...I shall read from a letter written by Mr. Jefferson in 1820.... It seems he had been presented by a gentleman of the name of Jarvis with a book, or essay, or periodical, called the "Republican," and he was writing in acknowledgement of the present, and noting some of its contents. After expressing the hope that the work will produce a favorable effect upon the minds of the young, he proceeds to say:

"That it will have this tendency may be expected, and for that reason I feel an urgency to note what I deem an error in it, the more requiring notice as your opinion is strengthened by that of many others. You seem in pages 84 and 148, to consider the judges as the ultimate arbiters of all constitutional questions—a very dangerous doctrine indeed and one which would place us under the despotism of an oligarchy. Our judges are as honest as other men, and not more so. They have, with others, the same passions for party, for power, and the privilege of their corps. Their maxim is, "boni judicis est ampliare jurisdictionem'; and their power is the more dangerous as they are in office for life, and not responsible, as the other functionaries are, to the elective control. The Constitution has erected no such single tribunal, knowing that to whatever hands confided, with the corruptions of time and party, its members would become despots. It has more wisely made all the departments co-equal and co-sovereign within themselves."

Thus we see the power claimed for the Supreme Court by Judge Douglas, Mr. Jefferson holds, would reduce us to the despotism of an oligarchy.

Now, I have said no more than this—in fact, never quite so much as this—at least I am sustained by Mr. Jefferson.

. . .

One more thing. Last night Judge Douglas tormented himself with horrors about my disposition to make negroes perfectly equal with white men in social and political relations. He did not stop to show that I have said any such thing, or that it legitimately follows from any thing I have said, but he rushes on with his assertions. I adhere to the Declaration of Independence. If Judge Douglas and his friends are not willing to stand by it, let them come up and amend it. Let them make it read that all men are created equal except negroes. Let us have it decided, whether the Declaration of Independence, in this blessed year of 1858, shall be thus amended.

. . .

My declarations upon this subject of negro slavery may be misrepresented, but can not be misunderstood. I have said that I do not understand the Declaration to mean that all men were created equal in all respects. They are not our equal in color; but I suppose that it does mean to declare that all men are equal in some respects; they are equal in their right to "life, liberty, and the pursuit of happiness." Certainly the negro is not our equal in color — perhaps not in many other respects; still, in the right to put into his mouth the bread that his own hands have earned, he is the equal of every other man, white or black. In pointing out that more has been given you, you can not be justified in taking away the little which has been given him. All I ask for the negro is that if you do not like him, let him alone. If God gave him but little, that little let him enjoy.

Walter F. Murphy

Who Shall Interpret?

So entrenched is the belief that the U.S. Supreme Court is the ultimate interpreter of the Constitution that the independent contributions of the other branches and the states are largely overlooked in the legal literature. In this essay, political scientist Walter Murphy explores the tradition of departmentalism: the responsibility of all three branches to interpret and apply the Constitution.

I. INTRODUCTION

...It is a fact of American political life that all public officials, from presidents to local police, often have to interpret the Constitution. Every public official takes an oath to uphold the Constitution, and the terms of the constitutional document are often broad. Deciding what policies government may legitimately pursue, whether to enact, sign, veto, or enforce a law, all create problems of interpretation. Even if one believes judges are the ultimate constitutional interpreters, government cannot halt and await a judicial decision whenever a constitutional problem arises.

The oath is also one that millions of private citizens have taken, and the Preamble lodges responsibility for the Constitution in "the people of the United States." Thus, it is fair for "the people," as its ultimate source of authority, to have an interpretive role. Indeed, one can plausibly argue, they have the duty, when they vote or utilize other means to influence public policy, to judge candidates' records and promises about constitutional interpretation.

· · ·

II. WHO SHALL INTERPRET THE CONSTITUTION?

The plain words of the document contain several different messages about WHO shall interpret. In conferring on Congress authority to make "all laws necessary and proper" to carry out powers delegated to the national government, Article I, Sec. 8, clearly implies that Congress (with the participation of the president since he is part of the legislative process) shall make judgments about the Constitution's meaning, for what laws are "proper" under the Constitution are sometimes far from manifest. There are similar terms in the Thirteenth, Fourteenth, Fifteenth, Nineteenth, Twenty-third, Twenty-fourth, and Twenty-sixth amendments.

In requiring the president to "preserve, protect, and defend the Constitution," Article II adds to his interpretive responsibilities. He could hardly fulfill those tasks without interpreting the Constitution to determine if it was being threatened or how to protect it....

The logic of institutional history as well as the words of the constitutional document also enmesh judges in constitutional interpretation. By extending "the judicial power" "to all cases, in law and equity, arising under this Constitution," Article III commands courts to participate in the interpretive process, as judges before and since John Marshall have modestly conceded.

But there is not a word in these clauses about whose views should prevail if the branches disagree....

· · ·

SOURCE: Walter F. Murphy, "Who Shall Interpret? The Quest for the Ultimate Constitutional Interpreter," 48 Review of Politics 401 (1986).

III. WHO IS THE AUTHORITATIVE INTERPRETER: THREE COMPETING THEORIES

Three principal theories claim to produce an answer to the question of WHO is the ultimate interpreter: judicial supremacy, legislative supremacy, and departmentalism. All, however, draw heavily on democratic theory; and much of the debate rests on the possibility of an appeal to "the people," though never so directly as in Jefferson's plan for national conventions.

A. Judicial Supremacy

Judicial supremacy is the most familiar theory. Its usual justification rests on the textual and functional grounds Marshall used in *Marbury v. Madison* (1803) for judicial review: (1) Article VI says the Constitution is law; (2) "it is emphatically the province and duty of the judicial department to say what the law is"; and thus (3) judicial review must be an integral part of the political system. Then follows a long step from judicial review — the authority of a court, when deciding cases, to refuse to give force to an act of a coordinate branch of government — to judicial supremacy, the obligation of coordinate officials not only to obey that ruling but to follow its reasoning in future deliberations....

On the other hand: (1) no constitutional text "expressly confine[s]" interpretation to the judiciary; (2) judicial review says nothing about the obligation of other branches of government to obey a court's decision or follow its reasoning; ...

B. Legislative Supremacy

Systematic assertions of legislative supremacy in constitutional interpretation have been infrequent, though they have at times been vigorously pushed, as after the Civil War when the Radical Republicans dominated Congress, impeached the president, and curbed the Court. Early on, some Jeffersonians had also pressed for congressional supremacy. Caesar Rodney of Delaware wrote in 1803: "Judicial supremacy may be made to bow before the strong arm of Legislative authority. We shall discover who is master of the ship." Threats of impeachment so frightened John Marshall that he was ready to modify judicial review:

> [T]he modern doctrine of impeachment should yield to an appellate jurisdiction in the legislature. A reversal of those legal opinions deemed unsound by the legislature would certainly better comport with the mildness of our character than a removal of the Judge who has rendered them unknowing of his fault.

This proposal has been several times revised — usually with the appellate jurisdiction resting in the Senate alone — but, of course, has never been adopted.

At bottom, any claim that congressional interpretation should prevail over judicial rests on legislators' connections to the people....

On the other hand, constitutionalism is wary of arguments that allow popularly elected officials final authority to define substantive rights....

C. Departmentalism

No president has ever pressed a claim to supremacy in constitutional interpretation. On the other hand, some presidents, like many legislators, have asserted equality.

Madison's position shifted as he faced various crises, but in the early days of the Republic he was clearly a departmentalist. His theory of allowing different social interests to dominate particular institutions and of pitting ambition against ambition and power against power pushes toward stalemates that can only be overcome by compromise, not adjudication. As he told the First Congress:

> There is not one Government... in the United States, in which provision is made for a particular authority to determine the limits of the constitutional division of power between the branches of the Government. In all systems, there are points which must be adjusted by the departments themselves, to which no one of them is competent.

. . .

V. CONCLUSION

The question of WHO shall interpret poses one of the fundamental problems with which any coherent constitutional theory must come to grips. The sort of analysis suggested here transforms the question from one that yields a universally applicable response, into a more complex set of queries about degrees of deference one institution owes another under varying circumstances. What emerges is a modified version of departmentalism.

. . .

There is a magnetic attraction to the notion of an ultimate constitutional interpreter, just as there is a magnetic pull to the idea of some passkey to constitutional interpretation that will, if properly turned, always open the door to truth, justice, and the American way. But finality, as Disraeli reminded us, "is not the language of politics." James Madison would have agreed.

SELECTED READINGS

BAKER, NANCY. Conflicting Loyalties: Law and Politics in the Attorney General's Office, 1789–1990. Lawrence, Kansas: University Press of Kansas, 1992.

BALL, HOWARD. Courts and Politics: The Federal Judicial System. Englewood Cliffs, N.J.: Prentice-Hall, 1980.

BAMBURGER, MICHAEL A. Reckless Legislation: How Lawmakers Ignore the Constitution. New Brunswick, N.J.: Rutgers University Press, 2000.

CAPLAN, LINCOLN. The Tenth Justice: The Solicitor General and the Rule of Law. New York: Knopf, 1987.

CHAYES, ABRAM. "The Role of the Judge in Public Law Litigation." 89 Harvard Law Review 1281 (1976).

CLAYTON, CORNELL W. The Politics of Justice: The Attorney General and the Making of Legal Policy. New York: M. E. Sharpe, Inc., 1992.

COOPER, PHILLIP J. Hard Judicial Choices: Federal District Court Judges and State and Local Officials. New York: Oxford University Press, 1988.

DEVINS, NEAL. Shaping Constitutional Values: Elected Government, the Supreme Court, and the Abortion Debate. Baltimore, Md.: Johns Hopkins University Press, 1996.

———, ed. Elected Branch Influences in Constitutional Decisionmaking, 56 Law & Contemp. Prob. (Autumn 1993).

EPSTEIN, LEE. Conservatives in Court. Knoxville: University of Tennessee Press, 1985.

FISHER, LOUIS. "Social Influences on Constitutional Law." 15 Journal of Political Science 7 1987.

———. "Constitutional Interpretation by Members of Congress." 63 North Carolina Law Review 707 (1985).

———. "Is the Solicitor General an Executive or a Judicial Agent? Caplan's Tenth Justice," 15 Law & Social Inquiry 305 (1990).

———. "The Judge as Manager," The Public Manager, Fall 1996, pp. 7–10.

———. Constitutional Dialogues: Interpretation as Political Process. Princeton, N.J.: Princeton University Press, 1988.

FISHER, LOUIS AND NEAL DEVINS. Political Dynamics of Constitutional Law. St. Paul, Minn.: West Publishing, 1996.

GINGER, ANN FAGAN. "Litigation as a Form of Political Action." 9 Wayne Law Review 458 (1963).

GRIFFITH, J. A. G. The Politics of the Judiciary. Glasgow: Fontana Press, 1985.

HARRIMAN, LINDA, AND JEFFREY D. STRAUSSMAN. "Do Judges Determine Budget Decisions? Federal Court Decisions in Prison Reform and State Spending for Corrections." 43 Public Administration Review 343 (1983).

HODDER-WILLIAMS, RICHARD. The Politics of the U.S. Supreme Court. London: George Allen & Unwin, 1980.

KMIEC, DOUGLAS W. The Attorney General's Lawyer: Inside the Meese Justice Department. New York: Praeger, 1992.

LASSER, WILLIAM. The Limits of Judicial Power: The Supreme Court in American Politics. Chapel Hill: University of North Carolina Press, 1988.

LATHAM, EARL. "The Supreme Court as a Political Institution." 31 Minnesota Law Review 205 (1947).

MURPHY, WALTER, AND C. HERMAN PRITCHETT, eds. Courts, Judges, and Politics. New York: Random House, 1986.

NEIER, ARYEH. Only Judgment: The Limits of Litigation in Social Change. Middletown, Conn.: Wesleyan University Press, 1982.

O'BRIEN, DAVID M. Storm Center: The Supreme Court in American Politics. New York: Norton, 1986.

O'CONNOR, KAREN, AND LEE EPSTEIN. "Amicus Curiae Participation in U.S. Supreme Court Litigation: An Appraisal of Hakman's "Forklore'." 16 Law and Society Review 311 (1981–1982).

PELTASON, JACK. Federal Courts in the Political Process. New York: Random House, 1955.

ROSENBLUM, VICTOR G. Law as a Political Instrument. New York: Random House, 1955.

SALOKAR, REBECCA MAE. The Solicitor General: The Politics of Law. Philadelphia: Temple University Press, 1992.

VOSE, CLEMENT E. Caucasians Only: The Supreme Court, the NAACP, and the Restrictive Covenant Cases. Berkeley: University of California Press, 1959.

WHITTINGTON, KEITH E. Constitutional Construction: Divided Powers and Constitutional Meaning. Cambridge, Mass.: Harvard University Press, 1999.

2

The Doctrine of Judicial Review

Judicial review in America survives a number of nagging, unanswered questions. By what right do life-tenured judges invalidate policies adopted by popularly elected officials? If judicial review is of such crucial importance for a written constitution, why did the framers omit it? Why is it based on implied, rather than explicit, power? If judicial review is essential to protect constitutional freedoms, how do other democratic nations survive without it?

At some point, judicial review assumes the characteristics of lawmaking. Constitutional interpretation is more than a technical exercise or display of judicial erudition. The power to interpret the law is the power to make the law. Judicial review can be another name for judicial legislation. As Bishop Hoadley announced in 1717: "Whosoever hath an absolute authority to interpret any written or spoken laws, it is he who is truly the lawgiver, to all intents and purposes, and not the person who first wrote or spoke them." James Bradley Thayer, 7 Harv. L. Rev. 129, 152 (1893).

Judicial review includes many activities. Courts may overturn a government action, find support for it, or refuse to rule at all. Judicial review applies to Congress, the chief executive, administrative agencies, state legislatures, and rulings of state courts. Although the holding of the Supreme Court is of utmost importance, it often serves as but one stage of an ongoing constitutional process shared with lower courts, the executive branch, and the legislature.

A. SOURCES OF JUDICIAL REVIEW AUTHORITY

When the chief executive or legislators make unpopular decisions, the voters may remove them at the next election. The ballot box represents a periodic test of the legitimacy of elected officers, a reaffirmation of authority they are quite happy to cite. The federal judiciary, however, cannot draw legitimacy from elections. When judges announce an unpopular decision, citizens want to know on what authority courts may overturn the judgments of elected officials who also take an oath to uphold the Constitution. Judges must be able to cite persuasive and authoritative sources: constitutional language, pre-*Marbury* precedents, principles announced by the Marshall Court, or convincing evidence that has accumulated since that time.

Constitutional Language

Article III, Section 1, of the Constitution provides that "The judicial Power of the United States, shall be vested in one Supreme Court, and in such inferior Courts as the Congress may from time to time ordain and establish." Section 2 extends the judicial power to various cases and controversies, but there is no specific grant of power to declare an act of Congress, the President, or state government unconstitutional. The absence of an explicit grant is not conclusive. An implied power may exist. For example, although the Constitution provides no authority for the President to assert executive privilege, remove appointees from office, issue executive orders with the force of law, or enter into international agreements without the advice and consent of the Senate, the Supreme Court has considered those powers implicit in Article

II.[1] Similarly, the Court has found an implied power for Congress to investigate, issue subpoenas, and exercise the power of contempt.[2]

The power of judicial review might be implied from two sources. Under Article III, Section 2, the judicial power extends to all cases *"arising under this Constitution,* the Laws of the United States, and Treaties made" (emphasis added). In most of the early drafts of the Constitution, the language *arising under* applied only to laws passed by Congress. When William Samuel Johnson moved to insert the words *this Constitution and the* before the word *Laws,* James Madison objected, stating that he "doubted whether it was not going too far to extend the jurisdiction of the Court generally to cases arising Under the Constitution, & whether it ought to be limited to cases of a Judiciary Nature. The right of expounding the Constitution in cases of this nature ought not to be given to that Department." Johnson's motion was agreed to without further discussion, "it being generally supposed that the jurisdiction given was constructively limited to cases of a Judiciary nature." 2 Farrand 430.

An intriguing bit of legislative history, but what did the framers mean by cases of a "judiciary nature"? However defined, evidently it was something less than full-blown judicial review. At the Virginia ratifying convention, Madison interpreted "arising under" to justify judicial review only against the states. 3 Elliot 532. Alexander Hamilton made the same point in Federalist No. 80. Under these readings, the purpose of judicial control was to control the states and protect federalism. It was not intended to control Congress and the President.

The power of judicial review might also be drawn from the Supremacy Clause in Article VI, which provides that the Constitution, federal laws "made in Pursuance thereof," and all treaties shall be the supreme law of the land, and "the Judges in every State shall be bound thereby, any Thing in the Constitution or Laws of any State to the Contrary notwithstanding." At a minimum, the Supremacy Clause requires federal courts to review the actions of state governments. It might also invite review of congressional statutes that are not "in pursuance" of the Constitution. However, judicial review over the coequal branches of Congress and the President represents a major leap and demands greater evidence. Justice Holmes once remarked: "I do not think the United States would come to an end if [the Supreme Court] lost [its] power to declare an act of Congress void. I do think the Union would be imperiled if we could not make that declaration as to the laws of the several States." Collected Legal Papers 295–96 (1920).

The Pre-*Marbury* Precedents

A number of precedents for judicial review before *Marbury* prepared the way for Marshall's famous opinion in 1803. British efforts in the 1760s to reestablish control over America provoked accusations by colonists that the laws of Parliament had violated the "common law" and the "law of reason" and were therefore void. These charges became important ingredients in the case presented to a "candid world" in 1776.

The best-known American challenge to an act of Parliament came in 1761 when James Otis argued the writs of assistance case in Boston. He claimed that British customs officials were not empowered by Parliament to use general search warrants. Even if Parliament had autho-

---

1. United States v. Nixon, 418 U.S. 683 (1974) (executive privilege); Myers v. United States, 272 U.S. 52 (1926) (removal power); Contractors Ass'n of Eastern Pa. v. Secretary of Labor, 442 F.2d 159 (3d Cir. 1971), cert. denied, 404 U.S. 854 (1971) (executive orders); and Dames & Moore v. Regan, 453 U.S. 654 (1981) (executive agreements).
2. McGrain v. Daugherty, 273 U.S. 135 (1927) (investigations); Eastland v. United States Servicemen's Fund, 421 U.S. 491, 505 (1975) (subpoenas); Anderson v. Dunn, 19 U.S. (6 Wheat.) 204, 228 (1821) (contempt power).

James Otis and Fundamental Law

This writ is against the fundamental principles of law. The privilege of the House. A man who is quiet, is as secure in his house, as a prince in his castle — notwithstanding all his debts and civil processes of any kind. But —

For flagrant crimes and in cases of great public necessity, the privilege may be infringed on. For felonies an officer may break, upon process and oath, that is, by a special warrant to search such a house, sworn to be suspected, and good grounds of suspicion appearing. . . .

As to Acts of Parliament. An act against the Constitution is void; an act against natural equity is void; and if an act of Parliament should be made, in the very words of this petition, it would be void. The executive Courts must pass such acts in disuse.

SOURCE: The Works of John Adams (Charles Francis Adams, ed.), Vol. II, pp. 521–22. See also pp. 523–25.

rized the writs of assistance, Otis said that the statute would be "against the Constitution," "against natural equity," and therefore void (see box). In 1766 a Virginia court held the Stamp Act unconstitutional. On the eve of the Declaration of Independence, a Massachusetts judge instructed the jury to treat acts of Parliament as violations of fundamental law and as "void" and "inoperative." Edward S. Corwin, The Doctrine of Judicial Review 32 (1914).

The proposition that courts could void an act of Parliament appears in Chief Justice Coke's opinion in *Dr. Bonham's Case* (1610). He said that when an act of Parliament "is against common right and reason, or repugnant, or impossible to be performed, the common law will controul it, and adjudge such Act to be void." 77 Eng. Rep. 646, 652. A few British judges in the seventeenth and eighteenth centuries cited Coke's argument, but the principle of judicial review never took root on English soil. Day v. Savadge, 80 Eng. Rep. 235, 237 (1614) and The City of London v. Wood, 88 Eng. Rep. 1592, 1602 (1702). In 1884 the Supreme Court noted: "notwithstanding what was attributed to Lord Coke in *Bonham's Case*... the omnipotence of Parliament over the common law was absolute, even against common right and reason." Hurtado v. California, 110 U.S. 516, 531 (1884).

For their understanding of British law the framers relied mainly on Blackstone's *Commentaries,* which states the case for parliamentary supremacy with singular clarity. For those who believed that acts of Parliament contrary to reason were void, he offered this advice:

But if the parliament will positively enact a thing to be done which is unreasonable, I know of no power that can control it: and the examples usually alleged in support of this sense of the rule do none of them prove, that, where the main object of a statute is unreasonable, the judges are at liberty to reject it; for that were to set the judicial power above that of the legislature, which would be subversive of all government. W. Blackstone, Commentaries, Book One, § 3, at 91 (Oxford 1775).

Although *Dr. Bonham's Case* provides inadequate support for the American concept of judicial review, it was accepted as good law and precedent by those who wanted to break with England. Intellectual justifications were needed to neutralize the appearance of impetuous and impulsive behavior. However, "voiding" the acts of Parliament did not automatically deliver the power of judicial review to American courts, especially those at the national level.

From independence to the framing of the Constitution, some of the state judges challenged the acts of their legislatures. Although scholars disagree on the strength of those precedents, decisions providing support for the theory of judicial review were handed down by judges in Virginia, New Jersey, New York, Connecticut, Rhode Island, and North Carolina. The language used by judges in holding state laws invalid was often more bold than the results they achieved. Charles Grove Haines, The American Doctrine of Judicial Supremacy 88–120 (1932).

B. THE FRAMERS' INTENT

By the time of the convention, some of the framers expected judicial review to be part of the new government. In reading their statements at the convention and during the ratification debates, it is important to keep their thoughts in context and recognize conflicting statements. The framers did not have a clear or fully developed theory of judicial review.

The framers wanted to replace the Articles of Confederation to make the central government more effective, resolve disputes among the states over legal and monetary systems, and limit legislative abuses. Each goal depended on the structure and power of the federal judiciary. Instead of the legislative supremacy that prevailed under the Articles of Confederation, the new Congress would be only one of three coordinate and coequal branches. Both the Virginia Plan, presented by Edmund Randolph, and the New Jersey Plan, advocated by William Paterson, called for the creation of an independent judiciary headed by a Supreme Court. Although the new judicial article left undecided such questions as whether to create lower federal courts or rely solely on state courts, it did grant broad authority to the Supreme Court.

The framers were worried that thirteen sets of state courts would announce contradictory rulings on matters of national concern. In Federalist No. 80, Alexander Hamilton said that thirteen independent courts of final jurisdiction "over the same causes, arising upon the same laws, is a hydra in government from which nothing but contradiction and confusion can proceed." The convention resolved that problem by adopting the Supremacy Clause. Judicial review over presidential and congressional actions, however, was a subject of much greater delicacy. By 1787 the framers had become alarmed about legislative overreaching. In Federalist No. 48, James Madison wrote that the "legislative department is everywhere extending the sphere of its activity and drawing all power into its impetuous vortex." Several delegates to the Philadelphia Convention expressed the same concern. 1 Farrand 254 (Wilson) and 2 Farrand 35 (Madison), 110 (Madison), and 288 (Mercer). However, giving the courts the final say over congressional acts was an extremely radical notion.

A common pastime of constitutional scholars is counting the heads of framers who favored judicial review. Depending on which year he wrote, Edward S. Corwin vacillated on the statistics, ranging from a high of seventeen framers to a low of five or six. Leonard D. Levy, ed., Judicial Review and the Supreme Court 3–4 (1967). Corwin uttered this scholar's lament in 1937 when he testified on the court-packing plan: "These people who say the framers intended [judicial review] are talking nonsense; and the people who say they did not intend it are talking nonsense. There is evidence on both sides." Senate Committee on the Judiciary, "Reorganization of the Federal Judiciary" (Part 2), 75th Cong., 1st Sess. 176 (1937). Other studies were flavored by a crusading spirit, either to "prove" the legitimacy of judicial review or to chop away at its foundations.[3] The issue remains unsettled; this very ambiguity adds an inhibiting force on judicial activism.

Council of Revision

Judicial review was discussed at the convention as a means of checking Congress and the states. The most important debate was over the veto of legislation passed by Congress. Ran-

---

3. For support of judicial review, see Charles A. Beard, The Supreme Court and the Constitution (1912), and Raoul Berger, Congress v. The Supreme Court (1969). Critics include Louis B. Boudin, Government by Judiciary (1932), and William W. Crosskey, Politics and the Constitution (1953).

dolph proposed a Council of Revision consisting of the "Executive and a convenient number of the National Judiciary...with authority to examine every act of the National Legislature before it shall operate, & every act of a particular Legislature before a Negative thereon shall be final; and that the dissent of the said Council shall amount to a rejection, unless the Act of the National Legislature be again passed...." 1 Farrand 21. Some commentators accept the elimination of the revisionary council as proof that the framers rejected judicial review. However, one of the arguments against the Council was the *availability* of judicial review. As reported by Madison: "Mr. Gerry doubts whether the Judiciary ought to form a part of it, as they will have a sufficient check agst. encroachments on their own department by their exposition of the laws, which involved a power of deciding on their Constitutionality. In some States the Judges had <actually> set aside laws as being agst. the Constitution. This was done too with general approbation." Id. at 97. Here is a clue of judicial review being exercised in cases of a "judiciary nature." The Court needed power to strike down congressional legislation that threatened the integrity or existence of the judiciary. Rufus King supported Gerry's argument after observing that the Justices of the Supreme Court "ought to be able to expound the law as it should come before them, free from the bias of having participated in its formation." This comment provides broad support for judicial review, whereas Gerry appeared to restrict it to legislative encroachments.

Congress Vetoing State Legislation

After debating a congressional veto over proposed state legislation, that idea was rejected for two reasons. The addition of the Supremacy Clause would presumably handle any conflicts between national law and state legislation. Moreover, the state courts could exercise judicial review to control legislative excesses. They "would not consider as valid any law contravening the Authority of the Union," and if such laws were not set aside by the judiciary they "may be repealed by a Nationl. law." 2 Farrand 27–28 (Sherman and Morris). Madison later said that a law "violating a constitution established by the people themselves, would be considered by the Judges as null & void." Id. at 93. These statements were clearly limited to judicial review at the *state*, not the national, level. A year later, writing to Thomas Jefferson, Madison denied that the Constitution empowered the Court to strike down acts of Congress (see box on next page). His comments support fluidity, not finality.

James Wilson, soon to be a member of the Supreme Court, defended the concept of judicial review at the Pennsylvania ratification convention. He said the legislature would be "kept within its prescribed bounds" by the judiciary. 2 Elliot 445. At the Connecticut ratifying convention, Oliver Ellsworth (destined to be the third Chief Justice of the Supreme Court) expected federal judges to void any legislative acts that were contrary to the Constitution. Id. at 196; see also Samuel Adams's comments in Massachusetts, id. at 131. At the Virginia ratifying convention, John Marshall anticipated that the federal judiciary would strike down unconstitutional legislative acts. Id. at 553; see also George Nicholas, id. at 443. The context of these remarks suggests that the availability of judicial review was used to reassure the states that national power would be held in check.

The *Federalist Papers* include several essays that speak strongly for judicial review. The principal essay, Hamilton's Federalist No. 78 (see reading), is designed partly to allay state fears about the power of the central government. The arguments in Federalist No. 78 were later borrowed by John Marshall to buttress his *Marbury* opinion. Hamilton's enthusiasm is somewhat suspect; he appears to have been a late convert to the cause of judicial review. His plan of government presented to the 1787 convention did not grant this power to the judiciary. 1 Farrand 282–93, 302–11; 3 Farrand 617–30. State laws contrary to the Constitution would be "utterly void," but the judiciary is not identified as the voiding agency. 1 Farrand 293.

James Madison on Judicial Review

A revisionary power [by the Council of Revision] is meant as a check to precipitate, to unjust, and to unconstitutional laws. These important ends would it is conceded be more effectually secured, without disarming the Legislature of its requisite authority, by requiring bills to be separately communicated to the Exec. & Judic'y depts. If either of these object, let ⅔, if both ¾ of each House be necessary to overrule the objection; and if either or both protest agst a bill as violating the Constitution, let it moreover be suspended notwithstanding the overruling proportion of the [legislative] Assembly, until there shall have been a subsequent election of the [House of Deputies] and a re-passage of the bill by ⅔ or ¾ of both Houses as the case may be. It sd not be allowed the Judges or [the] Executive to pronounce a law thus enacted unconstitu'l & invalid.

In the State Constitutions & indeed in the Fed'l one also, no provision is made for the case of a disagreement in expounding them; and as the Courts are generally the last in making [the] decision, it results to them by refusing or not refusing to execute a law, to stamp it with its final character. This makes the Judiciary Dept paramount in fact to the Legislature, which was never intended and can never be proper.

SOURCE: 5 Writings of James Madison 294 (Hunt ed. 1904).

In the years between ratification and *Marbury* v. *Madison,* the issue of judicial review was debated often in Congress, but not with any consistency. When Madison introduced the Bill of Rights in the House of Representatives, he predicted that once they were incorporated into the Constitution, "independent tribunals of justice will consider themselves in a peculiar manner the guardians of those rights; they will be an impenetrable bulwark against every assumption of power in the Legislative or Executive." 1 Annals of Congress 439 (June 8, 1789). But nine days later, during debate on the President's removal power, Madison denied that Congress should defer to the courts on this constitutional issue. He begged to know on what principle could it be contended "that any one department draws from the Constitution greater powers than another, in marking out the limits of the powers of the several departments?" If questions arose on the boundaries between the branches, he did not see "that any one of these independent departments has more right than another to declare their sentiments on that point." Id. at 500 (June 17, 1789). In 1791, when proponents of a national bank cited judicial review as a possible check on unconstitutional legislation, Madison was unpersuaded and voted against the bank. 3 Annals of Congress 1978–79 (February 4, 1791).

Alexander Hamilton
Federalist No. 78

We proceed now to an examination of the judiciary department of the proposed government.

In unfolding the defects of the existing Confederation, the utility and necessity of a federal judicature have been clearly pointed out....

Whoever attentively considers the different departments of power must perceive, that, in a government in which they are separated from each other, the judiciary, from the nature of its functions, will always be the least dangerous to the political rights of the Constitution; because it will be least in a capacity to annoy or injure them. The Executive not only dispenses the honors, but holds the sword of the community. The legislature not only commands the purse, but prescribes the rules by which the duties and rights of every citizen are to be regulated. The judiciary, on the contrary, has no influence over either the sword or the purse; no direction either of the strength or of the wealth of the society; and can take no active resolution whatever. It may truly be said to have neither FORCE nor WILL, but merely judgment; and must ultimately depend upon the aid of the executive arm even for the efficacy of its judgments....

The complete independence of the courts of justice is peculiarly essential in a limited Constitution. By a limited Constitution, I understand one which contains certain specified exceptions to the legislative authority; such, for instance, as that it shall pass no bills of attainder, no *ex-post-facto* laws, and the like. Limitations of this kind can be preserved in practice no other way than through the medium of courts of justice, whose duty it must be to declare all acts contrary to the manifest tenor of the Constitution void. Without this, all the reservations of particular rights or privileges would amount to nothing.

Some perplexity respecting the rights of the courts to pronounce legislative acts void, because contrary to the constitution, has arisen from an imagination that the doctrine would imply a superiority of the judiciary to the legislative power. It is urged that the authority which can declare the acts of another void, must necessarily be superior to the one whose acts may be declared void. As this doctrine is of great importance in all the American constitutions, a brief discussion of the ground on which it rests cannot be unacceptable.

There is no position which depends on clearer principles, than that every act of a delegated authority, contrary to the tenor of the commission under which it is exercised, is void. No legislative act, therefore, contrary to the Constitution, can be valid. To deny this, would be to affirm, that the deputy is greater than his principal; that the servant is above his master; that the representatives of the people are superior to the people themselves; that men acting by virtue of powers, may do not only what their powers do not authorize, but what they forbid.

If it be said that the legislative body are themselves the constitutional judges of their own powers, and that the construction they put upon them is conclusive upon the other departments, it may be answered, that this cannot be the natural presumption, where it is not to be collected from any particular provisions in the Constitution. It is not otherwise to be supposed, that the Constitution could intend to enable the representatives of the people to substitute their *will* to that of their constituents. It is far more rational to suppose, that the courts were designed to be an intermediate body between the people and the legislature, in order, among other things, to keep the latter within the limits assigned to their authority. The interpretation of the laws is the proper and peculiar province of the courts. A constitution is, in fact, and must be regarded by the judges, as a fundamental law. It therefore belongs to them to ascertain its meaning, as well as the meaning of any particular act proceeding from the legislative body. If there should happen to be an irreconcilable variance between the two, that which has the superior obligation and validity ought, of course, to be preferred; or, in other words, the Constitution ought to be preferred to the statute, the intention of the people to the intention of their agents.

Nor does this conclusion by any means suppose a superiority of the judicial to the legislative power. It only supposes that the power of the people is superior to both; and that where the will of the legislature, declared in its statutes, stands in opposition to that of the people, declared in the Constitution, the judges ought to be governed by the latter rather than the former. They ought to regulate their decisions by the fundamental laws, rather than by those which are not fundamental....

This independence of the judges is equally requisite to guard the Constitution and the rights of individuals from the effects of those ill humors, which the arts of designing men, or the influence of particular conjunctures, sometimes disseminate among the people themselves, and which, though they speedily give place to better information, and more deliberate reflection, have a tendency, in the meantime, to occasion dangerous innovations in the government, and serious oppressions of the minor party in the community.

C. THE ROAD TO *MARBURY*

Federal courts reviewed both national and state legislation prior to *Marbury*. In *Hayburn's Case* (1792), three circuit courts held divergent views on an act of Congress that appointed federal judges to serve as commissioners for claims settlement. Their decisions could be set aside by the Secretary of War. One of the courts agreed to serve. The other two believed that

---

Supreme Court Justices Inquire: May We Void a Legislative Act?

JUSTICE CHASE. Without giving an opinion, at this time whether this Court has jurisdiction to decide that any law made by Congress, contrary to the Constitution of the *United States* is void; I am fully satisfied that this court has no *jurisdiction* to determine that any law of any state *Legislature,* contrary to the Constitution of such *state,* is void....

I am under a necessity to give a *construction,* or explanation of the words, "*ex post facto law,*" because they have not any certain meaning attached to them. But I will not go farther than I feel myself bound to do; and if I ever exercise the jurisdiction I will not decide *any law to be void, but in a very clear case.*

JUSTICE IREDELL. If any act of Congress, or of the Legislature of a state, violates those constitutional provisions, it is unquestionably void; though, I admit, that as the authority to declare it void is of delicate and awful nature, the Court will never resort to that authority, but in a clear and urgent case.

SOURCE: Calder v. Bull, 3 Dall. 386, 392, 395, 399 (1798).

---

the statute was "unwarranted" because it required federal judges to perform nonjudicial duties and to render what was essentially an advisory opinion. The Supreme Court postponed decision until the next term; by that time Congress had repealed the offending sections and removed the Secretary's authority to veto decisions rendered by judges. 2 Dall. 409 (1792); 1 Stat. 243 (1792) and 1 Stat. 324 (1793). In 1794, a year after Congress repaired the statute, the Supreme Court decided that the original statute would have been unconstitutional if it sought to place nonjudicial powers on the circuit courts. United States v. Yale Todd (not published until 1851; 13 How. 51). The use of this 1794 case as a precedent for judicial review is rendered suspect by the fact that the statutory provision no longer existed.

Between 1791 and 1799, federal courts began to challenge and strike down a number of state laws. 1 Charles Warren, The Supreme Court in United States History 65–69 (1937). With regard to national legislation, in *Hylton* v. *United States* (1796) the Supreme Court upheld a congressional statute that imposed a tax on carriages. If the Court had authority to uphold an act of Congress, presumably it had authority to strike one down. Justice Chase said it was unnecessary "*at this time,* for me to determine, whether this court, *constitutionally* possesses the power to declare an act of Congress *void*... but if the court have such power, I am free to declare, that I will never exercise it, *but in a very clear case.*" 3 Dall. 171, 175 (1796). Two years later the Court upheld the constitutionality of another congressional act, this time involving the process of constitutional amendment. Hollingsworth v. Virginia, 3 Dall. 378 (1798).

Three other cases between 1795 and 1800 explored the authority of federal judges to declare state acts unconstitutional. In the first case, a circuit court decided that a Pennsylvania law was unconstitutional and void. Vanhorne's Lessee v. Dorrance, 2 Dall. 304 (1795). In 1798, Supreme Court Justices offered differing views on the existence and scope of judicial review (see box). In the third case, Justice Chase said that even if it were agreed that a statute contrary to the Constitution would be void, "it still remains a question, where the power resides to declare it void?" The "general opinion," he said, is that the Supreme Court could declare an act of Congress unconstitutional, "but there is no adjudication of the Supreme Court itself upon the point." Cooper v. Telfair, 4 Dall. 14, 19 (1800).

From 1789 to 1802, eleven state judiciaries exercised judicial review over state statutes. Charles Grove Haines, The American Doctrine of Judicial Supremacy, at 148–64. The assertion of power by the national judiciary was much more cautious, and yet even the Jeffersonian Republicans rebuked the federal courts for not striking down the repressive Alien and Sedition Acts of 1798. 1 Warren, The Supreme Court in United States History, at 215. In that same year Jefferson looked to the courts to protect basic rights: "the laws of the land, administered by upright judges, would protect you from any exercise of power unauthorized by the Constitution of the United States." 10 Writings of Thomas Jefferson 61 (Memorial ed. 1903).

Marshall Court Foundations

By 1801 the Supreme Court had yet to solidify its position as a coequal branch of government. It had upheld the constitutionality of a congressional statute. In a series of dicta, it gingerly explored the theory that it could hold one unconstitutional. In four bold decisions from 1803 to 1821, the Court held that it had the power to determine the constitutionality of statutes passed by Congress and state legislatures, as well as authority to review judgments by state courts in cases raising federal questions.

The election of 1800 marked a pivotal point for the nation. Although formally neutral between Britain and France, America rapidly divided into two warring camps. The Federalist party was pro-British; the Jeffersonian Republicans sympathized with the French. Efforts by the Adams administration to limit Republican criticism led to the Alien and Sedition Acts, further exacerbating partisan strife. When the Jeffersonians swept the elections of 1800, the Federalists looked for ways to salvage their dwindling political power.

Early in 1801, with a few weeks remaining for the Federalist Congress, two bills were passed to create a number of federal judges and justices of the peace in the District of Columbia. 2 Stat. 89, 103 (1801). Within a matter of days, President Adams nominated Federalists to the new posts, much to the outrage of Republicans. John Marshall was at that point serving as Secretary of State, although he had already been appointed to the Supreme Court for the next term. The commissions of office were processed, sent to the Senate, and confirmed. Some of the commissions, William Marbury's among them, were never delivered.

Upon assuming the presidency, Thomas Jefferson ordered that the commissions be withheld. The administration also urged Congress to repeal the Circuit Court Act (with its additional judgeships) and to block the anticipated 1802 term of the Supreme Court. Congress complied. 2 Stat. 132, 156 (1802). Partisan bitterness increased in the spring of 1801 when two Federalist judges instructed a district attorney to prosecute a newspaper that had published an attack on the judiciary. The jury refused to indict, but the Republicans saw this as additional evidence that the Federalists were engaged in a national conspiracy.[4] As part of a counterattack, the House of Representatives impeached District Judge John Pickering (a Federalist), contemplated the removal of Justice Chase from the Supreme Court, and seemed poised to remove other Federalist judges, including John Marshall.

In this tense political climate, William Marbury and his colleagues appealed to the former Attorney General, Charles Lee, for legal assistance. Lee brought the action directly to the Supreme Court under Section 13 of the Judiciary Act of 1789, which empowered the Court to issue writs of mandamus "in cases warranted by the principles and usages of law, to any courts appointed, or persons holding office, under the authority of the United States." Lee argued that the Court had jurisdiction under Section 13 because Madison was a person holding office (Secretary of State) under the authority of the United States. He asked the Court to issue a writ of mandamus, ordering Madison to deliver the commissions.

Marshall's options were circumscribed by one overpowering fact: whatever technical

---

4. George Lee Haskins and Herbert A. Johnson, 2 History of the Supreme Court of the United States: Foundations of Power: John Marshall 161–62 (1981).

ground he might use to rule against the administration, any order directing Madison to deliver the commissions was sure to be ignored. If the Court's order could be dismissed with impunity, the judiciary's power and prestige would suffer greatly. As Chief Justice Burger noted: "The Court could stand hard blows, but not ridicule, and the ale house would rock with hilarious laughter" had Marshall issued a mandamus ignored by Jefferson.[5] Marshall chose a tactic he used in future years. He would appear to absorb a short-term defeat in exchange for a long-term victory. The decision has been called "a masterwork of indirection, a brilliant example of Marshall's capacity to sidestep danger while seeking to court it, to advance in one direction while his opponents are looking in another." Robert G. McCloskey, The American Supreme Court 40 (1960).

The opinion acknowledged the merits of Marbury's case but denied that the Court had power to issue the mandamus. Through a strained reading, Marshall concluded that Section 13 expanded the original jurisdiction of the Court and thereby violated Article III of the Constitution. He maintained that Congress could alter the boundaries only of appellate jurisdiction. Announcing that the statute conflicted with the Constitution and that judges take an oath of office to support the Constitution, Marshall claimed that the power of constitutional interpretation was vested in the judiciary. MARBURY v. MADISON, 5 U.S. (1 Cr.) 137 (1803).

The decision in *Marbury* has stimulated a number of critiques. Marshall's analysis of original and appellate jurisdiction is less than compelling. He could have read Section 13 to connect mandamus action to appellate jurisdiction. Even if he related it to original jurisdiction, the Constitution did not explicitly prohibit Congress from adding to original jurisdiction. Furthermore, if the Court did indeed lack jurisdiction, why did Marshall reach further and explore the merits of Marbury's claim and expound on novel questions of judicial authority? Finally, given his previous involvement in the matter, there was strong reason for Marshall to disqualify himself (see reading by Van Alstyne).

Encircled by hostile political forces, Marshall decided that it was time to strike boldly for judicial independence. Instead of citing historical and legal precedents, all of which could have been challenged and picked apart by his opponents, Marshall reached to a higher plane and grounded his case on what appeared to be self-evident, universal principles. His decision seems to march logically and inexorably toward the only possible conclusion. *Marbury v. Madison* is famous for the proposition that the Court is supreme on constitutional questions, but it stands for a much more modest claim. Chief Justice Marshall stated that it is "emphatically the province and duty of the judicial department to say what the law is." 5 U.S. (1 Cr.) 137, 177 (1803). So it is, but the same can be said for Congress. Surely it is the province and duty of Congress to say what the law is. Moreover, the Court was not sufficiently powerful in 1803 to dictate to Congress or to the President.

Did Marshall believe that the Court was supreme on questions of constitutionality? Probably not. His behavior during the impeachment hearings of Judge Pickering and Justice Chase suggest that he was quite willing to share constitutional interpretations with the coequal branches. *Marbury* was issued on February 24, 1803. The House impeached Pickering on March 2, 1803, and the Senate convicted him on March 12, 1804. As soon as the House had impeached Pickering, it turned its guns on Chase. Under these precarious circumstances, Marshall wrote to Chase on January 23, 1805, suggesting that members of Congress did not have to impeach judges whenever they objected to their judicial opinions. Instead, Congress could simply review and reverse objectionable decisions through the legislative process. Marshall's

---

5. Warren E. Burger, "The Doctrine of Judicial Review: Mr. Marshall, Mr. Jefferson, and Mr. Marbury," in Mark W. Cannon and David M. O'Brien, eds., Views From the Bench 14 (1985).

Marshall Writes to Chase

Jan. 23, 1805

My dear Sir

. . .

Admitting it to be true that on legal principles Colo. Taylors testimony was admissible, it certainly constitutes a very extraordinary ground for an impeachment. According to the antient doctrine a jury finding a verdict against the law of the case was liable to an attaint; & the amount of the present doctrine seems to be that a Judge giving a legal opinion contrary to the opinion of the legislature is liable to impeachment.

As, for convenience & humanity the old doctrine of attaint has yielded to the silent, moderate but not less operative influence of new trials, I think the modern doctrine of impeachment should yield to an appellate jurisdiction in the legislature. A reversal of those legal opinions deemed unsound by the legislature would certainly better comport with the mildness of our character than [*would*] a removal of the Judge who has rendered them unknowing of his fault.

. . .

J. Marshall

SOURCE: 3 Albert J. Beveridge, The Life of John Marshall 177 (1919). Marshall dated the letter January 23, 1804, but modern scholarship fixes the date a year later; 6 The Papers of John Marshall 348 n.1 (Hobson ed. 1990). Like the rest of us, Marshall forgot to switch to the new year.

---

letter to Chase is somewhat ambiguous. He could have been referring to reversals of statutory interpretation, not constitutional interpretation, but given the temper of the times the latter seems more likely (see box).

Developments after *Marbury*

The power to strike down unconstitutional actions by coordinate branches of government was not used again until 1857, in *Dred Scott* v. *Sandford*, 60 U.S. (19 How.) 393. Judicial review of state actions, however, was more frequent. In two sets of decisions, the Court established its authority to review state statutes and state judicial decisions.

United States v. *Peters* (1809) and *Fletcher* v. *Peck* (1810) were decided in a difficult political period. Some states, reacting against the growth of national power, threatened secession and nullification. Richard Peters, a federal judge in Pennsylvania, was unable to compel state officials to obey a decree he had issued. The state legislature passed a law declaring the decree a usurpation of power and ordered the governor to resist any attempt to enforce it. Marshall then issued a mandamus ordering enforcement on the ground that state legislatures cannot interfere with the operation of the federal judicial process. 9 U.S. (5 Cr.) 115 (1809). The governor called out the militia to prevent a federal marshal from executing the court order. He also sought President Madison's assistance, but the state's resistance collapsed when Madison replied that the President "is not only unauthorized to prevent the execution of a decree sanctioned by the Supreme Court of the United States, but is expressly enjoined, by statute, to carry into effect any such decree where opposition may be made to it." Annals of Congress, 11th Cong. 2269.

In *Fletcher* v. *Peck* (1810), the Court struck down an act of a state legislature as unconstitutional. Several land companies had obtained a huge land grant at a bargain price from the Georgia legislature, offering bribes to a number of legislators. After elections, the new legislature revoked the land grant. In the meantime, innocent third parties had bought property from the corrupt land companies. Some of the purchasers challenged the revocation, claiming impairment of the obligations of a contract protected by Article I, Section 10, of the Constitution. Justice Marshall, recognizing the delicate task of reviewing state legislation, concluded that the revocation did constitute a violation of the Impairments Clause. 10 U.S. (6 Cr.) 87, 136–39 (1810) (see reading in Chapter 9).

A second pair of cases was decided after the War of 1812, following a substantial change in the Supreme Court's membership. The most important addition was Joseph Story. Though appointed by James Madison, he became as ardent a defender of national interests as Marshall. He wrote the decision that established the Court's authority to review state court decisions involving federal questions. MARTIN v. HUNTER'S LESSEE, 1 Wheat. 304 (1816). The dispute in *Martin* was between two private parties. In 1821, with a state as one of the parties, Marshall solidified the relationship of the Court to state courts and breathed new life into the Supremacy Clause. COHENS v. VIRGINIA, 6 Wheat. 264 (1821).

Marbury v. Madison

5 U.S. (1 Cr.) 137 (1803)

William Marbury and several colleagues were nominated by President John Adams to be justices of the peace in the District of Columbia. The Senate confirmed their names. Adams signed their commissions, and the seal of the United States was affixed to the commissions. However, in the confusion of the remaining days of the Adams administration, some of the commissions, including Marbury's, were not delivered. When President Thomas Jefferson entered office, he ordered that the commissions not be delivered. Marbury sued the Secretary of State, James Madison. The opinion in this case is written by Chief Justice John Marshall.

Opinion of the Court.

At the last term on the affidavits then read and filed with the clerk, a rule was granted in this case, requiring the secretary of state to show cause why a *mandamus* should not issue, directing him to deliver to William Marbury his commission as a justice of the peace for the county of Washington, in the district of Columbia.

No cause has been shown, and the present motion is for a *mandamus*. The peculiar delicacy of this case, the novelty of some of its circumstances, and the real difficulty attending the points which occur in it, require a complete exposition of the principles on which the opinion to be given by the court is founded.

. . .

The first object of inquiry is,

1st. Has the applicant a right to the commission he demands?

. . .

It appears, from the affidavits, that . . . a commission for William Marbury, as a justice of peace for the county of Washington, was signed by John Adams, then President of the United States; after which the seal of the United States was affixed to

it; but the commission has never reached the person for whom it was made out. . . .

The last act to be done by the president is the signature of the commission. He has then acted on the advice and consent of the senate to his own nomination. The time for deliberation has then passed. He has decided. His judgment, on the advice and consent of the senate concurring with his nomination, has been made, and the officer is appointed. This appointment is evidenced by an open, unequivocal act; and being the last act required from the person making it, necessarily excludes the idea of its being, so far as respects the appointment, an inchoate and incomplete transaction. . . .

The commission being signed, the subsequent duty of the secretary of state is prescribed by law, and not to be guided by the will of the president. He is to affix the seal of the United States to the commission, and is to record it.

This is not a proceeding which may be varied, if the judgment of the executive shall suggest one more eligible; but is a precise course accurately marked out by law, and is to be strictly pursued. It is the duty of the secretary of state to conform to the law, and in this he is an officer of the United States, bound to obey the laws. He acts, in this respect, as has been very properly stated at the bar, under the authority of law, and not by the instructions of the president. It is a ministerial act which the law enjoins on a particular officer for a particular purpose....

Mr. Marbury, then, since his commission was signed by the president, and sealed by the secretary of state, was appointed; and as the law creating the office, gave the officer a right to hold for five years, independent of the executive, the appointment was not revocable, but vested in the officer legal rights, which are protected by the laws of his country.

To withhold his commission, therefore, is an act deemed by the court not warranted by law, but violative of a vested legal right.

This brings us to the second inquiry; which is,

2dly, If he has a right, and that right has been violated, do the laws of his country afford him a remedy?

The very essence of civil liberty certainly consists in the right of every individual to claim the protection of the laws, whenever he receives an injury. One of the first duties of government is to afford that protection....

The government of the United States has been emphatically termed a government of laws, and not of men. It will certainly cease to deserve this high appellation, if the laws furnish no remedy for the violation of a vested legal right....

By the constitution of the United States, the president is invested with certain important political powers, in the exercise of which he is to use his own discretion, and is accountable only to his country in his political character and to his own conscience. To aid him in the performance of these duties, he is authorized to appoint certain officers, who act by his authority, and in conformity with his orders.

In such cases, their acts are his acts; and whatever opinion may be entertained of the manner in which executive discretion may be used, still there exists, and can exist, no power to control that discretion. The subjects are political. They respect the nation, not individual rights, and being intrusted to the executive, the decision of the executive is conclusive.... The acts of such an officer, as an officer, can never be examinable by the courts.

But when the legislature proceeds to impose on that officer other duties; when he is directed peremptorily to perform certain acts; when the rights of individuals are dependent on the performance of those acts; he is so far the officer of the law; is amenable to the laws for his conduct; and cannot at his discretion sport away the vested rights of others.

The conclusion from this reasoning is, that

where the heads of departments are the political or confidential agents of the executive, merely to execute the will of the president, or rather to act in cases in which the executive possesses a constitutional or legal discretion, nothing can be more perfectly clear than that their acts are only politically examinable. But where a specific duty is assigned by law, and individual rights depend upon the performance of that duty, it seems equally clear that the individual who considers himself injured, has a right to resort to the laws of his country for a remedy....

The question whether a right has vested or not, is, in its nature, judicial, and must be tried by the judicial authority....

It is, then, the opinion of the court,

1st. That by signing the commission of Mr. Marbury, the President of the United States appointed him a justice of peace for the county of Washington, in the district of Columbia; and that the seal of the United States, affixed thereto by the secretary of state, is conclusive testimony of the verity of the signature, and of the completion of the appointment; and that the appointment conferred on him a legal right to the office for the space of five years.

2dly. That, having this legal title to the office, he has a consequent right to the commission; a refusal to deliver which is a plain violation of that right, for which the laws of his country afford him a remedy.

It remains to be inquired whether,

3dly. He is entitled to the remedy for which he applies. This depends on,

1st. The nature of the writ applied for; and,

2dly. The power of this court.

1st. The nature of the writ.

Blackstone, in the 3d volume of his Commentaries, page 110, defines a *mandamus* to be "a command issuing in the king's name from the court of king's bench, and directed to any person, corporation, or inferior court of judicature within the king's dominions, requiring them to do some particular thing therein specified, which appertains to their office and duty, and which the court of king's bench has previously determined, or at least supposes, to be consonant to right and justice." ...

Still, to render the *mandamus* a proper remedy, the officer to whom it is to be directed, must be one to whom, on legal principles, such writ may be directed; and the person applying for it must be without any other specific and legal remedy.

1st. With respect to the officer to whom it would be directed. The intimate political relation subsisting between the President of the United States and the heads of departments, necessarily renders any legal investigation of the acts of one of those high officers peculiarly irksome, as well as delicate; and excites some hesitation with respect to the propriety of entering into such investigation. [*Judicial inquiry may*] be considered by some, as an attempt to intrude into the cabinet, and to intermeddle with the prerogatives of the executive.

It is scarcely necessary for the court to disclaim all pretensions to such a jurisdiction. An extravagance, so absurd and excessive, could not have been entertained for a moment. The province of the court is, solely, to decide on the rights of individuals, not to inquire how the executive, or executive officers, perform duties in which they have a discretion. Questions in their nature political, or which are, by the constitution and laws, submitted to the executive, can never be made in this court....

This, then, is a plain case for a *mandamus,* either to deliver the commission, or a copy of it from the record; and it only remains to be inquired,

Whether it can issue from this court.

The act to establish the judicial courts of the United States authorizes the supreme court "to issue writs of *mandamus,* in cases warranted by the principles and usages of law, to any courts appointed, or persons holding office, under the authority of the United States."

The secretary of state, being a person holding an office under the authority of the United States, is precisely within the letter of the description; and if this court is not authorized to issue a writ of *mandamus* to such an officer, it must be because the law is unconstitutional, and therefore absolutely incapable of conferring the authority, and assigning the duties which its words purport to confer and assign.

The constitution vests the whole judicial power of the United States in one supreme court, and such inferior courts as congress shall, from time to time, ordain and establish. This power is expressly extended to all cases arising under the laws of the United States; and, consequently, in some form, may be exercised over the present case; because the right claimed is given by a law of the United States.

In the distribution of this power it is declared that "the supreme court shall have original jurisdiction in all cases affecting ambassadors, other public ministers and consuls, and those in which a state shall be a party. In all other cases, the supreme court shall have appellate jurisdiction."

It has been insisted, at the bar, that as the orig-

inal grant of jurisdiction, to the supreme and inferior courts, is general, and the clause, assigning original jurisdiction to the supreme court, contains no negative or restrictive words, the power remains to the legislature, to assign original jurisdiction to that court in other cases than those specified in the article which has been recited; provided those cases belong to the judicial power of the United States.

If it had been intended to leave it in the discretion of the legislature to apportion the judicial power between the supreme and inferior courts according to the will of that body, it would certainly have been useless to have proceeded further than to have defined the judicial power, and the tribunals in which it should be vested. The subsequent part of the section is mere surplusage, is entirely without meaning, if such is to be the construction. If congress remains at liberty to give this court appellate jurisdiction, where the constitution has declared their jurisdiction shall be original; and original jurisdiction where the constitution has declared it shall be appellate; the distribution of jurisdiction, made in the constitution, is form without substance.

Affirmative words are often, in their operation, negative of other objects than those affirmed; and in this case, a negative or exclusive sense must be given to them, or they have no operation at all.

It cannot be presumed that any clause in the constitution is intended to be without effect; and, therefore, such a construction is inadmissible, unless the words require it.

If the solicitude of the convention, respecting our peace with foreign powers, induced a provision that the supreme court should take original jurisdiction in cases which might be supposed to affect them; yet the clause would have proceeded no further than to provide for such cases, if no further restriction on the powers of congress had been intended. That they should have appellate jurisdiction in all other cases, with such exceptions as congress might make, is no restriction; unless the words be deemed exclusive of original jurisdiction.

When an instrument organizing fundamentally a judicial system, divides it into one supreme, and so many inferior courts as the legislature may ordain and establish; then enumerates its powers, and proceeds so far to distribute them, as to define the jurisdiction of the supreme court by declaring the cases in which it shall take original jurisdiction, and that in others it shall take appellate jurisdiction; the plain import of the words seems to be, that in one class of cases its jurisdiction is original, and not appellate; in the other it is appellate, and not original. If any other construction would render the clause inoperative, that is an additional reason for rejecting such other construction, and for adhering to their obvious meaning.

To enable this court, then, to issue a *mandamus*, it must be shown to be an exercise of appellate jurisdiction, or to be necessary to enable them to exercise appellate jurisdiction.

It has been stated at the bar that the appellate jurisdiction may be exercised in a variety of forms, and that if it be the will of the legislature that a *mandamus* should be used for that purpose, that will must be obeyed. This is true, yet the jurisdiction must be appellate, not original.

It is the essential criterion of appellate jurisdiction, that it revises and corrects the proceedings in a cause already instituted, and does not create that cause. Although, therefore, a *mandamus* may be directed to courts, yet to issue such a writ to an officer for the delivery of a paper, is in effect the same as to sustain an original action for that paper, and, therefore, seems not to belong to appellate, but to original jurisdiction. Neither is it necessary in such a case as this, to enable the court to exercise its appellate jurisdiction.

The authority, therefore, given to the supreme court, by the act establishing the judicial courts of the United States, to issue writs of *mandamus* to public officers, appears not to be warranted by the constitution; and it becomes necessary to inquire whether a jurisdiction so conferred can be exercised.

The question, whether an act, repugnant to the constitution, can become the law of the land, is a question deeply interesting to the United States; but, happily, not of an intricacy proportioned to its interest. It seems only necessary to recognise certain principles, supposed to have been long and well established, to decide it.

That the people have an original right to establish, for their future government, such principles as, in their opinion, shall most conduce to their own happiness is the basis on which the whole American fabric has been erected. The exercise of this original right is a very great exertion; nor can it, nor ought it, to be frequently repeated. The principles, therefore, so established, are deemed fundamental. And as the authority from which they proceed is supreme, and can seldom act, they are designed to be permanent.

This original and supreme will organizes the government, and assigns to different departments their respective powers. It may either stop here, or establish certain limits not to be transcended by those departments.

The government of the United States is of the latter description. The powers of the legislature are defined and limited; and that those limits may not be mistaken, or forgotten, the constitution is written. To what purpose are powers limited, and to what purpose is that limitation committed to writing, if these limits may, at any time, be passed by those intended to be restrained? The distinction between a government with limited and unlimited powers is abolished, if those limits do not confine the persons on whom they are imposed, and if acts prohibited and acts allowed, are of equal obligation. It is a proposition too plain to be contested, that the constitution controls any legislative act repugnant to it; or, that the legislature may alter the constitution by an ordinary act.

Between these alternatives there is no middle ground. The constitution is either a superior paramount law, unchangeable by ordinary means, or it is on a level with ordinary legislative acts, and, like other acts, is alterable when the legislature shall please to alter it.

If the former part of the alternative be true, then a legislative act contrary to the constitution is not law: if the latter part be true, then written constitutions are absurd attempts, on the part of the people, to limit a power in its own nature illimitable.

Certainly all those who have framed written constitutions contemplate them as forming the fundamental and paramount law of the nation, and, consequently, the theory of every such government must be, that an act of the legislature, repugnant to the constitution, is void.

This theory is essentially attached to a written constitution, and, is consequently, to be considered, by this court, as one of the fundamental principles of our society. It is not therefore to be lost sight of in the further consideration of this subject.

If an act of the legislature, repugnant to the constitution, is void, does it, notwithstanding its invalidity, bind the courts, and oblige them to give it effect? Or, in other words, though it be not law, does it constitute a rule as operative as if it was a law? This would be to overthrow in fact what was established in theory; and would seem, at first view, an absurdity too gross to be insisted on. It shall, however, receive a more attentive consideration.

It is emphatically the province and duty of the judicial department to say what the law is. Those who apply the rule to particular cases, must of necessity expound and interpret that rule. If two laws conflict with each other, the courts must decide on the operation of each.

So if a law be in opposition to the constitution; if both the law and the constitution apply to a particular case, so that the court must either decide that case conformably to the law, disregarding the constitution; or conformably to the constitution, disregarding the law; the court must determine which of these conflicting rules governs the case. This is of the very essence of judicial duty.

If, then, the courts are to regard the constitution, and the constitution is superior to any ordinary act of the legislature, the constitution, and not such ordinary act, must govern the case to which they both apply.

Those, then, who controvert the principle that the constitution is to be considered, in court, as a paramount law, are reduced to the necessity of maintaining that courts must close their eyes on the constitution, and see only the law.

This doctrine would subvert the very foundation of all written constitutions. It would declare that an act which, according to the principles and theory of our government, is entirely void, is yet, in practice, completely obligatory. It would declare that if the legislature shall do what is expressly forbidden, such act, notwithstanding the express prohibition, is in reality effectual. It would be giving to the legislature a practical and real omnipotence, with the same breath which professes to restrict their powers within narrow limits. It is prescribing limits, and declaring that those limits may be passed at pleasure.

That it thus reduces to nothing what we have deemed the greatest improvement on political institutions, a written constitution, would of itself be sufficient, in America, where written constitutions have been viewed with so much reverence, for rejecting the construction. But the peculiar expressions of the constitution of the United States furnish additional arguments in favour of its rejection.

The judicial power of the United States is extended to all cases arising under the constitution.

Could it be the intention of those who gave this power, to say that in using it the constitution should not be looked into? That a case arising under the constitution should be decided without examining the instrument under which it arises?

This is too extravagant to be maintained.

In some cases, then, the constitution must be looked into by the judges. And if they can open it at all, what part of it are they forbidden to read or to obey?

There are many other parts of the constitution which serve to illustrate this subject.

It is declared that "no tax or duty shall be laid on articles exported from any state." Suppose a duty on the export of cotton, of tobacco, or of flour; and a suit instituted to recover it. Ought judgment to be rendered in such a case? ought the judges to close their eyes on the constitution, and only see the law?

The constitution declares "that no bill of attainder or *ex post facto* law shall be passed."

If, however, such a bill should be passed, and a person should be prosecuted under it; must the court condemn to death those victims whom the constitution endeavours to preserve?

"No person," says the constitution, "shall be convicted of treason unless on the testimony of two witnesses to the same overt act, or on confession in open court."

Here the language of the constitution is addressed especially to the courts. It prescribes, directly for them, a rule of evidence not to be departed from. If the legislature should change that rule, and declare *one* witness, or a confession *out* of court, sufficient for conviction, must the constitutional principle yield to the legislative act?

From these, and many other selections which might be made, it is apparent, that the framers of the constitution contemplated that instrument as a rule for the government of *courts,* as well as of the legislature.

Why otherwise does it direct the judges to take an oath to support it? This oath certainly applies in an especial manner, to their conduct in their official character. How immoral to impose it on them, if they were to be used as the instruments, and the knowing instruments, for violating what they swear to support!

The oath of office, too, imposed by the legislature, is completely demonstrative of the legislative opinion on this subject. It is in these words: "I do solemnly swear that I will administer justice without respect to persons, and do equal right to the poor and to the rich; and that I will faithfully and impartially discharge all the duties incumbent on me as   , according to the best of my abilities and understanding, agreeably to *the constitution* and laws of the United States."

Why does a judge swear to discharge his duties agreeably to the constitution of the United States, if that constitution forms no rule for his government? if it is closed upon him, and cannot be inspected by him?

If such be the real state of things, this is worse

than solemn mockery. To prescribe, or, to take this oath, becomes equally a crime.

It is also not entirely unworthy of observation, that in declaring what shall be the *supreme* law of the land, the *constitution* itself is first mentioned; and not the laws of the United States generally, but those only which shall be made in *pursuance* of the constitution, have that rank.

Thus, the particular phraseology of the constitution of the United States confirms and strengthens the principle, supposed to be essential to all written constitutions, that a law repugnant to the constitution is void; and that *courts,* as well as other departments, are bound by that instrument.

The rule must be discharged.

William W. Van Alstyne
A Critical Guide to *Marbury* v. *Madison*

The Court declares that the "first" issue presented by the case is: "Has the applicant a right to the commission he demands?" At least two criticisms of this beginning have been made. Both arise in answer to the question: Was Marbury's entitlement to the commission he demanded really the issue which the Court should have examined first? Arguably, it was not.

Surely the Court ought first determine whether it has any authority to decide any issues whatever respecting the merits of the case, *i.e.,* it should first resolve the preliminary question of its own jurisdiction. The Court's jurisdiction was ostensibly based on section 13 of the Judiciary Act of 1789 which Marbury alleged to empower the Court to issue a writ of mandamus in this sort of case. But if the Act did not in fact provide for such jurisdiction, or if it were invalid in attempting to provide for such jurisdiction, the Court would be without proper authority to consider the merits of Marbury's claim. . . .

. . . [T]here is clearly an "issue" of sorts which preceded any of those touched upon in the opinion. Specifically, it would appear that Marshall should have recused himself in view of his substantial involvement in the background of this controversy. Remember, too, that the Court thought it important to establish whether Marbury's commission had already been signed and sealed before it was withdrawn — to determine whether Marbury's interest had "vested" and whether Madison was refusing to carry out a merely ministerial duty, or whether the commission was sufficiently incomplete that matters of executive discretion were involved. Proof of the status of Marbury's commission not only involved circumstances within the Chief Justice's personal

knowledge, it was furnished in the Supreme Court by Marshall's own younger brother who had been with him in his office when, as Secretary of State, he had made out the commissions. Arguably the first issue, then, was the appropriateness of Marshall's participation in the decision.

MARBURY'S "RIGHT" TO THE COMMISSION

On the basis of the Act of 1801 providing for the appointment of justices of the peace for a five-year term plus findings of fact that the appointment had "vested," the Court held that Marbury had a "right" to the commission. The Act itself was based on the power of Congress granted by the Constitution in Article I, section 8, clause 17, "to exercise Legislation in all Cases whatsoever, over" the District of Columbia. Marshall concludes that once the commission had been signed and sealed by President Adams, Marbury's claim to the office was complete.

Marshall reasonably could have concluded, however, that no interest actually "vested" in Marbury prior to actual delivery of the commission. Jefferson evidently thought that the better conclusion, subsequently insisting that Marshall's decision on this point was a "perversion of law," and maintaining that "if there is any principle of law never yet contradicted, it is that delivery is one of the essentials to the validity of the deed." Even if Jefferson overstated the law, and even assuming authority could be found urging that certain interests "vest" prior to delivery, it would not necessarily be dispositive of this case. The Court is reviewing an aspect of executive power and passing judgment upon the propriety of conduct by a coordinate branch of government here, a consideration not present in an ordinary civil suit between private litigants. . . .

SOURCE: 1969 Duke L. J. 1. Footnotes omitted.

STATUTORY INTERPRETATION

Certainly the first question is the following one of statutory interpretation which was just barely treated in the opinion: Did section 13 of the Judiciary Act authorize this action to originate in the Supreme Court? The section provides:

"And be it further enacted, That the Supreme Court shall have exclusive jurisdiction of all controversies of a civil nature, where a state is a party, except between a state and its citizens; and except also between a state and citizens of other states, or aliens, in which latter case it shall have original but not exclusive jurisdiction. And shall have exclusively all such jurisdiction of suits or proceedings against ambassadors, or other public ministers, or their domestics, or domestic servants, as a court of law can have or exercise consistently with the law of nations; and original, but not exclusive jurisdiction of all suits brought by ambassadors, or other public ministers, or in which a consul, or vice consul, shall be a party. And the trial of issues in fact in the Supreme Court, in all actions at law against citizens of the United States, shall be by jury. The Supreme Court shall also have appellate jurisdiction from the circuit courts and courts of the several states, in the cases herein after specially provided for; and shall have power to issue writs of prohibition to the district courts, when proceeding as courts of admiralty and maritime jurisdiction, and writs of *mandamus,* in cases warranted by the principles and usages of law, to any courts appointed, or persons holding office, under the authority of the United States."*

Marshall quotes only the fragment at the end, perfunctorily notes that Madison holds office under the authority of the United States and therefore "is precisely within the letter of the description," and since he has already established that mandamus would otherwise be an appropriate remedy he quickly concludes that section 13 purports to authorize this case. But there is no discussion of whether this section *confers* original jurisdiction over suits seeking mandamus against persons holding office under the authority of the United States, or whether it merely authorizes mandamus to be so employed by the Court in cases properly *on appeal* or in aid of its original jurisdiction in cases involving foreign ministers or states. If it means only the latter, and if Marbury has no other basis for commencing his case in the Supreme Court, then the Court should simply dismiss the case for want of (statutory) jurisdiction and it need not, and ought not,

examine the constitutionality of section 13 under some other construction. An argument can be made, of course, that section 13 did not attempt to grant original jurisdiction in Marbury's case.

The section opens by describing the Court's original jurisdiction and then moves on to describe appellate jurisdiction ("hereinafter specially provided for"). Textually, the provision regarding mandamus says nothing expressly as to whether it is part of original or appellate jurisdiction or both, and the clause itself does not speak at all of "conferring jurisdiction" on the court. The grant of "power" to issue the writ, however, is juxtaposed with the section of appellate jurisdiction and, in fact, follows the general description of appellate jurisdiction in the same sentence, being separated only by a semicolon. No textual mangling is required to confine it to appellate jurisdiction. Moreover, no mangling is required even if it attaches both to original and to appellate jurisdiction, not as an enlargement of either, but simply as a specification of power which the Court is authorized to use in cases which are *otherwise* appropriately under consideration. Since this case is not otherwise within the specified type of original jurisdiction (*e.g.,* it is not a case in which a state is a party or a case against an ambassador), it should be dismissed....

JUDICIAL REVIEW

Assuming that section 13 of the Judiciary Act of 1789 does confer original jurisdiction in this case, is its constitutionality subject to judicial review? Marshall initially responds to this question, which, of course, is the issue which has made the case of historic importance, by posing his own rhetorical question: "whether an Act repugnant to the Constitution can become the law of the land." That it cannot is clear, he says, from the following considerations.

The people in an exercise of their "original right," established the government pursuant to a written constitution which defines and limits the powers of the legislature. A "legislative act contrary to the constitution is not law," therefore, as it is contrary to the original and supreme will which organized the legislature itself.

. . .

That the Constitution is a "written" one yields little or nothing as to whether acts of Congress may be given the force of positive law notwithstanding the opinion of judges, the executive, a minority or majority of the population, or even of

Congress itself (assuming that Congress might sometimes be pressed by political forces to adopt a law against its belief that it lacked power to do so) that such Acts are repugnant to the Constitution. That this is so is clear enough simply from the fact that even in Marshall's time (and to a great extent today), a number of nations maintained written constitutions and yet gave national legislative acts the full force of positive law without providing any constitutional check to guarantee the compatibility of those acts with their constitutions.

This observation, moreover, leads to the conclusion that Marshall presents a false dilemma in insisting that "[t]he constitution is *either* a superior paramount law, unchangeable by ordinary means, *or* it is on a level with ordinary legislative acts, and, like other acts, is alterable when the legislature shall please to alter it." Remember, the question he has posed is "whether an Act repugnant to the Constitution can become the law of the land." The question is not whether Congress can alter the Constitution by means other than those provided by Article V, and the case raises no issue concerning an alteration of any provision in the Constitution. We may assume that Congress cannot, by simple act, alter the Constitution and still we may maintain that an act which the Court or someone else *believes* to be repugnant to the Constitution shall be given the full force of positive law until repealed. Again, this is the situation which prevails in many other countries, and no absurdity is felt to exist where such a condition obtains.

. . .

Martin v. Hunter's Lessee

14 U.S. (1 Wheat.) 304 (1816)

A state district court upheld Martin's land claim, which was based on a treaty between America and Great Britain. The Virginia Court of Appeals, the highest court in that state, regarded the issue as solely one of state law and reversed the district court. The conflict escalated when the U.S. Supreme Court set aside the state ruling and the state court refused to obey. The Virginia Court of Appeals claimed that the Supreme Court had no authority to review its judgment, and to the extent that Section 25 of the Judiciary Act of 1789 attempted to extend the appellate jurisdiction of the Supreme Court to the state courts, the statute was unconstitutional. Chief Justice Marshall did not participate since he had earlier served as attorney for one of the parties.

STORY, J., delivered the opinion of the court.

. . .

The constitution of the United States was ordained and established, not by the states in their sovereign capacities, but emphatically, as the preamble of the constitution declares, by "the People of the United States." There can be no doubt, that it was competent to the people to invest the general government with all the powers which they might deem proper and necessary; to extend or restrain these powers according to their own good pleasure, and to give them a paramount and supreme authority. As little doubt can there be, that the people had a right to prohibit to the states the exercise of any powers which were, in their judgment, incompatible with the objects of the general compact; to make the powers of the state governments, in given cases, subordinate to those of the nation, or to reserve to themselves those sovereign authorities which they might not choose to delegate to either. The constitution was not, therefore, necessarily carved out of existing state sovereignties, nor a surrender of powers already existing in state institutions, for the powers of the states depend upon their own constitutions; and the people of every state had the right to modify and restrain them, according to their own views of policy or principle. On the other hand, it is perfectly clear, that the sovereign powers vested in the state governments, by their respective constitutions, remained unaltered and unimpaired, except so far as they were granted to the government of the United States....

...The constitution was for a new government, organized with new substantive powers, and not a mere supplementary charter to a government already existing. The confederation was a compact between states; and its structure and powers were wholly unlike those of the national government.

The constitution was an act of the people of the United States to supersede the confederation, and not to be engrafted on it, as a stock through which it was to receive life and nourishment....

This leads us to the consideration of the great question, as to the nature and extent of the appellate jurisdiction of the United States. We have already seen, that appellate jurisdiction is given by the constitution to the supreme court, in all cases where it has not original jurisdiction; subject, however, to such exceptions and regulations as congress may prescribe. It is, therefore, capable of embracing every case enumerated in the constitution, which is not exclusively to be decided by way of original jurisdiction. But the exercise of appellate jurisdiction is far from being limited, by the terms of the constitution, to the supreme court....

As, then, by the terms of the constitution, the appellate jurisdiction is not limited as to the supreme court, and as to this court, it may be exercised in all other cases than those of which it has original cognisance, what is there to restrain its exercise over state tribunals, in the enumerated cases? The appellate power is not limited by the terms of the third article to any particular courts. The words are, "the judicial power (which includes appellate power) shall extend to all cases," &c., and "in all other cases before mentioned the supreme court shall have appellate jurisdiction." It is the case, then, and not the court, that gives the jurisdiction....

If the constitution meant to limit the appellate jurisdiction to cases pending in the courts of the United States, it would necessarily follow, that the jurisdiction of these courts would, in all the cases enumerated in the constitution, be exclusive of state tribunals. How, otherwise, could the jurisdiction extend to *all* cases arising under the constitution, laws and treaties of the United States, or to *all* cases of admiralty and maritime jurisdiction? If some of these cases might be entertained by state tribunals, and no appellate jurisdiction as to them should exist, then the appellate power would not extend to *all,* but to *some,* cases....

But it is plain, that the framers of the constitution did contemplate that cases within the judicial cognisance of the United States, not only might, but would, arise in the state courts, in the exercise of their ordinary jurisdiction. With this view, the sixth article declares, that "this constitution, and the laws of the United States which shall be made in pursuance thereof, and all treaties made, or which shall be made, under the authority of the United States, shall be the supreme law of the land,

and the judges in every state shall be bound thereby, anything in the constitution or laws of any state to the contrary notwithstanding." It is obvious, that this obligation is imperative upon the state judges, in their official, and not merely in their private, capacities. From the very nature of their judicial duties, they would be called upon to pronounce the law applicable to the case in judgment. They were not to decide merely according to the laws or constitution of the state, but according to the constitution, laws and treaties of the United States — "the supreme law of the land." ...

. . .

It has been argued, that such an appellate jurisdiction over state courts is inconsistent with the genius of our governments, and the spirit of the constitution. That the latter was never designed to act upon state sovereignties, but only upon the people, and that if the power exists, it will materially impair the sovereignty of the states, and the independence of their courts. We cannot yield to the force of this reasoning; it assumes principles which we cannot admit, and draws conclusions to which we do not yield our assent.

...The courts of the United States can, without question, revise the proceedings of the executive and legislative authorities of the states, and if they are found to be contrary to the constitution, may declare them to be of no legal validity. Surely, the exercise of the same right over judicial tribunals is not a higher or more dangerous act of sovereign power.

Nor can such a right be deemed to impair the independence of state judges. It is assuming the very ground in controversy, to assert that they possess an absolute independence of the United States. In respect to the powers granted to the United States, they are not independent; they are expressly bound to obedience, by the letter of the constitution; and if they should unintentionally transcend their authority, or misconstrue the constitution, there is no more reason for giving their judgments an absolute and irresistible force, than for giving it to the acts of the other co-ordinate departments of state sovereignty....

It is further argued, that no great public mischief can result from a construction which shall limit the appellate power of the United States to cases in their own courts: first, because state judges are bound by an oath to support the constitution of the United States, and must be presumed to be men of learning and integrity; and secondly, because congress must have an unquestionable right [to] remove all cases within the scope of the judicial power from the state courts to the courts of the United States, at any time before final judgment, though not after final judgment. As to the first reason — admitting that the judges of the state courts are, and always will be, of as much learning, integrity and wisdom, as those of the courts of the United States (which we very cheerfully admit), it does not aid the argument. It is manifest, that the constitution has proceeded upon a theory of its own, and given or withheld powers according to the judgment of the American people, by whom it was adopted. We can only construe its powers, and cannot inquire into the policy or principles which induced the grant of them. The constitution has presumed (whether rightly or wrongly, we do not inquire), that state attachments, state prejudices, state jealousies, and state interests, might sometimes obstruct, or control, or be supposed to obstruct or control, the regular administration of justice....

This is not all. A motive of another kind, perfectly compatible with the most sincere respect for state tribunals, might induce the grant of appellate power over their decisions. That motive is the importance, and even necessity of uniformity of decisions throughout the whole United States, upon all subjects within the purview of the constitution. Judges of equal learning and integrity, in different states, might differently interpret the statute, or a treaty of the United States, or even the constitution itself: if there were no revising authority to control

these jarring and discordant judgments, and harmonize them into uniformity, the laws, the treaties and the constitution of the United States would be different, in different states, and might, perhaps, never have precisely the same construction, obligation or efficiency, in any two states. The public mischiefs that would attend such a state of things would be truly deplorable; and it cannot be believed, that they could have escaped the enlightened convention which formed the constitution. What, indeed, might then have been only prophecy, has now become fact; and the appellate jurisdiction must continue to be the only adequate remedy for such evils....

On the whole, the court are of opinion, that the appellate power of the United States does extend to cases pending in the state courts; and that the 25th section of the judiciary act, which authorizes the exercise of this jurisdiction in the specified cases, by a writ of error, is supported by the letter and spirit of the constitution. We find no clause in that instrument which limits this power; and we dare not interpose a limitation, where the people have not been disposed to create one.

. . .

It is the opinion of the whole court, that the judgment of the court of appeals of Virginia, rendered on the mandate in this cause, be reversed, and the judgment of the district court, held at Winchester, be, and the same is hereby affirmed.

Cohens v. Virginia

19 U.S. (6 Wheat.) 264 (1821)

This case involved the question of Supreme Court jurisdiction to review a criminal case in which the state itself was a party. The Cohen brothers were convicted by a Virginia court for selling lottery tickets, contrary to state law. The lottery had been established by an act of Congress to operate in the District of Columbia. The Cohens argued that state courts had no jurisdiction to review a congressional statute. The Virginia Court of Appeals, the state's highest court, rejected that defense and denied that the Supreme Court had power under the Constitution to review its ruling. Section 25 of the Judiciary Act of 1789 was again at issue.

Mr. Chief Justice MARSHALL delivered the opinion of the Court.

. . .

The counsel who opened the cause said, that the want of jurisdiction was shown by the subject matter of the case. The counsel who followed him said, that jurisdiction was not given by the judiciary act. The Court has bestowed all its attention on the arguments of both gentlemen, and supposes that their tendency is to show that this Court has no jurisdiction of the case, or, in other words, has no right to review the judgment of the State Court, because neither the constitution nor any law of the United States has been violated by that judgment.

The questions presented to the Court by the two first points made at the bar are of great magnitude, and may be truly said vitally to affect the Union. They exclude the inquiry whether the constitution and laws of the United States have been violated by the judgment which the plaintiffs in error seek to review; and maintain that, admitting such violation, it is not in the power of the government to apply a corrective. They maintain that the nation does not possess a department capable of restraining peaceably, and by authority of law, any attempts which may be made, by a part, against the legitimate powers of the whole; and that the government is reduced to the alternative of submitting to such attempts, or of resisting them by force. They maintain that the constitution of the United States has provided no tribunal for the final construction of itself, or of the laws or treaties of the nation; but that this power may be exercised in the last resort by the Courts of every State in the Union. That the constitution, laws, and treaties, may receive as many constructions as there are States; and that this is not a mischief, or, if a mischief, is irremediable....

1st. The first question to be considered is, whether the jurisdiction of this Court is excluded by the character of the parties, one of them being a State, and the other a citizen of that State?

The second section of the third article of the constitution defines the extent of the judicial power of the United States. Jurisdiction is given to the Courts of the Union in two classes of cases. In the first, their jurisdiction depends on the character of the cause, whoever may be the parties. This class comprehends "all cases in law and equity arising under this constitution, the laws of the United States, and treaties made, or which shall be made, under their authority." This clause extends the jurisdiction of the Court to all the cases described, without making in its terms any exception whatever, and without any regard to the condition of the party. If there be any exception, it is to be implied against the express words of the article.

In the second class, the jurisdiction depends entirely on the character of the parties. In this are comprehended "controversies between two or more States, between a State and citizens of another State," "and between a State and foreign States, citizens or subjects." If these be the parties, it is entirely unimportant what may be the subject of controversy. Be it what it may, these parties have a constitutional right to come into the Courts of the Union.

. . .

When we consider the situation of the government of the Union and of a State, in relation to each other; the nature of our constitution; the subordination of the State governments to that constitution; the great purpose for which jurisdiction over all cases arising under the constitution and laws of the United States, is confided to the judicial department; are we at liberty to insert in this general grant, an exception of those cases in which a State may be a party? Will the spirit of the constitution justify this attempt to control its words? We think it will not. We think a case arising under the constitution or laws of the United States, is cognizable in the Courts of the Union, whoever may be the parties to that case.

Had any doubt existed with respect to the just construction of this part of the section, that doubt would have been removed by the enumeration of those cases to which the jurisdiction of the federal Courts is extended, in consequence of the character of the parties.

...It would be hazarding too much to assert, that the judicatures of the States will be exempt from the prejudices by which the legislatures and people are influenced, and will constitute perfectly impartial tribunals. In many States the judges are dependent for office and for salary on the will of the legislature. The constitution of the United States furnishes no security against the universal adoption of this principle. When we observe the importance which that constitution attaches to the independence of judges, we are the less inclined to suppose that it can have intended to leave these constitutional questions to tribunals where this independence may not exist, in all cases where a State shall prosecute an individual who claims the protection of an act of Congress. These prosecutions may take place even without a legislative act. A person making a seizure under an act of Congress, may be indicted as a trespasser, if force has been employed, and of this a jury may judge. How extensive may be the mischief if the first decisions in such cases should be final!...

It is most true that this Court will not take jurisdiction if it should not: but it is equally true, that it must take jurisdiction if it should. The judiciary cannot, as the legislature may, avoid a measure because it approaches the confines of the constitution. We cannot pass it by because it is doubtful. With whatever doubts, with whatever difficulties, a case may be attended, we must decide it, if it be brought before us. We have no more right to decline the exercise of jurisdiction which is given, than to usurp that which is not given. The one or the other would

THE DOCTRINE OF JUDICIAL REVIEW

be treason to the constitution. Questions may occur which we would gladly avoid; but we cannot avoid them. All we can do is, to exercise our best judgment, and conscientiously to perform our duty. In doing this, on the present occasion, we find this tribunal invested with appellate jurisdiction in *all* cases arising under the constitution and laws of the United States. We find no exception to this grant, and we cannot insert one....

2d. The second objection to the jurisdiction of the Court is, that its appellate power cannot be exercised, in any case, over the judgment of a State Court.

This objection is sustained chiefly by arguments drawn from the supposed total separation of the judiciary of a State from that of the Union, and their entire independence of each other. The argument considers the federal judiciary as completely foreign to that of a State; and as being no more connected with it in any respect whatever, than the Court of a foreign State....

That the United States form, for many, and for most important purposes, a single nation, has not yet been denied. In war, we are one people. In making peace, we are one people. In all commercial regulations, we are one and the same people. In many other respects, the American people are one, and the government which is alone capable of controlling and managing their interests in all these respects, is the government of the Union....

In a government so constituted, is it unreasonable that the judicial power should be competent to give efficacy to the constitutional laws of the legislature? That department can decide on the validity of the constitution or law of a State, if it be repugnant to the constitution or to a law of the United States. Is it unreasonable that it should also be empowered to decide on the judgment of a State tribunal enforcing such unconstitutional law? Is it so very unreasonable as to furnish a justification for controling the words of the constitution?

We think it is not. We think that in a government acknowledgedly supreme, with respect to objects of vital interest to the nation, there is nothing inconsistent with sound reason, nothing incompatible with the nature of government, in making all its departments supreme, so far as re-

spects those objects, and so far as is necessary to their attainment. The exercise of the appellate power over those judgments of the State tribunals which may contravene the constitution or laws of the United States, is, we believe, essential to the attainment of those objects....

3d. We come now to the third objection, which, though differently stated by the counsel, is substantially the same. One gentleman has said that the judiciary act does not give jurisdiction in the case.

The cause was argued in the State Court, on a case agreed by the parties, which states the prosecution under a law for selling lottery tickets, which is set forth, and further states the act of Congress by which the City of Washington was authorized to establish the lottery. It then states that the lottery was regularly established by virtue of the act, and concludes with referring to the Court the questions, whether the act of Congress be valid? whether, on its just construction, it constitutes a bar to the prosecution? and, whether the act of Assembly, on which the prosecution is founded, be not itself invalid? These questions were decided against the operation of the act of Congress, and in favour of the operation of the act of the State.

If the 25th section of the judiciary act be inspected, it will at once be perceived that it comprehends expressly the case under consideration....

After having bestowed upon this question the most deliberate consideration of which we are capable, the Court is unanimously of opinion, that the objections to its jurisdiction are not sustained, and that the motion ought to be overruled.

Motion denied.

[Having ruled against Virginia's motion to dismiss the case for want of jurisdiction, the Court heard arguments on the merits of the Cohens' claim that the congressional sponsorship of the lottery barred a state prosecution for the sale of tickets. The Court affirmed the Virginia conviction by reasoning that the congressional statute was not a piece of national legislation but rather an exercise of congressional power over the District of Columbia. As local legislation, the lottery law did not override state penal laws.]

D. CONSTRAINTS ON JUDICIAL REVIEW

By the time of his visit to America in the 1830s, Alexis de Tocqueville could write of judicial review: "I am aware that a similar right has been sometimes claimed, but claimed in vain, by courts of justice in other countries, but in America it is recognized by all the authorities; and not a party, not so much as an individual, is found to contest it." 1 Alexis de Tocqueville, *Democracy in America* 100 (Bradley ed. 1951). In fact, judicial review was challenged at every level of government. State courts and state legislatures regularly challenged the jurisdiction of the Supreme Court, not only up to the Civil War but afterward as well. Charles Warren, 47 Am. L. Rev. 1, 161 (1913).

Justice John Gibson's dissent in *Eakin v. Raub* (1825) represents a trenchant rebuttal of Marshall's position on judicial review. Gibson, a Pennsylvania judge, conceded that the Supremacy Clause required judges to strike down state laws in conflict with the federal Constitution, but he rejected judicial review as a means of policing Congress and the President. Although a constitution was superior to a statute, that fact alone did not elevate judges to be the sole interpreters. The oath to support the Constitution was not unique to judges. The political branches had an equal right to put a construction on the Constitution. If a legislature were to abuse its powers and overstep the boundaries established by the Constitution, Gibson preferred that correction come at the hands of the people. Judicial errors were more difficult to correct, for they required constitutional amendment. EAKIN v. RAUB, 12 S. & R. 330, 343 (Pa. 1825). In subsequent years, Gibson resigned himself to a more generous definition of judicial review. Norris v. Clymer, 2 Pa. 277, 281 (1845).

Concern about judicial overreaching prompted some judges to advocate a philosophy of self-restraint. To temper criticism, they offered to presume the validity of government actions and to uphold the legislature in doubtful cases. Fletcher v. Peck, 10 U.S. 87, 128 (1810); Dartmouth College v. Woodward, 17 U.S. 517, 625 (1819). Similar guidelines were issued when reviewing lower court decisions. Judges comfortable with the legitimacy of judicial review wielded the power actively and aggressively. In a veto message in 1832, President Jackson vigorously asserted his own independent authority in interpreting the Constitution, even in the face of a contrary Supreme Court opinion. Similarly, President Lincoln sharply rejected the belief in judicial supremacy regarding constitutional analysis (see readings in Chapter One).

A major challenge to judicial review arose late in the nineteenth century when federal judges began to impose their own philosophies of economic laissez-faire. Repeatedly the courts struck down state and federal statutes designed to alleviate economic hardship. Legislative efforts to deal with monopoly, prices, minimum wages, maximum work hours, and organized labor were either rejected by the courts or severely restricted. The philosophy of judicial restraint, the presumption of legislative validity, and avoidance of decisions based on the wisdom of government action seemed virtually abandoned. The judges reached outside the Constitution to discover a "liberty of contract" that narrowed the scope of interstate commerce and the taxing power. These decisions stood in the path of progressive legislation and threatened effective government. Justice Stone lectured his colleagues in 1936 that courts "are not the only agency of government that must be assumed to have capacity to govern." United States v. Butler, 297 U.S. 1, 87 (1936).

Changes in the composition of the Supreme Court after 1937 removed the judicial impediment to economic regulation. The era of "substantive due process" appeared to be over. However, the Warren Court sparked another round of debate over judicial review, this time raising the claim that courts had tilted in a liberal direction. The opinions outlawing desegregation, requiring legislative reapportionment, providing right of counsel, and announcing novel constitutional rights of association and privacy—all supported the weak and politically disfranchised.

Activism vs. Self-Restraint

Critics who had called for judicial self-restraint during the 1930s now found themselves applauding the substantive results of the activist Warren Court. Others warned that the Court

---

Learned Hand on Judicial Restraint

...when the Constitution emerged from the Convention in September, 1787, the structure of the proposed government, if one looked to the text, gave no ground for inferring that the decisions of the Supreme Court, and *a fortiori* of the lower courts, were to be authoritative upon the Executive and the Legislature. Each of the three "departments" was an agency of a sovereign, the "People of the United States." Each was responsible to that sovereign, but not to one another; indeed, their "Separation" was still regarded as a condition of free government, whatever we may think of that notion now....

Each one of us must in the end choose for himself how far he would like to leave our collective fate to the wayward vagaries of popular assemblies. No one can fail to recognize the perils to which the last forty years have exposed such governments....For myself it would be most irksome to be ruled by a bevy of Platonic Guardians, even if I knew how to choose them, which I assuredly do not. If they were in charge, I should miss the stimulus of living in a society where I have, at least theoretically, some part in the direction of public affairs. Of course I know how illusory would be the belief that my vote determined anything; but nevertheless when I go to the polls I have a satisfaction in the sense that we are all engaged in a common venture.

SOURCE: Learned Hand, The Bill of Rights 27–28, 73–74 (1958).

---

risked losing popular support by issuing broad decisions in social and political areas. Reacting against Judge Learned Hand's plea in 1958 for judicial restraint (see box), Herbert Wechsler maintained that the issue was not whether judges possessed judicial review but rather how they exercised that authority. He objected to what he regarded as idiosyncratic, ad hoc, and poorly reasoned decisions and urged the courts to follow principled rules, deciding on grounds of "adequate neutrality and generality, tested not only by the instant application but by others that the principles imply." 73 Harv. L. Rev. 1, 15 (1959).

Many scholars agree that the Warren Court's opinions should have been better crafted to clarify statements of principles. If a majority opinion simply announced a result without adequately explaining the underlying argument, the courts would rule by fiat and decree. However, the concept of "neutral principles" has remained elusive and confusing. It appears to run counter to Holmes's dictum that "The life of the law has not been logic: it has been experience." The Common Law 1 (1881). In such areas as separation of church and state, separation of powers, and search-and-seizure operations, it is difficult to discover general principles that guide the Court. The judicial process has been characterized by starts and stops, direction and redirection, trial and error. Others point out that an insistence on principled decisions might prevent judges from discovering novel responses for unprecedented conditions. Charles E. Clark, 49 Va. L. Rev. 660, 665 (1963). Rigid adherence to fixed principles would prevent the tactical use of threshold arguments (such as standing, mootness, and ripeness) needed to protect the Court's prestige and effectiveness.

The post-Warren Court years were marked by continued controversy over the scope of judicial decisions. Presidents used rulings on such contentious issues as school desegregation, the death penalty, criminal procedures, and abortion as political rallying points. Courts were accused of deciding too many cases and overtaxing their institutional capacity. They were urged to limit court access in order to divert issues from the courthouse to the legislative arena.

Despite President Nixon's vow to nominate "strict constructionists" to the bench, the Burger Court continued to play an activist role. It created a constitutional right of "commercial free speech," struck down death-penalty statutes, initiated busing to overcome segregated schools, began the process of reversing sex discrimination, and authored the abortion decision. Many commentators viewed the abortion case as a revival of the era of "substantive due process" that prevailed before 1937. The Court's decision against the legislative veto in 1983, Justice White noted, struck down in "one fell swoop provisions in more laws enacted by Congress than the Court has cumulatively invalidated in its history." INS v. Chadha, 462 U.S. 919, 1002. The conditions that encourage judges to play an activist role were discussed by Justice Powell in a revealing interview in 1979 (see Powell reading).

Judicial Review and Democracy

Some critics of contemporary courts argue that the main objection to judicial review is that it runs counter to American democratic values. One study advised judges to limit their work to supporting broad participation in the democratic process and protecting minority rights. John Hart Ely, Democracy and Distrust (1980). Another study endorsed judicial review for protecting individual rights but proposed that the courts withdraw from almost all areas of federalism and separation of powers. Jesse H. Choper, Judicial Review and the National Political Process (1980).

It is tempting, but misleading, to call judicial review antidemocratic. The Constitution establishes a limited republic, not a direct or pure democracy. Popular sentiment is filtered through a system of representation. Majority vote is limited by various restrictions in the Constitution: candidates must be a certain age, Presidents may not serve a third term—regardless of what the people want. Although states range in population from less than a million to more than twenty million, each state receives the same number of Senators. Filibusters conducted by a minority of Senators can prevent the Senate from acting. Majority rule is further constrained by checks and balances, separation of powers, federalism, a bicameral legislature, and the Bill of Rights.

To the extent that the judiciary protects constitutional principles, it upholds the values of the people who drafted and ratified the Constitution. Throughout much of its history, however, the judiciary gave little support to civil liberties or civil rights. The record does not support the assertion that judicial review has been a force for protecting individual liberties. Henry W. Edgerton, 22 Corn. L. Q. 299 (1937). In a number of decisions over the past few decades affecting reapportionment, the right of association, and the "white primary" cases, it can be argued that the Supreme Court opened the door to broader public participation in the political process. In many ways the contemporary judiciary has helped strengthen democracy. Through its decisions, it performs an informing function previously associated with legislative bodies.

The judiciary performs other positive, legitimizing functions. Actions by executive and legislative officials are contested and brought before the courts for review. When upheld, citizens can see some standard at work other than the power of majorities and the raw force of politics. Alexander Bickel wrote: "The Court's prestige, the spell it casts as a symbol, enable it to entrench and solidify measures that may have been tentative in the conception or that are on the verge of abandonment in the execution." 75 Harv. L. Rev. 40, 48 (1961). But what happens when the Court faces a repressive executive or legislative action? If judges lend their support, as in the curfew and imprisonment of Japanese-Americans during World War II, the reputation of the judiciary as the guarantor of constitutional liberties is tarnished.

If the judiciary behaves in ways intolerable to the public, there are many methods available to legislators and executives to invoke court-curbing pressures. Presidential appointments and Senate confirmations supply a steady stream of influence by popularly elected public officials. Court decisions can be overturned by constitutional amendment, a process that is directly controlled by national and state legislatures. Short of such drastic remedies, judges remain sensitive and responsive to public opinion, notwithstanding traditional claims of judicial isolation from political forces. As witnessed by the "court-packing" effort of 1937 (discussed in the final chapter), there exists within the public a strong reservoir of support for the independence of the judiciary and the exercise of judicial review.

Statutory Restrictions on Judicial Review

By adopting explicit language in statutes, Congress may prohibit judicial review of agency actions. Thus, legislation in 1885 stated that decisions by the accounting officers of the Treasury Department regarding claims for property were to be treated as final determinations "and shall never thereafter be reopened or considered." A unanimous Court held that the statute conferred exclusive and final jurisdiction on the Treasury Department and that federal courts had no power to exercise judicial review over the agency's judgment. United States v. Babcock, 250 U.S. 328 (1919). Most decisions by the Secretary of Veterans Affairs on "questions of law and fact" affecting veterans' benefits "shall be final and conclusive and may not be reviewed by any other official or by any court..." 38 U.S.C. 511 (1994). The Court accepts the prohibition of judicial review on these questions of benefits or claims, providing there is no constitutional issue. Johnson v. Robison, 415 U.S. 361, 366–67 (1974). Legislation in 1988 subjected certain actions by the Department of Veterans Affairs to judicial review. 102 Stat. 4105 (1988). Under this authority, the Supreme Court reviewed a veteran's case in 1994. Brown v. Gardner, 513 U.S. 115 (1994).

The Administrative Procedure Act prohibits judicial review over agency action "committed to agency discretion by law." 5 U.S.C. 701(a)(2) (1994). When the Supreme Court determines that an agency action falls within that scope, it acknowledges that judicial review does not apply. Lincoln v. Vigil, 508 U.S. 182 (1993). If there is no explicit statutory language that precludes judicial review, courts will presume that federal court jurisdiction exists to hear challenges to agency procedures. McNary v. Haitian Refugee Center, Inc., 498 U.S. 479 (1991). Congress may authorize the Attorney General to make temporary orders that are not subject to judicial review. Touby v. United States, 500 U.S. 160 (1991).

In 1994 the Supreme Court again acknowledged the limits of judicial review. The Defense Base Closure and Realignment Act of 1990 established a commission to recommend the closing of unnecessary military bases. A unanimous Court ruled that commission recommendations were not a "final agency action" under the Administrative Procedure Act (APA) since the ultimate decision on closure rests with the President. Therefore the recommendations are not reviewable by the courts. "Where a statute, such as the 1990 Act, commits decisionmaking to the discretion of the President, judicial review of the President's action is not available." Dalton v. Specter, 511 U.S. 462, 477 (1994). An amendment by Senator Arlen Specter to subject base closures to judicial review was rejected a month later. 140 Cong. Rec. S7485–99 (daily ed. June 23, 1994). Two years earlier the Court had held that presidential actions are not reviewable under the APA because the President is not an "agency." Franklin v. Massachusetts, 505 U.S. 788 (1992).

Other executive actions are not subject to judicial review. When the Attorney General decides to go to the special division of federal judges for the appointment of an independent counsel, that decision is not reviewable "in any court." 28 U.S.C. 592(f) (1994). See Dellums v. Smith, 797 F.2d 817, 823 (9th Cir. 1986); Banzhaf v. Smith, 737 F.2d 1167 (D.C. Cir. 1984).

Eakin v. Raub: Gibson's Dissent

12 S. & R. 330 (Pa. 1825)

In this case, the Supreme Court of Pennsylvania reviews the constitutionality of a law passed by the state legislature. In a dissenting opinion, Justice John Gibson acknowledged that the Supremacy Clause required federal and state judges to invalidate state laws in conflict with the U.S. Constitution, but denied that the same power gave judges the right to invalidate actions by the legislative and executive branches unrelated to the Supremacy

Clause. Gibson's dissent represents one of the most coherent critiques of Chief Justice Marshall's reasoning in *Marbury v. Madison*.

GIBSON, J., dissenting. *[He questions the general power of courts to hold legislative acts unconstitutional.]* But it is said, that without *[the changes insisted on by the Supreme Court of Pennsylvania]*, the latter act would be unconstitutional; and, instead of controverting this, I will avail myself of it, to express an opinion which I have deliberately formed, on the abstract right of the judiciary to declare an unconstitutional act of the legislature void. It seems to me, there is a plain difference, hitherto unnoticed, between acts that are repugnant to the constitution of the particular state, and acts that are repugnant to the constitution of the *United States;* my opinion being, that the judiciary is bound to execute the former, but not the latter. I shall hereafter attempt to explain this difference, by pointing out the particular provisions in the constitution of the *United States,* on which it depends. I am aware, that a right to declare all unconstitutional acts void, without distinction as to either constitution, is generally held as a professional dogma; but I apprehend, rather as a matter of faith than of reason. I admit, that I once embraced the same doctrine, but without examination, and I shall, therefore, state the arguments that impelled me to abandon it, with great respect for those by whom it is still maintained. But I may premise, that it is not a little remarkable, that although the right in question has all along been claimed by the judiciary, no judge has ventured to discuss it, except Chief Justice MAR-SHALL (in *Marbury* v. *Madison, 1 Cranch* 176); and if the argument of a jurist so distinguished for the strength of his ratiocinative powers be found inconclusive, it may fairly be set down to the weakness of the position which he attempts to defend;...

The constitution of *Pennsylvania* contains no express grant of political powers to the judiciary. But to establish a grant by implication, the constitution is said to be a law of superior obligation; and consequently, that if it were to come into collision with an act of the legislature, the latter would have to give way; this is conceded. But it is a fallacy, to suppose, that they can come into collision *before the judiciary....*

The constitution and the *right* of the legislature to pass the act, may be in collision; but is that a legitimate subject for judicial determination? If it be, the judiciary must be a peculiar organ, to revise the proceedings of the legislature, and to correct its mistakes; and in what part of the constitution are we to look for this proud preeminence? Viewing the matter in the opposite direction, what would be thought of an act of assembly in which it should be declared that the supreme court had, in a particular case, put a wrong construction on the constitution of the *United States,* and that the judgment should therefore be reversed? It would, doubtless, be thought a usurpation of judicial power. But it is by no means clear, that to declare a law void, which has been enacted according to the forms prescribed in the constitution, is not a usurpation of legislative power. It is an act of sovereignty; and sovereignty and legislative power are said by Sir William *Blackstone* to be convertible terms. It is the business of the judiciary, to interpret the laws, not scan the authority of the lawgiver; and without the latter, it cannot take cognisance of a collision between a law and the constitution. So that, to affirm that the judiciary has a right to judge of the existence of such collision, is to take for granted the very thing to be proved;...

But it has been said to be emphatically the business of the judiciary, to ascertain and pronounce what the law is; and that this necessarily involves a consideration of the constitution. It does so: but how far? If the judiciary will inquire into anything beside the form of enactment, where shall it stop?...

The benefit of this maxim cannot be refused to the legislature, by those who advocate the other side, inasmuch as it is the foundation of their own hypothesis; for all respect is demanded for the acts of the judiciary. For instance, let it be supposed that the power to declare a law unconstitutional has been exercised. What is to be done? The legislature must acquiesce, although it may think the construction of the judiciary wrong. But why must it acquiesce? Only because it is bound to pay that respect to every other organ of the government, which it has a right to exact from each of them in turn. This is the argument. But it will not be pretended, that the legislature has not, at least, an equal right with the judiciary to put a construction on the constitution; nor that either of them is infallible; nor that either ought to be required to surrender its judgment to the other....I take it, then, the legislature is entitled to all the deference that is due to the judiciary; that its acts are, in no case, to be treated as *ipso facto* void, except where they would produce a revolution in the government; and that, to avoid them, requires the act of some tribunal competent, under the constitution (if any such there be), to pass on their validity. All that remains, therefore, is, to inquire whether the judiciary or the people are that tribunal.

Now, as the judiciary is not expressly constituted for that purpose, it must derive whatever authority of the sort it may possess, from the reasonableness and fitness of the thing. But, in theory, all the organs of the government are of equal capacity; or, if not equal, each must be supposed to have superior capacity only for those things which peculiarly belong to it; and as legislation peculiarly involves the consideration of those limitations which are put on the law-making power, and the interpretation of the laws when made, involves only the construction of the laws themselves, it follows, that the construction of the constitution, in this particular, belongs to the legislature, which ought, therefore, to be taken to have superior capacity to judge of the constitutionality of its own acts. But suppose, all to be of equal capacity, in every respect, why should one exercise a controlling power over the rest? That the judiciary is of superior rank, has never been pretended, although it has been said to be co-ordinate....

But the judges are sworn to support the constitution, and are they not bound by it as the law of the land? In some respects they are. In the very few cases in which the judiciary, and not the legislature, is the immediate organ to execute its provisions, they are bound by it, in preference to any act of assembly to the contrary; in such cases, the constitution is a rule to the courts. But what I have in view in this inquiry, is, the supposed right of the judiciary, to interfere, in cases where the constitution is to be carried into effect through the instrumentality of the legislature, and where that organ must necessarily first decide on the constitutionality of its own act. The oath to support the constitution is not peculiar to the judges, but is taken indiscriminately by every officer of the government... The official oath, then, relates only to the official conduct of the officer, and does not prove that he ought to stray from the path of his ordinary business, to search for violations of duty in the business of others; nor does it, as supposed, define the powers of the officer.

. . .

But it has been said, that this construction would deprive the citizen of the advantages which are peculiar to a written constitution, by at once declaring the power of the legislature, in practice, to be illimitable....

... I am of opinion, that it rests with the people, in whom full and absolute sovereign power resides, to correct abuses in legislation, by instructing their representatives to repeal the obnoxious act. What is wanting to plenary power in the government, is reserved by the people, for their own immediate use; and to redress an infringement of their rights in this respect, would seem to be an accessory of the power thus reserved. It might, perhaps, have been better to vest the power in the judiciary; as it might be expected, that its habits of deliberation, and the aid derived from the arguments of counsel, would more frequently lead to accurate conclusions. On the other hand, the judiciary is not infallible; and an error by it would admit of no remedy but a more distinct expression of the public will, through the extraordinary medium of a convention; whereas, an error by the legislature admits of a remedy by an exertion of the same will, in the ordinary exercise of the right of suffrage — a mode better calculated to attain the end, without popular excitement. It may be said, the people would probably not notice an error of their representatives. But they would as probably do so, as notice an error of the judiciary; and beside, it is a *postulate* in the theory of our government, and the very basis of the superstructure, that the people are wise, virtuous, and competent to manage their own affairs: and if they are not so, in fact, still, every question of this sort must be determined according to the principles of the constitution, as it came from the hands of its framers, and the existence of a defect which was not foreseen, would not justify those who administer the government, in applying a corrective in practice, which can be provided only by a convention.

. . .

But in regard to an act of assembly, which is found to be in collision with the constitution, laws or treaties of the *United States,* I take the duty of the judiciary to be exactly the reverse. By becoming parties to the federal constitution, the states have agreed to several limitations of their individual sovereignty, to enforce which, it was thought to be absolutely necessary, to prevent them from giving effect to laws in violation of those limitations, through the instrumentality of their own judges. Accordingly, it is declared in the fifth article and second section of the federal constitution, that "This constitution, and the laws of the *United States* which shall be made in pursuance thereof, and all treaties made, or which shall be made under the authority of the *United States,* shall be the *supreme* law of the land; and the *judges* in every *state* shall be BOUND thereby; anything in the *laws* or *constitution* of any *state* to the contrary notwithstanding."

This is an express grant of a political power, and it is conclusive, to show that no law of inferior obligation, as every state law must necessarily be, can be executed at the expense of the constitution, laws or treaties of the *United States....*

The Boundaries of Judicial Review:
Interview with Justice Powell

In an extraordinarily candid interview in 1979, Justice Lewis F. Powell discussed with Professor Harry M. Clor some of the considerations that determine the scope of judicial review and the reasons for judicial activism. The interview was published in the *Kenyon College Alumni Bulletin* (Summer 1979).

CLOR: I would like to begin with a rather broad and somewhat philosophic question. We can get more specific later on as you choose. This is a question about the role of the federal judiciary and particularly the Supreme Court in the American system of constitutional democracy. Do you see the Court as primarily a political institution, sharing responsibility for governing and making of public policy, or do you see it having a rather narrower function, simply to interpret the Constitution and the law?

POWELL: The judicial branch of government in the United States, of course, is a political branch in the broad sense. In view of the special role it has in our system, the Supreme Court is more than just an ordinary court. It is empowered to decide whether the other two branches of government live within the Constitution. You perhaps would know more accurately than I, but I do not think there is any other country in the world in which the judiciary has the power to invalidate decisions made by the legislative bodies of the country, both federal and state, and by the executive branch also. That's a rather awesome power and it's one that makes our system and our Court distinctive. A good many of the questions that involve constitutionality of statutes, and executive branch conduct, fairly can be viewed as political in the broadest sense. I suppose one could say our function, in that sense and to that degree, is politically oriented, yet basically we think of ourselves as judges guided by the Constitution as the law of the land.

CLOR: It is sometimes said that a certain judge or justice is a judicial statesman, or has acted in a statesmanlike way, which seems to suggest that something more is involved than just reading or interpreting the text of the Constitution or a law. Do you think there is such a thing as judicial statesmanship?

POWELL: Possibly, though in a limited sense. The Constitution was framed in rather sweeping language, some of which is susceptible to interpretations that not only *may* change but *have* changed over the decades. The clauses that people think about more frequently in this connection are the due process and equal protection clauses, the commerce clause and a number of other quite general phrases. The Court has to give meaning to those provisions of the Constitution, particularly the Bill of Rights, and as history demonstrates the views taken by the Court in one era do not necessarily survive a different era. That has happened with a good deal of frequency. The Constitution has been described, properly I think, as a sort of living political organism. The Court has helped, by its decisions, to keep the Constitution abreast of the vast changes that occur in the life of our nation.

CLOR: Do you think that judicial statesmanship, to the extent that there is such a thing, consists primarily of insight into the needs or demands of the times or into the changing conditions to which Constitutional clauses are to be applied?

POWELL: I'd rather not phrase it quite that way. It's well to bear in mind that the Court is composed of judges who are elected for life. We, therefore, are not directly responsible to the people in any political sense. This is both an asset and perhaps a liability. It could mean that the Court could move too far away from our democratic system. I don't think the Court has done that. Perhaps on very rare occasions. Yet, our independence does give the Court a freedom to make decisions that perhaps are necessary for our society, decisions that the legislative branch may be reluctant to make. The classic case that comes to mind is *Brown v. Board of Education*. The Congress had adequate authority under the Constitution to enact the sort of legislation that has been adopted since *Brown*. But it was the Supreme Court that finally decided in 1954 that segregation in our society must come to an end....

CLOR: One thing that fascinates me about the desegregation decision of *Brown v. Board of Education* is that the Court interpreted the equal protection clause quite differently from the earlier interpretation in 1896 of *Plessy v. Ferguson*. The Court virtually reversed its interpretation of the equal protection clause. How do you do that, Mr. Justice Powell?

POWELL: The Court has felt far freer to reverse Constitutional decisions than it has to reverse the interpretation of statutes. The Court's peculiar responsibility is to decide what the Constitution means. This country had moved a long ways by 1954 from the public mores and public perceptions that existed at the time of *Plessy v. Ferguson*. If you read the history of the post-Civil War, civil rights legislation, legislation that enacted Section 1983 of the statute which now produces a vast amount of litigation, I think you would have a hard time justifying the decision of our Court in 1954. One would have to strain to find an intention on the part of the Congress in 1866, and again in 1870 and 1871, to provide that there should be integration in education. Of course, there weren't very many public schools, but if the Court had gone strictly by what the Congress had intended, or probably intended, it would have reaffirmed *Plessy v. Ferguson*.

. . .

...The point I am making is that the Supreme Court perceived that vast changes had occurred not only in the United States but worldwide. It was long overdue to bring our Negro citizens into full citizenship.

CLOR: Does that mean the Court was remaking the Constitution, reading into the equal protection clause a meaning that it did not originally have?

POWELL: The Court cannot rely solely on what the founding fathers intended, or even on congressional intent when the Fourteenth Amendment was adopted. Conditions change as our country matures....

POWELL: ...As a matter of fact—and I don't assert this myself, but you've seen it in print—a good many people think the legislative branch bucks tough decisions to the judicial branch by drawing statutes in quite general and vague terms. Thus, a role sometimes viewed as legislative—I would not say "aristocratic"—is thrust upon us.

CLOR: The Congress hands the tough problem to the Court?

POWELL: It has been said a number of times that Congress does that, and perhaps if I were there I'd think it was a good idea on some issues. In this way members of Congress do not have to go on record on a tough issue.

. . .

E. METHODS OF CONSTITUTIONAL INTERPRETATION

Justice Jackson once remarked that "[n]othing has more perplexed generations of conscientious judges than the search in juridical science, philosophy and practice for objective and impersonal criteria for solution of politico-legal questions put to our courts." Vital Speeches, No. 24, Vol. XIX, at 759 (October 1, 1953). No completely satisfactory guide to judicial interpretation has ever been fashioned. Different techniques are available, including a dependence on literalism, natural law, history, and an eclectic approach.

Literalism

Advocates of strict constructionism (or what some scholars call "interpretivism") argue that judges should enforce only those norms that are stated or clearly implicit in the Constitution. Literalism is helpful on the easy issues (two Senators per state, minimum age of thirty-five for a President, and so forth), but those issues are so easy they do not provoke lawsuits. Other language in the Constitution is more vexing, such as the general phrases "due process" and "equal protection." Moreover, it would be inappropriate to take some phrases literally. In 1987 the Supreme Court noted that "it is well settled that the prohibition against impairing the obligation of contracts [Art. I, § 10] is not to be read literally." Keystone Bituminous Coal Assn. v. DeBenedictis, 480 U.S. 470, 502 (1987).

Attorney General Edwin Meese III, in a speech in 1985, advocated a "Jurisprudence of Original Intention." He argued that judges should restrict themselves to the original meaning of constitutional provisions. Justice Brennan, in a speech later that year, rejected the search for the framers' intent as "little more than arrogance cloaked as humility" (see reading).

Judges who offer interpretations that cannot be discovered within the "four corners" of the Constitution are considered activists or noninterpretivists. Most judges try to interpret the Constitution in accordance with the framers' intent, so far as that is possible, but in sifting through conflicting evidence they reach different conclusions. They also differ on whether the framers intended the Constitution to be interpreted statically or dynamically. Although some politicians equate strict constructionism with conservative law-and-order views, it can be applied equally well to liberal support for individual rights and religious freedom. Likewise, strict constructionism does not always mean judicial restraint. It can be synonymous, and often is, with judicial activism. Arthur J. Goldberg, Equal Justice 35–63 (1971). A recent example is the legislative veto case of 1983, which used strict constructionism with a vengeance to invalidate dozens of statutory provisions. INS v. Chadha, 462 U.S. 919 (1983).

An example of the literalist approach is Justice Black's position on the First Amendment, which provides that "Congress shall make no law...abridging the freedom of speech or of the press." Black insisted that those words mean precisely what they say. Allowing no exceptions, he accused his brethren of rewriting the Constitution to produce a new amendment: "Congress shall pass no law abridging freedom of speech, press, assembly, and petition, unless Congress and the Supreme Court reach the joint conclusion that on balance the interests of the government in stifling these freedoms is greater than the interest of the people in having them exercised." A Constitutional Faith 50 (1968). Black did not want judges deciding on such vague grounds as what is reasonable, fair, fundamental, or decent. He urged us "to follow what our Constitution says, not what judges think it should have said." Boddie v. Connecticut, 401 U.S. 371, 393 (1971). But the Constitution "says" nothing about segregated housing, segregated schools, an indigent's right to counsel, or many other issues that Black agreed to decide.

Extreme literalists demand that textual ambiguities be resolved solely by constitutional amendment instead of judicial interpretation. Although the literalist approach may have some superficial appeal, its impracticalities are immense. Madison went to great lengths in Federalist No. 44 to point out that a constitution, to survive, must be phrased in general terms. His comments were in support of the Necessary and Proper Clause of Article I, Section 8, which had been attacked for its vague grant of power to Congress. He said that the framers might have copied the Articles of Confederation, which prohibited the exercise of any power not *expressly* delegated by the states, or they might have attempted to enumerate congressional powers. The first alternative risked leaving the national government with insufficient power, whereas the second meant "a complete digest of laws on every subject to which the Constitution relates; accommodated not only to the existing state of things, but to all the possible changes which futurity may produce...." In 1819 Chief Justice John Marshall advanced the same argument in *McCulloch* v. *Maryland* (see box on next page).

Chief Justice Taney, in *Dred Scott* v. *Sandford* (1857), authored what is widely regarded as one of the major self-inflicted wounds on the Supreme Court. He did so by insisting that the meaning of "citizens" in Article III was restricted to what it meant in 1787: "No one, we presume, supposes that any change in public opinion or feeling, in relation to this unfortunate race [of blacks], in the civilized nations of Europe or in this country, should induce the court

Marshall on Constitutional Interpretation

...A constitution, to contain an accurate detail of all the subdivisions of which its great powers will admit, and of all the means by which they may be carried into execution, would partake of the prolixity of a legal code, and could scarcely be embraced by the human mind. It would probably never be understood by the public. Its nature, therefore, requires, that only its great outlines should be marked, its important objects designated, and the minor ingredients which compose those objects be deduced from the nature of the objects themselves....In considering this question, then, we must never forget, that it is a *constitution* we are expounding.

. . .

Let this be done in the case under consideration. The subject is the execution of those great powers on which the welfare of a nation essentially depends. It must have been the intention of those who gave these powers, to insure, as far as human prudence could insure, their beneficial execution. This could not be done by confiding the choice of means to such narrow limits as not to leave it in the power of Congress to adopt any which might be appropriate, and which were conducive to the end. This provision is made in a constitution intended to endure for ages to come, and, consequently, to be adapted to the various *crises* of human affairs. To have prescribed the means by which government should, in all future time, execute its powers, would have been to change, entirely, the character of the instrument, and give it the properties of a legal code....

. . .

We admit, as all must admit, that the powers of the government are limited, and that its limits are not to be transcended. But we think the sound construction of the constitution must allow to the national legislature that discretion, with respect to the means by which the powers it confers are to be carried into execution, which will enable that body to perform the high duties assigned to it, in the manner most beneficial to the people. Let the end be legitimate, let it be within the scope of the constitution, and all means which are appropriate, which are plainly adapted to that end, which are not prohibited, but consist with the letter and spirit of the constitution, are constitutional.

SOURCE: McCulloch v. Maryland, 17 U.S. 316, 407, 415, 421 (1819).

to give to the words of the Constitution a more liberal construction in their favor than they were intended to bear when the instrument was framed and adopted....[Constitutional language] must be construed now as it was understood at the time of its adoption. It is not only the same in words, but the same in meaning...." 60 U.S. at 426.

Justice Holmes rejected this reasoning. To him, a word "is not a crystal, transparent and unchanged, it is the skin of a living thought and may vary greatly in color and content according to the circumstances and the time in which it is used." Towne v. Eisner, 245 U.S. 418, 425 (1918). Literalism would place heavy demands on the amending process, subjecting the country to costly delays and uncertainties in response to issues never anticipated by the framers. Moreover, a literalist is at sea when two commands of the Constitution, such as free press and fair trial, collide. How is one constitutional principle to be balanced against another? What guides the Court in deciding between civil rights and state rights? When does government regulation give way to individual privacy? What weight should be given to protect a free press against searches and seizures by law enforcement officers? Where in the Constitution do we find answers to conflicts between workers and employers? Do certain rights, such as those enumerated in the First Amendment, have a "preferred" status?[6] Even if they do, are those rights subordinated to the needs of the government during time of national emergency?

---

6. Palko v. Connecticut, 302 U.S. 319, 326–27 (1937); Marsh v. Alabama, 326 U.S. 501, 509 (1946); Kovacs v. Cooper, 336 U.S. 77, 106 (1949) (Rutledge, J., dissenting).

Justice Iredell on Natural Law

If, then, a government, composed of legislative, executive and judicial departments, were established, by a constitution which imposed no limits on the legislative power, the consequence would inevitably be, that whatever the legislative power chose to enact, would be lawfully enacted, and the judicial power could never interpose to pronounce it void. It is true, that some speculative jurists have held, that a legislative act against natural justice must, in itself, be void; but I cannot think that, under such a government any court of justice would possess a power to declare it so....

...If...the legislature of the Union, or the legislature of any member of the Union, shall pass a law, within the general scope of their constitutional power, the court cannot pronounce it to be void, merely because it is, in their judgment, contrary to the principles of natural justice. The ideas of natural justice are regulated by no fixed standard: the ablest and the purest men have differed upon the subject; and all that the court could properly say, in such an event, would be, that the legislature (possessed of an equal right of opinion) had passed an act which, in the opinion of the judges, was inconsistent with the abstract principles of natural justice....

SOURCE: Calder v. Bull, 3 U.S. at 398–99 (1798).

Natural Law

Judges sometimes reach outside the Constitution to discover fundamental or universal principles to guide their decisions. This natural law approach, however, remains a continuing source of dispute. Writing in *Calder* v. *Bull* (1798), Justice Iredell urged his colleagues to base their decisions on constitutional grounds rather than on mere declarations of opinions regarding the laws of nature, which "are regulated by no fixed standard" (see box).

Justices react defensively to the charge that they merely read their own predilections into the Constitution, especially when interpreting such vague phrases as "due process," "equal protection," "unreasonable searches and seizures," and "cruel and unusual punishments." Nevertheless, Justices who oppose the death penalty argue that it violates the "human dignity" protected by the Constitution and is "no longer morally tolerable in our civilized society."[7] The law of defamation has been drawn not just from the First Amendment but from "our basic concept of the essential dignity and worth of every human being—a concept at the root of any decent system of ordered liberty." Rosenblatt v. Baer, 383 U.S. 75, 92 (1966).

Justice Frankfurter, remembered as the champion of judicial restraint, objected to those who called the interpretation of "due process" a mere matter of judicial caprice. Notwithstanding his general doctrine, he struck down actions that "shock the conscience" and "offend the community's sense of fair play and decency." Justice Black, a perennial critic of these opinions, charged that Frankfurter derived his standards basically from natural law, not constitutional law, and that such methods allowed judges to propound their own personal philosophies (see readings). In fact, the Constitution does have a "higher law" heritage.[8] From the very start, federal judges recognized that "there are certain great principles of justice, whose authority is universally acknowledged, that ought not to be entirely disregarded." Fletcher v. Peck, 10 U.S. at 132.

---

7. Furman v. Georgia, 408 U.S. 238, 270 (1972) (Brennan, J., dissenting); Gregg v. Georgia, 428 U.S. 153, 229 (1976) (Brennan, J., dissenting).

8. Edward S. Corwin, The "Higher Law" Background of American Constitutional Law (1928); J. A. C. Grant, "The Natural Law Background of Due Process," 31 Colum. L. Rev. 56 (1931).

Historical Development

To shed further light on constitutional meaning, judges turn to historical analysis. Justice O'Connor has said that when the intent of the framers is unclear, "we must employ both history and reason in our analysis." Wallace v. Jaffree, 472 U.S. 38, 81 (1985). The legal historian Willard Hurst regarded the general political, economic, and social history of the United States as "legally competent and relevant evidence for the interpretation of the Constitution." Edmond Cahn, ed., Supreme Court and Supreme Law 56 (1954). The meaning of "interstate commerce" could not be restricted to the methods of commerce available at the time the Constitution was adopted. The phrase had to keep pace with the progress of the country, extending from stagecoaches to steamboats, from railroads to the telegraph. Pensacola Telegraph Co. v. Western Union Telegraph Co., 96 U.S. 1, 9 (1877).

More than a century of practice became a justification for supporting the exercise of presidential power over the public lands despite the absence of any express or statutory authority: "long continued practice, known to and acquiesced in by Congress, would raise a presumption... of a recognised administrative power of the Executive in the management of the public lands."[9] Justice Holmes, writing in 1920, said that a case before the Court has to be considered "in the light of our whole experience and not merely in that of what was said a hundred years ago." Missouri v. Holland, 252 U.S. 416, 433 (1920). Holmes also remarked that "a page of history is worth a volume of logic." New York Trust Co. v. Eisner, 256 U.S. 345, 349 (1921).

Historical analysis is sometimes confined to discovering the intentions of the framers. Justice Jackson said despairingly at one point: "Just what our forefathers did envision, or would have envisioned had they foreseen modern conditions, must be divined from materials almost as enigmatic as the dreams Joseph was called upon to interpret for Pharaoh." Youngstown Co. v. Sawyer, 343 U.S. 579, 634 (1952). Efforts to discover the intent of the framers are complicated by incomplete and unreliable records. Which framers do we select, and during what periods of their lives? Do we reconstruct intentions partly from private letters, memoranda, and diaries? Do we focus on the debates at the Philadelphia Convention or also at the state ratifying conventions? How much British, American colonial, and early national history is applicable? Efforts by the Supreme Court to introduce historical evidence have been dismissed by some historians as mere law-office efforts: special pleading for a particular point of view. Alfred H. Kelly, 1965 Sup. Ct. Rev. 119.

The judiciary has been profoundly influenced by the prevailing views of social scientists, be they conservative or liberal. It has been customary for the Court to go outside the legal record and take judicial notice of writings by experts. The philosophy of Social Darwinism in the late nineteenth and twentieth centuries supplied part of the theoretical justification for a laissez-faire state. This doctrine, reshaped in the hands of judges, helped support their opposition to social and economic regulation. In time, laissez-faire principles were challenged by the "Brandeis brief," which introduced social and economic facts to justify regulation of factory and working conditions. The use of extralegal data helped undermine the Court's reliance on abstract reasoning about "liberty of contract." Paul L. Rosen, The Supreme Court and Social Science 23–101 (1972). Eventually, lawyers on both sides learned how to put together a Brandeis brief to support their case.

---

9. United States v. Midwest Oil Co., 236 U.S. 459, 472–74 (1915). See also Charles E. Miller, The Supreme Court and the Uses of History (1969); Paul Brest, "The Misconceived Quest for the Original Understanding," 60 B.U.L. Rev. 204 (1980); Frederick Bernays Wiener, Uses and Abuses of Legal History (1962); Sister Marie Carolyn Klinkhamer, "The Use of History in the Supreme Court, 1789–1935," 36 U. Det. L. J. 553 (1959); John Woodford, "The Blinding Light: The Uses of History in Constitutional Interpretation," 31 U. Chi. L. Rev. 502 (1964).

Eclecticism

If the Constitution is to guide future generations, there must be some flexibility in applying its language. Speaking of a New Deal dispute over the contract clause, the Supreme Court observed:

"It is no answer to say that this public need was not apprehended a century ago, or to insist that what the provision of the Constitution meant to the vision of that day it must mean to the vision of our time. If by the statement that what the Constitution meant at the time of its adoption it means to-day, it is intended to say that the great clauses of the Constitution must be confined to the interpretation which the framers, with the conditions and outlook of their time, would have placed upon them, the statement carries its own refutation." Home Bldg. & Loan Ass'n v. Blaisdell, 290 U.S. 398, 442–43 (1934).

In interpreting the Constitution, we look partly at the "judicial gloss" added by the courts. It is the responsibility of the judiciary to interpret the law, and under the doctrine of stare decisis (stand by the precedents) judges try to honor prior rulings. Nevertheless, sufficient variations and discord among existing precedents allow any number of directions for future decisions. Which elements of an opinion were essential for the result and therefore binding on subsequent courts? Which were peripheral (obiter dicta)? At what point do we comb concurring and dissenting opinions?

Judges hold different views about the doctrine of stare decisis. Some are more willing than others to break with prior holdings. The Supreme Court's practice is to apply stare decisis less rigidly to constitutional than to nonconstitutional cases. Glidden Co. v. Zdanok, 370 U.S. 530, 543 (1962). If the Court "errs" on nonconstitutional matters, legislatures may respond by passing a new statute. Errors of constitutional dimension, however, need attention by the judiciary. Burnet v. Coronado Oil & Gas Co., 285 U.S. 393, 406–07 (1932). Continuity is important for statutory law, for it permits citizens to arrange their business affairs with confidence. Courts should not disturb this sense of security and stability by needlessly disrupting the law. National Bank v. Whitney, 103 U.S. 99, 102 (1880). But errors of constitutional doctrine require correction. In the words of Justice Douglas, judges swear to support and defend the Constitution, "not the gloss which his predecessors may have put on it." 49 Colum. L. Rev. 735, 736 (1949).

Justice Roberts once complained that the Court's change of views "tends to bring adjudications of this tribunal into the same class as a restricted railroad ticket, good for this day and train only." Smith v. Allwright, 321 U.S. 649, 669 (1944). Justice Stewart argued that even if he believed the Court decided wrongly and he dissented at the time, subsequent rulings should be governed by what the majority decided. Donovan v. Dewey, 452 U.S. 594, 609 (1981). Many judges, however, would consider it irresponsible if they failed to correct a previous decision containing a mistake in constitutional law. The initial embarrassment of having the Court reverse itself is more than offset by the enhanced reputation of a Court willing to acknowledge its own errors. Justice Jackson declined to bind himself "hand and foot" to prior decisions, even when they were his own. He saw "no reason why I should be consciously wrong today because I was unconsciously wrong yesterday." Massachusetts v. United States, 333 U.S. 611, 639–40 (1948). Two years later, he penned an elegant justification for rejecting prior opinions that have lost their persuasive quality (see Jackson reading).

Outright reversal of a ruling is rare. More frequent is the practice of ignoring a precedent or "distinguishing" it from the pending case. These silent or tacit overrulings prompted Justice Black to remark of such cases: "Their interment is tactfully accomplished, without ceremony, eulogy, or report of their demise." Hood & Sons v. Du Mond, 336 U.S. 525, 555 (1949). Judges may argue that the current facts are different or simply reinterpret the precedent. Such techniques avoid the costs of overruling a precedent but also produce conflicting case law and uncertainty for those who must obey, interpret, enforce, and practice law.

After reviewing the various approaches to constitutional interpretation, Justice Cardozo described the judge's task as an eclectic exercise that blends in varying proportions the methods of philosophy, history, tradition, logic, and sociology. Rules are replaced by working hypotheses. The Nature of the Judicial Process (1921). The pressure of deadlines eliminates many options. Time, political constraints, and other limitations often make it impossible for judges to examine the entire record, pursue promising leads, review all the precedents, and produce original research.

Philip Bobbitt identified a broad range of techniques used by judges to interpret the Constitution. He suggested that if someone took colored pencils to mark through passages of a Supreme Court opinion, using a different color for each technique, the reader would end up with a multicolored picture. Constitutional Fate 93–94 (1982). This approach to the judicial art of opinion writing describes the work of judges whether they are "activists" or believers in original intent.

The Doctrine of Original Intent:
Attorney General Meese versus Justice Brennan

Reliance on the framers' intent to interpret the Constitution has been debated almost continuously. A particularly interesting exchange of views occurred in 1985. Attorney General Edwin Meese III, in a speech to the American Bar Association on July 9, 1985, advocated a "Jurisprudence of Original Intention." He insisted that the only legitimate method of constitutional interpretation consists of resurrecting the original meaning of constitutional provisions. In a speech delivered at Georgetown University on October 12, 1985, Justice William J. Brennan, Jr., rejected primary dependence on original intent. The task of judges, he said, is to adapt the Constitution to current problems and current needs.

ATTORNEY GENERAL MEESE:

The intended role of the judiciary generally, and the Supreme Court in particular, was to serve as the "bulwark of a limited constitution." The Founders believed that judges would not fail to regard the Constitution as fundamental law and would regulate their decisions by it. As the "faithful guardians of the Constitution," the judges were expected to resist any political effort to depart from the literal provisions of the Constitution. The standard of interpretation applied by the judiciary must focus on the text and the drafter's original intent.

. . .

In considering these areas of adjudication — Federalism, criminal law, and religion — one may conclude that far too many of the Court's opinions were, on the whole, mere policy choices rather than articulations of constitutional principle. The voting blocs and the arguments all reveal a greater allegiance to what the Court thinks constitutes sound public policy rather than a deference to what the Constitution, its text and intention, may demand.

One may also say that until there emerges a coherent jurisprudential stance, the work of the Court will continue in this ad hoc fashion. But that is not to argue for just *any* jurisprudence. In my opinion, a drift back toward the radical egalitarianism and expansive civil libertarianism of the Warren Court would once again be a threat to the notion of a limited but energetic government.

What, then, should a constitutional jurisprudence actually be? It should be a *jurisprudence of original intention*. By seeking to judge policies in light of principles, rather than remold principles in light of policies, the Court could avoid both the charge of incoherence *and* the charge of being either too conservative or too liberal.

A jurisprudence seriously aimed at the explication of original intention would produce defensible principles of government that would not be tainted by ideological predilection.

This belief in a *jurisprudence of original in-*

SOURCE: *South Texas Law Review,* Vol. 27, pp. 433–66 (1986). Footnotes omitted.

tention also reflects a deeply rooted commitment to the idea of democracy. The Constitution represents the consent of the governed to the structures and powers of the government. The Constitution is the fundamental will of the people; that is the reason the Constitution is the fundamental law. To allow the courts to govern simply by what it views at the time as fair and decent, is a scheme of government no longer popular; the idea of democracy has suffered. The permanence of the Constitution has been weakened. A constitution that is viewed as only what the judges say it is, is no longer a constitution in the true sense of the term.

Those who framed the Constitution chose their words carefully; they debated at great length the most minute points. The language they chose meant something. It is incumbent upon the Court to determine what that meaning was. This is not a shockingly new theory; nor is it arcane or archaic.

. . .

Our belief is that only the sense in which the Constitution was accepted and ratified by the nation, and only the sense in which laws were drafted and passed provide a solid foundation for adjudication. Any other standard suffers the defect of pouring new meaning into old words, thus creating new powers and new rights totally at odds with the logic of our Constitution and its commitment to the rule of law.

JUSTICE BRENNAN:

The amended Constitution of the United States entrenches the Bill of Rights and the Civil War amendments and draws sustenance from the bedrock principles of another great text, the Magna Carta. So fashioned, the Constitution embodies the aspiration to social justice, brotherhood, and human dignity that brought this nation into being. The Declaration of Independence, the Constitution, and the Bill of Rights solemnly committed the United States to be a country where the dignity and rights of all persons were equal before all authority. In all candor we must concede that part of this egalitarianism in America has been more pretension than realized fact. But we are an aspiring people, a people with faith in progress. Our amended Constitution is the lodestar for our aspirations. Like every text worth reading, it is not crystalline. The phrasing is broad and the limitations of its provisions are not clearly marked. Its majestic generalities and ennobling pronouncements are both luminous and obscure. This ambiguity, of course, calls forth interpretation, the interaction of reader and text. The encounter with the constitutional text has been, in many senses, my life's work. What is it we do when we interpret the Constitution? I will attempt to elucidate my approach to the text as well as my substantive interpretation.

. . .

...Our commitment to self-governance in a representative democracy must be reconciled with vesting in electorally unaccountable Justices the power to invalidate the expressed desires of representative bodies on the ground of inconsistency with higher law. Because judicial power resides in the authority to give meaning to the Constitution, the debate is really a debate about how to read the text, about constraints on what is legitimate interpretation.

There are those who find legitimacy in fidelity to what they call "the intentions of the Framers." In its most doctrinaire incarnation, this view demands that Justices discern exactly what the Framers thought about the question under consideration and simply follow that intention in resolving the case before them. It is a view that feigns self-effacing deference to the specific judgments of those who forged our original social compact. But in truth it is little more than arrogance cloaked as humility. It is arrogant to pretend that from our vantage we can gauge accurately the intent of the Framers on application of principle to specific, contemporary questions. All too often, sources of potential enlightenment such as records of the ratification debates provide sparse or ambiguous evidence of the original intention. Typically, all that can be gleaned is that the Framers themselves did not agree about the application or meaning of particular constitutional provisions and hid their differences in cloaks of generality. Indeed, it is far from clear whose intention is relevant—that of the drafters, the congressional disputants, or the ratifiers in the states—or even whether the idea of an original intention is a coherent way of thinking about a jointly drafted document drawing its authority from a general assent of the states. Apart from the problematic nature of the sources, our distance of two centuries cannot but work as a prism refracting all we perceive. One cannot help but speculate that the chorus of lamentations calling for interpretation faithful to "original intention"—and proposing nullification of interpretations that fail this quick litmus test—must inevitably come from persons who have no familiarity with the historical record.

· · ·

Current Justices read the Constitution in the only way that we can: as twentieth-century Americans. We look to the history of the time of framing and to the intervening history of interpretation. But the ultimate question must be: What do the words of the text mean in our time? For the genius of the Constitution rests not in any static meaning it might have had in a world that is dead and gone, but in the adaptability of its great principles to cope with current problems and current needs....

The Natural Law Debate: Frankfurter Against Black

In *Rochin* v. *California,* 342 U.S. 165 (1952), Justice Frankfurter overturned the actions of law enforcement officers who took a narcotics suspect to the hospital where an emetic was forced into his stomach against his will. He vomited two capsules containing morphine, and they were later admitted in evidence that led to his conviction. Frankfurter relied on the Due Process Clause of the Fourteenth Amendment to reverse the conviction. In a concurrence, Justice Black criticized Frankfurter for invoking natural law. Later, in *Griswold* v. *Connecticut,* 381 U.S. 479 (1965), in a case that struck down a state law banning contraceptives, Black's dissent summed up his views on the natural law approach.

MR. JUSTICE FRANKFURTER delivered the opinion of the Court.

...Regard for the requirements of the Due Process Clause "inescapably imposes upon this Court an exercise of judgment upon the whole course of the proceedings [resulting in a conviction] in order to ascertain whether they offend those canons of decency and fairness which express the notions of justice of English-speaking peoples even toward those charged with the most heinous offenses." *Malinski* v. *New York, supra,* at 416–417. These standards of justice are not authoritatively formulated anywhere as though they were specifics. Due process of law is a summarized constitutional guarantee of respect for those personal immunities which, as Mr. Justice Cardozo twice wrote for the Court, are "so rooted in the traditions and conscience of our people as to be ranked as fundamental"...or are "implicit in the concept of ordered liberty."...

· · ·

The vague contours of the Due Process Clause do not leave judges at large. We may not draw on our merely personal and private notions and disregard the limits that bind judges in their judicial function. Even though the concept of due process of law is not final and fixed, these limits are derived from considerations that are fused in the whole nature of our judicial process....

Due process of law thus conceived is not to be derided as resort to a revival of "natural law." To believe that this judicial exercise of judgment could be avoided by freezing "due process of law" at some fixed stage of time or thought is to suggest that the most important aspect of constitutional adjudication is a function for inanimate machines and not for judges, for whom the independence safeguarded by Article III of the Constitution was designed and who are presumably guided by established standards of judicial behavior. Even cybernetics has not yet made that haughty claim. To practice the requisite detachment and to achieve sufficient objectivity no doubt demands of judges the habit of self-discipline and self-criticism, incertitude that one's own views are incontestable and alert tolerance toward views not shared. But these are precisely the presuppositions of our judicial process. They are precisely the qualities society has a right to expect from those entrusted with ultimate judicial power.

· · ·

Applying these general considerations to the circumstances of the present case, we are compelled to conclude that the proceedings by which this conviction was obtained do more than offend some fastidious squeamishness or private sentimentalism about combatting crime too energetically. This is conduct that shocks the conscience. Illegally breaking into the privacy of the petitioner, the struggle to open his mouth and remove what was there, the forcible extraction of his stomach's contents—this course of proceeding by agents of government to obtain evidence is bound to offend even hardened sensibilities. They are methods too close to the rack and the screw to permit of constitutional differentiation....

. . .

MR. JUSTICE BLACK, concurring.

. . .

What the majority hold is that the Due Process Clause empowers this Court to nullify any state law if its application "shocks the conscience," offends "a sense of justice" or runs counter to the "decencies of civilized conduct." The majority emphasize that these statements do not refer to their own consciences or to their senses of justice and decency. For we are told that "we may not draw on our merely personal and private notions"; our judgment must be grounded on "considerations deeply rooted in reason and in the compelling traditions of the legal profession." We are further admonished to measure the validity of state practices, not by our reason, or by the traditions of the legal profession, but by "the community's sense of fair play and decency"; by the "traditions and conscience of our people"; or by "those canons of decency and fairness which express the notions of justice of English-speaking peoples." These canons are made necessary, it is said, because of "interests of society pushing in opposite directions."

If the Due Process Clause does vest this Court with such unlimited power to invalidate laws, I am still in doubt as to why we should consider only the notions of English-speaking peoples to determine what are immutable and fundamental principles of justice. Moreover, one may well ask what avenues of investigation are open to discover "canons" of conduct so universally favored that this Court should write them into the Constitution? All we are told is that the discovery must be made by an "evaluation based on a disinterested inquiry pursued in the spirit of science, on a balanced order of facts." ...

MR. JUSTICE BLACK [*dissenting in* Griswold].

The due process argument which my Brothers HARLAN and WHITE adopt here is based, as their opinions indicate, on the premise that this Court is vested with power to invalidate all state laws that it considers to be arbitrary, capricious, unreasonable, or oppressive, or on this Court's belief that a particular state law under scrutiny has no "rational or justifying" purpose, or is offensive to a "sense of fairness and justice." If these formulas based on "natural justice," or others which mean the same thing, are to prevail, they require judges to determine what is or is not constitutional on the basis of their own appraisal of what laws are unwise or unnecessary. The power to make such decisions is of course that of a legislative body....

. . .

...And so, I cannot rely on the Due Process Clause or the Ninth Amendment or any mysterious and uncertain natural law concept as a reason for striking down this state law. The Due Process Clause with an "arbitrary and capricious" or "shocking to the conscience" formula was liberally used by this Court to strike down economic legislation in the early decades of this century, threatening, many people thought, the tranquility and stability of the Nation. See, *e.g., Lochner* v. *New York,* 198 U. S. 45. That formula, based on subjective considerations of "natural justice," is no less dangerous when used to enforce this Court's views about personal rights than those about economic rights....

Stare Decisis

In the interest of consistency and predictability, judges prefer to decide cases in accordance with past rulings. This doctrine of stare decisis (stand by the precedents) has particular force when applied to statutory interpretation, but decisions are regularly reviewed and revised to take into account recent developments, new information, and better understanding. In a concurring opinion in *McGrath* v. *Kristensen,* 340 U.S. 162 (1950), Justice Jackson offered a candid, personal, and amusing justification for parting company with opinions that seem, upon reflection, unconvincing.

MR. JUSTICE JACKSON, concurring.

I concur in the judgment and opinion of the

Court. But since it is contrary to an opinion which, as Attorney General, I rendered in 1940, I owe some word of explanation. 39 Op. Atty. Gen. 504. I am entitled to say of that opinion what any discriminating reader must think of it—that it was as foggy as the statute the Attorney General was asked to interpret. It left the difficult border-line questions posed by the Secretary of War unanswered, covering its lack of precision with generalities which, however, gave off overtones of assurance that the Act applied to nearly every alien from a neutral country caught in the United States under almost any circumstances which required him to stay overnight.

The opinion did not at all consider aspects of our diplomatic history, which I now think, and should think I would then have thought, ought to be considered in applying any conscription Act to aliens.

. . .

Precedent, however, is not lacking for ways by which a judge may recede from a prior opinion that has proven untenable and perhaps misled others. See Chief Justice Taney, *License Cases*, 5 How. 504, recanting views he had pressed upon the Court as Attorney General of Maryland in *Brown* v. *Maryland*, 12 Wheat. 419. Baron Bramwell extricated himself from a somewhat similar embarrassment by saying, "The matter does not appear to me now as it appears to have appeared to me then." *Andrews* v. *Styrap*, 26 L. T. R. (N.S.) 704, 706. And Mr. Justice Story, accounting for his contradiction of his own former opinion, quite properly put the matter: "My own error, however, can furnish no ground for its being adopted by this Court...." *United States* v. *Gooding*, 12 Wheat. 460, 478. Perhaps Dr. Johnson really went to the heart of the matter when he explained a blunder in his dictionary—"Ignorance, sir, ignorance." But an escape less self-depreciating was taken by Lord Westbury, who, it is said, rebuffed a barrister's reliance upon an earlier opinion of his Lordship: "I can only say that I am amazed that a man of my intelligence should have been guilty of giving such an opinion." If there are other ways of gracefully and good-naturedly surrendering former views to a better considered position, I invoke them all.

SELECTED READINGS

AGRESTO, JOHN. The Supreme Court and Constitutional Democracy. Ithaca, N.Y.: Cornell University Press, 1984.

ALFANGE, DEAN, JR. "On Judicial Policymaking and Constitutional Change: Another Look at the "Original Intent' Theory of Constitutional Interpretation." 5 Hastings Constitutional Law Quarterly 603 (1978).

———. "Marbury v. Madison and Original Understandings of Judicial Review: In Defense of Traditional Wisdom," 1993 Supreme Court Review 329.

BERGER, RAOUL. Congress v. The Supreme Court. Cambridge, Mass.: Harvard University Press, 1969.

BICKEL, ALEXANDER M. The Least Dangerous Branch. New York: Bobbs-Merrill, 1962.

BISHIN, WILLIAM R. "Judicial Review in Democratic Theory." 50 Southern California Law Review 1099 (1977).

BLACK, CHARLES L., JR. The People and the Court. New York: Macmillan, 1960.

CARR, ROBERT K. The Supreme Court and Judicial Review. New York: Farrar and Rinehart, 1942.

COMMAGER, HENRY STEELE. Majority Rule and Minority Rights. New York: Oxford University Press, 1943.

CORWIN, EDWARD S. The Doctrine of Judicial Review. Princeton, N.J.: Princeton University Press, 1914.

———. "Court over Constitution. Princeton, N.J.: Princeton University Press, 1938.

DAHL, ROBERT A. "Decision-Making in a Democracy: The Role of the Supreme Court as a National Policy-Maker." 6 Journal of Public Law 279 (1957).

DUCAT, CRAIG R. Modes of Constitutional Interpretation. St. Paul, Minn.: West, 1978.

FISHER, LOUIS. "Methods of Constitutional Interpretation: The Limits of Original Intent." 18 Cumberland Law Review 43 (1987–1988).

———. "The Curious Belief in Judicial Supremacy." 25 Suffolk University Law Review 85 (1991).

HAINES, CHARLES GROVES. The American Doctrine of Judicial Supremacy. Berkeley: University of California Press, 1932.

HENKIN, LOUIS. "Some Reflections on Current Constitutional Controversy." 109 University of Pennsylvania Law Review 637 (1961).

JAFFE, LOUIS L. "The Right to Judicial Review." 71 Harvard Law Review 401, 769 (1958).

KURLAND, PHILIP B. Politics, the Constitution, and the Warren Court. Chicago: University of Chicago Press, 1970.

LEVY, LEONARD W. Original Intent and the Framers' Constitution. New York: Macmillan, 1988.

MILLER, ARTHUR S., AND RONALD F. HOWELL. "The Myth of Neutrality in Constitutional Adjudication." 27 University of Chicago Law Review 661 (1960).

NELSON, WILLIAM E. "Changing Conceptions of Judicial Review: The Evolution of Constitutional Theory in the States, 1790–1860." 120 University of Pennsylvania Law Review 1166 (1972).

O'BRIEN, DAVID M. "Judicial Review and Constitutional Politics: Theory and Practice." 48 University of Chicago Law Review 1052 (1981).

POLLAK, LOUIS H. "Racial Discrimination and Judicial Integrity: A Reply to Professor Wechsler." 108 University of Pennsylvania Law Review 1 (1959).

ROSTOW, EUGENE V. The Sovereign Prerogative. New Haven, Conn.: Yale University Press, 1962.

SCALIA, ANTONIN. A Matter of Interpretation: Federal Courts and the Law. Princeton, N.J.: Princeton University Press, 1997.

SNOWISS, SYLVIA. Judicial Review and the Law of the Constitution. New Haven, Conn.: Yale University Press, 1990.

WELLINGTON, HARRY H. "The Nature of Judicial Review." 91 Yale Law Journal 486 (1982).

WOLFE, CHRISTOPHER. The Rise of Modern Judicial Review. New York: Basic Books, 1986.

WRIGHT, J. SKELLY. "The Role of the Supreme Court in a Democratic Society — Judicial Activism or Restraint." 54 Cornell Law Review 1 (1968).

———. "Professor Bickel, the Scholarly Tradition, and the Supreme Court." 84 Harvard Law Review 769 (1971).

3

Threshold Requirements: Husbanding Power and Prestige

The scope of judicial review is circumscribed by rules of self-restraint fashioned by judges. Various court doctrines sketch out the minimum conditions needed to adjudicate a case. These thresholds (or "gatekeeping rules") do more than limit access by litigants. They shield judges from cases that threaten their independence and institutional effectiveness. They ration scarce judicial resources and postpone or avoid decisions on politically sensitive issues.

Chief Justice Marshall suggested that the boundaries for judicial action were quite fixed: "It is most true that this Court will not take jurisdiction if it should not: but it is equally true, that it must take jurisdiction if it should." Cohens v. Virginia, 6 Wheat. 264, 404 (1821). The record of the judiciary, however, is quite different. What the Court should or should not accept is largely a matter of judicial discretion. Reflecting on his work at the Supreme Court, Justice Brandeis confided: "The most important thing we do is not doing." Alexander M. Bickel, The Unpublished Opinions of Mr. Justice Brandeis 17 (1957). The deliberate withholding of judicial power often reflects the fact that courts lack ballot box legitimacy. While often couched in technical jargon, jurisdictional requirements implicate fundamental questions of democratic theory.

Judges invoke access rules to promote the adversary system, preserve public support, avoid conflicts with other branches of government, and provide flexibility of action for the judiciary. The doctrines used to pursue those goals include justiciability, standing, mootness, ripeness, political questions, and prudential considerations, all of which help protect an unelected and unrepresentative judiciary. Although efforts are made to distinguish these doctrines, inevitably they overlap. As noted by the Supreme Court: "The standing question thus bears close affinity to questions of ripeness—whether the harm asserted has matured sufficiently to warrant judicial intervention—and of mootness—whether the occasion for judicial intervention persists." Warth v. Seldin, 422 U.S. 490, 499 n.10 (1975).

A. CASES AND CONTROVERSIES

Article III of the Constitution limits the jurisdiction of federal courts to "cases" and "controversies." Courts must determine that they have jurisdiction to hear the case. Jurisdiction is granted both by the Constitution and by statute. Even after accepting jurisdiction, courts may decide that the subject matter is inappropriate for judicial consideration—what the courts call "nonjusticiable." This latter concept, at times synonymous with "political questions," is used to avoid collisions with Congress and the President. Baker v. Carr, 369 U.S. 186, 198, 208–34 (1962). It is also applied more broadly to cover issues outside the separation of powers. Flast v. Cohen, 392 U.S. 83, 95 (1968).

As a way to minimize error, miscalculation, and political conflict, courts adopt guidelines to avoid judgment on a large number of constitutional questions. These guidelines only provide very broad direction for judicial activity. If judges want to ignore them, they can. However, the rules supply a convenient list of justifications for refusing to decide a case. ASH-WANDER v. TVA, 297 U.S. 288 (1936).

To resolve a legal claim, courts need to know that parties have been adversely affected. Abstract or hypothetical questions, removed from a concrete factual setting, prevent courts from reaching an informed judgment. The words "cases" and "controversies" limit the federal courts "to questions presented in an adversary context and in a form historically viewed as capable of resolution through the judicial process." Flast v. Cohen, 392 U.S. at 95.

Adverseness

The adversary system seeks truth by having judges and juries observe a contest between two sets of professional advocates. It assumes that two antagonistic parties, each with a sufficient stake in the outcome, will marshal the best arguments to defend their interests. This clash between rival parties "sharpens the presentation of issues upon which the court so largely depends for illumination of difficult constitutional questions." Baker v. Carr, 369 U.S. at 204. A case brought by two parties with the same interest loses its adversary character. South Spring Gold Co. v. Amador Gold Co., 145 U.S. 300 (1892). Nor is there adverseness when two attorneys bring a collusive or "friendly suit" or when both parties agree on a constitutional issue and want the same result.[1]

Courts occasionally consider a case even when both parties agree on the issue. In *United States* v. *Lovett* (1946), the Justice Department agreed with the plaintiff that a provision in a congressional statute was unconstitutional. To protect its interests, Congress passed legislation to create a special counsel. Functioning officially as amicus curiae, the counsel in effect served as counsel for the United States to assure adverseness. 328 U.S. 303, 304 (1946). In other cases the courts have appointed a special counsel to satisfy the requirement for a genuinely adversary proceeding. Granville-Smith v. Granville-Smith, 349 U.S. 1, 4 (1955).

During the battle over the Watergate tapes, President Nixon's lawyers argued in court that a case or controversy did not exist because Special Prosecutor Leon Jaworski "was an employee of the executive branch and Nixon was his boss." The judge in that trial, John Sirica, remarked: "any fool could see that a more genuine controversy couldn't be imagined." John J. Sirica, To Set the Record Straight 224 (1979).

There appeared to be lack of adverseness in the legislative veto case decided by the Supreme Court in 1983. The plaintiff, Jagdish Rai Chadha, sued the Immigration and Naturalization Service (INS), charging that its statutory procedure for deportation was unconstitutional. The government agreed with him. The Ninth Circuit asked both the House of Representatives and the Senate to file briefs as amici curiae. The House argued that Chadha's case lacked the necessary adverseness because INS agreed that the statute was invalid and further argued that its appearance as amicus did not supply the adverseness needed for a case or controversy. The court rejected this reasoning because it would "implicitly approve the untenable result that all agencies could insulate unconstitutional orders and procedures from appellate review simply by agreeing that what they did was unconstitutional." Chadha v. INS, 634 F.2d 408, 420 (9th Cir. 1980).

In affirming the judgment of the Ninth Circuit, the Supreme Court also refused to regard the case as a "friendly, non-adversary, proceeding" between Chadha and the INS. As the Court noted, it would be "a curious result if, in the administration of justice, a person could be de-

---

1. United States v. Johnson, 319 U.S. 302 (1943). See also Lord v. Veazie, 49 U.S. 251 (1850), in which the plaintiff and defendant had the same interest, and Moore v. Board of Education, 402 U.S. 47 (1971). In some cases the Court will allow a president to sue his or her own company because the board of directors, backed by stockholders, voted against the president to create adverseness. Carter v. Carter Coal Co., 298 U.S. 238, 286–87 (1936).

Chief Justice Jay Explains the Court's Position on Issuing Advisory Opinions

8th August, 1793

[To President Washington:]

We have considered the previous question stated in a letter written by your direction to us by the Secretary of State on the 18th of last month, [regarding] the lines of separation drawn by the Constitution between the three departments of the government. These being in certain respects checks upon each other, and our being judges of a court in the last resort, are considerations which afford strong arguments against the propriety of our extra-judicially deciding the questions alluded to, especially as the power given by the Constitution to the President, of calling on the heads of departments for opinions, seems to have been *purposely* as well as expressly united to the *executive* departments.

We exceedingly regret every event that may cause embarrassment to your administration, but we derive consolation from the reflection that your judgment will discern what is right, and that your usual prudence, decision, and firmness will surmount every obstacle to the preservation of the rights, peace, and dignity of the United States.

SOURCE: 3 The Correspondence and Public Papers of John Jay 488–89 (H. Johnston ed. 1890).

nied access to the courts because the Attorney General of the United States agreed with the legal arguments asserted by the individual." From the moment of Congress's formal intervention as amicus, adverseness was "beyond doubt." Even prior to intervention there was "adequate Art. III adverseness." INS v. Chadha, 462 U.S. 919, 939 (1983).

Advisory Opinions

The case or controversy requirement was tested in 1790 when Secretary of the Treasury Alexander Hamilton sought the advice of Chief Justice John Jay. Resolutions adopted by the Virginia House of Representatives had challenged the right of the national government to assume state debts. Hamilton regarded this resistance as "the first symptom of a spirit which must either be killed or it will kill the Constitution of the United States" and urged that the "collective weight" of the three branches be employed to repudiate the resolutions. Jay replied that it was inadvisable to take any action. 1 Charles Warren, Supreme Court in United States History 52–53 (1937). Similar efforts by Secretary of State Jefferson in 1793 to obtain advisory opinions were rebuffed by the Court. The Justices considered it improper to make extrajudicial decisions, noting that the Constitution gives the President the express power to obtain opinions from the heads of the executive departments (see box).

This same period, however, yields conflicting evidence. Chief Justice Jay and his colleagues on the Court advised President Washington in 1790 that the statutory requirement for them to "ride circuit" (travel around the country hearing appellate cases) was unconstitutional. Robert A. Dahlquist, 14 Sw. U.L. Rev. 46, 50–54 (1983). And in *Hayburn's Case* (1792), two circuit courts explained to President Washington their constitutional objections to a statute passed by Congress.[2]

---

2. U.S. (2 Dall.) at 410–14 nn (1792). The statute was constitutionally objectionable because judicial decisions could be set aside by the Secretary of War, in effect converting a judicial decision into a mere advisory opinion. For similar reasons, the Court has opposed procedures that make its decisions dependent on executive and legislative actions before being carried out; Gordon v. United States, 117 U.S. 697 (1864).

In both of these disputes, however, the interests of the courts were directly involved: having to ride circuit and to perform nonjudicial duties.

The Supreme Court's formal position on advisory opinions appears in *Muskrat v. United States* (1911). Congress had authorized certain Indians to bring suit to determine the constitutionality of a statute. They were given expedited treatment by the Court of Claims and a right of appeal to the Supreme Court. Justice Day reviewed earlier instances in which federal judges decided that Congress could not impose nonjudicial duties on the courts. The suit, even though authorized by Congress, did not create a case or controversy between adverse parties. It was an effort to obtain the Court's opinion on the validity of congressional statutes. Day said it was inappropriate for the judiciary "to give opinions in the nature of advice concerning legislative action, a function never conferred upon it by the Constitution and against the exercise of which this court has steadily set its face from the beginning." 219 U.S. 346, 362 (1911). In 1948 the Court voiced its constitutional objections to a statute that allowed the President to override the judgment of a federal court. The procedure amounted to "an advisory opinion in its most obnoxious form." C. & S. Air Lines v. Waterman Corp., 333 U.S. 103, 113–14 (1948).

Nevertheless, judges find ways to offer advice to the political branches. Many of them have met with Presidents, legislators, and agency administrators to discuss matters that were being, or could be, litigated. Walter Murphy, The Elements of Judicial Strategy 132–55 (1964). As a nonjudicial function, the Judicial Conference performs an advisory role by commenting on pending legislation.

In their off-bench activities, federal judges have not hesitated to comment on the constitutionality of legislative proposals. After the Supreme Court in *INS v. Chadha* (1983) struck down the legislative veto, D.C. Circuit Judge Abner J. Mikva told a House committee that he did not think "there is any question" that a joint resolution of approval or disapproval, as a substitute for the discredited one-House and two-House vetoes, "would pass constitutional muster."[3]

Even in the course of writing an opinion, judges often resort to dicta to advise executive and legislative officers. For example, in *Duke Power Co. v. Carolina Environmental Study Group* (1978), Chief Justice Burger rejected a number of procedural attempts to postpone adjudication of the Price-Anderson Act. He said that any delay in interpreting the statute would frustrate one of its key purposes: "the elimination of doubts concerning the scope of private liability in the event of major nuclear accident." All parties would be adversely affected, he claimed, by deferring a decision. 438 U.S. 59, 82 (1978). Justice Stevens admitted that the decision would serve the national interest by removing doubts concerning the constitutionality of the Price-Anderson Act, but he did not include among judicial functions the duty to provide advisory opinions on important subjects:

> We are not statesmen; we are judges. When it is necessary to resolve a constitutional issue in the adjudication of an actual case or controversy, it is our duty to do so. But whenever we are persuaded by reasons of expediency to engage in the business of giving legal advice, we chip away a part of the foundation of our independence and our strength. Id. at 103 (concurring opinion).

A year later, Justice Stevens and three colleagues accused the Court of rendering an advisory opinion for the state of Massachusetts. In defense, Justice Powell explained that his decision merely provided "some guidance" to the state legislators. This exchange took place in two intriguing footnotes. BELLOTTI v. BAIRD, 443 U.S. 622 (1979). In 1994, a concurrence

---

3. "Legislative Veto After Chadha," hearings before the House Committee on Rules, 98th Cong., 2d Sess. 600 (1984).

by Justice O'Connor offered suggestions to New York State on how to create a school district for a religious minority without running into constitutional problems. Board of Ed. of Kiryas Joel v. Grumet, 512 U.S. 687, 717 (1994).

Declaratory Judgments

Parties uncertain of their legal rights want courts to determine those rights before injury is done. Otherwise, they might have to violate a law to bring a test case or forgo possible rights because of a fear of litigation. By issuing "declaratory judgments," courts can offer preventive relief. Representative Ralph Gilbert explained the advantages of declaratory judgments: "Under the present law [in 1928] you take a step in the dark and then turn on the light to see if you stepped into a hole. Under the declaratory law you turn on the light and then take a step." 69 Cong. Rec. 2030 (1928). Unlike other judgments, declaratory relief decides only legal rights; it does not determine damages or the right to coercive relief. To avoid the ban on advisory opinions, such judgments are limited to actual controversies. Also, declaratory judgments (unlike advisory opinions) are binding on the parties.

Before 1934, declaratory judgments had been issued by Great Britain, India, Scotland, Canada, Australia, and other nations. More than two dozen American states had adopted the practice. H. Rept. No. 1264, 73d Cong., 2d Sess. 1 (1934). Federal courts had also issued what were in effect declaratory judgments, because they determined rights and duties before a law was violated and even before a law had taken effect. Pierce v. Society of Sisters, 268 U.S. 510, 525 (1925); Village of Euclid v. Ambler Realty Co., 272 U.S. 365 (1926). To remove the legal uncertainty, Congress in 1934 passed the Declaratory Judgments Act. In "cases of actual controversy," it gives federal courts the power to declare "rights and other legal relations of any interested party petitioning for such declaration, whether or not further relief is or could be prayed, and such declaration shall have the force and effect of a final judgment or decree and be reviewable as such." 48 Stat. 955 (1934); 28 U.S.C. § 2201 (1982). In a unanimous decision, the Supreme Court upheld the constitutionality of this statute. Aetna Life Insurance Co. v. Haworth, 300 U.S. 227 (1937).

Ashwander v. TVA (The Brandeis Rules)

297 U.S. 288 (1936)

In a concurring opinion, Justice Brandeis reviewed the rules used by the courts to limit their exercise of judicial review. The rules are designed to avoid needless and potentially damaging (for the judiciary) conflicts with Congress.

The Court has frequently called attention to the "great gravity and delicacy" of its function in passing upon the validity of an act of Congress; and has restricted exercise of this function by rigid insistence that the jurisdiction of federal courts is limited to actual cases and controversies; and that they have no power to give advisory opinions. On this ground it has in recent years ordered the dismissal of several suits challenging the constitutionality of important acts of Congress....

The Court developed, for its own governance in the cases confessedly within its jurisdiction, a series of rules under which it has avoided passing upon a large part of all the constitutional questions pressed upon it for decision. They are:

1. The Court will not pass upon the constitutionality of legislation in a friendly, non-adversary, proceeding, declining because to decide such questions "is legitimate only in the last resort, and as a necessity in the determination of real, earnest and vital controversy between individuals. It never was the thought that, by means of a friendly suit, a party beaten in the legislature could transfer to the courts an inquiry as to the constitutionality of the legislative act." ...

2. The Court will not "anticipate a question of constitutional law in advance of the necessity of deciding it." ...

3. The Court will not "formulate a rule of con-

stitutional law broader than is required by the precise facts to which it is to be applied." ...

4. The Court will not pass upon a constitutional question although properly presented by the record, if there is also present some other ground upon which the case may be disposed of. This rule has found most varied application. Thus, if a case can be decided on either of two grounds, one involving a constitutional question, the other a question of statutory construction or general law, the Court will decide only the latter.... Appeals from the highest court of a state challenging its decision of a question under the Federal Constitution are frequently dismissed be-

cause the judgment can be sustained on an independent state ground....

5. The Court will not pass upon the validity of a statute upon complaint of one who fails to show that he is injured by its operation....

6. The Court will not pass upon the constitutionality of a statute at the instance of one who has availed himself of its benefits.

7. "When the validity of an act of the Congress is drawn in question, and even if a serious doubt of constitutionality is raised, it is a cardinal principle that this Court will first ascertain whether a construction of the statute is fairly possible by which the question may be avoided." ...

Bellotti v. Baird (Advisory Opinions)

443 U.S. 622 (1979)

A Massachusetts statute required parental consent before an abortion could be performed on an unmarried woman under the age of eighteen. If one or both parents refused, a judge could order the abortion "for good cause shown." The Court held that the statute unduly burdened the right to seek an abortion because it gave a judge the right to disapprove an abortion for a mature minor and required parental consultation or notification in every instance. Writing for the Court, Justice Powell suggested to Massachusetts what would be an acceptable judicial bypass procedure. Justice Stevens, joined by Justices Brennan, Marshall, and Blackmun, wrote a footnote that called Powell's opinion, in effect an advisory opinion. Powell prepared a footnote of his own to justify the direction he had given.

Justice Stevens:

Until and unless Massachusetts or another State enacts a less restrictive statutory scheme, this Court has no occasion to render an advisory opinion on the constitutionality of such a scheme. A real statute — rather than a mere outline of a possible statute — and a real case or controversy may well present questions that appear quite different from the hypothetical questions MR. JUSTICE POWELL has elected to address. Indeed, there is a certain irony in his suggestion that a statute that is intended to vindicate "the special interest of the State in encouraging an unmarried pregnant minor to seek the advice of her parents in making the important decision whether or not to bear a child," see *ante,* at 639, need not require notice to the parents of the minor's intended decision. That irony makes me wonder whether any legislature concerned with parental consultation would, in the absence of today's advisory opinion, have enacted a statute comparable to the one my Brethren have discussed.

Justice Powell:

The opinion of MR. JUSTICE STEVENS, concurring in the judgment, joined by three Members of the Court, characterizes this opinion as "advisory" and the questions it addresses as "hypothetical." Apparently, this is criticism of our attempt to provide some guidance as to how a State constitutionally may provide for adult involvement — either by parents or a state official such as a judge — in the abortion decisions of minors. In view of the importance of the issue raised, and the protracted litigation to which these parties already have been subjected, we think it would be irresponsible simply to invalidate § 12S without stating our views as to the controlling principles.

The statute before us today is the same one that was here in *Bellotti I.* The issues it presents were not then deemed "hypothetical." In a unanimous opinion, we remanded the case with directions that appropriate questions be certified to the Supreme Judicial Court of Massachusetts "concerning the meaning of [§ 12S] and the procedure it imposes." 428 U.S., at 151. We directed that this be done because, as stated in the opinion, we thought the construction of § 12S urged by appellants would "avoid or substantially modify the federal constitutional challenge to the statute." *Id.*, at 148. The central feature of § 12S was its provision that a state-court judge could make the ultimate decision, when necessary, as to the exercise by a minor of the right to an abortion. See *id.*, at 145. We held that this "would be fundamentally different from a statute that creates a

"'parental veto' [of the kind rejected in *Danforth.*]" *Ibid.* (footnote omitted). Thus, all Members of the Court agreed that providing for decisionmaking authority in a judge was not the kind of veto power held invalid in *Danforth.* The basic issues that were before us in *Bellotti I* remain in the case, sharpened by the construction of § 12S by the Supreme Judicial Court.

B. STANDING TO SUE

To satisfy the requirement of a case or controversy, parties bringing an action must have standing to sue. "Generalizations about standing to sue," Justice Douglas said with customary bluntness, "are largely worthless as such." Data Processing Service v. Camp, 397 U.S. 150, 151 (1970). Judges frequently accuse one another of circular reasoning. After the Supreme Court announced that the requirements of standing are met if a taxpayer has the "requisite personal stake in the outcome" of his or her suit, Justice Harlan chided the Court: "This does not, of course, resolve the standing problem; it merely restates it." Flast v. Cohen, 392 U.S. at 121 (dissenting opinion).

The reader forewarned, here are some generalizations. To demonstrate standing, parties must show injury to a legally protected interest, an injury that is real rather than abstract or hypothetical. O'Shea v. Littleton, 414 U.S. 488, 494 (1974). Injuries may be economic or noneconomic. Data Processing Service v. Camp, 397 U.S. at 154. They may be actual or threatened.[4] Injuries may afflict organizations as well as persons. Havens v. Realty Corp. v. Coleman, 455 U.S. 363, 379 n.19 (1982); Warth v. Seldin, 422 U.S. at 511. A "threatened" injury can be close cousin to the hypothetical. Five members of the Supreme Court in 1973 held that

---

The Elements of Standing

Over the years, our cases have established that the irreducible constitutional minimum of standing contains three elements. First, the plaintiff must have suffered an "injury in fact" — an invasion of a legally protected interest which is (a) concrete and particularized, see [*Allen v. Wright,* 468 U.S.] at 756; *Warth v. Seldin,* 422 U.S. 490, 508 (1975); *Sierra Club v. Morton,* 405 U.S. 727, 740–741, n. 16 (1972); and (b) "actual or imminent, not 'conjectural' or 'hypothetical,'" *Whitmore* [v. *Arkansas*], 495 U.S., at 155 (quoting *Los Angeles v. Lyons,* 461 U.S. 95, 102 (1983)). Second, there must be a causal connection between the injury and the conduct complained of — the injury has to be "fairly . . . trace[able] to the challenged action of the defendant, and not . . . th[e] result [of] the independent action of some third party not before the court." *Simon v. Eastern Kentucky Welfare Rights Org.,* 426 U.S. 26, 41–42 (1976). Third, it must be "likely," as opposed to merely "speculative," that the injury will be "redressed by a favorable decision." *Id.,* at 38, 43.

SOURCE: Lujan v. Defenders of Wildlife, 504 U.S. 555, 560–61 (1992).

---

4. Linda R.S. v. Richard D., 410 U.S. 614, 617 (1973); Gladstone, Realtors v. Village of Bellwood, 441 U.S. 91, 99 (1979); Muller Optical Co. v. EEOC, 574 F.Supp. 946, 950 (W.D. Tenn. 1983).

allegations of injury were sufficient to establish standing. Proof of actual injury was not necessary.[5] On the other hand, actual injury may be inadequate to establish standing if the Court wishes to defer to the states. City of Los Angeles v. Lyons, 461 U.S. 95 (1983). Occasionally, the Court summarizes the main elements of standing (see box on previous page).

Individuals, functioning in the role of private attorneys general, may have standing as "representatives of the public interest." Scenic Hudson Preservation Conf. v. FPC, 354 F.2d 608, 615–16 (2d Cir. 1965). This principle sometimes permits one party to assert the rights of third parties *(jus tertii)*. Federal courts are reluctant to resolve a controversy on the basis of the rights of third persons who are not parties to the litigation. "The courts depend on effective advocacy, and therefore should prefer to construe legal rights only when the most effective advocates of those rights are before them." Singleton v. Wulff, 428 U.S. 106, 113–14 (1976). When genuine obstacles prevent a third party from appearing in court (such as the need to maintain anonymity to avoid the loss of rights), the courts allow exceptions.[6]

Courts recognize that Congress can, by statute, confer standing upon an individual or a group, and courts may defer to Congress on such matters.[7] "Citizen suits" may be brought by private individuals to enforce federal laws, such as the Clean Water Act. Friends of Earth v. Laidlaw Environmental Servs., 120 S.Ct. 693 (2000). However, such statutory phrases as "any person aggrieved" or "adversely affected" allow the courts broad discretion in interpreting what Congress means by *standing*. Furthermore, Congress cannot compel the courts to grant standing for a suit that, in the opinion of judges, lacks the necessary ingredients of a case or controversy. Congressional efforts to confer standing are limited by the judiciary's exclusive responsibility to determine Article III requirements.[8] There is a fundamental difference between statutory standing and constitutional standing. In addition to the standing requirements of Article III (injury, etc.), the Court adopts a "prudential standing" rule that can favor not only the plaintiff seeking relief but also judicial power to referee disputes.[9]

Courts raise and lower the standing barrier depending on circumstances. In 1923 an individual taxpayer was denied standing to challenge the constitutionality of a federal statute that provided appropriations to the states for maternal and infant care. The taxpayer claimed that Congress had exceeded its Article I powers and had invaded territory reserved to the states by the Tenth Amendment. The Supreme Court decided that a federal taxpayer's interest in financing the program was "comparatively minute and indeterminable," and the effect on future taxation "so remote, fluctuating and uncertain" that there was no possibility of a direct injury to confer standing. FROTHINGHAM v. MELLON, 262 U.S. 447, 487 (1923).

---

5. United States v. SCRAP, 412 U.S. 669 (1973). Justice Stewart was satisfied with an "attenuated line of causation" linking litigant to an injury; id. at 688. Justices Blackmun and Brennan accepted allegations of harm as sufficient; id. at 699. Justice Douglas agreed with their position; id. at 703. Justice Marshall agreed with the holding on standing; id. at 724.

6. NAACP v. Alabama, 357 U.S. 449 (1958). See also Singleton v. Wulff, 428 U.S. at 114–16, and Note, "Standing to Assert Constitutional Jus Tertii," 88 Harv. L. Rev. 423 (1974). For a rejection of third-party suits, in this case involving one death row inmate attempting to intervene for another, see Whitmore v. Arkansas, 495 U.S. 149 (1990).

7. Sierra Club v. Morton, 405 U.S. 727, 732 n.3 (1972); Trafficante v. Metropolitan Life Ins., 409 U.S. 205, 209 (1972); Linda R.S. v. Richard D., 410 U.S. at 617 n.3; Warth v. Seldin, 422 U.S. at 501.

8. Data Processing Service v. Camp, 397 U.S. at 154; Simon v. Eastern Kentucky Welfare Rights Org., 426 U.S. 26, 41 n.22 (1976). For a strict reading of statutory authorization to bring suit, see Bread PAC v. FEC, 455 U.S. 577 (1982).

9. Here the courts determine whether the interest sought to be protected by the plaintiffs is *arguably* within the "zone of interests" to be protected by statute. The test is not whether a statute specifically intends to benefit a plaintiff; it is enough to find that the plaintiff's interests are arguably protected. National Credit Union Admin. v. First National Bank & Trust Co., 522 U.S. 479, 488–99 (1998); FEC v. Akins, 524 U.S. 11, 19–26 (1998).

The Party / Issue Dichotomy in *Flast*

The effort of the Court to distinguish between party and issue in *Flast* lost its crispness when the Justices tried to explain why Mrs. Flast had standing and Mrs. Frothingham did not. The Court looked to the substantive issues to determine whether a logical "nexus" existed between the status asserted and the claim adjudicated. The Court identified two aspects of nexus: "(1) the taxpayer must establish a logical link between his or her status and the legislative statute attacked, and (2) the taxpayer must connect his or her status with "the precise nature of the constitutional infringement alleged." 392 U.S. at 102. The Court concluded that both Frothingham and Flast satisfied the first but only Flast satisfied the second. Justice Harlan dissented, unable to understand how the Court could classify the Article I/Tenth Amendment position in *Frothingham* as too general, while accepting the First Amendment/Establishment Clause in *Flast* as sufficiently "precise."

The Court decided that it was time to retreat from the absolute barrier of *Frothingham* even if it could not adequately explain why. The party/issue distinction was unpersuasive. Even the questions of party and injury had become muddled. Did Mrs. Flast have to be a taxpayer to bring suit? Could she have had standing if she lived on interest from tax-exempt bonds and was therefore unable to show injury or a monetary stake? Such fundamental questions were left unanswered.

The *Flast* Doctrine

The Court's decision appeared to be driven largely by policy rather than by constitutional considerations. Lowering the barrier for standing meant increased casework for the judiciary. Other taxpayers could challenge federal statutes involving the outlay of public funds. Lowering the barrier might bring the administrative process to a standstill, as each disappointed party looked automatically to the courts for relief. The decision was criticized because it was unclear whether the Court had announced a constitutional bar to taxpayer suits (compelled by Article III limitations on federal court jurisdiction) or whether the Court had temporarily imposed a rule of self-restraint to be lifted in the future. In later years the Supreme Court admitted that *Frothingham* could be read either way. Flast v. Cohen, 392 U.S. at 92–93.

The Justice Department interpreted *Frothingham* as an absolute prohibition on taxpayer suits. The Supreme Court discarded that notion in a 1968 suit that involved a taxpayer's challenge to the use of public funds for religious schools. Such a doctrine would put the government in the position of conceding that a taxpayer lacked standing "even if Congress engaged in such palpably unconstitutional conduct as providing funds for the construction of churches for particular sects." FLAST v. COHEN, 392 U.S. 83, 98 n.17. The Court decided to liberalize the rule on standing but only at the cost of creating substantial doctrinal confusion. It claimed that standing focuses on the party, not the issue: "when standing is placed in issue in a case, the question is whether the person whose standing is challenged is a proper party to request an adjudication of a particular issue and not whether the issue is justiciable." Id. at 99–100. This distinction between party and issue was confusing (see box). By lowering the barrier for standing, the Supreme Court not only encouraged more lawsuits but invited collisions with other branches of government.

Separation of Powers Concerns

The Burger Court raised the requirements for standing. In 1972 it denied standing to an environmental group that wanted to prevent construction of a ski resort in a national park. The Court was deeply split; four Justices arrayed against three. Sierra Club v. Morton, 405 U.S. 727 (1972). In that same year it refused to decide whether the Army's surveillance of domestic activities constituted a chilling effect on First Amendment liberties. A majority of five Justices, with four dissenting, held that there was insufficient evidence of a direct injury to present a case for resolution in the courts.[10]

The close link between standing, issue, and limiting collisions with other branches is highlighted by a 1974 decision in which the Supreme Court denied standing to a taxpayer who challenged the constitutionality of covert spending by the Central Intelligence Agency. The Court specifically looked at the issues raised before dismissing the case on standing, even though the constitutional provision (the Statement and Account Clause) is quite as "precise" as the Establishment Clause at stake in *Flast*. More to the point, the Court noted that relief was available through the regular political process. What was dismissed on standing appeared to turn basically on questions of separation of power.[11] UNITED STATES v. RICHARDSON, 418 U.S. 166 (1974). In concurring in this 5 to 4 opinion, Justice Powell urged the Court to abandon *Flast*'s two-part "nexus" test as hopeless and warned that a failure by the judiciary to exercise self-restraint might provoke retaliation by the political branches. A relaxed standing policy, he said, would expand judicial power: "It seems to be inescapable that allowing unrestricted taxpayer or citizen standing would significantly alter the allocation of power at the national level, with a shift away from a democratic form of government." In 1997, under pressure of a lawsuit, the CIA released a figure of $26.6 billion for the budget of the intelligence community. Of that amount, the CIA portion was about $3 billion. In 1998, the CIA voluntarily released a figure of $26.7 billion for the community's budget, but in 1999 it again refused to disclose the aggregate budget. A lawsuit to obtain the budget total by invoking the Freedom of Information Act was dismissed in 1999. Aftergood v. CIA, Civ. No. 98-2107(TFH) (D.D.C. 1999).

The connection between standing and sensitive political issues was evident again in 1975 when the Court announced that the inquiry into standing "involves both constitutional limitations on federal-court jurisdiction and prudential limitations on its exercise.... In both dimensions it is founded in concern about the proper — and properly limited — role of the courts in a democratic society." Warth v. Seldin, 422 U.S. at 498. Prudential rules of standing are not constitutionally required, but they "serve to limit the role of the courts in resolving public disputes." Id. at 500. In a dissenting opinion joined by Justices White and Marshall, Justice Brennan picked additional holes in the Court's doctrine that standing was unrelated to the issue being litigated:

> While the Court gives lip service to the principle, often repeated in recent years, that "standing in no way depends on the merits of the plaintiff's contention that particular conduct is illegal," ... in fact the opinion, which tosses out of court almost every conceivable kind of plaintiff who could be injured by the activity claimed to be unconstitutional, can be explained only by an indefensible hostility to the claim on the merits.

The *Flast* doctrine was further shaken by *Valley Forge College* v. *Americans United* (1982), which denied plaintiffs standing to challenge the transfer of federal property to a Christian college. Justice Rehnquist, writing for the Court, first argued that the plaintiffs could not sue as taxpayers because the land was transferred under the Property Clause, not the Taxing and Spending Clause. He then denied that the Establishment Clause gave citizens a personal constitutional right to bring suit. Four Justices dissented, accusing the majority of using a "thresh-

---

10. Laird v. Tatum, 408 U.S. 1 (1972). Curiously, a year later the Court gave standing to five law students to bring an environmental suit against the Interstate Commerce Commission; United States v. SCRAP, 412 U.S. 669 (1973). Evidently, standing *does* depend on the issue.

11. See also Schlesinger v. Reservists to Stop the War, 418 U.S. 208 (1974), which denied plaintiffs standing to challenge the constitutionality of members of Congress who served in the military reserves, in apparent conflict with the Ineligibility Clause.

old question" to decide substantive issues and obfuscate legal rights. Valley Forge College v. Americans United, 454 U.S. 464 (1982). In 1984, the Court relied on separation of powers analysis to deny standing to black parents who challenged the government's desegregation policy. ALLEN v. WRIGHT, 468 U.S. 737 (1984).

In 1997, the Supreme Court issued an important decision regarding standing for members of Congress. Senator Robert C. Byrd and five other legislators brought suit to challenge the constitutionality of the Line Item Veto Act of 1996. Although Congress had by statute authorized such a lawsuit by members of Congress, the Court unanimously held that they lacked standing. The decision pointed out that Senator Byrd and his five colleagues were simply on the losing end of a vote to give the President a form of item-veto authority, and that both Houses of Congress had filed a brief upholding the constitutionality of the statute. The effect of the decision was to advise legislators who lose during the legislative process to seek remedies within Congress rather than turn to the courts for relief. Raines v. Byrd, 521 U.S. 811 (1997). See the reading for this case in Chapter One. A year later, when standing was established for two other plaintiffs, the Court declared the statute unconstitutional. Clinton v. City of New York, 524 U.S. 417 (1998). The reading for this decision appears in Chapter 6. Much of the confusion about the standing doctrine has its source in the Court's habit of spinning abstract theories that are, at bottom, techniques of deferring to the states and the elected branches.

Frothingham v. Mellon

262 U.S. 447 (1923)

The Commonwealth of Massachusetts and a taxpayer, Harriet Frothingham, challenged the constitutionality of a federal statute that provided appropriations to the states for maternal and infant care. They claimed that this use of the appropriations power exceeded the authority of Congress and invaded state power. The Court determined whether either party had sufficient standing to bring this type of lawsuit.

Mr. Justice Sutherland delivered the opinion of the Court.

These cases were argued and will be considered and disposed of together. The first is an original suit in this Court. The other was brought in the Supreme Court of the District of Columbia. That court dismissed the bill and its decree was affirmed by the District Court of Appeals. Thereupon the case was brought here by appeal. Both cases challenge the constitutionality of the Act of November 23, 1921, c. 135, 42 Stat. 224, commonly called the Maternity Act. Briefly, it provides for an initial appropriation and thereafter annual appropriations for a period of five years, to be apportioned among such of the several States as shall accept and comply with its provisions, for the purpose of coöperating with them to reduce maternal and infant mortality and protect the health of mothers and infants. It creates a bureau to administer the act in coöperation with state agencies, which are required to make such reports concerning their operations and expenditures as may be prescribed by the federal bureau. Whenever that bureau shall determine that funds have not been properly expended in respect of any State, payments may be withheld.

It is asserted that these appropriations are for purposes not national, but local to the States, and together with numerous similar appropriations constitute an effective means of inducing the States to yield a portion of their sovereign rights. It is further alleged that the burden of the appropriations provided by this act and similar legislation falls unequally upon the several States, and rests largely upon the industrial States, such as Massachusetts; that the act is a usurpation of power not granted to Congress by the Constitution—an attempted exercise of the power of local self-government reserved to the States by the Tenth Amendment; and that the defendants are proceeding to carry the act into operation. In the *Massachusetts* case it is alleged that the plaintiff's rights and powers as a sovereign State and the rights of its citizens have been invaded and usurped by these expenditures and acts; and that, although the State has not accepted the act, its constitutional rights are infringed by the passage thereof and the imposition upon the State of an illegal and unconstitutional option either to yield to the Federal Government a part of its reserved rights or lose the share which it would otherwise be entitled to receive of the moneys appropriated. In the *Frothingham* case plaintiff alleges that the effect of the statute will be to take her property, under the guise of taxation, without due process of law.

We have reached the conclusion that the cases must be disposed of for want of jurisdiction without considering the merits of the constitutional questions.

In the first case, the State of Massachusetts presents no justiciable controversy either in its own behalf or as the representative of its citizens. The appellant in the second suit has no such interest in the subject-matter, nor is any such injury inflicted or threatened, as will enable her to sue.

First. The State of Massachusetts in its own behalf, in effect, complains that the act in question invades the local concerns of the State, and is a usurpation of power, viz: the power of local self government reserved to the States.

Probably, it would be sufficient to point out that the powers of the State are not invaded, since the statute imposes no obligation but simply extends an option which the State is free to accept or reject. But we do not rest here. Under Article III, § 2, of the Constitution, the judicial power of this Court extends "to controversies . . . between a State and citizens of another State" and the Court has original jurisdiction "in all cases . . . in which a State shall be party." The effect of this is not to confer jurisdiction upon the Court merely because a State is a party, but only where it is a party to a proceeding of judicial cognizance. Proceedings not of a justiciable character are outside the contemplation of the constitutional grant. . . .

We come next to consider whether the suit may be maintained by the State as the representative of its citizens. To this the answer is not doubtful. We need not go so far as to say that a State may never intervene by suit to protect its citizens against any form of enforcement of unconstitutional acts of Congress; but we are clear that the right to do so does not arise here. Ordinarily, at least, the only way in which a State may afford protection to its citizens in such cases is through the enforcement of its own criminal statutes, where that is appropriate, or by opening its courts

to the injured persons for the maintenance of civil suits or actions. But the citizens of Massachusetts are also citizens of the United States. It cannot be conceded that a State, as *parens patriae,* may institute judicial proceedings to protect citizens of the United States from the operation of the statutes thereof. . . .

Second. The attack upon the statute in the *Frothingham* case is, generally, the same, but this plaintiff alleges in addition that she is a taxpayer of the United States; and her contention, though not clear, seems to be that the effect of the appropriations complained of will be to increase the burden of future taxation and thereby take her property without due process of law. The right of a taxpayer to enjoin the execution of a federal appropriation act, on the ground that it is invalid and will result in taxation for illegal purposes, has never been passed upon by this Court. In cases where it was presented, the question has either been allowed to pass *sub silentio* or the determination of it expressly withheld. . . .

. . . But the relation of a taxpayer of the United States to the Federal Government is very different. His interest in the moneys of the Treasury — partly realized from taxation and partly from other sources — is shared with millions of others; is comparatively minute and indeterminable; and the effect upon future taxation, of any payment out of the funds, so remote, fluctuating and uncertain, that no basis is afforded for an appeal to the preventive powers of a court of equity.

The administration of any statute, likely to produce additional taxation to be imposed upon a vast number of taxpayers, the extent of whose several liability is indefinite and constantly changing, is essentially a matter of public and not of individual concern. If one taxpayer may champion and litigate such a cause, then every other taxpayer may do the same, not only in respect of the statute here under review but also in respect of every other appropriation act and statute whose administration requires the outlay of public money, and whose validity may be questioned. The bare suggestion of such a result, with its attendant inconveniences, goes far to sustain the conclusion which we have reached, that a suit of this character cannot be maintained. It is of much significance that no precedent sustaining the right to maintain suits like this has been called to our attention, although, since the formation of the government, as an examination of the acts of Congress will disclose, a large number of statutes appropriating or involving the expenditure of moneys for non-federal purposes have been enacted and carried into effect.

The functions of government under our system are apportioned. To the legislative department has been committed the duty of making laws; to the executive the duty of executing them; and to the judiciary the duty of interpreting and applying them in cases properly brought before the courts. The general rule is that neither department may invade the province of the other and neither may control, direct or restrain the action of the other.... We have no power *per se* to review and annul acts of Congress on the ground that they are unconstitutional. That question may be considered only when the justification for some direct injury suffered or threatened, presenting a justiciable issue, is made to rest upon such an act. Then the power exercised is that of ascertaining and declaring the law applicable to the controversy. It amounts to little more than the negative power to disregard an unconstitutional enactment, which otherwise would stand in the way of the enforcement of a legal right. The party who invokes the power must be able to show not only that the statute is invalid but that he has sustained or is immediately in danger of sustaining some direct injury as the result of its enforcement, and not merely that he suffers in some indefinite way in common with people generally. If a case for preventive relief be presented the court enjoins, in effect, not the execution of the statute, but the acts of the official, the statute notwithstanding. Here the parties plaintiff have no such case. Looking through forms of words to the substance of their complaint, it is merely that officials of the executive department of the government are executing and will execute an act of Congress asserted to be unconstitutional; and this we are asked to prevent. To do so would be not to decide a judicial controversy, but to assume a position of authority over the governmental acts of another and co-equal department, an authority which plainly we do not possess.

No. 24, Original, dismissed.
No. 962 affirmed.

Flast v. Cohen

392 U.S. 83 (1968)

Taxpayers challenged the Elementary and Secondary Education Act of 1965 on the ground that it used federal funds to finance instruction and the purchase of educational materials for use in religious and sectarian schools, in violation of the Establishment and Free Exercise Clauses. A three-judge court ruled, on the basis of *Frothingham* v. *Mellon* (1923), that the taxpayers lacked standing to bring the suit. Florence Flast and other taxpayers brought this suit against Wilbur Cohen, Secretary of Health, Education and Welfare

MR. CHIEF JUSTICE WARREN delivered the opinion of the Court.

In *Frothingham* v. *Mellon,* 262 U.S. 447 (1923), this Court ruled that a federal taxpayer is without standing to challenge the constitutionality of a federal statute. That ruling has stood for 45 years as an impenetrable barrier to suits against Acts of Congress brought by individuals who can assert only the interest of federal taxpayers. In this case, we must decide whether the *Frothingham* barrier should be lowered when a taxpayer attacks a federal statute on the ground that it violates the Establishment and Free Exercise Clauses of the First Amendment.

Appellants filed suit in the United States District Court for the Southern District of New York to enjoin the allegedly unconstitutional expenditure of federal funds under Titles I and II of the Elementary and Secondary Education Act of 1965,... The complaint alleged that the seven appellants had as a common attribute that "each pay[s] income taxes of the United States," and it is clear from the complaint that the appellants were resting their standing to maintain the action solely on their status as federal taxpayers....

The gravamen of the appellants' complaint was that federal funds appropriated under the Act were being used to finance instruction in reading, arithmetic, and other subjects in religious schools, and to purchase textbooks and other instructional materials for use in such schools. Such expenditures were alleged to be in contravention of the Establishment and Free Exercise Clauses of the First Amendment. Appellants' constitutional attack focused on the statutory criteria which state and local authorities must meet to be eligible for federal grants under the Act.... The specific criterion ... attacked by the appellants is the requirement

"that, to the extent consistent with the number of educationally deprived children in the school district of the local educational agency who are enrolled in private elementary and secondary schools, such agency has made provision for including special educational services and arrangements (such as dual enrollment, educational radio and television, and mobile educational services and equipment) in which such children can participate ...." 20 U. S. C. § 241e (a)(2).

... A State wishing to participate in the program must submit a plan to the Commissioner [*of Education*] for approval, and the plan must

"provide assurance that to the extent consistent with law such library resources, textbooks, and other instructional materials will be provided on an equitable basis for the use of children and teachers in private elementary and secondary schools in the State...."

. . .

II.

This Court first faced squarely the question whether a litigant asserting only his status as a taxpayer has standing to maintain a suit in a federal court in *Frothingham* v. *Mellon, supra,* and that decision must be the starting point for analysis in this case.... The Court noted that a federal taxpayer's "interest in the moneys of the Treasury ... is comparatively minute and indeterminable" and that "the effect upon future taxation, of any payment out of the [Treasury's] funds, ... [is] remote, fluctuating and uncertain." *Id.,* at 487. As a result, the Court ruled that the taxpayer had failed to allege the type of "direct injury" necessary to confer standing. *Id.,* at 488.

Although the barrier *Frothingham* erected against federal taxpayer suits has never been breached, the decision has been the source of some confusion and the object of considerable criticism. The confusion has developed as commentators have tried to determine whether *Frothingham* establishes a constitutional bar to taxpayer suits or whether the Court was simply imposing a rule of self-restraint which was not constitutionally compelled. The conflicting viewpoints are reflected in the arguments made to this Court by the parties in this case. The Government has pressed upon us the view that *Frothingham* announced a constitutional rule, compelled by the Article III limitations on federal court jurisdiction

and grounded in considerations of the doctrine of separation of powers. Appellants, however, insist that *Frothingham* expressed no more than a policy of judicial self-restraint which can be disregarded when compelling reasons for assuming jurisdiction over a taxpayer's suit exist. The opinion delivered in *Frothingham* can be read to support either position. The concluding sentence of the opinion states that, to take jurisdiction of the taxpayer's suit, "would be not to decide a judicial controversy, but to assume a position of authority over the governmental acts of another and co-equal department, an authority which plainly we do not possess." 262 U.S., at 489. Yet the concrete reasons given for denying standing to a federal taxpayer suggest that the Court's holding rests on something less than a constitutional foundation. For example, the Court conceded that standing had previously been conferred on municipal taxpayers to sue in that capacity. However, the Court viewed the interest of a federal taxpayer in total federal tax revenues as "comparatively minute and indeterminable" when measured against a municipal taxpayer's interest in a smaller city treasury. *Id.,* at 486–487. This suggests that the petitioner in *Frothingham* was denied standing not because she was a taxpayer but because her tax bill was not large enough. In addition, the Court spoke of the "attendant inconveniences" of entertaining that taxpayer's suit because it might open the door of federal courts to countless such suits "in respect of every other appropriation act and statute whose administration requires the outlay of public money, and whose validity may be questioned." *Id.,* at 487. Such a statement suggests pure policy considerations.

To the extent that *Frothingham* has been viewed as resting on policy considerations, it has been criticized as depending on assumptions not consistent with modern conditions. For example, some commentators have pointed out that a number of corporate taxpayers today have a federal tax liability running into hundreds of millions of dollars, and such taxpayers have a far greater monetary stake in the Federal Treasury than they do in any municipal treasury. To some degree, the fear expressed in *Frothingham* that allowing one taxpayer to sue would inundate the federal courts with countless similar suits has been mitigated by the ready availability of the devices of class actions and joinder under the Federal Rules of Civil Procedure, adopted subsequent to the decision in *Frothingham.* Whatever the merits of the current debate over *Frothingham,* its very existence suggests that we should undertake a fresh examination of the limitations upon standing to sue in a federal court and the application of those limitations to taxpayer suits.

III.

The jurisdiction of federal courts is defined and limited by Article III of the Constitution. In terms relevant to the question for decision in this case, the judicial power of federal courts is constitutionally restricted to "cases" and "controversies." As is so often the situation in constitutional adjudication, those two words have an iceberg quality, containing beneath their surface simplicity submerged complexities which go to the very heart of our constitutional form of government. Embodied in the words "cases" and "controversies" are two complementary but somewhat different limitations. In part those words limit the business of federal courts to questions presented in an adversary context and in a form historically viewed as capable of resolution through the judicial process. And in part those words define the role assigned to the judiciary in a tripartite allocation of power to assure that the federal courts will not intrude into areas committed to the other branches of government....

...[T]he Government's position is that the constitutional scheme of separation of powers, and the deference owed by the federal judiciary to the other two branches of government within that scheme, present an absolute bar to taxpayer suits challenging the validity of federal spending programs. The Government views such suits as involving no more than the mere disagreement by the taxpayer "with the uses to which tax money is put." According to the Government, the resolution of such disagreements is committed to other branches of the Federal Government and not to the judiciary. Consequently, the Government contends that, under no circumstances, should standing be conferred on federal taxpayers to challenge a federal taxing or spending program. *[At this point the Court observes, in a footnote: "The logic of the Government's argument would compel it to concede that a taxpayer would lack standing even if Congress engaged in such palpably unconstitutional conduct as providing funds for the construction of churches for particular sects."]* An analysis of the function served by standing limitations compels a rejection of the Government's position.

... The fundamental aspect of standing is that it focuses on the party seeking to get his complaint before a federal court and not on the issues he wishes to have adjudicated. The "gist of the question of standing" is whether the party seeking relief has "alleged such a personal stake in the outcome of the controversy as to assure that concrete adverseness which sharpens the presentation of issues upon which the court so largely depends for illumination of difficult constitutional questions." *Baker v. Carr,* 369 U. S. 186, 204 (1962). In other words, when standing is placed in issue in a case, the question is whether the person whose standing is challenged is a proper party to request an adjudication of a particular issue and not whether the issue itself is justiciable. Thus, a party may have standing in a particular case, but the federal court may nevertheless decline to pass on the merits of the case because, for example, it presents a political question....

When the emphasis in the standing problem is placed on whether the person invoking a federal court's jurisdiction is a proper party to maintain the action, the weakness of the Government's argument in this case becomes apparent. The question whether a particular person is a proper party to maintain the action does not, by its own force, raise separation of powers problems related to improper judicial interference in areas committed to other branches of the Federal Government. Such problems arise, if at all, only from the substantive issues the individual seeks to have adjudicated.... A taxpayer may or may not have the requisite personal stake in the outcome, depending upon the circumstances of the particular case. Therefore, we find no absolute bar in Article III to suits by federal taxpayers challenging allegedly unconstitutional federal taxing and spending programs. There remains, however, the problem of determining the circumstances under which a federal taxpayer will be deemed to have the personal stake and interest that impart the necessary concrete adverseness to such litigation so that standing can be conferred on the taxpayer *qua* taxpayer consistent with the constitutional limitations of Article III.

IV.

The various rules of standing applied by federal courts have not been developed in the abstract. Rather, they have been fashioned with specific reference to the status asserted by the party whose standing is challenged and to the type of question he wishes to have adjudicated. We have noted that, in deciding the question of standing, it is not relevant that the substantive issues in the litigation might be nonjusticiable. However, our decisions establish that, in ruling on standing, it is both appropriate and necessary to look to the substantive issues for another purpose, namely, to determine whether there is a logical nexus between the status asserted and the claim sought to be adjudicated....

The nexus demanded of federal taxpayers has two aspects to it. First, the taxpayer must establish a logical link between that status and the type of legislative enactment attacked. Thus, a taxpayer will be a proper party to allege the unconstitutionality only of exercises of congressional power under the taxing and spending clause of Art. I, § 8, of the Constitution. It will not be sufficient to allege an incidental expenditure of tax funds in the administration of an essentially regulatory statute. This requirement is consistent with the limitation imposed upon state-taxpayer standing in federal courts in *Doremus* v. *Board of Education*, 342 U. S. 429 (1952). Secondly, the taxpayer must establish a nexus between that status and the precise nature of the constitutional infringement alleged. Under this requirement, the taxpayer must show that the challenged enactment exceeds specific constitutional limitations imposed upon the exercise of the congressional taxing and spending power and not simply that the enactment is generally beyond the powers delegated to Congress by Art. I, § 8. When both nexuses are established, the litigant will have shown a taxpayer's stake in the outcome of the controversy and will be a proper and appropriate party to invoke a federal court's jurisdiction.

The taxpayer-appellants in this case have satisfied both nexuses to support their claim of standing under the test we announce today. Their constitutional challenge is made to an exercise by Congress of its power under Art. I, § 8, to spend for the general welfare, and the challenged program involves a substantial expenditure of federal tax funds. In addition, appellants have alleged that the challenged expenditures violate the Establishment and Free Exercise Clauses of the First Amendment. Our history vividly illustrates that one of the specific evils feared by those who drafted the Establishment Clause and fought for its adoption was that the taxing and spending power would be used to favor one religion over another or to support religion in general.

. . .

The allegations of the taxpayer in *Frothingham* v. *Mellon, supra,* were quite different from those made in this case, and the result in *Frothingham* is consistent with the test of taxpayer standing announced today. The taxpayer in *Frothingham* attacked a federal spending program and she, therefore, established the first nexus required. However, she lacked standing because her constitutional attack was not based on an allegation that Congress, in enacting the Maternity Act of 1921, had breached a specific limitation upon its taxing and spending power. The taxpayer in *Frothingham* alleged essentially that Congress, by enacting the challenged statute, had exceeded the general powers delegated to it by Art. I, § 8, and that Congress had thereby invaded the legislative province reserved to the States by the Tenth Amendment. To be sure, Mrs. Frothingham made the additional allegation that her tax liability would be increased as a result of the allegedly unconstitutional enactment, and she framed that allegation in terms of a deprivation of property without due process of law. However, the Due Process Clause of the Fifth Amendment does not protect taxpayers against increases in tax liability, and the taxpayer in *Frothingham* failed to make any additional claim that the harm she alleged resulted from a breach by Congress of the specific constitutional limitations imposed upon an exercise of the taxing and spending power....

. . .

MR. JUSTICE DOUGLAS, concurring.

While I have joined the opinion of the Court, I do not think that the test it lays down is a durable one for the reasons stated by my BROTHER HARLAN....It would therefore be the part of wisdom, as I see the problem, to be rid of *Frothingham* here and now.

. . .

MR. JUSTICE STEWART, concurring.

I join the judgment and opinion of the Court, which I understand to hold only that a federal taxpayer has standing to assert that a specific expenditure of federal funds violates the Establishment Clause of the First Amendment....

MR. JUSTICE FORTAS, concurring.

I would confine the ruling in this case to the proposition that a taxpayer may maintain a suit to challenge the validity of a federal expenditure on the ground that the expenditure violates the Establishment Clause....

MR. JUSTICE HARLAN, dissenting.

The problems presented by this case are narrow and relatively abstract, but the principles by which they must be resolved involve nothing less than the proper functioning of the federal courts, and so run to the roots of our constitutional system. The nub of my view is that the end result of *Frothingham* v. *Mellon,* 262 U. S. 447, was correct, even though, like others, I do not subscribe to all of its reasoning and premises. Although I

therefore agree with certain of the conclusions reached today by the Court, I cannot accept the standing doctrine that it substitutes for *Frothingham,* for it seems to me that this new doctrine rests on premises that do not withstand analysis. Accordingly, I respectfully dissent.

. . .

United States v. Richardson

418 U.S. 166 (1974)

William B. Richardson, a taxpayer, sued to obtain the expenditures of the Central Intelligence Agency, which are not publicly reported. The taxpayer claimed that covert funding violated the Statement and Account Clause. In the majority opinion, which denied standing, Chief Justice Burger tried to preserve the doctrines set forth in *Flast* v. *Cohen.* Justice Powell, concurring, urged that the two-part "nexus" test in *Flast* be abandoned as intellectually incoherent.

MR. CHIEF JUSTICE BURGER delivered the opinion of the Court.

We granted certiorari in this case to determine whether the respondent has standing to bring an action as a federal taxpayer alleging that certain provisions concerning public reporting of expenditures under the Central Intelligence Agency Act of 1949 . . . violate Art. I, § 9, cl. 7, of the Constitution which provides:

"No Money shall be drawn from the Treasury, but in Consequence of Appropriations made by Law; and a regular Statement and Account of the Receipts and Expenditures of all public Money shall be published from time to time."

. . .

Although the recent holding of the Court in *Flast* v. *Cohen* . . . is a starting point in an examination of respondent's claim to prosecute this suit as a taxpayer, that case must be read with reference to its principal predecessor, *Frothingham* v. *Mellon,* 262 U. S. 447 (1923). In *Frothingham,* the injury alleged was that the congressional enactment challenged as unconstitutional would, if implemented, increase the complainant's future federal income taxes. Denying standing, the *Frothingham* Court rested on the "comparatively minute[,] remote, fluctuating and uncertain," *id.,* at 487, impact on the taxpayer, and the failure to allege the kind of direct injury required for standing.

. . .

II

Although the Court made it very explicit in

Flast that a "fundamental aspect of standing" is that it focuses primarily on the *party* seeking to get his complaint before the federal court rather than "on the issues he wishes to have adjudicated," *id.,* at 99, it made equally clear that

"in ruling on [taxpayer] standing, it is both appropriate and necessary to look to the substantive issues for another purpose, namely, to determine whether there is a logical nexus between the status asserted and the claim sought to be adjudicated." *Id.,* at 102.

We therefore turn to an examination of the issues sought to be raised by respondent's complaint to determine whether he is "a proper and appropriate party to invoke federal judicial power," *ibid.,* with respect to those issues.

We need not and do not reach the merits of the constitutional attack on the statute; our inquiry into the "substantive issues" is for the limited purpose indicated above. The mere recital of the respondent's claims and an examination of the statute under attack demonstrate how far he falls short of the standing criteria of *Flast* and how neatly he falls within the *Frothingham* holding left undisturbed. . . .

MR. JUSTICE POWELL, concurring.

I join the opinion of the Court because I am in accord with most of its analysis, particularly insofar as it relies on traditional barriers against federal taxpayer or citizen standing. And I agree that *Flast* v. *Cohen,* 392 U. S. 83 (1968), which set the boundaries for the arguments of the parties before us, is the most directly relevant precedent and quite correctly absorbs a major portion of the Court's attention. I write solely to indicate that I would go further than the Court and would lay to rest the approach undertaken in *Flast*. I would not overrule *Flast* on its facts, because it is now settled that federal taxpayer standing exists in Establishment Clause cases. I would not, however, perpetuate the doctrinal confusion inherent in the *Flast* two-part "nexus" test. That test is not a reliable indicator of when a federal taxpayer has standing, and it has no sound relationship to the question whether such a plaintiff, with no other interest at stake, should be allowed to bring suit against one of the branches of the Federal Government. In my opinion, it should be abandoned.

I

My difficulties with *Flast* are several. The opinion purports to separate the question of standing from the merits, *id.*, at 99–101, yet it abruptly returns to the substantive issues raised by a plaintiff for the purpose of determining "whether there is a logical nexus between the status asserted and the claim sought to be adjudicated." *Id.*, at 102. Similarly, the opinion distinguishes between constitutional and prudential limits on standing. *Id.*, at 92–94, 97. I find it impossible, however, to determine whether the two-part "nexus" test created in *Flast* amounts to a constitutional or a prudential limitation, because it has no meaningful connection with the Court's statement of the bare-minimum constitutional requirements for standing.

. . .

Relying on history, the Court [in *Flast*] identified the Establishment Clause as a specific constitutional limitation upon the exercise by Congress of the taxing and spending power conferred by Art. I, § 8....On the other hand, the Tenth Amendment, and apparently the Due Process Clause of the Fifth Amendment, were determined not to be such "specific" limitations. The bases for these determinations are not wholly clear, but it appears that the Court found the Tenth Amendment addressed to the interests of the States, rather than of taxpayers, and the Due Process Clause no protection against increases in tax liability. *Id.*, at 105.

In my opinion, Mr. Justice Harlan's critique of the *Flast* "nexus" test is unanswerable. As he pointed out, "the Court's standard for the determination of standing [*i.e.*, sufficiently concrete adverseness] and its criteria for the satisfaction of that standard are entirely unrelated." *Id.*, at 122. Assuming that the relevant constitutional inquiry is the intensity of the plaintiff's concern, as the Court initially posited, *id.*, at 99, the *Flast* criteria "are not in any sense a measurement of any plaintiff's interest in the outcome of any suit." *Id.*, at 121 (Harlan, J., dissenting). A plaintiff's incentive to challenge an expenditure does not turn on the "unconnected fact" that it relates to a regulatory rather than a spending program, *id.*, at 122, or on whether the constitutional provision on which he relies is a "specific limitation" upon Congress' spending powers. *Id.*, at 123.

The ambiguities inherent in the *Flast* "nexus" limitations on federal taxpayer standing are illustrated by this case. There can be little doubt about respondent's fervor in pursuing his case, both within administrative channels and at every level of the federal courts. The intensity of his interest appears to bear no relationship to the fact that, literally speaking, he is not challenging directly a congressional exercise of the taxing and spending power. On the other hand, if the involvement of the taxing and spending power has some relevance, it requires no great leap in reasoning to conclude that the Statement and Account Clause, Art. I, § 9, cl. 7, on which respondent relies, is inextricably linked to that power. And that Clause might well be seen as a "specific" limitation on congressional spending. Indeed, it could be viewed as the most democratic of limitations. Thus, although the Court's application of *Flast* to the instant case is probably literally correct, adherence to the *Flast* test in this instance suggests, as does *Flast* itself, that the test is not a sound or logical limitation on standing.

The lack of real meaning and of principled content in the *Flast* "nexus" test renders it likely that it will in time collapse of its own weight, as Mr. Justice Douglas predicted in his concurring opinion in that case. 392 U. S., at 107....

Relaxation of standing requirements is directly related to the expansion of judicial power. It seems to me inescapable that allowing unrestricted taxpayer or citizen standing would significantly alter the allocation of power at the national level, with a shift away from a democratic form of government. I also believe that repeated and essentially head-on confrontations between the life-tenured branch and the representative branches of government will not, in the long run, be beneficial to either. The public confidence essential to the former and the vitality critical to the latter may well erode if we do not exercise self-restraint in the utilization of our power to negative the actions of the other branches. We should be ever mindful of the contradictions that would arise if a democracy were to permit general oversight of the elected branches of government by a nonrepresentative, and in large measure insulated, judicial branch. Moreover, the argument that the Court should allow unrestricted taxpayer or citizen standing underestimates the ability of the representative branches of the Federal Government to respond to the citizen pressure that has been responsible in large measure for the current drift toward expanded standing. Indeed, taxpayer or citizen advocacy, given its potentially broad base, is precisely the type of leverage that in a democracy ought to be employed against the branches that were intended to be responsive to public attitudes about the appropriate operation of government....

The power recognized in *Marbury* v. *Madison,* 1 Cranch 137 (1803), is a potent one. Its prudent use seems to me incompatible with unlimited notions of taxpayer and citizen standing. Were we to utilize this power as indiscriminately as is now being urged, we may witness efforts by the representative branches drastically to curb its use....

. . .

MR. JUSTICE DOUGLAS, dissenting.

. . .

From the history of the [Statement and Account Clause] it is apparent that the Framers inserted it in the Constitution to give the public knowledge of the way public funds are expended. No one has a greater "personal stake" in policing this protective measure than a taxpayer. Indeed, if a taxpayer may not raise the question, who may do so? The Court states that discretion to release information is in the first instance "committed to the surveillance of Congress," and that the right of the citizenry to information under Art. I, §9, cl. 7, cannot be enforced directly, but only through the "[s]low, cumbersome, and unresponsive" electoral process. One has only to read constitutional history to realize that statement would shock Mason and Madison. Congress of course has discretion; but to say that it has the power to read the clause out of the Constitution when it comes to one or two or three agencies is astounding....

MR. JUSTICE STEWART, with whom MR. JUSTICE MARSHALL joins, dissenting.

. . .

On the merits, I presume that the Government's position would be that the Statement and Account Clause of the Constitution does not impose an affirmative duty upon it; that any such duty does not in any event run to Richardson; that any such duty is subject to legislative qualifications, one of which is applicable here; and that the question involved is political and thus not justiciable. Richardson might ultimately be thrown out of court on any one of these grounds, or some other. But to say that he might ultimately lose his lawsuit certainly does not mean that he had no standing to bring it.

For the reasons expressed, I believe that Richardson had standing to bring this action. Accordingly, I would affirm the judgment of the Court of Appeals.

MR. JUSTICE BRENNAN, dissenting [*at 235*].

The '"standing" of a plaintiff to be heard on a claim of invasion of his alleged legally protected right is established, in my view, by his good-faith allegation that " 'the challenged action has caused him injury in fact.' " *Barlow v. Collins,* 397 U. S. 159, 167–168 (1970) (concurring in the result and dissenting)....

Richardson plainly alleged injury in fact. My Brother STEWART demonstrates this in his analysis of Richardson's claimed right to have the budget of the Central Intelligence Agency published. The claim was not merely that failure to publish was a violation of the Constitution. The claim went further and alleged that this violation deprived Richardson, as an individual, and not as an inseparable part of the citizenry, of a right given him by Art. I, § 9, cl. 7. Moreover, his complaint, properly construed, alleged that the violations caused him injury not only in respect of his right as a citizen to know how Congress was spending the public fisc, but also in respect of his right as a voter to receive information to aid his decision how and for whom to vote. These claims may ultimately fail on the merits, but Richardson has "standing" to assert them.

Allen v. Wright

468 U.S. 737 (1984)

Inez Wright and several other black parents had children attending public schools in districts that were undergoing desegregation. They brought this nationwide class action against the federal government, alleging that the Internal Revenue Service (1) had not adopted sufficient standards and procedures to fulfill its obligation to deny tax-exempt status to racially discriminatory private schools, and (2) had thereby harmed the parents and interfered with their children's opportunity to receive an education in desegregated public schools. W. Wayne Allen, the head of a private school identified in the complaint, intervened as a defendant. With an eye to the separation of powers doctrine, the Court held that the parents lacked standing to sue.

JUSTICE O'CONNOR delivered the opinion of the Court.

. . .

II
A

Article III of the Constitution confines the federal courts to adjudicating actual "cases" and "controversies." As the Court explained in *Valley Forge Christian College v. Americans United for Separation of Church and State, Inc.*, 454 U.S. 464, 471–476 (1982), the "case or controversy" requirement defines with respect to the Judicial Branch the idea of separation of powers on which the Federal Government is founded. The several doctrines that have grown up to elaborate that requirement are "founded in concern about the proper—and properly limited—role of the courts in a democratic society." *Warth v. Seldin*, 422 U.S. 490, 498 (1975).

"All of the doctrines that cluster about Article III—not only standing but mootness, ripeness, political question, and the like—relate in part, and in different though overlapping ways, to an idea, which is more than an intuition but less than a rigorous and explicit theory, about the constitutional and prudential limits to the powers of an unelected, unrepresentative judiciary in our kind of government." *Vander Jagt v. O'Neill*, 226 U.S. App. D.C. 14, 26–27, 699 F.2d 1166, 1178–1179 (1983) (Bork, J., concurring).

The case-or-controversy doctrines state fundamental limits on federal judicial power in our system of government.

The Art. III doctrine that requires a litigant to have "standing" to invoke the power of a federal court is perhaps the most important of these doctrines....

...Like most legal notions, the standing concepts have gained considerable definition from developing case law. In many cases the standing question can be answered chiefly by comparing the allegations of the particular complaint to those made in prior standing cases. See, *e.g., Los Angeles v. Lyons*, *supra,* at 102–105. More important, the law of Art. III standing is built on a single basic idea—the idea of separation of powers. It is this fact which makes possible the gradual clarification of the law through judicial application. Of course, both federal and state courts have long experience in applying and elaborating in numerous contexts the pervasive and fundamental notion of separation of powers.

Determining standing in a particular case may be facilitated by clarifying principles or even clear rules developed in prior cases. Typically, however, the standing inquiry requires careful judicial examination of a complaint's allegations to ascertain whether the particular plaintiff is entitled to an adjudication of the particular claims asserted. Is the injury too abstract, or otherwise not appropriate, to be considered judicially cognizable? Is the line of causation between the illegal conduct and injury too attenuated? Is the prospect of obtaining relief from the injury as a result of a favorable ruling too speculative? These questions and any others relevant to the standing inquiry must be answered by reference to the Art. III notion that federal courts may exercise power only "in the last resort, and as a necessity," *Chicago & Grand Trunk R. Co. v. Wellman*, 143 U.S. 339, 345 (1892), and only when adjudication is "consistent with a system of separated powers and [the dispute is one] traditionally thought to be capable of resolution through the judicial process," *Flast v. Cohen*, 392 U.S. 83, 97 (1968). See *Valley Forge*, 454 U.S., at 472–473.

B

Respondents allege two injuries in their complaint to support their standing to bring this lawsuit. First, they say that they are harmed directly by the mere fact of Government financial aid to discriminatory private schools. Second, they say that the federal tax exemptions to racially discriminatory private schools in their communities impair their ability to have their public schools desegregated....

In the Court of Appeals, respondents apparently relied on the first injury. Thus, the court below asserted that "[t]he sole injury [respondents] claim is the denigration they suffer" as a result of the tax exemptions.... In this Court, respondents have not focused on this claim of injury. Here they stress the effect of the tax exemptions on their "equal educational opportunities,"... renewing reliance on the second injury described in their complaint.

Because respondents have not clearly disclaimed reliance on either of the injuries described in their complaint, we address both allegations of injury. We conclude that neither suffices to support respondents' standing. The first fails under clear precedents of this Court because it does not constitute judicially cognizable injury. The second fails because the alleged injury is not fairly traceable to the assertedly unlawful conduct of the IRS.

1

Respondent's first claim of injury can be interpreted in two ways. It might be a claim simply to have the Government avoid the violation of law alleged in respondents' complaint. Alternatively, it might be a claim of stigmatic injury, or denigration, suffered by all members of a racial group when the Government discriminates on the basis of race. Under neither interpretation is this claim of injury judicially cognizable.

. . .

The consequences of recognizing respondents' standing on the basis of their first claim of injury illustrate why our cases plainly hold that such injury is not judicially cognizable. If the abstract stigmatic injury were cognizable, standing would extend nationwide to all members of the particular racial groups against which the Government was alleged to be discriminating by its grant of a tax exemption to a racially discriminatory school, regardless of the location of that school. All such persons could claim the same sort of abstract stigmatic injury respondents assert in their first claim of injury. A black person in Hawaii could challenge the grant of a tax exemption to a racially discriminatory school in Maine. Recognition of standing in such circumstances would transform the federal courts into "no more than a vehicle for the vindication of the value interest of concerned bystanders." *United States v. SCRAP*, 412 U.S. 669, 687 (1973). Constitutional limits on the role of the federal courts preclude such a transformation.

2

It is in their complaint's second claim of injury that respondents allege harm to a concrete, personal interest that can support standing in some circumstances. The injury they identify—their children's diminished ability to receive an education in a racially integrated school—is, beyond any doubt, not only judicially cognizable but, as shown by cases from *Brown v. Board of Education*, 347 U.S. 483 (1954), to *Bob Jones University v. United States*, 461 U.S. 574 (1983), one of the most serious injuries recognized in our legal system. Despite the constitutional importance of curing the injury alleged injury by respondents, however, the federal judiciary may not redress it unless standing requirements are met. In this case, respondents' second claim of injury cannot support standing because the injury alleged is not fairly traceable to the Government conduct respondents challenge as unlawful.

The illegal conduct challenged by respondents is the IRS's grant of tax exemptions to some racially discriminatory schools. The line of causation between that conduct and desegregation of respondents' schools is attenuated at best. From the perspective of the IRS, the injury to respondents is highly indirect and "results form the independent action of some third party not before the court," *Simon v. Eastern Kentucky Welfare Rights Org.*, 426 U.S., at 42. As the Court pointed out in *Warth v. Seldin*, 422 U.S., at 505, "the indirectness of the injury...may make it substantially more difficult to meet the minimum requirement of Art. III...."

The diminished ability of respondents' children to receive a desegregated education would be fairly traceable to unlawful IRS grants of tax exemptions only if there were enough racially discriminatory private schools receiving tax exemptions in respondents' communities for withdrawal of those exemptions to make an appreciable difference in public school integration. Respondents have made no such allegation. It is, first, uncertain how many racially discriminatory private schools are in fact receiving tax exemptions. Moreover, it is entirely speculative, as respondents themselves conceded in the Court of Appeals... whether withdrawal of a tax exemption from any particular school would lead the school to change its policies. See 480 F. Supp., at 796. It is just as speculative whether any given parent of a child attending such a private school would decide to transfer the child to public school as a result of any changes in education or financial policy made by the private school once it was threatened with loss of tax-exempt status. It is also pure speculation whether, in a particular community, a large enough number of the numerous relevant school officials and parents would reach decisions that collectively would have a significant impact on the racial composition of the public schools.

The links in the chain of causation between the challenged Government conduct and the asserted injury are far too weak for the chain as a whole to sustain respondents' standing....

The idea of separation of powers that underlies standing doctrine explains why our cases preclude the conclusion that respondents' alleged injury "fairly can be traced to the challenged action" of the IRS. *Simon v. Eastern Kentucky Welfare Rights Org., supra,* at 41. That conclusion would pave the way generally for suits challenging, not specifically identifiable Government violations of law, but the particular programs agencies establish to carry out their legal obligations. Such suits, even when premised on allegations of several instances of violations of law, are rarely if ever appropriate for federal-court adjudication.

"Carried to its logical end, [respondents'] approach would have the federal courts as virtually continuing monitors of the wisdom and soundness of Executive action; such a role is appropriate for the Congress acting through its committees and the 'power of the purse'; it is not the role of the judiciary, absent actual present of immediately threatened injury resulting from unlawful governmental action." *Laird v. Tatum,* 408 U.S., at 15.

See also *Gilligan v. Morgan,* 413 U.S. 1, 14 (1973) (BLACKMUN, J., concurring).

The same concern for the proper role of the federal courts is reflected in cases like *O'Shea v. Littleton,* 414 U.S. 488 (1974), *Rizzo v. Goode,* 423 U.S. 362 (1976), and *Los Angeles v. Lyons,* 461 U.S. 95 (1983). In all three cases plaintiffs sought injunctive relief directed at certain systemwide law enforcement practices. The Court held in each case that, absent an allegation of a specific threat of being subject to the challenged practices, plaintiffs had no standing to ask for an injunction. Animating this Court's holdings was the principle that "[a] federal court... is not the proper forum to press" general complaints about the way in which government goes about its business. *Id.,* at 112.

Case-or-controversy considerations, the Court observed in *O'Shea v. Littleton, supra,* at 499, "obviously shade into into those determining whether the complaint states a sound basis for equitable relief." The latter set of considerations should therefore inform our judgment about whether respondents have standing. Most relevant to this case is the principle articulated in *Rizzo v. Goode, supra,* at 378–379:

"When a plaintiff seeks to enjoin the activity of a government agency, even within a unitary court system, his case must contend with 'the well-established rule that the Government has traditionally been granted the widest latitude in the "dispatch of its own internal affairs," *Cafeteria Workers v. McElroy,* 367 U.S. 886, 896 (1961),' quoted in *Sampson v. Murray,* 415 U.S. 61, 83 (1974)."

When transported into the Art. III context, that principle, grounded as it is in the idea of separation of powers, counsels against recognizing standing in a case brought, not to enforce specific legal obligations whose violation works a direct harm, but to seek a restructuring of the apparatus established by the Executive Branch to fulfill its legal duties. The Constitution, after all, assigns to the Executive Branch, and not to the Judicial Branch, the duty to "take Care that the Laws be faithfully executed." U.S. Const., Art. II, §3. We could not recognize respondents' standing in this case without running afoul of that structural principle.

· · ·

JUSTICE MARSHALL took no part in the decision of these cases.

JUSTICE BRENNAN, dissenting.

· · ·

JUSTICE STEVENS, with whom JUSTICE BLACKMUN joins, dissenting....

C. MOOTNESS

Mootness raises some of the same issues as standing and advisory opinions. Litigants able to establish standing at the outset of a case may find their personal stake diluted or eliminated by subsequent events. Because of a change in law or facts, the case or controversy may disappear and leave insufficient adverseness to guide the courts. If the action that triggered the complaint ceases, a court may have no means of granting relief.[12] At that point a decision could become, in effect, an advisory opinion.

A case is not mooted simply because one party discontinues a contested action. Judicial review cannot be circumvented merely through a strategy of starts and stops. If the controversy is likely to reappear, judicial scrutiny "ought not to be, as they might be, defeated, by short term orders, capable of repetition, yet evading review...."[13] Complaints about an election process, even after a particular election is over, may remain a continuing controversy that requires decision by the courts. Moore v. Ogilvie, 394 U.S. 814, 816 (1969).

If the judiciary is unprepared or unwilling to decide an issue, mootness is one avenue of escape. In 1952 the Supreme Court held that a public school Bible-reading case was moot because the child had graduated by the time the case had reached the Supreme Court. Although other students would be subjected to the same school policy in the future, the Court declared that "no decision we could render now would protect any rights she may once have had, and this Court does not sit to decide arguments after events have put them to rest." Doremus v. Board of Education, 342 U.S. 429, 433 (1952).

In a 1974 case, a white student denied admission to a law school claimed that the school's affirmative action policy discriminated against him, allowing minorities with lower test scores to enter. He was admitted after winning in trial court. By the time the case reached the

---

The Mootness Doctrine

The Court's refusal to hear moot cases was initially grounded in the common law doctrine that courts lack power to decide abstract questions in cases where no dispute exists. Courts have traditionally declined to hear cases in which neither party stands to gain or lose by a decision, on the theory that the state should not "be burdened with the expense of trying such unsubstantial controversies." Over the past decade, however, the Court has based its mootness decisions specifically on the case or controversy requirement of article III of the Constitution, a broad limitation which maintains the separation of powers by "assur[ing] that the federal courts will not intrude into areas committed to the other branches of government." The doctrine that courts will not hear moot cases thus serves two complementary purposes: it prevents the useless expenditure of judicial resources and assures that the courts will not intrude prematurely into policymaking in a manner that will unnecessarily constrain the other branches of government.

SOURCE: Note, "The Mootness Doctrine in the Supreme Court," 88 Harv. L. Rev. 373, 374–76 (1974) (footnotes omitted).

---

12. California v. San Pablo and Tulare Railroad Co., 149 U.S. 308 (1893); Jones v. Montague, 194 U.S. 147 (1904); Richardson v. McChesney, 218 U.S. 487 (1910). See also Sidney A. Diamond, "Federal Jurisdiction to Decide Moot Cases," 94 U. Pa. L. Rev. 125 (1946); United States v. Hamburg-American Co., 239 U.S. 466 (1916); United States v. Alaska S.S. Co., 253 U.S. 113 (1920); Brockington v. Rhodes, 396 U.S. 41 (1969); Hall v. Beals, 396 U.S. 45 (1969); Lewis v. Continental Bank Corp., 494 U.S. 472 (1990).

13. Southern Pacific Terminal Co. v. ICC, 219 U.S. 498, 515 (1911). See Washington v. Harper, 494 U.S. 210 (1990); United States v. Phosphate Export Corp., 393 U.S. 199, 203 (1968) and United States v. W. T. Grant Co., 345 U.S. 629, 632 (1953).

Supreme Court he was in his third and final year. The school assured the Court that he would be allowed to complete his legal studies regardless of the disposition of the case. The Court refused to reach the merits of the case, considering it moot. Four Justices dissented, predicting (correctly) that the issue would inevitably return to the Supreme Court. DeFUNIS v. ODE-GAARD, 416 U.S. 312 (1974). Within a few years another case challenging a university's affirmative action program found its way to the Supreme Court, in *Regents of the University of California* v. *Bakke* (1978), and this time the Court confronted the merits. 438 U.S. 265 (1978). For reading on *Bakke*, see chapter 15.

In *Roe* v. *Wade* (1973), plaintiffs argued that the Texas criminal abortion laws were unconstitutionally vague and infringed upon their right of privacy. The laws prohibited abortion except on medical advice to save the mother's life. Texas responded that one of the suits, brought by a pregnant single woman, was moot because her pregnancy had terminated. Justice Blackmun, writing for the majority, rejected that position:

> But when, as here, pregnancy is a significant fact in the litigation, the normal 266-day human gestation period is so short that the pregnancy will come to term before the usual appellate process is complete. If that termination makes a case moot, pregnancy litigation seldom will survive much beyond the trial stage, and appellate review will be effectively denied. Our law should not be that rigid. Pregnancy often comes more than once to the same woman, and in the general population, if man is to survive, it will always be with us. Pregnancy provides a classic justification for a conclusion of nonmootness. It truly could be "capable of repetition, yet evading review." 410 U.S. 113, 125 (1973).

In 1984, the Supreme Court had an opportunity to dismiss as moot an affirmative action case involving a court order for the dismissal or demotion of white employees who had more seniority than black employees who were retained. All white employees laid off as a result of the order were restored to duty a month later. Those demoted were later offered their old positions. Those facts did not prevent the Supreme Court in *Firefighters* v. *Stotts* from deciding the case and reversing the lower court actions. 467 U.S. 561, 568–72 (1984). Although some of the dissenters accused the majority of issuing an advisory opinion, the Court was evidently ready and willing to circumscribe the reach of affirmative action. The twists and turns of the mootness doctrine reflect the Court's effort to maintain a proper relationship with the other political branches.

In 2000, the Court held that the closing of a nude dancing club did not render the case moot. The city still needed to know whether its ordinance proscribing nudity in public places was constitutional and could be enforced. City of Erie v. Pap's A.M., 120 S.Ct. 1382 (2000).

DeFunis v. Odegaard

416 U.S. 312 (1974)

Marco DeFunis, Jr., was denied admission to the University of Washington Law School, although his test scores were higher than those of some of the minorities admitted. He was accepted after a trial court found in his favor and was in his third and final year when the case reached the Supreme Court. The question was whether the case should be dismissed on grounds of mootness.

PER CURIAM.

In 1971 the petitioner Marco DeFunis, Jr., applied for admission as a first-year student at the University of Washington Law School, a state-operated institution. The size of the incoming first-year class was to be limited to 150 persons, and

the Law School received some 1,600 applications for these 150 places. DeFunis was eventually notified that he had been denied admission. He thereupon commenced this suit in a Washington trial court, contending that the procedures and criteria employed by the Law School Admissions

Committee invidiously discriminated against him on account of his race in violation of the Equal Protection Clause of the Fourteenth Amendment to the United States Constitution.

DeFunis brought the suit on behalf of himself alone, and not as the representative of any class, against the various respondents, who are officers, faculty members, and members of the Board of Regents of the University of Washington. He asked the trial court to issue a mandatory injunction commanding the respondents to admit him as a member of the first-year class entering in September 1971, on the ground that the Law School admissions policy had resulted in the unconstitutional denial of his application for admission. The trial court agreed with his claim and granted the requested relief. DeFunis was, accordingly, admitted to the Law School and began his legal studies there in the fall of 1971. On appeal, the Washington Supreme Court reversed the judgment of the trial court and held that the Law School admissions policy did not violate the Constitution. By this time DeFunis was in his second year at the Law School.

He then petitioned this Court for a writ of certiorari, and MR. JUSTICE DOUGLAS, as Circuit Justice, stayed the judgment of the Washington Supreme Court pending the "final disposition of the case by this Court." By virtue of this stay, DeFunis has remained in law school, and was in the first term of his third and final year when this Court first considered his certiorari petition in the fall of 1973. Because of our concern that DeFunis' third-year standing in the Law School might have rendered this case moot, we requested the parties to brief the question of mootness before we acted on the petition. In response, both sides contended that the case was not moot. The respondents indicated that, if the decision of the Washington Supreme Court were permitted to stand, the petitioner could complete the term for which he was then enrolled but would have to apply to the faculty for permission to continue in the school before he could register for another term.

We granted the petition for certiorari on November 19, 1973, 414 U.S. 1038. The case was in due course orally argued on February 26, 1974.

In response to questions raised from the bench during the oral argument, counsel for the petitioner has informed the Court that DeFunis has now registered "for his final quarter in law school." Counsel for the respondents have made clear that the Law School will not in any way seek to abrogate this registration. In light of DeFunis' recent registration for the last quarter of his final law school year, and the Law School's assurance that his registration is fully effective, the insistent question again arises whether this case is not moot, and to that question we now turn.

The starting point for analysis is the familiar proposition that "federal courts are without power to decide questions that cannot affect the rights of litigants in the case before them." *North Carolina v. Rice*, 404 U.S. 244, 246 (1971).... Although as a matter of Washington state law it appears that this case would be saved from mootness by "the great public interest in the continuing issues raised by this appeal," 82 Wash. 2d 11, 23 n. 6, 507 P. 2d 1169, 1177 n. 6 (1973), the fact remains that under Art. III "[e]ven in cases arising in the state courts, the question of mootness is a federal one which a federal court must resolve before it assumes jurisdiction." *North Carolina v. Rice, supra,* at 246.

The respondents have represented that, without regard to the ultimate resolution of the issues in this case, DeFunis will remain a student in the Law School for the duration of any term in which he has already enrolled. Since he has now registered for his final term, it is evident that he will be given an opportunity to complete all academic and other requirements for graduation, and, if he does so, will receive his diploma regardless of any decision this Court might reach on the merits of this case. In short, all parties agree that DeFunis is now entitled to complete his legal studies at the University of Washington and to receive his degree from that institution. A determination by this Court of the legal issues tendered by the parties is no longer necessary to compel that result, and could not serve to prevent it. DeFunis did not cast his suit as a class action, and the only remedy he requested was an injunction commanding his admission to the Law School. He was not only accorded that remedy, but he now has also been irrevocably admitted to the final term of the final year of the Law School course. The controversy between the parties has thus clearly ceased to be "definite and concrete" and no longer "touch[es] the legal relations of parties having adverse legal interests." *Aetna Life Ins. Co. v. Haworth,* 300 U. S. 227, 240–241 (1937).

It matters not that these circumstances partially stem from a policy decision on the part of the respondent Law School authorities. The respondents, through their counsel, the Attorney General of the State, have professionally represented that in no event will the status of DeFunis now be affected by any view this Court might express on the merits of this controversy....

. . .

...[J]ust because this particular case did not reach the Court until the eve of the petitioner's graduation from law school, it hardly follows that the issue he raises will in the future evade review. If the admissions procedures of the Law School remain unchanged, there is no reason to suppose that a subsequent case attacking those procedures will not come with relative speed to this Court, now that the Supreme Court of Washington has spoken....

...[T]he judgment of the Supreme Court of Washington is vacated, and the cause is remanded for such proceedings as by that court may be deemed appropriate.

It is so ordered.

[Justice Douglas prepared a separate dissent.]

MR. JUSTICE BRENNAN, with whom MR. JUSTICE DOUGLAS, MR. JUSTICE WHITE, and MR. JUSTICE MARSHALL concur, dissenting.

I respectfully dissent. Many weeks of the school term remain, and petitioner may not receive his degree despite respondents' assurances that petitioner will be allowed to complete this term's schooling regardless of our decision. Any number of unexpected events—illness, economic necessity, even academic failure—might prevent his graduation at the end of the term. Were that misfortune to befall, and were petitioner required to register for yet another term, the prospect that he would again face the hurdle of the admissions

policy is real, not fanciful; for respondents warn that "Mr. DeFunis would have to take some appropriate action to request continued admission for the remainder of his law school education, and *some discretionary action by the University on such request would have to be taken.*" Respondents' Memorandum on the Question of Mootness 3–4 (emphasis supplied). Thus, respondents' assurances have not dissipated the possibility that petitioner might once again have to run the gantlet of the University's allegedly unlawful admissions policy....

. . .

Moreover, in endeavoring to dispose of this case as moot, the Court clearly disserves the public interest. The constitutional issues which are avoided today concern vast numbers of people, organizations, and colleges and universities, as evidenced by the filing of twenty-six *amicus curiae* briefs. Few constitutional questions in recent history have stirred as much debate, and they will not disappear. They must inevitably return to the federal courts and ultimately again to this Court. Cf. *Richardson* v. *Wright,* 405 U. S. 208, 212 (1972) (dissenting opinion). Because avoidance of repetitious litigation serves the public interest, that inevitability counsels against mootness determinations, as here, not compelled by the record....

. . .

D. RIPENESS

Just as a case brought too late can be moot, a case brought too early may not yet be ripe. Sometimes this results from a failure to exhaust administrative and state remedies. Plaintiffs must show that they have explored all avenues of relief before turning to the federal courts. Premature consideration by the courts does more than create unnecessary workload. It deprives judges of information needed for informed adjudication and forces them to deal at an abstract, speculative, and hypothetical level. The ripeness doctrine encourages settlement in the administrative arena (see box on next page).

Ripeness was at issue in a 1947 case brought by twelve federal employees against the Civil Service Commission. They wanted to prevent the Commission from enforcing a section of the Hatch Act that prohibited them from taking "any active part in political management or in political campaigns." The federal workers complained that the statute deprived them of their First Amendment rights of speech, press, and assembly. The Supreme Court regarded the employees' fears of losing their jobs as too speculative:

The power of courts, and ultimately of this Court, to pass upon the constitutionality of acts of Congress arises only when the interests of litigants require the use of this judicial authority for their protection against actual interference. A hypothetical threat is not

---

The Ripeness Doctrine

...The injunctive and declaratory judgment remedies are discretionary, and courts traditionally have been reluctant to apply them to administrative determinations unless these arise in the context of a controversy "ripe" for judicial resolution. Without undertaking to survey the intricacies of the ripeness doctrine it is fair to say that its basic rationale is to prevent the courts, through avoidance of premature adjudication, from entangling themselves in abstract disagreements over administrative policies, and also to protect the agencies from judicial interference until an administrative decision has been formalized and its effects felt in a concrete way by the challenging parties. The problem is best seen in a twofold aspect, requiring us to evaluate both the fitness of the issues for judicial decision and the hardship to the parties of withholding court consideration.

SOURCE: Abbott Laboratories v. Gardner, 387 U.S. 136, 148–49 (1967) (footnotes omitted).

---

enough. We can only speculate as to the kinds of political activity the appellants desire to engage in or as to the contents of their proposed public statements or the circumstances of their publication. It would not accord with judicial responsibility to adjudge, in a matter involving constitutionality, between the freedom of the individual and the requirements of public order except when definite rights appear upon the one side and definite prejudicial interferences upon the other. United Public Workers v. Mitchell, 330 U.S. 75, 90 (1947).

The situation of one of the federal employees, George P. Poole, was not hypothetical. He faced dismissal unless he could refute the charges of the Commission that his political activities had violated the Hatch Act. Accepting his suit as a justiciable case, the Court held that disciplinary action under the Hatch Act would not violate the Constitution. Justices Black and Douglas dissented, believing that the Court should have heard the cases of all twelve litigants. The threat of discharge, they said, was real rather than fanciful, immediate not remote. Douglas observed:

> ...[T]o require these employees first to suffer the hardship of a discharge is not only to make them incur a penalty; it makes inadequate, if not wholly illusory, any legal remedy which they might have. Men who must sacrifice their means of livelihood in order to test their jobs must either pursue prolonged and expensive litigation as unemployed persons or pull up their roots, change their life careers, and seek employment in other fields.

The issue of preventive relief often splits the courts. Should judges rule on a statute before its sanctions are invoked? A decision might offer relief to threatened individuals, but it also requires the courts to rule in advance of a concrete case or controversy. It forces judgments on hypothetical situations that raise remote and abstract issues. And yet judicial inaction can lead to irreparable harm to individuals once the statute is enforced. Longshoremen's Union v. Boyd, 347 U.S. 222, 224–26 (1954). Judicial review may be both necessary and appropriate to protect individuals before an agency enforces a regulation.[14]

The extreme point is reached when a suit lingers so long in the courts that it becomes "overripe." Justice Black described a case that bounced around for ten years before the Supreme Court sent it back to the lower courts "because of the staleness of the record." Hugo L. Black, A Constitutional Faith 17 (1968).

---

14. Abbott Laboratories v. Gardner, 387 U.S. 136 (1967). See also Toilet Goods Assn. v. Gardner, 387 U.S. 158 (1967) and Gardner v. Toilet Goods Assn., 387 U.S. 167 (1967).

Marking Time

As with mootness, disposing of a case on the ground of ripeness may delay but not necessarily avoid decision. In 1943 and 1961 the Supreme Court refused to rule on the constitutionality of Connecticut laws that prohibited married couples from using contraceptives or physicians from giving advice about their use. Tileston v. Ullman, 318 U.S. 44 (1943); Poe v. Ullman, 367 U.S. 497 (1961). Because the record suggested that the state was unlikely to prosecute offenders, the Court held that it lacked jurisdiction to decide hypothetical cases. In the 1961 case, the Court ignored the fact that the state had closed several birth control clinics. POE v. ULLMAN, 367 U.S. 497 (1961). After that decision, the state arrested physicians who had operated a birth control clinic in New Haven. They were found guilty and fined $100 each. In 1965 the Supreme Court held that they had standing and declared the Connecticut statute invalid under the "penumbra" of the Bill of Rights. Griswold v. Connecticut, 381 U.S. 479 (1965).

"Ripeness" may provide the means to sidestep momentarily a socially sensitive issue. Immediately after the Court had decided *Brown* v. *Board of Education* in 1954, it was faced with the constitutionality of a Virginia miscegenation statute. To strike down a law banning interracial marriages would stimulate the fears of critics of the decision who predicted that integrated schools would lead to "mongrelization" of the white race. The Court returned the case to the lower courts by citing the "inadequacy of the record" and the lack of a "properly-presented federal question." Naim v. Naim, 350 U.S. 891 (1955); 350 U.S. 985 (1956). In essence, the Court decided to buy some time. Years later, after the principle of desegregation had been safely established, the Court struck down the Virginia statute. Loving v. Virginia, 388 U.S. 1 (1967).

Judicial doctrine and political practicalities were joined in a 1978 case involving a congressional limitation on liability for accidents by private nuclear plants. A "hypothetical" issue, to be sure, but it was intuitively unappealing to insist that the courts await a nuclear catastrophe before deciding. The Court was satisfied that the test of ripeness had been met by two effects already evident from the operation of nuclear power plants: the emission of small quantities of radiation in the air and water, and an increase in the temperature of two lakes used for recreational purposes.[15]

Poe v. Ullman

367 U.S. 497 (1961)

A married couple, a married woman, and a doctor sued for declaratory relief against the threatened enforcement of Connecticut's birth control laws that prohibited married couples from using contraceptives and physicians from advising married couples about their use. Paul and Pauline Poe are the fictitious names of the plaintiffs, threatened with prosecution by the state's attorney, Abraham S. Ullman.

MR. JUSTICE FRANKFURTER announced the judgment of the Court and an opinion in which THE CHIEF JUSTICE, MR. JUSTICE CLARK and MR. JUSTICE WHITTAKER join.

These appeals challenge the constitutionality, under the Fourteenth Amendment, of Connecticut statutes which, as authoritatively construed by the Connecticut Supreme Court of Errors, prohibit the use of contraceptive devices and the giving of medical advice in the use of such devices. In proceedings seeking declarations of law, not on review of convictions for violation of the statutes, that court has ruled that these statutes would be applicable in the case of married couples and even under claim that conception would constitute a serious threat to the health or life of the female spouse....

---

15. Duke Power Co. v. Carolina Environment Study Group, 438 U.S. 69, 72–74, 81–82 (1978). Also on the need for courts to avoid premature decisions: Renne v. Geary, 501 U.S. 312 (1991); Socialist Labor Party v. Gilligan, 406 U.S. 583 (1972); Adler v. Board of Education, 342 U.S. 485, 497–508 (Frankfurter, J., dissenting).

...The State's Attorney intends to prosecute offenses against the State's laws, and claims that the giving of contraceptive advice and the use of contraceptive devices would be offenses forbidden by Conn. Gen. Stat. Rev., 1958, §§ 53–32 and 54–196....

Appellants' complaints in these declaratory judgment proceedings do not clearly, and certainly do not in terms, allege that appellee Ullman threatens to prosecute them for use of, or for giving advice concerning, contraceptive devices. The allegations are merely that, in the course of his public duty, he intends to prosecute any offenses against Connecticut law, and that he claims that use of and advice concerning contraceptives would constitute offenses. The lack of immediacy of the threat described by these allegations might alone raise serious questions of non-justiciability of appellants' claims. See *United Public Workers* v. *Mitchell,* 330 U.S. 75, 88. But even were we to read the allegations to convey a clear threat of imminent prosecutions, we are not bound to accept as true all that is alleged on the face of the complaint and admitted, technically, by demurrer, any more than the Court is bound by stipulation of the parties. *Swift & Co.* v. *Hocking Valley R. Co.,* 243 U.S. 281, 289. Formal agreement between parties that collides with plausibility is too fragile a foundation for indulging in constitutional adjudication.

The Connecticut law prohibiting the use of contraceptives has been on the State's books since 1879. Conn. Acts 1879, c. 78. During the more than three-quarters of a century since its enactment, a prosecution for its violation seems never to have been initiated, save in *State* v. *Nelson,* 126 Conn. 412, 11 A. 2d 856....

The fact that Connecticut has not chosen to press the enforcement of this statute deprives these controversies of the immediacy which is an indispensable condition of constitutional adjudication. This Court cannot be umpire to debates concerning harmless, empty shadows. To find it necessary to pass on these statutes now, in order to protect appellants from the hazards of prosecution, would be to close our eyes to reality....

Justiciability is of course not a legal concept with a fixed content or susceptible of scientific verification. Its utilization is the resultant of many subtle pressures, including the appropriateness of the issues for decision by this Court and the actual hardship to the litigants of denying them the relief sought. Both these factors justify withholding adjudication of the constitutional issue raised under the circumstances and in the manner in which they are now before the Court.

Dismissed.

MR. JUSTICE BLACK dissents because he believes that the constitutional questions should be reached and decided.

MR. JUSTICE BRENNAN, concurring in the judgment.

I agree that this appeal must be dismissed for failure to present a real and substantial controversy which unequivocally calls for adjudication of the rights claimed in advance of any attempt by the State to curtail them by criminal prosecution. I am not convinced, on this skimpy record, that these appellants as individuals are truly caught in an inescapable dilemma. The true controversy in this case is over the opening of birth-control clinics on a large scale; it is that which the State has prevented in the past, not the use of contraceptives by isolated and individual married couples....

MR. JUSTICE DOUGLAS, dissenting....

A public clinic dispensing birth-control information has indeed been closed by the State. Doctors and a nurse working in that clinic were arrested by the police and charged with advising married women on the use of contraceptives. That litigation produced *State* v. *Nelson,* 126 Conn. 412, 11 A. 2d 856, which upheld these statutes. That same police raid on the clinic resulted in the seizure of a quantity of the clinic's contraception literature and medical equipment and supplies. The legality of that seizure was in question in *State* v. *Certain Contraceptive Materials,* 126 Conn. 428, 11 A. 2d 863.

The Court refers to the *Nelson* prosecution as a "test case" and implies that it had little impact. Yet its impact was described differently by a contemporary observer who concluded his comment with this sentence: "This serious setback to the birth control movement [the *Nelson* case] led to the closing of all the clinics in the state, just as they had been previously closed in the state of Massachusetts." At oral argument, counsel for appellants confirmed that the clinics are still closed. In response to a question from the bench, he affirmed that "no public or private clinic" has dared give birth-control advice since the decision in the *Nelson* case....

When the Court goes outside the record to determine that Connecticut has adopted "The undeviating policy of nullification...of its anticontraceptive laws," it selects a particularly poor case in which to exercise such a novel power. This is not a law which is a dead letter. Twice since 1940, Connecticut has re-enacted these laws as part of general statutory revisions. Consistently, bills to remove the statutes from the books have been rejected by the legislature. In short, the statutes — far from being the accidental left-overs of another era — are the center of a continuing controversy in the State....

What are these people — doctor and patients — to do? Flout the law and go to prison? Violate the law surreptitiously and hope they will not get caught? By today's decision we leave them no other alternatives. It is not the choice they need have under the regime of the declaratory judgment and our constitutional system. It is not the choice worthy of a civilized society. A sick wife, a concerned husband, a conscientious doctor seek a dignified, discrete, orderly answer to the critical problem confronting them. We should not turn them away and make them flout the law and get arrested to have their constitutional rights determined....

MR. JUSTICE HARLAN, dissenting.

I am compelled, with all respect, to dissent from the dismissal of these appeals. In my view the course which the Court has taken does violence to established concepts of "justiciability," and unjustifiably leaves these appellants under the threat of unconstitutional prosecution.

· · ·

...I find it difficult to believe that doctors generally — and not just those operating specialized clinics — would continue openly to disseminate advice about contraceptives after *Nelson* in reliance on the State's supposed unwillingness to prosecute, or to consider that high-minded members of the profession would in consequence of such inaction deem themselves warranted in disrespecting this law so long as it is on the books. Nor can I regard as "chimerical" the fear of enforcement of these provisions that seems to have caused the disappearance of at least nine birth-control clinics. In short, I fear that the Court has indulged in a bit of sleight of hand to be rid of this case....

· · ·

MR. JUSTICE STEWART, dissenting.

For the reasons so convincingly advanced by both MR. JUSTICE DOUGLAS and MR. JUSTICE HARLAN, I join them in dissenting from the dismissal of these appeals. Since the appeals are nonetheless dismissed, my dissent need go no further. However, in refraining from a discussion of the constitutional issues, I in no way imply that the ultimate result I would reach on the merits of these controversies would differ from the conclusions of my dissenting Brothers.

E. POLITICAL QUESTIONS

The "political question" doctrine survives partly on circular reasoning. In *Marbury* v. *Madison,* Chief Justice Marshall claimed that "Questions in their nature political...can never be made in this court." 5 U.S. (1 Cr.) 137, at 170 (1803). Yet every question that reaches a court is, by its very nature, political. Justice Holmes, hearing a litigant claim that a question concerning a party primary was nonjusticiable because of its political character, said that such an objection "is little more than a play upon words." Nixon v. Herndon, 273 U.S. 536, 540 (1927).

Definitional problems are legion. After refusing to decide a war powers case in 1968, a federal judge declared: "Though it is not always a simple matter to define the meaning of the term "political question,' it is generally used to encompass all questions outside the sphere of judicial power." Velvel v. Johnson, 287 F.Supp. 846, 850 (D. Kans. 1968). That definition recalls this dictionary explanation: "violins are small cellos, and cellos are large violins." Roche, 49 Am. Pol. Sci. Rev. 762, 768 (1955).

Beyond questions of definition, there is some doubt whether a political question doctrine even exists in the sense that courts refuse to adjudicate certain issues. After reviewing political question cases, Louis Henkin concluded: "the Court does not refuse judicial review; it exercises it. It is not dismissing the case or the issue as nonjusticiable; it adjudicates it. It is not refusing to pass on the power of the political branches; it passes upon it, only to affirm that they had the power which had been challenged and that nothing in the Constitution prohibited the particular exercise of it." Henkin, 85 Yale L. J. 597, 606 (1976).

Criteria for Political Questions

1. A textually demonstrable constitutional commitment of the issue to a coordinate political department.

2. A lack of judicially discoverable and manageable standards for resolving it.

3. The impossibility of deciding without an initial policy determination of a kind clearly for nonjudicial discretion.

4. The impossibility of a court's undertaking independent resolution without expressing lack of the respect due coordinate branches of government.

5. An unusual need for unquestioning adherence to a political decision already made.

6. The potentiality of embarrassment from multifarious pronouncements by various departments on one question.

SOURCE: Baker v. Carr, 369 U.S. 186, 217 (1962).

In 1962 the Court identified the areas that are generally classified as political questions. BAKER v. CARR, 369 U.S. 186 (1962). Six criteria indicate the kinds of questions not subject to judicial resolution (see box).

The first criterion is "a textually demonstrable constitutional commitment of the issue to a coordinate political department." However, the very question of whether an issue has been textually committed to a coordinate branch requires judicial interpretation. Powell v. Mc-Cormack, 395 U.S. at 519. Moreover, the fact that an area *is* committed to Congress or the President does not automatically produce a political question. As the Supreme Court noted in 1983, "virtually every challenge to the constitutionality of a statute would be a political question" under that reasoning. INS v. Chadha, 462 U.S. 919, 941. The Court further pointed out:

> It is correct that this controversy may, in a sense, be termed "political." But the presence of constitutional issues with significant political overtones does not automatically invoke the political question doctrine. Resolution of litigation challenging the constitutional authority of one of the three branches cannot be evaded by courts because the issues have political implications in the sense urged by Congress. *Marbury* v. *Madison,* 1 Cranch 137 (1803), was also a "political" case, involving as it did claims under a judicial commission alleged to have been duly signed by the President but not delivered. Id. at 942–43.

During the Vietnam War period, several students at Kent State University in Ohio were killed after the governor had called out the National Guard. The students sought injunctive relief to prevent the governor from taking such actions in the future and to prevent the Guard from future violations of students' constitutional rights. Basically, the students wanted the courts to supervise the future training and operations of the Guard. The Supreme Court regarded those duties as vested solely in Congress by Article I, Section 8, Clause 16, which empowers Congress to provide "for organizing, arming, and disciplining the Militia, and for governing such Part of them as may be employed in the Service of the United States, reserving to the States respectively, the Appointment of the Officers, and the Authority of training the Militia according to the discipline prescribed by Congress." The Court said that such actions were meant to be exercised by the political branches: "it is difficult to conceive of an area of governmental activity in which the courts have less competence." Gilligan v. Morgan, 413 U.S. 1, 10 (1973).

The Court agreed that the concept of political questions was not of fixed content, and that "nonjusticiable" voting rights cases came to be accepted by the courts. But those cases, it said, "represented the Court's efforts to strengthen the political system by assuring a higher level of fairness and responsiveness to the political processes, not the assumption of a continuing judicial review of substantive political judgments entrusted expressly to the coordinate branches of government." Id. at 11. The judiciary accepts the exclusive responsibility of Congress to determine whether a state satisfies the language of Article IV, Section 4, which requires that the United States "shall guarantee to every State in this Union a Republican Form of Government." Luther v. Borden, 7 How. 1 (1849). In 1993 the Court held that the particular procedure used by the Senate to try impeachments, including the use of a committee to take testimony and gather evidence, is a nonjusticiable political question. Some of the Justices, however, were reluctant to say that Senate procedures for trying impeachments could never be reviewed by the courts. NIXON v. UNITED STATES, 506 U.S. 224 (1993).

The second criterion in *Baker v. Carr* is "a lack of judicially discoverable and manageable standards for resolving" a dispute. One example comes from *Coleman v. Miller* (1939). Thirteen years had elapsed before Kansas ratified the Child Labor Amendment. Was that too long a time for state action? The Court decided that it lacked statutory and constitutional criteria for judicial determination. The question of a reasonable time involved "an appraisal of a great variety of relevant conditions, political, social and economic, which can hardly be said to be within the appropriate range of evidence receivable in a court of justice...." 307 U.S. 433, 453 (1939).

Another example is *C. & S. Airlines v. Waterman Corp.* (1948). The courts were asked to review certain orders issued by the Civil Aeronautics Board involving overseas and foreign air transportation. The orders were subject to presidential review, possibly thrusting the courts into an advisory opinion role. However, the Supreme Court stated that the president, "both as Commander-in-Chief and as the Nation's organ for foreign affairs, has available intelligence services whose reports are not and ought not to be published to the world. It would be intolerable that courts, without the relevant information, should review and perhaps nullify actions of the Executive taken on information properly held secret." 333 U.S. 103, 111 (1948). The Court went on to say that "the very nature of executive decisions as to foreign policy is political, not judicial. Such decisions are wholly confided by our Constitution to the political departments of the government, Executive and Legislature." This statement is far too broad. As the Court later noted in *Baker v. Carr*: "it is error to suppose that every case or controversy which touches foreign relations lies beyond judicial cognizance." 369 U.S. at 211.

Certain matters of foreign policy are too sensitive for the courts to handle. When President Carter terminated the defense treaty with Taiwan, Senator Goldwater asked the courts to declare the termination invalid. The case reached the Supreme Court a few weeks before the scheduled termination. Justice Rehnquist attracted three other colleagues to his position that the issue represented a nonjusticiable political question. The Court was being asked to settle a dispute between the executive and legislative branches, "each of which has resources available to protect and assert its interests, resources not available to private litigants outside the judicial forum." Goldwater v. Carter, 444 U.S. at 1004. (See the reading on *Goldwater v. Carter* in Chapter 7.)

The third criterion is "the impossibility of deciding without an initial policy determination of a kind clearly for nonjudicial discretion." This criterion is laced with circularity and basically restates the issue. It would cover reapportionment in 1946 but not after 1962 (Colegrove v. Green, 328 U.S. 549 and Baker v. Carr, 369 U.S. 186).

The fourth criterion: "the impossibility of a court's undertaking independent resolution without expressing lack of the respect due coordinate branches of government." This factor exists in every case involving separation of powers, but it offers little guidance in resolving particular controversies. Whether in the Nixon tapes case *(United States v. Nixon)* or the exclusion of

The Exclusion of Adam Clayton Powell

Adam Clayton Powell, a flamboyant black Democrat from New York, served for twenty-two years in Congress and chaired the House Education and Labor Committee. He was re-elected in 1966 by a three-to-one majority, despite press reports that he had misallocated public funds and was unlawfully abusing the privileges of his office. He had also been held in criminal contempt of New York state courts in connection with a defamation suit against him.

Rather than expel Powell, a constitutional procedure that requires a two-thirds majority, the House decided on January 10, 1967 to postpone the seating of Powell until a special committee could investigate Powell's conduct. On March 1, the committee unanimously recommended that Powell be seated and then publicly censured and fined. The committee proposed this intermediate solution rather than risk an almost certain confrontation with the courts by excluding Powell.

In a fighting mood, the House decided that the courts would not intervene because of the political question. The committee's proposal failed by a vote of 202 to 222. A vote to exclude Powell passed by the overwhelming margin of 307 to 115. The D.C. Circuit upheld the exclusion. Writing for the court was Warren Burger, who a year later would become Chief Justice of the Supreme Court. Burger wanted to avoid a collision course with Congress. That courts "encounter some problems for which they can supply no solution is not invariably an occasion for regret or concern; this is an essential limitation in a system of divided powers." Powell v. McCormack, 395 F.2d 577, 605 (D.C. Cir. 1968).

When the case was taken to the Supreme Court, the House claimed "exclusive power" over the seating of members. In oral argument, House counsel Bruce Bromley insisted that the Court had no authority to restrain House action, no matter how audacious or unconstitutional. He claimed that "clearly unconstitutional, clearly improper" action would not be subject to judicial review. Yet in this confrontation the Supreme Court declared that Congress had overstepped its authority by excluding someone on factors other than the three qualifications specified in the Constitution: age, citizenship, and residency requirements. Powell v. McCormack, 395 U.S. 486 (1969). (See reading in Chapter 6.)

Adam Clayton Powell by the House of Representatives *(Powell v. McCormack),* the Court's judgment often challenges and overrides decisions made by coordinate branches (see box). Disrespect, in that sense, cannot be sufficient reason for creating a political question: "If it were, *every* judicial resolution of a constitutional challenge to a congressional enactment would be impermissible. Congress often explicitly considers whether bills violate constitutional provisions." United States v. Munoz-Flores, 495 U.S. 385, 390–91 (1990) (emphasis in original).

Criterion five: "an unusual need for unquestioning adherence to a political decision already made." Professor Henkin said that he did not know "of any case from which Justice Brennan might have derived such a principle." 85 Yale L. J. at 605–06 n.26. Some recent possibilities might include President Carter's termination of the Taiwan defense treaty and his handling of Iranian assets.[16]

The sixth criterion: "the potentiality of embarrassment from multifarious pronouncements by various departments on one question." Despite this guideline, the Supreme Court told the House of Representatives that Adam Clayton Powell should be seated. However, this criterion retains usefulness in matters regarding the recognition of foreign governments, political

---

16. Goldwater v. Carter, 444 U.S. 996 (1979); Dames & Moore v. Regan, 453 U.S. 654 (1981). See also Idaho v. Freeman, 529 F.Supp. 1107, 1140–41 (D. Idaho 1981), regarding Idaho's rescission of its vote to ratify the Equal Rights Amendment.

boundaries, envoys, the dates for beginning and ending wars, calling out the militia, and an alien's eligibility for federal benefits.[17]

Rules of self-restraint are part of the complex process of drawing limits on judicial power. Some scholars argue that prudence dictates restrictions on judicial activity. Others warn that the contemporary Court has confused the concept of justiciability and abdicated its duty to decide proper cases and controversies. The use of threshold requirements to avoid or delay judicial decision has sparked a number of lively debates, particularly one between Alexander M. Bickel and Gerald Gunther (see reading).

Baker v. Carr

369 U.S. 186 (1962)

In this case, in which the Supreme Court accepts jurisdiction over the apportionment of legislative seats, the Court sets forth the criteria for determining whether a case falls within the category of a "political question."

MR. JUSTICE BRENNAN delivered the opinion of the Court....

Our discussion, even at the price of extending this opinion, requires review of a number of political question cases, in order to expose the attributes of the doctrine — attributes which, in various settings, diverge, combine, appear, and disappear in seeming disorderliness. Since that review is undertaken solely to demonstrate that neither singly nor collectively do these cases support a conclusion that this apportionment case is nonjusticiable, we of course do not explore their implications in other contexts. That review reveals that in the Guaranty Clause cases and in the other "political question" cases, it is the relationship between the judiciary and the coordinate branches of the Federal Government, and not the federal judiciary's relationship to the States, which gives rise to the "political question."

We have said that "In determining whether a question falls within [the political question] category, the appropriateness under our system of government of attributing finality to the action of the political departments and also the lack of satisfactory criteria for a judicial determination are dominant considerations." *Coleman* v. *Miller,* 307 U. S. 433, 454–455. The nonjusticiability of a political question is primarily a function of the separation

of powers. Much confusion results from the capacity of the "political question" label to obscure the need for case-by-case inquiry. Deciding whether a matter has in any measure been committed by the Constitution to another branch of government, or whether the action of that branch exceeds whatever authority has been committed, is itself a delicate exercise in constitutional interpretation, and is a responsibility of this Court as ultimate interpreter of the Constitution. To demonstrate this requires no less than to analyze representative cases and to infer from them the analytical threads that make up the political question doctrine. We shall then show that none of those threads catches this case.

Foreign relations: There are sweeping statements to the effect that all questions touching foreign relations are political questions. Not only does resolution of such issues frequently turn on standards that defy judicial application, or involve the exercise of a discretion demonstrably committed to the executive or legislature; but many such questions uniquely demand single-voiced statement of the Government's views. Yet it is error to suppose that every case or controversy which touches foreign relations lies beyond judicial cognizance. Our cases in this field seem invariably to show a discriminating analysis of the particular question posed, in terms of the history of its management by the political branches, of its

---

17. Recognizing foreign governments: Rose v. Himely, 4 Cr. 241 (1808); Gelston v. Hoyt, 3 Wheat. 246 (1818). Political boundaries: Foster v. Neilson, 2 Pet. 253 (1829); Williams v. Suffolk Insurance Co., 13 Pet. 415 (1839). Envoys: Ex parte Hitz, 111 U.S. 766 (1884). Beginning and ending wars: Martin v. Mott, 12 Wheat. 19 (1827); Commercial Trust Co. v. Miller, 262 U.S. 51 (1923). Calling out the militia: Martin v. Mott, 12 Wheat. 19 (1827). Federal benefits: Mathews v. Diaz, 426 U.S. 67, 81–84 (1976).

susceptibility to judicial handling in the light of its nature and posture in the specific case, and of the possible consequences of judicial action....

While recognition of foreign governments so strongly defies judicial treatment that without executive recognition a foreign state has been called "a republic of whose existence we know nothing," and the judiciary ordinarily follows the executive as to which nation has sovereignty over disputed territory, once sovereignty over an area is politically determined and declared, courts may examine the resulting status and decide independently whether a statute applies to that area. Similarly, recognition of belligerency abroad is an executive responsibility, but if the executive proclamations fall short of an explicit answer, a court may construe them seeking, for example, to determine whether the situation is such that statutes designed to assure American neutrality have become operative. *The Three Friends,* 166 U.S. 1, 63, 66. Still again, though it is the executive that determines a person's status as representative of a foreign government, *Ex parte Hitz,* 111 U.S. 766, the executive's statements will be construed where necessary to determine the court's jurisdiction, *In re Baiz,* 135 U.S. 403. Similar judicial action in the absence of a recognizedly authoritative executive declaration occurs in cases involving the immunity from seizure of vessels owned by friendly foreign governments. Compare *Ex parte Peru,* 318 U.S. 578, with *Mexico v. Hoffman,* 324 U.S. 30, 34–35.

Dates of duration of hostilities: Though it has been stated broadly that "the power which declared the necessity is the power to declare its cessation, and what the cessation requires," *Commercial Trust Co. v. Miller,* 262 U.S. 51, 57, here too analysis reveals isolable reasons for the presence of political questions, underlying this Court's refusal to review the political departments' determination of when or whether a war has ended. Dominant is the need for finality in the political determination, for emergency's nature demands "A prompt and unhesitating obedience," *Martin v. Mott,* 12 Wheat. 19, 30 (calling up of militia). Moreover, "the cessation of hostilities does not necessarily end the war power. It was stated in *Hamilton v. Kentucky Distilleries & W. Co.,* 251 U.S. 146, 161, that the war power includes the power "to remedy the evils which have arisen from its rise and progress' and continues during that emergency. *Stewart v. Kahn,* 11 Wall, 493, 507." *Fleming v. Mohawk Wrecking Co.,* 331 U.S. 111, 116. But deference rests on reason, not habit....

Validity of enactments: In *Coleman v. Miller, supra,* this Court held that the questions of how long a proposed amendment to the Federal Constitution remained open to ratification, and what effect a prior rejection had on a subsequent ratification, were committed to congressional resolution and involved criteria of decision that necessarily escaped the judicial grasp. Similar considerations apply to the enacting process: "The respect due to coequal and independent departments," and the need for finality and certainty about the status of a statute contribute to judicial reluctance to inquire whether, as passed, it complied with all requisite formalities. *Field v. Clark,* 143 U.S. 649, 672, 676–677; see *Leser v. Garnett,* 258 U.S. 130, 137. But it is not true that courts will never delve into a legislature's records upon such a quest: If the enrolled statute lacks an effective date, a court will not hesitate to seek it in the legislative journals in order to preserve the enactment. *Gardner v. The Collector,* 6 Wall. 499. The political question doctrine, a tool of maintenance of governmental order, will not be so applied as to promote only disorder.

The status of Indian tribes: This Court's deference to the political departments in determining whether Indians are recognized as a tribe, while it reflects familiar attributes of political questions, *United States v. Holliday,* 3 Wall. 407, 419, also has a unique element in that "the relation of the Indians to the United States is marked by peculiar and cardinal distinctions which exist no where else.... [The Indians are] domestic dependent nations...in a state of pupilage. Their relation to the United States resembles that of a ward to his guardian." *The Cherokee Nation v. Georgia,* 5 Pet. 1, 16, 17. Yet, here too, there is no blanket rule. While " "It is for [Congress]...and not for the courts, to determine when the true interests of the Indian require his release from [the] condition of tutelage'..., it is not meant by this that Congress may bring a community or body of people within the range of this power by arbitrarily calling them an Indian tribe...." *United States v. Sandoval,* 231 U.S. 28, 46. Able to discern what is "distinctly Indian," *ibid.,* the courts will strike down any heedless extension of that label. They will not stand impotent before an obvious instance of a manifestly unauthorized exercise of power.

It is apparent that several formulations which vary slightly according to the settings in which the questions arise may describe a political question, although each has one or more elements which identify it as essentially a function of the separation of powers. Prominent on the surface of any case held to involve a political question is found a textually demonstrable constitutional commitment of the issue to a coordinate political department; or a lack of judicially discoverable and manageable standards for resolving it; or the impossibility of deciding without an initial policy determination of a kind clearly for nonjudicial discretion; or the impossibility of a court's undertaking independent resolution without expressing lack of the respect due coordinate branches of government; or an unusual need for unquestioning adherence to a political decision already made; or the potentiality of embarrassment from multifarious pronouncements by various departments on one question....

Republican form of government: Luther v. *Borden,* 7 How. 1, though in form simply an action for damages for trespass was, as Daniel Webster said in opening the argument for the defense,

"an unusual case." The defendants, admitting an otherwise tortious breaking and entering, sought to justify their action on the ground that they were agents of the established lawful government of Rhode Island, which State was then under martial law to defend itself from active insurrection; that the plaintiff was engaged in that insurrection; and that they entered under orders to arrest the plaintiff....

Clearly, several factors were thought by the Court in *Luther* to make the question there "political": the commitment to the other branches of the decision as to which is the lawful state government; the unambiguous action by the President, in recognizing the charter government as the lawful authority; the need for finality in the executive's decision; and the lack of criteria by which a court could determine which form of government was republican.

Nixon v. United States

506 U.S. 224 (1993)

Walter L. Nixon, Jr., a federal district judge, was convicted of federal crimes and sentenced to prison. The House of Representatives adopted articles of impeachment against him and the Senate, following Rule XI, sent the matter to a committee of Senators to hear evidence and report that evidence to the full Senate. After the Senate voted to convict Nixon, he sued on the ground that Senate Rule XI violates the constitutional language that places upon the Senate, and not a committee of the Senate, to "have the sole Power to try all Impeachments." A district court and appellate court held that his claim was nonjusticiable.

CHIEF JUSTICE REHNQUIST delivered the opinion of the Court.

. . .

A controversy is nonjusticiable — *i.e.*, involves a political question — where there is "a textually demonstrable constitutional commitment of the issue to a coordinate political department; or a lack of judicially discoverable and manageable standards for resolving it...." *Baker v. Carr,* 369 U.S. 186, 217 (1962). But the courts must, in the first instance, interpret the text in question and determine whether and to what extent the issue is textually committed. See *ibid.; Powell v. McCormack,* 396 U.S. 486, 519 (1969). As the discussion that follows makes clear, the concept of a textual commitment to a coordinate political department is not completely separate from the concept of a lack of judicially discoverable and manageable standards for resolving it; the lack of

judicially manageable standards may strengthen the conclusion that there is a textually demonstrable commitment to a coordinate branch.

In this case, we must examine Art I, §3, cl. 6, to determine the scope of authority conferred upon the Senate by the Framers regarding impeachment. It provides:

"The Senate shall have the sole Power to try all Impeachments. When sitting for that Purpose, they shall be on Oath or Affirmation. When the President of the United States is tried, the Chief Justice shall preside: And no Person shall be convicted without the Concurrence of two thirds of the Members present."

The language and structure of this Clause are revealing. The first sentence is a grant of authority to the Senate, and the word "sole" indicates that this authority is reposed in the Senate and nowhere else. The next two sentences specify requirements to which the Senate proceedings shall conform: The Senate shall be on oath or affirmation, a two-thirds vote is required to convict, and when the President is tried the Chief Justice shall preside.

Petitioner argues that the word "try" in the first sentence imposes by implication an additional requirement on the Senate in that the proceedings must be in the nature of a judicial trial. From there petitioner goes on to argue that this limitation precludes the Senate from delegating to a select committee the task of hearing the testimony of witnesses, as was done pursuant to Senate Rule XI. " '[T]ry' means more than simply 'vote on' or 'review' or 'judge.' In 1787 and today, trying a case means hearing the evidence, not scanning a cold record." Brief for Petitioner 25. Petitioner concludes from this that courts may review whether or not the Senate "tried" him before convicting him.

There are several difficulties with this position which lead us ultimately to reject it. The word "try," both in 1787 and later, has considerably broader meanings than those to which petitioner would limit it. Older dictionaries define try as "[t]o examine" or "[t]o examine as a judge." See 2 S. Johnson, A Dictionary of the English Language (1785). In more modern usage the term has various meanings. For example, try can mean "to examine or investigate judicially," "to conduct the trial of," or "to put to the test by experiment, investigation, or trial." Webster's Third New International Dictionary 2457 (1971). Petitioner submits that "try," as contained in T. Sheridan, Dictionary of the English Language (1796), means "to examine as a judge; to bring before a judicial tribunal." Based on the variety of definitions, however, we cannot say that the Framers used the word "try" as an implied limitation on the method by which the Senate might proceed in trying impeachments. "As a rule the Constitution speaks in general terms, leaving Congress to deal with subsidiary matters of detail as the public interests and changing conditions may require...." *Dillon v. Gloss*, 266 U.S. 368, 376 (1921).

The conclusion that the use of the word "try" in the first sentence of the Impeachment Trial Clause lacks sufficient precision to afford any judicially manageable standard of review of the Senate's actions is fortified by the existence of the three very specific requirements that the Constitution does impose on the Senate when trying impeachments: The Members must be under oath, a two-thirds vote is required to convict, and the Chief Justice presides when the President is tried. These limitations are quite precise, and their na-

ture suggests that the Framers did not intend to impose additional limitations on the form of the Senate proceedings by the use of the word "try" in the first sentence.

Petitioner devotes only two pages in his brief to negating the significance of the word "sole" in the first sentence of Clause 6. As noted above, that sentence provides that "[t]he Senate shall have the sole Power to try all Impeachments." We think that the word "sole" is of considerable significance. Indeed, the word "sole" appears only one other time in the Constitution—with respect to the House of Representatives' *sole* Power of Impeachment." Art. I, §2, cl. 5 (emphasis added). The commonsense meaning of the word "sole" is that the Senate alone shall have authority to determine whether an individual should be acquitted or convicted. The dictionary definition bears this out. "Sole" is defined as "having no companion," "solitary," "being the only one," and "functioning...independently and without assistance or interference." Webster's Third New International Dictionary 2168 (1971). If the courts may review the actions of the Senate in order to determine whether that body "tried" an impeached official, it is difficult to see how the Senate would be "functioning...independently and without assistance or interference."

Nixon asserts that the word "sole" has no substantive meaning. To support this contention, he argues that the word is nothing more than a mere "cosmetic edit" added by the Committee of Style after the delegates had approved the substance of the Impeachment Trial Clause. There are two difficulties with this argument. First, accepting as we must the proposition that the Committee of Style had no authority from the Convention to alter the meaning of the Clause, see 2 Records of the Federal Convention of 1787, p. 553 (M. Farrand ed. 1966) (hereinafter Farrand), we must presume that the Committee's reorganization or rephrasing accurately captured what the Framers meant in their unadorned language. See *Powell v. McCormack*, 395 U.S., at 538–539. That is, we must presume that the Committee did its job. This presumption is buttressed by the fact that the Constitutional Convention voted on, and accepted, the Committee of Style's linguistic version. See 2 Farrand 663–667. We agree with the Government that "the word 'sole' is entitled to no less weight than any other word of the text, because the Committee revision perfected what 'had been agreed to.' " Brief for Respondents 25. Second, carrying Nixon's argument to its logical conclusion would constrain us to say that the *second to last draft* would govern in every instance where the Committee of Style added an arguably substantive word. Such a result is at odds with the fact that the Convention passed the Committee's version, and with the well-established rule that the plain language of the enacted text is the best indicator of intent.

. . .

The Framers labored over the question of where the impeachment power should lie. Significantly, in at least two considered scenarios the power was placed with the Federal Judiciary. See 1 Farrand 21–22 (Virginia Plan); *id.*, at 244 (New Jersey Plan). Indeed, James Madison and the Committee of Detail proposed that the Supreme Court should have the power to determine impeachments. See 2 *id.*, at 551 (Madison); *id.*, at 178–179, 186 (Committee of Detail). Despite these proposals, the Convention ultimately decided that the Senate would have "the sole Power to try all Impeachments." Art. I, §3, cl. 6. According to Alexander Hamilton, the Senate was the "most fit depositary of this important trust" because its Members are representatives of the people. See The Federalist No. 65, p. 440 (J. Cooke ed. 1961). The Supreme Court was not the proper body because the Framers "doubted whether the members of that tribunal would, at all times, be endowed with so eminent a portion of fortitude as would be called for in the execution of so difficult a task" or whether the Court "would possess the degree of credit and authority" to carry out its judgment if it conflicted with the accusation brought by the Legislature—the people's representative. See *id.*, at 441. In addition, the Framers believed the Court was too small in number: "The awful discretion, which a court of impeachments must necessarily have, to doom to honor or to infamy the most confidential and the most distinguished characters of the community, forbids the commitment of the trust to a small number of persons." Id., at 441–442.

There are two additional reasons why the Judiciary, and the Supreme Court in particular, were not chosen to have any role in impeachments. First, the Framers recognized that most likely there would be two sets of proceedings for individuals who commit impeachable offenses—the impeachment trial and a separate criminal trial. In fact, the Constitution explicitly provides for two separate proceedings. See Art. I, §3, cl. 7. The Framers deliberately separated the two forums to avoid raising the specter of bias and to ensure independent judgments:

"Would it be proper that the persons, who had disposed of his fame and his most valuable rights as a citizen in one trial, should in another trial, for the same offence, be also the disposers of his life and his fortune? Would there not be the greatest reason to apprehend, that error in the first sentence would be the parent of error in the second sentence? That the strong bias of one decision would be apt to overrule the influence of any new lights, which might be brought to vary the complexion of another decision?" The Federalist No. 65, p. 442 (J. Cooke ed. 1961).

Certainly judicial review of the Senate's "trial" would introduce the same risk of bias as would participation in the trial itself.

Second, judicial review would be inconsistent with the Framers' insistence that our system be one of checks and balances. In our constitutional system, impeachment was designed to be the *only* check on the Judicial Branch by the Legislature. On the topic of judicial accountability, Hamilton wrote:

"The precautions for their responsibility are comprised in the article respecting impeachments. They are liable to be impeached for mal-conduct by the house of representatives, and tried by the senate, and if convicted, may be dismissed from office and disqualified for holding any other. *This is the only provision on the point, which is consistent with the necessary independence of the judicial character, and is the only one which we find in our own constitution in respect to our own judges"* Id., No. 79, at 532–533 (emphasis added).

Judicial involvement in impeachment proceedings, even if only for purposes of judicial review, is counterintuitive because it would eviscerate the "important constitutional check" placed on the Judiciary by the Framers. See *id.*, No. 81, at 545. Nixon's argument would place final reviewing authority with respect to impeachments in the hands of the same body that the impeachment process is meant to regulate.

. . .

In addition to the textual commitment argument, we are persuaded that the lack of finality and the difficulty of fashioning relief counsel against justiciability. See *Baker v. Carr,* 369 U.S., at 210. We agree with the Court of Appeals that opening the door of judicial review to the procedures used by the Senate in trying impeachments would "expose the political life of the country to months, or perhaps years, of chaos." ... This lack of finality would manifest itself most dramatically if the President were impeached.

The legitimacy of any successor, and hence his effectiveness, would be impaired severely, not merely while the judicial process was running its course, but during any retrial that a differently constituted Senate might conduct if its first judgment of conviction were invalidated. Equally uncertain is the question of what relief a court may give other than simply setting aside the judgment of conviction. Could it order the reinstatement of a convicted federal judge, or order Congress to create an additional judgeship if the seat had been filled in the interim?

Petitioner finally contends that a holding of nonjusticiability cannot be reconciled with our opinion in *Powell v. McCormack* 395 U.S. 486 (1969)....

Our conclusion in *Powell* was based on the fixed meaning of "[q]ualifications" set forth in Art. I, §2. The claim by the House that its power to "be the Judge of the Elections, Returns and Qualifications of its own Members" was a textual commitment of unreviewable authority was defeated by the existence of this separate provision specifying the only qualifications which might be imposed for House membership. The decision as to whether a Member satisfied these qualifications *was* placed with the House, but the decision as to what these qualifications consisted of was not.

In the case before us, there is no separate provision of the Constitution that could be defeated by allowing the Senate final authority to determine the meaning of the word "try" in the Impeachment Trial Clause. We agree with Nixon that courts possess power to review either legislative or executive action that transgresses identifiable textual limits. As we have made clear, "whether the action of [either the Legislative or Executive Branch] exceeds whatever authority has been committed, is itself a delicate exercise in constitutional interpretation, and is a responsibility of this Court as ultimate interpreter of the Constitution." *Baker v. Carr, supra,* at 211; accord, *Powell, supra,* at 521. But we conclude, after exercising that delicate responsibility, that the word "try" in the Impeachment Trial Clause does not provide an identifiable textual limit on the authority which is committed to the Senate.

For the foregoing reasons, the judgment of the Court of Appeals is

Affirmed

JUSTICE STEVENS, concurring.

For me, the debate about the strength of the inferences to be drawn from the use of the words "sole" and "try" is far less significant than the central fact that the Framers decided to assign the impeachment power to the Legislative Branch....Respect for a coordinate branch of the Government forecloses any assumption that improbable hypotheticals like those mentioned by JUSTICE WHITE and JUSTICE SOUTER will ever occur....

JUSTICE WHITE, with whom JUSTICE BLACKMUN joins, concurring in the judgment.

Petitioner contends that the method by which the Senate convicted him on two articles of impeachment violates Art. I, §3, cl. 6, of the Constitution, which mandates that the Senate "try" impeachments. The Court is of the view that the Constitution forbids us even to consider his contention. I find no such prohibition and would therefore reach the merits of the claim. I concur in the judgment because the Senate fulfilled its constitutional obligation to "try" petitioner.

I

It should be said at the outset that, as a practical matter, it will likely make little difference whether the Court's or my view controls this case. This is so because the Senate has very wide discretion in specifying impeachment trial procedures and because it is extremely unlikely that the Senate would abuse its discretion and insist on a procedure that could not be deemed a trial by reasonable judges. Even taking a wholly practical approach, I would prefer not to announce an unreviewable discretion in the Senate to ignore completely the constitutional direction to "try" impeachment cases. When asked at oral argument whether that direction would be satisfied if, after a House vote to impeach, the Senate, without any procedure whatsoever, unanimously found the accused guilty of being "a bad guy," counsel for the United States answered that the Government's theory "leads me to answer that question yes." Tr. of Oral Arg. 51. Especially in light of this advice from the Solicitor General, I would not issue an invitation to the Senate to find an excuse, in the name of other pressing business, to be dismissive of its critical role in the impeachment process.

Practicalities aside, however, since the meaning of a constitutional provision is at issue, my disagreement with the Court should be stated.

[II. A]

. . .

The majority's review of the historical record thus explains why the power to try impeachments properly resides with the Senate. It does not explain, however, the sweeping statement that the Judiciary was "not chosen to have any role in impeachments." *Ante,* at 234. Not a single word in the historical materials cited by the majority addresses judicial review of the Impeachment Trial Clause. And a glance at the arguments surrounding the Impeachment Clauses negates the majority's attempt to infer nonjusticiability from the Framers' arguments in support of the Senate's power to try impeachments.

. . .

. . . While the majority rejects petitioner's justiciability argument as espousing a view "inconsistent with the Framers' insistence that our system be one of checks and balances," *ante,* at 234, it is the Court's finding of nonjusticiability that truly upsets the Framers' careful design. In a truly balanced system, impeachments tried by the Senate would serve as a means of controlling the largely unaccountable Judiciary, even as judicial review would ensure that the Senate adhered to a minimal set of procedural standards in conducting impeachment trials.

B

The majority also contends that the term "try" does not present a judicially manageable standard. . . .
. . . The majority concludes that the term provides no "identifiable textual limit." Yet, as the Government itself conceded at oral argument, the term "try" is hardly so elusive as the majority would have it. See Tr. of Oral Arg. 51–52. Were the Senate, for example, to adopt the practice of automatically entering a judgment of conviction whenever articles of impeachment were delivered from the House, it is quite clear that the Senate will have failed to "try" impeachments. See *id.,* at 52. Indeed in this respect, "try" presents no greater, and perhaps fewer, interpretive difficulties

than some other constitutional standards that have been found amenable to familiar techniques of judicial construction, including, for example, "Commerce . . . among the several States," Art. I, §8, cl. 3, and "due process of law," Amdt. 6. . . . *Mathews v. Eldridge,* 424 U.S. 319, 334 (1976) (" " "[D]ue process," unlike some legal rules, is not a technical conception with a fixed content unrelated to time, place and circumstances' ") (quoting *Cafeteria & Restaurant Workers v. McElroy,* 367 U.S. 886, 895 (1961)).

III

The majority's conclusion that "try" is incapable of meaningful judicial construction is not without irony. One might think that if any class of concepts would fall within the definitional abilities of the Judiciary, it would be that class having to do with procedural justice. [On the basis of the historical record, White concludes that the Senate's use of a factfinding committee under Rule XI "is entirely compatible with the Constitution's command that the Senate 'try all impeachments.' "]

JUSTICE SOUTER, concurring in the judgment.

. . .

[Although Souter regards the Court as correct in dismissing this particular dispute as a political question, he can] envision different and unusual circumstances that might justify a more searching review of impeachment proceedings. If the Senate were to act in a manner seriously threatening the integrity of its results, convicting, say, upon a coin toss, or upon a summary determination that an officer of the United States was simply " "a bad guy,' " *ante,* at 239 (WHITE, J., concurring in judgment), judicial interference might well be appropriate. . . .

Virtues and Vices: Bickel versus Gunther

In a foreword entitled "The Passive Virtues," written for the 1960 term of the Supreme Court and published in the *Harvard Law Review* in 1961, Alexander M. Bickel urged the Court to avoid adjudication by making greater use of its doctrines on standing, case and controversy, ripeness, and political questions. A rebuttal, "The Subtle Vices of the "Passive Virtues' — A Comment on Principle and Expediency in Judicial Review," was prepared by Gerald Gunther and published in the January 1964 issue of the *Columbia Law Review.*

ALEXANDER M. BICKEL:

. . .

I.
"STANDING," "CASE AND CONTROVERSY," "RIPENESS," "POLITICAL QUESTION," AND THE RATIONALE OF *MARBURY* V. *MADISON*

In the beginning was the reasoning of *Marbury* v. *Madison,* against the background of *The Correspondence of the Justices* and *Hayburn's Case.* The background was faint, but it assumed sharper outline once *Marbury* v. *Madison* had been decided. If, as Marshall argued, the judiciary's power to construe and enforce the Constitution against the other departments is to be deduced from the obligation of the courts to decide cases conformably to law, which may sometimes be the Constitution, then it must follow that the power may be exercised only in a case. Marshall offered no other coherent justification for lodging it in the courts, and the text of the Constitution, whatever other supports it may or may not offer for Marshall's argument, extends the judicial power only "to all Cases" and "to Controversies." It follows that courts may make no pronouncements in the large and in the abstract, by way of opinions advising the other departments upon request; that they may give no opinions, even in a concrete case, which are advisory because they are not finally decisive, the power of ultimate disposition of the case having been reserved elsewhere; and that they may not decide noncases, which are not adversary situations and in which nothing of immediate consequence to the parties turns on the results. These are ideas at the heart of the reasoning in *Marbury* v. *Madison.* They constitute not so much limitations of the power of judicial review as necessary supports for the argument which established it. The words of art that are shorthand for these ideas are "case and controversy" and "standing."

It would seem also to follow from *Marbury* v. *Madison* that, except as stated, "all Cases" are justiciable and must be heard. Indeed Marshall, assuming the tone of absolute assertion that he deemed suitable when the Court's basic powers were in issue, said in *Cohens v. Virginia:*

"It is most true that this court will not take jurisdiction if it should not; but it is equally true, that it must take jurisdiction if it should. The judiciary cannot, as the legislature may, avoid a measure because it approaches the confines of the constitution. We cannot pass it by because it is doubtful. With whatever doubts, with whatever difficulties, a case may be attended, we must decide it if it be brought before us. We have no more right to decline the exercise of jurisdiction which is given, than to usurp that which is not given. The one or the other would be treason to the constitution."

But the doctrines of standing and case and controversy have in time come to mean also something entirely unrelated to the reasoning of *Marbury* v. *Madison.* They have encompassed numerous instances in which the Court did nothing else but to "decline the exercise of jurisdiction which is given...." And to this end they have been abetted by, or used interchangeably (and rather unanalytically) with, other doctrines, such as "ripeness" and "political question." This has caused great difficulties for those who would rest the institution of judicial review on the foundation of the opinion in *Marbury* v. *Madison,* or even on an independent, more scrupulous but quite similar process of deduction from the constitutional text.

. . .

...[O]nly by means of a play on words can the broad discretion that the courts have in fact exercised be turned into an act of constitutional interpretation. The political-question doctrine simply resists being domesticated in this fashion. There is something different about it, in kind, not in degree, from the general "interpretive process"; something greatly more flexible, something of prudence, not construction and not principle. And it is something that cannot exist within the four corners of *Marbury* v. *Madison.*

. . .

II.
THE POWER TO DECLINE THE EXERCISE OF JURISDICTION WHICH IS GIVEN

I have tried to show that the Supreme Court's well-established if imperfectly understood practice of declining on occasion to exercise the power of judicial review is difficult to reconcile with the strict-constructionist conception of the foundation of that power. If this were all what is called merely academic, it would be none the worse for it. Actually, however, important consequences are in play. Of course, no concept, strict-, loose-, or medium-constructionist, can get around the sheer necessity of limiting each year's business to what nine men can fruitfully deal with. But strict-constructionist compunctions cause the techniques for meeting this necessity to be viewed with misgiving and to be encumbered with fictive explanations. So are other techniques of avoiding adjudication, and I would suggest that herein lies at least part of the reason for the confusion and lack of direction that has characterized their development. Some of the confusion may be in the eye of the beholder, but not all....

Quite obviously, no society, certainly not a large and heterogeneous one, can fail in time to explode if it is deprived of the arts of compromise, if it knows no ways to muddle through. No good society can be unprincipled; and no viable society can be principle-ridden. But it is not true in our society that we are generally governed wholly by principle in some matters and indulge a rule of expediency exclusively in others. There is no such neat dividing line. There are exceptions, some of which are delineated by the political-question doctrine. Most often, however, and as often as not in matters of the widest and deepest concern such as the racial problem, both requirements exist most imperatively side by side: guiding principle and expedient compromise. The role of principle, when it cannot be the inflexible governing rule, is to affect the tendency of policies of expediency. And it is a potent role....

It follows that the techniques and allied devices for staying the Court's hand, as is avowedly true at least of certiorari, cannot themselves be principled in the sense in which we have a right to expect adjudications on the merits to be principled. They mark the point at which the Court gives the electoral institutions their head and itself stays out of politics, and there is nothing paradoxical in finding that here the Court is most a political animal. But this is not to concede unchanneled, undirected, unchartered discretion. It is not to concede judgment proceeding from impulse, hunch, sentiment, predilection, inarticulable and unreasoned. The antithesis of principle in an institution that represents decency and reason is not whim, nor even expediency, but prudence....

GERALD GUNTHER:

. . .

Principled adjudication is the standard—to a degree; it must be the standard—in some areas of constitutional decisions, to that degree only. There indeed lies the novelty and vulnerability of the Bickel thesis: the emphasis on principle as the highest Court duty, but only in a limited sphere of Court actions; the 100% insistence on principle, 20% of the time....

Bickel's targets are well chosen, his shots well aimed. But the prime interest here is not in his shooting gallery prowess but in his ammunition. Bickel is neither neo-realist nor absolutist. But Bickel's thesis must be examined in light of Bickel's warnings—warnings against polluting the decisional process through excessive preoccupation with the political market place; warnings against fostering menacing illusions, against suppressing candor; warnings against misrepresenting the is, against confusing the is with the ought. His critical premises are admirable: "the integrity of the Court's principled process should remain unimpaired"; "the Court does not involve itself in compromises and expedient actions." Do Bickel's creative contributions meet the standards of Bickel's devastating criticism?

II.

Principle and reason are hard taskmasters. Insistence on these essential ingredients is Bickel's starting point; but, as he contemplates their impact on the judicial process, unpalatable consequences loom ever larger. He cannot bear to abandon the requirement of principle in constitutional adjudication; he cannot bear the inexpedient results of unflinching adherence to principle.

He is put to an excruciating choice; his response is to avoid the choice, to seek escape routes.

He derives the philosophic basis for his ingenious solution from his contemplation of American democracy at large: "No good society can be unprincipled; and no viable society can be principle-ridden.... Our democratic system of government exists in this Lincolnian tension between principle and expediency, and within its judicial review must play its role." These cosmic observations may be sound; but their relevance and utility as applied to a specific process and institution, to judicial review and the Supreme Court, are questionable. And the inferences Bickel draws ultimately fail to satisfy: they rest on faulty perceptions of the adjudicatory process; and they yield guidelines which invite not accommodation but surrender of principle to expediency....

Bickel's ambitious survey of the avoidance techniques, his "passive virtues," is the most comprehensive we have had, and his examination of this tangled field is of significance quite independent of his purposes....

The result is a strange mixture. He covers an enormous range of techniques; he describes and applies his concepts with skill; he offers some fresh insights and much helpful clarification; yet the total product is essentially unpersuasive, profoundly disturbing, and ultimately subversive of the very values it professes to serve. Two major flaws, I submit, help to explain why so many superior parts add up to such an unsatisfying whole. First, the discrete analyses of the varied avoidance devices are too much influenced by Bickel's underlying premises and overriding purposes: in his anxiety to enlarge Court discretion not to adjudicate, some of the techniques are subjected to greater strains than they can bear. Second, as Bickel criticized some commentators as neo-realists, so it can be said that he suffers from the neo-

Brandeisian fallacy: invoking the well-known *Ashwander* statement by Brandeis, regarding avoidance of constitutional questions in adjudication, to assert an amorphous authority to withhold adjudication altogether—a power far broader than any suggested by the examples given by Brandeis, a discretion far wider than any that can be independently justified....

Of course the Court often may and should avoid "passing upon a large part of all of the constitutional questions pressed upon it for decision." Four of the seven Brandeis rules involve well-known instances of such avoidance—avoidance only of some or all of the constitutional questions argued, *not* avoidance of all decision on the merits of the case. Thus, when the Court does not "formulate a rule of constitutional law broader than is required by the precise facts," it merely narrows the constitutional ground of decision, but does not even avoid all constitutional decision. Similarly, when the Court does not decide a constitutional question presented by the case because there is a nonconstitutional ground "upon which the case may be disposed of," it only avoids constitutional decision, not a decision on the merits of the case. Nor, of course, does the Court withhold adjudication of the case when it makes a ruling on the constitutionality of a federal law unnecessary by finding a construction of the statute which is "fairly possible" and which avoids the constitutional doubts. These are all in a sense avoidance devices, and Bickel includes these and similar ones in his catalogue of techniques—but they are devices which go to the choice of the ground of decision of a case, not devices which avoid decision on the merits, not devices which "decline to exercise" the jurisdiction to decide....

· · ·

SELECTED READINGS

ALBERT, LEE A. "Justiciability and Theories of Judicial Review: A Remote Relationship." 50 Southern California Law Review 1139 (1977).

BRILMAYER, LEA. "The Jurisprudence of Article III: Perspectives on the "Case or Controversy' Requirement." 93 Harvard Law Review 297 (1979).

CONDON, DANIEL PATRICK. "The Generalized Grievance Restriction: Prudential Restraint or Constitutional Mandate?" 70 Georgetown Law Journal 1157 (1982).

HUGHES, GRAHAM. "Civil Disobedience and the Political Question Doctrine." 43 New York University Law Review 1 (1968).

JACKSON, R. BROOKE. "The Political Question Doctrine: Where Does It Stand After Powell v. McCormack, O'Brien v. Brown, and Gilligan v. Morgan?" 44 University of Colorado Law Review 477 (1973).

KATES, DON B., JR., AND WILLIAM T. BARKER. "Mootness in Judicial Proceedings: Toward a Coherent Theory." 62 California Law Review 1385 (1974).

LOGAN, DAVID A. "Standing to Sue: A Proposed Separation of Powers Analysis." 1984 Wisconsin Law Review 37.

MONAGHAN, HENRY P. "Constitutional Adjudication: The Who and When." 82 Yale Law Journal 1363 (1973).

MORRISON, ALAN B. "Rights Without Remedies: The Burger Court Takes the Federal Courts Out of the Business of Protecting Federal Rights." 30 Rutgers Law Review 841 (1977).

NAGEL, ROBERT F. "Political Law, Legalistic Politics: A Recent History of the Political Question Doctrine." 56 University of Chicago Law Review 643 (1989).

NICHOL, GENE R., JR. "Causation as a Standing Requirement: The Unprincipled Use of Judicial Restraint." 69 Kentucky Law Journal 185 (1980).

ORREN, KAREN. "Standing to Sue: Interest Group Conflict in the Federal Courts." 70 American Political Science Review 723 (1976).

POST, CHARLES GORDON, JR. The Supreme Court and Political Questions. Baltimore: The Johns Hopkins Press, 1936.

RADCLIFFE, JAMES E. The Case-or-Controversy Provision. University Park: Pennsylvania State University Press, 1978.

ROSENBLUM, VICTOR G. "Justiciability and Justice: Elements of Restraint and Indifference." 15 Catholic University Law Review 141 (1966).

SCALIA, ANTONIN. "The Doctrine of Standing as an Essential Element of the Separation of Powers." 17 Suffolk University Law Review 881 (1983).

SCHARPF, FRITZ W. "Judicial Review and the Political Question: A Functional Analysis." 75 Yale Law Journal 517 (1966).

SCOTT, KENNETH E. "Standing in the Supreme Court — A Functional Analysis." 86 Harvard Law Review 645 (1973).

SEDLER, ROBERT ALLEN. "Standing and the Burger Court: An Analysis and Some Proposals for Legislative Reform." 30 Rutgers Law Review 863 (1977).

STRUM, PHILIPPA. The Supreme Court and "Political Questions." University: University of Alabama Press, 1974.

TIGAR, MICHAEL E. "Judicial Power, the 'Political Question Doctrine,' and Foreign Relations." 17 UCLA Law Review 1135 (1970).

TUCKER, EDWIN W. "The Metamorphosis of the Standing to Sue Doctrine." 17 New York Law Forum 911 (1972).

TUSHNET, MARK V. "The Sociology of Article III: A Response to Professor Brilmayer." 93 Harvard Law Review 1698 (1980).

4

Judicial Organization

Questions of judicial organization can appear technical or esoteric, and yet organizational issues present questions of power. This chapter identifies the tangible constraints that operate on the judiciary: the power of Congress to create and monitor the federal court system, including the creation of legislative and specialized courts; the President's power to appoint judges and the Senate's power to confirm; questions of tenure, removal, and compensation of federal judges; and the extent to which judges can lobby for their causes.

A. FEDERAL COURT SYSTEM

Long before the American colonies declared their separation from England, the idea of an independent judiciary had secured a firm foothold. The Act of Settlement, passed by England in 1701, contributed to judicial autonomy by guaranteeing tenure for judges during good behavior. The power to constitute courts in the American colonies, however, was vested in the governor and council, creatures of the King. The assemblies were allowed to create courts only for small causes, subject always to the King's veto.[1]

The principle of judicial independence appears in several sections of the Declaration of Independence, which charged that the King had "obstructed the Administration of Justice, by refusing his Assent to Laws for establishing Judiciary Powers." Because of disputes between the British Crown and several of the colonies, laws establishing courts of justice were struck down repeatedly, sometimes eliminating courts for long stretches of time. Edward Dumbauld, The Declaration of Independence and What It Means Today 108–12 (1950). The Declaration of Independence also criticized the King for making judges "dependent on his Will alone, for the Tenure of their Offices, and the Amount and Payment of Their Salaries." Despite the Act of Settlement, the English government insisted that colonial judges serve at the King's pleasure. This policy provoked bitter resistance in New York, New Jersey, Pennsylvania, North Carolina, South Carolina, and Massachusetts, where colonial legislatures wanted judges to have tenure during good behavior. Id. at 112–15. Following the break with England, several American colonies included tenure and salary provisions in their constitutions to secure judicial independence.

Setting Up Federal Courts

After the colonies cut ties with England, state governments authorized vessels to prey on British shipping. A judicial system was needed to dispose of "prizes" taken during those raids. State admiralty courts made the initial determination, but appeals beyond that level required the attention of the Continental Congress. From 1776 to 1780, appeals were handled first by temporary committees and then by a standing committee, until Congress, in May 1780, created a "Court of Appeals in Cases of Capture." This tribunal, the first national judiciary, took

---

1. Julius Goebel, Jr., 1 History of the Supreme Court of the United States: Antecedents and Beginnings 12–13 (1971).

direction from the Continental Congress and even from the Secretary for Foreign Affairs.[2] The Court of Appeals continued to function until delegates arrived at Philadelphia in May 1787 to draft a new constitution.

The delegates to the Philadelphia Convention recognized the need for executive and judicial independence. They explored the possibility of setting up a Council of Revision, consisting of the executive and "a convenient number of the National Judiciary," to examine all bills from the legislature before they became law. Rejection by the Council could be overridden by the legislature. 1 Farrand 21. The convention turned down the proposal because the delegates wanted the Supreme Court to interpret the law without any prior participation. Id. at 97–98. The framers decided to vest the veto power exclusively in the President.

Article III of the Constitution created a separate judicial branch. The judges, both of the Supreme and inferior courts, "shall hold their Offices during good Behaviour, and shall, at stated Times, receive for their Services, a Compensation, which shall not be diminished during their Continuance in Office." The Constitution vests the judicial power of the United States "in one supreme Court, and in such inferior Courts as the Congress may from time to time ordain and establish." The word "may" implies that the establishment of lower courts is discretionary, and some members of the First Congress proposed to do only the minimum: staff and fund the Supreme Court and rely on the states for trial courts. The Judiciary Bill of 1789, as first drafted by the Senate, opted for federal trial (district) courts. An amendment to restrict those courts to cases of admiralty and maritime matters (like the Court of Appeals in Cases of Capture) was rejected. Warren, 37 Harv. L. Rev. 49, 67 (1923).

There were similar efforts in the House of Representatives to limit inferior courts to questions of admiralty. 1 Annals of Cong. 762, 777–78. These, too, were unsuccessful. Although there was some resistance to federal district courts, the House rejected the idea of relying on state courts. Id. at 783. Madison warned that the courts in many states "cannot be trusted with the execution of Federal laws." Because of limited tenure and possible salary reductions, some courts were too dependent on state legislatures. Making federal laws dependent on these courts "would throw us back into all the embarrassments which characterized our former situation." Id. at 812–13. By a vote of 31 to 11, the House decisively rejected a motion to establish only State Courts of Admiralty with no federal district courts. Id. at 834.

Creating Circuit Courts

The Judiciary Act of 1789 provided for a Chief Justice and five Associate Justices for the Supreme Court. It divided the United States into thirteen districts, with a federal judge for each district, and created three circuits to handle appellate cases: the eastern, middle, and southern circuits. The circuit courts met twice a year in each district and consisted of any two Justices of the Supreme Court and one district judge from that circuit. District judges could not vote in any case of appeal or error from their own decisions. Section 25 of the Judiciary Act also solidified federal control over the states by conferring upon the Supreme Court a supervisory role over state courts.

The Justices of the Supreme Court complained bitterly about their circuit court duties. In addition to handling cases on the Court's docket, Justices had to "ride circuit" by traveling around the country to hear appellate cases in the circuit courts. Riding circuit was an arduous and hazardous enterprise. Participation in circuit cases had another drawback: a Justice might have to review his own decision if the case reached the Supreme Court. All six Justices appealed to President Washington and Congress to reduce their labors. Congress offered mod-

---

2. Goebel, supra note 1, at 178–79; Henry J. Bourguignon, The First Federal Court: The Federal Appellate Prize Court of the American Revolution (1977).

est relief in 1793 by allowing the attendance of only one Justice for the holding of circuit court. 1 Am. State Papers 24, 52 (1834); 1 Stat. 333 (1793).

With six Justices to cover three circuits, each Justice now had to ride circuit only once a year. Pressure for relief resulted in the ill-fated Judiciary Act of 1801, which divided the country into six circuits and promised to terminate circuit riding by creating sixteen circuit judges. President John Adams elevated six district judges to those positions and also named three Senators and one Representative to the vacant district judgeships. Farrand, 5 Am. Hist. Rev. 682 (1900); 2 Stat. 89, §7 (1801).

Although the creation of circuit judges had been proposed for several years, the statute creating them was not signed until the closing days of the Adams administration. After President Adams hastily filled the positions and allotted them to loyal Federalists, the Jeffersonians condemned the "midnight judges bill" as unconscionable. They accused the Federalists of trying to accomplish through judicial appointments what had just been denied them in the national election. The Judiciary Act of 1801 also reduced the number of Supreme Court Justices from six to five, effective with the next vacancy. The reduction might have been justified because the work of the Justices had been cut back by eliminating circuit duties. Moreover, five Justices would avoid the possibility of tie votes. The Jeffersonians interpreted the statute less charitably. The reduction decreased Jefferson's opportunity to appoint his own candidate to the High Court. The new Congress promptly repealed the Judiciary Act of 1801 (see box).

Changes in the Number of Justices

The size of the Supreme Court fluctuated throughout the nineteenth century, keeping pace with the addition of new circuits. A seventh Justice was added in 1807 after the creation of a new judicial circuit. The size of the Supreme Court rose to nine in 1837, reflecting the westward expansion, and to ten by 1863 (to accommodate the Pacific Circuit). Three years later Congress lowered the permanent size of the Court to seven, although the membership never fell below eight. The reduction is often interpreted as a slap against President Andrew Johnson, depriving him of an opportunity to fill vacancies. The Radical Republicans feared that his appointees to the Court would oppose Reconstruction policies. S. Rept. No. 711, 75th

---

Congress "Fixes" the Meaning of the Constitution

[Congress passed legislation in 1802 to repeal the Judiciary Act of the previous year, in effect abolishing sixteen circuit judges and their salaries. A case challenging the right of Congress to abolish the circuit courts reached the Supreme Court in 1803, but Justice Paterson, writing for the Court, declined to overturn the statute.]

... Congress have constitutional authority to establish, from time to time, such inferior tribunals as they may think proper; and to transfer a cause from one such tribunal to another. In this last particular, there are no words in the constitution to prohibit or restrain the exercise of legislative power....

2d. Another reason for reversal is, that the judges of the supreme court have no right to sit as circuit judges, not being appointed as such, or, in other words, that they ought to have distinct commissions for that purpose. To this objection, which is of recent date, it is sufficient to observe, that practice, and acquiescence under it, for a period of several years, commencing with the organization of the judicial system, affords an irresistible answer, and has indeed fixed the construction. It is a contemporary interpretation of the most forcible nature. This practical exposition is too strong and obstinate to be shaken or controlled. Of course, the question is at rest, and ought not now to be disturbed.

SOURCE: Stuart v. Laird, 5 U.S. (1 Cr.) 298, 308 (1803).

Cong., 1st Sess. 13 (1937). His nomination of Henry Stanbery as an Associate Justice had to be withdrawn because Congress reduced the Court's size. However, Johnson signed the bill, and its legislative history does not suggest an attack on the Court. In fact, Chief Justice Salmon P. Chase, in pursuit of higher salaries for the Supreme Court, supported a reduction to seven members.[3] Legislation in 1869 brought the Court back to its present size of nine members.

Appellate Courts

A major step in judicial reorganization occurred in 1891 when Congress created a separate system of appellate courts, producing three tiers: district (trial) courts, circuit (appellate) courts, and the Supreme Court. A comprehensive "Judges Bill" in 1925 gave the Supreme Court greater discretion to grant or deny petitions of appeal from the lower courts.

In 1891 there were nine circuit courts of appeals. The Tenth Circuit, split from the Eighth, appeared in 1929. When the workload of the Fifth Circuit grew too large, Congress divided it in 1981, forming the Eleventh Circuit. Together with the D.C. Circuit, that made twelve courts of appeals. In 1982 Congress established the Court of Appeals for the Federal Circuit (CAFC), which inherits the work of the Court of Customs and Patent Appeals and hears cases coming from the U.S. Claims Court (later renamed Court of Federal Claims). Unlike the other twelve circuits, which cover a specific geographical area and possess general jurisdiction, the CAFC is nationwide and limited in subject matter jurisdiction (see map).

Three-Judge Courts

As a means of expediting action, Congress submits some disputes to a three-judge court consisting of a mix of district and appellate judges. 28 U.S.C. § 2284 (1994). Initially, these courts were established to limit the interference of federal courts with state statutes. Instead of allowing a single federal district judge to nullify a state law, Congress required three federal judges (including at least one circuit judge) to hear applications to enjoin the enforcement of state statutes on constitutional grounds. Their determinations are appealable directly to the Supreme Court. Note, 85 Yale L. J. 564 (1976). Three-judge courts place an administrative burden on the federal judiciary, requiring three judges to do what might be done by one. In 1976 Congress eliminated three-judge courts for certain situations. 90 Stat. 1119. Over the years, the jurisdiction of three-judge courts has been cut substantially. Stern, Gressman, Shapiro, and Geller, Supreme Court Practice 56–76 (1993).

Other Judicial Bodies

Congress has established various organizations to help the judiciary. In 1922 it created the Judicial Conference to coordinate the legislative requests and administrative actions of the federal courts. It had been the responsibility of the Justice Department to handle the administrative needs of the courts (including their budgets), creating an obvious separation of powers problem. In 1939 Congress established the Administrative Office of the United States Courts to take care of the managerial, research, statistical, and budgetary needs of the national judiciary. Also in 1939, Congress created judicial councils in each circuit to supervise the work of judges. In 1967 Congress created a Federal Judicial Center to study methods of improving judicial administration.

---

3. Charles Fairman, 6 History of the Supreme Court of the United States: Reconstruction and Reunion 163–71 (1971); Cong. Globe, 39th Cong. 3909 (July 18, 1866); Stanley I. Kutler, Judicial Power and Reconstruction Politics 48–63 (1968). As a U.S. Senator, Chase had proposed that no vacancies be filled until the Court's membership fell to six. He justified this smaller number because of reduced duties once Justices were relieved of their responsibilities for riding circuit. Cong. Globe, 33d Cong., 2d Sess. 216–17 (1855).

THE THIRTEEN FEDERAL JUDICIAL CIRCUITS

1st District also includes Puerto Rico

3d District also includes the U.S. Virgin Islands

9th District also includes Alaska, Hawaii, the Northern Mariana Islands, and Guam

B. LEGISLATIVE AND SPECIALIZED COURTS

In addition to "constitutional courts" established by Congress pursuant to Article III of the Constitution, Congress creates Article I courts to carry out legislative duties. Drawing on various sections of the Constitution, Congress has set up territorial courts, legislative courts, military courts, and the courts of the District of Columbia. Judges sitting on those courts are not automatically entitled to the rights of life tenure and irreducible compensation guaranteed to Article III federal judges.

Territorial Courts

Section 3 of Article IV gives Congress the power "to dispose of and make all needful Rules and Regulations respecting the Territory or other Property belonging to the United States." After Spain ceded Florida to the United States in 1819, Congress established a territorial government in Florida and its legislature created a court system that gave judges a term of four years. This system was challenged as a violation of the requirement in Article III that judges serve for life "during good Behaviour." The Supreme Court ruled that the territorial courts of Florida were not constitutional courts; they were legislative courts.[4]

---

4. American Ins. Co. v. Canter, 26 U.S. (1 Pet.) 511, 545 (1828). Also on territorial courts see Benner v. Porter, 9 How. 235 (1850); Hornbuckle v. Toombs, 18 Wall. 648 (1874); Reynolds v. United States, 98 U.S. 145 (1878); The "City of Panama," 101 U.S. 453 (1880); and Romeu v. Todd, 206 U.S. 358 (1907).

Is It Legislative or Judicial?

Two centuries of statutory activity illustrate the broad range of options available to Congress in handling the adjudication of certain federal questions. It may choose to resolve disputes within its own chambers, as it did initially with federal claims. In legislating on claims, it can create outside bodies and call on them to investigate and make nonbinding recommendations. Congress may decide to shift adjudicatory issues to executive agencies, as it did with the Board of General Appraisers. Finally, it can vest them in adjudicatory bodies and designate whether those courts should have Article I or Article III status. In cases brought before them, federal courts monitor these designations to assure that they comply with constitutional principles. Functions of government therefore float from one branch to another as Congress searches for the most effective means of discharging its duties. What is "legislative" at one stage becomes "administrative" at another and "judicial" still later.

Under its authority to govern territories, Congress established district courts in Puerto Rico, Guam, the Virgin Islands, the former Canal Zone, and the Northern Mariana Islands. The district court of Puerto Rico is classified as an Article III federal district court. Its judges hold office during good behavior; territorial judges serve eight-year terms. Similar to territorial courts are the consular courts established by Congress to carry out the constitutional powers regarding treaties and commerce with foreign nations. Ex parte Bakelite Corp., 279 U.S. 438, 451 (1929).

Legislative Courts

Congress has established a number of Article I legislative courts. It created the Court of Claims in 1855 to help Congress handle the large number of claims presented by citizens against the United States. The responsibility for determining these claims "belongs primarily to Congress as an incident of its power to pay the debts of the United States." Ex parte Bakelite, 279 U.S. at 452. At the beginning, the Court of Claims served an advisory role, but subsequent statutes made some of the judgments binding, gradually transforming the Court of Claims from an investigative to an adjudicatory body. In 1953 Congress made the Court of Claims an Article III court, giving it the constitutional protections of tenure and salary. 67 Stat. 226 (1953). However, legislation in 1982 gave the judges of the Claims Court a fourteen-year term, returning them to the status of an Article I Court. 96 Stat. 25 (1982). Legislation in 1992 changed its name to the Court of Federal Claims.

The United States Customs Court also illustrates the congressional need to delegate some of its constitutional responsibilities to other bodies. In 1890 Congress established within the Department of Treasury a Board of General Appraisers to review the decisions of appraisers and collectors at U.S. ports. In 1926 the Board was replaced by the United States Customs Court and in 1956 Congress made the Customs Court an Article III court. Its name was changed in 1980 to the Court of International Trade. 70 Stat. 532 (1956); 94 Stat. 1727 (1980).

Congress created a Court of Customs Appeal in 1909 to review final decisions of the Board of General Appraisers. The Court was established pursuant to the power of Congress to lay and collect duties on imports. Ex parte Bakelite, 279 U.S. at 458–59. The statute had been silent about judicial tenure. Congress granted the judges life tenure in 1930. 46 Stat. 590, 762 (1930). In 1958 Congress changed the court (by now called the Court of Customs and Patent Appeals) to an Article III court. Legislation in 1982 folded this court into the Court of Appeals for the Federal Circuit. 72 Stat. 848 (1958); 96 Stat. 25 (1982). These statutes illustrate the choices available to Congress in handling adjudicatory issues (see box).

The United States Tax Court was created in 1924 as the Board of Tax Appeals, placed within the Treasury Department as "an independent agency in the executive branch of the Government." 43 Stat. 338 (1924). Legislation in 1942 and 1969 changed the name of the Board to the "Tax Court of the United States" and gave it Article I status, 56 Stat. 957 (1942); 83 Stat. 30 (1969). All decisions of the Tax Court, other than small tax cases, are subject to review by the United States Court of Appeals and by the Supreme Court.

Military Courts

A third class of specialized courts derives from the power of Congress under Article I, Section 8, to "make Rules for the Government and Regulation of the land and naval Forces." Congress decided that criminal behavior in the military shall be tried by court-martial proceedings, not by courts established under Article III. The United States Court of Military Appeals, composed of three judges with fifteen-year terms, is an Article I court. Military courts need not satisfy all of the specific procedural protections offered by Article III courts.[5]

In 1969 the Supreme Court attempted to subject certain military questions to the jurisdiction of civilian courts. It held that a crime must be "service connected" to be under military jurisdiction. O'Callahan v. Parker, 395 U.S. 258 (1969). The service-connected doctrine became so confusing that the Court abandoned it in 1987. Jurisdiction of a court-martial now depends solely on the accused's status as a member of the armed forces. Solorio v. United States, 483 U.S. 435 (1987). Thus, the rights of servicemen result from action by Congress, not the courts.

District of Columbia Courts

Under Article I, Section 8, Congress exercises "exclusive Legislation in all Cases whatsoever, over such District." Initially, the Supreme Court regarded the District of Columbia courts as legislative, not constitutional.[6] In 1933 the Court reasoned that because the District was formed from territory belonging to Maryland and Virginia, District inhabitants should continue to enjoy their former constitutional rights and protections. D.C. courts were therefore considered constitutional courts established under Article III. O'Donoghue v. United States, 289 U.S. 516 (1933). There are two types of D.C. courts: federal courts (the U.S. District Court for the District of Columbia and the U.S. Court of Appeals for the D.C. Circuit) and local courts for the District (the Superior Court and the D.C. Court of Appeals). The former are Article III Courts; the latter can have Article I characteristics. The Court compared a District resident to that of a citizen in any other state charged with violating a state criminal law. Citizens in the D.C. courts are "no more disadvantaged and no more entitled to an Art. III judge than any other citizen of any of the 50 States who is tried for a strictly local crime." Palmore v. United States, 411 U.S. 389, 410 (1973).

Bankruptcy Courts

The demarcation between Article I and Article III courts remains a source of disagreement among Justices of the Supreme Court. In 1978, in an effort to handle thousands of bankruptcy cases, Congress established a bankruptcy court in each federal district. The judges of those courts were appointed by the President (subject to Senate advice and consent) for fourteen-

---

5. Palmore v. United States, 411 U.S. 389, 404 (1973). See Toth v. Quarles, 350 U.S. 11, 17–18 (1955). For additional material on military courts, see Chapter 7.

6. Keller v. Potomac Electric Power Co., 261 U.S. 428, 441–43 (1923); Postum Cereal Co. v. Calif. Fig Nut Co., 272 U.S. 693, 700 (1927); Ex parte Bakelite Corp., 279 U.S. 438, 450 (1929); Federal Radio Comm'n v. Gen'l Elec. Co., 281 U.S. 464, 468 (1930).

ROUTES TO THE SUPREME COURT

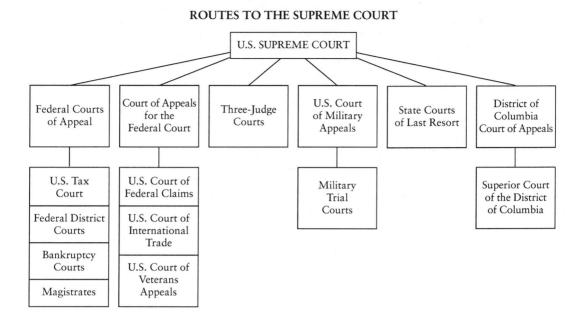

year terms and could be removed by the judicial council of the circuit. Their salaries could be decreased by Congress.

In 1982, the Supreme Court denied that Congress could establish specialized courts to carry out every one of its Article I powers. Although Congress has constitutional authority under Article I, Section 8, to establish "uniform Laws on the subject of Bankruptcies throughout the United States," this authority did not permit Congress to rely on a non-Article III court. Such reasoning, said the Court, "threatens to supplant completely our system of adjudication in independent Art. III tribunals and replace it with a system of 'specialized' legislative courts." The Court concluded that the Bankruptcy Act of 1978 had removed essential attributes of judicial power from the Article III district court and vested them in a non-Article III body. Northern Pipeline Const. Co. v. Marathon Pipe Line Co., 458 U.S. 50 (1982). Two years later, Congress passed legislation to reinstate the bankruptcy courts. The bankruptcy judges were made adjuncts of the district courts and given fourteen-year terms. 98 Stat. 2704 (1984).

The strict ruling on bankruptcy judges should not obscure the extent of adjudication that takes place outside Article III courts. In 1985 a unanimous Court upheld the arbitration provision of the Federal Insecticide, Fungicide, and Rodenticide Act. The Court decided that agency adjudication posed only a minimum threat to Article III judicial powers: "practical attention to substance rather than doctrinaire reliance on formal categories should inform application of Article III." Thomas v. Union Carbide Agric. Products Co., 473 U.S. 568, 587 (1985). A year later, the Court upheld another case of agency adjudication, again declining to "adopt formalistic and unbending rules." Commodity Futures Trading Comm'n v. Schor, 478 U.S. 833, 851 (1986).

Magistrates

In 1976 Congress created the office of U.S. magistrate to replace the earlier office of U.S. commissioner. Magistrates are appointed by district judges to serve for fixed terms. Their salaries, set by the Judicial Conference pursuant to statute, may be diminished by Congress. Magistrates are not Article III judges; they serve "as an integral part" of the U.S. District Court to hear and determine procedural motions, to hear motions for dismissal and for summary judgment, and to serve as special masters to research particular issues. In 1980 the Supreme Court upheld the authority of magistrates to conduct an evidentiary hearing, provided that the district judge makes a de novo (new) determination when the magistrate's findings or recommendations are contested. United States v. Raddatz, 447 U.S. 667 (1980).

C. THE APPOINTMENT PROCESS

The delegates at the Constitutional Convention condemned the British system of executive appointment, associating it with official corruption and debasement of the judiciary. At first they placed the power to select judges with Congress. Next, they considered vesting that responsibility solely in the Senate. Only late in the convention did they settle on joint action by the President and the Senate. 1 Farrand 21, 63, 119–28, 232–33; 2 Farrand 41–44, 80–83, 121. The President, under Article II of the Constitution, shall nominate "and by and with the Advice and Consent of the Senate, shall appoint... Judges of the supreme Court." The Constitution also permits Congress to vest the appointment of "inferior officers" in the President alone, in the courts, or in the heads of the executive departments.

Subjecting federal judges to presidential nomination and Senate confirmation creates an intensely political process. From an early date, Senators wielded considerable power in choosing nominees for federal judgeships. Members of the Supreme Court (especially Chief Justice Taft) have lobbied vigorously for their candidates. Other sectors of government are active. Private organizations participate. The American Bar Association (ABA) plays a key role. Its influence increased during the Truman administration when it established a special committee to judge the professional qualifications of candidates submitted by the Attorney General.

Nominating Panels

President Carter altered the selection process for appellate judges by establishing nominating panels. They were directed to recommend five candidates for each vacancy, allowing the President to select the nominee. As part of an accommodation, Senators continued to control nominations for district judges, although some opted for a panel system. When President Reagan took office, he abolished the judicial nominating commissions for appellate judges. The effect was to increase the Senate's influence. During the Bush and Clinton administrations, the nominating process for selecting federal judges followed a variety of practices: screening committees or panels to help Senators choose a nominee, recommendations from the state bar or lawyers associations, and an informal structure for interviewing and recommending candidates for judgeships.

How Nominations Affect Judicial Policy

The power to nominate Supreme Court Justices can produce sudden shifts in judicial policy. Slight changes in the composition of the Supreme Court have reversed previous rulings. In 1870 the Court reviewed a congressional statute that treated paper money as legal tender for discharging prior debts. Voting 4 to 3, the Court declared the statute unconstitutional. The partisanship that raged throughout the post-Civil War period did not bypass the courts. The four Justices in the majority were Democrats; the three dissenters were Republicans. In the lower federal courts, almost every Democratic judge pronounced the statute unconstitutional;

nearly every Republican judge sustained it. Hepburn v. Griswold, 8 Wall. (75 U.S.) 603 (1870); Fairman, 54 Harv. L. Rev. 1128, 1131 (1941).

The retirement of Justice Grier and the authorization by Congress the previous year of a new Justice allowed President Grant to appoint two members. His first two appointments were ill-starred. The Senate rejected his Attorney General, Ebenezer Hoar, while his second nominee, Edwin Stanton, died four days after being confirmed. Those nominations were made before the Court's decision. Grant had reason to believe that his next two appointments, submitted after the decision, would support the statute. William Strong, as a member of the Supreme Court of Pennsylvania, had already sustained the Legal Tender Act. Joseph P. Bradley appeared to be no less sympathetic. Fifteen months after the Legal Tender Act had been declared unconstitutional, the reconstituted Court upheld the Act by a 5–4 margin. Strong and Bradley joined the original three dissenters to form the majority; the four Justices who decided the case in 1870 now found themselves in the minority. Legal Tender Cases, 12 Wall. (79 U.S.) 457 (1871).

The transition from the Warren Court to the Burger Court also produced reversals of prior decisions (or efforts by the Court to "distinguish" prior holdings from current judicial policy). In 1971 a 5 to 4 majority — including two newcomers, Chief Justice Burger and Justice Blackmun — upheld a statutory procedure that stripped an individual of citizenship. The Court thus narrowed earlier holdings that citizenship could not be taken away unless voluntarily renounced. Justice Black objected that protections for American citizenship "should not be blown around by every passing political wind that changes the composition of this Court." Rogers v. Bellei, 401 U.S. 815, 837 (1971). No doubt Black was frustrated by policy shifts from the Warren Court to the Burger Court, but he himself had been part of the Roosevelt nominations after 1937 that helped chart a new course in constitutional interpretation. Changes in the Court's composition enable it to incorporate contemporary ideas and attitudes.

The Senate's Confirmation Record

The Senate has refused to confirm almost one out of every five presidential nominations to the Supreme Court. Twenty-five nominees have either been rejected, had their names submitted without Senate action, or been forced to withdraw. Most of those actions (eighteen) occurred before 1900. After the Senate rejected John J. Parker in 1930, confirmation of Supreme Court nominees seemed an automatic step. That pattern ended in 1968 when the Senate refused to advance Associate Justice Abe Fortas to the position of Chief Justice. Fortas, subjected to embarrassing questions about his acceptance of fees from private parties, eventually asked President Johnson to withdraw his nomination. Homer Thornberry, picked by Johnson to fill Fortas's seat as Associate Justice, then withdrew his name. A year later, with impeachment proceedings gearing up against him because of financial and personal improprieties, Fortas resigned from the Court.

The Supreme Court remained embroiled in political controversy in 1969 when the Senate rejected Nixon's nomination of Clement F. Haynsworth, Jr., to the Supreme Court. The ethical test applied by Republicans against Fortas was now used by Democrats against Haynsworth. A year later, the Senate rejected Nixon's next nominee, G. Harrold Carswell, who lacked the qualifications needed for Associate Justice. Nixon finally nominated Harry A. Blackmun, who was confirmed by a unanimous vote.

Probing a Nominee's Views

The emphasis given by Nixon to the sociopolitical views of judicial candidates merely underscores the entanglement of law and politics. Senators, too, in expressing their advice and con-

Ruth Bader Ginsburg on Abortion

Judge GINSBURG.... you asked me about my thinking on equal protection versus individual autonomy. My answer is that both are implicated. The decision whether or not to bear a child is central to a woman's life, to her well-being and dignity. It is a decision she must make for herself. When Government controls that decision for her, she is being treated as less than a fully adult human responsible for her own choices.

Senator [Hank] BROWN.... With regard to the equal protection argument, though, since this may well confer a right to choose on the woman, or could, would it also follow that the father would be entitled to a right to choose in this regard or [possess] some rights in this regard?

Judge GINSBURG. That was an issue left open in *Roe v. Wade* (1973). But if I recall correctly, it was put to rest in *Casey* (1992). In that recent decision, the Court dealt with a series of regulations. It upheld most of them, but it struck down one requiring notice to the husband....

The *Casey* majority understood that marriage and family life is not always all we might wish them to be. There are women whose physical safety, even their lives, would be endangered, if the law required them to notify their partner....

Senator BROWN. I was concerned that if the equal protection argument were relied on to ensure a right to choose, then looking for a sex-blind standard in this regard might also then convey rights in the father to this decision. Do you see that as following logically from the rights that can be conferred on the mother?

Judge GINSBURG. I will rest my answer on the *Casey* decision, which recognizes that it is her body, her life, and men, to that extent, are not similarly situated. They don't bear the child.

Senator BROWN. So the rights are not equal in this regard, because the interests are not equal?

Judge GINSBURG. It is essential to woman's equality with man that she be the decision-maker, that her choice be controlling....

SOURCE: "Nomination of Ruth Bader Ginsburg, To Be Associate Justice of the Supreme Court of the United States," hearings before the Senate Committee on the Judiciary, 103d Cong., 1st Sess. 207 (1993).

sent, feel at liberty to evaluate a nominee's political and constitutional philosophy in order to maintain a balance of views on the Court.[7]

As shown by the 1981 hearings on the nomination of Sandra Day O'Connor to the Court, her personal and judicial philosophy on the exceedingly sensitive issue of abortion was a matter of recurrent interest to Senators and one on which she was willing to state her views (see reading). O'Connor's willingness to discuss her opposition to abortion "as a matter of birth control or otherwise" can be compared to very different responses from Clarence Thomas and Ruth Bader Ginsburg during their confirmation hearings. At his hearings in 1991, Thomas was asked to comment on the position in *Roe* v. *Wade* that it is a woman's right to decide to terminate a pregnancy. He declined to discuss the issue: "I do not think that at this time that I could maintain my impartiality as a member of the judiciary and comment on that specific case" (page 127, Part 1, of hearings). Most nominees offer similar responses, regarding it as improper to discuss an issue that is likely to come before the Court. However, in hearings in 1993, Ruth Bader Ginsburg did not hesitate to express her view about a woman's right to choose (see box).

The Senate's rejection of two nominees by Nixon to the Supreme Court was duplicated in 1987. President Reagan nominated Judge Robert H. Bork, a conservative member of the D.C.

---

7. Senate Committee on the Judiciary, "Advice and Consent on Supreme Court Nominations," 94th Cong., 2d Sess. (Committee Print 1976). See L. A. Powe, Jr., "The Senate and the Court: Questioning a Nominee," 54 Tex. L. Rev. 891 (1976).

Circuit, to replace the more moderate Justice Powell. Everyone recognized the nomination as pivotal, especially after Reagan's selection of O'Connor in 1981, Antonin Scalia in 1986, and the elevation of Rehnquist as Chief Justice in 1986. Powell, a centrist, had supplied a swing vote on the Burger Court. The addition of Bork threatened to reverse a number of important decisions.

Major groups in the country mounted an intensive campaign against Bork, whose writings and speeches contained provocative views on civil rights, women's rights, the First Amendment, abortion, privacy, reapportionment, and criminal law. Four members of the ABA committee found him "not qualified." One voted "not opposed" (which means minimally qualified and not among the best available). Bork did not fare well during the hearings, and the White House committed a number of tactical blunders, such as trying to paint Bork as a moderate. The Senate voted 58 to 42 to reject Bork.

To replace Bork, a vindictive Reagan turned to Judge Douglas H. Ginsburg of the D.C. Circuit. The nomination unraveled almost hour by hour because of Ginsburg's thin credentials and questions of conflict of interest while he served in the Justice Department. Finally, after he admitted smoking marijuana into his thirties, while a professor of law, conservative support for his nomination took flight. The disclosure was particularly damaging because of Reagan's strong campaign against drugs and the administration's heavy emphasis on law and order. Within nine days of the nomination, Reagan received Ginsburg's request to withdraw his name. The next nominee, Judge Anthony Kennedy of the Ninth Circuit, sailed through the confirmation process without difficulty.

Another bruising battle occurred in 1991, when President Bush nominated Clarence Thomas to replace Justice Thurgood Marshall. After sensational hearings in which Anita F. Hill testified on alleged sexual harassment by Thomas when he served as chairman of the Equal Employment Opportunity Commission, the Senate confirmed him by the narrow vote of 52 to 48. Clinton's nominees encountered little opposition. Ruth Bader Ginsburg was confirmed by a vote of 96 to 3 and Stephen Breyer by a vote of 87 to 9.

Recess Appointments

The Senate is denied a role in the confirmation process when the President makes recess appointments to the Supreme Court. Under Article II, Section 2, the President "shall have Power to fill up all Vacancies that may happen during the Recess of the Senate, by granting Commissions which may expire at the End of their next Session." During the 1950s, President Eisenhower placed three men on the Supreme Court while the Senate recessed: Earl Warren, William J. Brennan, Jr., and Potter Stewart. All three joined the Court and participated in decisions before the Senate had an opportunity to review their qualifications and vote on their confirmation. In each case, the Senate gave its advice and consent, but the experience convinced most Senators that the procedure was unhealthy both for the Senate and the Court. How could federal judges serving under a recess appointment maintain total independence of mind? The anticipation of questions by a Senate committee during confirmation hearings might influence the direction and content of a nominee's decision.

In 1960 Senator Philip Hart introduced a resolution to discourage recess appointments to the courts. The Senate passed the resolution, 48 to 37, voting essentially along party lines. The resolution stated that the making of recess appointments to the Supreme Court may be inconsistent with the interests of the Court, the nominee, litigants before the Court, and the people of the United States. Such appointments should "not be made except under unusual circumstances and for the purpose of preventing or ending a demonstrable breakdown in the administration of the Court's business." 106 Cong. Rec. 18130–45 (1960). Although the resolution is not legally binding, no President after Eisenhower has made recess appointments to the Supreme Court. The President's constitutional authority to make recess appointments to federal courts was upheld in 1985.

United States v. Woodley, 751 F.2d 1008 (9th Cir. 1985), cert. denied, 475 U.S. 1048 (1986). However, the dissenters noted that although there have been approximately 300 judicial recess appointments since 1789, there has been only one such appointment since 1964. The fact that courts sanction the use of judicial recess appointments does not mean that the elected branches are obliged to accept the practice as constitutionally acceptable. The decision of the appellate court in 1985 functions more like an advisory opinion: It is constitutional if you want to do it. The final word on whether it is actually done lies with the President and the Senate.

Nomination Hearings of Sandra Day O'Connor

During the 1981 hearings on the nomination of Sandra Day O'Connor to be Associate Justice of the Supreme Court, Senators were interested in learning about the personal and philosophical views of the first woman nominated to the High Bench. Although the Senators wanted a nominee who would possess certain general qualities—integrity, honesty, technical knowledge, and proper judicial temperament—they also probed her position on the highly controversial issue of abortion, a question that had been decided already by the Court and was likely to be relitigated in the future. The selections below come from "Nomination of Sandra Day O'Connor," hearings before the Senate Committee on the Judiciary, 97th Cong., 1st Sess., September 9, 1981, pp. 60–63, 98, 106.

The CHAIRMAN [*Strom Thurmond*]. Judge O'Connor, there has been much discussion regarding your views on the subject of abortion. Would you discuss your philosophy on abortion, both personal and judicial, and explain your actions as a State senator in Arizona on certain specific matters: First, your 1970 committee vote in favor of House bill No. 20, which would have repealed Arizona's felony statutes on abortion. Then I have three other instances I will inquire about.

Judge O'CONNOR. Very well. May I preface my response by saying that the personal views and philosophies, in my view, of a Supreme Court Justice and indeed any judge should be set aside insofar as it is possible to do that in resolving matters that come before the Court.

Issues that come before the Court should be resolved based on the facts of that particular case or matter and on the law applicable to those facts, and any constitutional principles applicable to those facts. They should not be based on the personal views and ideology of the judge with regard to that particular matter or issue.

Now, having explained that, I would like to say that my own view in the area of abortion is that I am opposed to it as a matter of birth control or otherwise. The subject of abortion is a valid one, in my view, for legislative action subject to any constitutional restraints or limitations.

I think a great deal has been written about my vote in a Senate Judiciary Committee in 1970 on a bill called House bill No. 20, which would have

repealed Arizona's abortion statutes. Now in reviewing that, I would like to state first of all that that vote occurred some 11 years ago, to be exact, and was one which was not easily recalled by me, Mr. Chairman. In fact, the committee records when I looked them up did not reflect my vote nor that of other members, with one exception.

It was necessary for me, then, to eventually take time to look at news media accounts and determine from a contemporary article a reflection of the vote on that particular occasion. The bill did not go to the floor of the Senate for a vote; it was held in the Senate Caucus and the committee vote was a vote which would have taken it out of that committee with a recommendation to the full Senate.

The bill is one which concerned a repeal of Arizona's then statutes which made it a felony, punishable by from 2 to 5 years in prison, for anyone providing any substance or means to procure a miscarriage unless it was necessary to save the life of the mother. It would have, for example, subjected anyone who assisted a young woman who, for instance, was a rape victim in securing a D. & C. procedure within hours or even days of that rape.

At that time I believed that some change in Arizona statutes was appropriate, and had a bill been presented to me that was less sweeping than House bill No. 20, I would have supported that. It was not, and the news accounts reflect that I supported the committee action in putting the bill out of committee, where it then died in the caucus.

I would say that my own knowledge and awareness of the issues and concerns that many people have about the question of abortion has increased since those days. It was not the subject of a great deal of public attention or concern at the time it came before the committee in 1970. I would not have voted, I think, Mr. Chairman, for a simple repealer thereafter.

The CHAIRMAN. Now the second instance was your cosponsorship in 1973 of Senate bill No. 1190, which would have provided family planning services, including surgical procedures, even for minors without parental consent.

Judge O'CONNOR. Senate bill No. 1190 in 1973 was a bill in which the prime sponsor was from the city of Tucson, and it had nine other cosigners on the bill. I was one of those cosigners.

I viewed the bill as a bill which did not deal with abortion but which would have established as a State policy in Arizona, a policy of encouraging the availability of contraceptive information to people generally. The bill at the time, I think, was rather loosely drafted, and I can understand why some might read it and say, "What does this mean?"

That did not particularly concern me at the time because I knew that the bill would go through the committee process and be amended substantially before we would see it again. That was a rather typical practice, at least in the Arizona legislature. Indeed, the bill was assigned to a public health and welfare committee where it was amended in a number of respects.

It did not provide for any surgical procedure for an abortion, as has been reported inaccurately by some. The only reference in the bill to a surgical procedure was the following. It was one that said:

"A physician may perform appropriate surgical procedures for the prevention of conception upon any adult who requests such procedure in writing."

That particular provision, I believe, was subsequently amended out in committee but, be that as it may, it was in the bill on introduction.

Mr. Chairman, I supported the availability of contraceptive information to the public generally. Arizona had a statute or statutes on the books at that time, in 1973, which did restrict rather dramatically the availability of information about contraception to the public generally. It seemed to me that perhaps the best way to avoid having people who were seeking abortions was to enable people not to become pregnant unwittingly or without the intention of doing so.

The CHAIRMAN. The third instance, your 1974 vote against House Concurrent Memorial No.

2002, which urged Congress to pass a constitutional amendment against abortion.

Judge O'CONNOR. Mr. Chairman, as you perhaps recall, the *Rowe* [sic] v. *Wade* decision was handed down in 1973. I would like to mention that in that year following that decision, when concerns began to be expressed, I requested the preparation in 1973 of Senate bill No. 1333 which gave hospitals and physicians and employees the right not to participate in or contribute to any abortion proceeding if they chose not to do so and objected, notwithstanding their employment. That bill did pass the State Senate and became law.

The following year, in 1974, less than a year following the *Rowe* [sic] v. *Wade* decision, a House Memorial was introduced in the Arizona House of Representatives. It would have urged Congress to amend the Constitution to provide that the word person in the 5th and 14th amendments applies to the unborn at every stage of development, except in an emergency when there is a reasonable medical certainty that continuation of the pregnancy would cause the death of the mother. The amendment was further amended in the Senate Judiciary Committee.

I did not support the memorial at that time, either in committee or in the caucus.

. . .

I voted against it, Mr. Chairman, because I was not sure at that time that we had given the proper amount of reflection or consideration to what action, if any, was appropriate by way of a constitutional amendment in connection with the *Rowe* [sic] v. *Wade* decision.

. . .

The CHAIRMAN. Now the last instance is concerning a vote in 1974 against a successful amendment to a stadium construction bill which limited the availability of abortions.

Judge O'CONNOR. Also in 1974, which was an active year in the Arizona Legislature with regard to the issue of abortion, the Senate had originated a bill that allowed the University of Arizona to issue bonds to expand its football stadium. That bill passed the State Senate and went to the House of Representatives.

In the House it was amended to add a nongermane rider which would have prohibited the performance of abortions in any facility under the jurisdiction of the Arizona Board of Regents. When the measure returned to the Senate, at that time I was the Senate majority leader and I was very concerned because the whole subject had become one that was controversial within our own membership.

I was concerned as majority leader that we not encourage a practice of the addition of nongermane riders to Senate bills which we had passed without that kind of a provision. Indeed, Arizona's constitution has a provision which prohibits the putting together of bills or measures or riders dealing with more than one subject. I did oppose the addition by the House of the nongermane rider when it came back.

It might be of interest, though, to know, Mr. Chairman, that also in 1974 there was another Senate bill which would have provided for a medical assistance program for the medically needy. That was Senate bill No. 1165. It contained a provision that no benefits would be provided for abortions except when deemed medically necessary to save the life of the mother, or where the pregnancy had resulted from rape, incest, or criminal action. I supported that bill together with that provision and the measure did pass and become law....

PERSONAL PHILOSOPHY OF ABORTION

Senator DeConcini. Returning to the subject — and I am sure it probably will never end — of abortion, you have expressed your views a number of times here today and just now with Senator Dole. I wonder if you could share with us for just a few minutes not the voting record — I know you have had no judicial decisions on the subject matter that we could find — but your personal philosophy or feeling as to abortion so the record would be clear today?

Judge O'Connor. OK, Senator. Again let me preface a comment by saying that my personal views and beliefs in this area and in other areas have no place in the resolution of any legal issues that will come before the Court. I think these are matters that of necessity a judge must attempt to set aside in resolving the cases that come before the Court.

I have indicated to you the position that I have held for a long time — my own abhorrence of abortion as a remedy. It is a practice in which I would not have engaged, and I am not trying to criticize others in that process. There are many who have very different feelings on this issue. I recognize that, and I am sensitive to it.

. . .

D. TENURE, REMOVAL, AND COMPENSATION

Under Article III of the Constitution, judges "both of the supreme and inferior Courts, shall hold their Offices during good Behaviour." Article I gives the House of Representatives the sole power of impeachment and the Senate has the sole power to try all impeachments. A two-thirds majority of the Senate is required for conviction. Judges may be removed from office "on Impeachment for, and Conviction of, Treason, Bribery, or other high Crimes and Misdemeanors."

The impeachment process is cumbersome and suitable only for grave offenses. The need to remove judges for lesser offenses has long been recognized. In Federalist No. 79, Alexander Hamilton said that "insanity, without any formal or express provision, may be safely pronounced to be a virtual disqualification" for federal judges. However, he did not explain how judges would be removed for that cause. If insanity is a basis for removal, what of senility, incompetence, disability, alcoholism, laziness, and other deficiencies that may fall short of an impeachable offense?

19th Century Removal Efforts

The first example of a federal judge impeached and removed from office occurred in 1803 in the case of John Pickering. He was charged with misconduct in a trial and for being on the bench while intoxicated. Supreme Court Justice Samuel Chase was impeached in 1804 but acquitted. Actions were brought against a number of other federal judges, many of whom preferred to resign from office rather than defend themselves against the charges. Shipley, 35 Law & Contemp. Prob. 178, 190–91 (1970). Still other federal judges withdrew quietly from the bench before prosecutors could launch a full-scale investigation. Joseph Borkin, The Corrupt Judge (1962).

To encourage aged and infirm judges to leave the bench, Congress passed legislation in 1869 to authorize the payment of full salary to any federal judge who resigned at or after age 70 after completing at least ten years' service on the bench. 16 Stat. 44, § 5 (1869). For Justices with less than the required ten years, Congress has passed special statutes to provide full retirement benefits. 22 Stat. 2 (1882); Fairman, 51 Harv. L. Rev. 397 (1938).

Article I judges, such as territorial judges, have been removed by Presidents; these judges were not entitled to life tenure.[8] Article III judges are immune from removal, other than by impeachment. Nevertheless, they are subject to prosecution by the Justice Department for criminal offenses. The First Congress passed legislation providing that judges convicted of accepting a bribe "shall forever be disqualified to hold any office of honour, trust or profit under the United States." 1 Stat. 117, § 21 (1790). Moreover, any federal judge who engages in the practice of law "is guilty of a high misdemeanor." 28 U.S.C. § 454 (1994).

20th Century Removals

Criminal prosecutions have been used to drive corrupt judges from the bench. In 1973 Judge Otto Kerner, Jr., of the Seventh Circuit was found guilty of bribery, perjury, tax evasion, and other crimes, most of which occurred during his previous service as governor of Illinois. On appeal, Kerner argued that the Constitution provides only one way to remove a judge: impeachment. The Seventh Circuit decided that judicial immunity does not exempt judges from the operation of criminal laws and affirmed Kerner's conviction. United States v. Isaacs, 493 F.2d 1124 (7th Cir. 1974).

Kerner's prosecution largely concerned his actions before joining the bench. A different issue arose in the early 1980s when the Justice Department charged U.S. District Judge Alcee L. Hastings with criminal activities while sitting as a judge. The Eleventh Circuit decided in 1982 that Hastings could be prosecuted. United States v. Hastings, 681 F.2d 706 (11th Cir. 1982), cert. denied, 459 U.S. 1203 (1983). After a jury acquitted Hastings in 1983, a judicial inquiry panel conducted its own investigation into charges of misconduct. Hastings claimed that this inquiry undermined his independence as a federal judge, but the investigative and disciplinary procedure was upheld by the courts.[9]

As explained at the end of this section, Hastings was later impeached and removed by Congress. In 1984 U.S. District Judge Harry Claiborne was found guilty of income tax evasion. Two years later he was impeached and removed. In 1986 U.S. District Judge Walter L. Nixon, Jr., of Mississippi was convicted of lying to a federal grand jury; in 1989 he was impeached and removed.

Ineligibility Clause

Once nominated and appointed to the bench, a few judges have been vulnerable to the charge that they violated the "ineligibility clause" of the Constitution. Article I, Section 6, Clause 2, provides that no Senator or Representative "shall, during the Time for which he was elected, be appointed to any Civil Office under the Authority of the United States, which shall have been created, or the Emoluments whereof shall have been encreased during such time." Hugo Black's nomination to the Supreme Court in 1937 was challenged because a retirement system for the judiciary had been enacted that year while Black served as U.S. Senator. The Supreme Court avoided the issue by holding that the plaintiff lacked standing to bring suit. Ex parte Levitt, 302 U.S. 633 (1937).

A more recent challenge concerned Abner Mikva, a member of Congress nominated by Pres-

---

8. United States v. Guthrie, 58 U.S. (17 How.) 284, 288–89 (1854); 5 Op. Att'y Gen. 288, 291 (1851); and McAllister v. United States, 141 U.S. 174 (1891).

9. Hastings v. Judicial Conference of United States, 593 F.Supp. 1371 (D.D.C. 1984); In the Matter of Certain Complaints Under Investigation, 783 F.2d 1488 (11th Cir. 1986).

ident Carter to the D.C. Circuit. Working through Senator James McClure, who served as plaintiff, the National Rifle Association argued that the salaries of federal judges had been increased during Mikva's term in Congress. A three-judge court ruled that McClure lacked standing to challenge the validity of an appointment of a federal judge. The court said that McClure and his colleagues had an opportunity to vote against Mikva's confirmation. Senators on the losing side could not then ask the judiciary to reverse the Senate's action. *McClure v. Carter*, 513 F.Supp. 265 (D. Idaho 1981), aff'd sub nom. *McClure v. Reagan*, 454 U.S. 1025 (1981).

Judicial Council Sanctions

Statutory procedures are available for judges to retire on grounds of disability. If a judge fails to certify to the President his disability, a majority of the members of the judicial council of his circuit may sign a certificate of disability and submit it to the President. Once the President finds that the judge is "unable to discharge efficiently all the duties of his office by reason of permanent mental or physical disability," and that an additional judge is needed, the President may make the appointment with the advice and consent of the Senate. 28 U.S.C. § 372(b) (1994).

Each judicial council is authorized to make all necessary orders for the effective administration of court business. Judges "shall promptly carry into effect all orders of the judicial council." 28 U.S.C. § 332(d) (1994). The judicial council for the Tenth Circuit relied on this provision in the 1960s to order Judge Stephen S. Chandler of the Western District of Oklahoma to "take no action whatsoever in any case or proceeding now or hereafter pending in his court." The order did not remove Chandler from office; instead, it removed the office from him. In 1966 the Supreme Court denied an application to stay the council's order. *Chandler v. Judicial Council*, 382 U.S. 1003 (1966). The judicial council later modified its order, allowing Chandler to retain his cases but withholding any new assignments. The Supreme Court denied a motion by Chandler to nullify the new order. *Chandler v. Judicial Council*, 398 U.S. 74 (1970).

By 1979 all judicial councils had implemented rules for the processing of complaints against federal judges. Building on this system, Congress passed legislation in 1980 that assigns to the councils the responsibility for investigating charges against judges. The statute contemplates charges of inefficiency or ineffectiveness resulting from mental or physical disability (conditions that may not be impeachable). The legislation does not encompass complaints regarding the merits of a decision or the conduct of judges unconnected with their judicial duties.[10] The 1980 statute was upheld by a district court in 1984 and by the Eleventh Circuit in 1986. The latter court argued that investigation by judicial councils *increased* judicial independence (see box).[11]

The statute also allows a judicial council, after determining that a judge has engaged in conduct constituting one or more grounds for impeachment, to certify this determination for the Judicial Conference, which may then present a report to the House of Representatives for possible impeachment proceedings. This statutory procedure was upheld by a federal appellate court in 1987. *Hastings v. Judicial Conference of U.S.*, 829 F.2d 91 (D.C. Cir. 1987). The Judicial Conference invoked the statute in 1987 to vote unanimously for a recommendation to the House of Representatives that it consider impeaching U.S. District Court Judge Alcee L. Hastings. A year later, the House acted to impeach Hastings, and in 1989 he was removed by

---

10. 94 Stat. 2035 (1980). See S. Rept. No. 362, 96th Cong., 1st Sess. (1979) and H. Rept. No. 1313, 96th Cong., 2d Sess. (1980).

11. *Hastings v. Judicial Conference of the United States*, 593 F.Supp. 1371 (D.D.C. 1984). This decision was vacated in part and remanded in *Hastings v. Judicial Conference of the United States*, 770 F.2d 1093 (D.C. Cir. 1985). The appellate court ruled that the question of constitutionality of the 1980 statute was premature. The Eleventh Circuit not only upheld the statute but regarded it as a means of protecting judicial independence. *In the Matter of Certain Complaints Under Investigation*, 783 F.2d 1488 (11th Cir. 1986).

Judicial Councils Investigating Judges

... [W]e believe that Congress [in the 1980 statute] could reasonably have determined that some internal procedure for investigating complaints against members of the judiciary was not only in the public interest but was important to the continued independence of the judiciary as a whole. Judges have very substantial powers and are supported at public expense. Today, some kind of complaint procedure exists with respect to state judges in every state in the union. The judiciary as a whole, including the colleagues of complained-against judges, has an interest in seeing that non-frivolous complaints are looked into, to the end that the judge, and the system he exemplifies, be exonerated or, if not, that the public perceive that the system has undertaken to police itself, within constitutional limits, of course. Absent any form of judicial complaint procedure, courts would be virtually alone among public and professional occupations in lacking a means to clean house. The increase in the number of judges coupled with the increase in the complexity of judicial work and of courts, all suggest that some mechanism for looking into complaints is necessary and reasonable, if only to enable the courts themselves to sort out their own shortcomings and make the necessary administrative adjustments. In fact, a credible internal complaint procedure can be viewed as essential to maintaining the institutional independence of the courts. If judges cannot or will not keep their own house in order, pressures from the public and legislature might result in withdrawal of needed financial support or in the creation of investigatory mechanisms outside the judicial branch which, to a greater degree than the Act, would threaten judicial independence. Considerations of this sort were at the heart of the present legislation.

SOURCE: In the Matter of Certain Complaints Under Investigation, 783 F.2d 1488, 1507 (11th Cir. 1986).

the Senate. This was the first time a federal official had been impeached and removed from office for a crime after he had won acquittal.

Judges Nixon and Hastings continued to challenge their removals in court. Nixon brought an action claiming that his conviction in the Senate was void because he was not granted a trial before the full Senate. Instead, he was first examined by a twelve-member Senate committee. The lower courts held that the Senate's procedure was not justiciable. Nixon v. United States, 744 F.Supp. 9 (D.D.C. 1990); Nixon v. United States, 938 F.2d 239 (D.C. Cir. 1991). To the surprise of many, the Supreme Court granted cert to hear the case. Later, a federal district judge reviewed a similar complaint by Judge Hastings and decided that the Senate procedure violated elementary notions of fairness and due process associated with a trial. Hastings v. United States, 802 F.Supp. 491 (D.D.C. 1992). In 1993 the Supreme Court held that the Senate had sole discretion to choose the procedures to be used for impeachment, including the use of a committee to take testimony and gather evidence. Nixon v. United States, 506 U.S. 224 (1993). (This decision appears as a reading in Chapter 3, in the section on political questions.)

U.S. District Court Judge Robert Aguilar was convicted of illegally disclosing a wiretap. Although an appellate court reversed that conviction, Aguilar's conviction was reinstated by the Supreme Court in 1995. United States v. Aguilar, 515 U.S. 593 (1995). In 1996, the Justice Department dropped the charges in return for Aguilar's resignation. Legal Times, July 8, 1996, at 8.

Compensation

Judicial independence would count for little if the salaries of judges could be cut by legislators. Federal judges appointed to Article III courts are entitled to a compensation "which shall not be diminished during their Continuance in Office." In Federalist No. 79, Hamilton said that next to permanency in office "nothing can contribute more to the independence of the judges than a fixed provision for their support.... In the general course of human nature, a power over a man's subsistence amounts to a power over his will." That principle had been embodied in the Declaration of Independence, which attacked the British King for making colonial judges "dependent on his Will alone, for the Tenure of their Offices, and the Amount and Payment of their Salaries."

The No-Diminution Clause of the Constitution was challenged in 1802 when Congress repealed the Judiciary Act of the previous year. The effect was to abolish sixteen circuit judges and their salaries. Supporters of the repeal argued that it was irrational to expect a judge to hold office during good behavior and to continue receiving payment if the office no longer existed. A salary could not exist without an office. A case challenging the right of Congress to abolish the circuit courts reached the Supreme Court in 1803, but the Court declined to overturn the statute. Stuart v. Laird, 5 U.S. (1 Cr.) 298 (1803).

In 1920 the Supreme Court held that a federal income tax levied against Article III judges unconstitutionally diminished their salaries. Justice Holmes, in a dissent that would later become the majority position, denied that the No-Diminution Clause relieved federal judges "from the ordinary duties of a citizen." To require someone from the judicial branch to pay taxes like other people "cannot possibly be made an instrument to attack his independence as a judge." Evans v. Gore, 253 U.S. 245, 265 (1920). Nineteen years later the Supreme Court held that a federal tax could be applied to Article III judges. O'Malley v. Woodrough, 307 U.S. 277 (1939).

Nothing in this line of cases prevents Congress from giving judges a smaller pay raise than other federal employees or no increase at all. In 1964 members of Congress raised their pay by $7,500 while limiting the increase for Supreme Court Justices to $4,500. The legislative debate suggests that some members of Congress may have wanted to use the power of the purse to penalize the Court for its recent decisions. However, the smaller raise for the judiciary could be justified on other grounds: the more generous retirement system for the courts, the need for members of Congress to maintain two residences, and the extra costs they bear in traveling home to see constituents. 110 Cong. Rec. 17912, 18032–33 (1964).

As a way to protest their salary levels, 140 federal judges brought an action in the 1970s to argue that their salaries had been diminished unconstitutionally because pay had not kept pace with inflation. The courts dismissed this claim as meritless. Atkins v. United States, 556 F.2d 1028 (Ct. Cl. 1977), cert. denied, 434 U.S. 1009 (1978). Another case arose when Congress, in four consecutive years (1976–1979), passed statutes to stop or reduce authorized cost-of-living increases for all federal employees, including judges. A number of federal judges filed suit, claiming that these actions violated the No-Diminution Clause of the Constitution. In 1980 the Supreme Court held that Congress, under the provisions of the salary statutes, could disapprove scheduled pay increases for the judiciary provided it acted before October 1 of a new fiscal year (when they automatically took effect). The Court allowed two of the statutory actions taken prior to October 1 and struck down two others that came too late. United States v. Will, 449 U.S. 200 (1980).

As a result of this decision, judicial salaries moved well ahead of executive and legislative pay schedules. Congress retaliated in 1981 by passing legislation to require specific congressional authorization before any future pay raise for federal judges could take effect. The language effectively eliminated future automatic increases for the judiciary. 95 Stat. 1200, § 140 (1981). A subsequent statute allowed judicial salaries to be increased unless Congress, within a thirty-day period, passed a joint resolution of disapproval. 99 Stat. 1322, § 135 (1985). Congress used that procedure in 1989 to defeat a substantial raise for all federal officials, including judges. Later that year, however, it passed legislation that authorized pay increases for all three branches. 103 Stat. 1763–71 (1989).

Beginning in 1994, members of Congress denied themselves a cost-of-living increase. Since federal district judges are tied to the same salary as a member of Congress, the effect was to deny increases for the judiciary as well. Congress denied itself these increases in 1995 and

1996. When Congress voted itself a pay raise in 1997, it neglected to include judges. "Congress, but Not Judiciary, Receives an Increase in Pay," The New York Times, October 21, 1997, at A23. The following month Congress, in the Commerce-Justice appropriation bill, included a cost-of-living increase for federal judges. In 1999, federal judges had to go to court to win a cost-of-living pay increase. Williams v. United States, 48 F.Supp. 2d 52 (D.D.C. 1999).

E. JUDICIAL LOBBYING

To preserve their reputation for impartiality, objectivity, and independence, judges traditionally abstain from political activities that are the daily fare of executives and legislators. Judicial activities, both on and off the bench, are expected to be free from impropriety and the *appearance* of impropriety.

Before coming to the bench, most judges have been active in legislatures, government agencies, and other political activities. They are unlikely, upon confirmation, to adopt the manner and habits of a cloistered judge; nor should they. Legislation often has a direct bearing on the courts, justifying the active participation of judges at the bill-drafting and congressional-hearing stages. Canon 4 of the American Bar Association's Code of Judicial Conduct permits a judge to "appear at a public hearing before an executive or legislative body or official on matters concerning the law, the legal system, and the administration of justice, and he may otherwise consult with an executive or legislative body or official, but only on matters concerning the administration of justice" and never by casting doubt on his capacity to decide impartially any issue that may come before him. See 2 O.L.C. 30 (1978).

Frankfurter's Activities

With the 1982 release of *The Brandeis/Frankfurter Connection* by Bruce Allen Murphy, the public learned that Justice Brandeis, over a period of years, had secretly paid more than $50,000 to Felix Frankfurter to advance Brandeis's political agenda. The financial arrangement ended when Brandeis left the Court in 1939. Frankfurter joined the Court that year and remained deeply enmeshed in politics. He drafted legislative proposals for the Roosevelt administration, helped staff the upper echelons of the War Department, and assisted Roosevelt's reelection campaign in 1940.

The details of Frankfurter's activities were particularly ironic. As a member of the Court, he described himself as a "political eunuch," claiming that the Court "has no excuse for being unless it's a monastery." In 1944 he confided to a friend that "I have an austere and even sacerdotal view of the position of a judge on this Court, and that means I have nothing to say on matters that come within a thousand miles of what may fairly be called politics." Murphy, The Brandeis/Frankfurter Connection 9, 259–69. In a dissenting opinion, Frankfurter insisted that the authority of the Supreme Court depended on its "complete detachment, in fact and in appearance, from political entanglements." Baker v. Carr, 369 U.S. 186, 267 (1962). Despite such protestations, few Justices have been as politically active as Frankfurter.

Other Justices also participated in off-the-bench activities. The contacts between Brandeis and President Franklin D. Roosevelt had already been noted in the literature.[12] Taft, Frankfurter, Byrnes, and Fortas, while on the Court, met frequently with Presidents and discussed public issues.[13]

---

12. Philippa Strum, "Justice Brandeis and President Roosevelt," reprinted in Walter F. Murphy and C. Herman Pritchett, eds., Courts, Judges, and Politics 187–90 (1979).

13. See Max Freedman, ed., Roosevelt and Frankfurter: Their Correspondence (1967); John P. MacKenzie, The Appearance of Justice 1–33 (1974); and "Nonjudicial Activities of Supreme Court Justices and Other Federal Judges," hearings before the Senate Committee on the Judiciary, 91st Cong., 1st Sess. (1969).

Other Political Actions

Much earlier examples illustrate the difficulty that some members of the Supreme Court have had in drawing a line between law and politics. During the Court's first two decades, individual Justices campaigned for political candidates, ran for political office, and accepted political duties that came their way. Chief Justice John Jay was sent as special envoy to negotiate a treaty with England. Chief Justice Oliver Ellsworth followed that precedent by negotiating a treaty with France. Murphy, The Brandeis/Frankfurter Connection 345–63.

After Chief Justice Marshall issued his decision in *McCulloch* v. *Maryland* (1819), arguing in favor of broad implied powers for the federal government, a series of anonymous articles appeared in a Richmond newspaper attacking the decision and championing states' rights. The first few critiques were probably written by William Brockenbrough, a state judge from Virginia. Marshall could not bear to let the charges go unanswered. Working through his colleague Justice Bushrod Washington, Marshall penned a number of anonymous rebuttals (signed "A Friend of the Union") and published them in a Philadelphia newspaper. Four more critiques appeared in the Richmond newspaper, this time by Judge Spencer Roane of the Virginia Court of Appeals (using the pseudonym Hampden). Marshall answered those as well, signing them "A Friend of the Constitution." G. Gunther, ed., John Marshall's Defense of *McCulloch* v. *Maryland* (1969). Justice Story, while serving for more than twenty years as president of a Massachusetts branch of the United States Bank, tried to influence Treasury Department officials to secure large deposits in his bank and helped Daniel Webster draft a reply to President Jackson's veto of the Bank's charter in 1832.[14]

Many avenues are available to Justices who want to affect the course of political events. Public addresses, law review articles, and contacts with reporters, scholars, and magazine writers are methods of extending judicial influence beyond official actions. The Chief Justice prepares an annual "year-ender," summing up the problems, needs, and accomplishments of federal courts. He also delivers an annual report on the state of the judiciary, sometimes using these forums to criticize Congress for its actions and inactions. Proposals have been introduced for an annual "State of the Judiciary" address, to be delivered by the Chief Justice to a joint session of Congress. This proposal passed the Senate in 1980, but the House took no action. 126 Cong. Rec. 23397 (1980).

Judicial Conference

The Judicial Conference is the principal institutional body for preparing a legislative agenda. The organization dates back to 1922, when Congress directed the Chief Justice to call an annual conference of the senior circuit judges. The objective was to make a comprehensive survey of cases pending before the federal courts: their number and character, cases disposed of, and backlog. The potential for judicial lobbying did not go unnoticed. Representative Clarence F. Lea predicted that the Conference "will become the propaganda organization for legislation for the benefit of the Federal judiciary." 62 Cong. Rec. 203 (1921).

As the law now reads, the Chief Justice submits to Congress "an annual report of the proceedings of the Judicial Conference and its recommendations for legislation." 28 U.S.C. § 331 (1994). These reports are prepared for the spring and fall meetings of the Conference. Because the meetings are largely devoted to administrative and legislative matters rather than judicial duties, there has been pressure to open them to the public. Opponents of this reform

---

14. G. Edward White, The American Political Tradition 41 (1976); Gerald T. Dunne, Justice Joseph Story and the Rise of the Supreme Court 301–02, 328–31 (1970).

Rehnquist Lobbies the House

Chief Justice William H. Rehnquist yesterday took the unusual step of asking House members to reject a Senate-passed provision that would make most handgun murders a federal crime that carries the death penalty.

Rehnquist's lobbying effort against two provisions of the Senate's crime bill came as the House Judiciary Committee prepared for a drafting session Monday on its version of anti-crime legislation.

The Senate bill would authorize prosecution of handgun murders as federal crimes punishable by death. The provision introduced by Sen. Alfonse D'Amato (R-N.Y.) would apply to all murders committed with handguns that moved across state lines....

A statement accompanying Rehnquist's letter said the D'Amato amendments "will swamp the federal courts with routine cases that states are better equipped to handle, and will weaken the ability of the federal courts effectively to deal with difficult criminal cases that present uniquely federal issues."...

SOURCE: "Rehnquist Asks House Members to Reject Senate Handgun Bill," Washington Post, September 21, 1991, at A2.

proposal concede that the Conference is a creature of Congress and subject to further statutory change, but they argue that the principle of judicial independence should protect the proceedings of the Judicial Conference. The Conference came under fire in 1984 for improper lobbying, as well as a private group called the Federal Judges Association, but a GAO investigation found no legal violation. 63 Comp. Gen. 624 (1984).

Chief Justice Initiatives

The lobbying activities of Chief Justice Burger attracted press attention in 1978. On the eve of a Senate vote on the bankruptcy bill, he called Senator Dennis DeConcini and several other members of the Senate Judiciary Committee. DeConcini told reporters that Burger accused him of being "irresponsible" for supporting the legislation and said that the bill "was a political sale and he was going to the President and have him veto it." Calling the charge "a slap in the face of the entire Senate," DeConcini described Burger as being "very, very irate and rude." He "just screamed at me" and "not only lobbied, but pressured and attempted to be intimidating."[15] Representative Don Edwards, head of the House subcommittee responsible for the bankruptcy bill, said that he welcomed the views of judges but only when presented in "a scholarly, judicious way, in writing or in hearings, not in telephone calls once a bill has gone to the floor."[16]

As is customary for most members of the judiciary, Chief Justice Burger did not respond directly to DeConcini's charges. Within a month, however, while accepting an award in New York City, Burger defended his participation in the legislative process (see Burger reading). He also resisted activities he viewed as inappropriate. In 1981 a number of federal judges wanted to form an association to lobby Congress for higher salaries and fringe benefits. Interested judges would contribute $200 and list the members of Congress they felt comfortable contacting about judicial salaries. Burger advised the judges that the position of the federal judiciary should be expressed through the Judicial Conference.[17]

Chief Justice Rehnquist has taken a leading role in advocating legislation to reform appel-

---

15. "Senator Slams Burger on Move to Thwart Bill," National Law Journal, October 16, 1978; "Burger Wants Judges to Speak Up to Congress," Washington Post, October 26, 1978, at A13.
16. "Lobbying by Burger Provokes Criticism," New York Times, November 19, 1978, at 39.
17. "U.S. Judges Want Lobby; Burger Against Proposal," National Law Journal, June 29, 1981, at 2, 10.

late procedures for the death penalty. In 1989, instead of waiting for the Judicial Conference to submit its report and recommendations to Congress, Rehnquist took the initiative to send Congress a report prepared by a committee of federal judges he had appointed. Some judges interpreted his move as an end run around the Judicial Conference. Rehnquist's effort to expedite the legislative process was unsuccessful; serious divisions continued within Congress and the Judicial Conference on the proper legislative remedy. In 1991, Rehnquist intervened to ask members of the House of Representatives to reject a handgun bill because it would strain the federal courts (see box on previous page). In 2000, he urged Congress to end an eleven-year ban on speaking honoraria for federal judges.

Burger on Judicial Lobbying

On October 25, 1978, while accepting the Fordham-Stein Award in New York City, Chief Justice Burger delivered the following remarks on the proper boundaries of judicial intervention in the legislative process.

. . .

From time to time the question comes up as to whether the activities of those of our profession who are judges and who try to see that the needs of the courts are met in some way violate the concept of separation of powers.

I hope that you will not mind if I reflect with you tonight on the real meaning of the separation of powers in our tripartite constitutional system—and what it does not mean.

Justice Jackson had some relevant observations on this subject:

"While the Constitution diffuses power the better to secure liberty, it also contemplates that practice will integrate the dispersed powers into a workable government. It enjoins upon its branches separateness but interdependence, autonomy but reciprocity."

The separation of powers concept was never remotely intended to preclude cooperation, coordination, communication and joint efforts by the members of each branch with the members of the others. Examples of this are legion: The executive, represented by the Solicitor General, volunteers, or is invited by the Supreme Court, to file briefs advising the Supreme Court on questions of law. This happens countless times each term. Members of the Congress—sometimes singly, sometimes a dozen or more of them together—file briefs *amicus curiae* before the Court, advising us how a matter should be decided. These briefs are always welcomed by the Court.

We all remember that President Washington formally asked the Supreme Court for advice on certain policy questions but wisely the Court decided that it would not advise him on such matters. Justices have come to realize that they should avoid advising Presidents and the Congress on substantive policy questions but on matters relating to the courts there must be joint consultation. The separation of powers does not preclude such consultation.

From the beginning of the republic, members of the Congress have appeared as advocates before the Supreme Court. Indeed, they have been some of our great advocates, from Daniel Webster, Henry Clay and John Quincy Adams, and later William Seward. Webster was a Senator when he argued the famous *Dartmouth College* case. In more recent times other Senators, including Sam Ervin and William Saxbe, have appeared.

To be sure, there is a great and necessary tradition of insulation of judges and Justices from political activities generally. But participation in legislative and executive decisions which affect the judicial system is an absolute obligation of judges, as it is of lawyers. One manifestation of the desirable aloofness of judges from controversy is found in the tradition that they do not answer criticism or respond to attacks, no matter how scurrilous or unwarranted. But reasons for refusing to answer attacks must not be used as reasons to abdicate responsibility when Congress is legislating on matters directly affecting the courts. Indeed, the contrary is most emphatically true.

It is entirely appropriate for judges to comment upon issues which affect the courts. The Judicial Conference of the United States and the Administrative Office of the United States Courts receive requests from Congress from fifty to one hundred times each year to comment on pending bills.

Historically, the most valuable judicial improvements are made when the judiciary makes proposals and consults with Congress. Indeed, even after Congress acts, the President regularly requests the views of the Judicial Conference before he passes on legislation which relates to the federal courts. This has been going on for nearly two hundred years. It was more than forty years ago that Congress created the Judicial Conference of the United States, which as you know is made up of twenty-five judges from district courts, courts of appeals and special courts. It made the Chief Justice of the United States the chairman of that Conference. It meets approximately five or six days each year. It has committees dealing with special subjects—a committee on court administration, a committee on appellate rules, on criminal rules, on civil rules, on bankruptcy, on magistrates and similar subjects. These committees regularly confer with Congress and its staffs and the executive branch.

In creating the Judicial Conference, it was contemplated that the Conference would comment on legislation directly affecting the operation of the federal judicial system. The Conference has been doing that routinely for more than forty years. Any notion, therefore, that each of these branches should remain in solitary isolation or logic-tight compartments has no basis in reason, law, history or tradition....

SELECTED READINGS

ABRAHAM, HENRY J. Justices and Presidents: A Political History of Appointments to the Supreme Court. New York: Oxford University Press, 1974.

BALL, HOWARD. Courts and Politics: The Federal Judicial System. Englewood Cliffs, N.J.: Prentice-Hall, 1980.

BLACK, CHARLES L., JR. "A Note on Senatorial Consideration of Supreme Court Nominees." 79 Yale Law Journal 657 (1970).

BUSHNELL, ELEANORE. Crimes, Follies, and Misfortunes: The Federal Impeachment Trials. Champaign, Ill.: University of Illinois Press, 1992.

CARP, ROBERT A., AND C. K. ROWLAND. Policymaking and Politics in the Federal District Courts. Knoxville: University of Tennessee Press, 1983.

CHASE, HAROLD W. Federal Judges: The Appointing Process. Minneapolis: University of Minnesota, 1972.

DANELSKI, DAVID J. A Supreme Court Justice Is Appointed. New York: Random House, 1964.

EARLY, STEPHEN T., JR. Constitutional Courts of the U.S. Totowa, N.J.: Littlefield, Adams, 1977.

FISH, PETER GRAHAM. The Politics of Federal Judicial Administration. Princeton, N.J.: Princeton University Press, 1973.

GERHARDT, MICHAEL J. The Federal Impeachment Process: A Constitutional and Historical Analysis. Princeton University Press, 1996.

GROSSMAN, JOEL B. Lawyers and Judges: The ABA and the Politics of Judicial Selection. New York: Wiley, 1965.

HARRIS, JOSEPH P. The Advice and Consent of the Senate. Berkeley: University of California Press, 1953.

HAYNES, EVAN. The Selection and Tenure of Judges. Newark, N.J.: National Conference of Judicial Councils, 1944.

HOWARD, J. WOODFORD, JR. Courts of Appeals in the Federal Judicial System. Princeton, N.J.: Princeton University Press, 1981.

HULBARY, WILLIAM E., AND THOMAS G. WALKER. "The Supreme Court Selection Process: Presidential Motivations and Judicial Performance." 33 Western Political Quarterly 185 (1980).

KAHN, MICHAEL A. "The Politics of the Appointment Process: An Analysis of Why Learned Hand Was Never Appointed to the Supreme Court." 25 Stanford Law Review 251 (1973).

KURLAND, PHILIP B. "The Constitution and the Tenure of Federal Judges: Some Notes From History." 36 University of Chicago Law Review 665 (1969).

MASON, ALPHEUS THOMAS. "Extra-Judicial Work for Judges: The Views of Chief Justice Stone." 67 Harvard Law Review 193 (1953).

MURPHY, WALTER. "In His Own Image: Mr. Chief Justice Taft and Supreme Court Appointments." 1961 Supreme Court Review 159.

REHNQUIST, WILLIAM H. Grand Inquests: The Historical Impeachments of Justice Samuel Chase and President Andrew Johnson. New York: Morrow & Co., 1992.

SCHMIDHAUSER, JOHN R. "The Justices of the Supreme Court: A Collective Portrait." 3 Midwest Journal of Political Science 1 (1959).

———. Judges and Justices: The Federal Appellate Judiciary. Boston: Little, Brown, 1979.

SCIGLIANO, ROBERT. The Supreme Court and the Presidency. New York: The Free Press, 1971.

TRIBE, LAURENCE H. God Save This Honorable Court. New York: Random House, 1985.

WHEELER, RUSSELL. "Extrajudicial Activities of the Early Supreme Court." 1973 Supreme Court Review 123.

WINTERS, GLENN R., ed. Selected Readings: Judicial Selection and Tenure. Chicago: American Judicature Society, 1973.

5

Decision Making: Process and Strategy

Publication of *The Brethren: Inside the Supreme Court* in 1979 promised a rare glimpse into the inner sanctum of the Supreme Court. The authors claimed that for nearly two centuries the Supreme Court had made its decisions "in absolute secrecy." In fact, the deliberative process of the Court has been studied and scrutinized for years. Scholars have access to internal memoranda, conference notes, diaries, draft opinions, and correspondence by the Justices. Members of the Court and their law clerks publish widely. Drawing on those materials, we have a fairly detailed picture of the process that Justices use to make decisions.[1]

The Supreme Court begins its term on the first Monday in October and ends in late June or early July of the following year. A term is designated by the October date. (For example, the 2000 term began October 2, 2000.) During these approximately nine months, the Court selects cases, hears oral argument, writes opinions, and announces decisions. After recessing for the summer, the Justices continue to review petitions in preparation for the new term and decide emergency petitions brought to their attention. Although decisions by the Supreme Court require a quorum of six, in certain cases individual Justices may stay the execution and enforcement of lower court orders and give aggrieved parties time to petition the full Court for review. Each Justice performs other duties when assigned to one of the judicial circuits.

On rare occasions the Court convenes in the summer in special session to deal with urgent matters. For example, the Court met on June 18, 1953, to consider Justice Douglas' stay in the execution of Ethel and Julius Rosenberg, convicted of delivering atomic bomb information to the then Soviet Union. On June 19 the Court vacated the stay, and the Rosenbergs were executed that day. Another special session occurred on August 28, 1958, when the Court convened to consider a lower court order enforcing a desegregation plan for Little Rock High School. The Court unanimously upheld the lower court on September 12, three days before the school's scheduled opening. On July 8, 1974, the Court held oral argument on the Watergate tapes case, deciding on July 24 that President Nixon had to surrender the tapes to prosecutors. He resigned from office on August 9.

A. JURISDICTION: ORIGINAL AND APPELLATE

The Constitution assigns to the Supreme Court judicial power in "all Cases, in Law and Equity, arising under this Constitution, the Laws of the United States, and Treaties made, or which shall be made under their Authority...." The types of cases identified in the Constitu-

---

1. Bob Woodward and Scott Armstrong, The Brethren: Inside the Supreme Court 1 (1979). Of many commendable studies published before *The Brethren,* special note should be made of J. Woodford Howard, Jr., Mr. Justice Murphy 231–496 (1968); Walter F. Murphy, Elements of Judicial Strategy (1964); and Alpheus Thomas Mason, Harlan Fiske Stone: Pillar of the Law (1956). See also H. W. Perry, Jr., Deciding to Decide: Agenda Setting in the United States Supreme Court (1991); Bernard Schwartz, Decision: How the Supreme Court Decides Cases (1996); Edward Lazarus, Closed Chambers: The First Eyewitness Account of the Epic Struggles Inside the Supreme Court (1998).

tion affect (1) ambassadors, other public ministers, and consuls; (2) admiralty and maritime controversies; (3) controversies in which the United States is a party; and (4) controversies between two or more states, between a state and a citizen of another state, between citizens of different states, between citizens of the same state claiming lands under grants of different states, and between a state (or its citizens) and foreign states, citizens, or subjects.

This jurisdiction is divided between original and appellate. In all cases affecting ambassadors, other public ministers, and consuls, and those in which a state is a party, the Supreme Court has original jurisdiction. These cases may be taken directly to the Court without action by lower courts. Only rarely does a case of original jurisdiction concern ambassadors, diplomats, and consuls. Most of the cases involve litigation between states, such as disputes over boundaries and water rights. In the early days, original cases were tried before a jury in the Supreme Court. Georgia v. Brailsford, 3 U.S. (3 Dall.) 1 (1794). That practice was soon abandoned.

"Original" appears to imply exclusivity, suggesting that what is granted by the Constitution cannot be abridged or altered by Congress. Nevertheless, Congress has passed legislation that divides original jurisdiction into two categories: (1) original and exclusive jurisdiction, and (2) original but not exclusive jurisdiction. 28 U.S.C. § 1251 (1994). For the latter, lower federal courts share concurrent jurisdiction.

Congress has restricted the jurisdiction of federal courts by establishing criteria for "federal questions." Until 1980, certain federal court cases required at least $10,000 in dispute. The purpose was to reduce case congestion in federal courts. That amount was eliminated in 1980. 94 Stat. 2369. Congress wanted to resolve the anomaly faced by persons whose rights had been violated but were barred from the courts because they had not suffered a sufficient economic injury. Congress has established a dollar threshold of $50,000 for "diversity" jurisdiction (where federal courts consider cases involving state law if the parties are from different states). 28 U.S.C. § 1332 (1994).

Court jurisdiction may seem like a technical matter of interest only to specialists and practitioners of the law, but jurisdiction means political power. A question of jurisdiction provoked the first constitutional amendment adopted after the Bill of Rights. In 1793 the Court held that states could be sued in federal courts by citizens of another state. Chisholm v. Georgia, 2 Dall. (2 U.S.) 419. The public outcry was so deep and swift that the Eleventh Amendment, overriding *Chisholm*, passed both Houses of Congress in 1794 and was ratified in 1798. (Congressional efforts to withdraw jurisdiction from the courts are covered in the final chapter, "Efforts to Curb the Court.")

Dockets

Each year the Supreme Court receives about 7,000 petitions for review. A few cases concern original jurisdiction and are placed on the Original Docket. Original jurisdiction is used sparingly to protect the Court's workload with its appellate docket. The Court is especially reluctant to become a court of first instance and assume the fact-finding function of a trial court, a task for which the Court considers itself "ill-equipped." Ohio v. Wyandotte, 401 U.S. 493, 498 (1971). To assist in the handling of its original jurisdiction docket, the Court usually appoints special masters to study an issue and present recommendations.

Cases reach the Supreme Court by one of four routes. First, some parties come to the Court as a matter of statutory right. Congress has passed a number of statutes that provide for direct appeal, preferred treatment, and expedited action. In recent years, however, Congress has begun converting some of these statutes to discretionary review. H. Rept. No. 824 (Part 1), 97th Cong., 2d Sess. 6 (1982). The Court urged Congress to grant even greater discretion, and in 1988 Congress passed legislation to substantially eliminate the Court's mandatory or obligatory jurisdiction. 102 Stat. 662 (1988). To handle its workload, the Court often disposes of cases without written opinion.

Major Reasons for Granting Cert

1. Conflicts among federal appellate courts.
2. Conflicts between federal courts and state courts.
3. State or federal court's holding congressional statute unconstitutional.
4. Substantial constitutional, legal, or political issue.

5. Construction of important federal statute.
6. Submission of a petition by the Solicitor General.
7. Flagrant or egregious abuse of justice in the lower courts.

Writs of certiorari are a second route to the Supreme Court. By "granting cert" the Court calls up the records of a lower court, a decision that is wholly discretionary.

Third, petitions for review are submitted by indigents, including prison inmates, sometimes in the form of handwritten notes. These requests, called *in forma pauperis* (in the manner of a pauper), numbered a few dozen in 1930 but now range in the thousands each term. To discourage nuisance suits by indigents who file dozens of petitions and motions, the Court can require indigents to pay the normal $300 filing fee when they seek "extraordinary writs" in excess of normal requests. In re Sindram, 498 U.S. 177 (1991). Subsequently, the Court changed its rules to allow it to reject filings by indigents if filings are frivolous or malicious.

Fourth, an appellate court may submit a writ of certification to seek instruction on a question of law. 28 U.S.C. § 1254 (1994). This procedure is seldom used, for it forces the Court to decide questions of law without the guidance of findings and conclusions by the lower courts.

B. THE WRIT OF CERTIORARI

The Supreme Court controls its workload largely by exercising discretionary authority over cases coming to it for review. The discretionary writ of certiorari was initiated by the Evarts Act of 1891 and the Judicial Code of 1911, but the primary source of discretion awaited the "Judges Bill" of 1925. That statute eliminated direct review by the Supreme Court of decisions in the district courts and greatly expanded the use of the writ of certiorari. 43 Stat. 936 (1925).

Most of the decisions of the Supreme Court involve "cert" denials. Under Rule 10 of the Supreme Court, a review on writ of certiorari "is not a matter of right, but of judicial discretion" and will be granted "only for compelling reasons." Among the reasons listed in Rule 10 are conflicts among federal courts of appeals, between a federal court of appeals and a state court of last resort, and over federal questions decided by different state courts of last resort. Justices look for cases that pose questions of general importance: broad issues on the administration of the law, substantive constitutional questions, the construction of important federal statutes, and serious questions of public law. In a 1949 address, Chief Justice Vinson advised lawyers who prepare cert petitions to spend "a little less time discussing the merits of their cases and a little more time demonstrating why it is important that the Court should hear them. . . . If [a petition for certiorari] only succeeds in demonstrating that the decision below may be erroneous, it has not fulfilled its purpose." 69 S.Ct. vi (1949). Lawyers learn how to get the Court's attention (reading by Lauter).

Other factors explain why the Court grants cert. The literature on "cue theory" points to a key ingredient: the federal government's decision to seek review. The Court relies heavily on the seasoned judgment of the Solicitor General to bring only those cases that merit appeal. When that factor combines with other elements (the presence of a civil liberty issue, conflict between circuits, a lower court decision in which judges are divided), granting a petition is even more likely (see box).

At various times in its history, the Court has accepted an issue from a lower court because it appeared that the executive and legislative branches were unwilling to act. An appellate judge said that "waiting for the legislature is not productive. The legislature doesn't legislate. Courts have had to do a good deal of stuff that would be better for the legislature to have done. But it's better for courts to do them than no one." J. Woodford Howard, Jr., Courts of Appeals in the Federal Judicial System 163 n. (1981). Presumably the same attitude prevailed on the Supreme Court, but only recently have its members publicly admitted this function. Justice Powell said that judicial independence gives the Court "a freedom to make decisions that perhaps are necessary for our society, decisions that the legislative branch may be reluctant to make." Kenyon College Alumni Bulletin, Summer 1979, at 15. Justice Blackmun elaborated on that point in 1982. Asked whether desegregation was an example of where the courts had to do more because other branches did less, he replied:

> Well, one can come up with a lot of possible examples. That is one. One man, one vote is another one. And many of the sex discrimination cases perhaps are others. If one goes back twenty-five years, certainly things are different because of judicial intervention. I can remember when I was a law clerk a case came up concerning the possibility of a federal judge intervening in the administration of a prison and it was unheard of in those days. That was a problem for the prison administrative authorities. And now, of course, in recent years — and by that I mean twenty years anyway — there have been many instances where the courts, in effect, have taken constitutional rights inside the prison doors...." A Justice Speaks Out: A Conversation with Harry A. Blackmun," Cable News Network, Inc., conducted November 25, 1982, at 10–11.

Of the approximately 7,000 cases received each year, about one hundred are accepted for oral argument and full opinions. In other words, more than 95 percent of all petitions are denied. In evaluating the petitions, Justices dismiss many as frivolous and "dead-list" them (deny them "cert") without further deliberation. In recent years the Court has replaced the "dead list" with a "discuss list," which includes the cases deemed worthy of discussion. Any Justice can request that a case be added to the discuss list. Examples of frivolous petitions include: "Are Negroes in fact Indians and therefore entitled to Indians' exemptions from federal income taxes?"; "Are the federal income tax laws unconstitutional insofar as they do not provide a deduction for depletion of the human body?"; and "Does a ban on drivers turning right on a red light constitute an unreasonable burden on interstate commerce?" Brennan, 40 U. Chi. L. Rev. 473, 478 (1973). When an appeal or petition for writ of certiorari is frivolous, Rule 42.2 of the Supreme Court authorizes the award of appropriate damages to the party sued.

Screening Cert Petitions

Justices try to avoid cases where the legal issue is overpowered by emotional ingredients. When the Court reviewed cert petitions in 1975 to clarify the rights available to criminal defendants, it deliberately passed over the petition of someone who had been convicted of strangling, raping, and beheading a woman, followed by an attempt to skin her. Liva Baker, Miranda 105 (1983). It would have been impossible for the Court to announce legal principles in the midst of such ghastly circumstances.

In theory, Justices make a personal judgment on each of the thousands of petitions received annually. However, they depend on their law clerks to prepare memoranda that summarize the facts of a case and recommend acceptance or rejection. All of the Justices, with the exception of John Paul Stevens, participate in a "cert pool" to divvy up the work. They meet at a Friday conference to discuss and vote on the petitions that survive initial review. A single

Justice may set a case for decision at conference. As a symbol of unity, Justices shake hands upon entering the conference room. These gestures preserve an atmosphere of civility in an institution compelled to deal with some of the most fractious issues in society. Maintaining a measure of collegiality among nine strong personalities is no small feat. Members of the Court work together for long periods and under intense pressures.

To preserve confidentiality in the conference room, only the Justices are present. The junior Justice sits closest to the door, receiving and delivering messages that flow in and out of the room. Some political scientists reported that the rectangular table in the conference room had been chopped into three pieces by Chief Justice Burger and converted into an inverted U, supposedly to prevent the liberal Douglas from sitting opposite him in direct confrontation. Justice Powell reassured his readers in 1975 that the conference table "retains its pristine shape; there has been no hacking or sawing; the justices occupy their seats in the traditional order of seniority."[2] Visitors to the room find the table intact.

The Chief Justice begins the discussion of each case. He summarizes the facts, analyzes the law, and announces his proposed vote. He is followed by the other Justices, in order of seniority, from the senior Associate Justice down to the newest Justice. Before the Warren Court, voting was done in the opposite manner: the junior Justice voted first and the Chief Justice last. Toward the end of his service, Warren persuaded the Justices to vote in the same order as they had spoken.[3] Four votes are needed to grant certiorari. There have been cases where the Court grants cert and later, on the basis of changed circumstances, dismisses the writ of certiorari as "improvidently granted." Dismissing a case in this manner is sometimes called "digging a case" (dig—dismissed as improvidently granted).

Granting cert involves some tactical decisions by Justices. If five Justices are rigidly opposed, the four in favor of granting cert may decide against hearing the case because they know they will lose on the merits. If three Justices feel strongly that cert should be granted, sometimes another Justice will add the fourth vote ("join three"). For "defensive denials," Justices prefer to let some cases at lower levels, even if decided badly, to remain as a precedent only for a single circuit, instead of compounding the legal situation with a decision by the Supreme Court. If the Court is in transition from a liberal to a conservative body, a remaining liberal Justice may engage in defensive denials to prevent the Court from overturning liberal precedents. H. W. Perry, Jr., Deciding to Decide 98, 166–70, 198–207 (1991).

Justices must address a wide range of complex cases at each conference. Each Justice has a docket sheet to record each step of the process from deciding to hear a case to postconference voting. Conference notes provide a summary record of the arguments of each Justice on the merits of the case. Whoever is selected to draft the opinion can review the conference notes and weave an argument that will attract the maximum number of votes. At any point, however, votes may be changed before the opinion of the Court reaches its final stage.

In denying cert, the Court seldom offers an explanation. When it does, the reason is usually brief if not cryptic. More light is shed when Justices write a dissenting opinion on cert denials.

---

2. Lewis F. Powell, Jr., "Myths and Misconceptions About the Supreme Court," 61 A.B.A.J. 1344 (1975). See Glendon Schubert, Judicial Policy Making 134 (1977) and Howard Ball, Courts and Politics 254 (1980). For a discussion of some of the practices in conference, see William H. Rehnquist, "Sunshine in the Third Branch," 16 Washburn L. J. 559 (1977).

3. Walter F. Murphy and C. Herman Pritchett, eds., Courts, Judges, and Politics 657 (1979). This account is supported by a 1982 interview with Justice Blackmun; "A Justice Speaks Out: A Conversation with Harry A. Blackmun," Cable News Network, Inc., conducted November 25, 1982, at 21. In a 1963 article, Justice Brennan stated that voting began with the junior Justice; William J. Brennan, Jr., "Inside View of the High Court," New York Times Magazine, October 6, 1963, at 100. Justice Clark, in 1956, also said that the junior Justice voted first, 19 F.R.D. 303, 307, as did Justice Frankfurter in 1953, "Chief Justices I Have Known," 39 Va. L. Rev. 883, 903.

This practice, which has grown significantly in recent decades, complicates the Court's traditional position that cert denial means a refusal to take a case and nothing more. Darr v. Burford, 339 U.S. 200, 226 (1950). If dissenting Justices strongly voice their reasons and argue the merits, it may appear that the majority denying cert considered and rejected those arguments. Justices often differ on the significance to be attached to dissents on cert denials.[4] Speculation as to intent is hazardous. Even when Justices think that a lower court is wrong, they may vote to deny an application simply because they regard the federal question as insubstantial, poorly timed for review, or inappropriate because of the need for judicial restraint.

David Lauter

Certiorari Strategies

In the following article, "The Fine Art of Creating a Certiorari Petition," Lauter explains the considerations of obtaining four votes for a successful cert petition. The article appeared in the *National Law Journal,* December 10, 1984.

Several years ago, Bruce J. Ennis, then legal director of the American Civil Liberties Union, wrote a law review article about how to write a brief for the Supreme Court.

The theme of the piece was that a lawyer should not write for an abstract court, but should concentrate on catching the attention of each of the nine justices who actually will be reviewing the case.

Last week, Mr. Ennis, now in private practice in Washington, D.C.'s Ennis, Friedman, Bersoff & Ewing, provided an object lesson on how the job is done, persuading the Supreme Court to grant certiorari in a libel case involving a candidate for U.S. attorney, a man who didn't like him and a letter to President Reagan. *McDonald* v. *Smith, 84–476.*

The letter, written in 1980 by Robert McDonald, Mr. Ennis' client, told the president that he should not appoint David I. Smith to the U.S. attorney's job in Greensboro, N.C. Mr. Smith did not get the job, found out about the letter and sued for libel.

Mr. Ennis' argument, so far unsuccessful in federal district court and the 4th U.S. Circuit Court of Appeals, is that Mr. McDonald should be absolutely immune from civil liability for the letter under the First Amendment right to "petition the Government for a redress of grievances." The decisions rejecting that argument appear to be the first times the issue has been considered in federal court.

Mr. Ennis started out with the assumption that Justices William J. Brennan Jr. and Thurgood Marshall, who have been sympathetic to defense claims in libel cases, might be interested in hearing the case. Then he set about trying to find two more votes.

First, he noted, "the court has sort of gotten interested in libel issues again. From a law clerk's perspective it's a very juicy question and I thought the law clerks would push it."

The petition for certiorari made a particular point of emphasizing the venerable nature of the petition clause, arguing that the right to petition is far older than the rights of free speech and press. That argument, Mr. Ennis noted, was specially designed to appeal to the interest that several of the justices have in history. Justices John Paul Stevens and Lewis F. Powell Jr. frequently mention historical antecedents in their opinions as does Chief Justice Warren E. Burger.

In addition, the case posed an unusual conflict between state- and federal-court interpretations of constitutional law that Mr. Ennis hoped would appeal to several other justices.

Two state high courts within the 4th Circuit—West Virginia and Maryland—have held that petitions to the government cannot be the basis for a civil suit. With the 4th Circuit holding the other way, Mr. Ennis' petition argued, federal district courts in those two states sitting in diversity ac-

---

4. See differing views of Justices Blackmun and Marshall in United States v. Kras, 409 U.S. 434, 443, 460–61 (1973). Justices Stevens, Brennan, and Stewart objected when the Court gave a brief reason for denying cert ("for failure to file petition within time provided"); County of Sonoma v. Isbell, 439 U.S. 996 (1978). See also Peter Linzer, "The Meaning of Certiorari Denials," 79 Colum. L. Rev. 1127 (1979).

tions would be forced to follow the law of the circuit, rejecting the law of the state, implying "a premise that federal courts have greater wisdom, or at least authority, in interpreting the federal Constitution than do state courts."

"Justice [Sandra Day] O'Connor has written law review articles about the need to allow state court judges to make decisions," Mr. Ennis noted,

hoping that argument might particularly appeal to her. In addition, Justice William H. Rehnquist might be interested in the federalism aspect of the argument, he said.

Having now gotten the court's attention, Mr. Ennis, of course, faces the more difficult matter of winning the case. "It's a long way to go to convince this court to grant a new absolute right," he said.

C. FROM ORAL ARGUMENT TO DECISION

After a case receives four votes from Justices meeting in conference, it is transferred to the oral argument list. If Justices conclude that a question is clearly controlled by one of the Court's earlier decisions, they may summarily dispose of a lower court decision without oral argument or full briefing. One form of summary disposition is a per curiam opinion that grants cert but disposes of the merits without giving parties an opportunity to file briefs or argue before the Court. In 1980, for example, the Court decided a case involving press and speech restrictions on former government employees without hearing oral argument. Snepp v. United States, 444 U.S. 507. Summary disposition carries the risk of depriving the Court of crucial information. It can also suggest a "rush to judgment."

The Pentagon papers case of 1971 moved through the courts with extraordinary speed. Beginning with the *New York Times*'s publication of a secret Pentagon study on the origins and conduct of the Vietnam War, only seventeen days were consumed for action by two district courts, two appellate courts, and the Supreme Court. The *New York Times*'s petitions and motions were filed with the Supreme Court on June 24 at about 11 A.M. The government filed its motion later that evening. Oral argument took place on June 26. The record in the *Times* case did not arrive until 7 or 8 P.M. the previous evening. The briefs of the parties were received less than two hours before oral argument. Four days later the Court announced its decision, upholding the right of the press to publish material from the Pentagon study. Despite protests from several Justices, the Court moved quickly to protect the First Amendment right of the press to publish without prior restraint. New York Times v. United States, 403 U.S. 713 (1971).

Oral Argument

In preparation for oral argument, counsel for each side submits briefs and records that are distributed to each Justice. The Court hears oral argument in public session from Monday through Thursday, listening to cases from 10 A.M. to noon and from 1 to 3 P.M. On some days it is only from 10 to noon. Usually one hour is set aside for each case. Although briefs are important, members of the judiciary have noted that there are some judges "who listen better than they read and who are more receptive to the spoken than the written word." Harlan, 41 Corn. L. Q. 6 (1955). The impressions they receive during oral argument often carry with them into the conference room at the end of the week. Moreover, oral argument gives an opportunity for judges to explore with counsel key issues left undeveloped in the briefs.

During oral argument, the Chief Justice sits in the center of a raised bench with the senior Associate Justice to his right and the next ranking Justice to his left. Other Justices are arrayed by seniority alternately to his right and left, leaving the most junior Justice positioned farthest to his left. Some Justices rely on a "bench memorandum" prepared by law clerks to digest the facts and arguments of both sides and provide guidance during the questioning of counsel. Judicial styles differ at oral argument. Justice Douglas asked few questions and regarded many of the ones put forth by colleagues as attempts to lobby Justices for votes rather than to illuminate issues. William O. Douglas, The Court Years 181 (1981).

Writing Opinions

The number of full opinions each year is now about 80, down from the 140 to 150 annual rate of a few years ago (see figure on workload). To divide the time between hearing cases and writing opinions, the Court alternates between several weeks of oral argument and several weeks of recess to write opinions and study appeals and cert petitions. If the Chief Justice has voted with the majority in conference, he assigns the majority opinion either to himself or to another Justice. When the Chief Justice is in the minority, the senior Justice voting with the majority assigns the case. The decision by William Rehnquist to dissent in many cases during his first year as Chief Justice allowed Justice Brennan, a liberal colleague, to control assignment. The dissenters decide who shall write the dissenting opinion. Each Justice may write a separate opinion, concurrence, or dissent.

The assignment of opinions recognizes the need to distribute work load fairly, the different speeds with which Justices complete their research and writing, and the availability of exper-

SUPREME COURT'S WORKLOAD (1999–2000 TERM)

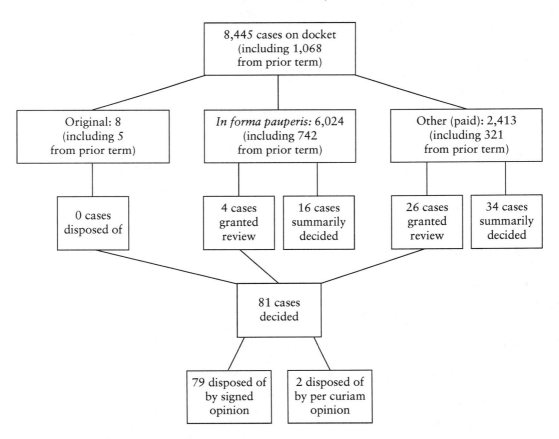

Source: 69 LW 3134 (August 15, 2000)

tise within the Court. Chief Justice Vinson, a former member of the House Ways and Means Committee and Secretary of the Treasury, preferred to handle tax cases. 49 Nw. U. L. Rev. 26, 31–32 (1954).

Although Justices are appointed for life and are immune from periodic campaigning for electoral office, they know that the ability to write acceptable opinions depends on sensitivity to the public. This consideration affects the assignment of opinions. In 1944 Chief Justice Stone initially assigned the Texas "white primary" case to Justice Frankfurter. Justice Jackson shared his misgivings with both Frankfurter and Stone, suggesting that because of "Southern sensibilities" it was unwise to have a Vienna-born Jew, raised in New England (the seat of the abolition movement), write the majority opinion striking down the Texas statute. With Frankfurter's consent, Stone transferred the assignment to Stanley Reed, a native-born Protestant and old-line Kentuckian. Reed was also a Democrat of long-standing, whereas Frankfurter's past ties to the Democratic party were suspect. Alpheus T. Mason, Harlan Fiske Stone: Pillar of the Law 614–15 (1968).

Recusal

Under English common law, judges could be disqualified for direct interest in a case but never for bias. Such an admission would have conceded the capacity for partiality or favoritism in a judge. Frank, 56 Yale L. J. 605, 609–10 (1947); Forer, 73 Harv. L. Rev. 1325, 1327 (1960). Many of the early Justices on the Supreme Court failed to recuse (remove) themselves from cases that, under today's standards, would call for disqualification. Justice Story decided cases involving the Bank of the United States while serving as president of a Massachusetts branch of it. Chief Justice Marshall wrote *Marbury* v. *Madison* after serving as the Secretary of State who had neglected to deliver the commission of office. However, Marshall withdrew from *Stuart* v. *Laird* (1803) because he had tried the case earlier in the circuit court.

Based on statutory guidelines, court decisions, judicial codes, and personal standards, judges withdraw from certain cases when they have a personal bias, when they previously served as counsel in the matter in controversy, and for other stated causes. 28 U.S.C. §§ 144, 455 (1994). Judges disqualify themselves to maintain the appearance of impartiality and due process. Chief Justice Stone and Justice Jackson did not take part in a 1942 decision because as former Attorneys General they had helped prosecute the case. United States v. Bethlehem Steel Corp., 315 U.S. 289, 309 (1942). Judge Haynsworth's failure to recuse himself in several cases in the Fourth Circuit became a key reason for the Senate's rejecting him for the Supreme Court in 1969.

Justice Jackson shocked the country in June 1946 by issuing a blistering attack on Justice Black. This extraordinary public revelation of a bitter feud between two members of the Supreme Court had its origins in a 1945 decision in which Black was part of a 5 to 4 majority upholding the right of coal miners. Jewell Ridge Corp. v. Local No. 6167, 325 U.S. 161 (1945). Jackson's dissent in that case quoted from a Senate debate in 1937 to show that Black, as a Senator, provided legislative history contrary to the majority's decision. It was also known that the chief counsel for the miners in the 1945 case was Black's former law partner.

The coal company petitioned for a rehearing, asking whether Black could render impartial justice given his connection with the legislation and the chief counsel. All members of the Court agreed that the motion for a rehearing should be denied, because the decision to disqualify oneself is purely a personal judgment to be made by each Justice. However, Jackson did not want to imply, by silence, that everyone on the Court supported Black's decision. When the Court denied the motion, Jackson wrote a concurring opinion, explaining that disqualification was not a decision for the full Court. Each Justice had to make that determination for himself. Frankfurter joined Jackson's concurrence. Jewell Ridge Coal Corp. v. Local No. 6167,

325 U.S. 897 (1945). Black's supporters were outraged by the concurrence because it drew attention to the issue of disqualification.

A newspaper article in May 1946 reported that Black regarded Jackson's concurrence as a gratuitous insult and a slur on Black's honor. The dispute was exacerbated by the pending selection of a Chief Justice by President Truman. Jackson hoped to be named; Black was dead-set against it. According to the newspaper story, Black threatened to resign if Truman selected Jackson as Chief Justice. Fleeson, "Supreme Court Feud," [Washington] Evening Star, May 16, 1946, at A-15. Black refused to comment on these newspaper stories.

While Jackson was in Nuremberg serving as Special Prosecutor for the Nazi trials, Truman nominated Fred Vinson to be Chief Justice. Jackson concluded that Black played a hand in denying him the promotion. From Nuremberg, Jackson cabled the Judiciary Committees to elaborate on the 1945 dispute. He said that after he announced his decision to write a concurrence on the petition for a rehearing, Black became "very angry" and said that any opinion that discussed the subject at all would mean "a declaration of war." Jackson told Black that he would "not stand for any more of his bullying and that, whatever I would otherwise do, I would now have to write my opinion to keep self-respect in the face of threats." Alluding to rumors that had been published critical of his role, Jackson remarked: "If war is declared on me I propose to wage it with the weapons of the open warrior, not those of the stealthy assassin." Jackson warned that if Black failed to disqualify himself in comparable situations in the future, "I will make my Jewell Ridge opinion look like a letter of recommendation by comparison." New York Times, June 11, 1946, at 2:6.

Justice Rehnquist was asked to recuse himself from *Laird* v. *Tatum* because he had earlier testified on the subject while serving as an official in the Justice Department. In a highly unusual memorandum, Rehnquist agreed that disqualification would have been required had he signed a pleading or brief in the case or actively participated in it. In two earlier cases he withdrew for those reasons. 409 U.S. 824, 828–29 (1972). However, he disagreed that testimony or the expression of one's views were adequate grounds for recusal. He also pointed out that disqualification of a Supreme Court Justice presents problems that do not exist in a lower court where one judge may substitute for another. Id. at 837–38. This issue resurfaced in 1986 during Rehnquist's nomination hearings to be Chief Justice.

Drafting Opinions

The process of writing opinions begins with the briefs prepared by opposing counsel, research by law clerks and library staff, and the knowledge that Justices acquire from decades of experience in public and private life. These drafts are printed within the Court building and circulated among the Justices. Comments are written on the drafts; memorandums are exchanged. Often, a forceful dissent may persuade members of the majority to change their position, creating a new majority from the old dissenting position. Chief Justice Vinson once remarked that an opinion circulated as a dissent "sometimes has so much in logic, reason, and authority to support it that it becomes the opinion of the Court." 69 S.Ct. x (1949). Draft opinions may be so influential in modifying the Court's final decision that they are never published. Alexander M. Bickel, The Unpublished Opinions of Mr. Justice Brandeis (1967). The threat of a dissent can force changes in the majority opinion.

The role of law clerks is sometimes described in lavish terms, as though they displace the functions of judges. Because of the growing importance of law clerks, Senator John Stennis suggested (perhaps whimsically) that it might be appropriate to subject them to confirmation by the Senate. 104 Cong. Rec. 8107–08 (1958). Publication of *The Brethren: Inside the Supreme Court* in 1979 catapulted clerks to a seemingly pivotal role in making judicial policy. However, this study depended heavily on interviews with clerks who no doubt found it tempting to embroider a bit on their contributions to public law. Edward Lazarus, a former Supreme Court law clerk, claimed that Justices "yield great and excessive power to immature, ideologically driven clerks, who in turn use that power to manipulate their bosses and the institution they ostensibly serve." Edward Lazarus, Closed Chambers 6 (1998).

Judges in the prime of life are unlikely to defer to the opinions of clerks fresh out of law school, however much the clerks may stimulate new ideas and approaches. Clerks come and go, but the persistence in decisions of a unique writing style is compelling evidence that judges do their own work. Nevertheless, clerks do more than check footnotes, review cert petitions, and perform minor editing tasks. Depending on the judge they work for, they might be asked to prepare a "prototype or aspirant opinion" to guide the thinking of the court. Frank M. Coffin, The Ways of a Judge 69 (1980). Because of heavy court workload, judges often let clerks do the preliminary draft of an opinion (see Coffin reading).

Personal Values and Attitudes

The legal profession no longer suggests that the sole duty of a judge is to place a constitutional provision beside a challenged statute to see whether the latter squares with the former. United States v. Butler, 297 U.S. 1, 62 (1936). Still, the belief that judges, in the act of deciding, are able to put aside their personal value systems retains a following. Justice Frankfurter made an eloquent plea for this concept of judicial deliberation:

> It is asked with sophomoric brightness, does a man cease to be himself when he becomes a Justice? Does he change his character by putting on a gown? No, he does not change his character. He brings his whole experience, his training, his outlook, his social, intellectual and moral environment with him when he takes a seat on the Supreme Bench. But a judge worth his salt is in the grip of his function. The intellectual habits of self-discipline which govern his mind are as much a part of him as the influence of the interest he may have represented at the bar, often much more so. 98 Proceedings Am. Phil. Soc. 233, 238 (1954).

It would be superficial to suggest that judges use their office simply to disseminate personal views, but decisions of individual judges flow at least in part from their own values and attitudes. Justice Miller, who served on the Supreme Court from 1862 to 1890, despaired of the fixed views and predispositions of those on the bench: "It is vain to contend with judges who have been at the bar the advocates for forty years of rail road companies, and all the forms of associated capital, when they are called upon to decide cases where such interests are in contest. All their training, all their feelings are from the start in favor of those who need no such influence." Charles Fairman, Mr. Justice Miller and the Supreme Court 374 (1939).

Although the votes of judges cannot be predicted with mathematical accuracy, attorneys are sophisticated enough to engage in "forum shopping" to find the court that augurs best for their client. Judicial independence and objectivity remain important values in the administration of justice, but by now it is routine to recognize definite alignments and alliances among judges. Even members of the judiciary acknowledge the existence of blocs. When Justice Blackmun joined the Supreme Court, he calculated that there were two Justices on the right, two on the left, and "five of us in the center." "A Justice Speaks Out: A Conversation with Harry A. Blackmun," Cable News Network, Inc., conducted November 25, 1982, at 22. Justice O'Connor's appearance in 1981 added another conservative voice to that of Chief Justice Burger and Justice Rehnquist. Blackmun, meanwhile, now found himself voting more frequently with the liberal bloc of Justices Brennan and Marshall. Blocs are not necessarily stable. They change over time and vary with the issue. During the Burger Court, Justices Blackmun, Powell, Stevens, and White formed part of a "floating center," casting the votes necessary to build a majority by joining either with the liberal votes of Brennan and Marshall or the conservative wing of Burger, O'Connor, and Rehnquist.

By the early 1990s, O'Connor was more often associated with a moderate center consisting also of Justices Kennedy and Souter. Justices Blackmun and Stevens were closely aligned with a more liberal bloc, while Justices Scalia and Thomas appeared to team up as a conservative bloc. After President Clinton's appointments of Ruth Bader Ginsburg and Stephen G. Breyer, the Court divided largely along the lines of five conservatives (Rehnquist, O'Connor, Scalia, Kennedy, and Thomas) and four moderate-liberals (Stevens, Souter, Ginsburg, and Breyer). Several justices played center roles, adding a fifth vote with one side to form a majority.

Communicating Clearly

Members of the judiciary sometimes complain that their decisions are distorted by the press. Mistakes and misconceptions by reporters are likely, given the time pressures between the announcement of a decision and the deadlines imposed by newspapers, magazines, and broadcast services. These pressures have been partly relieved by several changes over the past few decades. In 1965 the Supreme Court, instead of handing down all opinions on "Decision Monday," began delivering some of its decisions on other days of the week. The Court also started meeting at 10 A.M. rather than noon; these extra hours eased deadlines for reporters. To assure more accurate and sophisticated coverage, major newspapers and wire services began selecting reporters with law degrees or special training in the law.

Some of the "distortions" in the press come from Justices who use careless language in concurring and dissenting opinions, or from those who fail, in the statement for the Court, to correct misconceptions that appear in separate opinions. When the Supreme Court announced the School Prayer Decision in 1962, Justice Douglas's concurrence suggested that the decision would cover ceremonial observances of a religious nature, such as the Court's traditional invocation when it convenes and the offering of a daily prayer by a chaplain in Congress. Engel v. Vitale, 370 U.S. 421, 439–42 (1962). Such speculations, well beyond the issue before the Court, helped fuel public confusion and outrage. When opinions contain sharp crossfire between Justices, "news reporters and the public at large are likely to lose sight of the law in what appears (to the uninitiated at least) to be a battle of men and not of law." Newland, 17 West. Pol. Q. 15, 24–25 (1964). The prayer case was also grossly misrepresented by the president of the American Bar Association, who weighed in with the warning that the decision would require elimination of the motto "In God We Trust" from all coins. Id. at 28. The public impression never recovered from these irresponsible announcements.

The judiciary's ability to communicate accurately to the public requires a writing style that is precise and economical. Judges advise opinion writers to use familiar words and short sentences. They prefer simplicity, clarity, brevity, and a direct and vigorous style. Justice Jackson gloried in the "short Saxon word that pierces the mind like a spear and the simple figure that lights the understanding." 37 A.B.A.J. 801, 863–64 (1951). Nevertheless, judges have personal idiosyncrasies that produce affectation, ornate prose, and verbosity. Ambiguity is also likely when several strong-minded individuals must agree on a single statement.

In deciding a particular case, judges often stray from the central issue and add extraneous matter in the form of obiter dicta. Because these remarks are not necessary to the basic decision, they are not binding as legal precedent. Nevertheless, they can serve as the functional equivalent of an advisory opinion, supplying guidance to the future direction of legal thinking. In striking down a statute, a court might suggest to legislators how the law could be rewritten. Albertsworth, 23 Geo. L. J. 643, 650–63 (1935). As Griffin Bell noted during his service as a federal appellate judge, "the role of courts under our system of separation of powers and federalism may call such a practice into play in some situations." 15 J. Pub. L. 214, 217 (1966).

Coherence and "principled decision making" are difficult virtues to achieve for a multimembered Court that operates necessarily as a committee, attempting to stitch together a decision that can attract a majority. Compromises are needed. The difficulty is compounded by the practice of moving a step at a time, responding to the concrete case at hand. As noted by one scholar, the Court "is in the unenviable posture of a committee attempting to draft a horse by placing very short lines on a very large drawing-board at irregular intervals during which the membership of the committee constantly changes." Amsterdam, 58 Minn. L. Rev. 349, 350 (1974).

Finality of Decisions

Decisions by federal courts may embody broad policies of commerce, slavery and other issues that provoke other branches to restrict and reverse judicial judgements. However, the general rule is that the outcome of an individual case—for that litigant—is accepted by Congress and the President. For example, Abraham Lincoln challenged the political judgments in *Dred Scott* v. *Sandford* but did not propose to "disturb or resist the decision" regarding Dred Scott or Dred Scott's master (page 30). The larger issue—slavery, abortion, and so forth—is not so easily settled.

A decision in 1995 revisits the issue of the finality of judicial decisions. A case was pending in pretrial proceedings in federal district court when the Supreme Court, in 1991, held that litigation under a particular provision of the Securities Exchange Act must be commenced within one year after the discovery of facts constituting the violation and within three years after such violation. In effect, this was a judicial statute of limitations (setting a time period for prosecution). Following the Court's decision, the trial judge dismissed the case. Later in 1991, Congress revised the Securities Exchange Act to provide that any civil action pending at the time of the Court's decision would not be covered by the three-year limitation. In 1995, the Court held that this statute violated separation of powers by retroactively commanding federal courts to reopen final judgments. Plaut v. Spendthrift Farm, Inc., 514 U.S. 211 (1995). However, in 2000 the Court upheld a congressional statute that suspended certain federal court orders calling for remedies to prison conditions. Miller v. French, 120 S.Ct. 2246 (2000).

Frank M. Coffin
The Process of Writing a Decision

Every important appellate court decision is made by a group of equals. This fact reflects the shrewd judgment of the architects of our state and federal judicial systems that an appellate judge is no wiser than a trial judge. His only claim to superior judgment lies in numbers; three, five, seven, or nine heads are usually better than one.

This element of collegiality is not unique. As the very word implies, the governance of colleges and universities relies heavily on faculties. Boards of directors, committees, commissions, and legislative bodies act collegially. But there are differences. An appellate court is a small "college." The members may differ in seniority, but each holds rank equal to the others....

There is intimacy, continuity, and dynamism in the relations among judges, at least on the smaller courts. They do not come together just to vote. They interact with each other, influence each other, and have each other in mind almost from the time they first read briefs for the next session of court. In a sense, the relationship among judges who differ in their values and views is a bargaining one, yet it is a continuing negotiation, where each player lays his cards on the table just as soon as he discovers what cards he has. There is, on a serene court, no suggestion that anyone seeks to manipulate anyone else.

In short, there is a difference between arriving at a yes or no decision through majority vote and working up an opinion on a close case so that three or more judges of different sensitivities, values, and backgrounds can join not only in the result, but in the rationale, tone, nuances, and reservations. Although the task of building toward a unanimous opinion, or even of carpentering a majority, demands a certain amount of sacrifice of

Source: From Frank M. Coffin, The Ways of a Judge: Reflections from the Federal Appellate Bench (Boston: Houghton Mifflin, 1980), pp. 57–63. When this book was published, Coffin was Chief Judge of the First Circuit.

ego and substantive concession, collegiality has its solid satisfactions. One quickly realizes that he is not the only source of useful insights. He learns to rejoice when he sees an opinion he has written measurably strengthened by the suggestion of one of his colleagues. Then, too, decisions are sometimes unpleasant, hard, risky, controversial, when the public and the press are hot and quick in their criticism. On such occasions, the comfort of collegiality is a pearl of no little worth.

THE INTENSITY OF INDIVIDUAL INVOLVEMENT

One of the paradoxes about appellate courts is that there can coexist the kind of intimate collegiality I have sketched and a profound, almost antique individualism. Indeed, perhaps the collegiality is the more enduring because it feeds on, cherishes, and respects the individualism nourished by appellate courts. In any case I make so bold as to say that in this supertechnical, industrialized, computerized, organized age, appellate courts are among the last redoubts of individual work.

While reliance on machines and staff proliferates apace in corporations, legislatures, and executive bureaucracies, the appellate judge still lives and works in his chamber with his law clerks. Although, unlike his predecessor, he can no longer write the first draft of every opinion, he is, as we shall see, in the very heart of creation of every opinion at every stage.

The kind of individualism I refer to is not the individualism of style, flair, or color, though these, happily, are not absent. Rather, every work product of an appellate court, a judicial opinion, bears the individual trademarks of, and is freighted with, the personal scrutiny and reflection of each member to a greater extent than that of any other collegial body. An appellate court's work is the least delegable of that of any major public institution. . . .

Perhaps there are appellate judges who, on hearing the essential facts of such a case, can confidently announce a sound decision without pause. I have seen professors in the classroom so respond; also panelists, lecturers, and cocktail-party pundits. But I am thankful that nothing said under such circumstances affects the rights of parties.

Judges do have their share of excellent talkers. The best of them are called brilliant. Brilliance, however, seems to me more associated with the pyrotechnics of speech and writing; as the word suggests, it has to do with how thoughts can be made to shine and sparkle. Sound decision, on the other hand, is more than result; it is an edifice made up of rationale, tone, and direction. It is faithful to the past, settles the present, and foreshadows the future. Such a decision is rarely made quickly.

I see decision-making as neither a process that results in an early conviction based on instant exposure to competing briefs nor one in which the judge keeps an open mind through briefs, discussion in chambers, argument, and conference, and then summons up the will to decide. I see the process, rather, as a series of shifting biases. It is much like tracing the source of a river, following various minor tributaries, which are found to rise in swamps, returning to the channel, which narrows as one goes upstream.

One reads a good brief from the appellant; the position seems reasonable. But a good brief from appellee, bolstered perhaps by a trial judge's opinion, seems incontrovertible. Discussion with the law clerks in chambers casts doubt on any tentative position. Any such doubt may be demolished by oral argument, only to give rise to a new bias, which in turn may be shaken by the postargument conference among the judges. As research and writing reveal new problems, the tentative disposition of the panel of judges may appear wrong. The opinion is written and circulated, producing reactions from the other judges, which again change the thrust, the rationale, or even the result. Only when the process has ended can one say that the decision has been made, after as many as seven turns in the road. The guarantee of a judge's impartiality lies not in suspending judgment throughout the process but in recognizing that each successive judgment is tentative, fragile, and likely to be modified or set aside as a consequence of deepened insight. The nonlawyer looks on the judge as a model of decisiveness. The truth is more likely that the appellate judge in a difficult case is committed to the unpleasant state of prolonged indecisiveness.

D. UNANIMITY AND DISSENT

The Supreme Court initially followed the British practice of allowing each Justice to write opinions seriatim (in a series). Rather than announce a single opinion representing the collective position of the majority, the Justices delivered separate statements. Before John Marshall's appointment as Chief Justice, the Court had begun to deliver an opinion for the entire Court rather than a string of seriatim opinions. Marshall reinforced that direction, believing that a single decision strengthened the Court's power and dignity. He selected one Justice (often himself) to write the majority opinion. Dissents were rare. Jefferson delivered a stinging rebuke to the Chief Justice for departing from seriatim decisions: "An opinion is huddled up in conclave, perhaps by a majority of one, delivered as if unanimous, and with the silent acquiescence of lazy or timid associates, by a crafty chief judge, who sophisticates the law to his own mind, by the turn of his own reasoning." 15 Writings of Thomas Jefferson 298 (Memorial ed. 1904).

Jefferson's critique was written in 1820, about two decades after Marshall had joined the Court, and appeared to be triggered by Marshall's broad nationalist ruling in *McCulloch* v. *Maryland* (1819). Seriatim opinions had offered a definite benefit: each Justice was accountable for articulating the rationale behind a decision. However, Marshall wanted the Court to develop an institutional view, moving away from personal positions to a more generalized principle for the majority.

The harmony within the early Marshall Court depended partly on residential arrangements. The Justices lived together in the same boarding house on Capitol Hill, taking their meals at a common table. Justice Story described the members of the Marshall Court as "united as one.... We moot every question as we proceed, and ... conferences at our lodgings often come to a very quick, and, I trust, a very accurate opinion, in a few hours." James Sterling Young, The Washington Community 77 (1966).

This cohesiveness did not survive. Dissents became more frequent in later years of the Marshall Court and under future Chief Justices. At various times throughout history, however, members of the Court have placed a premium on unanimity. In 1922 Justice McReynolds wrote a majority opinion that provoked dissents from Brandeis, Clarke, and Pitney. Chief Justice Taft scheduled a reargument, and by the time he wrote the new majority opinion, Clarke and Pitney had retired. Taft sought Brandeis's views and eventually produced a unanimous opinion, with which McReynolds concurred.[5]

Concurrences and Per Curiam

At the urging of colleagues who fear that dissents will damage the corporate reputation of the Supreme Court, Justices have been willing to convert a dissent into a concurring opinion. Labeling it a concurrence, however, is often an inadequate mask to cover the dissenting view.[6] It is not unusual for Justices to concur in the judgment or result while shredding the logic, reasoning, and precedents contained in the opinion of the Court.[7] Justices also withhold dissents when the case is less significant to them. Such accommodations create a reservoir of good will, promote institutional harmony, and allow the acquiescent Justice to call upon a colleague at some future time for reciprocal favors—perhaps a fourth vote to grant certiorari. Walter F. Murphy, Elements of Judicial Strategy 52–53 (1964).

During preparation for *Brown* v. *Board of Education,* members of the Court felt strongly that unanimity was crucial in building public acceptance for desegregation. Discreet pressure was ap-

---

5. Alpheus Thomas Mason, "William Howard Taft," in Leon Friedman and Fred L. Israel, eds., 3 The Justices of the United States Supreme Court 2114 (1969), and Alexander M. Bickel, The Unpublished Opinions of Mr. Justice Brandeis, at 111–13. The case was Sonneborn Bros. v. Cureton, 262 U.S. 506 (1923).

6. Justice Murphy, under the urgings of colleagues, changed his dissent in *Hirabayashi* v. *United States* to a concurrence. See Murphy, supra note 1, at 46–47, and Howard, supra note 1, at 302–09.

7. Murphy v. Waterfront Comm'n, 378 U.S. 52, 80–92 (Harlan, J., concurring) (1964); Warden v. Hayden, 387 U.S. 294, 310–12 (Fortas, J., and Warren, C. J., concurring) (1967); Argersinger v. Hamlin, 407 U.S. 25, 41–44 (Burger, C. J., concurring) and 44–46 (Powell, J., concurring, joined by Rehnquist, J.) (1972).

plied to Justices to ward off concurring and dissenting opinions. Chief Justice Warren realized that once a Justice had announced his position, it would be more difficult for him to change his thinking, "so we decided that we could dispense with our usual custom of formally expressing our individual views at the first conference and would confine ourselves for a time to informal discussion of the briefs, the arguments made at the hearing, and our own independent research for each conference day, reserving our final opinions until the discussions were concluded." Warren, 239 Atlantic Monthly 35–36 (April 1977). By following this process, the Court agreed unanimously that the "separate but equal" doctrine had no place in public education.

In earlier rulings, the Court relied on per curiam opinions (unsigned opinions "for the court") to reduce friction. This technique permitted the Justices to present a united front and avoid details or legal interpretations that might have fractured the Court and communicated more information to the public than the Court thought prudent. In one of the early racial discrimination cases before *Brown*, Justice Frankfurter explained in a letter to Chief Justice Vinson that the per curiam "should set forth as briefly and as unargumentatively as possible" the Court's position. "In short," Frankfurter wrote, "our *per cur.* should avoid every possibility of serving as a target for contention...." Hutchinson, 68 Geo. L. J. 1, 9 (1979).

Unanimity to Make a Point

When Governor Orval Faubus and the Arkansas legislature fought to retain the state's system of segregated schools, the Supreme Court reaffirmed the principle it had enunciated in 1954. To underscore its unanimity, the names of all nine Justices were listed, including the three who had joined the Court since 1954. Frankfurter frustrated this strategy by insisting on a separate concurrence, agreeing to file it a week after the Court released its opinion. Cooper v. Aaron, 358 U.S. 1 (1958). Warren, Black, and Brennan were furious. Frankfurter's only justification for the extra statement was that he had a special responsibility to lecture Southern lawyers and law professors who had been his students at Harvard Law School. Bernard Schwartz, Super Chief 302–03 (1983).

In 1974, with President Nixon threatening to defy any judicial effort to make him surrender the Watergate tapes, the Supreme Court once again produced a unanimous ruling. United States v. Nixon, 418 U.S. 683 (1974). By forging a united front and rejecting Nixon's broad claim of executive privilege, the Court played a crucial role in bringing about his resignation. However, the very process of generating a unanimous opinion invited generalization at so high a plane that the result obfuscated the law of executive privilege.[8] This is an ever-present risk. Attracting a few additional votes may dilute legal principles to such an extent that some Justices in the original majority may decide to write concurring or even dissenting opinions.

Unanimity in these cases helped prepare the public for important rulings. In other situations, however, a multiplicity of opinions may be enlightening. In *Youngstown Co. v. Sawyer* (1952), every member of the six-man majority wrote a separate opinion discussing the limits of presidential power, which in this case concerned the seizure of steel mills. The country was therefore privy to nuances and complexities that would have been obscured by a broad ruling satisfactory to the majority. Multiplicity gave room for sophisticated explorations of the source and scope of executive powers. Concurring opinions may anticipate future developments in the direction of law.

---

8. Louis Henkin, "Executive Privilege: Mr. Nixon Loses but the Presidency Largely Prevails," 22 UCLA L. Rev. 40 (1974); William Van Alstyne, "A Political and Constitutional Review of *United States v. Nixon*," 22 UCLA L. Rev. 116 (1974).

Plurality Opinions

With the growth in the number of cases that determine constitutional issues, separate concurring and dissenting opinions have increased dramatically. Justice Rehnquist suggested that it "may well be that the nature of constitutional adjudication invites, at least, if it does not require, more separate opinions than does adjudication of issues of law in other areas." Rehnquist, 59 A.B.A.J. 361, 363 (1973). Of special concern is the Court's inability to prepare a decision that attracts a majority of the Justices. Instead, the Court delivers a plurality opinion that creates confusion in the lower courts and other branches of government. The number of plurality opinions by the Burger Court exceeded the number of all previous Courts. Note, 94 Harv. L. Rev. 1127 (1981); Davis & Reynolds, 1974 Duke L. J. 59.

In 1977, the Supreme Court announced a rule for determining the meaning of a plurality holding. Borrowing language from *Gregg v. Georgia* (1976), the Court stated: "When a fragmented Court decides a case and no single rationale explaining the result enjoys the assent of five Justices, 'the holding of the Court may be viewed as that position taken by those Members who concurred in the judgments on the narrowest grounds....' " Marks v. United States, 430 U.S. 188, 193 (1977). A scholar, after studying the application of the *Marks* rule, concluded that it was "insupportable and should be rejected." Mark Allen Thurmon, "When the Supreme Court Divides: Reconsidering the Precedential Value of Supreme Court Plurality Decisions," 42 Duke L. J. 419 (1992).

Dissents

Shortly before returning to the Supreme Court, this time as Chief Justice, Charles Evans Hughes wrote eloquently on the deliberative process of the judiciary. He recognized that a dissenting opinion can damage the appearance of justice that the public needs in a court of last resort. However, he felt it far more injurious to obtain unanimity by concealing genuine differences and personal convictions (see box). Following this tradition, Justice Douglas said that "[c]ertainty and unanimity in the law are possible both under the fascist and communist systems. They are not only possible; they are indispensable...." (see Douglas reading).

Dissents may force the majority to clarify and tighten its opinion. They can also serve as a precursor for a future majority holding. Justice Harlan's dissents in the *Civil Rights Cases* (1883), in *Plessy v. Ferguson* (1895), and in other race cases offered a broad interpretation of the Fourteenth Amendment in protecting the rights of blacks. This doctrine gained strength in some of the lower courts more than a half century later and foreshadowed the eventual overruling of *Plessy*. The dissents of Justice Holmes, especially in economic regulation cases, later carried the day for the Court. Justice Stone was a lone dissenter in the first flag-salute case in 1940, involving the religious freedoms of Jehovah's Witnesses. Two years later, three Justices from the majority (Black, Douglas, and Murphy) publicly announced that the decision "was wrongly decided." The following year, the Court reversed its 1940 ruling, vindicating Stone's position.[9] In 1942 the Court split 6 to 3, deciding that indigent defendants did not have a right to counsel in state court for all felonies. By 1963 the position of the three dissenters had been elevated to the majority position. Betts v. Brady, 316 U.S. 455, 474 (1942); Gideon v. Wainwright, 372 U.S. 335 (1963).

For a judicial body, dissent carries substantial costs. Justice Edward D. White, himself dissenting in an 1895 opinion, said that the "only purpose which an elaborate dissent can ac-

---

9. Minersville School District v. Gobitis, 310 U.S. 586 (1940); Jones v. Opelika, 316 U.S. 584, 624 (1942); West Virginia Board of Education v. Barnette, 319 U.S. 624 (1943).

Charles Evans Hughes on Dissent

There are some who think it desirable that dissents should not be disclosed as they detract from the force of the judgment. Undoubtedly, they do. When unanimity can be obtained without sacrifice of conviction, it strongly commends the decision to public confidence. But unanimity which is merely formal, which is recorded at the expense of strong, conflicting views, is not desirable in a court of last resort, whatever may be the effect upon public opinion at the time. This is so because what must ultimately sustain the court in public confidence is the character and independence of the judges. They are not there simply to decide cases, but to decide them as they think they should be decided, and while it may be regrettable that they cannot always agree, it is better that their independence should be maintained and recognized than that unanimity should be secured through its sacrifice. This does not mean that a judge should be swift to dissent, or that he should dissent for the sake of self-exploitation or because of a lack of that capacity for cooperation which is of the essence of any group action, whether judicial or otherwise. Independence does not mean cantankerousness and a judge may be a strong judge without being an impossible person. Nothing is more distressing on any bench than the exhibition of a captious, impatient, querulous spirit. We are fortunately free from this in our highest courts in Nation and State, much freer than in some of the days gone by. Dissenting opinions enable a judge to express his individuality. He is not under the compulsion of speaking for the court and thus of securing the concurrence of a majority. In dissenting, he is a free lance. A dissent in a court of last resort is an appeal to the brooding spirit of the law, to the intelligence of a future day, when a later decision may possibly correct the error into which the dissenting judge believes the court to have been betrayed.

SOURCE: Charles Evans Hughes, The Supreme Court of the United States 67–68 (1928).

---

complish, if any, is to weaken the effect of the opinion of the majority, and thus engender want of confidence in the conclusions of courts of last resort." Pollock v. Farmers' Loan & Trust Co., 157 U.S. 429, 608 (1895). Dissents detract from institutional unity and may exacerbate tensions within a court, which is by nature a collegial body. Those tensions are heightened by sarcastic dissents that question the integrity or intellectual ability of a fellow judge. Dissents can be especially irresponsible when they confuse or distort the holding of the Court (see Jackson reading).

Some members of the judiciary feel a special obligation to express their dissent when constitutional questions are at stake. Said Justice Moody in a 1908 dissent:

> Under ordinary circumstances, where the judgment rests exclusively, as it does here, upon a mere interpretation of the words of a law, which may be readily changed by the lawmaking branches of the Government, if they be so minded, a difference of opinion may well be left without expression. But where the judgment is a judicial condemnation of an act of a coordinate branch of our Government it is so grave a step that no member of the court can escape his own responsibility, or be justified in suppressing his own views, if unhappily they have not found expression in those of his associates. The Employers' Liability Cases, 207 U.S. 463, 504–05 (1908).

The choice between writing a dissent and joining the majority remains an individual matter. Although Justice Harlan dissented in *Miranda* v. *Arizona* (1966), the principle of stare decisis and the goal of institutional continuity and cohesiveness prompted him to acquiesce in future applications of *Miranda*. Orozco v. Texas, 394 U.S. 324, 328 (1969). Other Justices persist with their dissents.

William O. Douglas
The Dissent: A Safeguard of Democracy

All of us in recent years have heard and read many criticisms of the dissenting or concurring opinion. Separate opinions have often been deplored. Courts have been severely criticized for tolerating them. And that is why I rise to their defense.

About ten years ago when I took my seat on the bench, Chief Justice Hughes said this to me: "I think you will find after you have been on the bench for a while that in a great majority of the cases, perhaps in two-thirds of them, the judges will ultimately reach agreement and announce opinions that are unanimous. But in at least a third of the cases, agreement will not be possible. In those cases there will be dissents — no matter how carefully the judges were chosen — whether one President or several Presidents selected them."

Chief Justice Hughes spoke from a long experience both at the bar and in the conference room. In these days of uneasiness and confusion what he said to me is important not only to judges and lawyers but to everyone. It is indeed only when the meaning of his words is clear that the true nature of the judicial process is brought home to the community.

SEARCH FOR CERTAINTY

Holmes, perhaps better than anyone either before or after him, pointed out how illusory was the lawyer's search for certainty. Law is not what has been or is — law in the lawyer's sense is the prediction of things to come, the prediction of what decree will be written by designated judges on specified facts. In layman's language law is the prediction of what will happen to you if you do certain things. This was the lesson Holmes taught; and every lawyer on reflection knows that it is sound.

There are many reasons why this is so. No matter how clear and precise the code or other legal rule may be, the proof may be surrounded with doubt. And even though the proof is clear to the advocate, the credibility of the witnesses may raise serious questions for judge or jury. Uncertainty is increased when new and difficult problems under ambiguous statutes arise. And when

constitutional questions emerge, the case is, as we lawyers say, "at large." For the federal constitution, like most state constitutions, is not a code but a rule of action — a statement of philosophy and point of view, a summation of general principles, a delineation of the broad outlines of a regime which the Fathers designed for us.

These are the things that Holmes summed up when he described the lawyer's continuing and uncertain search for certainty. They indeed suggest why philosophers of the democratic faith will rejoice in the uncertainty of the law and find strength and glory in it.

Certainty and unanimity in the law are possible both under the fascist and communist systems. They are not only possible; they are indispensable; for complete subservience to the political regime is a *sine qua non* to judicial survival under either system. One cannot imagine the courts of Hitler engaged in a public debate over the principles of Der Fuehrer, with a minority of one or four deploring or denouncing the principles themselves. One cannot imagine a judge of a Communist court dissenting against the decrees of the Kremlin.

Disagreement among judges is as true to the character of democracy as freedom of speech itself. The dissenting opinion is as genuinely American as Otis' denunciation of the general warrants, as Thomas Paine's, Thomas Jefferson's, or James Madison's briefs for civil liberties....

LEGISLATIVE PROCESS ONE OF COMPROMISE

Those who have followed the legislative process can produce examples on end. That process is one of compromise — of qualifying absolutes, of creating exceptions to general rules. At times the process of compromise or conciliation involves well-nigh impossible adjustments. The clash of ideas may be so violent that a meeting of the minds seems out of the question. Where such cleavage is great and involves major issues, it may even tear a society apart. By the same token it can stop the legislative process or render it impotent, and thus deprive society of lawful and nonviolent means and methods of solving its problems. When the breach between the *pros* and *cons* is not too great, the legislative process functions. Even then, the compromise between competing ideas that emerges in the final legislation may be more ap-

SOURCE: Journal of the American Judicature Society, Vol. 32, pp. 104–07 (December 1948). Justice Douglas served on the Supreme Court from 1939 to 1975.

parent than real. For the legislative solution is often to write two opposing ideas into a statute. Without that solution enactment of the measure might, indeed, be impossible.

INTERPRETATION HAS LEGISLATIVE CHARACTERISTICS

And so the bill becomes the law and the law arrives before judges for interpretation. The battle that raged before the legislature is now transferred to the court. The passage of the legislation quieted the conflict only temporarily. It breaks out anew in the process of interpretation in the courts. A storm hits the court room, and the advocates take up the fight where the legislators left off. The same cleavage that appeared in legislative halls now shows up among the judges. Each side has eminent authority for its view since two conflicting ideas found their way into the legislation. It is therefore easy for judge or lawyer or editor to accuse the judge, who takes the opposing view, of usurping the role of the legislature. A more honest, a more objective view would concede that interpretation has legislative as well as judicial characteristics. It cannot be

otherwise where the legislature has left the choice of competing theories or ideas to the judges.

. . .

STARE DECISIS HAS SMALL PLACE IN CONSTITUTIONAL LAW

When we move to constitutional questions, uncertainty necessarily increases. A judge who is asked to construe or interpret the Constitution often rejects the gloss which his predecessors have put on it. For the gloss may, in his view, offend the spirit of the Constitution or do violence to it. That has been the experience of this generation and of all those that have preceded. It will likewise be the experience of those which follow. And so it should be. For it is the Constitution which we have sworn to defend, not some predecessor's interpretation of it. *Stare decisis* has small place in constitutional law. The Constitution was written for all time and all ages. It would lose its great character and become feeble, if it were allowed to become encrusted with narrow, legalistic notions that dominated the thinking of one generation.

Robert H. Jackson
The Limitation of Dissent

In argued cases, conferences are followed by the preparation and circulation of opinions by Justices designated by the Chief Justice when he is with the prevailing view and, if not, by the senior Associate who is. But any Justice is free to write as he will, and there may be one or more opinions concurring in the result but reaching it by different reasons, and there may be a dissenting opinion or opinions. This occasions complaint by laymen and the bar that they are required to piece all these contributions together in order to make out where the Supreme Court really stands as an institution.

All of this is at odds with the practice of most courts of continental Europe, which make it a rule to announce the decision in one statement only and to issue no dissents or concurrences. Moreover, their work is institutionalized and deper-

sonalized. The court's opinion bears the name of no author. Like our *per curiam* opinion, it may be the work of any member or of several in collaboration. This anonymity diminishes any temptation to exploit differences within the court, but it may also diminish the incentive for hard work on opinions. In any event, I am sure that not only Anglo-American tradition but judicial and professional opinion favors the identification of writers and the full disclosure of important differences within the Court. Mr. Jefferson would have required each Justice to write his reasons in every case, as proof that he gave it consideration and did not merely follow a leader.

The dissenting opinion strives to undermine the Court's reasoning and discredit its result. At its best, the dissent, as Mr. Hughes said, is "an appeal to the brooding spirit of the law, to the intelligence of a future day. . . ." But Judge Cardozo has written:

"... Comparatively speaking at least, the dissenter is irresponsible. The spokesman of the

SOURCE: From Justice Jackson's book, The Supreme Court in the American System of Government 16–19 (1955). Footnotes omitted.

court is cautious, timid, fearful of the vivid word, the heightened phrase. He dreams of an unworthy brood of scions, the spawn of careless *dicta,* disowned by the *ratio decidendi,* to which all legitimate offspring must be able to trace their lineage. The result is to cramp and paralyze. One fears to say anything when the peril of misunderstanding puts a warning finger to the lips. Not so, however, the dissenter. . . . For the moment, he is the gladiator making a last stand against the lions. The poor man must be forgiven a freedom of expression, tinged at rare moments with a touch of bitterness, which magnanimity as well as caution would reject for one triumphant."

Dissent has a popular appeal, for it is an underdog judge pleading for an underdog litigant. Of course, one party or the other must always be underdog in a lawsuit, the purpose of which really is to determine which one it shall be. But the tradition of great dissents built around such names as Holmes, Brandeis, Cardozo, and Stone is not due to the frequency or multiplicity of their dissents, but to their quality and the importance of the few cases in which they carried their disagreement beyond the conference table. Also, quite contrary to the popular notion, relatively few of all the dissents recorded in the Supreme Court have later become law, although some of these are of great importance.

There has been much undiscriminating eulogy of dissenting opinions. It is said they clarify the issues. Often they do the exact opposite. The technique of the dissenter often is to exaggerate the holding of the Court beyond the meaning of the majority and then to blast away at the excess. So the poor lawyer with a similar case does not know whether the majority opinion meant what it seemed to say or what the minority said it meant. Then, too, dissenters frequently force the majority to take positions more extreme than was originally intended. The classic example is the *Dred Scott Case,* in which Chief Justice Taney's extreme statements were absent in his original draft and were inserted only after Mr. Justice McLean, then a more than passive candidate for the presidency, raised the issue in dissent.

The *right of dissent* is a valuable one. Wisely used on well-chosen occasions, it has been of great service to the profession and to the law. But there is nothing good, for either the Court or the dissenter, in dissenting per se. Each dissenting opinion is a confession of failure to convince the writer's colleagues, and the true test of a judge is his influence in leading, not in opposing, his court.

E. CASELOAD BURDENS

The number of cases submitted to the Supreme Court increased dramatically in the twentieth century. In this era of "rights consciousness," a larger number of individuals and organizations go to court either to secure rights or to enforce rights already established by statute. The creation of additional district and appellate judgeships allows more plaintiffs and attorneys to enter the courts. Further aggravating the workload are dozens of statutes passed by Congress creating new causes of action, providing expedited methods of appeal, imposing duties on the judiciary, and awarding fees for attorneys.

In 1971 Chief Justice Burger appointed a group to study the growing caseload of the Supreme Court. Called the Freund Committee, the group recommended that Congress establish a seven-member National Court of Appeals to screen petitions filed with the Supreme Court and to certify 400 or so cases considered the most worthy. The Supreme Court would select from that list, but no appeal would be permitted from the cases rejected by the National Court of Appeals. The Committee's recommendation paralleled those announced earlier by Burger. U.S. News & World Report, December 14, 1970, at 43. The previous Chief Justice, Earl Warren, criticized the Committee's screening idea as a naive proposal from people who were unfamiliar with the Court's decisional process. He also objected to giving the National Court limited power to resolve conflicting decisions among the circuits. Warren, 28 Record Ass'n Bar of the City of N.Y. 627, 637, 642 (1973).

A second study, prepared by the Hruska Commission, was released in 1975. It, too, proposed a National Court of Appeals, but not to screen cases for the Supreme Court. A new court would be established to handle cases referred to it by the Supreme Court or appellate

TABLE 5.1 CASES DECIDED BY THE SUPREME COURT 1984–2000

	Disposed of by Signed Opinion	Disposed of by Per Curiam Opinion
1984–1985	159	11
1985–1986	161	10
1986–1987	164	10
1987–1988	151	9
1988–1989	156	12
1989–1990	143	3
1990–1991	121	4
1991–1992	120	3
1992–1993	111	4
1993–1994	93	6
1994–1995	91	3
1995–1996	87	3
1996–1997	87	3
1997–1998	93	1
1998–1999	84	4
1999–2000	81	2

courts. In 1983 Chief Justice Burger offered his own version of a National Court of Appeals. He suggested a temporary court, drawn from appellate judges in each circuit, to resolve conflicts between appellate courts. A major restructuring of the judicial system, he warned, was necessary to "avoid a breakdown of the system — or of some of the justices." Washington Post, February 7, 1983, at A-1.

The Court's docket is largely discretionary in character so to that extent its workload is self-imposed and self-inflicted. Moreover, the workload increases when the Court reaches out to decide matters that might have been left to state courts or to the process of slow percolation in the federal courts. In 1985 Justice Stevens (joined by Justices Brennan and Marshall) noted in dissent:

> Much of the Court's "burdensome" workload is a product of its own aggressiveness in this area [*of Fourth Amendment cases*]. By promoting the Supreme Court of the United States as the High Magistrate for every warrantless search and seizure, this practice has burdened the argument docket with cases presenting fact bound errors of minimal significance. It has also encouraged state legal officers to file petitions for certiorari in even the most frivolous search and seizure cases. California v. Carney, 471 U.S. 386, 396 (1985).

Justice Stevens made a similar point in two cases decided in 1990. Florida v. Wells, 495 U.S. 1, 12–13 (1990); Minnesota v. Olson, 495 U.S. 91, 101–02 (1990).

Justice Brennan was a persistent critic of proposals to allow a special court to screen cases for the Supreme Court. He called the screening function "second to none in importance." Brennan, 40 U. Chi. L. Rev. 473, 477 (1973). From his perspective, the dissenting opinions in denying cert represent an important foundation for the development of legal doctrine and the formation of future majority positions. He would not delegate to a separate court the responsibility for screening cases, a process he called "inherently subjective" in nature and one that helps educate Justices on contemporary issues. Id. at 480–81.

The workload problem could be relieved partly by withdrawing some nonjudicial duties from the Court. At present, the Chief Justice is a member of the Board of Regents of the Smithsonian Institution. He is also a trustee of the National Gallery of Art and of the Joseph H. Hirshhorn Museum and Sculpture Garden. He is responsible for appointing someone from the judicial branch to the National Historical Publications and Records Commission. Carrying out these extraneous duties seems to belie the claim that the Court is pressed to the limit with its caseload. In recent years, the Court decides fewer cases than in the past (see Table 5.1) and does not use the full amount of time available for oral argument.

SELECTED READINGS

BARTH, ALAN. Prophets with Honor: Great Dissents and Great Dissenters in the Supreme Court. New York: Knopf, 1974.

CASPER, GERHARD, AND RICHARD A. POSNER. The Workload of the Supreme Court. Chicago: American Bar Foundation, 1976.

ESTREICHER, SAMUEL, AND JOHN SEXTON. Redefining the Supreme Court's Role. New Haven: Yale University Press, 1986.

FRANK, JOHN P. Marble Palace: The Supreme Court in American Life. New York: Knopf, 1958.

HART, HENRY M., JR. "Foreword: The Time Chart of the Justices." 73 Harvard Law Review 84 (1959).

HARTNETT, EDWARD A. "Questioning Certiorari: Some Reflecitos Seventy-Five Years After the Judges' Bill." 100 Columbia Law Review 1643 (2000).

HELLMAN, ARTHUR D. "Caseload, Conflicts, and Decisional Capacity: Does the Supreme Court Need Help?" 67 Judicature 29 (1983).

HOWARD, J. WOODFORD, JR. Mr. Justice Murphy. Princeton, N.J.: Princeton University Press, 1968.

LAZARUS, EDWARD. Closed Chambers. New York: Times Books (1998).

MASON, ALPHEUS THOMAS. Harlan Fiske Stone: Pillar of the Law. New York: Viking, 1956.

MILLER, ARTHUR SELWYN, AND D. S. SASTRI. "Secrecy and the Supreme Court—On the Need for Piercing the Red Velour Curtain." 22 Buffalo Law Review 799 (1973). See also accompanying comments by Eugene Gressman; Joel B. Grossman; J. Woodford Howard, Jr.; Walter Probert; Glendon Schubert; and Roland Young.

MURPHY, WALTER F. Elements of Judicial Strategy. Chicago: University of Chicago Press, 1964.

NEWLAND, CHESTER A. "Personal Assistants to Supreme Court Justices: The Law Clerks." 40 Oregon Law Review 299 (1961).

O'BRIEN, DAVID M. Storm Center: The Supreme Court in American Politics. New York: Norton, 1986.

———, ed. Judges on Judging: Views from the Bench. Chatham, N.J.: Chatham House Publishers, 1997.

PELTASON, JACK W. Federal Courts in the Political Process. New York: Random House, 1955.

PERRY, H. W., JR. Deciding to Decide: Agenda Setting in the United States Supreme Court. Cambridge: Harvard University Press, 1991.

PROVINE, DORIS MARIE. Case Selection in the United States Supreme Court. Chicago: University of Chicago Press, 1980.

RICHARDSON, RICHARD J., AND KENNETH N. VINES. The Politics of Federal Courts: Lower Courts in the United States. Boston: Little, Brown, 1970.

ROHDE, DAVID W., AND HAROLD J. SPAETH. Supreme Court Decision Making. San Francisco: W. H. Freeman, 1976.

SCHWARTZ, BERNARD. Decision: How the Supreme Court Decides Cases. New York: Oxford University Press, 1996.

SPAETH, HAROLD J. Supreme Court Policy Making. San Francisco: W. H. Freeman, 1979.

STERN, ROBERT L., EUGENE GRESSMAN, AND STEPHEN M. SHAPIRO. Supreme Court Practice, 6th ed. Washington, D.C.: The Bureau of National Affairs, 1986.

SUNSTEIN, CASS. One Case at a Time: Judicial Minimalism on the Supreme Court. Cambridge, Mass.: Harvard University Press, 1999.

ULMER, S. SIDNEY. "Bricolage and Assorted Thoughts on Working in the Papers of the Supreme Court Justices." 35 Journal of Politics 286 (1973).

WESTIN, ALAN F., ed. The Supreme Court: Views from Inside. New York: Norton, 1961.

———. An Autobiography of the Supreme Court. New York: Macmillan, 1963.

WILKINSON, J. HARVIE, III. Serving Justice: A Supreme Court Clerk's View. New York: Charterhouse, 1974.

WOODWARD, BOB, AND SCOTT ARMSTRONG. The Brethren: Inside the Supreme Court. New York: Simon and Schuster, 1979.

6

Separation of Powers: Domestic Conflicts

The doctrine of separation of powers remains elusive. In both theory and practice it teems with subtleties, ironies, and apparent contradictions. Just what the framers intended remains a subject of continuing dispute, spawning a vast literature with varying interpretations. Even if we could agree on the "framers' intent," the relationships among the three branches of government have changed fundamentally in two centuries to produce novel arrangements and peculiar overlappings. Chapters 6 and 7 cover these general principles as well as specific clashes and controversies.

A. THE SEPARATION DOCTRINE

Critics of separated powers in America claim that this system produces intolerable deadlocks and inefficiency, especially for a twentieth-century government expected to exercise worldwide responsibilities. However, there is no necessary link between separated powers and inefficiency. The framers did not adopt a separation of powers to obstruct government. They wanted to create a system in 1787 that would operate more effectively and efficiently than the discredited Articles of Confederation, written in 1777 and ratified in 1781.

From One Branch to Three

Only one branch of national government existed before 1787: the Continental Congress. There was no executive or judiciary. Members of the Congress had to legislate and then serve on committees to administer and adjudicate what they had passed. Within a few years, the system proved to be so exhausting, inept, and embarrassing that it became necessary to delegate administrative and judicial duties to outside bodies. To relieve committees of administrative details, Congress turned to boards staffed by people outside the legislature. When these multiheaded boards failed to supply energy and accountability, Congress appointed single executive officers in 1781 to run the executive departments. These departments supplied a vital link in administrative structures between the Continental Congress and the national government established in 1787. Louis Fisher, President and Congress 1–27, 253–70 (1972).

The Continental Congress also established the beginnings of a national judiciary by setting up Courts of Admiralty to decide all controversies over naval captures and the distribution of war prizes. By 1780 Congress had created the Court of Appeals in Cases of Capture, which functioned until its last session on May 16, 1787, at the State House in Philadelphia across the hall from the room in which delegates were assembling for the Constitutional Convention.

Separation for Efficiency and Liberty

This separation of legislative, executive, and judicial functions reflects the framers' search for more efficient government. The separation was driven principally by events, not theory. In a striking phrase, the historian Francis Wharton said that the Constitution "did not make this distribution of power. It would be more proper to say that this distribution of power made the Constitution of the United States." 1 Francis Wharton, The Revolutionary Correspondence of the United States 663 (1889). Justice Brandeis spoke a half-truth when he claimed that the doctrine of separated powers was "adopted by the Convention of 1787, not to promote efficiency but to preclude the exercise of arbitrary power." Myers v. United States, 272 U.S. 52, 293 (1926). Efficiency was a key objective.

It is often said that powers are separated to preserve liberties. It is equally true that a rigid separation can *destroy* liberties. The historic swings in France between executive and legislative dominance suggest the danger of extreme separation. The French constitutions of 1791 and 1848, which established a pure separation of powers, ended in absolutism and reaction. M.J.C. Vile, Constitutionalism and the Separation of Powers 176–211 (1967). The framers wanted to avoid political fragmentation and paralysis of power. They knew that a rigid adherence to separated powers "in all cases would be subversive of the efficiency of the government, and result in the destruction of the public liberties." 1 Joseph Story, Commentaries on the Constitution of the United States 396 (1905 ed.). Justice Jackson described the complex elements that coexist in America's separation doctrine: "While the Constitution diffuses power the better to secure liberty, it also contemplates that practice will integrate the dispersed powers into a workable government. It enjoins upon its branches separateness but interdependence, autonomy but reciprocity." Youngstown Co. v. Sawyer, 343 U.S. 579, 635 (1952).

Implied Separation

Although the separation of powers doctrine is not expressly stated in the Constitution, it is implied in the allocation of legislative powers to the Congress in Article I, executive powers to the President in Article II, and judicial powers to the Supreme Court in Article III. Several provisions help reinforce the separation. Article I, Section 6, prohibits members of either House of Congress from holding any other civil office (the Incompatibility Clause). This provision has been difficult to litigate. In 1974 the Court denied standing to plaintiffs who challenged the right of members of Congress to hold a commission in the armed forces reserves. Schlesinger v. Reservists to Stop the War, 418 U.S. 208 (1974). The meaning of that clause is therefore left to the elected branches. Article I, Section 6, also prohibits members of Congress from being appointed to any federal office created during their term of office, or to any federal position whose salary has been increased during their term of office (the Ineligibility Clause). The framers were aware that members of the British Parliament had been corrupted by appointments to office from the Crown, but they were reluctant to exclude qualified and able people from public office. 1 Farrand 379–82, 386–90; 2 Farrand 283–84, 489–92.

To reconcile these conflicting goals, Congress has at times reduced the salary of an executive position to permit someone from the House or the Senate to be appointed to the post. For example, after Congress had increased the salary of the Secretary of State from $8,000 to $12,000, President Taft wanted to name Senator Philander Knox to that office in 1909. A special bill was drafted to reduce the compensation of the Secretary of State to the original figure. The bill inspired heated debate in the House of Representatives, 43 Cong. Rec. 2390–2404, 2408–15, but was enacted into law (35 Stat. 626). Knox was then nominated by President Taft and confirmed by the Senate. A similar situation arose in 1973 concerning the nomination of Senator William Saxbe as Attorney General after Congress had increased the salary of that office from $35,000 to $60,000. Legislation was enacted to keep Saxbe's compensation at $35,000. 87 Stat. 697 (1973). The debate offers a good example of the manner in which Congress engages in constitutional interpretation (see reading on Ineligibility Clause). Following these precedents, Congress passed legislation in 1980 (94 Stat. 343) and in 1993

(107 Stat. 4) to permit Senator Ed Muskie to become Secretary of State and Senator Lloyd Bentsen to become Secretary of the Treasury.

Other safeguards for the separation doctrine exist. Congress is prohibited from reducing the compensation of the President and members of the judiciary. United States v. Will, 449 U.S. 200 (1980). The Speech or Debate Clause, covered later in this chapter, provides legislative immunity to protect members of Congress from executive or judicial harassment.

Explicit Sharing

Several sections of the Constitution produce combinations, not separations, of the branches. The President may veto legislation, subject to a two-thirds override vote of each House. Some of the Anti-Federalists objected that the veto allowed the President to encroach upon the legislature. Alexander Hamilton, in Federalist No. 73, defended the qualified veto on two grounds: it protected the President's office against legislative "depredations," and it served as a check on bad laws. In signing legislation into law, Presidents often interpret provisions of a bill to avoid what they consider to be constitutional infirmities (see reading on signing statements).

Presidents also exercise a "pocket veto." The Constitution provides that any bill not returned by the President within ten days (Sundays excepted) shall become law unless the adjournment by Congress prevents the bill's return. In such cases, the bill does not become law and is pocket vetoed. Several decisions have effectively eliminated the use of a pocket veto *during* a congressional session.[1]

The remaining legal issue concerns the President's power to pocket veto a bill *between* the first and second sessions. This issue reached the Supreme Court but was dismissed in 1987 as moot. Barnes v. Kline, 759 F.2d 21 (D.C. Cir. 1985); Burke v. Barnes, 479 U.S. 361 (1987). This is another constitutional issue that requires interpretation by the elected branches. There is no question about the President's power to invoke the pocket veto at the end of the second session when Congress adjourns.

The Constitution contains other overlappings. The President nominates officers, but the Senate confirms. The President submits treaties that the Senate must approve. The House of Representatives may impeach executive and judicial officers, subject to the Senate's conviction in a trial presided over by the Chief Justice (for presidential impeachment). The courts decide criminal cases, but the President may pardon offenders. These mixtures led to complaints by several delegates at the state ratifying conventions. They objected that the branches of government had been intermingled instead of being kept separate. By the time of the Philadelphia Convention, however, the doctrine of separated powers had been overtaken by the system of checks and balances. One contemporary pamphleteer dismissed the separation doctrine, in its pure form, as a "hackneyed principle" and a "trite maxim." M.J.C. Vile, Constitutionalism and the Separation of Powers 153.

Madison devoted several of the essays in his *Federalist Papers* to the need for overlapping powers, claiming that the concept was superior to the impracticable partitioning of powers demanded by some of the Anti-Federalists (see readings). Alexander Hamilton, in Federalist No. 75, defended the combination of the executive with the Senate in the treaty process and bristled at "the trite topic of the intermixture of powers." Opponents were not satisfied. Three states—Virginia, North Carolina, and Pennsylvania—wanted a separation clause added to the national Bill of Rights. They proposed that neither branch could exercise the powers vested

---

1. Kennedy v. Sampson, 511 F.2d 430 (D.C. Cir. 1974); Wright v. United States, 302 U.S. 583 (1938). See also The Pocket Veto Case, 279 U.S. 655 (1929).

Is the Federal Government One of Enumerated Powers?

In exercising its power of judicial review, the Supreme Court frequently claims that the federal government is one of enumerated powers. In 1995, while striking down a congressional effort to regulate guns in schoolyards, it said: "We start with first principles. The Constitution creates a Federal Government of enumerated powers." United States v. Lopez, 514 U.S. 549, 552 (1995). Two years later, in invalidating the Religious Freedom Restoration Act, the Court announced: "Under our Constitution, the Federal Government is one of enumerated powers." Boerne v. Flores, 521 U.S. 507, 516 (1997).

Yet the federal government clearly exercises powers that are not enumerated, including the Court's own power of judicial review. Over the years, the Court has recognized a number of implied powers for all three branches. A more accurate statement would be that the federal government is one of enumerated powers plus those that are implied in the enumeration or

considered necessary for the effective functioning of government.

Article I, Section 5, provides that each House of Congress "may determine the Rules of its Proceedings [and] punish its Members for disorderly Behaviour." Article II, Section 2, states that the President "may require the Opinion, in writing, of the principal Officer in each of the executive Departments." Does any one doubt that Congress and the President could exercise those powers even if not enumerated?

Why does the Court speak about enumerated powers? Is it to impress upon the public that the federal government is subject to limits and that the Court is available to police the boundaries? Wouldn't that goal be satisfied by saying that the federal government is one of limited powers, which is surely the case? In these assertions about enumerated powers, is there risk that the Court may mislead the public and appear to be simplistic and false about fundamental principles?

in the others. Congress rejected that proposal as well as a substitute amendment to make the three departments "separate and distinct."[2]

Enumerated and Implied Powers

Strict constructionists regard the American Constitution as one of enumerated powers. They oppose the notion of implied powers, inherent powers, powers derived from custom, or any other extraconstitutional power not explicitly granted to one of the three branches. Although there is legitimate concern about the scope of implied powers, all three branches find it necessary to exercise powers not stated in the Constitution. Congress has the power to investigate as a necessary function of its legislative power; the President has the power to remove certain administrative officials to maintain executive accountability and responsibility; the Supreme Court has acquired the power to review legislative, executive, and state actions on questions of federal constitutionality. Nevertheless, the Court frequently insists that the federal government "is one of the enumerated powers" (see box).

The framers recognized the need for implied powers. Madison noted in Federalist No. 44: "No axiom is more clearly established in law, or in reason, than that whenever the end is required, the means are authorized; whenever a general power to do a thing is given, every particular power necessary for doing it is included." Congress is granted not merely the enumerated powers found within Article I but is also authorized to "make all Laws which shall be

2. Proposed by three states: 3 Elliot 280; 4 Elliot 116, 121; John Bach McMaster and Frederick D. Stone, eds., Pennsylvania and the Federal Constitution 475–77 (1888). Amendment language: Edward Dumbauld, The Bill of Rights and What It Means Today 174–75, 183, 199 (1957). Rejection: 1 Annals of Congress 435–36 (June 8, 1789) and 789–90 (August 18, 1789); 1 Senate Journals 64, 73–74 (1820).

necessary and proper for carrying into Execution the foregoing Powers, and all other Powers vested by this Constitution in the Government of the United States, or in any Department or Officer thereof." The history of the Tenth Amendment underscores the need for implied powers (page 335).[3]

The boundaries between the three branches of government are also strongly affected by the role of custom and acquiescence. When one branch engages in a certain practice and the other branches acquiesce, the practice gains legitimacy and can fix the meaning of the Constitution. Stuart v. Laird, 5 U.S. (1 Cr.) 299, 309 (1803). The President's power to remove officials was upheld in a 1903 ruling based largely on the "universal practice of the government for over a century." Shurtleff v. United States, 189 U.S. 311, 316 (1903). See also United States v. Midwest Oil Co., 236 U.S. 459, 469–71 (1915). Justice Frankfurter explained how executive power can grow when unchallenged: "A systematic, unbroken executive practice, long pursued to the knowledge of the Congress and never before questioned, engaged in by Presidents who have also sworn to uphold the Constitution, making as it were such exercise of power part of the structure of our government, may be treated as a gloss on 'executive Power' vested in the President by § 1 of Art. II." Youngstown Co. v. Sawyer, 343 U.S. 579, 610–611 (1952) (concurring opinion).[4]

Congress Interprets the Ineligibility Clause

During debate in 1973, Congress interpreted the Ineligibility (or Emoluments) Clause, which provides that no Senator or Representative shall, during the time for which he or she is elected, be appointed to any civil office "the Emoluments whereof shall have been encreased during such time." President Nixon wanted to nominate Senator William Saxbe to be Attorney General. Because of the constitutional prohibition, legislation was introduced with the support of the administration. The debate is an excellent example of the choice between the literal language of the Constitution and going behind the language to determine the framers' intent. The debate below occurred in the Senate on November 28, 1973, and can be found at 119 Cong. Rec. 38315–49. Senator Hiram Fong defended the bill; Senator Robert C. Byrd opposed it.

Mr. FONG. Mr. President, S. 2673 is a very simple bill. It merely sets the compensation and emoluments of the Office of Attorney General at that which existed on January 1, 1969. The proposed nomination of our colleague, Senator WILLIAM SAXBE, to the office of Attorney General has raised the question of the eligibility of a Member of Congress for appointment to a high executive office when the emoluments of that office have been increased during the term of the Member.

Senator SAXBE was elected a Senator from the State of Ohio. He took his oath January 4, 1969, and commenced his term of office....

The President transmitted to Congress on January 15, 1969, recommendations which included the increase of the salary of the Attorney General

---

3. Implied powers have been upheld in such cases as In re Neagle, 135 U.S. 1 (1890), which recognized the President's inherent authority to assign a U.S. marshal to protect a threatened federal judge, and In re Debs, 158 U.S. 1 (1895), supporting presidential use of military force to break a railroad strike.

4. The failure of Congress to repeal or revise a grant of statutory authority in the face of administrative interpretation has been held by the courts as "persuasive evidence" that the interpretation was intended by Congress. Zemel v. Rusk, 381 U.S. 1, 11 (1965). See also Dames & Moore v. Regan; 453 U.S. 654, 678–88 (1981); Norwegian Nitrogen Co. v. United States, 288 U.S. 294, 313 (1933); Costanzo v. Tillinghast, 287 U.S. 341, 345 (1932).

from $35,000 to $60,000 a year. On February 4, 1969, the Senate defeated Senate Resolution No. 82, which would have disapproved the Presidential recommendation. Senator SAXBE voted with the majority.

The pay raise, including that of the Attorney General, became effective shortly thereafter.

This is the increased emolument now making Senator SAXBE ineligible for appointment to the Office of Attorney General.

S. 2673 is designed to reduce the emolument of the Office of Attorney General to what it was at the time Senator SAXBE took office as Senator in 1969 and thus remove his ineligibility for appointment to that office.

. . .

2. APPOINTMENT TO OFFICE WHERE EMOLUMENT INCREASED

The relevant portion of the clause where an emolument has been increased states:

"No Senator or Representative shall, during the Time for which he was elected, be appointed to any civil Office under the Authority of the United States...the Emoluments whereof shall have been encreased during such time;"...

What has been permissible under this portion of this clause?

[Senator Fong explains that in two earlier instances, Senators were permitted to accept a Cabinet position although the salary of the Cabinet position had been increased during their term in office. In one case, Senator Morrill was confirmed for Secretary of State in 1876 after Congress had increased Cabinet officers from $8,000 to $10,000 in 1873 and reduced the salary a year later to $8,000. There was no challenge to his eligibility to serve. In 1909, Senator Knox was appointed Secretary of State after the salary for that position had been increased from $8,000 to $12,000 while Knox served as Senator. The Senate reduced Knox's salary as Secretary of State to what it was before his Senate term commenced and before the increase in pay.]

. . .

The [Ineligibility Clause]...was intended mainly to prevent two evils:

First. To protect legislators from unscrupulous executives using the enticement of public office to influence the actions of the legislators, and

Second. To avoid legislators viewing their elec-tion to Congress as a stepping stone to lucrative public office and utilizing their positions in the legislature as a means of creating offices or increasing the compensation of the offices they seek.

This being so, clearly the intent was not to prevent able and qualified Members of Congress from taking civil office.

Surely, the action of this Congress in reducing the emolument of the office of Attorney General from $60,000 to $35,000 cannot be said to be corruptive of the Members of this Congress nor can it be said that Senator SAXBE used his $42,500 Senate office as a stepping stone to a $35,000 office of Attorney General.

. . .

Mr. ROBERT C. BYRD. Mr. President, I yield myself such time as I may require.

. . .

On February 4, 1969, the Senate debated Senate Resolution 82, which would have disapproved the Presidential recommendation. The resolution was defeated; the pay raises, including that of the office of Attorney General, became effective shortly thereafter. Meanwhile, Mr. SAXBE's term of office as a U.S. Senator had begun on January 3, 1969 — about 6 weeks before the salary increase for the Attorney General became effective.

Hence, it seems clear beyond doubt that the proposed nomination of Mr. SAXBE, would fly squarely into the face of the prohibition contained in article I, section 6, clause 2 of the Constitution — which says, I repeat:

"No Senator or Representative shall, during the time for which he was elected, be appointed to any civil office under the authority of the United States, which shall have been created, or the emoluments whereof shall have been increased during such time;"...

Clearly, the emoluments of the Office of Attorney General were increased from $35,000 to $60,000 during the term for which Mr. SAXBE was elected — which term will not expire until January 3, 1975.

. . .

We, as legislators, have a responsibility to consider the constitutional aspects of the actions we take in the performance of our senatorial duties. We cannot be fully responsive to the high calling of our office by simply saying, "We will act to do thus and so; leave it to the courts to determine the constitutional rectitude of what we have done."

Ours is a higher duty. It is a duty that requires us — especially when great constitutional questions confront us in the first instance and on the first impression — to examine and to determine, according to our best lights, the constitutionality of actions we are called upon to take.

The nomination of Mr. SAXBE, under the circumstances peculiar to the nomination, fits almost squarely as a constitutional question heretofore essentially untested and unexplored.

Returning now to the matter before us: Can the constitutional bar be lifted by legislation? I say not.

. . .

I submit that the words of article I, section 6, clause 2, are clear, plain, simple, and easily understood by any citizen of this country.

. . .

[The Senate passed the bill, 75 to 16, and the House passed it on December 3. It became law on December 10, 1973 (P.L. 93-178, 87 Stat. 697)].

Presidential Signing Statements

When signing a bill into law, Presidents in recent years have adopted the practice of offering interpretations of various provisions in the bill to bring about what the President and his advisers consider a constitutional result. Below is the statement by President Bush on October 23, 1992, signing a defense authorization bill.

Today I am signing into law H.R. 5006, the "National Defense Authorization Act for Fiscal Year 1993."

. . .

I have signed this Act notwithstanding the reservations that I have regarding certain of its provisions. I am particularly concerned about provisions that purport to derogate the President's authority under the Constitution to conduct U.S. foreign policy, including negotiations with other countries. A number of provisions purport to establish foreign policy by providing that it shall be "the policy of the United States" or "the goal of the United States" to undertake specific diplomatic initiatives. Consistent with my responsibility under the Constitution for the conduct of diplomatic negotiations, and with established practice, I will construe these provisions to be precatory rather than mandatory. Other provisions purport to require reports to the Congress concerning diplomatic negotiations. I sign this bill with the understanding that these provisions do not detract from my constitutional authority to protect sensitive national security information.

. . .

I am also concerned that two provisions of H.R. 5006 might be construed to impinge on the President's authority as Commander in Chief and as head of the executive branch. Section 1303 purports to prohibit the use of appropriations to support a level of U.S. troops in Europe greater than 100,000 after October 1, 1995, and section 1302 purports to require a 40 percent cut in U.S. forces overseas after September 30, 1996, absent a war or national emergency. American forces abroad are a stabilizing influence in a volatile world and provide a ready means to protect American interests. Ill-considered cuts to America's forward presence diminish America's ability to help keep the peace in the future in various regions of the world. I shall construe these provisions consistent with my authority to deploy military personnel as necessary to fulfill my constitutional responsibilities.

. . .

I also note that section 330, under which the Secretary of Defense may "settle or defend" certain claims, should not be understood to detract from the Attorney General's plenary litigating authority. Accordingly, to the extent provided in current law, the Secretary of Defense will "settle or defend" claims in litigation through attorneys provided by the Department of Justice.

. . .

[Note: As enacted, H.R. 5006 is Public Law No. 102-484, approved October 23, 1992.]

Madison's Analysis of the Separation Doctrine

Some of the Anti-Federalists were astonished to find in the draft Constitution a variety of overlappings among the three branches of government: the President's power to veto legislation, the Senate's involvement in treaties and appointments, and other features of what we now call the system of checks and balances. In Federalist Nos. 47, 48, and 51, James Madison refutes these objections by reviewing the British Constitution, the theory of Montesquieu, and the practices adopted by the American states, all for the purpose of demonstrating that checks and balances are necessary to give the three branches adequate power to resist encroachments.

FEDERALIST NO. 47

Having reviewed the general form of the proposed government and the general mass of power allotted to it, I proceed to examine the particular structure of this government, and the distribution of this mass of power among its constituent parts.

One of the principal objections inculcated by the more respectable adversaries to the Constitution, is its supposed violation of the political maxim, that the legislative, executive, and judiciary departments ought to be separate and distinct. In the structure of the federal government, no regard, it is said, seems to have been paid to this essential precaution in favor of liberty. The several departments of power are distributed and blended in such a manner as at once to destroy all symmetry and beauty of form, and to expose some of the essential parts of the edifice to the danger of being crushed by the disproportionate weight of other parts.

No political truth is certainly of greater intrinsic value, or is stamped with the authority of more enlightened patrons of liberty, than that on which the objection is founded. The accumulation of all powers, legislative, executive, and judiciary, in the same hands, whether of one, a few, or many, and whether hereditary, self-appointed, or elective, may justly be pronounced the very definition of tyranny. Were the federal Constitution, therefore, really chargeable with the accumulation of power, or with a mixture of powers, having a dangerous tendency to such an accumulation, no further arguments would be necessary to inspire a universal reprobation of the system. I persuade myself, however, that it will be made apparent to every one, that the charge cannot be supported, and that the maxim on which it relies has been totally misconceived and misapplied. In order to form correct ideas on this important subject, it will be proper to investigate the sense in which the preservation of liberty requires that the three great departments of power should be separate and distinct.

The oracle who is always consulted and cited on this subject is the celebrated Montesquieu. If he be not the author of this invaluable precept in the science of politics, he has the merit at least of displaying and recommending it most effectually to the attention of mankind. Let us endeavor, in the first place, to ascertain his meaning on this point.

The British Constitution was to Montesquieu what Homer has been to the didactic writers on epic poetry. As the latter have considered the work of the immortal bard as the perfect model from which the principles and rules of the epic art were to be drawn, and by which all similar works were to be judged, so this great political critic appears to have viewed the Constitution of England as the standard, or to use his own expression, as the mirror of political liberty; and to have delivered, in the form of elementary truths, the several characteristic principles of that particular system. That we may be sure, then, not to mistake his meaning in this case, let us recur to the source from which the maxim was drawn.

On the slightest view of the British Constitution, we must perceive that the legislative, executive, and judiciary departments are by no means totally separate and distinct from each other. The executive magistrate forms an integral part of the legislative authority. He alone has the prerogative of making treaties with foreign sovereigns, which, when made, have, under certain limitations, the force of legislative acts. All the members of the judiciary department are appointed by him, can be removed by him on the address of the two Houses of Parliament, and form, when he pleases to consult them, one of his constitutional councils. One branch of the legislative department forms also a great constitutional council to the executive chief, as, on another hand, it is the sole depositary of judicial power in cases of impeachment, and is invested with the supreme appellate jurisdiction in all other cases. The judges, again, are so far connected with the legislative department as often to attend and participate in its deliberations, though not admitted to a legislative vote.

From these facts, by which Montesquieu was guided, it may clearly be inferred that, in saying "There can be no liberty where the legislative and executive powers are united in the same person, or body of magistrates," or, "if the power of judging be not separated from the legislative and executive powers," he did not mean that these departments ought to have no *partial agency* in, or no *control* over, the acts of each other. His meaning, as his own words import, and still more conclusively as illustrated by the example in his eye, can amount to no more than this, that where the *whole* power of one department is exercised by the same hands which possess the *whole* power of another department, the fundamental principles of a free constitution are subverted....

If we look into the constitutions of the several States, we find that, notwithstanding the emphatical and, in some instances, the unqualified terms in which this axiom has been laid down, there is not a single instance in which the several departments of power have been kept absolutely separate and distinct.

[Here Madison proceeds, state by state, to explain how the state constitutions mix the three powers of government.]

FEDERALIST NO. 48

It was shown in the last paper that the political apothegm there examined does not require that the legislative, executive, and judiciary departments should be wholly unconnected with each other. I shall undertake, in the next place, to show that unless these departments be so far connected and blended as to give to each a constitutional control over the others, the degree of separation which the maxim requires, as essential to a free government, can never in practice be duly maintained.

It is agreed on all sides, that the powers properly belonging to one of the departments ought not to be directly and completely administered by either of the other departments. It is equally evident, that none of them ought to possess, directly or indirectly, an overruling influence over the others, in the administration of their respective powers. It will not be denied, that power is of an encroaching nature, and that it ought to be effectually restrained from passing the limits assigned to it. After discriminating, therefore, in theory, the several classes of power, as they may in their nature be legislative, executive, or judiciary, the next and most difficult task is to provide some

practical security for each, against the invasion of the others. What this security ought to be, is the great problem to be solved.

Will it be sufficient to mark, with precision, the boundaries of these departments, in the constitution of the government, and to trust to these parchment barriers against the encroaching spirit of power? This is the security which appears to have been principally relied on by the compilers of most of the American constitutions. But experience assures us, that the efficacy of the provision has been greatly overrated; and that some more adequate defence is indispensably necessary for the more feeble, against the more powerful, members of the government. The legislative department is everywhere extending the sphere of its activity, and drawing all power into its impetuous vortex.

. . .

[Starting with Virginia, Madison details various examples of legislative usurpations of executive and judicial power. He also cites instances of executive encroachments.]

The conclusion which I am warranted in drawing from these observations is, that a mere demarcation on parchment of the constitutional limits of the several departments, is not a sufficient guard against those encroachments which lead to a tyrannical concentration of all the powers of government in the same hands.

FEDERALIST NO. 51

To what expedient, then, shall we finally resort, for maintaining in practice the necessary partition of power among the several departments, as laid down in the Constitution? The only answer that can be given is, that as all these exterior provisions are found to be inadequate, the defect must be supplied, by so contriving the interior structure of the government as that its several constituent parts may, by their mutual relations, be the means of keeping each other in their proper places....

In order to lay a due foundation for that separate and distinct exercise of the different powers of government, which to a certain extent is admitted on all hands to be essential to the preservation of liberty, it is evident that each department should have a will of its own; and consequently should be so constituted that the members of each should have as little agency as possible in the appointment of the members of the others....

It is equally evident, that the members of each

department should be as little dependent as possible on those of the others, for the emoluments annexed to their offices. Were the executive magistrate, or the judges, not independent of the legislature in this particular, their independence in every other would be merely nominal.

But the great security against a gradual concentration of the several powers in the same department, consists in giving to those who administer each department the necessary constitutional means and personal motives to resist encroachments of the others. The provision for defence must in this, as in all other cases, be made commensurate to the danger of attack. Ambition must be made to counteract ambition. The interest of the man must be connected with the constitutional rights of the place. It may be a reflection on

human nature, that such devices should be necessary to control the abuses of government. But what is government itself, but the greatest of all reflections on human nature? If men were angels, no government would be necessary. If angels were to govern men, neither external nor internal controls on government would be necessary. In framing a government which is to be administered by men over men, the great difficulty lies in this: you must first enable the government to control the governed; and in the next place oblige it to control itself. A dependence on the people is, no doubt, the primary control on the government; but experience has taught mankind the necessity of auxiliary precautions.

· · ·

B. PRESIDENTIAL POWER

Scholars have long debated the nature of executive power, in historical, philosophical, political, and constitutional terms. Do the words "executive power" in Article II suggest a grant to the President of broad, discretionary authority, of all powers conceivably executive in nature? Or is the executive power clause a reference to the subsequent enumeration of presidential power? In Federalist No. 69 and No. 70, Alexander Hamilton offered his views on the nature of executive power and compared it to the more comprehensive grant of power for the English king (see reading).

In a concurring opinion, Justice Robert H. Jackson denied that the executive power "is a grant in bulk of all conceivable power." Youngstown Co. v. Sawyer, 343 U.S. 579, 641 (1952). Yet it is widely acknowledged that the President possesses powers beyond those that are enumerated. For functional purposes, he enjoys some implied powers. As part of his administrative responsibilities and his duty to faithfully execute the laws under the Take Care Clause of Article II, he may exercise the power to remove executive officials. Myers v. United States, 272 U.S. 52 (1926). Similarly, the Court has recognized a limited executive privilege to retain information within the executive branch, as an attribute of the President's duties and responsibilities. United States v. Nixon, 418 U.S. 683 (1974).

Prerogative

Quite apart from the concept of enumerated and implied powers, each of which is grounded in the Constitution, do Presidents possess an extraconstitutional authority or prerogative power? May they act in response to an emergency—in the absence of law or even in conflict with it—for the public good? In *United States* v. *Curtiss-Wright Export Corp.*, for example, Justice George Sutherland asserted that authority over foreign affairs is not dependent upon a grant from the Constitution since the powers of external sovereignty are derived from the English Crown. 299 U.S. 304, 315–16. When President Harry S. Truman seized the steel mills in 1952, he invoked emergency powers and claimed that he could act "for whatever is for the best of the country." Public Papers of the Presidents, 1952–53, at 273. That interpretation was rejected by the Supreme Court. Youngstown Co. v. Sawyer, 343 U.S. 579 (1952).

Various scholars have embraced the claim of extra-constitutional executive powers and have located its modern expression in the Lockean Prerogative. Edward S. Corwin, The President:

Office and Powers, 1787–1948, at 10, 15–16, 6–7, 182 (3rd rev. ed. 1948), In the second of his *Two Treatises of Government* published in 1690, Locke stated that prerogative was the power "to act according to discretion, for the public good, without the prescription of the law and sometimes even against it." The executive does not possess the legal authority to act, but because he is perhaps best-positioned and best-equipped to act, he may choose to respond to the emergency, much like the man who, in Locke's single example of the prerogative to act against the law, pulls down "an innocent Man's House to stop the Fire, when the next to it is burning." Locke, Second Treatise, § 159. Neither the good citizen nor the executive acts under the color of law in the case of emergency; they simply act and accept the consequences. They can be spared punishment, if at all, through exoneration from the legislature in the way of retroactive authorization or by a pardon. If a President's explanation is unsatisfactory he may be impeached.

The method of retroactive authorization or indemnity maintains a semblance of constitutional government: the legislature and not the executive is the lawmaker. There is no evidence that the framers of the Constitution intended to incorporate the Lockean Prerogative in the Constitution. When President Lincoln took extraordinary actions at the start of the Civil War, while Congress was in recess, he acknowledged that some of his actions may have lacked legal authority and therefore turned to Congress for retroactive approval (see page 284).

Hamilton on Executive Power

In several essays in *The Federalist*, Alexander Hamilton hoped to allay the fears that the framers had defined executive power too broadly. In Federalist No. 69, he compared the power of the President to the much larger prerogatives of the King of England. How does contemporary presidential power compare with Hamilton's analysis? In Federalist No. 70, he defended energy in the executive as not only a leading characteristic of good government but also consistent with republican principles.

FEDERALIST NO. 69

I PROCEED now to trace the real characters of the proposed Executive, as they are marked out in the plan of the convention. This will serve to place in a strong light the unfairness of the representations which have been made in regard to it.

. . .

That magistrate is to be elected for *four* years; and is to be reeligible as often as the people of the United States shall think him worthy of their confidence. In these circumstances there is a total dissimilitude between *him* and a king of Great Britain, who in an *hereditary* monarch, possessing the crown as a patrimony descendible to his heirs forever; but there is a close analogy between *him* and a governor of New York, who is elected for *three* years, and is reeligible without limitation or intermission. If we consider how much less time would be requisite for establishing a dangerous influence in a single State, than for establishing a like influence throughout the United States, we must conclude that a duration of *four* years

for the Chief Magistrate of the Union is a degree of permanency far less to be dreaded in that office, than a duration of *three* years for a corresponding office in a single State.

The President of the United States would be liable to be impeached, tried, and, upon conviction of treason, bribery, or other high crimes or misdemeanors, removed from office; and would afterwards be liable to prosecution and punishment in the ordinary course of law. The person of the king of Great Britain is sacred and inviolable; there is no constitutional tribunal to which he is amenable; no punishment to which he can be subjected without involving the crisis of a national revolution....

The President of the United States is to have power to return a bill, which shall have passed the two branches of the legislature, for reconsideration; and the bill so returned is to become a law, if, upon that reconsideration, it be approved by two thirds of both houses. The king of Great Britain, on his part, has an absolute negative upon the acts of the two houses of Parliament. The disuse of that power for a considerable time past does not affect the reality of its existence; and is to be ascribed wholly to the crown's having found the means of substituting influence to authority, or the art of gaining a majority in one or the other of the two houses, to the necessity of exerting a prerogative which could seldom be exerted without hazarding some degree of national agitation....

The President is to be the "commander-in-chief of the army and navy of the United States, and of the militia of the several States, when called into the actual service of the United States. He is to have power to grant reprieves and pardons for offences against the United States, *except in cases of impeachment;* to recommend to the consideration of Congress such measures as he shall judge necessary and expedient; to convene, on extraordinary occasions, both houses of the legislature, or either of them, and, in case of disagreement between them *with respect to the time of adjournment,* to adjourn them to such time as he shall think proper; to take care that the laws be faithfully executed; and to commission all officers of the United States." In most of these particulars, the power of the President will resemble equally that of the king of Great Britain and of the governor of New York. The most material points of difference are these: — *First.* The President will have only the occasional command of such part of the militia of the nation as by legislative provision may be called into the actual service of the Union. The king of Great Britain and the governor of New York have at all times the entire command of all the militia within their several jurisdictions. In this article, therefore, the power of the President would be inferior to that of either the monarch or the governor. *Second.* The President is to be commander-in-chief of the army and navy of the United States. In this respect his authority would be nominally the same with that of the king of Great Britain, but in substance much inferior to it. It would amount to nothing more than the supreme command and direction of the military and naval forces, as first General and admiral of the Confederacy; while that of the British king extends to the *declaring* of war and to the *raising* and *regulating* of fleets and armies, — all which, by the Constitution under consideration, would appertain to the legislature.... *Third.* The power of the President, in respect to pardons, would extend to all cases, *except those of impeachment.* The governor of New York may pardon in all cases, even in those of impeachment, except for treason and murder. Is not the power of the governor, in this article, on a calculation of political consequences, greater than that of the

President?...*Fourth.* The President can only adjourn the national legislature in the single case of disagreement about the time of adjournment. The British monarch may prorogue or even dissolve the Parliament. The governor of New York may also prorogue the legislature of this State for a limited time; a power which, in certain situations, may be employed to very important purposes.

The President is to have power, with the advice and consent of the Senate, to make treaties, provided two thirds of the senators present concur. The king of Great Britain is the sole and absolute representative of the nation in all foreign transactions. He can of his own accord make treaties of peace, commerce, alliance, and of every other description....

The President is also to be authorized to receive ambassadors and other public ministers. This, though it has been a rich theme of declamation, is more a matter of dignity than of authority. It is a circumstance which will be without consequence in the administration of the government; and it was far more convenient that it should be arranged in this manner, than that there should be a necessity of convening the legislature, or one of its branches, upon every arrival of a foreign minister, though it were merely to take the place of a departed predecessor.

The President is to nominate, and, *with the advice and consent of the Senate,* to appoint ambassadors and other public ministers, judges of the Supreme Court, and in general all officers of the United States established by law, and whose appointments are not otherwise provided for by the Constitution. The king of Great Britain is emphatically and truly styled the fountain of honor. He not only appoints to all offices, but can create offices. He can confer titles of nobility at pleasure; and has the disposal of an immense number of church preferments. There is evidently a great inferiority in the power of the President, in this particular, to that of the British king;...

FEDERALIST NO. 70

THERE is an idea, which is not without its advocates, that a vigorous Executive is inconsistent with the genius of republican government. The enlightened well-wishers to this species of government must at least hope that the supposition is destitute of foundation; since they can never admit its truth, without at the same time admitting the condemnation of their own principles. Energy in the Executive is a leading character in the definition of good government. It is essential to the protection of the community against foreign attacks; it is not less essential to the steady administration of the laws; to the protection of property against those irregular and high-handed combinations which sometimes interrupt the ordinary course of justice; to the security of liberty against the enterprises and assaults of ambition, of faction, and of anarchy. Every man the least conversant in Roman story, knows how often that republic was obliged to take refuge in the absolute power of a single man, under the formidable title of Dictator, as well against the intrigues of ambitious individuals who aspired to the tyranny, and the seditions of whole classes of the community whose conduct threatened the existence of all government, as against the invasions of external enemies who menaced the conquest and destruction of Rome.

There can be no need, however, to multiply arguments or examples on this head. A feeble Executive implies a feeble execution of the government. A feeble execution is but another phrase for a bad execution; and a government ill executed, whatever it may be in theory, must be, in practice, a bad government.

Taking it for granted, therefore, that all men of sense will agree in the necessity of an energetic Executive, it will only remain to inquire, what are the ingredients which constitute this energy? How far can they be combined with those other ingredients which constitute safety in the republican sense? And how far does this combination characterize the plan which has been reported by the convention?

The ingredients which constitute energy in the Executive are, unity; duration; an adequate provision for its support; competent powers.

The ingredients which constitute safety in the republican sense are, a due dependence on the people; a due responsibility.

Those politicians and statesmen who have been the most celebrated for the soundness of their principles and for the justice of their views,

have declared in favor of a single Executive and a numerous legislature. They have, with great propriety, considered energy as the most necessary qualification of the former, and have regarded this as most applicable to power in a single hand; while they have, with equal propriety, considered the latter as best adapted to deliberation and wisdom, and best calculated to conciliate the confidence of the people and to secure their privileges and interests.

That unity is conducive to energy will not be disputed. Decision, activity, secrecy, and despatch will generally characterize the proceedings of one man in a much more eminent degree than the proceedings of any greater number; and in proportion as the number is increased, these qualities will be diminished.

. . .

The experience of other nations will afford little instruction on this head. As far, however, as it teaches any thing, it teaches us not to be enamoured of plurality in the Executive. . . .

. . . one of the weightiest objections to a plurality in the Executive, and which lies as much against the last as the first plan, is, that it tends to conceal faults and destroy responsibility. Responsibility is of two kinds — to censure and to punishment. The first is the more important of the two, especially in an elective office. Man, in public trust, will much oftener act in such a manner as to render him unworthy of being any longer trusted, than in such a manner as to make him obnoxious to legal punishment. But the multiplication of the Executive adds to the difficulty of detection in either case. It often becomes impossible, amidst mutual accusations, to determine on whom the blame or the punishment of a pernicious measure, or series of pernicious measures, ought really to fall. It is shifted from one to another with so much dexterity, and under such plausible appearances, that the public opinion is left in suspense about the real author. . . .

C. CREATING THE EXECUTIVE DEPARTMENTS

The Constitution establishes only a shell for government. It was left to the First Congress, by statute, to create executive departments and federal courts. In so doing, it necessarily debated and decided a number of fundamental constitutional issues. At that time, there was neither a functioning judiciary nor federal judicial precedents. From 1789 to the present, it has been primarily the responsibility of Congress to determine the structure of government, the pow-

Madison Describing Independence of Comptroller's Office

It will be necessary, said he, to consider the nature of this office, to enable us to come to a right decision on the subject; in analyzing its properties, we shall discover they are not purely of an Executive nature. It seems to me that they partake of a Judiciary quality as well as Executive; perhaps the latter obtains in the greater degree. The principal duty seems to be deciding upon the lawfulness and justice of the claims and accounts subsisting between the United States and particular citizens; this partakes

strongly of a judicial character, and there may be strong reasons why an officer of this kind should not hold his office at the pleasure of the Executive branch of the Government.

...I question very much whether [the President] can or ought to have any interference in the settling and adjusting the legal claims of individuals against the United States. The necessary examination and decision in such cases partake too much of the Judicial capacity to be blended with the Executive....

SOURCE: 1 Annals of Congress 611–12, 614 (1789).

ers and functions of agencies, limitations on the President's power to remove executive officials, the qualifications of appointees, and the level of funding.

Since each department had to be created by statute, the First Congress could have placed departments under a single individual or a board of commissioners. The experience under the Articles of Confederation convinced most legislators that the board system lacked responsibility, energy, and order. The House of Representatives in 1789 voted for single executives to head the departments. Congress treated the Secretary of Foreign Affairs and the Secretary of War as executive officials, which had been the practice under the Articles. In contrast, Congress regarded the Secretary of the Treasury partly as a *legislative* agent, reflecting the mixed record during the Articles when the duties shifted back and forth between a Superintendent of Finance and a Board of Treasury. The first Secretary of the Treasury, Alexander Hamilton, performed essentially as an arm of the President, not Congress, and so it has been ever since. Under President Andrew Jackson, Congress tried to treat the Secretary of the Treasury as a legislative agent. Jackson eventually prevailed in his argument that the Secretary is "wholly an executive officer," but he had to remove two Secretaries of the Treasury to effectuate his policy and was censured by the Senate for his action. Three years later the Senate ordered its resolution of censure expunged from the record. Louis Fisher, Constitutional Conflicts Between Congress and the President 55 (1997).

Hybrid Officers

Some of the officers within the Treasury Department had duties that were not wholly executive in nature. During debate on the Department in 1789, Madison admitted that the comptroller's office "seemed to bear a strong affinity" to the legislative branch, while its settlement and adjustment of legal claims "partake too much of the Judicial capacity to be blended with the Executive" (see box). When Congress created the General Accounting Office (GAO) in 1921, it transferred to it not merely the powers and duties of the comptroller but even the personnel. GAO has been called a mixed agency: "legislative" when it audits accounts and investigates programs, and "executive" when it approves payments and settles and adjusts accounts.[5]

---

5. United States ex rel. Brookfield Const. Co., Inc. v. Stewart, 234 F.Supp. 94, 99–100 (D.D.C. 1964), aff'd, 339 F.2d 754 (D.C. Cir. 1964).

This hybrid status was attacked by the Reagan administration in 1985 when it challenged the Comptroller General's authority to determine "bid protests." Disappointed bidders of government contracts could appeal to GAO and have the award of the contract delayed while GAO studied the dispute. The Justice Department regarded GAO as part of the legislative branch and therefore without authority to participate in executive duties. However, GAO's bid-protest powers were upheld in the lower courts.[6]

The confrontation heightened at the end of 1985 when Congress passed the Gramm-Rudman-Hollings Act. The statute, which required federal deficits to decline to zero by fiscal 1991, authorized the Comptroller General under certain circumstances to order program cuts to be carried out by the President through a "sequestration" process. The administration claimed that Congress could not give executive duties to a legislative officer. The Supreme Court in 1986 agreed that the Comptroller General's sequestration duties were unconstitutional because Congress could not vest executive functions in an officer removable by Congress. BOWSHER v. SYNAR, 478 U.S. 714 (1986).

Take Care Clause

Another dispute concerns the President's authority to supervise the officers within the executive branch. A careless reading of the Constitution gives the President the power to execute the laws. In fact, he is to "take Care that the Laws be faithfully executed" (Article II, Section 3). What happens if a statute places the execution of a program outside his control? Does this violate the principle of responsibility and accountability vested in a single executive? The short answer is that the heads of executive departments function only in part as political agents of the President. They also perform legal duties assigned to them by Congress. In *Marbury* v. *Madison* (1803), Chief Justice Marshall distinguished between two types of duties for a Cabinet head: ministerial and discretionary. The first duty allows Congress to direct a Secretary to carry out certain activities. The second duty is owed to the President alone. When a Secretary performs the first duty he is bound to obey the laws: "He acts ... under the authority of law, and not by the instructions of the president. It is a ministerial act which the law enjoins on a particular officer for a particular purpose." 5 U.S. (1 Cr.) 137, 157.

The concept of ministerial duties reappears in *Kendall* v. *United States,* 37 U.S. 522 (1838). Congress could mandate that certain payments be made, and neither the head of the executive department nor the President could deny or control these ministerial acts.[7]

In 1854 the Attorney General stated that when laws "define what is to be done by a given head of department, and how he is to do it, there the President's discretion stops...." 6 Op. Att'y Gen. 326, 341. Opinions by Attorneys General advised various Presidents of substantial political and legal constraints on their ability to intervene in certain departmental matters (see Attorney General reading). The President is responsible for seeing that administrative officers faithfully perform their duties, "but the statutes regulate and prescribe these duties, and he has no more power to add to, or subtract from, the duties imposed upon subordinate executive and administrative officers by the law, than those officers have to add or subtract from

---

6. See Ameron, Inc. v. U.S. Army Corps of Engineers, 607 F.Supp. 962 (D. N.J. 1985); 610 F.Supp. 750 (D. N.J. 1985); 787 F.2d 875 (3d Cir. 1986); 809 F.2d 979 (3d Cir. 1986). The statute was also upheld in Lear Siegler, Inc. v. Lehman, 842 F.2d 1102 (9th Cir. 1988). In response to a Justice Department request, the Supreme Court agreed to dismiss its writ of certiorari. 488 U.S. 918 (1988).

7. See also United States v. Schurz, 102 U.S. 378 (1880); United States v. Price, 116 U.S. 43 (1885); United States v. Louisville, 169 U.S. 249 (1898); and Clackamus County, Ore. v. McKay, 219 F.2d 479, 496 (D.C. Cir. 1954), vacated as moot, 349 U.S. 909 (1955).

his duties."[8] Departmental heads recognize the limitations that prevent them from interfering with decisions by administrative law judges (ALJs). Nash v. Califano, 613 F.2d 10 (2d Cir. 1980).

Federal courts invoked the ministerial-discretionary distinction on a regular basis during the Nixon administration to force the release of impounded funds. Cabinet heads were ordered to allocate or obligate funds. Berends v. Butz, 357 F.Supp. 143 (D. Minn. 1973); Train v. City of New York, 420 U.S. 35 (1975). Statutory duties also apply to the President. In 1974 an appellate court held that President Nixon had violated the law by refusing to carry out a statute on federal pay. He was directed to either submit to Congress the pay plan proposed by a salary commission or his own alternative plan. National Treasury Employees Union v. Nixon, 492 F.2d 587 (D.C. Cir. 1974).

Independent Commissions

Beginning in 1887, Congress created independent regulatory commissions and gave them some autonomy from presidential control. The Interstate Commerce Commission (ICC) was the first of these creatures, and since that time Congress has established other independent bodies, including the Federal Reserve System (1913), the Federal Trade Commission (1914), the Securities and Exchange Commission (1934), and the Commodity Futures Trading Commission (1975).

Compared to the single administrators who head the executive departments, commissions are multimember (collegial) bodies that are headed by at least three commissioners. Independence is secured in three ways: (1) the terms of the commissioners are staggered to insulate them from presidential elections, (2) the President's power to remove commissioners is limited by specified statutory grounds, and (3) restrictions are placed on the number of commissioners who may belong to the same political party.

Independent commissions often carry out judicial duties, which helps explain why commissions are collegial bodies. Just as we want appellate courts to consist of more than one judge to protect against "the idiosyncracies of a single individual," so do we want agencies that adjudicate to be multimember. Kenneth Culp Davis, Administrative Law of the Seventies 15 (1976). Even if the functions of these commissions were transferred to the regular executive departments, the judicial functions would still be set apart and insulated from presidential control.

Another odd body created by Congress is the U.S. Sentencing Commission, established in 1984 "as an independent commission in the judicial branch of the United States." Because of serious disparities among the sentences imposed by federal judges for similar offenses, this commission is responsible for devising more equitable sentencing guidelines. The seven voting members are appointed by the President with the advice and consent of the Senate. At least three members are federal judges. The Chairman of the Commission and other members are subject to removal by the President "only for neglect of duty or malfeasance in office or for other good cause shown." Of course, the President may only remove judges from the Commission, not from their judicial positions. The Supreme Court, voting 8 to 1, upheld the Commission against a number of challenges. It concluded that Congress had not delegated excessive legislative power to the Commission, nor had it violated separation of power principles by placing the Commission in the judicial branch and requiring federal judges to serve on the

---

8. 19 Op. Att'y Gen. 685, 686–87 (1890). See also 1 Op. Att'y Gen. 624 (1823); 1 Op. Att'y Gen. 636 (1824); 1 Op. Att'y Gen. 678 (1824); 1 Op. Att'y Gen. 705 (1825); 1 Op. Att'y Gen. 706 (1825); 2 Op. Att'y Gen. 480 (1831); 2 Op. Att'y Gen. 507 (1832); 2 Op. Att'y Gen. 544 (1832); 4 Op. Att'y Gen. 515 (1846); 5 Op. Att'y Gen. 287 (1851); 10 Op. Att'y Gen. 526 (1863); 11 Op. Att'y Gen. 14 (1864); 13 Op. Att'y Gen. 28 (1869); 18 Op. Att'y Gen. 31 (1884).

Could the President Use Constitutional Grounds to Veto an Independent Counsel Bill?

Suppose you work in the White House Counsel office and the President receives a bill to reauthorize the independent counsel statute. He tells you he has serious reservations about the bill, not merely policy concerns but constitutional issues as well. He concludes that the exercise of prosecuting authority by the independent counsel encroaches upon executive power and his obligations under the Constitution.

You remind him that the Supreme Court considered those issues in *Morrison* and yet upheld the statute on constitutional grounds. He reminds you that President Jackson vetoed the U.S. Bank bill despite *McCulloch* and says he does not feel bound by Court rulings when it comes to invoking the veto power to protect the prerogatives of his office. He feels an obligation to defend his own institution, regardless of what Congress or the courts do. In drafting his veto message, can you use constitutional arguments or has that issue already been settled by the Court's decision? For that matter, could Congress, in considering a bill to reauthorize the independent counsel, vote it down on constitutional grounds?

Commission and share their authority with nonjudges. Furthermore, it was not a constitutional violation to limit presidential removal for cause only. Mistretta v. United States, 488 U.S. 361 (1989).

Independent Counsel

Following the scandals of the Watergate period, Congress passed legislation in 1978 to establish an independent "special prosecutor" to investigate charges against the President, the Vice President, and high-level executive branch officials. Congress concluded that the Attorney General, as a key member of the President's cabinet, might face a conflict of interest in trying to prosecute a suspected top official. The special prosecutor, later called independent counsel, can be removed by the President only for "good cause" and is appointed by a special panel of federal judges.

The Justice Department attacked the statute as unconstitutional because it vested part of law enforcement in an officer not appointed by the President. Moreover, the removal feature was seen as an impermissible restriction on presidential power. However, the Supreme Court voted 7 to 1 to sustain the independent counsel. MORRISON v. OLSON, 487 U.S. 654 (1988). Although the independent counsel statute was reauthorized by Congress in 1994 for five years, objections continue to be heard, both on policy and constitutional grounds. If Congress reauthorizes the statute, could the President veto the bill on constitutional grounds after the procedure had been upheld by the Court in *Morrison* (see box)?

Each time Congress reauthorized the independent counsel statute—in 1983, 1987, and 1994—substantial reforms were adopted. Even with these changes, no doubt the potential for abuse is great for any prosecutor, including those in the Justice Department. When the office of independent counsel expired in 1999, Congress did not renew it.

The record of the independent counsel law does not support the claim that these individuals inevitably target a particular person and use unlimited funds to indict him. From 1978 to 1999, independent counsels investigated twenty controversies. No indictments were brought in twelve of the cases. When indictments and convictions were obtained, as with probes into corruption in executive departments (Housing and Urban Development, Agriculture) or into the Iran-Contra affair, the abuses were great and needed correction. Complaints have been made about the time that some investigations take and the level of expenditures (especially Lawrence Walsh's investigation of Iran-Contra and Kenneth Starr's investigation of White-water and other matters), but much of the delay and cost come from the complexity of the issues and the withholding of key documents by the administration. Some form of independent counsel—whether statutory or not—is needed because there are activities (particularly White House and presidential) that cannot be investigated by the Justice Department without creating an unacceptable conflict of interest.

Bowsher v. Synar

478 U.S. 714 (1986)

In an effort to gain control over the budget deficits that had mushroomed during the Reagan administration, Congress passed the Gramm-Rudman-Hollings Act in 1985. The statute established a multiyear schedule designed to bring the federal deficit to zero by 1991. If Congress and the President failed to abide by the statutory schedule, automatic cuts (called "sequestration") would occur. Under the sequestration process, the Comptroller General would receive budget estimates from the Office of Management and Budget (OMB) and the Congressional Budget Office (CBO) and proceed to draft the sequestration order, to be signed and issued by the President without change. The principal constitutional question was whether Congress could use the Comptroller General, generally thought to be within the legislative branch, to play a role in the execution of the laws. A three-judge federal court in 1986 held that the statute was unconstitutional as a violation of the separation of powers doctrine because the Comptroller General is removable only by a joint resolution initiated by Congress or by impeachment. Congressman Mike Synar filed the suit attacking the constitutionality of the Act. One of the defendants was Charles A. Bowsher, the Comptroller General.

CHIEF JUSTICE BURGER delivered the opinion of the Court.

The question presented by these appeals is whether the assignment by Congress to the Comptroller General of the United States of certain functions under the Balanced Budget and Emergency Deficit Control Act of 1985 violates the doctrine of separation of powers.

I

A

On December 12, 1985, the President signed into law the Balanced Budget and Emergency Deficit Control Act of 1985, ... popularly known as the "Gramm-Rudman-Hollings Act." The purpose of the Act is to eliminate the federal budget deficit. To that end, the Act sets a "maximum deficit amount" for federal spending for each of fiscal years 1986 through 1991. The size of that maximum deficit amount progressively reduces to zero in fiscal year 1991. If in any fiscal year the federal budget deficit exceeds the maximum deficit amount by more than a specified sum, the Act requires across-the-board cuts in federal spending to reach the targeted deficit level, with half of the cuts made to defense programs and the

other half made to non-defense programs. The Act exempts certain priority programs from these cuts. § 255.

These "automatic" reductions are accomplished through a rather complicated procedure, spelled out in § 251, the so-called "reporting provisions" of the Act. Each year, the Directors of the Office of Management and Budget (OMB) and the Congressional Budget Office (CBO) independently estimate the amount of the federal budget deficit for the upcoming fiscal year. If that deficit exceeds the maximum targeted deficit amount for that fiscal year by more than a specified amount, the Directors of OMB and CBO independently calculate, on a program-by-program basis, the budget reductions necessary to ensure that the deficit does not exceed the maximum deficit amount. The Act then requires the Directors to report jointly their deficit estimates and budget reduction calculations to the Comptroller General.

The Comptroller General, after reviewing the Directors' reports, then reports his conclusions to the President. § 251(b). The President in turn must issue a "sequestration" order mandating the spending reductions specified by the Comptroller General....

III

We noted recently that "[t]he Constitution sought to divide the delegated powers of the new Federal Government into three defined categories, Legislative, Executive, and Judicial." *INS v. Chadha,* 462 U.S. 919, 951 (1983). The declared purpose of separating and dividing the powers of government, of course, was to "diffus[e] power the better to secure liberty." *Youngstown Sheet & Tube Co. v. Sawyer,* 343 U.S. 579, 635 (1952) (Jackson, J., concurring). Justice Jackson's words echo the famous warning of Montesquieu, quoted by James Madison in The Federalist No. 47, that " 'there can be no liberty where the legislative and executive powers are united in the same person, or body of magistrates'...." The Federalist No. 47, p. 325 (J. Cooke ed. 1961).

. . .

The Constitution does not contemplate an active role for Congress in the supervision of officers charged with the execution of the laws it enacts. The President appoints "Officers of the United States" with the "Advice and Consent of the Senate...." Article II, § 2. Once the appointment has been made and confirmed, however, the Constitution explicitly provides for removal of Officers of the United States by Congress only upon impeachment by the House of Representatives and conviction by the Senate. An impeachment by the House and trial by the Senate can rest only on "Treason, Bribery or other high Crimes and Misdemeanors." Article II, § 4. A direct congressional role in the removal of officers charged with the execution of the laws beyond this limited one is inconsistent with separation of powers.

This was made clear in debate in the First Congress in 1789. *[The Court summarizes the holdings in* Myers v. United States, *272 U.S. 52 (1926),* Humphrey's Executor v. United States, *295 U.S. 602 (1935), and* Weiner v. United States, *357 U.S. 349 (1958).]*

In light of these precedents, we conclude that Congress cannot reserve for itself the power of removal of an officer charged with the execution of the laws except by impeachment. To permit the execution of the laws to be vested in an officer answerable only to Congress would, in practical terms, reserve in Congress control over the execution of the laws. As the District Court observed, "Once an officer is appointed, it is only the au-

thority that can remove him, and not the authority that appointed him, that he must fear and, in the performance of his functions, obey." 626 F.Supp., at 1401. The structure of the Constitution does not permit Congress to execute the laws; it follows that Congress cannot grant to an officer under its control what it does not possess.

. . .

IV

Appellants urge that the Comptroller General performs his duties independently and is not subservient to Congress. We agree with the District Court that this contention does not bear close scrutiny.

The critical factor lies in the provisions of the statute defining the Comptroller General's office relating to removability. Although the Comptroller General is nominated by the President from a list of three individuals recommended by the Speaker of the House of Representatives and the President pro tempore of the Senate, see 31 U.S.C. § 703(a)(2), and confirmed by the Senate, he is removable only at the initiative of Congress. He may be removed not only by impeachment but also by Joint Resolution of Congress "at any time" resting on any one of the following bases:

"(i) permanent disability;

"(ii) inefficiency;

"(iii) neglect of duty;

"(iv) malfeasance; or

"(v) a felony or conduct involving moral turpitude." 31 U.S.C. § 703(e)(1).

. . .

...The statute permits removal for "inefficiency," "neglect of duty," or "malfeasance." These terms are very broad and, as interpreted by Congress, could sustain removal of a Comptroller General for any number of actual or perceived transgressions of the legislative will....

...In constitutional terms, the removal powers over the Comptroller General's office dictate that he will be subservient to Congress.

. . .

Against this background, we see no escape from the conclusion that, because Congress had retained removal authority over the Comptroller General, he may not be entrusted with executive powers. The remaining question is whether the Comptroller General has been assigned such powers in the Balanced Budget and Emergency Deficit Control Act of 1985.

V

The primary responsibility of the Comptroller General under the instant Act is the preparation of a "report." This report must contain detailed estimates of projected federal revenues and expenditures. The report must also specify the reductions, if any, necessary to reduce the deficit to the target for the appropriate fiscal year. The reductions must be set forth on a program-by-program basis.

. . .

. . . [W]e view these functions as plainly entailing execution of the law in constitutional terms. Interpreting a law enacted by Congress to implement the legislative mandate is the very essence of "execution" of the law. Under § 251, the Comptroller General must exercise judgment concerning facts that affect the application of the Act. He must also interpret the provisions of the Act to determine precisely what budgetary calculations are required. Decisions of that kind are typically made by officers charged with executing a statute.

. . . [A]s *Chadha* makes clear, once Congress makes its choice in enacting legislation, its participation ends. Congress can thereafter control the execution of its enactment only indirectly — by passing new legislation. *Chadha*, 462 U.S., at 958. By placing the responsibility for execution of the Balanced Budget and Emergency Deficit Control Act in the hands of an officer who is subject to removal only by itself, Congress in effect has retained control over the execution of the Act and has intruded into the executive function. The Constitution does not permit such intrusion.

VI

[Appellants argued that rather than strike down the sequestration powers of the Comptroller General, the Court should nullify the provision of the Budget and Accounting Act of 1921 giving Congress authority to remove the Comptroller General. The Court rejected this option, concluding that this might make the Comptroller General subservient to the President, a result not intended by Congress.]

VII

No one can doubt that Congress and the President are confronted with fiscal and economic problems of unprecedented magnitude, but "the fact that a given law or procedure is efficient, convenient, and useful in facilitating functions of government, standing alone, will not save it if it is contrary to the Constitution. Convenience and efficiency are not the primary objectives — or the hallmarks — of democratic government . . ." *Chadha, supra,* 462 U.S., at 944.

We conclude the District Court correctly held that the powers vested in the Comptroller General under § 251 violate the command of the Constitution that the Congress play no direct role in the execution of the laws. Accordingly, the judgment and order of the District Court are affirmed.

Our judgment is stayed for a period not to exceed 60 days to permit Congress to implement the fallback provisions.

JUSTICE STEVENS, with whom JUSTICE MARSHALL joins, concurring in the judgment.

[They disagree that the power of Congress to remove the Comptroller General "represents the primary constitutional evil." They disagree also on the attempt to label the functions assigned to the Comptroller General as "executive." They view the statute as unconstitutional because it allows Congress, through the agency of the Comptroller General, to make policy that binds the nation without following the procedures mandated by Article I: passage of a bill by both Houses and presentment of the bill to the President. Stevens and Marshall also reject the premise in the majority opinion that a definite line distinguishes executive power from legislative power.]

. . .

JUSTICE WHITE dissenting.

The Court, acting in the name of separation of powers, takes upon itself to strike down the Gramm-Rudman-Hollings Act, one of the most novel and far-reaching legislative responses to a national crisis since the New Deal. The basis of the Court's action is a solitary provision of another statute that was passed over sixty years ago and has lain dormant since that time. I cannot concur in the Court's action. Like the Court, I will not purport to speak to the wisdom of the policies incorporated in the legislation the Court invalidates; that is a matter for the Congress and the Executive, *both* of which expressed their assent to the statute barely half a year ago. I will, however, address the wisdom of the Court's willingness to interpose its distressingly formalistic view of separation of powers as a bar to the attainment of governmental objectives through the means chosen by the Congress and the President in the legislative process established by the Constitution. Twice in the past four years I have expressed my view that the Court's recent efforts to police the separation of powers have rested on untenable constitutional propositions leading to regrettable results. See *Northern Pipeline Construction Co. v. Marathon Pipe Line Co.,* 458 U.S. 50, 92–118 (1982) (WHITE, J., dissenting); *INS v. Chadha,* 462 U.S. 919, 967–1003. (WHITE, J., dissenting). Today's result is even more misguided....

I

The Court's argument is straightforward: the Act vests the Comptroller General with "executive" powers, that is, powers to "[i]nterpre[t] a law enacted by Congress [in order] to implement the legislative mandate," *ante,* at 733; such powers may not be vested by Congress in itself or its agents, see *Buckley v. Valeo,* 424 U.S. 1, 120–141 (1976), for the system of government established by the Constitution for the most part limits Congress to a legislative rather than an executive or judicial role....

· · ·

It is evident (and nothing in the Court's opinion is to the contrary) that the powers exercised by the Comptroller General under the Gramm-Rudman Act are not such that vesting them in an officer not subject to removal at will by the President would in itself improperly interfere with Presidential powers. Determining the level of spending by the Federal Government is not by nature a function central either to the exercise of the President's enumerated powers or to his general duty to ensure execution of the laws; rather, appropriating funds is a peculiarly legislative function, and one expressly committed to Congress by Art. I, § 9, which provides that "[n]o Money shall be drawn from the Treasury, but in Consequence of Appropriations made by Law." ...

JUSTICE BLACKMUN dissenting.

The Court may be correct when it says that Congress cannot constitutionally exercise removal authority over an official vested with the budget-reduction powers that § 251 of the Balanced Budget and Emergency Deficit Control Act of 1985 gives to the Comptroller General. This, however, is not because "the removal powers over the Comptroller General's office dictate that he will be subservient to Congress," *ante,* at 730; I agree with JUSTICE WHITE that any such claim is unrealistic. Furthermore, I think it is clear under *Humphrey's Executor v. United States,* 295 U.S. 602 (1935), that "executive" powers of the kind delegated to the Comptroller General under the Deficit Control Act need not be exercised by an officer who serves at the President's pleasure; Congress certainly could prescribe the standards and procedures for removing the Comptroller General....

Attorney General Opinion on Ministerial Duties

As early as *Marbury v. Madison* (1803), the Supreme Court distinguished between two types of executive duties: ministerial and discretionary. For the latter, the duty of an executive official and adviser is to the President alone. For ministerial actions, however, the duty is to the statute, and the head of a department acts "under the authority of the law, and not by the instructions of the president. It is a ministerial act which the law enjoins on a particular officer for a particular purpose." 5 U.S. 137, 157. Beginning in 1823, Attorneys General regularly informed Presidents that they had no authority to interfere with certain statutory duties assigned by Congress to executive officers. The opinion below, by Attorney General William Wirt in 1823 (1 Op. Att'y Gen. 624), explains the law on ministerial duties to President Monroe. An opinion by Attorney General Cushing in 1854 (6 Op. Att'y Gen. 326), directed to President Pierce, also summarizes the law on ministerial duties.

SIR: I have examined the case of Major Joseph Wheaton, submitted by you for my opinion; and would proceed at once to the expression of an opinion on the merits of his claims, but that there is a preliminary inquiry which must be first made, and as to which I beg leave to ask your direction; and that is, whether it is proper for you to interfere in this case at all? I will suggest the considerations which strike me as rendering it improper.

I. It appears to me that you have no power to interfere.

The constitution of the United States requires

the President, in general terms, to take care that the laws be faithfully executed; that is, it places the officers engaged in the execution of the laws under his general superintendence: he is to see that they do their duty faithfully; and on their failure, to cause them to be displaced, prosecuted, or impeached, according to the nature of the case. In case of forcible resistance to the laws, too, so as to require the interposition of the power of the government to overcome the illegal resistance, he is to see that that power be furnished. But it could never have been the intention of the constitution, in assigning this general power to the President to take care that the laws be executed, that he should in person execute the laws himself. For example: if a marshal should either refuse to serve process altogether, or serve it irregularly, that the President should correct the irregularity, or supply the omission, by executing the process in person. To interpret this clause of the constitution so as to throw upon the President the duty of a personal interference in every specific case of an alleged or defective execution of the laws, and to call upon him to perform such duties himself, would be not only to require him to perform an impossibility himself, but to take upon himself the responsibility of all the subordinate executive officers of the government — a construction too absurd to be seriously contended for. But the requisition of the constitution is, that he shall *take care* that the *laws* be executed. If the laws, then, require a particular officer by name to perform a duty, not only is that officer bound to perform it, but no other officer can perform it without a violation of the law; and were the President to perform it, he would not only be not taking care that the laws were faithfully executed, but he would be violating them himself. The constitution assigns to Congress the power of designating the duties of particular officers: the President is only required to take care that they execute them faithfully....

Let us carry this principle to the laws which regulate the settlement of public accounts. In the original organization of the Treasury Department (vol. 2, Laws U.S., p. 48,) the duties of the officers are designated specifically. There was one Auditor and one Comptroller. The duty of the Auditor is declared to be to receive all public accounts; and, after examination, to certify the balance, and transmit the accounts, with the vouchers and certificate, to the Comptroller, for his decision thereon; with this *proviso:* that if any person be dissatisfied therewith, he may within six months appeal to the Comptroller against such settlement. Here the right of appeal stops; there is no proviso for an appeal to the President. With regard to the Comptroller, it directs that it shall be his duty to superintend the adjustment and preservation of all public accounts; to examine all accounts settled by the Auditor, and certify the balances arising thereon to the Register: no right of appeal from his decision to the President. With regard to the Register, it directs him "to receive from the Comptroller the accounts which shall have been *finally* adjusted, and to preserve such accounts with their vouchers and certificates." So the act of the 3d March, 1809, (vol. 4, Laws U.S., p. 221, sec. 2,) makes it the duty of the Comptroller to direct the Auditor and accountants forthwith to audit and settle any particular account; and to report such settlement for his revision and *final decision....* Thus, in every instance the decision of the Comptroller is declared to be *final;* and it is manifest that the law contemplates no farther examination by any officer, after such decision....

It would be strange, indeed, if it were otherwise. The office of President is ordained for very different purposes than that of settling individual accounts. The constitution has committed to him the care of the great interests of the nation, in all its foreign and domestic relations. *[For example, the President is charged with being the Commander in Chief, granting pardons, selecting ambassadors, making treaties, and so forth.]* How will it be possible for the President to perform these great duties, if he is also to exercise the appellate power of revising and correcting the settlement of all the individual accounts which pass through the hands of the accounting officers?...

Morrison v. Olson

487 U.S. 654 (1988)

The Ethics in Government Act of 1978, as amended, created an "independent counsel" to investigate high-ranking officials in the executive branch. Under the provisions of the statute, if the Attorney General concludes that the actions of an official exceed a certain

threshold, he or she applies to a panel of three federal judges who are authorized to appoint an independent counsel and to define the counsel's prosecutorial jurisdiction. The Attorney General may remove the independent counsel only "for cause." The statute was challenged in court on a number of constitutional grounds: the appointment power, the removal power, the separation of powers doctrine, and the President's obligation to see that the laws are faithfully executed. In this lawsuit, Independent Counsel Alexia Morrison investigated Theodore B. Olson, a former official with the Department of Justice. The statute was declared unconstitutional by a divided (2 to 1) panel of the D.C. Circuit.

CHIEF JUSTICE REHNQUIST delivered the opinion of the Court.

This case presents us with a challenge to the independent counsel provisions of the Ethics in Government Act of 1978, 28 U.S.C.A. §§ 49, 591 *et seq.* (1982 ed., Supp. V). We hold today that these provisions of the Act do not violate the Appointments Clause of the Constitution, Art. II, § 2, cl. 2, or the limitations of Article III, nor do they impermissibly interfere with the President's authority under Article II in violation of the constitutional principle of separation of powers.

I

Briefly stated, Title VI of the Ethics in Government Act... allows for the appointment of an "independent counsel" to investigate and, if appropriate, prosecute certain high ranking government officials for violations of federal criminal laws. The Act requires the Attorney General, upon receipt of information that he determines is "sufficient to constitute grounds to investigate whether any person [covered by the Act] may have violated any Federal criminal law," to conduct a preliminary investigation of the matter. When the Attorney General has completed this investigation, or 90 days has elapsed, he is required to report to a special court (the Special Division) created by the Act "for the purpose of appointing independent counsels." ... If the Attorney General determines that "there are no reasonable grounds to believe that further investigation is warranted," then he must notify the Special Division of this result. In such a case, "the division of the court shall have no power to appoint an independent counsel." § 592(b)(1). If, however, the Attorney General has determined that there are "reasonable grounds to believe that further investigation or prosecution is warranted," then he "shall apply to the division of the court for the appointment of an independent counsel." The Attorney General's application to the court "shall contain sufficient information to assist the [court] in selecting an independent counsel and in defining that independent counsel's prosecutorial jurisdiction."

§ 592(d). Upon receiving this application, the Special Division "shall appoint an appropriate independent counsel and shall define that independent counsel's prosecutorial jurisdiction." § 593(b).

With respect to all matters within the independent counsel's jurisdiction, the Act grants the counsel "full power and independent authority to exercise all investigative and prosecutorial functions and powers of the Department of Justice, the Attorney General, and any other officer or employee of the Department of Justice." § 594(a). The functions of the independent counsel include conducting grand jury proceedings and other investigations, participating in civil and criminal court proceedings and litigation, and appealing any decision in any case in which the counsel participates in an official capacity. §§ 594(a)(1)–(3)....

Two statutory provisions govern the length of an independent counsel's tenure in office. The first defines the procedure for removing an independent counsel. Section 596(a)(1) provides:

"An independent counsel appointed under this chapter may be removed from office, other than by impeachment and conviction, only by the personal action of the Attorney General and only for good cause, physical disability, mental incapacity, or any other condition that substantially impairs the performance of such independent counsel's duties."

If an independent counsel is removed pursuant to this section, the Attorney General is required to submit a report to both the Special Division and the Judiciary Committees of the Senate and the House "specifying the facts found and the ultimate grounds for such removal." § 596(a)(2)....

The other provision governing the tenure of the independent counsel defines the procedures for "terminating" the counsel's office. Under § 596(b)(1), the office of an independent counsel terminates when he notifies the Attorney General that he has completed or substantially completed any investigations or prosecutions undertaken pursuant to the Act. In addition, the Special Division, acting either on its own or on the suggestion of the Attorney General, may terminate the office of an independent counsel at any time if it finds that "the investigation of all matters within the prosecutorial jurisdiction of such independent counsel...have been completed or so substantially completed that it would be appropriate for the Department of Justice to complete such investigations and prosecutions." § 596(b)(2).

[Here the Court reviews the developments that led to the appointment of Alexia Morrison to investigate Theodore B. Olson. A report by the House Judiciary Committee in 1985 suggested that Mr. Olson, in his capacity as Assistant Attorney General for the Office of Legal Counsel, had given false and misleading testimony to Congress. After the committee requested the Attorney General to seek the appointment of an independent counsel to investigate the allegations against Olson and after the Attorney General completed a preliminary investigation, the Attorney General sought the appointment of an independent counsel and Ms. Morrison was selected.]

III

The Appointments Clause of Article II reads as follows:

"[The President] shall nominate, and by and with the Advice and Consent of the Senate, shall appoint Ambassadors, other public Ministers and Consuls, Judges of the Supreme Court, and all other Officers of the United States, whose Appointments are not herein otherwise provided for, and which shall be established by Law: but the Congress may by Law vest the Appointment of such inferior Officers, as they think proper, in the President alone, in the Courts of Law, or in the Heads of Departments." U.S. Const., Art. II, § 2, cl. 2.

The parties do not dispute that "[t]he Constitution for purposes of appointment...divides all its officers into two classes." *United States* v. *Germaine,* 99 U.S. (9 Otto) 508, 509 (1879). As we stated in *Buckley* v. *Valeo,* 424 U.S. 1, 132 (1976), "[p]rincipal officers are selected by the President with the advice and consent of the Senate. Inferior officers Congress may allow to be appointed by the President alone, by the heads of departments, or by the Judiciary." The initial question is, accordingly, whether appellant is an "inferior" or a "principal" officer. If she is the lat-

ter, as the Court of Appeals concluded, then the Act is in violation of the Appointments Clause.

The line between "inferior" and "principal" officers is one that is far from clear, and the Framers provided little guidance into where it should be drawn.... We need not attempt here to decide exactly where the line falls between the two types of officers, because in our view appellant clearly falls on the "inferior officer" side of that line. Several factors lead to this conclusion.

First, appellant is subject to removal by a higher Executive Branch official. Although appellant may not be "subordinate" to the Attorney General (and the President) insofar as she possesses a degree of independent discretion to exercise the powers delegated to her under the Act, the fact that she can be removed by the Attorney General indicates that she is to some degree "inferior" in rank and authority. Second, appellant is empowered by the Act to perform only certain, limited duties. An independent counsel's role is restricted primarily to investigation and, if appropriate, prosecution for certain federal crimes.... [T]his grant of authority does not include any authority to formulate policy for the Government or the Executive Branch....

Third, appellant's office is limited in jurisdiction. Not only is the Act itself restricted in applicability to certain federal officials suspected of certain serious federal crimes, but an independent counsel can only act within the scope of the jurisdiction that has been granted by the Special Division pursuant to a request by the Attorney General. Finally, appellant's office is limited in tenure. There is concededly no time limit on the appointment of a particular counsel. Nonetheless, the office of independent counsel is "temporary" in the sense that an independent counsel is appointed essentially to accomplish a single task, and when that task is over the office is terminated, either by the counsel herself or by action of the Special Division.... In our view, these factors relating to the "ideas of tenure, duration...and duties" of the independent counsel, *Germaine, supra,* at 511, are sufficient to establish that appellant is an "inferior" officer in the constitutional sense.

. . .

This does not, however, end our inquiry under the Appointments Clause. Appellees argue that even if appellant is an "inferior" officer, the Clause does not empower Congress to place the power to appoint such an officer outside the Executive Branch. They contend that the Clause does not contemplate congressional authorization of "interbranch appointments," in which an officer of one branch is appointed by officers of another branch. The relevant language of the Appointments Clause is worth repeating. It reads: "...but the Congress may by Law vest the Appointment of such inferior Officers, as they think proper, in the President alone, in the courts of Law, or in the Heads of Departments." On its face, the language of this "excepting clause" admits of no limitation on interbranch appointments. Indeed, the inclusion of "as they think proper" seems clearly to give Congress significant discretion to determine whether it is "proper" to vest the appointment of, for example, executive officials in the "courts of Law."...

We do not mean to say that Congress' power to provide for interbranch appointments of "inferior officers" is unlimited. In addition to separation of powers concerns, which would arise if such provisions for appointment had the potential to impair the constitutional functions assigned to one of the branches, *Siebold* itself suggested that Congress' decision to vest the appointment power in the courts would be improper if there was some "incongruity" between the functions normally performed by the courts and the performance of their duty to appoint.... We have recognized that courts may appoint private attorneys to act as prosecutor for judicial contempt judgments. See *Young* v. *United States ex rel. Vuitton et Fils S.A.,* 481 U.S. 787 (1987)....

IV

Appellees next contend that the powers vested in the Special Division by the Act conflict with Article III of the Constitution.... As a general rule, we have broadly stated that "executive or administrative duties of a nonjudicial nature may not be imposed on judges holding office under Art. III of the Constitution." *Buckley,* 424 U.S., at 123.... The purpose of this limitation is to help ensure the independence of the Judicial Branch and to prevent the judiciary from encroaching into areas reserved for the other branches....

Most importantly, the Act vests in the Special Division the power to choose who will serve as independent counsel and the power to define his or her jurisdiction. § 593(b). Clearly, once it is accepted that the Appointments Clause gives Congress the power to vest the appointment of officials such as the independent counsel in the "courts of Law," there can be no Article III objection to the Special Division's exercise of that

power, as the power itself derives from the Appointments Clause, a source of authority for judicial action that is independent of Article III. Appellees contend, however, that the Division's Appointments Clause powers do not encompass the power to define the independent counsel's jurisdiction. We disagree. In our view, Congress' power under the Clause to vest the "Appointment" of inferior officers in the courts may, in certain circumstances, allow Congress to give the courts some discretion in defining the nature and scope of the appointed official's authority....

We are more doubtful about the special Division's power to terminate the office of the independent counsel pursuant to § 596(b)(2). As appellees suggest, the power to terminate, especially when exercised by the Division on its own motion, is "administrative" to the extent that it requires the Special Division to monitor the progress of proceedings of the independent counsel and come to a decision as to whether the counsel's job is "completed." § 596(b)(2). It also is not a power that could be considered typically "judicial," as it has few analogues among the court's more traditional powers. Nonetheless, we do not, as did the Court of Appeals, view this provision as a significant judicial encroachment upon executive power or upon the prosecutorial discretion of the independent counsel.

...As we see it, "termination" may occur only when the duties of the counsel are truly "completed" or "so substantially completed" that there remains no need for any continuing action by the independent counsel. It is basically a device for removing from the public payroll an independent counsel who has served her purpose, but is unwilling to acknowledge the fact. So construed, the Special Division's power to terminate does not pose a sufficient threat of judicial intrusion into matters that are more properly within the Executive's authority to require that the Act be invalidated as inconsistent with Article III.

· · ·

V

We now turn to consider whether the Act is invalid under the constitutional principle of separation of powers. Two related issues must be addressed: The first is whether the provision of the Act restricting the Attorney General's power to remove the independent counsel to only those instances in which he can show "good cause," taken by itself, impermissibly interferes with the President's exercise of his constitutionally appointed functions. The second is whether, taken as a whole, the Act violates the separation of powers by reducing the President's ability to control the prosecutorial powers wielded by the independent counsel.

A

Two Terms ago we had occasion to consider whether it was consistent with the separation of powers for Congress to pass a statute that authorized a government official who is removable only by Congress to participate in what we found to be "executive powers." *Bowsher* v. *Synar,* 478 U.S. 714, 730 (1986). We held in *Bowsher* that "Congress cannot reserve for itself the power of removal of an officer charged with the execution of the laws except by impeachment." *Id.,* at 726. A primary antecedent for this ruling was our 1926 decision in *Myers* v. *United States,* 272 U.S. 52 (1926)....

Unlike both *Bowsher* and *Myers,* this case does not involve an attempt by Congress itself to gain a role in the removal of executive officials other than its established powers of impeachment and conviction. The Act instead puts the removal power squarely in the hands of the Executive Branch; an independent counsel may be removed from office, "only by the personal action of the Attorney General, and only for good cause." ...In our view, the removal provisions of the Act make this case more analogous to *Humphrey's Executor* v. *United States,* 295 U.S. 602 (1935), and *Wiener* v. *United States,* 357 U.S. 349 (1958), than to *Myers* or *Bowsher.*

. . .

Considering for the moment the "good cause" removal provision in isolation from the other parts of the Act at issue in this case, we cannot say that the imposition of a "good cause" standard for removal by itself unduly trammels on executive authority. There is no real dispute that the functions performed by the independent counsel are "executive" in the sense that they are law enforcement functions that typically have been undertaken by officials within the Executive Branch. As we noted above, however, the independent counsel is an inferior officer under the Appointments Clause, with limited jurisdiction and tenure and lacking policymaking or significant administrative authority. Although the counsel exercises no small amount of discretion and judgment in deciding how to carry out her duties under the Act, we simply do not see how the President's need to control the exercise of that discretion is so

central to the functioning of the Executive Branch as to require as a matter of constitutional law that the counsel be terminable at will by the President.

. . .

B

The final question to be addressed is whether the Act, taken as a whole, violates the principle of separation of powers by unduly interfering with the role of the Executive Branch....

We observe first that this case does not involve an attempt by Congress to increase its own powers at the expense of the Executive Branch. ... Unlike some of our previous cases, most recently *Bowsher* v. *Synar,* this case simply does not pose a "dange[r] of congressional usurpation of Executive Branch functions." 478 U.S., at 727; see also *INS* v. *Chadha,* 462 U.S. 919, 958 (1983)....

Similarly, we do not think that the Act works any *judicial* usurpation of properly executive functions. As should be apparent from our discussion of the Appointments Clause above, the power to appoint inferior officers such as independent counsels is not in itself an "executive" function in the constitutional sense, at least when Congress has exercised its power to vest the appointment of an inferior office in the "courts of Law."...

Finally, we do not think that the Act "impermissibly undermine[s]" the powers of the Executive Branch, *Schor, supra,* 478 U.S., at 856, or "disrupts the proper balance between the coordinate branches [by].prevent[ing] the Executive Branch from accomplishing its constitutionally assigned functions," *Nixon* v. *Administrator of General Services, supra,* 433 U.S., at 443. It is undeniable that the Act reduces the amount of control or supervision that the Attorney General and, through him, the President exercises over the investigation and prosecution of a certain class of alleged criminal activity. The Attorney General is not allowed to appoint the individual of his choice; he does not determine the counsel's jurisdiction; and his power to remove a counsel is limited. Nonetheless, the Act does give the Attorney General several means of supervising or controlling the prosecutorial powers that may be wielded by an independent counsel. Most importantly, the Attorney General retains the power to remove the counsel for "good cause," ...Notwithstanding the fact that the counsel is to some degree "independent" and free from Executive supervision to a greater extent than other federal prosecutors, in our view these features of the Act give the Executive Branch sufficient control over the independent counsel to ensure that the President is able to perform his constitutionally assigned duties.

. . .

Reversed.

JUSTICE KENNEDY took no part in the consideration or decision of this case.

JUSTICE SCALIA, dissenting.

. . . [T]he founders conspicuously and very consciously declined to sap the executive's strength in the same way they had weakened the legislature: by dividing the executive power. Proposals to have multiple executives, or a council of advisors with separate authority were rejected. . . . Thus, while "[a]ll legislative Powers herein granted shall be vested in a Congress of the United States, which shall consist of a Senate *and* House of Representatives," U.S. Const., Art I, § 1 (emphasis added), "[t]he executive Power shall be vested in *a President of the United States,*" Art. II, § 1, cl. 1 (emphasis added).

That is what this suit is about. Power. The allocation of power among Congress, the President and the courts in such fashion as to preserve the equilibrium the Constitution sought to establish — so that "a gradual concentration of the several powers in the same department," Federalist No. 51, p. 321 (J. Madison), can effectively be resisted. Frequently an issue of this sort will come before the Court clad, so to speak, in sheep's clothing: the potential of the asserted principle to effect important change in the equilibrium of power is not immediately evident, and must be discerned by a careful and perceptive analysis. But this wolf comes as a wolf.

I

[In this section, Justice Scalia reviews the history of Congress' investigation of the EPA scandal and concludes that the Attorney General, as a "practical matter," had no choice but to seek the appointment of an independent counsel to prosecute Olson.]

II

. . .

"The executive Power shall be vested in a President of the United States."

As I described at the outset of this opinion, this does not mean *some of* the executive power, but *all of* the executive power. It seems to me, therefore, that the decision of the Court of Appeals invalidating the present statute must be upheld on fundamental separation-of-powers principles if the following two questions are answered affirmatively: (1) Is the conduct of a criminal prosecution (and of an investigation to decide whether to prosecute) the exercise of purely executive power? (2) Does the statute deprive the President of the United States of exclusive control over the exercise of that power? Surprising to say, the Court appears to concede an affirmative answer to both questions, but seeks to avoid the inevitable conclusion that since the statute vests some purely executive power in a person who is not the President of the United States it is void.

The Court concedes that "[t]here is no real dispute that the functions performed by the independent counsel are "executive'," though it qualifies that concession by adding "in the sense that they are "law enforcement' functions that typically have been undertaken by officials within the Executive Branch." *Ante,* at 691. The qualifier adds nothing but atmosphere. In what *other* sense can one identify "the executive Power" that is supposed to be vested in the President (unless it includes everything the Executive Branch is given to do) *except* by reference to what has always and everywhere — if conducted by Government at all — been conducted never by the legislature, never by the courts, and always by the executive. . . .

As for the second question, whether the statute before us deprives the President of exclusive control over that quintessentially executive activity: The Court does not, and could not possibly, assert that it does not. That is indeed the whole object of the statute. Instead, the Court points out that the President, through his Attorney General, has at least *some* control. That concession is alone enough to invalidate the statute, but I cannot refrain from pointing out that the Court greatly exaggerates the extent of that "some" presidential control. "Most importan[t]" among these controls, the Court asserts, is the Attorney General's "power to remove the counsel for 'good cause.' " *Ante,* at 696. This is somewhat like referring to shackles as an effective means of locomotion. . . .

. . . It effects a revolution in our constitutional jurisprudence for the Court, once it has determined that (1) purely executive functions are at issue here, and (2) those functions have been given to a person whose actions are not fully within the supervision and control of the President, nonetheless to proceed further to sit in judgment of whether "the President's need to control the exercise of [the independent counsel's] discretion is *so central* to the functioning of the Executive Branch" as to require complete control, *ante,* at 691 (emphasis added), whether the conferral of his powers upon someone else *"sufficiently* deprives the President of control over the independent counsel to interfere impermissibly with [his] constitutional obligation to ensure the faithful execution of the laws," *ante,* at 693 (emphasis added), and whether "the Act give[s] the Executive Branch *sufficient* control over the independent counsel to ensure that the President is able to perform his constitutionally assigned duties," *ante,* at 696 (emphasis added). It is not for us to determine, and we have never presumed to determine, how much of the purely executive powers of government must be within the full control of the President. The Constitution prescribes that they *all* are.

The utter incompatibility of the Court's approach with our constitutional traditions can be made more clear, perhaps, by applying it to the powers of the other two Branches. Is it conceivable that if Congress passed a statute depriving itself of less than full and entire control over some insignificant area of legislation, we would inquire whether the matter was *"so central* to the functioning of the Legislative Branch" as really to require complete control, or whether the statute gives Congress *"sufficient* control over the surrogate legislator to ensure that Congress is able to perform its constitutionally assigned duties"? Of course we would have none of that. Once we determined that a purely legislative power was at issue we would require it to be exercised, wholly and entirely, by Congress. Or to bring the point closer to home, consider a statute giving to non-Article III judges just a tiny bit of purely judicial power in a relatively insignificant field, with substantial control, though not total control, in the courts—perhaps "clear error" review, which would be a fair judicial equivalent of the Attorney General's "for cause" removal power here. Is there any doubt that we would not pause to inquire whether the matter was *"so central* to the functioning of the Judicial Branch" as really to require complete control, or whether we retained *"sufficient* control over the matters to be decided that we are able to perform our constitutionally assigned duties"? We would say that our "constitutionally assigned duties" include *complete* control over all exercises of the judicial power—or, as the plurality opinion said in *Northern Pipeline Construction Co.* v. *Marathon Pipe Line Co.,* 458 U.S. 50, 58–59 (1982), that "[t]he inexorable command of [Article III] is clear and definite: The

judicial power of the United States must be exercised by courts having the attributes prescribed in Art. III."...

. . .

[In Sections III and IV, Scalia concludes that the independent counsel is a principal (not inferior) officer and, therefore, must be nominated by the President and confirmed by the Senate, and he agrees with the lower court's decision that the restrictions placed on the removal of the independent counsel violate established precedent.]

V

The purpose of the separation and equilibration of powers in general, and of the unitary Executive in particular, was not merely to assure effective government but to preserve individual freedom. Those who hold or have held offices covered by the Ethics in Government Act are entitled to that protection as much as the rest of us, and I conclude my discussion by considering the effect of the Act upon the fairness of the process they receive.

Only someone who has worked in the field of law enforcement can fully appreciate the vast power and the immense discretion that are placed in the hands of a prosecutor with respect to the objects of his investigation....

Under our system of government, the primary check against prosecutorial abuse is a political one. The prosecutors who exercise this awesome discretion are selected and can be removed by a President, whom the people have trusted enough to elect. Moreover, when crimes are not investigated and prosecuted fairly, nonselectively, with a reasonable sense of proportion, the President pays the cost in political damage to his administration. If federal prosecutors "pick people that [they] thin[k] [they] should get, rather than cases that need to be prosecuted," if they amass many more resources against a particular prominent individual, or against a particular class of political protestors, or against members of a particular political party, than the gravity of the alleged offenses or the record of successful prosecutions seems to warrant, the unfairness will come home to roost in the Oval Office. I leave it to the reader to recall the examples of this in recent years. That result, of course, was precisely what the Founders had in mind when they provided that all executive powers would be exercised by a *single* Chief Executive....

...How frightening it must be to have your own independent counsel and staff appointed, with nothing else to do but to investigate you until investigation is no longer worthwhile—with whether it is worthwhile not depending upon what such judgments usually hinge on, competing responsibilities. And to have that counsel and staff decide, with no basis for comparison, whether what you have done is bad enough, willful enough, and provable enough, to warrant an indictment. How admirable the constitutional system that provides the means to avoid such a distortion. And how unfortunate the judicial decision that has permitted it.

. . .

D. APPOINTMENTS AND REMOVALS

Three steps are required to fill offices created by Congress: (1) nomination by the President, (2) confirmation by the Senate, and (3) commissioning of the appointee by the President. For lesser officers, the Constitution permits Congress to dispense with the confirmation process and place the power of appointment directly in the President, the courts, or department heads.

In legal theory, the power to nominate is the "sole act of the president" and "completely voluntary." Marbury v. Madison, 5 U.S. at 155. Congress cannot designate the person to fill the office it creates. United States v. Ferreira, 54 U.S. (13 How.) 39, 50–51 (1852); Myers v. United States, 272 U.S. at 128. Nevertheless, it can stipulate the qualifications of appointees, and legislators frequently select the names of judges, U.S. attorneys, and marshals for their state. In such cases, the roles are reversed: Congress nominates and the President "advises and consents." If the names submitted by Congress are unacceptable, the White House and the Justice Department can object and request substitute proposals. Interest groups and professional organizations are also active in submitting names for consideration and evaluating those who are nominated.

There are limits to congressional intervention. In 1976 the Supreme Court reviewed a statute giving Congress the power to appoint four members to the Federal Election Commission, which monitors the financing and conduct of congressional and presidential elections. All six voting members (including two nominated by the President) required confirmation by the majority of *both* Houses of Congress. The Court ruled that Congress could not select officers responsible for carrying out executive and judicial duties. Such functions could be exercised only by "Officers of the United States" appointed pursuant to Article II, Section 2, Clause 2. For the Court, this meant either one of two constitutional options: nomination by the President, subject to the advice and consent of the Senate; or vesting the appointment power in the President alone, in the courts of law, or in department heads. Congress took the first option when it rewrote the statute. The decision explains how the appointment process is related to presidential responsibility and the separation doctrine. BUCKLEY v. VALEO, 424 U.S. 1 (1976).[9]

In *Buckley* v. *Valeo*, the Court noted that if an agency's powers are "essentially of an investigative and informative nature," Congress can appoint the agency officials. In reauthorizing the Civil Rights Commission in 1983, Congress passed legislation that gave it the right to appoint four of the eight members of the Commission. The President appointed the remaining four. 97 Stat. 1301 (1983). In signing the bill, President Reagan recognized that Con-

---

9. For recent analyses of the Appointments Clause, see Olympic Federal Savings and Loan Assn. v. Director, Office of Thrift Supervision, 732 F.Supp. 1183 (D.D.C. 1990), Freytag v. Commissioner, 501 U.S. 868 (1991), and Edmond v. United States, 520 U.S. 661 (1997).

Congressional Appointment of Executive Officials That Investigate

[*President Reagan's statement on signing the U.S. Commission on Civil Rights Act of 1983*]:

I have signed today H.R. 2230, establishing a new Commission on Civil Rights....

The bill I have signed today is, of course, a product of negotiation and compromise. While, as noted, I am pleased that the Commission has been re-created so that it may continue the missions assigned to it, the Department of Justice has raised concerns as to the constitutional implications of certain provisions of this legislation. I have appended a recitation of these reservations.

. . .

Statement by the Department of Justice

...The basic purpose of the old Commission on Civil Rights—to investigate, study, ap-

praise, and report on discrimination—would be maintained, and most of its current authorities would remain intact. However, because half of the members of the Commission will be appointed by the Congress, the Constitution does not permit the Commission to exercise responsibilities that may be performed only by "Officers of the United States" who are appointed in accordance with the Appointments Clause of the United States Constitution (Article II, Section 2, clause 2). Therefore, it should be clear that although the Commission will continue to perform investigative and informative functions, it may not exercise enforcement, regulatory, or other executive responsibilities that may be performed only by officers of the United States.

SOURCE: Public Papers of the Presidents, 1983 (II), at 1634–35.

gress operated within its powers because the essential functions of the Civil Rights Commission were investigative (see box).

Recess Appointments

The framers recognized that the Senate would not always be in session to give advice and consent to presidential nominations. To cover these periods, the President is authorized to make recess appointments: "The President shall have Power to fill up all Vacancies that may happen during the Recess of the Senate, by granting Commissions which shall expire at the End of their next Session" (Article II, Section 3, Clause 3). "Happen" is interpreted broadly to mean "happen to exist," even if a vacancy occurs while the Senate is in session. 1 Op. Att'y Gen. 631 (1823). The meaning of "recess" remains uncertain, although the Justice Department agrees that adjournments "for 5 or even 10 days" are too short to justify the use of the recess power. 3 Op. Att'y Gen. 20, 25 (1921); 3 O.L.C. 311, 314 (1979).

In 1863, when it appeared that Presidents were abusing the power to make recess appointments and were deliberately circumventing the Senate's confirmation role, Congress passed legislation to prohibit the use of funds to pay the salary of anyone appointed during a Senate recess to fill a vacancy that existed "while the Senate was in session and is by law required to be filled by and with the advice and consent of the Senate, until such appointee shall have been confirmed by the Senate." 12 Stat. 646 (1863). The law was liberalized in 1940 to permit payment under three conditions. 54 Stat. 751 (1940); 5 U.S.C. § 5503 (1994). Legislation has also been passed to prohibit funds to pay the salary of any recess appointee who is later rejected by the Senate. E.g., 113 Stat. 467, § 609 (1999); Fisher, Constitutional Conflicts 38–45. See also Chapter 4, pp. 132–33.

Removing Officials

Although the Constitution provides no express authority for the President to remove officials in the executive branch, it was agreed by the First Congress that responsible government requires the President to dismiss incompetent, corrupt, or unreliable administrators. If anything by nature is executive, Madison said, "it must be that power which is employed in superintending and seeing that the laws are faithfully executed." 1 Annals of Congress 500 (June 17, 1789).

These debates of 1789 were interpreted by Chief Justice Taft to leave not the "slightest doubt" that the power to remove officers appointed by the President and confirmed by the Senate is "vested in the President alone." MYERS v. UNITED STATES, 272 U.S. at 114. Taft reached too far; the debates reveal deep divisions among House members and close votes on the Senate side. Fisher, Constitutional Conflicts 49–54. Moreover, the debates in 1789 focused on the President's power to remove the Secretary of Foreign Affairs, which Congress conceded to be an agent of the President and executive in nature. Madison anticipated other types of officers in the executive branch who might have a mix of legislative and judicial duties, requiring greater independence from the President. 1 Annals of Congress 611–14 (June 29, 1789). See box on p. 184. Congress can place statutory limitations on the removal power, and the Supreme Court had recognized, before Taft made his sweeping claim, that Congress could identify the grounds for removal. Shurtleff v. United States, 189 U.S. 311 (1903).

A balance must be struck between the President's authority to remove executive officials and Congress's power under the Necessary and Proper Clause to create an office and attach conditions to it. Taft's decision was later modified to permit Congress to limit the President's power to remove commissioners with quasi-legislative and quasi-judicial powers. HUMPHREY'S EXECUTOR v. UNITED STATES 295 U.S. 602 (1935); Wiener v. United States, 357 U.S. 349 (1958). Depending on statutory language or commitments by the President and his subordinates to maintain an officer's independence, presidential power to remove officers may face other constraints.[10]

Beyond the occasional lawsuit are the more frequent interventions by Congress. Congress may remove an individual by abolishing the office. A term of office created by one statute can be reduced or eliminated by a subsequent statute, requiring the discharge of a federal employee. Crenshaw v. United States, 134 U.S. 99 (1890). Through the passage of nonbinding resolutions, committee investigations, the contempt power, and other pressures, Congress can precipitate a person's resignation or removal. Congress also intervenes to *protect* an officeholder, particularly a "whistleblower" who alerts Congress to agency deficiencies. Members intervene for reasons of simple justice and keeping open the channels of communication between agencies and Congress. Louis Fisher, "Congress and the Removal Power," 10 Congress & the Presidency 63 (1983).

Buckley v. Valeo

424 U.S. 1 (1976)

As part of the Federal Election Campaign Act amendments of 1974, which responded to the scandals during the election of 1972, Congress enacted a number of reforms, including the creation of the Federal Election Commission (FEC). Because Congress appointed some of the commissioners, the Supreme Court reviewed the framers' intent with respect to the

---

10. Nader v. Bork, 366 F.Supp. 104 (D.D.C. 1973); Borders v. Reagan, 518 F.Supp. 250 (D.D.C. 1981); Stephen Gettinger, "The Power Struggle Over Federal Parole," 8 Corrections Magazine 41 (1982); Berry v. Reagan, Civil Action No. 83-3182 (D.D.C. November 14, 1983).

Appointments Clause and the separation of powers theory. Senator James Buckley was one of several plaintiffs who brought this action against Francis Valeo, Secretary of the Senate.

PER CURIAM.

These appeals present constitutional challenges to the key provisions of the Federal Election Campaign Act of 1971 (Act), and related provisions of the Internal Revenue Code of 1954, all as amended in 1974.

. . .

IV. THE FEDERAL ELECTION COMMISSION

The 1974 amendments to the Act create an eight-member Federal Election Commission (Commission) and vest in it primary and substantial responsibility for administering and enforcing the Act. The question that we address in this portion of the opinion is whether, in view of the manner in which a majority of its members are appointed, the Commission may under the Constitution exercise the powers conferred upon it....

Chapter 14 of Title 2 makes the Commission the principal repository of the numerous reports and statements which are required by that chapter to be filed by those engaging in the regulated political activities. Its duties under § 438 (a) with respect to these reports and statements include filing and indexing, making them available for public inspection, preservation, and auditing and field investigations. It is directed to "serve as a national clearinghouse for information in respect to the administration of elections." § 438 (b).

Beyond these recordkeeping, disclosure, and investigative functions, however, the Commission is given extensive rulemaking and adjudicative powers. Its duty under § 438 (a)(10) is "to prescribe suitable rules and regulations to carry out the provisions of...chapter [14]." Under § 437d (a)(8) the Commission is empowered to make such rules "as are necessary to carry out the provisions of this Act." Section 437d(a)(9) authorizes it to "formulate general policy with respect to the administration of this Act" and enumerates sections of Title 18's Criminal Code, as to all of which provisions the Commission "has primary jurisdiction with respect to [their] civil enforcement." § 437c (b). The Commission is authorized under § 437f(a) to render advisory opinions with respect to activities possibly violating the Act, the Title 18 sections, or the campaign funding provisions of Title 26, the effect of which is that "[n]otwithstanding any other provision of law, any person with respect to whom an advisory opinion is rendered...who acts in good faith in accordance with the provisions and findings [thereof] shall be presumed to be in compliance with the [statutory provision] with respect to which such advisory opinion is rendered." § 437f(b). In the course of administering the provisions for Presidential campaign financing, the Commission may authorize convention expenditures which exceed the statutory limits....

The Commission's enforcement power is both direct and wide ranging. It may institute a civil action for (i) injunctive or other relief against "any acts or practices which constitute or will constitute a violation of this Act," § 437g (a)(5); (ii) declaratory or injunctive relief "as may be appropriate to implement or con[s]true any provisions" of Chapter 95 of Title 26, governing administration of funds for Presidential election campaigns and national party conventions...and (iii) "such injunctive relief as is appropriate to implement any provision" of Chapter 96 of Title 26, governing the payment of matching funds for Presidential primary campaigns.... If after the Commission's postdisbursement audit of candidates receiving payments under Chapter 95 or 96 it finds an overpayment, it is empowered to seek repayment of all funds due the Secretary of the Treasury.... In no respect do the foregoing civil actions require the concurrence of or participation by the Attorney General; conversely, the decision not to seek judicial relief in the above respects would appear to rest solely with the Commission. With respect to the referenced Title 18 sections, § 437g (a)(7) provides that if, after notice and opportunity for a hearing before it, the Commission finds an actual or threatened criminal violation, the Attorney General "upon request by the Commission...shall institute a civil action for relief." Finally, as "[a]dditional enforcement authority," § 456 (a) authorizes the Commission, after notice and opportunity for hearing, to make "a finding that a person...while a candidate for Federal office, failed to file" a required report of contributions or expenditures. If that finding is made within the applicable limitations period for prosecutions, the candidate is thereby "disqualified from becoming a candidate in any future election for Federal office for a period of time beginning on the date of such finding and ending one year after the expiration of the term of the Federal office for which such person was a candidate."

The body in which this authority is reposed

consists of eight members. The Secretary of the Senate and the Clerk of the House of Representatives are *ex officio* members of the Commission without the right to vote. Two members are appointed by the President *pro tempore* of the Senate "upon the recommendations of the majority leader of the Senate and the minority leader of the Senate." Two more are to be appointed by the Speaker of the House of Representatives, likewise upon the recommendations of its respective majority and minority leaders. The remaining two members are appointed by the President. Each of the six voting members of the Commission must be confirmed by the majority of both Houses of Congress, and each of the three appointing authorities is forbidden to choose both of their appointees from the same political party.

. . .

[After concluding that the Commission's composition was ripe for review, the Court analyzed the substantive issues.]

B. The Merits

Appellants urge that since Congress has given the Commission wide-ranging rulemaking and enforcement powers with respect to the substantive provisions of the Act, Congress is precluded under the principle of separation of powers from vesting in itself the authority to appoint those who will exercise such authority. Their argument is based on the language of Art. II, § 2, cl. 2, of the Constitution, which provides in pertinent part as follows:

"[The President] shall nominate, and by and with the Advice and Consent of the Senate, shall appoint . . . all other Officers of the United States, whose Appointments are not herein otherwise provided for, and which shall be established by Law: but the Congress may by Law vest the Appointment of such inferior Officers, as they think proper, in the President alone, in the Courts of Law, or in the Heads of Departments."

Appellants' argument is that this provision is the exclusive method by which those charged with executing the laws of the United States may be chosen. Congress, they assert, cannot have it both ways. If the Legislature wishes the Commission to exercise all of the conferred powers, then its members are in fact "Officers of the United States" and must be appointed under the Appointments Clause. But if Congress insists upon retaining the power to appoint, then the members of the Commission may not discharge those many functions

of the Commission which can be performed only by "Officers of the United States," as that term must be construed within the doctrine of separation of powers.

Appellee Commission and *amici* in support of the Commission urge that the Framers of the Constitution, while mindful of the need for checks and balances among the three branches of the National Government, had no intention of denying to the Legislative Branch authority to appoint its own officers. Congress, either under the Appointments Clause or under its grants of substantive legislative authority and the Necessary and Proper Clause in Art. I, is in their view empowered to provide for the appointment to the Commission in the manner which it did because the Commission is performing "appropriate legislative functions."

. . .

1. Separation of Powers

We do not think appellants' arguments based upon Art. II, § 2, cl. 2, of the Constitution may be so easily dismissed as did the majority of the Court of Appeals. Our inquiry of necessity touches upon the fundamental principles of the Government established by the Framers of the Constitution, and all litigants and all of the courts which have addressed themselves to the matter start on common ground in the recognition of the intent of the Framers that the powers of the three great branches of the National Government be largely separate from one another.

. . . [T]he Constitution by no means contemplates total separation of each of these three essential branches of Government. The President is a participant in the lawmaking process by virtue of his authority to veto bills enacted by Congress. The Senate is a participant in the appointive process by virtue of its authority to refuse to confirm persons nominated to office by the President. The men who met in Philadelphia in the summer of 1787 were practical statesmen, experienced in politics, who viewed the principle of separation of powers as a vital check against tyranny. But they likewise saw that a hermetic sealing off of the three branches of Government from one another would preclude the establishment of a Nation capable of governing itself effectively.

. . .

2. The Appointments Clause

The principle of separation of powers was not

simply an abstract generalization in the minds of the Framers: it was woven into the document that they drafted in Philadelphia in the summer of 1787....

It is in the context of these cognate provisions of the document that we must examine the language of Art. II. § 2, cl. 2, which appellants contend provides the only authorization for appointment of those to whom substantial executive or administrative authority is given by statute. Because of the importance of its language, we again set out the provision:

"[The President] shall nominate, and by and with the Advice and Consent of the Senate, shall appoint Ambassadors, other public Ministers and Consuls, Judges of the supreme Court, and all other Officers of the United States, whose Appointments are not herein otherwise provided for, and which shall be established by Law: but the Congress may by Law vest the Appointment of such inferior Officers, as they think proper, in the President alone, in the Courts of Law, or in the Heads of Departments."

The Appointments Clause could, of course, be read as merely dealing with etiquette or protocol in describing "Officers of the United States," but the drafters had a less frivolous purpose in mind....

We think that the term "Officers of the United States" ... is a term intended to have substantive meaning. We think its fair import is that any appointee exercising significant authority pursuant to the laws of the United States is an "Officer of the United States," and must, therefore, be appointed in the manner prescribed by § 2, cl. 2, of that Article.

. . .

Although two members of the Commission are initially selected by the President, his nominations are subject to confirmation not merely by the Senate, but by the House of Representatives as well. The remaining four voting members of the Commission are appointed by the President *pro tempore* of the Senate and by the Speaker of the House. While the second part of the Clause authorizes Congress to vest the appointment of the officers described in that part in "the Courts of Law, or in the Heads of Departments," neither the Speaker of the House nor the President *pro tempore* of the Senate comes within this language.

The phrase "Heads of Departments," used as it is in conjunction with the phrase "Courts of Law," suggests that the Departments referred to are themselves in the Executive Branch or at least have some connection with that branch. While the Clause expressly authorizes Congress to vest the appointment of certain officers in the "Courts of Law," the absence of similar language to include Congress must mean that neither Congress nor its officers were included within the language "Heads of Departments" in this part of cl. 2.

Thus with respect to four of the six voting members of the Commission, neither the President, the head of any department, nor the Judiciary has any voice in their selection.

. . .

Appellee Commission and *amici* contend somewhat obliquely that because the Framers had no intention of relegating Congress to a position below that of the co-equal Judicial and Executive Branches of the National Government, the Appointments Clause must somehow be read to include Congress or its officers as among those in whom the appointment power may be vested. But the debates of the Constitutional Convention, and the Federalist Papers, are replete with expressions of fear that the Legislative Branch of the National Government will aggrandize itself at the expense of the other two branches. The debates during the Convention, and the evolution of the draft version of the Constitution, seem to us to lend considerable support to our reading of the language of the Appointments Clause itself.

An interim version of the draft Constitution had vested in the Senate the authority to appoint Ambassadors, public Ministers, and Judges of the Supreme Court, and the language of Art. II as finally adopted is a distinct change in this regard. We believe that it was a deliberate change made by the Framers with the intent to deny Congress any authority itself to appoint those who were "Officers of the United States." The debates on the floor of the Convention reflect at least in part the way the change came about.

. . .

3. The Commission's Powers

Thus, on the assumption that all of the powers granted in the statute may be exercised by an agency whose members *have been* appointed in accordance with the Appointments Clause, the ultimate question is which, if any, of those powers may be exercised by the present voting Commissioners, none of whom *was* appointed as provided by that Clause. Our previous description of the statutory provisions...disclosed that the Commission's powers fall generally into three categories: functions relating to the flow of necessary information—receipt, dissemination, and investigation; functions with respect to the Commission's task of fleshing out the statute—rulemaking and advisory opinions; and functions necessary to ensure compliance with the statute and rules—informal procedures, administrative determinations and hearings, and civil suits.

Insofar as the powers confided in the Commission are essentially of an investigative and informative nature, falling in the same general category as those powers which Congress might delegate to one of its own committees, there can be no question that the Commission as presently constituted may exercise them....

But when we go beyond this type of authority to the more substantial powers exercised by the Commission, we reach a different result. The Commission's enforcement power, exemplified by its discretionary power to seek judicial relief, is authority that cannot possibly be regarded as merely in aid of the legislative function of Congress. A lawsuit is the ultimate remedy for a breach of the law, and it is to the President, and not to the Congress, that the Constitution entrusts the responsibility to "take Care that the Laws be faithfully executed." Art. II, § 3.

. . .

We hold that these provisions of the Act, vesting in the Commission primary responsibility for conducting civil litigation in the courts of the United States for vindicating public rights, violate Art. II, § 2, cl. 2, of the Constitution. Such functions may be discharged only by persons who are "Officers of the United States" within the language of that section.

. . .

MR. JUSTICE STEVENS took no part in the consideration or decision of these cases.

. . .

MR. CHIEF JUSTICE BURGER, concurring in part and dissenting in part.

...I agree with the Court that the members of the Federal Election Commission were unconstitutionally appointed. However, I disagree that we should give blanket *de facto* validation to all ac-

tions of the Commission undertaken until today. The issue is not before us and we cannot know what acts we are ratifying. I would leave this issue to the District Court to resolve if and when any challenges are brought.

. . .

MR. JUSTICE WHITE, concurring in part and dissenting in part.

...[I]t is plain that the FEC is the primary agency for the enforcement and administration of major parts of the election laws. It does not replace or control the executive agencies with respect to criminal prosecutions, but within the wide zone of its authority the FEC is independent of executive as well as congressional control except insofar as certain of its regulations must be laid before and not be disapproved by Congress.... With duties and functions such as these, members of the FEC are plainly "officers of the United States" as that term is used in Art. II, § 2, cl. 2.

It is thus not surprising that the FEC, in defending the legality of its members' appointments, does not deny that they are "officers of the United States" as that term is used in the Appointments Clause of Art. II. Instead, for reasons the Court outlines...its position appears to be that even if its members are officers of the United States, Congress may nevertheless appoint a majority of the FEC without participation by the President. This position that Congress may itself appoint the members of a body that is to administer a wide-ranging statute will not withstand examination in light of either the purpose and history of the Appointments Clause or of prior cases in this Court.

. . .

MR. JUSTICE MARSHALL, concurring in part and dissenting in part.

[Marshall concurred in the Court's opinion on FEC appointments.]

MR. JUSTICE BLACKMUN, concurring in part and dissenting in part.

[Blackmun concurred in the Court's opinion on FEC appointments.]

MR. JUSTICE REHNQUIST, concurring in part and dissenting in part.

[Rehnquist concurred in the Court's opinion on FEC appointments.]

Myers v. United States

272 U.S. 52 (1926)

A statute of 1876 provided that postmasters of the first, second, and third classes shall be appointed and may be removed by the President "by and with the advice and consent of the Senate." President Wilson removed Frank S. Myers, a postmaster of the first class, without seeking or obtaining Senate approval. The constitutional question was whether Congress could interfere with or restrict the President's power of removal, which the Solicitor General and the heirs of Myers argued was essential to preserve the President's responsibility as chief executive officer. The issue of the removal power was limited to officers subject to Senate confirmation.

MR. CHIEF JUSTICE TAFT delivered the opinion of the Court.

This case presents the question whether under the Constitution the President has the exclusive power of removing executive officers of the United States whom he has appointed by and with the advice and consent of the Senate.

Myers, appellant's intestate, was on July 21, 1917, appointed by the President, by and with the advice and consent of the Senate, to be a postmaster of the first class at Portland, Oregon, for a term of four years. On January 20, 1920, Myers' resignation was demanded. He refused the demand. On February 2, 1920, he was removed from office by order of the Postmaster General, acting by direction of the President....

By the 6th section of the Act of Congress of July 12, 1876, 19 Stat. 80, 81, c. 179, under which Myers was appointed with the advice and consent of the Senate as a first-class postmaster, it is provided that

"Postmasters of the first, second and third classes shall be appointed and may be removed by the President by and with the advice and consent of the Senate and shall hold their offices for four years unless sooner removed or suspended according to law."

The Senate did not consent to the President's removal of Myers during his term....

The question where the power of removal of executive officers appointed by the President by and with the advice and consent of the Senate was vested, was presented early in the first session of the First Congress. There is no express provision respecting removals in the Constitution, except as Section 4 of Article II, above quoted, provides for removal from office by impeachment. The subject was not discussed in the Constitutional Convention. Under the Articles of Confederation, Congress was given the power of appointing certain executive officers of the Confederation, and during the Revolution and while the Articles were given effect, Congress exercised the power of removal....

Consideration of the executive power was initiated in the Constitutional Convention by the seventh resolution in the Virginia Plan, introduced by Edmund Randolph. 1 Farrand, Records of the Federal Convention, 21. It gave to the Executive "all the executive powers of the Congress under the Confederation," which would seem therefore to have intended to include the power of removal which had been exercised by that body as incident to the power of appointment.

[Later modifications vested the executive in a single person, elected by an electoral college, with the power to appoint officers and the duty to see that all laws are faithfully observed.]

In the House of Representatives of the First Congress, on Tuesday, May 18, 1789, Mr. Madison moved in the Committee of the Whole that there should be established three executive departments — one of Foreign Affairs, another of the Treasury, and a third of War — at the head of each of which there should be a Secretary, to be appointed by the President by and with the advice and consent of the Senate, and to be removable by the President. The committee agreed to the establishment of a Department of Foreign Affairs, but a discussion ensued as to making the Secretary removable by the President. 1 Annals of Congress, 370, 371. "The question was now taken and carried, by a considerable majority, in favor of declaring the power of removal to be in the President." 1 Annals of Congress, 383.

On June 16, 1789, the House resolved itself into a Committee of the Whole on a bill proposed by Mr. Madison for establishing an executive department to be denominated the Department of Foreign Affairs, in which the first clause, after stating the title of the officer and describing his duties, had these words: "to be removable from office by the President of the United States." 1 Annals of Congress, 455. After a very full discussion the question was put: shall the words "to be removable by the President" be struck out? It was determined in the negative—yeas 20, nays 34. 1 Annals of Congress, 576.

On June 22, in the renewal of the discussion, "Mr. Benson moved to amend the bill, by altering the second clause, so as to imply the power of removal to be in the President alone. The clause enacted that there should be a chief clerk, to be appointed by the Secretary of Foreign Affairs, and employed as he thought proper, and who, in case of vacancy, should have the charge and custody of all records, books, and papers appertaining to the department. The amendment proposed that the chief clerk, "whenever the said principal officer shall be removed from office by the President of the United States, or in any other case of vacancy,' should during such vacancy, have the charge and custody of all records, books, and papers appertaining to the department." 1 Annals of Congress, 578.

"Mr. Benson stated that his objection to the clause "to be removable by the President' arose from an idea that the power of removal by the President hereafter might appear to be exercised by virtue of a legislative grant only, and consequently be subjected to legislative instability, when he was well satisfied in his own mind that it was fixed by a fair legislative construction of the Constitution." 1 Annals of Congress, 579.

"Mr. Benson declared, if he succeeded in this amendment, he would move to strike out the words in the first clause, "to be removable by the President' which appeared somewhat like a grant. Now, the mode he took would evade that point and establish a legislative construction of the Constitution. He also hoped his amendment would succeed in reconciling both sides of the House to the decision, and quieting the minds of gentlemen." 1 Annals of Congress, 578.

Mr. Madison admitted the objection made by the gentleman near him (Mr. Benson) to the words in the bill. He said: "They certainly may be construed to imply a legislative grant of the power. He wished everything like ambiguity expunged, and the sense of the House explicitly declared, and therefore seconded the motion. Gentlemen have all along proceeded on the idea that the Constitution vests the power in the President;

and what arguments were brought forward respecting the convenience or inconvenience of such disposition of the power, were intended only to throw light upon what was meant by the compilers of the Constitution. Now, as the words proposed by the gentleman from New York expressed to his mind the meaning of the Constitution, he should be in favor of them, and would agree to strike out those agreed to in the committee." 1 Annals of Congress, 578, 579.

Mr. Benson's first amendment to alter the second clause by the insertion of the italicized words, made that clause to read as follows:

"That there shall be in the State Department an inferior officer to be appointed by the said principal officer, and to be employed therein as he shall deem proper, to be called the Chief Clerk in the Department of Foreign Affairs, *and who, whenever the principal officer shall be removed from office by the President of the United States,* or in any other case of vacancy, shall, during such vacancy, have charge and custody of all records, books and papers appertaining to said department."

The first amendment was then approved by a vote of thirty to eighteen. 1 Annals of Congress, 580. Mr. Benson then moved to strike out in the first clause the words "to be removable by the President," in pursuance of the purpose he had already declared, and this second motion of his was carried by a vote of thirty-one to nineteen. 1 Annals of Congress, 585.

The bill as amended was ordered to be engrossed, and read the third time the next day, June 24, 1789, and was then passed by a vote of twenty-nine to twenty-two, and the Clerk was directed to carry the bill to the Senate and desire their concurrence. 1 Annals of Congress, 591.

It is very clear from this history that the exact question which the House voted upon was whether it should recognize and declare the power of the President under the Constitution to remove the Secretary of Foreign Affairs without the advice and consent of the Senate. That was what the vote was taken for. Some effort has been made to question whether the decision carries the result claimed for it, but there is not the slightest doubt, after an examination of the record, that the vote was, and was intended to be, a legislative declaration that the power to remove officers appointed by the President and the Senate vested in the President alone, and until the Johnson Impeachment trial in

1868, its meaning was not doubted even by those who questioned its soundness.

The discussion was a very full one. Fourteen out of the twenty-nine who voted for the passage of the bill, and eleven of the twenty-two who voted against the bill took part in the discussion. Of the members of the House, eight had been in the Constitutional Convention, and of these, six voted with the majority, and two, Roger Sherman and Elbridge Gerry, the latter of whom had refused to sign the Constitution, voted in the minority. After the bill as amended had passed the House, it was sent to the Senate, where it was discussed in secret session, without report. The critical vote there was upon the striking out of the clause recognizing and affirming the unrestricted power of the President to remove. The Senate divided by ten to ten, requiring the deciding vote of the Vice-President, John Adams, who voted against striking out, and in favor of the passage of the bill as it had left the House. Ten of the Senators had been in the Constitutional Convention, and of them six voted that the power of removal was in the President alone. The bill having passed as it came from the House was signed by President Washington and became a law. Act of July 27, 1789, 1 Stat. 28, c.4.

The bill was discussed in the House at length and with great ability. The report of it in the Annals of Congress is extended. James Madison was then a leader in the House, as he had been in the Convention. His arguments in support of the President's constitutional power of removal independently of Congressional provision, and without the consent of the Senate, were masterly, and he carried the House.

[Taft summarizes the reasons advanced by Madison and his associates for vesting the removal power in the President: the need to separate the legislature from the executive functions; the intention to create a strong President; the use of the removal power to permit the President to take responsibility for the conduct of the executive branch and to see that the laws are faithfully executed; the intention to make the power of removal incident to the power of appointment; and the need for the President to have full confidence in his subordinates. Nevertheless, Taft acknowledges that Congress can place certain duties in executive officers to make presidential removal inappropriate:]

...Of course there may be duties so peculiarly and specifically committed to the discretion of a particular officer as to raise a question whether the President may overrule or revise the officer's interpretation of his statutory duty in a particular instance. Then there may be duties of a quasi-judicial character imposed on executive officers and members of executive tribunals whose decisions after hearing affect interests of individuals, the discharge of which the President can not in a particular case properly influence or control. But even in such a case he may consider the decision after its rendition as a reason for removing the officer, on the ground that the discretion regularly entrusted to that officer by statute has not been on the whole intelligently or wisely exercised. Otherwise he does not discharge his own constitutional duty of seeing that the laws be faithfully executed.

. . .

For the reasons given, we must therefore hold that the provision of the law of 1876, by which the unrestricted power of removal of first class postmasters is denied to the President, is in violation of the Constitution, and invalid. This leads to an affirmance of the judgment of the Court of Claims.

. . .

Mr. Justice Holmes, dissenting.

My brothers McReynolds and Brandeis have discussed the question before us with exhaustive research and I say a few words merely to emphasize my agreement with their conclusion.

The arguments drawn from the executive power of the President, and from his duty to appoint officers of the United States (when Congress does not vest the appointment elsewhere), to take care that the laws be faithfully executed, and to commission all officers of the United States, seem to me spider's webs inadequate to control the dominant facts.

We have to deal with an office that owes its existence to Congress and that Congress may abolish tomorrow. Its duration and the pay attached to it while it lasts depend on Congress alone. Congress alone confers on the President the power to appoint to it and at any time may transfer the power to other hands. With such power over its own creation, I have no more trouble in believing that Congress has power to prescribe a term of life for it free from any interference than I have in accepting the undoubted power of Congress to decree its end. I have equally little trouble in accepting its power to prolong the tenure of an incumbent until Congress or the Senate shall have assented to his removal. The duty of the President to see that the laws be executed is a duty that does not go beyond the laws or require him to achieve more than Congress sees fit to leave within his power.

The separate opinion of MR. JUSTICE McREYNOLDS.

[In this sixty-two-page dissent, McReynolds reviews the succession of statutes that have limited the President's power of removal: civil service reforms; the laws creating commissions, boards, the Comptroller General, and the Board of Tax Appeals; and the general history of congressional control over postal affairs. He also refutes Taft's claim that a majority of the First Congress believed that the President's removal power was a constitutional grant. McReynolds pulls together his critique in the following section:]

X.

Congress has long and vigorously asserted its right to restrict removals and there has been no common executive practice based upon a contrary view. The President has often removed, and it is admitted that he may remove, with either the express or implied assent of Congress; but the present theory is that he may override the declared will of that body. This goes far beyond any practice heretofore approved or followed; it conflicts with the history of the Constitution, with the ordinary rules of interpretation, and with the construction approved by Congress since the beginning and emphatically sanctioned by this court. To adopt it would be revolutionary.

MR. JUSTICE BRANDEIS, dissenting.

[Brandeis followed with a fifty-six-page dissent, spelling out in great detail the power of Congress to fix the tenure of inferior officers and to limit the President's power of removal. Some of the statutes provided that removal shall be made only for specified causes. Others provided for removal only after a hearing. Congress also passed legislation restricting the President's power of nomination.]

. . .

The separation of the powers of government did not make each branch completely autonomous. It left each, in some measure, dependent upon the others, as it left to each power to exercise, in some respects, functions in their nature executive, legislative and judicial. Obviously the President cannot secure full execution of the laws, if Congress denies to him adequate means of doing so. Full execution may be defeated because Congress declines to create offices indispensable for that purpose. Or, because Congress, having created the office, declines to make the indispensable appropriation. Or, because Congress, having both created the office and made the appropriation, prevents, by restrictions which it imposes, the appointment of officials who in quality and character are indispensable to the efficient execution of the law.

. . .

Checks and balances were established in order that this should be "a government of laws and not of men." . . . The doctrine of the separation of powers was adopted by the Convention of 1787, not to promote efficiency but to preclude the exercise of arbitrary power. The purpose was, not to avoid friction, but, by means of the inevitable friction incident to the distribution of the governmental powers among three departments, to save the people from autocracy. . . .

Humphrey's Executor v. United States

295 U.S. 602 (1935)

William E. Humphrey, nominated by President Hoover for the Federal Trade Commission in 1931, was confirmed by the Senate. The Federal Trade Commission (FTC) Act allowed the President to remove a commissioner only for "inefficiency, neglect of duty, or malfeasance in office." In 1933 President Franklin D. Roosevelt asked Humphrey to resign, explaining that the administration's policies could be carried out only with commissioners supportive of Roosevelt's goals. When Humphrey refused to resign, Roosevelt removed him for policy reasons rather than the "for cause" reasons specified in the FTC Act. Humphrey's heirs brought suit to recover his salary. In this decision, the Court reviews its broad ruling in *Myers* regarding the scope of the President's removal power.

MR. JUSTICE SUTHERLAND delivered the opinion of the Court.

Plaintiff brought suit in the Court of Claims against the United States to recover a sum of money alleged to be due the deceased for salary as a Federal Trade Commissioner from October 8, 1933, when the President undertook to remove him from office, to the time of his death on February 14, 1934....

William E. Humphrey, the decedent, on December 10, 1931, was nominated by President Hoover to succeed himself as a member of the Federal Trade Commission, and was confirmed by the United States Senate. He was duly commissioned for a term of seven years expiring September 25, 1938; and, after taking the required oath of office, entered upon his duties. On July 25, 1933, President Roosevelt addressed a letter to the commissioner asking for his resignation, on the ground "that the aims and purposes of the Administration with respect to the work of the Commission can be carried out most effectively with personnel of my own selection," but disclaiming any reflection upon the commissioner personally or upon his services. The commissioner replied, asking time to consult his friends. After some further correspondence upon the subject, the President on August 31, 1933, wrote the commissioner expressing the hope that the resignation would be forthcoming and saying:

"You will, I know, realize that I do not feel that your mind and my mind go along together on either the policies or the administering of the Federal Trade Commission, and, frankly, I think it is best for the people of this country that I should have a full confidence."

The commissioner declined to resign; and on October 7, 1933, the President wrote him:

"Effective as of this date you are hereby removed from the office of Commissioner of the Federal Trade Commission."

Humphrey never acquiesced in this action, but continued thereafter to insist that he was still a member of the commission, entitled to perform its duties and receive the compensation provided by law at the rate of $10,000 per annum. Upon these and other facts set forth in the certificate, which we deem it unnecessary to recite, the following questions are certified:

"1. Do the provisions of section 1 of the Federal Trade Commission Act, stating that "any commissioner may be removed by the President for inefficiency, neglect of duty, or malfeasance in office,' restrict or limit the power of the President to remove a commissioner except upon one or more of the causes named?

"If the foregoing question is answered in the affirmative, then—

"2. If the power of the President to remove a commissioner is restricted or limited as shown by the foregoing interrogatory and the answer made thereto, is such a restriction or limitation valid under the Constitution of the United States?"

The Federal Trade Commission Act...creates a commission of five members to be appointed by the President by and with the advice and consent of the Senate, and § 1 provides:

"Not more than three of the commissioners shall be members of the same political party. The first commissioners appointed shall continue in office for terms of three, four, five, six, and seven years, respectively, from the date of the taking effect of this Act, the term of each to be designated by the President, but their successors shall be appointed for terms of seven years, except that any person chosen to fill a vacancy shall be appointed only for the unexpired term of the commissioner whom he shall succeed. The commission shall choose a chairman from its own membership. No commissioner shall engage in any other business, vocation, or employment. Any commissioner may be removed by the President for inefficiency, neglect of duty, or malfeasance in office...."

. . .

First. The question first to be considered is whether, by the provisions of § 1 of the Federal Trade Commission Act already quoted, the President's power is limited to removal for the specific causes enumerated therein. The negative contention of the government is based principally upon the decision of this court in *Shurtleff* v. *United States,* 189 U. S. 311. That case involved the power of the President to remove a general appraiser of merchandise appointed under the Act of June 10, 1890, 26 Stat. 131. Section 12 of the act provided for the appointment by the President, by and with the advice and consent of the Senate, of nine general appraisers of merchandise, who "may be removed from office at any time by the President for inefficiency, neglect of duty, or malfeasance in office." The President removed Shurtleff without assigning any cause therefor.

The Court of Claims dismissed plaintiff's petition to recover salary, upholding the President's power to remove for causes other than those stated. In this court Shurtleff relied upon the maxim *expressio unius est exclusio alterius;* but this court held that, while the rule expressed in the maxim was a very proper one and founded upon justifiable reasoning in many instances, it "should not be accorded controlling weight when to do so would involve the alteration of the universal practice of the government for over a century and the consequent curtailment of the powers of the executive in such an unusual manner." What the court meant by this expression appears from a reading of the opinion. That opinion—after saying that no term of office was fixed by the act and that, with the exception of judicial officers provided for by the Constitution, no civil officer had ever held office by life tenure since the foundation of the government—points out that to construe the statute as contended for by Shurtleff would give the appraiser the right to hold office during his life or until found guilty of some act specified in the statute, the result of which would be a complete revolution in respect of the general tenure of office, effected by implication with regard to that particular office only.

...The situation here presented is plainly and wholly different. The statute fixes a term of office, in accordance with many precedents. The first commissioners appointed are to continue in office for terms of three, four, five, six, and seven years, respectively; and their successors are to be appointed for terms of seven years—any commissioner being subject to removal by the President for inefficiency, neglect of duty, or malfeasance in office. The words of the act are definite and unambiguous.

...[I]f the intention of Congress that no removal should be made during the specified term except for one or more of the enumerated causes were not clear upon the face of the statute, as we think it is, it would be made clear by a consideration of the character of the commission and the legislative history which accompanied and preceded the passage of the act.

The commission is to be non-partisan; and it must, from the very nature of its duties, act with entire impartiality. It is charged with the enforcement of no policy except the policy of the law. Its duties are neither political nor executive, but predominantly quasi-judicial and quasi-legislative.

Like the Interstate Commerce Commission, its members are called upon to exercise the trained judgment of a body of experts "appointed by law and informed by experience."...

The legislative reports in both houses of Congress clearly reflect the view that a fixed term was necessary to the effective and fair administration of the law. In the report to the Senate (No. 597, 63d Cong., 2d Sess., pp. 10–11) the Senate Committee on Interstate Commerce, in support of the bill which afterwards became the act in question, after referring to the provision fixing the term of office at seven years, so arranged that the membership would not be subject to complete change at any one time, said:

"The work of this commission will be of a most exacting and difficult character, demanding persons who have experience in the problems to be met—that is, a proper knowledge of both the public requirements and the practical affairs of industry. It is manifestly desirable that the terms of the commissioners shall be long enough to give them an opportunity to acquire the expertness in dealing with these special questions concerning industry that comes from experience."

The report declares that one advantage which the commission possessed over the Bureau of Corporations (an executive subdivision in the Department of Commerce which was abolished by the act) lay in the fact of its independence, and that it was essential that the commission should not be open to the suspicion of partisan direction. The report quotes (p. 22) a statement to the committee by Senator Newlands, who reported the bill, that the tribunal should be of high character and "independent of any department of the government.... a board or commission of dignity, permanence, and ability, independent of executive authority, except in its selection, and independent in character."

The debates in both houses demonstrate that the prevailing view was that the commission was not to be "subject to anybody in the government but...only to the people of the United States"; free from "political domination or control" or the "probability or possibility of such a thing"; to be "separate and apart from any existing department of the government—not subject to the orders of the President."

More to the same effect appears in the debates, which were long and thorough and contain nothing to the contrary....

Thus, the language of the act, the legislative reports, and the general purposes of the legislation as reflected by the debates, all combine to demonstrate the Congressional intent to create a body of experts who shall gain experience by length of service—a body which shall be independent of executive authority, *except in its selection,* and free to exercise its judgment without the leave or hindrance of any other official or any department of the government. To the accomplishment of these purposes, it is clear that Congress was of opinion that length and certainty of tenure would vitally contribute. And to hold that, nevertheless, the members of the commission continue in office at the mere will of the President, might be to thwart, in large measure, the very ends which Congress sought to realize by definitely fixing the term of office.

We conclude that the intent of the act is to limit the executive power of removal to the causes enumerated, the existence of none of which is claimed here; and we pass to the second question.

Second. To support its contention that the removal provision of § 1, as we have just construed it, is an unconstitutional interference with the executive power of the President, the government's chief reliance is *Myers* v. *United States,* 272 U. S. 52...the narrow point actually decided was only that the President had power to remove a postmaster of the first class, without the advice and consent of the Senate as required by act of Congress. In the course of the opinion of the court, expressions occur which tend to sustain the government's contention, but these are beyond the point involved and, therefore, do not come within the rule of *stare decisis.* In so far as they are out of harmony with the views here set forth, these expressions are disapproved....

The office of a postmaster is so essentially unlike the office now involved that the decision in the *Myers* case cannot be accepted as controlling our decision here. A postmaster is an executive officer restricted to the performance of executive functions. He is charged with no duty at all related to either the legislative or judicial power. The actual decision in the *Myers* case finds support in the theory that such an officer is merely one of the units in the executive department and, hence, inherently subject to the exclusive and illimitable power of removal by the Chief Executive, whose subordinate and aid he is....

The Federal Trade Commission is an administrative body created by Congress to carry into effect legislative policies embodied in the statute in accordance with the legislative standard therein prescribed, and to perform other specified duties as a legislative or as a judicial aid. Such a body cannot in any proper sense be characterized as an arm or an eye of the executive. Its duties are performed without executive leave and, in the contemplation of the statute, must be free from executive control. In administering the provisions of the statute in respect of "unfair methods of competition"—that is to say in filling in and administering the details embodied by that general standard—the commission acts in part quasi-legislatively and in part quasi-judicially. In making investigations and reports thereon for the information of Congress under § 6, in aid of the legislative power, it acts as a legislative agency. Under § 7, which authorizes the commission to act as a master in chancery under rules prescribed by the court, it acts as an agency of the judiciary. To the extent that it exercises any executive function—as distinguished from executive power in the constitutional sense—it does so in the discharge and effectuation of its quasi-legislative or quasi-judicial powers, or as an agency of the legislative or judicial departments of the government.

If Congress is without authority to prescribe causes for removal of members of the trade commission and limit executive power of removal accordingly, that power at once becomes practically all-inclusive in respect of civil officers with the exception of the judiciary provided for by the Constitution.... We are thus confronted with the serious question whether not only the members of these quasi-legislative and quasi-judicial bodies, but the judges of the legislative Court of Claims, exercising judicial power (*Williams* v. *United States,* 289 U. S. 553, 565–567), continue in office only at the pleasure of the President.

We think it plain under the Constitution that illimitable power of removal is not possessed by the President in respect of officers of the character of those just named. The authority of Congress, in creating quasi-legislative or quasi-judicial agencies, to require them to act in discharge of their duties independently of executive control cannot well be doubted; and that authority includes, as an appropriate incident, power to fix the period during which they shall continue in office, and to forbid their removal except for cause in the meantime. For it is quite evident that one who holds his office only during the pleasure of another, cannot be depended upon to maintain an attitude of independence against the latter's will.

The fundamental necessity of maintaining each of the three general departments of government entirely free from the control or coercive influence, direct or indirect, of either of the others, has often been stressed and is hardly open to serious question. So much is implied in the very fact of the separation of the powers of these departments by the Constitution; and in the rule which recognizes their essential co-equality....

...A reading of the debates [*in 1789*] shows that the President's illimitable power of removal was not considered in respect of other than executive officers. And it is pertinent to observe that when, at a later time, the tenure of office for the Comptroller of the Treasury was under consideration, Mr. Madison quite evidently thought that, since the duties of that office were not purely of an executive nature but partook of the judiciary quality as well, a different rule in respect of executive removal might well apply. 1 Annals of Congress, cols. 611–612.

. . .

The result of what we now have said is this: Whether the power of the President to remove an officer shall prevail over the authority of Congress to condition the power by fixing a definite term and precluding a removal except for cause, will depend upon the character of the office; the *Myers* decision, affirming the power of the President

alone to make the removal, is confined to purely executive officers; and as to officers of the kind here under consideration, we hold that no removal can be made during the prescribed term for which the officer is appointed, except for one or more of the causes named in the applicable statute.

To the extent that, between the decision in the *Myers* case, which sustains the unrestrictable power of the President to remove purely executive officers, and our present decision that such power does not extend to an office such as that here involved, there shall remain a field of doubt, we leave such cases as may fall within it for future consideration and determination as they may arise.

In accordance with the foregoing, the questions submitted are answered.

Question No. 1, Yes.
Question No. 2, Yes.

Mr. Justice McReynolds agrees that both questions should be answered in the affirmative. A separate opinion in *Myers* v. *United States*, 272 U. S. 178, states his views concerning the power of the President to remove appointees.

E. DELEGATION OF LEGISLATIVE POWER

The boundaries between the legislative and executive branches are often obscured by large grants of power delegated by Congress. This delegation supposedly violates a fundamental principle, dating back to John Locke. The legislature "cannot transfer the power of making laws to any other hands, for it being but a delegated power from the people, they who have it cannot pass it over to others." John Locke, Second Treatise on Civil Government, § 141. This concept is embodied in the ancient maxim *delegata potestas non potest delegari* ("delegated power cannot be delegated").

The non-delegation principle is essential at least in preventing Congress from transferring its legislative power to private groups. In 1936 the Supreme Court struck down a statute partly because it delegated power to representatives of the coal industry to set up a code of mandatory regulations. This was "legislative delegation in its most obnoxious form; for it is not even delegation to an official or an official body, presumptively disinterested, but to private persons whose interests may be and often are adverse to the interests of others in the same business." Carter v. Carter Coal Co., 298 U.S. 238, 311 (1936).

With the exception of two cases handed down in 1935, Congress has encountered little opposition from the courts in delegating legislative power to the President, executive agencies, and independent commissions. In sustaining these delegations, the judiciary typically waxes eloquent about the serious breach were Congress ever to transfer its legislative power to other parties, after which it finds a way to uphold the delegation. Field v. Clark, 143 U.S. 649, 692 (1891) and HAMPTON & CO. v. UNITED STATES 276 U.S. 394, 406 (1928).

The courts justify vast delegations of legislative power after satisfying themselves that the

Standardless Delegations

Broad delegations have been upheld in many cases because of the structure provided for independent commissions. They operate on a multi-member (collegial) basis, which supplies a check on possible abuses. Moreover, the term of commissioners are lengthy and staggered. Congress limits the number of commissioners who may belong to the same political party and restricts the ability of the President to remove commissioners. Finally, standardless delegations have been upheld when the accumulated customs of a regulated industry and the practices developed by states have served to narrow the discretion of a federal agency. Fahey v. Mallonee, 332 U.S. 245, 250, 253 (1947). See also Chapter 5 of Louis Fisher, The Politics of Shared Power (1998).

Standardless delegations have been upheld when the legislative history supplies guidelines for administrative action. A massive delegation of wage-price controls to President Nixon in 1970 was justified by guidelines placed in committee reports and the legislative history. A three-judge court claimed that whether legislative purposes are included in committee reports or the public law "is largely a matter of drafting style." Amalgamated Meat Cutters & Butcher Work. v. Connally, 337 F.Supp. 737, 750 (D.D.C. 1971) (three-judge court). However, agencies are not as tightly bound by legislative history and nonstatutory controls.

---

powers are confined either by congressional guidelines or procedural safeguards. Statutory guidelines are often absent, however, when Congress orders the Interstate Commerce Commission to protect the "public interest," directs the Federal Trade Commission to police "unfair methods of competition," supplies the standard of "public convenience, interest, or necessity" for the Federal Communications Commission, and requires the Securities and Exchange Commission to ensure that corporations do not "unduly or unnecessarily complicate the structure" or "unfairly or inequitably distribute voting power among security holders."[11] The structure of these commissions supplies some built-in safeguards (see box).

The NRA Cases

The two occasions on which the Supreme Court struck down a delegation of legislative authority to the President involved the National Industrial Recovery Act (NIRA), which authorized industrial and trade associations to draw up codes that minimized competition, raised prices, and restricted production. If the President found the codes unacceptable, he could prescribe his own and enforce them as law. In the first case, the Court held that Congress had failed to establish guidelines or congressional policy to control the President's actions. Panama Refining v. Ryan, 293 U.S. 388 (1935). Although Justice Cardozo argued in the first decision that Congress had supplied adequate standards, in the second he protested: "This is delegation running riot." SCHECHTER CORP. v. UNITED STATES, 295 U.S. at 553. The drafting of the NIRA was dominated by industries and trade associations; executive officials appeared to have little interest in constitutional questions or procedural safeguards. Peter H. Irons, The New Deal Lawyers 22–107 (1982).

During the course of this litigation, the Court discovered that the government had brought

---

11. The "public interest" guideline was upheld in ICC v. Goodrich Transit Co., 224 U.S. 194, 214–15 (1912), Intermountain Rate Cases, 234 U.S. 476, 486–88 (1914), Avent v. United States, 266 U.S. 127, 130 (1924), and N.Y. Central Securities Co. v. United States, 287 U.S. 12, 24–25 (1932). "Unfair method of competition" passed muster in FTC v. Gratz, 253 U.S. 421, 427–28 (1920), while "public convenience" survived judicial scrutiny in FCC v. Pottsville Broadcasting Co., 309 U.S. 134, 137–88 (1940). The SEC guideline was upheld in American Power Co. v. SEC, 329 U.S. 90, 104–06 (1946).

an indictment and taken an appeal only to learn, to its embarrassment, that the regulation justifying this action had been repealed by an executive order. Panama Refining Co. v. Ryan, 293 U.S. at 412–13. The House Judiciary Committee in 1935 condemned the "utter chaos" regarding the publication and distribution of administrative rules and pronouncements. H. Rept. No. 280, 74th Cong., 1st Sess. 1–2 (1935). Congress passed legislation that year to provide for publication in a "Federal Register" of all presidential and agency documents having the effect of law. 49 Stat. 500 (1935).

Other reforms are embodied in the Administrative Procedure Act (APA) of 1946, which establishes standards for agency rulemaking to assure fairness and openness. Agencies are required to give notice and a hearing before issuing a rule or regulation. Findings of fact are supplied for the record; procedures exist for appeal. Through such procedural standards, Congress tries to eliminate or minimize the opportunity for executive caprice and arbitrariness. The APA relies on the doctrine of separated powers by prohibiting investigative or prosecuting personnel from participating in agency adjudications. 5 U.S.C. §§ 553–54 (1994).

The standards for delegation need not be stricter when the power to tax is involved. Skinner v. Mid-America Pipeline Co., 490 U.S. 212 (1989). Also in 1989, all nine Justices rejected a claim that Congress had delegated excessively in creating the U.S. Sentencing Commission. Mistretta v. United States, 488 U.S. 361 (1989). Unanimous decisions in 1991 and 1996 dismissed the argument that Congress had unconstitutionally delegated its legislative power. Touby v. United States, 500 U.S. 160 (1991); Loving v. United States, 517 U.S. 748 (1996).

Presidential Legislation

Agency regulations are not supposed to be a substitute for the general policy-making that Congress supplies in the form of a public law. 6 Op. Att'y Gen. 10 (1853). Agency rulemaking draws its authority from power granted directly or indirectly by Congress.[12] The situation is different when the President "legislates" by issuing executive orders and proclamations. Here the President draws not necessarily on statutory authority but on power he believes is his under the Constitution.

Executive orders and proclamations are subject to legislative and judicial controls. When Congress objected to an executive order used by President Nixon to rejuvenate the Subversive Activities Control Board, Congress used its power of the purse to prohibit the agency from using any funds to carry out the order. As a result, the agency eventually disappeared. Fisher, Constitutional Conflicts 112–13. The federal courts have also been active in declaring proclamations and executive orders illegal.[13]

---

12. Chrysler Corp. v. Brown, 441 U.S. 281, 306–08 (1979). See Lincoln Electric Co. v. Commissioner of Int. Rev., 190 F.2d 326, 330 (6th Cir. 1951); American Broadcasting Co. v. United States, 110 F.Supp. 374, 384 (S.D. N.Y. 1953), aff'd, 347 U.S. 284 (1954); and Independent Meat Packers Ass'n v. Butz, 526 F.2d 228, 234–36 (8th Cir. 1975), cert. denied, 424 U.S. 966 (1976).

13. Chamber of Commerce of U.S. v. Reich, 74 F.3d 1322 (D.C. Cir. 1996); Independent Gasoline Marketers Council v. Duncan, 492 F.Supp. 614, 620–21 (D.D.C. 1980); Kaplan v. Johnson, 409 F.Supp. 190, 206 (N.D.Ill. 1976); Cole v. Young, 351 U.S. 536, 555 (1956); Youngstown Co. v. Sawyer, 343 U.S. 579 (1952); Schechter Corp. v. United States, 295 U.S. 495, 525–26 (1935); Panama Refining Co. v. Ryan, 295 U.S. 388, 433 (1935); United States v. Symonds, 120 U.S. 46 (1887); Little v. Barreme, 2 Cr. 170 (1804). See Louis Fisher, Constitutional Conflicts Between Congress and the President 106–18 (1997).

Hampton & Co. v. United States

276 U.S. 394 (1928)

The Tariff Act of 1922 empowered the President to increase or decrease duties in order to equalize the differences between the costs of producing at home and those in competing foreign countries. The Act established certain criteria to be taken into account in determining the differences, fixed the limits for increases and decreases, and required the Tariff Commission to first investigate before any duties could be changed. The major issue before the Court was whether the Act constituted an invalid delegation of legislative power to the President. J.W. Hampton, Jr. & Company, an importer, challenged the Constitutionality of this statute.

MR. CHIEF JUSTICE TAFT delivered the opinion of the Court.

J. W. Hampton, Jr., & Company made an importation into New York of barium dioxide, which the collector of customs assessed at the dutiable rate of six cents per pound. This was two cents per pound more than that fixed by statute, par. 12, ch. 356, 42 Stat. 858, 860. The rate was raised by the collector by virtue of the proclamation of the President, 45 Treas. Dec. 669, T. D. 40216, issued under, and by authority of, § 315 of Title III of the Tariff Act of September 21, 1922, ch. 356, 42 Stat. 858, 941, which is the so-called flexible tariff provision. Protest was made and an appeal was taken under § 514, . . . The pertinent parts of § 315 of Title III . . . are as follows:

"Section 315(a). That in order to regulate the foreign commerce of the United States and to put into force and effect the policy of the Congress by this Act intended, whenever the President, upon investigation of the differences in costs of production of articles wholly or in part the growth or product of the United States and of like or similar articles wholly or in part the growth or product of competing foreign countries, shall find it thereby shown that the duties fixed in this Act do not equalize the said differences in costs of production in the United States and the principal competing country he shall, by such investigation, ascertain said differences and determine and proclaim the changes in classifications or increases or decreases in any rate of duty provided in this Act shown by said ascertained differences in such costs of production necessary to equalize the same. Thirty days after the date of such proclamation or proclamations, such changes in classification shall take effect, . . . the total increase or decrease of such rates of duty shall not exceed 50 per centum of the rates specified in Title I of this Act, or in any amendatory Act. . . .

"(c). That in ascertaining the differences in costs

of production, under the provisions of subdivisions (a) and (b) of this section, the President, in so far as he finds it practicable, shall take into consideration (1) the differences in conditions in production, including wages, costs of material, and other items in costs of production of such or similar articles in the United States and in competing foreign countries; (2) the differences in the wholesale selling prices of domestic and foreign articles in the principal markets of the United States; (3) advantages granted to a foreign producer by a foreign government, or by a person, partnership, corporation, or association in a foreign country; and (4) any other advantages or disadvantages in competition.

"Investigations to assist the President in ascertaining differences in costs of production under this section shall be made by the United States Tariff Commission, and no proclamation shall be issued under this section until such investigation shall have been made. The commission shall give reasonable public notice of its hearings and shall give reasonable opportunity to parties interested to be present, to produce evidence, and to be heard. The commission is authorized to adopt such reasonable procedure, rules, and regulations as it may deem necessary."

. . .

The issue here is as to the constitutionality of § 315, upon which depends the authority for the proclamation of the President and for two of the six cents per pound duty collected from the petitioner. The contention of the taxpayers is twofold—first, they argue that the section is invalid in that it is a delegation to the President of the legislative power, which by Article I, § 1 of the Constitution, is vested in Congress, the power being that declared in § 8 of Article I, that the Congress shall have power to lay and collect taxes, duties, imposts and excises. The second objection is that, as § 315 was enacted with the avowed intent and for the purpose of protecting the industries of the United States, it is invalid because the Constitution gives power to lay such taxes only for revenue.

First. It seems clear what Congress intended by § 315. Its plan was to secure by law the imposition of customs duties on articles of imported merchandise which should equal the difference between the cost of producing in a foreign country the articles in question and laying them down for sale in the United States, and the cost of producing and selling like or similar articles in the United States, so that the duties not only secure revenue but at the same time enable domestic producers to compete on terms of equality with foreign producers in the markets of the United States. It may be that it is difficult to fix with exactness this difference, but the difference which is sought in the statute is perfectly clear and perfectly intelligible. Because of the difficulty in practically determining what that difference is, Congress seems to have doubted that the information in its possession was such as to enable it to make the adjustment accurately, and also to have apprehended that with changing conditions the difference might vary in such a way that some readjustments would be necessary to give effect to the principle on which the statute proceeds....

The well-known maxim *"Delegata potestas non potest delegari,"* applicable to the law of agency in the general and common law, is well understood and has had wider application in the construction of our Federal and State Constitutions than it has in private law. The Federal Constitution and State Constitutions of this country divide the governmental power into three branches.... [I]t is a breach of the National fundamental law if Congress gives up its legislative power and transfers it to the President, or to the Judicial branch, or if by law it attempts to invest itself or its members with either executive power or judicial power. This is not to say that the three branches are not co-ordinate parts of one government and that each in the field of its duties may not invoke the action of the two other branches in so far as the action invoked shall not be an assumption of the constitutional field of action of another branch. In determining what it may do in seeking assistance from another branch, the extent and character of that assistance must be fixed according to common sense and the inherent necessities of the governmental co-ordination.

The field of Congress involves all and many varieties of legislative action, and Congress has

found it frequently necessary to use officers of the Executive Branch, within defined limits, to secure the exact effect intended by its acts of legislation, by vesting discretion in such officers to make public regulations interpreting a statute and directing the details of its execution, even to the extent of providing for penalizing a breach of such regulations....

Congress may feel itself unable conveniently to determine exactly when its exercise of the legislative power should become effective, because dependent on future conditions, and it may leave the determination of such time to the decision of an Executive,... As Judge Ranney of the Ohio Supreme Court in *Cincinnati, Wilmington and Zanesville Railroad Co.* v. *Commissioners,* 1 Ohio St. 77, 88, said in such a case:

"The true distinction, therefore, is, between the delegation of power to make the law, which necessarily involves a discretion as to what it shall be, and conferring an authority or discretion as to its execution, to be exercised under and in pursuance of the law. The first cannot be done; to the latter no valid objection can be made." See also *Moers* v. *Reading,* 21 Penn. St. 188, 202; *Locke's Appeal,* 72 Penn. St. 491, 498.

Again, one of the great functions conferred on Congress by the Federal Constitution is the regulation of interstate commerce and rates to be exacted by interstate carriers for the passenger and merchandise traffic. The rates to be fixed are myriad. If Congress were to be required to fix every rate, it would be impossible to exercise the power at all. Therefore, common sense requires that in the fixing of such rates, Congress may provide a Commission, as it does, called the Interstate Commerce Commission, to fix those rates, after hearing evidence and argument concerning them from interested parties, all in accord with a general rule that Congress first lays down, that rates shall be just and reasonable considering the service given, and not discriminatory....

It is conceded by counsel that Congress may use executive officers in the application and enforcement of a policy declared in law by Congress, and authorize such officers in the application of the Congressional declaration to enforce it by regulation equivalent to law. But it is said that this never has been permitted to be done where Congress has exercised the power to levy taxes and fix customs duties. The authorities make no such distinction. The same principle that permits Congress to exercise its rate making power in interstate commerce, by declaring the rule which shall prevail in the legislative fixing of rates, and enables it to remit to a rate-making body created in accordance with its provisions the fixing of such rates, justifies a similar provision for the fixing of customs duties on imported merchandise. If Congress shall lay down by legislative act an intelligible principle to which the person or body authorized to fix such rates is directed to conform, such legislative action is not a forbidden delegation of legislative power.... This conclusion is amply sustained by a case in which there was no advisory commission furnished the President—a case to which this Court gave the fullest consideration nearly forty years ago. In *Field* v. *Clark,* 143 U. S. 649, 680, the third section of the Act of October 1, 1890 [*authorized the President to suspend the provisions of the statute relating to the free introduction of certain articles "for such time as he shall deem just."*]

...What the President was required to do was merely in execution of the act of Congress. It was not the making of law. He was the mere agent of the law-making department to ascertain and declare the event upon which its expressed will was to take effect.

Second. The second objection to § 315 is that the declared plan of Congress, either expressly or by clear implication, formulates its rule to guide the President and his advisory Tariff Commission as one directed to a tariff system of protection that will avoid damaging competition to the country's industries by the importation of goods from other countries at too low a rate to equalize foreign and domestic competition in the markets of the United States. It is contended that the only power of Congress in the levying of customs duties is to create revenue, and that it is unconstitutional to frame the customs duties with any other view than that of revenue raising. It undoubtedly is true that during the political life of this country there has been much discussion between parties as to the wisdom of the policy of protection, and we may go further and say as to its constitutionality, but no historian, whatever his view of the wisdom of the policy of protection, would contend that Congress, since the first revenue Act, in 1789, has not assumed that it was within its power in making provision for the collection of revenue, to put taxes upon importations and to vary the subjects of such taxes or rates in an effort to encourage the growth of the industries of the Nation by protecting home production against foreign competition. It is enough to point out that the second act adopted by the Congress of the United States, July 4, 1789, ch. 2, 1 Stat. 24, contained the following recital.

"SEC. 1. Whereas it is necessary for the support of government, for the discharge of the debts of the United States, and the encouragement and protection of manufactures, that duties be laid on goods, wares and merchandises imported: Be it enacted, etc."

In this first Congress sat many members of the Constitutional Convention of 1787. This Court has repeatedly laid down the principle that a contemporaneous legislative exposition of the Constitution when the founders of our Government and framers of our Constitution were actively participating in public affairs, long acquiesced in, fixes the construction to be given its provisions....

Affirmed.

Schechter Corp. v. United States

295 U.S. 495 (1935)

In *Panama Refining Co.* v. *Ryan,* 293 U.S. 388 (1935), the Supreme Court struck down part of the National Industrial Recovery Act as an invalid delegation of legislative power from Congress to the President. The statute placed upon industrial and trade associations the responsibility for drawing up codes to minimize competition, raise prices, and restrict production. If the President regarded the codes as unacceptable, he could prescribe his own codes and enforce them by law. *Panama Refining* held that a section of the statute governing controls on petroleum production failed to establish criteria to govern the President's course. Only Justice Cardozo dissented. In *Schechter,* the "sick chicken" case, the Court examines the constitutionality of the remainder of the statute.

MR. CHIEF JUSTICE HUGHES delivered the opinion of the Court.

Petitioners...were convicted in the District Court of the United States for the Eastern District of New York on eighteen counts of an indictment charging violations of what is known as the "Live Poultry Code," and on an additional count for conspiracy to commit such violations. By demurrer to the indictment and appropriate motions on the trial, the defendants contended (1) that the Code had been adopted pursuant to an unconstitutional delegation by Congress of legislative power; (2) that it attempted to regulate intrastate transactions which lay outside the authority of Congress; and (3) that in certain provisions it was repugnant to the due process clause of the Fifth Amendment.

[The Court described New York City as the largest live-poultry market in the United States, 96 percent of the poultry coming from other states. The Schechter Corporation usually purchased their live poultry from a market in New York City or at the railroad terminals serving the City, but occasionally they bought in Philadelphia. They trucked the poultry to their slaughterhouse markets in Brooklyn for sale to retail dealers and butchers. They did not sell the poultry in interstate commerce.]

The "Live Poultry Code" was promulgated under § 3 of the National Industrial Recovery Act. That section...authorizes the President to approve "codes of fair competition." Such a code may be approved for a trade or industry, upon application by one or more trade or industrial associations or groups, if the President finds (1) that such associations or groups "impose no inequitable restrictions on admission to membership therein and are truly representative," and (2) that such codes are not designed "to promote monopolies or to eliminate or oppress small enterprises and will not operate to discriminate against them, and will tend to effectuate the policy" of Title I of the Act. Such codes "shall not permit monopolies or monopolistic practices." As a condition of his approval, the President may "impose such conditions (including requirements for the making of reports and the keeping of accounts) for the protection of consumers, competitors, employees, and others, and in furtherance of the public interest, and may provide such exceptions to and exemptions from the provisions of such code as the President in his discretion deems necessary to effectuate the policy herein declared." Where such a code has not been approved, the President may prescribe one, either on his own

motion or on complaint. Violation of any provision of a code (so approved or prescribed) "in any transaction in or affecting interstate or foreign commerce" is made a misdemeanor punishable by a fine of not more than $500 for each offense, and each day the violation continues is to be deemed a separate offense.

The "Live Poultry Code" was approved by the President on April 13, 1934....

[The Code fixed the number of hours for workdays, the minimum pay, the minimum number of employees, and prohibited the employment of any person under sixteen years of age. The Code was administered through an "industry advisory committee" selected by trade associations and members of the industry. A "code supervisor" was appointed with the approval of the committee by agreement between the Secretary of Agriculture and the Administrator for Industrial Recovery.]

First. Two preliminary points are stressed by the Government with respect to the appropriate approach to the important questions presented. We are told that the provision of the statute authorizing the adoption of codes must be viewed in the light of the grave national crisis with which Congress was confronted. Undoubtedly, the conditions to which power is addressed are always to be considered when the exercise of power is challenged. Extraordinary conditions may call for extraordinary remedies. But the argument necessarily stops short of an attempt to justify action which lies outside the sphere of constitutional authority. Extraordinary conditions do not create or enlarge constitutional power. The Constitution established a national government with powers deemed to be adequate, as they have proved to be both in war and peace, but these powers of the national government are limited by the constitutional grants....

The further point is urged that the national crisis demanded a broad and intensive coöperative effort by those engaged in trade and industry, and that this necessary coöperation was sought to be fostered by permitting them to initiate the adoption of codes. But the statutory plan is not simply one for voluntary effort. It does not seek merely to endow voluntary trade or industrial associations or groups with privileges or immunities. It involves the coercive exercise of the lawmaking power. The codes of fair competition which the statute attempts to authorize are codes of laws. If valid, they place all persons within their reach under the obligation of positive law, binding equally those who assent and those who do not assent. Violations of the provisions of the codes are punishable as crimes.

Second. The question of the delegation of legislative power. We recently had occasion to review the pertinent decisions and the general principles which govern the determination of this question. *Panama Refining Co. v. Ryan,* 293 U. S. 388. The Constitution provides that "All legislative powers herein granted shall be vested in a Congress of the United States, which shall consist of a Senate and House of Representatives." Art I, § 1. And the Congress is authorized "To make all laws which shall be necessary and proper for carrying into execution" its general powers. Art. I, § 8, par. 18. The Congress is not permitted to abdicate or to transfer to others the essential legislative functions with which it is thus vested. We have repeatedly recognized the necessity of adapting legislation to complex conditions involving a host of details with which the national legislature cannot deal directly. We pointed out in the *Panama Company* case that the Constitution has never been regarded as denying to Congress the necessary resources of flexibility and practicality, which will enable it to perform its function in laying down policies and establishing standards, while leaving to selected instrumentalities the making of subordinate rules within prescribed limits and the determination of facts to which the policy as declared by the legislature is to apply. But we said that the constant recognition of the necessity and validity of such provisions, and the wide range of administrative authority which has been developed by means of them, cannot be allowed to obscure the limitations of the authority to delegate, if our constitutional system is to be maintained. *Id.,* p. 421.

Accordingly, we look to the statute to see whether Congress has overstepped these limitations,—whether Congress in authorizing "codes of fair competition" has itself established the standards of legal obligation, thus performing its essential legislative function, or, by the failure to enact such standards, has attempted to transfer that function to others.

The aspect in which the question is now presented is distinct from that which was before us in the case of the *Panama Company.* There, the subject of the statutory prohibition was defined. National Industrial Recovery Act, § 9 (c). That subject was the transportation in interstate and foreign commerce of petroleum and petroleum products which are produced or withdrawn from storage in excess of the amount permitted by state authority. The question was with respect to the range of discretion given to the President in prohibiting that transportation. *Id.,* pp. 414, 415, 430. As to the "codes of fair competition," under § 3 of the Act, the question is more fundamental. It is whether there is any adequate definition of the subject to which the codes are to be addressed.

What is meant by "fair competition" as the term is used in the Act? Does it refer to a category established in the law, and is the authority to make codes limited accordingly? Or is it used as a convenient designation for whatever set of laws the formulators of a code for a particular trade or industry may propose and the President may approve (subject to certain restrictions), or the President may himself prescribe, as being wise and beneficent provisions for the government of the trade or industry in order to accomplish the broad purposes of rehabilitation, correction and expansion which are stated in the first section of Title I?

The Act does not define "fair competition." . . .

The Government urges that the codes will "consist of rules of competition deemed fair for each industry by representative members of that industry—by the persons most vitally concerned and most familiar with its problems." Instances are cited in which Congress has availed itself of such assistance; as *e.g.,* in the exercise of its authority over the public domain, with respect to the recognition of local customs or rules of miners as to mining claims, or, in matters of a more or less technical nature, as in designating the standard height of drawbars. But would it be seriously contended that Congress could delegate its legislative authority to trade or industrial associations or groups so as to empower them to enact the laws they deem to be wise and beneficent for the rehabilitation and expansion of their trade or industries? Could trade or industrial associations or groups be constituted legislative bodies for that purpose because such associations or groups are familiar with the problems of their enterprises? And, could an effort of that sort be made valid by such a preface of generalities as to permissible aims as we find in section 1 of title I? The answer is obvious. Such a delegation of legislative power is unknown to our law and is utterly inconsistent with the constitutional prerogatives and duties of Congress.

The question, then, turns upon the authority which § 3 of the Recovery Act vests in the President to approve or prescribe. If the codes have standing as penal statutes, this must be due to the effect of the executive action. But Congress cannot delegate legislative power to the President to exercise an unfettered discretion to make whatever laws he thinks may be needed or advisable for the rehabilitation and expansion of trade or industry....

...Section 3 of the Recovery Act is without precedent. It supplies no standards for any trade, industry or activity. It does not undertake to prescribe rules of conduct to be applied to particular states of fact determined by appropriate administrative procedure. Instead of prescribing rules of conduct, it authorizes the making of codes to prescribe them. For that legislative undertaking, § 3 sets up no standards, aside from the statement of the general aims of rehabilitation, correction and expansion described in section one. In view of the scope of that broad declaration, and of the nature of the few restrictions that are imposed, the discretion of the President in approving or prescribing codes, and thus enacting laws for the government of trade and industry throughout the country, is virtually unfettered. We think that the code-making authority thus conferred is an unconstitutional delegation of legislative power.

· · ·

MR. JUSTICE CARDOZO, concurring.

The delegated power of legislation which has found expression in this code is not canalized within banks that keep it from overflowing. It is unconfined and vagrant, if I may borrow my own words in an earlier opinion. *Panama Refining Co. v. Ryan,* 293 U. S. 388, 440.

This court has held that delegation may be unlawful though the act to be performed is definite and single, if the necessity, time and occasion of performance have been left in the end to the discretion of the delegate. *Panama Refining Co. v. Ryan, supra.* I thought that ruling went too far. I pointed out in an opinion that there had been "no grant to the Executive of any roving commission to inquire into evils and then, upon discovering them, do anything he pleases." 293 U. S. at p. 435. Choice, though within limits, had been given him "as to the occasion, but none whatever as to the means." *Ibid.* Here, in the case before us, is an attempted delegation not confined to any single act nor to any class or group of acts identified or described by reference to a standard. Here in effect is a roving commission to inquire into evils and upon discovery correct them.

...This is delegation running riot. No such plenitude of power is susceptible of transfer....

I am authorized to state that MR. JUSTICE STONE joins in this opinion.

F. CONGRESSIONAL OVERSIGHT

Congress maintains control over delegated power through a variety of methods: the power to appropriate funds, changes in authorization language, reliance on nonstatutory controls, and different forms of the "legislative veto" (which retains some vitality even after the Supreme Court declared it unconstitutional in 1983). Another form of control, the power to investigate, is covered in the next section.

Power of the Purse

In Federalist No. 58, James Madison regarded the power of the purse as the "most complete and effectual weapon with which any constitution can arm the immediate representatives of the people, for obtaining a redress of every grievance, and for carrying into effect every just and salutary measure." Article I, Section 9, of the Constitution places this weapon squarely in the hands of Congress: "No Money shall be drawn from the Treasury, but in Consequence of Appropriations made by Law."

There are relatively few restrictions on this power of the purse. Congress cannot lawfully use its funding power to establish a religion.[14] It may not diminish the compensation of federal judges. It may neither increase nor decrease the compensation of the President during his term in office. It may not include language in appropriations bills to deny funds to named "subver-

---

14. U.S. Constitution, Amend. I; Flast v. Cohen, 392 U.S. 83, 104–05 (1968). However, plaintiffs who challenge federal assistance to religious institutions may be unable to establish standing as a litigant; Valley Forge College v. Americans United, 454 U.S. 464 (1982).

sives," for such legislative punishment is a bill of attainder prohibited by Article III, Section 3. United States v. Lovett, 328 U.S. 303 (1946); Blitz v. Donovan, 538 F.Supp. 1119 (D.D.C. 1982). A proviso in an appropriations bill may not interfere with the President's power to issue a pardon or prescribe for the judiciary the effect of a pardon. United States v. Klein, 13 Wall. 128 (1872); Hart v. United States, 118 U.S. 62 (1886).

For the most part, Congress may invoke the power of the purse to control almost every facet of executive activity. Appropriations can be lump sum or itemized. If lump sum (to give administrators discretion), congressional committees can insist on an informal veto over certain agency actions. Congress can attach "riders" or conditions to appropriations bills to prohibit the use of funds for specified purposes. Executive officials may object to "micromanagement" by legislators, but Congress has the constitutional authority to control administrative activity in minute detail.

Presidents share the power of the purse in several ways. The Budget and Accounting Act of 1921 gave the President authority to submit a national budget each year. Through this submission the President has an important means of setting the legislative agenda for Congress. Moreover, Presidents and their assistants are generally given some discretion in withholding funds (impoundment), transferring funds from one appropriation account to another, and "reprogramming" funds within an account. Louis Fisher, Presidential Spending Power (1975).

In response to abuses by the Nixon administration, Congress passed the Impoundment Control Act of 1974 to limit presidential actions to two types of impoundment: *rescission* (terminating funds), which requires the approval of Congress within forty-five days of continuous session, and *deferral* (delay of spending), which could have been disapproved by either House. When the legislative veto was invalidated by *INS* v. *Chadha* in 1983, it was later decided that the President's authority to make policy deferrals fell with the legislative veto because they were inseverable. City of New Haven v. United States, 809 F.2d 900 (D.C. Cir. 1987). This decision restricted the President to submitting routine deferrals to Congress.

The Item Veto

In 1996, Congress passed the Line Item Veto Act to strengthen the President's power to rescind funds. Instead of requiring the approval of Congress (the procedure established in 1974), presidential rescissions would take effect within 30 days unless Congress passed a bill or joint resolution of disapproval. The President could then veto the disapproval legislation, forcing each House to muster a two-thirds majority to override the veto. It is actually a misnomer to call this statute an "item veto." Presidents would still be left with the same choice they have had since 1789: either sign the whole bill or veto the whole bill. If the President signed a bill, the new procedure became available to cancel not only appropriated funds but also new entitlements and limited tax benefits.

In 1997, a constitutional challenge to the statute was turned back by the Supreme Court, which held that the plaintiffs (members of Congress) lacked standing to bring the suit. Raines v. Byrd, 521 U.S. 811 (1997). (See the reading on this decision in Chapter 1.) A year later the Court granted standing to other plaintiffs and ruled that the Line Item Veto Act violates the Presentment Clause. Clinton v. City of New York, 524 U.S. 417 (1998). Problems with the decision suggest that the item veto could return in some other form (see box on next page).

Enactment of Authorizations

With the exception of the offices of the President, the Vice President, and the Supreme Court, every other agency of government depends on Congress for its existence. In creating an agency, Congress determines its mission, structure, personnel, and ceilings for appropriations. It is for

The Item Veto: Will It Return?

By a 6–3 vote, the Supreme Court in 1998 decided that the Line Item Veto Act of 1996 was unconstitutional because it violated the Presentment Clause. That central part of the decision suggests that the issue was essentially procedural: to cancel law, the two branches have to follow the standard legislative process, including presentment of a bill to the President for his signature or veto. In a sense, the Court adhered to language in *Chadha*: "Amendment and repeal of statutes, no less than enactment, must conform with Art. I." 462 U.S. at 954. But *Chadha* was about Congress intervening in the executive process without complying with the lawmaking requirements of bicameralism and presentment. The item veto statute represented a grant of power to the President with no congressional interference other than an opportunity to disapprove the President's cancellations, and the disapproval measure complied fully with bicameralism and presentment.

The Court admitted, as it had to, that previous legislation had delegated to the President substantial authority to suspend and alter statutory language, particularly in tariffs and duties. Conceding the point, the Court noted that the statutes identified "all relate to foreign trade, and this Court has recognized that in the foreign affairs arena" the President has considerable discretion. The argument appears to turn from strict procedural matters (Presentment Clause) to the substance of law being altered (foreign versus domestic policy).

The Court ends by saying that any presidential power to alter legislation must come not by legislation but by constitutional amendment. However, there are a number of statutory options to create a new type of "item veto" that would comply fully with presentment. One is "separate enrollment (breaking large appropriations bills into tiny pieces). Another is to appropriate sums "not exceeding" a specified amount, allowing the President to withhold much or all of the money. Another option: a statute directs the President to carry out a program unless he determines that it is unnecessary.

Congress to decide whether the agency has a permanent authorization or must return to Congress every year or every few years for reauthorization. Through its action on authorization bills, Congress can redirect agency activities, require reports to Congress, redefine missions, or reorganize the agency out of existence.

Nonstatutory Controls

Although agencies are subject to authorization and appropriation actions through public law, much of the congressional control is maintained outside the statutory process. Committee reports, committee hearings, correspondence from review committees, and other nonstatutory techniques allow Congress to monitor and direct agency activity without passing another public law. Because these controls are informal and not legally binding, the system functions on a "keep the faith" attitude. Agencies receive lump-sum funds and broad authority from Congress; in return, they acquiesce to a multitude of nonstatutory controls. Agencies follow these controls for practical, not legal, reasons. Violation of congressional trust may result in budget cutbacks, restrictive statutory language, and line-item appropriations. Agencies may ignore nonstatutory controls but only "at the peril of strained relations with the Congress." 55 Comp. Gen. 307, 319, 325–26 (1975). See also 55 Comp. Gen. 812 (1976) and 1 O.L.C. 133 (1977).

Legislative Vetoes

During the 1930s, executive officials wanted to "make law" without passage of a statute. President Hoover obtained authority to reorganize the executive branch without having to submit a bill to Congress for hearings, amendments, and enactment by both Houses. Congress agreed only on the condition that either House could reject a reorganization plan by passing a resolution of disapproval. Through this accommodation was born the "legislative veto." Congress experimented with the one-House veto, the two-House veto (passage of a concurrent resolution), and even a committee veto. Fisher, Constitutional Conflicts 141–49.

This procedure obviously departs from the Presentment Clause in Article I, Section 7, which provides that "Every Order, Resolution, or Vote to which the Concurrence of the Senate and House of Representatives may be necessary (except on a question of Adjournment)" shall be presented to the President. Legislative vetoes are not presented to the President. President Hoover accepted the compromise because it simplified executive reorganization. This quid pro quo was extended to other areas, including immigration, arms sales, the war power, impoundment, and agency regulations. Eventually, the Justice Department and the White House decided that the bargain no longer favored the executive branch. A test case, involving an immigration statute, was soon on its way to the Supreme Court.

In the 1930s the executive branch had prevailed upon Congress to delegate discretionary authority over the deportation of aliens. Congress agreed to allow the Attorney General to suspend deportations provided that the suspensions were subject to a one-House legislative veto. Congress exercised this power on numerous occasions. The test case arose in 1975 when the House of Representatives disapproved the suspension of deportation for six aliens, including Jagdish Rai Chadha. After exhausting his administrative remedies in the Immigration and Naturalization Service, he won a court victory in the Ninth Circuit in 1980. The Supreme Court granted certiorari and twice heard the case on oral argument.

INS v. Chadha

In a sweeping decision handed down in 1983, the Supreme Court declared the legislative veto unconstitutional. All legislative vetoes were unconstitutional because they violated the Presentment Clause. In addition, the one-House veto was unconstitutional because it violated the principle of bicameralism (which requires action by both Houses). Chief Justice Burger, writing for the majority, said that whenever congressional action has the "purpose and effect of altering the legal rights, duties and relations of persons" outside the legislative branch, Congress must act through both Houses in a bill presented to the President. INS v. CHADHA, 462 U.S. 919 (1983).

The Court's opinion suffers from a number of deficiencies. It claimed that the convenience of the legislative veto could not overcome the framers' view that efficiency was not a primary objective or hallmark of democratic government, and yet the framers ranked efficiency highly. The Court also argued that the legislative veto threatened the independence of the President by evading his veto power, but Presidents encouraged the legislative veto to obtain greater authority. Under the legislative veto procedure, Congress could not amend a President's proposal. The general veto was therefore not needed for presidential self-defense. More importantly, the decision did not, and could not, eliminate the conditions that gave rise to the legislative veto: the desire of executive officials for broad delegations of power, and the insistence of Congress that it control those delegations without having to pass another public law. The executive-legislative accommodations that prevailed before *Chadha* continue to exist, sometimes in forms that are indistinguishable from the legislative veto supposedly struck down by the Court (see Fisher reading).

Recent Disputes

In 1989 the Bush administration entered into an accommodation with Congress which was criticized as an unconstitutional legislative veto. To obtain funds for the Nicaraguan contras, Secretary of State James A. Baker, III agreed to give four committees of Congress and con-

The Baker Accord

April 28, 1989

Dear Mr. Speaker:

Pursuant to the bipartisan agreement on Central America between the Executive and the Congress, the Congress has now voted to extend humanitarian assistance to the Nicaraguan Resistance at current levels through February 28, 1990. This assistance has been authorized and appropriated but will not be obligated beyond November 30, 1989, except in the context of consultation among the Executive, the Senate Majority and Minority leaders, the Speaker of the House of Representatives and the Majority and Minority leaders, and the rel-

evant authorization and appropriation committees, and only if affirmed via letters from the Bipartisan Leadership of Congress and the relevant House and Senate authorization and appropriations committees.

This bipartisan accord on Central America represents a unique agreement between the Executive and Legislative Branches. Thus, it is the intention of the parties that this agreement in no way establishes any precedent for the Executive or the Legislative Branch regarding the authorization and appropriation process.

Sincerely yours,
James A. Baker, III

gressional leaders a veto power over the release of some of the funds. White House Counsel C. Boyden Gray objected that the agreement appeared to be unconstitutional under *Chadha,* as did former federal judge Robert H. Bork. However, Baker's agreement did not appear in a public law. It was an informal, nonstatutory, "side agreement" that is not covered by *Chadha* (see box). Four members of the House of Representatives challenged the "Baker Accord" as unconstitutional, but their suit was dismissed by a federal district court. Burton v. Baker, 723 F.Supp. 1550 (D.D.C. 1990).

In 1991 the Court relied on *Chadha* to strike down a statutory provision enacted by Congress in 1986 that gave a board of review (composed of nine members of Congress) a veto over decisions made by a regional authority responsible for two airports serving the District of Columbia. The Court held that the veto power violated the doctrine of separation of powers. Metropolitan Washington Airports Auth. v. Noise Abatement Citizens, 501 U.S. 252 (1991). Congress enacted remedial legislation later that year, reconstituting the board of review and giving it the power to recommend but not to veto. The new statute authorized Congress to pass a joint resolution of disapproval to reject actions by the regional authority. Joint resolutions satisfy the requirements of *Chadha* (bicameralism and presentment). 105 Stat. 2197, Title VII (1991). This new law didn't satisfy the courts either. The D.C. Circuit held that the board of review acted as an agent of Congress and that it exercised federal power in violation of the separation of powers doctrine. When this ruling was appealed to the Supreme Court, cert was denied. Hechinger v. Metro. Wash. Airports Authority, 36 F.3d 97 (D.C. Cir. 1994), cert. denied, 513 U.S. 1126 (1995).

Clinton v. City of New York,

524 U.S. 417 (1998)

After President Clinton had exercised his authority under the Line Item Veto Act by canceling certain items, two plaintiffs claiming injury challenged the constitutionality of the statute. A district court ruled that the Act's cancellation procedures violate the Present-

ment Clause. Having granted the plaintiffs standing, the Supreme Court turned to the constitutional question: May Congress grant the President discretionary authority to amend or cancel certain provisions in budget legislation?

JUSTICE STEVENS delivered the opinion of the Court.

The Line Item Veto Act (Act)...was enacted in April 1996 and became effective on January 1, 1997....

[In Sections I, II, and III, Stevens reviews the canceled items that are at issue in this case, states the injuries claimed by the plaintiffs, decides that the plaintiffs (the City of New York and a farmers' cooperative) were "individuals" entitled to bring an expedited matter to the Court, and concludes that the plaintiffs had standing.]

IV

The Line Item Veto Act gives the President the power to "cancel in whole" three types of provisions that have been signed into law: "(1) any dollar amount of discretionary budget authority; (2) any item of new direct spending; or (3) any limited tax benefit."...It is undisputed that the New York case involves an "item of new direct spending" and that the Snake River case involves a "limited tax benefit" as those terms are defined in the Act....

The Act requires the President to adhere to precise procedures whenever he exercises his cancellation authority. In identifying items for cancellation he must consider the legislative history, the purposes, and other relevant information about the items....He must determine, with respect to each cancellation, that it will "(i) reduce the Federal budget deficit; (ii) not impair any essential Government functions; and (iii) not harm the national interest."...Moreover, he must transmit a special message to Congress notifying it of each cancellation within five calendar days (excluding Sundays) after the enactment of the canceled provision....

A cancellation takes effect upon receipt by Congress of the special message from the President....If, however, a "disapproval bill" pertaining to a special message is enacted into law, the cancellations set forth in that message become "null and void."...

The effect of a cancellation is plainly stated in § 691e, which defines the principal terms used in the Act. With respect to both an item of new direct spending and a limited tax benefit, the cancellation prevents the item "from having legal force or effect."...

In both legal and practical effect, the President has amended two Acts of Congress by repealing a portion of each. "[R]epeal of statutes, no less than enactment, must conform with Art. I." *INS v. Chadha*, 462 U. S. 919, 954 (1983). There is no provision in the Constitution that authorizes the President to enact, to amend, or to repeal statutes. Both Article I and Article II assign responsibilities to the President that directly relate to the lawmaking process, but neither addresses the issue presented by these cases. The President "shall from time to time give to the Congress Information on the State of the Union, and recommend to their Consideration such Measures as he shall judge necessary and expedient...." Art. II, § 3. Thus, he may initiate and influence legislative proposals. Moreover, after a bill has passed both Houses of Congress, but "before it become[s] a Law," it must be presented to the President. If he approves it, "he shall sign it, but if not he shall return it, with his Objections to that House in which it shall have originated, who shall enter the Objections at large on their Journal, and proceed to reconsider it." Art. I, § 7, cl. 2. His "return" of a bill, which is usually described as a "veto," is subject to being overridden by a two-thirds vote in each House.

There are important differences between the President's "return" of a bill pursuant to Article I, § 7, and the exercise of the President's cancellation authority pursuant to the Line Item Veto Act. The constitutional return takes place *before* the bill becomes law; the statutory cancellation occurs *after* the bill becomes law. The constitutional return is of the entire bill; the statutory cancellation is of only a part. Although the Constitution expressly authorizes the President to play a role in the process of enacting statutes, it is silent on the subject of unilateral Presidential action that either repeals or amends parts of duly enacted statutes.

There are powerful reasons for construing constitutional silence on this profoundly important issue as equivalent to an express prohibition. The procedures governing the enactment of statutes set forth in the text of Article I were the product of the great debates and compromises that produced the Constitution itself. Familiar historical materials provide abundant support for the conclusion that the power to enact statutes may only "be exercised in accord with a single, finely wrought and exhaustively considered, procedure." *Chadha,*

462 U. S., at 951. Our first President understood the text of the Presentment Clause as requiring that he either "approve all the parts of a Bill, or reject it in toto." What has emerged in these cases from the President's exercise of his statutory cancellation powers, however, are truncated versions of two bills that passed both Houses of Congress. They are not the product of the "finely wrought" procedure that the Framers designed.

At oral argument, the Government suggested that the cancellations at issue in these cases do not effect a "repeal" of the canceled items because under the special "lockbox" provisions of the Act, a canceled item "retain[s] real, legal budgetary effect" insofar as it prevents Congress and the President from spending the savings that result from the cancellation.... The text of the Act expressly provides, however, that a cancellation prevents a direct spending or tax benefit provision "from having legal force or effect."... That a canceled item may have "real, legal budgetary effect" as a result of the lockbox procedure does not change the fact that by canceling the items at issue in these cases, the President made them entirely inoperative as to appellees....

V

The Government advances two related arguments to support its position that despite the unambiguous provisions of the Act, cancellations do not amend or repeal properly enacted statutes in violation of the Presentment Clause. First, relying primarily on *Field v. Clark,* 143 U. S. 649 (1892), the Government contends that the cancellations were merely exercises of discretionary authority granted to the President by the Balanced Budget Act and the Taxpayer Relief Act read in light of the previously enacted Line Item Veto Act. Second, the Government submits that the substance of the authority to cancel tax and spending items "is, in practical effect, no more and no less than the power to 'decline to spend' specified sums of money, or to 'decline to implement' specified tax measures."... Neither argument is persuasive.

In *Field v. Clark*, the Court upheld the constitutionality of the Tariff Act of 1890. *[The statute contained a "free list" of almost 300 specific articles that were exempted from import duties, but authorized the President to suspend the exemption for certain articles whenever he decided that the country exporting those products imposed duties on the agricultural products of the United States that he deemed to be "reciprocally unequal and unreasonable." Stevens identifies what he considered*

to be three critical differences between the President's power to suspend the exemption from import duties and the President's power under the Line Item Veto Act.] First, the exercise of the suspension power was contingent upon a condition that did not exist when the Tariff Act was passed: the imposition of "reciprocally unequal and unreasonable" import duties by other countries. In contrast, the exercise of the cancellation power within five days after the enactment of the Balanced Budget and Tax Reform Acts necessarily was based on the same conditions that Congress evaluated when it passed those statutes. Second, under the Tariff Act, when the President determined that the contingency had arisen, he had a duty to suspend; in contrast, while it is true that the President was required by the Act to make three determinations before he canceled a provision,... those determinations did not qualify his discretion to cancel or not to cancel. Finally, whenever the President suspended an exemption under the Tariff Act, he was executing the policy that Congress had embodied in the statute. In contrast, whenever the President cancels an item of new direct spending or a limited tax benefit he is rejecting the policy judgment made by Congress and relying on his own policy judgment. Thus, the conclusion in *Field v. Clark* that the suspensions mandated by the Tariff Act were not exercises of legislative power does not undermine our opinion that cancellations pursuant to the Line Item Veto Act are the functional equivalent of partial repeals of Acts of Congress that fail to satisfy Article I, § 7.

The Government's reliance upon other tariff and import statutes, discussed in *Field,* that contain provisions similar to the one challenged in *Field* is unavailing for the same reasons. Some of those statutes authorized the President to "suspen[d] and discontinu[e]" statutory duties upon his determination that discriminatory duties imposed by other nations had been abolished....

The cited statutes all relate to foreign trade, and this Court has recognized that in the foreign affairs arena, the President has "a degree of discretion and freedom from statutory restriction which would not be admissible were domestic affairs alone involved." *United States v. Curtiss-Wright Export Corp., 299 U. S. 304, 320 (1936)....*

Neither are we persuaded by the Government's contention that the President's authority to cancel new direct spending and tax benefit items is no greater than his traditional authority to decline to spend appropriated funds. The Government has reviewed in some detail the series of statutes in which Congress has given the Executive broad discretion over the expenditure of appropriated funds. For example, the First Congress appropriated "sum[s] not exceeding" specified amounts to be spent on various Government operations.... In those statutes, as in later years, the President was given wide discretion with respect to both the amounts to be spent and how the money would be allocated among different functions. It is argued that the Line Item Veto Act merely confers comparable discretionary authority over the expenditure of appropriated funds. The critical difference between this statute and all of its predecessors, however, is that unlike any of them, this Act gives the President the unilateral power to change the text of duly enacted statutes. None of the Act's predecessors could even arguably have been construed to authorize such a change.

VI

. . .

If there is to be a new procedure in which the President will play a different role in determining the final text of what may "become a law," such change must come not by legislation but through the amendment procedures set forth in Article V of the Constitution....

The judgment of the District Court is affirmed.

It is so ordered.

JUSTICE KENNEDY, concurring.

[Kennedy emphasizes the structural issues present in this case. "Liberty is always at stake when one or more of the branches seek to transgress the separation of powers." Concentration of power in the hands of a single branch "is a threat to liberty." Liberty is protected not only by the Bill of Rights but by the principles of separation of powers, federalism, and checks and balances.]

It is no answer, of course, to say that Congress surrendered its authority by its own hand; nor does it suffice to point out that a new statute, signed by the President or enacted over his veto, could restore to Congress the power it now seeks to relinquish. That a congressional cession of power is voluntary does not make it innocuous. The Constitution is a compact enduring for more than our time, and one Congress cannot yield up its own powers, much less those of other Congresses to follow.... Abdication of responsibility is not part of the constitutional design....

JUSTICE SCALIA, with whom JUSTICE O'CONNOR joins, and with whom JUSTICE BREYER joins as to Part III, concurring in part and dissenting in part.

...[U]nlike the Court I find the President's cancellation of spending items to be entirely in accord with the Constitution.

I

[In this section, Scalia argues that the statute's expedited-review provision, which makes that procedure available to "[any Member of Congress or any individual adversely affected by [the Act]," does not apply to the plaintiffs: corporations, cooperatives, and governmental entities. The single exception is Mike Cranney, who joined the complaint with the farmers' cooperative. Scalia would deny expedited-review to the plaintiffs and subject them to certiorari review.]

[In Sections II and III, Scalia examines whether the plaintiffs have standing to bring their suit. He concludes that the farmers' cooperative lacked standing, but agreed that the New York plaintiffs had standing. However, he did not agree that the President's cancellation of this item violated the Presentment Clause.]

The Presentment Clause requires, in relevant part, that "[e]very Bill which shall have passed the House of Representatives and the Senate, shall, before it becomes a Law, be presented to the President of the United States; If he approve he shall sign it, but if not he shall return it," U. S. Const., Art. I, § 7, cl. 2. There is no question that enactment of the Balanced Budget Act complied with these requirements: the House and Senate passed the bill, and the President signed it into law. It was only *after* the requirements of the Presentment Clause had been satisfied that the President exercised his authority under the Line Item Veto Act to cancel the spending item. Thus, the Court's problem with the Act is not that it authorizes the President to veto parts of a bill and sign others into law, but rather that it authorizes him to "cancel"—prevent from "having legal force or effect"—certain parts of duly enacted statutes.

Article I, § 7 of the Constitution obviously prevents the President from cancelling a law that Congress has not authorized him to cancel. Such action cannot possibly be considered part of his execution of the law, and if it is legislative action, as the Court observes, " 'repeal of statutes, no less than enactment, must conform with Art. I.' "... quoting from *INS v. Chadha*, 462 U. S. 919, 954 (1983).

But that is not this case. It was certainly arguable, as an original matter, that Art. I, § 7 also prevents the President from cancelling a law which itself *authorizes* the President to cancel it. But as the Court acknowledges, that argument has long since been made and rejected. In 1809, Congress passed a law authorizing the President to cancel trade restrictions against Great Britain and France if either revoked edicts directed at the United States... The Tariff Act of 1890 authorized the President to "suspend, by proclamation to that effect" certain of its provisions if he determined that other countries were imposing "reciprocally unequal and unreasonable" duties.... This Court upheld the constitutionality of that Act in *Field v. Clark,* 143 U. S. 649 (1892), reciting the history since 1798 of statutes conferring upon the President the power to, *inter alia,* "discontinue the prohibitions and restraints hereby enacted and declared," ... "suspend the operation of the aforesaid act," ...and "declare the provisions of this act to be inoperative," ....

As much as the Court goes on about Art. I, § 7, therefore, that provision does not demand the result the Court reaches....

I turn, then, to the crux of the matter: whether Congress's authorizing the President to cancel an item of spending gives him a power that our history and traditions show must reside exclusively in the Legislative Branch. I may note, to begin with, that the Line Item Veto Act is not the first statute to authorize the President to "cancel" spending items. In *Bowsher v. Synar* 478 U. S. 714 (1986), we addressed the constitutionality of the Balanced Budget and Emergency Deficit Control Act of 1985 [*Gramm-Rudman Act*], which required the President, if the federal budget deficit exceeded a certain amount, to issue a "sequestration" order mandating spending reductions specified by the Comptroller General.... The effect of sequestration was that "amounts sequestered...shall be *permanently cancelled,*" ...(emphasis added). We held that the Act was unconstitutional, not because it impermissibly gave the Executive legislative power, but because it gave the Comptroller General, an officer of the Legislative Branch over whom Congress retained removal power, "the ultimate authority to determine the budget cuts to be made," 478 U. S., at 733, "functions...*plainly entailing execution of the law in constitutional terms.*" ...(emphasis added)....

Insofar as the degree of political, "law-making" power conferred upon the Executive is concerned, there is not a dime's worth of difference between Congress's authorizing the President to *cancel* a spending item, and Congress's authorizing money to be spent on a particular item at the President's discretion. And the latter has been done since the Founding of the Nation. From 1789–1791, the First Congress made lump-sum appropriations for the entire Government—"sum[s] not exceeding" specified amounts for broad purposes.... From a very early date Congress also made permissive individual appropriations, leaving the decision whether to spend the money to the President's unfettered discretion. In 1803, it appropriated $50,000 for the President to build "not exceeding fifteen gun boats, to be armed, manned and fitted out, and employed for such purposes as in his opinion the public service may require," ...

The short of the matter is this: Had the Line Item Veto Act authorized the President to "decline to spend" any item of spending contained in the Balanced Budget Act of 1997, there is not the slightest doubt that authorization would have been constitutional. What the Line Item Veto Act does instead—authorizing the President to "cancel" an item of spending—is technically different. But the technical difference does *not* relate to the technicalities of the Presentment Clause, which have been fully complied with; and the doctrine of unconstitutional delegation, which *is* at issue here, is preeminently *not* a doctrine of technicalities. The title of the Line Item Veto Act, which was perhaps designed to simplify for public comprehension, or perhaps merely to comply with the terms of a campaign pledge, has succeeded in faking out the Supreme Court. The President's action it authorizes in fact is not a line-item veto and thus does not offend Art. I, § 7; and insofar as the substance of that action is concerned, it is no different from what Congress has permitted the President to do since the formation of the Union.

. . .

JUSTICE BREYER, with whom JUSTICE O'CONNOR and JUSTICE SCALIA join as to Part III, dissenting.

I agree with the Court that the parties have standing, but I do not agree with its ultimate conclusion. In my view the Line Item Veto Act does not violate any specific textual constitutional command, nor does it violate any implicit Separation of Powers principle. Consequently, I believe that the Act is constitutional.

II

I approach the constitutional question before

us with three general considerations in mind. *First,* the Act represents a legislative effort to provide the President with the power to give effect to some, but not to all, of the expenditure and revenue-diminishing provisions contained in a single massive appropriations bill. And this objective is constitutionally proper.

When our Nation was founded, Congress could easily have provided the President with this kind of power. In that time period, our population was less than four million,... federal employees numbered fewer than 5,000,... annual federal budget outlays totaled approximately $4 million,... and the entire operative text of Congress's first general appropriations law read as follows:

"Be it enacted... [t]hat there be appropriated for the service of the present year, to be paid out of the monies which arise, either from the requisitions heretofore made upon the several states, or from the duties on import and tonnage, the following sums, viz. A sum not exceeding two hundred and sixteen thousand dollars for defraying the expenses of the civil list, under the late and present government; a sum not exceeding one hundred and thirty-seven thousand dollars for defraying the expenses of the department of war; a sum not exceeding one hundred and ninety thousand dollars for discharging the warrants issued by the late board of treasury, and remaining unsatisfied; and a sum not exceeding ninety-six thousand dollars for paying the pensions to invalids." Act of Sept. 29, 1789, ch. 23, § 1, 1 Stat. 95.

At that time, a Congress, wishing to give a President the power to select among appropriations, could simply have embodied each appropriation in a separate bill, each bill subject to a separate Presidential veto.

Today, however, our population is about 250 million,... the Federal Government employs more than four million people,... the annual federal budget is $1.5 trillion,... and a typical budget appropriations bill may have a dozen titles, hundreds of sections, and spread across more than 500 pages of the Statutes at Large.... Congress cannot divide such a bill into thousands, or tens of thousands, of separate appropriations bills, each one of which the President would have to sign, or to veto, separately. Thus, the question is whether the Constitution permits Congress to choose a particular novel *means* to achieve this same, constitutionally legitimate, *end.*

Second, the case in part requires us to focus upon the Constitution's generally phrased structural provisions, provisions that delegate all "legislative" power to Congress and vest all "executive" power in the President.... The Court, when applying these provisions, has interpreted them generously in terms of the institutional arrangements that they permit.... [*These cases call*] attention to the genius of the Framers' pragmatic vision, which this Court has long recognized in cases that find constitutional room for necessary institutional innovation.

Third, we need not here referee a dispute among the other two branches....

· · ·

III

...When the President "canceled" the two appropriation measures now before us, he did not *repeal* any law nor did he *amend* any law. He simply *followed* the law, leaving the statutes, as they are literally written, intact.

To understand why one cannot say, *literally speaking,* that the President has repealed or amended any law, imagine how the provisions of law before us might have been, but were not, written. Imagine that the canceled New York health care tax provision at issue here... had instead said the following:

<u>Section One.</u> Taxes... that were collected by the State of New York from a health care provider before June 1, 1997 and for which a waiver of provisions [requiring payment] have been sought... are deemed to be permissible health care related taxes... *provided however that the President may prevent the just-mentioned provision from having legal force or effect if he determines x, y and z.* (Assume x, y and z to be the same determinations required by the Line Item Veto Act).

Whatever a person might say, or think, about the constitutionality of this imaginary law, there is one thing the English language would prevent one from saying. One could not say that a President who "prevent[s]" the deeming language from "having legal force or effect"... has either *repealed* or *amended* this particular hypothetical statute. Rather, the President has *followed* that law to the letter. He has exercised the power it explicitly delegates to him. He has executed the law, not repealed it.

· · ·

INS v. Chadha

462 U.S. 919 (1983)

Congress authorized the Attorney General to suspend the deportation of aliens. Suspensions, however, were subject to the disapproval of either House. Along with a list of 340 names, the Attorney General suspended the deportation of Jagdish Rai Chadha, an East Indian born in Kenya and who held a British passport. In 1975 the House of Representatives adopted a resolution disapproving six names, including that of Chadha. He moved to suspend the deportation proceedings on the ground that the portion of the statute giving Congress a one-House veto was unconstitutional. In 1980 the Ninth Circuit held that the legislative veto violated the doctrine of separation of powers. The Supreme Court twice held oral argument before deciding the case.

CHIEF JUSTICE BURGER delivered the opinion of the Court.

We granted certiorari [*to consider*] a challenge to the constitutionality of the provision in § 244(c)(2) of the Immigration and Nationality Act, 66 Stat. 216, as amended, 8 U. S. C. § 1254(c)(2), authorizing one House of Congress, by resolution, to invalidate the decision of the Executive Branch, pursuant to authority delegated by Congress to the Attorney General of the United States, to allow a particular deportable alien to remain in the United States.

I

Chadha is an East Indian who was born in Kenya and holds a British passport. He was lawfully admitted to the United States in 1966 on a nonimmigrant student visa. His visa expired on June 30, 1972. On October 11, 1973, the District Director of the Immigration and Naturalization Service ordered Chadha to show cause why he should not be deported for having "remained in the United States for a longer time than permitted."... Chadha conceded that he was deportable for overstaying his visa and the hearing was adjourned to enable him to file an application for suspension of deportation under § 244(a)(1) of the Act....

[The immigration judge suspended Chadha's deportation, and a report of the suspension was transmitted. Acting under § 244(c)(2) of the Act, and without debate or recorded vote, the House of Representatives disapproved Chadha's suspension. Before addressing the constitutionality of the one-House veto, the Court concluded that (1) it had jurisdiction to entertain the INS appeal, (2) the legislative veto could be severed from the Act without affecting the Attorney General's authority to suspend deportations, (3) Chadha had standing to bring the suit, (4) there was no reason

to avoid the constitutional issue because Chadha might have alternative means of relief, (5) the Ninth Circuit had jurisdiction to decide the case, (6) the case represented a genuine case or controversy with the necessary concrete adverseness, and (7) the case did not constitute a nonjusticiable political question.]

III
A

We turn now to the question whether action of one House of Congress under § 244(c)(2) violates strictures of the Constitution. We begin, of course, with the presumption that the challenged statute is valid....

By the same token, the fact that a given law or procedure is efficient, convenient, and useful in facilitating functions of government, standing alone, will not save it if it is contrary to the Constitution. Convenience and efficiency are not the primary objectives—or the hallmarks—of democratic government and our inquiry is sharpened rather than blunted by the fact that congressional veto provisions are appearing with increasing frequency in statutes which delegate authority to executive and independent agencies:

"Since 1932, when the first veto provision was enacted into law, 295 congressional veto-type procedures have been inserted in 196 different statutes as follows: from 1932 to 1939, five statutes were affected; from 1940–49, nineteen statutes; between 1950–59, thirty-four statutes; and from 1960–69, forty-nine. From the year 1970 through 1975, at least one hundred sixty-three such provisions were included in eighty-nine laws." Abourezk, The Congressional Veto: A Contemporary Response to Executive Encroachment on Legislative Prerogatives, 52 Ind. L. Rev. 323, 324 (1977).

* * *

Explicit and unambiguous provisions of the Constitution prescribe and define the respective functions of the Congress and of the Executive in the legislative process. Since the precise terms of those familiar provisions are critical to the resolution of these cases, we set them out verbatim. Article I provides:

"All legislative Powers herein granted shall be vested in a Congress of the United States, which shall consist of a Senate *and* House of Representatives." Art. I, § 1. (Emphasis added.)

"Every Bill which shall have passed the House of Representatives *and* the Senate, *shall,* before it becomes a law, be presented to the President of the United States..." Art. I, § 7, cl. 2. (Emphasis added.)

"*Every* Order, Resolution, or Vote to which the Concurrence of the Senate and House of Representatives may be necessary (except on a question of Adjournment) *shall be* presented to the President of the United States; and before the Same shall take Effect, *shall be* approved by him, or being disapproved by him, *shall be* repassed by two thirds of the Senate and House of Representatives, according to the Rules and Limitations prescribed in the Case of a Bill." Art. I, § 7, cl. 3. (Emphasis added.)

. . .

B
The Presentment Clauses

The records of the Constitutional Convention reveal that the requirement that all legislation be presented to the President before becoming law was uniformly accepted by the Framers. Presentment to the President and the Presidential veto were considered so imperative that the draftsmen took special pains to assure that these requirements could not be circumvented. During the final debate on Art. I, § 7, cl. 2, James Madison expressed concern that it might easily be evaded by the simple expedient of calling a proposed law a "resolution" or "vote" rather than a "bill." 2 Farrand 301–302. As a consequence, Art. I, § 7, cl. 3...was added....

The decision to provide the President with a limited and qualified power to nullify proposed legislation by veto was based on the profound conviction of the Framers that the powers conferred on Congress were the powers to be most carefully circumscribed....

C
Bicameralism

The bicameral requirement of Art. I, §§ 1, 7, was of scarcely less concern to the Framers than was the Presidential veto and indeed the two concepts are interdependent. By providing that no law could take effect without the concurrence of the prescribed majority of the Members of both Houses, the Framers reemphasized their belief, already remarked upon in connection with the Presentment Clauses, that legislation should not be enacted unless it has been carefully and fully considered by the Nation's elected officials....

. . .

We see therefore that the Framers were acutely conscious that the bicameral requirement and the Presentment Clauses would serve essential constitutional functions. The President's participation in the legislative process was to protect the Executive Branch from Congress and to protect the whole people from improvident laws. The division of the Congress into two distinctive bodies assures that the legislative power would be exercised only after opportunity for full study and debate in separate settings.... It emerges clearly that the prescription for legislative action in Art. I, §§ 1, 7, represents the Framers' decision that the legislative power of the Federal Government be exercised in accord with a single, finely wrought and exhaustively considered, procedure.

IV

The Constitution sought to divide the delegated powers of the new Federal Government into three defined categories, Legislative, Executive, and Judicial, to assure, as nearly as possible, that each branch of government would confine itself to its assigned responsibility. The hydraulic pressure inherent within each of the separate Branches to exceed the outer limits of its power, even to accomplish desirable objectives, must be resisted.

Although not "hermetically" sealed from one another, *Buckley* v. *Valeo,* 424 U. S., at 121, the powers delegated to the three Branches are functionally identifiable. When any Branch acts, it is presumptively exercising the power the Constitution has delegated to it....

Examination of the action taken here by one House pursuant to § 244(c)(2) reveals that it was essentially legislative in purpose and effect. In purporting to exercise power defined in Art. I, § 8, cl. 4, to "establish an uniform Rule of Naturalization," the House took action that had the purpose and effect of altering the legal rights, duties, and relations of persons, including the Attorney General, Executive Branch officials and Chadha, all outside the Legislative Branch. Section 244(c)(2) purports to authorize one House of Congress to require the Attorney General to deport an individual alien whose deportation otherwise would be canceled under § 244. The one-House veto operated in these cases to overrule the Attorney General and mandate Chadha's deportation; absent the House action, Chadha would remain in the United States. Congress has *acted* and its action has altered Chadha's status.

· · ·

[The Court acknowledges that the Constitution in some cases authorizes one House of Congress to act alone without the check of the President's veto: the power of the House of Representatives to initiate impeachment, the Senate's power to try impeachments, the Senate's action on appointments, and the Senate's action on treaties.]

The veto authorized by § 244(c)(2) doubtless has been in many respects a convenient shortcut; the "sharing" with the Executive by Congress of its authority over aliens in this manner is, on its face, an appealing compromise. In purely practical terms, it is obviously easier for action to be taken by one House without submission to the President; but it is crystal clear from the records of the Convention, contemporaneous writings and debates, that the Framers ranked other values higher than efficiency. The records of the Convention and debates in the states preceding ratification underscore the common desire to define and limit the exercise of the newly created federal powers affecting the states and the people. There is unmistakable expression of a determination that legislation by the national Congress be a step-by-step, deliberate and deliberative process.

The choices we discern as having been made in the Constitutional Convention impose burdens on governmental processes that often seem clumsy, inefficient, even unworkable, but those hard choices were consciously made by men who had lived under a form of government that permitted arbitrary governmental acts to go unchecked. There is no support in the Constitution or decisions of this Court for the proposition that the cumbersomeness and delays often encountered in complying with explicit constitutional standards may be avoided, either by the Congress or by the President. See *Youngstown Sheet & Tube Co. v. Sawyer*, 343 U. S. 579 (1952). With all the obvious flaws of delay, untidiness, and potential for abuse, we have not yet found a better way to preserve freedom than by making the exercise of power subject to the carefully crafted restraints spelled out in the Constitution.

V

We hold that the congressional veto provision in § 244(c)(2) is severable from the Act and that it is unconstitutional. Accordingly, the judgment of the Court of Appeals is

Affirmed.

JUSTICE POWELL, concurring in the judgment.

The Court's decision, based on the Presentment Clauses, Art. I, § 7, cls. 2 and 3, apparently will invalidate every use of the legislative veto. The breadth of this holding gives one pause. Congress has included the veto in literally hundreds of statutes, dating back to the 1930's. Congress clearly views this procedure as essential to controlling the delegation of power to administrative agencies. One reasonably may disagree with Congress' assessment of the veto's utility, but the respect due its judgment as a coordinate branch of Government cautions that our holdings should be no more extensive than necessary to decide these cases. In my view, the cases may be decided on a narrower ground. When Congress finds that a particular person does not satisfy the statutory criteria for permanent residence in this country it has assumed a judicial function in violation of the principle of separation of powers. Accordingly, I concur only in the judgment.

· · ·

JUSTICE WHITE, dissenting.

Today the Court not only invalidates § 244(c)(2) of the Immigration and Nationality Act, but also sounds the death knell for nearly 200 other statutory provisions in which Congress has reserved a "legislative veto." For this reason, the Court's decision is of surpassing importance. And it is for this reason that the Court would have been well advised to decide the cases, if possible, on the narrower grounds of separation of powers, leaving for full consideration the constitutionality of other congressional review statutes operating on such varied matters as war powers and agency rulemaking, some of which concern the independent regulatory agencies.

The prominence of the legislative veto mechanism in our contemporary political system and its importance to Congress can hardly be over-stated. It has become a central means by which Congress secures the accountability of executive and independent agencies. Without the legislative veto, Congress is faced with a Hobson's choice: either to refrain from delegating the necessary authority, leaving itself with a hopeless task of writing laws with the requisite specificity to cover endless special circumstances across the entire policy landscape, or in the alternative, to abdicate its lawmaking function of the Executive Branch and independent agencies. To choose the former leaves major national problems unresolved; to opt for the latter risks unaccountable policymaking by those not elected to fill that role. Accordingly, over the past five decades, the legislative veto has been placed in nearly 200 statutes. The device is known in every field of governmental concern: reorganization, budgets, foreign affairs, war powers, and regulation of trade, safety, energy, the environment, and the economy.

I

[White explains that the legislative veto arose in 1929 when President Hoover sought authority to reorganize the executive branch and expressed willingness to have Congress check his actions by exercising a one-House veto. In subsequent actions, the two branches applied this quid pro quo to other areas. The result was that the President gained new authority and Congress held a legislative veto to control the delegated authority.]

The history of the legislative veto also makes clear that it has not been a sword with which Congress has struck out to aggrandize itself at the expense of the other branches—the concerns of Madison and Hamilton. Rather, the veto has been a means of defense, a reservation of ultimate authority necessary if Congress is to fulfill its designated role under Art. I as the Nation's lawmaker. While the President has often objected to particular legislative vetoes, generally those left in the hands of congressional Committees, the Executive has more often agreed to legislative review as the price for a broad delegation of authority. To be sure, the President may have preferred unrestricted power, but that could be precisely why Congress thought it essential to retain a check on the exercise of delegated authority.

. . .

III

. . .

The central concern of the presentment and bicameralism requirements of Art. I is that when a departure from the legal status quo is undertaken, it is done with the approval of the President and both Houses of Congress—or, in the event of a Presidential veto, a two-thirds majority in both Houses. This interest is fully satisfied by the operation of § 244(c)(2). The President's approval is found in the Attorney General's action in recommending to Congress that the deportation order for a given alien be suspended. The House and the Senate indicate their approval of the Executive's action by not passing a resolution of disapproval within the statutory period. Thus, a change in the legal status quo—the deportability of the alien—is consummated only with the approval of each of the three relevant actors. The disagreement of any one of the three maintains the alien's pre-existing status: the Executive may choose not to recommend suspension; the House and Senate may each veto the recommendation. The effect on the rights and obligations of the affected individuals and upon the legislative system is precisely the same as if a private bill were introduced but failed to receive the necessary approval....

V

I regret that I am in disagreement with my colleagues on the fundamental questions that these cases present. But even more I regret the destructive scope of the Court's holding. It reflects a profoundly different conception of the Constitution than that held by the courts which sanctioned the modern administrative state. Today's decision strikes down in one fell swoop provisions in more laws enacted by Congress than the Court has cumulatively invalidated in its history....

JUSTICE REHNQUIST, with whom JUSTICE WHITE joins, dissenting.

[Rehnquist states his belief that Congress did not intend the one-House veto to be severable from § 244(c)(2). Because the Court had held the legislative veto unconstitutional, Rehnquist would strike down the delegated authority as well.]

Louis Fisher

Legislative Vetoes After *Chadha*

After the Supreme Court in *INS* v. *Chadha* (1983) held the legislative veto unconstitutional, Congress continued to place legislative vetoes in bills and Presidents continued to sign them into law. Many of these new statutory controls required executive agencies to seek the approval of specific congressional committees before implementing an agency action. The various methods available to Congress for finding substitutes for the legislative veto, and in fact for using legislative vetoes, are explored by Louis Fisher in "Judicial Misjudgments About the Lawmaking Process: The Legislative Veto Case," 45 Pub. Adm. Rev. 705 (Special Issue, November 1985). A more recent analysis appears in Louis Fisher, "The Legislative Veto: Invalidated, It Survives," 56 Law & Contemp. Prob. 273 (Autumn 1993).

In past years the Supreme Court has damaged its reputation by issuing decisions based on misconceptions about the political and economic system. After trying to impose archaic and mechanical concepts about federalism, the taxing power, the commerce power, and other clauses of the Constitution, the court was forced to retreat from pronouncements that were simply unacceptable for a developing nation. To minimize what Charles Evans Hughes once called the court's penchant for "self-inflicted wounds," justices evolved a number of rules to limit their exercise of judicial review. One mainstay is the principle that the court will not "formulate a rule of constitutional law broader than is required by the precise facts to which it is to be applied."

That guideline was not followed in 1983 when the Supreme Court issued *INS* v. *Chadha*, which declared the legislative veto unconstitutional in all its forms. The court announced that future congressional efforts to alter "the legal rights, duties and relations of persons" outside the legislative branch must follow the full lawmaking process: passage of a bill or joint resolution by both Houses and presentment of that measure to the president for his signature or veto. The court lectured Congress that it could no longer rely on the legislative veto as "a convenient shortcut" to control executive agencies. Instead, "legislation by the national Congress [must] be a step-by-step, deliberate and deliberative process." According to the court, the framers insisted that "the legislative power of the Federal Government be exercised in accord with a single, finely wrought and exhaustively considered, procedure."

A HISTORY OF ACCOMMODATIONS

All three branches reached agreement long ago

that the step-by-step, deliberate and deliberative process is not appropriate for each and every exercise of the legislative power. Despite occasional invocations of the non-delegation doctrine, the court itself has accepted the inevitable delegation of legislative power to executive agencies and independent commissions. Administrative bodies routinely "make law" through the rulemaking process. Efforts are made to subject this lawmaking activity to procedural safeguards, but the persistence of the Administrative State is ample proof that the theoretical model of legislative action envisioned by the framers applies only in the most general sense to the 20th century.

Notwithstanding 50 years of delicate accommodations between the executive and legislative branches regarding the legislative veto, the Supreme Court decided to strike it down in one fell swoop. In his dissent, Justice White claimed that the court "sounds the death knell for nearly 200 other statutory provisions in which Congress has reserved a 'legislative veto.'" Although White demonstrated better than his colleagues an appreciation of the realities and subtleties of lawmaking in contemporary times, he too framed the issue too starkly. He argued that without the legislative veto, Congress "is faced with a Hobson's choice: either to refrain from delegating the necessary authority, leaving itself with a hopeless task of writing laws with the requisite specificity to cover endless special circumstances across the entire policy landscape, or in the alternative, to abdicate its lawmaking function to the Executive Branch and independent agencies." In fact, Congress and the agencies have access to a number of middle-range options that serve much the same purpose as the legislative veto. In some cases, current practices are difficult to distinguish from what supposedly vanished with the death knell.

· · ·

THE PERSISTENCE OF
LEGISLATIVE VETOES

It came as a surprise to some observers that Congress continued to place legislative vetoes in bills after the court's decision and President Reagan continued to sign the bills into law. In the 16 months between *Chadha* and the adjournment of the 98th Congress, an additional 53 legislative vetoes were added to the books.

[By the end of the 106th Congress, which adjourned at the end of 2000, the list of new legislative vetoes had increased to more than four hundred.]

A flagrant case of non-compliance? A sign of disrespect for the courts? An alarming challenge to the time-honored belief that the Supreme Court has the last word on constitutional questions? Perhaps, but the court painted with too broad a brush and offered a simplistic solution that is unacceptable to the political branches. Its decision will be eroded by open defiance and subtle evasion. Neither consequence is attractive, but much of the responsibility for this condition belongs on the doorstep of the court.

Some of the legislative vetoes enacted since *Chadha* are easy to spot. Most of them vest control in the appropriations committees. For example, construction grants by the Environmental Protection Agency are subject to the approval of the appropriations committees (97 Stat. 226). The approval of the appropriations committees is required before exceeding certain dollar amounts in the National Flood Insurance Fund (97 Stat. 227)....

Other legislative vetoes are more subtle. A continuing resolution provided that foreign assistance funds allocated to each country "shall not exceed those provided in fiscal year 1983 or those provided in the budget estimates for each country, whichever are lower, unless submitted through the regular reprogramming procedures of the Committees on Appropriations" (97 Stat. 736). Those procedures provide for committee prior-approval. The District of Columbia Appropriation Act for fiscal 1984 prohibited funds from being obligated or spent by reprogramming "except pursuant to advance approval of the reprogramming granted according to the procedure set forth" in two House reports, both of which require prior approval by the appropriations committees (97 Stat. 827).

One year after *Chadha*, President Reagan received the HUD-Independent Agencies Appropriations bill which contained a number of committee vetoes. In his signing statement, he took note of those vetoes and asked Congress to stop adding provisions that the Supreme Court had held to be unconstitutional. He said that "the time has come, with more than a year having passed since the Supreme Court's decision in *Chadha*, to make clear that legislation containing legislative veto devices that comes to me for my approval or disapproval will be implemented in a manner consistent with the *Chadha* decision." The clear import was that the administration did not feel bound by the statutory requirements to seek the approval of congressional committees before implementing certain actions.

The House Appropriations Committee responded to the president's statement by reviewing an agreement it had entered into with NASA four years previously. Caps were set on various NASA programs, usually at the level requested in the president's budget. The agreement allowed NASA to exceed the caps with the approval of the appropriations committees. The House Appropriations Committee thought that the procedure had "worked well during the past four years, and has provided a mechanism by which the Congress and the Committee can be assured that funds are used solely for the purpose for which they were appropriated." Because of Reagan's statement and the threat to ignore committee controls, the committee said it was necessary to repeal the accommodation that had lasted for four years. Repeal language was inserted in the second supplemental bill for fiscal 1984. Both sides stood to lose. The appropriations committees would not be able to veto NASA proposals; NASA would not be able to exceed ceilings without enacting new language in a separate appropriation bill.

Neither NASA nor the appropriations committees wanted to enact a separate public law just to exceed a cap. To avoid this kind of administrative rigidity, NASA Administrator James M. Beggs wrote to both committees on August 9, 1984. His letter reveals the pragmatic sense of give-and-take that is customary between executive agencies and congressional committees. His letter also underscores the impracticality and unreality of the doctrines enunciated by the Supreme Court in *Chadha*:

"We have now operated under the present operating plan and reprogramming procedures for several years and have found them to be workable. In light of the constitutional questions raised concerning the legislative veto provisions included in P.L. 98-371 [the HUD-Independent Agencies Appropriations Act], however, the House Committee on Appropriations has proposed in H.R. 6040, the FY 1984 general supplemental, deletion of all Committee approval provisions, leaving inflexible, binding funding limitations on several programs. Without some procedure for adjustment, other than a subsequent separate legislative enactment, these ceilings could seriously impact the ability of NASA to meet unforeseen technical changes or problems that are inherent in challenging R&D programs. We believe that the present legislative procedure could be converted by this letter into an informal agreement by NASA not to exceed amounts for Committee designated programs without the approval of the Committees on Appropriations. This agreement would assume that both the statutory funding ceilings and the Committee approval mechanisms would be deleted from the FY 1985 legislation, and that it would not be the normal practice to include either mechanism in future appropriations bills. Further, the agreement would assume that future program ceiling amounts would be identified by the Committees in the Conference Report accompanying NASA's annual appropriations act and confirmed by NASA in its submission of the annual operating plan. NASA would not expend any funds over the ceilings identified in the Conference Report for these programs without the prior approval of the Committees."

In short, the agency would continue to honor legislative vetoes. But they would be informal rather than statutory. Beggs ended his letter by as-suring the appropriations committees that NASA "will comply with any ceilings imposed by the Committees without the need for legislative ceilings which could cause serious damage to NASA's ongoing programs." By converting the legislative veto to an informal and non-statutory status, NASA is not legally bound by the agreement. Violation of the agreement, however, could provoke the appropriations committees to place caps in the appropriation bill and force the agency to lift them only through the enactment of another public law.

. . .

CONCLUSIONS

Through its misreading of history, congressional procedures, and executive-legislative relations, the Supreme Court has commanded the political branches to follow a lawmaking process that is impracticable and unworkable. Neither agencies nor committees want the static model of government offered by the court. The inevitable result is a record of non-compliance, subtle evasion, and a system of lawmaking that is now more convoluted, cumbersome, and covert than before. In many cases the court's decision simply drives underground a set of legislative and committee vetoes that had previously operated in plain sight. No one should be misled if the number of legislative vetoes placed in statutes gradually declines over the years. Fading from view will not mean disappearance. In one form or another legislative vetoes will remain an important method for reconciling legislative and executive interests.

G. INVESTIGATIONS AND EXECUTIVE PRIVILEGE

The impact of implied powers is nowhere more evident than in the struggle for information. Although the Constitution does not expressly give Congress the power to investigate, the Supreme Court in 1927 announced that a legislative body "cannot legislate wisely or effectively in the absence of information respecting the conditions which the legislation is intended to affect or change." McGrain v. Daugherty, 273 U.S. 135, 175. Similarly, the Constitution does not give the President the privilege of withholding information from Congress, and yet in 1974 the Court decided that the President's interest in withholding information to protect confidentiality with his advisers is implied in the Constitution: "to the extent this interest relates to the effective discharge of a President's powers, it is constitutionally based." United States v. Nixon, 418 U.S. 683, 711 (1974).

There is an inevitable collision when Congress attempts to carry out its investigative function and the President invokes executive privilege. Which branch should surrender to the other? Major confrontations require some type of compromise, prodded by Congress's power to punish for contempt and the judiciary's ability to steer both branches toward an acceptable accommodation.

Congressional Investigations

Congress relies on its investigative power to enact legislation; to oversee the administration of programs; to inform the public; and to protect its integrity, dignity, reputation, and privileges. To enforce each of these responsibilities, each House of Congress possesses an inherent power to punish for contempt. Without the power to punish for contempt, Congress would be left "exposed to every indignity and interruption that rudeness, caprice, or even conspiracy, may mediate against it." Anderson v. Dunn, 6 Wheat. 204, 228 (1821).

This decision in 1821 limited the power of Congress to punish for contempt. Each House had to exercise the least possible power adequate to the end proposed (in this case the power to imprison) and the duration of punishment could not exceed the life of the legislative body (that is, imprisonment had to terminate with congressional adjournment). Because of those restrictions, Congress decided in 1857 to use the judiciary to enforce its investigative power. Failure to appear or refusal to answer pertinent questions can lead to a contempt vote in either House, which requires a U.S. attorney to seek an indictment by a grand jury and conviction in the courts. 11 Stat. 155 (1957), codified at 2 U.S.C. §§ 192–94 (1994). This law, as amended, was upheld in In re Chapman, 166 U.S. 661 (1897). Congress created a third option in 1978. If an individual from the private sector refuses to comply with a Senate subpoena (an order requiring certain action under threat of punishment), the Senate may request a court order to require compliance with the subpoena. Failure to obey the court order can lead to civil contempt. The sanction is lifted once the individual complies with the Senate's request. 28 U.S.C. § 1364 (1994).

Because of such spectacles as the McCarthy hearings of the 1950s, which deteriorated into a witch hunt for "subversives," congressional investigations are often associated with careless and damaging intrusions into personal lives. Most investigations, however, are conducted in a responsible manner and pose no threat to individual liberties or the separation of powers. In fact, congressional investigations often enhance individual liberties by challenging and exposing abuses by the executive barnch or the private sector.

Prodded by the adverse publicity from the 1950s, Congress adopted a set of procedures for committee investigations to assure fairness. The courts also insisted that committee hearings be properly authorized by Congress and their scope defined. United States v. Rumely, 345 U.S. 41 (1953); Gojack v. United States, 384 U.S. 702 (1966). In 1957, in what was considered a sharp rebuke to Congress, the Court held that fundamental fairness demanded that a witness be given adequate guidance in deciding the pertinency of a question. There was no congressional power "to expose for the sake of exposure." WATKINS v. UNITED STATES, 354 U.S. 178 (1957). The tone of the decision, together with other judicial rulings during that period, triggered a groundswell of opposition from legislators. Various bills were introduced to curb the Court. In the face of this political pressure, the Supreme Court, two years later, retreated from its position. It now adopted a generous "balancing test" that allowed the government's interest in self-preservation to outweigh the individual's right to remain silent. BARENBLATT v. UNITED STATES, 360 U.S. 109 (1959).

When the activities of an organization did not raise questions of subversion and communism, at least directly, the courts were more likely to protect the rights of association. This is the teaching of a 1958 case, in which a state's attorney general attempted to obtain the membership list of a civil rights organization, the NAACP. Such publicity could have discouraged individuals from joining and participating in exposed groups. The principles announced in this case give greater support to the rights of speech, assembly, and association. NAACP v. Alabama, 357 U.S. 449 (1958). See also Gibson v. Florida Legislative Investigation Committee, 372 U.S. 539 (1963).

Immunity for Witnesses

Witnesses may invoke the Fifth Amendment privilege against self-incrimination. Quinn v. United States, 349 U.S. 155 (1955) and Empsak v. United States, 349 U.S. 190 (1955). An immunity procedure is available to force testimony while at the same time recognizing Fifth Amendment rights. Witnesses may receive full immunity or partial immunity. For the latter, a witness can be compelled to testify and later be prosecuted so long as the witness's testimony (or evidence derived from it) is not used in the prosecution.[15]

Colonel Oliver North received partial immunity—also called "use immunity"—when he testified before the Iran-Contra hearings in 1987. He was later convicted of three felonies: obstructing the investigation by Congress, mutilating government documents, and taking an illegal gratuity. The charges were subsequently dismissed because of his testimony. Under the new and more stringent standard imposed by the courts, prosecutors must show that a defendant's testimony could have had no influence on the witnesses called to a trial. Otherwise, the witnesses are "tainted" and their remarks may not be used to convict (see chapter 13, pp. 726–27).

Over the years, the Court has attempted to establish guidelines for congressional investigations. In 1881 it struck down an investigation and a contempt action because the matter was already pending before a court. Kilbourn v. Thompson, 103 U.S. 168, 182. Such a doctrine would put congressional investigations on the back burner for years while awaiting the outcome of a lawsuit. Executive agencies could sidetrack an embarrassing committee hearing simply by filing suit and pursuing appeals. Congress may decide to defer its investigation until the completion of a criminal trial or refuse to wait for the results of long, drawn-out litigation. The latter course was followed during the Reagan administration when Congress investigated corruption within the Environmental Protection Agency. In such circumstances, Congress has the right to proceed, even at the cost of postponing a trial.[16]

Initially, the courts held that congressional investigations must relate to some legislative purpose. Congress should not conduct "fruitless" inquiries without the prospect of legislation. Kilbourn v. Thompson, 103 U.S. at 194–95. Later, however, the Court admitted that a "potential" for legislation is sufficient. McGrain v. Daugherty, 273 U.S. at 177. Even this is too restrictive a test. Committee efforts to oversee executive agencies may take researchers up "blind alleys" and into nonproductive enterprises: "To be a valid legislative inquiry there need be no predictable end result." Eastland v. United States Servicemen's Fund, 421 U.S. 491, 509 (1975) (see box on next page). Attorney General William French Smith incorrectly stated that congressional requests for information are on stronger ground if Congress has specific legislation in mind than when it simply probes as part of a general oversight effort.[17]

A decision by the Supreme Court in 1995 limited the ability of the Justice Department to prosecute lawmakers and government officials for lying to Congress. Section 1001 of Title 18 criminalizes unsworn false statements in any matter within the jurisdiction of any "department or agency" of the United States. In holding that Section 1001 did not apply to federal courts, the Court also overruled a 1955 case that had applied Section 1001 to a former Member' of Congress who had made a false statement to the Disbursing Office of the House of

---

15. 18 U.S.C. §§ 6001–05 (1994). The immunity procedure, as a substitute for the Fifth Amendment, was upheld in Ullmann v. United States, 350 U.S. 422 (1956); Kastigar v. United States, 406 U.S. 441 (1972); and Application of U.S. Senate Select Com. on Pres. Cam. Act., 361 F.Supp. 1270 (D.D.C. 1973).

16. Delaney v. United States, 199 F.2d 107, 114–15 (1st Cir. 1952). See also Hutcheson v. United States, 369 U.S. 599, 612–13, 623–24 (1962), Sinclair v. United States, 279 U.S. 263, 295 (1929), and Fisher, Constitutional Conflicts Between Congress and the President 160–72 (1997).

17. "Executive Privilege: Legal Opinions Regarding Claim of President Ronald Reagan in Response to a Subpoena Issued to James G. Watt, Secretary of the Interior," prepared for the use of the House Committee on Energy and Commerce, 97th Cong., 1st Sess. 3 (Comm. Print November 1981).

Evolving Judicial Standards for Congressional Investigations

Congress could not conduct "fruitless" inquiries without the prospect for legislation. Kilbourn v. Thompson, 103 U.S. 168, 194–195 (1881)

"Potential" for legislation is sufficient. Mc-Grain v. Daugherty, 273 U.S. 135, 177 (1927)

Witnesses must understand the pertinency of a question. Watkins v. United States, 354 U.S. 178 (1957)

A "balancing test" permits the government's interest in self-preservation to outweigh an individual's right to remain silent. Barenblatt v. United States, 360 U.S. 109 (1959)

Investigation can lead up "blind alleys" with no predictable legislative result. Eastland v. United States Servicemen's Fund, 421 U.S. 491, 509 (1975)

Representatives. The effect of the 1995 ruling was to limit the Justice Department's ability to prosecute only those individuals who committed perjury to Congress (for lying under oath). Hubbard v. United States, 514 U.S. 695 (1995). Congress responded to *Hubbard* by enacting legislation a year later that reinstated criminal penalties for making false statements to Congress. 110 Stat. 3459 (1996).

Impeachment

The ultimate form of the investigative power is impeachment. The President, Vice President, and all civil officers of the United States shall be removed from office upon "Impeachment for, and Conviction of, Treason, Bribery, or other high Crimes and Misdemeanors" (Article II, Section 4). Treason is defined in Article III, Section 3, while bribery has a fairly clear statutory meaning. What constitutes "other high Crimes and Misdemeanors"? The framers rejected vague grounds for impeachment, such as "maladministration," because this would be equivalent to having the President serve at the pleasure of Congress. 3 Farrand 65–66, 550. However, impeachment need not require indictable crimes or specific statutory offenses. In Federalist No. 65, Alexander Hamilton included "political crimes" (abuses in office or violation of the public trust) as legitimate grounds for impeachment. Madison also supported impeachment for political abuses or neglect of office. 1 Annals of Congress 372–73 (May 19, 1789). The purpose of impeachment is to remove someone from office, not to punish for a crime. Impeachable conduct need not be criminal. That was the conclusion of the House Committee on the Judiciary during the impeachment proceedings of Richard Nixon. In 1993 the Supreme Court upheld the Senate's practice of conducting an impeachment trial in two stages: fact-finding by a 12-member committee followed by action by the full Senate. Nixon v. United States, 506 U.S. 224 (1993). For a reading on this decision, see chapter 3.

The impeachment of President Bill Clinton highlighted several issues about the process. The House of Representatives, voting largely along party grounds on December 19, 1998, adopted two articles of impeachment, one on perjury and the other on obstruction of justice. Voting on February 12, 1999, the Senate "acquitted" Clinton on both articles. With regard to the perjury article, 45 Senators voted "guilty" and 55 voted "not guilty." The vote on obstruction of justice was only 50 to 50, far short of the two-thirds required for removal.

The votes were distorted because the Senate currently votes simultaneously on two separate issues: guilt and removal. From 1789 to 1936, the Senate voted first for guilt and next for removal, allowing Senators to hold someone guilty of the charges brought against them but then decide that the person should not be removed from office. After 1936 the two issues were collapsed into a single vote. Many Senators who voted "not guilty" explained that Clinton was indeed guilty.

For example, Senator Robert C. Byrd (D-W.Va.) voted "not guilty" on both articles although he thought that Clinton's behavior constituted "an impeachable offense, a political high crime or misdemeanor against the state." Not wanting to remove Clinton, Byrd had only one choice: to vote "not guilty," after judging him guilty on both counts. Other Senators, including Susan Collins (R-Me.), Olympia Snowe (R-Me.), James Jeffords (R-Vt.), Fred Thompson (R-Tenn.), Ted Stevens (R-Alas.), and Slade Gorton (R-Wash.), concluded that Clinton was guilty on one or both articles but voted "not guilty" because they thought removal was unwarranted.

Senator Snowe put it this way: "Acquittal is not exoneration." John Breaux, a Democrat from Louisiana, voted against the articles but cautioned that his vote "is not a vote on the innocence of this President. He is not innocent." Bob Kerrey, Democrat from Nebraska, added: "While there is plenty of blame to go around in this case, the person responsible for it going this far is the President of the United States."

Secondly, the votes on the two articles turned on factors that had nothing to do with the evidence presented. Some legislators cited public polls of Clinton's popularity as reason to vote against impeachment and removal. Had Clinton been less popular, would that factor (unrelated to the evidence) been adequate grounds for supporting his impeachment and removal? Moreover, lawmakers pointed to the buoyant stock market, low unemployment, and modest inflation as reasons for keeping Clinton in office. Had economic conditions turned sour, would that have justified Clinton's impeachment and removal from office? Obviously many lawmakers found it difficult to focus on the substance of the two articles.

Executive Privilege

President George Washington and his cabinet complied with a request by the House of Representatives in 1792 for papers regarding a military defeat but also concluded that it would be appropriate in the future to refuse documents "the disclosure of which would injure the public." 1 Writings of Thomas Jefferson 303–05 (Mem. ed. 1903). In general, Presidents agree to make papers and documents available for impeachment inquiries or congressional investigations into administrative corruption. While upholding a very broad theory of executive privilege in 1982, Attorney General Smith said he would not try to "shield documents [from Congress] which contain evidence of criminal or unethical conduct by agency officials from proper review." H. Rept. No. 968, 97th Cong., 2d Sess. 41 (1982).

If executive officials refuse congressional requests for information, a move by Congress to cite the person for contempt is often an effective way to get the official's attention and cooperation. For example, in 1982 the House of Representatives voted 259 to 105 to hold Anne Gorsuch, administrator of the Environmental Protection Agency, in contempt. In an unprecedented action, the U.S. Attorney did not take the contempt citation to the grand jury, as required by statute. Instead, the administration asked a district court to declare the House action an unconstitutional intrusion into the President's authority to withhold information from Congress. After this tactic failed, the documents were released. United States v. House of Representatives, 556 F. Supp. 150 (D.D.C. 1983). Use of subpoenas and threats of contempt citations led to the release of several documents by the Clinton administration. Louis Fisher, Constitutional Conflicts between Congress and the President 166–67, 183 (1997).

The major executive privilege case — *United States* v. *Nixon* — did not involve a congressional request for executive documents. The request came from the courts as part of the effort to prosecute Watergate crimes. A unanimous Court rejected the argument that the decision to release such documents is up to the President, not the courts. To permit Nixon absolute control over the documents would have prevented the judiciary from carrying out its duties. UNITED STATES v. NIXON, 418 U.S. 683 (1974).

Conflicts between the executive and legislative branches are sometimes resolved with the assistance of federal judges. A deadlock between a House committee and the Justice Department during the 1970s, regarding the release of "national security" information, was eventually broken through the efforts of Judge Harold Leventhal. He convinced each branch that a compromise worked out between them would be better than a solution dictated by the courts. Practical accommodations are required instead of rigid abstractions about the power of Congress to investigate or the power of the President to withhold information (see readings for AT&T cases).

Presidential Immunity

Although the Constitution does not provide an express immunity for the President, the courts have developed a doctrine of official immunity for executive officials and the President. Unless executive employees enjoyed an immunity for their official actions, they could not be expected to administer laws vigorously and effectively. Barr v. Matteo, 360 U.S. 564 (1959); Gregoire v. Biddle, 177 F.2d 579 (2d Cir. 1949). In 1982, the Supreme Court held that the President is entitled to absolute immunity, in civil suits, regarding all of his official acts. Nixon v. Fitzgerald, 457 U.S. 731 (1982). A qualified immunity is available for presidential aides. Harlow v. Fitzgerald, 457 U.S. 800 (1982); Mitchell v. Forsyth, 472 U.S. 511 (1985).

A separate question is whether the President is entitled to immunity from civil liability for *unofficial* acts: acts committed in a personal capacity rather than as President. This issue arose when Paula Corbin Jones brought a lawsuit against Bill Clinton for an incident that occurred before he became President. She claimed that in 1991, at a conference held at a hotel in Little Rock, Clinton (at that time governor of Arkansas) sexually harassed and assaulted her. Clinton's attorneys argued that the President should have a temporary immunity while serving in office and that the case should not go forward until he left office. In 1997, a unanimous Court decided that the Constitution does not afford the President temporary immunity in this case. CLINTON v. JONES, 520 U.S. 681 (1997). The case was dismissed in 1998 when a district judge held that there were "no genuine issues for trial in this case." After Jones appealed, Clinton agreed to settle the case by giving her $850,000.

The Supreme Court's prediction that the case could go forward without substantially burdening President Clinton has been much maligned. However, the resulting burden had less to do with Jones than to new allegations concerning Clinton's relationship with White House intern Monica Lewinsky and serious charges of possible White House efforts to lie, suborn witnesses, and obstruct justice.

Watkins v. United States

354 U.S. 178 (1957)

Beginning in the early 1950s, congressional committees conducted searching inquiries into left-wing activities of American citizens. The atmosphere of the cold war permitted little toleration of "disloyal" thoughts and conduct. In this case, the House Committee on Un-American Activities called John Watkins, a labor organizer, to testify. He agreed to describe his past participation in the Communist party and identify current members. However, he refused to answer questions about those who had left the movement. His refusal led to conviction for contempt of Congress. A panel of the D.C. Circuit reversed the conviction, but the full bench, sitting *en banc*, affirmed the conviction.

Mr. Chief Justice Warren delivered the opinion of the Court.

This is a review by certiorari of a conviction under 2 U. S. C. § 192 for "contempt of Congress." The misdemeanor is alleged to have been committed during a hearing before a congressional investigating committee. It is not the case of a truculent or contumacious witness who refuses to answer all questions or who, by boisterous or discourteous conduct, disturbs the decorum of the committee room. Petitioner was prosecuted for refusing to make certain disclosures which he asserted to be beyond the authority of the committee to demand. The controversy thus rests upon fundamental principles of the power of the Congress and the limitations upon that power. We approach the questions presented with conscious awareness of the far-reaching ramifications that can follow from a decision of this nature.

On April 29, 1954, petitioner appeared as a witness in compliance with a subpoena issued by a Subcommittee of the Committee on Un-American Activities of the House of Representatives. The Subcommittee elicited from petitioner a description of his background in labor union activities.…

Petitioner's name had been mentioned by two witnesses who testified before the Committee at prior hearings. In September 1952, one Donald O. Spencer admitted having been a Communist from 1943 to 1946. He declared that he had been recruited into the Party with the endorsement and prior approval of petitioner, whom he identified as the then District Vice-President of the Farm Equipment Workers. Spencer also mentioned that petitioner had attended meetings at which only card-carrying Communists were admitted. A month before petitioner testified, one Walter Rumsey stated that he had been recruited into the Party by petitioner. Rumsey added that he had paid Party dues to, and later collected dues from, petitioner, who had assumed the name, Sam Brown. Rumsey told the Committee that he left the Party in 1944.

Petitioner answered these allegations freely and without reservation. His attitude toward the inquiry is clearly revealed from the statement he made when the questioning turned to the subject of his past conduct, associations and predilections:

"I am not now nor have I ever been a card-carrying member of the Communist Party. Rumsey was wrong when he said I had recruited him into the party, that I had received his dues, that I paid dues to him, and that I had used the alias Sam Brown.

"Spencer was wrong when he termed any meetings which I attended as closed Communist Party meetings.

"I would like to make it clear that for a period of time from approximately 1942 to 1947 I cooperated with the Communist Party and participated in Communist activities to such a degree that some persons may honestly believe that I was a member of the party.

"I have made contributions upon occasions to Communist causes. I have signed petitions for Communist causes. I attended caucuses at an FE convention at which Communist Party officials were present."

. . .

The Subcommittee, too, was apparently satisfied with petitioner's disclosures. After some further discussion elaborating on the statement, counsel for the Committee turned to another aspect of Rumsey's testimony. Rumsey had identified a group of persons whom he had known as members of the Communist Party, and counsel began to read this list of names to petitioner. Petitioner stated that he did not know several of the persons. Of those whom he did know, he refused to tell whether he knew them to have been members of the Communist Party. He explained to the Subcommittee why he took such a position:

"I am not going to plead the fifth amendment, but I refuse to answer certain questions that I believe are outside the proper scope of your committee's activities. I will answer any questions which this committee puts to me about myself. I will also answer questions about those persons whom I knew to be members of the Communist Party and whom I believe still are. I will not, however, answer any questions with respect to others with whom I associated in the past. I do not believe that any law in this country requires me to testify about persons who may in the past have been Communist Party members or otherwise engaged in Communist Party activity but who to my best knowledge and belief have long since removed themselves from the Communist movement.

"I do not believe that such questions are relevant to the work of this committee nor do I believe that this committee has the right to undertake the public exposure of persons because of their past activities. I may be wrong, and the committee may have this power, but until and unless a court of law so holds and directs me to answer,

I most firmly refuse to discuss the political activities of my past associates."

The Chairman of the Committee submitted a report of petitioner's refusal to answer questions to the House of Representatives. H. R. Rep. No. 1579, 83d Cong., 2d Sess. The House directed the Speaker to certify the Committee's report to the United States Attorney for initiation of criminal prosecution. H. Res. 534, 83d Cong., 2d Sess. A seven-count indictment was returned. Petitioner waived his right to jury trial and was found guilty on all counts by the court. The sentence, a fine of $100 and one year in prison, was suspended, and petitioner was placed on probation.

An appeal was taken to the Court of Appeals for the District of Columbia. The conviction was reversed by a three-judge panel, one member dissenting. Upon rehearing *en banc,* the full bench affirmed the conviction....

We start with several basic premises on which there is general agreement. The power of the Congress to conduct investigations is inherent in the legislative process. That power is broad. It encompasses inquiries concerning the administration of existing laws as well as proposed or possibly needed statutes. It includes surveys of defects in our social, economic or political system for the purpose of enabling the Congress to remedy them. It comprehends probes into departments of the Federal Government to expose corruption, inefficiency or waste. But, broad as is this power of inquiry, it is not unlimited. There is no general authority to expose the private affairs of individuals without justification in terms of the functions of the Congress. This was freely conceded by the Solicitor General in his argument of this case. *["Now, we don't claim on behalf of the Government that there is any right to expose for the purposes of exposure. And I don't know that Congress has ever claimed any such right. But we do say, in the same breath, that there is a right to inform the public at the same time you inform the Congress."]* Nor is the Congress a law enforcement or trial agency. These are functions of the executive and judicial departments of government. No inquiry is an end in itself; it must be related to, and in furtherance of, a legitimate task of the Congress. Investigations conducted solely for the personal aggrandizement of the investigators or to "punish" those investigated are indefensible.

It is unquestionably the duty of all citizens to cooperate with the Congress in its efforts to obtain the facts needed for intelligent legislative action. It is their unremitting obligation to respond to subpoenas, to respect the dignity of the Congress and its committees and to testify fully with respect to matters within the province of proper investigation. This, of course, assumes that the constitutional rights of witnesses will be respected by the Congress as they are in a court of justice. The Bill of Rights is applicable to investigations as to all forms of governmental action. Witnesses cannot be compelled to give evidence against themselves. They cannot be subjected to unreasonable search and seizure. Nor can the First Amendment freedoms of speech, press, religion, or political belief and association be abridged.

[The Court describes the English Parliament's abuse of its contempt power, which was immune even from judicial review. Citizens who made comments critical of Parliament could be punished, fined, and imprisoned. Parliamentary probes were eventually replaced by investigations conducted by Royal Commissions of Inquiry, comprised of experts who rarely had the authority to compel the testimony of witnesses or the production of documents.]

The history of contempt of the legislature in this country is notably different from that of England. In the early days of the United States, there lingered the direct knowledge of the evil effects of absolute power. Most of the instances of use of compulsory process by the first Congresses concerned matters affecting the qualification or integrity of their members or came about in inquiries dealing with suspected corruption or mismanagement of government officials. Unlike the English practice, from the very outset the use of contempt power by the legislature was deemed subject to judicial review.

. . .

It is not surprising, from the fact that the Houses of Congress so sparingly employed the power to conduct investigations, that there have been few cases requiring judicial review of the power. The Nation was almost one hundred years old before the first case reached this Court to challenge the use of compulsory process as a legislative device *[Kilbourn v. Thompson, 103 U.S. 168 (1881). Relatively few congressional investigations thereafter were contested in the courts.]* ...

In the decade following World War II, there appeared a new kind of congressional inquiry unknown in prior periods of American history. Principally this was the result of the various investigations into the threat of subversion of the United States Government, but other subjects of congressional interest also contributed to the changed scene. This new phase of legislative inquiry involved a broad-scale intrusion into the lives and affairs of private citizens. It brought before the courts novel questions of the appropriate limits of congressional inquiry....

. . .

We have no doubt that there is no congressional power to expose for the sake of exposure. The public is, of course, entitled to be informed concerning the workings of its government. That cannot be inflated into a general power to expose where the predominant result can only be an invasion of the private rights of individuals. But a solution to our problem is not to be found in testing the motives of committee members for this purpose. Such is not our function. Their motives alone would not vitiate an investigation which had been instituted by a House of Congress if that assembly's legislative purpose is being served.

. . .

The authorizing resolution of the Un-American Activities Committee was adopted in 1938.... It defines the Committee's authority as follows:

"The Committee on Un-American Activities, as a whole or by subcommittee, is authorized to make from time to time investigations of (1) the extent, character, and objects of un-American propaganda activities in the United States, (2) the diffusion within the United States of subversive and un-American propaganda that is instigated from foreign countries or of a domestic origin and attacks the principle of the form of government as guaranteed by our Constitution, and (3) all other questions in relation thereto that would aid Congress in any necessary remedial legislation."

It would be difficult to imagine a less explicit authorizing resolution. Who can define the meaning of "un-American"? What is that single, solitary "principle of the form of government as guaranteed by our Constitution"? There is no need to dwell upon the language, however. At one time, perhaps, the resolution might have been read narrowly to confine the Committee to the subject of propaganda. The events that have transpired in the fifteen years before the interrogation of petitioner make such a construction impossible at this date.

The members of the Committee have clearly demonstrated that they did not feel themselves restricted in any way to propaganda in the narrow sense of the word. Unquestionably the Committee conceived of its task in the grand view of its name. Un-American activities were its target, no matter how or where manifested....

Combining the language of the resolution with the construction it has been given, it is evident that the preliminary control of the Committee exercised by the House of Representatives is slight or non-existent. No one could reasonably deduce from the charter the kind of investigation that the Committee was directed to make.

[The Court offers these guidelines: In order for a reviewing court to determine whether a committee investigation is fulfilling a legislative purpose, the committee's activity must be properly authorized by resolution. In order for a witness to understand the pertinency of a question directed by a committee member or committee staff, and to avoid being held in contempt, the witness must have knowledge of the subject of the inquiry and the pertinency of a question to that inquiry. This knowledge can come from the authorizing resolution, remarks by committee members, and the nature of the proceedings.]

...Unless the subject matter has been made to appear with undisputable clarity, it is the duty of the investigative body, upon objection of the witness on grounds of pertinency, to state for the record the subject under inquiry at that time and the manner in which the propounded questions are pertinent thereto. To be meaningful, the explanation must describe what the topic under inquiry is and the connective reasoning whereby the precise questions asked relate to it.

The statement of the Committee Chairman in this case, in response to petitioner's protest, was woefully inadequate to convey sufficient information as to the pertinency of the questions to the subject under inquiry. Petitioner was thus not accorded a fair opportunity to determine whether he was within his rights in refusing to answer, and his conviction is necessarily invalid under the Due Process Clause of the Fifth Amendment.

The judgment of the Court of Appeals is reversed, and the case is remanded to the District Court with instructions to dismiss the indictment.

It is so ordered.

MR. JUSTICE BURTON and MR. JUSTICE WHITTAKER took no part in the consideration or decision of this case.

MR. JUSTICE FRANKFURTER, concurring.

. . .

MR. JUSTICE CLARK, dissenting.

As I see it the chief fault in the majority opinion is its mischievous curbing of the informing function of the Congress. While I am not versed in its procedures, my experience in the Executive Branch of the Government leads me to believe that the requirements laid down in the opinion for the operation of the committee system of inquiry are both unnecessary and unworkable....

Barenblatt v. United States

360 U.S. 109 (1959)

The Court's "lecture" to Congress in *Watkins* v. *United States* (1957) was one of several cases that convinced many members of Congress that the judiciary was overstepping its bounds. A number of court-curbing bills were introduced and acted upon. There is reason to believe that the Court recognized a serious collision with Congress and moved in this case, as well as others, to reduce the friction. Lloyd Barenblatt, a college professor, refused to answer certain questions put to him by a subcommittee of the House Committee on Un-American Activities. For his refusal he was convicted, fined, and sentenced to six months in prison.

MR. JUSTICE HARLAN delivered the opinion of the Court.

Once more the Court is required to resolve the conflicting constitutional claims of congressional power and of an individual's right to resist its exercise. The congressional power in question concerns the internal process of Congress in moving within its legislative domain; it involves the utilization of its committees to secure "testimony needed to enable it efficiently to exercise a legislative function belonging to it under the Constitution." *McGrain* v. *Daugherty*, 273 U. S. 135, 160....

Broad as it is, the power is not, however, without limitations. Since Congress may only investigate into those areas in which it may potentially legislate or appropriate, it cannot inquire into matters which are within the exclusive province of one of the other branches of the Government. Lacking the judicial power given to the Judiciary, it cannot inquire into matters that are exclusively the concern of the Judiciary. Neither can it supplant the Executive in what exclusively belongs to the Executive. And the Congress, in common with all branches of the Government, must exercise its powers subject to the limitations placed by the Constitution on governmental action, more particularly in the context of this case the relevant limitations of the Bill of Rights.

. . .

We here review petitioner's conviction under 2 U.S.C. § 192 for contempt of Congress, arising from his refusal to answer certain questions put to him by a Subcommittee of the House Committee on Un-American Activities during the course of an inquiry concerning alleged Communist infiltration into the field of education.

[Section 192 provides: "Every person who having been summoned as a witness by the authority of either House of Congress to give testimony or to produce papers upon any matter under inquiry before either House, or any joint committee established by a joint or concurrent resolution of the two Houses of Congress, or any committee of either House of Congress, willfully makes default, or who, having appeared, refuses to answer any question pertinent to the question under inquiry, shall be deemed guilty of a misdemeanor, punishable by a fine of not more than $1,000 nor less than $100 and imprisonment in a common jail for not less than one month nor more than twelve months."]

. . .

Pursuant to a subpoena, and accompanied by counsel, petitioner on June 28, 1954, appeared as a witness before this congressional Subcommittee.

After answering a few preliminary questions and testifying that he had been a graduate student and teaching fellow at the University of Michigan from 1947 to 1950 and an instructor in psychology at Vassar College from 1950 to shortly before his appearance before the Subcommittee, petitioner objected generally to the right of the Subcommittee to inquire into his "political" and "religious" beliefs or any "other personal and private affairs" or "associational activities," upon grounds set forth in a previously prepared memorandum which he was allowed to file with the Subcommittee. Thereafter petitioner specifically declined to answer each of the following five questions:

"Are you now a member of the Communist Party? [Count One.]

"Have you ever been a member of the Communist Party? [Count Two.]

"Now, you have stated that you knew Francis Crowley. Did you know Francis Crowley as a member of the Communist Party? [Count Three.]

"Were you ever a member of the Haldane Club of the Communist Party while at the University of Michigan? [Count Four.]

"Were you a member while a student of the University of Michigan Council of Arts, Sciences, and Professions?" [Count Five.]

In each instance the grounds of refusal were those set forth in the prepared statement. Petitioner expressly disclaimed reliance upon "the Fifth Amendment."

. . .

...As we conceive the ultimate issue in this case to be whether petitioner could properly be convicted of contempt for refusing to answer questions relating to his participation in or knowledge of alleged Communist Party activities at educational institutions in this country, we find it unnecessary to consider the validity of his conviction under the Third and Fifth Counts, the only ones involving questions which on their face do not directly relate to such participation or knowledge.

Petitioner's various contentions resolve themselves into three propositions: First, the compelling of testimony by the Subcommittee was neither legislatively authorized nor constitutionally permissible because of the vagueness of Rule XI of the House of Representatives, Eighty-third Congress, the charter of authority of the parent Committee. Second, petitioner was not adequately apprised of the pertinency of the Subcommittee's questions to the subject matter of the

inquiry. Third, the questions petitioner refused to answer infringed rights protected by the First Amendment.

[After deciding that Rule XI was not constitutionally infirm on the ground of vagueness, that the questions put to Barenblatt were clearly pertinent, and that he had been adequately informed, the Court turns to the First Amendment issue.]

CONSTITUTIONAL CONTENTIONS.

Our function, at this point, is purely one of constitutional adjudication in the particular case and upon the particular record before us, not to pass judgment upon the general wisdom or efficacy of the activities of this Committee in a vexing and complicated field.

The precise constitutional issue confronting us is whether the Subcommittee's inquiry into petitioner's past or present membership in the Communist Party transgressed the provisions of the First Amendment, which of course reach and limit congressional investigations. *Watkins, supra,* at 197.

The Court's past cases establish sure guides to decision. Undeniably, the First Amendment in some circumstances protects an individual from being compelled to disclose his associational relationships. However, the protections of the First Amendment, unlike a proper claim of the privilege against self-incrimination under the Fifth Amendment, do not afford a witness the right to resist inquiry in all circumstances. Where First Amendment rights are asserted to bar governmental interrogation resolution of the issue always involves a balancing by the courts of the competing private and public interests at stake in the particular circumstances shown. These principles were recognized in the *Watkins* case, where, in speaking of the First Amendment in relation to congressional inquiries, we said (at p. 198): "It is manifest that despite the adverse effects which follow upon compelled disclosure of private matters, not all such inquiries are barred....The critical element is the existence of, and the weight to be ascribed to, the interest of the Congress in demanding disclosures from an unwilling witness." ...

...[I]n stating in the *Watkins* case, p. 200, that "there is no congressional power to expose for the sake of exposure," we at the same time declined to inquire into the "motives of committee members," and recognized that their "motives alone would not vitiate an investigation which had been instituted by a House of Congress if that assembly's legislative purpose is being served." Having scrutinized this record we cannot say that the unanimous panel of the Court of Appeals which first considered this case was wrong in concluding that "the primary purposes of the inquiry were in aid of legislative processes." 240 F. 2d, at 881. Certainly this is not a case like *Kilbourn* v. *Thompson,* 103 U.S. 168, 192, where "the House of Representatives not only exceeded the limit of its own authority, but assumed a power which could only be properly exercised by another branch of the government, because it was in its nature clearly judicial." See *McGrain* v. *Daugherty,* 273 U. S. 135, 171. The constitutional legislative power of Congress in this instance is beyond question.

. . .

We conclude that the balance between the individual and the governmental interests here at stake must be struck in favor of the latter, and that therefore the provisions of the First Amendment have not been offended.

We hold that petitioner's conviction for contempt of Congress discloses no infirmity, and that the judgment of the Court of Appeals must be

Affirmed.

MR. JUSTICE BLACK, with whom THE CHIEF JUSTICE and MR. JUSTICE DOUGLAS concur, dissenting.

. . .

...I cannot agree with this disposition of the case for I believe that the resolution establishing the House Un-American Activities Committee and the questions that Committee asked Barenblatt violate the Constitution in several respects. (1) Rule XI creating the Committee authorizes such a sweeping, unlimited, all-inclusive and undiscriminating compulsory examination of witnesses in the field of speech, press, petition and assembly that it violates the procedural requirements of the Due Process Clause of the Fifth Amendment. (2) Compelling an answer to the questions asked Barenblatt abridges freedom of speech and association in contravention of the First Amendment. (3) The Committee proceedings were part of a legislative program to stigmatize and punish by public identification and exposure all witnesses considered by the Committee to be guilty of Communist affiliations, as well as all witnesses who refused to answer Committee ques-

tions on constitutional grounds; the Committee was thus improperly seeking to try, convict, and punish suspects, a task which the Constitution expressly denies to Congress and grants exclusively to the courts, to be exercised by them only after indictment and in full compliance with all the safeguards provided by the Bill of Rights.

. . .

II.

The First Amendment says in no equivocal language that Congress shall pass no law abridging freedom of speech, press, assembly or petition. The activities of this Committee, authorized by Congress, do precisely that, through exposure, obloquy and public scorn....

(A) I do not agree that laws directly abridging First Amendment freedoms can be justified by a congressional or judicial balancing process....

To apply the Court's balancing test under such circumstances is to read the First Amendment to say "Congress shall pass no law abridging freedom of speech, press, assembly and petition, unless Congress and the Supreme Court reach the joint conclusion that on balance the interest of the Government in stifling these freedoms is greater than the interest of the people in having them exercised." ...

But even assuming what I cannot assume, that some balancing is proper in this case, I feel that the Court after stating the test ignores it completely. At most it balances the right of the Government to preserve itself, against Barenblatt's right to refrain from revealing Communist affiliations. Such a balance, however, mistakes the factors to be weighed. In the first place, it completely leaves out the real interest in Barenblatt's silence, the interest of the people as a whole in being able to join organizations, advocate causes and make political "mistakes" without later being subjected to governmental penalties for having dared to think for themselves. It is this right, the right to err politically, which keeps us strong as a Nation. For no number of laws against communism can have as much effect as the personal conviction which comes from having heard its arguments and rejected them, or from having once accepted its tenets and later recognized their worthlessness. Instead, the obloquy which results from investigations such as this not only stifles "mistakes" but prevents all but the most courageous from hazarding any views which might at some later time become disfavored. This result, whose importance cannot be overestimated, is doubly crucial when it affects the universities, on which we must largely rely for the experimentation and development of new ideas essential to our country's welfare. It is these interests of society, rather than Barenblatt's own right to silence, which I think the Court should put on the balance against the demands of the Government, if any balancing process is to be tolerated....

. . .

Ultimately all the questions in this case really boil down to one—whether we as a people will try fearfully and futilely to preserve democracy by adopting totalitarian methods, or whether in accordance with our traditions and our Constitution we will have the confidence and courage to be free.

I would reverse this conviction.

MR. JUSTICE BRENNAN, dissenting.

I would reverse this conviction. It is sufficient that I state my complete agreement with my Brother BLACK that no purpose for the investigation of Barenblatt is revealed by the record except exposure purely for the sake of exposure. This is not a purpose to which Barenblatt's rights under the First Amendment can validly be subordinated. An investigation in which the processes of lawmaking and law-evaluating are submerged entirely in exposure of individual behavior—in adjudication, of a sort, through the exposure process—is outside the constitutional pale of congressional inquiry. *Watkins* v. *United States,* 354 U. S. 178, 187, 200; see also *Sweezy* v. *New Hampshire,* 354 U. S. 234; *NAACP* v. *Alabama,* 357 U. S. 449; *Uphaus* v. *Wyman, ante,* p. 82 (dissenting opinion).

United States v. Nixon

418 U.S. 683 (1974)

The Special Prosecutor investigating the Watergate affair filed a motion for a subpoena to produce certain tapes and documents relating to conversations and meetings between President Nixon and others. President Nixon, claiming executive privilege, filed a motion to quash the subpoena. A district judge rejected that motion and issued an order for an *in camera* examination of the subpoenaed material. This order was stayed pending appellate review.

MR. CHIEF JUSTICE BURGER delivered the opinion of the Court.

This litigation presents for review the denial of a motion, filed in the District Court on behalf of the President of the United States, in the case of *United States* v. *Mitchell* (D. C. Crim. No. 74-110), to quash a third-party subpoena *duces tecum* issued by the United States District Court for the District of Columbia, pursuant to Fed. Rule Crim. Proc. 17 (c). The subpoena directed the President to produce certain tape recordings and documents relating to his conversations with aides and advisers. The court rejected the President's claims of absolute executive privilege, of lack of jurisdiction, and of failure to satisfy the requirements of Rule 17 (c). The President appealed to the Court of Appeals. We granted both the United States' petition for certiorari before judgment (No. 73-1766), and also the President's cross-petition for certiorari before judgment (No. 73-1834), because of the public importance of the issues presented and the need for their prompt resolution. 417 U. S. 927 and 960 (1974).

On March 1, 1974, a grand jury of the United States District Court for the District of Columbia returned an indictment charging seven named individuals [*Attorney General John N. Mitchell, White House aides H. R. Haldeman and John D. Ehrlichman, Charles W. Colson, Robert C. Mardian, Kenneth W. Parkinson, and Gordon Strachan. The latter four were either on the White House staff or with the Committee for the Re-election of the President.*] with various offenses, including conspiracy to defraud the United States and to obstruct justice. Although he was not designated as such in the indictment, the grand jury named the President, among others, as an unindicted coconspirator. On April 18, 1974, upon motion of the Special Prosecutor, see n. 8, *infra,* a subpoena *duces tecum* was issued pursuant to Rule 17 (c) to the President by the United States District Court and made returnable on May 2, 1974. This subpoena required the production, in advance of the September 9 trial date, of certain tapes, memoranda, papers, transcripts, or other writings relating to certain precisely identified meetings between the

President and others. The Special Prosecutor was able to fix the time, place, and persons present at these discussions because the White House daily logs and appointment records had been delivered to him. On April 30, the President publicly released edited transcripts of 43 conversations; portions of 20 conversations subject to subpoena in the present case were included. On May 1, 1974, the President's counsel filed a "special appearance" and a motion to quash the subpoena under Rule 17 (c). This motion was accompanied by a formal claim of privilege.

. . .

II. JUSTICIABILITY

In the District Court, the President's counsel argued that the court lacked jurisdiction to issue the subpoena because the matter was an intra-branch dispute between a subordinate and superior officer of the Executive Branch and hence not subject to judicial resolution. That argument has been renewed in this Court with emphasis on the contention that the dispute does not present a "case" or "controversy" which can be adjudicated in the federal courts. The President's counsel argues that the federal courts should not intrude into areas committed to the other branches of Government. He views the present dispute as essentially a "jurisdictional" dispute within the Executive Branch which he analogizes to a dispute between two congressional committees. Since the Executive Branch has exclusive authority and absolute discretion to decide whether to prosecute a case, *Confiscation Cases,* 7 Wall. 454 (1869); *United States* v. *Cox,* 342 F. 2d 167, 171 (CA5), cert. denied *sub nom. Cox* v. *Hauberg,* 381 U. S. 935 (1965), it is contended that a President's decision is final in determining what evidence is to be used in a given criminal case. Although his counsel concedes that the President has delegated certain specific powers to the Special Prosecutor, he has not "waived nor delegated to the Special Prosecutor the President's duty to claim privilege as to all materials . . . which fall within the President's inherent authority to refuse to disclose to any executive officer." Brief for the President 42. The Special Prosecutor's demand for the items therefore presents, in the view of the President's counsel, a political question under *Baker* v. *Carr,* 369 U. S. 186 (1962), since it involves a "textually demonstrable" grant of power under Art. II.

The mere assertion of a claim of an "intra-branch dispute," without more, has never operated to defeat federal jurisdiction; justiciability does not depend on such a surface inquiry. In *United States* v. *ICC,* 337 U. S. 426 (1949), the Court observed, "courts must look behind names that symbolize the parties to determine whether a justiciable case or controversy is presented." *Id.,* at 430.

. . .

[The Court reviews the following facts: under authority of Article II, Section 2, Congress vested in the Attorney General the power to conduct criminal litigation and to appoint subordinate officers; acting pursuant to statutory authority, the Attorney General delegated authority to a Special Prosecutor with unique authority and tenure; the regulation delegating this authority gave the Special Prosecutor explicit power to contest claims of executive privilege; this regulation had the force of law and had not been amended or revoked.]

In light of the uniqueness of the setting in which the conflict arises, the fact that both parties are officers of the Executive Branch cannot be viewed as a barrier to justiciability. It would be inconsistent with the applicable law and regulation, and the unique facts of this case to conclude other than that the Special Prosecutor has standing to bring this action and that a justiciable controversy is presented for decision.

. . .

IV. THE CLAIM OF PRIVILEGE

A

. . . [W]e turn to the claim that the subpoena should be quashed because it demands "confidential conversations between a President and his close advisors that it would be inconsistent with the public interest to produce." App. 48a. The first contention is a broad claim that the separation of powers doctrine precludes judicial review of a President's claim of privilege. The second contention is that if he does not prevail on the claim of absolute privilege, the court should hold as a matter of constitutional law that the privilege prevails over the subpoena *duces tecum.*

In the performance of assigned constitutional duties each branch of the Government must initially interpret the Constitution, and the interpretation of its powers by any branch is due great respect from the others. The President's counsel, as we have noted, reads the Constitution as providing an absolute privilege of confidentiality for all Presidential communications. Many decisions of this Court, however, have unequivocally reaffirmed the holding of *Marbury* v. *Madison,* 1 Cranch 137 (1803), that "[i]t is emphatically the province and duty of the judicial department to say what the law is." *Id.,* at 177.

No holding of the Court has defined the scope of judicial power specifically relating to the enforcement of a subpoena for confidential Presidential communications for use in a criminal prosecution, but other exercises of power by the Executive Branch and the Legislative Branch have been found invalid as in conflict with the Constitution. *Powell* v. *McCormack,* 395 U. S. 486 (1969); *Youngstown Sheet & Tube Co.* v. *Sawyer,* 343 U. S. 579 (1952).

Notwithstanding the deference each branch must accord the others, the "judicial Power of the United States" vested in the federal courts by Art. III, § 1, of the Constitution can no more be shared with the Executive Branch than the Chief Executive, for example, can share with the Judiciary the veto power, or the Congress share with the Judiciary the power to override a Presidential veto. Any other conclusion would be contrary to the basic concept of separation of powers and the checks and balances that flow from the scheme of a tripartite government. The Federalist, No. 47, p. 313 (S. Mittell ed. 1938). We therefore reaffirm that it is the province and duty of this Court "to say what the law is" with respect to the claim of privilege presented in this case. *Marbury* v. *Madison, supra,* at 177.

B

In support of his claim of absolute privilege, the President's counsel urges two grounds, one of which is common to all governments and one of which is peculiar to our system of separation of powers. The first ground is the valid need for protection of communications between high Government officials and those who advise and assist them in the performance of their manifold duties; the importance of this confidentiality is too plain to require further discussion. Human experience teaches that those who expect public dissemination of their remarks may well temper candor with a concern for appearances and for their own interests to the detriment of the decisionmaking process. Whatever the nature of the privilege of confidentiality of Presidential communications in the exercise of Art. II powers, the privilege can be said to derive from the supremacy of each branch within its own assigned area of constitutional duties. Certain powers and privileges flow from the nature of enumerated powers; the protection of the confidentiality of Presidential communications has similar constitutional underpinnings.

The second ground asserted by the President's counsel in support of the claim of absolute privilege rests on the doctrine of separation of powers. Here it is argued that the independence of the Executive Branch within its own sphere, *Humphrey's Executor* v. *United States,* 295 U. S. 602, 629–630 (1935); *Kilbourn* v. *Thompson,* 103 U. S. 168, 190–191 (1881), insulates a President from a judicial subpoena in an ongoing criminal prosecution, and thereby protects confidential Presidential communications.

However, neither the doctrine of separation of powers, nor the need for confidentiality of high-level communications, without more, can sustain an absolute, unqualified Presidential privilege of immunity from judicial process under all circumstances. The President's need for complete candor and objectivity from advisers calls for great deference from the courts. However, when the privilege depends solely on the broad, undifferentiated claim of public interest in the confidentiality of such conversations, a confrontation with other values arises. Absent a claim of need to protect military, diplomatic, or sensitive national security secrets, we find it difficult to accept the argument that even the very important interest in confidentiality of Presidential communications is significantly diminished by production of such material for *in camera* inspection with all the protection that a district court will be obliged to provide.

The impediment that an absolute, unqualified privilege would place in the way of the primary constitutional duty of the Judicial Branch to do justice in criminal prosecutions would plainly conflict with the function of the courts under Art. III. In designing the structure of our Government and dividing and allocating the sovereign power among three co-equal branches, the Framers of the Constitution sought to provide a comprehensive system, but the separate powers were not intended to operate with absolute independence.

"While the Constitution diffuses power the better to secure liberty, it also contemplates that practice will integrate the dispersed powers into a workable government. It enjoins upon its branches separateness but interdependence, autonomy but reciprocity." *Youngstown Sheet & Tube Co.* v. *Sawyer,* 343 U. S., at 635 (Jackson, J., concurring).

To read the Art. II powers of the President as providing an absolute privilege as against a subpoena essential to enforcement of criminal statutes on no more than a generalized claim of the public interest in confidentiality of nonmilitary and nondiplomatic discussions would upset the constitutional balance of "a workable government" and gravely impair the role of the courts under Art. III.

C

Since we conclude that the legitimate needs of the judicial process may outweigh Presidential privilege, it is necessary to resolve those competing interests in a manner that preserves the essential functions of each branch. The right and indeed the duty to resolve that question does not free the Judiciary from according high respect to the representations made on behalf of the President. *United States* v. *Burr,* 25 F. Cas. 187, 190, 191–192 (No. 14,694) (CC Va. 1807).

The expectation of a President to the confidentiality of his conversations and correspondence, like the claim of confidentiality of judicial deliberations, for example, has all the values to which we accord deference for the privacy of all citizens and, added to those values, is the necessity for protection of the public interest in candid, objective, and even blunt or harsh opinions in Presidential decisionmaking. A President and those who assist him must be free to explore alternatives in the process of shaping policies and making decisions and to do so in a way many would be unwilling to express except privately. These are the considerations justifying a presumptive privilege for Presidential communications. The privilege is fundamental to the operation of Government and inextricably rooted in the separation of powers under the Constitution....

But this presumptive privilege must be considered in light of our historic commitment to the rule of law. This is nowhere more profoundly manifest than in our view that "the twofold aim [of criminal justice] is that guilt shall not escape or innocence suffer." *Berger* v. *United States,* 295 U. S., at 88. We have elected to employ an adversary system of criminal justice in which the parties contest all issues before a court of law. The need to develop all relevant facts in the adversary system is both fundamental and comprehensive. The ends of criminal justice would be defeated if judgments were to be founded on a partial or speculative presentation of the facts. The very integrity of the judicial system and public confidence in the system depend on full disclosure of all the facts, within the framework of the rules of evidence. To ensure that justice is done, it is imperative to the function of courts that compulsory process be available for the production of evidence needed either by the prosecution or by the defense.

. . .

In this case the President challenges a subpoena served on him as a third party requiring the production of materials for use in a criminal prosecution; he does so on the claim that he has a privilege against disclosure of confidential communications. He does not place his claim of privilege on the ground they are military or diplomatic secrets. As to these areas of Art. II duties the courts have traditionally shown the utmost deference to Presidential responsibilities....

. . .

In this case we must weigh the importance of the general privilege of confidentiality of Presidential communications in performance of the President's responsibilities against the inroads of such a privilege on the fair administration of criminal justice. *[The Court, in a footnote, adds: "We are not here concerned with the balance between the President's generalized interest in confidentiality and the need for relevant evidence in civil litigation, nor with that between the confidentiality interest and congressional demands for information, nor with the President's interest in preserving state secrets. We address only the conflict between the President's assertion of a generalized privilege of confidentiality and the constitutional need for relevant evidence in criminal trials."]* The interest in preserving confidentiality is weighty indeed and entitled to great respect. However, we cannot conclude that advisers will be moved to temper the candor of their remarks by the infrequent occasions of disclosure because of the possibility that such conversations will be called for in the context of a criminal prosecution.

On the other hand, the allowance of the privilege to withhold evidence that is demonstrably relevant in a criminal trial would cut deeply into the guarantee of due process of law and gravely impair the basic function of the courts. A President's acknowledged need for confidentiality in the communications of his office is general in nature, whereas the constitutional need for production of relevant evidence in a criminal proceeding is specific and central to the fair adjudication of a particular criminal case in the administration of justice. Without access to specific facts a criminal prosecution may be totally frustrated. The President's broad interest in confidentiality of communications will not be vitiated by disclosure of a limited number of conversations preliminarily shown to have some bearing on the pending criminal cases.

We conclude that when the ground for asserting privilege as to subpoenaed materials sought for use in a criminal trial is based only on the generalized interest in confidentiality, it cannot prevail over the fundamental demands of due process of law in the fair administration of criminal justice. The generalized assertion of privilege must yield to the demonstrated, specific need for evidence in a pending criminal trial.

. . .

Since this matter came before the Court during the pendency of a criminal prosecution, and on representations that time is of the essence, the mandate shall issue forthwith.

Affirmed.

MR. JUSTICE REHNQUIST took no part in the consideration or decision of these cases.

Negotiating Executive Privilege: The AT&T Cases

Executive documents are routinely shared with Congress, including documents that are highly classified and confidential. When there is a conflict between the executive and legislative branches, accommodations are usually discovered that avoid litigation. Even when a case is brought to court, the usual resolution is to force the two branches to find an intermediate position that will satisfy executive as well as congressional interests. The two cases below, involving national-security wiretaps, illustrate the practical efforts to iron out executive-legislative collisions. In a series of steps, Judge Harold Leventhal helped resolve a dispute between the Justice Department and a congressional committee. The two cases are *United States* v. *AT&T*, 551 F.2d 384 (D.C. Cir. 1976) and *United States* v. *AT&T*, 567 F.2d 121 (D.C. Cir. 1977). The first selection is from the 1976 case.

LEVENTHAL, Circuit Judge.

This unusual case involves a portentous clash between the executive and legislative branches, the executive branch asserting its authority to maintain tight control over information related to our national security, and the legislative branch asserting its authority to gather information necessary for the formulation of new legislation.

In the name of the United States, the Justice Department sued to enjoin the American Telephone and Telegraph Co. (AT&T) from complying with a subpoena of a subcommittee of the House of Representatives issued in the course of an investigation into warrantless "national security" wiretaps. Congressman Moss, chairman of the subcommittee, intervened on behalf of the House, the real defendant in interest since AT&T, while prepared to comply with the subpoena in the absence of a protective court order, has no stake in the controversy beyond knowing whether its legal obligation is to comply with the subpoena or not. The District Court issued the injunction requested by plaintiff and Chairman Moss appeals.

The case presents difficult problems, preliminary questions of jurisdiction and justiciability (application of the political question doctrine) and

the ultimate issue on the merits of resolving or balancing the constitutional powers asserted by the legislative and executive branches.

In order to avoid a possibly unnecessary constitutional decision, we suggest the outlines of a possible settlement which may meet the mutual needs of the congressional and executive parties, without requiring a judicial resolution of a head-on confrontation, and we remand without decision at this time in order to permit exploration of this solution by the parties, under District Court guidance if needed.

If the parties reach an impasse this will be reported to us by the District Court. We would then be confronted with the need to enter an order disposing of the appeal pending.

I. BACKGROUND

The controversy arose out of an investigation by the Subcommittee on Oversight and Investigations of the House Committee on Interstate and Foreign Commerce. The Subcommittee was interested in determining the nature and extent of warrantless wiretapping in the United States for asserted national security purposes. It was concerned with the possible abuse of that power and its effect on privacy and other interests of U.S.

citizens, and with the possible need for limiting legislation.

The warrantless wiretaps which became the focus of this part of the investigation used facilities provided by AT&T upon its receipt from the FBI of "request" letters. Each request letter specified a target line to be tapped, identified by telephone number, address, or other numerical designation. The letter requested a "leased line" to carry the tapped communications from the target location to a designated monitoring station manned by federal agents.

On June 22, 1976, the Subcommittee authorized and the Committee Chairman issued a subpoena requiring the president of AT&T to turn over to the Subcommittee copies of all national security request letters sent to AT&T and its subsidiaries by the FBI as well as records of such taps prior to the time when the practice of sending such letters was initiated. After the subpoena was issued, AT&T stood ready to comply.

At this point the White House approached Subcommittee Chairman John Moss in search of an alternative arrangement meeting the Subcommittee's information needs. The basic thrust of the ensuing negotiations between the Subcommittee and the Justice Department was to substitute, for the request letters, expurgated copies of the backup memoranda upon which the Attorney General based his decision to authorize the warrantless taps. These memoranda, providing information on the purpose and nature of the surveillance, might have been more informative to Congress than the request letters, which merely contained numerical identification of the line to be tapped. The Justice Department agreed, at least informally and tentatively, to provide the Subcommittee staff expurgated copies of the backup memo pertaining to foreign intelligence taps, with all information which would identify the target replaced by generic description, such as "Middle Eastern diplomat." The negotiations came close to success, but broke down over the issue of verification by the Subcommittee of the accuracy of the executive's generic descriptions by inspection of a sample of the original memoranda.

. . .

III. QUESTIONS PRESENTED

. . .

D. Clash of Absolutes

In this case we are faced with patently conflicting assertions of absolute authority. Each branch of government claims that as long as it is exercising its authority for a legitimate purpose, its actions are unreviewable by the courts.

1. Congressional Investigatory Power

Congress relies on the Speech or Debate Clause, as interpreted in *Eastland* v. *United States Servicemen's Fund*, 421 U.S. 491, 95 S.Ct. 1813, 44 L.Ed.2d 324 (1975) in support of its contention that its subpoena power cannot be impeded by the Executive. *Eastland* held that, even on an allegation of infringement of First Amendment rights, the courts could not interfere with a subpoena concerning a legitimate area of congressional investigation. . . .

2. Executive National Security Power

The Justice Department claims the President retains ultimate authority to decide what risks to national security are acceptable. Thus, where documents are subpoenaed by Congress, the court's role would be at an end once it determined that there was some risk to national security. At that point, it would have to defer to the President. . . .

E. Strength of the Constitutional Interests

1. Executive

The President asserts the power to maintain the secrecy of information pertaining to national security and finds this power inherent in the responsibility given him in article II of the Constitution for foreign and military affairs. . . .

. . .

There is constitutional power, under the Necessary and Proper Clause, in the federal government to keep national security information secret. This is typically a government power, to be exercised by the legislative and executive branches acting together. . . .

2. Congressional

Congressional power to investigate and acquire information by subpoena is on a firm constitutional basis. . . .

F. Balancing by the Courts

A court seeking to balance the legislative and executive interests asserted here would face severe problems in formulating and applying standards. Granted that the subpoenas are clearly within the proper legislative investigatory sphere, it is difficult to "weigh" Congress's need for the request letters. Congress's power to monitor executive actions is implicit in the appropriations power. Here, for instance, if the President has the inherent power claimed to block the subpoena, how is Congress to assure that appropriated funds are not being used for illegal warrantless domestic electronic surveillance?

As to the danger to national security, a court would have to consider the Subcommittee's track record for security, the likelihood of a leak if other members of the House sought access to the material. In addition to this delicate and possibly unseemly determination, the court would have to weigh the effect of a leak on intelligence activities and diplomatic relations. Finally, the court would have to consider the reasonableness of the alternatives offered by the parties and decide which would better reconcile the competing constitutional interests.

IV. REASONS FOR EXPLORATION OF SETTLEMENT

Before moving on to a decision of such nerve-center constitutional questions, we pause to allow for further efforts at a settlement. We think that suggestion is particularly appropriate in this case and may well be productive.... The legislative and executive branches have a long history of settlement of disputes that seemed irreconcilable. There was almost a settlement in 1976. It may well be attainable in 1977.

Furthermore, our own reflections may be of some assistance. As a prelude to settlement conference, it may be helpful if we review pertinent considerations:

1. This dispute between the legislative and executive branches has at least some elements of the political-question doctrine. A court decision selects a victor, and tends thereafter to tilt the scales. A compromise worked out between the branches is most likely to meet their essential needs and the country's constitutional balance.

. . .

[1977 decision:]

LEVENTHAL, Circuit Judge:

This case brings to us for a second time conflicting assertions by the executive and legislative branches, contentions that require the third branch to decide whether its constitutional mandate to decide controversies extends to such a conflict, and if so what measure of judicial resolution is sound and appropriate.

. . .

When we first came to the case, we developed a novel and somewhat gingerly approach for the delicate problem of accommodating the needs and powers of two coordinate branches in a situation where each claimed absolute authority.... To the extent possible, we wished to avoid a resolution that might disturb the balance of power between the two branches and inaccurately reflect their true needs....

Negotiation has narrowed but not bridged the gap between the parties. Accordingly, we must adopt a somewhat more traditional approach. We begin by deciding that complete judicial abstention on political question grounds is not warranted. In addressing the merits, however, we continue to move cautiously. Taking full account of the negotiating positions, we have chartered the course that we think is most likely to accommodate the substantial needs of the parties. Doubtless, neither will be satisfied. But in our view there is good reason to believe that the procedure set forth in this opinion will prove feasible in practice, with such adjustments and refinements as may be evolved by the parties and the district court....

. . .

The framers, rather than attempting to define and allocate all governmental power in minute detail, relied, we believe, on the expectation that where conflicts in scope of authority arose between the coordinate branches, a spirit of dynamic compromise would promote resolution of the dispute in the manner most likely to result in efficient and effective functioning of our governmental system. Under this view, the coordinate branches do not exist in an exclusively adversary relationship to one another when a conflict in authority arises. Rather, each branch should take cognizance of an implicit constitutional mandate to seek optimal accommodation through a realistic evaluation of the needs of the conflicting branches in the particular fact situation. This aspect of our constitutional scheme avoids the mischief of polarization of disputes....

[The case was dismissed on December 21, 1978, after the Justice Department and the subcommittee amicably resolved their differences.]

Clinton v. Jones

520 U.S. 681 (1997)

Paula Corbin Jones sued President Clinton for sexual harassment and assault for an incident that occurred in 1991, when Clinton served as governor of Arkansas. While recognizing that she would have a right to pursue the lawsuit after he left the presidency, Clinton moved to dismiss the case on grounds of presidential immunity. A federal appellate court held that a President enjoys absolute immunity only for official, not unofficial, acts. Jones v. Clinton, 72 F.3d 1354 (8th Cir. 1996). The Supreme Court agreed to hear the case.

JUSTICE STEVENS delivered the opinion of the Court.

This case raises a constitutional and a prudential question concerning the Office of the President of the United States. Respondent, a private citizen, seeks to recover damages from the current occupant of that office based on actions allegedly taken before his term began. The President submits that in all but the most exceptional cases the Constitution requires federal courts to defer such litigation until his term ends and that, in any event, respect for the office warrants such a stay. Despite the force of the arguments supporting the President's submissions, we conclude that they must be rejected.

I

Petitioner, William Jefferson Clinton, was elected to the Presidency in 1992, and reelected in 1996. His term of office expires on January 20, 2001. In 1991 he was the Governor of the State of Arkansas. Respondent, Paula Corbin Jones, is a resident of California. In 1991 she lived in Arkansas, and was an employee of the Arkansas Industrial Development Commission.

On May 6, 1994, she commenced this action in the United States District Court for the Eastern District of Arkansas by filing a complaint naming petitioner and Danny Ferguson, a former Arkansas State Police officer, as defendants. The complaint alleges two federal claims, and two state law claims over which the federal court has jurisdiction because of the diverse citizenship of the parties. As the case comes to us, we are required to assume the truth of the detailed—but as yet untested—factual allegations in the complaint.

Those allegations principally describe events that are said to have occurred on the afternoon of May 8, 1991, during an official conference held at the Excelsior Hotel in Little Rock, Arkansas. The Governor delivered a speech at the conference; respondent—working as a state employee—staffed the registration desk. She alleges that Ferguson persuaded her to leave her desk and to visit the Governor in a business suite at the hotel, where he made "abhorrent" sexual advances that she vehemently rejected. She further claims that her superiors at work subsequently dealt with her in a hostile and rude manner, and changed her duties to punish her for rejecting those advances. Finally, she alleges that after petitioner was elected President, Ferguson defamed her by making a statement to a reporter that implied she had accepted petitioner's alleged overtures, and that various persons authorized to speak for the President publicly branded her a liar by denying that the incident had occurred.

Respondent seeks actual damages of $75,000, and punitive damages of $100,000. Her complaint contains four counts. The first charges that petitioner, acting under color of state law, deprived her of rights protected by the Constitution, in violation of Rev. Stat. § 1979, 42 U.S.C. § 1983. The second charges that petitioner and Ferguson engaged in a conspiracy to violate her federal rights, also actionable under federal law. See Rev. Stat. § 1980, 42 U.S.C. § 1985. The third is a state common law claim for intentional infliction of emotional distress, grounded primarily on the incident at the hotel. The fourth count, also based on state law, is for defamation, embracing both the comments allegedly made to the press by Ferguson and the statements of petitioner's agents. Inasmuch as the legal sufficiency of the claims has not yet been challenged, we assume, without deciding, that each of the four counts states a cause of action as a matter of law. With the exception of the last charge, which arguably may involve conduct within the outer perimeter of the President's official responsibilities, it is perfectly clear that the alleged misconduct of petitioner was unrelated to any of his official duties as President of the United States and, indeed, occurred before he was elected to that office.

II

In response to the complaint, petitioner promptly advised the District Court that he intended to file a motion to dismiss on grounds of Presidential immunity, and requested the court to defer all other pleadings and motions until after the immunity issue was resolved....

IV

Petitioner's principal submission—that "in all but the most exceptional cases"... the Constitution affords the President temporary immunity from civil damages litigation arising out of events that occurred before he took office— cannot be sustained on the basis of precedent.

Only three sitting Presidents have been defendants in civil litigation involving their actions prior to taking office. Complaints against Theodore Roosevelt and Harry Truman had been dismissed before they took office; the dismissals were affirmed after their respective inaugurations. Two companion cases arising out of an automobile accident were filed against John F. Kennedy in 1960 during the Presidential campaign. After taking office, he unsuccessfully argued that his status as Commander in Chief gave him a right to a stay under the Soldiers' and Sailors' Civil Relief Act of 1940, 50 U.S.C.App. §§ 501–525. The motion for a stay was denied by the District Court, and the matter was settled out of court. Thus, none of those cases sheds any light on the constitutional issue before us.

The principal rationale for affording certain public servants immunity from suits for money damages arising out of their official acts is inapplicable to unofficial conduct. In cases involving prosecutors, legislators, and judges we have repeatedly explained that the immunity serves the public interest in enabling such officials to perform their designated functions effectively without fear that a particular decision may give rise to personal liability....

This reasoning provides no support for an immunity for *unofficial* conduct. As we explained in [Nixon v.] Fitzgerald, "the sphere of protected action must be related closely to the immunity's justifying purposes." Id., at 755. Because of the President's broad responsibilities, we recognized in that case an immunity from damages claims arising out of official acts extending to the "outer perimeter of his authority." Id., at 757, But we have never suggested that the President, or any other official, has an immunity that extends beyond the scope of any action taken in an official capacity. See id, at

759 (Burger, C. J., concurring) (noting that "a President, like Members of Congress, judges, prosecutors, or congressional aides— all having absolute immunity—are not immune for acts outside official duties"); see also id. at 761, n 4.

. . .

VI

Petitioner's strongest argument supporting his immunity claim is based on the text and structure of the Constitution. He does not contend that the occupant of the Office of the President is "above the law," in the sense that his conduct is entirely immune from judicial scrutiny. The President argues merely for a postponement of the judicial proceedings that will determine whether he violated any law. His argument is grounded in the character of the office that was created by Article II of the Constitution, and relies on separation of powers principles that have structured our constitutional arrangement since the founding.

As a starting premise, petitioner contends that he occupies a unique office with powers and responsibilities so vast and important that the public interest demands that he devote his undivided time and attention to his public duties. He submits that—given the nature of the office—the doctrine of separation of powers places limits on the authority of the Federal Judiciary to interfere with the Executive Branch that would be transgressed by allowing this action to proceed.

We have no dispute with the initial premise of the argument. Former presidents, from George Washington to George Bush, have consistently endorsed petitioner's characterization of the office.... As Justice Jackson has pointed out, the Presidency concentrates executive authority "in a single head in whose choice the whole Nation has a part, making him the focus of public hopes and expectations. In drama, magnitude and finality his decisions so far overshadow any others that almost alone he fills the public eye and ear." *Youngstown Sheet & Tube Co. v. Sawyer,* 343 U.S., at 653 (Jackson, J., concurring)....

It does not follow, however, that separation of powers principles would be violated by allowing this action to proceed....

...in this case there is no suggestion that the Federal Judiciary is being asked to perform any function that might in some way be described as "executive." Respondent is merely asking the courts to exercise their core Article III jurisdiction to decide cases and controversies. Whatever the outcome of this case, there is no possibility that the decision will curtail the scope of the official powers of the Executive Branch. The litigation of questions that relate entirely to the unofficial conduct of the individual who happens to be the President poses no perceptible risk of misallocation of either judicial power or executive power.

Rather than arguing that the decision of the case will produce either an aggrandizement of judicial power or a narrowing of executive power, petitioner contends that—as a by-product of an otherwise traditional exercise of judicial power—burdens will be placed on the President that will hamper the performance of his official duties. We have recognized that "[e]ven when a branch does not arrogate power to itself ... the separation-of-powers doctrine requires that a branch not impair another in the performance of its constitutional duties." Loving v. United States, 517 U.S. 748, 757 (1996); see also Nixon v. Administrator of General Services, 433 U.S. 425, 443 (1977). As a factual matter, petitioner contends that this particular case—as well as the potential additional litigation that an affirmance of the Court of Appeals judgment might spawn—may impose an unacceptable burden on the President's time and energy, and thereby impair the effective performance of his office.

Petitioner's predictive judgment finds little support in either history or the relatively narrow compass of the issues raised in this particular case. As we have already noted, in the more than 200-year history of the Republic, only three sitting Presidents have been subjected to suits for their private actions.... If the past is any indicator, it seems unlikely that a deluge of such litigation will ever engulf the Presidency. As for the case at hand, if properly managed by the District Court, it appears to us highly unlikely to occupy any substantial amount of petitioner's time.

Of greater significance, petitioner errs by presuming that interactions between the Judicial Branch and the Executive, even quite burdensome interactions, necessarily rise to the level of constitutionally forbidden impairment of the Executive's ability to perform its constitutionally mandated functions. "[O]ur ... system imposes upon the Branches a degree of overlapping responsibility, a duty of interdependence as well as independence the absence of which 'would preclude the establishment of a Nation capable of governing itself effectively.'" Mistretta, 488 U.S., at 381 (quoting Buckley, 424 U.S., at 121). As Madison explained, separation of powers does not mean that the branches "ought to have no *partial agency* in, or no *controul* over the acts of each other."...

First, we have long held that when the President takes official action, the Court has the authority to determine whether he has acted within the law. Perhaps the most dramatic example of such a case is our holding that President Truman exceeded his constitutional authority when he issued an order directing the Secretary of Commerce to take possession of and operate most of the Nation's steel mills in order to avert a national catastrophe. *Youngstown Sheet & Tube Co. v. Sawyer* 343 U.S. 579 (1952)....

Second, it is also settled that the President is subject to judicial process in appropriate circumstances. Although Thomas Jefferson apparently thought otherwise, Chief Justice Marshall, when presiding in the treason trial of Aaron Burr, ruled that a subpoena *duces tecum* could be directed to the President. *United States v. Burr*, 25 F. Cas. 30 (No. 14,692d) (C.C.Va. 1807). We unequivocally and emphatically endorsed Marshall's position when we held that President Nixon was obligated to comply with a subpoena commanding him to produce certain tape recordings of his conversations with his aides. *United States v. Nixon,* 418 U.S. 683 (1974). As we explained, "neither the doctrine of separation of powers, nor the need for confidentiality of high-level communications, without more, can sustain an absolute, unqualified Presidential privilege of immunity from judicial process under all circumstances." *Id.,* at 706.

Sitting Presidents have responded to court orders to provide testimony and other information with sufficient frequency that such interactions between the Judicial and Executive Branches can scarcely be thought a novelty. President Monroe responded to written interrogatories,...President Nixon—as noted above—produced tapes in response to a subpoena *duces tecum,* see *United States v. Nixon*, President Ford complied with an order to give a deposition in a criminal trial, *United States v. Fromme*, 405 F.Supp. 578 (E.D.Cal.1975), and President Clinton has twice given videotaped testimony in criminal proceedings....Moreover, sitting Presidents have also voluntarily complied with judicial requests for testimony. President Grant gave a lengthy deposition in a criminal case under such circumstances,...and President Carter similarly gave videotaped testimony for use at a criminal trial, *ibid.*

In sum, "[i]t is settled law that the separation-of-powers doctrine does not bar every exercise of jurisdiction over the President of the United

States." *Fitzgerald,* 457 U.S., at 753–754. If the Judiciary may severely burden the Executive Branch by reviewing the legality of the President's official conduct, and if it may direct appropriate process to the President himself, it must follow that the federal courts have power to determine the legality of his unofficial conduct. The burden on the President's time and energy that is a mere by-product of such review surely cannot be considered as onerous as the direct burden imposed by judicial review and the occasional invalidation of his official actions. We therefore hold that the doctrine of separation of powers does not require federal courts to stay all private actions against the President until he leaves office.

... we turn to the question whether the District Court's decision to stay the trial until after petitioner leaves office was an abuse of discretion.

VII

The Court of Appeals described the District Court's discretionary decision to stay the trial as the "functional equivalent" of a grant of temporary immunity. 72 F.3d, at 1361, n. 9. Concluding that petitioner was not constitutionally entitled to such an immunity, the court held that it was error to grant the stay. *Ibid.* Although we ultimately conclude that the stay should not have been granted, we think the issue is more difficult than the opinion of the Court of Appeals suggests.

Strictly speaking the stay was not the functional equivalent of the constitutional immunity that petitioner claimed, because the District Court ordered discovery to proceed. Moreover, a stay of either the trial or discovery might be justified by considerations that do not require the recognition of any constitutional immunity. The District Court has broad discretion to stay proceedings as an incident to its power to control its own docket.... Although we have rejected the argument that the potential burdens on the President violate separation of powers principles, those burdens are appropriate matters for the District Court to evaluate in its management of the case. The high respect that is owed to the office of the Chief Executive, though not justifying a rule of categorical immunity, is a matter that should inform the conduct of the entire proceeding, including the timing and scope of discovery.

Nevertheless, we are persuaded that it was an abuse of discretion for the District Court to defer the trial until after the President leaves office. Such a lengthy and categorical stay takes no account whatever of the respondent's interest in bringing the case to trial. The complaint was filed within the statutory limitations period—albeit near the end of that period—and delaying trial would increase the danger of prejudice resulting from the loss of evidence, including the inability of witnesses to recall specific facts, or the possible death of a party.

The decision to postpone the trial was, furthermore, premature.... In this case, at the stage at which the District Court made its ruling, there was no way to assess whether a stay of trial after the completion of discovery would be warranted. Other than the fact that a trial may consume some of the President's time and attention, there is nothing in the record to enable a judge to assess the potential harm that may ensue from scheduling the trial promptly after discovery is concluded. We think the District Court may have given undue weight to the concern that a trial might generate unrelated civil actions that could conceivably hamper the President in conducting the duties of his office. If and when that should occur, the court's discretion would permit it to manage those actions in such fashion (including deferral of trial) that interference with the President's duties would not occur. But no such impingement upon the President's conduct of his office was shown here.

VIII

We add a final comment on two matters that are discussed at length in the briefs: the risk that our decision will generate a large volume of politically motivated harassing and frivolous litigation, and the danger that national security concerns might prevent the President from explaining a legitimate need for a continuance.

We are not persuaded that either of these risks is serious. Most frivolous and vexatious litigation is terminated at the pleading stage or on summary judgment, with little if any personal involvement by the defendant. See Fed. Rules Civ. Proc. 12, 56. Moreover, the availability of sanctions provides a significant deterrent to litigation directed at the President in his unofficial capacity for purposes of political gain or harassment. History indicates that the likelihood that a significant number of such cases will be filed is remote. Although scheduling problems may arise; there is no reason to assume that the District Courts will be either unable to accommodate the President's needs or unfaithful to the tradition—especially in matters involving national security—of giving "the utmost deference to Presidential responsibilities." Several Presidents, including petitioner, have given testimony without jeopardizing the Nations's security. See *supra,* at 1649. In short, we have confidence in the ability of our federal judges to deal with both of these concerns.

If Congress deems it appropriate to afford the President stronger protection, it may respond with appropriate legislation....

The Federal District Court has jurisdiction to decide this case. Like every other citizen who properly invokes that jurisdiction, respondent has a right to an orderly disposition of her claims. Accordingly, the judgment of the Court of Appeals is affirmed.

It is so ordered.

[Justice Breyer prepared a lengthy concurring opinion in which he discussed the specific situation when a President "sets forth and explains a conflict between judiciary proceeding and public duties." Under this circumstance, a federal district judge might schedule a trial in such a way that it interferes with the President's discharge of his public duties. Breyer's concurrence emphasizes the importance of the President's office and the danger of having a single judge "second guess" a President's needs.]

H. CONGRESSIONAL MEMBERSHIP AND PREROGATIVES

Under Article I, Section 5, each House of Congress "may determine the rules of its proceedings, punish its members for disorderly behavior, and, with the concurrence of two thirds, expel a member." Each House is also "the judge of the elections, returns and qualifications of its own members." Qualifications for office are set forth in Article I, Sections 2 and 3: age (twenty-five for Representatives and thirty for Senators), citizenship (seven years for Representatives and nine years for Senators), and residency (members must be "inhabitants" of the state in which they are chosen). The custom is for Representatives to also reside in the district for which they are elected.

On a few occasions the House of Representatives has refused to seat someone elected to office. A prominent example was Victor Berger of Wisconsin, a Socialist denied his seat in 1919 because he had been convicted for opposing World War I. A case that eventually reached the Supreme Court involved Adam Clayton Powell, a flamboyant black Congressman from New York. He was reelected in 1966, but the House refused to seat him, in part because of criminal proceedings against him. Many observers thought that the issue was clearly a political question to be decided solely by the House, but in 1969 the Supreme Court held that neither House could deny a seat to a duly elected member who satisfied the qualifications for office specified in the Constitution: age, citizenship, and residency. Congress could not add to that list of qualifications. POWELL v. McCORMACK, 395 U.S. 486 (1969). (See box on "The Exclusion of Adam Clayton Powell" in chapter 3, page 109).

If the House wanted to exclude Powell, it had to first seat him and then expel him by the two-thirds majority required by the Constitution. Previously, the Court had held that the Georgia legislature had violated Julian Bond's First Amendment rights by refusing to seat him because he had expressed his opposition to the Vietnam War. Bond v. Floyd, 385 U.S. 116 (1966). In addition to expulsion, Congress may censure a member for dishonorable or disreputable behavior.

Term Limits

A number of states adopted constitutional amendments and other measures to place term limits on legislators not only in state government but in Congress as well. An amendment to the Arkansas Constitution, limiting members of Congress to three terms in the House of Representatives and two terms in the Senate, was declared unconstitutional by the Supreme Court in 1995. Relying primarily on *Powell v. McCormack*, the court held that the Arkansas provision violated the U.S. Constitution by adding to the qualifications established for members of Congress. U.S. Term Limits, Inc. v. Thornton, 514 U.S. 779 (1995).

Also in 1995, the U.S. House of Representatives voted on a constitutional amendment to limit Representatives and Senators to a certain number of terms. Some of the proposals would have limited the terms of Representatives to six years and Senators to twelve, while others imposed limits of twelve years on both chambers. All of these amendments were voted down, including the basic Republican amendment (a lifetime limit of twelve years for both Houses), which lost on a vote of 227 to 204—a two-thirds majority being required for a constitutional amendment. A constitutional amendment stalled in the Senate in 1996 because of a filibuster. Another House effort in 1997 to amend the Constitution to impose term limits attracted the support of only 217 to 211.

Speech or Debate Clause

Article I, Section 6, provides that "for any Speech or Debate in either House," Senators and Representatives "shall not be questioned in any other Place." The courts have consistently held that the immunities offered by this Clause exist not simply for the personal or private benefit of members "but to protect the integrity of the legislative process by insuring the independence of individual legislators." United States v. Brewster, 408 U.S. 501, 507 (1972). It protects members from executive or judicial harassment. United States v. Johnson, 383 U.S. 177 (1966). The Clause covers not only words spoken in debate but also anything required to conduct legislative business: remarks made in the course of committee hearings; speeches printed in the *Congressional Record,* even when not delivered; and information acquired by congressional staff. Other activities, which the courts call "political" rather than "legislative," are not protected: contacts with executive agencies, assistance to constituents seeking federal contracts, the preparation of news releases and newsletters, and speeches or documents delivered outside the Congress (see box). Some of these issues were analyzed by the Court in GRAVEL v. UNITED STATES, 408 U.S. 606 (1972).

Speech or Debate Clause

Covers

Words spoken in debate and anything in relation to legislative business. Kilbourn v. Thompson, 103 U.S. 168, 204 (1881).

Remarks in committee hearings and committee reports. Gravel v. United States, 408 U.S. 606 (1972); Doe v. McMillan, 412 U.S. 306 (1973).

Speeches in *Congressional Record,* whether delivered or not. Hutchinson v. Proxmire, 433 U.S. 111, 116 n.3 (1979).

Congressional aides when carrying out legislative tasks. Gravel v. United States, 408 U.S. 606 (1972).

Judges may not inquire into the motivation for a Congressman's speech. United States v. Johnson, 383 U.S. 169, 176–77 (1966).

Does Not Cover

Criminal actions that are peripherally related to some legislative function. United States v. Brewster, 408 U.S. 501, 521 (1972).

"Errands" for constituents, making appointments with executive agencies, and assistance in securing federal contracts. United States v. Brewster, at 513.

Newsletters to constituents, news releases, and speeches delivered outside Congress. United States v. Brewster, at 513; Hutchinson v. Proxmire.

Private publications by members of Congress. Gravel v. United States, at 625; Doe v. McMillan, at 314–15.

Contacts with executive branch. United States v. Johnson, at 172; Gravel v. United States, at 625.

To protect its prerogatives, Congress has not hesitated to engage in direct confrontations with the judiciary. In 1970 the House Committee on Internal Security prepared a report entitled "Limited Survey of Honoraria Given Guest Speakers for Engagements at Colleges and Universities." By including the names of leftist or antiwar speakers and the amounts they received, the committee hoped that alumni would complain about the use of college funds and threaten to withhold future contributions. The ACLU obtained a copy of the galleys of the committee report and asked a federal judge to issue an injunction prohibiting its publication. U.S. District Judge Gesell did just that, ordering the Public Printer and the Superintendent of Documents not to print the report or even any "fascimile" of it. He suggested that Congress could print the report in the *Congressional Record* if it wanted to. Hentoff v. Ichord, 318 F.Supp. 1175 (D.D.C. 1970).

The House of Representatives responded with a resolution that told everyone, including the courts, to get out of the way. During debate on the resolution, it was pointed out that Congress does not print committee reports in the *Congressional Record*. Supporters of the resolution argued that Judge Gesell's order violated the Speech and Debate Clause and interfered with the authority of each House to determine the rules of its proceedings and to publish them. After the resolution passed by a large bipartisan margin of 302 to 54, the report was printed without any further judicial involvement. 116 Cong. Rec. 41358–74 (1970); H. Rept. No. 1732, 91st Cong., 2d Sess. (1970).

Article I, Section 6, also provides that members of Congress "shall in all cases, except treason, felony and breach of the peace, be privileged from arrest during their attendance at the session of their respective houses, and in going to and returning from the same." Immunity from arrest during sessions of the legislature can be traced back to struggles between the English Parliament and the King.

Powell v. McCormack

395 U.S. 486 (1969)

Adam Clayton Powell had served New York's 18th Congressional District since 1945. After his reelection in 1966, the House of Representatives passed a resolution refusing to seat him. By that point Powell had been charged with a number of offenses, including misappropriation of public funds and illegal salary payments for his wife. Also, he had been held in contempt in a New York defamation suit. After the exclusion vote, Powell and thirteen voters of his congressional district sued John W. McCormack, Speaker of the House, and several other House officials. A district court said it lacked jurisdiction to hear the case; the D.C. Circuit held that it had jurisdiction but that the case was nonjusticiable.

Mr. Chief Justice Warren delivered the opinion of the Court.

In November 1966, petitioner Adam Clayton Powell, Jr., was duly elected from the 18th Congressional District of New York to serve in the United States House of Representatives for the 90th Congress. However, pursuant to a House resolution, he was not permitted to take his seat. Powell (and some of the voters of his district) then filed suit in Federal District Court, claiming that the House could exclude him only if it found he failed to meet the standing requirements of age, citizenship, and residence contained in Art. I, § 2, of the Constitution—requirements the House specifically found Powell met—and thus had excluded him unconstitutionally. The District Court dismissed petitioners' complaint "for want of jurisdiction of the subject matter." A panel of the Court of Appeals affirmed the dismissal, although on somewhat different grounds, each judge filing a separate opinion. We have determined that it was error to dismiss the complaint and that petitioner Powell is entitled to a declaratory judgment that he was unlawfully excluded from the 90th Congress.

I.
FACTS.

During the 89th Congress, a Special Subcommittee on Contracts of the Committee on House Administration conducted an investigation into the expenditures of the Committee on Education and Labor, of which petitioner Adam Clayton Powell, Jr., was chairman. The Special Subcommittee issued a report concluding that Powell and certain staff employees had deceived the House authorities as to travel expenses. The report also indicated there was strong evidence that certain illegal salary payments had been made to Powell's wife at his direction. See H. R. Rep. No. 2349, 89th Cong., 2d Sess., 6–7 (1966). No formal action was taken during the 89th Congress. However, prior to the organization of the 90th Congress, the Democratic members-elect met in caucus and voted to remove Powell as chairman of the Committee on Education and Labor. See H. R. Rep. No. 27, 90th Cong., 1st Sess., 1–2 (1967).

When the 90th Congress met to organize in January 1967, Powell was asked to step aside while the oath was administered to the other members-elect. Following the administration of the oath to the remaining members, the House discussed the procedure to be followed in determining whether Powell was eligible to take his seat. After some debate, by a vote of 363 to 65 the House adopted House Resolution No. 1, which provided that the Speaker appoint a Select Committee to determine Powell's eligibility. 113 Cong. Rec. 26–27. Although the resolution prohibited Powell from taking his seat until the House acted on the Select Committee's report, it did provide that he should receive all the pay and allowances due a member during the period.

The Select Committee, composed of nine lawyer-members, issued an invitation to Powell to testify before the Committee. The invitation letter stated that the scope of the testimony and investigation would include Powell's qualifications as to age, citizenship, and residency; his involvement in a civil suit (in which he had been held in contempt); and "[m]atters of . . . alleged official misconduct since January 3, 1961." . . . Powell appeared at the Committee hearing held on February 8, 1967. . . . [He was willing to] give information relating only to his age, citizenship, and residency; upon the advice of counsel, he refused to answer other questions.

. . . [O]n February 23, 1967, the Committee issued its report, finding that Powell met the standing qualifications of Art. I § 2 H. R. Rep. No. 27,

90th Cong., 1st Sess., 31 (1967). However, the Committee further reported that Powell had asserted an unwarranted privilege and immunity from the processes of the courts of New York; that he had wrongfully diverted House funds for the use of others and himself; and that he had made false reports on expenditures of foreign currency to the Committee on House Administration. *Id.,* at 31–32. The Committee recommended that Powell be sworn and seated as a member of the 90th Congress but that he be censured by the House, fined $40,000 and be deprived of his seniority. *Id.,* at 33.

The report was presented to the House on March 1, 1967, and the House debated the Select Committee's proposed resolution. At the conclusion of the debate, by a vote of 222 to 202 the House rejected a motion to bring the resolution to a vote. An amendment to the resolution was then offered; it called for the exclusion of Powell and a declaration that his seat was vacant. The Speaker ruled that a majority vote of the House would be sufficient to pass the resolution if it were so amended. 113 Cong. Rec. 5020. After further debate, the amendment was adopted by a vote of 248 to 176. Then the House adopted by a vote of 307 to 116 House Resolution No. 278 in its amended form, thereby excluding Powell and directing that the Speaker notify the Governor of New York that the seat was vacant.

Powell and 13 voters of the 18th Congressional District of New York subsequently instituted this suit in the United States District Court for the District of Columbia. Five members of the House of Representatives were named as defendants *[including John W. McCormack, Speaker of the House, and several House officials.]*

. . . While the case was pending on our docket, the 90th Congress officially terminated and the 91st Congress was seated. In November 1968, Powell was again elected as the representative of the 18th Congressional District of New York and he was seated by the 91st Congress. The resolution seating Powell also fined him $25,000. . . .

Respondents press upon us a variety of arguments to support the court below; they will be considered in the following order. (1) Events occurring subsequent to the grant of certiorari have rendered this litigation moot. (2) The Speech or Debate Clause of the Constitution, Art. I, § 6, insulates respondents' action from judicial review. (3) The decision to exclude petitioner Powell is supported by the power granted to the House of Representatives to expel a member. (4) This Court lacks subject matter jurisdiction over petitioners' action. (5) Even if subject matter jurisdiction is present, this litigation is not justiciable either under the general criteria established by this Court or because a political question is involved.

II.
MOOTNESS.

After certiorari was granted, respondents filed a memorandum suggesting that two events which occurred subsequent to our grant of certiorari require that the case be dismissed as moot. On January 3, 1969, the House of Representatives of the 90th Congress officially terminated, and petitioner Powell was seated as a member of the 91st Congress. 115 Cong. Rec. H22 (daily ed., January 3, 1969). Respondents insist that the gravamen of petitioners' complaint was the failure of the 90th Congress to seat petitioner Powell and that, since the House of Representatives is not a continuing body and Powell has now been seated, his claims are moot. Petitioners counter that three issues remain unresolved and thus this litigation presents a "case or controversy" within the meaning of Art. III: (1) whether Powell was unconstitutionally deprived of his seniority by his exclusion from the 90th Congress; (2) whether the resolution of the 91st Congress imposing as "punishment" a $25,000 fine is a continuation of respondents' allegedly unconstitutional exclusion, . . . and (3) whether Powell is entitled to salary withheld after his exclusion from the 90th Congress. We conclude that Powell's claim for back salary remains viable even though he has been seated in the 91st Congress and thus find it unnecessary to determine whether the other issues have become moot.

. . .

III.
SPEECH OR DEBATE CLAUSE.

Respondents assert that the Speech or Debate Clause of the Constitution, Art. I, § 6, is an absolute bar to petitioners' action. This Court has on four prior occasions—*Dombrowski* v. *Eastland,* 387 U. S. 82 (1967); *United States* v. *Johnson,* 383 U. S. 169 (1966); *Tenney* v. *Brandhove,* 341 U. S. 367 (1951); and *Kilbourn* v. *Thompson,* 103 U. S. 168 (1881)—been called upon to determine if allegedly unconstitutional action taken by legislators or legislative employees is insulated from judicial review by the Speech or Debate Clause. . . .

The Speech or Debate Clause, adopted by the Constitutional Convention without debate or opposition, finds its roots in the conflict between Parliament and the Crown culminating in the Glorious Revolution of 1688 and the English Bill of Rights of 1689. Drawing upon this history, we concluded in *United States* v. *Johnson* . . . that the purpose of this clause was "to prevent intimidation [of legislators] by the executive and accountability before a possibly hostile judiciary." . . .

Our cases make it clear that the legislative immunity created by the Speech or Debate Clause performs an important function in representative government. It insures that legislators are free to represent the interests of their constituents without fear that they will be later called to task in the courts for that representation. . . .

Legislative immunity does not, of course, bar all judicial review of legislative acts. That issue was settled by implication as early as 1803, see *Marbury* v. *Madison,* 1 Cranch 137, and expressly in *Kilbourn* v. *Thompson,* the first of this Court's cases interpreting the reach of the Speech or Debate Clause *[involving the constitutionality of a House Resolution ordering the arrest and imprisonment of a recalcitrant witness who had refused to respond to a subpoena issued by a House investigating committee.]* . . .

That House employees are acting pursuant to express orders of the House does not bar judicial review of the constitutionality of the underlying legislative decision. *Kilbourn* decisively settles this question, since the Sergeant at Arms was held liable for false imprisonment even though he did nothing more than execute the House Resolution that Kilbourn be arrested and imprisoned. . . . [T]hough this action may be dismissed against the Congressmen petitioners are entitled to maintain their action against House employees and to judicial review of the propriety of the decision to exclude petitioner Powell. . . .

IV.
EXCLUSION OR EXPULSION.

The resolution excluding petitioner Powell was adopted by a vote in excess of two-thirds of the 434 Members of Congress—307 to 116. 113 Cong. Rec. 5037–5038. Article I, § 5, grants the House authority to expel a member "with the Concurrence of two thirds." Respondents assert that the House may expel a member for any reason whatsoever and that, since a two-thirds vote was obtained, the procedure by which Powell was denied his seat in the 90th Congress should be regarded as an expulsion, not an exclusion. . . .

[The Court reviewed the legislative proceedings of

Powell's exclusion. The chairman of the Select Committee posed a parliamentary inquiry to determine whether a two-thirds vote was necessary. The Speaker replied that action by a majority vote would be in accordance with the rules. The Court also notes that the House has determined that a member should not be expelled for action taken during a prior Congress.]

V.
SUBJECT MATTER JURISDICTION.

[The Court holds that there is jurisdiction to hear the case and that the case is justiciable. Judicial power extends to all cases "arising under" the Constitution. A suit arises under the Constitution if a claim will be sustained if the Constitution is given one construction and will be defeated if it is given another construction.]

VI.
JUSTICIABILITY.

Having concluded that the Court of Appeals correctly ruled that the District Court had jurisdiction over the subject matter, we turn to the question whether the case is justiciable....

A. *General Considerations.*

In deciding generally whether a claim is justiciable, a court must determine whether "the duty asserted can be judicially identified and its breach judicially determined, and whether protection for the right asserted can be judicially molded." *Baker v. Carr, supra,* at 198. Respondents do not seriously contend that the duty asserted and its alleged breach cannot be judicially determined. If petitioners are correct, the House had a duty to seat Powell once it determined he met the standing requirements set forth in the Constitution. It is undisputed that he met those requirements and that he was nevertheless excluded.

Respondents do maintain, however, that this case is not justiciable because, they assert, it is impossible for a federal court to "mold effective relief for resolving this case." Respondents emphasize that petitioners asked for coercive relief against the officers of the House, and, they contend, federal courts cannot issue mandamus or injunctions compelling officers or employees of the House to perform specific official acts. Respondents rely primarily on the Speech or Debate Clause to support this contention.

We need express no opinion about the appropriateness of coercive relief in this case, for petitioners sought a declaratory judgment, a

form of relief the District Court could have issued. The Declaratory Judgment Act, 28 U. S. C. § 2201, provides that a district court may "declare the rights...of any interested party... whether or not further relief is or could be sought." ...We thus conclude that in terms of the general criteria of justiciability, this case is justiciable.

B. *Political Question Doctrine.*

1. *Textually Demonstrable Constitutional Commitment.*

Respondents maintain that even if this case is otherwise justiciable, it presents only a political question. It is well established that the federal courts will not adjudicate political questions.... In *Baker v. Carr, supra,* we noted that political questions are not justiciable primarily because of the separation of powers within the Federal Government. After reviewing our decisions in this area, we concluded that on the surface of any case held to involve a political question was at least one of the following formulations:

"a textually demonstrable constitutional commitment of the issue to a coordinate political department; or a lack of judicially discoverable and manageable standards for resolving it; or the impossibility of deciding without an initial policy determination of a kind clearly for nonjudicial discretion; or the impossibility of a court's undertaking independent resolution without expressing lack of the respect due coordinate branches of government; or an unusual need for unquestioning adherence to a political decision already made; or the potentiality of embarrassment from multifarious pronouncements by various departments on one question." 369 U. S., at 217.

Respondents' first contention is that this case presents a political question because under Art. I, § 5, there has been a "textually demonstrable constitutional commitment" to the House of the "adjudicatory power" to determine Powell's qualifications. Thus it is argued that the House, and the House alone, has power to determine who is qualified to be a member.

In order to determine whether there has been a textual commitment to a co-ordinate department of the Government, we must interpret the Constitution. In other words, we must first determine what power the Constitution confers upon the House through Art. I, § 5, before we can determine to what extent, if any, the exercise of that power is subject to judicial review....

In order to determine the scope of any "textual commitment" under Art. I, § 5, we necessarily must determine the meaning of the phrase to "be the Judge of the Qualifications of its own Members." *[Here the Court analyzes in detail British and American precedents before the Philadelphia Convention, the debates at the Convention, and post-Convention debates (especially Hamilton's Federalist No. 60, which argues that the qualifications of Members of Congress "are defined and fixed ... and are unalterable by the legislature"). On the basis of these historical materials, the Court concludes that the House may not exclude someone who meets the requirements for membership expressly prescribed by the Constitution. After seating such a person, the House may expel, but only after securing the two-thirds majority required by the Constitution.]*

2. Other Considerations.

Respondents' alternate contention is that the case presents a political question because judicial resolution of petitioners' claim would produce a "potentially embarrassing confrontation between coordinate branches" of the Federal Government. But, as our interpretation of Art. I, § 5, discloses, a determination of petitioner Powell's right to sit would require no more than an interpretation of the Constitution. Such a determination falls within the traditional role accorded courts to interpret the law, and does not involve a "lack of the respect due [a] coordinate [branch] of government," nor does it involve an "initial policy determination of a kind clearly for nonjudicial discretion." *Baker v. Carr,* 369 U. S. 186, at 217. Our system of government requires that federal courts on occasion interpret the Constitution in a manner at variance with the construction given the document by another branch. The alleged conflict that such an adjudication may cause cannot justify the courts' avoiding their constitutional responsibility. See *United States v. Brown,* 381 U. S. 437, 462 (1965); *Youngstown Sheet & Tube Co. v. Sawyer,* 343 U. S. 579, 613–614 (1952) (Frankfurter, J., concurring); *Myers v. United States,* 272 U. S. 52, 293 (1926) (Brandeis, J., dissenting).

Nor are any of the other formulations of a political question "inextricable from the case at bar." *Baker v. Carr, supra,* at 217. Petitioners seek a determination that the House was without power to exclude Powell from the 90th Congress, which, we have seen, requires an interpretation of the Constitution—a determination for which clearly there are "judicially ... manageable standards." Finally, a judicial resolution of petitioners' claim will not result in "multifarious pronouncements by various departments on one question." For, as we noted in *Baker v. Carr, supra,* at 211, it is the responsibility of this Court to act as the ultimate interpreter of the Constitution. *Marbury v. Madison,* 1 Cranch 137 (1803). Thus, we conclude that petitioners' claim is not barred by the political question doctrine, and, having determined that the claim is otherwise generally justiciable, we hold that the case is justiciable.

Mr. Justice Douglas *[concurring].*

· · ·

MR. JUSTICE STEWART, dissenting.

I believe that events which have taken place since certiorari was granted in this case on November 18, 1968, have rendered it moot, and that the Court should therefore refrain from deciding the novel, difficult, and delicate constitutional questions which the case presented at its inception.

· · ·

II.

The passage of time and intervening events have ... made it impossible to afford the petitioners the principal relief they sought in this case. If any aspect of the case remains alive, it is only Congressman Powell's individual claim for the salary of which he was deprived by his absence from the 90th Congress. But even if that claim can be said to prevent this controversy from being moot, which I doubt, there is no need to reach the fundamental constitutional issues that the Court today undertakes to decide.

This Court has not in the past found that an incidental claim for back pay preserves the controversy between a legislator and the legislative body which evicted him, once the term of his eviction has expired....

There are, then substantial questions as to whether, on his salary claim, Powell could obtain relief against any or all of these respondents. On the other hand, if he was entitled to a salary as a member of the 90th Congress, he has a certain and completely satisfactory remedy in an action for a money judgment against the United States in the Court of Claims....

Gravel v. United States

408 U.S. 606 (1972)

Senator Mike Gravel read to his subcommittee from classified documents (the Pentagon Papers), which he then placed in the public records. The press reported that he had arranged to have the Papers privately published. A grand jury investigating possible violations of federal law issued a subpoena to one of Gravel's aides. Gravel intervened, maintaining that the subpoena would violate the Speech or Debate Clause. The lower courts held that the Clause protects all legislative acts, including legislative work done by congressional aides. The district court ruled that the Clause does not cover private publications. The appellate court agreed but concluded that Gravel and his aide could not be questioned about private publications because of a common-law privilege.

Opinion of the Court by MR. JUSTICE WHITE, announced by MR. JUSTICE BLACKMUN.

These cases arise out of the investigation by a federal grand jury into possible criminal conduct with respect to the release and publication of a classified Defense Department study entitled History of the United States Decision-Making Process on Viet Nam Policy. This document, popularly known as the Pentagon Papers, bore a Defense security classification of Top Secret-Sensitive. The crimes being investigated included the retention of public property or records with intent to convert (18 U. S. C. § 641), the gathering and transmitting of national defense information (18 U. S. C. § 793), the concealment or removal of public records or documents (18 U. S. C. § 2071), and conspiracy to commit such offenses and to defraud the United States (18 U. S. C. § 371).

Among the witnesses subpoenaed were Leonard S. Rodberg, an assistant to Senator Mike Gravel of Alaska and a resident fellow at the Institute of Policy Studies, and Howard Webber, Director of M. I. T. Press. Senator Gravel, as intervenor, filed motions to quash the subpoenas and to require the Government to specify the particular questions to be addressed to Rodberg. He asserted that requiring these witnesses to appear and testify would violate his privilege under the Speech or Debate Clause of the United States Constitution, Art. I, § 6, cl. 1.

It appeared that on the night of June 29, 1971, Senator Gravel, as Chairman of the Subcommittee on Buildings and Grounds of the Senate Public Works Committee, convened a meeting of the subcommittee and there read extensively from a copy of the Pentagon Papers. He then placed the entire 47 volumes of the study in the public record. Rodberg had been added to the Senator's staff earlier in the day and assisted Gravel in preparing for and conducting the hearing. Some weeks later there were press reports that Gravel had arranged for the papers to be published by Beacon Press and that members of Gravel's staff had talked with Webber as editor of M. I. T. Press.

. . .

I

Because the claim is that a Member's aide shares the Member's constitutional privilege, we consider first whether and to what extent Senator Gravel himself is exempt from process or inquiry by a grand jury investigating the commission of a crime. Our frame of reference is Art. I, § 6, cl. 1, of the Constitution:

"The Senators and Representatives shall receive a Compensation for their Services, to be ascertained by Law, and paid out of the Treasury of the United States. They shall in all Cases, except Treason, Felony and Breach of the Peace, be privileged from Arrest during their Attendance at the Session of their respective Houses, and in going to and returning from the same; and for any Speech or Debate in either House, they shall not be questioned in any other Place."

The last sentence of the Clause provides Members of Congress with two distinct privileges. Except in cases of "Treason, Felony and Breach of the Peace," the Clause shields Members from arrest while attending or traveling to and from a session of their House. History reveals, and prior cases so hold, that this part of the Clause exempts Members from arrest in civil cases only. "When the Constitution was adopted, arrests in civil suits were still common in America. It is only to such arrests that the provision applies." *Long* v. *Ansell*, 293 U. S. 76, 83 (1934) (footnote omitted). "Since...the terms treason, felony and breach of the peace, as used in the constitutional provision relied upon, excepts from the operation of the privilege all criminal offenses, the conclusion results that the claim of privilege of exemption from arrest and sentence was without merit...." *Williamson v. United States,* 207 U. S. 425, 446 (1908). Nor does freedom from arrest confer immunity on a Member from service of process as a defendant in civil matters, *Long v. Ansell, supra,* at 82–83, or as a witness in a criminal case. "The constitution gives to every man, charged with an offence, the benefit of compulsory process, to secure the attendance of his witnesses. I do not know of any privilege to exempt members of congress from the service, or the obligations, of a *subpoena,* in such cases." *United States v. Cooper,* 4 Dall. 341 (1800) (Chase, J., sitting on Circuit). It is, therefore, sufficiently plain that the constitutional freedom from arrest does not exempt Members of Congress from the operation of the ordinary criminal laws, even though imprisonment may prevent or interfere with the performance of their duties as Members. *Williamson v. United States, supra;* cf. *Burton v. United States,* 202 U. S. 344 (1906). Indeed, implicit in the narrow scope of the privilege of freedom from arrest is, as Jefferson noted, the judgment that legislators ought not to stand above the law they create but ought generally to be bound by it as are ordinary persons. T. Jefferson, Manual of Parliamentary Practice, S. Doc. No. 92-1, p. 437 (1971).

In recognition, no doubt, of the force of this part of § 6, Senator Gravel disavows any assertion of general immunity from the criminal law. But he points out that the last portion of § 6 affords Members of Congress another vital privilege— they may not be questioned in any other place for any speech or debate in either House. The claim is not that while one part of § 6 generally permits prosecutions for treason, felony, and breach of the peace, another part nevertheless broadly forbids them. Rather, his insistence is that the Speech or Debate Clause at the very least protects him from criminal or civil liability and from questioning elsewhere than in the Senate, with respect to the events occurring at the subcommittee hearing at which the Pentagon Papers were introduced into the public record. To us this claim is incontrovertible. The Speech or Debate Clause was designed to assure a co-equal branch of the government wide freedom of speech, debate, and deliberation without intimidation or threats from the Executive Branch. It thus protects Members against prosecutions that directly impinge upon or threaten the legislative process. We have no doubt that Senator Gravel may not be made to answer—either in terms of questions or in terms of defending himself from prosecution—for the events that occurred at the subcommittee meeting. Our decision is made easier by the fact that the United States appears to have abandoned whatever position it took to the contrary in the lower courts.

Even so, the United States strongly urges that because the Speech or Debate Clause confers a privilege only upon "Senators and Representatives," Rodberg himself has no valid claim to constitutional immunity from grand jury inquiry. In our view, both courts below correctly rejected this position. We agree with the Court of Appeals that for the purpose of construing the privilege a Member and his aide are to be "treated as one," *United States v. Doe,* 455 F. 2d, at 761; ... it is literally impossible, in view of the complexities of the modern legislative process, with Congress almost constantly in session and matters of legislative concern constantly proliferating, for Members of Congress to perform their legislative tasks without the help of aides and assistants; that the day-to-day work of such aides is so critical to the Members' performance that they must be treated as the latter's alter egos; and that if they are not so recognized, the central role of the Speech or Debate Clause—to prevent intimidation of legislators by the Executive and accountability before a possibly hostile judiciary, *United States v. Johnson,* 383 U. S. 169, 181 (1966)—will inevitably be diminished and frustrated.

. . .

Nor can we agree with the United States that our conclusion is foreclosed by *Kilbourn v. Thompson, supra, Dombrowski v. Eastland,* 387 U. S. 82 (1967), and *Powell v. McCormack,* 395 U. S. 486 (1969), where the speech or debate privilege was held unavailable to certain House and committee employees. Those cases do not hold that persons other than Members of Congress are beyond the protection of the Clause when they perform or aid in the performance of legislative acts....

None of these three cases adopted the simple proposition that immunity was unavailable to congressional or committee employees because they were not Representatives or Senators; rather, immunity was unavailable because they engaged in illegal conduct that was not entitled to Speech or Debate Clause protection. The three cases reflect a decidedly jaundiced view towards extending the Clause so as to privilege illegal or unconstitutional conduct beyond that essential to foreclose executive control of legislative speech or debate and associated matters such as voting and committee reports and proceedings....

II

We are convinced also that the Court of Appeals correctly determined that Senator Gravel's alleged arrangement with Beacon Press to publish the Pentagon Papers was not protected speech or debate within the meaning of Art. I, § 6, cl. 1, of the Constitution.

Historically, the English legislative privilege was not viewed as protecting republication of an otherwise immune libel on the floor of the House....

...[T]he [Speech or Debate] Clause has not been extended beyond the legislative sphere. That Senators generally perform certain acts in their official capacity as Senators does not necessarily make all such acts legislative in nature. Members of Congress are constantly in touch with the Executive Branch of the Government and with administrative agencies—they may cajole, and exhort with respect to the administration of a federal statute—but such conduct, though generally done, is not protected legislative activity. *United States* v. *Johnson* decided at least this much. "No argument is made, nor do we think that it could be successfully contended, that the Speech or Debate Clause reaches conduct, such as was involved in the attempt to influence the Department of Justice, that is in no wise related to the due functioning of the legislative process." 383 U. S., at 172. Cf. *Burton* v. *United States*, 202 U. S., at 367–368.

Legislative acts are not all-encompassing. The heart of the Clause is speech or debate in either House. Insofar as the Clause is construed to reach other matters, they must be an integral part of the deliberative and communicative processes by which Members participate in committee and House proceedings with respect to the consideration and passage or rejection of proposed legislation or with respect to other matters which the Constitution places within the jurisdiction of either House. As the Court of Appeals put it, the courts have extended the privilege to matters beyond pure speech or debate in either House, but "only when necessary to prevent indirect impairment of such deliberations." *United States* v. *Doe*, 455 F. 2d, at 760.

Here, private publication by Senator Gravel through the cooperation of Beacon Press was in no way essential to the deliberations of the Senate;...

...The Speech or Debate Clause does not in our view extend immunity to Rodberg, as a Senator's aide, from testifying before the grand jury about the arrangement between Senator Gravel and Beacon Press or about his own participation, if any, in the alleged transaction, so long as legislative acts of the Senator are not impugned.

. . .

MR. JUSTICE STEWART, dissenting in part.

The Court today holds that the Speech or Debate Clause does not protect a Congressman from being forced to testify before a grand jury about sources of information used in preparation for legislative acts. This critical question was not embraced in the petitions for certiorari. It was not dealt with in the written briefs. It was addressed only tangentially during the oral arguments. Yet it is a question with profound implications for the effective functioning of the legislative process. I cannot join in the Court's summary resolution of so vitally important a constitutional issue.

. . .

Under the Court's ruling, a Congressman may be subpoenaed by a vindictive Executive to testify about informants who have not committed crimes and who have no knowledge of crime. Such compulsion can occur, because the judiciary has traditionally imposed virtually no limitations on the grand jury's broad investigatory powers; grand jury investigations are not limited in scope to specific criminal acts, and standards of materiality and relevance are greatly relaxed. But even if the Executive had reason to believe that a Member of Congress had knowledge of a specific probable violation of law, it is by no means clear to me that the Executive's interest in the administration of justice must *always* override the public interest in having an informed Congress....

MR. JUSTICE DOUGLAS, dissenting.

I would construe the Speech or Debate Clause to insulate Senator Gravel and his aides from inquiry concerning the Pentagon Papers, and Beacon Press from inquiry concerning publication of them, for that publication was but another way of informing the public as to what had gone on in the privacy of the Executive Branch concerning the conception and pursuit of the so-called "war" in Vietnam. Alternatively, I would hold that Beacon Press is protected by the First Amendment from prosecution or investigations for publishing or undertaking to publish the Pentagon Papers.

. . .

MR. JUSTICE BRENNAN, with whom MR. JUS-
TICE DOUGLAS, and MR. JUSTICE MARSHALL,
join, dissenting.

...My concern is with the narrow scope accorded the Speech or Debate Clause by today's decision. I fully agree with the court that a Congressman's immunity under the Clause must also be
extended to his aides if it is to be at all effective....

I

In holding that Senator Gravel's alleged
arrangement with Beacon Press to publish the Pentagon Papers is not shielded from extra-senatorial
inquiry by the Speech or Debate Clause, the Court
adopts what for me is a far too narrow view of the
legislative function. The Court seems to assume

that words spoken in debate or written in congressional reports are protected by the Clause, so that
if Senator Gravel had recited part of the Pentagon
Papers on the Senate floor or copied them into a
Senate report, those acts could not be questioned
"in any other Place." Yet because he sought a
wider audience, to publicize information deemed
relevant to matters pending before his own committee, the Senator suddenly loses his immunity
and is exposed to grand jury investigation and possible prosecution for the republication....

Thus, the Court excludes from the sphere of
protected legislative activity a function that I had
supposed lay at the heart of our democratic system. I speak, of course, of the legislator's duty to
inform the public about matters affecting the administration of government....

CONCLUSIONS

Most of the conflicts between Congress and the President are resolved through informal negotiations and accommodations. Rarely does an issue enter the judicial arena. When it does,
the courts are reluctant to set hard-and-fast rules in such complex areas as executive privilege, delegation, and congressional investigations. An emphasis is placed on middle-ground
remedies that protect the essential interests of each branch. Beyond the statutory framework
agreed to by executive and legislative officials, the two branches have evolved an elaborate
system of informal, nonstatutory agreements that satisfy the competing needs of executive
flexibility and congressional control. In this important sense, the meaning of separation of
powers depends heavily on nonjudicial interpretations by the executive and legislative
branches. Louis Fisher, "Separation of Powers: Interpretation Outside the Courts," 18 Pepperdine L. Rev. 57 (1990).

In recent decades, the Supreme Court has fluctuated between conflicting theories of separated powers. At times, it adopts a flexible, pragmatic model that tolerates an overlapping
of powers. On other occasions, it embraces a rigid, formalistic view, announcing that the
separation between the branches must be kept pure and immaculate. There is also substantial evidence that the Burger Court used a different methodology depending on the issue, resorting to fixed and original principles to strike down congressional actions but accepting
executive actions as within the permissible bounds of an evolving, dynamic Constitution.
The Rehnquist Court appears to be moving back to a pragmatic reading of the separation
doctrine.[18]

---

18. See Erwin Chermerinsky, "A Paradox Without a Principle: A Comment on the Burger Court's Jurisprudence
in Separation of Powers Cases," 60 S.Cal. L.Rev. 1083 (1987). For two significant Rehnquist Court opinions, see the
independent counsel case of Morrison v. Olson, 487 U.S. 654 (1988) and the U.S. Sentencing Commission case of
Mistretta v. United States, 488 U.S. 361 (1989). Flexible models were used by the Burger Court in United States v.
Nixon, 418 U.S. 683 (1974) and Nixon v. Administrator of General Services, 433 U.S. 425 (1977). Rigid theories
were presented in Northern Pipeline Co. v. Marathon Pipe Line Co., 458 U.S. 50 (1982); INS v. Chadha, 462 U.S.
919 (1983); and Bowsher v. Synar, 478 U.S. 714 (1986).

SELECTED READINGS

BARBER, SOTIRIOS A. The Constitution and the Delegation of Congressional Power. Chicago: University of Chicago Press, 1975.

BESSETTE, JOSEPH M., AND JEFFREY TULIS, eds. The Presidency in the Constitutional Order. Baton Rouge: Louisiana State University Press, 1981.

BRECKENRIDGE, ADAM CARLYLE. The Executive Privilege, Lincoln: University of Nebraska Press, 1974.

COOPER, PHILLIP J. "By Order of the President: Administration by Executive Order and Proclamation." 18 Administration & Society 233 (1986).

CRAIG, BARBARA HINKSON. Chadha. New York: Oxford University Press, 1988.

FISHER, LOUIS. The Politics of Shared Power: Congress and the Executive. College Station,Tex.: Texas A&M University Press, 4th ed., 1998.

———. Constitutional Conflicts Between Congress and the President. Lawrence: University Press of Kansas, 4th ed., 1997.

———. "Invoking Executive Privilege: Navigating Ticklish Political Waters." 8 William & Mary Bill of Rights Journal 583 (2000).

GLENNON, MICHAEL J. "The Use of Custom in Resolving Separation of Powers Disputes." 64 Boston University Law Review 109 (1984).

GOLDWIN, ROBERT A. AND ART KAUFMAN, eds. Separation of Powers—Does It Still Work? Washington, D.C.: American Enterprise Institute, 1986.

GWYN, W.B. "The Meaning of Separation of Powers." Tulane Series in Political Science, Vol. IX (1965).

HAMILTON, JAMES. The Power to Probe: A Study of Congressional Investigations. New York: Random House, 1976.

HARRIS, JOSEPH P. The Advice and Consent of the Senate: A Study of the Confirmation of Appointments by the United States Senate. Berkeley: University of California Press, 1953.

KADEN, ALAN SCOTT. "Judicial Review of Executive Action in Domestic Affairs." 80 Columbia Law Review 1535 (1980).

KAISER, FREDERICK M. "Congressional Control of Executive Actions in the Aftermath of the Chadha Decision." 36 Administrative Law Review 239 (1984).

McGOWAN, CARL "Congress, Court and Control of Delegated Powers." 77 Columbia Law Review 1119 (1977).

ROSENBERG, MORTON. "Beyond the Limits of Executive Power: Presidential Control of Agency Rulemaking Under Executive Order 12,291." 80 Michigan Law Review 193 (1981).

STATHIS, STEPHEN W. "Executive Cooperation: Presidential Recognition of the Investigative Authority of Congress and the Courts." 3 Journal of Law & Politics 183 (1986).

VILE, M.J.C. Constitutionalism and the Separation of Powers. London: Oxford University Press, 1967.

WINTERTON, GEORGE. "The Concept of Extra-Constitutional Executive Power in Domestic Affairs." 7 Hastings Constitutional Law Quarterly 1 (1979).

7

Separation of Powers: Emergencies and Foreign Affairs

The doctrine of separated powers has its share of subtleties and puzzles in domestic disputes. Even more enigmatic is the doctrine's application to external affairs and emergency powers. This chapter begins by examining efforts to distinguish between external and internal affairs. It analyzes the scope of the "executive prerogative," which some Presidents cite as authority to exercise powers not expressly stated in the Constitution, even when their actions are contrary to laws passed by Congress. Other sections explore the scope of treaties and executive agreements, the war power, and questions of citizenship.

A. EXTERNAL AND INTERNAL AFFAIRS

Those who believe that the lion's share of authority in foreign affairs belongs with the President rely heavily on Justice Sutherland's decision in *United States* v. *Curtiss-Wright Corp.* (1936). The case could have been confined to a single question: May Congress delegate to the President the authority to prohibit the shipment of arms or munitions to any country in South America whenever he decided that the material would promote domestic violence? The Court agreed that legislation over the international field must often accord to the President greater discretion than would be admissible for domestic affairs. But Sutherland went beyond the issue of delegation to add pages of obiter dicta to describe the far-reaching dimensions of executive power in foreign affairs. He assigned to the President a number of powers not found in the Constitution. *Curtiss-Wright* is cited frequently to justify not only broad grants of legislative power to the President but also the exercise of inherent, extraconstitutional powers. UNITED STATES v. CURTISS-WRIGHT CORP., 299 U.S. 304 (1936).

Curtiss-Wright echoed positions Sutherland had taken as a United States Senator and as a member of the Senate Foreign Relations Committee. It closely tracks his article, "The Internal and External Powers of the National Government," printed as Senate Document No. 417 in 1910, which claimed that national sovereignty "inhered in the United States from the beginning" rather than in the colonies or the states. His book, *Constitutional Power and World Affairs* (1919), promoted the same themes.

In *Curtiss-Wright,* Sutherland refers to Congressman John Marshall's remark in 1800 that the President is the "sole organ of the nation in its external relations," implying that the President makes foreign policy unilaterally. That would be powerful evidence, given Marshall's elevation a year later to be Chief Justice of the Supreme Court. However, when read in context, Marshall only meant that the President communicates to other nations U.S. foreign policy *after* it has been adopted jointly by the executive and legislative branches (either by treaty or by statute). Marshall clearly meant that the President was the "sole organ" in *implementing,* not formulating, foreign policy (see box on next page).

Sutherland believed that foreign and domestic affairs were fundamentally different because the powers of external sovereignty passed from the Crown "not to the colonies severally, but

Marshall's "Sole Organ" Remark

[*The following statement by Congressman John Marshall, during legislative debate in 1800, came in response to a proposal to impeach President John Adams for interfering with judicial proceedings underway in the trial of Jonathan Robbins. Pursuant to an extradition treaty, Adams had agreed to return Robbins to England.*]

The [dispute] was in its nature a national demand made upon the nation. The parties were the two nations. They cannot come into court to litigate their claims, nor can a court decide on them. Of consequence, the demand is not a case for judicial cognizance.

The President is the sole organ of the nation in its external relations, and its sole representative with foreign nations. Of consequence, the demand of a foreign nation can only be made on him.

He possesses the whole Executive power. He holds and directs the force of the nation. Of con-

sequence, any act to be performed by the force of the nation is to be performed through him.

He is charged to execute the laws. A treaty is declared to be a law. He must then execute a treaty, where he, and he alone, possesses the means of executing it.

The treaty, which is a law, enjoins the performance of a particular object. The person who is to perform this object is marked out by the Constitution, since the person is named who conducts the foreign intercourse, and is to take care that the laws be faithfully executed. The means by which it is to be performed, the force of the nation, are in the hands of this person. Ought not this person to perform the object, although the particular mode of using the means has not been prescribed? Congress, unquestionably, may prescribe the mode, and Congress may devolve on others the whole execution of the contract; but, till this be done, it seems the duty of the Executive department to execute the contract by any means it possesses.

SOURCE: Annals of Cong., 6th Cong. 613–14 (1800).

to the colonies in their collective and corporate capacity as the United States of America." However, from 1774 to 1788 the colonies and states operated as sovereign entities, not as parts of a collective body. They acted free and independent of one another. The creation of the Continental Congress did not disturb the sovereign capacity of the states to make treaties, borrow money, solicit arms, lay embargoes, collect tariff duties, and conduct separate military campaigns.

Even if the power of external sovereignty had somehow passed intact from the Crown to the "United States," the Constitution divides that power between Congress and the President. The President and the Senate share the treaty power. Congress has the responsibility to raise and support military forces, to lay and collect duties on foreign trade, to regulate commerce with foreign nations, and to fund the armed services. Contemporary conditions make it increasingly difficult to draw a crisp line between external and internal affairs. Oil embargoes imposed by foreign governments have an immediate impact on America's economy, raising the price at home and producing long lines at the neighborhood gas station. The President's decision to ship or withhold wheat from the Soviet Union has a major effect on farming communities. Trade policies are both international and domestic in scope. As President Bush noted in 1991: "I guess my bottom line... is you can't separate foreign policy from domestic." Public Papers of the Presidents, 1991 (II), at 1629. In his first inaugural address, in 1993, President Clinton remarked: "There is no longer a clear division between what is foreign and what is domestic." There never was.

The contemporary Supreme Court continues to look more sympathetically on delegation that involves external affairs. Even Chief Justice Rehnquist, the strongest advocate of the nondelegation doctrine on the present Court, adopts a different standard for international crises, "the nature of which Congress can hardly have been expected to anticipate in any detail." Dames & Moore v. Regan, 453 U.S. 654, 669 (1981). He agrees that Congress "is permitted to legislate both with greater breadth and with greater flexibility" when a statute governs military affairs. Rostker v. Goldberg, 453 U.S. 57, 66 (1981), quoting Parker v. Levy, 417 U.S. 733, 756 (1974). More importantly, *Curtiss-Wright* is used to support the existence of independent, implied, and inherent powers for the President.[1]

Officials of the Reagan administration took a number of actions known collectively as the Iran-Contra affair: sending arms to Iran, diverting funds to the Contras in Nicaragua, and soliciting funds from private donors and foreign countries because Congress refused to appropriate funds for the Contras. Some defenders of these executive actions pointed to *Curtiss-Wright* as legal justification. A report, prepared jointly by the House and the Senate, rejects this reliance on *Curtiss-Wright* (see reading "Congress Interprets *Curtiss-Wright:* The Iran-Contra Report").

Right to Travel

Claiming both constitutional and statutory authority, Presidents and their administrations use the control over passports and visas to restrict travel by foreigners to this country and by Americans to other countries. Administrations advance a number of foreign policy and national security justifications, while opponents of restraints on foreign travel raise First Amendment issues of access to information and right of association. There is broad agreement among both groups that the government is justified in banning travel to regions affected by pestilence or war.

The interesting fact about these cases is that the Court generally decides them on statutory grounds. This keeps the door fully open for participation by Congress and the President in shaping the law on the right to travel. In 1958 the Supreme Court reviewed the State Department's action in withholding passports from several Americans because of their association with the Communist party. Although the Court referred to the right to travel as part of a citizen's constitutional "liberty" that could not be denied without due process of law, it avoided the constitutional issue and held that the Secretary of State had exceeded the authority delegated to him by Congress. Kent v. Dulles, 357 U.S. 116 (1958); Dayton v. Dulles, 357 U.S. 144 (1958). Legislation was introduced to strengthen the authority of the Secretary of State, but none of the bills passed Congress.

In 1964 the Court struck down a congressional provision that prevented individuals from applying for a passport if they belonged to a "Communist-action" or "Communist-front" organization. If they already held a passport, it would be revoked. The Court decided that the provision was too broad and indiscriminate in restricting the right to travel. Aptheker v. United States, 378 U.S. 500 (1964). A year later, however, the Court upheld the authority of the State Department to impose *area* restrictions (in this case, involving Cuba). The Court argued that it was permissible to deny all citizens the right to travel to a certain country, in contrast to the 1958 case which involved an individual's belief or association. Zemel v. Rusk, 381 U.S. 1 (1965).

Subsequent cases circumscribed the State Department's authority to impose area restrictions.[2] Moreover, in 1978 Congress passed legislation to limit area restrictions. In the spirit of the Helsinki Accords of 1975, which encouraged the free movement of people and ideas, Congress adopted the following amendment to the Passport Act: "Unless authorized by law, a passport may not be designated as restricted for travel to or for use in any country other than a country with which the United States is at war, where armed hostilities are in progress, or where there is imminent danger to the public health or the physical safety of United States travellers." 92 Stat. 971, § 124 (1978); 22 U.S.C. § 211a (1994).

---

1. United States v. Pink, 315 U.S. 203, 229 (1942); Knauff v. Shaughnessy, 338 U.S. 537, 542 (1950); United States v. Mazurie, 419 U.S. 544, 566–67 (1975).

2. On area restrictions, see also United States v. Laub, 385 U.S. 475 (1967); Travis v. United States, 385 U.S. 491 (1967); Lynd v. Rusk, 389 F.2d 940 (D.C. Cir. 1967). Congress can limit welfare payments to recipients who travel abroad for thirty days or more; Califano v. Aznavorian, 439 U.S. 170 (1978).

Recent cases have given broad support to executive restrictions on foreign travel. In 1981 the Court upheld the authority of the Secretary of State to revoke the passport of Philip Agee, a former CIA employee who had announced his intention to identify undercover CIA agents and intelligence sources in foreign countries. The Court said that the revocation inhibited Agee's action, not his speech. The Secretary's decision was based on a departmental regulation, a broad interpretation of the 1978 amendments, and the "silence" of Congress in acquiescing to the Department's action. Specific authorization from Congress, said the Court, was not required. HAIG v. AGEE, 453 U.S. 280 (1981). The broadness of this ruling suggests that an administration may prevent the foreign travel of anyone who is apt to question or embarrass the President's foreign policy.

In 1984 the Court upheld (5 to 4) a Treasury Department regulation that prohibited general tourist and business travel to Cuba. The Reagan administration decided to retaliate against Cuba for its political and military interventions in Latin America and in Africa. Congress had passed the International Emergency Economic Powers Act in 1977 to limit the President's power, but the Court read the Act broadly to permit the sanctions against Cuba. Regan v. Wald, 468 U.S. 222 (1984).

In recent years Congress has revisited the McCarran-Walter Act of 1952, which kept aliens out of the country because of their political and economic beliefs. 66 Stat. 184–86 (1952). Under that authority, a number of noted writers and political figures have been denied entrance into the United States to speak. In 1990 Congress revised McCarran-Walter to make it more difficult to exclude aliens for their beliefs, statements, and associations. 104 Stat. 5071 (1990).

United States v. Curtiss-Wright Corp.

299 U.S. 304 (1936)

In 1935, in the *Panama Refining* and *Schechter* cases, the Supreme Court struck down the National Industrial Recovery Act and its delegation of legislative power to the President. The *Curtiss-Wright* case involves the delegation of legislative power to the President in foreign rather than domestic affairs. In 1934 Congress authorized the President to place an embargo on the sale of arms and munitions to countries engaged in armed conflict in South America if the President determined that an embargo would contribute to the establishment of peace. Justice Sutherland, writing for the Court, upholds the statute partly on the distinction he drew between external and internal affairs.

MR. JUSTICE SUTHERLAND delivered the opinion of the Court.

On January 27, 1936, an indictment was returned in the court below, the first count of which charges that appellees, beginning with the 29th day of May, 1934, conspired to sell in the United States certain arms of war, namely fifteen machine guns, to Bolivia, a country then engaged in armed conflict in the Chaco, in violation of the Joint Resolution of Congress approved May 28, 1934, and the provisions of a proclamation issued on the same day by the President of the United States pursuant to authority conferred by § 1 of the resolution....

. . .

First. It is contended that by the Joint Resolution, the going into effect and continued operation of the resolution was conditioned (a) upon the President's judgment as to its beneficial effect upon the reestablishment of peace between the countries engaged in armed conflict in the Chaco; (b) upon the making of a proclamation, which was left to his unfettered discretion, thus constituting an attempted substitution of the President's will for that of Congress; (c) upon the making of a proclamation putting an end to the operation of the resolution, which again was left to the President's unfettered discretion; and (d) further, that the extent of its operation in particular cases was subject to limitation and exception by the President, controlled by no standard. In each of these particulars, appellees urge that Congress abdicated its essential functions and delegated them to the Executive.

Whether, if the Joint Resolution had related solely to internal affairs it would be open to the challenge that it constituted an unlawful delegation of legislative power to the Executive, we find it unnecessary to determine. The whole aim of the resolution is to affect a situation entirely external to the United States, and falling within the category of foreign affairs. The determination which we are called to make, therefore, is whether the Joint Resolution, as applied to that situation, is vulnerable to attack under the rule that forbids a delegation of the law-making power. In other words, assuming (but not deciding) that the challenged delegation, if it were confined to internal affairs, would be invalid, may it nevertheless be sustained on the ground that its exclusive aim is to afford a remedy for a hurtful condition within foreign territory?

It will contribute to the elucidation of the question if we first consider the differences between the powers of the federal government in respect of foreign or external affairs and those in respect of domestic or internal affairs. That there are differences between them, and that these differences are fundamental, may not be doubted.

The two classes of powers are different, both in respect of their origin and their nature. The broad statement that the federal government can exercise no powers except those specifically enumerated in the Constitution, and such implied powers as are necessary and proper to carry into effect the enumerated powers, is categorically true only in respect of our internal affairs. In that field, the primary purpose of the Constitution was to carve from the general mass of legislative powers *then possessed by the states* such portions as it was thought desirable to vest in the federal government, leaving those not included in the enumeration still in the states. *Carter* v. *Carter Coal Co.,* 298 U.S. 238, 294. That this doctrine applies only to powers which the states had, is self evident. And since the states severally never possessed international powers, such powers could not have been carved from the mass of state powers but obviously were transmitted to the United States from some other source. During the colonial period, those powers were possessed exclusively by and were entirely under the control of the Crown. By the Declaration of Independence, "the Representatives of the United States of America" declared the United [not the several] Colonies to be free and independent states, and as such to have "full Power to levy War, conclude Peace, contract Alliances, establish Commerce

and to do all other Acts and Things which Independent States may of right do."

As a result of the separation from Great Britain by the colonies acting as a unit, the powers of external sovereignty passed from the Crown not to the colonies severally, but to the colonies in their collective and corporate capacity as the United States of America. Even before the Declaration, the colonies were a unit in foreign affairs, acting through a common agency — namely the Continental Congress, composed of delegates from the thirteen colonies. That agency exercised the powers of war and peace, raised an army, created a navy, and finally adopted the Declaration of Independence. Rulers come and go; governments end and forms of government change; but sovereignty survives. A political society cannot endure without a supreme will somewhere. Sovereignty is never held in suspense. When, therefore, the external sovereignty of Great Britain in respect of the colonies ceased, it immediately passed to the Union. *See Penhallow* v. *Doane,* 3 Dall. 54, 80–81. That fact was given practical application almost at once. The treaty of peace, made on September 23, 1783, was concluded between his Brittanic Majesty and the "United States of America." 8 Stat. — European Treaties — 80.

The Union existed before the Constitution, which was ordained and established among other things to form "a more perfect Union." Prior to that event, it is clear that the Union, declared by the Articles of Confederation to be "perpetual," was the sole possessor of external sovereignty and in the Union it remained without change save in so far as the Constitution in express terms qualified its exercise....

Not only, as we have shown, is the federal power over external affairs in origin and essential character different from that over internal affairs, but participation in the exercise of the power is significantly limited. In this vast external realm, with its important, complicated, delicate and manifold problems, the President alone has the power to speak or listen as a representative of the nation. He *makes* treaties with the advice and consent of the Senate; but he alone negotiates. Into the field of negotiation the Senate cannot intrude; and Congress itself is powerless to invade it. As Marshall said in his great argument of March 7, 1800, in the House of Representatives, "The President is the sole organ of the nation in its external relations, and its sole representative with foreign nations." Annals, 6th Cong., col. 613. The Senate Committee on Foreign Relations at a very early day in our history (February 15, 1816), reported to the Senate, among other things, as follows:

"The President is the constitutional representative of the United States with regard to foreign nations. He manages our concerns with foreign nations and must necessarily be most competent to determine when, how, and upon what subjects negotiation may be urged with the greatest prospect of success. For his conduct he is responsible to the Constitution. The committee consider this responsibility the surest pledge for the faithful discharge of his duty. They think the interference of the Senate in the direction of foreign negotiations calculated to diminish that responsibility and thereby to impair the best security for the national safety. The nature of transactions with foreign nations, moreover, requires caution and unity of design, and their success frequently depends on secrecy and dispatch." U. S. Senate, Reports, Committee on Foreign Relations, vol. 8, p. 24.

It is important to bear in mind that we are here dealing not alone with an authority vested in the President by an exertion of legislative power, but with such an authority plus the very delicate, plenary and exclusive power of the President as the sole organ of the federal government in the field of international relations — a power which does not require as a basis for its exercise an act of Congress, but which, of course, like every other governmental power, must be exercised in subordination to the applicable provisions of the Constitution. It is quite apparent that if, in the maintenance of our international relations, embarrassment — perhaps serious embarrassment — is to be avoided and success for our aims achieved, congressional legislation which is to be made effective through negotiation and inquiry within the international field must often accord to the President a degree of discretion and freedom from statutory restriction which would not be admissible were domestic affairs alone involved. Moreover, he, not Congress, has the better opportunity of knowing the conditions which prevail in foreign countries, and especially is this true in time of war. He has his confidential sources of information. He has his agents in the form of diplomatic, consular and other officials. Secrecy in respect of information gathered by them may be highly necessary, and the premature disclosure of it productive of harmful results. Indeed, so clearly is this true that the first President refused

to accede to a request to lay before the House of Representatives the instructions, correspondence and documents relating to the negotiation of the Jay Treaty — a refusal the wisdom of which was recognized by the House itself and has never since been doubted. In his reply to the request, President Washington said:

"The nature of foreign negotiations requires caution, and their success must often depend on secrecy; and even when brought to a conclusion a full disclosure of all the measures, demands, or eventual concessions which may have been proposed or contemplated would be extremely impolitic; for this might have a pernicious influence on future negotiations, or produce immediate inconveniences, perhaps danger and mischief, in relation to other powers. The necessity of such caution and secrecy was one cogent reason for vesting the power of making treaties in the President, with the advice and consent of the Senate, the principle on which that body was formed confining it to a small number of members. To admit, then, a right in the House of Representatives to demand and to have as a matter of course all the papers respecting a negotiation with a foreign power would be to establish a dangerous precedent." 1 Messages and Papers of the Presidents, p. 194.

[Sutherland neglected to point out that Washington had already submitted the documents to the Senate. It could also have been noted that when treaties require implementing legislation and appropriations, as most do, Presidents have submitted treaty documents to both Houses of Congress.]

. . .

We deem it unnecessary to consider, *seriatim,* the several clauses which are said to evidence the unconstitutionality of the Joint Resolution as involving an unlawful delegation of legislative power. It is enough to summarize by saying that, both upon principle and in accordance with precedent, we conclude there is sufficient warrant for the broad discretion vested in the President to determine whether the enforcement of the statute will have a beneficial effect upon the reëstablishment of peace in the affected countries; whether he shall make proclamation to bring the resolution into operation; whether and when the resolution shall cease to operate and to make proclamation accordingly; and to prescribe limitations and exceptions to which the enforcement of the resolution shall be subject.

. . .

The judgment of the court below must be reversed and the cause remanded for further proceedings in accordance with the foregoing opinion.

Reversed.

MR. JUSTICE MCREYNOLDS does not agree. He is of opinion that the court below reached the right conclusion and its judgment ought to be affirmed.

MR. JUSTICE STONE took no part in the consideration or decision of this case.

Congress Interprets *Curtiss-Wright*: The Iran-Contra Report

Several witnesses before the Iran-Contra Committees in 1987 testified that the actions by the Reagan administration could be justified in terms of *United States* v. *Curtiss-Wright Corp.* (1936), which they claimed recognized broad powers for the President in foreign affairs. The majority report rejected this position. The passage below appeared in *Iran-Contra Affair*, H. Rept. No. 100–433, S. Rept. No. 100–216, 100th Cong., 1st Sess., 388–90 (November 1987).

In urging a broad interpretation of presidential power, various witnesses before these Committees invoked the Supreme Court's 1936 decision in *United States* v. *Curtiss-Wright Export Corporation*. Their reliance on this case is misplaced.

In *Curtiss-Wright,* Congress, by statute, had delegated to the President the power to prohibit the sale of arms to countries in an area of South America if the President believed the prohibition would promote peace. The Curtiss-Wright Corporation claimed that the power to make this determination was a legislative power that Congress could not delegate to the President.

Witnesses at the hearings misread this case to justify their claim that the President had broad inherent foreign policy powers to the virtual exclusion of Congress. *Curtiss-Wright* did not present any such issue. The case involved the question of the powers of the President in foreign policy where Congress expressly authorizes him to act; it did not involve the question of the President's foreign policy powers when Congress expressly forbids him to act.

In *Curtiss-Wright,* the Court upheld broad delegations by Congress of power to the President in matters of foreign affairs. Writing for the Court, Justice Sutherland said that legislation within "the international field must often accord to the President a degree of discretion and freedom from statutory restriction which would not be admissible were domestic affairs alone involved."

In language frequently seized on by those seeking to claim that the President's role in foreign policy is exclusive, Justice Sutherland noted that the President was acting not only with a delegation of power by the legislature, but also with certain powers the Constitution gave directly to him:

"It is important to bear in mind that we are here dealing not alone with an authority vested in the President by an exertion of legislative power, but with such an authority plus the very delicate, plenary and exclusive power of the President as the sole organ of the federal government in the field of international relations—a power which does not require as a basis for its exercise an act of Congress, but which, of course, like every other governmental power, must be exercised in subordination to applicable provisions of the Constitution."

Some have tried to interpret this passage as stating that the President may act in foreign affairs against the will of Congress. But that is not what it says. As Justice Jackson later observed, the most that can be drawn from Justice Sutherland's language is the intimation "that the President might act in external affairs without congressional authority, but not that he might act contrary to an Act of Congress." More recently, in *Dames & Moore* v. *Regan,* the Supreme Court cautioned that the broad language in *Curtiss-Wright* must be viewed only in context of that case. Writing for the majority, Justice (now Chief Justice) Rehnquist expressed the Court's view of the appropriate relationship between the executive and the legislative branches in the conduct of foreign policy:

"When the President acts pursuant to an express or implied authorization from Congress, he exercises not only his powers but also those delegated by Congress. In such a case the executive action 'would be supported by the strongest presumptions and widest latitude of judicial interpretation, and the burden of persuasion would rest heavily upon any who might attack it.'... When the President acts in the absence of congressional authorization he may enter a 'zone of twilight in which he and Congress may have concurrent authority, or in which its distribution is uncertain.'... In such a case, the analysis becomes more complicated, and the validity of the President's action, at least so far as separation-of-powers principles are concerned, hinges on a consideration of all the circumstances which might shed light on the views of the Legislative Branch toward such action, including 'congressional inertia, indifference or quiescence.'... Finally, when the President acts in contravention of the will of Congress, 'his power is at its lowest ebb' and the Court can sustain his actions 'only by disabling the Congress from action on the subject.'"

Similarly, in 1981, the D.C. Circuit cautioned against undue reliance on the quoted passage from *Curtiss-Wright:* "To the extent that denominating the President as the 'sole organ' of the United States in international affairs constitutes a blanket endorsement of plenary Presidential power over any matter extending beyond the borders of this country, we reject that characterization."

In calling the President the "sole organ" of the Nation in its relations with other countries, Justice Sutherland quoted from a speech by John Marshall in 1800 when Marshall was a Member of the House of Representatives: "As Marshall said in his great argument of March 7, 1800, in the House of Representatives, 'The President is the sole organ of the nation in its external relations, and its sole representative with foreign nations.' Annals, 6th Cong., col. 613."

The reader might assume from this passage that Marshall advocated an exclusive, independent power for the President in the area of foreign affairs, free from legislative control. When his statement is placed in the context of the "great argument of March 7, 1800," however, it is clear that Marshall regarded the President as simply carrying out the law as established by statute or treaty. The House had been debating a decision by President John Adams to turn over to England a person charged with murder. Some members thought the President should be impeached for encroaching upon the judiciary, since the case was already pending in court. Marshall replied that President Adams was executing a treaty approved by the Senate that had the force of law.

Haig v. Agee

453 U.S. 280 (1981)

In this case, the "right to travel" collides with the President's interests over foreign policy and national security. Philip Agee, a former employee of the Central Intelligence Agency, had announced a campaign to expose CIA officers and agents. His activities abroad resulted in the identification of CIA agents and intelligence sources in foreign countries. After Secretary of State Alexander Haig revoked his passport, Agee filed suit claiming that the regulation cited by Haig had not been authorized by Congress and was impermissibly overbroad. Agee also argued that the passport revocation violated his freedom to travel and his First Amendment right to criticize governmental policies. Moreover, he charged that the failure to accord him a hearing before the revocation constituted a violation of procedural due process under the Fifth Amendment. The district court and the D.C. Circuit agreed that the regulation exceeded Haig's authority.

CHIEF JUSTICE BURGER delivered the opinion of the Court.

The question presented is whether the President, acting through the Secretary of State, has authority to revoke a passport on the ground that the holder's activities in foreign countries are causing or are likely to cause serious damage to the national security or foreign policy of the United States.

I

A

Philip Agee, an American citizen, currently resides in West Germany. From 1957 to 1968, he was employed by the Central Intelligence Agency. He held key positions in the division of the Agency that is responsible for covert intelligence gathering in foreign countries. In the course of his duties at the Agency. Agee received training in clandestine operations, including the methods used to protect the identities of intelligence employees and sources of the United States overseas. He served in undercover assignments abroad and came to know many Government employees and other persons supplying information to the United States. The relationships of many of these people to our Government are highly confidential; many are still engaged in intelligence gathering.

In 1974, Agee called a press conference in London to announce his "campaign to fight the United States CIA wherever it is operating." He declared his intent "to expose CIA officers and agents and to take the measures necessary to drive them out of the countries where they are operating." Since 1974, Agee has, by his own assertion, devoted consistent effort to that program, and he has traveled extensively in other countries in order to carry it out. To identify CIA personnel in a particular country, Agee goes to the target country and consults sources in local diplomatic circles whom he knows from his prior service in the United States Government. He recruits collaborators and trains them in clandestine techniques designed to expose the "cover" of CIA employees and sources. Agee and his collaborators have repeatedly and publicly identified individuals and organizations located in foreign countries as undercover CIA agents, employees, or sources. The record reveals that the identifications divulge classified information, violate Agee's express contract not to make any public statements about Agency matters without prior clearance by the Agency, have prejudiced the ability of the United States to obtain intelligence, and have been followed by episodes of violence against the persons and organizations identified.

In December 1979, the Secretary of State revoked Agee's passport and delivered an explanatory notice to Agee in West Germany. The notice states in part:

"The Department's action is predicated upon a determination made by the Secretary under the provisions of [22 CFR] Section 51.70 (b)(4) that your activities abroad are causing or are likely to cause serious damage to the national security or the foreign policy of the United States...."

The notice also advised Agee of his right to an ad-ministrative hearing and offered to hold such a hearing in West Germany on 5 days' notice.

Agee at once filed suit against the Secretary. He alleged that the regulation invoked by the Secretary, 22 CFR § 51.70 (b)(4) (1980), has not been authorized by Congress and is invalid; that the regulation is impermissibly overbroad; that the revocation prior to a hearing violated his Fifth Amendment right to procedural due process; and that the revocation violated a Fifth Amendment liberty interest in a right to travel and a First Amendment right to criticize Government policies. He sought declaratory and injunctive relief, and he moved for summary judgment on the question of the authority to promulgate the regulation and on the constitutional claims.

[The district court held that the regulation exceeded the statutory powers of the Secretary under the Passport Act and ordered the Secretary to restore Agee's passport. The D.C. Circuit held that the Secretary was required to show that Congress had authorized the regulation either by an express delegation or by an implied approval. The Court found that the regulation exceeded authority granted by Congress.]

II

The principal question before us is whether the statute authorizes the action of the Secretary pursuant to the policy announced by the challenged regulation.

A

1

Although the historical background that we develop later is important, we begin with the language of the statute.... The Passport Act of 1926 provides in pertinent part:

"The Secretary of State may grant and issue passports, and cause passports to be granted, issued, and verified in foreign countries by diplomatic representatives of the United States... under such rules as the President shall designate and prescribe for and on behalf of the United States, and no other person shall grant, issue, or verify such passports." 22 U. S. C. § 211a (1976 ed., Supp. IV).

This language is unchanged since its original enactment in 1926.

The Passport Act does not in so many words confer upon the Secretary a power to revoke a passport. Nor, for that matter, does it expressly authorize denials of passport applications. Neither, however, does any statute expressly limit those powers. It is beyond dispute that the Secretary has the power to deny a passport for reasons not specified in the statutes. For example, in *Kent* v. *Dulles,* 357 U. S. 116 (1958), the Court recognized congressional acquiescence in Executive policies of refusing passports to applicants "participating in illegal conduct, trying to escape the toils of the law, promoting passport frauds, or otherwise engaging in conduct which would violate the laws of the United States." *Id.,* at 127. In *Zemel,* the Court held that "the weightiest considerations of national security" authorized the Secretary to restrict travel to Cuba at the time of the Cuban missile crisis. 381 U. S., at 16. Agee concedes that if the Secretary may deny a passport application for a certain reason, he may revoke a passport on the same ground.

2

Particularly in light of the "broad rule-making authority granted in the [1926] Act," *Zemel,* 381 U.S., at 12, a consistent administrative construction of that statute must be followed by the courts " "unless there are compelling indications that it is wrong." " *E. I. du Pont de Nemours & Co.* v. *Collins,* 432 U. S. 46, 55 (1977), quoting *Red Lion Broadcasting Co.* v. *FCC,* 395 U. S. 367, 381 (1969); see *Zemel, supra,* at 11. This is especially so in the areas of foreign policy and national security, where congressional silence is not to be equated with congressional disapproval. In *United States* v. *Curtiss-Wright Export Corp.,* 299 U. S. 304 (1936), the volatile nature of problems confronting the Executive in foreign policy and national defense was underscored:

"In this vast external realm, with its important, complicated, delicate and manifold problems, the President alone has the power to speak or listen as a representative of the nation.... As Marshall said in his great argument of March 7, 1800, in the House of Representatives, "The President is the sole organ of the nation in its external relations, and its sole representative with foreign nations."" *Id.,* at 319.

Applying these considerations to statutory construction, the *Zemel* Court observed:

"[B]ecause of the changeable and explosive nature of contemporary international relations, and the fact that the Executive is immediately privy to information which cannot be swiftly presented to, evaluated by, and acted upon by the legislature,

Congress—in giving the Executive authority over matters of foreign affairs—must of necessity paint with a brush broader than that it customarily wields in domestic areas." 381 U. S., at 17 (emphasis supplied).

Matters intimately related to foreign policy and national security are rarely proper subjects for judicial intervention. In *Harisiades* v. *Shaughnessy,* 342 U. S. 580 (1952), the Court observed that matters relating "to the conduct of foreign relations...are so exclusively entrusted to the political branches of government as to be largely immune from judicial inquiry or interference." *Id.,* at 589; accord, *Chicago & Southern Air Lines, Inc.* v. *Waterman S.S. Corp.,* 333 U. S. 103, 111 (1948).

B

1

A passport is, in a sense, a letter of introduction in which the issuing sovereign vouches for the bearer and requests other sovereigns to aid the bearer....

...As a travel control document, a passport is both proof of identity and proof of allegiance to the United States. Even under a travel control statute, however, a passport remains in a sense a document by which the Government vouches for the bearer and for his conduct.

The history of passport controls since the earliest days of the Republic shows congressional recognition of Executive authority to withhold passports on the basis of substantial reasons of national security and foreign policy....

. . .

[Here follows a series of actions by the President and the Secretary of State asserting their authority to deny passports for reasons of national security. The Court concludes that Congress, in the Passport Act of 1926, adopted these administrative constructions. In addition to this "congressional acquiescence," the Court argues that a statute enacted in 1978 is "weighty evidence" that Congress approved of executive interpretations.]

III

Agee also attacks the Secretary's action on three constitutional grounds: first, that the revocation of his passport impermissibly burdens his freedom to travel; second, that the action was intended to penalize his exercise of free speech and deter his criticism of Government policies and practices; and third, that failure to accord him a prerevocation hearing violated his Fifth Amendment right to procedural due process.

In light of the express language of the passport regulations, which permits their application only in cases involving likelihood of "serious damage" to national security or foreign policy, these claims are without merit.

Revocation of a passport undeniably curtails travel, but the freedom to travel abroad with a "letter of introduction" in the form of a passport issued by the sovereign is subordinate to national security and foreign policy considerations; as such, it is subject to reasonable governmental regulation....

. . .

We reverse the judgment of the Court of Appeals and remand for further proceedings consistent with this opinion.

Reversed and remanded.

JUSTICE BLACKMUN, concurring.

There is some force, I feel, in Justice Brennan's observations ... that today's decision cannot be reconciled fully with all the reasoning of *Zemel* v. *Rusk*, 381 U. S. 1 (1965), and, particularly, of *Kent* v. *Dulles*, 357 U. S. 116 (1958), and that the Court is cutting back somewhat upon the opinions in those cases *sub silentio*. I would have preferred to have the Court disavow forthrightly the aspects of *Zemel* and *Kent* that may suggest that evidence of a long-standing Executive policy or construction in this area is not probative of the issue of congressional authorization. Nonetheless, believing this is what the Court in effect has done, I join its opinion.

JUSTICE BRENNAN, with whom JUSTICE MARSHALL joins, dissenting.

Today the Court purports to rely on prior decisions of this Court to support the revocation of a passport by the Secretary of State. Because I believe that such reliance is fundamentally misplaced, and that the Court instead has departed from the express holdings of those decisions, I dissent.

. . .

II

This is not a complicated case. The Court has twice articulated the proper mode of analysis for determining whether Congress has delegated to the Executive Branch the authority to deny a passport under the Passport Act of 1926. *Zemel* v. *Rusk*, 381 U. S. 1 (1965); *Kent* v. *Dulles*, 357 U.S. 116 (1958). The analysis is hardly confusing, and I expect that had the Court faithfully applied it, today's judgment would affirm the decision below.

. . .

... [C]learly neither *Zemel* nor *Kent* holds that a longstanding Executive *policy* or *construction* is sufficient proof that Congress has implicitly authorized the Secretary's action. The cases hold that an administrative *practice* must be demonstrated; in fact *Kent* unequivocally states that mere *construction* by the Executive—no matter how longstanding and consistent—is *not* sufficient....

... Only when Congress had maintained its silence in the face of a consistent and substantial pattern of actual passport denials or revocations—where the parties will presumably object loudly, perhaps through legal action, to the Secretary's exercise of discretion—can this Court be sure that Congress is aware of the Secretary's actions and has implicitly approved that exercise of discretion. Moreover, broad statements by the Executive Branch relating to its discretion in the passport area lack the precision of definition that would follow from concrete applications of that discretion in specific cases. Although Congress might register general approval of the Executive's overall policy, it still might disapprove of the Executive's pattern of applying that broad rule in specific categories of cases.

. . .

B. EXECUTIVE PREROGATIVE

Theodore Roosevelt and William Howard Taft supposedly championed opposite theories of presidential power. Roosevelt asserted that it was the President's right and duty to do "anything that the needs of the Nation demanded, unless such action was forbidden by the Constitution or by the laws." 20 Works of Theodore Roosevelt 347 (1926). Through this theory the President could enter and occupy any vacuum. In contrast, Taft maintained that the President "can exercise no power which cannot be fairly and reasonably traced to some specific grant of power or justly implied and included within such express grant as proper and necessary to its exercise. Such specific grant must be either in the Federal Constitution or in an act of Congress passed in pursuance thereof." William Howard Taft, Our Chief Magistrate and His Powers 139–40 (1916).

This passage appears to make Taft an advocate of enumerated powers, but he did not believe that every use of presidential power required a specific constitutional or statutory grant. He recognized the need for implied powers: powers that can be "fairly and reasonably traced" or "justly implied." He even adds a "necessary and proper" clause for the President. His book on the presidency promotes a broad view of executive power: incidental powers to remove officers, inferable powers to protect the lives and property of American citizens living abroad, powers created by custom, and emergency powers (such as Lincoln's suspension of the writ of habeas corpus during the Civil War). Taft concluded that executive power was limited "so far as it is possible to limit such a power consistent with that discretion and promptness of action that are essential to preserve the interests of the public in times of emergency, or legislative neglect or inaction."

Lincoln's Initiatives

Taft's formulation follows what is known as the Lockean prerogative: the executive's power to act for the public good in the absence of law and sometimes even against it. Lincoln claimed this authority in April 1861 while Congress was in recess. He issued proclamations calling forth state militias, suspended the writ of habeas corpus, and placed a blockade on the rebellious states. He told Congress that his actions, "whether strictly legal or not," were necessary for the public good. 7 Richardson, Messages and Papers of the Presidents 3225. Congress subsequently passed a statute legalizing his proclamations "as if they had been issued and done under the previous express authority and direction of the Congress of the United States." 12 Stat. 326 (1861). Legislative sanction is an essential ingredient of the prerogative. In times of emergency, the executive may act outside the law but must submit his case to the legislature and the people for approval (see box opposite).

Lincoln's suspension of the writ of habeas corpus ran directly counter to a decision by Chief Justice Taney, sitting as a circuit judge in Baltimore. Taney concluded that Lincoln had no power to issue the writ and that the prisoner, John Merryman, should be set free. But Taney recognized that he could not prevail in a direct confrontation with the President on this issue during an emergency period. With some resignation, Taney said he exercised "all the power which the constitution and laws confer upon me, but that power has been resisted by a force too strong for me to overcome." Ex parte Merryman, 17 Fed. Case No. 9,487 (1861), at 153. Lincoln had the legal support of his Attorney General. 10 Op. Att'y Gen. 74, 81 (1861).

Lincoln's use of emergency power to justify the blockade on Southern states was upheld by a sharply divided Supreme Court. In a 5 to 4 decision, the Court held that Lincoln could take the actions he did despite the absence of a declaration of war by Congress. The President was bound to meet the emergency "in the shape it presented itself, without waiting for Congress to baptize it with a name; and no name given to it by him or them could change the fact." THE PRIZE CASES, 2 Black (67 U.S.) 635, 669 (1863). Not until the war was over and Lincoln was dead did the Supreme Court breathe some life into the privilege of the writ of habeas corpus. EX PARTE MILLIGAN, 4 Wall. (71 U.S.) 2 (1866). In response to *Milligan*, Congress passed legislation to limit the Court's jurisdiction to hear cases involving martial law and military trials (see the section on withdrawing jurisdiction in the final chapter "Efforts to Curb

Lincoln's Exercise of the Prerogative

...These measures, whether strictly legal or not, were ventured upon under what appeared to be a popular demand and a public necessity; trusting then as now that Congress would readily ratify them. It is believed that nothing has been done beyond the constitutional competency of Congress.

Soon after the first call for militia, it was considered a duty to authorize the commanding general in proper cases, according to his discretion, to suspend the privilege of the writ of *habeas corpus,* or, in other words, to arrest and detain, without resort to the ordinary processes and forms of law, such individuals as he might deem dangerous to the public safety. This authority has purposely been exercised but very sparingly. Nevertheless, the legality and propriety of what has been done under it are questioned, and the attention of the country has been called to the proposition that one who is sworn to "take care that the laws be faithfully executed" should not himself violate them. Of course some consideration was given to the questions of power and propriety before this matter was acted upon. The whole of the laws which were required to be faithfully executed

were being resisted, and failing of execution in nearly one third of the States. Must they be allowed to finally fail of execution, even had it been perfectly clear that by the use of the means necessary to their execution some single law, made in such extreme tenderness of the citizen's liberty, that practically it relieves more of the guilty than of the innocent, should to a very limited extent be violated? To state the question more directly: are all the laws *but one* to go unexecuted, and the Government itself go to pieces, lest that one be violated? Even in such a case, would not the official oath be broken if the government should be overthrown, when it was believed that disregarding the single law would tend to preserve it? [*Here Lincoln explains why it was appropriate for him to suspend the writ of habeas corpus, in a "dangerous emergency," even though the language for suspension appears in Article I.*]

No more extended argument is now offered, as an opinion, at some length, will probably be presented by the Attorney General. Whether there shall be any legislation upon the subject, and if any, what, is submitted entirely to the better judgment of Congress.

SOURCE: Message to Congress, July 4, 1861.

---

the Court"). In the years following the Civil War, the Court was reluctant to challenge the powers of commander in chief. Mississippi v. Johnson, 4 Wall. 475 (1867).

FDR, Truman, and Nixon

A notorious use of emergency power was President Roosevelt's decision during World War II to put a curfew on more than 100,000 Americans of Japanese descent (about two-thirds of whom were natural-born U.S. citizens) and then place them in detention camps. A unanimous Supreme Court sustained the curfew, although Justice Murphy remarked that it "bears a melancholy resemblance to the treatment accorded to the members of the Jewish race in Germany and in other parts of Europe." Hirabayashi v. United States, 320 U.S. 81 (1943). Putting Japanese-Americans in detention camps split the Court, the Justices voting 6–3 to uphold this action. The dissents by Murphy and Jackson, objecting that the exclusion order resulted from racism, were particularly vehement. KOREMATSU v. UNITED STATES, 323 U.S. 214, 243 (1944).[3] Congress passed legislation in 1988 to offer the nation's apology for this tragic episode and to provide cash reparations to survivors and their families. 102 Stat. 903 (1988).

---

3. See also Yasui v. United States, 320 U.S. 115 (1943); Ex parte Endo, 323 U.S. 283 (1944); Eugene V. Rostow, "The Japanese American Cases—A Disaster," 54 Yale L. J. 489 (1945); Nanette Dembitz, "Racial Discrimination and the Military Judgment: The Supreme Court's Korematsu and Endo Decisions," 45 Colum. L. Rev. 175 (1945); Peter Irons, Justice at War: The Story of the Japanese American Internment Cases (1983).

President Truman used the emergency power in 1952 to seize steel mills during the Korean War. The Supreme Court overturned his action, but the 6 to 3 decision revealed almost as many positions as there were Justices. All six Justices in the majority wrote separate opinions, each taking a slightly different view of emergency power. Only Justices Black and Douglas advocated a doctrine of express and enumerated powers. The other seven Justices, in four concurrences and three dissents, recognized that implied and emergency powers might have to be invoked. Jackson developed a theory of constitutional powers that had three scenarios. Presidential authority reaches its highest level when the President acts pursuant to congressional authorization. His power is at its "lowest ebb" when he takes measures incompatible with the will of Congress. In between these two categories lay a "zone of twilight" in which Congress neither grants nor denies authority. In such circumstances, "congressional inertia, indifference or quiescence may sometimes, at least as a practical matter, enable, if not invite, measures of independent presidential responsibility." YOUNGSTOWN CO. v. SAWYER, 343 U.S. 579, 637 (1952). Jackson's opinion underscores the fact that the Constitution is often shaped not by textual interpretations from the courts but by a political dialectic among the branches.

The concept of "national security" often becomes an umbrella term to justify a broad range of emergency actions by the President. The Nixon administration was especially active in invoking the term. It asked the courts to enjoin two newspapers from publishing the Pentagon Papers, a confidential report that the administration had prepared to study the origins and conduct of the Vietnam War. The report had been leaked to the newspapers, raising the question of prior restraint on a free press. The Supreme Court decided against the administration. The word "security," warned Justice Black, "is a broad, vague generality whose contours should not be invoked to abrogate the fundamental law embodied in the First Amendment." NEW YORK TIMES CO. v. UNITED STATES, 403 U.S. 713, 719 (1971). Erwin N. Griswold, who served as Solicitor General at the time of the Pentagon Papers case, and who argued in oral argument that publication of the documents would damage national security, admitted in 1989 that no such damage had occurred (see Griswold reading). Although First Amendment freedoms were protected in the Pentagon Papers case, the Court upheld the right of the Central Intelligence Agency to require its employees to sign secrecy agreements promising not to publish information about the agency without the Director's prior approval. Snepp v. United States, 444 U.S. 507 (1980).

National Security Wiretaps

Beginning in the 1920s, a succession of administrations resorted to wiretapping for the purpose of controlling domestic crime and protecting national security. The Communications Act of 1934 made it a crime to intercept and divulge wire or radio communications, but President Roosevelt in 1940 instructed his Attorney General that wiretapping should continue for "grave matters involving the defense of the nation." Francis Biddle, In Brief Authority 167 (1962). The tension between the statute and Roosevelt's instruction was relieved in part by the practice of intercepting but not divulging communications or using them in court for evidence.

The Omnibus Crime Control Act of 1968 allowed domestic wiretaps if authorized by judicial warrants. The government claimed that warrantless surveillances for "national security" purposes were lawful as a reasonable exercise of presidential power. A section of the 1968 Act stated that nothing in the statute limited the President's constitutional power to protect against the overthrow of the government or against "any other clear and present danger to the structure or existence of the Government." A unanimous decision by the Supreme Court in 1972 held that the section merely disclaimed congressional intent to define presidential powers in matters affecting national security and did not authorize warrantless national security surveillances. Moreover, the Fourth Amendment required prior judicial approval for surveillances of *domestic* organizations. The Court carefully avoided the question of surveillances over foreign powers, whether within or outside the country. United States v. United States District Court, 407 U.S. 297 (1972).

Congress passed legislation in 1978 to restrict presidential actions. A court order is now required to engage in electronic surveillance within the United States for purposes of obtaining foreign intelligence information. A special court, appointed by the Chief Justice, reviews applications submitted by government attorneys. 93 Stat. 1783 (1978).

Congress enacted legislation in the 1970s to limit the President's use of emergency powers. A number of statutes had contained latent or dormant authority for the President, ready to spring to life whenever he issued a proclamation declaring the nation to be in a state of emergency. Legislation in 1977 and 1978 terminated emergency authorities and subjected future emergencies to procedural safeguards and congressional control. 90 Stat. 1255 (1976); 91 Stat. 1625 (1977). Congressional control depended partly on a concurrent resolution of disapproval, but the Supreme Court declared the legislative veto unconstitutional in *INS* v. *Chadha* (1983). It insisted that whenever Congress wants to control the executive branch, it must comply with bicameralism (action by both Houses) and presentment (presenting a bill or joint resolution to the President). Two years later Congress satisfied the Court ruling by changing the control to a joint resolution of disapproval. 99 Stat. 448, § 801 (1985).

The Prize Cases

2 Black (67 U.S.) 635 (1863)

Among other emergency actions in 1861, President Lincoln declared a blockade of ports controlled by persons in armed rebellion against the government. The owners of the captured ships and cargo (prize, or captured property), brought suit in federal court. To justify the blockade and seizure of neutral vessels, a state of war had to exist, but Congress had made no such declaration. Under what constitutional authority did Lincoln act? Does a state of war require a formal declaration? Three Lincoln appointees—Swayne, Miller, and Davis—joined Grier and Wayne to uphold presidential power.

Mr. Justice GRIER. There are certain propositions of law which must necessarily affect the ultimate decision of these cases, and many others, which it will be proper to discuss and decide before we notice the special facts peculiar to each.

They are, 1st. Had the President a right to institute a blockade of ports in possession of persons in armed rebellion against the Government, on the principles of international law, as known and acknowledged among civilized States?

2d. Was the property of persons domiciled or residing within those States a proper subject of capture on the sea as "enemies' property?"

I. Neutrals have a right to challenge the existence of a blockade *de facto,* and also the authority of the party exercising the right to institute it. They have a right to enter the ports of a friendly nation for the purposes of trade and commerce, but are bound to recognize the rights of a belligerent engaged in actual war, to use this mode of coercion, for the purpose of subduing the enemy.

That a blockade *de facto* actually existed, and

was formally declared and notified by the President on the 27th and 30th of April, 1861, is an admitted fact in these cases.

That the President, as the Executive Chief of the Government and Commander-in-chief of the Army and Navy, was the proper person to make such notification, has not been, and cannot be disputed.

The right of prize and capture has its origin in the *"jus belli,"* and is governed and adjudged under the law of nations. To legitimate the capture of a neutral vessel or property on the high seas, a war must exist *de facto,* and the neutral must have a knowledge or notice of the intention of one of the parties belligerent to use this mode of coercion against a port, city, or territory, in possession of the other.

Let us enquire whether, at the time this blockade was instituted, a state of war existed which would justify a resort to these means of subduing the hostile force.

War has been well defined to be, "That state in which a nation prosecutes its right by force."

The parties belligerent in a public war are independent nations. But it is not necessary to constitute war, that both parties should be acknowledged as independent nations or sovereign States. A war may exist where one of the belligerents, claims sovereign rights as against the other.

Insurrection against a government may or may not culminate in an organized rebellion, but a civil war always begins by insurrection against the lawful authority of the Government. A civil war is never solemnly declared; it becomes such by its accidents — the number, power, and organization of the persons who originate and carry it on. When the party in rebellion occupy and hold in a hostile manner a certain portion of territory; have declared their independence; have cast off their allegiance; have organized armies; have commenced hostilities against their former sovereign, the world acknowledges them as belligerents, and the contest a *war....*

As a civil war is never publicly proclaimed, *eo nomine,* against insurgents, its actual existence is a fact in our domestic history which the Court is bound to notice and to know.

The true test of its existence, as found in the writings of the sages of the common law, may be thus summarily stated: "When the regular course of justice is interrupted by revolt, rebellion, or insurrection, so that the Courts of Justice cannot be kept open, *civil war exists* and hostilities may be prosecuted on the same footing as if those opposing the Government were foreign enemies invading the land."

By the Constitution, Congress alone has the power to declare a national or foreign war. It cannot declare war against a State, or any number of States, by virtue of any clause in the Constitution. The Constitution confers on the President the whole Executive power. He is bound to take care that the laws be faithfully executed. He is Commander-in-chief of the Army and Navy of the United States, and of the militia of the several States when called into the actual service of the United States. He has no power to initiate or declare a war either against a foreign nation or a domestic State. But by the Acts of Congress of February 28th, 1795, and 3d of March, 1807, he is authorized to call out the militia and use the military and naval forces of the United States in case of invasion by foreign nations, and to suppress insurrection against the government of a State or of the United States.

If a war be made by invasion of a foreign nation, the President is not only authorized but bound to resist force by force. He does not initiate the war, but is bound to accept the challenge without waiting for any special legislative authority. And whether the hostile party be a foreign invader, or States organized in rebellion, it is none the less a war, although the declaration of it be *"unilateral."* Lord Stowell (1 Dodson, 247) observes, "It is not the less a war on *that account,* for war may exist without a declaration on either side. It is so laid down by the best writers on the law of nations. A declaration of war by one country only, is not a mere challenge to be accepted or refused at pleasure by the other."

The battles of Palo Alto and Resaca de la Palma had been fought before the passage of the Act of Congress of May 13th, 1846, which recognized *"a state of war as existing by the act of the Republic of Mexico."* This act not only provided for the future prosecution of the war, but was itself a vindication and ratification of the Act of the President in accepting the challenge without a previous formal declaration of war by Congress.

This greatest of civil wars was not gradually developed by popular commotion, tumultuous assemblies, or local unorganized insurrections. However long may have been its previous conception, it nevertheless sprung forth suddenly from the parent brain, a Minerva in the full panoply of *war.* The President was bound to meet it in the shape it presented itself, without waiting for Congress to baptize it with a name; and no name given to it by him or them could change the fact.

. . .

Whether the President in fulfilling his duties, as Commander-in-chief, in suppressing an insurrection, has met with such armed hostile resistance, and a civil war of such alarming proportions as will compel him to accord to them the character of belligerents, is a question to be decided *by him,* and this Court must be governed by the decisions and acts of the political department of the Government to which this power was entrusted. "He must determine what degree of force the crisis demands." The proclamation of blockade is itself official and conclusive evidence to the Court that a state of war existed which demanded and authorized a recourse to such a measure, under the circumstances peculiar to the case.

The correspondence of Lord Lyons with the Secretary of State admits the fact and concludes the question.

If it were necessary to the technical existence of a war, that it should have a legislative sanction, we find it in almost every act passed at the extraordinary session of the Legislature of 1861, which was wholly employed in enacting laws to enable the Government to prosecute the war with vigor and efficiency. And finally, in 1861, we find Congress *"ex majore cautela"* and in anticipation of such astute objections, passing an act "approving, legalizing, and making valid all the acts, proclamations, and orders of the President, &c., as if they had been *issued and done under the previous express authority* and direction of the Congress of the United States."

. . .

The objection made to this act of ratification, that it is *expost facto,* and therefore unconstitutional and void, might possibly have some weight on the trial of an indictment in a criminal Court. But precedents from that source cannot be received as authoritative in a tribunal administering public and international law.

On this first question therefore we are of the opinion that the President had a right, *jure belli,* to institute a blockade of ports in possession of the States in rebellion, which neutrals are bound to regard.

. . .

[The Court then decides whether the property of all persons residing within the territory of the states in rebellion, captured on the high seas, is to be treated as "enemies' property" whether the owner be in arms against the government or not.]

Mr. Justice NELSON dissenting.

. . .

We are of opinion . . . that, according to the very terms of the proclamation, neutral ships were entitled to a warning by one of the blockading squadron and could be lawfully seized only on the second attempt to enter or leave the port.

It is remarkable, also, that both the President and the Secretary, in referring to the blockade, treat the measure, not as a blockade under the law of nations, but as a restraint upon commerce at the interdicted ports under the municipal laws of the Government.

. . .

This power *[of announcing war]* in all civilized nations is regulated by the fundamental laws or municipal constitution of the country.

By our Constitution this power is lodged in Congress. Congress shall have power "to declare war, grant letters of marque and reprisal, and make rules concerning captures on land and water."

. . .

. . . But we are asked, what would become of the peace and integrity of the Union in case of an insurrection at home or invasion from abroad if this power could not be exercised by the President in the recess of Congress, and until that body could be assembled?

The framers of the Constitution fully comprehended this question, and provided for the contingency. Indeed, it would have been surprising if they had not, as a rebellion had occurred in the State of Massachusetts while the Convention was in session, and which had become so general that it was quelled only by calling upon the military power of the State. The Constitution declares that Congress shall have power "to provide for calling forth the militia to execute the laws of the Union, suppress insurrections, and repel invasions." Another clause, "that the President shall be Commander-in-chief of the Army and Navy of the United States, and of the militia of the several States when called into the actual service of the United States;" and, again, "He shall take care that the laws shall be faithfully executed." Congress passed laws on this subject in 1792 and 1795. 1 United States Laws, pp. 264, 424.

[In 1807 Congress passed additional legislation authorizing the President to call forth the militia to suppress insurrection.]

. . .

The Acts of 1795 and 1807 did not, and could not under the Constitution, confer on the President the power of declaring war against a State of this Union, or of deciding that war existed, and upon that ground authorize the capture and confiscation of the property of every citizen of the State whenever it was found on the waters. . . . This great power over the business and property of the citizen is reserved to the legislative department by the express words of the Constitution. It cannot be delegated or surrendered to the Executive. . . .

. . .

Upon the whole, after the most careful consideration of this case which the pressure of other duties has admitted, I am compelled to the conclusion that no civil war existed between this Government and the States in insurrection till recognized by the Act of Congress 13th of July, 1861; that the President does not possess the power under the Constitution to declare war or recognize its existence within the meaning of the law of nations, which carries with it belligerent rights, and thus change the country and all its citizens from a state of peace to a state of war; that this power belongs exclusively to the Congress of the United States, and, consequently, that the President had no power to set on foot a blockade under the law of nations, and that the capture of the vessel and cargo in this case, and in all cases before us in which the capture occurred before the 13th of July, 1861, for breach of blockade, or as enemies' property, are illegal and void, and that the decrees of condemnation should be reversed and the vessel and cargo restored.

Mr. Chief Justice TANEY, Mr. Justice CATRON and Mr. Justice CLIFFORD, concurred in the dissenting opinion of Mr. Justice NELSON.

Ex parte Milligan

4 Wall. (71 U.S.) 2 (1866)

Lambdin P. Milligan, a U.S. citizen from Indiana, was arrested by the military in 1864 on charges of conspiracy, found guilty before a military commission, and sentenced to be hanged. He presented a petition of habeas corpus to the federal courts, asking to be discharged from unlawful imprisonment because the military had no jurisdiction over him. He insisted that he was entitled to trial by jury in a civilian court. The question was whether the President, in times of emergency, could suspend the writ of habeas corpus and declare martial law.

Mr. Justice DAVIS delivered the opinion of the court.

On the 10th day of May, 1865, Lambdin P. Milligan presented a petition to the Circuit Court of the United States for the District of Indiana, to be discharged from an alleged unlawful imprisonment....

. . .

The importance of the main question presented by this record cannot be overstated; for it involves the very framework of the government and the fundamental principles of American liberty.

During the late wicked Rebellion, the temper of the times did not allow that calmness in deliberation and discussion so necessary to a correct conclusion of a purely judicial question. *Then,* considerations of safety were mingled with the exercise of power; and feelings and interests prevailed which are happily terminated. *Now* that the public safety is assured, this question, as well as all others, can be discussed and decided without passion or the admixture of any element not required to form a legal judgment. We approach the investigation of this case, fully sensible of the magnitude of the inquiry and the necessity of full and cautious deliberation.

. . .

The controlling question in the case is this:

Upon the *facts* stated in Milligan's petition, and the exhibits filed, had the military commission mentioned in it *jurisdiction,* legally, to try and sentence him? Milligan, not a resident of one of the rebellious states, or a prisoner of war, but a citizen of Indiana for twenty years past, and never in the military or naval service, is, while at his home, arrested by the military power of the United States, imprisoned, and, on certain criminal charges preferred against him, tried, convicted, and sentenced to be hanged by a military commission, organized under the direction of the military commander of the military district of Indiana. Had this tribunal the *legal* power and authority to try and punish this man?

No graver question was ever considered by this court, nor one which more nearly concerns the rights of the whole people; for it is the birthright of every American citizen when charged with crime, to be tried and punished according to law.

[The Court reviews such fundamental constitutional rights as grand jury, trial by jury, confrontation of witnesses against the accused, obtaining witnesses in the accused's favor, and assistance of counsel.]

Time has proven the discernment of our ancestors; for even these provisions, expressed in such plain English words, that it would seem the ingenuity of man could not evade them, are *now,* after the lapse of more than seventy years, sought to be avoided. Those great and good men foresaw that troublous times would arise, when rulers and people would become restive under restraint, and seek by sharp and decisive measures to accomplish ends deemed just and proper; and that the principles of constitutional liberty would be in peril, unless established by irrepealable law. The history of the world had taught them that what was done in the past might be attempted in the future. The Constitution of the United States is a law for rulers and people, equally in war and in peace, and covers with the shield of its protection all classes of men, at all times, and under all circumstances. No doctrine, involving more pernicious consequences, was ever invented by the wit of man than that any of its provisions can be suspended during any of the great exigencies of government. Such a doctrine leads directly to anarchy or despotism, but the theory of necessity on which it is based is false; for the government, within the Constitution, has all the powers granted to it, which are necessary to preserve its existence; as has been happily proved by the result of the great effort to throw off its just authority.

. . .

This court has judicial knowledge that in Indiana the Federal authority was always unopposed, and its courts always open to hear criminal accusations and redress grievances; and no usage of war could sanction a military trial there for any offence whatever of a citizen in civil life, in nowise connected with the military service. Congress could grant no such power; and to the honor of our national legislature be it said, it has never been provoked by the state of the country even to attempt its exercise. One of the plainest constitutional provisions was, therefore, infringed when Milligan was tried by a court not ordained and established by Congress, and not composed of judges appointed during good behavior.

. . .

This nation, as experience has proved, cannot always remain at peace, and has no right to expect that it will always have wise and humane rulers, sincerely attached to the principles of the Constitution. Wicked men, ambitious of power, with hatred of liberty and contempt of law, may fill the place once occupied by Washington and Lincoln; and if this right is conceded, and the calamities of war again befall us, the dangers to human liberty are frightful to contemplate. . . .

It is essential to the safety of every government that, in a great crisis, like the one we have just passed through, there should be a power somewhere of suspending the writ of *habeas corpus*. . . . The Constitution . . . does not say after a writ of *habeas corpus* is denied a citizen, that he shall be tried otherwise than by the course of the common law; if it had intended this result, it was easy by the use of direct words to have accomplished it. . . .

. . . Martial rule can never exist where the courts are open, and in the proper and unobstructed exercise of their jurisdiction. . . .

The CHIEF JUSTICE delivered the following opinion.

Four members of the court, concurring with their brethren in the order heretofore made in this cause, but unable to concur in some important particulars with the opinion which has just been read, think it their duty to make a separate statement of their views of the whole case.

We do not doubt that the Circuit Court for the District of Indiana had jurisdiction of the petition of Milligan for the writ of *habeas corpus*.

. . .

It is clear . . . that the Circuit Court was bound to hear Milligan's petition for the writ of *habeas corpus*, called in the act an order to bring the prisoner before the judge or the court, and to issue the writ, or, in the language of the act, to make the order.

The first question, therefore — Ought the writ to issue? — must be answered in the affirmative.

And it is equally clear that he was entitled to the discharge prayed for.

It must be borne in mind that the prayer of the petition was not for an absolute discharge, but to be delivered from military custody and imprisonment, and if found probably guilty of any offence, to be turned over to the proper tribunal for inquiry and punishment; or, if not found thus probably guilty, to be discharged altogether.

. . .

That the third question, namely: Had the military commission in Indiana, under the facts stated, jurisdiction to try and sentence Milligan? must be answered negatively is an unavoidable inference from affirmative answers to the other two.

. . .

But the opinion which has just been read goes further; and as we understand it, asserts not only that the military commission held in Indiana was not authorized by Congress, but that it was not in the power of Congress to authorize it; from which it may be thought to follow, that Congress has no power to indemnify the officers who composed the commission against liability in civil courts for acting as members of it.

We cannot agree to this.

We agree in the proposition that no department of the government of the United States — neither President, nor Congress, nor the Courts — possesses any power not given by the Constitution.

We assent, fully, to all that is said, in the opinion, of the inestimable value of the trial by jury, and of the other constitutional safeguards of civil liberty. And we concur, also, in what is said of the writ of *habeas corpus,* and of its suspension, with two reservations: (1.) That, in our judgment, when the writ is suspended, the Executive is authorized to arrest as well as to detain; and (2.) that there are cases in which, the privilege of the writ being suspended, trial and punishment by military commission, in states where civil courts are open, may be authorized by Congress, as well as arrest and detention.

We think that Congress had power, though not

exercised, to authorize the military commission which was held in Indiana.

. . .

Congress has the power not only to raise and support and govern armies but to declare war. It has, therefore, the power to provide by law for carrying on war. This power necessarily extends to all legislation essential to the prosecution of war with vigor and success, except such as interferes with the command of the forces and the conduct of campaigns....

We cannot doubt that, in such a time of public danger, Congress had power, under the Constitution, to provide for the organization of a military commission, and for trial by that commission of persons engaged in this conspiracy. The fact that the Federal courts were open was regarded by Congress as a sufficient reason for not exercising the power; but that fact could not deprive Congress of the right to exercise it....

. . .

Mr. Justice WAYNE, Mr. Justice SWAYNE, and Mr. Justice MILLER concur with me in these views.

Korematsu v. United States

323 U.S. 214 (1944)

Under authority of President Roosevelt's Executive Order 9066 and a congressional statute enacted in 1942, the Commanding General of the Western Defense Command issued an order directing the exclusion of all Japanese-Americans from a West Coast military area. Exclusion meant imprisonment in barbed wire stockades, called assembly centers, until the individuals could be transported inland to "relocation centers" under military guard. The military order, covering both aliens and U.S. citizens, was based on the belief of Commanding General J.L. DeWitt that all individuals of Japanese descent were "subversive" and belonged to an "enemy race" whose "racial strains are undiluted." Fred Korematsu, an American citizen of Japanese descent, was convicted for violating the exclusion order. His conviction was affirmed by the Ninth Circuit.

MR. JUSTICE BLACK delivered the opinion of the Court.

The petitioner, an American citizen of Japanese descent, was convicted in a federal district court for remaining in San Leandro, California, a "Military Area," contrary to Civilian Exclusion Order No. 34 of the Commanding General of the Western Command, U. S. Army, which directed that after May 9, 1942, all persons of Japanese ancestry should be excluded from that area. No question was raised as to petitioner's loyalty to the

United States. The Circuit Court of Appeals affirmed, and the importance of the constitutional question involved caused us to grant certiorari.

It should be noted, to begin with, that all legal restrictions which curtail the civil rights of a single racial group are immediately suspect. That is not to say that all such restrictions are unconstitutional. It is to say that courts must subject them to the most rigid scrutiny. Pressing public necessity may sometimes justify the existence of such restrictions; racial antagonism never can.

. . .

Exclusion Order No. 34, which the petitioner knowingly and admittedly violated, was one of a number of military orders and proclamations, all of which were substantially based upon Executive Order No. 9066, 7 Fed. Reg. 1407. That order, issued after we were at war with Japan, declared that "the successful prosecution of the war requires every possible protection against espionage and against sabotage to national-defense material, national-defense premises, and national-defense utilities...."

One of the series of orders and proclamations, a curfew order, which like the exclusion order here was promulgated pursuant to Executive Order 9066, subjected all persons of Japanese ancestry in prescribed West Coast military areas to remain in their residences from 8 P.M. to 6 A.M. As is the case with the exclusion order here, that prior curfew order was designed as a "protection against espionage and against sabotage." In *Hirabayashi* v. *United States,* 320 U.S. 81, we sustained a conviction obtained for violation of the curfew order. The Hirabayashi conviction and this one thus rest on the same 1942 Congressional Act and the same basic executive and military orders, all of which orders were aimed at the twin dangers of espionage and sabotage.

The 1942 Act was attacked in the *Hirabayashi* case as an unconstitutional delegation of power; it was contended that the curfew order and other orders on which it rested were beyond the war powers of the Congress, the military authorities and of the President, as Commander in Chief of the Army; and finally that to apply the curfew order against none but citizens of Japanese ancestry amounted to a constitutionally prohibited discrimination solely on account of race. To these questions, we gave the serious consideration which their importance justified. We upheld the curfew order as an exercise of the power of the government to take steps necessary to prevent espionage and sabotage in an area threatened by Japanese attack.

In the light of the principles we announced in the *Hirabayashi* case, we are unable to conclude that it was beyond the war power of Congress and the Executive to exclude those of Japanese ancestry from the West Coast war area at the time they did. True, exclusion from the area in which one's home is located is a far greater deprivation than constant confinement to the home from 8 P.M. to 6 A.M. Nothing short of apprehension by the proper military authorities of the gravest imminent danger to the public safety can constitutionally justify either. But exclusion from a threatened area, no less than curfew, has a definite and close relationship to the prevention of espionage and sabotage. The military authorities, charged with the primary responsibility of defending our shores, concluded that curfew provided inadequate protection and ordered exclusion. They did so, as pointed out in our *Hirabayashi* opinion, in accordance with Congressional authority to the military to say who should, and who should not, remain in the threatened areas.

. . .

...[W]e are not unmindful of the hardships imposed by it upon a large group of American citizens. Cf. *Ex parte Kawato,* 317 U.S. 69, 73. But hardships are part of war, and war is an aggregation of hardships. All citizens alike, both in and out of uniform, feel the impact of war in greater or lesser measure. Citizenship has its responsibilities as well as its privileges, and in time of war the burden is always heavier. Compulsory exclusion of large groups of citizens from their homes, except under circumstances of direst emergency and peril, is inconsistent with our basic governmental institutions. But when under conditions of modern warfare our shores are threatened by hostile forces, the power to protect must be commensurate with the threatened danger.

. . .

It is said that we are dealing here with the case of imprisonment of a citizen in a concentration camp solely because of his ancestry, without evidence or inquiry concerning his loyalty and good disposition towards the United States. Our task would be simple, our duty clear, were this a case involving the imprisonment of a loyal citizen in a concentration camp because of racial prejudice. Regardless of the true nature of the assembly and relocation centers—and we deem it unjustifiable to call them concentration camps with all the ugly connotations that term implies—we are dealing specifically with nothing but an exclusion order. To cast this case into outlines of racial prejudice, without reference to the real military dangers which were presented, merely confuses the issue. Korematsu was not excluded from the Military Area because of hostility to him or his race. He *was* excluded because we are at war with the Japanese Empire, because the properly constituted military authorities feared an invasion of our West

Coast and felt constrained to take proper security measures, because they decided that the military urgency of the situation demanded that all citizens of Japanese ancestry be segregated from the West Coast temporarily, and finally, because Congress, reposing its confidence in this time of war in our military leaders — as inevitably it must — determined that they should have the power to do just this. There was evidence of disloyalty on the part of some, the military authorities considered that the need for action was great, and time was short. We cannot — by availing ourselves of the calm perspective of hindsight — now say that at that time these actions were unjustified.

Affirmed.

MR. JUSTICE FRANKFURTER, concurring.

. . .

MR. JUSTICE ROBERTS.

I dissent, because I think the indisputable facts exhibit a clear violation of Constitutional rights.

This is not a case of keeping people off the streets at night as was *Hirabayashi* v. *United States,* 320 U.S. 81, nor a case of temporary exclusion of a citizen from an area for his own safety or that of the community, nor a case of offering him an opportunity to go temporarily out of an area where his presence might cause danger to himself or to his fellows. On the contrary, it is the case of convicting a citizen as a punishment for not submitting to imprisonment in a concentration camp, based on his ancestry, and solely because of his ancestry, without evidence or inquiry concerning his loyalty and good disposition towards the United States. If this be a correct statement of the facts disclosed by this record, and facts of which we take judicial notice, I need hardly labor the conclusion that Constitutional rights have been violated.

. . .

MR. JUSTICE MURPHY, dissenting.

This exclusion of "all persons of Japanese ancestry, both alien and non-alien," from the Pacific Coast area on a plea of military necessity in the absence of martial law ought not to be approved. Such exclusion goes over "the very brink of constitutional power" and falls into the ugly abyss of racism.

In dealing with matters relating to the prosecution and progress of a war, we must accord great respect and consideration to the judgments of the military authorities who are on the scene and who have full knowledge of the military facts. The scope of their discretion must, as a matter of necessity and common sense, be wide. And their judgments ought not to be overruled lightly by those whose training and duties ill-equip them to deal intelligently with matters so vital to the physical security of the nation.

At the same time, however, it is essential that there be definite limits to military discretion, especially where martial law has not been declared. Individuals must not be left impoverished of their constitutional rights on a plea of military necessity that has neither substance nor support. Thus, like other claims conflicting with the asserted constitutional rights of the individual, the military claim must subject itself to the judicial process of having its reasonableness determined and its conflicts with other interests reconciled. . . .

The judicial test of whether the Government, on a plea of military necessity, can validly deprive an individual of any of his constitutional rights is whether the deprivation is reasonably related to a public danger that is so "immediate, imminent, and impending" as not to admit of delay and not to permit the intervention of ordinary constitutional processes to alleviate the danger. . . . Yet no reasonable relation to an "immediate, imminent, and impending" public danger is evident to support this racial restriction which is one of the most sweeping and complete deprivations of constitutional rights in the history of this nation in the absence of martial law.

. . .

That this forced exclusion was the result in good measure of this erroneous assumption of racial guilt rather than bona fide military necessity is evidenced by the Commanding General's Final Report on the evacuation from the Pacific Coast area. In it he refers to all individuals of Japanese descent as "subversive," as belonging to "an enemy race" whose "racial strains are undiluted," and as constituting "over 112,000 potential enemies . . . at large today" along the Pacific Coast. In support of this blanket condemnation of all persons of Japanese descent, however, no reliable evidence is cited to show that such individuals were generally disloyal, or had generally so conducted themselves in this area as to constitute a special menace to defense installations or war industries, or had otherwise by their behavior furnished reasonable ground for their exclusion as a group.

. . .

The military necessity which is essential to the validity of the evacuation order thus resolves itself into a few intimations that certain individuals actively aided the enemy, from which it is inferred that the entire group of Japanese Americans could not be trusted to be or remain loyal to the United States. No one denies, of course, that there were some disloyal persons of Japanese descent on the Pacific Coast who did all in their power to aid their ancestral land. Similar disloyal activities have been engaged in by many persons of German, Italian and even more pioneer stock in our country. But to infer that examples of individual disloyalty prove group disloyalty and justify discriminatory action against the entire group is to deny that under our system of law individual guilt is the sole basis for deprivation of rights....

. . .

I dissent, therefore, from this legalization of racism. Racial discrimination in any form and in any degree has no justifiable part whatever in our democratic way of life. It is unattractive in any setting but it is utterly revolting among a free people who have embraced the principles set forth in the Constitution of the United States. All residents of this nation are kin in some way by blood or culture to a foreign land. Yet they are primarily and necessarily a part of the new and distinct civilization of the United States. They must accordingly be treated at all times as the heirs of the American experiment and as entitled to all the rights and freedoms guaranteed by the Constitution.

MR. JUSTICE JACKSON, dissenting.

Korematsu was born on our soil, of parents born in Japan. The Constitution makes him a citizen of the United States by nativity and a citizen of California by residence. No claim is made that he is not loyal to this country. There is no suggestion that apart from the matter involved here he is not law-abiding and well disposed. Korematsu, however, has been convicted of an act not commonly a crime. It consists merely of being present in the state whereof he is a citizen, near the place where he was born, and where all his life he has lived.

. . .

Now, if any fundamental assumption underlies our system, it is that guilt is personal and not inheritable. Even if all of one's antecedents had been convicted of treason, the Constitution forbids its penalties to be visited upon him, for it provides that "no attainder of treason shall work corruption of blood, or forfeiture except during the life of the person attained." But here is an attempt to make an otherwise innocent act a crime merely because this prisoner is the son of parents as to whom he had no choice, and belongs to a race from which there is no way to resign....

. . .

Youngstown Co. v. Sawyer

343 U.S. 579 (1952)

In April 1952, to avert a nationwide strike of steelworkers that threatened U.S. military needs in the Korean War, President Truman issued an executive order directing Secretary of Commerce Sawyer to seize and operate most of the steel mills. The order was not based on specific statutory authority. In fact, Truman decided not to use the statutory remedy available in the Taft-Hartley Act of 1947, which was enacted into law over his veto. In court, the administration justified the executive order on the basis of inherent presidential power (see pages 12–13). The district court issued a preliminary injunction against the seizure, rejecting the theory of inherent power, but the D.C. Circuit stayed this injunction pending review by the Supreme Court.

MR. JUSTICE BLACK delivered the opinion of the Court.

We are asked to decide whether the President was acting within his constitutional power when he issued an order directing the Secretary of Commerce to take possession of and operate most of the Nation's steel mills. The mill owners argue that the President's order amounts to lawmaking, a legislative function which the Constitution has expressly confided to the Congress and not to the President. The Government's position is that the order was made on findings of the President that his action was necessary to avert a national catastrophe which would inevitably result from a stoppage of steel production, and that in meeting this grave emergency the President was acting within the aggregate of his constitutional powers as the Nation's Chief Executive and the Commander in Chief of the Armed Forces of the United States....

. . .

I.

[The Court rejects the administration's argument that the case should be resolved on nonconstitutional grounds. The constitutional question is "ripe for determination on the record presented."]

II.

The President's power, if any, to issue the order must stem either from an act of Congress or from the Constitution itself. There is no statute that expressly authorizes the President to take possession of property as he did here. Nor is there any act of Congress to which our attention has been directed from which such a power can fairly be implied. Indeed, we do not understand the Government to rely on statutory authorization for this seizure....

. . .

Moreover, the use of the seizure technique to solve labor disputes in order to prevent work stoppages was not only unauthorized by any congressional enactment; prior to this controversy, Congress had refused to adopt that method of settling labor disputes. When the Taft-Hartley Act was under consideration in 1947, Congress rejected an amendment which would have authorized such governmental seizures in cases of emergency. Apparently it was thought that the technique of seizure, like that of compulsory arbitration, would interfere with the process of collective bargaining. Consequently, the plan Congress adopted in that Act did not provide for seizure under any circumstances. Instead, the plan sought to bring about settlements by use of the customary devices of mediation, conciliation, investigation by boards of inquiry, and public reports. In some instances temporary injunctions were authorized to provide cooling-off periods. All this failing, unions were left free to strike after a secret vote by employees as to whether they wished to accept their employers' final settlement offer.

It is clear that if the President had authority to issue the order he did, it must be found in some provision of the Constitution. And it is not

claimed that express constitutional language grants this power to the President. The contention is that presidential power should be implied from the aggregate of his powers under the Constitution. Particular reliance is placed on provisions in Article II which say that "The executive Power shall be vested in a President..."; that "he shall take Care that the Laws be faithfully executed"; and that he "shall be Commander in Chief of the Army and Navy of the United States."

The order cannot properly be sustained as an exercise of the President's military power as Commander in Chief of the Armed Forces. The Government attempts to do so by citing a number of cases upholding broad powers in military commanders engaged in day-to-day fighting in a theater of war. Such cases need not concern us here. Even though "theater of war" be an expanding concept, we cannot with faithfulness to our constitutional system hold that the Commander in Chief of the Armed Forces has the ultimate power as such to take possession of private property in order to keep labor disputes from stopping production. This is a job for the Nation's lawmakers, not for its military authorities.

Nor can the seizure order be sustained because of the several constitutional provisions that grant executive power to the President. In the framework of our Constitution, the President's power to see that the laws are faithfully executed refutes the idea that he is to be a lawmaker. The Constitution limits his functions in the lawmaking process to the recommending of laws he thinks wise and the vetoing of laws he thinks bad. And the Constitution is neither silent nor equivocal about who shall make laws which the President is to execute. The first section of the first article says that "All legislative Powers herein granted shall be vested in a Congress of the United States...." After granting many powers to the Congress, Article I goes on to provide that Congress may "make all Laws which shall be necessary and proper for carrying into Execution the foregoing Powers, and all other Powers vested by this Constitution in the Government of the United States, or in any Department or Officer thereof."

The President's order does not direct that a congressional policy be executed in a manner prescribed by Congress—it directs that a presidential policy be executed in a manner prescribed by the President. The preamble of the order itself, like that of many statutes, sets out reasons why the President believes certain policies should be adopted, proclaims these policies as rules of conduct to be followed, and again, like a statute, authorizes a government official to promulgate additional rules and regulations consistent with the policy proclaimed and needed to carry that policy into execution. The power of Congress to adopt such public policies as those proclaimed by the order is beyond question. It can authorize the taking of private property for public use. It can make laws regulating the relationships between employers and employees, prescribing rules designed to settle labor disputes, and fixing wages and working conditions in certain fields of our economy. The Constitution does not subject this lawmaking power of Congress to presidential or military supervision or control.

It is said that other Presidents without congressional authority have taken possession of private business enterprises in order to settle labor disputes. But even if this be true, Congress has not thereby lost its exclusive constitutional authority to make laws necessary and proper to carry out the powers vested by the Constitution "in the Government of the United States, or any Department or Officer thereof."

The Founders of this Nation entrusted the lawmaking power to the Congress alone in both good and bad times. It would do no good to recall the historical events, the fears of power and the hopes for freedom that lay behind their choice. Such a review would but confirm our holding that this seizure order cannot stand.

The judgment of the District Court is

Affirmed.

. . .

MR. JUSTICE FRANKFURTER, concurring.

...Not so long ago it was fashionable to find our system of checks and balances obstructive to effective government. It was easy to ridicule that system as outmoded — too easy. The experience through which the world has passed in our own day has made vivid the realization that the Framers of our Constitution were not inexperienced doctrinaires. These long-headed statesmen had no illusion that our people enjoyed biological or psychological or sociological immunities from the hazards of concentrated power. It is absurd to see a dictator in a representative product of the sturdy democratic traditions of the Mississippi Valley. The accretion of dangerous power does not come in a day. It does come, however slowly, from the generative force of unchecked disregard of the restrictions that fence in even the most disinterested assertion of authority.

. . .

The issue before us can be met, and therefore should be, without attempting to define the President's powers comprehensively....

...Deeply embedded traditional ways of conducting government cannot supplant the Constitution or legislation, but they give meaning to the words of a text or supply them. It is an inadmissibly narrow conception of American constitutional law to confine it to the words of the Constitution and to disregard the gloss which life has written upon them. In short, a systematic, unbroken, executive practice, long pursued to the knowledge of the Congress and never before questioned, engaged in by Presidents who have also sworn to uphold the Constitution, making as it were such exercise of power part of the structure of our government, may be treated as a gloss on "executive Power" vested in the President by § 1 of Art. II.

. . .

MR. JUSTICE DOUGLAS, concurring.

. . .

The method by which industrial peace is achieved is of vital importance not only to the parties but to society as well. A determination that sanctions should be applied, that the hand of the law should be placed upon the parties, and that the force of the courts should be directed against them, is an exercise of legislative power. In some nations that power is entrusted to the executive branch as a matter of course or in case of emergencies. We chose another course. We chose to place the legislative power of the Federal Government in the Congress.

. . .

MR. JUSTICE JACKSON, concurring in the judgment and opinion of the Court.

. . .

A judge, like an executive adviser, may be surprised at the poverty of really useful and unambiguous authority applicable to concrete problems of executive power as they actually present themselves. Just what our forefathers did envision, or would have envisioned had they foreseen modern conditions, must be divined from materials almost as enigmatic as the dreams Joseph was called upon to interpret for Pharaoh. A century and a half of partisan debate and scholarly speculation yields no net result but only supplies more or less apt quotations from respected sources on each side of any question. They largely cancel each other. And court decisions are indecisive because of the judicial practice of dealing with the largest questions in the most narrow way.

The actual art of governing under our Constitution does not and cannot conform to judicial definitions of the power of any of its branches based on isolated clauses or even single Articles torn from context. While the Constitution diffuses power the better to secure liberty, it also contemplates that practice will integrate the dispersed powers into a workable government. It enjoins upon its branches separateness but interdependence, autonomy but reciprocity. Presidential powers are not fixed but fluctuate, depending upon their disjunction or conjunction with those of Congress. We may well begin by a somewhat over-simplified grouping of practical situations in which a President may doubt, or others may challenge, his powers, and by distinguishing roughly the legal consequences of this factor of relativity.

1. When the President acts pursuant to an express or implied authorization of Congress, his authority is at its maximum, for it includes all that he possesses in his own right plus all that Congress can delegate. In these circumstances, and in these only, may he be said (for what it may be worth) to personify the federal sovereignty. If his act is held unconstitutional under these circumstances, it usually means that the Federal Government as an undivided whole lacks power. A seizure executed by the President pursuant to an Act of Congress would be supported by the strongest of presumptions and the widest latitude of judicial interpretation, and the burden of persuasion would rest heavily upon any who might attack it.

2. When the President acts in absence of either a congressional grant or denial of authority, he can only rely upon his own independent powers, but there is a zone of twilight in which he and Congress may have concurrent authority, or in which its distribution is uncertain. Therefore, congressional inertia, indifference or quiescence may sometimes, at least as a practical matter, enable, if not invite, measures on independent presidential responsibility. In this area, any actual test of power is likely to depend on the imperatives of events and contemporary imponderables rather than on abstract theories of law.

3. When the President takes measures incompatible with the expressed or implied will of Congress, his power is at its lowest ebb, for then he can rely only upon his own constitutional powers minus any constitutional powers of Congress over the matter. Courts can sustain exclusive presidential control in such a case only by disabling the Congress from acting upon the subject. Presidential claim to a power at once so conclusive and preclusive must be scrutinized with caution, for what is at stake is the equilibrium established by our constitutional system.

. . .

We should not use this occasion to circumscribe, much less to contract, the lawful role of the President as Commander in Chief. I should indulge the widest latitude of interpretation to sustain his exclusive function to command the instruments of national force, at least when turned against the outside world for the security of our society. But, when it is turned inward, not because of rebellion but because of a lawful economic struggle between industry and labor, it should have no such indulgence....

...I have no illusion that any decision by this Court can keep power in the hands of Congress if it is not wise and timely in meeting its problems. A crisis that challenges the President equally, or perhaps primarily, challenges Congress. If not good law, there was worldly wisdom in the maxim attributed to Napoleon that "The tools belong to the man who can use them." We may say that power to legislate for emergencies belongs in the hands of Congress, but only Congress itself can prevent power from slipping through its fingers.

...With all its defects, delays and inconveniences, men have discovered no technique for long preserving free government except that the Executive be under the law, and that the law be made by parliamentary deliberations.

Such institutions may be destined to pass away. But it is the duty of the Court to be last, not first, to give them up.

MR. JUSTICE BURTON, concurring in both the opinion and judgment of the Court.

. . .

...The present situation is not comparable to that of an imminent invasion or threatened attack. We do not face the issue of what might be the President's constitutional power to meet such catastrophic situations. Nor is it claimed that the current seizure is in the nature of a military command addressed by the President, as Commander-in-Chief, to a mobilized nation waging, or imminently threatened with, total war.

· · ·

Mr. Justice Clark, concurring in the judgment of the Court.

· · ·

...In my view...the Constitution does grant to the President extensive authority in times of grave and imperative national emergency. In fact, to my thinking, such a grant may well be necessary to the very existence of the Constitution itself. As Lincoln aptly said, "[is] it possible to lose the nation and yet preserve the Constitution?" In describing this authority I care not whether one calls it "residual," "inherent," "moral," "implied," "aggregate," "emergency," or otherwise....

I conclude that where Congress has laid down specific procedures to deal with the type of crisis confronting the President, he must follow those procedures in meeting the crisis; but that in the absence of such action by Congress, the President's independent power to act depends upon the gravity of the situation confronting the nation. I cannot sustain the seizure in question because here... Congress had prescribed methods to be followed by the President in meeting the emergency at hand.

· · ·

Mr. Chief Justice Vinson, with whom Mr. Justice Reed and Mr. Justice Minton join, dissenting.

· · ·

I.

In passing upon the question of Presidential powers in this case, we must first consider the context in which those powers were exercised.

Those who suggest that this is a case involving extraordinary power should be mindful that these are extraordinary times. A world not yet recovered from the devastation of World War II has been forced to face the threat of another and more terrifying global conflict.

Accepting in full measure its responsibility in the world community, the United States was instrumental in securing adoption of the United Nations Charter, approved by the Senate by a vote of 89 to 2. The first purpose of the United Nations is to "maintain international peace and security, and to that end: to take effective collective measures for the prevention and removal of threats to the peace, and for the suppression of acts of aggression or other breaches of the peace,..." In 1950, when the United Nations called upon member nations "to render every assistance" to repel aggression in Korea, the United States furnished its vigorous support. For almost two full years, our armed forces have been fighting in Korea, suffering casualties of over 108,000 men. Hostilities have not abated. The "determination of the United Nations to continue its action in Korea to meet the aggression" has been reaffirmed. Congressional support of the action in Korea has been manifested by provisions for increased military manpower and equipment and for economic stabilization, as hereinafter described.

· · ·

Congress recognized the impact of these defense programs upon the economy. Following the attack in Korea, the President asked for authority to requisition property and to allocate and fix priorities for scarce goods. In the Defense Production Act of 1950, Congress granted the powers requested and, *in addition,* granted power to stabilize prices and wages and to provide for settlement of labor disputes arising in the defense program. The Defense Production Act was extended in 1951, a Senate Committee noting that in the dislocation caused by the programs for purchase of military equipment "lies the seed of an economic disaster that might well destroy the military might we are straining to build." Significantly, the Committee examined the problem "in terms of just one commodity, steel," and found "a graphic picture of the over-all inflationary danger growing out of reduced civilian supplies and rising incomes."...

VI.

The diversity of views expressed in the six opinions of the majority, the lack of reference to authoritative precedent, the repeated reliance upon prior dissenting opinions, the complete disregard of the uncontroverted facts showing the gravity of the emergency and the temporary nature of the taking all serve to demonstrate how far afield one must go to affirm the order of the District Court.

The broad executive power granted by Article II to an officer on duty 365 days a year cannot, it is said, be invoked to avert disaster. Instead, the President must confine himself to sending a message to Congress recommending action. Under this messenger-boy concept of the Office, the President cannot even act to preserve legislative programs from destruction so that Congress will have something left to act upon....

New York Times Co. v. United States

403 U.S. 713 (1971)

The Nixon administration brought action in federal court to prevent publication in the *New York Times* and the *Washington Post* of certain materials collectively called the Pentagon Papers. The documents consisted of a classified study prepared by the Defense Department, entitled "History of U.S. Decision-Making Process on Viet Nam Policy." The administration claimed that publication of the materials would be injurious to national security. The newspapers argued that the First Amendment protected against prior restraint on the right to publish.

PER CURIAM.

We granted certiorari in these cases in which the United States seeks to enjoin the New York Times and the Washington Post from publishing the contents of a classified study entitled "History of U.S. Decision-Making Process on Viet Nam Policy."...

"Any system of prior restraints of expression comes to this Court bearing a heavy presumption against its constitutional validity." *Bantam Books, Inc.* v. *Sullivan,* 372 U.S. 58, 70 (1963); see also *Near* v. *Minnesota,* 283 U.S. 697 (1931). The Government "thus carries a heavy burden of showing justification for the imposition of such a restraint." *Organization for a Better Austin* v. *Keefe,* 402 U.S. 415, 419 (1971). The District Court for the Southern District of New York in the *New York Times* case and the District Court for the District of Columbia and the Court of Appeals for the District of Columbia Circuit in the *Washington Post* case held that the Government had not met that burden. We agree.

The judgment of the Court of Appeals for the District of Columbia Circuit is therefore affirmed. The order of the Court of Appeals for the Second Circuit is reversed and the case is remanded with directions to enter a judgment affirming the judgment of the District Court for the Southern District of New York. The stays entered June 25, 1971, by the Court are vacated. The judgments shall issue forthwith.

So ordered.

MR. JUSTICE BLACK, with whom MR. JUSTICE DOUGLAS joins, concurring.

I adhere to the view that the Government's case against the Washington Post should have been dismissed and that the injunction against the New York Times should have been vacated without oral argument when the cases were first presented to this Court. I believe that every moment's continuance of the injunctions against these newspapers amounts to a flagrant, indefensible, and continuing violation of the First Amendment....

...Madison and the other Framers of the First Amendment, able men that they were, wrote in language they earnestly believed could never be misunderstood: "Congress shall make no law... abridging the freedom... of the press...." Both the history and language of the First Amendment support the view that the press must be left free to publish news, whatever the source, without censorship, injunctions, or prior restraints.

In the First Amendment the Founding Fathers gave the free press the protection it must have to fulfill its essential role in our democracy. The press was to serve the governed, not the governors. The Government's power to censor the press was abolished so that the press would remain forever free to censure the Government. The press was protected so that it could bare the secrets of government and inform the people. Only a free and unrestrained press can effectively expose deception in government. And paramount among the responsibilities of a free press is the duty to prevent any part of the government from deceiving the people and sending them off to distant lands to die of foreign fevers and foreign shot and shell. In my view, far from deserving condemnation for their courageous reporting, the New York Times, the Washington Post, and other newspapers should be commended for serving the purpose that the Founding Fathers saw so clearly. In revealing the workings of government that led to the Vietnam war, the newspapers nobly did precisely that which the Founders hoped and trusted they would do.

. . .

...[T]he Government argues in its brief that in spite of the First Amendment, "[t]he authority of the Executive Department to protect the nation against publication of information whose disclosure would endanger the national security stems from two interrelated sources: the constitutional power of the President over the conduct of foreign affairs and his authority as Commander-in-Chief."

. . .

The word "security" is a broad, vague generality whose contours should not be invoked to abrogate the fundamental law embodied in the First Amendment. The guarding of military and diplomatic secrets at the expense of informed representative government provides no real security for our Republic. . . .

MR. JUSTICE DOUGLAS, with whom MR. JUSTICE BLACK joins, concurring.

. . .

The dominant purpose of the First Amendment was to prohibit the widespread practice of governmental suppression of embarrassing information. It is common knowledge that the First Amendment was adopted against the widespread use of the common law of seditious libel to punish the dissemination of material that is embarrassing to the powers-that-be. . . .

MR. JUSTICE BRENNAN, concurring.

I

I write separately in these cases only to emphasize what should be apparent: that our judgments in the present cases may not be taken to indicate the propriety, in the future, of issuing temporary stays and restraining orders to block the publication of material sought to be suppressed by the Government. So far as I can determine, never before has the United States sought to enjoin a newspaper from publishing information in its possession. . . .

II

. . . [O]nly governmental allegation and proof that publication must inevitably, directly, and immediately cause the occurrence of an event kindred to imperiling the safety of a transport already at sea can support even the issuance of an interim restraining order. . . .

MR. JUSTICE STEWART, with whom MR. JUSTICE WHITE joins, concurring.

. . .

. . . If the Constitution gives the Executive a large degree of unshared power in the conduct of foreign affairs and the maintenance of our national defense, then under the Constitution the Ex-

ecutive must have the largely unshared duty to determine and preserve the degree of internal security necessary to exercise that power successfully. It is an awesome responsibility, requiring judgment and wisdom of a high order. I should suppose that moral, political, and practical considerations would dictate that a very first principle of that wisdom would be an insistence upon avoiding secrecy for its own sake. For when everything is classified, then nothing is classified, and the system becomes one to be disregarded by the cynical or the careless, and to be manipulated by those intent on self-protection or self-promotion. . . .

. . . [I]n the cases before us we are asked neither to construe specific regulations nor to apply specific laws. We are asked, instead, to perform a function that the Constitution gave to the Executive, not the Judiciary. We are asked, quite simply, to prevent the publication by two newspapers of material that the Executive Branch insists should not, in the national interest, be published. I am convinced that the Executive is correct with respect to some of the documents involved. But I cannot say that disclosure of any of them will surely result in direct, immediate, and irreparable damage to our Nation or its people. That being so, there can under the First Amendment be but one judicial resolution of the issues before us. I join the judgments of the Court.

MR. JUSTICE WHITE, with whom MR. JUSTICE STEWART joins, concurring.

I concur in today's judgments, but only because of the concededly extraordinary protection against prior restraints enjoyed by the press under our constitutional system. I do not say that in no circumstances would the First Amendment permit an injunction against publishing information about government plans or operations. Nor, after examining the materials the Government characterizes as the most sensitive and destructive, can I deny that revelation of these documents will do substantial damage to public interests. Indeed, I am confident that their disclosure will have that result. But I nevertheless agree that the United States has not satisfied the very heavy burden that it must meet to warrant an injunction against publication in these cases, at least in the absence of express and appropriately limited congressional authorization for prior restraints in circumstances such as these.

. . .

MR. JUSTICE MARSHALL, concurring.

The Government contends that the only issue

in these cases is whether in a suit by the United States, "the First Amendment bars a court from prohibiting a newspaper from publishing material whose disclosure would pose a "grave and immediate danger to the security of the United States."" Brief for the United States 7. With all due respect, I believe the ultimate issue in these cases is even more basic than the one posed by the Solicitor General. The issue is whether this Court or the Congress has the power to make law.

...The Government argues that in addition to the inherent power of any government to protect itself, the President's power to conduct foreign affairs and his position as Commander in Chief give him authority to impose censorship on the press to protect his ability to deal effectively with foreign nations and to conduct the military affairs of the country....

It would, however, be utterly inconsistent with the concept of separation of powers for this court to use its power of contempt to prevent behavior that Congress has specifically declined to prohibit. There would be a similar damage to the basic concept of these co-equal branches of Government if when the Executive Branch has adequate authority granted by Congress to protect "national security" it can choose instead to invoke the contempt power of a court to enjoin the threatened conduct. The Constitution provides that Congress shall make laws, the President execute laws, and courts interpret laws. *Youngstown Sheet & Tube Co. v. Sawyer,* 343 U. S. 579 (1952). It did not provide for government by injunction in which the courts and the Executive Branch can "make law" without regard to the action of Congress.

. . .

MR. CHIEF JUSTICE BURGER, dissenting.

...In these cases, the imperative of a free and unfettered press comes into collision with another imperative, the effective functioning of a complex modern government and specifically the effective exercise of certain constitutional powers of the Executive. Only those who view the First Amendment as an absolute in all circumstances — a view I respect, but reject — can find such cases as these to be simple or easy.

These cases are not simple for another and more immediate reason. We do not know the facts of the cases. No District Judge knew all the facts. No Court of Appeals judge knew all the facts. No member of this Court knows all the facts.

Why are we in this posture, in which only those judges to whom the First Amendment is absolute and permits of no restraint in any circumstances or for any reason, are really in a position to act?

I suggest we are in this posture because these cases have been conducted in unseemly haste....

. . .

MR. JUSTICE HARLAN, with whom THE CHIEF JUSTICE and MR. JUSTICE BLACKMUN join, dissenting.

These cases forcefully call to mind the wise admonition of Mr. Justice Holmes, dissenting in *Northern Securities Co. v. United States,* 193 U. S. 197, 400–401 (1904):

"Great cases like hard cases make bad law. For great cases are called great, not by reason of their real importance in shaping the law of the future, but because of some accident of immediate overwhelming interest which appeals to the feelings and distorts the judgment. These immediate interests exercise a kind of hydraulic pressure which makes what previously was clear seem doubtful, and before which even well settled principles of law will bend."

With all respect, I consider that the Court has been almost irresponsibly feverish in dealing with these cases.

Both the Court of Appeals for the Second Circuit and the Court of Appeals for the District of Columbia Circuit rendered judgment on June 23. The New York Times' petition for certiorari, its motion for accelerated consideration thereof, and its application for interim relief were filed in this Court on June 24 at about 11 A.M. The application of the United States for interim relief in the *Post* case was also filed here on June 24 at about 7:15 P.M. This Court's order setting a hearing before us on June 26 at 11 A.M., a course which I joined only to avoid the possibility of even more peremptory action by the Court, was issued less than 24 hours before. The record in the *Post* case was filed with the Clerk shortly before 1 P.M. on June 25; the record in the *Times* case did not arrive until 7 or 8 o'clock that same night. The briefs of the parties were received less than two hours before argument on June 26.

This frenzied train of events took place in the name of the presumption against prior restraints created by the First Amendment. Due regard for the extraordinarily important and difficult questions involved in these litigations should have led the Court to shun such a precipitate timetable.

. . .

MR. JUSTICE BLACKMUN, dissenting.

. . .

With such respect as may be due to the contrary view, this, in my opinion, is not the way to try a lawsuit of this magnitude and asserted importance. It is not the way for federal courts to adjudicate, and to be required to adjudicate, issues that allegedly concern the Nation's vital welfare....

Erwin N. Griswold

How Sensitive Were the "Pentagon Papers"?

In the administration's brief to the Supreme Court on *New York Times Co. v. United States,* Solicitor General Erwin N. Griswold described all of the materials in the forty-seven volumes as classified "Top Secret-Sensitive," "Top Secret," or "Secret." By the time the case reached the Court, the administration wanted to bar only the publication of a smaller number of documents, the disclosure of which would pose a "grave and immediate danger to the security of the United States." During oral argument, Griswold told the Court that the broaching of one of the documents "would be of extraordinary seriousness to the security of the United States." Publication of the documents, according to Griswold, "will affect lives. It will affect the process of the termination of the war. It will affect the process of recovering prisoners of war." Later in the oral argument he warned the Court that publication would interfere with the conduct of "delicate negotiations now in process, or contemplated for the future." Yet in an article for the *Washington Post* on February 15, 1989, entitled "Secrets Not Worth Keeping" (p. A25), he admits that publication produced no trace of a threat to the national security. As he explains, the principal concern of classifiers "is not with national security, but rather with government embarrassment of one sort or another."

It may be relevant at this time to recount some details of events which attracted widespread attention several years ago. The occasion was the presentation of the Pentagon Papers case *(New York Times* v. *United States* and *United States* v. *Washington Post)* before the United States Supreme Court, and the year was 1971.

At that time, I held the office of solicitor general of the United States. The government then in office, under the presidency of Richard Nixon, was determined to do everything in its power to prevent the press from publishing some 47 volumes of mimeographed papers preserved primarily in the office of the Secretary of Defense in the Pentagon, and thus known as the Pentagon Papers. These papers were *in toto* classified as Top Secret....

It was my responsibility to represent the interests of the United States before the Supreme Court. Everything happened very fast. The U.S. Court of Appeals for the District of Columbia decided the case on Thursday, June 24, 1971. On Friday, at noon, I was advised by Chief Justice Warren Burger that the case would be heard by the Supreme Court on Saturday morning, June 26, and that "briefs will be exchanged between the parties in the courtroom immediately before the argument."

At that time, no briefs had been written, and, indeed, I had never seen the *outside* of the Pentagon Papers. I immediately arranged for a set of the papers to be brought to my office. It was obvious that I could not read all of the materials in the time available. In this situation, I arranged to have three high officials, one each from the Defense Department, the State Department and the National Security Agency come to my office. I asked them to tell me what items in the 47 volumes were really bad — what items, if disclosed, would be a real threat to the security of the United States.

This produced a total of about 40 items over which these officers expressed concern. I then read each of these items, but quickly came to the conclusion that most of them presented no serious threat to national security, and that there was simply no prospect that the Supreme Court would ban the publication of all of these items. Eventually, I reduced the list to a total of 11 items. My deputy, Daniel M. Friedman, wrote the main or "open" brief for the United States, while I wrote the "secret" brief, contending that these 11 items presented a threat to the national security.

. . .

So, I went ahead and presented the case before the court, relying only on the 11 items. As is well known, we lost, by a six-to-three vote, with three members of the majority saying there could never be a prior restraint, while three others said that a prior restraint would be appropriate in a proper case, but that there was no adequate threat to national security in this case.

Accordingly, the newspapers printed many items from the Pentagon Papers. And within a few weeks, under the auspices of Sen. Mike Gravel of Alaska, the entire contents of all the papers were printed. I have never seen any trace of a threat to

the national security from the publication. Indeed, I have never seen it even suggested that there was such an actual threat. . . .

It quickly becomes apparent to any person who has considerable experience with classified material that there is massive overclassification and that the principal concern of the classifiers is not with national security, but rather with governmental embarrassment of one sort or another. There may be some basis for short-term classification while plans are being made, or negotiations are going on, but apart from details of weapons systems, there is very rarely any real risk to current national security from the publication of facts relating to transactions in the past, even the fairly recent past. . . .

C. TREATIES AND EXECUTIVE AGREEMENTS

Under Article VI of the Constitution, federal statutes made pursuant to the Constitution, and all treaties "shall be the supreme Law of the Land." State judges are bound by those actions, "any Thing in the Constitution or Laws of any State to the Contrary Notwithstanding." In passing legislation to carry out a treaty, Congress may act in ways that might not have been sustained in the form of a freestanding statute. See Missouri v. Holland (page 342).

The President makes treaties "by and with the Advice and Consent of the Senate." The process of treaty making need not be divided into two exclusive and sequential stages: negotiation solely by the President, followed by Senate advice and consent. When President Washington first communicated with the Senate regarding the appropriate procedure for treaties, he considered oral communications with Senators "indispensably necessary." Treaties seemed to him "of a legislative nature," inviting deliberation in the Senate's chamber. 30 Writings of Washington 373, 378. On August 22, 1789, he met with Senators to secure their advice and consent to an Indian treaty. The Senators felt uncomfortable in his presence and disliked having to rely solely on information provided by the Secretary of War, who was present. Washington returned two days later and obtained the Senate's consent, but he decided against a repeat performance.

This incident has been misinterpreted to suggest that Washington negotiated all future treaties without Senate involvement. In fact, he continued to seek the Senate's advice by written communications rather than personal appearances. Senators were asked to approve the appointment of treaty negotiators and even to advise on their negotiating instructions. Far from being a "presidential monopoly," the negotiation of treaties has often been shared with the Senate in order to obtain legislative understanding and support. Presidential insistence to "go it alone" in negotiating treaties has often had disastrous results. Fisher, Constitutional Conflicts Between Congress and the President 228–32 (1997).

Role of the House

Although the Senate is the only House of Congress with a constitutional role in the treaty process, the House of Representatives plays a crucial role. As early as 1796, members of the House of Representatives insisted that the House possessed "a discretionary power of carrying the Treaty into effect, or refusing it their sanction." Annals of Congress, 4th Cong., 1st Session. 426–28. Certain powers delegated to Congress as a whole, such as the authority to regulate foreign commerce or to set tariffs, could not be exercised through the treaty-making power. The general power of appropriating funds to execute a treaty represents another constraint on the President and the Senate. When two-thirds of the Senate fails to ratify a treaty, Presidents have turned to Congress as a whole to accomplish the same purpose by obtaining a simple majority vote in both Houses for a joint resolution. The annexation of Texas and Hawaii and the adoption of the St. Lawrence Seaway plan were accomplished in this manner. The position of the House of Representatives is enhanced when treaties contain language requiring that funds be made available through the normal procedures of Congress, including prior authorization and annual appropriations. This language requires action not only by the Senate Foreign Relations Committee and the House International Relations Committee but also by both Appropriations Committees.

Treaty Termination

The constitutional issue of treaty termination was raised in 1978 when President Jimmy Carter terminated a defense treaty with Taiwan. The Senate considered a resolution that would have required the approval of the Senate or both Houses of Congress before the President could terminate any defense treaty, but final action was never taken on the measure. A federal district judge decided that some form of congressional concurrence was required, either the approval of a majority of both Houses or the consent of two-thirds of the Senate. Goldwater v. Carter, 481 F.Supp. 949, 963–64 (D.D.C. 1979). This decision was rejected by an appellate court and the Supreme Court, in part because of the failure of Congress to confront the President directly. In the words of Justice Jackson from the Steel Seizure Case, Carter had acted in a "zone of twilight." Goldwater v. Carter, 617 F.2d 697 (D.C. Cir. 1979); GOLDWATER v. CARTER, 444 U.S. 996 (1979). The Justices of the Supreme Court split along so many lines that their opinions shed little light on future treaty terminations. Congress has yet to pass legislation to define executive and legislative roles in this matter.

Executive Agreements

Treaties differ from executive agreements in several regards. Treaties require the advice and consent of the Senate; executive agreements do not. Treaties (unlike executive agreements) may supersede prior conflicting statutes. United States v. Schooner Peggy, 5 U.S. (1 Cr.) 103 (1801). Otherwise, officials in the executive branch have considerable latitude in entering into international compacts either by treaty or by executive agreement. Among the more controversial executive agreements are the destroyers-bases deal with Great Britain in 1940, the Yalta and Potsdam agreements of 1945, the Vietnam peace agreement of 1973, the Sinai agreements of 1975, and recent military-base agreements with Spain, Diego Garcia, and Bahrain.

The vast majority of executive agreements are based on statutory authority or treaty language. Although these agreements may lack what the Supreme Court calls the "dignity" of a treaty, since they do not require Senate approval, they are nevertheless valid international compacts. Altman & Co. v. United States, 224 U.S. 583, 600–01 (1912).[4] In addition to statutory and treaty authority, the executive branch claims four sources of constitutional authority that allow the President to enter into executive agreements: (1) his duty as chief executive to represent the nation in foreign affairs, (2) his authority to receive ambassadors and other public ministers, (3) his authority as commander in chief, and (4) his duty to "take care that the laws be faithfully executed." 11 FAM [Foreign Affairs Manual] 721.2(b)(3) (October 25, 1974). The scope of these unilateral initiatives has been narrowed by judicial and congressional actions.

---

4. In United States v. Pink, 315 U.S. 203, 230 (1942), the Court regarded executive agreements as having a "similar dignity" with treaties. For an opinion by Acting Attorney General McGranery in 1946 upholding the legality of an executive agreement made pursuant to a joint resolution, see 40 Op. Att'y Gen. 469.

Congressional Oversight of Executive Agreements

The Committee on Foreign Relations, to which was referred the bill (S. 596) to require that international agreements other than treaties, hereafter entered into by the United States, be transmitted to the Congress within 60 days after the execution thereof, having considered the same, reports favorably thereon without amendment and recommends that the bill do pass.

. . .

As the committee has discovered, there have been numerous agreements contracted with foreign governments in recent years, particularly agreements of a military nature, which remain wholly unknown to Congress and to the people. A number of these agreements have been uncovered by the Symington Subcommittee on Security Agreements and Commitments Abroad, including, for example, an agreement with Ethiopia in 1960, agreements with Laos in 1963, with Thailand in 1964 and again in 1967, with Korea in 1966, and certain secret annexes to the Spanish bases agreement.

Section 112(a) of title I of the United States Code now requires the Secretary of State to compile and publish all international agreements other than treaties concluded by the United States during each calendar year. The executive, however, has long made it a practice to withhold those agreements which, in its judgment, are of a "sensitive" nature. Such agreements, often involving military arrangements with foreign countries, are frequently not only "sensitive" but exceedingly significant as broadened commitments for the United States. Although they are sometimes characterized as "contingency plans," they may in practice involve the United States in war. For this reason the committee attaches the greatest importance to the establishment of a legislative requirement that all such agreements be submitted to Congress.

... Whatever objection on security grounds the executive might have to the submission of such information to Congress is met by the provision of the bill which authorizes the President, at his option, to transmit certain agreements not to the Congress as a whole, but to the two foreign affairs committees "under an appropriate injunction of secrecy to be removed only upon due notice from the President."

SOURCE: S. Rept. No. 92–591, 92d Cong., 2d Sess. (1972).

Few would deny that the President has constitutional authority to recognize foreign governments. President Roosevelt's recognition of Soviet Russia led to the "Litvinov Assignment" in 1933 and subsequent property claims in the courts. His decision was upheld by the Supreme Court. United States v. Belmont, 301 U.S. 324 (1937); United States v. Pink, 315 U.S. 203 (1942). Left undecided was the President's power to enter into agreements that violate such constitutional provisions as the Due Process and Just Compensation Clauses of the Fifth Amendment. Under certain circumstances, the use of the recognition power by the President may invade the war prerogatives of Congress. President Andrew Jackson made that argument in declining to recognize the independence of Texas, fearing that such action would result in war with Mexico and undercut the legitimate constitutional role of Congress. Louis Fisher, Presidential War Power, at 30.

The State Department concedes that an executive agreement cannot be "inconsistent with legislation enacted by Congress in the exercise of its constitutional authority." 11 FAM 721.2(b)(3) (1974). For example, an agreement cannot survive if it conflicts with a commercial statute concerning another country. Foreign commerce is "subject to regulation, so far as this country is concerned, by Congress alone." United States v. Guy W. Capps, Inc., 204 F.2d 655, 660 (4th Cir. 1953), aff'd on other grounds, 348 U.S. 296 (1955). Other executive agreements have been struck down because they violate the Just Compensation Clause or deprive an accused of trial by jury. Seery v. United States, 127 F.Supp. 601 (Ct. Cl. 1955); Reid v. Covert, 354 U.S. 1 (1957).

The Iranian hostage crisis of 1979 produced a series of extraordinary moves by President Carter, including the freezing of Iran's assets in America and the suspension of claims pending in American courts. Although the Supreme Court found no specific authority for the suspension of claims, legal justifications were discovered somewhere in the combination of past presidential practices to settle claims by executive agreement, the history of "implicit" congressional approval, and the failure of Congress to contest the Iranian agreement. The Court, straining to uphold an agreement it could not possibly overturn, limited the reach of its opinion by confining it to the specific circumstances in the case. DAMES & MOORE v. REGAN, 453 U.S. 654 (1981).

A number of secret agreements have been entered into without the knowledge of Congress. Many of these agreements were of an economic or military nature, committing the United States to various obligations (see box). Legislation in 1972 (the Case Act) requires the Secretary of State to transmit to Congress within sixty days the text of "any international agreement, other than a treaty," to which the United States is a party. If the President decides that publication would be prejudicial to national security, he may transmit an agreement to the Senate Committee on Foreign Relations and the House Committee on International Relations under an injunction of secrecy removable only by the President. 86 Stat. 619 (1972); 1 U.S.C. § 112b (1994). Because the executive branch circumvented the statute by calling some agreements "arrangements," Congress passed legislation to tighten the reporting statute. 91 Stat. 224, § 5 (1977); 92 Stat. 993, § 708 (1978). Legislative control is strengthened even more by requiring that Congress approve certain agreements or appropriate funds to carry them out.

Goldwater v. Carter

444 U.S. 996 (1979)

On December 15, 1978, President Carter terminated a defense treaty with Taiwan. Under the terms of the treaty, either party could end the pact after giving the other country a year's notice. By the time the case had traveled through the district court and the appellate court, the treaty was about to be terminated. Senator Barry Goldwater argued that a treaty, being law, required legislative action for its repeal. Acting without oral argument, the Court dismissed the complaint by Goldwater. Having disposed of the issue in summary fashion, several Justices filed separate statements setting forth their individual views.

MR. JUSTICE POWELL, concurring in the judgment.

Although I agree with the result reached by the Court, I would dismiss the complaint as not ripe for judicial review.

I

This Court has recognized that an issue should not be decided if it is not ripe for judicial review. *Buckley* v. *Valeo*, 424 U.S. 1, 113–114 (1976) *(per curiam)*. Prudential considerations persuade me that a dispute between Congress and the President is not ready for judicial review unless and until each branch has taken action asserting its constitutional authority. Differences between the President and the Congress are commonplace under our system. The differences should, and almost invariably do, turn on political rather than legal considerations. The Judicial Branch should not decide issues affecting the allocation of power between the President and Congress until the political branches reach a constitutional impasse. Otherwise, we would encourage small groups or even individual Members of Congress to seek judicial resolution of issues before the normal political process has the opportunity to resolve the conflict.

In this case, a few Members of Congress claim that the President's action in terminating the treaty with Taiwan has deprived them of their constitutional role with respect to a change in the supreme law of the land. Congress has taken no official action. In the present posture of this case, we do not know whether there ever will be an actual confrontation between the Legislative and Executive Branches. Although the Senate has considered a resolution declaring that Senate approval is necessary for the termination of any mutual defense treaty, see 125 Cong. Rec. 13672,

13695–13697 (1979), no final vote has been taken on the resolution. See *id.*, at 32522–32531. Moreover, it is unclear whether the resolution would have retroactive effect. See *id.*, at 13711–13721; *id.*, at 15210. It cannot be said that either the Senate or the House has rejected the President's claim. If the Congress chooses not to confront the President, it is not our task to do so. I therefore concur in the dismissal of this case.

II

MR. JUSTICE REHNQUIST suggests, however, that the issue presented by this case is a nonjusticiable political question which can never be considered by this Court. I cannot agree.

[Justice Powell concludes that if this case were ready for review, it would satisfy the criteria established by Baker *v.* Carr *(1962) for cases that the Court may properly decide.]*

III

In my view, the suggestion that this case presents a political question is incompatible with this Court's willingness on previous occasions to decide whether one branch of our Government has impinged upon the power of another. See *Buckley v. Valeo,* 424 U.S., at 138; *United States v. Nixon, supra,* at 707; *The Pocket Veto Case,* 279 U.S. 655, 676–678 (1929); *Myers v. United States,* 272 U.S. 52 (1926). Under the criteria enunciated in *Baker v. Carr,* we have the responsibility to decide whether both the Executive and Legislative Branches have constitutional roles to play in termination of a treaty. If the Congress, by appropriate formal action, had challenged the President's authority to terminate the treaty with Taiwan, the resulting uncertainty could have serious consequences for our country. In that situation, it would be the duty of this Court to resolve the issue.

MR. JUSTICE REHNQUIST, with whom THE CHIEF JUSTICE, MR. JUSTICE STEWART, and MR. JUSTICE STEVENS join, concurring in the judgment.

I am of the view that the basic question presented by the petitioners in this case is "political" and therefore nonjusticiable because it involves the authority of the President in the conduct of our country's foreign relations and the extent to which the Senate or the Congress is authorized to negate the action of the President....

· · ·

I believe it follows *a fortiori* from [Coleman v. Miller, 307 U.S. 433 (1939)] that the controversy in the instant case is a nonjusticiable political dispute that should be left for resolution by the Executive and Legislative Branches of the Government. Here, while the Constitution is express as to the manner in which the Senate shall participate in the ratification of a treaty, it is silent as to that body's participation in the abrogation of a treaty. In this respect the case is directly analogous to *Coleman, supra....*

I think that the justifications for concluding that the question here is political in nature are even more compelling than in *Coleman* because it involves foreign relations — specifically a treaty commitment to use military force in the defense of a foreign government if attacked. In *United States v. Curtiss-Wright Corp.,* 299 U.S. 304 (1936), this Court said:

"Whether, if the Joint Resolution had related solely to internal affairs it would be open to the challenge that it constituted an unlawful delegation of legislative power to the Executive, we find it unnecessary to determine. The whole aim of the resolution is to affect a situation entirely external to the United States, and falling within the category of foreign affairs...." *Id.,* at 315.

The present case differs in several important respects from *Youngstown Sheet & Tube Co. v. Sawyer,* 343 U.S. 579 (1952), cited by petitioners as authority both for reaching the merits of this dispute and for reversing the Court of Appeals. In *Youngstown,* private litigants brought a suit contesting the President's authority under his war powers to seize the Nation's steel industry, an action of profound and demonstrable domestic impact. Here, by contrast, we are asked to settle a dispute between coequal branches of our Government, each of which has resources available to protect and assert its interests, resources not available to private litigants outside the judicial forum. Moreover, as in *Curtiss-Wright,* the effect of this action, as far as we can tell, is "entirely external to the United States, and [falls] within the category of foreign affairs." Finally, as already noted, the situation presented here is closely akin to that presented in *Coleman,* where the Constitution spoke only to the procedure for ratification of an amendment, not to its rejection.

Having decided that the question presented in this action is nonjusticiable, I believe that the appropriate disposition is for this Court to vacate the decision of the Court of Appeals and remand with instructions for the District Court to dismiss the complaint....

MR. JUSTICE BLACKMUN, with whom MR. JUSTICE WHITE joins, dissenting in part.

In my view, the time factor and its importance are illusory; if the President does not have the power to terminate the treaty (a substantial issue that we should address only after briefing and oral argument), the notice of intention to terminate surely has no legal effect. It is also indefensible, without further study, to pass on the issue of justiciability or on the issues of standing or ripeness. While I therefore join in the grant of the petition for certiorari, I would set the case for oral argument and give it the plenary consideration it so obviously deserves.

MR. JUSTICE BRENNAN, dissenting.

I respectfully dissent from the order directing the District Court to dismiss this case, and would affirm the judgment of the Court of Appeals in-so-far as it rests upon the President's well-established authority to recognize, and withdraw recognition from, foreign governments....

In stating that this case presents a nonjusticiable "political question," MR. JUSTICE REHNQUIST, in my view, profoundly misapprehends the political-question principle as it applies to matters of foreign relations. Properly understood, the political-question doctrine restrains courts from reviewing an exercise of foreign policy judgment by the coordinate political branch to which authority to make that judgment has been "constitutional[ly] commit[ted]." *Baker v. Carr,* 369 U.S. 186, 211–213, 217 (1962). But the doctrine does not pertain when a court is faced with the *antecedent* question whether a particular branch has been constitutionally designated as the repository of political decisionmaking power. Cf. *Powell v. McCormack,* 395 U.S. 486, 519–521 (1969). The issue of decisionmaking authority must be resolved as a matter of constitutional law, not political discretion; accordingly, it falls within the competence of the courts.

The constitutional question raised here is prudently answered in narrow terms. Abrogation of the defense treaty with Taiwan was a necessary incident to Executive recognition of the Peking Government, because the defense treaty was predicated upon the now-abandoned view that the Taiwan Government was the only legitimate political authority in China. Our cases firmly establish that the Constitution commits to the President alone the power to recognize, and withdraw recognition from, foreign regimes.... That mandate being clear, our judicial inquiry into the treaty rupture can go no further....

Dames & Moore v. Regan

453 U.S. 654 (1981)

After Iran seized American hostages in 1979, President Carter declared a national emergency and blocked the removal or transfer of all Iranian property subject to the jurisdiction of the United States. He also authorized certain judicial proceedings to handle resulting disputes brought by private parties seeking access to Iranian assets. When the American hostages were released on January 20, 1981, the United States and Iran entered into an agreement that required the termination of all legal proceedings in U.S. courts involving claims of U.S. nationals against Iran. Those claims would be submitted to binding arbitration before an Iran-United States Claims Tribunal. In this case, a private party seeks to prevent enforcement of various executive orders and regulations issued to implement the agreement with Iran. The basic question of this case is whether the administration exceeded statutory and constitutional powers. A private company, Dames & Moore, sued Secretary of the Treasury Donald Regan.

JUSTICE REHNQUIST delivered the opinion of the Court.

The questions presented by this case touch fundamentally upon the manner in which our Republic is to be governed....

[*This*] dispute involves various Executive Orders and regulations by which the President nullified attachments and liens on Iranian assets in the United States, directed that these assets be transferred to Iran, and suspended claims against Iran that may be presented to an International Claims Tribunal. This action was taken in an effort to comply with an Executive Agreement between the United States and Iran....

But before turning to the facts and law which we believe determine the result in this case, we stress that the expeditious treatment of the issues involved by all of the courts which have considered the President's actions makes us acutely aware of the necessity to rest decision on the narrowest possible ground capable of deciding the case. *Ashwander* v. *TVA,* 297 U.S. 288, 347 (1936) (Brandeis, J., concurring)....

I

On November 4, 1979, the American Embassy in Tehran was seized and our diplomatic personnel were captured and held hostage. In response to that crisis, President Carter, acting pursuant to the International Emergency Economic Powers Act, ... (hereinafter IEEPA), declared a national emergency on November 14, 1979, and blocked the removal or transfer of "all property and interests in property of the Government of Iran, its instrumentalities and controlled entities and the Central Bank of Iran which are or become subject to the jurisdiction of the United States...." ... On November 15, 1979, the Treasury Department's Office of Foreign Assets Control issued a regulation providing that "[u]nless licensed or authorized ... any attachment, judgment, decree, lien, execution, garnishment, or other judicial process is null and void with respect to any property in which on or since [November 14, 1979,] there existed an interest of Iran." ...

On November 26, 1979, the President granted a general license authorizing certain judicial proceedings against Iran but which did not allow the "entry of any judgment or of any decree or order of similar or analogous effect...." § 535.504 (a). On December 19, 1979, a clarifying regulation was issued stating that "the general authorization for judicial proceedings contained in § 535.504 (a) includes pre-judgment attachment." § 535.418.

On December 19, 1979, petitioner Dames & Moore filed suit in the United States District Court for the Central District of California against the Government of Iran, the Atomic Energy Organization of Iran, and a number of Iranian banks. In its complaint, petitioner alleged that its wholly owned subsidiary, Dames & Moore International, S. R. L., was a party to a written contract with the Atomic Energy Organization, and that the sub-

sidiary's entire interest in the contract had been assigned to petitioner. Under the contract, the subsidiary was to conduct site studies for a proposed nuclear power plant in Iran. As provided in the terms of the contract, the Atomic Energy Organization terminated the agreement for its own convenience on June 30, 1979. Petitioner contended, however, that it was owed $3,436,694.30 plus interest for services performed under the contract prior to the date of termination. The District Court issued orders of attachment directed against property of the defendants, and the property of certain Iranian banks was then attached to secure any judgment that might be entered against them.

On January 20, 1981, the Americans held hostage were released by Iran pursuant to an Agreement entered into the day before.... The Agreement stated that "[i]t is the purpose of [the United States and Iran] ... to terminate all litigation as between the Government of each party and the nationals of the other, and to bring about the settlement and termination of all such claims through binding arbitration." ... In furtherance of this goal, the Agreement called for the establishment of an Iran-United States Claims Tribunal which would arbitrate any claims not settled within six months. Awards of the Claims Tribunal are to be "final and binding" and "enforceable ... in the courts of any nation in accordance with its laws." ... Under the Agreement, the United States is obligated

"to terminate all legal proceedings in United States courts involving claims of United States persons and institutions against Iran and its state enterprises, to nullify all attachments and judgments obtained therein, to prohibit all further litigation based on such claims, and to bring about the termination of such claims through binding arbitration." ...

In addition, the United States must "act to bring about the transfer" by July 19, 1981, of all Iranian assets held in this country by American banks.... One billion dollars of these assets will be deposited in a security account in the Bank of England, to the account of the Algerian Central Bank, and used to satisfy awards rendered against Iran by the Claims Tribunal. *Ibid.*

On January 19, 1981, President Carter issued a series of Executive Orders implementing the terms of the agreement.

[On February 24, 1981, President Reagan issued an executive order in which he "ratified" the January 19 executive orders. Meanwhile, a federal district court awarded Dames & Moore the

amount claimed under the contract plus interest. Later, the company filed an action seeking to prevent enforcement of the executive orders and Treasury Department regulations implementing the agreement with Iran.]

II

[In this section, Justice Rehnquist finds Justice Jackson's concurring opinion in Youngstown Co. v. Sawyer *(1952), classifying presidential actions into three general categories, to be analytically useful but somewhat too general to apply. Presidential action in any particular case does not fall "neatly in one of three pigeonholes, but rather at some point along a spectrum running from explicit congressional authorization to explicit congressional prohibition. This is particularly true as respects cases such as the one before us. . . ."]*

III

In nullifying post-November 14, 1979, attachments and directing those persons holding blocked Iranian funds and securities to transfer them to the Federal Reserve Bank of New York for ultimate transfer to Iran, President Carter cited five sources of express or inherent power. The Government, however, has principally relied on § 203 of the IEEPA. . . .

[Dames and Moore argued that the Court should ignore the plain language of this statute and examine its legislative history and the history of the Trading With the Enemy Act (TWEA), which reveals that IEEPA "was not intended to give the President such extensive power over the assets of a foreign state during times of national emergency."

The Court disagreed, refusing to read out of IEEPA the meaning of certain words. To the Court, nothing in the history of that statute or of the TWEA requires such a result.] To the contrary, we think both the legislative history and cases interpreting the TWEA fully sustain the broad authority of the Executive when acting under this congressional grant of power.

IV

Although we have concluded that the IEEPA constitutes specific congressional authorization to the President to nullify the attachments and order the transfer of Iranian assets, there remains the question of the President's authority to suspend claims pending in American courts. Such claims have, of course, an existence apart from the attachments which accompanied them. In terminat-

ing these claims through Executive Order No. 12294, the President purported to act under authority of both the IEEPA and 22 U. S. C. § 1732, the so-called "Hostage Act." 46 Fed. Reg. 14111 (1981).

We conclude that although the IEEPA authorized the nullification of the attachments, it cannot be read to authorize the suspension of the claims. The claims of American citizens against Iran are not in themselves transactions involving Iranian property or efforts to exercise any rights with respect to such property. . . . *[The Court also concludes that the Hostage Act does not provide specific authorization to the President to suspend claims in American courts.]*

Concluding that neither the IEEPA nor the Hostage Act constitutes specific authorization of the President's action suspending claims, however, is not to say that these statutory provisions are entirely irrelevant to the question of the validity of the President's action. We think both statutes highly relevant in the looser sense of indicating congressional acceptance of a broad scope for executive action in circumstances such as those presented in this case. As noted in Part III, . . . the IEEPA delegates broad authority to the President to act in times of national emergency with respect to property of a foreign country. The Hostage Act similarly indicates congressional willingness that the President have broad discretion when responding to the hostile acts of foreign sovereigns. . . .

Although we have declined to conclude that the IEEPA or the Hostage Act directly authorizes the President's suspension of claims for the reasons noted, we cannot ignore the general tenor of Congress' legislation in this area in trying to determine whether the President is acting alone or at least with the acceptance of Congress. As we have noted, Congress cannot anticipate and legislate with regard to every possible action the President may find it necessary to take or every possible situation in which he might act. Such failure of Congress specifically to delegate authority does not, "especially . . . in the areas of foreign policy and national security," imply "congressional disapproval" of action taken by the Executive. *Haig* v. *Agee, ante,* at 291. On the contrary, the enactment of legislation closely related to the question of the President's authority in a particular case which evinces legislative intent to accord the President broad discretion may be considered to "invite" "measures on independent presidential responsibility." *Youngstown,* 343 U. S., at 637 (Jackson, J., concurring). At least this is so where there is no contrary indication of legislative intent and when, as here, there is a history of congressional acquiescence in conduct of the sort engaged in by the President. It is to that history which we now turn.

Not infrequently in affairs between nations, outstanding claims by nationals of one country against the government of another country are "sources of friction" between the two sovereigns. *United States v. Pink,* 315 U. S. 203, 225 (1942). To resolve these difficulties, nations have often entered into agreements settling the claims of their respective nationals. As one treatise writer puts it, international agreements settling claims by nationals of one state against the government of another "are established international practice reflecting traditional international theory." L. Henkin, Foreign Affairs and the Constitution 262 (1972). Consistent with that principle, the United States has repeatedly exercised its sovereign authority to settle the claims of its nationals against foreign countries. Though those settlements have sometimes been made by treaty, there has also been a longstanding practice of settling such claims by executive agreement without the advice and consent of the Senate....

Crucial to our decision today is the conclusion that Congress has implicitly approved the practice of claim settlement by executive agreement....

...[T]he legislative history of the IEEPA further reveals that Congress has accepted the authority of the Executive to enter into settlement agreements. Though the IEEPA was enacted to provide for some limitation on the President's emergency powers, Congress stressed that "[n]othing in this act is intended...to interfere with the authority of the President to [block assets], or to impede the settlement of claims of U. S. citizens against foreign countries." S. Rep. No. 95-466, p. 6 (1977); 50 U. S. C. § 1706 (a)(1) (1976 ed., Supp. III).

In addition to congressional acquiescence in the President's power to settle claims, prior cases of this Court have also recognized that the President does have some measure of power to enter into executive agreements without obtaining the advice and consent of the Senate. *[The Court cites United States v. Pink, 315 U.S. 203 (1942) and Ozanic v. United States, 188 F.2d 228, 231 (2d Cir. 1951).]*

...[W]e do not believe that the President has

attempted to divest the federal courts of jurisdiction. Executive Order No. 12294 purports only to "suspend" the claims, not divest the federal court of "jurisdiction." As we read the Executive Order, those claims not within the jurisdiction of the Claims Tribunal will "revive" and become judicially enforceable in United States courts....

In light of all of the foregoing—the inferences to be drawn from the character of the legislation Congress has enacted in the area, such as the IEEPA and the Hostage Act, and from the history of acquiescence in executive claims settlement—we conclude that the President was authorized to suspend pending claims pursuant to Executive Order No. 12294....

Just as importantly, Congress has not disapproved of the action taken here. Though Congress has held hearings on the Iranian Agreement itself, Congress has not enacted legislation, or even passed a resolution, indicating its displeasure with the Agreement. Quite the contrary, the relevant Senate Committee has stated that the establishment of the Tribunal is "of vital importance to the United States." S. Rep. No. 97-71, p. 5 (1981). We are thus clearly not confronted with a situation in which Congress has in some way resisted the exercise of Presidential authority.

Finally, we re-emphasize the narrowness of our decision. We do not decide that the President possesses plenary power to settle claims, even as against foreign governmental entities....But where, as here, the settlement of claims has been determined to be a necessary incident to the resolution of a major foreign policy dispute between our country and another, and where, as here, we can conclude that Congress acquiesced in the President's action, we are not prepared to say that the President lacks the power to settle such claims.

. . .

JUSTICE STEVENS, concurring in part.

. . .

JUSTICE POWELL, concurring in part and dissenting in part.

. . .

D. THE WAR POWER

Congress is given specific power in the Constitution to declare war and to provide for the armed forces. Congress has declared war five times: the War of 1812 against England, the Mexican War in 1846, the Spanish-American War in 1898, World War I in 1917, and World War II in 1941.[5] Congress may also pass legislation to *authorize* military action against another nation, as it did with the Quasi-War against France in 1798. The Supreme Court recognized the constitutionality of undeclared wars, which the Court called limited, partial, imperfect, or "quasi" wars. Bas v. Tingy, 4 U.S. (4 Dall.) 36 (1800); Talbot v. Seeman, 5 U.S. (1 Cr.) 1 (1801). In the second case, Chief Justice Marshall recognized the broad constitutional authority of Congress to decide to initiate hostilities, whether by declaration or not: "The whole powers of war being, by the constitution of the United States, vested in congress, the acts of that body can alone be resorted to as our guides in this inquiry." 5 U.S. at 28.

Article I, Section 2, makes the President "Commander in Chief of the Army and Navy of the United States, and of the Militia of the several States, when called into the actual Service of the United States." Scholars disagree whether this merely confers a title (commander in chief) or implies additional powers for the President. Where the power begins and ends has mystified the courts. Youngstown Co. v. Sawyer, 343 U.S. 579, 641 (1952). The Justice Department has argued that the President is commander in chief not because he is necessarily skilled in the art of war but because it preserves civilian supremacy over the military. 10 Op. Att'y Gen. 74, 79 (1861).

The delegates at the Philadelphia Convention recognized an implied power for the President to "repel sudden attacks." When it was proposed that Congress be empowered to "make war," Charles Pinckney objected that legislative proceedings "were too slow" for the safety of the country in an emergency. Madison and Elbridge Gerry successfully inserted "declare" for "make," thereby "leaving to the Executive the power to repel sudden attacks" (see box on next page). The President's independent power was therefore limited to *defensive* actions. Offensive actions were reserved to Congress, to be decided through its deliberative processes. At the Pennsylvania ratifying convention, James Wilson expressed the prevailing sentiment that the system of checks and balances "will not hurry us into war; it is calculated to guard against it. It will not be in the power of a single man, or a single body of men, to involve us in such distress; for the important power of declaring war is vested in the legislature at large." 2 Elliot 528.

In the early decades, Presidents and their military advisers recognized that the decision to take the country to war lay with Congress. As President Jefferson told Congress on December 8, 1801, anything "beyond the line of defense" depended on legislative judgment. Fisher, Presidential War Power, at 13–25. Court decisions during this period also acknowledged the supremacy of Congress in authorizing war and setting boundaries for the President. Little v. Barreme, 6 U.S. (2 Cr.) 169, 179 (1804); United States v. Smith, 27 Fed. Cas. 1192, 1229–30 (C.C.N.Y. 1806)(No. 16,342).

When Congress delegates to the President its power to call forth the militia to suppress insurrections or to repel invasions, the decision to use force belongs solely to the President. In order to respond effectively to emergencies and avoid divided control, the power to respond is centered in the commander in chief. Martin v. Mott, 25 U.S. (12 Wheat.) 19 (1827). The Supreme Court stated in 1850 that the President as commander in chief "is authorized to direct the movements of the naval and military forces placed by law at his command, and to employ them in the manner he may deem most effectual to harass and conquer and subdue the

---

5. Actually, there were multiple declarations during the two world wars: two declarations for World War I (against Germany and Austria-Hungary) and six declarations for World War II (Japan, Germany, Italy, Bulgaria, Hungary, and Rumania).

The Framers Debating to "Declare War"

[*On August 17, 1787, the delegates at the Constitutional Convention debated giving Congress the power to "make war."*]

Mr Pinkney opposed the vesting this power in the Legislature. Its proceedings were too slow. It wd. meet but once a year. The Hs. of Reps. would be too numerous for such deliberations. The Senate would be the best depositary, being more acquainted with foreign affairs, and most capable of proper resolutions. If the States are equally represented in Senate, so as to give no advantage to large States, the power will notwithstanding be safe, as the small have their all at stake in such cases as well as the large States. It would be singular for one — authority to make war, and another peace.

Mr Butler. The Objections agst the Legislature lie in a great degree agst the Senate. He was for vesting the power in the President, who will have all the requisite qualities, and will not make war but when the Nation will support it.

Mr. M(adison) and Mr Gerry moved to insert *"declare,"* striking out *"make"* war; leaving to the Executive the power to repel sudden attacks.

Mr Sharman thought it stood very well. The Executive shd. be able to repel and not to commence war. "Make" better than "declare" the latter narrowing the power too much.

Mr Gerry never expected to hear in a republic a motion to empower the Executive alone to declare war.

Mr Elseworth. there is a material difference between the cases of making *war,* and making *peace.* It shd. be more easy to get out of war, than into it. War also is a simple and overt declaration. peace attended with intricate & secret negociations.

Mr. Mason was agst giving the power of war to the Executive, because not (safely) to be trusted with it; or to the Senate, because not so constructed as to be entitled to it. He was for clogging rather than facilitating war; but for facilitating peace. He preferred *"declare"* to *"make"*.

On the Motion to insert *declare* — in place of *Make,* (it was agreed to.)

N. H. no. Mas. abst. Cont. no.* Pa ay. Del. ay. Md. ay. Va. ay. N. C. ay. S. C. ay. Geo — ay. [Ayes — 7; noes — 2; absent — I.]

*On the remark by Mr. King that *"make"* war might be understood to "conduct" it which was an Executive function, Mr. Elseworth gave up his objection (and the vote of Cont was changed to — ay.)

---

enemy." Fleming v. Page, 50 U.S. (9 How.) 602, 614. Notice that the power to move forces is "placed by *law* at his command." How much does the President depend on Congress to provide the authorizations and appropriations necessary for military action? Under the Constitution, it is the responsibility of Congress to raise and support the military forces, to make military regulations, to provide for calling up the militia to suppress insurrections and to repel invasions, and to provide for the organization and disciplining of the militia. Art. I, § 8.

Article I, Section 8, assigns to Congress and the states different responsibilities over the militia (the part-time fighting force). Congress provides for organizing, arming, and disciplining the militia, while the states appoint the officers and retain authority for training the militia "according to the discipline prescribed by Congress." Congress may authorize the President to order members of the National Guard to active duty for purposes of training outside the United States, during time of peace, without either the consent of state governors or the declaration of a national emergency. Perpich v. Department of Defense, 496 U.S. 334 (1990).

Military Courts

The use of military courts during the Civil War in states where federal courts were open and operating had been curbed by *Ex parte Milligan* (page 290). The issue returned during and after World War II. A unanimous Court in 1942 held that aliens who entered the country with the intention of committing sabotage could be tried by military commission. Alien offenders against the law of war were not entitled to trial by jury before a civilian court. Ex parte Quirin,

317 U.S. 1 (1942). This exception did not allow governors to operate under martial law and substitute military for judicial trials of civilians who were not charged with violations of the law of war. Duncan v. Kahanamoku, 327 U.S. 304 (1946). Nor may the military arrest someone who has been honorably discharged and try that person before a court-martial. Prosecution must be conducted by civilian courts. Toth v. Quarles, 350 U.S. 11 (1955).

In 1969 the Supreme Court attempted to subject certain military questions to the jurisdiction of civilian courts. It held that to be under military jurisdiction, a crime must be "service connected." Otherwise, members of the military were entitled to a civilian trial, including the constitutional right to indictment by grand jury and trial by jury. O'Callahan v. Parker, 395 U.S. 258 (1969). So confusing was the service-connected doctrine that the Court abandoned it in 1987. Jurisdiction of a court-martial now depends solely on the accused's status as a member of the armed forces. The Court announced that Congress "has primary responsibility for the delicate task of balancing the rights of servicemen against the needs of the military." Solorio v. United States, 483 U.S. 435, 447 (1987).

War Powers Resolution

Presidential war powers have expanded because of several developments. The idea of "defensive war" was originally limited to protective actions against the borders of the United States or ships at sea. After World War II, defensive war assumed a much broader meaning. American bases were spread throughout the world; military commitments were added to defense pacts and treaties. Under these agreements, an attack on an ally could be interpreted as an attack on the United States. Presidents also used military force on numerous occasions to protect American lives and property, often stretching those objectives to achieve foreign policy or military objectives, as in the Dominican Republic in 1965, Cambodia in 1970, Grenada in 1983, and Panama in 1989. The bombing of Libya in 1986 was defended as an antiterrorist response.

The exercise of presidential war power by Lyndon Johnson and Richard Nixon provoked Congress to pass legislation in an effort to curb executive initiatives and promote collective efforts between Congress and the President. The War Powers Resolution of 1973 has three main provisions: presidential consultation with Congress, presidential reports to Congress, and congressional termination of military action. The purpose of the Resolution, as stated in § 2(a), is "to insure that the collective judgment" of both branches will apply to the introduction of U.S. forces into hostilities. Yet an examination of other sections, together with executive interpretations, judicial decisions, and congressional behavior, supplies ample evidence that collective judgment is by no means assured. WAR POWERS RESOLUTION.

The President is to consult with Congress "in every possible instance." This language obviously leaves considerable discretion to the President on both the form and timing of consultation. The framers of the Resolution did not expect the President to consult with 535 legislators, but whom should he contact? The leadership? The chairmen and ranking members of designated committees? Selected advisers? Congress has yet to select a group that can work with the President on an emergency basis. It is agreed that consultation means more than being briefed. Consultation means an opportunity to influence a pending decision. H. Rept. No. 287, 93d Cong., 1st Sess. 6–7 (1973).

The Resolution requires that the President, after introducing forces into hostilities, report to Congress within forty-eight hours. Precisely what conditions require a report is unclear from the legislation, and if a report is delayed, so are the mechanisms for congressional control. Under the Resolution, military action must terminate within sixty days after the report unless Congress (1) declares war or enacts a specific authorization, (2) extends by law the sixty-day period, or (3) is physically unable to meet as a result of an armed attack on the

United States. The President may extend the period by an additional thirty days if he determines that force is needed to protect and remove American troops.

Congress has two means of control: (1) a decision not to support the President during the sixty-to-ninety day period or (2) passage of a concurrent resolution at any time to direct the President to remove forces engaged in hostilities. The first mechanism has little meaning because the clock for the sixty-to-ninety day period begins to run only when the President reports under a very specific section: Section 4(a)(1). President Ford was the only President to report under that section — in the *Mayaguez* capture in 1975 — but by the time he reported the operation was over. Thus, the clock that was intended to limit the President never ticks.

The force of a concurrent resolution has been weakened by two developments. The executive branch takes the position that if the President has power to put men into combat, "that power could not be taken away by concurrent resolution because the power is constitutional in nature." "War Powers: A Test of Compliance," hearings before the House Committee on International Relations, 94th Cong., 1st Sess. 91 (1975). Executive officials argue that the President has a number of constitutional reasons for using military force without congressional approval, such as rescuing Americans living abroad, rescuing foreign nationals under certain circumstances, and protecting U.S. embassies and legations. Id. at 90–91.

Moreover, the Supreme Court in 1983 struck down all one-House and two-House (concurrent) resolutions as legislative vetoes that have no binding effect on the executive branch. INS v. Chadha, 462 U.S. 919. Still, passage of a concurrent resolution would mean that a majority of legislators in each House opposed the President's actions. It is difficult to conceive of a President persisting after that vote. Also, if Congress complied with *Chadha* by passing a joint resolution of disapproval, the President could veto that and Congress would now need a two-thirds majority in each House to stop a presidential war.

Members of Congress have gone to court to contest military initiatives by the President, but these efforts are regularly turned aside by federal judges on the ground that the determination of what constitutes hostilities or imminent hostilities is essentially a fact-finding matter reserved to Congress, not the courts. Crockett v. Reagan, 558 F.Supp. 893 (D.D.C. 1982), aff'd, 720 F.2d 1355 (D.C. Cir. 1983), cert. denied, 467 U.S. 1251 (1984).[6] When President Reagan sent ships into the Persian Gulf in 1987 without reporting to Congress under the War Powers Resolution, 110 members of the House of Representatives took the matter to court. Similar to the other cases, a district court declined to accept jurisdiction and dismissed the case. Lowry v. Reagan, 676 F.Supp. 333 (D.D.C. 1987).

The War Powers Resolution does not cover "paramilitary" (covert) operations. Beginning in 1974 and continuing through the Reagan years, Congress enacted a number of statutes and amendments to restrict covert actions. Part of the accommodation of a 1980 statute required the President to fully inform the House and Senate Intelligence Committees in a "timely fashion" of covert operations in foreign countries. Congress discovered in November 1986 that President Reagan had been sending arms to Iran for ten months, without any notification to Congress. As a result, the Senate passed legislation in 1988 to tighten the requirement so that notification could be delayed for no more than forty-eight hours, but the House of Representatives did not act on the bill. Legislation in 1991 clarified the reporting requirements for covert operations. Presidents are now expected to inform the intelligence committees in advance on almost all such operations. 105 Stat. 441–45 (1991).

---

6. See also Sanchez-Espinoza v. Reagan, 568 F.Supp. 596 (D.D.C. 1983), aff'd, Sanchez-Espinoza v. Reagan, 770 F.2d 202 (D.C. Cir. 1985) (Nicaragua); Conyers v. Reagan, 578 F.Supp. 324 (D.D.C. 1984), dismissed as moot, Conyers v. Reagan, 765 F.2d 1124 (D.C. Cir. 1985) (Grenada).

Actions by Bush and Clinton

The principle of "collective judgment" contemplated in § 2(a) of the War Powers Resolution was sorely tested in 1990, when President Bush claimed that he could mount an offensive operation against Iraq without any congressional authorization. After Iraq's invasion of Kuwait on August 2, 1990, Bush sent U.S. troops to Saudi Arabia to defend that country, deter further Iraqi aggression, and maintain access to Middle East oil. He also put together a 28-nation coalition aligned against Iraq and was successful in obtaining a number of United Nations resolutions condemning Iraq. In November, Bush announced a substantial increase in the number of U.S. troops, giving him the capability of acting offensively against Iraq. The Bush administration argued that it could shift from a defensive posture to an offensive operation without first obtaining authorization from Congress. Two lawsuits challenging the constitutionality of Bush's action were avoided by two federal courts. Ange v. Bush, 752 F.Supp. 509 (D.D.C. 1990); DELLUMS v. BUSH, 752 F.Supp. 1141 (D.D.C. 1990). The latter, however, rejected many of the arguments advanced by the Bush administration with regard to presidential war powers. Perhaps with an eye to that decision, on January 8, 1991, Bush asked Congress to pass legislation supporting military action in the Persian Gulf. After three days of intense debate, Congress passed the legislation. 105 Stat. 3 (1991). Because of the authorizing statute, a major constitutional crisis was averted.

In his eight years in office, President Clinton engaged in a remarkable amount of military activity without ever seeking authority from Congress. He sent cruise missiles into Iraq, conducted military operations in Somalia, threatened to invade Haiti, ordered air strikes in Bosnia, dispatched 20,000 ground troops to Bosnia, and sent cruise missiles into Sudan and Afghanistan. In each case he argued that he had no constitutional obligation other than to consult with members of Congress before taking military action. Like Bush in Iraq, he pointed to authority obtained from resolutions passed by the UN Security Council. In addition, he cited authorizing actions by the North Atlantic Council (NATO) for ordering air strikes in Bosnia. Louis Fisher, "Sidestepping Congress: Presidents Acting Under the UN and NATO," 47 Case Western Reserve L. Rev. 1237 (1997).

Clinton's major military initiative was going to war against Yugoslavia in 1999. Here there was no claim of acting in a defensive manner or to protect American lives. It was an unambiguous, unvarnished example of taking the country from a state of peace to a state of war, without ever asking Congress for authority. Congress took a number of votes, but none of them authorized what Clinton did and none of them prohibited him from doing what he did. An effort by a member of Congress to litigate the constitutionality of the war in Yugoslavia was unsuccessful. CAMPBELL v. CLINTON, 203 F.3d 19 (D.C. Cir. 2000). However, the decision by a federal appellate court revealed different views by judges on a member's standing to bring such a case and the competence of courts to decide questions of war.

The War Powers Resolution has been criticized ever since it was enacted. An effort by the House of Representatives in 1995 to repeal it failed on a vote of 201 to 217. 142 Cong. Rec. H5655-74 (daily ed. June 7, 1995). Much of the motivation behind that attempt reflected the belief that the Resolution interferes with the President's constitutional duties. However, some scholars support repeal because the Resolution delegates to the President powers that the Constitution lodges with Congress, especially the decision to initiate war.[7]

---

7. Louis Fisher & David Gray Adler, "The War Powers Resolution: Time to Say Goodbye," 113 Pol. Sci. Q. 1 (1998); Michael J. Glennon, "Too Far Apart: Repeal the War Powers Resolution," 50 U. Miami L. Rev. 17 (1995); Edward Keynes, "The War Powers Resolution: A Bad Idea Whose Time Has Come and Gone," 23 U. Toledo L. Rev. 343 (1992).

War Powers Resolution

After several years of hearings and floor action, Congress passed legislation in 1973 to provide a framework for "collective judgment" between Congress and the President in the exercise of the war power. Although President Nixon vetoed the bill, he was overridden by both Houses and the bill became law. It establishes procedures for the introduction of U.S. forces into combat and sets forth a number of important policies in Section 8. The legislation, P.L. 93-148, is found at 87 Stat. 555 (1973), 50 U.S.C. § 1541–48 (1994).

JOINT RESOLUTION

Concerning the war powers of Congress and the President.

Resolved by the Senate and House of Representatives of the United States of America in Congress assembled,

Short Title

SECTION 1. This joint resolution may be cited as the "War Powers Resolution".

Purpose and Policy

SEC. 2. (a) It is the purpose of this joint resolution to fulfill the intent of the framers of the Constitution of the United States and insure that the collective judgment of both the Congress and the President will apply to the introduction of United States Armed Forces into hostilities, or into situations where imminent involvement in hostilities is clearly indicated by the circumstances, and to the continued use of such forces in hostilities or in such situations.

(b) Under article I, section 8, of the Constitution, it is specifically provided that the Congress shall have the power to make all laws necessary and proper for carrying into execution, not only its own powers but also all other powers vested by the Constitution in the Government of the United States, or in any department or officer thereof.

(c) The constitutional powers of the President as Commander-in-Chief to introduce United States Armed Forces into hostilities, or into situations where imminent involvement in hostilities is clearly indicated by the circumstances, are exercised only pursuant to (1) a declaration of war, (2) specific statutory authorization, or (3) a national emergency created by attack upon the United States, its territories or possessions, or its armed forces.

Consultation

SEC. 3. The President in every possible instance shall consult with Congress before introducing United States Armed Forces into hostilities or into situations where imminent involvement in hostil-

ities is clearly indicated by the circumstances, and after every such introduction shall consult regularly with the Congress until United States Armed Forces are no longer engaged in hostilities or have been removed from such situations.

Reporting

SEC. 4. (a) In the absence of a declaration of war, in any case in which United States Armed Forces are introduced —

(1) into hostilities or into situations where imminent involvement in hostilities is clearly indicated by the circumstances;

(2) into the territory, airspace or waters of a foreign nation, while equipped for combat, except for deployments which relate solely to supply, replacement, repair, or training of such forces; or

(3) in numbers which substantially enlarge United States Armed Forces equipped for combat already located in a foreign nation;

the President shall submit within 48 hours to the Speaker of the House of Representatives and to the President pro tempore of the Senate a report, in writing, setting forth —

(A) the circumstances necessitating the introduction of United States Armed Forces;

(B) the constitutional and legislative authority under which such introduction took place; and

(C) the estimated scope and duration of the hostilities or involvement.

(b) The President shall provide such other information as the Congress may request in the fulfillment of its constitutional responsibilities with respect to committing the Nation to war and to the use of United States Armed Forces abroad.

(c) Whenever United States Armed Forces are introduced into hostilities or into any situation described in subsection (a) of this section, the President shall, so long as such armed forces continue to be engaged in such hostilities or situation, report to the Congress periodically on the status of such hostilities or situation as well as on the scope and duration of such hostilities or situation, but in no event shall he report to the Congress less often than once every six months.

Congressional Action

SEC. 5. (a) Each report submitted pursuant to section 4(a) (1) shall be transmitted to the Speaker of the House of Representatives and to the President pro tempore of the Senate on the same calendar day....

(b) Within sixty calendar days after a report is submitted or is required to be submitted pursuant to section 4(a) (1), whichever is earlier, the President shall terminate any use of United States Armed Forces with respect to which such report was submitted (or required to be submitted), unless the Congress (1) has declared war or has enacted a specific authorization for such use of United States Armed Forces, (2) has extended by law such sixty-day period, or (3) is physically unable to meet as a result of an armed attack upon the United States. Such sixty-day period shall be extended for not more than an additional thirty days if the President determines and certifies to the Congress in writing that unavoidable military necessity respecting the safety of United States Armed Forces requires the continued use of such armed forces in the course of bringing about a prompt removal of such forces.

(c) Notwithstanding subsection (b), at any time that United States Armed Forces are engaged in hostilities outside the territory of the United States, its possessions and territories without a declaration of war or specific statutory authorization, such forces shall be removed by the President if the Congress so directs by concurrent resolution.

Congressional Priority Procedures for Joint Resolution or Bill

SEC. 6 *[Provides for expedited consideration of a joint resolution or bill introduced pursuant to Section 5(b). Deadlines are established for committee and floor action, unless the House or Senate determine otherwise by yeas and nays. The objective is to complete action not later than the expiration of the sixty-day period.]*

Congressional Priority Procedures for Concurrent Resolution

SEC. 7. *[Provides for expedited consideration of a concurrent resolution introduced pursuant to Section 5(c). Deadlines are established for committee and floor action, unless the House or Senate determine otherwise by yeas and nays. The objective is to complete action within forty-eight days.]*

Interpretation of Joint Resolution

SEC. 8. (a) Authority to introduce United States Armed Forces into hostilities or into situations wherein involvement in hostilities is clearly indicated by the circumstances shall not be inferred—

(1) from any provision of law (whether or not in effect before the date of the enactment of this joint resolution), including any provision contained in any appropriation Act, unless such provision specifically authorizes the introduction of United States Armed Forces into hostilities or into such situations and states that it is intended to constitute specific statutory authorization within the meaning of this joint resolution; or

(2) from any treaty heretofore or hereafter ratified unless such treaty is implemented by legislation specifically authorizing the introduction of United States Armed Forces into hostilities or into such situations and stating that it is intended to constitute specific statutory authorization within the meaning of this joint resolution.

(b) Nothing in this joint resolution shall be construed to require any further specific statutory authorization to permit members of United States Armed Forces to participate jointly with members of the armed forces of one or more foreign countries in the headquarters operations of high-level military commands which were established prior to the date of enactment of this joint resolution and pursuant to the United Nations Charter or any treaty ratified by the United States prior to such date.

(c) For purposes of this joint resolution, the term "introduction of United States Armed Forces" includes the assignment of members of such armed forces to command, coordinate, participate in the movement of, or accompany the regular or irregular military forces of any foreign country or government when such military forces are engaged, or there exists an imminent threat that such forces will become engaged, in hostilities.

(d) Nothing in this joint resolution—

(1) is intended to alter the constitutional authority of the Congress or of the President, or the provisions of existing treaties; or

(2) shall be construed as granting any authority to the President with respect to the introduction of United States Armed Forces into hostilities or into situations wherein involvement in hostilities is clearly indicated by the circumstances which authority he would not have had in the absence of this joint resolution.

Separability Clause

SEC. 9. If any provision of this joint resolution or the application thereof to any person or circumstance is held invalid, the remainder of the joint resolution and the application of such pro-vision to any other person or circumstance shall not be affected thereby.

Effective Date

SEC. 10. This joint resolution shall take effect on the date of its enactment.

Dellums v. Bush

752 F.Supp. 1141 (D.D.C. 1990)

After President Bush introduced U.S. troops into the Persian Gulf to create the potential for taking offensive action against Iraq, Congressman Ronald Dellums and fifty-three other members of Congress brought suit requesting an injunction to prevent President Bush from going to war without first securing a declaration of war or other explicit congressional authorization. Although the district court declined to issue the injunction, it issued a significant opinion rejecting many of the theories of presidential power advanced by the administration.

HAROLD H. GREENE, District Judge.

This is a lawsuit by a number of members of Congress who request an injunction directed to the President of the United States to prevent him from initiating an offensive attack against Iraq without first securing a declaration of war or other explicit congressional authorization for such action.

I

The factual background is, briefly, as follows. On August 2, 1990, Iraq invaded the neighboring country of Kuwait. President George Bush almost immediately sent United States military forces to the Persian Gulf area to deter Iraqi aggression and to preserve the integrity of Saudi Arabia. The United States, generally by presidential order and at times with congressional concurrence, also took other steps, including a blockade of Iraq, which were approved by the United Nations Security Council, and participated in by a great many other nations.

On November 8, 1990, President Bush announced a substantial increase in the Persian Gulf military deployment, raising the troop level significantly above the 230,000 then present in the area. At the same time, the President stated that the objective was to provide "an adequate *offensive* military option" should that be necessary to achieve such goals as the withdrawal of Iraqi forces from Kuwait. Secretary of Defense Richard Cheney likewise referred to the ability of the additional military forces "to conduct *offensive* military operations."

The House of Representatives and the Senate have in various ways expressed their support for the President's past and present actions in the Persian Gulf. However, the Congress was not asked for, and it did not take, action pursuant to Article I, Section 8, Clause 11 of the Constitution "to declare war" on Iraq. On November 19, 1990, the congressional plaintiffs brought this action, which proceeds on the premise that the initiation of offensive United States military action is imminent, that such action would be unlawful in the absence of a declaration of war by the Congress, and that a war without concurrence by the Congress would deprive the congressional plaintiffs of the voice to which they are entitled under the Constitution. The Department of Justice, acting on behalf of the President, is opposing the motion for preliminary injunction, and it has also moved to dismiss. Plaintiffs thereafter moved for summary judgment.

The Department raises a number of defenses to the lawsuit—most particularly that the complaint presents a non-justiciable political question, that plaintiffs lack standing to maintain the action, that their claim violates established canons of equity jurisprudence, and that the issue of the proper allocation of the war making powers between the branches is not ripe for decision. These will now be considered seriatim.

II POLITICAL QUESTION

It is appropriate first to sketch out briefly the constitutional and legal framework in which the current controversy arises. Article, I, Section 8, Clause 11 of the Constitution grants to the Congress the power "To declare War." To the extent that this unambiguous direction requires construction or explanation, it is provided by the framers' comments that they felt it to be unwise to entrust the momentous power to involve the nation in a war to the President alone; Jefferson explained that he desired "an effectual check to the Dog of war"; James Wilson similarly expressed the expectation that this system would guard against hostilities being initiated by a single man. Even Abraham Lincoln, while a Congressman, said more than half a century later that *"no one man* should hold the power of bringing" war upon us.

The congressional power to declare war does not stand alone, however, but it is accompanied by powers granted to the President. Article II, Section 1, Clause 1 and Section 2 provide that "[t]he executive powers shall be vested in a President of the United States of America," and that "[t]he President shall be Commander in Chief of the Army and Navy...."

It is the position of the Department of Justice on behalf of the President that the simultaneous existence of all these provisions renders it impossible to isolate the war-declaring power. The Department further argues that the design of the Constitution is to have the various war- and military-related provisions construed and acting together, and that their harmonization is a political rather than a legal question. In short, the Department relies on the political question doctrine.

That doctrine is premised both upon the separation of powers and the inherent limits of judicial abilities.... In relation to the issues involved in this case, the Department of Justice expands on its basic theme, contending that by their very nature the determination whether certain types of military actions require a declaration of war is not justiciable, but depends instead upon delicate judgments by the political branches. On that view, the question whether an offensive action taken by American armed forces constitutes an act of war (to be initiated by a declaration of war) or an "offensive military attack" (presumably undertaken by the President in his capacity as commander-in-chief) is not one of objective fact but involves an exercise of judgment based upon all the vagaries of foreign affairs and national security.... Indeed, the Department contends that there are no judicially discoverable and manageable standards to apply....

This claim on behalf of the Executive is far too sweeping to be accepted by the courts. If the Executive had the sole power to determine that any particular offensive military operation, no matter

how vast, does not constitute war-making but only an offensive military attack, the congressional power to declare war will be at the mercy of a semantic decision by the Executive. Such an "interpretation" would evade the plain language of the Constitution, and it cannot stand.

. . .

...[T]he Department goes on the suggest that the issue in this case is still political rather than legal, because in order to resolve the dispute the Court would have to inject itself into foreign affairs, a subject which the Constitution commits to the political branches. That argument, too, must fail.

While the Constitution grants to the political branches, and in particular to the Executive, responsibility for conducting the nation's foreign affairs, it does not follow that the judicial power is excluded from the resolution of cases merely because they may touch upon such affairs. The court must instead look at "the particular question posed" in the case. *Baker v. Carr,* 369 U.S. at 211.... In fact, courts are routinely deciding cases that touch upon or even have a substantial impact on foreign and defense policy....

. . .

...[T]he Court has no hesitation in concluding that an offensive entry into Iraq by several hundred thousand United States servicemen under the conditions described above could be described as a "war" within the meaning of Article I, Section 8, Clause 11, of the Constitution. To put it another way: the Court is not prepared to read out of the Constitution the clause granting to the Congress, and to it alone, the authority "to declare war."

III STANDING

The Department of Justice argues next that the plaintiffs lack "standing" to pursue this action.

. . .

With close to 400,000 United States troops stationed in Saudi Arabia, with all troop rotation and leave provisions suspended, and with the President having acted vigorously on his own as well as through the Secretary of State to obtain from the United Nations Security Council a resolution authorizing the use of all available means to remove Iraqi forces from Kuwait, including the use of force, it is disingenuous for the Department to characterize plaintiffs' allegations as to the imminence of the threat of offensive military action for standing purposes as "remote and conjectural,"....For these reasons, the Court concludes that the plaintiffs have adequately alleged a threat of injury in fact necessary to support standing.

IV REMEDIAL DISCRETION

Another issue raised by the Department which must be addressed briefly is the application to this case of the doctrine of "remedial" discretion developed by the Court of Appeals for this Circuit. *[i.e., courts will dismiss a case brought by a congressional plaintiff who could obtain substantial relief from fellow legislators through the enactment, repeal, or amendment of a statute.]*

. . .

The plaintiffs in this case do not have a remedy available from their fellow legislators. While action remains open to them which would make the issues involved more concrete, and hence make the matter ripe for review by the Court, these actions would not remedy the threatened harm plaintiffs assert. A joint resolution counselling the President to refrain from attacking Iraq without a congressional declaration of war would not be likely to stop the President from initiating such military action if he is persuaded that the Constitution affirmatively gives him the power to act otherwise.

Plaintiffs in the instant case, therefore, cannot gain "substantial relief" by persuasion of their colleagues alone. The "remedies" of cutting off funding to the military or impeaching the President are not available to these plaintiffs either politically or practically. Additionally, these "remedies" would not afford the relief sought by the plaintiffs — which is the guarantee that they will have the opportunity to debate and vote on the wisdom of initiating a military attack against Iraq before the United States military becomes embroiled in belligerency with that nation.

V RIPENESS

Although, as discussed above, the Court rejects several of defendant's objections to the maintenance of this lawsuit, and concludes that, in principle, an injunction may issue at the request of Members of Congress to prevent the conduct of a war which is about to be carried on without congressional authorization, it does not follow that these plaintiffs are entitled to relief at this junc-

ture. For the plaintiffs are met with a significant obstacle to such relief: the doctrine of ripeness.

. . .

In the context of this case, there are two aspects to ripeness, which the Court will now explore.

A. *Actions By the Congress*

No one knows the position of the Legislative Branch on the issue of war or peace with Iraq; certainly no one, including this Court, is able to ascertain the congressional position on that issue on the basis of this lawsuit brought by fifty-three members of the House of Representatives and one member of the U.S. Senate. It would be both premature and presumptuous for the Court to render a decision on the issue of whether a declaration of war is required at this time or in the near future when the Congress itself has provided no indication whether it deems such a declaration either necessary, on the one hand, or imprudent, on the other.

. . .

...In short, unless the Congress as a whole, or by a majority, is heard from, the controversy here cannot be deemed ripe; it is only if the majority of the Congress seeks relief from an infringement on its constitutional war-declaration power that it may be entitled to receive it.

B. *Actions Taken By the Executive*

The second half of the ripeness issue involves the question whether the Executive Branch of government is so clearly committed to immediate military operations that may be equated with a "war" within the meaning of Article I, Section 8, Clause 11, of the Constitution that a judicial decision may properly be rendered regarding the application of that constitutional provision to the current situation.

Plaintiffs assert that the matter is currently ripe for judicial action because the President himself has stated that the present troop build-up is to provide an adequate offensive military option in the area. His successful effort to secure passage of United Nations Resolution 678, which authorizes the use of "all available means" to oust Iraqi forces remaining in Kuwait after January 15, 1991, is said to be an additional fact pointing toward the Executive's intention to initiate military hostilities against Iraq in the near future.

The Department of Justice, on the other hand, points to statements of the President that the troops already in Saudi Arabia are a peacekeeping force to prove that the President might not initiate more offensive military actions. In addition, and more realistically, it is possible that the meetings set for later this month and next between President Bush and the Foreign Minister of Iraq, Tariq Aziz, in Washington, and Secretary of State James Baker and Saddam Hussein in Baghdad, may result in a diplomatic solution to the present situation, and in any event under the U.N. Security Council resolution there will not be resort to force before January 15, 1991.

. . .

...[A]n injunction will be issued only if, on both of the aspects of the doctrine discussed above, the Court could find that the controversy is ripe for judicial decision. That situation does not, or at least not yet, prevail, and plaintiffs' request for a preliminary injunction will therefore not be granted.

For the reasons stated, it is this 13th day of December, 1990

ORDERED that plaintiffs' motion for preliminary injunction be and it is hereby denied.

Campbell v. Clinton

203 F.3d 19 (D.C. Cir. 2000)*

Congressman Tom Campbell, joined by several other members of Congress, filed a lawsuit seeking a declaration that President Clinton violated the War Powers Clause of the Constitution and the War Powers Resolution by committing U.S. forces to hostilities in Yugoslavia without obtaining authority from Congress. After a district court granted the President's motion to dismiss, Campbell brought this appeal. The D.C. circuit considered several issues, including Campbell's standing to bring the suit and the competence of courts to decide questions of war.

SILBERMAN, Circuit Judge:

A number of congressmen, led by Tom Campbell of California, filed suit claiming that the President violated the War Powers Resolution and the War Powers Clause of the Constitution by directing U.S. forces' participation in the recent NATO campaign in Yugoslavia. The district court dismissed for lack of standing. We agree with the district court and therefore affirm.

I.

On March 24, 1999, President Clinton announced the commencement of NATO air and cruise missile attacks on Yugoslav targets. Two days later he submitted to Congress a report, "consistent with the War Powers Resolution," detailing the circumstances necessitating the use of armed forces, the deployment's scope and expected duration, and asserting that he had "taken these actions pursuant to [his] authority...as Commander in Chief and Chief Executive." On April 28, Congress voted on four resolutions re-

---

* The text for this case was obtained in electronic form from Westlaw and is reproduced by permission of the West Group.

lated to the Yugoslav conflict: It voted down a declaration of war 427 to 2 and an "authorization" of the air strikes 213 to 213, but it also voted against requiring the President to immediately end U.S. participation in the NATO operation and voted to fund that involvement. The conflict between NATO and Yugoslavia continued for 79 days, ending on June 10 with Yugoslavia's agreement to withdraw its forces from Kosovo and allow deployment of a NATO-led peacekeeping force....

II.

The government does not respond to appellants' claim on the merits. Instead the government challenges the jurisdiction of the federal courts to adjudicate this claim on three separate grounds: the case is moot; appellants lack standing, as the district court concluded; and the case is nonjusticiable. Since we agree with the district court that the congressmen lack standing it is not necessary to decide whether there are other jurisdictional defects.

The question whether congressmen have standing in federal court to challenge the lawfulness of actions of the executive was answered, at least in large part, in the Supreme Court's recent

decision in *Raines v. Byrd*, 521 U.S. 811...
(1997). *Raines* involved a constitutional challenge
to the President's authority under the short-lived
Line Item Veto Act....the Court held that petitioners in the case lacked "legislative standing" to
challenge the Act. The Court noted that petitioners already possessed an adequate political remedy, since they could vote to have the Line Item
Veto Act repealed, or to provide individual spending bills with a statutory exemption....

Thereafter in *Chenoweth v. Clinton*, 181 F.3d
112, 115 (D.C.Cir.1999), emphasizing the separation-of-powers problems inherent in legislative
standing, we held that congressmen had no standing to challenge the President's introduction of a
program through executive order rather than
statute. As in *Raines*, appellants contended that
the President's action inflicted an institutional injury upon Congress, in this case by circumventing
its legislative authority, but, we said,

"It is uncontested that the Congress could terminate the [contested program] were a sufficient
number in each House so inclined. Because the
parties' dispute is therefore fully susceptible to political resolution, we would [under circuit prece-
dent] dismiss the complaint to avoid 'meddl[ing]
in the internal affairs of the legislative branch.'
Applying *Raines*, we would reach the same conclusion...."

There remains, however, a soft spot in the legal
barrier against congressional legal challenges to
executive action, and it is a soft spot that appellants sought to penetrate. [*Here Judge Silberman
analyzes a 1939 decision by the Supreme Court,
Coleman v. Miller, and the Court's interpretation
of that decision in Raines as to whether an executive action "nullified" a legislator's vote.*]

It is, to be sure, not readily apparent what the
Supreme Court meant by that word. It would
seem the Court used nullify to mean treating a
vote that did not pass as if it had, or vice versa.
The "nullification" alleged in this case therefore
differs from *Coleman* in a significant respect. In
that case state officials endorsed a defeated ratification, treating it as approved, while the President
here did not claim to be acting pursuant to the defeated declaration of war or a statutory authorization, but instead "pursuant to [his] constitutional authority to conduct U.S. foreign relations
and as Commander-in-Chief and Chief Executive."...The Court did not suggest in *Raines* that
the President "nullifies" a congressional vote and
thus legislators have standing whenever the gov-

ernment does something Congress voted against,
still less that congressmen would have standing
anytime a President allegedly acts in excess of
statutory authority. As the government correctly
observes, appellants' statutory argument, although cast in terms of the nullification of a recent
vote, essentially is that the President violated the
quarter-century old War Powers Resolution. Similarly, their constitutional argument is that the
President has acted illegally—in excess of his authority—because he waged war in the constitutional sense without a congressional delegation.
Neither claim is analogous to a *Coleman* nullification.

We think the key to understanding the Court's
treatment of *Coleman* and its use of the word nullification is its implicit recognition that a ratification vote on a constitutional amendment is an unusual situation. It is not at all clear whether once
the amendment was "deemed ratified," see
Raines, 521 U.S. at 822, the Kansas Senate could
have done anything to reverse that position. We
think that must be what the Supreme Court implied when it said the *Raines* plaintiffs could not
allege that the "[Line Item Veto Act] would nullify their votes in the future," and that, after all, a
majority of senators and congressmen could always repeal the Line Item Veto Act....The *Coleman* senators, by contrast, may well have been
powerless to rescind a ratification of a constitutional amendment that they claimed had been defeated. In other words, they had no legislative
remedy. Under that reading—which we think explains the very narrow possible *Coleman* exception to *Raines*—appellants fail because they continued, after the votes, to enjoy ample legislative
power to have stopped prosecution of the "war."

In this case, Congress certainly could have
passed a law forbidding the use of U.S. forces in
the Yugoslav campaign; indeed, there was a measure—albeit only a concurrent resolution—introduced to require the President to withdraw U.S.
troops. Unfortunately, however, for those congressmen who, like appellants, desired an end to
U.S. involvement in Yugoslavia, this measure was
defeated by a 139 to 290 vote. Of course, Congress always retains appropriations authority and
could have cut off funds for the American role in
the conflict. Again there was an effort to do so but
it failed; appropriations were authorized. And
there always remains the possibility of impeachment should a President act in disregard of Congress' authority on these matters.

· · ·

Accordingly, the district court is affirmed; appellants lack standing.

SILBERMAN, Circuit Judge, concurring:

Appellants argued that we should consider in our standing analysis that if congressmen lack standing only military personnel might be able to challenge a President's arguably unlawful use of force, and it would be undesirable to put the armed forces in such a position. Although that is not a consideration that bears on standing, ... that argument leads me to observe that, in my view, no one is able to bring this challenge because the two claims are not justiciable. We lack "judicially discoverable and manageable standards" for addressing them, and the War Powers Clause claim implicates the political question doctrine. See *Baker v. Carr*, 369 U.S. 186, 217 (1962).

Prior litigation under the WPR has turned on the threshold test whether U.S. forces are engaged in hostilities or are in imminent danger of hostilities. But the question posed by appellants— whether the President's refusal to discontinue American activities in Yugoslavia violates the WPR— necessarily depends on the statute having been triggered in the first place. It has been held that the statutory threshold standard is not precise enough and too obviously calls for a political judgment to be one suitable for judicial determinations.... I think that is correct....

Nor is the constitutional claim justiciable. Appellants contend this case is governed by *Mitchell v. Laird*, 488 F.2d 611, 614 (D.C.Cir.1973), where we said that "[t]here would be no insuperable difficulty in a court determining whether" the Vietnam conflict constituted a war in the Constitutional sense. *See also Dellums v. Bush*, 752 F.Supp. 1141, 1146 (D.D.C.1990) ("[T]he Court has no hesitation in concluding that an offensive entry into Iraq by several hundred thousand United States servicemen ... could be described as a 'war' within the meaning ... of the Constitution."). But a careful reading of both cases reveals that the language upon which appellants rely is only dicta....

RANDOLPH, Circuit Judge, concurring in the judgment:

The majority opinion [*by Silberman and Tatel, on standing*] does not, I believe, correctly analyze plaintiffs' standing to sue. It misconceives the holding of *Raines v. Byrd* ... and conflicts with the law of this circuit. I believe plaintiffs lack standing, at least to litigate their constitutional claim, but for reasons the majority opinion neglects. I also believe that the case is moot, an optional disposition of the appeal. The serious questions about the constitutionality of the War Powers Resolution must therefore be put off for still another day.

I.[B] STANDING

The majority opinion analyzes standing rather differently than I do. It says plaintiffs lack standing to pursue their statutory claim because "they continued, after the votes, to enjoy ample legislative power to have stopped prosecution of the 'war.' " ...

The majority has, I believe, confused the right to vote in the future with the nullification of a vote in the past, a distinction *Raines* clearly made. *See* 521 U.S. at 824. To say that your vote was not nullified because you can vote for other legislation in the future is like saying you did not lose yesterday's battle because you can fight again tomorrow. The Supreme Court did not engage in such illogic....

. . .

TATEL, Circuit Judge, concurring:

Although I agree with Judge Silberman that *Raines v. Byrd* ... as interpreted by this court in *Chenoweth v. Clinton* ... deprives plaintiffs of standing to bring this action, I do not share his view that the case poses a nonjusticiable political question.... In my view, were this case brought by plaintiffs with standing, we could determine whether the President, in undertaking the air campaign in Yugoslavia, exceeded his authority under the Constitution or the War Powers Resolution.

To begin with, I do not agree that courts lack judicially discoverable and manageable standards for "determining the existence of a 'war.' " ... Whether the military activity in Yugoslavia amounted to "war" within the meaning of the Declare War Clause ... is no more standardless than any other question regarding the constitutionality of government action. Precisely what police conduct violates the Fourth Amendment guarantee "against unreasonable searches and seizures?" When does government action amount to "an establishment of religion" prohibited by the First Amendment? When is an election district so bizarrely shaped as to violate the Fourteenth Amendment guarantee of "equal protection of the laws?" Because such constitutional terms are not self-defining, standards for answering these questions have evolved, as legal standards always do, through years of judicial decisionmaking. Courts have proven no less capable of developing standards to resolve war powers challenges.

Since the earliest years of the nation, courts have not hesitated to determine when military action constitutes "war." In *Bas v. Tingy*, 4 U.S. (4 Dall.) 37 (1800), the Supreme Court had to decide whether hostilities between France and the United States amounted to a state of war in order to resolve disputes over captured ships....

More recent cases have also recognized the competence of courts to determine whether a state of war exists. Responding to a challenge to the constitutionality of the Vietnam War, this circuit confronted "the critical question ... whether the hostilities in Indo-China constitute *in the Constitutional sense* a 'war,' both within and beyond the meaning of that term in Article I, Section 8, Clause 11." *Mitchell v. Laird*, 488 F.2d 611, 614 (D.C.Cir.1973) (emphasis added). The court found "no insuperable difficulty in a court deter-

mining whether," given the extent of the hostilities, "there has been a war in Indo-China." ... courts are competent to adjudge the existence of war and the allocation of war powers between the President and Congress....

Nor is the question nonjusticiable because the President, as Commander in Chief, possesses emergency authority to use military force to defend the nation from attack without obtaining prior congressional approval. Judge Silberman's suggestion notwithstanding, ... President Clinton does not claim that the air campaign was necessary to protect the nation from imminent attack. In his report to Congress, the President explained that the military action was "in response to the FRY government's continued campaign of violence and repression against the ethnic Albanian population in Kosovo." ... [H]e never claimed that an emergency required him to act without congressional authorization; in fact, the Kosovo issue had been festering for years....

E. RIGHTS OF CITIZENSHIP

All three branches have been active in determining questions of citizenship and aliens. Article I, Section 8, Clause 4, gives Congress the power to establish a "uniform Rule of Naturalization." However, Congress has conferred jurisdiction upon the courts to naturalize aliens as citizens, and the executive branch has been active in asserting its notion of prerogatives concerning both citizenship and aliens.

Part of the controversy concerns the ability of aliens to obtain citizenship if they oppose war. In 1929 the Supreme Court held that the government was entitled to deny a woman an application for naturalization because, as a pacifist, she answered that she "would not take up arms personally" to defend the country. The Court said that the duty of citizens to defend the country against enemies was a "fundamental principle" of the Constitution. United States v. Schwimmer, 279 U.S. 644, 650 (1929). In one of his famous dissents, Justice Holmes noted that the woman was more than fifty years of age and could not bear arms if she wanted to. He added:

> ... [I]f there is any principle of the Constitution that more imperatively calls for attachment than any other it is the principle of free thought—not free thought for those who agree with us but freedom for the thought that we hate....I would suggest that the Quakers have done their share to make the country what it is, that many citizens agree with the applicant's belief and that I had not supposed hitherto that we regretted our inability to expel them because they believe more than some of us do in the teachings of the Sermon on the Mount.

Two years later, the Court again upheld the government's action in denying an application for citizenship from someone who would not promise to bear arms in defense of the United States unless he believed the war to be morally justified. He based his belief not on pacifism but on the principles of Christianity. The Court acknowledged that Congress could, as it had, relieve the conscientious objector from the obligation to bear arms, but this policy applied only to citizens, not to aliens seeking citizenship. The dissenters in this 5 to 4 decision argued that Congress had never expressly required that aliens promise to bear arms as a condition of obtaining citizenship and that courts should not act on the basis of implications. United States v. Macintosh, 283 U.S. 605, 623–24 (1931); United States v. Bland, 283 U.S. 636 (1931).

These decisions were shaken and finally overturned by cases in the 1940s. The first concerned someone who had been granted citizenship in 1927 but the government began proceedings in 1939 to cancel the citizenship, claiming that during the five years before naturalization the man had been affiliated with certain Communist organizations. The government charged that he had obtained citizenship by "fraud." The Court held that it was not enough for the government to prevail on a bare preponderance of the evidence. The evidence had to be clear, unequivocal, and convincing. The government could not sustain this higher burden. Schneiderman v. United States, 320 U.S. 118 (1943).

In 1946 the Court overruled its earlier decisions in *Schwimmer, Macintosh,* and *Bland.* It held that an alien who is willing to take the oath of allegiance and to serve in the army as a noncombatant but who, because of religious beliefs, is unwilling to bear arms in defense of the country, may be admitted nonetheless to citizenship. The Court pointed out that many citizens — nurses, engineers, doctors, chaplains, litter bearers — contribute to the war effort without bearing arms. Girouard v. United States, 328 U.S. 61, 64 (1946).

In 1958 the Court decided whether a native-born American could be stripped of his citizenship because he had been convicted by court-martial for wartime desertion. The Army had sentenced him to three years of hard labor, forfeited his pay and allowances, and gave him a dishonorable discharge. When he later applied for a passport, it was denied because a congressional statute required loss of citizenship for wartime desertion or a dishonorable discharge. The Court held that a person must voluntarily renounce or abandon citizenship. Citizenship was not "a license that expires upon misbehavior." Trop v. Dulles, 356 U.S. 86, 92 (1958). Denationalization violated the Eighth Amendment because it resulted in "the total destruction of the individual's status in organized society. It is a form of punishment more primitive than torture, for it destroys for the individual the political existence that was centuries in the development." Id. at 101.

The Court divided 5 to 4 on this case and split by the same margin in a companion case that upheld the power of Congress to strip someone of citizenship if he or she votes in a foreign political election. The Court deferred to Congress on this occasion because of foreign policy considerations and the possibility of serious international embarrassment. Perez v. Brownell, 356 U.S. 44 (1958). The dissenters maintained that citizenship "*is* man's basic right for it is nothing less than the right to have rights. Remove this priceless possession and there remains a stateless person, disgraced and degraded in the eyes of his countrymen."

Another 5–4 decision in 1963 held that Congress could not use expatriation as punishment for draft evaders without providing for the procedural safeguards in the Fifth and Sixth Amendments: indictment, notice, confrontation, jury trial, assistance of counsel, and compulsory process for obtaining witnesses. Kennedy v. Mendoza-Martinez, 372 U.S. 144 (1963). Obviously, this decision was inconsistent with the result five years before in *Perez,* which permitted expatriation without criminal trial, and the Court was parting company from earlier decisions that had ruled expatriation unconstitutional under the Eighth Amendment. Another ruling in 1964 struck down a statutory provision because it favored native-born citizens over naturalized citizens. Schneider v. Rusk, 377 U.S. 163 (1964).

The confusion continued in 1967 with a 5–4 decision overruling *Perez.* This brought the Court back to where it was in 1958: citizenship could be renounced only voluntarily. Even acting under the foreign affairs power, Congress has no power to divest a person of his or her citizenship. Afroyim v. Rusk, 387 U.S. 253 (1967). However, this decision and *Schneider* were "distinguished" in 1971 when the Court allowed citizenship to be lost under certain conditions. If someone acquires citizenship by being born abroad to parents, one of whom is an

American citizen, citizenship can be retained only by satisfying residency requirements established by Congress. Rogers v. Bellei, 401 U.S. 815 (1971).[8]

CONCLUSIONS

Much of the debate on the allocation of foreign affairs powers between Congress and the President revolves around two competing models. Under the *Curtiss-Wright* model, the President is blessed with extraconstitutional, inherent powers. The necessities of international affairs and diplomacy make the President the dominant figure. On the other hand, the *Steel Seizure Case* assumes that Congress is the basic lawmaker in both domestic and foreign affairs. Inherent powers are denied, although congressional inertia, silence, or acquiescence may invite independent and conclusive actions by the executive.

The lesson to be drawn from either model is that Congress has ample powers to legislate for emergencies, at home or abroad, but those powers must be exercised. Congressional influence depends on its willingness to act and to take responsibility. Presidential influence, at least for long-term commitments, cannot survive on assertions of inherent power. The President needs the support and understanding of both Congress and the public.

SELECTED READINGS

ADLER, DAVID GRAY, AND LARRY N. GEORGE, eds. The Constitution and the Conduct of American Foreign Policy. Lawrence, Kans.: University Press of Kansas, 1996.

BOROSAGE, ROBERT L. "Para-Legal Authority and Its Perils." 40 Law and Contemporary Problems 166 (1976).

COHEN, RICHARD. "Self-Executing Executive Agreements: A Separation of Powers Problem." 24 Buffalo Law Review 137 (1974).

EDGAR, HAROLD, AND BENNO C. SCHMIDT, JR. "Curtiss-Wright Comes Home: Executive Power and National Security Secrecy." 21 Harvard Civil Rights — Civil Liberties Law Review 349 (1986).

ELY, JOHN HART. War and Responsibility: Constitutional Lessons of Vietnam and Its Aftermath. Princeton: Princeton University Press, 1993.

FARBER, DANIEL A. "National Security, the Right to Travel, and the Courts." 1981 Supreme Court Review 263.

FISHER, LOUIS. Presidential War Power. Lawrence, Kans.: University Press of Kansas, 1995.

FRANCK, THOMAS M., AND EDWARD WEISBAND. Foreign Policy by Congress. New York: Oxford University Press, 1979.

———— and Michael J. Glennon. Foreign Relations and National Security Law. St. Paul, Minn.: West, 1987.

GLENNON, MICHAEL J. Constitutional Diplomacy. Princeton: Princeton University Press, 1990.

HENKIN, LOUIS. Foreign Affairs and the Constitution. New York: Oxford University Press, 1996.

HURTGEN, JAMES R. "The Case for Presidential Prerogative." 7 University of Toledo Law Review 59 (1975).

KOH, HAROLD HONGJU. The National Security Constitution. New Haven: Yale University Press, 1990.

LOFGREN, CHARLES A. "U.S. v. Curtiss-Wright Export Corporation: An Historical Reassessment." 83 Yale Law Journal 1 (1973).

————. "War-Making Under the Constitution: The Original Understanding." 81 Yale Law Journal 672 (1972).

MARCUS, MAEVA. Truman and the Steel Seizure Case: The Limits of Presidential Power. New York: Columbia University Press, 1977.

MURPHY, JOHN F. "Treaties and International Agreements Other Than Treaties: Constitutional Allocation of Power and Responsibility

---

8. See also Fedorenko v. United States, 449 U.S. 490 (1981); John P. Roche, "The Expatriation Cases: "Breathes There the Man, With Soul So Dead...'?" 1963 Sup. Ct. Rev. 325; P. Allan Dionisopoulos, "Afroyim v. Rusk: The Evolution, Uncertainty and Implications of a Constitutional Principle," 55 Minn. L. Rev. 235 (1970).

Among the President, the House of Representatives, and the Senate." 23 University of Kansas Law Review 221 (1975).

O'DONNELL, THOMAS A. "Illumination or Elimination of the "Zone of Twilight'? Congressional Acquiescence and Presidential Authority in Foreign Affairs." 51 Cincinnati Law Review 95 (1982).

OHLY, D. CHRISTOPHER. "Advice and Consent: International Executive Claims Settlement Agreements." 5 Californian Western International Law Journal 271 (1975).

PAUST, JORDAN J. "Is the President Bound by the Supreme Law of the Land?—Foreign Affairs and National Security Reexamined." 9 Hastings Constitutional Law Quarterly 719 (1982).

REVELEY, W. TAYLOR, III. War Powers of the President and Congress. Charlottesville: University Press of Virginia, 1981.

ROVINE, ARTHUR W. "Separation of Powers and International Executive Agreements." 52 Indiana Law Review 297 (1977).

SILVERSTEIN, GORDON. Imbalance of Powers: Constitutional Interpretation and the Making of American Foreign Policy. New York: Oxford University Press, 1997.

SOFAER, ABRAHAM D. War, Foreign Affairs and Constitutional Power: The Origins. Cambridge, Mass.: Ballinger Publishing, 1976.

STEVENS, CHARLES J. "The Use and Control of Executive Agreements: Recent Congressional Initiatives." 20 Orbis 905 (1977).

8

Federal-State Relations

Federalism divides political power and sovereignty between the national government and the states. As a broad principle it cuts across almost every constitutional issue, including law enforcement, civil liberties, civil rights, sex discrimination, voting rights, reapportionment, privacy, and welfare payments. This chapter focuses on six topics: the principle of federalism, state immunity against suits, the Commerce Clause, the spending and taxing power, the doctrines of preemption and abstention, and the application of the Bill of Rights to the states.

Under Chief Justice Marshall, the Supreme Court gave broad support to congressional efforts to exercise its commerce powers. Later, the Court attempted to restrain Congress, but a variety of judicial doctrines did little more than slow the growth of national power. Congress developed its own independent view of federal-state relations. The meaning of federalism has been shaped more by Congress than by the courts. As the Supreme Court noted in 1946: "the history of judicial limitation of congressional power over commerce, when exercised affirmatively, has been more largely one of retreat than of ultimate victory." Prudential Ins. Co. v. Benjamin, 328 U.S. 408, 415.

A. THE PRINCIPLE OF FEDERALISM

In Federalist No. 39, James Madison responded to the criticism that the Constitution had improperly created a national government instead of a federal form (a confederation of sovereign states). Madison identified some features of the Constitution that gave it a national character; other provisions vested power directly in the states. He concluded that the proposed Constitution "is, in strictness, neither a national nor a federal Constitution, but a composition of both."

Independence from England left the thirteen American states without a central government. Under the Articles of Confederation, drafted in 1777 and ratified in 1781, each state retained "its sovereignty, freedom and independence" except for a few powers expressly delegated to the national government. The weakness of the confederation became of increasing concern, forcing the states to seek some form of regional cooperation to deal with commercial problems. Representatives of Virginia and Maryland met in 1785 at the home of George Washington, but it was decided that an interstate compact would be of more value if it included additional states. Consequently, all states were invited to Annapolis in 1786 to discuss commercial issues. Poor attendance and the need to address other problems led to the convention at Philadelphia the following year "to devise such further provisions as shall appear to them necessary to render the constitution of the Federal Government adequate to the exigencies of the Union."

What emerged from Philadelphia was an entirely new structure of government that divided power functionally (among three separate branches) and spatially (between the national government and the states). The Constitution rejected Montesquieu's theory that republican government could flourish only in small countries. He believed that as the size of the country increased, popular control had to be surrendered, yielding power to aristocracies in moderate-sized countries and to monarchies in large countries. Madison turned this theory on its head in Federalist No. 10 by arguing that republican government was unlikely to survive in a small territory, because a dominant faction would oppress the minority. "Extend the sphere," however, "and you take in a greater variety of parties and interests; you make it less probable that a majority of the whole will have a common motive to invade the rights of other citizens." Dividing this large territory into distinct states added further stability. As Hamilton said in Federalist No. 28, the national government and the states could check the usurpations of each other: "The people, by throwing themselves into either scale, will infallibly make it preponderate. If their rights are invaded by either, they can make use of the other as the instrument of redress."

The Virginia Plan

The Virginia Plan submitted to the Philadelphia Convention called for a strong central government. The rival New Jersey Plan, espousing a confederation with power left largely to the states, attracted little support. The eventual compromise gave the central government power to collect taxes, regulate commerce, declare war, and other express functions, including the Necessary and Proper Clause to carry into effect the enumerated powers. The power of Congress was divided between two chambers: a House of Representatives elected by the people, with its membership based on population; and a Senate elected by state legislatures, with two Senators for each state. This struck an accommodation between the preference of the big states (representation by population) and the demand of the small states (equal voting power for each state).

The Virginia Plan proposed a congressional veto over all state laws "contravening in the opinion of the National Legislature the articles of Union." Although this provision was initially agreed to without debate or dissent, it was later eliminated. 1 Farrand 21, 54. Instead, the Constitution assigns specific powers to Congress, expressly prohibits the states from exercising certain powers, and allows states to exercise other powers if Congress consents (see Table 8.1).

New States and Territories

The Constitution provides for the admission of new states in Article IV, Section 3: "[N]o new State shall be formed or erected within the Jurisdiction of any other State; nor any State be formed by the Junction of two or more States, or Parts of States, without the consent of the legislatures of the States concerned as well as of the Congress." An exception to this provision occurred in 1861, after South Carolina fired on Fort Sumter. Several states, including Virginia, voted to secede from the Union. The western counties of Virginia nullified the Virginia ordinance of secession and agreed to form a new state. In 1863 President Lincoln issued a proclamation making West Virginia the thirty-fifth state. For territory acquired from other countries (such as from the Louisiana Purchase or the Mexican War), Congress converted those lands to territories and later to states.

The Supremacy Clause

National powers are further reinforced by the Supremacy Clause in Article IV, Section 2: "This Constitution, and the laws of the United States which shall be made in pursuance thereof; and all treaties made, or which shall be made, under the authority of the United States, shall be the supreme law of the land; and the judges in every State shall be bound thereby, anything in the constitution or laws of any State to the contrary notwithstanding." Early in its history, the Supreme Court decided that in cases of conflict between state law and a treaty, the latter prevails. Ware v. Hylton, 3 U.S. (3 Dall.) 198 (1796).

In 2000, the Supreme Court applied the Supremacy Clause to a Massachusetts law that

TABLE 8.1   NATIONAL AND STATE POWERS UNDER THE CONSTITUTION*

National Powers	State Powers	Prohibited State Powers	State Powers if Congress Consents
Tax	Tax	—	—
Lay duties on imports and exports	Exercise police power	Tax articles from other states	Lay duties on imports and exports
Borrow money	Borrow money	—	—
Regulate foreign commerce	—	—	—
Regulate interstate commerce	Regulate intrastate commerce	—	—
Establish courts	Establish courts	—	—
Make treaties	—	Make treaties	Make compacts with other states
Coin money	—	Coin money	—
Emit bills of credit	—	Emit bills of credit	—
Declare war	—	Declare war	Engage in war
Raise and support military	—	—	Keep troops in time of peace
Grant letters of marque and reprisal	—	Grant letters of marque and reprisal	—

*The national powers identified above are found in Art. I, § 8, and Art. II. State powers are proscribed by Art. I, § 10. Under Art. I, §§ 9 and 10, both Congress and the states are prohibited from passing bills of attainder, ex post facto laws, and laws that grant titles of nobility. In addition, states may not pass laws that impair obligation of contracts.

barred state entities from buying goods or services from companies doing business with Burma. Congress later imposed sanctions on Burma, but delegated to the President substantial discretion to lift the sanctions if Burma made progress in human rights and democracy. A nonprofit corporation, representing several companies affected by the state law, sued on the basis that Massachusetts infringed on the federal foreign affairs power, violated the Foreign Commerce Clause, and was preempted by the federal statute. The Supreme Court held that the state law was invalid under the Supremacy Clause. Crosby v. National Foreign Trade Council, 120 S.Ct. 2288 (2000).

The Property Clause

State sovereignty is qualified by the power of Congress under the Property Clause "to dispose of and make all needful Rules and Regulations respecting the Territory or other Property belonging to the United States" (Art. IV, § 3, Cl. 2). Under this grant of authority, Congress exercises control over vast stretches of public land located inside the states, particularly those in the West. Kleppe v. New Mexico, 426 U.S. 529 (1976).

Privileges and Immunities

State sovereignty is also limited by the Privileges and Immunities Clause: "The Citizens of each State shall be entitled to all Privileges and Immunities of Citizens in the several States" (Art.

IV, § 2). Along with the Commerce Clause, this was intended to create a "national economic union." Supreme Court of New Hampshire v. Piper, 470 U.S. 274, 280 (1985).[1]

The protection of privileges and immunities also appears in Section 1 of the Fourteenth Amendment: "No State shall make or enforce any law which shall abridge the privileges or immunities of citizens of the United States." In 1999, the Supreme Court resurrected this part of the Fourteenth Amendment by striking down a California statute that limited the maximum welfare benefits available to a family that had resided in the state for less than twelve months. Such families would receive the amount paid by the state of their prior residence. Voting 7 to 2, the Court ruled that this durational residence requirement discriminated against citizens who were entitled to enjoy the privileges and immunities of citizens in the states that they visit. Saenz v. Roe, 526 U.S. 489 (1999).

The Privileges and Immunities Clause of the Fourteenth Amendment had little use ever since the Court decided the *Slaughter-House Cases* in 1873. The Court had struck down durational residency requirements for welfare benefits in earlier cases, but only by finding a "right to travel" in the equal protection guarantee of the Fourteenth Amendment. Shapiro v. Thompson, 394 U.S. 618 (1969). Thirteen years later, in a concurring opinion, Justice O'Connor found a right to travel in the privileges and immunities protection of Article IV, § 2. Zobel v. Williams, 457 U.S. 55 (1982). In his dissent to the 1999 opinion, Chief Justice Rehnquist objected to the Court "unearthing from its tomb" the Privileges and Immunities Clause of the Fourteenth Amendment.

The National Guard

Questions of federalism also concern control over National Guard units. Under Article I, Section 8, Congress may call forth the "militia" (part-time military forces) to suppress insurrections and repel invasions. Congress may also provide for "organizing, arming, and disciplining" the militia and "for governing such Part of them" when called into service for the federal government. The states appoint the officers and have authority for "training the Militia according to the discipline prescribed by Congress." In 1990 a unanimous Court held that a state governor's consent is not needed for training the National Guard in foreign countries. Perpich v. Department of Defense, 496 U.S. 334 (1990).

Nullification and Secession

National powers were regularly threatened by state efforts to secede from the Union or to assert the doctrines of interposition and nullification. After the Federalist party passed the Alien and Sedition Acts, the Jeffersonian Republicans protested this exercise of national power. Jefferson's draft of the Kentucky Resolutions of 1798 stated that unauthorized actions by the federal government were "void, and of no force." Here was the doctrine of nullification. The Virginia Resolutions of 1798, which Madison helped write, used somewhat softer language. In cases where the federal government overstepped its powers, the states "have the right and are in duty bound to interpose for arresting the progress of the evil, and for maintaining within their respective limits the authorities, rights, and liberties appertaining to them." Some years later the Federalists complained about Republican policies in the national government. Meeting at the Hartford Convention of 1814, Federalists considered secession and registered the opposition of New England states to the measures taken by Republicans. In 1832 South Carolina's ordinance of nullification maintained that the tariff acts enacted by Congress were "null, void, and no law."

---

1. See also Hicklin v. Orbeck, 437 U.S. 518 (1978); Baldwin v. Montana Fish and Game Comm'n, 436 U.S. 371 (1978); Austin v. New Hampshire, 420 U.S. 656 (1975); Toomer v. Witsell, 334 U.S. 385 (1948).

The spirit of nullification led eventually to the South's secession from the Union and the start of the Civil War. In 1869 the Supreme Court determined that the rebel states never left the Union: "The Constitution, in all its provisions, looks to an indestructible Union, composed of indestructible States." Texas v. White, 7 Wall. (74 U.S.) 700, 725. In admitting new states to the Union, Congress cannot impose conditions that would make a state unequal to others. It cannot, for example, dictate to a state the location of its capital. Coyle v. Oklahoma, 221 U.S. 559 (1911).

The Tenth Amendment

Throughout the nineteenth and twentieth centuries, there have been efforts to reassert the notion of sovereign states by relying on the Tenth Amendment, which provides that the powers "not delegated to the United States by the Constitution, nor prohibited by it to the States, are reserved to the States respectively, or to the people." The Articles of Confederation had given greater protection to the states, which retained all powers except those "expressly delegated" to the national government. When that phrase was proposed for the Tenth Amendment, Madison objected to the word "expressly" because the functions and responsibilities of the federal government could not be delineated with such precision. It was impossible to confine a government to the exercise of express powers, for there "must necessarily be admitted powers by implication, unless the Constitution descended to recount every minutiae." 1 Annals of Cong. 761 (Aug. 18, 1789). On the strength of his argument, Congress eliminated the word "expressly." Moreover, the Necessary and Proper Clause affords Congress the power to pass laws to carry into execution the express powers.

Chief Justice Marshall relied on this legislative history and constitutional text when he upheld the power of Congress to establish a national bank, even though such power is not expressly included in the Constitution. This endorsement of incidental or implied powers signaled a major advance for both national and congressional powers. McCULLOCH v. MARYLAND, 17 U.S. (4 Wheat.) 315 (1819). In upholding the national bank, Marshall followed closely the reasoning and justification first set forth by legislative and executive officials when they developed constitutional grounds for the bank in 1791 (see box, next page).

The idea that the Tenth Amendment contains substantive powers for the states is revived on occasion when the Supreme Court tries to rewrite the Constitution by shoehorning the word "expressly" into the Tenth Amendment. Lane County v. Oregon, 74 U.S. (7 Wall.) 71, 76 (1868); Hammer v. Dagenhart, 247 U.S. 251, 275 (1918). Most decisions, however, accept the Amendment as merely declaratory of a general relationship between the federal government and the states. In 1920, the Court denied that the treaty power was restricted in any way "by some invisible radiation from the general terms of the Tenth Amendment." MISSOURI v. HOLLAND, 252 U.S. 416, 434. A decade later, the Court held that the Tenth Amendment added nothing to the Constitution as originally ratified. United States v. Sprague, 282 U.S. 716, 733 (1931). Justice Stone dismissed the Tenth Amendment in 1941 as a "truism," rephrasing it to read "that all is retained which has not been surrendered." United States v. Darby, 312 U.S. 100, 124. As a declaratory statement, however, the Amendment "is not without significance." Fry v. United States, 421 U.S. 542, 547 n.7 (1975). The Tenth Amendment has been cited in recent cases to uphold state powers (pp. 384–86).

The Eleventh Amendment

States were fearful that they would be sued by citizens from other states or citizens from foreign countries. At the Virginia ratifying convention, Madison insisted that the Supreme Court's jurisdiction over controversies between a state and citizens of another state did not give individuals the power to call any state into court. A citizen might initiate an action, but federal

Nonjudicial Officials Determine Constitutionality of U.S. Bank

Responding to a request by the House of Representatives, Secretary of the Treasury Alexander Hamilton prepared a report on the establishment of a national bank and submitted it on December 13, 1790. 2 Annals of Cong. 2082–2112. Much of the legislative debate the following year focused on the constitutional authority of Congress to use implied powers to create the bank. The Senate acted first, passing the bank bill on January 20, 1791.

During House debate, Madison argued against the constitutionality of the bank on the ground that it was not an enumerated power of Congress, although this contradicted the position he had taken two years earlier on the Tenth Amendment. Fisher Ames challenged Madison's theory of enumerated powers by saying that if the power to raise armies had not been given expressly to Congress, it would have been implied by other parts of the Constitution. Theodore Sedgwick reminded the House that Madison, in 1789, had convinced a majority of members that the President had the power to remove executive officials, even though that power is not specifically stated in the Constitution. 2 Annals of Cong. 1955, 1960. Elias Boudinot pointed to Madison's essay in Federalist No. 44, which offered a broad interpretation of the Necessary and Proper Clause available to Congress to discharge its powers. Id. at 1977. The House passed the bill, 39 to 20.

After the bill cleared Congress, President George Washington asked Cabinet members to comment on the constitutionality of the legislation. Attorney General Edmund Randolph and Secretary of State Thomas Jefferson concluded that Congress lacked the constitutional power to grant a corporate charter for a national bank. Secretary of the Treasury Hamilton prepared a detailed analysis, defending the power of Congress to act in this area. Having drafted the bank bill, he was hardly in a position to view the matter with detachment or objectivity, but all the major players, including Madison, Randolph, and Jefferson, had well-formed attachments and predilections. Having digested the three constitutional opinions from his Cabinet members, Washington signed the bill. When the issue was later brought before the Supreme Court for adjudication, Chief Justice Marshall borrowed wholesale from Hamilton's interpretation of implied powers, sovereignty, and the Necessary and Proper Clause. See 8 The Papers of Alexander Hamilton 97–134 (Harold C. Syrett ed. 1965).

courts would have jurisdiction only if a state consented to be a party. 3 Elliot 533. In Federalist No. 81, Hamilton claimed that states would be shielded by the general principle of immunity: "It is inherent in the nature of sovereignty not to be amenable to the suit of an individual *without its consent.*"

One of the first cases brought to the Supreme Court involved a suit by Dutch bankers to recover funds from Maryland. In this case, the state's Attorney General voluntarily appeared. Vanstophorst v. Maryland, 2 Dall. 401 (1791). The issue of state immunity reached explosive proportions when two citizens from South Carolina, acting as executors of a British creditor, filed suit against Georgia. In 1793 the Supreme Court decided that the suit was consistent with Article III, Section 2, which gave the federal courts jurisdiction over controversies "between a State and Citizens of another State." Chisholm v. Georgia, 2 U.S. (2 Dall.) 419. To prevent a rash of citizen suits, Congress and the states promptly overturned the Court's ruling by ratifying the Eleventh Amendment: "The Judicial power of the United States shall not be construed to extend to any suit in law or equity, commenced or prosecuted against one of the United States by Citizens of another State, or by Citizens or Subjects of any foreign state." Although the Amendment does not expressly bar suits against a state by its own citizens, the Court has consistently held that a state is subject to such suits if it consents.[2]

As interpreted by the Court, however, the Eleventh Amendment does not give states total immunity from suits filed by citizens from other states. The doctrine that a state may not be sued in its own courts without its consent does not provide absolute immunity from suits in the courts of another state. Nevada v. Hall, 440 U.S. 410 (1979). Moreover, the Eleventh Amendment has been substantially narrowed by the Fourteenth Amendment. The Eleventh Amendment only prohibits suits directed against the *states*. Suits are allowed against state *officers* who are charged with denying due process or equal protection under the Fourteenth Amendment. The theory is that an officer acting illegally is functioning as an individual rather than a state official. Ex parte Young, 209 U.S. 123 (1908); Smyth v. Ames, 169 U.S. 466, 518–519 (1898).[3]

This theory does not support a suit against a state official who is used simply as a conduit to recover money from the state. Even if not named in such a case, the state is the real party and is entitled to sovereign immunity. Ford Motor Co. v. Department of Treasury, 323 U.S. 459 (1945); Alabama v. Pugh, 438 U.S. 781 (1978).

State governments regularly invoke sovereign immunity to protect their budgets. In 1974 the Supreme Court held that a suit could not force a state to make retroactive payments for a program it administered for the aged, blind, and disabled. Although the suit was filed against various state officials who administered the program, the funds for retroactive payments would come from the state. The fact that the program was funded equally by state and federal funds was insufficient to establish state consent to be sued in federal courts. Edelman v. Jordan, 415 U.S. 651, 673 (1974). Two years later the Court decided that whenever there is a collision between the Eleventh Amendment and Section 5 of the Fourteenth Amendment, which grants Congress authority to enforce "by appropriate legislation" the substantive provisions of the Fourteenth Amendment, the congressional statute prevails. This policy allows suits against states even for retroactive payments from their treasuries. Fitzpatrick v. Bitzer, 427 U.S. 445 (1976). Principles of federalism "that might otherwise be an obstacle to congressional authority are necessarily overridden by the power to enforce the Civil War Amendments "by appropriate legislation.' Those Amendments were specifically designed as an expansion of federal power and an intrusion on state sovereignty." Rome v. United States, 446 U.S. 156, 179 (1980). Unless Congress expresses in unmistakable terms its intent to abrogate the Eleventh Amendment, states may not be sued in federal court without their consent. Atascadero State Hospital v. Scanlon, 473 U.S. 234 (1985); Dellmuth v. Muth, 491 U.S. 223 (1989).

Other than its enforcement powers under the Fourteenth Amendment, may Congress use its Article I powers to abrogate the Eleventh Amendment? The Court has held that Congress may use the Commerce Clause to set aside the sovereign immunity of states. Dennis v. Higgins, 498 U.S. 439 (1991); Pennsylvania v. Union Gas Co., 491 U.S. 1 (1989). In the 1990s, the Court began to place some limits on the Commerce Clause (pages 385–86). The Court has also ruled that the Bankruptcy Code, based on the Article I power of Congress to establish uniform laws for bankruptcies, does not abrogate the states' Eleventh Amendment immunity. Hoffman v. Connecticut Income Maint. Dept., 492 U.S. 96 (1989). A series of decisions in the

---

2. Blatchford v. Native Village of Noatak, 501 U.S. 775 (1991). Employees v. Missouri Public Health Dept., 411 U.S. 279, 280 (1973); Great Northern Life Ins. Co. v. Read, 322 U.S. 47, 51 (1944); Duhne v. New Jersey, 251 U.S. 311 (1920); Hans v. Louisiana, 134 U.S. 1 (1890). The theory that the Eleventh Amendment forbids federal courts to hear suits against a state by a citizen of that state was rejected by four Justices in Atascadero State Hospital v. Scanlon, 473 U.S. 234 (1985) and Welch v. Texas Dept. of Highways, 483 U.S. 468 (1987).

3. See Truax v. Raich, 239 U.S. 33 (1915); William A. Fletcher, "A Historical Interpretation of the Eleventh Amendment: A Narrow Construction of an Affirmative Grant of Jurisdiction Rather than a Prohibition Against Jurisdiction," 35 Stan. L. Rev. 1033 (1983); Doyle Mathis, "The Eleventh Amendment: Adoption and Interpretation," 2 Ga. L. Rev. 207 (1968).

1980s and 1990s revealed a Court sharply split over the meaning and application of the Eleventh Amendment. Four decisions found the Court divided 5 to 4.[4] In 1996, a badly-fractured Supreme Court held that Congress lacked authority under the Indian Commerce Clause to abrogate the states' Eleventh Amendment immunity from lawsuits. Seminole Tribe of Florida v. Florida, 517 U.S. 44 (1996). Three decisions in 1999 protected the states against unconsented suits brought against them (see pages 386–87).

McCulloch v. Maryland

17 U.S. (4 Wheat.) 315 (1819)

Congress passed legislation in 1816 to create a Bank of the United States. The power to incorporate a national bank is not expressly granted in the Constitution. On the issue whether an implied power existed, Chief Justice Marshall supplies a broad interpretation of the meaning of the Constitution. In 1818 Maryland passed legislation to impose a tax on all banks or branches of banks in the state not chartered by the legislature. James W. McCulloch, the Bank's cashier in Baltimore, refused to pay the tax. The dispute gave Marshall an opportunity to define the relationship between the national government and the states, interpret the Necessary and Proper Clause, and judge the validity of a state tax on a federal instrumentality.

March 7th, 1819. MARSHALL Ch. J., delivered the opinion of the court. — In the case now to be determined, the defendant, a sovereign state, denies the obligation of a law enacted by the legislature of the Union, and the plaintiff, on his part, contests the validity of an act which has been passed by the legislature of that state. The constitution of our country, in its most interesting and vital parts, is to be considered; the conflicting powers of the government of the Union and of its members, as marked in that constitution, are to be discussed; and an opinion given, which may essentially influence the great operations of the government. No tribunal can approach such a question without a deep sense of its importance, and of the awful responsibility involved in its decision....

The first question made in the cause is — has congress power to incorporate a bank? It has been truly said, that this can scarcely be considered as an open question, entirely unprejudiced by the former proceedings of the nation respecting it....

The power now contested was exercised by the first congress elected under the present constitution. The bill for incorporating the Bank of the United States did not steal upon an unsuspecting legislature, and pass unobserved. Its principle was completely understood, and was opposed with equal zeal and ability. After being resisted, first, in the fair and open field of debate, and afterwards, in the executive cabinet, with as much persevering talent as any measure has ever experienced, and being supported by arguments which convinced minds as pure and as intelligent as this country can boast, it became a law. The original act was permitted to expire; but a short experience of the embarrassments to which the refusal to revive it exposed the government, convinced those who were most prejudiced against the measure of its necessity, and induced the passage of the present law. It would require no ordinary share of intrepidity, to assert that a measure adopted under these circumstances, was a bold and plain usurpation, to which the constitution gave no countenance. These observations belong to the cause; but they are not made under the impression, that, were the question entirely new, the law would be found irreconcilable with the constitution.

In discussing this question, the counsel for the state of Maryland have deemed it of some importance, in the construction of the constitution, to consider that instrument, not as emanating from the people, but as the act of sovereign and independent states. The powers of the general government, it has been said, are delegated by the

4. Seminole Tribe of Florida v. Florida, 517 U.S. 44 (1996); Hess v. Port Authority Trans-Hudson Corp., 513 U.S. 30 (1994); Welch v. Texas Dept. of Highways, 483 U.S. 468 (1987); Pennhurst State School & Hosp. v. Halderman, 465 U.S. 89 (1984).

states, who alone are truly sovereign; and must be exercised in subordination to the states, who alone possess supreme dominion. It would be difficult to sustain this proposition. The convention which framed the constitution was indeed elected by the state legislatures. But the instrument, when it came from their hands, was a mere proposal, without obligation, or pretensions to it. It was reported to the then existing congress of the United States, with a request that it might "be submitted to a convention of delegates, chosen in each state by the people thereof, under the recommendation of its legislature, for their assent and ratification." This mode of proceeding was adopted; and by the convention, by congress, and by the state legislatures, the instrument was submitted to the *people.* They acted upon it in the only manner in which they can act safely, effectively and wisely, on such a subject, by assembling in convention. It is true, they assembled in their several states—and where else should they have assembled? No political dreamer was ever wild enough to think of breaking down the lines which separate the states, and of compounding the American people into one common mass. Of consequence, when they act, they act in their states. But the measures they adopt do not, on that account, cease to be the measures of the people themselves, or become the measures of the state governments.

From these conventions, the constitution derives its whole authority. The government proceeds directly from the people; is "ordained and established," in the name of the people; and is declared to be ordained, "in order to form a more perfect union, establish justice, insure domestic tranquility, and secure the blessings of liberty to themselves and to their posterity." The assent of the states, in their sovereign capacity, is implied, in calling a convention, and thus submitting that instrument to the people. But the people were at perfect liberty to accept or reject it; and their act was final. It required not the affirmance, and could not be negatived, by the state governments. The constitution, when thus adopted, was of complete obligation, and bound the state sovereignties.

. . .

This government is acknowledged by all, to be one of enumerated powers. The principle, that it can exercise only the powers granted to it, would seem too apparent, to have required to be enforced by all those arguments, which its enlightened friends, while it was depending before the people, found it necessary to urge; that principle is now universally admitted. But the question respecting the extent of the powers actually granted, is perpetually arising, and will probably continue to arise, so long as our system shall exist. In discussing these questions, the conflicting powers of the general and state governments must be brought into view, and the supremacy of their respective laws, when they are in opposition, must be settled.

If any one proposition could command the universal assent of mankind, we might expect it would be this—that the government of the Union, though limited in its powers, is supreme within its sphere of action. This would seem to result, necessarily, from its nature. It is the government of all; its powers are delegated by all; it represents all, and acts for all.... The government of the United States, then, though limited in its powers, is supreme; and its laws, when made in pursuance of the constitution, form the supreme law of the land, "anything in the constitution or laws of any state to the contrary notwithstanding."

Among the enumerated powers, we do not find that of establishing a bank or creating a corporation. But there is no phrase in the instrument which, like the articles of confederation, excludes incidental or implied powers; and which requires that everything granted shall be expressly and minutely described. Even the 10th amendment, which was framed for the purpose of quieting the excessive jealousies which had been excited, omits the word "expressly," and declares only, that the powers "not delegated to the United States, nor prohibited to the states, are reserved to the states or to the people;" thus leaving the question, whether the particular power which may become the subject of contest, has been delegated to the one government, or prohibited to the other, to depend on a fair construction of the whole instrument. The men who drew and adopted this amendment had experienced the embarrassments resulting from the insertion of this word in the articles of confederation, and probably omitted it, to avoid those embarrassments. A constitution, to contain an accurate detail of all the subdivisions of which its great powers will admit, and of all the means by which they may be carried into execution, would partake of the prolixity of a legal code, and could scarcely be embraced by the human mind. It would, probably, never be understood by the public. Its nature, therefore, requires, that only its great outlines should be marked, its important objects designated, and the minor ingredients which compose those objects, be deduced from the nature of the objects themselves. That this idea was entertained by the framers of the American constitution, is not only to be inferred from the nature of the instrument, but from the language. Why else were some of the limitations, found in the 9th section of the 1st article, introduced? It is also, in some degree, warranted, by their having omitted to use any restrictive term which might prevent its receiving a fair and just interpretation. In considering this question, then, we must never forget that it is a *constitution* we are expounding.

Although, among the enumerated powers of government, we do not find the word "bank" or "incorporation," we find the great powers, to lay and collect taxes; to borrow money; to regulate commerce; to declare and conduct a war; and to raise and support armies and navies. The sword and the purse, all the external relations, and no inconsiderable portion of the industry of the nation, are intrusted to its government. It can never be pretended, that these vast powers draw after them others of inferior importance, merely because they are inferior. Such an idea can never be advanced. But it may with great reason be contended, that a government, intrusted with such ample powers, on the due execution of which the happiness and prosperity of the nation so vitally depends, must also be intrusted with ample means for their execution....

· · ·

...[T]he constitution of the United States has not left the right of congress to employ the necessary means, for the execution of the powers conferred on the government, to general reasoning. To its enumeration of powers is added, that of making "all laws which shall be necessary and proper, for carrying into execution the foregoing powers, and all other powers vested by this constitution, in the government of the United States, or in any department thereof." The counsel for the state of Maryland have urged various arguments, to prove that this clause, though, in terms, a grant of power, is not so, in effect; but is really restrictive of the general right, which might otherwise be implied, of selecting means for executing the enumerated powers. In support of this proposition, they have found it necessary to contend, that this clause was inserted for the purpose of conferring on congress the power of making laws. That, without it, doubts might be entertained, whether congress could exercise its powers in the form of legislation.

But could this be the object for which it was inserted? A government is created by the people, having legislative, executive and judicial powers. Its legislative powers are vested in a congress, which is to consist of a senate and house of representatives.... Could it be necessary to say, that a legislature should exercise legislative powers, in the shape of legislation? After allowing each house to prescribe its own course of proceeding, after describing the manner in which a bill should become a law, would it have entered into the mind of a single member of the convention, that an express power to make laws was necessary, to enable the legislature to make them? That a legislature, endowed with legislative powers, can legislate, is a proposition too self-evident to have been questioned.

But the argument on which most reliance is placed, is drawn from that peculiar language of this clause. Congress is not empowered by it to make all laws, which may have relation to the powers conferred on the government, but such only as may be *"necessary and proper"* for carrying them into execution. The word *"necessary"* is considered as controlling the whole sentence, and as limiting the right to pass laws for the execution of the granted powers, to such as are indispensable, and without which the power would be nugatory. That it excludes the choice of means, and leaves to congress, in each case, that only which is most direct and simple.

Is it true, that this is the sense in which the word "necessary" is always used? Does it always import an absolute physical necessity, so strong, that one thing to which another may be termed necessary, cannot exist without that other? We think it does not. If reference be had to its use, in the common affairs of the world, or in approved authors, we find that it frequently imports no more than that one thing is convenient, or useful, or essential to another. To employ the means necessary to an end, is generally understood as employing any means calculated to produce the end, and not as being confined to those single means, without which the end would be entirely unattainable....

Let this be done in the case under consideration. The subject is the execution of those great powers on which the welfare of a nation essentially depends. It must have been the intention of those who gave these powers, to insure, so far as human prudence could insure, their beneficial execution. This could not be done, by confiding the choice of means to such narrow limits as not to leave it in the power of congress to adopt any which might be appropriate, and which were conducive to the end. This provision is made in a constitution, intended to endure for ages to come, and consequently, to be adapted to the various *crises* of human affairs. To have prescribed the means by which government should, in all future time, execute its powers, would have been to change, entirely, the character of the instrument, and give it the properties of a legal code. It would have been an unwise attempt to provide, by immutable rules, for exigencies which, if foreseen at all, must have been seen dimly, and which can be best provided for as they occur. To have declared, that the best means shall not be used, but those alone, without which the power given would be nugatory, would have been to deprive the legislature of the capacity to avail itself of experience, to exercise its reason, and to accommodate its legislation to circumstances.

. . .

[Marshall rejects Maryland's argument that the Necessary and Proper Clause was intended to abridge the powers of Congress.]

1st. The clause is placed among the powers of congress, not among the limitations on those powers. 2d. Its terms purport to enlarge, not to diminish the powers vested in the government. It purports to be an additional power, not a restriction on those already granted. No reason has been, or can be assigned, for thus concealing an intention to narrow the discretion of the national legislature, under words which purport to enlarge it....

We admit, as all must admit, that the powers of the government are limited, and that its limits are not to be transcended. But we think the sound construction of the constitution must allow to the national legislature that discretion, with respect to the means by which the powers it confers are to be carried into execution, which will enable that body to perform the high duties assigned to it, in the manner most beneficial to the people. Let the end be legitimate, let it be within the scope of the constitution, and all means which are appropriate, which are plainly adapted to that end, which are not prohibited, but consist with the letter and spirit of the constitution, are constitutional.

That a corporation must be considered as a means not less usual, not of higher dignity, not more requiring a particular specification than other means, has been sufficiently proved....

. . .

It being the opinion of the court, that the act incorporating the bank is constitutional; and that the power of establishing a branch in the state of Maryland might be properly exercised by the bank itself, we proceed to inquire—

2. Whether the state of Maryland may, without violating the constitution, tax that branch? That the power of taxation is one of vital importance; that it is retained by the states; that it is not abridged by the grant of a similar power to the government of the Union; that it is to be concurrently exercised by the two governments—are truths which have never been denied. But such is the paramount character of the constitution, that its capacity to withdraw any subject from the action of even this power, is admitted. The states are expressly forbidden to lay any duties on imports or exports, except what may be absolutely necessary for executing their inspection laws. If the obligation of this prohibition must be conceded—if it may restrain a state from the exercise of its taxing power on imports and exports—the same paramount character would seem to restrain, as it certainly may restrain, a state from such other exercise of this power, as is in its nature incompatible with, and repugnant to, the constitutional laws of the Union. A law, absolutely repugnant to another, as entirely repeals that other as if express terms of repeal were used.

On this ground, the counsel for the bank places its claim to be exempted from the power of a state to tax its operations. There is no express provision for the case, but the claim has been sustained on a principle which so entirely pervades the constitution, is so intermixed with the materials which compose it, so interwoven with its web, so blended with its texture, as to be incapable of being separated from it, without rending it into shreds. This great principle is, that the constitution and the laws made in pursuance thereof are supreme; that they control the constitution and laws of the respective states, and cannot be controlled by them. From this, which may be almost termed an axiom, other propositions are deduced as corollaries, on the truth or error of which, and on their application to this case, the cause has been supposed to depend. These are, 1st. That a power to create implies a power to preserve: 2d. That a power to destroy, if wielded by a different hand, is hostile to, and incompatible with these powers to create and to preserve: 3d. That where this repugnancy exists, that authority which is supreme must control, not yield to that over which it is supreme.

These propositions, as abstract truths, would, perhaps, never be controverted. Their application to this case, however, has been denied; and both in maintaining the affirmative and the negative, a splendor of eloquence, and strength of argument, seldom, if ever, surpassed, have been displayed.

The power of congress to create, and of course, to continue, the bank, was the subject of the preceding part of this opinion; and is no longer to be considered as questionable. That the power of taxing it by the states may be exercised so as to destroy it, is too obvious to be denied. But taxation is said to be an absolute power, which acknowledges no other limits than those expressly prescribed in the constitution, and like sovereign power of every other description, is intrusted to the discretion of those who use it. But the very terms of this argument admit, that the sovereignty of the state, in the article of taxation itself, is subordinate to, and may be controlled by the constitution of the United States. How far it has been controlled by that instrument, must be a question of construction. In making this construction, no principle, not declared, can be admissible, which would defeat the legitimate operations of a supreme government. It is of the very essence of supremacy, to remove all obstacles to its action within its own sphere, and so to modify every power vested in subordinate governments, as to exempt its own operations from their own influence. This effect need not be stated in terms. It is so involved in the declaration of supremacy, so necessarily implied in it, that the expression of it could not make it more certain. We must, therefore, keep it in view, while construing the constitution.

. . .

The sovereignty of a state extends to everything which exists by its own authority, or is introduced by its permission; but does it extend to those means which are employed by congress to carry into execution powers conferred on that body by the people of the United States? We think it demonstrable, that it does not. Those powers are not given by the people of a single state. They are given by the people of the United States, to a government whose laws, made in pursuance of the constitution, are declared to be supreme. Consequently, the people of a single state cannot confer a sovereignty which will extend over them.

. . .

The court has bestowed on this subject its most deliberate consideration. The result is a conviction that the states have no power, by taxation or otherwise, to retard, impede, burden, or in any manner control, the operations of the constitutional laws enacted by congress to carry into execution the powers vested in the general government. This is, we think, the unavoidable consequence of that supremacy which the constitution has declared. We are unanimously of opinion, that the law passed by the legislature of Maryland, imposing a tax on the Bank of the United States, is unconstitutional and void.

. . .

Missouri v. Holland

252 U.S. 416 (1920)

The United States and Great Britain entered into a treaty in 1916 to protect migratory birds in the United States and Canada. Congress passed legislation in 1918 to enforce the treaty, providing for prohibitions on the killing, capturing, or selling of any of the migratory birds included within the terms of the treaty, except as permitted by regulations compatible with the treaty. Ray P. Holland, U.S. Game Warden, threatened to arrest and prosecute citizens of Missouri for violating the Migratory Bird Treaty Act. Missouri claimed that the treaty and the statute invaded the rights reserved to the states by the Tenth Amendment. A federal district court upheld the congressional act.

MR. JUSTICE HOLMES delivered the opinion of the court.

This is a bill in equity brought by the State of Missouri to prevent a game warden of the United States from attempting to enforce the Migratory Bird Treaty Act of July 3, 1918, c. 128, 40 Stat. 755, and the regulations made by the Secretary of Agriculture in pursuance of the same. The ground of the bill is that the statute is an unconstitutional interference with the rights reserved to the States by the Tenth Amendment, and that the acts of the defendant done and threatened under that authority invade the sovereign right of the State and contravene its will manifested in statutes. The State also alleges a pecuniary interest, as owner of the wild birds within its borders and otherwise, admitted by the Government to be sufficient, but it is enough that the bill is a reasonable and proper means to assert the alleged quasi sovereign rights of a State....

...It is unnecessary to go into any details, because, as we have said, the question raised is the general one whether the treaty and statute are void as an interference with the rights reserved to the States.

To answer this question it is not enough to refer to the Tenth Amendment, reserving the powers not delegated to the United States, because by Article II, § 2, the power to make treaties is delegated expressly, and by Article VI treaties made under the authority of the United States, along with the Constitution and laws of the United States made in pursuance thereof, are declared the supreme law of the land. If the treaty is valid there can be no dispute about the validity of the statute under Article I, § 8, as a necessary and proper means to execute the powers of the Government. The language of the Constitution as to the supremacy of treaties being general, the question before us is narrowed to an inquiry into the ground upon which the present supposed exception is placed.

It is said that a treaty cannot be valid if it infringes the Constitution, that there are limits, therefore, to the treatymaking power, and that one such limit is that what an act of Congress could not do unaided, in derogation of the powers reserved to the States, a treaty cannot do. An earlier act of Congress that attempted by itself and not in pursuance of a treaty to regulate the killing of migratory birds within the States had been held bad in the District Court. *United States* v. *Shauver*, 214 Fed. Rep. 154. *United States* v. *McCullagh*, 221 Fed. Rep. 288. Those decisions were supported by arguments that migratory birds were owned by the States in their sovereign capacity for the benefit of their people, and that under cases like *Geer* v. *Connecticut*, 161 U. S. 519, this control was one that Congress had no power to displace. The same argument is supposed to apply now with equal force.

Whether the two cases cited were decided rightly or not they cannot be accepted as a test of the treaty power. Acts of Congress are the supreme law of the land only when made in pursuance of the Constitution, while treaties are declared to be so when made under the authority of the United States. It is open to question whether the authority of the United States means more than the formal acts prescribed to make the convention. We do not mean to imply that there are no qualifications to the treaty-making power; but they must be ascertained in a different way. It is obvious that there may be matters of the sharpest exigency for the national well being that an act of Congress could not deal with but that a treaty followed by such an act could, and it is not lightly to be assumed that, in matters requiring national action, "a power which must belong to and somewhere reside in every civilized government" is not to be found. *Andrews* v. *Andrews*, 188 U.S. 14, 33. What was said in that case with regard to the powers of the States applies with equal force to the powers of the nation in cases where the States individually are incompetent to act. We are not yet discussing the particular case before us but only are considering the validity of the test proposed. With regard to that we may add that when we are dealing with words that also are a constituent act, like the Constitution of the United States, we must realize that they have called into life a being the development of which could not have been foreseen completely by the most gifted of its begetters. It was enough for them to realize or to hope that they had created an organism; it has taken a century and has cost their successors much sweat and blood to prove that they created a nation. The case before us must be considered in the light of our whole experience and not merely in that of what was said a hundred years ago. The treaty in question does not contravene any prohibitory words to be found in the Constitution. The only question is whether it is forbidden by some invisible radiation from the general terms of the Tenth Amendment. We must consider what this country has become in deciding what that Amendment has reserved.

The State as we have intimated founds its claim of exclusive authority upon an assertion of title to migratory birds, an assertion that is embodied in statute. No doubt it is true that as between a State and its inhabitants the State may regulate the killing and sale of such birds, but it does not follow that its authority is exclusive of paramount powers. To put the claim of the State upon title is to lean upon a slender reed. Wild birds are not in the possession of anyone; and possession is the beginning of ownership. The whole foundation of the State's rights is the presence within their jurisdiction of birds that yesterday had not arrived, tomorrow may be in another State and in a week a thousand miles away. If we are to be accurate we cannot put the case of the State upon higher ground than that the treaty deals with creatures that for the moment are within the state borders, that it must be carried out by officers of the United States within the same territory, and that but for the treaty the State would be free to regulate this subject itself.

As most of the laws of the United States are carried out within the States and as many of them deal with matters which in the silence of such laws the State might regulate, such general grounds are not enough to support Missouri's claim. Valid treaties of course "are as binding within the territorial limits of the States as they are elsewhere throughout the dominion of the United States." *Baldwin* v. *Franks*, 120 U. S. 678, 683. No doubt the great body of private relations usually fall within the control of the State, but a treaty may override its power....

Here a national interest of very nearly the first magnitude is involved. It can be protected only by national action in concert with that of another power. The subject-matter is only transitorily within the State and has no permanent habitat therein. But for the treaty and the statute there soon might be no birds for any powers to deal with. We see nothing in the Constitution that compels the Government to sit by while a food supply is cut off and the protectors of our forests and our crops are destroyed. It is not sufficient to rely upon the States. The reliance is vain, and were it otherwise, the question is whether the United States is forbidden to act. We are of opinion that the treaty and statute must be upheld. *Carey* v. *South Dakota*, 250 U. S. 118.

Decree affirmed.

MR. JUSTICE VAN DEVANTER and MR. JUSTICE PITNEY dissent.

B. THE COMMERCE CLAUSE

The Commerce Clause has produced many collisions between the legislative and judicial branches, often pitting the power of Congress to advance its national agenda against judicial constraints that favored business or state interests. Although the Court in many instances blocked national efforts to regulate the economy, over the long run a persistent Congress prevailed with its independent interpretation of the Commerce Clause. Today, the scope of the commerce power is left largely to Congress. In recent years, Congress has invoked the Commerce Clause to enact civil rights legislation, a subject treated in Chapter 15.

Commercial friction among the states during the 1770s and 1780s generated pressure for stronger national powers. The Continental Congress had no power to raise revenue or to regulate commerce among the states. Its power to conclude treaties with foreign nations meant little unless it could control commerce coming into state ports. With each state guarding its sphere of sovereignty, thirteen conflicting systems of commercial regulation and duty schedules governed trade in the country. These commercial disputes led to the Annapolis Convention in 1786 and the Philadelphia Convention a year later. Among the enumerated duties given to Congress was the power to "regulate commerce with foreign nations, and among the several States, and with the Indian tribes." Art. I, § 8, Cl. 2.

The scope of the Commerce Clause reached the Supreme Court in *Gibbons v. Ogden* (1824). The decision by Chief Justice Marshall is significant for three reasons. First, although Marshall was a strong defender of private property and contractual rights, he advanced a broad interpretation of the power of Congress to regulate commerce. Commerce was more than discrete transactions; it was intercourse. Congress had the power to regulate economic life in the nation to promote the free flow of interstate commerce, including actions within state borders that interfered with that flow. Second, his decision averted potential economic warfare among the states, which would have revived the destructive practices operating before the Constitution. Third, the decision represents one of the most articulate rebuttals of "strict constructionism." GIBBONS v. OGDEN, 22 U.S. (9 Wheat.) 1 (1824).

Three years later, Marshall again supported national power by striking down a Maryland statute because it violated two constitutional provisions: the prohibition on states to lay a duty on imports and the power of Congress to regulate interstate commerce. To distinguish between congressional and state powers. Marshall developed the "original package" concept. States could not tax an import in its original form or package, but after the imported article became "incorporated and mixed up with the mass of property in the country," it was vulnerable to state taxes. Brown v. Maryland, 25 U.S. (12 Wheat.) 419, 441 (1827). Those decisions, however, did not mean that the national government had exclusive control over the commerce power. In areas where Congress had not exercised its commerce power, Marshall recognized the authority of states to regulate commerce within their own borders. Willson v. Black-bird Creek Marsh Co., 27 U.S. (2 Pet.) 244 (1829).

Concurrent Powers

Other cases elaborated on the jurisdiction between the national and state governments. The broad nationalistic interpretation of Marshall was supplanted by more restrictive rulings from the Taney Court. A decision in 1837 permitted states to adopt regulations for passengers arriving from foreign countries. The Court considered packages, not people, as subjects of commerce. States could exercise the "police power" to protect the general welfare of their citizens. New York v. Miln, 36 U.S. (11 Pet.) 102 (1837). Under this doctrine of concurrent powers, states could regulate commerce within their borders unless preempted by Congress. For example, if Congress authorized the importation of liquor from foreign countries, states had to accept the liquor in its "original package." Once the cask became part of retail or domestic traffic, the state police power justified the imposition of taxes, licenses, or total prohibition of liquor. The same reasoning applied to liquor shipped from neighboring states. License Cases, 46 U.S. (5 How.) 504 (1847). The Supreme Court even allowed states to collect "fees" from foreign vessels by distinguishing fees from the imposts and duties forbidden by Article I, Section 10. The regulation of foreign commerce was not an exclusive power of Congress. States could exercise concurrent jurisdiction over portions of that power, especially when invited by Congress. COOLEY v. BOARD OF WARDENS, 53 U.S. (12 How.) 299 (1852). During this same period, however, the Court denied states the right to impose taxes on alien passengers arriving at state ports, even when states used "health" as a justification. Passenger Cases, 48 U.S. (7 How.) 282 (1849).

The Supreme Court also created the doctrine of exclusive jurisdictions. Under the theory of "dual federalism," the states and the national government exercised mutually exclusive powers. "The powers which one possesses, the other does not." United States v. Cruikshank, 92 U.S. (2 Otto.) 542, 550 (1876). In 1890 the Court ruled that a state's prohibition of intoxicating liquors could not be applied to original packages or kegs. The power of Congress over commerce, even if not expressly stated in a statute, appeared to override state police powers and local options. The Court qualified its opinion by saying that the states could not exclude incoming articles "without congressional permission." Leisy v. Hardin, 135 U.S. 100, 125 (1890).

Congress promptly overturned the decision by passing legislation that made intoxicating liquors, upon their arrival in a state or territory, subject to the police powers "to the same extent and in the same manner as though such liquids or liquors had been produced in such State or Territory, and shall not be exempt therefrom by reason of being introduced therein in original packages or otherwise." 26 Stat. 313 (1890). The Supreme Court upheld the constitutionality of this statute. In re Rahrer, 140 U.S. 545 (1891). Excerpts from the congressional debate are reprinted on pages 353–55. Three years later, the Court reviewed a state statute that prohibited the sale of oleomargarine that had been colored to look like butter, including oleomargarine manufactured outside the state. The Court supported the statute even though Congress had previously legislated on oleomargarine. Plumley v. Massachusetts, 155 U.S. 461 (1894).

May Congress Annul the Court's Decision?

Mr. Justice McLEAN dissenting....

After a very tedious and minute investigation of the facts of the case, which embraced the reports of practical engineers, depositions from the most experienced river men, statements of the stages of water in the river throughout the year, and also after a full consideration of the legal principles applicable to the matter in controversy, six of the members of this tribunal, two only dissenting, were brought to the conclusion that the bridge was a material obstruction to the navigation of the river....

The decree in the Wheeling bridge case was the result of a judicial investigation, founded upon facts ascertained in the course of the hearing. It was strictly a judicial question. The complaint was an obstruction of commerce, by the bridge, to the injury of the complainant, and the court found the fact to be as alleged in the bill. It was said by Chief Justice Marshall, many years ago, that congress could do many things,

but that it could not alter a fact. This it has attempted to do in the above act....

From the organization of the legislative power, it is unfitted for the discharge of judicial duties; and the same may be said of this court in regard to legislation. It may therefore happen, that, when either trenches upon the appropriate powers of the other, their acts are inoperative and void....

Mr. Justice GRIER....

I concur with my brother McLean, that congress cannot annul or vacate any decree of this court; that the assumption of such a power is without precedent, and, as a precedent for the future, it is of dangerous example.

Mr. Justice WAYNE....

...Whatever congress may have intended by the act of August, 1852, I do not think it admits of the interpretation given to it by the majority of the court; and if it does, then my opinion is that the act would be unconstitutional....

Source: Pennsylvania v. Wheeling and Belmont Bridge Co., 18 How. (59 U.S.) 421, 437–40, 449, 450 (1856).

Dormant Commerce Clause

In cases when Congress does not exercise its commerce power, that authority is silent or dormant. In such situations the Court may decide that a state action is forbidden by the Commerce Clause. However, if Congress then enacts legislation to permit the state action, the Court will acquiesce to the congressional policy. For example, in 1852 the Supreme Court held that the height of a bridge in Pennsylvania made it "a nuisance." Congress quickly passed legislation declaring the bridges at issue to be "lawful structures" and the Court subsequently ruled that the bridge was no longer an unlawful obstruction.[5] In separate dissents, Justices McLean, Grier, and Wayne argued that Congress could not annul or vacate a court decree and that the 1852 statute was improperly an exercise of judicial, not legislative, power (see box).

Those positions have never been adopted by the Court, which noted in 1946: "whenever Congress' judgment has been uttered affirmatively to contradict the Court's previously expressed view that specific action taken by the states in Congress' silence was forbidden by the commerce clause, this body has accommodated its previous judgment to Congress' expressed approval." Prudential Ins. Co. v. Benjamin, 326 U.S. 408, 425 (1946). In 1985, the Court said

---

5. Pennsylvania v. Wheeling &c. Bridge Co., 13 How. (54 U.S.) 518 (1852); 10 Stat. 112, § 6 (1852); Pennsylvania v. Wheeling and Belmont Bridge Co., 18 How. (59 U.S.) 421 (1856).

that when Congress "so chooses, state actions which it plainly authorizes are invulnerable to constitutional attack under the Commerce Clause."[6]

The give-and-take between Congress and the judiciary is illustrated by the insurance cases. In 1869, the Supreme Court held that states could regulate insurance because it was not a "transaction of commerce." Paul v. Virginia, 8 Wall. 168. That holding, along with 150 years of precedents, was overturned in 1944 when the Court interpreted the transaction of insurance business across state lines as interstate commerce subject to congressional regulation. The Court said that Congress had not intended to exempt the insurance business from the Sherman Antitrust Act. United States v. South-Eastern Underwriters Assn., 322 U.S. 533 (1944). Congress quickly passed the McCarran Act, essentially reversing the Court by authorizing states to regulate insurance. 59 Stat. 33 (1945). Acting under cover of this statute, states were once again allowed to regulate and tax the business of insurance. Prudential Ins. Co. v. Benjamin, 328 U.S. 408 (1946).

Antitrust Policy

In an effort to curb the concentration of economic power after the Civil War, Congress passed the Sherman Antitrust Act in 1890 to prohibit combinations and conspiracies that restrained trade. Through a series of rulings, the Supreme Court largely nullified the law's effectiveness. In 1895 the Court held that the Act did not apply to monopolies engaged in the *manufacture* of items necessary for life. Through this reasoning the Act exempted (by judicial fiat) the "Sugar Trust": the American Sugar Refining Company, which was incorporated in New Jersey and controlled about 98 percent of the sugar refining business in the country. The Court argued that manufacturing precedes commerce and is not part of it and that the power to regulate the manufacture of a "necessary of life" belongs to the police power of the states. The Court regarded the sugar monopoly's restraint on trade as "indirect," not direct. United States v. E.C. Knight Co., 156 U.S. 1 (1895).

The Court narrowly upheld the application of the Sherman Antitrust Act to holding companies that rival railroad companies had established to combine their forces and restrain interstate commerce. Northern Securities Co. v. United States, 193 U.S. 197 (1904). The Act was gravely weakened in 1911 when the Court adopted the "rule of reason" doctrine. Previously, the Court had applied the literal and strict language of the Act, which made no exceptions. It prohibited *every* contract, combination, or conspiracy in restraint of interstate or foreign trade. *Every* person engaged in such activity was guilty of a misdemeanor. In this early period, the Court refused to limit the Act to "unreasonable" restraints of trade. United States v. Trans-Missouri Freight Assn., 166 U.S. 290, 327–41 (1897); United States v. Joint Traffic Assn., 171 U.S. 505, 573–78 (1898). If companies entered into contracts that restrained interstate or foreign commerce to any extent, Congress could nullify the contracts. Addyston Pipe & Steel Co. v. United States, 175 U.S. 211 (1899).

Matters changed abruptly in 1911 with the "rule of reason." The Sherman Act was judicially amended to prohibit only *unreasonable* or *undue* restraints. In a dissent, Justice Harlan condemned the use of judicial construction to amend the Constitution and rewrite statutes. Standard Oil Co. v. United States, 221 U.S. 1, 105 (1911); United States v. American Tobacco Co., 221 U.S. 106 (1911). Judgments of "reasonable" rates are now exercised by administrative agencies, not the judiciary. Moreover, the Court has long since abandoned the artificial

---

6. Northeast Bancorp v. Board of Governors, FRS, 472 U.S. 159, 174 (1985). In a concurrence in 1995, Justices Kennedy and O'Connor conceded that "if we invalidate a state law, Congress can in effect overturn our judgment." United States v. Lopez, 514 U.S. 549, 580 (1995). See also Julian N. Eule, "Laying the Dormant Commerce Clause to Rest," 91 Yale L. J. 425 (1982); William Cohen, "Congressional Power to Validate Unconstitutional State Laws: A Forgotten Solution to an Old Enigma," 35 Stan. L. Rev. 387 (1983).

separation between "manufacturing" and "commerce." Mandeville Farms v. Sugar Co., 334 U.S. 219, 229 (1948).

Gibbons v. Ogden

22 U.S. (9 Wheat.) 1 (1824)

New York granted to Robert R. Livingston and Robert Fulton the exclusive privilege to operate steamboats on all waters within the jurisdiction of the state. Other states enacted similar laws, and soon friction emerged as states required out-of-state boats to pay substantial fees to be admitted. The retaliation that resulted was similar to the commercial warfare among the states prior to the adoption of the Constitution. This case involved the issue of whether New York could require a steamboat operating between New York and New Jersey to secure a New York license. Was this within the power of a state or did it infringe on the commerce power given to Congress? Thomas Gibbons and Aaron Ogden had been partners, operating a steamboat between New Jersey and New York, but they became antagonists in this tangled suit.

March 2d, 1824. MARSHALL, Ch. J., ... The appellant contends, that this decree [*by New York*] is erroneous, because the laws which purport to give the exclusive privilege it sustains, are repugnant to ... that clause in the constitution which authorizes congress to regulate commerce [*and*] to that which authorizes congress to promote the progress of science and useful arts.

. . .

... [R]eference has been made to the political situation of these states, anterior to its formation. It has been said, that they were sovereign, were completely independent, and were connected with each other only by a league. This is true. But when these allied sovereigns converted their league into a government, when they converted their congress of ambassadors, deputed to deliberate on their common concerns, and to recommend measures of general utility, into a legislature, empowered to enact laws on the most interesting subjects, the whole character in which the states appear, underwent a change, the extent of which must be determined by a fair consideration of the instrument by which that change was effected.

This instrument contains an enumeration of powers expressly granted by the people to their government. It has been said, that these powers ought to be construed strictly. But why ought they to be so construed? Is there one sentence in the constitution which gives countenance to this rule? In the last of the enumerated powers, that which grants, expressly, the means for carrying all others into execution, congress is authorized "to make all laws which shall be necessary and proper" for the purpose. But this limitation on the means which may be used, is not extended to the powers which are conferred; nor is there one sentence in the constitution, which has been pointed out by the gentlemen of the bar, or which we have been able to discern, that prescribes this rule. We do not, therefore, think ourselves justified in adopting it. What do gentlemen mean, by a strict construction? If they contend only against that enlarged construction, which would extend words beyond their natural and obvious import, we might question the application of the term, but should not controvert the principle. If they contend for that narrow construction which, in support of some theory not to be found in the constitution, would deny to the government those powers which the words of the grant, as usually understood, import, and which are consistent with the general views and objects of the instrument — for that narrow construction, which would cripple the government, and render it unequal to the objects for which it is declared to be instituted, and to which the powers given, as fairly understood, render it competent — then we cannot perceive the propriety of this strict construction, nor adopt it as the rule by which the constitution is to be expounded....

The words are, "congress shall have power to regulate commerce with foreign nations, and among the several states, and with the Indian tribes."

The subject to be regulated is commerce; and our constitution being, as was aptly said at the bar, one of enumeration, and not of definition, to ascertain the extent of the power, it becomes necessary to settle the meaning of the word. The counsel for the appellee would limit it to traffic, to buying and selling, or the interchange of commodities, and do not admit that it comprehends navigation. This would restrict a general term, applicable to many objects, to one of its significations. Commerce, undoubtedly, is traffic, but it is something more—it is intercourse. It describes the commercial intercourse between nations, and parts of nations, in all its branches, and is regulated by prescribing rules for carrying on that intercourse. The mind can scarcely conceive a system for regulating commerce between nations, which shall exclude all laws concerning navigation, which shall be silent on the admission of the vessels of the one nation into the ports of the other.... All America understands, and has uniformly understood, the word "commerce," to comprehend navigation. It was so understood, and must have been so understood, when the constitution was framed. The power over commerce, including navigation, was one of the primary objects for which the people of America adopted their government, and must have been contemplated in forming it. The convention must have used the word in that sense, because all have understood it in that sense; and the attempt to restrict it comes too late.

If the opinion that "commerce," as the word is used in the constitution, comprehends navigation also, requires any additional confirmation, that additional confirmation is, we think, furnished by the words of the instrument itself.... The 9th section of the last article declares, that "no preference shall be given, by any regulation of commerce or revenue, to the ports of one state over those of another." This clause cannot be understood as applicable to those laws only which are passed for the purposes of revenue, because it is expressly applied to commercial regulations; and the most obvious preference which can be given to one port over another, in regulating commerce, relates to navigation. But the subsequent part of the sentence is still more explicit. It is, "nor shall vessels bound to or from one state, be obliged to enter, clear or pay duties in another." These words have a direct reference to navigation.

The universally acknowledged power of the government to impose embargoes, must also be considered as showing, that all America is united in that construction which comprehends navigation in the word commerce. Gentlemen have said, in argument, that this is a branch of the war-making power, and that an embargo is an instrument of war, not a regulation of trade. That it may be, and often is, used as an instrument of war, cannot be denied.... But all embargoes are

not of this description.... When congress imposed that embargo which, for a time, engaged the attention of every man in the United States, the avowed object of the law was, the protection of commerce, and the avoiding of war. By its friends and its enemies, it was treated as a commercial, not as a war measure....

The word used in the constitution, then, comprehends, and has been always understood to comprehend, navigation within its meaning; and a power to regulate navigation, is as expressly granted, as if that term had been added to the word "commerce."

To what commerce does this power extend? The constitution informs us, to commerce "with foreign nations, and among the several states, and with the Indian tribes."

It has, we believe, been universally admitted, that these words comprehend every species of commercial intercourse between the United States and foreign nations. No sort of trade can be carried on between this country and any other, to which this power does not extend. It has been truly said, that commerce, as the word is used in the constitution, is a unit, every part of which is indicated by the term.

If this be the admitted meaning of the word, in its application to foreign nations, it must carry the same meaning throughout the sentence, and remain a unit, unless there be some plain intelligible cause which alters it.

The subject to which the power is next applied, is to commerce, "among the several states." The word "among" means intermingled with. A thing which is among others, is intermingled with them. Commerce among the states, cannot stop at the external boundary line of each state, but may be introduced into the interior.

It is not intended to say, that these words comprehend that commerce, which is completely internal, which is carried on between man and man in a state, or between different parts of the same state, and which does not extend to or affect other states. Such a power would be inconvenient, and is certainly unnecessary.

Comprehensive as the word "among" is, it may very properly be restricted to that commerce which concerns more states than one. The phrase is not one which would probably have been selected to indicate the completely interior traffic of a state, because it is not an apt phrase for that purpose; and the enumeration of the particular classes of commerce to which the power was to be extended, would not have been made, had the intention been to extend the power to every description. The enumeration presupposes something not enumerated; and that something, if we regard the language or the subject of the sentence, must be the exclusively internal commerce of a state....

But in regulating commerce with foreign nations, the power of congress does not stop at the jurisdictional lines of the several states. It would be a very useless power, if it could not pass those lines. The commerce of the United States with foreign nations, is that of the whole United States; every district has a right to participate in it. The deep streams which penetrate our country in every direction, pass through the interior of almost every state in the Union, and furnish the means of exercising this right. If congress has the power to regulate it, that power must be exercised whenever the subject exists. If it exists within the states, if a foreign voyage may commence or terminate at a port within a state, then the power of congress may be exercised within a state.

This principle is, if possible, still more clear, when applied to commerce "among the several states." They either join each other, in which case they are separated by a mathematical line, or they are remote from each other, in which case other states lie between them. What is commerce "among" them; and how is it to be conducted? Can a trading expedition between two adjoining states, commence and terminate outside of each? And if the trading intercourse be between two states remote from each other, must it not commence in one, terminate in the other, and probably pass through a third? Commerce among the states must, of necessity, be commerce with the states....

We are now arrived at the inquiry—what is this power?

It is the power to regulate; that is, to prescribe the rule by which commerce is to be governed. This power, like all others vested in congress, is complete in itself, may be exercised to its utmost extent, and acknowledges no limitations, other than are prescribed in the constitution. These are expressed in plain terms, and do not affect the questions which arise in this case, or which have been discussed at the bar. If, as has always been understood, the sovereignty of congress, though limited to specified objects, is plenary as to those objects, the power over commerce with foreign nations, and among the several states, is vested in congress as absolutely as it would be in a single government, having in its constitution the same restrictions on the exercise of the power as are

found in the constitution of the United States. The wisdom and the discretion of congress, their identity with the people, and the influence which their constituents possess at elections, are, in this, as in many other instances, as that, for example, of declaring war, the sole restraints on which they have relied, to secure them from its abuse. They are the restraints on which the people must often rely solely, in all representative governments.

The power of congress, then, comprehends navigation, within the limits of every state in the Union; so far as that navigation may be, in any manner, connected with "commerce with foreign nations, or among the several states, or with the Indian tribes." It may, of consequence, pass the jurisdictional line of New York, and act upon the very waters to which the prohibition now under consideration applies.

. . .

...When...each government exercises the power of taxation, neither is exercising the power of the other. But when a state proceeds to regulate commerce with foreign nations, or among the several states, it is exercising the very power that is granted to congress, and is doing the very thing which congress is authorized to do. There is no analogy, then, between the power of taxation and the power of regulating commerce.

[Marshall concludes that the licenses for the steamboats operated by Gibbons, which were granted under an act of Congress, gave full authority to those vessels to navigate the waters of the United States, notwithstanding any law of New York to the contrary. Conflicting New York laws were unconstitutional and void.]

Powerful and ingenious minds, taking, as postulates, that the powers expressly granted to the government of the Union, are to be contracted, by construction, into the narrowest possible compass, and that the original powers of the states are retained, if any possible construction will retain them, may, by a course of well-digested, but refined and metaphysical reasoning, founded on these premises, explain away the constitution of our country, and leave it, a magnificent structure, indeed, to look at, but totally unfit for use. They may so entangle and perplex the understanding, as to obscure principles, which were before thought quite plain, and induce doubts where, if the mind were to pursue its own course, none would be perceived. In such a case, it is peculiarly necessary to recur to safe and fundamental principles, to sustain those principles, and, when sustained, to make them the tests of the arguments to be examined.

JOHNSON, Justice. — The judgment entered by the court in this cause, has my entire approbation; but having adopted my conclusions on views of the subject materially different from those of my brethren, I feel it incumbent on me to exhibit those views....

Cooley v. Board of Wardens

53 U.S. 299 (1852)

A Pennsylvania law provided that all vessels of a certain description coming into state port should employ pilots to assure safety. If they refused they were required to pay a pilotage fee. Aaron Cooley argued that the state law was a regulation of foreign commerce and therefore an action solely within the authority of Congress, which had passed legislation in 1789 regarding the regulation of ports. Was this area of commerce within the exclusive domain of Congress, or could states exercise concurrent jurisdiction? Did foreign commerce demand uniformity or permit local diversity?

Mr. Justice CURTIS delivered the opinion of the court.

. . .

We think this particular regulation concerning half-pilotage fees, is an appropriate part of a general system of regulations of this subject. Testing it by the practice of commercial States and countries legislating on this subject, we find it has usually been deemed necessary to make similar provisions. Numerous laws of this kind are cited in the learned argument of the counsel for the defendant in error; and their fitness, as a part of a system of pilotage, in many places, may be inferred from their existence in so many different States and countries. Like other laws they are framed to meet the most usual cases, *quæ frequentius accidunt;* they rest upon the propriety of securing lives and property exposed to the perils of a dangerous navigation, by taking on board a person peculiarly skilled to encounter or avoid them;...

. . .

That the power to regulate commerce includes the regulation of navigation, we consider settled. And when we look to the nature of the service performed by pilots, to the relations which that service and its compensations bear to navigation between the several States, and between the ports of the United States and foreign countries, we are brought to the conclusion, that the regulation of the qualifications of pilots, of the modes and times of offering and rendering their services, of the responsibilities which shall rest upon them, of the powers they shall possess, of the compensation they may demand, and of the penalties by which their rights and duties may be enforced, do constitute regulations of navigation, and consequently of commerce, within the just meaning of this clause of the Constitution.

. . .

It becomes necessary, therefore, to consider whether this law of Pennsylvania, being a regulation of commerce, is valid.

The act of Congress of the 7th of August, 1789, sect. 4, is as follows:

"That all pilots in the bays, inlets, rivers, harbors, and ports of the United States shall continue to be regulated in conformity with the existing laws of the States, respectively, wherein such pilots may be, or with such laws as the States may respectively hereafter enact for the purpose, until further legislative provision shall be made by Congress."

If the law of Pennsylvania, now in question, had been in existence at the date of this act of Congress, we might hold it to have been adopted by Congress, and thus made a law of the United States, and so valid. Because this act does, in effect, give the force of an act of Congress, to the then existing State laws on this subject, so long as they should continue unrepealed by the State which enacted them.

But the law on which these actions are founded was not enacted till 1803. What effect then can be attributed to so much of the act of 1789, as declares, that pilots shall continue to be regulated in conformity, "with such laws as the States may respectively hereafter enact for the purpose, until further legislative provision shall be made by Congress"?

...The grant of commercial power to Congress does not contain any terms which expressly exclude the States from exercising an authority over its subject-matter. If they are excluded it must be because the nature of the power, thus granted to Congress, requires that a similar authority should not exist in the States....

...The act of 1789 contains a clear and authoritative declaration by the first Congress, that the nature of this subject is such, that until Congress should find it necessary to exert its power, it should be left to the legislation of the States; that it is local and not national; that it is likely to be the best provided for, not by one system, or plan of regulations, but by as many as the legislative discretion of the several States should deem applicable to the local peculiarities of the ports within their limits.

Viewed in this light, so much of this act of 1789 as declares that pilots shall continue to be regulated "by such laws as the States may respectively hereafter enact for that purpose," instead of being held to be inoperative, as an attempt to confer on the States a power to legislate, of which the Constitution had deprived them, is allowed an appropriate and important signification. It manifests the understanding of Congress, at the outset of the government, that the nature of this subject is not such as to require its exclusive legislation. The practice of the States, and of the national government, has been in conformity with this declaration, from the origin of the national government to this time; and the nature of the subject when examined, is such as to leave no doubt of the superior fitness and propriety, not to say the absolute necessity, of different systems of regulation, drawn from local knowledge and experience, and conformed to local wants....

It is the opinion of a majority of the court that the mere grant to Congress of the power to regulate commerce, did not deprive the States of power to regulate pilots, and that although Congress has legislated on this subject, its legislation manifests an intention, with a single exception, not to regulate this subject, but to leave its regulation to the several States....

We are of opinion that this State law was enacted by virtue of a power, residing in the State to legislate; that it is not in conflict with any law of Congress; that it does not interfere with any system which Congress has established by making regulations, or by intentionally leaving individuals to their own unrestricted action; that this law is therefore valid, and the judgment of the Supreme Court of Pennsylvania in each case must be affirmed.

Mr. Justice McLean and Mr. Justice Wayne dissented; and Mr. Justice Daniel, although he concurred in the judgment of the court, yet dissented from its reasoning.

Mr. Justice McLEAN.

It is with regret that I feel myself obliged to dissent from the opinion of a majority of my brethren in this case.

. . .

Why did Congress pass the act of 1789, adopting the pilot-laws of the respective States? Laws they unquestionably were, having been enacted by the States before the adoption of the Constitution....

Congress adopted the pilot-laws of the States, because it was well understood, they could have had no force, as regulations of foreign commerce or of commerce among the States, if not so adopted. By their adoption they were made acts of Congress, and ever since they have been so considered and enforced.

Each State regulates the commerce within its limits; which is not within the range of federal powers. So far, and no farther could effect have been given to the pilot laws of the States, under the Constitution. But those laws were only adopted "until further legislative provisions shall be made by Congress."

This shows that Congress claimed the whole commercial power on this subject, by adopting the pilot laws of the States, making them acts of Congress; and also by declaring that the adoption was only until some further legislative provision could be made by Congress.

Can Congress annul the acts of a State passed within its admitted sovereignty? No one, I suppose, could sustain such a proposition. State sovereignty can neither be enlarged nor diminished by an act of Congress. It is not known that Congress has ever claimed such a power.

If the States had not the power to enact pilot laws, as connected with foreign commerce, in 1789, when did they get it? It is an exercise of sovereign power to legislate. In this respect the Constitution is the same now as in 1789, and also the power of a State is the same....

I think the charge of half-pilotage is correct under the circumstances, and I only object to the power of the State to pass the law. Congress, to whom the subject peculiarly belongs, should have been applied to, and no doubt it would have adopted the act of the State.

Mr. Justice DANIEL.

I agree with the majority in their decision, that the judgments of the Supreme Court of Pennsylvania in these cases, should be affirmed, though I cannot go with them in the process or argument by which their conclusion has been reached.... The true question here is, whether the power to enact pilot-laws is appropriate and necessary, or rather most appropriate and necessary to the State or the federal governments. It being conceded that this power has been exercised by the States from their very dawn of existence; that it can be practi-

cally and beneficially applied by the local authorities only; it being conceded, as it must be, that the power to pass pilot-laws, as such, has not been in any express terms delegated to Congress, and does not necessarily conflict with the right to establish commercial regulations, I am forced to conclude that this is an original and inherent power in the States, and not one to be merely tolerated, or held subject to the sanction of the federal government.

. . .

Congress Overturns *Leisy v. Hardin*

In *Leisy* v. *Hardin,* 135 U.S. 100 (1890), the Supreme Court held that an Iowa law violated the Commerce Clause by prohibiting the sale of intoxicating liquors except for pharmaceutical, medicinal, chemical, or sacramental purposes. The law applied to "original packages" or kegs, unbroken and unopened, from the importer. Under the decision, based on Chief Justice Marshall's decision in *Brown* v. *Maryland* (1827), states were forbidden from regulating commerce between the states "without congressional permission." Within a matter of months, Congress passed legislation to override the Court. Portions of the Senate debate are reproduced here (21 Cong. Rec. 4642, 4954–55, 4964) as well as the statute (26 Stat. 313). The statute was upheld in *In re Rahrer,* 140 U.S. 545 (1891).

Mr. WILSON, of Iowa. From the Committee on the Judiciary I report favorably, with an amendment, the bill (S. 398) subjecting imported liquors to the provisions of the laws of the several States....

. . .

Mr. HOAR. I desire to make a brief statement in regard to the matter. This bill is rendered necessary, in the opinion of the committee, by the late decision of the Supreme Court of the United States, which holds, as I understand it, that intoxicating liquor manufactured in one State, conveyed into another, and there sold by the manufacturer or his agent, is protected by the Constitution of the United States from any regulation or prohibition of that sale by the State law on the ground that such prohibition or regulation is an interference with the regulation of commerce between the States. The court, in their opinion, say that the States can not pass such prohibitory or regulating statutes without the permission of Congress, which is understood to imply an opinion on the part of the court that Congress may give that permission, and that with that permission the States may pass the regulation or prohibitory enactment which they see fit.

. . .

[Mr. WILSON, of Iowa.]

...Mr. President, that State, which I in part represent in this body, elected as its policy the prohibition of the manufacture and sale of intoxicating liquors. The people of the State are satisfied with it; they desire the enforcement of their law; but, since the decision from which I have read an extract was announced, agents of distilleries and breweries in other States of the Union are already traversing Iowa and organizing "the original-package saloon" within the State, and there is no limitation as to what "the original package" may be. It may be a pint or a half-pint bottle of whisky; it may be a bottle or a keg of beer; it may be in any quantity and whatsoever form of package agreed upon between the manufacturer of another State and the agent that he may send to transact his business in Iowa.

All the States of this Union do not want prohibition. Some of them want license; some of them want local option; they have various desires in this respect. Some of them may want unrestrained traffic in the sale of intoxicants. The State of Iowa does not want that. She wants her present policy; at least, she should have an opportunity to administer it until her people determine to adopt something else in its place; and so with all the States.

Mr. BUTLER. The Senator from Iowa will allow me to interrupt him for an inquiry.

Mr. WILSON, of Iowa. Certainly.

Mr. BUTLER. Does the Senator hold that under the decision of the Supreme Court the State of Iowa would have the right, after the package gets into that State, to prevent the sale or take control of it in any way after it crosses the line?

Mr. WILSON, of Iowa. Undoubtedly the decision of the Supreme Court protects every package that may be transported into that State from abroad, from foreign countries or from other States, until it shall have passed from the hands of the importer and thereby become mingled with the common property of the State.

Mr. BUTLER. Then the State has the right to interpose by its laws and prevent the sale or any disposition of the article imported?

Mr. WILSON, of Iowa. After it shall have passed from the hands of the importer or his agent. But under this decision, whatever package may be introduced there — for instance, the brewer in Illinois, the distiller in Illinois or any other State may arrange to send his package in there, even in the shape of a vial containing a single drink, and organize his saloon on that basis, the importer holding possession, protected by the decision of the Supreme Court, until that package shall pass from his possession into the hands of his customer and that customer may drink a single drink of whisky in that original-package saloon in the good State of Iowa, and in spite of her laws.

. . .

Mr. EDMUNDS....

Now, let us begin with the Supreme Court. The Supreme Court of the United States is an independent and co-ordinate branch of the Government. Its mission is to decide causes between parties, and its decision of causes between parties all good order and government require shall be carried out and respected as between parties. But, as it regards the Congress of the United States, its opinions are of no more value to us than ours are to it. We are just as independent of the Supreme Court of the United States as it is of us, and every judge will admit it.

Suppose we think that this court has gone wrong and has made a mistake in deciding a given case between A and B that involves the safety and happiness of all the people of the United States in their respective States covering a continent, and that an internal policy may be good for the Pacific coast and bad for a State on the Atlantic coast, are

we to stop and say that is the end of the law and the mission of civilization in the United States for that reason? I take it not. It may be that when the next case comes up on a further and wider consideration the very gentlemen who now compose the court, differing as some of them did with the majority, may come to the conclusion that they had been led into an error and that they may still hold that the States of the United States in respect of what shall be done in those States and not among them is a matter that the Constitution leaves to those States to regulate as they will.

So I do not feel absolutely condemned and overpersuaded and feel myself as put in a box by what the Supreme Court of the United States have so recently said. It is their mission to decide causes between parties as they think they ought to be decided; and, as they have often done, it may be their mission next year to change their opinion and say that the rule ought to be the other way. So I do not feel deeply embarrassed by the fact that the Supreme Court of the United States has taken the largest step that in the whole hundred years of the Republic has ever been taken toward the centralization of power somewhere, either in the Supreme Court or in Congress, one or the other.

I do not believe, for one, in the centralization of power. I believe in its segregation and separation in every respect that concerns the internal affairs of the body of the people in every one of the States, leaving out of the question those universal human rights that everybody agrees are intrinsic in man and citizen.

So I am not greatly disturbed in respect of what the Supreme Court of the United States have said and done, except so far as it makes it now the mission of Congress to exert its power upon the subjects according to the light that it thought it had shone upon it, in order to preserve the internal policy and police of every State for itself, whether you call it an independent right or the execution of a national power under agencies that Congress provides, whichever way you choose to state it.

[Statute (26 Stat. 313)]:

Be it enacted by the Senate and House of Representatives of the United States of America in Congress assembled, That all fermented, distilled, or other intoxicating liquors or liquids transported into any State or Territory or remaining therein for use, consumption, sale or storage therein, shall upon arrival in such State or Territory be subject to the operation and effect of the laws of such State or Territory enacted in the exercise of its police powers, to the same extent and in the same manner as though such liquids or liquors had been produced in such State or Territory, and shall not be exempt therefrom by reason of being introduced therein in original packages or otherwise.

Approved, August 8, 1890.

C. NATIONALIZATION OF THE ECONOMY

Fundamental changes in economic structures over the past century gradually washed away many traditional boundaries between intrastate and interstate commerce. Judicial doctrines of dual federalism and concurrent powers lost ground to a gradual centralization of authority in the national government.

In 1886, the Supreme Court struck down an Illinois railroad statute because it affected, even for the part of the journey within the state, commerce among the states. Wabash, &c., Railway Co. v. Illinois, 118 U.S. 557 (1886). This decision made national regulation imperative, and Congress responded a year later by creating the Interstate Commerce Commission. Another decision allowed Congress to prohibit national and interstate traffic in lottery tickets even if its motivation—such as morality—competed with the state police power. CHAMPION v. AMES (Lottery Case), 188 U.S. 321 (1903). Two years later, a unanimous Court upheld a congressional statute that prevented a company from restraining trade even when the company's cattle came to rest within a stockyard of a particular state. The movement of cattle from state to state created a "current of commerce" subject to congressional control. Swift & Co. v. United States, 196 U.S. 375, 399 (1905). In later years, the Court evoked a similar image, calling the stockyards a temporary resting place for cattle moving interstate, serving as "a throat through which the current of commerce flows." Stafford v. Wallace, 258 U.S. 495, 516 (1922).

These decisions supported congressional regulation only in selected areas: railroads, morals, and health. For example, in 1914 the Supreme Court rejected artificial distinctions between *intrastate* and *interstate* by holding that Congress could regulate actions inside a state that were *related* to interstate commerce. Through this reasoning, it allowed a congressional commission to set railroad rates within a state. Shreveport Rate Case, 234 U.S. 342. Under the Commerce Clause, Congress could establish an eight-hour day for all railroad workers engaged in interstate commerce, especially when needed to resolve a nationwide strike. Wilson v. New, 243 U.S. 332 (1917). Other decisions upheld the power of Congress to seize and condemn prohibited articles, to forbid the interstate transportation of women engaged in prostitution, and to make it a crime to transport stolen motor vehicles in interstate or foreign commerce.[7] During time of war, commercial operations normally regulated by the states fall within the domain of the national government.[8]

Child Labor Legislation

This pattern of sustaining congressional power did not apply to factory conditions, hours, or wages. In 1916 Congress passed legislation to prevent the products of child labor from being shipped interstate. Legislators concluded that the bill was constitutional and consistent with recent Supreme Court rulings that permitted Congress to use the Commerce Clause to regu-

---

7. Hipolite Egg Co. v. United States, 220 U.S. 45 (1911) (seizing and condemning articles); Hoke v. United States, 227 U.S. 308 (1913) and Caminetti v. United States, 242 U.S. 470 (1917) (White Slave Traffic Act); Brooks v. United States, 267 U.S. 432 (1925) (stolen cars). See also Atlantic Coast Line v. Riverside Mills, 219 U.S. 186 (1911).

8. Case v. Bowles, 327 U.S. 92, 102 (1946); Dakota Cent. Tel. Co. v. South Dakota, 250 U.S. 163 (1919); Northern Pac. Ry. Co. v. North Dakota, 250 U.S. 135 (1919).

Solicitor General Beck Defends Child Labor Bill

The belief that the judiciary is fully empowered to sit in judgment upon the motives or objectives of other branches of the Government is a mischievous one, in that it so lowers the sense of constitutional morality among the people that neither in the legislative branch of the Government nor among the people is there as strong a purpose as formerly to maintain their constitution form of Government.

. . .

The erroneous idea that this court is the sole guardian and protector of our constitutional form of government has inevitably led to an impairment, both with the people and with their representatives, of what may be called the constitutional conscience.

... The prevalent disposition seems to be to ignore constitutional questions by shifting them to the Supreme Court, in the belief that that court will exercise the full powers of revision, which I have tried to show the Framers of the Constitution did not intend this court to have. The result may be an exaltation of this court, as a tribunal of extraordinary power; but, in the matter of constitutionalism, it inevitably leads to an impairment of the powers and duties of Congress and, above all, to the impairment of the popular conscience; for, in the last analysis, the Constitution will last in substance as long as the people believe in it and are willing to struggle for it.

Source: Brief on Behalf of Appellants and Plaintiff in Error, Bailey v. Drexel Furniture Co., Nos. 590, 657, U.S. Supreme Court, October Term, 1921, at 54–55; 21 Landmark Briefs 59–60.

late public health and morals. However, the Court held that the law exceeded the commerce power and invaded responsibilities left to the states. HAMMER v. DAGENHART, 247 U.S. 251 (1918). Within a matter of days, members of Congress confronted the Court by introducing new measures to regulate child labor. 56 Cong. Rec. 8341 (1918). The strategy this time was to use the taxing power by levying an excise tax on the net profits of persons employing child labor. Id. at 11560. Some members of Congress thought that the Court's decision had settled the issue and that Congress had no business reopening it. Senator Henry Cabot Lodge (R-Mass.), a leading conservative, denied that another legislative attempt at ending the "great evil" of child labor was inappropriate. 57 Cong. Rec. 611 (1918).

When this statute was brought before the Supreme Court, Solicitor General James M. Beck prepared a brief that defended the tax. He also urged the Court to exercise political prudence when reviewing, and possibly overturning, the considered efforts of the coequal branches, Congress and the President (see box). Nevertheless, the Court struck down this second statute as well. BAILEY v. DREXEL FURNITURE CO. [Child Labor Tax Case], 259 U.S. 20 (1922). Not until 1941, after the composition of the Court had been drastically altered and restrictive judicial doctrines abandoned, was child labor legislation upheld. UNITED STATES v. DARBY, 312 U.S. 100 (1941).

Judicial efforts to curb other economic reforms adopted by Congress and the states are treated in Chapter 9. Courts restricted state use of the "police power," relied on a fictional "liberty of contract" to invalidate other statutes, and used substantive due process to strike down legislative efforts to establish maximum hours and minimum wages. These judicial doctrines came to an end in 1937.

Champion v. Ames
(Lottery Case)

188 U.S. 321 (1903)

Many of the states tried to suppress the buying and selling of lottery tickets but found themselves helpless in controlling lotteries in interstate commerce. Congress passed legislation in 1895 to prohibit lottery tickets from interstate or foreign commerce. Charles Champion was charged with violating the act. The Court confronted three principal issues. Is the selling of lottery tickets subject to regulation under the Commerce Clause? Does the power to regulate commerce include the authority to prohibit it? May Congress exercise a national "police power" to protect citizens from immoral transactions, or is that responsibility reserved to the states?

MR. JUSTICE HARLAN, after making the foregoing statement of facts, delivered the opinion of the court.

The appellant insists that the carrying of lottery tickets from one State to another State by an express company engaged in carrying freight and packages from State to State, although such tickets may be contained in a box or package, does not constitute, and cannot by any act of Congress be legally made to constitute, *commerce* among the States within the meaning of the clause of the Constitution of the United States providing that Congress shall have power "to regulate commerce with foreign nations, and among the several States, and with the Indian tribes;" consequently, that Congress cannot make it an offence to cause such tickets to be carried from one State to another.

. . .

What is the import of the word "commerce" as used in the Constitution? It is not defined by that instrument. Undoubtedly, the carrying from one State to another by independent carriers of things or commodities that are ordinary subjects of traffic, and which have in themselves a recognized value in money, constitutes interstate commerce....

. . .

It was said in argument that lottery tickets are not of any real or substantial value in themselves, and therefore are not subjects of commerce. If that were conceded to be the only legal test as to what are to be deemed subjects of the commerce that may be regulated by Congress, we cannot accept as accurate the broad statement that such tickets are of no value. Upon their face they showed that the lottery company offered a large capital prize, to be paid to the holder of the ticket winning the prize at the drawing advertised to be held at Asuncion, Paraguay. Money was placed on deposit in different banks in the United States to be applied by the agents representing the lottery company to the prompt payment of prizes. These tickets were the subject of traffic; they could have been sold; and the holder was assured that the company would pay to him the amount of the prize drawn....

We are of opinion that lottery tickets are subjects of traffic and therefore are subjects of commerce, and the regulation of the carriage of such tickets from State to State, at least by independent carriers, is a regulation of commerce among the several States.

But it is said that the statute in question does not regulate the carrying of lottery tickets from State to State, but by punishing those who cause them to be so carried Congress in effect prohibits such carrying; that in respect of the carrying from one State to another of articles or things that are, in fact, or according to usage in business, the subjects of commerce, the authority given Congress was not to *prohibit,* but only to *regulate....*

. . .

...Are we prepared to say that a provision which is, in effect, a *prohibition* of the carriage of such articles from State to State is not a fit or appropriate mode for the *regulation* of that particular kind of commerce? If lottery traffic, *carried on through interstate commerce,* is a matter of which Congress may take cognizance and over which its power may be exerted, can it be possible that it must tolerate the traffic, and simply regulate the manner in which it may be carried on? Or may not Congress, for the protection of the people of all the States, and under the power to regulate interstate commerce, devise such means, within the scope of the Constitution, and not prohibited by it, as will drive that traffic out of commerce among the States?

. . .

If a State, when considering legislation for the suppression of lotteries within its own limits, may properly take into view the evils that inhere in the raising of money, in that mode, why may not Congress, invested with the power to regulate commerce among the several States, provide that such commerce shall not be polluted by the carrying of lottery tickets from one State to another? In this connection it must not be forgotten that the power of Congress to regulate commerce among the States is plenary, is complete in itself, and is subject to no limitations except such as may be found in the Constitution. What provision in that instrument can be regarded as limiting the exercise of the power granted? What clause can be cited which, in any degree, countenances the suggestion that one may, of right, carry or cause to be carried from one State to another that which will harm the public morals? *[The Court dismisses the argument that the constitutional provision that no person shall be deprived of liberty without due process of law implies the right to introduce into commerce an article that is injurious to the public morals.]*

If it be said that the act of 1895 is inconsistent with the Tenth Amendment, reserving to the States respectively or to the people the powers not delegated to the United States, the answer is that the power to regulate commerce among the States has been expressly delegated to Congress.

Besides, Congress, by that act, does not assume to interfere with traffic or commerce in lottery tickets carried on exclusively within the limits of any State, but has in view only commerce of that kind among the several States. It has not assumed to interfere with the completely internal affairs of any State, and has only legislated in respect of a matter which concerns the people of the United States....

. . .

... We decide nothing more in the present case than that lottery tickets are subjects of traffic among those who choose to sell or buy them; that the carriage of such tickets by independent carriers from one State to another is therefore interstate commerce; that under its power to regulate commerce among the several States Congress —

subject to the limitations imposed by the Constitution upon the exercise of the powers granted — has plenary authority over such commerce, and may prohibit the carriage of such tickets from State to State; and that legislation to that end, and of that character, is not inconsistent with any limitation or restriction imposed upon the exercise of the powers granted to Congress.

The judgment is

Affirmed.

MR. CHIEF JUSTICE FULLER, with whom concur MR. JUSTICE BREWER, MR. JUSTICE SHIRAS and MR. JUSTICE PECKHAM, dissenting.

. . .

The power of the State to impose restraints and burdens on persons and property in conservation and promotion of the public health, good order and prosperity is a power originally and always belonging to the States, not surrendered by them to the General Government nor directly restrained by the Constitution of the United States, and essentially exclusive, and the suppression of lotteries as a harmful business falls within this power, commonly called of police. *Douglas* v. *Kentucky,* 168 U. S. 488.

It is urged, however, that because Congress is empowered to regulate commerce between the several States, it, therefore, may suppress lotteries by prohibiting the carriage of lottery matter. Congress may indeed make all laws necessary and proper for carrying the powers granted to it into execution, and doubtless an act prohibiting the carriage of lottery matter would be necessary and proper to the execution of a power to suppress lotteries; but that power belongs to the States and not to Congress. To hold that Congress has general police power would be to hold that it may accomplish objects not entrusted to the General Government, and to defeat the operation of the Tenth Amendment, declaring that: "The powers not delegated to the United States by the Constitution, nor prohibited by it to the States, are reserved to the States respectively, or to the people."

. . .

Hammer v. Dagenhart

247 U.S. 251 (1918)

In 1916, Congress passed legislation to prohibit the transportation in interstate commerce of goods made at a factory where children under the age of fourteen years worked, or children between the ages of fourteen and sixteen worked more than eight hours a day, or more than six days a week, or after 7 p.m. or before 6 a.m. Roland H. Dagenhart filed this suit on his own behalf and for his two minor sons who were employed in a cotton mill. After a district court declared the statute unconstitutional, the U.S. Attorney, W.C. Hammer, brought an appeal to the Supreme Court.

MR. JUSTICE DAY delivered the opinion of the court.

. . .

The attack upon the act rests upon three propositions: First: It is not a regulation of interstate and foreign commerce; Second: It contravenes the Tenth Amendment to the Constitution; Third: It conflicts with the Fifth Amendment to the Constitution.

The controlling question for decision is: Is it within the authority of Congress in regulating commerce among the States to prohibit the transportation in interstate commerce of manufactured goods, the product of a factory in which, within thirty days prior to their removal therefrom, children . . . have been employed. . . .

The power essential to the passage of this act, the Government contends, is found in the commerce clause of the Constitution which authorizes Congress to regulate commerce with foreign nations and among the States.

In *Gibbons* v. *Ogden,* 9 Wheat. 1, Chief Justice Marshall, speaking for this court, and defining the extent and nature of the commerce power, said, "It is the power to regulate; that is, to prescribe the rule by which commerce is to be governed." In other words, the power is one to control the means by which commerce is carried on, which is directly the contrary of the assumed right to forbid commerce from moving and thus destroy it as to particular commodities. But it is insisted that adjudged cases in this court establish the doctrine that the power to regulate given to Congress incidentally includes the authority to prohibit the movement of ordinary commodities and therefore that the subject is not open for discussion. The cases demonstrate the contrary. They rest upon the character of the particular subjects dealt with and the fact that the scope of governmental authority, state or national, possessed over

them is such that the authority to prohibit is as to them but the exertion of the power to regulate.

The first of these cases is *Champion* v. *Ames,* 188 U.S. 321, the so-called *Lottery Case,* in which it was held that Congress might pass a law having the effect to keep the channels of commerce free from use in the transportation of tickets used in the promotion of lottery schemes. In *Hipolite Egg Co.* v. *United States,* 220 U.S. 45, this court sustained the power of Congress to pass the Pure Food and Drug Act which prohibited the introduction into the States by means of interstate commerce of impure foods and drugs. In *Hoke* v. *United States,* 227 U. S. 308, this court sustained the constitutionality of the so-called "White Slave Traffic Act" whereby the transportation of a woman in interstate commerce for the purpose of prostitution was forbidden. . . .

In each of these instances the use of interstate transportation was necessary to the accomplishment of harmful results. In other words, although the power over interstate transportation was to regulate, that could only be accomplished by prohibiting the use of the facilities of interstate commerce to effect the evil intended.

This element is wanting in the present case. The thing intended to be accomplished by this statute is the denial of the facilities of interstate commerce to those manufacturers in the States who employ children within the prohibited ages. The act in its effect does not regulate transportation among the States, but aims to standardize the ages at which children may be employed in mining and manufacturing within the States. The goods shipped are of themselves harmless. . . .

. . .

It is further contended that the authority of Congress may be exerted to control interstate commerce in the shipment of child-made goods because of the effect of the circulation of such goods in other States where the evil of this class of labor has been recognized by local legislation, and the right to thus employ child labor has been more rigorously restrained than in the State of production. In other words, that the unfair competition, thus engendered, may be controlled by closing the channels of interstate commerce to manufacturers in those States where the local laws do not meet what Congress deems to be the more just standard of other States.

There is no power vested in Congress to require the States to exercise their police power so as to prevent possible unfair competition. Many causes may coöperate to give one State, by reason of local laws or conditions, an economic advantage over others. The Commerce Clause was not intended to give to Congress a general authority to equalize such conditions. In some of the States laws have been passed fixing minimum wages for women, in others the local law regulates the hours of labor of women in various employments. Business done in such States may be at an economic disadvantage when compared with States which have no such regulations; surely, this fact does not give Congress the power to deny transportation in interstate commerce to those who carry on business where the hours of labor and the rate of compensation for women have not been fixed by a standard in use in other States and approved by Congress.

The grant of power to Congress over the subject of interstate commerce was to enable it to regulate such commerce, and not to give it authority to control the States in their exercise of the police power over local trade and manufacture.

The grant of authority over a purely federal matter was not intended to destroy the local power always existing and carefully reserved to the States in the Tenth Amendment to the Constitution.

. . .

In our view the necessary effect of this act is, by means of a prohibition against the movement in interstate commerce of ordinary commercial commodities, to regulate the hours of labor of children in factories and mines within the States, a purely state authority. Thus the act in a twofold sense is repugnant to the Constitution. It not only transcends the authority delegated to Congress over commerce but also exerts a power as to a purely local matter to which the federal authority does not extend. The far reaching result of upholding the act cannot be more plainly

indicated than by pointing out that if Congress can thus regulate matters entrusted to local authority by prohibition of the movement of commodities in interstate commerce, all freedom of commerce will be at an end, and the power of the States over local matters may be eliminated, and thus our system of government be practically destroyed.

For these reasons we hold that this law exceeds the constitutional authority of Congress. It follows that the decree of the District Court must be

Affirmed.

MR. JUSTICE HOLMES, dissenting.

. . . The objection urged against the power *[of Congress]* is that the States have exclusive control over their methods of production and that Congress cannot meddle with them, and taking the proposition in the sense of direct intermeddling I agree to it and suppose that no one denies it. But if an act is within the powers specifically conferred upon Congress, it seems to me that it is not made any less constitutional because of the indirect effects that it may have, however obvious it may be that it will have those effects, and that we are not at liberty upon such grounds to hold it void.

The first step in my argument is to make plain what no one is likely to dispute — that the statute in question is within the power expressly given to Congress if considered only as to its immediate effects and that if invalid it is so only upon some collateral ground. The statute confines itself to prohibiting the carriage of certain goods in interstate or foreign commerce. Congress is given power to regulate such commerce in unqualified terms. It would not be argued today that the power to regulate does not include the power to prohibit. . . .

The question then is narrowed to whether the exercise of its otherwise constitutional power by Congress can be pronounced unconstitutional because of its possible reaction upon the conduct of the States in a matter upon which I have admitted that they are free from direct control. I should have thought that matter had been disposed of so fully as to leave no room for doubt. I should have thought that the most conspicuous decisions of this Court had made it clear that the power to regulate commerce and other constitutional powers could not be cut down or qualified by the fact that it might interfere with the carrying out of the domestic policy of any State.

The manufacture of oleomargarine is as much

a matter of state regulation as the manufacture of cotton cloth. Congress levied a tax upon the compound when colored so as to resemble butter that was so great as obviously to prohibit the manufacture and sale. In a very elaborate discussion the present Chief Justice excluded any inquiry into the purpose of an act which apart from that purpose was within the power of Congress. *McCray v. United States,* 195 U. S. 27....

The notion that prohibition is any less prohibition when applied to things now thought evil I do not understand. But if there is any matter upon which civilized countries have agreed—far more unanimously than they have with regard to intoxicants and some other matters over which this country is now emotionally aroused—it is the evil of premature and excessive child labor. I should have thought that if we were to introduce our own moral conceptions where in my opinion they do not belong, this was preëminently a case for upholding the exercise of all its powers by the United States.

But I had thought that the propriety of the exercise of a power admitted to exist in some cases was for the consideration of Congress alone and that this Court always had disavowed the right to intrude its judgment upon questions of policy or morals. It is not for this Court to pronounce when prohibition is necessary to regulation if it ever may be necessary—to say that it is permissible as against strong drink but not as against the product of ruined lives.

The act does not meddle with anything belonging to the States. They may regulate their internal affairs and their domestic commerce as they like. But when they seek to send their products across the state line they are no longer within their rights. If there were no Constitution and no Congress their power to cross the line would depend upon their neighbors. Under the Constitution such commerce belongs not to the States but to Congress to regulate. It may carry out its views of public policy whatever indirect effect they may have upon the activities of the States....

MR. JUSTICE MCKENNA, MR. JUSTICE BRANDEIS AND MR. JUSTICE CLARKE concur in this opinion.

Bailey v. Drexel Furniture Co.
(Child Labor Tax Case)

259 U.S. 20 (1922)

After the Supreme Court in *Hammer* v. *Dagenhart* (1918) struck down the attempt by Congress to use the Commerce Clause to regulate child labor, Congress passed legislation in 1919 to levy a tax on goods produced by child labor. The Court in this case reviews the power of Congress to use its taxing power as a regulatory device to eliminate the evils of child labor. J.W. Bailey, an IRS collector, assessed the Drexel Furniture Company $6,312.79 for employing a boy under the age of fourteen during the 1919 tax year.

MR. CHIEF JUSTICE TAFT delivered the opinion of the court.

This case presents the question of the constitutional validity of the Child Labor Tax Law....

. . .

The law is attacked on the ground that it is a regulation of the employment of child labor in the States—an exclusively state function under the Federal Constitution and within the reservations of the Tenth Amendment. It is defended on the ground that it is a mere excise tax levied by the Congress of the United States under its broad power of taxation conferred by § 8, Article I, of the Federal Constitution. We must construe the law and interpret the intent and meaning of Congress from the language of the act. The words are to be given their ordinary meaning unless the context shows that they are differently used. Does this law impose a tax with only that incidental restraint and regulation which a tax must inevitably involve? Or does it regulate by the use of the so-called tax as a penalty? If a tax, it is clearly an excise. If it were an excise on a commodity or other thing of value we might not be permitted under previous decisions of this court to infer solely from its heavy burden that the act intends a prohibition instead of a tax. But this act is more. It provides a heavy exaction for a departure from a detailed and specified course of conduct in business. That course of business is that employers shall employ in mines and quarries, children of an age greater than sixteen years; in mills and factories, children of an age greater than fourteen years, and shall prevent children of less than sixteen years in mills and factories from working more than eight hours a day or six days in the week. If an employer departs from this prescribed course of business, he is to pay to the Government one-tenth of his entire net income in the business for a full year. The amount is not to be proportioned in any degree to the extent or frequency of the departures, but is to be paid by the employer in full measure whether he employs five hundred children for a year, or employs only one for a day. Moreover, if he does not know the child is within the named age limit, he is not to pay; that is to say, it is only where he knowingly departs from the prescribed course that payment is to be exacted. Scienter is associated with penalties not with taxes. The employer's factory is to be subject to inspection at any time not only by the taxing officers of the Treasury, the Department normally charged with the collection of taxes, but also by the Secretary of Labor and his subordinates whose normal function is the advancement and protection of the welfare of the workers. In the light of these features of the act, a court must be blind not to see that the so-called tax is imposed to stop the employment of children within the age limits prescribed. Its prohibitory and regulatory effect and purpose are palpable. All others can see and understand this. How can we properly shut our minds to it?

It is the high duty and function of this court in cases regularly brought to its bar to decline to recognize or enforce seeming laws of Congress, dealing with subjects not entrusted to Congress but left or committed by the supreme law of the land to the control of the States. We can not avoid the duty even though it require us to refuse to give effect to legislation designed to promote the highest good. The good sought in unconstitutional legislation is an insidious feature because it leads citizens and legislators of good purpose to promote it without thought of the serious breach it will make in the ark of our covenant or the harm which will come from breaking down recognized standards. In the maintenance of local self government, on the one hand, and the national power, on the other, our country has been able to endure and prosper for near a century and a half.

Out of a proper respect for the acts of a coördinate branch of the Government, this court has gone far to sustain taxing acts as such, even though there has been ground for suspecting from the weight of the tax it was intended to destroy its subject. But, in the act before us, the presumption of validity cannot prevail, because the proof of the contrary is found on the very face of its provisions. Grant the validity of this law, and all that Congress would need to do, hereafter, in seeking to take over to its control any one of the great number of subjects of public interest, jurisdiction of which the States have never parted with, and which are reserved to them by the Tenth Amendment, would be to enact a detailed measure of complete regulation of the subject and enforce it by a so-called tax upon departures from it. To give such magic to the word "tax" would be to break down all constitutional limitation of the powers of Congress and completely wipe out the sovereignty of the States.

The difference between a tax and a penalty is sometimes difficult to define and yet the consequences of the distinction in the required method of their collection often are important.... Taxes are occasionally imposed in the discretion of the legislature on proper subjects with the primary motive of obtaining revenue from them and with the incidental motive of discouraging them by making their continuance onerous. They do not lose their character as taxes because of the incidental motive. But there comes a time in the extension of the penalizing features of the so-called tax when it loses its character as such and becomes a mere penalty with the characteristics of regulation and punishment. Such is the case in the law before us. Although Congress does not invalidate the contract of employment or expressly declare that the employment within the mentioned ages is illegal, it does exhibit its intent practically to achieve the latter result by adopting the criteria of wrongdoing and imposing its principal consequence on those who transgress its standard.

The case before us can not be distinguished from that of *Hammer* v. *Dagenhart*, 247 U.S. 251. Congress there enacted a law to prohibit transportation in interstate commerce of goods made at a factory in which there was employment of children within the same ages and for the same number of hours a day and days in a week as are penalized by the act in this case. This court held the law in that case to be void. It said:

"In our view the necessary effect of this act is, by means of a prohibition against the movement in interstate commerce of ordinary commercial commodities, to regulate the hours of labor of children in factories and mines within the States, a purely state authority."

In the case at the bar, Congress in the name of a tax which on the face of the act is a penalty seeks to do the same thing, and the effort must be equally futile.

The analogy of the *Dagenhart Case* is clear. The congressional power over interstate commerce is, within its proper scope, just as complete and unlimited as the congressional power to tax, and the legislative motive in its exercise is just as free from judicial suspicion and inquiry. Yet when Congress threatened to stop interstate commerce in ordinary and necessary commodities, unobjectionable as subjects of transportation, and to deny the same to the people of a State in order to coerce them into compliance with Congress's regulation of state concerns, the court said this was not in fact regulation of interstate commerce, but rather that of State concerns and was invalid. So here the so-called tax is a penalty to coerce people of a State to act as Congress wishes them to act in respect of a matter completely the business of the state government under the Federal Constitution....

. . .

For the reasons given, we must hold the Child Labor Tax Law invalid and the judgment of the District Court is

Affirmed.

MR. JUSTICE CLARKE dissents.

United States v. Darby

312 U.S. 100 (1941)

The Fair Labor Standards Act of 1938 provided for minimum wages and maximum hours for employees engaged in the production of goods for interstate commerce. The statute forced the Court to rethink its doctrine on "manufacture." If manufacture is not of itself interstate commerce, would the shipment of manufactured goods interstate bring it within the authority of Congress to regulate? The statute also excluded the products of child labor from interstate commerce, requiring the Court to revisit its holding in *Hammer* v. *Dagenhart* (1918), which had struck down the use of the Commerce Clause to regulate child labor. In this case, the government prosecutes Fred W. Darby, owner of a lumber company, for violating the 1938 statute.

MR. JUSTICE STONE delivered the opinion of the Court.

The two principal questions raised by the record in this case are, *first,* whether Congress has constitutional power to prohibit the shipment in interstate commerce of lumber manufactured by employees whose wages are less than a prescribed minimum or whose weekly hours of labor at that wage are greater than a prescribed maximum, and, *second,* whether it has power to prohibit the employment of workmen in the production of goods "for interstate commerce" at other than prescribed wages and hours. A subsidiary question is whether in connection with such prohibitions Congress can require the employer subject to them to keep records showing the hours worked each day and week by each of his employees including those engaged "in the production and manufacture of goods to-wit, lumber, for 'interstate commerce.'"

. . .

The indictment charges that appellee is engaged, in the State of Georgia, in the business of acquiring raw materials, which he manufactures into finished lumber with the intent, when manufactured, to ship it in interstate commerce to customers outside the state, and that he does in fact so ship a large part of the lumber so produced. There are numerous counts charging appellee with the shipment in interstate commerce from Georgia to points outside the state of lumber in the production of which, for interstate commerce, appellee has employed workmen at less than the prescribed minimum wage or more than the prescribed maximum hours without payment to them of any wage for overtime. Other counts charge the employment by appellee of workmen in the production of lumber for interstate commerce at wages at less than 25 cents an hour or for more than the maximum hours per week without payment to them of the prescribed overtime wage. Still another count charges appellee with failure to keep records showing the hours worked each day a week by each of his employees....

The demurrer, so far as now relevant to the appeal, challenged the validity of the Fair Labor Standards Act under the Commerce Clause and the Fifth and Tenth Amendments. The district court quashed the indictment in its entirety upon the broad grounds that the Act, which it interpreted as a regulation of manufacture within the states, is unconstitutional. It declared that manufacture is not interstate commerce and that the regulation by the Fair Labor Standards Act of wages and hours of employment of those engaged in the manufacture of goods which it is intended at the time of production "may or will be" after production "sold in interstate commerce in part or in whole" is not within the congressional power to regulate interstate commerce.

. . .

The prohibition of shipment of the proscribed goods in interstate commerce....

While manufacture is not of itself interstate commerce, the shipment of manufactured goods interstate is such commerce and the prohibition of such shipment by Congress is indubitably a regulation of the commerce. The power to regulate commerce is the power "to prescribe the rule by which commerce is governed." *Gibbons* v. *Ogden,* 9 Wheat. 1, 196. It extends not only to those regulations which aid, foster and protect the commerce, but embraces those which prohibit it....It is conceded that the power of Congress to prohibit transportation in interstate commerce includes noxious articles,...stolen articles,...kidnapped persons,...and articles such as intoxicating liquor or convict made goods, traffic in which is forbidden or restricted by the laws of the state of destination....

But it is said that the present prohibition falls within the scope of none of these categories; that while the prohibition is nominally a regulation of the commerce its motive or purpose is regulation of wages and hours of persons engaged in manufacture, the control of which has been reserved to the states and upon which Georgia and some of the states of destination have placed no restriction;...

The power of Congress over interstate commerce "is complete in itself, may be exercised to its utmost extent, and acknowledges no limitations other than are prescribed in the Constitution." *Gibbons* v. *Ogden, supra,* 196. That power can neither be enlarged nor diminished by the exercise or non-exercise of state power....Congress, following its own conception of public policy concerning the restrictions which may appropriately be imposed on interstate commerce, is free to ex-

clude from the commerce articles whose use in the states for which they are destined it may conceive to be injurious to the public health, morals or welfare, even though the state has not sought to regulate their use....

Such regulation is not a forbidden invasion of state power merely because either its motive or its consequence is to restrict the use of articles of commerce within the states of destination; and is not prohibited unless by other Constitutional provisions. It is no objection to the assertion of the power to regulate interstate commerce that its exercise is attended by the same incidents which attend the exercise of the police power of the states....

In the more than a century which has elapsed since the decision of *Gibbons* v. *Ogden,* these principles of constitutional interpretation have been so long and repeatedly recognized by this Court as applicable to the Commerce Clause, that there would be little occasion for repeating them now were it not for the decision of this Court twenty-two years ago in *Hammer* v. *Dagenhart,* 247 U.S. 251. In that case it was held by a bare majority of the Court over the powerful and now classic dissent of Mr. Justice Holmes setting forth the fundamental issues involved, that Congress was without power to exclude the products of child labor from interstate commerce. The reasoning and conclusion of the Court's opinion there cannot be reconciled with the conclusion which we have reached, that the power of Congress under the Commerce Clause is plenary to exclude any article from interstate commerce subject only to the specific prohibitions of the Constitution.

Hammer v. *Dagenhart* has not been followed. The distinction on which the decision was rested that Congressional power to prohibit interstate commerce is limited to articles which in themselves have some harmful or deleterious property—a distinction which was novel when made and unsupported by any provision of the Constitution—has long since been abandoned....

The conclusion is inescapable that *Hammer* v. *Dagenhart* was a departure from the principles which have prevailed in the interpretation of the Commerce Clause both before and since the decision and that such vitality, as a precedent, as it then had has long since been exhausted. It should be and now is overruled.

. . .

Our conclusion is unaffected by the Tenth Amendment which provides: "The powers not delegated to the United States by the Constitution, nor prohibited by it to the States, are reserved to the States respectively, or to the people." The amendment states but a truism that all is retained which has not been surrendered. There is nothing in the history of its adoption to suggest that it was more than declaratory of the relationship between the national and state governments as it had been established by the Constitution before the amendment or that its purpose was other than to allay fears that the new national government might seek to exercise powers not granted, and that the states might not be able to exercise fully their reserved powers....

Reversed.

D. THE NEW DEAL WATERSHED

During the New Deal, the Supreme Court at first resisted, but eventually capitulated, to a wholesale expansion of congressional power over commerce. Initially, the Court prohibited Congress from regulating commercial activities that were regarded as production and manufacture, as "local" or intrastate, or that affected commerce only "indirectly." These formulas were variations of dual federalism. By 1936 the Court began to embrace what it had accepted intermittently in the past: Congress could regulate intrastate activities that had a substantial relation to interstate commerce.

In two cases in 1935, the Court declared unconstitutional the National Industrial Recovery Act (NIRA) of 1933. A provision involving production quotas for petroleum products was struck down as an excessive delegation of legislative power to the President. Panama Refining Co. v. Ryan, 293 U.S. 388 (1935). The remainder of the NIRA was invalidated a few months later when a unanimous Court decided that the statute violated the delegation doctrine and exceeded Congress's power to regulate commerce. The Court refused to apply the "current of commerce" concept to intrastate commerce that involved purchases or transportation of goods outside the state. Once a commodity became "commingled with the mass of property within the State," the flow of interstate commerce ceased. Schechter Corp. v. United States, 295 U.S. 495, 543 (1935).

The Court struck down the Railroad Retirement Act, which transferred funds from railroad carriers to retirees. The Court, refusing to justify the statute under the Commerce Clause, treated it as a taking of property requiring just compensation. Railroad Retirement Board v. Alton R. Co., 295 U.S. 330 (1935). Also invalidated was the Bituminous Coal Conservation Act of 1935, which relied on the Commerce Clause to regulate mining and the distribution of coal. The Court said that the commerce power did not permit Congress to control the conditions in which coal is produced (such as labor conditions) before coal became an article of commerce. Labor conditions affected commerce only "indirectly." Production and manufacture did not constitute commerce, said the Court, even when done with intent to sell or transport the commodities out of the state. CARTER v. CARTER COAL CO., 298 U.S. 238 (1936). The processing tax of the Agricultural Adjustment Act was declared unconstitutional in *United States* v. *Butler* (see reading at pages 408–11).

The Court Switches

After Roosevelt's election in 1936 and his attempt to pack the judiciary, the Supreme Court began to accommodate New Deal legislation. Without a change in the Court's composition, but with Chief Justice Hughes and Justice Roberts now solidly supporting the three liberals (Brandeis, Cardozo, and Stone), the Court upheld the National Labor Relations Act. The Court accepted Congress's argument that labor disputes directly burdened or obstructed interstate or foreign commerce and could be regulated by the Commerce Clause. The Act gave employees in industry a fundamental right to organize and engage in collective bargaining.

Stages of Federalism

1. Nationalism (1789–1835). National powers are read broadly to include implied as well as explicit powers. Generous interpretation of Commerce Clause. Dominated by *McCulloch v. Maryland* (1819) and *Gibbons v. Ogden* (1824). Opportunity for states in some areas to exercise concurrent power over commerce.

2. Dual Federalism (1835–1937). National and state governments have mutually exclusive powers. Within their own spheres they are supreme and independent. Congress may not exercise power over production or manufacturing because they are "local" and intrastate.

Congress could not regulate economic activities that affected commerce only "indirectly."

3. Cooperative Federalism (1937–present). Businesses "affected with a public interest" or with a substantial relation to interstate commerce may be regulated by Congress. Relying on the spending power, Congress makes grants to states and imposes conditions on those funds. Congress may preempt state regulation but, until it does, states may regulate with standards that differ from federal requirements. In the 1990s, the Supreme Court handed down a number of decisions that revitalized dual federalism.

Any intrastate activity that had a close and substantial relationship to interstate commerce could be brought within the control of Congress. To enforce the Act, Congress established a National Labor Relations Board (NLRB) with the power to prevent any person from engaging in unfair labor practices "affecting commerce." NLRB v. JONES & LAUGHLIN, 301 U.S. 1 (1937).

In 1939 the Court sustained the Agricultural Adjustment Act, which used marketing controls to limit the amount of commodities that could be sold. Through the use of quotas, Congress hoped to stabilize prices and limit production. Farmers who exceeded their allotment had to pay a penalty at the warehouses, the "throat" where commodities entered "the stream of commerce." Mulford v. Smith, 307 U.S. 38, 47 (1939). Wheat marketing quotas, even for wheat not intended for commerce but for consumption on the farm, were upheld three years later by a unanimous Court. WICKARD v. FILBURN, 317 U.S. 111 (1942). The Fair Labor Standards Act of 1938 was upheld, allowing Congress to regulate the wages and hours of manufacturing employees. The Court rejected the argument that manufacturing was an intrastate activity and therefore outside the Commerce Clause. Congress could regulate intrastate activities where they have a "substantial effect" on interstate commerce. United States v. Darby, 312 U.S. 100, 119 (1941).

Through these decisions the United States entered into its third and current stage of "cooperative federalism" (see box). Although by the late 1930s the Court had largely bowed to the judgments of Congress on economic regulation and the scope of the Commerce Clause, the new Roosevelt Court signaled its intention to give greater scrutiny to constitutional provisions that protect individual rights and liberties. In a famous footnote written by Justice Stone in a 1938 case, the Court suggested that it might have a special responsibility to protect "discrete and insular minorities," especially when the political processes that supposedly safeguard minority rights have been curtailed. United States v. Carolene Products Co., 304 U.S. 144, 153 n.4 (1938). This footnote foreshadowed the Court's later activism in such areas as religious liberty, racial discrimination, and criminal rights. (The *Carolene* footnote appears in Chapter 15, p. 851.)

After the Court's retreat in 1937, it continued to monitor federal-state legislation over the economy. State efforts to limit the length of railroad cars traveling interstate could not be justified for reasons of safety or the police power. Even when Congress had not regulated an area, state actions that interfered with interstate commerce were not permitted under the Commerce

Clause. SOUTHERN PACIFIC CO. v. ARIZONA 325 U.S. 761 (1945). Although states may impose burdensome regulations in the interest of local health and safety, they may not restrain interstate commerce for the purpose of advancing their own commercial interests or promoting local economic advantages. Hood v. Du Mond, 336 U.S. 525 (1949). The Supreme Court has developed a number of criteria to indicate when state actions burden interstate commerce, but the enforcement and implementation of these judicial tests depend largely on congressional action. Commonwealth Edison Co. v. Montana, 453 U.S. 609 (1981).

Scope of Independent State Action

These decisions did not permit Congress to preempt every area of commerce that might affect interstate activities. States could still control local conditions and affect interstate commerce incidentally while protecting their citizens' welfare. Milk Board v. Eisenberg Co., 306 U.S. 346 (1939). Even when 90 to 95 percent of a state's product was shipped in interstate or foreign commerce, states could adopt marketing and price-stabilization programs in the interest of the "safety, health and well-being of local communities," especially when the activity "may never be adequately dealt with by Congress." Parker v. Brown, 317 U.S. 341, 362–63 (1943).[9] To protect their environmental and natural resources, states may enact regulations even when the incidental effect creates some burden on interstate commerce. Minnesota v. Clover Leaf Creamery Co., 449 U.S. 456 (1981).

The commerce power allows Congress to control such local activity as loan sharking (using threats and extortion to collect loans). Although local, these techniques are part of organized crime that affect interstate and foreign commerce. Perez v. United States, 402 U.S. 146 (1971). The breadth of the New Deal revolution is reflected in two decisions in 1981 that upheld congressional regulation of surface coal mining. The statute authorized states to propose a program of environmental protection to meet minimum federal standards. If states failed to prepare a program, they would be forced to adopt a federal plan. A unanimous Court upheld the statute. Hodel v. Virginia Surface Mining & Recl. Assn., 452 U.S. 264 (1981); Hodel v. Indiana, 452 U.S. 314 (1981). [As explained in Section F, several decisions by the Court in the 1990s limited power of Congress over the states.]

Other decisions gave states substantial leeway to look for new sources of revenue. The Supreme Court held in 1991 that states may adopt a single business tax (a value-added tax) without violating the Due Process Clause or the Commerce Clause. Trinova Corp. v. Michigan Dept. of Treasury, 498 U.S. 358 (1991). A 1992 ruling marked a first step toward allowing states to force mail-order companies to collect taxes from out-of-state shoppers. Quill Corp. v. North Dakota, 504 U.S. 298 (1992). The mail-order business had grown from $2.4 billion a year in 1967, when the Court first blocked state taxes on such sales, to an estimated $183 billion by 1989. In 1994, the Court ruled that states could tax corporations not merely on their earnings within the state but also on their worldwide income. Barclays Bank v. Franchise Tax Bd. of Cal., 512 U.S. 298 (1994).

While the Court and Congress supported these state initiatives, some state activities still run afoul of the Commerce Clause. Two decisions in 1992 limited the authority of states to dispose of hazardous waste and other materials. Chemical Waste Management, Inc. v. Hunt, 504 U.S. 334 (1992); Fort Gratiot Landfill v. Mich. Dept. of Nat. Res., 504 U.S. 353 (1992). A 1994 decision held that an Oregon law—subjecting waste generated in other states to a discriminatory surcharge approximately three times higher than that imposed on waste gener-

---

9. See also Carter v. Virginia, 321 U.S. 131 (1944) for the power of states to regulate shipments entering into and passing out of their borders, and Milk Board v. Eisenberg Co., 306 U.S. 346, 351 (1939) for the ability of states to regulate local conditions even when they incidentally or indirectly involve interstate commerce.

ated within the state—was invalid under the Commerce Clause. Oregon Waste Systems v. Dept. of Env. Quality, 511 U.S. 93 (1994). In that same year, the Court ruled that a local ordinance on solid waste discriminated against interstate commerce because it favored the local station and squelched competition. C&A Carbone, Inc. v. Clarkstown, 511 U.S. 383 (1994). A unanimous Court in 1996 ruled that a North Carolina "intangibles tax" discriminated against interstate commerce by favoring purely domestic corporations over those involved in interstate commerce. Fulton Corp. v. Faulkner, 516 U.S. 325 (1996). Another unanimous ruling in 1999 held that an Alabama franchise tax violated the Commerce Clause. South Central Bell Telephone Co. v. Alabama, 526 U.S. 160 (1999).

Carter v. Carter Coal Co.

298 U.S. 238 (1936)

After the Supreme Court in 1935 struck down the National Industrial Recovery Act, Congress relied on the Commerce Clause to pass legislation to regulate mining and the distribution of coal. The legislation authorized a commission to regulate maximum and minimum prices of coal and to regulate the workers engaged in coal production. Could Congress control the conditions in which coal was produced before it became an article of interstate commerce, or were production and manufacturing purely within the control of states?

MR. JUSTICE SUTHERLAND delivered the opinion of the Court.

The purposes of the "Bituminous Coal Conservation Act of 1935," involved in these suits, as declared by the title, are to stabilize the bituminous coal-mining industry and promote its interstate commerce; to provide for cooperative marketing of bituminous coal; to levy a tax on such coal and provide for a drawback under certain conditions; to declare the production, distribution, and use of such coal to be affected with a national public interest; to conserve the national resources of such coal; to provide for the general welfare, and for other purposes. C. 824, 49 Stat. 991. The constitutional validity of the act is challenged in each of the suits.

. . .

The general rule with regard to the respective powers of the national and the state governments under the Constitution, is not in doubt. The states were before the Constitution; and, consequently, their legislative powers antedated the Constitution. Those who framed and those who adopted that instrument meant to carve from the general mass of legislative powers, then possessed by the states, only such portions as it was thought wise to confer upon the federal government; and in order that there should be no uncertainty in respect of what was taken and what was left, the national powers of legislation were not aggregated but enumer-

ated—with the result that what was not embraced by the enumeration remained vested in the states without change or impairment....

...Since the validity of the act depends upon whether it is a regulation of interstate commerce, the nature and extent of the power conferred upon Congress by the commerce clause becomes the determinative question in this branch of the case....

As used in the Constitution, the word "commerce" is the equivalent of the phrase "intercourse for the purposes of trade," and includes transportation, purchase, sale, and exchange of commodities between the citizens of the different states. And the power to regulate commerce embraces the instruments by which commerce is carried on....

That commodities produced or manufactured within a state are intended to be sold or transported outside the state does not render their production or manufacture subject to federal regulation under the commerce clause....

We have seen that the word "commerce" is the equivalent of the phrase "intercourse for the purposes of trade." Plainly, the incidents leading up to and culminating in the mining of coal do not constitute such intercourse. The employment of men, the fixing of their wages, hours of labor and working conditions, the bargaining in respect of these things—whether carried on separately or collectively—each and all constitute intercourse for the purposes of production, not of trade....

A consideration of the foregoing, and of many cases which might be added to those already cited, renders inescapable the conclusion that the effect of the labor provisions of the act, including those in respect of minimum wages, wage agreements, collective bargaining, and the Labor Board and its powers, primarily falls upon production and not upon commerce; and confirms the further resulting conclusion that production is a purely local activity. It follows that none of these essential antecedents of production constitutes a transaction in or forms any part of interstate commerce.... Everything which moves in interstate commerce has had a local origin. Without local production somewhere, interstate commerce, as now carried on, would practically disappear. Nevertheless, the local character of mining, of manufacturing and of crop growing is a fact, and remains a fact, whatever may be done with the products.

. . .

Whether the effect of a given activity or condition is direct or indirect is not always easy to determine. The word "direct" implies that the activity or condition invoked or blamed shall operate proximately — not mediately, remotely, or collaterally — to produce the effect. It connotes the absence of an efficient intervening agency or condition. And the extent of the effect bears no logical relation to its character. The distinction between a direct and an indirect effect turns, not upon the magnitude of either the cause or the effect, but entirely upon the manner in which the effect has been brought about. If the production by one man of a single ton of coal intended for interstate sale and shipment, and actually so sold and shipped, affects interstate commerce indirectly, the effect does not become direct by multiplying the tonnage, or increasing the number of men employed, or adding to the expense or complexities of the business, or by all combined. It is quite true that rules of law are sometimes qualified by considerations of degree, as the government argues. But the matter of degree has no bearing upon the question here, since that question is not — What is the *extent* of the local activity or condition, or the *extent* of the effect produced upon interstate commerce? but — What is the *relation* between the activity or condition and the effect?

Much stress is put upon the evils which come from the struggle between employers and employees over the matter of wages, working conditions, the right of collective bargaining, etc., and the resulting strikes, curtailment and irregularity of production and effect on prices; and it is insisted that interstate commerce is *greatly* affected thereby. But, in addition to what has just been said, the conclusive answer is that the evils are all local evils over which the federal government has no legislative control. The relation of employer and employee is a local relation. At common law, it is one of the domestic relations. The wages are paid for the doing of local work. Working conditions are obviously local conditions. . . .

Separate opinion of Mr. Chief Justice Hughes.

I agree that the stockholders were entitled to bring their suits; that, in view of the question whether any part of the Act could be sustained, the suits were not premature; that the so-called tax is not a real tax, but a penalty; that the constitutional power of the Federal Government to impose this penalty must rest upon the commerce clause, as the Government concedes; that production — in this case mining — which precedes commerce, is not itself commerce; and that the power to regulate commerce among the several States is not a power to regulate industry within the State.

. . .

But that is not the whole case. The Act also provides for the regulation of the prices of bituminous coal sold in interstate commerce and prohibits unfair methods of competition in interstate commerce. Undoubtedly transactions in carrying on interstate commerce are subject to the federal power to regulate that commerce and the control of charges and the protection of fair competition in that commerce are familiar illustrations of the exercise of the power, as the Interstate Commerce Act, the Packers and Stockyards Act, and the Anti-Trust Acts abundantly show. . . .

Whether the policy of fixing prices of commodities sold in interstate commerce is a sound policy is not for our consideration. The question of that policy, and of its particular applications, is for Congress. The exercise of the power of regulation is subject to the constitutional restriction of the due process clause, and if in fixing rates, prices or conditions of competition, that requirement is transgressed, the judicial power may be invoked to the end that the constitutional limitation may be maintained. . . .

Upon what ground, then, can it be said that

this plan for the regulation of transactions in interstate commerce in coal is beyond the constitutional power of Congress? The Court reaches that conclusion in the view that the invalidity of the labor provisions requires us to condemn the Act in its entirety. I am unable to concur in that opinion. I think that the express provisions of the Act preclude such a finding of inseparability.

. . .

MR. JUSTICE CARDOZO (dissenting in Nos. 636, 649 and 650, and in No. 651 concurring in the result).

. . .

First: I am satisfied that the Act is within the power of the central government in so far as it provides for minimum and maximum prices upon sales of bituminous coal in the transactions of interstate commerce and in those of intrastate commerce where interstate commerce is directly or intimately affected. Whether it is valid also in other provisions that have been considered and con-

demned in the opinion of the court, I do not find it necessary to determine at this time. . . .

Congress was not condemned to inaction in the face of price wars and wage wars so pregnant with disaster. Commerce had been choked and burdened; its normal flow had been diverted from one state to another; there had been bankruptcy and waste and ruin alike for capital and for labor. The liberty protected by the Fifth Amendment does not include the right to persist in this anarchic riot. . . . There is testimony in these records, testimony even by the assailants of the statute, that only through a system of regulated prices can the industry be stabilized and set upon the road of orderly and peaceful progress. . . . An evil existing, and also the power to correct it, the lawmakers were at liberty to use their own discretion in the selection of the means.

. . .

I am authorized to state that MR. JUSTICE BRANDEIS and MR. JUSTICE STONE join in this opinion.

NLRB v. Jones & Laughlin

301 U.S. 1 (1937)

In the National Labor Relations Act of 1935, Congress concluded that labor disputes had a direct burden on interstate or foreign commerce and could be regulated by the Commerce Clause. Even activities taking place within a state, if they had a close and substantial relationship to interstate commerce, could be brought within the control of Congress. Under the shadow of Roosevelt's court-packing plan, the Court decided whether this exertion of national power invaded the rights reserved to the states.

MR. CHIEF JUSTICE HUGHES delivered the opinion of the Court.

In a proceeding under the National Labor Relations Act of 1935, the National Labor Relations Board found that the respondent, Jones & Laughlin Steel Corporation, had violated the Act by engaging in unfair labor practices affecting commerce. . . . The unfair labor practices charged were that the corporation was discriminating against members of the union with regard to hire and tenure of employment, and was coercing and intimidating its employees in order to interfere with their self-organization. The discriminatory and coercive action alleged was the discharge of certain employees.

The National Labor Relations Board, sustaining the charge, ordered the corporation to cease and desist from such discrimination and coercion, to offer reinstatement to ten of the employees

named, to make good their losses in pay, and to post for thirty days notices that the corporation would not discharge or discriminate against members, or those desiring to become members, of the labor union. . . .

. . .

Contesting the ruling of the Board, the respondent argues (1) that the Act is in reality a regulation of labor relations and not of interstate commerce; (2) that the Act can have no application to the respondent's relations with its production employees because they are not subject to regulation by the federal government; and (3) that the provisions of the Act violate § 2 of Article III and the Fifth and Seventh Amendments of the Constitution of the United States.

. . . Jones & Laughlin Steel Corporation . . . is organized under the laws of Pennsylvania and has its principal office at Pittsburgh. It is engaged in the business of manufacturing iron and steel in plants situated in Pittsburgh and nearby Aliquippa, Pennsylvania. It manufactures and distributes a widely diversified line of steel and pig iron, being the fourth largest producer of steel in the United States. With its subsidiaries — nineteen in number — it is a completely integrated enterprise, owning and operating ore, coal and limestone properties, lake and river transportation facilities and terminal railroads located at its manufacturing plants. It owns or controls mines in Michigan and Minnesota. It operates four ore steamships on the Great Lakes, used in the transportation of ore to its factories. It owns coal mines in Pennsylvania. It operates towboats and steam barges used in carrying coal to its factories. It owns limestone properties in various places in Pennsylvania and West Virginia. It owns the Monongahela connecting railroad which connects the plants of the Pittsburgh works and forms an interconnection with the Pennsylvania, New York Central and Baltimore and Ohio Railroad systems. It owns the Aliquippa and Southern Railroad Company which connects the Aliquippa works with the Pittsburgh and Lake Erie, part of the New York Central system. Much of its product is shipped to its warehouses in Chicago, Detroit, Cincinnati and Memphis, — to the last two places by means of its own barges and transportation equipment. In Long Island City, New York, and in New Orleans it operates structural steel fabricating shops in connection with the warehousing of semi-finished materials sent from its works. Through one of its wholly-owned subsidiaries it owns, leases and operates stores, warehouses and yards for the distribution of equipment and supplies for drilling and operating oil and gas wells and for pipe lines, refineries and pumping stations. It has sales offices in twenty cities in the United States and a wholly-owned subsidiary which is devoted exclusively to distributing its product in Canada. Approximately 75 per cent. of its product is shipped out of Pennsylvania.

Summarizing these operations, the Labor Board concluded that the works in Pittsburgh and Aliquippa "might be likened to the heart of a self-contained, highly integrated body. They draw in the raw materials from Michigan, Minnesota, West Virginia, Pennsylvania in part through arteries and by means controlled by the respondent; they transform the materials and then pump them

out to all parts of the nation through the vast mechanism which the respondent has elaborated."

. . .

First. The scope of the Act. — The Act is challenged in its entirety as an attempt to regulate all industry, thus invading the reserved powers of the States over their local concerns....

There can be no question that the commerce thus contemplated by the Act (aside from that within a Territory or the District of Columbia) is interstate and foreign commerce in the constitutional sense. The Act also defines the term "affecting commerce" (§ 2 (7)):

"The term "affecting commerce' means in commerce, or burdening or obstructing commerce or the free flow of commerce, or having led or tending to lead to a labor dispute burdening or obstructing commerce or the free flow of commerce."

This definition is one of exclusion as well as inclusion. The grant of authority to the Board does not purport to extend to the relationship between all industrial employees and employers. Its terms do not impose collective bargaining upon all industry regardless of effects upon interstate or foreign commerce. It purports to reach only what may be deemed to burden or obstruct that commerce and, thus qualified, it must be construed as contemplating the exercise of control within constitutional bounds. It is a familiar principle that acts which directly burden or obstruct interstate or foreign commerce, or its free flow, are within the reach of the congressional power....

Second. The unfair labor practices in question. — The unfair labor practices found by the Board are those defined in § 8, subdivisions (1) and (3). These provide:

Sec. 8. It shall be an unfair labor practice for an employer —

"(1) To interfere with, restrain, or coerce employees in the exercise of the rights guaranteed in section 7."

"(3) By discrimination in regard to hire or tenure of employment or any term or condition of employment to encourage or discourage membership in any labor organization:..."

Section 8, subdivision (1), refers to § 7, which is as follows:

"Sec. 7. Employees shall have the right to self-organization, to form, join, or assist labor organizations, to bargain collectively through representatives of their own choosing, and to engage in concerted activities, for the purpose of collective bargaining or other mutual aid or protection."

Thus, in its present application, the statute goes no further than to safeguard the right of employees to self-organization and to select representatives of their own choosing for collective bargaining or other mutual protection without restraint or coercion by their employer.

That is a fundamental right. Employees have as clear a right to organize and select their representatives for lawful purposes as the respondent has to organize its business and select its own officers and agents. Discrimination and coercion to prevent the free exercise of the right of employees to self-organization and representation is a proper subject for condemnation by competent legislative authority. Long ago we stated the reason for labor organizations. We said that they were organized out of the necessities of the situation; that a single employee was helpless in dealing with an employer; that he was dependent ordinarily on his daily wage for the maintenance of himself and family; that if the employer refused to pay him the wages that he thought fair, he was nevertheless unable to leave the employ and resist arbitrary and unfair treatment; that union was essential to give laborers opportunity to deal on an equality with their employer....

Third. The application of the Act to employees engaged in production. — The principle involved. — Respondent says that whatever may be said of employees engaged in interstate commerce, the industrial relations and activities in the manufacturing department of respondent's enterprise are not subject to federal regulation. The argument rests upon the proposition that manufacturing in itself is not commerce....

...Although activities may be intrastate in character when separately considered, if they have such a close and substantial relation to interstate commerce that their control is essential or appropriate to protect that commerce from burdens and obstructions, Congress cannot be denied the power to exercise that control....

Fourth. Effects of the unfair labor practice in respondent's enterprise. — Giving full weight to respondent's contention with respect to a break in the complete continuity of the "stream of commerce" by reason of respondent's manufacturing operations, the fact remains that the stoppage of those operations by industrial strife would have a most serious effect upon interstate commerce. In view of respondent's far-flung activities, it is idle to say that the effect would be indirect or remote. It is obvious that it would be immediate and might be catastrophic. We are asked to shut our eyes to the plainest facts of our national life and to deal with the question of direct and indirect effects in an intellectual vacuum....

Experience has abundantly demonstrated that the recognition of the right of employees to self-organization and to have representatives of their own choosing for the purpose of collective bargaining is often an essential condition of industrial peace. Refusal to confer and negotiate has been one of the most prolific causes of strife. This is such an outstanding fact in the history of labor disturbances that it is a proper subject of judicial notice and requires no citation of instances....

. . .

Our conclusion is that the order of the Board was within its competency and that the Act is valid as here applied. The judgment of the Circuit Court of Appeals is reversed and the cause is remanded for further proceedings in conformity with this opinion.

Reversed.

[On the same day, the Court handed down other decisions that upheld actions by the National Labor Relations Board.]

MR. JUSTICE MCREYNOLDS delivered the following dissenting opinion in the cases preceding:

MR. JUSTICE VAN DEVANTER, MR. JUSTICE SUTHERLAND, MR. JUSTICE BUTLER and I are unable to agree with the decisions just announced.

. . .

The Constitution still recognizes the existence of states with indestructible powers; the Tenth Amendment was supposed to put them beyond controversy.

We are told that Congress may protect the "stream of commerce" and that one who buys raw material without the state, manufactures it therein, and ships the output to another state is in that stream. Therefore it is said he may be prevented from doing anything which may interfere with its flow.

This, too, goes beyond the constitutional limitations heretofore enforced. If a man raises cattle and regularly delivers them to a carrier for interstate shipment, may Congress prescribe the conditions under which he may employ or discharge helpers on the ranch? The products of a mine pass daily into interstate commerce; many things are brought to it from other states. Are the owners and the miners within the power of Congress in respect of the miners' tenure and discharge? May a mill owner be prohibited from closing his factory or discontinuing his business because so to do would stop the flow of products to and from his plant in interstate commerce? May employees in a factory be restrained from quitting work in a body because this will close the factory and thereby stop the flow of commerce? May arson of a factory be made a Federal offense whenever this would interfere with such flow? If the business cannot continue with the existing wage scale, may Congress command a reduction? If the ruling of the Court just announced is adhered to these questions suggest some of the problems certain to arise.

. . .

Wickard v. Filburn

317 U.S. 111 (1942)

In 1941 Congress amended the Agricultural Adjustment Act of 1938 to increase the penalty on excess production. Roscoe Filburn, a farmer, received a wheat allotment of 11 acres for his 1941 crop but sowed 23 acres, planning to use the extra crop for home consumption. He was penalized for the excess production and brought suit against Secretary of Agriculture Claude Wickard. This case examines the power of Congress to control production, even within a state, to increase the price of wheat.

MR. JUSTICE JACKSON delivered the opinion of the Court.

. . .

II

It is urged that under the Commerce Clause of the Constitution, Article I, § 8, clause 3, Congress does not possess the power it has in this instance sought to exercise. The question would merit little consideration since our decision in *United States v. Darby*, 312 U.S. 100, sustaining the federal power to regulate production of goods for commerce, except for the fact that this Act extends federal regulation to production not intended in any part for commerce but wholly for consumption on the farm. The Act includes a definition of "market" and its derivatives, so that as related to wheat, in addition to its conventional meaning, it also means to dispose of "by feeding (in any form) to poultry or livestock which, or the products of which, are sold, bartered, or exchanged, or to be so disposed of." Hence, marketing quotas not only embrace all that may be sold without penalty but also what may be consumed on the premises. Wheat produced on excess acreage is designated as "available for marketing" as so defined, and the penalty is imposed thereon. Penalties do not depend upon whether any part of the wheat, either within or without the quota, is sold or intended to be sold. The sum of this is that the Federal Government fixes a quota including all that the farmer may harvest for sale or for his own farm needs, and declares that wheat produced on excess acreage may neither be disposed of nor used except upon payment of the penalty, or except it is stored as required by the Act or delivered to the Secretary of Agriculture.

Appellee says that this is a regulation of production and consumption of wheat. Such activities are, he urges, beyond the reach of Congressional power under the Commerce Clause, since they are local in character, and their effects upon interstate commerce are at most "indirect." In answer the Government argues that the statute regulates neither production nor consumption, but only marketing; and, in the alternative, that if the Act does go beyond the regulation of marketing it is sustainable as a "necessary and proper" implementation of the power of Congress over interstate commerce.

The Government's concern lest the Act be held to be a regulation of production or consumption, rather than of marketing, is attributable to a few dicta and decisions of this Court which might be understood to lay it down that activities such as "production," "manufacturing," and "mining" are strictly "local" and, except in special circumstances which are not present here, cannot be regulated under the commerce power because their effects upon interstate commerce are, as matter of law, only "indirect." Even today, when this power has been held to have great latitude, there is no decision of this Court that such activities may be regulated where no part of the product is intended for interstate commerce or intermingled with the subjects thereof. We believe that a review of the course of decision under the Commerce Clause will make plain, however, that questions of the power of Congress are not to be decided by reference to any formula which would give controlling force to nomenclature such as "production" and "indirect" and foreclose consideration of the actual effects of the activity in question upon interstate commerce.

At the beginning Chief Justice Marshall described the federal commerce power with a breadth never yet exceeded. *Gibbons* v. *Ogden, 9* Wheat. 1, 194–195. He made emphatic the embracing and penetrating nature of this power by warning that effective restraints on its exercise must proceed from political rather than from judicial processes. *Id.* at 197.

For nearly a century, however, decisions of this Court under the Commerce Clause dealt rarely with questions of what Congress might do in the exercise of its granted power under the Clause, and almost entirely with the permissibility of state activity which it was claimed discriminated against or burdened interstate commerce. During this period there was perhaps little occasion for the affirmative exercise of the commerce power, and the influence of the Clause on American life and law was a negative one, resulting almost wholly from its operation as a restraint upon the powers of the states. In discussion and decision the point of reference, instead of being what was "necessary and proper" to the exercise by Congress of its granted power, was often some concept of sovereignty thought to be implicit in the status of statehood. Certain activities such as "production," "manufacturing," and "mining" were occasionally said to be within the province of state governments and beyond the power of Congress under the Commerce Clause.

It was not until 1887, with the enactment of the Interstate Commerce Act, that the interstate commerce power began to exert positive influence in American law and life. This first important federal resort to the commerce power was followed in 1890 by the Sherman Anti-Trust Act and, thereafter, mainly after 1903, by many others. These statutes ushered in new phases of adjudication, which required the Court to approach the interpretation of the Commerce Clause in the light of an actual exercise by Congress of its power thereunder.

When it first dealt with this new legislation, the Court adhered to its earlier pronouncements, and allowed but little scope to the power of Congress.

United States v. *Knight Co., 156* U.S. 1. These earlier pronouncements also played an important part in several of the five cases in which this Court later held that Acts of Congress under the Commerce Clause were in excess of its power.

Even while important opinions in this line of restrictive authority were being written, however, other cases called forth broader interpretations of the Commerce Clause destined to supersede the earlier ones, and to bring about a return to the principles first enunciated by Chief Justice Marshall in *Gibbons* v. *Ogden, supra.*

Not long after the decision of *United States* v. *Knight Co., supra,* Mr. Justice Holmes, in sustaining the exercise of national power over intrastate activity, stated for the Court that "commerce among the States is not a technical legal conception, but a practical one, drawn from the course of business." *Swift & Co.* v. *United States, 196* U.S. 375, 398. It was soon demonstrated that the effects of many kinds of intrastate activity upon interstate commerce were such as to make them a proper subject of federal regulation. In some cases sustaining the exercise of federal power over intrastate matters the term "direct" was used for the purpose of stating, rather than of reaching, a result; in others it was treated as synonymous with "substantial" or "material"; and in others it was not used at all. Of late its use has been abandoned in cases dealing with questions of federal power under the Commerce Clause.

In the *Shreveport Rate Cases, 234* U. S. 342, the Court held that railroad rates of an admittedly intrastate character and fixed by authority of the state might, nevertheless, be revised by the Federal Government because of the economic effects which they had upon interstate commerce. The opinion of Mr. Justice Hughes found federal intervention constitutionally authorized because of "matters having such a close and substantial relation to interstate traffic that the control is essential or appropriate to the security of that traffic, to the efficiency of the interstate service, and to the maintenance of conditions under which interstate commerce may be conducted upon fair terms and without molestation or hindrance." *Id.* at 351.

The Court's recognition of the relevance of the economic effects in the application of the Commerce Clause, exemplified by this statement, has made the mechanical application of legal formulas no longer feasible. Once an economic measure of the reach of the power granted to Congress in the Commerce Clause is accepted, questions of federal power cannot be decided simply by finding the activity in question to be "production," nor can consideration of its economic effects be foreclosed by calling them "indirect." ...

Whether the subject of the regulation in question was "production," "consumption," or "marketing" is, therefore, not material for purposes of deciding the question of federal power before us. That an activity is of local character may help in a doubtful case to determine whether Congress intended to reach it. The same consideration might help in determining whether in the absence of Congressional action it would be permissible for the state to exert its power on the subject matter, even though in so doing it to some degree affected interstate commerce. But even if appellee's activity be local and though it may not be regarded as commerce, it may still, whatever its nature, be reached by Congress if it exerts a substantial economic effect on interstate commerce, and this irrespective of whether such effect is what might at some earlier time have been defined as "direct" or "indirect."

. . .

It is well established by decisions of this Court that the power to regulate commerce includes the power to regulate the prices at which commodities in that commerce are dealt in and practices affecting such prices. One of the primary purposes of the Act in question was to increase the market price of wheat, and to that end to limit the volume thereof that could affect the market. It can hardly be denied that a factor of such volume and variability as home-consumed wheat would have a substantial influence on price and market conditions. This may arise because being in marketable condition such wheat overhangs the market and, if induced by rising prices, tends to flow into the market and check price increases. But if we assume that it is never marketed, it supplies a need of the man who grew it which would otherwise be reflected by purchases in the open market. Homegrown wheat in this sense competes with wheat in commerce. The stimulation of commerce is a use of the regulatory function quite as definitely as prohibitions or restrictions thereon. This record leaves us in no doubt that Congress may properly have considered that wheat consumed on the farm where grown, if wholly outside the scheme of regulation, would have a substantial effect in defeating and obstructing its purpose to stimulate trade therein at increased prices.

. . .

Southern Pacific Co. v. Arizona

325 U.S. 761 (1945)

This case examines the authority of states to regulate commerce concurrently with national controls. The power of Congress to regulate interstate commerce does not totally prohibit states from enacting legislation to protect the health and safety of their citizens. Here the Court weighs competing, and sometimes conflicting, interests: Arizona's decision to limit the length of trains and the national interest in uniform and efficient railway service.

MR. CHIEF JUSTICE STONE delivered the opinion of the Court.

The Arizona Train Limit Law of May 16, 1912, ... makes it unlawful for any person or corporation to operate within the state a railroad train of more than fourteen passenger or seventy freight cars, and authorizes the state to recover a money penalty for each violation of the Act. The questions for decision are whether Congress has, by legislative enactment, restricted the power of the states to regulate the length of interstate trains as a safety measure and, if not, whether the statute contravenes the commerce clause of the Federal Constitution.

In 1940 the State of Arizona brought suit in the Arizona Superior Court against appellant, the Southern Pacific Company, to recover the statutory penalties for operating within the state two interstate trains, one a passenger train of more than fourteen cars, and one a freight train of more than seventy cars. Appellant answered, admitting the train operations, but defended on the ground that the statute offends against the commerce clause and the due process clause of the Fourteenth Amendment and conflicts with federal legislation....

. . .

Although the commerce clause conferred on the national government power to regulate commerce, its possession of the power does not exclude all state power of regulation. Ever since

Willson v. *Black-Bird Creek Marsh Co.,* 2 Pet. 245, and *Cooley* v. *Board of Wardens,* 12 How. 299, it has been recognized that, in the absence of conflicting legislation by Congress, there is a residuum of power in the state to make laws governing matters of local concern which nevertheless in some measure affect interstate commerce or even, to some extent, regulate it.... When the regulation of matters of local concern is local in character and effect, and its impact on the national commerce does not seriously interfere with its operation, and the consequent incentive to deal with them nationally is slight, such regulation has been generally held to be within state authority....

But ever since *Gibbons* v. *Ogden,* 9 Wheat. 1, the states have not been deemed to have authority to impede substantially the free flow of commerce from state to state, or to regulate those phases of the national commerce which, because of the need of national uniformity, demand that their regulation, if any, be prescribed by a single authority....

For a hundred years it has been accepted constitutional doctrine that the commerce clause, without the aid of Congressional legislation, thus affords some protection from state legislation inimical to the national commerce, and that in such cases, where Congress has not acted, this Court, and not the state legislature, is under the commerce clause the final arbiter of the competing demands of state and national interests....

Congress has undoubted power to redefine the distribution of power over interstate commerce. It may either permit the states to regulate the commerce in a manner which would otherwise not be permissible,... or exclude state regulation even of matters of peculiarly local concern which nevertheless affect interstate commerce....

But in general Congress has left it to the courts to formulate the rules thus interpreting the commerce clause in its application, doubtless because it has appreciated the destructive consequences to the commerce of the nation if their protection were withdrawn...and has been aware that in their application state laws will not be invalidated without the support of relevant factual material which will "afford a sure basis" for an informed judgment.... Meanwhile, Congress has accommodated its legislation, as have the states, to these rules as an established feature of our constitutional system. There has thus been left to the states wide scope for the regulation of matters of local state concern, even though it in some measure affects the commerce, provided it does not materially restrict the free flow of commerce across state lines, or inter-

fere with it in matters with respect to which uniformity of regulation is of predominant national concern.

Hence the matters for ultimate determination here are the nature and extent of the burden which the state regulation of interstate trains, adopted as a safety measure, imposes on interstate commerce, and whether the relative weights of the state and national interests involved are such as to make inapplicable the rule, generally observed, that the free flow of interstate commerce and its freedom from local restraints in matters requiring uniformity of regulation are interests safeguarded by the commerce clause from state interference.

. . .

The findings show that the operation of long trains, that is trains of more than fourteen passenger and more than seventy freight cars, is standard practice over the main lines of the railroads of the United States, and that, if the length of trains is to be regulated at all, national uniformity in the regulation adopted, such as only Congress can prescribe, is practically indispensable to the operation of an efficient and economical national railway system. On many railroads passenger trains of more than fourteen cars and freight trains of more than seventy cars are operated, and on some systems freight trains are run ranging from one hundred and twenty-five to one hundred and sixty cars in length. Outside of Arizona, where the length of trains is not restricted, appellant runs a substantial proportion of long trains. In 1939 on its comparable route for through traffic through Utah and Nevada from 66 to 85% of its freight trains were over seventy cars in length and over 43% of its passenger trains included more than fourteen passenger cars.

In Arizona, approximately 93% of the freight traffic and 95% of the passenger traffic is interstate. Because of the Train Limit Law appellant is required to haul over 30% more trains in Arizona than would otherwise have been necessary. The record shows a definite relationship between operating costs and the length of trains, the increase in length resulting in a reduction of operating costs per car. The additional cost of operation of trains complying with the Train Limit Law in Arizona amounts for the two railroads traversing that state to about $1,000,000 a year. The reduction in train lengths also impedes efficient operation. More locomotives and more manpower are required; the necessary conversion and reconversion of train lengths at terminals and the delay caused by breaking up and remaking long trains upon entering and leaving the state in order to comply with the law, delays the traffic and diminishes its volume moved in a given time, especially when traffic is heavy.

. . .

The unchallenged findings leave no doubt that the Arizona Train Limit Law imposes a serious burden on the interstate commerce conducted by appellant. It materially impedes the movement of appellant's interstate trains through that state and interposes a substantial obstruction to the national policy proclaimed by Congress, to promote adequate, economical and efficient railway transportation service. Interstate Commerce Act, preceding § 1, 54 Stat. 899....

The trial court found that the Arizona law had no reasonable relation to safety, and made train operation more dangerous. Examination of the evidence and the detailed findings makes it clear that this conclusion was rested on facts found which indicate that such increased danger of accident and personal injury as may result from the greater length of trains is more than offset by the increase in the number of accidents resulting from the larger number of trains when train lengths are reduced....

...Here examination of all the relevant factors makes it plain that the state interest is outweighed by the interest of the nation in an adequate, economical and efficient railway transportation service, which must prevail.

Reversed.

MR. JUSTICE RUTLEDGE concurs in the result.

MR. JUSTICE BLACK, dissenting.

. . .

...[T]he determination of whether it is in the interest of society for the length of trains to be governmentally regulated is a matter of public policy. Someone must fix that policy—either the Congress, or the state, or the courts. A century and a half of constitutional history and government admonishes this Court to leave that choice to the elected legislative representatives of the people themselves, where it properly belongs both on democratic principles and the requirements of efficient government.

. . .

MR. JUSTICE DOUGLAS, dissenting.

. . .

...My view has been that the courts should intervene only where the state legislation discriminated against interstate commerce or was out of harmony with laws which Congress had enacted....It seems to me particularly appropriate that that course be followed here. For Congress has given the Interstate Commerce Commission broad powers of regulation over interstate carriers. The Commission is the national agency which has been entrusted with the task of promoting a safe, adequate, efficient, and economical transportation service. It is the expert on this subject. It is in a position to police the field. And if its powers prove inadequate for the task, Congress, which has paramount authority in this field, can implement them.

. . .

E. FROM *NATIONAL LEAGUE* TO *GARCIA*

One of the most contentious issues of federalism in recent decades involves the extension of federal hours-and-wages standards to state employees. The Supreme Court halted this trend toward national control in *National League of Cities* v. *Usery* (1976) but reversed itself nine years later in *Garcia* v. *San Antonio Metropolitan Transit Authority* (1985), giving Congress almost total power under the Commerce Clause. In *Garcia*, the Court announced that the protection of federalism depends largely on the political process operating within Congress.

The Fair Labor Standards Act of 1938 expressly exempted all states and their political divisions from the federal minimum-wage and overtime provisions. In 1966 Congress extended federal minimum wages and overtime pay to state-operated hospitals and schools. Two years later the Court upheld that legislation as rationally based, deciding that Congress had prop-

The Hapless, Hopeless Effort to Implement *National League*

In 1981, a unanimous Court rejected a district court's argument that land use regulation was a "traditional governmental function" reserved to the states under *National League*. The Court held that *National League* applied to "states as states" and not to private business operations within a state. Hodel v. Virginia Surface Mining & Recl. Assn., 452 U.S. 264 (1981). A year later, a 5–4 Court rejected a district court's attempt to use *National League* to prohibit Congress from regulating retail sales of electricity and natural gas. The district court said this area of economic regulation was traditional; the Court said it was not. FERC v. Mississippi, 456 U.S. 742 (1982). In that same year, the Court rejected a Second Circuit's conclusion that a state-owned railroad engaged in interstate commerce represented a traditional governmental function. A unanimous Court said that the operation of railroads "has traditionally been a function of private industry, not state or local governments." United Transportation Union v. Long Island R. Co., 455 U.S. 678, 686 (1982).

In 1981 a federal district court held that the Age Discrimination in Employment Act passed by Congress in 1967 violated the Tenth Amendment theory articulated in *National League*. The case involved Wyoming's mandatory retirement of game wardens at the age of 55. Game wardens seemed to fit the categories of police protection, parks, and recreation, all of which *National League* specifically classified as a traditional state function. Nevertheless, a 5–4 Court reversed the district court. EEOC v. Wyoming, 460 U.S. 226 (1983). Significantly, Justice Blackmun (who had given Rehnquist a fifth vote in *National League*) provided the fifth vote in this case. Although the Wyoming case did not override *National League,* many legal interpreters concluded that little life remained in the 1976 ruling.

erly taken into account the effect on interstate competition and the promotion of labor peace. Maryland v. Wirtz, 392 U.S. 183 (1968). Building on that decision, in 1975 the Court upheld the short-term power of the President to stabilize wages and salaries of state employees. Fry v. United States, 421 U.S. 542, 549–59.

A year later, however, Justice Rehnquist attracted four other votes to his position that federal minimum-wage and maximum-hour provisions could not displace state powers in such "traditional governmental functions" as fire prevention, police protection, sanitation, public health, and parks and recreation. Amendments to the Fair Labor Standards Act in 1974 had extended the wage-and-hour provisions to almost all state employees. The 5–4 decision by Rehnquist overruled *Wirtz* by holding that the 1974 amendments threatened the independent existence of states. Justice Blackmun, in a tentative concurrence, supplied the fifth vote. The dissents were sharply worded. For the first time in four decades, the Court had invalidated a statute passed by Congress pursuant to the Commerce Clause. NATIONAL LEAGUE OF CITIES v. USERY, 426 U.S. 833 (1976).

Rehnquist's bifurcation between traditional and nontraditional governmental functions could not be applied with confidence or consistency either in the lower courts or in the Supreme Court itself. When lower courts found a function to be "traditional" and thus within the realm of state sovereignty, the Court would frequently reverse on the ground that the function was actually nontraditional and beyond the protection offered in *National League* (see box).

One of the curious facts about *National League* is that when the Supreme Court remanded the case to a three-judge district court, the district court did not try to determine the difference between traditional and nontraditional functions. Instead, it asked the Labor Department to identify nontraditional state functions. It did so, providing a list of traditional functions as well. Included in the Department's list of nontraditional functions was "local mass transit systems," a decision that prompted new litigation and a challenge to *National League*.

National League Is Overturned

Justice Blackmun's majority opinion in the mass transit case nullified the decision with which he had concurred less than ten years before. He pointed to the difficulty that courts had experienced in distinguishing between "traditional" and "nontraditional" state functions. The effect of his 5–4 decision was to leave the protection of federalism largely to the political process of Congress. GARCIA v. SAN ANTONIO METROPOLITAN TRANSIT AUTHORITY, 469 U.S. 528 (1985).

Garcia threatened the states with massive budgetary obligations. Most state employees were already receiving at least the minimum wage, but the cost of meeting the overtime provisions of the Fair Labor Standards Act could have reached several billion dollars, much of it for firefighters and police in local government. To prevent that cost from being transferred to the states, Congress passed legislation to postpone the effective date of *Garcia* (decided February 19, 1985) to April 15, 1986, and permitted the use of compensatory time as a substitute for paying overtime. 99 Stat. 787 (1985).

National League of Cities v. Usery

426 U.S. 833 (1976)

This case marks an effort by Justice Rehnquist to devise a doctrine to protect states' rights against federal intrusion. In 1974 Congress amended the Fair Labor Standards Act to extend minimum wage and maximum hour provisions to cover almost all employees of states and their political divisions. The National League of Cities, supported by a number of cities and states, brought an action against Secretary of Labor W.J. Usery, Jr., challenging the validity of the 1974 amendments and seeking declaratory and injunctive relief. A three-judge district court dismissed the complaint for failure to state a claim upon which relief might be granted.

MR. JUSTICE REHNQUIST delivered the opinion of the Court.

Nearly 40 years ago Congress enacted the Fair Labor Standards Act, and required employers covered by the Act to pay their employees a minimum hourly wage and to pay them at one and one-half times their regular rate of pay for hours worked in excess of 40 during a workweek.…

The original Fair Labor Standards Act passed in 1938 specifically excluded the States and their political subdivisions from its coverage.…

I

In a series of amendments beginning in 1961 Congress began to extend the provisions of the Fair Labor Standards Act to some types of public employees. The 1961 amendments to the Act extended its coverage to persons who were employed in "enterprises" engaged in commerce or in the production of goods for commerce. And in 1966, with the amendment of the definition of employers under the Act, the exemption heretofore extended to the States and their political subdivisions was removed with respect to employees

of state hospitals, institutions, and schools. We nevertheless sustained the validity of the combined effect of these two amendments in *Maryland v. Wirtz*, 392 U.S. 183 (1968).

In 1974, Congress again broadened the coverage of the Act.…By its 1974 amendments,… Congress has now entirely removed the exemption previously afforded States and their political subdivisions, substituting only the Act's general exemption for executive, administrative, or professional personnel, …which is supplemented by provisions excluding from the Act's coverage those individuals holding public elective office or serving such an officeholder in one of several specific capacities.… The Act thus imposes upon almost all public employment the minimum wage and maximum hour requirements previously restricted to employees engaged in interstate commerce.…

II

It is established beyond peradventure that the Commerce Clause of Art. I of the Constitution is a grant of plenary authority to Congress. That authority is, in the words of Mr. Chief Justice Marshall in *Gibbons* v. *Ogden,* 9 Wheat. 1 (1824), "the power to regulate; that is, to prescribe the rule by which commerce is to be governed." *Id.,* at 196.

. . .

Appellants in no way challenge these decisions establishing the breadth of authority granted Congress under the commerce power. Their contention, on the contrary, is that when Congress seeks to regulate directly the activities of States as public employers, it transgresses an affirmative limitation on the exercise of its power akin to other commerce power affirmative limitations contained in the Constitution....

This Court has never doubted that there are limits upon the power of Congress to override state sovereignty, even when exercising its otherwise plenary powers to tax or to regulate commerce which are conferred by Art. I of the Constitution. In *Wirtz,* for example, the Court took care to assure the appellants that it had "ample power to prevent...'the utter destruction of the State as a sovereign political entity,'" which they feared. 392 U.S., at 196. Appellee Secretary in this case, both in his brief and upon oral argument, has agreed that our federal system of government imposes definite limits upon the authority of Congress to regulate the activities of the States as States by means of the commerce power.... In *Fry, supra,* the Court recognized that an express declaration of this limitation is found in the Tenth Amendment:

"While the Tenth Amendment has been characterized as a 'truism,' stating merely that 'all is retained which has not been surrendered,' *United States* v. *Darby,* 312 U.S. 100, 124 (1941), it is not without significance. The Amendment expressly declares the constitutional policy that Congress may not exercise power in a fashion that impairs the States' integrity or their ability to function effectively in a federal system." 421 U. S., at 547 n. 7.

. . .

One undoubted attribute of state sovereignty is the States' power to determine the wages which shall be paid to those whom they employ in order to carry out their governmental functions, what hours those persons will work, and what compensation will be provided where these employees may be called upon to work overtime. The question we must resolve here, then, is whether these determinations are "functions essential to separate and independent existence'"...so that Congress may not abrogate the States' otherwise plenary authority to make them.

. . .

Judged solely in terms of increased costs in dollars, *[the Act makes]* a significant impact on the functioning of the governmental bodies involved. The Metropolitan Government of Nashville and Davidson County, Tenn., for example, asserted that the Act will increase its costs of providing essential police and fire protection, without any increase in service or in current salary levels, by $938,000 per year....The State of California, which must devote significant portions of its budget to fire-suppression endeavors, estimated that application of the Act to its employment practices will necessitate an increase in its budget of between $8 million and $16 million.

Increased costs are not, of course, the only adverse effects which compliance with the Act will visit upon state and local governments, and in turn upon the citizens who depend upon those governments. In its complaint in intervention, for example, California asserted that it could not comply with the overtime costs (approximately $750,000 per year) which the Act required to be paid to California Highway Patrol cadets during their academy training program. California reported that it had thus been forced to reduce its academy training program from 2,080 hours to only 960 hours, a compromise undoubtedly of substantial importance to those whose safety and welfare may depend upon the preparedness of the California Highway Patrol.

. . .

Our examination of the effect of the 1974 amendments, as sought to be extended to the States and their political subdivisions, satisfies us that both the minimum wage and the maximum hour provisions will impermissibly interfere with the integral governmental functions of these bodies....[E]ven if we accept appellee's assessments concerning the impact of the amendments, their application will nonetheless significantly alter or displace the States' abilities to structure employer-employee relationships in such areas as fire prevention, police protection, sanitation, public health, and parks and recreation. These activities are typical of those performed by state and local governments in discharging their dual functions of administering the public law and furnishing public services. Indeed, it is functions such as these which governments are created to provide, services such as these which the States have traditionally afforded their citizens. We hold that insofar as the challenged amendments operate to directly displace the States' freedom to structure integral operations in areas of traditional governmental functions, they are not within the authority granted Congress by Art. I, § 8, cl. 3.

. . .

The judgment of the District Court is accordingly reversed, and the cases are remanded for further proceedings consistent with this opinion.

So ordered.

MR. JUSTICE BLACKMUN, concurring.

The Court's opinion and the dissents indicate the importance and significance of this litigation as it bears upon the relationship between the Federal Government and our States. Although I am not untroubled by certain possible implications of the Court's opinion — some of them suggested by the dissents — I do not read the opinion so despairingly as does my Brother BRENNAN. In my view, the result with respect to the statute under challenge here is necessarily correct. I may misinterpret the Court's opinion, but it seems to me that it adopts a balancing approach, and does not outlaw federal power in areas such as environmental protection, where the federal interest is demonstrably greater and where state facility compliance with imposed federal standards would be essential.... With this understanding on my part of the Court's opinion, I join it.

MR. JUSTICE BRENNAN, with whom MR. JUSTICE WHITE and MR. JUSTICE MARSHALL join, dissenting.

The Court concedes, as of course it must, that Congress enacted the 1974 amendments pursuant to its exclusive power under Art. I, § 8, cl. 3, of the Constitution "[t]o regulate Commerce... among the several States." It must therefore be surprising that my Brethren should choose this bicentennial year of our independence to repudiate principles governing judicial interpretation of our Constitution settled since the time of Mr. Chief Justice John Marshall, discarding his postulate that the Constitution contemplates that restraints upon exercise by Congress of its plenary commerce power lie in the political process and not in the judicial process. For 152 years ago Mr. Chief Justice Marshall enunciated that principle to

which, until today, his successors on this Court have been faithful.

"[T]he power over commerce... is vested in Congress as absolutely as it would be in a single government, having in its constitution the same restrictions on the exercise of the power as are found in the constitution of the United States. *The wisdom and the discretion of Congress, their identity with the people, and the influence which their constituents possess at elections, are... the sole restraints on which they have relied, to secure them from its abuse. They are the restraints on which the people must often rely solely, in all representative governments.*" Gibbons v. Ogden, 9 Wheat. 1, 197 (1824) (emphasis added).

. . .

Today's repudiation of this unbroken line of precedents that firmly reject my Brethren's ill-conceived abstraction can only be regarded as a transparent cover for invalidating a congressional judgment with which they disagree. The only analysis even remotely resembling that adopted today is found in a line of opinions dealing with the Commerce Clause and the Tenth Amendment that ultimately provoked a constitutional crisis for the Court in the 1930's. *E. g., Carter v. Carter Coal Co.,* 298 U. S. 238 (1936); *United States v. Butler,* 297 U. S. 1 (1936); *Hammer v. Dagenhart,* 247 U. S. 251 (1918).... It may have been the eventual abandonment of that overly restrictive construction of the commerce power that spelled defeat for the Court-packing plan, and preserved the integrity of this institution....

. . .

A sense of the enormous impact of States' political power is gained by brief reference to the federal budget. The largest estimate by any of the appellants of the cost impact of the 1974 amendments — $1 billion — pales in comparison with the financial assistance the States receive from the Federal Government. In fiscal 1977 the President's proposed budget recommends $60.5 billion in federal assistance to the States, exclusive of loans....

MR. JUSTICE STEVENS, dissenting.

The Court holds that the Federal Government may not interfere with a sovereign State's inherent right to pay a substandard wage to the janitor at the state capitol. The principle on which the holding rests is difficult to perceive.

The Federal Government may, I believe, require the State to act impartially when it hires or fires the janitor, to withhold taxes from his paycheck, to observe safety regulations when he is performing his job, to forbid him from burning too much soft coal in the capitol furnace, from dumping untreated refuse in an adjacent waterway, from overloading a state-owned garbage truck, or from driving either the truck or the Governor's limousine over 55 miles an hour. Even though these and many other activities of the capitol janitor are activities of the State *qua* State,

I have no doubt that they are subject to federal regulation.

I agree that it is unwise for the Federal Government to exercise its power in the ways described in the Court's opinion....

My disagreement with the wisdom of this legislation may not, of course, affect my judgment with respect to its validity. On this issue there is no dissent from the proposition that the Federal Government's power over the labor market is adequate to embrace these employees....

Garcia v. San Antonio Metro. Transit Auth.

469 U.S. 528 (1985)

The federalism doctrine of *National League of Cities* (1976) rested on a narrow 5 to 4 decision, with Justice Blackmun's concurrence supplying the fifth vote. The doctrine's attempt to distinguish between "traditional" and "nontraditional" governmental functions produced vast confusion in the lower courts. Blackmun eventually concluded that the doctrine was unsound and unworkable. By switching sides, he created a new 5 to 4 majority to overturn *National League of Cities*. The *Garcia* case began in 1979 when the Department of Labor issued an opinion that the operations of the San Antonio Metropolitan Transit Authority (SAMTA) were not immune from the minimum-wage and overtime requirements of the Fair Labor Standards Act. SAMTA filed an action in federal district court, seeking declaratory relief. On the same day, Joe G. Garcia and several other SAMTA employees brought suit against SAMTA for overtime pay under the Fair Labor Standards Act.

JUSTICE BLACKMUN delivered the opinion of the Court.

. . .

In the present cases, a Federal District Court concluded that municipal ownership and operation of a mass-transit system is a traditional governmental function and thus, under *National League of Cities*, is exempt from the obligations imposed by the FLSA. Faced with the identical question, three Federal Courts of Appeals and one state appellate court have reached the opposite conclusion.

Our examination of this "function" standard applied in these and other cases over the last eight years now persuades us that the attempt to draw the boundaries of state regulatory immunity in terms of "traditional governmental function" is not only unworkable but is also inconsistent with established principles of federalism and, indeed, with those very federalism principles on which *National League of Cities* purported to rest. That case, accordingly, is overruled.

I

The history of public transportation in San Antonio, Tex., is characteristic of the history of local mass transit in the United States generally. Passenger transportation for hire within San Antonio originally was provided on a private basis by a local transportation company. In 1913, the Texas Legislature authorized the State's municipalities to regulate vehicles providing carriage for hire.... Two years later, San Antonio enacted an ordinance setting forth franchising, insurance, and safety requirements for passenger vehicles operated for hire. The city continued to rely on such publicly regulated private mass transit until 1959, when it purchased the privately owned San Antonio Transit Company and replaced it with a public authority known as the San Antonio Transit System (SATS). SATS operated until 1978, when the city transferred its facilities and equipment to appellee San Antonio Metropolitan Transit Authority (SAMTA), a public mass-transit authority organized on a countywide basis....

As did other localities, San Antonio reached the

point where it came to look to the Federal Government for financial assistance in maintaining its public mass transit. SATS managed to meet its operating expenses and bond obligations for the first decade of its existence without federal or local financial aid. By 1970, however, its financial position had deteriorated to the point where federal subsidies were vital for its continued operation....

The principal federal program to which SATS and other mass-transit systems looked for relief was the Urban Mass Transportation Act of 1964 (UMTA),... which provides substantial federal assistance to urban mass-transit programs.... SATS received its first UMTA subsidy, a $4.1 million capital grant, in December 1970. From then until February 1980, SATS and SAMTA received over $51 million in UMTA grants—more than $31 million in capital grants, over $20 million in operating assistance, and a minor amount in technical assistance. During SAMTA's first two fiscal years, it received $12.5 million in UMTA operating grants, $26.8 million from sales taxes, and only $10.1 million from fares. Federal subsidies and local sales taxes currently account for about 75 percent of SAMTA's operating expenses.

. . .

II

...The District Court voiced a common concern: "Despite the abundance of adjectives, identifying which particular state functions are immune *[from regulation under the Fair Labor Standards Act]* remains difficult." 557 F. Supp., at 447. Just how troublesome the task has been is revealed by the results reached in other federal cases.... We find it difficult, if not impossible, to identify an organizing principle that places each of the cases in the first group *[protected under National League of Cities]* on one side of a line and each of the cases in the second group *[not protected]* on the other side. The constitutional distinction between licensing drivers *[protected]* and regulating traffic *[not protected]*, for example, or between operating a highway authority *[protected]* and operating a mental health facility *[not protected]*, is elusive at best.

. . .

We believe, however, that there is a more fundamental problem at work here.... The essence of our federal system is that within the realm of authority left open to them under the Constitution, the States must be equally free to engage in any activity that their citizens choose for the common weal, no matter how unorthodox or unnecessary anyone else—including the judiciary—deems state involvement to be. Any rule of state immunity that looks to the "traditional," "integral," or "necessary" nature of governmental functions inevitably invites an unelected federal judiciary to make decisions about which state policies it favors and which ones it dislikes.... In the words of Justice Black:

"There is not, and there cannot be, any unchanging line of demarcation between essential and non-essential governmental functions. Many governmental functions of today have at some time in the past been nongovernmental. The genius of our government provides that, within the sphere of constitutional action, the people—acting not through the courts but through their elected legislative representatives—have the power to determine as conditions demand, what services and functions the public welfare requires." *Helvering v. Gerhardt,* 304 U.S., at 427 (concurring opinion).

We therefore now reject, as unsound in principle and unworkable in practice, a rule of state immunity from federal regulation that turns on a judicial appraisal of whether a particular governmental function is "integral" or "traditional."...

. . .

IV

This analysis makes clear that Congress' action in affording SAMTA employees the protections of the wage and hour provisions of the FLSA contravened no affirmative limit on Congress' power under the Commerce Clause. The judgment of the District Court therefore must be reversed.

Of course, we continue to recognize that the States occupy a special and specific position in our constitutional system and that the scope of Congress' authority under the Commerce Clause must reflect that position. But the principal and basic limit on the federal commerce power is that inherent in all congressional action—the built-in restraints that our system provides through state participation in federal governmental action. The political process ensures that laws that unduly burden the States will not be promulgated. In the factual setting of these cases the internal safeguards of the political process have performed as intended.

. . .

National League of Cities v. *Usery,* 426 U. S. 833 (1976), is overruled. The judgment of the District Court is reversed, and these cases are remanded to that court for further proceedings consistent with this opinion.

It is so ordered.

JUSTICE POWELL, with whom THE CHIEF JUSTICE, JUSTICE REHNQUIST, and JUSTICE O'CONNOR join, dissenting.

. . .

I

There are, of course, numerous examples over the history of this Court in which prior decisions have been reconsidered and overruled. There have been few cases, however, in which the principle of *stare decisis* and the rationale of recent decisions were ignored as abruptly as we now witness. . . .

. . .

Whatever effect the Court's decision may have in weakening the application of *stare decisis,* it is likely to be less important than what the Court has done to the Constitution itself. A unique feature of the United States is the *federal* system of government guaranteed by the Constitution and implicit in the very name of our country. Despite some genuflecting in the Court's opinion to the concept of federalism, today's decision effectively reduces the Tenth Amendment to meaningless rhetoric when Congress acts pursuant to the Commerce Clause. . . .

[II.B]

Today's opinion does not explain how the States' role in the electoral process guarantees that particular exercises of the Commerce Clause power will not infringe on residual state sovereignty. Members of Congress are elected from the various States, but once in office they are Members of the Federal Government. . . .

More troubling than the logical infirmities in the Court's reasoning is the result of its holding, *i.e.,* that federal political officials, invoking the Commerce Clause, are the sole judges of the limits of their own power. This result is inconsistent with the fundamental principles of our constitutional system. See, *e.g.,* The Federalist No. 78 (Hamilton). At least since *Marbury* v. *Madison,* 1 Cranch 137, 177 (1803), it has been the settled province of the federal judiciary "to say what the law is" with respect to the constitutionality of Acts of Congress. . . .

JUSTICE REHNQUIST, dissenting.

. . .

JUSTICE O'CONNOR, with whom JUSTICE POWELL and JUSTICE REHNQUIST join, dissenting.

The Court today surveys the battle scene of federalism and sounds a retreat. Like JUSTICE POWELL, I would prefer to hold the field and, at the very least, render a little aid to the wounded. . . .

. . .

. . . With the abandonment of *National League of Cities,* all that stands between the remaining essentials of state sovereignty and Congress is the latter's underdeveloped capacity for self-restraint.

. . .

F. STATE POWERS REVIVED

Although *Garcia* shifted much of the guardian role of federalism to the states, the Supreme Court continues to use the Tenth Amendment and other constitutional provisions to protect state powers. Whereas the Court in *Garcia* was willing to leave federalism largely to the political process, in the 1990s and 2000 the Court moved aggressively to curb congressional authority and favor state sovereignty.

In 1991 the Court held that Missouri's constitution—providing a mandatory retirement age of 70 for most state judges—does not violate the Age Discrimination in Employment Act (ADEA) of 1967. As a sovereign state, Missouri's range of action is protected by the Tenth Amendment and the Guarantee Clause of Art. IV, § 4. The authority of states to determine the qualification of their officials lies at the heart of representative government. This decision seemed to rest largely on constitutional grounds, and yet the Court was also involved in statutory interpretation, leaving the door open for Congress to rewrite the ADEA so that it explicitly covers state judges. Gregory v. Ashcroft, 501 U.S. 452, 467 (1991).

A year later, the Court relied on the Tenth Amendment to invalidate part of a 1985 congressional statute designed to force states to find disposal sites for low-level radioactive waste. The 6–3 decision ruled that the statutory provision (forcing states to take possession of the waste if they failed to discover other solutions) was an invalid effort by Congress to commandeer the states' legislative processes and thus inconsistent with the Tenth Amendment. The Court said that states are not "mere political subdivisions" of the United States, nor are state governments regional offices or administrative agencies of the federal government. New York v. United States, 505 U.S. 144, 188 (1992). In terms of public policy, the decision was not too significant. Rather than try to draft new legislation that would satisfy the Court, Congress decided to rely on the existing compacts that states had created to dispose of low-level radioactive waste.

Gun Controls

In 1995, the Supreme Court struck down a congressional statute that banned guns within 1,000 feet of a school. Divided 5 to 4, the Court ruled that Congress had exceeded its authority under the Commerce Clause. The majority held that the statute had nothing to do with commerce or any sort of economic enterprise. UNITED STATES v. LOPEZ, 514 U.S. 549 (1995). Some commentators regarded the decision as one of the most important rulings in recent decades, but it may have been a case where Congress simply failed to present adequate findings to show an interstate commerce link with guns on school playgrounds.

Within two weeks of the Court's decision, President Clinton submitted legislation to Congress to amend the earlier statute by requiring the federal government to prove that the firearm has "moved in or the possession of such firearm otherwise affects interstate or foreign commerce." Public Papers of the Presidents, 1995, I, at 678. Congress enacted legislation in 1996, finding that crime at the local level "is exacerbated by the interstate movement of drugs, guns, and criminal gangs," that the occurrence of violent crime in school zones has resulted in a decline in the quality of education, and that it has the power under the interstate commerce clause to enact the legislation. The statutory language provides that "It shall be unlawful for any individual knowingly to possess a firearm that has moved in or that otherwise affects interstate or foreign commerce at a place that the individual knows, or has reasonable cause to believe, is a school zone." 110 Stat. 3009–369, § 657 (1996).

Term Limits and Indian Casinos

Federalism was an issue in the term limits case decided by the Supreme Court in 1995. A number of states had adopted constitutional amendments or other measures to place term limits on legislators not only from the states but in Congress as well. Arkansas, for example, amended its constitution to limit members of Congress to three terms in the House of Representatives and to two terms in the Senate. Relying primarily on *Powell* v. *McCormack*, 395 U.S. 486 (1969), the Court held that the Arkansas provision violated the U.S. Constitution by adding to the qualifications established for members of Congress. U.S. Term Limits, Inc. v. Thornton, 514 U.S. 779 (1995). The fifth vote in this 5 to 4 decision was supplied in a concurrence by Justice Kennedy, who invoked principles of federalism to strike down the Arkansas amendment: "That the States may not invade the sphere of federal sovereignty is as incontestable, in my view, as the corollary proposition that the Federal Government must be held within the boundaries of its own power when it intrudes upon matters reserved to the States." Id. at 841.

Again divided 5 to 4, the Court in 1996 ruled that Congress lacked authority under the Indian Commerce Clause to abrogate the states' Eleventh Amendment immunity from lawsuits.

At issue was the Indian Gaming Regulatory Act, which allowed Indian tribes to sue states in federal court in disputes between tribes and states regarding gaming operations. Gambling in Indian casinos had grown to a $4 billion a year business. While overruling the opinion in *Pennsylvania* v. *Union Gas Co.* (1989) that the Commerce Clause can trump state sovereign immunity, the Court left in place the holding in *Fitzpatrick* v. *Bitzer* (1976) that Congress can override state immunity when it legislates pursuant to the Fourteenth Amendment. Four Justices joined two lengthy dissents. Seminole Tribe of Florida v. Florida, 517 U.S. 44 (1996).

Gun Controls Again

In another 5 to 4 ruling, the Court in 1997 relied largely on its understanding of federalism to strike down a key portion of the 1993 Brady gun control law. That statute required state and local law enforcement officers to conduct background checks on prospective handgun purchasers. Relying heavily on its 1992 decision in *New York,* the Court held that state legislatures "are *not* subject to federal direction." Printz v. United States, 521 U.S. 898 (1997). The Court cited the Tenth Amendment as ground for invalidating the statutory provision. Id. at 919. It also pointed to *New York*'s standard that Congress cannot compel the states to enact or enforce a federal regulatory program and cannot "circumvent that prohibition by conscripting the States's officers directly." Id. at 935. Concurrences by Justices O'Connor and Thomas agreed that the Brady Act violated the Tenth Amendment. The dissenters looked to Hamilton's essay in Federalist No. 27 and to statutes of the early Congresses as evidence that Congress may require state courts and other state officials to implement federal law.

The Court's decision is not expected to have a substantial effect on governmental policy. Most states already require background checks and the federal government is developing a system that can do the work currently left to local law enforcement officials. Beginning on November 30, 1998, gun dealers will be required to check the names of prospective buyers against a computerized list of offenders prepared by the FBI.

Lawsuits Against the States

A trio of 5–4 decisions on June 23, 1999, placed additional curbs on congressional power to expose states to private lawsuits without state consent. Although the rulings attracted broad attention, much of the interest was directed to the continued division of Justices on federalism. Split along political lines, the majority consisted of the conservative-moderate wing (Rehnquist, O'Connor, Kennedy, Scalia, and Thomas), while the dissents came from moderate-liberals (Stevens, Souter, Ginsburg, and Breyer). Writing for the *New York Times*, Linda Greenhouse remarked that "the fault line that runs through the current Court as a all but unbridgeable gulf has to do not with the higher-profile issues of race, religion, abortion or due precess, but with federalism." N.Y. Times, June 24, 1999, at A22.

Two of the decisions affected the application of federal law to states. In the first, Congress had amended the Lanham Act to subject states to suits for false and misleading advertising. The Court ruled that the statute abrogated state sovereign immunity because Florida had not expressly consented to being sued in federal court and Congress had not acted validly under its enforcement powers under the Fourteenth Amendment. College Savings Bank v. Florida Prepaid Postsecondary, 527 U.S. 666 (1999).

The second decision covered a 1992 amendment to federal law that expressly abrogated the states' sovereign immunity from claims of patent infringement. The Court ruled that this amendment could not be upheld as an exercise of Congress' power under the Fourteenth Amendment because it was not properly "remedial" and it lacked proportionality. To invoke the Fourteenth Amendment, Congress must identify state conduct that transgresses the substantive provisions of the Amendment. Florida Prepaid Postsecondary v. College Sav., 527 U.S. 627 (1999).

The decision that drew most of the interest involved a suit brought against a state for violating the overtime provision of the Fair Labor Standards Act. The Court held that any effort by Congress to authorize private actions against the states *in state court*, without the consent of the states, is an unconstitutional abrogation of state sovereign immunity. ALDEN v. MAINE, 527 U.S. 706 (1999).

Continuing its string of 5–4 decisions on federalism, in 2000 the Court ruled that state workers — discriminated against because of their age — could not sue under federal law in the states. The Eleventh Amendment, said the majority, prevented such suits against state employers. The Court held that Congress, in the Age Discrimination in Employment Act of 1967 (ADEA), had stated a clear intent to abrogate the states' immunity but that the abrogation exceeded congressional authority under Section 5 of the Fourteenth Amendment. Kimel v. Florida Bd. of Regents, 120 S.Ct. 631 (2000).

On the following day, in a rare unanimous decision involving federalism, the Court upheld a congressional statute (the Driver's Privacy Protection Act of 1994) that prohibited states from disclosing the personal information that drivers provide when obtaining a license. As a result of the decision, states may not sell addresses, telephone numbers, and other information included in the license application. Congress passed the 1994 statute after the death of a woman who had been killed by a stalker who had obtained her address from the motor vehicles division. The Court held that Congress acted properly under its powers to regulate interstate commerce. Reno v. Condon, 120 S.Ct. 666 (2000).

Another blow to congressional power came in 2000 when the Court held that a provision in the Violence Against Women Act of 1994 could not be sustained under the Commerce Clause or Section 5 of the Fourteenth Amendment. The provision permitted victims of rape, domestic violence and other crimes "motivated by gender" to sue their attackers in federal court. Unlike the Guns in the Schoolyard Act, Congress had amassed findings and compiled a record to demonstrate the scope of the problem. Similar to other federalism rulings, the Court was split 5 to 4. UNITED STATES v. MORRISON, 120 S.Ct. 1740 (2000).

Federalism was at stake in 2000 when the Court reversed the Supreme Court of Florida's order for a manual recount to decide the presidential election. Although critics accused the majority of inconsistently championing federalism in most matters but not in this one, the Court was faced with issues of Art. II, § 1, cl. 2, of the United States Constitution and compliance with 3 U.S.C. § 5 (see Chapter 18 for further details). As Chief Justice Rehnquist and Justices Scalia and Thomas noted in their concurrence, the Court's "inquiry does not imply a disrespect for state *courts* but rather a respect for the constitutionally prescribed role of state *legislatures.*" Bush v. Gore, 121 S.Ct. 525, 535 (2000).

[Also struck down largely on grounds of federalism was the Religious Freedom Restoration Act of 1993, treated in Chapter 12; Boerne v. Flores, 521 U.S. 507 (1997).]

Contract with America

The Republican "Contract with America," announced on September 24, 1994, pledged a smaller federal government and a larger role for the states. Republican victories in the elections that fall gave them control of both Houses of Congress, converting the Contract into a blueprint for legislative action. Several planks of the Contract were devoted to federalism.

The Contract guaranteed "the first ever vote on a constitutional amendment" to establish term limits for members of Congress. Republicans wanted to eliminate the "lifetime job" for members of Congress. However, in 1995 the House of Representatives rejected several proposed term limits. Some of the proposals would have limited the terms of Representatives to six years and Senators to twelve, while others imposed limits of twelve years on both chambers. All of the amendments failed, including the basic Republican amendment (a lifetime limit of twelve years for both Houses), which lost on a vote of 227 to 204—a two-thirds majority being required for a constitutional amendment. 141 Cong. Rec. 9748 (1995).

Another federalism initiative dealt with "unfunded mandates." The Contract promised to do away with the practice of the federal government imposing expensive mandates on the states without providing federal funds. Legislation was enacted into law on March 22, 1995, but it did not terminate unfunded mandates. Many of the mandates concerning civil rights, the disabled, and other categories were specifically exempted. For other mandates, the statute merely created a procedure that requires the Congressional Budget Office to identify any bill that creates an unfunded mandate of $50 million or higher on the states. If CBO issues such an estimate, a member of Congress is entitled to make a point of order against the provision, but the point of order can be overridden by a simple majority in either chamber. Although the legislation may make Congress more sensitive and responsive to the issue of unfunded mandates, previous mandates can continue and new ones can be added. 109 Stat. 48 (1995).

The Federalism Act of 1999 (H.R. 2245) was introduced to require Congress and executive officials to follow new procedures when the federal government intends to preempt state powers. Federalism impact assessments would be necessary. The bill went nowhere because some organizations, like the U.S. Chamber of Congress, argue that one-size-fits-all national laws are less costly for businesses. Also, labor and environmental groups would rather work through a single Congress than fifty states.

United States v. Lopez

514 U.S. 549 (1995)

Congress enacted legislation in 1990 [§ 922(q)] to forbid "any individual knowingly to possess a firearm at a place that [he] knows...is a school zone." The Fifth Circuit held that, in light of what it characterized as insufficient congressional findings and legislative history, the provision was invalid as beyond Congress' power under the Commerce Clause. Alfonso Lopez, Jr., a 12th-grade student, arrived at his high school carrying a concealed handgun and five bullets.

CHIEF JUSTICE REHNQUIST delivered the opinion of the Court.

In the Gun-Free School Zones Act of 1990, Congress made it a federal offense "for any individual knowingly to possess a firearm at a place that the individual knows, or has reasonable cause to believe, is a school zone."...The Act neither regulates a commercial activity nor contains a requirement that the possession be connected in any way to interstate commerce. We hold that the Act exceeds the authority of Congress "[t]o regulate Commerce...among the several States...." U. S. Const., Art. I, § 8, cl. 3.

. . .

We start with first principles. The Constitution creates a Federal Government of enumerated powers. See Art. I, § 8. As James Madison wrote, "[t]he powers delegated by the proposed Constitution to the federal government are few and de-

fined. Those which are to remain in the State governments are numerous and indefinite." The Federalist No. 45, pp. 292–293 (C. Rossiter ed. 1961). This constitutionally mandated division of authority "was adopted by the Framers to ensure protection of our fundamental liberties." *Gregory v. Ashcroft,* 501 U. S. 452, 458 (1991) (internal quotation marks omitted). "Just as the separation and independence of the coordinate branches of the Federal Government serve to prevent the accumulation of excessive power in any one branch, a healthy balance of power between the States and the Federal Government will reduce the risk of tyranny and abuse from either front." *Ibid.*

The Constitution delegates to Congress the power "[t]o regulate Commerce with foreign Nations, and among the several States, and with the Indian Tribes." Art. I, § 8, cl. 3. The Court, through Chief Justice Marshall, first defined the nature of Congress' commerce power in *Gibbons v. Ogden,* 9 Wheat. 1, 189–190 (1824):

"Commerce, undoubtedly, is traffic, but it is something more: it is intercourse. It describes the commercial intercourse between nations, and parts of nations, in all its branches, and is regulated by prescribing rules for carrying on that intercourse."

The commerce power "is the power to regulate; that is, to prescribe the rule by which commerce is to be governed. This power, like all others vested in congress, is complete in itself, may be exercised to its utmost extent, and acknowledges no limitations, other than are prescribed in the constitution." *Id.,* at 196. The *Gibbons* Court, however, acknowledged that limitations on the commerce power are inherent in the very language of the Commerce Clause.

"It is not intended to say that these words comprehend that commerce, which is completely internal, which is carried on between man and man in a State, or between different parts of the same State, and which does not extend to or affect other States. Such a power would be inconvenient, and is certainly unnecessary.
"Comprehensive as the word 'among' is, it may very properly be restricted to that commerce which concerns more States than one.... The enumeration presupposes something not enumerated; and that something, if we regard the language, or the subject of the sentence, must be the exclusively internal commerce of a State." *Id.,* at 194–195.

For nearly a century thereafter, the Court's Commerce Clause decisions dealt but rarely with the extent of Congress' power, and almost entirely with the Commerce Clause as a limit on state legislation that discriminated against interstate commerce *[Chief Justice Rehnquist summarizes the Court's holdings in cases that recognized a broad power in Congress to regulate commerce, including* NLRB *v.* Jones & Laughlin Steel Corp. *(1937),* United States *v.* Darby *(1941), and* Wickard *v.* Filburn *(1942).]*

But even these modern-era precedents which have expanded congressional power under the Commerce Clause confirm that this power is subject to outer limits. In *Jones & Laughlin Steel,* the Court warned that the scope of the interstate commerce power "must be considered in the light of our dual system of government and may not be extended so as to embrace effects upon interstate commerce so indirect and remote that to embrace them, in view of our complex society, would effectually obliterate the distinction between what is national and what is local and create a completely centralized government." 301 U. S., at 37; see also

Darby, supra, at 119–120 (Congress may regulate intrastate activity that has a "substantial effect" on interstate commerce); *Wickard, supra,* at 125 (Congress may regulate activity that "exerts a substantial economic effect on interstate commerce"). Since that time, the Court has heeded that warning and undertaken to decide whether a rational basis existed for concluding that a regulated activity sufficiently affected interstate commerce....

Consistent with this structure, we have identified three broad categories of activity that Congress may regulate under its commerce power.... First, Congress may regulate the use of the channels of interstate commerce.... Second, Congress is empowered to regulate and protect the instrumentalities of interstate commerce, or persons or things in interstate commerce, even though the threat may come only from intrastate activities.... Finally, Congress' commerce authority includes the power to regulate those activities having a substantial relation to interstate commerce,... *i.e.,* those activities that substantially affect interstate commerce,...

Within this final category, admittedly, our case law has not been clear whether an activity must "affect" or "substantially affect" interstate commerce in order to be within Congress' power to regulate it under the Commerce Clause.... We conclude, consistent with the great weight of our case law, that the proper test requires an analysis of whether the regulated activity "substantially affects" interstate commerce.

We now turn to consider the power of Congress, in the light of this framework, to enact § 922(q). The first two categories of authority may be quickly disposed of: § 922(q) is not a regulation of the use of the channels of interstate commerce, nor is it an attempt to prohibit the interstate transportation of a commodity through the channels of commerce; nor can § 922(q) be justified as a regulation by which Congress has sought to protect an instrumentality of interstate commerce or a thing in interstate commerce. Thus, if § 922(q) is to be sustained, it must be under the third category as a regulation of an activity that substantially affects interstate commerce.

. . .

Section 922(q) is a criminal statute that by its terms has nothing to do with "commerce" or any sort of economic enterprise, however broadly one might define those terms. Section 922(q) is not an essential part of a larger regulation of economic activity, in which the regulatory scheme could be undercut unless the intrastate activity were regulated. It cannot, therefore, be sustained under our cases upholding regulations of activities that arise out of or are connected with a commercial transaction, which viewed in the aggregate, substantially affects interstate commerce.

. . .

Although as part of our independent evaluation of constitutionality under the Commerce Clause we of course consider legislative findings, and indeed even congressional committee findings, regarding effect on interstate commerce, ... the Government concedes that "[n]either the statute nor its legislative history contain[s] express congressional findings regarding the effects upon interstate commerce of gun possession in a school zone." ... We agree with the Government that Congress normally is not required to make formal findings as to the substantial burdens that an activity has on interstate commerce.... But to the extent that congressional findings would enable us to evaluate the legislative judgment that the activity in question substantially affected interstate commerce, even though no such substantial effect was visible to the naked eye, they are lacking here.

. . .

The Government's essential contention, *in fine*, is that we may determine here that § 922(q) is valid because possession of a firearm in a local school zone does indeed substantially affect interstate commerce.... The Government argues that possession of a firearm in a school zone may result in violent crime and that violent crime can be expected to affect the functioning of the national economy in two ways. First, the costs of violent crime are substantial, and, through the mechanism of insurance, those costs are spread throughout the population.... Second, violent crime reduces the willingness of individuals to travel to areas within the country that are perceived to be unsafe.... The Government also argues that the presence of guns in schools poses a substantial threat to the educational process by threatening the learning environment. A handicapped educational process, in turn, will result in a less productive citizenry. That, in turn, would have an adverse effect on the Nation's economic well-being As a result, the Government argues that Congress cpuld rationally have concluded that § 922(q) substantially affects interstate commerce.

We pause to consider the implications of the Government's arguments. The Government admits, under its "costs of crime" reasoning, that Congress could regulate not only all violent crime, but all activities that might lead to violent crime, regardless of how tenuously they relate to interstate commerce.... Similarly, under the Government's "national productivity" reasoning, Congress could regulate any activity that it found was related to the economic productivity of individual citizens: family law (including marriage, divorce, and child custody), for example. Under the theories that the Government presents in support of § 922(q), it is difficult to perceive any limitation on federal power, even in areas such as criminal law enforcement or education where States historically have been sovereign. Thus, if we were to accept the Government's arguments, we are hard pressed to posit any activity by an individual that Congress is without power to regulate.

Although JUSTICE BREYER argues that acceptance of the Government's rationales would not authorize a general federal police power, he is unable to identify any activity that the States may regulate but Congress may not....

For the foregoing reasons the judgment of the Court of Appeals is

Affirmed.

JUSTICE KENNEDY, with whom JUSTICE O'CONNOR joins, concurring.

. . .

While it is doubtful that any State, or indeed any reasonable person, would argue that it is wise policy to allow students to carry guns on school premises, considerable disagreement exists about how best to accomplish that goal. In this circumstance, the theory and utility of our federalism are revealed, for the States may perform their role as laboratories for experimentation to devise various solutions where the best solution is far from clear....

The statute now before us forecloses the States from experimenting and exercising their own judgment in an area to which States lay claim by right of history and expertise, and it does so by regulating an activity beyond the realm of commerce in the ordinary and usual sense of that term. The tendency of this statute to displace state regulation in areas of traditional state concern is evident from its territorial operation. There are over 100,000 elementary and secondary schools in the United States....

JUSTICE THOMAS, concurring.

...Although I join the majority, I write separately to observe that our case law has drifted far from the original understanding of the Commerce Clause. In a future case, we ought to temper our Commerce Clause jurisprudence in a manner that both makes sense of our more recent case law and is more faithful to the original understanding of that Clause.

We have said that Congress may regulate not only "Commerce...among the several States," U.S. Const., Art. I, § 8, cl. 3, but also anything that has a "substantial effect" on such commerce. This test, if taken to its logical extreme, would give Congress a "police power" over all aspects of American life....

. . .

In an appropriate case, I believe that we must further reconsider our "substantial effects" test with an eye toward constructing a standard that reflects the text and history of the Commerce Clause without totally rejecting our more recent Commerce Clause jurisprudence.

. . .

IV

...When asked at oral argument if there were *any* limits to the Commerce Clause, the Government was at a loss for words.... Likewise, the principal dissent insists that there are limits, but it cannot muster even one example....

JUSTICE STEVENS, dissenting.

. . .

JUSTICE SOUTER, dissenting.

In reviewing congressional legislation under the Commerce Clause, we defer to what is often a merely implicit congressional judgment that its regulation addresses a subject substantially affecting interstate commerce "if there is any rational basis for such a finding...."

...The modern respect for the competence and primacy of Congress in matters affecting commerce developed only after one of this Court's most chastening experiences, when it perforce repudiated an earlier and untenably expansive conception of judicial review in derogation of congressional commerce power. A look at history's sequence will serve to show how today's decision tugs the Court off course, leading it to suggest opportunities for further developments that would

be at odds with the rule of restraint to which the Court still wisely states adherence.

. . .

II

...it seems fair to ask whether the step taken by the Court today does anything but portend a return to the untenable jurisprudence from which the Court extricated itself almost 60 years ago. The answer is not reassuring. To be sure, the occasion for today's decision reflects the century's end, not its beginning But if it seems anomalous that the Congress of the United States has taken to regulating school yards, the Act in question is still probably no more remarkable than state regulation of bake shops 90 years ago....

JUSTICE BREYER, with whom JUSTICE STEVENS, JUSTICE SOUTER, and JUSTICE GINSBURG join, dissenting.

The issue in this case is whether the Commerce Clause authorizes Congress to enact a statute that makes it a crime to possess a gun in, or near, a school.... In my view, the statute falls well within the scope of the commerce power as this Court has understood that power over the last half century.

I

In reaching this conclusion, I apply three basic principles of Commerce Clause interpretation. First, the power to "regulate Commerce... among the several States," U. S. Const., Art. I, § 8, cl. 3, encompasses the power to regulate local activities insofar as they significantly affect interstate commerce....

...I use the word "significant" because the word "substantial" implies a somewhat narrower power than recent precedent suggests.... But to speak of "substantial effect" rather than "significant effect" would make no difference in this case.

Second, in determining whether a local activity will likely have a significant effect upon interstate commerce, a court must consider, not the effect of an individual act (a single instance of gun possession), but rather the cumulative effect of all similar instances (*i.e.,* the effect of all guns possessed in or near schools)....

Third, the Constitution requires us to judge the connection between a regulated activity and interstate commerce, not directly, but at one remove. Courts must give Congress a degree of leeway in determining the existence of a significant factual connection between the regulated activity and interstate commerce — both because the Constitution delegates the commerce power directly to Congress and because the determination requires an empirical judgment of a kind that a legislature is more likely than a court to make with accuracy. The traditional words "rational basis" capture this leeway....

II

Applying these principles to the case at hand, we must ask whether Congress could have had a *rational basis* for finding a significant (or substantial) connection between gun-related school violence and interstate commerce. Or, to put the question in the language of the *explicit* finding that Congress made when it amended this law in 1994: Could Congress rationally have found that "violent crime in school zones," through its effect

on the "quality of education," significantly (or substantially) affects "interstate" or "foreign commerce"? 18 U.S.C. §§ 922(q)(1)(F), (G). As long as one views the commerce connection, not as a "technical legal conception," but as "a practical one," *Swift & Co. v. United States,* 196 U.S. 376, 398 (1905) (Holmes, J.), the answer to this question must be yes. Numerous reports and studies—generated both inside and outside government—make clear that Congress could reasonably have found the empirical connection that its law, implicitly or explicitly, asserts. *[Breyer supplies an Appendix of materials to document this point.]*

. . .

Alden v. Maine

527 U.S. 706 (1999)*

John H. Alden and other probation officers from the state of Maine brought this action against the state for violating the overtime provisions of the Fair Labor Standards Act (FLSA). After the state courts dismissed their lawsuit, the Supreme Court granted cert. The issue, which split the Court 5 to 4, was whether Congress under its Article I powers could subject states to suits by private parties in state court without the consent of the state.

JUSTICE KENNEDY delivered the opinion of the Court.

In 1992, petitioners, a group of probation officers, filed suit against their employer, the State of Maine, in the United States District Court for the District of Maine. The officers alleged the State had violated the overtime provisions of the Fair Labor Standards Act of 1938 (FLSA)...and sought compensation and liquidated damages. While the suit was pending, this Court decided *Seminole Tribe of Fla.* v. *Florida,* 517 U.S. 44 (1996), which made it clear that Congress lacks power under Article I to abrogate the States' sovereign immunity from suits commenced or prosecuted in the federal courts. Upon consideration of *Seminole Tribe,* the District Court dismissed petitioners' action, and the Court of Appeals affirmed.... Petitioners then filed the same action in

state court. The state trial court dismissed the suit on the basis of sovereign immunity, and the Maine Supreme Judicial Court affirmed....

We hold that the powers delegated to Congress under Article I of the United States Constitution do not include the power to subject nonconsenting States to private suits for damages in state courts. We decide as well that the State of Maine has not consented to suits for overtime pay and liquidated damages under the FLSA. On these premises we affirm the judgment sustaining dismissal of the suit.

I

The Eleventh Amendment makes explicit reference to the States' immunity from suits "commenced or prosecuted against one of the United States by Citizens of another State, or by Citizens or Subjects of any Foreign State."...We have, as a result, sometimes referred to the States' immunity from suit as "Eleventh Amendment immunity." The phrase is convenient shorthand but

---

* The text for this case was obtained in electronic form from Westlaw and is reproduced by permission of the West Group.

something of a misnomer, for the sovereign immunity of the States neither derives from nor is limited by the terms of the Eleventh Amendment. Rather, as the Constitution's structure, and its history, and the authoritative interpretations by this Court make clear, the States' immunity from suit is a fundamental aspect of the sovereignty which the States enjoyed before the ratification of the Constitution, and which they retain today ... except as altered by the plan of the Convention or certain constitutional Amendments.

A

Although the Constitution establishes a National Government with broad, often plenary authority over matters within its recognized competence, the founding document "specifically recognizes the States as sovereign entities." *Seminole Tribe of Fla. v. Florida, supra*, at 71, n. 15; accord, *Blatchford v. Native Village of Noatak*, 501 U.S. 775, 779 (1991) ("[T]he States entered the federal system with their sovereignty intact")....

The federal system established by our Constitution preserves the sovereign status of the States in two ways. First, it reserves to them a substantial portion of the Nation's primary sovereignty, together with the dignity and essential attributes inhering in that status. The States "form distinct and independent portions of the supremacy, no more subject, within their respective spheres, to the general authority than the general authority is subject to them, within its own sphere." The Federalist No. 39, p. 245 (C. Rossiter ed. 1961) (J. Madison).

Second, even as to matters within the competence of the National Government, the constitutional design secures the founding generation's rejection of "the concept of a central government that would act upon and through the States" in favor of "a system in which the State and Federal Governments would exercise concurrent authority over the people—who were, in Hamilton's words, 'the only proper objects of government.'" *Printz, supra*, at 919–920 (quoting The Federalist No. 15, at 109); accord, *New York, supra*, at 166 ("The Framers explicitly chose a Constitution that confers upon Congress the power to regulate individuals, not States")....

B

The generation that designed and adopted our federal system considered immunity from private suits central to sovereign dignity. When the Constitution was ratified, it was well established in English law that the Crown could not be sued without consent in its own courts....

Although the American people had rejected other aspects of English political theory, the doctrine that a sovereign could not be sued without its consent was universal in the States when the Constitution was drafted and ratified....

The ratification debates, furthermore, underscored the importance of the States' sovereign immunity to the American people. Grave concerns were raised by the provisions of Article III which extended the federal judicial power to controversies between States and citizens of other States or foreign nations. As we have explained:

"Unquestionably the doctrine of sovereign immunity was a matter of importance in the early days of independence. Many of the States were heavily indebted as a result of the Revolutionary War. They were vitally interested in the question whether the creation of a new federal sovereign, with courts of its own, would automatically subject them, like lower English lords, to suits in the courts of the 'higher' sovereign." [*Nevada v. Hall*, 440 U.S. 410 (1979)] at 418 (footnote omitted).

The leading advocates of the Constitution assured the people in no uncertain terms that the Constitution would not strip the States of sovereign immunity. [*Kennedy quotes Alexander Hamilton in Federalist No. 81 that "[i]t is inherent in the nature of sovereignty not to be amenable to the suit of an individual without its consent." Kennedy cites similar positions by James Madison and John Marshall at the Virginia ratifying convention. He also reviews the "outrage" that greeted the Supreme Court's decision in Chisholm v. Georgia (1793) that a private citizen may sue a state without its consent and the resulting Eleventh Amendment that overturned that decision.]*

II

In this case we must determine whether Congress has the power, under Article I, to subject nonconsenting States to private suits in their own courts....

[A.1]

Article I, § 8 grants Congress broad power to enact legislation in several enumerated areas of national concern. The Supremacy Clause, furthermore, provides:

"This Constitution, and the Laws of the United

States which shall be made in Pursuance thereof..., shall be the supreme Law of the Land; and the Judges in every State shall be bound thereby, any Thing in the Constitution or Laws of any state to the Contrary notwithstanding." U.S. Const., Art. VI.

It is contended that, by virtue of these provisions, where Congress enacts legislation subjecting the States to suit, the legislation by necessity overrides the sovereign immunity of the States.

. . .

The Constitution, by delegating to Congress the power to establish the supreme law of the land when acting within its enumerated powers, does not foreclose a State from asserting immunity to claims arising under federal law merely because that law derives not from the State itself but from the national power.... We reject any contention that substantive federal law by its own force necessarily overrides the sovereign immunity of the States....

. . .

The dissenting opinion seeks to reopen these precedents, contending that state sovereign immunity must derive either from the common law (in which case the dissent contends it is defeasible by statute) or from natural law (in which case the dissent believes it cannot bar a federal claim).... As should be obvious to all, this is a false dichotomy....

Although the sovereign immunity of the States derives at least in part from the common-law tradition, the structure and history of the Constitution make clear that the immunity exists today by constitutional design. The dissent has provided no persuasive evidence that the founding generation regarded the States' sovereign immunity as defeasible by federal statute....

[B.4]

Although the Constitution grants broad powers to Congress, our federalism requires that Congress treat the States in a manner consistent with their status as residuary sovereigns and joint participants in the governance of the Nation.... The founding generation thought it "neither becoming nor convenient that the several States of the Union, invested with that large residuum of sovereignty which had not been delegated to the United States, should be summoned as defendants

to answer the complaints of private persons." *In re Ayers,* 123 U.S., at 505....

Petitioners contend that immunity from suit in federal court suffices to preserve the dignity of the States. Private suits against nonconsenting States, however, present "the indignity of subjecting a State to the coercive process of judicial tribunals at the instance of private parties," *In re Ayers, supra,* at 505.... regardless of the forum. Not only must a State defend or default but also it must face the prospect of being thrust, by federal fiat and against its will, into the disfavored status of a debtor, subject to the power of private citizens to levy on its treasury or perhaps even government buildings or property which the State administers on the public's behalf.

. . .

It is unquestioned that the Federal Government retains its own immunity from suit not only in state tribunals but also in its own courts. In light of our constitutional system recognizing the essential sovereignty of the States, we are reluctant to conclude that the States are not entitled to a reciprocal privilege.

. . .

In light of history, practice, precedent, and the structure of the Constitution, we hold that the States retain immunity from private suit in their own courts, an immunity beyond the congressional power to abrogate by Article I legislation.

III

[This section explains that the constitutional privilege of a state to assert sovereign immunity in its own courts "does not confer upon the State a concomitant right to disregard the Constitution or valid federal law. The States and their officers are bound by obligations imposed by the Constitution and by federal statutes that comport with the constitutional design. We are unwilling to assume the States will refuse to honor the Constitution or obey the binding laws of the United States." Sovereign immunity "does not bar all judicial review of state compliance with the Constitution and valid federal law." Many states have enacted statutes consenting to a wide variety of suits. Moreover, in adopting the Fourteenth Amendment, "the people required the States to surrender a portion of the sovereignty that had been preserved to them by the original Constitution, so that Congress may authorize private suits against nonconsenting States pursuant to its § 5

enforcement power.... " *The principle of sovereign immunity bars suits against states "but not lesser entities," such as suits prosecuted against a municipal corporation or other governmental entity that is not an arm of the State. Sovereign immunity does not bar all suits against state officers.]*

IV

The sole remaining question is whether Maine has waived its immunity.... Although petitioners contend the State has discriminated against federal rights by claiming sovereign immunity from this FLSA suit, there is no evidence that the State has manipulated its immunity in a systematic fashion to discriminate against federal causes of action. To the extent Maine has chosen to consent to certain classes of suits while maintaining its immunity from others, it has done no more than exercise a privilege of sovereignty concomitant to its constitutional immunity from suit. The State, we conclude, has not consented to suit.

V

...The State of Maine has not questioned Congress' power to prescribe substantive rules of federal law to which it must comply. Despite an initial good-faith disagreement about the requirements of the FLSA, it is conceded by all that the State has altered its conduct so that its compliance with federal law cannot now be questioned. The Solicitor General of the United States has appeared before this Court, however, and asserted that the federal interest in compensating the States' employees for alleged past violations of federal law is so compelling that the sovereign State of Maine must be stripped of its immunity and subjected to suit in its own courts by its own employees. Yet, despite specific statutory authorization, see 29 U.S.C. § 216(c), the United States apparently found the same interests insufficient to justify sending even a single attorney to Maine to prosecute this litigation. The difference between a suit by the United States on behalf of the employees and a suit by the employees implicates a rule that the National Government must itself deem the case of sufficient importance to take action against the State; and history, precedent, and the structure of the Constitution make clear that, under the plan of the Convention, the States have consented to suits of the first kind but not of the second. The judgment of the Supreme Judicial Court of Maine is

Affirmed.

JUSTICE SOUTER, with whom JUSTICE STEVENS, JUSTICE GINSBURG, and JUSTICE BREYER join, dissenting.

. . .

I

The Court rests its decision principally on the claim that immunity from suit was "a fundamental aspect of the sovereignty which the States enjoyed before the ratification of the Constitution,"..., an aspect which the Court understands to have survived the ratification of the Constitution in 1788 and to have been "confirm[ed]" and given constitutional status,... by the adoption of the Tenth Amendment in 1791....

...The Court's principal rationale for today's result, then, turns on history: was the natural law conception of sovereign immunity as inherent in any notion of an independent State widely held in the United States in the period preceding the ratification of 1788 (or the adoption of the Tenth Amendment in 1791)?

The answer is certainly no. There is almost no evidence that the generation of the Framers thought sovereign immunity was fundamental in the sense of being unalterable. Whether one looks at the period before the framing, to the ratification controversies, or to the early republican era, the evidence is the same. Some Framers thought sovereign immunity was an obsolete royal prerogative inapplicable in a republic; some thought sovereign immunity was a common-law power defeasible, like other common-law rights, by statute; and perhaps a few thought, in keeping with a natural law view distinct from the common-law conception, that immunity was inherent in a sovereign because the body that made a law could not logically be bound by it. Natural law thinking on the part of a doubtful few will not, however, support the Court's position.

A

The American Colonies did not enjoy sovereign immunity, that being a privilege understood in English law to be reserved for the Crown alone;... If a colonial lawyer had looked into Blackstone for the theory of sovereign immunity, as indeed many did, he would have found nothing clearly suggesting that the Colonies as such enjoyed any immunity from suit....

B

Starting in the mid-1760's, ideas about sovereignty in colonial America began to shift as Americans argued that, lacking a voice in Parliament, they had not in any express way consented to being taxed.... The story of the subsequent development of conceptions of sovereignty is complex and uneven; here, it is enough to say that by the time independence was declared in 1776, the locus of sovereignty was still an open question, except that almost by definition, advocates of independence denied that sovereignty with respect to the American Colonies remained with the King in Parliament.

As the concept of sovereignty was unsettled, so was that of sovereign immunity. Some States appear to have understood themselves to be without immunity from suit in their own courts upon independence.... Other new States understood themselves to be inheritors of the Crown's common-law sovereign immunity and so enacted statutes authorizing legal remedies against the State parallel to those available in England....

Around the time of the Constitutional Convention, then, there existed among the States some diversity of practice with respect to sovereign immunity; but despite a tendency among the state constitutions to announce and declare certain inalienable and natural rights of men and even of the collective people of a State,... no State declared that sovereign immunity was one of those rights....

C

At the Constitutional Convention, the notion of sovereign immunity, whether as natural law or as common law, was not an immediate subject of debate, and the sovereignty of a State in its own courts seems not to have been mentioned. This comes as no surprise, for although the Constitution required state courts to apply federal law, the Framers did not consider the possibility that federal law might bind States, say, in their relations with their employees. In the subsequent ratification debates, however, the issue of jurisdiction over a State did emerge in the question whether States might be sued on their debts in federal court, and on this point, too, a variety of views emerged and the diversity of sovereign immunity conceptions displayed itself.

The only arguable support for the Court's absolutist view that I have found among the leading participants in the debate surrounding ratification was the one already mentioned, that of Alexander Hamilton in The Federalist No. 81, where he described the sovereign immunity of the States in language suggesting principles associated with natural law...

. . .

...From a canvass of... opinion expressed at the ratifying conventions, one thing is certain. No one was espousing an indefeasible, natural law view of sovereign immunity. The controversy over the enforceability of state debts subject to state law produced emphatic support for sovereign immunity from eminences as great as Madison and Marshall, but neither of them indicated adherence to any immunity conception outside the common law.

. . .

E

If the natural law conception of sovereign immunity as an inherent characteristic of sovereignty enjoyed by the States had been broadly accepted at the time of the founding, one would expect to find it reflected somewhere in the five opinions delivered by the Court in *Chisholm* v. *Georgia*, 2 Dall. 419 (1793). Yet that view did not appear in any of them....

. . .

...Not a single Justice suggested that sovereign immunity was an inherent and indefeasible right of statehood, and neither counsel for Georgia before the Circuit Court... nor Justice Iredell seems even to have conceived the possibility that the new Tenth Amendment produced the equivalent of such a doctrine....

[III]

. . .

Least of all is it to the point for the Court to suggest that because the Framers would be surprised to find States subjected to a federal-law suit in their own courts under the commerce power, the suit must be prohibited by the Constitution....

If the Framers would be surprised to see States subjected to suit in their own courts under the commerce power, they would be astonished by the reach of Congress under the Commerce Clause generally. The proliferation of Government, State and Federal, would amaze the Framers, and the administrative state with its reams of regulations would leave them rubbing their eyes. But the Framers' surprise at, say, the FLSA, or the Federal Communications Commission, or the Federal Reserve Board is no threat to the constitutionality of any one of them...

[IV.B]

[*In this section Souter charges that it is "whimsy" for the Court to argue that the United States may bring suit in federal court against a state for damages under the FLSA, because the Secretary of Labor lacks the enforcement staff to litigate the interests of some 4.7 million employees of the fifty states.*]

V

The Court has swung back and forth with regrettable disruption on the enforceability of the FLSA against the States, but if the present majority had a defensible position one could at least accept its decision with an expectation of stability ahead. As it is, any such expectation would be naive. The resemblance of today's state sovereign immunity to the *Lochner* era's industrial due process is striking. The Court began this century by imputing immutable constitutional status to a conception of economic self-reliance that was never true to industrial life and grew insistently fictional with the years, and the Court has chosen to close the century by conferring like status on a conception of state sovereign immunity that is true neither to history nor to the structure of the Constitution. I expect the Court's late essay into immunity doctrine will prove the equal of its earlier experiment in laissez-faire, the one being as unrealistic as the other, as indefensible, and probably as fleeting.

United States v. Morrison

120 S.Ct. 1740 (2000)*

Christy Brzonkala, a student at the Virginia Polytechnic Institute, charged two students with assaulting and raping her in 1994. Although the school's Judicial Committee initially found one of the students, Antonio Morrison, guilty of sexual assault (later changing the charge to "using abusive language") and sentenced him to suspension for two semesters, the university later set aside Morrison's punishment. Brzonkala sued the students and Virginia Tech in federal court, complaining that the attack violated 42 U.S.C. § 13981 (part of the Violence Against Women Act of 1994). She also charged that Virginia Tech violated Title IX. A district court dismissed the Title IX claim and concluded that Congress lacked authority under either the Commerce Clause or Section 5 of the Fourteenth Amendment to enact § 13981. The Fourth Circuit, sitting en banc, affirmed the district court's conclusion that Congress lacked constitutional authority to enact § 13981.

CHIEF JUSTICE REHNQUIST delivered the opinion of the Court.

In these cases we consider the constitutionality of 42 U.S.C. § 13981, which provides a federal civil remedy for the victims of gender-motivated violence.... Believing that these cases are controlled by our decisions in *United States* v. *Lopez*, 514 U.S. 549 (1995), *United States* v. *Harris*, 106 U.S. 629 (1883), and the *Civil Rights Cases*, 109 U.S. 3 (1883), we affirm.

I

Petitioner Christy Brzonkala enrolled at Virginia Polytechnic Institute (Virginia Tech) in the fall of 1994. In September of that year, Brzonkala met respondents Antonio Morrison and James Crawford, who were both students at Virginia Tech and members of its varsity football team. Brzonkala alleges that, within 30 minutes of meeting Morrison and Crawford, they assaulted and repeatedly raped her....

[*Brzonkala filed a complaint against the two students. After several actions by the university's judicial committee, Virginia Tech's senior vice president and provost set aside any punishment*

---

* The text for this case was obtained in electronic form from Westlaw and is reproduced by permission of the West Group.

for Morrison. After learning that Morrison would be returning to Virginia Tech, Brzonkala dropped out of the university and sued Morrison, Crawford, and Virginia Tech, claiming a violation of § 13981 and Title IX.]

Section 13981 was part of the Violence Against Women Act of 1994. . . . It states that "[a]ll persons within the United States shall have the right to be free from crimes of violence motivated by gender." . . .

Section 13981 defines a "crim[e] of violence motivated by gender" as "a crime of violence committed because of gender or on the basis of gender, and due, at least in part, to an animus based on the victim's gender." . . .

. . . [S]ubsection (e)(3) provides a § 13981 litigant with a choice of forums: Federal and state courts "shall have concurrent jurisdiction" over complaints brought under the section.

. . . Congress explicitly identified the sources of federal authority on which it relied in enacting § 13981. It said that a "federal civil rights cause of action" is established "[p]ursuant to the affirmative power of Congress . . . under section 5 of the Fourteenth Amendment to the Constitution, as well as under section 8 of Article I of the Constitution." . . .

II

. . . Brzonkala and the United States rely upon the third clause of [*section 8*], which gives Congress power "[t]o regulate Commerce with foreign Nations, and among the several States, and with the Indian Tribes."

. . .

As we observed in *Lopez*, modern Commerce Clause jurisprudence has "identified three broad categories of activity that Congress may regulate under its commerce power." . . . "First, Congress may regulate the use of the channels of interstate commerce." . . . "Second, Congress is empowered to regulate and protect the instrumentalities of interstate commerce, or persons or things in interstate commerce, even though the threat may come only from intrastate activities." . . . "Finally, Congress' commerce authority includes the power to regulate those activities having a substantial relation to interstate commerce, . . . *i.e.*, those activities that substantially affect interstate commerce." . . .

Petitioners do not contend that these cases fall within either of the first two of these categories of Commerce Clause regulation. They seek to sustain § 13981 as a regulation of activity that sub-

stantially affects interstate commerce. . . . we agree that this is the proper inquiry.

Since *Lopez* most recently canvassed and clarified our case law governing this third category of Commerce Clause regulation, it provides the proper framework for conducting the required analysis of § 13981. [*Rehnquist explains that the Court held that the Gun-Free School Zones Act of 1990 exceeded Congress' authority under the Commerce Clause because (1) the Act had "nothing to do with 'commerce' or any sort of economic enterprise," (2) the Act contained no express jurisdictional element to limit its reach to a discrete set of firearm possessions connected to interstate commerce, (3) neither the statutory language nor the legislative history contained express congressional findings regarding the effects upon interstate commerce of gun possession in a school zone, and (4) the link between gun possession and a substantial effect on interstate commerce was so attenuated that Congress might regulate not only all violent crime "but all activities that might lead to crime, regardless of how tenuously they relate to interstate commerce."]*

With these principles underlying our Commerce Clause jurisprudence as reference points, the proper resolution of the present cases is clear. Gender-motivated crimes of violence are not, in any sense of the phrase, economic activity. . . .

Like the Gun-Free School Zones Act at issue in *Lopez*, § 13981 contains no jurisdictional element establishing that the federal cause of action is in pursuance of Congress' power to regulate interstate commerce. Although *Lopez* makes clear that such a jurisdictional element would lend support to the argument that § 13981 is sufficiently tied to interstate commerce, Congress elected to cast § 13981's remedy over a wider, and more purely intrastate, body of violent crime.

In contrast with the lack of congressional findings that we faced in *Lopez*, § 13981 is supported by numerous findings regarding the serious impact that gender-motivated violence has on victims and their families. . . . But the existence of congressional findings is not sufficient, by itself, to sustain the constitutionality of Commerce Clause legislation. . . . " '[w]hether particular operations affect interstate commerce sufficiently to come under the constitutional power of Congress to regulate them is ultimately a judicial rather than a legislative question, and can be settled finally only by this Court'." 514 U.S., at 557, n. 2 (quoting *Heart of Atlanta Motel*, 379 U.S., at 273 (Black, J., concurring)).

In these cases, Congress' findings are substantially weakened by the fact that they rely so heavily on a method of reasoning that we have already rejected as unworkable if we are to maintain the Constitution's enumeration of powers. Congress found that gender-motivated violence affects interstate commerce

"by deterring potential victims from traveling interstate, from engaging in employment in interstate business, and from transacting with business, and in places involved in interstate commerce; ... by diminishing national productivity, increasing medical and other costs, and decreasing the supply of and the demand for interstate products." ...

... If accepted, petitioners' reasoning would allow Congress to regulate any crime as long as the nationwide, aggregated impact of that crime has substantial effects on employment, production, transit, or consumption. Indeed, if Congress may regulate gender-motivated violence, it would be able to regulate murder or any other type of violence since gender-motivated violence, as a subset of all violent crime, is certain to have lesser economic impacts than the larger class of which it is a part.

Petitioners' reasoning, moreover, will not limit Congress to regulating violence but may, as we suggested in *Lopez*, be applied equally as well to family law and other areas of traditional state regulation since the aggregate effect of marriage, divorce, and childrearing on the national economy is undoubtedly significant. Congress may have recognized this specter when it expressly precluded § 13981 from being used in the family law context....

We accordingly reject the argument that Congress may regulate noneconomic, violent criminal conduct based solely on that conduct's aggregate effect on interstate commerce. The Constitution requires a distinction between what is truly national and what is truly local.... The regulation and punishment of intrastate violence that is not directed at the instrumentalities, channels, or goods involved in interstate commerce has always been the province of the States....

III

[W]e address petitioners' alternative argument that the section's civil remedy should be upheld as an exercise of Congress' remedial power under § 5 of the Fourteenth Amendment.... The principles governing an analysis of congressional legislation under § 5 are well settled. Section 5 states that Congress may " 'enforce,' by 'appropriate legislation' the constitutional guarantee that no State shall deprive any person of 'life, liberty or property, without due process of law,' nor deny any person 'equal protection of the laws.' " *City of Boerne* v. *Flores*, 521 U.S. 507, 517 (1997)....

Petitioners' § 5 argument is founded on an assertion that there is pervasive bias in various state justice systems against victims of gender-motivated violence. This assertion is supported by a voluminous congressional record....

... However, the language and purpose of the Fourteenth Amendment place certain limitations on the manner in which Congress may attack discriminatory conduct. These limitations are necessary to prevent the Fourteenth Amendment from obliterating the Framers' carefully crafted balance of power between the States and the National Government. Foremost among these limitations is the time-honored principle that the Fourteenth Amendment, by its very terms, prohibits only state action. [*Here Rehnquist discusses* United States v. Harris, *106 U.S. 629 (1883) and the* Civil Rights Cases, *109 U.S. 3 (1883) for the proposition that Congress' § 5 power cannot be directed exclusively against the actions of private persons. He rejects the argument that* United States v. Guest, *383 U.S. 745 (1966) and* District of Columbia v. Carter, *409 U.S. 418 (1973) overruled these longstanding limitations on Congress' § 5 authority.*]

For these reasons, we conclude that Congress' power under § 5 does not extend to the enactment of § 13981.

IV

Petitioner Brzonkala's complaint alleges that she was the victim of a brutal assault. But Congress' effort in § 13981 to provide a federal civil remedy can be sustained neither under the Commerce Clause nor under § 5 of the Fourteenth Amendment. If the allegations here are true, no civilized system of justice could fail to provide her a remedy for the conduct of respondent Morrison. But under our federal system that remedy must be provided by the Commonwealth of Virginia, and not by the United States. The judgment of the Court of Appeals is

Affirmed.

JUSTICE THOMAS, concurring.

... I write separately only to express my view that the very notion of a "substantial effects" test under the Commerce Clause is inconsistent with the original understanding of Congress' powers and with this Court's early Commerce Clause cases. By continuing to apply this rootless and malleable standard, however circumscribed, the Court has encouraged the Federal Government to persist in its view that the Commerce Clause has virtually no limits....

JUSTICE SOUTER, with whom JUSTICE STEVENS, JUSTICE GINSBURG, and JUSTICE BREYER join, dissenting.

The Court says both that it leaves Commerce Clause precedent undisturbed and that the Civil Rights Remedy of the Violence Against Women Act of 1994 ... exceeds Congress's power under that Clause. I find the claims irreconcilable and respectfully dissent. *[In a footnote, Souter explains that by finding the law a valid exercise of Commerce Clause power, he has no occasion to analyze the Fourteenth Amendment claim.]*

I

Our cases, which remain at least nominally undisturbed, stand for the following propositions. Congress has the power to legislate with regard to activity that, in the aggregate, has a substantial effect on interstate commerce....

One obvious difference from *United States* v. *Lopez* ... is the mountain of data assembled by Congress, here showing the effects of violence against women on interstate commerce. Passage of the Act in 1994 was preceded by four years of hearings, which included testimony from physicians and law professors; from survivors of rape and domestic violence; and from representatives of state law enforcement and private business. The record includes reports on gender bias from task forces in 21 States, and we have the benefit of specific factual findings in the eight separate Reports issued by Congress and its committees over the long course leading to enactment....

With respect to domestic violence, Congress received evidence for the following findings: ["Three out of four American women will be victims of violent crimes sometime during their life." ... "Violence is the leading cause of injuries to women ages 15 to 44 ..." ... "An estimated 4 million American women are battered each year by their husbands or partners." ... "Over 1 million women in the United States seek medical assistance each year for injuries sustained [from] their husbands or other partners." ...]

The evidence as to rape was similarly extensive, supporting these conclusions: ["[The incidence of] rape rose four times as fast as the total national crime rate over the past 10 years." ... "According to one study, close to half a million girls now in high school will be raped before they graduate." ... "[One hundred twenty-five thousand] college women can expect to be raped during this—or any—year." ...]

Congress thereby explicitly stated the predicate for the exercise of its Commerce Clause power. Is its conclusion irrational in view of the data amassed? True, the methodology of particular studies may be challenged, and some of the figures arrived at may be disputed. But the sufficiency of the evidence before Congress to provide a rational basis for the finding cannot seriously be questioned....

II

The Act would have passed muster at any time between *Wickard* in 1942 and *Lopez* in 1995, a period in which the law enjoyed a stable understanding that congressional power under the Commerce Clause, complemented by the authority of the Necessary and Proper Clause, Art. I. § 8 cl. 18, extended to all activity that, when aggregated, has a substantial effect on interstate commerce....

The fact that the Act does not pass muster before the Court today is therefore proof, to a degree that *Lopez* was not, that the Court's nominal adherence to the substantial effects test is merely that. Although a new jurisprudence has not emerged with any distinctness, it is clear that some congressional conclusions about obviously substantial, cumulative effects on commerce are being assigned lesser values than the once-stable doctrine would assign them. These devaluations are accomplished not by any express repudiation of the substantial effects test or its application through the aggregation of individual conduct, but by supplanting rational basis scrutiny with a new criterion of review.

· · ·

A

... In the half century following the modern activation of the commerce power with passage of the Interstate Commerce Act in 1887, this Court from time to time created categorical enclaves beyond congressional reach by declaring such activities as "mining," "production," "manufacturing," and union membership to be outside the definition of "commerce" and by limiting application of the effects test to "direct" rather than "indirect" commercial consequences....

Since adherence to these formalistically contrived confines of commerce power in large measure provoked the judicial crisis of 1937, one might reasonably have doubted that Members of this Court would ever again toy with a return to the days before *NLRB* v. *Jones & Laughlin Steel Corp.*, 301 U.S. 1 (1937), which brought the earlier and nearly disastrous experiment to an end. And yet today's decision can only be seen as a step toward recapturing the prior mistakes....

B

The Court finds it relevant that the statute addresses conduct traditionally subject to state prohibition under domestic criminal law, a fact said to have some heightened significance when the violent conduct in question is not itself aimed directly at interstate commerce or its instrumentalities.... Again, history seems to be recycling, for the theory of traditional state concern as grounding a limiting principle has been rejected previously, and more than once. It was disapproved in *Darby*, 312 U.S., at 123–124, and held insufficient standing alone to limit the commerce power in *Hodel*, 452 U.S., at 276–277.... *Garcia* v. *San Antonio Metropolitan Transit Authority*, 469 U.S. 528 (1985)...held that the concept of "traditional governmental function"...was incoherent, there being no explanation that would make sense of the multifarious decisions placing some functions on one side of the line, some on the other....

The objection to reviving traditional state spheres of action as a consideration in commerce analysis, however, not only rests on the portent of incoherence, but is compounded by a further defect just as fundamental. The defect, in essence, is the majority's rejection of the Founders' considered judgment that politics, not judicial review, should mediate between state and national interests as the strength and legislative jurisdiction of the National Government inevitably increased through the expected growth of the national economy....

C

...Today's majority...finds no significance whatever in the state support for the Act based upon the States' acknowledged failure to deal adequately with gender-based violence in state courts, and the belief of their own law enforcement agencies that national action is essential.

The National Association of Attorneys General supported the Act unanimously,...and Attorneys General from 38 States urged Congress to enact the Civil Rights Remedy, representing that "the current system for dealing with violence against women is inadequate,"...

...[W]hen the Civil Rights Remedy was challenged in court, the States came to its defense. Thirty-six of them and the Commonwealth of Puerto Rico have filed an amicus brief in support of petitioners in these cases, and only one State has taken respondents' side....

JUSTICE BREYER, with whom JUSTICE STEVENS joins, and with whom JUSTICE SOUTER and JUSTICE GINSBURG join as to Part I-A, dissenting.

* * *

G. THE SPENDING AND TAXING POWERS

The pattern of federal spending and taxing powers has been similar to the Commerce Clause. The courts initially placed constraints on congressional power and offered protection to "local" activities in the states. Over time, however, these constraints have been largely removed because the judiciary recognizes the need for national powers and regulation.

The Constitution speaks clearly on only one aspect of the taxing power: "No tax or duty shall be laid on articles exported from any State" (Art. I, § 9). Other tax questions have provoked extensive litigation. Difficulties in distinguishing between direct and indirect taxes created major conflicts between Congress and the judiciary. Indirect taxes must follow the rule of uniformity: "The Congress shall have Power to lay and collect Taxes, Duties, Imposts, and Excises, to pay the Debts and provide for the common Defense and general Welfare of the United States; but all Duties, Imposts and Excises shall be uniform throughout the United States" (Art. I, § 8). The rule of uniformity protects states from discriminatory actions by the national government, although federal taxes do not have to fall equally on each state, nor is Congress barred from adopting tax exemptions for certain regions. United States v. Psasynski, 462 U.S. 74 (1983).

Direct taxes are covered in Article I, Section 9: "No capitation, or other direct, tax shall be laid, unless in proportion to the census or enumeration herein before directed to be taken." Capitation taxes, or "head taxes," have never been enacted by Congress. Other direct taxes must be levied among the states in accordance with the rule of apportionment. The question of a direct tax was first decided by the Supreme Court in 1796. A carriage tax imposed by Congress was attacked as a direct tax, requiring that it be apportioned among the states on the basis of population. A unanimous Court, however, ruled that the tax was indirect. The decision appeared to limit direct taxes to two kinds: a capitation or poll tax, imposed without regard to property, and a tax on land. Hylton v. United States, 3 Dall. 171, 175 (1796). From 1798 to 1816 the federal government imposed direct taxes on real estate and slaves. In 1861 the federal tax applied to real estate only. Veazie Bank v. Fenno, 75 U.S. (8 Wall.) 533, 543 (1869). Federal taxes on currency and bank circulation were not considered a direct tax. Id. at 546–47.

Income Tax

In 1881 a unanimous Court again limited the meaning of direct taxes to capitation taxes and taxes on real estate. The Court interpreted the federal income tax of 1864, as amended in 1865, as an indirect tax. Springer v. United States, 102 U.S. 586 (1881). In 1895, after a hundred years of agreement on the meaning of direct taxes, the Court reversed direction and struck down a federal income tax, treating it as a direct tax to be apportioned on the basis of population. The statute was invalidated in two steps. The first decision held that the tax on rents or income of real estate was a direct tax and violated the Constitution by not following the apportionment rule. Pollock v. Farmers' Loan & Trust Co., 157 U.S. 429 (1895). A second decision struck down the income tax, in part because the Court concluded that invalidation of the other taxes left a tax scheme that Congress could not have intended. POLLOCK v. FARMERS' LOAN & TRUST CO., 158 U.S. 601, 637 (1895).

The Court acted under the shadow of class warfare and threats of socialism. During oral argument, Joseph H. Choate warned the Justices that the tax was "communistic in its purposes and tendencies." 157 U.S. at 532. After the first hearing, the Court split 4 to 4 on the question of the income tax. Upon rehearing, a 5 to 4 decision invalidated the tax. The member missing from the first decision, Justice Jackson, voted to *sustain* the tax in the second case. All things being equal, this should have yielded a 5–4 tally supporting the income tax. One Justice obviously switched his vote. Who he was, and why he switched, has never been revealed. Because of the vote switching and razor-thin majority, the decision became known as one of three "self-inflicted wounds" on the Court (the other two being *Dred Scott* in 1857 and the Legal Tender Cases of 1870). Charles Evans Hughes, The Supreme of the United States 54 (1928). It was not until 1913 that Congress and the states overrode *Pollock* by passing the Sixteenth Amendment.

The income tax cases marked an unusual setback for the power of Congress to tax. In 1904 the Court held that the judiciary would not limit the taxing power simply because it had been exercised in an unwise, oppressive, or injurious manner. Nor could the courts inquire into the motive or purpose of Congress in passing a tax, or discover a limitation in the Due Process Clause of the Fifth Amendment. Congressional abuses in such cases had to be corrected by the voters. McCray v. United States, 195 U.S. 27 (1904). In 1911 a unanimous Court upheld a corporation income tax passed by Congress. The Court called it an excise, not a direct, tax and said it complied with the rule of uniformity. Flint Stone Tracy Co., 220 U.S. 107 (1911). When Congress tried to use the taxing power to regulate matters the Court considered within the police power of the states, the congressional statute was declared invalid. Bailey v. Drexel Furniture Co. (Child Labor Tax Case), 259 U.S. 20 (1922); Hill v. Wallace, 259 U.S. 44 (1922).

New Deal Cases

The question of Congress intruding upon "local" matters within the jurisdiction of the states resulted in the invalidation of several New Deal statutes. In 1936 the Supreme Court struck down a so-called excise tax in the Bituminous Coal Conservation Act of 1935 because it coerced coal producers to submit to the price-fixing and labor provisions of the Act. Carter v. Carter Coal Co., 298 U.S. 238, 288–89 (1936). Also in 1936, the Court declared unconstitutional a "processing tax" enacted by Congress as part of the Agricultural Adjustment Act. In return for limiting their acreage and crops, farmers received payments from this tax. The Court held that the power of taxation exists to support government, not to expropriate money from one group to benefit another as part of a general regulatory scheme. Moreover, the Court held that the tax was coercive on farmers and invaded state powers by trying to regulate the "local" matter of agriculture. The decision suggests that had Congress explicitly invoked its commerce power, the Act might have been sustained. In writing the opinion for the Court, Justice Roberts unveiled his famous mechanical formula for determining the constitutionality of a statute. UNITED STATES v. BUTLER, 297 U.S. 1 (1936).

Spending and Regulatory Power

Roberts abandoned his conservative brethren a year later by joining a 5 to 4 decision upholding Title IX of the Social Security Act. Congress imposed a tax on employers to support a national unemployment compensation plan. Funds from state unemployment laws were paid over to the Secretary of the Treasury and credited to an unemployment trust fund. Title IX was upheld even though it seemed to conflict with *Butler* by pressuring states to adopt unemployment compensation laws as part of a regulatory, and not merely revenue-raising, effort. STEWARD MACHINE CO. v. DAVIS, 301 U.S. 548 (1937). Congress responded to *Butler* by passing the Soil Conservation and Domestic Allotment Act of 1936 and the Agricultural Adjustment Act of 1938. These statutes avoided the processing tax but pursued the same objective of controlling production by relying on the federal appropriations power and the Commerce Clause.

By attaching conditions to federal funds, Congress can regulate certain state activities. States acquiesce by accepting federal strings with the funds. Oklahoma v. CSC, 330 U.S. 127, 143–44 (1947). Federal grants to states have grown over the years, representing a substantial percentage of state budgets (see Table 8.2). Thus, Congress may direct the Secretary of Transportation to withhold a percentage of federal funds from states that allow persons under twenty-one to buy alcoholic beverages. SOUTH DAKOTA v. DOLE, 483 U.S. 203 (1987). The Court has accepted the use of the spending power to impose racial and ethnic criteria as a condition attached to federal grants (a 10 percent "set-aside" for minority businesses). Fullilove v. Klutznick, 448 U.S. 448 (1980), reprinted in Chapter 15. If the conditions are offensive to state interests, there is no obligation to accept the funds.

The states and the federal government are generally free to exercise their taxing power if they proceed on a rational basis and do not resort to classifications that are "palpably arbitrary." Allied Stores of Ohio v. Bowers, 358 U.S. 522, 527 (1959); Lehnhausen v. Lake Shore Auto Parts Co., 410 U.S. 356 (1973). Congress has had mixed results in using the taxing power to regulate narcotics, gambling, liquor, and firearms. The application of the taxing power to narcotics has been repeatedly upheld.[10] The Court has held that because a federal liquor tax operated not as a tax but as a penalty, it usurped the police powers of the states.

---

10. United States v. Doremus, 249 U.S. 86 (1919); Nigro v. United States, 276 U.S. 332 (1928); United States v. Sanchez, 340 U.S. 42 (1950). Questions have been raised in some cases as to whether compliance with these laws automatically exposes someone to the risk of self-incrimination. Leary v. United States, 395 U.S. 6 (1969); United States v. Covington, 395 U.S. 57 (1969); Minor v. United States, 396 U.S. 87 (1969).

TABLE 8.2   FEDERAL GRANTS TO STATES (in billions)

Fiscal Year	Amount	Percent of Total State-Local Outlays
1955	$ 3.1	10.1
1960	7.0	13.8
1965	11.0	14.9
1970	21.8	16.7
1975	47.0	20.6
1980	83.0	21.7
1985	106.1	17.7
1990	136.8	16.1
1991	154.1	17.1
1992	179.2	18.3
1993	198.6	19.1
1994	215.4	19.6
1995	228.7	19.6
1996	234.8	19.2
1997	244.6	19.0

SOURCE: Governments Division, Bureau of the Census, U.S. Department of Commerce.

United States v. Constantine, 296 U.S. 287 (1935); United States v. Kesterson, 296 U.S. 299 (1935).

The taxing power has been used to regulate firearms, with the Court pointing out that every tax "is in some measure regulatory." Sonzinsky v. United States, 300 U.S. 506, 513 (1937). Such statutes, however, cannot force gun dealers to incriminate themselves. Haynes v. United States, 390 U.S. 85 (1968). The same issue applies to federal taxes on gambling. At first, the Court determined that federal taxes and requirements to register with the Internal Revenue Service did not violate the Self-Incrimination Clause. United States v. Kahriger, 345 U.S. 22 (1953); Lewis v. United States, 348 U.S. 419 (1955). The Court later held that such statutes unconstitutionally compel gamblers to incriminate themselves. Marchetti v. United States, 390 U.S. 39 (1968); Grosso v. United States, 390 U.S. 62 (1968).

Intergovernmental Tax Immunity

The theory of dual federalism, which created exclusive jurisdictions for the federal government and the states, spawned the sister doctrine of intergovernmental tax immunity. Chief Justice Marshall struck down a state tax on the U.S. Bank by arguing extravagantly that the power to tax is the power to destroy. McCulloch v. Maryland, 17 U.S. (4 Wheat.) 315 (1819). If states could not tax federal instrumentalities, presumably the federal government could not tax state activities, and indeed the Court reached that conclusion in 1871 by holding that Congress could not tax the salary of a state judge. Justice Bradley, in a solitary dissent, objected to the doctrine that "the general government is to be regarded in any sense foreign or antagonistic to the State governments, their officers, or people." He correctly predicted that the decision would lead to impractical and mischievous results. Collector v. Day, 78 U.S. (11 Wall.) 113, 128–29 (1871).

The doctrine of intergovernmental tax immunity did not exempt state activities from federal taxation when states entered the field of ordinary business operations. Nongovernmental functions are taxed in the same manner as private businesses. South Carolina v. United States, 199 U.S. 437 (1905). The doctrine was shaken in 1928 when four Justices dissented against a rigid application of reciprocal tax immunity. In one of the dissents, Justice Holmes remarked: "The power to tax is not the power to destroy while this Court sits." Panhandle Oil Co. v. Knox, 277 U.S. 218, 223 (1928). By 1939 the Court decided to overrule *Collector v. Day* to the extent that it recognized "an implied constitutional immunity from income taxation of the salaries of officers or employees of the national or a state government or their instrumentalities." Graves v. N.Y. ex rel. O'Keefe, 306 U.S. 466, 486 (1939).

Congressional legislation also changed the substance of intergovernmental tax immunity. Beginning in 1864, Congress allowed the states to tax certain activities of national banks. 13 Stat. 111 (1864); see 12 U.S.C. § 548 (1994). Any changes in state taxation of national banks must come from Congress, not from the courts. First Agricultural Nat'l Bank v. State Tax Comm'n, 392 U.S. 339, 346 (1968). Recent decisions have struck down state taxes on military installations operated by the federal government, but the judgment in these cases turned not on abstract constitutional doctrines but on congressional intent (the Buck Act of 1940).[11]

A decision in 1989 struck down state laws that impose discriminatory taxes on state and federal workers. Michigan taxed federal government pensions but exempted state and local government retirees. The 8–1 ruling affected more than a dozen states, especially Virginia. Davis v. Michigan Dept. of Treasury, 489 U.S. 803 (1989). Virginia changed its law to treat all pensions the same, but federal and military pensioners sued the state to recover taxes paid earlier. In 1993 the Court ruled that the *Davis* decision must be applied retroactively, exposing Virginia and fifteen other states to a potential cost of $1.8 billion in refunds. Harper v. Virginia Dept. of Taxation, 509 U.S. 86 (1993). Also relying on the *Davis* precedent, a unanimous Court in 1992 held invalid a Kansas law that taxed federal military retirement benefits while exempting benefits received by other retirees. Barker v. Kansas, 503 U.S. 594 (1992). A decision in 1994 made it more difficult for states to avoid paying tax refunds to federal retirees. Reich v. Collins, 513 U.S. 106 (1994).[12]

Pollock v. Farmers' Loan & Trust Co.

158 U.S. 601 (1895)

The Constitution retained for the states the power of direct taxation. The federal government could also invoke that power, but only on the condition that such taxes be apportioned among the states in accordance with their numbers. Congress passed an income tax in 1894. The task for the Court was to distinguish between direct and indirect taxes and to specify the conditions for the latter. Earlier in 1895, the Court decided that the statute's tax on rents or income of real estate represented a direct tax and was therefore unconstitutional for failure to follow the apportionment rule. Pollock v. Farmers' Loan

---

11. United States v. Tax Comm'n of Mississippi, 421 U.S. 599 (1975); United States v. State Tax Comm'n of Mississippi, 412 U.S. 363 (1973). Massachusetts v. United States, 435 U.S. 444 (1978), held that a registration tax by Congress in the Airport and Airway Revenue Act of 1970 did not violate the tax immunity of states. South Carolina v. Baker, 485 U.S. 505 (1988), upheld a congressional statute that removed the federal tax exemption for interest earned on nonregistered (bearer) state and local bonds. A state sales or use tax on a federal bankruptcy liquidation sale has been upheld. California Equalization Bd. v. Sierra Summit, 490 U.S. 844 (1989).

12. Tax liabilities of states were also affected by two decisions in 1990. In the first decision, a unanimous Court held that states must pay refunds or make adjustments for taxes that were collected unconstitutionally. Due process requires a state to give taxpayers a meaningful opportunity to obtain relief from such taxes. McKesson Corp. v. Florida Alcohol & Tobacco Div., 496 U.S. 18 (1990). In the second decision, a 5–4 Court ruled that a 1987 decision striking down a Pennsylvania tax as discriminatory could not be applied retroactively to force Arkansas (with a similar law) to repay taxes collected before the 1987 decision. The Court reasoned that Arkansas had no way of foreseeing the 1987 ruling. American Trucking Assns., Inc. v. Smith, 496 U.S. 167 (1990).

& Trust Co., 157 U.S. 429 (1895). That left one remaining issue from the statute: the income tax. Charles Pollock, a stockholder in Farmers' Loan & Trust, sued the company to prevent it from paying the income tax.

MR. CHIEF JUSTICE FULLER delivered the opinion of the court.

... [T]he Constitution divided Federal taxation into two great classes, the class of direct taxes, and the class of duties, imposts, and excises; and prescribed two rules which qualified the grant of power as to each class.

The power to lay direct taxes apportioned among the several States in proportion to their representation in the popular branch of Congress, a representation based on population as ascertained by the census, was plenary and absolute; but to lay direct taxes without apportionment was forbidden. The power to lay duties, imposts, and excises was subject to the qualification that the imposition must be uniform throughout the United States.

Our previous decision was confined to the consideration of the validity of the tax on the income from real estate, and on the income from municipal bonds. The question thus limited was whether such taxation was direct or not, in the meaning of the Constitution; and the court went no farther, as to the tax on the income from real estate, than to hold that it fell within the same class as the source whence the income was derived, that is, that a tax upon the realty and a tax upon the receipts therefrom were alike direct; while as to the income from municipal bonds, that could not be taxed because of want of power to tax the source, and no reference was made to the nature of the tax as being direct or indirect.

We are now permitted to broaden the field of inquiry, and to determine to which of the two great classes a tax upon a person's entire income, whether derived from rents, or products, or otherwise, of real estate, or from bonds, stocks, or other forms of personal property, belongs; and we are unable to conclude that the enforced subtraction from the yield of all the owner's real or personal property, in the manner prescribed, is so different from a tax upon the property itself, that it is not a direct, but an indirect tax, in the meaning of the Constitution.

. . .

The founders anticipated that the expenditures of the States, their counties, cities, and towns, would chiefly be met by direct taxation on accumulated property, while they expected that those of the Federal government would be for the most part met by indirect taxes. And in order that the power of direct taxation by the general government should not be exercised, except on necessity; and, when the necessity arose, should be so exercised as to leave the States at liberty to discharge their respective obligations, and should not be so exercised, unfairly and discriminatingly, as to particular States or otherwise, by a mere majority vote, possibly of those whose constituents were intentionally not subjected to any part of the burden, the qualified grant was made. Those who made it knew that the power to tax involved the power to destroy....

It is said that a tax on the whole income of property is not a direct tax in the meaning of the Constitution, but a duty, and, as a duty, leviable without apportionment, whether direct or indirect. We do not think so. Direct taxation was not restricted in one breath, and the restriction blown to the winds in another.

. . .

According to the census, the true valuation of real and personal property in the United States in 1890 was $65,037,091,197, of which real estate with improvements thereon made up $39,544,544,333. Of course, from the latter must be deducted, in applying these selections, all unproductive property and all property whose net yield does not exceed four thousand dollars; but, even with such deductions, it is evident that the income from realty formed a vital part of the scheme for taxation embodied therein. If that be stricken out, and also the income from all invested personal property, bonds, stocks, investments of all kinds, it is obvious that by far the largest part of the anticipated revenue would be eliminated, and this would leave the burden of the tax to be borne by professions, trades, employments, or vocations; and in that way what was intended as a tax on capital would remain in substance a tax on occupations and labor. We cannot believe that such was the intention of Congress. We do not mean to say that an act laying by apportionment a direct tax on all real estate and personal property, or the income thereof, might not also lay excise taxes on business, privileges, employments, and vocations. But this is not such an act; and the scheme must be considered as a whole. Being invalid as to the greater part, and falling, as the tax would, if any part were held valid, in a direction which could not have been contemplated except in connection with the taxation considered as an entirety, we are constrained to conclude that sections twenty-seven to thirty-seven, inclusive, of the act, which became a law without the signature of the President on August 28, 1894, are wholly inoperative and void.

Our conclusions may, therefore, be summed up as follows:

First. We adhere to the opinion already announced, that, taxes on real estate being indisputably direct taxes, taxes on the rents or income of real estate are equally direct taxes.

Second. We are of opinion that taxes on personal property, or on the income of personal property, are likewise direct taxes.

Third. The tax imposed by sections twenty-seven to thirty-seven, inclusive, of the act of 1894, so far as it falls on the income of real estate and of personal property, being a direct tax within the meaning of the Constitution, and, therefore, unconstitutional and void because not apportioned according to representation, all those sections, constituting one entire scheme of taxation, are necessarily invalid.

The decrees hereinbefore entered in this court will be vacated; the decrees below will be reversed, and the cases remanded, with instructions to grant the relief prayed.

MR. JUSTICE HARLAN dissenting.

. . .

What are "direct taxes" within the meaning of the Constitution? In the convention of 1787, Rufus King asked what was the precise meaning of *direct* taxation, and no one answered. Madison Papers, 5 Elliott's Debates, 451. The debates of that famous body do not show that any delegate attempted to give a clear, succinct definition of what, in his opinion, was a direct tax. Indeed, the report of those debates, upon the question now before us, is very meagre and unsatisfactory....

A question so difficult to be answered by able statesmen and lawyers directly concerned in the organization of the present government, can now, it seems, be easily answered, after a reexamination of documents, writings, and treatises on political economy, all of which, without any exception worth noting, have been several times directly brought to the attention of this court. And whenever that has been done the result al-

ways, until now, has been that a duty on incomes, derived from taxable subjects, of whatever nature, was held not to be a direct tax within the meaning of the Constitution, to be apportioned among the States on the basis of population, but could be laid, according to the rule of uniformity, upon individual citizens, corporations, and associations without reference to numbers in the particular States in which such citizens, corporations, or associations were domiciled....

. . .

...The recent civil war, involving the very existence of the nation, was brought to a successful end, and the authority of the Union restored, in part, by the use of vast amounts of money raised under statutes imposing duties on incomes derived from every kind of property, real and personal, not by the unequal rule of apportionment among the States on the basis of numbers, but by the rule of uniformity, operating upon individuals and corporations in all the States. And we are now asked to declare—and the judgment this day rendered in effect declares—that the enormous sums thus taken from the people, and so used, were taken in violation of the supreme law of the land....

. . .

In my judgment—to say nothing of the disregard of the former adjudications of this court, and of the settled practice of the government—this decision may well excite the gravest apprehensions. It strikes at the very foundations of national authority, in that it denies to the general government a power which is, or may become, vital to the very existence and preservation of the Union in a national emergency,...

MR. JUSTICE BROWN dissenting.

. . .

It is difficult to overestimate the importance of these cases. I certainly cannot overstate the regret I feel at the disposition made of them by the court. It is never a light thing to set aside the deliberate will of the legislature, and in my opinion it should never be done, except upon the clearest proof of its conflict with the fundamental law. Respect for the Constitution will not be inspired by a narrow and technical construction which shall limit or impair the necessary powers of Congress. Did the reversal of these cases involve merely the striking down of the inequitable features of this law, or even the whole law, for its want of uniformity, the consequences would be less serious; but as it implies a declaration that every income tax must be laid according to the rule of apportionment, the decision involves nothing less than a surrender of the taxing power to the moneyed class. . . .

MR. JUSTICE JACKSON dissenting.

. . .

The decision disregards the well-established canon of construction to which I have referred, that an act passed by a coördinate branch of the government has every presumption in its favor, and should never be declared invalid by the courts unless its repugnancy to the Constitution is clear beyond all reasonable doubt. It is not a matter of conjecture; it is the established principle that it must be clear beyond a reasonable doubt. . . .

The practical operation of the decision is not only to disregard the great principles of equality in taxation, but the further principle that in the imposition of taxes for the benefit of the government the burdens thereof should be imposed upon those having most *ability* to bear them. This decision, in effect, works out a directly opposite result, in relieving the citizens having the greater *ability*, while the burdens of taxation are made to fall most heavily and oppressively upon those having the least ability. . . . Considered in all its bearings, this decision is, in my judgment, the most disastrous blow ever struck at the constitutional power of Congress. . . .

MR. JUSTICE WHITE dissenting.

. . .

United States v. Butler

297 U.S. 1 (1936)

Processors of farm products challenged the "processing and floor taxes" included in the Agricultural Adjustment Act of 1933. The question was whether a tax could expropriate money from one group, to be expended by another, as a necessary means for regulation. The suit was brought by William M. Butler and the Hoosac Mills Corporation. Questions of state power were involved, as well as the distinction between "local" and "national" methods of agriculture.

MR. JUSTICE ROBERTS delivered the opinion of the Court.

In this case we must determine whether certain provisions of the Agricultural Adjustment Act, 1933, conflict with the Federal Constitution.

Title I of the statute is captioned "Agricultural Adjustment." Section 1 recites that an economic emergency has arisen, due to disparity between the prices of agricultural and other commodities, with consequent destruction of farmers' purchasing power and breakdown in orderly exchange, which, in turn, have affected transactions in agricultural commodities with a national public interest and burdened and obstructed the normal currents of commerce, calling for the enactment of legislation.

[Section 8 empowered the Secretary of Agriculture to enter into agreements with agricultural producers for the purpose of reducing acreage and production, thus supporting prices by limiting supply. In connection with this reduction on production, the Secretary was authorized to provide producers with "rental or benefit payments" and to issue licenses for processors engaged in the handling ("in the current of interstate or foreign commerce") of agricultural commodities and products.]

Section 9 (a) enacts:

"To obtain revenue for extraordinary expenses incurred by reason of the national economic emergency, there shall be levied processing taxes as hereinafter provided. When the Secretary of Agriculture determines that rental or benefit payments are to be made with respect to any basic agricultural commodity, he shall proclaim such determination, and a processing tax shall be in effect with respect to such commodity from the beginning of the marketing year therefor next following the date of such proclamation. The processing tax shall be levied, assessed, and collected upon the first domestic processing of the commodity, whether of domestic production or imported, and shall be paid by the processor. . . ."

[Section 16 authorized the Secretary of Agriculture to impose a "floor tax" on the sale of agricultural products.]

· · ·

The tax can only be sustained by ignoring the avowed purpose and operation of the act, and holding it a measure merely laying an excise upon processors to raise revenue for the support of government. Beyond cavil the sole object of the legislation is to restore the purchasing power of agricultural products to a parity with that prevailing in an earlier day; to take money from the processor and bestow it upon farmers who will reduce their acreage for the accomplishment of the proposed end, and, meanwhile to aid these farmers during the period required to bring the prices of their crops to the desired level.

· · ·

It is inaccurate and misleading to speak of the exaction from processors prescribed by the challenged act as a tax, or to say that as a tax it is subject to no infirmity. A tax, in the general understanding of the term, and as used in the Constitution, signifies an exaction for the support of the Government. The word has never been thought to connote the expropriation of money from one group for the benefit of another. We may concede that the latter sort of imposition is constitutional when imposed to effectuate regulation of a matter in which both groups are interested and in respect of which there is a power of legislative regulation. But manifestly no justification for it can be found unless as an integral part of such regulation. The exaction cannot be wrested out of its setting, denominated an excise for raising revenue and legalized by ignoring its purpose as a mere instrumentality for bringing about a desired end. To do this would be to shut our eyes to what all others than we can see and understand. *Child Labor Tax Case*, 259 U.S. 20, 37.

We conclude that the act is one regulating agricultural production; that the tax is a mere incident of such regulation and that the respondents have standing to challenge the legality of the exaction.

· · ·

Second. The Government asserts that even if the respondents may question the propriety of the appropriation embodied in the statute their attack must fail because Article I, § 8 of the Constitution authorizes the contemplated expenditure of the funds raised by the tax. This contention presents the great and the controlling question in the case.…

There should be no misunderstanding as to the function of this court in such a case. It is sometimes said that the court assumes a power to overrule or control the action of the people's representatives. This is a misconception. The Constitution is the supreme law of the land ordained and established by the people. All legislation must conform to the principles it lays down. When an act of Congress is appropriately challenged in the courts as not conforming to the constitutional mandate the judicial branch of the Government has only one duty, — to lay the article of the Constitution which is invoked beside the statute which is challenged and to decide whether the latter squares with the former.…

· · ·

Article I, § 8, of the Constitution vests sundry powers in the Congress. But two of its clauses have any bearing upon the validity of the statute under review.

The third clause endows the Congress with power "to regulate Commerce … among the several States." Despite a reference in its first section to a burden upon, and an obstruction of the normal currents of commerce, the act under review does not purport to regulate transactions in interstate or foreign commerce. Its stated purpose is the control of agricultural production, a purely local activity, in an effort to raise the prices paid the farmer. Indeed, the Government does not attempt to uphold the validity of the act on the basis of the commerce clause, which, for the purpose of the present case, may be put aside as irrelevant.

The clause thought to authorize the legislation, — the first, — confers upon the Congress power "to lay and collect Taxes, Duties, Imposts and Excises, to pay the Debts and provide for the common Defence and general Welfare of the United States.…" It is not contended that this provision grants power to regulate agricultural production upon the theory that such legislation would promote the general welfare. The Government concedes that the phrase "to provide for the general welfare" qualifies the power "to lay and collect taxes." The view that the clause grants power to provide for the general welfare, independently of the taxing power, has never been authoritatively accepted. Mr. Justice Story points out that if it were adopted "it is obvious that under color of the generality of the words, to 'provide for the common defence and general welfare,' the government of the United States is, in reality, a government of general and unlimited powers, notwithstanding the subsequent enumeration of specific powers." The true construction undoubtedly is that the only thing granted is the power to tax for the purpose of providing funds for payment of the nation's debts and making provision for the general welfare.

Nevertheless the Government asserts that warrant is found in this clause for the adoption of the Agricultural Adjustment Act. The argument is that Congress may appropriate and authorize the spending of moneys for the "general welfare"; that the phrase should be liberally construed to cover anything conducive to national welfare; that decision as to what will promote such welfare rests with Congress alone, and the courts may not review its determination; and finally that the appropriation under attack was in fact for the general welfare of the United States.

[Here Roberts analyzes the constitutional phrase "general welfare," concluding that the words "cannot be meaningless" and must have been "intended to limit and define the granted power to raise and to expend money." He summarizes Madison's position that the phrase amounted to nothing more than a reference to the other powers enumerated, and that the grant of power to tax and spend for the general welfare must be confined to the enumerated powers granted to Congress. Hamilton maintained that the general welfare clause conferred a power separate and distinct from the powers later enumerated. Story agreed with Hamilton. Roberts says that "the reading advocated by Mr. Justice Story is the correct one." Nevertheless, the broader construction "leaves the power to spend subject to limitations," and part of those limitations is that "the powers of taxation and appropriation extend only to matters of national, as distinguished from local welfare."]

. . .

We are not now required to ascertain the scope of the phrase "general welfare of the United States" or to determine whether an appropriation in aid of agriculture falls within it. Wholly apart from that question, another principle embedded in our Constitution prohibits the enforcement of the Agricultural Adjustment Act. The act invades the reserved rights of the states. It is a statutory plan to regulate and control agricultural production, a matter beyond the powers delegated to the federal government. The tax, the appropriation of the funds raised, and the direction for their disbursement, are but parts of the plan. They are but means to an unconstitutional end.

. . .

Third. If the taxing power may not be used as the instrument to enforce a regulation of matters of state concern with respect to which the Congress has no authority to interfere, may it, as in the present case, be employed to raise the money necessary to purchase a compliance which the Congress is powerless to command? The Government asserts that whatever might be said against the validity of the plan if compulsory, it is constitutionally sound because the end is accomplished by voluntary co-operation. There are two sufficient answers to the contention. The regulation is not in fact voluntary. The farmer, of course, may refuse to comply, but the price of such refusal is the loss of benefits. The amount offered is intended to be sufficient to exert pressure on him to agree to the proposed regulation. The power to confer or withhold unlimited benefits is the power to coerce or destroy. If the cotton grower elects not to accept the benefits, he will receive less for his crops; those who receive payments will be able to undersell him. The result may well be financial ruin. . . . This is coercion by economic pressure. The asserted power of choice is illusory.

. . .

But if the plan were one for purely voluntary co-operation it would stand no better so far as federal power is concerned. At best it is a scheme for purchasing with federal funds submission to federal regulation of a subject reserved to the states.

. . .

MR. JUSTICE STONE, dissenting.

. . . The power of courts to declare a statute unconstitutional is subject to two guiding principles of decision which ought never to be absent from judicial consciousness. One is that courts are concerned only with the power to enact statutes, not with their wisdom. The other is that while unconstitutional exercise of power by the executive and legislative branches of the government is subject to judicial restraint, the only check upon our own exercise of power is our own sense of self-restraint. For the removal of unwise laws from the statute books appeal lies not to the courts but to the ballot and to the processes of democratic government.

. . .

...Courts are not the only agency of government that must be assumed to have capacity to govern. Congress and the courts both unhappily may falter or be mistaken in the performance of their constitutional duty. But interpretation of our great charter of government which proceeds on any assumption that the responsibility for the preservation of our institutions is the exclusive concern of any one of the three branches of government, or that it alone can save them from destruction is far more likely, in the long run, "to obliterate the constituent members" of "an indestructible union of indestructible states" than the frank recognition that language, even of a constitution, may mean what it says: that the power to tax and spend includes the power to relieve a nationwide economic maladjustment by conditional gifts of money.

MR. JUSTICE BRANDEIS and MR. JUSTICE CARDOZO join in this opinion.

Steward Machine Co. v. Davis

301 U.S. 548 (1937)

Title IX of the Social Security Act of 1935 imposed an "excise tax" on employers, the proceeds to go into the U.S. Treasury to establish an unemployment compensation fund. Credit against the tax (up to 90 percent) would be given to employers who contributed under a state unemployment law. Questions: Did the tax unconstitutionally attempt to coerce the states to adopt their own unemployment compensation legislation, to be approved by the Federal Government? Could Title IX be interpreted as a "cooperative plan" into which states freely entered because of benefits available to them? If the credit gave the states motive and temptation, was that the same as coercion? The Steward Machine Company brought this action against Harwell G. Davis, Collector of Internal Revenue.

MR. JUSTICE CARDOZO delivered the opinion of the Court.

The validity of the tax imposed by the Social Security Act on employers of eight or more is here to be determined.

. . .

The assault on the statute proceeds on an extended front. Its assailants take the ground that the tax is not an excise; that it is not uniform throughout the United States as excises are required to be; that its exceptions are so many and arbitrary as to violate the Fifth Amendment; that its purpose was not revenue, but an unlawful invasion of the reserved powers of the states; and that the states in submitting to it have yielded to coercion and have abandoned governmental functions which they are not permitted to surrender.

The objections will be considered seriatim with such further explanation as may be necessary to make their meaning clear.

First. The tax, which is described in the statute as an excise, is laid with uniformity throughout the United States as a duty, an impost or an excise upon the relation of employment.

. . .

The subject matter of taxation open to the power of the Congress is as comprehensive as that open to the power of the states, though the method of apportionment may at times be different. "The Congress shall have power to lay and collect taxes, duties, imposts and excises." Art. 1, § 8. If the tax is a direct one, it shall be apportioned according to the census or enumeration. If it is a duty, impost, or excise, it shall be uniform throughout the United States. Together, these classes include every form of tax appropriate to sovereignty.... Whether the tax is to be classified as an "excise" is in truth not of critical importance. If not that, it is an "impost"...or a "duty"....A capitation or other "direct" tax it certainly is not....

2. The tax being an excise, its imposition must conform to the canon of uniformity. There has been no departure from this requirement. According to the settled doctrine the uniformity exacted is geographical, not intrinsic....

Second. The excise is not invalid under the provisions of the Fifth Amendment by force of its exemptions.

The statute does not apply, as we have seen, to employers of less than eight. It does not apply to agricultural labor, or domestic service in a private home or to some other classes of less importance. Petitioner contends that the effect of these restrictions is an arbitrary discrimination vitiating the tax.

. . .

The classifications and exemptions directed by the statute now in controversy have support in considerations of policy and practical convenience that cannot be condemned as arbitrary. . . .

Third. The excise is not void as involving the coercion of the States in contravention of the Tenth Amendment or of restrictions implicit in our federal form of government.

. . .

To draw the line intelligently between duress and inducement there is need to remind ourselves of facts as to the problem of unemployment that are now matters of common knowledge. . . . During the years 1929 to 1936, when the country was passing through a cyclical depression, the number of the unemployed mounted to unprecedented heights. Often the average was more than 10 million; at times a peak was attained of 16 million or more. Disaster to the breadwinner meant disaster to dependents. Accordingly the roll of the unemployed, itself formidable enough, was only a partial roll of the destitute or needy. The fact developed quickly that the states were unable to give the requisite relief. The problem had become national in area and dimensions. There was need of help from the nation if the people were not to starve. It is too late today for the argument to be heard with tolerance that in a crisis so extreme the use of the moneys of the nation to relieve the unemployed and their dependents is a use for any purpose narrower than the promotion of the general welfare. . . . The nation responded to the call of the distressed. . . .

. . . Before Congress acted, unemployment compensation insurance was still, for the most part, a project and no more. Wisconsin was the pioneer. Her statute was adopted in 1931. At times bills for such insurance were introduced elsewhere, but they did not reach the stage of law. In 1935, four states (California, Massachusetts, New Hampshire and New York) passed unemployment laws on the eve of the adoption of the Social Security Act, and two others did likewise after the federal act and later in the year. The statutes differed to some extent in type, but were directed to a common end. In 1936, twenty-eight other states fell in line, and eight more the present year. But if states had been holding back before the passage of the

federal law, inaction was not owing, for the most part, to the lack of sympathetic interest. Many held back through alarm lest, in laying such a toll upon their industries, they would place themselves in a position of economic disadvantage as compared with neighbors or competitors. . . . Two consequences ensued. One was that the freedom of a state to contribute its fair share to the solution of a national problem was paralyzed by fear. The other was that in so far as there was failure by the states to contribute relief according to the measure of their capacity, a disproportionate burden, and a mountainous one, was laid upon the resources of the Government of the nation.

The Social Security Act is an attempt to find a method by which all these public agencies may work together to a common end. Every dollar of the new taxes will continue in all likelihood to be used and needed by the nation as long as states are unwilling, whether through timidity or for other motives, to do what can be done at home. . . .

Who then is coerced through the operation of this statute? Not the taxpayer. He pays in fulfillment of the mandate of the local legislature. Not the state. Even now she does not offer a suggestion that in passing the unemployment law she was affected by duress. . . . For all that appears she is satisfied with her choice, and would be sorely disappointed if it were now to be annulled. The difficulty with the petitioner's contention is that it confuses motive with coercion. . . . In like manner every rebate from a tax when conditioned upon conduct is in some measure a temptation. But to hold that motive or temptation is equivalent to coercion is to plunge the law in endless difficulties. . . .

Fourth. The statute does not call for a surrender by the states of powers essential to their quasi-sovereign existence.

. . .

. . . The states are at liberty, upon obtaining the consent of Congress, to make agreements with one another. Constitution, Art. I, § 10, par. 3. . . . We find no room for doubt that they may do the like with Congress if the essence of their statehood is maintained without impairment. . . .

Separate opinion of MR. JUSTICE McREYNOLDS.

That portion of the Social Security legislation here under consideration, I think, exceeds the power granted to Congress. It unduly interferes with the orderly government of the State by her own people and otherwise offends the Federal Constitution.

. . .

Separate opinion of MR. JUSTICE SUTHERLAND.

With most of what is said in the opinion just handed down, I concur....

But the question with which I have difficulty is whether the administrative provisions of the act invade the governmental administrative powers of the several states reserved by the Tenth Amendment. A state may enter into contracts; but a state cannot, by contract or statute, surrender the execution, or a share in the execution, of any of its governmental powers either to a sister state or to the federal government, any more than the federal government can surrender the control of any of its governmental powers to a foreign nation....

MR. JUSTICE VAN DEVANTER joins in this opinion.

MR. JUSTICE BUTLER, dissenting.

I think that the objections to the challenged enactment expressed in the separate opinions of MR. JUSTICE MCREYNOLDS and MR. JUSTICE SUTHERLAND are well taken. I am also of opinion that, in principle and as applied to bring about and to gain control over state unemployment compensation, the statutory scheme is repugnant to the Tenth Amendment...

South Dakota v. Dole

483 U.S. 203 (1987)

Congress passed legislation in 1984 directing the Secretary of Transportation to withhold a percentage of federal highway funds from states that refuse to adopt age twenty-one as the minimum drinking age. An issue before the Court was the extent to which Congress can use its spending power, and more particularly conditions attached to federal funds, to achieve national objectives. South Dakota challenged the constitutionality of the statute and brought suit against Secretary of Transportation Elizabeth Dole. A district court dismissed the complaint and the Eighth Circuit affirmed.

CHIEF JUSTICE REHNQUIST delivered the opinion of the Court.

. . .

In this Court, the parties direct most of their efforts to defining the proper scope of the Twenty-first Amendment. Relying on our statement in *California Retail Liquor Dealers Assn. v. Midcal Aluminum, Inc.,* 445 U.S. 97, 110 (1980), that the "Twenty-first Amendment grants the States virtually complete control over whether to permit importation or sale of liquor and how to structure the liquor distribution system," South Dakota asserts that the setting of minimum drinking ages is clearly within the "core powers" reserved to the States under § 2 of the Amendment....

...Despite the extended treatment of the question by the parties, however, we need not decide in this case whether that Amendment would prohibit an attempt by Congress to legislate directly a national minimum drinking age. Here, Congress has acted indirectly under its spending power to encourage uniformity in the States' drinking ages. As we explain below, we find this legislative effort within constitutional bounds even if Congress may not regulate drinking ages directly.

The Constitution empowers Congress to "lay and collect Taxes, Duties, Imposts, and Excises, to pay the Debts and provide for the common Defence and general Welfare of the United States." Art. I, § 8, cl. 1. Incident to this power, Congress may attach conditions on the receipt of federal funds, and has repeatedly employed the power "to further broad policy objectives by conditioning receipt of federal moneys upon compliance by the recipient with federal statutory and administrative directives." *Fullilove v. Klutznick,* 448 U.S. 448, 474 (1980) (Opinion of Burger, C.J.).... The breadth of this power was made clear in *United States v. Butler,* 297 U.S. 1, 66 (1936), where the Court, resolving a longstanding debate over the scope of the Spending Clause, determined that "the power of Congress to authorize expenditure of public moneys for public purposes is not limited by the direct grants of legislative power found in the Constitution." Thus, objectives not thought to be within Article I's "enumerated legislative fields," *id.,* at 65, may nevertheless be attained through the use of the spending power and the conditional grant of federal funds.

The spending power is of course not unlimited, *Pennhurst State School and Hospital* v. *Halderman*, 451 U.S. 1, 17, and n. 13 (1981), but is instead subject to several general restrictions articulated in our cases. The first of these limitations is derived from the language of the Constitution itself: the exercise of the spending power must be in pursuit of "the general welfare." ... In considering whether a particular expenditure is intended to serve general public purposes, courts should defer substantially to the judgment of Congress. ... Second, we have required that if Congress desires to condition the States' receipt of federal funds, it "must do so unambiguously ..., enabl[ing] the States to exercise their choice knowingly, cognizant of the consequences of their participation." ... Third, our cases have suggested (without significant elaboration) that conditions on federal grants might be illegitimate if they are unrelated "to the federal interest in particular national projects or programs." ... Finally, we have noted that other constitutional provisions may provide an independent bar to the conditional grant of federal funds. ...

South Dakota does not seriously claim that § 158 is inconsistent with any of the first three restrictions mentioned above. ... Congress found that the differing drinking ages in the States created particular incentives for young persons to combine their desire to drink with their ability to drive, and that this interstate problem required a national solution. The means it chose to address this dangerous situation were reasonably calculated to advance the general welfare. The conditions upon which States receive the funds, moreover, could not be more clearly stated by Congress. See 23 U.S.C. § 158 (1982 ed., Supp. III). And the State itself, rather than challenging the germaneness of the condition to federal purposes, admits that it "has never contended that the congressional action was ... unrelated to a national concern in the absence of the Twenty-first Amendment." ... Indeed, the condition imposed by Congress is directly related to one of the main purposes for which highway funds are expended — safe interstate travel. See 23 U.S.C. § 101(b). This goal of the interstate highway system had been frustrated by varying drinking ages among the States. A presidential commission appointed to study alcohol-related accidents and fatalities on the Nation's highways concluded that the lack of uniformity in the States' drinking ages

created "an incentive to drink and drive" because "young persons commut[e] to border States where the drinking age is lower." Presidential Commission on Drunk Driving, Final Report 11 (1983). By enacting § 158, Congress conditioned the receipt of federal funds in a way reasonably calculated to address this particular impediment to a purpose for which the funds are expended.

The remaining question about the validity of § 158 — and the basic point of disagreement between the parties — is whether the Twenty-first Amendment constitutes an "independent constitutional bar" to the conditional grant of federal funds. *Lawrence County* v. *Lead-Deadwood School Dist., supra,* at 269–270. Petitioner, relying on its view that the Twenty-first Amendment prohibits *direct* regulation of drinking ages by Congress, asserts that "Congress may not use the spending power to regulate that which it is prohibited from regulating directly under the Twenty-first Amendment." ... But our cases show that this "independent constitutional bar" limitation on the spending power is not of the kind petitioner suggests. *United States* v. *Butler,* 297 U.S., at 66, for example, established that the constitutional limitations on Congress when exercising its spending power are less exacting than those on its authority to regulate directly.

. . .

These cases establish that the "independent constitutional bar" limitation on the spending power is not, as petitioner suggests, a prohibition on the indirect achievement of objectives which Congress is not empowered to achieve directly. Instead, we think that the language in our earlier opinions stands for the unexceptionable proposition that the power may not be used to induce the States to engage in activities that would themselves be unconstitutional. Thus, for example, a grant of federal funds conditioned on invidiously discriminatory state action or the infliction of cruel and unusual punishment would be an illegitimate exercise of the Congress' broad spending power. But no such claim can be or is made here. Were South Dakota to succumb to the blandishments offered by Congress and raise its drinking age to 21, the State's action in so doing would not violate the constitutional rights of anyone.

Our decisions have recognized that in some circumstances the financial inducement offered by Congress might be so coercive as to pass the point at which "pressure turns into compulsion." *Steward Machine Co.* v. *Davis, supra,* 301 U.S., at

590. Here, however, Congress has directed only that a State desiring to establish a minimum drinking age lower than 21 lose a relatively small percentage of certain federal highway funds. Petitioner contends that the coercive nature of this program is evident from the degree of success it has achieved. We cannot conclude, however, that a conditional grant of federal money of this sort is unconstitutional simply by reason of its success in achieving the congressional objective.

When we consider, for a moment, that all South Dakota would lose if she adheres to her chosen course as to a suitable minimum drinking age is 5% of the funds otherwise obtainable under specified highway grant programs, the argument as to coercion is shown to be more rhetoric than fact....

JUSTICE BRENNAN, dissenting.

I agree with JUSTICE O'CONNOR that regulation of the minimum age of purchasers of liquor falls squarely within the ambit of those powers reserved to the States by the Twenty-first Amendment.... Since States possess this constitutional power, Congress cannot condition a federal grant in a manner that abridges this right. The Amendment, itself, strikes the proper balance between federal and state authority. I therefore dissent.

JUSTICE O'CONNOR, dissenting.

[The National Minimum Drinking Age Amend-

ment] is an attempt to regulate the sale of liquor, an attempt that lies outside Congress' power to regulate commerce because it falls within the ambit of § 2 of the Twenty-first Amendment.

. . .

...the Court's application of the requirement that the condition imposed be reasonably related to the purpose for which the funds are expended, is cursory and unconvincing....

...[I]f the purpose of § 158 is to deter drunken driving, it is far too over- and under-inclusive. It is over-inclusive because it stops teenagers from drinking even when they are not about to drive on interstate highways. It is under-inclusive because teenagers pose only a small part of the drunken driving problem in this Nation. See, *e.g.,* 130 Cong. Rec. S8216 (June 26, 1984) (remarks of Sen. Humphrey) ("Eighty-four percent of all highway fatalities involving alcohol occur among those whose ages exceed 21"); *id.,* at S8219 (remarks of Sen. McClure) ("Certainly, statistically, if you use that one set of statistics, then the mandatory drinking age ought to be raised at least to 30"); *ibid.* (remarks of Sen. Symms) ("most of the studies point out that the drivers of age 21–24 are the worst offenders").

. . .

H. PREEMPTION AND ABSTENTION

Federal-state relationships are shaped by two cross-cutting doctrines. Under the preemption doctrine, certain matters have such a national character that federal laws must supersede state laws. The abstention doctrine works in the opposite direction. As an exercise of discretionary authority, federal courts relinquish jurisdiction under various circumstances in order to avoid needless friction with the administration of state affairs. Both doctrines are complex and change over time.

The Preemption Doctrine

The preemption doctrine draws its force from the Supremacy Clause of Article VI of the Constitution, which declares that all laws made in pursuance to the Constitution and all treaties made under the authority of the United States shall be the "supreme Law of the Land." Federal actions of this character are superior to any conflicting provision of a state constitution or law. When Congress exercises its express powers, as it does by adopting uniform laws of bankruptcy, national legislation preempts state legislation. Perez v. Campbell, 402 U.S. 637 (1971). If compliance with both federal and state regulations in interstate commerce is a physical impossibility, federal law also preempts state law. Florida Lime & Avocado Growers, Inc. v. Paul, 373 U.S. 132, 142–43 (1963). Some of the enumerated powers of Congress are obviously exclusive, such as the power to exercise "exclusive Legislation" over the District of

Smith Reacts to Court Decisions

Mr. [*Howard*] SMITH of Virginia.... I do want to make 1 or 2 comments on...a bill of which I am an author, H.R. 3, to correct a decision of the Supreme Court of the United States in the Steve Nelson and other cases....

...[T]he Supreme Court has assumed out of a clear sky to say what the Congress intended when the Congress has not said it. If anything is to be done upon this subject, I think it is very important that we have a general law which will simply say that when Congress means to do away with State laws the Congress shall say so. [102 Cong. Rec. 6385 (1956)]

Mr. SMITH of Virginia.... This bill...just does two things. It says to the Supreme Court—

First. Do not undertake to read the minds of the Congress; we, in the Congress, think ourselves more capable of knowing our minds than the Supreme Court has proved itself capable of

in the past; and we will do our own mind reading; and we are telling you that when we get ready to repeal a State law or preempt a field, we will say so and we will not leave it to the Supreme Court to guess whether we are or not. That is No. 1.

Second. The other thing this bill does is to say that the Supreme Court must not knock down State laws unless they are in irreconcilable conflict with a Federal law.... [104 Cong. Rec. 14139–40 (1958)]

[The House of Representatives passed legislation of this nature in 1958, but no action was taken by the Senate. The House again passed legislation in 1959, but by that time the Supreme Court, in Uphaus v. Wyman, *360 U.S. 72, had decided that states could proceed with prosecutions for sedition against the state itself.]*

Columbia and the power "to coin money," which Art. I, § 10, expressly prohibits for the states.

The preemption doctrine also covers powers not expressly stated. In the area of foreign affairs, including regulation of aliens, state statutes may not stand "as an obstacle to the accomplishment and execution of the full purposes and objectives of Congress." Hines v. Davidowitz, 312 U.S. 52, 67 (1941). In 1956 the Supreme Court invalidated a state sedition law because the Smith Act, passed by Congress, regulated the same subject. The Court concluded that it had been the intent of Congress to occupy the whole field of sedition. PENNSYLVANIA v. NELSON, 350 U.S. 497, 504. The author of the Smith Act promptly denied that he had ever intended the result reached by the Court (see box). Congressional committees reported legislation to permit federal-state concurrent jurisdiction in the area of sedition and subversion and to prohibit courts from using intent or implication to decide preemption.[13] Although these bills were never enacted, in the midst of their consideration the Court held that a state could investigate subversive activities against itself. To this extent state and federal sedition laws could coexist. Uphaus v. Wyman, 360 U.S. 72, 76 (1959). A potential legislative-judicial clash was thus averted. In matters affecting foreign affairs and international relations, the courts have excluded state involvement. Zschernig v. Miller, 389 U.S. 429, 436 (1968). However, state governments maintain direct contact with both private and government officials in foreign countries in order to promote export trade and foreign investments.

Congress has used its preemption power to regulate major areas of environmental law. The Water Quality Act of 1965, the Air Quality Act of 1967, and the Clean Water Act of 1972 il-

---

13. H. Rept. No. 2576, 84th Cong., 2d Sess. (1956); S. Rept. No. 2117, 84th Cong., 2d Sess. (1956); S. Rept. No. 2230, 84th Cong., 2d Sess. (1956); H. Rept. No. 1878, 85th Cong., 2d Sess. (1958); 104 Cong. Rec. 13844–65, 13993–14023, 14138–62 (1958); H. Rept. No. 422, 86th Cong., 1st Sess. (1959); 105 Cong. Rec. 11486–508, 11625–67, 11789–808 (1959).

lustrate this trend toward national standards. States can attempt to forestall federal controls by forming interstate compacts to handle problems of a regional nature. These compacts, however, require the approval of Congress if they tend to increase the political power of the states or encroach upon the Supremacy Clause. Cuyler v. Adams, 449 U.S. 433, 440 (1981).

The field of nuclear energy has been largely preempted by Congress, especially over questions of safety and plant construction. States retain authority over economic questions, such as the need for additional plants, the type of facility to be licensed, land use, and setting rates. Pacific Gas & Elec. v. Energy Resources Comm'n, 461 U.S. 190, 212 (1983). The exclusive authority of the federal government over safety questions was compromised a year later when the Court allowed a jury to award punitive damages against a company in a case where Karen Silkwood, a laboratory analyst, was contaminated by plutonium. Silkwood v. Kerr-McGee Corp., 464 U.S. 238 (1984). State law claims were also allowed in a later nuclear-safety case; English v. General Electric Co., 496 U.S. 72 (1990). Recent preemption cases involve pension plans. In response to pension benefits lost by employees because of bankruptcies, mergers, and theft, Congress passed the Employee Retirement Income Security Act of 1974 (ERISA). With certain exceptions, the statute preempts all state laws that "relate to" any employee benefit plan. The Supreme Court has given a broad reading to the statute's preemption clause.[14]

The dominant role of Congress in determining preemption was emphasized by Justice Rehnquist in 1986 during his confirmation hearings to be Chief Justice. He said that Congress "is probably the ultimate decider as to what the proper relationship between State and Federal law is in most situations. . . . How much is going to be Federal law in any area in which the Congress power reaches and how much is going to be State law, really in the last analysis, depends upon Congress." "Nomination of Justice William Hubbs Rehnquist," hearings before the Senate Committee on the Judiciary, 99th Cong., 2d Sess., 131 (1986). His judgment has been supported by subsequent cases.[15]

The Abstention Doctrine

The abstention doctrine helps refute the periodic, apocalyptic announcements that "federalism is dead." To cultivate comity and mutual respect between the national and state levels, federal courts abstain in some areas. It would be impossible and self-destructive for federal courts to intervene in every state matter. The policy of abstention can be traced back to a congressional statute in 1793: "nor shall a writ of injunction [by federal courts] be granted to stay proceedings in any court of a state." 1 Stat. 335, § 5.

---

14. Ingersoll-Rand Co. v. McClendon, 498 U.S. 133 (1990); FMC v. Holliday, 498 U.S. 52 (1990); Metropolitan Life Ins. Co. v. Massachusetts, 471 U.S. 724 (1985); Shaw v. Delta Air Lines, 463 U.S. 85 (1983); Alessi v. Raybestos-Manhattan, Inc., 451 U.S. 504 (1981). Other preemption cases include California Coastal Comm'n v. Granite Rock Co., 480 U.S. 572 (1987); Exxon Corp. v. Governor of Maryland, 437 U.S. 117 (1978); Ray v. Atlantic Richfield Co., 435 U.S. 151 (1978). For a case in which federal regulations did not preempt state and local regulation because Congress had not expressed that intent, see Hillsborough County v. Automated Medical Labs, 471 U.S. 707 (1985).

15. United States v. Locke, 120 S.Ct. 1135 (2000) (federal law preempts state regulation of oil tankers); Barnett Bank of Marion County, N.A. v. Nelson, 517 U.S. 25 (1996) (federal statute preempts state statute that prevented a national bank from selling insurance in a small town); Cipollone v. Liggett Group, Inc., 505 U.S. 504 (1992) (federal legislation does not preempt state law damages actions, although it does preempt state mandates for particular warnings on cigarette labels or in cigarette advertisements); Gade v. National Solid Wastes Management Assn., 505 U.S. 88 (1992) (federal law prohibits states from adopting additional training requirements for workers handling hazardous waste); Morales v. Trans World Airlines, Inc., 504 U.S. 374 (1992) (federal law preempts state regulation of airline fare advertising to protect consumers); Wisconsin Public Intervenor v. Mortier, 504 U.S. 374 (1991) (federal law does not preempt regulation of pesticides by local governments); United Steelworkers of America v. Rawson, 495 U.S. 362 (1990) (federal labor law preempts tort claim in state court); California v. FERC, 495 U.S. 490 (1990) (federal law preempts states from requiring flow rates for water in hydroelectric projects that are higher than federal standards, even for the purpose of protecting fish and wildlife).

The Fourteenth Amendment opened the door to a much larger federal role. After the Supreme Court in *Ex parte Young* (1908) suggested that federal courts would intervene extensively in state affairs, Congress acted to limit judicial interference. Instead of allowing a single federal judge to strike down a state statute or enjoin its operation, Congress required a three-judge court to hear and decide such actions.[16] The policy of abstention crystallized as court doctrine in 1941. A unanimous Supreme Court held that it should withhold judgment until state courts reach a definitive construction of a state statute. Federal courts should avoid "needless friction with state policies" and promote "harmonious relation between state and federal authority" by waiting until the highest state court has disposed of a constitutional issue. Railroad Commission v. Pullman, 312 U.S. 496, 500–01. Acting under this authority, the Supreme Court has returned cases to state courts to permit interpretation of questions that were not considered or resolved.[17]

Abstention is a general policy and can be waived. Abstention is inappropriate where state statutes are vulnerable on their face for abridging free expression or discouraging protected activities. Federal courts intervene in these cases to prevent state officials from invoking a statute in bad faith, with no hope for success, simply to harass minorities or their organizations. This exception to the abstention doctrine is aimed at statutes that are so vague or overbroad that they threaten First Amendment freedoms. Dombrowski v. Pfister, 380 U.S. 479 (1965); Zwickler v. Koota, 389 U.S. 241 (1967). In the case of a pending state criminal proceeding, federal courts intervene only under extraordinary circumstances: where the danger of irreparable loss is both great and immediate and where the threat to federally protected rights cannot be eliminated during the course of the trial. Younger v. Harris, 401 U.S. 37 (1971); Samuels v. Mackell, 401 U.S. 66 (1971). The policy of noninterference also applies to certain state civil proceedings. Huffman v. Pursue, Ltd., 420 U.S. 592 (1975).

Noninterference by the Supreme Court in state matters often provokes biting dissents that regard federalism as a cloak used to cover constitutional violations by state officials. Justice Brennan, for example, remarked: "Under the banner of vague, undefined notions of equity, comity, and federalism, the Court has embarked upon the dangerous course of condoning both isolated . . . and systematic . . . violations of civil liberties." Juidice v. Vail, 430 U.S. 327, 346 (1977). See also the dissents in Paul v. Davis, 424 U.S. 693 (1976), and Rizzo v. Goode, 423 U.S. 362 (1976).

Pennsylvania v. Nelson

350 U.S. 497 (1956)

Steve Nelson was convicted for violating the Pennsylvania Sedition Act. The question here is whether Congress, by passing the Smith Act of 1940, preempted the enforcement of state sedition acts.

MR. CHIEF JUSTICE WARREN delivered the opinion of the Court.

The respondent Steve Nelson, an acknowledged member of the Communist Party, was convicted in the Court of Quarter Sessions of Allegheny County, Pennsylvania, of a violation of the Pennsylvania Sedition Act and sentenced to

imprisonment for twenty years and to a fine of $10,000 and to costs of prosecution in the sum of $13,000. The Superior Court affirmed the conviction. 172 Pa. Super. 125, 92 A. 2d 431. The Supreme Court of Pennsylvania, recognizing but not reaching many alleged serious trial errors and conduct of the trial court infringing upon respon-

---

16. 36 Stat. 557, § 17 (1910); 36 Stat. 1162, § 266 (1911); 37 Stat. 1013 (1913); 38 Stat. 220 (1913). These statutes are codified at 28 U.S.C. § 2284 (1994).

17. Reetz v. Bozanich, 397 U.S. 82 (1970); Henry v. Mississippi, 379 U.S. 443 (1965); Meridian v. Southern Bell T. & T. Co., 358 U.S. 639 (1959); Musser v. Utah, 333 U.S. 95 (1948).

dent's right to due process of law, decided the case on the narrow issue of supersession of the state law by the Federal Smith Act. In its opinion, the court stated:

"And, while the Pennsylvania statute proscribes sedition against either the Government of the United States or the Government of Pennsylvania, it is only alleged sedition against the United States with which the instant case is concerned. Out of all the voluminous testimony, we have not found, nor has anyone pointed to, a single word indicating a seditious act or even utterance directed against the Government of Pennsylvania."

The precise holding of the court, and all that is before us for review, is that the Smith Act of 1940, as amended in 1948, which prohibits the knowing advocacy of the overthrow of the Government of the United States by force and violence, supersedes the enforceability of the Pennsylvania Sedition Act which proscribes the same conduct.

. . .

It should be said at the outset that the decision in this case does not affect the right of States to enforce their sedition laws at times when the Federal Government has not occupied the field and is not protecting the entire country from seditious conduct. The distinction between the two situations was clearly recognized by the court below. Nor does it limit the jurisdiction of the States where the Constitution and Congress have specifically given them concurrent jurisdiction, as was done under the Eighteenth Amendment and the Volstead Act. *United States* v. *Lanza,* 260 U. S. 377. Neither does it limit the right of the State to protect itself at any time against sabotage or attempted violence of all kinds. Nor does it prevent the State from prosecuting where the same act constitutes both a federal offense and a state offense under the police power....

...In this case, we think that each of several tests of supersession is met.

First, "[t]he scheme of federal regulation [is] so pervasive as to make reasonable the inference that Congress left no room for the States to supplement it." *Rice* v. *Santa Fe Elevator Corp.,* 331 U. S., at 230. The Congress determined in 1940 that it was necessary for it to re-enter the field of antisubversive legislation, which had been abandoned by it in 1921. In that year, it enacted the Smith Act which proscribes advocacy of the overthrow of any government — federal, state or local — by force and violence and organization of and knowing membership in a group which so advocates. *[The Court also summarizes the Internal Security Act of 1950 and the Communist Control Act of 1954.]*

We examine these Acts only to determine the congressional plan. Looking to all of them in the aggregate, the conclusion is inescapable that Congress has intended to occupy the field of sedition. Taken as a whole, they evince a congressional plan which makes it reasonable to determine that no room has been left for the States to supplement it....

Second, the federal statutes "touch a field in which the federal interest is so dominant that the federal system [must] be assumed to preclude enforcement of state laws on the same subject." *Rice* v. *Santa Fe Elevator Corp.,* 331 U. S., at 230, citing *Hines* v. *Davidowitz, supra.* Congress has devised an all-embracing program for resistance to the various forms of totalitarian aggression....

Third, enforcement of state sedition acts presents a serious danger of conflict with the administration of the federal program. Since 1939, in order to avoid a hampering of uniform enforcement of its program by sporadic local prosecutions, the Federal Government has urged local authorities not to intervene in such matters, but to turn over to the federal authorities immediately and unevaluated all information concerning subversive activities.

. . .

The judgment of the Supreme Court of Pennsylvania is

Affirmed.

Mr. Justice Reed, with whom Mr. Justice Burton and Mr. Justice Minton join, dissenting.

. . .

Congress has not, in any of its statutes relating to sedition, specifically barred the exercise of state power to punish the same Acts under state law. And, we read the majority opinion to assume for this case that, absent federal legislation, there is no constitutional bar to punishment of sedition against the United States by both a State and the Nation....

First, the Court relies upon the pervasiveness of the antisubversive legislation embodied in the Smith Act of 1940, 18 U.S.C. § 2385, the Internal Security Act of 1950, 64 Stat. 987, and the Communist Control Act of 1954, 68 Stat. 775. It asserts that these Acts in the aggregate mean that Congress has occupied the "field of sedition" to the exclusion of the States....

We cannot agree that the federal criminal sanctions against sedition directed at the United States are of such a pervasive character as to indicate an intention to void state action.

Secondly, the Court states that the federal sedition statutes touch a field "in which the federal interest is so dominant" they must preclude state laws on the same subject. This concept is suggested in a comment on *Hines* v. *Davidowitz*, 312 U.S. 52, in the *Rice* case, at 230. The Court in *Davidowitz* ruled that federal statutes compelling alien registration preclude enforcement of state statutes requiring alien registration. We read *Davidowitz* to teach nothing more than that, when the Congress provided a single nation-wide integrated system of regulation so complete as that for aliens' registration (with fingerprinting, a scheduling of activities, and continuous information as to their residence), the Act bore so directly on our foreign relations as to make it evident that Congress intended only one uniform national alien registration system.

· · ·

Thirdly, the Court finds ground for abrogating Pennsylvania's antisedition statute because, in the Court's view, the State's administration of the Act may hamper the enforcement of the federal law.... The Court's attitude as to interference seems to us quite contrary to that of the Legislative and Executive Departments. Congress was advised of the existing state sedition legislation when the Smith Act was enacted and has been kept current with its spread. No declaration of exclusiveness followed....

Finally, and this one point seems in and of itself decisive, there is an independent reason for reversing the Pennsylvania Supreme Court. The Smith Act appears in Title 18 of the United States Code, which Title codifies the federal criminal laws. Section 3231 of that Title provides:

"Nothing in this title shall be held to take away or impair the jurisdiction of the courts of the several States under the laws thereof."

That declaration springs from the federal character of our Nation. It recognizes the fact that maintenance of order and fairness rests primarily with the States. The section was first enacted in 1825 and has appeared successively in the federal criminal laws since that time. This Court has interpreted the section to mean that States may provide concurrent legislation in the absence of explicit congressional intent to the contrary....

· · ·

I. NATIONALIZATION OF THE BILL OF RIGHTS

Two months before the first Congress met, James Madison supported constitutional amendments to provide "for all essential rights, particularly the rights of Conscience in the fullest latitude, the freedom of the press, trials by jury, security against general warrants &c." 5 The Writings of James Madison 320 (letter to George Eve, January 2, 1789). The responsibility for moving these amendments through the House of Representatives fell to Madison, who argued that a Bill of Rights would remove apprehensions that the people felt toward the new national government. 1 Annals of Congress 431–33 (1789). He also wanted to place restrictions on the states and proposed that "[n]o State shall violate the equal rights of conscience, of the freedom of the press, or the trial by jury in criminal cases." Id. at 435. The states "are as liable to attack these invaluable privileges as the General Government...." Id. at 441. As finally drafted and ratified, however, the first ten amendments to the Constitution—the Bill of Rights—limited only the federal government.

In 1833 the Supreme Court reaffirmed that the Bill of Rights restrained only the federal government, not the states. At issue was the Just Compensation Clause of the Fifth Amendment. Barron v. Baltimore, 32 U.S. (7 Pet.) 243. The same conclusion was reached by the Court twenty-five years later. Withers v. Buckley, 20 How. (61 U.S.) 84, 89–90 (1858). However, the Civil War and passage of the Fourteenth Amendment in 1868 worked a fundamental change in federal-state relations. The Amendment prohibited states from making or enforcing any law "which shall abridge the privileges or immunities of citizens of the United States; nor shall any State deprive any person of life, liberty, or property, without due process of law; nor deny to any person within its jurisdiction the equal protection of the laws." The Due Process Clause would become the vehicle for applying most of the Bill of Rights to the states.

The idea of imposing a national standard on the states was rejected by the Supreme Court in 1873 when it held that the primary purpose of the Civil War amendments (the Thirteenth, Fourteenth, and Fifteenth Amendments) was to guarantee freedom for blacks. Moreover, privileges and immunities were to be protected by the states, not the national government. Slaughter-House Cases, 16 Wall. 36, 77–79. Other decisions during this period also refused to apply the Bill of Rights to the states.[18] However, the Equal Protection Clause of the Fourteenth Amendment was available to prevent states from acting in a discriminatory or arbitrary manner. Yick Wo v. Hopkins, 118 U.S. 356 (1886).

The Incorporation Doctrine

By the end of the century, the Court had decided that certain portions of the Bill of Rights should be applied to the states. The Court began with the Just Compensation Clause of the Fifth Amendment, reflecting the judiciary's commitment at that time to business and corporate interests. Missouri Pacific Railway Co. v. Nebraska, 164 U.S. 403 (1896); Chicago, B. & Q. Railway Co. v. Chicago, 166 U.S. 226 (1897). Thus began the process of "incorporating" the Bill of Rights into the Due Process Clause of the Fourteenth Amendment and extending these guarantees to the states. Although in 1904 the Court held that the Confrontation Clause of the Sixth Amendment did not apply to the states (West v. Louisiana, 194 U.S. 258), and four years later refused to extend the Self-Incrimination Clause of the Fifth Amendment to the states (Twining v. New Jersey, 211 U.S. 78), within a few decades the Court began the step-by-step process of bringing the states under the Bill of Rights. Almost every provision of the Bill of Rights now covers the states (see Table 8.3). This process is sometimes called the doctrine of absorption or the selective incorporation of the Bill of Rights.

Selective incorporation reflects a contest between two schools of thought. The second Justice Harlan believed that courts have a duty to see that due process follows principles consistent with the people's "traditions and conscience." In re Gault, 387 U.S. 1, 67 (1967). Justice Black opposed this philosophy because it requires judges to impose personal notions of natural law. Duncan v. Louisiana, 391 U.S. 145, 168 (1968). To limit judicial activism, at least in the incremental form supported by Harlan, Black promoted the wholesale incorporation of the Bill of Rights. ADAMSON v. CALIFORNIA, 332 U.S. 46, 75 (1947). Ironically, Black's activism probably exceeded Harlan's. Almost all of the Bill of Rights has been incorporated, with little opposition from contemporary members of the Supreme Court (see Rehnquist's testimony).

The selective incorporation of the Bill of Rights does not always mean that a national standard has been forced upon the states. For example, the First Amendment applies to all states, and yet court rulings on obscenity allow wide discretion to accommodate local community

---

18. Pervear v. Commonwealth, 5 Wall. (72 U.S.) 475 (1867); Twitchell v. The Commonwealth, 7 Wall. (74 U.S.) 321 (1869); The Justices v. Murray, 9 Wall. (76 U.S.) 274 (1870); Walker v. Sauvinet, 92 U.S. (2 Otto.) 90, 92 (1876); United States v. Cruikshank, 92 U.S. 542, 552 (1876); Hurtado v. California, 110 U.S. 516, 538 (1884); Presser v. Illinois, 116 U.S. 252, 265 (1886); Spies v. Illinois, 123 U.S. 131, 166 (1887); In re Kemmler, 136 U.S. 436, 446 (1890); McElvaine v. Brush, 142 U.S. 155, 158 (1891); O'Neil v. Vermont, 144 U.S. 323, 332 (1892). See also Maxwell v. Dow, 176 U.S. 581 (1900), which declined to apply the guarantees of the Fifth and Sixth Amendments to the states.

TABLE 8.3   INCORPORATION OF BILL OF RIGHTS

Amendment	Clause	Decision
First	Congress shall make no law respecting an establishment of religion, ...	Everson v. Board of Education, 330 U.S. 1, 15 (1947).
	or prohibiting the free exercise thereof; ...	Cantwell v. Connecticut, 310 U.S. 296, 303 (1940).
	or abridging the freedom of speech, ...	Gitlow v. New York, 268 U.S. 652, 666 (1925); Fiske v. Kansas, 274 U.S. 380, 387 (1927).
	or of the press; ...	Near v. Minnesota, 283 U.S. 697, 707 (1931). See also Gitlow v. New York, 268 U.S. 652, 666 (1925).
	or the right of the people peaceably to assemble, and to petition the Government for a redress of grievances.	DeJonge v. Oregon, 299 U.S. 352, 364 (1937).
Second	A well regulated Militia, being necessary to the security of a free State, the right of the people to keep and bear arms, shall not be infringed.	—
Third	No soldier shall, in time of peace be quartered in any house, without the consent of the Owner, nor in time of war, but in a manner to be prescribed by law.	—
Fourth	The right of the people to be secure in their persons, houses, papers, and effects, against unreasonable searches and seizures, shall not be violated, and no Warrants shall issue, but upon probable cause, supported by Oath or affirmation, and particularly describing the place to be searched, and the persons or things to be seized.	Wolf v. Colorado, 338 U.S. 25, 27–28 (1949); Mapp v. Ohio, 367 U.S. 643, 655 (1961); Ker v. California, 374 U.S. 23 (1963).
Fifth	No person shall be held to answer for a capital, or otherwise infamous crime, unless on a presentment or indictment of a Grand Jury, except in cases arising in the land or naval forces, or in the Militia, when in actual service in time of War or public danger; ...	—
	nor shall any person be subject for the same offence to be twice put in jeopardy of life or limb; ...	Benton v. Maryland, 395 U.S. 784, 787 (1969).
	nor shall be compelled in any Criminal Case to be a witness against himself; ...	Malloy v. Hogan, 378 U.S. 1, 3 (1964).
	nor be deprived of life, liberty, or property, without due process of law; ...	[Parallel to Fourteenth Amendment.]
	nor shall private property be taken for public use, without just compensation.	Missouri Pacific Railway Co. v. Nebraska, 164 U.S. 403, 417 (1896); Chicago, B. & Q. R.R. Co. v. Chicago, 166 U.S. 226, 241 (1897).

TABLE 8.3   INCORPORATION OF BILL OF RIGHTS *continued*

Amendment	Clause	Decision
Sixth	In all criminal prosecutions, the accused shall enjoy the right to a speedy and public trial,...	In re Oliver, 333 U.S. 257, 273 (1948) [right to public trial] and Klopfer v. North Carolina, 386 U.S. 213, 222 (1967) [right to speedy trial].
	by an impartial jury of the State and district wherein the crime shall have been committed, which district shall have been previously ascertained by law, and to be informed of the nature and cause of the accusation;...	Duncan v. Louisiana, 391 U.S. 145, 149 (1968); Parker v. Gladden, 385 U.S. 363–64 (1966). See also Irvin v. Dowd, 366 U.S. 717 (1961) and Turner v. Louisiana, 379 U.S. 466 (1965).
	to be confronted with the witness against him;...	Pointer v. Texas, 380 U.S. 400, 403 (1965).
	to have compulsory process for obtaining witnesses in his favor;...	Washington v. Texas, 388 U.S. 14, 19 (1967).
	and to have the Assistance of Counsel for his defence.	Powell v. Alabama, 287 U.S. 45, 67–68 (1932) [counsel for young and illiterate in a capital case]; Gideon v. Wainright, 372 U.S. 335, 344 (1963) [counsel for felony trials]; Douglas v. California, 372 U.S. 353, 357–58 (1963) [counsel for first appeals]; Argersinger v. Hamlin, 407 U.S. 25 (1972) [counsel for felony or misdemeanor trials involving jail term].
Seventh	In suits at common law, where the value in Controversy shall exceed twenty dollars, the right of trial by jury shall be preserved, and no fact tried by a jury, shall be otherwise re-examined in any Court of the United States, than according to the rules of the common law.	—
Eighth	Excessive bail shall not be required...	Schilb v. Kuebel, 404 U.S. 357, 365 (1971).
	nor excessive fines imposed...	—
	nor cruel and unusual punishment inflicted.	Robinson v. California, 370 U.S. 660, 666 (1962).
Ninth	The enumeration in the Constitution, of certain rights, shall not be construed to deny or disparage others retained by the people.	Griswold v. Connecticut, 381 U.S. 479 484 (1965) [also invoked other parts of the Bill of Rights].
Tenth	The powers not delegated to the United States by the Constitution, nor prohibited by it to the States, are reserved to the States respectively, or to the people.	—

standards. Miller v. California, 413 U.S. 15, 30–34 (1973). The right to a jury trial applies to the states, but states are at liberty to depart from federal standards by establishing juries with less than twelve members and by accepting nonunanimous verdicts (page 706). Also, state courts can insulate themselves from national standards by basing their rulings not on the U.S.

Constitution but on rights guaranteed in their state constitutions. State courts are able to interpret individual liberties more expansively than the federal government. PruneYard Shopping Center v. Robins, 447 U.S. 74, 81 (1980); Collins et al., 13 Hast. Const. L. Q. 599 (1986). Other chapters offer specific examples in which state courts, relying on their own constitutions, reject constitutional doctrines advanced by the U.S. Supreme Court.

Adamson v. California
332 U.S. 46 (1947)

Admiral Dewey Adamson was convicted of a murder charge and sentenced to death. Under California's constitution and its penal laws, Adamson's failure to explain or to deny evidence against him could be commented on by the court and by counsel and considered by the court and the jury. The immediate question was whether this procedure violated the guaranty in the Fifth Amendment that no person "shall be compelled in any criminal case to be a witness against himself." The Court held that his privilege is not inherent in the right to a fair trial and is not protected by the Due Process Clause of the Fourteenth Amendment. In his dissent, Justice Black lays the groundwork for arguing that the entire Bill of Rights should be incorporated in the Due Process Clause of the Fourteenth Amendment and applied against the states.

MR. JUSTICE REED delivered the opinion of the Court.

... The provisions of California law which were challenged in the state proceedings as invalid under the Fourteenth Amendment to the Federal Constitution are those of the state constitution and penal code.... They permit the failure of a defendant to explain or to deny evidence against him to be commented upon by court and by counsel and to be considered by court and jury. The defendant did not testify....

In the first place, appellant urges that the provision of the Fifth Amendment that no person "shall be compelled in any criminal case to be a witness against himself" is a fundamental national privilege or immunity protected against state abridgment by the Fourteenth Amendment or a privilege or immunity secured, through the Fourteenth Amendment, against deprivation by state action because it is a personal right, enumerated in the federal Bill of Rights.

Secondly, appellant relies upon the due process of law clause of the Fourteenth Amendment to invalidate the provisions of the California law....

... It is settled law that the clause of the Fifth Amendment, protecting a person against being compelled to be a witness against himself, is not made effective by the Fourteenth Amendment as a protection against state action on the ground that freedom from testimonial compulsion is a right of national citizenship, or because it is a personal privilege or immunity secured by the Federal Constitution as one of the rights of man that are listed in the Bill of Rights.

The reasoning that leads to those conclusions starts with the unquestioned premise that the Bill of Rights, when adopted, was for the protection of the individual against the federal government and its provisions were inapplicable to similar actions done by the states. *Barron v. Baltimore,* 7 Pet. 243; *Feldman v. United States,* 322 U.S. 487, 490. With the adoption of the Fourteenth Amendment, it was suggested that the dual citizenship recognized by its first sentence ["All persons born or naturalized in the United States, and subject to the jurisdiction thereof, are citizens of the United States and of the State wherein they reside"] secured for citizens federal protection for their elemental privileges and immunities of state citizenship. The *Slaughter-House Cases* decided, contrary to the suggestion, that these rights, as privileges and immunities of state citizenship, remained under the sole protection of the state governments....

Appellant secondly contends that if the privilege against self-incrimination is not a right protected by the privileges and immunities clause of the Fourteenth Amendment against state action, this privilege, to its full scope under the Fifth Amendment, inheres in the right to a fair trial. A right to a fair trial is a right admittedly protected by the due process clause of the Fourteenth Amendment. Therefore, appellant argues, the due process clause of the Fourteenth Amendment protects his privilege against self-incrimination. The due process clause of the Fourteenth Amendment, however, does not draw all the rights of the federal Bill of Rights under its protection. That contention was made and rejected in *Palko* v. *Connecticut,* 302 U. S. 319, 323...

MR. JUSTICE FRANKFURTER, concurring.

. . .

Between the incorporation of the Fourteenth Amendment into the Constitution and the beginning of the present membership of the Court—a period of seventy years—the scope of that Amendment was passed upon by forty-three judges. Of all these judges, only one, who may respectfully be called an eccentric exception, ever indicated the belief that the Fourteenth Amendment was a shorthand summary of the first eight Amendments theretofore limiting only the Federal Government, and that due process incorporated those eight Amendments as restrictions upon the powers of the States....

. . .

Indeed, the suggestion that the Fourteenth Amendment incorporates the first eight Amendments as such is not unambiguously urged. Even the boldest innovator would shrink from suggesting to more than half the States that they may no longer initiate prosecutions without indictment by grand jury, or that thereafter all the States of the Union must furnish a jury of twelve for every case involving a claim above twenty dollars. There is suggested merely a selective incorporation of the first eight Amendments into the Fourteenth Amendment. Some are in and some are out, but we are left in the dark as to which are in and which are out. Nor are we given the calculus for determining which go in and which stay out. If the basis of selection is merely that those provisions of the first eight Amendments are incorporated which commend themselves to individual justices as indispensable to the dignity and happiness of a free man, we are thrown back to a merely subjective test....

MR. JUSTICE BLACK, dissenting.

. . .

This decision reasserts a constitutional theory spelled out in *Twining* v. *New Jersey,* 211 U. S. 78, that this Court is endowed by the Constitution with boundless power under "natural law" peri-

odically to expand and contract constitutional standards to conform to the Court's conception of what at a particular time constitutes "civilized decency" and "fundamental liberty and justice." Invoking this *Twining* rule, the Court concludes that although comment upon testimony in a federal court would violate the Fifth Amendment, identical comment in a state court does not violate today's fashion in civilized decency and fundamentals and is therefore not prohibited by the Federal Constitution as amended.

. . .

My study of the historical events that culminated in the Fourteenth Amendment, and the expressions of those who sponsored and favored, as well as those who opposed its submission and passage, persuades me that one of the chief objects that the provisions of the Amendment's first section, separately, and as a whole, were intended to accomplish was to make the Bill of Rights applicable to the states. With full knowledge of the import of the *Barron* decision, the framers and backers of the Fourteenth Amendment proclaimed its purpose to be to overturn the constitutional rule that case had announced. This historical purpose has never received full consideration or exposition in any opinion of this Court interpreting the Amendment.

. . .

...I am attaching to this dissent an appendix which contains a résumé, by no means complete, of the Amendment's history. In my judgment that history conclusively demonstrates that the language of the first section of the Fourteenth Amendment, taken as a whole, was thought by those responsible for its submission to the people, and by those who opposed its submission, sufficiently explicit to guarantee that thereafter no state could deprive its citizens of the privileges and protections of the Bill of Rights. Whether this Court ever will, or whether it now should, in the light of past decisions, give full effect to what the Amendment was intended to accomplish is not necessarily essential to a decision here. However that may be, our prior decisions, including *Twining,* do not prevent our carrying out that purpose, at least to the extent of making applicable to the states, not a mere part, as the Court has, but the full protection of the Fifth Amendment's provision against compelling evidence from an accused to convict him of crime. And I further contend that the "natural law" formula which the Court uses to reach its conclusion in this case should be abandoned as an incongruous excrescence on our Constitution. I believe that formula to be itself a violation of our Constitution, in that it subtly conveys to courts, at the expense of legislatures, ultimate power over public policies in fields where no specific provision of the Constitution limits legislative power....

. . .

...I fear to see the consequences of the Court's practice of substituting its own concepts of decency and fundamental justice for the language of the Bill of Rights as its point of departure in interpreting and enforcing that Bill of Rights. If the choice must be between the selective process of the *Palko* decision applying some of the Bill of Rights to the States, or the *Twining* rule applying none of them, I would choose the *Palko* selective process. But rather than accept either of these choices, I would follow what I believe was the original purpose of the Fourteenth Amendment— to extend to all the people of the nation the com-

plete protection of the Bill of Rights. To hold that this Court can determine what, if any, provisions of the Bill of Rights will be enforced, and if so to what degree, is to frustrate the great design of a written Constitution.

. . .

MR. JUSTICE DOUGLAS joins in this opinion.

[*At this point, Black inserts a thirty-one-page appendix describing the origin and legislative history of the Fourteenth Amendment, concluding that the Bill of Rights applies to the states. He also quotes from Justices who believed that the Privileges and Immunities Clause of the Fourteenth Amendment applies to the states.*]

MR. JUSTICE MURPHY, with whom MR. JUSTICE RUTLEDGE concurs, dissenting.

. . .

The Incorporation Doctrine: Testimony by Justice Rehnquist

In 1986, during Senate hearings for his nomination for Chief Justice of the Supreme Court, Justice Rehnquist was asked by Senator Arlen Specter about the "incorporation doctrine": the gradual incorporation of the Bill of Rights into the Due Process Clause of the Fourteenth Amendment to be applied against the states. Originally, the Bill of Rights restricted only the federal government. Attorney General Edwin Meese III, as one of the more vocal critics of the incorporation doctrine, had written that "nowhere else has the principle of Federalism been dealt such a politically violent and constitutionally suspect blow as by the theory of incorporation." Meese, "The Supreme Court of the United States: Bulwark of a Limited Constitution," 27 So. Tex. L. Rev. 455, 463–64 (1986). The testimony below comes from "Nomination of Justice William Hubbs Rehnquist," hearings before the Senate Committee on the Judiciary, 99th Cong., 2d Sess., 191–92, 350–51, 356 (1986).

Justice REHNQUIST.... [I]f you are looking at the language of the due process clause, as I recall it, Senator, it says: "No State shall deprive any person of life, liberty or property without due process of law."

And the question then becomes, you know, as you know perfectly well, what is included under liberty, or, what provisions from the Bill of Rights are carried over by that language? And I would say that, from the language itself, it is not evident that any particular provisions are carried over, not inexorable; but if you look at the word liberty, and you wonder what kind of liberty are they talking about, surely one liberty was freedom of speech, freedom of the press.

So, it seems to me it is quite natural to carry those over. But I do not know that the language of the due process clause, nor necessarily, what I happen to recall about the debates, and that sort of thing, necessarily indicates that the full rigors of the first amendment as applied to Congress, necessarily were to be applied to the States.

Senator SPECTER. Well, the difficulty with that, it seems to me—and I am just probing to get your line of reasoning on it—is that it is so speculative. If you are picking out a portion of the first amendment, the freedom of speech—if you seek to avoid putting your own personal views, as they arise in a case, which I know you have testified in the 1971 proceedings, that you are very much opposed to—how can you really separate the various aspects of something as fundamental as speech?

Isn't it really all in there? Once you say that the due process clause incorporates freedom of speech under the first amendment, isn't that all there is to it? How can you separate any of it out as not incorporated?

Justice REHNQUIST. Well, if you say that the due process clause incorporates and makes applicable against the States, the first amendment in haec verba, so to speak, the question is answered. If it does that, it does carry it over in precisely the terms that it is applicable to Congress against the State.

But I think the argument on the other side, is that—and I think this is made very well in Justice Jackson's dissent in the *Beauharnais* case—is that there was a good deal of understanding of what freedom of speech meant at the time the Constitution was adopted, that was undoubtedly applicable against the States, but that there were perhaps slightly more latitude allowed to the States than were allowed to the Federal Government.

Justice Harlan took that position in his opinion in the *Roth* case. That the States could proscribe certain kinds of obscenity but that the Federal Government could not.

Senator SPECTER. Mr. Justice Rehnquist, at the risk of asking questions which may come before the Court, I think these are pretty well established principles, but, there is considerable concern on the part of this Senator about the applicability of the due process clause of the 14th amendment to certain fundamental liberties, as embodied in the first 10 amendments.

And I would like to ask your view as to the inclusion of the free exercise of religion in *Cantwell* v. *Connecticut*. It was a unanimous opinion. Does that matter rest, so far as you are concerned?

Justice REHNQUIST. Most certainly, yes.

Senator SPECTER. And the establishment clause in *Everson* v. *Board of Education?*

Justice REHNQUIST. No. I think I criticized the *Everson* case in my dissent in Wallace against Jaffrey, not for the result it reached at all, but for its use of the term "wall of separation between church and state," which I felt was simply not historically justified.

. . .

Senator SPECTER. . . . Is there any question in your mind that the due process clause of the 14th amendment incorporates freedom of speech?

Justice REHNQUIST. Other than the point I made yesterday. It, obviously, incorporates freedom of speech. I took the position in a couple of opinions I wrote in following Justice Jackson and Justice Harlan that some of the details might be different as applied against the States as opposed to the Federal Government.

Senator SPECTER. Would you repeat the distinction you see as to the scope of the due process clause incorporating the establishment clause of the first amendment?

Justice REHNQUIST. No; I think that is settled by the *Everson* case.

Senator SPECTER. All right.

There is no question that the due process clause of the 14th amendment incorporates freedom of the press under the first amendment?

Justice REHNQUIST. I do not think so.

Senator SPECTER. Are the rights of assembly and petition incorporated by the due process clause of the 14th amendment?

Justice REHNQUIST. Yes; I think they are.

Senator SPECTER. Is the search and seizure clause of the fourth amendment incorporated by the due process clause of the fourteenth amendment?

Justice REHNQUIST. That was held in *Mapp* v. *Ohio.*

Senator SPECTER. Do you agree with that? Do you believe it is a decided matter?

Justice REHNQUIST. It is certainly a settled matter, yes.

Senator SPECTER. Is double jeopardy under the fifth amendment incorporated in the due process clause of the 14th amendment?

Justice REHNQUIST. I think that was in the— Senator, I am going to draw back a little. Because in a case like *Benton* v. *Maryland* that came to the Court where—before I got there. I did not participate in that case. I have followed *Benton* v. *Maryland* many times when I have been on the Court. But to say whether I agree with a case that was decided before I came on the Court, I think it is better to phrase it that my record in voting on the case has certainly shown that I have followed that case.

Senator SPECTER. Well, I am not asking whether you agree with it. I am asking whether you consider it a settled issue that the incorporation doctrine covers that issue.

The concern I have is whether the incorporation doctrine is going to be undercut. Although I do not think that you and I have any difference of opinion on this, I just want to be sure.

Justice REHNQUIST. I think in a case—I cannot remember—a case coming up from Montana, I took the—Justice Stewart joined my opinion, I joined Justice Stewart's opinion—saying that some of the nuances of the double jeopardy clause should not apply the same to the States as to the Federal Government.

I think this was a case involving when the trial started, for the purposes of—when jeopardy attached. And the rule in the Federal cases was when a witness is first sworn. But Montana had a wholly different procedure. And it just seemed that a fair translation of the Federal rule to the State rule would not give you an identical situation.

. . .

Senator SPECTER.... I had gone through a number of the provisions of the Bill of Rights on the incorporation doctrine, Mr. Justice Rehnquist, because I think it is important to lay to rest the conclusion that the 14th amendment due process clause does incorporate certain provisions of the Bill of Rights.

I have only gone over the ones which have been incorporated. I have not gone into the ones which have not been, because I do not want to move into a lot of areas of the law which are not settled.

There are two remaining areas I want to ask you about. Do you regard it as settled law that the speedy trial provision is incorporated under the due process clause of the 14th amendment?

Justice REHNQUIST. Yes, I think that is settled law, and my opinions reflect it.

Senator SPECTER. What about the cruel and unusual punishment provision of the eighth amendment, is that incorporated into the due process clause of the 14th amendment?

Justice REHNQUIST. Again, my opinions reflect the fact.

CONCLUSIONS

Areas in which state and local governments were once virtually supreme, including agriculture, mining, manufacturing, and labor, eventually gave way to federal controls when transportation systems and economic markets assumed a national character. Over time, much of intrastate commerce became interstate commerce. Issues long identified with local government, including education, health, welfare, and law enforcement, are now largely a matter of federal-state cooperation. The federal taxing power, magnified by the Sixteenth Amendment and the income tax, ushered in hundreds of federal grant programs.

The Supreme Court likes to characterize itself as a guardian of federalism, but its doctrines in this area are often vague and unworkable. One scholar, Mark Tushnet, remarked: "Every time the Supreme Court has wandered into the federalism forest, it has gotten lost." 47 Vand. L. Rev. 1623, 1624 (1994). Moreover, the Court' incorporation doctrine has done much to undermine state independence and to centralize national power.

Although litigation continues to define federal-state relations, it operates mostly at the margins. Basic questions of federalism are left to the determination of Congress. During his confirmation hearings in 1986 to be Associate Justice to the Supreme Court, Antonin Scalia testified that "the primary defender of the constitutional balance, the Federal Government versus the states...the primary institution to strike the right balance is the Congress.... On the basis of the court's past decisions...the main protection for that is in the policymaking area, is in the Congress. The court's struggles to prescribe what is the proper role of the Federal Government vis-à-vis the State have essentially been abandoned for quite a while." "Nomination of Judge Antonin Scalia," hearings before the Senate Committee on the Judiciary, 99th Cong., 2d Sess., 81–82 (1986).

Scalia testified one year after the Court, in *Garcia*, seemed to signal that it would no longer intervene to police the boundaries between the national government and the states, but would leave that determination chiefly to Congress. However, during the 1990s, in a series of cases, the Court has reentered the field to challenge congressional statutes and to breathe additional life into the Tenth Amendment and the Eleventh Amendment.

SELECTED READINGS

ABRAMS, KATHRYN. "On Reading and Using the Tenth Amendment." 93 Yale Law Journal 723 (1984).

ADLER, MATTHEW D. AND SETH F. KREIMER. "The New Etiquette of Federalism: New York, Printz, and Yeskey." 1998 Supreme Court Review 71.

ALFANGE, DEAN, JR. "Congressional Regulation of the 'States Qua States': From National League of Cities to EEOC v. Wyoming." 1983 Supreme Court Review 215.

ANDERSON, WILLIAM. The Nation and the States: Rivals or Partners? Minneapolis: University of Minnesota Press, 1955.

BENSON, PAUL R., JR. The Supreme Court and the Commerce Clause, 1937–1970. New York: Dunellen, 1970.

BRENNAN, WILLIAM J., JR. "The Bill of Rights and the States." 36 New York University Law Review 761 (1961).

BRIGHTON, ROBERT CHARLES, JR. "Separating Myth from Reality in Federalism Decisions: A Perspective of American Federalism — Past and Present." 35 Vanderbilt Law Review 161 (1982).

CORWIN, EDWARD S. The Commerce Power Versus States' Rights. Princeton, N.J.: Princeton University Press, 1936.

———. "The Passing of Dual Federalism." 36 Virginia Law Review 1 (1950).

FAIRMAN, CHARLES. "Does the Fourteenth Amendment Incorporate the Bill of Rights?" 2 Stanford Law Review 5 (1949).

FISHER, LOUIS. "How the States Shape Constitutional Law." 15 State Legislatures 37 (August 1989).

GIBBONS, JOHN J. "The Eleventh Amendment and State Sovereign Immunity: A Reinterpretation." 83 Columbia Law Review 1889 (1983).

GREEN, JOHN RAYBURN. "The Bill of Rights, the Fourteenth Amendment, and the Supreme Court." 46 Michigan Law Review 869 (1948).

HENKIN, LOUIS. "'Selective Incorporation' in the Fourteenth Amendment." 73 Yale Law Journal 74 (1963).

HOWARD, A.E. DICK. "The States and the Supreme Court." 31 Catholic University Law Review 380 (1982).

KRAMER, LARRY D. "Putting the Politics Back into the Political Safeguards of Federalism." 100 Columbia Law Review 215 (2000).

LESSIG, LAWRENCE. "Translating Federalism: United States v. Lopez," 1995 Supreme Court Review 125.

LOFGREN, CHARLES A. "The Origins of the Tenth Amendment: History, Sovereignty, and the Problem of Constitutional Intention," in Ronald K.L. Collins, ed., Constitutional Government in America. Durham, N.C.: Carolina Academic Press, 1980.

MERRITT, DEBORAH JONES. "Commerce!," 94 Michigan Law Review 674 (1995).

MICHELMAN, FRANK I. "States' Rights and States' Roles: Permutations of 'Sovereignty' in National League of Cities v. Usery." 86 Yale Law Journal 1165 (1977).

MORRISON, STANLEY. "Does the Fourteenth Amendment Incorporate the Bill of Rights?" 2 Stanford Law Review 140 (1949).

NAGEL, ROBERT F. "Federalism as a Fundamental Value: National League of Cities in Perspective." 1981 Supreme Court Review 81.

NEUBORNE, BURT. "The Myth of Parity." 90 Harvard Law Review 1105 (1977).

SCHMIDHAUSER, JOHN R. The Supreme Court as Final Arbiter in Federal-State Relations, 1789–1957. Chapel Hill: University of North Carolina Press, 1958.

SHAPIRO, DAVID L. "Wrong Terms: The Eleventh Amendment and the Pennhurst Case." 98 Harvard Law Review 61 (1984).

VILE, M.J.C. The Structure of American Federalism. London: Oxford University Press, 1961.

WELLS, MICHAEL. "The Role of Comity in the Law of Federal Courts." 60 North Carolina Law Review 59 (1981).

WISE, CHARLES AND ROSEMARY O'LEARY. "Is Federalism Dead or Alive in the Supreme Court? Implications for Public Administrators." 52 Public Administration Review 559 (1992).

9

Economic Liberties

From the late nineteenth century to the 1930s, the courts struck down efforts by Congress and state legislatures to ease the harshness of industrial conditions. Statutes that established maximum hours or minimum wages were declared unconstitutional interferences with property rights, due process, and "liberty of contract." State legislatures attempted to use the "police power" to protect public health and safety. In many of these cases the courts held that government existed to protect life, liberty, and property, with property accorded the greatest protection. Over those decades the judiciary promoted an exceptionally narrow definition of property and restricted the government's ability to protect the health and safety of citizens. This chapter also analyzes two other issues involving economic rights: the Contract Clause (prohibiting states from impairing the obligation of contracts) and the Taking Clause (providing that private property shall not be taken for public use without just compensation).

A. THE MEANING OF PROPERTY

Few words evoke more powerful emotions than *property.* Pierre Proudhon, the French anarchist of the nineteenth century, equated property with theft. Jesus warned that it would be easier for a camel to pass through the eye of a needle than for a rich man to enter the kingdom of God. Others elevated property to a position of reverence and respect. Machiavelli advised a prince not to take property, for "men forget more easily the death of their father than the loss of their patrimony."

Many of us have been taught from childhood to think of property as tangible objects: land, buildings, personal property, business, and wealth. The word itself, however, suggests a larger meaning. It derives from *proprius,* which means something private or peculiar to oneself. This general concept embraces intangible possessions, including reputation, ideas, and religious opinions. As a result of court decisions in recent decades, property rights have expanded to cover welfare payments, job rights, garnishment procedures, unemployment compensation, and environmental rights. Property in America acquires specific meaning from custom, statutes, and court decisions.

Property, as a legal creation, fluctuates in meaning over time. Before the War of Independence, a landed aristocracy in America was protected by *entail* (making land inalienable) and *primogeniture* (transferring land to the eldest son). Gradually those laws were abolished. Up until the Civil War, property extended to black slaves, who were auctioned off at the market, bought and sold as human merchandise. Congress enacted fugitive slave laws to return "property" to its owners. In *Dred Scott* v. *Sandford* (1857), Chief Justice Taney said that the right of property in a slave was "distinctly and expressly affirmed in the Constitution. The right to traffic in it, like an ordinary article of merchandise and property, was guaranteed to the citizens of the United States, in every State that might desire it, for twenty years." 60 U.S. at 451.

Well into the twentieth century, the courts continued to treat wives as the property of the husband. The concept of *coverture,* described by Blackstone more than two centuries ago, maintained its influence. Upon marriage, a woman's legal existence was submerged into that of the husband. Marriage made husband and wife "one person in law." Under the husband's "wing, protection, and *cover,* she performs every thing." Performance included availability for sex, making it legally impossible in some states for a man to rape his wife. Adultery with a man's wife was considered a violation of the *husband's* property rights. Tinker v. Colwell, 193 U.S. 473 (1904).

Locke and Madison

To the framers of the Constitution, property represented a broad concept. They knew that when John Locke spoke of property, he meant "lives, liberties and estates" — not simply the latter. To Locke, individuals possessed property in their persons as well as in their goods. Every man had a property in the labor of his body and the work of his hands. The act of labor invested part of one's personality in an object.

James Madison developed a comprehensive view of property. In Federalist No. 10, he spoke of the "diversity in the faculties of men, from which the rights of property originate." Because mankind consists of different and unequal faculties, different and unequal kinds of property result. But Madison did not say that the most important function of government was to protect property. Rather, the "protection of these faculties is the first object of government." Consistent with that notion, the Constitution authorizes Congress to "promote the progress of science and useful arts, by securing for limited times to authors and inventors the exclusive right to their respective writings and discoveries." Art. I, § 8, Cl. 8. Madison's views are elaborated in an essay written in 1792. People had property in their opinions, in the free communication of ideas, in religious beliefs, and the free use of faculties and "free choice of the objects on which to employ them." Because conscience is the "most sacred of all property," it is a greater violation to invade a man's conscience than to invade his home (see Madison reading).

This broad view of property rights was obscured by the Supreme Court during America's industrial growth in the nineteenth century. The Court invoked the Due Process Clause of the Fifth and Fourteenth Amendments to control the substantive content of federal and state legislation. In upholding the right of business to operate free of government control, the Court was said to protect property. But it did not protect property in its larger sense, including the community's interest in health and safety. Walton Hamilton and Irene Till explained that it is "incorrect to say that the judiciary protected property; rather they called that property to which they accorded protection." 12 Encycl. Soc. Sci. 536 (1934).

Property has come to represent a "bundle of rights." Kaiser Aetna v. United States, 444 U.S. 164, 176 (1979). These rights have little in common except that they are asserted by persons and enforced by government. Felix S. Cohen, for many years a gifted lecturer at the Yale Law School, underscored the enforcement aspect by proposing that the following label be affixed to all property: "To the world: "Keep off X unless you have my permission, which I may grant or withhold.' Signed: Private citizen. Endorsed: The state." 9 Rutgers L. Rev. 347, 374 (1954). Although legislative actions and judicial decisions help determine the boundaries of property, the state does not create interests. The active, driving force behind property is the individual who remains conscious of rights and insists on their protection.

Madison's Essay on Property

This term in its particular application means "that dominion which one man claims and exercises over the external things of the world, in exclusion of every other individual."

In its larger and juster meaning, it embraces every thing to which a man may attach a value and have a right; and *which leaves to every one else the like advantage.*

In the former sense, a man's land, or merchandize, or money is called his property.

In the latter sense, a man has property in his opinions and the free communication of them.

He has a property of peculiar value in his religious opinions, and in the profession and practice dictated by them.

He has property very dear to him in the safety and liberty of his person.

He has an equal property in the free use of his faculties and free choice of the objects on which to employ them.

In a word, as a man is said to have a right to his property, he may be equally said to have a property in his rights.

Where an excess of power prevails, property of no sort is duly respected. No man is safe in his opinions, his person, his faculties or his possessions.

Where there is an excess of liberty, the effect is the same, tho' from an opposite cause.

Government is instituted to protect property of every sort; as well that which lies in the various rights of individuals, as that which the term particularly expresses. This being the end of government, that alone is a *just* government, which *impartially* secures to every man, whatever is his *own.*

According to this standard of merit, the praise of affording a just security to property, should be sparingly bestowed on a government which, however scrupulously guarding the possessions of individuals, does not protect them in the enjoyment and communication of their opinions, in which they have an equal, and in the estimation of some, a more valuable property.

More sparingly should this praise be allowed to a government, where a man's religious rights are violated by penalties, or fettered by tests, or taxed by a hierarchy. Conscience is the most sacred of all property; other property depending in part on positive law, the exercise of that, being a natural and inalienable right. To guard a man's house as his castle, to pay public and enforce private debts with the most exact faith, can give no title to invade a man's conscience which is more sacred than his castle, or to withhold from it that debt of protection, for which the public faith is pledged, by the very nature and original conditions of the social pact.

That is not a just government, nor is property secure under it, where the property which a man has in his personal safety and personal liberty, is violated by arbitrary seizures of one class of citizens for the service of the rest. A magistrate issuing warrants to a press gang, would be in his proper functions in Turkey or Indostan, under appellations proverbial of the most compleat despotism.

That is not a just government, nor is property secure under it, where arbitrary restrictions, exemptions, and monopolies deny to part of its citizens that free use of their faculties, and free choice of their occupations, which not only constitute their property in the general sense of the word; but are the means of acquiring property strictly so called. What must be the spirit of legislation where a manufacturer of linen cloth is forbidden to bury his own child in a linen shroud, in order to favour his neighbor who manufactures woolen cloth; where the manufacturer and wearer of woolen cloth are again forbidden the economical use of buttons of that material, in favor of the manufacturer of buttons of other materials!

A just security to property is not afforded by that government under which unequal taxes oppress one species of property and reward another species: where arbitrary taxes invade the domestic sanctuaries of the rich, and excessive taxes grind the faces of the poor; where the keenness and competitions of want are deemed an insufficient spur to labor, and taxes are again applied by an unfeeling policy, as another spur; in violation of that sacred property, which Heaven, in decreeing man to earn his bread by the sweat of his brow, kindly reserved to him, in the small repose that could be spared from the supply of his necessities.

If there be a government then which prides itself on maintaining the inviolability of property; which provides that none shall be taken *directly* even for public use without indemnification to the owner, and yet *directly* violates the property which individuals have in their opinions, their re-

SOURCE: This essay, by James Madison, appeared in *The National Gazette*, March 29, 1792, and was reprinted in *The Writings of James Madison*, edited by Gaillard Hunt, Vol. 6, pp. 101–03.

ligion, their persons, and their faculties; nay more, which *indirectly* violates their property, in their actual possessions, in the labor that acquires their daily subsistence, and in the hallowed remnant of time which ought to relieve their fatigues and soothe their cares, the inference will have been anticipated, that such a government is not a pattern for the United States.

If the United States mean to obtain or deserve the full praise due to wise and just governments, they will equally respect the rights of property, and the property in rights: they will rival the government that most sacredly guards the former; and by repelling its example in violating the latter, will make themselves a pattern to that and all other governments.

B. THE CONTRACT CLAUSE

The Constitution prohibits any state from passing any law "impairing the Obligation of Contracts." Art. I, § 10. Objections were raised at the Philadelphia Convention that this provision was far too broad and impractical, 2 Farrand 439–40, and so it has proven to be. Madison stated in Federalist No. 44 that the constitutional prohibitions against bills of attainder, ex post facto laws, and laws impairing the obligation of contracts were added in the interest of "personal security and private rights" and to protect the people from the "fluctuating policy which had directed the public councils." However, under the police power and emergency conditions, state actions that impair the obligation of contracts have been upheld repeatedly by the courts. As the Supreme Court noted in 1987, "it is well settled that the prohibition against impairing the obligation of contracts is not to be read literally." Keystone Bituminous Coal Assn. v. DeBenedictis, 480 U.S. 470, 502 (1987). The Contract Clause is invoked only when there has been a *substantial* impairment of a contractual relationship.[1]

The prohibition against ex post facto laws might have been used to protect contracts and property rights, but in 1798 the Court restricted this constitutional provision to criminal statutes. The Court said that "Every *ex post facto* law must necessarily be retrospective; but every retrospective law is not an *ex post facto* law." CALDER v. BULL, 3 U.S. (3 Dall.) 385, 390 (1798).

The first major case involving the Contract Clause arose in Georgia. The state legislature, in what became known as the "Yazoo Land Fraud," sold vast tracts of land in 1795 to four companies. With a single exception, every legislator voting for the measure sold his vote either for money or for shares of stock in the companies. In response to this blatant bribery, a mob marched on the state capital and threatened the lives of the lawmakers. Benjamin Wright, The Contract Clause of the Constitution 21 (1938). Public outrage forced the new legislature a year later to rescind the statute. Did this repeal of a corrupt statute violate the contractual rights of speculators and prospective settlers who purchased land from the companies?

Writing for the Supreme Court, Chief Justice Marshall held that the legislature of 1795 possessed constitutional authority to pass the initial statute. The innocent third parties who bought land from the companies, he said, were not responsible for legislative corruption or fraud. On a good-faith basis they had entered into contracts with the companies. Marshall further pointed out that it was inappropriate to expect courts to annul a statute by inquiring into the purity of legislative motives. FLETCHER v. PECK, 10 U.S. (6 Cr.) 87 (1810). This decision made it clear that the Contract Clause covered not only "private contracts" but "state contracts" as well (see box). Another reading of the Contract Clause in defense of property rights was announced in *New Jersey* v. *Wilson*, which extended the contract clause to grants

---

1. General Motors Corp. v. Romein, 503 U.S. 181, 186 (1992); Energy Reserves Group, Inc. v. Kansas Power & Light Co., 459 U.S. 400, 411 (1983); Allied Structural Steel Co. v. Spannaus, 438 U.S. 234, 244 (1978).

Doctrine of Vested Rights

...[L]egislative acts interfering with an individual's property or diminishing its value were constitutionally suspect, and this led to the third main contribution of *Fletcher* v. *Peck,* the instrumental conclusion that courts had a duty to void state laws tampering with either private or public contracts. Marshall's opinion, to be sure, made much of the great "delicacy" of voiding a law, but it did not flinch from the "solemn obligation" to declare the repeal act unconstitutional. Together, these three assumptions—the inclusion of public grants under the limitations of the contract clause, the primacy of vested property as a constitutional value, and the judicial duty to void legislative impairments of contract rights—summarize one of the most influential doctrines of American constitutionalism. Edward S. Corwin called it the "Doctrine of Vested Rights." "Setting out with the assumption that the property right is fundamental," Corwin wrote, it "treats any law impairing *vested rights,* whatever its intention, as a bill of pains and penalties, and so, void." This doctrine, which was fully asserted for the first time in the case that grew out of the Yazoo land fraud, dominated American constitutional law during much of the nineteenth century and the first third of the twentieth.

SOURCE: C. Peter Magrath, Yazoo, Law and Politics in the New Republic: The Case of *Fletcher* v. *Peck* 103 (1966).

of tax immunity. 11 U.S. (7 Cr.) 164 (1812). The overriding theme over history has been a balancing between the right of private property and the right of government to regulate property for the general public.

The Dartmouth College case of 1819 stands as a famous legal landmark. The college had been created in 1754 as a charity school to instruct Indians in the Christian religion. In 1769 it was chartered by the British crown as a private corporation. The college continued to be funded entirely by private donations. In 1816 New Hampshire passed legislation to increase the number of trustees in the college and thereby transfer control to appointees of the governor.

In his decision for the Court, Chief Justice Marshall said that the British parliament could have annulled the charter at any time. New Hampshire could have altered the charter after the break with England and before ratification of the U.S. Constitution. However, the Contract Clause prohibited the state from impairing the contract of a "private eleemosynary institution": an institution created by private parties, sustained by private funds, and devoted to charitable goals. Marshall explained that had the college been created by the legislature and supported by public funds, the state could have altered the contract. Under those circumstances the college would have existed as a public corporation to satisfy a public purpose. Dartmouth, however, had a right to continue under its private charter without interference by the state. Otherwise, Marshall warned, all charitable and educational institutions would fall under the control of government. DARTMOUTH COLLEGE v. WOODWARD, 17 U.S. (4 Wheat.) 517 (1819).

This case has few applications today. The line between "public" and "private" is less clear, and even private institutions are subject to state regulation and control. Henry J. Friendly, The Dartmouth College Case and the Public-Private Penumbra (1969). Nevertheless, the case established important limits on the power of government to interfere with academic freedom and acts of incorporation. It also reassured Federalist property holders who feared the reach of majority rule and state legislatures.

Rights of the Community

The Charles River Bridge case of 1837 illustrates that the right of contract is never absolute. In 1785 the legislature of Massachusetts incorporated a company to build a bridge and take tolls. About four decades later it created another company to build a bridge nearby. The second bridge took tolls for a few years and then became free. Travelers, of course, switched to the new bridge and proprietors of the first bridge complained that the legislature had impaired the obligations of a contract. The Supreme Court, balancing the rights of property against the rights reserved to the states, held that a state law may be retrospective in character and alter rights formerly vested by law without violating the Contract Clause. Although corporations are given certain rights by law, the community also has rights in a dynamic economy to improved public accommodations and travel. CHARLES RIVER BRIDGE v. WARREN BRIDGE, 36 U.S. (11 Pet.) 419 (1837).

The principle of *Charles River* has been affirmed in many cases. The Contract Clause does not prevent a state from granting a right and repealing or modifying that right in future years. A legislature may grant a monopoly and decide at a later time that it is in the interest of the state to abolish the monopoly and allow other companies to enter the field. Slaughter-House Cases, 83 U.S. (16 Wall.) 36 (1873); Butchers' Union Co. v. Crescent City Co., 111 U.S. 746 (1884). In matters affecting public health, public safety, or public morals, one legislature may not bind future legislatures.[2]

Private contracts are subject to government control. The right of an owner of a building to contract with tenants may be limited by rent-control laws. Block v. Hirsh, 256 U.S. 135 (1921). Although contracts may create rights of property, when they concern a subject matter within the control of Congress "they have a congenital infirmity." Norman v. Baltimore & Ohio R. Co., 294 U.S. 240, 307–08 (1935), cited in Connolly v. Pension Benefit Guaranty Corp., 475 U.S. 211, 223–24 (1986).

If a state passes a bankruptcy law to relieve debtors of their liabilities, does this impair the obligation of contracts? The Supreme Court in an early case decided that states are not prevented from passing bankruptcy laws unless Congress preempts the field by passing a uniform law authorized by Article I, Section 8, Clause 4. In this particular case, the Court determined that the state law did impair the obligation of contracts. Sturges v. Crowninshield, 17 U.S. (4 Wheat.) 120 (1819). The following decade the Court again held that congressional inaction on uniform bankruptcy laws permitted the states to legislate on the subject. Moreover, states could pass laws discharging a debtor from liability if the law preceded the contract. If a bankruptcy act operated prospectively, it did not violate the Contract Clause. Ogden v. Saunders, 25 U.S. (12 Wheat.) 212 (1827). Contracts are then entered into in light of the bankruptcy policy established by law.

The Minnesota Moratorium

The question of a retrospective law was decided by the Supreme Court in 1934. A 5–4 decision upheld a Minnesota law, passed during the Great Depression, that gave homeowners a delay of up to two years in meeting their mortgage payments. Although the law clearly impaired contracts entered into prior to the statute, both the state court and the Supreme Court agreed that the police power had sufficient scope in an emergency to set aside, for a limited period, the Contract Clause. HOME BLDG. & LOAN ASSN. v. BLAISDELL, 290 U.S. 398 (1934). A year later, by a 5 to 4 vote, the Court upheld the power of Congress to abrogate the "gold clauses" in private contracts. To prevent a run on the banks and the hoarding of gold, President Franklin D. Roosevelt and Congress had taken emergency actions in 1933 to prevent individuals from requiring payment in gold or a particular kind of coin.[3] In several other

---

2. Stone v. Mississippi, 101 U.S. 814 (1880); Fertilizing Co. v. Hyde Park, 97 U.S. 659 (1879); Beer Co. v. Massachusetts, 97 U.S. 25 (1878).

3. Norman v. B.&O. R. Co., 294 U.S. 240 (1935). For other "gold clause" cases, see Nortz v. United States, 294 U.S. 317 (1935) and Perry v. United States, 294 U.S. 330 (1935).

cases, where state actions were not restricted to an emergency period, statutes were declared invalid under the Contract Clause.[4]

The Contract Clause does not carry the same importance today as it did in the era of *Fletcher* and *Dartmouth College.* As a limitation on state power, it has been largely replaced by the Due Process and Equal Protection Clauses of the Fourteenth Amendment. There are still circumstances, however, where the Contract Clause is successfully invoked to strike down a state statute. A contemporary case involved the Port Authority of New York and New Jersey. In 1962 the two states passed a statutory covenant that prevented the Authority from subsidizing rail passenger transportation by using revenues and reserves pledged as security for bonds issued by the Authority. In 1974 the two states repealed the statutory covenant. Although the New Jersey courts upheld the repeal as a valid exercise of the police power, the Supreme Court in 1977 ruled that the repeal violated the Contract Clause by eliminating an important security provision for bondholders. United States Trust Co. v. New Jersey, 431 U.S. 1 (1977).

The three dissenters in this 4–3 decision accused the Court of "dusting off" the Contract Clause and giving it a meaning broader than intended by the framers. According to their analysis and some other studies, the Contract Clause was conceived of "primarily as protection for economic transactions entered into by purely private parties, rather than obligations involving the State itself." Id. at 45. This philosophy would allow each new legislature to rescind the policies of the previous legislature. The problem is that state obligations frequently involve investments by private parties, as in the Port Authority case.

A year later, the Court struck down a Minnesota law for violating the Contract Clause, pointing out that the police power did not give the states unlimited authority to abridge existing contractual relationships. Moreover, the Minnesota law did not deal with grave economic or social emergencies, as in the 1934 *Blaisdell* case. Justices Brennan, White, and Marshall dissented from what they regarded as the Court's extension of the Contract Clause beyond its original intent. Allied Structural Steel Co. v. Spannaus, 438 U.S. 234 (1978).

Calder v. Bull

3 U.S. (3 Dall.) 385 (1798)

The Constitution prohibits any state from passing any law "impairing the Obligation of Contracts." The Constitution also prohibits states from passing ex post facto laws, which might apply to protect contracts and property rights. The issue in this case is whether the prohibition against ex post facto laws applies only to criminal statutes. Caleb Bull and his wife attempted to appeal a probate court ruling over a will, only to find that the time for their appeal had expired. After they convinced the Connecticut legislature to revise the law and lengthen the time for appeal, and prevailed in the lawsuit, John Calder and his wife protested that the new law violated the Ex Post Facto Clause.

CHASE, Justice. — The decision of one question determines (in my opinion) the present dispute. I shall, therefore, state from the record no more of the case, than I think necessary for the consideration of that question only.

The legislature of Connecticut, on the 2d Thursday of May 1795, passed a resolution or

law, which, for the reasons assigned, set aside a decree of the Court of Probate for Hartford, on the 21st of March 1793, which decree disapproved of the will of Normand Morrison (the grandson), made the 21st of August 1779, and refused to record the said will; and granted a new hearing by the said court of probate, with liberty

---

4. Treigle v. Acme Homestead Assn., 297 U.S. 189 (1936); Worthen Co. v. Kavanaugh, 295 U.S. 56 (1935); Worthen Co. v. Thomas, 292 U.S. 426 (1934). But see also El Paso v. Simmons, 379 U.S. 497 (1965); East New York Bank v. Hahn, 326 U.S. 230 (1945); Faitoute Co. v. Asbury Park, 316 U.S. 502 (1942); Veix v. Sixth Ward Assn., 310 U.S. 32 (1940).

of appeal therefrom, in six months. A new hearing was had, in virtue of this resolution or law, before the said court of probate, who, on the 27th of July 1795, approved the said will, and ordered it to be recorded. At August 1795, appeal was then had to the superior court at Hartford, who, at February term 1796, affirmed the decree of the court of probate. Appeal was had to the supreme court of errors of Connecticut, who, in June 1796, adjudged that there were no errors. More than eighteen months elapsed from the decree of the court of probate (on the 1st of March 1793), and thereby Caleb Bull and wife were barred of all right of appeal, by a statute of Connecticut. There was no law of that state whereby a new hearing or trial, before the said court of probate, might be obtained. Calder and wife claimed the premises in question, in right of the wife, as heiress of N. Morrison, physician; Bull and wife claimed under the will of N. Morrison, the grandson.

The counsel for the plaintiffs in error contend, that the said resolution or law of the legislature of Connecticut, granting a new hearing, in the above case, is an *ex post facto* law, prohibited by the constitution of the United States; that any law of the federal government, or of any of the state government, contrary to the constitution of the United States, is void; and that this court possesses the power to declare such law void.

. . .

The effect of the resolution or law of Connecticut, above stated, is to revise a decision of one of its inferior courts, called the court of probate for Hartford, and to direct a new hearing of the case by the same court of probate, that passed the decree against the will of Normand Morrison. By the existing law of Connecticut, a right to recover certain property had vested in Calder and wife (the appellants), in consequence of a decision of a court of justice, but in virtue of a subsequent resolution or law, and the new hearing thereof, and the decision in consequence, this right to recover certain property was divested, and the right to the property declared to be in Bull and wife, the appellees. The sole inquiry is, whether this resolution or law of Connecticut, having such operation, is an *ex post facto* law, within the prohibition of the federal constitution?

Whether the legislature of any of the states can revise and correct by law, a decision of any of its courts of justice, although not prohibited by the constitution of the state, is a question of very great importance, and not necessary now to be de-

termined; because the resolution or law in question does not go so far. I cannot subscribe to the omnipotence of a state legislature, or that it is absolute and without control; although its authority should not be expressly restrained by the constitution, or fundamental law of the state. The people of the United States erected their constitutions or forms of government, to establish justice, to promote the general welfare, to secure the blessings of liberty, and to protect their persons and property from violence. The purposes for which men enter into society will determine the nature and terms of the social compact; and as they are the foundation of the legislative power, they will decide what are the proper objects of it. The nature, and ends of legislative power will limit the exercise of it. This fundamental principle flows from the very nature of our free republican governments, that no man should be compelled to do what the laws do not require; nor to refrain from acts which the laws permit. There are acts which the federal, or state legislature cannot do, without exceeding their authority. There are certain vital principles in our free republican governments, which will determine and overrule an apparent and flagrant abuse of legislative power; as to authorize manifest injustice by positive law; or to take away that security for personal liberty, or private property, for the protection whereof the government was established. An act of the legislature (for I cannot call it a law), contrary to the great first principles of the social compact, cannot be considered a rightful exercise of legislative authority. The obligation of a law, in governments established on express compact, and on republican principles, must be determined by the nature of the power on which it is founded.

. . .

The constitution of the United States, article I., section 9, prohibits the legislature of the United States from passing any *ex post facto* law; and, in § 10, lays several restrictions on the authority of the legislatures of the several states; and, among them, "that no state shall pass any *ex post facto* law."

It may be remembered, that the legislatures of several of the states, to wit, Massachusetts, Pennsylvania, Delaware, Maryland, and North and South Carolina, are expressly prohibited, by their state constitutions, from passing any *ex post facto* law.

I shall endeavor to show what law is to be considered an *ex post facto* law, within the words and meaning of the prohibition in the federal constitution. The prohibition, "that no state shall pass any *ex post facto* law," necessarily requires some explanation; for, naked and without explanation, it is unintelligible, and means nothing.... [T]he plain and obvious meaning and intention of the prohibition is this: that the legislatures of the several states, shall not pass laws, after a fact done by a subject or citizen, which shall have relation to such fact, and shall punish him for having done it. The prohibition, considered in this light, is an additional bulwark in favor of the personal security of the subject, to protect his person from punishment by legislative acts, having a retrospective operation. I do not think it was inserted, to secure the citizen in his private rights of either property or contracts. The prohibitions not to make anything but gold and silver coin a tender in payment of debts, and not to pass any law impairing the obligation of contracts, were inserted to secure private rights; but the restriction not to pass any *ex post facto* law, was to secure the person of the subject from injury or punishment, in consequence of such law. If the prohibition against making *ex post facto* laws was intended to secure personal rights from being affected or injured by such laws, and the prohibition is sufficiently extensive for that object, the other restraints I have enumerated, were unnecessary, and therefore, improper; for both of them are retrospective.

I will state what laws I consider *ex post facto* laws, within the words and the intent of the prohibition. 1st. Every law that makes an action done before the passing of the law, and which was innocent when done, criminal; and punishes such action. 2d. Every law that aggravates a crime, or makes it greater than it was, when committed. 3d. Every law that changes the punishment, and inflicts a greater punishment, than the law annexed to the crime, when committed. 4th. Every law that alters the legal rules of evidence, and receives less, or different testimony, than the law required at the time of the commission of the offence, in order to convict the offender. All these, and similar laws, are manifestly unjust and oppressive. In my opinion, the true distinction is between *ex post facto* laws, and retrospective laws. Every *ex post facto* law must necessarily be retrospective; but every retrospective law is not an *ex post facto* law: the former only are prohibited. Every law that takes away or impairs rights vested, agreeable to existing laws, is retrospective, and is generally unjust, and may be oppressive; and it is a good general rule, that a law should have no retrospect: but

there are cases in which laws may justly, and for the benefit of the community, and also of individuals, relate to a time antecedent to their commencement; as statutes of oblivion or of pardon. They are certainly retrospective, and literally both concerning and after the facts committed. But I do not consider any law *ex post facto*, within the prohibition, that mollifies the rigor of the criminal law: but only those that create or aggravate the crime; or increase the punishment, or change the rules of evidence, for the purpose of conviction....

. . .

I am of opinion, that the decree of the supreme court of errors of Connecticut be affirmed, with costs.

PATERSON, Justice.—

...[T]he words of the constitution of the United States are, "That no state shall pass any bill of attainder, *ex post facto* law, or law impairing the obligation of contracts." Article I., § 10. Where is the necessity or use of the latter words, if a law impairing the obligation of contracts, be comprehended within the terms *ex post facto* law? It is obvious, from the specification of contracts in the last member of the clause, that the framers of the constitution did not understand or use the words in the sense contended for on the part of the plaintiffs in error. They understood and used the words in their known and appropriate signification, as referring to crimes, pains and penalties, and no further....

. . .

IREDELL, Justice.—Though I concur in the general result of the opinions which have been delivered, I cannot entirely adopt the reasons that are assigned upon the occasion.

...[I]t has been the policy of all the American states, which have, individually, framed their state constitutions, since the revolution, and of the people of the United States, when they framed the federal constitution, to define with precision the objects of the legislative power, and to restrain its exercise within marked and settled boundaries. If any act of congress, or of the legislature of a state, violates those constitutional provisions, it is unquestionably void; though, I admit, that as the authority to declare it void is of a delicate and awful nature, the court will never resort to that authority, but in a clear and urgent case. If, on the other hand, the legislature of the Union, or the legislature of any member of the Union, shall pass a law, within the general scope of their constitutional power, the court cannot pronounce it to be void, merely because it is, in their judgment, contrary to the principles of natural justice. The ideas of natural justice are regulated by no fixed standard: the ablest and the purest men have differed upon the subject; and all that the court could properly say, in such an event, would be, that the legislature (possessed of an equal right of opinion) had passed an act which, in the opinion of the judges, was inconsistent with the abstract principles of natural justice....

CUSHING, Justice.—The case appears to me to be clear of all difficulty, taken either way. If the act is a judicial act, it is not touched by the federal constitution: and if it is a legislative act, it is maintained and justified by the ancient and uniform practice of the state of Connecticut.

Judgment affirmed.

Fletcher v. Peck

10 U.S. (6 Cr.) 87 (1810)

In 1803 John Peck sold to Robert Fletcher a tract of land lying along the Mississippi River. The land dated back to an act of the Georgia legislature in 1795 and had changed hands often since that time. Because of corruption associated with the statute, a new legislature in 1796 rescinded the land grant. Fletcher went to court in Massachusetts, claiming a breach of contract: that the legislature never had authority to sell and dispose of the land. Did the rescinding legislation nullify the contractual rights of innocent third parties who had purchased land and sold it, or were they protected by the Contract Clause?

MARSHALL, Ch. J. delivered the opinion of the court as follows:

. . .

The question, whether a law be void for its repugnancy to the constitution, is, at all times, a question of much delicacy, which ought seldom, if ever, to be decided in the affirmative, in a doubtful case. The court, when impelled by duty to render such a judgment, would be unworthy of its station, could it be unmindful of the solemn obligations which that station imposes. But it is not on slight implication and vague conjecture that the legislature is to be pronounced to have transcended its powers, and its acts to be considered as void. The opposition between the constitution and the law should be such that the judge feels a clear and strong conviction of their incompatibility with each other.

In this case the court can perceive no such opposition. In the constitution of Georgia, adopted in the year 1789, the court can perceive no restriction on the legislative power, which inhibits the passage of the act of 1795. The court cannot say that, in passing that act, the legislature has transcended its powers, and violated the constitution.

. . .

The 2d count assigns, in substance, as a breach of this covenant, that the original grantees from the state of Georgia promised and assured divers members of the legislature, then sitting in general assembly, that if the said members would assent to, and vote for, the passing of the act, and if the said bill should pass, such members should have a share of, and be interested in, all the lands purchased from the said state by virtue of such law. And that divers of the said members, to whom the said promises were made, were unduly influenced thereby, and, under such influence, did vote for the passing of the said bill; by reason whereof the said law was a nullity, &c. and so the title of the state of Georgia did not pass to the said Peck, &c.

. . .

That corruption should find its way into the governments of our infant republics, and contaminate the very source of legislation, or that impure motives should contribute to the passage of a law, or the formation of a legislative contract, are circumstances most deeply to be deplored. How far a court of justice would, in any case, be competent, on proceedings instituted by the state itself, to vacate a contract thus formed, and to annul rights acquired, under that contract, by third persons having no notice of the improper means by which it was obtained, is a question which the court would approach with much circumspection. It may well be doubted how far the validity of a law depends upon the motives of its framers, and how far the particular inducements, operating on members of the supreme sovereign power of a state, to the formation of a contract by that power, are examinable in a court of justice. If the principle be conceded, that an act of the supreme sovereign power might be declared null by a court, in consequence of the means which procured it, still would there be much difficulty in saying to what extent those means must be applied to produce this effect. Must it be direct corruption, or would interest or undue influence of any kind be sufficient? Must the vitiating cause operate on a majority, or on what number of the members? Would the act be null, whatever might be the wish of the nation, or would its obligation or nullity depend upon the public sentiment?

If the majority of the legislature be corrupted, it may well be doubted, whether it be within the province of the judiciary to control their conduct, and, if less than a majority act from impure motives, the principle by which judicial interference would be regulated, is not clearly discerned.

Whatever difficulties this subject might present, when viewed under aspects of which it may be susceptible, this court can perceive none in the particular pleadings now under consideration.

This is not a bill brought by the state of Georgia, to annul the contract, nor does it appear to the court, by this count, that the state of Georgia is dissatisfied with the sale that has been made. The case, as made out in the pleadings, is simply this. One individual who holds lands in the state of Georgia, under a deed convenanting that the title of Georgia was in the grantor, brings an action of covenant upon this deed, and assigns, as a breach, that some of the members of the legislature were induced to vote in favour of the law, which constituted the contract, by being promised an interest in it, and that therefore the act is a mere nullity.

This solemn question cannot be brought thus collaterally and incidentally before the court. It would be indecent, in the extreme, upon a private contract, between two individuals, to enter into an inquiry respecting the corruption of the sovereign power of a state. If the title be plainly deduced from a legislative act, which the legislature might constitutionally pass, if the act be clothed with all the requisite forms of a law, a court, sitting as a court of law, cannot sustain a suit brought by one individual against another founded on the allegation that the act is a nullity, in consequence of the impure motives which influenced certain members of the legislature which passed the law.

. . .

The third count recites the undue means practised on certain members of the legislature, as stated in the second count, and then alleges that, in consequence of these practices, and of other causes, a subsequent legislature passed an act annulling and rescinding the law under which the conveyance to the original grantees was made, declaring that conveyance void, and asserting the title of the state to the lands it contained. The count proceeds to recite at large, this rescinding act, and concludes with averring that, by reason of this act, the title of the said Peck in the premises was constitutionally and legally impaired, and rendered null and void.

. . . [T]here are certain great principles of justice, whose authority is universally acknowledged, that ought not to be entirely disregarded.

. . . Titles, which, according to every legal test, are perfect, are acquired with that confidence which is inspired by the opinion that the purchaser is safe. If there be any concealed defect, arising from the conduct of those who had held the property long before he acquired it, of which he had no notice, that concealed defect cannot be set up against him. He has paid his money for a title good at law, he is innocent, whatever may be the guilt of others, and equity will not subject him to the penalties attached to that guilt. All titles would be insecure, and the intercourse between man and man would be very seriously obstructed, if this principle be overturned.

. . .

In this case the legislature may have had ample proof that the original grant was obtained by practices which can never be too much reprobated, and which would have justifed its abrogation so far as respected those to whom crime was imputable. But the grant, when issued, conveyed an estate in fee-simple to the grantee, clothed with all the solemnities which law can bestow. This estate was transferrable; and those who purchased parts of it were not stained by that guilt which infected the original transaction. . . .

The principle asserted is, that one legislature is competent to repeal any act which a former legislature was competent to pass; and that one legislature cannot abridge the powers of a succeeding legislature.

The correctness of this principle, so far as respects general legislation, can never be controverted. But, if an act be done under a law, a succeeding legislature cannot undo it. The past cannot be recalled by the most absolute power.

Conveyances have been made, those conveyances have vested legal estates, and, if those estates may be seized by the sovereign authority, still, that they originally vested is a fact, and cannot cease to be a fact.

When, then, a law is in its nature a contract, when absolute rights have vested under that contract, a repeal of the law cannot devest those rights; ...

The validity of this rescinding act, then, might well be doubted, were Georgia a single sovereign power. But Georgia cannot be viewed as a single, unconnected, sovereign power, on whose legislature no other restrictions are imposed than may be found in its own constitution. She is a part of a large empire; she is a member of the American union; and that union has a constitution the supremacy of which all acknowledge, and which imposes limits to the legislatures of the several states, which none claim a right to pass. The constitution of the United States declares that no state shall pass any bill of attainder, *ex post facto* law, or law impairing the obligation of contracts.

. . .

A bill of attainder may affect the life of an individual, or may confiscate his property, or may do both.

In this form the power of the legislature over the lives and fortunes of individuals is expressly restrained. What motive, then, for implying, in words which import a general prohibition to impair the obligation of contracts, an exception in favour of the right to impair the obligation of those contracts into which the state may enter?

The state legislatures can pass no *ex post facto* law. An *ex post facto* law is one which renders an act punishable in a manner in which it was not punishable when it was committed. Such a law may inflict penalties on the person, or may

inflict pecuniary penalties which swell the public treasury. The legislature is then prohibited from passing a law by which a man's estate, or any part of it, shall be seized for a crime which was not declared, by some previous law, to render him liable to that punishment. Why, then, should violence be done to the natural meaning of words for the purpose of leaving to the legislature the power of seizing, for public use, the estate of an individual in the form of a law annulling the title by which he holds that estate? The court can perceive no sufficient grounds for making this distinction. This rescinding act would have the effect of an *ex post facto* law. It forfeits the estate of Fletcher for a crime not committed by himself, but by those from whom he purchased. ...

It is, then, the unanimous opinion of the court, that, in this case, the estate having passed into the hands of a purchaser for a valuable consideration, without notice, the state of Georgia was restrained, either by general principles which are common to our free institutions, or by the particular provisions of the constitution of the United States, from passing a law whereby the estate of the plaintiff in the premises so purchased could be constitutionally and legally impaired and rendered null and void.

. . .

JOHNSON, J. In this case I entertain, on two points, an opinion different from that which has been delivered by the court.

I do not hesitate to declare that a state does not possess the power of revoking its own grants. But I do it on a general principle, on the reason and nature of things: a principle which will impose laws even on the deity.

. . .

Dartmouth College v. Woodward

17 U.S. (4 Wheat.) 517 (1819)

Dartmouth College functioned as a private school, funded entirely by private donations. New Hampshire passed legislation in 1816 to increase the number of trustees at the college and thereby transfer control to appointees of the governor. The constitutional question was whether the Contract Clause prohibited the state from impairing the contract of a "private eleemosynary institution." The old trustees of Dartmouth College brought this suit against William H. Woodward, the secretary-treasurer of Dartmouth who sided with the new trustees.

February 2d, 1819. The opinion of the court was delivered by MARSHALL, Ch. J.—This is an

action of trover, brought by the Trustees of Dartmouth College against William H. Woodward, in the state court of New Hampshire, for the book of records, corporate seal, and other corporate property, to which the plaintiffs allege themselves to be entitled. A special verdict, after setting out the rights of the parties, finds for the defendant, if certain acts of the legislature of New Hampshire, passed on the 27th of June, and on the 18th of December 1816, be valid, and binding on the trustees, without their assent, and not repugnant to the constitution of the United States; otherwise, it finds for the plaintiffs. The superior court of judicature of New Hampshire rendered a judgment upon this verdict for the defendant, which judgment has been brought before this court by writ of error. The single question now to be considered is, do the acts to which the verdict refers violate the constitution of the United States?

This court can be insensible neither to the magnitude nor delicacy of this question. The validity of a legislative act is to be examined; and the opinion of the highest law tribunal of a state is to be revised—an opinion which carries with it intrinsic evidence of the diligence, of the ability, and the integrity, with which it was formed. On more than one occasion, this court has expressed the cautious circumspection with which it approaches the consideration of such questions; and has declared, that in no doubtful case, would it pronounce a legislative act to be contrary to the constitution. But the American people have said, in the constitution of the United States, that "no state shall pass any bill of attainder, *ex post facto* law, or law impairing the obligation of contracts." In the same instrument, they have also said, "that the judicial power shall extend to all cases in law and equity arising under the constitution." On the judges of this court, then, is imposed the high and solemn duty of protecting, from even legislative violation, those contracts which the constitution of our country has placed beyond legislative control; and, however irksome the task may be, this is a duty from which we dare not shrink.

The title of the plaintiffs originates in a charter dated the 13th day of December, in the year 1769, incorporating twelve persons therein mentioned, by the name of "The Trustees of Dartmouth College," granting to them and their successors the usual corporate privileges and powers, and authorizing the trustees, who are to govern the college, to fill up all vacancies which may be created in their own body.

The defendant claims under three acts of the legislature of New Hampshire, the most material

of which was passed on the 27th of June 1816, and is entitled, "an act to amend the charter, and enlarge and improve the corporation of Dartmouth College." Among other alterations in the charter, this act increases the number of trustees to twenty-one, gives the appointment of the additional members to the executive of the state, and creates a board of overseers, with power to inspect and control the most important acts of the trustees. This board consists of twenty-five persons. The president of the senate, the speaker of the house of representatives, of New Hampshire, and the governor and lieutenant-governor of Vermont, for the time being, are to be members *ex officio*. The board is to be completed by the governor and council of New Hampshire, who are also empowered to fill all vacancies which may occur. The acts of the 18th and 26th of December are supplemental to that of the 27th of June, and are principally intended to carry that act into effect. The majority of the trustees of the college have refused to accept this amended charter, and have brought this suit for the corporate property, which is in possession of a person holding by virtue of the acts which have been stated.

It can require no argument to prove, that the circumstances of this case constitute a contract. An application is made to the crown for a charter to incorporate a religious and literary institution. In the application, it is stated, that large contributions have been made for the object, which will be conferred on the corporation, as soon as it shall be created. The charter is granted, and on its faith the property is conveyed. Surely, in this transaction every ingredient of a complete and legitimate contract is to be found. The points for consideration are, 1. Is this contract protected by the constitution of the United States? 2. Is it impaired by the acts under which the defendant holds?

1. On the first point, it has been argued, that the word "contract," in its broadest sense, would comprehend the political relations between the government and its citizens, would extend to offices held within a state, for state purposes, and to many of those laws concerning civil institutions, which must change with circumstances, and be modified by ordinary legislation; which deeply concern the public, and which, to preserve good government, the public judgment must control. That even marriage is a contract, and its obligations are affected by the laws respecting divorces. That the clause in the constitution, if construed in its greatest latitude, would prohibit these laws. Taken in its broad, unlimited sense, the clause

would be an unprofitable and vexatious interference with the internal concerns of a state, would unnecessarily and unwisely embarrass its legislation, and render immutable those civil institutions, which are established for purposes of internal government, and which, to subserve those purposes, ought to vary with varying circumstances. That as the framers of the constitution could never have intended to insert in that instrument, a provision so unnecessary, so mischievous, and so repugnant to its general spirit, the term "contract" must be understood in a more limited sense. That it must be understood as intended to guard against a power, of at least doubtful utility, the abuse of which had been extensively felt; and to restrain the legislature in future from violating the right to property. That, anterior to the formation of the constitution, a course of legislation had prevailed in many, if not in all, of the states, which weakened the confidence of man in man, and embarrassed all transactions between individuals, by dispensing with a faithful performance of engagements. To correct this mischief, by restraining the power which produced it, the state legislatures were forbidden "to pass any law impairing the obligation of contracts," that is, of contracts respecting property, under which some individual could claim a right to something beneficial to himself; and that, since the clause in the constitution must in construction receive some limitation, it may be confined, and ought to be confined, to cases of this description; to cases within the mischief it was intended to remedy.

...If the act of incorporation be a grant of political power, if it create a civil institution, to be employed in the administration of the government, or if the funds of the college be public property, or if the state of New Hampshire, as a government, be alone interested in its transactions, the subject is one in which the legislature of the state may act according to its own judgment, unrestrained by any limitation of its power imposed by the constitution of the United States.

But if this be a private eleemosynary institution, endowed with a capacity to take property, for objects unconnected with government, whose funds are bestowed by individuals, on the faith of the charter; if the donors have stipulated for the future disposition and management of those funds, in the manner prescribed by themselves; there may be more difficulty in the case....

[After determining that the funds of Dartmouth College consisted entirely of private donations, Chief Justice Marshall raises broader issues.]

...Are the trustees and professors public officers, invested with any portion of political power, partaking in any degree in the administration of civil government, and performing duties which flow from the sovereign authority? That education is an object of national concern, and a proper subject of legislation, all admit. That there may be an institution, founded by government, and placed entirely under its immediate control, the officers of which would be public officers, amenable exclusively to government, none will deny. But is Dartmouth College such an institution? Is education altogether in the hands of government? Does every teacher of youth become a public officer, and do donations for the purpose of education necessarily become public property, so far that the will of the legislature, not the will of the donor, becomes the law of the donation? These questions are of serious moment to society, and deserve to be well considered.

. . .

From this review of the charter, it appears, that Dartmouth College is an eleemosynary institution, incorporated for the purpose of perpetuating the application of the bounty of the donors, to the specified objects of that bounty; that its trustees or governors were originally named by the founder, and invested with the power of perpetuating themselves; that they are not public officers, nor is it a civil institution, participating in the administration of government; but a charity school, or a seminary of education, incorporated for the preservation of its property, and the perpetual application of that property to the objects of its creation.

. . .

The opinion of the court, after mature deliberation, is, that this is a contract, the obligation of which cannot be impaired, without violating the constitution of the United States. This opinion appears to us to be equally supported by reason, and by the former decisions of this court.

2. We next proceed to the inquiry, whether its obligation has been impaired by those acts of the legislature of New Hampshire, to which the special verdict refers?

From the review of this charter, which has been taken, it appears that the whole power of governing the college, of appointing and removing tutors, of fixing their salaries, of directing the course of study to be pursued by the students, and of filling up vacancies created in their own body, was vested in the trustees. On the part of the crown, it was expressly stipulated, that this corporation, thus constituted, should continue for ever; and that the number of trustees should for ever consist of twelve, and no more. By this contract, the crown was bound, and could have made no violent alteration in its essential terms, without impairing its obligation.

By the revolution, the duties, as well as the powers, of government devolved on the people of New Hampshire. It is admitted, that among the latter was comprehended the transcendent power of parliament, as well as that of the executive department. It is too clear, to require the support of argument, that all contracts and rights respecting property, remained unchanged by the revolution. The obligations, then, which were created by the charter to Dartmouth College, were the same in the new, that they had been in the old government. The power of the government was also the same. A repeal of this charter, at any time prior to the adoption of the present constitution of the United States, would have been an extraordinary and unprecedented act of power, but one which could have been contested only by the restrictions upon the legislature, to be found in the constitution of the state. But the constitution of the United States has imposed this additional limitation, that the legislature of a state shall pass no act "impairing the obligation of contracts."

. . .

It results from this opinion, that the acts of the legislature of New Hampshire, which are stated in the special verdict found in this cause, are repugnant to the constitution of the United States; and that the judgment on this special verdict ought to have been for the plaintiffs. The judgment of the state court must, therefore, be reversed.

WASHINGTON, Justice.—[Concurred.]

JOHNSON, Justice, concurred, for the reasons stated by the Chief Justice.

LIVINGSTON, Justice, concurred, for the reasons stated by the Chief Justice, and Justices WASHINGTON and STORY.

Story, Justice.—[Concurred.]

DUVALL, Justice, dissented.

Charles River Bridge v. Warren Bridge

36 U.S. (11 Pet.) 419 (1837)

In 1785 the legislature of Massachusetts incorporated a company ("The Proprietors of the Charles River Bridge") to build a bridge and accept tolls. Decades later it established "The Proprietors of the Warren Bridge" to build a bridge nearby; over the course of time this bridge became free to travelers. The first bridge filed a lawsuit, claiming that the legislature had impaired the obligation of a contract. This significant decision by Chief Justice Taney balances the rights of private property against the public's need for economic development.

TANEY, Ch. J., delivered the opinion of the court.—The questions involved in this case are of the gravest character, and the court have given to them the most anxious and deliberate consideration. The value of the right claimed by the plaintiffs is large in amount; and many persons may, no doubt, be seriously affected in their pecuniary interests, by any decision which the court may pronounce; and the questions which have been raised as to the power of the several states, in relation to the corporations they have chartered, are pregnant with important consequences; not only to the individuals who are concerned in the corporate franchises, but to the communities in which they exist. The court are fully sensible, that it is their duty, in exercising the high powers conferred on them by the constitution of the United States, to deal with these great and extensive interests, with the utmost caution; guarding, so far as they have the power to do so, the rights of property, and at the same time, carefully abstaining from any encroachment on the rights reserved to the states.

. . .

The plaintiffs in error insist, mainly, upon two grounds: 1st. That by virtue of the grant of 1650, Harvard College was entitled, in perpetuity, to the right of keeping a ferry between Charlestown and Boston; that this right was exclusive; and that the legislature had not the power to establish another ferry on the same line of travel, because it would infringe the rights of the college; and that these rights, upon the erection of the bridge in the place of the ferry, under the charter of 1785, were transferred to, and became vested in "The Proprietors of the Charles River Bridge;" and that under, and by virtue of this transfer of the ferry-right, the rights of the bridge company were as exclusive in that line of travel, as the rights of the ferry. 2d. That independently of the ferry-right, the acts of the legislature of Massachusetts, of 1785 and 1792, by their true construction, necessarily implied, that the legislature would not authorize another bridge, and especially, a free one, by the side of this, and placed in the same line of travel, whereby the franchise granted to the "Proprietors of the Charles River Bridge" should be rendered of no value; and the plaintiffs in error contend, that the grant of the ferry to the college, and of the charter to the proprietors of the bridge, are both contracts on the part of the state; and that the law authorizing the erection of the Warren bridge in 1828, impairs the obligation of one or both of these contracts.

... [I]t is apparent, that the plaintiffs in error cannot sustain themselves here, either upon the ferry-right, or the charter to the bridge; upon the ground, that vested rights of property have been divested by the legislature. And whether they claim under the ferry-right, or the charter to the bridge, they must show that the title which they claim, was acquired by contract, and that the terms of that contract have been violated by the charter to the Warren bridge. In other words, they must show, that the state had entered into a contract with them, or those under whom they claim, not to establish a free bridge at the place where the Warren bridge is erected. Such, and such only, are the principles upon which the plaintiffs in error can claim relief in this case.

. . .

But upon what ground can the plaintiffs in error contend, that the ferry-rights of the college have been transferred to the proprietors of the bridge? If they have been thus transferred, it must be by some mode of transfer known to the law; and the evidence relied on to prove it, can be pointed out in the record. How was it transferred? It is not suggested, that there ever was, in point of fact, a deed of conveyance executed by the college to the bridge company. Is there any evidence in the record, from which such a conveyance may,

upon legal principle, be presumed? The testimony before the court, so far from laying the foundation for such a presumption, repels it, in the most positive terms....

. . .

This brings us to the act of the legislature of Massachusetts, of 1785, by which the plaintiffs were incorporated by the name of "The Proprietors of the Charles River Bridge;" and it is here, and in the law of 1792, prolonging their charter, that we must look for the extent and nature of the franchise conferred upon the plaintiffs. Much has been said in the argument of the principles of construction by which this law is to be expounded, and what undertakings, on the part of the state, may be implied. The court think there can be no serious difficulty on that head. It is the grant of certain franchises, by the public, to a private corporation, and in a matter where the public interest is concerned....

... [T]he object and end of all government is to promote the happiness and prosperity of the community by which it is established; and it can never be assumed, that the government intended to diminish its power of accomplishing the end for which it was created. And in a country like ours, free, active and enterprising, continually advancing in numbers and wealth, new channels of communication are daily found necessary, both for travel and trade, and are essential to the comfort, convenience and prosperity of the people. A state ought never to be presumed to surrender this power, because, like the taxing power, the whole community have an interest in preserving it undiminished. And when a corporation alleges, that a state has surrendered, for seventy years, its power of improvement and public accommodation, in a great and important line of travel, along which a vast number of its citizens must daily pass, the community have a right to insist, in the language of this court, above quoted, "that its abandonment ought not to be presumed, in a case, in which the deliberate purpose of the state to abandon it does not appear." The continued existence of a government would be of no great value, if, by implications and presumptions, it was disarmed of the powers necessary to accomplish the ends of its creation, and the functions it was designed to perform, transferred to the hands of privileged corporations.... While the rights of private property are sacredly guarded, we must not forget, that the community also have rights, and that the happiness and well-being of every citizen depends on their faithful preservation.

Adopting the rule of construction above stated as the settled one, we proceed to apply it to the charter of 1785, to the proprietors of the Charles River bridge. This act of incorporation is in the usual form, and the privileges such as are commonly given to corporations of that kind. It confers on them the ordinary faculties of a corporation, for the purpose of building the bridge; and establishes certain rates of toll, which the company are authorized to take: this is the whole grant. There is no exclusive privilege given to them over the waters of Charles river, above or below their bridge; no right to erect another bridge themselves, nor to prevent other persons from erecting one; no engagement from the state, that another shall not be erected; and no undertaking not to sanction competition, nor to make improvements that may diminish the amount of its income. Upon all these subjects, the charter is silent; and nothing is said in it about a line of travel, so much insisted on in the argument, in which they are to have exclusive privileges. No words are used, from which an intention to grant any of these rights can be inferred; if the plaintiff is entitled to them, it must be implied, simply, from the nature of the grant; and cannot be inferred, from the words by which the grant is made.

The relative position of the Warren bridge has already been described. It does not interrupt the passage over the Charles River bridge, nor make the way to it, or from it, less convenient. None of the faculties or franchises granted to that corporation, have been revoked by the legislature; and its right to take the tolls granted by the charter remains unaltered. In short, all the franchises and rights of property, enumerated in the charter, and there mentioned to have been granted to it, remain unimpaired. But its income is destroyed by the Warren bridge; which, being free, draws off the passengers and property which would have gone over it, and renders their franchise of no value. This is the gist of the complainant; for it is not pretended, that the erection of the Warren bridge would have done them any injury, or in any degree affected their right of property, if it had not diminished the amount of their tolls. In order, then, to entitle themselves to relief, it is necessary to show, that the legislature contracted not to do the act of which they complain; and that they impaired, or in other words, violated, that contract, by the erection of the Warren bridge.

The inquiry, then, is, does the charter contain such a contract on the part of the state? Is there any such stipulation to be found in that instrument? It must be admitted on all hands, that there is none; no words that even relate to another bridge, or to the diminution of their tolls, or to the line of travel. . . .

Indeed, the practice and usage of almost every state in the Union, old enough to have commenced the work of internal improvement, is opposed to the doctrine contended for on the part of the plaintiffs in error. Turnpike roads have been made in succession, on the same line of travel; the later ones interfering materially with the profits of the first. These corporations have, in some instances, been utterly ruined by the introduction of newer and better modes of transportation and traveling. In some cases, railroads have rendered the turnpike roads on the same line of travel so entirely useless, that the franchise of the turnpike corporation is not worth preserving. Yet in none of these cases have the corporation supposed that their privileges were invaded, or any contract violated on the part of the state. . . .

The judgment of the supreme judicial court of the commonwealth of Massachusetts, dismissing the plaintiffs' bill, must, therefore, be affirmed, with costs.

McLEAN, Justice. *[Favored dismissing the case for lack of jurisdiction.]*

BALDWIN, Justice. — *[Concurred.]*

STORY, Justice. *(Dissenting.)*

. . .

But it has been argued, and the argument has been pressed in every form which ingenuity could suggest, that if grants of this nature are to be construed liberally, as conferring any exclusive rights on the grantees, it will interpose an effectual barrier against all general improvements of the country. For myself, I profess not to feel the cogency of this argument, either in its general application to the grant of franchises, or in its special application to the present grant. This is a subject upon which different minds may well arrive at different conclusions, both as to policy and principle. Men may, and will, complexionally differ upon topics of this sort, according to their natural and acquired habits of speculation and opinion. For my own part, I can conceive of no surer plan to arrest all public improvements, founded on private capital and enterprise, than to make the outlay of that capital uncertain and questionable, both as to security and as to productiveness. No man will hazard his capital in any enterprise, in which, if there be a loss, it must be borne exclusively by himself; and if there be success, he has not the slightest security of enjoying the rewards of that success, for a single moment. If the government means to invite its citizens to enlarge the public comforts and conveniences, to establish bridges, or turnpikes, or canals, or railroads, there must be some pledge, that the property will be safe; that the enjoyment will be co-extensive with the grant; and that success will not be the signal of a general combination to overthrow its rights and to take away its profits....

. . .

Upon the whole, my judgment is, that the act of the legislature of Massachusetts granting the charter of Warren Bridge, is an act impairing the obligation of the prior contract and grant to the proprietors of Charles River bridge; and, by the constitution of the United States, it is, therefore, utterly void....

THOMPSON, Justice.—The opinion delivered by my brother, Mr. Justice STORY, I have read over and deliberately considered. On this full consideration, I concur entirely in all the principles and reasonings contained in it; and I am of opinion, the decree of the supreme judicial court of Massachusetts should be reversed.

Home Bldg. & Loan Assn. v. Blaisdell
290 U.S. 398 (1934)

A Minnesota statute, enacted in 1933, declared that the Great Depression created an emergency demanding an exercise of the police power to protect the public and promote the general welfare. It temporarily extended the time allowed by existing law for redeeming real property from foreclosure and sale under existing mortgages. It became known as the Minnesota Mortgage Moratorium Law. At issue was Article I, § 10, of the U.S. Constitution, which provides that no state shall pass any law "impairing the Obligation of Contracts." Could this constitutional prohibition be waived during time of emergency? A married couple, John H. and Rosella Blaisdell, complained that the Minnesota statute deprived them of their rights under a lawful private mortgage contract by arbitrarily changing its terms.

MR. CHIEF JUSTICE HUGHES delivered the opinion of the Court.

Appellant contests the validity of Chapter 339 of the Laws of Minnesota of 1933, p. 514, approved April 18, 1933, called the Minnesota Mortgage Moratorium Law, as being repugnant to the contract clause (Art. I, § 10) and the due process and equal protection clauses of the Fourteenth Amendment, of the Federal Constitution....

[The Law provided for judicial relief with respect to foreclosures of mortgages and execution sales of real estate. Sales could be postponed and redemption periods extended. The Law remained in effect "only during the continuance of the emergency and in no event beyond May 1, 1935." The Court was concerned with the provisions authorizing the district court of the county to extend the period of redemption from foreclosure sales.]

Invoking the relevant provision of the statute, appellees applied to the District Court of Hennepin County for an order extending the period of redemption from a foreclosure sale. Their petition stated that they owned a lot in Minneapolis

which they had mortgaged to appellant; that the mortgage contained a valid power of sale by advertisement and that by reason of their default the mortgage had been foreclosed and sold to appellant on May 2, 1932, for $3700.98; that appellant was the holder of the sheriff's certificate of sale; that because of the economic depression appellees had been unable to obtain a new loan or to redeem, and that unless the period of redemption were extended the property would be irretrievably lost; and that the reasonable value of the property greatly exceeded the amount due on the mortgage including all liens, costs and expenses.

On the hearing, appellant objected to the introduction of evidence upon the ground that the statute was invalid under the federal and state constitutions, and moved that the petition be dismissed. The motion was granted and a motion for a new trial was denied. On appeal, the Supreme Court of the State reversed the decision of the District Court....

[The trial court extended the period of redemption to May 1, 1935, and ordered Blaisdell to pay

the loan association a certain amount each month over that period.]

The state court upheld the statute as an emergency measure. Although conceding that the obligations of the mortgage contract were impaired, the court decided that what it thus described as an impairment was, notwithstanding the contract clause of the Federal Constitution, within the police power of the State as that power was called into exercise by the public economic emergency which the legislature had found to exist....

In determining whether the provision for this temporary and conditional relief exceeds the power of the State by reason of the clause in the Federal Constitution prohibiting impairment of the obligations of contracts, we must consider the relation of emergency to constitutional power, the historical setting of the contract clause, the development of the jurisprudence of this Court in the construction of that clause, and the principles of construction which we may consider to be established.

Emergency does not create power. Emergency does not increase granted power or remove or diminish the restrictions imposed upon power granted or reserved. The Constitution was adopted in a period of grave emergency. Its grants of power to the Federal Government and its limitations of the power of the States were determined in the light of emergency and they are not altered by emergency. What power was thus granted and what limitations were thus imposed are questions which have always been, and always will be, the subject of close examination under our constitutional system.

While emergency does not create power, emergency may furnish the occasion for the exercise of power. "Although an emergency may not call into life a power which has never lived, nevertheless emergency may afford a reason for the exertion of a living power already enjoyed." *Wilson v. New,* 243 U.S. 332, 348.... [E]mergency would not permit a State to have more than two Senators in the Congress, or permit the election of President by a general popular vote without regard to the number of electors to which the States are respectively entitled, or permit the States to "coin money" or to "make anything but gold and silver coin a tender in payment of debts." But where constitutional grants and limitations of power are set forth in general clauses, which afford a broad outline, the process of construction is essential to fill in the details. That is true of the contract clause....

In the construction of the contract clause, the debates in the Constitutional Convention are of little aid. But the reasons which led to the adoption of that clause, and of the other prohibitions of Section 10 of Article I, are not left in doubt and have frequently been described with eloquent emphasis. The widespread distress following the revolutionary period, and the plight of debtors, had called forth in the States an ignoble array of legislative schemes for the defeat of creditors and the invasion of contractual obligations. Legislative interferences had been so numerous and extreme that the confidence essential to prosperous trade had been undermined and the utter destruction of credit was threatened. "The sober people of America" were convinced that some "thorough reform" was needed which would "inspire a general prudence and industry, and give a regular course to the business of society." *The Federalist,* No. 44. It was necessary to interpose the restraining power of a central authority in order to secure the foundations even of "private faith."...

But full recognition of the occasion and general purpose of the clause does not suffice to fix its precise scope. Nor does an examination of the details of prior legislation in the States yield criteria which can be considered controlling. To ascertain the scope of the constitutional prohibition we examine the course of judicial decisions in its application. These put it beyond question that the prohibition is not an absolute one and is not to be read with literal exactness like a mathematical formula....

Not only is the constitutional provision qualified by the measure of control which the State retains over remedial processes, but the State also continues to possess authority to safeguard the vital interests of its people. It does not matter that legislation appropriate to that end "has the result of modifying or abrogating contracts already in effect." *Stephenson v. Binford,* 287 U.S. 251, 276. Not only are existing laws read into contracts in order to fix obligations as between the parties, but the reservation of essential attributes of sovereign power is also read into contracts as a postulate of the legal order. The policy of protecting contracts against impairment presupposes the maintenance of a government by virtue of which contractual relations are worth while,—a government which retains adequate authority to secure the peace and good order of society. This principle of harmonizing the constitutional prohibition with the necessary residuum of state power has had progressive recognition in the decisions of this Court.

While the charters of private corporations constitute contracts, a grant of exclusive privilege is not to be implied as against the State. *Charles River Bridge* v. *Warren Bridge,* 11 Pet. 420. And all contracts are subject to the right of eminent domain. *West River Bridge* v. *Dix,* 6 How. 507. The reservation of this necessary authority of the State is deemed to be a part of the contract....

It is no answer to say that this public need was not apprehended a century ago, or to insist that what the provision of the Constitution meant to the vision of that day it must mean to the vision of our time. If by the statement that what the Constitution meant at the time of its adoption it means to-day, it is intended to say that the great clauses of the Constitution must be confined to the interpretation which the framers, with the conditions and outlook of their time, would have placed upon them, the statement carries its own refutation. It was to guard against such a narrow conception that Chief Justice Marshall uttered the memorable warning — "We must never forget that it is a *constitution* we are expounding" (*McCulloch* v. *Maryland,* 4 Wheat. 316, 407) — "a constitution intended to endure for ages to come, and consequently, to be adapted to the various *crises* of human affairs." *Id.,* p. 415. When we are dealing with the words of the Constitution, said this Court in *Missouri* v. *Holland,* 252 U.S. 416, 433, "we must realize that they have called into life a being the development of which could not have been foreseen completely by the most gifted of its begetters.... The case before us must be considered in the light of our whole experience and not merely in that of what was said a hundred years ago."

. . .

We are of the opinion that the Minnesota statute as here applied does not violate the contract clause of the Federal Constitution. Whether the legislation is wise or unwise as a matter of policy is a question with which we are not concerned.

. . .

MR. JUSTICE SUTHERLAND, dissenting.

Few questions of greater moment than that just decided have been submitted for judicial inquiry during this generation. He simply closes his eyes to the necessary implications of the decision who fails to see in it the potentiality of future gradual but ever-advancing encroachments upon the sanctity of private and public contracts. The effect of the Minnesota legislation, though serious enough in itself, is of trivial significance compared with the far more serious and dangerous inroads

upon the limitations of the Constitution which are almost certain to ensue as a consequence naturally following any step beyond the boundaries fixed by that instrument. And those of us who are thus apprehensive of the effect of this decision would, in a matter so important, be neglectful of our duty should we fail to spread upon the permanent records of the court the reasons which move us to the opposite view.

A provision of the Constitution, it is hardly necessary to say, does not admit of two distinctly opposite interpretations. It does not mean one thing at one time and an entirely different thing at another time. If the contract impairment clause, when framed and adopted, meant that the terms of a contract for the payment of money could not be altered *in invitum* by a state statute enacted for the relief of hardly pressed debtors to the end and with the effect of postponing payment or enforcement during and because of an economic or financial emergency, it is but to state the obvious to say that it means the same now.... The true rule was forcefully declared in *Ex parte Milligan,* 4 Wall. 2, 120–121, in the face of circumstances of national peril and public unrest and disturbance far greater than any that exist today.... [I]n words the power and truth of which have become increasingly evident with the lapse of time, there was laid down the rule without which the Constitution would cease to be the "supreme law of the land," binding equally upon governments and governed at all times and under all circumstances, and become a mere collection of political maxims to be adhered to or disregarded according to the prevailing sentiment or the legislative and judicial opinion in respect of the supposed necessities of the hour:

"The Constitution of the United States is a law for rulers and people, equally in war and in peace, and covers with the shield of its protection all classes of men, at all times, and under all circumstances. No doctrine, involving more pernicious consequences, was ever invented by the wit of man than that any of its provisions can be suspended during any of the great exigencies of government. Such a doctrine leads directly to anarchy or despotism,..."

Chief Justice Taney, in *Dred Scott* v. *Sandford,* 19 How. 393, 426, said that while the Constitution remains unaltered it must be construed now as it was understood at the time of its adoption; that it is not only the same in words but the same in meaning, "and as long as it continues to exist in its present form, it speaks not only in the same words, but with the same meaning and intent with which it spoke when it came from the hands of its framers, and was voted on and adopted by the people of the United States. Any other rule of construction would abrogate the judicial character of this court, and make it the mere reflex of the popular opinion or passion of the day." ...

The provisions of the Federal Constitution, undoubtedly, are pliable in the sense that in ap-propriate cases they have the capacity of bringing within their grasp every new condition which falls within their meaning. But, their *meaning* is changeless; it is only their *application* which is extensible. ...

. . .

I am authorized to say that MR. JUSTICE VAN DEVANTER, MR. JUSTICE MCREYNOLDS and MR. JUSTICE BUTLER concur in this opinion.

C. THE TAKING CLAUSE

Under the Fifth Amendment, private property shall not "be taken for public use, without just compensation." This is referred to variously as the Taking Clause, the Public Use Clause, or the Just Compensation Clause. Under the Due Process Clause of the Fourteenth Amendment, as well as under their own constitutions, states are also forbidden from taking private property for public use without just compensation. Chicago, B. & Q. R.R. Co. v. Chicago, 166 U.S. 226, 236–37, 241 (1897). The taking of property constitutes an exercise of the power of eminent domain, which gives the sovereign the right to condemn or expropriate private property for a public purpose upon payment of just compensation.

The decision to invoke the power of eminent domain is purely a legislative function. Whether compensation is "just" or whether property has been taken for "public use" are questions that might be taken to the courts. Every deprivation of property does not require compensation. PruneYard Shopping Center v. Robins, 447 U.S. 74, 82 (1980). Even when compensation must be paid, a plethora of 5–4 decisions by the Supreme Court demonstrate fundamental disagreements about the proper method of calculating what is "just."[5]

The Scope of Property

The dimensions of land property are of broad and changing scope. The ancient *ad coelum* doctrine gave landowners control of their property downward to the core of the earth and upward to the heavens. A landowner's rights to the column of air above his land led to successful actions against overhanging eaves, protruding structures, and the firing of projectiles or the stringing of wires across someone's land. Portsmouth Co. v. United States, 260 U.S. 327 (1922). Another case involved a deed under which a coal company conveyed land surface to homeowners but reserved the right to remove all the coal under the property. Any damages to the surface resulting from mining were waived. The homeowners tried to prevent the company from burrowing under their property and removing supporting structures for their house and land. Despite the existence of a state statute passed after the deed, forbidding mining that would cause land under a home to sink, an 8–1 decision by the Supreme Court held that the police power could not protect shortsighted homeowners who acquired only surface rights. Pennsylvania Coal Co. v. Mahon, 260 U.S. 393 (1922).

Homeowners in the vicinity of transportation systems may be entitled to some compensation for damages. Landowners next to a railroad tunnel had no right to be compensated for normal operations (vibration from trains and the emission of smoke, cinders, and gases). However, they were entitled to the recovery of some damages if fans within the tunnel pumped ad-

---

5. United States v. Fuller, 409 U.S. 488 (1973); Almota Farmers Elevator & Whse. Co. v. United States, 409 U.S. 470 (1973); United States v. Cors, 337 U.S. 325 (1949); United States ex rel. TVA v. Powelson, 319 U.S. 266 (1943).

ditional smoke and gases onto their property. Richards v. Washington Terminal Co., 233 U.S. 546 (1914). If military bombers skim so close to a person's home and chicken farm that chickens are killed by crashing into the walls from fright and homeowners are unable to sleep, the flights constitute a "taking" of property requiring just compensation. United States v. Causby, 328 U.S. 256 (1946). See also Griggs v. Allegheny County, 369 U.S. 84 (1962).[6]

War, Regulation, and Zoning

Under conditions of war, private property may be demolished to prevent use by the enemy. Compensation need not be given to the owner. United States v. Caltex, 344 U.S. 149 (1952). Through its power to regulate commerce and other matters, Congress may diminish the value of private property without triggering the Taking Clause. The Supreme Court noted in 1986 that Congress "routinely creates burdens for some that directly benefit others." In setting minimum wages, controlling prices, or regulating other actions, "it cannot be said that the Taking Clause is violated whenever legislation requires one person to use his or her assets for the benefit of another." Connolly v. Pension Benefit Guaranty Corp., 475 U.S. at 223. Statutes may be interpreted as merely regulatory rather than a taking. FCC v. Florida Power Corp., 480 U.S. 245 (1987). When property is diminished without a taking, the decision to provide compensation is a question for the legislative branch, not the courts. Batten v. United States, 306 F.2d 580, 585 (10th Cir. 1962).

Zoning laws may restrict, diminish, or destroy the value of property, but they do not necessarily represent a taking. Communities use zoning ordinances as part of the police power to promote public health, safety, and morals. Restrictions are placed on the height of buildings and the materials and methods of construction, and certain industries are excluded from residential areas. These regulations usually do not represent unconstitutional deprivations of property or takings.[7] Zoning ordinances that attempted to segregate neighborhoods on the basis of race have been struck down as unconstitutional. Buchanan v. Warley, 245 U.S. 60 (1917). Moreover, zoning ordinances that arbitrarily or unreasonably interfere with a family's right to remain as a unit within their home have been declared unconstitutional. Moore v. East Cleveland, 431 U.S. 494 (1977).

Zoning ordinances apply equally to all property owners in a designated area. However, laws passed to preserve historic buildings and neighborhoods affect only particular property owners. Any alterations to these structures must be approved by local officials or commissions. In a case decided by the Supreme Court in 1978, a company claimed that the application of New York City's landmarks law to the Grand Central Terminal constituted a taking of property in violation of the Fifth and Fourteenth Amendments. The decision, which denied that property had been taken, reveals the difficulty the Court has experienced in defining the meaning of the Taking Clause. PENN CENTRAL TRANSP. CO. v. NEW YORK CITY, 438 U.S. 104 (1978).

Although the Taking Clause of the Fifth Amendment applies to the states, state courts may reach a different result by deciding cases entirely upon their own constitutions. For example,

---

6. Other "taking" cases include Andrus v. Allard, 444 U.S. 51 (1979); United States v. Reynolds, 397 U.S. 14 (1970); YMCA v. United States, 395 U.S. 85 (1969); Goldblatt v. Hempstead, 369 U.S. 590 (1962); Armstrong v. United States, 364 U.S. 40 (1960); United States v. Central Eureka Mining Co., 357 U.S. 155 (1958); Berman v. Parker, 348 U.S. 26 (1954); United States v. Petty Motor Co., 327 U.S. 372 (1946); Miller v. Schoene, 276 U.S. 272 (1928); Hadacheck v. Sebastian, 239 U.S. 394 (1915).

7. San Diego Gas & Electric Co. v. San Diego, 450 U.S. 621 (1981); Agins v. Tiburon, 447 U.S. 255 (1980); Village of Belle Terre v. Boraas, 416 U.S. 1 (1974); Zahn v. Bd. of Public Works, 274 U.S. 325 (1927); Euclid v. Ambler Co., 272 U.S. 365 (1926); Welch v. Swasey, 214 U.S. 91 (1909). See also MacDonald, Sommer & Frates v. Yolo County, 477 U.S. 340 (1986) and Williamson Planning Comm'n v. Hamilton Bank, 473 U.S. 172 (1985), for the ripeness hurdle that can prevent courts from reaching the taking issue.

Recent Taking Cases

A state may not force landlords to permit a company to install cable television in return for nominal payments (such as a one-time one-dollar payment). The permanent physical occupation of an owner's property constitutes a taking and requires just compensation.	Loretto v. Teleprompter Manhattan CATV Corp., 458 U.S. 419 (1972).
If a private developer deepens a pond to form a marina and connects it to a navigable bay used by the public, the marina loses its character as a private property. However, if the government wishes to make the marina a public aquatic park, it must pay just compensation.	Kaiser Aetna v. United States, 444 U.S. 164 (1979).
Company data supplied to the government in the form of trade secrets can be treated as property entitled to protection under the Taking Clause.	Ruckelshaus v. Monsanto Co., 467 U.S. 986 (1984).
Coal companies failed to show that a taking had occurred when a state required that 50 percent of the coal beneath statutorily protected structures had to be kept in place to provide surface support.	Keystone Bituminous Coal Assn. v. DeBenedictis, 480 U.S. 470 (1987).
"Temporary" takings are impermissible. Once a taking has been determined, government must compensate the owner for the period during which the taking was effective.	First English Evangelical Lutheran Church v. Los Angeles County, 482 U.S. 304 (1987).
As a condition for permitting someone to replace a small bungalow on their beachfront lot with a larger house, a state may not insist that the owners allow the public to pass across their beach, which was located between two public beaches.	Nollan v. California Coastal Commission, 483 U.S. 825 (1987).

in 1991 the Supreme Court of Pennsylvania held that there had been an unconstitutional taking when a historical preservation commission for Philadelphia designated a theater building as historic over the objections of its owner. The Court decided that the costs associated with preserving historic buildings should be borne by all taxpayers rather than by the individual property owner. United Artists v. Historical Com'n, 595 A.2d 6 (Pa. 1991).

Contemporary Disputes

Recent cases highlight the complexity and broad reach of the Taking Clause (see box). In a controversial case in 1984, the Court held that the use of eminent domain to condemn land as a means of redistributing private property and combating oligarchy is a valid "public use." HAWAII HOUSING AUTHORITY v. MIDKIFF, 467 U.S. 229 (1984).

Several cases in 1992 promised to provide greater protection to property owners under the Taking Clause, but the merits were not squarely reached. In one case a unanimous Court merely held that a rent-control ordinance did not amount to a *physical* taking of the property of owners of a mobile home park. The Court concluded that the ordinance might have caused a *regulatory* taking, but that issue was not properly before the Court. Yee v. Escondido, 503 U.S. 519 (1992). A more significant ruling that year narrowed the rights of states to rely on regulatory takings that completely deprive individuals of the economic use of their property. In this case an individual bought two oceanfront lots with the intent to build homes on them, but two years later the South Carolina legislature passed environmental regulations that prohibited development of the property. As a result of the Court's ruling, South Carolina had to identify nuisance and property laws in force at the time the oceanfront lots were purchased. To be exempt from compensating a property owner, the state would have to claim more than a general public interest or an interest in preventing serious public harm. Lucas v. South Carolina Coastal Council, 505 U.S. 1003 (1992). As explained in the next section, this case took odd turns when it went back to South Carolina.

A 1994 ruling by the Supreme Court broadened property rights by announcing that land use requirements may be "takings." The 5–4 decision dealt with the practice of local governments giving property owners a permit for building a development only on the condition that they donate part of their land for parks, bike paths, and other public purposes. These conditions will now be valid only if the local government makes "some sort of individualized determination that the required dedication is related both in nature and extent to the impact of the proposed development." Dolan v. City of Tigard, 512 U.S. 374, 391 (1994). Other recent decisions on the taking of property include Babbitt v. Youpee, 519 U.S. 234 (1997); Suitum v. Tahoe Regional Planning Agency, 520 U.S. 725 (1997); Phillips v. Washington Legal Foundation, 524 U.S. 156 (1998); Eastern Enterprises v. Apfel, 524 U.S. 498 (1998); and City of Monterey v. Del Monte Dunes, 526 U.S. 687 (1999). The last three were 5–4 decisions, underscoring the Court's inability to agree on constitutional principles.

Following the Trail

As with other Supreme Court decisions, one never knows how big a gap will emerge between what the Court says and what happens next. *Lucas* v. *South Carolina Coastal Council* (1992) supposedly featured a collision between two forces, with the state ("the Environmentalist") preventing David Lucas from doing any construction on his two beachfront lots. After the Court reversed and remanded, South Carolina was unable to prove that the building contemplated by Lucas would constitute a common law nuisance. A settlement of $1.5 million paid Lucas $425,000 for each lot and covered his interest and legal fees. After deducting mortgage and costs, he walked away with less than $100,000. What did South Carolina do with the two lots? Keep them pristine and untouched by the worker's hand? Not at all. First it rejected a bid from one of Lucas's neighbors, who offered $315,000 for one of the lots to prevent any building on it. The state then accepted $392,500 per lot from a construction company which intended to develop the property, precisely what the state had prohibited Lucas from doing. Thus, a case that started out with South Carolina adamantly opposed to any construction on oceanfront property did a full reverse after the Court's opinion. Gideon Kanner, "Not with a Bang, but a Giggle: The Settlement of the Lucas Case," in David L. Callies, ed., Takings 308–11 (1996).

Congressional Action

Congress has considered legislation in recent years to require federal agencies to determine whether their regulatory activities amount to a taking of private property. The purpose is either to compel government to compensate property owners or to force agencies to scale back their regulations. The Senate passed this type of requirement in 1991, building on Executive Order 12630 issued by President Reagan in 1988, but the Senate language was not enacted. 137 Cong. Rec. S7539–62 (daily ed. June 12, 1991); 53 Fed. Reg. 8859 (1988).

The "Contract with America," announced by more than three hundred Republican candidates for the U.S. House of Representatives on September 27, 1994, called for a number of reforms to limit government and expand individual rights. One of the provisions sought to protect private property owners by compensating them for all but very small reductions in the value of their property that were caused by government regulation. The draft bill provided that a private property owner "is entitled" to receive compensation and the head of an agency "shall pay" a private property owner any compensation required.

However, when it became apparent that full compensation for such losses would add heavily to the federal deficit and complicate other Republican goals (such as a balanced budget), the bill was modified by removing the concept of an entitlement. As passed by the House, the private property bill stated that the federal government "shall" compensate anyone whose private property had been diminished in value by at least twenty percent. Yet the government's liability was sharply reduced by other language in the bill. No compensation would be made if an agency's primary purpose was to prevent an identifiable hazard to public health or safety, or if the owner's proposed use of land would have been a nuisance. Moreover, if a citizen presented a claim, the agency had the option of paying the amount or seeking reimbursement from another agency that shared responsibility. If an agency said that it had no money to pay the claim, the only obligation at that point would be for the agency head to ask Congress for an appropriation. Congress would have no obligation (except perhaps a moral one) to appropriate anything. The Senate never acted on the bill or any variation of it.

In 1997, the House passed a bill to expedite access to the federal courts for private parties claiming a violation of the Taking Clause. 143 Cong. Rec. H8938–64 (daily ed. October 22, 1997). The Senate did not bring this bill up for a vote. In 1998, the House passed another version of this legislation. 144 Cong. Rec. H1085–94, H1135–40 (daily ed. March 11–12, 1998). The Senate failed to act on this bill either. Opponents objected that federal courts would make decisions better left to local zoning authorities and state courts. In 2000, the House passed legislation for expedited access to federal courts to challenge deprivations of private property by governmental actions. 146 Cong. Rec. H1089-114 (daily ed. March 16, 2000).

Penn Central Transp. Co. v. New York City

438 U.S. 104 (1978)

New York City passed legislation to protect historic landmarks and neighborhoods from quick decisions that might destroy or fundamentally alter their character. The law authorized a commission to designate a building to be a "landmark" on a particular "landmark site." The Grand Central Terminal, owned by the Penn Central Transportation Co., was designated a landmark and the block it occupies as a "landmark site." When the commission rejected Penn Central's plans to construct a multistory office building over the terminal, Penn Central brought suit in state court claiming that the application of the landmarks law had "taken" its property without just compensation in violation of the Fifth and Fourteenth Amendments and arbitrarily deprived it of its property without due process of law in violation of the Fourteenth Amendment. In this decision the Court attempts to identify principles that establish when state regulatory burdens become a "taking."

MR. JUSTICE BRENNAN delivered the opinion of the Court.

. . .

II

The issues presented by appellants are (1) whether the restrictions imposed by New York City's law upon appellants' exploitation of the Terminal site effect a "taking" of appellants' property for a public use within the meaning of the Fifth Amendment, which of course is made applicable to the States through the Fourteenth Amendment, see *Chicago, B. & Q. R. Co. v. Chicago,* 166 U.S. 226, 239 (1897), and, (2), if so, whether the transferable development rights afforded appellants constitute "just compensation" within the meaning of the Fifth Amendment. We need only address the question whether a "taking" has occurred.

A

Before considering appellants' specific contentions, it will be useful to review the factors that have shaped the jurisprudence of the Fifth Amendment injunction "nor shall private property be taken for public use, without just compensation." The question of what constitutes a "taking" for purposes of the Fifth Amendment has proved to be a problem of considerable difficulty. While this Court has recognized that the "Fifth Amendment's guarantee ... (is) designed to bar Government from forcing some people alone to bear public burdens which, in all fairness and justice, should be borne by the public as a whole," *Armstrong* v. *United States,* 364 U.S. 40, 49 (1960), this Court, quite simply, has been unable to develop any "set formula" for determining when "justice and fairness" require that economic injuries caused by public action be compensated by the government, rather than remain disproportionately concentrated on a few persons....

In engaging in these essentially ad hoc, factual inquiries, the Court's decisions have identified several factors that have particular significance. The economic impact of the regulation on the claimant and, particularly, the extent to which the regulation has interfered with distinct investment-backed expectations are, of course, relevant considerations.... So, too, is the character of the governmental action. A "taking" may more readily be found when the interference with property can be characterized as a physical invasion by government, see, *e. g., United States* v. *Causby,* 328 U.S. 256 (1946), than when interference arises from some public program adjusting the benefits and burdens of economic life to promote the common good.

"Government hardly could go on if to some extent values incident to property could not be diminished without paying for every such change in the general law," *Pennsylvania Coal Co.* v. *Mahon,* 260 U.S. 393, 413 (1922), and this Court has accordingly recognized, in a wide variety of contexts, that government may execute laws or programs that adversely affect recognized economic values. Exercises of the taxing power are one obvious example. A second are the decisions in which this Court has dismissed "taking" challenges on the ground that, while the challenged government action caused economic harm, it did not interfere with interests that were sufficiently bound up with the reasonable expectations of the claimant to constitute "property" for Fifth Amendment purposes....

More importantly for the present case, in instances in which a state tribunal reasonably concluded that "the health, safety, morals, or general welfare" would be promoted by prohibiting particular contemplated uses of land, this Court has upheld land-use regulations that destroyed or adversely affected recognized real property interests. See *Nectow* v. *Cambridge,* 277 U.S. 183, 188 (1928). Zoning laws are, of course, the classic example....

Zoning laws generally do not affect existing uses of real property, but "taking" challenges have also been held to be without merit in a wide variety of situations when the challenged governmental actions prohibited a beneficial use to which individual parcels had previously been devoted and thus caused substantial individualized harm. *Miller* v. *Schoene,* 276 U.S. 272 (1928), is illustrative. In that case, a state entomologist, acting pursuant to a state statute, ordered the claimants to cut down a large number of ornamental red cedar trees because they produced cedar rust fatal to apple trees cultivated nearby. Although the statute provided for recovery of any expense incurred in removing the cedars, and permitted claimants to use the felled trees, it did not provide compensation for the value of the standing trees or for the resulting decrease in market value of the properties as a whole. A unanimous Court held that this latter omission did not render the statute invalid. The Court held that the State might properly make "a choice between the preservation of one class of property and that of the other" and since the apple industry was important in the State involved, concluded that the State had not exceeded "its constitutional powers by deciding upon the destruction of one class of property [without compensation] in order to save another which, in the judgment of the legislature, is of greater value to the public." *Id.,* at 279.

. . .

B

In contending that the New York City law has "taken" their property in violation of the Fifth and Fourteenth Amendments, appellants make a series of arguments, which, while tailored to the facts of this case, essentially urge that any substantial restriction imposed pursuant to a landmark law must be accompanied by just compensation if it is to be constitutional....

... Appellants ... do not dispute that a showing of diminution in property value would not establish a "taking" if the restriction had been imposed as a result of historic-district legislation, see generally *Maher* v. *New Orleans*, 516 F. 2d 1051 (CA5 1975), but appellants argue that New York City's regulation of individual landmarks is fundamentally different from zoning or from historic-district legislation because the controls imposed by New York City's law apply only to individuals who own selected properties.

Stated baldly, appellants' position appears to be that the only means of ensuring that selected owners are not singled out to endure financial hardship for no reason is to hold that any restriction imposed on individual landmarks pursuant to the New York City scheme is a "taking" requiring the payment of "just compensation." Agreement with this argument would, of course, invalidate not just New York City's law, but all comparable landmark legislation in the Nation. We find no merit in it.

... It is, of course, true that the Landmarks Law has a more severe impact on some landowners than on others, but that in itself does not mean that the law effects a "taking." Legislation designed to promote the general welfare commonly burdens some more than others....

. . .

C

Rejection of appellants' broad arguments is not, however, the end of our inquiry, for all we thus far have established is that the New York City law is not rendered invalid by its failure to provide "just compensation" whenever a landmark owner is restricted in the exploitation of property interests, such as air rights, to a greater extent than provided for under applicable zoning laws. We now must consider whether the interference with appellants' property is of such a magnitude that "there must be an exercise of eminent domain and compensation to sustain [it]." *Pennsylvania Coal Co.* v. *Mahon*, 260 U.S., at 413....

... [T]he New York City law does not interfere in any way with the present uses of the Terminal. Its designation as a landmark not only permits but contemplates that appellants may continue to use the property precisely as it has been used for the past 65 years: as a railroad terminal containing office space and concessions....

... While the Commission's actions in denying applications to construct an office building in excess of 50 stories above the Terminal may indicate that it will refuse to issue a certificate of appropriateness for any comparably sized structure, nothing the Commission has said or done suggests an intention to prohibit *any* construction above the Terminal....

On this record, we conclude that the application of New York City's Landmarks Law has not effected a "taking" of appellants' property. The restrictions imposed are substantially related to the promotion of the general welfare and not only permit reasonable beneficial use of the landmark site but also afford appellants opportunities further to enhance not only the Terminal site proper but also other properties.

Affirmed.

MR. JUSTICE REHNQUIST, with whom THE CHIEF JUSTICE and MR. JUSTICE STEVENS join, dissenting.

Of the over one million buildings and structures in the city of New York, appellees have singled out 400 for designation as official landmarks. The owner of a building might initially be pleased that his property has been chosen by a distinguished committee of architects, historians, and city planners for such a singular distinction. But he may well discover, as appellant Penn Central Transportation Co. did here, that the landmark designation imposes upon him a substantial cost, with little or no offsetting benefit except for the honor of the designation....

Only in the most superficial sense of the word can this case be said to involve "zoning." Typical zoning restrictions may, it is true, so limit the prospective uses of a piece of property as to diminish the value of that property in the abstract because it may not be used for the forbidden purposes. But any such abstract decrease in value will more than likely be at least partially offset by an increase in value which flows from similar restrictions as to use on neighboring properties. All property owners in a designated area are placed under the same restrictions, not only for the benefit of the municipality as a whole but also for the common benefit of one another....

I

The Fifth Amendment provides in part: "nor shall private property be taken for public use, without just compensation." In a very literal sense, the actions of appellees violated this constitutional prohibition. Before the city of New York declared Grand Central Terminal to be a landmark, Penn Central could have used its "air rights" over the Terminal to build a multistory office building, at an apparent value of several million dollars per year. Today, the Terminal cannot be modified in *any* form, including the erection of additional stories, without the permission of the Landmark Preservation Commission, a permission which appellants, despite good-faith attempts, have so far been unable to obtain. Because the Taking Clause of the Fifth Amendment has not always been read literally, however, the constitutionality of appellees' actions requires a closer scrutiny of this Court's interpretation of the three key words in the Taking Clause — "property," "taken," and "just compensation."

A

Appellees do not dispute that valuable property rights have been destroyed. And the Court has frequently emphasized that the term "property" as used in the Taking Clause includes the entire "group of rights inhering in the citizen's [ownership]." *United States* v. *General Motors Corp.,* 323 U.S. 373 (1945)....

B

Appellees have thus destroyed — in a literal sense, "taken" — substantial property rights of Penn Central. While the term "taken" might have been narrowly interpreted to include only physical seizures of property rights, "the construction of the phrase has not been so narrow. The courts have held that the deprivation of the former owner rather than the accretion of a right or interest to the sovereign constitutes the taking." *Id.,* at 378....

. . .

Hawaii Housing Authority v. Midkiff

467 U.S. 229 (1984)

How much may legislatures exercise their police powers without "taking" property in violation of the Fifth and Fourteenth Amendments? Such questions necessarily involve a sharing of judgments and jurisdiction by legislatures and courts. In this case, the Hawaii Legislature enacted a land reform act in 1967 in an effort to reduce the social and economic evils of a land oligopoly that could be traced back to the early high chiefs of the Hawaiian Islands. The statute created a land condemnation scheme and provoked a suit that claimed a violation of constitutional rights. Frank Midkiff, a landowner, filed suit to have the land reform act declared unconstitutional as a violation of the Taking Clause. The Ninth Circuit agreed that it was a taking.

JUSTICE O'CONNOR delivered the opinion of the Court.

. . .

I

A

The Hawaiian Islands were originally settled by Polynesian immigrants from the western Pacific. These settlers developed an economy around a feudal land tenure system in which one island high chief, the ali'i nui, controlled the land and assigned it for development to certain subchiefs. The subchiefs would then reassign the land to other lower ranking chiefs, who would administer the land and govern the farmers and other tenants working it. All land was held at the will of the ali'i nui and eventually had to be returned to his trust. There was no private ownership of land....

Beginning in the early 1800's, Hawaiian leaders and American settlers repeatedly attempted to divide the lands of the kingdom among the crown, the chiefs, and the common people. These efforts proved largely unsuccessful, however, and the land remained in the hands of a few. In the mid-1960's, after extensive hearings, the Hawaii Legislature discovered that, while the State and Federal Governments owned almost 49% of the State's land, another 47% was in the hands of only 72 private landowners.... The legislature further found that 18 landholders, with tracts of 21,000 acres or more, owned more than 40% of this land and that on Oahu, the most urbanized of the islands, 22 landowners owned 72.5% of the fee simple titles.... The legislature concluded that concentrated land ownership was responsible for skewing the State's residential fee simple market, inflating land prices, and injuring the public tranquility and welfare.

To redress these problems, the legislature decided to compel the large landowners to break up their estates.... To accommodate the needs of both lessors and lessees, the Hawaii Legislature enacted the Land Reform Act of 1967 (Act), Haw. Rev. Stat., ch. 516, which created a mechanism for condemning residential tracts and for transferring ownership of the condemned fees simple to existing lessees. By condemning the land in question, the Hawaii Legislature intended to make the land sales involuntary, thereby making the federal tax consequences less severe while still facilitating the redistribution of fees simple....

Under the Act's condemnation scheme, tenants living on single-family residential lots within developmental tracts at least five acres in size are entitled to ask the Hawaii Housing Authority (HHA) to condemn the property on which they live.... When 25 eligible tenants, or tenants on half the lots in the tract, whichever is less, file appropriate applications, the Act authorizes HHA to hold a public hearing to determine whether acquisition by the State of all or part of the tract will "effectuate the public purposes" of the Act.... If HHA finds that these public purposes will be served, it is authorized to designate some or all of the lots in the tract for acquisition. It then acquires, at prices set either by condemnation trial or by negotiation between lessors and lessees, the former fee owners' full "right, title, and interest" in the land....

After compensation has been set, HHA may sell the land titles to tenants who have applied for fee simple ownership.... If HHA does not sell the lot to the tenant residing there, it may lease the lot or sell it to someone else, provided that public notice has been given....

·   ·   ·

III

The majority of the Court of Appeals next determined that the Act violates the "public use" requirement of the Fifth and Fourteenth Amendments. On this argument, however, we find ourselves in agreement with the dissenting judge in the Court of Appeals.

A

The starting point for our analysis of the Act's constitutionality is the Court's decision in *Berman* v. *Parker*, 348 U.S. 26 (1954). In *Berman*, the Court held constitutional the District of Columbia Redevelopment Act of 1945. That Act provided both for the comprehensive use of the eminent domain power to redevelop slum areas and for the possible sale or lease of the condemned lands to private interests. In discussing whether the takings authorized by that Act were for a "public use," *id.*, at 31, the Court stated:

"We deal, in other words, with what traditionally has been known as the police power. An attempt to define its reach or trace its outer limits is fruitless, for each case must turn on its own facts. The definition is essentially the product of legislative determinations addressed to the purposes of government, purposes neither abstractly nor historically capable of complete definition. Subject to specific constitutional limitations, when the legislature has spoken, the public interest has been declared in terms well-nigh conclusive. In such cases the legislature, not the judiciary, is the main guardian of the public needs to be served by social legislation, whether it be Congress legislating concerning the District of Columbia ... or the States legislating concerning local affairs.... This principle admits of no exception merely because the power of eminent domain is involved...." *Id.*, at 32 (citations omitted).

The Court explicitly recognized the breadth of the principle it was announcing, noting:

"Once the object is within the authority of Congress, the right to realize it through the exercise of eminent domain is clear. For the power of eminent domain is merely the means to the end.... Once the object is within the authority of Congress, the means by which it will be attained is also for Congress to determine. Here one of the means chosen is the use of private enterprise for redevelopment of the area. Appellants argue that this makes the project a taking from one businessman for the benefit of another businessman. But the means of executing the project are for Congress and Congress alone to determine, once the public purpose has been established." *Id.*, at 33.

The "public use" requirement is thus coterminous with the scope of a sovereign's police powers.

There is, of course, a role for courts to play in reviewing a legislature's judgment of what constitutes a public use, even when the eminent domain power is equated with the police power. But the Court in *Berman* made clear that it is "an extremely narrow" one. *id.*, at 32. The Court in

Berman cited with approval the Court's decision in *Old Dominion Co.* v. *United States,* 269 U.S. 55, 66 (1925), which held that deference to the legislature's "public use" determination is required "until it is shown to involve an impossibility." The *Berman* Court also cited to *United States ex rel. TVA* v. *Welch,* 327 U.S. 546, 552 (1946), which emphasized that "[a]ny departure from this judicial restraint would result in courts deciding on what is and is not a governmental function and in their invalidating legislation on the basis of their view on that question at the moment of decision, a practice which has proved impracticable in other fields." In short, the Court has made clear that it will not substitute its judgment for a legislature's judgment as to what constitutes a public use "unless the use be palpably without reasonable foundation." *United States* v. *Gettysburg Electric R. Co.,* 160 U.S. 668, 680 (1896).

To be sure, the Court's cases have repeatedly stated that "one person's property may not be taken for the benefit of another private person without a justifying public purpose, even though compensation be paid." *Thompson* v. *Consolidated Gas Corp.,* 300 U.S. 55, 80 (1937).... Where the exercise of the eminent domain power is rationally related to a conceivable public purpose, the Court has never held a compensated taking to be proscribed by the Public Use Clause....

On this basis, we have no trouble concluding that the Hawaii Act is constitutional. The people of Hawaii have attempted, much as the settlers of the original 13 Colonies did, to reduce the perceived social and economic evils of a land oligopoly traceable to their monarchs. The land oligopoly has, according to the Hawaii Legislature, created artificial deterrents to the normal functioning of the State's residential land market and forced thousands of individual homeowners to lease, rather than buy, the land underneath their homes. Regulating oligopoly and the evils associated with it is a classic exercise of a State's police powers.... We cannot disapprove of Hawaii's exercise of this power.

Nor can we condemn as irrational the Act's approach to correcting the land oligopoly problem. The Act presumes that when a sufficiently large number of persons declare that they are willing but unable to buy lots at fair prices the land market is malfunctioning. When such a malfunction is signalled, the Act authorizes HHA to condemn lots in the relevant tract. The Act limits the number of lots any one tenant can purchase and authorizes HHA to use public funds to ensure that the market dilution goals will be achieved. This is a comprehensive and rational approach to identifying and correcting market failure.

. . .

B

... The fact that a state legislature, and not the Congress, made the public use determination does not mean that judicial deference is less appropriate. Judicial deference is required because, in our system of government, legislatures are better able to assess what public purposes should be advanced by an exercise of the taking power. State legislatures are as capable as Congress of making such determinations within their respective spheres of authority. See *Berman* v. *Parker,* 348 U.S., at 32. Thus, if a legislature, state or federal, determines there are substantial reasons for an exercise of the taking power, courts must defer to its determination that the taking will serve a public use.

IV

The State of Hawaii has never denied that the Constitution forbids even a compensated taking of property when executed for no reason other than to confer a private benefit on a particular private party. A purely private taking could not withstand the scrutiny of the public use requirement; it would serve no legitimate purpose of government and would thus be void. But no purely private taking is involved in these cases. The Hawaii Legislature enacted its Land Reform Act not to benefit a particular class of identifiable individuals but to attack certain perceived evils of concentrated property ownership in Hawaii — a legitimate public purpose. Use of the condemnation power to achieve this purpose is not irrational. Since we assume for purposes of these appeals that the weighty demand of just compensation has been met, the requirements of the Fifth and Fourteenth Amendments have been satisfied. Accordingly, we reverse the judgment of the Court of Appeals, and remand these cases for further proceedings in conformity with this opinion.

It is so ordered.

JUSTICE MARSHALL took no part in the consideration or decision of these cases.

D. THE POLICE POWER

The courts of the nineteenth century permitted legislatures and municipalities broad discretion to use the "police power" to regulate public health and safety. The power of states to "impose restraints and burdens upon persons and property in conservation and promotion of the public health, good order and prosperity, is a power originally and always belonging to the States, not surrendered by them to the general government nor directly restrained by the Constitution of the United States, and essentially exclusive." In re Rahrer, 140 U.S. 545, 554 (1891). The police power may serve malign as well as benign purposes. In 1896, the Supreme Court held that Louisiana could use its police power to provide for "separate but equal" accommodations for whites and blacks in railway coaches. Plessy v. Ferguson, 163 U.S. 537, 544 (1896).

In a major case in 1873, a 5–4 decision by the Supreme Court upheld a monopoly that Louisiana had granted to a slaughterhouse. The Court ruled that the statute represented a valid police regulation for the health and comfort of the people. The decision proved pivotal for two other reasons. First, it concluded that the privileges and immunities under the Fourteenth Amendment were to be protected by the states, not the national government. Second, the powerful dissents influenced future proponents of property rights and liberty of contract. SLAUGHTER-HOUSE CASES, 83 U.S. (16 Wall.) 36 (1873). Just as the police power could justify a monopoly, so could the same state a few years later invoke that power to abolish the monopoly and reintroduce competition. Butchers' Union Co. v. Crescent City Co., 111 U.S. 746 (1884).

There were some hints at the state level that legislative efforts to control business activities could be curbed by the courts. Wynehamer v. People, 13 N.Y. 378 (1856). However, the Supreme Court provided broad support for state regulatory efforts. An Illinois law setting maximum charges for storing grain in warehouses and elevators was upheld in 1877 as a legitimate exercise of state authority to regulate businesses affected with a public interest. MUNN v. ILLINOIS, 94 U.S. 113 (1877). Other cases during this period supported use of the police power for economic regulation. Fertilizing Co. v. Hyde Park, 97 U.S. 659 (1879); Patterson v. Kentucky, 97 U.S. 501 (1879); Beer Co. v. Massachusetts, 97 U.S. 25 (1878).

A unanimous decision in 1885 upheld a law prohibiting public laundries from operating from 10 P.M. to 6 A.M. Barbier v. Connolly, 113 U.S. 27. A year later, the Court upheld the power of a state railroad commission to fix freight and passenger rates. Railroad Commission Cases, 116 U.S. 307, 347, 353 (1886). A unanimous ruling in 1887 allowed states to prohibit the manufacture and sale of intoxicating liquors within the state. It belonged to the legislative branch "to exert what are known as the police powers of the State, and to determine, primarily, what measures are appropriate or needful for the protection of the public morals, the public health, or the public safety." Mugler v. Kansas, 123 U.S. 623, 661.

Judicial Limits

In 1890 the Supreme Court declared unconstitutional a Minnesota law not because it exceeded the police power but because the judiciary of that state had decided that the reasonableness of rates established by a railroad and warehouse commission was final and conclusive, prohibiting review by the courts. This case did not prevent regulation by the state. It merely required the courts to determine whether the rates satisfied due process of law. Chicago, Milwaukee and St. Paul Railway Co. v. Minnesota, 134 U.S. 418 (1890). Also that year, the Court invalidated a Minnesota police power statute because it interfered with commerce among the states and thus invaded the province of Congress. Minnesota v. Barber, 136 U.S. 313.

In 1897 a unanimous Supreme Court used the magic phrase "liberty to contract" and spoke strongly about a citizen's right to be free to earn his livelihood. Allgeyer v. Louisiana, 165 U.S.

The Police Power

...While this [police] power is inherent in all governments, it has doubtless been greatly expanded in its application during the past century, owing to an enormous increase in the number of occupations that are dangerous, or so far detrimental to the health of employés as to demand special precautions for their well-being and protection, or the safety of adjacent property. While this court has held...that the police power cannot be put forward as an excuse for oppressive and unjust legislation, it may be lawfully resorted to for the purpose of preserving the public health, safety or morals, or the abatement of public nuisances, and a large discretion "is necessarily vested in the legislature to determine not only what the interests of the public require, but what measures are necessary for the protection of such interests."...

While this power is necessarily inherent in every form of government, it was, prior to the adoption of the Constitution, but sparingly used in this country. As we were then almost purely an agricultural people, the occasion for any special protection of a particular class did not exist. Certain profitable employments, such as lotteries and the sale of intoxicating liquors, which were then considered to be legitimate, have since fallen under the ban of public opinion, and are now either altogether prohibited, or made subject to stringent police regulations. The power to do this has been repeatedly affirmed by this court....

While the business of mining coal and manufacturing iron began in Pennsylvania as early as 1716, and in Virginia, North Carolina and Massachusetts even earlier than this, both mining and manufacturing were carried on in such a limited way and by such primitive methods that no special laws were considered necessary, prior to the adoption of the Constitution, for the protection of the operatives; but, in the vast proportions which these industries have since assumed, it has been found that they can no longer be carried on with due regard to the safety and health of those engaged in them, without special protection against the dangers necessarily incident to these employments....

SOURCE: Holden v. Hardy, 169 U.S. 366, 391–93 (1898).

578, 589, 591. This general philosophy did not prevent the Court the next year from upholding an eight-hour day for workers in coal mines and smelters. The Court flatly rejected the idea that workers and employers stood on equal footing in reaching a contract. Holden v. Hardy, 169 U.S. 366, 397 (1898). The Court perceptively noted that the police power had been greatly expanded in the nineteenth century because of the growth of dangerous occupations (see box). In 1903 the Court upheld an eight-hour law in Kansas covering all persons employed by the state or local governments, including work contracted by the state. Atkin v. Kansas, 191 U.S. 207.

Slaughter-House Cases

16 Wall. 36 (1873)

The legislature of Louisiana passed an act granting to a corporation, which it created, the exclusive right for twenty-five years to operate slaughterhouses. The corporation operated within three parishes, including the city of New Orleans, and prohibited other persons from competing with the corporation. The constitutional issue was whether this exclusive grant of monopoly privilege was a police regulation for the health and comfort of the people or whether it violated the constitutional rights of other citizens to exercise their trade and occupation. The Supreme Court's decision is significant because it is the first interpretation of the Civil War Amendments, especially the reach and purpose of the Fourteenth Amendment and the power of the federal government to direct state activities.

Mr. Justice MILLER, now, April 14th, 1873, delivered the opinion of the court.

. . .

It is . . . the slaughter-house privilege, which is mainly relied on to justify the charges of gross injustice to the public, and invasion of private right.

It is not, and cannot be successfully controverted, that it is both the right and the duty of the legislative body—the supreme power of the State or municipality—to prescribe and determine the localities where the business of slaughtering for a great city may be conducted. To do this effectively it is indispensable that all persons who slaughter animals for food shall do it in those places *and nowhere else.*

The statute under consideration defines these localities and forbids slaughtering in any other. It does not, as has been asserted, prevent the butcher from doing his own slaughtering. On the contrary, the Slaughter-House Company is required, under a heavy penalty, to permit any person who wishes to do so, to slaughter in their houses; and they are bound to make ample provision for the convenience of all the slaughtering for the entire city. The butcher then is still permitted to slaughter, to prepare, and to sell his own meats; but he is required to slaughter at a specified place and to pay a reasonable compensation for the use of the accommodations furnished him at that place.

. . .

It cannot be denied that the statute under consideration is aptly framed to remove from the more densely populated part of the city, the noxious slaughter-houses, and large and offensive collections of animals necessarily incident to the slaughtering business of a large city, and to locate them where the convenience, health, and comfort of the people require they shall be located. And it must be conceded that the means adopted by the act for this purpose are appropriate, are stringent, and effectual. . . .

. . .

The plaintiffs in error accepting this issue, allege that the statute is a violation of the Constitution of the United States in these several particulars:

That it creates an involuntary servitude forbidden by the thirteenth article of amendment;

That it abridges the privileges and immunities of citizens of the United States;

That it denies to the plaintiffs the equal protection of the laws; and,

That it deprives them of their property without due process of law; contrary to the provisions of the first section of the fourteenth article of amendment.

This court is thus called upon for the first time to give construction to these articles.

. . .

The most cursory glance at these articles *[the Thirteenth, Fourteenth, and Fifteenth Amendments]* discloses a unity of purpose, when taken in connection with the history of the times, which cannot fail to have an important bearing on any question of doubt concerning their true meaning. Nor can such doubts, when any reasonably exist, be safely and rationally solved without a reference to that history; . . .

The institution of African slavery, as it existed in about half the States of the Union, and the contests pervading the public mind for many years, between those who desired its curtailment and ultimate extinction and those who desired additional safeguards for its security and perpetuation, culminated in the effort, on the part of most of the States in which slavery existed, to separate from the Federal government, and to resist its authority. This constituted the war of the rebellion, and whatever auxiliary causes may have contributed to bring about this war, undoubtedly the overshadowing and efficient cause was African slavery.

. . . [T]he war being over, those who had succeeded in re-establishing the authority of the Federal government were . . . determined to place this main and most valuable result *[emancipation]* in the Constitution of the restored Union as one of its fundamental articles. Hence the thirteenth article of amendment of that instrument. Its two short sections seem hardly to admit of construction, so vigorous is their expression and so appropriate to the purpose we have indicated.

"1. Neither slavery nor involuntary servitude, except as a punishment for crime, whereof the party shall have been duly convicted, shall exist within the United States or any place subject to their jurisdiction.

"2. Congress shall have power to enforce this article by appropriate legislation."

. . .

[The Court summarizes the adoption of the Fourteenth Amendment, as a response to the "black

codes" used by southern states to suppress blacks, and the Fifteenth Amendment.]

We repeat, then, in the light of this recapitulation of events, almost too recent to be called history, but which are familiar to us all; and on the most casual examination of the language of these amendments, no one can fail to be impressed with the one pervading purpose found in them all, lying at the foundation of each, and without which none of them would have been even suggested; we mean the freedom of the slave race, the security and firm establishment of that freedom, and the protection of the newly-made freeman and citizen from the oppressions of those who had formerly exercised unlimited dominion over him. It is true that only the fifteenth amendment, in terms, mentions the negro by speaking of his color and his slavery. But it is just as true that each of the other articles was addressed to the grievances of that race, and designed to remedy them as the fifteenth.

We do not say that no one else but the negro can share in this protection. Both the language and spirit of these articles are to have their fair and just weight in any question of construction. Undoubtedly while negro slavery alone was in the mind of the Congress which proposed the thirteenth article, it forbids any other kind of slavery, now or hereafter. If Mexican peonage or the Chinese coolie labor system shall develop slavery of the Mexican or Chinese race within our territory, this amendment may safely be trusted to make it void....

The first section of the fourteenth article, to which our attention is more specially invited, opens with a definition of citizenship....

"All persons born or naturalized in the United States, and subject to the jurisdiction thereof, are citizens of the United States and of the State wherein they reside."

. . .

It is quite clear, then, that there is a citizenship of the United States, and a citizenship of a State, which are distinct from each other, and which depend upon different characteristics or circumstances in the individual.

We think this distinction and its explicit recognition in this amendment of great weight in this argument, because the next paragraph of this same section, which is the one mainly relied on by the plaintiffs in error, speaks only of privileges and immunities of citizens of the United States, and does not speak of those of citizens of the several

States. The argument, however, in favor of the plaintiffs rests wholly on the assumption that the citizenship is the same, and the privileges and immunities guaranteed by the clause are the same.

The language is, "No State shall make or enforce any law which shall abridge the privileges or immunities of citizens of *the United States.*" It is a little remarkable, if this clause was intended as a protection to the citizen of a State against the legislative power of his own State, that the word citizen of the State should be left out when it is so carefully used, and used in contradistinction to citizens of the United States, in the very sentence which precedes it....

. . .

Fortunately we are not without judicial construction of this clause of the Constitution. The first and the leading case on the subject is that of *Corfield* v. *Coryell,* decided by Mr. Justice Washington in the Circuit Court for the District of Pennsylvania in 1823.

"The inquiry," he says, "is, what are the privileges and immunities of citizens of the several States? We feel no hesitation in confining these expressions to those privileges and immunities which are *fundamental;* which belong of right to the citizens of all free governments, and which have at all times been enjoyed by citizens of the several States which compose this Union, from the time of their becoming free, independent, and sovereign. What these fundamental principles are, it would be more tedious than difficult to enumerate. They may all, however, be comprehended under the following general heads: protection by the government, with the right to acquire and possess property of every kind, and to pursue and obtain happiness and safety, subject, nevertheless, to such restraints as the government may prescribe for the general good of the whole."

. . .

...Was it the purpose of the fourteenth amendment, by the simple declaration that no State should make or enforce any law which shall abridge the privileges and immunities of *citizens of the United States,* to transfer the security and protection of all the civil rights which we have mentioned, from the States to the Federal government? And where it is declared that Congress shall have the power to enforce that article, was it intended to bring within the power of Congress the entire domain of civil rights heretofore belonging exclusively to the States?

. . .

. . . [S]uch a construction followed by the reversal of the judgments of the Supreme Court of Louisiana in these cases, would constitute this court a perpetual censor upon all legislation of the States, on the civil rights of their own citizens, with authority to nullify such as it did not approve as consistent with those rights, as they existed at the time of the adoption of this amendment. The argument we admit is not always the most conclusive which is drawn from the consequences urged against the adoption of a particular construction of an instrument. But when, as in the case before us, these consequences are so serious, so far-reaching and pervading, so great a departure from the structure and spirit of our institutions; when the effect is to fetter and degrade the State governments by subjecting them to the control of Congress, in the exercise of powers heretofore universally conceded to them of the most ordinary and fundamental character; when in fact it radically changes the whole theory of the relations of the State and Federal governments to each other and of both these governments to the people; the argument has a force that is irresistible, in the absence of language which expresses such a purpose too clearly to admit of doubt.

We are convinced that no such results were intended by the Congress which proposed these amendments, nor by the legislatures of the States which ratified them.

. . .

"All persons born or naturalized in the United States, and subject to the jurisdiction thereof, are citizens of the United States and of the State wherein they reside. No State shall make or enforce any law which shall abridge the privileges or immunities of citizens of the United States; nor shall any State deprive any person of life, liberty, or property without due process of law, nor deny to any person within its jurisdiction the equal protection of its laws."

The argument has not been much pressed in these cases that the defendant's charter deprives the plaintiffs of their property without due process of law, or that it denies to them the equal protection of the law. The first of these paragraphs has been in the Constitution since the adoption of the fifth amendment, as a restraint upon the Federal power. It is also to be found in

some form of expression in the constitutions of nearly all the States, as a restraint upon the power of the States. This law, then, has practically been the same as it now is during the existence of the government, except so far as the present amendment may place the restraining power over the States in this matter in the hands of the Federal government.

We are not without judicial interpretation, therefore, both State and National, of the meaning of this clause. And it is sufficient to say that under no construction of that provision that we have ever seen, or any that we deem admissible, can the restraint imposed by the State of Louisiana upon the exercise of their trade by the butchers of New Orleans be held to be a deprivation of property within the meaning of that provision.

"Nor shall any State deny to any person within its jurisdiction the equal protection of the laws."

In the light of the history of these amendments, and the pervading purpose of them, which we have already discussed, it is not difficult to give a meaning to this clause. The existence of laws in the States where the newly emancipated negroes resided, which discriminated with gross injustice and hardship against them as a class, was the evil to be remedied by this clause, and by it such laws are forbidden.

. . .

The judgments of the Supreme Court of Louisiana in these cases are

Affirmed.

Mr. Justice FIELD, dissenting:

. . .

The act of Louisiana presents the naked case, unaccompanied by any public considerations, where a right to pursue a lawful and necessary calling, previously enjoyed by every citizen, and in connection with which a thousand persons were daily employed, is taken away and vested exclusively for twenty-five years, for an extensive district and a large population, in a single corporation, or its exercise is for that period restricted to the establishments of the corporation, and there allowed only upon onerous conditions.

. . .

[After reviewing a number of court decisions, Field concludes:] In all these cases there is a recognition of the equality of right among citizens in the pursuit of the ordinary avocations of life, and a declaration that all grants of exclusive privileges, in contravention of this equality, are against common right, and void.

This equality of right, with exemption from all disparaging and partial enactments, in the lawful pursuits of life, throughout the whole country, is the distinguishing privilege of citizens of the United States. To them, everywhere, all pursuits, all professions, all avocations are open without other restrictions than such as are imposed equally upon all others of the same age, sex, and condition.... [I]t is to me a matter of profound regret that its validity is not recognized by a majority of this court, for by it the right of free labor, one of the most sacred and imprescriptible rights of man, is violated....

I am authorized by the CHIEF JUSTICE, Mr. Justice SWAYNE, and Mr. Justice BRADLEY, to state that they concur with me in this dissenting opinion.

Mr. Justice BRADLEY, also dissenting:

...in my judgment, the right of any citizen to follow whatever lawful employment he chooses to adopt (submitting himself to all lawful regulations) is one of his most valuable rights, and one which the legislature of a State cannot invade, whether restrained by its own constitution or not.

. . .

...[T]he Declaration of Independence, which was the first political act of the American people in their independent sovereign capacity, lays the foundation of our National existence upon this broad proposition: "That all men are created equal; that they are endowed by their Creator with certain inalienable rights; that among these are life, liberty, and the pursuit of happiness." Here again we have the great threefold division of the rights of freemen, asserted as the rights of man. Rights to life, liberty, and the pursuit of happiness are equivalent to the rights of life, liberty, and property. These are the fundamental rights which can only be taken away by due process of law,...

Mr. Justice SWAYNE, dissenting:

. . .

Munn v. Illinois

94 U.S. 113 (1877)

This case illustrates the need to balance two conflicting interests: the property rights of private individuals against the duty of the state to regulate economic conditions for the public good. Although economic regulation is sometimes regarded as a phenomenon of the twentieth century, this case makes clear that it has been customary "from time immemorial." Statutes regulating private property do not necessarily deprive an owner of his property without due process of law. When the owner of property devotes it to a use "in which the public has an interest," the owner must submit to some degree of public control. The issue in this case concerns a law passed by Illinois fixing the maximum rate for storing grain in warehouses in Chicago and other places in the state. Ira Munn, owner of a number of grain warehouses, challenged the state law.

Mr. CHIEF JUSTICE WAITE delivered the opinion of the court.

The question to be determined in this case is whether the general assembly of Illinois can, under the limitations upon the legislative power of the States imposed by the Constitution of the United States, fix by law the maximum of charges for the storage of grain in warehouses at Chicago and other places in the State....

It is claimed that such a law is repugnant—

1. To that part of sect. 8, art. 1, of the Constitution of the United States which confers upon Congress the power "to regulate commerce with foreign nations and among the several States;"

2. To that part of sect. 9 of the same article which provides that "no preference shall be given by any regulation of commerce or revenue to the ports of one State over those of another;" and

3. To that part of amendment 14 which ordains that no State shall "deprive any person of

life, liberty, or property, without due process of law, nor deny to any person within its jurisdiction the equal protection of the laws."

We will consider the last of these objections first.

Every statute is presumed to be constitutional. The courts ought not to declare one to be unconstitutional, unless it is clearly so. If there is doubt, the expressed will of the legislature should be sustained.

The Constitution contains no definition of the word "deprive," as used in the Fourteenth Amendment. To determine its signification, therefore, it is necessary to ascertain the effect which usage has given it, when employed in the same or a like connection.

While this provision of the amendment is new in the Constitution of the United States, as a limitation upon the powers of the States, it is old as a principle of civilized government. It is found in Magna Charta, and, in substance if not in form, in nearly or quite all the constitutions that have been from time to time adopted by the several States of the Union. By the Fifth Amendment, it was introduced into the Constitution of the United States as a limitation upon the powers of the national government, and by the Fourteenth, as a guaranty against any encroachment upon an acknowledged right of citizenship by the legislatures of the States. ... Under these *[police]* powers the government regulates the conduct of its citizens one towards another, and the manner in which each shall use his own property, when such regulation becomes necessary for the public good. In their exercise it has been customary in England from time immemorial, and in this country from its first colonization, to regulate ferries, common carriers, hackmen, bakers, millers, wharfingers, innkeepers, &c., and in so doing to fix a maximum of charge to be made for services rendered, accommodations furnished, and articles sold....

From this it is apparent that, down to the time of the adoption of the Fourteenth Amendment, it was not supposed that statutes regulating the use, or even the price of the use, of private property necessarily deprived an owner of his property without due process of law. Under some circumstances they may, but not under all....

This brings us to inquire as to the principles upon which this power of regulation rests, in order that we may determine what is within and what without its operative effect. Looking, then, to the common law, from whence came the right which the Constitution protects, we find that

when private property is "affected with a public interest, it ceases to be *juris privati* only."... Property does become clothed with a public interest when used in a manner to make it of public consequence, and affect the community at large. When, therefore, one devotes his property to a use in which the public has an interest, he, in effect, grants to the public an interest in that use, and must submit to be controlled by the public for the common good, to the extent of the interest he has thus created. He may withdraw his grant by discontinuing the use; but, so long as he maintains the use, he must submit to the control.

. . .

But we need not go further. Enough has already been said to show that, when private property is devoted to a public use, it is subject to public regulation. It remains only to ascertain whether the warehouses of these plaintiffs in error, and the business which is carried on there, come within the operation of this principle.

For this purpose we accept as true the statements of fact contained in the elaborate brief of one of the counsel of the plaintiffs in error. From these it appears that "the great producing region of the West and North-west sends its grain by water and rail to Chicago, where the greater part of it is shipped by vessel for transportation to the seaboard by the Great Lakes, and some of it is forwarded by railway to the Eastern ports.... Vessels, to some extent, are loaded in the Chicago harbor, and sailed through the St. Lawrence directly to Europe.... The quantity [of grain] received in Chicago has made it the greatest grain market in the world. This business has created a demand for means by which the immense quantity of grain can be handled or stored, and these have been found in grain warehouses, which are commonly called elevators, because the grain is elevated from the boat or car, by machinery operated by steam, into the bins prepared for its reception, and elevated from the bins, by a like process, into the vessel or car which is to carry it on.... In this way the largest traffic between the citizens of the country north and west of Chicago and the citizens of the country lying on the Atlantic coast north of Washington is in grain which passes through the elevators of Chicago. In this way the trade in grain is carried on by the inhabitants of seven or eight of the great States of the West with four or five of the States lying on the sea-shore, and forms the largest part of inter-state commerce in these States....

...[I]t is apparent that all the elevating facilities through which these vast productions "of seven or eight great States of the West" must pass on the way "to four or five of the States on the sea-shore" may be a "virtual" monopoly.

Under such circumstances it is difficult to see why, if the common carrier, or the miller, or the ferryman, or the innkeeper, or the wharfinger, or the baker, or the cartman, or the hackney-coachman, pursues a public employment and exercises "a sort of public office," these plaintiffs in error do not. They stand, to use again the language of their counsel, in the very "gateway of commerce," and take toll from all who pass. Their business most certainly "tends to a common charge, and is become a thing of public interest and use." ... Certainly, if any business can be clothed "with a public interest, and cease to be *juris privati* only," this has been. It may not be made so by the operation of the Constitution of Illinois or this statute, but it is by the facts.

We also are not permitted to overlook the fact that, for some reason, the people of Illinois, when they revised their Constitution in 1870, saw fit to make it the duty of the general assembly to pass laws "for the protection of producers, shippers, and receivers of grain and produce," art. 13, sect. 7; ... This indicates very clearly that during the twenty years in which this peculiar business had been assuming its present "immense proportions," something had occurred which led the whole body of the people to suppose that remedies such as are usually employed to prevent abuses by virtual monopolies might not be inappropriate here.... Of the propriety of legislative interference within the scope of legislative power, the legislature is the exclusive judge.

. . .

It is insisted, however, that the owner of property is entitled to a reasonable compensation for its use, even though it be clothed with a public interest, and that what is reasonable is a judicial and not a legislative question.

As has already been shown, the practice has been otherwise. In countries where the common law prevails, it has been customary from time immemorial for the legislature to declare what shall be a reasonable compensation under such circumstances, or, perhaps more properly speaking, to fix a maximum beyond which any charge made would be unreasonable. Undoubtedly, in mere private contracts, relating to matters in which the public has no interest, what is reasonable must be

ascertained judicially. But this is because the legislature has no control over such a contract....

We know that *[the police power]* is a power which may be abused; but that is no argument against its existence. For protection against abuses by legislatures the people must resort to the polls, not to the courts.

. . .

We come now to consider the effect upon this statute of the power of Congress to regulate commerce.

It was very properly said in the case of the *State Tax on Railway Gross Receipts,* 15 Wall. 293, that "it is not every thing that affects commerce that amounts to a regulation of it, within the meaning of the Constitution." The warehouses of these plaintiffs in error are situated and their business carried on exclusively within the limits of the State of Illinois. They are used as instruments by those engaged in State as well as those engaged in inter-state commerce, but they are no more necessarily a part of commerce itself than the dray or the cart by which, but for them, grain would be transferred from one railroad station to another. Incidentally they may become connected with inter-state commerce, but not necessarily so. Their regulation is a thing of domestic concern, and, certainly, until Congress acts in reference to their inter-state relations, the State may exercise all the powers of government over them, even though in so doing it may indirectly operate upon commerce outside its immediate jurisdiction....

Judgment affirmed.

MR. JUSTICE FIELD and MR. JUSTICE STRONG dissented.

MR. JUSTICE FIELD. I am compelled to dissent from the decision of the court in this case, and from the reasons upon which that decision is founded. The principle upon which the opinion of the majority proceeds is, in my judgment, subversive of the rights of private property, heretofore believed to be protected by constitutional guaranties against legislative interference, and is in conflict with the authorities cited in its support.

. . .

...[I]t would seem from its opinion that the court holds that property loses something of its private character when employed in such a way as to be generally useful....

If this be sound law, if there be no protection,

either in the principles upon which our republican government is founded, or in the prohibitions of the Constitution against such invasion of private rights, all property and all business in the State are held at the mercy of a majority of its legislature. The public has no greater interest in the use of buildings for the storage of grain than it has in the use of buildings for the residences of families, nor, indeed, any thing like so great an interest; and, according to the doctrine announced, the legislature may fix the rent of all tenements used for residences, without reference to the cost of their erection. . . . The public is interested in the manufacture of cotton, woollen, and silken fabrics, in the construction of machinery, in the printing and publication of books and periodicals, and in the making of utensils of every variety, useful and ornamental; indeed, there is hardly an enterprise or business engaging the attention and labor of any considerable portion of the community, in which the public has not an interest in the sense in which that term is used by the court in its opinion; and the doctrine which allows the legislature to interfere with and regulate the charges which the owners of property thus employed shall make for its use, that is, the rates at which all these different kinds of business shall be carried on, has never before been asserted, so far as I am aware, by any judicial tribunal in the United States.

. . .

MR. JUSTICE STRONG. . . .

E. SUBSTANTIVE DUE PROCESS

By 1903 the Court had sustained an eight-hour day for the public sector and for certain industries in the private sector (coal mining and smelting). Over the next three decades the courts regularly invalidated legislative efforts to establish maximum hours or minimum wages — efforts the judiciary regarded as an unconstitutional interference with the "liberty of contract." Lawyers from the corporate sector helped translate the philosophy of laissez-faire into legal terms and constitutional doctrine. One of the intellectual pillars was Thomas M. Cooley, whose *Constitutional Limitations* appeared in 1868. Cooley emphasized limits on legislative authority in order to protect personal liberty and private property. Herbert Spencer's *Social Statics* (1851) counseled against government efforts to protect the weak, preferring instead a kind of Darwinian struggle for survival of the "fittest." Christopher G. Tiedeman's *Treatise on the Limitations of the Police Power* (1886) also developed the theory of laissez-faire and liberty of contract. See Benjamin R. Twiss, Lawyers and the Constitution (1942).

The climate of the years following the Civil War promoted the pursuit of material goals, especially after the heavy sacrifices demanded by the war. Elitism by corporate leaders could not be justified on tradition (feudalism) or the will of God (Calvinism). Neither belief system fitted an age devoted to materialist thinking, scientific discovery, and industrial capitalism. Justification took the form of Social Darwinism: the belief in ruthless individualism in which only the strongest were allowed to survive. Material success became the overriding value. The American Bar Association, founded in 1878, campaigned to limit legislative interference with property rights. The specter of "socialism" and "communism" gave added force and urgency to these efforts.

The *Lochner* Era

Judicial tolerance of the police power came to an abrupt halt in 1905 when the Court invalidated a New York law limiting bakery workers to sixty hours a week or ten hours a day. Justice Peckham, writing for a 5–4 majority, converted the general right to make a contract into laissez-faire rigidity. He found no "reasonable ground" to interfere with the liberty of a person to contract for as many hours of work as desired. LOCHNER v. NEW YORK, 198 U.S. 45, 57 (1905). The statute seemed to him to serve no purpose in safeguarding public health or the health of the worker. Such laws were "mere meddlesome interferences" with the rights of an individual to enter into contracts. Lawyers who opposed the law argued that it was not a health measure but rather "a labor law" to promote paternalism.

In their dissent, Justices Harlan, White, and Day reviewed previous holdings of the Court that had interpreted the police power generously to support economic regulation. They cited statistical studies to show the need for remedial legislation. Peckham's opinion was so flavored with conservative business doctrines that Justice Holmes, in his dissent, accused the majority of deciding "upon an economic theory which a large part of the country does not entertain." The Constitution, he said, is "not intended to embody a particular economic theory, whether of paternalism and the organic relation of the citizen to the state or of *laissez faire*." However, laissez-faire did not mean a free market. Corporations were busily involved in forming pools, trusts, "community of interests," and other devices to protect themselves from competition. The marketplace of many competing units was becoming a relic of the past.

Sociological Data

The Court equivocated on the principle of laissez-faire. In 1908 it struck down a congressional statute that made it unlawful for the railroads to fire workers because of their union membership. A 6–2 decision maintained the fiction of *Lochner* that the employer and employee had "equality of right" to enter into a contract, "and any legislation that disturbs that equality is an arbitrary interference with the liberty of contract over which no government can legally justify in a free land." Adair v. United States, 208 U.S. 161, 175 (1908). See also Coppage v. Kansas, 236 U.S. 1 (1915).

Also in 1908, however, the Court sustained Oregon's ten-hour day for women. The statistical record referred to by the dissenters in *Lochner* supplied a good tactical clue for Louis D. Brandeis, who argued the case for Oregon. His sister-in-law, Josephine Goldmark, was closely associated with the National Consumers' League, which had long advocated improved working conditions. She supervised an intensive search of library holdings and helped produce a brief of 113 pages, almost all of which consisted of copious data extracted from sociological studies supporting the need for limiting working hours for women. The Court called attention to what is now known as the "Brandeis brief": a compilation of state and foreign statutes that imposed restrictions on the hours of labor required of women, followed by extracts from more than ninety reports of committees, bureaus of statistics, commissioners of hygiene, and inspectors of factories. These studies, drawn primarily from Europe, concluded that long hours of labor "are dangerous for women, primarily because of their special physical organization." Muller v. Oregon, 208 U.S. 412, 419–20 n.1 (1908).

Could the constitutional principle announced in *Lochner* be displaced by public opinion and sociological data? The Court engaged in a bit of judicial doubletalk:

> The legislation and opinions referred to in the margin may not be, technically speaking, authorities, and in them is little or no discussion of the constitutional question presented to us for determination, yet they are significant of a widespread belief that woman's physical structure, and the functions she performs in consequence thereof, justify special legislation restricting or qualifying the conditions under which she should be permitted to toil. Constitutional questions, it is true, are not settled by even a consensus of present public opinion, for it is the peculiar value of a written constitution that it places in unchanging form limitations upon legislative action, and thus gives a permanence and stability to popular government which otherwise would be lacking. At the same time, when a question of fact is debated and debatable, and the extent to which a special constitutional limitation goes is affected by the truth in respect to that fact, a widespread

and long continued belief concerning it is worthy of consideration. We take judicial cognizance of all matters of general knowledge.[8]

"Liberty of contract" did not prevent the Court in 1911 from unanimously upholding an Iowa statute that prohibited certain contracts by railroad companies, or delivering another unanimous opinion three years later to sustain a New York law requiring certain industries to pay employees semimonthly and in cash. Chicago, Burlington & Quincy R.R. Co. v. McGuire, 219 U.S. 543 (1911) and Erie R.R. Co. v. Williams, 233 U.S. 685 (1914). Rent-control laws were also upheld, preventing a landlord from freely contracting with his or her tenants. Block v. Hirsh, 256 U.S. 135 (1921).

In 1917 the Court upheld the constitutionality of Oregon's ten-hour day for men and women, including a provision for overtime pay. Brandeis was now on the Court as an Associate Justice. Because of his previous involvement in litigating this type of case, he did not participate in the decision. Felix Frankfurter of the Harvard Law School argued the case for Oregon and prepared a "Brandeis brief" that contained an array of facts and statistics to demonstrate the effects of overtime on the physical and moral health of the worker. His brief reviewed industrial conditions and labor experiences in England and the United States. A 5–3 Court sustained the statute. Bunting v. Oregon, 243 U.S. 426 (1917).

Frankfurter was again lead counsel in defending a congressional statute that provided for minimum wages for women and children in the District of Columbia. Despite his lengthy sociological brief, the Court held the statute invalid. Writing for a 5–3 majority, Justice Sutherland found the mass of data compiled by Frankfurter "interesting but only mildly persuasive." ADKINS v. CHILDREN'S HOSPITAL, 261 U.S. 525, 560 (1923). Because of progress in contractual, political, and civil status of women since the *Muller* decision of 1908, Sutherland said that the continuation of protective legislation could not be justified. Although the Court had sustained statutes setting maximum hours, the minimum wage law seemed dangerous territory to the majority. What was next, Sutherland asked, maximum wages? In one of the dissents, Chief Justice Taft thought that the line drawn between hours and wages was imaginary. Justice Holmes's dissent described how the phrase "due process of law" had evolved into the "dogma, Liberty of Contract."

The Great Depression

Between 1923 and 1934, the Court repeatedly struck down statutes on the ground that the activity regulated was not "affected with a public interest."[9] At the same time, new areas of economic life were becoming national in scope and gradually brought within Congress' power over interstate commerce (see Chapter 8). Finally, the onset of the Great Depression of 1929 shattered the theory of a self-correcting free economy.

The philosophy of *Adkins* survived as late as 1936; although a decision that year striking down New York's minimum wage law for women and children could muster only a 5–4 majority. "Freedom of contract," said the Court, "is the general rule and restraint the exception."

---

8. Muller v. Oregon, 208 U.S. 412, 420–21 (1908). For unanimous rulings that upheld other state statutes setting maximum hours for women, see Bosley v. McLaughlin, 236 U.S. 385 (1915); Miller v. Wilson, 236 U.S. 373 (1915); and Riley v. Massachusetts, 232 U.S. 671 (1914). A 5–4 Court upheld a congressional statute setting an eight-hour day for railroad workers engaged in interstate commerce; Wilson v. New, 243 U.S. 332 (1917).

9. New State Ice Co. v. Liebmann, 285 U.S. 262 (1932); Williams v. Standard Oil Co., 278 U.S. 235 (1929); Ribnik v. McBride, 277 U.S. 350 (1928); Tyson & Brother v. Banton, 273 U.S. 418 (1927); Wolff Co. v. Industrial Court, 262 U.S. 522 (1923).

Morehead v. N.Y. ex rel. Tipaldo, 298 U.S. 587, 610–11. Chief Justice Hughes dissented, joined by Brandeis, Stone, and Cardozo. Stone, in a separate dissent, criticized the basis on which the majority had declared the New York law invalid: "It is difficult to imagine any grounds, other than our own personal economic predilections, for saying that the contract of employment is any the less an appropriate subject of legislation than are scores of others, in dealing with which this Court has held that legislatures may curtail individual freedom in the public interest." Stone emphasized the changes that had occurred in economic conditions: "In the years that have intervened since the *Adkins* case we have had opportunity to learn that a wage is not always the resultant of free bargaining between employers and employees; that it may be one forced upon employees by their economic necessities and upon employers by the most ruthless of their competitors.... Because of their nature and extent these are public problems. A generation ago they were for the individual to solve; today they are the burden of the nation."

Liberty-of-Contract Doctrine Abandoned

Adkins was finally overruled in 1937. Sutherland, Van Devanter, McReynolds, and Butler, who had provided four of the majority votes in *Morehead,* dissented. Roberts, the fifth member of that majority, now joined the four dissenters from *Morehead* to uphold a minimum wage law for women and minors in the state of Washington. WEST COAST HOTEL CO. v. PARRISH, 300 U.S. 379 (1937). Since the Washington case was decided about two months after President Franklin D. Roosevelt had unveiled his court-packing plan (see the section on the court-packing plan in the concluding chapter), much has been made of Roberts's "switch in time that saved nine." However, Roberts had already broken with his doctrinaire laissez-faire colleagues. He wrote the 5–4 opinion in *Nebbia* v. *New York,* 291 U.S. 502 (1934), which upheld a price-setting statute. With his support, the Court was prepared to sustain minimum wage legislation in the fall of 1936 but had delayed its ruling because Justice Stone was ill.[10]

Justice Sutherland, speaking for the four dissenters in *West Coast Hotel,* assailed the theory that decisions of the Supreme Court should be reconsidered because of economic conditions: "the meaning of the Constitution does not change with the ebb and flow of economic events." His phrase "ebb and flow" suggests a seasonal if not spasmodic quality, which seems offensive to a constitution grounded on fundamental principles. However, the record of the Court on economic regulation was decidedly one of ebb and flow. Over a period of about four decades, the Court had tried to impose a liberty-of-contract theory at a time when power was shifting dramatically from the employee to the employer. A countervailing force was needed, and the elected branches intervened to redress the imbalance. Liberals welcomed the decision in *West Coast Hotel* as did conservatives, because it averted a serious threat to the Court's independence and prestige (see box on next page).

By 1941 the composition of the Court had been radically altered, especially with Reed, Murphy, and Black replacing Sutherland, Butler, and Van Devanter. A unanimous Court that year upheld a congressional statute setting minimum wages and maximum hours for men and women. The statute was within the power of Congress to regulate interstate commerce and to protect public health, morals, and welfare. No conflict was found with the due process of law or with the rights of states under the Tenth Amendment. United States v. Darby, 312 U.S. 100 (1941). Another unanimous decision in 1941 overruled the laissez-faire doctrine of *Rib-*

---

10. Felix Frankfurter, "Mr. Justice Roberts," 104 U. Pa. L. Rev. 311 (1955); 2 Merlo J. Pusey, Charles Evans Hughes 757 (1963). For a challenge to Roberts' recollection of key events in 1936, see Clement E. Vose, Constitutional Change 228–34 (1972).

Political Reaction to *West Coast Hotel*

The effect of this decision was far-reaching in law and in economics, but its immediate repercussions were political. The Administration forces had to like the decision, for it was what they had long contended the law to be. It stimulated the movement in both state and nation to "put a floor under wages" and a "ceiling over hours," and a law to prescribe minimum wages and maximum hours in interstate commerce was soon proposed to Congress. But the liberals had a good deal to say about judicial strangling for fifteen years of such legislation in both state and nation by what was now conceded to be a blunder of the Court....

The conservatives liked the decision. They knew the former one [*Adkins*] took ground too reactionary to be held. The timing of the yielding was a boon to them. It removed a great deal of pressure for reform of the Court, and they made much of the argument that the Court did not need reforming, but could and would reform itself. At any rate the Court had made a bold turn in direction. The doctrine of "freedom of contract," which had menaced all types of legislation to regulate the master and servant relation, had been uprooted so definitely that it could hardly be expected to thrive again. Labor was free from the shackles of a fictitious freedom.

SOURCE: Robert H. Jackson, The Struggle for Judicial Supremacy 211–12 (1941).

---

nik v. *McBride*. Olsen v. Nebraska, 313 U.S. 236 (1941). A combination of social, economic, and political forces had finally reversed the constitutional doctrines of the Court. In the future, decisions about economic or social philosophy would be left largely to legislatures, not to the courts. FERGUSON v. SKRUPA, 372 U.S. 726 (1963). See also Williamson v. Lee Optical Co., 348 U.S. 483, 488 (1955) and Day-Brite Lighting, Inc. v. Missouri, 342 U.S. 421 (1952).

Lochner v. New York

198 U.S. 45 (1905)

New York passed a law prohibiting employees from working in bakeries more than sixty hours a week or ten hours a day. The statute, sustained by the state courts, was similar to other labor laws passed by states to protect workers from industrial conditions that threatened health and safety. The case represented a conflict between two values: the police power of the state to regulate economic activities versus the "liberty" protected by the Fourteenth Amendment to contract without unreasonable interference by the state. Joseph Lochner, a bakery owner, claimed that the New York law violated the U.S. Constitution.

MR. JUSTICE PECKHAM, after making the foregoing statement of the facts, delivered the opinion of the court.

The indictment, it will be seen, charges that the plaintiff in error violated the one hundred and tenth section of article 8, chapter 415, of the Laws of 1897, known as the labor law of the State of New York, in that he wrongfully and unlawfully required and permitted an employé working for him to work more than sixty hours in one week.... The mandate of the statute that "no employé shall be required or permitted to work," is the substantial equivalent of an enactment that "no employé shall contract or agree to work," more than ten

hours per day, and as there is no provision for special emergencies the statute is mandatory in all cases. It is not an act merely fixing the number of hours which shall constitute a legal day's work, but an absolute prohibition upon the employer, permitting, under any circumstances, more than ten hours work to be done in his establishment. The employé may desire to earn the extra money, which would arise from his working more than the prescribed time, but this statute forbids the employer from permitting the employé to earn it.

The statute necessarily interferes with the right of contract between the employer and employés, concerning the number of hours in which the latter may labor in the bakery of the employer. The general right to make a contract in relation to his business is part of the liberty of the individual protected by the Fourteenth Amendment of the Federal Constitution. *Allgeyer* v. *Louisiana,* 165 U.S. 578. Under that provision no State can deprive any person of life, liberty or property without due process of law. The right to purchase or to sell labor is part of the liberty protected by this amendment, unless there are circumstances which exclude the right. There are, however, certain powers, existing in the sovereignty of each State in the Union, somewhat vaguely termed police powers, the exact description and limitation of which have not been attempted by the courts. Those powers, broadly stated and without, at present, any attempt at a more specific limitation, relate to the safety, health, morals and general welfare of the public....

The State, therefore, has power to prevent the individual from making certain kinds of contracts, and in regard to them the Federal Constitution offers no protection. If the contract be one which the State, in the legitimate exercise of its police power, has the right to prohibit, it is not prevented from prohibiting it by the Fourteenth Amendment. Contracts in violation of a statute, either of the Federal or state government, or a contract to let one's property for immoral purposes, or to do any other unlawful act, could obtain no protection from the Federal Constitution, as coming under the liberty of person or of free contract....

. . .

It must, of course, be conceded that there is a limit to the valid exercise of the police power by the State. There is no dispute concerning this general proposition. Otherwise the Fourteenth Amendment would have no efficacy and the legislatures of the States would have unbounded power, and it would be enough to say that any piece of legislation was enacted to conserve the morals, the health or the safety of the people; such legislation would be valid, no matter how absolutely without foundation the claim might be. The claim of the police power would be a mere pretext—become another and delusive name for the supreme sovereignty of the State to be exercised free from constitutional restraint. This is not contended for. In every case that comes before this court, therefore, where legislation of this character is concerned and where the protection of the Federal Constitution is sought, the question necessarily arises: Is this a fair, reasonable and appropriate exercise of the police power of the State, or is it an unreasonable, unnecessary and arbitrary interference with the right of the individual to his personal liberty or to enter into those contracts in relation to labor which may seem to him appropriate or necessary for the support of himself and his family? Of course the liberty of contract relating to labor includes both parties to it. The one has as much right to purchase as the other to sell labor.

This is not a question of substituting the judgment of the court for that of the legislature. If the act be within the power of the State it is valid, although the judgment of the court might be totally opposed to the enactment of such a law. But the question would still remain: Is it within the police power of the State? and that question must be answered by the court.

The question whether this act is valid as a labor law, pure and simple, may be dismissed in a few words. There is no reasonable ground for interfering with the liberty of person or the right of free contract, by determining the hours of labor, in the occupation of a baker. There is no contention that bakers as a class are not equal in intelligence and capacity to men in other trades or manual occupations, or that they are not able to assert their rights and care for themselves without the protecting arm of the State, interfering with their independence of judgment and of action. They are in no sense wards of the State. Viewed in the light of a purely labor law, with no reference whatever to the question of health, we think that a law like the one before us involves neither the safety, the morals nor the welfare of the public, and that the interest of the public is not in the slightest degree affected by such an act. The law must be upheld, if at all, as a law pertaining to the health of the individual engaged in the occupation of a baker. It does not affect any other portion of the public than those who are engaged in that occupation. Clean and wholesome bread does not depend upon whether the baker works but ten hours per day or only sixty hours a week. The limitation of the hours of labor does not come within the police power on that ground.

. . .

We think that there can be no fair doubt that the trade of a baker, in and of itself, is not an unhealthy one to that degree which would authorize the legislature to interfere with the right to labor, and with the right of free contract on the part of the individual, either as employer or employé. In looking through statistics regarding all trades and occupations, it may be true that the trade of a baker does not appear to be as healthy as some other trades, and is also vastly more healthy than still others. To the common understanding the trade of a baker has never been regarded as an unhealthy one. Very likely physicians would not recommend the exercise of that or of any other trade as a remedy for ill health. Some occupations are more healthy than others, but we think there are none which might not come under the power of the legislature to supervise and control the hours of working therein, if the mere fact that the occupation is not absolutely and perfectly healthy is to confer that right upon the legislative department of the Government. It might be safely affirmed that almost all occupations more or less affect the health....

... The act is not, within any fair meaning of the term, a health law, but is an illegal interference with the rights of individuals, both employers and employés, to make contracts regarding labor upon such terms as they may think best, or which they may agree upon with the other parties to such contracts. Statutes of the nature of that under review, limiting the hours in which grown and intelligent men may labor to earn their living, are mere meddlesome interferences with the rights of the individual, and they are not saved from condemnation by the claim that they are passed in the exercise of the police power....

... In our judgment it is not possible in fact to discover the connection between the number of hours a baker may work in the bakery and the healthful quality of the bread made by the workman. The connection, if any exists, is too shadowy and thin to build any argument for the interference of the legislature. If the man works ten hours a day it is all right, but if ten and a half or eleven his health is in danger and his bread may be unhealthful, and, therefore, he shall not be permitted to do it. This, we think, is unreasonable and entirely arbitrary. When assertions such as we have advertised to become necessary in order to give, if possible, a plausible foundation for the contention that the law is a "health law," it gives rise to at least a suspicion that there was some other motive dominating the legislature than the purpose to subserve the public health or welfare.

. . .

MR. JUSTICE HARLAN, with whom MR. JUSTICE WHITE and MR. JUSTICE DAY concurred, dissenting.

. . .

It is plain that this statute was enacted in order to protect the physical well-being of those who work in bakery and confectionery establishments. It may be that the statute had its origin, in part, in the belief that employers and employés in such establishments were not upon an equal footing, and that the necessities of the latter often compelled them to submit to such exactions as unduly taxed their strength. Be this as it may, the statute must be taken as expressing the belief of the people of New York that, as a general rule, and in the case of the average man, labor in excess of sixty hours during a week in such establishments may endanger the health of those who thus labor. Whether or not this be wise legislation it is not the province of the court to inquire. Under our systems of government the courts are not concerned with the wisdom or policy of legislation. So that in determining the question of power to interfere with liberty of contract, the court may inquire whether the means devised by the State are germane to an end which may be lawfully accomplished and have a real or substantial relation to the protection of health, as involved in the daily work of the persons, male and female, engaged in bakery and confectionery establishments. But when this inquiry is entered upon I find it impossible, in view of common experience, to say that there is here no real or substantial relation between the means employed by the State and the end sought to be accomplished by its legislation.... Therefore I submit that this court will transcend its functions if it assumes to annul the statute of New York....

[Justice Harlan summarizes a number of studies that describe the health hazards of working in a bakery, including the inhalation of flour dust that causes inflammation of the lungs and the bronchial tubes.]

MR. JUSTICE HOLMES dissenting.

. . .

This case is decided upon an economic theory which a large part of the country does not entertain. If it were a question whether I agreed with that theory, I should desire to study it further and long before making up my mind. But I do not conceive that to be my duty, because I strongly believe that my agreement or disagreement has nothing to do with the right of a majority to embody their opinions in law. It is settled by various decisions of this court that state constitutions and state laws may regulate life in many ways which we as legislators might think as injudicious or if you like as tyrannical as this, and which equally with this interfere with the liberty to contract. Sunday laws and usury laws are ancient examples. A more modern one is the prohibition of lotteries. The liberty of the citizen to do as he likes so long as he does not interfere with the liberty of others to do the same, which has been a shibboleth for some well-known writers, is interfered with by school laws, by the Post Office, by every state or municipal institution which takes his money for purposes thought desirable, whether he likes it or not. The Fourteenth Amendment does not enact Mr. Herbert Spencer's Social Statics. The other day we sustained the Massachusetts vaccination law. *Jacobson* v. *Massachusetts,* 197 U.S. 11. United States and state statutes and decisions cutting down the liberty to contract by way of combination are familiar to this court. *Northern Securities Co.* v. *United States,* 193 U.S. 197. Two years ago we upheld the prohibition of sales of stock on margins or for future delivery in the constitution of California. *Otis* v. *Parker,* 187 U.S. 606. The decision sustaining an eight hour law for miners is still recent. *Holden* v. *Hardy,* 169 U.S. 366. Some of these laws embody convictions or prejudices which judges are likely to share. Some may not. But a constitution is not intended to embody a particular economic theory, whether of paternalism and the organic relation of the citizen to the State or of *laissez faire*. It is made for people of fundamentally differing views, and the accident of our finding certain opinions natural and familiar or novel and even shocking ought not to conclude our judgment upon the question whether statutes embodying them conflict with the Constitution of the United States.

General propositions do not decide concrete cases. The decision will depend on a judgment or intuition more subtle than any articulate major premise. But I think that the proposition just stated, if it is accepted, will carry us far toward the end. Every opinion tends to become a law. I think that the word liberty in the Fourteenth Amendment is perverted when it is held to prevent the natural outcome of a dominant opinion, unless it can be said that a rational and fair man necessarily would admit that the statute proposed would infringe fundamental principles as they have been understood by the traditions of our people and our law. It does not need research to show that no such sweeping condemnation can be passed upon the statute before us. A reasonable man might think it a proper measure on the score of health. Men whom I certainly could not pronounce unreasonable would uphold it as a first instalment of a general regulation of the hours of work. Whether in the latter aspect it would be open to the charge of inequality I think it unnecessary to discuss.

Adkins v. Children's Hospital

261 U.S. 525 (1923)

In 1918 Congress passed a law setting minimum wages for women and children in the District of Columbia. As in other cases, the question was one of balancing the police power of Congress to regulate health and safety with the right of individuals to conduct their own affairs without legislative interference. Children's Hospital and a female elevator operator at a hotel brought this case to prevent enforcement of the act by Jesse C. Adkins and the two other members of a wage board.

Mr. Justice Sutherland delivered the opinion of the Court.

The question presented for determination by these appeals is the constitutionality of the Act of September 19, 1918, providing for the fixing of minimum wages for women and children in the District of Columbia. 40 Stat. 960, c. 174.

[The act authorized a three-member wage board to investigate wages for women and minors and to order changes in wages after giving public notice and holding a public hearing. Questions of fact determined by the board could not be appealed.]

. . .

The statute now under consideration is attacked upon the ground that it authorizes an unconstitutional interference with the freedom of contract included within the guaranties of the due process clause of the Fifth Amendment. That the right to contract about one's affairs is a part of the liberty of the individual protected by this clause, is settled by the decisions of this Court and is no longer open to question.... Within this liberty are contracts of employment of labor: In making such contracts, generally speaking, the parties have an equal right to obtain from each other the best terms they can as the result of private bargaining.

. . .

There is, of course, no such thing as absolute freedom of contract. It is subject to a great variety of restraints. But freedom of contract is, nevertheless, the general rule and restraint the exception; and the exercise of legislative authority to abridge it can be justified only by the existence of exceptional circumstances. Whether these circumstances exist in the present case constitutes the question to be answered. It will be helpful to this end to review some of the decisions where the interference has been upheld and consider the grounds upon which they rest.

[Justice Sutherland reviews cases in which the Court upheld statutes fixing rates and charges to be exacted on businesses impressed with a public interest; statutes relating to contracts for the performance of public work; statutes prescribing the character, methods, and time for payment of wages; and statutes fixing hours of labor.]

. . .

In the *Muller Case* the validity of an Oregon statute, forbidding the employment of any female in certain industries more than ten hours during any one day was upheld. The decision proceeded upon the theory that the difference between the sexes may justify a different rule respecting hours of labor in the case of women than in the case of men. It is pointed out that these consist in differences of physical structure, especially in respect of the maternal functions, and also in the fact that historically woman has always been dependent upon man, who has established his control by superior physical strength. The cases of *Riley, Miller* and *Bosley* follow in this respect the *Muller Case*. But the ancient inequality of the sexes, otherwise than physical, as suggested in the *Muller Case* (p. 421) has continued "with diminishing intensity." In view of the great — not to say revolutionary — changes which have taken place since that utterance, in the contractual, political and civil status of women, culminating in the Nineteenth Amendment, it is not unreasonable to say that these dif-

ferences have now come almost, if not quite, to the vanishing point. In this aspect of the matter, while the physical differences must be recognized in appropriate cases, and legislation fixing hours or conditions of work may properly take them into account, we cannot accept the doctrine that women of mature age, *sui juris,* require or may be subjected to restrictions upon their liberty of contract which could not lawfully be imposed in the case of men under similar circumstances. To do so would be to ignore all the implications to be drawn from the present day trend of legislation, as well as that of common thought and usage, by which woman is accorded emancipation from the old doctrine that she must be given special protection or be subjected to special restraint in her contractual and civil relationships....

If now, in the light furnished by the foregoing exceptions to the general rule forbidding legislative interference with freedom of contract, we examine and analyze the statute in question, we shall see that it differs from them in every material respect. It is not a law dealing with any business charged with a public interest or with public work, or to meet and tide over a temporary emergency. It has nothing to do with the character, methods or periods of wage payments. It does not prescribe hours of labor or conditions under which labor is to be done. It is not for the protection of persons under legal disability or for the prevention of fraud. It is simply and exclusively a price-fixing law, confined to adult women (for we are not now considering the provisions relating to minors), who are legally as capable of contracting for themselves as men....

The standard furnished by the statute for the guidance of the board is so vague as to be impossible of practical application with any reasonable degree of accuracy. What is sufficient to supply the necessary cost of living for a woman worker and maintain her in good health and protect her morals is obviously not a precise or unvarying sum — not even approximately so. The amount will depend upon a variety of circumstances: the individual temperament, habits of thrift, care, ability to buy necessaries intelligently, and whether the woman live alone or with her family. To those who practice economy, a given sum will afford comfort, while to those of contrary habit the same sum will be wholly inadequate.... The relation between earnings and morals is not capable of standardization. It cannot be shown that well paid women safeguard their morals more carefully than those who are poorly paid....

It is said that great benefits have resulted from the operation of such statutes, not alone in the District of Columbia but in the several States, where they have been in force. A mass of reports, opinions of special observers and students of the subject, and the like, has been brought before us in support of this statement, all of which we have found interesting but only mildly persuasive....

Finally, it may be said that if, in the interest of the public welfare, the police power may be invoked to justify the fixing of a minimum wage, it may, when the public welfare is thought to require it, be invoked to justify a maximum wage. The power to fix high wages connotes, by like course of reasoning, the power to fix low wages. If, in the face of the guaranties of the Fifth Amendment, this form of legislation shall be legally justified, the field for the operation of the police power will have been widened to a great and dangerous degree....

It follows from what has been said that the act in question passes the limit prescribed by the Constitution, and, accordingly, the decrees of the court below are

Affirmed.

MR. JUSTICE BRANDEIS took no part in the consideration or decision of these cases.

MR. CHIEF JUSTICE TAFT, dissenting.

. . .

Legislatures in limiting freedom of contract between employee and employer by a minimum wage proceed on the assumption that employees, in the class receiving least pay, are not upon a full level of equality of choice with their employer and in their necessitous circumstances are prone to accept pretty much anything that is offered. They are peculiarly subject to the overreaching of the harsh and greedy employer. The evils of the sweating system and of the long hours and low wages which are characteristic of it are well known. Now, I agree that it is a disputable question in the field of political economy how far a statutory requirement of maximum hours or minimum wages may be a useful remedy for these evils, and whether it may not make the case of the oppressed employee worse than it was before. But it is not the function of this Court to hold congressional acts invalid simply because they are passed to carry out economic views which the Court believes to be unwise or unsound.

. . .

[Chief Justice Taft cites earlier cases in which the Court upheld legislation setting maximum hours.]

...I assume that the conclusion in this case rests on the distinction between a minimum of wages and a maximum of hours in the limiting of liberty to contract. I regret to be at variance with the Court as to the substance of this distinction. In absolute freedom of contract the one term is as important as the other, for both enter equally into the consideration given and received, a restriction as to one is not any greater in essence than the other, and is of the same kind. One is the multiplier and the other the multiplicand.

If it be said that long hours of labor have a more direct effect upon the health of the employee than the low wage, there is very respectable authority from close observers, disclosed in the record and in the literature on the subject quoted at length in the briefs, that they are equally harmful in this regard. Congress took this view and we can not say it was not warranted in so doing.

. . .

I am not sure from a reading of the opinion whether the Court thinks the authority of *Muller* v. *Oregon* is shaken by the adoption of the Nineteenth Amendment. The Nineteenth Amendment did not change the physical strength or limitations of women upon which the decision in *Muller* v. *Oregon* rests. The Amendment did give women political power and makes more certain that legislative provisions for their protection will be in accord with their interests as they see them. But I don't think we are warranted in varying constitutional construction based on physical differences between men and women, because of the Amendment.

. . .

But for my inability to agree with some general observations in the forcible opinion of MR. JUSTICE HOLMES who follows me, I should be silent and merely record my concurrence in what he says. It is perhaps wiser for me, however, in a case of this importance, separately to give my reasons for dissenting.

I am authorized to say that MR. JUSTICE SANFORD concurs in this opinion.

MR. JUSTICE HOLMES, dissenting.

The question in this case is the broad one, Whether Congress can establish minimum rates of wages for women in the District of Columbia with due provision for special circumstances, or whether we must say that Congress has no power to meddle with the matter at all. To me, notwithstanding the deference due to the prevailing judgment of the Court, the power of Congress seems absolutely free from doubt. The end, to remove conditions leading to ill health, immorality and the deterioration of the race, no one would deny to be within the scope of constitutional legislation. The means are means that have the approval of Congress, of many States, and of those governments from which we have learned our greatest lessons. When so many intelligent persons, who have studied the matter more than any of us can, have thought that the means are effective and are worth the price, it seems to me impossible to deny that the belief reasonably may be held by reasonable men....

The earlier decisions upon the same words in the Fourteenth Amendment began within our memory and went no farther than an unpretentious assertion of the liberty to follow the ordinary callings. Later that innocuous generality was expanded into the dogma, Liberty of Contract.

Contract is not specially mentioned in the text that we have to construe. It is merely an example of doing what you want to do, embodied in the word liberty. But pretty much all law consists in forbidding men to do some things that they want to do, and contract is no more exempt from law than other acts....

I confess that I do not understand the principle on which the power to fix a minimum for the wages of women can be denied by those who admit the power to fix a maximum for their hours of work. I fully assent to the proposition that here as elsewhere the distinctions of the law are distinctions of degree, but I perceive no difference in the kind or degree of interference with liberty, the only matter with which we have any concern, between the one case and the other. The bargain is equally affected whichever half you regulate. *Muller* v. *Oregon,* I take it, is as good law today as it was in 1908. It will need more than the Nineteenth Amendment to convince me that there are no differences between men and women, or that legislation cannot take those differences into account....

West Coast Hotel Co. v. Parrish

300 U.S. 379 (1937)

This case overruled *Adkins* v. *Children's Hospital* (1923) and, with it, the doctrine that courts can continually second-guess legislative judgments about the need for statutes governing minimum wages, maximum hours, and other aspects of industrial working conditions. Similarly, this case rejects the exalted notion of "liberty of contract," which presupposed an equality of power between employer and employee to work out a mutually satisfactory contract. The issue before the Court in this case was a statute of the state of Washington providing for the establishment of minimum wages for women. Elsie Parrish, an employee of the West Coast Hotel Company, sued to recover wages owed her under the state law.

MR. CHIEF JUSTICE HUGHES delivered the opinion of the Court.

. . .

The appellant relies upon the decision of this Court in *Adkins* v. *Children's Hospital,* 261 U.S. 525, which held invalid the District of Columbia Minimum Wage Act, which was attacked under the due process clause of the Fifth Amendment. On the argument at bar, counsel for the appellees attempted to distinguish the *Adkins* case upon the ground that the appellee was employed in a hotel and that the business of an innkeeper was affected with a public interest. That effort at dis-

tinction is obviously futile, as it appears that in one of the cases ruled by the *Adkins* opinion the employee was a woman employed as an elevator operator in a hotel. *Adkins* v. *Lyons,* 261 U.S. 525, at p. 542.

The recent case of *Morehead* v. *New York ex rel. Tipaldo,* 298 U.S. 587, came here on certiorari to the New York court, which had held the New York minimum wage act for women to be invalid. A minority of this Court thought that the New York statute was distinguishable in a material feature from that involved in the *Adkins* case, and that for that and other reasons the New York statute should be sustained. But the Court of Appeals of New York had said that it found no material difference between the two statutes, and this Court held that the "meaning of the statute" as fixed by the decision of the state court "must be accepted here as if the meaning had been specifically expressed in the enactment." *Id., p. 609.* That view led to the affirmance by this Court of the judgment in the *Morehead* case, as the Court considered that the only question before it was whether the *Adkins* case was distinguishable and that reconsideration of that decision had not been sought. Upon that point the Court said: "The petition for the writ sought review upon the ground that this case [*Morehead*] is distinguishable from that one [*Adkins*]. No application has been made for reconsideration of the constitutional question there decided. The validity of the principles upon which that decision rests is not challenged. This court confines itself to the ground upon which the writ was asked or granted.... Here the review granted was no broader than that sought by the petitioner.... He is not entitled and does not ask to be heard upon the question whether the *Adkins* case should be overruled. He maintains that it may be distinguished on the ground that the statutes are vitally dissimilar." *Id., pp. 604, 605.*

We think that the question which was not deemed to be open in the *Morehead* case is open and is necessarily presented here. The Supreme Court of Washington has upheld the minimum wage statute of that State. It has decided that the statute is a reasonable exercise of the police power of the State. In reaching that conclusion the state court has invoked principles long established by this Court in the application of the Fourteenth Amendment. The state court has refused to regard the decision in the *Adkins* case as determinative and has pointed to our decisions both before and since that case as justifying its position. We are of the opinion that this ruling of the state court demands on our part a reëxamination of the *Adkins* case. The importance of the question, in which many States having similar laws are concerned, the close division by which the decision in the *Adkins* case was reached, and the economic conditions which have supervened, and in the light of which the reasonableness of the exercise of the protective power of the State must be considered, make it not only appropriate, but we think imperative, that in deciding the present case the subject should receive fresh consideration.

. . .

The principle which must control our decision is not in doubt. The constitutional provision invoked is the due process clause of the Fourteenth Amendment governing the States, as the due process clause invoked in the *Adkins* case governed Congress. In each case the violation alleged by those attacking minimum wage regulation for women is deprivation of freedom of contract. What is this freedom? The Constitution does not speak of freedom of contract. It speaks of liberty and prohibits the deprivation of liberty without due process of law. In prohibiting that deprivation the Constitution does not recognize an absolute and uncontrollable liberty. Liberty in each of its phases has its history and connotation. But the liberty safeguarded is liberty in a social organization which requires the protection of law against the evils which menace the health, safety, morals and welfare of the people. Liberty under the Constitution is thus necessarily subject to the restraints of due process, and regulation which is reasonable in relation to its subject and is adopted in the interests of the community is due process.

This essential limitation of liberty in general governs freedom of contract in particular. More than twenty-five years ago we set forth the applicable principle in these words, after referring to the cases where the liberty guaranteed by the Fourteenth Amendment had been broadly described:

"But it was recognized in the cases cited, as in many others, that freedom of contract is a qualified and not an absolute right. There is no absolute freedom to do as one wills or to contract as one chooses. The guaranty of liberty does not withdraw from legislative supervision that wide department of activity which consists of the making of contracts, or deny to government the power to provide restrictive safeguards. Liberty implies the absence of arbitrary restraint, not immunity from reasonable regulations and prohibitions imposed in the interests of the community." *Chicago, B. & Q. R. Co. v. McGuire,* 219 U.S. 549, 567.

This power under the Constitution to restrict freedom of contract has had many illustrations. That it may be exercised in the public interest with respect to contracts between employer and employee is undeniable....

The point that has been strongly stressed that adult employees should be deemed competent to make their own contracts was decisively met nearly forty years ago in *Holden* v. *Hardy, supra,* where we pointed out the inequality in the footing of the parties....

· · ·

It is manifest that this established principle is peculiarly applicable in relation to the employment of women in whose protection the State has a special interest. That phase of the subject received elaborate consideration in *Muller* v. *Oregon* (1908), 208 U.S. 412, where the constitutional authority of the State to limit the working hours of women was sustained....

[After reviewing the dissents of Justice Holmes and Chief Justice Taft in Adkins, *and citing cases after* Adkins *that upheld state statutes on economic regulation, the Court concludes:]*

With full recognition of the earnestness and vigor which characterize the prevailing opinion in the *Adkins* case, we find it impossible to reconcile that ruling with these well-considered declarations. What can be closer to the public interest than the health of women and their protection from unscrupulous and overreaching employers? And if the protection of women is a legitimate end of the exercise of state power, how can it be said that the requirement of the payment of a minimum wage fairly fixed in order to meet the very necessities of existence is not an admissible means to that end? The legislature of the State was clearly entitled to consider the situation of women in employment, the fact that they are in the class receiving the least pay, that their bargaining power is relatively weak, and that they are the ready victims of those who would take advantage of their necessitous circumstances....

There is an additional and compelling consideration which recent economic experience has brought into a strong light. The exploitation of a class of workers who are in an unequal position with respect to bargaining power and are thus relatively defenceless against the denial of a living wage is not only detrimental to their health and well being but casts a direct burden for their support upon the community. What these workers lose in wages the taxpayers are called upon to pay. The bare cost of living must be met. We may take judicial notice of the unparalleled demands for relief which arose during the recent period of depression and still continue to an alarming extent despite the degree of economic recovery which has been achieved.... The community is not bound to provide what is in effect a subsidy for unconscionable employers....

· · ·

Our conclusion is that the case of *Adkins* v.

Children's Hospital, supra, should be, and it is, overruled. The judgment of the Supreme Court of the State of Washington is

Affirmed.

Mr. Justice Sutherland, dissenting:

Mr. Justice Van Devanter, Mr. Justice McReynolds, Mr. Justice Butler and I think the judgment of the court below should be reversed.

· · ·

The suggestion that the only check upon the exercise of the judicial power, when properly invoked, to declare a constitutional right superior to an unconstitutional statute is the judge's own faculty of self-restraint, is both ill considered and mischievous. Self-restraint belongs in the domain of will and not of judgment. The check upon the judge is that imposed by his oath of office, by the Constitution and by his own conscientious and informed convictions; and since he has the duty to make up his own mind and adjudge accordingly, it is hard to see how there could be any other restraint....

It is urged that the question involved should now receive fresh consideration, among other reasons, because of "the economic conditions which have supervened"; but the meaning of the Constitution does not change with the ebb and flow of economic events. We frequently are told in more general words that the Constitution must be construed in the light of the present. If by that it is meant that the Constitution is made up of living words that apply to every new condition which they include, the statement is quite true. But to say, if that be intended, that the words of the Constitution mean today what they did not mean when written—that is, that they do not apply to a situation now to which they would have applied then—is to rob that instrument of the essential element which continues it in force as the people have made it until they, and not their official agents, have made it otherwise.

· · ·

Coming, then, to a consideration of the Washington statute, it first is to be observed that it is in every substantial respect identical with the statute involved in the *Adkins* case. Such vices as existed in the latter are present in the former. And if the *Adkins* case was properly decided, as we who join in this opinion think it was, it necessarily follows that the Washington statute is invalid.

. . .

The Washington statute, like the one for the District of Columbia, fixes minimum wages for adult women. Adult men and their employers are left free to bargain as they please; and it is a significant and an important fact that all state statutes to which our attention has been called are of like character. The common-law rules restricting the power of women to make contracts have, under our system, long since practically disappeared.

Women today stand upon a legal and political equality with men. There is no longer any reason why they should be put in different classes in respect of their legal right to make contracts; nor should they be denied, in effect, the right to compete with men for work paying lower wages which men may be willing to accept. And it is an arbitrary exercise of the legislative power to do so.

. . .

Ferguson v. Skrupa

372 U.S. 726 (1963)

For a period of about four or five decades, ending in 1937, the Supreme Court overturned dozens of statutes enacted by Congress and state legislatures to ameliorate the conditions of industrialization. Laws establishing minimum wages and maximum hours, regulating child labor, and governing other aspects of industrial society were struck down. In this decision, the Court explains that such matters in the future will be left essentially to legislatures, not courts. Frank C. Skrupa, in the business of "debt adjusting," brought this action against the Attorney General of Kansas, William M. Ferguson.

MR. JUSTICE BLACK delivered the opinion of the Court.

In this case, properly here on appeal under 28 U.S.C. § 1253, we are asked to review the judgment of a three-judge District Court enjoining, as being in violation of the Due Process Clause of the Fourteenth Amendment, a Kansas statute making it a misdemeanor for any person to engage "in the business of debt adjusting" except as an incident to "the lawful practice of law in this state." The statute defines "debt adjusting" as "the making of a contract, express or implied, with a particular debtor whereby the debtor agrees to pay a certain amount of money periodically to the person engaged in the debt adjusting business who shall for a consideration distribute the same among certain specified creditors in accordance with a plan agreed upon."

The complaint, filed by appellee Skrupa doing business as "Credit Advisors," alleged that Skrupa was engaged in the business of "debt adjusting" as defined by the statute, that his business was a "useful and desirable" one, that his business activities were not "inherently immoral or dangerous" or in any way contrary to the public welfare, and that therefore the business could not be "absolutely prohibited" by Kansas. The three-judge court heard evidence by Skrupa tending to show the usefulness and desirability of his business and evidence

by the state officials tending to show that "debt adjusting" lends itself to grave abuses against distressed debtors, particularly in the lower income brackets, and that these abuses are of such gravity that a number of States have strictly regulated "debt adjusting" or prohibited it altogether....

The only case discussed by the court below as support for its invalidation of the statute was *Commonwealth* v. *Stone*, 191 Pa. Super. 117, 155 A. 2d 453 (1959), in which the Superior Court of Pennsylvania struck down a statute almost identical to the Kansas act involved here....[T]he Pennsylvania court relied heavily on *Adams* v. *Tanner*, 244 U.S. 590 (1917), which held that the Due Process Clause forbids a State to prohibit a business which is "useful" and not "inherently immoral or dangerous to public welfare."

Both the District Court in the present case and the Pennsylvania court in *Stone* adopted the philosophy of *Adams* v. *Tanner*, and cases like it, that it is the province of courts to draw on their own views as to the morality, legitimacy, and usefulness of a particular business in order to decide whether a statute bears too heavily upon that business and by so doing violates due process. Under the system of government created by our Constitution, it is up to legislatures, not courts, to decide on the wisdom and utility of legislation. There was a time when the Due Process Clause was used by this Court to strike down laws which were thought unreasonable, that is, unwise or incompatible with some particular economic or social philosophy. In this manner the Due Process Clause was used, for example, to nullify laws prescribing maximum hours for work in bakeries, *Lochner* v. *New York,* 198 U.S. 45 (1905), outlawing "yellow dog" contracts, *Coppage* v. *Kansas,* 236 U.S. 1 (1915), setting minimum wages for women, *Adkins* v. *Children's Hospital,* 261 U.S. 525 (1923), and fixing the weight of loaves of bread, *Jay Burns Baking Co.* v. *Bryan,* 264 U.S. 504 (1924). This intrusion by the judiciary into the realm of legislative value judgments was strongly objected to at the time, particularly by Mr. Justice Holmes and Mr. Justice Brandeis....

The doctrine that prevailed in *Lochner, Coppage, Adkins, Burns,* and like cases — that due process authorizes courts to hold laws unconstitutional when they believe the legislature has acted unwisely — has long since been discarded. We have returned to the original constitutional proposition that courts do not substitute their social and economic beliefs for the judgment of legislative bodies, who are elected to pass laws....

...We conclude that the Kansas Legislature was free to decide for itself that legislation was needed to deal with the business of debt adjusting.

Unquestionably, there are arguments showing that the business of debt adjusting has social utility, but such arguments are properly addressed to the legislature, not to us. We refuse to sit as a "superlegislature to weigh the wisdom of legislation," and we emphatically refuse to go back to the time when courts used the Due Process Clause "to strike down state laws, regulatory of business and industrial conditions, because they may be unwise, improvident, or out of harmony with a particular school of thought." Nor are we able or willing to draw lines by calling a law "prohibitory" or "regulatory." Whether the legislature takes for its textbook Adam Smith, Herbert Spencer, Lord Keynes, or some other is no concern of ours. The Kansas debt adjusting statute may be wise or unwise. But relief, if any be needed, lies not with us but with the body constituted to pass laws for the State of Kansas.

. . .

Reversed.

MR. JUSTICE HARLAN concurs in the judgment on the ground that this state measure bears a rational relation to a constitutionally permissible objective. See *Williamson* v. *Lee Optical Co.,* 348 U.S. 483, 491.

CONCLUSIONS

The protection of economic rights is not the province solely of the courts. Legislators and executives (at both the national and state levels) make the initial determination in balancing the rights of property owners against the interests of communities and society. The historical record demonstrates that when the judiciary invokes artificial doctrines to prevent legislative action ("liberty of contract" and other slogans), the persistence of social and political pressures has been sufficient, over time, to prevail. The main struggle over economic rights is fought out within the political branches through the electoral process. Aside from a few pivotal decisions, courts generally play a marginal role at the very edges of these conflicts.

An artificial line between property rights and human rights continues to be drawn. With forceful prose, Justice Stewart attempted to join the two concepts:

[T]he dichotomy between personal liberties and property rights is a false one. Property does not have rights. People have rights. The right to enjoy property without unlawful deprivation, no less than the right to speak or the right to travel, is in truth a "personal" right, whether the "property" in question be a welfare check, a home, or a savings account. In fact, a fundamental interdependence exists between the personal right to liberty and the personal right in property. Neither could have meaning without the other. Lynch v. Household Finance Corp., 405 U.S. 538, 552 (1972).

SELECTED READINGS

ACKERMAN, BRUCE. Private Property and the Constitution. New Haven, Conn.: Yale University Press, 1977.

BERGER, LAWRENCE. "A Policy Analysis of the Taking Problem." 49 New York University Law Review 165 (1974).

BLUME, LAWRENCE, AND DANIEL L. RUBINFELD. "Compensation for Takings: An Economic Analysis." 72 California Law Review 569 (1984).

BRIGHAM, JOHN. "Property & the Supreme Court: Do the Justices Make Sense?" 16 Polity 242 (1983).

CALLIES, DAVID L., et al. Cases and Materials on Land Use. St. Paul, Minn.: West Group, 1999.

———, ed. Takings: Land-Development Conditions and Regulatory Takings after *Dolan* and *Lucas*. Section of State and Local Government Law, American Bar Association, 1996.

COHEN, FELIX S. "Dialogue on Private Property." 9 Rutgers Law Review 357 (1954).

DUNHAM, ALLISON. "Griggs v. Allegheny County in Perspective: Thirty Years of Supreme Court Expropriation Law." 1962 Supreme Court Review 63.

ELY, JAMES W., JR. The Guardian of Every Other Right: A Constitutional History of Property Rights. New York: Oxford University Press, 1992.

EPSTEIN, RICHARD A. Takings: Private Property and the Power of Eminent Domain. Cambridge, Mass.: Harvard University Press, 1985.

HALE, ROBERT L. "The Supreme Court and the Contract Clause." 57 Harvard Law Review 512, 621, 852 (1944).

HORWITZ, MORTON J. "The Transformation in the Conception of Property in American Law." 40 University of Chicago Law Review 248 (1973).

HUMBACH, JOHN A. "A Unifying Theory for the Just-Compensation Cases: Takings, Regulation and Public Use." 34 Rutgers Law Review 243 (1982).

JOHNSON, CORWIN W. "Compensation for Invalid Land-Use Regulations." 15 Georgia Law Review 559 (1981).

LERNER, MAX. "The Supreme Court and American Capitalism." 42 Yale Law Journal 668 (1933).

LEVY, LEONARD W. "Property As a Human Right." 5 Constitutional Commentary 169 (1988).

McCLOSKEY, ROBERT G. "Economic Due Process and the Supreme Court: An Exhumation and Reburial." 1962 Supreme Court Review 34.

MANDELKER, DANIEL R. "Land Use Takings: The Compensation Issue." 8 Hastings Constitutional Law Quarterly 491 (1981).

MENDELSON, WALLACE. "B.F. Wright on the Contract Clause: A Progressive Misreading of the Marshall-Taney Era," 38 Western Political Quarterly 262 (1985).

MICHELMAN, FRANK I. "Property, Utility, and Fairness: Comments on the Ethical Foundations of 'Just Compensation' Law." 80 Harvard Law Review 1165 (1967).

OAKES, JAMES L. " 'Property Rights' in Constitutional Analysis Today." 56 Washington Law Review 583 (1981).

REICH, CHARLES A. "The New Property." 73 Yale Law Journal 733 (1964).

ROSE, CAROL M. "Mahon Reconsidered: Why the Takings Issue Is Still a Muddle." 57 Southern California Law Review 561 (1984).

SALLET, JONATHAN B. "Regulatory 'Takings' and Just Compensation: The Supreme Court's Search for a Solution Continues." 18 Urban Lawyer 635 (1986).

SAX, JOSEPH L. "Takings and the Police Power." 74 Yale Law Journal 36 (1964).

———. "Takings, Private Property, and Public Rights." 81 Yale Law Journal 149 (1971).

STOEBUCK, WILLIAM B. "Police Power, Takings, and Due Process." 37 Washington and Lee Law Review 1057 (1980).

WRIGHT, BENJAMIN F., JR. The Contract Clause of the Constitution. Cambridge, Mass.: Harvard University Press, 1938.

10

Free Speech in a Democratic Society

The foundations for a free and open society are recognized in the First Amendment: "Congress shall make no law respecting an establishment of religion, or prohibiting the free exercise thereof; or abridging the freedom of speech, or of the press; or the right of the people peaceably to assemble, and to petition the Government for a redress of grievances." Through these words the framers attempted to secure the freedom of conscience and the free communication of ideas. To Justice Cardozo, the freedom of thought and speech forms "the matrix, the indispensable condition, of nearly every other form of freedom." Palko v. Connecticut, 302 U.S. 319, 327 (1937).

Free speech fulfills a number of personal, social, and political functions. In part, it strengthens individual growth and self-fulfillment. In the words of Justice Brandeis, it exists to "make men free to develop their faculties." Whitney v. California, 274 U.S. 357, 375 (1927). The First Amendment protects the "marketplace" of ideas, the promotion of knowledge, and the search for truth. Finally, the First Amendment "serves to ensure that the individual citizen can effectively participate in and contribute to our republican system of self-government." Globe Newspaper Co. v. Superior Court, 457 U.S. 596, 604 (1982). In this sense, it reinforces the full political debate needed in a vigorous and healthy democratic society.

Only by tolerating different ideas and beliefs can democracy function and survive, especially in a culture as heterogeneous and heterodox as the United States. The history of America is largely the repudiation of orthodoxy by the spirit of individualism and nonconformism. In a famous dissent in 1929, Justice Holmes said that "if there is any principle of the Constitution that more imperatively calls for attachment than any other it is the principle of free thought — not free thought for those who agree with us but freedom for the thought that we hate." United States v. Schwimmer, 279 U.S. 644, 654–55 (1929). Zechariah Chafee, Jr., a major influence on free-speech doctrines, put it differently: "The real value of freedom of speech is not to the minority that wants to talk, but to the majority that does not want to listen." Zechariah Chafee, Jr., Free Speech in the United States ix (1941).

Even if the Constitution lacked a First Amendment, representative government requires that citizens be free to discuss government and debate its policies. Some forms of speech make government impossible, such as actions that disrupt legislatures and courts. The following sections identify the major tests used to scrutinize governmental limitations placed on speech.

A. FREE SPEECH AND NATIONAL SECURITY

In certain periods of our history, speech has been suppressed and punished. The heavy hand of the majority fell against sympathizers with France during the 1790s; labor organizers, anarchists, and socialists in the late nineteenth and early twentieth centuries; opponents of World War I; the Communists during and after World War II; and those who spoke out against the Vietnam War. Throughout these periods, the Supreme Court attempted to fashion doctrines to protect pure speech but not action, activity, and advocacy. Distinctions between these categories remain opaque.

Sedition

In 1798 the Federalist party passed the notorious Alien and Sedition Acts to silence the opposition within the United States, particularly Republicans and "Francophiles." The Alien Acts increased the years of residence for aliens seeking citizenship, authorized deportation of "dangerous" aliens, and imposed other sanctions. 1 Stat. 566, 570, 577 (1798). The Sedition Act prohibited any person from printing or uttering "any false, scandalous and malicious" statement against the federal government, either House of Congress, or the President. 1 Stat. 596, § 2 (1798). This statute is analyzed more closely in the next chapter.

Not until the United States entered World War I did Congress pass another sedition act. Section 3 of the Espionage Act of 1917 prohibited acts that interfered with or obstructed military recruitment or morale. When opponents of the war released pamphlets that attacked conscription and urged opposition to the draft, the government responded with criminal prosecutions. A unanimous Supreme Court upheld the indictments on the basis of wartime conditions and circumstances. Writing for the Court, Justice Holmes penned his famous admonition against "shouting fire in a theatre" and offered his "clear and present danger" test. SCHENCK v. UNITED STATES, 249 U.S. 47 (1919). Holmes offered a poor analogy. Shouting a *false statement* in a crowded theater to produce panic has nothing to do with circulating a leaflet that expresses an *opinion* about a war.

The Court issued similar rulings against war protesters that same month. Frohwerk v. United States, 249 U.S. 204 (1919); Debs v. United States, 249 U.S. 211 (1919). This line of cases developed the "bad tendency" test to curb speech that posed threats or a danger to society. Under this test, there need be no clear and present danger. The mere tendency to create evil justifies suppression.

In a penetrating critique in the *Harvard Law Review* in 1919, Zechariah Chafee, Jr., argued that the First Amendment declared a national policy "in favor of the public discussion of all public questions. Such a declaration should make Congress reluctant and careful in the enactment of all restrictions upon utterance, even though the courts will not refuse to enforce them as unconstitutional." Chafee claimed that the framers adopted the First Amendment to give "the right of unrestricted discussion of public affairs," not only in time of peace but more importantly during war (see box on next page). The First Amendment protected not merely an individual's interest in speaking out but society's interest in hearing criticism and vigorous debate.

Following the appearance of this article, Holmes and Brandeis dissented in a free-speech case later that year. Five antiwar activists had been convicted for criticizing U.S. involvement in World War I, encouraging resistance, and urging workers not to produce war materials. Holmes wrote one of his memorable dissents, appealing for tolerance and the "free trade in ideas." ABRAMS v. UNITED STATES, 250 U.S. 616 (1919). The clear-and-present-danger test supposedly favors free speech more than the bad-tendency test, but these standards are applied unevenly.

The Sedition Act of 1918 made it illegal to utter "any disloyal, profane, scurrilous, or abusive language" about the form of government, the Constitution, soldiers and sailors, the flag, or uniform of the armed forces. State laws that declared it a misdemeanor to teach or advocate that citizens should not assist the United States in carrying on a war with its enemies were upheld. Gilbert v. Minnesota, 254 U.S. 325 (1920). A New York law punished persons for advocating the overthrow of government. The Court sustained the statute, treating such advocacy as "a call to action" rather than abstract doctrine. GITLOW v. NEW YORK, 268 U.S. 652 (1925). Holmes and Brandeis dissented, objecting that "[e]very idea is an incitement." In *Gitlow,* the Court also ruled that freedoms of speech and press are among the personal rights and liberties protected by the Due Process Clause of the Fourteenth Amendment and are therefore applied against the states. Just three years before, the Court had held that the Fourteenth

Free Speech During Wartime

...It is sometimes argued that the Constitution gives Congress the power to declare war, raise armies, and support a navy, that one provision of the Constitution cannot be used to break down another provision, and consequently freedom of speech cannot be invoked to break down the war power. I would reply that the First Amendment is just as much a part of the Constitution as the war clauses, and that it is equally accurate to say that the war clauses cannot be invoked to break down freedom of speech. The truth is that all provisions of the Constitution must be construed together so as to limit each other. In war as in peace, this process of mutual adjustment must include the Bill of Rights. There are those who believe that the Bill of Rights can be set aside in war time at the uncontrolled will of the government. The first ten amendments were drafted by men who had just been through a war. Two of these amendments expressly apply in war....

The First Amendment protects two kinds of interests in free speech. There is an individual interest, the need of many men to express their opinions on matters vital to them if life is to be worth living, and a social interest in the attainment of truth, so that the country may not only adopt the wisest course of action but carry it out in the wisest way. This social interest is especially important in war time. Even after war has been declared there is bound to be a confused mixture of good and bad arguments in its support, and a wide difference of opinion as to its objects. Truth can be sifted out from falsehood only if the government is vigorously and constantly cross-examined, so that the fundamental issues of the struggle may be clearly defined, and the war may not be diverted to improper ends, or conducted with an undue sacrifice of life and liberty, or prolonged after its just purposes are accomplished. Legal proceedings prove that an opponent makes the best cross-examiner. Consequently it is a disastrous mistake to limit criticism to those who favor the war....

SOURCE: Zechariah Chafee, Jr., "Freedom of Speech in War Time," 32 Harv. L. Rev. 932, 955, 958 (1919).

Amendment did *not* impose upon the states an obligation to confer the right of free speech. Prudential Ins. Co. v. Cheek, 259 U.S. 530, 538, 542–43 (1922).

In two decisions in 1927, the Court tackled the issue of syndicalism: the doctrine that workers could use force to seize control of the economy and the government. A unanimous Court upheld California's statute against criminal syndicalism, but Justice Brandeis in his concurrence prepared a masterful essay on the principles of free speech. WHITNEY v. CALIFORNIA, 274 U.S. 357 (1927). Another unanimous opinion that year struck down Kansas's syndicalism statute because it punished class struggles unrelated to crime, violence, or other unlawful acts. Fiske v. Kansas, 274 U.S. 380 (1927). A California statute making it a felony to display a red flag to symbolize opposition to government was declared unconstitutionally vague. Stromberg v. California, 283 U.S. 359 (1931). Also on the ground of vagueness, the Court invalidated a Georgia statute that made it a crime to attempt to incite insurrection or resistance by force. Herndon v. Lowry, 301 U.S. 242 (1937).

National security interests were invoked during the Vietnam War to restrain free speech. A series of cases in 1968 and 1969 involved draft-card burning, the wearing of black arm bands to protest the war, and flag burning, all covered in a later section on symbolic speech (pages 528–30). In addition, in 1970 a unanimous Court struck down a congressional statute that imposed criminal penalties for the unauthorized wearing of an American military uniform except for a theatrical or motion picture production that does not discredit the armed forces. The statute, applied against a skit that expressed opposition to American involvement in the Vietnam War, imposed an unconstitutional restraint on free speech by singling out for punishment productions that were unfavorable to the military. Schacht v. United States, 398 U.S. 58 (1970). (The Pentagon Papers case, one of the key decisions on national security and the First Amendment, is discussed in Chapters 7 and 11.)

The Communist Cases

Following World War II, Congress placed a number of restrictions on members of the Communist party. The Labor Management Relations Act of 1947 required union officers to file a non-Communist affidavit. 61 Stat. 146, 9(h). The purpose was to remove obstructions to commerce from "political strikes" instigated by Communists. The Court, by a 4 to 2 vote, held that the statute bore a reasonable relation to the "evil" it was designed to reach and did not interfere with speech or thought. The statute, said the Court, was designed to regulate *conduct* and "Congress, not the courts, is primarily charged with determination of the need for regulation of activities affecting interstate commerce." American Communications Assn. v. Douds, 339 U.S. 382, 400 (1950). There was no actual conduct, however. The mere threat or capability of obstructing commerce was considered adequate grounds for the statute.

A year later, the Court decided the constitutionality of the Smith Act of 1940, which made it unlawful for any person to advocate the violent overthrow of "any government in the United States" or to conspire to advocate such violence. Divided 6 to 2, the Court upheld the statute against the charge that it violated the First Amendment because of indefiniteness. Although the Smith Act was aimed at potential conduct rather than actual conduct, the Court responded to the free-speech issue by saying that the statute was "directed at advocacy, not discussion." DENNIS v. UNITED STATES, 341 U.S. 494, 502 (1951). "We hold that the statute may be applied where there is a 'clear and present danger' of the substantive evil which the legislature had the right to prevent." Id. at 512. In his concurrence, Frankfurter conceded the difficulty of distinguishing between protected speech and unprotected advocacy: "It is true that there is no divining rod by which we may locate 'advocacy.' Exposition of ideas readily merges into advocacy." Id. at 545.

Dennis was severely circumscribed in 1957 when the Court reversed the convictions of fourteen Communists charged with advocating and teaching the overthrow of the United States government by force and violence. The Court held that the Smith Act did not prohibit advocacy and teaching of forcible overthrow as an abstract principle. As interpreted by the Court, the statute proscribed only the "advocacy of action to that end." The meaning of that phrase remains vague, but the effect has been to extend greater protection to pure advocacy. YATES v. UNITED STATES, 354 U.S. 298 (1957). From *Schenck* to contemporary cases, the Supreme Court experiments with a number of shifting tests and doctrines on free speech (see box on next page).

Both Congress and the courts were involved in monitoring, and finally abolishing, the Subversive Activities Control Board (SACB), which had been authorized to order groups to register with the Attorney General as a "Communist-action" organization. An effort to adjudicate the statute was turned aside in 1956 because of alleged perjuries committed by three government witnesses. Communist Party v. SACB, 351 U.S. 115 (1956). Five years later the Court, with a 5 to 4 vote, affirmed the Board's finding that the Communist party was a Communist-action organization and therefore required to register with the Attorney General. Sidestepping such constitutional issues as free speech, bill of attainder, and self-incrimination, the Court concluded that the statute was "regulatory" rather than "prohibitory." Communist Party v. SACB, 367 U.S. 1 (1961). On that same day, in two decisions, the Court held that mere membership in the Communist party did not violate the Smith Act. Punishment could be applied only against members who actively advanced the party's aims. It is therefore no longer a crime to advocate, as an abstract doctrine, the forcible overthrow of government. Scales v. United States, 367 U.S. 203 (1961); Noto v. United States, 367 U.S. 290 (1961).

Other cases during this period also relaxed the pattern of rigid anticommunism. In 1965 the Court held that a congressional statute making it a crime for a Communist party member to serve as union officer constituted a bill of attainder. United States v. Brown, 381 U.S. 437.

Free Speech Tests

Clear and Present Danger	Government may suppress speech only when it represents a clear and present danger to society. "The question in every case is whether the words used are used in such circumstances and are of such a nature as to create a clear and present danger that they will bring about the substantive evils that Congress has a right to prevent." Schenck v. United States, 249 U.S. 47, 52 (1919).
Bad Tendency	Even a "tendency" to obstruct government justifies prosecution. Debs v. United States, 249 U.S. 211, 216 (1919). Government can extinguish a spark before it becomes a flame. Gitlow v. New York, 268 U.S. 652, 669 (1925).
Preferred Position	"Freedom of press, freedom of speech, freedom of religion are in a preferred position." Murdock v. Pennsylvania, 319 U.S. 105, 115 (1943); Jones v. Opelika, 316 U.S. 584, 608 (1942) (Stone, J., dissenting).
Action, not Advocacy	Constitution permits pure advocacy and teaching of forcible overthrow of government by force and violence. What is proscribed is advocacy of action. Yates v. United States, 354 U.S. 298 (1957); Brandenburg v. Ohio, 395 U.S. 444, 447 (1969).
Ad Hoc Balancing	Government may suppress speech when its own interests outweigh those of an individual. Barenblatt v. United States, 360 U.S. 109 (1959).

In the same year, a unanimous Court struck down the registration feature as a violation of the Self-Incrimination Clause because information submitted to the Attorney General could be used as evidence toward a criminal prosecution. Albertson v. SACB, 382 U.S. 70 (1965).

Congress rejuvenated the Subversive Activities Control Board in 1968 by authorizing it to determine, through hearings, whether individuals and organizations were Communist. The following year an appellate court declared that the new procedure violated the First Amendment freedom of association. Boorda v. SACB, 421 F.2d 1142 (D.C. Cir. 1969), cert. denied, 397 U.S. 1042 (1970). With the Board facing extinction, President Nixon issued an executive order expanding its power and field of inquiry. After Congress used its power of the purse to deny funds to carry out the executive order, the Board went out of business. Fisher, Constitutional Conflicts Between Congress and the President 112–13 (1997).

Schenck v. United States

249 U.S. 47 (1919)

Charles T. Schenck, general secretary of the Socialist party, was charged with violating the Espionage Act of 1917. The government claimed that the printing and circulation of 15,000 leaflets, which attacked the draft for World War I, caused insubordination in the military forces and obstructed the recruitment and enlistment of soldiers. Writing for a unanimous Court, Justice Holmes formulated his "clear and present danger" test for deciding First Amendment questions.

MR. JUSTICE HOLMES delivered the opinion of the court.

This is an indictment in three counts. The first charges a conspiracy to violate the Espionage Act of June 15, 1917, c. 30, § 3, 40 Stat. 217, 219, by causing and attempting to cause insubordination, &c., in the military and naval forces of the United States, and to obstruct the recruiting and enlistment service of the United States, when the United States was at war with the German Empire, to-wit, that the defendants wilfully conspired to have printed and circulated to men who had been called and accepted for military service under the Act of May 18, 1917, a document set forth and alleged to be calculated to cause such insubordination and obstruction. The count alleges overt acts in pursuance of the conspiracy, ending in the distribution of the document set forth. The second count alleges a conspiracy to commit an offence against the United States, to-wit, to use the mails for the transmission of matter declared to be nonmailable by Title XII, § 2 of the Act of June 15, 1917, to-wit, the above mentioned document, with an averment of the same overt acts. The third count charges an unlawful use of the mails for the transmission of the same matter and otherwise as above. The defendants were found guilty on all the counts. They set up the First Amendment to the Constitution forbidding Congress to make any law abridging the freedom of speech, or of the press, and bringing the case here on that ground have argued some other points also of which we must dispose.

. . .

The document in question upon its first printed side recited the first section of the Thirteenth Amendment, said that the idea embodied in it was violated by the Conscription Act and that a conscript is little better than a convict. In impassioned language it intimated that conscription was despotism in its worst form and a monstrous wrong against humanity in the interest of Wall Street's chosen few. It said "Do not submit to intimidation," but in form at least confined itself to peaceful measures such as a petition for the repeal of the act. The other and later printed side of the sheet was headed "Assert Your Rights." It stated reasons for alleging that any one violated the Constitution when he refused to recognize "your right to assert your opposition to the draft," and went on "If you do not assert and support your rights, you are helping to deny or disparage rights which it is the solemn duty of all citizens and residents of the United States to retain." It described the arguments on the other side as coming from cunning politicians and a mercenary capitalist press, and even silent consent to the conscription law as helping to support an infamous conspiracy. It denied the power to send our citizens away to foreign shores to shoot up the people of other lands, and added that words could not express the condemnation such cold-blooded ruthlessness deserves, &c., &c., winding up "You must do your share to maintain, support and uphold the rights of the people of this country." Of course the document would not have been sent unless it had been intended to have some effect, and we do not see what effect it could be expected to have upon persons subject to the draft except to influence them to obstruct the carrying of it out. The defendants do not deny that the jury might find against them on this point.

But it is said, suppose that that was the tendency of this circular, it is protected by the First Amendment to the Constitution. Two of the strongest expressions are said to be quoted respectively from well-known public men. It well may be that the prohibition of laws abridging the freedom of speech is not confined to previous restraints, although to prevent them may have been the main purpose, as intimated in *Patterson* v. *Colorado,* 205 U.S. 454, 462. We admit that in many places and in ordinary times the defendants in saying all that was said in the circular would have been within their constitutional rights. But the character of every act depends upon the circumstances in which it is done. *Aikens* v. *Wisconsin,* 195 U. S. 194, 205, 206. The most stringent protection of free speech would not protect a man in falsely shouting fire in a theatre and causing a panic. It does not even protect a man from an injunction against uttering words that may have all the effect of force. *Gompers* v. *Bucks Stove & Range Co.,* 221 U. S. 418, 439. The question in every case is whether the words used are used in such circumstances and are of such a nature as to create a clear and present danger that they will bring about the substantive evils that Congress has a right to prevent. It is a question of proximity and degree. When a nation is at war many things that might be said in time of peace are such a hindrance to its effort that their utterance will not be endured so long as men fight and that no Court could regard them as protected by any constitutional right. It seems to be admitted that if an actual obstruction of the recruiting service were proved, liability for words that produced that effect might be enforced. The statute of 1917 in § 4 punishes conspiracies to obstruct as well as actual obstruction. If the act, (speaking, or circulating a paper,) its tendency and the intent with which it is done are the same, we perceive no ground for saying that success alone warrants making the act a crime. . . .

. . .

Judgments affirmed.

Abrams v. United States

250 U.S. 616 (1919)

In another prosecution under the Espionage Act, the government charged five defendants with printing and circulating leaflets that opposed U.S. involvement in World War I. The five defendants, all born in Russia, were Jacob Abrams, Hyman Lachowsky, Samuel Lipman, Hyman Rosansky, and Mollie Steimer. The dissent by Justice Holmes, considering his opinion in *Schenck* earlier in the year, is especially significant.

MR. JUSTICE CLARKE delivered the opinion of the court.

On a single indictment, containing four counts, the five plaintiffs in error, hereinafter designated the defendants, were convicted of conspiring to violate provisions of the Espionage Act of Congress (§ 3, Title I, of Act approved June 15, 1917, as amended May 16, 1918, 40 Stat. 553).

Each of the first three counts charged the defendants with conspiring, when the United States was at war with the Imperial Government of Germany, to unlawfully utter, print, write and publish: In the first count, "disloyal, scurrilous and abusive language about the form of Government of the United States;" in the second count, language "intended to bring the form of Government of the United States into contempt, scorn, contumely and disrepute;" and in the third count, language "intended to incite, provoke and encourage resistance to the United States in said war." The charge in the fourth count was that the defendants conspired "when the United States was at war with the Imperial German Government, ... unlawfully and willfully, by utterance, writing, printing and publication, to urge, incite and advocate curtailment of production of things and products, to wit, ordnance and ammunition, necessary and essential to the prosecution of the war." The offenses were charged in the language of the act of Congress.

It was charged in each count of the indictment that it was a part of the conspiracy that the defendants would attempt to accomplish their unlawful purpose by printing, writing and distributing in the City of New York many copies of a leaflet or circular, printed in the English language, and of another printed in the Yiddish language, copies of which, properly identified, were attached to the indictment.

All of the five defendants were born in Russia. They were intelligent, had considerable schooling, and at the time they were arrested they had lived in the United States terms varying from five to ten years, but none of them had applied for naturalization. Four of them testified as witnesses in their own behalf and of these, three frankly avowed that they were "rebels," "revolutionists," "anarchists," that they did not believe in government in any form, and they declared that they had no interest whatever in the Government of the United States. The fourth defendant testified that he was a "socialist" and believed in "a proper kind of government, not capitalistic," but in his classification the Government of the United States was "capitalistic."

It was admitted on the trial that the defendants had united to print and distribute the described circulars and that five thousand of them had been printed and distributed about the 22d day of August, 1918. . . . The circulars were distributed some by throwing them from a window of a building where one of the defendants was employed and others secretly, in New York City.

. . .

The first of the two articles attached to the indictment is conspicuously headed, "The Hypocrisy of the United States and her Allies." After denouncing President Wilson as a hypocrite and a coward because troops were sent into Russia, it proceeds to assail our Government in general, saying:

"His [the President's] shameful, cowardly silence about the intervention in Russia reveals the hypocrisy of the plutocratic gang in Washington and vicinity."

It continues:

"He [the President] is too much of a coward to come out openly and say: 'We capitalistic nations cannot afford to have a proletarian republic in Russia.'"

Among the capitalistic nations Abrams testified the United States was included.

Growing more inflammatory as it proceeds, the circular culminates in:

"The Russian Revolution cries: Workers of the World! Awake! Rise! Put down your enemy and mine!

"Yes! friends, there is only one enemy of the workers of the world and that is CAPITALISM."

This is clearly an appeal to the "workers" of this country to arise and put down by force the Government of the United States which they characterize as their "hypocritical," "cowardly" and "capitalistic" enemy.

It concludes:

"Awake! Awake, you Workers of the World!

"REVOLUTIONISTS."

The second of the articles was printed in the Yiddish language and in the translation is headed, "Workers—Wake up." After referring to "his Majesty, Mr. Wilson, and the rest of the gang; dogs of all colors!", it continues:

"Workers, Russian emigrants, you who had the least belief in the honesty of *our* Government,"

which defendants admitted referred to the United States Government,

"must now throw away all confidence, must spit in the face the false, hypocritic, military propaganda which has fooled you so relentlessly, calling forth your sympathy, your help, to the prosecution of the war."

The purpose of this obviously was to persuade the persons to whom it was addressed to turn a deaf ear to patriotic appeals in behalf of the Government of the United States, and to cease to render it assistance in the prosecution of the war.

It goes on:

"With the money which you have loaned, or are going to loan them, they will make bullets not only for the Germans, but also for the Workers Soviets of Russia. *Workers in the ammunition factories, you are producing bullets, bayonets, cannon, to murder not only the Germans, but also your dearest, best, who are in Russia and are fighting for freedom.*"

It will not do to say, as is now argued, that the only intent of these defendants was to prevent injury to the Russian cause. Men must be held to have intended, and to be accountable for, the effects which their acts were likely to produce. Even if their primary purpose and intent was to aid the cause of the Russian Revolution, the plan of action which they adopted necessarily involved, before it could be realized, defeat of the war program of the United States....

. . .

...[T]he plain purpose of their propaganda was to excite, at the supreme crisis of the war, disaffection, sedition, riots, and, as they hoped, revolution, in this country for the purpose of embarrassing and if possible defeating the military plans of the Government in Europe. A technical distinction may perhaps be taken between disloyal and abusive language applied to the *form* of our government or language intended to bring the *form* of our government into contempt and disrepute, and language of like character and intended to produce like results directed against the President and Congress, the agencies through which that form of government must function in time of war. But it is not necessary to a decision of this case to consider whether such distinction is vital or merely formal, for the language of these circulars was obviously intended to provoke and to encourage resistance to the United States in the war, as the third count runs, and, the defendants, in terms, plainly urged and advocated a resort to a general strike of workers in ammunition factories for the purpose of curtailing the production of ordnance and munitions necessary and essential to the prosecution of the war as is charged in the fourth count. Thus it is clear not only that some evidence but that much persuasive evidence was before the jury tending to prove that the defendants were guilty as charged in both the third and fourth counts of the indictment and under the long established rule of law hereinbefore stated the judgment of the District Court must be

Affirmed.

MR. JUSTICE HOLMES dissenting.

. . .

I never have seen any reason to doubt that the questions of law that alone were before this Court in the cases of *Schenck, Frohwerk* and *Debs*, 249 U.S. 47, 204, 211, were rightly decided. I do not doubt for a moment that by the same reasoning that would justify punishing persuasion to murder, the United States constitutionally may punish speech that produces or is intended to produce a clear and imminent danger that it will bring about forthwith certain substantive evils that the United States constitutionally may seek to prevent. The power undoubtedly is greater in time of war than in time of peace because war opens dangers that do not exist at other times.

But as against dangers peculiar to war, as against others, the principle of the right to free speech is always the same. It is only the present danger of immediate evil or an intent to bring it about that warrants Congress in setting a limit to the expression of opinion where private rights are not concerned. Congress certainly cannot forbid all effort to change the mind of the country. Now nobody can suppose that the surreptitious publishing of a silly leaflet by an unknown man, without more, would present any immediate danger that its opinions would hinder the success of the government arms or have any appreciable tendency to do so....

. . .

In this case sentences of twenty years imprisonment have been imposed for the publishing of two leaflets that I believe the defendants had as much right to publish as the Government has to publish the Constitution of the United States now vainly invoked by them. Even if I am technically wrong and enough can be squeezed from these poor and puny anonymities to turn the color of legal litmus paper; I will add, even if what I think the necessary intent were shown; the most nominal punishment seems to me all that possibly could be inflicted, unless the defendants are to be made to suffer not for what the indictment alleges but for the creed that they avow—a creed that I believe to be the creed of ignorance and immaturity when honestly held, as I see no reason to doubt that it was held here, but which, although made the subject of examination at the trial, no one has a right even to consider in dealing with the charges before the Court.

Persecution for the expression of opinions seems to me perfectly logical. If you have no doubt of your premises or your power and want a certain result with all your heart you naturally express your wishes in law and sweep away all opposition. To allow opposition by speech seems to indicate that you think the speech impotent, as when a man says that he has squared the circle, or that you do not care whole-heartedly for the result, or that you doubt either your power or your premises. But when men have realized that time has upset many fighting faiths, they may come to believe even more than they believe the very foundations of their own conduct that the ultimate good desired is better reached by free trade in ideas—that the best test of truth is the power of the thought to get itself accepted in the competition of the market, and that truth is the only ground upon which their wishes safely can be carried out. That at any rate is the theory of our Constitution. It is an experiment, as all life is an experiment. Every year if not every day we have to wager our salvation upon some prophecy based upon imperfect knowledge. While that experiment is part of our system I think that we should be eternally vigilant against attempts to check the expression of opinions that we loathe and believe to be fraught with death, unless they so imminently threaten immediate interference with the lawful and pressing purposes of the law that an immediate check is required to save the country. I wholly disagree with the argument of the Government that the First Amendment left the common law as to seditious libel in force. History seems to me against the notion. I had conceived that the United States through many years had shown its repentance for the Sedition Act of 1798, by repaying fines that it imposed....

MR. JUSTICE BRANDEIS concurs with the foregoing opinion.

Gitlow v. New York

268 U.S. 652 (1925)

Benjamin Gitlow, a member of the left-wing section of the Socialist party, was convicted for violating the New York laws of criminal anarchy (advocating the violent overthrow of the government). This case represents a step in the incorporation of part of the First Amendment into the Due Process Clause of the Fourteenth Amendment, thus including the freedoms of speech and press among those protected from impairment by the states.

MR. JUSTICE SANFORD delivered the opinion of the Court.

Benjamin Gitlow was indicted in the Supreme Court of New York, with three others, for the statutory crime of criminal anarchy. New York Penal Laws, §§ 160, 161. He was separately tried, convicted, and sentenced to imprisonment....

The contention here is that the statute, by its

terms and as applied in this case, is repugnant to the due process clause of the Fourteenth Amendment. Its material provisions are:

"§ 160. *Criminal anarchy defined.* Criminal anarchy is the doctrine that organized government should be overthrown by force or violence, or by assassination of the executive head or of any of the executive officials of government, or by any unlawful means. The advocacy of such doctrine either by word of mouth or writing is a felony.

"§ 161. *Advocacy of criminal anarchy.* Any person who:

"1. By word of mouth or writing advocates, advises or teaches the duty, necessity or propriety of overthrowing or overturning organized government by force or violence, or by assassination of the executive head or of any of the executive officials of government, or by any unlawful means; or,

"2. Prints, publishes, edits, issues or knowingly circulates, sells, distributes or publicly displays any book, paper, document, or written or printed matter in any form, containing or advocating, advising or teaching the doctrine that organized government should be overthrown by force, violence or any unlawful means...,

" 'Is guilty of a felony and punishable' by imprisonment or fine, or both."

The indictment was in two counts. The first charged that the defendant had advocated, advised and taught the duty, necessity and propriety of overthrowing and overturning organized government by force, violence and unlawful means, by certain writings therein set forth entitled "The Left Wing Manifesto"; the second that he had printed, published and knowingly circulated and distributed a certain paper called "The Revolutionary Age," containing the writings set forth in the first count advocating, advising and teaching the doctrine that organized government should be overthrown by force, violence and unlawful means.

. . .

There was no evidence of any effect resulting from the publication and circulation of the Manifesto.

No witnesses were offered in behalf of the defendant.

Extracts from the Manifesto are set forth in the margin. Coupled with a review of the rise of Socialism, it condemned the dominant "moderate Socialism" for its recognition of the necessity of the democratic parliamentary state; repudiated its policy of introducing Socialism by legislative measures; and advocated, in plain and unequivocal language, the necessity of accomplishing the "Communist Revolution" by a militant and "revolutionary Socialism," based on "the class struggle" and mobilizing the "power of the proletariat in action," through mass industrial revolts developing into mass political strikes and "revolutionary mass action," for the purpose of conquering and destroying the parliamentary state and establishing in its place, through a "revolutionary dictatorship of the proletariat," the system of Communist Socialism....

The precise question presented, and the only question which we can consider under this writ of error, then is, whether the statute, as construed and applied in this case by the state courts, deprived the defendant of his liberty of expression in violation of the due process clause of the Fourteenth Amendment.

The statute does not penalize the utterance or publication of abstract "doctrine" or academic discussion having no quality of incitement to any concrete action. It is not aimed against mere historical or philosophical essays. It does not restrain the advocacy of changes in the form of government by constitutional and lawful means. What it prohibits is language advocating, advising or teaching the overthrow of organized government by unlawful means. These words imply urging to action. Advocacy is defined in the Century Dictionary as: "1. The act of pleading for, supporting, or recommending; active espousal." It is not the abstract "doctrine" of overthrowing organized government by unlawful means which is denounced by the statute, but the advocacy of action for the accomplishment of that purpose. It was so construed and applied by the trial judge, who specifically charged the jury that: "A mere grouping of historical events and a prophetic deduction from them would neither constitute advocacy, advice or teaching of a doctrine for the overthrow of government by force, violence or unlawful means. [And] if it were a mere essay on the subject, as suggested by counsel, based upon deductions from alleged historical events, with no teaching, advice or advocacy of action, it would not constitute a violation of the statute...."

The Manifesto, plainly, is neither the statement of abstract doctrine nor, as suggested by counsel, mere prediction that industrial disturbances and revolutionary mass strikes will result spontaneously in an inevitable process of evolution in the economic system. It advocates and urges in fervent language mass action which shall progressively foment industrial disturbances and through political mass strikes and revolutionary mass action overthrow and destroy organized parliamentary government. It concludes with a call to action in these words: "The proletariat revolution and the Communist reconstruction of society — *the struggle for these* — is now indispensable.... The Communist International calls the proletariat of the world to the final struggle!" This is not the expression of philosophical abstraction, the mere prediction of future events; it is the language of direct incitement.

. . .

For present purposes we may and do assume that freedom of speech and of the press — which are protected by the First Amendment from abridgment by Congress — are among the fundamental personal rights and "liberties" protected by the due process clause of the Fourteenth Amendment from impairment by the States....

By enacting the present statute the State has determined, through its legislative body, that utterances advocating the overthrow of organized government by force, violence and unlawful means, are so inimical to the general welfare and involve such danger of substantive evil that they may be penalized in the exercise of its police power. That determination must be given great weight.... The State cannot reasonably be required to measure the danger from every such utterance in the nice balance of a jeweler's scale. A single revolutionary spark may kindle a fire that, smouldering for a time, may burst into a sweeping and destructive conflagration....

And finding, for the reasons stated, that the statute is not in itself unconstitutional, and that it has not been applied in the present case in derogation of any constitutional right, the judgment of the Court of Appeals is

Affirmed.

Mr. Justice Holmes, dissenting.

Mr. Justice Brandeis and I are of opinion that this judgment should be reversed. The general principle of free speech, it seems to me, must be taken to be included in the Fourteenth Amendment, in view of the scope that has been given to the word 'liberty' as there used, although perhaps it may be accepted with a somewhat larger latitude of interpretation than is allowed to Congress by the sweeping language that governs or ought to govern the laws of the United States. If I am right, then I think that the criterion sanctioned by the full Court in *Schenck* v. *United States,* 249 U.S. 47, 52, applies. "The question in every case is whether the words used are used in such circumstances and are of such a nature as to create a clear and present danger that they will bring about the substantive evils that [the State] has a right to prevent." It is true that in my opinion this criterion was departed from in *Abrams* v. *United States,* 250 U.S. 616, but the convictions that I expressed in that case are too deep for it to be possible for me as yet to believe that it and *Schaefer* v. *United States,* 251 U.S. 466, have settled the law. If what I think the correct test is applied, it is manifest that there was no present danger of an attempt to overthrow the government by force on the part of the admittedly small minority who shared the defendant's views. It is said that this manifesto was more than a theory, that it was an incitement. Every idea is an incitement. It offers itself for belief and if believed it is acted on unless some other belief outweighs it or some failure of energy stifles the movement at its birth. The only difference between the expression of an opinion and an incitement in the narrower sense is the speaker's enthusiasm for the result. Eloquence may set fire to reason. But whatever may be thought of the redundant discourse before us it had no chance of starting a present conflagration. If in the long run the beliefs expressed in proletarian dictatorship are destined to be accepted by the dominant forces of the community, the only meaning of free speech is that they should be given their chance and have their way.

If the publication of this document had been laid as an attempt to induce an uprising against government at once and not at some indefinite time in the future it would have presented a different question. The object would have been one with which the law might deal, subject to the doubt whether there was any danger that the publication could produce any result, or in other words, whether it was not futile and too remote from possible consequences. But the indictment alleges the publication and nothing more.

Whitney v. California

274 U.S. 357 (1927)

Charlotte Anita Whitney was prosecuted for violating California's Criminal Syndicalism Act, which covered efforts of trade unions and industrial workers to gain control of production through general strikes, sabotage, violence, or other criminal means. She was found guilty of having organized and participated in a group assembled to advocate, teach, aid, and abet criminal syndicalism. A unanimous Court upheld the Act, but the case is remembered primarily because of the eloquent exposition of First Amendment values in the concurrence by Brandeis.

MR. JUSTICE SANFORD delivered the opinion of the Court.

By a criminal information filed in the Superior Court of Alameda County, California, the plaintiff in error was charged, in five counts, with violations of the Criminal Syndicalism Act of that State....

. . .

The following facts, among many others, were established on the trial by undisputed evidence: The defendant, a resident of Oakland, in Alameda County, California, had been a member of the Local Oakland branch of the Socialist Party. This Local sent delegates to the national convention of the Socialist Party held in Chicago in 1919, which resulted in a split between the "radical" group and the old-wing Socialists. The "radicals" — to whom the Oakland delegates adhered — being ejected, went to another hall, and formed the Communist Labor Party of America. Its Constitution provided for the membership of persons subscribing to the principles of the Party and pledging themselves to be guided by its Platform, and for the formation of state organizations conforming to its Platform as the supreme declaration of the Party. In its "Platform and Program" the Party declared that it was in full harmony with "the revolutionary working class parties of all countries" and adhered to the principles of Communism laid down in the Manifesto of the Third International at Moscow, and that its purpose was "to create a unified revolutionary working class movement in America," organizing the workers as a class, in a revolutionary class struggle to conquer the capitalist state.... advocated, as the most important means of capturing state power, the action of the masses, proceeding from the shops and factories, the use of the political machinery of the capitalist state being only secondary; the organization of the workers into "revolutionary industrial unions"; propaganda pointing out their revolutionary nature and possibilities; and great industrial battles showing the value of the strike as a political weapon....

. . .

2. It is clear that the Syndicalism Act is not repugnant to the due process clause by reason of vagueness and uncertainty of definition. It has no substantial resemblance to the statutes held void for uncertainty under the Fourteenth and Fifth Amendments... because not fixing an ascertainable standard of guilt. The language of § 2, subd. 4, of the Act, under which the plaintiff in error was convicted, is clear; the definition of "criminal syndicalism" specific.

. . .

3. Neither is the Syndicalism Act repugnant to the equal protection clause, on the ground that, as its penalties are confined to those who advocate a resort to violent and unlawful methods as a means of changing industrial and political conditions, it arbitrarily discriminates between such persons and those who may advocate a resort to these methods as a means of maintaining such conditions.

. . .

4. Nor is the Syndicalism Act as applied in this case repugnant to the due process clause as a restraint of the rights of free speech, assembly, and association.

That the freedom of speech which is secured by the Constitution does not confer an absolute right to speak, without responsibility, whatever one may choose, or an unrestricted and unbridled license giving immunity for every possible use of language and preventing the punishment of those who abuse this freedom; and that a State in the exercise of its police power may punish those who abuse this freedom by utterances inimical to the public welfare, tending to incite to crime, disturb the public peace, or endanger the foundations of organized government and threaten its overthrow by unlawful means, is not open to question. *Gitlow v. New York,* 268 U.S. 652, 666–668, and cases cited.

. . .

The order dismissing the writ of error will be vacated and set aside, and the judgment of the Court of Appeal

Affirmed.

MR. JUSTICE BRANDEIS; concurring.

. . .

This Court has not yet fixed the standard by which to determine when a danger shall be deemed clear; how remote the danger may be and yet be deemed present; and what degree of evil shall be deemed sufficiently substantial to justify resort to abridgement of free speech and assembly as the means of protection. To reach sound conclusions on these matters, we must bear in mind why a State is, ordinarily, denied the power to prohibit dissemination of social, economic and political doctrine which a vast majority of its citizens believes to be false and fraught with evil consequence.

Those who won our independence believed that the final end of the State was to make men free to develop their faculties; and that in its government the deliberative forces should prevail over the arbitrary. They valued liberty both as an end and as a means. They believed liberty to be the secret of happiness and courage to be the secret of liberty. They believed that freedom to think as you will and to speak as you think are means indispensable to the discovery and spread of political truth; that without free speech and assembly discussion would be futile; that with them, discussion affords ordinarily adequate protection against the dissemination of noxious doctrine; that the greatest menace to freedom is an inert people; that public discussion is a political duty; and that this should be a fundamental principle of the American government. They recognized the risks to which all human institutions are subject. But they knew that order cannot be secured merely through fear of punishment for its infraction; that it is hazardous to discourage thought, hope and imagination; that fear breeds repression; that repression breeds hate; that hate menaces stable government; that the path of safety lies in the opportunity to discuss freely supposed grievances

and proposed remedies; and that the fitting remedy for evil counsels is good ones. Believing in the power of reason as applied through public discussion, they eschewed silence coerced by law — the argument of force in its worst form. Recognizing the occasional tyrannies of governing majorities, they amended the Constitution so that free speech and assembly should be guaranteed.

Fear of serious injury cannot alone justify suppression of free speech and assembly. Men feared witches and burnt women. It is the function of speech to free men from the bondage of irrational fears. To justify suppression of free speech there must be reasonable ground to fear that serious evil will result if free speech is practiced. There must be reasonable ground to believe that the danger apprehended is imminent. There must be reasonable ground to believe that the evil to be prevented is a serious one. Every denunciation of existing law tends in some measure to increase the probability that there will be violation of it. Condonation of a breach enhances the probability. Expressions of approval add to the probability. Propagation of the criminal state of mind by teaching syndicalism increases it. Advocacy of law-breaking heightens it still further. But even advocacy of violation, however reprehensible morally, is not a justification for denying free speech where the advocacy falls short of incitement and there is nothing to indicate that the advocacy would be immediately acted on. The wide difference between advocacy and incitement, between preparation and attempt, between assembling and conspiracy, must be borne in mind. In order to support a finding of clear and present danger it must be shown either that immediate serious violence was to be expected or was advocated, or that the past conduct furnished reason to believe that such advocacy was then contemplated.

Those who won our independence by revolution were not cowards. They did not fear political change. They did not exalt order at the cost of liberty. To courageous, self-reliant men, with confidence in the power of free and fearless reasoning applied through the processes of popular government, no danger flowing from speech can be deemed clear and present, unless the incidence of the evil apprehended is so imminent that it may befall before there is opportunity for full discussion. If there be time to expose through discussion the falsehood and fallacies, to avert the evil by the processes of education, the remedy to be applied is more speech, not enforced silence. Only an emergency can justify repression. Such must be the rule if authority is to be reconciled with freedom. Such, in my opinion, is the command of the Constitution. It is therefore always open to Americans to challenge a law abridging free speech and as-

sembly by showing that there was no emergency justifying it.

. . .

MR. JUSTICE HOLMES joins in this opinion.

Dennis v. United States

341 U.S. 494 (1951)

Eugene Dennis and other leaders of the American Communist party were indicted and found guilty under the Smith Act for willfully and knowingly conspiring to teach and advocate the overthrow of the U.S. government by force or violence. The question before the courts was whether the statute violated First Amendment rights. To do that, the Supreme Court had to give clearer meaning to the *Schenck* test of "clear and present danger."

MR. CHIEF JUSTICE VINSON announced the judgment of the Court and an opinion in which MR. JUSTICE REED, MR. JUSTICE BURTON and MR. JUSTICE MINTON join.

Petitioners were indicted in July, 1948, for violation of the conspiracy provisions of the Smith Act.... We granted certiorari, 340 U. S. 863, limited to the following two questions: (1) Whether either § 2 or § 3 of the Smith Act, inherently or as construed and applied in the instant case, violates the First Amendment and other provisions of the Bill of Rights; (2) whether either § 2 or § 3 of the Act, inherently or as construed and applied in the instant case, violates the First and Fifth Amendments because of indefiniteness.

Sections 2 and 3 of the Smith Act, 54 Stat. 671, 18 U.S.C. (1946 ed.) §§ 10, 11 (see present 18 U.S.C. § 2385), provide as follows:

"SEC. 2. (a) It shall be unlawful for any person—

"(1) to knowingly or willfully advocate, abet, advise, or teach the duty, necessity, desirability, or propriety of overthrowing or destroying any government in the United States by force or violence, or by the assassination of any officer of any such government;

"(2) with intent to cause the overthrow or destruction of any government in the United States, to print, publish, edit, issue, circulate, sell, distribute, or publicly display any written or printed matter advocating, advising, or teaching the duty, necessity, desirability, or propriety of overthrowing or destroying any government in the United States by force or violence;

"(3) to organize or help to organize any society, group, or assembly of persons who teach, ad-

vocate, or encourage the overthrow or destruction of any government in the United States by force or violence; or to be or become a member of, or affiliate with, any such society, group, or assembly of persons, knowing the purposes thereof.

"(b) For the purposes of this section, the term 'government in the United States' means the Government of the United States, the government of any State, Territory, or possession of the United States, the government of the District of Columbia, or the government of any political subdivision of any of them.

"SEC. 3. It shall be unlawful for any person to attempt to commit, or to conspire to commit, any of the acts prohibited by the provisions of this title."

. . .

[T]he Court of Appeals held that the record supports the following broad conclusions: By virtue of their control over the political apparatus of the Communist Political Association, petitioners were able to transform that organization into the Communist Party; that the policies of the Association were changed from peaceful cooperation with the United States and its economic and political structure to a policy which had existed before the United States and the Soviet Union were fighting a common enemy, namely, a policy which worked for the overthrow of the Government by force and violence; that the Communist Party is a highly disciplined organization, adept at infiltration into strategic positions, use of aliases, and double-meaning language; that the Party is rigidly controlled; that Communists, unlike other political parties, tolerate no dissension from the policy laid down by the guiding forces, but that the approved program is slavishly followed by the members of the Party; that the literature of the Party and the statements and activities of its leaders, petitioners here, advocate, and the general goal of the Party was, during the period in question, to achieve a successful overthrow of the existing order by force and violence.

I.

[The trial judge charged the jury that the Smith Act required an unlawful intent. The Court agreed with this interpretation.]

II.

The obvious purpose of the statute is to protect existing Government, not from change by peaceable, lawful and constitutional means, but from change by violence, revolution and terrorism. That it is within the *power* of the Congress to protect the Government of the United States from armed rebellion is a proposition which requires little discussion. Whatever theoretical merit there may be to the argument that there is a "right" to rebellion against dictatorial governments is without force where the existing structure of the government provides for peaceful and orderly change. We reject any principle of governmental helplessness in the face of preparation for revolution, which principle, carried to its logical conclusion, must lead to anarchy. No one could conceive that it is not within the power of Congress to prohibit acts intended to overthrow the Government by force and violence. The question with which we are concerned here is not whether Congress has such *power,* but whether the *means* which it has employed conflict with the First and Fifth Amendments to the Constitution.

One of the bases for the contention that the means which Congress has employed are invalid takes the form of an attack on the face of the statute on the grounds that by its terms it prohibits academic discussion of the merits of Marxism-Leninism, that it stifles ideas and is contrary to all concepts of a free speech and a free press.

. . .

The very language of the Smith Act negates the interpretation which petitioners would have us impose on that Act. It is directed at advocacy, not discussion. Thus, the trial judge properly charged the jury that they could not convict if they found that petitioners did "no more than pursue peace-

ful studies and discussions or teaching and advocacy in the realm of ideas." ...

III.

. . .

No important case involving free speech was decided by this Court prior to *Schenck* v. *United States,* 249 U. S. 47 (1919). Writing for a unanimous Court, Justice Holmes stated that the "question in every case is whether the words used are used in such circumstances and are of such a nature as to create a clear and present danger that they will bring about the substantive evils that Congress has a right to prevent." 249 U. S. at 52....

...[T]he literal problem which is presented is what has been meant by the use of the phrase "clear and present danger" of the utterances bringing about the evil within the power of Congress to punish.

Obviously, the words cannot mean that before the Government may act, it must wait until the *putsch* is about to be executed, the plans have been laid and the signal is awaited. If Government is aware that a group aiming at its overthrow is attempting to indoctrinate its members and to commit them to a course whereby they will strike when the leaders feel the circumstances permit, action by the Government is required....

. . .

...[T]his analysis disposes of the contention that a conspiracy to advocate, as distinguished from the advocacy itself, cannot be constitutionally restrained, because it comprises only the preparation. It is the existence of the conspiracy which creates the danger.... If the ingredients of the reaction are present, we cannot bind the Government to wait until the catalyst is added.

IV.

[The trial judge instructed the jury that if the defendants were found guilty of violating the Smith Act, he would determine as a matter of law that there was sufficient danger of a substantive evil that Congress has a right to prevent. The Court agreed that this was a question of law for a judge to decide.]

V.

There remains to be discussed the question of vagueness — whether the statute as we have interpreted it is too vague, not sufficiently advising those who would speak of the limitations upon their activity. It is urged that such vagueness contravenes the First and Fifth Amendments....

We agree that the standard as defined is not a neat, mathematical formulary. Like all verbalizations it is subject to criticism on the score of indefiniteness. But petitioners themselves contend that the verbalization "clear and present danger" is the proper standard. We see no difference, from the standpoint of vagueness, whether the standard of "clear and present danger" is one contained *in haec verba* within the statute, or whether it is the judicial measure of constitutional applicability....

We hold that §§ 2 (a) (1), 2 (a) (3) and 3 of the Smith Act do not inherently, or as construed or applied in the instant case, violate the First Amendment and other provisions of the Bill of Rights, or the First and Fifth Amendments because of indefiniteness. Petitioners intended to overthrow the Government of the United States as speedily as the circumstances would permit. Their conspiracy to organize the Communist Party and to teach and advocate the overthrow of the Government of the United States by force and violence created a "clear and present danger" of an attempt to overthrow the Government by force and violence. They were properly and constitutionally convicted for violation of the Smith Act. The judgments of conviction are

Affirmed.

MR. JUSTICE CLARK took no part in the consideration or decision of this case.

MR. JUSTICE FRANKFURTER, concurring in affirmance of the judgment.

. . .

I.

[Frankfurter discusses the need to weigh the interests of free speech against those of national security.]

But how are competing interests to be assessed? Since they are not subject to quantitative ascertainment, the issue necessarily resolves itself into asking, who is to make the adjustment? — who is to balance the relevant factors and ascertain which interest is in the circumstances to prevail? Full responsibility for the choice cannot be given to the courts. Courts are not representative bodies....

Primary responsibility for adjusting the interests which compete in the situation before us of necessity belongs to the Congress....

MR. JUSTICE JACKSON, concurring.

. . .

IV.

. . .

While I think there was power in Congress to enact this statute and that, as applied in this case, it cannot be held unconstitutional, I add that I have little faith in the long-range effectiveness of this conviction to stop the rise of the Communist movement. Communism will not go to jail with these Communists. No decision by this Court can forestall revolution whenever the existing government fails to command the respect and loyalty of the people and sufficient distress and discontent is allowed to grow up among the masses....

MR. JUSTICE BLACK, dissenting.

. . .

...These petitioners were not charged with an attempt to overthrow the Government. They were not charged with overt acts of any kind designed to overthrow the Government. They were not even charged with saying anything or writing anything designed to overthrow the Government. The charge was that they agreed to assemble and to talk and publish certain ideas at a later date: The indictment is that they conspired to organize the Communist Party and to use speech or newspapers and other publications in the future to teach and advocate the forcible overthrow of the Government. No matter how it is worded, this is a virulent form of prior censorship of speech and press, which I believe the First Amendment forbids. I would hold § 3 of the Smith Act authorizing this prior restraint unconstitutional on its face and as applied.

. . .

MR. JUSTICE DOUGLAS, dissenting.

If this were a case where those who claimed protection under the First Amendment were teaching the techniques of sabotage, the assassination of the President, the filching of documents from public files, the planting of bombs, the art of street warfare, and the like, I would have no doubts. The freedom to speak is not absolute; the teaching of methods of terror and other seditious conduct should be beyond the pale along with obscenity and immorality. This case was argued as if those were the facts. The argument imported much seditious conduct into the record. That is easy and it has popular appeal, for the activities of Communists in plotting and scheming against the free world are common knowledge. But the fact is that no such evidence was introduced at the trial....

. . .

There was a time in England when the concept of constructive treason flourished. Men were punished not for raising a hand against the king but for thinking murderous thoughts about him. The Framers of the Constitution were alive to that

abuse and took steps to see that the practice would not flourish here. Treason was defined to require overt acts — the evolution of a plot against the country into an actual project. The present case is not one of treason. But the analogy is close when the illegality is made to turn on intent, not on the nature of the act. We then start probing men's minds for motive and purpose; they become entangled in the law not for what they did but *for what they thought*; they get convicted not for what they said but for the purpose with which they said it.

. . .

Yates v. United States

354 U.S. 298 (1957)

Leaders of the Communist party in California, including Oleta O'Connor Yates, were indicted and convicted under the Smith Act. This case allowed the Supreme Court to revisit its holding in *Dennis* v. *United States* (1951) and provide greater protection to First Amendment freedoms.

MR. JUSTICE HARLAN delivered the opinion of the Court.

We brought these cases here to consider certain questions arising under the Smith Act which have not heretofore been passed upon by this Court, and otherwise to review the convictions of these petitioners for conspiracy to violate that Act. Among other things, the convictions are claimed to rest upon an application of the Smith Act which is hostile to the principles upon which its constitutionality was upheld in *Dennis* v. *United States,* 341 U. S. 494.

These 14 petitioners stand convicted, after a jury trial in the United States District Court for the Southern District of California, upon a single count indictment charging them with conspiring (1) to advocate and teach the duty and necessity of overthrowing the Government of the United States by force and violence, and (2) to organize, as the Communist Party of the United States, a society of persons who so advocate and teach, all with the intent of causing the overthrow of the Government by force and violence as speedily as circumstances would permit....

In the view we take of this case, it is necessary for us to consider only the following of petitioners' contentions: (1) that the term "organize" as used in the Smith Act was erroneously construed by the two lower courts; (2) that the trial court's instructions to the jury erroneously excluded from the case the issue of "incitement to action"; (3)

that the evidence was so insufficient as to require this Court to direct the acquittal of these petitioners....

I. THE TERM "ORGANIZE."

One object of the conspiracy charged was to violate the third paragraph of 18 U. S. C. § 2385, which provides:

"Whoever organizes or helps or attempts to organize any society, group, or assembly of persons who teach, advocate, or encourage the overthrow or destruction of any [government in the United States] by force or violence ... [s]hall be fined not more than $10,000 or imprisoned not more than ten years, or both...."

Petitioners claim that "organize" means to "establish," "found," or "bring into existence," and that in this sense the Communist Party was organized by 1945 at the latest. On this basis petitioners contend that this part of the indictment, returned in 1951, was barred by the three-year statute of limitations. The Government, on the other hand, says that "organize" connotes a continuing process which goes on throughout the life of an organization, and that, in the words of the trial court's instructions to the jury, the term includes such things as "the recruiting of new members and the forming of new units, and the regrouping or expansion of existing clubs, classes and other units of any society, party, group or other organization." The two courts below accepted the Government's position. We think, however, that petitioners' position must prevail....

...In these circumstances we should follow the familiar rule that criminal statutes are to be strictly construed and give to "organize" its narrow meaning, that is, that the word refers only to acts entering into the creation of a new organization, and not to acts thereafter performed in carrying on its activities, even though such acts may loosely be termed "organizational."...

II. INSTRUCTIONS TO THE JURY.

Petitioners contend that the instructions to the jury were fatally defective in that the trial court refused to charge that, in order to convict, the jury must find that the advocacy which the defendants conspired to promote was of a kind calculated to "incite" persons to action for the forcible overthrow of the Government. It is argued that advocacy of forcible overthrow as mere *abstract doctrine* is within the free speech protection of the First Amendment; that the Smith Act, consistently with that constitutional provision, must be taken as proscribing only the sort of advocacy which incites to illegal *action;* and that the trial court's charge, by permitting conviction for mere advocacy, unrelated to its tendency to produce forcible action, resulted in an unconstitutional application of the Smith Act. The Government, which at the trial also requested the court to charge in terms of "incitement," now takes the position, however, that the true constitutional dividing line is not between inciting and abstract advocacy of forcible overthrow, but rather between advocacy as such, irrespective of its inciting qualities, and the mere discussion or exposition of violent overthrown as an abstract theory.

. . .

We are thus faced with the question whether the Smith Act prohibits advocacy and teaching of forcible overthrow as an abstract principle, divorced from any effort to instigate action to that end, so long as such advocacy or teaching is engaged in with evil intent. We hold that it does not.

The distinction between advocacy of abstract doctrine and advocacy directed at promoting unlawful action is one that has been consistently recognized in the opinions of this Court....

...The legislative history of the Smith Act and related bills shows beyond all question that Congress was aware of the distinction between the advocacy or teaching of abstract doctrine and the advocacy or teaching of action, and that it did not intend to disregard it. The statute was aimed at the advocacy and teaching of concrete action for the forcible overthrow of the Government, and not of principles divorced from action.

. . .

We recognize that distinctions between advocacy or teaching of abstract doctrines, with evil intent, and that which is directed to stirring people to action, are often subtle and difficult to grasp, for in a broad sense, as Mr. Justice Holmes said in his dissenting opinion in *Gitlow, supra,* 268 U. S., at 673: "Every idea is an incitement." But the very subtlety of these distinctions required the most clear and explicit instructions with reference to them, for they concerned an issue which went to the very heart of the charges against these petitioners. The need for precise and understandable instructions on this issue is further emphasized by the equivocal character of the evidence in this record, with which we deal in Part III of this opinion. Instances of speech that could be considered to amount to "advocacy of action" are so few and far between as to be almost completely overshadowed by the hundreds of instances in the record in which overthrow, if mentioned at all, occurs in the course of doctrinal disputation so remote from action as to be almost wholly lacking in probative value. Vague references to "revolutionary" or "militant" action of an unspecified character, which are found in the evidence, might in addition be given too great weight by the jury in the absence of more precise instructions. Particularly in light of this record, we must regard the trial court's charge in this respect as furnishing wholly inadequate guidance to the jury on this central point in the case....

III. THE EVIDENCE.

The determinations already made require a reversal of these convictions. Nevertheless, in the exercise of our power under 28 U. S. C. § 2106 to "direct the entry of such appropriate judgment... as may be just under the circumstances," we have conceived it to be our duty to scrutinize this lengthy record with care, in order to determine whether the way should be left open for a new trial of all or some of these petitioners. Such a judgment, we think, should, on the one hand, foreclose further proceedings against those of the petitioners as to whom the evidence in this record would be palpably insufficient upon a new trial, and should, on the other hand, leave the Government free to retry the other petitioners under proper legal standards, especially since it is by no means clear that certain aspects of the evidence against them could not have been clarified to the advantage of the Government had it not been under a misapprehension as to the burden cast upon it by the Smith Act....

[The Court concludes that the evidence against five defendants was so clearly insufficient that their acquittal should be ordered. Nine defendants could be retried.]

. . .

MR. JUSTICE BURTON, concurring in the result.

I agree with the result reached by the Court, and with the opinion of the Court except as to its interpretation of the term "organize" as used in the Smith Act. As to that, I agree with the interpretation given it by the Court of Appeals. 225 F. 2d 146.

MR. JUSTICE BRENNAN and MR. JUSTICE WHITTAKER took no part in the consideration or decision of this case.

MR. JUSTICE BLACK, with whom MR. JUSTICE DOUGLAS joins, concurring in part and dissenting in part.

I.

I would reverse every one of these convictions and direct that all the defendants be acquitted. In my judgment the statutory provisions on which these prosecutions are based abridge freedom of speech, press and assembly in violation of the First Amendment to the United States Constitution....

. . .

MR. JUSTICE CLARK, dissenting.

. . .

I would affirm the convictions. However, the Court has freed five of the convicted petitioners and ordered new trials for the remaining nine. As to the five, it says that the evidence is "clearly insufficient." I agree with the Court of Appeals, the District Court, and the jury that the evidence showed guilt beyond a reasonable doubt....

B. ASSOCIATIONAL RIGHTS

The Constitution does not expressly provide for a right of association. Gradually, however, the First Amendment and the "liberty" interest secured by the Fourteenth Amendment have been interpreted to protect a person's right to associate with others who share similar ideas, interests, and goals. Self-government is more than Self. In many ways, America is a nation of joiners. Americans band together to seek friendship, cooperation, and concerted action.

Associational rights were heavily litigated throughout the 1940s and 1950s, usually involving a person's membership in the Communist party or in organizations considered subversive to the national interest. For a time, these memberships were punished by government. In 1943 Congress passed legislation to deny salaries to three federal officials suspected of "subversive" activities (see reading). This statute was struck down by the Supreme Court as a bill of attainder. United States v. Lovett, 328 U.S. 303 (1946). However, the Court upheld Maryland's requirement that state candidates for office, before being placed on the ballot, take an oath or sign an affidavit that they were not engaged in an attempt to overthrow the government by force or violence and were not knowingly members of an organization engaged in such attempts. Gerende v. Election Board, 341 U.S. 56 (1951). Municipalities could require public employees to execute affidavits disclosing whether or not they were, or ever had been, members of Communist organizations. Garner v. Los Angeles Board, 341 U.S. 716 (1951). States were allowed to bar employment in public schools for any member of an organization advocating the overthrow of government by force, violence, or unlawful means. Adler v. Board of Education, 342 U.S. 485 (1952).

These cases provoked dissents from Justices who regarded these state laws as constitu-

Freedom of Association

... Petitioner argues that in view of the facts and circumstances shown in the record, the effect of compelled disclosure of the membership lists will be to abridge the rights of its rank-and-file members to engage in lawful association in support of their common beliefs. It contends that governmental action which, although not directly suppressing association, nevertheless carries this consequence, can be justified only upon some overriding valid interest of the State.

Effective advocacy of both public and private points of view, particularly controversial ones, is undeniably enhanced by group association, as this Court has more than once recognized by remarking upon the close nexus between the freedoms of speech and assembly.... It is beyond debate that freedom to engage in association for the advancement of beliefs and ideas is an inseparable aspect of the "liberty" assured by the Due Process Clause of the Fourteenth Amendment, which embraces freedom of speech.... Of course, it is immaterial whether the beliefs sought to be advanced by association pertain to political, economic, religious or cultural matters, and state action which may have the effect of curtailing the freedom to associate is subject to the closest scrutiny.

SOURCE: NAACP v. Alabama, 357 U.S. 449, 460–61 (1958).

---

tionally offensive. In part, they objected to the use of "guilt by association" to punish people, often without even a hearing. The Court did manage to strike down "loyalty oaths" that required state employees to vow that they had not been a member of "Communist front" or "subversive" organizations. Such laws violated due process because membership might have been innocent and unknowing. Wieman v. Updegraff, 344 U.S. 183 (1952). By a 5 to 4 margin, the Court invalidated a city charter that stripped city employees of their jobs if they invoked the Self-Incrimination Clause before a legislative committee inquiring into their official conduct. These summary dismissals, said the Court, violated due process and made a mockery of the Fifth Amendment. Slochower v. Board of Education, 350 U.S. 551 (1956). The Court also used the Due Process Clause to protect attorneys who were refused permission to take the bar examination, or who were not allowed to practice after passing the bar, because of their associations with Communist organizations. Schware v. Board of Bar Examiners, 353 U.S. 232 (1957); Konigsberg v. State Bar, 353 U.S. 252 (1957).[1]

The Court's record on associational freedom for Communist and subversive organizations during this period was mixed.[2] The right of association in the NAACP was a different matter. When Alabama tried to obtain the membership list of the NAACP's state chapter, a unanimous Court held that members had a constitutional right to associate freely with others as part of the "liberty" protected by the Fourteenth Amendment (see box). Another unanimous ruling rejected compulsory disclosure of NAACP memberships as an unconstitutional interference with the freedom of association.[3] Minor parties, such as the Socialist Workers party,

---

1. But see the confusing array of cases since that time: Konigsberg v. State Bar, 366 U.S. 36 (1961); In re Anastaplo, 366 U.S. 82 (1961); Baird v. State Bar of Arizona, 401 U.S. 1 (1971); In re Stolar, 401 U.S. 23 (1971); Law Students' Research Council v. Wadmond, 401 U.S. 154 (1971); In re Primus, 436 U.S. 412 (1978).

2. Sweezy v. New Hampshire, 354 U.S. 234 (1957); Beilan v. Board of Education, 357 U.S. 399 (1958); Lerner v. Casey, 357 U.S. 468 (1958); Nelson v. Los Angeles County, 362 U.S. 1 (1960); Shelton v. Tucker, 364 U.S. 479 (1960).

3. Bates v. Little Rock, 361 U.S. 516 (1960). See also NAACP v. Button, 371 U.S. 415 (1963) and Gibson v. Florida Legislative Comm., 372 U.S. 539 (1963). In 1928 the Court allowed states to obtain the membership lists of the Ku Klux Klan, because its conduct was "inimical to personal rights and public welfare." Bryant v. Zimmerman, 278 U.S. 63, 75 (1928).

need not report the names of campaign contributors if it results in harassment and reprisals. Brown v. Socialist Workers '74 Campaign Comm., 459 U.S. 87 (1982).

By the 1960s, the Supreme Court was striking down loyalty oaths because they were so vague as to violate due process.[4] The objection to "guilt by association" gained a Court majority by 1966. Elfbrandt v. Russell, 384 U.S. 11 (1966). In 1967 a 6 to 2 majority struck down a congressional statute that sought to punish any worker at a defense facility who belonged to a Communist organization. The Court held that the statute abridged the right of association by reaching too broadly to include inactive members or those employed in nonsensitive jobs. United States v. Robel, 389 U.S. 258 (1967).

In 1992 an 8–1 Court held that it was unconstitutional to use a defendant's membership in a white racist gang during a sentencing proceeding unless that evidence was relevant to the crime committed. Otherwise, the introduction of that evidence violates the First Amendment right of association. In this case, the murderer was white as was the victim. Dawson v. Delaware, 503 U.S. 159 (1992).

Congress Seeks to Remove "Subversives" from FDR's Administration

In an emergency appropriations bill in 1943, Congress debated an amendment designed to withhold federal salaries from three named individuals: Goodwin B. Watson and William E. Dodd, Jr., of the Federal Communications Commission, and Robert Morse Lovett, governor of the Virgin Islands. They were among a group of federal officials labeled by Congressman Martin Dies as "irresponsible, unrepresentative, crackpot, radical bureaucrats." 89 Cong. Rec. 479 (1943). The debate in the House of Representatives shows most members willing to use the power of the purse to punish individuals for their opinions and associations. A few members opposed the amendment, regarding it as a violation of the First Amendment, a usurpation of the President's removal power, and a bill of attainder forbidden by the Constitution. The debate below is taken from 89 Cong. Rec. 4482–87, 4546–58, 4581–4605.

Mr. CELLER. Mr. Chairman, we are going to vote this afternoon, I presume, on the so-called amendment offered by the Kerr committee. In that connection, I fear that we are embarking upon something rather dangerous. We should think very deeply before we vote approval of the so-called ouster of liberals from various executive departments of the Government.

As I view it, this is an attempt to discharge certain men in the Government service because of their opinions. It is primarily just that.

. . .

Mr. OUTLAND. Mr. Chairman, this proposal to remove certain men from the Government service by means of an amendment to an appropriation bill is extremely dangerous. In my judgment, it violates our American concepts of fair play, freedom of speech, and direct action. It sets up no definite standards as to what is subversive and

opens wide the path of intolerance. Under the principle here implied, for example, a Cabinet member could be removed from his position by having Congress disapprove his social or economic views, and then follow up such disapproval by an amendment such as we are discussing today.

. . .

And what is the basis for this contemplated action? It is simply that they have belonged to organizations or spoken before groups which do not meet with the approval of certain Members of Congress. Thus it becomes a matter solely of opinion, not of law, and we have prided ourselves that in this democracy of ours we are governed by laws, not by the whims of men. Such action smacks far more of the tactics of the Nazis and the Fascists, against whom we are fighting, than of the spirit of American justice and fair play.

---

4. Cramp v. Bd. of Public Instruction, 368 U.S. 278 (1961); Baggett v. Bullitt, 377 U.S. 360 (1964); Keyishian v. Board of Regents, 385 U.S. 589 (1967).

. . .

Mr. COFFEE. . . . What is this crime of which these men are guilty? It is that either they have been the sponsors of some organization, have addressed some organization, donated to some organization which someone, somewhere, somehow said in his opinion was inimical or acting in a manner inimical to the best interests of the United States. There is not a finding anywhere in the report of the Kerr committee that any of the gentlemen so characterized was guilty of advocating the overthrow of the American Government by force and violence. There is no charge anywhere in the committee or in the hearings to the effect that any of these distinguished intellectuals advocated the overthrow of this Government.

. . .

We in Congress are sitting here as judge, as jury, and as prosecutor. . . . We are attempting to do something today which is unconstitutional. We are attempting to impeach men by methods other than impeachment. . . . [This] has the effect of a bill of attainder, one of the fundamental things against which our colonial forefathers sought separation from the mother country 160 years ago.

. . .

Mr. DIRKSEN. . . . The real issue is whether or not this body, that is charged under the Constitution as the keeper of the purse, without whose action not one dollar can go out of the Federal Treasury, can, under that authority, spell out that power to determine who shall be on the pay roll and who shall not.

. . .

Their freedom of speech is not involved. Dr. Dodd can go down on Marshall Square tonight and make any kind of a speech he wants to, but I am not going to see him on the pay roll of the Federal Government, the recipient of the taxpayers' money, and do it. That is a different thing.

Mr. KERR. . . . This Congress has the right to say to whom the people's money shall be paid. Congress will not be denied and should never be denied that right. The question involved here is one that simply involves that proposition and that statement.

. . .

Mr. HOLIFIELD. . . . I do not know whether

these three men are loyal American citizens or not. I do not believe that such a determination is the prerogative of a Member of Congress or a committee thereof. The transcript of the testimony before the committee was withheld, or unavailable, to the general membership until the time of voting. We were asked to vote on a punitive legislative amendment which was directed against three individuals. In my opinion, any legislation passed by Congress should be general in its impact and not directed either for or against an individual. The civil and Federal courts are the proper places to determine the punishment of an individual. . . .

Mr. MARCANTONIO. . . . We have a most fantastic situation. We are to vote on an amendment to an appropriation bill, to expel three people from the Federal Government without a single word of the hearings before us. All we have before us is what we are told by the gentlemen who are on the committee. How can any Member do justice to these men without having before us what they said to the committee in their own defense?

. . .

Mr. BURDICK. Mr. Chairman, many here bemoan the fact that a few Members have seen fit to raise the question of the constitutional right of the Congress to pass a law denying the salary of an officer and thus deprive him of his right to hold office. If ever there was a constitutional question involved in any legislation, it is involved in this amendment. One of the cornerstones of our democracy is attacked — the right of free speech and the freedom of the press. If free speech can be denied in this case, it can, by the same token, be denied in any case.

. . .

In my opinion — and I almost feel like apologizing for expressing this opinion for fear that my salary may be taken away — this Congress does not have the constitutional right to legislate any citizen out of his property, or his salary, which is the same thing, merely because he has expressed an opinion which is not approved by a majority of this Congress.

. . .

Mr. HOBBS. Mr. Chairman, I am exceedingly loath to oppose the pending amendment. I honor and respect the judgment both of our great Committee on Appropriations and also the special subcommittee on whose reports this amendment stands. I am devoted to the men who compose those committees and in many cases I would bow to their superior wisdom. But in a case such as this, wherein the amendment is clearly unconstitutional, in my opinion, I simply cannot follow their leadership, much as I would like to.

The pending amendment is a bill of pains and penalties within the meaning of the constitutional prohibition:

"No bill of attainder...shall be passed (art. I,...sec. 9)."

"A bill of attainder is a legislative act which inflicts punishment without a judicial trial. If the punishment be less than death, it is a bill of pains and penalties. As the term 'bill of attainder' is used in the Federal Constitution, it includes both bills of attainder particularly, and bills of pains and penalties. (*Cummings* v. *Missouri* (71 U.S. (4 Wall.) 277, 18 L. Ed. 356); *Drehman* v. *Stifle* (75 U.S. (8 Wall.), 595, 601, 19 L. Ed. 508); *Pierce* v. *Carskadon* (83 U.S. (16 Wall.), 234, 239, 21 L. Ed. 276)."

If, then, the amendment now being considered inflicts punishment, it is a bill of pains and penalties, since there has been no judicial trial....

[President Roosevelt signed the bill containing this amendment, but later explained that he did so because the bill provided emergency appropriations during the recess of Congress. In noting that the three individuals were being disqualified for federal employment because of "political opinions" attributed to them, he regarded the provision as "not only unwise and discriminatory, but unconstitutional as a bill of attainder," which he said the Supreme Court had defined as "a legislative act which inflicts punishment without judicial trial." Public Papers and Addresses of Franklin D. Roosevelt, 1943 Volume, at 386. It was on that ground that the provision was held unconstitutional by the Court of Claims in Lovett v. United States, 66 F. Supp. 142 (Ct. Cl. 1945), *and by the Supreme Court in* United States v. Lovett, 328 U.S. 303 (1946).]

C. THE REGULATION OF SPEECH

The Free Speech Clause has never been interpreted to confer an absolute right. Although speech is constitutionally protected, government may adopt regulations to protect other societal interests. The scope of free speech depends on three variables: time, place, and manner. Citizens are not at liberty to commit perjury, to libel, or to infringe on copyrights. There is no constitutional right to "insist upon a street meeting in the middle of Times Square at the rush hour as a form of freedom of speech or assembly." Cox v. Louisiana, 379 U.S. 536, 554 (1965). To prevent the clogging of sidewalks and public streets, licenses may be required for parades and public processions. Cox v. New Hampshire, 312 U.S. 569 (1941). Sound trucks equipped with amplifiers and capable of generating "loud and raucous noises" may be prohibited. Kovacs v. Cooper, 336 U.S. 77 (1949); Saia v. New York, 334 U.S. 558 (1948). A mailer's right to communicate stops at the mailbox of an addressee who objects to what is being sent. Rowan v. Post Office Dept., 397 U.S. 728 (1970).

The scope of free speech depends partly on where it is exercised. The Supreme Court has identified three places: the traditional public forum (public parks), a public forum designated by the government (state universities), and the nonpublic forum (private homes). For the first two, restrictions on free speech are subject to heightened scrutiny by the courts (see box on next page). The right of free speech applies to public forums. I have a right to express my views at a public assembly, not in your living room. When the state applies restrictions to speech, the general rule is that they be "content neutral." Government is not supposed to be a censor. When regulations are imposed to limit speech, they cannot be "overbroad," pulling within their reach speech that is both protected and unprotected. Even for public parks, however, government may adopt "guidelines" to regulate the noise from rock concerts that disturbs park users and nearby apartment residents. Provided that the regulation is content neutral and narrowly tailored to serve "significant governmental interest," reasonable limits may be im-

---

Forums for Speech

Traditional public forum (example: public park)	Subject to strict scrutiny by the courts (must be narrowly drawn to achieve a compelling state interest).
Public forum designated by the government (example: state university)	Also subject to strict-scrutiny analysis.
Remaining public property (example: airport terminal)	Regulation is permitted if reasonable.

---

posed on speech. Ward v. Rock Against Racism, 491 U.S. 781 (1989). The Supreme Court has decided a number of cases involving access to abortion clinics (pp. 1018–20).

Content Neutral

The concept "content neutral" is a central principle for safeguarding free speech. When public officials issue licenses or permits to allow groups to conduct peaceful demonstrations, permission should not depend on what will be said and expressed. In 1992, a 5–4 Court struck down a Georgia law that allowed county administrators to adjust a $1,000 fee for a permit to conduct a parade or assembly on public property. The Court decided that the law was facially unconstitutional because it failed to provide standards to guide administrators and appeared to allow administrators to adjust the fee based on the content of the speech. The fee could be varied to reflect the estimated cost of maintaining public order, implying that controversial or unpopular groups might have to pay more. Forsyth County, Ga. v. Nationalist Movement, 505 U.S. 123 (1992).

The Supreme Court has stated that regulation and suppression "are not the same, either in purpose or result, and courts of justice can tell the difference." Poulos v. New Hampshire, 345 U.S. 395, 408 (1953). Regulation can become a code word to suppress speech that is unpopular with the majority or objectionable to local authorities. To compel labor organizers to obtain a card from a state official before soliciting memberships may simply be a guise to discourage trade unionism. Thomas v. Collins, 323 U.S. 516 (1945). It is legitimate to require speakers to fill out applications before using city parks for group meetings, but not when the applications are denied for arbitrary or discriminatory reasons, such as against a disliked minority sect or an objectionable speech. Under these conditions, the requirement for a license or permit constitutes forbidden censorship and prior restraint.

As a regulatory device, "breach of the peace" statutes can translate easily into suppression of speech. A 1963 case involved high school and college students who had been convicted for gathering peacefully on the grounds of the South Carolina legislature to express their grievances about state laws concerning black citizens. By an 8 to 1 vote, the Court held that the state had infringed the rights of free speech, free assembly, and freedom to petition for a redress of grievances. EDWARDS v. SOUTH CAROLINA, 372 U.S. 229 (1963).[5]

More narrowly, 5–4, the Court reversed the convictions of five black males who participated in an orderly, nondisruptive sit-in at a branch library to protest segregation. The Court

---

5. See also Shuttlesworth v. Birmingham, 394 U.S. 147 (1969); Poulos v. New Hampshire, 345 U.S. 395 (1953); Fowler v. Rhode Island, 345 U.S. 67 (1953); Kunz v. New York, 340 U.S. 290 (1951); Niemotko v. Maryland, 340 U.S. 268 (1951).

Solicitation of Funds

In 1980 the Court struck down a village ordinance that required charitable organizations to use at least 75 percent of their receipts for "charitable purposes" to be eligible for door-to-door or on-street solicitation of contributions. Charitable appeals involve a variety of speech interests: communication of information, dissemination of views and ideas, and advocacy of causes. Schaumburg v. Citizens for Better Environ, 444 U.S. 620 (1980). See also Cornelius v. NAACP Legal Defense & Ed. Fund, 473 U.S. 788 (1985); Secretary of State of Md. v. J.H. Munson Co., 467 U.S. 947 (1984); Breard v. Alexandria, 341 U.S. 622 (1951); Martin v. Struthers, 319 U.S. 141 (1943).

A 5–4 Court in 1990 upheld a federal regulation that prohibits solicitation on the premises of a post office. The regulation was considered a "reasonable" restriction on First Amendment rights and was not subjected to strict-scrutiny analysis. United States v. Kokinda, 497 U.S. 720 (1990). In 1992 the Court ruled that an airport terminal operated by a public authority is not a "public forum," permitting the authority to ban solicitation of money within the terminals. Such bans need only satisfy a reasonableness standard. The airports involved in this case—Kennedy, La Guardia, and Newark—permit solicitation on the sidewalks outside the terminal buildings. Although the Court decided 6–3 that prohibitions on solicitations were reasonable, a different 5–4 majority said that airports must permit groups to hand out literature. Some airports continue to permit solicitations within their terminals but restrict them to certain areas and hours. Int'l Society for Krishna Consciousness v. Lee, 505 U.S. 672. Also in 1992, a 5–3 Court upheld a Tennessee law that prohibited the solicitation of votes and the display of campaign materials within 100 feet of the entrance to polling places on election day. The Court concluded that the statute was narrowly tailored to serve a compelling state interest in preventing voter intimidation and election fraud. Burson v. Freeman, 504 U.S. 191 (1992).

protected their freedom of speech, assembly, and the right to petition. Brown v. Louisiana, 383 U.S. 131 (1966).

Speech is subject to greater restraint when the question is one not of orderly demonstrations, conducted without obstructing the functions of government, but rather disruptive sit-ins and trespasses. The Supreme Court upheld the convictions of students who demonstrated on the premises of a jail. ADDERLEY v. FLORIDA, 385 U.S. 39 (1966). Similarly, sit-in demonstrations, kneel-in demonstrations, and mass street parades may not continue in defiance of a temporary injunction issued by a judicial authority. Walker v. City of Birmingham, 388 U.S. 307 (1967).

Overly broad breach-of-the-peace statutes, directed against actions that "agitate" or arouse citizens "from a state of repose ... to disquiet," are by their very nature antagonistic to the First Amendment. One function of the Free Speech Clause "is to invite dispute. It may indeed best serve its high purpose when it induces a condition of unrest, creates dissatisfaction with conditions as they are, or even stirs people to anger. Speech is often provocative and challenging." Cox v. Louisiana, 379 U.S. 536, 551–52 (1965), citing Terminiello v. Chicago, 337 U.S. 1, 4 (1949). A unanimous Court in 1969 struck down a state statute that made it illegal to advocate crime or violence to accomplish reform. In this case, involving a gathering of the Ku Klux Klan, the Court held that government may not forbid advocacy unless it is directed to incite imminent lawless action. BRANDENBURG v. OHIO, 395 U.S. 444 (1969). The Court carefully monitors laws that restrict the solicitation of funds (see box).

Expressive Content

Freedom of speech also includes the right not to support an ideology. In 1977 the Supreme Court struck down a requirement in New Hampshire that noncommercial vehicles carry license tags bearing the state motto, "Live Free or Die." Jehovah's Witnesses considered the motto repugnant to their moral, religious, and political beliefs. The Court held that a state may not force an individual to advertise an ideological message, using a car as a "mobile billboard." The First Amendment protects the freedom to speak and not to speak. Wooley v. Maynard, 430 U.S. 705 (1977).

In 1995, a unanimous Court upheld the right of the organizers of Boston's St. Patrick's Day parade to exclude gay marchers. To the Court, a parade is a "public drama" to make a collective point. The organizers had a right to exclude a group that would have altered the expressive content of the parade. Hurley v. Irish-American Gay Group of Boston, 515 U.S. 557 (1995).

Hurley became the basis for deciding a conflict between a New Jersey law that prohibits discrimination against sexual orientation and the right of the Boy Scouts of America to expel an adult Scout who had announced that he is gay. The Boy Scouts, a private organization engaged in instilling its system of values in young people, asserted that homosexual conduct is inconsistent with the values it seeks to promote. James Dale, whose membership was revoked, is a gay rights activist. Unlike the unanimous ruling in *Hurley*, the Court split 5 to 4 in deciding that the New Jersey law violated the Boy Scouts' First Amendment right of expressive association. Although the Scout Oath and Law do not mention sexuality or sexual orientation, the Court interpreted the terms "morally straight" and "clean" as opposition to homosexual conduct, a position the Boy Scouts have adopted ever since 1978. Dale's presence in the Boy Scouts would force the organization to send a message that it accepts homosexual conduct as a legitimate form of behavior. Boy Scouts of America v. Dale, 120 S.Ct. 2446 (2000).

Justice Stevens' dissent, joined by Souter, Ginsburg, and Breyer, argued that the New Jersey law did not impose any "serious burdens" on the Boy Scouts or force the organization to communicate any message it did not want to endorse. He claimed that the Boy Scouts had never take a clear and unequivocal position of homosexuality. Further, Stevens disagreed that Dale's membership sent a message comparable to that of the gay marchers in *Hurley*.

Although the Boy Scouts prevailed in court, it might be penalized by corporations and state governments that withdraw their support for fear that continued assistance could imply tolerance for discrimination against gays. The Clinton administration announced that it would not close federal lands to Boy Scout Jamborees. How the rest of society will react remains an open question.

Dues and Fees

The Court has scrutinized various dues and fees to determine when they present First Amendment problems. In 1977, the Court upheld a Michigan requirement that nonunion members pay a "service charge" to the union, but also placed restrictions on the use of the funds. The union could use the money for collective bargaining, contract administration, and grievance-adjustment purposes, but it could not force nonunion employees to contribute to ideological causes they oppose. Abood v. Detroit Board of Education, 431 U.S. 209 (1977).

A unanimous Court in 1990 extended the principle in *Abood* by holding that lawyers cannot be compelled to pay state bar dues used to support political or ideological causes to which they do not subscribe. Keller v. State Bar of California, 496 U.S. 1 (1990). In 1991, in another clarification of *Abood,* the Court ruled 8 to 1 that public employee unions cannot charge nonmembers for political lobbying and public relations campaigns unless those efforts are directly related to ratification of a contract. Lehnert v. Ferris Faculty Assn., 500 U.S. 507 (1991).

Other decisions have clarified the use of dues and fees. In 1995, the Court held that the University of Virginia had denied students their right of free speech by using student fees to finance the printing of student publications but withholding funds from "Wide Awake," a Christian newspaper. Rosenberger v. University of Virginia, 515 U.S. 819 (1995). The Court was divided 5 to 4 in this case, but in 2000 it was unanimous in holding that public colleges can require students to pan an activity fee even when the funds are used to support political advocacy by groups and some students object to the message. Christian law students at the University of Wisconsin objected that the activity fee had been used to fund student organizations supportive of gay rights and other liberal causes. The Court argued that the fees helped promote an open dialogue among students. This type of activity fees is constitutional provided it is applied neutrally and does not favor one viewpoint over another. Board of Regents of University of Wisconsin v. Southworth, 120 S.Ct. 1346 (2000).

Public Employees

The right of free speech for public employees poses unique problems. After much litigation to the contrary, it is now settled that public employees have a constitutional right to comment upon matters "of public concern." Pickering v. Board of Education, 391 U.S. 563 (1968). They do not forfeit First Amendment freedoms when they engage in private communications with their employers, even when the exchange is considered insulting, hostile, loud, and arrogant. Givhan v. Western Line Consol. School Dist., 439 U.S. 410 (1979). Public employees are prohibited by the Hatch Act from participating in certain political party activities. When Presidents Theodore Roosevelt and William Howard Taft imposed a "gag order" to prohibit federal employees from lobbying Congress, Congress responded with legislation that gave civil servants the right to petition Congress and to furnish information to either House. 37 Stat. 556, § 6 (1912); 48 Cong. Rec. 4513, 5201, 5223, 5235, 10671 (1912).

Beyond these general guideposts, the scope of free speech for public employees is uncertain. In 1983, a 5–4 Court upheld the removal of public employees who object to internal office conditions and attempt to organize opposition to superiors, even when the reasons for dismissal are alleged to be mistaken or unreasonable. Connick v. Myers, 461 U.S. 138 (1983). Four years later, again by a 5–4 vote, the Court overturned the removal of a public employee who remarked to a coworker, after learning of the assassination attempt on President Reagan, "If they go for him again, I hope they get him." Justice Powell, the swing vote, explained that this offhand remark by a clerical employee was insufficiently disruptive of the office to justify dismissal. Rankin v. McPherson, 483 U.S. 378 (1987).

The degree of free speech available to public workers split the Court in 1994. In ruling that a public employer must first investigate an incident before firing someone and have "reasonable" grounds for the dismissal, the Court's plurality decision (joined by four Justices) precipitated concurrences from four colleagues and drew two dissents. Waters v. Churchill, 511 U.S. 661 (1994). In a 1995 ruling striking down a federal law that prohibited most executive branch employees from accepting outside income for speeches and articles, three Justices dissented and a fourth dissented in part. The Court found the law especially offensive because it prevented employees from accepting compensation even when the subject of the speech or article had no connection to the employee's official duties. United States v. National Treasury Employees Union, 513 U.S. 454 (1995).[6] (Additional discussion on the First Amendment rights of public employees appears in the earlier section on associational rights.)

With regard to free speech in the armed forces, the Court generally treats the military as a

---

6. For other free speech cases involving public employees, see Branti v. Finkel, 445 U.S. 507 (1980); Mt. Healthy City Board of Ed. v. Doyle, 429 U.S. 274 (1977); Elrod v. Burns, 427 U.S. 347 (1976); Perry v. Sindermann, 408 U.S. 593 (1972). O'Hare Truck Service, Inc. v. Northlake, 518 U.S. 712 (1996), builds on *Elrod* and *Burns* to extend the right of political expression to those who contract for government services. That ruling was reinforced by Board of Comm'rs, Wabaunsee Cty. v. Umbehr, 518 U.S. 668 (1996).

separate enclave of constitutional law, permitting restrictions on speech that would be impermissible in civilian society. Elementary rights of circulating petitions and listening to speeches by political candidates are denied in the interests of military discipline and order.[7]

After protecting the free-speech rights of public employees in a number of cases that restricted the use of patronage to dismiss government workers (note 6), the Court in 1990 extended that principle to four new personnel actions: promotion, transfer, hiring, and recall (bringing someone back after a layoff). In a hotly contested 5–4 decision, the Court held that personnel actions in those areas cannot be based on party affiliation and party support. Other than cases where party affiliation is an "appropriate requirement" for the position involved (the Court gave no clue as to what that means), patronage is an impermissible infringement on public employees' First Amendment rights. It appears that this decision will have more impact on state and local governments than on the Federal Government. For the dissenters, Justice Scalia excoriated the Court for usurping a "policy question to be decided by the people's representatives." He also flagged a conspicuous irony: most Justices of the Supreme Court owe their appointment to patronage. Presidents almost always appoint judges from their own party. Rutan v. Republican Party of Illinois, 497 U.S. 62 (1990).

In 1998, a unanimous Court held that federal employees can be disciplined for lying about misconduct. Unlike in criminal trials where defendants need not testify, federal workers have an obligation to answer questions. In agency investigations, federal employees have a right to be heard but not a right to lie. LaChance v. Erickson, 522 U.S. 262 (1998).

"Fighting Words"

The Supreme Court created, and subsequently altered, the "fighting-words" doctrine. A unanimous decision in 1942 upheld a state law that prohibited speech in public that is offensive or derisive of another person. The statutory purpose was to prevent a breach of the peace. Chaplinsky v. New Hampshire, 315 U.S. 568 (1942). That decision was undercut in 1949 when the Court, divided 5–4, struck down a Chicago ordinance that prohibited any breach of the peace. The trial court had interpreted the ordinance to prohibit any speech that "stirs the public to anger" and "invites disputes." The Court declared that a function of free speech is to invite disputes:

> "It may indeed best serve its high purpose when it induces a condition of unrest, creates dissatisfaction with conditions as they are, or even stirs people to anger. Speech is often provocative and challenging. It may strike at prejudices and preconceptions and have profound unsettling effects as it presses for acceptance of an idea." Terminiello v. Chicago, 337 U.S. 1, 4 (1949).

The fighting-words doctrine was kept alive two years later when the Court split 6–3 in upholding a New York statute that prohibited incitement of a breach of the peace. The Court supported intervention by the police to prevent a riot. Feiner v. New York, 340 U.S. 315 (1951). The following year, a 5–4 decision upheld an Illinois statute that made it illegal to publish anything that exposed the citizens of any race, color, creed, or religion to contempt, derision, or obloquy. At issue was the distribution of racist leaflets that portrayed blacks as depraved, criminal, and unchaste. Beauharnais v. Illinois, 343 U.S. 250 (1952).

In light of recent cases, little remains of the fighting-words doctrine. In 1971 a 5–4 Court overturned the conviction of Paul Robert Cohen, who had been sentenced to thirty days for

---

7. United States v. Albertini, 472 U.S. 675 (1985); Secretary of Navy v. Huff, 444 U.S. 453 (1980); Brown v. Glines, 444 U.S. 348 (1980); Greer v. Spock, 424 U.S. 828 (1976); Parker v. Levy, 417 U.S. 733 (1974). But see Flower v. United States, 407 U.S. 197 (1972).

wearing, in a county courthouse, a jacket bearing the words "Fuck the Draft." Unlike its decisions in cases involving obscenity and pornography, the Court found itself unable to "distinguish this from any other offensive word." COHEN v. CALIFORNIA, 403 U.S. 15, 25 (1971).[8]

A year later, the Court agreed to set aside the conviction of someone who had said to a police officer: "White son of a bitch, I'll kill you." The Court found the state law, making it a misdemeanor to use "opprobrious words or abusive language, tending to cause a breach of the peace," unconstitutionally vague and overbroad. Gooding v. Wilson, 405 U.S. 518 (1972). When an eighteen-year-old at a small public gathering remarked that if inducted into the army and made to carry a rifle "the first man I want to get in my sights is L.B.J. [President Lyndon B. Johnson]," the Court held that the context of this remark made it political hyperbole rather than a knowing and willful threat against the President. Watts v. United States, 394 U.S. 705 (1969).

An issue of exceptional emotional intensity involved the request of American Nazis to march in Skokie, Illinois, a village with thousands of Holocaust survivors. They wanted to march in their uniforms, display the swastika, and distribute literature promoting hatred against Jews. After many court rulings, they eventually held a rally in Chicago's Marquette Park. National Socialist Party v. Skokie, 432 U.S. 43 (1977); Collin v. Smith, 447 F.Supp. 676 (N.D. Ill. 1978), aff'd, 578 F.2d 1197 (7th Cir. 1978), cert. denied, 439 U.S. 916 (1978).

Another emotional issue, decided by the Supreme Court in 1992, focused on a St. Paul, Minnesota, "hate crimes law" used to prosecute someone for burning a cross on a black family's lawn. The law prohibited the display of a symbol that one knows or has reason to know "arouses anger, alarm or resentment in others on the basis of race, color, creed, religion or gender." The Court struck down the law as a violation of free speech, but the Justices could not agree on their reasoning. R.A.V. v. ST. PAUL, 505 U.S. 377 (1992). On such free speech doctrines as "discrete categories" and "overbreadth," the Justices sharply disagree (see box on next page). The decision is expected to cast doubt on the constitutionality of other laws that prohibit cross burning; laws that impose heavier penalties for such crimes as vandalism, arson, and assault that are motivated by racial, religious, or other bias; and campus speech codes that punish students for offensive remarks. Although the St. Paul ordinance was held invalid, individuals guilty of cross burning, swastika displays, and other actions could have been prosecuted under other Minnesota statutes that prohibit terroristic threats, arson, and criminal damage to property.

Building on *R.A.V. v. St. Paul,* a unanimous Court in 1993 decided that states may impose heavier prison sentences when assailants select their victims on the basis of race, religion, or other biases. In this case, a group of black teenagers in Wisconsin beat up a white youth after discussing the racially charged movie *Mississippi Burning*. The Court distinguished this case from the St. Paul ordinance by holding that the latter was explicitly directed at expression, whereas the Wisconsin law aimed only at conduct. Wisconsin v. Mitchell, 508 U.S. 476 (1993).

---

8. Yet the Court distinguishes language well enough to use code by referring to articles entitled "M——f—— Acquitted" and organizations known as "Up Against the Wall, M——f——." Papish v. University of Missouri Curators, 410 U.S. 667 (1973). Similar cases include Rosenfeld v. New Jersey, 408 U.S. 901 (1972); Lewis v. City of New Orleans, 408 U.S. 913 (1972); Brown v. Oklahoma, 408 U.S. 914 (1972); Cason v. City of Columbus, 409 U.S. 1053 (1972). For other obscenity/breach-of-the-peace cases, see Hess v. Indiana, 414 U.S. 105 (1973) and Lewis v. City of New Orleans, 415 U.S. 130 (1974).

Judicial Guidelines for Free Speech Cases

The Supreme Court often uses three tests to determine the constitutionality of governmental efforts to restrict free speech:

1. *Discrete Categories (content-based).* Certain categories of expression may be prohibited on the basis of their content: shouting "fire" in a crowded theatre [Schenck v. United States, 249 U.S. 47, 52 (1919)]; "fighting words" [Chaplinsky v. New Hampshire, 315 U.S. 568, 572 (1942)]; defamation [Beauharnais v. Illinois, 343 U.S. 250 (1952)]; child pornography [New York v. Ferber, 458 U.S. 747 (1982)]. In these cases the expressive content is either of no value or of de minimis value to society.

2. *Overbreadth Doctrine.* Governmental actions are invalid if they prohibit not only unprotected expression but protected expression as well. Schaumburg v. Citizens for a Better Environment, 444 U.S. 620, 634 (1980). The "possible harm to society in permitting some unprotected speech to go unpunished is outweighed by the possibility that protected speech of others may be muted ...." Broadrick v. Oklahoma, 413 U.S. 601, 612 (1973).

3. *Void for Vagueness.* A law is invalid on its face if it is so vague that persons "of common intelligence must necessarily guess at its meaning and differ as to its application." Connally v. General Construction Co., 269 U.S. 385, 391 (1926). Examples include loyalty oaths [Baggett v. Bullitt, 377 U.S. 360 (1964)] and a city ordinance that forbids three or more persons from meeting on sidewalks and acting in a manner "annoying" to persons passing by [Coates v. City of Cincinnati, 402 U.S. 611 (1971)].

Edwards v. South Carolina

372 U.S. 229 (1963)

Feeling aggrieved by the laws of South Carolina, 187 black high school and college students assembled peacefully on the grounds of the state legislature. When told by police officers that they must disperse within fifteen minutes or face arrest, they sang patriotic and religious songs. Although there was no violence or threat of violence on their part, they were arrested and convicted of the common-law crime of breach of the peace. James Edwards, a student, is one of the petitioners in this case.

MR. JUSTICE STEWART delivered the opinion of the Court.

The petitioners, 187 in number, were convicted in a magistrate's court in Columbia, South Carolina, of the common-law crime of breach of the peace. Their convictions were ultimately affirmed by the South Carolina Supreme Court, 239 S. C. 339, 123 S. E. 2d 247. We granted certiorari, 369 U. S. 870, to consider the claim that these convictions cannot be squared with the Fourteenth Amendment of the United States Constitution.

There was no substantial conflict in the trial evidence. Late in the morning of March 2, 1961, the petitioners, high school and college students of the Negro race, met at the Zion Baptist Church in Columbia. From there, at about noon, they walked in separate groups of about 15 to the South Carolina State House grounds, an area of two city blocks open to the general public. Their purpose was "to submit a protest to the citizens of South Carolina, along with the Legislative Bodies of South Carolina, our feelings and our dissatisfaction with the present condition of discriminatory actions against Negroes, in general, and to let them know that we were dissatisfied and that we would like for the laws which prohibited Negro privileges in this State to be removed."

Already on the State House grounds when the petitioners arrived were 30 or more law enforcement officers, who had advance knowledge that the petitioners were coming. Each group of petitioners entered the grounds through a driveway and parking area known in the record as the "horseshoe." As they entered, they were told by the law enforcement officials that "they had a right, as a citizen, to go through the State House grounds, as any other citizen has, as long as they were peaceful." During the next half hour or 45 minutes, the petitioners, in the same small groups, walked single file or two abreast in an orderly way through the grounds, each group carrying placards bearing such messages as "I am proud to be a Negro" and "Down with segregation."

During this time a crowd of some 200 to 300 onlookers had collected in the horseshoe area and on the adjacent sidewalks. There was no evidence to suggest that these onlookers were anything but curious, and no evidence at all of any threatening remarks, hostile gestures, or offensive language on the part of any member of the crowd. The City Manager testified that he recognized some of the onlookers, whom he did not identify, as "possible trouble makers," but his subsequent testimony made clear that nobody among the crowd actually caused or threatened any trouble. There was no obstruction of pedestrian or vehicular traffic within the State House grounds. No vehicle was prevented from entering or leaving the horseshoe area. Although vehicular traffic at a nearby street intersection was slowed down somewhat, an officer was dispatched to keep traffic moving. There were a number of bystanders on the public sidewalks adjacent to the State House grounds, but they all moved on when asked to do so, and there was no impediment of pedestrian traffic. Police protection at the scene was at all times sufficient to meet any foreseeable possibility of disorder.

In the situation and under the circumstances thus described, the police authorities advised the petitioners that they would be arrested if they did not disperse within 15 minutes. Instead of dispersing, the petitioners engaged in what the City Manager described as "boisterous," "loud," and "flamboyant" conduct, which, as his later testimony made clear, consisted of listening to a "religious harangue" by one of their leaders, and loudly singing "The Star Spangled Banner" and other patriotic and religious songs, while stamping their feet and clapping their hands. After 15 minutes had passed, the police arrested the petitioners and marched them off to jail.

Upon this evidence the state trial court convicted the petitioners of breach of the peace, and imposed sentences ranging from a $10 fine or five days in jail, to a $100 fine or 30 days in jail. In affirming the judgments, the Supreme Court of South Carolina said that under the law of that State the offense of breach of the peace "is not susceptible of exact definition," but that the "general definition of the offense" is as follows:

"In general terms, a breach of the peace is a vi-

olation of public order, a disturbance of the public tranquility, by any act or conduct inciting to violence . . . , it includes any violation of any law enacted to preserve peace and good order. It may consist of an act of violence or an act likely to produce violence. It is not necessary that the peace be actually broken to lay the foundation for a prosecution for this offense. If what is done is unjustifiable and unlawful, tending with sufficient directness to break the peace, no more is required. Nor is actual personal violence an essential element in the offense. . . .

"By 'peace,' as used in the law in this connection, is meant the tranquility enjoyed by citizens of a municipality or community where good order reigns among its members, which is the natural right of all persons in political society." 239 S. C., at 343–344, 123 S. E. 2d, at 249.

The petitioners contend that there was a complete absence of any evidence of the commission of this offense, and that they were thus denied one of the most basic elements of due process of law. . . . Whatever the merits of this contention, we need not pass upon it in the present case. The state courts have held that the petitioners' conduct constituted breach of the peace under state law, and we may accept their decision as binding upon us to that extent. But it nevertheless remains our duty in a case such as this to make an independent examination of the whole record. . . . And it is clear to us that in arresting, convicting, and punishing the petitioners under the circumstances disclosed by this record, South Carolina infringed the petitioners' constitutionally protected rights of free speech, free assembly, and freedom to petition for redress of their grievances.

It has long been established that these First Amendment freedoms are protected by the Fourteenth Amendment from invasion by the States. . . . The circumstances in this case reflect an exercise of these basic constitutional rights in their most pristine and classic form. The petitioners felt aggrieved by laws of South Carolina which allegedly "prohibited Negro privileges in this State." They peaceably assembled at the site of the State Government and there peaceably expressed their grievances "to the citizens of South Carolina, along with the Legislative Bodies of South Carolina." Not until they were told by police officials that they must disperse on pain of arrest did they do more. Even then, they but sang patriotic and religious songs after one of their leaders had delivered a "religious harangue." There was no violence or threat of violence on their part, or on the part of any member of the crowd watching them. Police protection was "ample."

This, therefore, was a far cry from the situation in *Feiner* v. *New York,* 340 U. S. 315, where two policemen were faced with a crowd which was "pushing, shoving and milling around," *id.,* at 317, where at least one member of the crowd "threatened violence if the police did not act," *id.,* at 317, where "the crowd was pressing closer around petitioner and the officer," *id.,* at 318, and where "the speaker passes the bounds of argument or persuasion and undertakes incitement to riot." *Id.,* at 321. And the record is barren of any evidence of "fighting words." See *Chaplinsky* v. *New Hampshire,* 315 U. S. 568.

We do not review in this case criminal convictions resulting from the evenhanded application of a precise and narrowly drawn regulatory statute evincing a legislative judgment that certain specific conduct be limited or proscribed. If, for example, the petitioners had been convicted upon evidence that they had violated a law regulating traffic, or had disobeyed a law reasonably limiting the periods during which the State House grounds were open to the public, this would be a different case.... These petitioners were convicted of an offense so generalized as to be, in the words of the South Carolina Supreme Court, "not susceptible of exact definition." And they were convicted upon evidence which showed no more than that the opinions which they were peaceably expressing were sufficiently opposed to the views of the majority of the community to attract a crowd and necessitate police protection.

The Fourteenth Amendment does not permit a State to make criminal the peaceful expression of unpopular views. "[A] function of free speech under our system of government is to invite dispute. It may indeed best serve its high purpose when it induces a condition of unrest, creates dissatisfaction with conditions as they are, or even stirs people to anger. Speech is often provocative and challenging. It may strike at prejudices and preconceptions and have profound unsettling effects as it presses for acceptance of an idea. That is why freedom of speech . . . is . . . protected against censorship or punishment, unless shown likely to produce a clear and present danger of a serious substantive evil that rises far above public inconvenience, annoyance, or unrest.... There is no room under our Constitution for a more restrictive view. For the alternative would lead to standard-

ization of ideas either by legislatures, courts, or dominant political or community groups." *Terminiello* v. *Chicago,* 337 U. S. 1, 4–5. As in the *Terminiello* case, the courts of South Carolina have defined a criminal offense so as to permit conviction of the petitioners if their speech "stirred people to anger, invited public dispute, or brought about a condition of unrest. A conviction resting on any of those grounds may not stand." *Id.,* at 5.

As Chief Justice Hughes wrote in *Stromberg* v. *California,* "The maintenance of the opportunity for free political discussion to the end that government may be responsive to the will of the people and that changes may be obtained by lawful means, an opportunity essential to the security of the Republic, is a fundamental principle of our constitutional system. A statute which upon its face, and as authoritatively construed, is so vague and indefinite as to permit the punishment of the fair use of this opportunity is repugnant to the guaranty of liberty contained in the Fourteenth Amendment...." 283 U. S. 359, 369.

For these reasons we conclude that these criminal convictions cannot stand.

Reversed.

Mr. Justice Clark, dissenting.

The convictions of the petitioners, Negro high school and college students, for breach of the peace under South Carolina law are accepted by the Court "as binding upon us to that extent" but are held violative of "petitioners' constitutionally protected rights of free speech, free assembly, and freedom to petition for redress of their grievances." Petitioners, of course, had a right to peaceable assembly, to espouse their cause and to petition, but in my view the manner in which they exercised those rights was by no means the passive demonstration which this Court relates; rather, as the City Manager of Columbia testified, "a dangerous situation was really building up" which South Carolina's courts expressly found had created "an actual interference with traffic and an imminently threatened disturbance of the peace of the community." Since the Court does not attack the state courts' findings and accepts the convictions as "binding" to the extent that the petitioners' conduct constituted a breach of the peace, it is difficult for me to understand its understatement of the facts and reversal of the convictions.

. . .

Adderley v. Florida

385 U.S. 39 (1966)

Harriett Louise Adderley and thirty-one other college students were members of a group of about 200 who demonstrated against their schoolmates' arrest and perhaps segregation in jail. They assembled on a nonpublic jail driveway, which they blocked. Adjacent to the county jail premises they sang, clapped, and danced. The sheriff, the jail's custodian, advised them that they were trespassing on county property and would have to leave or be arrested. They refused and were convicted under a Florida trespass statute for "trespass with a malicious and mischievous intent."

MR. JUSTICE BLACK delivered the opinion of the Court.

Petitioners, Harriett Louise Adderley and 31 other persons, were convicted by a jury in a joint trial in the County Judge's Court of Leon County, Florida, on a charge of "trespass with a malicious and mischievous intent" upon the premises of the county jail contrary to § 821.18 of the Florida statutes set out below. ["Every trespass upon the property of another, committed with a malicious and mischievous intent, the punishment of which is not specially provided for, shall be punished by imprisonment not exceeding three months, or by fine not exceeding one hundred dollars." Fla. Stat. § 821.18 (1965).] Petitioners, apparently all students of the Florida A. & M. University in Tallahassee, had gone from the school to the jail about a mile away, along with many other students, to "demonstrate" at the jail their protests of arrests of other protesting students the day before, and perhaps to protest more generally against state and local policies and practices of racial segregation, including segregation of the jail. The county sheriff, legal custodian of the jail and jail grounds, tried to persuade the students to leave the jail grounds. When this did not work, he notified them that they must leave, that if they did not leave he would arrest them for trespassing, and that if they resisted he would charge them with that as well. Some of the students left but others, including petitioners, remained and they were arrested. On appeal the convictions were affirmed by the Florida Circuit Court and then by the Florida District Court of Appeal, 175 So. 2d 249. That being the highest state court to which they could appeal, petitioners applied to us for certiorari contending that, in view of petitioners' purpose to protest against jail and other segregation policies, their conviction denied them "rights of free speech, assembly, petition, due process of law and equal protection of the laws as guaranteed by the Fourteenth Amendment to the Constitution of the United States." ...

I.

Petitioners have insisted from the beginning of this case that it is controlled by and must be reversed because of our prior cases of *Edwards* v. *South Carolina,* 372 U. S. 229, and *Cox* v. *Louisiana,* 379 U. S. 536, 559. We cannot agree.

The *Edwards* case, like this one, did come up when a number of persons demonstrated on public property against their State's segregation policies. They also sang hymns and danced, as did the demonstrators in this case. But here the analogies to this case end. In *Edwards,* the demonstrators went to the South Carolina State Capitol grounds to protest. In this case they went to the jail. Traditionally, state capitol grounds are open to the public. Jails, built for security purposes, are not. The demonstrators at the South Carolina Capitol went in through a public driveway and as they entered they were told by state officials there that they had a right as citizens to go through the State House grounds as long as they were peaceful. Here the demonstrators entered the jail grounds through a driveway used only for jail purposes and without warning to or permission from the sheriff. More importantly, South Carolina sought to prosecute its State Capitol demonstrators by charging them with the common-law crime of breach of the peace. This Court in *Edwards* took pains to point out at length the indefinite, loose, and broad nature of this charge; indeed, this Court pointed out at p. 237, that the South Carolina Supreme Court had itself declared that the "breach of the peace" charge is "not susceptible of exact definition." South Carolina's power to prosecute, it was emphasized at p. 236, would have been different had the State proceeded under a "precise and narrowly drawn regulatory statute evincing a legislative judgment that certain specific conduct be limited or proscribed" such as, for example, "limiting the periods during which the State House grounds were open to the public...." The South Carolina breach-of-the-peace statute was thus struck down as being so broad and all-embracing as to jeopardize speech, press, assembly and petition, under the constitutional doctrine enunciated in *Cantwell* v. *Connecticut,* 310 U. S. 296, 307–308, and followed in many subsequent cases. And it was on this same ground of vagueness that in *Cox* v. *Louisiana, supra,* at 551–552, the Louisiana breach-of-the-peace law used to prosecute Cox was invalidated.

The Florida trespass statute under which these petitioners were charged cannot be challenged on this ground. It is aimed at conduct of one limited kind, that is, for one person or persons to trespass upon the property of another with a malicious and mischievous intent. There is no lack of notice in this law, nothing to entrap or fool the unwary.

Petitioners seem to argue that the Florida trespass law is void for vagueness because it requires a trespass to be "with a malicious and mischievous intent...." But these words do not broaden the scope of trespass so as to make it cover a multitude of types of conduct as does the common-law breach-of-the-peace charge. On the contrary, these words narrow the scope of the offense. The trial court charged the jury as to their meaning and petitioners have not argued that this definition, set out below, [" 'Malicious' means wrongful, you remember back in the original charge, the State has to prove beyond a reasonable doubt there was a malicious and mischievous intent. The word 'malicious' means that the wrongful act shall be done voluntarily, unlawfully and without excuse or justification. The word 'malicious' that is used in these affidavits does not necessarily allege nor require the State to prove that the defendant had actual malice in his mind at the time of the alleged trespass. Another way of stating the definition of 'malicious' is by 'malicious' is meant the act was done knowingly and willfully and without any legal justification.

" 'Mischievous,' which is also required, means that the alleged trespass shall be inclined to cause petty and trivial trouble, annoyance and vexation to others in order for you to find that the alleged trespass was committed with mischievous intent."] is not a reasonable and clear definition of the terms. The use of these terms in the statute, instead of contributing to uncertainty and misunderstanding, actually makes its meaning more understandable and clear.

· · ·

IV.

...petitioners' summary of facts, as well as that of the Circuit Court, shows an abundance of facts to support the jury's verdict of guilty in this case.

In summary both these statements show testimony ample to prove this: Disturbed and upset by the arrest of their schoolmates the day before, a large number of Florida A. & M. students assembled on the school grounds and decided to march down to the county jail. Some apparently wanted to be put in jail too, along with the students already there. A group of around 200 marched from the school and arrived at the jail singing and clapping. They went directly to the jail-door entrance where they were met by a deputy sheriff, evidently surprised by their arrival. He asked them to move back, claiming they were blocking the entrance to the jail and fearing that they might attempt to enter the jail. They moved back part of the way, where they stood or sat, singing, clapping and dancing, on the jail driveway and on an adjacent grassy area upon the jail premises. This particular jail entrance and driveway were not normally used by the public, but by the sheriff's department for transporting prisoners to and from the courts several blocks away and by commercial concerns for servicing the jail. Even after their partial retreat, the demonstrators continued to block vehicular passage over this driveway up to the entrance of the jail. Someone called the sheriff who was at the moment apparently conferring with one of the state court judges about incidents connected with prior arrests for demonstrations. When the sheriff returned to the jail, he immediately inquired if all was safe inside the jail and was told it was. He then engaged in a conversation with two of the leaders. He told them that they were trespassing upon jail property and that he would give them 10 minutes to leave or he would arrest them. Neither of the leaders did anything to disperse the crowd, and one of them told the sheriff that they wanted to get arrested. A local minister talked with some of the demonstrators and told them not to enter the jail, because they could not arrest themselves, but just to remain where they were. After about 10 minutes, the sheriff, in a voice loud enough to be heard by all, told the demonstrators that he was the legal custodian of the jail and its premises, that they were trespassing on county property in violation of the law, that they should all leave forthwith or he would arrest them, and that if they attempted to resist arrest, he would charge them with that as a separate offense. Some of the group then left.

Others, including all petitioners, did not leave. Some of them sat down. In a few minutes, realizing that the remaining demonstrators had no intention of leaving, the sheriff ordered his deputies to surround those remaining on jail premises and placed them, 107 demonstrators, under arrest. The sheriff unequivocally testified that he did not arrest any persons other than those who were on the jail premises. Of the three petitioners testifying, two insisted that they were arrested before they had a chance to leave, had they wanted to, and one testified that she did not intend to leave. The sheriff again explicitly testified that he did not arrest any person who was attempting to leave.

Under the foregoing testimony the jury was authorized to find that the State had proven every essential element of the crime, as it was defined by the state court. That interpretation is, of course, binding on us, leaving only the question of whether conviction of the state offense, thus defined, unconstitutionally deprives petitioners of their rights to freedom of speech, press, assembly or petition. We hold it does not. The sheriff, as jail custodian, had power, as the state courts have here held, to direct that this large crowd of people get off the grounds. There is not a shred of evidence in this record that this power was exercised, or that its exercise was sanctioned by the lower courts, because the sheriff objected to what was being sung or said by the demonstrators or because he disagreed with the objectives of their protest. The record reveals that he objected only to their presence on that part of the jail grounds reserved for jail uses. There is no evidence at all that on any other occasion had similarly large groups of the public been permitted to gather on this portion of the jail grounds for any purpose. Nothing in the Constitution of the United States prevents Florida from even-handed enforcement of its general trespass statute against those refusing to obey the sheriff's order to remove themselves from what amounted to the curtilage of the jailhouse. The State, no less than a private owner of property, has power to preserve the property under its control for the use to which it is lawfully dedicated.... The United States Constitution does not forbid a State to control the use of its own property for its own lawful nondiscriminatory purpose.

These judgments are

Affirmed.

MR. JUSTICE DOUGLAS with whom THE CHIEF JUSTICE, MR. JUSTICE BRENNAN, and MR. JUSTICE FORTAS concur, dissenting.

...With all respect...the Court errs in treating the case as if it were an ordinary trespass case or an ordinary picketing case.

The jailhouse, like an executive mansion, a legislative chamber, a courthouse, or the statehouse itself *(Edwards v. South Carolina, supra)* is one of the seats of government, whether it be the Tower of London, the Bastille, or a small county jail. And when it houses political prisoners or those who many think are unjustly held, it is an obvious center for protest. The right to petition for the redress of grievances has an ancient history and is not limited to writing a letter or sending a telegram to a congressman; it is not confined to appearing before the local city council, or writing letters to the President or Governor or Mayor. See *N. A. A. C. P. v. Button,* 371 U. S. 415, 429–431. Conventional methods of petitioning may be, and often have been, shut off to large groups of our citizens. Legislators may turn deaf ears; formal complaints may be routed endlessly through a bureaucratic maze; courts may let the wheels of justice grind very slowly. Those who do not control television and radio, those who cannot afford to advertise in newspapers or circulate elaborate pamphlets may have only a more limited type of access to public officials. Their methods should not be condemned as tactics of obstruction and harassment as long as the assembly and petition are peaceable, as these were.

. . .

Brandenburg v. Ohio

395 U.S. 444 (1969)

Charles Brandenburg, a Ku Klux Klan leader, was convicted under an Ohio criminal law for advocating crime or violence as a means of accomplishing industrial or political reform. Neither the indictment nor the trial judge's instructions to the jury refined the statute's definition of the crime in terms of mere advocacy as distinguished from incite-

ment to imminent lawless action. His conviction was affirmed by the intermediate Ohio appellate court without opinion.

PER CURIAM.

The appellant, a leader of a Ku Klux Klan group, was convicted under the Ohio Criminal Syndicalism statute for "advocat[ing] ... the duty, necessity, or propriety of crime, sabotage, violence, or unlawful methods of terrorism as a means of accomplishing industrial or political reform" and for "voluntarily assembl[ing] with any society, group, or assemblage of persons formed to teach or advocate the doctrines of criminal syndicalism." Ohio Rev. Code Ann. § 2923.13. He was fined $1,000 and sentenced to one to 10 years' imprisonment....

The record shows that a man, identified at trial as the appellant, telephoned an announcer-reporter on the staff of a Cincinnati television station and invited him to come to a Ku Klux Klan "rally" to be held at a farm in Hamilton County. With the cooperation of the organizers, the reporter and a cameraman attended the meeting and filmed the events. Portions of the films were later broadcast on the local station and on a national network.

The prosecution's case rested on the films and on testimony identifying the appellant as the person who communicated with the reporter and who spoke at the rally. The State also introduced into evidence several articles appearing in the film, including a pistol, a rifle, a shotgun, ammunition, a Bible, and a red hood worn by the speaker in the films.

One film showed 12 hooded figures, some of whom carried firearms. They were gathered around a large wooden cross, which they burned. No one was present other than the participants and the newsmen who made the film. Most of the words uttered during the scene were incomprehensible when the film was projected, but scattered phrases could be understood that were derogatory of Negroes and, in one instance, of Jews. Another scene on the same film showed the appellant, in Klan regalia, making a speech. The speech, in full, was as follows:

"This is an organizers' meeting. We have had quite a few members here today which are — we have hundreds, hundreds of members throughout the State of Ohio. I can quote from a newspaper clipping from the Columbus, Ohio Dispatch, five weeks ago Sunday morning. The Klan has more members in the State of Ohio than does any other organization. We're not a revengent organization, but if our President, our Congress, our Supreme Court, continues to suppress the white, Caucasian race, it's possible that there might have to be some revengeance taken.

"We are marching on Congress July the Fourth, four hundred thousand strong. From there we are dividing into two groups, one group to march on St. Augustine, Florida, the other group to march into Mississippi. Thank you."

The second film showed six hooded figures one of whom, later identified as the appellant, repeated a speech very similar to that recorded on the first film. The reference to the possibility of "revengeance" was omitted, and one sentence was added: "Personally, I believe the nigger should be returned to Africa, the Jew returned to Israel." Though some of the figures in the films carried weapons, the speaker did not.

The Ohio Criminal Syndicalism Statute was enacted in 1919. From 1917 to 1920, identical or quite similar laws were adopted by 20 States and two territories. E. Dowell, A History of Criminal Syndicalism Legislation in the United States 21 (1939). In 1927, this Court sustained the constitutionality of California's Criminal Syndicalism Act, Cal. Penal Code §§ 11400–11402, the text of which is quite similar to that of the laws of Ohio. *Whitney* v. *California,* 274 U. S. 357 (1927). The Court upheld the statute on the ground that, without more, "advocating" violent means to effect political and economic change involves such danger to the security of the State that the State may outlaw it. Cf. *Fiske* v. *Kansas,* 274 U. S. 380 (1927). But *Whitney* has been thoroughly discredited by later decisions. See *Dennis* v. *United States,* 341 U. S. 494, at 507 (1951). These later decisions have fashioned the principle that the constitutional guarantees of free speech and free press do not permit a State to forbid or proscribe advocacy of the use of force or of law violation except where such advocacy is directed to inciting or producing imminent lawless action and is likely to incite or produce such action....

Measured by this test, Ohio's Criminal Syndicalism Act cannot be sustained. The Act punishes persons who "advocate or teach the duty, necessity, or propriety" of violence "as a means of accomplishing industrial or political reform"; or who publish or circulate or display any book or paper containing such advocacy; or who "justify" the commission of violent acts "with intent to exemplify, spread or advocate the propriety of the doctrines of criminal syndicalism"; or who "voluntarily assemble" with a group formed "to teach or advocate the doctrines of criminal syndicalism." Neither the indictment nor the trial judge's instructions to the jury in any way refined the statute's bald definition of the crime in terms of mere advocacy not distinguished from incitement to imminent lawless action.

Accordingly, we are here confronted with a statute which, by its own words and as applied, purports to punish mere advocacy and to forbid, on pain of criminal punishment, assembly with others merely to advocate the described type of action. Such a statute falls within the condemnation of the First and Fourteenth Amendments. The contrary teaching of *Whitney* v. *California, supra,* cannot be supported, and that decision is therefore overruled.

Reversed.

Mr. Justice Black, concurring.

I agree with the views expressed by Mr. Justice Douglas in his concurring opinion in this case that the "clear and present danger" doctrine should have no place in the interpretation of the First Amendment. I join the Court's opinion, which, as I understand it, simply cites *Dennis* v. *United States,* 341 U. S. 494 (1951), but does not indicate any agreement on the Court's part with the "clear and present danger" doctrine on which *Dennis* purported to rely.

Mr. Justice Douglas, concurring.

While I join the opinion of the Court, I desire to enter a *caveat.*

. . .

...I see no place in the regime of the First Amendment for any "clear and present danger" test, whether strict and tight as some would make it, or free-wheeling as the Court in *Dennis* rephrased it.

When one reads the opinions closely and sees when and how the "clear and present danger" test has been applied, great misgivings are aroused. First, the threats were often loud but always puny and made serious only by judges so wedded to the *status quo* that critical analysis made them nervous. Second, the test was so twisted and perverted in *Dennis* as to make the trial of those teachers of Marxism an all-out political trial which was part and parcel of the cold war that has eroded substantial parts of the First Amendment.

. . .

The line between what is permissible and not subject to control and what may be made impermissible and subject to regulation is the line between ideas and overt acts.

. . .

Cohen v. California

403 U.S. 15 (1971)

Paul Robert Cohen was convicted of violating a California law that prohibited "maliciously and willfully disturb[ing] the peace or quiet of any neighborhood or person... by... offensive conduct." In a corridor of the Los Angeles Courthouse, he wore a jacket bearing the words "Fuck the Draft." The issue before the Supreme Court was whether the state had a compelling reason to override First Amendment interests by making the simple display of this single four-letter expletive a criminal offense.

Mr. Justice Harlan delivered the opinion of the Court.

This case may seem at first blush too inconsequential to find its way into our books, but the issue it presents is of no small constitutional significance.

Appellant Paul Robert Cohen was convicted in the Los Angeles Municipal Court of violating that part of California Penal Code § 415 which prohibits "maliciously and willfully disturb[ing] the peace or quiet of any neighborhood or person... by... offensive conduct..." He was given 30 days' imprisonment. The facts upon which his conviction rests are detailed in the opinion of the Court of Appeal of California, Second Appellate District, as follows:

"On April 26, 1968, the defendant was observed in the Los Angeles County Courthouse in the corridor outside of division 20 of the municipal court wearing a jacket bearing the words 'Fuck the Draft' which were plainly visible. There were women and children present in the corridor. The defendant was arrested. The defendant testified that he wore the jacket knowing that the words were on the jacket as a means of informing the public of the depth of his feelings against the Vietnam War and the draft.

"The defendant did not engage in, nor threaten to engage in, nor did anyone as the result of his conduct in fact commit or threaten to commit any act of violence. The defendant did not make any loud or unusual noise, nor was there any evidence that he uttered any sound prior to his arrest." 1 Cal. App. 3d 94, 97–98, 81 Cal. Rptr. 503, 505 (1969).

In affirming the conviction the Court of Appeal held that "offensive conduct" means "behavior which has a tendency to provoke *others* to acts of violence or to in turn disturb the peace," and that the State had proved this element because, on the facts of this case, "[i]t was certainly reasonably foreseeable that such conduct might cause others to rise up to commit a violent act against the person of the defendant or attempt to forcibly remove his jacket." 1 Cal. App. 3d, at 99–100, 81 Cal. Rptr., at 506. The California Supreme Court declined review by a divided vote....

. . .

I

In order to lay hands on the precise issue which this case involves, it is useful first to canvass various matters which this record does *not* present.

The conviction quite clearly rests upon the asserted offensiveness of the *words* Cohen used to convey his message to the public. The only "conduct" which the State sought to punish is the fact of communication. Thus, we deal here with a conviction resting solely upon "speech," cf. *Stromberg* v. *California,* 283 U. S. 359 (1931), not upon any separately identifiable conduct....

Appellant's conviction, then, rests squarely upon his exercise of the "freedom of speech" protected from arbitrary governmental interference by the Constitution and can be justified, if at all, only as a valid regulation of the manner in which he exercised that freedom, not as a permissible prohibition on the substantive message it conveys. This does not end the inquiry, of course, for the First and Fourteenth Amendments have never been thought

to give absolute protection to every individual to speak whenever or wherever he pleases, or to use any form of address in any circumstances that he chooses. In this vein, too, however, we think it important to note that several issues typically associated with such problems are not presented here.

In the first place, Cohen was tried under a statute applicable throughout the entire State. Any attempt to support this conviction on the ground that the statute seeks to preserve an appropriately decorous atmosphere in the courthouse where Cohen was arrested must fail in the absence of any language in the statute that would have put appellant on notice that certain kinds of otherwise permissible speech or conduct would nevertheless, under California law, not be tolerated in certain places. See *Edwards* v. *South Carolina,* 372 U. S. 229, 236–237, and n. 11 (1963). Cf. *Adderley* v. *Florida,* 385 U. S. 39 (1966). No fair reading of the phrase "offensive conduct" can be said sufficiently to inform the ordinary person that distinctions between certain locations are thereby created. *[Here the Court adds a footnote: "It is illuminating to note what transpired when Cohen entered a courtroom in the building. He removed his jacket and stood with it folded over his arm. Meanwhile, a policeman sent the presiding judge a note suggesting that Cohen be held in contempt of court. The judge declined to do so and Cohen was arrested by the officer only after he emerged from the courtroom. App. 18–19."]*

In the second place, as it comes to us, this case cannot be said to fall within those relatively few categories of instances where prior decisions have established the power of government to deal more comprehensively with certain forms of individual expression simply upon a showing that such a form was employed. This is not, for example, an obscenity case. Whatever else may be necessary to give rise to the States' broader power to prohibit obscene expression, such expression must be, in some significant way, erotic. *Roth* v. *United States,* 354 U. S. 476 (1957). It cannot plausibly be maintained that this vulgar allusion to the Selective Service System would conjure up such psychic stimulation in anyone likely to be confronted with Cohen's crudely defaced jacket.

This Court has also held that the States are free to ban the simple use, without a demonstration of additional justifying circumstances, of so-called "fighting words," those personally abusive epithets which, when addressed to the ordinary citizen, are, as a matter of common knowledge, inherently likely to provoke violent reaction.

Chaplinsky v. *New Hampshire,* 315 U. S. 568 (1942). While the four-letter word displayed by Cohen in relation to the draft is not uncommonly employed in a personally provocative fashion, in this instance it was clearly not "directed to the person of the hearer." *Cantwell* v. *Connecticut,* 310 U. S. 296, 309 (1940). No individual actually or likely to be present could reasonably have regarded the words on appellant's jacket as a direct personal insult. Nor do we have here an instance of the exercise of the State's police power to prevent a speaker from intentionally provoking a given group to hostile reaction. Cf. *Feiner* v. *New York,* 340 U. S. 315 (1951); *Terminiello* v. *Chicago,* 337 U. S. 1 (1949). There is, as noted above, no showing that anyone who saw Cohen was in fact violently aroused or that appellant intended such a result.

Finally, in arguments before this Court much has been made of the claim that Cohen's distasteful mode of expression was thrust upon unwilling or unsuspecting viewers, and that the State might therefore legitimately act as it did in order to protect the sensitive from otherwise unavoidable exposure to appellant's crude form of protest. Of course, the mere presumed presence of unwitting listeners or viewers does not serve automatically to justify curtailing all speech capable of giving offense. See, *e. g., Organization for a Better Austin* v. *Keefe,* 402 U. S. 415 (1971). While this Court has recognized that government may properly act in many situations to prohibit intrusion into the privacy of the home of unwelcome views and ideas which cannot be totally banned from the public dialogue, *e. g., Rowan* v. *Post Office Dept.,* 397 U. S. 728 (1970), we have at the same time consistently stressed that "we are often 'captives' outside the sanctuary of the home and subject to objectionable speech." *Id., at* 738. The ability of government, consonant with the Constitution, to shut off discourse solely to protect others from hearing it is, in other words, dependent upon a showing that substantial privacy interests are being invaded in an essentially intolerable manner. Any broader view of this authority would effectively empower a majority to silence dissidents simply as a matter of personal predilections.

In this regard, persons confronted with Cohen's jacket were in a quite different posture than, say, those subjected to the raucous emissions of sound trucks blaring outside their residences. Those in the Los Angeles courthouse could effectively avoid further bombardment of their sensibilities simply by averting their eyes....

II

... The constitutional right of free expression is powerful medicine in a society as diverse and populous as ours. It is designed and intended to remove governmental restraints from the arena of public discussion, putting the decision as to what views shall be voiced largely into the hands of each of us, in the hope that use of such freedom will ultimately produce a more capable citizenry and more perfect polity and in the belief that no other approach would comport with the premise of individual dignity and choice upon which our political system rests. See *Whitney* v. *California,* 274 U. S. 357, 375–377 (1927) (Brandeis, J., concurring).

To many, the immediate consequence of this freedom may often appear to be only verbal tumult, discord, and even offensive utterance. These are, however, within established limits, in truth necessary side effects of the broader enduring values which the process of open debate permits us to achieve. That the air may at times seem filled with verbal cacophony is, in this sense, not a sign of weakness but of strength. We cannot lose sight of the fact that, in what otherwise might seem a trifling and annoying instance of individual distasteful abuse of a privilege, these fundamental societal values are truly implicated....

Against this perception of the constitutional policies involved, we discern certain more particularized considerations that peculiarly call for reversal of this conviction. First, the principle contended for by the State seems inherently boundless. How is one to distinguish this from any other offensive word? Surely the State has no right to cleanse public debate to the point where it is grammatically palatable to the most squeamish among us. Yet no readily ascertainable general principle exists for stopping short of that result were we to affirm the judgment below. For, while the particular four-letter word being litigated here is perhaps more distasteful than most others of its genre, it is nevertheless often true that one man's vulgarity is another's lyric. Indeed, we think it is largely because governmental officials cannot make principled distinctions in this area that the Constitution leaves matters of taste and style so largely to the individual.

Additionally, we cannot overlook the fact, because it is well illustrated by the episode involved here, that much linguistic expression serves a dual communicative function: it conveys not only ideas capable of relatively precise, detached explication, but otherwise inexpressible emotions as well. In fact, words are often chosen as much for their emotive as their cognitive force. We cannot sanction the view that the Constitution, while solicitous of the cognitive content of individual speech, has little or no regard for that emotive function which, practically speaking, may often be the more important element of the overall message sought to be communicated....

Finally, and in the same vein, we cannot indulge the facile assumption that one can forbid particular words without also running a substantial risk of suppressing ideas in the process. Indeed, governments might soon seize upon the censorship of particular words as a convenient guise for banning the expression of unpopular views. We have been able, as noted above, to discern little social benefit that might result from running the risk of opening the door to such grave results.

It is, in sum, our judgment that, absent a more particularized and compelling reason for its actions, the State may not, consistently with the First and Fourteenth Amendments, make the simple public display here involved of this single four-letter expletive a criminal offense. Because that is the only arguably sustainable rationale for the conviction here at issue, the judgment below must be

Reversed.

MR. JUSTICE BLACKMUN, with whom THE CHIEF JUSTICE and MR. JUSTICE BLACK join.

I dissent, and I do so for two reasons:

1. Cohen's absurd and immature antic, in my view, was mainly conduct and little speech.... Further, the case appears to me to be well within the sphere of *Chaplinsky* v. *New Hampshire,* 315 U. S. 568 (1942), where Mr. Justice Murphy, a known champion of First Amendment freedoms, wrote for a unanimous bench. As a consequence, this Court's agonizing over First Amendment values seems misplaced and unnecessary.

2. I am not at all certain that the California Court of Appeal's construction of § 415 is now the authoritative California construction. The Court of Appeal filed its opinion on October 22, 1969. The Supreme Court of California declined review by a four-to-three vote on December 17. See 1 Cal. App. 3d, at 104. A month later, on January 27, 1970, the State Supreme Court in another case construed § 415, evidently for the first time. *In re Bushman,* 1 Cal. 3d 767, 463 P. 2d 727. Chief Justice Traynor, who was among the dissenters to his court's refusal to take Cohen's case, wrote the majority opinion. He held that § 415 "is not unconstitutionally vague and overbroad" and further said:

"[T]hat part of Penal Code section 415 in question here makes punishable only wilful and malicious conduct that is violent and endangers public safety and order or that creates a clear and present danger that others will engage in violence of that nature.

"...[It] does not make criminal any nonviolent act unless the act incites or threatens to incite others to violence...." 1 Cal. 3d, at 773–774, 463 P. · 2d, at 731.

Cohen was cited in *Bushman,* 1 Cal. 3d, at 773, 463 P. 2d, at 730, but I am not convinced that its description there and *Cohen* itself are completely consistent with the "clear and present danger" standard enunciated in *Bushman.* Inasmuch as this Court does not dismiss this case, it ought to be remanded to the California Court of Appeal for reconsideration in the light of the subsequently rendered decision by the State's highest tribunal in *Bushman.*

MR. JUSTICE WHITE concurs in Paragraph 2 of MR. JUSTICE BLACKMUN's dissenting opinion.

R.A.V. v. St. Paul

505 U.S. 377 (1992)

A teenager (identified here by his initials R.A.V.) and his friends were charged with burning a cross on a black family's lawn. The City of St. Paul, Minnesota, charged them under its Bias-Motivated Crime Ordinance, which prohibits the display of a symbol one knows or has reason to know "arouses anger, alarm or resentment" in others on the basis of race, color, creed, religion or gender. This language drew comparison to the fighting-words doctrine of *Chaplinsky* v. *New Hampshire* (1942) and raised questions whether the ordinance was, on its face, unconstitutional because it attempted to silence speech on the basis of its content. The case is remarkable for the deep divisions within the Court on First Amendment analysis.

JUSTICE SCALIA delivered the opinion of the Court.

In the predawn hours of June 21, 1990, petitioner and several other teenagers allegedly assembled a crudely-made cross by taping together broken chair legs. They then allegedly burned the cross inside the fenced yard of a black family that lived across the street from the house where petitioner was staying. Although this conduct could have been punished under any of a number of laws *[terroristic threats, arson, criminal damage to property]*, one of the two provisions under which respondent city of St. Paul chose to charge petitioner (then a juvenile) was the St. Paul Bias-Motivated Crime Ordinance, St. Paul, Minn. Legis. Code § 292.02 (1990), which provides:

"Whoever places on public or private property a symbol, object, appellation, characterization or graffiti, including, but not limited to, a burning cross or Nazi swastika, which one knows or has reasonable grounds to know arouses anger, alarm or resentment in others on the basis of race, color, creed, religion or gender commits disorderly conduct and shall be guilty of a misdemeanor."

Petitioner moved to dismiss this count on the ground that the St. Paul ordinance was substantially overbroad and impermissibly content-based and therefore facially invalid under the First Amendment....

I

In construing the St. Paul ordinance, we are bound by the construction given to it by the Minnesota court.... Accordingly, we accept the Minnesota Supreme Court's authoritative statement that the ordinance reaches only those expressions that constitute "fighting words" within the meaning of *Chaplinsky*. 464 N. W. 2d, at 510–511. Petitioner and his *amici* urge us to modify the scope of the *Chaplinsky* formulation, thereby invalidating the ordinance as "substantially overbroad," *Broadrick* v. *Oklahoma,* 413 U. S. 601, 610 (1973). We find it unnecessary to consider this issue. Assuming, *arguendo,* that all of the expression reached by the ordinance is proscribable under the "fighting words" doctrine, we nonetheless conclude that the ordinance is facially unconstitutional in that it prohibits otherwise permitted speech solely on the basis of the subjects the speech addresses.

The First Amendment generally prevents government from proscribing speech, see, *e.g., Cantwell* v. *Connecticut,* 310 U. S. 296, 309–311

(1940), or even expressive conduct, see, *e.g., Texas* v. *Johnson,* 491 U. S. 397, 406 (1989), because of disapproval of the ideas expressed. Content-based regulations are presumptively invalid.... From 1791 to the present, however, our society, like other free but civilized societies, has permitted restrictions upon the content of speech in a few limited areas, which are "of such slight social value as a step to truth that any benefit that may be derived from them is clearly outweighed by the social interest in order and morality." *Chaplinsky, supra,* at 572. We have recognized that "the freedom of speech" referred to by the First Amendment does not include a freedom to disregard these traditional limitations. See, *e.g., Roth* v. *United States,* 354 U. S. 476 (1957) (obscenity); *Beauharnais* v. *Illinois,* 343 U. S. 250 (1952) (defamation); *Chaplinsky* v. *New Hampshire, supra,* ("fighting words"); ...

We have sometimes said that these categories of expression are "not within the area of constitutionally protected speech," *Roth, supra,* at 483; *Beauharnais, supra,* at 266; *Chaplinsky, supra,* at 571–572, or that the "protection of the First Amendment does not extend" to them, *Bose Corp.* v. *Consumers Union of United States, Inc.,* 466 U. S. 485, 504 (1984); *Sable Communications of Cal., Inc.* v. *FCC,* 492 U. S. 115, 124 (1989). Such statements must be taken in context, however, and are no more literally true than is the occasionally repeated shorthand characterizing obscenity "as not being speech at all," Sunstein, Pornography and the First Amendment, 1986 Duke L. J. 589, 615, n. 146. What they mean is that these areas of speech can, consistently with the First Amendment, be regulated *because of their constitutionally proscribable content* (obscenity, defamation, etc.)—not that they are categories of speech entirely invisible to the Constitution, so that they may be made the vehicles for content discrimination unrelated to their distinctively proscribable content. Thus, the government may proscribe libel; but it may not make the further content discrimination of proscribing *only* libel critical of the government....

II

Applying these principles to the St. Paul ordinance, we conclude that, even as narrowly construed by the Minnesota Supreme Court, the ordinance is facially unconstitutional. Although the phrase in the ordinance, "arouses anger, alarm or resentment in others," has been limited by the Minnesota Supreme Court's construction to reach only those symbols or displays that amount to "fighting words," the remaining, unmodified terms make clear that the ordinance applies only to "fighting words" that insult, or provoke violence, "on the basis of race, color, creed, religion or gender." Displays containing abusive invective, no matter how vicious or severe, are permissible unless they are addressed to one of the specified disfavored topics. Those who wish to use "fighting words" in connection with other ideas — to express hostility, for example, on the basis of political affiliation, union membership, or homosexuality — are not covered. The First Amendment does not permit St. Paul to impose special prohibitions on those speakers who express views on disfavored subjects. . . .

In its practical operation, moreover, the ordinance goes even beyond mere content discrimination, to actual viewpoint discrimination. Displays containing some words — odious racial epithets, for example — would be prohibited to proponents of all views. But "fighting words" that do not themselves invoke race, color, creed, religion, or gender — aspersions upon a person's mother, for example — would seemingly be usable *ad libitum* in the placards of those arguing *in favor* of racial, color, etc. tolerance and equality, but could not be used by that speaker's opponents. One could hold up a sign saying, for example, that all "anti-Catholic bigots" are misbegotten; but not that all "papists" are, for that would insult and provoke violence "on the basis of religion." St. Paul has no such authority to license one side of a debate to fight freestyle, while requiring the other to follow Marquis of Queensbury Rules.

. . . [T]he reason why fighting words are categorically excluded from the protection of the First Amendment is not that their content communicates any particular idea, but that their content embodies a particularly intolerable (and socially unnecessary) *mode* of expressing *whatever* idea the speaker wishes to convey. St. Paul has not singled out an especially offensive mode of expression — it has not, for example, selected for prohibition only those fighting words that communicate ideas in a threatening (as opposed to a merely obnoxious) manner. Rather, it has proscribed fighting words of whatever manner that communicate messages of racial, gender, or religious intolerance. Selectivity of this sort creates the possibility that the city is seeking to handicap the expression of particular ideas. That possibility would alone be enough to render the ordinance presumptively invalid, but St. Paul's comments and concessions in this case elevate the possibility to a certainty.

. . .

Let there be no mistake about our belief that burning a cross in someone's front yard is reprehensible. But St. Paul has sufficient means at its disposal to prevent such behavior without adding the First Amendment to the fire.

The judgment of the Minnesota Supreme Court is reversed, and the case is remanded for proceedings not inconsistent with this opinion.

It is so ordered.

JUSTICE WHITE, with whom JUSTICE BLACKMUN and JUSTICE O'CONNOR join, and with whom JUSTICE STEVENS joins except as to Part I(A), concurring in the judgment.

I agree with the majority that the judgment of the Minnesota Supreme Court should be reversed. However, our agreement ends there.

This case could easily be decided within the contours of established First Amendment law by holding, as petitioner argues, that the St. Paul ordinance is fatally overbroad because it criminalizes not only unprotected expression but expression protected by the First Amendment. See Part II, *infra*. Instead, "find[ing] it unnecessary" to consider the questions upon which we granted review, . . . the Court holds the ordinance facially unconstitutional on a ground that was never presented to the Minnesota Supreme Court, a ground that has not been briefed by the parties before this Court, a ground that requires serious departures from the teaching of prior cases and is inconsistent with the plurality opinion in *Burson v. Freeman,* 504 U. S. 191 (1992), which was joined by two of the five Justices in the majority in the present case.

. . . [I]n the present case, the majority casts aside long-established First Amendment doctrine without the benefit of briefing and adopts an untried theory. This is hardly a judicious way of proceeding, and the Court's reasoning in reaching its result is transparently wrong.

I

A

This Court's decisions have plainly stated that expression falling within certain limited categories so lacks the values the First Amendment was designed to protect that the Constitution affords no protection to that expression. *Chaplinsky v. New Hampshire,* 315 U. S. 568 (1942), made the point in the clearest possible terms:

"There are certain well-defined and narrowly

limited classes of speech, the prevention and punishment of which have never been thought to raise any Constitutional problem.... It has been well observed that such utterances are no essential part of any exposition of ideas, and are of such slight social value as a step to truth that any benefit that may be derived from them is clearly outweighed by the social interest in order and morality." *Id.,* at 571–572.

See also *Bose Corp.* v. *Consumers Union of United States, Inc.,* 466 U. S. 485, 504 (1984) (citing *Chaplinsky*).

Thus, as the majority concedes,... this Court has long held certain discrete categories of expression to be proscribable on the basis of their content. For instance, the Court has held that the individual who falsely shouts "fire" in a crowded theatre may not claim the protection of the First Amendment. *Schenck* v. *United States,* 249 U. S. 47, 52 (1919). The Court has concluded that neither child pornography, nor obscenity, is protected by the First Amendment. *New York* v. *Ferber,* 458 U. S. 747, 764 (1982); *Miller* v. *California,* 413 U. S. 15, 20 (1973); *Roth* v. *United States,* 354 U. S. 476, 484–485 (1957). And the Court has observed that, "[l]eaving aside the special considerations when public officials [and public figures] are the target, a libelous publication is not protected by the Constitution." *Ferber, supra,* at 763 (citations omitted).

All of these categories are content based. But the Court has held that the First Amendment does not apply to them because their expressive content is worthless or of *de minimis* value to society. *Chaplinsky, supra,* at 571–572....

Today, however, the Court announces that earlier Courts did not mean their repeated statements that certain categories of expression are "not within the area of constitutionally protected speech."... The present Court submits that such clear statements "must be taken in context" and are not "literally true." ...

To the contrary, those statements meant precisely what they said: The categorical approach is a firmly entrenched part of our First Amendment jurisprudence....

. . .

C

... [I]f the majority were to give general application to the rule on which it decides this case, today's decision would call into question the constitutionality of the statute making it illegal to threaten the life of the President. 18 U. S. C. § 871.

See *Watts* v. *United States,* 394 U. S. 705 (1969) *(per curiam).* Surely, this statute, by singling out certain threats, incorporates a content-based distinction; it indicates that the Government especially disfavors threats against the President as opposed to threats against all others....

. . .

III

Today, the Court has disregarded two established principles of First Amendment law without providing a coherent replacement theory. Its decision is an arid, doctrinaire interpretation, driven by the frequently irresistible impulse of judges to tinker with the First Amendment. The decision is mischievous at best and will surely confuse the lower courts. I join the judgment, but not the folly of the opinion.

JUSTICE BLACKMUN, concurring in the judgment.

I regret what the Court has done in this case. The majority opinion signals one of two possibilities: it will serve as precedent for future cases, or it will not. Either result is disheartening.

In the first instance, by deciding that a State cannot regulate speech that causes great harm unless it also regulates speech that does not (setting law and logic on their heads), the Court seems to abandon the categorical approach, and inevitably to relax the level of scrutiny applicable to content-based laws. As JUSTICE WHITE points out, this weakens the traditional protections of speech. If all expressive activity must be accorded the same protection, that protection will be scant. The simple reality is that the Court will never provide child pornography or cigarette advertising the level of protection customarily granted political speech. If we are forbidden from categorizing, as the Court has done here, we shall reduce protection across the board. It is sad that in its effort to reach a satisfying result in this case, the Court is willing to weaken First Amendment protections.

In the second instance is the possibility that this case will not significantly alter First Amendment jurisprudence, but, instead, will be regarded as an aberration—a case where the Court manipulated doctrine to strike down an ordinance whose premise it opposed, namely, that racial threats and verbal assaults are of greater harm than other fighting words. I fear that the Court has been distracted from its proper mission by the temptation to decide the issue over "politically correct speech" and "cultural diversity," neither of which is presented here. If this is the meaning of today's opinion, it is perhaps even more regrettable.

. . .

JUSTICE STEVENS, with whom JUSTICE WHITE and JUSTICE BLACKMUN join as to Part I, concurring in the judgment.

. . .

III

...I disagree with both the Court's and part of JUSTICE WHITE's analysis of the constitutionality St. Paul ordinance. Unlike the Court, I do not believe that all content-based regulations are equally infirm and presumptively invalid; unlike JUSTICE WHITE, I do not believe that fighting words are wholly unprotected by the First Amendment. To the contrary, I believe our decisions establish a more complex and subtle analysis, one that considers the content and context of the regulated speech, and the nature and scope of the restriction on speech. Applying this analysis and assuming *arguendo* (as the Court does) that the St. Paul ordinance is *not* overbroad, I conclude that such a selective, subject-matter regulation on proscribable speech is constitutional.

. . .

D. FORMS OF SPEECH

The Supreme Court recognizes categories of speech that would have been novel if not inscrutable to the framers. These forms include symbolic speech, "speech plus," commercial speech, and broadcasting rights. Several free-speech issues are covered in Chapter 18: campaign financing (where the Court has decided that "money is speech") and ballot initiatives.

Symbolic Speech and Flag Desecration

Ideas spread by symbols as well as by words. A California statute made it a felony to display a red flag "as a sign, symbol or emblem of opposition to organized government." By a 7–1 majority, the Supreme Court in 1931 held the statute unconstitutionally vague and repugnant to the guaranty of liberty contained in the Fourteenth Amendment. Stromberg v. California, 283 U.S. 359 (1931). There are obvious limits to symbolic speech and "expressive conduct." As Justice Rehnquist noted in a dissent: "One who burns down the factory of a company whose products he dislikes can expect his First Amendment defense to a consequent arson prosecution to be given short shrift by the courts." Smith v. Goguen, 415 U.S. 566, 594 (1974).

A spectacular form of symbolic speech occurred in a 1968 case involving the burning of a draft card to protest the Vietnam War. The act violated a federal statute that applied to any person "who forges, alters, knowingly destroys, knowingly mutilates, or in any manner changes" a draft card. A 7–1 Court held that the statute did not unconstitutionally abridge free speech; government has a legitimate interest in preserving draft cards; and the act of burning a draft card is not "symbolic speech" protected by the First Amendment. United States v. O'Brien, 391 U.S. 367 (1968). On the other hand, school children were permitted to wear black arm bands to protest the Vietnam War. Their conduct, which the Court called "closely akin to 'pure speech,'" had been quiet and nondisruptive. Tinker v. Des Moines School Dist., 393 U.S. 503, 505 (1969), reprinted in Chapter 16.

States and the federal government have adopted a number of laws to prohibit desecration and abuse of the American flag. A 1907 decision by the Supreme Court involved a Nebraska law that punished the desecration of the flag and the use of the flag to advertise the sale of articles. An exception was made for newspapers, periodicals, or books if disconnected from any advertisement. The Court, voting 8–1, upheld the statute's application against a company that printed the flag on a bottle of beer. Halter v. Nebraska, 205 U.S. 34 (1907). A Massachusetts law, prohibiting anyone from publicly treating the flag "contemptuously," was held void for vagueness when used to convict an individual who wore a small U.S. flag sewn to the seat of his blue jeans. Smith v. Goguen, 415 U.S. 566 (1974).

More difficult to resolve are cases where the flag is used to communicate opposition to the government and its policies. In 1967 opponents of the Vietnam War burned flags in New York City's Central Park. Congress responded the next year with legislation providing that whoever "knowingly casts contempt upon any flag of the United States by publicly mutilating, defacing, defiling, burning, or trampling upon it shall be fined not more than $1,000 or imprisoned for not more than one year, or both." 82 Stat. 291. The legislative history reveals that Congress intended to punish the war protesters.

A conviction for flag burning was set aside by the Supreme Court in 1969 because the punishment was directed not only for acts against the flag but for words as well. Street v. New York, 394 U.S. 576 (1969). Another flag case involved a conviction for taping a peace symbol to an American flag and hanging it upside down to protest the Vietnam War. The purpose was to associate the flag with peace, not war. The Court, by a 6–3 majority, held that the state law infringed on protected expression: "there can be little doubt that appellant communicated through the use of symbols." Spence v. Washington, 418 U.S. 405, 410 (1974).

During the 1988 presidential campaign, George Bush and Michael Dukakis clashed on the issue of whether public school teachers could be compelled to order students to pledge allegiance to the flag. Dukakis had vetoed such a bill as governor of Massachusetts, relying on an advisory opinion by the Massachusetts Supreme Court. Bush claimed that he would have found a way to sign the bill. Thereafter the two candidates tried to see who could stand in front of more flags and sound more patriotic.

The flag issue returned with full force the next year when the Supreme Court, divided 5–4, held that a conviction for flag desecration (burning the flag during a protest) was contrary to the First Amendment. The majority regarded the action as "expressive conduct" protected by the Constitution. TEXAS v. JOHNSON, 491 U.S. 397 (1989). The decision triggered a flurry of bills and constitutional amendments, with President Bush's support, to overturn the decision.

In response to *Texas* v. *Johnson,* Congress passed the Flag Protection Act of 1989. The basic purpose was to comply with *Johnson* by making the federal statute "content neutral." The major change was to delete from the 1968 statute the words "casts contempt." The new law read: "Whoever knowingly mutilates, defaces, physically defiles, burns, maintains on the floor or ground, or tramples upon any flag of the United States shall be fined under this title or imprisoned for not more than one year, or both." 103 Stat. 777. Sponsors of this legislation argued that the Court would uphold a statute that merely protected the physical integrity of the flag by focusing solely on conduct and not on the message being conveyed by the flag burner. The bill passed the House by a vote of 380 to 38; the Senate margin was 91 to 9. On October 19, 1989, the Senate rejected a proposed constitutional amendment to permit Congress to outlaw flag desecration. The 51 to 48 margin in favor of the amendment fell 15 votes short of the required two-thirds of those present and voting.

The 1989 statute provided for expedited review by the courts: a district court decision would be appealed directly to the Supreme Court. Two district courts ruled that flag-burning represents an expression of political dissent and is protected by the First Amendment. United States v. Haggerty, 731 F.Supp. 415 (W.D. Wash. 1990); United States v. Eichman, 731 F. Supp. 1123 (D.D.C. 1990). Divided 5 to 4, the Supreme Court held the congressional statute unconstitutional. The government's interest in protecting the physical integrity of the flag could not justify its infringement on First Amendment rights. United States v. Eichman, 496 U.S. 310 (1990).

Immediately following the decision, President Bush renewed his call for a constitutional amendment to protect the flag, but the House of Representatives on June 21 rejected the amendment by a vote of 254 to 177, or 34 votes shy of the necessary two-thirds. On June 26, the Senate also voted down the amendment, 58 to 42, which was 9 votes short. The time consumed by Congress to pass the new law and have it tested in the courts was sufficient to take the steam out of the campaign to amend the Constitution and thus avoid the first alteration of the Bill of Rights. See Charles Tiefer, "The Flag-Burning Controversy of 1989–90: Congress' Valid Role in Constitutional Dialogue," 29 Harv. J. on Legis. 357 (1992). A constitutional amendment to prohibit flag desecration passed the House in 1995, this time by more than a two-thirds margin (312 to 120). The amendment was narrowly defeated in the Senate 63 to 36 (three votes short). In 1997, more than two-thirds of the House voted for a constitutional amendment to prohibit flag desecration (310 to 114), but the Senate took no action. The Senate vote in 2000 was 63 to 37 (four votes short).

[The issue of symbolic speech also includes nude dancing, treated in the next chapter under obscenity.]

"Speech Plus"

The term "speech plus" refers to speech mixed with conduct. For example, picketing is "free speech *plus,* the plus being physical activity that may implicate traffic and related matters." Amalgamated Food Employees v. Logan Plaza, 391 U.S. 308, 326 (1968). To promote an idea or cause, individuals gather together and carry placards, distribute leaflets, and ask passersby to sign petitions. In 1940 the Court held that picketing is protected by the constitutional freedoms of speech, peaceable assembly, and the right to petition government for redress of grievances. Thornhill v. Alabama, 310 U.S. 88 (1940).[9] A unanimous Court in 1937 held that peaceable assembly cannot be made a crime. De Jonge v. Oregon, 299 U.S. 353 (1937). This case also applied the right of peaceable assembly, guaranteed under the federal Constitution, to the states. See also Hague v. C.I.O., 307 U.S. 496 (1939).

After the *Thornhill* decision in 1940, the Court conducted a gradual retreat from the right to picket. The state not only could regulate picketing to protect against violence and the destruction of property but also could prohibit peaceful picketing to further state interests, especially dealing with labor conditions. Picketing could be enjoined to prevent efforts to restrain trade, Giboney v. Empire Storage, 336 U.S. 490 (1949).[10] In recent years, decisions have been more supportive of peaceful demonstrations and picketing.[11] However, when picketers concentrate on a single household, government may prohibit such picketing in order to protect the privacy of a homeowner. Frisby v. Schultz, 487 U.S. 474 (1988).

If picketing is done on private property, which constitutional interest should prevail? An early case involved the right of a company town to require a permit before anyone could distribute literature. The Supreme Court ruled that since the town's shopping district was freely accessible to the general public, the town's public nature overshadowed its private claim. The right to distribute literature was therefore upheld. Marsh v. Alabama, 326 U.S. 501 (1946).

From this simple company-town issue came the conundrum of free speech in shopping centers. The Court might well have asked plaintively: "Oh, Founding Fathers, where are you

---

9. Other picketing cases during this period include: New Negro Alliance v. Grocery Co., 303 U.S. 552 (1938); Milk Wagon Drivers Union v. Meadowmoor Co., 312 U.S. 287 (1941); A.F. of L. v. Swing, 312 U.S. 321 (1941); Hotel Employees' Local v. Board, 315 U.S. 437 (1942); Carpenters Union v. Ritter's Cafe, 315 U.S. 722 (1942); Allen-Bradley Local v. Board, 315 U.S. 742 (1942); Bakery Drivers Local v. Wohl, 315 U.S. 769 (1942).

10. Injunctions against peaceful picketing were also upheld in International Brotherhood of Teamsters v. Hanke, 339 U.S. 470 (1950); Building Service Union v. Gazzam, 339 U.S. 532 (1950); and International Brotherhood of Teamsters v. Vogt, Inc., 354 U.S. 284 (1957).

11. Gregory v. Chicago, 394 U.S. 111 (1969); Coates v. City of Cincinnati, 402 U.S. 611 (1971); Police Department of Chicago v. Mosley, 408 U.S. 92 (1972); Grayned v. City of Rockford, 408 U.S. 104 (1972); Carey v. Brown, 447 U.S. 455 (1980); NAACP v. Claiborne Hardware Co., 458 U.S. 886 (1982).

Independent State Interpretations

When federal courts decide that the U.S. Constitution does not protect a contested right, state judges may protect that same right by independently interpreting their own constitutions. Although the U.S. Supreme Court has decided that the federal constitution does not guarantee the right of free speech in a shopping center, the states below have upheld free speech rights in privately owned shopping centers and private universities. State constitutions not only include the negative placed in the U.S. Constitution (no law shall abridge the freedom of speech) but also the positive. For example, the Colorado Constitution provides that "every person shall be free to speak, write or publish whatever he will on any subject" (Art. II, § 10).

California	Robins v. PruneYard Shopping Center, 592 P.2d 341 (1979).
Colorado	Bock v. Westminster Mall Co., 819 P.2d 55 (1991).
New Jersey	State v. Schmid, 423 A.2d 615 (1980).
Pennsylvania	Commonwealth v. Tate, 432 A.2d 1382 (1981).
Washington	Alderwood Assoc. v. Wash. Envir. Council, 635 P.2d 108 (1981).

when we need you?" In 1968 the Court divided 6–3 in ruling that peaceful picketing of a business enterprise within a shopping center did not violate property rights. The Court followed the reasoning of *Marsh* but cautioned in a footnote that its decision was limited to picketing that was directly related to shopping center activities. Amalgamated Food Employees v. Logan Valley Plaza, 391 U.S. 308, 320 n.9 (1968).

The footnote helped justify a modification in 1972. The distribution of handbills inside a shopping center was held to be a violation of property rights. The handbills (protesting the Vietnam War and the draft) had no relation to the purpose of the shopping center. Lloyd Corp. v. Tanner, 407 U.S. 551 (1972). Confusion became rampant four years later when the Court denied striking members of a union the right to enter a shopping center to picket against their employer. Presumably, this kind of picketing was protected by *Logan Valley,* but the Court said that its new doctrine was based on *statutory* grounds, even though it also reached out to dispose of constitutional issues. The Justices couldn't even agree whether *Lloyd* had overruled *Logan Valley.* Hudgens v. NLRB, 424 U.S. 507 (1976).

In 1980 the Supreme Court reviewed a case in which a privately owned shopping center prohibited visitors or tenants from engaging in any publicly expressive activity (including circulation of petitions) that was not directly related to the commercial purposes of the center. The California courts upheld the rights of students to petition on unrelated matters. The Supreme Court, in a unanimous ruling, affirmed that decision. State courts can make independent and authoritative determinations, under their own constitutions, on the balance between free speech and property rights in shopping centers. PRUNEYARD SHOPPING CENTER v. ROBINS, 447 U.S. 74 (1980). Thus, rights not available through the federal courts can be protected by state courts interpreting state constitutions (see box). In 1991 the Justices of the Colorado Supreme Court reviewed the "tortuous history" of the U.S. Supreme Court's jurisprudence on free speech and decided to go their own way. They were urged to follow "the twists and turns of this federal road to the end" but declined. "We are unpersuaded by the United States Supreme Court's various reasonings in this line of cases. . . . The definitive word was left to the state courts to write." Bock v. Westminster Mall Co., 819 P.2d 55, 58 (Colo. 1991).

Texas v. Johnson

491 U.S. 397 (1989)

As a means of protesting against the policies of the Reagan administration and American corporations, Gregory Lee Johnson burned an American flag in front of Dallas City Hall in 1984. He was convicted under Texas law for desecrating a flag, but the Texas Court of Criminal Appeals reversed the conviction on the ground that it was inconsistent with the First Amendment. The Supreme Court dealt with the issue of whether Johnson's action was "expressive conduct" protected by the Constitution.

JUSTICE BRENNAN delivered the opinion of the Court.

After publicly burning an American flag as a means of political protest, Gregory Lee Johnson was convicted of desecrating a flag in violation of Texas law. This case presents the question whether his conviction is consistent with the First Amendment. We hold that it is not.

I

While the Republican National Convention was taking place in Dallas in 1984, respondent Johnson participated in a political demonstration dubbed the "Republican War Chest Tour." As explained in literature distributed by the demonstrators and in speeches made by them, the purpose of this event was to protest the policies of the Reagan administration and of certain Dallas-based corporations....

The demonstration ended in front of Dallas City Hall, where Johnson unfurled the American flag, doused it with kerosene, and set it on fire. While the flag burned, the protestors chanted, "America, the red, white, and blue, we spit on you." After the demonstrators dispersed, a witness to the flag-burning collected the flag's remains and buried them in his backyard. No one was physically injured or threatened with injury, though several witnesses testified that they had been seriously offended by the flag-burning.

. . .

II

Johnson was convicted of flag desecration for burning the flag rather than for uttering insulting words. This fact somewhat complicates our consideration of his conviction under the First Amendment. We must first determine whether Johnson's burning of the flag constituted expressive conduct, permitting him to invoke the First Amendment in challenging his conviction.... If his conduct was expressive, we next decide whether the State's regulation is related to the suppression of free expression....

. . .

The State of Texas conceded for purposes of its oral argument in this case that Johnson's conduct was expressive conduct.... Johnson burned an American flag as part—indeed, as the culmination—of a political demonstration that coincided with the convening of the Republican Party and its renomination of Ronald Reagan for President. The expressive, overtly political nature of this conduct was both intentional and overwhelmingly apparent. At his trial, Johnson explained his reasons for burning the flag as follows: "The American Flag was burned as Ronald Reagan was being renominated as President. And a more powerful statement of symbolic speech, whether you agree with it or not, couldn't have been made at that time. It's quite a just position [juxtaposition]. We had new patriotism and no patriotism." ...

III

The Government generally has a freer hand in restricting expressive conduct than it has in restricting the written or spoken word.... It may not, however, proscribe particular conduct *because* it has expressive elements. "[W]hat might be termed the more generalized guarantee of freedom of expression makes the communicative nature of conduct an inadequate *basis* for singling out that conduct for proscription. A law *directed* at the communicative nature of conduct must, like a law directed at speech itself, be justified by the substantial showing of need that the First Amendment requires." ...

Thus, although we have recognized that where " 'speech' and 'nonspeech' elements are combined in the same course of conduct, a sufficiently important governmental interest in regulating the nonspeech element can justify incidental limitations on First Amendment freedoms," [*United States v. O'Brien (burning of a draft card)*] we have limited the applicability of *O'Brien*'s relatively lenient standard to those cases in which "the governmental interest is unrelated to the suppression of free expression...."

In order to decide whether *O'Brien*'s test applies here, therefore, we must decide whether Texas has asserted an interest in support of Johnson's conviction that is unrelated to the suppression of expression. If we find that an interest asserted by the State is simply not implicated on the facts before us, we need not ask whether *O'Brien*'s test applies.... The State offers two separate interests to justify this conviction: preventing breaches of the peace, and preserving the flag as a symbol of nationhood and national unity. We hold that the first interest is not implicated on this record and that the second is related to the suppression of expression.

A

Texas claims that its interest in preventing breaches of the peace justifies Johnson's conviction for flag desecration. However, no disturbance of the peace actually occurred or threatened to occur because of Johnson's burning of the flag....

The State's position, therefore, amounts to a claim that an audience that takes serious offense at particular expression is necessarily likely to disturb the peace and that the expression may be prohibited on this basis. Our precedents do not countenance such a presumption. On the contrary, they recognize that a principal "function of free speech under our system of government is to invite dispute. It may indeed best serve its high purpose when it induces a condition of unrest, creates dissatisfaction with conditions as they are, or even stirs people to anger." *Terminiello* v. *Chicago*, 337 U. S. 1, 4 (1949)....

Nor does Johnson's expressive conduct fall within that small class of "fighting words" that are "likely to provoke the average person to retaliation, and thereby cause a breach of the peace." *Chaplinsky* v. *New Hampshire*, 315 U. S. 568, 574 (1942). No reasonable onlooker would have regarded Johnson's generalized expression of dissatisfaction with the policies of the Federal Government as a direct personal insult or an invitation to exchange fisticuffs....

We thus conclude that the State's interest in maintaining order is not implicated on these facts....

B

The State also asserts an interest in preserving the flag as a symbol of nationhood and national unity. In *Spence*, we acknowledged that the Government's interest in preserving the flag's special symbolic value "is directly related to expression in the context of activity" such as affixing a peace symbol to a flag. 418 U.S., at 414, n. 8. We are equally persuaded that this interest is related to expression in the case of Johnson's burning of the flag. The State, apparently, is concerned that such conduct will lead people to believe either that the flag does not stand for nationhood and national unity, but instead reflects other, less positive concepts, or that the concepts reflected in the flag do not in fact exist, that is, we do not enjoy unity as a Nation....

IV

It remains to consider whether the State's interest in preserving the flag as a symbol of nationhood and national unity justifies Johnson's conviction.

...Johnson was not, we add, prosecuted for the expression of just any idea; he was prosecuted for his expression of dissatisfaction with the policies of this country, expression situated at the core of our First Amendment values....

Moreover, Johnson was prosecuted because he knew that his politically charged expression would cause "serious offense." If he had burned the flag as a means of disposing of it because it was dirty or torn, he would not have been convicted of flag desecration under this Texas law: federal law designates burning as the preferred means of disposing of a flag "when it is in such condition that it is no longer a fitting emblem for display," 36 U. S. C. § 176(k), and Texas has no quarrel with this means of disposal.... The Texas law is thus not aimed at protecting the physical integrity of the flag in all circumstances, but is designed instead to protect it only against impairments that would cause serious offense to others. Texas concedes as much: "Section 42.09(b) reaches only those severe acts of physical abuse of the flag carried out in a way likely to be offensive. The statute mandates intentional or knowing abuse, that is, the kind of mistreatment that is not innocent, but rather is intentionally designed to seriously offend other individuals."...

Whether Johnson's treatment of the flag violated Texas law thus depended on the likely communicative impact of his expressive conduct....

...According to Texas, if one physically treats the flag in a way that would tend to cast doubt on either the idea that nationhood and national unity are the flag's referents or that national unity actually exists, the message conveyed thereby is a harmful one and therefore may be prohibited.

If there is a bedrock principle underlying the First Amendment, it is that the Government may not prohibit the expression of an idea simply because society finds the idea itself offensive or disagreeable. . . .

. . . We reject the suggestion, urged at oral argument by counsel for Johnson, that the Government lacks "any state interest whatsoever" in regulating the manner in which the flag may be displayed. Tr. of Oral Arg. 38. Congress has, for example, enacted precatory regulations describing the proper treatment of the flag, see 36 U. S. C. §§ 173–177, and we cast no doubt on the legitimacy of its interest in making such recommendations. To say that the Government has an interest in encouraging proper treatment of the flag, however, is not to say that it may criminally punish a person for burning a flag as a means of political protest. . . .

· · ·

We are tempted to say, in fact, that the flag's deservedly cherished place in our community will be strengthened, not weakened, by our holding today. Our decision is a reaffirmation of the principles of freedom and inclusiveness that the flag best reflects, and of the conviction that our toleration of criticism such as Johnson's is a sign and source of our strength. Indeed, one of the proudest images of our flag, the one immortalized in our own national anthem, is of the bombardment it survived at Fort McHenry. It is the Nation's resilience, not its rigidity, that Texas sees reflected in the flag—and it is that resilience that we reassert today.

The way to preserve the flag's special role is not to punish those who feel differently about these matters. It is to persuade them that they are wrong. . . . We can imagine no more appropriate response to burning a flag than waving one's own, no better way to counter a flag-burner's message than by saluting the flag that burns, no surer means of preserving the dignity even of the flag that burned than by—as one witness here did—according its remains a respectful burial. We do not consecrate the flag by punishing its desecration, for in doing so we dilute the freedom that this cherished emblem represents.

V

Johnson was convicted for engaging in expres-

sive conduct. The State's interest in preventing breaches of the peace does not support his conviction because Johnson's conduct did not threaten to disturb the peace. Nor does the State's interest in preserving the flag as a symbol of nationhood and national unity justify his criminal conviction for engaging in political expression. The judgment of the Texas Court of Criminal Appeals is therefore

Affirmed.

JUSTICE KENNEDY, concurring.

I write not to qualify the words JUSTICE BRENNAN chooses so well, for he says with power all that is necessary to explain our ruling. I join his opinion without reservation, but with a keen sense that this case, like others before us from time to time, exacts its personal toll. This prompts me to add to our pages these few remarks.

The case before us illustrates better than most that the judicial power is often difficult in its exercise. We cannot here ask another branch to share responsibility, as when the argument is made that a statute is flawed or incomplete. For we are presented with a clear and simple statute to be judged against a pure command of the Constitution. The outcome can be laid at no door but ours.

The hard fact is that sometimes we must make decisions we do not like. We make them because they are right, right in the sense that the law and the Constitution, as we see them, compel the result. . . .

· · ·

CHIEF JUSTICE REHNQUIST, with whom JUSTICE WHITE and JUSTICE O'CONNOR join, dissenting.

. . . For more than 200 years, the American flag has occupied a unique position as the symbol of our Nation, a uniqueness that justifies a governmental prohibition against flag burning in the way respondent Johnson did here.

[Here Rehnquist includes various poems, resolutions, and anthems in praise of the flag, written by Ralph Waldo Emerson, Francis Scott Key, and John Greenleaf Whittier. He reviews also the role played by the flag in World War II (with the marines raising the flag on Mount Suribachi at Iwo Jima) and in the Korean War. He further explains that Congress passed the Flag Desecration Act of 1968 because flag burnings had undermined the morale of American troops in Vietnam.]

The American flag, then, throughout more than

200 years of our history, has come to be the visible symbol embodying our Nation. It does not represent the views of any particular political party, and it does not represent any particular political philosophy. The flag is not simply another "idea" or "point of view" competing for recognition in the marketplace of ideas. Millions and millions of Americans regard it with an almost mystical reverence regardless of what sort of social, political, or philosophical beliefs they may have....

. . .

...Johnson was free to make any verbal denunciation of the flag that he wished; indeed, he was free to burn the flag in private. He could publicly burn other symbols of the Government or effigies of political leaders. He did lead a march through the streets of Dallas, and conducted a rally in front of the Dallas City Hall. He engaged in a "die-in" to protest nuclear weapons. He shouted out various slogans during the march, including: "Reagan, Mondale which will it be? Either one means World War III"; "Ronald Reagan, killer of the hour, Perfect example of U. S. power"; and "red, white and blue, we spit on you,

you stand for plunder, you will go under."... For none of these acts was he arrested or prosecuted; it was only when he proceeded to burn publicly an American flag stolen from its rightful owner that he violated the Texas statute....

. . .

The result of the Texas statute is obviously to deny one in Johnson's frame of mind one of many means of "symbolic speech." Far from being a case of "one picture being worth a thousand words," flag burning is the equivalent of an inarticulate grunt or roar that, it seems fair to say, is most likely to be indulged in not to express any particular idea, but to antagonize others....

JUSTICE STEVENS, dissenting.

The value of the flag as a symbol cannot be measured.... [I]n my considered judgment, sanctioning the public desecration of the flag will tarnish its value — both for those who cherish the ideas for which it waves and for those who desire to don the robes of martyrdom by burning it....

PruneYard Shopping Center v. Robins

447 U. S. 74 (1980)

The question of free speech in a shopping center raises two competing interests: the values of the First Amendment and protection to private property. In this case, Michael Robins and other high school students distributed pamphlets and asked passersby to sign petitions in opposition to a United Nations resolution against Zionism. The activity occurred in PruneYard, a privately owned shopping center in Campbell, California. This case is of special interest because it illustrates that individual rights may receive greater protection under a state constitution than under the federal Constitution.

MR. JUSTICE REHNQUIST delivered the opinion of the Court.

We postponed jurisdiction of this appeal from the Supreme Court of California to decide the important federal constitutional questions it presented. Those are whether state constitutional provisions, which permit individuals to exercise free speech and petition rights on the property of a privately owned shopping center to which the public is invited, violate the shopping center owner's property rights under the Fifth and Fourteenth Amendments or his free speech rights under the First and Fourteenth Amendments.

I

Appellant PruneYard is a privately owned

shopping center in the city of Campbell, Cal. It covers approximately 21 acres — 5 devoted to parking and 16 occupied by walkways, plazas, sidewalks, and buildings that contain more than 65 specialty shops, 10 restaurants, and a movie theater. The PruneYard is open to the public for the purpose of encouraging the patronizing of its commercial establishments. It has a policy not to permit any visitor or tenant to engage in any publicly expressive activity, including the circulation of petitions, that is not directly related to its commercial purposes....

Appellees are high school students who sought to solicit support for their opposition to a United Nations resolution against "Zionism." On a Saturday afternoon they set up a card table in a corner of PruneYard's central courtyard. They distributed pamphlets and asked passersby to sign petitions, which were to be sent to the President and Members of Congress. Their activity was peaceful and orderly and so far as the record indicates was not objected to by PruneYard's patrons.

Soon after appellees had begun soliciting signatures, a security guard informed them that they would have to leave because their activity violated PruneYard regulations. The guard suggested that they move to the public sidewalk at the PruneYard's perimeter. Appellees immediately left the premises and later filed this lawsuit in the California Superior Court of Santa Clara County. They sought to enjoin appellants from denying them access to the PruneYard for the purpose of circulating their petitions.

The Superior Court held that appellees were not entitled under either the Federal or California Constitution to exercise their asserted rights on the shopping center property.... The California Court of Appeal affirmed.

The California Supreme Court reversed, holding that the California Constitution protects "speech and petitioning, reasonably exercised, in shopping centers even when the centers are privately owned." 23 Cal. 3d 899, 910, 592 P. 2d 341, 347 (1979)....

... Before this Court, appellants contend that their constitutionally established rights under the Fourteenth Amendment to exclude appellees from adverse use of appellants' private property cannot be denied by invocation of a state constitutional provision or by judicial reconstruction of a State's laws of private property. We postponed consideration of the question of jurisdiction until the hearing of the case on the merits. 444 U. S. 949. We now affirm.

. . .

III

Appellants first contend that *Lloyd Corp. v. Tanner,* 407 U. S. 551 (1972), prevents the State from requiring a private shopping center owner to provide access to persons exercising their state constitutional rights of free speech and petition when adequate alternative avenues of communication are available. *Lloyd* dealt with the question whether under the Federal Constitution a privately owned shopping center may prohibit the distribution of handbills on its property when the hand-billing is unrelated to the shopping center's operations. *Id.,* at 552. The shopping center had adopted a strict policy against the distribution of handbills within the building complex and its malls, and it made no exceptions to this rule. *Id.,* at 555. Respondents in *Lloyd* argued that because the shopping center was open to the public, the First Amendment prevents the private owner from enforcing the handbilling restriction on shopping center premises. *Id.,* at 564. In rejecting this claim we substantially repudiated the rationale of *Food Employees v. Logan Valley Plaza,* 391 U. S. 308 (1968), which was later overruled in *Hudgens v. NLRB,* 424 U. S. 507 (1976). We stated that property does not "lose its private character merely because the public is generally invited to use it for designated purposes," and that "[t]he essentially private character of a store and its privately owned abutting property does not change by virtue of being large or clustered with other stores in a modern shopping center." 407 U. S., at 569.

Our reasoning in *Lloyd,* however, does not *ex proprio vigore* limit the authority of the State to exercise its police power or its sovereign right to adopt in its own Constitution individual liberties more expansive than those conferred by the Federal Constitution.... In *Lloyd, supra,* there was no state constitutional or statutory provision that had been construed to create rights to the use of private property by strangers, comparable to those found to exist by the California Supreme Court here....

IV

Appellants next contend that a right to exclude others underlies the Fifth Amendment guarantee against the taking of property without just compensation and the Fourteenth Amendment guarantee against the deprivation of property without due process of law.

It is true that one of the essential sticks in the bundle of property rights is the right to exclude others. *Kaiser Aetna v. United States,* 444 U. S. 164, 179–180 (1979). And here there has literally been a "taking" of that right to the extent that the California Supreme Court has interpreted the State Constitution to entitle its citizens to exercise free expression and petition rights on shopping center property. But it is well established that "not every destruction or injury to property by governmental action has been held to be a 'taking' in the constitutional sense." *Armstrong v. United States,* 364 U. S. 40, 48 (1960).... *[The Court rejects the claim that there had been a "taking" or that property had been denied without due process of law.]*

V

Appellants finally contend that a private property owner has a First Amendment right not to be forced by the State to use his property as a forum for the speech of others. They state that in *Wooley* v. *Maynard,* 430 U. S. 705 (1977), this Court concluded that a State may not constitutionally require an individual to participate in the dissemination of an ideological message by displaying it on his private property in a manner and for the express purpose that it be observed and read by the public. This rationale applies here, they argue, because the message of *Wooley* is that the State may not force an individual to display any message at all.

Wooley, however, was a case in which the government itself prescribed the message, required it to be displayed openly on appellee's personal property that was used "as part of his daily life," and refused to permit him to take any measures to cover up the motto even though the Court found that the display of the motto served no important state interest. Here, by contrast, there are a number of distinguishing factors. Most important, the shopping center by choice of its owner is not limited to the personal use of appellants. It is instead a business establishment that is open to the public to come and go as they please. The views expressed by members of the public in passing out pamphlets or seeking signatures for a petition thus will not likely be identified with those of the owner. Second, no specific message is dictated by the State to be displayed on appellants' property. There consequently is no danger of governmental discrimination for or against a particular message. Finally, as far as appears here appellants can expressly disavow any connection with the message by simply posting signs in the area where the speakers or handbillers stand. Such signs, for example, could disclaim any sponsorship of the message and could explain that the persons are communicating their own messages by virtue of state law.

. . .

We conclude that neither appellants' federally recognized property rights nor their First Amendment rights have been infringed by the California Supreme Court's decision recognizing a right of appellees to exercise state-protected rights of expression and petition on appellants' property. The judgment of the Supreme Court of California is therefore

Affirmed.

MR. JUSTICE BLACKMUN *[concurring]* ....

MR. JUSTICE MARSHALL, concurring.

. . .

...I applaud the court's decision, which is a part of a very healthy trend of affording state constitutional provisions a more expansive interpretation than this Court has given to the Federal Constitution....

MR. JUSTICE WHITE, concurring in part and concurring in the judgment.

I join MR. JUSTICE POWELL's concurring opinion but with these additional remarks.

. . .

I agree that on the record before us there was not an unconstitutional infringement of appellants' property rights. But it bears pointing out that the Federal Constitution does not require that a shopping center permit distributions or solicitations on its property. Indeed, *Hudgens* v. *NLRB,* 424 U. S. 507 (1976), and *Lloyd Corp.* v. *Tanner,* 407 U. S. 551 (1972), hold that the First and Fourteenth Amendments do not prevent the property owner from excluding those who would demonstrate or communicate on his property. Insofar as the Federal Constitution is concerned, therefore, a State may decline to construe its own constitution so as to limit the property rights of the shopping center owner.

. . .

MR. JUSTICE POWELL, with whom MR. JUSTICE WHITE joins, concurring in part and in the judgment.

Although I join the judgment, I do not agree with all of the reasoning in Part V of the Court's opinion. I join Parts I–IV on the understanding that our decision is limited to the type of shopping center involved in this case. Significantly different questions would be presented if a State authorized strangers to picket or distribute leaflets in privately owned, freestanding stores and commercial premises. Nor does our decision today apply to all "shopping centers." This generic term may include retail establishments that vary widely in size, location, and other relevant characteristics. Even large establishments may be able to show that the number or type of persons wishing to

speak on their premises would create a substantial annoyance to customers that could be eliminated only by elaborate, expensive, and possibly

unenforceable time, place, and manner restrictions....

E. COMMERCIAL SPEECH

Free speech has come to include "speech" related to commercial activities. Initially unprotected under the Constitution, commercial speech is now safeguarded by the courts. In part,
this reflects the growing appreciation that commercial speech is part of the free flow of information necessary for informed choice and democratic participation.

The concept of commercial speech appeared in a 1942 case involving a municipal ordinance
that prohibited the distribution in the streets of printed handbills bearing commercial advertising matter. The disputed handbill in this case was double-faced: half consisting of a protest
against the city's police (protected speech), the other half containing an advertisement. The
Court held unanimously that such artifices could not so easily evade the prohibition of the ordinance. Although the Constitution protects the dissemination of opinion by handbills, it "imposes no such restraint on government as respects purely commercial advertising." Valentine
v. Chrestensen, 316 U.S. 52, 54 (1942).

Other cases explored the notion of commercial speech,[12] but a major step occurred in 1974
when the Supreme Court narrowly upheld (by a 5–4 vote) a city's policy of allowing commercial, religious, and civic advertising in its transit system but prohibiting ads for political
candidates. The four dissenters argued that once the city opened a forum for communication
by accepting ads, it could not discriminate "among forum uses solely on the basis of message
content." Lehman v. City of Shaker Heights, 418 U.S. 298, 310 (1974).

Free Flow of Information

The value of commercial speech was etched sharply a year later when the Supreme Court, divided 5–4, struck down a state law that made it a misdemeanor for anyone to sell or circulate newspapers that contain ads encouraging abortions. Decided in the shadow of the abortion cases of 1973, the Court held that the statute infringed upon constitutionally protected
speech. At issue was not merely the right of newspapers to publish commercial material but
the right of the reader to make informed choices. Bigelow v. Virginia, 421 U.S. 809 (1975).

A similar point was made concerning the right of professionals to advertise their services.
In earlier cases, the Court had sustained laws that prohibited certain occupations, such as den-
tists, from advertising. Semler v. Dental Examiners, 294 U.S. 608 (1935). In 1976, however,
an 8–1 Supreme Court decision rejected a state law that declared it unprofessional conduct
for a licensed pharmacist to advertise the prices of prescription drugs. The Court explained
that it was not just a matter of trade but of health and the free flow of information. Virginia
State Board of Pharmacy v. Virginia Citizens Consumer Council, 425 U.S. 748 (1976). See
also Linmark Associates v. Willingboro, 431 U.S. 85 (1977).

Building on this line of cases, in 1977 the Court declared unconstitutional a state rule that
prohibited attorneys from advertising in newspapers or other media. The Court protected

---

12. In Capital Broadcasting Co. v. Acting Attorney General, 405 U.S. 1000 (1972), the Supreme Court summarily
affirmed a district court decision's sustaining the constitutionality of 15 U.S.C. § 1335, which prohibited the electronic media from carrying cigarette advertising. The district court called this form of communication commercial
speech. See also Pittsburgh Press Co. v. Human Rel. Comm'n, 413 U.S. 376, 384–85 (1973).

commercial speech on these grounds: "The listener's interest is substantial; the consumer's concern for the free flow of commercial speech often may be far keener than his concern for urgent political dialogue. Moreover, significant societal interests are served by such speech. Advertising, though entirely commercial, may often carry information of import to significant issues of the day." Bates v. State Bar of Arizona, 433 U.S. 350, 364 (1977).[13] The right to advertise does not protect lawyers from being disciplined by the bar for soliciting clients in person. Ohralik v. Ohio State Bar Assn., 436 U.S. 447 (1978).

The Court showed its concern for the free flow of information in 1978. Split 5–4, it held that a Massachusetts statute violated the First Amendment because it restricted business corporations from making contributions or expenditures to influence votes on questions submitted to the people. Some of the dissenters objected that the Court should have deferred to legislatures "in the context of the political arena where the expertise of legislators is at its peak and that of judges is at its very lowest." First National Bank of Boston v. Bellotti, 435 U.S. 765, 804 (1978).

In 1983 unanimous Court struck down a congressional statute that prohibited the mailing of unsolicited advertisements for contraceptives. The Court held that the statute violated commercial speech protected by the First Amendment: "where—as in this case—a speaker desires to convey truthful information relevant to important social issues such as family planning and the prevention of venereal disease, we have previously found the First Amendment interest served by such speech paramount." Bolger v. Youngs Drug Products Corp., 463 U.S. 60, 69 (1983).

A unanimous ruling in 1995 declared unconstitutional a federal law abridging a brewer's right to provide the public with accurate information about the alcoholic content of malt beverages. Rubin v. Coors Brewing Co., 514 U.S. 476 (1995). A year later another unanimous Court struck down a Rhode Island ban on the advertising of liquor prices, ruling that the states' authority under the 21st Amendment does not override the First Amendment free speech guarantee. Writing for the Court, Justice Stevens said that the First Amendment "directs us to be especially skeptical of regulations that seek to keep people in the dark for what the government perceives to be their own good." 44 Liquormart, Inc. v. Rhode Island, 517 U.S. 484, 503 (1996). There was no majority agreement, however, on the meaning of commercial speech.

Regulating the Economy

Commercial speech involves conflicts between state efforts to regulate the economy and the interest of businesses to promote their activities. A New York law prohibited an electric utility from placing ads to encourage the use of electricity. The law reflected concern at that time over insufficient fuel supply because of Middle East oil embargoes. By an 8–1 majority, the Court held that the law violated the First Amendment. Although the utility exercised a monopoly over electricity, it faced competition from oil and gas. Central Hudson Gas & Elec. v. Public Service Comm'n, 447 U.S. 557 (1980). This case suggested that government had to use the "least restrictive means" in regulating commercial speech, but the Court held in 1989 that only a reasonable "fit" is required between the legislature's ends to regulate commercial speech and the means it chooses. Board of Trustees, State Univ. of N.Y. v. Fox, 492 U.S. 469 (1989).

In 1997, when it looked like marketing orders issued by the U.S. Agriculture Department might run afoul of the standards for commercial speech announced in *Central Hudson*, the Court

---

13. Additional guidelines on advertising by lawyers: In re R.M.J., 455 U.S. 191 (1982); Zauderer v. Office of Disciplinary Counsel, 471 U.S. 626 (1985); Shapero v. Kentucky Bar Assn., 486 U.S. 466 (1988); Peel v. Attorney Disciplinary Comm'n of Ill., 496 U.S. 91 (1990). A ruling in 1995, splitting the Court 5 to 4, upheld a Florida bar rule that prohibited personal-injury lawyers from sending targeted direct-mail solicitations to victims or their relatives until 30 days following an accident or disaster. Florida Bar v. Went For It, Inc., 515 U.S. 618 (1995).

held that the legal question was not free speech or the First Amendment but "rather [it] is simply a question of economic policy for Congress and the Executive to resolve," and that Congress had sufficient authority to sanction these marketing orders through its power to regulate commerce. Glickman v. Wileman Bros. & Elliott, 521 U.S. 457, 468, 476 (1997). Four dissenters attacked the Court for failing to follow the tests issued in *Central Hudson* and other decisions.

Some states have tried to regulate billboards. The city of San Diego, in an effort to eliminate dangerous distractions to pedestrians and motorists and improve the appearance of city streets, placed restrictions on billboards and outdoor advertising displays. However, it made exceptions for on-site advertising (signs on the property of the business) and twelve other categories. Because the city seemed to afford greater protection to commercial (on-site) speech than to noncommercial speech, the ordinance was held invalid. Metromedia, Inc. v. San Diego, 453 U.S. 490 (1981). Restrictions that are totally neutral, such as the prohibition against the posting of all signs on public property, have been upheld. Cities may decide that a total ban is necessary to prevent visual clutter and to reduce traffic hazards. Because the ban is total, there is no hint of censorship or suppression of particular views. City Council v. Taxpayers for Vincent, 466 U.S. 789 (1984).

Metromedia and *Vincent* guided the Court in 1994 when it unanimously struck down a city ordinance that prohibited residents from putting political or personal signs in their yards. In this case a woman placed an 8.5 by 11-inch sign in the second story window of her home stating, "For Peace in the Gulf." The Court held that the ordinance, intended to minimize the "visual clutter" associated with such signs, violated her right to free speech. Ladue, City of v. Gilleo, 512 U.S. 43 (1994).

A 1986 decision on commercial speech dealt with gambling. A Puerto Rican statute legalized certain forms of casino gambling to promote tourism but prohibited gambling rooms from advertising to the public in Puerto Rico. A sharply divided (5–4) Court sustained the statute, rejecting the argument that once Puerto Rico chose to legalize casino gambling it was prohibited by the First Amendment from restricting advertising. Posadas de Puerto Rico Assoc. v. Tourism Co., 478 U.S. 328 (1986). However, in 1999 the Court held unanimously that a federal law, prohibiting radio and TV advertising of casino gambling, could not be applied to states where such gambling is legal. Federal law in this area had become too "pierced by exemptions and inconsistencies" to be applied coherently. Greater New Orleans Broadcasting v. United States, 527 U.S. 173, 190 (1999).

F. BROADCASTING RIGHTS

In theory, there is no limit to the number of newspapers. Radio and television stations, however, compete for a finite number of public airwaves. Acting under the Commerce Clause, Congress established the Federal Communications Commission (FCC) to allocate this limited space. It grants licenses for a specific number of years, subject to various conditions supplied by statute and agency regulation. The FCC may revoke or suspend a license if a station violates these conditions. No one has a free-speech right to use public airwaves without a license. National Broadcasting Co. v. United States, 319 U.S. 190 (1943).

In 1949 the FCC developed a "fairness doctrine" to require broadcasters to present public issues and give each side of an issue fair coverage. 13 FCC 1246 (1949). Although Congress never explicitly authorized this doctrine, a unanimous Court held that the agency regulation was consistent with congressional policy and did not violate the First Amendment. Red Lion Broadcasting Co. v. FCC, 395 U.S. 367 (1969). Next, there was the question of whether broadcasters are required to accept paid editorial advertisements. The Court again deferred to the judgments of the FCC and Congress that no such requirement exists. Columbia Broadcasting System v. Democratic National Committee, 412 U.S. 94 (1973). Congress and the FCC formulated the policy, accepted by the courts, that political candidates are entitled to "reasonable access" to broadcasting stations to promote their campaigns for federal office. CBS, Inc. v. FCC, 453 U.S. 367 (1981). Some congressional initiatives were struck down, such as the requirement that stations receiving federal funds could not editorialize. FCC v. League of Women Voters of California, 468 U.S. 364 (1984).

Conditions are imposed on radio and television programs that would be intolerable for newspapers. For example, Congress requires that if one political candidate is given time on the air, opponents must receive "equal opportunities." 47 U.S.C. § 315(a) (1994). In 1970 Congress prohibited the advertisement of cigarettes on radio or television. 84 Stat. 87 (1970). It later applied the same restriction to little cigars. 15 U.S.C. § 1335 (1994). In 1986 the ban was extended to smokeless tobacco (snuff). 100 Stat. 32, § 3(f); 15 U.S.C. 4402(f) (1994).

In 1998, the Court ruled 6 to 3 that public TV stations have the right to choose which political candidates may appear in debates that are broadcast. Ralph Forbes, a former member of the American Nazi Party who ran in 1992 as an independent candidate, was excluded from a TV debate that included Republican and Democratic candidates for Arkansas' Third Congressional District. Although Forbes lost his opportunity to present his views, the Court was concerned that requiring TV stations to invite all candidates, no matter how minor or marginal, might lead broadcasters to cancel such programs. Adopting that policy "does not promote speech but represses it." Arkansas Educ. Television Com'n v. Forbes, 523 U.S. 666, 682 (1998).

The Court gives two reasons for subjecting broadcasting to more severe restrictions than newspapers: the pervasive presence of the broadcast media and its unique access to children. The FCC was therefore allowed to prohibit the playing of "indecent" material in the afternoon (George Carlin's monologue on "seven dirty words"). The same material, in a different place or at another time, might have received First Amendment protection. FCC v. PACIFICA FOUNDATION 438 U.S. 726, 748–51 (1978). Ever since 1948, Congress has prohibited anyone from uttering "any obscene, indecent, or profane language" by means of radio communication. 18 U.S.C. § 1464 (1994).

Following the *Pacifica* decision, the FCC continued to restrict its enforcement efforts against indecent broadcasts to programs before 10 P.M. Under the Reagan administration, however, the Commission pushed the "safe harbor" period up to 12 midnight. Before that standard could be implemented, Congress intervened in 1988 to order the FCC to promulgate regulations on indecent broadcasts to cover the full 24 hours a day. 102 Stat. 2228, § 608 (1988). The Commission promulgated a new rule prohibiting all broadcasts of indecent materials, but that was declared a violation of the First Amendment. Action for Children's Television v. FCC, 932 F.2d 1504 (D.C. Cir. 1991), cert. denied, 503 U.S. 913–14 (1992). Congress passed legislation to require the FCC to promulgate regulations that will prohibit indecent programming from 6 A.M. to midnight, except for stations that go off the air before midnight, which may broadcast such material beginning at 10 P.M. 106 Stat. 954, § 16 (1992).

Cable TV and Internet

Congressional legislation in 1992 to regulate cable TV led to a decision by the Supreme Court two years later holding that cable is entitled to free speech protection. However, the standard applied is not strict scrutiny but rather an intermediate level of scrutiny. The intermediate level offers greater protection than for broadcasters, who are regulated more strictly because of the scarcity of channels resulting from frequencies in the electromagnetic spectrum. Turner Broadcasting Systems, Inc. v. FCC, 512 U.S. 622 (1994).

Other parts of the 1992 statute reached the Supreme court in 1996. A deeply divided Court (six Justices dissented with parts of the Court's opinion) ruled that cable TV operators may ban indecent programming from certain commercial channels but it was inconsistent with the First Amendment to ban such material from "public access" channels used by local governments and community groups. The Court also struck down a provision that required cable operators to allow access to "patently offensive" programming only when individuals request, in writing, this material. The application of this complex ruling, particularly with fast-paced technological changes, is very uncertain. Denver Area Educ. Telecom. Consortium v. FCC, 518 U.S. 727 (1996). A year later the Court, with a 5–4 majority, held that Congress could require cable systems to carry local broadcast TV stations (the "must carry" rule). The Court rejected the cable industry's argument that the 1992 congressional statute was a form of government-compelled speech that violated the First Amendment. The majority essentially deferred to Congress in reconciling "the complex and fast-changing field of television." Turner Broadcasting Systems, Inc. v. FCC, 520 U.S. 180, 224 (1997).

There was no deference to congressional judgment in another 1997 decision regarding the Internet. The Court held that two provisions of the Communications Decency Act of 1996 violated the First Amendment. One provision prohibited the knowing transmission on the Internet of obscene or indecent messages to any recipient under 18 years of age. The other provision prohibited the knowing sending or displaying of patently offensive messages in a manner that made it available to anyone under 18 years of age. The Court, with a 7 to 2 majority, decided that Congress had suppressed speech that adults had a constitutional right to receive. In contrast to the more restrictive rights of broadcasters, it appeared that the Court was extending to online communications the same level of free speech protections allowed for the print media, such as newspapers and magazines. RENO v. ACLU, 521 U.S. 844 (1997). These provisions of the statute were struck down partly because of alternatives that exist: software programs ("filters") that allow parents to screen out objectionable material. After the Court's decision, President Clinton stated: "With the right technology and rating systems, we can help ensure that our children don't end up in the red light districts of cyberspace." Public Papers of the Presidents, 1997, I, at 829.

In 1999, the Court affirmed a lower court ruling that upheld a federal law that makes it a crime to transmit e-mails that are obscene, lewd, or intended to annoy other people. The statute was upheld on the understanding that the Justice Department would prosecute only cases of obscenity and not messages that are indecent or merely annoying. ApolloMedia Corp. v. Reno, 526 U.S. 1061 (1999). However, in 2000 the Court ruled that congressional legislation on cable television was unconstitutional because it required providers of sexually explicit material to "fully scramble" their signals or offer the programs only when children are unlikely to be watching. Divided 5 to 4, the court found that the statute violated the First Amendment because government had failed to show that the statutory remedy was the least restrictive way of preventing children from watching such material. United States v. Playboy Entertainment Group, Inc., 120 S.Ct. 1878 (2000).

The Fairness Doctrine

Broadcasting rights fluctuate with technology. In 1973 the Court explained that the problems of regulating broadcasting "are rendered more difficult because the broadcast industry is dynamic in terms of technological change; solutions adequate a decade ago are not necessarily so now, and those acceptable today may well be outmoded 10 years hence." Columbia Broadcasting System v. Democratic National Committee, 412 U.S. 94, 102 (1973). The fairness doctrine depends largely on the limited number of access points available to licensees. If outlets increased because of technology, the doctrine's rationale would be undermined. In a footnote to a 1984 decision, the Court recognized that the emergence of cable and satellite television created new channels for the public. However, "without some signal from Congress or the FCC" that technological development required revision of broadcasting regulation, the Court was not prepared to challenge the fairness doctrine. FCC v. League of Women Voters of California, 468 U.S. 364, 377–78 n.11 (1984). See also n.12 at 378–79.

The FCC chairman in the Reagan administration criticized the fairness doctrine as unconstitutional and threatened to abolish it. In 1985 a Commission report concluded that the doctrine violates the First Amendment and no longer serves the public interest. However, it declined to initiate a new rule to eliminate or modify the doctrine. On the basis of that report, a party brought suit and asked the D.C. Circuit to consider the constitutionality of the doctrine. The D.C. Circuit refused on the ground that the report did not constitute "agency action" subject to judicial review. Radio-Television News Directors Ass'n v. FCC, 809 F.2d 860 (D.C. Cir. 1987). On the same day, the D.C. Circuit returned a case to the FCC because it had failed to give adequate consideration to a station owner's constitutional arguments regarding the fairness doctrine. The Commission regarded Congress and the courts as more appropriate arenas for deciding the constitutional question. The D.C. Circuit, however, thought it might benefit from the FCC's analysis, even if the Commission felt political pressure from Congress to avoid a final conclusion. Meredith Corp. v. FCC, 809 F.2d 863, 872 (D.C. Cir. 1987). It noted that federal officials are not only bound by the Constitution but also take an oath to support and defend it: "To enforce a Commission-generated policy that the Commission itself believes is unconstitutional may well constitute a violation of that oath...." Id. at 874.

Congress passed legislation in 1987 to codify the fairness doctrine, but President Reagan vetoed the bill. He stated that the doctrine was antagonistic to the First Amendment and was no longer justified because of new media outlets, such as cable television. Public Papers of the Presidents, 1987, I, at 690. The FCC unanimously abolished the fairness doctrine, claiming that it represented an unconstitutional restriction on free speech. Bills have been introduced in Congress to reinstate the fairness doctrine.

FCC v. Pacifica Foundation

438 U.S. 726 (1978)

A radio station of Pacifica Foundation made an afternoon broadcast of George Carlin's satiric monologue "Filthy Words," which listed and repeated a variety of colloquial uses of "words you couldn't say on the public airwaves." A father who heard the broadcast while driving with his young son complained to the Federal Communications Commission (FCC), which later issued a declaratory order granting the complaint. Although the FCC did not impose formal sanctions, it stated that the order would be placed in the station's license file and that if subsequent complaints were received it would decide whether to invoke sanctions, including a decision not to renew the license. The FCC also announced that it had the power to regulate indecent broadcasting. The D.C. Circuit reversed the FCC's action, partly on the ground that it was censorship and the agency rule was overbroad.

MR. JUSTICE STEVENS delivered the opinion of the Court (Parts I, II, III, and IV-C) and an opinion in which THE CHIEF JUSTICE and MR. JUSTICE REHNQUIST joined (Parts IV-A and IV-B).

This case requires that we decide whether the Federal Communications Commission has any power to regulate a radio broadcast that is indecent but not obscene.

A satiric humorist named George Carlin recorded a 12-minute monologue entitled "Filthy Words" before a live audience in a California theater. He began by referring to his thoughts about

"the words you couldn't say on the public, ah, airwaves, um, the ones you definitely wouldn't say, ever." He proceeded to list those words and repeat them over and over again in a variety of colloquialisms. The transcript of the recording, which is appended to this opinion, indicates frequent laughter from the audience.

At about 2 o'clock in the afternoon on Tuesday, October 30, 1973, a New York radio station, owned by respondent Pacifica Foundation, broadcast the "Filthy Words" monologue. A few weeks later a man, who stated that he had heard the broadcast while driving with his young son, wrote a letter complaining to the Commission. He stated that, although he could perhaps understand the "record's being sold for private use, I certainly cannot understand the broadcast of same over the air that, supposedly, you control."

The complaint was forwarded to the station for comment. In its response, Pacifica explained that the monologue had been played during a program about contemporary society's attitude toward language and that, immediately before its broadcast, listeners had been advised that it included "sensitive language which might be regarded as offensive to some." Pacifica characterized George Carlin as "a significant social satirist" who "like Twain and Sahl before him, examines the language of ordinary people.... Carlin is not mouthing obscenities, he is merely using words to satirize as harmless and essentially silly our attitudes towards those words." Pacifica stated that it was not aware of any other complaints about the broadcast.

On February 21, 1975, the Commission issued a declaratory order granting the complaint and holding that Pacifica "could have been the subject of administrative sanctions." 56 F.C.C. 2d 94, 99. The Commission did not impose formal sanctions, but it did state that the order would be "associated with the station's license file, and in the event that subsequent complaints are received, the Commission will then decide whether it should utilize any of the available sanctions it has been granted by Congress." *[Congress has empowered the FCC to revoke a station's license, issue a cease and desist order, or impose a monetary forfeiture. The FCC can also deny a license renewal and grant a short-term renewal.]*

In its memorandum opinion the Commission stated that it intended to "clarify the standards which will be utilized in considering" the growing number of complaints about indecent speech on the airwaves. *Id.,* at 94. Advancing several reasons for treating broadcast speech differently from other forms of expression, the Commission found a power to regulate indecent broadcasting in two statutes: 18 U. S. C. § 1464 (1976 ed.), which forbids the use of "any obscene, indecent, or profane language by means of radio communications," and 47 U. S. C. § 303 (g), which requires the Commission to "encourage the larger and more effective use of radio in the public interest."

. . .

...[T]he Commission concluded that certain words *[in Carlin's broadcast]* depicted sexual and excretory activities in a patently offensive manner, noted that they "were broadcast at a time when children were undoubtedly in the audience (i. e., in the early afternoon)," and that the prerecorded language, with these offensive words "repeated over and over," was "deliberately broadcast." *Id.,* at 99. In summary, the Commission stated: "We therefore hold that the language as broadcast was indecent and prohibited by 18 U. S. C. § 1464." *Ibid.*

. . .

The United States Court of Appeals for the District of Columbia Circuit reversed, with each of the three judges on the panel writing separately....

. . .

II

The relevant statutory questions are whether the Commission's action is forbidden "censorship" within the meaning of 47 U. S. C. § 326 and whether speech that concededly is not obscene may be restricted as "indecent" under the authority of 18 U. S. C. § 1464 (1976 ed.). The questions are not unrelated, for the two statutory provisions have a common origin. Nevertheless, we analyze them separately.

Section 29 of the Radio Act of 1927 provided:

"Nothing in this Act shall be understood or construed to give the licensing authority the power of censorship over the radio communications or signals transmitted by any radio station, and no regulation or condition shall be promulgated or fixed by the licensing authority which shall interfere with the right of free speech by means of radio communications. No person within the jurisdiction of the United States shall utter any obscene, indecent, or profane language by means of radio communication." 44 Stat. 1172.

The prohibition against censorship unequivocally denies the Commission any power to edit proposed broadcasts in advance and to excise material considered inappropriate for the airwaves. The prohibition, however, has never been construed to deny the Commission the power to review the content of completed broadcasts in the performance of its regulatory duties.

During the period between the original enactment of the provision in 1927 and its re-enactment in the Communications Act of 1934, the courts and the Federal Radio Commission held that the section deprived the Commission of the power to subject "broadcasting matter to scrutiny prior to its release," but they concluded that the Commission's "undoubted right" to take note of past program content when considering a licensee's renewal application "is not censorship."

. . .

We conclude, therefore, that § 326 does not limit the Commission's authority to impose sanctions on licensees who engage in obscene, indecent, or profane broadcasting.

III

The only other statutory question presented by this case is whether the afternoon broadcast of the "Filthy Words" monologue was indecent within the meaning of § 1464. Even that question is narrowly confined by the arguments of the parties.

The Commission identified several words that referred to excretory or sexual activities or organs, stated that the repetitive, deliberate use of those words in an afternoon broadcast when children are in the audience was patently offensive, and held that the broadcast was indecent. Pacifica takes issue with the Commission's definition of indecency, but does not dispute the Commission's preliminary determination that each of the components of its definition was present. Specifically, Pacifica does not quarrel with the conclusion that this afternoon broadcast was patently offensive. Pacifica's claim that the broadcast was not indecent within the meaning of the statute rests entirely on the absence of prurient appeal.

The plain language of the statute does not support Pacifica's argument. The words "obscene, indecent, or profane" are written in the disjunctive, implying that each has a separate meaning. Prurient appeal is an element of the obscene, but the normal definition of "indecent" merely refers to nonconformance with accepted standards of morality.

. . .

Because neither our prior decisions nor the language or history of § 1464 supports the conclusion that prurient appeal is an essential component of indecent language, we reject Pacifica's construction of the statute. When that construction is put to one side, there is no basis for disagreeing with the Commission's conclusion that indecent language was used in this broadcast.

IV

Pacifica makes two constitutional attacks on the Commission's order. First, it argues that the Commission's construction of the statutory language broadly encompasses so much constitutionally protected speech that reversal is required even if Pacifica's broadcast of the "Filthy Words" monologue is not itself protected by the First Amendment. Second, Pacifica argues that inasmuch as the recording is not obscene, the Constitution forbids any abridgment of the right to broadcast it on the radio.

A

The first argument fails because our review is limited to the question whether the Commission has the authority to proscribe this particular broadcast. As the Commission itself emphasized, its order was "issued in a specific factual context." 59 F. C. C. 2d, at 893. That approach is appropriate for courts as well as the Commission when regulation of indecency is at stake for indecency is largely a function of context—it cannot be adequately judged in the abstract.

. . .

B

When the issue is narrowed to the facts of this case, the question is whether the First Amendment denies government any power to restrict the public broadcast of indecent language in any circumstances. For if the government has any such power, this was an appropriate occasion for its exercise.

The words of the Carlin monologue are unquestionably "speech" within the meaning of the First Amendment. It is equally clear that the Commission's objections to the broadcast were based in part on its content. The order must therefore fall if, as Pacifica argues, the First Amendment prohibits all governmental regulation that depends on the content of speech. Our past cases demonstrate, however, that no such absolute rule is mandated by the Constitution.

. . .

In this case it is undisputed that the content of Pacifica's broadcast was "vulgar," "offensive," and "shocking." Because content of that character is not entitled to absolute constitutional protection under all circumstances, we must consider its context in order to determine whether the

Commission's action was constitutionally permissible.

. . .

C

We have long recognized that each medium of expression presents special First Amendment problems, *Joseph Burstyn, Inc. v. Wilson,* 343 U. S. 495, 502–503. And of all forms of communication, it is broadcasting that has received the most limited First Amendment protection. Thus, although other speakers cannot be licensed except under laws that carefully define and narrow official discretion, a broadcaster may be deprived of his license and his forum if the Commission decides that such an action would serve "the public interest, convenience, and necessity." . . .

The reasons for these distinctions are complex, but two have relevance to the present case. First, the broadcast media have established a uniquely pervasive presence in the lives of all Americans. Patently offensive, indecent material presented over the airwaves confronts the citizen, not only in public, but also in the privacy of the home, where the individual's right to be left alone plainly outweighs the First Amendment rights of an intruder. *Rowan v. Post Office Dept.,* 397 U. S. 728. Because the broadcast audience is constantly tuning in and out, prior warnings cannot completely protect the listener or viewer from unexpected program content. . . .

Second, broadcasting is uniquely accessible to children, even those too young to read. Although Cohen's *[Paul Cohen, who entered a courthouse wearing a jacket with the words "Fuck the Draft"; Cohen v. California, 403 U.S. 15 (1971)]* written message might have been incomprehensible to a first grader, Pacifica's broadcast could have enlarged a child's vocabulary in an instant. . . .

. . .

The judgment of the Court of Appeals is reversed.

It is so ordered.

MR. JUSTICE POWELL, with whom MR. JUSTICE BLACKMUN joins, concurring in part and concurring in the judgment.

I join Parts I, II, III, and IV-C of MR. JUSTICE STEVENS' opinion. The Court today reviews only the Commission's holding that Carlin's monologue was indecent "as broadcast" at two o'clock in the afternoon, and not the broad sweep of the Commission's opinion. . . .

MR. JUSTICE BRENNAN, with whom MR. JUSTICE MARSHALL joins, dissenting.

I agree with MR. JUSTICE STEWART that, under *Hamling v. United States,* 418 U. S. 87 (1974), and *United States v. 12 200-ft. Reels of Film,* 413 U. S. 123 (1973), the word "indecent" in 18 U. S. C. § 1464 (1976 ed.) must be construed to prohibit only obscene speech. . . .

. . .

The Court's balance, of necessity, fails to accord proper weight to the interests of listeners who wish to hear broadcasts the FCC deems offensive. It permits majoritarian tastes completely to preclude a protected message from entering the homes of a receptive, unoffended minority. No decision of this Court supports such a result. . . .

MR. JUSTICE STEWART, with whom MR. JUSTICE BRENNAN, MR. JUSTICE WHITE, and MR. JUSTICE MARSHALL join, dissenting.

The Court today recognizes the wise admonition that we should "avoid the unnecessary decision of [constitutional] issues." *Ante,* at 734. But it disregards one important application of this salutary principle — the need to construe an Act of Congress so as to avoid, if possible, passing upon its constitutionality. It is apparent that the constitutional questions raised by the order of the Commission in this case are substantial. Before deciding them, we should be certain that it is necessary to do so.

The statute pursuant to which the Commission acted, 18 U. S. C. § 1464 (1976 ed.), makes it a federal offense to utter "any obscene, indecent, or profane language by means of radio communication." The Commission held, and the Court today agrees, that "indecent" is a broader concept than "obscene" as the latter term was defined in *Miller v. California,* 413 U. S. 15, because language can be "indecent" although it has social, political, or artistic value and lacks prurient appeal. 56 F. C. C. 2d 94, 97–98. But this construction of § 1464, while perhaps plausible, is by no means compelled. To the contrary, I think that "indecent" should properly be read as meaning no more than "obscene." Since the Carlin monologue concededly was not "obscene," I believe that the Commission lacked statutory authority to ban it. . . .

Reno v. ACLU

521 U.S. 844 (1997)

Congress passed the Communications Decency Act (CDA) of 1996 to protect minors from harmful material on the Internet. Several parties, including the ACLU, brought this suit against Attorney General Janet Reno. A three-judge panel entered a preliminary injunction against enforcement of the statutory provisions challenged under the First Amendment. Under the special review provisions of the CDA, the government appealed the case directly to the Supreme Court.

JUSTICE STEVENS delivered the opinion of the Court.

At issue is the constitutionality of two statutory provisions enacted to protect minors from "indecent" and "patently offensive" communications on the Internet. Notwithstanding the legitimacy and importance of the congressional goal of protecting children from harmful materials, we agree with the three-judge District Court that the statute abridges "the freedom of speech" protected by the First Amendment.

I

The District Court made extensive findings of fact, most of which were based on a detailed stipulation prepared by the parties....

The Internet

The Internet is an international network of interconnected computers. It is the outgrowth of what began in 1969 as a military program called "ARPANET," ...

The internet has experienced "extraordinary growth." The number of "host" computers — those that store information and relay communications — increased from about 300 in 1981 to approximately 9,400,000 by the time of the trial in 1996. Roughly 60% of these hosts are located in the United States. About 40 million people used the Internet at the time of trial, a number that is expected to mushroom to 200 million by 1999.

Individuals can obtain access to the Internet from many different sources, generally hosts themselves or entities with a host affiliation. Most colleges and universities provide access for their students and faculty; many corporations provide their employees with access through an office network; many communities and local libraries provide free access; and an increasing number of storefront "computer coffee shops" provide access for a small hourly fee. Several major national "online services" such as America Online, CompuServe, the Microsoft Network, and Prodigy offer access to their own extensive proprietary network as well as a link to the much larger resources of the Internet. These commercial online services had almost 12 million individual subscribers at the time of trial.

Anyone with access to the Internet may take advantage of a wide variety of communication and information retrieval methods. These methods are constantly evolving and difficult to categorize precisely. But, as presently constituted, those most relevant to this case are electronic mail ("e-mail"), automatic mailing list services ("mail exploders," sometimes referred to as "listservs"), "newsgroups," "chat rooms," and the "World Wide Web." All of these methods can be used to transmit text; most can transmit sound, pictures, and moving video images. Taken together, these tools constitute a unique medium — known to its users as "cyberspace" — located in no particular geographical location but available to anyone, anywhere in the world, with access to the Internet.

. . .

From the publishers' point of view, [*the Internet*] constitutes a vast platform from which to address and hear from a world-wide audience of millions of readers, viewers, researchers, and buyers. Any person or organization with a computer connected to the Internet can "publish" information....

Sexually Explicit Material

Sexually explicit material on the Internet includes text, pictures, and chat and "extends from the modestly titillating to the hardest-core."...

Some of the communications over the Internet that originate in foreign countries are also sexually explicit.

Though such material is widely available, users seldom encounter such content accidentally. "A document's title or a description of the document will usually appear before the document itself... and in many cases the user will receive detailed information about a site's content before he or she need take the step to access the document. Almost all sexually explicit images are preceded by warnings as to the content." For that reason, the "odds are slim" that a user would enter a sexually explicit site by accident. Unlike communications received by radio or television, "the receipt of information on the Internet requires a series of affirmative steps more deliberate and directed than merely turning a dial. A child requires some sophistication and some ability to read to retrieve material and thereby to use the Internet unattended."

Systems have been developed to help parents control the material that may be available on a home computer with Internet access. A system may either limit a computer's access to an approved list of sources that have been identified as containing no adult material, it may block designated inappropriate sites, or it may attempt to block messages containing identifiable objectionable features. "Although parental control software currently can screen for certain suggestive words or for known sexually explicit sites, it cannot now screen for sexually explicit images." Nevertheless, the evidence indicates that "a reasonably effective method by which parents can prevent their children from accessing sexually explicit and other material which parents may believe is inappropriate for their children will soon be available."

Age Verification

The problem of age verification differs for different uses of the Internet. The District Court categorically determined that there "is no effective way to determine the identity or the age of a user who is accessing material through e-mail, mail exploders, newsgroups or chat rooms." The Government offered no evidence that there was a reliable way to screen recipients and participants in such fora for age. Moreover, even if it were technologically feasible to block minors' access to newsgroups and chat rooms containing discussions of art, politics or other subjects that potentially elicit "indecent" or "patently offensive" contributions, it would not be possible to block their access to that material and "still allow them access to the remaining content, even if the overwhelming majority of that content was not indecent."

Technology exists by which an operator of a Web site may condition access on the verification of requested information such as a credit card number or an adult password. Credit card verification is only feasible, however, either in connection with a commercial transaction in which the card is used, or by payment to a verification agency.

Using credit card possession as a surrogate for proof of age would impose costs on non-commercial Web sites that would require many of them to shut down. For that reason, at the time of the trial, credit card verification was "effectively unavailable to a substantial number of Internet content providers." ... Moreover, the imposition of such a requirement "would completely bar adults who do not have a credit card and lack the resources to obtain one from accessing any blocked material."

Commercial pornographic sites that charge their users for access have assigned them passwords as a method of age verification. The record does not contain any evidence concerning the reliability of these technologies. Even if passwords are effective for commercial purveyors of indecent material, the District Court found that an adult password requirement would impose significant burdens on noncommercial sites, both because they would discourage users from accessing their sites and because the cost of creating and maintaining such screening systems would be "beyond their reach."

· · ·

II

The Telecommunications Act of 1996, Pub.L. 104–104, 110 Stat. 56, was an unusually important legislative enactment. As stated on the first of its 103 pages, its primary purpose was to reduce regulation and encourage "the rapid deployment of new telecommunications technologies." The major components of the statute have nothing to do with the Internet; ...

[*Title V — known as the Communications Decency Act (CDA) — contained two provisions challenged in this case.*]

The first, 47 U.S.C.A. § 223(a) (Supp. 1997), prohibits the knowing transmission of obscene or indecent messages to any recipient under 18 years of age [*The statute provided for fines and up to two years in prison.*]

The breadth of these prohibitions is qualified by two affirmative defenses.... One covers those who take "good faith, reasonable, effective, and appropriate actions" to restrict access by minors to the prohibited communications. § 223(e)(5)(A). The other covers those who restrict access to covered material by requiring certain designated forms of age proof, such as a verified credit card or an adult identification number or code. § 223(e)(5)(B).

· · ·

IV

In arguing for reversal, the Government contends that the CDA is plainly constitutional under three of our prior decisions: (1) *Ginsberg v. New York,* 390 U.S. 629 (1968); (2) *FCC v. Pacifica Foundation,* 438 U.S. 726 (1978); and (3) *Renton v. Playtime Theatres, Inc.,* 475 U.S. 41 (1986). A close look at these cases, however, raises — rather than relieves — doubts concerning the constitutionality of the CDA.

In *Ginsberg,* we upheld the constitutionality of a New York statute that prohibited selling to minors under 17 years of age material that was considered obscene as to them even if not obscene as to adults. [*The Court gives four reasons why the statute upheld in* Ginsberg *was narrower than the CDA: the New York prohibition did not bar parents from purchasing the magazines for their children; the New York statute applied only to commercial transactions whereas the CDA contained no such limitation; the New York statute cabined its definition of material that is harmful to minors with the requirement that it be "utterly without redeeming social importance for minors," whereas the CDA failed to provide any definition of the term "indecent" and omitted any requirement that the "patently offensive" material lack serious literary, artistic, political, or scientific value; the New York statute defined a minor as a person under the age of 17, whereas the CDA applied to those under 18.*]

In *Pacifica,* we upheld a declaratory order of the Federal Communications Commission, holding that the broadcast of a recording of a 12-minute monologue entitled "Filthy Words" that had previously been delivered to a live audience "could have been the subject of administrative sanctions." [*The Court found these distinctions between* Pacifica *and the CDA: the order in* Pacifica *targeted a specific broadcast whereas the CDA's broad categorical prohibition is not limited to particular times; unlike the CDA, the FCC's declaratory order was not punitive; the FCC's order applied to a medium that had received the most limited First Amendment protection. The Internet has no comparable history.*]

In *Renton,* we upheld a zoning ordinance that kept adult movie theatres out of residential neighborhoods. The ordinance was aimed, not at the content of the films shown in the theaters, but rather at the "secondary effects" — such as crime and deteriorating property values — that these theaters fostered: "It is th[e] secondary effect which these zoning ordinances attempt to avoid, not the dissemination of 'offensive' speech." 475 U.S. at 49 (quoting *Young v. American Mini Theatres, Inc.,* 427 U.S. 50, 71, n. 34 (1976). According to the Government, the CDA is constitutional because it constitutes a sort of "cyberzoning" on the Internet. But the CDA applies broadly to the entire universe of cyberspace. And the purpose of the CDA is to protect children from the primary effects of "indecent" and "patently offensive" speech, rather than any "secondary" effect of such speech. Thus, the CDA is a content-based blanket restriction on speech, and, as such, cannot be "properly analyzed as a form of time, place, and manner regulation." 475 U.S., at 46. ...

V

[*In this section the Court explains that the Internet is not as "invasive" as radio and television. Users seldom encounter content "by accident." Also, unlike congressional regulation of the broadcast spectrum, the Internet cannot be considered a "scarce" expressive commodity.*]

VI

Regardless of whether the CDA is so vague that it violates the Fifth Amendment, the many ambiguities concerning the scope of its coverage render it problematic for purposes of the First Amendment. For instance, each of the two parts of the CDA uses a different linguistic form. The first uses the word "indecent," 47 U.S.C.A. § 223(a) (Supp.1997), while the second speaks of material that "in context, depicts or describes, in terms patently offensive as measured by contemporary community standards, sexual or excretory activities or organs," § 223(d). Given the absence of a definition of either term, this difference in language will provoke uncertainty among speakers about how the two standards relate to each other and just what they mean. Could a speaker confidently assume that a serious discussion about birth control practices, homosexuality, the First Amendment issues raised by the Appendix to our *Pacifica* opinion, or the consequences of prison rape would not violate the CDA? This uncertainty undermines the likelihood that the CDA has been carefully tailored to the congressional goal of protecting minors from potentially harmful materials.

The vagueness of the CDA is a matter of special concern for two reasons. First, the CDA is a content-based regulation of speech. The vagueness of such a regulation raises special First Amendment concerns because of its obvious chilling effect on free speech. ...Second, the CDA is a criminal statute. In addition to the opprobrium and stigma of a criminal conviction, the CDA threatens violators with penalties including up to two years in prison for each act of violation. The severity of criminal sanctions may well cause speakers to remain silent rather than communicate even arguably unlawful words, ideas, and images....

· · ·

VII

We are persuaded that the CDA lacks the precision that the First Amendment requires when a statute regulates the content of speech. In order to deny minors access to potentially harmful speech, the CDA effectively suppresses a large amount of speech that adults have a constitutional right to receive and to address to one another. That burden on adult speech is unacceptable if less restrictive alternatives would be at least as effective in achieving the legitimate purpose that the statute was enacted to serve.

· · ·

X

[*In this section the Court declines the government's invitation for the Court to sever from the CDA the words or phrases that the Court finds unconstitutional. Drawing on language from an earlier decision, it says that it "will not rewrite a ... law to conform it to constitutional requirements."*]

XI

In this Court, though not in the District Court, the Government asserts that—in addition to its interest in protecting children—its "[e]qually significant" interest in fostering the growth of the Internet provides an independent basis for upholding the constitutionality of the CDA....The Government apparently assumes that the unregulated availability of "indecent" and "patently offensive" material on the Internet is driving countless citizens away from the medium because of the risk of exposing themselves or their children to harmful material.

We find this argument singularly unpersuasive. The drastic expansion of this new marketplace of ideas contradicts the factual basis of this contention....

For the foregoing reasons, the judgment of the district court is affirmed.

It is so ordered.

JUSTICE O'CONNOR with whom THE CHIEF JUSTICE joins, concurring in the judgment in part and dissenting in part.

[*They agree with the Court that the "display" provision cannot pass muster but conclude that the "indecency transmission" and "specific person" provisions would not be unconstitutional in all of their applications. They would sustain those provisions "to the extent they apply to the transmission of Internet communications where the party initiating the communication knows that all of the recipients are minors."*]

CONCLUSIONS

The concept of "free speech" emerged from political developments in America and the needs of self-government and self-development. From the laconic formulation in the First Amendment, the right of free speech has become more specialized and complex, expanding to include such twentieth-century technology as broadcasting rights. Various tests have been fashioned to draw a line between liberty and licentiousness, none with much success. There is general agreement on giving broad scope to pure advocacy of ideas, even if threatening to government, and applying restrictions only when advocacy takes the form of action and conduct. For the most part, pure speech—even "fighting words"—is tolerated as part of the process of peaceful political change.

Debates on free speech frequently concentrate on the meaning of judicial rulings, but the real safeguards for free speech lie in the attitudes of the general public. As Chafee wrote: "The victories of liberty of speech must be won in the mind before they are won in the courts." Zechariah Chafee, Jr., Free Speech in the United States 325 (1941). Through his writings he "often stressed the fact that the ultimate security for free and fruitful discussion lies in the tolerance of private citizens." Id. at x.

Other dimensions of the First Amendment are examined in the next chapter: the right of a free press, the natural tensions between a free press and a fair trial, and the bedeviled areas of libel and obscenity.

SELECTED READINGS

ANASTAPLO, GEORGE. The Constitutionalist: Notes on the First Amendment. Dallas, Tex.: Southern Methodist University Press, 1971.

BARRON, JEROME A., AND C. THOMAS DIENES. Handbook of Free Speech and Free Press. Boston: Little, Brown, 1979.

BERNS, WALTER. Freedom, Virtue, & the First Amendment. Baton Rouge: Louisiana State University Press, 1957.

——— The First Amendment and the Future of American Democracy. Chicago: Gateway Editions, 1985.

BORK, ROBERT H. "Neutral Principles and Some First Amendment Problems." 47 Indiana Law Journal 1 (1971).

BRENNAN, WILLIAM J., JR. "The Supreme Court and the Meiklejohn Interpretation of the First Amendment." 79 Harvard Law Review 1 (1965).

CAHN, EDMUND. "Mr. Justice Black and First Amendment Absolutes: A Public Interview." 37 New York University Law Review 549 (1962).

CHAFEE, ZECHARIAH, JR. "Freedom of Speech in War Time." 32 Harvard Law Review 932 (1919).

———. Free Speech in the United States. Cambridge, Mass.: Harvard University Press, 1941.

COOPER, PHILLIP J. "The Supreme Court, the First Amendment, and Freedom of Information." 46 Public Administration Review 622 (Nov./Dec. 1986).

DORSEN, NORMAN, AND JOEL GORA. "Free Speech, Property, and the Burger Court: Old Values, New Balances." 1982 Supreme Court Review 195.

EMERSON, THOMAS I. The System of Freedom of Expression. New York: Random House, 1970.

———. "First Amendment Doctrine and the Burger Court," 68 California Law Review 422 (1980).

FELLMAN, DAVID. The Constitutional Right of Association. Chicago: University of Chicago Press, 1963.

FISS, OWEN M. The Irony of Free Speech. Cambridge, Mass.: Harvard University Press, 1996.

FRIENDLY, FRED W. The Good Guys, the Bad Guys, and the First Amendment: Free Speech vs. Fairness in Broadcasting. New York: Random House, 1975.

GREENEWALT, KENT. Fighting Words: Individuals, Communities, and Liberties of Speech. Princeton: Princeton University Press, 1995.

HAIMAN, FRANKLYN S. Speech and Law in a Free Society. Chicago: University of Chicago Press, 1981.

HENTOFF, NAT. Free Speech for Me — But Not for Thee. New York: HarperCollins, 1992.

KALVEN, HARRY, JR. "The Concept of the Public Forum: Cox v. Louisiana." 1965 Supreme Court Review 1.

MEIKLEJOHN, ALEXANDER. "The First Amendment Is an Absolute." 1961 Supreme Court Review 245.

———. Political Freedom: The Constitutional Powers of the People. New York: Oxford University Press, 1965.

MENDELSON, WALLACE. "Clear and Present Danger — From Schenck to Dennis." 52 Columbia Law Review 313 (1952).

MURPHY, PAUL L. The Meaning of Freedom of Speech. Westport, Conn.: Greenwood Publishing, 1972.

O'BRIEN, DAVID M. The Public's Right to Know: The Supreme Court and the First Amendment. New York: Praeger, 1981.

RABBAN, DAVID M. Free Speech in Its Forgotten Years. New York: Cambridge University Press, 1997.

SCHIRO, RICHARD. "Commercial Speech: The Demise of a Chimera." 1976 Supreme Court Review 45.

SHAPIRO, MARTIN. Freedom of Speech: The Supreme Court and Judicial Review. Englewood Cliffs, N.J.: Prentice-Hall, 1966.

SMOLLA, RODNEY A. Free Speech in an Open Society. New York: Alfred A. Knopf, 1992.

11

Freedom of the Press

The Supreme Court generally treats free speech and free press as complementary parts of a larger value designed to promote "freedom of expression." At times, it even demotes freedom of the press, making it a subordinate right derived from freedom of speech. Such formulations distort the historical record. The right to a free press has stronger roots than the right to free speech. Of the eleven original states that adopted revolutionary constitutions, nine protected freedom of press and only one (Pennsylvania) protected speech.

Freedom of the press implies two rights: the right to publish without prior restraint, and the right to publish without prosecution or penalty for the views advanced. The first right is nearly inviolable. A heavy presumption lies against any governmental effort to restrain a publication. The second right is more circumscribed, permitting action against publishers who print materials considered libelous or obscene. A separate issue involves the collision that occurs between the sometimes competing interests of a free press and a fair trial.

A. THE EVOLUTION OF PRESS FREEDOMS

Many of the battles for individual liberty from the sixteenth to the eighteenth centuries in England centered around the struggle for a free press. Government officials and church authorities tried to suppress writings that threatened their control. Both prosecutions and persecutions were used to silence critics and free thinkers. Authors were punished for views considered to be seditious or heretical. In time, a system of censorship developed to prevent such writings from being published. One of the early protests against censorship and prior restraint came from the pen of the poet John Milton, especially *AREOPAGITICA* (1644).

English law eventually prohibited prior restraint on publications. As explained by William Blackstone, the liberty of the press "consists in laying no *previous* restraints upon publications, and not in freedom from censure for criminal matter when published." The right to publish was protected, but if an individual published material found to be "improper, mischievous or illegal, he must take the consequence of his own temerity." 4 Blackstone, Commentaries *151–52. These categories encourage the publication only of innocuous material. English law also permitted the government to punish whoever published "seditious libel," another vague realm that invites action against whoever offends or annoys the government.

Zenger's Trial

The trial of John Peter Zenger in 1735 represents a watershed in the fight for a free press in America. William Cosby, New York's royal governor, became embroiled in a local power struggle. The *New-York Weekly Journal* was established to oppose the royal newspaper, the *New-York Gazette*. Zenger, serving as the printer for the opposition newspaper, helped run the first independent journal in America. A series of articles in the *New-York Weekly Journal* promoted the theory of a free press and attacked the Cosby administration.

Cosby placed Zenger in prison for seditious libel. However, a grand jury decided against

Andrew Hamilton's Appeal to the Jury

... Gentlemen of the Jury, it is to you we must now appeal, for Witness, to the Truth of the Facts we have offered, and are denied the Liberty to prove; ...

... I beg Leave to insist, that the Right of complaining or remonstrating is natural; And the Restraint upon this natural Right is the law only, and that those Restraints can only extend to what is *false*; For as it is Truth alone which can excuse or justify any Man for complaining of a bad Administration, I as frankly agree, that nothing ought to excuse a man who raises a false Charge or Accusation, even against a private Person, and that no manner of Allowance ought to be made to him who does so against a publick Magistrate. *Truth* ought to govern the whole Affair of Libels, ...

I am truely very unequal to such an Undertaking on many Accounts. And you see I labour under the Weight of many Years, and am born down with great Infirmities of Body; yet Old and Weak as I am, I should think of it my Duty, if required, to go to the utmost Part of the Land, where my Service could be of any Use in assisting to quench the Flame of Prosecutions upon Informations, set on Foot by the Government, to deprive a People of the Right of Remonstrating (and complaining too) of the arbitrary Attempts of Men in Power. Men who injure and oppress the People under the Administration provoke them to cry out and complain; and then make that very Complaint the Foundation for new Oppressions and Prosecutions. I wish I could say there were no Instances of this Kind. But to conclude; the Question before the Court and you, Gentlemen of the Jury, is not of small nor private Concern, it is not the Cause of a poor Printer, nor of *New-York* alone, which you are now trying: No! It may in its Consequence, affect every Freeman that lives under a British Government on the main of *America*. It is the best Cause. It is the Cause of Liberty; and I make no Doubt but your upright Conduct, this Day, will not only entitle you to the Love and Esteem of your Fellow-Citizens; but every Man who prefers Freedom to a Life of Slavery will bless and honour You, as Men who have baffled the Attempt of Tyranny; and by an impartial and uncorrupt Verdict, have laid a noble Foundation for securing to ourselves, our Posterity, and our Neighbours, That, to which Nature and the Laws of our Country have given us a Right—The Liberty—both of exposing and opposing arbitrary Power (in these Parts of the World, at least) by speaking and writing Truth.

SOURCE: Leonard W. Levy, ed., Freedom of the Press from Zenger to Jefferson 48, 54, 58–59 (1996).

indicting Zenger, and the New York Assembly refused to carry out the request of Cosby's Council that several issues of the *New-York Weekly Journal* be burned. In 1735 Zenger was again imprisoned for seditious libel. Another grand jury rejected indictment. The New York attorney general relied on an information, as an alternative to grand jury action, to charge Zenger for publishing "false, scandalous, malicious, and seditious" libels. Andrew Hamilton, a famous trial attorney in America, argued that Zenger's newspapers had not published "false" material. He said that Zenger had published the truth and had the right to do so. The trial judge advised Hamilton that truth was not a defense under the law; the material was libel even if true. Hamilton appealed to the jury to uphold the cause of liberty and a free press (see box). The jury returned a verdict of not guilty. Although the law had not changed, the jury action planted a seed to make truth a defense in a libel case. The threat of seditious libel virtually disappeared in America after Zenger's trial.

The Framers' Intent

Except for brief periods in our history, America has placed a high value on the importance of a free press. Leonard Levy, a leading scholar of the First Amendment, wrote an influential work in 1960 in which he challenged the prevailing belief that the framers were deeply committed to press freedoms. In *Legacy of Suppression,* he made three major points: the First Amendment was not intended to prevent the state from suppressing seditious libel; American legislatures, especially during the colonial period, were "far more oppressive" than common-law courts; and the Bill of Rights was more the "chance product of political expediency" than a principled commitment to personal liberties. Moreover, Levy concluded that the Jeffersonians, strident critics of the Sedition Act of 1798, were not much more tolerant of political dissent than the Federalists had been.

In a revision of this work in 1985, entitled *Emergence of a Free Press,* Levy examined new evidence and concluded that the American experience with a free press was broad in scope. "Press criticism of government policies and politicians, on both state and national levels, during the war [of Independence] and in the peaceful years of the 1780s and 1790s, raged as contemptuously and scorchingly as it had against Great Britain in the period between the Stamp Act and the battle of Lexington." The presses in the states operated "as if the law of seditious libel did not exist." He explained that if one examines American *practices* rather than American law and theory, there exists not a legacy of suppression but rather a "legacy of liberty" (p. x).

The Sedition Act

A period of suppression certainly includes the Sedition Act of 1798, which provided penalties for writing, printing, uttering, or publishing "false, scandalous and malicious" statements against the federal government, either House of Congress, or the President. 1 Stat. 596, § 2. Still, the principle from the Zenger trial prevailed. Any person prosecuted under the act had the right to "give in evidence in his defence, the truth of the matter contained in the publication charged as a libel." Moreover, the jury had the right to "determine the law and the fact." Id., § 3. The debate on the Sedition Act demonstrates that the principle of a free press was strongly held at that time (see reading). The statute was so unpopular that it fatally wounded its sponsor, the Federalist party, and expired under its own terms in 1801.

The constitutionality of the Sedition Act was never determined in the courts. Instead, it was decided by the people in the national elections of 1800, which drove the Federalist party out of office and into oblivion. President Jefferson called the Sedition Act a "nullity" and pardoned every person prosecuted under it (see box on page 24 of Chapter 1). He believed that prosecution for seditious libel could be done only by the states, not the federal government. Later, Congress pronounced the statute "unconstitutional, null, and void," and appropriated funds to reimburse those who had been subjected to fines (see reading on pages 25–26 of Chapter 1). The Supreme Court later acknowledged that the Sedition Act was struck down not by a court of law but by "the court of history." New York Times Co. v. Sullivan, 376 U.S. 254, 276 (1964).

John Milton
Areopagitica (1644)

In this classic defense of a free press, Milton appeals to the Parliament of England to reject licenses for printing. He had learned of an order that would prohibit the printing of any book, pamphlet, or paper unless first approved and licensed. His essay is one of the most compelling arguments against using prior restraint to suppress written materials.

If ye be thus resolved, as it were injury to think ye were not, I know not what should withhold me from presenting ye with a fit instance wherein to show both that love of truth which ye eminently profess, and that uprightness of your judgment which is not wont to be partial to yourselves; by judging over again that order which ye have ordained *to regulate printing: that no book, pam-*

phlet, or paper shall be henceforth printed, unless the same be first approved and licensed by such, or at least one of such, as shall be thereto appointed. For that part which preserves justly every man's copy to himself, or provides for the poor, I touch not; only wish they be not made pretences to abuse and persecute honest and painful men who offend not in either of these particulars. But that other clause of licensing books, which we thought had died with his brother *quadragesimal* and *matrimonial* when the prelates expired, I shall now attend with such a homily as shall lay before ye, first, the inventors of it to be those whom ye will be loth to own; next, what is to be thought in general of reading; whatever sort the books be; and that this order avails nothing to the suppressing of scandalous, seditious, and libelous books, which were mainly intended to be suppressed; last, that it will be primely to the discouragement of all learning, and the stop of truth, not only by disexercising and blunting our abilities in what we know already, but by hindering and cropping the discovery that might be yet further made both in religious and civil wisdom.

I deny not but that it is of greatest concernment in the church and commonwealth to have a vigilant eye how books demean themselves, as well as men, and thereafter to confine, imprison, and do sharpest justice on them as malefactors. For books are not absolutely dead things, but do contain a potency of life in them to be as active as that soul was whose progeny they are; nay, they do preserve as in a vial the purest efficacy and extraction of that living intellect that bred them. I know they are as lively, and as vigorously productive, as those fabulous dragon's teeth; and being sown up and down, may chance to spring up armed men. And yet, on the other hand, unless wariness be used, as good almost kill a man as kill a good book: who kills a man kills a reasonable creature, God's image; but he who destroys a good book, kills reason itself, kills the image of God, as it were, in the eye. Many a man lives a burden to the earth; but a good book is the precious life-blood of a master spirit, embalmed and treasured up on purpose to a life beyond life....

. . .

...If we think to regulate printing, thereby to rectify manners, we must regulate all recreations and pastimes, all that is delightful to man. No music must be heard, no song be set or sung, but what is grave and Doric. There must be licensing dancers, that no gesture, motion, or deportment be taught our youth, but what by their allowance shall be thought honest; for such Plato was provided of. It will ask more than the work of twenty licensers to examine all the lutes, the violins, and the guitars in every house; they must not be suffered to prattle as they do, but must be licensed what they may say. And who shall silence all the airs and madrigals that whisper softness in chambers?...

Next, what more national corruption, for which England hears ill abroad, than household gluttony? Who shall be the rectors of our daily rioting? And what shall be done to inhibit the multitudes that frequent those houses where drunkenness is sold and harbored? Our garments also should be referred to the licensing of some more sober workmasters, to see them cut into a less wanton garb. Who shall regulate all the mixed conversation of our youth, male and female together, as is the fashion of this country?...

. . .

What should ye do then, should ye suppress all this flowery crop of knowledge and new light sprung up and yet springing daily in this city? Should ye set an oligarchy of twenty engrossers over it, to bring a famine upon our minds again, when we shall know nothing but what is measured to us by their bushel? Believe it, Lords and Commons, they who counsel ye to such a suppressing do as good as bid ye suppress yourselves; and I will soon show how. If it be desired to know the immediate cause of all this free writing and free speaking, there cannot be assigned a truer than your own mild and free and humane government; it is the liberty, Lords and Commons, which your own valorous and happy counsels have purchased us, liberty which is the nurse of all great wits. This is that which hath rarefied and enlightened our spirits like the influence of heaven; this is that which hath enfranchised, enlarged, and lifted up our apprehensions degrees above themselves. Ye cannot make us now less capable, less knowing, less eagerly pursuing of the truth, unless ye first make yourselves, that made us so, less the lovers, less the founders of our true liberty. We can grow ignorant again, brutish, formal, and slavish, as ye found us; but you then must first become that which ye cannot be, oppressive, arbitrary, and tyrannous, as they were from whom ye have freed us....

House Debate on the Sedition Act of 1798

When John Adams was elected President in 1796, there was concern that the United States might be drawn into war against France. To control foreigners in this country and a press that lashed out against the administration's policy, Congress passed the Alien and Sedition Acts of 1798. The Sedition Act declared that if any person "shall write, print, utter or publish...any false, scandalous and malicious writing or writings against the government of the United States, or either house of the Congress of the United States, or the President of the United States, with intent to defame the said government, or either house of the said Congress, or the said President, or to bring them, or either of them, into contempt or disrepute; or to excite against them, or either of them, the hatred of the good people of the United States, or to stir up sedition," the person would be subject to fines and imprisonment. The debate below, from the House of Representatives, is taken from 8 Annals of Congress 2093–94, 2097, 2105, 2109, 2139–40, 2147–48, 2152, 2164. Jeffersonian Republicans are identified as Democrats. The bill passed the House, 44 to 41.

[MR. ALLEN, Federalist of Connecticut]—I hope this bill will not be rejected. If ever there was a nation which required a law of this kind, it is this. Let gentlemen look at certain papers printed in this city and elsewhere, and ask themselves whether an unwarrantable and dangerous combination does not exist to overturn and ruin the Government by publishing the most shameless falsehoods against the Representatives of the people of all denominations, that they are hostile to free Governments and genuine liberty, and of course to the welfare of this country; that they ought, therefore, to be displaced, and that the people ought to raise an *insurrection* against the Government.

...Permit me to read a paragraph from "The Time-Piece," a paper printed in New York:

"When such a character attempts by antiquated and exploded sophistry, by Jesuitical arguments, to extinguish the sentiment of liberty, 'tis fit the mask should be torn off from this meaner species of aristocracy than history has condescended to record; where a person without patriotism, without philosophy, without a taste for the fine arts, building his pretensions on a gross and indigested compilation of statutes and precedents, is jostled into the Chief Magistracy by the ominous combination of old Tories with old opinions, and old Whigs with new, 'tis fit this mock Monarch, with his Court, composed of Tories and speculators,..."

Gentlemen contend for the liberty of opinions and of the press. Let me ask them whether they seriously think the liberty of the press authorizes such publications? The President of the United States is here called "a person without patriotism, without philosophy, and a mock monarch," and the free election of the people is pronounced "a jostling him into the Chief Magistracy by the ominous combination of old Tories with old opinions, and old Whigs with new."

If this be not a conspiracy against Government and people, I know not what to understand from *[such writing]*...The freedom of the press and opinions was never understood to give the right of publishing falsehoods and slanders, nor of exciting sedition, insurrection, and slaughter, with impunity. A man was always answerable for the malicious publication of falsehood; and what more does this bill require?

. . .

[EDWARD LIVINGSTON, Democrat from New York.]...The gentleman...has said, that provided the law is clear and well defined, and the trial by jury is preserved, he knew of no law which could infringe the liberty of the press. If this be true, Congress might restrict all printing at once. We have, said he, nothing to do but to make the law precise, and then we may forbid a newspaper to be printed, and make it death for any man to attempt it!

If this be the extent to which this bill goes, it is...an abridgment of the liberty of the press, which the Constitution has said shall not be abridged....

[ALBERT GALLATIN, Democrat from Pennsylvania.] Was the gentleman afraid, or rather was Administration afraid, that in this instance error could not be successfully opposed by truth? The

American Government had heretofore subsisted, it had acquired strength, it had grown on the affection of the people, it had been fully supported without the assistance of laws similar to the bill now on the table. It had been able to repel opposition by the single weapon of argument. And at present, when out of ten presses in the country nine were employed on the side of Administration, such is their want of confidence in the purity of their own views and motives, that they even fear the unequal contest, and require the help of force in order to suppress the limited circulation of the opinions of those who did not approve all their measures.

. . .

[JOHN NICHOLAS, Democrat from Virginia] rose, he said, to ask an explanation of the principles upon which this bill is founded. He confessed it was strongly impressed upon his mind, that it was not within the powers of the House to act upon this subject. He looked in vain amongst the enumerated powers given to Congress in the Constitution, for an authority to pass a law like the present; but he found what he considered as an express prohibition against passing it. . . .

Gentlemen have said that this bill is not to restrict the liberty of the press but its licentiousness. He wished gentlemen to inform him where they drew the line between this liberty and licentiousness of which they speak; he wished to know where the one commenced and the other ended? Will they say the one is truth, and the other falsehood! Gentlemen cannot believe for a moment that such a definition will satisfy the inquiry. The great difficulty which has existed in all free Governments, would, long since, have been done away, if it could have been effected by a simple declaration of this kind. It has been the object of all regulations with respect to the press, to destroy the only means by which the people can examine and become acquainted with the conduct of persons employed in their Government. . . .

. . .

[HARRISON GRAY OTIS, Federalist from Massachusetts.] It was, therefore, most evident to his mind, that the Constitution of the United States,

prior to the amendments that have been added to it, secured to the National Government the cognizance of all the crimes enumerated in the bill, and it only remained to be considered whether those amendments divested it of this power. The amendment quoted by the gentleman from Virginia is in these words: "Congress shall make no law abridging the freedom of speech and of the press." The terms "freedom of speech and of the press," he supposed, were a phraseology perfectly familiar in the jurisprudence of every State, and of a certain and technical meaning. It was a mode of expression which we had borrowed from the only country in which it had been tolerated, and he pledged himself to prove that the construction which he should give to those terms, should be consonant not only to the laws of that country, but to the laws and judicial decisions of many of the States composing the Union. . . . although in several of the State constitutions, the liberty of speech and of the press were guarded by the most express and unequivocal language, the Legislatures and Judicial departments of those States had adopted the definitions of the English law, and provided for the punishment of defamatory and seditious libels. . . .

. . .

After having given this short sketch of the features of this bill, Mr. *[Gallatin]* said . . . that laws against writings of this kind had uniformly been one of the most powerful engines used by tyrants to prevent the diffusion of knowledge, to throw a veil on their folly or their crimes, to satisfy those mean passions which always denote little minds, and to perpetuate their own tyranny. The principles of the law of political libels were to be found in the rescripts of the worst Emperors of Rome, in the decisions of the Star Chamber. Princes of elevated minds, Governments actuated by pure motives, had ever despised the slanders of malice, and listened to the animadversions made on their conduct. They knew that the proper weapon to combat error was truth, and that to resort to coercion and punishments in order to suppress writings attacking their measures, was to confess that these could not be defended by any other means.

. . .

B. REGULATING THE PRESS

Like other First Amendment freedoms, the press is subject to regulations. Initially, state actions that abridged the press were not subject to redress in the federal courts. Those matters were left to state and local judgments. Patterson v. Colorado, 205 U.S. 454 (1907); Fox v. Washington, 236 U.S. 273 (1915). In 1931, however, the Court held that a free press is within the liberty safeguarded by the Due Process Clause of the Fourteenth Amendment. The case involved Minnesota's effort to suppress the "malicious, scandalous and defamatory" articles of Jay Near, an indefatigable critic of corruption in the Minneapolis government. The effect of the state law, said the Court, was to put a publisher under censorship. Except for certain conditions that did not apply in this case, the government could not impose censorship or prior restraint on newspapers and other publications. NEAR v. MINNESOTA, 283 U.S. 697 (1931).

Following this decision, the Court identified a number of unconstitutional regulations on the press. Although publications can be taxed like any other business, taxes may not be applied to discriminate against newspapers, limit their circulation, or subject publications to penalties that amount to previous restraint. Grosjean v. American Press Co., 297 U.S. 233 (1936). The Court has struck down tax systems that pose the risk of discrimination or suppression. Arkansas Writers' Project, Inc. v. Ragland, 481 U.S. 221 (1987); Minneapolis Star v. Minnesota Comm'r of Rev., 460 U.S. 575 (1983). Although states may not single out the press and apply discriminatory taxes, it may tax cable television operations while exempting newspapers and magazines provided there is no intent to censor the expressive activities of cable TV. Thus, some media may be taxed differently from others. Leathers v. Medlock, 499 U.S. 439 (1991).

In 1991, a unanimous court struck down a New York law designed to prevent criminals from profiting from books and movies about their illegal actions. Payments criminals received for books or other works would be placed in a fund to compensate victims of crimes. In this case, New York's "Son of Sam" law was applied to a book called *Wiseguy,* which described the activities of a Mafia foot soldier. The book was later turned into the hit movie, *GoodFellas.* The Court held that the law was "significantly overinclusive" and would have prevented the publication of such works as Thoreau's *Civil Disobedience* and Saint Augustine's *Confessions,* both of which described the author's illegal actions. Simon & Schuster v. New York Crime Victims Bd., 502 U.S. 105 (1991).

Government cannot require licenses to distribute literature; this is a form of censorship. Pamphlets and leaflets have been "historic weapons in the defense of liberty." Lovell v. Griffin, 303 U.S. 444, 452 (1938). Government may not require people to print their name and address on a handbill. Anonymity is often necessary for the communication of ideas, as witnessed by the fictitious names of those who wrote the *Federalist Papers.* Talley v. California, 362 U.S. 60, 65 (1960). The principle in *Talley* was reiterated by the Court in 1995 when it said that anonymous pamphleteering "is a shield from the tyranny of the majority." McIntyre v. Ohio Elections Comm'n, 514 U.S. 334, 357 (1995).

It is unconstitutional to ban the distribution of handbills by arguing that their prohibition prevents littering of the streets. The purpose of keeping the streets clean "is insufficient to justify an ordinance which prohibits a person rightfully on a public street from handing literature to one willing to receive it. Any burden imposed upon the city authorities in cleaning and caring for the streets as an indirect consequence of such distribution results from the constitutional protection of the freedom of speech and press." Schneider v. State, 308 U.S. 147, 162 (1939). See also Jamison v. Texas, 318 U.S. 413 (1943). The distribution of informational literature is an essential part of a free press and a democratic society. Organization for a Better Austin v. Keefe, 402 U.S. 415 (1971). (See box on next page for other decisions regulating the press.)

Legislatures retain some latitude in regulating the content of newspapers. In 1973 the Court upheld a Pittsburgh ordinance that prohibited newspapers from printing ads that listed job

Regulating the Press

Acceptable regulations

Government may punish those who call at a home, for the purpose of distributing literature, when the occupant posts an unwillingness to be disturbed. Martin v. Struthers, 319 U.S. 141 (1943).

Uninvited door-to-door canvassing by a publisher's representative can be proscribed as an invasion of privacy. Breard v. Alexandria, 341 U.S. 622 (1951).

Publishers are not exempt from agency subpoena powers. Okla. Press Pub. Co. v. Walling, 327 U.S. 186 (1946).

Prison officials may prohibit interviews between prison inmates and reporters who attempt to investigate and publicize prison conditions. Houchins v. KQED, Inc., 438 U.S. 1 (1978); Saxbe v. Washington Post, 417 U.S. 843 (1974); Pell v. Procunier, 417 U.S. 817 (1974).

Invalid regulations

Although Congress may exclude certain materials from the mails, the Postmaster General cannot act as a censor by deciding which items are mailable and which are not. Hannegan v. Esquire, Inc., 327 U.S. 146 (1946).

Laws may not prohibit the distribution of magazines on such vague grounds that they consist of bloody and lustful criminal deeds. Winters v. New York, 333 U.S. 507 (1948).

Statutes on "corrupt practices" (prohibiting electioneering or soliciting of votes on election day) cannot be applied against newspapers that publish views on election day. Mills v. Alabama, 384 U.S. 214 (1966).

Public officials may not be given "unbridled discretion" in granting or denying applications from newspapers to place newsracks on public property. Lakewood, City of, v. Plain Dealer Pub. Co., 486 U.S. 750 (1988).

---

opportunities under headings of "Male Interest" and "Female Interest." Such labels perpetuated sex discrimination and unequal pay. Pittsburgh Press Co. v. Human Rel. Comm'n, 413 U.S. 376 (1973). Advertisements in newspapers can be regulated because they are "classic examples of commercial speech." Id. at 385. The Court said it had "no doubt that a newspaper constitutionally could be forbidden to publish a want ad proposing a sale of narcotics or soliciting prostitutes." Id. at 388.

A unique case arose in 1997, in which a publisher was held liable in a civil suit for publishing a hit-man manual. The publisher, Paladin Press, acknowledged that it realized that its book, *Hit Man: A Technical Manual for Independent Contractors,* would be used by criminals and would-be criminals in the solicitation, planning, and commission of murder and murder for hire. A contract killer relied on the 130-page manual to kill someone's wife, eight-year-old child, and the child's nurse. The First Amendment did not bar a wrongful death action against Paladin. Rice v. Paladin Enterprises Inc., 128 F.3d 233 (4th Cir. 1997), cert. denied, 523 U.S. 1074 (1998). On March 21, 1999, Paladin Press agreed to a multi-million dollar settlement.

Regulating News Coverage

Regulation of newspaper advertisements does not permit regulation of news coverage. A unanimous Court in 1974 held that government may not compel a newspaper to print a response from a political candidate to a critical editorial. Although "access advocates" argued that chain newspapers and nationwide wire services no longer provided a true marketplace of diverse opinions, the Court refused to permit the government to dictate to the press the contents of its news stories and editorials. Miami Herald Publishing Co. v. Tornillo, 418 U.S. 241 (1974). Another unanimous opinion in 1978 struck down a Virginia statute that made it a crime to divulge information regarding proceedings before a state judicial review commission that received complaints about judges' disability or misconduct. The Court held that the First

Amendment does not permit the criminal punishment of third persons (in this case the press), who were strangers to the proceedings, from publishing truthful information. Landmark Communications, Inc. v. Virginia, 435 U.S. 829 (1978). Building on *Landmark Communications,* the Court in 1990 unanimously struck down a Florida law that prohibited witnesses before a state grand jury from ever disclosing their testimony in any manner. A reporter wanted to do a story based in part on his testimony before a grand jury. The Court held that the state law violated the First Amendment to the extent that it prohibited grand jury witnesses from disclosing their testimony after the grand jury's term had ended. Butterworth v. Smith, 494 U.S. 624 (1990).

In 1989, the Court reversed a ruling that imposed compensatory and punitive damages against a newspaper that printed the name of a rape victim. Although the publication violated a state law, the woman's full name had appeared in a police report available to the press. The Florida Star v. B.J.F. 491 U.S. 524 (1989). Similarly, a newspaper is free to publish a rape victim's name that was obtained from judicial records open to public inspection. Cox Broadcasting Co. v. Cohn, 420 U.S. 469 (1975). If an individual gives a newspaper information after receiving a promise of confidentiality and the newspaper later identifies the individual, the First Amendment does not prevent the person from suing the newspaper for damages on the ground that a promise had been breached. Cohen v. Cowles Media Co., 501 U.S. 663 (1991).

The interests of a free press suffered a major setback in 1978 when the Court decided that law enforcement officials could obtain a warrant and come onto the premises of a newspaper to conduct a search for evidence regarding another party. Zurcher v. Stanford Daily, 436 U.S. 547 (1978). After the press appealed to Congress for help, legislation was enacted in 1980 to direct police to use subpoenas as a less intrusive method of obtaining documents. The congressional response is described in greater detail in Chapter 14 (pages 771, 772–73).

National Security

In 1931, in striking down Minnesota's law as a prior restraint on the press, the Court noted that censorship would be constitutional under certain conditions. "No one would question but that a government might prevent actual obstruction to its recruiting service or the publication of the sailing dates of transports or the number and location of troops." Near v. Minnesota, 283 U.S. at 716. The Nixon administration thought this type of critical need had arrived when it sought an injunction to prevent the publication of a classified study entitled "History of U.S. Decision-Making Process on Viet Nam Policy." The administration argued that publication of these materials (the "Pentagon Papers") would be injurious to national security. However, the Supreme Court, with a 6–3 majority in *New York Times Co. v. United States* (1971), held that the administration had failed to meet the "heavy burden" of justifying prior restraint on a publication. A brief per curiam opinion preceded a collection of concurrences and dissents. (The decision is reprinted in Chapter 7.)

Several years later, the Carter administration attempted to prevent the publication in *The Progressive* magazine of an article that claimed to describe the design of an H-bomb. A federal district court judge issued a preliminary injunction against the publication, recognizing that this was the first instance of prior restraint to his knowledge. Balanced against a free press was this consideration: "A mistake against the United States could pave the way for thermonuclear annihilation for us all. In that event, our right to life is extinguished and the right to publish becomes moot." United States v. Progressive, 467 F.Supp. 990, 996 (W.D. Wis. 1979). As it turned out, essentially the same material appeared in another publication, without a nuclear holocaust, and the case was dismissed. 610 F.2d 819 (7th Cir. 1979); Morland v. Sprecher, 443 U.S. 709 (1979). *The Progressive* published the article in its November 1979 issue.

Questions of press and national security are at issue when the CIA and other federal agen-

---

Shield Law

Newspaper, radio or television broadcasting station personnel need not disclose source of information.—No person shall be compelled to disclose in any legal proceeding or trial before any court, or before any grand or petit jury, or before the presiding officer of any tribunal, or his agent or agents, or before the general assembly, or any committee thereof, or before any city or county legislative body, or any committee thereof, or elsewhere, the source of any information procured or obtained by him, and published in a newspaper or by a radio or television broadcasting station by which he is engaged or employed, or with which he is connected.

SOURCE: Kentucky Revised Statutes, Annotated, § 421.100 (1992). (1649d-1: amend. Acts 1952, ch. 121.)

---

cies require employees, as a condition of employment, to sign a statement agreeing not to publish anything relating to the agency without first submitting the manuscript and obtaining approval. This condition applies both during and after employment. Frank Snepp, a former CIA employee, published a critical evaluation of the agency without first seeking approval. Although the book contained no classified information, the Supreme Court affirmed a lower court's injunction on future writings by Snepp, requiring that he submit manuscripts to the CIA. Snepp was also ordered to give the government his earnings from the book (*Decent Interval*) he published without CIA's clearance. Snepp v. United States, 444 U.S. 507 (1980).[1]

Reporter's Privilege

A landmark ruling in 1972 involved the question of whether newspaper reporters can be compelled to respond to a grand jury subpoena and answer questions. Reporters argue that their sources are privileged and cannot be revealed without destroying their access to informers who demand anonymity. They also express concern that the forced disclosure of information to grand juries will make them appear to be agents of government. However, a 5–4 Court decided that the need to investigate and prosecute criminal charges overrides a reporter's rights, including the protection of confidential sources. BRANZBURG v. HAYES, 408 U.S. 665 (1972). Some of the states already had "shield laws" to protect reporters from court orders. Other state laws protecting reporters were added after *Branzburg*. As of 2000, thirty-one states and the District of Columbia have such laws (see box). The Supreme Court conceded that Congress has the power to enact similar legislation. Id. at 706.

Free-press conflicts are not always between the government and a publisher. At times, they involve one publisher against another, with the issue decided largely on statutory, not constitutional, grounds. In one case, President Gerald Ford signed a contract with Harper & Row to publish his memoirs. Harper & Row then negotiated a prepublication agreement with *Time* magazine to print parts of the manuscript. Shortly before the scheduled release of *Time*'s article, there appeared an unauthorized article in *The Nation* magazine, including at least 300 to 400 words verbatim from the unpublished Ford manuscript. In interpreting the Copyright Act passed by Congress, the Supreme Court held that *The Nation*'s article was not a "fair use" sanctioned by the statute. Harper & Row v. Nation Enterprises, 471 U.S. 539 (1985).

---

1. See also United States v. Marchetti, 466 F.2d 1309 (4th Cir. 1972), cert. denied, 409 U.S. 1063 (1972); Knopf v. Colby, 509 F.2d 1362 (4th Cir. 1975), cert. denied, 421 U.S. 992 (1975).

Near v. Minnesota

283 U.S. 697 (1931)

A Minnesota law provided that anyone engaged in the business of publishing "a malicious, scandalous and defamatory newspaper, magazine, or other periodical" was guilty of a nuisance and subject to a suit by the state. The periodicals could be abated and their publishers enjoined from future violations. The punishment of contempt was available for disobeying an injunction. The state prosecuted Jay Near for publishing the *Saturday Press*, a hardhitting newspaper that focused largely on corruption and racketeering in Minneapolis. Many of his attacks were directed at the mayor and police chief.

MR. CHIEF JUSTICE HUGHES delivered the opinion of the Court.

Chapter 285 of the Session Laws of Minnesota for the year 1925 provides for the abatement, as a public nuisance, of a "malicious, scandalous and defamatory newspaper, magazine or other periodical." Section one of the Act is as follows:

"Section 1. Any person who, as an individual, or as a member or employee of a firm, or association or organization, or as an officer, director, member or employee of a corporation, shall be engaged in the business of regularly or customarily producing, publishing or circulating, having in possession, selling or giving away.

(a) an obscene, lewd and lascivious newspaper, magazine, or other periodical, or

(b) a malicious, scandalous and defamatory newspaper, magazine or other periodical, is guilty of a nuisance, and all persons guilty of such nuisance may be enjoined, as hereinafter provided.

. . .

"In actions brought under (b) above, there shall be available the defense that the truth was published with good motives and for justifiable ends and in such actions the plaintiff shall not have the right to report *(sic)* to issues or editions of periodicals taking place more than three months before the commencement of the action."

. . .

Under this statute, clause (b), the County Attorney of Hennepin County brought this action to enjoin the publication of what was described as a "malicious, scandalous and defamatory newspaper, magazine and periodical," known as "The Saturday Press," published by the defendants in the city of Minneapolis. The complaint alleged that the defendants, on September 24, 1927, and on eight subsequent dates in October and November, 1927, published and circulated editions of that periodical which were "largely devoted to malicious, scandalous and defamatory articles" concerning Charles G. Davis, Frank W. Brunskill, the Minneapolis Tribune, the Minneapolis Journal, Melvin C. Passolt, George E. Leach, the Jewish Race, the members of the Grand Jury of Hennepin County impaneled in November, 1927, and then holding office, and other persons, as more fully appeared in exhibits annexed to the complaint, consisting of copies of the articles described and constituting 327 pages of the record. While the complaint did not so allege, it appears from the briefs of both parties that Charles G. Davis was a special law enforcement officer employed by a civic organization, that George E. Leach was Mayor of Minneapolis, that Frank W. Brunskill was its Chief of Police, and that Floyd B. Olson (the relator in this action) was County Attorney.

Without attempting to summarize the contents of the voluminous exhibits attached to the complaint, we deem it sufficient to say that the articles charged in substance that a Jewish gangster was in control of gambling, bootlegging and racketeering in Minneapolis, and that law enforcing officers and agencies were not energetically performing their duties. Most of the charges were directed against the Chief of Police; he was charged with gross neglect of duty, illicit relations with gangsters, and with participation in graft. The County Attorney was charged with knowing the existing conditions and with failure to take adequate measures to remedy them. The Mayor was accused of inefficiency and dereliction. One member of the grand jury was stated to be in sympathy with the gangsters. A special grand jury and a special prosecutor were demanded to deal with the situation in general, and, in particular, to investigate an attempt to assassinate one Guilford, one of the original defendants, who, it appears from the articles, was shot by gangsters after the first issue of the periodical had been published. There is no question but that the articles made serious accusations against the public officers named and others in connection with the prevalence of crimes and the failure to expose and punish them.

. . .

[The state court found Near's newspaper in violation of the statute and ordered that publication be ceased.]

This statute, for the suppression as a public nuisance of a newspaper or periodical, is unusual, if not unique, and raises questions of grave importance transcending the local interests involved in the particular action. It is no longer open to doubt that the liberty of the press, and of speech, is within the liberty safeguarded by the due process clause of the Fourteenth Amendment from invasion by state action. It was found impossible to conclude that this essential personal liberty of the citizen was left unprotected by the general guaranty of fundamental rights of person and property.... In maintaining this guaranty, the authority of the State to enact laws to promote the health, safety, morals and general welfare of its people is necessarily admitted....

. . .

First. The statute is not aimed at the redress of individual or private wrongs. Remedies for libel remain available and unaffected.... In the present action there was no allegation that the matter published was not true. It is alleged, and the statute requires the allegation, that the publication was "malicious." But, as in prosecutions for libel, there is no requirement of proof by the State of malice in fact as distinguished from malice inferred from the mere publication of the defamatory matter. The judgment in this case proceeded upon the mere proof of publication. The statute permits the defense, not of the truth alone, but only that the truth was published with good motives and for justifiable ends. It is apparent that under the statute the publication is to be regarded as defamatory if it injures reputation, and that it is scandalous if it circulates charges of reprehensible conduct, whether criminal or otherwise, and the publication is thus deemed to invite public reprobation and to constitute a public scandal. The *[state]* court sharply defined the purpose of the statute, bringing out the precise point, in these words: "There is no constitutional right to publish a fact merely because it is true. It is a matter of common knowledge that prosecutions under the criminal libel statutes do not result in efficient repression or suppression of the evils of scandal. Men who are the victims of such assaults seldom resort to the courts. This is especially true if their sins are exposed and the only question relates to whether it was done with good motives and for justifiable ends. This law is not for the protection of the person attacked nor to punish the wrongdoer. It is for the protection of the public welfare."

Second. The statute is directed not simply at the circulation of scandalous and defamatory statements with regard to private citizens, but at the continued publication by newspapers and periodicals of charges against public officers of corruption, malfeasance in office, or serious neglect of duty. Such charges by their very nature create a public scandal. They are scandalous and defamatory within the meaning of the statute, which has its normal operation in relation to publications dealing prominently and chiefly with the alleged derelictions of public officers.

Third. The object of the statute is not punishment, in the ordinary sense, but suppression of the offending newspaper or periodical. The reason for the enactment, as the state court has said, is that prosecutions to enforce penal statutes for libel do not result in "efficient repression or suppression of the evils of scandal."...

Fourth. The statute not only operates to suppress the offending newspaper or periodical but to put the publisher under an effective censorship. When a newspaper or periodical is found to be "malicious, scandalous and defamatory," and is suppressed as such, resumption of publication is punishable as a contempt of court by fine or imprisonment.... Whether he would be permitted again to publish matter deemed to be derogatory to the same or other public officers would depend upon the court's ruling....

The question is whether a statute authorizing such proceedings in restraint of publication is consistent with the conception of the liberty of the press as historically conceived and guaranteed. In determining the extent of the constitutional protection, it has been generally, if not universally, considered that it is the chief purpose of the guaranty to prevent previous restraints upon publication. The struggle in England, directed against the legislative power of the licenser, resulted in renunciation of the censorship of the press. The liberty deemed to be established was thus described by Blackstone: "The liberty of the press is indeed essential to the nature of a free state; but this consists in laying no *previous* restraints upon publications, and not in freedom from censure for criminal matter when published. Every freeman has an undoubted right to lay what sentiments he pleases before the public; to forbid this, is to destroy the freedom of the press; but if he publishes what is improper, mischievous or illegal, he must take the consequence of his own temerity." 4 Bl. Com. 151, 152; see Story on the Constitution, §§ 1884, 1889....

. . .

The objection has also been made that the principle as to immunity from previous restraint is stated too broadly, if every such restraint is deemed to be prohibited. That is undoubtedly true; the protection even as to previous restraint is not absolutely unlimited.... No one would question but that a government might prevent actual obstruction to its recruiting service or the publication of the sailing dates of transports or the number and location of troops. On similar grounds, the primary requirements of decency may be enforced against obscene publications. The security of the community life may be protected against incitements to acts of violence and the overthrow by force of orderly government....

The fact that for approximately one hundred and fifty years there has been almost an entire absence of attempts to impose previous restraints upon publications relating to the malfeasance of public officers is significant of the deep-seated conviction that such restraints would violate constitutional right. Public officers, whose character and conduct remain open to debate and free discussion in the press, find their remedies for false accusations in actions under libel laws providing for redress and punishment, and not in proceedings to restrain the publication of newspapers and periodicals. The general principle that the constitutional guaranty of the liberty of the press gives immunity from previous restraints has been approved in many decisions under the provisions of state constitutions.

The importance of this immunity has not lessened. While reckless assaults upon public men, and efforts to bring obloquy upon those who are endeavoring faithfully to discharge official duties, exert a baleful influence and deserve the severest condemnation in public opinion, it cannot be said that this abuse is greater, and it is believed to be less, than that which characterized the period in which our institutions took shape. Meanwhile, the administration of government has become more complex, the opportunities for malfeasance and corruption have multiplied, crime has grown to most serious proportions, and the danger of its protection by unfaithful officials and of the impairment of the fundamental security of life and property by criminal alliances and official neglect, emphasizes the primary need of a vigilant and courageous press, especially in great cities. The fact that the liberty of the press may be abused by miscreant purveyors of scandal does not make any the less necessary the immunity of the press from previous restraint in dealing with official misconduct. Subsequent punishment for such abuses as may exist is the appropriate remedy, consistent with constitutional privilege.

. . .

For these reasons we hold the statute, so far as it authorized the proceedings in this action under clause (b) of section one, to be an infringement of the liberty of the press guaranteed by the Fourteenth Amendment. We should add that this decision rests upon the operation and effect of the statute, without regard to the question of the truth of the charges contained in the particular periodical. The fact that the public officers named in this case, and those associated with the charges of official dereliction, may be deemed to be impeccable, cannot affect the conclusion that the statute imposes an unconstitutional restraint upon publication.

Judgment reversed.

MR. JUSTICE BUTLER, dissenting.

. . .

It is of the greatest importance that the States shall be untrammeled and free to employ all just and appropriate measures to prevent abuses of the liberty of the press.

. . .

MR. JUSTICE VAN DEVANTER, MR. JUSTICE MCREYNOLDS, and MR. JUSTICE SUTHERLAND concur in this opinion.

Branzburg v. Hayes

408 U.S. 665 (1972)

In this case, the needs of a free press and criminal prosecution collide. Paul M. Branzburg, a former reporter with the Louisville *Courier-Journal*, was called before a county grand jury after he wrote an article describing how two men made hashish from marijuana. He refused to identify them. Also involved in this case were Paul Pappas, a reporter-cameraman, and Earl Caldwell, a reporter for the *New York Times*, who refused to testify about their coverage of the Black Panthers. This action by Branzburg is against John P. Hayes, a Kentucky trial judge.

Opinion of the Court by MR. JUSTICE WHITE, announced by THE CHIEF JUSTICE.

The issue in these cases is whether requiring newsmen to appear and testify before state or federal grand juries abridges the freedom of speech and press guaranteed by the First Amendment. We hold that it does not.

I

. . . [T]he Courier-Journal carried a story under petitioner's by-line describing in detail his observations of two young residents of Jefferson County synthesizing hashish from marihuana, an activity which, they asserted, earned them about $5,000 in three weeks. The article included a photograph of a pair of hands working above a laboratory table on which was a substance identified by the caption as hashish. The article stated that petitioner had promised not to reveal the identity of the two hashish makers. Petitioner was shortly subpoenaed by the Jefferson County grand jury; he appeared, but refused to identify the individuals he had seen possessing marihuana or the persons he had seen making hashish from marihuana. A state trial court judge ordered petitioner to answer these questions and rejected his contention that the Kentucky reporters' privilege statute, Ky. Rev. Stat. § 421.100 (1962), the First Amendment of the United States Constitution, or §§ 1, 2, and 8 of the Kentucky Constitution authorized his refusal to answer. Petitioner then sought prohibition and mandamus in the Kentucky Court of Appeals on the same grounds, but the Court of Appeals denied the petition. . . .

The second case involving petitioner Branzburg arose out of his later story published on January 10, 1971, which described in detail the use of drugs in Frankfort, Kentucky. The article reported that in order to provide a comprehensive survey of the "drug scene" in Frankfort, petitioner had "spent two weeks interviewing several dozen drug users in the capital city" and had seen some of them smoking marihuana. A num-

ber of conversations with and observations of several unnamed drug users were recounted. Subpoenaed to appear before a Franklin County grand jury "to testify in the matter of violation of statutes concerning use and sale of drugs," petitioner Branzburg moved to quash the summons; the motion was denied, although an order was issued protecting Branzburg from revealing "confidential associations, sources or information" but requiring that he "answer any questions which concern or pertain to any criminal act, the commission of which was actually observed by [him]." Prior to the time he was slated to appear before the grand jury, petitioner sought mandamus and prohibition from the Kentucky Court of Appeals, arguing that if he were forced to go before the grand jury or to answer questions regarding the identity of informants or disclose information given to him in confidence, his effectiveness as a reporter would be greatly damaged. The Court of Appeals once again denied the requested writs. . . .

. . .

II

Petitioners Branzburg and Pappas and respondent Caldwell press First Amendment claims that may be simply put: that to gather news it is often necessary to agree either not to identify the source of information published or to publish only part of the facts revealed, or both; that if the reporter is nevertheless forced to reveal these confidences to a grand jury, the source so identified and other confidential sources of other reporters will be measurably deterred from furnishing publishable information, all to the detriment of the free flow of information protected by the First Amendment. Although the newsmen in these cases do not claim an absolute privilege against official interrogation in all circumstances, they assert that the reporter should not be forced either to appear or to testify before a grand jury or at trial until and unless sufficient grounds are shown for believing that the reporter possesses information relevant to a crime the grand jury is investigating, that the information the reporter has is unavailable from other sources, and that the need for the information is sufficiently compelling to override the claimed invasion of First Amendment interests occasioned by the disclosure. Principally relied upon are prior cases emphasizing the importance of the First Amendment guarantees to individual development and to our system of representative government, decisions requiring that official action with adverse impact on First Amendment rights be justified by a public interest that is "compelling" or "paramount," and those precedents establishing the principle that justifiable governmental goals may not be achieved by unduly broad means having an unnecessary impact on protected rights of speech, press, or association. The heart of the claim is that the burden on news gathering resulting from compelling reporters to disclose confidential information outweighs any public interest in obtaining the information.

We do not question the significance of free speech, press, or assembly to the country's welfare. Nor is it suggested that news gathering does not qualify for First Amendment protection; without some protection for seeking out the news, freedom of the press could be eviscerated. But these cases involve no intrusions upon speech or assembly, no prior restraint or restriction on what the press may publish, and no express or implied command that the press publish what it prefers to withhold. No exaction or tax for the privilege of publishing, and no penalty, civil or criminal, related to the content of published material is at issue here. The use of confidential sources by the press is not forbidden or restricted; reporters remain free to seek news from any source by means within the law. No attempt is made to require the press to publish its sources of information or indiscriminately to disclose them on request.

The sole issue before us is the obligation of reporters to respond to grand jury subpoenas as other citizens do and to answer questions relevant to an investigation into the commission of crime. Citizens generally are not constitutionally immune from grand jury subpoenas; and neither the First Amendment nor any other constitutional provision protects the average citizen from disclosing to a grand jury information that he has received in confidence....

. . .

...[T]he great weight of authority is that newsmen are not exempt from the normal duty of appearing before a grand jury and answering questions relevant to a criminal investigation. At common law, courts consistently refused to recognize the existence of any privilege authorizing a newsman to refuse to reveal confidential information to a grand jury.

. . .

A number of States have provided newsmen a statutory privilege of varying breadth, but the majority have not done so, and none has been provided by federal statute. Until now the only testimonial privilege for unofficial witnesses that is rooted in the Federal Constitution is the Fifth Amendment privilege against compelled self-incrimination. We are asked to create another by interpreting the First Amendment to grant newsmen a testimonial privilege that other citizens do not enjoy. This we decline to do. Fair and effective law enforcement aimed at providing security for the person and property of the individual is a fundamental function of government, and the grand jury plays an important, constitutionally mandated role in this process. On the records now before us, we perceive no basis for holding that the public interest in law enforcement and in ensuring effective grand jury proceedings is insufficient to override the consequential, but uncertain, burden on news gathering that is said to result from insisting that reporters, like other citizens, respond to relevant questions put to them in the course of a valid grand jury investigation or criminal trial.

. . .

There remain those situations where a source is not engaged in criminal conduct but has information suggesting illegal conduct by others. Newsmen frequently receive information from such sources pursuant to a tacit or express agreement to withhold the source's name and suppress any information that the source wishes not published. Such informants presumably desire anonymity in order to avoid being entangled as a witness in a criminal trial or grand jury investigation. They may fear that disclosure will threaten their job security or personal safety or that it will simply result in dishonor or embarrassment.

The argument that the flow of news will be diminished by compelling reporters to aid the grand jury in a criminal investigation is not irrational, nor are the records before us silent on the matter.

But we remain unclear how often and to what extent informers are actually deterred from furnishing information when newsmen are forced to testify before a grand jury. The available data indicate that some newsmen rely a great deal on confidential sources and that some informants are particularly sensitive to the threat of exposure and may be silenced if it is held by this Court that, ordinarily, newsmen must testify pursuant to subpoenas, but the evidence fails to demonstrate that there would be a significant constriction of the flow of news to the public if this Court reaffirms the prior common-law and constitutional rule regarding the testimonial obligations of newsmen. Estimates of the inhibiting effect of such subpoenas on the willingness of informants to make disclosures to newsmen are widely divergent and to a great extent speculative. It would be difficult to canvass the views of the informants themselves; surveys of reporters on this topic are chiefly opinions of predicted informant behavior and must be viewed in the light of the professional self-interest of the interviewees. . . .

Accepting the fact, however, that an undetermined number of informants not themselves implicated in crime will nevertheless, for whatever reason, refuse to talk to newsmen if they fear identification by a reporter in an official investigation, we cannot accept the argument that the public interest in possible future news about crime from undisclosed, unverified sources must take precedence over the public interest in pursuing and prosecuting those crimes reported to the press by informants and in thus deterring the commission of such crimes in the future.

. . .

At the federal level, Congress has freedom to determine whether a statutory newsman's privilege is necessary and desirable and to fashion standards and rules as narrow or broad as deemed necessary to deal with the evil discerned and, equally important, to refashion those rules as experience from time to time may dictate. There is also merit in leaving state legislatures free, within First Amendment limits, to fashion their own standards in light of the conditions and problems with respect to the relations between law enforcement officials and press in their own areas. It goes without saying, of course, that we are powerless to bar state courts from responding in their own way and construing their own constitutions so as to recognize a newsman's privilege, either qualified or absolute.

. . .

Mr. Justice POWELL, concurring.

I add this brief statement to emphasize what seems to me to be the limited nature of the Court's holding. The Court does not hold that newsmen, subpoenaed to testify before a grand jury, are without constitutional rights with respect to the gathering of news or in safeguarding their sources. Certainly, we do not hold, as suggested in Mr. Justice STEWART's dissenting opinion, that state and federal authorities are free to "annex" the news media as "an investigative arm of government." . . .

Mr. Justice DOUGLAS, dissenting in No. 70-57, *United States* v. *Caldwell.*

Caldwell, a black, is a reporter for the New York Times and was assigned to San Francisco with the hope that he could report on the activities and attitudes of the Black Panther Party. Caldwell in time gained the complete confidence of its members and wrote in-depth articles about them.

. . .

It is my view that there is no "compelling need" that can be shown which qualifies the reporter's immunity from appearing or testifying before a grand jury, unless the reporter himself is implicated in a crime. His immunity in my view is therefore quite complete, . . . [I]n my view a newsman has an absolute right not to appear before a grand jury, . . .

. . .

I would also reverse the judgments in No. 70-85, *Branzburg* v. *Hayes,* and No. 70-94, *In re Pappas,* for the reasons stated in the above dissent in No. 70-57, *United States* v. *Caldwell.*

Mr. Justice STEWART, with whom Mr. Justice BRENNAN and Mr. Justice MARSHALL join, dissenting.

The Court's crabbed view of the First Amendment reflects a disturbing insensitivity to the critical role of an independent press in our society. The question whether a reporter has a constitutional right to a confidential relationship with his source is of first impression here, but the principles that should guide our decision are as basic as any to be found in the Constitution. While Mr. Justice POWELL's enigmatic concurring opinion gives some hope of a more flexible view in the future, the Court in these cases holds that a newsman has no First Amendment right to protect his sources when called before a grand jury. . . .

I

The reporter's constitutional right to a confidential relationship with his source stems from the broad societal interest in a full and free flow of information to the public. It is this basic concern that underlies the Constitution's protection of a free press, ... because the guarantee is "not for the benefit of the press so much as for the benefit of all of us." *Time, Inc. v. Hill,* 385 U.S. 374, 389.

. . .

C. FREE PRESS VERSUS FAIR TRIAL

The *Branzburg* decision, requiring reporters to testify before a grand jury, is only one of many collisions between the press and the judiciary. A more frequent confrontation is when the press wants to cover a trial and a judge wants to close it. For the most part, the Supreme Court has supported the press and the public in such conflicts, but the record is filled with erratic turns and refashioned doctrines. In these contests, the Court is sensitive to public opinion and the needs of a democratic society.

One of the early cases concerned a newspaper charged with contempt of court because of its unflattering stories about a judge's conduct in a pending case. The contempt was upheld by the Supreme Court. Toledo Newspaper Co. v. United States, 247 U.S. 402 (1918). This decision was later overturned in Nye v. United States, 313 U.S. 33 (1941). Both decisions were efforts to interpret a congressional statute that restricted the power of judges to punish for contempt. 4 Stat. 487 (1831); 18 U.S.C. § 401. The right of the press to publish comments about pending litigation without being held in contempt of court was also upheld in another case in 1941. The Court observed that the "assumption that respect for the judiciary can be won by shielding judges from published criticism wrongly appraises the character of American public opinion." Bridges v. California, 314 U.S. 252, 270 (1941).

There have been many such cases. In 1946 a unanimous Court reversed a state court's action that held a newspaper in contempt for criticizing a trial judge and impugning his integrity. Pennekamp v. Florida, 328 U.S. 331 (1946). Judges claim that newspaper stories can obstruct the fair and impartial administration of justice in pending cases. However, the general record is to protect the freedom of the press, even when state judges are elected for short terms and lack the independence of life-tenured federal judges. Craig v. Harney, 331 U.S. 367 (1947). If misleading and inflammatory newspaper stories create a prejudicial climate and make a fair trial impossible, cases can be postponed, transferred to a different place, and convictions can be reversed.[2]

The confrontation between a free press and a fair trial reaches its highest pitch when judges issue gag orders to prohibit public comment about a pending trial. In 1976 a unanimous Court reversed the decision of a Nebraska state court judge who, in anticipation of a trial for a multiple murder, restrained newspapers, broadcasters, journalists, news media associations, and national newswire services from publishing or broadcasting statements by the accused to law enforcement officers. The ban extended to statements to third parties, except members of the press. The Supreme Court held that the heavy burden imposed as a condition of prior restraint had not been met. NEBRASKA PRESS ASSN. v. STUART, 427 U.S. 539 (1976). When court proceedings are open to the public, a judge may not enjoin the news media from publishing the name or photograph of someone charged with an offense. Oklahoma Publishing Co. v. District Court, 430 U.S. 308 (1977).

---

2. Shepherd v. Florida, 341 U.S. 50 (1951); Estes v. Texas, 381 U.S. 532 (1965); Sheppard v. Maxwell, 384 U.S. 333 (1966).

Justices Respond to *Gannett*

After the decision in *Gannett Co. v. De-Pasquale* (1979), some judges began to close their courtrooms not only for pretrial proceedings but also for the trial itself. Several Justices of the Supreme Court made appearances before the public to explain that *Gannett* was being misinterpreted. In an interview, Chief Justice Burger noted that *Gannett* was limited to pretrial proceedings, wondering whether judges around the country were "reading newspaper reports of what we said" rather than the opinion itself. In a separate appearance, Justice Powell denied that the Court had any ill feelings toward the press: "Instead of having any hostility toward you, we are dependent on you very much." In this panel session at the American Bar Association's annual meeting, Powell added: "We are totally dependent on the media to interpret what we do. That's all the public knows about us." Justice

Blackmun, who wrote a lengthy dissent in *Gannett*, told a group of federal judges in South Dakota that "despite what my colleague, the Chief Justice has said," the opinion authorized the closing of full trials. At yet a fourth public meeting, Justice Stevens conceded that the possibility that judges might be granting requests too casually to close entire trials to the public "may justify the adoption of new court rules, or even new legislation." In making this comment in Tucson, Ariz., Stevens seemed to underscore Blackmun's comment that Chief Justice Burger was reading *Gannett* too narrowly. It was highly unusual, and possibly unprecedented, for four Justices to comment publicly about a Court opinion. These remarks seemed to guarantee that the Court would quickly revisit *Gannett*, which is what the Justices did in *Richmond Newspapers, Inc. v. Virginia* (1980).

SOURCES: New York Times, August 9, 1979, at A17; August 11, 1979, at 43; August 14, 1979, at A13; September 4, 1979, at A15; September 9, 1979, at 41.

From *Gannett* to *Richmond Newspapers*

The dialectic between judicial decisions and public opinion is captured vividly in two back-to-back cases in 1979 and 1980. In the first, a 5 to 4 decision by the Supreme Court supported a trial judge's ruling to close a pretrial hearing to the public and the press. The motion had been made by defendants without objection by the prosecutor. In upholding the need to protect the fair-trial rights of defendants, the Court held that the public has no constitutional right of access to pretrial proceedings. The Court said that the constitutional guarantee of a public trial is for the benefit of the defendant, not the public: "we hold that members of the public have no constitutional right under the Sixth and Fourteenth Amendments to attend criminal trials." GANNETT CO. v. DePASQUALE, 443 U.S. 368, 391 (1979). In a concurrence, Chief Justice Burger said that the Sixth Amendment right to public trial applied strictly to the trial, not to pretrial proceedings. Two other concurrences, by Powell and Rehnquist, undercut the strength of the majority opinion.

In response to the Court's fragmented and disjointed opinion, some judges around the country began to close their courtrooms to the public, not only for pretrial proceedings but for the entire trial and even sentencing. In some cases, they allowed the public in but kept the press out. The press mounted a vigorous counterattack. Critics of the decision claimed that it denied citizens the right to keep government accountable and maintain democratic control. Members of the Supreme Court, including Burger, Powell, Blackmun, and Stevens, took the unusual step of telling audiences around the country that *Gannett* had been "misread" to permit unacceptable restraints on the press (see box).

Within a year, a 7–1 Supreme Court decided to limit the damage of *Gannett* by announcing a more sympathetic understanding of the public's need to attend trials. The Court held that the public's right of access to criminal trials is implicit in the First Amendment. Open trials promote many interests: the yearning to see justice done, the public education that comes from attending a trial, the maintenance of public trust in the judicial system, and the opportunity to check the fairness and accuracy of judicial proceedings. RICHMOND NEWSPAPERS, INC. v. VIRGINIA, 448 U.S. 555 (1980). The guarantee of public proceedings in criminal trials has been extended to cover even the *voir dire* screening of potential jurors. Press-Enterprise Co. v. Superior Court of Cal., 464 U.S. 501 (1984). There is also a right of access to preliminary hearings for criminal proceedings. Press-Enterprise Co. v. Superior Court, 478 U.S. 1 (1986).

Public access has reached the point where some judicial proceedings are televised. A unanimous Supreme Court held that the Constitution does not prohibit states from experimenting with televised trials. Chandler v. Florida, 449 U.S. 560 (1981). Chief Justice Burger opposed televising Supreme Court proceedings, but some members of the Rehnquist Court seem more supportive of this prospect. In 1988 Chief Justice Rehnquist and Justices White and Kennedy attended a brief demonstration of how filming could be done of Supreme Court proceedings, but there has been no change in the Court's policy against cameras. Lower federal courts may experiment with television coverage of civil cases.[3]

Nebraska Press Assn. v. Stuart

427 U.S. 539 (1976)

A Nebraska state trial judge, anticipating a trial for a multiple murder that had attracted widespread news coverage, entered an order that restrained newspapers, broadcasters, journalists, news media associations, and national newswire services from publishing or broadcasting accounts of confessions or admissions made by the accused to law enforcement officers or third parties. An exception was made for confessions or admissions made to the press. The question was whether the order by Judge Stuart, intended to prevent pretrial publicity that might jeopardize a fair trial, violated the constitutional guarantee of a free press.

Mr. Chief Justice Burger delivered the opinion of the Court.

The respondent State District Judge entered an order restraining the petitioners from publishing or broadcasting accounts of confessions or admissions made by the accused or facts "strongly implicative" of the accused in a widely reported murder of six persons. We granted certiorari to decide whether the entry of such an order on the showing made before the state court violated the constitutional guarantee of freedom of the press.

. . .

III

The problems presented by this case are almost as old as the Republic. Neither in the Constitution nor in contemporaneous writings do we find that the conflict between these two important rights was anticipated, yet it is inconceivable that the authors of the Constitution were unaware of the potential conflicts between the right to an unbiased jury and the guarantee of freedom of the press.…

The speed of communication and the pervasiveness of the modern news media have exacerbated these problems, however, as numerous appeals demonstrate. The trial of Bruno Hauptmann in a small New Jersey community for the abduction and murder of the Charles Lindberghs' infant child probably was the most widely covered trial up to that time, and the nature of the coverage produced widespread public reaction. Criticism

---

3. "Cameras Roll Into Federal Court Again," Legal Times, May 6, 1996, at 14; Jonathan Groner, "Who Rules? Which Rules?: Cameras-in-Court Decision Tests Power of Judicial Conference," Legal Times, March 11, 1996, at 1; Linda Greenhouse, "Reversing Course, Judicial Panel Allows Televising Appeals Courts," The New York Times, March 13, 1996, at A1; Joe Sexton, "U.S. Judge Allows Cameras at Hearing," The New York Times, March 2, 1996, at 22.

was directed at the "carnival" atmosphere that pervaded the community and the courtroom itself. Responsible leaders of press and the legal profession—including other judges—pointed out that much of this sorry performance could have been controlled by a vigilant trial judge and by other public officers subject to the control of the court....

The excesses of press and radio and lack of responsibility of those in authority in the *Hauptmann* case and others of that era led to efforts to develop voluntary guidelines for courts, lawyers, press, and broadcasters. See generally J. Lofton, Justice and the Press 117–130 (1966). The effort was renewed in 1965 when the American Bar Association embarked on a project to develop standards for all aspects of criminal justice, including guidelines to accommodate the right to a fair trial and the rights of a free press. See Powell, The Right to a Fair Trial, 51 A. B. A. J. 534 (1965). The resulting standards, approved by the Association in 1968, received support from most of the legal profession....

In practice, of course, even the most ideal guidelines are subjected to powerful strains when a case such as Simants' *[arrested for the six murders in Sutherland, Neb.]* arises, with reporters from many parts of the country on the scene. Reporters from distant places are unlikely to consider themselves bound by local standards. They report to editors outside the area covered by the guidelines, and their editors are likely to be guided only by their own standards....

IV

The Sixth Amendment in terms guarantees "trial, by an impartial jury..." in federal criminal prosecutions. Because "trial by jury in criminal cases is fundamental to the American scheme of justice," the Due Process Clause of the Fourteenth Amendment guarantees the same right in state criminal prosecutions. *Duncan* v. *Louisiana,* 391 U. S. 145, 149 (1968).

. . .

In the overwhelming majority of criminal trials, pretrial publicity presents few unmanageable threats to this important right. But when the case is a "sensational" one tensions develop between the right of the accused to trial by an impartial jury and the rights guaranteed others by the First Amendment. The relevant decisions of this Court, even if not dispositive, are instructive by way of background.

In *Irvin* v. *Dowd,* ... the defendant was convicted of murder following intensive and hostile news coverage. The trial judge had granted a defense motion for a change of venue, but only to an adjacent county, which had been exposed to essentially the same news coverage. At trial, 430 persons were called for jury service; 268 were excused because they had fixed opinions as to guilt. Eight of the 12 who served as jurors thought the defendant guilty, but said they could nevertheless render an impartial verdict. On review the Court vacated the conviction and death sentence and remanded to allow a new trial for, "[w]ith his life at stake, it is not requiring too much that petitioner be tried in an atmosphere undisturbed by so huge a wave of public passion...." 366 U. S., at 728.

Similarly, in *Rideau* v. *Louisiana,* 373 U. S. 723 (1963), the Court reversed the conviction of a defendant whose staged, highly emotional confession had been filmed with the cooperation of local police and later broadcast on television for three days while he was awaiting trial, saying "[a]ny subsequent court proceedings in a community so pervasively exposed to such a spectacle could be but a hollow formality." *Id.,* at 726. And in *Estes* v. *Texas,* 381 U. S. 532 (1965), the Court held that the defendant had not been afforded due process where the volume of trial publicity, the judge's failure to control the proceedings, and the telecast of a hearing and of the trial itself "inherently prevented a sober search for the truth." *Id.,* at 551. See also *Marshall* v. *United States,* 360 U. S. 310 (1959).

. . .

V

The First Amendment provides that "Congress shall make no law...abridging the freedom...of the press," and it is "no longer open to doubt that the liberty of the press, and of speech, is within the liberty safeguarded by the due process clause of the Fourteenth Amendment from invasion by state action." *Near* v. *Minnesota ex rel. Olson,* 283 U. S. 697, 707 (1931). See also *Grosjean* v. *American Press Co.,* 297 U. S. 233, 244 (1936). The Court has interpreted these guarantees to afford special protection against orders that prohibit the publication or broadcast of particular information or commentary—orders that impose a "previous" or "prior" restraint on speech. None of our decided cases on prior restraint involved restrictive orders entered to protect a defendant's right to a fair and impartial jury, but the opinions on prior restraint have a common thread relevant to this case.

In *Near* v. *Minnesota ex rel. Olson, supra,* the Court held invalid a Minnesota statute providing for the abatement as a public nuisance of any "malicious, scandalous and defamatory newspaper, magazine or other periodical." ...

. . .

The Court relied on *Patterson* v. *Colorado ex rel. Attorney General,* 205 U. S. 454, 462 (1907): "[T]he main purpose of [the First Amendment] is 'to prevent all such *previous restraints* upon publications as had been practiced by other governments.' "

[*Burger reviews other cases holding that any prior restraint on expression comes to the Court with a "heavy presumption" against its constitutional validity:* Organization for a Better Austin *v.* Keefe, 402 U. S. 415 (1971); New York Times Co. *v.* United States, 403 U. S. 713 (1971).]

... Truthful reports of public judicial proceedings have been afforded special protection against subsequent punishment. See *Cox Broadcasting Corp.* v. *Cohn,* 420 U. S. 469, 492–493 (1975); see also, *Craig* v. *Harney,* 331 U.S. 367, 374 (1947). For the same reasons the protection against prior restraint should have particular force as applied to reporting of criminal proceedings, whether the crime in question is a single isolated act or a pattern of criminal conduct.

"A responsible press has always been regarded as the handmaiden of effective judicial administration, especially in the criminal field. Its function in this regard is documented by an impressive record of service over several centuries. The press does not simply publish information about trials but guards against the miscarriage of justice by subjecting the police, prosecutors, and judicial processes to extensive public scrutiny and criticism." *Sheppard* v. *Maxwell,* 384 U. S., at 350.

. . .

VI

We turn now to the record in this case ... To do so, we must examine the evidence before the trial judge when the order was entered to determine (a) the nature and extent of pretrial news coverage; (b) whether other measures would be likely to mitigate the effects of unrestrained pretrial publicity; and (c) how effectively a restraining order would operate to prevent the threatened danger.

The precise terms of the restraining order are also important. We must then consider whether the record supports the entry of a prior restraint on publication, one of the most extraordinary remedies known to our jurisprudence.

A

. . .

Our review of the pretrial record persuades us that the trial judge was justified in concluding that there would be intense and pervasive pretrial publicity concerning this case. He could also reasonably conclude, based on common human experience, that publicity might impair the defendant's right to a fair trial. He did not purport to say more, for he found only "a clear and present danger that pre-trial publicity *could* impinge upon the defendant's right to a fair trial." (Emphasis added.) His conclusion as to the impact of such publicity on prospective jurors was of necessity speculative, dealing as he was with factors unknown and unknowable.

B

We find little in the record that goes to another aspect of our task, determining whether measures short of an order restraining all publication would have insured the defendant a fair trial. ...

We have therefore examined this record to determine the probable efficacy of the measures short of prior restraint on the press and speech. There is no finding that alternative measures would not have protected Simants' rights, and the Nebraska Supreme Court did no more than imply that such measures might not be adequate. Moreover, the record is lacking in evidence to support such a finding.

C

We must also assess the probable efficacy of prior restraint on publication as a workable method of protecting Simants' right to a fair trial, and we cannot ignore the reality of the problems of managing and enforcing pretrial restraining orders. The territorial jurisdiction of the issuing court is limited by concepts of sovereignty. ...

... [T]he events disclosed by the record took place in a community of 850 people. It is reasonable to assume that, without any news accounts being printed or broadcast, rumors would travel swiftly by word of mouth. One can only speculate on the accuracy of such reports, given the generative propensities of rumors; they could well be more damaging than reasonably accurate news accounts. But plainly a whole community cannot be restrained from discussing a subject intimately affecting life within it.

Given these practical problems, it is far from clear that prior restraint on publication would have protected Simants' rights.

. . .

E

. . .

Of necessity our holding is confined to the record before us. But our conclusion is not simply a result of assessing the adequacy of the showing made in this case; it results in part from the problems inherent in meeting the heavy burden of demonstrating, in advance of trial, that without prior restraint a fair trial will be denied. The practical problems of managing and enforcing restrictive orders will always be present. In this sense, the record now before us is illustrative rather than exceptional....

...We hold that, with respect to the order entered in this case prohibiting reporting or commentary on judicial proceedings held in public, the barriers have not been overcome; to the extent that this order restrained publication of such material, it is clearly invalid. To the extent that it prohibited publication based on information gained from other sources, we conclude that the heavy burden imposed as a condition to securing a prior restraint was not met and the judgment of the Nebraska Supreme Court is therefore

Reversed.

MR. JUSTICE WHITE, concurring.

. . .

MR. JUSTICE POWELL, concurring.

. . .

MR. JUSTICE BRENNAN, with whom MR. JUSTICE STEWART and MR. JUSTICE MARSHALL join, concurring in the judgment.

. . .

MR. JUSTICE STEVENS, concurring in the judgment.

. . .

Gannett Co. v. DePasquale

443 U.S. 368 (1979)

At a pretrial hearing on a motion to suppress allegedly involuntary confessions and certain physical evidence, two defendants in a state prosecution for second-degree murder, robbery, and grand larceny requested that the public be excluded from the hearing. They argued that adverse publicity had jeopardized their ability to receive a fair trial. The District Attorney did not oppose the motion, nor did a reporter for the Gannett publishers. Judge DePasquale granted the motion. In response to the reporter's letter the next day asserting a right to cover the hearing and requesting access to the transcript, the judge refused to grant Gannett immediate access to the transcript, ruling that the interests of the press and the public were outweighed by defendants' right to a fair trial.

MR. JUSTICE STEWART delivered the opinion of the Court.

The question presented in this case is whether members of the public have an independent constitutional right to insist upon access to a pretrial judicial proceeding, even though the accused, the prosecutor, and the trial judge all have agreed to the closure of that proceeding in order to assure a fair trial.

I

[Wayne Clapp disappeared after he had ac- *companied two men, Greathouse and Jones, on a fishing outing. The boat they used was laced with bullet holes, suggesting a violent death for Clapp. Two Gannett newspapers covered the story, including the arrest of Greathouse, Jones, and Greathouse's wife. The newspapers reported the indictments of the two men and the woman and their arraignments. Defense attorneys were given ninety days to file pretrial motions. During that period, Greathouse and Jones moved to suppress statements made to the police and to suppress physical evidence seized.]*

The motions to suppress came on before Judge DePasquale on November 4. At this hearing, defense attorneys argued that the unabated buildup of adverse publicity had jeopardized the ability of the defendants to receive a fair trial. They thus requested that the public and the press be excluded from the hearing. The District Attorney did not oppose the motion. Although Carol Ritter, a reporter employed by the petitioner, was present in the courtroom, no objection was made at the time of the closure motion. The trial judge granted the motion.

The next day, however, Ritter wrote a letter to the trial judge asserting a "right to cover this hearing," and requesting that "we ... be given access to the transcript." The judge responded later the same day. He stated that the suppression hearing had concluded and that any decision on immediate release of the transcript had been reserved. The petitioner then moved the court to set aside its exclusionary order.

[The judge refused to vacate his order. The New York Supreme Court, Appellate Division, vacated the order, but the New York Court of Appeals upheld the exclusion of the press and the public from the pretrial proceeding.]

II

[Shortly before the entry of judgment by the Appellate Division, both defendants pleaded guilty to lesser offenses and a transcript of the suppression hearing was made available to Gannett. In this section the Court holds that, notwithstanding the availability of the transcript, the controversy is not moot.]

III

This Court has long recognized that adverse publicity can endanger the ability of a defendant to receive a fair trial....

Publicity concerning pretrial suppression hearings such as the one involved in the present case poses special risks of unfairness. The whole purpose of such hearings is to screen out unreliable or illegally obtained evidence and insure that this evidence does not become known to the jury. Cf. *Jackson v. Denno*, 378 U.S. 368. Publicity concerning the proceedings at a pretrial hearing, however, could influence public opinion against a defendant and inform potential jurors of inculpatory information wholly inadmissible at the actual trial.

The danger of publicity concerning pretrial suppression hearings is particularly acute, because it may be difficult to measure with any degree of certainty the effects of such publicity on the fairness of the trial. After the commencement of the trial itself, inadmissible prejudicial information about a defendant can be kept from a jury by a variety of means. When such information is publicized during a pretrial proceeding, however, it may never be altogether kept from potential jurors. Closure of pretrial proceedings is often one of the most effective methods that a trial judge can employ to attempt to insure that the fairness of a trial will not be jeopardized by the dissemination of such information throughout the community before the trial itself has even begun. Cf. *Rideau v. Louisiana*, 373 U.S. 723.

IV

A

The Sixth Amendment, applicable to the States through the Fourteenth, surrounds a criminal trial with guarantees such as the rights to notice, confrontation, and compulsory process that have as their overriding purpose the protection of the accused from prosecutorial and judicial abuses. Among the guarantees that the Amendment provides to a person charged with the commission of a criminal offense, and to him alone, is the "right to a speedy and public trial, by an impartial jury." The Constitution nowhere mentions any right of access to a criminal trial on the part of the public; its guarantee, like the others enumerated, is personal to the accused....

. . .

B

While the Sixth Amendment guarantees to a defendant in a criminal case the right to a public trial, it does not guarantee the right to compel a private trial.... [T]he issue is whether members of the public have an enforceable right to a public trial that can be asserted independently of the parties in the litigation.

There can be no blinking the fact that there is a strong societal interest in public trials. Openness in court proceedings may improve the quality of testimony, induce unknown witnesses to come forward with relevant testimony, cause all trial participants to perform their duties more conscientiously, and generally give the public an opportunity to observe the judicial system....

Recognition of an independent public interest in the enforcement of Sixth Amendment guarantees is a far cry, however, from the creation of a constitutional right on the part of the public. In an adversary system of criminal justice, the public interest in the administration of justice is protected by the participants in the litigation.…

V

In arguing that members of the general public have a constitutional right to attend a criminal trial, despite the obvious lack of support for such a right in the structure or text of the Sixth Amendment, the petitioner and *amici* rely on the history of the public-trial guarantee. This history, however, ultimately demonstrates no more than the existence of a common-law rule of open civil and criminal proceedings.

A

. . .

…The history upon which the petitioner and *amici* rely totally fails to demonstrate that the Framers of the Sixth Amendment intended to create a constitutional right in strangers to attend a pretrial proceeding, when all that they actually did was to confer upon the accused an explicit right to demand a public trial.…

B

But even if the Sixth and Fourteenth Amendments could properly be viewed as embodying the common-law right of the public to attend criminal trials, it would not necessarily follow that the petitioner would have a right of access under the circumstances of this case. For there exists no persuasive evidence that at common law members of the public had any right to attend pretrial proceedings; indeed, there is substantial evidence to the contrary.…

. . .

For these reasons, we hold that members of the public have no constitutional right under the Sixth and Fourteenth Amendments to attend criminal trials.

VI

The petitioner also argues that members of the press and the public have a right of access to the pretrial hearing by reason of the First and Fourteenth Amendments.…

Several factors lead to the conclusion that the actions of the trial judge here were consistent with any right of access the petitioner may have had under the First and Fourteenth Amendments.…

[T]he trial court found that the representatives of the press did have a right of access of constitutional dimension, but held, under the circumstances of this case, that this right was outweighed by the defendants' right to a fair trial.…

Furthermore, any denial of access in this case was not absolute but only temporary. Once the danger of prejudice had dissipated, a transcript of the suppression hearing was made available. The press and the public then had a full opportunity to scrutinize the suppression hearing. Unlike the case of an absolute ban on access, therefore, the press here had the opportunity to inform the public of the details of the pretrial hearing accurately and completely. Under these circumstances, any First and Fourteenth Amendment right of the petitioner to attend a criminal trial was not violated.

VII

We certainly do not disparage the general desirability of open judicial proceedings. But we are not asked here to declare whether open proceedings represent beneficial social policy, or whether there would be a constitutional barrier to a state law that imposed a stricter standard of closure than the one here employed by the New York courts. Rather, we are asked to hold that the Constitution itself gave the petitioner an affirmative right of access to this pretrial proceeding, even though all the participants in the litigation agreed that it should be closed to protect the fair-trial rights of the defendants.

For all of the reasons discussed in this opinion, we hold that the Constitution provides no such right. Accordingly, the judgment of the New York Court of Appeals is affirmed.

It is so ordered.

Mr. Chief Justice Burger, concurring.

I join the opinion of the Court, but I write separately to emphasize my view of the nature of the proceeding involved in today's decision. By definition, a hearing on a motion before trial to suppress evidence is not a *trial;* it is a *pre*trial hearing.

…[D]uring the last 40 years in which the pretrial processes have been enormously expanded, it has never occurred to anyone, so far as I am aware, that a pretrial deposition or pretrial interrogatories were other than wholly private to the litigants. A pretrial deposition does not become part of a "trial" until and unless the contents of the deposition are offered in evidence.…

MR. JUSTICE POWELL, concurring.

. . .

MR. JUSTICE REHNQUIST, concurring.

. . . [L]ower courts should not assume that after today's decision they must adhere to the procedures employed by the trial court in this case or to those advanced by MR. JUSTICE POWELL in his separate opinion in order to avoid running afoul of the First Amendment. To the contrary, in my view and, I think, in the view of a majority of this Court, the lower courts are under no constitutional constraint either to accept or reject those procedures. They remain, in the best tradition of our federal system, free to determine for themselves the question whether to open or close the proceeding. . . .

MR. JUSTICE BLACKMUN, with whom MR. JUSTICE BRENNAN, MR. JUSTICE WHITE, and MR. JUSTICE MARSHALL join, concurring in part and dissenting in part.

. . .

Today's decision, as I view it, is an unfortunate one. . . . That rule is to the effect that if the defense and the prosecution merely agree to have the public excluded from a suppression hearing, and the trial judge does not resist—as trial judges may be prone not to do, since nonresistance is easier than resistance—closure shall take place, and there is nothing in the Sixth Amendment that prevents that happily agreed upon event. The result is that the important interests of the public and the press (as a part of that public) in open judicial proceedings are rejected and cast aside as of little value or significance.

Because I think this easy but wooden approach is without support either in legal history or in the intendment of the Sixth Amendment, I dissent.

. . .

D

[Blackmun acknowledges that the Sixth Amendment speaks only of a public "trial," but argues that the pretrial suppression hearing often is a decisive stage for the defendant and the prosecution. He concludes that the Sixth and Fourteenth Amendments prohibit a state from conducting a pretrial suppression hearing in private, even at the request of the accused, "unless full and fair consideration is first given to the public's interest, protected by the Amendments, in open trials."]

Richmond Newspapers, Inc. v. Virginia

448 U.S. 555 (1980)

After three trials on a murder charge had been either reversed on appeal or had resulted in mistrials, a Virginia court granted the motion of the defense counsel to close the trial to the public and to the press. At the fourth trial, the defendant moved that the trial be closed to the public. The prosecutor did not object, and the judge closed the trial. Richmond Newspapers, Inc., appealed.

MR. CHIEF JUSTICE BURGER announced the judgment of the Court and delivered an opinion, in which MR. JUSTICE WHITE and MR. JUSTICE STEVENS joined.

The narrow question presented in this case is whether the right of the public and press to attend criminal trials is guaranteed under the United States Constitution.

. . .

II

We begin consideration of this case by noting that the precise issue presented here has not previously been before this Court for decision. In *Gannett Co. v. DePasquale, supra,* the Court was not required to decide whether a right of access to *trials,* as distingushed from hearings on *pretrial* motions, was constitutionally guaranteed. The Court held that the Sixth Amendment's guarantee to the accused of a public trial gave neither the public nor the press an enforceable right of access to a *pretrial* suppression hearing. . . .

In prior cases the Court has treated questions involving conflicts between publicity and a defendant's right to a fair trial; . . . But here for the first time the Court is asked to decide whether a criminal trial itself may be closed to the public upon the unopposed request of a defendant, without any demonstration that closure is required to protect the defendant's superior right to a fair trial, or that some other overriding consideration requires closure.

. . .

B

...[T]he historical evidence demonstrates conclusively that at the time when our organic laws were adopted, criminal trials both here and in England had long been presumptively open. This is no quirk of history; rather, it has long been recognized as an indispensable attribute of an Anglo-American trial. Both Hale in the 17th century and Blackstone in the 18th saw the importance of openness to the proper functioning of a trial; it gave assurance that the proceedings were conducted fairly to all concerned, and it discouraged perjury, the misconduct of participants, and decisions based on secret bias or partiality....

...The early history of open trials in part reflects the widespread acknowledgment, long before there were behavioral scientists, that public trials had significant community therapeutic value. Even without such experts to frame the concept in words, people sensed from experience and observation that, especially in the administration of criminal justice, the means used to achieve justice must have the support derived from public acceptance of both the process and its results.

When a shocking crime occurs, a community reaction of outrage and public protest often follows. See H. Weihofen, The Urge to Punish 130–131 (1956). Thereafter the open processes of justice serve an important prophylactic purpose, providing an outlet for community concern, hostility, and emotion. Without an awareness that society's responses to criminal conduct are underway, natural human reactions of outrage and protest are frustrated and may manifest themselves in some form of vengeful "self-help," as indeed they did regularly in the activities of vigilante "committees" on our frontiers....

Civilized societies withdraw both from the victim and the vigilante the enforcement of criminal laws, but they cannot erase from people's consciousness the fundamental, natural yearning to see justice done — or even the urge for retribution. The crucial prophylactic aspects of the administration of justice cannot function in the dark;... where the trial has been concealed from public

view an unexpected outcome can cause a reaction that the system at best has failed and at worst has been corrupted....

C

. . .

Despite the history of criminal trials being presumptively open since long before the Constitution, the State presses its contention that neither the Constitution nor the Bill of Rights contains any provision which by its terms guarantees to the public the right to attend criminal trials. Standing alone, this is correct, but there remains the question whether, absent an explicit provision, the Constitution affords protection against exclusion of the public from criminal trials.

III

A

The First Amendment, in conjunction with the Fourteenth, prohibits governments from "abridging the freedom of speech, or of the press; or the right of the people peaceably to assemble, and to petition the Government for a redress of grievances." These expressly guaranteed freedoms share a common core purpose of assuring freedom of communication on matters relating to the functioning of government. Plainly it would be difficult to single out any aspect of government of higher concern and importance to the people than the manner in which criminal trials are conducted;...

The Bill of Rights was enacted against the backdrop of the long history of trials being presumptively open. Public access to trials was then regarded as an important aspect of the process itself;...In guaranteeing freedoms such as those of speech and press, the First Amendment can be read as protecting the right of everyone to attend trials so as to give meaning to those explicit guarantees....

C

The State argues that the Constitution nowhere spells out a guarantee for the right of the public to attend trials, and that accordingly no such right is protected. The possibility that such a contention could be made did not escape the notice of the Constitution's draftsmen; they were concerned that some important rights might be thought disparaged because not specifically guaranteed. It was even argued that because of this danger no Bill of Rights should be adopted. See, *e. g.,* The Federalist No. 84 (A. Hamilton). In a letter to Thomas Jefferson in October 1788, James Madison explained why he, although "in favor of a bill of rights," had "not viewed it in an important light" up to that time: "I conceive that in a certain degree . . . the rights in question are reserved by the manner in which the federal powers are granted." He went on to state that "there is great reason to fear that a positive declaration of some of the most essential rights could not be obtained in the requisite latitude." 5 Writings of James Madison 271 (G. Hunt ed. 1904).

But arguments such as the State makes have not precluded recognition of important rights not enumerated. Notwithstanding the appropriate caution against reading into the Constitution rights not explicitly defined, the Court has acknowledged that certain unarticulated rights are implicit in enumerated guarantees. For example, the rights of association and of privacy, the right to be presumed innocent, and the right to be judged by a standard of proof beyond a reasonable doubt in a criminal trial, as well as the right to travel, appear nowhere in the Constitution or Bill of Rights. Yet these important but unarticulated rights have nonetheless been found to share constitutional protection in common with explicit guarantees. The concerns expressed by Madison and others have thus been resolved; fundamental rights, even though not expressly guaranteed, have been recognized by the Court as indispensable to the enjoyment of rights explicitly defined.

We hold that the right to attend criminal trials is implicit in the guarantees of the First Amendment; without the freedom to attend such trials, which people have exercised for centuries, important aspects of freedom of speech and "of the press could be eviscerated." *Branzburg,* 408 U. S., at 681.

. . .

Mr. Justice Powell took no part in the consideration or decision of this case.

Mr. Justice White, concurring.

. . .

Mr. Justice Stevens, concurring.

. . .

Mr. Justice Brennan, with whom Mr. Justice Marshall joins, concurring in the judgment.

. . .

Mr. Justice Stewart, concurring in the judgment.

. . .

Mr. Justice Blackmun, concurring in the judgment.

. . .

Mr. Justice Rehnquist, dissenting.

In the Gilbert and Sullivan operetta "Iolanthe," the Lord Chancellor recites:

"The Law is the true embodiment
of everything that's excellent,
It has no kind of fault or flaw,
And I, my Lords, embody the Law."

It is difficult not to derive more than a little of this flavor from the various opinions supporting the judgment in this case. The opinion of The Chief Justice states:

"[H]ere for the first time the Court is asked to decide whether a criminal trial itself may be closed to the public upon the unopposed request of a defendant, without any demonstration that closure is required to protect the defendant's superior right to a fair trial, or that some other overriding consideration requires closure." *Ante,* at 564.

The opinion of Mr. Justice Brennan states:

"Read with care and in context, our decisions must therefore be understood as holding only that any privilege of access to governmental information is subject to a degree of restraint dictated by the nature of the information and countervailing interests in security or confidentiality.' *Ante,* at 586.

For the reasons stated in my separate concurrence in *Gannett Co. v. DePasquale,* 443 U. S. 368, 403 (1979), I do not believe that either the First or Sixth Amendment, as made applicable to the States by the Fourteenth, requires that a State's reasons for denying public access to a trial, where both the prosecuting attorney and the defendant have consented to an order of closure approved by the judge, are subject to any additional constitutional review at our hands. And

I most certainly do not believe that the Ninth Amendment confers upon us any such power to review orders of state trial judges closing trials in such situations....

. . .

D. LIBEL LAW

The press and the media face a battery of costly suits brought by individuals who claim damage to their reputations. Making publishers fully liable for errors that injure others would lead to self-censorship and a diminished free press. In balancing the values between the rights of a free press and safeguards against defamation, the Supreme Court recognizes that the First Amendment "requires that we protect some falsehood in order to protect speech that matters." Gertz v. Robert Welch, Inc., 418 U.S. 323, 341 (1974).

Defamation takes the form of *slander* (oral defamation) and *libel* (written defamation). In addition to defamation of a person, there can also be "product disparagement." Bose Corp. v. Consumers Unions of U.S., Inc., 466 U.S. 485 (1984). In 1998, a federal judge ruled that Texas cattlemen had no right to sue Oprah Winfrey for her televised remarks about the potential effects of "mad cow disease" on the safety of beef. In winning the case, Winfrey spent close to a million dollars in her defense.

British libel law permitted punishment of any writing that tended to bring into disrepute the government or established religion or was likely to provoke a breach of the peace. Truth was not a defense in criminal libel; "the provocation, and not the falsity, is the thing to be punished criminally." 4 Blackstone, Commentaries 150. Contemporary courts recognize truth as a defense, but libel law is engulfed by confusion and tenuous distinctions.

Public Officials

Although the relationship between malice and defamation was explored in the nineteenth century, White v. Nicholls, 44 U.S. (3 How.) 266 (1845), the benchmark libel case dates from 1964. In response to an advertisement in the *New York Times,* charging Alabama police with acts of terrorism and violence against civil rights demonstrators, a state official responsible for the police brought a libel suit against the newspaper and four civil rights leaders. In a unanimous decision, the Court held that the official could not recover damages unless he could prove that the defamatory information in the advertisement was made with "actual malice," which the Court defined as "knowledge that it was false or with reckless disregard of whether it was false or not." NEW YORK TIMES CO. v. SULLIVAN, 376 U.S. 254, 280 (1964).

Following *Sullivan,* a series of cases have limited the reach of defamation suits. For example, a Louisiana defamation statute permitted critics of public officials to be punished not only for false statements made with ill will but even true statements made with ill will. A district attorney in Louisiana, during a news conference, accused state judges of being lazy and inefficient and of hampering his efforts to enforce the laws. He was convicted of violating the state defamation statute. A unanimous Supreme Court held that the Constitution limits state power to impose sanctions for criticism of the official conduct of public officials. Punishment applied only to false statements made with knowledge of their falsity or with reckless disregard of whether they are true or false. "Truth may not be the subject of either civil or criminal sanctions where discussion of public affairs is concerned." Garrison v. Louisiana, 379 U.S. 64, 74 (1964). Concurrences by Justices Black, Douglas, and Goldberg objected to *any* punishment for criticizing public officials. Black and Douglas claimed that fines and jail sentences for "malicious" statements marked a return to the Sedition Act of 1798 and a revival of the law of seditious libel.

In 1966 the Court reversed another libel suit that had awarded damages to an individual employed by three county commissioners. He claimed that a newspaper column accused him of fiscal mismanagement, but the Court ruled that any implication of wrongdoing had not been directed to him personally. Rosenblatt v. Baer, 383 U.S. 75 (1966). Three concurrences by Douglas, Stewart, and Black argued that the Constitution bars any libel actions against government officials.

Public Figures

Apart from libel suits involving government officials, the Court reviews cases in which private individuals seek damages for defamation or invasion of privacy. A libel suit was brought by James Hill, who had been held hostage in his home, along with his family, by escaped convicts. His ordeal helped inspire a novel and later a play, called *The Desperate Hours*. In writing about the play, *Life* magazine related it specifically to the Hill incident and called the play a reenactment. Hill was awarded damages. The Court reversed the judgment with instructions that damages could be given only upon proof that *Life* was knowingly or recklessly false. There had to be calculated falsehoods. Mere negligence, said the Court, would put an intolerable burden on the press. Time, Inc. v. Hill, 385 U.S. 374 (1967).

This case developed the public-figure doctrine by distinguishing between private citizens (like James Hill) who desired anonymity and those who, because of their prominence in sports, entertainment, and other fields, were "public figures." The latter had a reduced right of privacy. The public-figure doctrine was used in another case in 1967. Libel damages were allowed for an athletic director accused in a magazine article of "fixing" a football game. The falsehood inflicted substantial damage on his reputation and resulted from deficient investigative and reporting techniques. Curtis Publishing Co. v. Butts, 388 U.S. 130 (1967). The Court has issued other guidelines to clarify the public-figure doctrine. Harte-Hanks Communications v. Connaughton, 491 U.S. 657 (1989).

Public Concern

In 1971 a plurality of Supreme Court Justices was ready to float another doctrine. They said that the First Amendment's impact on state libel laws depended not so much on whether the plaintiff was a public official, a public figure, or a private individual, but whether the defamation concerns "an issue of public or general concern." Rosenbloom v. Metromedia, 403 U.S. 29, 44 (1971). Under the latter test, the rights of a free press require special protection and tolerance. In his concurrence, Justice White attempted to summarize the multiple and evolving doctrines of the Court. Public officers and public figures had to prove either knowing or reckless disregard of the truth. Other plaintiffs had to prove at least negligent falsehood, "but if the publication about them was in an area of legitimate public interest, then they too must prove deliberate or reckless error."

This new formulation did not sit well. Why should a private individual be forced to satisfy the rigorous requirement of knowing-or-reckless falsity simply because the defamatory falsehood became an issue of public or general interest? Within a few years the Court abandoned the *Rosenbloom* doctrine because it gave insufficient protection to private individuals. The Court recognized that public officials and public figures have more opportunities to use the media to rebut defamation. Private individuals are "more vulnerable to injury, and the state interest in protecting them is correspondingly greater." GERTZ v. ROBERT WELCH, INC., 418 U.S. 323, 344 (1974). Although states must follow the knowing-or-reckless-disregard test for public officials and public figures, they "should retain substantial latitude in their efforts to enforce a legal remedy for defamatory falsehood injurious to the reputation of a private individual." In discarding the doctrine of "public or general concern," the Court doubted the wisdom of committing such tasks to the conscience of judges.

Libel Doctrines

1. *Actual Malice.* Public officials or public figures may recover damages if there is "actual malice" (knowledge that the statements are false or made with reckless disregard of whether they were false or not). New York Times Co. v. Sullivan, 376 U.S. 254, 280 (1964).

2. *Public Figure.* Certain individuals who are prominent in public life (because of sports, entertainment, and so forth) have a reduced right of privacy. Time, Inc. v. Hill, 385 U.S. 374, 384–86 (1967). Their defamation suits must meet a higher standard of proof than for a private citizen.

3. *Public Concern.* Libel actions are more difficult to win if the information published relates to an issue of public or general concern. Rosenbloom v. Metromedia, 403 U.S. 29, 44 (1971). The Court later backed away from that test. Gertz v. Robert Welch, Inc., 418 U.S. 323 (1974).

4. *Fact vs. Opinion.* There is no wholesale exemption for what might be called "opinion." Expressions of opinion may often imply an assertion of objective fact. Milkovich v. Lorain Journal Co., 497 U.S. 1 (1990).

In *Gertz,* the Court suggested that statements of "opinion" might be exempt from defamation suits. In 1990 the Court focused specifically on the issue of whether a columnist can be sued for expressing an opinion. The Court denied that a dichotomy exists between fact and opinion, refusing to create a wholesale defamation exemption for anything that might be labeled an opinion. Expressions of opinion, said the Court, may often imply an assertion of objective fact. The 7–2 decision permits libel suits if opinions contain or imply "false and defamatory" facts. Milkovich v. Lorain Journal Co., 497 U.S. 1 (1990). A year later the Court ruled that writers may be sued for fabricating quotations if the injurious words are significantly different from what was actually said. Manufactured quotations can be the basis for a libel suit if the writer makes a "material change in the meaning" of someone's statement. Under this test, writers still have substantial flexibility to alter a speaker's words without fear of a libel suit. Masson v. New Yorker Magazine, Inc., 501 U.S. 496 (1991).

This heightened solicitude for private individuals who seek damages in libel suits has been reinforced over the years. A series of cases adopted a narrow definition of "public figure," thus allowing private individuals who might be prominent locally a better chance of collecting on a libel suit.[4] However, in 1985 the Court resurrected the public-concern doctrine. In a 5–4 decision, it held that speech on matters of "purely private concern" is entitled to less First Amendment protection than speech involving public concern. Once it is determined that there is a lack of public concern in a libel action, plaintiffs may be awarded damages without having to show actual malice. Dun & Bradstreet, Inc. v. Greenmoss Builders, 472 U.S. 749 (1985). The dissenters objected that the majority had provided "almost no guidance as to what constitutes a protected matter of public concern." The public-concern doctrine was used a year later in another 5–4 decision. The Court held that when a newspaper publishes speech of public concern about a private figure, the individual cannot recover libel damages without showing that the statements are false. Philadelphia Newspapers, Inc. v. Hepps, 475 U.S. 767 (1986). Libel cases are governed by a number of doctrines (see box).

---

4. Wolston v. Reader's Digest Assn., Inc., 443 U.S. 157 (1979); Hutchinson v. Proxmire, 443 U.S. 111 (1979); Time, Inc. v. Firestone, 424 U.S. 448 (1976). In *Hutchinson,* the Court noted: "Clearly, those charged with defamation cannot, by their own conduct, create their own defense by making the claimant a public figure." 443 U.S. at 135.

The Heavy Cost of Litigation

Although *Sullivan* made it more difficult for public officials and public figures to win libel verdicts against the press, nothing in that decision prevented the filing of a suit and forcing the press to exhaust funds and resources to defend itself. Celebrities claiming injury sued the press and the media for large sums. For example, General William C. Westmoreland filed a $120 million suit against CBS-TV and its weekly program "60 Minutes" for charging that he and his command had misled the public, the Congress, and the President about enemy troop strength in Vietnam in order to advance the political argument that the war was being won. Ariel Sharon, former Israeli Defense Minister, sued *Time* magazine for $50 million for suggesting that he had encouraged the massacre of hundreds of Lebanese in the Sabra and Shatila refugee camps.

Westmoreland agreed to drop the case in 1985, before verdict, in return for a joint statement in which CBS expressed its respect for his "long and faithful service to his country" and Westmoreland gave his esteem for CBS's "distinguished journalistic tradition." In a separate statement, CBS said it stood by the fairness and accuracy of the program. Also in 1985, a jury in New York issued a split verdict on Sharon, concluding that *Time* had acted negligently and carelessly but not with actual malice or reckless disregard for the truth. In a separate action in Israel, Sharon and *Time* announced an out-of-court settlement in 1986 in which *Time* admitted that its story was "erroneous" and agreed to pay part of Sharon's legal fees. The legal expenses for CBS and *Time* to defend their interests were vast.

A decision by the Supreme Court in 1988 sparked an unusual amount of interest in libel law. A jury had awarded $200,000 to the Reverend Jerry Falwell, founder of the Moral Majority, for damages inflicted by an advertisement in *Hustler* magazine. The ad was a takeoff on a Campari liqueur campaign in which celebrities discussed "their first time." The parody portrays Falwell as a drunkard having sex with his mother in an outhouse. Although the jury said the parody was not libelous because it was patently unbelievable, it assessed damages for the "emotional distress" suffered by Falwell. A unanimous Court ruled that public figures and public officials unable to prove libel cannot recover damages for parodies, no matter how outrageous, that might cause emotional distress. "Outrageousness" was too subjective a test and would interfere with the free flow of ideas protected by the First Amendment. HUSTLER MAGAZINE v. FALWELL, 485 U.S. 46 (1988).

The original purpose of the actual-malice test was to safeguard the press by erecting a high shield. How does a plaintiff determine that a falsehood results from malice? What steps must be taken to show that a publisher has "knowledge" or acts with "reckless disregard" in issuing false statements? May plaintiffs interview and depose employees of a newspaper or broadcasting station to discover the state of mind of those who edit, produce, and publish stories? Would this threaten a free press? In 1979 a 6–3 Court held that the First Amendment does not prohibit a plaintiff in a libel case from inquiring into the editorial process. Herbert v. Lando, 441 U.S. 153 (1979).

A 1985 libel case offers a rare example where the Court was able to speak with a unanimous voice. In letters to President Reagan, someone had written false and derogatory statements about a person being considered for U.S. attorney. The author of the letters claimed that the Petition Clause of the First Amendment gave him absolute immunity from liability. The Court held that statements made in a petition are not entitled to greater constitutional protection than other First Amendment expressions. McDonald v. Smith, 472 U.S. 479 (1985).

The law on libel has become so confused and costly for plaintiffs and defendants that alternatives to adjudication are being explored. One approach is to bar lawsuits if a complainant receives a retraction or an opportunity to reply in a newspaper or broadcast outlet. If the complainant fails to receive that satisfaction, either side could ask a court for a declaratory judgment on the truth or falsity of the statement at issue. Vague standards, including "actual malice" and "public figure," could be eliminated.

New York Times Co. v. Sullivan

376 U.S. 254 (1964)

An advertisement in the *New York Times* included statements, some of them false, about actions that Alabama police had taken against civil rights demonstrators. L.B. Sullivan, who supervised the police, brought a libel action against the newspaper and four civil rights leaders. After he won a jury award in the state courts, a unanimous Supreme Court held that the law applied by the Alabama courts gave insufficient protection to free speech and free press. The Court developed the actual-malice test for recovering damages in a defamation suit.

MR. JUSTICE BRENNAN delivered the opinion of the Court.

We are required in this case to determine for the first time the extent to which the constitutional protections for speech and press limit a State's power to award damages in a libel action brought by a public official against critics of his official conduct.

Respondent L. B. Sullivan is one of the three elected Commissioners of the City of Montgomery, Alabama. He testified that he was "Commissioner of Public Affairs and the duties are supervision of the Police Department, Fire Department, Department of Cemetery and Department of Scales." He brought this civil libel action against the four individual petitioners, who are Negroes and Alabama clergymen, and against petitioner the New York Times Company, a New York corporation which publishes the New York Times, a daily newspaper. A jury in the Circuit Court of Montgomery County awarded him damages of $500,000, the full amount claimed, against all the petitioners, and the Supreme Court of Alabama affirmed. 273 Ala. 656, 144 So. 2d 25.

Respondent's complaint alleged that he had been libeled by statements in a full-page advertisement that was carried in the New York Times on March 29, 1960. Entitled "Heed Their Rising Voices," the advertisement began by stating that "As the whole world knows by now, thousands of Southern Negro students are engaged in widespread non-violent demonstrations in positive affirmation of the right to live in human dignity as guaranteed by the U. S. Constitution and the Bill of Rights." It went on to charge that "in their efforts to uphold these guarantees, they are being met by an unprecedented wave of terror by those who would deny and negate that document which the whole world looks upon as setting the pattern

for modern freedom...." Succeeding paragraphs purported to illustrate the "wave of terror" by describing certain alleged events. The text concluded with an appeal for funds for three purposes: support of the student movement, "the struggle for the right-to-vote," and the legal defense of Dr. Martin Luther King, Jr., leader of the movement, against a perjury indictment then pending in Montgomery.

The text appeared over the names of 64 persons, many widely known for their activities in public affairs, religion, trade unions, and the performing arts. Below these names, and under a line reading "We in the south who are struggling daily for dignity and freedom warmly endorse this appeal," appeared the names of the four individual petitioners and of 16 other persons....

Of the 10 paragraphs of text in the advertisement, the third and a portion of the sixth were the basis of respondent's claim of libel. They read as follows:

Third paragraph:

"In Montgomery, Alabama, after students sang 'My Country, 'Tis of Thee' on the State Capitol steps, their leaders were expelled from school, and truckloads of police armed with shotguns and tear-gas ringed the Alabama State College Campus. When the entire student body protested to state authorities by refusing to re-register, their dining hall was padlocked in an attempt to starve them into submission."

Sixth paragraph:

"Again and again the Southern violators have answered Dr. King's peaceful protests with intimidation and violence. They have bombed his home almost killing his wife and child. They have assaulted his person. They have arrested him seven times — for 'speeding,' 'loitering' and similar 'offenses.' And now they have charged him with 'perjury' — a *felony* under which they could imprison him for *ten years*...."

Although neither of these statements mentions respondent by name, he contended that the word "police" in the third paragraph referred to him as the Montgomery Commissioner who supervised the Police Department, so that he was being accused of "ringing" the campus with police. He further claimed that the paragraph would be read as imputing to the police, and hence to him, the padlocking of the dining hall in order to starve the students into submission. As to the sixth paragraph, he contended that since arrests are ordinarily made by the police, the statement "They have arrested [Dr. King] seven times" would be read as referring to him; he further contended that the "They" who did the arresting would be equated with the "They" who committed the other described acts and with the "Southern violators." Thus, he argued, the paragraph would be read as accusing the Montgomery police, and hence him, of answering Dr. King's protests with "intimidation and violence," bombing his home, assaulting his person, and charging him with perjury. Respondent and six other Montgomery residents testified that they read some or all of the statements as referring to him in his capacity as Commissioner.

It is uncontroverted that some of the statements contained in the two paragraphs were not accurate descriptions of events which occurred in Montgomery. Although Negro students staged a demonstration on the State Capitol steps, they sang the National Anthem and not "My Country, 'Tis of Thee." Although nine students were expelled by the State Board of Education, this was not for leading the demonstration at the Capitol, but for demanding service at a lunch counter in the Montgomery County Courthouse on another day. Not the entire student body, but most of it, had protested the expulsion, not by refusing to register, but by boycotting classes on a single day; virtually all the students did register for the ensuing semester. The campus dining hall was not padlocked on any occasion, and the only students who may have been barred from eating there were the few who had neither signed a preregistration application nor requested temporary meal tickets. Although the police were deployed near the campus in large numbers on three occasions, they did not at any time "ring" the campus, and they were

not called to the campus in connection with the demonstration on the State Capitol steps, as the third paragraph implied. Dr. King had not been arrested seven times, but only four; and although he claimed to have been assaulted some years earlier in connection with his arrest for loitering outside a courtroom, one of the officers who made the arrest denied that there was such an assault.

On the premise that the charges in the sixth paragraph could be read as referring to him, respondent was allowed to prove that he had not participated in the events described. Although Dr. King's home had in fact been bombed twice when his wife and child were there, both of these occasions antedated respondent's tenure as Commissioner, and the police were not only not implicated in the bombings, but had made every effort to apprehend those who were. Three of Dr. King's four arrests took place before respondent became Commissioner. Although Dr. King had in fact been indicted (he was subsequently acquitted) on two counts of perjury, each of which carried a possible five-year sentence, respondent had nothing to do with procuring the indictment.

Respondent made no effort to prove that he suffered actual pecuniary loss as a result of the alleged libel....

. . .

Alabama law denies a public officer recovery of punitive damages in a libel action brought on account of a publication concerning his official conduct unless he first makes a written demand for a public retraction and the defendant fails or refuses to comply. Alabama Code, Tit. 7, § 914. Respondent served such a demand upon each of the petitioners. None of the individual petitioners responded to the demand, primarily because each took the position that he had not authorized the use of his name on the advertisement and therefore had not published the statements that respondent alleged had libeled him. The Times did not publish a retraction in response to the demand, but wrote respondent a letter stating, among other things, that "we ... are somewhat puzzled as to how you think the statements in any way reflect on you," and "you might, if you desire, let us know in what respect you claim that the statements in the advertisement reflect on you." Respondent filed this suit a few days later without answering the letter. The Times did, however, subsequently publish a retraction of the advertisement upon the demand of Governor John Patterson of Alabama, who asserted that the publication charged him with "grave misconduct and...improper actions and omissions as Governor of Alabama and Ex-Officio Chairman of the State Board of Education of Alabama." When asked to explain why there had been a retraction for the Governor but not for respondent, the Secretary of the Times testified: "We did that because we didn't want anything that was published by The Times to be a reflection on the State of Alabama and the Governor was, as far as we could see, the embodiment of the State of Alabama and the proper representative of the State and, furthermore, we had by that time learned more of the actual facts which the ad purported to recite and, finally, the ad did refer to the action of the State authorities and the Board of Education presumably of which the Governor is the ex-officio chairman...." On the other hand, he testified that he did not think that "any of the language in there referred to Mr. Sullivan."

. . .

II.

Under Alabama law as applied in this case, a publication is "libelous per se" if the words "tend to injure a person...in his reputation" or to "bring [him] into public contempt"; the trial court stated that the standard was met if the words are such as to "injure him in his public office, or impute misconduct to him in his office, or want of official integrity, or want of fidelity to a public trust...." ...Unless [the defendant] can discharge the burden of proving truth, general damages are presumed, and may be awarded without proof of pecuniary injury. A showing of actual malice is apparently a prerequisite to recovery of punitive damages, and the defendant may in any event forestall a punitive award by a retraction meeting the statutory requirements. Good motives and belief in truth do not negate an inference of malice, but are relevant only in mitigation of punitive damages if the jury chooses to accord them weight....

The question before us is whether this rule of liability, as applied to an action brought by a public official against critics of his official conduct, abridges the freedom of speech and of the press that is guaranteed by the First and Fourteenth Amendments.

. . .

The general proposition that freedom of expression upon public questions is secured by the First Amendment has long been settled by our decisions. The constitutional safeguard, we have said, "was fashioned to assure unfettered interchange of ideas for the bringing about of political and social changes desired by the people." *Roth v. United States,* 354 U. S. 476, 484....

. . .

Thus we consider this case against the background of a profound national commitment to the principle that debate on public issues should be uninhibited, robust, and wide-open, and that it may well include vehement, caustic, and sometimes unpleasantly sharp attacks on government and public officials....The present advertisement, as an expression of grievance and protest on one of the major public issues of our time, would seem clearly to qualify for the constitutional protection. The question is whether it forfeits that protection by the falsity of some of its factual statements and by its alleged defamation of respondent.

. . .

Injury to official reputation affords no more warrant for repressing speech that would otherwise be free than does factual error. Where judicial officers are involved, this Court has held that concern for the dignity and reputation of the courts does not justify the punishment as criminal contempt of criticism of the judge or his decision. *Bridges* v. *California,* 314 U. S. 252. This is true even though the utterance contains "half-truths" and "misinformation."...If judges are to be treated as "men of fortitude, able to thrive in a hardy climate,"...surely the same must be true of other government officials, such as elected city commissioners. Criticism of their official conduct does not lose its constitutional protection merely because it is effective criticism and hence diminishes their official reputations.

If neither factual error nor defamatory content suffices to remove the constitutional shield from criticism of official conduct, the combination of the two elements is no less inadequate. This is the lesson to be drawn from the great controversy over the Sedition Act of 1798, 1 Stat. 596, which first crystallized a national awareness of the central meaning of the First Amendment....

Although the Sedition Act was never tested in this Court, the attack upon its validity has carried the day in the court of history. Fines levied in its prosecution were repaid by Act of Congress on the ground that it was unconstitutional....Jefferson, as President, pardoned those who had been convicted and sentenced under the Act and remitted their fines....

· · ·

The constitutional guarantees require, we think, a federal rule that prohibits a public official from recovering damages for a defamatory falsehood relating to his official conduct unless he proves that the statement was made with "actual malice" — that is, with knowledge that it was false or with reckless disregard of whether it was false or not....

III.

...[W]e consider that the proof presented to show actual malice lacks the convincing clarity which the constitutional standard demands, and hence that it would not constitutionally sustain the judgment for respondent under the proper rule of law. The case of the individual petitioners requires little discussion. Even assuming that they could constitutionally be found to have authorized the use of their names on the advertisement, there was no evidence whatever that they were aware of any erroneous statements or were in any way reckless in that regard. The judgment against them is thus without constitutional support.

As to the Times, we similarly conclude that the facts do not support a finding of actual malice. The statement by the Times' Secretary that, apart from the padlocking allegation, he thought the advertisement was "substantially correct," affords no constitutional warrant for the Alabama Supreme Court's conclusion that it was a "cavalier ignoring of the falsity of the advertisement [from which] the jury could not have but been impressed with the bad faith of The Times, and its maliciousness inferable therefrom." The statement does not indicate malice at the time of the publication; even if the advertisement was not "substantially correct" — although respondent's own proofs tend to show that it was — that opinion was at least a reasonable one, and there was no evidence to impeach the witness' good faith in holding it. The Times' failure to retract upon respondent's demand, although it later retracted upon the demand of Governor Patterson, is likewise not adequate evidence of malice for constitutional purposes. Whether or not a failure to retract may ever constitute such evidence, there are two reasons why it does not here. *First,* the letter

written by the Times reflected a reasonable doubt on its part as to whether the advertisement could reasonably be taken to refer to respondent at all. *Second,* it was not a final refusal, since it asked for an explanation on this point — a request that respondent chose to ignore....

Finally, there is evidence that the Times published the advertisement without checking its accuracy against the news stories in the Times' own files. The mere presence of the stories in the files does not, of course, establish that the Times "knew" the advertisement was false, since the state of mind required for actual malice would have to be brought home to the persons in the Times' organization having responsibility for the publication of the advertisement. With respect to the failure of those persons to make the check, the record shows that they relied upon their knowledge of the good reputation of many of those whose names were listed as sponsors of the advertisement, and upon the letter from A. Philip Randolph, known to them as a responsible individual, certifying that the use of the names was authorized....

The judgment of the Supreme Court of Alabama is reversed and the case is remanded to that court for further proceedings not inconsistent with this opinion.

Reversed and remanded.

MR. JUSTICE BLACK, with whom MR. JUSTICE DOUGLAS joins, concurring.

...I vote to reverse exclusively on the ground that the Times and the individual defendants had an absolute, unconditional constitutional right to publish in the Times advertisement their criticisms of the Montgomery agencies and officials....

MR. JUSTICE GOLDBERG, with whom MR. JUSTICE DOUGLAS joins, concurring in the result.

· · ·

In my view, the First and Fourteenth Amendments to the Constitution afford to the citizen and to the press an absolute, unconditional privilege to criticize official conduct despite the harm which may flow from excesses and abuses....

Gertz v. Robert Welch, Inc.

418 U.S. 323 (1974)

An article appearing in a magazine published by Robert Welch, Inc., claimed that a murder trial was part of a Communist conspiracy to discredit the local police. The article falsely stated that Elmer Gertz, an attorney who represented the parents of a youth killed by the police, had a criminal record and labeled him a "Communist-fronter." This case prompted the Court to revisit its holdings on the protections of private individuals who are subject to defamatory falsehoods.

MR. JUSTICE POWELL delivered the opinion of the Court.

This Court has struggled for nearly a decade to define the proper accommodation between the law of defamation and the freedoms of speech and press protected by the First Amendment. With this decision we return to that effort....

I

In 1968 a Chicago policeman named Nuccio shot and killed a youth named Nelson. The state authorities prosecuted Nuccio for the homicide and ultimately obtained a conviction for murder in the second degree. The Nelson family retained petitioner Elmer Gertz, a reputable attorney, to represent them in civil litigation against Nuccio.

Respondent publishes American Opinion, a monthly outlet for the views of the John Birch Society. Early in the 1960's the magazine began to warn of a nationwide conspiracy to discredit local law enforcement agencies and create in their stead a national police force capable of supporting a Communist dictatorship. As part of the continuing effort to alert the public to this assumed danger, the managing editor of American Opinion commissioned an article on the murder trial of Officer Nuccio. For this purpose he engaged a regular contributor to the magazine. In March 1969 respondent published the resulting article under the title "FRAME-UP: Richard Nuccio And The War On Police." The article purports to demonstrate that the testimony against Nuccio at his criminal trial was false and that his prosecution was part of the Communist campaign against the police.

In his capacity as counsel for the Nelson family in the civil litigation, petitioner attended the coroner's inquest into the boy's death and initiated actions for damages, but he neither discussed Officer Nuccio with the press nor played any part in the criminal proceeding. Notwithstanding petitioner's remote connection with the prosecution of Nuccio, respondent's magazine portrayed him as an architect of the "frame-up." According to the article, the police file on petitioner took "a

big, Irish cop to lift." The article stated that petitioner had been an official of the "Marxist League for Industrial Democracy, originally known as the Intercollegiate Socialist Society, which has advocated the violent seizure of our government." It labeled Gertz a "Leninist" and a "Communist-fronter." It also stated that Gertz had been an officer of the National Lawyers Guild, described as a Communist organization that "probably did more than any other outfit to plan the Communist attack on the Chicago police during the 1968 Democratic Convention."

These statements contained serious inaccuracies. The implication that petitioner had a criminal record was false. Petitioner had been a member and officer of the National Lawyers Guild some 15 years earlier, but there was no evidence that he or that organization had taken any part in planning the 1968 demonstrations in Chicago. There was also no basis for the charge that petitioner was a "Leninist" or a "Communist-fronter." And he had never been a member of the "Marxist League for Industrial Democracy" or the "Intercollegiate Socialist Society."

The managing editor of American Opinion made no effort to verify or substantiate the charges against petitioner....

[Robert Welch, Inc., asserted that Gertz was a public official or a public figure and that the article concerned an issue of public interest and concern. Relying on New York Times Co. v. Sullivan *(1964), the publisher claimed that Gertz had to prove "actual malice" — that the publisher had knowledge the article was false or operated with reckless disregard whether it was false or not. The magazine's managing editor submitted an affidavit denying any knowledge of the falsity of the statements and stating that he had relied on the author's reputation for accuracy.]*

II

The principal issue in this case is whether a newspaper or broadcaster that publishes defamatory falsehoods about an individual who is neither a public official nor a public figure may claim a constitutional privilege against liability for the injury inflicted by those statements. The Court considered this question on the rather different set of facts presented in *Rosenbloom v. Metromedia, Inc.*, 403 U. S. 29 (1971).

...The eight Justices who participated in *Rosenbloom* announced their views in five separate opinions, none of which commanded more than three votes....

In affirming the trial court's judgment in the instant case, the Court of Appeals relied on MR. JUSTICE BRENNAN's conclusion for the *Rosenbloom* plurality that "all discussion and communication involving matters of public or general concern," 403 U. S., at 44, warrant the protection from liability for defamation accorded by the rule originally enunciated in *New York Times Co. v. Sullivan,* 376 U. S. 254 (1964)....

...MR. JUSTICE BRENNAN took the *New York Times* privilege one step further. He concluded that its protection should extend to defamatory falsehoods relating to private persons if the statements concerned matters of general or public interest. He abjured the suggested distinction between public officials and public figures on the one hand and private individuals on the other. He focused instead on society's interest in learning about certain issues: "If a matter is a subject of public or general interest, it cannot suddenly become less so merely because a private individual is involved, or because in some sense the individual did not 'voluntarily' choose to become involved."...

III

We begin with the common ground. Under the First Amendment there is no such thing as a false idea. However pernicious an opinion may seem, we depend for its correction not on the conscience of judges and juries but on the competition of other ideas. But there is no constitutional value in false statements of fact....

Although the erroneous statement of fact is not worthy of constitutional protection, it is nevertheless inevitable in free debate. As James Madison pointed out in the Report on the Virginia Resolutions of 1798: "Some degree of abuse is inseparable from the proper use of every thing; and in no instance is this more true than in that of the press."...And punishment of error runs the risk of inducing a cautious and restrictive exercise of the constitutionally guaranteed freedoms of speech and press. Our decisions recognize that a rule of strict liability that compels a publisher or broadcaster to guarantee the accuracy of his factual assertions may lead to intolerable self-censorship....

The need to avoid self-censorship by the news media is, however, not the only societal value at issue. If it were, this Court would have embraced long ago the view that publishers and broadcasters enjoy an unconditional and indefeasible immunity from liability for defamation....

The legitimate state interest underlying the law of libel is the compensation of individuals for the harm inflicted on them by defamatory falsehood. We would not lightly require the State to abandon this purpose,...

...The first remedy of any victim of defamation is self-help—using available opportunities to contradict the lie or correct the error and thereby to minimize its adverse impact on reputation. Public officials and public figures usually enjoy significantly greater access to the channels of effective communication and hence have a more realistic opportunity to counteract false statements than private individuals normally enjoy. Private individuals are therefore more vulnerable to injury, and the state interest in protecting them is correspondingly greater.

More important than the likelihood that private individuals will lack effective opportunities for rebuttal, there is a compelling normative consideration underlying the distinction between public and private defamation plaintiffs. An individual who decides to seek governmental office must accept certain necessary consequences of that involvement in public affairs. He runs the risk of closer public scrutiny than might otherwise be the case....

Those classed as public figures stand in a similar position. Hypothetically, it may be possible for someone to become a public figure through no purposeful action of his own, but the instances of truly involuntary public figures must be exceedingly rare. For the most part those who attain this status have assumed roles of especial prominence in the affairs of society....

Even if the foregoing generalities do not obtain in every instance, the communications media are entitled to act on the assumption that public officials and public figures have voluntarily exposed themselves to increased risk of injury from defamatory falsehood concerning them. No such assumption is justified with respect to a private individual....private individuals are not only more vulnerable to injury than public officials and public figures; they are also more deserving of recovery.

For these reasons we conclude that the States should retain substantial latitude in their efforts to enforce a legal remedy for defamatory falsehood injurious to the reputation of a private individual. The extension of the *New York Times* test proposed by the *Rosenbloom* plurality would abridge this legitimate state interest to a degree that we find unacceptable. And it would occasion the additional difficulty of forcing state and federal judges to decide on an *ad hoc* basis which publications address issues of "general or public interest" and which do not—to determine, in the words of MR. JUSTICE MARSHALL, "what information is relevant to self-government." *Rosenbloom v. Metromedia, Inc.,* 403 U. S., at 79. We doubt the wisdom of committing this task to the conscience of judges. Nor does the Constitution require us to draw so thin a line between the drastic alternatives of the *New York Times* privilege and the common law of strict liability for defamatory error....

We hold that, so long as they do not impose liability without fault, the States may define for themselves the appropriate standard of liability for a publisher or broadcaster of defamatory falsehood injurious to a private individual....

V

[In this section the Court denies Welch's contention that Gertz is a "public official" or a "public figure" because he had been active in community and professional affairs.]

MR. JUSTICE BLACKMUN, concurring.

. . .

MR. CHIEF JUSTICE BURGER, dissenting.

The doctrines of the law of defamation have had a gradual evolution primarily in the state courts. In *New York Times Co. v. Sullivan,* 376 U. S. 254 (1964), and its progeny this Court entered this field.

Agreement or disagreement with the law as it has evolved to this time does not alter the fact that it has been orderly development with a consistent basic rationale. In today's opinion the Court abandons the traditional thread so far as the ordinary private citizen is concerned and introduces the concept that the media will be liable for neg-ligence in publishing defamatory statements with respect to such persons....

MR. JUSTICE DOUGLAS, dissenting.

The Court describes this case as a return to the struggle of "defin[ing] the proper accommodation between the law of defamation and the freedoms of speech and press protected by the First Amendment." It is indeed a struggle, once described by Mr. Justice Black as "the same quagmire" in which the Court "is now helplessly struggling in the field of obscenity." *Curtis Publishing Co. v. Butts,* 388 U. S. 130, 171 (concurring opinion). I would suggest that the struggle is a quite hopeless one, for, in light of the command of the First Amendment, no "accommodation" of its freedoms can be "proper" except those made by the Framers themselves.

. . .

MR. JUSTICE BRENNAN, dissenting.

...I adhere to my view expressed in *Rosenbloom v. Metromedia, Inc., supra,* that we strike the proper accommodation between avoidance of media self-censorship and protection of individual reputations only when we require States to apply the *New York Times Co. v. Sullivan,* 376 U.S. 254 (1964), knowing-or-reckless-falsity standard in civil libel actions concerning media reports of the involvement of private individuals in events of public or general interest.

. . .

MR. JUSTICE WHITE, dissenting.

...The States must now struggle to discern the meaning of such ill-defined concepts as "liability without fault" and to fashion novel rules for the recovery of damages. These matters have not been briefed or argued by the parties and their workability has not been seriously explored. Nevertheless, yielding to the apparently irresistible impulse to announce a new and different interpretation of the First Amendment, the Court discards history and precedent in its rush to refashion defamation law in accordance with the inclinations of a perhaps evanescent majority of the Justices.

. . .

Hustler Magazine v. Falwell

485 U.S. 46 (1988)

Jerry Falwell, a nationally known minister and commentator on politics and public affairs, filed a libel suit against the *Hustler* magazine and its publisher, Larry C. Flynt. The suit sought to recover damages for libel and intentional infliction of emotional distress arising from the publication of an advertisement parody that displayed Falwell as a drunkard having sex with his mother in an outhouse. The jury rejected the libel claim on the ground that the parody was not believable, but it ruled in Falwell's favor on the emotional distress claim. The Fourth Circuit affirmed the ruling.

CHIEF JUSTICE REHNQUIST delivered the opinion of the Court.

Petitioner Hustler Magazine, Inc., is a magazine of nationwide circulation. Respondent Jerry Falwell, a nationally known minister who has been active as a commentator on politics and public affairs, sued petitioner and its publisher, petitioner Larry Flynt, to recover damages for invasion of privacy, libel, and intentional infliction of emotional distress....

The inside front cover of the November 1983 issue of Hustler Magazine featured a "parody" of an advertisement for Campari Liqueur that contained the name and picture of respondent and was entitled "Jerry Falwell talks about his first time." This parody was modeled after actual Campari ads that included interviews with various celebrities about their "first times." Although it was apparent by the end of each interview that this meant the first time they sampled Campari, the ads clearly played on the sexual double entendre of the general subject of "first times." Copying the form and layout of these Campari ads, Hustler's editors chose respondent as the featured celebrity and drafted an alleged "interview" with him in which he states that his "first time" was during a drunken incestuous rendezvous with his mother in an outhouse. The Hustler parody portrays respondent and his mother as drunk and immoral, and suggests that respondent is a hypocrite who preaches only when he is drunk. In small print at the bottom of the page, the ad contains the disclaimer, "ad parody—not to be taken seriously." The magazine's table of contents also lists the ad as "Fiction; Ad and Personality Parody."

Soon after the November issue of Hustler became available to the public, respondent brought this diversity action in the United States District Court for the Western District of Virginia against Hustler Magazine, Inc., Larry C. Flynt, and Flynt Distributing Co. Respondent stated in his complaint that publication of the ad parody in Hustler entitled him to recover damages for libel, invasion of privacy, and intentional infliction of emotional distress. The case proceeded to trial. At the close of the evidence, the District court granted a directed verdict for petitioners on the invasion of privacy claim. The jury then found against respondent on the libel claim, specifically finding that the ad parody could not "reasonably be understood as describing actual facts about [respondent] or actual events in which [he] participated."... The jury ruled for respondent on the intentional infliction of emotional distress claim, however, and stated that he should be awarded $100,000 in compensatory damages, as well as $50,000 each in punitive damages from petitioners....

. . .

This case presents us with a novel question involving First Amendment limitations upon a State's authority to protect its citizens from the intentional infliction of emotional distress. We must decide whether a public figure may recover damages for emotional harm caused by the publication of an ad parody offensive to him, and doubtless gross and repugnant in the eyes of most. Respondent would have us find that a State's interest in protecting public figures from emotional distress is sufficient to deny First Amendment protection to speech that is patently offensive and is intended to inflict emotional injury, even when that speech could not reasonably have been interpreted as stating actual facts about the public figure involved. This we decline to do.

At the heart of the First Amendment is the recognition of the fundamental importance of the free flow of ideas and opinions on matters of public interest and concern.... We have therefore been particularly vigilant to ensure that individual expressions of ideas remain free from governmentally imposed sanctions....

The sort of robust political debate encouraged by the First Amendment is bound to produce speech that is critical of those who hold public office or those public figures who are "intimately involved in the resolution of important public questions or, by reason of their fame, shape events in areas of concern to society at large." ... Such criticism, inevitably, will not always be reasoned or moderate; public figures as well as public officials will be subject to "vehement, caustic, and sometimes unpleasantly sharp attacks," ...

Of course, this does not mean that *any* speech about a public figure is immune from sanction in the form of damages. Since *New York Times Co. v. Sullivan, supra,* we have consistently ruled that a public figure may hold a speaker liable for the damage to reputation caused by publication of a defamatory falsehood, but only if the statement was made "with knowledge that it was false or with reckless disregard of whether it was false or not." *Id.,* 376 U.S., at 279–280. False statements of fact are particularly valueless; they interfere with the truth-seeking function of the marketplace of ideas, and they cause damage to an individual's reputation that cannot easily be repaired by counterspeech, however persuasive or effective. See *Gertz,* 418 U.S., at 340, 344, n. 9. But even though falsehoods have little value in and of themselves, they are "nevertheless inevitable in free debate," *id.,* at 340, and a rule that would impose strict liability on a publisher for false factual assertions would have an undoubted "chilling" effect on speech relating to public figures that does have constitutional value. "Freedoms of expression require 'breathing space.'" *Philadelphia Newspapers, Inc. v. Hepps,* 475 U.S. 767, 772 (1986) (quoting *New York Times,* 376 U.S., at 272). This breathing space is provided by a constitutional rule that allows public figures to recover for libel or defamation only when they can prove *both* that the statement was false and that the statement was made with the requisite level of culpability.

Respondent argues, however, that a different standard should apply in this case because here the State seeks to prevent not reputational damage, but the severe emotional distress suffered by the person who is the subject of an offensive publication.... In respondent's view, and in the view of the Court of Appeals, so long as the utterance was intended to inflict emotional distress, was outrageous, and did in fact inflict serious emotional distress, it is of no constitutional import whether the statement was a fact or an opinion, or whether it was true or false. It is the intent to cause injury that is the gravamen of the tort, and

the State's interest in preventing emotional harm simply outweighs whatever interest a speaker may have in speech of this type.

Generally speaking the law does not regard the intent to inflict emotional distress as one which should receive much solicitude, and it is quite understandable that most if not all jurisdictions have chosen to make it civilly culpable where the conduct in question is sufficiently "outrageous." But in the world of debate about public affairs, many things done with motives that are less than admirable are protected by the First Amendment. In *Garrison v. Louisiana,* 379 U.S. 64 (1964), we held that even when a speaker or writer is motivated by hatred or illwill his expression was protected by the First Amendment....

. . .

Were we to hold otherwise, there can be little doubt that political cartoonists and satirists would be subjected to damages awards without any showing that their work falsely defamed its subject. Webster's defines a caricature as "the deliberately distorted picturing or imitating of a person, literary style, etc. By exaggerating features or mannerisms for satirical effect." Webster's New Unabridged Twentieth Century Dictionary of the English Language 275 (2d ed. 1979). The appeal of the political cartoon or caricature is often based on exploration of unfortunate physical traits or politically embarrassing events—an exploration often calculated to injure the feelings of the subject of the portrayal. The art of the cartoonist is often not reasoned or evenhanded, but slashing and onesided....

. . .

Despite their sometimes caustic nature, from the early cartoon portraying George Washington as an ass down to the present day, graphic depictions and satirical cartoons have played a prominent role in public and political debate. Nast's castigation of the Tweed Ring, Walt McDougall's characterization of presidential candidate James G. Blaine's banquet with the millionaires at Delmonico's as "The Royal Feast of Belshazzar," and numerous other efforts have undoubtedly had an effect on the course and outcome of contemporaneous debate. Lincoln's tall, gangling posture, Teddy Roosevelt's glasses and teeth, and Franklin D. Roosevelt's jutting jaw and cigarette holder have been memorialized by political cartoons with an effect that could not have been obtained by the photographer or the portrait artist. From the viewpoint of history it is clear that our political discourse would have been considerably poorer without them.

Respondent contends, however, that the caricature in question here was so "outrageous" as to distinguish it from more traditional political cartoons. There is no doubt that the caricature of respondent and his mother published in Hustler is at best a distant cousin of the political cartoons described above, and a rather poor relation at that. If it were possible by laying down a principled standard to separate the one from the other, public discourse would probably suffer little or no harm. But we doubt that there is any such standard, and we are quite sure that the pejorative description "outrageous" does not supply one. "Outrageousness" in the area of political and social discourse has an inherent subjectiveness about it which would allow a jury to impose liability on the basis of the jurors' tastes or views, or perhaps on the basis of their dislike of a particular expression. An "outrageousness" standard thus runs afoul of our longstanding refusal to allow damages to be awarded because the speech in question may have an adverse emotional impact on the audience....

Admittedly, these oft-repeated First Amendment principles, like other principles, are subject to limitations. We recognized in *Pacifica Foundation,* that speech that is " 'vulgar,' 'offensive,' and 'shocking' " is "not entitled to absolute constitutional protection under all circumstances." 438 U.S., at 747. In *Chaplinsky* v. *New Hampshire,* 315 U.S. 568 (1942), we held that a state could lawfully punish an individual for the use of insulting " 'fighting' words—those which by their very utterance inflict injury or tend to incite an immediate breach of the peace.".... But the sort of expression involved in this case does not seem to us to be governed by any exception to the general First Amendment principles stated above.

We conclude that public figure and public officials may not recover for the tort of intentional infliction of emotional distress by reason of publications such as the one here at issue without showing in addition that the publication contains a false statement of fact which was made with "actual malice," *i.e.,* with knowledge that the statement was false or with reckless disregard as to whether or not it was true....

Here it is clear that respondent Falwell is a "public figure" for purposes of First Amendment law. The jury found against respondent on his libel claim when it decided that the Hustler ad parody could not "reasonably be understood as describing actual facts about [respondent] or actual events in which [he] participated.".... The Court of Appeals interpreted the jury's finding to be that the ad parody "was not reasonably believable,".... and in accordance with our custom we accept this finding. Respondent is thus relegated to his claim for damages awarded by the jury for the intentional infliction of emotional distress by "outrageous" conduct. But for reasons heretofore stated this claim cannot, consistently with the First Amendment, form a basis for the award of damages when the conduct in question is the publication of a caricature such as the ad parody involved here. The judgment of the Court of Appeals is accordingly

Reversed.

JUSTICE KENNEDY took no part in the consideration or decision of this case.

JUSTICE WHITE concurring in the judgment.

As I see it, the decision in *New York Times* v. *Sullivan,* 376 U.S. 254 (1964), has little to do with this case, for here the jury found that the ad contained no assertion of fact. But I agree with the Court that the judgment below, which penalized the publication of the parody, cannot be squared with the First Amendment.

E. OBSCENITY

I write about obscenity and pornography with heavy heart and wry amusement. Readers are unlikely to comprehend judicial declamations on prurient interest, lascivious matter, lewdness, lust, socially redeeming values, and contemporary community standards. Students are baffled to encounter plaintiffs called "12 200-ft Reels of Super 8 mm. Film." Still, this is an important area of First Amendment law, and there is some instruction in the Court's willingness to adjudicate and offer guidance for an overwhelmingly thankless task. The Court is regularly accused of delving into metaphysics and functioning like an ecclesiastical court.

Under English law, the test of obscenity was defined as the tendency of the written matter "to deprave and corrupt those whose minds are open to such immoral influences, and into whose hands a publication of this sort may fall." Regina v. Hicklin, L.R. 3 Q.B. 360, 371 (1868). In the United States, the issue of obscenity did not occupy much time for the national government. It was not until 1873 that Congress passed the Comstock Act to make it illegal to sell, lend, give away, or exhibit any obscene writings or pictures. The statute also prohibited the mailing of obscene materials. 17 Stat. 598–600. These and other statutes led to several Supreme Court decisions before the century was out.[5] The Supreme Court found it necessary to distinguish between coarse and vulgar writings (not covered by the statute) and lewd, lascivious, and obscene writings which were made illegal. Swearingen v. United States, 161 U.S. 446 (1896). In addition to these prohibited categories, Congress outlawed the mailing of "filthy" books. 35 Stat. 1129, § 211 (1909); United States v. Limehouse, 285 U.S. 424 (1932). A major case in 1931, upholding the rights of a free press, said that "the primary requirements of decency may be enforced against obscene publications." Near v. Minnesota, 283 U.S. 697, 716 (1931).

Significant principles were established in the lower federal courts. In 1913 Judge Learned Hand rejected the English precedent in *Hicklin*. He did not believe that society was content in reducing "our treatment of sex to the standard of a child's library in the supposed interest of a salacious few. . . ." United States v. Kennerly, 209 F. 119, 121 (S.D.N.Y. 1913). Further driving home his point: "To put thought in leash to the average conscience of the time is perhaps tolerable, but to fetter it by the necessities of the lowest and least capable seems a fatal policy." With regard to a challenge to James Joyce's *Ulysses,* a district judge held that the courts must determine whether an author *intended* a book to be obscene. The judge concluded that *Ulysses* was a sincere and honest book and that Joyce did not intend to excite sexual impulses or lustful thoughts. United States v. One Book Called "Ulysses," 5 F.Supp. 182 (S.D.N.Y. 1933). Another judge allowed a book to enter the country on the ground that a reading of it "would not stir the sex impulses of any person with a normal mind." United States v. One Book Entitled "Contraception," 51 F.2d 525, 528 (S.D.N.Y. 1931).

The Supreme Court's preoccupation with the issue of obscenity began in the 1950s. In a censorship case involving a New York law banning "sacrilegious" movies, a unanimous Court held that the statute violated two constitutional principles: the presumption against prior restraint and the forbidden use of religious objectives to pursue state policy. Joseph Burstyn, Inc. v. Wilson, 343 U.S. 495 (1952). In 1957 another unanimous ruling struck down a Michigan statute that sought to keep "obscene" books from the general public when the book would have a potentially deleterious effect on youth. As the Court noted, the law would "reduce the adult population of Michigan to reading only what is fit for children." Butler v. Michigan, 352 U.S. 380, 383 (1957).

Fragmented Decisions

These two unanimous rulings encouraged the Court's foray into obscenity law, but subsequent cases scattered the Justices in different directions with conflicting theories. Justice Harlan later observed: "The subject of obscenity has produced a variety of views among the members of the Court unmatched in any other course of constitutional interpretation." Interstate Circuit

---

5. United States v. Chase, 135 U.S. 255 (1890); Grimm v. United States, 156 U.S. 604 (1895); Rosen v. United States, 161 U.S. 29 (1895); Andrews v. United States, 162 U.S. 420 (1896); Price v. United States, 165 U.S. 311 (1897); Dunlop v. United States, 165 U.S. 486 (1897).

v. Dallas, 390 U.S. 676 (1968). The Court split 5–4 in 1957 in upholding a state law that allowed a court, without a jury trial, to enjoin further distribution of obscene books and order their destruction. Kingsley Books, Inc. v. Brown, 354 U.S. 436 (1957). In a pivotal case the same year, the Court unveiled a set of new doctrines: obscenity is not within the area of constitutionally protected speech or press; sex and obscenity are not synonymous; the test for obscenity is whether "to the average person, applying contemporary community standards, the dominant theme of the material taken as a whole appeals to prurient interest." The dissenters attacked these vague, ill-defined standards. ROTH v. UNITED STATES, 354 U.S. 476 (1957).

To appreciate the complaint of the dissenters, look up *prurient* in the dictionary. Read also the meandering opinions, none of them attracting a majority, in Manual Enterprises v. Day, 370 U.S. 479 (1962). Justice Clark, dissenting, said of this 6 to 1 decision that "those in the majority like ancient Gaul are split into three parts...." In Jacobellis v. Ohio, 378 U.S. 184 (1964), a 6–3 decision generated five opinions by those in the majority. In one of the concurrences, Justice Stewart uttered his famous test for hard-core pornography: "I know it when I see it."

In two 1959 decisions, the Court managed a unanimous ruling on one case and an 8–1 majority on the other. In the first, it held that the denial of a license to show a motion picture (*Lady Chatterly's Lover*) violated the First Amendment freedom to advocate ideas. The movie had been banned because it presented adultery as being right and desirable under certain circumstances. Kingsley Pictures Corp. v. Regents, 360 U.S. 684 (1959). In his concurrence, Justice Black said that if the nation embarked on the road of censorship, "this Court is about the most inappropriate Supreme Court of Censors that could be found." In the other case, the Court ruled that a city ordinance was unconstitutional because its effect would allow a store owner to sell only the books he had inspected. Under this scheme, restrictions affected the distribution of constitutionally protected as well as obscene literature. Smith v. California, 361 U.S. 147 (1959).

The question of prior restraint returned in 1961, producing a 5–4 decision that upheld the examination of movies before their showing. Licensing could be used to suppress ideas—not only obscene but social and political views as well. The issue was not the standards for censorship but the act of censorship itself. Times Film Corp. v. Chicago, 365 U.S. 43 (1961). The Court supported the screening of movies, a procedure that would be intolerable for newspapers or even broadcasting. The Court later insisted on procedural safeguards whenever films are required to be submitted to a censor.[6]

Revisiting *Roth*

The tests announced in *Roth* begged for clarification. What are "contemporary community standards"? For Justices Brennan and Goldberg, the phrase referred not to state and local communities but to society at large. Jacobellis v. Ohio, 378 U.S. 184, 193 (1964). Chief Justice Warren and Justice Clark, in dissent, believed that "contemporary community standards" meant community standards, not a national standard. Two years later, in a dissent, Justice Black said he was uncertain whether the community standards referred to were worldwide, nationwide, sectionwide, statewide, countrywide, precinctwide, or townshipwide. Ginzburg v. United States, 383 U.S. 463, 479–80 (1966).

What is obscenity? *Roth* said that sex and obscenity are not synonymous. The Court has also held that obscenity means more than vulgarity. To be obscene, an expression must be erotic. Cohen v. California, 403 U.S. 15, 20 (1971). In 1985 the Court found it necessary to distinguish between "lust," which it called a normal sexual response, and the categories of

---

6. Freedman v. Maryland, 380 U.S. 51 (1965); Teitel Film Corp. v. Cusack, 390 U.S. 139 (1968); Southeastern Promotions, Ltd. v. Conrad, 420 U.S. 546 (1975); Vance v. Universal Amusement Co., 445 U.S. 308 (1980).

lasciviousness or prurient interest that involve a morbid interest in sex. Brockett v. Spokane Arcades, Inc., 472 U.S. 491 (1985). What is lascivious? What is prurient? What is morbid? Also, cities may not outlaw pornography on the ground that it discriminates against women by portraying them as sex objects. The state may not declare one perspective right and silence opponents. Hudnut v. American Booksellers Assn., Inc., 475 U.S. 1001 (1986); 771 F.2d 323.

Nudity, depending on the context, is not necessarily obscene.[7] The Court struck down as overbroad a state law that made it a punishable offense for a drive-in movie to exhibit films showing nudity when the screen is visible from a public street or place. The Court pointed out that the law would bar even "a baby's buttocks, the nude body of a war victim, or scenes from a culture in which nudity is indigenous." Erznoznik v. City of Jacksonville, 422 U.S. 205, 213 (1975). A 6–3 Court deferred to the states on the question of whether nude entertainment could take place simultaneously with the dispensing of liquor. The decision depended partly on the authority of states under the Twenty-First Amendment to control liquor.[8]

An interesting twist to *Roth* is that its author, Justice Brennan, later took the lead in restricting its scope. Writing an opinion in 1966 joined by Chief Justice Warren and Justice Fortas, he said that even if a book had (1) prurient appeal and (2) was patently offensive to contemporary community standards, it also had to be found (3) *"utterly* without redeeming social value" to be banned. All three elements had to be met. Memoirs v. Massachusetts, 383 U.S. 413, 418–19 (1966). In one of the dissents, Justice Harlan noted: "The central development that emerges from the aftermath of *Roth* ... is that no stable approach to the obscenity problem has yet been devised by this Court." He also doubted whether the utterly-without-redeeming test had "any meaning at all."

On the same day, a 5–4 Court affirmed the conviction of someone who had "pandered" to the erotic interests of readers by mailing literature at first from Intercourse and Blue Ball, Pennsylvania, and finally settling on Middlesex, New Jersey. Ginzburg v. United States, 383 U.S. 463 (1966). These promotional and advertising techniques appeared to be the decisive factors in justifying the person's conviction. Justice Douglas, dissenting, reminded his brethren of advertisements in national magazines "chock-full of thighs, ankles, calves, bosoms, eyes, and hair, to draw the potential buyer's attention to lotions, tires, food, liquor, clothing, autos, and even insurance policies."[9]

The *Miller* Standards

By 1973 the legal meaning of *obscenity* had run in so many directions that the Court needed to formulate new standards. This it did by rejecting the *Memoirs* test that a work must be *"utterly* without redeeming social value." Moreover, the Court said it was not necessary to employ a "national standard." The values of a "forum community" (such as a state) will do. New guidelines for obscenity were announced: (1) whether the "average person, applying contem-

---

7. Kois v. California, 408 U.S. 229 (1972); Jenkins v. Georgia, 418 U.S. 153, 161 (1974); Schad v. Mount Ephraim, 452 U.S. 61 (1981).

8. California v. La Rue, 409 U.S. 109 (1972). See also New York State Liquor Authority v. Bellanca, 452 U.S. 714 (1981) and Newport v. Iacobucci, 479 U.S. 92 (1986).

9. For other cases during this period, see Mishkin v. New York, 383 U.S. 502 (1966); Redrup v. New York, 386 U.S. 767 (1967); Interstate Circuit v. Dallas, 390 U.S. 676 (1968); Rabeck v. New York, 391 U.S. 462 (1968). For instructive articles on obscenity, see Harry Kalven, Jr., "The Metaphysics of the Law of Obscenity," 1960 Sup. Ct. Rev. 1; Louis Henkin, "Morals and the Constitution: The Sin of Obscenity," 63 Colum. L. Rev. 391 (1963); Earl Finbar Murphy, "The Value of Pornography," 10 Wayne L. Rev. 655 (1964); C. Peter Magrath, "The Obscenity Cases: Grapes of Roth," 1966 Sup. Ct. Rev. 7.

Obscenity Doctrines

ROTH v. UNITED STATES
(1957)

Obscenity is not within the area of constitutionally protected speech or press. The test for obscenity is whether "to the average person, applying contemporary community standards, the dominant theme of the material taken as a whole appeals to prurient interest."

MEMOIRS v. MASSACHUSETTS
(1966)

It must be established that (1) the dominant theme of the material taken as a whole appeals to a prurient interest in sex; (2) the material is patently offensive because it affronts contemporary community standards relating to the description or representation of sexual matters; and (3) the material is utterly without redeeming social value. All three elements had to be met.

MILLER v. CALIFORNIA
(1973)

Three guidelines: (1) whether the average person, applying contemporary community standards, would find that the work, taken as a whole, appeals to the prurient interest; (2) whether the work depicts or describes, in a patently offensive way, sexual conduct specifically defined by the applicable state law; and (3) whether the work, taken as a whole, lacks "serious literary, artistic, political, or scientific value."

porary community standards," would find that the work, taken as a whole, appeals to the prurient interest; (2) whether the work depicts or describes, in a patently offensive way, sexual conduct specifically defined by the applicable state law; and (3) whether the work, taken as a whole, lacks "serious literary, artistic, political, or scientific value." MILLER v. CALIFORNIA, 413 U.S. 15 (1973). One of the four dissents came from Justice Brennan, author of *Roth*. He elaborated on his objections while dissenting in another case the same day. PARIS ADULT THEATRE I v. SLATON, 413 U.S. 49 (1973). Obscenity doctrines have changed significantly from case to case (see box).

The forum-community test does not mean that a jury can operate without limits, allowing it to convict someone for showing a woman with a bare midriff. Jenkins v. Georgia, 418 U.S. 153, 161 (1974). One judge, who was reversed, told the jury that community standards on obscene films meant whatever should not be seen with their mothers sitting next to them. Liles v. Oregon, 425 U.S. 963, 966 (1975). In 1987 the Court held that only the first two prongs of the *Miller* test should be decided by juries on "contemporary community standards." Whether a work has literary, artistic, political, or scientific value need not obtain majority approval to merit protection. The value of a work does not vary from community to community. Pope v. Illinois, 481 U.S. 497 (1987).

Some of the states have refused to adopt the three tests of *Miller* v. *California*. For example, the Oregon Supreme Court said that it could not justify the prosecution of someone who failed to meet such a vague notion as contemporary standards. State citizens would be forced to guess about a future jury's estimate of contemporary state standards of "prurience." The state court also explained that the *Miller* guidelines ran counter to Oregon's political and social culture, which was "dedicated to founding a free society unfettered by the governmental imposition of some people's views of morality on the free expression of others." State v. Henry, 732 P.2d 9, 16 (Ore. 1987).

In 1969 a unanimous Court held that the private possession of obscene materials by adults at home cannot be made a crime. Adults may read and watch what they like in the privacy of their own home. Stanley v. Georgia, 394 U.S. 557 (1969) (see reading in Chapter 17). The *Stanley* doctrine does not justify the mailing of obscene materials to adults, the attempt to bring in obscene materials at a port of entry, or the importation of obscene matter intended for an adult's private use.[10] Moreover, states may outlaw the possession or viewing of child pornography even in the privacy of one's home. Osbourne v. Ohio, 495 U.S. 103 (1990).

Watching obscene films at home does not create a right to watch them at public theaters. Paris Adult Theatre I v. Slaton, 413 U.S. 49 (1973). Cities may use their zoning authority to disperse adult movie theaters, even if the distinction demands content-based regulation. Young v. American Mini Theatres, 427 U.S. 50 (1976). Cities may also adopt zoning ordinances to keep adult movie theaters away from residential areas, churches, parks, and schools. Renton v. Playtime Theatres, Inc., 475 U.S. 41 (1986). A unanimous Court in 1990 held that cities may prohibit motels from renting rooms for less than ten hours, on the theory that short-time periods indicate that the rooms are being used for prostitution. In this same case, the Court divided 6–3 when it required city regulations on sexually oriented businesses to contain procedural safeguards to avoid violations of the First Amendment. FW/PBS, Inc. v. Dallas, 493 U.S. 215 (1990).

Dial-a-Porn

Congress has been active in legislating against "dial-a-porn": sexually explicit messages available over the telephone. Legislation in 1983 prohibited any party in the District of Columbia or in interstate or foreign communication from providing by telephone, either directly or through use of a recording device, "any obscene or indecent communication for commercial purposes" to any person under eighteen years of age. 97 Stat. 1469, § 8 (1983). The statute had two problems. The provider of these messages had no way of knowing the age of the caller. The FCC, responsible for implementing this statute, found it nearly impossible to enforce it. Second, by permitting persons over eighteen to receive these messages with their consent, the statute in effect legalized dial-a-porn.

Congress passed new legislation in 1988 to completely ban dial-a-porn services, regardless of the age of the caller. 102 Stat. 424, § 6101 (1988). The Court later held that Congress may prohibit the interstate transmission of obscene commercial telephone messages, but that the ban on *indecent* messages violated the First Amendment. There were no legislative findings to justify the conclusion that Congress was unable to devise constitutionally acceptable and less restrictive means to achieve the government's legitimate interest in protecting minors. The statute, therefore, was not drawn in a sufficiently narrow manner. Sable Communications of Cal. v. FCC, 492 U.S. 115 (1989).

In response, Congress rewrote the statute to require telephone companies to block access to sexually explicit messages unless customers ask in writing to receive them. Dial-a-porn companies attacked the statute as a violation of free press, but in 1992 the Supreme Court refused to hear a challenge to an appellate court that upheld the amended statutory language. Dial Information Services Corp. of New York v. Barr, 502 U.S. 1072 (1992); 938 F.2d 1535 (2d Cir. 1991).

NEA Grants

Congress passed legislation in 1989 in response to public outcries against the use of public funds to support photographic exhibits (showing the work of Robert Mapplethorpe and Andres Serrano) that many found to be obscene and sacrilegious. Under the terms of the statute, funds appropriated to the National Endowment for the Arts (NEA) and the National Endowment for the Humanities (NEH) could not be used to promote materials considered by the endowments to be obscene *and,* taken as a whole, without serious literary, artistic, political, or scientific value. Substantial debate in both Houses of Congress resulted in adopting

---

10. United States v. Reidel, 402 U.S. 351 (1971); United States v. Thirty-Seven Photographs, 402 U.S. 363 (1971); United States v. 12 200-ft Reels of Super 8 mm. Film, 413 U.S. 123 (1973); United States v. Orito, 413 U.S. 139 (1973).

statutory language that would avoid government censorship and violation of the First Amendment. 103 Stat. 741, § 304 (1989). The restriction was removed the following year.

In two highly controversial cases in 1990, juries in Cincinnati, Ohio, and Fort Lauderdale, Florida, decided that an art gallery and the rap band 2 Live Crew were not guilty of obscenity charges. These cases underscore the point that "obscenity" often depends more on the intuition and judgment of jurors than on Supreme Court guidelines. Regardless of what standards are announced by the Court, jurors have the "final word" in deciding whether a book, movie, art exhibit, or musical production belongs in their neighborhood.

The issue of NEA funding returned to the Court in 1998. Legislation passed by Congress in 1990 required the agency to ensure that "artistic excellence and artistic merit are the criteria by which [grant] applications are judged, taking into consideration general standards of decency and respect for the diverse beliefs and values of the American public." The Ninth Circuit held that this language, on its face, impermissibly discriminated on the basis of viewpoint and was void for vagueness under the First and Fifth Amendments. The Supreme Court, however, found that the language was facially valid and did not interfere with First Amendment rights and did not violate vagueness principles. An 8–1 Court held that the statutory provision merely added "considerations" and did not prevent awards to projects that might be "indecent" or "disrespectful." As for vagueness, all NEA grants are inescapably subjective, including giving awards for "artistic excellence" and "artistic merit." Many government programs that award scholarships and grants depend on general criteria such as "excellence" and "superior ability." National Endowment for Arts v. Finley, 524 U.S. 569 (1998). In their concurrence, Justices Scalia and Thomas said that the statutory language was constitutional even if it was viewpoint discrimination. They pointed out that the four individuals denied funding by the NEA may pursue their free expression at any time, but without the public paying for it.

Nude Dancing

In 1991, the Court splintered in several directions in passing judgment on an Indiana law that required public dancers in entertainment establishments to wear pasties and a G-string. A 5–4 majority upheld the statute but could not offer coherent reasons for doing so. Chief Justice Rehnquist, joined by Justices O'Connor and Kennedy, concluded that the state's police power (protecting public health, safety, and morals) was sufficient to override whatever expressive conduct the dancers hoped to achieve under the First Amendment. They said the statute was directed at public nudity, not erotic dancing. Justice Souter, in a concurrence, agreed that there was a First Amendment issue but offered different reasons for upholding the statute. The fifth member of the majority, Justice Scalia, denied that the statute implicated a First Amendment interest. Barnes v. Glen Theatre, Inc., 501 U.S. 560 (1991). It is uncertain how the majority would react to the prosecution of those who produce *Hair* or *Equus,* two plays that feature totally nude scenes.

The Court revisited this issue in 2000, ruling that cities and states may ban nude dancing to combat crime and "other negative secondary effects." The 6 to 3 opinion upheld a city ordinance that required dancers in clubs to wear pasties and a G-string. Writing for a plurality of four, Justice O'Connor said that the ordinance — *on its face* — represented a general prohibition on public nudity and therefore regulated conduct, not expression. It did not, she said, specifically target nudity that contained an erotic message. However, statements by the city attorney and other city officials indicate that the ordinance was aimed at nude dancing in clubs and was not intended to apply to "legitimate" theater productions. O'Connor concluded that the city's interest in combating negative secondary effects overrode whatever expressive message there might be in nude dancing. Scalia and Thomas, concurring in the judgment, regarded the case as moot but pointed out that the ordinance did not contain any exception for productions like *Hair* or *Equus*; nevertheless, the city was unlikely to enforce the ban on such plays. Scalia and Thomas would have upheld an ordinance directed solely at nude dancing without trying to identify "secondary effects." Souter dissented in part, concluding that the city's evidentiary record failed to justify the ordinance. In their dissent, Stevens and Ginsburg objected to the secondary-effects test to ban what they considered to be protected First Amendment expression, and pointed to the case record to show that the ordinance was targeting nude dancing and not public nudity in general. City of Erie v. Pap's A.M., 120 S.Ct. 1382 (2000).

Child Pornography

One of the few areas of agreement in obscenity law is the need to treat children differently from adults. With regard to minors, states may restrict minors under seventeen years of age from reading materials that are not obscene for adults. Ginsberg v. New York, 390 U.S. 629 (1968). Literature can be restricted if there is a "tendency of widely circulated books of this category to reach the impressionable young and have a continuing impact." Kaplan v. California, 413 U.S. 115, 120 (1973). There are continuing disputes as to how booksellers should be required to display sexual publications harmful to juveniles. Virginia v. American Booksellers Assn., 484 U.S. 383 (1988).

In one of the rare unanimous decisions on obscenity, in 1982 the Court upheld a state law directed at child pornography. The statute prohibited persons from knowingly promoting a "sexual performance" by a child under sixteen by distributing material describing such a performance. Sexual performance was defined as actual or simulated sexual intercourse, deviate sexual intercourse, sexual bestiality, masturbation, sado-masochistic abuse, or lewd exhibition of the genitals. NEW YORK v. FERBER, 458 U.S. 747 (1982). Congress passed legislation in 1978 to make it a federal crime to use children under sixteen for the production of pornographic materials. The law applies to the sale and distribution of obscene materials, mailed or transported in interstate or foreign commerce, that depict children in sexually explicit conduct. 92 Stat. 7 (1978). Those restrictions were strengthened in 1984 by raising the age to eighteen and relying on *Ferber* to remove the requirement in existing law that child pornography be proven "obscene" before convictions could be obtained. 98 Stat. 204 (1984). Amendments in 1986 and 1988 further tightened the statutory prohibitions against child pornography. 100 Stat. 3510 (1986); 102 Stat. 4485–4503 (Subtitle N) (1988).

The 1988 legislation was struck down because the requirements for recordkeeping by producers of visual materials of sexually explicit conduct placed an excessive burden on First Amendment rights. Records had to be kept for all models, regardless of age. American Library Ass'n v. Thornburgh, 713 F.Supp. 469 (D.D.C. 1989). Congress rewrote the statue in 1990, but the revised language was also found unconstitutional, again on the ground that the recordkeeping requirement was not narrowly tailored to protect children from being used in pornographic materials. American Library Ass'n v. Barr, 794 F.Supp. 412 (D.D.C. 1992).

In 1990, a 6–3 decision by the Supreme Court broadened state power to curb child pornography. States may now outlaw the possession or viewing of child pornography even in the privacy of one's own home. The majority concluded that a law passed by Ohio was a legitimate effort to protect the victims of child pornography by eliminating the market at all levels of the distribution chain. Eighteen other states had adopted similar laws. In their dissent, Justices Brennan, Marshall, and Stevens regarded the Ohio statute as overbroad, permitting prosecution for innocuous and constitutionally protected conduct. The majority conceded that such instances could arise because the statute "may have been imprecise at its fringes." Nevertheless, they rejected the overbreadth challenge, partly on the ground that state courts have the ability to narrow state statutes so that they apply only to unprotected conduct. Osborne v. Ohio, 495 U.S. 103 (1990).

Some of the efforts to combat obscenity raise Fourth Amendment issues. Police officers may not make ad hoc decisions to search newsstands and seize "obscene" materials.[11] Before issuing a warrant to seize allegedly obscene materials, a magistrate must make some kind of inquiry into the factual basis for the allegation. Lee Art Theatre v. Virginia, 392 U.S. 636 (1968). However, an adversary hearing is not required prior to a seizure. Heller v. New York, 413 U.S. 483 (1973).

[For efforts to regulate indecent broadcasts and to ban the dissemination to minors (under age 18) of "indecent" or "patently offensive" material on the Internet, see pages 541–42 in Chapter 10.]

Roth v. United States

354 U.S. 476 (1957)

In this decision, the Supreme Court for the first time sets forth the major doctrines regarding obscenity. Two cases are involved. The *Roth* case (referred to as No. 582) concerns the constitutionality of a federal statute used to convict Roth for mailing an obscene book and obscene circulars and advertising. The companion case, *Alberts* v. *California* (No. 61), deals with a California law that made it a misdemeanor to keep for sale or to advertise material that is "obscene or indecent."

MR. JUSTICE BRENNAN delivered the opinion of the Court.

The constitutionality of a criminal obscenity statute is the question in each of these cases. In *Roth,* the primary constitutional question is whether the federal obscenity statute violates the provision of the First Amendment that "Congress shall make no law ... abridging the freedom of speech, or of the press...." In *Alberts,* the primary constitutional question is whether the obscenity provisions of the California Penal Code invade the freedoms of speech and press as they may be incorporated in the liberty protected from state action by the Due Process Clause of the Fourteenth Amendment.

. . .

The dispositive question is whether obscenity is utterance within the area of protected speech and press. Although this is the first time the question has been squarely presented to this Court, either under the First Amendment or under the Fourteenth Amendment, expressions found in numerous opinions indicate that this Court has always assumed that obscenity is not protected by the freedoms of speech and press....

The guaranties of freedom of expression in effect in 10 of the 14 States which by 1792 had ratified the

Constitution, gave no absolute protection for every utterance. Thirteen of the 14 States provided for the prosecution of libel, and all of those States made either blasphemy or profanity, or both, statutory crimes. As early as 1712, Massachusetts made it criminal to publish "any filthy, obscene, or profane song, pamphlet, libel or mock sermon" in imitation or mimicking of religious services.... Thus, profanity and obscenity were related offenses.

. . .

... [I]mplicit in the history of the First Amendment is the rejection of obscenity as utterly without redeeming social importance. This rejection for that reason is mirrored in the universal judgment that obscenity should be restrained, reflected in the international agreement of over 50 nations, in the obscenity laws of all of the 48 States, and in the 20 obscenity laws enacted by the Congress from 1842 to 1956.... We hold that obscenity is not within the area of constitutionally protected speech or press.

. . .

However, sex and obscenity are not synonymous. Obscene material is material which deals with sex in a manner appealing to prurient interest. The portrayal of sex, *e.g.,* in art, literature and

---

11. Marcus v. Search Warrant, 367 U.S. 717 (1961); A Quantity of Books v. Kansas, 378 U.S. 205 (1964); Roade v. Kentucky, 413 U.S. 496 (1973).

scientific works, is not itself sufficient reason to deny material the constitutional protection of freedom of speech and press. Sex, a great and mysterious motive force in human life, has indisputably been a subject of absorbing interest to mankind through the ages; it is one of the vital problems of human interest and public concern....

The early leading standard of obscenity allowed material to be judged merely by the effect of an isolated excerpt upon particularly susceptible persons. *Regina* v. *Hicklin,* [1868] L. R. 3 Q. B. 360. Some American courts adopted this standard but later decisions have rejected it and substituted this test: whether to the average person, applying contemporary community standards, the dominant theme of the material taken as a whole appeals to prurient interest. The *Hicklin* test, judging obscenity by the effect of isolated passages upon the most susceptible persons, might well encompass material legitimately treating with sex, and so it must be rejected as unconstitutionally restrictive of the freedoms of speech and press. On the other hand, the substituted standard provides safeguards adequate to withstand the charge of constitutional infirmity.

Both trial courts below sufficiently followed the proper standard. Both courts used the proper definition of obscenity. In addition, in the *Alberts* case, in ruling on a motion to dismiss, the trial judge indicated that, as the trier of facts, he was judging each item as a whole as it would affect the normal person, and in *Roth,* the trial judge instructed the jury as follows:

"...The test is not whether it would arouse sexual desires or sexual impure thoughts in those comprising a particular segment of the community, the young, the immature or the highly prudish or would leave another segment, the scientific or highly educated or the so-called worldly-wise and sophisticated indifferent and unmoved....

"The test in each case is the effect of the book, picture or publication considered as a whole, not upon any particular class, but upon all those whom it is likely to reach. In other words, you determine its impact upon the average person in the community. The books, pictures and circulars must be judged as a whole, in their entire context, and you are not to consider detached or separate portions in reaching a conclusion. You judge the circulars, pictures and publications which have been put in evidence by present-day standards of the community. You may ask yourselves does it offend the common conscience of the community by present-day standards.

. . .

"In this case, ladies and gentlemen of the jury, you and you alone are the exclusive judges of what the common conscience of the community is, and in determining that conscience you are to consider the community as a whole, young and old, educated and uneducated, the religious and the irreligious—men, women and children."

It is argued that the statutes do not provide reasonably ascertainable standards of guilt and therefore violate the constitutional requirements of due process. *Winters* v. *New York,* 333 U. S. 507. The federal obscenity statute makes punishable the mailing of material that is "obscene, lewd, lascivious, or filthy...or other publication of an indecent character." The California statute makes punishable, *inter alia,* the keeping for sale or advertising material that is "obscene or indecent." The thrust of the argument is that these words are not sufficiently precise because they do not mean the same thing to all people, all the time, everywhere.

Many decisions have recognized that these terms of obscenity statutes are not precise. This Court, however, has consistently held that lack of precision is not itself offensive to the requirements of due process. "...[T]he Constitution does not require impossible standards"; all that is required is that the language "conveys sufficiently definite warning as to the proscribed conduct when measured by common understanding and practices...." *United States* v. *Petrillo,* 332 U. S. 1, 7–8....

In summary, then, we hold that these statutes, applied according to the proper standard for judging obscenity, do not offend constitutional safeguards against convictions based upon protected material, or fail to give men in acting adequate notice of what is prohibited.

. . .

The judgments are

Affirmed.

MR. CHIEF JUSTICE WARREN, concurring in the result.

I agree with the result reached by the Court in these cases, but, because we are operating in a field of expression and because broad language used here may eventually be applied to the arts and sciences and freedom of communication generally, I would limit our decision to the facts before us and to the validity of the statutes in question as applied.

. . .

MR. JUSTICE HARLAN, concurring in the result in No. 61, and dissenting in No. 582.

I regret not to be able to join the Court's opinion. I cannot do so because I find lurking beneath its disarming generalizations a number of problems which not only leave me with serious misgivings as to the future effect of today's decisions, but which also, in my view, call for different results in these two cases.

I.

My basic difficulties with the Court's opinion are threefold. First, the opinion paints with such a broad brush that I fear it may result in a loosening of the tight reins which state and federal courts should hold upon the enforcement of obscenity statutes. Second, the Court fails to discriminate between the different factors which, in my opinion, are involved in the constitutional adjudication of state and federal obscenity cases. Third, relevant distinctions between the two obscenity statutes here involved, and the Court's own definition of "obscenity," are ignored.

. . .

II.

I concur in the judgment of the Court in No. 61, *Alberts* v. *California*.

. . .

III.

I dissent in No. 582, *Roth* v. *United States*.

We are faced here with the question whether the federal obscenity statute, as construed and applied in this case, violates the First Amendment to the Constitution. To me, this question is of quite a different order than one where we are dealing with state legislation under the Fourteenth Amendment. I do not think it follows that state and federal powers in this area are the same, and that just because the State may suppress a particular utterance, it is automatically permissible for the Federal Government to do the same.…

…[T]he interests which obscenity statutes purportedly protect are primarily entrusted to the care, not of the Federal Government, but of the States. Congress has no substantive power over sexual morality.…

MR. JUSTICE DOUGLAS, with whom MR. JUSTICE BLACK concurs, dissenting.

When we sustain these convictions, we make the legality of a publication turn on the purity of thought which a book or tract instills in the mind of the reader. I do not think we can approve that standard and be faithful to the command of the First Amendment, which by its terms is a restraint on Congress and which by the Fourteenth is a restraint on the States.

. . .

By these standards punishment is inflicted for thoughts provoked, not for overt acts nor antisocial conduct. This test cannot be squared with our decisions under the First Amendment. Even the ill-starred *Dennis* case conceded that speech to be punishable must have some relation to action which could be penalized by government.…

The tests by which these convictions were obtained require only the arousing of sexual thoughts. Yet the arousing of sexual thoughts and desires happens every day in normal life in dozens of ways. Nearly 30 years ago a questionnaire sent to college and normal school women graduates asked what things were most stimulating sexually. Of 409 replies, 9 said "music"; 18 said "pictures"; 29 said "dancing"; 40 said "drama"; 95 said "books"; and 218 said "man."…

. . .

Any test that turns on what is offensive to the community's standards is too loose, too capricious, too destructive of freedom of expression to be squared with the First Amendment. Under that test, juries can censor, suppress, and punish what they don't like, provided the matter relates to "sexual impurity" or has a tendency "to excite lustful thoughts." This is community censorship in one of its worst forms. It creates a regime where in the battle between the literati and the Philistines, the Philistines are certain to win.…

Miller v. California

413 U.S. 15 (1973)

After thrashing about in a number of cases on obscenity and pornography, the Court in this case sets forth general principles that have helped to guide subsequent decisions. An interesting feature of this case is that Justice Brennan, author of *Roth* v. *United States* and several other decisions attempting to explain the principles used by courts to restrict obscenity, dissents in both *Miller* and the companion case, *Paris Adult Theatre I.* In those dissents Brennan argues that judicial standards for obscenity have not protected First Amendment rights and that the concept of obscenity cannot be defined with sufficient specificity by the courts to provide fair notice to persons vulnerable to prosecution. California prosecuted Marvin Miller for distributing obscene matter.

MR. CHIEF JUSTICE BURGER delivered the opinion of the Court.

This is one of a group of "obscenity-pornography" cases being reviewed by the Court in a re-examination of standards enunciated in earlier cases involving what Mr. Justice Harlan called "the intractable obscenity problem." *Interstate Circuit, Inc.* v. *Dallas,* 390 U. S. 676, 704 (1968) (concurring and dissenting).

. . .

I

This case involves the application of a State's criminal obscenity statute to a situation in which sexually explicit materials have been thrust by aggressive sales action upon unwilling recipients who had in no way indicated any desire to receive such materials. This Court has recognized that the States have a legitimate interest in prohibiting dissemination or exhibition of obscene material when the mode of dissemination carries with it a significant danger of offending the sensibilities of unwilling recipients or of exposure to juveniles.... The dissent of MR. JUSTICE BRENNAN reviews the background of the obscenity problem, but since the Court now undertakes to formulate standards more concrete than those in the past, it is useful for us to focus on two of the landmark cases in the somewhat tortured history of the Court's obscenity decisions. In *Roth* v. *United States,* 354 U. S. 476 (1957), the Court sustained a conviction under a federal statute punishing the mailing of "obscene, lewd, lascivious or filthy...." materials. The key to that holding was the Court's rejection of the claim that obscene materials were protected by the First Amendment. Five Justices joined in the opinion stating:

"All ideas having even the slightest redeeming social importance — unorthodox ideas, con-

troversial ideas, even ideas hateful to the prevailing climate of opinion — have the full protection of the [First Amendment] guaranties, unless excludable because they encroach upon the limited area of more important interests. But implicit in the history of the First Amendment is the rejection of obscenity as utterly without redeeming social importance...."

. . .

Nine years later, in *Memoirs* v. *Massachusetts,* 383 U. S. 413 (1966), the Court veered sharply away from the *Roth* concept and, with only three Justices in the plurality opinion, articulated a new test of obscenity. The plurality held that under the *Roth* definition

"as elaborated in subsequent cases, three elements must coalesce: it must be established that (a) the dominant theme of the material taken as a whole appeals to a prurient interest in sex; (b) the material is patently offensive because it affronts contemporary community standards relating to the description or representation of sexual matters; and (c) the material is utterly without redeeming social value." *Id.,* at 418.

. . .

While *Roth* presumed "obscenity" to be "utterly without redeeming social importance," *Memoirs* required that to prove obscenity it must be affirmatively established that the material is *"utterly* without redeeming social value." Thus, even as they repeated the words of *Roth,* the *Memoirs* plurality produced a drastically altered test that called on the prosecution to prove a negative, *i.e.,* that the material was *"utterly* without redeeming social value" — a burden virtually impossible to discharge under our criminal standards of proof....

Apart from the initial formulation in the *Roth* case, no majority of the Court has at any given time been able to agree on a standard to determine what constitutes obscene, pornographic material subject to regulation under the States' police power....

The case we now review was tried on the theory that the California Penal Code § 311 approximately incorporates the three-stage *Memoirs* test, *supra.* But now the *Memoirs* test has been abandoned as unworkable by its author *[Brennan],* and no Member of the Court today supports the *Memoirs* formulation.

II

...[W]e now confine the permissible scope of such regulation to works which depict or describe sexual conduct. That conduct must be specifically defined by the applicable state law, as written or authoritatively construed. A state offense must also be limited to works which, taken as a whole, appeal to the prurient interest in sex, which portray sexual conduct in a patently offensive way, and which, taken as a whole, do not have serious literary, artistic, political, or scientific value.

The basic guidelines for the trier of fact must be: (a) whether "the average person, applying contemporary community standards" would find that the work, taken as a whole, appeals to the prurient interest, *Kois* v. *Wisconsin, supra,* at 230, quoting *Roth* v. *United States, supra,* at 489; (b) whether the work depicts or describes, in a patently offensive way, sexual conduct specifically defined by the applicable state law; and (c) whether the work, taken as a whole, lacks serious literary, artistic, political, or scientific value. We do not adopt as a constitutional standard the *"utterly* without redeeming social value" test of *Memoirs* v. *Massachusetts,* 383 U. S., at 419; that concept has never commanded the adherence of more than three Justices at one time.

. . .

We emphasize that it is not our function to propose regulatory schemes for the States. That must await their concrete legislative efforts. It is possible, however, to give a few plain examples of what a state statute could define for regulation under part (b) of the standard announced in this opinion, *supra:*

(a) Patently offensive representations or descriptions of ultimate sexual acts, normal or perverted, actual or simulated.

(b) Patently offensive representations or de-

scriptions of masturbation, excretory functions, and lewd exhibition of the genitals.

. . .

It is certainly true that the absence, since *Roth,* of a single majority view of this Court as to proper standards for testing obscenity has placed a strain on both state and federal courts. But today, for the first time since *Roth* was decided in 1957, a majority of this Court has agreed on concrete guidelines to isolate "hard core" pornography from expression protected by the First Amendment....

. . .

III

Under a National Constitution, fundamental First Amendment limitations on the powers of the States do not vary from community to community, but this does not mean that there are, or should or can be, fixed, uniform national standards of precisely what appeals to the "prurient interest" or is "patently offensive." These are essentially questions of fact, and our Nation is simply too big and too diverse for this Court to reasonably expect that such standards could be articulated for all 50 States in a single formulation, even assuming the prerequisite consensus exists....

. . .

It is neither realistic nor constitutionally sound to read the First Amendment as requiring that the people of Maine or Mississippi accept public depiction of conduct found tolerable in Las Vegas, or New York City.

. . .

IV

The dissenting Justices sound the alarm of repression. But, in our view, to equate the free and robust exchange of ideas and political debate with commercial exploitation of obscene material demeans the grand conception of the First Amendment and its high purposes in the historic struggle for freedom....

There is no evidence, empirical or historical, that the stern 19th century American censorship of public distribution and display of material relating to sex, see *Roth* v. *United States, supra,* at 482–485, in any way limited or affected expression of serious literary, artistic, political, or scientific ideas. On the contrary, it is beyond any question that the era following Thomas Jefferson to Theodore Roosevelt was an "extraordinarily vigorous period," not just in economics and politics, but in *belles lettres* and in "the outlying fields of social and political philosophies." We do not see the harsh hand of censorship of ideas—good or bad, sound or unsound—and "repression" of political liberty lurking in every state regulation of commercial exploitation of human interest in sex.

. . .

In sum, we (a) reaffirm the *Roth* holding that obscene material is not protected by the First Amendment; (b) hold that such material can be regulated by the States, subject to the specific safeguards enunciated above, without a showing that the material is *"utterly* without redeeming social value"; and (c) hold that obscenity is to be determined by applying "contemporary community standards,"...not "national standards."...

Vacated and remanded.

MR. JUSTICE DOUGLAS, dissenting.

I

Today we leave open the way for California to send a man to prison for distributing brochures that advertise books and a movie under freshly written standards defining obscenity which until today's decision were never the part of any law.

The Court has worked hard to define obscenity and concededly has failed. In *Roth* v. *United States,* 354 U. S. 476, it ruled that "[o]bscene material is material which deals with sex in a manner appealing to prurient interest." *Id.,* at 487. Obscenity, it was said, was rejected by the First Amendment because it is "utterly without redeeming social importance." *Id.,* at 484. The presence of a "prurient interest" was to be determined by "contemporary community standards." *Id.,* at 489. That test, it has been said, could not be determined by one standard here and another standard there, *Jacobellis* v. *Ohio,* 378 U. S. 184, 194, but "on the basis of a national standard." *Id.,* at 195. My BROTHER STEWART in *Jacobellis* commented that the difficulty of the Court in giving content to obscenity was that it was "faced

with the task of trying to define what may be indefinable." *Id.,* at 197.

. . .

Obscenity cases usually generate tremendous emotional outbursts. They have no business being in the courts. If a constitutional amendment authorized censorship, the censor would probably be an administrative agency. Then criminal prosecutions could follow as, if, and when publishers defied the censor and sold their literature. Under that regime a publisher would know when he was on dangerous ground. Under the present regime—whether the old standards or the new ones are used—the criminal law becomes a trap. A brand new test would put a publisher behind bars under a new law improvised by the courts after the publication. That was done in *Ginzburg* and has all the evils of an *ex post facto* law.

. . .

MR. JUSTICE BRENNAN, with whom MR. JUSTICE STEWART and MR. JUSTICE MARSHALL join, dissenting.

In my dissent in *Paris Adult Theatre I* v. *Slaton, post,* p. 73, decided this date, I noted that I had no occasion to consider the extent of state power to regulate the distribution of sexually oriented material to juveniles or the offensive exposure of such material to unconsenting adults. In the case before us, appellant was convicted of distributing obscene matter in violation of California Penal Code § 311.2, on the basis of evidence that he had caused to be mailed unsolicited brochures advertising various books and a movie. I need not now decide whether a statute might be drawn to impose, within the requirements of the First Amendment, criminal penalties for the precise conduct at issue here. For it is clear that under my dissent in *Paris Adult Theatre I,* the statute under which the prosecution was brought is unconstitutionally overbroad, and therefore invalid on its face....

Paris Adult Theatre I v. Slaton

413 U.S. 49 (1973)

Lewis R. Slaton, a district attorney, prosecuted the owners of two theaters to enjoin the showing of two allegedly obscene films. The trial judge viewed the films and held that the showing of the films in commercial theaters to consenting adults, with reasonable precautions taken to exclude minors, was constitutionally permissible. The Georgia Supreme

Court reversed, holding that the films constituted "hard core" pornography not within the protection of the First Amendment. This case is significant because of the extensive dissent by Justice Brennan, author of the decision that first excluded obscenity from First Amendment protection, *Roth* v. *United States*.

Mr. Chief Justice Burger delivered the opinion of the Court.

Petitioners are two Atlanta, Georgia, movie theaters and their owners and managers, operating in the style of "adult" theaters....

. . .

I

It should be clear from the outset that we do not undertake to tell the States what they must do, but rather to define the area in which they may chart their own course in dealing with obscene material. This Court has consistently held that obscene material is not protected by the First Amendment as a limitation on the state police power by virtue of the Fourteenth Amendment....

Georgia case law permits a civil injunction of the exhibition of obscene materials.... While this procedure is civil in nature, and does not directly involve the state criminal statute proscribing exhibition of obscene material, the Georgia case law permitting civil injunction does adopt the definition of "obscene materials" used by the criminal statute. Today, in *Miller* v. *California, supra,* we have sought to clarify the constitutional definition of obscene material subject to regulation by the States, and we vacate and remand this case for reconsideration in light of *Miller.*

. . .

II

We categorically disapprove the theory, apparently adopted by the trial judge, that obscene, pornographic films acquire constitutional immunity from state regulation simply because they are exhibited for consenting adults only. This holding was properly rejected by the Georgia Supreme Court. Although we have often pointedly recognized the high importance of the state interest in regulating the exposure of obscene materials to juveniles and unconsenting adults,... this Court has never declared these to be the only legitimate state interests permitting regulation of obscene material. The States have a long-recognized legitimate interest in regulating the use of obscene material in local commerce and in all places of public accommodation, as long as these regulations do not run afoul of specific constitutional prohibitions.

In particular, we hold that there are legitimate state interests at stake in stemming the tide of commercialized obscenity, even assuming it is feasible to enforce effective safeguards against exposure to juveniles and to passersby.... These include the interest of the public in the quality of life and the total community environment, the tone of commerce in the great city centers, and, possibly, the public safety itself. The Hill-Link Minority Report of the Commission on Obscenity and Pornography indicates that there is at least an arguable correlation between obscene material and crime....

. . .

But, it is argued, there are no scientific data which conclusively demonstrate that exposure to obscene material adversely affects men and women or their society. It is urged on behalf of the petitioners that, absent such a demonstration, any kind of state regulation is "impermissible." We reject this argument. It is not for us to resolve empirical uncertainties underlying state legislation, save in the exceptional case where that legislation plainly impinges upon rights protected by the Constitution itself....

. . .

The States, of course, may follow...a "laissez-faire" policy and drop all controls on commercialized obscenity, if that is what they prefer, just as they can ignore consumer protection in the marketplace, but nothing in the Constitution *compels* the States to do so with regard to matters falling within state jurisdiction....

. . .

Finally, petitioners argue that conduct which directly involves "consenting adults" only has, for that sole reason, a special claim to constitutional protection. Our Constitution establishes a broad range of conditions on the exercise of power by the States, but for us to say that our Constitution incorporates the proposition that conduct involving consenting adults only is always beyond state regulation, is a step we are unable to take. Commercial exploitation of depictions, descriptions, or exhibitions of obscene conduct on commercial premises open to the adult public falls within a State's broad power to regulate commerce and protect the public environment. The issue in this context goes beyond whether someone, or even the majority, considers the conduct depicted as "wrong" or "sinful." The States have the power to make a morally neutral judgment that public exhibition of obscene material, or commerce in such material, has a tendency to injure the community as a whole, to endanger the public safety, or to jeopardize, in Mr. Chief Justice Warren's words, the States' "right . . . to maintain a decent society." *Jacobellis* v. *Ohio,* 378 U. S., at 199 (dissenting opinion).

. . .

Vacated and remanded.

MR. JUSTICE DOUGLAS, dissenting.

. . .

I am sure I would find offensive most of the books and movies charged with being obscene. But in a life that has not been short, I have yet to be trapped into seeing or reading something that would offend me. I never read or see the materials coming to the Court under charges of "obscenity," because I have thought the First Amendment made it unconstitutional for me to act as a censor. I see ads in bookstores and neon lights over theaters that resemble bait for those who seek vicarious exhilaration. As a parent or a priest or as a teacher I would have no compunction in edging my children or wards away from the books and movies that did no more than excite man's base instincts. But I never supposed that government was permitted to sit in judgment on one's tastes or beliefs—save as they involved action within the reach of the police power of government.

I applaud the effort of my Brother BRENNAN to forsake the low road which the Court has followed in this field. The new regime he would inaugurate is much closer than the old to the policy of abstention which the First Amendment proclaims. . . .

MR. JUSTICE BRENNAN, with whom MR. JUSTICE STEWART and MR. JUSTICE MARSHALL join, dissenting.

. . . I am convinced that the approach initiated 16 years ago in *Roth* v. *United States,* 354 U. S. 476 (1957), and culminating in the Court's decision today, cannot bring stability to this area of the law without jeopardizing fundamental First Amendment values, and I have concluded that the time has come to make a significant departure from that approach.

. . .

III

Our experience with the *Roth* approach has certainly taught us that the outright suppression of obscenity cannot be reconciled with the fundamental principles of the First and Fourteenth Amendments. . . .

. . . [A]fter 16 years of experimentation and debate I am reluctantly forced to the conclusion that none of the available formulas, including the one announced today, can reduce the vagueness to a tolerable level while at the same time striking an acceptable balance between the protections of the First and Fourteenth Amendments, on the one hand, and on the other the asserted state interest in regulating the dissemination of certain sexually oriented materials. Any effort to draw a constitutionally acceptable boundary on state power must resort to such indefinite concepts as "prurient interest," "patent offensiveness," "serious literary value," and the like. The meaning of these concepts necessarily varies with the experience, outlook, and even idiosyncrasies of the person defining them. Although we have assumed that obscenity does exist and that we "know it when [we] see it," *Jacobellis* v. *Ohio, supra,* at 197 (STEWART, J., concurring), we are manifestly unable to describe it in advance except by reference to concepts so elusive that they fail to distinguish clearly between protected and unprotected speech.

. . .

IV

1. The approach requiring the smallest deviation from our present course would be to draw a new line between protected and unprotected speech, still permitting the States to suppress all material on the unprotected side of the line. In my view, clarity cannot be obtained pursuant to this approach except by drawing a line that resolves all doubt in favor of state power and against the guarantees of the First Amendment. . . .

2. The alternative adopted by the Court today recognizes that a prohibition against any depiction or description of human sexual organs could not be reconciled with the guarantees of the First Amendment. But the Court does retain the view that certain sexually oriented material can be con-

sidered obscene and therefore unprotected by the First and Fourteenth Amendments. To describe that unprotected class of expression, the Court adopts a restatement of the *Roth-Memoirs* definition of obscenity: "The basic guidelines for the trier of fact must be: (a) whether "the average person, applying contemporary community standards' would find that the work, taken as a whole, appeals to the prurient interest...(b) whether the work depicts or describes, in a patently offensive way, sexual conduct specifically defined by the applicable state law, and (c) whether the work, taken as a whole, lacks serious literary, artistic, political, or scientific value." *Miller* v. *California, ante,* at 24. In apparent illustration of "sexual conduct," as that term is used in the test's second element, the Court identifies "(a) [p]atently offensive representations or descriptions of ultimate sexual acts, normal or perverted, actual or simulated," and "(b) [p]atently offensive representations or descriptions of masturbation, excretory functions, and lewd exhibition of the genitals." *Id.,* at 25.

The differences between this formulation and the three-pronged *Memoirs* test are, for the most part, academic. The first element of the Court's test is virtually identical to the *Memoirs* requirement that "the dominant theme of the material taken as a whole [must appeal] to a prurient interest in sex." 383 U. S., at 418. Whereas the second prong of the *Memoirs* test demanded that the material be "patently offensive because it affronts contemporary community standards relating to the description or representation of sexual matters," *ibid.,* the test adopted today requires that the material describe, "in a patently offensive way, sexual conduct specifically defined by the applicable state law." *Miller* v. *California, ante,* at 24. The third component of the *Memoirs* test is that the material must be "utterly without redeeming social value." 383 U. S., at 418. The Court's rephrasing requires that the work, taken as a whole, must be proved to lack "serious literary, artistic, political, or scientific value." *Miller, ante,* at 24.

. . .

3. I have also considered the possibility of reducing our own role, and the role of appellate courts generally, in determining whether particular matter is obscene. Thus, we might conclude that juries are best suited to determine obscenity *vel non* and that jury verdicts in this area should not be set aside except in cases of extreme departure from prevailing standards. Or, more generally, we might adopt the position that where a lower federal or state court has conscientiously applied the constitutional standard, its finding of obscenity will be no more vulnerable to reversal by this Court than any finding of fact.... [W]hile it would mitigate the institutional stress produced by the *Roth* approach, it would neither offer nor produce any cure for the other vices of vagueness. Far from providing a clearer guide to permissible primary conduct, the approach would inevitably lead to even greater uncertainty and the consequent due process problems of fair notice. And the approach would expose much protected, sexually oriented expression to the vagaries of jury determinations....

4. Finally, I have considered the view, urged so forcefully since 1957 by our Brothers Black and Douglas, that the First Amendment bars the suppression of any sexually oriented expression. That position would effect a sharp reduction, although perhaps not a total elimination, of the uncertainty that surrounds our current approach. Nevertheless, I am convinced that it would achieve that desirable goal only by stripping the States of power to an extent that cannot be justified by the commands of the Constitution....

V

Our experience since *Roth* requires us not only to abandon the effort to pick out obscene materials on a case-by-case basis, but also to reconsider a fundamental postulate of *Roth*: that there exists a definable class of sexually oriented expression that may be totally suppressed by the Federal and State Governments....

. . .

New York v. Ferber

458 U.S. 747 (1982)

A New York statute prohibited persons from knowingly promoting a sexual performance by a child under the age of sixteen by distributing material that depicts such a performance. The statute defined "sexual performance." Paul Ira Ferber was convicted for sell-

ing films depicting young boys masturbating. The highest New York court reversed the conviction by holding that the statute violated the First Amendment because it was both underinclusive and overbroad.

JUSTICE WHITE delivered the opinion of the Court.

At issue in this case is the constitutionality of a New York criminal statute which prohibits persons from knowingly promoting sexual performances by children under the age of 16 by distributing material which depicts such performances.

I

In recent years, the exploitive use of children in the production of pornography has become a serious national problem. The Federal Government and 47 States have sought to combat the problem with statutes specifically directed at the production of child pornography. At least half of such statutes do not require that the materials produced be legally obscene. Thirty-five States and the United States Congress have also passed legislation prohibiting the distribution of such materials; 20 States prohibit the distribution of material depicting children engaged in sexual conduct without requiring that the material be legally obscene.

New York is one of the 20. In 1977, the New York Legislature enacted Article 263 of its Penal Law. N. Y. Penal Law, Art. 263 (McKinney 1980). Section 263.05 criminalizes as a class C felony the use of a child in a sexual performance:

"A person is guilty of the use of a child in a sexual performance if knowing the character and content thereof he employs, authorizes or induces a child less than sixteen years of age to engage in a sexual performance or being a parent, legal guardian or custodian of such child, he consents to the participation by such child in a sexual performance."

A "[s]exual performance" is defined as "any performance or part thereof which includes sexual conduct by a child less than sixteen years of age." § 263.00(1). "Sexual conduct" is in turn defined in § 263.00(3):

" 'Sexual conduct' means actual or simulated sexual intercourse, deviate sexual intercourse, sexual bestiality, masturbation, sado-masochistic abuse, or lewd exhibition of the genitals."

A performance is defined as "any play, motion picture, photograph or dance" or "any other visual representation exhibited before an audience." § 263.00(4).

At issue in this case is § 263.15, defining a class D felony:

"A person is guilty of promoting a sexual performance by a child when, knowing the character and content thereof, he produces, directs or promotes any performance which includes sexual conduct by a child less than sixteen years of age."

· · ·

II

The Court of Appeals proceeded on the assumption that the standard of obscenity incorporated in § 263.10, which follows the guidelines enunciated in *Miller* v. *California*, 413 U. S. 15 (1973), constitutes the appropriate line dividing protected from unprotected expression by which to measure a regulation directed at child pornography. It was on the premise that "nonobscene adolescent sex" could not be singled out for special treatment that the court found § 263.15 "strikingly underinclusive." Moreover, the assumption that the constitutionally permissible regulation of pornography could not be more extensive with respect to the distribution of material depicting children may also have led the court to conclude that a narrowing construction of § 263.15 was unavailable.

The Court of Appeals' assumption was not unreasonable in light of our decisions. This case, however, constitutes our first examination of a statute directed at and limited to depictions of sexual activity involving children. We believe our inquiry should begin with the question of whether a State has somewhat more freedom in proscribing works which portray sexual acts or lewd exhibitions of genitalia by children.

· · ·

B

The *Miller* standard, like its predecessors, was an accommodation between the State's interests in protecting the "sensibilities of unwilling recipients" from exposure to pornographic material and the dangers of censorship inherent in unabashedly content-based laws. Like obscenity statutes, laws directed at the dissemination of child pornography run the risk of suppressing protected expression by allowing the hand of the censor to become unduly heavy. For the following reasons, however, we are persuaded that the States are entitled to greater leeway in the regulation of pornographic depictions of children.

First. It is evident beyond the need for elaboration that a State's interest in "safeguarding the physical and psychological well-being of a minor" is "compelling." *Globe Newspaper Co.* v. *Superior Court,* 457 U. S. 596, 607 (1982). "A democratic society rests, for its continuance, upon the healthy, well-rounded growth of young people into full maturity as citizens." *Prince* v. *Massachusetts,* 321 U. S. 158, 168 (1944)....

...The legislative judgment, as well as the judgment found in the relevant literature, is that the use of children as subjects of pornographic materials is harmful to the physiological, emotional, and mental health of the child. That judgment, we think, easily passes muster under the First Amendment.

Second. The distribution of photographs and films depicting sexual activity by juveniles is intrinsically related to the sexual abuse of children in at least two ways. First, the materials produced are a permanent record of the children's participation and the harm to the child is exacerbated by their circulation. Second, the distribution network for child pornography must be closed if the production of material which requires the sexual exploitation of children is to be effectively controlled. Indeed, there is no serious contention that the legislature was unjustified in believing that it is difficult, if not impossible, to halt the exploitation of children by pursuing only those who produce the photographs and movies. While the production of pornographic materials is a low-profile, clandestine industry, the need to market the resulting products requires a visible apparatus of distribution. The most expeditious if not the only practical method of law enforcement may be to dry up the market for this material by imposing severe criminal penalties on persons selling, advertising, or otherwise promoting the product....

Respondent does not contend that the State is unjustified in pursuing those who distribute child pornography. Rather, he argues that it is enough for the State to prohibit the distribution of materials that are legally obscene under the *Miller* test. While some States may find that this approach properly accommodates its interests, it does not

follow that the First Amendment prohibits a State from going further. The *Miller* standard, like all general definitions of what may be banned as obscene, does not reflect the State's particular and more compelling interest in prosecuting those who promote the sexual exploitation of children. Thus, the question under the *Miller* test of whether a work, taken as a whole, appeals to the prurient interest of the average person bears no connection to the issue of whether a child has been physically or psychologically harmed in the production of the work. Similarly, a sexually explicit depiction need not be "patently offensive" in order to have required the sexual exploitation of a child for its production. In addition, a work which, taken on the whole, contains serious literary, artistic, political, or scientific value may nevertheless embody the hardest core of child pornography. "It is irrelevant to the child [who has been abused] whether or not the material ... has a literary, artistic, political or social value." Memorandum of Assemblyman Lasher in Support of § 263.15. We therefore cannot conclude that the *Miller* standard is a satisfactory solution to the child pornography problem.

Third. The advertising and selling of child pornography provide an economic motive for and are thus an integral part of the production of such materials, an activity illegal throughout the Nation....

Fourth. The value of permitting live performances and photographic reproductions of children engaged in lewd sexual conduct is exceedingly modest, if not *de minimis.* We consider it unlikely that visual depictions of children performing sexual acts or lewdly exhibiting their genitals would often constitute an important and necessary part of a literary performance or scientific or educational work....

Fifth. Recognizing and classifying child pornography as a category of material outside the protection of the First Amendment is not incompatible with our earlier decisions. When a definable class of material, such as that covered by § 263.15, bears so heavily and pervasively on the welfare of children engaged in its production, we think the balance of competing interests is clearly struck and that it is permissible to consider these materials as without the protection of the First Amendment.

. . .

III

It remains to address the claim that the New York statute is unconstitutionally overbroad because it would forbid the distribution of material with serious literary, scientific, or educational value or material which does not threaten the harms sought to be combated by the State. Respondent prevailed on that ground below, and it is to that issue that we now turn.

The New York Court of Appeals recognized that overbreadth scrutiny has been limited with respect to conduct-related regulation, *Broadrick v. Oklahoma,* 413 U. S. 601 (1973), but it did not apply the test enunciated in *Broadrick* because the challenged statute, in its view, was directed at "pure speech." The court went on to find that § 263.15 was fatally overbroad: "[T]he statute would prohibit the showing of any play or movie in which a child portrays a defined sexual act, real or simulated, in a nonobscene manner. It would also prohibit the sale, showing, or distributing of medical or educational materials containing photographs of such acts. Indeed, by its terms, the statute would prohibit those who oppose such portrayals from providing illustrations of what they oppose." 52 N. Y. 2d, at 678, 422 N. E. 2d, at 525.

. . .

A

The traditional rule is that a person to whom a statute may constitutionally be applied may not challenge that statute on the ground that it may conceivably be applied unconstitutionally to others in situations not before the Court....

The scope of the First Amendment overbreadth doctrine, like most exceptions to established principles, must be carefully tied to the circumstances in which facial invalidation of a statute is truly warranted. Because of the wide-reaching effects of striking down a statute on its face at the request of one whose own conduct may be punished despite the First Amendment, we have recognized that the overbreadth doctrine is "strong medicine" and have employed it with hesitation, and then "only as a last resort." *Broadrick,* 413 U.S., at 613. We have, in consequence, insisted that the overbreadth involved be "substantial" before the statute involved will be invalidated on its face.

. . .

B

Applying these principles, we hold that § 263.15 is not substantially overbroad. We consider this the paradigmatic case of a state statute whose legitimate reach dwarfs its arguably impermissible applications. New York, as we have held, may constitutionally prohibit dissemination of material specified in § 263.15. While the reach of the statute is directed at the hard core of child pornography, the Court of Appeals was understandably concerned that some protected expression, ranging from medical textbooks to pictorials in the National Geographic would fall prey to the statute. How often, if ever, it may be necessary to employ children to engage in conduct clearly within the reach of § 263.15 in order to produce educational, medical, or artistic works cannot be known with certainty. Yet we seriously doubt, and it has not been suggested, that these arguably impermissible applications of the statute amount to more than a tiny fraction of the materials within the statute's reach....

IV

Because § 263.15 is not substantially overbroad, it is unnecessary to consider its application to material that does not depict sexual conduct of a type that New York may restrict consistent with the First Amendment. As applied to Paul Ferber and to others who distribute similar material, the statute does not violate the First Amendment as applied to the States through the Fourteenth. The judgment of the New York Court of Appeals is reversed, and the case is remanded to that court for further proceedings not inconsistent with this opinion.

So ordered.

JUSTICE BLACKMUN concurs in the result.

JUSTICE O'CONNOR, concurring.

. . .

JUSTICE BRENNAN, with whom JUSTICE MARSHALL joins, concurring in the judgment.

. . .

JUSTICE STEVENS, concurring in the judgment.

. . .

CONCLUSIONS

The decision by the Warren Court in *New York Times Co.* v. *Sullivan* (1964) appeared to be a ringing endorsement for a free press. Debate on public issues was to be "uninhibited, robust, and wide-open." However, the language and rationale of *Sullivan* paved the way for a series of rulings by the Burger Court that exposed the press to costly settlements and lawsuits in libel cases. There continues to be a presumption against prior restraint, but self-censorship by the press is a possible consequence of expensive litigation. Moreover, the Burger Court held that newsrooms could be searched by law enforcement officials (*Zurcher* in 1978) and reporters could be jailed for refusing to disclose confidential sources (*Branzburg* in 1972). With some starts and stops, the Burger Court generally supported press freedoms with regard to open trials and access to court proceedings. Questions of obscenity and pornography continue to perplex and divide the Court. It is strange that the United States seems preoccupied with the effect of obscenity and pornography on citizens, especially children, while it appears to be less concerned about the level of violence on television. Studies indicate a causal relationship between televised violence and later aggressive behavior in children.

Freedom of the press depends on the relationship that exists between the government and the citizen. Does government extend the right of a free press to the people or do the people instruct the government on its rights and powers? Remarks by James Madison during House debate in 1794 provide an important context for this question. The House was considering a censure of certain societies involved in an insurrection in western Pennsylvania (the Whiskey Rebellion). Madison warned that opinions could not be the object of legislation. Congressional resolutions of censure might extend improperly to the liberties of speech and of the press, he said, and then concluded: "If we advert to the nature of Republican Government, we shall find that the censorial power is in the people over the Government, and not in the Government over the people." 4 Annals of Congress 934 (1794).

SELECTED READINGS

ANDERSON, DAVID A. "The Origins of the Press Clause." 30 UCLA Law Review 455 (1983).

BARRON, JEROME A. Freedom of the Press for Whom? Bloomington: Indiana University Press, 1973.

BERNS, WALTER. "Freedom of the Press and the Alien and Sedition Laws: A Reappraisal." 1970 Supreme Court Review 109.

BEZANSON, RANDALL P., ET AL. Libel Law and the Press: Myth and Reality. New York: The Free Press, 1987.

BLANCHARD, MARGARET A. "The Institutional Press and its First Amendment Privileges." 1978 Supreme Court Review 225.

BLASI, VINCENT. "Toward a Theory of Prior Restraint: The Central Linkage." 66 Minnesota Law Review 11 (1981).

BURANELLI, VINCENT. The Trial of Peter Zenger. New York: New York University Press, 1957.

EMERSON, THOMAS I. "The Doctrine of Prior Restraint." 20 Law and Contemporary Problems 648 (1955).

EMERY, EDWIN. The Press and America. Englewood Cliffs, N.J.: Prentice-Hall, 1984.

FRIENDLY, FRED W. Minnesota Rag. New York: Random House, 1981.

GERALD, J. EDWARD. The Press and the Constitution, 1931–1947. Minneapolis, Minn.: University of Minnesota Press, 1948.

HUDON, EDWARD G. Freedom of Speech and Press in America. Washington, D.C.: Public Affairs Press, 1963.

KALVEN, HARRY, JR. "The Reasonable Man and the First Amendment: Hill, Butts, and Walker." 1967 Supreme Court Review 267.

———. "The New York Times Cases: A Note on the 'Central Meaning of the First Amendment'." 1964 Supreme Court Review 191.

LAWHORNE, CLIFTON O. Defamation and Public Officials. Carbondale: Southern Illinois University Press, 1971.

———. The Supreme Court and Libel. Carbondale: Southern Illinois University Press, 1981.

LEVY, LEONARD W. Emergence of a Free Press. New York: Oxford University Press, 1985.

————, ED. Freedom of the Press from Zenger to Jefferson. Durham, N.C.: Carolina Academic Press, 1996.

LEWIS, ANTHONY. Make No Law: The Sullivan Case and the First Amendment. New York: Vintage Books, 1991.

LINDE, HANS. "Courts and Censorship." 66 Minnesota Law Review 171 (1981).

LOFTON, JOHN. The Press as Guardian of the First Amendment. Columbia: University of South Carolina Press, 1980.

MACKINNON, CATHERINE A. Only Words. Cambridge, Mass.: Harvard University Press, 1993.

MURPHY, PAUL L. "Near v. Minnesota in the Context of Historical Developments." 66 Minnesota Law Review 95 (1981).

NELSON, HAROLD L., ED. Freedom of the Press: From Hamilton to the Warren Court. Indianapolis, Ind.: Bobbs-Merrill, 1967.

SHAPIRO, MARTIN, ED. The Pentagon Papers and the Courts: A Study in Foreign Policy-Making and Freedom of the Press. San Francisco: Chandler Publishing, 1972.

SMITH, JAMES MORTON. Freedom's Fetters: The Alien and Sedition Laws and American Civil Liberties. Ithaca, N.Y.: Cornell University Press, 1956.

SMITH, JEFFERY A. War and Press Freedom: The Problem of Prerogative Power. New York: Oxford University Press, 1999.

UNGAR, SANFORD J. The Papers & The Papers. New York: Dutton, 1972.

12

Religious Freedom

The religion clauses in the First Amendment contain two distinct objectives: "Congress shall make no law respecting an establishment of religion or prohibiting the free exercise thereof." These clauses—the Establishment Clause and the Free Exercise Clause—sometimes overlap and compete. Satisfying one clause may violate the other. If Congress grants a tax exemption for church property, is that establishment of religion? Taxing the property, however, might interfere with free exercise. When Congress provides chaplains for soldiers in the armed forces, is that an act of establishment? Yet denying soldiers access to ministers or rabbis would interfere with free exercise, especially for soldiers assigned to remote outposts. It is well established that the government may accommodate religious practices in various ways without violating the Establishment Clause.

These complexities are not solved by invoking metaphors about the "wall of separation" between church and state. In upholding state assistance of transportation to parochial schools, Justice Black claimed that the First Amendment "has erected a wall between church and state. That wall must be kept high and impregnable. We could not approve the slightest breach. New Jersey has not breached it here." Everson v. Board of Education, 330 U.S. 1, 18 (1947). In fact, a breach did occur in this case. A year later, in a concurring opinion, Justice Jackson questioned the Court's reasoning and predicted correctly that the Court would make "the legal 'wall of separation between church and state' as winding as the famous serpentine wall designed by Mr. Jefferson for the University he founded." McCollum v. Board of Education, 333 U.S. 203, 238 (1948). Justice Reed advised: "A rule of law should not be drawn from a figure of speech." Id. at 247.

A complete wall between church and state is neither possible nor desirable. Religious organizations have a right to lobby and petition government for various programs and activities. Ministers may serve in the legislature and hold other public offices. McDaniel v. Paty, 435 U.S. 618 (1978). Sectarian schools are obliged to teach the secular subjects specified by the state and must adhere to state health and safety standards. "Some relationship between government and religious organizations is inevitable.... Fire inspections, building and zoning regulations, and state requirements under compulsory school-attendance laws are examples of necessary and permissible contacts." Lemon v. Kurtzman, 403 U.S. 602, 614 (1971).

How are the religion clauses to be interpreted? On several occasions the Supreme Court has recognized that the clauses "had the same objective and were intended to provide the same protection against governmental intrusion on religious liberty as the Virginia statute." Everson v. Board of Education, 330 U.S. at 13. See also Reynolds v. United States, 98 U.S. 145, 162–164 (1878). The Virginia Statute for Establishing Religious Freedom—the handiwork of Thomas Jefferson and James Madison—provides valuable guidance in understanding the motivations behind the religion clauses. However, it is true that six states (Connecticut, Georgia, Maryland, Massachusetts, New Hampshire, and South Carolina) continued to provide assistance to established churches after 1786. In 1833 Massachusetts became the last state to end support to established religions. It is also the case that the first Congress enacted the Northwest Territory Ordinance, Article III of which provides: "Religion, morality, and knowledge, being necessary to good government and the happiness of mankind, schools and the means of education shall forever be encouraged." 1 Stat. 52 (1789).

A. THE VIRGINIA STATUTE

Religious liberties, which form the basis for political and social rights, had their origin in the long struggle to separate church and state. The three-volume study by Anson Phelps Stokes documents this development: "the study of American history shows that this actual separation, especially in the states, was generally the precursor, and always the surest support of public opinion in guaranteeing freedom of conscience and worship." 1 Stokes, Church and State in the United States 646 (1950). The Virginia statute of 1786 declared "that no man shall be compelled to frequent or support any religious worship, place, or ministry whatsoever, nor shall be enforced, restrained, molested, or burthened in his body or goods, nor shall otherwise suffer on account of his religious opinions or belief...." The preamble provided: "to compel a man to furnish contributions of money for the propagation of opinions which he disbelieves, is sinful and tyrannical." The author of the statute was Jefferson; the man who enacted it into Virginia law was Madison. Both men regarded religion and its free exercise as a fundamental human right into which the state could not intrude. Wrote Jefferson: "our rulers can have authority over such natural rights, only as we have submitted to them. The rights of conscience we never submitted, we could not submit." 3 Writings of Thomas Jefferson 263 (Ford ed.).

Neither Madison nor Jefferson had patience for sectarian battles, narrow creeds, or doctrinal wrangling. For them, religion was more of a general moral code to be practiced, not preached. "On the dogmas of religion," wrote Jefferson, "as distinguished from moral principles, all mankind, from the beginning of the world to this day, have been quarrelling, fighting, burning and torturing one another, for abstractions unintelligible to themselves and to all others, and absolutely beyond the comprehension of the human mind. Were I to enter on that arena, I should only add an unit to the number of Bedlamites." 10 Writings of Thomas Jefferson 67–68 (Ford ed.).

As with other colonies, Virginians suffered from religious cruelty and intolerance among different sects. Madison deplored the "diabolical, hell-conceived principle of persecution" that raged about him in 1774. 1 Writings of James Madison 21 (Hunt ed.). Baptists, Presbyterians, Catholics, Quakers, and other minority groups were whipped, fined, imprisoned, and forced to support the established Anglican Church. Between 1776 and 1786, Virginia moved a step at a time to establish religious freedom. The state Bill of Rights in 1776 proclaimed that religion "can be directed only by reason and conviction, not by force or violence, and therefore all men are equally entitled to the free exercise of religion, according to the dictates of conscience."

General Assessment Bill

Oppressive laws against dissenters nevertheless remained on the books. In December 1776 Virginia repealed its laws directed against heretics and nonattendance and exempted dissenters from giving financial support to the Anglican Church. Another step toward disestablishment occurred in 1779 when Virginia repealed all laws requiring even the members of the Anglican Church to support their own ministry. As a substitute for this preferential treatment, the Anglican Church pressed for a general tax to benefit all Christian religions. Bills were introduced to obtain public funds for teachers of Christianity. The final version allowed taxpayers to designate which church should receive their share of the tax and even gave the nonreligious taxpayer the option of directing taxes to general educational purposes.

Proponents of the general assessment claimed that Christianity and public morals would be handicapped without state financial aid, but the Baptists and some Presbyterians, who would have benefited financially from the bill, opposed the general assessment. Madison, in his famous "Memorial and Remonstrance Against Religious Assessments," insisted that religion be left to the conviction and conscience of the individual. Religion consisted in voluntary acts "wholly exempt" from the state's jurisdiction. He protested against religious assessments partly because "experience witnesseth that ecclesiastical establishments, instead of maintaining the purity and efficacy of Religion, have had a contrary operation. . . . What have been its fruits? More or less in all places, pride and indolence in the Clergy; ignorance and servility in the laity; in both, superstition, bigotry and persecution." 2 Writings of James Madison 187 (Hunt ed.).

The force and logic of Madison's detailed attack, emphasizing the inherent incompatibility between private religious beliefs and public financial support, led to the defeat of the general assessment bill. Virginia thereby prohibited religious aid even on a nonpreferential basis. Madison seized the opportunity to reintroduce Jefferson's Statute for Establishing Religious Freedom, which passed in January 1786 (see reading on Virginia statute). Many of those principles appear in the House debate in 1789 on the Bill of Rights (see reading). Years later, in evaluating religious institutions in Virginia after they had been denied public funds, Madison remarked that "it is impossible to deny that Religion prevails with more zeal, and a more exemplary priesthood than it ever did when established and patronised by Public authority." 9 Writings of James Madison 102 (Hunt ed.). A resolution passed by Congress in 1988 contains this Madisonian sentiment: "religion is most free when it is observed voluntarily at private initiative, uncontaminated by Government interference and unconstrained by majority preference." 102 Stat. 1772 (1988).

The Philadelphia Convention

When the delegates assembled at the constitutional convention in Philadelphia, there were very few comments about religion. On May 29, 1787, Charles Pinckney's draft constitution included a provision that the national legislature "shall pass no law on the subject of Religion." 3 Farrand 599. However, his plan was never acted upon. The subject of religion was not addressed except for debate on a national university and two provisions in Article VI. Three days before adjournment, Madison and Pinckney moved to give Congress the power "to establish an University, in which no preferences or distinctions should be allowed on account of religion." With little discussion the motion was defeated, 6 to 4, with one state divided. 2 Farrand 616.

Article VI provides that members of Congress, members of state legislatures, and all executive and judicial officers — both federal and state — "shall be bound by Oath or Affirmation, to support this Constitution; but no religious Test shall ever be required as a Qualification to any Office or public Trust under the United States." Unlike and affirmation, an oath is generally understood to be directed to a deity or divine authority. Quakers, Mennonites, and other denominations objected to oaths on various grounds, including the Biblical injunction "Swear not at all" (Matthew 5:34). Using affirmation as an option accommodated their religious beliefs.

Whereas the oath/affirmation requirement applies to all public officials — state and federal — the test ban covers only federal officials. Several state constitutions included a religious test, requiring officeholders to profess faith in Jesus Christ, God, Protestantism, or the Christian religion. Many of those religious tests were removed from the state constitutions from 1789 to 1793. A religious test in Maryland's constitution reached the Supreme Court in 1961. Roy Torcaso, appointed to the office of Notary Public, refused to comply with the constitutional requirement that he declare a belief in the existence of God. The Court held that the religious test invaded his "freedom of belief and religion and therefore cannot be enforced against him." Torcaso v. Watkins, 367 U.S. 488, 496 (1961).

Virginia Statute for Establishing Religious Freedom (1786)

James Madison, Thomas Jefferson, and George Mason were in the forefront of Virginians who challenged the established Anglican Church and sought to secure religious liberty for all citizens. For them, religious belief was a natural right entrusted to the conscience of the individual and could not be the subject of state interference or coercion. That principle was included in the state Bill of Rights in 1776. Three years later, Virginia repealed its law requiring members of the Anglican Church to support their own ministry. The Church advocated a general tax to benefit all Christian religions, but Madison and others were successful in defeating the bill. Madison was then able to pass, in 1786, Jefferson's Statute for Establishing Religious Freedom. The bill is reproduced from William Waller Hening, *The Statutes at Large: Being a Collection of All the Laws of Virginia,* Vol. XII, pp. 84–86 (1823).

I. WHEREAS Almighty God hath created the mind free; that all attempts to influence it by temporal punishments or burthens, or by civil incapacitations, tend only to beget habits of hypocrisy and meanness, and are a departure from the plan of the Holy author of our religion, who being Lord both of body and mind, yet chose not to propagate it by coercions on either, as was in his Almighty power to do; that the impious presumption of legislators and rulers, civil as well as ecclesiastical, who being themselves but fallible and uninspired men, have assumed dominion over the faith of others, setting up their own opinions and modes of thinking as the only true and infallible, and as such endeavouring to impose them on others, hath established and maintained false religions over the greatest part of the world, and through all time; that to compel a man to furnish contributions of money for the propagation of opinions which he disbelieves, is sinful and tyrannical; that even the forcing him to support this or that teacher of his own religious persuasion, is depriving him of the comfortable liberty of giving his contributions to the particular pastor, whose morals he would make his pattern, and whose powers he feels most persuasive to righteousness, and is withdrawing from the ministry those temporary rewards, which proceeding from an approbation of their personal conduct, are an additional incitement to earnest and unremitting labours for the instruction of mankind; that our civil rights have no dependence on our religious opinions, any more than our opinions in physics or geometry; that therefore the proscribing any citizen as unworthy the public confidence by laying upon him an incapacity of being called to offices of trust and emolument, unless he profess or renounce this or that religious opinion, is depriving him injuriously of those privileges and advantages to which in common with his fellow-citizens he has a natural right; that it tends only to corrupt the principles of that religion it is meant to encourage, by bribing with a monopoly of wordly honours and emoluments, those who will externally profess and conform to it; that though indeed these are criminal who do not withstand such temptation, yet neither are those innocent who lay the bait in their way; that to suffer the civil magistrate to intrude his powers into the field of opinion, and to restrain the profession or propagation of principles on supposition of their ill tendency, is a dangerous fallacy, which at once destroys all religious liberty, because he being of course judge of that tendency will make his opinions the rule of judgment, and approve or condemn the sentiments of others only as they shall square with or differ from his own; that it is time enough for the rightful purposes of civil government, for its officers to interfere when principles break out into overt acts against peace and good order; and finally, that truth is great and will prevail if left to herself, that she is the proper and sufficient antagonist to error, and has nothing to fear from the conflict, unless by human interposition disarmed of her natural weapons, free argument and debate, errors ceasing to be dangerous when it is permitted freely to contradict them:

II. *Be it enacted by the General Assembly,* That no man shall be compelled to frequent or support any religious worship, place, or ministry whatsoever, nor shall be enforced, restrained, molested, or burthened in his body or goods, nor shall otherwise suffer on account of his religious opinions or belief; but that all men shall be free to profess, and by argument to maintain, their opinion in matters of religion, and that the same shall in no wise diminish, enlarge, or affect their civil capacities.

III. And though we well know that this assembly elected by the people for the ordinary purposes of legislation only, have no power to restrain the acts of succeeding assemblies, constituted with powers equal to our own, and that therefore to declare this act to be irrevocable would be of no effect in law; yet we are free to declare, and do declare, that the rights hereby asserted are of the natural rights of mankind, and that if any act shall be hereafter passed to repeal the present, or to narrow its operation, such act will be an infringement of natural right.

House Debate on the Religion Clauses (1789)

On June 8, 1789, Congressman James Madison proposed the following language as part of a list of amendments to the Constitution: "The civil rights of none shall be abridged on account of religious belief or worship, nor shall any national religion be established, nor shall the full and equal rights of conscience be in any manner, or on any pretext, infringed." He also recommended the following restriction on the states: "No State shall violate the equal rights of conscience, or the freedom of the press, or the trial by jury in criminal cases." 1 Annals of Congress 434, 435. After Madison's proposals were reworked by a special committee, on August 15 the House debated the Religion Clauses. The passages below are taken from 1 Annals of Congress 729–31, 766, 913.

The House again went into a Committee of the Whole on the proposed amendments to the Constitution, Mr. BOUDINOT in the Chair.

The fourth proposition being under consideration, as follows:

Article 1. Section 9. Between paragraphs two and three insert "no religion shall be established by law, nor shall the equal rights of conscience be infringed."

Mr. SYLVESTER had some doubts of the propriety of the mode of expression used in this paragraph. He apprehended that it was liable to a construction different from what had been made by the committee. He feared it might be thought to have a tendency to abolish religion altogether.

Mr. VINING suggested the propriety of transposing the two members of the sentence.

Mr. GERRY said it would read better if it was, that no religious doctrine shall be established by law.

Mr. SHERMAN thought the amendment altogether unnecessary, inasmuch as Congress had no authority whatever delegated to them by the Constitution to make religious establishments; he would, therefore, move to have it struck out.

Mr. CARROLL. — As the rights of conscience are, in their nature, of peculiar delicacy, and will little bear the gentlest touch of governmental hand; and as many sects have concurred in opinion that they are not well secured under the present Constitution, he said he was much in favor of adopting the words. He thought it would tend more towards conciliating the minds of the people to the Government than almost any other amendment he had heard proposed. He would not contend with gentlemen about the phraseology, his object was to secure the substance in such a manner as to satisfy the wishes of the honest part of the community.

Mr. MADISON said, he apprehended the meaning of the words to be, that Congress should not establish a religion, and enforce the legal observation of it by law, nor compel men to worship God in any manner contrary to their conscience. Whether the words are necessary or not, he did not mean to say, but they had been required by some of the State Conventions, who seemed to entertain an opinion that under the clause of the Constitution, which gave power to Congress to make all laws necessary and proper to carry into execution the Constitution, and the laws made under it, enabled them to make laws of such a nature as might infringe the rights of conscience, and establish a national religion; to prevent these effects he presumed the amendment was intended, and he thought it was well expressed as the nature of the language would admit.

Mr. HUNTINGTON said that he feared, with the gentleman first up on this subject, that the words might be taken in such latitude as to be extremely hurtful to the cause of religion. He understood the amendment to mean what had been expressed by the gentleman from Virginia; but others might find it convenient to put another construction upon it. The ministers of their congregations to the Eastward were maintained by the contributions of those who belonged to their society; the expense of building meeting-houses was contributed in the same manner. These things were regulated by by-laws. If an action was brought before a Federal Court on any of these cases, the person who had neglected to perform his engagements could not be compelled to do it; for a support of ministers or building of places of worship might be construed into a religious establishment.

By the charter of Rhode Island, no religion could be established by law; he could give a history of the effects of such a regulation; indeed the people were now enjoying the blessed fruits of it. He hoped, therefore, the amendment would be made in such a way as to secure the rights of conscience, and a free exercise of the rights of religion, but not to patronise those who professed no religion at all.

Mr. MADISON thought, if the word "national" was inserted before religion, it would satisfy the minds of honorable gentlemen. He believed that the people feared one sect might obtain a preeminence, or two combine together, and establish a religion to which they would compel others to conform. He thought if the word "national" was introduced, it would point the amendment directly to the object it was intended to prevent.

Mr. LIVERMORE was not satisfied with that amendment; but he did not wish them to dwell long on the subject. He thought it would be better if it were altered, and made to read in this manner, that Congress shall make no laws touching religion, or infringing the rights of conscience.

Mr. GERRY did not like the term national, proposed by the gentleman from Virginia, and he hoped it would not be adopted by the House. It brought to his mind some observations that had taken place in the conventions at the time they were considering the present Constitution. It had been insisted upon by those who were called anti-federalists, that this form of Government consolidated the Union; the honorable gentleman's motion shows that he considers it in the same light. Those who were called anti-federalists at that time, complained that they had injustice done them by the title, because they were in favor of a Federal Government, and the others were in favor of a national one; the federalists were for ratifying the Constitution as it stood, and the others not until amendments were made. Their names then

ought not to have been distinguished by federalists and anti-federalists, but rats and anti-rats.

Mr. MADISON withdrew his motion, but observed that the words "no national religion shall be established by law," did not imply that the Government was a national one; the question was then taken on Mr. LIVERMORE's motion, and passed in the affirmative, thirty-one for, and twenty against it.

. . .

[August 20, 1789:]

On motion of Mr. AMES, the fourth amendment was altered so as to read "Congress shall make no law establishing religion, or to prevent the free exercise thereof, or to infringe the rights of conscience." This being adopted.

[The Senate considered a number of changes and also combined the clauses of religion, speech, press, assembly, and petition to produce this language: "Congress shall make no law establishing articles of faith or a mode of worship, or prohibiting the free exercise of religion, or abridging the freedom of speech, or the press, or the right of the people peaceably to assemble, and petition the government for the redress of grievances."]

[September 24, 1789:]

The House proceeded to consider the report of a Committee of Conference, on the subject-matter of the amendments depending between the two Houses to the several articles of amendment to the Constitution of the United States, as proposed by this House: whereupon, it was resolved, that they recede from their disagreement to all the amendments; provided that the two articles, which, by the amendments of the Senate, are now proposed to be inserted as the third and eighth articles, shall be amended to read as follows:

"Art. 3. Congress shall make no law respecting an establishment of religion, or prohibiting a free exercise thereof, or abridging the freedom of speech, or of the press, or the right of the people peaceably to assemble, and to petition the Government for a redress of grievances."

B. FREE EXERCISE CLAUSE

Many religious fundamentalists believe that government has a positive duty to promote religion. Under their interpretation, the First Amendment seems to extend religious rights only

Free Exercise of Religion

Protected (Belief)

The truth of a religious belief (avoiding heresy trials). United States v. Ballard, 322 U.S. 78 (1944).

Property disputes that turn on the question of church doctrine or ecclesiastical law, an area that is beyond the bounds of civil courts. Watson v. Jones, 13 Wall. 679 (1872); Jones v. Wolf, 443 U.S. 595 (1979); Presbyterian Church v. Hull Church, 393 U.S. 440, 449 (1969).

Government may not interfere with the selection of clergy to head a church. Nedroff v. St. Nicholas Cathedral, 344 U.S. 94 (1952); Serbian Orthodox Diocese v. Milovojevich, 426 U.S. 696 (1976).

Unprotected (Practice)

Mormon's belief in polygamy. Reynolds v. United States, 98 U.S. 145 (1878); Davis v. Beason, 133 U.S. 333 (1890); Mormon Church v. United States, 136 U.S. (1890).

Transporting a woman across state lines to enter into a plural marriage, even if motivated by religious belief. Cleveland v. United States, 329 U.S. 14 (1946).

Handling poisonous reptiles as part of a church service. Lawson v. Commonwealth, 164 S.W.2d 972 (Ky. 1942); State v. Massey, 51 S.E.2d 179 (N.C. 1949), appeal dismissed for want of a substantial federal question sub nom. Bunn v. North Carolina, 336 U.S. 942 (1949); State ex rel. Swann v. Pack, 527 S.W.2d 99 (Tenn. 1975), cert. denied, 424 U.S. 954 (1976).

to the believer and the orthodox. Although a treaty with Tripoli in 1796 stated that the United States "is not in any sense founded on the Christian religion" (8 Stat. 155, Art. XI), dicta from a few decisions of the Supreme Court suggest the contrary. The history of the country, said the Court in 1892, confirms that "this is a Christian nation." Church of the Holy Trinity v. United States, 143 U.S. 457, 471. Writing for the Court in 1952, Justice Douglas said "We are a religious people whose institutions presuppose a Supreme Being." Zorach v. Clauson, 343 U.S. 306, 313. The religious complexity of the United States has led some speakers to refer to "Judeo-Christian" values, but even that term excludes increasingly large populations of Moslems, Hindus, Buddhists, and other religions.

Congressional statutes have endorsed religious belief. Congress has required the inscription "In God We Trust" on coins and paper money.[1] After World War II, Congress engaged in ideological fencing with Soviet Russia by promoting spiritualism over materialism and theism over atheism. It directed the President to "set aside and proclaim a suitable day each year, other than a Sunday, as a National Day of Prayer, on which the people of the United States may turn to God in prayer and meditation at churches, in groups, and as individuals." 66 Stat. 64 (1952); 36 U.S.C. § 169h. Two years later it added the words "under God" to the pledge of allegiance. 68 Stat. 249 (1954); 36 U.S.C. § 172. This flourish of religiosity culminated in a law making "In God We Trust" the national motto. 70 Stat. 732 (1956); 36 U.S.C. § 186. An appellate court concluded that the national motto and the slogan on coinage and currency merely reflected a patriotic or ceremonial quality and had "no theological or ritualistic impact." Aronow v. United States, 432 F.2d 242, 243 (9th Cir. 1970). See also O'Hair v. Blumenthal, 462 F.Supp. 19 (W.D. Tex. 1978).

The executive branch joined in this quest for piety. In 1955 President Eisenhower advised the American Legion: "Without God, there could be no American form of Government, nor an American way of life. Recognition of the Supreme Being is the first — the most basic — ex-

---

1. E.g., 13 Stat. 518, § 5 (1865); 35 Stat. 164 (1908); 69 Stat. 290 (1955); 31 U.S.C. §§ 5112(d)(1), 5114(b).

pression of Americanism." 1955 Public Papers of the Presidents 274. Recent Presidents, including Richard Nixon, Gerald Ford, Jimmy Carter, and Ronald Reagan, actively used their office to promote religion and prayer.

These congressional and presidential affirmations of religion have been tempered by court decisions calling for neutrality on the part of government—not just between religions but between religion and irreligion. "The law knows no heresy, and is committed to the support of no dogma, the establishment of no sect." Watson v. Jones, 13 Wall. 679, 728 (1872). Neither a state nor the federal government "can force [or] influence a person to go to or to remain away from church against his will or force him to profess a belief or disbelief in any religion. No person can be punished for entertaining or professing religious beliefs or disbeliefs, for church attendance or non-attendance." Everson v. Board of Education, 330 U.S. 1, 15–16 (1947). Justice Jackson, who sent his own children to sectarian schools, warned that the "day that this country ceases to be free for irreligion it will cease to be free for religion—except for the sect that can win political power." Zorach v. Clauson, 343 U.S. at 306 (dissenting opinion).

Chaplains

Beginning in 1774, the Continental Congress authorized Rev. Jacob Duché to open Congress with prayers. Congress appropriated funds to pay him and his successors, as well as chaplains to serve military troops and to assist in military hospitals. The First Congress built on those precedents by electing chaplains to serve in the House and Senate.

Conscientious Objectors

The First Congress considered giving an exemption from military service for conscientious objectors. In the militia bill of 1790, lawmakers debated exempting persons conscientiously scrupulous of bearing arms, allowing them to pay a certain amount in lieu of military service. After a fair amount of discussion, it was decided to shift that issue to the states. 1 Annals of Cong. 1869–73, 1874–75 (1790). In what became the Second Amendment, the House added this provision: "but no one religiously scrupulous of bearing arms shall be compelled to render military service in person." However, the Senate deleted that language. 1 S. Journal 63–64, 71, 77 (1789).

Congress passed legislation in 1917 to exempt ministers of religion and theological students from military service. Conscientious objectors were relieved from military action but had to serve in a noncombatant role. The Court held that these laws did not violate the religion clauses. Selective Draft Law Cases, 245 U.S. 366 (1918). State universities were permitted to require male students to take a course in military science and tactics, even if such courses offended the beliefs of conscientious and religious objectors. The Court reasoned that the students were not compelled to attend a state university. If they chose to matriculate, they had to comply with the conditions imposed. Hamilton v. Regents, 293 U.S. 245 (1934).

As a result of subsequent statutes and decisions, an individual can now be exempt from combat duty without professing a belief in a Supreme Being. Congress exempted from military combat persons whose religious training and belief made them conscientiously opposed to participating in war in any form. As used in the statute, religious training and belief meant "an individual's belief in a relation to a Supreme Being involving duties superior to those arising from any human relation, but [not including] essentially political, sociological or philosophical views or a merely personal code." 62 Stat. 613 (1948). The Court held that the test of "religious belief" is whether it is a sincere and meaningful belief occupying in the individual's life a place parallel to that filled by the God of those explicitly eligible for the exemption. United States v. Seeger, 380 U.S. 163 (1965). Congress rewrote the statute two years later by eliminating the phrase "a relation to a Supreme Being involving duties superior to those arising from any human relation." 81 Stat. 104 (1967); 50 U.S.C. app. § 456(j). Persons may be classified as conscientious objectors even when they do not affirm or deny belief in a Supreme Being.[2]

The congressional requirement that a religious objector be conscientiously opposed to war "in any form" does not apply to a Jehovah's Witness who indicates a willingness to fight in defense of "his ministry, Kingdom Interests and...his fellow brethren." The weapons of this warfare are spiritual, not carnal. He is willing to engage in a "theocratic war" if Jehovah so commands. The congressional statute refers to military conflicts in our time, not a fight at Armageddon. Sicurella v. United States, 348 U.S. 385 (1955).

The Flag-Salute Cases

Periodically, government has prosecuted and harassed minorities whose beliefs did not directly threaten public order. For example, a number of states in the 1930s adopted laws that compelled school children to salute the flag. The Jehovah's Witnesses complained that saluting a secular symbol offended their religious faith. Nonetheless, the compulsory flag salute survived several test cases.[3]

In 1937, a federal district judge in Pennsylvania found these statutes unconstitutional. If someone on the basis of sincere religious beliefs defied a statute, the individual's rights would prevail unless the state demonstrated that the statute was necessary for the public safety, health, morals, property, or personal rights. The district judge thought that other courts had given insufficient weight to the value of religious liberty. Moreover, he distinguished between the compulsory military courses in state universities sanctioned by Regents v. Hamilton, 293 U.S. 245 (1934), and the compulsory flag salute imposed on children in grade school and high school. Students attend state universities on their own volition; attendance at the elementary and secondary school level is mandatory. The judge appealed to the heritage of his state: "We may well recall that William Penn, the founder of Pennsylvania, was expelled from Oxford University for his refusal for conscience' sake to comply with regulations not essentially dissimilar [to the compulsory flag salute], and suffered, more than once, imprisonment in England because of his religious convictions. The commonwealth he founded was intended as a haven for all those persecuted for conscience' sake." Gobitis v. Minersville School Dist., 21 F.Supp. 581, 585 (E.D. Pa. 1937).

Although the religion clauses of the First Amendment had not yet been applied to the states, the federal judge held that the "liberty protected by the due process clause of the Fourteenth Amendment undoubtedly includes the liberty to entertain any religious belief, to practice any religious principle, and to do any act or refrain from doing any act, on conscientious grounds, which does not endanger the public safety, violate the laws of morality or property, or infringe on personal rights." Id. at 587. This judgment was supported by another decision from the same judge, Gobitis v. Minersville School Dist., 24 F.Supp. 271 (1938), and by a federal appellate court, Minersville School Dist. v. Gobitis, 108 F.2d 683 (3d Cir. 1939).

The Supreme Court granted certiorari to review the Pennsylvania flag-salute case. Before issuing its decision, in another case it upheld the right of a Jehovah's Witness who had been prosecuted for violating a state law that prohibited the solicitation of money, services, subscriptions "or any valuable thing" unless approved in advance by a public official. Jesse Cantwell had gone from house to house to solicit money, sell books, and play records on a portable phonograph. Some of the records included attacks on Roman Catholics. A unani-

---

2. Welsh v. United States, 398 U.S. 333, 337 (1970). See also Gillette v. United States, 401 U.S. 437 (1971) and Clay v. United States, 403 U.S. 698 (1971). Inconsistent statements can cast legitimate doubt on the sincerity of a religious objector. Witmer v. United States, 348 U.S. 375 (1955).

3. Leoles v. Landers, 192 S.E. 218; 302 U.S. 656 (1937); Hering v. State Board of Education, 189 A. 629; 303 U.S. 624 (1938); Gabrielli v. Knickerbocker, 82 P.2d 391; 306 U.S. 621 (1939); Johnson v. Deerfield, 25 F.Supp. 918; 306 U.S. 621 (1939).

mous Court struck down the state law as a violation of the free exercise of religion. The Court also held that the religion clauses in the First Amendment applied to the states. Cantwell v. Connecticut, 310 U.S. 296, 303 (1940).

Two weeks later, the Supreme Court seemed to reverse course when it upheld Pennsylvania's compulsory flag-salute law. Justice Frankfurter, writing for an 8–1 majority, wrote a decision deeply flawed by contradictions, ipse dixits, and double-talk. The logic appeared to rest on two assumptions: liberty requires unifying sentiments, and national unity promotes national security. Only Justice Stone dissented. Several Justices in the majority would soon wish they had. MINERSVILLE SCHOOL DISTRICT v. GOBITIS, 310 U.S. 586 (1940).

The decision was excoriated by law journals, the press, and religious organizations. Roman Catholics, although often the prime target of attacks from Jehovah's Witnesses, found Frankfurter's opinion intolerable. A few months after Frankfurter's decision, Justice Douglas told Frankfurter that Justice Black was having second thoughts. Sarcastically, Frankfurter asked whether Black had spent the summer reading the Constitution. "No," Douglas replied, "he has been reading the papers." H. N. Hirsch, The Enigma of Felix Frankfurter 152 (1981).

By 1942 three members of the *Gobitis* majority publicly apologized for their votes. Justices Black, Douglas, and Murphy now announced that the 1940 case "was wrongly decided." Jones v. Opelika, 316 U.S. 584, 624. Frankfurter's decision thus commanded at best a slim majority, and two members of the *Gobitis* Court had been replaced by Justices Jackson and Rutledge. The 8–1 majority evaporated so quickly that a federal district judge in 1942 determined that *Gobitis* was no longer binding even though it had yet to be overruled. He calculated that of the seven remaining Justices on the Supreme Court who had participated in *Gobitis*, "four have given public expression to the view that it is unsound." Barnette v. West Virginia State Board of Ed., 47 F.Supp. 251, 253 (S.D. W.Va. 1942).

The Court overruled *Gobitis* in 1943, almost three years to the date that it was announced. Justice Jackson wrote for a 6–3 majority. Only Justices Roberts and Reed agreed with Frankfurter that *Gobitis* was properly decided. In a lengthy and passionate dissent, Frankfurter sought to vindicate his views. WEST VIRGINIA STATE BOARD OF EDUCATION v. BARNETTE, 319 U.S. 624 (1943). Jackson wrote a moving and powerful defense of religious freedom and the Bill of Rights, but credit for the liberalized decision belongs to citizens who refused to accept the Court's 1940 pronouncements on the meaning of the Constitution, minority rights, and religious liberty.

Accommodating Religious Beliefs

While the flag-salute cases were being litigated in the 1940s, the Court decided other important issues of religious freedom. A Jehovah's Witness had been convicted for violating a Texas ordinance that required a permit to solicit orders and sell books. The Court held unanimously that the ordinance represented "administrative censorship in an extreme form" and abridged the freedom of religion, press, and speech guaranteed by the Fourteenth Amendment. Largent v. Texas, 318 U.S. 418, 422 (1943). Similarly, it struck down a Pennsylvania ordinance requiring a license tax for those who canvass or solicit orders for books, paintings, pictures, wares, or merchandise. Once again a Jehovah's Witness had been convicted. The Court held that these constraints on missionary evangelism violated the constitutional liberties of speech, press, and religion. Murdock v. Pennsylvania, 319 U.S. 105 (1943). Other state efforts to impose a license tax on the selling of religious merchandise or to require a town's permission before "peddling" religious literature were struck down.[4] A state may not permit one religious

---

4. Douglas v. Jeannette, 319 U.S. 157 (1943); Follett v. McCormick, 321 U.S. 573 (1944); Tucker v. Texas, 326 U.S. 517 (1946).

organization to conduct services in a public park while denying that same privilege to another religious group. Fowler v. Rhode Island, 345 U.S. 67 (1953).

The state's interest in regulating religious activity is strengthened when a child is involved. In 1944 the Court upheld a Massachusetts statute that prohibited minors (boys under twelve, girls under eighteen) from selling newspapers, magazines, or other articles in public places. A nine-year-old had helped in the distribution of Jehovah's Witness literature. By a 5–4 vote, the Court upheld the conviction of the youth's guardian on the ground that the state has a special interest in protecting children. Prince v. Massachusetts, 321 U.S. 158. As the child matures, however, the state's interest declines. In 1972 the Supreme Court decided the case of members of the Amish religious order who had been convicted for violating Wisconsin's requirement that children attend school until age sixteen. The parents argued that sending their children to public or private schools after the eighth grade endangered the salvation of both parent and child by exposing the children to material, competitive, and modern values. The Court found that the religious interests of the Amish outweighed the interests of the state. Wisconsin v. Yoder, 406 U.S. 205 (1972).

Congress exempts self-employed Amish from paying social security taxes because they have a religiously based obligation to provide for their fellow members. 26 U.S.C. § 1402(g) (1994). The Supreme Court held that the exemption applies only to self-employed individuals, not to all employers and employees who are Amish. To the Court, the accommodation in the *Yoder* case was less disruptive than allowing various exceptions to the social security system. "Because the broad public interest in maintaining a sound tax system is of such a high order, religious belief in conflict with the payment of taxes affords no basis for resisting the tax." United States v. Lee, 455 U.S. 252, 260 (1982). Congress, finding the Court's interpretation too narrow, broadened the exemption for the Amish. 102 Stat. 3781–83, §8007 (1988).

The question of taxing religious organizations returned in 1990, when a unanimous Court held that it was constitutional for California to subject religious materials sold by a Louisiana religious organization to two taxes: a sales tax for sales within California and a use tax for mail-order sales. The Court regarded the taxes not as a tax on the right to disseminate religious information, ideas, or beliefs, but rather as a neutral tax on retail purchases, just as Bibles sold in a secular bookstore are taxed. The Louisiana organization (operated by Jimmy Swaggart) was not being singled out for special or burdensome treatment. Swaggart Ministries v. Cal. Bd. of Equalization, 493 U.S. 378 (1990).

Other cases illustrate the constant need to reach accommodations between state interests and religious belief. Minnesota required religious organizations at a state fair to sell and distribute religious literature and to solicit funds only at an assigned location within the fairgrounds. Members of those organizations were free to walk around and discuss religious matters in face-to-face contacts. A Krishna group claimed that the rule restricted its religious practices and its ability to proselytize for new members and financial support. The Court agreed that a state, in an effort to control the flow of crowds at a large fair, can restrict the sale of literature and solicitation of funds. Heffron v. Int'l Soc. for Krishna Consciousness, 452 U.S. 640 (1981).

A 1986 decision illustrates how the First Amendment is shaped not merely by court opinions but by legislative action as well. An Air Force regulation provided that headgear may not be worn indoors except by armed security police in the performance of their duties. An Air Force officer (an Orthodox Jew and ordained rabbi) claimed that the regulation prevented him from wearing his yarmulke (skullcap) and therefore infringed on his freedom to exercise his religious beliefs. The Supreme Court, split 5–4, upheld the regulation as necessary for military discipline, unity, and order. In one of the dissents, Justice Brennan claimed that the Court's response "is to abdicate its role as primary expositor of the Constitution and protector of individual liberties in favor of credulous deference to unsupported assertions of military necessity." GOLDMAN v. WEINBERGER, 475 U.S. 503, 514 (1986). Fortunately, other institutions of government are capable of protecting individual liberties, Congress among them. As Brennan later noted: "Guardianship of this precious liberty *[of religious freedom]* is not the exclusive domain of federal courts. It is the responsibility as well of the States and of the other branches of the Federal Government." Id. at 523. Congress passed legislation in 1987 to permit military personnel to wear conservative, unobtrusive religious apparel indoors, provided that it does not interfere with their military duties (see reading of floor debate).

[A number of state laws governing Sunday worship and Sunday closings implicate both religion clauses: free exercise and establishment. In one of these cases, *Employment Division* v. *Smith* (1990), the Court abandoned its usual test that states must show a "compelling governmental interest" in restricting the free exercise of religion. Congress passed legislation in 1993 to challenge that decision, but in 1997 the Court held this statute to be unconstitutional. Congress enacted new legislation in 2000 (page 641).]

Minersville School District v. Gobitis

310 U.S. 586 (1940)

Pennsylvania required students in public schools to participate in a daily ceremony of saluting the national flag while reciting in unison a pledge of allegiance to it "and to the Republic for which it stands; one Nation indivisible, with liberty and justice for all." Failure to abide by this requirement resulted in the expulsion of Jehovah's Witnesses, who believed that this gesture of respect for the flag was forbidden by Biblical commands. Two students, Lillian and William Gobitis, brought this case with their father against school authorities.

MR. JUSTICE FRANKFURTER delivered the opinion of the Court.

A grave responsibility confronts this Court whenever in course of litigation it must reconcile the conflicting claims of liberty and authority. But when the liberty invoked is liberty of conscience, and the authority is authority to safeguard the nation's fellowship, judicial conscience is put to its severest test. Of such a nature is the present controversy.

... The Gobitis family are affiliated with "Jehovah's Witnesses," for whom the Bible as the Word of God is the supreme authority. The children had been brought up conscientiously to believe that such a gesture of respect for the flag was forbidden by command of Scripture. *[A footnote refers to these verses from Chapter 20 of Exodus: "3. Thou shalt have no other gods before me. 4. Thou shalt not make unto thee any graven image, or any likeness of any thing that is in heaven above, or that is in the earth beneath, or that is in the water under the earth. 5. Thou shalt not bow down thyself to them, nor serve them:..."]*

The Gobitis children were of an age for which Pennsylvania makes school attendance compulsory. Thus they were denied a free education, and

their parents had to put them into private schools. To be relieved of the financial burden thereby entailed, their father, on behalf of the children and in his own behalf, brought this suit. He sought to enjoin the authorities from continuing to exact participation in the flag-salute ceremony as a condition of his children's attendance at the Minersville school....

We must decide whether the requirement of participation in such a ceremony, exacted from a child who refuses upon sincere religious grounds, infringes without due process of law the liberty guaranteed by the Fourteenth Amendment.

. . .

...When does the constitutional guarantee *[of religious freedom]* compel exemption from doing what society thinks necessary for the promotion of some great common end, or from a penalty for conduct which appears dangerous to the general good?...

...Our present task, then, as so often the case with courts, is to reconcile two rights in order to prevent either from destroying the other. But, because in safeguarding conscience we are dealing with interests so subtle and so dear, every possible leeway should be given to the claims of religious faith.

[*Frankfurter refers to earlier cases in which political authority was upheld over conscientious scruples, including laws against bigamy (contrary to Mormonism), drafting conscientious objectors for noncombatant roles, and requiring military training for all male university students.*]

... Even if it were assumed that freedom of speech goes beyond the historic concept of full opportunity to utter and to disseminate views, however heretical or offensive to dominant opinion, and includes freedom from conveying what may be deemed an implied but rejected affirmation, the question remains whether school children, like the Gobitis children, must be excused from conduct required of all the other children in the promotion of national cohesion. We are dealing with an interest inferior to none in the hierarchy of legal values. National unity is the basis of national security. To deny the legislature the right to select appropriate means for its attainment presents a totally different order of problem from that of the propriety of subordinating the possible ugliness of littered streets to the free expression of opinion through distribution of handbills. Compare *Schneider v. State,* 308 U. S. 147.

. . .

Unlike the instances we have cited, the case before us is not concerned with an exertion of legislative power for the promotion of some specific need or interest of secular society — the protection of the family, the promotion of health, the common defense, the raising of public revenues to defray the cost of government. But all these specific activities of government presuppose the existence of an organized political society. The ultimate foundation of a free society is the binding tie of cohesive sentiment. Such a sentiment is fostered by all those agencies of the mind and spirit which may serve to gather up the traditions of a people, transmit them from generation to generation, and thereby create that continuity of a treasured common life which constitutes a civilization. "We live by symbols." The flag is the symbol of our national unity, transcending all internal differences, however large, within the framework of the Constitution. This Court has had occasion to say that "... the flag is the symbol of the Nation's power, the emblem

of freedom in its truest, best sense.... it signifies government resting on the consent of the governed; liberty regulated by law; the protection of the weak against the strong; security against the exercise of arbitrary power; and absolute safety for free institutions against foreign aggression." *Halter* v. *Nebraska,* 205 U. S. 34, 43. And see *United States* v. *Gettysburg Electric Ry. Co.,* 160 U. S. 668.

. . .

The wisdom of training children in patriotic impulses by those compulsions which necessarily pervade so much of the educational process is not for our independent judgment. Even were we convinced of the folly of such a measure, such belief would be no proof of its unconstitutionality. For ourselves, we might be tempted to say that the deepest patriotism is best engendered by giving unfettered scope to the most crochety beliefs. Perhaps it is best, even from the standpoint of those interests which ordinances like the one under review seek to promote, to give to the least popular sect leave from conformities like those here in issue. But the courtroom is not the arena for debating issues of educational policy. It is not our province to choose among competing considerations in the subtle process of securing effective loyalty to the traditional ideals of democracy, while respecting at the same time individual idiosyncrasies among a people so diversified in racial origins and religious allegiances. So to hold would in effect make us the school board for the country. That authority has not been given to this Court, nor should we assume it.

We are dealing here with the formative period in the development of citizenship. Great diversity of psychological and ethical opinion exists among us concerning the best way to train children for their place in society. Because of these differences and because of reluctance to permit a single, iron-cast system of education to be imposed upon a nation compounded of so many strains, we have held that, even though public education is one of our most cherished democratic institutions, the Bill of Rights bars a state from compelling all children to attend the public schools. *Pierce* v. *Society of Sisters,* 268 U. S. 510. But it is a very different thing for this Court to exercise censorship over the conviction of legislatures that a particular program or exercise will best promote in the minds of children who attend the common schools an attachment to the institutions of their country.

What the school authorities are really asserting is the right to awaken in the child's mind considerations as to the significance of the flag contrary to those implanted by the parent....

Judicial review, itself a limitation on popular government, is a fundamental part of our constitutional scheme. But to the legislature no less than to courts is committed the guardianship of deeply-cherished liberties. See *Missouri, K. & T. Ry. Co. v. May,* 194 U. S. 267, 270. Where all the effective means of inducing political changes are left free from interference, education in the abandonment of foolish legislation is itself a training in liberty. To fight out the wise use of legislative authority in the forum of public opinion and before legislative assemblies rather than to transfer such a contest to the judicial arena, serves to vindicate the self-confidence of a free people.

Reversed.

MR. JUSTICE MCREYNOLDS concurs in the result.

MR. JUSTICE STONE, dissenting:

. . .

History teaches us that there have been but few infringements of personal liberty by the state which have not been justified, as they are here, in the name of righteousness and the public good, and few which have not been directed, as they are now, at politically helpless minorities.... *[While]* expressions of loyalty, when voluntarily given, may promote national unity, it is quite another matter to say that their compulsory expression by children in violation of their own and their parents' religious convictions can be regarded as playing so important a part in our national unity as to leave school boards free to exact it despite the constitutional guarantee of freedom of religion. The very terms of the Bill of Rights preclude, it seems to me, any reconciliation of such compulsions with the constitutional guaranties by a legislative declaration that they are more important to the public welfare than the Bill of Rights.

. . .

... We have previously pointed to the importance of a searching judicial inquiry into the legislative judgment in situations where prejudice against discrete and insular minorities may tend to curtail the operation of those political processes ordinarily to be relied on to protect minorities. See *United States* v. *Carolene Products Co.,* 304 U. S. 144, 152, note 4. And until now we have not hesitated similarly to scrutinize legislation restricting the civil liberty of racial and religious minorities although no political process was affected. *Meyer* v. *Nebraska,* 262 U. S. 390; *Pierce* v. *Society of Sisters, supra; Farrington* v. *Tokushige,* 273 U. S. 284. Here we have such a small minority entertaining in good faith a religious belief, which is such a departure from the usual course of human conduct, that most persons are disposed to regard it with little toleration or concern. In such circumstances careful scrutiny of legislative efforts to secure conformity of belief and opinion by a compulsory affirmation of the desired belief, is especially needful if civil rights are to receive any protection. Tested by this standard, I am not prepared to say that the right of this small and helpless minority, including children having a strong religious conviction, whether they understand its nature or not, to refrain from an expression obnoxious to their religion, is to be overborne by the interest of the state in maintaining discipline in the schools.

The Constitution expresses more than the conviction of the people that democratic processes must be preserved at all costs. It is also an expression of faith and a command that freedom of mind and spirit must be preserved, which government must obey, if it is to adhere to that justice and moderation without which no free government can exist. For this reason it would seem that legislation which operates to repress the religious freedom of small minorities, which is admittedly within the scope of the protection of the Bill of Rights, must at least be subject to the same judicial scrutiny as legislation which we have recently held to infringe the constitutional liberty of religious and racial minorities.

With such scrutiny I cannot say that the inconveniences which may attend some sensible adjustment of school discipline in order that the religious convictions of these children may be spared, presents a problem so momentous or pressing as to outweigh the freedom from compulsory violation of religious faith which has been thought worthy of constitutional protection.

West Virginia State Board of Education v. Barnette

319 U.S. 624 (1943)

Justice Frankfurter's opinion in *Gobitis* met with strong criticism from the legal community, the press, civil liberties groups, and religious organizations. In *Jones v. Opelika* (1942), three members of Frankfurter's 8 to 1 majority stated that the decision "was wrongly decided." That reduced the majority to 5 to 4, and changes in the Court's composition since *Gobitis* pointed to a probable overturning of Frankfurter's decision. One of the new members of the Court, Justice Jackson, wrote for a 6 to 3 majority striking down the compulsory flag salute. Frankfurter prepared an emotional dissent; only two other members of the *Gobitis* majority, Roberts and Reed, adhered to the views expressed by that Court. Walter Barnette, a Jehovah's Witness, challenged a West Virginia statute on the ground that it violated his and his children's religious beliefs.

MR. JUSTICE JACKSON delivered the opinion of the Court.

. . .

The Board of Education on January 9, 1942, adopted a resolution containing recitals taken largely from the Court's *Gobitis* opinion and ordering that the salute to the flag become "a regular part of the program of activities in the public schools," that all teachers and pupils "shall be required to participate in the salute honoring the Nation represented by the Flag; provided, however, that refusal to salute the Flag be regarded as an act of insubordination, and shall be dealt with accordingly."

The resolution originally required the "commonly accepted salute to the Flag" which it defined. Objections to the salute as "being too much like Hitler's" were raised by the Parent and Teachers Association, the Boy and Girl Scouts, the Red Cross, and the Federation of Women's Clubs. Some modification appears to have been made in deference to these objections, but no concession was made to Jehovah's Witnesses. What is now required is the "stiff-arm" salute, the saluter to keep the right hand raised with palm turned up while the following is repeated: "I pledge allegiance to the Flag of the United States of America and to the Republic for which it stands; one Nation, indivisible, with liberty and justice for all."

Failure to conform is "insubordination" dealt with by expulsion. Readmission is denied by statute until compliance. Meanwhile the expelled child is "unlawfully absent" and may be proceeded against as a delinquent. His parents or guardians are liable to prosecution, and if convicted are subject to fine not exceeding $50 and jail term not exceeding thirty days.

. . .

The freedom asserted by these appellees does not bring them into collision with rights asserted by any other individual. It is such conflicts which most frequently require intervention of the State to determine where the rights of one end and those of another begin. But the refusal of these persons to participate in the ceremony does not interfere with or deny rights of others to do so. Nor is there any question in this case that their behavior is peaceable and orderly. The sole conflict is between authority and rights of the individual. . . .

. . .

[Jackson analyzes several premises that formed the foundation for Gobitis.*]*

1. It was said that the flag-salute controversy confronted the Court with "the problem which Lincoln cast in memorable dilemma: 'Must a government of necessity be too *strong* for the liberties of its people, or too *weak* to maintain its own existence?'" and that the answer must be in favor of strength. *Minersville School District* v. *Gobitis, supra,* at 596.

We think these issues may be examined free of pressure or restraint growing out of such considerations.

It may be doubted whether Mr. Lincoln would have thought that the strength of government to maintain itself would be impressively vindicated by our confirming power of the State to expel a handful of children from school. Such oversimplification, so handy in political debate, often lacks the precision necessary to postulates of judicial reasoning. If validly applied to this problem, the utterance cited would resolve every issue of power in favor of those in authority and would require us to override every liberty thought to weaken or delay execution of their policies.

Government of limited power need not be anemic government. Assurance that rights are secure tends to diminish fear and jealousy of strong government, and by making us feel safe to live under it makes for its better support. Without promise of a limiting Bill of Rights it is doubtful if our Constitution could have mustered enough strength to enable its ratification....

2. It was also considered in the *Gobitis* case that functions of educational officers in States, counties and school districts were such that to interfere with their authority "would in effect make us the school board for the country."...

The Fourteenth Amendment, as now applied to the States, protects the citizen against the State itself and all of its creatures—Boards of Education not excepted. These have, of course, important, delicate, and highly discretionary functions, but none that they may not perform within the limits of the Bill of Rights. That they are educating the young for citizenship is reason for scrupulous protection of Constitutional freedoms of the individual, if we are not to strangle the free mind at its source and teach youth to discount important principles of our government as mere platitudes.

. . .

3. The *Gobitis* opinion reasoned that this is a field "where courts possess no marked and certainly no controlling competence," that it is committed to the legislatures as well as the courts to guard cherished liberties and that it is constitutionally appropriate to "fight out the wise use of legislative authority in the forum of public opinion and before legislative assemblies rather than to transfer such a contest to the judicial arena," since all the "effective means of inducing political changes are left free."...

The very purpose of a Bill of Rights was to withdraw certain subjects from the vicissitudes of political controversy, to place them beyond the reach of majorities and officials and to establish them as legal principles to be applied by the courts. One's right to life, liberty, and property, to free speech, a free press, freedom of worship and assembly, and other fundamental rights may not be submitted to vote; they depend on the outcome of no elections.

. . .

...[W]e act in these matters not by authority of our competence but by force of our commissions. We cannot, because of modest estimates of our competence in such specialties as public education, withhold the judgment that history authenticates as the function of this Court when liberty is infringed.

4. Lastly, and this is the very heart of the *Gobitis* opinion, it reasons that "National unity is the basis of national security," that the authorities have "the right to select appropriate means for its attainment," and hence reaches the conclusion that such compulsory measures toward "national unity" are constitutional....Upon the verity of this assumption depends our answer in this case.

National unity as an end which officials may foster by persuasion and example is not in question. The problem is whether under our Constitution compulsion as here employed is a permissible means for its achievement.

Struggles to coerce uniformity of sentiment in support of some end thought essential to their time and country have been waged by many good as well as by evil men. Nationalism is a relatively recent phenomenon but at other times and places the ends have been racial or territorial security, support of a dynasty or regime, and particular plans for saving souls. As first and moderate methods to attain unity have failed, those bent on its accomplishment must resort to an ever-increasing severity. As governmental pressure toward unity becomes greater, so strife becomes more bitter as to whose unity it shall be. Probably no deeper division of our people could proceed from any provocation than from finding it necessary to choose what doctrine and whose program public educational officials shall compel youth to unite in embracing. Ultimate futility of such attempts to compel coherence is the lesson of every such effort from the Roman drive to stamp out Christianity as a disturber of its pagan unity, the Inquisition, as a means to religious and dynastic unity, the Siberian exiles as a means to Russian unity, down to the fast failing efforts of our present totalitarian enemies. Those who begin coercive elimination of dissent soon find themselves exterminating dissenters. Compulsory unification of opinion achieves only the unanimity of the graveyard.

It seems trite but necessary to say that the First Amendment to our Constitution was designed to avoid these ends by avoiding these beginnings. There is no mysticism in the American concept of the State or of the nature or origin of its authority. We set up government by consent of the governed, and the Bill of Rights denies those in power any legal opportunity to coerce that consent. Authority here is to be controlled by public opinion, not public opinion by authority.

The case is made difficult not because the principles of its decision are obscure but because the flag involved is our own. Nevertheless, we apply the limitations of the Constitution with no fear that freedom to be intellectually and spiritually diverse or even contrary will disintegrate the social organization. To believe that patriotism will not flourish if patriotic ceremonies are voluntary and spontaneous instead of a compulsory routine is to make an unflattering estimate of the appeal of our institutions to free minds. We can have intellectual individualism and the rich cultural diversities that we owe to exceptional minds only at the price of occasional eccentricity and abnormal attitudes. When they are so harmless to others or to the State as those we deal with here, the price is not too great. But freedom to differ is not limited to things that do not matter much. That would be a mere shadow of freedom. The test of its substance is the right to differ as to things that touch the heart of the existing order.

If there is any fixed star in our constitutional constellation, it is that no official, high or petty, can prescribe what shall be orthodox in politics, nationalism, religion, or other matters of opinion or force citizens to confess by word or act their faith therein. If there are any circumstances which permit an exception, they do not now occur to us.

We think the action of the local authorities in compelling the flag salute and pledge transcends constitutional limitations on their power and invades the sphere of intellect and spirit which it is the purpose of the First Amendment to our Constitution to reserve from all official control.

The decision of this Court in *Minersville School District* v. *Gobitis* and the holdings of those few *per curiam* decisions which preceded and foreshadowed it are overruled, and the judgment enjoining enforcement of the West Virginia Regulation is

Affirmed.

MR. JUSTICE ROBERTS and MR. JUSTICE REED adhere to the views expressed by the Court in *Minersville School District* v. *Gobitis,* 310 U. S.

586, and are of the opinion that the judgment below should be reversed.

MR. JUSTICE BLACK and MR. JUSTICE DOUGLAS, concurring:

. . .

MR. JUSTICE MURPHY, concurring:

. . .

MR. JUSTICE FRANKFURTER, dissenting:

One who belongs to the most vilified and persecuted minority in history is not likely to be insensible to the freedoms guaranteed by our Constitution. Were my purely personal attitude relevant I should wholeheartedly associate myself with the general libertarian views in the Court's opinion, representing as they do the thought and action of a lifetime. But as judges we are neither Jew nor Gentile, neither Catholic nor agnostic. We owe equal attachment to the Constitution and are equally bound by our judicial obligations whether we derive our citizenship from the earliest or the latest immigrants to these shores. As a member of this Court I am not justified in writing my private notions of policy into the Constitution, no matter how deeply I may cherish them or how mischievous I may deem their disregard. The duty of a judge who must decide which of two claims before the Court shall prevail, that of a State to enact and enforce laws within its general competence or that of an individual to refuse obedience because of the demands of his conscience, is not that of the ordinary person. It can never be emphasized too much that one's own opinion about the wisdom or evil of a law should be excluded altogether when one is doing one's duty on the bench. The only opinion of our own even looking in that direction that is material is our opinion whether legislators could in reason have enacted such a law. In the light of all the circumstances, including the history of this question in this Court, it would require more daring than I possess to deny that reasonable legislators could have taken the action which is before us for review....

Goldman v. Weinberger

475 U.S. 503 (1986)

Captain Goldman, an Orthodox Jew and an ordained rabbi, brought suit against Secretary of Defense Weinberger, claiming that an Air Force regulation prevented him from wearing his yarmulke (skullcap) indoors and infringed on his First Amendment freedom to exercise his religious belief. A federal district court granted an injunction against the

Air Force, prohibiting it from denying Goldman the right to wear a yarmulke while in uniform; the D.C. Circuit reversed the decision.

JUSTICE REHNQUIST delivered the opinion of the Court.

Petitioner S. Simcha Goldman contends that the Free Exercise Clause of the First Amendment to the United States Constitution permits him to wear a yarmulke while in uniform, notwithstanding an Air Force regulation mandating uniform dress for Air Force personnel....

. . .

Until 1981, petitioner was not prevented from wearing his yarmulke on the base. He avoided controversy by remaining close to his duty station in the health clinic and by wearing his service cap over the yarmulke when out of doors. But in April 1981, after he testified as a defense witness at a court-martial wearing his yarmulke but not his service cap, opposing counsel lodged a complaint with Colonel Joseph Gregory, the Hospital Commander, arguing that petitioner's practice of wearing his yarmulke was a violation of Air Force Regulation (AFR) 35-10. This regulation states in pertinent part that "[h]eadgear will not be worn... [w]hile indoors except by armed security police in the performance of their duties." AFR 35-10, ¶ 1-6.h(2)(f) (1980).

Colonel Gregory informed petitioner that wearing a yarmulke while on duty does indeed violate AFR 35-10, and ordered him not to violate this regulation outside the hospital. Although virtually all of petitioner's time on the base was spent in the hospital, he refused. Later, after petitioner's attorney protested to the Air Force General Counsel, Colonel Gregory revised his order to prohibit petitioner from wearing the yarmulke even in the hospital....

. . .

Petitioner argues that AFR 35-10, as applied to him, prohibits religiously motivated conduct and should therefore be analyzed under the standard enunciated in *Sherbert* v. *Verner,* 374 U.S. 398, 406 (1963).... But we have repeatedly held that "the military is, by necessity, a specialized society separate from civilian society." *Parker* v. *Levy,* 417 U.S. 733, 743 (1974)....

Our review of military regulations challenged on First Amendment grounds is far more deferential than constitutional review of similar laws or regulations designed for civilian society. The military need not encourage debate or tolerate

protest to the extent that such tolerance is required of the civilian state by the First Amendment; to accomplish its mission the military must foster instinctive obedience, unity, commitment, and esprit de corps....

The considered professional judgment of the Air Force is that the traditional outfitting of personnel in standardized uniforms encourages the subordination of personal preferences and identities in favor of the overall group mission. Uniforms encourage a sense of hierarchical unity by tending to eliminate outward individual distinctions except for those of rank....

To this end, the Air Force promulgated AFR 35-10, a 190-page document, which states that "Air Force members will wear the Air Force uniform while performing their military duties, except when authorized to wear civilian clothes on duty." AFR § 35-10, ¶ 1-6 (1980). The rest of the document describes in minute detail all of the various items of apparel that must be worn as part of the Air Force uniform. It authorizes a few individualized options with respect to certain pieces of jewelry and hair style, but even these are subject to severe limitations....

Petitioner Goldman contends that the Free Exercise Clause of the First Amendment requires the Air Force to make an exception to its uniform dress requirements for religious apparel unless the accoutrements create a "clear danger" of undermining discipline and esprit de corps. He asserts that in general, visible but "unobtrusive" apparel will not create such a danger and must therefore be accommodated. He argues that the Air Force failed to prove that a specific exception for his practice of wearing an unobtrusive yarmulke would threaten discipline. He contends that the Air Force's assertion to the contrary is mere *ipse dixit,* with no support from actual experience or a scientific study in the record, and is contradicted by expert testimony that religious exceptions to AFR 35-10 are in fact desirable and will increase morale by making the Air Force a more humane place.

But whether or not expert witnesses may feel that religious exceptions to AFR 35-10 are desirable is quite beside the point. The desirability of dress regulations in the military is decided by the appropriate military officials, and they are under no constitutional mandate to abandon their considered professional judgment. Quite obviously, to the extent the regulations do not permit the wearing of religious apparel such as a yarmulke, a practice described by petitioner as silent devotion akin to prayer, military life may be more objectionable for petitioner and probably others. But the First Amendment does not require the military to accommodate such practices in the face of its view that they would detract from the uniformity sought by the dress regulations. The Air Force has drawn the line essentially between religious apparel which is visible and that which is not, and we hold that those portions of the regulations challenged here reasonably and even-handedly regulate dress in the interest of the military's perceived need for uniformity. The First Amendment therefore does not prohibit them from being applied to petitioner even though their effect is to restrict the wearing of the headgear required by his religious beliefs.

The judgment of the Court of Appeals is

Affirmed.

JUSTICE STEVENS, with whom JUSTICE WHITE and JUSTICE POWELL join, concurring.

Captain Goldman presents an especially attractive case for an exception from the uniform regulations that are applicable to all other Air Force personnel.... Nevertheless, as the case has been argued, I believe we must test the validity of the Air Force's rule not merely as it applies to Captain Goldman but also as it applies to all service personnel who have sincere religious beliefs that may conflict with one or more military commands.

... The very strength of Captain Goldman's claim creates the danger that a similar claim on behalf of a Sikh or a Rastafarian might readily be dismissed as "so extreme, so unusual, or so fad-dish an image that public confidence in his ability to perform his duties will be destroyed." ... The Air Force has no business drawing distinctions between such persons when it is enforcing commands of universal application.

As the Court demonstrates, the rule that is challenged in this case is based on a neutral, completely objective standard—visibility. It was not motivated by hostility against, or any special respect for, any religious faith. An exception for yarmulkes would represent a fundamental departure from the true principle of uniformity that supports that rule. For that reason, I join the Court's opinion and its judgment.

JUSTICE BRENNAN, with whom JUSTICE MARSHALL joins, dissenting.

Simcha Goldman invokes this Court's protection of his First Amendment right to fulfill one of the traditional religious obligations of a male Orthodox Jew—to cover his head before an omnipresent God. The Court's response to Goldman's request is to abdicate its role as principal expositor of the Constitution and protector of individual liberties in favor of credulous deference to unsupported assertions of military necessity. I dissent.

. . .

JUSTICE BLACKMUN, dissenting.

. . .

JUSTICE O'CONNOR, with whom JUSTICE MARSHALL joins, dissenting.

. . .

Congress Reverses *Goldman*

After the Supreme Court's decision in *Goldman* v. *Weinberger* (1986), legislation was immediately introduced to permit members of the armed forces to wear religious apparel indoors if the item is neat and conservative. The legislation permitted the Secretary of Defense to prohibit the wearing of an item of religious apparel if it interfered with the performance of military duties. The House passed the legislation in 1986, but it failed in the Senate. Both Houses acted on the legislation in 1987, and the provision was enacted into law. 101 Stat. 1086–87, § 508 (1987). Excerpts from the congressional debate appear below. 133 Cong. Rec. 11851–53, 25250–60 (1987).

Mrs. SCHROEDER....

Mr. Chairman, the amendment permits the wearing of "neat and conservative" religious apparel—that is, Jewish yarmulkes and Sikh turbans—so long as the apparel does not interfere with the performance of military duties.

The "neat and conservative" standard was drawn from existing Air Force regulations, which use that term to define what jewelry members of the military may wear.

The military services have opposed any such legislation.

The Army — but not the other services — accepted Sikhs with turbans from the late 1940's to the early 1960's. When they stopped accepting Sikhs, they grandfathered those then in service. At least one Sikh remains on active duty. As near as can be learned from the limited records, the Army ceased accepting Sikhs when it was told it must either accept all nonuniform religious apparel — turbans, yarmulkes, saffron robes, dreadlocks, etc. — or none, but could not pick and choose among religious faiths.

Yarmulkes have never been formally permitted — although some have been worn without objection over the years....

. . .

Mr. DORNAN of California. Mr. Chairman, I rise in support of this amendment.

I cannot think of any religious devotion more unobtrusive than wearing a yarmulke. There are people who have more hair, times 10, than a tiny little skull cap and it can be worn under jet fighter helmets, under garrison hats, under helmets, it can even be worn under a regular flight cap.

I am receiving mail, I have received six letters just within the last 2 weeks, from Americans of Sikh heritage. It is their religious devotion not to ever cut any of their bodily hair. Those beards we see are probably 2 feet long wound up and inside that turban is as much hair as they can grow. They point out how honorably they have served the British Empire, that at one time as 4 percent of the population, they were more than 35 percent of the officer and NCO corps in the British Indian Army and that percentage is still 10 times higher than their numbers in India now. This is in spite of some religious conflict.

Is there some specificity in this where it leaves — I would like to ask the gentlewoman to respond — where it leaves the military some leeway, Rastafarian hair or something, but where we can be specific in our legislative dialog that this has nothing to do with restricting something as precious, but as tiny and small, as the wearing of a yarmulke by orthodox people?

I yield to the gentlewoman from Colorado.

Mrs. SCHROEDER. Mr. Chairman, I thank the gentleman and I am very honored that the gentleman is backing this amendment.

Yes, indeed, what we are saying here is that the Secretary concerned may prohibit the wearing of any item of religious apparel if the circumstances are that the Secretary determines that the wearing of the item would interfere with the performance of the Member's military duties.

I think if they say it interferes and could make that case, yes; so if some one appeared saying they wanted to say wear a robe and fly an airplane and you could be concerned about getting the robe caught up in the puddles, yes; outside of that, a yarmulke, no.

. . .

Mr. SOLARZ. Mr. Chairman, I thank the gentlewoman for yielding.

The only really serious concerns that have been expressed about this amendment have to do with the extent to which they might permit members of the armed forces to wear bizarre forms of apparel that could undermine military discipline.

I think it is important for the Members to know that the armed forces of Canada, the armed forces of the United Kingdom, the armed forces of New Zealand, all permit people in their military not only to wear yarmulkes, but also, if they are Sikhs, to wear turbans.

I need hardly remind you that the most effective military force in the Middle East, the Israel Defense Forces, permits its members to wear yarmulkes. I do not think it has handicapped their ability to overcome their enemies in battle.

. . .

The CHAIRMAN. The question is on the amendment offered by the gentlewoman from Colorado [Mrs. SCHROEDER].

The amendment was agreed to.

[Senate action:]

Mr. LAUTENBERG. Mr. President, today I am offering an amendment to permit the wearing of neat and conservative religious apparel in the military. Under my amendment, such apparel would be permitted only if it does not interfere with the performance of military duty.

. . .

...[T]his amendment, and this issue, is broader than any one religion. It concerns the right of people of all faiths to serve their country without having to forsake their religious beliefs and practices, it would affirm the religious and ethnic diversity that have made America strong, not weak.

The primary philosophical objection to this amendment has been that wearing visible items of religious apparel may threaten the military uniformity necessary in building unit cohesion. While I appreciate and agree with the importance of unit cohesion and esprit de corps in the Armed Forces, I do not believe that wearing neat and conservative religious apparel threatens this principle.

To the contrary, it would strengthen morale by affirming that the military is a humane and tolerant institution....

Although uniformity is claimed as an important value, the services easily permit other manifestations of religious diversity. Service members attend Christian, Islamic, Jewish, and other religious services. Barracks mates see Mormons wearing temple garments, and Catholics wearing crosses and scapulars. It is obvious that our services are made up of people from different faiths and ethnic backgrounds, and that diversity is America's greatest asset. It is no secret, nor should it be.

. . .

Our citizens in uniform should not be deprived of their basic constitutional rights, such as the free exercise of religion, the minute they enter the military. There must be a compelling and supportable argument justifying such a prohibition. None has been made.

Some of the services have argued that the neat and conservative standard will be hard to apply, forcing them to make delicate and difficult distinctions between religious garb. But the services have a successful record of using the neat and conservative standard to distinguish acceptable from unacceptable jewelry. If we can make this distinction for neat and conservative jewelry, why can't we make it for religious apparel.

Certainly, the wearing of apparel central to the practice of one's religious beliefs is more important and worthy of review than the wearing of jewelry. The Air Force permits the wearing of up to three rings and one identification bracelet of neat and conservative but nonuniform design. This jewelry is permitted even if, as it is often the case with rings, it associates the wearer with a denominational school or a religious or secular fraternal organization. These items are not deemed to be unacceptably divisive. I cannot see why religious apparel that is neat and conservative would be.

. . .

Mr. MURKOWSKI. I thank the Senator from Ohio.

Mr. President, I rise as the ranking minority member of the Committee on Veterans' Affairs. At the request of numerous organizations representing service members and veterans of all faiths, I feel compelled to express my concern regarding the amendment of the Senator from New Jersey, which would allow service members to wear religious apparel while in uniform. The American Legion, with over 2.5 million members, and the Military Coalition, representing 16 of the largest organizations for military personnel, do not support the amendment of the Senator from New Jersey.

. . .

Mr. President, I suggest to my colleagues that this amendment creates many more problems than it solves. The issue is not religious freedoms. The issue is whether we write into law an arbitrary standard and then tell our military leaders to apply it as best as they can. Right now, they apply a very logical, neutral standard. I suggest to my colleagues that they ought to be permitted to continue to apply that visibility standard.

. . .

Mr. GLENN. Mr. President, I yield myself such time as I may require.

Mr. President, I truly regret having to rise to oppose the amendment by the distinguished Senator from New Jersey....

[Senator Glenn placed in the Record a letter from the Secretary of Defense, Caspar Weinberger, opposing the amendment on the ground that it would force commanders to apply subjective criteria ("neat and conservative") in distinguishing among religious apparel. Senator Glenn also placed in the Record a "20-star letter" from the Joint Chiefs of Staff, opposing the amendment. The letter, signed by the chairman of the Joint Chiefs, the general of the Air Force, the general of the Army, the general of the Marine Corps, and the admiral of the Navy, adds up to five four-star officers.]

Mr. ADAMS. Mr. President, I intend to vote for this amendment but I do not do so with enthusiasm. My lack of enthusiasm springs from two sources. First, in my view, this is an issue which should never have gone to the courts and never come before the Congress. In the past, the military services have been able to accommodate individuals on a case by case basis. Those informal agreements seem to have served everyone's interest. I just wish that we were able to return to a time when people spoke with each other instead of sued each other. Second, I have to tell you that I was shocked by the level of lobbying that has gone on about this issue. I have had more calls from constituents on this issue than I had on SDI [*Strategic Defense Initiative*]; I had more requests for visits from DOD on this issue than I did on a comprehensive test ban. There are some really vital issues that need to be addressed in this bill—and while this issue is important, the fate of the nation does not hang on it. . . .

[After defeating a motion to table the amendment, which lost 42 to 55, the Senate agreed to the amendment, 55 to 42.]

C. ESTABLISHMENT CLAUSE

The church-state docket since the 1940s has been dominated by two issues: (1) the appropriation of public funds to support sectarian schools and (2) government encouragement of prayer and religious instruction in public schools. Other cases, however, helped define the boundaries of the Establishment Clause.

In 1899 the Supreme Court upheld the appropriation of funds by Congress to a hospital operated by the Catholic Church. The Court denied that the statute violated the Establishment Clause. Religious ownership did not, by itself, make the hospital religious or sectarian. The character of an institution is measured by the charter creating it. There was no allegation that the hospital was confined to members of the Catholic Church or that the hospital had violated its charter to serve the poor. Bradfield v. Roberts, 175 U.S. 291. The Court also held that a congressional appropriation to educate Indians in sectarian schools did not violate the Establishment Clause. The tribal and trust funds used for this purpose were not general public moneys. They belonged to the Indians as compensation for lands that they had ceded to the United States. Quick Bear v. Leupp, 210 U.S. 50 (1908).

A series of cases from 1947 to 1970 tested the extent to which government could provide financial assistance to sectarian schools (section D in this chapter). By 1971, the Court was ready to develop what is called the "*Lemon* test" to guide its rulings on church-state questions (see box).

Equal Access

In a 1981 case, a state university allowed student secular groups to meet in university buildings but denied the same privilege to student religious groups. The university reasoned that giving permission to the latter would violate the Establishment Clause. The Supreme Court, voting 8–1, disagreed. State efforts to comply with the Establishment Clause do not permit discrimination against the religious speech of the student group seeking access to buildings for their meetings. Widmar v. Vincent, 454 U.S. 263 (1981).

The *Lemon* Test

In *Lemon v. Kurtzman*, 403 U.S. 602, 612–13 (1971), the Court established a three-prong test to determine the constitutionality of legislation regarding church-state relations, especially the Establishment Clause. These three principles are quite broad, giving the Court substantial discretion in applying them. For some erosion of the *Lemon* test, see p. 665.

1. The statute must have a secular legislative purpose.

2. Its principal or primary effect must be one that neither advances nor inhibits religion.

3. It must not foster excessive entanglement with religion.

In response to *Widmar,* Congress passed the "Equal Access" bill to prohibit any public secondary school receiving federal funds from denying equal access to students who wish to conduct a meeting devoted to religious objectives. Such meetings are to be voluntary, student-initiated, and without sponsorship by the school. If schools allow one or more non-curricular clubs (clubs unrelated to regular courses) to meet on school property during noninstructional time, they cannot refuse to allow other groups to meet simply because of "the religious, political, philosophical, or other content of the speech at such meetings." 98 Stat. 1302 (1984). In 1990, the Court upheld this statute against challenges that it violated the Establishment Clause. Eight Justices agreed that, in this case, a public high school had allowed such clubs as Subsurfers and a chess group to meet after school and should not have prohibited a Christian club from meeting. Writing for the Court, Justice O'Connor attracted only three other Justices (Rehnquist, White, and Blackmun) to her analysis of the Establishment Clause. Westside Community Bd. of Ed. v. Mergens, 496 U.S. 226 (1990).

The Court had earlier held that high school students may form religious groups and meet in school rooms. Bender v. Williamsport Area School Dist., 475 U.S. 534 (1986). If states permit school property to be used after hours for social, civic, and recreational purposes, they may not discriminate on the basis of religious viewpoint. Lamb's Chapel v. Center Moriches School Dist., 508 U.S. 384 (1993).

Building on *Widmar v. Vincent* and *Lamb's Chapel,* the Court in 1995 held that the University of Virginia denied students their right of free speech when it helped finance the printing of student publications but withheld payment from "Wide Awake," a Christian newspaper. The university argued that funding the newspaper would have violated the Establishment Clause, but a 5–4 majority ruled that no violation exists when a university subsidizes publications on a religion-neutral basis. The Court found it significant that the financial assistance came from student fees rather than from a tax levied by the State, but admitted that the payment of student fees is also mandatory. Rosenberger v. University of Virginia, 515 U.S. 819 (1995).

Other Conflicts

A Minnesota law provided that only religious organizations receiving more than half of their total contributions from members or affiliated organizations would be exempt from the registration and reporting requirements of a charitable solicitation statute. A 5–4 Supreme Court held that the statute violated the Establishment Clause because it set up an official denominational preference. The 50 percent rule was not "closely fitted" to the state's asserted interest in preventing fraudulent solicitations. Moreover, the statute presented too great a risk of politicizing religion. Different religious organizations would jockey for support within the legislature to obtain exemptions. Larson v. Valente, 456 U.S. 228 (1982).

In that same year the Court held that a Massachusetts statute violated the Establishment Clause by vesting in the governing bodies of churches the power to prevent issuance of liquor licenses within a 500-foot radius of the churches. The Court regarded the statute as a delegation of legislative zoning power to a nongovernmental entity. Not only was the churches' power under the statute standardless, calling for no reasons or findings for action, but the "mere appearance of a joint exercise of legislative authority by Church and State provides a significant symbolic benefit to religion in the minds of some by reason of the power conferred." Larkin v. Grendel's Den, Inc., 459 U.S. 116, 125–26 (1982).

The Continuing Saga of Kiryas Joel

In 1994, the Court relied on *Larkin v. Grendel's Den* to strike down a public school district that New York had created solely for the disabled children of a small village of Hasidic Jews. New

York drew the school district to coincide with the population of Kiryas Joel, a Satmar Hasidic enclave about 40 miles north of New York City. The Court, divided 6 to 3, ruled that the school district violated the Establishment Clause. Board of Ed. of Kiryas Joel v. Grumet, 512 U.S. 687 (1994). New York responded to the decision by passing a statute that allowed any municipality meeting certain criteria to form its own school district. Kiryas Joel met the criteria. In fact, out of 1,546 municipalities in New York State, it was the *only* one to qualify. In 1995, a state trial court upheld the new law but was reversed a year later by the State Appellate Division. The state's highest court, the Court of Appeals, also struck down this second attempt to create a district for Kiryas Joel. Defying the courts, the state legislature passed legislation on August 4, 1997, creating a special public school district for the Hasidic sect. The legislators said that the new legislation was applicable to other municipalities, not just Kiryas Joel, but the benefits appeared to favor only Kiryas Joel. "Defying Courts, Lawmakers Approve School District for Hasidim," New York Times, August 5, 1997, at A19. This third attempt to preserve the Hasidic school district was also rejected by New York Courts. In 1999, the Supreme Court refused to hear an appeal from Kiryas Joel. Pataki v. Grumet, 120 S.Ct. 363 (1999).

Crèches and Menorahs

The Court has had a difficult time deciding whether public officials can erect crèches and menorahs on public property. In 1984, the Court split 5–4 in reviewing a crèche case from the city of Pawtucket, Rhode Island, which annually erected a Christmas display, including a crèche, or Nativity scene. In upholding the city, the Court offended some religious groups by reasoning that the crèche could be displayed because it had a "secular purpose." LYNCH v. DONNELLY, 465 U.S. 668 (1984). The decision opened the door to other governmental practices. The issue returned to the Court in 1989 in two forms: the constitutionality of a crèche on the grand staircase of the Allegheny County Courthouse and an 18-foot Chanukah menorah (candelabrum) plus a 45-foot decorated Christmas tree placed just outside the City-County Building. In a muddled decision, offering few intelligible principles to guide the lower courts (or state legislatures), the Court struck down the crèche display by the vote of 5 to 4 and upheld the menorah/Christmas tree display 6 to 3. ALLEGHENY COUNTY v. GREATER PITTSBURGH ACLU, 492 U.S. 573 (1989).

To reach this result, the majority concluded that the combination of a Jewish menorah and a Christmas tree somehow recognized "cultural diversity," with little appreciation that the attempt to transform a religious symbol to a cultural event would be offensive to many Jews. By noting that Christmas and Chanukah "are part of the same winter-holiday season, which has attained a secular status in our society," Justice Blackmun's opinion for the majority appeared to secularize, if not Christianize, a Jewish holiday. With regard to the crèche display, Justice Blackmun argued that it offended the Constitution in part because it stood alone, surrounded by a floral decoration, whereas the crèche in *Lynch v. Donnelly* was mixed with a Santa Claus house, reindeer pulling Santa's sleigh, candy-striped poles, a Christmas tree, carolers, and cutout figures representing such characters as a clown, an elephant, and a teddy bear. Would the addition of some of those objects have saved the crèche in Pittsburgh? No one knows. It is not even clear whether the menorah/Christmas tree combination would be constitutional had the two symbols been transposed, placing the menorah directly in front of the entrance to the City-County Building with the Christmas tree positioned to the side, or making the menorah 45-feet high alongside a smaller Christmas tree. Finally, if municipalities are free to celebrate Christian and Jewish holidays, what of other sects and of nonbelievers? Does the goal of "cultural diversity" require representation for those groups? Instead of disposing of such questions, the Court virtually invited any number of variations to revisit the judiciary.

One such variation, decided by the Court in 1995, involved Ohio prohibiting the Ku Klux

Klan from placing a large wooden cross in front of the state capitol. In the past, state officials had allowed in that public forum the display of a Christmas tree and a menorah. The state argued that the Klan's cross, given the proximity to the seat of government, might imply that the cross bore the state's approval. The Court decided that the Klan's display was private religious speech entitled to protection under the First Amendment. However, the plurality opinion by Justice Scalia (joined by Rehnquist, Kennedy, and Thomas) was followed by three concurrences: one by Thomas, another by O'Connor (joined by Souter and Breyer) and a third by Souter (joined by O'Connor and Breyer), making it difficult to locate agreement on any general principles that might guide future cases. Stevens and Ginsburg wrote separate dissenting opinions. Capitol Sq. Review Bd. v. Pinette, 515 U.S. 753 (1995).

The crèche/menorah issue continues to percolate in the lower courts. City officials of Jersey City, N.J., erected on the city hall plaza a holiday display containing a crèche and menorah. After a federal district court issued an injunction against the display, it was modified by adding plastic figures of Frosty the Snowman and Santa Claus and a red wooden sled. That satisfied the district judge, who decided that the secular figures somehow "demystified" and "desanctified" the religious meaning of the crèche and menorah. The Third Circuit, however, ruled that the display violated the Establishment Clause. ACLU v. Schundler, 104 F.3d 1435 (3d Cir. 1997), cert. denied, 520 U.S. 1265 (1997).

Sunday Worship

In laws governing Sunday worship and Sunday closings, state interests must be balanced against an individual's preference to worship on a day other than Sunday (so-called Sabbatarians). In one case, a Seventh-Day Adventist had been fired because she would not work on Saturday, the Sabbath day of her faith. She was later denied unemployment compensation benefits on the ground that she would not accept suitable work when offered. The Court held that the state law violated her religious freedoms. This law was vulnerable on First Amendment grounds because the state expressly saved the Sunday worshipper from having to make the kind of choice faced by the Seventh-Day Adventist. Sherbert v. Verner, 374 U.S. 398, 406 (1963). Government may not put an employee in the predicament of choosing between fidelity to religious beliefs and access to public benefits. Hobbie v. Unemployment Appeals Comm'n of Fla., 480 U.S. 136 (1987); Thomas v. Review Bd., Ind. Empl. Sec. Div., 450 U.S. 707 (1981). It is not necessary to belong to an established religious sect that forbids work on Sundays. A sincere, personal religious belief is sufficient. Frazee v. Employment Security Dept., 489 U.S. 829 (1989).

These cases were decided on constitutional grounds. Other cases revolve around statutory questions, including the intent of Congress when it passes legislation to prohibit religious discrimination. One provision states that employers have an obligation to "reasonably accommodate to an employee's . . . religious observance or practice without undue hardship on the conduct of the employer's business." 42 U.S.C. § 2000e(j) (1994). Congress added this provision after courts had "come down on both sides" of the rights of Sabbatarians. The language was intended to "resolve by legislation . . . that which the courts apparently have not resolved." 118 Cong. Rec. 705–06 (1972). These cases turn on questions of what burden of proof should be placed on the employee to prove discrimination. Ansonia Board of Education v. Philbrook, 479 U.S. 60 (1986). Congress also exempted religious organizations from the prohibition on religious discrimination in employment. 42 U.S.C. § 2000e-1 (1994). The purpose was to shield religious organizations from liability in the case of employment suits. A unanimous Court in 1987 held that this exemption does not offend the Establishment Clause. Corporation of Presiding Bishop v. Amos, 483 U.S. 327 (1987).

Although states may not discriminate against Sabbatarians, they might err by going in the opposite direction to promote their religious practice. In 1985 the Court held that a Connecticut law violated the Establishment Clause because it provided that no person "who states that a particular day of the week is observed as his Sabbath may be required by his employer to work on such day. An employee's refusal to work on his Sabbath shall not constitute grounds for his dismissal." The Court struck down the statute because it lacked neutrality in religious matters. Estate of Thornton v. Caldor, Inc., 472 U.S. 703. What began as an effort to accommodate the free exercise of religion ended up violating the Establishment Clause.

Religious Freedom Restoration Act (RFRA)

A decision by the Court in 1990, regarding unemployment compensation benefits, prompted Congress in 1993 to pass legislation that overrode the Court. In 1997, the Court declared that the statute was unconstitutional, pushing the matter back to Congress to consider alternative legislation. The 1990 decision concerned two members of the Native American Church who had been fired by a private organization because they ingested peyote, a hallucinogenic drug. They took the drug as part of a religious, sacramental exercise. Eating the peyote plant, which embodies their deity, is an act of worship and communion. Their application for unemployment compensation was denied by Oregon under a state law that disqualifies employees who are fired for work-related "misconduct." Remaining drug-free was a condition of their employment.

The Court, divided 6 to 3, held that the Free Exercise Clause permits a state to prohibit sacramental peyote use and to deny unemployment benefits to persons fired for such use. State law may prohibit the possession and use of a drug even if it incidentally prohibits a religious practice. The Court distinguished this case from other unemployment-benefit cases by noting that the religious conduct in those cases was not prohibited by law. Oregon law made it a criminal offense to possess or use peyote. Four Justices — O'Connor in her concurrence and Blackmun, Brennan, and Marshall in their dissents — rejected the Court's opinion that states need not demonstrate a "compelling government interest" to justify general prohibitions that affect the free exercise of religion. Oregon remained free to make an exemption for the use of peyote by members of the Native American Church. About two dozen states had statutory or judicially-crafted exemptions for the religious use of peyote. EMPLOYMENT DIVISION v. SMITH, 494 U.S. 872 (1990). The Oregon legislature repaired some of the damage of the Court's decision by enacting a bill that protects the sacramental use of peyote by the Native American Church. Oregon Laws, Chap. 329, June 24, 1991.

Smith provided a framework for the Court to analyze ordinances that a Florida city council passed to prohibit the Santeria religion from sacrificing animals as a form of devotion. Animals are killed to nurture a personal relationship with spirits. Since the ordinances were aimed specifically at the Santeria religion (even to the point of exempting kosher slaughter), the *Smith* test did not apply. The ordinances were not general and neutral. Thus, the ordinances had to be justified by a compelling governmental interest and had to be narrowly tailored to advance that interest. A unanimous Court found the ordinances to be overbroad and underinclusive. Even were the governmental interests compelling, the ordinances were not drawn narrowly enough to accomplish those purposes. To the Court, the ordinances were aimed at suppressing a religious exercise. Church of Lukumi Babalu Aye v. Hialeah, 508 U.S. 520 (1993). In a concurrence, Justice Souter expressed his doubt whether *Smith* merited the Court's continued adherence.

A number of religious groups urged Congress to pass legislation that would grant greater religious freedom than recognized in *Smith*. The purpose was to reinstate the previous standard (compelling governmental interest) for testing federal, state, and local laws. Proponents of the bill believed that the Court's ruling threatened a number of religious practices, including the use of ceremonial wine, the practice of kosher slaughter, and the Hmong (Laotian) religious objection to autopsy. In 1993, Congress passed the Religious Freedom Restoration Act (RFRA). (See reading for congressional debate.)

RFRA provided that governments may substantially burden a person's religious exercise only if they demonstrate a compelling interest and use the least restrictive means of furthering that interest. The statute restored the compelling interest test of *Sherbert* v. *Verner*, 374 U.S. 398 (1963) and *Wisconsin* v. *Yoder*, 406 U.S. 205 (1972). 107 Stat. 1488 (1993). A year later, Congress passed legislation to legalize the use of peyote by Native Americans for ceremonial purposes. No Indian may be penalized or discriminated against for such use, including the denial of benefits under public assistance programs. 108 Stat. 3125 (1994).

Whatever the Court decided to do with RFRA, it would acknowledge the central role of majoritarian politics in protecting religious rights. If it upheld the statute, it would recognize that religious groups, in concert with Congress, could define religious freedom more generously than the Court. If it struck it down, it would merely reaffirm the 1990 *Smith* holding, which itself depended on the majoritarian process to protect religion. As the Court noted in *Smith*: "It may fairly be said that leaving accommodation to the political process will place at a relative disadvantage those religious practices that are not widely engaged in; but that unavoidable consequence of democratic government must be preferred to a system in which each conscience is a law unto itself or in which judges weigh the social importance of all laws against the centrality of all religious beliefs." 494 U.S. at 890.

In 1997, the Court ruled that Congress exceeded the scope of its enforcement power under Section 5 of the Fourteenth Amendment in enacting RFRA. In many ways, Congress had asked for a black eye by attempting to reimpose a constitutional standard (*Sherbert* v. *Verner*) that the Court itself had rejected in *Smith*. The Court could not sit still and have Congress ram *Sherbert* down its throat. But the reasoning and premises in the Court's decision were superficial, unpersuasive, and internally inconsistent (see box on next page). They invite continued challenges and legislative activity. Although the Court strongly hinted that it has the last and final word in deciding the meaning of the Constitution, it in fact left the door wide open for future congressional action. BOERNE v. FLORES, 521 U.S. 507 (1997). In 1998, the Eighth Circuit held that RFRA was constitutional as applied to the federal government. In re Young, 141 F.3d 854 (8th Cir. 1998), cert. denied, sub nom. Christians v. Crystal Evangelical Free Church, 525 U.S. 811 (1998).

"Son of RFRA"

On June 9, 1998, a "Son of RFRA" bill was introduced, relying this time on congressional prerogatives over spending and commerce. The bill passed the House the following year by a vote of 306 to 118. By the time the bill cleared both chambers, it had been restricted to provide two kinds of protections. First, it offers religious groups protection in land-use disputes, such as zoning issues (the kind that triggered *Boerne* v. *Flores*). Second, the bill makes it easier for prisoners or other persons confined in state-run institutions to practice their faith. The bill applies to any organization that receives federal money, including state and local prisons that get federal construction and maintenance funds. Finally, the bill relies on congressional power over interstate commerce, because construction materials are shipped between states for the renovation of buildings owned by religious organizations. President Clinton signed the bill on September 22, 2000. 114 Stat. 803 (2000).

Sunday Closing Laws

Sunday closing laws (or "blue laws") were challenged in court as a violation of the Establishment Clause. A major case involved a Maryland law that prohibited the sale on Sunday of all merchandise except the retail sale of tobacco products, confectionaries, milk, bread, fruit, gasoline, oils, greases, drugs, medicines, newspapers, and periodicals. After litigation began, the state legislature allowed other exceptions. In reviewing the history of Sunday closing laws, an 8–1 majority for the Supreme Court found that the original motivation had gradually

Analysis of *Boerne* v. *Flores*

In deciding that Congress exceeded its power under Section 5 of the Fourteenth Amendment, the Court reasoned that Section 5 is limited to "enforcement" and "remedial" actions. It then charges: "Legislation which alters the meaning of the Free Exercise Clause cannot be said to be enforcing the Clause. Congress does not enforce a constitutional right by changing what the right is." 521 U.S. at 519. But in enacting RFRA, Congress did not alter the meaning of the Free Exercise Clause any more than the Court alters the meaning of that Clause with its rulings, especially when it reverses itself.

The Court acknowledged, as it had to, that the line between remedial actions and substantive constitutional changes is difficult to draw and that Congress must have "wide latitude" in determining where it lies. It suggests that RFRA was invalid because it failed to show a "congruence and proportionality between the injury to be prevented or remedied and the means adopted to that end." That suggests that a redrafted bill — with greater congruence and proportionality — might pass muster. Is that the Court's intent? Similarly, the Court says that RFRA's legislative record "lacks examples of modern instances of generally applicable laws passed because of religious bigotry." Id. at 530. Is that the problem? If Congress, with findings, could identify recent examples of religious persecution, would that justify RFRA?

The Court injected some unintended humor with this grave admonition: "Shifting legislative majorities could change the Constitution and effectively circumvent the difficult and detailed amendment process contained in Article V." Id. at 529. The same result flows from Court decisions that reflect shifting judicial majorities or changes in the way that a Justice analyzes an issue. Two days before the Court invalidated RFRA it overruled a decision from 1985 that had limited federal assistance to parochial schools. Agostini v. Felton, 521 U.S. 203 (1997), reversing Aguilar v. Felton, 473 U.S. 402 (1985).

The Court concluded with the suggestion that constitutional interpretation is a judicial monopoly: "Our national experience teaches that the Constitution is preserved best when each part of the government respects both the Constitution and the proper actions and determinations of the other branches. When the Court has interpreted the Constitution, it has acted within the province of the Judicial Branch, which embraces the duty to say what the law is." Id. at 535–36. Nothing in two hundred years of constitutional practice and construction (or "national experience") supports such a static formulation.

---

changed from a religious character to a secular purpose in setting aside a day for rest and recreation. The fact that the day was Sunday, "a day of particular significance for the dominant Christian sects, does not bar the State from achieving its secular goals." McGowan v. Maryland, 366 U.S. 420, 445 (1961). The secularization of Sunday was evident in the repeal of earlier laws that had a distinctly religious purpose, such as banning bingo games, pinball machines, slot machines, dancing, and the sale of alcoholic beverages. Id. at 423–24, 448.

Corporations, claiming economic injury, were unsuccessful in challenging the Sunday closing laws. Two Guys v. McGinley, 366 U.S. 582 (1961). The effect of those laws raised more difficult questions when applied to Jewish businesses that closed Friday evening and all day Saturday to observe the Sabbath. The state forced them to close on Sunday as well. Dividing 6–3 on this issue, the Court reasoned that the law did not inconvenience all members of the Orthodox Jewish faith, but only those who chose to work on Sunday. Dodging the question of why Sunday would be selected as the official day of rest, the Court argued that any law was likely to result in an economic disadvantage to some religious sect. Braunfeld v. Brown, 366 U.S. 599 (1961). A Massachusetts law allowing kosher markets to sell kosher meats until 10 A.M. on Sunday was upheld 6–3, even though plaintiffs argued that it was economically impractical for them to stay open from Saturday at sundown until 10 A.M. on Sunday. These laws

State Closing Laws

Although the U.S. Supreme Court upheld Sunday closing laws, some of the states changed their laws to permit businesses to operate on Sunday if religious convictions forced them to close on another day. The Supreme Court of Pennsylvania concluded that state laws on Sunday closings were so "riddled with exception after exception" that they violated the equal protection of the laws. Kroger Co. v. O'Hara Tp., 392 A.2d 266, 273 (Pa. 1978). The Supreme Court of Pennsylvania could find no fair and substantial relationship between the objective of providing a uniform day of rest and recreation and in "permitting the sale of novelties but not Bibles and bathing suits; in permitting the sale of fresh meat patties but not frozen meat patties; or in permitting the installation of an electric meter but not a T.V. antenna." Id. at 275.

The Supreme Court of Connecticut found the state's Sunday closing laws too arbitrary, discriminatory, and unreasonable to satisfy the requirements of equal protection and due process. It cited a comic strip showing a customer asking the proprietor of a drugstore for a snow shovel, a roll of film, a hairnet, and a box of candy. When the customer finally asked whether he had any wood stoves the proprietor replied indignantly: "Wood Stoves?... in a DRUG store?" Caldor's, Inc. v. Bedding Barn, Inc., 417 A.2d 343, 353 n.9 (Conn. 1979).

were saved because they had lost their original religious character. Gallagher v. Crown Kosher Market, 366 U.S. 617 (1961). See also Arlan's Dept. Store v. Kentucky, 371 U.S. 218 (1962). The doctrinal confusion of these federal rulings convinced some state legislatures and state courts to adopt more coherent policies under their own constitutions (see box).

Teenage Chastity

In 1988 the Supreme Court decided an important case involving the use of federal funds to discourage adolescent, premarital sex. The statute, known formally as the Adolescent Family Life Act of 1981 and informally as the Teenage Chastity Act, authorized federal grants to public and private groups, including religious organizations. The Court acknowledged that some of the funds had been spent by religious groups impermissibly to promote religious doctrines. Nevertheless, a 5 to 4 Court held that the statute, *on its face,* did not violate the Establishment Clause. It remanded the case to the district court to determine whether the Act, *as applied,* violates the Clause. Bowen v. Kendrick, 487 U.S. 589 (1988).

The remand put pressure on the government to negotiate with the plaintiffs to show that the law, as applied, had no *Lemon* problems. The government took time for this review. The plaintiffs were in no hurry. They wanted the government to do whatever was necessary to avoid constitutional violations. The district judge gave the government time to negotiate draft settlement agreements with the plaintiffs. Finally, in 1993, the parties agreed to settle out of court all matters related to the litigation.

Lynch v. Donnelly

465 U.S. 668 (1984)

Each year the city of Pawtucket, R.I., set up a Christmas display in a park owned by a nonprofit organization and located in the city's shopping district. In addition to such objects as a Santa Clause house, a Christmas tree, and a banner that read "SEASONS GREETINGS," the display included a crèche (nativity scene). The crèche had been included in this display for forty years or more. Daniel Donnelly brought an action in federal court, challenging the inclusion of the crèche as a violation of the Establishment

Clause. The defendant was Dennis Lynch, Mayor of Pawtucket. The district court upheld the challenge and permanently enjoined the city from including the crèche in the display. The First Circuit affirmed.

CHIEF JUSTICE BURGER delivered the opinion of the Court.

We granted certiorari to decide whether the Establishment Clause of the First Amendment prohibits a municipality from including a crèche, or Nativity scene, in its annual Christmas display.

I

Each year, in cooperation with the downtown retail merchants' association, the city of Pawtucket, R.I., erects a Christmas display as part of its observance of the Christmas holiday season. The display is situated in a park owned by a non-profit organization and located in the heart of the shopping district. The display is essentially like those to be found in hundreds of towns or cities across the Nation—often on public grounds—during the Christmas season. The Pawtucket display comprises many of the figures and decorations traditionally associated with Christmas, including, among other things, a Santa Claus house, reindeer pulling Santa's sleigh, candy-striped poles, a Christmas tree, carolers, cutout figures representing such characters as a clown, an elephant, and a teddy bear, hundreds of colored lights, a large banner that reads "SEASONS GREETINGS," and the crèche at issue here. All components of this display are owned by the city.

The crèche, which has been included in the display for 40 or more years, consists of the traditional figures, including the Infant Jesus, Mary and Joseph, angels, shepherds, kings, and animals, all ranging in height from 5" to 5'. In 1973, when the present crèche was acquired, it cost the city $1,365; it now is valued at $200. The erection and dismantling of the crèche costs the city about $20 per year; nominal expenses are incurred in lighting the crèche. No money has been expended on its maintenance for the past 10 years.

. . .

II

A

This Court has explained that the purpose of the Establishment and Free Exercise Clauses of the First Amendment is

"to prevent, as far as possible, the intrusion of

either [the church or the state] into the precincts of the other." *Lemon v. Kurtzman,* 403 U.S. 602, 614 (1971).

At the same time, however, the Court has recognized that

"total separation is not possible in an absolute sense. Some relationship between government and religious organizations is inevitable." *Ibid.*

. . .

B

The Court's interpretation of the Establishment Clause has comported with what history reveals was the contemporaneous understanding of its guarantees. A significant example of the contemporaneous understanding of that Clause is found in the events of the first week of the First Session of the First Congress in 1789. In the very week that Congress approved the Establishment Clause as part of the Bill of Rights for submission to the states, it enacted legislation providing for paid Chaplains for the House and Senate. In *Marsh v. Chambers,* 463 U.S. 783 (1983), we noted that 17 Members of that First Congress had been Delegates to the Constitutional Convention where freedom of speech, press, and religion and antagonism toward an established church were subjects of frequent discussion. We saw no conflict with the Establishment Clause when Nebraska employed members of the clergy as official legislative Chaplains to give opening prayers at sessions of the state legislature. *Id.,* at 791.

. . .

C

[Burger provides other examples of official acknowledgment of religion: making Thanksgiving, with its religious overtones, a national holiday; giving federal employees a holiday for Christmas; putting "In God We Trust" on currency; including "One nation under God" in the Pledge of Allegiance; using public revenue to display religious paintings in art galleries; decorating the Supreme Court with religious motifs; and having Congress direct the President to proclaim a National Day of Prayer.]

III

. . .

The District Court inferred from the religious nature of the crèche that the city has no secular purpose for the display. In so doing, it rejected the city's claim that its reasons for including the crèche are essentially the same as its reasons for sponsoring the display as a whole. The District Court plainly erred by focusing almost exclusively on the crèche. When viewed in the proper context of the Christmas Holiday season, it is apparent that, on this record, there is insufficient evidence to establish that the inclusion of the crèche is a purposeful or surreptitious effort to express some kind of subtle governmental advocacy of a particular religious message. In a pluralistic society a variety of motives and purposes are implicated. The city, like the Congresses and Presidents, however, has principally taken note of a significant historical religious event long celebrated in the Western World. The crèche in the display depicts the historical origins of this traditional event long recognized as a National Holiday. . . .

The narrow question is whether there is a secular purpose for Pawtucket's display of the crèche. The display is sponsored by the city to celebrate the Holiday and to depict the origins of that Holiday. These are legitimate secular purposes. The District Court's inference, drawn from the religious nature of the crèche, that the city has no secular purpose was, on this record, clearly erroneous.

The District Court found that the primary effect of including the crèche is to confer a substantial and impermissible benefit on religion in general and on the Christian faith in particular. Comparisons of the relative benefits to religion of different forms of governmental support are elusive and difficult to make. But to conclude that the primary effect of including the crèche is to advance religion in violation of the Establishment Clause would require that we view it as more beneficial to and more an endorsement of religion, for example, than expenditure of large sums of public money for textbooks supplied throughout the country to students attending church-sponsored schools, *Board of Education* v. *Allen, supra;* expenditure of public funds for transportation of students to church-sponsored schools, *Everson* v. *Board of Education, supra;* federal grants for college buildings of church-sponsored institutions of higher education combining secular and religious education, *Tilton* v. *Richardson,* 403 U.S. 672 (1971); noncategorical grants to church-spon-

sored colleges and universities, *Roemer* v. *Board of Public Works,* 426 U.S. 736 (1976); and the tax exemptions for church properties sanctioned in *Walz* v. *Tax Comm'n,* 397 U.S. 664 (1970). It would also require that we view it as more of an endorsement of religion than the Sunday Closing Laws upheld in *McGowan* v. *Maryland,* 366 U.S. 420 (1961); the release time program for religious training in *Zorach* v. *Clauson,* 343 U.S. 306 (1952); and the legislative prayers upheld in *Marsh* v. *Chambers,* 463 U.S. 783 (1983).

. . .

IV

. . .

The Court has acknowledged that the "fears and political problems" that gave rise to the Religion Clauses in the 18th century are of far less concern today. *Everson,* 330 U.S., at 8. We are unable to perceive the Archbishop of Canterbury, the Bishop of Rome, or other powerful religious leaders behind every public acknowledgment of the religious heritage long officially recognized by the three constitutional branches of government. Any notion that these symbols pose a real danger of establishment of a state church is farfetched indeed.

V

That this Court has been alert to the constitutionally expressed opposition to the establishment of religion is shown in numerous holdings striking down statutes or programs as violative of the Establishment Clause. . . . Taken together these cases abundantly demonstrate the Court's concern to protect the genuine objectives of the Establishment Clause. It is far too late in the day to impose a crabbed reading of the Clause on the country.

VI

We hold that, notwithstanding the religious significance of the crèche, the city of Pawtucket has not violated the Establishment Clause of the First Amendment. Accordingly, the judgment of the Court of Appeals is reversed.

It is so ordered.

JUSTICE O'CONNOR, concurring.

I concur in the opinion of the Court. I write separately to suggest a clarification of our Establishment Clause doctrine. . . .

[Justice O'Connor argues that the government can run afoul of the Establishment Clause in two

principal ways: (1) excessive entanglement with religious institutions and (2) endorsement or approval of religion. In this case she found neither entanglement nor endorsement.]

JUSTICE BRENNAN, with whom JUSTICE MARSHALL, JUSTICE BLACKMUN, and JUSTICE STEVENS join, dissenting.

...the Court properly looks for guidance to the settled test announced in *Lemon* v. *Kurtzman,* 403 U.S. 602 (1971), for assessing whether a challenged governmental practice involves an impermissible step toward the establishment of religion....

I

...After reviewing the Court's opinion, I am convinced that this case appears hard not because the principles of decision are obscure, but because the Christmas holiday seems so familiar and agreeable. Although the Court's reluctance to disturb a community's chosen method of celebrating such an agreeable holiday is understandable, that cannot justify the Court's departure from controlling precedent....

A

...

Applying the three-part *[Lemon]* test to Pawtucket's crèche, I am persuaded that the city's inclusion of the crèche in its Christmas display simply does not reflect a "clearly secular... purpose."...

...[A]s was true in *Larkin* v. *Grendel's Den, Inc.,* 459 U.S. 116, 123–124 (1982), all of Pawtucket's "valid secular objectives can be readily accomplished by other means." Plainly, the city's interest in celebrating the holiday and in promoting both retail sales and goodwill are fully served by the elaborate display of Santa Claus, reindeer, and wishing wells that are already a part of Pawtucket's annual Christmas display. More importantly, the nativity scene, unlike every other element of the Hodgson Park display, reflects a sectarian exclusivity that the avowed purposes of celebrating the holiday season and promoting re-

tail commerce simply do not encompass. To be found constitutional, Pawtucket's seasonal celebration must at least be nondenominational and not serve to promote religion. The inclusion of a distinctively religious element like the crèche, however, demonstrates that a narrower sectarian purpose lay behind the decision to include a nativity scene. That the crèche retained this religious character for the people and municipal government of Pawtucket is suggested by the Mayor's testimony at trial in which he stated that for him, as well as others in the city, the effort to eliminate the nativity scene from Pawtucket's Christmas celebration "is a step towards establishing another religion, non-religion that it may be." App. 100. Plainly, the city and its leaders understood that the inclusion of the crèche in its display would serve the wholly religious purpose of "keep[ing] 'Christ in Christmas.' " 525 F. Supp. 1150, 1173 (RI 1981)....

Finally, it is evident that Pawtucket's inclusion of a crèche as part of its annual Christmas display does pose a significant threat of fostering "excessive entanglement." As the Court notes,...the District Court found no administrative entanglement in this case, primarily because the city had been able to administer the annual display without extensive consultation with religious officials.... Of course, there is no reason to disturb that finding, but it is worth noting that after today's decision, administrative entanglements may well develop. Jews and other non-Christian groups, prompted perhaps by the Mayor's remark that he will include a Menorah in future displays, can be expected to press government for inclusion of their symbols, and faced with such requests, government will have to become involved in accommodating the various demands....

. . .

JUSTICE BLACKMUN, with whom JUSTICE STEVENS joins, dissenting.

. . .

Allegheny County v. Greater Pittsburgh ACLU

492 U.S. 573 (1989)

Two holiday displays on public property in downtown Pittsburgh prompted this lawsuit: a crèche depicting the Christian nativity scene (placed on the Grand Staircase of the Allegheny County Courthouse) and an 18-foot Chanukah menorah, or candelabrum,

(placed just outside the City-County Building next to the city's 45-foot decorated Christmas tree). The crèche was donated by the Holy Name Society, a Roman Catholic group, and the menorah is owned by Chabad, a Jewish group. The ACLU objected that the displays violated the Establishment Clause. The District Court denied relief, relying on *Lynch* v. *Donnelly* (1984), but the Third Circuit reversed. This case is of interest because of the continuing inability of the Court to present a coherent doctrine governing these displays.

JUSTICE BLACKMUN announced the judgment of the Court and delivered the opinion of the Court with respect to Parts III-A, IV, and V, an opinion with respect to Parts I and II, in which JUSTICE STEVENS and JUSTICE O'CONNOR join, an opinion with respect to Part III-B, in which JUSTICE STEVENS joins, an opinion with respect to Part VII, in which JUSTICE O'CONNOR joins, and an opinion with respect to Part VI.

This litigation concerns the constitutionality of two recurring holiday displays located on public property in downtown Pittsburgh. The first is a crèche placed on the Grand Staircase of the Allegheny County Courthouse. The second is a Chanukah menorah placed just outside the City-County Building, next to a Christmas tree and a sign saluting liberty. The Court of Appeals for the Third Circuit ruled that each display violates the Establishment Clause of the First Amendment because each has the impermissible effect of endorsing religion. 842 F. 2d 655 (1988). We agree that the crèche display has that unconstitutional effect but reverse the Court of Appeals' judgment regarding the menorah display.

I

A

The county courthouse is owned by Allegheny County and is its seat of government. It houses the offices of the county commissioners, controller, treasurer, sheriff, and clerk of court. Civil and criminal trials are held there.... The "main," "most beautiful," and "most public" part of the courthouse is its Grand Staircase, set into one arch and surrounded by others, with arched windows serving as a backdrop....

Since 1981, the county has permitted the Holy Name Society, a Roman Catholic group, to display a crèche in the county courthouse during the Christmas holiday season.... As observed in this Nation, Christmas has a secular, as well as a religious, dimension.

The crèche in the county courthouse, like other crèches, is a visual representation of the scene in the manger in Bethlehem shortly after the birth of Jesus, as described in the Gospels of Luke and Matthew. The crèche includes figures of the infant Jesus, Mary, Joseph, farm animals, shepherds, and wise men, all placed in or before a wooden representation of a manger, which has at its crest an angel bearing a banner that proclaims "Gloria in Excelsis Deo!"

During the 1986–1987 holiday season, the crèche was on display on the Grand Staircase from November 26 to January 9.... It had a wooden fence on three sides and bore a plaque stating: "This Display Donated by the Holy Name Society." Sometime during the week of December 2, the county placed red and white poinsettia plants around the fence.... The county also placed a small evergreen tree, decorated with a red bow, behind each of the two endposts of the fence.... These trees stood alongside the manger backdrop and were slightly shorter than it was. The angel thus was at the apex of the crèche display. Altogether, the crèche, the fence, the poinsettias, and the trees occupied a substantial amount of space on the Grand Staircase. No figures of Santa Claus or other decorations appeared on the Grand Staircase....

B

The City-County Building is separate and a block removed from the county courthouse and, as the name implies, is jointly owned by the city of Pittsburgh and Allegheny County. The city's portion of the building houses the city's principal offices, including the mayor's.... The city is responsible for the building's Grant Street entrance which has three rounded arches supported by columns....

For a number of years, the city has had a large Christmas tree under the middle arch outside the Grant Street entrance. Following this practice, city employees on November 17, 1986, erected a 45-foot tree under the middle arch and decorated it with lights and ornaments.... A few days later, the city placed at the foot of the tree a sign bearing the mayor's name and entitled "Salute to Liberty." Beneath the title, the sign stated:

"During this holiday season, the city of Pittsburgh salutes liberty. Let these festive lights remind us that we are the keepers of the flame of liberty and our legacy of freedom." JEV 41.

At least since 1982, the city has expanded its Grant Street holiday display to include a symbolic representation of Chanukah, an 8-day Jewish holiday that begins on the 25th day of the Jewish lunar month of Kislev.... The 25th of Kislev usually occurs in December, and thus Chanukah is the annual Jewish holiday that falls closest to Christmas Day each year. In 1986, Chanukah began at sundown on December 26....

According to Jewish tradition, on the 25th of Kislev in 164 B.C.E. (before the common era (165 B.C.)), the Maccabees rededicated the Temple of Jerusalem after recapturing it from the Greeks, or, more accurately, from the Greek-influenced Seleucid Empire, in the course of a political rebellion....

The Talmud explains the lamp-lighting ritual as a commemoration of an event that occurred during the rededication of the Temple. The Temple housed a seven-branch menorah, which was to be kept burning continuously.... When the Maccabees rededicated the Temple, they had only enough oil to last for one day. But, according to the Talmud, the oil miraculously lasted for eight days (the length of time it took to obtain additional oil).... To celebrate and publicly proclaim this miracle, the Talmud prescribes that it is a mitzvah (*i.e.,* a religious deed or commandment),... for Jews to place a lamp with eight lights just outside the entrance to their homes or in a front window during the eight days of Chanukah....

Chanukah, like Christmas, is a cultural event as well as a religious holiday.... Indeed, the Chanukah story always has had a political or national, as well as a religious, dimension: it tells of national heroism in addition to divine intervention. Also, Chanukah, like Christmas, is a winter holiday; according to some historians, it was associated in ancient times with the winter solstice. Just as some Americans celebrate Christmas without regard to its religious significance, some nonreligious American Jews celebrate Chanukah as an expression of ethnic identity, and "as a cultural or national event, rather than as a specifically religious event."...

... [S]ome have suggested that the proximity of Christmas accounts for the social prominence of Chanukah in this country. Whatever the reason, Chanukah is observed by American Jews to an extent greater than its religious importance would indicate: in the hierarchy of Jewish holidays, Chanukah ranks fairly low in religious signifi-

cance. This socially heightened status of Chanukah reflects its cultural or secular dimension.

. . .

IV

We turn first to the county's crèche display. There is no doubt, of course, that the crèche itself is capable of communicating a religious message.... Indeed, the crèche in this lawsuit uses words, as well as the picture of the nativity scene, to make its religious meaning unmistakably clear. "Glory to God in the Highest!" says the angel in the crèche — Glory to God because of the birth of Jesus. This praise to God in Christian terms is indisputably religious — indeed sectarian — just as it is when said in the Gospel or in a church service.

Under the Court's holding in *Lynch,* the effect of a crèche display turns on its setting. Here, unlike in *Lynch,* nothing in the context of the display detracts from the crèche's religious message. The *Lynch* display comprised a series of figures and objects, each group of which had its own focal point. Santa's house and his reindeer were objects of attention separate from the crèche, and had their specific visual story to tell. Similarly, whatever a "talking" wishing well may be, it obviously was a center of attention separate from the crèche. Here, in contrast, the crèche stands alone: it is the single element of the display on the Grand Staircase.

The floral decoration surrounding the crèche cannot be viewed as somehow equivalent to the secular symbols in the overall *Lynch* display. The floral frame, like all good frames, serves only to draw one's attention to the message inside the frame. The floral decoration surrounding the crèche contributes to, rather than detracts from, the endorsement of religion conveyed by the crèche....

Furthermore, the crèche sits on the Grand Staircase, the "main" and "most beautiful part" of the building that is the seat of county government.... No viewer could reasonably think that it occupies this location without the support and approval of the government....

In sum, *Lynch* teaches that government may celebrate Christmas in some manner and form, but not in a way that endorses Christian doctrine. Here, Allegheny County has transgressed this line. It has chosen to celebrate Christmas in a way that has the effect of endorsing a patently Christian message: Glory to God for the birth of Jesus Christ. Under *Lynch,* and the rest of our cases, nothing more is required to demonstrate a violation of the Establishment Clause. The display of the crèche in this context, therefore, must be permanently enjoined.

. . .

VI

The display of the Chanukah menorah in front of the City-County Building may well present a closer constitutional question. The menorah, one must recognize, is a religious symbol: it serves to commemorate the miracle of the oil as described in the Talmud. But the menorah's message is not exclusively religious. The menorah is the primary visual symbol for a holiday that, like Christmas, has both religious and secular dimensions.

Moreover, the menorah here stands next to a Christmas tree and a sign saluting liberty. While no challenge has been made here to the display of the tree and the sign, their presence is obviously relevant in determining the effect of the menorah's display. The necessary result of placing a menorah next to a Christmas tree is to create an "overall holiday setting" that represents both Christmas and Chanukah—two holidays, not one....

...Because government may celebrate Christmas as a secular holiday, it follows that government may also acknowledge Chanukah as a secular holiday. Simply put, it would be a form of discrimination against Jews to allow Pittsburgh to celebrate Christmas as a cultural tradition while simultaneously disallowing the city's acknowledgment of Chanukah as a contemporaneous cultural tradition.

Accordingly, the relevant question for Establishment Clause purposes is whether the combined display of the tree, the sign, and the menorah has the effect of endorsing both Christian and Jewish faiths, or rather simply recognizes that both Christmas and Chanukah are part of the same winter-holiday season, which has attained a secular status in our society. Of the two interpretations of this particular display, the latter seems far more plausible and is also in line with *Lynch*.

...[A] 40-foot Christmas tree was one of the objects that validated the crèche in *Lynch*. The widely accepted view of the Christmas tree as the preeminent secular symbol of the Christmas holiday season serves to emphasize the secular component of the message communicated by other elements of an accompanying holiday display, including the Chanukah menorah.

The tree, moreover, is clearly the predominant element in the city's display. The 45-foot tree occupies the central position beneath the middle archway in front of the Grant Street entrance to the City-County Building; the 18-foot menorah is positioned to one side. Given this configuration, it is much more sensible to interpret the meaning of the menorah in light of the tree, rather than vice versa. In the shadow of the tree, the menorah is readily understood as simply a recognition that Christmas is not the only traditional way of observing the winter-holiday season. In these circumstances, then, the combination of the tree and the menorah communicates, not a simultaneous endorsement of both the Christian and Jewish faiths, but instead, a secular celebration of Christmas coupled with an acknowledgment of Chanukah as a contemporaneous alternative tradition.

. . .

VII

Lynch v. *Donnelly* confirms, and in no way repudiates, the longstanding constitutional principle that government may not engage in a practice that has the effect of promoting or endorsing religious beliefs. The display of the crèche in the county courthouse has this unconstitutional effect. The display of the menorah in front of the City-County Building, however, does not have this effect, given its "particular physical setting."

The judgment of the Court of Appeals is affirmed in part and reversed in part, and the cases are remanded for further proceedings.

It is so ordered.

[Justice O'Connor, with whom Justices Brennan and Stevens join in Part II of her opinion, concurs in part and concurs in the judgment of Justice Blackmun's opinion for the Court. Justice Brennan, joined by Justices Marshall and Stevens, writes a separate opinion concurring in part and dissenting in part. He would have held both displays in violation of the Establishment Clause.]

JUSTICE KENNEDY, with whom THE CHIEF JUSTICE, JUSTICE WHITE, and JUSTICE SCALIA join, concurring in the judgment in part and dissenting in part.

The majority holds that the County of Allegheny violated the Establishment Clause by displaying a crèche in the county courthouse,... This view of the Establishment Clause reflects an unjustified hostility toward religion, a hostility inconsistent with our history and our precedents, and I dissent from this holding. The crèche display is constitutional,...

II

...It cannot be disputed that government, if it chooses, may participate in sharing with its citizens the joy of the holiday season, by declaring public holidays, installing or permitting festive displays, sponsoring celebrations and parades, and providing holiday vacations for its employees. All levels of our government do precisely that. As we said in *Lynch,* "Government has long recognized—indeed it has subsidized—holidays with religious significance." 465 U. S., at 676.

. . .

Employment Division v. Smith

494 U.S. 872 (1990)

Oregon law prohibited sacramental use of the drug peyote. Alfred Smith and Galen Black were fired from their jobs because they ingested peyote at a ceremony of the Native American Church. Their application for unemployment compensation was denied on the ground that they had been discharged for work-related "misconduct." Divided 6 to 3, the Supreme Court upheld the state's action against the charge that it violated the Free Exercise Clause. This case is significant because four Justices—the three dissenters and Justice O'Connor in her concurrence—objected to the Court's dismissal of the compelling interest test. The Oregon Supreme Court held that Oregon law prohibits religiously inspired use of peyote but concluded that the prohibition was invalid under the Free Exercise Clause.

JUSTICE SCALIA delivered the opinion of the Court.

This case requires us to decide whether the Free Exercise Clause of the First Amendment permits the State of Oregon to include religiously inspired peyote use within the reach of its general criminal prohibition on use of that drug, and thus permits the State to deny unemployment benefits to persons dismissed from their jobs because of such religiously inspired use.

. . .

II

Respondents' claim for relief rests on our decisions in *Sherbert* v. *Verner, supra, Thomas* v. *Review Board, Indiana Employment Security Div., supra,* and *Hobbie* v. *Unemployment Appeals Comm'n of Florida,* 480 U.S. 136 (1987), in which we held that a State could not condition the availability of unemployment insurance on an individual's willingness to forgo conduct required by his religion. As we observed in *Smith I* [485 U.S. 660 (1988)], however, the conduct at issue in those cases was not prohibited by law.... Now that the Oregon Supreme Court has confirmed that Oregon does prohibit the religious use of peyote, we proceed to consider whether that prohibition is permissible under the Free Exercise Clause.

A

...The free exercise of religion means, first and foremost, the right to believe and profess whatever religious doctrine one desires....

But the "exercise of religion" often involves not only belief and profession but the performance of (or abstention from) physical acts: assembling with others for a worship service, participating in sacramental use of bread and wine, proselytizing, abstaining from certain foods or certain modes of transportation. It would be true, we think (though no case of ours has involved the point), that a state would be "prohibiting the free exercise [of religion]" if it sought to ban such acts or abstentions only when they are engaged in for religious reasons, or only because of the religious belief that they display. It would doubtless be unconstitutional, for example, to ban the casting of "statutes that are to be used for worship purposes," or to prohibit bowing down before a golden calf.

Respondents in the present case, however, seek to carry the meaning of "prohibiting the free exercise [of religion]" one large step further. They contend that their religious motivation for using peyote places them beyond the reach of a criminal law that is not specifically directed at their religious practice, and that is concededly constitutional as applied to those who use the drug for other reasons.... As a textual matter, we do not think the words must be given that meaning. It is no more necessary to regard the collection of a general tax, for example, as "prohibiting the free exercise [of religion]" by those citizens who believe support of organized government to be sinful, than it is to regard the same tax as "abridging the freedom...of the press" of those publishing companies that must pay the tax as a condition of staying in business. It is a permissible reading of the text, in the one case as in the other, to say that if prohibiting the exercise of religion (or burdening the activity of printing) is not the object of the tax but merely the incidental effect of a generally applicable and otherwise valid provision, the First Amendment has not been offended....

Our decisions reveal that the latter reading is the correct one. We have never held that an individual's religious beliefs excuse him from compliance with an otherwise valid law prohibiting conduct that the State is free to regulate. *[Here Justice Scalia refers to* Reynolds *v.* United States, *98 U.S. 145 (1879), which rejected the claim that criminal laws against polygamy could not be constitutionally applied to those whose religion commanded the practice.]*

. . .

The only decisions in which we have held that the First Amendment bars application of a neutral, generally applicable law to religiously motivated action have involved not the Free Exercise Clause alone, but the Free Exercise Clause in conjunction with other constitutional protections, such as freedom of speech and of the press....

...There being no contention that Oregon's drug law represents an attempt to regulate religious beliefs, the communication of religious beliefs, or the raising of one's children in those beliefs, the rule to which we have adhered ever since *Reynolds* plainly controls....

B

Respondents argue that even though exemption from generally applicable criminal laws need not automatically be extended to religiously motivated actors, at least the claim for a religious exemption must be evaluated under the balancing test set forth in *Sherbert* v. *Verner,* 374 U.S. 398 (1963). Under the *Sherbert* test, governmental actions that substantially burden a religious practice must be justified by a compelling governmental interest.... Applying that test we have, on three occasions, invalidated state unemployment compensation rules that conditioned the availability of benefits upon an applicant's willingness to work under conditions forbidden by his religion.

[Sherbert, Thomas v. Review Bd, and Hobbie v. Unemployment Appeals.] We have never invalidated any governmental action on the basis of the *Sherbert* test except the denial of unemployment compensation....In recent years we have abstained from applying the *Sherbert* test (outside the unemployment compensation field) at all. *[Scalia cites* Bowen v. Roy, *476 U.S. 693 (1986),* Lyng v. *Northwest Indian Cemetery Protective Assn., 485 U.S. 439 (1988),* Goldman v. *Weinberger, 475 U.S. 503 (1986), and* O'Lone v. *Estate of Shabazz, 482 U.S. 342 (1987).]*

Even if we were inclined to breathe into *Sherbert* some life beyond the unemployment compensation field, we would not apply it to require exemptions from a generally applicable criminal law....

The "compelling governmental interest" requirement seems benign, because it is familiar from other fields [such as race and speech]. What it produces in those other fields — equality of treatment, and an unrestricted flow of contending speech — are constitutional norms; what it would produce here — a private right to ignore generally applicable laws — is a constitutional anomaly.

Nor is it possible to limit the impact of respondents' proposal by requiring a "compelling state interest" only when the conduct prohibited is "central" to the individual's religion. Cf. *Lyng* v. *Northwest Indian Cemetery Protective Assn.,* 485 U.S., at 474–476 (BRENNAN, J., dissenting). It is no more appropriate for judges to determine the "centrality" of religious beliefs before applying a "compelling interest" test in the free exercise field, than it would be for them to determine the "importance" of ideas before applying the "compelling interest" test in the free speech field....

...The rule respondents favor would open the prospect of constitutionally required religious exemptions from civic obligations of almost every conceivable kind — *[ranging from compulsory military service, to the payment of taxes, to health and safety regulation such as manslaughter and child neglect laws, compulsory vaccination laws, drug laws, and traffic laws; to social welfare legislation such as minimum wage laws, child labor laws, animal cruelty laws, environmental protection laws, and laws providing for equality of opportunity for the races]*. The First Amendment's protection of religious liberty does not require this.

Values that are protected against government interference through enshrinement in the Bill of Rights are not thereby banished from the political process. Just as a society that believes in the negative protection accorded to the press by the First Amendment is likely to enact laws that affirmatively foster the dissemination of the printed word, so also a society that believes in the negative protection accorded to religious belief can be expected to be solicitous of that value in its legislation as well. It is therefore not surprising that a number of States have made an exception to their drug laws for sacramental peyote use.... It may fairly be said that leaving accommodation to the political process will place at a relative disadvantage those religious practices that are not widely engaged in; but that unavoidable consequence of democratic government must be preferred to a system in which each conscience is a law unto itself or in which judges weigh the social importance of all laws against the centrality of all religious beliefs.

Because respondents' ingestion of peyote was prohibited under Oregon law, and because that prohibition is constitutional, Oregon may, consistent with the Free Exercise Clause, deny respondents unemployment compensation when their dismissal results from use of the drug. The decision of the Oregon Supreme Court is accordingly reversed.

It is so ordered.

JUSTICE O'CONNOR, with whom JUSTICE BRENNAN, JUSTICE MARSHALL, and JUSTICE BLACKMUN join as to Parts I and II, concurring in the judgment.

Although I agree with the result the Court reaches in this case, I cannot join its opinion. In my view, today's holding dramatically departs from well-settled First Amendment jurisprudence, appears unnecessary to resolve the question presented, and is incompatible with our Nation's fundamental commitment to individual religious liberty.

. . .

II

...the Court holds that where the law is a generally applicable criminal prohibition, our usual free exercise jurisprudence does not even apply.... To reach this sweeping result, however, the Court must not only give a strained reading of the First Amendment but must also disregard our consistent application of free exercise doctrine to cases involving generally applicable regulations that burden religious conduct.

A

...a law that prohibits certain conduct—conduct that happens to be an act of worship for someone—manifestly does prohibit that person's free exercise of his religion. A person who is barred from engaging in religiously motivated conduct is barred from exercising his religion....

...The compelling interest test effectuates the First Amendment's command that religious liberty is an independent liberty, that it occupies a preferred position, and that the Court will not permit encroachments upon this liberty, whether direct or indirect, unless required by clear and compelling governmental interests "of the highest order," *Yoder, supra,* at 215....

B

. . .

Finally, the Court today suggests that the disfavoring of minority religions is an "unavoidable consequence" under our system of government and that accommodation of such religions must be left to the political process.... In my view, however, the First Amendment was enacted precisely to protect the rights of those whose religious practices are not shared by the majority and may be viewed with hostility. The history of our free exercise doctrine amply demonstrates the harsh impact majoritarian rule has had on unpopular or emerging religious groups such as the Jehovah's Witnesses and the Amish....

III

[In this section, Justice O'Connor concludes that Oregon has a compelling interest in prohibiting the possession of peyote by its citizens and that uniform application of Oregon's criminal prohibition is essential in accomplishing the overriding interest of Oregon in preventing the physical harm caused by the use of a Schedule I controlled substance. Granting a selective exemption for Native Americans "would seriously impair" Oregon's compelling interest.]

JUSTICE BLACKMUN, with whom JUSTICE BRENNAN and JUSTICE MARSHALL join, dissenting.

. . .

I

In weighing the clear interest of respondents Smith and Black (hereinafter respondents) in the free exercise of their religion against Oregon's asserted interest in enforcing its drug laws, it is important to articulate in precise terms the state interest involved....

The State proclaims an interest in protecting the health and safety of its citizens from the dangers of unlawful drugs. It offers, however, no evidence that the religious use of peyote has ever harmed anyone....

The State also seeks to support its refusal to make an exception for religious use of peyote by invoking its interest in abolishing drug trafficking. There is, however, practically no illegal traffic in peyote....Peyote simply is not a popular drug; its distribution for use in religious rituals has nothing to do with the vast and violent traffic in illegal narcotics that plagues this country.

Finally, the State argues that granting an exception for religious peyote use would erode its interest in the uniform, fair, and certain enforcement of its drug laws. The State fears that, if it grants an exemption for religious peyote use, a flood of other claims to religious exemptions will follow....This argument, however, could be made in almost any free exercise case....

Congress Reacts to *Smith*

In response to *Employment Division* v. *Smith* (1990), members of Congress introduced the Religious Freedom Restoration Act to give greater protection to religious liberty than afforded by the Supreme Court. In 1993, Congress passed the bill. Excerpts of the floor debate in the House of Representatives, demonstrating that the "majoritarian" branch of Congress can often be more sensitive and protective of minority rights than the Court, are included below. Source: 139 Cong. Rec. 9680–82 (1993).

Mr. *[Jack]* BROOKS *[chairman of the House Judiciary Committee].* Mr. Speaker, I yield myself such time as I may consume.

Mr. Speaker, H.R. 1308, the Religious Freedom Restoration Act of 1993, reflects a commitment to one of our most cherished freedoms — the right to practice one's faith without undue interference at the hands of the Government. It will restore the standard for addressing claims under the free exercise clause of the first amendment as it was prior to the Supreme Court's Smith decision in 1990. Under longstanding constitutional principles, any governmental burden on the free exercise of religion was subject to the strictest test of constitutional scrutiny. In order to satisfy the free exercise clause, Government had to demonstrate that it had a compelling State interest in burdening the free exercise of religion and that it used the least restrictive means of furthering that interest.

In Smith, the Supreme Court abandoned the compelling State interest test in favor of a much weaker standard of review. H.R. 1308 statutorily reinstates the strict test that was in place prior to Smith.

The Supreme Court's decision 3 years ago transformed a most hallowed liberty into a mundane concept with little more status than a fishing license — thus subjecting religious freedom to the whims of Government officials. That, indeed, has been the sorry legacy of the Court's view of this matter. Passage of this legislation is the only means to restore substance to the constitutional guarantee of religious freedom.

...I want to note the unprecedented coalition of religious denominations and civil rights groups who have united to stand up for the liberty given meaning by this bill. I am proud of how such marvelous diversity was united by a shared view of the place and role of religion in our society. I urge the approval of this legislation.

. . .

Mr. *[Hamilton]* FISH. Mr. Speaker, the ability of men and women of faith to freely practice their religion as guaranteed by the first amendment was seriously threatened by the 1990 decision of the U.S. Supreme Court in Employment Services Division versus Smith. In response to the Smith decision, a broad and unprecedented coalition of religious groups including the American Jewish Congress, the Church of Jesus Christ of Latterday Saints, the Christian Life Commission of the Southern Baptist Convention, and the National Council of Churches have come together to support enactment of the Religious Freedom Restoration Act.

. . .

Since Smith was decided in 1990, individuals seeking to practice their religion, unhampered by Government action, have largely been without recourse. The Religious Freedom Restoration Act will provide them with a means to challenge Government regulations which unnecessarily burden the free exercise of religion.

The legislation will guarantee that all Americans, regardless of their particular creed or oath, are able to enjoy the right to worship and practice their faith, from unnecessary Government intrusion.

. . .

Mr. *[Don]* EDWARDS of California....

This is a very, very important bill. People say, "Well, why is it so important?"

Let me just point out things that have happened that violate religious freedom, since the 1990 Smith decision.

Autopsies have been unnecessarily and wrongly performed upon the Hmong and Jewish deceased in violation of strong religious feelings that autopsies should not be performed.

For example, the Amish in Minnesota. It is an important part of their religious freedom that their buggies—we have seen them, Mr. Speaker, the buggies of the Amish, driving along the country roads—be very plain. That has religious significance to the Amish.

And yet the State of Minnesota, I believe, or maybe it was the local ordinance, required the Amish to put a light on the buggies, a fluorescent light, in violation of the religious freedom of the Amish people. And they had to finally seek State help, the State constitution, to rescue them from this violation.

And so here is another case. I think it is important to see the examples of why this bill is needed. A Federal investigator was fired because it was against his religion to do a certain investigation of a pacifist group.

. . .

Mr. *[Henry]* HYDE....

When this legislation was considered by the Subcommittee on Civil and Constitutional Rights and the full Judiciary Committee in the 102d Congress, I offered several amendments. These amendments were designed to address concerns I had with respect to abortion-related claims, third-party challenges to church-run social service programs, and challenges to the tax-exempt status of religious institutions. Since that time, my concerns have been resolved either through explicit statutory changes or through committee report language.

A major issue of contention in the 102d Congress was whether the bill was a true restoration of the law as it existed prior to Smith or whether it sought to impose a more stringent statutory standard. Of course, the label restoration is inappropriate in this context since the Congress writes laws—it does not and cannot overrule the Supreme Court's interpretation of the Constitution. *[But may not Congress, by statute, protect religious liberties left unprotected by the Court? In that way Congress engages in constitutional interpretation.]*

Boerne v. Flores

521 U.S. 507 (1997)

Local zoning authorities of the City of Boerne, Texas, denied a Catholic Archbishop a building permit to enlarge a church subject to an ordinance governing historic preservation. P.F. Flores, the Archbishop, brought this suit to challenge the ordinance under the Religious Freedom Restoration Act (RFRA). A district court held that Congress had exceeded the scope of its enforcement power under Section 5 of the Fourteenth Amendment, but that decision was reversed by the Fifth Circuit, which found RFRA to be constitutional.

JUSTICE KENNEDY delivered the opinion of the Court.

A decision by local zoning authorities to deny a church a building permit was challenged under the Religious Freedom Restoration Act of 1993 (RFRA), 107 Stat. 1488, 42 U.S.C. § 2000bb *et. seq.* The case calls into question the authority of

Congress to enact RFRA. We conclude the statute exceeds Congress' power.

I

Situated on a hill in the city of Boerne, Texas, some 28 miles northwest of San Antonio, is St. Peter Catholic Church. Built in 1923, the church's structure replicates the mission style of the region's earlier history. The church seats about 230 worshippers, a number too small for its growing parish. Some 40 to 60 parishioners cannot be accommodated at some Sunday masses. In order to meet the needs of the congregation the Archbishop of San Antonio gave permission to the parish to plan alterations to enlarge the building.

A few months later, the Boerne City Council passed an ordinance authorizing the city's Historic Landmark Commission to prepare a preservation plan with proposed historic landmarks and districts. Under the ordinance, the Commission must preapprove construction affecting historic landmarks or buildings in a historic district.

Soon afterwards, the Archbishop applied for a building permit so construction to enlarge the church could proceed. City authorities, relying on the ordinance and the designation of a historic district (which, they argued, included the church), denied the application. The Archbishop brought this suit challenging the permit denial...

The complaint contained various claims, but to this point the litigation has centered on RFRA and the question of its constitutionality. The Archbishop relied upon RFRA as one basis for relief from the refusal to issue the permit. The District Court concluded that by enacting RFRA Congress exceeded the scope of its enforcement power under § 5 of the Fourteenth Amendment. The court certified its order for interlocutory appeal and the Fifth Circuit reversed, finding RFRA to be constitutional. 73 F.3d 1352 (1996). We granted certiorari, 519 U.S. 926 (1996), and now reverse.

II

[*The Court reviews its ruling in* Employment Division v. Smith *(1990) and the decision by Congress to enact RFRA in direct response to* Smith.]

III

A

Under our Constitution, the Federal Government is one of enumerated powers. *M'Culloch v. Maryland,* 4 Wheat. 316, 405 (1819); see also The Federalist No. 45, p. 292 (C. Rossiter ed. 1961) (J. Madison). The judicial authority to determine the constitutionality of laws, in cases and controversies, is based on the premise that the "powers of the legislature are defined and limited; and that those limits may not be mistaken, or forgotten, the constitution is written." *Marbury v. Madison,* 1 Cranch 137, 176 (1803).

Congress relied on its Fourteenth Amendment enforcement power in enacting the most far reaching and substantial of RFRA's provisions,... The Fourteenth Amendment provides, in relevant part:

"Section 1.... No State shall make or enforce any law which shall abridge the privileges or immunities of citizens of the United States; nor shall any State deprive any person of life, liberty, or property, without due process of law; nor deny to any person within its jurisdiction the equal protection of the laws.

. . .

"Section 5. The Congress shall have power to enforce, by appropriate legislation, the provisions of this article."

The parties disagree over whether RFRA is a proper exercise of Congress' § 5 power "to enforce" by "appropriate legislation" the constitutional guarantee that no State shall deprive any person of "life, liberty, or property, without due process of law" nor deny any person "equal protection of the laws."

In defense of the Act respondent contends, with support from the United States as *amicus,* that RFRA is permissible enforcement legislation. Congress, it is said, is only protecting by legislation one of the liberties guaranteed by the Fourteenth Amendment's Due Process Clause, the free exercise of religion, beyond what is necessary under *Smith.* It is said the congressional decision to dispense with proof of deliberate or overt discrimination and instead concentrate on a law's effects accords with the settled understanding that § 5 includes the power to enact legislation designed to prevent as well as remedy constitutional violations. It is further contended that Congress' § 5 power is not limited to remedial or preventive legislation.

All must acknowledge that § 5 is "a positive grant of legislative power" to Congress, *Katzenbach v. Morgan,* 384 U.S. 641, 651 (1966). In *Ex parte Virginia,* 100 U.S. 339, 345–346 (1879), we explained the scope of Congress' § 5 power in the following broad terms:

"Whatever legislation is appropriate, that is, adapted to carry out the objects the amendments have in view, whatever tends to enforce submission to the prohibitions they contain, and to secure to all persons the enjoyment of perfect equality of civil rights and the equal protection of the laws against State denial or invasion, if not prohibited, is brought within the domain of congressional power."

Legislation which deters or remedies constitutional violations can fall within the sweep of Congress' enforcement power even if in the process it prohibits conduct which is not itself unconstitutional and intrudes into "legislative spheres of autonomy previously reserved to the States." *Fitzpatrick v. Bitzer,* 427 U.S. 445, 455 (1976). For example, the Court upheld a suspension of literacy tests and similar voting requirements under Congress' parallel power to enforce the provisions of the Fifteenth Amendment, see U.S. Const., Amdt. 15, § 2, as a measure to combat racial discrimination in voting, *South Carolina v. Katzenbach,* 383 U.S. 301, 308 (1966), despite the facial constitutionality of the tests under *Lassiter v. Northampton County Bd. of Elections,* 360 U.S. 45 (1959). We have also concluded that other measures protecting voting rights are within Congress' power to enforce the Fourteenth and Fifteenth Amendments, despite the burdens those measures placed on the State....

It is also true, however, the "[a]s broad as the congressional enforcement power is, it is not unlimited." *Oregon v. Mitchell,* [400 U.S.] at 128, (opinion of Black, J.). In assessing the breadth of § 5's enforcement power, we begin with its text. Congress has been given the power "to enforce" the "provisions of this article." We agree with respondent, of course, that Congress can enact legislation under § 5 enforcing the constitutional right to the free exercise of religion. The "provisions of this article," to which § 5 refers, include the Due Process Clause of the Fourteenth Amendment. Congress' power to enforce the Free Exercise Clause follows from our holding in *Cantwell v. Connecticut,* 310 U.S. 296, 303 (1940), that the "fundamental concept of liberty embodied in [the Fourteenth Amendment's Due Process Clause] embraces the liberties guaranteed by the First Amendment." ...

Congress' power under § 5, however, extends only to "enforc[ing]" the provisions of the Fourteenth Amendment. The Court has described this power as "remedial," *South Carolina v. Katzenbach, supra,* at 326. The design of the Amendment and the text of § 5 are inconsistent with the suggestion that Congress has the power to decree the substance of the Fourteenth Amendment's restrictions on the States. Legislation which alters the meaning of the Free Exercise Clause cannot be said to be enforcing the Clause. Congress does not

enforce a constitutional right by changing what the right is. It has been given the power "to enforce," not the power to determine what constitutes a constitutional violation. Were it not so, what Congress would be enforcing would no longer be, in any meaningful sense, the "provisions of [the Fourteenth Amendment]."

While the line between measures that remedy or prevent unconstitutional actions and measures that make a substantive change in the governing law is not easy to discern, and Congress must have wide latitude in determining where it lies, the distinction exists and must be observed. There must be a congruence and proportionality between the injury to be prevented or remedied and the means adopted to that end. Lacking such a connection, legislation may become substantive in operation and effect. History and our case law support drawing that distinction, one apparent from the text of the Amendment.

1

The Fourteenth Amendment's history confirms the remedial, rather than substantive, nature of the Enforcement Clause [*Here the Court reviews the work of the Joint Committee on Reconstruction, which drafted what would become the Fourteenth Amendment in January 1866. Floor debate criticized the draft for giving Congress the power to intrude into traditional areas of state sovereignty. The House voted to table the proposal. The Joint Committee drafted new language. Instead of the original language, giving Congress the power "to make all laws which shall be necessary and proper to secure to the citizens of each State all privileges and immunities of citizens in the several States, and to all persons in the several States equal protection in the rights of life, liberty, and property," the revised text provided that Congress "shall have power to enforce, by appropriate legislation, the provisions of this article." According to the Court, Congress' power "was no longer plenary but remedial." In the words of a study by Horace E. Flack,* The Adoption of the Fourteenth Amendment *(1908), the early draft gave "Congress, and not the courts, [the power] to judge whether or not any of the privileges or immunities were not secured to citizens in the several States."*]

2

The remedial and preventive nature of Congress' enforcement power, and the limitation inherent in the power, were confirmed in our earliest cases on the Fourteenth Amendment. In the

Civil Rights Cases, 109 U.S. 3 (1883), the Court invalidated sections of the Civil Rights Act of 1875 which prescribed criminal penalties for denying to any person "the full enjoyment of" public accommodations and conveyances, on the grounds that it exceeded Congress' power by seeking to regulate private conduct. The Enforcement Clause, the Court said, did not authorize Congress to pass "general legislation upon the rights of the citizen, but corrective legislation; that is, such as may be necessary and proper for counteracting such laws as the States may adopt or enforce, and which, by the amendment, they are prohibited from making or enforcing...." *Id.,* at 13–14....

[The Court proceeds to analyze such cases as South Carolina v. Katzenbach to explain the remedial nature of Section 5 in dealing with racial discrimination. In such cases Congress had before it a historical record of discriminatory treatment of racial minorities.]

3

Any suggestion that Congress has a substantive, non-remedial power under the Fourteenth Amendment is not supported by our case law. In *Oregon v. Mitchell, supra,* at 112, a majority of the Court concluded Congress had exceeded its enforcement powers by enacting legislation lowering the minimum age of voters from 21 to 18 in state and local elections. The five Members of the Court who reached this conclusion explained that the legislation intruded into an area reserved by the Constitution to the States....

There is language in our opinion in *Katzenbach v. Morgan,* 384 U.S. 641 (1966), which could be interpreted as acknowledging a power in Congress to enact legislation that expands the rights contained in § 1 of the Fourteenth Amendment. This is not a necessary interpretation, however, or even the best one.... As Justice Stewart explained in *Oregon v. Mitchell, supra,* at 296, interpreting *Morgan* to give Congress the power to interpret the Constitution "would require an enormous extension of that decision's rationale."

If Congress could define its own powers by altering the Fourteenth Amendment's meaning, no longer would the Constitution be "superior paramount law, unchangeable by ordinary means." it would be "on a level with ordinary legislative acts, and, like other acts,... alterable when the legislature shall please to alter it." *Marbury v. Madison,* 1 Cranch, at 177. Under this approach, it is difficult to conceive of a principle that would limit congressional power.... Shifting legislative majorities could change the Constitution and effectively circumvent the difficult and detailed amendment process contained in Article V.

We now turn to consider whether RFRA can be considered enforcement legislation under § 5 of the Fourteenth Amendment.

B

Respondent contends that RFRA is a proper exercise of Congress' remedial or preventive power. The Act, it is said, is a reasonable means of protecting the free exercise of religion as defined by *Smith.* It prevents and remedies laws which are enacted with the unconstitutional object of targeting religious beliefs and practices.... To avoid the difficulty of proving such violations, it is said, Congress can simply invalidate any law which imposes a substantial burden on a religious practice unless it is justified by a compelling interest and is the least restrictive means of accomplishing that interest. If Congress can prohibit laws with discriminatory effects in order to prevent racial discrimination in violation of the Equal Protection Clause.... then it can do the same, respondent argues, to promote religious liberty.

While preventive rules are sometimes appropriate remedial measures, there must be a congruence between the means used and the ends to be achieved....

A comparison between RFRA and the Voting Rights Act is instructive. In contrast to the record which confronted Congress and the judiciary in the voting rights cases, RFRA's legislative record lacks examples of modern instances of generally applicable laws passed because of religious bigotry. The history of persecution in the country detailed in the hearings mentions no episodes occurring in the past 40 years....

Regardless of the state of the legislative record, RFRA cannot be considered remedial, preventive legislation, if those terms are to have any meaning. RFRA is so out of proportion to a supposed remedial or preventive object that it cannot be understood as responsive to, or designed to prevent, unconstitutional behavior. It appears, instead, to attempt a substantive change in constitutional protections....

The reach and scope of RFRA distinguish it from other measures passed under Congress' enforcement power, even in the area of voting rights. In *South Carolina v. Katzenbach,* the challenged provisions were confined to those regions of the country where voting discrimination had been most flagrant, see 383 U.S., at 315, and affected a discrete class of state laws, *i.e.,* state voting laws.... The provisions restricting and banning literacy tests, upheld in *Katzenbach v. Morgan,* ... and *Oregon v. Mitchell,* ... attacked a particular type of voting qualification....

The stringent test RFRA demands of state laws reflects a lack of proportionality or congruence between the means adopted and the legitimate end to be achieved. If an objector can show a substantial burden on his free exercise, the State must demonstrate a compelling governmental interest and show that the law is the least restrictive means of furthering its interest....

. . .

When Congress acts within its sphere of power and responsibilities, it has not just the right but the duty to make its own informed judgment on the meaning and force of the Constitution.... Our national experience teaches that the Constitution is preserved best when each part of the government respects both the Constitution and the proper actions and determinations of the other branches. When the Court has interpreted the Constitution, it has acted within the province of the Judicial Branch, which embraces the duty to say what the law is. *Marbury v. Madison,* 1 Cranch, at 177. When the political branches of the Government act against the background of a judicial interpretation of the Constitution already issued, it must be understood that in later cases and controversies the Court will treat its precedents with the respect due them under settled principles, including *stare decisis,* and contrary expectations must be disappointed. RFRA was designed to control cases and controversies, such as the one before us; but as the provisions of the federal statute here invoked are beyond congressional authority, it is this Court's precedent, not RFRA, which must control.

. . .

... The judgment of the Court of Appeals sustaining the Act's constitutionality is reversed.

It is so ordered

JUSTICE STEVENS, concurring.

. . .

JUSTICE SCALIA, with whom JUSTICE STEVENS joins, concurring in part.

I write to respond briefly to the claim of JUSTICE O'CONNOR's dissent... that historical materials support a result contrary to the one reached in *Employment Div., Dept. of Human Resources of Oregon v. Smith,* ... The dissent's extravagant claim that the historical record shows *Smith* to have been wrong should be compared with the assessment of the most prominent scholarly critic of *Smith,* who, after an extensive review of the historical record, was willing to venture no more than that "constitutionally compelled exemptions [from generally applicable laws regulating conduct] were *within the contemplation* of the framers and ratifiers as a *possible interpretation* of the free exercise clause. McConnell, The Origins and Historical Understanding of Free Exercise of Religion, 103 Harv. L. Rev. 1409, 1415 (1990) (emphasis added)....

... The issue presented by *Smith* is, quite simply, whether the people, through their elected representatives, or rather this Court, shall control the outcome of those concrete cases. For example, shall it be the determination of this Court, or rather of the people, whether (as the dissent apparently believes,...) church construction will be exempt from zoning laws? The historical evidence put forward by the dissent does nothing to undermine the conclusion we reached in *Smith:* It shall be the people.

JUSTICE O'CONNOR, with whom JUSTICE BREYER joins except as to a portion of Part I, dissenting.

. . .

I

I agree with much of the reasoning set forth in Part III-A of the Court's opinion. Indeed, if I agreed with the Court's standard in *Smith,* I would join the opinion. As the Court's careful and thorough historical analysis shows, Congress lacks the "power to decree the *substance* of the Fourteenth Amendment's restrictions on the States." ... (emphasis added). Rather, its power under § 5 of the Fourteenth Amendment extends only to *enforcing* the Amendment's provisions. In short, Congress lacks the ability independently to define or expand the scope of constitutional rights by statute.... This recognition does not, of course, in any way diminish Congress' obligation to draw its own conclusions regarding the Constitution's meaning. Congress, no less than this Court, is called upon to consider the requirements of the Constitution and to act in accordance with its dictates. But when it enacts legislation in furtherance of its delegated powers, Congress must make its judgments consistent with this Court's exposition of the Constitution and with the limits placed on its legislative authority by provisions such as the Fourteenth Amendment.

[The rest of O'Connor's dissent attacks Scalia's opinion for the Court in Smith. *She argues that* Smith *is "gravely at odds" with earlier free exercise precedents and introduces historical material to dispute Scalia's analysis.]*

JUSTICE SOUTER, dissenting.

To decide whether the Fourteenth Amendment gives Congress sufficient power to enact the Religious Freedom Restoration Act, the Court measures the legislation against the free-exercise standard of *Employment Div., Dept. of Human Resources of Oregon v. Smith,* . . . I have serious

doubts about the precedential value of the *Smith* rule and its entitlement to adherence. These doubts are intensified today by the historical arguments going to the original understanding of the Free Exercise Clause presented in JUSTICE O'CONNOR's opinion, . . . this case should be set down for reargument permitting plenary reexamination of the issue. . . .

JUSTICE BREYER, dissenting.

I agree with JUSTICE O'CONNOR that the Court should direct the parties to brief the question whether *Employment Div., Dept. of Human Resources of Oregon v. Smith,* . . . was correctly decided, and set this case for reargument. . . .

D. FINANCIAL ASSISTANCE TO SECTARIAN SCHOOLS

Before the *Everson* case of 1947, litigation on sectarian schools was limited to such questions as their right to exist. Pierce v. Society of Sisters, 268 U.S. 510 (1925). Other cases dealt with the liberty of private schools to teach certain subjects, such as German. Meyer v. Nebraska, 262 U.S. 390 (1923). Financial aid became an issue when Louisiana used public funds to supply school books to children in private schools, including sectarian schools. A unanimous Supreme Court sustained this legislation on the ground that the books were not religious (they were the same books used by public school students) and that the books benefited children and the state, not the religious schools. The state's interest in education, said the Court, justified the assistance. Cochran v. Board of Education, 281 U.S. 370 (1930). This "child-benefit" theory became the basis for upholding other forms of state assistance to sectarian schools. In time, the Court came to recognize that this theory opened the door to almost unlimited public funding of religious schools.

Transportation, Textbooks, and Tax Exemptions

In 1947, a sharply divided Supreme Court upheld a New Jersey statute that reimbursed parents for the cost of sending their children to parochial schools on public buses. The 5–4 decision also declared that the Establishment Clause was applicable to the states, just as *Cantwell* in 1940 had applied the Free Exercise Clause to the states. Justice Black's opinion for the Court made a number of unrealistic claims about separating church and state. He said that neither a state nor the federal government "can pass laws which aid one religion, aid all religions, or prefer one religion over another." EVERSON v. BOARD OF EDUCATION, 330 U.S. 1, 15. Yet, New Jersey aided parochial schools by reimbursing transportation costs, and later Court decisions would uphold other forms of assistance. Congress has even passed laws to assist particular religions, such as the social security exemption for the Amish. Black also asserted: "No tax in any amount, large or small, can be levied to support any religious activities or institutions. . . ." In fact, taxpayer funds have been used to provide transportation, textbooks, and other types of state and federal aid to religious institutions. Finally, Black claimed that neither a state nor the federal government "can, openly or secretly, participate in the affairs of any religious organizations or groups and *vice versa.*" This, too, was superficial. Government may establish health, safety, and curricula standards for sectarian schools, and religious organizations may lobby legislatures, the courts, and the agencies. Four Justices dissented from Black's opinion. Justice Douglas, who joined with Black, later admitted doubts about *Everson.* Engel v. Vitale, 370 U.S. 421, 443 (1962); Walz v. Tax Commission, 397 U.S. 664, 703 (1970).

The next step in supporting financial assistance to sectarian schools came in 1968. A New York law required textbooks to be "lent" free of charge to all students in grades 7 through 12, including children attending private and sectarian schools. A 6–3 decision by the Court held that the statute was constitutional because the benefit was to parents and children, not to schools. Board of Education v. Allen, 392 U.S. 236. The child-benefit theory would look less appealing five years later when the Court struck down a Mississippi law that authorized the lending of books to all-white, nonsectarian private schools. The state argued that the statute benefited children, not schools. The Court dismissed this claim as a way to rationalize state assistance to segregated schools. Norwood v. Harrison, 413 U.S. 455 (1973). The Court was willing to preserve a legal fiction on church-state questions while facing reality on racial segregation.

Interestingly, the opinion for the Court in *Allen* defended the textbook assistance partly on the basis of *Everson,* and yet Black, the author of *Everson,* dissented along with Douglas and Fortas. Black now realized what he had invited with his child-benefit theory in the transportation case: "It requires no prophet to foresee that on the argument used to support this law others could be upheld providing for state or federal government funds to buy property on which to erect religious school buildings or to erect the buildings themselves, to pay the salaries of the religious school teachers, and finally to have the sectarian religious groups cease to rely on voluntary contributions of members of their sects while waiting for the Government to pick up all the bills for the religious schools." 392 U.S. at 253. A number of state courts, interpreting highly specific and restrictive language in their constitutions, refused to uphold transportation and textbook assistance to sectarian schools. They specifically rejected the child-benefit theory embraced by the Supreme Court (see box on next page).

In 1970 the Court upheld tax exemptions to religious organizations for properties used solely for religious worship. The Court decided 8–1 that the exemption was not aimed at establishing, sponsoring, or supporting religion; tax exemption created only a minimal and remote involvement between church and state; and government involvement would be far greater with taxation. Apparently decisive for the Court was the persistence of tax exemptions to religious bodies for almost two centuries. Walz v. Tax Commission, 397 U.S. 664, 677. The thrust of *Walz* was limited in 1989 when the Court struck down as a violation of the Establishment Clause a Texas law that exempted religious publications from sales taxes. However, the meaning of this decision was diluted by several concurring opinions. Texas Monthly, Inc. v. Bullock, 489 U.S. 1 (1989). Two years earlier the Court had held that tax systems may not be used to discriminate or suppress. Arkansas Writers' Project, Inc. v. Ragland, 481 U.S. 221 (1987).

Seeking Limits on Assistance

In 1971, the Court attempted to stem the flow of financial assistance to sectarian schools by striking down laws in two states. Pennsylvania had given state funds to nonpublic elementary and secondary schools by reimbursing teachers' salaries, textbooks, and institutional materials in secular subjects. Rhode Island paid teachers in nonpublic elementary schools a supplement of 15 percent of their annual salaries. By a 7–0 vote in the Pennsylvania case and a 7–1 vote in the Rhode Island case, the Court found that these forms of assistance violated the religion clauses. Three tests were developed to determine constitutionality: (1) the statute must have a secular legislative purpose, (2) its principal or primary effect must be one that neither advances nor inhibits religion, and (3) it must not foster excessive entanglement with religion. LEMON v. KURTZMAN, 403 U.S. 602, 612–13 (1971). This three-prong test is frequently waived or ignored by the courts. For example, the government often passes laws that seek to

The States Limit Assistance

A number of states have refused to accept decisions by the U.S. Supreme Court upholding public assistance to sectarian schools (transportation in *Everson v. Board of Education* and textbooks in *Board of Education v. Allen*). State constitutions are frequently quite specific in prohibiting the appropriation of public funds for any religious worship or instruction. The Alaska Supreme Court dismissed the U.S. Supreme Court's decision in *Everson* as "unpersuasive." Matthews v. Quinton, 362 P.2d 932, 936 (Alas.

1961). Many state courts rejected the doctrinal basis for upholding public assistance to sectarian schools: the "child-benefit" theory. The California Supreme Court said that in most instances this theory "leads to results which are logically indefensible." California Teachers Ass'n v. Riles, 632 P.2d 953, 962 (Cal. 1981). Other state courts, despite restrictive language in their constitutions, have upheld transportation and textbooks for sectarian schools. The following states have invalidated such assistance:

Alaska	Matthews v. Quinton, 362 P.2d 932 (1961), cert. denied, 368 U.S. 517 (1962) (transportation).
California	California Teachers Ass'n v. Riles, 632 P.2d 953 (1981) (textbooks).
Delaware	Opinion of the Justices, 216 A.2d 668 (1966) (transportation).
Hawaii	Spears v. Honda, 449 P.2d 130 (1969) (transportation).
Idaho	Epeldi v. Engelking, 488 P.2d 860 (1971), cert. denied, 406 U.S. 957 (1972) (transportation).
Kentucky	Fannin v. Williams, 655 S.W.2d 480 (1983) (textbooks); Fiscal Court of Jefferson City v. Brady, 885 S.W.2d 681 (1994) (transportation).
Massachusetts	Bloom v. School Committee of Springfield, 379 N.E.2d 578 (1978) (textbooks).
Michigan	In re Advisory Op. re Const. of 1974 PA 242, 228 N.W.2d 772 (1975) (textbooks).
Missouri	McVey v. Hawkins, 258 S.W.2d 927 (1953) (transportation); Paster v. Tussey, 512 S.W.2d 97 (1974), cert. denied sub nom. Reynolds v. Paster, 419 U.S. 1111 (1975) (textbooks).
Nebraska	Gaffney v. State Department of Education, 220 N.W.2d 550 (1974) (textbooks).
Oklahoma	Board of Education for Ind. Sch. Dist. No. 52 v. Antone, 384 P.2d 911 (1963); Gurney v. Ferguson, 122 P.2d 1002 (1941), cert. denied, 317 U.S. 588 (1942), rehearing denied, 317 U.S. 707 (1942) (transportation).
Oregon	Dickman v. School District No. 62C, 366 P.2d 533 (1961), cert. denied, 371 U.S. 823 (1962) (textbooks).
South Dakota	McDonald v. School Bd. of Yankton, Etc., 246 N.W.2d 93 (1976) (textbooks).
Washington	Visser v. Nooksack Valley School Dist. No. 506, 207 P.2d 198 (1949) (transportation).
Wisconsin	State v. Nusbaum, 115 N.W.2d 761 (1962); State v. Milquet, 192 N.W. 392 (1923) (transportation).

accommodate religious practices (in the form of various exemptions), and these laws are generally sustained even though their primary effect is to advance religion.

On the same day that the Court struck down the Pennsylvania and Rhode Island statutes, it upheld by a 5–4 vote a congressional statute that provided construction grants for church-related colleges and universities. The money was spent for buildings that had a nonreligious purpose: libraries; a science building; a language laboratory; and a music, drama, and arts building. The Court decided that there was less religious indoctrination in colleges than in elementary and secondary schools, where student minds are more impressionable. It ruled, however, that the congressional provision allowing the religious use of these buildings after twenty years to be a violation of the religion clauses. Tilton v. Richardson, 403 U.S. 672, 683–84 (1971).

In subsequent decisions the Court confronted new forms of financial assistance to sectarian schools. New York appropriated $28 million to reimburse nonpublic schools for expenses related to examinations, record keeping, and reports mandated by the state. The Court held that this aid contravened the Establishment Clause. There was no audit to determine whether state payments exceeded costs by the schools, nor any evaluation to see whether the tests were free of religious instruction. The schools had argued that the state should be permitted to pay for any activity mandated by state law or regulation, but the Court rejected this theory because it could require state payments for minimum lighting or sanitary facilities for all school buildings. Levitt v. Committee for Public Education, 413 U.S. 472, 481 (1973). A later effort by New York to reimburse nonpublic schools for expenses incurred before the Court's decision was declared unconstitutional. New York v. Cathedral Academy, 434 U.S. 125 (1977).

A case in 1973 concerned another type of financial assistance to sectarian schools. A South Carolina statute authorized the issuance of revenue bonds that benefited a Baptist-controlled college. Using *Lemon*'s three-part test, the Court held 6–3 that the statute did not violate the Establishment Clause. The Court said the Act had a secular purpose (benefiting higher education), its primary effect did not advance or inhibit religion, and there was no excessive entanglement with religion. *Tilton* was cited to support state assistance to schools at the university level. The Court found that the Baptist college had no significant religious orientation. The three dissenters viewed the state as deeply involved in the fiscal affairs of the college, even to the extent of fixing tuition rates as part of the state's duty to assure sufficient revenues to meet bond and interest obligations. Hunt v. McNair, 413 U.S. 734, 753 (1973).

Tuition Assistance and Vouchers

A New York statute provided direct money grants to qualifying nonpublic schools. The money was used to maintain and repair facilities and equipment, to reimburse low-income parents who sent their children to nonpublic elementary and secondary schools, and to provide tax relief for parents failing to qualify for tuition reimbursement. The Supreme Court held that all three forms of assistance violated the Establishment Clause, even if the tuition grants went to the parents rather than directly to the schools. All of the Justices agreed that the maintenance and repair provision was unconstitutional. Chief Justice Burger and Justices White and Rehnquist would have upheld the reimbursement and tax relief provisions. Committee for Public Education v. Nyquist, 413 U.S. 756 (1973).

The Court tried to explain why tax exemptions were permissible in *Walz* (they were "indirect and incidental") while the tax credits at stake in the New York statutes were unconstitutional. The decisive element was that the granting of new tax benefits, in contrast to the extension of tax exemptions, "would tend to increase rather than limit the involvement between Church and State." The Court had to weigh the "potentially divisive political effect of an aid program." Support for maintenance and repair and the grants for tuition would require appropriations each year, opening the door to continuing strife between church and state. Id. at 793–97.

In short, the Court had to do more than interpret constitutional text and case law. It had to make a political judgment about the level of tension and confrontation likely to result from government assistance to sectarian schools. It was for this reason that it also struck down a Pennsylvania statute that reimbursed parents for a portion of tuition expenses incurred in sending their children to nonpublic schools. More than 90 percent of the nonpublic schools were sectarian. The Court rejected the contention that tuition assistance went to parents rather than to schools. Sloan v. Lemon, 413 U.S. 825 (1973).

Waiting in the wings is another constitutional issue: Whether government can provide parents with vouchers to subsidize their children's education at private and sectarian schools. State and federal courts have handed down a number of decisions, some upholding vouchers, others striking them down. If the U.S. Supreme Court were to uphold a voucher system, state courts could still invalidate them as contrary to the state constitution.

"Lending" Textbooks and School Equipment

In other decisions involving financial assistance to sectarian schools the Court split 6–3 or 5–4. Lengthy concurrences made it difficult to chart the positions of individual Justices. A 1975 decision responded to a Pennsylvania statute that authorized "auxiliary services" and textbook loans to all children enrolled in nonpublic elementary and secondary schools. The state could loan instructional materials and equipment. Auxiliary services included counseling, testing, psychological services, and speech and hearing therapy; instructional materials included periodicals, photographs, maps, charts, recordings, and films; instructional equipment embraced such items as projectors, recorders, and laboratory paraphernalia. A 6–3 Court, made more complex by Justices concurring in part and dissenting in part, held that everything but textbook loans violated the Establishment Clause. The Court continued to believe that textbook loans benefited parents and children, not schools. Meek v. Pittenger, 421 U.S. 349, 361. [To the extent that *Meek* assumed that placing public employees on parochial school grounds inevitably results in state-sponsored indoctrination or constitutes a symbolic union between government and religion, *Meek* is overruled by Agostini v. Felton, 521 U.S. 203, 223 (1997).]

Would it have made a constitutional difference if instructional materials and equipment had been "lent" to parents and children rather than to schools? Justice Brennan, joined by Justices Douglas and Marshall, said it was "pure fantasy" to treat the textbook program as a loan to students: "The whole business is handled by the school and public authorities and neither parents nor children have a say. The guidelines make crystal clear that the nonpublic school, not its pupils, is the motivating force behind the textbook loan, and that virtually the entire loan transaction is to be, and is in fact, conducted between officials of the nonpublic school, on the one hand, and officers of the State on the other." 421 U.S. at 379–80.

A year later the Court, divided 5–4, upheld a Maryland grant of state funds to colleges and universities that refrained from awarding "only seminarian or theological degrees." Funds could not be used for sectarian purposes. The four colleges were affiliated with the Roman Catholic Church. The federal district court had found that the religious colleges were not "pervasively sectarian" or substantially involved in indoctrination. In one of the dissents, Justice Stevens expressed concern about "the pernicious tendency of a state subsidy to tempt religious schools to compromise their religious mission without wholly abandoning it." Roemer v. Maryland Public Works Bd., 426 U.S. 736, 775 (1976).

Ohio authorized various forms of aid to nonpublic schools, most of which were sectarian. Splitting in various directions, the Court upheld the provisions extending assistance for secular textbooks, standardized testing and scoring, diagnostic services, and therapeutic and remedial services. It struck down the portions of the law relating to instructional materials, instructional equipment, and providing transportation and services for field trips. The state statute "loaned" the instructional materials and equipment to the pupils or their parents, but the Court dismissed this mechanism as a patent effort to exploit the *Meek* holding. Parents and students were being used as a conduit to funnel assistance to the schools. Wolman v. Walter, 433 U.S. 229, 250 (1977). Justice Marshall, who had voted with the majority in *Allen* to uphold textbook loans, now announced that it should be overruled and a new line drawn between church and state. Id. at 256–59.

Reimbursements

In 1980 the Supreme Court reviewed a New York law similar to the payment system declared unconstitutional in *Levitt* in 1973. The law directed payment to nonpublic schools for their costs in complying with certain state-mandated requirements, including testing, reporting, and recordkeeping. The new law provided for state auditing to assure that public funds would be used only for secular purposes (a safeguard absent from the law struck down in *Levitt*). A 5–4 decision held that the statute did not violate the Establishment Clause. Justice Blackmun's dissent, joined by Brennan and Marshall, pointed out that the "state-mandated" requirements would have been performed by the schools, with or without reimbursement. Justice Stevens, also dissenting, criticized the Court's opinion as "another in a long line of cases making largely ad hoc decisions about what payments may or may not be constitutionally made to nonpublic schools." He said the Court's rationale could be used to justify state subsidies for fire drills or the construction and maintenance of fireproof classrooms. Moreover, he advised that "the entire enterprise of trying to justify various types of subsidies to nonpublic schools should be abandoned." Committee for Public Education v. Regan, 444 U.S. 646, 671 (1980).

A Parade of 5–4 Decisions

Two decisions in 1985 demonstrate the profound disagreement within the Court on public assistance to sectarian schools. One decision, with Justices divided 5–4, held invalid a New York program that used federal funds to pay the salaries of public school employees who taught in parochial schools. Although the state monitored the content of federally funded classes to avoid the advancement of religion (part of the *Lemon* test), the Court held that this very involvement produced excessive entanglement of church and state. Aguilar v. Felton, 473 U.S. 402. Twelve years later the Court (again divided 5–4) decided that *Aguilar* erred in concluding that New York City's program resulted in an excessive entanglement between church and state. In the years following *Aguilar*, the parties affected by that decision told the Court that the 1985 ruling could not be squared with subsequent changes to Establishment Clause jurisprudence. In 1997, the Court agreed that *Aguilar* was no longer good law and reversed it. Agostini v. Felton, 521 U.S. 203 (1997).

Why did the Court reverse itself between 1985 and 1997? The switch can be explained partly by changing composition. Of the five Justices in the *Aguilar* majority, only Justice Stevens remained on the Court in 1997. Joining him on the dissenting side in 1997 were three newcomers: Souter, Ginsburg, and Breyer. Of the four dissenters in 1985, two remained to decide *Agostini*: Rehnquist and O'Connor. They formed a majority by combining with three Justices who had joined the Court: Scalia, Kennedy, and Thomas.

But it was more than a change in composition. From the start, *Aguilar* never made much sense. By prohibiting public school teachers from entering parochial schools, the Court created the need for mobile classrooms, other "neutral sites," and a reliance on computer and telecommunications technologies, all of which were more costly. Starting in 1988, Congress appropriated "capital expenses" to finance this alternative instruction. Instead of limiting public assistance to parochial schools, *Aguilar* led to greater expenditures. *Agostini* again raises questions about the utility of the three-prong *Lemon* test (see box on next page).

The other decision from 1985 involved a complicated Michigan program that used public funds to teach nonpublic school students in classrooms located in and leased from nonpublic schools. A "shared time" program offered secular classes during the regular school day. The teachers were full-time employees of the public schools, but a "significant portion" had previously taught in nonpublic schools. A second program, called "community education," was voluntary and offered secular classes after school. These teachers were part-time public school

Problems with the *Lemon* Test

In Lemon v. Kurtzman, 403 U.S. 602, 612–13 (1971), the Court established a three-prong test for determining church-state issues, especially the Establishment Clause: (1) the statute must have a secular legislative purpose, (2) its principal or primary effect must be one that neither advances nor inhibits religion, and (3) it must not foster excessive entanglement with religion.

On some church-state issues, such as the use of chaplains by legislative bodies, the Court would have had to strike down the practice had it followed *Lemon*. Instead, the Court simply ignored the three-part test and relied on historical precedents to uphold the use of chaplains in legislatures. Marsh v. Chambers, 463 U.S. 783 (1983).

In a dissent in 1985, Justice Rehnquist pointed to problems with the first and third prongs. The secular purpose test "has proved mercurial in application" in part because it depends upon what legislators pub in the legislative history and what they leave out. That is, legislative purpose can be easily manipulated to hide intentions. The entanglement test, he said, can create an "insoluble paradox" because the Court requires that aid to parochial schools be closely watched so that it is not put to sectarian use, and yet the very effort to supervise might create an entanglement issue. Wallace v. Jaffree, 472 U.S. 38, 108–09. Justice O'Connor also questioned the utility of the entanglement test. Aguilar v. Felton, 473 U.S. 402, 422 (1983).

In upholding public aid to sectarian schools in 1997, the Court submerged the entanglement test into the primary effect test. Instead of separate guidelines, the two tests were combined. Agostini v. Felton, 521 U.S. 203, 232–33 (1997).

In recent decisions, the Court has resolved a number of Establishment Clause cases with little or no reference to the *Lemon* test. Rosenberger v. University of Virginia, 515 U.S. 819 (1995); Capitol Square Review Bd. v. Pinette, 515 U.S. 753 (1995); Board of Education of Kiryas Joel v. Grumet, 512 U.S. 687 (1994); Zobrest v. Catalina Foothills Sch. Dist., 509 U.S. 1 (1993); Lee v. Weisman, 505 U.S. 577 (1992).

employees generally employed in the nonpublic schools in which the classes were held. Most of the nonpublic schools were sectarian religious schools. A 5–4 decision held that both programs had the primary effect of advancing religion. Grand Rapids School District v. Ball, 473 U.S. 373. In deciding *Agostini* in 1997, the 5–4 Court said that it was abandoning the presumption in *Ball* that placing public employees on parochial school grounds inevitably results in state-sponsored indoctrination or constitutes a symbolic union between government and religion. 521 U.S. at 223.

In 2000, the Court was again badly divided on the issue of providing financial assistance to sectarian schools. Six Justices agreed that it was constitutional to provide computers and related instructional materials to religious schools, but two of those Justices objected to the breadth of the opinion written by the other four. Three Justices prepared a lengthy dissent. Mitchell v. Helms, 120 S.Ct. 2530 (2000).

Other Disputes

Federal assistance to sectarian schools may also implicate the Property Clause, which empowers Congress "to dispose of and make all needful Rules and Regulations respecting the Territory or other Property belonging to the United States." Art. IV, § 3, Cl. 2. Pursuant to this Clause, Congress passed a law governing the disposition of surplus federal property and the government transferred a military hospital to a church-related college. An organization favoring church-state separation filed suit on the ground that the transfer violated the Establishment Clause. A 5–4 decision by the Supreme Court held that the organization lacked stand-

Court Decisions Involving Financial Assistance to Sectarian Schools

Assistance Sustained

Transportation. Everson v. Board of Education, 330 U.S. 1 (1947).

Textbooks. Board of Education v. Allen, 392 U.S. 236 (1968).

Tax exemptions. Walz v. Tax Commission, 397 U.S. 664 (1970).

Construction grants for colleges. Tilton v. Richardson, 403 U.S. 672 (1971).

Revenue bonds for colleges. Hunt v. McNair, 413 U.S. 734 (1973).

State grants to colleges. Roemer v. Maryland Public Works Bd., 426 U.S. 736 (1976).

Standardized testing and scoring; diagnostic services; therapeutic and remedial services. Wolman v. Walter, 433 U.S. 229 (1977).

Testing, reporting, and record keeping (with state auditing). Committee for Public Education v. Regan, 444 U.S. 646 (1980).

"Surplus" federal property for colleges. Valley Forge College v. Americans United, 454 U.S. 464 (1982).

Tax deductions for expenses incurred in providing tuition, textbooks, and transportation. Mueller v. Allen, 463 U.S. 388 (1983).

State aid under a rehabilitation program used to finance training at a Christian college. Witters v. Wash. Dept. of Services for Blind, 474 U.S. 481 (1986).

Providing sign-language interpreter to a deaf child enrolled in a sectarian high school. Zobrest v. Catalina Foothills School Dist., 509 U.S. 1 (1993)

Salaries for public school employees teaching in parochial schools. Agostini v. Felton, 521 U.S. 203 (1997).

Computers and related instructional materials. Mitchell v. Helms, 120 S.Ct. 2530 (2000).

Assistance Invalidated

Teachers' salaries. Lemon v. Kurtzman, 403 U.S. 602 (1971).

Examinations, record keeping, and reports (without state auditing). Levitt v. Committee for Public Education, 413 U.S. 472 (1973).

Maintenance and repair of facilities and equipment; reimbursements for low-income parents; tax relief for parents not qualifying for tuition reimbursement. Committee for Public Education v. Nyquist, 413 U.S. 756 (1973).

Reimbursements for tuition expenses. Sloan v. Lemon, 413 U.S. 825 (1973).

Counseling, testing, psychological services, and speech and hearing therapy; instructional materials including periodicals, photographs, maps, charts, recordings, and films; instructional equipment including projectors, recorders, and laboratory paraphernalia. Meek v. Pittenger, 421 U.S. 349 (1975). To the extent that *Meek* assumes that placing public employees on parochial school grounds inevitably results in state-sponsored indoctrination or constitutes a symbolic union between government and religion, *Meek* is overruled by Agostini v. Felton, 521 U.S. 203, 223 (1997). *Meek* was also weakened by *Mitchell* v. *Helms*, 120 S.Ct. 2530 (2000).

Instructional materials, instructional equipment, and transportation and services for field trips. Wolman v. Walter, 433 U.S. 229 (1977). *Wolman* was weakened by *Mitchell* v. *Helms*, 120 S.Ct. 2530 (2000).

---

ing to bring the suit. Moreover, the Court reasoned that the transfer was not pursuant to the Taxing and Spending Clause, under which the parties might have had standing, but under the Property Clause. Relying on a legal fiction, the majority claimed that the source of the complaint was not a congressional action but rather an agency action to transfer a parcel of federal property. Through this rationale the parties were unable to challenge the action under the

Establishment Clause. The dissenters accused the majority of engaging in a "dissembling exercise." Valley Forge College v. Americans United, 454 U.S. 464, 493 (1982).

Tax deductions are another source of state assistance to sectarian schools. A Minnesota law allowed taxpayers, in computing their state income tax, to deduct expenses incurred in providing tuition, textbooks, and transportation for their children attending elementary and secondary schools, including schools of a sectarian nature. Another 5–4 decision by the Supreme Court held that the statute did not violate the Establishment Clause. It met the three-part *Lemon* test, even though the law helped fund sectarian textbooks. Mueller v. Allen, 463 U.S. 388 (1983).

In 1986, in a rare unanimous ruling regarding government assistance to sectarian schools, the Court held that state aid under a rehabilitation program to finance an individual's training at a Christian college did not advance religion in a way inconsistent with the Establishment Clause. The assistance was defended on the ground that it went to the student, who then transmitted it to an institution of his or her choice. The majority opinion made no mention of *Mueller,* which four concurring Justices thought should have formed the basis for the decision. Witters v. Wash. Dept. of Services for Blind, 474 U.S. 481 (1986). When the case went back to the state of Washington, the state supreme court reached the opposite conclusion. Looking to the state constitution, which prohibits the use of any public monies for religious instruction, it held that the funds could not go to the student. Witters v. State Com'n for the Blind, 771 P.2d 1119 (Wash. 1989). The kinds of assistance that are permitted to religious institutions and those that are prohibited form a complicated and sometimes incomprehensible pattern (see box on previous page).

Building on *Witters,* in 1993 the Court (this time divided 5–4) ruled that the Establishment Clause does not prevent a public school from providing a sign-language interpreter to a deaf child enrolled in a sectarian high school. Even when a sectarian school receives a financial benefit, the government program is permissible if it neutrally provides benefits to a broad class of citizens defined without reference to religion. Zobrest v. Catalina Foothills School Dist., 509 U.S. 1 (1993). The four dissenters objected that the majority should have returned the case to the lower courts to decide statutory and regulatory questions first before reaching the constitutional issue.

Everson v. Board of Education

330 U.S. 1 (1947)

Acting under a New Jersey statute, the township of Ewing reimbursed parents for money spent in transporting their children to school. Part of the money went to children attending Catholic schools. Arch R. Everson, a taxpayer in the local school district, filed suit challenging the right of the Board of Education of the Township of Ewing to reimburse parents of parochial school students. The New Jersey Supreme Court held the statute unconstitutional, but was reversed by the New Jersey Court of Errors and Appeals.

MR. JUSTICE BLACK delivered the opinion of the Court.

[Everson alleged that the statute and township resolution violated the Due Process Clause of the Fourteenth Amendment by authorizing the state to tax the private property of some and bestow it upon others, to be used for their own private purposes. Black rejects this argument and turns to the question of the Establishment Clause.]

Second. The New Jersey statute is challenged as a "law respecting an establishment of religion." The First Amendment, as made applicable to the states by the Fourteenth, *Murdock v. Pennsylvania,* 319 U. S. 105, commands that a state "shall make no law respecting an establishment of religion, or prohibiting the free exercise thereof...." These words of the First Amendment reflected in the minds of early Americans a vivid mental picture of conditions and practices which they fervently wished to stamp out in order to preserve liberty for themselves and for their posterity. Doubtless their goal has not been entirely reached; but so far has the Nation moved toward it that the expression "law respecting an establishment of religion," probably does not so vividly remind present-day Americans of the evils, fears, and political problems that caused that expression to be written into our Bill of Rights....

[Black reviews the experiences and efforts of the early settlers to establish religious freedom. After summarizing the efforts of Jefferson and Madison in Virginia to enact the Bill for Religious Liberty and the subsequent adoption of the First Amendment, Black focuses on the meaning of the Establishment Clause.]

The "establishment of religion" clause of the First Amendment means at least this: Neither a state nor the Federal Government can set up a church. Neither can pass laws which aid one religion, aid all religions, or prefer one religion over another. Neither can force nor influence a person to go to or to remain away from church against his will or force him to profess a belief or disbelief in any religion. No person can be punished for entertaining or professing religious beliefs or disbeliefs, for church attendance or nonattendance. No tax in any amount, large or small, can be levied to support any religious activities or institutions, whatever they may be called, or whatever form they may adopt to teach or practice religion. Neither a state nor the Federal Government can, openly or secretly, participate in the affairs of any religious organizations or groups and *vice versa*. In the words of Jefferson, the clause against establishment of religion by law was intended to erect "a wall of separation between church and State." *Reynolds* v. *United States, supra* at 164.

We must consider the New Jersey statute in accordance with the foregoing limitations imposed by the First Amendment.... New Jersey cannot consistently with the "establishment of religion" clause of the First Amendment contribute tax-raised funds to the support of an institution which teaches the tenets and faith of any church. On the other hand, other language of the amendment commands that New Jersey cannot hamper its citizens in the free exercise of their own religion.... While we do not mean to intimate that a state could not provide transportation only to children attending public schools, we must be careful, in protecting the citizens of New Jersey against state-established churches, to be sure that we do not inadvertently prohibit New Jersey from extending its general state law benefits to all its citizens without regard to their religious belief.

Measured by these standards, we cannot say that the First Amendment prohibits New Jersey from spending tax-raised funds to pay the bus fares of parochial school pupils as a part of a general program under which it pays the fares of pupils attending public and other schools. It is undoubtedly true that children are helped to get to church schools. There is even a possibility that some of the children might not be sent to the church schools if the parents were compelled to pay their children's bus fares out of their own pockets when transportation to a public school would have been paid for by the State. The same possibility exists where the state requires a local transit company to provide reduced fares to school children including those attending parochial schools, or where a municipally owned transportation system undertakes to carry all school children free of charge. Moreover, state-paid policemen, detailed to protect children going to and from church schools from the very real hazards of traffic, would serve much the same purpose and accomplish much the same result as state provisions intended to guarantee free transportation of a kind which the state deems to be best for the school children's welfare. And parents might refuse to risk their children to the serious danger of traffic accidents going to and from parochial schools, the approaches to which were not protected by policemen. Similarly, parents might be reluctant to permit their children to attend schools which the state had cut off from such general government services as ordinary police and fire protection, connections for sewage disposal, public highways and sidewalks. Of course, cutting off church schools from these services, so separate and so indisputably marked off from the religious function, would make it far more difficult for the schools to operate. But such is obviously not the purpose of the First Amendment. That Amendment requires the state to be a neutral in its relations with groups of religious believers and non-believers; it does not require the state to be their adversary. State power is no more to be used so as to handicap religions than it is to favor them.

This Court has said that parents may, in the discharge of their duty under state compulsory education laws, send their children to a religious rather than a public school if the school meets the secular educational requirements which the state has power to impose. See *Pierce* v. *Society of Sisters,* 268 U. S. 510. It appears that these parochial schools meet New Jersey's requirements. The State contributes no money to the schools. It does not support them. Its legislation, as applied, does no more than provide a general program to help parents get their children, regardless of their religion, safely and expeditiously to and from accredited schools.

The First Amendment has erected a wall between church and state. That wall must be kept high and impregnable. We could not approve the slightest breach. New Jersey has not breached it here.

Affirmed.

MR. JUSTICE JACKSON, dissenting.

I find myself, contrary to first impressions, unable to join in this decision. I have a sympathy, though it is not ideological, with Catholic citizens who are compelled by law to pay taxes for public schools, and also feel constrained by conscience and discipline to support other schools for their own children. Such relief to them as this case involves is not in itself a serious burden to taxpayers and I had assumed it to be as little serious in principle. Study of this case convinces me otherwise. The Court's opinion marshals every argument in favor of state aid and puts the case in its most favorable light, but much of its reasoning confirms my conclusions that there are no good grounds upon which to support the present legislation. In fact, the undertones of the opinion, advocating complete and uncompromising separation of Church from State, seem utterly discordant with its conclusion yielding support to their commingling in educational matters. The case which irresistibly comes to mind as the most fitting precedent is that of Julia who, according to Byron's reports, "whispering 'I will ne'er consent,'—consented."

I.

The Court sustains this legislation by assuming two deviations from the facts of this particular case; first, it assumes a state of facts the record does not support, and secondly, it refuses to consider facts which are inescapable on the record.

The Court concludes that this "legislation, as applied, does no more than provide a general program to help parents get their children, regardless of their religion, safely and expeditiously to and from accredited schools," and it draws a comparison between "state provisions intended to guarantee free transportation" for school children with services such as police and fire protection, and implies that we are here dealing with "laws authorizing new types of public services...." This hypothesis permeates the opinion. The facts will not bear that construction.

The Township of Ewing is not furnishing transportation to the children in any form; it is not operating school busses itself or contracting for their operation; and it is not performing any public service of any kind with this taxpayer's money. All school children are left to ride as ordinary paying passengers on the regular busses operated by the public transportation system. What the Township does, and what the taxpayer complains of, is at stated intervals to reimburse parents for the fares paid, provided the children attend either public schools or Catholic Church schools. This expenditure of tax funds has no possible effect on the child's safety or expedition in transit. As passengers on the public busses they travel as fast and no faster, and are as safe and no safer, since their parents are reimbursed as before.

In addition to thus assuming a type of service that does not exist, the Court also insists that we must close our eyes to a discrimination which does exist. The resolution which authorizes disbursement of this taxpayer's money limits reimbursement to those who attend public schools and Catholic schools. That is the way the Act is applied to this taxpayer.

The New Jersey Act in question makes the character of the school, not the needs of the children, determine the eligibility of parents to reimbursement.... [U]nder the Act and resolution brought to us by this case, children are classified according to the schools they attend and are to be aided if they attend the public schools or private Catholic schools, and they are not allowed to be aided if they attend private secular schools or private religious schools of other faiths.

. . .

III.

. . .

It seems to me that the basic fallacy in the Court's reasoning, which accounts for its failure to apply the principles it avows, is in ignoring the essentially religious test by which beneficiaries of this expenditure are selected. A policeman protects a Catholic, of course—but not because he is a Catholic; it is because he is a man and a member of our society. The fireman protects the Church school—but not because it is a Church school; it is because it is property, part of the assets of our society. Neither the fireman nor the policeman has to ask before he renders aid "Is this man or building identified with the Catholic Church?" But before these school authorities draw a check to reimburse for a student's fare they must ask just that question, and if the school is a Catholic one they may render aid because it is such, while if it is of any other faith or is run for profit, the help must be withheld....

MR. JUSTICE FRANKFURTER joins in this opinion.

MR. JUSTICE RUTLEDGE, with whom MR. JUSTICE FRANKFURTER, MR. JUSTICE JACKSON and MR. JUSTICE BURTON agree, dissenting.

. . .

...New Jersey's statute sustained is the first, if indeed it is not the second breach to be made by this Court's action. That a third, and a fourth, and still others will be attempted, we may be sure. For just as *Cochran* v. *Board of Education,* 281 U. S. 370, has opened the way by oblique ruling *[supplying secular textbooks to religious schools]* for this decision, so will the two make wider the breach for a third. Thus with time the most solid freedom steadily gives way before continuing corrosive decision.

. . .

Lemon v. Kurtzman

403 U.S. 602 (1971)

A number of states passed legislation providing financial assistance to church-related elementary and secondary schools, going far beyond the initial support of transportation and textbooks. These state initiatives required the Court to establish guidelines and principles to distinguish permissible from impermissible aid. This case involves legislation enacted by Rhode Island and Pennsylvania. In the lead case, Alton J. Lemon, a citizen and taxpayer of Pennsylvania as well as a parent of a child attending a public school in Pennsylvania, brings suit against David H. Kurtzman, Superintendent of Public Instruction of Pennsylvania. A three-judge federal court held that the Pennsylvania law violated neither the Establishment nor the Free Exercise Clause of the First Amendment.

MR. CHIEF JUSTICE BURGER delivered the opinion of the Court.

. . .

Pennsylvania has adopted a statutory program that provides financial support to nonpublic elementary and secondary schools by way of reimbursement for the cost of teachers' salaries, textbooks, and instructional materials in specified secular subjects. Rhode Island has adopted a statute under which the State pays directly to teachers in nonpublic elementary schools a supplement of 15% of their annual salary. Under each statute state aid has been given to church-related educational institutions. We hold that both statutes are unconstitutional.

I

THE RHODE ISLAND STATUTE

The Rhode Island Salary Supplement Act was enacted in 1969. It rests on the legislative finding that the quality of education available in nonpublic elementary schools has been jeopardized by the rapidly rising salaries needed to attract competent and dedicated teachers. The Act au-

thorizes state officials to supplement the salaries of teachers of secular subjects in nonpublic elementary schools by paying directly to a teacher an amount not in excess of 15% of his current annual salary. As supplemented, however, a nonpublic school teacher's salary cannot exceed the maximum paid to teachers in the State's public schools, and the recipient must be certified by the state board of education in substantially the same manner as public school teachers.

In order to be eligible for the Rhode Island salary supplement, the recipient must teach in a nonpublic school at which the average per-pupil expenditure on secular education is less than the average in the State's public schools during a specified period. Appellant State Commissioner of Education also requires eligible schools to submit financial data. If this information indicates a per-pupil expenditure in excess of the statutory limitation, the records of the school in question must be examined in order to assess how much of the expenditure is attributable to secular education and how much to religious activity.

The Act also requires that teachers eligible for salary supplements must teach only those subjects that are offered in the State's public schools. They must use "only teaching materials which are used in the public schools." Finally, any teacher applying for a salary supplement must first agree in writing "not to teach a course in religion for so long as or during such time as he or she receives any salary supplements" under the Act.

. . .

A three-judge federal court...found that Rhode Island's nonpublic elementary schools accommodated approximately 25% of the State's pupils. About 95% of these pupils attended schools affiliated with the Roman Catholic church. To date some 250 teachers have applied for benefits under the Act. All of them are employed by Roman Catholic schools.

. . .

THE PENNSYLVANIA STATUTE

Pennsylvania has adopted a program that has some but not all of the features of the Rhode Island program. The Pennsylvania Nonpublic Elementary and Secondary Education Act was passed in 1968 in response to a crisis that the Pennsylvania Legislature found existed in the State's nonpublic schools due to rapidly rising costs. The statute affirmatively reflects the legislative conclusion that the State's educational goals could appropriately be fulfilled by government support of "those purely secular educational objectives achieved through nonpublic education...."

The statute authorizes appellee state Superintendent of Public Instruction to "purchase" specified "secular educational services" from nonpublic schools. Under the "contracts" authorized by the statute, the State directly reimburses nonpublic schools solely for their actual expenditures for teachers' salaries, textbooks, and instructional materials. A school seeking reimbursement must maintain prescribed accounting procedures that identify the "separate" cost of the "secular educational service." These accounts are subject to state audit....

There are several significant statutory restrictions on state aid. Reimbursement is limited to courses "presented in the curricula of the public schools." It is further limited "solely" to courses in the following "secular" subjects: mathematics, modern foreign languages, physical science, and physical education. Textbooks and instructional materials included in the program must be approved by the state Superintendent of Public Instruction. Finally, the statute prohibits reimbursement for any course that contains "any subject matter expressing religious teaching, or the morals or forms of worship of any sect."

...The State has now entered into contracts with some 1,181 nonpublic elementary and secondary schools with a student population of some 535,215 pupils—more than 20% of the total number of students in the State. More than 96% of these pupils attend church-related schools, and most of these schools are affiliated with the Roman Catholic church.

. . .

II

In *Everson* v. *Board of Education,* 330 U.S. 1 (1947), this Court upheld a state statute that reimbursed the parents of parochial school children for bus transportation expenses. There Mr. Justice Black, writing for the majority, suggested that the decision carried to "the verge" of forbidden territory under the Religion Clauses. *Id.,* at 16. Candor compels acknowledgment, moreover, that we can only dimly perceive the lines of demarcation in this extraordinarily sensitive area of constitutional law.

The language of the Religion Clauses of the First Amendment is at best opaque, particularly when compared with other portions of the Amendment. Its authors did not simply prohibit the establishment of a state church or a state religion, an area history shows they regarded as very important and fraught with great dangers. Instead they commanded that there should be "no law *respecting* an establishment of religion." A law may be one "respecting" the forbidden objective while falling short of its total realization. A law "respecting" the proscribed result, that is, the establishment of religion, is not always easily identifiable as one violative of the Clause. A given law might not *establish* a state religion but nevertheless be one "respecting" that end in the sense of being a step that could lead to such establishment and hence offend the First Amendment.

In the absence of precisely stated constitutional prohibitions, we must draw lines with reference to the three main evils against which the Establishment Clause was intended to afford protection: "sponsorship, financial support, and active involvement of the sovereign in religious activity." *Walz* v. *Tax Commission,* 397 U.S. 664, 668 (1970).

Every analysis in this area must begin with consideration of the cumulative criteria developed by the Court over many years. Three such tests may be gleaned from our cases. First, the statute must have a secular legislative purpose; second, its principal or primary effect must be one that neither advances nor inhibits religion, *Board of Education v. Allen*, 392 U.S. 236, 243 (1968); finally, the statute must not foster "an excessive government entanglement with religion." *Walz, supra,* at 674.

Inquiry into the legislative purposes of the Pennsylvania and Rhode Island statutes affords no basis for a conclusion that the legislative intent was to advance religion. On the contrary, the statutes themselves clearly state that they are intended to enhance the quality of the secular education in all schools covered by the compulsory attendance laws. There is no reason to believe the legislatures meant anything else....

The two legislatures, however, have also recognized that church-related elementary and secondary schools have a significant religious mission and that a substantial portion of their activities is religiously oriented. They have therefore sought to create statutory restrictions designed to guarantee the separation between secular and religious educational functions and to ensure that State financial aid supports only the former. All these provisions are precautions taken in candid recognition that these programs approached, even if they did not intrude upon, the forbidden areas under the Religion Clauses. We need not decide whether these legislative precautions restrict the principal or primary effect of the programs to the point where they do not offend the Religion Clauses, for we conclude that the cumulative impact of the entire relationship arising under the statutes in each State involves excessive entanglement between government and religion.

III

. . .

(A) RHODE ISLAND PROGRAM

The District court made extensive findings on the grave potential for excessive entanglement that inheres in the religious character and purpose of the Roman Catholic elementary schools of Rhode Island, to date the sole beneficiaries of the Rhode Island Salary Supplement Act.

. . .

We need not and do not assume that teachers in parochial schools will be guilty of bad faith or any conscious design to evade the limitations imposed by the statute and the First Amendment.

We simply recognize that a dedicated religious person, teaching in a school affiliated with his or her faith and operated to inculcate its tenets, will inevitably experience great difficulty in remaining religiously neutral. Doctrines and faith are not inculcated or advanced by neutrals....

... The State must be certain, given the Religion Clauses, that subsidized teachers do not inculcate religion — indeed the State here has undertaken to do so. To ensure that no trespass occurs, the State has therefore carefully conditioned its aid with pervasive restrictions. An eligible recipient must teach only those courses that are offered in the public schools and use only those texts and materials that are found in the public schools. In addition the teacher must not engage in teaching any course in religion.

A comprehensive, discriminating, and continuing state surveillance will inevitably be required to ensure that these restrictions are obeyed and the First Amendment otherwise respected. Unlike a book, a teacher cannot be inspected once so as to determine the extent and intent of his or her personal beliefs and subjective acceptance of the limitations imposed by the First Amendment. These prophylactic contacts will involve excessive and enduring entanglement between state and church.

There is another area of entanglement in the Rhode Island program that gives concern. The statute excludes teachers employed by nonpublic schools whose average per-pupil expenditures on secular education equal or exceed the comparable figures for public schools. In the event that the total expenditures of an otherwise eligible school exceed this norm, the program requires the government to examine the school's records in order to determine how much of the total expenditures is attributable to secular education and how much to religious activity. This kind of state inspection and evaluation of the religious content of a religious organization is fraught with the sort of entanglement that the Constitution forbids....

(B)

Pennsylvania Program *[The Court found similar problems of excessive entanglement: providing state aid to sectarian schools established to propagate a particular religious faith; state restrictions and surveillance to ensure that teachers play a strictly nonideological role; reimbursement contingent on state approval of courses and teaching materials; and state auditing of a parochial school's financial records.]*

. . .

The judgment of the Rhode Island District Court in No. 569 and No. 570 is affirmed. The judgment of the Pennsylvania District Court in No. 89 is reversed, and the case is remanded for further proceedings consistent with this opinion.

MR. JUSTICE MARSHALL took no part in the consideration or decision of No. 89 *[the Pennsylvania case]*.

MR. JUSTICE DOUGLAS, whom MR. JUSTICE BLACK joins, concurring.

. . .

MR. JUSTICE MARSHALL, who took no part in the consideration or decision of No. 89,...while intimating no view as to the continuing vitality of *Everson* v. *Board of Education,* 330 U.S. 1 (1947), concurs in MR. JUSTICE DOUGLAS' opinion covering Nos. 569 and 570 *[the Rhode Island cases]*.

MR. JUSTICE BRENNAN *[concurring]*.

. . .

MR. JUSTICE WHITE, concurring in the judgments in No. 153 *[Tilton v. Richardson, which sustained federal construction grants to sectarian universities]* and No. 89 and dissenting in Nos. 569 and 570.

. . .

The Court strikes down the Rhode Island statute on its face....The Court...finds that impermissible "entanglement" will result from administration of the program. The reasoning is a curious and mystifying blend, but a critical factor appears to be an unwillingness to accept the District Court's express findings that on the evidence before it none of the teachers here involved mixed religious and secular instruction. Rather, the District Court struck down the Rhode Island statute because it concluded that activities outside the secular classroom would probably have a religious content and that support for religious education therefore necessarily resulted from the financial aid to the secular programs, since that aid generally strengthened the parochial schools and increased the number of their students.

. . .

The Court thus creates an insoluble paradox for the State and the parochial schools. The State cannot finance secular instruction if it permits religion to be taught in the same classroom; but if it exacts a promise that religion not be so taught— a promise the school and its teachers are quite willing and on this record able to give—and enforces it, it is then entangled in the "no entanglement" aspect of the Court's Establishment Clause jurisprudence.

. . .

E. RELIGIOUS INSTRUCTION AND PRAYERS

Beginning in 1948, the Supreme Court has had to referee an extraordinarily divisive and emotional issue: efforts to introduce religious instruction and prayers into public schools. Especially with regard to the prayer issue, the Supreme Court has been vilified for "driving God out of the classroom," but these critiques often misunderstand the Court's rulings.

Religious Instruction

A 1948 case dealt with an Illinois law that allowed religious teachers to give religious instruction in public school buildings once a week. Parents could excuse their children from secular classes to attend religious instruction. The Court held, 8–1, that use of the state's tax-supported public schools for compulsory education to enable sectarian groups to give religious instruction to students in public school buildings violated the religion clauses. In a concurring opinion, joined by Justices Jackson, Rutledge, and Burton, Justice Frankfurter spoke about the dangers of coercing children: "The law of imitation operates, and non-conformity is not an outstanding characteristic of children. The result is an obvious pressure upon children to attend." McCollum v. Board of Education, 333 U.S. 203, 227.

Advocates of religious instruction next proposed that it be done outside the school building. New York City permitted its public schools to release students during school hours, on written requests from their parents, to go to religious centers for religious instruction or devotional exercises. Students not released stayed in the public school classrooms. The churches providing the instruction reported the names of children released for instruction but who failed to appear. The Supreme Court, divided 6–3, held that the "released time" program did not violate the religion clauses. Writing for the majority, Justice Douglas said that when the state "encourages religious instruction or cooperates with religious authorities by adjusting the schedule of public events to sectarian needs, it follows the best of our traditions. For it then respects the religious nature of our people and accommodates the public service to their spiritual needs." Zorach v. Clauson, 343 U.S. 306, 313–14 (1952). This "accommodationist" stance conflicts with the Court's frequent call for neutrality.

Justice Black, who had adopted the accommodationist position when he upheld reimbursement of transportation costs in *Everson,* dissented in the released-time case. He accused the Court of abandoning the neutrality principle by endorsing a law that helped "religious sects get attendants presumably too unenthusiastic to go unless moved to do so by the pressure of this state machinery." Frankfurter, dissenting, agreed with this criticism of the majority's opinion. Jackson, in the third dissent, put the matter forcefully: "Here schooling is more or less suspended during the 'released time' so the nonreligious attendants will not forge ahead of the churchgoing absentees. But it serves as a temporary jail for a pupil who will not go to Church. It takes more subtlety of mind than I possess to deny that this is governmental constraint in support of religion."

Prayers in Public Schools

If the Court attempted to accommodate religious groups in *Zorach,* in 1962 it set off a storm still raging by holding that a New York "Regents' Prayer" was unconstitutional. State law directed that the following prayer be said aloud by each class of a public school at the beginning of each day: "Almighty God, we acknowledge our dependence upon Thee, and we beg Thy blessings upon us, our parents, our teachers and our Country." The 6–1 decision, written by Black, argued that the Establishment Clause "must at least mean that in this country it is no part of the business of government to compose official prayers for any group of the American people to recite as a part of a religious program carried on by government." ENGEL v. VITALE, 370 U.S. 421, 425. Douglas' concurrence offered unfortunate and unnecessary speculations about the use of prayers in opening the business of the Supreme Court and of Congress. Stewart's dissent also strayed from the issue before the Court. He did not want to deny school children their "wish" to recite the prayer or to interfere with those "who want to begin their day by joining in prayer," but the issue was not the desire of children to pray on their own initiative. It was the constitutionality of a state composing an official prayer mandated for minors in public schools.

A number of newspapers incorrectly reported that the Court had banned prayer, when in fact it had banned *official* prayer. There was strong pressure to pass a constitutional amendment to nullify the Court's decision. That movement stalled when congressional hearings revealed broad support by Protestant, Catholic, and Jewish organizations for the Court's ruling (see reading).

A year later, the Court decided 8–1 that states may not require that passages from the Bible be read or that the Lord's Prayer be recited in the public schools at the beginning of each day, even if individual students may be excused upon written request of their parents. The Court did not bar the study of the Bible or of religion "when presented objectively as part of a secular program of education." Abington School Dist. v. Schempp, 374 U.S. 203, 225 (1963). Stewart was again the lone dissenter.

Evolutionism vs. Creationism

States have been active in prohibiting the teaching of evolution in the schools. Tennessee's "monkey law," adopted in 1925, led to the famous *Scopes* case in 1927. Scopes v. State, 289 S.W. 363 (Tenn. 1927). When the issue of anti-evolution laws reached the Supreme Court in 1968, a unanimous Court struck down Arkansas's statute making it unlawful for a teacher in any state-supported school or university to teach or use a textbook that claimed that mankind evolved from a lower order of animals. The statute violated the Establishment Clause because a particular religious group considered the evolution theory in conflict with the Book of Genesis. Epperson v. Arkansas, 393 U.S. 97.

In 1987 a 7–2 Court held invalid Louisiana's "Creationism Act," which prohibited the teaching of the theory of evolution in public elementary and secondary schools unless accompanied by instruction in the theory of "creation science." The latter, based on the Book of Genesis, opposes the theory of evolution. The Court rejected the state's assertion that the statute furthered "academic freedom." The legislative record revealed a bias in favor of creationism and religious doctrine. EDWARDS v. AGUILLARD, 482 U.S. 578 (1987). Other cases in the lower courts concerned challenges to textbooks that allegedly promote the "religion" of secular humanism.[5] In 1999, the Kansas Board of Education voted to delete any mention of evolution from the state's science curriculum and from any state assessment test. The curriculum allows for the teaching of "micro-evolution" (genetic adaptation). Elections in 2000 to the Kansas school board appeared to reinstate the teaching of evolution.

The Court Fragments

The votes on these cases show a remarkable strength for the majority of the Supreme Court: 8–1 in *McCollum*, 6–1 in *Engel*, 8–1 in *Abington*, unanimous in *Epperson*, and 7–2 in *Edwards*. Only in *Zorach* was the Court seriously divided (6–3).

No such agreement marks other decisions on religious instruction and prayer. In 1980 the Court split 5–4 in holding that a Kentucky statute requiring the posting of a copy of the Ten Commandments on the wall of each public school classroom violated the Establishment Clause. Although the copies were purchased with private funds, the mere posting provided official state support for religion. Portions of the Ten Commandments could have been regarded as secular in purpose (the parts concerning honoring one's parents, killing, adultery, stealing, false witness, and covetousness), but other sections were clearly religious in nature (worshiping the Lord God alone, avoiding idolatry, not using the Lord's name in vain, and observing the Sabbath). Stone v. Graham, 449 U.S. 39, 41–42. The dissenters were Chief Justice Burger and Justices Blackmun, Stewart, and Rehnquist.

In 1983 the Court divided 6–3 in upholding the practice of the Nebraska legislature to begin each of its sessions with a prayer by a chaplain paid by the state with the legislature's approval. The Court noted that Congress has followed the same practice without interruption for almost 200 years, and that precedents dating back to the First Congress, which drafted the Bill of Rights, shed important light on what the framers intended by the Establishment Clause. Marsh v. Chambers, 463 U.S. 783. As Justice Brennan noted in his dissent, the his-

---

5. A federal judge in Tennessee held that a state requirement for all students in grades 1 through 8 to use a prescribed set of reading textbooks was unconstitutional because the books contained "secular humanist" teachings that offended Christian beliefs. Mozert v. Hawkins County Public Schools, 647 F.Supp. 1194 (E.D. Tenn. 1986). His decision was overturned by a unanimous panel of the Sixth Circuit; 827 F.2d 1058 (6th Cir. 1987), cert. denied, 484 U.S. 1066 (1988). A federal judge in Alabama also banned textbooks from public schools in the state because they promoted the "religion" of secular humanism. Smith v. Board of Com'rs of Mobile County, 655 F.Supp. 939 (S.D. Ala. 1987). His decision was reversed by the Eleventh Circuit; 827 F.2d 684 (11th Cir. 1987).

torical analogy allowed the Court to violate *Lemon*'s three-part test. The Nebraska statute had a religious, not a secular, purpose; its principal or primary effect advanced religion; and it fostered government entanglement with religion.

While the Nebraska chaplain case was wending its way through the courts, a separate challenge concerned chaplains in the U.S. Senate and the U.S. House of Representatives. A district judge held in 1981 that the taxpayer had no standing to bring the suit. Murray v. Morton, 505 F.Supp. 144 (D.D.C. 1981). However, the appellate court reinstated the suit and sent the case back to the trial judge for a decision on the merits. Murray v. Buchanan, 674 F.2d 14 (D.C. Cir. 1982). Three weeks later the House of Representatives passed a resolution viewing with "deep concern" the appellate court decision and expressing in strong terms the constitutional power of the House "to determine the rules of its proceedings, to select officers, and otherwise to control its internal affairs." The resolution also stated that the decision of the appellate court "implies a lack of respect due a coordinate branch concerning matters committed to it by the Constitution." The resolution passed by the vote of 388 to zero. 128 Cong. Rec. 5890–96 (1982). The case was then heard by the D.C. Circuit, sitting en banc. Because of the Supreme Court's decision in *Marsh* v. *Chambers,* the D.C. Circuit held that the complaint against the House and Senate chaplains "retains no vitality" and dismissed the case. Murray v. Buchanan, 720 F.2d 689 (D.C. Cir. 1983) (en banc).

A 1985 decision saw the Court again badly fractured on questions of prayer. The case concerned Alabama's one-minute period of silence in all public schools "for meditation or voluntary prayer." A 6–3 Court, this time using the *Lemon* test, found that the state law violated the religion clauses because the purpose of the statute was to advance religion. WALLACE v. JAFFREE, 472 U.S. 38 (1985). A New Jersey "moment of silence" statute reached the Supreme Court in 1987, but the case was dismissed because the parties bringing the case no longer had standing. Karcher v. May, 484 U.S. 72 (1987).

The constitutionality of graduation prayers split the Court 5–4 in 1992. The case involved the practice in Rhode Island middle and high schools of inviting members of the clergy to give invocations and benedictions at school graduation ceremonies. School officials advised speakers that the invocations and benedictions should be nonsectarian. Because of that fact, the Court concluded that state officials were directing the performance of a formal religious exercise, resulting in a state-sponsored and state-directed activity. The school principal selected the religious participant and provided guidelines on the content of the prayer. Such activities were proscribed by *Engel* v. *Vitale* and earlier decisions. The fact that graduation exercise were "voluntary" did not permit school officials to use indirect coercion against students and parents who wanted to attend a very significant event but objected to religious exercises. The Court distinguished between the school prayers at issue in this case (involving young people subject to indoctrination and peer pressure) with the prayers earlier allowed in adult institutions such as the Nebraska legislature and the U.S. Congress. LEE v. WEISMAN, 505 U.S. 577 (1992).

States continued to use other methods to bring prayers into graduation exercises. A Texas school district permitted public high school seniors to choose student volunteers to deliver nonsectarian, nonproselytizing invocations at their graduation ceremonies. Unlike *Lee* v. *Weisman,* outside clergy were not invited nor did school officials become involved in directing or monitoring the content of these prayers. The Fifth Circuit upheld the Texas practice in 1992; a year later the Supreme Court let this decision stand without comment. Jones v. Clear Creek Independent School Dist., 977 F.2d 963 (5th Cir. 1992), cert. denied, 508 U.S. 967 (1993). The District of Columbia decided in 1993 to permit student-led prayers at graduation exercises. Washington Post, June 17, 1993, at D1.

The issue of school prayer returned to the Court in 2000 when it ruled, 6 to 3, that prayers led by students at high school football games are unconstitutional when they are officially sanctioned. Rejecting the arguments that the prayers were voluntary and private, the Court

President Clinton's Memorandum on Religious Expression in Public Schools

. . .

I share the concern and frustration that many Americans feel about situations where the protections accorded by the First Amendment are not recognized or understood. This problem has manifested itself in our Nation's public schools. It appears that some school officials, teachers and parents have assumed that religious expression of any type is either inappropriate, or forbidden altogether, in public schools.

As our courts have affirmed, however, nothing in the First Amendment converts our public schools into religion-free zones, or requires all religious expression to be left behind at the schoolhouse door. While the government may not use schools to coerce the consciences of our students, or to convey official endorsement of religion, the government's schools also may not discriminate against private religious expression during the school day.

I have been advised by the Department of Justice and the Department of Education that the First Amendment permits—and protects—a greater degree of religious expression in public schools than many Americans may now understand....The following principles are among those that apply to religious expression in our schools:

Student prayer and religious discussion: The Establishment Clause of the First Amendment does not prohibit purely private religious speech by students. Students therefore have the same right to engage in individual or group prayer and religious instruction during the school day as they do to engage in other comparable activity. For example, students may read their Bibles or other scriptures, say grace before meals, and pray before tests to the same extent they may engage in comparable non-disruptive activities. Local school authorities possess substantial discretion to impose rules of order and other pedagogical restrictions on student activities, but they may not structure or administer such rules to discriminate against religious activity or speech.

Generally, students may pray in a nondisruptive manner when not engaged in school activities or instruction, and subject to the rules that normally pertain to the applicable setting. Specifically, students in informal settings, such as cafeterias and hallways, may pray and discuss their religious views with each other, subject to the same rules or order as apply to other student activities and speech. Students may also speak to, and attempt to persuade, their peers about religious topics just as they do with regard to political topics. School officials, however, should intercede to stop student speech that constitutes harassment aimed at a student or a group of students....

Graduation prayer and baccalaureates: Under current Supreme Court decisions, school officials may not mandate or organize prayer at graduation, nor organize religious baccalaureate ceremonies. If a school generally opens its facilities to private groups, it must make its facilities available on the same terms to organizers of privately sponsored religious baccalaureate services. A school may not extent preferential treatment to baccalaureate ceremonies and may in some instances be obliged to disclaim official endorsement of such ceremonies.

Official neutrality regarding religious activity: Teachers and school administrators, when acting in those capacities, are representatives of the state and are prohibited by the establishment clause from soliciting or encouraging religious activity, and from participating in such activity with students. Teachers and administrators also are prohibited from discouraging activity because of its religious content, and from soliciting or encouraging antireligious activity.

Teaching about religion: Public schools may not provide religious instruction, but they may teach *about* religion, including the Bible or other scripture: the history of religion, comparative religion, the Bible (or other scripture)-as-literature, and the role of religion in the history of the United States and other countries are all permissible public school subjects....

SOURCE: Public Papers of the Presidents, 1995, II, 1083–85.

regarded the prayers as "authorized by a government policy and take place on government property at government-sponsored school-related events." SANTA FE INDEPENDENT SCHOOL DIST. v. DOE, 120 S.Ct. 2266 (2000). Although school authorities cannot organize student-led prayers to be given over the public address system, nothing can stop students from standing up to give prayers at the start of a football game, or other sporting event, if the prayers seem spontaneous and undirected.

Responses by Congress and the President

Although President Reagan lost no time in 1981 in stating that the Court had "ruled wrongly" on school prayer, his administration never confronted the Court on *Engel*. Instead, Justice Department officials merely argued in favor of a moment of silence or voluntary prayer. Reagan never embraced state-mandated school prayers. While remarking in 1982 that "God should [never] have been expelled from the classroom," his proposed constitutional amendment simply proposed that nothing should be construed to prohibit individual or group prayer in public schools and that no person shall be required to participate in prayer. Public Papers of the Presidents, 1982, I, 603, 647–48. This language did not repudiate *Engel*; it supported it.

Several times Congress has considered legislation to permit voluntary prayer by school children. These bills sometimes propose that federal courts be denied jurisdiction to enter any judgment, decree, or order denying or restricting voluntary prayer in any public school. Such bills have never been adopted. In 1971, the House of Representatives voted 240 to 162 for an amendment to permit voluntary prayer or meditation in public buildings. The vote was 28 votes shy of the two-thirds needed. Reagan's proposed constitutional amendment for voluntary prayer failed in 1984, eleven votes short. In June 1998, the House of Representatives voted 224 to 203 for a constitutional amendment to permit voluntary prayer. The effort fell short by 61 votes. The proposed language was fully consistent with *Engel* because government was not to "initiate or designate school prayers." For all the fulmination against the Court's ruling in 1962, religious groups remain largely in support of that decision.

In 1995, in an effort to take some of the steam out of a proposed school prayer amendment, President Bill Clinton issued a memorandum to clarify the rights of public school children to religious expression. As he notes, children may engage in individual or group prayer and religious discussion during the school day and participate in events, before and after school, with religious content (see box on previous page). Studies indicate that students in public schools are active in prayer clubs and other religious activities, and a number of public schools offer classes that study the Bible as history and literature. States are experimenting with ways of posting the Ten Commandments without violating the Establishment Clause.

Engel v. Vitale

370 U.S. 421 (1962)

The New York Board of Regents composed a prayer to be recited in public schools. A group of parents brought action against the state. The parent named first in the suit was Steven I. Engel, who sued William J. Vitale and other members of the Board of Education of Union Free School District. The New York courts upheld the "Regents' prayer," provided that pupils were not compelled to join in the prayer over their objections or the objections of their parents.

MR. JUSTICE BLACK delivered the opinion of the Court.

The respondent Board of Education of Union Free School District No. 9, New Hyde Park, New

York, acting in its official capacity under state law, directed the School District's principal to cause the following prayer to be said aloud by each class in the presence of a teacher at the beginning of each school day:

"Almighty God, we acknowledge our dependence upon Thee, and we beg Thy blessings upon us, our parents, our teachers and our Country."

This daily procedure was adopted on the recommendation of the State Board of Regents, a governmental agency created by the State Constitution to which the New York Legislature has granted broad supervisory, executive, and legislative powers over the State's public school system. These state officials composed the prayer which they recommended and published as a part of their "Statement on Moral and Spiritual Training in the Schools," saying: "We believe that this Statement will be subscribed to by all men and women of good will, and we call upon all of them to aid in giving life to our program."

. . .

We think that by using its public school system to encourage recitation of the Regents' prayer, the State of New York has adopted a practice wholly inconsistent with the Establishment Clause. There can, of course, be no doubt that New York's program of daily classroom invocation of God's blessings as prescribed in the Regents' prayer is a religious activity. It is a solemn avowal of divine faith and supplication for the blessings of the Almighty....

The petitioners contend among other things that the state laws requiring or permitting use of the Regents' prayer must be struck down as a violation of the Establishment Clause because that prayer was composed by governmental officials as a part of a governmental program to further religious beliefs. For this reason, petitioners argue, the State's use of the Regents' prayer in its public school system breaches the constitutional wall of separation between Church and State. We agree with that contention since we think that the constitutional prohibition against laws respecting an establishment of religion must at least mean that in this country it is no part of the business of government to compose official prayers for any group of the American people to recite as a part of a religious program carried on by government.

It is a matter of history that this very practice of establishing governmentally composed prayers for religious services was one of the reasons which caused many of our early colonists to leave England and seek religious freedom in America. The Book of Common Prayer, which was created under governmental direction and which was approved by Acts of Parliament in 1548 and 1549, set out in minute detail the accepted form and content of prayer and other religious ceremonies to be used in the established, tax-supported Church of England. The controversies over the Book and what should be its content repeatedly threatened to disrupt the peace of that country as the accepted forms of prayer in the established church changed with the views of the particular ruler that happened to be in control at the time....

It is an unfortunate fact of history that when some of the very groups which had most strenuously opposed the established Church of England found themselves sufficiently in control of colonial governments in this country to write their own prayers into law, they passed laws making their own religion the official religion of their respective colonies....

. . .

There can be no doubt that New York's state prayer program officially establishes the religious beliefs embodied in the Regents' prayer. The respondents' argument to the contrary, which is largely based upon the contention that the Regents' prayer is "non-denominational" and the fact that the program, as modified and approved by state courts, does not require all pupils to recite the prayer but permits those who wish to do so to remain silent or be excused from the room, ignores the essential nature of the program's constitutional defects. Neither the fact that the prayer may be denominationally neutral nor the fact that its observance on the part of the students is voluntary can serve to free it from the limitations of the Establishment Clause, as it might from the Free Exercise Clause, of the First Amendment, both of which are operative against the States by virtue of the Fourteenth Amendment.... When the power, prestige and financial support of government is placed behind a particular religious belief, the indirect coercive pressure upon religious minorities to conform to the prevailing officially approved religion is plain. But the purposes underlying the Establishment Clause go much further than that. Its first and most immediate purpose rested on the belief that a union of government and religion tends to destroy government and to degrade religion. The history of governmentally established religion, both in England and in this country, showed that whenever government had allied itself with one particular form of religion, the inevitable result had been that it had incurred the hatred, disrespect and even contempt of those who held contrary beliefs. That same history showed that many people had lost their respect for any religion that had relied upon the support of government to spread its faith. The Establishment Clause thus stands as an expression of principle on the part of the Founders of our Constitution that religion is too personal, too sacred, too holy, to permit its "unhallowed perversion" by a civil magistrate. Another purpose of the Establishment Clause rested upon an awareness of the historical fact that governmentally established religions and religious persecutions go hand in hand. . . .

It has been argued that to apply the Constitution in such a way as to prohibit state laws respecting an establishment of religious services in public schools is to indicate a hostility toward religion or toward prayer. Nothing, of course, could be more wrong. The history of man is inseparable from the history of religion. . . . It is neither sacrilegious nor antireligious to say that each separate government in this country should stay out of the business of writing or sanctioning official prayers and leave that purely religious function to the people themselves and to those the people choose to look to for religious guidance.

. . .

The judgment of the Court of Appeals of New York is reversed and the cause remanded for further proceedings not inconsistent with this opinion.

Reversed and remanded.

MR. JUSTICE FRANKFURTER took no part in the decision of this case.

MR. JUSTICE WHITE took no part in the consideration or decision of this case.

MR. JUSTICE DOUGLAS, concurring.

. . .

MR. JUSTICE STEWART, dissenting.

. . . I cannot see how an "official religion" is established by letting those who want to say a prayer say it. On the contrary, I think that to deny the wish of these school children to join in reciting this prayer is to deny them the opportunity of sharing in the spiritual heritage of our Nation.

The Court's historical review of the quarrels over the Book of Common Prayer in England

throws no light for me on the issue before us in this case. England had then and has now an established church. Equally unenlightening, I think, is the history of the early establishment and later rejection of an official church in our own States. For we deal here not with the establishment of a state church, which would, of course, be constitutionally impermissible, but with whether school children who want to begin their day by joining in prayer must be prohibited from doing so. Moreover, I think that the Court's task, in this as in all areas of constitutional adjudication, is not responsibly aided by the uncritical invocation of metaphors like the "wall of separation," a phrase nowhere to be found in the Constitution. What is relevant to the issue here is not the history of an established church in sixteenth century England or in eighteenth century America, but the history of the religious traditions of our people, reflected in countless practices of the institutions and officials of our government.

At the opening of each day's Session of this Court we stand, while one of our officials invokes the protection of God. Since the days of John Marshall our Crier has said, "God save the United States and this Honorable Court." Both the Senate and the House of Representatives open their daily Sessions with prayer. Each of our Presidents, from George Washington to John F. Kennedy, has upon assuming his Office asked the protection and help of God.

The Court today says that the state and federal governments are without constitutional power to prescribe any particular form of words to be recited by any group of the American people on any subject touching religion. One of the stanzas of "The Star-Spangled Banner," made our National Anthem by Act of Congress in 1931, contains these verses:

> "Blest with victory and peace, may the
>   heav'n rescued land
> Praise the Pow'r that hath made and pre-
>   served us a nation!
> Then conquer we must, when our cause it is
>   just,
> And this be our motto 'In God is our Trust.' "

In 1954 Congress added a phrase to the Pledge of Allegiance to the Flag so that it now contains the words "one Nation *under God,* indivisible, with liberty and justice for all." In 1952 Congress enacted legislation calling upon the President each year to proclaim a National Day of Prayer. Since

1865 the words "IN GOD WE TRUST" have been impressed on our coins.

Countless similar examples could be listed, but there is no need to belabor the obvious. It was all summed up by this Court just ten years ago in a single sentence: "We are a religious people whose institutions presuppose a Supreme Being." *Zorach* v. *Clauson,* 343 U. S. 306, 313.

. . .

Congressional Hearings on School Prayer (1964)

After the Supreme Court in *Engel* v. *Vitale* (1962) struck down state efforts to require students in public schools to recite an official state prayer, many members of Congress introduced constitutional amendments to permit school prayer. Some legislators may have assumed that their initiative would appeal to organized religion, but hearings conducted in 1964 by the House Judiciary Committee revealed broad opposition by Protestant, Catholic, and Jewish organizations. The groups testifying against a constitutional amendment included the American Baptist Convention, the American Jewish Congress, the American Lutheran Church, the Episcopal Church, the National Council of Churches of Christ, the Synagogue Council of America, and the United Presbyterian Church. The testimony below is by Dr. Edwin H. Tuller, General Secretary, American Baptist Convention, speaking on behalf of the National Council of Churches. These hearings underscore the linkage between constitutional law and the attitudes and values of the private sector.

DR. TULLER:...As a result of the Supreme Court decision on the regents' prayer, many constitutional amendments had been proposed by Members of Congress at the time the general board *[of the National Council of Churches]* met, which do not differ appreciably from those now before this committee. In reference to such efforts to rewrite the first amendment, the general board said:

"We express the conviction that the first amendment to our Constitution *in its present wording* has provided the framework within which responsible citizens and our courts have been able to afford maximum protection for the religious liberty of all our citizens." [Emphasis added.]

The general board did not single out a specific proposed amendment for comment, but they were in effect rejecting the current proposals to rewrite the first amendment.

Many people assume that church leaders would of course favor anything designed to "aid religion," and some do not understand why they do not favor prayer and Bible reading in public schools. "What harm can it do"? they ask. It is not possible to know the mind of all members of the general board, but some of them expressed their convictions in debate or discussion on such points as these:

(a) Public institutions belong to all citizens, whatever their religious beliefs or lack of them; it is not right for the majority to impose religious beliefs or practices on the minority in public institutions when adequate provisions are available for those who desire to do so to express such beliefs and follow such practices in nonpublic settings with others of like mind;

(b) Because of American religious variety, our public schools are particularly inappropriate places for corporate religious exercises. Young and impressionable children from a wide variety of religious backgrounds and from no religious background at all, are present not by choice, but by compulsion of law and are not genuinely free to decide for themselves whether or not they will participate. Many of them are thus compelled to choose between the religious or (nonreligious) intentions of their parents and the expectations of their teachers and fellow pupils;

(c) In such a setting, children are almost always not given a genuinely free choice by glib use of the words "voluntary participation," when the whole atmosphere of the classroom is one of compliance and conformity to group activities.

When the teacher (or a group of pupils) selects a prayer or Bible reading, and all or most of the class members participate in it, at a time and in a procedure instituted by the teacher as the adult bearer of the authority of the public school, it is a rare child indeed who will isolate himself from his fellows by declining to participate. Thus a subtle but no less effective form of duress is present which should never blight the act of worship.

If a completely spontaneous effort should arise among devout children of a fairly uniform religious heritage, we doubt that police action of any community would interfere. We equally doubt that the Bill of Rights has to be amended to permit this possibility, since it already guarantees the "free exercise" of religion.

(d) Who is to compose the prayers, and who is to select the Scriptures? What form of the Lord's Prayer will be used, and which version of the Bible? In those who take their faith seriously, these things are important. They do not consider all prayers or Scriptures interchangeable. Many devout Christians do not want their children to conclude that their transactions with the Most High are something routine, casual, and indiscriminate, in the same category with algebra and spelling;

(e) What a nonsectarian theistic majority can require today in the way of a regents prayer or Bible reading "without comment" a sectarian majority can require tomorrow in the way of an Augsburg Confession, a "Hail, Mary" or a theistic tract. These things are best not subject to a majority decision, but left to the free choice of each person at the time and place his conscience directs;

(f) Religious practices that are nonsectarian are too vague and generalized to have much meaning or effect for character development or moral motivation; whereas practices which are specific or demanding enough to effect character or motivation are unacceptable to some and therefore sectarian.

As the pronouncement says:

"Major faith groups have not agreed on a formulation of religious beliefs common to all. Even if they had done so, such a body of religious doctrine would tend to become a substitute for the more demanding commitments of historic faiths."

The United Presbyterian General Assembly has said:

"Bible reading and prayers as devotional acts in public schools tend toward indoctrination or meaningless ritual and should be omitted for both reasons." ("Relations Between Church and State," p. 7.)

(g) Protestants believe that prayer can be effectively addressed to God by any believer at any time and in any place. It does not have to be oral or formal, it does not have to be in unison or collective, it does not require a set garb or posture. Any and all children can pray to God in public schools or anywhere else at any time, and no one can stop them.

It is not necessary, however, that the children who happen to be assigned to the same classroom should stop what they are doing to pray with them. God will hear and answer the prayer of one child, though his petition be uttered in the secret places of his inmost self. The effectiveness and the availability of prayer are not enhanced by the intervention of the agencies of the public school or government; in fact, the reverse is as likely to be the case.

(h) Many Christians see in routine formal corporate rituals in public schools at least the danger against which their Lord warned in the Sermon on the Mount—that what begins as a spontaneous and sincere outpouring of devotion can become a public display of hypocrisy, making a show of piety.

For these reasons and others, the leadership of the major Protestant churches, men and women who have given their lives to seek the will of God and attempt to do it, and who have been entrusted by their fellow seekers with position of responsibility and trust, are not convinced, by and large, that God desires an attenuated and conventional worship administered in public school classrooms by the State.

They are not requesting or demanding it on behalf of the churches and churchmen whom they have been called to lead. And most of them are opposed to jeopardizing our long cherished freedom to worship God as conscience dictates by tampering with the first amendment.

Edwards v. Aguillard

482 U.S. 578 (1987)

Don Aguillard and other parents of children attending public schools in Louisiana, together with teachers and religious leaders, brought this suit against Governor Edwin W.

Edwards and Louisiana officials. They challenged a state law that prohibited the teaching of the theory of evolution in public elementary and secondary schools unless accompanied by instruction in the theory of "creation science" (the biblical belief in the abrupt appearance of life in complex form). The plaintiffs attacked the statute as a violation of the Establishment Clause because it promoted a particular religious belief. A federal district court held the statute unconstitutional. The Fifth Circuit affirmed.

JUSTICE BRENNAN delivered the opinion of the Court.

The question for decision is whether Louisiana's "Balanced Treatment for Creation-Science and Evolution-Science in Public School Instruction" Act (Creationism Act), La.Rev.Stat. Ann. §§ 17:286.1– 17:286.7 (West 1982), is facially invalid as violative of the Establishment Clause of the First Amendment.

I

The Creationism Act forbids the teaching of the theory of evolution in public schools unless accompanied by instruction in "creation science." § 17:286.4A. No school is required to teach evolution or creation science. If either is taught, however, the other must also be taught. *Ibid.* The theories of evolution and creation science are statutorily defined as "the scientific evidences for [creation or evolution] and inferences from those scientific evidences." §§ 17.286.3(2) and (3).

. . .

III

Lemon's first prong focuses on the purpose that animated adoption of the Act. "The purpose prong of the *Lemon* test asks whether government's actual purpose is to endorse or disapprove of religion." . . . In this case, the petitioners have identified no clear secular purpose for the Louisiana Act.

True, the Act's stated purpose is to protect academic freedom. La.Rev.Stat.Ann. § 17:286.2 (West 1982). This phrase might, in common parlance, be understood as referring to enhancing the freedom of teachers to teach what they will. The Court of Appeals, however, correctly concluded that the Act was not designed to further that goal. We find no merit in the State's argument that the "legislature may not [have] use[d] the terms 'academic freedom' in the correct legal sense. They might have [had] in mind, instead, a basic concept of fairness; teaching all of the evidence." Tr. of Oral Arg. 60. Even if "academic freedom" is read to mean "teaching all of the evidence" with respect to the origin of human beings, the Act does not further this purpose. The goal of providing a more comprehensive science curriculum is not furthered either by outlawing the teaching of evolution or by requiring the teaching of creation science.

A

While the Court is normally deferential to a State's articulation of a secular purpose, it is required that the statement of such purpose be sincere and not a sham. . . .

It is clear from the legislative history that the purpose of the legislative sponsor, Senator Bill Keith, was to narrow the science curriculum. During the legislative hearings, Senator Keith stated: "My preference would be that neither [creationism nor evolution] be taught." 2 App. E621. Such a ban on teaching does not promote—indeed, it undermines—the provision of a comprehensive scientific education.

It is equally clear that requiring schools to teach creation science with evolution does not advance academic freedom. The Act does not grant teachers a flexibility that they did not already possess to supplant the present science curriculum with the presentation of theories, besides evolution, about the origin of life. Indeed, the Court of Appeals found that no law prohibited Louisiana public schoolteachers from teaching any scientific theory. 765 F.2d, at 1257. As the president of the Louisiana Science Teachers Association testified, "[a]ny scientific concept that's based on established fact can be included in our curriculum already, and no legislation allowing this is necessary." 2 App. E616. The Act provides Louisiana schoolteachers with no new authority. Thus the stated purpose is not furthered by it.

. . .

Furthermore, the goal of basic "fairness" is hardly furthered by the Act's discriminatory preference for the teaching of creation science and against the teaching of evolution. While requiring that curriculum guides be developed for creation science, the Act says nothing of comparable guides for evolution. La.Rev.Stat.Ann. § 17:286.7A (West 1982). Similarly, research services are supplied for creation science but not for evolution. § 17:286.7B. Only "creation scientists" can serve on the panel that supplies the resource services. *Ibid.* The Act forbids school boards to discriminate against anyone who "chooses to be a creation-scientist" or to teach "creationism," but fails to protect those who choose to teach evolution or any other noncreation science theory, or who refuse to teach creation science. § 17:286.4C.

. . .

B

. . . [W]e need not be blind in this case to the legislature's preeminent religious purpose in enacting this statute. There is a historic and contemporaneous link between the teachings of certain religious denominations and the teaching of evolution. It was this link that concerned the Court in *Epperson* v. *Arkansas,* 393 U.S. 97 (1968). . . .

Senator Keith's leading expert on creation science, Edward Boudreaux, testified at the legislative hearings that the theory of creation science included belief in the existence of a supernatural creator. See 1 App. E421–422 (noting that "creation scientists" point to high probability that life was "created by an intelligent mind"). Senator Keith also cited testimony from other experts to support the creation-science view that "a creator [was] responsible for the universe and everything in it." . . .

V

The Louisiana Creationism Act advances a religious doctrine by requiring either the banishment of the theory of evolution from public school classrooms or the presentation of a religious viewpoint that rejects evolution in its entirety. The Act violates the Establishment Clause of the First Amendment because it seeks to employ the symbolic and financial support of government to achieve a religious purpose. The judgment of the Court of Appeals therefore is

Affirmed.

JUSTICE POWELL, with whom JUSTICE O'CONNOR joins, concurring.

I write separately to note certain aspects of the legislative history, and to emphasize that nothing in the Court's opinion diminishes the traditionally broad discretion accorded state and local school officials in the selection of the public school curriculum.

. . .

JUSTICE WHITE, concurring in the judgment.

. . .

JUSTICE SCALIA, with whom THE CHIEF JUSTICE joins, dissenting.

Even if I agreed with the questionable premise that legislation can be invalidated under the Establishment Clause on the basis of its motivation alone, without regard to its effects, I would still find no justification for today's decision. The Louisiana legislators who passed the "Balanced Treatment for Creation-Science and Evolution-Science Act" (Balanced Treatment Act), La.Rev. Stat.Ann. §§ 17:286.1–17:286.7 (West 1982), each of whom had sworn to support the Constitution, were well aware of the potential Establishment Clause problems and considered that aspect of the legislation with great care. After seven hearings and several months of study, resulting in substantial revision of the original proposal, they approved the Act overwhelmingly and specifically articulated the secular purpose they meant it to serve. Although the record contains abundant evidence of the sincerity of that purpose (the only issue pertinent to this case), the Court today holds, essentially on the basis of "its visceral knowledge regarding what *must* have motivated the legislators," 778 F.2d 225, 227 (CA5 1985) (Gee, J., dissenting) (emphasis added), that the members of the Louisiana Legislature knowingly violated their oaths and then lied about it. . . .

I

This case arrives here in the following posture: The Louisiana Supreme Court has never been given an opportunity to interpret the Balanced Treatment Act, State officials have never attempted to implement it, and it has never been the subject of a full evidentiary hearing. We can only guess at its meaning. We know that it forbids instruction in either "creation-science" or "evolution-science" without instruction in the other, § 17:286.4A, but the parties are sharply divided over what creation science consists of. Appellants insist that it is a collection of educationally valuable scientific data that has been censored from classrooms by an embarrassed scientific establishment. Appellees insist it is not science at all but thinly veiled religious doctrine. Both interpretations of the intended meaning of that phrase find considerable support in the legislative history.

At least at this stage in the litigation, it is plain

to me that we must accept appellants' view of what the statute means. To begin with, the statute itself *defines* "creation-science" as "the *scientific evidences* for creation and inferences from those *scientific evidences.*" § 17:286.3(2) (emphasis added). If, however, that definition is not thought sufficiently helpful, the means by which the Louisiana Supreme Court will give the term more precise content is quite clear—and again, at this stage in the litigation, favors the appellants' view. "Creation science" is unquestionably a "term of art," see Brief for 72 Nobel Laureates, et al. as *Amici Curiae* 20, and thus, under Louisiana law, is "to be interpreted according to [its] received meaning and acceptation with the learned in the art, trade or profession to which [it] refer[s]." La.Civ. Code Ann., Art. 15 (West 1952). The only

evidence in the record of the "received meaning and acceptation" of "creation science" is found in five affidavits filed by appellants. In those affidavits, two scientists, a philosopher, a theologian, and an educator, all of whom claim extensive knowledge of creation science, swear that it is essentially a collection of scientific data supporting the theory that the physical universe and life within it appeared suddenly and have not changed substantially since appearing.... These experts insist that creation science is a strictly scientific concept that can be presented without religious reference.... At this point, then, we must assume that the Balanced Treatment Act does *not* require the presentation of religious doctrine.

. . .

Wallace v. Jaffree

472 U.S. 38 (1985)

Alabama passed legislation authorizing a one-minute period of silence in all public schools "for meditation or voluntary prayer." It also authorized teachers to lead "willing students" in a prescribed prayer to "Almighty God...the Creator and Supreme Judge of the world." A federal district court upheld the statute, concluding that Alabama could establish a state religion if it wanted to. This ruling was reversed by the Eleventh Circuit. Ishmael Jaffree, a citizen of Alabama and parent of children in public schools, initiated the suit. The appellant is George C. Wallace, Governor of Alabama.

JUSTICE STEVENS delivered the opinion of the Court.

At an early stage of this litigation, the constitutionality of three Alabama statutes was questioned: (1) § 16-1-20, enacted in 1978, which authorized a 1-minute period of silence in all public schools "for meditation"; (2) § 16-1-20.1, enacted in 1981, which authorized a period of silence "for meditation or voluntary prayer"; and (3) § 16-1-20.2, enacted in 1982, which authorized teachers to lead "willing students" in a prescribed prayer to "Almighty God...the Creator and Supreme Judge...of the world."

. . .

...[T]he narrow question for decision is whether § 16-1-20.1, which authorizes a period of silence for "meditation or voluntary prayer," is a law respecting the establishment of religion within the meaning of the First Amendment.

. . .

III

. . .

It is the first of these three *[Lemon]* criteria that is most plainly implicated by this case. As the District Court correctly recognized, no consideration of the second or third criteria is necessary if a statute does not have a clearly secular purpose. For even though a statute that is motivated in part by a religious purpose may satisfy the first criterion,...the First Amendment requires that a statute must be invalidated if it is entirely motivated by a purpose to advance religion.

In applying the purpose test, it is appropriate to ask "whether government's actual purpose is to endorse or disapprove of religion." In this case, the answer to that question is dispositive. For the record not only provides us with an unambiguous affirmative answer, but it also reveals that the enactment of § 16-1-20.1 was not motivated by any clearly secular purpose—indeed, the statute had *no* secular purpose.

IV

The sponsor of the bill that became § 16-1-20.1, Senator Donald Holmes, inserted into the legislative record — apparently without dissent — a statement indicating that the legislation was an "effort to return voluntary prayer" to the public schools. Later Senator Holmes confirmed this purpose before the District Court. In response to the question whether he had any purpose for the legislation other than returning voluntary prayer to public schools, he stated: "No, I did not have no other purpose in mind." The State did not present evidence of *any* secular purpose.

The unrebutted evidence of legislative intent contained in the legislative record and in the testimony of the sponsor of § 16-1-20.1 is confirmed by a consideration of the relationship between this statute and the two other measures that were considered in this case. The District Court found that the 1981 statute and its 1982 sequel had a common, nonsecular purpose. The wholly religious character of the later enactment is plainly evident from its text. When the differences between § 16-1-20.1 and its 1978 predecessor, § 16-1-20, are examined, it is equally clear that the 1981 statute has the same wholly religious character.

There are only three textual differences between § 16-1-20.1 and § 16-1-20: (1) the earlier statute applies only to grades one through six, whereas § 16-1-20.1 applies to all grades; (2) the earlier statute uses the word "shall" whereas § 16-1-20.1 uses the word "may"; (3) the earlier statute refers only to "meditation" whereas § 16-1-20.1 refers to "meditation or voluntary prayer." The first difference is of no relevance in this litigation because the minor appellees were in kindergarten or second grade during the 1981–1982 academic year. The second difference would also have no impact on this litigation because the mandatory language of § 16-1-20 continued to apply to grades one through six. Thus, the only significant textual difference is the addition of the words "or voluntary prayer."

The legislative intent to return prayer to the public schools is, of course, quite different from merely protecting every student's right to engage in voluntary prayer during an appropriate moment of silence during the schoolday. The 1978 statute already protected that right, containing nothing that prevented any student from engaging in voluntary prayer during a silent minute of meditation. Appellants have not identified any secular purpose that was not fully served by § 16-1-20 before the enactment of § 16-1-20.1. Thus, only two conclusions are consistent with the text of § 16-1-20.1: (1) the statute was enacted to convey a message of State endorsement and promotion of prayer; or (2) the statute was enacted for no purpose. No one suggests that the statute was nothing but a meaningless or irrational act.

We must, therefore, conclude that the Alabama Legislature intended to change existing law and that it was motivated by the same purpose that the Governor's answer to the second amended complaint expressly admitted; that the statement inserted in the legislative history revealed; and that Senator Holmes' testimony frankly described. The legislature enacted § 16-1-20.1, despite the existence of § 16-1-20 for the sole purpose of expressing the State's endorsement of prayer activities for one minute at the beginning of each schoolday. The addition of "or voluntary prayer" indicates that the State intended to characterize prayer as a favored practice. Such an endorsement is not consistent with the established principle that the government must pursue a course of complete neutrality toward religion.

. . .

The judgment of the Court of Appeals is affirmed.

It is so ordered.

JUSTICE POWELL, concurring.

I concur in the Court's opinion and judgment that Ala. Code § 16-1-20.1 (Supp. 1984) violates the Establishment Clause of the First Amendment. My concurrence is prompted by Alabama's persistence in attempting to institute state-sponsored prayer in the public schools by enacting three successive statutes. I agree fully with JUSTICE O'CONNOR's assertion that some moment-of-silence statutes may be constitutional, a suggestion set forth in the Court's opinion as well....

JUSTICE O'CONNOR, concurring in the judgment.

...I agree with the judgment of the Court that, in light of the findings of the courts below and the history of its enactment, § 16-1-20.1 of the Alabama Code violates the Establishment Clause of the First Amendment. In my view, there can be little doubt that the purpose and likely effect of this subsequent enactment is to endorse and sponsor voluntary prayer in the public schools. I write separately to identify the peculiar features of the Alabama law that render it invalid, and to explain why moment of silence laws in other States do not necessarily manifest the same infirmity. I also write to explain why neither history nor the Free Exercise Clause of the First Amendment validates the Alabama law struck down by the Court today.

I

. . .

It once appeared that the Court had developed a workable standard by which to identify impermissible government establishments of religion. See *Lemon* v. *Kurtzman,* 403 U.S. 602 (1971).... Despite its initial promise, the *Lemon* test has proven problematic. The required inquiry into "entanglement" has been modified and questioned, see *Mueller* v. *Allen,* 463 U.S. 388, 403, n. 11 (1983), and in one case we have upheld state action against an Establishment Clause challenge without applying the *Lemon* test at all. *Marsh* v. *Chambers,* 463 U. S. 783 (1983). The author of *Lemon* himself apparently questions the test's general applicability. See *Lynch* v. *Donnelly,* 465 U. S. 668, 679 (1984). JUSTICE REHNQUIST today suggests that we abandon *Lemon* entirely....

Perhaps because I am new to the struggle, I am not ready to abandon all aspects of the *Lemon* test. I do believe, however, that the standards announced in *Lemon* should be reexamined and refined in order to make them more useful in achieving the underlying purpose of the First Amendment....

. . .

II

...When the intent of the Framers is unclear, I believe we must employ both history and reason in our analysis. The primary issue raised by JUSTICE REHNQUIST's dissent is whether the historical fact that our Presidents have long called for public prayers of Thanks should be dispositive on the constitutionality of prayer in public schools. I think not. At the very least, Presidential Proclamations are distinguishable from school prayer in that they are received in a noncoercive setting and are primarily directed at adults, who presumably are not readily susceptible to unwilling religious indoctrination....

CHIEF JUSTICE BURGER, dissenting.

. . .

I make several points about today's curious holding.

(a) It makes no sense to say that Alabama has "endorsed prayer" by merely enacting a new statute "to specify expressly that voluntary prayer is *one* of the authorized activities during a moment of silence," ... (O'CONNOR, J., concurring in judgment) (emphasis added). To suggest that a moment-of-silence statute that includes the word "prayer" unconstitutionally endorses religion, while one that simply provides for a moment of silence does not, manifests not neutrality but hostility toward religion....

Curiously, the opinions do not mention that *all* of the sponsor's statements relied upon—including the statement "inserted" into the Senate Journal—were made *after* the legislature had passed the statute; indeed, the testimony that the Court finds critical was given well over a year after the statute was enacted. As even the appellees concede, ... there is not a shred of evidence that the legislature as a whole shared the sponsor's motive or that a majority in either house was even aware of the sponsor's view of the bill when it was passed....

JUSTICE WHITE, dissenting.

For the most part agreeing with the opinion of THE CHIEF JUSTICE, I dissent from the Court's judgment invalidating Ala. Code § 16-1-20.1 (Supp. 1984). Because I do, it is apparent that in my view the First Amendment does not proscribe either (1) statutes authorizing or requiring in so many words a moment of silence before classes begin or (2) a statute that provides, when it is initially passed, for a moment of silence for meditation or prayer....

JUSTICE REHNQUIST, dissenting.

[Rehnquist devotes fifteen pages to the history of the adoption of the Bill of Rights, especially the Religion Clauses in the First Amendment. He concludes that the Amendment was designed to prohibit the establishment of a national religion, and perhaps to prevent discrimination among sects, but did not require neutrality on the part of government between religion and irreligion. He also critiques the three-part test of Lemon v. Kurtzman.*]*

These difficulties arise because the *Lemon* test has no more grounding in the history of the First Amendment than does the wall theory upon which it rests. The three-part test represents a determined effort to craft a workable rule from a historically faulty doctrine; but the rule can only be as sound as the doctrine it attempts to service. The three-part test has simply not provided adequate standards for deciding Establishment Clause cases, as this Court has slowly come to realize. Even worse, the *Lemon* test has caused this Court to fracture into unworkable plurality opinions, . . . depending upon how each of the three factors applies to a certain state action. The results from our school services cases show the difficulty we have encountered in making the *Lemon* test yield principled results.

. . .

Lee v. Weisman

505 U.S. 577 (1992)

Principals of the public middle and high schools in Providence, Rhode Island, were permitted to invite members of the clergy to give invocations and benedictions at school graduation ceremonies. Robert E. Lee, a principal, invited a rabbi to offer prayers at a middle school graduation. Daniel Weisman, father of a daughter (Deborah) scheduled to graduate at those exercises, filed a suit to prevent school officials from including prayers in that ceremony. After that motion was denied, Daniel Weisman sought a permanent injunction to bar Lee and other public school officials from inviting clergy to deliver invocations and benedictions at future graduations, including Deborah's high school graduation. A federal district court enjoined Lee from continuing the practice on the ground that it violated the Establishment Clause, and the First Circuit affirmed.

JUSTICE KENNEDY delivered the opinion of the Court.

. . .

I

A

. . .

It has been the custom of Providence school officials to provide invited clergy with a pamphlet entitled "Guidelines for Civic Occasions," prepared by the National Conference of Christians and Jews. The Guidelines recommend that public prayers at nonsectarian civic ceremonies be composed with "inclusiveness and sensitivity," though they acknowledge that "[p]rayer of any kind may be inappropriate on some civic occasions." App. 20–21. The principal gave Rabbi Gutterman the pamphlet before the graduation and advised him the invocation and benediction should be nonsectarian. Agreed Statement of Facts ¶ 17, *id.,* at 13.

Rabbi Gutterman's prayers were as follows:

"INVOCATION

"God of the Free, Hope of the Brave:
"For the legacy of America where diversity is celebrated and the rights of minorities are protected, we thank You. May these young men and women grow up to enrich it.

"For the liberty of America, we thank You. May these new graduates grow up to guard it.

"For the political process of America in which all its citizens may participate, for its court system where all may seek justice we thank You. May those we honor this morning always turn to it in trust.

"For the destiny of America we thank You. May the graduates of Nathan Bishop Middle School so live that they might help to share it.

"May our aspirations for our country and for these young people, who are our hope for the future, be richly fulfilled.

AMEN"

"BENEDICTION

"O God, we are grateful to You for having endowed us with the capacity for learning which we have celebrated on this joyous commencement.

"Happy families give thanks for seeing their children achieve an important milestone. Send Your blessings upon the teachers and administrators who helped prepare them.

"The graduates now need strength and guidance for the future, help them to understand that we are not complete with academic knowledge alone. We must each strive to fulfill what You require of us all: To do justly, to love mercy, to walk humbly.

"We give thanks to You, Lord, for keeping us alive, sustaining us and allowing us to reach this special, happy occasion.

AMEN"

. . .

II

These dominant facts mark and control the confines of our decision: State officials direct the performance of a formal religious exercise at promotional and graduation ceremonies for secondary schools. Even for those students who object to the religious exercise, their attendance and participation in the state-sponsored religious activity are in a fair and real sense obligatory, though the school district does not require attendance as a condition for receipt of the diploma.

. . . [T]he controlling precedents as they relate to prayer and religious exercise in primary and secondary public schools compel the holding here that the policy of the city of Providence is an unconstitutional one. . . . The government involvement with religious activity in this case is pervasive, to the point of creating a state-sponsored and state-directed religious exercise in a public school. Conducting this formal religious observance conflicts with settled rules pertaining to prayer exercises for students, and that suffices to determine the question before us.

The principle that government may accommodate the free exercise of religion does not supersede the fundamental limitations imposed by the Establishment Clause. It is beyond dispute that, at a minimum, the Constitution guarantees that government may not coerce anyone to support or participate in religion or its exercise, or otherwise act in a way which "establishes a [state] religion or religious faith, or tends to do so." *Lynch, supra,* at 678; see also *Allegheny County, supra,* at 591 quoting *Everson* v. *Board of Education of Ewing,* 330 U. S. 1, 15–16 (1947). The State's involvement in the school prayers challenged today violates these central principles.

That involvement is as troubling as it is undenied. A school official, the principal, decided that an invocation and a benediction should be given; this is a choice attributable to the State, and from a constitutional perspective it is as if a state statute decreed that the prayers must occur. The principal

chose the religious participant, here a rabbi, and that choice is also attributable to the State. The reason for the choice of a rabbi is not disclosed by the record, but the potential for divisiveness over the choice of a particular member of the clergy to conduct the ceremony is apparent.

Divisiveness, of course, can attend any state decision respecting religions, and neither its existence nor its potential necessarily invalidates the State's attempts to accommodate religion in all cases. The potential for divisiveness is of particular relevance here though, because it centers around an overt religious exercise in a secondary school environment where, as we discuss below, . . . subtle coercive pressures exist and where the student had no real alternative which would have allowed her to avoid the fact or appearance of participation.

The State's role did not end with the decision to include a prayer and with the choice of clergyman. Principal Lee provided Rabbi Gutterman with a copy of the "Guidelines for Civic Occasions," and advised him that his prayers should be nonsectarian. Through these means the principal directed and controlled the content of the prayer. Even if the only sanction for ignoring the instructions were that the rabbi would not be invited back, we think no religious representative who valued his or her continued reputation and effectiveness in the community would incur the State's displeasure in this regard. It is a cornerstone principle of our Establishment Clause jurisprudence that "it is no part of the business of government to compose official prayers for any group of the American people to recite as a part of a religious program carried on by government," *Engel* v. *Vitale,* 370 U. S. 421, 425 (1962), and that is what the school officials attempted to do.

Petitioners argue, and we find nothing in the case to refute it, that the directions for the content of the prayers were a good-faith attempt by the school to ensure that the sectarianism which is so often the flashpoint for religious animosity be removed from the graduation ceremony. . . . The question is not the good faith of the school in attempting to make the prayer acceptable to most persons, but the legitimacy of its undertaking that enterprise at all when the object is to produce a prayer to be used in a formal religious exercise which students, for all practical purposes, are obliged to attend.

. . .

. . . There can be no doubt that for many, if not most, of the students at the graduation, the act of standing or remaining silent was an expression of participation in the Rabbi's prayer. That was the very point of the religious exercise. It is of little comfort to a dissenter, then, to be told that for her the act of standing or remaining in silence signifies mere respect, rather than participation. What matters is that, given our social conventions, a reasonable dissenter in this milieu could believe that the group exercise signified her own participation or approval of it.

Finding no violation under these circumstances would place objectors in the dilemma of participating, with all that implies, or protesting. We do not address whether that choice is acceptable if the affected citizens are mature adults, but we think the State may not, consistent with the Establishment Clause, place primary and secondary school children in this position. Research in psychology supports the common assumption that adolescents are often susceptible to pressure from their peers towards conformity, and that the influence is strongest in matters of social convention.…

There was a stipulation in the District Court that attendance at graduation and promotional ceremonies is voluntary.… Petitioners and the United States, as *amicus,* made this a center point of the case, arguing that the option of not attending the graduation excuses any inducement or coercion in the ceremony itself. The argument lacks all persuasion. Law reaches past formalism. And to say a teenage student has a real choice not to attend her high school graduation is formalistic in the extreme. True, Deborah could elect not to attend commencement without renouncing her diploma; but we shall not allow the case to turn on this point. Everyone knows that in our society and in our culture high school graduation is one of life's most significant occasions. A school rule which excuses attendance is beside the point. Attendance may not be required by official decree, yet it is apparent that a student is not free to absent herself from the graduation exercise in any real sense of the term "voluntary," for absence would require forfeiture of those intangible benefits which have motivated the student through youth and all her high school years. Graduation is a time for family and those closest to the student to celebrate success and express mutual wishes of gratitude and respect, all to the end of impressing upon the young person the role that it is his or her right and duty to assume in the community and all of its diverse parts.

The importance of the event is the point the school district and the United States rely upon to argue that a formal prayer ought to be permitted, but it becomes one of the principal reasons why their argument must fail. Their contention, one of considerable force were it not for the constitutional constraints applied to state action, is that the prayers are an essential part of these ceremonies because for many persons an occasion of this significance lacks meaning if there is no recognition, however brief, that human achievements cannot be understood apart from their spiritual essence. We think the Government's position that this interest suffices to force students to choose between compliance or forfeiture demonstrates fundamental inconsistency in its argumentation. It fails to acknowledge that what for many of Deborah's classmates and their parents was a spiritual imperative was for Daniel and Deborah Weisman religious conformance compelled by the State. While in some societies the wishes of the majority might prevail, the Establishment Clause of the First Amendment is addressed to this contingency and rejects the balance urged upon us. The Constitution forbids the State to exact religious conformity from a student as the price of attending her own high school graduation. This is the calculus the Constitution commands.

. . .

For the reasons we have stated, the judgment of the Court of Appeals is

Affirmed.

Justice Blackmun, with whom Justice Stevens and Justice O'Connor join, concurring.

Nearly half a century of review and refinement of Establishment Clause jurisprudence has distilled one clear understanding: Government may neither promote nor affiliate itself with any religious doctrine or organization, nor may it obtrude itself in the internal affairs of any religious institution. The application of these principles to the present case mandates the decision reached today by the Court.

. . .

Justice Souter, with whom Justice Stevens and Justice O'Connor join, concurring.

[Souter argues against the school of thought that the Establishment Clause permits "nonpreferential" state promotion of religion. He accepts it as "settled principle that the Establishment Clause forbids support for religion in general no less than support for one religion or some."]

JUSTICE SCALIA, with whom THE CHIEF JUSTICE, JUSTICE WHITE, and JUSTICE THOMAS join, dissenting.

Three Terms ago, I joined an opinion recognizing that the Establishment Clause must be construed in light of the "[g]overnment policies of accommodation, acknowledgment, and support for religion [that] are an accepted part of our political and cultural heritage." That opinion affirmed that "the meaning of the Clause is to be determined by reference to historical practices and understandings." It said that "[a] test for implementing the protections of the Establishment Clause that, if applied with consistency, would invalidate longstanding traditions cannot be a proper reading of the Clause." *Allegheny County* v. *Greater Pittsburgh ACLU,* 492 U. S. 573, 657, 670 (1989) (KENNEDY, J., concurring in judgment in part and dissenting in part).

These views of course prevent me from joining today's opinion, which is conspicuously bereft of any reference to history. In holding that the Establishment Clause prohibits invocations and benedictions at public-school graduation ceremonies, the Court—with nary a mention that it is doing so—lays waste a tradition that is as old as public-school graduation ceremonies themselves, and that is a component of an even more longstanding American tradition of nonsectarian prayer to God at public celebrations generally. As its instrument of destruction, the bulldozer of its social engineering, the Court invents a boundless, and boundlessly manipulable, test of psychological coercion.... Today's opinion shows more forcefully than volumes of argumentation why our Nation's protection, that fortress which is our Constitution, cannot possibly rest upon the changeable philosophical predilections of the Justices of this Court, but must have deep foundations in the historic practices of our people.

. . .

II

The Court presumably would separate graduation invocations and benedictions from other instances of public "preservation and transmission of religious beliefs" on the ground that they involve "psychological coercion." I find it a sufficient embarrassment that our Establishment Clause jurisprudence regarding holiday displays, see *Allegheny County* v. *Greater Pittsburgh ACLU,* 492 U. S. 573 (1989), has come to "requir[e] scrutiny more commonly associated with interior decorators than with the judiciary." *American Jewish Congress* v. *Chicago,* 827 F. 2d 120, 129 (Easterbrook, J., dissenting). But interior decorating is a rock-hard science compared to psychology practiced by amateurs. A few citations of "[r]esearch in psychology" that have no particular bearing upon the precise issue here, ... cannot disguise the fact that the Court has gone beyond the realm where judges know what they are doing. The Court's argument that state officials have "coerced" students to take part in the invocation and benediction at graduation ceremonies is, not to put too fine a point on it, incoherent.

. . .

Santa Fe Independent Sch. Dist. v. Doe

120 S.Ct. 2266 (2000)*

In Texas, before each home varsity football game, a student of Santa Fe High School delivered a prayer. Mormon and Catholic students, along with their mothers, challenged this practice as a violation of the Establishment Clause. While the suit was pending, the school district altered the procedure for deciding whether a prayer should be delivered. A district court ruled that the prayer must be nonsectarian and nonproselytizing. The Fifth Circuit held that the student-led and student-initiated prayer, even as modified, was invalid.

---

* The text for this case was obtained in electronic form from Westlaw and is reproduced by permission from West Group.

JUSTICE STEVENS delivered the opinion of the Court.

Prior to 1995, the Santa Fe High School student who occupied the school's elective office of student council chaplain delivered a prayer over the public address system before each varsity football game for the entire season. This practice, along with others, was challenged in District Court as a violation of the Establishment Clause of the First Amendment. While these proceedings were pending in the District Court, the school district adopted a different policy that permits, but does not require, prayer initiated and led by a student at all home games. The District Court entered an order modifying that policy to permit only nonsectarian, nonproselytizing prayer. The Court of Appeals held that, even as modified by the District Court, the football prayer policy was invalid. We granted the school district's petition for certiorari to review that holding.

I

The Santa Fe Independent School District (District) is a political subdivision of the State of Texas,... Respondents are two sets of current or former students and their respective mothers. One family is Mormon and the other is Catholic. The District Court permitted respondents (Does) to litigate anonymously to protect them from intimidation or harassment.

...In their complaint the Does alleged that the District had engaged in several proselytizing practices, such as promoting attendance at a Baptist revival meeting, encouraging membership in religious clubs, chastising children who held minority religious beliefs, and distributing Gideon Bibles on school premises. They also alleged that the District allowed students to read Christian invocations and benedictions from the stage at graduation ceremonies, and to deliver overtly Christian prayers over the public address system at home football games.

[*The district court entered an interim order, requiring that prayer at graduation exercises be "non-denominational" and that it be presented by a senior student or students selected by members of the graduating class.*] The text of the prayer was to be determined by the students, without scrutiny or preapproval by school officials. References to particular religious figures "such as Mohammed, Jesus, Buddha, or the like" would be permitted "as long as the general thrust of the prayer is non-proselytizing."...

[*The district court subsequently adopted other policies, including the use of a secret ballot to decide whether to include an invocation and benediction as part of a graduation exercise, and to elect by secret ballot, from a list of student volunteers, students to deliver nonsectarian, nonproselytizing invocations and benedictions. Similar guidelines were provided for prayer at football games. The court later eliminated the requirement that invocations, benedictions, and prayers be nonsectarian and nonproselytizing, and substituted "messages" and "statements" for the word "prayer." Fifth Circuit precedents held that student-led prayer that was approved by a vote of the students and was nonsectarian and nonproselytizing was permissible at high school graduation ceremonies. However, the Fifth Circuit regarded school-encouraged prayer at school-related sporting events as constitutionally impermissible for two reasons: they were far less solemn and far more frequent.*]

II

...In *Lee* v. *Weisman*, 505 U.S. 577 (1992), we held that a prayer delivered by a rabbi at a middle school graduation ceremony violated that Clause. Although this case involves student prayer at a different type of school function, our analysis is properly guided by the principles that we endorsed in *Lee*.

As we held in that case:

"The principle that government may accommodate the free exercise of religion does not supersede the fundamental limitations imposed by the Establishment Clause. It is beyond dispute that, at a minimum, the Constitution guarantees that government may not coerce anyone to support or participate in religion or its exercise, or otherwise act in a way which 'establishes a [state] religion or religious faith, or tends to do so.' " *Id.*, at 587 (citations omitted) (quoting *Lynch* v. *Donnelly*, 465 U.S. 668, 678 (1984)).

In this case the District first argues that this principle is inapplicable to its October policy because the messages are private student speech, not public speech.... we are not persuaded that the pregame invocations should be regarded as "private speech."

These invocations are authorized by a government policy and take place on government property at government-sponsored school-related events. Of course, not every message delivered under such circumstances is the government's own. We have held, for example, that an individual's contribution to a government-created forum was not government speech. See *Rosenberger v. Rector and Visitors of Univ. of Va.*, 515 U.S. 819 (1995). Although the District relies heavily on *Rosenberger* and similar cases involving such forums, it is clear that the pregame ceremony is not the type of forum discussed in those cases. The Santa Fe school officials simply do not "evince either 'by policy or by practice,' any intent to open the [pregame ceremony] to 'indiscriminate use,'... by the student body generally." *Hazelwood School Dist.* v. *Kuhlmeier*, 484 U.S. 260, 270 (1988) (quoting *Perry Ed. Assn.* v. *Perry Local Educators' Assn.*, 460 U.S. 37, 47 (1983)). Rather, the school allows only one student, the same student for the entire season, to give the invocation. The statement or invocation, moreover, is subject to particular regulations that confine the content and topic of the student's message, ...

...Santa Fe's student election system ensures that only those messages deemed "appropriate" under the District's policy may be delivered. That is, the majoritarian process implemented by the District guarantees, by definition, that minority candidates will never prevail and that their views will be effectively silenced.

. . .

Moreover, the District has failed to divorce itself from the religious content in the invocations. It has not succeeded in doing so, either by claiming that its policy is " 'one of neutrality rather than endorsement' " or by characterizing the individual student as the "circuit-breaker" in the process. Contrary to the District's repeated assertions that it has adopted a "hands-off" approach to the pregame invocation, the realities of the situation plainly reveal that its policy involves both perceived and actual endorsement of religion. In this case, as we found in *Lee*, the "degree of school involvement" makes it clear that the pregame prayers bear "the imprint of the State and thus put school-age children who objected in an untenable position." 505 U.S., at 590.

The District has attempted to disentangle itself from the religious messages by developing the two-step student election process. The text of the October policy, however, exposes the extent of the school's entanglement. The elections take place at all only because the school "board *has chosen to permit* students to deliver a brief invocation and/or message." App. 104 (emphasis added). The elections thus "shall" be conducted "by the high school student council" and "[u]pon advice

and direction of the high school principal." *Id.*, at 104–105. The decision whether to deliver a message is first made by majority vote of the entire student body, followed by a choice of the speaker in a separate, similar majority election. Even though the particular words used by the speaker are not determined by those votes, the policy mandates that the "statement or invocation" be "consistent with the goals and purposes of this policy," which are "to solemnize the event, to promote good sportsmanship and student safety, and to establish the appropriate environment for the competition." *Ibid.*

In addition to involving the school in the selection of the speaker, the policy, by its terms, invites and encourages religious messages. The policy itself states that the purpose of the message is "to solemnize the event." A religious message is the most obvious method of solemnizing an event. Moreover, the requirements that the message "promote good citizenship" and "establish the appropriate environment for competition" further narrow the types of message deemed appropriate, suggesting that a solemn, yet nonreligious, message, such as commentary on United States foreign policy, would be prohibited. Indeed, the only type of message that is expressly endorsed in the text is an "invocation"–a term that primarily describes an appeal for divine assistance....

. . .

School sponsorship of a religious message is impermissible because it sends the ancillary message to members of the audience who are nonadherents "that they are outsiders, not full members of the political community, and an accompanying message to adherents that they are insiders, favored members of the political community." *Lynch v. Donnelly*, 465 U.S., at 688 (1984) (O'CONNOR, J., concurring). The delivery of such a message—over the school's public address system, by a speaker representing the student body, under the supervision of school faculty, and pursuant to a school policy that explicitly and implicitly encourages public prayer—is not properly characterized as "private" speech.

III

The District next argues that its football policy is distinguishable from the graduation prayer in *Lee* because it does not coerce students to participate in religious observances. Its argument has two parts: first, that there is no impermissible government coercion because the pregame messages are the product of student choices; and second, that there is really no coercion at all because attendance at an extracurricular event, unlike a graduation ceremony, is voluntary.

The reasons just discussed explaining why the alleged "circuit-breaker" mechanism of the dual elections and student speaker do not turn public speech into private speech also demonstrate why these mechanisms do not insulate the school from the coercive element of the final message....

The District further argues that attendance at the commencement ceremonies at issue in *Lee* "differs dramatically" from attendance at high school football games, which it contends "are of no more than passing interest to many students" and are "decidedly extracurricular," thus dissipating any coercion.... Attendance at a high school football game, unlike showing up for class, is certainly not required in order to receive a diploma. Moreover, we may assume that the District is correct in arguing that the informal pressure to attend an athletic event is not as strong as a senior's desire to attend her own graduation ceremony.

There are some students, however, such as cheerleaders, members of the band, and, of course, the team members themselves, for whom seasonal commitments mandate their attendance, sometimes for class credit. The District also minimizes the importance to many students of attending and participating in extracurricular activities as part of a complete educational experience. As we noted in *Lee*, "[l]aw reaches past formalism." 505 U.S., at 595. To assert that high school students do not feel immense social pressure, or have a truly genuine desire, to be involved in the extracurricular event that is American high school football is "formalistic in the extreme." *Ibid.*

... [N]othing in the Constitution as interpreted by this Court prohibits any public school student from voluntarily praying at any time before, during, or after the schoolday. But the religious liberty protected by the Constitution is abridged when the State affirmatively sponsors the particular religious practice of prayer.

IV

Finally, the District argues repeatedly that the Does have made a premature facial challenge to the October policy that necessarily must fail. The District emphasizes, quite correctly, that until a student actually delivers a solemnizing message under the latest version of the policy, there can be no certainty that any of the statements or invoca-

tions will be religious. Thus, it concludes, the October policy necessarily survives a facial challenge.

... [T]he simple enactment of this policy, with the purpose and perception of school endorsement of student prayer, was a constitutional violation. We need not wait for the inevitable to confirm and magnify the constitutional injury.... [E]ven if no Santa Fe High School student were ever to offer a religious message, the October policy fails a facial challenge because the attempt by the District to encourage prayer is also at issue. Government efforts to endorse religion cannot evade constitutional reproach based solely on the remote possibility that those attempts may fail.

. . .

The judgment of the Court of Appeals is, accordingly, affirmed.

It is so ordered.

CHIEF JUSTICE REHNQUIST, with whom JUSTICE SCALIA and JUSTICE THOMAS join, dissenting.

The Court distorts existing precedent to conclude that the school district's student-message program is invalid on its face under the Establishment Clause. But even more disturbing than its holding is the tone of the Court's opinion; it bristles with hostility to all things religious in public life. Neither the holding nor the tone of the opinion is faithful to the meaning of the Establishment Clause, when it is recalled that George Washington himself, at the request of the very Congress which passed the Bill of Rights, proclaimed a day of "public thanksgiving and prayer, to be observed by acknowledging with grateful hearts the many and signal favors of Almighty God." ...

We do not learn until late in the Court's opinion that respondents in this case challenged the district's student-message program at football games before it had been put into practice. As the Court explained in *United States v. Salerno*, 481 U.S. 739, 745 (1987), the fact that a policy might "operate unconstitutionally under some conceivable set of circumstances is insufficient to render it wholly invalid." ... While there is an exception to this principle in the First Amendment overbreadth context because of our concern that people may refrain from speech out of fear of prosecution,... there is no similar justification for Establishment Clause cases. No speech will be "chilled" by the existence of a government policy that might unconstitutionally endorse religion over nonreligion. Therefore, the question is not whether the district's policy *may be* applied in violation of the Establishment Clause, but whether it inevitably will be.

...[W]ith respect to the policy's purpose, the Court holds that "the simple enactment of this policy, with the purpose and perception of school endorsement of student prayer, was a constitutional violation."...But the policy itself has plausible secular purposes: "[T]o solemnize the event, to promote good sportsmanship and student safety, and to establish the appropriate environ-ment for the competition."...Where a governmental body "expresses a plausible secular purpose" for an enactment, "courts should generally defer to that stated intent." *Wallace, supra,* at 74–75 (O'CONNOR, J., concurring in judgment);...The Court grants no deference to—and appears openly hostile toward—the policy's stated purposes, and wastes no time in concluding that they are a sham.

. . .

F. NINE JUSTICES IN SEARCH OF A MODEL

The Court has experimented with a number of tests and models in trying to referee church-state disputes. The child-benefit theory, adopted in *Everson,* was partly abandoned after states used it to justify an increasing array of financial assistance to sectarian schools. The three-part *Lemon* test has been somewhat more durable, because its generality allows the Court to re-shape it or ignore it for individual cases. Does a statute have a "secular legislative purpose"? "Secular" is often redefined to meet the case at hand. Is the "principal or primary effect" of a statute such that it neither "advances nor inhibits" religion? Does the statute foster "excessive entanglement" with religion? These formulations give the Court ample room to maneu-ver. The tests can even conflict. As Chief Justice Rehnquist noted in one dissent, the entangle-ment test presents a "Catch-22" paradox. Aid must be supervised by the state to avoid religious content in state-funded secular classes, "but the supervision itself is held to cause an entanglement." Aguilar v. Felton, 473 U.S. at 421.

If the *Lemon* test presents difficulties for the Court, it can switch to a different model and justify a religious practice on the historical record. It used this approach in upholding tax ex-emptions in *Walz* and state chaplains in *Marsh.* In the latter case, Justice Brennan objected to the Court's sanctioning of a contemporary practice simply because it was done at the time of the First Congress: "Legislators, influenced by the passions and exigencies of the moment, the pressure of constituents and colleagues, and the press of business, do not always pass sober constitutional judgment on every piece of legislation they enact, and this must be assumed to be as true of the Members of the First Congress as any other." He also noted that the Court often recognizes that the practices in place "at the time any particular guarantee was enacted into the Constitution do not necessarily fix forever the meaning of that guarantee." Marsh v. Chambers, 463 U.S. at 814–15, 816.

Another test is to distinguish between state aid to primary and secondary schools and state aid to colleges and universities. A more tolerant judicial attitude toward the latter, on the ground that college students are less likely to be indoctrinated to a particular religious creed, was used to sustain financial assistance in *Tilton, Hunt,* and *Roemer.* It was on this basis that the Court in *Lee* v. *Weisman* held invalid invocations and benedictions by clergy at public middle and high schools, while recognizing that adults are frequently exposed to prayers at public ceremonies.

The Court has not consistently adopted a policy of "neutrality" toward religions. The ma-jority in several cases openly follows a principle of supporting religious belief. Justice Douglas justified the released-time program in *Zorach* because it "encourages religious instruction" and therefore "follows the best of our traditions." When Chief Justice Burger wrote the opin-ion in 1970 upholding tax exemptions to religious organizations, he claimed that the exemp-tion was "neither the advancement nor the inhibition of religion; it is neither sponsorship nor hostility." Yet, a page later, he explained that the state has an "affirmative policy" to consider religious groups "as beneficial and stabilizing influences in community life...." Walz v. Tax Commission, 397 U.S. 664, 672–73. An affirmative and supportive attitude is also reflected in his commitment to a "benevolent neutrality" toward churches and religious exercises. Id. at 676–77. Such remarks appear to make the Court a partisan for one side.

Justice Black warned in *Engel* v. *Vitale* that a union of government and religion injures both parties because it "tends to destroy government and to degrade religion." The cost has been substantial for religion. Its "secularization" has reduced the phrase "In God We Trust" (found on coins, in the national anthem, and in the national motto) to patriotic rather than theological significance. According to the reasoning in *Lynch* v. *Donnelly,* even the crèche has been secularized as part of the Christmas season. Pressure for prayer in public schools risks the formulation of bland language to satisfy all sects. In their quest for state and federal funds, some religious schools are tempted to surrender autonomy and to dilute the sectarian content of their courses.

SELECTED READINGS

BLANCHARD, PAUL. God and Man in Washington. Boston: Beacon Press, 1960.

BROWN, ERNEST J. "Quis Custodiet Ipsos Custodes? — The School-Prayer Cases." 1963 Supreme Court Review 1.

CAHN, EDMUND. "The "Establishment of Religion' Puzzle." 36 New York University Law Review 1274 (1961).

CHOPER, JESSE H. "The Religion Clauses of the First Amendment: Reconciling the Conflict." 41 University of Pittsburgh Law Review 673 (1980).

CORD, ROBERT L. Separation of Church and State: Historical Fact and Current Fiction. New York: Lambeth Press, 1982.

DOLBEARE, KENNETH M., AND PHILLIP E. HAMMOND. The School Prayer Decisions. Chicago: University of Chicago Press, 1971.

EVANS, BETTE NOVIT. Interpreting the Free Exercise of Religion: The Constitution and American Pluralism. Chapel Hill, N.C.: University of North Carolina Press, 1997.

GIANNELLA, DONALD A. "Religious Liberty, Nonestablishment, and Doctrinal Development: The Religious Liberty Guarantee." 80 Harvard Law Review 1381 (1967).

———. "Religious Liberty, Nonestablishment, and Doctrinal Development: The Nonestablishment Principle." 81 Harvard Law Review 513 (1968).

———. "Lemon and Tilton: The Bitter and the Sweet of Church-State Entanglement." 1971 Supreme Court Review 147.

GREENAWALT, KENT. "All or Nothing at All: The Defeat of Selective Conscientious Objection." 1971 Supreme Court Review 31.

———. "Quo Vadis: The Status and Prospects of 'Tests' Under the Religion Clauses," 1995 Supreme Court Review 323.

KATZ, WILBUR G. "Radiations from Church Tax Exemption." 1970 Supreme Court Review 93.

KAUPER, PAUL G. Religion and the Constitution. Baton Rouge: Louisiana State University Press, 1964.

———. "Church Autonomy and the First Amendment: The Presbyterian Church Case." 1969 Supreme Court Review 347.

KELLY, DEAN M., ED. Government Intervention in Religious Affairs. New York: Pilgrim Press, 1982.

KURLAND, PHILIP B. Religion and the Law: Of Church and State and the Supreme Court. Chicago: Aldine Publishing, 1962.

———. "The Regents' Prayer Case: "Full of Sound and Fury, Signifying...'" 1962 Supreme Court Review 1.

LEVY, LEONARD W. The Establishment Clause: Religion and the First Amendment. Chapel Hill, N.C.: University of North Carolina Press, 1994.

MORGAN, RICHARD E. The Supreme Court and Religion. New York: The Free Press, 1972.

———. "The Establishment Clause and Sectarian Schools: A Final Installment?" 1973 Supreme Court Review 57.

OAKS, DALLIN H., ED. The Wall between Church and State. Chicago: University of Chicago Press, 1963.

PETERS, SHAWN FRANCIS. Judging Jehovah's Witnesses: Religious Persecution and the Dawn of the Rights Revolution. Lawrence: University Press of Kansas, 2000.

PFEFFER, LEO. Church, State, and Freedom. Boston: Beacon Press, 1967.

SORAUF, FRANK J. The Wall of Separation: The Constitutional Politics of Church and State. Princeton, N.J.: Princeton University Press, 1976.

STOKES, ANSON PHELPS. Church and State in the United States. 3 vols. New York: Harper & Row, 1950.

VAN ALSTYNE, WILLIAM W. "Constitutional Separation of Church and State: The Quest for a Coherent Position." 57 American Political Science Review 865 (1963).

WITTE, JOHN JR. Religion and the American Constitutional Experiment. Boulder, Colo.: Westview Press, 2000.

13

Rights of the Accused

Probably no area of constitutional law harbors as many public misconceptions and suspicions as the rights available to the accused. The public wonders how many rights flow from the Constitution and how many from the pen of a judge. The right to a jury trial is generally understood and supported. Juries form an independent check between the government and the defendant. The writ of habeas corpus is another constitutional protection for those unlawfully detained by government. The Bill of Rights contains additional safeguards: use of a grand jury to indict suspects; protections against double jeopardy and self-incrimination; the right to a speedy and public trial by an impartial jury; the right to confront witnesses and obtain witnesses for the defendant; the right to have assistance of counsel; and prohibitions against excessive bail, excessive fines, and cruel and unusual punishment. Still other rights derive from congressional statutes and judicial decisions.

To the popular mind, "legal technicalities" permit known criminals to go free. Public fears and ignorance are easily exploited during political campaigns dominated by law-and-order themes. Candidates routinely attack the courts for handcuffing the police. Strong emotions thus cast a dark shadow across basic values of procedural due process and the right to a fair trial. Although Americans are quick to condemn violations of human rights in other countries, they often attack the operation of due process at home. Yet Justice Frankfurter reminded us that "the history of liberty has largely been the history of observance of procedural safeguards." McNabb v. United States, 318 U.S. 332, 347 (1943).

Criminal litigation is largely a matter for state courts. The vast bulk of criminal offenses are handled at the state, not the national, level. This chapter reviews developments of criminal law by Congress and the federal courts. It also identifies areas in which state courts either took the lead or departed from federal standards.

A. THE CONCEPT OF DUE PROCESS

Due process is generally traced to the Magna Carta of 1215, in which the English king promised not to proceed against a freeman "unless by the lawful judgment of his peers or by the law of the land." Due process became equivalent to the laws passed by the English Parliament. In America, however, legislative enactments are subjected to the scrutiny of the courts. Murray's Lessee v. Hoboken Land & Improvement Co., 18 How. 272, 276 (1856).

Due process relies partly on the written guarantees in the Constitution. Under the Fifth Amendment, which originally applied only to the federal government, no person shall be "deprived of life, liberty, or property, without due process of law." The Fourteenth Amendment applies the same standard to the states. At a minimum, "due process" generally means that an accused must be given notice of a charge and adequate opportunity to appear and be heard.[1] The right to be heard does not include the right to make false statements with respect

---

1. In a series of rulings, the Supreme Court has held that due process does not in every instance require advance notice and hearing. For example, see Gilbert v. Homar, 520 U.S. 924 (1997), decided by a unanimous Court.

to charges, whether one lies under oath (perjury) or not under oath (false statements). LaChance v. Erickson, 522 U.S. 262 (1998), Brogan v. United States, 522 U.S. 398 (1998). Other amendments, from the Fourth through the Eighth, supply additional substance to due process.

Due process also depends on American values of fairness. The Constitution does not specify the standards required to convict, but the requirement that guilt of a criminal charge be proved "beyond a reasonable doubt" is part of custom dating back to the early years of our nation. In re Winship, 397 U.S. 358, 361 (1970). The reasonable-doubt standard "is indispensable to command the respect and confidence of the community in applications of the criminal law. It is critical that the moral force of the criminal law not be diluted by a standard of proof that leaves people in doubt whether innocent men are being condemned." Id. at 364. The requirement of proof beyond a reasonable doubt in a criminal case is "bottomed on a fundamental value determination of our society that it is far worse to convict an innocent man than to let a guilty man go free." Id. at 372 (Harlan, J., concurring). Civil litigation, on the other hand, permits proof by a preponderance of the evidence. Id. at 371.[2] A presumption of innocence favors the accused. A defendant is innocent until proved guilty. The burden of establishing guilt rests on the prosecution "from the beginning to the end of the trial." Agnew v. United States, 165 U.S. 36, 49–50 (1897).

A fair trial cannot be conducted in the presence of a mob-dominated jury. A jury cannot deliberate fairly and reach a just conclusion when threatened by violence from a mob bent on lynching the accused. Such trials violate fundamental notions of due process. A case decided by the Supreme Court in 1915 concerned Leo Frank, who had been charged with the murder of a thirteen-year-old girl. His trial was dominated by angry crowds, chanting "Hang the Jew." After the Supreme Court upheld the conduct of his trial, he was taken from prison by an armed mob and lynched. Frank v. Mangum, 237 U.S. 309 (1915). In 1986, the Georgia Board of Pardons and Paroles gave Frank a posthumous pardon.

Even before assistance of counsel was recognized as a constitutional right in state criminal cases, the Supreme Court held in 1932 that due process required counsel for a defendant facing a death sentence. POWELL v. ALABAMA, 287 U.S. 45 (1932). Due process is denied when witnesses are whipped and tortured until they testify against the accused. Moore v. Dempsey, 261 U.S. 86, 89 (1923). Confessions have been extorted by law officers who used violence and brutality. In one case, a black suspect was repeatedly hanged by a rope to the limb of a tree and tied to the tree and whipped until he confessed. Other defendants were stripped and beaten to obtain confessions. These convictions were reversed on the ground that coerced confessions are inherently suspect as evidence. Brown v. Mississippi, 297 U.S. 278 (1936).

Even if a confession can be corroborated by independent evidence, the state violates due process if it uses methods that are inquisitorial and threatening. Rogers v. Richmond, 365 U.S. 534 (1961). These forms of persecution are generally inflicted upon "the poor, the ignorant, the numerically weak, the friendless, and the powerless." Chambers v. Florida, 309 U.S. 227, 237–38 (1940). Coercion can involve psychological compulsion, not merely physical beatings.

---

2. The standard of "beyond a reasonable doubt" was reemphasized in Sullivan v. Louisiana, 508 U.S. 275 (1993) and given further guidance in Victor v. Nebraska, 511 U.S. 1 (1994). In 1996, a unanimous Court reaffirmed an individual's right not to stand trial unless the person comprehends the charges brought by prosecutors. A defendant should have to prove incompetence only by the less demanding standard of a "preponderance" of the evidence. Cooper v. Oklahoma, 517 U.S. 348 (1996).

Miller v. Fenton, 474 U.S. 104 (1985). Confessions might result improperly from a "truth serum" administered by a police physician. Townsend v. Sain, 372 U.S. 293 (1963).[3]

In addition to judicial guidance, due process is defined by congressional actions that revise the criminal code. Through statutory activity, Congress provides standards for culpability; identifies grounds (such as insanity) to defend against prosecution; establishes a structure for sentencing; and sets forth the rules for pretrial and trial procedures, admissibility of evidence, and contempt of court. Congress reviews the Federal Rules of Criminal Procedure submitted by the Supreme Court. These rules, governing such matters as alibis, plea bargaining, and pretrial motions, may be revised or delayed by Congress. Rules of evidence, dealing with privileges, witnesses, and testimony, are also subject to congressional review and action.

Habeas Corpus

Under Article I, Section 9, the privilege of the writ of habeas corpus "shall not be suspended, unless when in Cases of Rebellion or Invasion the public Safety may require it." Through use of this "great writ," judges may determine whether someone is being imprisoned illegally. Authorities who receive the writ (*habeas corpus* means "you have the body") must justify the legality of a detention. Over time, the purpose of the writ has been expanded from protecting rights before conviction to giving relief after conviction. The Warren Court used the writ to enforce Bill of Rights protections in state courts, both broadening federal power over the states and adding substantially to the Court's work load. Fay v. Noia, 372 U.S. 391 (1963). The Burger Court attempted to cut back the scope of the writ. Wainwright v. Sykes, 433 U.S. 72 (1977); Francis v. Henderson, 425 U.S. 536 (1976). Congress has passed legislation to limit the availability of habeas corpus relief for state and federal prisoners. The Court has also been active in limiting the opportunity for prisoners to obtain habeas corpus relief. Restrictions have been placed on death row inmates who want their claims heard in federal court after unsuccessful appeals in state court (pages 754–55).

Entrapment

Due process becomes an issue in questions of entrapment, when law enforcement officers instigate a crime by trickery and deception. Through such actions they help manufacture or stimulate a crime that might not have occurred without their intervention. Entrapment tactics should not be confused with "sting" operations, in which law officers use deceit to ensnare those who have *already* committed a crime.

As an example of entrapment, government officials lured a citizen into violating the law by making repeated and persistent solicitations, taking advantage of sentiment and friendship to encourage and provoke a crime. The Supreme Court held that the officials implanted in the mind of an innocent person the disposition to commit an offense. Sorrells v. United States, 287 U.S. 435 (1932). In another case, the Court limited law enforcement to the prevention of crime and the apprehension of criminals: "Manifestly, that function does not include the manufacturing of crime." Sherman v. United States, 356 U.S. 369, 372 (1958). The Court attempts to distinguish between two tests: subjective (the defendant's predisposition to commit a crime) and objective (the tactics used by law enforcement officers to instigate a crime). The Supreme

---

3. For other coerced confessions that were overturned, see Arizona v. Fulminante, 499 U.S. 279 (1991); Clewis v. Texas, 386 U.S. 707 (1967); Haynes v. Washington, 373 U.S. 503 (1963); Culombe v. Connecticut, 367 U.S. 568 (1961); Reck v. Pate, 367 U.S. 433 (1961); Spano v. New York, 360 U.S. 315 (1959); Payne v. Arkansas, 356 U.S. 560 (1958); Leyra v. Denno, 347 U.S. 556 (1954); Watts v. Indiana, 338 U.S. 49 (1949); Malinski v. New York, 324 U.S. 401 (1945); Ashcraft v. Tennessee, 322 U.S. 143 (1944); White v. Texas, 310 U.S. 530 (1940); and Wan v. United States, 266 U.S. 1 (1924). See also Stein v. New York, 346 U.S. 156 (1953), overruled by Jackson v. Denno, 378 U.S. 368 (1964).

Court has offered the vague standard that entrapment is no defense unless the government's conduct "is so outrageous" as to violate due process. United States v. Russell, 411 U.S. 423, 431 (1973).[4] This decision, parting company with *Sorrells* and *Sherman,* opened the door to governmental abuses.

In 1992, the Court returned to the traditional test by holding that the government must prove beyond a reasonable doubt that the accused was predisposed to commit a crime. Government agents may not excite someone's interest in pornographic material banned by law and pressure that person into purchasing the literature. Jacobson v. United States, 503 U.S. 540 (1992). The Court has devised many technical definitions of entrapment, some of them quite subtle in determining "predisposition." But if a juror decides that prosecutors have abused their powers by encouraging someone to commit a crime that would not have happened without the government's intervention, the last word on the meaning of entrapment (at least in that case) is with the juror.

Powell v. Alabama

287 U.S. 45 (1932)

In this famous trial known as the "Scottsboro case," Ozie Powell and several other black youths in Alabama were charged with raping two white girls. The boys were found guilty and given the death sentence. The case involves basic questions of due process, including the right to a fair trial, assistance of counsel, and the exclusion of blacks from the jury.

MR. JUSTICE SUTHERLAND delivered the opinion of the Court.

These cases were argued together and submitted for decision as one case.

The petitioners, hereinafter referred to as defendants, are negroes charged with the crime of rape, committed upon the persons of two white girls....

. . .

In this court the judgments are assailed upon the grounds that the defendants, and each of them, were denied due process of law and the equal protection of the laws, in contravention of the Fourteenth Amendment, specifically as follows: (1) they were not given a fair, impartial and deliberate trial; (2) they were denied the right of counsel, with the accustomed incidents of consultation and opportunity of preparation for trial; and (3) they were tried before juries from which qualified members of their own race were systematically excluded. These questions were properly raised and saved in the courts below.

The only one of the assignments which we shall consider is the second, in respect of the denial of counsel; ...

The record shows that on the day when the offense is said to have been committed, these defendants, together with a number of other negroes, were upon a freight train on its way through Alabama. On the same train were seven white boys and the two white girls. A fight took place between the negroes and the white boys, in the course of which the white boys, with the exception of one named Gilley, were thrown off the train. A message was sent ahead, reporting the fight and asking that every negro be gotten off the train. The participants in the fight, and the two girls, were in an open gondola car. The two girls testified that each of them was assaulted by six different negroes in turn, and they identified the seven defendants as having been among the number. None of the white boys was called to testify, with the exception of Gilley, who was called in rebuttal.

Before the train reached Scottsboro, Alabama,

---

4. See also Mathews v. United States, 485 U.S. 58 (1988); Hampton v. United States, 425 U.S. 484 (1976); Osborn v. United States, 385 U.S. 323 (1966); Hoffa v. United States, 385 U.S. 293 (1966); Lewis v. United States, 385 U.S. 206 (1966); Massiah v. United States, 377 U.S. 201 (1964); Lopez v. United States, 373 U.S. 427 (1963); Raley v. Ohio, 360 U.S. 423 (1959); United States v. Twigg, 588 F.2d 373 (3d Cir. 1978); United States v. Archer, 486 F.2d 670 (2d Cir. 1973).

a sheriff's posse seized the defendants and two other negroes. Both girls and the negroes then were taken to Scottsboro, the county seat. Word of their coming and of the alleged assault had preceded them, and they were met at Scottsboro by a large crowd. It does not sufficiently appear that the defendants were seriously threatened with, or that they were actually in danger of, mob violence; but it does appear that the attitude of the community was one of great hostility....

... [W]e confine ourselves, as already suggested, to the inquiry whether the defendants were in substance denied the right of counsel, and if so, whether such denial infringes the due process clause of the Fourteenth Amendment.

First. The record shows that immediately upon the return of the indictment defendants were arraigned and pleaded not guilty. Apparently they were not asked whether they had, or were able to employ, counsel, or wished to have counsel appointed; or whether they had friends or relatives who might assist in that regard if communicated with. That it would not have been an idle ceremony to have given the defendants reasonable opportunity to communicate with their families and endeavor to obtain counsel is demonstrated by the fact that, very soon after conviction, able counsel appeared in their behalf. This was pointed out by Chief Justice Anderson in the course of his dissenting opinion. "They were non-residents," he said, "and had little time or opportunity to get in touch with their families and friends who were scattered throughout two other states, and time has demonstrated that they could or would have been represented by able counsel had a better opportunity been given by a reasonable delay in the trial of the cases, judging from the number and activity of counsel that appeared immediately or shortly after their conviction.".…

It is hardly necessary to say that, the right to counsel being conceded, a defendant should be afforded a fair opportunity to secure counsel of his own choice. Not only was that not done here, but such designation of counsel as was attempted was either so indefinite or so close upon the trial as to amount to a denial of effective and substantial aid in that regard....

It thus will be seen that until the very morning of the trial no lawyer had been named or definitely designated to represent the defendants. Prior to that time, the trial judge had "appointed all the members of the bar" for the limited "purpose of arraigning the defendants." Whether they would represent the defendants thereafter if no counsel appeared in their behalf, was a matter of speculation only, or, as the judge indicated, of mere anticipation on the part of the court. Such a designation, even if made for all purposes, would, in our opinion, have fallen far short of meeting, in any proper sense, a requirement for the appointment of counsel. How many lawyers were members of the bar does not appear; but, in the very nature of things, whether many or few, they would not, thus collectively named, have been given that clear appreciation of responsibility or impressed with that individual sense of duty which should and naturally would accompany the appointment of a selected member of the bar, specifically named and assigned.

... The defendants, young, ignorant, illiterate, surrounded by hostile sentiment, haled back and forth under guard of soldiers, charged with an atrocious crime regarded with especial horror in the community where they were to be tried, were thus put in peril of their lives within a few moments after counsel for the first time charged with any degree of responsibility began to represent them.

. . .

What, then, does a hearing include? Historically and in practice, in our own country at least, it has always included the right to the aid of counsel when desired and provided by the party asserting the right. The right to be heard would be, in many cases, of little avail if it did not comprehend the right to be heard by counsel. Even the intelligent and educated layman has small and sometimes no skill in the science of law. If charged with crime, he is incapable, generally, of determining for himself whether the indictment is good or bad. He is unfamiliar with the rules of evidence. Left without the aid of counsel he may be put on trial without a proper charge, and convicted upon incompetent evidence, or evidence irrelevant to the issue or otherwise inadmissible. He lacks both the skill and knowledge adequately to prepare his defense, even though he have a perfect one. He requires the guiding hand of counsel at every step in the proceedings against him. Without it, though he be not guilty, he faces the danger of conviction because he does not know how to establish his innocence. If that be true of men of intelligence, how much more true is it of the ignorant and illiterate, or those of feeble intellect. If in any case, civil or criminal, a state or federal court were arbitrarily to refuse to hear a party by counsel, employed by and appearing for him, it reasonably may not be doubted that such a refusal would be a denial of a hearing, and, therefore, of due process in the constitutional sense.

. . .

In the light of the facts outlined in the forepart of this opinion — the ignorance and illiteracy of the defendants, their youth, the circumstances of public hostility, the imprisonment and the close surveillance of the defendants by the military forces, the fact that their friends and families were all in other states and communication with them necessarily difficult, and above all that they stood in deadly peril of their lives — we think the failure of the trial court to give them reasonable time and opportunity to secure counsel was a clear denial of due process.

But passing that, and assuming their inability, even if opportunity had been given, to employ counsel, as the trial court evidently did assume, we are of opinion that, under the circumstances just stated, the necessity of counsel was so vital and imperative that the failure of the trial court to make an effective appointment of counsel was likewise a denial of due process within the meaning of the Fourteenth Amendment. Whether this would be so in other criminal prosecutions, or under other circumstances, we need not determine. All that it is necessary now to decide, as we do decide, is that in a capital case, where the defendant is unable to employ counsel, and is incapable adequately of making his own defense because of ignorance, feeble mindedness, illiteracy, or the like, it is the duty of the court, whether requested or not, to assign counsel for him as a necessary requisite of due process of law; and that duty is not discharged by an assignment at such a time or under such circumstances as to preclude the giving of effective aid in the preparation and trial of the case....

The judgments must be reversed and the causes remanded for further proceedings not inconsistent with this opinion.

Judgments reversed.

MR. JUSTICE BUTLER, dissenting.

. . .

MR. JUSTICE MCREYNOLDS concurs in this opinion.

B. GRAND JURIES AND JURY TRIALS

Procedural safeguards include indictment by a grand jury and trial by regular (petit) jury. The Fifth Amendment provides that "no person shall be held for a capital, or otherwise infamous crime, unless on a presentment or indictment of a grand jury, except in cases arising in the land or naval forces, or in the militia, when in actual service in time of war or public danger." Definitions of "infamous" vary from one age to another, depending on the severity of the punishment. An offense punishable by death must be prosecuted by indictment; offenses punishable by imprisonment exceeding one year or at hard labor must also be prosecuted by indictment unless the defendant waives indictment and requests prosecution by information.[5] The grand jury procedure in the Fifth Amendment is one of the few provisions in the Bill of Rights that has not been incorporated into the Due Process Clause of the Fourteenth Amendment and applied against the states.

The Grand Jury

Grand juries are meant to check government. In England, they acquired an independence "free from control by the Crown or judges." Costello v. United States, 350 U.S. 359, 362 (1956). Before initiating a criminal trial in America, a federal prosecutor must convince a body of laypersons (usually 23 members) that sufficient evidence exists to try a suspect. If satisfied by the evidence, twelve or more jurors may indict, which is a formal charge recommending that the person be brought to trial. When the evidence justifies a criminal trial, grand jurors pre-

---

5. Rule 7 of the Rules of Criminal Procedure; Smith v. United States, 360 U.S. 1 (1959); Ex parte Wilson, 114 U.S. 417 (1885). Prosecution by information is taken at the initiative of a prosecutor under sworn oath.

sent an indictment or "true bill" detailing the charges. A trial is limited to the charges identified in the indictment. A trial judge may not broaden the charges and allow a jury to decide
questions outside the scope of the indictment.

State grand juries vary in size. The requirement for a grand jury applies only to the federal
government. In 1884 the Supreme Court held that the Due Process Clause of the Fourteenth
Amendment cannot be used to require states to indict by grand jury. Instead, states may prosecute upon a district attorney's "information," which consists of a prosecutor's accusation
under oath.[6]

Grand juries do not follow the same procedural or evidentiary rules as a trial court. Witnesses, asked questions under oath, are not accompanied by their attorney. A judge is not present in the grand jury room. The rules of evidence, which normally require that questions be
relevant and material, do not apply in the grand jury room. The public and the press are excluded. Records, transcripts, and materials are largely secret.[7] The proceedings are not adversary hearings to adjudicate guilt or innocence. They merely determine whether criminal
proceedings should be instituted. Unlike a regular trial, grand jurors may decide that
"hearsay" evidence is sufficient grounds to indict. Costello v. United States, 350 U.S. at 362.
In a 5–4 decision in 1992, the Court held that an otherwise valid indictment may not be dismissed on the ground that the government failed to disclose to the grand jury "substantial ex-
culpatory evidence" in its possession. United States v. Williams, 504 U.S. 36 (1992).

Grand juries are subject to the test of impartiality required for trial juries. Congress took
the initiative in 1875 by prohibiting the use of race to exclude citizens from service as grand
or petit jurors. 18 Stat. 336, § 4; 18 U.S.C. § 243 (1994). The Court upheld that statute and
has continued to strike down the systematic exclusion of blacks from grand juries.[8] Exclusion
of Mexican-Americans from grand juries and regular juries is unconstitutional. Hernandez v.
Texas, 347 U.S. 475 (1954). Even inadequate representation of a class, such as Mexican-Americans, is unconstitutional. Castaneda v. Partida, 430 U.S. 482 (1977).

Witnesses before a grand jury may invoke the Fifth Amendment privilege against self-incrimination. Counselman v. Hitchcock, 142 U.S. 547 (1892). This privilege is overridden if
the government grants immunity to the witness (pages 726–27). Witnesses who then refuse
to answer questions may be jailed for contempt of court. Witnesses may not refuse to answer
because questions are based on illegally obtained evidence. United States v. Calandra, 414 U.S.
338 (1974). The First Amendment does not protect newspaper reporters from responding to
a grand jury subpoena and answering questions. Branzburg v. Hayes, 408 U.S. 665 (1972).
This judicial doctrine can be modified by Congress, but Congress has yet to pass such legislation. A number of states have enacted shield laws to protect reporters from grand jury inquiries
(page 562).

Grand juries are supposed to be independent checks on a prosecutor's allegations, but at
times they become pawns in the hands of zealous and politically motivated prosecutors. Justice Douglas once said in dissent: "It is, indeed, common knowledge that the grand jury, hav-

---

6. Hurtado v. California, 110 U.S. 516 (1884); Maxwell v. Dow, 176 U.S. 581 (1900); Lem Wood v. Oregon, 229
U.S. 586 (1913).

7. Under the general rule of secrecy of Rule 6(e) of the Federal Rules of Criminal Procedure, access to grand jury
materials is severely restricted, even for government attorneys. United States v. Baggot, 463 U.S. 476 (1983); United
States v. Sells Engineering, Inc., 463 U.S. 418 (1983); Illinois v. Abbott & Associates, Inc., 460 U.S. 557 (1983); Douglas Oil Co. v. Petrol Stops Northwest, 441 U.S. 211 (1979); Pittsburgh Plate Glass Co. v. United States, 360 U.S.
395 (1959); United States v. Procter & Gamble, 356 U.S. 677 (1958).

8. E.g., Ex parte Virginia, 100 U.S. 339 (1880); Strauder v. West Virginia, 100 U.S. 303, 308 (1880). See also
Vasquez v. Hillery, 474 U.S. 254 (1986); Rose v. Mitchell, 443 U.S. 545 (1979); Alexander v. Louisiana, 405 U.S. 625
(1972); Arnold v. North Carolina, 376 U.S. 773 (1964); Eubanks v. Louisiana, 356 U.S. 584 (1958); Pierre v.
Louisiana, 306 U.S. 354 (1939).

ing been conceived as a bulwark between the citizen and the Government, is now a tool of the Executive." United States v. Mara, 410 U.S. 19, 23 (1973). Indiscriminate use of grand juries can smear the reputation of an individual targeted by an administration. At times, the grand jury can be unleashed against radical, nonconformist, and unpopular groups, and exploited to harass and intimidate political opposition. But federal prosecutors must marshal sufficient information to gain the support of grand juries, and service on a grand jury allows citizens to feel that they are part of government decisions and understand them.

Jury Trials

Article III, Section 2, provides that the "Trial of all Crimes, except in Cases of Impeachment, shall be by Jury." Under the Sixth Amendment, for all criminal prosecutions the accused is entitled to "an impartial jury." Although the system of jury trials is often under attack, it offers a valuable opportunity for ordinary citizens to participate in the administration of justice. Their involvement can prevent the government's use of arbitrary power. Alexis de Tocqueville praised the jury for its ability to educate people in civic affairs: "By obliging men to turn their attention to other affairs than their own, it rubs off that private selfishness which is the rust of society." 1 Democracy in America 295 (Bradley ed. 1951).

An accused may waive the right to a jury trial and be tried by the court. A defendant waives a jury trial in writing with the approval of the court and the consent of the government. Due process is denied when a suspect is tried before a judge who has a direct, personal, substantial, and pecuniary interest in deciding against the defendant. Tumey v. Ohio, 272 U.S. 510 (1927). Defendants may forgo a trial by entering into a "plea bargain" with the prosecutor. Most criminal cases are disposed of by pleas of guilty. By pleading guilty to a lesser charge, the defendant avoids the risk of a heavier sentence if convicted at trial. Plea bargaining places great power in the hands of a prosecutor, who can use this tool in a coercive and arbitrary manner by threatening to indict for a higher crime if the accused refuses to plead guilty.

Federal juries "shall be of 12," but a verdict may be rendered with less than 12 if one or more jurors are excused after the trial begins. A jury verdict in federal courts must be unanimous. State juries may follow different procedures. The constitutional guarantee of trial by jury does not require a state to provide an accused with a jury of twelve for noncapital cases. The Supreme Court regards twelve as a common-law number and a "historical accident." Williams v. Florida, 399 U.S. 78, 88–89 (1970). However, a jury for a criminal trial in the states must number at least six. BALLEW v. GEORGIA, 435 U.S. 223 (1978).

For noncapital cases, states may allow nonunanimous jury verdicts. APODACA v. OREGON, 406 U.S. 404 (1972). If the jury consists of only six persons, a nonunanimous verdict in a state criminal trial for nonpetty offenses violates the Sixth and Fourteenth Amendments. Burch v. Louisiana, 441 U.S. 130 (1979).

The right to a jury trial does not extend to every criminal proceeding. Offenses that are "petty" (as defined by congressional statute) are tried without a jury. Cheff v. Schnackenberg, 384 U.S. 373, 379–80 (1966); District of Columbia v. Clawans, 300 U.S. 617, 624 (1937). The right to a jury trial depends on the potential penalty, not the category of offense. Thus, if someone faces a two-year prison sentence for a "misdemeanor," a jury trial is required. DUNCAN v. LOUISIANA, 391 U.S. 145 (1968). No offense can be regarded as "petty" if imprisonment of more than six months is authorized. Baldwin v. New York, 399 U.S. 66 (1970); Blanton v. North Las Vegas, 489 U.S. 538 (1989). However, in 1996 the Court (divided 5 to 4) held that someone is not entitled to a jury trial even when facing an aggregate prison term greater than six months. What counts, said the Court, was the legislature's judgment that the offense is petty. Lewis v. United States, 518 U.S. 343 (1996).

Jury Nullification

For the most part, jurors follow the law as explained by prosecutors and judges. On some occasions—and often highly important ones—jurors rely on their own conscience in deciding what is constitutional and proper. In their own way, jurors sense and articulate what is due process, equal protection, free speech, unreasonable searches and seizures, and cruel and unusual punishments. In exercising independent judgment, jurors at various times have represented the best and the worst of democracy. Jeffrey Abramson, We, the Jury (1994). Jurors help draw a line around permissible governmental behavior, no matter what legislators enact, prosecutors bring, or judges decide.

"Jury nullification" remains a controversial issue. The term means that jurors may acquit even when they are convinced that the defendant is guilty as charged. At such times, jurors refuse to be bound by the facts of the case or the judge's instruction of the law, and instead vote their conscience. Members of a minority might do this to protest majority policy. But the philosophy of jury nullification is broader than that. In the words of one study, juries "might be the last outpost of a skeptical citizenry that is wary of too much power in the hands of public officials, and nullification introduces a degree of unpredictability that requires prosecutors always to remember who has the last word about who is punished." Leipold, "Rethinking Jury Nullification," 82 Va. L. Rev. 253, 324 (1996).

The Seventh Amendment

The Seventh Amendment contains this language: "In suits at common law, where the value in controversy shall exceed twenty dollars, the right of trial by jury shall be preserved...." The purpose was to guarantee a jury not only for criminal trials but for civil trials as well. Nevertheless, the reach of the Seventh Amendment has been severely limited. First, it has not been applied to the states. Walker v. Sauvinet, 92 U.S. (12 Otto.) 90, 92 (1876). Second, the trial of civil cases may be conducted before a jury of six persons rather than the twelve required for other federal trials. Colgrove v. Battin, 413 U.S. 149 (1973). Third, the Seventh Amendment does not prevent Congress from assigning to an administrative agency the task of adjudicating violations of federal statutes that create new "public rights" involving the government in its sovereign capacity. The Seventh Amendment "preserved" only the rights to a jury trial in existence at that time. Atlas Roofing Co. v. Occupational Safety Comm'n, 430 U.S. 442 (1977). More than a hundred federal statutes allow civil penalties to be imposed in excess of twenty dollars without a jury trial. 132 Cong. Rec. 24867–69 (1986). Fourth, there is no Seventh Amendment right to a jury trial against the federal government. Galloway v. United States, 319 U.S. 372, 388 (1943).[9] Fifth, the Seventh Amendment right to a jury trial does not extend to patent claim construction. This decision concludes that judges are better suited than juries to give meaning to patent terms. Markman v. Westview Instruments, Inc., 517 U.S. 370 (1996).

Discrimination in Jury Selection

Racial and gender discrimination in jury formation has been a persistent problem in America. Congress passed legislation in 1875 to prohibit the use of race as a factor in selecting jurors.

---

9. Other important Seventh Amendment cases include Gasperini v. Center for Humanities, Inc., 518 U.S. 415 (1996); Granfinanciera v. Nordberg, 492 U.S. 33 (1989); Tull v. United States, 481 U.S. 412 (1987); Lehman v. Nakshian, 453 U.S. 156 (1981); and Dimick v. Schiedt, 293 U.S. 474 (1935). For a critique of adjudication by executive agencies rather than by Article III courts, see Sun, "Congressional Delegation of Adjudicatory Power to Federal Agencies and the Right to Trial by Jury," 1988 Duke L. J. 539.

State Courts Reject *Swain*

Following the Supreme Court's decision in *Swain v. Alabama* (1965), several state courts regarded the ruling as defective, unworkable, and too prejudicial to the rights of defendants. They decided that prosecutors should have a much heavier burden when they use peremptory challenges to affect the racial composition of a jury.

The Supreme Court of California announced that Swain "provides less protection to California residents than the rule we now adopt." People v. Wheeler, 583 P.2d 748, 767 (Cal. 1978). The 1965 decision furnished "no protection whatsoever" to the first defendant who suffered discrimination, and subsequent defendants had little likelihood of collecting the evidence needed to show a pattern of prosecutorial abuse. Research would not reveal which of the excused jurors were black. Id. at 767–68.

The Supreme Judicial Court of Massachusetts was persuaded by California's decision, noting that *Swain* imposed "Sisyphean burdens" on defendants. Commonwealth v. Soares, 387 N.E.2d 499, 509 n.10 (Mass. 1979), cert. denied, 444 U.S. 881 (1979). In light of the extensive criticism of *Swain* in the law reviews "and in recognition of the negligible protection that decision offers to a defendant asserting the right to trial by jury of peers, we take this opportunity to depart from applying its rule perfunctorily, and choose instead to examine this problem from a new vantage point." Id. at 510 n.12.

The Supreme Court of Florida concluded that the *Swain* test was so burdensome that it "has seldom if ever been met." State v. Neil, 457 So.2d 481, 483 (Fla. 1984). While not embracing fully either the California or the Massachusetts approach, the Florida court decided that "an alternative to *Swain* is needed." Id. at 485. The New Mexico Court of Appeals indicated that two alternatives were available: *Swain* or the California-Massachusetts rationale supported by the New Mexico Constitution. State v. Crespin, 612 P.2d 716 (N.M. 1980).

Note: The U.S. Supreme Court overturned Swain in Batson v. Kentucky, 476 U.S. 79 (1986).

---

18 Stat. 336, § 4; 18 U.S.C. § 243 (1994). The Supreme Court has held that due process is denied when blacks are consistently and wholly excluded from jury service. Norris v. Alabama, 294 U.S. 587 (1935). Although these principles existed for almost a century, Congress had to pass legislation in 1968 to supply additional safeguards against discrimination in the selection of jurors (both grand and petit). 82 Stat. 54. Yet the problem of racial exclusion continued.[10] It was not until 1975 that the Supreme Court held that the exclusion of women from petit juries violated the right to a jury trial. Taylor v. Louisiana, 419 U.S. 522 (1975).

In 1965 the Supreme Court reviewed the practice of prosecutors who use "peremptory strikes" (eliminating potential jurors without stating a reason). The Court held that a prosecutor's reliance on peremptory challenges to strike all six blacks, even though it produced an all-white jury, did not constitute racial discrimination unless it could be shown that the prosecutor had engaged in this practice for many years. Swain v. Alabama, 380 U.S. 202 (1965). The Court's ruling provoked strong critiques in the law reviews and was rejected by a number of state courts, which put a much heavier burden on prosecutors to justify peremptory challenges along racial lines. These courts refused to accept the *Swain* rationale (see box). The law reviews were uniformly critical of *Swain*. In 1983, in a case denying certiorari to revisit *Swain,* two Justices dissented and three other Justices appeared ready to reconsider the merits of *Swain,* especially in light of its unfriendly reception in the states. Justice Stevens noted:

---

10. See McCray v. New York, 461 U.S. 961 (1983); Peters v. Kiff, 407 U.S. 493 (1972); Carter v. Jury Commission, 396 U.S. 320 (1970).

"In my judgment it is a sound exercise of discretion for the Court to allow the various States to serve as laboratories in which the issue receives further study before it is addressed by this Court." McCray v. New York, 461 U.S. 961, 963 (1983).

Under these pressures, the Court decided to overturn *Swain* in 1986. The Court held that a prosecutor may not use racial reasons and peremptory challenges to strike all black persons to produce an all-white jury. A prosecutor may not use peremptory challenges on the assumption that black jurors cannot impartially consider a state's case against a black. It is no longer necessary, as under *Swain,* for the defendant to prove discrimination by the prosecutor. If a minority defendant objects to a prosecutor's peremptory challenges, the burden falls on the prosecutor to convince the judge that the exclusions are not racially motivated. Batson v. Kentucky, 476 U.S. 79 (1986).

Batson has undergone other refinements. A case in 1990 involved a *white* defendant who objected to the exclusion of blacks from his jury. The Court, split 5 to 4, held that white defendants have standing to object to peremptory challenges that exclude blacks from a jury, but that the Sixth Amendment's "fair cross section" requirement does not prevent either side from using peremptory strikes to exclude racial or other groups. The Court said that the Sixth Amendment does not assure a *representative* jury but rather an *impartial* one. Because the petitioner in this case was a white man, an equal protection issue was not raised. Holland v. Illinois, 493 U.S. 474 (1990).[11]

In 1991 the Court revisited the question of excluding black jurors from a white person's trial. This time a 7–2 Court held that a white person has a right under the Equal Protection Clause to object to the state's use of peremptory challenges to remove blacks from a jury. It no longer matters whether the defendant and the excluded jurors are of the same race. Reaching back to the Civil Rights Act passed by Congress in 1875, which prohibited the exclusion of blacks from juries, the Court said that racial discrimination in jury selection casts doubt on the integrity of the judicial process. Powers v. Ohio, 499 U.S. 400 (1991). That decision was later reinforced when the Court, divided 6–3, held that private litigants in civil cases cannot exclude potential jurors because of their race. *Batson* applied to peremptory strikes by the prosecution; it now applies to the defendant's attorney as well. Edmonson v. Leeville Concrete Co., 500 U.S. 614 (1991). That principle was extended to criminal cases in 1992. Neither prosecutors nor defendants may use racially discriminatory peremptory challenges to keep people off juries. Georgia v. McCollum, 505 U.S. 42 (1992). Justice Thomas in a concurrence, and Justices O'Connor and Scalia in their dissents, were concerned that this extension would weaken the rights of criminal defendants.

As a further clarification of *Batson,* the Court in 1991 explained that prosecutors may use peremptory challenges to exclude Hispanics from jury service when the prosecutor can explain that the basis for the exclusion was race-neutral. There may be legitimate reasons for excluding potential jurors who happen to be Hispanic or of some other race. Hernandez v. New York, 500 U.S. 352 (1991). Another peremptory challenge case was decided in Trevino v. Texas, 503 U.S. 562 (1992).

Lawyers may not use gender to exclude people from serving on a jury. Sex stereotyping (women on juries are likely to vote a certain way on accused rapists, paternity suits, etc.) is no longer permissible. J.E.B. v. Alabama ex rel. T.B., 511 U.S. 127 (1994). The Court also tampered with *Batson* by ruling that prosecutors may strike potential jurors for reasons that do not make sense so long as the action is race-neutral (e.g., striking jurors because they have long hair, a mustache, or a goatee type beard). Purkett v. Elem, 514 U.S. 765 (1995). In 1998,

---

11. In 1991, the Court held that state courts could not rule that a defendant's allegation of an equal protection violation under *Swain* failed to raise a *Batson* claim, nor could state courts adopt a procedural rule after a defendant's trial that prohibited federal judicial review of an equal protection claim. Ford v. Georgia, 498 U.S. 411 (1991).

the Court ruled that white criminal defendants who have been indicted by grand juries from which black people have been excluded may challenge the constitutionality of the indictment. Campbell v. Louisiana, 523 U.S. 392 (1998).

Ballew v. Georgia
435 U.S. 223 (1978)

In 1972, in *Apodaca* v. *Oregon*, the Supreme Court decided that jury verdicts in the states need not be unanimous as in federal courts. The Court also had to resolve questions about the *size* of a jury. *Williams* v. *Florida* (1970) determined that jury trials in the states need not follow the common-law number of twelve. Could it be six? Less than six? What was the magic minimum number for a constitutional trial by jury? In this case, Claude Davis Ballew argued that Georgia's law allowing a jury of five for a criminal trial was unconstitutional.

MR. JUSTICE BLACKMUN announced the judgment of the Court and delivered an opinion in which MR. JUSTICE STEVENS joined.

This case presents the issue whether a state criminal trial to a jury of only five persons deprives the accused of the right to trial by jury guaranteed to him by the Sixth and Fourteenth Amendments. Our resolution of the issue requires an application of principles enunciated in *Williams* v. *Florida*, 399 U.S. 78 (1970), where the use of a six-person jury in a state criminal trial was upheld against similar constitutional attack.

I

. . .

Petitioner *[Ballew]* was brought to trial in the Criminal Court of Fulton County. After a jury of 5 persons had been selected and sworn, petitioner moved that the court impanel a jury of 12 persons. ... That court, however, tried its misdemeanor cases before juries of five persons pursuant to Ga. Const., Art. 6 § 16, ¶ 1, ... and to ... Ga. Laws.... Petitioner contended that for an obscenity trial, a jury of only five was constitutionally inadequate to assess the contemporary standards of the community.... He also argued that the Sixth and Fourteenth Amendments required a jury of at least six members in criminal cases....

The motion for a 12-person jury was overruled, and the trial went on to its conclusion before the 5-person jury that had been impaneled....

. . .

...We granted certiorari. 429 U. S. 1071

(1977). Because we now hold that the five-member jury does not satisfy the jury trial guarantee of the Sixth Amendment, as applied to the States through the Fourteenth, we do not reach the other issues.

II

The Fourteenth Amendment guarantees the right of trial by jury in all state nonpetty criminal cases. *Duncan* v. *Louisiana*, 391 U. S. 145, 159–162 (1968). The Court in *Duncan* applied this Sixth Amendment right to the States because "trial by jury in criminal cases is fundamental to the American scheme of justice." *Id.*, at 149. The right attaches in the present case because the maximum penalty for violating § 26-2101, as it existed at the time of the alleged offenses, exceeded six months' imprisonment....

In *Williams* v. *Florida*, 399 U. S., at 100, the Court reaffirmed that the "purpose of the jury trial, as we noted in *Duncan*, is to prevent oppression by the Government. 'Providing an accused with the right to be tried by a jury of his peers gave him an inestimable safeguard against the corrupt or overzealous prosecutor and against the compliant, biased, or eccentric judge.' *Duncan* v. *Louisiana*, [391 U. S.,] at 156." See *Apodaca* v. *Oregon*, 406 U. S. 404, 410 (1972) (opinion of WHITE, J.). This purpose is attained by the participation of the community in determinations of guilt and by the application of the common sense of laymen who, as jurors, consider the case. *Williams* v. *Florida*, 399 U. S., at 100.

Williams held that these functions and this purpose could be fulfilled by a jury of six members. As the Court's opinion in that case explained at some length, *id.*, at 86–90, common-law juries included 12 members by historical accident, "unrelated to the great purposes which gave rise to the jury in the first place." *Id.,* at 89–90. The Court's earlier cases that had *assumed* the number 12 to be constitutionally compelled were set to one side because they had not considered history and the function of the jury. *Id.,* at 90–92. Rather than requiring 12 members, then, the Sixth Amendment mandated a jury only of sufficient size to promote group deliberation, to insulate members from outside intimidation, and to provide a representative cross-section of the community. *Id.,* at 100. Although recognizing that by 1970 little empirical research had evaluated jury performance, the Court found no evidence that the reliability of jury verdicts diminished with six-member panels. Nor did the Court anticipate significant differences in result, including the frequency of "hung" juries. *Id.,* at 101–102, and nn. 47 and 48. Because the reduction in size did not threaten exclusion of any particular class from jury roles, concern that the representative or cross-section character of the jury would suffer with a decrease to six members seemed "an unrealistic one." *Id.,* at 102. As a consequence, the six-person jury was held not to violate the Sixth and Fourteenth Amendments.

III

When the Court in *Williams* permitted the reduction in jury size — or, to put it another way, when it held that a jury of six was not unconstitutional — it expressly reserved ruling on the issue whether a number smaller than six passed constitutional scrutiny....

First, recent empirical data suggest that progressively smaller juries are less likely to foster effective group deliberation. At some point, this decline leads to inaccurate fact-finding and incorrect application of the common sense of the community to the facts. Generally, a positive correlation exists between group size and the quality of both group performance and group productivity. A variety of explanations have been offered for this conclusion. Several are particularly applicable in the jury setting. The smaller the group, the less likely are members to make critical contributions necessary for the solution of a given problem. Because most juries are not permitted to take notes...memory is important for accurate jury deliberations. As juries decrease in size, then, they are less likely to have members who remember each of the important pieces of evidence or argu-

ment. Furthermore, the smaller the group, the less likely it is to overcome the biases of its members to obtain an accurate result. When individual and group decisionmaking were compared, it was seen that groups performed better because prejudices of individuals were frequently counterbalanced, and objectivity resulted. Groups also exhibited increased motivation and self-criticism. All these advantages, except, perhaps, self-motivation, tend to diminish as the size of the group diminishes. Because juries frequently face complex problems laden with value choices, the benefits are important and should be retained. In particular, the counterbalancing of various biases is critical to the accurate application of the common sense of the community to the facts of any given case.

Second, the data now raise doubts about the accuracy of the results achieved by smaller and smaller panels. Statistical studies suggest that the risk of convicting an innocent person (Type I error) rises as the size of the jury diminishes. Because the risk of not convicting a guilty person (Type II error) increases with the size of the panel, an optimal jury size can be selected as a function of the interaction between the two risks. Nagel and Neef concluded that the optimal size, for the purpose of minimizing errors, should vary with the importance attached to the two types of mistakes. After weighting Type I error as 10 times more significant than Type II, perhaps not an unreasonable assumption, they concluded that the optimal jury size was between six and eight. As the size diminished to five and below, the weighted sum of errors increased because of the enlarging risk of the conviction of innocent defendants.

[Here Justice Blackmun draws extensively on statistical studies and results that relate jury size to "correct" decisions, hung juries, and representation on the jury by minority groups in the community.]

IV

While we adhere to, and reaffirm our holding in *Williams* v. *Florida,* these studies, most of which have been made since *Williams* was decided in 1970, lead us to conclude that the purpose and functioning of the jury in a criminal trial is seriously impaired, and to a constitutional degree, by a reduction in size to below six members. We readily admit that we do not pretend to discern a clear line between six members and five. But the assembled data raise substantial doubt about the reliability and appropriate representation of panels smaller than six. Because of the fundamental importance of the jury trial to the American system of criminal justice, any further reduction that promotes inaccurate and possibly biased decisionmaking, that causes untoward differences in verdicts, and that prevents juries from truly representing their communities, attains constitutional significance.

. . .

Petitioner, therefore, has established that his trial on criminal charges before a five-member jury deprived him of the right to trial by jury guaranteed by the Sixth and Fourteenth Amendments.

VI

The judgment of the Court of Appeals is reversed, and the case is remanded for further proceedings not inconsistent with this opinion.

It is so ordered.

MR. JUSTICE STEVENS, concurring.

. . .

MR. JUSTICE WHITE, concurring in the judgment.

. . .

MR. JUSTICE POWELL, with whom THE CHIEF JUSTICE and MR. JUSTICE REHNQUIST join, concurring in the judgment.

...I have reservations as to the wisdom—as well as the necessity—of MR. JUSTICE BLACKMUN's heavy reliance on numerology derived from statistical studies. Moreover, neither the validity nor the methodology employed by the studies cited was subjected to the traditional testing mechanisms of the adversary process. The studies relied on merely represent unexamined findings of persons interested in the jury system.

For these reasons I concur only in the judgment.

MR. JUSTICE BRENNAN, with whom MR. JUSTICE STEWART and MR. JUSTICE MARSHALL join.

. . .

Apodaca v. Oregon

406 U.S. 404 (1972)

After the Court had agreed in *Duncan* v. *Louisiana* (1968) that a criminal defendant is entitled to a jury trial in the states, the Court faced a related issue. Could jury verdicts be less than unanimous, even though unanimity is required in the federal courts? Distinctions were necessary between capital and noncapital crimes. Robert Apodaca and two other men were convicted by Oregon jurors who returned less-than-unanimous verdicts.

MR. JUSTICE WHITE announced the judgment of the Court and an opinion in which THE CHIEF JUSTICE, MR. JUSTICE BLACKMUN, and MR. JUSTICE REHNQUIST joined.

...[A]ll three sought review in this Court upon a claim that conviction of crime by a less-than-unanimous jury violates the right to trial by jury in criminal cases specified by the Sixth Amendment and made applicable to the States by the Fourteenth. See *Duncan* v. *Louisiana,* 391 U. S. 145 (1968). We granted certiorari to consider this claim, 400 U. S. 901 (1970), which we now find to be without merit.

In *Williams* v. *Florida,* 399 U. S. 78 (1970), we had occasion to consider a related issue: whether the Sixth Amendment's right to trial by jury requires that all juries consist of 12 men. After considering the history of the 12-man requirement and the functions it performs in contemporary society, we concluded that it was not of constitu-

tional stature. We reach the same conclusion today with regard to the requirement of unanimity.

I

Like the requirement that juries consist of 12 men, the requirement of unanimity arose during the Middle Ages and had become an accepted feature of the common-law jury by the 18th century. But, as we observed in *Williams,* "the relevant constitutional history casts considerable doubt on the easy assumption...that if a given feature existed in a jury at common law in 1789, then it was necessarily preserved in the Constitution." *Id.,* at 92–93. The most salient fact in the scanty history of the Sixth Amendment, which we reviewed in full in *Williams,* is that, as it was introduced by James Madison in the House of Representatives, the proposed Amendment provided for trial

"by an impartial jury of freeholders of the vicinage, with the requisite of unanimity for conviction, of the right of challenge, and other accustomed requisites...." 1 Annals of Cong. 435 (1789).

Although it passed the House with little alteration, this proposal ran into considerable opposition in the Senate, particularly with regard to the vicinage requirement of the House version. The draft of the proposed Amendment was returned to the House in considerably altered form, and a conference committee was appointed. That committee refused to accept not only the original House language but also an alternate suggestion by the House conferees that juries be defined as possessing "the accustomed requisites." Letter from James Madison to Edmund Pendleton, Sept. 23, 1789, in 5 Writings of James Madison 424 (G. Hunt ed. 1904). Instead, the Amendment that ultimately emerged from the committee and then from Congress and the States provided only for trial

"by an impartial jury of the State and district wherein the crime shall have been committed, which district shall have been previously ascertained by law...."

As we observed in *Williams,* one can draw conflicting inferences from this legislative history. One possible inference is that Congress eliminated references to unanimity and to the other "accustomed requisites" of the jury because those requisites were thought already to be implicit in the very concept of jury. A contrary explanation, which we found in *Williams* to be the more plausible, is that the deletion was intended to have some substantive effect. See 399 U. S., at 96–97. Surely one fact that is absolutely clear from this history is that, after a proposal had been made to specify precisely which of the common-law requisites of the jury were to be preserved by the Constitution, the Framers explicitly rejected the proposal and instead left such specification to the future. As in *Williams,* we must accordingly consider what is meant by the concept "jury" and determine whether a feature commonly associated with it is constitutionally required. And, as in *Williams,* our inability to divine "the intent of the Framers" when they eliminated references to the "accustomed requisites" requires that in determining what is meant by a jury we must turn to other than purely historical considerations.

II

Our inquiry must focus upon the function served by the jury in contemporary society. Cf. *Williams* v. *Florida, supra,* at 99–100. As we said

in *Duncan,* the purpose of trial by jury is to prevent oppression by the Government by providing a "safeguard against the corrupt or overzealous prosecutor and against the compliant, biased, or eccentric judge." *Duncan* v. *Louisiana,* 391 U. S., at 156. "Given this purpose, the essential feature of a jury obviously lies in the interposition between the accused and his accuser of the commonsense judgment of a group of laymen...." *Williams* v. *Florida, supra,* at 100. A requirement of unanimity, however, does not materially contribute to the exercise of this commonsense judgment. As we said in *Williams,* a jury will come to such a judgment as long as it consists of a group of laymen representative of a cross section of the community who have the duty and the opportunity to deliberate, free from outside attempts at intimidation, on the question of a defendant's guilt. In terms of this function we perceive no difference between juries required to act unanimously and those permitted to convict or acquit by votes of 10 to two or 11 to one. Requiring unanimity would obviously produce hung juries in some situations where nonunanimous juries will convict or acquit. But in either case, the interest of the defendant in having the judgment of his peers interposed between himself and the officers of the State who prosecute and judge him is equally well served.

. . .

IV

Petitioners also cite quite accurately a long line of decisions of this Court upholding the principle that the Fourteenth Amendment requires jury panels to reflect a cross section of the community.... They then contend that unanimity is a necessary precondition for effective application of the cross-section requirement, because a rule permitting less than unanimous verdicts will make it possible for convictions to occur without the acquiescence of minority elements within the community.

There are two flaws in this argument. One is petitioners' assumption that every distinct voice in the community has a right to be represented on every jury and a right to prevent conviction of a defendant in any case. All that the Constitution forbids, however, is systematic exclusion of identifiable segments of the community from jury panels and from the juries ultimately drawn from those panels; a defendant may not, for example, challenge the makeup of a jury merely because no members of his race are on the jury, but must prove that his race has been systematically excluded.... No group, in short, has the right to block convictions; it has only the right to partici-pate in the overall legal processes by which crim-inal guilt and innocence are determined.

We also cannot accept petitioners' second as-sumption—that minority groups, even when they are represented on a jury, will not ade-quately represent the viewpoint of those groups simply because they may be outvoted in the final result. They will be present during all delibera-tions, and their views will be heard. We cannot assume that the majority of the jury will refuse to weigh the evidence and reach a decision upon ra-tional grounds, just as it must now do in order to obtain unanimous verdicts, or that a majority will deprive a man of his liberty on the basis of prejudice when a minority is presenting a rea-sonable argument in favor of acquittal. We sim-ply find no proof for the notion that a majority will disregard its instructions and cast its votes for guilt or innocence based on prejudice rather than the evidence.

We accordingly affirm the judgment of the Court of Appeals of Oregon.

It is so ordered.

[Blackmun and Powell wrote concurring opin-ions. Douglas, Brennan, and Marshall wrote dis-senting opinions.]

Mr. Justice Stewart, with whom Mr. Jus-tice Brennan and Mr. Justice Marshall join, dissenting.

In *Duncan* v. *Louisiana,* 391 U. S. 145, the Court squarely held that the Sixth Amendment right to trial by jury in a federal criminal case is made wholly applicable to state criminal trials by the Fourteenth Amendment. Unless *Duncan* is to be overruled, therefore, the only relevant question here is whether the Sixth Amendment's guarantee of trial by jury embraces a guarantee that the ver-dict of the jury must be unanimous. The answer to that question is clearly "yes," as my Brother Powell has cogently demonstrated in that part of his concurring opinion that reviews almost a cen-tury of Sixth Amendment adjudication.

Until today, it has been universally understood that a unanimous verdict is an essential element of a Sixth Amendment jury trial.....

I would follow these settled Sixth Amendment precedents and reverse the judgment before us.

Duncan v. Louisiana

391 U.S. 145 (1968)

Gary Duncan was sentenced to sixty days in prison and fined $150 for simple battery. His request for a jury trial was denied. In this case, the Court decides whether trial by jury in criminal cases is so fundamental to the American scheme of justice that it must be avail-able in state courts as well as in federal courts.

Mr. Justice White delivered the opinion of the Court.

Appellant, Gary Duncan, was convicted of simple battery in the Twenty-fifth Judicial District Court of Louisiana. Under Louisiana law simple battery is a misdemeanor, punishable by a maxi-mum of two years' imprisonment and a $300 fine. Appellant sought trial by jury, but because the Louisiana Constitution grants jury trials only in cases in which capital punishment or imprison-ment at hard labor may be imposed, the trial judge denied the request. Appellant was convicted and sentenced to serve 60 days in the parish prison and pay a fine of $150.....

I

The Fourteenth Amendment denies the States the power to "deprive any person of life, liberty, or property, without due process of law." In re-

solving conflicting claims concerning the meaning of this spacious language, the Court has looked increasingly to the Bill of Rights for guidance; many of the rights guaranteed by the first eight Amendments to the Constitution have been held to be protected against state action by the Due Process Clause of the Fourteenth Amendment.....

The test for determining whether a right ex-tended by the Fifth and Sixth Amendments with respect to federal criminal proceedings is also pro-tected against state action by the Fourteenth Amendment has been phrased in a variety of ways in the opinions of this Court. The question has been asked whether a right is among those " 'fun-damental principles of liberty and justice which lie at the base of all our civil and political institu-tions,' " *Powell* v. *Alabama,* 287 U.S. 45, 67 (1932); whether it is "basic in our system of ju-risprudence," *In re Oliver,* 333 U. S. 257, 273

(1948); and whether it is "a fundamental right, essential to a fair trial," *Gideon* v. *Wainwright,* 372 U.S. 335, 343–344 (1963).... The claim before us is that the right to trial by jury guaranteed by the Sixth Amendment meets these tests. The position of Louisiana, on the other hand, is that the Constitution imposes upon the States no duty to give a jury trial in any criminal case, regardless of the seriousness of the crime or the size of the punishment which may be imposed. Because we believe that trial by jury in criminal cases is fundamental to the American scheme of justice, we hold that the Fourteenth Amendment guarantees a right of jury trial in all criminal cases which—were they to be tried in a federal court—would come within the Sixth Amendment's guarantee. Since we consider the appeal before us to be such a case, we hold that the Constitution was violated when appellant's demand for jury trial was refused.

The history of trial by jury in criminal cases has been frequently told. It is sufficient for present purposes to say that by the time our Constitution was written, jury trial in criminal cases had been in existence in England for several centuries and carried impressive credentials traced by many to Magna Carta. Its preservation and proper operation as a protection against arbitrary rule were among the major objectives of the revolutionary settlement which was expressed in the Declaration and Bill of Rights of 1689....

Jury trial came to America with English colonists, and received strong support from them. Royal interference with the jury trial was deeply resented. Among the resolutions adopted by the First Congress of the American Colonies (the Stamp Act Congress) on October 19, 1765—resolutions deemed by their authors to state "the most essential rights and liberties of the colonists"—was the declaration:

"That trial by jury is the inherent and invaluable right of every British subject in these colonies."

The First Continental Congress, in the resolve of October 14, 1774, objected to trials before judges dependent upon the Crown alone for their salaries and to trials in England for alleged crimes committed in the colonies; the Congress therefore declared:

"That the respective colonies are entitled to the common law of England, and more especially to the great and inestimable privilege of being tried by their peers of the vicinage, according to the course of that law."

The Declaration of Independence stated solemn objections to the King's making "Judges dependent on his Will alone, for the tenure of their offices, and the amount and payment of their salaries," to his "depriving us in many cases, of the benefits of Trial by Jury," and to his "transporting us beyond Seas to be tried for pretended offenses." The Constitution itself, in Art. III, § 2, commanded:

"The Trial of all Crimes, except in Cases of Impeachment, shall be by Jury; and such Trial shall be held in the State where the said Crimes shall have been committed."

Objections to the Constitution because of the absence of a bill of rights were met by the immediate submission and adoption of the Bill of Rights. Included was the Sixth Amendment which, among other things, provided:

"In all criminal prosecutions, the accused shall enjoy the right to a speedy and public trial, by an impartial jury of the State and district wherein the crime shall have been committed."

The constitutions adopted by the original States guaranteed jury trial. Also, the constitution of every State entering the Union thereafter in one form or another protected the right to jury trial in criminal cases.

Even such skeletal history is impressive support for considering the right to jury trial in criminal cases to be fundamental to our system of justice....

II.

Louisiana's final contention is that even if it must grant jury trials in serious criminal cases, the conviction before us is valid and constitutional because here the petitioner was tried for simple battery and was sentenced to only 60 days in the parish prison. We are not persuaded. It is doubtless true that there is a category of petty crimes or offenses which is not subject to the Sixth Amendment jury trial provision and should not be subject to the Fourteenth Amendment jury trial requirement here applied to the States. Crimes carrying possible penalties up to six months do not require a jury trial if they otherwise qualify as petty offenses, *Cheff* v. *Schnackenberg,* 384 U. S. 373 (1966). But the penalty authorized for a particular crime is of major relevance in determining whether it is serious or not and may in itself, if severe enough, subject the trial to the mandates of the Sixth Amendment. *District of Columbia* v. *Clawans*, 300 U. S. 617 (1937)....

In determining whether the length of the authorized prison term or the seriousness of other punishment is enough in itself to require a jury trial, we are counseled by *District of Columbia* v. *Clawans, supra,* to refer to objective criteria, chiefly the existing laws and practices in the Nation. In the federal system, petty offenses are defined as those punishable by no more than six months in prison and a $500 fine. In 49 of the 50 States crimes subject to trial without a jury, which occasionally include simple battery, are punishable by no more than one year in jail. Moreover, in the late 18th century in America crimes triable without a jury were for the most part punishable by no more than a six-month prison term, although there appear to have been exceptions to this rule. We need not, however, settle in this case the exact location of the line between petty offenses and serious crimes. It is sufficient for our purposes to hold that a crime punishable by two years in prison is, based on past and contemporary standards in this country, a serious crime and not a petty offense. Consequently, appellant was entitled to a jury trial and it was error to deny it.

The judgment below is reversed and the case is remanded for proceedings not inconsistent with this opinion.

[Fortas wrote a concurring opinion. Black, joined by Douglas, wrote a concurrence disputing the position taken in Harlan's dissent, which objects to the selective incorporation of the Bill of Rights into the Fourteenth Amendment and prefers reliance on the Due Process Clause. Black objects to this approach because due process has "no permanent meaning [and shifts] from time to time in accordance with judges' predilections and understandings of what is best for the country."]

Mr. Justice Harlan, whom Mr. Justice Stewart joins, dissenting.

Every American jurisdiction provides for trial by jury in criminal cases. The question before us is not whether jury trial is an ancient institution, which it is; nor whether it plays a significant role in the administration of criminal justice, which it does; nor whether it will endure, which it shall. The question in this case is whether the State of Louisiana, which provides trial by jury for all felonies, is prohibited by the Constitution from trying charges of simple battery to the court alone. In my view, the answer to that question, mandated alike by our constitutional history and by the longer history of trial by jury, is clearly "no."

The States have always borne primary responsibility for operating the machinery of criminal justice within their borders, and adapting it to their particular circumstances. In exercising this responsibility, each State is compelled to conform its procedures to the requirements of the Federal Constitution. The Due Process Clause of the Fourteenth Amendment requires that those procedures be fundamentally fair in all respects. It does not, in my view, impose or encourage nationwide uniformity for its own sake; it does not command adherence to forms that happen to be old; and it does not impose on the States the rules that may be in force in the federal courts except where such rules are also found to be essential to basic fairness.

The Court's approach to this case is an uneasy and illogical compromise among the views of various Justices on how the Due Process Clause should be interpreted. The Court does not say that those who framed the Fourteenth Amendment intended to make the Sixth Amendment applicable to the States. And the Court concedes that it finds nothing unfair about the procedure by which the present appellant was tried. Nevertheless, the Court reverses his conviction: it holds, for some reason not apparent to me, that the Due Process Clause incorporates the particular clause of the Sixth Amendment that requires trial by jury in federal criminal cases—including, as I read its opinion, the sometimes trivial accompanying baggage of judicial interpretation in federal contexts.

. . .

C. ELEMENTS OF A FAIR TRIAL

Justice Jackson once remarked that he would rather live under Soviet law enforced by American procedures than under American law enforced by Soviet procedures. Leonard W. Levy, The Origins of the Fifth Amendment ix (1986 ed.) Procedural protections are essential curbs against governmental abuses and arbitrary action. The procedural safeguards treated in this section include a speedy and public trial, protections against double jeopardy, and the right to confront witnesses and call witnesses for the defense.

Speedy and Public Trial

The Sixth Amendment provides that in all criminal prosecutions the accused "shall enjoy the right to a speedy and public trial, by an impartial jury of the State and district wherein the crime shall have been committed, which district shall have been previously ascertained by law, and to be informed of the nature and cause of the accusation...." The needs of public justice may require delays, however. "While justice should be administered with dispatch, the essential ingredient is orderly expedition and not mere speed." Smith v. United States, 360 U.S. 1, 10 (1959).

When a trial is repeatedly and indefinitely postponed, an indicted person is subjected to public scorn without an opportunity to be exonerated in the courts. Under such conditions, a defendant is denied a speedy trial, a right now applied against the states. Klopfer v. North Carolina, 386 U.S. 213 (1967). In cases in which defendants failed to assert the right to a speedy trial and delays did not seriously prejudice their case, five years could elapse between an arrest and a trial without violating the Speedy Trial Clause. Barker v. Wingo, 407 U.S. 514 (1972).

Congress passed the Speedy Trial Act in 1974 in an effort to prevent these delays in federal court. Charges can be dismissed unless the person is brought to trial within 100 days of arrest. The statute establishes deadlines for indictment and arraignment. Certain delays can be excluded in computing the 100 days. 88 Stat. 2076 (1975); 18 U.S.C. §§ 3161–74 (1994). Congress has made subsequent amendments to the Speedy Trial Act. See United States v. Rojas-Contreras, 474 U.S. 231 (1985). Moreover, the Court has held that the time during which an accused is not under indictment or under official restraint (subject to bail or in jail) is excluded when determining a speedy trial claim. Under these tests, the government has been permitted to prosecute charges that are ten years old. United States v. Loud Hawk, 474 U.S. 302 (1986). In some jurisdictions, such as the District of Columbia, suspects have been held a year or more in jail while awaiting trial. Washington Post, April 4, 1987, p. A-1. In 1992 a 5–4 Court ruled that the government may not bring a person to trial eight and one-half years after indictment, particularly when the government is to blame for the delay. Doggett v. United States, 505 U.S. 647 (1992).

The constitutional right to a "public trial" protects an individual from secret proceedings where there is no opportunity to secure counsel, prepare a defense, cross-examine witnesses, or summon witnesses for the accused. The Anglo-American distrust of secret trials has been traced to the Spanish Inquisition, the English Star Chamber, and the French *lettre de cachet*. In re Oliver, 333 U.S. 257, 268–69 (1948). Public trials restrain potential abuses of judicial power. Id. at 270. This constitutional protection in the Bill of Rights has been applied to the states. Id. at 273. There have been occasions, however, where a judge has excluded the public while adjudging someone guilty of criminal contempt for refusing to answer questions. Levine v. United States, 362 U.S. 610 (1960). Moreover, there is a constant tension between a judge's interest in closing a trial and the right of the public and the press to attend (see pages 569–80).

Double Jeopardy

Under the Fifth Amendment, a person shall not be subject "for the same offense to be twice put in jeopardy of life or limb." Litigation exposes a raft of complex issues. What is the "same offense"? What is "jeopardy"? The law of double jeopardy consists of several rules, each rule "marooned in a sea of exceptions." 75 Yale L. J. 262, 263 (1965). The Supreme Court admits that its decisions in this area are "a veritable Sargasso Sea." Albernaz v. United States, 450 U.S. 333, 343 (1981).

As first proposed by Madison in 1789, the Double Jeopardy Clause provided: "No person shall be subject, except in cases of impeachment, to more than one punishment or one trial for the same offence." 1 Annals of Congress 434. Some members of the House of Representatives objected that the limitation of "one trial" would prevent a convicted person from obtaining a second trial if the first was deficient. Id. at 753. The Senate changed the language to its present form. S. Jour., 1st Cong., 1st Sess. 71, 77.

The underlying purpose of the Double Jeopardy Clause is to prohibit the government from making repeated attempts to convict an individual, "subjecting him to embarrassment, expense and ordeal and compelling him to live in a continuing state of anxiety and insecurity." Green v. United States, 355 U.S. 184, 187 (1957). Acquittal acts as an absolute bar on a second trial. United States v. DiFrancesco, 449 U.S. 117, 129 (1980). The meaning of "acquittal," however, often divides the Court.[12]

There is no double jeopardy in trying someone twice for the same offense if the jury is unable to reach a verdict, the jury is discharged, or an appeals court returns the case to the trial court because of defects in the original indictment.[13] Even so, by the time a judge discharges the jury the accused might already have been placed in "jeopardy." When does jeopardy attach? When the jury is empaneled and sworn? The first witness sworn? The first evidence introduced? On such questions the Court splinters to produce 5–4 and 6–3 decisions.[14]

Other difficulties spring from jurisdictional questions. May a state and the federal government (two sovereigns) prosecute someone for the same act? In three unanimous rulings, the Supreme Court held that a person may be prosecuted for the same act under federal law and state law. The theory is that there are two distinct offenses rather than the "same offense" under the Fifth Amendment.[15]

When this theory was reaffirmed in 1959, the Court split 5–4. The dissenters regarded double prosecutions as constitutionally repulsive, particularly when the federal government, after losing a case, helps a state try the person for the same offense. Bartkus v. Illinois, 359 U.S. 121 (1959). Because of inherent tribal sovereignty, an Indian can be tried in Tribal Court and in federal court for the same incident. United States v. Wheeler, 435 U.S. 313 (1978). Two states may prosecute a person for the same criminal activity. Heath v. Alabama, 474 U.S. 82 (1985). This theory of "dual sovereignty" does not allow double prosecutions *within* a state: once by the state and again by a municipality. Cities are not sovereign entities. Waller v. Florida, 406 U.S. 916 (1972).

In 1997, a unanimous Court held that the Double Jeopardy Clause permitted the government to fine someone for fraud or other regulatory wrongdoing and later resort to the criminal process by prosecute the person for the same offense. The first action was civil, the second criminal. It would be double jeopardy only when imposing multiple criminal punishments for the same offense. Hudson v. United States, 522 U.S. 93 (1997). Similarly, although O.J. Simpson was acquitted in a criminal trial for the deaths of Nicole Brown Simpson and Ronald Goldman, their families successfully brought a civil suit charging Simpson with wrongful death. Lemrick Nelson, Jr., was cleared in 1992 of state criminal charges that he killed Yankel Rosenbaum in Brooklyn. Yet five years later he was convicted of violating Rosenbaum's civil rights. See Yale Kamisar, "Call It Double Jeopardy," New York Times, February 14, 1997, at A37.

---

12. United States v. Scott, 437 U.S. 82 (1978); United States v. Sisson, 399 U.S. 267 (1970).

13. United States v. Ball, 163 U.S. 662, 672 (1896); Thompson v. United States, 155 U.S. 271 (1894); Logan v. United States, 144 U.S. 263, 297–98 (1892).

14. Crist v. Bretz, 437 U.S. 28 (1978); Illinois v. Somerville, 410 U.S. 458 (1973); United States v. Jorn, 400 U.S. 470 (1971); Downum v. United States, 372 U.S. 734 (1963); Gori v. United States, 367 U.S. 364 (1961).

15. Jerome v. United States, 318 U.S. 101 (1943); Herbert v. Louisiana, 272 U.S. 312 (1926); United States v. Lanza, 260 U.S. 377 (1922).

Double Jeopardy Rulings

1. If someone is found guilty and an appeals court orders a new trial, the trial court may not impose a stiffer penalty than the one the defendant received the first time. Arizona v. Rumsey, 467 U.S. 203 (1984); Price v. Georgia, 398 U.S. 323 (1970); Green v. United States, 355 U.S. 184 (1957).

2. If someone is charged with robbing six poker players and is acquitted in a trial involving one of the players, the government may not proceed to prosecute him for robbing one of the other players. Ashe v. Swenson, 397 U.S. 436 (1970). See also Simpson v. Florida, 403 U.S. 384 (1971).

3. The federal government may introduce at trial the statement of someone who testified at an earlier trial against the same defendant, even though the defendant was acquitted in the first trial. The Court reasoned that the government was not relitigating the facts of the earlier case. Dowling v. United States, 493 U.S. 342 (1990).

4. An individual pleaded guilty to driving while intoxicated and failing to keep to the right of the median. Later he was indicted for manslaughter, homicide, and assault. To prove those charges, the government had to depend on the charges for which he had already pled guilty. The Court held that the Double Jeopardy Clause bars a subsequent prosecution if, to establish an essential element of an offense charged, the government will seek to prove conduct for which the defendant has already been prosecuted. Grady v. Corbin, 495 U.S. 508 (1990). Three years later the Court reversed *Grady* to permit the prosecution of a man charged with assaulting his wife even though he had been earlier convicted of contempt of court for the same attack., United States v. Dixon, 509 U.S. 688 (1993).

5. Someone was found guilty of attempting to manufacture an illegal drug based on evidence concerning the shipment of chemicals and equipment to him. The person was later charged with conspiracy, relying in part on the earlier conviction. The Court held that the Double Jeopardy Clause does not bar the prosecution of two crimes different in time and place. United States v. Felix, 503 U.S. 378 (1992).*

---

* For other recent rulings, in 1994 the Court split 5 to 4 in holding that Montana could not convict marijuana farmers of drug crimes and later use the state law to collect an estimated $900,000 in taxes on the marijuana grown. Montana Dept. of Revenue v. Kurth Ranch, 511 U.S. 767 (1994). The Court agreed 8 to 1 that double jeopardy principles do not prevent prosecution for a crime even if the same criminal behavior had been used to increase the defendant's prison sentence for a different offense. Witte v. United States, 515 U.S. 389 (1995). A rare unanimous Court held that a district court had erred in sentencing someone to concurrent life sentences for the same offense. Rutledge v. United States, 517 U.S. 292 (1996). The Court held (8 to 1) that civil forfeiture is not "punishment" for double jeopardy purposes. Government may both prosecute someone for criminal violations and later seize their property. United States v. Ursery, 518 U.S. 267 (1996). See also Monge v. California, 524 U.S. 721 (1998).

Decisions on double jeopardy initially dealt with the federal government or its territories.[16] In 1937 the Court reviewed a state prosecution of an individual who had been sentenced to life imprisonment but, upon retrial, was sentenced to death. The Court denied that double jeopardy represented a fundamental principle of liberty and justice that must be applied against the states. PALKO v. CONNECTICUT, 302 U.S. 319 (1937). This decision was overturned in 1969 when the Court held that the double jeopardy provision in the Fifth Amendment is fundamental to our constitutional heritage and enforceable against the states through the Fourteenth Amendment. Benton v. Maryland, 395 U.S. 784 (1969). Other decisions attempted to define the confused contours of the Double Jeopardy Clause, raising issues of exquisite complexity and subtlety (see box).

The issue of imposing a more severe sentence when a defendant is convicted in a second

---

16. Diaz v. United States, 223 U.S. 442 (1912); Serra v. Mortiga, 204 U.S. 470 (1907); Kepner v. United States, 195 U.S. 100 (1904); United States v. Ball, 163 U.S. 662 (1896).

trial has occupied both Congress and the courts. In 1969 the Supreme Court decided that there is no constitutional bar to imposing a more severe sentence on reconviction, provided the sentencing judge is not motivated by vindictiveness. The guarantee against double jeopardy, however, requires that punishment already exacted must be fully credited to the new sentence. North Carolina v. Pearce, 395 U.S. 711, 718 (1969); Chaffin v. Stynchcombe, 412 U.S. 17 (1973). If someone is convicted and successfully moves for a new trial because of prosecutorial misconduct, upon reconviction the judge may impose a heavier sentence. Texas v. McCullough, 475 U.S. 134 (1986).

These cases deal with new sentences after a new trial. In 1970 Congress authorized increases in an *existing* sentence; appellate courts may review and increase a trial court's sentence for "dangerous special offenders." 84 Stat. 950, § 3576. The Supreme Court upheld this procedure in United States v. DiFrancesco, 449 U.S. 117 (1980). Legislation in 1984 permits appellate courts to increase existing sentences for offenses in areas other than organized crime. 98 Stat. 2011, § 3742 (1984). The basis for such statutes is that the scope of punishment is a matter for legislatures, not courts. Missouri v. Hunter, 459 U.S. 359, 368 (1983). Legislatures may authorize multiple punishments and consecutive sentences. Although a person may not be punished more than once for the same offense, a single incident can violate more than one statutory provision and lead to cumulative punishment. These statutes do not violate double jeopardy.[17]

"Megan's Law," named after a 7-year-old girl raped and murdered by a twice-convinced sex offender, is a New Jersey statute that requires authorities to notify communities of convicted persons who move to their neighborhoods. Most of the other states, including the District of Columbia, have adopted similar statutes. The claim that such statutes impose a second punishment and violate the Double Jeopardy Clause was rejected by the Third Circuit in 1997. W.P. v. Verniero, 127 F.3d 298 (3d Cir. 1997), cert. denied, 522 U.S. 1109–10 (1998). In 1997, a 5–4 ruling by the Supreme Court held that locking up a repeat sex offender in a mental institution does not violate the double-jeopardy protection. Kansas v. Hendricks, 521 U.S. 346 (1997).

Right of Confrontation

The Sixth Amendment provides that in all criminal prosecutions the accused has the right to "be confronted with the witnesses against him [and] to have compulsory process for obtaining witnesses in his favor." In 1965 the Supreme Court held that the right of confrontation and cross-examination is a fundamental right made obligatory on the states by the Fourteenth Amendment. Pointer v. Texas, 380 U.S. 400 (1965); Douglas v. Alabama, 380 U.S. 415 (1965). Two years later, the Court also applied against the states the right of an accused to have compulsory process for obtaining witnesses. Washington v. Texas, 388 U.S. 14 (1967). The Confrontation and Compulsory Process Clauses give an accused a fair opportunity to present a defense.[18]

In 1988 the Court struck down a state law permitting children who claim they are victims of sexual abuse to testify in court behind screens. Coy v. Iowa, 487 U.S. 1012 (1988). Despite *Coy*, in 1990 a 5–4 Court upheld a Maryland law that allowed a child witness in a sexual abuse case to testify against a defendant at trial, outside the defendant's physical presence, by

---

17. Jones v. Thomas, 491 U.S. 376 (1989); Garrett v. United States, 471 U.S. 773 (1985); Albernaz v. United States, 450 U.S. 333 (1981); Illinois v. Vitale, 447 U.S. 410 (1980); Whalen v. United States, 445 U.S. 684 (1980); Gore v. United States, 357 U.S. 386 (1958); Blockburger v. United States, 284 U.S. 299 (1932). See also Brown v. Ohio, 432 U.S. 161 (1977), which held that a person could not be prosecuted for "joyriding" and then later for auto theft if the latter offense includes the former. This holding seems eroded by Ohio v. Johnson, 457 U.S. 493 (1984).

18. Pennsylvania v. Ritchie, 480 U.S. 39 (1987); Crane v. Kentucky, 476 U.S. 683 (1986); Lee v. Illinois, 476 U.S. 530 (1986).

one-way closed circuit television. The child, prosecutor, and defense counsel were in another room; the defendant remained in electronic communication with counsel. The Court held that the Confrontation Clause does not guarantee criminal defendants an absolute right to a face-to-face meeting with the witnesses against them at trial. The Maryland procedure passed constitutional muster because it was necessary to further an important public policy (protecting children from courtroom trauma) and it otherwise assured the testimony's reliability. Writing for the dissenters, Justice Scalia accused the Court of using cost-benefit analysis to read out of the Constitution an explicit guarantee. Maryland v. Craig, 497 U.S. 836 (1990). The Court also divided 5–4 in deciding that a two-and-one-half-year-old girl's statement to her pediatrician that her father sexually abused her could not be used at trial. The Court concluded that there was no guarantee that the pediatrician's hearsay testimony was trustworthy. Idaho v. Wright, 497 U.S. 805 (1990). In 1992 the Court again explored the necessity of producing children (victims of a sexual assault) at trial. White v. Illinois, 502 U.S. 346 (1992).

In 1991, the Court divided 7–2 in upholding Michigan's rape-shield statute that requires defendants to give notice ten days in advance of an intent to introduce evidence of a defendant's past sexual conduct with the victim. Although the statute implicates the Sixth Amendment to the extent that it diminishes a defendant's ability to present evidence and confront adverse witnesses, the Court held that the statute serves a valid legislative purpose that rape victims are protected against surprise, harassment, and unnecessary invasions of privacy. Michigan v. Lucas, 500 U.S. 145 (1991).

Under certain circumstances, a disruptive defendant may be removed from the courtroom without violating his constitutional right to be present and to confront witnesses against him. Illinois v. Allen, 397 U.S. 337 (1970). A trial court's ruling in violation of the Confrontation Clause may even be tolerated if the Supreme Court finds the error "harmless." Delaware v. Van Arsdall, 475 U.S. 673 (1986). Other exceptions to the Confrontation Clause include the use of out-of-court statements in conspiracy trials (permitting hearsay evidence).[19] It is also possible to admit prior-recorded testimony at a trial without the opportunity for confrontation if two conditions are met: the evidence is reliable and the state has made an effort to locate the witness.[20]

Palko v. Connecticut

302 U.S. 319 (1937)

In this opinion, which concerns the Double Jeopardy Clause, Justice Cardozo looks more broadly to determine the respective responsibilities of the federal government and the states and to identify the individual rights "found to be implicit in the concept of ordered liberty." Frank Palko was found guilty of second-degree murder and sentenced to life imprisonment. Upon retrial, he was convicted of first-degree murder and sentenced to be executed.

MR. JUSTICE CARDOZO delivered the opinion of the Court.

A statute of Connecticut permitting appeals in criminal cases to be taken by the state is challenged by appellant as an infringement of the Fourteenth Amendment of the Constitution of the

United States. Whether the challenge should be upheld is now to be determined.

Appellant was indicted in Fairfield County, Connecticut, for the crime of murder in the first degree. A jury found him guilty of murder in the second degree, and he was sentenced to confine-

---

19. Bourjaily v. United States, 483 U.S. 171 (1987); United States v. Inadi, 475 U.S. 387 (1986); Dutton v. Evans, 400 U.S. 74 (1970).

20. Ohio v. Roberts, 448 U.S. 56 (1980); Mancusi v. Stubbs, 408 U.S. 204 (1972); Barber v. Page, 390 U.S. 719 (1968).

ment in the state prison for life. Thereafter the State of Connecticut, with the permission of the judge presiding at the trial, gave notice of appeal to the Supreme Court of Errors.... [T]he Supreme Court of Errors reversed the judgment and ordered a new trial. *State v. Palko,* 121 Conn. 669; 186 Atl. 657. It found that there had been error of law to the prejudice of the state (1) in excluding testimony as to a confession by defendant; (2) in excluding testimony upon cross-examination of defendant to impeach his credibility, and (3) in the instructions to the jury as to the difference between first and second degree murder.

Pursuant to the mandate of the Supreme Court of Errors, defendant was brought to trial again. Before a jury was impaneled and also at later stages of the case he made the objection that the effect of the new trial was to place him twice in jeopardy for the same offense, and in so doing to violate the Fourteenth Amendment of the Constitution of the United States. Upon the overruling of the objection the trial proceeded. The jury returned a verdict of murder in the first degree, and the court sentenced the defendant to the punishment of death. The Supreme Court of Errors affirmed the judgment of conviction.... The case is here upon appeal. 28 U. S. C., § 344.

1. The execution of the sentence will not deprive appellant of his life without the process of law assured to him by the Fourteenth Amendment of the Federal Constitution.

The argument for appellant is that whatever is forbidden by the Fifth Amendment is forbidden by the Fourteenth also. The Fifth Amendment, which is not directed to the states, but solely to the federal government, creates immunity from double jeopardy. No person shall be "subject for the same offense to be twice put in jeopardy of life or limb." The Fourteenth Amendment ordains, "nor shall any State deprive any person of life, liberty, or property, without due process of law." To retry a defendant, though under one indictment and only one, subjects him, it is said, to double jeopardy in violation of the Fifth Amendment, if the prosecution is one on behalf of the United States. From this the consequence is said to follow that there is a denial of life or liberty without due process of law, if the prosecution is one on behalf of the People of a State....

We have said that in appellant's view the Fourteenth Amendment is to be taken as embodying the prohibitions of the Fifth. His thesis is even broader. Whatever would be a violation of the original bill of rights (Amendments I to VIII) if

done by the federal government is now equally unlawful by force of the Fourteenth Amendment if done by a state. There is no such general rule.

The Fifth Amendment provides, among other things, that no person shall be held to answer for a capital or otherwise infamous crime unless on presentment or indictment of a grand jury. This court has held that, in prosecutions by a state, presentment or indictment by a grand jury may give way to informations at the instance of a public officer. *Hurtado* v. *California,* 110 U. S. 516; *Gaines* v. *Washington,* 277 U. S. 81, 86. The Fifth Amendment provides also that no person shall be compelled in any criminal case to be a witness against himself. This court has said that, in prosecutions by a state, the exemption will fail if the state elects to end it. *Twining* v. *New Jersey,* 211 U. S. 78, 106, 111, 112. Cf. *Snyder* v. *Massachusetts, supra,* p. 105; *Brown* v. *Mississippi,* 297 U. S. 278, 285. The Sixth Amendment calls for a jury trial in criminal cases and the Seventh for a jury trial in civil cases at common law where the value in controversy shall exceed twenty dollars. This court has ruled that consistently with those amendments trial by jury may be modified by a state or abolished altogether.... As to the Fourth Amendment, one should refer to *Weeks* v. *United States,* 232 U. S. 383, 398, and as to other provisions of the Sixth, to *West* v. *Louisiana,* 194 U. S. 258.

On the other hand, the due process clause of the Fourteenth Amendment may make it unlawful for a state to abridge by its statutes the freedom of speech which the First Amendment safeguards against encroachment by the Congress, ... or the like freedom of the press, ... or the free exercise of religion, ... or the right of peaceable assembly, without which speech would be unduly trammeled, ... or the right of one accused of crime to the benefit of counsel, *Powell* v. *Alabama,* 287 U. S. 45. In these and other situations immunities that are valid as against the federal government by force of the specific pledges of particular amendments have been found to be implicit in the concept of ordered liberty, and thus, through the Fourteenth Amendment, become valid as against the states.

The line of division may seem to be wavering and broken if there is a hasty catalogue of the cases on the one side and the other. Reflection and analysis will induce a different view. There emerges the perception of a rationalizing principle which gives to discrete instances a proper order and coherence. The right to trial by jury and the immunity from prosecution except as the result of an indictment may have value and importance. Even so, they are not of the very essence of a scheme of ordered liberty. To abolish them is not to violate a "principle of justice so rooted in the traditions and conscience of our people as to be ranked as fundamental." *Snyder v. Massachusetts, supra,* p. 105; *Brown v. Mississippi, supra,* p. 285; *Hebert v. Louisiana,* 272 U. S. 312, 316. Few would be so narrow or provincial as to maintain that a fair and enlightened system of justice would be impossible without them. What is true of jury trials and indictments is true also, as the cases show, of the immunity from compulsory self-incrimination. *Twining v. New Jersey, supra.* This too might be lost, and justice still be done. Indeed, today as in the past there are students of our penal system who look upon the immunity as a mischief rather than a benefit, and who would limit its scope, or destroy it altogether. No doubt there would remain the need to give protection against torture, physical or mental. *Brown v. Mississippi, supra.* Justice, however, would not perish if the accused were subject to a duty to respond to orderly inquiry. The exclusion of these immunities and privileges from the privileges and immunities protected against the action of the states has not been arbitrary or casual. It has been dictated by a study and appreciation of the meaning, the essential implications, of liberty itself.

We reach a different plane of social and moral values when we pass to the privileges and immunities that have been taken over from the earlier articles of the federal bill of rights and brought within the Fourteenth Amendment by a process of absorption. These in their origin were effective against the federal government alone. If the Fourteenth Amendment has absorbed them, the process of absorption has had its source in the belief that neither liberty nor justice would exist if they were sacrificed. *Twining v. New Jersey, supra,* p. 99. This is true, for illustration, of freedom of thought, and speech. Of that freedom one may say that it is the matrix, the indispensable condition, of nearly every other form of freedom. With rare aberrations a pervasive recognition of that truth can be traced in our history, political and legal. So it has come about that the domain of liberty, withdrawn by the Fourteenth Amendment from encroachment by the states, has been enlarged by latter-day judgments to include liberty of the mind as well as liberty of action. The extension became, indeed, a logical imperative when once it was recognized, as long ago it was, that liberty is something more than exemption from physical restraint, and that even in the field of substantive rights and duties the legislative judgment, if oppressive and arbitrary, may be overridden by the courts. Cf. *Near v. Minnesota ex rel. Olson, supra; De Jonge v. Oregon, supra.* Fundamental too in the concept of due process, and so in that of liberty, is the thought that condemnation shall be rendered only after trial. *Scott v. McNeal,* 154 U. S. 34; *Blackmer v. United States,* 284 U. S. 421. The hearing, moreover, must be a real one, not a sham or a pretense. *Moore v. Dempsey,* 261 U. S. 86; *Mooney v. Holohan,* 294 U. S. 103. For that reason, ignorant defendants in a capital case were held to have been condemned unlawfully when in truth, though not in form, they were refused the aid of counsel. *Powell v. Alabama, supra,* pp. 67, 68....

Our survey of the cases serves, we think, to justify the statement that the dividing line between them, if not unfaltering throughout its course, has been true for the most part to a unifying principle. On which side of the line the case made out by the appellant has appropriate location must be the next inquiry and the final one. Is that kind of double jeopardy to which the statute has subjected him a hardship so acute and shocking that our polity will not endure it? Does it violate those "fundamental principles of liberty and justice which lie at the base of all our civil and political institutions"? *Hebert v. Louisiana, supra.* The answer surely must be "no."... The state is not attempting to wear the accused out by a multitude of cases with accumulated trials. It asks no more than this, that the case against him shall go on until there shall be a trial free from the corrosion of substantial legal error....

2. The conviction of appellant is not in derogation of any privileges or immunities that belong to him as a citizen of the United States.

There is argument in his behalf that the privileges and immunities clause of the Fourteenth Amendment as well as the due process clause has been flouted by the judgment.

Maxwell v. Dow, supra, p. 584, gives all the answer that is necessary.

The judgment is

Affirmed.

MR. JUSTICE BUTLER dissents.

D. SELF-INCRIMINATION

Procedural due process includes other protections for the accused: prompt arraignment before a magistrate and the privilege against self-incrimination. These issues triggered some of
the most bitterly contested rulings by the Supreme Court: *Mallory* v. *United States* (1957), *Escobedo* v. *Illinois* (1964), and *Miranda* v. *Arizona* (1966). The latter two cases are analyzed
in the next section on "Assistance of Counsel."

Prompt Arraignment

Congress and state legislatures have required police officers to take an accused to the nearest
judicial officer for arraignment. If officers ignore this procedure and detain the suspect for
days in order to extract a confession, the evidence can be excluded by the courts. McNabb v.
United States, 318 U.S. 332 (1943). These rulings conform to legislative policy, such as the
rule adopted by Congress that requires an arrested person to be taken before a committing
magistrate "without unnecessary delay." MALLORY v. UNITED STATES, 354 U.S. 449
(1957). Congress responded to *Mallory* by making confessions admissible if the defendant is
arraigned within six hours. 82 Stat. 210 (1968); 18 U.S.C. § 3501(c) (1994).

At the state level, persons arrested without a warrant were expected to be brought before
a neutral magistrate, who would determine whether there was probable cause for detention.
Gerstein v. Pugh, 420 U.S. 103 (1975). That standard was clarified in 1991 by a 5–4 Court
that decided that persons arrested without a warrant may be held for up to 48 hours before
being brought before a magistrate. A delay of that length can be challenged if the arrested person can prove that the delay was unreasonable. Riverside, County of, v. McLaughlin, 500 U.S.
44 (1991). The Court later held that the 48-hour rule applied retroactively to all pending cases
at the time of *McLaughlin*. Powell v. Nevada, 511 U.S. 79 (1994).

Privilege against Self-Incrimination

The Fifth Amendment provides that no person "shall be compelled in any Criminal Case to
be a witness against himself." The purpose of this privilege is to prevent repressive and arbitrary methods of prosecution, such as "the horror of Star Chamber proceedings" in England.
Quinn v. United States, 349 U.S. 155, 161 (1955). Government officials may not pry incriminating evidence from the lips of the accused. Prosecutors are "forced to search for independent evidence instead of relying upon proof extracted from individuals by force of law." United
States v. White, 322 U.S. 694, 698 (1944).

The privilege against self-incrimination is not automatic or self-executing. It can be waived
and "must be deemed waived" if a witness does not assert it in a timely manner. Vajtauer v.
Comm'n of Immigration, 273 U.S. 103 (1927). Although the privilege against self-incrimination can be waived, even vague and ambiguous references to the "Fifth Amendment" are sufficient to invoke its protection.[21] If a defendant voluntarily takes the stand, he or she may be
cross-examined as any other witness, thereby risking the disclosure of incriminating information. Brown v. United States, 356 U.S. 148 (1958). Once a defendant offers to be a witness,
"his credibility may be impeached, his testimony may be assailed, and is to be weighed as that
of any other witness." Reagan v. United States, 157 U.S. 301, 305 (1895).

In federal proceedings, an accused may request the court to instruct the jury that a defendant's failure to testify does not create a presumption of guilt and must not be used by the jury
against him or her. Bruno v. United States, 308 U.S. 287 (1939). In some of the states, however,
courts and prosecutors were allowed to comment on a defendant's failure to explain or to deny

---

21. Quinn v. United States, 349 U.S. at 162–64; Emspak v. United States, 349 U.S. 190 (1955).

evidence against him or her. The court or the jury could take that into consideration. Adamson v. California, 332 U.S. 46 (1947) (reprinted in Chapter 8). In this case and in *Twining* v. *New Jersey*, 211 U.S. 78 (1908), the Court applied the Self-Incrimination Clause only to the federal government, not to the states. In 1964 the Court held that the privilege against self-incrimination is incorporated in the Due Process Clause of the Fourteenth Amendment and therefore applicable to the states. Malloy v. Hogan, 378 U.S. 1 (1964). Subsequent cases have attempted to explain when it is appropriate to comment on a defendant's failure to testify.[22]

Problems of federalism provoked the extension of the Self-Incrimination Clause to the states. In 1944, the Court held that a person could be compelled under a state immunity statute to give testimony and the information could be used later in federal court to convict him. Feldman v. United States, 322 U.S. 487 (1944). This placed the witness in a no-win situation. Agreeing to testify could bring conviction in federal court; refusal to testify risked state imprisonment for contempt of court. This dilemma was resolved in 1964 when a unanimous Court held that one jurisdiction within the federal system may not compel a witness (granted immunity) to give testimony that might incriminate him under the laws of another jurisdiction. Murphy v. Waterfront Comm'n, 378 U.S. 52 (1964).

What does the privilege protect? An early case held that seizure of a person's private books and papers, to be used as evidence in court, was the same as compelling the person to be a witness against himself or herself. Boyd v. United States, 116 U.S. 616 (1886). This sweeping interpretation was narrowed by subsequent decisions. Official or business records, including union records, are not protected by the Fourth or Fifth Amendments. The privilege against self-incrimination is a personal one and applies only to natural individuals, not to corporations or organizations.[23] Individuals cannot refuse to file a tax return simply because the government might discover income from criminal activities.

Drivers involved in an accident can be required to stop and provide their name and address, even at the risk of criminal liability. California v. Byers, 402 U.S. 424 (1971). Initially, the Court decided that federal requirements that gamblers register with the IRS did not violate the Self-Incrimination Clause, United States v. Kahriger, 345 U.S. 22 (1953) and Lewis v. United States, 348 U.S. 419 (1955). The Court later reversed itself and held that such statutes unconstitutionally compel gamblers to incriminate themselves. Marchetti v. United States, 390 U.S. 39 (1968); Grosso v. United States, 390 U.S. 62 (1968). It is unconstitutional to require a group to register and file a list of its members if that information can be used as evidence toward a criminal prosecution. Albertson v. SACB, 382 U.S. 70 (1965). Witnesses may not be asked to exercise this constitutional privilege at the cost of losing their jobs.[24]

In 1998, the Court held that a resident alien cannot invoke the Self-Incrimination Clause to withhold information from the U.S. government out of fear that disclosure might lead to prosecution by a foreign nation. Although an alien is a "person" under the Fifth Amendment,

---

22. If the defendant's attorney is concerned about jury misconceptions regarding the defendant's silence, the judge has an obligation, upon the attorney's request, to instruct the jury that the accused's decision not to testify cannot be used as an inference of guilt. Carter v. Kentucky, 450 U.S. 288 (1981). Instruction can possibly stimulate adverse inferences by calling attention to a defendant's silence. Lakeside v. Oregon, 435 U.S. 333 (1978). Earlier, in *Griffin* v. *California*, 380 U.S. 609 (1965), the Court held that state courts were not allowed to comment on a defendant's failure to testify.

23. Braswell v. United States, 487 U.S. 99 (1988); United States v. Doe, 465 U.S. 605 (1984); Fisher v. United States, 425 U.S. 391 (1976); Bellis v. United States, 417 U.S. 85 (1974); Campbell Painting Co. v. Reid, 392 U.S. 286 (1968); United States v. White, 322 U.S. 694 (1944); Wilson v. United States, 221 U.S. 361 (1911); Hale v. Henkel, 201 U.S. 43 (1906).

24. Lefkowitz v. Turley, 414 U.S. 70 (1973); Sanitation Men v. Sanitation Comm'n, 392 U.S. 280 (1968); Gardner v. Broderick, 392 U.S. 273 (1968); Garrity v. New Jersey, 385 U.S. 493 (1967); Slochower v. Board of Education, 350 U.S. 551 (1956). Lawyers who invoke their privilege against self-incrimination should not face disbarment as a result. Sperack v. Klein, 385 U.S. 511 (1967), overturning Cohen v. Hurley, 366 U.S. 117 (1961).

the Clause applies to prosecution of criminal cases in the United States, not in foreign countries. United States v. Balsys, 524 U.S. 666 (1998).

Nontestimonial Evidence

Novel issues suggest the difficulty of relying solely on "framers' intent." The Court has held that the extraction of blood by a physician in a hospital does not offend due process. A blood sample, containing alcohol, can be used to convict someone for involuntary manslaughter. Breithaupt v. Abram, 352 U.S. 432 (1957). A blood test, regarded as "physical or real" evidence rather than testimonial evidence, is unprotected by the Fifth Amendment. Blood may be extracted even if the patient refuses. Schmerber v. California, 384 U.S. 757 (1966). If someone arrested for drunk driving refuses to take a blood-alcohol test, the refusal may be used against him at trial without offending the Self-Incrimination Clause. South Dakota v. Neville, 459 U.S. 553 (1983). Police may videotape drunk-driving suspects and use evidence of their slurred speech against them at trial without first advising them of their constitutional rights. The Court considers slurred-speech evidence "non-testimonial" and therefore unprotected by the Self-Incrimination Clause and not requiring a *Miranda* warning. Pennsylvania v. Muniz, 496 U.S. 582 (1990). Handwriting samples may be taken of a suspect without violating the Self-Incrimination Clause. Gilbert v. California, 388 U.S. 263 (1967). An accused may be compelled to be present at a police lineup and utter the words of the person who committed the crime. United States v. Wade, 388 U.S. 218, 221–23 (1967).

A 1990 case concerned a woman held in civil contempt for refusing to produce to state authorities her infant son, who had been the subject of child abuse. The state feared that the child was abused or even dead. She claimed that the contempt order violated the Self-Incrimination Clause. A 7–2 Court held that she could not invoke the Clause under these circumstances, but did not decide whether the state could use her refusal in a subsequent criminal proceeding. Baltimore Dept. of Soc. Serv. v. Bouknight, 493 U.S. 549 (1990).

Immunity

Congress has enacted legislation to compel persons to testify by granting them immunity from prosecution. The Interstate Commerce Act of 1887 compelled persons to testify and produce documents. The claim of a witness that such testimony or evidence "may tend to criminate... shall not excuse such witness from testifying," but the evidence or testimony "shall not be used against such person on the trial of any criminal proceeding." 24 Stat. 383, § 12 (1887). The statute was revised two years later. 25 Stat. 858, § 3.

The Supreme Court held that this procedure did not conform to the Self-Incrimination Clause because it did not give a witness *absolute* immunity against future prosecution. Counselman v. Hitchcock, 142 U.S. 547 (1892). Congress rewrote the statute to provide that no person compelled to testify "shall be prosecuted or subjected to any penalty or forfeiture for or on account of any transaction, matter or thing, concerning which he may testify...." 27 Stat. 443 (1893). This is called "transactional immunity," offering complete immunity for the transaction (offense). In a 5–4 decision, the Supreme Court upheld this statute and rejected a literal interpretation of the Constitution. It concluded that compelled testimony, in the company of absolute immunity, met the essential purpose of the Self-Incrimination Clause, even if the testimony exposed the witness to public disgrace. Brown v. Walker, 161 U.S. 591, 595 (1896).[25]

---

25. Under certain statutes, if a witness appears in response to a subpoena and gives testimony, this action by itself may provide total immunity and prevent prosecution regardless of whether the witness claims the privilege against self-incrimination. United States v. Monia, 317 U.S. 424 (1943). See also Smith v. United States, 337 U.S. 137 (1949); Shapiro v. United States, 335 U.S. 1 (1948); United States v. Hoffman, 335 U.S. 77 (1948).

Compelled Testimony and Tainted Witnesses

In 1972 the Supreme Court held that Congress can compel testimony from an unwilling witness who invokes the Self-Incrimination Clause by conferring "use" (limited) immunity. However, the prosecution has the burden of proving affirmatively that evidence introduced at trial is derived from a legitimate source "wholly independent" of the compelled testimony. The prosecutor may not rely on information that is "directly or indirectly" derived from compelled testimony. Kastigar v. United States, 406 U.S. 441, 453, 460 (1972). At a "Kastigar hearing," trial judges must determine whether testimony given in court is tainted by immunized testimony presented to Congress.

The convictions of Lt. Col. Oliver North and Vice Admiral John Poindexter, stemming from the Iran-Contra affair, were overturned on appeal because independent counsel Lawrence E. Walsh had failed to show that the testimony of witnesses at the trials had not been impermissibly tainted by exposure to the immunized testimony of North and Poindexter to Congress.

In the North case, the D.C. Circuit adopted a heightened standard for use immunity. It held that a prohibited "use" occurs whenever a witness's testimony is in any way "shaped, altered, or affected" by immunized testimony. United States v. North, 910 F.2d 843, 863 (D.C. Cir. 1990). It returned the case to the trial court, requiring it to review the testimony of each witness "line-by-line and item-by-item." Id. at 872. That standard proved too onerous for the prosecution, and North's conviction was thrown out.

Poindexter's conviction was also overturned because the D.C. Circuit decided that independent counsel Walsh had not carried his burden of showing that Poindexter's compelled testimony was not used against him at his trial. When North testified at Poindexter's trial, he said he could not separate in his mind (1) what he knew after watching Poindexter's immunized testimony to Congress and (2) what he knew before from his own unrefreshed memory. United States v. Poindexter, 951 F.2d 369 (D.C. Cir. 1991), cert. denied, 506 U.S. 1021 (1992).

In 1954 Congress authorized the granting of immunity by a grand jury, by a majority of one House, or by a two-thirds majority of a congressional committee. Applications are made for a court order to compel testimony. Refusal to testify can result in contempt of court and imprisonment. 68 Stat. 745. The Court upheld this statute in Ullmann v. United States, 350 U.S. 422 (1956). The immunity procedure was codified in 1970 (84 Stat. 926) and appears in 18 U.S.C. §§ 6001–05 (1994). The immunity offered is called "use immunity" or "limited immunity." No testimony or other information compelled under a court order, or any information "directly or indirectly" derived from the testimony or other information, "may be used against the witness in any criminal case." 18 U.S.C. § 6002. Use immunity provides less protection than transactional immunity. A witness given use immunity may still be prosecuted for the crime on the basis of evidence obtained from independent sources. However, as the Iran-Contra cases of Lt. Col. Oliver North and Vice Admiral John Poindexter illustrate, the granting of limited immunity by Congress for the purpose of taking testimony at hearings makes it extremely difficult for the prosecution to demonstrate that the testimony of witnesses at trial has not been tainted by the compelled testimony (see box). The Supreme Court has held that the scope of use immunity under Section 6002 is coextensive with the Self-Incrimination Clause. Kastigar v. United States, 406 U.S. 441 (1972).

Mallory v. United States

354 U.S. 449 (1957)

Federal law officers arrested Andrew Mallory on charges of rape and proceeded to question him until he confessed about seven hours later. The issue was whether the police should have taken him before a magistrate "without unnecessary delay" in accordance with the Federal

Rules of Criminal Procedure. Some of the issues in this case were later crystallized in *Gideon* v. *Wainwright* (1963), *Escobedo* v. *Illinois* (1964), and *Miranda* v. *Arizona* (1966).

MR. JUSTICE FRANKFURTER delivered the opinion of the Court.

Petitioner was convicted of rape in the United States District Court for the District of Columbia, and, as authorized by the District Code, the jury imposed a death sentence. The Court of Appeals affirmed, one judge dissenting. 98 U. S. App. D. C. 406, 236 F. 2d 701. Since an important question involving the interpretation of the Federal Rules of Criminal Procedure was involved in this capital case, we granted the petition for certiorari. 352 U.S. 877.

The rape occurred at six p. m. on April 7, 1954, in the basement of the apartment house inhabited by the victim....

Petitioner and one of his grown nephews disappeared from the apartment house shortly after the crime was committed. The former was apprehended the following afternoon between two and two-thirty p. m. and was taken, along with his older nephews, also suspects, to police headquarters. At least four officers questioned him there in the presence of other officers for thirty to forty-five minutes, beginning the examination by telling him, according to his testimony, that his brother had said that he was the assailant. Petitioner strenuously denied his guilt. He spent the rest of the afternoon at headquarters, in the company of the other two suspects and his brother a good part of the time. About four p. m. the three suspects were asked to submit to "lie detector" tests, and they agreed. The officer in charge of the polygraph machine was not located for almost two hours, during which time the suspects received food and drink. The nephews were then examined first. Questioning of petitioner began just after eight p. m. Only he and the polygraph operator were present in a small room, the door to which was closed.

Following almost an hour and one-half of steady interrogation, he "first stated that he could have done this crime, or that he might have done it. He finally stated that he was responsible...." (Testimony of polygraph operator, R. 70.) Not until ten p. m., after petitioner had repeated his confession to other officers, did the police attempt to reach a United States Commissioner for the purpose of arraignment. Failing in this, they obtained petitioner's consent to examination by the deputy coroner, who noted no indicia of physical or psychological coercion. Petitioner was then confronted by the complaining witness and

"[p]ractically every man in the Sex Squad," and in response to questioning by three officers, he repeated the confession. Between eleven-thirty p. m. and twelve-thirty a. m. he dictated the confession to a typist. The next morning he was brought before a Commissioner. At the trial, which was delayed for a year because of doubt about petitioner's capacity to understand the proceedings against him, the signed confession was introduced in evidence.

The case calls for the proper application of Rule 5 (a) of the Federal Rules of Criminal Procedure, promulgated in 1946, 327 U. S. 821. That Rule provides:

"(a) APPEARANCE BEFORE THE COMMISSIONER. An officer making an arrest under a warrant issued upon a complaint or any person making an arrest without a warrant shall take the arrested person without unnecessary delay before the nearest available commissioner or before any other nearby officer empowered to commit persons charged with offenses against the laws of the United States. When a person arrested without a warrant is brought before a commissioner or other officer, a complaint shall be filed forthwith."

This provision has both statutory and judicial antecedents for guidance in applying it. The requirement that arraignment be "without unnecessary delay" is a compendious restatement, without substantive change, of several prior specific federal statutory provisions.... Nearly all the States have similar enactments.

In *McNabb* v. *United States,* 318 U. S. 332, 343–344, we spelled out the important reasons of policy behind this body of legislation:

"The purpose of this impressively pervasive requirement of criminal procedure is plain.... The awful instruments of the criminal law cannot be entrusted to a single functionary. The complicated process of criminal justice is therefore divided into different parts, responsibility for which is separately vested in the various participants upon whom the criminal law relies for its vindication. Legislation such as this, requiring that the police must with reasonable promptness show legal cause for detaining arrested persons, constitutes an important safeguard—not only in assuring protection for the innocent but also in securing conviction of the guilty by methods that commend themselves to a progressive and self-confident society. For this procedural requirement checks resort to those reprehensible practices known as the 'third degree' which, though universally rejected as indefensible, still find their way into use. It aims to avoid all the evil implications of secret interrogation of persons accused of crime."

Since such unwarranted detention led to tempting utilization of intensive interrogation, easily gliding into the evils of "the third degree," the Court held that police detention of defendants beyond the time when a committing magistrate was readily accessible constituted "willful disobedience of law." In order adequately to enforce the congressional requirement of prompt arraignment, it was deemed necessary to render inadmissible incriminating statements elicited from defendants during a period of unlawful detention.

. . .

The circumstances of this case preclude a holding that arraignment was "without unnecessary delay." Petitioner was arrested in the early afternoon and was detained at headquarters within the vicinity of numerous committing magistrates. Even though the police had ample evidence from other sources than the petitioner for regarding the petitioner as the chief suspect, they first questioned him for approximately a half hour. When this inquiry of a nineteen-year-old lad of limited intelligence produced no confession, the police asked him to submit to a "lie-detector" test. He was not told of his rights to counsel or to a pre-liminary examination before a magistrate, nor was he warned that he might keep silent and "that any statement made by him may be used against him." After four hours of further detention at headquarters, during which arraignment could easily have been made in the same building in which the police headquarters were housed, petitioner was examined by the lie-detector operator for another hour and a half before his story began to waver. Not until he had confessed, when any judicial caution had lost its purpose, did the police arraign him.

We cannot sanction this extended delay, resulting in confession, without subordinating the general rule of prompt arraignment to the discretion of arresting officers in finding exceptional circumstances for its disregard. In every case where the police resort to interrogation of an arrested person and secure a confession, they may well claim, and quite sincerely, that they were merely trying to check on the information given by him. Against such a claim and the evil potentialities of the practice for which it is urged stands Rule 5 (a) as a barrier. Nor is there an escape from the constraint laid upon the police by that Rule in that two other suspects were involved for the same crime. Presumably, whomever the police arrest they must arrest on "probable cause." It is not the function of the police to arrest, as it were, at large and to use an interrogating process at police headquarters in order to determine whom they should charge before a committing magistrate on "probable cause."

Reversed and remanded.

E. ASSISTANCE OF COUNSEL

The Sixth Amendment entitles a person "to have the Assistance of Counsel for his defence." Without counsel, an accused is unable to exercise effectively the rights available in the Constitution: the privilege to remain silent, to cross-examine witnesses, to challenge biased jurors, and a variety of subtle questions of law that tax the resourcefulness even of seasoned lawyers. "A layman is usually no match for the skilled prosecutor whom he confronts in the court room. He needs the aid of counsel lest he be the victim of overzealous prosecutors, of the law's complexity, or his own ignorance or bewilderment." Williams v. Kaiser, 323 U.S. 471, 476 (1945). A defendant may proceed without counsel if the decision is voluntary and the defendant is aware of the dangers and disadvantages of self-representation.[26]

The Court has held that government, in its fight against drug dealers and racketeers, may seize assets from those operations that criminal defendants intended to use to pay their

---

26. Faretta v. California, 422 U.S. 806 (1975); McKaskle v. Wiggins, 465 U.S. 168 (1984). Under certain circumstances, judges may deny the defendant's choice of lawyer. Wheat v. United States, 486 U.S. 153 (1988).

lawyers. The constitutional right to have assistance of counsel is not violated when government seizes ill-gotten gains. United States v. Monsanto, 491 U.S. 600 (1989); Caplin & Drysdale v. United States, 491 U.S. 617 (1989).

The question of providing an attorney for indigent defendants was decided partly by the Supreme Court in 1932 when it held that the Due Process Clause of the Fourteenth Amendment requires the appointment of counsel for someone accused of a capital crime. If a defendant is incapable of making his own defense because of "ignorance, feeblemindedness, illiteracy, or the like, it is the duty of the court, whether requested or not, to assign counsel for him as a necessary requisite of due process of law." Powell v. Alabama, 287 U.S. 45, 71 (1932). Six years later, the Court held that indigents charged with a crime in a federal court are entitled by the Sixth Amendment to have the assistance of counsel unless that right is intelligently and competently waived. Johnson v. Zerbst, 304 U.S. 458 (1938).

From *Betts* to *Gideon*

The question of providing counsel in a *state* court vexed the Court for more than two decades. In 1942 it ruled that a state's refusal to appoint counsel for an indigent in a criminal proceeding did not deny due process. Betts v. Brady, 316 U.S. 455 (1942). The Court divided 6–3 in this case, and dozens and dozens of subsequent decisions whittled away at the majority position. The denial of counsel in a state court brought four dissents in 1946. Carter v. Illinois, 329 U.S. 173. The Court agreed unanimously in 1954 that due process was violated when a state judge denied a defendant the opportunity to obtain counsel on a separate accusation regarding his habitual criminal record. Chandler v. Fretag, 348 U.S. 3. The Court split 5 to 4 in two cases in 1957 and 1959 in which counsel had been denied in a state proceeding. In re Groban, 352 U.S. 330; Anonymous v. Baker, 360 U.S. 287.

In 1960 the Court held that lack of counsel for an indigent in a state case deprived the accused of due process. As the two dissenters noted, the Court did not even mention *Betts v. Brady,* although the decision "cuts serious inroads into that holding." Hudson v. North Carolina, 363 U.S. 697, 704 (1960). A year later a unanimous Court ruled that due process had been violated by denying counsel to an indigent, ignorant, and mentally ill black. This was a noncapital felony case. Again, the opinion of the Court made no mention of *Betts.* McNeal v. Culver, 365 U.S. 109, 117 (1961). In two other noncapital felony cases, a unanimous Court held that the denial of counsel violated due process. Chewning v. Cunningham, 368 U.S. 443 (1962); Carnley v. Cochran, 369 U.S. 506 (1962). *Betts,* left dangling by a thread, was allowed to fall in 1963. A unanimous Court held that the Sixth Amendment right of assistance of counsel is incorporated in the Due Process Clause of the Fourteenth Amendment and applied against the states. GIDEON v. WAINWRIGHT, 372 U.S. 335 (1963). This decision provoked other rulings on the right of counsel (see box).

The Supreme Court received great credit for issuing *Gideon,* yet it lagged behind many states that had already recognized that government has a constitutional responsibility to provide counsel for indigents prosecuted by the state. The Supreme Court of Indiana in 1854 held that a "civilized community" could not put a citizen in jeopardy and withhold counsel from the poor. Webb v. Baird, 6 Ind. 13 (1854). In 1859 the Wisconsin Supreme Court called it a "mockery" to promise a pauper a fair trial and then tell him he must employ his own counsel. Carpenter v. Dane, 9 Wis. 249 (1859). Congress passed legislation in 1892 to provide counsel to represent poor persons and extended that provision in 1910. 27 Stat. 252 (1892); 36 Stat. 866 (1910).

No sooner had the Court forged a unanimous front to produce *Gideon,* it split 5–4 on a case that still divides the nation. Danny Escobedo was held in police headquarters for questioning regarding the fatal shooting of his brother-in-law. Although he asked to see his lawyer, who was in the building, the police rejected his request and eventually obtained a damaging

Assistance of Counsel

The Supreme Court's decision in *Gideon v. Wainwright* (1963), requiring states to appoint counsel for indigent defendants, precipitated a number of other decisions to define at what stage of a prosecution the assistance of counsel is needed.

Required

Assistance of counsel for a first appeal. Douglas v. California, 372 U.S. 353 (1963); Evitts v. Lucey, 469 U.S. 387 (1985).

Post-indictment lineups. United States v. Wade, 388 U.S. 218 (1967); Gilbert v. California, 388 U.S. 263 (1967).

Preliminary hearings. Coleman v. Alabama, 399 U.S. 1 (1970). This includes any adversary proceeding before trial in which the government seeks incriminating testimony. Brewer v. Williams, 430 U.S. 387, 401 (1977); Maine v. Moulton, 474 U.S. 159, 170 (1985).

Post-trial proceedings, such as sentencing. Mempa v. Rhay, 389 U.S. 128 (1967).

Assistance of counsel is needed if a sentence involves some imprisonment, whether the offense is classified as felony, misdemeanor, or petty. Argersinger v. Hamlin, 407 U.S. 25 (1972); Scott v. Illinois, 440 U.S. 367 (1979).

Assistance of psychiatrist for indigents whose main defense is insanity. Ake v. Oklahoma, 470 U.S. 68 (1985).

Not required

Counsel for additional appeals, such as a petition for certiorari to the U.S. Supreme Court. Ross v. Moffitt, 417 U.S. 600 (1974).

Pre-indictment "showup" at police station. Kirby v. Illinois, 406 U.S. 682 (1972).

Under certain circumstances, a suspect may be brought before a witness for the purpose of identification without the assistance of counsel. Stovall v. Denno, 388 U.S. 293 (1967); Kirby v. Illinois, 406 U.S. 682 (1972). This is not allowed, however, if the prosecutor uses a suggestive manner in presenting a suspect to the witness. Moore v. Illinois, 434 U.S. 220 (1971).

The right to counsel is not violated when an attorney refuses to agree to a defendant's desire to present perjured testimony. Nix v. Whiteside, 475 U.S. 157 (1986).

Counsel for death-row inmates seeking postconviction relief. Murray v. Giarrantano, 492 U.S. 1 (1989).

Post-indictment photographic display to allow witness to identify offender. United States v. Ash, 413 U.S. 300 (1973).

statement. The Court held that Escobedo had been denied the assistance of counsel in violation of the Sixth and Fourteenth Amendments. ESCOBEDO v. ILLINOIS, 378 U.S. 478 (1964). Recent cases have explored the criteria needed for "effective" assistance of counsel.[27]

The *Miranda* Warning

Building on cases involving coerced confessions, self-incrimination, and right to counsel, the Supreme Court in 1966 handed down the controversial *Miranda* ruling. The decision announced a cluster of constitutional rights for defendants who are held in police custody and cut off from the outside world. The atmosphere and environment of incommunicado interrogation was held to be inherently intimidating and hostile to the privilege against self-incrimination. To prevent compulsion by law enforcement officials, the person in custody must

---

27. Lockhart v. Fretwell, 506 U.S. 364 (1993); Lozada v. Deeds, 498 U.S. 430 (1991); Burger v. Kemp, 483 U.S. 776 (1987); Strictland v. Washington, 466 U.S. 688 (1984); United States v. Cronic, 466 U.S. 648 (1984); Jones v. Barnes, 463 U.S. 745 (1983); Wainwright v. Torna, 455 U.S. 586 (1982); Cuyler v. Sullivan, 446 U.S. 335 (1980); Holloway v. Arkansas, 435 U.S. 475 (1978).

be clearly informed—before interrogation—of the following: the right to remain silent, anything said may be used in court, the right to consult with an attorney and to have a lawyer present during interrogation, and the right to have a lawyer appointed if the accused is indigent. MIRANDA v. ARIZONA, 384 U.S. 436 (1966).

The decision did not rest solely on constitutional grounds. The Court invited Congress to contribute its handiwork: "Our decision in no way creates a constitutional straitjacket which will handicap sound efforts at reform, nor is it intended to have this effect. We encourage Congress and the States to continue their laudable search for increasingly effective ways of protecting the rights of the individual while promoting efficient enforcement of our criminal laws." Id. at 467. Congress passed legislation in 1968 to allow for the admissibility of confessions if voluntarily given. Trial judges would determine the issue of voluntariness after taking into consideration all the circumstances surrounding the confession, including five elements identified by Congress. 82 Stat. 210 (1968); 18 U.S.C. § 3501(a)(b) (1994).

Miranda has been bitterly attacked for restricting the efforts of law enforcement officials. However, the Supreme Court correctly noted that its holding was not "an innovation in our jurisprudence." 384 U.S. at 442. Indeed, *Miranda*-type warnings had been given routinely by federal agents in the past. McNabb v. United States, 318 U.S. 332, 336 (1943). They had been given by state officials, as the Court noted in *Michigan* v. *Tucker,* 417 U.S. 433, 447 (1974). Long before *Miranda,* state police recognized that an individual has a constitutional right to remain silent and that suspects must be told that anything said could be used against them in court. Haley v. Ohio, 332 U.S. 596, 598, 604 (1948).

Neither *Miranda* nor *Escobedo* was given full retroactivity. Johnson v. New Jersey, 384 U.S. 719 (1966). When applied to future prosecutions, the reversal of a conviction because of a *Miranda* violation does not mean that the suspect goes free. The state can try the case again without the tainted evidence. Orozco v. Texas, 394 U.S. 324 (1969).

In 1999, the Fourth Circuit held that *Miranda* was not a constitutional holding and that the statute Congress enacted in 1968 was the final say on the question of admissibility of a defendant's statement. The Supreme Court reversed the Fourth Circuit in 2000, ruling that *Miranda* was a constitutional decision and could not be overruled by Congress. DICKERSON v. UNITED STATES, 120 S.Ct. 2326 (2000).

When Is Someone in Custody?

Since 1966, *Miranda* has been modified by an evergrowing number of exceptions. Although an accused's statement to police may be rendered inadmissible under *Miranda,* it can be used to impeach the credibility of an accused who chooses to take the stand in his or her own defense. *Miranda* is not a license to commit perjury. Harris v. New York, 401 U.S. 222 (1971); Oregon v. Hass, 420 U.S. 714 (1975). If a defendant takes the stand and tells the jury a story that is inconsistent with what he told the police after being given *Miranda* warnings, cross-examination may probe these conflicting statements. Anderson v. Charles, 447 U.S. 404 (1980).

The reach of the *Miranda* rule is circumscribed by specific conditions. It does not apply to testimony before a grand jury. United States v. Mandujano, 425 U.S. 564 (1976). It applies only after a person is taken into custody. The Court admits that the definition of custody is "a slippery one" and presents "murky and difficult questions" of when it begins. Oregon v. Elstad, 470 U.S. 298, 309, 316 (1985). Although a person in custody is entitled to *Miranda* rights regardless of the nature of the offense (felony or misdemeanor), there is no need to read these rights for routine roadside stops by traffic cops. Berkemer v. McCarty, 468 U.S. 420 (1984). Moreover, if incriminating information can be obtained before a person is taken into custody and given the *Miranda* warning, the information is admissible as evidence. Oregon v. Mathiason, 429 U.S. 492 (1977). Police therefore have an incentive to talk to a suspect without placing him under arrest and reading the *Miranda* rights, in the hopes of uncovering incriminating evidence or eliciting a confession. California v. Beheler, 463 U.S. 1121 (1983). Convicted felons who are required to report to probation officers and be truthful "in all matters" are not considered "in custody." Therefore, any statements they make of an incriminating nature may be used against them in court. Minnesota v. Murphy, 465 U.S. 420 (1984).[28]

Once in Custody

Even after a person is in custody and advised of his *Miranda* rights, police officers may engage in a conversation between themselves that leads to an incriminating statement from the suspect. Such conversations are permissible if they are not "interrogations" (questioning intended to elicit an incriminating response). Rhode Island v. Innis, 446 U.S. 291 (1980). How do the courts distinguish between conversations and interrogations and decide whether the police intended to provoke an incriminating response?

Police questioning may expand for other reasons. After a suspect is given a *Miranda* warning and declines to comment, police may suspend questioning for a "significant" period, give another warning, and obtain incriminating information that is admissible as evidence. Michigan v. Mosley, 423 U.S. 96 (1975). Once an accused asks for counsel, the police may not return and interrogate him without counsel unless he voluntarily "initiates" the communication. Edwards v. Arizona, 451 U.S. 477 (1981).[29]

Edwards led to some confusion in the lower courts. Did *Edwards* only protect an accused between the time he invokes his right to counsel and consults counsel but not afterward? Is the protection of *Edwards* terminated or suspended simply because a suspect consults with counsel? In 1991 the Court ruled that the protection does not end but continues. It does not pass "in and out of existence." Minnick v. Mississippi, 498 U.S. 146, 154 (1991).

Further Erosion of *Miranda*

The opportunity for the police to question a suspect split the Court 5 to 4 in 1990. After a suspect told the police that he did not know whether he should talk to his lawyer, an officer said that it was unnecessary. He then made a statement that was later used to impeach his testimony, a procedure the Court upheld. Michigan v. Harvey, 494 U.S. 344 (1990). Another decision in 1990 held that the police may place an undercover agent in jail, posing as a fellow inmate, and it is not necessary to give *Miranda* warnings to a cellmate before eliciting an incriminating response. The essential ingredients that require *Miranda* warnings are a "police dominated atmosphere," coercion, and compulsion. An 8–1 Court decided that those conditions are not present in a jail cell block. Illinois v. Perkins, 496 U.S. 292 (1990).

In another *Miranda* interpretation in 1991, a 6–3 Court distinguished between the Fifth Amendment right to counsel set forth in *Miranda* and the Sixth Amendment right to counsel required by the Constitution. Thus, a suspect who is represented in court triggers the Sixth

---

28. In 1995, the Court reviewed a confession of murder that resulted from a two-hour, tape-recorded session at Alaska state trooper headquarters. The state trial and appellate courts determined that the suspect was not "in custody" when he confessed. Statutory law provides that state-court fact findings shall be presumed to be correct, but the Court held that the issue whether a suspect is "in custody" (and therefore entitled to *Miranda* warnings) presents a mixed question of law and fact warranting independent review by federal courts. Thompson v. Keohane, 516 U.S. 99 (1995).

29. See also Michigan v. Jackson, 475 U.S. 625 (1986); Shea v. Louisiana, 470 U.S. 51 (1985); Smith v. Illinois, 469 U.S. 91 (1984); Solem v. Stumes, 465 U.S. 638 (1984); Wyrick v. Fields, 459 U.S. 42 (1982). Further refinements depend on what kind of communication the accused "initiates": a substantive discussion about the crime or merely a routine request for a drink of water or use of the telephone. Oregon v. Bradshaw, 462 U.S. 1039 (1983). A refusal to make a written statement without counsel need not be interpreted to exclude an oral statement that is incriminating. Connecticut v. Barrett, 479 U.S. 523 (1987). See also Colorado v. Spring, 479 U.S. 564 (1987).

Amendment right to counsel but not the Fifth Amendment right. The Sixth Amendment right is "offense-specific." As a result, someone represented by a lawyer in court for one crime may be questioned by the police about a separate offense. Representation for one crime does not prevent the police from advising the suspect of his *Miranda* rights and obtaining incriminating statements about another crime. McNeil v. Wisconsin, 501 U.S. 171 (1991). In the future, counsel for defendants will have to state specifically that they are invoking their clients' *Miranda* rights.

In a major weakening of the *Miranda* doctrine in 1985, the Court held that if police officers violate *Miranda* procedures by obtaining a confession before reading a suspect his rights, the mistake may be cured by reading the rights later and obtaining a confession a second time. The suspect, having let the "cat out of the bag" with the first confession, may be more inclined to repeat it. OREGON v. ELSTAD, 470 U.S. 298 (1985). A year later, the Court clarified that the involuntariness of a confession after a *Miranda* warning derives only from police coercion, not from a defendant's mental condition (such as being told by the "voice of God" to confess). Colorado v. Connolly, 479 U.S. 157 (1986).

There is also a "public safety" exception to the *Miranda* rule. Its literal language may be waived if there is concern for the public safety. Thus, when an officer frisks a suspect and discovers an empty shoulder holster, it is appropriate to ask where the gun is before making formal arrest and reading the *Miranda* rights. New York v. Quarles, 467 U.S. 649 (1984). Moreover, a 5–4 Court decided that the warning need not be given in the exact form described in *Miranda,* but simply must reasonably convey to a suspect his or her rights. Thus, informing a suspect that an attorney would be appointed "if and when you go to court" does not render the warning inadequate. Duckworth v. Eagan, 492 U.S. 195 (1989).

Gideon v. Wainwright

372 U.S. 335 (1963)

In *Betts* v. *Brady* (1942), the Supreme Court held that an indigent defendant was not entitled to be appointed counsel for noncapital cases. That doctrine was undercut repeatedly in cases after *Betts*. Clarence Earl Gideon, sentenced to five years in the Florida state prison, had to defend himself at the trial without benefit of counsel. From his prison cell, with a handwritten note, he petitioned the Supreme Court to overturn *Betts*.

MR. JUSTICE BLACK delivered the opinion of the Court.

Petitioner was charged in a Florida state court with having broken and entered a poolroom with intent to commit a misdemeanor. This offense is a felony under Florida law. Appearing in court without funds and without a lawyer, petitioner asked the court to appoint counsel for him, whereupon the following colloquy took place:

"THE COURT: Mr. Gideon, I am sorry, but I cannot appoint Counsel to represent you in this case. Under the laws of the State of Florida, the only time the Court can appoint Counsel to represent a Defendant is when that person is charged with a capital offense. I am sorry, but I will have to deny your request to appoint Counsel to defend you in this case.

"THE DEFENDANT: The United States Supreme Court says I am entitled to be represented by Counsel."

Put to trial before a jury, Gideon conducted his defense about as well as could be expected from a layman. He made an opening statement to the jury, cross-examined the State's witnesses, presented witnesses in his own defense, declined to testify himself, and made a short argument "emphasizing his innocence to the charge contained in the Information filed in this case." The jury returned a verdict of guilty, and petitioner was sentenced to serve five years in the state prison. Later, petitioner filed in the Florida Supreme Court this habeas corpus petition attacking his conviction and sentence on the ground that the trial court's refusal to appoint counsel for him denied him rights "guaranteed by the Constitution and the Bill of Rights by the United States Government." Treating the petition for habeas corpus as properly before it, the State Supreme Court, "upon consideration thereof" but without an opinion, denied all relief. Since 1942, when *Betts* v. *Brady,* 316 U. S. 455, was decided by a divided Court, the problem of a defendant's federal constitutional right to counsel in a state court has been a continuing source of controversy and litigation in both state and federal courts. To give this problem another review here, we granted certiorari. 370 U.S. 908. Since Gideon was proceeding *in forma pauperis,* we appointed counsel to represent him and requested both sides to discuss in their briefs and oral arguments the following: "Should this Court's holding in *Betts* v. *Brady,* 316 U.S. 455, be reconsidered?"

I.

The facts upon which Betts claimed that he had been unconstitutionally denied the right to have counsel appointed to assist him are strikingly like the facts upon which Gideon here bases his federal constitutional claim. Betts was indicted for robbery in a Maryland state court. On arraignment, he told the trial judge of his lack of funds to hire a lawyer and asked the court to appoint one for him. Betts was advised that it was not the practice in that county to appoint counsel for indigent defendants except in murder and rape cases. He then pleaded not guilty, had witnesses summoned, cross-examined the State's witnesses, examined his own, and chose not to testify himself. He was found guilty by the judge, sitting without a jury, and sentenced to eight years in prison. Like Gideon, Betts sought release by habeas corpus, alleging that he had been denied the right to assistance of counsel in violation of the Fourteenth Amendment. Betts was denied any relief, and on review this Court affirmed. It was held that a refusal to appoint counsel for an indigent defendant charged with a felony did not necessarily violate the Due Process Clause of the Fourteenth Amendment,...

II.

The Sixth Amendment provides, "In all criminal prosecutions, the accused shall enjoy the right... to have the Assistance of Counsel for his defence." We have construed this to mean that in federal courts counsel must be provided for defendants unable to employ counsel unless the right is competently and intelligently waived. Betts argued that this right is extended to indigent defendants in state courts by the Fourteenth Amendment. In response the Court stated that,

while the Sixth Amendment laid down "no rule for the conduct of the States, the question recurs whether the constraint laid by the Amendment upon the national courts expresses a rule so fundamental and essential to a fair trial, and so, to due process of law, that it is made obligatory upon the States by the Fourteenth Amendment." 316 U.S., at 465....

. . .

We accept *Betts* v. *Brady*'s assumption, based as it was on our prior cases, that a provision of the Bill of Rights which is "fundamental and essential to a fair trial" is made obligatory upon the States by the Fourteenth Amendment. We think the Court in *Betts* was wrong, however, in concluding that the Sixth Amendment's guarantee of counsel is not one of these fundamental rights. Ten years before *Betts* v. *Brady,* this Court, after full consideration of all the historical data examined in *Betts,* had unequivocally declared that "the right to the aid of counsel is of this fundamental character." *Powell* v. *Alabama,* 287 U. S. 45, 68 (1932). While the Court at the close of its *Powell* opinion did by its language, as this Court frequently does, limit its holding to the particular facts and circumstances of that case, its conclusions about the fundamental nature of the right to counsel are unmistakable. Several years later, in 1936, the Court reemphasized what it had said about the fundamental nature of the right to counsel in this language:

"We concluded that certain fundamental rights, safeguarded by the first eight amendments against federal action, were also safeguarded against state action by the due process of law clause of the Fourteenth Amendment, and among them the fundamental right of the accused to the aid of counsel in a criminal prosecution." *Grosjean* v. *American Press Co.,* 297 U. S. 233, 243–244 (1936).

And again in 1938 this Court said:

"[The assistance of counsel] is one of the safeguards of the Sixth Amendment deemed necessary to insure fundamental human rights of life and liberty.... The Sixth Amendment stands as a constant admonition that if the constitutional safeguards it provides be lost, justice will not 'still be done.'" *Johnson* v. *Zerbst,* 304 U. S. 458, 462 (1938). To the same effect, see *Avery* v. *Alabama,* 308 U. S. 444 (1940), and *Smith* v. *O'Grady,* 312 U.S. 329 (1941).

In light of these and many other prior decisions of this Court, it is not surprising that the *Betts* Court, when faced with the contention that "one charged with crime, who is unable to obtain counsel, must be furnished counsel by the State," conceded that "[e]xpressions in the opinions of this court lend color to the argument...." 316 U.S., at 462–463. The fact is that in deciding as it did—that "appointment of counsel is not a fundamental right, essential to a fair trial"—the Court in *Betts* v. *Brady* made an abrupt break with its own well-considered precedents. In returning to these old precedents, sounder we believe than the new, we but restore constitutional principles established to achieve a fair system of justice. Not only these precedents but also reason and reflection require us to recognize that in our adversary system of criminal justice, any person hauled into court, who is too poor to hire a lawyer, cannot be assured a fair trial unless counsel is provided for him. This seems to us to be an obvious truth. Governments, both state and federal, quite properly spend vast sums of money to establish machinery to try defendants accused of crime. Lawyers to prosecute are everywhere deemed essential to protect the public's interest in an orderly society. Similarly, there are few defendants charged with crime, few indeed, who fail to hire the best lawyers they can get to prepare and present their defenses. That government hires lawyers to prosecute and defendants who have the money hire lawyers to defend are the strongest indications of the widespread belief that lawyers in criminal courts are necessities, not luxuries. The right of one charged with crime to counsel may not be deemed fundamental and essential to fair trials in some countries, but it is in ours. From the very beginning, our state and national constitutions and laws have laid great emphasis on procedural and substantive safeguards designed to assure fair trials before impartial tribunals in which every defendant stands equal before the law. This noble ideal cannot be realized if the poor man charged with crime has to face his accusers without a lawyer to assist him. A defendant's need for a lawyer is nowhere better stated than in the moving words of Mr. Justice Sutherland in *Powell* v. *Alabama:*

"The right to be heard would be, in many cases, of little avail if it did not comprehend the right to be heard by counsel. Even the intelligent and educated layman has small and sometimes no skill in the science of law. If charged with crime, he is incapable, generally, of determining for himself whether the indictment is good or bad. He is unfamiliar with the rules of evidence. Left without the aid of counsel he may be put on trial without a proper charge, and convicted upon incompetent evidence, or evidence irrelevant to the issue or otherwise inadmissible. He lacks both the skill and knowledge adequately to prepare his defense, even though he have a perfect one. He requires the guiding hand of counsel at every step in the proceedings against him. Without it, though he be not guilty, he faces the danger of conviction because he does not know how to establish his innocence." 287 U.S., at 68–69.

The Court in *Betts* v. *Brady* departed from the sound wisdom upon which the Court's holding in *Powell* v. *Alabama* rested. Florida, supported by two other States, has asked that *Betts* v. *Brady* be left intact. Twenty-two States, as friends of the Court, argue that *Betts* was "an anachronism when handed down" and that it should now be overruled. We agree.

The judgment is reversed and the cause is remanded to the Supreme Court of Florida for further action not inconsistent with this opinion.

Reversed.

MR. JUSTICE DOUGLAS. *[concurring opinion]*...

MR. JUSTICE CLARK, concurring in the result....

MR. JUSTICE HARLAN, concurring.

. . .

Escobedo v. Illinois

378 U.S. 478 (1964)

Danny Escobedo, a twenty-two-year-old of Mexican extraction, was arrested in connection with the fatal shooting of his brother-in-law. Although his lawyer was in police head-

quarters, the lawyer was denied access to see his client. The question was whether the refusal by the police to allow Escobedo to consult with his lawyer constituted a denial of the right to counsel.

MR. JUSTICE GOLDBERG delivered the opinion of the Court.

The critical question in this case is whether, under the circumstances, the refusal by the police to honor petitioner's request to consult with his lawyer during the course of an interrogation constitutes a denial of "the Assistance of Counsel" in violation of the Sixth Amendment to the Constitution as "made obligatory upon the States by the Fourteenth Amendment," *Gideon* v. *Wainwright,* 372 U. S. 335, 342, and thereby renders inadmissible in a state criminal trial any incriminating statement elicited by the police during the interrogation.

On the night of January 19, 1960, petitioner's brother-in-law was fatally shot. In the early hours of the next morning, at 2:30 a. m., petitioner was arrested without a warrant and interrogated. Petitioner made no statement to the police and was released at 5 that afternoon pursuant to a state court writ of habeas corpus obtained by Mr. Warren Wolfson, a lawyer who had been retained by petitioner.

On January 30, Benedict DiGerlando, who was then in police custody and who was later indicted for the murder along with petitioner, told the police that petitioner had fired the fatal shots. Between 8 and 9 that evening, petitioner and his sister, the widow of the deceased, were arrested and taken to police headquarters. En route to the police station, the police "had handcuffed the defendant behind his back," and "one of the arresting officers told defendant that DiGerlando had named him as the one who shot" the deceased. Petitioner testified, without contradiction, that the "detectives said they had us pretty well, up pretty tight, and we might as well admit to this crime," and that he replied, "I am sorry but I would like to have advice from my lawyer." A police officer testified that although petitioner was not formally charged "he was in custody" and "couldn't walk out the door."

Shortly after petitioner reached police headquarters, his retained lawyer arrived. The lawyer described the ensuing events in the following terms:

"On that day I received a phone call [from "the mother of another defendant"] and pursuant to that phone call I went to the Detective Bureau at 11th and State. The first person I talked to was the Sergeant on duty at the Bureau Desk, Sergeant Pidgeon. I asked Sergeant Pidgeon for permission to speak to my client, Danny Escobedo.... Sergeant Pidgeon made a call to the Bureau lockup and informed me that the boy had been taken from the lockup to the Homicide Bureau. This was between 9:30 and 10:00 in the evening. Before I went anywhere, he called the Homicide Bureau and told them there was an attorney waiting to see Escobedo. He told me I could not see him. Then I went upstairs to the Homicide Bureau. There were several Homicide Detectives around and I talked to them. I identified myself as Escobedo's attorney and asked permission to see him. They said I could not.... The police officer told me to see Chief Flynn who was on duty. I identified myself to Chief Flynn and asked permission to see my client. He said I could not.... I think it was approximately 11:00 o'clock. He said I couldn't see him because they hadn't completed questioning.... [F]or a second or two I spotted him in an office in the Homicide Bureau. The door was open and I could see through the office.... I waved to him and he waved back and then the door was closed, by one of the officers at Homicide. There were four or five officers milling around the Homicide Detail that night. As to whether I talked to Captain Flynn any later that day, I waited around for another hour or two and went back again and renewed by [*sic*] request to see my client. He again told me I could not.... I filed an official complaint with Commissioner Phelan of the Chicago Police Department. I had a conversation with every police officer I could find. I was told at Homicide that I couldn't see him and I would have to get a writ of habeas corpus. I left the Homicide Bureau and from the Detective Bureau at 11th and State at approximately 1:00 A.M. [Sunday morning] I had no opportunity to talk to my client that night. I quoted to Captain Flynn the Section of the Criminal Code which allows an attorney the right to see his client."

Petitioner testified that during the course of the interrogation he repeatedly asked to speak to his lawyer and that the police said that his lawyer "didn't want to see" him. The testimony of the police officers confirmed these accounts in substantial detail.

Notwithstanding repeated requests by each, petitioner and his retained lawyer were afforded no opportunity to consult during the course of the entire interrogation.

[During the interrogation, Escobedo made an incriminating statement and was later convicted of murder.]

The interrogation here was conducted before petitioner was formally indicted. But in the context of this case, that fact should make no difference. When petitioner requested, and was denied, an opportunity to consult with his lawyer, the investigation had ceased to be a general investigation of "an unsolved crime." *Spano v. New York,* 360 U. S. 315, 327 (STEWART, J., concurring). Petitioner had become the accused, and the purpose of the interrogation was to "get him" to confess his guilt despite his constitutional right not to do so. At the time of his arrest and throughout the course of the interrogation, the police told petitioner that they had convincing evidence that he had fired the fatal shots. Without informing him of his absolute right to remain silent in the face of this accusation, the police urged him to make a statement....

It is argued that if the right to counsel is afforded prior to indictment, the number of confessions obtained by the police will diminish significantly, because most confessions are obtained during the period between arrest and indictment, and "any lawyer worth his salt will tell the suspect in no uncertain terms to make no statement to police under any circumstances." *Watts v. Indiana,* 338 U. S. 49, 59 (Jackson, J., concurring in part and dissenting in part). This argument, of course, cuts two ways. The fact that many confessions are obtained during this period points up its critical nature as a "stage when legal aid and advice" are surely needed.... The right to counsel would indeed be hollow if it began at a period when few confessions were obtained. There is necessarily a direct relationship between the importance of a stage to the police in their quest for a confession and the criticalness of that stage to the accused in his need for legal advice. Our Constitution, unlike some others, strikes the balance in favor of the right of the accused to be advised by his lawyer of his privilege against self-incrimination. See Note, 73 Yale L. J. 1000, 1048–1051 (1964).

... This Court also has recognized that "history amply shows that confessions have often been extorted to save law enforcement officials the trouble and effort of obtaining valid and independent evidence...." *Haynes v. Washington,* 373 U. S. 503, 519.

We have also learned the companion lesson of history that no system of criminal justice can, or should, survive if it comes to depend for its continued effectiveness on the citizens' abdication through unawareness of their constitutional rights. No system worth preserving should have to *fear* that if an accused is permitted to consult with a lawyer, he will become aware of, and exercise, these rights. If the exercise of constitutional rights will thwart the effectiveness of a system of law enforcement, then there is something very wrong with that system.

We hold, therefore, that where, as here, the investigation is no longer a general inquiry into an unsolved crime but has begun to focus on a particular suspect, the suspect has been taken into police custody, the police carry out a process of interrogations that lends itself to eliciting incriminating statements, the suspect has requested and been denied an opportunity to consult with his lawyer, and the police have not effectively warned him of his absolute constitutional right to remain silent, the accused has been denied "the Assistance of Counsel" in violation of the Sixth Amendment to the Constitution as "made obligatory upon the States by the Fourteenth Amendment," *Gideon v. Wainwright,* 372 U. S., at 342, and that no statement elicited by the police during the interrogation may be used against him at a criminal trial.

. . .

The judgment of the Illinois Supreme Court is reversed and the case remanded for proceedings not inconsistent with this opinion.

Reversed and remanded.

MR. JUSTICE HARLAN, dissenting.

I would affirm the judgment of the Supreme Court of Illinois on the basis of *Cicenia v. Lagay,* 357 U. S. 504, decided by this Court only six years ago. Like my Brother WHITE, ... I think the rule announced today is most ill-conceived and that it seriously and unjustifiably fetters perfectly legitimate methods of criminal law enforcement.

MR. JUSTICE STEWART, dissenting.

I think this case is directly controlled by *Cicenia v. Lagay,* 357 U. S. 504, and I would therefore affirm the judgment.

. . .

MR. JUSTICE WHITE, with whom MR. JUSTICE CLARK and MR. JUSTICE STEWART join, dissenting.

. . .

...The only "inquisitions" the Constitution forbids are those which compel incrimination. Escobedo's statements were not compelled and the Court does not hold that they were.

This new American judges' rule, which is to be applied in both federal and state courts, is perhaps thought to be a necessary safeguard against the possibility of extorted confessions. To this extent it reflects a deep-seated distrust of law enforcement officers everywhere, unsupported by relevant data or current material based upon our own experience. Obviously law enforcement officers can make mistakes and exceed their authority, as today's decision shows that even judges can do, but I have somewhat more faith than the Court evidently has in the ability and desire of prosecutors and of the power of the appellate courts to discern and correct such violations of the law.

Miranda v. Arizona

384 U.S. 436 (1966)

Prior to 1966, Supreme Court decisions had established a number of rights for individuals taken into police custody: defendants had to be arraigned before a neutral magistrate; indigent defendants had a right to court-appointed counsel; confessions could not be coerced. In this landmark decision, the Court announced the rights available to an accused during police interrogation to protect his or her constitutional privilege against self-incrimination. Ernesto Miranda confessed to a crime during police interrogation without requesting the assistance of counsel.

Mr. Chief Justice Warren delivered the opinion of the Court.

The cases before us raise questions which go to the roots of our concepts of American criminal jurisprudence: the restraints society must observe consistent with the Federal Constitution in prosecuting individuals for crime. More specifically, we deal with the admissibility of statements obtained from an individual who is subjected to custodial police interrogation and the necessity for procedures which assure that the individual is accorded his privilege under the Fifth Amendment to the Constitution not to be compelled to incriminate himself.

. . .

I.

The constitutional issue we decide in each of these cases is the admissibility of statements obtained from a defendant questioned while in custody or otherwise deprived of his freedom of action in any significant way. In each, the defendant was questioned by police officers, detectives, or a prosecuting attorney in a room in which he was cut off from the outside world. In none of these cases was the defendant given a full and effective warning of his rights at the outset of the interrogation process. In all the cases, the questioning elicited oral admissions, and in three of them, signed statements as well which were admitted at their trials. They all thus share salient features—incommunicado interrogation of individuals in a police-dominated atmosphere, resulting in self-incriminating statements without full warnings of constitutional rights.

An understanding of the nature and setting of this in-custody interrogation is essential to our decisions today. The difficulty in depicting what transpires at such interrogations stems from the fact that in this country they have largely taken place incommunicado. From extensive factual studies undertaken in the early 1930's, including the famous Wickersham Report to Congress by a Presidential Commission, it is clear that police violence and the "third degree" flourished at that time. In a series of cases decided by this Court long after these studies, the police resorted to physical brutality—beating, hanging, whipping—and to sustained and protracted questioning incommunicado in order to extort confessions....

The examples given above are undoubtedly the exception now, but they are sufficiently widespread to be the object of concern. Unless a proper limitation upon custodial interrogation is achieved—such as these decisions will advance—there can be no assurance that practices of this nature will be eradicated in the foreseeable future....

Again we stress that the modern practice of in-custody interrogation is psychologically rather than physically oriented. As we have stated before, "Since *Chambers* v. *Florida,* 309 U. S. 227, this Court has recognized that coercion can be mental as well as physical, and that the blood of the accused is not the only hallmark of an unconstitutional inquisition." *Blackburn* v. *Alabama,* 361 U.S. 199, 206 (1960)....

The officers are told by the manuals that the "principal psychological factor contributing to a successful interrogation is *privacy* — being alone with the person under interrogation." The efficacy of this tactic has been explained as follows:

"If at all practicable, the interrogation should take place in the investigator's office or at least in a room of his own choice. The subject should be deprived of every psychological advantage. In his own home he may be confident, indignant, or recalcitrant. He is more keenly aware of his rights and more reluctant to tell of his indiscretions or criminal behavior within the walls of his home. Moreover his family and other friends are nearby, their presence lending moral support. In his own office, the investigator possesses all the advantages. The atmosphere suggests the invincibility of the forces of the law."

To highlight the isolation and unfamiliar surroundings, the manuals instruct the police to display an air of confidence in the suspect's guilt and from outward appearance to maintain only an interest in confirming certain details. The guilt of the subject is to be posited as a fact. The interrogator should direct his comments toward the reasons why the subject committed the act, rather than court failure by asking the subject whether he did it. Like other men, perhaps the subject has had a bad family life, had an unhappy childhood, had too much to drink, had an unrequited desire for women. The officers are instructed to minimize the moral seriousness of the offense, to cast blame on the victim or on society. These tactics are designed to put the subject in a psychological state where his story is but an elaboration of what the police purport to know already — that he is guilty. Explanations to the contrary are dismissed and discouraged.

. . .

It is obvious that such an interrogation environment is created for no purpose other than to subjugate the individual to the will of his examiner. This atmosphere carries its own badge of intimidation. To be sure, this is not physical intimidation, but it is equally destructive of human dignity. The current practice of incommunicado

interrogation is at odds with one of our Nation's most cherished principles — that the individual may not be compelled to incriminate himself. Unless adequate protective devices are employed to dispel the compulsion inherent in custodial surroundings, no statement obtained from the defendant can truly be the product of his free choice.

. . .

III.

Today, then, there can be no doubt that the Fifth Amendment privilege is available outside of criminal court proceedings and serves to protect persons in all settings in which their freedom of action is curtailed in any significant way from being compelled to incriminate themselves. We have concluded that without proper safeguards the process of in-custody interrogation of persons suspected or accused of crime contains inherently compelling pressures which work to undermine the individual's will to resist and to compel him to speak where he would not otherwise do so freely. In order to combat these pressures and to permit a full opportunity to exercise the privilege against self-incrimination, the accused must be adequately and effectively apprised of his rights and the exercise of those rights must be fully honored.

It is impossible for us to foresee the potential alternatives for protecting the privilege which might be devised by Congress or the States in the exercise of their creative rule-making capacities. Therefore we cannot say that the Constitution necessarily requires adherence to any particular solution for the inherent compulsions of the interrogation process as it is presently conducted. Our decision in no way creates a constitutional straitjacket which will handicap sound efforts at reform, nor is it intended to have this effect. We encourage Congress and the States to continue their laudable search for increasingly effective ways of protecting the rights of the individual while promoting efficient enforcement of our criminal laws. However, unless we are shown other procedures which are at least as effective in apprising accused persons of their right of silence and in assuring a continuous opportunity to exercise it, the following safeguards must be observed.

At the outset, if a person in custody is to be subjected to interrogation, he must first be informed in clear and unequivocal terms that he has the right to remain silent. For those unaware of the privilege, the warning is needed simply to make them aware of it — the threshold requirement for an intelligent decision as to its exercise.

More important, such a warning is an absolute prerequisite in overcoming the inherent pressures of the interrogation atmosphere....

The warning of the right to remain silent must be accompanied by the explanation that anything said can and will be used against the individual in court. This warning is needed in order to make him aware not only of the privilege, but also of the consequences of forgoing it....

The circumstances surrounding in-custody interrogation can operate very quickly to overbear the will of one merely made aware of his privilege by his interrogators. Therefore, the right to have counsel present at the interrogation is indispensable to the protection of the Fifth Amendment privilege under the system we delineate today....

In order fully to apprise a person interrogated of the extent of his rights under this system then, it is necessary to warn him not only that he has the right to consult with an attorney, but also that if he is indigent a lawyer will be appointed to represent him. Without this additional warning, the admonition of the right to consult with counsel would often be understood as meaning only that he can consult with a lawyer if he has one or has the funds to obtain one....

Over the years the Federal Bureau of Investigation has compiled an exemplary record of effective law enforcement while advising any suspect or arrested person, at the outset of an interview, that he is not required to make a statement, that any statement may be used against him in court, that the individual may obtain the services of an attorney of his own choice and, more recently, that he has a right to free counsel if he is unable to pay....

MR. JUSTICE CLARK, dissenting in Nos. 759, 760, and 761, and concurring in the result in No. 584.

It is with regret that I find it necessary to write in these cases. However, I am unable to join the majority because its opinion goes too far on too little, while my dissenting brethren do not go quite far enough. Nor can I join in the Court's criticism of the present practices of police and investigatory agencies as to custodial interrogation. The materials it refers to as "police manuals" are, as I read them, merely writings in this field by pro-

fessors and some police officers. Not one is shown by the record here to be the official manual of any police department, much less in universal use in crime detection. Moreover, the examples of police brutality mentioned by the Court are rare exceptions to the thousands of cases that appear every year in the law reports....

MR. JUSTICE HARLAN, whom MR. JUSTICE STEWART and MR. JUSTICE WHITE join, dissenting.

I believe the decision of the Court represents poor constitutional law and entails harmful consequences for the country at large. How serious these consequences may prove to be only time can tell....

...There can be little doubt that the Court's new code would markedly decrease the number of confessions. To warn the suspect that he may remain silent and remind him that his confession may be used in court are minor obstructions. To require also an express waiver by the suspect and an end to questioning whenever he demurs must heavily handicap questioning. And to suggest or provide counsel for the suspect simply invites the end of the interrogation....

...The foray which the Court makes today brings to mind the wise and farsighted words of Mr. Justice Jackson in *Douglas* v. *Jeannette,* 319 U. S. 157, 181 (separate opinion): "This Court is forever adding new stories to the temples of constitutional law, and the temples have a way of collapsing when one story too many is added."

MR. JUSTICE WHITE, with whom MR. JUSTICE HARLAN and MR. JUSTICE STEWART join, dissenting.

...There is, in my view, every reason to believe that a good many criminal defendants who otherwise would have been convicted on what this Court has previously thought to be the most satisfactory kind of evidence will now, under this new version of the Fifth Amendment, either not be tried at all or will be acquitted if the State's evidence, minus the confession, is put to the test of litigation.

· · ·

Dickerson v. United States

120 S.Ct. 2326 (2000)*

Charles Thomas Dickerson was charged with conspiracy to commit bank robbery and other offenses. His motion, to suppress a statement he had made on the ground that it was obtained in violation of *Miranda*, was granted by a district court. The Fourth Circuit reversed the suppression order. It agreed with the district court that Dickerson had not received *Miranda* warnings before making his statement, but also held that *Miranda* was not a constitutional holding and that a statute enacted by Congress to modify *Miranda* was the final say on the question of admissibility of the statement.

CHIEF JUSTICE REHNQUIST delivered the opinion of the Court.

In *Miranda* v. *Arizona*, 384 U.S. 436 (1966), we held that certain warnings must be given before a suspect's statement made during custodial interrogation could be admitted in evidence. In the wake of that decision, Congress enacted 18 U.S.C. §3501, which in essence laid down a rule that the admissibility of such statements should turn only on whether or not they were voluntarily made. We hold that *Miranda*, being a constitutional decision of this Court, may not be in effect overruled by an Act of Congress, and we decline to overrule *Miranda* ourselves. We therefore hold that *Miranda* and its progeny in this Court govern the admissibility of statements made during custodial interrogation in both state and federal courts.

...Prior to *Miranda*, we evaluated the admissibility of a suspect's confession under a voluntariness test. The roots of this test developed in the common law, as the courts of England and then the United States recognized that coerced confessions are inherently untrustworthy.... Over time, our cases recognized two constitutional bases for the requirement that a confession be voluntary to be admitted into evidence: the Fifth Amendment right against self-incrimination and the Due Process Clause of the Fourteenth Amendment. See, *e.g.*, *Bram* v. *United States*, 168 U.S. 532, 542 (1897) (stating that the voluntariness test "is controlled by that portion of the Fifth Amendment...commanding that no person 'shall be compelled in any criminal case to be a

witness against himself' "); *Brown* v. *Mississippi*, 297 U.S. 278 (1936) (reversing a criminal conviction under the Due Process Clause because it was based on a confession obtained by physical coercion).

While *Bram* was decided before *Brown* and its progeny, for the middle third of the 20th century our cases based the rule against admitting coerced confessions primarily, if not exclusively, on notions of due process.... Those cases refined the test into an inquiry that examines "whether a defendant's will was overborne" by the circumstances surrounding the giving of a confession. *Schneckloth [v. Bustamonte]*, 412 U.S., at 226....

We have never abandoned this due process jurisprudence, and thus continue to exclude confessions that were obtained involuntarily....

In *Miranda*, we noted that the advent of modern custodial police interrogation brought with it an increased concern about confessions obtained by coercion.... We concluded that the coercion inherent in custodial interrogation blurs the line between voluntary and involuntary statements, and thus heightens the risk that an individual will not be "accorded his privilege under the Fifth Amendment...not to be compelled to incriminate himself."...Accordingly, we laid down "concrete constitutional guidelines for law enforcement agencies and courts to follow."...

Two years after *Miranda* was decided, Congress enacted §3501. That section provides, in relevant part:

"(a) In any criminal prosecution brought by the United States or by the District of Columbia, a confession...shall be admissible in evidence if it is voluntarily given. Before such confession is received in evidence, the trial judge shall, out of the

* The text for this case was obtained in electronic form from Westlaw and is reproduced by permission of the West Group.

presence of the jury, determine any issue as to voluntariness. If the trial judge determines that the confession was voluntarily made it shall be admitted in evidence and the trial judge shall permit the jury to hear relevant evidence on the issue of voluntariness and shall instruct the jury to give such weight to the confession as the jury feels it deserves under all the circumstances.

"(b) The trial judge in determining the issue of voluntariness shall take into consideration all the circumstances surrounding the giving of the confession, ..."

... Congress may not legislatively supersede our decisions interpreting and applying the Constitution. See, *e.g., City of Boerne* v. *Flores*, 521 U.S. 507, 517–521 (1997). This case therefore turns on whether the *Miranda* Court announced a constitutional rule or merely exercised its supervisory authority to regulate evidence in the absence of congressional direction. Recognizing this point, the Court of Appeals surveyed *Miranda* and its progeny to determine the constitutional status of the *Miranda* decision.... Relying on the fact that we have created several exceptions to *Miranda*'s warnings requirement and that we have repeatedly referred to the *Miranda* warnings as "prophylactic," *New York* v. *Quarles*, 467 U.S. 649, 653 (1984), and "not themselves rights protected by the Constitution," *Michigan* v. *Tucker*, 417 U.S. 433, 444 (1974), the Court of Appeals concluded that the protections announced in *Miranda* are not constitutionally required....

We disagree with the Court of Appeals' conclusion, although we concede that there is language in some of our opinions that supports the view taken by that court. But first and foremost of the factors on the other side—that *Miranda* is a constitutional decision—is that both *Miranda* and two of its companion cases applied the rule to proceedings in state courts—to wit, Arizona, California, and New York.... Since that time, we have consistently applied *Miranda*'s rule to prosecutions arising in state courts....

The *Miranda* opinion itself begins by stating that the Court granted certiorari "to explore some facets of the problems... of applying the privilege against self-incrimination to in-custody interrogation, *and to give concrete constitutional guidelines for law enforcement agencies and courts to follow.*" 384 U.S., at 441–442 (emphasis added). In fact, the majority opinion is replete with statements indicating that the majority thought it was announcing a constitutional rule....

Additional support for our conclusion that *Miranda* is constitutionally based is found in the *Miranda* Court's invitation for legislative action to protect the constitutional right against coerced self-incrimination. After discussing the "compelling pressures" inherent in custodial police interrogation, the *Miranda* Court concluded that, "[i]n order to combat these pressures and to permit a full opportunity to exercise the privilege against self-incrimination, the accused must be adequately and effectively appraised of his rights and the exercise of those rights must be fully honored." *Id.*, at 467. However, the Court emphasized that it could not foresee "the potential alternatives for protecting the privilege which might be devised by Congress or the States," and it accordingly opined that the Constitution would not preclude legislative solutions that differed from the prescribed *Miranda* warnings but which were "at least as effective in apprising accused persons of their right of silence and in assuring a continuous opportunity to exercise it." *Ibid.*

[*Note 6 provides*: The Court of Appeals relied in part on our statement that the *Miranda* decision in no way "creates a 'constitutional straightjacket.'" ... However, a review of our opinion in *Miranda* clarifies that this disclaimer was intended to indicate that the Constitution does not require police to administer the particular *Miranda* warnings, not that the Constitution does not require a procedure that is effective in securing Fifth Amendment rights.]

The Court of Appeals also relied on the fact that we have, after our *Miranda* decision, made exceptions from its rule in cases such as *New York* v. *Quarles*... and *Harris* v. *New York*... But we have also broadened the application of the *Miranda* doctrine in cases such as *Doyle* v. *Ohio*... and *Arizona* v. *Roberson*, ... These decisions illustrate the principle—not that *Miranda* is not a constitutional rule—but that no constitutional rule is immutable....

. . .

Whether or not we would agree with *Miranda*'s reasoning and its resulting rule, were we addressing the issue in the first instance, the principles of *stare decisis* weigh heavily against overruling it now....

We do not think there is such justification for overruling *Miranda*. *Miranda* has become embedded in routine police practice to the point where the warnings have become part of our national culture....

In sum, we conclude that *Miranda* announced a constitutional rule that Congress may not supersede legislatively. Following the rule of *stare decisis*, we decline to overrule *Miranda* ourselves. The judgment of the Court of Appeals is therefore

Reversed.

JUSTICE SCALIA, with whom JUSTICE THOMAS joins, dissenting.

Those to whom judicial decisions are an unconnected series of judgments that produce either favored or disfavored results will doubtless greet today's decision as a paragon of moderation, since it declines to overrule *Miranda* v. *Arizona*, 384 U.S. 436 (1966). Those who understand the judicial process will appreciate that today's decision is not a reaffirmation of *Miranda*, but a radical revision of the most significant element of *Miranda* (as of all cases): the rationale that gives it a permanent place in our jurisprudence.

Marbury v. *Madison* ... held that an Act of Congress will not be enforced by the courts if what it prescribes violates the Constitution of the United States. That was the basis on which *Miranda* was decided. One will search today's opinion in vain, however, for a statement (surely simple enough to make) that what 18 U.S.C. §3501 prescribes—the use at trial of a voluntary confession, even when a *Miranda* warning or its equivalent has failed to be given—violates the Constitution. The reason the statement does not appear is not only (and perhaps not so much) that it would be absurd, inasmuch as §3501 excludes from trial precisely what the Constitution excludes from trial, viz., compelled confessions; but also that Justices whose votes are needed to compose today's majority are on record as believing that a violation of *Miranda* is not a violation of the Constitution.... And so, to justify today's agreed-upon result, the Court must adopt a significant new, if not entirely comprehensible, principle of constitutional law. As the Court chooses to describe that principle, statutes of Congress can be disregarded, not only when what they prescribe violates the Constitution, but when what they prescribe contradicts a decision of this Court that "announced a constitutional rule," ... As I shall discuss in some detail, the only thing that can possibly mean in the context of this case is that this Court has the power, not merely to apply the Constitution but to expand it, imposing what it regards as useful "prophylactic" restrictions upon Congress and the States. That is an immense and frightening antidemocratic power, and it does not exist.

. . .

II

. . .

The issue ... is not whether court rules are "mutable"; they assuredly are. It is not whether, in the light of "various circumstances," they can be "modifi[ed]"; they assuredly can. The issue is whether, *as mutated and modified*, they must *make sense*. The requirement that they do so is the only thing that prevents this Court from being some sort of nine-headed Caesar, giving thumbs-up or thumbs-down to whatever outcome, case by case, suits or offends its collective fancy....

Finally, the Court asserts that *Miranda* must be a "constitutional decision" announcing a "constitutional rule," and thus immune to congressional modification, because we have since its inception applied it to the States. If this argument is meant as an invocation of *stare decisis*, it fails because, though it is true that our cases applying *Miranda* against the States must be reconsidered if *Miranda* is not required by the Constitution, it is likewise true that our cases (discussed above) based on the principle that *Miranda* is *not* required by the Constitution will have to be reconsidered if it *is*. So the *stare decisis* argument is a wash....

IV

... I am not convinced by petitioner's argument that *Miranda* should be preserved because the decision occupies a special place in the "public's consciousness." ... As far as I am aware, the public is not under the illusion that we are infallible. I see little harm in admitting that we made a mistake in taking away from the people the ability to decide for themselves what protections (beyond those required by the Constitution) are reasonably affordable in the criminal investigatory process....

* * *

Today's judgment converts *Miranda* from a milestone of judicial overreaching into the very Cheops' Pyramid (or perhaps the Sphinx would be a better analogue) of judicial arrogance....

I dissent from today's decision, and, until §3501 is repealed, will continue to apply it in all cases where there has been a sustainable finding that the defendant's confession was voluntary.

Oregon v. Elstad

470 U.S. 298 (1985)

Police officers picked up Michael James Elstad at his home as a suspect in a burglary. Without being given the warnings required by *Miranda* v. *Arizona* (1966), he made an incriminating statement. At the station house, after he was advised of and waived his *Miranda* rights, he executed a written confession. Should his confession have been excluded from trial because his first incriminating statement, before the *Miranda* warnings, had let "the cat out of the bag"? Does *Miranda* protect a suspect only after he is officially in custody? When is a person in custody? Elstad's conviction was reversed by the Oregon Court of Appeals.

JUSTICE O'CONNOR delivered the opinion of the Court.

This case requires us to decide whether an initial failure of law enforcement officers to administer the warnings required by *Miranda* v. *Arizona,* 384 U.S. 436 (1966), without more, "taints" subsequent admissions made after a suspect has been fully advised of and has waived his *Miranda* rights....

I

In December 1981, the home of Mr. and Mrs. Gilbert Gross, in the town of Salem, Polk County, Ore., was burglarized. Missing were art objects and furnishings valued at $150,000. A witness to the burglary contacted the Polk County Sheriff's Office, implicating respondent Michael Elstad, an 18-year-old neighbor and friend of the Grosses' teenage son. Thereupon, Officers Burke and McAllister went to the home of respondent Elstad, with a warrant for his arrest. Elstad's mother answered the door. She led the officers to her son's room where he lay on his bed, clad in shorts and listening to his stereo. The officers asked him to get dressed and to accompany them into the living room. Officer McAllister asked respondent's mother to step into the kitchen, where he explained that they had a warrant for her son's arrest for the burglary of a neighbor's residence. Officer Burke remained with Elstad in the living room. He later testified:

"I sat down with Mr. Elstad and I asked him if he was aware of why Detective McAllister and myself were there to talk with him. He stated no, he had no idea why we were there. I then asked him if he knew a person by the name of Gross, and he said yes, he did, and also added that he heard that there was a robbery at the Gross house. And at that point I told Mr. Elstad that I felt he was involved in that, and he looked at me and stated, 'Yes, I was there.' "...

Elstad was transported to the Sheriff's headquarters and approximately one hour later, Officers Burke and McAllister joined him in McAllister's office. McAllister then advised respondent for the first time of his *Miranda* rights, reading from a standard card. Respondent indicated he understood his rights, and, having these rights in mind, wished to speak with the officers. Elstad gave a full statement, explaining that he had known that the Gross family was out of town and had been paid to lead several acquaintances to the Gross residence and show them how to gain entry through a defective sliding glass door. The statement was typed, reviewed by respondent, read back to him for correction, initialed and signed by Elstad and both officers. As an afterthought, Elstad added and initialed the sentence, "After leaving the house Robby & I went back to [the] van & Robby handed me a small bag of grass."...Respondent concedes that the officers made no threats or promises either at his residence or at the Sheriff's office.

Respondent was charged with first-degree burglary. He was represented at trial by retained counsel. Elstad waived his right to a jury, and his case was tried by a Circuit Court Judge. Respondent moved at once to suppress his oral statement and signed confession. He contended that the statement he made in response to questioning at his house "let the cat out of the bag," citing *United States* v. *Bayer,* 331 U.S. 532 (1947), and tainted the subsequent confession as "fruit of the poisonous tree," citing *Wong Sun* v. *United States,* 371 U.S. 471 (1963). The judge ruled that the statement, "I was there," had to be excluded because the defendant had not been advised of his *Miranda* rights. The written confession taken after Elstad's arrival at the Sheriff's office, however, was admitted in evidence. The court found:

"[H]is written statement was given freely, voluntarily and knowingly by the defendant after he had waived his right to remain silent and have counsel present which waiver was evidenced by the card which the defendant had signed. [It] was not tainted in any way by the previous brief statement between the defendant and the Sheriff's Deputies that had arrested him." ...

Elstad was found guilty of burglary in the first degree. He received a 5-year sentence and was ordered to pay $18,000 in restitution.

. . .

II

The arguments advanced in favor of suppression of respondent's written confession rely heavily on metaphor. One metaphor, familiar from the Fourth Amendment context, would require that respondent's confession, regardless of its integrity, voluntariness, and probative value, be suppressed as the "tainted fruit of the poisonous tree" of the *Miranda* violation. A second metaphor questions whether a confession can be truly voluntary once the "cat is out of the bag." Taken out of context, each of these metaphors can be misleading. They should not be used to obscure fundamental differences between the role of the Fourth Amendment exclusionary rule and the function of *Miranda* in guarding against the prosecutorial use of compelled statements as prohibited by the Fifth Amendment. The Oregon court assumed and respondent here contends that a failure to administer *Miranda* warnings necessarily breeds the same consequences as police infringement of a constitutional right, so that evidence uncovered following an unwarned statement must be suppressed as "fruit of the poisonous tree." We believe this view misconstrues the nature of the protections afforded by *Miranda* warnings and therefore misreads the consequences of police failure to supply them.

A

. . .

Because *Miranda* warnings may inhibit persons from giving information, this Court has determined that they need be administered only after the person is taken into "custody" or his freedom has otherwise been significantly restrained. *Miranda* v. *Arizona,* 384 U.S., at 478. Unfortunately, the task of defining "custody" is a slippery one, and "policemen investigating serious crimes [cannot realistically be expected to] make no errors whatsoever." *Michigan* v. *Tucker, supra,* at 446. If errors are made by law enforcement officers in administering the prophylactic *Miranda* procedures, they should not breed the same irremediable consequences as police infringement of the Fifth Amendment itself. It is an unwarranted extension of *Miranda* to hold that a simple failure to administer the warnings, unaccompanied by any actual coercion or other circumstances calculated to undermine the suspect's ability to exercise his free will, so taints the investigatory process that a subsequent voluntary and informed waiver is ineffective for some indeterminate period. Though *Miranda* requires that the unwarned admission must be suppressed, the admissibility of any subsequent statement should turn in these circumstances solely on whether it is knowingly and voluntarily made.

B

The Oregon court, however, believed that the unwarned remark compromised the voluntariness of respondent's later confession. It was the court's view that the prior *answer* and not the unwarned questioning impaired respondent's ability to give a valid waiver and that only lapse of time and change of place could dissipate what it termed the "coercive impact" of the inadmissible statement. When a prior statement is actually coerced, the time that passes between confessions, the change in place of interrogations, and the change in identity of the interrogators all bear on whether that coercion has carried over into the second confession. ... The failure of police to administer *Miranda* warnings does not mean that the statements received have actually been coerced, but only that courts will presume the privilege against compulsory self-incrimination has not been intelligently exercised.... [A] careful and thorough administration of *Miranda* warnings serves to cure the condition that rendered the unwarned statement inadmissible.

...We must conclude that, absent deliberately coercive or improper tactics in obtaining the initial statement, the mere fact that a suspect has made an unwarned admission does not warrant a presumption of compulsion. A subsequent administration of *Miranda* warnings to a suspect who has given a voluntary but unwarned statement ordinarily should suffice to remove the conditions that precluded admission of the earlier statement. In such circumstances, the finder of fact may reasonably conclude that the suspect made a rational and intelligent choice whether to waive or invoke his rights.

. . .

IV

. . .

...We hold today that a suspect who has once responded to unwarned yet uncoercive questioning is not thereby disabled from waiving his rights and confessing after he has been given the requisite *Miranda* warnings.

The judgment of the Court of Appeals of Oregon is reversed, and the case is remanded for further proceedings not inconsistent with this opinion.

It is so ordered.

JUSTICE BRENNAN, with whom JUSTICE MARSHALL joins, dissenting.

...[T]he Court has engaged of late in a studied campaign to strip the *Miranda* decision piecemeal and to undermine the rights *Miranda* sought to secure. Today's decision not only extends this effort a further step, but delivers a potentially crippling blow to *Miranda* and the ability of courts to safeguard the rights of persons accused of crime....

JUSTICE STEVENS, dissenting.

The Court concludes its opinion with a carefully phrased statement of its holding:

"We hold today that a suspect who has once responded to unwarned yet uncoercive questioning is not thereby disabled from waiving his rights and confessing after he has been given the requisite *Miranda* warnings."...

I

The desire to achieve a just result in this particular case has produced an opinion that is somewhat opaque and internally inconsistent. If I read it correctly, its conclusion rests on two untenable premises: (1) that the respondent's first confession was not the product of coercion; and (2) that no constitutional right was violated when respondent was questioned in a tranquil, domestic setting.

. . .

F. THE EIGHTH AMENDMENT

The Eighth Amendment, borrowing language from the English Bill of Rights of 1689, provides that "[e]xcessive bail shall not be required, nor excessive fines imposed, nor cruel and unusual punishments inflicted." The first two clauses produce relatively few cases for the Supreme Court. The last six words have generated a massive caseload on the death penalty, an issue that is extraordinarily complex and divisive.

Excessive Bail

To gain freedom while awaiting trial, a defendant may have to put up money for a bail bond to guarantee his presence at the trial. Meeting bail allows the accused to prepare a defense and prevents the infliction of punishment prior to conviction. Excessive bail destroys both rights. The level of bail is monitored by criminal rules adopted by Congress and occasional judicial rulings. Stack v. Boyle, 342 U.S. 1 (1952).

Bail may be denied totally for capital cases. Even for noncapital cases, there are instances where bail is refused. Carlson v. Landon, 342 U.S. 524 (1952). In 1966, Congress passed legislation to remove the inequity of holding persons too poor to raise bail. Defendants charged with noncapital offenses shall be released on their own "personal recognizance" unless a court determines that release will not assure the defendant's later appearance in court. 80 Stat. 214 (1966); 18 U.S.C. §§ 3141–56 (1994). Additional legislation in 1984 requires courts to keep suspects in jail if the government demonstrates by clear and convincing evidence that release will not "reasonably assure" the safety of the community. 98 Stat. 1978–80. This statute on pretrial detention ("preventive detention") was upheld in *United States* v. *Salerno,* 481 U.S. 739 (1987). With a 6–3 majority in 1990, the Court held that the failure of the government to comply with the prompt-hearing provision of the Bail Reform Act of 1984 does not require the release of a person who should be, under the terms of that statute, detained. United States v. Montalvo-Murillo, 495 U.S. 711 (1990). The question of excessive bail is sometimes addressed not in terms of the Eighth Amendment but on grounds of equal protection and due process. Schilb v. Kuebel, 404 U.S. 357 (1971).

Excessive Fines

This section of the Constitution was rarely litigated in the past. For example, see Ex parte Watkins, 7 Pet. 568 (1833). In contemporary times, the question of excessive fines is more likely attacked under the Equal Protection and Due Process Clauses. In 1970 the Supreme Court unanimously struck down on equal protection grounds a state statute that subjected indigents to additional imprisonment if they failed to pay a fine. Williams v. Illinois, 399 U.S. 235 (1970). See also Tate v. Short, 401 U.S. 395 (1971).

A 7–2 ruling by the Supreme Court in 1989 held that the Excessive Fines Clause does not protect businesses against multimillion dollar awards of punitive damages in civil disputes between private parties. The Clause is restricted to cases in which the government prosecutes a case and has an interest in recovering damages. Every member of the Court (the majority opinion by Blackmun, the concurrence by Brennan and Marshall, and the partial dissent by O'Connor and Stevens) indicated that punitive damage awards may still be limited under the Due Process Clause of the Fourteenth Amendment. Browning-Ferris Industries v. Kelco Disposal, 492 U.S. 257 (1989).

In 1991 the Court provided some guidelines on due process restrictions on punitive damages awards. Pacific Mutual Life Ins. Co. v. Haslip, 499 U.S. 1 (1991). Two years later it upheld a jury's award of $10 million in punitive damages when there had been actual damages of only $19,000. Although six Justices sustained the large punitive damages award, they could not form a majority of the Court behind any particular reasoning. TXO Production Corp. v. Alliance Resources Corp., 509 U.S. 443 (1993). Also in 1993, the Court ruled that the Excessive Fines Clause limits the power of the federal government to seize homes and businesses (civil forfeiture proceedings) to combat illegal drug trafficking. Austin v. United States, 509 U.S. 602 (1993). Since that time, the Court has decided that other federal government seizures violate the Excessive Fines Clause (see section in next chapter or civil forfeitures, pp. 787–88).

In 1994 the Court held that Oregon's constitution, which prohibited judicial review of the amount of punitive damages awarded by a jury "unless the Court can affirmatively say there is no evidence to support the verdict," violated the Due Process Clause. Honda Motor Co. v. Oberg, 512 U.S. 415 (1994). Two years later the Court for the first time overturned a punitive-damage award. An Alabama physician, after purchasing a new BMW automobile, discovered that the car had been repainted. A jury awarded him $4 million as punishment to BMW for fraud and breach of contract for failing to disclose the repainting; an appeals court lowered the amount to $2 million. The Supreme Court, divided 5 to 4, ruled that the $2 million punitive damages award was grossly excessive and violated the Due Process Clause. BMW of North America, Inc. v. Gore, 517 U.S. 559 (1996). The decision raised the expectation that Congress would revisit the issue of establishing national standards for punitive damages. On

May 2, 1996, President Clinton vetoed a bill passed by the Republican Congress to limit the liability of companies that make faulty products. He argued that the bill intruded on state authority over tort law and disadvantaged consumers. The House sustained the veto.

Cruel and Unusual Punishments

The meaning of "cruel and unusual" varies from one American culture to another. A congressional statute in 1790 required the death penalty for forgery. 1 Stat. 115, § 14. Today, that penalty would be considered disproportionate to the crime. In 1879 the Supreme Court decided that public shooting was not cruel and unusual, although forms of torture (dragged to the place of execution, embowelled alive, beheaded, quartered, or burned alive) exceeded constitutional limits. Wilkerson v. Utah, 99 U.S. 130 (1879). The framers would have regarded electrocution as "unusual," if not inconceivable, but in 1890 the Court found it constitutionally inoffensive. In re Kemmler, 136 U.S. 436 (1890). Throughout this period the Court held consistently that the states were not bound by the Eighth Amendment.[30]

Even for most of the twentieth century, the Eighth Amendment added little to the Supreme Court's docket. It invoked the amendment in 1910 to strike down the sentence of someone given fifteen years at hard labor and kept in chains day and night for falsifying a public document. The Court said that punishment must be graduated and proportioned to the offense committed. Weems v. United States, 217 U.S. 349 (1910). In 1947 the Court held that states could try a second time to electrocute someone after they had bungled the first effort. To the 5–4 majority, a second attempt was neither double jeopardy nor cruel and unusual punishment. Francis v. Resweber, 329 U.S. 459 (1947).

The extent to which "cruel and unusual" is culturally determined and varies with the times can be seen in two cases decided in 1958 and 1962. In the first, the Court interpreted the Eighth Amendment in light of the "evolving standards of decency that mark the progress of a maturing society." Trop v. Dulles, 356 U.S. 86, 101 (1958). Stripping a native-born American of his citizenship because of wartime desertion constituted cruel and unusual punishment. Four years later the Court, guided by "contemporary human knowledge," decided that it was cruel and unusual to punish someone for the mere status of being a narcotics addict when the person was not under the influence of narcotics at the time of arrest. Robinson v. California, 370 U.S. 660, 666 (1962). This decision incorporated the Cruel and Unusual Punishment Clause into the Fourteenth Amendment and applied it to the states. In 1968 the Court refused to extend the narcotics decision to strike down a conviction for public drunkenness. It distinguished being drunk in public from the general status of having a narcotics addiction. Powell v. Texas, 392 U.S. 514, 532 (1968).

In 1992, the Court rejected the claim that execution by cyanide gas, which takes eight to ten minutes before the victim dies by suffocation, is cruel and unusual punishment. Gomez v. U.S. Dist. Court for N.D. of Cal., 503 U.S. 653 (1992). In 1999, the Court denied cert to a constitutional challenge against Florida's use of the electric chair as the sole means of execution. The chair had malfunctioned a number of times. Lopez v. Singletary, 525 U.S. 1116 (1999). The next year Florida passed legislation to provide death by lethal injection as an alternative procedure. The Court also denied cert to consider the claim that spending two decades on death row constitutes cruel and unusual punishment. Knight v. Florida, 120 S.Ct. 459 (1999).

The overwhelming number of cases on the Eighth Amendment have been decided since 1970. In a series of cases from 1970 to 1973, the Court held that a guilty plea is not invalid

---

30. O'Neil v. Vermont, 144 U.S. 323 (1892); In re Kemmler, 136 U.S. 436 (1890); Pervear v. The Commonwealth, 5 Wall. (72 U.S.) 475 (1867).

or coerced simply because the accused wants to avoid a possible death penalty.[31] In 1971 the Court handed down the first of many long-winded, discursive explorations of the death penalty, deciding in this case that juries could be given absolute discretion to choose between life imprisonment and death and that juries can decide both guilt and punishment (death) in a single unitary proceeding. Due process did not require a bifurcated trial. McGautha v. California, 402 U.S. 183 (1971).

The number of prisoners executed declined sharply in the 1950s and 1960s. By the late 1960s and early 1970s, there were no persons executed in any of the states. In 1972 the Supreme Court of California declared the death penalty a violation of the state constitutional ban against cruel or unusual punishments. Within nine months, however, the voters of California amended the state constitution to reinstate the death penalty. People v. Anderson, 493 P.2d 880 (Cal. 1972), cert. denied, 406 U.S. 958 (1972); Cal. Const. Art. I, § 27. This collision between a judicial ruling and public opinion would soon occur at the national level.

The *Furman* Challenge

In 1972 the Court abruptly struck down death-penalty statutes in Georgia and Texas as cruel and unusual because of the erratic nature of their application. A brief one-page per curiam — announcing the result — served as a preface for more than two hundred pages of concurrences and dissents. Only two Justices (Brennan and Marshall) regarded the death penalty unconstitutional in all cases. The opinions for the 5–4 majority focused on the arbitrariness and inequalities in state practices: the increasing rarity of executions and the application of that punishment to blacks more than whites, to men more than women, and to the poor more than the rich. FURMAN v. GEORGIA, 408 U.S. 238 (1972).

The Court's holding confronted explicit language in the Constitution, which acknowledges the death penalty four times. The Fifth Amendment requires a presentment or indictment by grand jury for persons accused of a "capital, or otherwise infamous crime." The Double Jeopardy Clause refers to taking "life or limb." Also in the Fifth Amendment, no person shall be deprived of "life, liberty, or property" without due process of law. Under the Fourteenth Amendment, no state shall deprive any person of "life, liberty, or property" without due process of law. One could argue that *acknowledging* the death penalty in the Constitution does not mandate it or even favor it.

The Public Answers

Following the *Furman* decision, the majority of states immediately reinstituted the death penalty for certain kinds of crime. This public endorsement of capital punishment put pressure on the Court to modify *Furman*. In the first of five decisions handed down on July 2, 1976, the Court reviewed the changes in Georgia's statute following *Furman* and upheld, 7–2, the new procedure. GREGG v. GEORGIA, 428 U.S. 153 (1976). The Court noted that the position of Justices Brennan and Marshall in *Furman*, that the Eighth Amendment prohibits the death penalty, had been "undercut substantially" by state actions from 1972 to 1976 to enact statutes calling for the death penalty. Id. at 179. Moreover, in 1974 Congress enacted legislation providing the death penalty for aircraft piracy that results in death. Id. at 179–80. The "evolving standards of decency" (Warren's language in *Trop v. Dulles*) still tolerated and supported executions. In this and the companion cases, the Court attempted to identify the factors and criteria that are necessary for states to invoke the death penalty. Proffitt v. Florida, 428 U.S. 242 (1976); Jurek v. Texas, 428 U.S. 262 (1976); Woodson v. North Carolina, 428

---

31. Tollett v. Henderson, 411 U.S. 258 (1973); North Carolina v. Alford, 400 U.S. 25 (1970); Parker v. North Carolina, 397 U.S. 790 (1970); Brady v. North Carolina, 397 U.S. 742 (1970).

U.S. 280 (1976); Roberts v. Louisiana, 428 U.S. 325 (1976). These cases require states to establish a capital-sentencing procedure that weighs aggravating factors against mitigating factors.

Although the death penalty is once again available, executions are often postponed or avoided because the Court finds defects in sentencing procedures or discovers due process problems.[32] The Court has gradually broadened the scope of the death penalty to include not only those who intend to kill but also those who serve as accomplices to a murder. Compare Tison v. Arizona, 481 U.S. 137 (1987) with Cabana v. Bullock, 474 U.S. 376 (1986) and Enmund v. Florida, 458 U.S. 782 (1982).

Aggravating and Mitigating Factors

The Court is often divided 5 to 4 on how judges and juries should weigh and reweigh aggravating and mitigating circumstances in reaching a death sentence. Clemons v. Mississippi, 494 U.S. 738 (1990); Boyde v. California, 494 U.S. 370 (1990); Blystone v. Pennsylvania, 494 U.S. 299 (1990). Two other death penalty cases in 1990 produced 5–4 splits on the Court. Lewis v. Jeffers, 497 U.S. 764 (1990); Walton v. Arizona, 497 U.S. 639 (1990). Even after David Souter replaced William Brennan, Jr., on the Court, the Justices remain divided 5–4 on some death penalty cases. A decision in 1991 held that the Florida Supreme Court had failed to consider whether mitigating circumstances in a case would have resulted in a life sentence rather than a death penalty. Parker v. Dugger, 498 U.S. 308 (1991). Another 5–4 decision held that the sentencing procedure followed by a state judge violated the Due Process Clause. Lankford v. Idaho, 500 U.S. 110 (1991).

The 1992 Court included Clarence Thomas as a replacement for Thurgood Marshall, who, along with Justice Brennan, had been a steadfast opponent of the death penalty. A 1992 decision, with Scalia, Rehnquist, and Thomas dissenting, ruled that a murder defendant in a capital case has the right to question potential jurors whether they would automatically impose a death sentence if they returned a guilty verdict. Such jurors must be excluded: "A juror who will automatically vote for the death penalty in every case will fail in good faith to consider the evidence of aggravating and mitigating circumstances as the instructions require him to do." Morgan v. Illinois, 504 U.S. 719, 729 (1992). The Court had previously, in *Witherspoon v. Illinois*, 391 U.S. 510 (1968), given prosecutors the same right to question jurors. The Court divided 5–4 in 1993 in holding that a judge had properly instructed a jury on the future dangerousness of a youthful defendant, who was later sentenced to death. Johnson v. Texas, 509 U.S. 350 (1993).

In 1994 the Court held that a sentencing jury, in choosing between death or life imprisonment, must be told that if sentenced to life the defendant would not be eligible for parole under state law. Otherwise, the jury might more readily accept the prosecutor's argument that the

---

32. In 2000, the Court halted a man's execution in Alabama, perhaps to give the Court an opportunity to decide the constitutionality of electrocution. In re Tarver, 120 S.Ct. 1005 (2000). In 1994 the Court, split 5 to 4, held that federal judges may stop a scheduled execution to give a state prisoner time to obtain a lawyer to challenge the constitutionality of a sentence. McFarland v. Scott, 512 U.S. 849 (1994). The Court divided 5 to 4 a year later in holding that state prosecutors had wrongly suppressed evidence favorable to a defendant, who was sentenced to death. He was entitled to a new trial. Kyles v. Whitley, 514 U.S. 419 (1995). See also McCoy v. North Carolina, 494 U.S. 433 (1990); South Carolina v. Gathers, 490 U.S. 805 (1989); Mills v. Maryland, 486 U.S. 367 (1988); Satterwhite v. Texas, 486 U.S. 249 (1988); Booth v. Maryland, 482 U.S. 496 (1987); Skipper v. South Carolina, 476 U.S. 1 (1986); Caldwell v. Mississippi, 472 U.S. 320 (1985); Eddings v. Oklahoma, 455 U.S. 104 (1982); Godfrey v. Georgia, 446 U.S. 420 (1980); Bell v. Ohio, 438 U.S. 637 (1978); Lockett v. Ohio, 438 U.S. 586 (1978); Roberts v. Louisiana, 431 U.S. 633 (1977); Gardner v. Florida, 430 U.S. 349 (1977). A separate issue is the exclusion of jurors who are unwilling or unable to take an oath that a mandatory death penalty or life imprisonment will not affect their deliberations. This practice was struck down in Witherspoon v. Illinois, 391 U.S. 510 (1968) and Adams v. Texas, 448 U.S. 38 (1980).

defendant is so dangerous that he must be executed. That argument is undercut when jurors understand that the defendant will not be released on parole. Simmons v. South Carolina, 512 U.S. 154 (1994).

Victims' Rights

A death penalty case in 1991 split the court 6 to 3 with regard to the introduction of "victim-impact" evidence about the character of a murder and its effects on survivors. In two earlier 5–4 decisions—Booth v. Maryland, 482 U.S. 497 (1987) and South Carolina v. Gaithers, 490 U.S. 805 (1989)—the Court had ruled such evidence inadmissible at a capital sentencing hearing. Yet the Court in 1991 decided that the Eighth Amendment does not prohibit juries, in considering the death penalty, from hearing victim-impact evidence. Prosecutors may now describe the emotional impact of a murder on the victim's family. Payne v. Tennessee, 501 U.S. 808 (1991).

Congress passed legislation in 1997 to allow certain relatives of the victims of the 1995 Oklahoma City bombing to attend the trial of the accused bombers. The new law prevents federal judges from barring from the courtroom individuals who plan to testify during the sentencing phase of the trial. 111 Stat. 12 (1997). Judge Richard Matsch, the presiding judge in the Oklahoma case, had previously ruled that people who intended to testify at sentencing time could not sit in on the trial. Legislation in 1996 also dealt with the victims of crimes. 110 Stat. 1227–47 (1996).

Proportionality

At times, the Court decides whether executions are justified for a certain class of crimes. In 1977 it found the death penalty disproportionate punishment for the crime of raping an adult woman. The gradual abandonment of that penalty by most states was accepted by the Court as persuasive evidence of contemporary public judgment. Coker v. Georgia, 433 U.S. 584, 593–96 (1977). Under the principle of proportionality, life imprisonment for certain nonviolent crimes contravenes the Eighth Amendment. Solem v. Helm, 463 U.S. 277 (1983).

Solem was weakened in 1991 when a 5–4 Court decided that a mandatory life term in prison, without possibility of parole, for possessing about 1 ½ pounds of cocaine was not unconstitutional. Two members of the majority, Scalia and Rehnquist, would override Solem and declare that the Eighth Amendment contains no proportionality guarantee. Sentencing would be purely a matter of legislative prerogative. The other three members of the majority (Kennedy, O'Connor, and Souter) continue to recognize a proportionality principle but concluded that it was not breached in this case. Harmelin v. Michigan, 501 U.S. 957 (1991).

In affirming a death sentence, state courts are not required to compare the sentence to others to determine if it is disproportionate. The Court tolerates what it calls "aberrational outcomes" in the application of the death penalty. Pulley v. Harris, 465 U.S. 37, 54 (1984). The Court has held that the execution of prisoners who are insane violates the Eighth Amendment. Ford v. Wainwright, 477 U.S. 399 (1986). The issue of executing the retarded or mentally incapacitated continues to divide the nation. A 5–4 decision by the Supreme Court in 1989 held that the Eighth Amendment does not categorically bar execution of the mentally retarded. The majority cited a lack of "objective indicators" from society to prohibit such executions. The "clearest and most reliable objective evidence of contemporary values," it said, are the statutes passed by legislative bodies in this country. The Court also looked to data concerning the actions of sentencing jurors. Penry v. Lynaugh, 492 U.S. 302, 331 (1989).

Statistics demonstrate that the death penalty is applied disproportionately to blacks who kill whites, compared to whites who kill blacks or each race killing one of its own. Nevertheless, the Court refused in 1987 to find a constitutional violation to this pattern. Discretion in sentencing need not mean discrimination. Discretionary judgments by jurors, even when they reveal a strong racial bias at an aggregate level, did not convince the Court that racial discrimination exists for a *particular* case. The Court held that legislatures are better qualified to evaluate and respond to statistical studies regarding racial discrimination in sentencing. Mc-CLESKEY v. KEMP, 481 U.S. 278, 319 (1987). In response to this decision, Congress considered legislation that would create a federal right to be free from race discrimination in cases of capital punishment. Language was included in a 1994 statute to ensure that race is not considered by jurors in deciding a death sentence. 108 Stat. 1996 (1994).

Legislative Procedures

Congress has considered a number of bills to establish procedures for imposing the death penalty. At the time of *Furman* v. *Georgia* (1972), federal law authorized capital punishment for such crimes as espionage and treason. Congress tried to pass legislation to remove arbitrary and capricious results. In 1988 Congress passed legislation to provide constitutional procedures for implementing the death penalty in cases involving certain drug-related murders and the killing of law enforcement officers. 102 Stat. 4387 (1988). The Federal Death Penalty Act of 1994 authorized capital punishment for dozens of federal crimes. The procudures under this statute were upheld by the Supreme Court in 1999, divided 5 to 4. Jones v. United States, 527 U.S. 373 (1999). Other procedures are included in the Antiterrorism and Effective Death Penalty Act of 1996. 110 Stat. 1214. The record shows that questions of the death penalty are largely in the hands of legislatures and public opinion (see Powell reading).

A unanimous Court in 1996 upheld the constitutionality of the military's death penalty. At the same time, it found nothing objectionable in terms of separation of powers for Congress to delegate to the President the discretion to identify aggravating factors in capital murder cases. Loving v. United States, 517 U.S. 748 (1996).

Questions of cruel and unusual punishment sometimes concern unusually heavy sentences. The Supreme Court held that conviction for three felonies totaling $229.11 could be punished by a mandatory life sentence. Rummel v. Estelle, 445 U.S. 263 (1980). Following the policy of deferring to the legislature for the level of punishment, the Court sustained a forty-year sentence for someone convicted for possessing and selling marijuana. Hutto v. Davis, 454 U.S. 370 (1982).

To correct vast inequities and disparities in sentencing, Congress created a Sentencing Commission in 1984 and received its recommendations in 1987. Because of the composition of the Commission (a mixture of judges and nonjudges subject to removal from the Commission by the President), and because the recommendations became law without any congressional action, suits were filed raising a number of constitutional issues. In 1989 the Court upheld the Sentencing Commission and the procedure used to enact its recommendations into law. Justice Scalia was the sole dissenter in this 8–1 decision, which not only upheld the delegation of legislative authority to the Commission and the assignment of extrajudicial duties to judges but also endorsed the creation of independent agencies that are not directly under the President's control. Mistretta v. United States, 488 U.S. 361 (1989).

State Options

Operating under their own constitutions, states have a range of choices in supporting or prohibiting capital punishment. Thirty-eight states have a death penalty, but most of the executions occur in a handful of states, particularly Texas, Virginia, Florida, Missouri, and Louisiana. The use of new evidence to exonerate death-row inmates has prompted a number of states to review their capital punishment procedures. In 2000, Governor George H. Ryan of Illinois announced that he would block executions until the procedures in his state were

Habeas Corpus Relief for Death-Row Inmates

A series of Supreme Court rulings beginning in 1990 have limited the ability of death-row inmates to use the writ of habeas corpus to seek federal review of state court convictions. Three decisions in 1990 curbed prisoner access to federal review. Those decisions, building on Teague v. Lane, 489 U.S. 288 (1989), involve the issue of whether "new rules" by the Court can be applied retroactively to challenge a conviction. Divided 5 to 4 in these cases, the Court refused to apply new rules retroactively to overturn convictions for a capital crime. Butler v. McKellar, 494 U.S. 407 (1990); Saffle v. Parks, 494 U.S. 484 (1990); Sawyer v. Smith, 497 U.S. 227 (1990). Another 5–4 decision in 1996 used the new-rule analysis to deny a death-row inmate the right to have his conviction reviewed in federal court. Gray v. Netherland, 518 U.S. 152 (1996).

In 1991 the Court clarified its standards for determining when a petitioner abuses the writ of habeas corpus. To disprove abuse, a petitioner must explain why a claim was not raised at an earlier time and must identify the prejudice that would result in denying the writ, such as a fundamental miscarriage of justice or the conviction of an innocent person. McCleskey v. Zant, 499 U.S. 467 (1991). A year later, the Court turned aside the effort of a death-row prisoner to get a second chance in federal court to prove that he did not deserve the death penalty for his crimes. Sawyer v. Whitley, 505 U.S. 333 (1992).

In 1993, a 6–3 Court held that prisoners who have exhausted their appeals and later produce new evidence, have no right to be heard in a federal court unless the evidence offers a truly persuasive claim of their innocence. Herrera v. Collins, 506 U.S. 390 (1993).

A 5–4 decision in 1995 permitted a state prisoner to file a second federal habeas petition to avoid a sentence of death. He was allowed to introduce new evidence that he was wrongly convicted. Schlup v. Delo, 513 U.S. 298 (1995). In 1996, a unanimous Court held that a federal court had erred in dismissing a death row inmate's first federal appeal alleging violation of constitutional rights. The Court said that if a district judge cannot dismiss a first habeas petition on the merits before the scheduled execution, the court must postpone the execution and address the merits. Lonchar v. Thomas, 517 U.S. 314 (1996). In 1998, the Court split 5 to 4 in holding that a lower court had erroneously granted habeas corpus relief to a death-row inmate. Calderon v. Coleman, 525 U.S. 141 (1998).

thoroughly investigated. Legislatures in other states have voted down moratoriums on capital punishment.

Habeas Corpus Relief

The death penalty continues to preoccupy and divide the Court. Recent decisions have made it more difficult for death row inmates to seek federal review of their conviction in state courts. The result is that prisoners are less likely to obtain habeas corpus relief and the pace of executions has quickened (see box).

The Antiterrorism and Effective Death Penalty Act of 1996 includes a provision that cuts back on inmates' ability to appeal to the Supreme Court in successive habeas petitions. After their first appeal, prisoners would need the approval of a three-judge panel before presenting their habeas petition to a trial court. 110 Stat. 1217–26 (1996). This part of the law was challenged as an unconstitutional restriction on the appellate jurisdiction of the Supreme court. A unanimous Court held that the statute did not violate the Constitution because the Court could still entertain original habeas petitions (those filed in the first instance with the Court). Under Court rules, petitions for an original writ of habeas corpus are granted only under "exceptional circumstances." The Act only removed the Court's authority to consider an appeal or a cert petition to review a decision of the three-judge panel. Felker v. Turpin, 518 U.S. 651

(1996). Two years later the Court held that the 1996 statute does not prevent an inmate from claiming he is insane and should not be executed. This type of habeas corpus petition is not limited to a single appeal. Stewart v. Martinez-Villareal, 523 U.S. 637 (1998). In 2000, the Court offered further guidance in interpreting the 1996 statute and the scope of federal court review of state court actions in capital cases. Williams v. Taylor, 120 S.Ct. 1479 (2000); Williams v. Taylor, 120 S.Ct. 1495 (2000).

[For criminal procedures regarding juveniles (including the death penalty) and the rights of prisoners, see Chapter 16.]

Furman v. Georgia

408 U.S. 238 (1972)

William Henry Furman was convicted of murder in Georgia and sentenced to death. Another petitioner was sentenced to death after being convicted of rape in Georgia. A third petitioner was sentenced to death in Texas for the crime of rape. The Court was asked whether the death penalty in these cases constituted cruel and unusual punishment and was therefore unconstitutional.

PER CURIAM.

... Certiorari was granted limited to the following question: "Does the imposition and carrying out of the death penalty in [these cases] constitute cruel and unusual punishment in violation of the Eighth and Fourteenth Amendments?" 403 U.S. 952 (1971). The Court holds that the imposition and carrying out of the death penalty in these cases constitute cruel and unusual punishment in violation of the Eighth and Fourteenth Amendments. The judgment in each case is therefore reversed insofar as it leaves undisturbed the death sentence imposed, and the cases are remanded for further proceedings.

So ordered.

MR. JUSTICE DOUGLAS, MR. JUSTICE BRENNAN, MR. JUSTICE STEWART, MR. JUSTICE WHITE, and MR. JUSTICE MARSHALL have filed separate opinions in support of the judgments. THE CHIEF JUSTICE, MR. JUSTICE BLACKMUN, MR. JUSTICE POWELL, and MR. JUSTICE REHNQUIST have filed separate dissenting opinions.

MR. JUSTICE DOUGLAS, concurring.

. . .

The words "cruel and unusual" certainly include penalties that are barbaric. But the words, at least when read in light of the English proscription against selective and irregular use of penalties, suggest that it is "cruel and unusual" to apply the death penalty — or any other penalty — selectively to minorities whose numbers are few, who are outcasts of society, and who are unpopular, but whom society is willing to see suffer though it would not countenance general application of the same penalty across the board....

There is increasing recognition of the fact that the basic theme of equal protection is implicit in "cruel and unusual" punishments. "A penalty ... should be considered 'unusually' imposed if it is administered arbitrarily or discriminatorily." The same authors add that "[t]he extreme rarity with which applicable death penalty provisions are put to use raises a strong inference of arbitrariness." The President's Commission on Law Enforcement and Administration of Justice recently concluded:

"Finally there is evidence that the imposition of the death sentence and the exercise of dispensing power by the courts and the executive follow discriminatory patterns. The death sentence is disproportionately imposed and carried out on the poor, the Negro, and the members of unpopular groups."

. . .

MR. JUSTICE BRENNAN, concurring.

II

. . .

In determining whether a punishment comports with human dignity, we are aided also by a second principle inherent in the Clause — that the State must not arbitrarily inflict a severe punishment. This principle derives from the notion that the State does not respect human dignity when, without reason, it inflicts upon some people a severe punishment that it does not inflict upon others. Indeed, the very words "cruel and unusual punishments" imply condemnation of the arbitrary infliction of severe punishment....

III

. . .

The question...is whether the deliberate infliction of death is today consistent with the command of the Clause that the State may not inflict punishments that do not comport with human dignity. I will analyze the punishment of death in terms of the principles set out above and the cumulative test to which they lead: It is a denial of human dignity for the State arbitrarily to subject a person to an unusually severe punishment that society has indicated it does not regard as acceptable, and that cannot be shown to serve any penal purpose more effectively than a significantly less drastic punishment. Under these principles and this test, death is today a "cruel and unusual" punishment.

. . .

In comparison to all other punishments today, then, the deliberate extinguishment of human life by the State is uniquely degrading to human dignity. I would not hesitate to hold, on that ground alone, that death is today a "cruel and unusual" punishment, were it not that death is a punishment of longstanding usage and acceptance in this country. I therefore turn to the second principle — that the State may not arbitrarily inflict an unusually severe punishment.

The outstanding characteristic of our present practice of punishing criminals by death is the infrequency with which we resort to it. The evidence is conclusive that death is not the ordinary punishment for any crime.

There has been a steady decline in the infliction of this punishment in every decade since the 1930's, the earliest period for which accurate statistics are available. In the 1930's, executions averaged 167 per year; in the 1940's, the average was 128; in the 1950's, it was 72; and in the years 1960–1962, it was 48. There have been a total of 46 executions since then, 36 of them in 1963–1964. Yet our population and the number of capital crimes committed have increased greatly over the past four decades....

When the punishment of death is inflicted in a trivial number of the cases in which it is legally available, the conclusion is virtually inescapable that it is being inflicted arbitrarily. Indeed, it smacks of little more than a lottery system....

MR. JUSTICE STEWART, concurring.

The penalty of death differs from all other forms of criminal punishment, not in degree but in kind. It is unique in its total irrevocability. It is unique in its rejection of rehabilitation of the convict as a basic purpose of criminal justice. And it is unique, finally, in its absolute renunciation of all that is embodied in our concept of humanity.

For these and other reasons, at least two of my Brothers have concluded that the infliction of the death penalty is constitutionally impermissible in all circumstances under the Eighth and Fourteenth Amendments. Their case is a strong one. But I find it unnecessary to reach the ultimate question they would decide....

. . .

These death sentences are cruel and unusual in the same way that being struck by lightning is cruel and unusual. For, of all the people convicted of rapes and murders in 1967 and 1968, many just as reprehensible as these, the petitioners are among a capriciously selected random handful upon whom the sentence of death has in fact been imposed...the Eighth and Fourteenth Amendments cannot tolerate the infliction of a sentence of death under legal systems that permit this unique penalty to be so wantonly and so freakishly imposed.

For these reasons I concur in the judgments of the Court.

MR. JUSTICE WHITE, concurring.

. . .

The imposition and execution of the death penalty are obviously cruel in the dictionary sense. But the penalty has not been considered cruel and unusual punishment in the constitutional sense because it was thought justified by the social ends it was deemed to serve. At the moment that it ceases realistically to further these purposes, however, the emerging question is whether its imposition in such circumstances would violate the Eighth Amendment. It is my view that it would, for its imposition would then be the pointless and needless extinction of life with only marginal contributions to any discernible social or public purposes....

MR. JUSTICE MARSHALL concurring.

[After rejecting the traditional purposes conceivably served by capital punishment (retribution, deterrence, prevention of repetitive criminal acts, encouragement of guilty pleas and confessions,

eugenics, and economy), Marshall turns to other considerations.]

VI

...[C]apital punishment is imposed discriminatorily against certain identifiable classes of people; there is evidence that innocent people have been executed before their innocence can be proved; and the death penalty wreaks havoc with our entire criminal justice system.…

Regarding discrimination, it has been said that "[i]t is usually the poor, the illiterate, the underprivileged, the member of the minority group — the man who, because he is without means, and is defended by a court-appointed attorney — who becomes society's sacrificial lamb.…" Indeed, a look at the bare statistics regarding executions is enough to betray much of the discrimination. A total of 3,859 persons have been executed since 1930, of whom 1,751 were white and 2,066 were Negro. Of the executions, 3,334 were for murder; 1,664 of the executed murderers were white and 1,630 were Negro; 455 persons, including 48 whites and 405 Negroes, were executed for rape. It is immediately apparent that Negroes were executed far more often than whites in proportion to their percentage of the population. Studies indicate that while the higher rate of execution among Negroes is partially due to a higher rate of crime, there is evidence of racial discrimination.…

There is also overwhelming evidence that the death penalty is employed against men and not women. Only 32 women have been executed since 1930, while 3,827 men have met a similar fate.…

MR. CHIEF JUSTICE BURGER, with whom MR. JUSTICE BLACKMUN, MR. JUSTICE POWELL, and MR. JUSTICE REHNQUIST join, dissenting.

At the outset it is important to note that only two members of the Court, MR. JUSTICE BRENNAN and MR. JUSTICE MARSHALL, have concluded that the Eighth Amendment prohibits capital punishment for all crimes and under all circumstances.…

I

If we were possessed of legislative power, I would either join with MR. JUSTICE BRENNAN and MR. JUSTICE MARSHALL or, at the very least, restrict the use of capital punishment to a small category of the most heinous crimes. Our constitutional inquiry, however, must be divorced from personal feelings as to the morality and efficacy of the death penalty, and be confined to the meaning and applicability of the uncertain language of the Eighth Amendment.…

...[I]t disregards the history of the Eighth Amendment and all the judicial comment that has followed to rely on the term "unusual" as affecting the outcome of these cases. Instead, I view these cases as turning on the single question whether capital punishment is "cruel" in the constitutional sense. The term "unusual" cannot be read as limiting the ban on "cruel" punishments or as somehow expanding the meaning of the term "cruel." For this reason I am unpersuaded by the facile argument that since capital punishment has always been cruel in the everyday sense of the word, and has become unusual due to decreased use, it is, therefore, now "cruel and unusual."

. . .

MR. JUSTICE BLACKMUN, dissenting.

[Blackman expresses his "abhorrence" for the death penalty and states that if he were a legislator he would vote against the death penalty and that if he were a governor he would be "sorely tempted" to exercise executive clemency. But he concludes that the Court oversteps its constitutional duties by striking down the Georgia and Texas statutes.]

MR. JUSTICE POWELL, with whom THE CHIEF JUSTICE, MR. JUSTICE BLACKMUN, and MR. JUSTICE REHNQUIST join, dissenting.

. . .

In terms of the constitutional role of this Court, the impact of the majority's ruling is all the greater because the decision encroaches upon an area squarely within the historic prerogative of the legislative branch — both state and federal — to protect the citizenry through the designation of penalties for prohibitable conduct. It is the very sort of judgment that the legislative branch is competent to make and for which the judiciary is ill-equipped.…

MR. JUSTICE REHNQUIST, with whom THE CHIEF JUSTICE, MR. JUSTICE BLACKMUN, and MR. JUSTICE POWELL join, dissenting.

. . .

...The most expansive reading of the leading constitutional cases does not remotely suggest that this Court has been granted a roving commission, either by the Founding Fathers or by the framers of the Fourteenth Amendment, to strike down laws that are based upon notions of policy or morality suddenly found unacceptable by a majority of this Court.…

. . .

Gregg v. Georgia

428 U.S. 153 (1976)

After the Supreme Court in *Furman v. Georgia* (1972) declared the death penalty unconstitutional as practiced in Georgia and Texas, more than thirty states reinstituted the death penalty. But these states added new procedures in an effort to minimize the arbitrariness of the death sentence. On July 2, 1976, the Court handed down five decisions that reviewed these new state laws. In this case, Troy Leon Gregg was charged with committing armed robbery and murder. He was convicted, and the jury returned a sentence of death.

Judgment of the Court, and opinion of Mr. Justice Stewart, Mr. Justice Powell, and Mr. Justice Stevens, announced by Mr. Justice Stewart.

The issue in this case is whether the imposition of the sentence of death for the crime of murder under the law of Georgia violates the Eighth and Fourteenth Amendments.

I

The petitioner, Troy Gregg, was charged with committing armed robbery and murder. In accordance with Georgia procedure in capital cases, the trial was in two stages, a guilt stage and a sentencing stage. *[The jury found Gregg guilty of two counts of armed robbery and two counts of murder. At the penalty stage, which took place before the same jury, neither the prosecutor nor Gregg's lawyer offered any additional evidence. The trial judge instructed the jury that it could recommend either a death sentence or a life prison sentence on each count. The jury could consider the facts and circumstances, if any, presented by the parties in mitigation or aggravation. To impose the death penalty, the jury had to first find beyond a reasonable doubt one of these aggravating circumstances: (1) that the murder was committed while Gregg was engaged in the armed robbery, (2) that Gregg committed the offense of murder for the purpose of receiving money and the automobile taken during the murder, or (3) the offense of murder was "outrageously and wantonly vile, horrible and inhuman" in that it involved the "depravity" of Gregg's mind.]*

[The jury found the first and second of these circumstances and returned verdicts of death on each count. The Supreme Court of Georgia affirmed the convictions and the imposition of the death sentences for murder.]

. . .

III

We address initially the basic contention that the

punishment of death for the crime of murder is, under all circumstances, "cruel and unusual" in violation of the Eighth and Fourteenth Amendments of the Constitution. In Part IV of this opinion, we will consider the sentence of death imposed under the Georgia statutes at issue in this case.

. . .

B

. . . [I]n assessing a punishment selected by a democratically elected legislature against the constitutional measure, we presume its validity. We may not require the legislature to select the least severe penalty possible so long as the penalty selected is not cruelly inhumane or disproportionate to the crime involved. And a heavy burden rests on those who would attack the judgment of the representatives of the people.

This is true in part because the constitutional test is intertwined with an assessment of contemporary standards and the legislative judgment weighs heavily in ascertaining such standards. "[I]n a democratic society legislatures, not courts, are constituted to respond to the will and consequently the moral values of the people." *Furman v. Georgia, supra,* at 383 (Burger, C. J., dissenting). . . .

C

In the discussion to this point we have sought to identify the principles and considerations that guide a court in addressing an Eighth Amendment claim. We now consider specifically whether the sentence of death for the crime of murder is a *per se* violation of the Eighth and Fourteenth Amendments to the Constitution. We note first that history and precedent strongly support a negative answer to this question.

. . .

The most marked indication of society's endorsement of the death penalty for murder is the legislative response to *Furman.* The legislatures of at least 35 States have enacted new statutes that provide for the death penalty for at least some crimes that result in the death of another person. And the Congress of the United States, in 1974, enacted a statute providing the death penalty for aircraft piracy that results in death. These recently adopted statutes have attempted to address the concerns expressed by the Court in *Furman* primarily (i) by specifying the factors to be weighed and the procedures to be followed in deciding when to impose a capital sentence, or (ii) by making the death penalty mandatory for specified crimes. But all of the post-*Furman* statutes make clear that capital punishment itself has not been rejected by the elected representatives of the people.

In the only statewide referendum occurring since *Furman* and brought to our attention, the people of California adopted a constitutional amendment that authorized capital punishment, in effect negating a prior ruling by the Supreme Court of California in *People* v. *Anderson,* 6 Cal. 3d 628, 493 P. 2d 880, cert. denied, 406 U. S. 958 (1972), that the death penalty violated the California Constitution.

The jury also is a significant and reliable objective index of contemporary values because it is so directly involved.... [T]he actions of juries in many States since *Furman* are fully compatible with the legislative judgments, reflected in the new statutes, as to the continued utility and necessity of capital punishment in appropriate cases. At the close of 1974 at least 254 persons had been sentenced to death since *Furman,* and by the end of March 1976, more than 460 persons were subject to death sentences.

. . .

... [W]e cannot say that the judgment of the Georgia Legislature that capital punishment may be necessary in some cases is clearly wrong. Considerations of federalism, as well as respect for the ability of a legislature to evaluate, in terms of its particular State, the moral consensus concerning the death penalty and its social utility as a sanction, require us to conclude, in the absence of more convincing evidence, that the infliction of death as a punishment for murder is not without justification and thus is not unconstitutionally severe.

... [W]e cannot say that the punishment is invariably disproportionate to the crime. It is an extreme sanction, suitable to the most extreme of crimes.

We hold that the death penalty is not a form of punishment that may never be imposed, regard-less of the circumstances of the offense, regardless of the character of the offender, and regardless of the procedure followed in reaching the decision to impose it.

IV

We now consider whether Georgia may impose the death penalty on the petitioner in this case.

A

... [T]he concerns expressed in *Furman* that the penalty of death not be imposed in an arbitrary or capricious manner can be met by a carefully drafted statute that ensures that the sentencing authority is given adequate information and guidance. As a general proposition these concerns are best met by a system that provides for a bifurcated proceeding at which the sentencing authority is apprised of the information relevant to the imposition of sentence and provided with standards to guide its use of the information.

We do not intend to suggest that only the above-described procedures would be permissible under *Furman* or that any sentencing system constructed along these general lines would inevitably satisfy the concerns of *Furman,* for each distinct system must be examined on an individual basis. Rather, we have embarked upon this general exposition to make clear that it is possible to construct capital-sentencing systems capable of meeting *Furman*'s constitutional concerns.

B

We now turn to consideration of the constitutionality of Georgia's capital-sentencing procedures. In the wake of *Furman,* Georgia amended its capital punishment statute, but chose not to narrow the scope of its murder provisions.... Thus, now as before *Furman,* in Georgia "[a] person commits murder when he unlawfully and with malice aforethought, either express or implied, causes the death of another human being." Ga. Code Ann., § 26-1101 (a) (1972). All persons convicted of murder "shall be punished by death or by imprisonment for life." § 26-1101 (c) (1972).

Georgia did act, however, to narrow the class of murderers subject to capital punishment by specifying 10 statutory aggravating circumstances, one of which must be found by the jury to exist beyond a reasonable doubt before a death sentence can ever be imposed. In addition, the jury is authorized to consider any other appropriate aggravating or mitigating circumstances. § 27-2534.1 (b) (Supp. 1975). The jury is not required to find any mitigating circumstance in order to make a recommendation of mercy that is binding on the trial court, see § 27-2302 (Supp. 1975), but it must find a *statutory* aggravating circumstance before recommending a sentence of death.

These procedures require the jury to consider the circumstances of the crime and the criminal before it recommends sentence. No longer can a Georgia jury do as Furman's jury did: reach a finding of the defendant's guilt and then, without guidance or direction, decide whether he should live or die. Instead, the jury's attention is directed to the specific circumstances of the crime: Was it committed in the course of another capital felony? Was it committed for money? Was it committed upon a peace officer or judicial officer? Was it committed in a particularly heinous way or in a manner that endangered the lives of many persons? In addition, the jury's attention is focused on the characteristics of the person who committed the crime: Does he have a record of prior convictions for capital offenses? Are there any special facts about this defendant that mitigate against imposing capital punishment (*e.g.*, his youth, the extent of his cooperation with the police, his emotional state at the time of the crime). As a result, while some jury discretion still exists, "the discretion to be exercised is controlled by clear and objective standards so as to produce non-discriminatory application." *Coley* v. *State*, 231 Ga. 829, 834, 204 S. E. 2d 612, 615 (1974).

As an important additional safeguard against arbitrariness and caprice, the Georgia statutory scheme provides for automatic appeal of all death sentences to the State's Supreme Court. That court is required by statute to review each sentence of death and determine whether it was imposed under the influence of passion or prejudice, whether the evidence supports the jury's finding of a statutory aggravating circumstance, and whether the sentence is disproportionate compared to those sentences imposed in similar cases....

V

...[W]e hold that the statutory system under which Gregg was sentenced to death does not violate the Constitution. Accordingly, the judgment of the Georgia Supreme Court is affirmed.

It is so ordered.

MR. JUSTICE WHITE, with whom THE CHIEF JUSTICE and MR. JUSTICE REHNQUIST join, concurring in the judgment.

. . .

Statement of THE CHIEF JUSTICE and MR. JUSTICE REHNQUIST:

We concur in the judgment and join the opinion of MR. JUSTICE WHITE, agreeing with its analysis that Georgia's system of capital punishment comports with the Court's holding in *Furman* v. *Georgia*, 408 U. S. 238 (1972).

MR. JUSTICE BLACKMUN, concurring in the judgment.

. . .

MR. JUSTICE BRENNAN, dissenting.

. . .

The fatal constitutional infirmity in the punishment of death is that it treats "members of the human race as nonhumans, as objects to be toyed with and discarded. [It is] thus inconsistent with the fundamental premise of the Clause that even the vilest criminal remains a human being possessed of common human dignity."...

MR. JUSTICE MARSHALL, dissenting.

In *Furman* v. *Georgia*, 408 U. S. 238, 314 (1972) (concurring opinion), I set forth at some length my views on the basic issue presented to the Court in these cases. The death penalty, I concluded, is a cruel and unusual punishment prohibited by the Eighth and Fourteenth Amendments. That continues to be my view.

. . .

McCleskey v. Kemp

481 U.S. 278 (1987)

Warren McCleskey, a black, was convicted of murder and two counts of armed robbery. After his conviction and death sentence were affirmed by the Georgia Supreme Court, he petitioned for habeas corpus relief. A federal district court concluded that he failed to support his claim that Georgia's death sentencing process was unconstitutional. The Eleventh

Circuit affirmed. The Supreme Court here reviews the question whether the Eighth Amendment was violated because of evidence that the death penalty in Georgia is imposed more often on black defendants and killers of white victims than on white defendants and killers of black victims. The other party in this case is Ralph Kemp, an official in the Georgia prison system.

JUSTICE POWELL delivered the opinion of the Court.

This case presents the question whether a complex statistical study that indicates a risk that racial considerations enter into capital sentencing determinations proves that petitioner McCleskey's capital sentence is unconstitutional under the Eighth or Fourteenth Amendment.

I

McCleskey, a black man, was convicted of two counts of armed robbery and one count of murder in the Superior Court of Fulton County, Georgia, on October 12, 1978. McCleskey's convictions arose out of the robbery of a furniture store and the killing of a white police officer during the course of the robbery....

. . .

[McCleskey filed a petition for a writ of habeas corpus, claiming that the Georgia capital sentencing process is administered in a racially discriminatory manner in violation of the Eighth and Fourteenth Amendments to the United States Constitution.] In support of his claim, McCleskey proffered a statistical study performed by Professors David C. Baldus, George Woodworth, and Charles Pulaski (the Baldus study) that purports to show a disparity in the imposition of the death sentence in Georgia based on the race of the murder victim and, to a lesser extent, the race of the defendant. The Baldus study is actually two sophisticated statistical studies that examine over 2,000 murder cases that occurred in Georgia during the 1970s. The raw numbers collected by Professor Baldus indicate that defendants charged with killing white persons received the death penalty in 11% of the cases, but defendants charged with killing blacks received the death penalty in only 1% of the cases. The raw numbers also indicate a reverse racial disparity according to the race of the defendant: 4% of the black defendants received the death penalty, as opposed to 7% of the white defendants.

Baldus also divided the cases according to the combination of the race of the defendant and the race of the victim. He found that the death penalty was assessed in 22% of the cases involving black defendants and white victims; 8% of the cases involving white defendants and white victims; 1% of the cases involving black defendants and black victims; and 3% of the cases involving white defendants and black victims. Similarly, Baldus found that prosecutors sought the death penalty in 70% of the cases involving black defendants and white victims; 32% of the cases involving white defendants and white victims; 15% of the cases involving black defendants and black victims; and 19% of the cases involving white defendants and black victims.

Baldus subjected his data to an extensive analysis, taking account of 230 variables that could have explained the disparities on nonracial grounds. One of his models concludes that, even after taking account of 39 nonracial variables, defendants charged with killing white victims were 4.3 times as likely to receive a death sentence as defendants charged with killing blacks. According to this model, black defendants were 1.1 times as likely to receive a death sentence as other defendants. Thus, the Baldus study indicates that black defendants, such as McCleskey, who kill white victims have the greatest likelihood of receiving the death penalty. [The District Court held that the Baldus study failed to support McCleskey's claim and dismissed the petition. The Eleventh Circuit affirmed the dismissal, concluding that the statistical evidence confirms rather than condemns the Georgia system.]

II

McCleskey's first claim is that the Georgia capital punishment statute violates the Equal Protection Clause of the Fourteenth Amendment. He argues that race has infected the administration of Georgia's statute in two ways: persons who murder whites are more likely to be sentenced to death than persons who murder blacks, and black murderers are more likely to be sentenced to death than white murderers. As a black defendant who killed a white victim, McCleskey claims that the Baldus study demonstrates that he was discriminated against because of his race and because of the race of his victim. In its broadest form, McCleskey's claim of discrimination extends to every actor in the Georgia capital sentencing process, from the prosecutor who sought the death penalty and the jury that imposed the sentence, to the State itself that enacted the capital punishment statute and allows it to remain in effect despite its allegedly discriminatory application. We agree with the Court of Appeals, and every other court that has considered such a challenge, that this claim must fail.

A

Our analysis begins with the basic principle that a defendant who alleges an equal protection violation has the burden of proving "the existence of purposeful discrimination." *Whitus* v. *Georgia,* 385 U.S. 545, 550 (1967). A corollary to this principle is that a criminal defendant must prove that the purposeful discrimination "had a discriminatory effect" on him. *Wayte* v. *United States,* 470 U.S. 598, 608 (1985). Thus, to prevail under the Equal Protection Clause, McCleskey must prove that the decision-makers in *his* case acted with discriminatory purpose. He offers no evidence specific to his own case that would support an inference that racial considerations played a part in his sentence. Instead, he relies solely on the Baldus study. McCleskey argues that the Baldus study compels an inference that his sentence rests on purposeful discrimination. McCleskey's claim that these statistics are sufficient proof of discrimination, without regard to the facts of a particular case, would extend to all capital cases in Georgia, at least where the victim was white and the defendant is black.

The Court has accepted statistics as proof of intent to discriminate in certain limited contexts. First, this Court has accepted statistical disparities as proof of an equal protection violation in the selection of the jury venire in a particular district. Although statistical proof normally must present a "stark" pattern to be accepted as the sole proof of discriminatory intent under the Constitution, *Arlington Heights* v. *Metropolitan Housing Dev. Corp.,* 429 U.S. 252, 266 (1977), "[b]ecause of the nature of the jury-selection task, ... we have permitted a finding of constitutional violation even when the statistical pattern does not approach [such] extremes." *Id.,* at 266, n. 13. Second, this Court has accepted statistics in the form of multiple regression analysis to prove statutory violations under Title VII. *Bazemore* v. *Friday,* 478 U.S. 385, 400–401 (1986) (opinion of BRENNAN, J., concurring in part).

But the nature of the capital sentencing decision, and the relationship of the statistics to that decision, are fundamentally different from the corresponding elements in the venire-selection or Title VII cases. Most importantly, each particular decision to impose the death penalty is made by a petit jury selected from a properly constituted venire. Each jury is unique in its composition, and the Constitution requires that its decision rest on consideration of innumerable factors that vary according to the characteristics of the individual defendant and the facts of the particular capital offense....

... Because discretion is essential to the criminal justice process, we would demand exceptionally clear proof before we would infer that the discretion has been abused. The unique nature of the decisions at issue in this case also counsel against adopting such an inference from the disparities indicated by the Baldus study. Accordingly, we hold that the Baldus study is clearly insufficient to support an inference that any of the decisionmakers in McCleskey's case acted with discriminatory purpose.

. . .

V

... McCleskey's arguments are best presented to the legislative bodies. It is not the responsibility — or indeed even the right — of this Court to determine the appropriate punishment for particular crimes. It is the legislatures, the elected representatives of the people, that are "constituted to respond to the will and consequently the moral values of the people." *Furman* v. *Georgia,* 408 U.S., at 383 (Burger, C.J., dissenting). Legislatures also are better qualified to weigh and "evaluate the results of statistical studies in terms of their own local conditions and with a flexibility of approach that is not available to the courts," *Gregg* v. *Georgia, supra,* at 186....

VI

Accordingly, we affirm the judgment of the Court of Appeals for the Eleventh Circuit.

It is so ordered.

JUSTICE BRENNAN, with whom JUSTICE MARSHALL joins, and with whom JUSTICE BLACKMUN and JUSTICE STEVENS join in all but Part I, dissenting.

. . .

V

. . .

The Court's decision today will not change what attorneys in Georgia tell other Warren McCleskeys about their chances of execution. Nothing will soften the harsh message they must convey, nor alter the prospect that race undoubtedly will continue to be a topic of discussion. McCleskey's evidence will not have obtained judicial acceptance, but that will not affect what is said on death row. However many criticisms of today's decision may be rendered, these painful conversations will serve as the most eloquent dissents of all.

JUSTICE BLACKMUN, with whom JUSTICE MARSHALL and JUSTICE STEVENS join and with whom JUSTICE BRENNAN joins in all but Part IV-B, dissenting.

The Court today sanctions the execution of a man despite his presentation of evidence that establishes a constitutionally intolerable level of racially based discrimination leading to the imposition of his death sentence. I am disappointed with the Court's action not only because of its denial of constitutional guarantees to petitioner McCleskey individually, but also because of its departure from what seems to me to be well-developed constitutional jurisprudence.

JUSTICE BRENNAN has thoroughly demonstrated, *ante,* that, if one assumes that the statistical evidence presented by petitioner McCleskey is valid, as we must in light of the Court of Appeals' assumption, there exists in the Georgia capital-sentencing scheme a risk of racially based discrimination that is so acute that it violates the Eighth Amendment....

. . .

JUSTICE STEVENS, with whom JUSTICE BLACKMUN joins, dissenting.

. . .

In this case it is claimed—and the claim is supported by elaborate studies which the Court properly assumes to be valid—that the jury's sentencing process was likely distorted by racial prejudice. The studies demonstrate a strong probability that McCleskey's sentencing jury ... was influenced by the fact that McCleskey is black and his victim was white, and that this same outrage would not have been generated if he had killed a member of his own race. This sort of disparity is constitutionally intolerable....

. . .

Justice Lewis Powell, Jr.
The Death Penalty and Public Opinion

Following his retirement from the Supreme Court, Justice Lewis Powell, Jr., delivered a speech on capital punishment on August 7, 1988, at the American Bar Association's annual meeting in Toronto. He cited language from the Constitution and statutes from the First Congress to indicate that the Founding Fathers approved capital punishment. After summarizing the Court's holdings in *Furman* v. *Georgia* (1972) and *Gregg* v. *Georgia* (1976), he concluded that the decision on capital punishment was basically in the hands of legislatures and public opinion. The excerpts below are taken from "Death Penalty? Society Has Ruled," *Legal Times,* August 15, 1988, pp. 12, 13.

Since *Gregg,* the Supreme Court has decided—with full opinions—a number of capital cases. In view of the finality of capital punishment, appellate courts—including the Supreme Court—have reviewed each case with great care. Although protective refinements have been enunciated, *Gregg* remains the law. We have recognized, in accordance with Chief Justice Warren's opinion in *Trop* v. *Dulles,* that the Eighth Amendment "must draw its meaning from evolving standards of decency that mark the progress of a maturing society."

Thus, our constitutional decisions have been informed by contemporary judgments of society as evidenced by decisions of state legislatures and sentencing decisions of juries. Thirty-seven states now have capital punishment statutes enacted since the *Furman* decision. In 33 of these states, death sentences have been imposed. Although no federal death sentences have been imposed in recent years, several federal criminal statutes authorize a penalty of death, and Congress has recently been considering imposition of the death penalty for certain murders committed in connection with drug violations. And juries continue to impose the sentence of death.

The evidence, therefore, is compelling that a large majority of our people consider that for certain crimes, capital punishment is appropriate. In the face of this evidence, it would be difficult for a court—even the Supreme Court—to conclude that the legislatures of a great majority of the states and the Congress are mistaken as to contemporary standards of decency in our society.

. . .

...As a co-author of *Gregg* and recently the author of *McCleskey* (v. *Kemp*], I adhere to the view that the death penalty lawfully may be imposed under our Constitution. My concerns relate to the way the system malfunctions and to the shocking murder rate that prevails in our country. In view of the unambiguous public support for capital punishment, one would think that the time has come for Congress to give thoughtful consideration to making reasonable changes in the federal law governing review of criminal convictions. It is now evident that our unique system of multiple and dual collateral review is abused, particularly in capital cases. If capital punishment cannot be enforced, even where innocence is not an issue and the fairness of the trial is not seriously questioned, perhaps Congress and the state legislatures should take a serious look at whether retention of a punishment that is not being enforced is in the public interest.

G. THE RIGHT TO BEAR ARMS

The right to bear arms fits awkwardly in a chapter devoted to the rights of the accused. However, the Second Amendment is debated so widely, and with such intensity and emotion, that it merits discussion. What was the purpose of this amendment? Is the right to bear arms so fundamental that government is powerless to regulate it? What types of restrictions on guns are appropriate and constitutional?

Adoption of the Second Amendment

At face value, the Second Amendment appears to protect a *collective* right (a well-regulated militia), not a personal right: "A well regulated Militia, being necessary to the security of a free State, the right of the people to keep and bear Arms, shall not be infringed." However, that issue is confused somewhat by the legislative history of the amendment. Madison's proposal on June 8, 1789, starts with individual rights: "The right of the people to keep and bear arms shall not be infringed; a well armed and well regulated militia being the best security of a free country; but no person religiously scrupulous of bearing arms shall be compelled to render military service in person." 1 Annals of Cong. 434 (1789).

Through this language, Madison drew upon principles from English history and the American states. Individuals needed arms to participate as citizen-soldiers in a well-regulated militia. These temporary fighting forces, created in periods of emergency, were intended to avoid the dangers of a standing army. Joyce Lee Malcolm, To Keep and Bear Arms 1–3, 146–49 (1996 ed.). This argument has little application to the contemporary reliance on a standing army.

Madison's language changed as it moved through Congress. By the time his proposal emerged from a select committee, the emphasis had shifted from personal rights to individuals operating within a militia: "A well regulated militia, composed of the body of the people, being the best security of a free state, the right of the people to keep and bear arms shall not be infringed; but no person religiously scrupulous shall be compelled to bear arms." 1 Annals of Cong. 749. The Senate dropped the provision on conscientious objectors and perfected other language. 1 Journal of the First Session of the Senate 71, 77 (1820).

It could be argued that the purpose of the Bill of Rights as a whole is to protect *personal* rights, not collective rights.[33] Even if one accepts that position, the individual rights identified in the first ten amendments are not absolute. Various limits operate on speech, press, religion, and other rights. The right to bear arms does not mean that every individual may possess a howitzer or rocket launcher; there is no constitutional right to bring a handgun into a classroom.

Federal Legislation

In 1934, Congress passed legislation to restrict the transportation of sawed-off shotguns (with a barrel less than eighteen inches long) in interstate commerce. 48 Stat. 1236 (1934). A unanimous Court upheld that statute against the claim that it violated the Second Amendment. The Court found no evidence that sawed-off shotguns had "some reasonable relationship to the preservation or efficiency of a well regulated militia." United States v. Miller, 307 U.S. 174, 178 (1939). The Court related the Second Amendment to the power of Congress, in Article I, to call forth the militia and to see that it is properly organized, armed, and disciplined. Id. The rest of the decision also focused on the right to bear arms as a collective responsibility rather than an individual right to use weapons for hunting or other purposes.

Congress has passed other legislation to control firearms. A major gun control bill was enacted in 1968, following the fatal shootings of Martin Luther King, Jr. and Robert F. Kennedy. 82 Stat. 1213 (1968). A separate statute, the Omnibus Crime Control and Safe Streets Act, included a section on firearms. 82 Stat. 225–35 (1968). Two decades later, during the Reagan administration, Congress passed the Firearms Owners' Protection Act, which eased somewhat the restrictions in the 1968 legislation. 100 Stat. 449 (1986). See also 100 Stat. 766 (1986). In 1993, the Brady bill provided a five-day waiting period for handgun purchases. 107 Stat. 1536 (1993). Legislation in 1994 added a ban on semiautomatic weapons. 108 Stat. 1996–2010 (1994). Because of the paucity of federal court decisions on the Second Amendment, the scope of "gun rights" is left largely to the elected branches operating at the national level and in the states.

State Actions

The Second Amendment applies to the national government, not to the states. Individual states may therefore interpret their own constitutional provisions to enact restrictions on weapons. In 2000, for example, the Massachusetts attorney general announced that consumer protection laws would be used to prohibit the sale of cheap handguns ("Saturday Night Specials") and to require safety locks for all handguns sold in the state. Also in 2000, Maryland passed legislation to require childproof locks for handguns.[34]

---

33. William Van Alstyne, "The Second Amendment and the Personal Right to Arms," 43 Duke L. J. 1236 (1994); 1 Laurence H. Tribe, American Constitutional Law 897–98 n.211 (2000).

34. The literature on the Second Amendment is vast, but interested readers may want to start with Robert J. Spitzer, The Politics of Gun Control (2d ed. 1998); David E. Young, ed., The Origin of the Second Amendment (2 ed. 1995); Sanford Levinson, "The Embarrassing Second Amendment," 99 Yale L. J. 661 (1989); and Stephen P. Halbrook, That Every Man Be Armed (1984).

SELECTED READINGS

AMAR, AKHIL REED. The Constitution and Criminal Procedure: First Principles. New Haven, Conn.: Yale University Press, 1997.

BAKER, LIVA. Miranda: Crime, Law and Politics. New York: Atheneum, 1983.

BEDAU, HUGO ADAM. ed. The Death Penalty in America. New York: Oxford University Press, 1982.

BLACK, CHARLES L. Capital Punishment: The Inevitability of Caprice and Mistake. New York: Norton, 1974.

BODENHAMER, DAVID J. Fair Trial: Rights of the Accused in American History. New York: Oxford University Press, 1992.

CLARK, LEROY D. The Grand Jury: The Use and Abuse of Political Power. New York: Quadrangle, 1975.

EDWARDS, GEORGE J., JR. The Grand Jury. New York: AMS Press, 1973. Originally published in 1906.

FELLMAN, DAVID. The Defendant's Rights Today. Madison: University of Wisconsin Press, 1976.

FRANKEL, MARVIN E., AND GARY P. NAFTALIS. The Grand Jury. New York: Hill and Wang, 1975.

GOLDSTEIN, ABRAHAM S. The Passive Judiciary: Prosecutorial Discretion and the Guilty Plea. Baton Rouge: Louisiana State University Press, 1981.

GRAHAM, FRED P. The Self-Inflicted Wound. New York: Macmillan, 1970.

LEHMAN, GODFREY D. We the Jury . . . The Impact of Jurors on Our Basic Freedoms. Amherst, N.Y.: Prometheus Books, 1997.

LEVY, LEONARD W. Origins of the Fifth Amendment. New York: Macmillan, 1986.

———. Against the Law: The Nixon Court and Criminal Justice. New York: Harper Torchbooks, 1976.

———. The Palladium of Justice: Origins of Trial by Jury. Chicago: Ivan R. Dee, 1999.

LEWIS, ANTHONY. Gideon's Trumpet. New York: Vintage, 1964.

MANSFIELD, JOHN H. "The Albertson Case: Conflict between the Privilege Against Self-Incrimination and the Government's Need for Information." 1966 Supreme Court Review 103.

MEDALIE, RICHARD J. From Escobedo to Miranda: The Anatomy of a Supreme Court Decision. Washington, D.C.: Lerner Law Book Co., 1966.

MELTSNER, MICHAEL. Cruel and Unusual: The Supreme Court and Capital Punishment. New York: William Morrow, 1974.

POLSBY, DANIEL D. "The Death of Capital Punishment? Furman v. Georgia." 1972 Supreme Court Review 1.

SEIDMAN, LOUIS MICHAEL. "The Supreme Court, Entrapment, and Our Criminal Justice Dilemma." 1981 Supreme Court Review 111.

SELLIN, THORSTEN. The Penalty of Death. Beverly Hills, Calif.: Sage Publications, 1980.

SIGLER, JAY A. Double Jeopardy: The Development of a Legal and Social Policy. Ithaca, N.Y.: Cornell University Press, 1969.

SPERLICH, PETER W. "Trial by Jury: It May Have a Future." 1978 Supreme Court Review 191.

STEPHENS, OTIS H., JR. The Supreme Court and Confessions of Guilt. Knoxville: University of Tennessee Press, 1973.

WAY, H. FRANK. Criminal Justice and the American Constitution. North Scituate, Mass.: Duxbury Press, 1980.

WESTEN, PETER, AND RICHARD DRUBEL. "Toward a General Theory of Double Jeopardy." 1978 Supreme Court Review 81.

YASUDA, TED K. "Entrapment as a Due Process Defense: Developments after Hampton v. United States." 57 Indiana Law Journal 89 (1982).

YOUNGER, RICHARD D. The People's Panel: The Grand Jury in the United States, 1634–1941. Providence, R.I.: Brown University Press, 1963.

14

Search and Seizure

No area of constitutional law is more unsettled, and unsettling, than Supreme Court decisions on search and seizure. The Court must apply eighteenth-century principles to such twentieth-century practices as automobile and aerial searches, the use of trained dogs to detect drugs, wiretaps of phone calls, and increasingly sophisticated methods of electronic eavesdropping. Congress has had to legislate to protect the privacy of communication by cellular phones; e-mail privacy remains a difficult issue. All three branches of government have been active in defining the contours and content of the Fourth Amendment.

A. EXPECTATIONS OF PRIVACY

Several statutes passed by the First Congress affected what we know today as Fourth Amendment interests, but the Amendment itself was not ratified until 1791. Indeed, it would be years before the federal courts handed down decisions interpreting the Fourth Amendment. In the meantime, Congress had to form its own judgments on the permissible limits of governmental searches and seizures.

Congress did not have to wait for the drafting of the Fourth Amendment to understand private citizens' resentment of governmental intrusion. The insistence on privacy at home, captured in the maxim "a man's house is his castle," had been expressed for thousands of years.[1] The expectation of privacy within one's home is found in biblical law, the *Talmud*, and the *Code of Hammurabi*. The members of the First Congress were aware of this heritage.

The Fourth Amendment is difficult to interpret in isolation because it often implicates other sections of the Constitution. The Fourth and Fifth Amendments "throw great light on each other. For the 'unreasonable searches and seizures' condemned in the Fourth Amendment are almost always made for the purpose of compelling a man to give evidence against himself, which in criminal cases is condemned by the Fifth Amendment...." Boyd v. United States, 116 U.S. 616, 633 (1886). The two Amendments sometimes "run almost into each other." Id. at 630. Cases lie at the "crossroads" of the Fourth and Fifth Amendments. Brown v. Illinois, 422 U.S. 590, 591 (1975). Searches and seizures also invoke more general constitutional interests, such as the privacy of the individual. In 1965 the Court asked: "Would we allow the police to search the sacred precincts of marital bedrooms for telltale signs of the use of contraceptives? The very idea is repulsive to the notions of privacy surrounding the marriage relationship." Griswold v. Connecticut, 381 U.S. 479, 485–86.

These complexities are compounded by the language of the Fourth Amendment: "The right of the people to be secure in their persons, houses, papers, and effects, against unreasonable searches and seizures, shall not be violated and no Warrants shall issue, but upon probable cause, supported by Oath or affirmation, and particularly describing the place to be searched, and the persons or things to be seized." It is more than a problem of defining "unreasonable"

---

1. Nelson B. Lasson, The History and Development of the Fourth Amendment to the United States Constitution 13 (1937).

and "probable cause." Should the Amendment be taken as a unit, requiring warrants to make a search and seizure reasonable? There are too many exceptions to the warrant requirement to accept that construction.

Does the Amendment split into two discrete halves, allowing warrantless searches and seizures (provided they are "reasonable") in the first clause, followed by a second clause that describes warrants if used? Some Justices appear to emphasize the first clause to the exclusion of the second, insisting on "reasonableness" but not warrants. Florida v. Royer, 460 U.S. 491, 520 (1983) (Rehnquist dissenting). Justices White and Rehnquist and Chief Justice Burger have argued that it was "not generally considered 'unreasonable' at common law for officers to break doors in making warrantless felony arrests." According to their reading, the second clause "does not purport to alter colonial practice." Payton v. New York, 445 U.S. 573, 610 (1980) (dissenting opinion). This interpretation overlooks the decisive break by America with British and colonial practices. Justice Bradley summarized the conditions that preceded the rupture with England:

> In order to ascertain the nature of the proceedings intended by the Fourth Amendment to the Constitution under the terms "unreasonable searches and seizures," it is only necessary to recall the contemporary or then recent history of the controversies on the subject, both in this country and in England. The practice had obtained in the colonies of issuing writs of assistance to the revenue officers, empowering them, in their discretion, to search suspected places for smuggled goods, which James Otis pronounced "the worst instrument of arbitrary power, the most destructive of English liberty, and the fundamental principles of law, that ever was found in an English law book;" since they placed "the liberty of every man in the hands of every petty officer." This was in February, 1761, in Boston, and the famous debate in which it occurred was perhaps the most prominent event which inaugurated the resistance of the colonies to the oppressions of the mother country. "Then and there," said John Adams, "then and there was the first scene of the first act of opposition to the arbitrary claims of Great Britain. Then and there the child Independence was born." Boyd v. United States, 116 U.S. at 625.

In 1772, a Committee of Correspondence in Boston prepared *The Rights of the Colonists* and added a long list of British actions that had infringed those rights. Collectors and other "petty officers" boarded vessels and entered homes and shops in the search for illegal merchandise: "Our houses and even our bed chambers, are exposed to be ransacked, our boxes chests & trunks broke open ravaged and plundered by wretches, whom no prudent man would venture to employ even as menial servants." 1 The Roots of the Bill of Rights 206 (Bernard Schwartz ed. 1980). By the time of independence, American states had begun to adopt their own bills of rights. Most of these included protections against unreasonable searches and seizures (see box on next page).

Although Americans were outraged by writs of assistance and the general search warrant, it has been settled practice throughout our history that warrants are not required for every search and seizure. Various exceptions exist, and the list lengthens with each passing decade. The following sections cover the warrant requirement, the exceptions to it, the technological problems of electronic eavesdropping, and the Court's doctrine of excluding illegally obtained evidence (the exclusionary rule).

B. ARREST AND SEARCH WARRANTS

It is customary for the Court to reiterate that "searches conducted outside the judicial process, without prior approval by judge or magistrate, are *per se* unreasonable under the Fourth Amendment—subject only to a few specifically established and well-delineated exceptions."

Early State Provisions on Search and Seizure

The Virginia Bill of Rights of 1776: "general warrants, whereby an officer or messenger may be commanded to search suspected places without evidence of a fact committed, or to seize any person or persons not named, or whose offence is not particularly described and supported by evidence, are grievous and oppressive, and ought not to be granted."

The Declaration of Rights issued by Pennsylvania in 1776: "[T]he people have a right to hold themselves, their houses, papers, and possessions free from search and seizure, and therefore warrants without oaths or affirmation first made, affording a sufficient foundation for them, and whereby any officer or messenger may be commanded or required to search suspected places, or to seize any person or persons, his or their property, not particularly described are contrary to that right, and ought not to be granted."

The Massachusetts Declaration of Rights of 1780: "Every subject has a right to be secure from all unreasonable searches, and seizures, of his person, his houses, his papers, and all his possessions. All warrants, therefore, are contrary to this right, if the cause or foundation of them be not previously supported by oath or affirmation, and if the order in the warrant to a civil officer, to make search in suspected places, or to arrest one or more suspected persons, or to seize their property, be not accompanied with a special designation of the persons or objects of search, arrest, or seizure; and no warrant ought to be issued but in cases, and with the formalities prescribed by the laws."

The early constitutions of Maryland, New Hampshire, North Carolina, and Vermont also included safeguards against arbitrary searches and seizures.

Katz v. United States, 389 U.S. 347, 357 (1967). These "exceptions" have grown rapidly over the years.

For most of the Court's history, it has been axiomatic that the safeguards built into the Fourth Amendment depend upon warrants issued upon probable cause "by a neutral and detached magistrate." Constitutional liberties are not secure when relying on the judgments of the officer "engaged in the often competitive enterprise of ferreting out crime." To allow warrantless action by a law enforcement officer "would reduce the Amendment to a nullity and leave the people's homes secure only in the discretion of police officers." Johnson v. United States, 333 U.S. 10, 14 (1948). However, in recent decades the Court has upheld warrantless seizures even when there is sufficient time for the police to seek a warrant from a magistrate.

Grounds for Issuing a Warrant

To obtain a search warrant, a law enforcement officer must state in an affidavit the reasons for the search. The reasons must show probable cause; mere suspicion or belief is insufficient ground. If an affidavit merely asserts an officer's belief in the truth of statements made by others, without adequate reason to support the statements, the affidavit does not justify a search warrant. Grau v. United States, 287 U.S. 124 (1932). Before authorizing a warrant, a magistrate is supposed to find probable cause from facts or circumstances presented in the affidavit. Nathanson v. United States, 290 U.S. 41 (1933). These standards were substantially weakened in 1984 when the Court adopted the "good-faith" test that allowed the admission of evidence obtained from a search warrant even after it was later found to be unsupported by probable cause. United States v. Leon, 468 U.S. 897 (see pages 814–15, 824–27).

Since searches are sometimes conducted incident to an arrest, an arrest warrant must also be based on an officer's personal knowledge and belief that someone has committed a crime. Giordenello v. United States, 357 U.S. 480 (1958). In determining probable cause and reasonable grounds, warrants may be based on information and hearsay supplied by informers who have a record of providing reliable tips and when officers verify the information through their own observations.[2] If a warrant is deficient in some respect, the resulting search and seizure can be declared invalid.

The Fourth Amendment requires that a search warrant "particularly describe" the items to be seized. A magistrate may not authorize an open-ended search warrant and leave to the discretion of officials (even when he accompanies them) the decision of what objects to seize when they arrive. The warrant must specify the things to be seized at the time the warrant is issued, not after the search and seizure are complete. Lo-Ji Sales, Inc. v. New York, 442 U.S. 319 (1979).[3] Under some circumstances, a defective warrant can nonetheless produce a valid conviction. In one case, several men transported stolen goods to a retail store, which was searched under a defective warrant. The men were unable to contest the admission of the seized evidence because they had no legitimate expectation of privacy or interest of any kind in the store. Brown v. United States, 411 U.S. 223 (1973). Warrants are not required to search students. New Jersey v. T.L.O., 469 U.S. 325 (1985) (reprinted in Chapter 16).

In 1980 the Supreme Court struck down a New York law that authorized police officers to enter a private residence without a warrant and with force, if necessary, to make a routine felony arrest. The statute allowed them to seize evidence after entry. The Court held that, absent "exigent circumstances," officers may not enter a home without a warrant. It is a basic principle of the Fourth Amendment that searches and seizures inside a home without a warrant are "presumptively unreasonable." Payton v. New York, 445 U.S. 573, 586 (1980). The Supreme Court cited *Payton* in a 1990 decision in holding, 7 to 2, that the police had no exigent circumstances to justify their warrantless entry into a house where a robbery suspect was an overnight guest. There was no risk that he would escape and he had a legitimate expectation of privacy as a guest. Minnesota v. Olson, 495 U.S. 91 (1990). [*Payton* was weakened in another 1990 decision, *New York* v. *Harris* (see page 815)].

Although an overnight guest is protected by the Fourth Amendment, the same privilege does not extend to someone who is present in a person's house or apartment for a couple of hours (to bag cocaine). Minnesota v. Carter, 525 U.S. 83 (1998).

A warrantless nighttime entry into a home to arrest someone for a noncriminal, nonjailable traffic offense is prohibited by the Fourth Amendment. Welsh v. Wisconsin, 466 U.S. 740 (1984). Without consent or exigent circumstances, a law enforcement officer with an arrest warrant may not legally search for that person in the home of a third party (a party not suspected of a crime) without first obtaining a search warrant. The Court explained the broad potential for abuse. In one case the police, armed with an arrest warrant for two fugitives, searched 300 homes. Steagald v. United States, 451 U.S. 204, 215 (1981).

---

2. Draper v. United States, 358 U.S. 307 (1959); Rugendorf v. United States, 376 U.S. 528 (1964). The magistrate must understand some of the underlying circumstances relied on by the informer and some of the underlying circumstances that prompt an officer to conclude that an informer is creditable and his or her information reliable. Aguilar v. Texas, 378 U.S. 108 (1964); United States v. Harris, 403 U.S. 573 (1971). A magistrate cannot authorize a warrant simply by accepting an informer's unsubstantiated tip. Spinelli v. United States, 393 U.S. 410 (1969); Whiteley v. Warden, 401 U.S. 560 (1971). These rules evolved into the "totality of the circumstances" approach, under which a magistrate may use independent police work to corroborate an informer's tip. Illinois v. Gates, 462 U.S. 213 (1983); Massachusetts v. Upton, 466 U.S. 727 (1984). Also on the importance of corroborating an informer's tip: Florida v. J.L., 120 S.Ct. 1375 (2000); Alabama v. White, 496 U.S. 325 (1990).

3. Searches have been declared unreasonable when federal agents falsely claim to have a search warrant, Go-Bart Co. v. United States, 282 U.S. 344 (1931), or when a search warrant has expired, Sgro v. United States, 287 U.S. 206 (1932). If an officer deliberately misleads a magistrate by making false statements and those statements are necessary to find probable cause, a defendant is entitled to challenge the truthfulness of the affidavit. If the defendant prevails, the search warrant is declared void and the fruits of the search are excluded. Franks v. Delaware, 438 U.S. 154 (1978). On the other hand, if factual inaccuracies do not destroy the integrity of an affidavit, the resulting search is permitted. Rugendorf v. United States, 376 U.S. 528 (1964).

Congressional Initiatives

The question of third-party searches arose in a 1978 case involving a police search of a student newspaper that had taken photographs of a clash between demonstrators and police. A search warrant was issued to obtain the photographs and learn the identities of those who had assaulted police officers. The Court held that police are not prevented from issuing a search warrant simply because the owner of a place is not reasonably suspected of criminal involvement. A warrant could be properly drafted to protect the interests of a free press. Zurcher v. Stanford Daily, 436 U.S. 547. The Court invited the other two branches to participate by noting that the Fourth Amendment "does not prevent or advise against legislative or executive efforts to establish nonconstitutional protections against possible abuses of the search warrant procedure...." Id. at 567. Although Congress could not pass legislation to weaken the Fourth Amendment, it could act to strengthen its protections. S. Rept. No. 96-874, at 4.

The Court's decision was denounced by newspapers as "a first step toward a police state," an assault that "stands on its head the history of both the first and the fourth amendments," and a threat to the "privacy rights of the law-abiding." S. Rept. No. 874, 96th Cong., 2d Sess. 5 (1980). In an amicus brief, Solicitor General Wade H. McCree argued that the use of a warrant to search third parties was constitutional and that there was no need to adopt a "subpoena-first" policy to obtain materials, even if the parties were newspapers with a First Amendment interest. After the uproar that greeted the Court's decision, the Carter administration realized that it had miscalculated. McCree had a reputation for composing clever limericks. Robert J. Havel, at that time Deputy Director of Public Information for the Justice Department, applied his own hand to this craft:

> A solicitor known fondly as Wade
> Filed a brief supporting a raid
> By police on the premises
> Of a newspaper nemesis
> Said the press, what a big egg Wade laid.

Congress responded by passing a bill that limited newsroom searches. With certain exceptions, it required the use of a subpoena instead of a search warrant to obtain documentary materials from those who disseminate newspapers, books, broadcasts, or other similar forms of public communication. 94 Stat. 1879 (1980). The "dialogue" between Congress and the Court on constitutional matters is captured nicely in the floor debates (see reading).

The subpoena-first policy offers several advantages to newspapers. A subpoena involves a court hearing where the newspaper can state its case; search warrants are issued without any possibility of influence by a newspaper. Moreover, a subpoena allows the newspaper to produce the specific document requested, rather than having police officers enter the premises of a newsroom and disrupt operations while searching through file cabinets, desks, and wastebaskets.

Subpoenas have been used to obtain microfilms of checks, deposit slips, and other records from a bank account. In 1976 the Supreme Court held that a Fourth Amendment interest could not be vindicated in court by challenging such a subpoena. The Court treated the materials as business records of a bank, not private papers of a person. The Court did not consider checks as confidential communications; the checks were regarded as negotiable instruments used in commercial transactions. The depositor took the risk that third parties could convey sensitive information to the government. United States v. Miller, 425 U.S. 435 (1976).

In short, private parties could not look to the courts for the protection of Fourth Amendment interests. Justice Brennan noted in a dissent that a depositor "reveals many aspects of his personal affairs, opinions, habits and associations. Indeed, the totality of bank records provides a virtual current biography." See also California Bankers Assn. v. Shultz, 416 U.S. 21

(1974). Congress responded by passing the Right to Financial Privacy Act of 1978. The statute allows notice to depositors before access is given to governmental agencies to review their financial records; gives the depositor an opportunity to challenge governmental access; and sets forth requirements for administrative subpoena or summons, search warrants, and judicial subpoena. The government can delay notice to the depositor only by obtaining an order from a judge or magistrate. 92 Stat. 3697. In this manner, certain Fourth Amendment safeguards rendered unavailable by the Supreme Court were secured by congressional action. The congressional debate on the Financial Privacy Act is reprinted in Chapter 17.

Congress Responds to *Zurcher* v. *Stanford Daily*

In *Zurcher* v. *Stanford Daily*, 436 U.S. 547 (1978), the Supreme Court upheld the right of law enforcement officers to use a search warrant on the premises of a newspaper. The newspaper was not a suspected party to a crime. It was a "third party," and in previous cases third-party searches were subject to substantial restraints. This use of a search warrant against a newspaper created a collision between two values: First Amendment rights versus law enforcement needs. In response to *Zurcher,* Congress passed legislation in 1980 to offer greater protection to First Amendment interests. The debate below, from the House of Representatives, is taken from 126 Cong. Rec. 26561–64, 26567 (1980).

Mr. KASTENMEIER. Mr. Speaker, I move to suspend the rules and pass the bill (H.R. 3486) to limit governmental search and seizure of materials possessed by persons involved in first amendment activities, . . .

Mr. Speaker, sometimes a longstanding principle of constitutional jurisprudence is thrown into doubt by a decision of the Supreme Court which—while it may answer a narrow question based on specific facts—leaves Government officials and members of the public in doubt as to how to interpret the law. When this occurs it is often best for Congress to step in to fill the void, rather than to await the results of many years of potential litigation which will again redefine the principle. This is the case with respect to the matter before us today—legislation to redefine a portion of the law of search and seizure in response to the Supreme Court's decision in Zurcher against Stanford Daily in 1978.

Prior to Stanford Daily, the long established interpretation of the fourth amendment had held that a search warrant was considered to meet the constitutional ban on general searches only if the evidence sought constituted contraband, or fruits or instrumentalities of a crime. This rule was modified in 1967 in Warden against Hayden to permit searches for mere evidence, but the facts of that case involved evidence obtained incidental to an arrest.

In the Stanford Daily case the Supreme Court swept away 200 years of jurisprudence greatly limiting searches directed against innocent third parties. The opinion of the Court, delivered by Mr. Justice White, set forth a new theory governing third party searches—identifying the standard to be applied in issuing such warrants as one of "reasonableness." Further, while recognizing that any reasonableness requirement must be established with "scrupulous exactitude," where a newspaper was involved, the Court's opinion did not conclude that the first amendment placed any additional restraints on such searches.

The public and congressional response to the Supreme Court's decision was immediate. Newspaper editorials appeared all over the country condemning the Court's decision. And in Congress numerous members, of every ideological and political stripe, introduced remedial legislation. Meanwhile, the President ordered the Attorney General to study the issue and make a legislative recommendation to him. After consultation with constitutional scholars, civil libertarians, law enforcement authorities, and Cabinet officers, the President recommended H.R. 3486, the bill before us today.

As introduced the bill before you protected third parties from arbitrary searches only where first amendment interests were involved. However, with the exception of the Department of Justice, not a single witness in favor of the legislation testified that the protections of the bill should be limited to the press alone. In fact, the representatives of media organizations were among the strongest proponents of expanding the legislation to protect all innocent third parties from arbitrary search and seizure. A great deal of apprehension was expressed about singling out the press for special treatment.

As a result, when the committee met for markup it was agreed that the legislation should be extended to provide guidance to Federal law enforcement officials as to the circumstances under which search warrants should be used to obtain information from innocent third parties other than those engaged in first amendment activities. However, because of the constitutional and policy implications of regulating the police powers of State and local authorities, the committee decided to limit the applicability of any broader third party provisions of the bill to searches by Federal officials only. Of course, we would hope that State legislatures would follow suit, and indeed eight States have already enacted similar legislation. With respect to searches directed against persons preparing materials for broadcast or publication, we retained the features of the original bill—which apply to State and local as well as Federal officials. The justification involved is the historic obligation of the Federal Government to protect the free speech values of the first amendment.

. . .

Mr. HYDE. Mr. Speaker, I rise in reluctant support of this legislation. Since the moment it emerged from the Subcommittee on Courts, Civil Liberties, and the Administration of Justice, I opposed a provision then contained in section 3 of the bill and which was designed to extend the "subpena-first" rule to "all innocent third parties." At that time, I offered an amendment to strike that section and fully intended to join with my colleague from the other side, Mr. DANIELSON from California, in offering an amendment on the floor to remove that portion of the bill. The Justice Department has since withdrawn its support for this amendment and so I will not offer it.

As has been stated, this legislation is principally designed to protect the public's right to know. It is not designed to make a sweeping change in constitutional law regarding the probable cause standard contained in the fourth amendment. In Zurcher against Stanford Daily, 436 U.S. 597 (1978), the Court held that the fourth amendment's minimal requirement for the issuance of a search warrant is probable cause to believe the evidence exists where you wish to search. Congress, of course, has the power to broaden and build upon that standard. This is what we have done with the creation of the "subpena first" rule now contained in the bill. By this procedure, law enforcement authorities must seek a subpena first before resorting to the issuance of a search warrant....

C. EXCEPTIONS TO THE WARRANT REQUIREMENT

Law enforcement officials may make warrantless arrests and searches by relying on ten exceptions: (1) border searches, (2) consent, (3) "hot pursuit" and no-knock entry, (4) the "plain-view" doctrine, (5) automobiles, (6) "stop and frisk," (7) search incident to arrest, (8) administrative inspections, (9) drug tests, and (10) civil forfeiture. Each exception has its own unique, evolutionary history of complex line drawing.

Border Searches

Long before the Supreme Court discovered exceptions to the warrant requirement, Congress and the executive branch decided that warrants were not necessary for border searches. As the Supreme Court noted in 1985: "Since the founding of our Republic, Congress has granted the Executive plenary authority to conduct routine searches and seizures at the border, without probable cause or a warrant, in order to regulate the collection of duties and to prevent the introduction of contraband into this country." United States v. Montoya de Hernandez, 473 U.S. 531, 535 (1985). A statute in 1789 authorized federal officials to enter any ship or vessel suspected of having concealed goods or merchandise and to search and seize such goods. 1 Stat. 43, § 24. Under contemporary law, any officer authorized to board or search vessels may examine any person on whom he "shall suspect there is merchandise which is subject to duty, or shall have been introduced into the United States in any manner contrary to law...

and to search any trunk or envelope, wherever found, in which he may have a reasonable cause to suspect there is merchandise which was imported contrary to law." Such merchandise shall be seized and held for trial. 19 U.S.C. § 482 (1994).

These laws reflect the judgment of the legislative and executive branches that the expectation of privacy in the interior of the country does not apply to the borders where smuggling and illegal entry are chronic problems. The authority of the United States to search baggage "of arriving international travelers is based on its inherent sovereign authority to protect its territorial integrity." Torres v. Puerto Rico, 442 U.S. 465, 472–473 (1979). Common carriers (such as airlines) have a right to inspect packages to assure that they do not contain contraband or explosive substances. Illinois v. Andreas, 463 U.S. 765, 769 n.1 (1983). When customs officials have reasonable cause to suspect that incoming international mail contains contraband, they may open envelopes and examine the substance inside. The letter itself may not be read without a search warrant. United States v. Ramsey, 431 U.S. 606 (1977); 19 C.F.R. § 145.3. Officers of the Immigration and Naturalization Service are authorized to conduct a warrantless search of any person seeking admission to the United States if the officer has "reasonable cause" to suspect that grounds exist for excluding the person from the United States. 8 U.S.C. § 1357(c) (1994). (Border searches for illegal aliens are discussed in the section entitled "Automobiles.")

The First Congress established a number of precedents for warrantless searches and seizures at the border. 1 Stat. 164, § 31; 19 U.S.C. § 1581(a). Upon reviewing the constitutionality of a statute that authorized warrantless border searches, Justice Rehnquist traced the law back to 1790 and agreed that "the enactment of this statute by the same Congress that promulgated the constitutional Amendments that ultimately became the Bill of Rights gives the statute an important historical pedigree." United States v. Villamonte-Marquez, 462 U.S. 579, 585 (1983). Acting under this statutory authority, customs officials may board vessels without any suspicion of wrongdoing. All persons coming into the United States from foreign countries "shall be liable to detention and search" by authorized federal officers or agents. 19 U.S.C. § 1582 (1994).

Border officials must now contend with smugglers who swallow drug capsules or cocaine-filled balloons and condoms. When officials suspected one woman of being a "balloon swallower," attempting what is called alimentary canal smuggling, they held her for sixteen hours during which time they considered sending her home, performing an x-ray (which she refused), and conducting a test to check her claim of being pregnant (the test proved negative). Nature eventually took its course; she discharged 88 cocaine-filled balloons over a four-day period. Considering the circumstances, the Court regarded the officials' actions as permissible under the Fourth Amendment. United States v. Montoya de Hernandez, 473 U.S. 531 (1985).

A decision by the Supreme Court in 1990 addressed the question of whether the Fourth Amendment applies to a search and seizure by U.S. agents in a foreign country. The Drug Enforcement Administration (DEA), working with Mexican officials, searched the Mexican residences of a Mexican suspect and seized certain documents. A district court held that the DEA agents had failed to justify searching the premises without a warrant. The Ninth Circuit affirmed. However, a 6–3 Court held that the Fourth Amendment does not apply to searches and seizures by U.S. agents of property owned by a nonresident alien and located in a foreign country. Although no judicial remedies are available to limit these actions by U.S. agents, the Court noted: "If there are to be restrictions on searches and seizures which occur incident to such American action, they must be imposed by the political branches through diplomatic understanding, treaty, or legislation." Justice Stevens, who concurred in the judgment, disagreed with the Court's sweeping opinion but agreed that the search conducted by U.S. agents was not "unreasonable" under the Fourth Amendment. He also stated that the Warrant Clause had no application to searches of noncitizens' homes in foreign jurisdictions because American magistrates have no power to authorize such searches. United States v. Verdugo-Urquidez, 494 U.S. 259 (1990).

Two years later the Court went even further by holding that the U.S. government may *kid-*

Elected Branch Response to *Alvarez-Machain*

On the very day that the Supreme Court decided *Alvarez-Machain*, Press Secretary Marlin Fitzwater attempted to defuse the impact of the ruling by announcing that the United States strongly believes in "fostering respect for international rules of law, including in particular the principles of respect for territorial integrity and sovereign equality of states." Neither Alvarez-Machain's arrest nor the Court's decision reflected any change in U.S. policy "to cooperate with foreign states in achieving law enforcement objectives." Public Papers of the Presidents, 1992–93, I, at 940–41.

Within a week of the Court's ruling, a subcommittee of the House Judiciary Committee held hearings on the legality of abducting foreign nationals. The experts who testified were strongly critical of the Court's decision and the practice of transborder abductions. "Kidnapping Suspects Abroad," hearings before the Subcommittee on Civil and Constitutional Rights of the House Committee on the Judiciary, 102d Cong., 2d Sess. (1992). Legislation was proposed to prohibit international kidnapping. Because of the critical response to the Court's ruling, negotiations began between U.S. and Mexican government officials. President Bush announced to the Mexican government that the United States would not engage in transborder abductions, although leaving open the possibility that abductions might occur in extreme cases.

Negotiations between the United States and Mexico continued with the Clinton administration, resulting on November 24, 1994, in the Treaty to Prohibit Transborder Abductions. However, the treaty was never submitted to the U.S. Senate. For further details, see William J. Aceves, "The Legality of Transborder Abductions: A Study of *United States* v. *Alvarez-Machain*," 3 Southwestern Journal of Law & Trade in the Americas 101 (1996).

nap people from foreign countries to bring them here for trial. Voting 6–3, the Court concluded that the abduction did not violate an extradition treaty between the United States and Mexico. Writing for the majority, Chief Justice Rehnquist noted that the treaty "says nothing about the obligations of the United States and Mexico to refrain from forcible abductions of people from the territory of the other nation, or the consequences under the Treaty if such an abduction occurs." United States v. Alvarez-Machain, 504 U.S. 655, 663 (1992). Under this interpretation, the treaty would have to prohibit kidnappings explicitly. In his dissent, Justice Stevens said that Rehnquist's reasoning would permit the United States "to torture or simply to execute a person rather than to attempt extradition," because these options are not explicitly prohibited by the treaty either. Stevens also warned that the U.S. example invites other countries to attempt their own kidnappings. The decision provoked the charge from domestic critics and foreign countries that U.S. Presidents could act in defiance of international law, an impression that the Bush and Clinton administrations attempted to dispel (see box). (Border-search cases are also discussed at the end of the section entitled "Automobiles.")

Consent

The protections of the Fourth Amendment may be waived if a person's consent is voluntary and without coercion. Consent is not granted when one submits to authority. Johnson v. United States, 333 U.S. 10, 13 (1948). In one case, government agents entered a suspect's home without a search warrant or arrest warrant but with his wife's permission. The Court held that his constitutional rights had not been waived when his wife, under implied coercion, allowed the agents to enter. Amos v. United States, 255 U.S. 313 (1921). Under other circumstances the Court has allowed a wife or third party to admit officers to make a full search and find incriminating evidence if the consent has been given voluntarily. United States v. Matlock, 415 U.S. 164 (1974).

Following the reasoning in *Matlock,* a 6–3 Court in 1990 decided that evidence from a warrantless search could be introduced at trial if the police were allowed to enter a home by someone they "reasonably believed" had authority to consent to the search, even if it was later discovered that the person *lacked* authority. Illinois v. Rodriguez, 497 U.S. 177 (1990). In 1991 another 6–3 decision by the Court held that police officers looking for illicit drugs may board buses and ask passengers for permission to search their bags. The Court considered such encounters "consensual" if passengers felt free to disregard the police and go about their business. The dissenters argued that passengers would feel intimidated by the police and unable to assert their constitutional rights fully. Florida v. Bostick, 501 U.S. 429 (1991). On the other hand, the Court has held that bus passengers have a legitimate expectation of privacy that their carry-on bags will not be manipulated by law enforcement officers in their search for contraband. Bond v. United States, 120 S.Ct. 1462 (2000).

The use of undercover agents complicates the notion of consent. A federal narcotics agent, by misrepresenting his identity and expressing his willingness to buy narcotics, was invited into the home of a drug dealer. There was no question of entrapment; the agent did not encourage or stimulate a crime. The Court decided that the dealer, by opening his home as a place of illegal business, had surrendered any expectation of privacy. Lewis v. United States, 385 U.S. 206 (1966).

"Hot Pursuit" and No-Knock Entry

A 1967 decision by the Supreme Court dealt with an armed robbery suspect who, police learned, had entered a certain house. The police arrived minutes later and were told at the door of the house, by the suspect's wife, that she had no objection to their searching the house. Her consent alone did not justify the resulting search. The police acted reasonably by entering the house and searching for the suspect and for weapons that he had used in the robbery or might use against them. The Fourth Amendment did not require the police to delay the investigation and endanger their lives or the lives of others. "Speed here was essential, and only a thorough search of the house for persons and weapons could have insured that [the suspect] was the only man present and that the police had control of all weapons which could be used against them or to effect an escape." Warden v. Hayden, 387 U.S. 294, 298–99.

The Court also expanded the police power by rejecting the "mere evidence" rule. Previous decisions had allowed police to seize the instrumentalities of a crime (weapons, stolen property) but prohibited the seizure of "merely evidentiary materials." The Court now rejected that distinction by allowing the officers to seize certain clothing items that were later used to convict the suspect. The Court held that privacy is not disturbed to any greater degree by a search directed to a purely evidentiary object than by a search directed to an instrumentality, fruit, or contraband. Id. at 301–02.

Another case concerned a woman suspected of selling narcotics. When the police approached her to make an arrest, she was standing in the doorway holding a paper bag. As she retreated into the house they followed, finding envelopes containing heroin and marked money. The Court held that standing in the doorway put her in a "public place" with no expectation of privacy. United States v. Santana, 427 U.S. 38 (1976).

It is now established that under the reasonableness requirement of the Fourth Amendment law enforcement officers must *generally* announce their presence and their authority before entering a home. However, the Court recognizes that under some circumstances (e.g., the belief that evidence might be destroyed if advance notice is given) the "knock and announce" principle is not always required. Wilson v. Arkansas, 514 U.S. 927 (1995). No-knock entry may be necessary to prevent the destruction of evidence, Richards v. Wisconsin, 520 U.S. 385 (1997), even when property is damaged by the entry, United States v. Ramirez, 523 U.S. 65 (1998).

"Plain-View" Doctrine

Following a brutal murder of a fourteen-year-old girl, the police went to the suspect's home to question him. On later visits they questioned his wife and eventually arrested him. The police searched his car without a warrant, arguing that it was an instrumentality of the crime and could be seized on his property "because it was in plain view." The Supreme Court reviewed previous holdings on the plain-view doctrine and concluded that the police officer in each of them had a justification for an intrusion "in the course of which he came inadvertently across a piece of evidence incriminating the accused." There has to be some valid reason for the officer's presence, for otherwise the doctrine would invite a general exploratory search without a warrant. When the police know in advance the location of the evidence and intend to seize it, a warrant should be obtained. In this case the police had ample opportunity to obtain a warrant and failed to do so, making the seizure and subsequent search of the car unconstitutional. COOLIDGE v. NEW HAMPSHIRE, 403 U.S. 443, 464–73 (1971).

The issue of "inadvertence" in *Coolidge* was replayed in 1990 in a 7–2 opinion of the Court. A police officer, having obtained a search warrant to look for property stolen during an armed robbery, did not find the goods but saw weapons in plain view and seized them. The Court held that the Fourth Amendment does not prohibit the warrantless seizure of evidence in plain view even though the discovery of the evidence was not inadvertent. The Court reached this conclusion despite the Fourth Amendment requirement that warrants "particularly describ[e] the place to be searched, and the persons or things to be seized." Horton v. California, 496 U.S. 128 (1990).

The plain-view doctrine allows limited searches and seizures following a fire. In one case, after a fire had been brought under control, firefighters discovered containers of a flammable liquid. A police detective took some pictures, and the fire chief and the detective removed the containers. Subsequent visits produced additional evidence and information. At no time was there a warrant. The Supreme Court upheld the removal of the containers without a warrant, as well as materials taken the following morning, but later visits (some coming a month later) required a warrant. A burning building is "an exigency of sufficient proportions" to permit a warrantless entry, and once inside the building firefighters "may seize evidence of arson that is in plain view." Michigan v. Tyler, 436 U.S. 499, 509 (1978). Nevertheless, people retain significant privacy interests in their fire-damaged home. Arson investigators may not conduct a warrantless search of the entire house simply because of a fire. Michigan v. Clifford, 464 U.S. 287 (1984). Some of the state courts have rejected the U.S. Supreme Court's doctrine on "plain view" (see box on p. 22).

Actions by private parties can put items in "plain view." While examining a damaged package, employees of a private freight carrier saw a white powder and notified the Drug Enforcement Administration. A DEA agent arrived, tested the powder, and determined that it was cocaine. The Court allowed the warrantless search and seizure because the actions of private individuals had placed the powder essentially in plain view of the agent. United States v. Jacobsen, 466 U.S. 109 (1984).[4] In 1988 the Court ruled that police do not need a warrant to look through trash left on a curb for a pickup, and through that examination discover evidence that supports a search warrant for narcotics use. The owner of the trash has no reasonable expectation of privacy. California v. Greenwood, 486 U.S. 35 (1988). Some state

---

4. When a private carrier mistakenly delivers a package to the wrong person, who opens it, the government may not exceed the scope of the private search. A partial invasion of privacy does not justify a total invasion by the government. Walter v. United States, 447 U.S. 649 (1980).

State Courts Examine the Merits of *Greenwood*

After the Supreme Court in *California* v. *Greenwood* (1988) upheld a police search of trash left out for a pickup, some state courts required law enforcement officials to obtain a warrant first before searching garbage. In reaching that conclusion in 1990, the New Jersey Supreme Court noted that when it interprets the state constitution, "we look for direction to the United States Supreme Court, ... But although that Court may be a polestar that guides us as we navigate the New Jersey Constitution, we bear ultimate responsibility for the safe passage of our ship. Our eyes must not be so fixed on that star that we risk the welfare of our passengers on the shoals of constitutional doctrine. In interpreting the New Jersey Constitution, we must look in front of us as well as above us."

The New Jersey Supreme Court pointed out that for "most of our country's history, the primary source of protection of individual rights has been state constitutions, not the federal Bill of Rights." Whenever the U.S. Constitution offers citizens less protection than a state constitution, "we have not merely the authority to give full effect to the State protection, we have a duty to do so." State v. Hempele, 576 A.2d 793, 800 (N.J. 1990). The Supreme Court of Washington also held, contrary to *Greenwood*, that the removal of garbage by law enforcement officials for the purpose of obtaining evidence is an unreasonable intrusion upon private affairs. State v. Boland, 800 P.2d 1112 (Wash. 1990).

---

courts, interpreting their own constitutions, decided that *Greenwood* intrudes too much on privacy interests (see box).

Related to the plain-view exception is the "open-field" doctrine, which permits police officers to enter and search a field without a warrant. Hester v. United States, 265 U.S. 57 (1924). The term "effects" in the Fourth Amendment is considered less inclusive than property, permitting law enforcement officers to bypass locked gates and "No Trespassing" signs to discover marijuana growing in open fields. The Court reasons that open fields are accessible to the public and to the police in ways that a home, office, or commercial structure are not. Oliver v. United States, 466 U.S. 170 (1984). Similarly, police may cross a series of fences to look in a barn that is not considered to be protected by the Fourth Amendment. United States v. Dunn, 480 U.S. 294 (1987).

Two cases in 1986 expanded the government's authority under the open-field or plain-view doctrines. In one, the Court upheld the authority of the Environmental Protection Agency to use aerial observation and photography to implement the Clean Air Act. Without a warrant, EPA took aerial photographs of an industrial plant complex. Dow Chemical Co. v. United States, 476 U.S. 227 (1986). In the second, law enforcement officers flew over a suspect's house at an altitude of 1,000 feet and identified marijuana plants growing in the yard. On the basis of these observations, a search warrant was obtained. The Court, divided 5–4, ruled that the suspect had no expectation of privacy from *all* observations of his backyard. CALIFORNIA v. CIRAOLO, 476 U.S. 207 (1986). This case invited variations on the theme, such as flying over at even lower altitudes or using police helicopters to hover over a suspect's home or outside an apartment window. In 1989 the Court (again divided 5–4) upheld the use of police helicopters to conduct surveillance from a height of 400 feet above a greenhouse in a residential backyard. Florida v. Riley, 488 U.S. 445 (1989).

Automobiles

No exception to the warrant requirement contains as many permutations and perturbations as the exception for automobiles. The automobile exception illustrates how the constitutionality of an issue can be shaped initially by the executive and legislative branches. From an early date, congressional statutes and Attorney General opinions agreed that government agents could make warrantless searches and seizures of ships, automobiles, and other vehicles that could be easily moved outside the jurisdiction of an officer by the time he obtained a warrant. 1 Stat. 43, § 24 (1789); 26 Op. Att'y Gen. 243 (1907). This justification appears in the first Supreme Court decision on automobile searches. If law enforcement officers had probable cause to stop a car, they could search it without a warrant and seize its contents without violating the Fourth Amendment. The Court regarded its decision as consistent with the intent of Congress in the National Prohibition Act.[5]

The Court struggled to find reasonable boundaries for car searches. If evidence is in plain sight of an officer who has a right to be in a position of viewing it, the material can be introduced in evidence without a warrant.[6] Incriminating evidence can be taken from the exterior of an automobile without a search warrant. Cardwell v. Lewis, 417 U.S. 583 (1974). Even when a car is impounded at a police station or towed to a garage, with no risk of its being moved or its contents taken, a warrantless search of the *interior* is valid. The Court argues that such searches are necessary to inventory the vehicle's contents and to prevent dangerous weapons or materials from falling into the hands of vandals.[7] If inventory searches are insufficiently regulated to prevent "a general rummaging in order to discover incriminating evidence," the evidence will be suppressed. Florida v. Wells, 495 U.S. 1 (1990).

Leather Briefcases vs. Cardboard Boxes. These cases suggest that expectations of privacy for the contents of an automobile are severely limited. Other decisions, however, imply that the right to privacy exists for such items as personal luggage, especially when fortified by double locks. United States v. Chadwick, 433 U.S. 1 (1977); Arkansas v. Sanders, 442 U.S. 753 (1979). This line of argument was ill-fated. Justice Blackmun warned that left "hanging in limbo, and probably soon to be litigated, are the briefcase, the wallet, the package, the paper bag, and every other kind of container." 442 U.S. at 768. Within a few years the Court decided that officers needed a search warrant before opening packages wrapped in green opaque plastic. Clearly the Court did not want to make what might appear to be class distinctions, upholding the right of privacy for a leather briefcase but denying it for a cardboard box: "What one person may put into a suitcase, another may put into a paper bag." Robbins v. California, 453 U.S. 420, 426 (1981). Justice Powell criticized the law on automobile searches as "intolerably confusing." Id. at 430.

The latitude for automobile searches continues to widen. As an incident to a lawful arrest, a police officer may reach into the interior of a car, remove a jacket, and unzip one of the pockets to discover cocaine. The search is valid because it is incident to a lawful custodial arrest. New York v. Belton, 453 U.S. 454 (1981). However, if a police officer stopped a car without probable cause or reasonable suspicion, the seizure of contraband—even if in plain view— is unreasonable under the Fourth Amendment. An individual's right of privacy outweighs a police officer's decision to make random spot checks. Delaware v. Prouse, 440 U.S. 648 (1979). If passengers in an automobile are unable to show ownership of the car or its contents, they have no standing to raise vicarious Fourth Amendment challenges to the search.

---

5. Carroll v. United States, 267 U.S. 132 (1925). See also Husty v. United States, 282 U.S. 694 (1931) and Brinegar v. United States, 338 U.S. 160 (1949). If a car could have been searched on the streets, officers may follow it into a garage and search it there. Scher v. United States, 305 U.S. 251 (1938).

6. Texas v. Brown, 460 U.S. 730 (1983); Colorado v. Bannister, 449 U.S. 1 (1980); Harris v. United States, 390 U.S. 234 (1968).

7. See Colorado v. Bertine, 479 U.S. 367 (1987); Illinois v. Lafayette, 462 U.S. 640 (1983); Michigan v. Thomas, 458 U.S. 259 (1982); South Dakota v. Opperman, 428 U.S. 364, 369 (1976); Texas v. White, 423 U.S. 67 (1975); Cady v. Dombrowski, 413 U.S. 433, 448 (1973); Chambers v. Maroney, 399 U.S. 42 (1970).

The *Ross* Doctrine

Police with probable cause stopped a car, searched the driver, and searched the interior of the car. After arresting the driver, they opened the car's trunk and discovered a closed brown paper bag. Inside they found glassine bags containing a white powder, later determined to be heroin. They drove the car to police headquarters and conducted another warrantless search, opening a zippered leather pouch.

The Supreme Court held that police officers who have legitimately stopped an automobile and have probable cause to believe that it contains contraband may conduct a warrantless search that is as thorough as a magistrate could authorize by warrant. United States v. Ross, 456 U.S. 798 (1982). The Court insisted that the decision was "faithful to the interpretation of the Fourth Amendment that the Court has followed with substantial consistency through-

out our history." Id. at 824. And yet it effectively repealed the Fourth Amendment warrant requirement for automobile searches and the traditional reliance on a neutral and detached magistrate. The Court did not explain why a search warrant could not be obtained after arresting a suspect and immobilizing the car.

In 1999, the Court (divided 7 to 2) upheld the search of an automobile when police had probable cause that it contained illegal drugs. Under those circumstances, it was not necessary to obtain a search warrant, even if there was time. Maryland v. Dyson, 527 U.S. 465 (1999).

State courts may reject the *Ross* doctrine by adopting standards that offer owners of automobiles greater protection against searches and seizures. E.g., State v. Ringer, 674 P.2d 1240 (Wash. 1983).

Rakas v. Illinois, 439 U.S. 128 (1978). The major expansion of automobile searches came in 1982 (see box). UNITED STATES v. ROSS, 456 U.S. 798.

Ross did not decide whether the Fourth Amendment requires the police to obtain a warrant to open a package in an automobile when they lack probable cause to search the entire car. In 1991, a 6–3 court held that when a police search extends only to a container within an automobile and police have probable cause to believe that the container holds contraband or evidence, they may search the container without a warrant. The curious result of this decision is that a container can be searched within a car without a warrant and yet not on a public street. California v. Acevedo, 500 U.S. 565 (1991). Another 1991 decision ruled that when an individual gives a police officer consent to search a car, the officer may search all items within the car, including a folded paper bag. Florida v. Jimeno, 500 U.S. 248 (1991). In 1991 the Supreme Court of Vermont rejected *Acevedo* and held that the type of seizure at issue in that case was impermissible under the state constitution. State v. Savva, 616 A.2d 774 (Vt. 1991).

The Court now allows the government to seize trucks suspected of containing marijuana and wait three days to search the packages, without ever bothering to obtain a search warrant. United States v. Johns, 469 U.S. 478 (1985). When police have probable cause that an automobile is contraband and it is sitting in a public place, they may seize it without a warrant. Florida v. White, 526 U.S. 559 (1999). The freedom of police officers to search a car extends to mobile motor homes parked in a lot. The Court has largely replaced the mobility rationale of *Carroll* with the argument that the expectation of privacy in a car or motor home is significantly less than for a home or office. New York v. Class, 475 U.S. 106 (1986); California v. Carney, 471 U.S. 386 (1985).

Minor Traffic Violations. In 1996, a unanimous Court ruled that police officers may stop motorists for minor traffic violations and use that opportunity to search for evidence of drug trafficking. The drugs can be seized and used for prosecution even if the officers had no probable cause to suspect illegal drug-dealing activity. Whren v. United States, 517 U.S. 805 (1996).

Also in 1996, the Court held that when police officers stop motorists for speeding violations they need not tell them they are "free to go" before questioning them on other matters or searching their cars for drugs. Ohio v. Robinette, 519 U.S. 33 (1996). Justice Ginsburg in a concurrence and Justice Stevens in a dissent pointed out that states, in interpreting their constitutions, could prevent the type of search condoned by the Supreme Court. When a car is lawfully stopped, a police officer may not only order the driver to step out of the car but the passengers as well. Maryland v. Wilson, 519 U.S. 408 (1997); Pennsylvania v. Mimms, 434 U.S. 106 (1977).

A unanimous Court in 1998 held that police may not stop a motorist for speeding and use that occasion to conduct a full search of the car. The police officer issued the person a citation rather than arresting him. Knowles v. Iowa, 526 U.S. 113 (1998). A year later, the Court reviewed a case in which a patrol officer stopped someone who had been speeding and driving with a faulty break light. The officer noticed a hypodermic syringe in the shirt pocket of the driver, who admitted that he used the syringe to take drugs. At that point the officer had probable cause to search the automobile. However, he also looked into the passenger's purse and found drugs and drug paraphernalia. Divided 6 to 3, the Court upheld looking into the purse, reading *Ross* broadly to argue that the search was justified because otherwise the driver could hide contraband in a passenger's belongings. Wyoming v. Houghton, 526 U.S. 295 (1999).

Checkpoints. Several automobile cases concern the use of roving patrols and checkpoints near the Mexican border to discover contraband or illegal aliens. Unless there is probable cause or consent, a roving patrol may not conduct a warrantless search of a car twenty-five air miles north of the Mexican border. Almeida-Sanchez v. United States, 413 U.S. 266 (1973). The Court later held that this decision should not be applied retroactively since border patrols had been acting on the basis of a federal statute, administrative regulations, and previous court decisions. United States v. Peltier, 422 U.S. 531 (1975). A roving patrol may not stop vehicles near the Mexican border and question the occupants about their citizenship and immigration status simply because they appear to be of Mexican ancestry. If an officer's observations lead him to suspect that a vehicle contains illegal aliens, he may stop a car briefly and investigate the circumstances that provoked his suspicion. United States v. Brignoni-Ponce, 422 U.S. 873 (1975); United States v. Cortez, 449 U.S. 411 (1981).

Fixed checkpoints present a different issue. Patrol officers at these sites, which are located away from the border, may stop vehicles and inquire about citizenship. In the absence of consent or probable cause, however, officers may not search the interior of a vehicle. For this purpose there is no difference between a checkpoint and a roving patrol. United States v. Ortiz, 422 U.S. 891 (1975); United States v. Martinez-Fuerte, 428 U.S. 543 (1976). In 1990 a 6–3 decision by the Court held that highway sobriety checkpoints are constitutional. Although roadblocks to catch drunk drivers are seizures under the Fourth Amendment, they are a "reasonable" technique for responding to "alcohol-related death and mutilation on the Nation's roads." Michigan State Police Dept. v. Sitz, 496 U.S. 444, 451 (1990).

"Stop and Frisk"

Many of the exceptions to the warrant requirement refer to "exigent circumstances." Other emergency situations also permit search and seizure without a warrant. The Court has held that a police officer has a right to "stop and frisk" an individual who is behaving suspiciously, even though there is no probable cause to make an arrest. Whenever a "reasonably prudent officer" believes that his safety or that of others is endangered, he may make a reasonable search for weapons of the person he thinks armed and dangerous, regardless of whether he has probable cause for arrest or an absolute certainty that the individual is armed. The Court recognizes that officers on the beat may have to take swift action based upon on-the-spot decisions. TERRY v. OHIO, 392 U.S. 1 (1968).[8]

Terry now permits "protective sweeps" in private homes when the searching officer acts with an arrest warrant and has reasonable belief that areas to be swept may harbor individuals posing a danger to the police. Maryland v. Buie, 494 U.S. 325 (1990). A *Terry* investigatory stop upheld, based on an anonymous tip corroborated by independent police work, was upheld in Alabama v. White, 496 U.S. 325 (1990). A unanimous Court in 1993 upheld a *Terry*-stop to seize *nonthreatening* contraband. Minnesota v. Dickerson, 508 U.S. 366 (1993). The Fourth Amendment limits on-the-spot decisions by police who use deadly force against unarmed, fleeing suspects. Tennessee v. Garner, 471 U.S. 1 (1985).

Brief stops to question a suspect are permissible if police have a reasonable suspicion that is grounded in specific and articulable facts. Reid v. United States, 448 U.S. 438 (1980); United States v. Hensley, 469 U.S. 221 (1985). Individuals suspected of criminal activity can be detained for periods as long as 40 minutes when the delay is attributable mainly to their evasive actions. United States v. Sharpe, 470 U.S. 675 (1985). Detentions of 90 minutes are not justified as a *Terry*-type investigative stop, United States v. Place, 462 U.S. 696 (1983), but detention can last for much longer periods at the border when smuggling is suspected, United States v. Montoya de Hernandez, 473 U.S. 531 (1985). These decisions do not justify detaining a suspect or bringing him or her to police headquarters on less than probable cause with the hope of discovering incriminating evidence.[9]

Suspicious activities and furtive movements may be sufficient reason for an officer to apprehend someone and frisk the suspect for possible weapons or burglar's tools. Sibron v. New York, 392 U.S. 40, 66 (1968). However, unless there is reasonable suspicion based on objective facts that an individual is engaged or has engaged in criminal conduct, an officer may not require someone to identify himself or herself and may not make an arrest if identification is refused.[10] A warrant to search a bartender does not justify frisking everyone in the tavern. Ybarra v. Illinois, 444 U.S. 85 (1979).

May the police pursue a fleeing suspect and offer drugs discarded during the chase as evidence in court? The Court held that the fleeing suspect was not "seized" when he dropped the drugs. Assuming that the officer's pursuit constituted a "show of authority" ordering the person to stop, the person did not comply with the order and therefore was not seized until finally tackled. Because the suspect did not submit to the officer's authority, the abandoned drugs were not the fruit of a seizure and could be introduced as evidence. California v. Hodari D., 499 U.S. 621 (1991). A year later, the Supreme Court of Hawaii declined to adopt this definition of seizure, preferring to give greater protection to Hawaiian citizens (see box on next page). Attempted but failed seizures of a person, as in a high-speed police chase, are beyond the scope of the Fourth Amendment. County of Sacramento v. Lewis, 523 U.S. 833 (1998).

Two decisions in 2000 added refinements to *Terry*. The Court held that a defendant's unprovoked flight from police, in an area of heavy narcotics trafficking, supported a reasonable suspicion that he was involved in criminal activity. His behavior therefore justified a stop and frisk. A separate statement by Stevens, Souter, Ginsburg, and Breyer pointed out that flight can be entirely innocent. Illinois v. Wardlow, 120 S.Ct. 673 (2000). In the second decision, the

---

    8. See also United States v. Sokolow, 490 U.S. 1 (1989); Michigan v. Long, 463 U.S. 1032 (1983); Michigan v. Summers, 452 U.S. 692 (1981); Pennsylvania v. Mimms, 434 U.S. 106 (1977); Adams v. Williams, 407 U.S. 143 (1972).

    9. Florida v. Royer, 460 U.S. 491 (1983); Taylor v. Alabama, 457 U.S. 687 (1982); Dunaway v. New York, 442 U.S. 200 (1979); Morales v. New York 396 U.S. 102 (1969).

    10. Kolender v. Lawson, 461 U.S. 352 (1983); Michigan v. DeFillippo, 443 U.S. 31 (1979); Brown v. Texas, 443 U.S. 47 (1979).

Independent Standards under the Constitution of Hawaii

... [W]e decline to adopt the definition of seizure employed by the United States Supreme Court in *Hodari D.* and, instead, choose to afford greater protection to our citizens....

We cannot allow the police to randomly "encounter" individuals without any objective basis for suspecting them of misconduct and then place them in a coercive environment in order to develop reasonable suspicion to justify their detention. This investigative technique is based on the proposition that an otherwise innocent person, who comes under police scrutiny for no good reason, is not innocent unless he or she convinces the police that he or she is. Such a procedure is anathema to our constitutional freedoms. For these reasons, we hold that the police conduct violated [the defendant's] right to be secure against unreasonable seizures guaranteed by article I, section 7 of the Hawaii Constitution.

SOURCE: State v. Quino, 840 P.2d 358, 362, 365 (Hawaii 1992).

Court ruled that police may not stop and frisk someone merely on the basis of an anonymous tip that he is carrying a gun. Yet the Court left open the door to accepting anonymous tips in other situations: tips about someone carrying a bomb, and conditions in airports, schools, and other public places. Florida v. J.L., 120 S.Ct. 1375 (2000).

Search Incident to Arrest

Police officers may conduct a search incident to a valid arrest. However, allowing a warrantless search and seizure whenever there is an arrest risks swallowing the general principle of the Fourth Amendment in an exception. Trupiano v. United States, 334 U.S. 699, 708 (1948). Otherwise, the government could justify an arrest because of a search and a search because of an arrest. Johnson v. United States, 333 U.S. 10, 16–17 (1948). For a reaffirmation of the reasoning in *Johnson,* see Smith v. Ohio, 494 U.S. 541 (1990).

A lawful arrest may be followed by a search of the persons and premises in order to find and seize things connected with the crime. Agnello v. United States, 269 U.S. 20 (1925). Although a search warrant for intoxicating liquors and articles for their manufacture may not be used to seize a ledger and bills of account, if the latter are in plain view they may be picked up as an incident of an arrest. Marron v. United States, 275 U.S. 192 (1927).

What are the limits of a search for articles that are not in plain view? An arrest should not be used as a pretext to conduct a general and exploratory search for incriminating information. Nevertheless, in 1947 the Supreme Court allowed an arrest warrant to justify a five-hour search of an apartment. Beneath clothes in a bedroom bureau drawer, federal agents found a sealed envelope marked "personal papers." They tore it open and found several draft cards used to convict the suspect. The Court claimed that the search was incident to the arrest, although the draft cards were unrelated to the crimes for which the suspect had been arrested. Harris v. United States, 331 U.S. 145. Three years later, the Court allowed government agents with an arrest warrant to search a suspect's desk, safe, and file cabinets to seize 573 forged stamps. The search and seizure were considered incident to a lawful arrest. United States v. Rabinowitz, 339 U.S. 56 (1950).

These decisions were overturned in *Chimel* (1969), discussed later, but first the Court disposed of other issues. It decided that an arrest warrant could not be used to search and seize items in a room if the suspect was not there. United States v. Jeffers, 324 U.S. 48 (1951). Nor could an arrest warrant justify an indiscriminate search and seizure even after an arrest. Kremen v. United States, 353 U.S. 346 (1957). When law requires police officers to make an arrest only after giving notice of their authority and purpose, or when statutes prohibit an unannounced entering of a home, actions contrary to the law invalidate an arrest and the seizure of incriminating goods. Sabbath v. United States, 391 U.S. 585 (1968); Miller v. United States, 357 U.S. 301 (1958).[11]

A search incident to an arrest must be closely connected in time and place. A warrantless search is not incident to an arrest that occurs two days later, Stoner v. California, 376 U.S. 483 (1964); or when an arrest occurs in one place and the police attempt to use it to search a home blocks away, James v. Louisiana, 382 U.S. 36 (1965); or when the police arrest a person outside the individual's house and take the person inside for the purpose of conducting a warrantless search, Shipley v. California, 395 U.S. 818 (1969) and Vale v. Louisiana, 399 U.S. 30 (1970). However, when a formal arrest quickly follows a search, it may not be "particularly important that the search preceded the arrest rather than vice versa." Rawlings v. Kentucky, 448 U.S. 98, 111 (1980).

In 1969 the Supreme Court tried to limit the reach of searches that are incident to an arrest. The case involved police officers who arrived at a home with an arrest warrant but not a search warrant. The suspect's wife allowed them to enter. When the suspect arrived, he was arrested but he specifically denied the police the right to "look around." They did so anyway, searching the entire house, attic, garage, and small workshop. The Court reversed the conviction, holding that an arresting officer may search a person to discover and remove weapons and may search the area within the immediate control of the suspect, who might grab a weapon or destroy evidence. A broader search requires a search warrant. CHIMEL v. CALIFORNIA, 395 U.S. 752.

When a suspect is detained with probable cause, even though not arrested, it is permissible for the police in the course of questioning at a station house to take samples from the person's fingernails. Although there was no search warrant and the suspect objected, the search was considered an appropriate action to preserve highly evanescent evidence. Cupp v. Murphy, 412 U.S. 291 (1973). In the case of a lawful custodial arrest, a full search of the person is reasonable under the Fourth Amendment. Police may search outer clothing to remove weapons, search elsewhere for evidence, and inventory possessions as part of the process of booking someone.[12]

Administrative Inspections

Congressional statutes authorize many types of warrantless inspections by federal officers, and in almost every case of a challenged statute the Supreme Court has upheld the legislative judgment. Beginning with the First Congress, statutes have required certain businesses to have their records available for federal inspectors. Legislation in 1791 provided that the books of distilleries shall "lie open" for inspection officers to take notes. 1 Stat. 207, § 35. Contemporary law authorizes federal inspectors to enter distilleries during business hours to examine records and documents. 26 U.S.C. § 5146(b) (1994). The Narcotics Drug Act of 1914 required persons who dispensed narcotics to prepare orders on IRS (Internal Revenue Service) forms and make them available to official inspectors. United States v. Doremus, 249 U.S. 86 (1919). During business hours, federal inspectors may enter the premises of any firearms or ammunition importer, manufacturer, dealer, or collector to examine records and documents. 18 U.S.C. § 923(g) (1994).

---

11. If there is neither reasonable grounds nor probable cause to make an arrest, incriminating statements or materials may not be introduced as evidence. United States v. Crews, 445 U.S. 463 (1980); Davis v. Mississippi, 394 U.S. 721 (1969); Recznik v. City of Lorain, 393 U.S. 166 (1968); Beck v. Ohio, 379 U.S. 89 (1964); Wong Sun v. United States, 371 U.S. 471 (1963). Without probable cause, consent, or judicial authorization, police may not bring someone to headquarters to obtain incriminating evidence. Hayes v. Florida, 470 U.S. 811 (1985); Taylor v. Alabama, 457 U.S. 687 (1982); Dunaway v. New York, 442 U.S. 200 (1979).

12. United States v. Robinson, 414 U.S. 218 (1973); Gustafson v. Florida, 414 U.S. 260 (1973); United States v. Edwards, 415 U.S. 800 (1974); Illinois v. Lafayette, 462 U.S. 640 (1983).

Standards for Administrative Inspections

In 1967 the Supreme Court placed restrictions on warrantless inspections of homes and businesses. The Court pointed out that inspections by city officials were not merely "civil" in nature. A refusal to allow an inspection, combined with the discovery of conditions that violate local ordinances, rendered the person subject to criminal process. Unless an emergency required immediate access, owners of homes and businesses had a constitutional right to insist that inspectors first obtain a search warrant. Nevertheless, the warrant need not conform to the Fourth Amendment standard of probable cause. "Reasonableness" or a "suitable" warrant would suffice. Camera v. Municipal Court, 387 U.S. 523 (1967); See v. City of Seattle, 387 U.S. 541 (1967). Although government employees are entitled to Fourth Amendment protections and have a legitimate expectation of privacy in their office, desk, and file cabinets, employers may, without a warrant, conduct a search of the office if there are reasonable grounds related to work or work-related misconduct. O'Connor v. Ortega, 480 U.S. 709 (1987).

With the growth of federal regulatory activities, the courts began to monitor the scope of agency inspections. In 1924 the Supreme Court rejected the argument of the Federal Trade Commission (FTC) that it had unlimited right of access to company records. The spirit and letter of the Fourth Amendment counseled against the belief that Congress intended to authorize a "fishing expedition" into private papers on the possibility that they may disclose a crime. FTC v. American Tobacco Co., 264 U.S. 298. However, when federal agents used heavy-handed tactics to investigate a black market operation in gasoline, the Court sustained the warrantless search because the agents found gasoline ration coupons, which the Court regarded as public documents, not private property. Davis v. United States, 328 U.S. 582 (1946). Similarly, the Court held that the terms of a government contract allowed federal agents to audit a contractor's books at any time during business hours. By agreeing to permit inspection of office accounts and records in order to obtain the government's business, a contractor voluntarily waived privacy rights. Zap v. United States, 328 U.S. 624 (1946).

Beginning in 1950, the Supreme Court upheld the right of government inspectors to enter private homes to inspect for unsanitary conditions. District of Columbia v. Little, 339 U.S. 1 (1950). Home owners who refused to allow health inspectors to enter could be convicted. Ironically, this meant that someone suspected of criminal activity had a constitutional right to object to warrantless searches of his home, while no such right existed for those not suspected of crime but who merely objected to health inspectors entering. Frank v. Maryland, 359 U.S. 360, 378 (1959). See also Ohio ex rel. Eaton v. Price, 360 U.S. 246 (1959), and Eaton v. Price, 364 U.S. 263 (1960). A few years later the Court began placing some limits on administrative inspections, but adopted lowered standards to justify a warrant (see box).

Certain businesses (liquor, narcotics, firearms) are particularly susceptible to warrantless inspections. The Court acknowledges that Congress "has broad authority to fashion standards of reasonableness for searches and seizures" in the liquor industry. Colonnade Catering Corp. v. United States, 397 U.S. 72, 77 (1970). Congress also authorized warrantless searches of firearms stores during business hours, and the Court upheld this provision against the charge that it violated the Fourth Amendment. United States v. Biswell, 406 U.S. 311 (1972). Without a warrant, state health inspectors may enter a corporation's outdoor premises in the daylight, without its knowledge or consent, for the purpose of making tests of smoke emitted from chimneys. Air Pollution Variance Bd. v. Western Alfalfa, 416 U.S. 861 (1974).

This pattern of judicial support for congressional judgments on administrative inspections came to a sudden halt in 1978 when a 5–3 Court held that warrantless inspections of company work areas, in search of safety and health hazards, intruded on Fourth Amendment rights. The Court struck down these OSHA (Occupational Safety and Health Administration) inspections in part because they affected every industry involved in interstate commerce, in contrast to such specific industries as liquor and firearms. The Court held that OSHA inspectors require a warrant, though probable cause was not necessary. Marshall v. Barlow's, Inc., 436 U.S. 307 (1978). The three dissenters (Stevens, Blackmun, and Rehnquist) maintained that the Fourth Amendment had no application to "routine, regulatory inspections of commercial premises" and objected to the Court's substituting its judgment for Congress' on the inspection procedure needed to effectuate the purposes of the statute.

The rationale of the Court's decision in *Barlow's* was quickly tested by litigation on the Federal Mine Safety and Health Amendments Act of 1977. The statute required federal officials to inspect underground mines at least four times a year and surface mines at least twice a year to ensure compliance with safety and health standards. Inspectors had a right to enter without advance notice and did not need a warrant. A federal court, relying on *Barlow's,* held that the statute violated the rights of private companies, who could refuse entry to federal inspectors. Marshall v. Dewey, 493 F.Supp. 963 (E.D. Wis. 1980).

The district court's trust in Supreme Court precedents was misplaced. An 8–1 majority of the Supreme Court reversed, holding that Congress had properly determined that warrantless searches were needed to further the regulatory scheme for mine inspections. Congress had "broad authority" to regulate commercial enterprises engaged in interstate commerce. In language that appeared to undermine its holding in *Barlow's,* the Court maintained that its previous decisions on administrative inspections

> make clear that a warrant may not be constitutionally required when Congress has reasonably determined that warrantless searches are necessary to further a regulatory scheme and the federal regulatory presence is sufficiently comprehensive and defined that the owner of commercial property cannot help but be aware that his property will be subject to periodic inspections undertaken for specific purposes. Donovan v. Dewey, 452 U.S. 594, 600 (1981).

The scope of warrantless inspections of "closely regulated" industries was extended in 1987 to permit police officers to enter junkyards to discover stolen automobiles and parts. New York v. Burger, 482 U.S. 691 (1987).

Businesses open to the general public do not have the same expectations of privacy as people who live at home or work in offices. Detectives may enter a bookstore, purchase a magazine, and use that as evidence to arrest the owner for selling obscene materials. Examining the books and magazines offered for sale is not a "search" nor is the purchase a "seizure." The bookstore owner had no "reasonable expectation of privacy in areas of the store where the public was invited to enter and to transact business." Maryland v. Macon, 472 U.S. 463, 469 (1985).

Drug Tests

Mandatory drug tests for government employees have been reviewed by the courts for compliance with the Fourth Amendment. Two decisions in 1989 by the Supreme Court began the process of establishing some boundaries. In the first case, decided by a 7–2 majority, the Court upheld federal regulations that require blood and urine tests for railroad employees following major train accidents. Such tests are considered reasonable even though they are warrantless and there is no reasonable suspicion that any particular employee is impaired. Skinner v. Railway Labor Executives' Assn., 489 U.S. 602 (1989). In the second case, the Court divided 5–4 in upholding a Customs Service requirement of urine tests for all employees seeking transfer or promotion to positions having a direct involvement in drug interdiction or that involve the carrying of firearms. National Treasury Employees Union v. Von Raab, 489 U.S. 656 (1989). In 1989 the Court also upheld Conrail's policy of requiring its employees to undergo physical examinations periodically and upon return from leave. Urinalysis drug screening is part of the exam. Consol. Rail Corp. v. Railway Labor Executives, 491 U.S. 299 (1989).

In 1990 the Court refused to review challenges to two lower-court decisions that upheld random drug testing of two groups of federal workers. The first case involved the Army's compulsory drug-testing program for drug counselors. National Federation of Federal Employees v. Cheney, 493 U.S. 1056 (1990); National Federation of Federal Employees v. Cheney, 884 F.2d 603 (D.C. Cir. 1989). The second involved a program in the Justice Department to perform random drug testing of employees who hold top secret, national-security clearances. Bell v. Thornburgh, 493 U.S. 1056 (1990); Harmon v. Thornburgh, 878 F.2d 484 (D.C. Cir. 1989). In 1995, the Court upheld an Oregon school district's policy that required junior high boys and girls who wanted to participate in sports to provide urine samples as a method for determining drug use. Vernonia School Dist. v. Acton, 515 U.S. 646 (1995). This case is discussed more fully in Chapter 16, p. 966.

In 1997, the Court decided a case in which candidates for high office in Georgia challenged the constitutionality of a statute that required them to submit to and pass drug tests to qualify for state office. Divided 8 to 1, the Court held that the state law did not fit within the category of constitutionally permissible suspicionless searches. The exceptions allowed for drug testing for those involved in drug interdiction, the carrying of firearms, student athletics, customs employees, railway employees, and other areas did not apply here. Chandler v. Miller, 520 U.S. 305 (1997). A year later, the Court denied an appeal by two government economists who objected to a policy that required them to take random drug tests because they had access to the Old Executive Office Building, which is on White House grounds. Stigile v. Clinton, 110 F.3d 801 (D.C. Cir. 1997), cert. denied, 522 U.S. 1147 (1998).

Civil Forfeiture

Congress and the Supreme Court have begun to place some restrictions on the government's ability to seize property (with or without a warrant) as part of civil forfeiture procedures used in the war on drugs. Unlike criminal forfeiture, civil forfeiture does not require criminal conviction of the property owner. In fact, an owner's acquittal does not prevent the government from seizing houses, automobiles, boats, and other property. Under civil forfeiture proceedings, the government does not have to adhere to constitutionally required safeguards needed in criminal prosecutions. The standard for civil forfeiture is guilty until proven innocent. The burden of proof is on the property owner, not the government.

A 1993 ruling now requires a hearing before U.S. marshals can seize property. United States v. James Daniel Good Real Property, 510 U.S. 43 (1993). Other restrictions have been imposed by the Court: United States v. Parcel of Rumson, N.J., Land, 507 U.S. 111 (1993); Austin v. United States, 509 U.S. 602 (1993). However, in 1996 the Court (divided 5 to 4) held that a state may use forfeiture proceedings to seize a car used by a husband for sexual activities with a prostitute even though the car was jointly owned by the husband and his wife. The Court ruled that she was not entitled to innocent owner defense nor was the forfeiture of her interest in the car a taking of private property for public use in violation of the Taking Clause. Bennis v. Michigan, 516 U.S. 442 (1996). Also in 1996, the Court ruled that the government may prosecute someone for criminal violations and also seize their property without violating the constitutional provision regarding double jeopardy. Even though the civil forfeiture arises from the same offense leading to criminal prosecution, the Court (divided 8 to 1) found no constitutional objection. Civil forfeiture, it said, is not "punishment" for double jeopardy purposes. United States v. Ursery, 518 U.S. 267 (1996).

Divided 5–4 in 1998, the Court ruled that the federal government could not seize and keep the money of someone who tried to take funds out of the country simply because the person failed to fill out a Customs Service form properly. A Syrian immigrant tried to take $357,000 out of the country without declaring it on the form that requires someone to report the transportation of more than $10,000 outside the United States. The Court held that the forfeiture violated the Excessive Fines Clause. United States v. Bajakajian, 524 U.S. 321 (1998).

In 2000, Congress passed the Civil Asset Forfeiture Reform Act, which places restrictions on law enforcement officials. A coalition of civil libertarians, business executives, and conservatives argued that too many innocent citizens had their rights violated by the campaign against drugs and other crimes. Government prosecutors must now satisfy a burden of proof (preponderance of the evidence) before seizing property, and indigent defendants will receive free representation. The government must also reimburse property owners for their legal expenses if they successfully challenge the seizure of their assets. 114 Stat. 202 (2000).

Coolidge v. New Hampshire
403 U.S. 443 (1971)

This case involves what the Court called a "particularly brutal murder" of a fourteen-year-old girl. Edward Coolidge was charged with the murder. The case illustrates the need to have warrants issued by a "neutral and detached magistrate" and to have searches and seizures conducted pursuant to judicial process. Also discussed in this case is the plain-view doctrine and the scope of searches and seizures that are incident to an arrest. The Court divided 5–4 on most of the issues, but a precise count is impossible because several of the Justices never discussed or joined in sections of the majority opinion.

MR. JUSTICE STEWART delivered the opinion of the Court.*

. . .

Pamela Mason, a 14-year-old girl, left her home in Manchester, New Hampshire, on the evening of January 13, 1964, during a heavy snowstorm, apparently in response to a man's telephone call for a babysitter. Eight days later, after a thaw, her body was found by the side of a major north-south highway several miles away. She had been murdered. The event created great alarm in the area, and the police immediately began a massive investigation.

On January 28, having learned from a neighbor that the petitioner, Edward Coolidge, had been away from home on the evening of the girl's disappearance, the police went to his house to question him. They asked him, among other things, if he owned any guns, and he produced three, two shotguns and a rifle. They also asked

---

* Parts II-A, II-B, and II-C of this opinion are joined only by MR. JUSTICE DOUGLAS, MR. JUSTICE BRENNAN, and MR. JUSTICE MARSHALL.

whether he would take a lie-detector test concerning his account of his activities on the night of the disappearance. He agreed to do so on the following Sunday, his day off. The police later described his attitude on the occasion of this visit as fully "cooperative." His wife was in the house throughout the interview.

On the following Sunday, a policeman called Coolidge early in the morning and asked him to come down to the police station for the trip to Concord, New Hampshire, where the lie-detector test was to be administered. That evening, two plainclothes policemen arrived at the Coolidge house, where Mrs. Coolidge was waiting with her mother-in-law for her husband's return. These two policemen were not the two who had visited the house earlier in the week, and they apparently did not know that Coolidge had displayed three guns for inspection during the earlier visit. The plain-clothesmen told Mrs. Coolidge that her husband was in "serious trouble" and probably would not be home that night. They asked Coolidge's mother to leave, and proceeded to question Mrs. Coolidge. During the course of the interview they obtained from her four guns belonging to Coolidge, and some clothes that Mrs. Coolidge thought her husband might have been wearing on the evening of Pamela Mason's disappearance.

Coolidge was held in jail on an unrelated charge that night, but he was released the next day. During the ensuing two and a half weeks, the State accumulated a quantity of evidence to support the theory that it was he who had killed Pamela Mason. On February 19,...the Manchester police chief made formal application, under oath, for the arrest and search warrants. The complaint supporting the warrant for a search of Coolidge's Pontiac automobile, the only warrant that concerns us here, stated that the affiant "has probable cause to suspect and believe, and does suspect and believe, and herewith offers satisfactory evidence, that there are certain objects and things used in the commission of said offense, now kept, and concealed in or upon a certain vehicle, to wit: 1951 Pontiac two-door sedan...." The warrants were then signed and issued by the Attorney General himself, acting as a justice of the peace. Under New Hampshire law in force at that time, all justices of the peace were authorized to issue search warrants....

. . .

The police arrested Coolidge in his house on the day the warrant issued.... [A]bout two and a half hours after Coolidge had been taken into custody the cars were towed to the police station. It appears that at the time of the arrest the cars were parked in the Coolidge driveway, and that although dark had fallen they were plainly visible both from the street and from inside the house where Coolidge was actually arrested. The 1951 Pontiac was searched and vacuumed on February 21, two days after it was seized, again a year later, in January 1965, and a third time in April 1965.

At Coolidge's subsequent jury trial on the charge of murder, vacuum sweepings, including particles of gun powder, taken from the Pontiac were introduced in evidence against him, as part of an attempt by the State to show by microscopic analysis that it was highly probable that Pamela Mason had been in Coolidge's car. Also introduced in evidence was one of the guns taken by the police on their Sunday evening visit to the Coolidge house—a .22-caliber Mossberg rifle, which the prosecution claimed was the murder weapon. Conflicting ballistics testimony was offered on the question whether the bullets found in Pamela Mason's body had been fired from this rifle. Finally, the prosecution introduced vacuum sweepings of the clothes taken from the Coolidge house that same Sunday evening, and attempted to show through microscopic analysis that there was a high probability that the clothes had been in contact with Pamela Mason's body. Pretrial motions to suppress all this evidence were referred by the trial judge to the New Hampshire Supreme Court, which ruled the evidence admissible. 106 N.H. 186, 208 A.2d 322. The jury found Coolidge guilty and he was sentenced to life imprisonment. The New Hampshire Supreme Court affirmed the judgment of conviction, 109 N. H. 403, 260 A. 2d 547, and we granted certiorari to consider the constitutional questions raised by the admission of this evidence against Coolidge at his trial. 399 U.S. 926.

I

The petitioner's first claim is that the warrant authorizing the seizure and subsequent search of his 1951 Pontiac automobile was invalid because not issued by a "neutral and detached magistrate." Since we agree with the petitioner that the warrant was invalid for this reason, we need not consider his further argument that the allegations under oath supporting the issuance of the warrant were so conclusory as to violate relevant constitutional standards....

The classic statement of the policy underlying the warrant requirement of the Fourth Amendment is that of Mr. Justice Jackson, writing for the Court in *Johnson* v. *United States,* 333 U.S. 10, 13–14:

"The point of the Fourth Amendment, which often is not grasped by zealous officers, is not that it denies law enforcement the support of the usual inferences which reasonable men draw from evidence. Its protection consists in requiring that those inferences be drawn by a neutral and detached magistrate instead of being judged by the officer engaged in the often competitive enterprise of ferreting out crime. Any assumption that evidence sufficient to support a magistrate's disinterested determination to issue a search warrant will justify the officers in making a search without a warrant would reduce the Amendment to a nullity and leave the people's homes secure only in the discretion of police officers.... When the right of privacy must reasonably yield to the right of search is, as a rule, to be decided by a judicial officer, not by a policeman or government enforcement agent."

. . .

In this case, the determination of probable

cause was made by the chief "government enforcement agent" of the State — the Attorney General — who was actively in charge of the investigation and later was to be chief prosecutor at the trial.... the whole point of the basic rule so well expressed by Mr. Justice Jackson is that prosecutors and policemen simply cannot be asked to maintain the requisite neutrality with regard to their own investigations — the "competitive enterprise" that must rightly engage their single-minded attention....

II

The State proposes three distinct theories to bring the facts of this case within one or another of the exceptions to the warrant requirement....

A

The State's first theory is that the seizure on February 19 and subsequent search of Coolidge's Pontiac were "incident" to a valid arrest. We assume that the arrest of Coolidge inside his house was valid, so that the first condition of a warrantless "search incident" is met.... And since the events in issue took place in 1964, we assess the State's argument in terms of the law as it existed before *Chimel* v. *California*, 395 U.S. 752, which substantially restricted the "search incident" exception to the warrant requirement, but did so only prospectively. *Williams* v. *United States,* 401 U.S. 646. But even under pre-*Chimel* law, the State's position is untenable.

The leading case in the area before *Chimel* was *United States* v. *Rabinowitz,* 339 U.S. 56, which was taken to stand "for the proposition, *inter alia,* that a warrantless search 'incident to a lawful arrest' may generally extend to the area that is considered to be in the 'possession' or under the 'control' of the person arrested." *Chimel, supra,* at 760. In this case, Coolidge was arrested inside his house; his car was outside in the driveway. The car was not touched until Coolidge had been removed from the scene. It was then seized and taken to the station, but it was not actually searched until two days later.

First, it is doubtful whether the police could have carried out a contemporaneous search of the car under *Rabinowitz* standards. For this Court has repeatedly held that, even under *Rabinowitz,* "[a] search may be incident to an arrest ' "only if it is substantially contemporaneous with the arrest and is confined to the *immediate* vicinity of the arrest...." ' " These cases make it clear beyond any question that a lawful pre-*Chimel* arrest of a

suspect outside his house could never by itself justify a warrantless search inside the house. There is nothing in search-incident doctrine (as opposed to the special rules for automobiles and evidence in "plain view," to be considered below) that suggests a different result where the arrest is made inside the house and the search outside and at some distance away.

. . .

B

The second theory put forward by the State to justify a warrantless seizure and search of the Pontiac car is that under *Carroll* v. *United States,* 267 U.S. 132, the police may make a warrantless search of an automobile whenever they have probable cause to do so, and, under our decision last Term in *Chambers* v. *Maroney,* 399 U.S. 42, whenever the police may make a legal contemporaneous search under *Carroll,* they may also seize the car, take it to the police station, and search it there. But even granting that the police had probable cause to search the car, the application of the *Carroll* case to these facts would extend it far beyond its original rationale.

. . .

The word "automobile" is not a talisman in whose presence the Fourth Amendment fades away and disappears. And surely there is nothing in this case to invoke the meaning and purpose of the rule of *Carroll* v. *United States* — no alerted criminal bent on flight, no fleeting opportunity on an open highway after a hazardous chase, no contraband or stolen goods or weapons, no confederates waiting to move the evidence, not even the inconvenience of a special police detail to guard the immobilized automobile. In short, by no possible stretch of the legal imagination can this be made into a case where "it is not practicable to secure a warrant," *Carroll, supra,* at 153, and the "automobile exception," despite its label, is simply irrelevant.

. . .

C

The State's third theory in support of the warrantless seizure and search of the Pontiac car is that the car itself was an "instrumentality of the crime," and as such might be seized by the police on Coolidge's property because it was in plain view. Supposing the seizure to be thus lawful, the case of *Cooper* v. *California*, 386 U.S. 58, is said to support a subsequent warrantless search at the station house, with or without probable cause. Of course, the distinction between an "instrumentality of crime" and "mere evidence" was done away with by *Warden* v. *Hayden,* 387 U.S. 294, and we may assume that the police had probable cause to seize the automobile. But, for the reasons that follow, we hold that the "plain view" exception to the warrant requirement is inapplicable to this case.

. . .

What the "plain view" cases have in common is that the police officer in each of them had a prior justification for an intrusion in the course of which he came inadvertently across a piece of evidence incriminating the accused. The doctrine serves to supplement the prior justification— whether it be a warrant for another object, hot pursuit, search incident to lawful arrest, or some other legitimate reason for being present unconnected with a search directed against the accused—and permits the warrantless seizure. Of course, the extension of the original justification is legitimate only where it is immediately apparent to the police that they have evidence before them; the "plain view" doctrine may not be used to extend a general exploratory search from one object to another until something incriminating at last emerges.

. . .

In the light of what has been said, it is apparent that the "plain view" exception cannot justify the police seizure of the Pontiac car in this case. The police had ample opportunity to obtain a valid warrant; they knew the automobile's exact description and location well in advance; they intended to seize it when they came upon Coolidge's property. And this is not a case involving contraband or stolen goods or objects dangerous in themselves.

The seizure was therefore unconstitutional, and so was the subsequent search at the station house. Since evidence obtained in the course of the search was admitted at Coolidge's trial, the judgment must be reversed and the case remanded to the New Hampshire Supreme Court. *Mapp* v. *Ohio,* 367 U.S. 643.

. . .

MR. JUSTICE HARLAN, concurring.

. . .

MR. CHIEF JUSTICE BURGER, dissenting in part and concurring in part.

. . .

MR. JUSTICE BLACK, concurring and dissenting.

. . . Believing that the search and seizure here was reasonable and that the Fourth Amendment properly construed contains no such exclusionary rule, I dissent.

. . .

MR. JUSTICE BLACKMUN joins MR. JUSTICE BLACK in Parts II and III of this opinion and in that portion of Part I thereof which is to the effect that the Fourth Amendment supports no exclusionary rule.

MR. JUSTICE WHITE, with whom THE CHIEF JUSTICE joins, concurring and dissenting.

I would affirm the judgment. In my view, Coolidge's Pontiac was lawfully seized as evidence of the crime in plain sight and thereafter was lawfully searched under *Cooper* v. *California,* 386 U.S. 58 (1967)....

. . .

California v. Ciraolo

476 U.S. 207 (1986)

California police received an anonymous telephone tip that Dante Ciraolo was growing marijuana in his backyard, which was enclosed by two fences and shielded from view at ground level. Using a private airplane, the police flew over his house at an altitude of 1,000 feet and readily identified marijuana plants growing in the yard. After obtaining a search warrant, the marijuana plants were seized. The California trial court denied Ciraolo's mo-

tion to suppress the evidence of the search, but the California Court of Appeal reversed on the ground that the warrantless aerial observation violated the Fourth Amendment.

CHIEF JUSTICE BURGER delivered the opinion of the Court.

We granted certiorari to determine whether the Fourth Amendment is violated by aerial observation without a warrant from an altitude of 1,000 feet of a fenced-in backyard within the curtilage of a home.

I

On September 2, 1982, Santa Clara Police received an anonymous telephone tip that marijuana was growing in respondent's backyard. Police were unable to observe the contents of respondent's yard from ground level because of a 6-foot outer fence and a 10-foot inner fence completely enclosing the yard. Later that day, Officer Shutz, who was assigned to investigate, secured a private plane and flew over respondent's house at an altitude of 1,000 feet, within navigable airspace; he was accompanied by Officer Rodriguez. Both officers were trained in marijuana identification. From the overflight, the officers readily identified marijuana plants 8 feet to 10 feet in height growing in a 15- by 25-foot plot in respondent's yard; they photographed the area with a standard 35mm camera.

On September 8, 1982, Officer Shutz obtained a search warrant on the basis of an affidavit describing the anonymous tip and their observations; a photograph depicting respondent's house, the backyard, and neighboring homes was attached to the affidavit as an exhibit. The warrant was executed the next day and 73 plants were seized; it is not disputed that these were marijuana.

After the trial court denied respondent's motion to suppress the evidence of the search, respondent pleaded guilty to a charge of cultivation of marijuana. The California Court of Appeal reversed, however, on the ground that the warrantless aerial *observation* of respondent's yard which led to the issuance of the warrant violated the Fourth Amendment....

. . .

II

The touchstone of Fourth Amendment analysis is whether a person has a "constitutionally protected reasonable expectation of privacy." *Katz* v. *United States,* 389 U.S. 347, 360 (1967) (Harlan, J., concurring). *Katz* posits a two-part inquiry: first, has the individual manifested a subjective expectation of privacy in the object of the challenged search? Second, is society willing to recognize that expectation as reasonable? See *Smith* v. *Maryland,* 442 U.S. 735, 740 (1979).

Clearly—and understandably—respondent has met the test of manifesting his own subjective intent and desire to maintain privacy as to his unlawful agricultural pursuits. However, we need not address that issue, for the State has not challenged the finding of the California Court of Appeal that respondent had such an expectation. It can reasonably be assumed that the 10-foot fence was placed to conceal the marijuana crop from at least street-level views....

Yet a 10-foot fence might not shield these plants from the eyes of a citizen or a policeman perched on the top of a truck or a 2-level bus. Whether respondent therefore manifested a subjective expectation of privacy from *all* observations of his backyard, or whether instead he manifested merely a hope that no one would observe his unlawful gardening pursuits, is not entirely clear in these circumstances. Respondent appears to challenge the authority of government to observe his activity from any vantage point or place if the viewing is motivated by a law enforcement purpose, and not the result of a casual, accidental observation.

We turn, therefore, to the second inquiry under *Katz, i.e.,* whether that expectation is reasonable. In pursuing this inquiry, we must keep in mind that "[t]he test of legitimacy is not whether the individual chooses to conceal assertedly 'private' activity," but instead "whether the government's intrusion infringes upon the personal and societal values protected by the Fourth Amendment." *Oliver, supra,* at 181–183.

Respondent argues that because his yard was in the curtilage of his home, no governmental aerial observation is permissible under the Fourth Amendment without a warrant. The history and genesis of the curtilage doctrine is instructive. "At common law, the curtilage is the area to which extends the intimate activity associated with the 'sanctity of a man's home and the privacies of life.'" *Oliver, supra,* at 180 (quoting *Boyd* v. *United States,* 116 U.S. 616, 630 (1886)). See 4 Blackstone, Commentaries *225. The protection afforded the curtilage is essentially a protection of families and personal privacy in an area intimately linked to the home, both physically and psychologically, where privacy expectations are most heightened. The claimed area here was immediately adjacent to a suburban home, surrounded by high double fences. This close nexus to the home would appear to encompass this small area within the curtilage. Accepting, as the State does, that this yard and its crop fall within the curtilage, the question remains whether naked-eye observation of the curtilage by police from an aircraft lawfully operating at an altitude of 1,000 feet violates an expectation of privacy that is reasonable.

That the area is within the curtilage does not itself bar all police observation. The Fourth Amendment protection of the home has never been extended to require law enforcement officers to shield their eyes when passing by a home on public thoroughfares. Nor does the mere fact that an individual has taken measures to restrict some views of his activities preclude an officer's observations from a public vantage point where he has a right to be and which renders the activities clearly visible....

The observations by Officers Shutz and Rodriguez in this case took place within public navigable airspace, see 49 U.S.C. App. § 1304, in a physically nonintrusive manner; from this point they were able to observe plants readily discernible to the naked eye as marijuana. That the observation from aircraft was directed at identifying the plants and the officers were trained to recognize marijuana is irrelevant. Such observation is precisely what a judicial officer needs to provide a basis for a warrant. Any member of the public flying in this airspace who glanced down could have seen everything that these officers observed. On this record, we readily conclude that respondent's expectation that his garden was protected from such observation is unreasonable and is not an expectation that society is prepared to honor.

· · ·

Reversed.

JUSTICE POWELL with whom JUSTICE BRENNAN, JUSTICE MARSHALL, and JUSTICE BLACKMUN join, dissenting.

Concurring in *Katz* v. *United States,* 389 U.S.

347 (1967), Justice Harlan warned that any decision to construe the Fourth Amendment as proscribing only physical intrusions by police onto private property "is, in the present day, bad physics as well as bad law, for reasonable expectations of privacy may be defeated by electronic as well as physical invasion." *Id.,* at 362. Because the Court today ignores that warning in an opinion that departs significantly from the standard developed in *Katz* for deciding when a Fourth Amendment violation has occurred, I dissent.

· · ·

III

A

· · ·

The Court's holding... must rest solely on the fact that members of the public fly in planes and may look down at homes as they fly over them.... The Court does not explain why it finds this fact to be significant. One may assume that the Court believes that citizens bear the risk that air travelers will observe activities occurring within backyards that are open to the sun and air. This risk, the Court appears to hold, nullifies expectations of privacy in those yards even as to purposeful police surveillance from the air....

This line of reasoning is flawed. First, the actual risk to privacy from commercial or pleasure aircraft is virtually nonexistent. Travelers on commercial flights, as well as private planes used for business or personal reasons, normally obtain at most a fleeting, anonymous, and nondiscriminating glimpse of the landscape and buildings over which they pass. The risk that a passenger on such a plane might observe private activities, and might connect those activities with particular people, is simply too trivial to protect against. It is no accident that, as a matter of common experience, many people build fences around their residential areas, but few build roofs over their backyards....

· · ·

United States v. Ross

456 U.S. 798 (1982)

Police officers conducted a warrantless search of the interior of a car belonging to Albert Ross, even after the car had been taken to police headquarters and impounded. After a

federal district court denied Ross's motion to suppress the evidence found in the car, he was convicted for possessing heroin with intent to distribute it. The Court of Appeals reversed by holding that the officers had probable cause to stop and search the car, including its trunk, without a warrant, but they should not have opened a paper bag or leather pouch discovered in the trunk.

JUSTICE STEVENS delivered the opinion of the Court.

In *Carroll* v. *United States,* 267 U.S. 132, the Court held that a warrantless search of an automobile stopped by police officers who had probable cause to believe the vehicle contained contraband was not unreasonable within the meaning of the Fourth Amendment. The Court in *Carroll* did not explicitly address the scope of the search that is permissible. In this case, we consider the extent to which police officers — who have legitimately stopped an automobile and who have probable cause to believe that contraband is concealed somewhere within it — may conduct a probing search of compartments and containers within the vehicle whose contents are not in plain view. We hold that they may conduct a search of the vehicle that is as thorough as a magistrate could authorize in a warrant "particularly describing the place to be searched."

I

In the evening of November 27, 1978, an informant who had previously proved to be reliable telephoned Detective Marcum of the District of Columbia Police Department and told him that an individual known as "Bandit" was selling narcotics kept in the trunk of a car parked at 439 Ridge Street. The informant stated that he had just observed "Bandit" complete a sale and that "Bandit" had told him that additional narcotics were in the trunk. The informant gave Marcum a detailed description of "Bandit" and stated that the car was a "purplish maroon" Chevrolet Malibu with District of Columbia license plates.

Accompanied by Detective Cassidy and Sergeant Gonzales, Marcum immediately drove to the area and found a maroon Malibu parked in front of 439 Ridge Street. A license check disclosed that the car was registered to Albert Ross; a computer check on Ross revealed that he fit the informant's description and used the alias "Bandit." In two passes through the neighborhood the officers did not observe anyone matching the informant's description. To avoid alerting persons on the street, they left the area.

The officers returned five minutes later and observed the maroon Malibu turning off Ridge Street onto Fourth Street. They pulled alongside the Malibu, noticed that the driver matched the informant's description, and stopped the car. Marcum and Cassidy told the driver — later identified as Albert Ross, the respondent in this action — to get out of the vehicle. While they searched Ross, Sergeant Gonzales discovered a bullet on the car's front seat. He searched the interior of the car and found a pistol in the glove compartment. Ross then was arrested and handcuffed. Detective Cassidy took Ross' keys and opened the trunk, where he found a closed brown paper bag. He opened the bag and discovered a number of glassine bags containing a white powder. Cassidy replaced the bag, closed the trunk, and drove the car to headquarters.

At the police station Cassidy thoroughly searched the car. In addition to the "lunch-type" brown paper bag, Cassidy found in the trunk a zippered red leather pouch. He unzipped the pouch and discovered $3,200 in cash. The police laboratory later determined that the powder in the paper bag was heroin. No warrant was obtained.

Ross was charged with possession of heroin with intent to distribute, in violation of 21 U.S.C. § 841(a). Prior to trial, he moved to suppress the heroin found in the paper bag and the currency found in the leather pouch. After an evidentiary hearing, the District Court denied the motion to suppress. The heroin and currency were introduced in evidence at trial and Ross was convicted.

A three-judge panel of the Court of Appeals reversed the conviction. It held that the police had probable cause to stop and search Ross' car and that, under *Carroll* v. *United States, supra,* and *Chambers* v. *Maroney,* 399 U.S. 42, the officers lawfully could search the automobile — including its trunk — without a warrant. The court considered separately, however, the warrantless search of the two containers found in the trunk. On the basis of *Arkansas* v. *Sanders,* 442 U.S. 753, the court concluded that the constitutionality of a warrantless search of a container found in an automobile depends on whether the owner possesses a reasonable expectation of privacy in its contents. Applying that test, the court held that the warrantless search of the paper bag was valid but the search of the leather pouch was not. The court remanded for a new trial at which the items taken from the paper bag, but not those from the leather pouch, could be admitted.

The entire Court of Appeals then voted to rehear the case en banc. A majority of the court rejected the panel's conclusion that a distinction of constitutional significance existed between the two containers found in respondent's trunk; it held that the police should not have opened either container without first obtaining a warrant....

The en banc Court of Appeals considered, and rejected, the argument that it was reasonable for the police to open both the paper bag and the leather pouch because they were entitled to conduct a warrantless search of the entire vehicle in which the two containers were found....

. . .

IV

In *Carroll* itself, the whiskey that the prohibition agents seized was not in plain view. It was discovered only after an officer opened the rumble seat and tore open the upholstery of the lazyback. The Court did not find the scope of the search unreasonable. Having stopped Carroll and Kiro on a public road and subjected them to the indignity of a vehicle search — which the Court found to be a reasonable intrusion on their privacy because it was based on probable cause that their vehicle was transporting contraband — prohibition agents were entitled to tear open a portion of the roadster itself. The scope of the search was no greater than a magistrate could have authorized by issuing a warrant based on the probable cause that justified the search. Since such a warrant could have authorized the agents to open the rear portion of the roadster and to rip the upholstery in their search for concealed whiskey, the search was constitutionally permissible.

. . .

A lawful search of fixed premises generally extends to the entire area in which the object of the search may be found and is not limited by the possibility that separate acts of entry or opening may be required to complete the search. Thus, a warrant that authorizes an officer to search a home for illegal weapons also provides authority to open closets, chests, drawers, and containers in which the weapon might be found. A warrant to open a footlocker to search for marihuana would also authorize the opening of packages found in-

side. A warrant to search a vehicle would support a search of every part of the vehicle that might contain the object of the search. When a legitimate search is under way, and when its purpose and its limits have been precisely defined, nice distinctions between closets, drawers, and containers, in the case of a home, or between glove compartments, upholstered seats, trunks, and wrapped packages, in the case of a vehicle, must give way to the interest in the prompt and efficient completion of the task at hand.

This rule applies equally to all containers, as indeed we believe it must. One point on which the Court was in virtually unanimous agreement in *Robbins* was that a constitutional distinction between "worthy" and "unworthy" containers would be improper. Even though such a distinction perhaps could evolve in a series of cases in which paper bags, locked trunks, lunch buckets, and orange crates were placed on one side of the line or the other, the central purpose of the Fourth Amendment forecloses such a distinction. For just as the most frail cottage in the kingdom is absolutely entitled to the same guarantees of privacy as the most majestic mansion, so also may a traveler who carries a toothbrush and a few articles of clothing in a paper bag or knotted scarf claim an equal right to conceal his possessions from official inspection as the sophisticated executive with the locked attaché case.

...[A]n individual's expectation of privacy in a vehicle and its contents may not survive if probable cause is given to believe that the vehicle is transporting contraband. Certainly the privacy interests in a car's trunk or glove compartment may be no less than those in a movable container. An individual undoubtedly has a significant interest that the upholstery of his automobile will not be ripped or a hidden compartment within it opened. These interests must yield to the authority of a search, however, which — in light of *Carroll* — does not itself require the prior approval of a magistrate. The scope of a warrantless search based on probable cause is no narrower — and no broader — than the scope of a search authorized by a warrant supported by probable cause. Only the prior approval of the magistrate is waived; the search otherwise is as the magistrate could authorize.

The scope of a warrantless search of an automobile thus is not defined by the nature of the container in which the contraband is secreted. Rather, it is defined by the object of the search and the places in which there is probable cause to believe that it may be found....

V

...We hold that the scope of the warrantless search authorized by that exception is no broader and no narrower than a magistrate could legitimately authorize by warrant. If probable cause justifies the search of a lawfully stopped vehicle, it justifies the search of every part of the vehicle and its contents that may conceal the object of the search.

The judgment of the Court of Appeals is reversed. The case is remanded for further proceedings consistent with this opinion.

It is so ordered.

JUSTICE BLACKMUN, concurring.

. . .

JUSTICE POWELL, concurring.

. . .

JUSTICE WHITE, dissenting.

I would not overrule *Robbins* v. *California,* 453 U.S. 420 (1981). For the reasons stated by Justice Stewart in that case, I would affirm the judgment of the Court of Appeals. I also agree with much of JUSTICE MARSHALL's dissent in this case.

JUSTICE MARSHALL, with whom JUSTICE BRENNAN joins, dissenting.

The majority today not only repeals all realistic limits on warrantless automobile searches, it repeals the Fourth Amendment warrant requirement itself. By equating a police officer's estimation of probable cause with a magistrate's, the Court utterly disregards the value of a neutral and detached magistrate....

I

. . .

The only convincing explanation I discern for the majority's broad rule is expediency: it assists police in conducting automobile searches, ensuring that the private containers into which criminal suspects often place goods will no longer be a Fourth Amendment shield. See *ante,* at 820. "When a legitimate search is under way," the Court instructs us, "nice distinctions between... glove compartments, upholstered seats, trunks, and wrapped packages...must give way to the interest in the prompt and efficient completion of the task at hand." *Ante,* at 821. No "nice distinctions" are necessary, however, to comprehend the well-recognized differences between movable containers (which, even after today's decision, would be subject to the warrant requirement if located outside an automobile), and the automobile itself, together with its integral parts. Nor can I pass by the majority's glib assertion that the "prompt and efficient completion of the task at hand" is paramount to the Fourth Amendment interests of our citizens. I had thought it well established that "the mere fact that law enforcement may be made more efficient can never by itself justify disregard of the Fourth Amendment." *Mincey* v. *Arizona,* 437 U.S., at 393.

. . .

Terry v. Ohio

392 U.S. 1 (1968)

The Fourth Amendment standard of probable cause for searches and seizures was relaxed in this case to permit a "stop and frisk" of three individuals who had been behaving suspiciously. The pat down by the police officer produced concealed weapons used to convict John Terry and his companion. The Ohio Supreme Court dismissed their appeal. As a result of this case, the *Terry*-stop has become a legitimate technique available for law enforcement officers.

MR. CHIEF JUSTICE WARREN delivered the opinion of the Court.

This case presents serious questions concerning the role of the Fourth Amendment in the confrontation on the street between the citizen and the policeman investigating suspicious circumstances.

Petitioner Terry was convicted of carrying a concealed weapon and sentenced to the statutorily prescribed term of one to three years in the penitentiary. Following the denial of a pretrial motion to suppress, the prosecution introduced in evidence two revolvers and a number of bullets seized from Terry and a codefendant, Richard Chilton, by Cleveland Police Detective Martin

McFadden. At the hearing on the motion to suppress this evidence, Officer McFadden testified that while he was patrolling in plain clothes in downtown Cleveland at approximately 2:30 in the afternoon of October 31, 1963, his attention was attracted by two men, Chilton and Terry, standing on the corner of Huron Road and Euclid Avenue. He had never seen the two men before, and he was unable to say precisely what first drew his eye to them. However, he testified that he had been a policeman for 39 years and a detective for 35 and that he had been assigned to patrol this vicinity of downtown Cleveland for shoplifters and pickpockets for 30 years. He explained that he had developed routine habits of observation over the years and that he would "stand and watch people or walk and watch people at many intervals of the day." He added: "Now, in this case when I looked over they didn't look right to me at the time."

His interest aroused, Officer McFadden took up a post of observation in the entrance to a store 300 to 400 feet away from the two men. "I get more purpose to watch them when I seen their movements," he testified. He saw one of the men leave the other one and walk southwest on Huron Road, past some stores. The man paused for a moment and looked in a store window, then walked on a short distance, turned around and walked back toward the corner, pausing once again to look in the same store window. He rejoined his companion at the corner, and the two conferred briefly. Then the second man went through the same series of motions, strolling down Huron Road, looking in the same window, walking on a short distance, turning back, peering in the store window again, and returning to confer with the first man at the corner. The two men repeated this ritual alternately between five and six times apiece—in all, roughly a dozen trips. At one point, while the two were standing together on the corner, a third man approached them and engaged them briefly in conversation. This man then left the two others and walked west on Euclid Avenue. Chilton and Terry resumed their measured pacing, peering, and conferring. After this had gone on for 10 to 12 minutes, the two men walked off together, heading west on Euclid Avenue, following the path taken earlier by the third man.

By this time Officer McFadden had become thoroughly suspicious. He testified that after observing their elaborately casual and oft-repeated reconnaissance of the store window on Huron Road, he suspected the two men of "casing a job, a stick-up," and that he considered it his duty as a police officer to investigate further. He added that he feared "they may have a gun." Thus, Officer McFadden followed Chilton and Terry and saw them stop in front of Zucker's store to talk to the same man who had conferred with them earlier on the street corner. Deciding that the situation was ripe for direct action, Officer McFadden approached the three men, identified himself as a police officer and asked for their names. At this point his knowledge was confined to what he had observed. He was not acquainted with any of the three men by name or by sight, and he had received no information concerning them from any other source. When the men "mumbled something" in response to his inquiries, Officer McFadden grabbed petitioner Terry, spun him around so that they were facing the other two, with Terry between McFadden and the others, and patted down the outside of his clothing. In the left breast pocket of Terry's overcoat Officer McFadden felt a pistol. He reached inside the overcoat pocket, but was unable to remove the gun. At this point, keeping Terry between himself and the others, the officer ordered all three men to enter Zucker's store. As they went in, he removed Terry's overcoat completely, removed a .38-caliber revolver from the pocket and ordered all three men to face the wall with their hands raised. Officer McFadden proceeded to pat down the outer clothing of Chilton and the third man, Katz. He discovered another revolver in the outer pocket of Chilton's overcoat, but no weapons were found on Katz. The officer testified that he only patted the men down to see whether they had weapons, and that he did not put his hands beneath the outer garments of either Terry or Chilton until he felt their guns. So far as appears from the record, he never placed his hands beneath Katz' outer garments. Officer McFadden seized Chilton's gun, asked the proprietor of the store to call a police wagon, and took all three men to the station, where Chilton and Terry were formally charged with carrying concealed weapons.

. . .

I.

...No judicial opinion can comprehend the protean variety of the street encounter, and we can only judge the facts of the case before us. Nothing we say today is to be taken as indicating approval of police conduct outside the legitimate investigative sphere. Under our decision, courts still retain their traditional responsibility to guard against police conduct which is overbearing or harassing, or which trenches upon personal security without the objective evidentiary justification which the Constitution requires. When such conduct is identified, it must be condemned by the judiciary and its fruits must be excluded from evidence in criminal trials. And, of course, our approval of legitimate and restrained investigative conduct undertaken on the basis of ample factual justification should in no way discourage the employment of other remedies than the exclusionary rule to curtail abuses for which that sanction may prove inappropriate.

Having thus roughly sketched the perimeters of the constitutional debate over the limits on police investigative conduct in general and the background against which this case presents itself, we turn our attention to the quite narrow question posed by the facts before us: whether it is always unreasonable for a policeman to seize a person and subject him to a limited search for weapons unless there is probable cause for an arrest....

II.

Our first task is to establish at what point in this encounter the Fourth Amendment becomes relevant. That is, we must decide whether and when Officer McFadden "seized" Terry and whether and when he conducted a "search." There is some suggestion in the use of such terms as "stop" and "frisk" that such police conduct is outside the purview of the Fourth Amendment because neither action rises to the level of a "search" or "seizure" within the meaning of the Constitution. We emphatically reject this notion. It is quite plain that the Fourth Amendment governs "seizures" of the person which do not eventuate in a trip to the station house and prosecution for crime — "arrests" in traditional terminology. It must be recognized that whenever a police officer accosts an individual and restrains his freedom to walk away, he has "seized" that person. And it is nothing less than sheer torture of the English language to suggest that a careful exploration of the outer surfaces of a person's clothing all over his or her body in an attempt to find weapons is not a "search." Moreover, it is simply fantastic to urge that such a procedure performed in public by a policeman while the citizen stands helpless, perhaps facing a wall with his hands raised, is a "petty indignity." It is a serious intrusion upon the sanctity of the person, which may inflict great in-

dignity and arouse strong resentment, and it is not to be undertaken lightly.

. . .

In this case there can be no question, then, that Officer McFadden "seized" petitioner and subjected him to a "search" when he took hold of him and patted down the outer surfaces of his clothing. We must decide whether at that point it was reasonable for Officer McFadden to have interfered with petitioner's personal security as he did. And in determining whether the seizure and search were "unreasonable" our inquiry is a dual one — whether the officer's action was justified at its inception, and whether it was reasonably related in scope to the circumstances which justified the interference in the first place.

III.

If this case involved police conduct subject to the Warrant Clause of the Fourth Amendment, we would have to ascertain whether "probable cause" existed to justify the search and seizure which took place. However, that is not the case.... [W]e deal here with an entire rubric of police conduct — necessarily swift action predicated upon the on-the-spot observations of the officer on the beat — which historically has not been, and as a practical matter could not be, subjected to the warrant procedure....

. . .

Our evaluation of the proper balance that has to be struck in this type of case leads us to conclude that there must be a narrowly drawn authority to permit a reasonable search for weapons for the protection of the police officer, where he has reason to believe that he is dealing with an armed and dangerous individual, regardless of whether he has probable cause to arrest the individual for a crime. The officer need not be absolutely certain that the individual is armed; the issue is whether a reasonably prudent man in the circumstances would be warranted in the belief that his safety or that of others was in danger.... And in determining whether the officer acted reasonably in such circumstances, due weight must be given, not to his inchoate and unparticularized suspicion or "hunch," but to the specific reasonable inferences which he is entitled to draw from the facts in light of his experience....

IV.

We must now examine the conduct of Officer

McFadden in this case to determine whether his search and seizure of petitioner were reasonable, both at their inception and as conducted. He had observed Terry, together with Chilton and another man, acting in a manner he took to be preface to a "stick-up." We think on the facts and circumstances Officer McFadden detailed before the trial judge a reasonably prudent man would have been warranted in believing petitioner was armed and thus presented a threat to the officer's safety while he was investigating his suspicious behavior. The actions of Terry and Chilton were consistent with McFadden's hypothesis that these men were contemplating a daylight robbery—which, it is reasonable to assume, would be likely to involve the use of weapons—and nothing in their conduct from the time he first noticed them until the time he confronted them and identified himself as a police officer gave him sufficient reason to negate that hypothesis. Although the trio had departed the original scene, there was nothing to indicate abandonment of an intent to commit a robbery at some point. Thus, when Officer McFadden approached the three men gathered before the display window at Zucker's store he had observed enough to make it quite reasonable to fear that they were armed; and nothing in their response to his hailing them, identifying himself as a police officer, and asking their names served to dispel that reasonable belief. We cannot say his decision at that point to seize Terry and pat his clothing for weapons was the product of a volatile or inventive imagination, or was undertaken simply as an act of harassment; the record evidences the tempered act of a policeman who in the course of an investigation had to make a quick decision as to how to protect himself and others from possible danger, and took limited steps to do so.

. . .

V.

We conclude that the revolver seized from Terry was properly admitted in evidence against him. At the time he seized petitioner and searched him for weapons, Officer McFadden had reasonable grounds to believe that petitioner was armed and dangerous, and it was necessary for the protection of himself and others to take swift measures to discover the true facts and neutralize the threat of harm if it materialized. The policeman carefully restricted his search to what was appropriate to the discovery of the particular items which he sought. Each case of this sort will, of course, have to be decided on its own facts. We merely hold today that where a police officer observes unusual conduct which leads him reasonably to conclude in light of his experience that criminal activity may be afoot and that the persons with whom he is dealing may be armed and presently dangerous, where in the course of investigating this behavior he identifies himself as a policeman and makes reasonable inquiries, and where nothing in the initial stages of the encounter serves to dispel his reasonable fear for his own or others' safety, he is entitled for the protection of himself and others in the area to conduct a carefully limited search of the outer clothing of such persons in an attempt to discover weapons which might be used to assault him. Such a search is a reasonable search under the Fourth Amendment, and any weapons seized may properly be introduced in evidence against the person from whom they were taken.

Affirmed.

MR. JUSTICE BLACK concurs in the judgment and the opinion except where the opinion quotes from and relies upon this Court's opinion in *Katz v. United States* and the concurring opinion in *Warden v. Hayden.*

MR. JUSTICE HARLAN, concurring.

. . .

MR. JUSTICE WHITE, concurring.

. . .

MR. JUSTICE DOUGLAS, dissenting.

. . .

To give the police greater power than a magistrate is to take a long step down the totalitarian path. Perhaps such a step is desirable to cope with modern forms of lawlessness. But if it is taken, it should be the deliberate choice of the people through a constitutional amendment. . . .

Chimel v. California

395 U.S. 752 (1969)

In this decision, the Supreme Court attempted to limit the scope of a search that is made incident to an arrest. Police officers, armed with an arrest warrant but not a search warrant, were admitted to Ted Steven Chimel's home by his wife. They served him with the arrest warrant when he arrived and proceeded to search the entire house, finding evidence that led to his conviction for burglary. The conviction was upheld by the state courts.

MR. JUSTICE STEWART delivered the opinion of the Court.

This case raises basic questions concerning the permissible scope under the Fourth Amendment of a search incident to a lawful arrest.

The relevant facts are essentially undisputed. Late in the afternoon of September 13, 1965, three police officers arrived at the Santa Ana, California, home of the petitioner with a warrant authorizing his arrest for the burglary of a coin shop. The officers knocked on the door, identified themselves to the petitioner's wife, and asked if they might come inside. She ushered them into the house, where they waited 10 or 15 minutes until the petitioner returned home from work. When the petitioner entered the house, one of the officers handed him the arrest warrant and asked for permission to "look around." The petitioner objected, but was advised that "on the basis of the lawful arrest," the officers would nonetheless conduct a search. No search warrant had been issued.

Accompanied by the petitioner's wife, the officers then looked through the entire three-bedroom house, including the attic, the garage, and a small workshop. In some rooms the search was relatively cursory. In the master bedroom and sewing room, however, the officers directed the petitioner's wife to open drawers and "to physically move contents of the drawers from side to side so that [they] might view any items that would have come from [the] burglary." After completing the search, they seized numerous items—primarily coins, but also several medals, tokens, and a few other objects. The entire search took between 45 minutes and an hour.

At the petitioner's subsequent state trial on two charges of burglary, the items taken from his house were admitted into evidence against him, over his objection that they had been unconstitutionally seized. He was convicted, and the judgments of conviction were affirmed by both the California Court of Appeal, 61 Cal. Rptr. 714, and the California Supreme Court, 68 Cal. 2d 436, 439 P. 2d 333. Both courts accepted the petitioner's contention that the arrest warrant was invalid because the supporting affidavit was set out in conclusory terms, but held that since the arresting officers had procured the warrant "in good faith," and since in any event they had had sufficient information to constitute probable cause for the petitioner's arrest, that arrest had been lawful. From this conclusion the appellate courts went on to hold that the search of the petitioner's home had been justified, despite the absence of a search warrant, on the ground that it had been incident to a valid arrest. We granted certiorari in order to consider the petitioner's substantial constitutional claims. 393 U.S. 958.

Without deciding the question, we proceed on the hypothesis that the California courts were correct in holding that the arrest of the petitioner was valid under the Constitution. This brings us directly to the question whether the warrantless search of the petitioner's entire house can be constitutionally justified as incident to that arrest. The decisions of this Court bearing upon that question have been far from consistent, as even the most cursory review makes evident.

. . .

In 1950...came *United States* v. *Rabinowitz,* 339 U. S. 56, the decision upon which California primarily relies in the case now before us. In *Rabinowitz,* federal authorities had been informed that the defendant was dealing in stamps bearing forged overprints. On the basis of that information they secured a warrant for his arrest, which they executed at his one-room business office. At the time of the arrest, the officers "searched the desk, safe, and file cabinets in the office for about an hour and a half," *id.,* at 59, and seized 573 stamps with forged overprints. The stamps were admitted into evidence at the defendant's trial, and this Court affirmed his conviction, rejecting the contention that the warrantless search had been unlawful. The Court held that the search in its entirety fell within the principle giving law enforcement authorities "[t]he right 'to search the place where the arrest is made in order to find and seize things connected with the crime....' " *Id.,* at 61....

Rabinowitz has come to stand for the proposition, *inter alia,* that a warrantless search "incident to a lawful arrest" may generally extend to the area that is considered to be in the "possession" or under the "control" of the person arrested. And it was on the basis of that proposition that the California courts upheld the search of the petitioner's entire house in this case. That doctrine, however, at least in the broad sense in which it was applied by the California courts in this case, can withstand neither historical nor rational analysis.

Even limited to its own facts, the *Rabinowitz* decision was, as we have seen, hardly founded on an unimpeachable line of authority. As Mr. Justice Frankfurter commented in dissent in that case, the "hint" contained in *Weeks* was, without persuasive justification, "loosely turned into dictum and finally elevated to a decision." 339 U.S., at 75. And the approach taken in cases such as *Go-Bart, Lefkowitz,* and *Trupiano* was essentially disregarded by the *Rabinowitz* Court.

Nor is the rationale by which the State seeks here to sustain the search of the petitioner's house supported by a reasoned view of the background and purpose of the Fourth Amendment. Mr. Justice Frankfurter wisely pointed out in his *Rabinowitz* dissent that the Amendment's proscription of "unreasonable searches and seizures" must be read in light of "the history that gave rise to the words" — a history of "abuses so deeply felt by the Colonies as to be one of the potent causes of the Revolution...." 339 U. S., at 69. The Amendment was in large part a reaction to the general warrants and warrantless searches that had so alienated the colonists and had helped speed the movement for independence. In the scheme of the Amendment, therefore, the requirement that "no Warrants shall issue, but upon probable cause," plays a crucial part. As the Court put it in *McDonald* v. *United States,* 335 U. S. 451:

"We are not dealing with formalities. The presence of a search warrant serves a high function. Absent some grave emergency, the Fourth Amendment has interposed a magistrate between the citizen and the police. This was done not to shield criminals nor to make the home a safe haven for illegal activities. It was done so that an objective mind might weigh the need to invade that privacy in order to enforce the law. The right of privacy was deemed too precious to entrust to the discretion of those whose job is the detection of crime and the arrest of criminals.... And so the Constitution requires a magistrate to pass on the desires of the police before they violate the privacy of the home. We cannot be true to that constitutional requirement and excuse the absence of a search warrant without a showing by those who seek exemption from the constitutional mandate that the exigencies of the situation made that course imperative." *Id.,* at 455–456.

. . .

Only last Term in *Terry* v. *Ohio,* 392 U. S. 1, we emphasized that "the police must, whenever practicable, obtain advance judicial approval of searches and seizures through the warrant procedure,"... and that "[t]he scope of [a] search must be 'strictly tied to and justified by' the circumstances which rendered its initiation permissible."... The search undertaken by the officer in that "stop and frisk" case was sustained under that test, because it was no more than a "protective ... search for weapons."...

A similar analysis underlies the "search incident to arrest" principle, and marks its proper extent. When an arrest is made, it is reasonable for the arresting officer to search the person arrested in order to remove any weapons that the latter might seek to use in order to resist arrest or effect his escape. Otherwise, the officer's safety might well be endangered, and the arrest itself frustrated. In addition, it is entirely reasonable for the arresting officer to search for and seize any evidence on the arrestee's person in order to prevent its concealment or destruction. And the area into which an arrestee might reach in order to grab a weapon or evidentiary items must, of course, be governed by a like rule. A gun on a table or in a drawer in front of one who is arrested can be as dangerous to the arresting officer as one concealed in the clothing of the person arrested. There is ample justification, therefore, for a search of the arrestee's person and the area "within his immediate control" — construing that phrase to mean the area from within which he might gain possession of a weapon or destructible evidence.

There is no comparable justification, however, for routinely searching any room other than that in which an arrest occurs — or, for that matter, for searching through all the desk drawers or other closed or concealed areas in that room itself. Such searches, in the absence of well-recognized exceptions, may be made only under the authority of a search warrant. The "adherence to judicial processes" mandated by the Fourth Amendment requires no less.

. . .

Application of sound Fourth Amendment principles to the facts of this case produces a clear result. The search here went far beyond the petitioner's person and the area from within which he might have obtained either a weapon or something that could have been used as evidence against him. There was no constitutional justification, in the absence of a search warrant, for extending the search beyond that area. The scope of the search was, therefore, "unreasonable" under the Fourth and Fourteenth Amendments, and the petitioner's conviction cannot stand.

Reversed.

MR. JUSTICE HARLAN, concurring.

. . .

MR. JUSTICE WHITE, with whom MR. JUSTICE BLACK joins, dissenting.

Few areas of the law have been as subject to shifting constitutional standards over the last 50 years as that of the search "incident to an arrest." There has been a remarkable instability in this whole area, which has seen at least four major shifts in emphasis. Today's opinion makes an untimely fifth. In my view, the Court should not now abandon the old rule.

. . .

D. ELECTRONIC EAVESDROPPING

The framers were well aware that eavesdropping could intrude upon personal privacy. The use of *electronic* eavesdropping, however, forced Congress and the Supreme Court to interpret eighteenth-century language in the Fourth Amendment in light of the latest technological advances. The use of wiretapping by law enforcement officials requires the active involvement of all three branches.

The Court first confronted electronic eavesdropping when it considered the use of wiretaps by prohibition agents in the 1920s to monitor and intercept telephone calls. Small wires were inserted in telephone wires leading from residences. Taps could be made in the streets near the houses or in the basement of large office buildings. In a bitterly divided 5–4 decision, the Court reasoned that there was no violation of the Fourth Amendment because the taps did not *enter* the premises. Hence, there was neither "search" nor "seizure." This wooden assessment provoked a scathing dissent from Justice Brandeis, who accurately predicted that technology would overwhelm the Fourth Amendment unless the Court met the challenge with open eyes. OLMSTEAD v. UNITED STATES, 277 U.S. 438 (1928).

Chief Justice Taft, writing for the majority, invited Congress to establish boundaries for wiretapping: "Congress may of course protect the secrecy of telephone messages by making them, when intercepted, inadmissible in evidence in federal criminal trials, by direct legislation, and thus depart from the common law of evidence." Id. at 465–66. Section 605 of the Federal Communications Act of 1934 was intended to fill that gap by making it a crime to intercept or to use any wire or radio communication. Because of that statute, the government could not introduce as trial evidence any information obtained from a wiretap.[13] This restriction, however, did not prevent the government from using wiretaps to "induce" people whose conversations had been overheard to turn state's evidence and appear as witnesses for the government. Goldstein v. United States, 316 U.S. 114 (1942).

Executive Practices

In the 1930s the executive branch followed a divided policy on wiretapping. The Bureau of Investigation (later the Federal Bureau of Investigation) regarded wiretapping as unethical and

---

13. Nardone v. United States, 302 U.S. 379 (1937); Weiss v. United States, 308 U.S. 321 (1939); Nardone v. United States, 308 U.S. 338 (1939).

Roosevelt's Confidential Memo on Wiretapping

[To Attorney General Robert H. Jackson, May 21, 1940]

I am convinced that the Supreme Court never intended any dictum in the particular case which it decided to apply to grave matters involving the defense of the Nation.

It is, of course, well known that certain other nations have been engaged in the organization of propaganda of so-called "fifth columns" in other countries and in preparation for sabotage, as well as in actual sabotage.

You are, therefore, authorized and directed in such cases as you may approve, after investigation of the need in each case, to authorize the necessary investigating agents that they are at liberty to secure information by listening devices direct to the conversation or other communications of persons suspected of subversive activities against the Government of the United States, including suspected spies. You are requested furthermore to limit these investigations so conducted to a minimum and to limit them in so far as possible to aliens.

SOURCE: Francis Biddle, In Brief Authority 167 (1962).

impermissible under the regulations of the Attorney General. The Bureau of Prohibition, located within the Department of the Treasury, freely admitted to using wiretapping. Congress considered, but never passed, statutory prohibitions on wiretapping by the Bureau of Prohibition. The Bureau was abolished after the states ratified the Twenty-First Amendment in 1933, repealing the constitutional prohibition on liquor.

In the early 1940s, committee reports from the House of Representatives recommended that certain federal agencies be authorized to wiretap for purposes of national security, including investigations into sabotage, treason, seditious conspiracy, espionage, and violations of the neutrality law. The House passed such a bill in 1940, but the Senate took no action. After the attack on Pearl Harbor on December 7, 1941, the House passed legislation to authorize wiretapping for national security purposes. Again, the Senate refused to take up the bill.

Denied statutory authority for wiretapping, the executive branch took matters into its own hands. On March 18, 1940, Attorney General Robert H. Jackson issued the following order to the Bureau of Investigation: "Wire tapping: Telephone or telegraph wires shall not be tapped unless prior authorization of the Director of the Bureau has been secured." 86 Cong. Rec. A1471 (1940). On May 21, 1940, President Franklin D. Roosevelt sent a confidential memorandum to Jackson that permitted wiretapping in selected areas (see box).

Technological Advances

Until *Olmstead* was overturned in 1967, the Court wrestled with new forms of technological intrusion. Federal agents used a "detectaphone" to overhear telephone conversations. This instrument, when placed against the wall of a room, could pick up sound waves on the other side of the wall. A receiver amplified the sound waves and allowed agents to listen to phone conversations. The Court held that there was neither a "communication" nor an "interception" within the meaning of Section 605. Relying on *Olmstead,* the Court found no violation of the Fourth Amendment. Goldman v. United States, 316 U.S. 129 (1942). Undercover agents, equipped with a radio transmitter, were allowed to stand in a laundry and engage a suspect in conversation. His self-incriminating statements were picked up by a radio receiver and used to convict him. The Court ruled that there was neither "search" nor "seizure" because the government did not trespass when it entered the suspect's store. On Lee v. United States, 343 U.S. 747 (1952).

The ingenuity of investigators and police easily outpaced the Court's interpretation of the

Fourth Amendment. Using a key made by a locksmith, state police entered the home of a suspect and installed a concealed microphone in the hall. A hole was bored in the roof to allow wires to transmit sounds to a neighboring garage. The police returned later and moved the microphone to a bedroom and came back a third time to move it to a closet. Although a trespass and probably a burglary had been committed, the Court found no violation of Section 605 and upheld the action. Irvine v. California, 347 U.S. 128 (1954). The Court blithely noted: "All that was heard through the microphone was what an eavesdropper, hidden in the hall, the bedroom, or the closet, might have heard." Id. at 131.

Other variations of electronic eavesdropping blossomed. Police officers used an extension phone in an adjoining room to listen to a conversation. They had the consent of the subscriber (who was a party to the conversation) but not the consent of the sender, which Section 605 required. Nevertheless, the Court held that the contents of the communication were admissible in a federal criminal trial because there was no "interception" within the meaning of Section 605. The Court remarked that every party to a telephone conversation takes the risk that the other party may have an extension phone, allowing others to overhear the conversation. Rathbun v. United States, 355 U.S. 107, 111 (1957). The use of a four-party line, with one line connected to a phone that permits the police to hear and record all conversations without lifting the receiver, violated Section 605 because it intercepted and divulged a communication. Lee v. Florida, 392 U.S. 378 (1968). The police deliberately arranged to have the four-party line connected to a suspect's house, whereas in *Rathbun* the extension phone had not been installed just for the police.

In another case, government agents pushed an electronic listening device through the wall of an adjoining house until it touched the heating duct of a suspect's house. Through the use of this "spike mike," officers with earphones listened to conversations taking place on both floors of the house. The Court held that this physical penetration into the suspect's house violated the Fourth Amendment. Silverman v. United States, 365 U.S. 505 (1961). Three years later, the Court reversed a state court decision that had upheld the use of evidence obtained by a small microphone that had been stuck in a wall, penetrating to the depth of a thumb tack. Clinton v. Virginia, 377 U.S. 158; 130 S.E.2d 437.

On some occasions federal judges were asked to authorize an electronic device to record conversations. For example, a lawyer was suspected of wanting to bribe a prospective member of a federal jury. He had hired a Nashville policeman to investigate backgrounds of potential jurors, unaware that the policeman had also agreed to report to federal agents any illegal activities he observed. The district court authorized the placement of a tape recorder on the policeman to record future conversations about bribe efforts. The Court upheld the admissibility of these conversations, which led to the lawyer's conviction. Osborn v. United States, 385 U.S. 323 (1966).

Judicial Restrictions

Two decisions in 1967 placed major constraints on electronic eavesdropping. A New York law was struck down because it permitted the installation of recording devices without requiring the police to specify that a particular crime had been or was being committed. Also, the police failed to particularly describe the conversations sought. The broad sweep of the statute violated the Fourth Amendment. Berger v. New York, 388 U.S. 41. Also in 1967, the Court finally overturned the "trespass" doctrine of *Olmstead* and *Goldman*. By a 7–1 vote, the Court declared unconstitutional the placing of electronic listening and recording devices on the outside of public telephone booths to obtain incriminating evidence. Although there was no physical entrance into the area occupied by the suspect, he had a legitimate expectation of privacy within the phone booth. In a broadly principled decision capable of accommodating technological ingenuity, the Court held that the Fourth Amendment "protects people, not places." KATZ v. UNITED STATES, 389 U.S. 347, 351.

In response to *Katz,* Congress passed legislation in 1968 requiring law enforcement officers to obtain a warrant before placing taps on phones or installing bugs (concealed microphones). If an "emergency" exists, communications can be intercepted for up to forty-eight hours without a warrant in cases involving organized crime or national security. Warrants are limited to specific periods of time. After a wire intercept is terminated, the person monitored is informed of the fact and date of the entry. 82 Stat. 212; 18 U.S.C. §§ 2510–20.

Judicial activity after 1968 concentrated more on statutory construction than on constitutional interpretation. A number of cases examined the government's compliance with the wiretap statute.[14] The Court decided that the Fourth Amendment and congressional legislation protect the *content* of communications, not the numbers dialed from a phone. Smith v. Maryland, 442 U.S. 735 (1979). Although the wiretap law does not explicitly authorize covert entry to install bugging equipment, the Court has held that the language and purpose of the statute implicitly authorize such action without violating the Fourth Amendment. Dalia v. United States, 441 U.S. 238 (1979). (For judicial and congressional action on electronic surveillance for "national security" purposes, see pages 286–87.)

Court doctrines and congressional statutes are periodically tested and outstripped by new technology. "Beepers" (battery-operated radio transmitters) allow law enforcement officers to follow cars and locate illegal operations. United States v. Knotts, 460 U.S. 276 (1983). The use of a beeper to monitor the movement of articles within a private residence, however, is not permitted under the Fourth Amendment. United States v. Karo, 468 U.S. 705 (1984). Other developments include electronic mail, cellular and cordless phones, night vision cameras, parabolic microphones to pick up conversations in homes or offices, satellite communication systems, and closed-circuit video cameras.

These innovations made it necessary for Congress to rethink and rewrite the law on electronic eavesdropping. Federal judges appealed to Congress to pass legislation that would clarify Fourth Amendment law. United States v. Torres, 751 F.2d 875, 885–86 (7th Cir. 1984). Congress passed legislation in 1986 to modernize the restrictions on electronic eavesdropping. During the debate in the House of Representatives, the floor manager, Congressman Robert Kastenmeier, noted: "We may provide the forum to balance the privacy rights of citizens with the legitimate law enforcement needs of the Government; or we abdicate that role to ad hoc decisions made by the courts and the executive branch." 132 Cong. Rec. 14886 (1986). Congress passed additional legislation in 1994 to help police wiretappers keep pace with advancing technology. 108 Stat. 4279 (1994).

Olmstead v. United States

277 U.S. 438 (1928)

Roy Olmstead and several accomplices were convicted of violating the National Prohibition Act by importing and selling liquor. On the basis of evidence obtained by wiretapping telephone conversations, indictments were handed down against more than seventy individuals involved in an extensive operation that reached across the Canadian border. The Ninth Circuit upheld the convictions.

---

14. E.g., United States v. Ojeda Rios, 495 U.S. 257 (1990); Scott v. United States, 436 U.S. 128 (1978); United States v. New York Telephone Co., 434 U.S. 159 (1977); United States v. Donovan, 429 U.S. 413 (1977); United States v. Chavez, 416 U.S. 562 (1974); United States v. Giordano, 416 U.S. 505 (1974); United States v. Kahn, 415 U.S. 143 (1974).

MR. CHIEF JUSTICE TAFT delivered the opinion of the Court.

· · ·

The information which led to the discovery of the conspiracy and its nature and extent was largely obtained by intercepting messages on the telephones of the conspirators by four federal prohibition officers. Small wires were inserted along the ordinary telephone wires from the residences of four of the petitioners and those leading from the chief office. The insertions were made without trespass upon any property of the defendants. They were made in the basement of the large office building. The taps from house lines were made in the streets near the houses.

The gathering of evidence continued for many months. Conversations of the conspirators of which refreshing stenographic notes were currently made, were testified to by the government witnesses. They revealed the large business transactions of the partners and their subordinates. Men at the wires heard the orders given for liquor by customers and the acceptances; they became auditors of the conversations between the partners. All this disclosed the conspiracy charged in the indictment. Many of the intercepted conversations were not merely reports but parts of the criminal acts. The evidence also disclosed the difficulties to which the conspirators were subjected, the reported news of the capture of vessels, the arrest of their men and the seizure of cases of liquor in garages and other places. It showed the dealing by Olmstead, the chief conspirator, with members of the Seattle police, the messages to them which secured the release of arrested members of the conspiracy, and also direct promises to officers of payments as soon as opportunity offered.

· · ·

The [*Fourth*] Amendment itself shows that the search is to be of material things—the person, the house, his papers or his effects. The description of the warrant necessary to make the proceeding lawful, is that it must specify the place to be searched and the person or *things* to be seized.

It is urged that the language of Mr. Justice Field in *Ex parte Jackson,* already quoted, offers an analogy to the interpretation of the Fourth Amendment in respect of wire tapping. But the analogy fails. The Fourth Amendment may have proper application to a sealed letter in the mail because of the constitutional provision for the Postoffice Department and the relations between the Government and those who pay to secure protection of their sealed letters. See Revised Statutes, §§ 3978 to 3988, whereby Congress monopolizes the carriage of letters and excludes from that business everyone else, and § 3929 which forbids any postmaster or other person to open any letter not addressed to himself. It is plainly within the words of the Amendment to say that the unlawful rifling by a government agent of a sealed letter is a search and seizure of the sender's papers or effects. The letter is a paper, an effect, and in the custody of a Government that forbids carriage except under its protection.

The United States takes no such care of telegraph or telephone messages as of mailed sealed letters. The Amendment does not forbid what was done here. There was no searching. There was no seizure. The evidence was secured by the use of the sense of hearing and that only. There was no entry of the houses or offices of the defendants.

By the invention of the telephone, fifty years ago, and its application for the purpose of extending communications, one can talk with another at a far distant place. The language of the Amendment can not be extended and expanded to include telephone wires reaching to the whole world from the defendant's house or office. The intervening wires are not part of his house or office any more than are the highways along which they are stretched.

This Court in *Carroll* v. *United States,* 267 U.S. 132, 149, declared:

"The Fourth Amendment is to be construed in the light of what was deemed an unreasonable search and seizure when it was adopted and in a manner which will conserve public interests as well as the interests and rights of individual citizens."

Justice Bradley in the *Boyd* case, and Justice Clark in the *Gouled* case, said that the Fifth Amendment and the Fourth Amendment were to be liberally construed to effect the purpose of the framers of the Constitution in the interest of liberty. But that can not justify enlargement of the language employed beyond the possible practical meaning of houses, persons, papers, and effects, or so to apply the words search and seizure as to forbid hearing or sight.

Hester v. *United States,* 265 U.S. 57, held that the testimony of two officers of the law who trespassed on the defendant's land, concealed themselves one hundred yards away from his house and saw him come out and hand a bottle of whiskey to another, was not inadmissible. While there was a trespass, there was no search of person, house, papers or effects....

Congress may of course protect the secrecy of telephone messages by making them, when intercepted, inadmissible in evidence in federal criminal trials, by direct legislation, and thus depart from the common law of evidence. But the courts may not adopt such a policy by attributing an enlarged and unusual meaning to the Fourth Amendment. The reasonable view is that one who installs in his house a telephone instrument with connecting wires intends to project his voice to those quite outside, and that the wires beyond his house and messages while passing over them are not within the protection of the Fourth Amendment. Here those who intercepted the projected voices were not in the house of either party to the conversation.

. . .

A standard which would forbid the reception of evidence if obtained by other than nice ethical conduct by government officials would make society suffer and give criminals greater immunity than has been known heretofore. In the absence of controlling legislation by Congress, those who realize the difficulties in bringing offenders to justice may well deem it wise that the exclusion of evidence should be confined to cases where rights under the Constitution would be violated by admitting it.

The statute of Washington, adopted in 1909, provides (Remington Compiled Statutes, 1922, § 2656-18) that:

"Every person...who shall intercept, read or in any manner interrupt or delay the sending of a message over any telegraph or telephone line... shall be guilty of a misdemeanor."

This statute does not declare that evidence obtained by such interception shall be inadmissible, and by the common law, already referred to, it would not be. *People* v. *McDonald,* 177 App. Div. (N.Y.) 806. Whether the State of Washington may prosecute and punish federal officers violating this law and those whose messages were intercepted may sue them civilly is not before us. But clearly a statute, passed twenty years after the admission of the State into the Union can not affect the rules of evidence applicable in courts of the United States in criminal cases. Chief Justice Taney, in *United States* v. *Reid,* 12 How. 361, 363, construing the 34th section of the Judiciary Act, said:

"But it could not be supposed, without very plain words to show it, that Congress intended to give the states the power of prescribing the rules of evidence in trials for offenses against the United States. For this construction would place the criminal jurisprudence of one sovereignty under the control of another." See also *Withaup* v. *United States,* 127 Fed. 530, 534.

The judgments of the Circuit Court of Appeals are affirmed. The mandates will go down forthwith under Rule 31.

Affirmed.

MR. JUSTICE HOLMES:

...But I think, as MR. JUSTICE BRANDEIS says, that apart from the Constitution the Government ought not to use evidence obtained and only obtainable by a criminal act. There is no body of precedents by which we are bound, and which confines us to logical deduction from established rules. Therefore we must consider the two objects of desire, both of which we cannot have, and make up our minds which to choose. It is desirable that criminals should be detected, and to that end that all available evidence should be used. It also is desirable that the Government should not itself foster and pay for other crimes, when they are the means by which the evidence is to be obtained. If it pays its officers for having got evidence by crime I do not see why it may not as well pay them for getting it in the same way, and I can attach no importance to protestations of disapproval if it knowingly accepts and pays and announces that in future it will pay for the fruits. We have to choose, and for my part I think it a less evil that some criminals should escape than that the Government should play an ignoble part.

. . .

MR. JUSTICE BRANDEIS, dissenting.

. . .

When the Fourth and Fifth Amendments were adopted, "the form that evil had theretofore taken," had been necessarily simple. Force and violence were then the only means known to man by which a Government could directly effect self-incrimination. It could compel the individual to testify—a compulsion effected, if need be, by torture. It could secure possession of his papers and other articles incident to his private life—a seizure effected, if need be, by breaking and entry. Protection against such invasion of "the sanctities of a man's home and the privacies of life" was provided in the Fourth and Fifth Amendments by specific language. *Boyd* v. *United States,* 116 U.S. 616, 630. But "time works changes, brings into existence new conditions and purposes." Subtler and more far-reaching means of invading privacy have become available to the Government. Discovery and invention have made it possible for the Government, by means far more effective than stretching upon the rack, to obtain disclosure in court of what is whispered in the closet.

Moreover, "in the application of a constitution, our contemplation cannot be only of what has been but of what may be." The progress of science in furnishing the Government with means of espionage is not likely to stop with wire-tapping. Ways may some day be developed by which the Government, without removing papers from secret drawers, can reproduce them in court, and by which it will be enabled to expose to a jury the most intimate occurrences of the home. Advances in the psychic and related sciences may bring means of exploring unexpressed beliefs, thoughts and emotions.

. . .

The protection guaranteed by the *[Fourth and Fifth]* Amendments is much broader in scope. The makers of our Constitution undertook to secure conditions favorable to the pursuit of happiness. They recognized the significance of man's spiritual nature, of his feelings and of his intellect. They knew that only a part of the pain, pleasure and satisfactions of life are to be found in material things. They sought to protect Americans in their beliefs, their thoughts, their emotions and their sensations. They conferred, as against the Government, the right to be let alone—the most comprehensive of rights and the right most valued by civilized men. To protect that right, every unjustifiable intrusion by the Government upon the privacy of the individual, whatever the means employed, must be deemed a violation of the Fourth Amendment. And the use, as evidence in a criminal proceeding, of facts ascertained by such intrusion must be deemed a violation of the Fifth.

Applying to the Fourth and Fifth Amendments the established rule of construction, the defendants' objections to the evidence obtained by wire-tapping must, in my opinion, be sustained. It is, of course, immaterial where the physical connection with the telephone wires leading into the defendants' premises was made. And it is also immaterial that the intrusion was in aid of law enforcement. Experience should teach us to be most on our guard to protect liberty when the Government's purposes are beneficent. Men born to freedom are naturally alert to repel invasion of their liberty by evil-minded rulers. The greatest dangers to liberty lurk in insidious encroachment by men of zeal, well-meaning but without understanding.

. . .

Decency, security and liberty alike demand that government officials shall be subjected to the same rules of conduct that are commands to the citizen. In a government of laws, existence of the government will be imperilled if it fails to observe the law scrupulously. Our Government is the potent, the omnipresent teacher. For good or for ill, it teaches the whole people by its example. Crime is contagious. If the Government becomes a lawbreaker, it breeds contempt for law; it invites every man to become a law unto himself; it invites anarchy. To declare that in the administration of the criminal law the end justifies the means—to declare that the Government may commit crimes in order to secure the conviction of a private criminal—would bring terrible retribution. Against that pernicious doctrine this Court should resolutely set its face.

MR. JUSTICE BUTLER, dissenting.

. . .

MR. JUSTICE STONE, dissenting.

. . .

Katz v. United States

389 U.S. 347 (1967)

Charles Katz was convicted for transmitting information on bets and wagers by telephone across state lines. FBI agents overheard his phone conversations by attaching an electronic

listening and recording device to the top of a public telephone booth he used. The Ninth Circuit affirmed his conviction, finding that there was no Fourth Amendment violation since there was "no physical entrance into the area occupied by" Katz.

MR. JUSTICE STEWART delivered the opinion of the Court.

...[T]he parties have attached great significance to the characterization of the telephone booth from which the petitioner placed his calls. The petitioner has strenuously argued that the booth was a "constitutionally protected area." The Government has maintained with equal vigor that it was not. But this effort to decide whether or not a given "area," viewed in the abstract, is "constitutionally protected" deflects attention from the problem presented by this case. For the Fourth Amendment protects people, not places. What a person knowingly exposes to the public, even in his own home or office, is not a subject of Fourth Amendment protection.... But what he seeks to preserve as private, even in an area accessible to the public, may be constitutionally protected....

The Government stresses the fact that the telephone booth from which the petitioner made his calls was constructed partly of glass, so that he was as visible after he entered it as he would have been if he had remained outside. But what he sought to exclude when he entered the booth was not the intruding eye—it was the uninvited ear. He did not shed his right to do so simply because he made his calls from a place where he might be seen. No less than an individual in a business office, in a friend's apartment, or in a taxicab, a person in a telephone booth may rely upon the protection of the Fourth Amendment. One who occupies it, shuts the door behind him, and pays the toll that permits him to place a call is surely entitled to assume that the words he utters into the mouthpiece will not be broadcast to the world. To read the Constitution more narrowly is to ignore the vital role that the public telephone has come to play in private communication.

The Government contends, however, that the activities of its agents in this case should not be tested by Fourth Amendment requirements, for the surveillance technique they employed involved no physical penetration of the telephone booth from which the petitioner placed his calls. It is true that the absence of such penetration was at one time thought to foreclose further Fourth Amendment inquiry, *Olmstead* v. *United States,* 277 U.S. 438, 457, 464, 466; *Goldman* v. *United States,* 316 U.S. 129, 134–136, for that Amendment was thought to limit only searches and seizures of tangible property. But "[t]he premise that property interests control the right of the Government to search and seize has been discredited." *Warden* v. *Hayden,* 387 U.S. 294, 304. Thus, although a closely divided Court supposed in *Olmstead* that surveillance without any trespass and without the seizure of any material object fell outside the ambit of the Constitution, we have since departed from the narrow view on which that decision rested. Indeed, we have expressly held that the Fourth Amendment governs not only the seizure of tangible items, but extends as well to the recording of oral statements, overheard without any "technical trespass under...local property law." *Silverman* v. *United States,* 365 U.S. 505, 511. Once this much is acknowledged, and once it is recognized that the Fourth Amendment protects people — and not simply "areas" — against unreasonable searches and seizures, it becomes clear that the reach of that Amendment cannot turn upon the presence or absence of a physical intrusion into any given enclosure.

We conclude that the underpinnings of *Olmstead* and *Goldman* have been so eroded by our subsequent decisions that the "trespass" doctrine there enunciated can no longer be regarded as controlling. The Government's activities in electronically listening to and recording the petitioner's words violated the privacy upon which he justifiably relied while using the telephone booth and thus constituted a "search and seizure" within the meaning of the Fourth Amendment. The fact that the electronic device employed to achieve that end did not happen to penetrate the wall of the booth can have no constitutional significance.

The question remaining for decision, then, is whether the search and seizure conducted in this case complied with constitutional standards. In that regard, the Government's position is that its agents acted in an entirely defensible manner: They did not begin their electronic surveillance until investigation of the petitioner's activities had established a strong probability that he was using the telephone in question to transmit gambling information to persons in other States, in violation of federal law. Moreover, the surveillance was limited, both in scope and in duration, to the specific purpose of establishing the contents of the petitioner's unlawful telephonic communications. The agents confined their surveillance to the brief periods during which he used the telephone booth, and they took great care to overhear only the conversations of the petitioner himself.

Accepting this account of the Government's actions as accurate, it is clear that this surveillance was so narrowly circumscribed that a duly authorized magistrate, properly notified of the need for such investigation, specifically informed of the basis on which it was to proceed, and clearly apprised of the precise intrusion it would entail, could constitutionally have authorized, with appropriate safeguards, the very limited search and seizure that the Government asserts in fact took place....

The Government urges that, because its agents relied upon the decisions in *Olmstead* and *Goldman,* and because they did no more here than they might properly have done with prior judicial sanction, we should retroactively validate their conduct. That we cannot do. It is apparent that the agents in this case acted with restraint. Yet the inescapable fact is that this restraint was imposed by the agents themselves, not by a judicial officer. They were not required, before commencing the search, to present their estimate of probable cause for detached scrutiny by a neutral magistrate. They were not compelled, during the conduct of the search itself, to observe precise limits established in advance by a specific court order. Nor were they directed, after the search had been completed, to notify the authorizing magistrate in detail of all that had been seized. In the absence of such safeguards, this Court has never sustained a search upon the sole ground that officers reasonably expected to find evidence of a particular crime and voluntarily confined their activities to the least intrusive means consistent with that end.... [S]earches conducted outside the judicial process, without prior approval by judge or magistrate, are *per se* unreasonable under the Fourth Amendment — subject only to a few specifically established and well-delineated exceptions.

It is difficult to imagine how any of those exceptions could ever apply to the sort of search and seizure involved in this case. Even electronic surveillance substantially contemporaneous with an individual's arrest could hardly be deemed an "incident" of that arrest. Nor could the use of electronic surveillance without prior authorization be justified on grounds of "hot pursuit." And, of course, the very nature of electronic surveillance precludes its use pursuant to the suspect's consent.

The Government does not question these basic principles. Rather, it urges the creation of a new exception to cover this case. It argues that surveillance of a telephone booth should be exempted from the usual requirement of advance authorization by a magistrate upon a showing of probable cause. We cannot agree. Omission of such authorization

"bypasses the safeguards provided by an objective predetermination of probable cause, and substitutes instead the far less reliable procedure of an after-the-event justification for the . . . search, too likely to be subtly influenced by the familiar shortcomings of hindsight judgment." *Beck* v. *Ohio,* 379 U.S. 89, 96.

And bypassing a neutral predetermination of the *scope* of a search leaves individuals secure from Fourth Amendment violations "only in the discretion of the police." *Id.,* at 97.

These considerations do not vanish when the search in question is transferred from the setting of a home, an office, or a hotel room to that of a telephone booth. Wherever a man may be, he is entitled to know that he will remain free from unreasonable searches and seizures. The government agents here ignored "the procedure of antecedent justification . . . that is central to the Fourth Amendment," a procedure that we hold to be a constitutional precondition of the kind of electronic surveillance involved in this case. Because the surveillance here failed to meet that condition, and because it led to the petitioner's conviction, the judgment must be reversed.

It is so ordered.

Mr. Justice MARSHALL took no part in the consideration or decision of this case.

Mr. Justice DOUGLAS, with whom Mr. Justice BRENNAN joins, concurring.

While I join the opinion of the Court, I feel compelled to reply to the separate concurring opinion of my Brother WHITE, which I view as a wholly unwarranted green light for the Executive Branch to resort to electronic eavesdropping without a warrant in cases which the Executive Branch itself labels "national security" matters.

Neither the President nor the Attorney General is a magistrate. In matters where they believe national security may be involved they are not detached, disinterested, and neutral as a court or magistrate must be....

Mr. Justice HARLAN, concurring.

. . .

MR. JUSTICE WHITE, concurring.

I agree that the official surveillance of petitioner's telephone conversations in a public booth must be subjected to the test of reasonableness under the Fourth Amendment and that on the record now before us the particular surveillance undertaken was unreasonable absent a warrant properly authorizing it....

...We should not require the warrant procedure and the magistrate's judgment if the President of the United States or his chief legal officer, the Attorney General, has considered the requirements of national security and authorized electronic surveillance as reasonable.

MR. JUSTICE BLACK, dissenting.

. . .

Tapping telephone wires, of course, was an unknown possibility at the time the Fourth Amendment was adopted. But eavesdropping (and wiretapping is nothing more than eavesdropping by telephone) was, as even the majority opinion in *Berger, supra,* recognized, "an ancient practice which at common law was condemned as a nuisance. 4 Blackstone, Commentaries 168. In those days the eavesdropper listened by naked ear under the eaves of houses or their windows, or beyond their walls seeking out private discourse." 388 U.S., at 45. There can be no doubt that the Framers were aware of this practice, and if they had desired to outlaw or restrict the use of evidence obtained by eavesdropping, I believe that they would have used the appropriate language to do so in the Fourth Amendment. They certainly would not have left such a task to the ingenuity of language-stretching judges....

E. THE EXCLUSIONARY RULE

The "exclusionary rule" refers to a general doctrine that excludes illegally obtained evidence from trial. The rule is shaped by Court doctrine as well as by congressional and executive actions. Sometimes the Court invites action by Congress. Olmstead v. United States, 277 U.S. 438, 465–66 (1928). The wiretap statute of 1968 prohibits the admissibility of any evidence "in any trial, hearing or other proceeding in or before any court, grand jury, department, offices, agency, regulatory body, legislative committee, or other authority of the United States, a state, or a political subdivision thereof" if the disclosure of that information violates the statute. 18 U.S.C. § 2514.

The exclusion of coerced confessions dates back to common-law practice; the exclusion of evidence and documents obtained by illegal searches and seizures is largely a twentieth-century development. The practice at the state level allowed pertinent evidence even if law enforcement officers had acted illegally. Courts did not take notice of how documents or articles were seized. Judges considered only the competence of the evidence, not the method by which it was obtained. Adams v. New York, 192 U.S. 585 (1904). There were some exceptions at the state level. The Iowa Supreme Court announced in 1903 that the admission of evidence illegally obtained would "emasculate" the constitutional guaranty in the state constitution against unreasonable searches and seizures. State v. Sheridan, 96 N.W. 730, 731 (Iowa 1903).

The Federal Exclusionary Rule

The exclusionary rule originated at the federal level in 1914, when the Supreme Court ruled unanimously that papers illegally seized by federal officers may not be introduced in court as evidence. The details of the case demonstrate that the Court was reacting to the record of law enforcement officials who were willing and able to convict people by any means: unlawful seizures, forced confessions, and other violations of constitutional rights. WEEKS v. UNITED STATES, 232 U.S. 383.

Because the decision did not address papers illegally seized by private parties or state and local officers, federal agents could still profit from violations committed by others. When private parties stole documents and gave them to the federal government for prosecution, a suit had to be directed against the private party. On the theory that the government was not responsible for the wrongful seizure, it could use the stolen papers for grand jury action. Burdeau v. McDowell, 256 U.S. 465 (1921). Similarly, federal agents could use the fruits of an illegal search and seizure committed by state officers as long as the federal government did not participate or cooperate in the illegal actions. Byars v. United States, 273 U.S. 28 (1927); Gambino v. United States, 275 U.S. 310 (1927). The crux of the Court's doctrine was "that a search is a search by a federal official if he had a hand in it; it is not a search by a federal official if evidence secured by state authorities is turned over to the federal authorities on a silver platter." Lustig v. United States, 338 U.S. 74, 79 (1949).

When federal officers violated congressional policy by failing to take suspects to the nearest U.S. commissioner or judicial officer for arraignment and instead held them for several days to obtain incriminating evidence, the Court set aside the convictions and held that the illegally obtained information was inadmissible. McNabb v. United States, 318 U.S. 332 (1943). These convictions were overturned because federal agents violated the Federal Rules of Criminal Procedure devised by Congress to assure that an arrested person is taken before a committing magistrate "without unnecessary delay." Mallory v. United States, 354 U.S. 449 (1957).

Application to the States?

In 1949 the Court held squarely that the doctrine of *Weeks*, which made illegally obtained evidence inadmissible in federal courts, was not imposed on the states by the Fourteenth Amendment. In a strange opinion, Justice Frankfurter spoke eloquently about an individual's constitutional right to be protected from arbitrary intrusions by state police; he offered little, however, in the way of practical relief. He suggested two ways to restrain the states from making illegal searches and seizures: "the remedies of private action" against the offending officer, and "the internal discipline of the police, under the eyes of an alert public opinion." He also thought that Congress could pass a statute under Section 5 of the Fourteenth Amendment to make *Weeks* binding on the states. Wolf v. Colorado, 338 U.S. 25, 33 (1949). In his dissenting opinion, Justice Murphy dismissed Frankfurter's remedies as unrealistic. Murphy, who had served previously as Attorney General under President Franklin D. Roosevelt, remarked: "Little need be said concerning the possibilities of criminal prosecution. Self-scrutiny is a lofty ideal, but its exaltation reaches new heights if we expect a District Attorney to prosecute himself or his associates for well-meaning violations of the search and seizure clause during a raid the District Attorney or his associates have ordered." Murphy concluded that only one remedy existed to deter violations of the Fourth Amendment: a rule to exclude illegally obtained evidence. In a separate dissent, Justice Rutledge agreed that without the exclusionary rule the Fourth Amendment was "a dead letter."

Two years later, the Supreme Court advised lower federal courts not to intervene in state criminal proceedings to suppress evidence even when there were claims that the evidence had been obtained by unlawful search and seizure. Stefanelli v. Minard, 342 U.S. 117 (1951). But when state officers used methods that seemed to the Court "too close to the rack and the screw," evidence was excluded as a violation of the Due Process Clause. The actions of county sheriffs in entering a home without a warrant, forcing their way into a suspect's bedroom, struggling with him to extract capsules he had placed in his mouth, and then taking him to a hospital where "stomach pumping" caused him to vomit two capsules containing morphine, seemed to the Court "conduct that shocks the conscience." Rochin v. California, 342 U.S. 165, 172 (1952). Nevertheless, local police continued to obtain evidence that would have been inadmissible in federal court. Schwartz v. Texas, 344 U.S. 199 (1952); Irvine v. California, 347 U.S. 128 (1954). The practical result was that the Court applied the exclusionary rule in ad hoc fashion to the states whenever a majority of the Court felt sufficiently revolted by local police actions.

A 1960 decision laid the groundwork for overturning *Wolf* and applying *Weeks* to the states. State law enforcement officers had conducted an illegal search and seizure. Because federal agents were not involved, evidence admitted in federal court was used to convict the defendant. The Supreme Court decided that the silver-platter doctrine had become intolerable and that it did not matter to the victim of police abuse "whether his constitutional right has been invaded by a federal agent or by a state officer." Elkins v. United States, 364 U.S. 206, 215 (1960). The decision responded to practical problems of federalism. If the fruit of an unlawful search by state agents could not be admitted in a federal trial, there would be no inducement "to subterfuge and evasion with respect to federal-state cooperation in criminal investigation." Id. at 222.

Mapp v. Ohio

A year later the Court applied the exclusionary rule to the states. The decision was not so much a federal imposition on the states as a recognition that they were already heading in that direction. Prior to the *Wolf* case in 1949, about one-third of the states supported the exclusionary rule. By 1961, additional states had conceded that the only effective remedy to official lawlessness was the exclusion of evidence illegally obtained. The remedies presented by Frankfurter in *Wolf* now seemed to the Court an exercise in "obvious futility." MAPP v. OHIO, 367 U.S. 643, 652 (1961). The Court applied the exclusionary rule to the states for several reasons: to deter unlawful conduct by the government; to provide effective protection to a person's constitutional right to privacy under the Fourth Amendment; to eliminate the double standard practiced by the federal government and the states; and to preserve judicial integrity by forcing the government to obey its own laws.

Mapp was criticized for placing a federal straitjacket on the diverse needs of state police and prosecutors. In fact, *Mapp* has accommodated a variety of circumstances and conditions at both the state and federal level. In 1971 the Court held that a defendant's statement, although ruled inadmissible as evidence, could nevertheless be used by the state to impeach a suspect's credibility if he or she chooses to testify. The exclusionary rule does not give a defendant the right to commit perjury. Harris v. New York, 401 U.S. 222 (1971). In 1974 the Court denied that a grand jury witness could invoke the exclusionary rule as grounds for not testifying. When a grand jury subpoenas an individual for questioning, the person cannot refuse because the evidence at issue was seized illegally. The Court considered the deterrent effect on police misconduct too speculative and minimal to impede the grand jury's role. United States v. Calandra, 414 U.S. 338 (1974).

Erosion of Exclusionary Rule

The largest loophole in the exclusionary rule is the "good faith" defense, which has been actively explored by all three branches. In 1976 the Court held that evidence seized by a state officer acting in good faith (who nonetheless violated the Fourth and Fourteenth Amendments) is admissible in a *civil* proceeding by the federal government. The Court, pointing out that the exclusionary rule was intended to deter state officers from overzealous criminal investigations, questioned the deterrent effect of excluding evidence at a federal civil proceeding. The societal cost of excluding the evidence seemed too high to the Court. The supervision of law enforcement "is properly the duty of the Executive and Legislative Branches." United States v. Janis, 428 U.S. 433, 459 (1976). Justice Stewart, dissenting, expressed concern that the Court was reviving the silver-platter doctrine. On the same day, the Court reviewed a number of state court criminal convictions based on evidence that allegedly was illegally obtained. Notwithstanding the fact that the Fourth Amendment claims might have been meritorious had they been asserted originally, the Court held that federal courts should not consider such petitions

Exceptions to Exclusionary Rule

1. "Good faith" actions for civil cases. United States v. Janis, 428 U.S. 433 (1976).

2. "Good faith" actions for criminal cases. United States v. Leon, 468 U.S. 897 (1984); Segura v. United States, 468 U.S. 796 (1984); Illinois v. Krull, 480 U.S. 340 (1987). (States may reject good-faith doctrine.)

3. Habeas corpus petitions appealing state convictions are denied if the exclusionary rule issue has been fully litigated in the state courts. Stone v. Powell, 428 U.S. 465 (1976).

4. Illegally obtained evidence may be used to impeach a witness's credibility. United States v. Havens, 446 U.S. 620 (1978). That doctrine does not apply to the testimonies of all defense witnesses. James v. Illinois, 493 U.S. 307 (1990).

5. Illegally obtained evidence taken from a third person may be used to convict someone else. United States v. Payner, 447 U.S. 727 (1980); United States v. Salvucci, 448 U.S. 83 (1980).

6. Use of illegally obtained information may be used when it would have been discovered anyway (the "inevitable discovery" exception). Nix v. Williams, 467 U.S. 431 (1984).

7. Second confessions are allowed after a first confession is illegally obtained. New York v. Harris, 495 U.S. 14 (1990).

8. Grand jury witnesses may not invoke the exclusionary rule and refuse to testify because the evidence at issue was seized illegally. United States v. Calandra, 414 U.S. 338 (1974).

9. Exclusionary rule does not apply in parole revocation hearings. Pennsylvania Bd. of Probation v. Scott, 524 U.S. 357 (1998).

when a defendant has already been afforded an opportunity to litigate that claim in a state court. STONE v. POWELL, 428 U.S. 465.

The extent to which the exclusionary rule can be circumvented is evident in several cases. After federal agents had participated in a break-in and theft of papers belonging to a third party, the government used this evidence to convict someone else of falsifying his federal income tax. The Court held that the convicted person had no standing to contest the illegal and unconstitutional search of another party. United States v. Payner, 447 U.S. 727 (1980). Similarly, the Court discarded an earlier ruling that persons charged with crimes of possession had "automatic standing" to challenge illegal searches, without regard to whether they had an expectation of privacy in the place searched. The Court now held that defendants charged with crimes of possession may only claim the benefits of the exclusionary rule if their own Fourth Amendment rights had been violated. United States v. Salvucci, 448 U.S. 83 (1980).

United States v. Leon

The Court continues to carve out other exceptions to the exclusionary rule. If information is obtained from a suspect in violation of the constitutional right to have counsel and that information would have been discovered anyway without a constitutional violation, the evidence is admissible. Under this "inevitable discovery" exception to the exclusionary rule, prosecutors need not prove good faith of police or the absence of bad faith. Nix v. Williams, 467 U.S. 431, 445 (1984). When a search results from a defective warrant, the incriminating evidence obtained from that search is admissible on the ground that the mistake was made by the judge issuing the warrant, not the police officer. The Court reasoned that suppression of the evidence would have no deterrent effect on the police who thought they were acting in "good faith" that the warrant was valid. Massachusetts v. Shepperd, 468 U.S. 981 (1984); UNITED STATES v. LEON, 468 U.S. 897 (1984). The same reasoning applies to a search conducted by police pursuant to a statute later found to be unconstitutional. Illinois v. Krull, 480 U.S. 340 (1987). Illegal police conduct in the form of a warrantless entry is effectively excused

States Reject *Leon* Good-Faith Test

In *United States* v. *Leon* (1984), the Supreme Court held that evidence would not have to be excluded at trial if police officers were operating in "good faith" that a warrant was valid even if it were later determined that the warrant was defective. A number of state courts have refused to adopt the *Leon* test, preferring to grant individuals greater rights under the state constitution than are presently available under the U.S. Constitution as interpreted by the U.S. Supreme Court:

Connecticut	State v. Marsala, 579 A.2d 58 (1990)
Massachusetts	Commonwealth v. Upton, 476 N.E.2d 548 (1985)
Michigan	People v. Sundling, 395 N.W.2d 308 (1986)
Minnesota	State v. Herbst, 395 N.W.2d 399 (1986)
New Jersey	State v. Novembrino, 519 A.2d 820 (1987)
New York	People v. Bigelow, 488 N.E.2d 451 (1985)
North Carolina	State v. Carter, 370 S.E.2d 553 (1988)
Pennsylvania	Commonwealth v. Edmunds, 586 A.2d 887 (1991)
Wisconsin	State v. Grawien, 367 N.W.2d 816 (1985)

unless it can be shown that the officers acted in bad faith by purposely delaying the obtaining of a warrant. Segura v. United States, 468 U.S. 796 (1984).

The Court divided 5 to 4 in a 1990 case involving a warrantless entry by police into a suspect's home. The suspect was read his *Miranda* rights and made an admission of guilt. After arrest and a trip to the police station, he was read his *Miranda* rights again and made another statement of guilt. The Court held that the second statement could be admitted into evidence, even though the first was obtained in violation of *Payton* v. *New York,* 445 U.S. 573 (1980). The majority denied that admission of the second statement provided an incentive for the police to violate *Payton.* New York v. Harris, 495 U.S. 14 (1990). In 1995, the Court held that the exclusionary rule does not require the suppression of evidence seized in violation of the Fourth Amendment when the error results from clerical errors by court employees. Similar to the reasoning in *Leon,* the Court said that the purpose of the exclusionary rule is to deter misconduct by police, not court employees, and that since court employees are not direct adjuncts to law enforcement officers devoted to ferreting out crimes, court employees have no stake in the outcome of particular prosecutions. Arizona v. Evans, 514 U.S. 1 (1995).

The exclusionary rule has been narrowed by the Supreme Court to the point where it exists solely to deter police misconduct. United States v. Leon, 468 U.S. at 916. Largely ignored are other important objectives of the rule identified so carefully in *Weeks* and *Mapp:* protecting an individual's right to privacy; eliminating the double standard between the federal government and the states; shielding the judiciary from the taint of official lawlessness; and forcing the government to obey its own laws. As the Court gradually dilutes the meaning of the exclusionary rule, constitutional rights are now more likely to be protected at the state level. A number of state courts have refused to adopt the *Leon* good-faith doctrine for the state constitution (see box).

By grounding the exclusionary rule almost exclusively on the rationale that it deters unlawful police conduct, the doctrine is simply a judicial choice of remedies cast in the form of a rule of evidence rather than a doctrine that is constitutionally anchored. Congress may therefore pass legislation to modify the rule. In 1995, the House passed the Exclusionary Rule Reform Act, which incorporated the good-faith exception. 141 Cong. Rec. 4064–85 (1995). However, the Senate did not act on the bill. Enactment of this exception would place an extraordinary and unrealistic demand on the sensitivity of law enforcement officers to respect constitutional rights and limits. Law enforcers would have to police themselves instead of having their actions monitored by a neutral and detached magistrate. Unless Congress can pass an effective tort remedy to punish officers who violate constitutional rights, the exclusionary rule will remain a necessary constraint on official lawlessness.[15]

Weeks v. United States

232 U.S. 383 (1914)

Without a search warrant, police entered the home of Fremont Weeks and took certain papers used to convict him of transporting lottery tickets through the mails. Weeks filed a petition for the return of his private papers and possessions. The Supreme Court confronted the question of whether illegal and unauthorized actions by the government could produce evidence admissible in a criminal prosecution. A federal district court required the return to Weeks of property that was not pertinent to the charge against him but permitted the District Attorney to retain papers to be used in evidence in the trial.

MR. JUSTICE DAY delivered the opinion of the court.

. . .

The defendant was arrested by a police officer, so far as the record shows, without warrant, at the Union Station in Kansas City, Missouri, where he was employed by an express company. Other police officers had gone to the house of the defendant and being told by a neighbor where the key was kept, found it and entered the house. They searched the defendant's room and took possession of various papers and articles found there, which were afterwards turned over to the United States Marshal. Later in the same day police officers returned with the Marshal, who thought he might find additional evidence, and, being admitted by someone in the house, probably a boarder, in response to a rap, the Marshal searched the defendant's room and carried away certain letters and envelopes found in the drawer of a chiffonier. Neither the marshal nor the police officers had a search warrant.

. . .

Upon the introduction of such papers during the trial, the defendant objected on the ground that the papers had been obtained without a search warrant and by breaking open his home, in violation of the Fourth and Fifth Amendments to the Constitution of the United States, which objection was overruled by the court. Among the papers retained and put in evidence were a number of lottery tickets and statements with reference to the lottery, taken at the first visit of the police to the defendant's room, and a number of letters written to the defendant in respect to the lottery, taken by the Marshal upon his search of defendant's room.

. . .

The history of [the Fourth] Amendment is given with particularity in the opinion of Mr. Justice Bradley, speaking for the court in *Boyd* v. *United States* 116 U.S. 616. As was there shown, it took its origin in the determination of the framers of the Amendments to the Federal Constitution to provide for that instrument a Bill of Rights, securing to the American people, among other things, those safeguards which had grown up in England to protect the people from unreasonable searches and seizures, such as were permitted under the general warrants issued under authority of the Government by which there had been invasions of the home and privacy of the citizens and the seizure of their private papers in support of charges, real or imaginary, made against them. Such practices had also received sanction under warrants and seizures under the

---

15. In 1971, the Supreme Court held that violations of the Fourth Amendment by federal agents give rise to a cause of action for damages resulting from unconstitutional conduct. Bivens v. Six Unknown Fed. Narcotics Agents, 403 U.S. 388 (1971). Even the Attorney General acting in the realm of national security is not absolutely immune for violating the Fourth Amendment. Mitchell v. Forsyth, 472 U.S. 511 (1989). Other cases on the liability of law enforcement officers for damages include Malley v. Briggs, 475 U.S. 335 (1986) and Anderson v. Creighton, 483 U.S. 635 (1967). In 1999, the Court held that police can be sued for allowing media "ride-alongs" with law enforcement officers, particularly when reporters and photographers enter private homes. Wilson v. Layne, 526 U.S. 603 (1999).

so-called writs of assistance, issued in the American colonies. See 2 Watson on the Constitution, 1414 *et seq.* Resistance to these practices had established the principle which was enacted into the fundamental law in the Fourth Amendment, that a man's house was his castle and not to be invaded by any general authority to search and seize his goods and papers. Judge Cooley, in his Constitutional Limitations, pp. 425, 426, in treating of this feature of our Constitution, said: "The maxim that "every man's house is his castle,' is made a part of our constitutional law in the clauses prohibiting unreasonable searches and seizures, and has always been looked upon as of high value to the citizen." "Accordingly," says Lieber in his work on Civil Liberty and Self-Government, 62, in speaking of the English law in this respect, "no man's house can be forcibly opened, or he or his goods be carried away after it has thus been forced, except in cases of felony, and then the sheriff must be furnished with a warrant, and take great care lest he commit a trespass. This principle is jealously insisted upon." In *Ex parte Jackson,* 96 U.S. 727, 733, this court recognized the principle of protection as applicable to letters and sealed packages in the mail, and held that consistently with this guaranty of the right of the people to be secure in their papers against unreasonable searches and seizures such matter could only be opened and examined upon warrants issued on oath or affirmation particularly describing the thing to be seized, "as is required when papers are subjected to search in one's own household."

. . .

The effect of the Fourth Amendment is to put the courts of the United States and Federal officials, in the exercise of their power and authority, under limitations and restraints as to the exercise of such power and authority, and to forever secure the people, their persons, houses, papers and effects against all unreasonable searches and seizures under the guise of law. This protection reaches all alike, whether accused of crime or not, and the duty of giving to it force and effect is obligatory upon all entrusted under our Federal system with the enforcement of the laws. The tendency of those who execute the criminal laws of the country to obtain conviction by means of unlawful seizures and enforced confessions, the latter often obtained after subjecting accused persons to unwarranted practices destructive of rights secured by the Federal Constitution, should find no sanction in the judg-

ments of the courts which are charged at all times with the support of the Constitution and to which people of all conditions have a right to appeal for the maintenance of such fundamental rights.

What then is the present case? Before answering that inquiry specifically, it may be well by a process of exclusion to state what it is not. It is not an assertion of the right on the part of the Government, always recognized under English and American law, to search the person of the accused when legally arrested to discover and seize the fruits or evidences of crime. This right has been uniformly maintained in many cases. . . . Nor is it the case of testimony offered at a trial where the court is asked to stop and consider the illegal means by which proofs, otherwise competent, were obtained—of which we shall have occasion to treat later in this opinion. Nor is it the case of burglar's tools or other proofs of guilt found upon his arrest within the control of the accused.

The case in the aspect in which we are dealing with it involves the right of the court in a criminal prosecution to retain for the purposes of evidence the letters and correspondence of the accused, seized in his house in his absence and without his authority, by a United States Marshal holding no warrant for his arrest and none for the search of his premises. . . . If letters and private documents can thus be seized and held and used in evidence against a citizen accused of an offense, the protection of the Fourth Amendment declaring his right to be secure against such searches and seizures is of no value, and, so far as those thus placed are concerned, might as well be stricken from the Constitution. The efforts of the courts and their officials to bring the guilty to punishment, praiseworthy as they are, are not to be aided by the sacrifice of those great principles established by years of endeavor and suffering which have resulted in their embodiment in the fundamental law of the land. The United States Marshal could only have invaded the house of the accused when armed with a warrant issued as required by the Constitution, upon sworn information and describing with reasonable particularity the thing for which the search was to be made. Instead, he acted without sanction of law, doubtless prompted by the desire to bring further proof to the aid of the Government, and under color of his office undertook to make a seizure of private papers in direct violation of the constitutional prohibition against such action. Under such circumstances, without sworn information and particular description, not even an order of court would have justified such procedure, much less was it within the authority of the United States Marshal to thus invade the house and privacy of the accused.

. . .

We therefore reach the conclusion that the letters in question were taken from the house of the accused by an official of the United States acting under color of his office in direct violation of the constitutional rights of the defendant; that having made a seasonable application for their return, which was heard and passed upon by the court, there was involved in the order refusing the application a denial of the constitutional rights of the accused, and that the court should have restored these letters to the accused. In holding them and permitting their use upon the trial, we think prejudicial error was committed. As to the papers and property seized by the policemen, it

does not appear that they acted under any claim of Federal authority such as would make the Amendment applicable to such unauthorized seizures. The record shows that what they did by way of arrest and search and seizure was done before the finding of the indictment in the Federal court, under what supposed right or authority does not appear. What remedies the defendant may have against them we need not inquire, as the Fourth Amendment is not directed to individual misconduct of such officials. Its limitations reach the Federal Government and its agencies. *Boyd Case,* 116 U.S., *supra,* and see *Twining* v. *New Jersey,* 211 U. S. 78.

It results that the judgment of the court below must be reversed, and the case remanded for further proceedings in accordance with this opinion.

Reversed.

Mapp v. Ohio

367 U.S. 643 (1961)

Dollree Mapp was convicted for possessing obscene materials. Cleveland police had arrived at her home looking for a bombing suspect. Without a search warrant, they forced their way in and proceeded to search the entire house, including dresser drawers, suitcases, photo albums, personal papers, and a trunk in the basement. Although the Supreme Court of Ohio admitted that the materials had been "unlawfully seized during an unlawful search," it upheld her conviction.

Mr. Justice Clark delivered the opinion of the Court.

. . .

On May 23, 1957, three Cleveland police officers arrived at appellant's residence in that city pursuant to information that "a person [was] hiding out in the home, who was wanted for questioning in connection with a recent bombing, and that there was a large amount of policy paraphernalia being hidden in the home." Miss Mapp and her daughter by a former marriage lived on the top floor of the two-family dwelling. Upon their arrival at that house, the officers knocked on the door and demanded entrance but appellant, after telephoning her attorney, refused to admit them without a search warrant. They advised their headquarters of the situation and undertook a surveillance of the house.

The officers again sought entrance some three hours later when four or more additional officers arrived on the scene. When Miss Mapp did not

come to the door immediately, at least one of the several doors to the house was forcibly opened and the policemen gained admittance. Meanwhile Miss Mapp's attorney arrived, but the officers, having secured their own entry, and continuing in their defiance of the law, would permit him neither to see Miss Mapp nor to enter the house. It appears that Miss Mapp was halfway down the stairs from the upper floor to the front door when the officers, in this highhanded manner, broke into the hall. She demanded to see the search warrant. A paper, claimed to be a warrant, was held up by one of the officers. She grabbed the "warrant" and placed it in her bosom. A struggle ensued in which the officers recovered the piece of paper and as a result of which they handcuffed appellant because she had been "belligerent" in resisting their official rescue of the "warrant" from her person. Running roughshod over appellant, a policeman "grabbed" her, "twisted [her] hand," and she "yelled [and] pleaded with him" because "it was hurting." Appellant, in handcuffs, was then forcibly taken upstairs to her bedroom where the officers searched a dresser, a chest of drawers, a closet and some suitcases. They also looked into a photo album and through personal papers belonging to the appellant. The search spread to the rest of the second floor including the child's bedroom, the living room, the kitchen and a dinette. The basement of the building and a trunk found therein were also searched. The obscene materials for possession of which she was ultimately convicted were discovered in the course of that widespread search.

At the trial no search warrant was produced by the prosecution, nor was the failure to produce one explained or accounted for. At best, "There is, in the record, considerable doubt as to whether there ever was any warrant for the search of defendant's home." 170 Ohio St., at 430, 166 N. E. 2d, at 389. The Ohio Supreme Court believed a "reasonable argument" could be made that the conviction should be reversed "because the 'methods' employed to obtain the [evidence]...were such as to 'offend "a sense of justice,"'" but the court found determinative the fact that the evidence had not been taken "from defendant's person by the use of brutal or offensive physical force against defendant." 170 Ohio St., at 431, 166 N. E. 2d, at 389–390.

The State says that even if the search were made without authority, or otherwise unreasonably, it is not prevented from using the unconstitutionally seized evidence at trial, citing *Wolf* v. *Colorado,* 338 U. S. 25 (1949), in which this Court did indeed hold "that in a prosecution in a State court for a State crime the Fourteenth Amendment does not forbid the admission of evidence obtained by an unreasonable search and seizure."...

I.

Seventy-five years ago, in *Boyd* v. *United States,* 116 U. S. 616, 630 (1886), considering the Fourth and Fifth Amendments as running "almost into each other" on the facts before it, this Court held that the doctrines of those Amendments

"apply to all invasions on the part of the government and its employés of the sanctity of a man's home and the privacies of life. It is not the breaking of his doors, and the rummaging of his drawers, that constitutes the essence of the offence; but it is the invasion of his indefeasible right of personal security, personal liberty and private property.... Breaking into a house and opening boxes and drawers are circumstances of ag-

gravation; but any forcible and compulsory extortion of a man's own testimony or of his private papers to be used as evidence to convict him of crime or to forfeit his goods, is within the condemnation...[of those Amendments]."

The Court noted that

"constitutional provisions for the security of person and property should be liberally construed.... It is the duty of courts to be watchful for the constitutional rights of the citizen, and against any stealthy encroachments thereon." At p. 635.

. . .

II.

In 1949, 35 years after *Weeks* was announced, this Court, in *Wolf* v. *Colorado, supra,* again for the first time, discussed the effect of the Fourth Amendment upon the States through the operation of the Due Process Clause of the Fourteenth Amendment. It said:

"[W]e have no hesitation in saying that were a State affirmatively to sanction such police incursion into privacy it would run counter to the guaranty of the Fourteenth Amendment." At p. 28.

Nevertheless, after declaring that the "security of one's privacy against arbitrary intrusion by the police" is "implicit in 'the concept of ordered liberty' and as such enforceable against the States through the Due Process Clause," cf. *Palko* v. *Connecticut,* 302 U. S. 319 (1937), and announcing that it "stoutly adhere[d]" to the *Weeks* decision, the Court decided that the *Weeks* exclusionary rule would not then be imposed upon the States as "an essential ingredient of the right." 338 U. S., at 27–29. The Court's reasons for not considering essential to the right to privacy, as a curb imposed upon the States by the Due Process Clause, that which decades before had been posited as part and parcel of the Fourth Amendment's limitation upon federal encroachment of individual privacy, were bottomed on factual considerations.

While they are not basically relevant to a decision that the exclusionary rule is an essential ingredient of the Fourth Amendment as the right it embodies is vouchsafed against the States by the Due Process Clause, we will consider the current validity of the factual grounds upon which *Wolf* was based.

The Court in *Wolf* first stated that "[t]he contrariety of views of the States" on the adoption of the exclusionary rule of *Weeks* was "particularly impressive" (at p. 29); and, in this connection, that it could not "brush aside the experience of States which deem the incidence of such conduct by the police too slight to call for a deterrent remedy ... by overriding the [States'] relevant rules of evidence." At pp. 31–32. While in 1949, prior to the *Wolf* case, almost two-thirds of the States were opposed to the use of the exclusionary rule, now, despite the *Wolf* case, more than half of those since passing upon it, by their own legislative or judicial decision, have wholly or partly adopted or adhered to the *Weeks* rule.... Significantly, among those now following the rule is California, which, according to its highest court, was "compelled to reach that conclusion because other remedies have completely failed to secure compliance with the constitutional provisions...." *People* v. *Cahan,* 44 Cal. 2d 434, 445, 282 P. 2d 905, 911 (1955). In connection with this California case, we note that the second basis elaborated in *Wolf* in support of its failure to enforce the exclusionary doctrine against the States was that "other means of protection" have been afforded "the right to privacy." 338 U.S., at 30. The experience of California that such other remedies have been worthless and futile is buttressed by the experience of other States. The obvious futility of relegating the Fourth Amendment to the protection of other remedies has, moreover, been recognized by this Court since *Wolf.* See *Irvine* v. *California,* 347 U. S. 128, 137 (1954).

Likewise, time has set its face against what *Wolf* called the "weighty testimony" of *People* v. *Defore,* 242 N. Y. 13, 150 N. E. 585 (1926). There Justice (then Judge) Cardozo, rejecting adoption of the *Weeks* exclusionary rule in New York, had said that "[t]he Federal rule as it stands is either too strict or too lax." 242 N. Y., at 22, 150 N. E., at 588. However, the force of that reasoning has been largely vitiated by later decisions of this Court. These include the recent discarding of the "silver platter" doctrine which allowed federal judicial use of evidence seized in violation of the Constitution by state agents, *Elkins* v. *United States, supra;* ...

It, therefore, plainly appears that the factual considerations supporting the failure of the *Wolf* Court to include the *Weeks* exclusionary rule when it recognized the enforceability of the right to privacy against the States in 1949, while not basically relevant to the constitutional consideration, could not, in any analysis, now be deemed controlling.

. . .

IV.

Since the Fourth Amendment's right of privacy has been declared enforceable against the States through the Due Process Clause of the Fourteenth, it is enforceable against them by the same sanction of exclusion as is used against the Federal Government. Were it otherwise, then just as without the *Weeks* rule the assurance against unreasonable federal searches and seizures would be "a form of words," valueless and undeserving of mention in a perpetual charter of inestimable human liberties, so too, without that rule the freedom from state invasions of privacy would be so ephemeral and so neatly severed from its conceptual nexus with the freedom from all brutish means of coercing evidence as not to merit this Court's high regard as a freedom "implicit in the concept of ordered liberty."

. . .

V.

Moreover, our holding that the exclusionary rule is an essential part of both the Fourth and Fourteenth Amendments is not only the logical dictate of prior cases, but it also makes very good sense. There is no war between the Constitution and common sense. Presently, a federal prosecutor may make no use of evidence illegally seized, but a State's attorney across the street may, although he supposedly is operating under the enforceable prohibitions of the same Amendment. Thus the State, by admitting evidence unlawfully seized, serves to encourage disobedience to the Federal Constitution which it is bound to uphold. Moreover, as was said in *Elkins,* "[t]he very essence of a healthy federalism depends upon the avoidance of needless conflict between state and federal courts." 364 U.S., at 221.... In nonexclusionary States, federal officers, being human, were by it invited to and did, as our cases indicate, step across the street to the State's attorney with their unconstitutionally seized evidence. Prosecution on the basis of that evidence was then had in a state court in utter disregard of the enforceable Fourth Amendment. If the fruits of an unconstitutional search had been inadmissible in both state and federal courts, this inducement to evasion would have been sooner eliminated....

. . .

There are those who say, as did Justice (then Judge) Cardozo, that under our constitutional exclusionary doctrine "[t]he criminal is to go free because the constable has blundered." *People* v. *Defore*, 242 N. Y., at 21, 150 N. E., at 587. In some cases this will undoubtedly be the result. But, as was said in *Elkins*, "there is another consideration—the imperative of judicial integrity." 364 U. S., at 222. The criminal goes free, if he must, but it is the law that sets him free. Nothing can destroy a government more quickly than its failure to observe its own laws, or worse, its disregard of the charter of its own existence.... Nor can it lightly be assumed that, as a practical matter, adoption of the exclusionary rule fetters law enforcement. Only last year this Court expressly considered that contention and found that "pragmatic evidence of a sort" to the contrary was not wanting. *Elkins* v. *United States, supra*, at 218. The Court noted that

"The federal courts themselves have operated under the exclusionary rule of *Weeks* for almost half a century; yet it has not been suggested either that the Federal Bureau of Investigation has thereby been rendered ineffective, or that the administration of criminal justice in the federal courts has thereby been disrupted. Moreover, the experience of the states is impressive.... The movement towards the rule of exclusion has been halting but seemingly inexorable." *Id.*, at 218–219.

The ignoble shortcut to conviction left open to the State tends to destroy the entire system of constitutional restraints on which the liberties of the people rest. Having once recognized that the right to privacy embodied in the Fourth Amendment is enforceable against the States, and that the right to be secure against rude invasions of privacy by state officers is, therefore, constitutional in origin, we can no longer permit that right to remain an empty promise. Because it is enforceable in the same manner and to like effect as other basic rights secured by the Due Process Clause, we can no longer permit it to be revocable at the whim of any police officer who, in the name of law enforcement itself, chooses to suspend its enjoyment. Our decision, founded on reason and truth, gives to the individual no more than that which the Constitution guarantees him, to the police officer no less than that to which honest law enforcement is entitled, and, to the courts, that judicial integrity so necessary in the true administration of justice.

The judgment of the Supreme Court of Ohio is reversed and the cause remanded for further proceedings not inconsistent with this opinion.

Reversed and remanded.

Mr. Justice Black, concurring.

. . .

Mr. Justice Douglas, concurring.

. . .

Memorandum of Mr. Justice Stewart.

. . .

Mr. Justice Harlan, whom Mr. Justice Frankfurter and Mr. Justice Whittaker join, dissenting.

In overruling the *Wolf* case the Court, in my opinion, has forgotten the sense of judicial restraint which, with due regard for *stare decisis,* is one element that should enter into deciding whether a past decision of this Court should be overruled. Apart from that I also believe that the *Wolf* rule represents sounder Constitutional doctrine than the new rule which now replaces it.

. . .

The preservation of a proper balance between state and federal responsibility in the administration of criminal justice demands patience on the part of those who might like to see things move faster among the States in this respect. Problems of criminal law enforcement vary widely from State to State.... For us the question remains, as it has always been, one of state power, not one of passing judgment on the wisdom of one state course or another....

Stone v. Powell

428 U.S. 465 (1976)

Lloyd Powell, convicted of criminal offenses in a state court, claimed that evidence used to convict him had been obtained by an illegal search and seizure. In an action against the

warden, W. T. Stone, he sought relief in a federal district court by filing a petition for a writ of federal habeas corpus. This case examines the following question: Should a federal court consider a claim that evidence has been illegally obtained and introduced when the convicted person already litigated that claim in the state courts? Also at issue is the scope of the exclusionary rule.

MR. JUSTICE POWELL delivered the opinion of the Court.

. . .

I

We summarize first the relevant facts and procedural history of these cases.

A

Respondent Lloyd Powell was convicted of murder in June 1968 after trial in a California state court. At about midnight on February 17, 1968, he and three companions entered the Bonanza Liquor Store in San Bernardino, Cal., where Powell became involved in an altercation with Gerald Parsons, the store manager, over the theft of a bottle of wine. In the scuffling that followed Powell shot and killed Parsons' wife. Ten hours later an officer of the Henderson, Nev., Police Department arrested Powell for violation of the Henderson vagrancy ordinance, and in the search incident to the arrest discovered a .38-caliber revolver with six expended cartridges in the cylinder.

Powell was extradited to California and convicted of second-degree murder in the Superior Court of San Bernardino County. Parsons and Powell's accomplices at the liquor store testified against him. A criminologist testified that the revolver found on Powell was the gun that killed Parsons' wife. The trial court rejected Powell's contention that testimony by the Henderson police officer as to the search and the discovery of the revolver should have been excluded because the vagrancy ordinance was unconstitutional. In October 1969, the conviction was affirmed by a California District Court of Appeal. Although the issue was duly presented, that court found it unnecessary to pass upon the legality of the arrest and search because it concluded that the error, if any, in admitting the testimony of the Henderson officer was harmless beyond a reasonable doubt under *Chapman* v. *California,* 386 U. S. 18 (1967). The Supreme Court of California denied Powell's petition for habeas corpus relief.

In August 1971 Powell filed an amended petition for a writ of federal habeas corpus under 28 U. S. C. § 2254 in the United States District Court for the Northern District of California, contending that the testimony concerning the .38-caliber revolver should have been excluded as the fruit of an illegal search. He argued that his arrest had been unlawful because the Henderson vagrancy ordinance was unconstitutionally vague, and that the arresting officer lacked probable cause to believe that he was violating it. The District Court concluded that the arresting officer had probable cause and held that even if the vagrancy ordinance was unconstitutional, the deterrent purpose of the exclusionary rule does not require that it be applied to bar admission of the fruits of a search incident to an otherwise valid arrest. In the alternative, that court agreed with the California District Court of Appeal that the admission of the evidence concerning Powell's arrest, if error, was harmless beyond a reasonable doubt.

In December 1974, the Court of Appeals for the Ninth Circuit reversed. 507 F. 2d 93. The court concluded that the vagrancy ordinance was unconstitutionally vague, that Powell's arrest was therefore illegal, and that although exclusion of the evidence would serve no deterrent purpose with regard to police officers who were enforcing statutes in good faith, exclusion would serve the public interest by deterring legislators from enacting unconstitutional statutes. *Id.,* at 98. After an independent review of the evidence the court concluded that the admission of the evidence was not harmless error since it supported the testimony of Parsons and Powell's accomplices. *Id.,* at 99.

. . .

II

The authority of federal courts to issue the writ of habeas corpus *ad subjiciendum* was included in the first grant of federal-court jurisdiction, made by the Judiciary Act of 1789, c. 20, § 14, 1 Stat. 81, with the limitation that the writ extend only to prisoners held in custody by the United States....

In 1867 the writ was extended to state prisoners. Act of Feb. 5, 1867, c. 28, § 1, 14 Stat. 385. Under the 1867 Act federal courts were authorized to give relief in "all cases where any person may be restrained of his or her liberty in violation of the constitution, or of any treaty or law of the United States...."

. . .

The discussion in *Kaufman* [v. *United States,* 394 U. S. 217 (1969)] of the scope of federal habeas corpus rests on the view that the effectuation of the Fourth Amendment, as applied to the States through the Fourteenth Amendment, requires the granting of habeas corpus relief when a prisoner has been convicted in state court on the basis of evidence obtained in an illegal search or seizure since those Amendments were held in *Mapp* v. *Ohio,* 367 U. S. 643 (1961), to require exclusion of such evidence at trial and reversal of conviction upon direct review. Until these cases we have not had occasion fully to consider the validity of this view.... Upon examination, we conclude, in light of the nature and purpose of the Fourth Amendment exclusionary rule, that this view is unjustified. We hold, therefore, that where the State has provided an opportunity for full and fair litigation of a Fourth Amendment claim, the Constitution does not require that a state prisoner be granted federal habeas corpus relief on the ground that evidence obtained in an unconstitutional search or seizure was introduced at his trial.

III

Decisions prior to *Mapp* advanced two principal reasons for application of the rule in federal trials. The Court in *Elkins,* for example, in the context of its special supervisory role over the lower federal courts, referred to the "imperative of judicial integrity," suggesting that exclusion of illegally seized evidence prevents contamination of the judicial process. 364 U. S., at 222.

... While courts, of course, must ever be concerned with preserving the integrity of the judicial process, this concern has limited force as a justification for the exclusion of highly probative evidence. The force of this justification becomes minimal where federal habeas corpus relief is sought by a prisoner who previously has been afforded the opportunity for full and fair consideration of his search-and-seizure claim at trial and on direct review.

The primary justification for the exclusionary rule then is the deterrence of police conduct that violates Fourth Amendment rights....

IV

We turn now to the specific question presented by these cases. Respondents allege violations of Fourth Amendment rights guaranteed them through the Fourteenth Amendment. The question is whether state prisoners—who have been afforded the opportunity for full and fair consideration of their reliance upon the exclusionary rule with respect to seized evidence by the state courts at trial and on direct review—may invoke their claim again on federal habeas corpus review. The answer is to be found by weighing the utility of the exclusionary rule against the costs of extending it to collateral review of Fourth Amendment claims.

The costs of applying the exclusionary rule even at trial and on direct review are well known: the focus of the trial, and the attention of the participants therein, are diverted from the ultimate question of guilt or innocence that should be the central concern in a criminal proceeding. Moreover, the physical evidence sought to be excluded is typically reliable and often the most probative information bearing on the guilt or innocence of the defendant. As Mr. Justice Black emphasized in his dissent in *Kaufman:*

"A claim of illegal search and seizure under the Fourth Amendment is crucially different from many other constitutional rights; ordinarily the evidence seized can in no way have been rendered untrustworthy by the means of its seizure and indeed often this evidence alone establishes beyond virtually any shadow of a doubt that the defendant is guilty." 394 U. S., at 237.

Application of the rule thus deflects the truthfinding process and often frees the guilty. The disparity in particular cases between the error committed by the police officer and the windfall afforded a guilty defendant by application of the rule is contrary to the idea of proportionality that is essential to the concept of justice. Thus, although the rule is thought to deter unlawful police activity in part through the nurturing of respect for Fourth Amendment values, if applied indiscriminately it may well have the opposite effect of generating disrespect for the law and administration of justice. These long-recognized costs of the rule persist when a criminal conviction is sought to be overturned on collateral review on the ground that a search-and-seizure claim was erroneously rejected by two or more tiers of state courts.

. . .

We adhere to the view that these considerations support the implementation of the exclusionary rule at trial and its enforcement on direct appeal of state-court convictions. But the additional contribution, if any, of the consideration of search-and-seizure claims of state prisoners on collateral review is small in relation to the costs....

In sum, we conclude that where the State has provided an opportunity for full and fair litigation of a Fourth Amendment claim, a state prisoner may not be granted federal habeas corpus relief on the ground that evidence obtained in an unconstitutional search or seizure was introduced at his trial. In this context the contribution of the exclusionary rule, if any, to the effectuation of the Fourth Amendment is minimal and the substantial societal costs of application of the rule persist with special force.

Accordingly, the judgments of the Courts of Appeals are

Reversed.

MR. CHIEF JUSTICE BURGER, concurring.

I concur in the Court's opinion. By way of dictum, and somewhat hesitantly, the Court notes that the holding in this case leaves undisturbed the exclusionary rule as applied to criminal trials. For reasons stated in my dissent in *Bivens v. Six Unknown Fed. Narcotics Agents,* 403 U. S. 388, 411 (1971), it seems clear to me that the exclusionary rule has been operative long enough to demonstrate its flaws. The time has come to modify its reach,...

. . .

MR. JUSTICE BRENNAN, with whom MR. JUSTICE MARSHALL concurs, dissenting.

. . .

IV

...[I]t is a matter for Congress, not this Court, to prescribe what federal courts are to review state prisoners' claims of constitutional error committed by state courts. Until this decision, our cases have never departed from the construction of the habeas statutes as embodying a congressional intent that, however substantive constitutional rights are delineated or expanded, those rights may be asserted as a procedural matter under federal habeas jurisdiction. Employing the transparent tactic that today's is a decision construing the Constitution, the Court usurps the authority—vested by the Constitution in the Congress—to reassign federal judicial responsibility for reviewing state prisoners' claims of failure of state courts to redress violations of their Fourth Amendment rights....

. . .

MR. JUSTICE WHITE, dissenting.

For many of the reasons stated by MR. JUSTICE BRENNAN, I cannot agree that the writ of habeas corpus should be any less available to those convicted of state crimes where they allege Fourth Amendment violations than where other constitutional issues are presented to the federal court....

United States v. Leon

468 U.S. 897 (1984)

The question in this case is whether the exclusionary rule covers the actions of law enforcement officers who believe they are acting in "good faith" by obtaining a search warrant but later discover that the warrant is invalid. The search involved drug trafficking by Alberto Leon and his associates. The District Court rejected the government's good-faith defense and suppressed the evidence against Leon. The Ninth Circuit affirmed.

JUSTICE WHITE delivered the opinion of the Court.

This case presents the question whether the Fourth Amendment exclusionary rule should be modified so as not to bar the use in the prosecution's case in chief of evidence obtained by officers acting in reasonable reliance on a search warrant issued by a detached and neutral magistrate but ultimately found to be unsupported by probable cause....

I

In August 1981, a confidential informant of unproven reliability informed an officer of the

Burbank Police Department that two persons known to him as "Armando" and "Patsy" were selling large quantities of cocaine and methaqualone from their residence at 620 Price Drive in Burbank, Cal. The informant also indicated that he had witnessed a sale of methaqualone by "Patsy" at the residence approximately five months earlier and had observed at that time a shoebox containing a large amount of cash that belonged to "Patsy." He further declared that "Armando" and "Patsy" generally kept only small quantities of drugs at their residence and stored the remainder at another location in Burbank.

On the basis of this information, the Burbank police initiated an extensive investigation focusing first on the Price Drive residence and later on two other residences as well. Cars parked at the Price Drive residence were determined to belong to respondents Armando Sanchez, who had previously been arrested for possession of marihuana, and Patsy Stewart, who had no criminal record. During the course of the investigation, officers observed an automobile belonging to respondent Ricardo Del Castillo, who had previously been arrested for possession of 50 pounds of marihuana, arrive at the Price Drive residence. The driver of that car entered the house, exited shortly thereafter carrying a small paper sack, and drove away. A check of Del Castillo's probation records led the officers to respondent Alberto Leon, whose telephone number Del Castillo had listed as his employer's. Leon had been arrested in 1980 on drug charges, and a companion had informed the police at that time that Leon was heavily involved in the importation of drugs into this country. Before the current investigation began, the Burbank officers had learned that an informant had told a Glendale police officer that Leon stored a large quantity of methaqualone at his residence in Glendale. During the course of this investigation, the Burbank officers learned that Leon was living at 716 South Sunset Canyon in Burbank.

Subsequently, the officers observed several persons, at least one of whom had prior drug involvement, arriving at the Price Drive residence and leaving with small packages; observed a variety of other material activity at the two residences as well as at a condominium at 7902 Via Magdalena; and witnessed a variety of relevant activity involving respondents' automobiles. The officers also observed respondents Sanchez and Stewart board separate flights for Miami. The pair later returned to Los Angeles together, consented to a search of their luggage that revealed only a small amount of marihuana, and left the airport. Based on these and other observations summarized in the affidavit, App. 34, Officer Cyril Rombach of the Burbank Police Department, an experienced and well-trained narcotics investigator, prepared an application for a warrant to search 620 Price Drive, 716 South Sunset Canyon, 7902 Via Magdalena, and automobiles registered to each of the respondents for an extensive list of items believed to be related to respondents' drug-trafficking activities. Officer Rombach's extensive application was reviewed by several Deputy District Attorneys.

A facially valid search warrant was issued in September 1981 by a State Superior Court Judge. The ensuing searches produced large quantities of drugs at the Via Magdalena and Sunset Canyon addresses and a small quantity at the Price Drive residence. Other evidence was discovered at each of the residences and in Stewart's and Del Castillo's automobiles. Respondents were indicted by a grand jury in the District Court for the Central District of California and charged with conspiracy to possess and distribute cocaine and a variety of substantive counts.

The respondents then filed motions to suppress the evidence seized pursuant to the warrant. The District Court held an evidentiary hearing and, while recognizing that the case was a close one, . . . granted the motions to suppress in part. It concluded that the affidavit was insufficient to establish probable cause, but did not suppress all of the evidence as to all of the respondents because none of the respondents had standing to challenge all of the searches. In response to a request from the Government, the court made clear that Officer Rombach had acted in good faith, but it rejected the Government's suggestion that the Fourth Amendment exclusionary rule should not apply where evidence is seized in reasonable, good-faith reliance on a search warrant.

The District Court denied the Government's motion for reconsideration, . . . and a divided panel of the Court of Appeals for the Ninth Circuit affirmed. . . .

We have concluded that, in the Fourth Amendment context, the exclusionary rule can be modified somewhat without jeopardizing its ability to perform its intended functions. Accordingly, we reverse the judgment of the Court of Appeals.

II

Language in opinions of this Court and of individual Justices has sometimes implied that the exclusionary rule is a necessary corollary of the Fourth Amendment,...or that the rule is required by the conjunction of the Fourth and Fifth Amendments.... These implications need not detain us long. The Fifth Amendment theory has not withstood critical analysis or the test of time, see *Andresen v. Maryland,* 427 U. S. 463 (1976), and the Fourth Amendment "has never been interpreted to proscribe the introduction of illegally seized evidence in all proceedings or against all persons." *Stone v. Powell,* 428 U. S. 465, 486 (1976).

A

The substantial social costs exacted by the exclusionary rule for the vindication of Fourth Amendment rights have long been a source of concern. "Our cases have consistently recognized that unbending application of the exclusionary sanction to enforce ideals of governmental rectitude would impede unacceptably the truth-finding functions of judge and jury." *United States v. Payner,* 447 U. S. 727, 734 (1980). An objectionable collateral consequence of this interference with the criminal justice system's truth-finding function is that some guilty defendants may go free or receive reduced sentences as a result of favorable plea bargains. Particularly when law enforcement officers have acted in objective good faith or their transgressions have been minor, the magnitude of the benefit conferred on such guilty defendants offends basic concepts of the criminal justice system....

III

...To the extent that proponents of exclusion rely on its behavioral effects on judges and magistrates *[to authorize proper warrants],* their reliance is misplaced. First, the exclusionary rule is designed to deter police misconduct rather than to punish the errors of judges and magistrates. Second, there exists no evidence suggesting that judges and magistrates are inclined to ignore or subvert the Fourth Amendment or that lawlessness among these actors requires application of the extreme sanction of exclusion.

...[M]ost important, we discern no basis, and are offered none, for believing that exclusion of evidence seized pursuant to a warrant will have a significant deterrent effect on the issuing judge or magistrate. Many of the factors that indicate that the exclusionary rule cannot provide an effective "special" or "general" deterrent for individual offending law enforcement officers apply as well to

judges or magistrates. And, to the extent that the rule is thought to operate as a "systemic" deterrent on a wider audience, it clearly can have no such effect on individuals empowered to issue search warrants. Judges and magistrates are not adjuncts to the law enforcement team; as neutral judicial officers, they have no stake in the outcome of particular criminal prosecutions. The threat of exclusion thus cannot be expected significantly to deter them. Imposition of the exclusionary sanction is not necessary meaningfully to inform judicial officers of their errors, and we cannot conclude that admitting evidence obtained pursuant to a warrant while at the same time declaring that the warrant was somehow defective will in any way reduce judicial officers' professional incentives to comply with the Fourth Amendment, encourage them to repeat their mistakes, or lead to the granting of all colorable warrant requests.

B

If exclusion of evidence obtained pursuant to a subsequently invalidated warrant is to have any deterrent effect, therefore, it must alter the behavior of individual law enforcement officers or the policies of their departments. One could argue that applying the exclusionary rule in cases where the police failed to demonstrate probable cause in the warrant application deters future inadequate presentations or "magistrate shopping" and thus promotes the ends of the Fourth Amendment. Suppressing evidence obtained pursuant to a technically defective warrant supported by probable cause also might encourage officers to scrutinize more closely the form of the warrant and to point out suspected judicial errors. We find such arguments speculative and conclude that suppression of evidence obtained pursuant to a warrant should be ordered only on a case-by-case basis and only in those unusual cases in which exclusion will further the purposes of the exclusionary rule.

. . .

[White reviews previous cases that concluded that the exclusionary rule is most justified when a law enforcement officer knows the search was unconstitutional. Where the officer's conduct is objectively reasonable, White said that the exclusion of evidence will not further the ends of the exclusionary rule in any appreciable way. Excluding evidence under these circumstances would not affect future conduct except to make the officer less willing to do his duty.]

This is particularly true, we believe, when an officer acting with objective good faith has obtained a search warrant from a judge or magistrate and acted within its scope. In most such cases, there is no police illegality and thus nothing to deter. It is the magistrate's responsibility to determine whether the officer's allegations establish probable cause and, if so, to issue a warrant comporting in form with the requirements of the Fourth Amendment.... Penalizing the officer for the magistrate's error, rather than his own, cannot logically contribute to the deterrence of Fourth Amendment violations.

C

Suppression... remains an appropriate remedy if the magistrate or judge in issuing a warrant was misled by information in an affidavit that the affiant knew was false or would have known was false except for his reckless disregard of the truth. *Franks* v. *Delaware,* 438 U. S. 154 (1978). The exception we recognize today will also not apply in cases where the issuing magistrate wholly abandoned his judicial role in the manner condemned in *Lo-Ji Sales, Inc.* v. *New York,* 442 U. S. 319 (1979); in such circumstances, no reasonably well trained officer should rely on the warrant. Nor would an officer manifest objective good faith in relying on a warrant based on an affidavit "so lacking in indicia of probable cause as to render official belief in its existence entirely unreasonable." ... Finally, depending on the circumstances of the particular case, a warrant may be so facially deficient—*i. e.*, in failing to particularize the place to be searched or the things to be seized—that the executing officers cannot reasonably presume it to be valid....

. . .

Accordingly, the judgment of the Court of Appeals is

Reversed.

JUSTICE BLACKMUN, concurring.

. . .

JUSTICE BRENNAN, with whom JUSTICE MARSHALL joins, dissenting.

...[I]n case after case, I have witnessed the Court's gradual but determined strangulation of the rule. It now appears that the Court's victory over the Fourth Amendment is complete....

The Court seeks to justify this result on the ground that the "costs" of adhering to the exclusionary rule in cases like those before us exceed the "benefits." But the language of deterrence and of cost/benefit analysis, if used indiscriminately, can have a narcotic effect. It creates an illusion of technical precision and ineluctability. It suggests that not only constitutional principle but also empirical data support the majority's result. When the Court's analysis is examined carefully, however, it is clear that we have not been treated to an honest assessment of the merits of the exclusionary rule, but have instead been drawn into a curious world where the "costs" of excluding illegally obtained evidence loom to exaggerated heights and where the "benefits" of such exclusion are made to disappear with a mere wave of the hand.

The majority ignores the fundamental constitutional importance of what is at stake here. While the machinery of law enforcement and indeed the nature of crime itself have changed dramatically since the Fourth Amendment became part of the Nation's fundamental law in 1791, what the Framers understood then remains true today—that the task of combating crime and convicting the guilty will in every era seem of such critical and pressing concern that we may be lured by the temptations of expediency into forsaking our commitment to protecting individual liberty and privacy....

JUSTICE STEVENS ... dissenting ...

IV

... Under the majority's new rule, even when the police know their warrant application is probably insufficient, they retain an incentive to submit it to a magistrate, on the chance that he may take the bait. No longer must they hesitate and seek additional evidence in doubtful cases....

CONCLUSIONS

From 1789 to the present, members of Congress and Presidents have been deeply involved in the development of Fourth Amendment law. Often they had to explore search and seizure issues without guidance from judicial rulings. With few exceptions, the courts have accepted congressional judgments as consistent with the Fourth Amendment. On some occasions, even after the Supreme Court has decided a Fourth Amendment issue, Congress has reentered the field and significantly modified what the Court has done. In these areas the "law" of search and seizure is defined as much by the *United States Code* as by the *United States Reports*.

While it is important to understand the purpose of the Fourth Amendment in restricting governmental searches, reliance on the "framers' intent" offers only limited assistance. The framers did not anticipate or discuss the types of cases that now bedevil the courts. Is it a permissible search and seizure to extract blood from someone to prove intoxication? Breithaupt v. Abram, 352 U.S. 432 (1957); Schmerber v. California, 384 U.S. 757 (1966). May a state force a suspect to undergo surgery to remove a bullet lodged in his chest and then introduce the bullet into evidence? Winston v. Lee, 470 U.S. 753 (1985). Answers to these questions ("yes" for the first, "no" for the second) require the Court each time to balance individual and government rights within the particular fact patterns of a case.

The scope of the Fourth Amendment has broadened considerably since the framers first drafted the language. Although the Amendment refers to the "right of the people" to be secure, it also protects corporations from unlawful search and seizure.[16] Through a series of decisions, the Amendment now applies to the states.

Over the years, the Court has adopted a balancing test that weighs a suspect's right against the needs of government and society. As the Court noted in 1983: "We must balance the nature and quality of the intrusion on the individual's Fourth Amendment interests against the importance of the governmental interests alleged to justify the intrusion." United States v. Place, 462 U.S. 696, 703. This attitude severely weakens the Fourth Amendment. Instead of serving as a restriction on government, which was the original purpose, the contemporary test is whether the government's interest or society's interest will prevail over a particular suspect. An individual can expect little protection from the Constitution when the odds are so heavily stacked.

A more appropriate balance is not one suspect against the government or against society but rather the interest of society against governmental misconduct and overreaching. The former test can produce a crude cost/benefit analysis with "a narcotic effect," creating "an illusion of technical precision and ineluctability." United States v. Leon, 468 U.S. at 929 (Brennan, J., dissenting). To the extent that the court balances an individual's interest against society's interest in law enforcement, it performs essentially a legislative judgment, inviting a sharing of power with Congress and the executive.

As with other branches, Congress can make major mistakes when it interprets the Fourth Amendment. However, the impulsiveness with which Congress sometimes moves in wrong directions allows it just as easily to reverse course and repeal the offending statute. For example, in 1970 Congress passed two ill-considered measures that authorized law enforcement officers to break and enter private dwellings and businesses. 84 Stat. 630–31; 84 Stat. 1274, § 509. Serious doubts about the constitutionality of these bills, combined with shocking reports of federal agents breaking into the wrong homes, prompted Congress four years later to repeal both provisions. 88 Stat. 1455, §§ 3, 4. Compare that performance with the twelve years it took the Court in *Mapp* to overturn *Wolf,* or the thirty-nine years needed for *Katz* to reverse *Olmstead.*

---

16. G.M. Leasing Corp. v. United States, 429 U.S. 338, 353 (1977); Essgee Co. v. United States, 262 U.S. 151 (1923); Silverthorne Lumber Co. v. United States, 251 U.S. 385 (1920).

SELECTED READINGS

ALLEN, FRANCIS A. "Federalism and the Fourth Amendment: A Requiem for Wolf." 1961 Supreme Court Review 1.

AMSTERDAM, ANTHONY G. "Perspectives on the Fourth Amendment." 58 Minnesota Law Review 349 (1974).

ERVIN, SAM J., JR. "The Exclusionary Rule: An Essential Ingredient of the Fourth Amendment." 1983 Supreme Court Review 283.

FISHER, EDWARD C. Search and Seizure. Evanston, Ill.: Northwestern University Press, 1970.

FISHER, LOUIS. "Congress and the Fourth Amendment." 21 Georgia Law Review 107 (Special Issue 1986).

KAMISAR, YALE. "Is the Exclusionary Rule an "Illogical' or "Unnatural' Interpretation of the Fourth Amendment?" 62 Judicature 66 (1978).

———. "The Exclusionary Rule in Historical Perspective: The Struggle to Make the Fourth Amendment More Than "An Empty Blessing'." 62 Judicature 337 (1979).

KAPLAN, JOHN. "The Limits of the Exclusionary Rule." 26 Stanford Law Review 1027 (1974).

KITCH, EDMUND W. "Katz v. United States: The Limits of the Fourth Amendment." 1968 Supreme Court Review 133.

LAFAVE, WAYNE C. " 'Case-by-Case Adjudication' Versus 'Standardized Procedures': The Robinson Dilemma." 1974 Supreme Court Review 127.

——— Search and Seizure: A Treatise on the Fourth Amendment. 4 vols. St. Paul, Minn.: West, 1987.

LANDYNSKI, JACOB W. Search and Seizure and the Supreme Court. Baltimore: Johns Hopkins University Press, 1966.

LEVY, LEONARD W. A License to Steal: The Forfeiture of Property. Chapel Hill, N.C.: University of North Carolina Press, 1996.

———. "Origins of the Fourth Amendment." 114 Political Science Quarterly 79 (1999).

OAKS, DALLIN H. "Studying the Exclusionary Rule in Search and Seizure." 37 University of Chicago Law Review 665 (1970).

POSNER, RICHARD A. "Rethinking the Fourth Amendment." 1981 Supreme Court Review 49.

SCHLESINGER, STEVEN R. Exclusionary Injustice. New York: Marcel Dekker, 1977.

SKLANSKY, DAVID A. "Traffic Stops, Minority Motorists, and the Future of the Fourth Amendment." 1997 Supreme Court Review 271.

STEWART, POTTER. "The Road to Mapp v. Ohio and Beyond: The Origins, Development and Future of the Exclusionary Rule in Search-and-Seizure Cases." 83 Columbia Law Review 1365 (1983).

TRAYNOR, ROGER J. "Mapp v. Ohio at Large in the Fifty States." 1962 Duke Law Journal 319.

U.S. CONGRESS. "The Exclusionary Rule Bills." Hearings before the Senate Committee on the Judiciary, 97th Cong., 1st and 2d Sess. (1981, 1982).

WHITE, JAMES B. "The Fourth Amendment as a Way of Talking about People: A Study of Robinson and Matlock." 1974 Supreme Court Review 165.

WILKEY, MALCOLM RICHARD. "The Exclusionary Rule: Why Suppress Valid Evidence?," 62 Judicature 214 (1978).

———. "A Call for Alternatives to the Exclusionary Rule: Let Congress and the Courts Speak." 62 Judicature 351 (1979).

15

Racial Discrimination

No issue has dominated American constitutional law as much as the question of race, beginning with slavery and discrimination against blacks, followed by recent efforts to heal the wounds of racism. Two earlier chapters addressed the issue of race: First Amendment questions in Chapter 10 (sit-in and demonstration cases) and rights of the accused in Chapter 13 (jury composition and the death penalty). The sections on voting rights and reapportionment in Chapter 18 deal heavily with racial questions. This chapter concentrates on slavery, the Civil War amendments, school desegregation, racial discrimination in housing, desegregation of public facilities, and issues of employment and affirmative action.

A. SLAVERY

At the time the framers met at the Philadelphia Convention, slavery was an established institution in the southern states. Recognizing that reality in the Constitution while laying the groundwork for abolishing slavery represented a matter of delicate tactics and compromise. How could the framers reconcile slavery with the principles in the Declaration of Independence? For this there could be no compromise. A nation could not proclaim that "all men are created equal" and at the same time condone slavery. Thomas Jefferson's original draft of the Declaration of Independence contained a sharp condemnation of slavery:

> [*King George III*] has waged cruel war against human nature itself, violating its most sacred rights of life & liberty in the persons of a distant people who never offended him, captivating & carrying them into slavery in another hemisphere, or to incur miserable death in their transportation thither, this piratical warfare, the opprobrium of *infidel* powers, is the warfare of the CHRISTIAN king of Great Britain, determined to keep open a market where MEN should be bought & sold, he has prostituted his negative [*veto*] for suppressing every legislative attempt to prohibit or to restrain this execrable commerce: and that this assemblage of horrors might want no fact of distinguished die, he is now exciting those very people to rise in arms among us, and to purchase that liberty of which *he* has deprived them, by murdering the people upon whom *he* also obtruded them; thus paying off former crimes committed against the *liberties* of one people, with crimes which he urges them to commit against the *lives* of another.

Because of opposition from southern delegates in the Continental Congress, that passage was struck from Jefferson's draft. However, the Northwest Ordinance of 1787, which governed the territory northwest of the Ohio River, contained this forthright declaration in Article 6: "There shall be neither slavery nor involuntary servitude in the said territory, otherwise than in the punishment of crimes whereof the party shall have been duly convicted. . . ."

Constitutional Language

Although the word "slavery" does not appear in the Constitution drafted at Philadelphia in 1787, it is implied in several places. First, Article V provides that no amendment to the Constitution prior to 1808 "shall in any Manner affect the first and fourth Clauses in the Ninth Section of the first Article...." The first clause in Section 9 states that the "Migration or Importation of such Persons as any of the States now existing shall think proper to admit" shall not be prohibited by Congress before 1808. This grace period for the slave trade prompted Madison to remark: "Twenty years will produce all the mischief that can be apprehended from the liberty to import slaves. So long a term will be more dishonorable to the National Character than to say nothing about it in the Constitution." 2 Farrand 415. The first clause in Section 9 also permitted a tax or duty on imported slaves "not exceeding ten dollars for each Person." The delegates divided on the merits of this language. Some regarded it as offensive to tax slaves as though they were incoming goods or articles of merchandise. Others thought that a tax might discourage the importation of slaves. The modest level of the tax suggests that the objective was revenue more than prohibition. 2 Farrand 416. Madison "thought it wrong to admit in the Constitution the idea that there could be property in men." 2 Farrand 417.

Slavery also became mixed with the question of apportioning taxes and Representatives among the states. The fourth clause in Section 9 prohibits capitation or other direct taxes unless in proportion to population. How was population to be measured? Should slaves be counted like whites, giving the southern states additional representation because of their "peculiar institution"? Alternatively, should representation be based solely on free inhabitants? William Paterson of New Jersey, objecting to any credit to the south for slaves, did not want to give "an indirect encouragemt. of the slave trade." 1 Farrand 561.

As with other matters, the framers reached a compromise. Under Article I, Representatives and direct taxes were apportioned among the states "according to their respective Numbers, which shall be determined by adding to the whole Number of free Persons, including those bound to Service for a Term of Years, and excluding Indians not taxed, three fifths of all other Persons." The three-fifths formula had been devised by the Continental Congress to deal with taxes. As picked up by the framers, the formula seems to imply that they regarded blacks as three-fifths of a person, or subhuman, but the fraction had a different effect. It penalized the states for practicing slavery. Their number of Representatives was reduced from what it would have been by freeing blacks.

Finally, Article IV, Section 2, provided that persons "held to Service or Labour" in one state shall be delivered back to that state in case they escaped to another. At the Virginia ratifying convention, Madison explained that this clause was inserted to "enable owners of slaves to reclaim them." 3 Farrand 325. This part of the Constitution became the basis for the fugitive slave laws passed by Congress.

Early Legislation

The 1790 census showed 757,363 blacks in the United States, or 19.3 percent of the population. Of these, 59,466 were free. States in excess of 20 percent slaves included South Carolina, Virginia, Georgia, Maryland, North Carolina, and Delaware. Slave-holding plantations were not profitable, but the situation changed dramatically in 1793 with Eli Whitney's invention of the cotton gin. The machine made it easier to separate the fiber from the seed, allowing plantation owners to export much greater quantities. Beginning in 1794, Congress passed various bills to regulate and restrict the slave trade. It enacted legislation in 1807 to stop the slave trade altogether, effective January 1, 1808. However, slaves continued to enter the country illegally, requiring additional legislation.[1]

Opposition to slavery came from the public, not from judicial, executive, or legislative actions. Individual Americans, untutored in the fine points of constitutional law, viewed slavery as repugnant to fundamental political and legal principles, especially those embedded in the Declaration of Independence. The essential antislavery documents were private writings and speeches, not court decisions or legislative statutes. William M. Wiecek, The Sources of Antislavery Constitutionalism in America, 1760–1848 (1977). Citizens felt a strong duty to express their opinions on constitutional rights. They deferred neither to courts nor legislatures. Americans of the mid-nineteenth century "were not inclined to leave to private lawyers any more than to public men the conception, execution, and interpretation of public law. The conviction was general that no aristocracy existed with respect to the Constitution. Like politics, with which it was inextricably joined, the Constitution was everyone's business." Harold M. Hyman, A More Perfect Union 6 (1975).

Legislation in the early decades contained conflicting values on slavery. Naturalization was permitted only for "free white person[s]." 1 Stat. 103, § 1 (1790); 1 Stat. 414, § 1 (1795). However, several early statutes governing the territories of Mississippi and Louisiana prohibited slavery. 1 Stat. 550, § 7 (1798); 2 Stat. 286, § 10 (1804).

Congress passed legislation to implement the constitutional provision on runaway slaves. The Fugitive Slave Act of 1793 authorized the return of slaves to their owners. 1 Stat. 302. The Supreme Court decided that congressional action preempted fugitive slave laws passed by the states. Prigg v. Pennsylvania, 16 Pet. 539 (1842). In response, many of the northern states repealed their laws, making it more difficult to capture runaways and forcing Congress to amend the Fugitive Slave Act in 1850. 9 Stat. 462. A unanimous Court upheld the constitutionality of this statute. Ableman v. Booth, 21 How. 506 (1859).

During this period, Congress attempted to maintain a balance between free states and slave states. The Ordinance of 1787 had prohibited slavery in the Northwest Territory (the Ohio country). Land acquired by the Louisiana Purchase threatened to upset the balance of slave and nonslave states. As a remedy, the Missouri Compromise Act of 1820 admitted Missouri as a slave state but prohibited slavery in future states north of the 36° 30′ line.

That compromise was upended when the United States acquired a vast tract of new territory after the Mexican War (1848). In response, Congress enacted the Compromise of 1850, but the statute largely dodged the issue of slavery. Senator Stephen Douglas reignited the issue by proposing that states unable under the 1820 Missouri Compromise Act to have slaves could elect to have them if their citizens so chose. The resulting Kansas-Nebraska Act of 1854 repealed the Missouri Compromise and left the decision of slavery to the new territories (and future states), a policy known as the doctrine of congressional noninterference or popular sovereignty. Political leadership was desperately needed at the national level to moderate the passions, but neither Congress nor the President was willing to confront the matter. Instead, they tossed the smoldering issue to the Supreme Court, encouraging it to resolve the dispute.

The *Dred Scott* Case

Elected President in 1856, James Buchanan wanted to mention the subject of slavery in his inaugural address but was uncertain of the Court's plans to decide the pending case of *Dred Scott* v. *Sandford*. In an extraordinary revelation of internal Court proceedings, Justices Catron and Grier wrote to Buchanan that the Court was indeed ready to decide the matter and that

---

1. 1 Stat. 347 (1794); 2 Stat. 70 (1800); 2 Stat. 205 (1803); 2 Stat. 426 (1807). Additional legislation was needed after 1808: 3 Stat. 450 (1818); 3 Stat. 532 (1819); 3 Stat. 600, §§ 4, 5 (1820).

Buchanan's Inaugural Address (1857)
(Excerpts)

We have recently passed through a Presidential contest in which the passions of our fellow-citizens were excited to the highest degree by questions of deep and vital importance; but when the people proclaimed their will the tempest at once subsided and all was calm.

The voice of the majority, speaking in the manner prescribed by the Constitution, was heard, and instant submission followed. Our own country could alone have exhibited so grand and striking a spectacle of the capacity of man for self-government.

What a happy conception, then, was it for Congress to apply this simple rule, that the will of the majority shall govern, to the settlement of the question of domestic slavery in the Territories! Congress is neither "to legislate slavery into any Territory or State nor to exclude it therefrom, but to leave the people thereof perfectly free to form and regulate their domestic institutions in their own way, subject only to the Constitution of the United States."

As a natural consequence, Congress has also prescribed that when the Territory of Kansas shall be admitted as a State it "shall be received into the Union with or without slavery, as their constitution may prescribe at the time of their admission."

A difference of opinion has arisen in regard to the point of time when the people of a Territory shall decide this question for themselves.

This is, happily, a matter of but little practical importance. Besides, it is a judicial question, which legitimately belongs to the Supreme Court of the United States, before whom it is now pending, and will, it is understood, be speedily and finally settled. To their decision, in common with all good citizens, I shall cheerfully submit, whatever this may be....

Buchanan should mention that fact in his address. Catron advised Buchanan to say that because of the "high and independent character" of the Court, "it will decide & settle a controversy which has so long and seriously agitated the country, and which *must* ultimately be decided by the Supreme Court." In a separate letter, Grier even gave Buchanan details on how the Court would split and along what lines. 10 The Works of James Buchanan 106–08 (J. Moore ed. 1910). Fortified by these confidential communications, Buchanan included within his inaugural address the naive expectation that the explosive issue of slavery could be decided solely and finally by the Supreme Court (see box).

Dred Scott, a slave from Missouri, argued that he had become free by following his master to a free state (Illinois) and to a free territory (Upper Louisiana). The principal issue was whether Scott, after returning to Missouri, was a citizen capable of suing in the federal courts. Did his stay on free soil give him this right? The Court held that Scott (and all other black slaves and their descendants) was not a citizen of the United States or of Missouri. Chief Justice Taney refused to allow contemporary social beliefs to change the meaning of the Constitution by making citizens of blacks. No one, he said, "supposes that any change in public opinion or feeling, in relation to this unfortunate race, in the civilized nations of Europe or in this country, should induce the court to give to the words of the Constitution a more liberal construction in their favor than they were intended to bear when the instrument was framed and adopted." DRED SCOTT v. SANDFORD, 19 How. 393, 426 (1857). Taney also ruled that Congress was without power to prevent the spread of slavery to the territories in the West.

The press divided widely in their response to Taney's decision. The *New York Tribune* remarked: "The decision, we need hardly say, is entitled to just as much moral weight as would be the judgment of a majority of those congregated in any Washington bar-room." Newspapers in the south, of course, accepted Taney's decision as the last word. According to the *Louisville Democrat*, the decision "is right, and the argument unanswerable, we presume, but whether or not, what this tribunal decides the Constitution to be, that it is; and all patriotic men will acquiesce."

Unlike Buchanan, who expressed a willingness to accept any decision of the Court, regardless of its merits, the people took sides. A historic challenge came in Illinois in 1858, when Senator Douglas debated a largely unknown challenger, Abraham Lincoln. Douglas supported *Dred Scott* without reservation. Lincoln accepted the decision only as it affected the particular parties; he repudiated the larger policy questions decided by the Court (see reading in Chapter 1).

The Court had miscalculated wildly. Concurring in Taney's opinion, Justice Wayne referred to the constitutional issues as so divisive "that the peace and harmony of the country required the settlement of them by judicial decision." Id. at 455. In his inaugural address, Buchanan had spoken confidently that the Dred Scott case was at the Supreme Court, where the issue of slavery would be "speedily and finally settled." Instead, the country lurched into a bloody civil war that left, out of a population of about 30 million, more than 600,000 dead and another 400,000 wounded.

Dred Scott v. Sandford

60 U.S. (19 How.) 393 (1857)

Dred Scott, a Negro slave, belonged to Dr. Emerson, who in 1834 took him from Missouri to the free state of Illinois. In 1836 Dr. Emerson took Dred Scott to a military post in the territory known as Upper Louisiana, situated north of 36 degrees, 30 minutes, also a free territory. In 1838 they returned to Missouri. Dred Scott and his wife and two daughters were later sold to John F.A. Sanford (incorrectly spelled in the case as Sandford). Dred Scott brought an action in the Circuit Court of the United States, claiming that as a result of his stay in free territory he was a citizen of Missouri capable of suing for his freedom. The case might have been confined to the question whether the Circuit Court had jurisdiction to hear the case or whether Dred Scott was a citizen. Instead, the issues were broadened to include the power of Congress to exclude slavery in the territories.

Mr. Chief Justice TANEY delivered the opinion of the Court.

. . .

The question is simply this: Can a negro, whose ancestors were imported into this country, and sold as slaves, become a member of the political community formed and brought into existence by the Constitution of the United States, and as such become entitled to all the rights, and privileges, and immunities, guarantied by that instrument to the citizen? One of which rights is the privilege of suing in a court of the United States in the cases specified in the Constitution.

It will be observed, that the plea applies to that class of persons only whose ancestors were negroes of the African race, and imported into this country, and sold and held as slaves. The only matter in issue before the court, therefore, is, whether the descendants of such slaves, when they shall be emancipated, or who are born of parents who had become free before their birth, are citizens of a State, in the sense in which the word citizen is used in the Constitution of the United States....

. . .

In discussing this question, we must not confound the rights of citizenship which a State may confer within its own limits, and the rights of citizenship as a member of the Union. It does not by any means follow, because he has all the rights and privileges of a citizen of a State, that he must be a citizen of the United States. He may have all of the rights and privileges of the citizen of a State, and yet not be entitled to the rights and privileges of a citizen in any other State. For previous to the adoption of the Constitution of the United States, every State had the undoubted right to confer on whomsoever it pleased the character of citizen, and to endow him with all its rights....

The question then arises, whether the provisions of the Constitution, in relation to the personal rights and privileges to which the citizen of a State should be entitled, embraced the negro African race, at that time in this country, or who might afterwards be imported, who had then or should afterwards be made free in any State; and to put it in the power of a single State to make him a citizen of the United States, and endue him with the full rights of citizenship in every other State without their consent? Does the Constitution of the United States act upon him whenever he shall be made free under the laws of a State, and raised there to the rank of a citizen, and immediately clothe him with all the privileges of a citizen in every other State, and in its own courts?

The court think the affirmative of these propositions cannot be maintained. And if it cannot, the plaintiff in error could not be a citizen of the State of Missouri, within the meaning of the Constitution of the United States, and, consequently, was not entitled to sue in its courts.

. . .

It becomes necessary, therefore, to determine who were citizens of the several States when the Constitution was adopted. And in order to do this, we must recur to the Governments and institutions of the thirteen colonies, when they separated from Great Britain and formed new sovereignties, and took their places in the family of independent nations. We must inquire who, at that time, were recognised as the people or citizens of a State, whose rights and liberties had been outraged by the English Government; and who declared their independence, and assumed the powers of Government to defend their rights by force of arms.

In the opinion of the court, the legislation and histories of the times, and the language used in the Declaration of Independence, show, that neither the class of persons who had been imported as slaves, nor their descendants, whether they had become free or not, were then acknowledged as a part of the people, nor intended to be included in the general words used in that memorable instrument.

It is difficult at this day to realize the state of public opinion in relation to that unfortunate race, which prevailed in the civilized and enlightened portions of the world at the time of the Declaration of Independence, and when the Constitution of the United States was framed and adopted. But the public history of every European nation displays it in a manner too plain to be mistaken.

They had for more than a century before been regarded as beings of an inferior order, and alto-gether unfit to associate with the white race, either in social or political relations; and so far inferior, that they had no rights which the white man was bound to respect; and that the negro might justly and lawfully be reduced to slavery for his benefit. He was bought and sold, and treated as an ordinary article of merchandise and traffic, whenever a profit could be made by it. This opinion was at that time fixed and universal in the civilized portion of the white race. It was regarded as an axiom in morals as well as in politics, which no one thought of disputing, or supposed to be open to dispute; and men in every grade and position in society daily and habitually acted upon it in their private pursuits, as well as in matters of public concern, without doubting for a moment the correctness of this opinion.

. . .

[Colonial laws and the state of feeling toward blacks] show that a perpetual and impassable barrier was intended to be erected between the white race and the one which they had reduced to slavery, and governed as subjects with absolute and despotic power, and which they then looked upon as so far below them in the scale of created beings, that intermarriages between white persons and negroes or mulattoes were regarded as unnatural and immoral, and punished as crimes, not only in the parties, but in the person who joined them in marriage. And no distinction in this respect was made between the free negro or mulatto and the slave, but this stigma, of the deepest degradation, was fixed upon the whole race.

. . .

[The Declaration of Independence] proceeds to say: "We hold these truths to be self-evident: that all men are created equal; that they are endowed by their Creator with certain unalienable rights; that among them is life, liberty, and the pursuit of happiness; that to secure these rights, Governments are instituted, deriving their just powers from the consent of the governed."

The general words above quoted would seem to embrace the whole human family, and if they were used in a similar instrument at this day would be so understood. But it is too clear for dispute that the enslaved African race were not intended to be included, and formed no part of the people who framed and adopted this declaration; . . .

[Taney states that the words "people" and "citizens" in the U.S. Constitution excluded the negro race and refers to the provisions permitting the

slave trade until 1808 and requiring states to return escaped persons held in labor or service. He also discusses the movement in some states, after 1787, to abolish slavery, and the persistence of laws in slaveholding states treating blacks as an inferior class. He cites a law passed by Congress in 1790 limiting the right of becoming citizens "to aliens being free white persons."]

No one, we presume, supposes that any change in public opinion or feeling, in relation to this unfortunate race, in the civilized nations of Europe or in this country, should induce the court to give to the words of the Constitution a more liberal construction in their favor than they were intended to bear when the instrument was framed and adopted. Such an argument would be altogether inadmissible in any tribunal called on to interpret it. If any of its provisions are deemed unjust, there is a mode prescribed in the instrument itself by which it may be amended; but while it remains unaltered, it must be construed now as it was understood at the time of its adoption. It is not only the same in words, but the same in meaning, and delegates the same powers to the Government, and reserves and secures the same rights and privileges to the citizen; and as long as it continues to exist in its present form, it speaks not only in the same words, but with the same meaning and intent with which it spoke when it came from the hands of its framers, and was voted on and adopted by the people of the United States. Any other rule of construction would abrogate the judicial character of this court, and make it the mere reflex of the popular opinion or passion of the day. This court was not created by the Constitution for such purposes. Higher and graver trusts have been confided to it, and it must not falter in the path of duty.

. . .

. . . [U]pon a full and careful consideration of the subject, the court is of opinion, that, upon the facts stated in the plea of abatement, Dred Scott was not a citizen of Missouri within the meaning of the Constitution of the United States, and not entitled as such to sue in its courts; and, consequently, that the Circuit Court had no jurisdiction of the case, and that the judgment on the plea in abatement is erroneous.

[Taney next turns to the question whether Dred Scott became free by living in a free state or territory. This raised the issue whether Congress was

empowered to pass legislation to exclude slavery from certain lands.]

In considering this part of the controversy, two questions arise: 1. Was he, together with his family, free in Missouri by reason of the stay in the territory of the United States herein-before mentioned? And 2. If they were not, is Scott himself free by reason of his removal to Rock Island, in the State of Illinois, as stated in the above admission?

We proceed to examine the first question.

The act of Congress, upon which the plaintiff relies, declares that slavery and involuntary servitude, except as a punishment for crime, shall be forever prohibited in all that part of the territory ceded by France, under the name of Louisiana, which lies north of thirty-six degrees thirty minutes north latitude, and not included within the limits of Missouri *[the Missouri Compromise Act of 1820]*. And the difficulty which meets us at the threshold of this part of the inquiry is, whether Congress was authorized to pass this law under any of the powers granted to it by the Constitution; for if the authority is not given by that instrument, it is the duty of this court to declare it void and inoperative, and incapable of conferring freedom upon any one who is held as a slave under the laws of any one of the States.

The counsel for the plaintiff has laid much stress upon that article in the Constitution which confers on Congress the power "to dispose of and make all needful rules and regulations respecting the territory or other property belonging to the United States;" but, in the judgment of the court, that provision has no bearing on the present controversy, and the power there given, whatever it may be, is confined, and was intended to be confined, to the territory which at that time belonged to, or was claimed by, the United States, and was within their boundaries as settled by the treaty with Great Britain, and can have no influence upon a territory afterwards acquired from a foreign Government. It was a special provision for a known and particular territory, and to meet a present emergency, and nothing more.

. . .

The language used in the clause, the arrangement and combination of the powers, and the somewhat unusual phraseology it uses, when it speaks of the political power to be exercised in the government of the territory, all indicate the design and meaning of the clause to be such as we have mentioned. It does not speak of *any* territory, nor of *Territories,* but uses language which, according to its legitimate meaning, points to a particular thing. The power is given in relation only to *the* territory of the United States—that is, to a territory then in existence, and then known or claimed as the territory of the United States....

Now, as we have already said in an earlier part of this opinion, upon a different point, the right of property in a slave is distinctly and expressly affirmed in the Constitution. The right to traffic in it, like an ordinary article of merchandise and property, was guaranteed to the citizens of the United States, in every State that might desire it, for twenty years. And the Government in express terms is pledged to protect it in all future time, if the slave escapes from his owner. This is done in plain words—too plain to be misunderstood. And no word can be found in the Constitution which gives Congress a greater power over slave property, or which entitles property of that kind to less protection than property of any other description. The only power conferred is the power coupled with the duty of guarding and protecting the owner in his rights.

Upon these considerations, it is the opinion of the court that the act of Congress which prohibited a citizen from holding and owning property of this kind in the territory of the United States north of the line therein mentioned, is not warranted by the Constitution, and is therefore void; and that neither Dred Scott himself, nor any of his family, were made free by being carried into this territory; even if they had been carried there by the owner, with the intention of becoming a permanent resident.

. . .

[*Justices Wayne, Nelson, Grier, Daniel, Campbell, and Catron wrote separate concurring opinions.*]

Mr. Justice McLEAN and Mr. Justice CURTIS dissented.

Mr. Justice McLEAN dissenting.

. . .

In the argument, it was said that a colored citizen would not be an agreeable member of society. This is more a matter of taste than of law. Several of the States have admitted persons of color to the right of suffrage, and in this view have recognised them as citizens; and this has been done in the slave as well as the free States. On the question of citizenship, it must be admitted that we have not been very fastidious. Under the late treaty with Mexico, we have made citizens of all grades, combinations, and colors. The same was done in the admission of Louisiana and Florida....

. . .

...[I]f we are to turn our attention to the dark ages of the world, why confine our view to colored slavery? On the same principles, white men were made slaves. All slavery has its origin in power, and is against right.

The power of Congress to establish Territorial Governments, and to prohibit the introduction of slavery therein, is the next point to be considered.

. . .

The prohibition of slavery north of thirty-six degrees thirty minutes, and of the State of Missouri, contained in the act admitting that State into the Union, was passed by a vote of 134, in the House of Representatives, to 42. Before Mr. Monroe signed the act, it was submitted by him to his Cabinet, and they held the restriction of slavery in a Territory to be within the constitutional powers of Congress. It would be singular, if in 1804 Congress had power to prohibit the introduction of slaves in Orleans Territory from any other part of the Union, under the penalty of freedom to the slave, if the same power, embodied in the Missouri compromise, could not be exercised in 1820.

But this law of Congress, which prohibits slavery north of Missouri and of thirty-six degrees thirty minutes, is declared to have been null and void by my brethren. And this opinion is founded mainly, as I understand, on the distinction drawn between the [*Northwest*] ordinance of 1787 and the Missouri compromise line. In what does the distinction consist? The ordinance, it is said, was a compact entered into by the confederated States before the adoption of the Constitution; and that in the cession of territory authority was given to establish a Territorial Government.

It is clear that the ordinance did not go into operation by virtue of the authority of the Confederation, but by reason of its modification and adoption by Congress under the Constitution. It seems to be supposed, in the opinion of the court, that the articles of cession placed it on a different footing from territories subsequently acquired. I am unable to perceive the force of this distinction.

That the ordinance was intended for the government of the Northwestern Territory, and was limited to such Territory, is admitted. It was extended to Southern Territories, with modifications, by acts of Congress, and to some Northern Territories. But the ordinance was made valid by the act of Congress, and without such act could have been of no force. It rested for its validity on the act of Congress, the same, in my opinion, as the Missouri compromise line.

If Congress may establish a Territorial Government in the exercise of its discretion, it is a clear principle that a court cannot control that discretion. This being the case, I do not see on what ground the act is held to be void. It did not purport to forfeit property, or take it for public purposes. It only prohibited slavery; in doing which, it followed the ordinance of 1787.

. . .

Mr. Justice CURTIS dissenting.

. . .

It has been often asserted that the Constitution was made exclusively by and for the white race. It has already been shown that in five of the thirteen original States, colored persons then possessed the elective franchise, and were among those by whom the Constitution was ordained and established. If so, it is not true, in point of fact, that the Constitution was made exclusively by the white race. And that it was made exclusively for the white race is, in my opinion, not only an assumption not warranted by anything in the Constitution, but contradicted by its opening declaration, that it was ordained and established by the people of the United States, for themselves and their posterity. And as free colored persons were then citizens of at least five States, and so in every sense part of the people of the United States, they were among those for whom and whose posterity the Constitution was ordained and established.

. . .

I dissent, therefore, from that part of the opinion of the majority of the court, in which it is held that a person of African descent cannot be a citizen of the United States; and I regret I must go further, and dissent both from what I deem their assumption of authority to examine the constitutionality of the act of Congress commonly called the Missouri compromise act, and the grounds and conclusions announced in their opinion.

. . . On so grave a subject as this, I feel obliged to say that, in my opinion, such an exertion of judicial power transcends the limits of the authority of the court, . . .

B. CIVIL WAR AMENDMENTS

During the war, Congress and President Lincoln took steps to eradicate slavery and its evils. Many of their actions in 1862 and 1863 eviscerated the two main principles announced by Chief Justice Taney in *Dred Scott:* Congress could not prohibit slavery in the territories, and blacks could not be citizens. Several years later that decision was formally overturned by the three Civil War amendments, ratified from 1865 to 1870. But Congress and the Attorney General took action before those amendments.

In 1862 Congress passed a number of statutes directed against slavery. It offered financial compensation to states that agreed to gradually abolish slavery, abolished slavery in the District of Columbia, and prohibited slavery in the territories (thus rejecting a central tenet of *Dred Scott*). 12 Stat. 617, 376, 432 (1862). During debate on the latter statute, no one even referred to the Court's decision. Congress never doubted its own independent constitutional power to prohibit slavery in the territories, with or without the Court. Congress also passed legislation that freed slaves from all those who committed treason against the United States or incited or engaged in any rebellion or insurrection against the United States. 12 Stat. 589 (1862). On January 1, 1863, Lincoln issued his Emancipation Proclamation.

The second main element of *Dred Scott* was discredited in 1862 when Attorney General Bates released a long opinion stating that neither color nor race could deny American blacks the right of citizenship. He pointed out that "freemen of all colors" had voted in some of the states. The idea of denying citizenship on the ground of color was received by other nations "with incredulity, if not disgust." The Constitution, Bates said, was "silent about *race* as it is about *color.*" With regard to *Dred Scott,* he held that the case, "as it stands of record, does not determine, nor purport to determine," the question of blacks to be citizens. What Chief Justice Taney said about citizenship was pure dicta and "of no authority as a judicial decision." Bates concluded: "the *free man of color,...* if born in the United States, is a citizen of the United States." 10 Op. Att'y Gen. 382 (1862).

Constitutional Amendments

Following the war, Congress passed the Thirteenth Amendment, adopted in 1865, to abolish the institution of slavery. The Fourteenth Amendment, ratified in 1868, provided for the equality of whites and blacks before the law. The Fifteenth Amendment, ratified in 1870, gave blacks the right to vote. Under the express language of these Amendments, Congress was empowered to enforce them "by appropriate legislation."

The Fourteenth Amendment had been foreshadowed by the Civil Rights Act of 1866. After passage of the Thirteenth Amendment, a number of southern states enacted "Black Codes" to keep the newly freed slaves in a subordinate status economically, politically, and culturally. The 1866 statute made all persons born in the United States, excluding Indians not taxed, citizens of the United States. Such citizens, "of every race and color," had the same right in every state and territory "to make and enforce contracts, to sue, be parties, and give evidence, to inherit, purchase, lease, sell, hold, and convey real and personal property, and to full and equal benefit of all laws and proceedings for the security of person and property, as is enjoyed by white citizens...." 14 Stat. 27, § 1 (1866). President Andrew Johnson vetoed the bill, claiming that the power to confer the right of state citizenship "is just as exclusively with the several States as the power to confer the right of Federal citizenship is with Congress." He objected to forcing this policy on the southern states and questioned whether blacks, newly emerged from slavery, had the "requisite qualifications to entitle them to all the privileges and immunities of citizens of the United States." 8 Richardson 3604. Congress overrode the veto, making the Civil Rights Act law on April 9, 1866. Similar objectives were incorporated in the Fourteenth Amendment, passed by Congress on June 13, 1866, and ratified by the states on July 20, 1868.

Public Accommodations

Legislation in 1875 attempted to close the gap between the Declaration of Independence and the Constitution. The preamble of the statute read: "Whereas, it is essential to just government we recognize the equality of all men before the law...." 18 Stat. 335. The statute provided for equality of all races in using public accommodations: inns, "conveyances" (transportation), theaters, and other places of public amusement. One of the sponsors, Congressman Benjamin Butler (R-Mass.), forcefully rejected the argument of opponents who claimed that the bill attempted to impose a national standard of "social equality" among blacks and whites (see box on next page). This landmark legislation would be struck down by the Supreme Court in 1883 as a federal encroachment on the states and an interference with private relationships.

Before issuing that decision, the Court handled other questions of race. State efforts to deny blacks the right to participate as jurors were struck down as a violation of the Equal Protection Clause of the Fourteenth Amendment. In doing so, however, the Court betrayed a prevailing attitude: "the colored race, as a race, was abject and ignorant, and in that condition was unfitted to command the respect of those who had superior intelligence. Their training had left them mere children, and as such they needed the protection which a wise government extends to those who are unable to protect themselves." Strauder v. West Virginia, 100 U.S.

Equal Access and "Social Equality"

[Opponents of the Civil Rights Act of 1875 claimed that the goal of giving blacks equal access to public accommodations was meant to enforce "social equality" among the races. Congressman Benjamin Butler (R-Mass.) eloquently rejected that claim, but it was later used by the Supreme Court in the *Civil Rights Cases* (1883) to declare the legislation unconstitutional.]

Mr. [Benjamin] BUTLER [R-Mass.].... It seems to me wholly illogical, as I know it to be wholly unjust and wrong [to deny blacks equal access to public accommodations]. The colored men are either American citizens or they are not. The Constitution, for good or for evil, for right or for wrong, has made them American citizens; and the moment they were clothed with that attribute of citizenship they stood on a political and legal equality with every other citizen, be he whom he may. And I repel and repudiate the idea that there is any intention by the provisions of any one of these bills to make any social equality. That is simply an argument to the prejudice.

Social equality is not effected or affected by law. It can only come from the voluntary will of each person. Each man can in spite of the law, and does in spite of the law, choose his own associates.

But it is said we put them into the cars. The men that are put into the cars and the women that are put into the cars I trust are not my associates. There are many white men and white women whom I should prefer not to associate with who have a right to ride in the cars. That is not a question of society at all; it is a question of a common right in a public conveyance.

And so in regard of places of amusement, in regard to theaters. I do not understand that a theater is a social gathering. I do not understand that men gather there for society, except the society they choose to make each for himself. So in regard to inns....

... There is not a white man [in] the South that would not associate with the negro — all that is required by this bill — if that negro were his servant. He would eat with him, suckle from her, play with her or him as children, be together with them in every way, provided they were slaves. There never has been an objection to such an association. But the moment that you elevate this black man to citizenship from a slave, then immediately he becomes offensive. That is why I say that this prejudice is foolish, unjust, illogical, and ungentlemanly.

SOURCE: 3 Cong. Rec. 939–40 (1875).

303, 306 (1880). The Equal Protection Clause was available to offer that protection. As the Court later admitted, however, that Clause was "[v]irtually strangled in infancy by post-civil-war judicial reactionism." Regents of the University of California v. Bakke, 438 U.S. 265, 291 (1978), quoting with approval a law review article.

The Court recognized the authority of Congress, under Section 5 of the Fourteenth Amendment, to enact appropriate legislation to enforce the amendment. State judges who excluded blacks from grand and petit juries could be indicted for violating federal law. The purpose of the Civil War amendments was to "raise the colored race from that condition of inferiority and servitude in which most of them had previously stood, into perfect equality of civil rights with all other persons within the jurisdiction of the States." Ex parte Virginia, 100 U.S. 339, 344–45 (1880). When states excluded blacks from grand juries on the ground that they were "utterly unqualified by want of intelligence, experience, or moral integrity," the Court dismissed the indictments issued by the grand jury. Neal v. Delaware, 103 U.S. 370, 394 (1880). However, when Alabama prohibited interracial cohabitation or marriage and imposed heavier penalties for interracial cohabitation than for cohabitation by those of the same race, a unanimous Court discovered no violation of the Equal Protection Clause of the Fourteenth Amendment. Pace v. Alabama, 106 U.S. 583 (1883).

Civil Rights Cases (1883)

The major case from this period was the Court's decision to strike down the Civil Rights Act of 1875, which had made all public accommodations available regardless of race. The Court held that Section 5 of the Fourteenth Amendment empowered Congress only to enforce the prohibitions placed upon the states. Congress could regulate only "state action," not discrimination by private parties. The Court suggested that Congress might invoke the commerce power to regulate rights in public conveyances passing from one state to another, but that question was not before the Court. Justice Harlan issued the sole dissent, pointing out that for centuries the common law had prohibited private parties from acting in a discriminatory fashion toward travelers who needed access to inns and restaurants. Because of the Court's action, what could have been accomplished in 1875 had to await the Civil Rights Act of 1964. CIVIL RIGHTS CASES, 109 U.S. 3 (1883).

The Court initially believed that the "one pervading purpose" of the Civil War amendments was to free enslaved blacks and protect their freedoms. Slaughter-House Cases, 16 Wall. 36, 71 (1873), reprinted in Chapter 9. Although the Fourteenth Amendment appeared to give limited protection to blacks, a unanimous Court in 1886 declared a San Francisco ordinance discriminatory against Chinese operators of laundries. Announced as a fire-prevention measure, the ordinance required all laundries in wooden buildings to obtain a permit. Local authorities denied permission to a majority of Chinese, but all of the non-Chinese laundries, except for one, were allowed to continue. The Court found the ordinance "purely arbitrary" and a violation of the Equal Protection Clause of the Fourteenth Amendment. Yick Wo v. Hopkins, 118 U.S. 356 (1886).

Yick Wo illustrates that the Fourteenth Amendment, intended to grant rights to newly freed blacks, applies literally to "all persons." Yick Wo was not a U.S. citizen; he was still a subject of the Emperor of China. However, the Fourteenth Amendment protects all persons, not all citizens. As the nation filled with immigrants, the Equal Protection Clause of the Fourteenth Amendment was extended "to all ethnic groups seeking protection from official discrimination": Celtic Irish, Chinese, Austrian resident aliens, Japanese, and Mexican-Americans. Regents of the University of California v. Bakke, 438 U.S. at 292. Similarly, although Congress passed civil rights legislation in 1866 and 1870 to protect blacks (currently §§ 1981 and 1982), those statutory provisions apply to all groups subjected to discrimination solely because of their ancestry or ethnic characteristics, including Jews and Arabs. Shaare Tefila Congregation v. Cobb, 481 U.S. 615 (1987); Saint Francis College v. Al-Khazraji, 481 U.S. 604 (1987).

Separate but Equal

The Fourteenth Amendment extended civil rights to blacks, but a number of states (not only in the South) invoked the police power to require separate facilities. Racial segregation applied to transportation, education, housing, parks, hospitals, restaurants, hotels, theaters, waiting rooms, and bathrooms. Statutes and ordinances even required separate phone booths for blacks and whites and separate textbooks. Black and white prostitutes had to be kept in separate districts. Regents of the University of California v. Bakke, 438 U.S. at 393.

When states attempted to require shared accommodations for public transportation, a unanimous Court held that these statutes, to the extent that they regulated interstate commerce, were unconstitutional and void. Hall v. DeCuir, 95 U.S. 485 (1878). Mississippi passed a law in 1888 that required all railroads (other than streetcars) carrying passengers within the state to provide equal, but separate, accommodations for whites and blacks. A 7–2 Court ruled that the statute did not violate the Commerce Clause because the law applied solely to commerce within the state. Louisville &c. Railway Co. v. Mississippi, 133 U.S. 587 (1890).

In 1896 the Supreme Court upheld a Louisiana statute that required railroads to provide equal, but separate, accommodations for white and black passengers. At that time, the tide of public opinion ran strongly against the policy of shared accommodations. The Court said that "in the nature of things" it could not have been intended to force the commingling of the two races. Laws requiring their separation "do not necessarily imply the inferiority of either race to the other" and were within the police power of the states. Justice Harlan was the sole dissenter. PLESSY v. FERGUSON, 163 U.S. 537, 544 (1896).

The separate-but-equal doctrine saddled state governments with heavy financial costs, requiring duplicate facilities for whites and blacks. In 1914 a unanimous Court upheld an Oklahoma statute that required separate-but-equal train accommodations for whites and blacks. As it was restricted to intrastate commerce, the Court found no constitutional infirmity. However, it rejected the railroads' contention that they could provide dining and Pullman (sleeper) cars for whites only, because there were insufficient blacks to justify separate cars. States had to bear the expense of separate facilities. McCabe v. A., T. & S.F. Ry. Co., 235 U.S. 151 (1914).

Bus and train systems changed from intrastate to interstate, making it difficult for states to defend a separate-but-equal policy. In 1941 a unanimous Court held that the treatment of a black on an interstate journey—denying him the right to use an available seat in a Pullman car after he had paid a first-class fare and requiring him to leave that car and ride in a second-class car—was unjust and violated the Interstate Commerce Act. Moreover, the Court found that the accommodations for black passengers were substantially inferior to those for white passengers. Mitchell v. United States, 313 U.S. 80 (1941).

A Virginia statute required all passenger motor vehicle carriers, both interstate and intrastate, to separate the races. A black was convicted for refusing to move to the back of an interstate bus that traveled from Virginia through the District of Columbia to Baltimore, Maryland. A 7–1 Court held the statute invalid because it interfered with interstate commerce and disrupted the uniformity and convenience required for national travel. To comply with the Virginia law, black passengers traveling from the north would have to change their seats once they entered Virginia. Morgan v. Virginia, 328 U.S. 373 (1946). Finally, a unanimous Court in 1950 decided that an interstate railroad's separation of races in the dining car violated the Interstate Commerce Act, which made it unlawful for a railroad in interstate commerce "to subject any particular person . . . to any undue or unreasonable prejudice or disadvantage in any respect whatsoever." The Court thus disposed of this issue on statutory, not constitutional, grounds. Henderson v. United States, 339 U.S. 816 (1950). Therefore, before the Court handed down its Desegregation Decision in 1954, a combination of factors had chipped away at the policy of separate-but-equal facilities for transportation. The next section on school desegregation identifies other decisions, before 1954, that undermined the separate-but-equal doctrine.

Civil Rights Cases

109 U.S. 3 (1883)

Congress passed the Civil Rights Act of 1875 to extend to blacks the full and equal enjoyment of public accommodations, including inns, transportation on land and water, theaters, and other places of amusement. The statute also provided penalties for anyone who denied these privileges to black people. Owners of hotels, theaters, and a railroad were indicted. The question for the Court was whether the Thirteenth and Fourteenth Amendments prohibited only state action or private action as well.

MR. JUSTICE BRADLEY delivered the opinion of the court. After stating the facts in the above language he continued:

It is obvious that the primary and important question in all the cases is the constitutionality of the law: for if the law is unconstitutional none of the prosecutions can stand.

The sections of the law referred to provide as follows:

"SEC. 1. That all persons within the jurisdiction of the United States shall be entitled to the full and equal enjoyment of the accommodations, advantages, facilities, and privileges of inns, public conveyances on land or water, theatres, and other places of public amusement; subject only to the conditions and limitations established by law, and applicable alike to citizens of every race and color, regardless of any previous condition of servitude.

"SEC. 2. That any person who shall violate the foregoing section ... shall for every such offence forfeit and pay the sum of five hundred dollars to the person aggrieved thereby, to be recovered in an action of debt, with full costs; and shall also, for every such offence, be deemed guilty of a misdemeanor, and, upon conviction thereof, shall be fined not less than five hundred nor more than one thousand dollars, or shall be imprisoned not less than thirty days nor more than one year...."

. . .

Has Congress constitutional power to make such a law? Of course, no one will contend that the power to pass it was contained in the Constitution before the adoption of the last three amendments. The power is sought, first, in the Fourteenth Amendment, and the views and arguments of distinguished Senators, advanced whilst the law was under consideration, claiming authority to pass it by virtue of that amendment, are the principal arguments adduced in favor of the power. We have carefully considered those arguments, as was due to the eminent ability of those who put them forward, and have felt, in all its force, the weight of authority which always invests a law that Congress deems itself competent to pass. But the responsibility of an independent judgment is now thrown upon this court; and we are bound to exercise it according to the best lights we have.

The first section of the Fourteenth Amendment (which is the one relied on), after declaring who shall be citizens of the United States, and of the several States, is prohibitory in its character, and prohibitory upon the States. It declares that:

"No State shall make or enforce any law which shall abridge the privileges or immunities of citizens of the United States; nor shall any State deprive any person of life, liberty, or property without due process of law; nor deny to any person within its jurisdiction the equal protection of the laws."

It is State action of a particular character that is prohibited. Individual invasion of individual rights is not the subject-matter of the amendment. It has a deeper and broader scope. It nullifies and makes void all State legislation, and State action of every kind, which impairs the privileges and immunities of citizens of the United States, or which injures them in life, liberty or property without due process of law, or which denies to any of them the equal protection of the laws. It not only does this, but, in order that the national will, thus declared, may not be a mere *brutum fulmen,* the last section of the amendment invests Congress with power to enforce it by appropriate legislation. To enforce what? To enforce the prohibition. To adopt appropriate legislation for correcting the effects of such prohibited State laws and State acts, and thus to render them effectually null, void, and innocuous. This is the legislative power conferred upon Congress, and this is the whole of it. It does not invest Congress with power to legislate upon subjects which are within the domain of State legislation; but to provide modes of relief against State legislation, or State action, of the kind referred to. It does not authorize Congress to create a code of municipal law for the regulation of private rights; but to provide modes of redress against the operation of State laws, and the action of State officers executive or judicial, when these are subversive of the fundamental rights specified in the amendment....

. . .

We have discussed the question presented by the law on the assumption that a right to enjoy equal accommodation and privileges in all inns, public conveyances, and places of public amusement, is one of the essential rights of the citizen which no State can abridge or interfere with. Whether it is such a right, or not, is a different question which, in the view we have taken of the validity of the law on the ground already stated, it is not necessary to examine.

We have also discussed the validity of the law in reference to cases arising in the States only; and not in reference to cases arising in the Territories or the District of Columbia, which are subject to the plenary legislation of Congress in every branch of municipal regulation. Whether the law would be a valid one as applied to the Territories and the District is not a question for consideration in the cases before us; they all being cases arising within the limits of States. And whether Congress, in the exercise of its power to regulate commerce amongst the several States, might or might not pass a law regulating rights in public conveyances passing from one State to another, is also a question which is not now before us, as the sections in question are not conceived in any such view.

But the power of Congress to adopt direct and primary, as distinguished from corrective legislation, on the subject in hand, is sought, in the second place, from the Thirteenth Amendment, which abolishes slavery. This amendment declares "that neither slavery, nor involuntary servitude, except as a punishment for crime, whereof the party shall have been duly convicted, shall exist within the United States, or any place subject to their jurisdiction;" and it gives Congress power to enforce the amendment by appropriate legislation.

. . .

. . . [I]t is assumed, that the power vested in Congress to enforce the article by appropriate legislation, clothes Congress with power to pass all laws necessary and proper for abolishing all badges and incidents of slavery in the United States: and upon this assumption it is claimed, that this is sufficient authority for declaring by law that all persons shall have equal accommodations and privileges in all inns, public conveyances, and places of amusement; the argument being, that the denial of such equal accommodations and privileges is, in itself, a subjection to a species of servitude within the meaning of the amendment. . . .

Now, conceding, for the sake of the argument, that the admission to an inn, a public conveyance, or a place of public amusement, on equal terms with all other citizens, is the right of every man and all classes of men, is it any more than one of those rights which the states by the Fourteenth Amendment are forbidden to deny to any person? And is the Constitution violated until the denial of the right has some State sanction or authority? Can the act of a mere individual, the owner of the inn, the public conveyance or place of amuse-

ment, refusing the accommodation, be justly regarded as imposing any badge of slavery or servitude upon the applicant, or only as inflicting an ordinary civil injury, properly cognizable by the laws of the State, and presumably subject to redress by those laws until the contrary appears?

After giving to these questions all the consideration which their importance demands, we are forced to the conclusion that such an act of refusal has nothing to do with slavery or involuntary servitude, and that if it is violative of any right of the party, his redress is to be sought under the laws of the State; or if those laws are adverse to his rights and do not protect him, his remedy will be found in the corrective legislation which Congress has adopted, or may adopt, for counteracting the effect of State laws, or State action, prohibited by the Fourteenth Amendment. It would be running the slavery argument into the ground to make it apply to every act of discrimination which a person may see fit to make as to the guests he will entertain, or as to the people he will take into his coach or cab or car, or admit to his concert or theatre, or deal with in other matters of intercourse or business. . . .

When a man has emerged from slavery, and by the aid of beneficent legislation has shaken off the inseparable concomitants of that state, there must be some stage in the progress of his elevation when he takes the rank of a mere citizen, and ceases to be the special favorite of the laws, and when his rights as a citizen, or a man, are to be protected in the ordinary modes by which other men's rights are protected. There were thousands of free colored people in this country before the abolition of slavery, enjoying all the essential rights of life, liberty and property the same as white citizens; yet no one, at that time, thought that it was any invasion of his personal status as a freeman because he was not admitted to all the privileges enjoyed by white citizens, or because he was subjected to discriminations in the enjoyment of accommodations in inns, public conveyances and places of amusement. Mere discriminations on account of race or color were not regarded as badges of slavery. If, since that time, the enjoyment of equal rights in all these respects has become established by constitutional enactment, it is not by force of the Thirteenth Amendment (which merely abolishes slavery), but by force of the Thirteenth and Fifteenth Amendments.

. . .

. . . [T]he answer to be given will be that the first and second sections of the act of Congress of March 1st, 1875, entitled "An Act to protect all citizens in their civil and legal rights," are unconstitutional and void, and that judgment should be rendered upon the several indictments in those cases accordingly.

And it is so ordered.

Mr. Justice Harlan dissenting.

The opinion in these cases proceeds, it seems to me, upon grounds entirely too narrow and artificial. I cannot resist the conclusion that the substance and spirit of the recent amendments of the Constitution have been sacrificed by a subtle and ingenious verbal criticism....

...It remains now to inquire what are the legal rights of colored persons in respect of the accommodations, privileges and facilities of public conveyances, inns and places of public amusement?

First, as to public conveyances on land and water. *[Earlier cases ruled that]* railroads are public highways, established by authority of the State for the public use; that they are none the less public highways, because controlled and owned by private corporations; that it is a part of the function of government to make and maintain highways for the conveyance of the public; that no matter who is the agent, or what is the agency, the function performed is *that of the State;*...

Second, *as to inns. The same general observations which have been made as to railroads are applicable to inns. The word "inn" has a technical legal signification. It means, in the act of 1875, just what it meant at common law. A mere private boarding-house is not an inn, nor is its keeper subject to the responsibilities, or entitled to the privileges of a common innkeeper. "To constitute one an innkeeper, within the legal force of that term, he must keep a house of entertainment or lodging for all travellers or wayfarers who might choose to accept the same, being of good character or conduct."* Redfield on Carriers, etc., § 575. *Says Judge Story:*

"An innkeeper may be defined to be the keeper of a common inn for the lodging and entertainment of travellers and passengers, their horses and attendants. An innkeeper is bound to take in all travellers and wayfaring persons, and to entertain them, if he can accommodate them, for a reasonable compensation; and he must guard their goods with proper diligence....If an innkeeper improperly refuses to receive or provide for a guest, he is liable to be indicted therefor....They (carriers of passengers) are no more

at liberty to refuse a passenger, if they have sufficient room and accommodations, than an innkeeper is to refuse suitable room and accommodations to a guest." Story on Bailments, §§ 475–6.

. . .

...[A] keeper of an inn is in the exercise of a quasi public employment. The law gives him special privileges and he is charged with certain duties and responsibilities to the public. The public nature of his employment forbids him from discriminating against any person asking admission as a guest on account of the race or color of that person.

Third. As to places of public amusement. It may be argued that the managers of such places have no duties to perform with which the public are, in any legal sense, concerned, or with which the public have any right to interfere; and, that the exclusion of a black man from a place of public amusement, on account of his race, or the denial to him, on that ground, of equal accommodations at such places, violates no legal right for the vindication of which he may invoke the aid of the courts. My answer is, that places of public amusement, within the meaning of the act of 1875, are such as are established and maintained under direct license of the law. The authority to establish and maintain them comes from the public. The colored race is a part of that public. The local government granting the license represents them as well as all other races within its jurisdiction. A license from the public to establish a place of public amusement, imports, in law, equality of right, at such places, among all the members of that public....

...I agree that government has nothing to do with social, as distinguished from technically legal, rights of individuals. No government ever has brought, or ever can bring, its people into social intercourse against their wishes. Whether one person will permit or maintain social relations with another is a matter with which government has no concern. I agree that if one citizen chooses not to hold social intercourse with another, he is not and cannot be made amenable to the law for his conduct in that regard; for no legal right of a citizen is violated by the refusal of others to maintain merely social relations with him, even upon grounds of race. What I affirm is that no State, nor the officers of any State, nor any corporation or individual wielding power under State authority for the public benefit or the public convenience, can, consistently either with the freedom established by the fundamental law, or with that equality of civil rights which now belongs to every citizen, discriminate against freemen or citizens, in those rights, because of their race, or because they once labored under the disabilities of slavery imposed upon them as a race. The rights which Congress, by the act of 1875, endeavored to secure and protect are legal, not social rights. The right, for instance, of a colored citizen to use the accommodations of a public highway, upon the same terms as are permitted to white citizens, is no more a social right than his right, under the law, to use the public streets of a city or a town, or a turnpike road, or a public market, or a post office, or his right to sit in a public building with others, of whatever race, for the purpose of hearing the political questions of the day discussed....

. . .

My brethren say, that when a man has

emerged from slavery, and by the aid of beneficent legislation has shaken off the inseparable concomitants of that state, there must be some stage in the progress of his elevation when he takes the rank of a mere citizen, and ceases to be the special favorite of the laws, and when his rights as a citizen, or a man, are to be protected in the ordinary modes by which other men's rights are protected. It is, I submit, scarcely just to say that the colored race has been the special favorite of the laws. The statute of 1875, now adjudged to be unconstitutional, is for the benefit of citizens of every race and color. What the nation, through Congress, has sought to accomplish in reference to that race, is—what had already been done in every State of the Union for the white race—to secure and protect rights belonging to them as freemen and citizens; nothing more....

Plessy v. Ferguson

163 U.S. 537 (1896)

After the Civil War, and despite the Thirteenth and Fourteenth Amendments, some of the states began to adopt segregationist policies by creating "separate-but-equal" facilities for blacks and whites. Eventually, the policy extended to schools, transportation, parks, and other public accommodations. This case involved a Louisiana law that required separate railway cars for whites and blacks. Homer A. Plessy, one-eighth black, was arrested for attempting to sit in a railroad coach reserved for whites. He appealed an order by a state judge, John Ferguson.

MR. JUSTICE BROWN, after stating the case, delivered the opinion of the court.

This case turns upon the constitutionality of an act of the General Assembly of the State of Louisiana, passed in 1890, providing for separate railway carriages for the white and colored races. Acts 1890, No. 111, p. 152.

The first section of the statute enacts "that all railway companies carrying passengers in their coaches in this State, shall provide equal but separate accommodations for the white, and colored races, by providing two or more passenger coaches for each passenger train, or by dividing the passenger coaches by a partition so as to secure separate accommodations: *Provided,* That this section shall not be construed to apply to street railroads. No person or persons, shall be admitted to occupy seats in coaches, other than, the ones assigned, to them on account of the race they belong to."

[Sections two and three provided for fines and imprisonment for those who failed to comply with

the statute, with a proviso that "nothing in this act shall be construed as applying to nurses attending children of the other race."]

The information filed in the criminal District Court charged in substance that Plessy, being a passenger between two stations within the State of Louisiana, was assigned by officers of the company to the coach used for the race to which he belonged, but he insisted upon going into a coach used by the race to which he did not belong. Neither in the information nor plea was his particular race or color averred.

The petition for the writ of prohibition averred that petitioner was seven eighths Caucasian and one eighth African blood; that the mixture of colored blood was not discernible in him, and that he was entitled to every right, privilege and immunity secured to citizens of the United States of the white race; and that, upon such theory, he took possession of a vacant seat in a coach where passengers of the white race were accommodated, and was ordered by the conductor to vacate said coach and take a seat in another assigned to persons of the colored race, and having refused to comply with such demand he was forcibly ejected with the aid of a police officer, and imprisoned in the parish jail to answer a charge of having violated the above act.

The constitutionality of this act is attacked upon the ground that it conflicts both with the Thirteenth Amendment of the Constitution, abolishing slavery, and the Fourteenth Amendment, which prohibits certain restrictive legislation on the part of the States.

1. That it does not conflict with the Thirteenth Amendment, which abolished slavery and involuntary servitude, except as a punishment for crime, is too clear for argument. Slavery implies involuntary servitude—a state of bondage; the ownership of mankind as a chattel, or at least the control of the labor and services of one man for the benefit of another, and the absence of a legal right to the disposal of his own person, property and services. This amendment was said in the *Slaughter-house cases,* 16 Wall. 36, to have been intended primarily to abolish slavery, as it had been previously known in this country, and that it equally forbade Mexican peonage or the Chinese coolie trade, when they amounted to slavery or involuntary servitude, and that the use of the word "servitude" was intended to prohibit the use of all forms of involuntary slavery, of whatever class or name. It was intimated, however, in that case that this amendment was regarded by the statesmen of that day as insufficient to protect the colored race from certain laws which had been enacted in the Southern States, imposing upon the colored race onerous disabilities and burdens, and curtailing their rights in the pursuit of life, liberty and property to such an extent that their freedom was of little value; and that the Fourteenth Amendment was devised to meet this exigency.

So, too, in the *Civil Rights cases,* 109 U.S. 3, 24, it was said that the act of a mere individual, the owner of an inn, a public conveyance or place of amusement, refusing accommodations to colored people, cannot be justly regarded as imposing any badge of slavery or servitude upon the applicant, but only as involving an ordinary civil injury, properly cognizable by the laws of the State, and presumably subject to redress by those laws until the contrary appears....

A statute which implies merely a legal distinction between the white and colored races—a distinction which is founded in the color of the two races, and which must always exist so long as white men are distinguished from the other race by color—has no tendency to destroy the legal equality of the two races, or reëstablish a state of involuntary servitude. Indeed, we do not understand that the Thirteenth Amendment is strenuously relied upon by the plaintiff in error in this connection.

2. By the Fourteenth Amendment, all persons born or naturalized in the United States, and subject to the jurisdiction thereof, are made citizens of the United States and of the State wherein they reside; and the States are forbidden from making or enforcing any law which shall abridge the privileges or immunities of citizens of the United States, or shall deprive any person of life, liberty or property without due process of law, or deny to any person within their jurisdiction the equal protection of the laws.

The proper construction of this amendment was first called to the attention of this court in the *Slaughter-house cases,* 16 Wall. 36, which involved, however, not a question of race, but one of exclusive privileges. The case did not call for any expression of opinion as to the exact rights it was intended to secure to the colored race, but it was said generally that its main purpose was to establish the citizenship of the negro; to give definitions of citizenship of the United States and of the States, and to protect from the hostile legislation of the States the privileges and immunities of citizens of the United States, as distinguished from those of citizens of the States.

The object of the amendment was undoubtedly to enforce the absolute equality of the two races before the law, but in the nature of things it could not have been intended to abolish distinctions based upon color, or to enforce social, as distinguished from political equality, or a commingling of the two races upon terms unsatisfactory to either. Laws permitting, and even requiring, their separation in places where they are liable to be brought into contact do not necessarily imply the inferiority of either race to the other, and have been generally, if not universally, recognized as within the competency of the state legislatures in the exercise of their police power. The most common instance of this is connected with the establishment of separate schools for white and colored children, which has been held to be a valid exercise of the legislative power even by courts of States where the political rights of the colored race have been longest and most earnestly enforced.

. . .

So far, then, as a conflict with the Fourteenth Amendment is concerned, the case reduces itself to the question whether the statute of Louisiana is a reasonable regulation, and with respect to this there must necessarily be a large discretion on the part of the legislature. In determining the question of reasonableness it is at liberty to act with reference to the established usages, customs and traditions of the people, and with a view to the promotion of their comfort, and the preservation of the public peace and good order. Gauged by this standard, we cannot say that a law which authorizes or even requires the separation of the two races in public conveyances is unreasonable, or more obnoxious to the Fourteenth Amendment than the acts of Congress requiring separate schools for colored children in the District of Columbia, the constitutionality of which does not seem to have been questioned, or the corresponding acts of state legislatures.

We consider the underlying fallacy of the plaintiff's argument to consist in the assumption that the enforced separation of the two races stamps the colored race with a badge of inferiority. If this be so, it is not by reason of anything found in the act, but solely because the colored race chooses to put that construction upon it. The argument necessarily assumes that if, as has been more than once the case, and is not unlikely to be so again, the colored race should become the dominant power in the state legislature, and should enact a law in precisely similar terms, it would thereby relegate the white race to an inferior position. We imagine that the white race, at least, would not acquiesce in this assumption. The argument also assumes that social prejudices may be overcome by legislation, and that equal rights cannot be secured to the negro except by an enforced commingling of the two races. We cannot accept this proposition. If the two races are to meet upon terms of social equality, it must be the result of natural affinities, a mutual appreciation of each other's merits and a voluntary consent of individuals. . . . If the civil and political rights of both races be equal one cannot be inferior to the other civilly or politically. If one race be inferior to the other socially, the Constitution of the United States cannot put them upon the same plane.

It is true that the question of the proportion of colored blood necessary to constitute a colored person, as distinguished from a white person, is one upon which there is a difference of opinion in the different States, some holding that any visible admixture of black blood stamps the person as belonging to the colored race, (*State* v. *Chavers, 5*

Jones, [N.C.] 1, p. 11); others that it depends upon the preponderance of blood, (*Gray* v. *State,* 4 Ohio, 354; *Monroe* v. *Collins,* 17 Ohio St. 665); and still others that the predominance of white blood must only be in the proportion of three fourths. (*People* v. *Dean,* 14 Michigan, 406; *Jones* v. *Commonwealth,* 80 Virginia, 538.) But these are questions to be determined under the laws of each State and are not properly put in issue in this case. Under the allegations of his petition it may undoubtedly become a question of importance whether, under the laws of Louisiana, the petitioner belongs to the white or colored race.

The judgment of the court below is, therefore,

Affirmed.

MR. JUSTICE HARLAN dissenting.

. . .

However apparent the injustice of such legislation may be, we have only to consider whether it is consistent with the Constitution of the United States.

That a railroad is a public highway, and that the corporation which owns or operates it is in the exercise of public functions, is not, at this day, to be disputed. . . .

In respect of civil rights, common to all citizens, the Constitution of the United States does not, I think, permit any public authority to know the race of those entitled to be protected in the enjoyment of such rights. Every true man has pride of race, and under appropriate circumstances when the rights of others, his equals before the law, are not to be affected, it is his privilege to express such pride and to take such action based upon it as to him seems proper. But I deny that any legislative body or judicial tribunal may have regard to the race of citizens when the civil rights of those citizens are involved. . . .

. . .

It was said in argument that the statute of Louisiana does not discriminate against either race, but prescribes a rule applicable alike to white and colored citizens. But this argument does not meet the difficulty. Every one knows that the statute in question had its origin in the purpose, not so much to exclude white persons from railroad cars occupied by blacks, as to exclude colored people from coaches occupied by or assigned to white persons. . . .

The white race deems itself to be the dominant race in this country. And so it is, in prestige, in achievements, in education, in wealth and in power. So, I doubt not, it will continue to be for all time, if it remains true to its great heritage and holds fast to the principles of constitutional liberty. But in view of the Constitution, in the eye of the law, there is in this country no superior, dominant, ruling class of citizens. There is no caste here. Our Constitution is color-blind, and neither knows nor tolerates classes among citizens. In respect of civil rights, all citizens are equal before the law. The humblest is the peer of the most powerful. The law regards man as man, and takes no account of his surroundings or of his color when his civil rights as guaranteed by the supreme law of the land are involved. It is, therefore, to be regretted that this high tribunal, the final expositor of the fundamental law of the land, has reached the conclusion that it is competent for a State to regulate the enjoyment by citizens of their civil rights solely upon the basis of race.

In my opinion, the judgment this day rendered will, in time, prove to be quite as pernicious as the decision made by this tribunal in the *Dred Scott case*.... The recent amendments of the Constitution, it was supposed, had eradicated these principles from our institutions. But it seems that we have yet, in some of the States, a dominant race — a superior class of citizens, which assumes to regulate the enjoyment of civil rights, common to all citizens, upon the basis of race. The present decision, it may well be apprehended, will not only stimulate aggressions, more or less brutal and irritating, upon the admitted rights of colored citizens, but will encourage the belief that it is possible, by means of state enactments, to defeat the beneficent purposes which the people of the United States had in view when they adopted the recent amendments of the Constitution, by one of which the blacks of this country were made citizens of the United States and of the States in which they respectively reside, and whose privileges and immunities, as citizens, the States are forbidden to abridge. Sixty millions of whites are in no danger from the presence here of eight millions of blacks. The destinies of the two races, in this country, are indissolubly linked together, and the interests of both require that the common government of all shall not permit the seeds of race hate to be planted under the sanction of law. What can more certainly arouse race hate, what more certainly create and perpetuate a feeling of distrust between these races, than state enact-

ments, which, in fact, proceed on the ground that colored citizens are so inferior and degraded that they cannot be allowed to sit in public coaches occupied by white citizens? That, as all will admit, is the real meaning of such legislation as was enacted in Louisiana.

. . .

There is a race so different from our own that we do not permit those belonging to it to become citizens of the United States. Persons belonging to it are, with few exceptions, absolutely excluded from our country. I allude to the Chinese race. But by the statute in question, a Chinaman can ride in the same passenger coach with white citizens of the United States, while citizens of the black race in Louisiana, many of whom, perhaps, risked their lives for the preservation of the Union, who are entitled, by law, to participate in the political control of the State and nation, who are not excluded, by law or by reason of their race, from public stations of any kind, and who have all the legal rights that belong to white citizens, are yet declared to be criminals, liable to imprisonment, if they ride in a public coach occupied by citizens of the white race....

The arbitrary separation of citizens, on the basis of race, while they are on a public highway, is a badge of servitude wholly inconsistent with the civil freedom and the equality before the law established by the Constitution. It cannot be justified upon any legal grounds.

If evils will result from the commingling of the two races upon public highways established for the benefit of all, they will be infinitely less than those that will surely come from state legislation regulating the enjoyment of civil rights upon the basis of race. We boast of the freedom enjoyed by our people above all other peoples. But it is difficult to reconcile that boast with a state of the law which, practically, puts the brand of servitude and degradation upon a large class of our fellow-citizens, our equals before the law. The thin disguise of "equal" accommodations for passengers in railroad coaches will not mislead any one, nor atone for the wrong this day done.

. . .

MR. JUSTICE BREWER did not hear the argument or participate in the decision of this case.

The *Carolene* Footnote

[In 1938, at a time when the Supreme Court was withdrawing its scrutiny of economic regulation, Justice Stone wrote a footnote indicating that the Court had a special duty to safeguard minority rights. United States v. Carolene Products Co., 304 U.S. 144, 153 n.4 (1938). His formulation later evolved into a "strict scrutiny" analysis for protecting fundamental rights, including issues of race discrimination.]

There may be narrower scope for operation of the presumption of constitutionality when legislation appears on its face to be within a specific prohibition of the Constitution, such as those of the first ten amendments, which are deemed equally specific when held to be embraced within the Fourteenth....

It is unnecessary to consider now whether legislation which restricts those political processes which can ordinarily be expected to bring about repeal of undesirable legislation, is to be subjected to more exacting judicial scrutiny under the general prohibitions of the Fourteenth Amendment than are most other types of legislation *[restrictions upon the right to vote, to disseminate information, and interferences with political organizations and peaceable assembly].*

Nor need we enquire whether similar considerations enter into the review of statutes directed at particular religious...or national... or racial minorities...; whether prejudice against discrete and insular minorities may be a special condition, which tends seriously to curtail the operation of those political processes ordinarily to be relied upon to protect minorities, and which may call for a correspondingly more searching judicial inquiry....

C. SCHOOL DESEGREGATION

Like transportation, the policy of separate-but-equal in education became increasingly impractical. Various forces helped erode this practice long before the Court struck it down in 1954. Part of the shift toward desegregation reflected a mobile society, with each state receiving new visitors and new challenges to its customs. Another factor was foreign policy. Competition with international communism after World War II put pressure on the United States to abolish segregation and bring practices in line with American ideals.

Plessy reinforced the separate-but-equal doctrine in many fields, including education. A unanimous Court in 1899 ruled that schools, even if segregated, were a matter belonging to the states. The opinion was written by Justice Harlan, the lone dissenter in *Plessy*. Cumming v. Board of Education, 175 U.S. 528 (1899). States were permitted to outlaw integrated education in private colleges. Berea College v. Kentucky, 211 U.S. 45 (1908). A unanimous ruling held that states had discretion to assign Chinese children to attend public schools with blacks. Gong Lum v. Rice, 275 U.S. 78 (1927).

Opponents of *Plessy* decided to file lawsuits to attack the most vulnerable area: segregated graduate schools. The timing was propitious. During the late 1930s, the courts began to abandon use of the Due Process Clause to protect property interests ("substantive due process") and relied more on the Equal Protection Clause to defend individual rights. Regents of the University of California v. Bakke, 438 U.S. at 291–92. This attitude was expressed most forcefully in a famous footnote by Justice Stone. In reviewing the standards for judicial review and the choice between activism and restraint, he suggested that the courts might have a special responsibility for protecting "discrete and insular minorities," particularly when political processes relied upon to protect minorities have been curtailed (see box). Although this footnote has never been adopted as the holding of the Court, it expressed a solicitude that captures much of the Court's work in racial discrimination since 1938.

Beginning in 1936, Court decisions on the separate-but-equal policy in higher education gradually painted *Plessy* into an ever-narrowing corner. In one case, black applicants were denied admission to the law school at the University of Maryland. As compensation, the state offered to pay their tuition to a law school outside the state. A unanimous appellate court in Maryland ruled that this policy violated the Equal Protection Clause. Blacks would encounter greater costs traveling to another state and paying additional living expenses. Moreover, an education outside the state would not adequately prepare blacks who intended to practice in Maryland. Pearson v. Murray, 182 A. 593 (Md. 1936). Missouri also wanted to pay black students their tuition costs for a law school education in an adjacent state. The Supreme Court, divided 7–2, held that this policy violated the Equal Protection Clause by creating a privilege for white law students (able to attend the Missouri law school) that was denied to blacks. Missouri ex rel. Gaines v. Canada, 305 U.S. 337 (1938). See also Sipuel v. Board of Regents, 332 U.S. 631 (1948) and Fisher v. Hurst, 333 U.S. 147 (1948).

The next effort to preserve *Plessy* was to create a separate law school for blacks within the state. A unanimous Court in 1950 concluded that the school for blacks did not satisfy the separate-but-equal standard. The University of Texas Law School, attended by whites, was superior in terms of its professional staff, library, law review, moot court facilities, scholarship funds, distinguished alumni, tradition, and prestige. Sweatt v. Painter, 339 U.S. 629 (1950). Oklahoma agreed to admit blacks to the state university but separated them from white students. Blacks had to sit in a special seat in the classroom, a special table in the library, and a special table in the cafeteria. Once again, a unanimous Court found this in violation of the Equal Protection Clause. The restrictions on the black student impaired and inhibited "his ability to study, to engage in discussions and exchange views with other students, and, in general, to learn his profession." McLaurin v. Oklahoma State Regents, 339 U.S. 637 (1950). *Plessy*'s days were clearly numbered.

Brown v. Board of Education

These cases laid the groundwork for the desegregation case of 1954. Other influences were important. The horrors of racism in Nazi Germany, sending millions of Jews to their death in gas chambers and concentration camps, showed the results of preaching a "master race." After the war, President Truman took steps to eliminate discrimination in federal government and to abolish segregation in the armed forces. The United States, which emerged as a world leader after World War II, could not fight world communism while maintaining racial segregation at home. The NAACP's brief observed: "Survival of our country in the present international situation is inevitably tied to resolution of this domestic issue." The federal government's amicus brief in 1952 explained in great detail the harmful effects of American segregation on the foreign policy of the executive branch. Racial discrimination affected American blacks and dark-skinned visitors from other countries, furnishing "grist for the Communist propaganda mills" (see reading).

By the time of the desegregation case of 1954, seventeen states and the District of Columbia required segregated schools. Four other states permitted segregation as a local option. The Supreme Court admitted that in approaching the problem of school segregation "we cannot turn the clock back to 1868 when the [Fourteenth] Amendment was adopted, or even to 1896 when *Plessy* v. *Ferguson* was written." BROWN v. BOARD OF EDUCATION, 347 U.S. 483, 492 (1954). The unanimous decision was the result of much internal bargaining (see box on next page). Segregation, said the Court, generated a feeling of inferiority among black children: "Whatever may have been the extent of psychological knowledge at the time of *Plessy* v. *Ferguson,* this finding [of inequality] is amply supported by modern authority." Following this sentence was a famous footnote, the wisdom of which has been

Building a Unanimous Court

In 1952 and through most of 1953, the Supreme Court appeared to be split down the middle on the constitutionality of segregated schools. Four Justices (Black, Douglas, Burton, and Minton) were ready to overrule *Plessy*. Five Justices (Vinson, Reed, Frankfurter, Jackson, and Clark) either supported *Plessy* or were loath to abandon it. Chief Justice Vinson died on September 8, 1953, and was replaced by Earl Warren. There now seemed to be a 5–4 majority to reverse *Plessy*. Moreover, Clark indicated he was ready to shift sides, giving Warren a 6–3 majority. What could Warren do to attract Reed, Frankfurter, and Jackson and present a united front?

Two of the Southerners on the Court (Clark and Reed) indicated they might join a unanimous decision if enforcement could be done in different ways, and different times, by the states. Jackson and Frankfurter also wanted a flexible remedy. Frankfurter recalled a phrase from Justice Holmes and used it to argue that states could enforce *Brown* "with all deliberate speed" (close to an oxymoron). These vague formulations, helpful in producing a unanimous ruling, also encouraged years of minimal compliance from the states. The broad constitutional rights announced in 1954 were undermined a year later in the implementing decision.

SOURCES: S. Sidney Ulmer, "Earl Warren and the *Brown* Decision," 33 J. Pol. 689, 691–92 (1971); Richard Kluger, Simple Justice 589–614, 682–87, 696–99, 742–45 (1975); William O. Douglas, The Court Years 113 (1980); Bernard Schwartz, Super Chief, 72–127 (1983); and Philip Elman, "The Solicitor General's Office, Justice Frankfurter, and Civil Rights Litigation, 1946–1960: An Oral History," 100 Harv. L. Rev. 817, 842–43 (1987).

extensively debated, citing seven psychological and sociological studies on the effects of discrimination and segregation on children.[2]

In striking down segregated schools in the states, the Court relied on the Equal Protection Clause of the Fourteenth Amendment. What could be used to overturn segregation in the nation's capital? The Fifth Amendment, applicable to the District of Columbia, does not contain an equal protection clause. It would have been intolerable for the Court to invalidate segregated schools in the states and allow them to operate in the District of Columbia. The Court finessed the problem by holding that racial segregation in the D.C. public schools denied black children the due process of law guaranteed by the Fifth Amendment. The concepts of equal protection and due process, "both stemming from our American ideal of fairness, are not mutually exclusive." BOLLING v. SHARPE, 347 U.S. 497, 499 (1954).

In 1955 the Court announced guidelines for implementing its desegregation decision. How quickly were states to make the transition? The Court largely deferred to local school authorities in determining the appropriate course, leaving to federal courts the duty of considering whether school authorities were acting in good faith to comply with desegregation. Several phrases from the Court—including "practical flexibility," "as soon as practicable," "a prompt and reasonable start," and "all deliberate speed"—gave a green light to obstruction and procrastination. BROWN v. BOARD OF EDUCATION, 349 U.S. 294 (1955).

2. See Abraham L. Davis, The United States Supreme Court and the Uses of Social Science Data 48–61, 65–74, 95–118 (1973); William B. Ball, "Lawyers and Social Sciences—Guiding the Guides," 5 Vill. L. Rev. 215 (1959–60); Kenneth B. Clark, "The Desegregation Cases: Criticism of the Social Scientist's Role," 5 Vill. L. Rev. 224 (1959–60); Herbert Garfinkel, "Social Science Evidence and the School Desegregation Cases," 21 J. Pol. 37 (1959); Jack Greenberg, "Social Scientists Take the Stand," 54 Mich. L. Rev. 953 (1956); Edmond Cahn, "Jurisprudence," 30 N.Y.U. L. Rev. 150 (1955).

Political Resistance

In issuing its desegregation decision, the Supreme Court obviously did not have the last word. The Justice Department had given strong encouragement to the Court to strike down segregated schools, but that was during the Truman administration. The amicus brief filed by the Justice Department after Dwight D. Eisenhower became President was not as strong. Eisenhower failed to give full support to the *Brown* decision, perhaps reflecting his belief in states' rights and limited government. In any event, the record after 1954 was marred by massive state resistance and acts of violence against blacks. A major confrontation occurred in Arkansas, when Governor Orval Faubus defied three court orders to integrate the Little Rock Central High School. On September 24, 1957, President Eisenhower sent in armed troops to prevent the obstruction of justice. In a radio and television address to the nation, Eisenhower spoke of the harm done to America's prestige and influence in the world, noting that "enemies are gloating over this incident." Public Papers of the Presidents, 1957, at 694. In 1958, after calling a special term in August, the Court affirmed the lower court orders in the Little Rock crisis. COOPER v. AARON, 358 U.S. 1 (1958).

The Court's insistence on desegregation in 1954 and its announcement of judiciary supremacy in 1958 did little to integrate public schools. As late as 1964, the Court complained that there "has been entirely too much deliberation and not enough speed" in enforcing *Brown* v. *Board of Education.* Griffin v. School Bd., 377 U.S. 218, 229 (1964). The act of finality needed more than a Court decision. The resolution required the concerted action of the elected branches: Congress and the President. A federal appellate court noted in 1966: "A national effort, bringing together Congress, the executive and the judiciary may be able to make meaningful the right of Negro children to equal educational opportunities. *The courts acting alone have failed.*" United States v. Jefferson County Board of Education, 372 F.2d 836, 847 (5th Cir. 1966) (emphasis in original). Three federal statutes, passed in 1957, 1960, and 1964, put the nation on course in eliminating segregation in public facilities. [The Voting Rights Act of 1965 is analyzed in Chapter 18.]

Federal Legislation

The Civil Rights Act of 1957 was the first civil rights measure passed since 1875. It established a Commission on Civil Rights to investigate allegations of discrimination, authorized the President to appoint an additional Assistant Attorney General to head a new Civil Rights Division in the Justice Department, and set fines for those convicted in cases arising from the statute. 71 Stat. 634. The broad investigative powers of the Commission were upheld by the Supreme Court. Hannah v. Larche, 363 U.S. 420 (1960). The Civil Rights Act of 1960 strengthened existing laws on obstruction of court orders, provided criminal penalties for acts of violence and destruction, and authorized court-appointed "referees" to monitor voting rights. 74 Stat. 86.

The major step was the Civil Rights Act of 1964, the most far-reaching civil rights statute since the Reconstruction Era. Public pressure for legislative action included sit-ins, demonstrations, picketing, and boycotts. For the first time on a civil rights bill, Senators were able to vote cloture and stop a filibuster. The legislation passed by top-heavy majorities of 289–126 in the House and 73–27 in the Senate. Bipartisan support was solid. The House voted 153–91 Democrat and 136–35 Republican. The party split in the Senate was 46–21 for Democrats and 27–6 for Republicans. Major factions throughout the country had united to give the final word. 78 Stat. 241.

The statute provided new guarantees for black voters and created a Community Relations Service to help resolve civil rights problems. The most significant sections concerned public accommodations, termination of federal funds, and discrimination in employment. Title IV dealt with desegregation of public education, including elementary, secondary, and higher education. Title VI provided for nondiscrimination in federally assisted programs. If parties receiving federal funds refused to voluntarily comply with the statute, agencies could terminate funds. Termination of assistance was subject to judicial review. Title VII, on equal employment opportunity, outlawed employment practices based on race, color, religion, sex, or national origin. The Act created the Equal Employment Opportunity Commission (EEOC) to enforce the law.

Title VI, threatening a cutoff of federal funds from states that continued racial discrimination in schools, became more significant as the level of federal assistance increased. The Elementary and Secondary Education Act of 1965 provided large federal grants to school districts. It was the first general school aid in the nation's history. School districts now had to decide what they wanted most: segregated schools or federal funds.

De Facto Segregation and Busing

For much of the 1950s and 1960s, smug northerners pretended that segregation was a problem only for the South. Little notice was taken of northern school systems that were segregated in fact (de facto) rather than by law (de jure). Increasingly, inner-city blacks were encircled by white suburbs. What was to be done when segregated schools resulted not from state laws but from residential patterns?

Busing was one possibility. Although busing today is associated with efforts to integrate schools, it can be used just as easily to *promote* segregation. In eastern Virginia, where there was no residential segregation, school buses were used heavily to criss-cross students from one corner of the county to another to maintain all-white and all-black schools. Green v. County School Board, 391 U.S. 430, 432 (1968). The Court said that where it was possible to identify a "white school" or a "black school," a prima facie case existed to show deprivation of constitutional rights. Id. at 435.

In 1971 a unanimous Court held that district courts had broad power to fashion remedies for desegregated schools. To achieve greater racial balance, judges could alter school district zones, reassign teachers, and bus students. SWANN v. CHARLOTTE-MECKLENBURG BD. OF ED., 402 U.S. 1 (1971). A unanimous Court also struck down state antibusing laws. North Carolina State Board of Education v. Swann, 402 U.S. 43 (1971).

These rulings appeared to clash with language in the Civil Rights Act of 1964, which defined *desegregation* as the assignment of students to public schools without regard to their race, color, religion, or national origin, and stated that desegregation "shall not mean the assignment of students to public schools in order to overcome racial imbalance." 78 Stat. 246, § 401(b). In fact, race was regularly taken into account by courts to devise desegregation plans. The Civil Rights Act of 1964 did not empower any federal official or court "to issue any order seeking to achieve a racial balance in any school by requiring the transportation of pupils...." 78 Stat. 248, § 407(a). The Court sidestepped this potential conflict by arguing that the busing provision in the statute was directed at de facto, not de jure, segregation. Swann v. Charlotte-Mecklenburg, 402 U.S. at 17–18.

Within a few years busing was used to integrate schools in non-southern states. A Supreme Court decision in 1973 involved the school system in Denver, Colorado. Parents of black children charged that the school board maintained a segregated system through the use of student attendance zones, school-site selection, and a neighborhood school policy. A 7–1 Court found that the school board intended school segregation in one area, thereby practicing de jure segregation, and that the burden appropriately shifted to the board to prove that other segregated schools were not also the result of intentional actions. Several Justices dismissed the difference between de jure and de facto segregation, preferring that whenever segregated public schools exist there is prima facie evidence of a constitutional violation by the school board. This test avoided the question of whether segregation resulted from "intent" (de jure) or "effect" (de facto). Keyes v. School District No. 1, Denver, Colo., 413 U.S. 189 (1973).

Another non-southern school system scrutinized by the Court was in Detroit. Black families claimed that schools had been racially segregated because of official policies. The lower courts concluded that a Detroit-only solution was inadequate; widespread busing, reaching to outlying districts, would be necessary. The string of unanimous or near-unanimous decisions by the Supreme Court on school segregation now shattered. Divided 5 to 4, the Court dismissed the remedies adopted by the lower courts. It decided that a cross-district busing plan would disrupt school district lines, violate the tradition of local school control, and thrust judges into the role of "school superintendent" for which they are unqualified. The district court had ordered the school board to obtain at least 295 school buses, with the cost borne by the state. The Supreme Court concluded that a metropolitan area remedy punished outlying districts with no showing that they had committed constitutional violations. MIL-LIKEN v. BRADLEY, 418 U.S. 717 (1974). In a follow-up case for Detroit, a unanimous Court agreed that lower courts can order compensatory or remedial educational programs for schoolchildren subjected to past acts of de jure segregation. Assistance included reading instruction, in-service teacher training, testing, and counseling. Milliken v. Bradley, 433 U.S. 267 (1977).

The Supreme Court scrutinized two other northern school systems, in Columbus and Dayton, Ohio. The Court decided that there had been de jure segregation, requiring officials to take affirmative action in desegregating the school system. Justice Powell had already expressed opposition to widespread busing as a remedy. Chief Justice Burger agreed that it "is becoming increasingly doubtful that massive public transportation really accomplishes the desirable objectives sought." Columbus Board of Education v. Penick, 443 U.S. 449, 469 (1979). In a dissent, Justice Powell warned that parents resentful of court-ordered integration might withdraw their children from public schools by relocating their families ("white flight") or turning to private schools. Either choice would produce resegregation of public schools. Id. at 484. See also Dayton Board of Education v. Brinkman, 433 U.S. 406 (1977), and Dayton Board of Education v. Brinkman, 443 U.S. 526 (1979).

Opposition to Busing

In addition to placing antibusing language in the Civil Rights Act of 1964, Congress prohibited the use of appropriated funds to bus students for racial balance. However, these restrictions controlled federal agencies, not the courts. States were affected by some limitations that prohibited agencies from forcing states to bus students as a condition for receiving federal funds.[3] In prohibiting the forced busing of students, Congress sometimes softened the language by adding: "Except as required by the Constitution." 84 Stat. 48, §§ 408, 409 (1970). Congress, issuing findings that busing was sometimes harmful, specified appropriate remedies. Yet, it also stated that its actions were "not intended to modify or diminish the authority" of U.S. courts to enforce the Fifth and Fourteenth Amendments. 88 Stat. 515, § 203(b) (1974), codified at 20 U.S.C. § 1702(b) (1994). Other limitations applied directly to the courts. 88

---

3. 81 Stat. 441, § 16 (1967); 82 Stat. 995, § 409 (1968); 84 Stat. 805, §§ 209, 210 (1970); 85 Stat. 107, §§ 309, 310 (1971); 90 Stat. 21–22, §§ 207–09 (1976); 90 Stat. 1433–34, §§ 206–08 (1976); 92 Stat. 1585–86, §§ 207–09 (1978).

Stat. 517, § 215 (1974), codified at 20 U.S.C. § 1714 (1994). The riders on appropriations bills expired at the end of each fiscal year; other restrictions on busing became part of permanent law.[4]

In 1982, the Court reviewed a statewide initiative in Washington designed to prohibit the use of mandatory busing to achieve integrated public schools. Split 5 to 4, the Court held that the initiative violated the Equal Protection Clause. Washington v. Seattle School Dist. No. 1, 458 U.S. 457 (1982). A combination of dissenting Justices, public opposition, and restrictions by Congress eventually forced the courts to abandon widespread busing as a remedy for desegregation. Black parents as well as white parents objected to having their children transported on buses for long distances. They preferred other solutions, including "compensatory schools" or "magnet schools" that offered extra teachers, computers, better laboratories, and other resources. With the support of the Supreme Court, some cities abandoned busing as a means of racially integrating their schools. Riddick v. School Bd. of City of Norfolk, 784 F.2d 521 (4th Cir. 1986) (en banc), cert. denied, 479 U.S. 938 (1986). In 1998, a federal judge in Maryland finally ordered an end to mandatory busing in Prince George's County, a 26-year-old policy that was opposed by both white and black parents. By 1996, nearly 92 percent of bused students were black, and many were sent to predominantly black schools outside their neighborhoods. In 1999, in the area where busing began, a federal judge ruled that busing was no longer necessary for the Charlotte-Mecklenburg School District because evidence of intentional discrimination had disappeared.

Return to Segregated Schools?

A 1991 ruling by the Supreme Court, divided 5–3, reversed an appellate court decision that made it difficult for schools to terminate desegregation decrees. The Court held that a district court, in determining whether a school board had complied with a desegregation decree, must decide whether the board complied in good faith with the decree since it was entered and whether, in light of every facet of school operations, the vestiges of past de jure segregation had been eliminated to the extent practicable. Under this ruling, desegregation decrees could be lifted even if a school district is heading toward a more segregated, dual system. Board of Ed. of Oklahoma City v. Dowell, 498 U.S. 237 (1991).

The trend toward accepting largely all-white or all-black schools was also furthered by a 1992 unanimous ruling by the Supreme Court. It held that when racial imbalance in schools is the result of population shifts, school districts and federal judges are not required to adopt "awkward, inconvenient, and even bizarre" measures (language borrowed from *Swann* v. *Charlotte-Mecklenburg*) to achieve integrated schools. Massive busing was not considered a viable option by either the parties, the district court, or the Supreme Court. A school district has a duty to eliminate segregation that is de jure, not de facto. Federal courts have the authority to relinquish supervision and control of school districts even if full compliance with desegregation plans has not been achieved in every area of school operations. Freeman v. Pitts, 503 U.S. 467 (1992).

At the university level, the Court continued to put pressure on state schools to eliminate racial segregation. An 8–1 ruling in 1992 requires state officials to do more than simply declare that historically white and black colleges are open to students of any race. A race-neutral admissions policy does not necessarily satisfy a state's obligation. Certain policies, such as setting higher minimum test scores at white colleges or providing less state funding for black colleges, may have the effect of perpetuating segregated institutions. This case involved Mis-

---

4. 80 Stat. 1264, § 205(f) (1966), codified at 42 U.S.C. § 3335(f) (1994); 84 Stat. 169, § 422 (1970), codified at 20 U.S.C. § 1232a (1994); 86 Stat. 371–373, Title VIII (1972), codified at 20 U.S.C. §§ 1651–56 (1994); 88 Stat. 514–521, Title II (1974), codified at 20 U.S.C. §§ 1701–58 (1994).

A Return to "Separate but Equal"?

Because of neighborhood housing patterns, a retreat from busing, and court decisions that are dismantling desegregation plans, public schools are returning to a de facto segregated status. Researchers at the Harvard Graduate School of Education found that from 1991 to 1994, the percentage of minority students in schools with a substantial white enrollment fell appreciably. Hispanic students are now more likely than black students to be isolated in schools that are largely minority and poor. Seg-

regated schools are developing in the suburbs just as they did in the inner cities.

Some analysts believe that the trend toward resegregation reflects the view of many parents and educators, both white and minority, that integrated schools are no longer a paramount educational goal. Some minority parents seek out ethnic identification for their children or put the emphasis on safety, neighborhood schools, and good education rather than an integrated environment.

SOURCE: "Schools See Re-Emergence of 'Separate but Equal,'" The New York Times, April 8, 1997, at A10; see also "After 45 Years, Resegregation Emerges In Schools, Study Finds," The New York Times, June 13, 1999, at 31.

---

sissippi, where more than 99 percent of white students attend five large white colleges (averaging between 80 and 91 percent white students), and the racial composition at three other colleges ranges from 92 to 99 percent black. A number of other states are affected by this ruling. United States v. Fordice, 505 U.S. 717 (1992).

Desegregation was frustrated by other tactics. "Freedom of choice" plans permitted whites to attend all-black schools and blacks to attend all-white schools. Predictably, whites did not attend black schools, and few blacks attended white schools. The Court struck down these plans as inadequate remedies for desegregation.[5] "Transfer plans" allowed students to transfer from a school where they would be in a racial minority back to a former segregated school. A unanimous Court declared this procedure invalid. Goss v. Board of Education, 373 U.S. 683 (1963). Also, states were not permitted to create new school districts that had the effect of producing a refuge for white students. United States v. Scotland Neck Bd. of Educ., 407 U.S. 484 (1972).

In 1990 the Court issued an extraordinary decision that endorsed the power of federal judges to order local governmental bodies to increase taxes to pay for a court-ordered school desegregation plan. Missouri v. Jenkins, 495 U.S. 33 (1990). This 5 to 4 decision was undercut five years later when the Court, divided again 5 to 4, held that a federal judge had exceeded his authority in ordering pay raises for school personnel and increased funding for remedial programs in inner-city public schools, the same schools at issue in the 1990 ruling. The judge had ordered extra spending on the predominantly black Kansas City public schools so that they might attract white students from the suburbs. Missouri v. Jenkins, 515 U.S. 70 (1995). In 1997, a federal appellate court scrapped a wide-ranging school desegregation decree because many of its remedies were unjustified and an abuse of judicial discretion. People Who Care v. Rockford Bd. of Ed., 111 F.3d 528 (7th Cir. 1997); see also People Who Care v. Rockford Bd of Ed., 171 F.3d 1083 (7th Cir. 1999). In 2000, the Supreme Court refused to hear a lower court ruling that prohibited public schools from making enrollment decisions based on race. Montgomery County Public Schools v. Eisenberg, 120 S. Ct. 1420 (2000). Recent studies show a return to segregated schools (see box).

---

5. Wright v. Council of City of Emporia, 407 U.S. 451 (1972); Monroe v. Board of Commissioners, 391 U.S. 450 (1968); Raney v. Board of Education, 391 U.S. 443 (1968); Green v. County School Board, 391 U.S. 430 (1968).

Private Schools

Southern states attempted to avoid integrated education by closing public schools with white and black enrollment and setting up "private schools" operated for white students only. County funds provided tuition funds for the private schools, euphemistically called a "freedom of choice" program. Federal courts enjoined the counties from paying tuition grants or giving tax credits as long as public schools remained closed. The Supreme Court supported those rulings and announced, in 1964, that its slogan "all deliberate speed" had produced too much deliberation and not enough speed. Griffin v. School Board, 377 U.S. 218, 229 (1964). The time for deliberate speed "has run out." Id. at 234.[6] The IRS denied tax-exempt status to private schools with racially discriminatory admissions policies. See Prince Edward School Foundation v. Commissioner of Internal Revenue, 478 F.Supp. 107 (D.D.C. 1979), cert. denied, 450 U.S. 944 (1981). Some of these schools, such as the Prince Edward Academy in Virginia, regained tax-exempt status after announcing that they were open to all races.

In Mississippi the number of virtually all-white private secular schools increased substantially after the desegregation ruling in 1954. In 1973 a unanimous Court held that Mississippi could not give free textbooks to private schools that practiced racial or other invidious discrimination. Norwood v. Harrison, 413 U.S. 455 (1973). Another ruling involved private schools that had been set up in Virginia shortly after the 1954 desegregation decision. These schools excluded qualified children solely because they were black. A 7–2 Court held that federal law prohibited racial discrimination in the making and enforcement of private contracts practiced by these schools. Runyon v. McCrary, 427 U.S. 160 (1976).

In 1970 the IRS announced that it would not give tax-exempt status to private schools that practiced racial discrimination. That policy persisted until 1982 when the Reagan administration said that the IRS had exceeded its statutory powers. A year later, an 8–1 Court sustained the IRS. The national policy of nondiscrimination could not support the granting of tax-exemption to institutions that adopt racial policies. Tax-exemption is a benefit given to organizations that provide a public benefit. Bob Jones University v. United States, 461 U.S. 574 (1983). In other cases, suits brought against the IRS for failing to deny tax-exempt status to racially discriminatory private schools have been set aside for lack of standing by plaintiffs. Allen v. Wright, 468 U.S. 737 (1984).

Government's Brief in *Brown*

In an amicus brief filed December 1952 in the case of *Brown* v. *Board of Education,* the Justice Department explained the interest of the President and the executive branch in abolishing racial discrimination. The importance of civil rights transcended domestic politics. The persistence of segregation in America undermined its claim to democratic values and provided an easy target for exploitation by communist nations. The selection below is from 49 Landmark Briefs 116–21.

I

The Interest of the United States

...The cases at bar do not involve isolated acts of racial discrimination by private individuals or groups. On the contrary, it is contended in these cases that public school systems established in the states of Kansas, South Carolina, Virginia, and Delaware, and in the District of Columbia, unconstitutionally discriminate against Negroes solely because of their color.

This contention raises questions of the first importance in our society. For racial discriminations

---

6. Other rejections of the "all deliberate speed" formula include Alexander v. Board of Education, 396 U.S. 1218 (1969); Keyes v. Denver School District, 396 U.S. 1215 (1969); Alexander v. Board of Education, 396 U.S. 19 (1969).

imposed by law, or having the sanction or support of government, inevitably tend to undermine the foundations of a society dedicated to freedom, justice, and equality. The proposition that all men are created equal is not mere rhetoric. It implies a rule of law — an indispensable condition to a civilized society — under which all men stand equal and alike in the rights and opportunities secured to them by their government. Under the Constitution every agency of government, national and local, legislative, executive, and judicial, must treat each of our people as an *American,* and not as a member of a particular group classified on the basis of race or some other constitutional irrelevancy. The color of a man's skin — like his religious beliefs, or his political attachments, or the country from which he or his ancestors came to the United States — does not diminish or alter his legal status or constitutional rights. "Our Constitution is color-blind, and neither knows nor tolerates classes among citizens."

The problem of racial discrimination is particularly acute in the District of Columbia, the nation's capital. This city is the window through which the world looks into our house. The embassies, legations, and representatives of all nations are here, at the seat of the Federal Government. Foreign officials and visitors naturally judge this country and our people by their experiences and observations in the nation's capital; and the treatment of colored persons here is taken as the measure of our attitude toward minorities generally. The President has stated that "The District of Columbia should be a true symbol of American freedom and democracy for our own people, and for the people of the world." Instead, as the President's Committee on Civil Rights found, the District of Columbia "is a graphic illustration of a failure of democracy." The Committee summarized its findings as follows:

"For Negro Americans, Washington is not just the nation's capital. It is the point at which all public transportation into the South becomes "Jim Crow.' If he stops in Washington, a Negro may dine like other men in the Union Station, but as soon as he steps out into the capital, he leaves such democratic practices behind. With very few exceptions, he is refused service at downtown restaurants, he may not attend a downtown movie or play, and he has to go into the poorer section of the city to find a night's lodging. The Negro who decides to settle in the District must often find a home in an overcrowded, substandard area. He must often take a job below the level of his ability. He must send his children to the inferior public schools set aside for Negroes and entrust his family's health to medical agencies which give inferior service. In addition, he must endure the countless daily humiliations that the system of segregation imposes upon the one-third of Washington that is Negro.

. . .

"The shamefulness and absurdity of Washington's treatment of Negro Americans is highlighted by the presence of many dark-skinned foreign visitors. Capital custom not only humiliates colored citizens, but is a source of considerable embarrassment to these visitors.... Foreign officials are often mistaken for American Negroes and refused food, lodging and entertainment. However, once it is established that they are not Americans, they are accommodated."

It is in the context of the present world struggle between freedom and tyranny that the problem of racial discrimination must be viewed. The United States is trying to prove to the people of the world, of every nationality, race, and color, that a free democracy is the most civilized and most secure form of government yet devised by man. We must set an example for others by showing firm determination to remove existing flaws in our democracy.

The existence of discrimination against minority groups in the United States has an adverse effect upon our relations with other countries. Racial discrimination furnishes grist for the Communist propaganda mills, and it raises doubts even among friendly nations as to the intensity of our devotion to the democratic faith....

Brown v. Board of Education

347 U.S. 483 (1954)

After chipping away at the foundations of *Plessy* v. *Ferguson,* a unanimous Court in this case resolved that the "separate but equal" doctrine has no place in the field of education.

In deciding that the history of the Fourteenth Amendment is inconclusive as to its intended effect on public education, the Court held that the use of race to segregate white and black children in the public schools is a denial to black children of the equal protection of the laws guaranteed by the Fourteenth Amendment. In this case, Linda Brown was prohibited from attending a white public school in Topeka, Kansas. She was one of several plaintiffs.

MR. CHIEF JUSTICE WARREN delivered the opinion of the Court.

These cases come to us from the States of Kansas, South Carolina, Virginia, and Delaware. They are premised on different facts and different local conditions, but a common legal question justifies their consideration together in this consolidated opinion.

In each of the cases, minors of the Negro race, through their legal representatives, seek the aid of the courts in obtaining admission to the public schools of their community on a nonsegregated basis. In each instance, they had been denied admission to schools attended by white children under laws requiring or permitting segregation according to race. This segregation was alleged to deprive the plaintiffs of the equal protection of the laws under the Fourteenth Amendment. In each of the cases other than the Delaware case, a three-judge federal district court denied relief to the plaintiffs on the so-called "separate but equal" doctrine announced by this Court in *Plessy v. Ferguson,* 163 U.S. 537. Under that doctrine, equality of treatment is accorded when the races are provided substantially equal facilities, even though these facilities be separate. In the Delaware case, the Supreme Court of Delaware adhered to that doctrine, but ordered that the plaintiffs be admitted to the white schools because of their superiority to the Negro schools.

The plaintiffs contend that segregated public schools are not "equal" and cannot be made "equal," and that hence they are deprived of the equal protection of the laws. Because of the obvious importance of the question presented, the Court took jurisdiction. Argument was heard in the 1952 Term, and reargument was heard this Term on certain questions propounded by the Court.

Reargument was largely devoted to the circumstances surrounding the adoption of the Fourteenth Amendment in 1868. It covered exhaustively consideration of the Amendment in Congress, ratification by the states, then existing practices in racial segregation, and the views of proponents and opponents of the Amendment. This discussion and our own investigation convince us that, although these sources cast some light, it is not enough to resolve the problem with which we are faced. At best, they are inconclusive. The most avid proponents of the post-War Amendments undoubtedly intended them to remove all legal distinctions among "all persons born or naturalized in the United States." Their opponents, just as certainly, were antagonistic to both the letter and the spirit of the Amendments and wished them to have the most limited effect. What others in Congress and the state legislatures had in mind cannot be determined with any degree of certainty.

An additional reason for the inconclusive nature of the Amendment's history, with respect to segregated schools, is the status of public education at that time. In the South, the movement toward free common schools, supported by general taxation, had not yet taken hold. Education of white children was largely in the hands of private groups. Education of Negroes was almost nonexistent, and practically all of the race were illiterate. In fact, any education of Negroes was forbidden by law in some states. Today, in contrast, many Negroes have achieved outstanding success in the arts and sciences as well as in the business and professional world. It is true that public school education at the time of the Amendment had advanced further in the North, but the effect of the Amendment on Northern States was generally ignored in the congressional debates. Even in the North, the conditions of public education did not approximate those existing today. The curriculum was usually rudimentary; ungraded schools were common in rural areas; the school term was but three months a year in many states; and compulsory school attendance was virtually unknown. As a consequence, it is not surprising that there should be so little in the history of the Fourteenth Amendment relating to its intended effect on public education.

In the first cases in this Court construing the Fourteenth Amendment, decided shortly after its adoption, the Court interpreted it as proscribing all state-imposed discriminations against the Negro race. The doctrine of "separate but equal" did not make its appearance in this Court until 1896 in the case of *Plessy v. Ferguson, supra,* involving not education but transportation. American courts have since labored with the doctrine for over half a century. In this Court, there have been six cases involving the "separate but equal" doctrine in the field of public education. In *Cumming v. County Board of Education,* 175 U.S. 528, and *Gong Lum v. Rice,* 275 U.S. 78, the validity of the doctrine itself was not challenged. In more recent cases, all on the graduate school level, inequality was found in that specific benefits enjoyed by white students were denied to Negro students of the same educational qualifications. *Missouri ex rel. Gaines v. Canada,* 305 U.S. 337; *Sipuel v. Oklahoma,* 332 U.S. 631; *Sweatt v. Painter,* 339 U.S. 629; *McLaurin v. Oklahoma State Regents,* 339 U.S. 637. In none of these cases was it necessary to re-examine the doctrine to grant relief to the Negro plaintiff. And in *Sweatt v. Painter, supra,* the Court expressly reserved decision on the question whether *Plessy v. Ferguson* should be held inapplicable to public education.

In the instant cases, that question is directly presented. Here, unlike *Sweatt v. Painter,* there are findings below that the Negro and white schools involved have been equalized, or are being equalized, with respect to buildings, curricula, qualifications and salaries of teachers, and other "tangible" factors. Our decision, therefore, cannot turn on merely a comparison of these tangible factors in the Negro and white schools involved in each of the cases. We must look instead to the effect of segregation itself on public education.

In approaching this problem, we cannot turn the clock back to 1868 when the Amendment was adopted, or even to 1896 when *Plessy v. Ferguson* was written. We must consider public education in the light of its full development and its present place in American life throughout the Nation. Only in this way can it be determined if segregation in public schools deprives these plaintiffs of the equal protection of the laws.

Today, education is perhaps the most important function of state and local governments. Compulsory school attendance laws and the great expenditures for education both demonstrate our recognition of the importance of education to our democratic society. It is required in the performance of our most basic public responsibilities, even service in the armed forces. It is the very foundation of good citizenship. Today it is a principal instrument in awakening the child to cultural values, in preparing him for later professional training, and in helping him to adjust normally to his environment. In these days, it is doubtful that any child may reasonably be expected to succeed in life if he is denied the opportunity of an education.

Such an opportunity, where the state has undertaken to provide it, is a right which must be made available to all on equal terms.

We come then to the question presented: Does segregation of children in public schools solely on the basis of race, even though the physical facilities and other "tangible" factors may be equal, deprive the children of the minority group of equal educational opportunities? We believe that it does.

In *Sweatt v. Painter, supra,* in finding that a segregated law school for Negroes could not provide them equal educational opportunities, this Court relied in large part on "those qualities which are incapable of objective measurement but which make for greatness in a law school." In *McLaurin v. Oklahoma State Regents, supra,* the Court, in requiring that a Negro admitted to a white graduate school be treated like all other students, again resorted to intangible considerations: "... his ability to study, to engage in discussions and exchange views with other students, and, in general, to learn his profession." Such considerations apply with added force to children in grade and high schools. To separate them from others of similar age and qualifications solely because of their race generates a feeling of inferiority as to their status in the community that may affect their hearts and minds in a way unlikely ever to be undone. The effect of this separation on their educational opportunities was well stated by a finding in the Kansas case by a court which nevertheless felt compelled to rule against the Negro plaintiffs:

"Segregation of white and colored children in public schools has a detrimental effect upon the colored children. The impact is greater when it has the sanction of the law; for the policy of separating the races is usually interpreted as denoting the inferiority of the negro group. A sense of inferiority affects the motivation of a child to learn. Segregation with the sanction of law, therefore, has a tendency to [retard] the educational and mental development of negro children and to deprive them of some of the benefits they would receive in a racial[ly] integrated school system."

Whatever may have been the extent of psychological knowledge at the time of *Plessy v. Ferguson,* this finding is amply supported by modern authority. *[Here the Court adds its famous footnote 11: K. B. Clark, Effect of Prejudice and Discrimination on Personality Development (Midcentury White House Conference on Children and Youth, 1950); Witmer and Kotinsky, Personality in the Making (1952), c. VI; Deutscher and*

Chein, The Psychological Effects of Enforced Segregation: A Survey of Social Science Opinion, 26 J. Psychol. 259 (1948); Chein, What are the Psychological Effects of Segregation Under Conditions of Equal Facilities?, 3 Int. J. Opinion and Attitude Res. 229 (1949); Brameld, Educational Costs, in Discrimination and National Welfare (MacIver, ed., 1949), 44–48; Frazier, The Negro in the United States (1949), 674–681. And see generally Myrdal, An American Dilemma (1944).] Any language in *Plessy* v. *Ferguson* contrary to this finding is rejected.

We conclude that in the field of public education the doctrine of "separate but equal" has no place. Separate educational facilities are inherently unequal. Therefore, we hold that the plaintiffs and others similarly situated for whom the actions have been brought are, by reason of the segregation complained of, deprived of the equal protection of the laws guaranteed by the Fourteenth Amendment. This disposition makes unnecessary any discussion whether such segregation also violates the Due Process Clause of the Fourteenth Amendment.

Because these are class actions, because of the wide applicability of this decision, and because of the great variety of local conditions, the formulation of decrees in these cases presents problems of considerable complexity. On reargument, the consideration of appropriate relief was necessarily subordinated to the primary question — the constitutionality of segregation in public education. We have now announced that such segregation is a denial of the equal protection of the laws. In order that we may have the full assistance of the parties in formulating decrees, the cases will be restored to the docket, and the parties are requested to present further argument on Questions 4 and 5 previously propounded by the Court for the reargument this Term. The Attorney General of the United States is again invited to participate. The Attorneys General of the states requiring or permitting segregation in public education will also be permitted to appear as *amici curiae* upon request to do so by September 15, 1954, and submission of briefs by October 1, 1954.

It is so ordered.

Bolling v. Sharpe

347 U.S. 497 (1954)

In *Brown* v. *Board of Education* (1954), the Supreme Court struck down "separate but equal" public schools in the states, relying on the Equal Protection Clause of the Fourteenth Amendment. What was to be done about segregated schooling in the District of Columbia, which is not subject to the Fourteenth Amendment? The Court could invoke the Fifth Amendment, which did apply to the District of Columbia, but the Fifth Amendment lacks an Equal Protection Clause. Politically, the Court could not invalidate segregated schools in the states and allow them to operate in D.C. In this case the Court discovers a solution. Spottswood Thomas Bolling and other students from a junior high school brought this action against C. Melvin Sharpe and the other members of the D.C. Board of Education.

MR. CHIEF JUSTICE WARREN delivered the opinion of the Court.

This case challenges the validity of segregation in the public schools of the District of Columbia. The petitioners, minors of the Negro race, allege that such segregation deprives them of due process of law under the Fifth Amendment. They were refused admission to a public school attended by white children solely because of their race. They sought the aid of the District Court for the District of Columbia in obtaining admission. That court dismissed their complaint. The Court granted a writ of certiorari before judgment in the Court of Appeals because of the importance of the constitutional question presented. 344 U. S. 873.

We have this day held that the Equal Protection Clause of the Fourteenth Amendment prohibits the states from maintaining racially segregated public schools. The legal problem in the District of Columbia is somewhat different, however. The Fifth Amendment, which is applicable in the District of Columbia, does not contain an equal protection clause as does the Fourteenth Amendment which applies only to the states. But the concepts of equal protection and due process, both stemming from our American ideal of fairness, are not mutually exclusive. The "equal protection of the laws" is a more explicit safeguard of prohibited unfairness than "due process of law," and, therefore, we do not imply that the two are always interchangeable phrases. But, as this Court has recognized, discrimination may be so unjustifiable as to be violative of due process.

Classifications based solely upon race must be scrutinized with particular care, since they are contrary to our traditions and hence constitutionally suspect. As long ago as 1896, this Court declared the principle "that the Constitution of the United States, in its present form, forbids, so far as civil and political rights are concerned, discrimination by the General Government, or by the States, against any citizen because of his race." And in *Buchanan v. Warley*, 245 U.S. 60, the Court held that a statute which limited the right of a property owner to convey his property to a person of another race was, as an unreasonable discrimination, a denial of due process of law.

Although the Court has not assumed to define "liberty" with any great precision, that term is not confined to mere freedom from bodily re-straint. Liberty under law extends to the full range of conduct which the individual is free to pursue, and it cannot be restricted except for a proper governmental objective. Segregation in public education is not reasonably related to any proper governmental objective, and thus it imposes on Negro children of the District of Columbia a burden that constitutes an arbitrary deprivation of their liberty in violation of the Due Process Clause.

In view of our decision that the Constitution prohibits the states from maintaining racially segregated public schools, it would be unthinkable that the same Constitution would impose a lesser duty on the Federal Government. We hold that racial segregation in the public schools of the District of Columbia is a denial of the due process of law guaranteed by the Fifth Amendment to the Constitution.

. . .

It is so ordered.

Brown v. Board of Education

349 U.S. 294 (1955)

In the first *Brown* case, called *Brown I,* the Court held that racial discrimination in public schools is unconstitutional. Having announced the constitutional principle, the Court had to issue instructions on the means used to implement its ruling. This case, called *Brown II,* has been heavily criticized for deferring too much to local school districts and thus delaying implementation of *Brown I.*

MR. CHIEF JUSTICE WARREN delivered the opinion of the Court.

These cases were decided on May 17, 1954. The opinions of that date, declaring the fundamental principle that racial discrimination in public education is unconstitutional, are incorporated herein by reference. All provisions of federal, state, or local law requiring or permitting such discrimination must yield to this principle. There remains for consideration the manner in which relief is to be accorded.

Because these cases arose under different local conditions and their disposition will involve a variety of local problems, we requested further argument on the question of relief. In view of the nationwide importance of the decision, we invited the Attorney General of the United States and the Attorneys General of all states requiring or permitting racial discrimination in public education to present their views on that question. The par-ties, the United States, and the States of Florida, North Carolina, Arkansas, Oklahoma, Maryland, and Texas filed briefs and participated in the oral argument.

These presentations were informative and helpful to the Court in its consideration of the complexities arising from the transition to a system of public education freed of racial discrimination. The presentations also demonstrated that substantial steps to eliminate racial discrimination in public schools have already been taken, not only in some of the communities in which these cases arose, but in some of the states appearing as *amici curiae,* and in other states as well. Substantial progress has been made in the District of Columbia and in the communities in Kansas and Delaware involved in this litigation. The defendants in the cases coming to us from South Carolina and Virginia are awaiting the decision of this Court concerning relief.

Full implementation of these constitutional principles may require solution of varied local school problems. School authorities have the primary responsibility for elucidating, assessing, and solving these problems; courts will have to consider whether the action of school authorities constitutes good faith implementation of the governing constitutional principles. Because of their proximity to local conditions and the possible need for further hearings, the courts which originally heard these cases can best perform this judicial appraisal. Accordingly, we believe it appropriate to remand the cases to those courts.

In fashioning and effectuating the decrees, the courts will be guided by equitable principles. Traditionally, equity has been characterized by a practical flexibility in shaping its remedies and by a facility for adjusting and reconciling public and private needs. These cases call for the exercise of these traditional attributes of equity power. At stake is the personal interest of the plaintiffs in admission to public schools as soon as practicable on a nondiscriminatory basis. To effectuate this interest may call for elimination of a variety of obstacles in making the transition to school systems operated in accordance with the constitutional principles set forth in our May 17, 1954, decision. Courts of equity may properly take into account the public interest in the elimination of such obstacles in a systematic and effective manner. But it should go without saying that the vitality of these constitutional principles cannot be allowed to yield simply because of disagreement with them.

While giving weight to these public and private considerations, the courts will require that the defendants make a prompt and reasonable start toward full compliance with our May 17, 1954, ruling. Once such a start has been made, the courts may find that additional time is necessary to carry out the ruling in an effective manner. The burden rests upon the defendants to establish that such time is necessary in the public interest and is consistent with good faith compliance at the earliest practicable date. To that end, the courts may consider problems related to administration, arising from the physical condition of the school plant, the school transportation system, personnel, revision of school districts and attendance areas into compact units to achieve a system of determining admission to the public schools on a nonracial basis, and revision of local laws and regulations which may be necessary in solving the foregoing problems. They will also consider the adequacy of any plans the defendants may propose to meet these problems and to effectuate a transition to a racially nondiscriminatory school system. During this period of transition, the courts will retain jurisdiction of these cases.

The judgments below, except that in the Delaware case, are accordingly reversed and the cases are remanded to the District Courts to take such proceedings and enter such orders and decrees consistent with this opinion as are necessary and proper to admit to public schools on a racially nondiscriminatory basis with all deliberate speed the parties to these cases. The judgment in the Delaware case — ordering the immediate admission of the plaintiffs to schools previously attended only by white children — is affirmed on the basis of the principles stated in our May 17, 1954, opinion, but the case is remanded to the Supreme Court of Delaware for such further proceedings as that Court may deem necessary in light of this opinion.

It is so ordered.

Cooper v. Aaron

358 U.S. 1 (1958)

Federal courts approved a plan of gradual desegregation of the races in the public schools in Little Rock, Arkansas, to admit black children to a previously all-white high school at the beginning of the 1957–58 school year. The state legislature and Governor Orval Faubus opposed the plan, leading to threats of mob violence. John Aaron, a black student prevented from attending the high school, brought this case against William G. Cooper, a member of the Board of Directors of the Little Rock school district.

Opinion of the Court by THE CHIEF JUSTICE, MR. JUSTICE BLACK, MR. JUSTICE FRANKFURTER, MR. JUSTICE DOUGLAS, MR. JUSTICE BURTON, MR. JUSTICE CLARK, MR. JUSTICE HARLAN, MR. JUSTICE BRENNAN, and MR. JUSTICE WHITTAKER.

As this case reaches us it raises questions of

the highest importance to the maintenance of our federal system of government. It necessarily involves a claim by the Governor and Legislature of a State that there is no duty on state officials to obey federal court orders resting on this Court's considered interpretation of the United States Constitution. Specifically it involves actions by the Governor and Legislature of Arkansas upon the premise that they are not bound by our holding in *Brown v. Board of Education,* 347 U. S. 483....

On May 20, 1954, three days after the first *Brown* opinion the Little Rock District School Board adopted, and on May 23, 1954, made public, a statement of policy entitled "Supreme Court Decision — Segregation in Public Schools." In this statement the Board recognized that

"It is our responsibility to comply with Federal Constitutional Requirements and we intend to do so when the Supreme Court of the United States outlines the method to be followed."

Thereafter the Board undertook studies of the administrative problems confronting the transition to a desegregated public school system at Little Rock. It instructed the Superintendent of Schools to prepare a plan for desegregation, and approved such a plan on May 24, 1955, seven days before the second *Brown* opinion. The plan provided for desegregation at the senior high school level (grades 10 through 12) as the first stage. Desegregation at the junior high and elementary levels was to follow. It was contemplated that desegregation at the high school level would commence in the fall of 1957, and the expectation was that complete desegregation of the school system would be accomplished by 1963. Following the adoption of this plan, the Superintendent of Schools discussed it with a large number of citizen groups in the city. As a result of these discussions, the Board reached the conclusion that "a large majority of the residents" of Little Rock were of "the belief ... that the Plan, although objectionable in principle," from the point of view of those supporting segregated schools, "was still the best for the interests of all pupils in the District."

Upon challenge by a group of Negro plaintiffs desiring more rapid completion of the desegregation process, the District Court upheld the School Board's plan, *Aaron v. Cooper,* 143 F. Supp. 855. The Court of Appeals affirmed 243 F. 2d 361. Review of that judgment was not sought here.

While the School Board was thus going forward with its preparation for desegregating the Little Rock school system, other state authorities, in contrast, were actively pursuing a program designed to perpetuate in Arkansas the system of racial segregation which this Court had held violated the Fourteenth Amendment. First came, in November 1956, an amendment to the State Constitution flatly commanding the Arkansas General Assembly to oppose "in every Constitutional manner the Un-constitutional desegregation decisions of May 17, 1954 and May 31, 1955 of the United States Supreme Court," Ark. Const., Amend. 44, and, through their initiative, a pupil assignment law, Ark. Stat. 80-1519 to 80-1524. Pursuant to this state constitutional command, a law relieving school children from compulsory attendance at racially mixed schools, Ark. Stat. 80-1525, and a law establishing a State Sovereignty Commission, Ark. Stat. 6-801 to 6-824, were enacted by the General Assembly in February 1957.

The School Board and the Superintendent of Schools nevertheless continued with preparations to carry out the first stage of the desegregation program. Nine Negro children were scheduled for admission in September 1957 to Central High School, which has more than two thousand students. Various administrative measures, designed to assure the smooth transition of this first stage of desegregation, were undertaken.

On September 2, 1957, the day before these Negro students were to enter Central High, the school authorities were met with drastic opposing action on the part of the Governor of Arkansas who dispatched units of the Arkansas National Guard to the Central High School grounds and placed the school "off limits" to colored students. As found by the District Court in subsequent proceedings, the Governor's action had not been requested by the school authorities, and was entirely unheralded. The findings were these:

"Up to this time [September 2], no crowds had gathered about Central High School and no acts of violence or threats of violence in connection with the carrying out of the plan had occurred. Nevertheless, out of an abundance of caution, the school authorities had frequently conferred with the Mayor and Chief of Police of Little Rock about taking appropriate steps by the Little Rock police to prevent any possible disturbances or acts of violence in connection with the attendance of the 9 colored students at Central High School. The Mayor considered that the Little Rock police force could adequately cope with any incidents which might arise at the opening of school. The Mayor, the Chief of Police, and the school authorities made no request to the Governor or any representative of his for State assistance in maintaining peace and order at Central High School. Neither the Governor nor any other official of the State government consulted with the Little Rock authorities about whether the Little Rock police were prepared to cope with any incidents which might arise at the school, about any need for State assistance in maintaining peace and order, or about stationing the Arkansas National Guard at Central High School." *Aaron v. Cooper,* 156 F. Supp. 220, 225.

The Board's petition for postponement in this proceeding states: "The effect of that action [of the Governor] was to harden the core of opposition to the Plan and cause many persons who theretofore had reluctantly accepted the Plan to believe there was some power in the State of Arkansas which, when exerted, could nullify the Federal law and permit disobedience of the decree of this [District] Court, and from that date hostility to the Plan was increased and criticism of the officials of the [School] District has become more bitter and unrestrained." The Governor's action caused the School Board to request the Negro students on September 2 not to attend the high school "until the legal dilemma was solved." The next day, September 3, 1957, the Board petitioned the District Court for instructions, and the court, after a hearing, found that the Board's request of the Negro students to stay away from the high school had been made because of the stationing of the military guards by the state authorities. The court determined that this was not a reason for departing from the approved plan, and ordered the School Board and Superintendent to proceed with it.

On the morning of the next day, September 4, 1957, the Negro children attempted to enter the high school but, as the District Court later found, units of the Arkansas National Guard "acting pursuant to the Governor's order, stood shoulder to shoulder at the school grounds and thereby forcibly prevented the 9 Negro students ... from entering," as they continued to do every school day during the following three weeks. 156 F. Supp., at 225.

[On the basis of an investigation by the U.S. attorney, the district court found that the school board's plan had been obstructed by Faubus and enjoined him from further interference.]

The next school day was Monday, September 23, 1957. The Negro children entered the high school that morning under the protection of the Little Rock Police Department and members of the Arkansas State Police. But the officers caused the children to be removed from the school during the morning because they had difficulty controlling a large and demonstrating crowd which had gathered at the high school. 163 F. Supp., at 16. On September 25, however, the President of the United States dispatched federal troops to Central High School and admission of the Negro students to the school was thereby effected. Regular army troops continued at the high school until November 27, 1957. They were then replaced by federalized National Guardsmen who remained throughout the balance of the school year. Eight of the Negro students remained in attendance at the school throughout the school year.

We come now to the aspect of the proceedings presently before us. On February 20, 1958, the School Board and the Superintendent of Schools filed a petition in the District Court seeking a postponement of their program for desegregation. Their position in essence was that because of extreme public hostility, which they stated had been engendered largely by the official attitudes and actions of the Governor and the Legislature, the maintenance of a sound educational program at Central High School, with the Negro students in attendance, would be impossible. The Board therefore proposed that the Negro students already admitted to the school be withdrawn and sent to segregated schools, and that all further steps to carry out the Board's desegregation program be postponed for a period later suggested by the Board to be two and one-half years.

[After the district court granted the relief requested by the school board, the Eighth Circuit reversed. The Supreme Court convened in special term on August 28, 1958, to hear oral argument. On September 12, the Court affirmed the judgment of the Eighth Circuit.]

In affirming the judgment of the Court of Appeals which reversed the District Court we have accepted without reservation the position of the School Board, the Superintendent of Schools, and their counsel that they displayed entire good faith in the conduct of these proceedings and in dealing with the unfortunate and distressing sequence of events which has been outlined. We likewise have accepted the findings of the District Court as to the conditions at Central High School during the 1957–1958 school year, and also the findings that the educational progress of all the students, white and colored, of that school has suffered and will continue to suffer if the conditions which prevailed last year are permitted to continue.

The significance of these findings, however, is to be considered in light of the fact, indisputably revealed by the record before us, that the conditions they depict are directly traceable to the actions of legislators and executive officials of the State of Arkansas, taken in their official capacities, which reflect their own determination to resist this Court's decision in the *Brown* case and which have brought about violent resistance to that decision in Arkansas....

The controlling legal principles are plain. The command of the Fourteenth Amendment is that no "State" shall deny to any person within its jurisdiction the equal protection of the laws. "A State acts by its legislative, its executive, or its judicial authorities. It can act in no other way. The constitutional provision, therefore, must mean that no agency of the State, or of the officers or agents by whom its powers are exerted, shall deny to any person within its jurisdiction the equal protection of the laws. Whoever, by virtue of public position under a State government,... denies or takes away the equal protection of the laws, violates the constitutional inhibition; and as he acts in the name and for the State, and is clothed with the State's power, his act is that of the State. This must be so, or the constitutional prohibition has no meaning." *Ex parte Virginia,* 100 U. S. 339, 347....

What has been said, in the light of the facts developed, is enough to dispose of the case. However, we should answer the premise of the actions of the Governor and Legislature that they are not bound by our holding in the *Brown* case. It is necessary only to recall some basic constitutional propositions which are settled doctrine.

Article VI of the Constitution makes the Constitution the "supreme Law of the Land." In 1803, Chief Justice Marshall, speaking for a unanimous Court, referring to the Constitution as "the fundamental and paramount law of the nation," declared in the notable case of *Marbury* v. *Madison,* 1 Cranch 137, 177, that "It is emphatically the province and duty of the judicial department to say what the law is." This decision declared the basic principle that the federal judiciary is supreme in the exposition of the law of the Constitution, and that principle has ever since

been respected by this Court and the Country as a permanent and indispensable feature of our constitutional system. It follows that the interpretation of the Fourteenth Amendment enunciated by this Court in the *Brown* case is the supreme law of the land, and Art. VI of the Constitution makes it of binding effect on the States "any Thing in the Constitution or Laws of any State to the Contrary notwithstanding." Every state legislator and executive and judicial officer is solemnly committed by oath taken pursuant to Art. VI, cl. 3, "to support this Constitution."...

No state legislator or executive or judicial officer can war against the Constitution without violating his undertaking to support it. Chief Justice Marshall spoke for a unanimous Court in saying that: "If the legislatures of the several states may, at will, annul the judgments of the courts of the United States, and destroy the rights acquired under those judgments, the constitution itself becomes a solemn mockery...." *United States v. Peters,* 5 Cranch 115, 136. A Governor who asserts a power to nullify a federal court order is similarly restrained. If he had such power, said Chief Justice Hughes, in 1932, also for a unanimous Court, "it is manifest that the fiat of a state Governor, and not the Constitution of the United States, would be the supreme law of the land; that the restrictions of the Federal Constitution upon the exercise of state power would be but impotent phrases...." *Sterling v. Constantin,* 287 U. S. 378, 397–398.

It is, of course, quite true that the responsibility for public education is primarily the concern of the States, but it is equally true that such responsibilities, like all other state activity, must be exercised consistently with federal constitutional requirements as they apply to state action. The Constitution created a government dedicated to equal justice under law. The Fourteenth Amendment embodied and emphasized that ideal. State support of segregated schools through any arrangement, management, funds, or property cannot be squared with the Amendment's command that no State shall deny to any person within its jurisdiction the equal protection of the laws....

Concurring opinion of MR. JUSTICE FRANK-FURTER.

. . .

Swann v. Charlotte-Mecklenburg Bd. of Ed.

402 U.S. 1 (1971)

By 1971 there had been little progress in desegregating public schools, despite the Supreme Court's historic decision in 1954. School boards were under pressure from the courts to come forward with desegregation plans *now*. In this case, the Court focuses on remedies available to federal courts to produce a unitary school system free of state-imposed segregation. James Swann and other black students challenged the desegregation plans of Charlotte-Mecklenberg, North Carolina.

MR. CHIEF JUSTICE BURGER delivered the opinion of the Court.

We granted certiorari in this case to review important issues as to the duties of school authorities and the scope of powers of federal courts under this Court's mandates to eliminate racially separate public schools established and maintained by state action. *Brown* v. *Board of Education,* 347 U.S. 483 (1954) *(Brown I).*

This case and those argued with it arose in States having a long history of maintaining two sets of schools in a single school system deliberately operated to carry out a governmental policy to separate pupils in schools solely on the basis of race. That was what *Brown* v. *Board of Education* was all about. These cases present us with the problem of defining in more precise terms than heretofore the scope of the duty of school authorities and district courts in implementing *Brown I* and the mandate to eliminate dual systems and establish unitary systems at once....

I

The Charlotte-Mecklenburg school system, the 43d largest in the Nation, encompasses the city of Charlotte and surrounding Mecklenburg County, North Carolina. The area is large — 550 square miles — spanning roughly 22 miles east-west and 36 miles north-south. During the 1968–1969 school year the system served more than 84,000 pupils in 107 schools. Approximately 71% of the pupils were found to be white and 29% Negro. As of June 1969 there were approximately 24,000 Negro students in the system, of whom 21,000 attended schools within the city of Charlotte. Two-thirds of those 21,000 — approximately 14,000 Negro students — attended 21 schools which were either totally Negro or more than 99% Negro.

[Litigation produced a number of desegregation plans by the school board; by a court-appointed expert; by the U.S. Department of Health, Education, and Welfare; and by four members of the school board. From these plans the Court issued new guidelines for school authorities and courts.]

III

. . .

The school authorities argue that the equity powers of federal district courts have been limited by Title IV of the Civil Rights Act of 1964, 42 U.S.C. § 2000c.... Section 2000c (b) defines "desegregation" as it is used in Title IV:

" 'Desegregation' means the assignment of students to public schools and within such schools without regard to their race, color, religion, or national origin, but 'desegregation' shall not mean the assignment of students to public schools in order to overcome racial imbalance."

Section 2000c-6, authorizing the Attorney General to institute federal suits, contains the following proviso:

"[N]othing herein shall empower any official or court of the United States to issue any order seeking to achieve a racial balance in any school by requiring the transportation of pupils or students from one school to another or one school district to another in order to achieve such racial balance, or otherwise enlarge the existing power of the court to insure compliance with constitutional standards."

On their face, the sections quoted purport only to insure that the provisions of Title IV of the Civil Rights Act of 1964 will not be read as granting new powers. The proviso in § 2000c-6 is in terms designed to foreclose any interpretation of the Act as expanding the *existing* powers of federal courts to enforce the Equal Protection Clause. There is no suggestion of an intention to restrict those powers or withdraw from courts their historic equitable remedial powers. The legislative history of Title IV indicates that Congress was concerned that the Act might be read as creating a right of action under the Fourteenth Amendment in the situation of so-called "de facto segregation," where racial imbalance exists in the schools but with no showing that this was brought about by discriminatory action of state authorities. In short, there is nothing in the Act that provides us material assistance in answering the question of remedy for state-imposed segregation in violation of *Brown I*. The basis of our decision must be the prohibition of the Fourteenth Amendment that no State shall "deny to any person within its jurisdiction the equal protection of the laws."

IV

[The Court reviews the major principles identified in previous cases regarding remedies for segregated school systems.]

V

The central issue in this case is that of student assignment, and there are essentially four problem areas:

(1) to what extent racial balance or racial quotas may be used as an implement in a remedial order to correct a previously segregated system;

(2) whether every all-Negro and all-white school must be eliminated as an indispensable part of a remedial process of desegregation;

(3) what the limits are, if any, on the rearrangement of school districts and attendance zones, as a remedial measure; and

(4) what the limits are, if any, on the use of transportation facilities to correct state-enforced racial school segregation.

(1) *Racial Balances or Racial Quotas.*

The constant theme and thrust of every holding from *Brown I* to date is that state-enforced separation of races in public schools is discrimination that violates the Equal Protection Clause. The remedy commanded was to dismantle dual school systems.

. . .

In this case it is urged that the District Court has imposed a racial balance requirement of 71%–29% on individual schools. The fact that no such objective was actually achieved—and would appear to be impossible—tends to blunt that claim....

. . .

We see therefore that the use made of mathematical ratios was no more than a starting point in the process of shaping a remedy, rather than an inflexible requirement. From that starting point the District Court proceeded to frame a decree that was within its discretionary powers, as an equitable remedy for the particular circumstances. As we said in *Green*, a school authority's remedial plan or a district court's remedial decree is to be judged by its effectiveness. Awareness of the racial composition of the whole school system is likely to be a useful starting point in shaping a remedy to correct past constitutional violations. In sum, the very limited use made of mathematical ratios was within the equitable remedial discretion of the District Court.

(2) *One-race Schools.*

The record in this case reveals the familiar phenomenon that in metropolitan areas minority groups are often found concentrated in one part of the city. In some circumstances certain schools may remain all or largely of one race until new schools can be provided or neighborhood patterns change. Schools all or predominately of one race in a district of mixed population will require close scrutiny to determine that school assignments are not part of state-enforced segregation.

. . .

(3) *Remedial Altering of Attendance Zones.*

The maps submitted in these cases graphically demonstrate that one of the principal tools employed by school planners and by courts to break up the dual school system has been a frank—and sometimes drastic—gerrymandering of school districts and attendance zones. An additional step was pairing, "clustering," or "grouping" of schools with attendance assignments made deliberately to accomplish the transfer of Negro students out of formerly segregated Negro schools and transfer of white students to formerly all-Negro schools. More often than not, these zones are neither compact nor contiguous; indeed they may be on opposite ends of the city. As an interim corrective measure, this cannot be said to be beyond the broad remedial powers of a court.

. . .

(4) *Transportation of Students.*

The scope of permissible transportation of students as an implement of a remedial decree has never been defined by this Court and by the very nature of the problem it cannot be defined with precision. No rigid guidelines as to student transportation can be given for application to the infinite variety of problems presented in thousands of situations. Bus transportation has been an integral part of the public education system for years, and was perhaps the single most important factor in the transition from the one-room schoolhouse to the consolidated school. Eighteen million of the Nation's public school children, approximately 39%, were transported to their schools by bus in 1969–1970 in all parts of the country.

The importance of bus transportation as a normal and accepted tool of educational policy is readily discernible in this and the companion case.[Davis v. School Comm'rs of Mobile County, 402 U.S. 33 (1971).] The Charlotte school authorities did not purport to assign students on the basis of geographically drawn zones until 1965 and then they allowed almost unlimited transfer privileges. The District Court's conclusion that assignment of children to the school nearest their home serving their grade would not produce an effective dismantling of the dual system is supported by the record.

Thus the remedial techniques used in the District Court's order were within that court's power to provide equitable relief; implementation of the decree is well within the capacity of the school authority.

The decree provided that the buses used to implement the plan would operate on direct routes. Students would be picked up at schools near their homes and transported to the schools they were to attend. The trips for elementary school pupils average about seven miles and the District Court found that they would take "not over 35 minutes at the most." This system compares favorably with the transportation plan previously operated in Charlotte under which each day 23,600 students on all grade levels were transported an average of 15 miles one way for an average trip requiring over an hour....

VI

The Court of Appeals, searching for a term to define the equitable remedial power of the district courts, used the term "reasonableness." In *Green, supra,* this Court used the term "feasible" and by implication, "workable," "effective," and "realistic" in the mandate to develop "a plan that promises realistically to work, and...to work *now.*" On the facts of this case, we are unable to conclude that the order of the District Court is not reasonable, feasible and workable....

. . .

For the reasons herein set forth, the judgment of the Court of Appeals is affirmed as to those parts in which it affirmed the judgment of the District Court. The order of the District Court, dated August 7, 1970, is also affirmed.

It is so ordered.

Milliken v. Bradley

418 U.S. 717 (1974)

Ronald Bradley and other parents and students in Detroit, Michigan, brought an action against Governor William G. Milliken. They alleged that the Detroit public school system was racially segregated as a result of the official policies and actions of state and city officials. A district court, concluding that official acts had created and perpetuated school segregation, ordered the Detroit Board of Education to submit Detroit-only desegregation plans. The court also ordered the state officials to submit desegregation plans encompassing the three-county metropolitan area, despite the fact that the 85 outlying school districts in these three counties were not parties to the action and there was no claim that they had committed constitutional violations. The district court ruled that Detroit-only plans were inadequate to accomplish desegregation and that it was proper to consider metropolitan plans. The Sixth Circuit affirmed that a metropolitan plan was the only feasible solution and was within the district court's equity powers.

MR. CHIEF JUSTICE BURGER delivered the opinion of the Court.

We granted certiorari in these consolidated cases to determine whether a federal court may impose a multidistrict, areawide remedy to a single-district *de jure* segregation problem absent any finding that the other included school districts have failed to operate unitary school systems within their districts....

I

[After the case bounced back and forth between the district court and the Sixth Circuit, the district court concluded that governmental actions had contributed to residential segregation and therefore school segregation. Moreover, school segregation had been perpetuated by optional attendance zones created by the Detroit Board of Education, allowing white students to escape black schools. Busing was used to transport black students to distant black schools rather than have them attend closer white schools. With one exception, created by the burning of a white school, white children were not bused to predominantly black schools. As a remedy, the district court designated 53 of the 85 suburban school districts plus Detroit as the "desegregation area" and ordered the Detroit Board of Education to purchase or lease "at least" 295 school buses to produce a desegregation plan for the metropolitan area. The Sixth Circuit agreed that any solution less comprehensive than a metropolitan area plan would be ineffective.]

II

. . .

Viewing the record as a whole, it seems clear that the District Court and the Court of Appeals shifted the primary focus from a Detroit remedy to the metropolitan area only because of their conclusion that total desegregation of Detroit would not produce the racial balance which they perceived as desirable....

In *Swann,* which arose in the context of a single independent school district, the Court held:

"If we were to read the holding of the District Court to require, as a matter of substantive constitutional right, any particular degree of racial balance or mixing, that approach would be disapproved and we would be obliged to reverse." 402 U.S., at 24.

The clear import of this language from *Swann* is that desegregation, in the sense of dismantling a dual school system, does not require any particular racial balance in each "school, grade or classroom." See *Spencer v. Kugler,* 404 U.S. 1027 (1972).

...No single tradition in public education is more deeply rooted than local control over the operation of schools; local autonomy has long been thought essential both to the maintenance of community concern and support for public schools and to quality of the educational process. See *Wright v. Council of the City of Emporia,* 407 U.S., at 469. Thus, in *San Antonio School District v. Rodriguez,* 411 U.S. 1, 50 (1973), we observed that local control over the educational process affords citizens an opportunity to participate in decisionmaking, permits the structuring of school programs to fit local needs, and encourages "experimentation, innovation, and a healthy competition for educational excellence."

. . .

...[A]n interdistrict remedy might be in order where the racially discriminatory acts of one or more school districts caused racial segregation in an adjacent district, or where district lines have been deliberately drawn on the basis of race. In such circumstances an interdistrict remedy would be appropriate to eliminate the interdistrict segregation directly caused by the constitutional violation. Conversely, without an interdistrict violation and interdistrict effect, there is no constitutional wrong calling for an interdistrict remedy.

The record before us, voluminous as it is, contains evidence of *de jure* segregated conditions only in the Detroit schools; indeed, that was the theory on which the litigation was initially based and on which the District Court took evidence.... With no showing of significant violation by the 53 outlying school districts and no evidence of any interdistrict violation or effect, the court went beyond the original theory of the case as framed by the pleadings and mandated a metropolitan area remedy. To approve the remedy ordered by the court would impose on the outlying districts, not shown to have committed any constitutional violation, a wholly impermissible remedy based on a standard not hinted at in *Brown I* and *II* or any holding of this Court.

. . .

IV

. . .

We conclude that the relief ordered by the District Court and affirmed by the Court of Appeals was based upon an erroneous standard and was unsupported by record evidence that acts of the outlying districts effected the discrimination found to exist in the schools of Detroit. Accordingly, the judgment of the Court of Appeals is reversed and the case is remanded for further proceedings consistent with this opinion leading to prompt formulation of a decree directed to eliminating the segregation found to exist in Detroit city schools, a remedy which has been delayed since 1970.

Reversed and remanded.

MR. JUSTICE STEWART, concurring.

. . .

MR. JUSTICE DOUGLAS, dissenting.

. . .

When we rule against the metropolitan area remedy we take a step that will likely put the problems of the blacks and our society back to the period that antedated the "separate but equal" regime of *Plessy* v. *Ferguson,* 163 U.S. 537. The reason is simple.

The inner core of Detroit is now rather solidly black; and the blacks, we know, in many instances are likely to be poorer, just as were the Chicanos in *San Antonio School District* v. *Rodriguez,* 411 U.S. 1. By that decision the poorer school districts must pay their own way. It is therefore a foregone conclusion that we have now given the States a formula whereby the poor must pay their own way.

Today's decision, given *Rodriguez,* means that there is no violation of the Equal Protection Clause though the schools are segregated by race and though the black schools are not only "separate" but "inferior."

. . .

MR. JUSTICE WHITE, with whom MR. JUSTICE DOUGLAS, MR. JUSTICE BRENNAN, and MR. JUSTICE MARSHALL join, dissenting.

The District Court and the Court of Appeals found that over a long period of years those in charge of the Michigan public schools engaged in various practices calculated to effect the segregation of the Detroit school system. The Court does not question these findings, nor could it reasonably do so. Neither does it question the

obligation of the federal courts to devise a feasible and effective remedy. But it promptly cripples the ability of the judiciary to perform this task, . . .

MR. JUSTICE MARSHALL, with whom MR. JUSTICE DOUGLAS, MR. JUSTICE BRENNAN, and MR. JUSTICE WHITE join, dissenting.

In *Brown* v. *Board of Education,* 347 U.S. 483 (1954), this Court held that segregation of children in public schools on the basis of race deprives minority group children of equal educational opportunities and therefore denies them the equal protection of the laws under the Fourteenth Amendment. . . .

After 20 years of small, often difficult steps toward that great end, the Court today takes a giant step backwards. Notwithstanding a record showing widespread and pervasive racial segregation in the educational system provided by the State of Michigan for children in Detroit, this Court holds that the District Court was powerless to require the State to remedy its constitutional violation in any meaningful fashion. . . .

I

The great irony of the Court's opinion and, in my view, its most serious analytical flaw may be gleaned from its concluding sentence, in which the Court remands for "prompt formulation of a decree directed to eliminating the segregation found to exist in Detroit city schools, a remedy which has been delayed since 1970." . . . The majority, however, seems to have forgotten the District Court's explicit finding that a Detroit-only decree, the only remedy permitted under today's decision, "would not accomplish desegregation."

. . .

III

. . .

Desegregation is not and was never expected to be an easy task. Racial attitudes ingrained in our Nation's childhood and adolescence are not quickly thrown aside in its middle years. But just as the inconvenience of some cannot be allowed to stand in the way of the rights of others, so public opposition, no matter how strident, cannot be permitted to divert this Court from the enforcement of the constitutional principles at issue in this case. Today's holding, I fear, is more a reflection of a perceived public mood that we have gone far enough in enforcing the Constitution's guarantee of equal justice than it is the product of neutral principles of law. In the short run, it may seem to be the easier course to allow our great metropolitan areas to be divided up each into two cities—one white, the other black—but it is a course, I predict, our people will ultimately regret. I dissent.

D. DESEGREGATING OTHER ACTIVITIES

Aside from schools and transportation, other facilities and activities available to the public have been the subject of segregation laws: housing, parks and playgrounds, golf courses, swimming pools, beaches, courtrooms, restaurants, and marriage. All three branches have searched for remedies.

Race and Housing

Public schools remain segregated because of housing patterns, both within the city and between the city and the suburbs. Some of these patterns result from discriminatory actions by public officials and private homeowners. The process of breaking down racial barriers depends on a combination of judicial rulings, presidential leadership, congressional enactments, state initiatives, and racial tolerance by private homeowners.

Compared to the tenacious hold of the separate-but-equal doctrine in the fields of education, transportation, and public accommodations, it is surprising to find a number of early judicial rulings against segregated housing. In *Buchanan* v. *Warley* (1917), a unanimous Court struck down a city ordinance that prohibited blacks from occupying houses in blocks controlled by whites. Such restrictions, said the Court, exceeded the police power and invaded the Fourteenth Amendment's right to acquire, enjoy, and use property. The case was not so much a vindication of racial equality; rather, it supported the freedom of whites to sell their property without interference. The Court based its decision not only on the Fourteenth Amendment but also on the Civil Rights Acts passed by Congress in 1866 and 1870.[7]

Of major importance is a unanimous opinion by the Court in 1948. Private parties in St. Louis, Missouri, agreed to exclude blacks from buying or occupying residences. The Court held that the agreements (restrictive covenants) did not themselves violate the Fourteenth Amendment. However, it would be a constitutional violation for the state courts to enforce them. SHELLEY v. KRAEMER, 334 U.S. 1 (1948). See also Hurd v. Hodge, 334 U.S. 25 (1948), and Barrows v. Jackson, 346 U.S. 249 (1953).

The principle of *Shelley* also prohibited discrimination against blacks in state-owned buildings. A restaurant in a building owned by Delaware refused to serve blacks. The building, constructed with public funds for public purposes, was owned and operated by the state, which leased part of it to a private operator for a restaurant. The Court held that this made the state a joint participant in operating the restaurant. The proscriptions of the Fourteenth Amendment applied to the restaurant just as though they were "binding covenants" written into the lease itself. Burton v. Wilmington Pkg. Auth., 365 U.S. 715 (1961).

The Fair Housing Act

In 1962 President Kennedy issued Executive Order 11063 to prohibit racial, ethnic, and religious discrimination in federally owned and assisted housing. The Civil Rights Act of 1964 prohibited racial discrimination in federally assisted programs, including public housing. In

---

7. Buchanan v. Warley, 245 U.S. 60, 78–79 (1917). See also Corrigan v. Buckley, 271 U.S. 323 (1926); Benjamin v. Tyler, 273 U.S. 668 (1927); Richmond, City of v. Deans, 281 U.S. 704 (1930).

1968 Congress passed the Fair Housing Act to prohibit the use of race, color, religion, or national origin in the sale or rental of most housing. Passage came in the turmoil of urban riots and widespread violence. One week before the House took its final vote to support open housing, Martin Luther King, Jr., was assassinated. 82 Stat. 81 (1968).

While Congress debated this legislation, an open-housing case reached the Supreme Court. An interracial couple had been denied the right to buy a house in suburban St. Louis. Two months after enactment of the fair housing bill, a 7–2 Court held that federal law (dating back to the Civil Rights Act of 1866) prohibited every racially motivated refusal to rent or sell property. The Court ruled that Congress had authority under the Thirteenth Amendment to pass the 1866 legislation. The Amendment forbade not only slavery but also the "badges and the incidents of slavery." Congress may prohibit both state action and private action that restrict the right of blacks to purchase, lease, and use property. JONES v. MAYER CO., 392 U.S. 409 (1968).

A year later, the Court held that questions of fair housing may not be put to voters for approval. The rights of minorities cannot be delegated to referenda results. Hunter v. Erickson, 393 U.S. 385 (1969). When the issue is not fair housing but simply low-rent public housing, states may put such matters to the people in the form of a referendum. The question here is not racial but rather income class (poor versus rich). James v. Valtierra, 402 U.S. 137 (1971). The Court also held that "private social clubs" may not use racial discrimination to prevent white owners from leasing their homes to blacks. These practices violate congressional policy dating back to 1866. Sullivan v. Little Hunting Park, 396 U.S. 229 (1969).

Subsequent cases reviewed segregation in public housing projects. Black tenants in Chicago claimed that the housing authority, supported by the Department of Housing and Urban Development (HUD), had deliberately selected public housing sites to avoid placing blacks in white neighborhoods. A unanimous Court agreed that metropolitan-area remedies, covering both city and suburbs, might be necessary to alleviate the effects of segregated housing. Area-wide action was justified in this case because HUD itself had violated the Constitution and statutes. Hills v. Gautreaux, 425 U.S. 284 (1976).

Enforcing Fair Housing

Segregated housing persists throughout the country. Studies conducted by sending white, black, and Hispanic "testers" to real estate offices reveal that discrimination continues to be practiced against blacks and dark-skinned Hispanics. Havens Realty Corp. v. Coleman, 455 U.S. 363 (1982). The Fair Housing Act of 1968 was never effectively enforced. To strengthen the Act, Congress passed legislation in 1988 to give the executive branch new authority to bring lawsuits when mediation efforts fail. The law permits government to seek large monetary damages for victims of housing discrimination. 102 Stat. 1619 (1988). The 1988 statute removed a $1,000 limit on punitive damage awards in housing bias cases. As a result, a settlement in Maryland in 1990 resulted in the payment of $225,000 by a development company, while a settlement earlier that year in California produced a payment of $450,000 by a Los Angeles apartment complex. Washington Post, April 13, 1990, at B1; February 20, 1990, at A2. In 1995, a Wisconsin property insurer accused of discriminating against minorities agreed to pay a record $14.5 million to seven black plaintiffs—the first time the Justice Department has used the Fair Housing Act against property insurers. Washington Post, April 8, 1995, at E1.

In 1990 the Court restricted the power of federal judges to force compliance with a housing desegregation plan. Split 5–4, the Court held that a district judge had abused his power by levying individual fines against four members of the city council of Yonkers, New York, for refusing to pass legislation needed to settle the discrimination suit. The majority decided

Integrated Public Facilities

Beaches and bathhouses. Dawson v. Mayor, 220 F.2d 386 (4th Cir. 1955), aff'd, 350 U.S. 877 (1955).

Golf courses, parks, playgrounds, community centers. Holmes v. City of Atlanta, 223 F.2d 93 (5th Cir. 1955), aff'd, 350 U.S. 879 (1955); Watson v. Memphis, 373 U.S. 526 (1963).

Buses. Browder v. Gayle, 142 F.Supp. 707 (M.D. Ala. 1956), aff'd, 352 U.S. 903 (1956) [explicitly overruling *Plessy v. Ferguson*].

Courtrooms. Johnson v. Virginia, 373 U.S. 61 (1963).

Bus terminal restaurants (interstate). Boynton v. Virginia, 364 U.S. 454 (1960).

Public accommodations covered by the Civil Rights Act of 1964. Heart of Atlanta Motel v. United States, 379 U.S. 241 (1964); Katzenbach v. McClung, 379 U.S. 294 (1964).

that the fines would be permissible only if a much larger fine against the *city* proved ineffective. Spallone v. United States, 493 U.S. 265 (1990).

Public Accommodations

Following *Brown* v. *Board of Education,* federal courts struck down a number of laws that discriminated on the basis of race. These cases affected public beaches and bathhouses, golf courses and parks, buses, courtrooms, and restaurants (see box). Blacks sat at lunch counters to challenge the policy of owners to deny them service. A cluster of cases pushed restaurants in the direction of abandoning that policy, but these cases also implied that the final word on this issue would have to come from legislatures, not courts.[8]

Mounting pressure for action finally culminated in passage of the Civil Rights Act of 1964. One of its sections on public accommodations barred discrimination on grounds of race, color, religion, or national origin if the operations affected interstate commerce or discrimination was supported by state action. Activities covered within this section included restaurants; cafeterias; lunchrooms; lunch counters; soda fountains; gas stations; movies; theaters; concert halls; sports arenas; stadiums; or any inn, hotel, motel, or lodging house for transient guests other than units with five or less rooms. This section did not apply to private clubs. Congressional action on public accommodations appeared to contradict the *Civil Rights Cases* of 1883, which had never been overruled by the Supreme Court. Congress avoided this potential conflict by basing the statute not only on the Civil War amendments but also on the Commerce Clause (see reading).

The public accommodation section was sustained in two unanimous rulings by the Court. The first involved a large motel in Atlanta, Georgia, used by interstate travelers. The Court supported the public accommodation provision as a valid exercise of congressional power under the Commerce Clause. HEART OF ATLANTA MOTEL v. UNITED STATES, 379 U.S. 241 (1964). The second case concerned a restaurant in Birmingham, Alabama. Although it catered to local white customers and provided a take-out service for blacks, it served food obtained from interstate commerce and was therefore within the reach of the Commerce Power as exercised by Congress. The Act specifically covers restaurants where "a substantial por-

---

8. Bouie v. City of Columbia, 378 U.S. 347 (1964); Bell v. Maryland, 378 U.S. 226 (1964); Avent v. North Carolina, 373 U.S. 375 (1963); Gober v. City of Birmingham, 373 U.S. 374 (1963); Lombard v. Louisiana, 373 U.S. 267 (1963); Shuttlesworth v. City of Birmingham, 373 U.S. 262 (1963); Peterson v. City of Greenville, 373 U.S. 244 (1963); Turner v. City of Memphis, 369 U.S. 350 (1962); Garner v. Louisiana, 368 U.S. 157 (1961).

tion" of the food served "has moved in commerce." Katzenbach v. McClung, 379 U.S. 294 (1964).

Private Facilities

The public accommodations title of the Civil Rights Act of 1964 did not apply to "a private club or other establishment not in fact open to the public," other than the facilities covered by the title (Section 201(e)). Several decisions fleshed out the scope of that section. Even when a facility is privately owned, action by the state to enforce a private policy of racial segregation violates the Equal Protection Clause of the Fourteenth Amendment. Griffin v. Maryland, 378 U.S. 130 (1964). When private individuals or groups exercise powers or perform functions governmental in nature, such as establishing a park for whites only, they become agencies or instrumentalities of the state and are subject to the restrictions of the Fourteenth Amendment. Evans v. Newton, 382 U.S. 296 (1966).

As with school segregation, opponents of racial equality tried a number of tactics. Residents of Virginia opened playground facilities and a community park for whites only. A 6–3 Court held that this nonstock corporation, acting as a "private social club," practiced racial discrimination in violation of federal law. Sullivan v. Little Hunting Park, 396 U.S. 229 (1969). A unanimous Court in 1973 ruled that a recreational association violated congressional policy by limiting the use of its swimming pool to white members and their white guests. The Court considered this case indistinguishable from *Sullivan*. Tillman v. Wheaton-Haven Recreation Assn., 410 U.S. 431 (1973).

A different result was reached in a 1972 case. A black guest at a private club had been denied service in the dining room and bar solely because of his race. Did the issuance of a state liquor license make the discriminatory practices "state action"? The Court, divided 6–3, relied on the *Civil Rights Cases* of 1883 to distinguish between discriminatory action by the state, which is prohibited by the Equal Protection Clause, and discriminatory action by private parties, against which the Clause erects no shield. The Court was reluctant to conclude that the provision of state benefits or services, including such necessities as electricity, water, and police and fire protection, was sufficient to implicate the state and automatically convert a private entity into state action. MOOSE LODGE NO. 107 v. IRVIS, 407 U.S. 163 (1972). Private companies and schools that receive almost all of their funds from public sources do not necessarily perform a "state action." Randell-Baker v. Kohn, 457 U.S. 830 (1982).

Marriage and Cohabitation

In 1955 the Court received a miscegenation case from Virginia. Rather than strike down a law against mixed marriages, the Court decided to dodge this socially explosive issue. The Court's ruling on desegregation in 1954 had been criticized by opponents who predicted that integrated schools would produce "mongrelization" of the white race. A state court, in upholding the Virginia statute, said that natural law forbade interracial marriage: "the social amalgamation which leads to a corruption of races is as clearly divine as that which imparted to them different natures." Naim v. Naim, 87 S.E.2d 749, 752 (Va. 1955). State regulation of marriages was necessary to prevent "a mongrel breed of citizens." Id. at 756.

The Supreme Court quickly returned the case to Virginia, giving time for its ruling on desegregation to establish itself as the law of the land. Naim v. Naim, 350 U.S. 891 (1955). A unanimous ruling in 1964 held that Florida's statute prohibiting the cohabitation of unmarried interracial couples, singling them out for punishment, was a denial of equal protection. McLaughlin v. Florida, 379 U.S. 184 (1964). By 1967, with the Civil Rights Act of 1964 in place, the Court was prepared to strike down miscegenation laws and did so unanimously. It pointed out that fourteen states in the previous fifteen years had repealed laws prohibiting interracial marriages. Contemporary public opinion, operating through legislatures, thus played a part. The Court rejected the argument that the state law should be upheld because the framers of the Fourteenth Amendment did not intend to prohibit miscegenation laws. "Under our Constitution, the freedom to marry, or not marry, a person of another race resides with the individual and cannot be infringed by the State." Loving v. Virginia, 388 U.S. 1, 12 (1967).

Shelley v. Kraemer

334 U.S. 1 (1948)

Private agreements, known as restrictive covenants, were used in Missouri to prevent blacks from owning property. Private agreements, standing alone, usually do not violate the Fourteenth Amendment, which is directed against actions by state governments. The question in this case was whether a connection existed between private agreements and the state of Missouri. The Kraemers, a couple in the neighborhood subject to the terms of the restrictive covenant, brought suit to prevent the Shelleys, a black couple, from taking possession of property. The trial court denied the relief but was reversed by the Supreme Court of Missouri.

MR. CHIEF JUSTICE VINSON delivered the opinion of the Court.

These cases present for our consideration questions relating to the validity of court enforcement of private agreements, generally described as restrictive covenants, which have as their purpose the exclusion of persons of designated race or color from the ownership or occupancy of real property. Basic constitutional issues of obvious importance have been raised.

The first of these cases comes to this Court on certiorari to the Supreme Court of Missouri. On February 16, 1911, thirty out of a total of thirty-nine owners of property fronting both sides of Labadie Avenue between Taylor Avenue and Cora Avenue in the city of St. Louis, signed an agreement, which was subsequently recorded, providing in part:

"...[T]he said property is hereby restricted to the use and occupancy for the term of Fifty (50) years from this date, so that it shall be a condition all the time and whether recited and referred to as [sic] not in subsequent conveyances and shall attach to the land as a condition precedent to the sale of the same, that hereafter no part of said property or any portion thereof shall be, for said term of Fifty-years, occupied by any person not of the Caucasian race, it being intended hereby to restrict the use of said property for said period of time against the occupancy as owners or tenants of any portion of said property for resident or other purpose by people of the Negro or Mongolian Race."

The entire district described in the agreement included fifty-seven parcels of land. The thirty owners who signed the agreement held title to forty-seven parcels, including the particular parcel involved in this case. At the time the agreement was signed, five of the parcels in the district were owned by Negroes. One of those had been occupied by Negro families since 1882, nearly thirty years before the restrictive agreement was executed. The trial court found that owners of seven out of nine homes on the south side of Labadie Avenue, within the restricted district and "in the immediate vicinity" of the premises in question, had failed to sign the restrictive agreement in 1911. At the time this action was brought, four of the premises were occupied by Negroes, and had been so occupied for periods ranging from twenty-three to sixty-three years. A fifth parcel had been occupied by Negroes until a year before this suit was instituted.

On August 11, 1945, pursuant to a contract of sale, petitioners Shelley, who are Negroes, for valuable consideration received from one Fitzgerald a warranty deed to the parcel in question. The trial court found that petitioners had no actual knowledge of the restrictive agreement at the time of the purchase.

On October 9, 1945, respondents, as owners of other property subject to the terms of the restrictive covenant, brought suit in the Circuit Court of the city of St. Louis praying that petitioners Shelley be restrained from taking possession of the property and that judgment be entered divesting title out of petitioners Shelley and revesting title in the immediate grantor or in such other person as the court should direct. . . .

I.

Whether the equal protection clause of the Fourteenth Amendment inhibits judicial enforcement by state courts of restrictive covenants based on race or color is a question which this Court has not heretofore been called upon to consider. Only two cases have been decided by this Court which in any way have involved the enforcement of such agreements. The first of these was the case of *Corrigan* v. *Buckley,* 271 U.S. 323 (1926). There, suit was brought in the courts of the District of Columbia to enjoin a threatened violation of certain restrictive covenants relating to lands situated in the city of Washington. . . . It is apparent that that case, which had originated in the federal courts and involved the enforcement of covenants on land located in the District of Columbia, could present no issues under the Fourteenth Amendment; for that Amendment by its terms applies only to the States. Nor was the question of the validity of court enforcement of the restrictive covenants under the Fifth Amendment properly before the Court, as the opinion of this Court specifically recognizes. . . .

The second of the cases involving racial restrictive covenants was *Hansberry* v. *Lee,* 311 U.S. 32 (1940). *[As disposed of by the Court, the issues presented by* Shelley v. Kraemer *were not reached.]*

It is well, at the outset, to scrutinize the terms of the restrictive agreements involved in these cases. In the Missouri case, the covenant declares that no part of the affected property shall be "occupied by any person not of the Caucasian race, it being intended hereby to restrict the use of said property . . . against the occupancy as owners or tenants of any portion of said property for resident or other purpose by people of the Negro or Mongolian Race." Not only does the restriction seek to proscribe use and occupancy of the affected properties by members of the excluded class, but as construed by the Missouri courts, the agreement requires that title of any person who uses his property in violation of the restriction shall be divested. . . .

It cannot be doubted that among the civil rights intended to be protected from discriminatory state action by the Fourteenth Amendment are the rights to acquire, enjoy, own and dispose of property. Equality in the enjoyment of property rights was regarded by the framers of that Amendment as an essential pre-condition to the realization of other basic civil rights and liberties which the Amendment was intended to guarantee. Thus,

§ 1978 of the Revised Statutes, derived from § 1 of the Civil Rights Act of 1866 which was enacted by Congress while the Fourteenth Amendment was also under consideration, provides:

"All citizens of the United States shall have the same right, in every State and Territory, as is enjoyed by white citizens thereof to inherit, purchase, lease, sell, hold, and convey real and personal property."

This Court has given specific recognition to the same principle. *Buchanan* v. *Warley,* 245 U.S. 60 (1917).

It is likewise clear that restrictions on the right of occupancy of the sort sought to be created by the private agreements in these cases could not be squared with the requirements of the Fourteenth Amendment if imposed by state statute or local ordinance. We do not understand respondents to urge the contrary. . . .

. . . [T]he present cases . . . do not involve action by state legislatures or city councils. Here the particular patterns of discrimination and the areas in which the restrictions are to operate, are determined, in the first instance, by the terms of agreements among private individuals. Participation of the State consists in the enforcement of the restrictions so defined. The crucial issue with which we are here confronted is whether this distinction removes these cases from the operation of the prohibitory provisions of the Fourteenth Amendment.

Since the decision of this Court in the *Civil Rights Cases,* 109 U.S. 3 (1883), the principle has become firmly embedded in our constitutional law that the action inhibited by the first section of the Fourteenth Amendment is only such action as may fairly be said to be that of the States. That Amendment erects no shield against merely private conduct, however discriminatory or wrongful.

We conclude, therefore, that the restrictive agreements standing alone cannot be regarded as violative of any rights guaranteed to petitioners by the Fourteenth Amendment. So long as the purposes of those agreements are effectuated by voluntary adherence to their terms, it would appear clear that there has been no action by the State and the provisions of the Amendment have not been violated. Cf. *Corrigan* v. *Buckley, supra.*

But here there was more. These are cases in which the purposes of the agreements were secured only by judicial enforcement by state courts of the restrictive terms of the agreements. The respondents urge that judicial enforcement of private agreements does not amount to state action; or, in any event, the participation of the State is so attenuated in character as not to amount to state action within the meaning of the Fourteenth Amendment. Finally, it is suggested, even if the States in these cases may be deemed to have acted in the constitutional sense, their action did not deprive petitioners of rights guaranteed by the Fourteenth Amendment. We move to a consideration of these matters.

II.

That the action of state courts and judicial officers in their official capacities is to be regarded as action of the State within the meaning of the Fourteenth Amendment, is a proposition which has long been established by decisions of this Court....

...[T]he examples of state judicial action which have been held by this Court to violate the Amendment's commands are not restricted to situations in which the judicial proceedings were found in some manner to be procedurally unfair. It has been recognized that the action of state courts in enforcing a substantive common-law rule formulated by those courts, may result in the denial of rights guaranteed by the Fourteenth Amendment, even though the judicial proceedings in such cases may have been in complete accord with the most rigorous conceptions of procedural due process....

The short of the matter is that from the time of the adoption of the Fourteenth Amendment until the present, it has been the consistent ruling of this Court that the action of the States to which the Amendment has reference includes action of state courts and state judicial officials....

III.

Against this background of judicial construction, extending over a period of some three-quarters of a century, we are called upon to consider whether enforcement by state courts of the restrictive agreements in these cases may be deemed to be the acts of those States; and, if so, whether that action has denied these petitioners the equal protection of the laws which the Amendment was intended to insure.

We have no doubt that there has been state action in these cases in the full and complete sense of the phrase. The undisputed facts disclose that petitioners were willing purchasers of properties upon which they desired to establish homes. The owners of the properties were willing sellers; and contracts of sale were accordingly consummated. It is clear that but for the active intervention of the state courts, supported by the full panoply of state power, petitioners would have been free to occupy the properties in question without restraint.

. . .

We hold that in granting judicial enforcement of the restrictive agreements in these cases, the States have denied petitioners the equal protection of the laws and that, therefore, the action of the state courts cannot stand....

. . .

For the reasons stated, the judgment of the Supreme Court of Missouri and the judgment of the Supreme Court of Michigan must be reversed.

Reversed.

MR. JUSTICE REED, MR. JUSTICE JACKSON, and MR. JUSTICE RUTLEDGE took no part in the consideration or decision of these cases.

Jones v. Mayer Co.

392 U.S. 409 (1968)

Joseph Lee Jones, a black, claimed in court that the Alfred H. Mayer Company had refused to sell him a home solely because of his race. He relied in part on 42 U.S.C. § 1982, which provides that all citizens "shall have the same right, in every State and Territory, as is enjoyed by white citizens thereof to inherit, purchase, lease, sell, hold, and convey real and personal property." The district court dismissed the complaint and the Eighth Circuit affirmed, concluding that section 1982 applies only to state action and does not reach private refusals to sell.

MR. JUSTICE STEWART delivered the opinion of the Court.

In this case we are called upon to determine the scope and the constitutionality of an Act of Congress, 42 U.S.C. § 1982....

...We hold that § 1982 bars *all* racial discrimination, private as well as public, in the sale or rental of property, and that the statute, thus construed, is a valid exercise of the power of Congress to enforce the Thirteenth Amendment.

I.

At the outset, it is important to make clear precisely what this case does *not* involve. Whatever else it may be, 42 U.S.C. § 1982 is not a comprehensive open housing law. In sharp contrast to the Fair Housing Title (Title VIII) of the Civil Rights Act of 1968, Pub. L. 90-284, 82 Stat. 81, the statute in this case deals only with racial discrimination and does not address itself to discrimination on grounds of religion or national origin. It does not deal specifically with discrimination in the provision of services or facilities in connection with the sale or rental of a dwelling. It does not prohibit advertising or other representations that indicate discriminatory preferences. It does not refer explicitly to discrimination in financing arrangements or in the provision of brokerage services. It does not empower a federal administrative agency to assist aggrieved parties. It makes no provision for intervention by the Attorney General. And, although it can be enforced by injunction, it contains no provision expressly authorizing a federal court to order the payment of damages.

. . .

[There are] vast differences between, on the one hand, a general statute applicable only to racial discrimination in the rental and sale of property and enforceable only by private parties acting on their own initiative, and, on the other hand, a detailed housing law, applicable to a broad range of discriminatory practices and enforceable by a complete arsenal of federal authority. Having noted these differences, we turn to a consideration of § 1982 itself.

II.

This Court last had occasion to consider the scope of 42 U.S.C. § 1982 in 1948, in *Hurd* v. *Hodge*, 334 U.S. 24. That case arose when property owners in the District of Columbia sought to enforce racially restrictive covenants against the Negro purchasers of several homes on their block. *[The Court held that Section 1982 was designed to prevent this kind of discrimination, but a federal court had assisted in the enforcement of the racially restrictive agreement. Thus,* Hurd *did not present the question whether "purely private*

discrimination, unaided by any action on the part of the government, would violate § 1982 if its effect were to deny a citizen the right to rent or buy property solely because of his race or color."]

III.

We begin with the language of the statute itself. In plain and unambiguous terms, § 1982 grants to all citizens, without regard to race or color, "the same right" to purchase and lease property "as is enjoyed by white citizens." . . .

On its face, therefore, § 1982 appears to prohibit *all* discrimination against Negroes in the sale or rental of property — discrimination by private owners as well as discrimination by public authorities. Indeed, even the respondents seem to concede that, if § 1982 "means what it says" — to use the words of the respondents' brief — then it must encompass every racially motivated refusal to sell or rent and cannot be confined to officially sanctioned segregation in housing. Stressing what they consider to be the revolutionary implications of so literal a reading of § 1982, the respondents argue that Congress cannot possibly have intended any such result. Our examination of the relevant history, however, persuades us that Congress meant exactly what it said.

IV.

In its original form, 42 U.S.C. § 1982 was part of § 1 of the Civil Rights Act of 1866. That section was cast in sweeping terms:

"Be it enacted by the Senate and House of Representatives of the United States of America in Congress assembled, That all persons born in the United States and not subject to any foreign power, . . . are hereby declared to be citizens of the United States; and such citizens, of every race and color, without regard to any previous condition of slavery or involuntary servitude, . . . shall have the same right, in every State and Territory in the United States, to make and enforce contracts, to sue, be parties, and give evidence, to inherit, purchase, lease, sell, hold, and convey real and personal property, and to full and equal benefit of all laws and proceedings for the security of person and property, as is enjoyed by white citizens, and shall be subject to like punishment, pains, and penalties, and to none other, any law, statute, ordinance, regulation, or custom, to the contrary notwithstanding."

The crucial language for our purposes was that which guaranteed all citizens "the same right, in every State and Territory in the United States,... to inherit, purchase, lease, sell, hold, and convey real and personal property...as is enjoyed by white citizens...." To the Congress that passed the Civil Rights Act of 1866; it was clear that the right to do these things might be infringed not only by "State or local law" but also by "custom, or prejudice." Thus, when Congress provided in § 1 of the Civil Rights Act that the right to purchase and lease property was to be enjoyed equally throughout the United States by Negro and white citizens alike, it plainly meant to secure that right against interference from any source whatever, whether governmental or private.

Indeed, if § 1 had been intended to grant nothing more than an immunity from *governmental* interference, then much of § 2 would have made no sense at all. For that section, which provided fines and prison terms for certain individuals who deprived others of rights "secured or protected" by § 1, was carefully drafted to exempt private violations of § 1 from the criminal sanctions it imposed. There would, of course, have been no private violations to exempt if the only "right" granted by § 1 had been a right to be free of discrimination by public officials. Hence the structure of the 1866 Act, as well as its language, points to the conclusion urged by the petitioners in this case — that § 1 was meant to prohibit *all* racially motivated deprivations of the rights enumerated in the statute, although only those deprivations perpetrated "under color of law" were to be criminally punishable under § 2.

. . .

Nor was the scope of the 1866 Act altered when it was re-enacted in 1870, some two years after the ratification of the Fourteenth Amendment. It is quite true that some members of Congress supported the Fourteenth Amendment "in order to eliminate doubt as to the constitutional validity of the Civil Rights Act as applied to the States." *Hurd* v. *Hodge,* 334 U.S. 24, 32–33. But it certainly does not follow that the adoption of the Fourteenth Amendment or the subsequent readoption of the Civil Rights Act were meant somehow to *limit* its application to state action. The legislative history furnishes not the slightest factual basis for any such speculation, and the conditions prevailing in 1870 make it highly implausible. For by that time most, if not all, of the former Confederate States, then under the control of "reconstructed" legislatures, had formally repudiated racial discrimination, and the focus of

congressional concern had clearly shifted from hostile statutes to the activities of groups like the Ku Klux Klan, operating wholly outside the law.

Against this background, it would obviously make no sense to assume, without any historical support whatever, that Congress made a silent decision in 1870 to exempt private discrimination from the operation of the Civil Rights Act of 1866....

V.

The remaining question is whether Congress has power under the Constitution to do what § 1982 purports to do: to prohibit all racial discrimination, private and public, in the sale and rental of property. Our starting point is the Thirteenth Amendment, for it was pursuant to that constitutional provision that Congress originally enacted what is now § 1982. The Amendment consists of two parts. Section 1 states:

"Neither slavery nor involuntary servitude, except as a punishment for crime whereof the party shall have been duly convicted, shall exist within the United States, or any place subject to their jurisdiction."

Section 2 provides:

"Congress shall have power to enforce this article by appropriate legislation."

As its text reveals, the Thirteenth Amendment "is not a mere prohibition of State laws establishing or upholding slavery, but an absolute declaration that slavery or involuntary servitude shall not exist in any part of the United States." *Civil Rights Cases,* 109 U.S. 3, 20. It has never been doubted, therefore, "that the power vested in Congress to enforce the article by appropriate legislation," *ibid.,* includes the power to enact laws "direct and primary, operating upon the acts of individuals, whether sanctioned by State legislation or not." *Id.,* at 23.

Thus, the fact that § 1982 operates upon the unofficial acts of private individuals, whether or not sanctioned by state law, presents no constitutional problem....

...Surely Congress has the power under the Thirteenth Amendment rationally to determine what are the badges and the incidents of slavery, and the authority to translate that determination into effective legislation. Nor can we say that the determination Congress has made is an irrational one.... when racial discrimination herds men into ghettos and makes their ability to buy property turn on the color of their skin, then it too is a relic of slavery.

. . .

...The judgment is

Reversed.

MR. JUSTICE DOUGLAS, concurring.

. . .

MR. JUSTICE HARLAN, whom MR. JUSTICE WHITE joins, dissenting.

. . .

...I believe that the Court's construction of § 1982 as applying to purely private action is al-most surely wrong, and at the least is open to se-rious doubt. The issues of the constitutionality of § 1982, as construed by the Court, and of lia-bility under the Fourteenth Amendment alone, also present formidable difficulties. Moreover, the political processes of our own era have, since the date of oral argument in this case, given birth to a civil rights statute embodying "fair housing" provisions which would at the end of this year make available to others, though apparently not to the petitioners themselves, the type of relief which the petitioners now seek. It seems to me that this latter factor so diminishes the public im-portance of this case that by far the wisest course would be for this Court to refrain from decision and to dismiss the writ as improvidently granted.

Congress Interprets the Commerce Clause

Congressional action on the public accommodations section of the Civil Rights Act of 1964 was jeopardized by the Supreme Court's decision in the *Civil Rights Cases* of 1883. In that case, the Court struck down an earlier congressional effort, based on the Four-teenth Amendment, to pass legislation on public accommodations. Rather than risk a head-on collision with the Court, Congress selected another instrument to achieve its ends: the Commerce Clause. The language below is from Senate Report No. 872, 88th Cong., 2d Sess. 12–14 (1964).

At the outset a formidable obstacle to a favor-able determination on S. 1732 appeared to be an 1883 decision by the U.S. Supreme Court holding unconstitutional an 1875 statute providing crimi-nal penalties for denials of service by public facil-ities or accommodations on account of race, color, or religion. This 1875 law was expressly based on the 14th amendment, but the Supreme Court could not find the requisite "State action" in de-nials of service by privately owned establishments. There is a large body of legal thought that believes the Court would either reverse the earlier decision if the question were again presented or that changed circumstances in the intervening 80 years would make it possible for the earlier decision to be distinguished. That question, however, was not before the committee, for the instant measure is based on the commerce clause (art. 1, sec. 8, clause 3) of the Constitution. The majority opinion of the Court in the 1883 decision carefully stated that they were not foreclosing a statute based on the broad powers of Congress such as are found in the commerce clause. Mr. Justice Bradley wrote:

"Of course, these remarks do not apply to those cases in which Congress is clothed with di-rect and plenary powers of legislation over the whole subject, accompanied with an express or implied denial of such power to the States, as in the regulation of commerce with foreign nations, and among the several States and with the Indian tribes, the coining of money, the establishment of post offices and post roads, the declaring of war, etc. In these cases Congress has power to pass laws for regulating the subjects specified in every detail, and the conduct and transactions of individuals in respect thereof." (109 U.S. 3, 18 (1883))

Attached as an appendix to this report is a brief prepared at the request of the committee by Prof. Paul Freund of the Harvard Law School, a noted authority on the Constitution. In this doc-ument Professor Freund concludes that the law proposed by S. 1732 is consistent with the Con-stitution and the decisions thereunder by the Supreme Court. In the judgment of the committee it would be upheld on review. Similar conclusions were reached by almost all legal scholars or prac-titioners consulted by the committee or inquired of by witnesses appearing before the committee. Professor Freund wrote: "The commerce power is clearly adequate and appropriate. No impropri-ety need be felt in using the commerce clause as a response to a deep moral concern." Where social injustices occur in commercial activities the commerce clause has been used to prevent discrimination; it has been used to prohibit racial discrimination; and it has been used to reach intrastate activities if they have a substantial effect (individually or cumulatively) upon commerce. The committee concludes that there is sufficient authority in the Constitution to uphold S. 1732.

Congress, in the exercise of its plenary power over interstate commerce, may regulate commerce or that which affects it for other than purely economic goals.

"The motive and purpose of a regulation of interstate commerce are matters for the legislative judgment upon the exercise of which the Constitution places no restriction and over which the courts are given no control." (Mr. Justice Stone in *United States* v. *Darby*, 312 U.S. 100, 115 (1941))

The fact that S. 1732 would accomplish socially oriented objectives by aid of the commerce clause powers would not detract from its validity. There are many instances in which Congress has discouraged practices which it deems evil, dangerous, or unwise by a regulation of interstate commerce. Examples of this are found in Federal legislation keeping the channels of commerce free from the transportation of tickets used in lottery schemes, sustained in *Champion* v. *Ames,* 188 U.S. 321 (1903); the Pure Food and Drug Act, sustained in *Hipolite Egg Co.* v. *United States,* 220 U.S. 45 (1911); the "White Slave Traffic Act," upheld in *Hoke* v. *United States,* 227 U.S. 308 (1913); strict regulation of the transportation of intoxicating liquors, sustained in *Clark Distilling Co.* v. *Western Maryland Railway Co.,* 242 U.S. 311 (1917); and the Fair Labor Standards Act, imposing wages and hours requirements, sustained in *United States* v. *Darby,* 312 U.S. 100 (1941).

Heart of Atlanta Motel v. United States

379 U.S. 241 (1964)

Title II of the Civil Rights Act of 1964 prohibits racial discrimination in places of public accommodation affecting interstate commerce. Establishments covered by the Act include inns, hotels, restaurants, cafeterias, and movie theaters. The appellant in this case, the Heart of Atlanta Motel located in Atlanta, Georgia, restricted its clientele to white persons. The motel claimed that the statute exceeded Congress' power under the Commerce Clause and violated other parts of the Constitution. A three-judge court upheld the constitutionality of Title II.

Mr. Justice Clark delivered the opinion of the Court.

. . .

1. THE FACTUAL BACKGROUND AND CONTENTIONS OF THE PARTIES.

The case comes here on admissions and stipulated facts. Appellant owns and operates the Heart of Atlanta Motel which has 216 rooms available to transient guests. The motel is located on Courtland Street, two blocks from downtown Peachtree Street. It is readily accessible to interstate highways 75 and 85 and state highways 23 and 41. Appellant solicits patronage from outside the State of Georgia through various national advertising media, including magazines of national circulation; it maintains over 50 billboards and highway signs within the State, soliciting patronage for the motel; it accepts convention trade from outside Georgia and approximately 75% of its registered guests are from out of State. Prior

to passage of the Act the motel had followed a practice of refusing to rent rooms to Negroes, and it alleged that it intended to continue to do so. In an effort to perpetuate that policy this suit was filed.

The appellant contends that Congress in passing this Act exceeded its power to regulate commerce under Art. I, § 8, cl. 3, of the Constitution of the United States; that the Act violates the Fifth Amendment because appellant is deprived of the right to choose its customers and operate its business as it wishes, resulting in a taking of its liberty and property without due process of law and a taking of its property without just compensation; and, finally, that by requiring appellant to rent available rooms to Negroes against its will, Congress is subjecting it to involuntary servitude in contravention of the Thirteenth Amendment.

The appellees counter that the unavailability to Negroes of adequate accommodations interferes significantly with interstate travel, and that Congress, under the Commerce Clause, has power to remove such obstructions and restraints; that the Fifth Amendment does not forbid reasonable regulation and that consequential damage does not constitute a "taking" within the meaning of that amendment; that the Thirteenth Amendment claim fails because it is entirely frivolous to say that an amendment directed to the abolition of human bondage and the removal of widespread disabilities associated with slavery places discrimination in public accommodations beyond the reach of both federal and state law.

. . .

3. TITLE II OF THE ACT.

This Title is divided into seven sections beginning with § 201 (a) which provides that:

"All persons shall be entitled to the full and equal enjoyment of the goods, services, facilities, privileges, advantages, and accommodations of any place of public accommodation, as defined in this section, without discrimination or segregation on the ground of race, color, religion, or national origin."

There are listed in § 201 (b) four classes of business establishments, each of which "serves the public" and "is a place of public accommodation" within the meaning of § 201 (a) "if its operations affect commerce, or if discrimination or segregation by it is supported by State action." The covered establishments are:

"(1) any inn, hotel, motel, or other establishment which provides lodging to transient guests, other than an establishment located within a building which contains not more than five rooms for rent or hire and which is actually occupied by the proprietor of such establishment as his residence;

"(2) any restaurant, cafeteria . . . [not here involved];

"(3) any motion picture house . . . [not here involved];

"(4) any establishment . . . which is physically located within the premises of any establishment otherwise covered by this subsection, or . . . within the premises of which is physically located any such covered establishment . . . [not here involved]."

Section 201 (c) defines the phrase "affect commerce" as applied to the above establishments. It first declares that "any inn, hotel, motel, or other

establishment which provides lodging to transient guests" affects commerce *per se.* Restaurants, cafeterias, etc., in class two affect commerce only if they serve or offer to serve interstate travelers or if a substantial portion of the food which they serve or products which they sell have "moved in commerce." . . .

4. APPLICATION OF TITLE II TO HEART OF ATLANTA MOTEL.

It is admitted that the operation of the motel brings it within the provisions of § 201 (a) of the Act and that appellant refused to provide lodging for transient Negroes because of their race or color and that it intends to continue that policy unless restrained.

The sole question posed is, therefore, the constitutionality of the Civil Rights Act of 1964 as applied to these facts. The legislative history of the Act indicates that Congress based the Act on § 5 and the Equal Protection Clause of the Fourteenth Amendment as well as its power to regulate interstate commerce under Art. I, § 8, cl. 3, of the Constitution.

The Senate Commerce Committee made it quite clear that the fundamental object of Title II was to vindicate "the deprivation of personal dignity that surely accompanies denials of equal access to public establishments." At the same time, however, it noted that such an objective has been and could be readily achieved "by congressional action based on the commerce power of the Constitution." S. Rep. No. 872, *supra,* at 16–17. Our study of the legislative record, made in the light of prior cases, has brought us to the conclusion that Congress possessed ample power in this regard, and we have therefore not considered the other grounds relied upon. This is not to say that the remaining authority upon which it acted was not adequate, a question upon which we do not pass, but merely that since the commerce power is sufficient for our decision here we have considered it alone. Nor is § 201 (d) or § 202, having to do with state action, involved here and we do not pass upon either of those sections.

5. THE CIVIL RIGHTS CASES, 109 U.S. 3 (1883), AND THEIR APPLICATION.

In light of our ground for decision, it might be well at the outset to discuss the *Civil Rights Cases, supra,* which declared provisions of the Civil Rights Act of 1875 unconstitutional. 18

Stat. 335, 336. We think that decision inapposite, and without precedential value in determining the constitutionality of the present Act. Unlike Title II of the present legislation, the 1875 Act broadly proscribed discrimination in "inns, public conveyances on land or water, theaters, and other places of public amusement," without limiting the categories of affected businesses to those impinging upon interstate commerce. In contrast, the applicability of Title II is carefully limited to enterprises having a direct and substantial relation to the interstate flow of goods and people, except where state action is involved. Further, the fact that certain kinds of businesses may not in 1875 have been sufficiently involved in interstate commerce to warrant bringing them within the ambit of the commerce power is not necessarily dispositive of the same question today. Our populace had not reached its present mobility, nor were facilities, goods and services circulating as readily in interstate commerce as they are today....

6. THE BASIS OF CONGRESSIONAL ACTION.

While the Act as adopted carried no congressional findings the record of its passage through each house is replete with evidence of the burdens that discrimination by race or color places upon interstate commerce.... This testimony included the fact that our people have become increasingly mobile with millions of people of all races traveling from State to State; that Negroes in particular have been the subject of discrimination in transient accommodations, having to travel great distances to secure the same; that often they have been unable to obtain accommodations and have had to call upon friends to put them up overnight...; and that these conditions had become so acute as to require the listing of available lodging for Negroes in a special guidebook which was itself "dramatic testimony to the difficulties" Negroes encounter in travel....

7. THE POWER OF CONGRESS OVER INTERSTATE TRAVEL.

The power of Congress to deal with these obstructions depends on the meaning of the Commerce Clause....

It is said that the operation of the motel here is of a purely local character. But, assuming this to be true, "[i]f it is interstate commerce that feels the pinch, it does not matter how local the operation which applies the squeeze." *United States v.*

Women's Sportswear Mfrs. Assn., 336 U.S. 460, 464 (1949). See *Labor Board v. Jones & Laughlin Steel Corp., supra.* As Chief Justice Stone put it in *United States v. Darby, supra:*

"The power of Congress over interstate commerce is not confined to the regulation of commerce among the states. It extends to those activities intrastate which so affect interstate commerce or the exercise of the power of Congress over it as to make regulation of them appropriate means to the attainment of a legitimate end, the exercise of the granted power of Congress to regulate interstate commerce. See *McCulloch v. Maryland,* 4 Wheat. 316, 421." At 118.

Thus the power of Congress to promote interstate commerce also includes the power to regulate the local incidents thereof, including local activities in both the States or origin and destination, which might have a substantial and harmful effect upon that commerce. One need only examine the evidence which we have discussed above to see that Congress may — as it has — prohibit racial discrimination by motels serving travelers, however "local" their operations may appear.

Nor does the Act deprive appellant of liberty or property under the Fifth Amendment. The commerce power invoked here by the Congress is a specific and plenary one authorized by the Constitution itself. The only questions are: (1) whether Congress had a rational basis for finding that racial discrimination by motels affected commerce, and (2) if it had such a basis, whether the means it selected to eliminate that evil are reasonable and appropriate. If they are, appellant has no "right" to select its guests as it sees fit, free from governmental regulation.

. . .

We find no merit in the remainder of appellant's contentions, including that of "involuntary servitude." As we have seen, 32 States prohibit racial discrimination in public accommodations. These laws but codify the common-law innkeeper rule which long predated the Thirteenth Amendment....

We, therefore, conclude that the action of the Congress in the adoption of the Act as applied here to a motel which concededly serves interstate travelers is within the power granted it by the Commerce Clause of the Constitution, as interpreted by this Court for 140 years. It may be argued that Congress could have pursued other methods to eliminate the obstructions it found in interstate commerce caused by racial discrimination. But this is a matter of policy that rests entirely with the Congress not with the courts. How obstructions in commerce may be removed — what means are to be employed — is within the sound and exclusive discretion of the Congress. It is subject only to one caveat — that the means chosen by it must be reasonably adapted to the end permitted by the Constitution. We cannot say that its choice here was not so adapted. The Constitution requires no more.

Affirmed.

[Justices Black, Douglas, and Goldberg wrote separate concurring opinions.]

Moose Lodge No. 107 v. Irvis

407 U.S. 163 (1972)

K. Leroy Irvis, a black guest of a member of Moose Lodge No. 107, was refused service at the club's dining room and bar solely because of his race. In suing for injunctive relief, he contended that the discrimination was "state action" and thus a violation of the Equal Protection Clause of the Fourteenth Amendment. He argued that a connection existed between the private club and the state because the Pennsylvania liquor board had issued the lodge a private club liquor license. A three-judge district court found the lodge's membership and guest practices discriminatory and agreed that there was state action.

MR. JUSTICE REHNQUIST delivered the opinion of the Court.

Appellee Irvis, a Negro (hereafter appellee), was refused service by appellant Moose Lodge, a local branch of the national fraternal organization located in Harrisburg, Pennsylvania. Appellee then brought this action under 42 U.S.C. § 1983 for injunctive relief in the United States District Court for the Middle District of Pennsylvania. He claimed that because the Pennsylvania liquor board had issued appellant Moose Lodge a private club license that authorized the sale of alcoholic beverages on its premises, the refusal of service to him was "state action" for the purposes of the Equal Protection Clause of the Fourteenth Amendment....

I

The District Court in its opinion found that "a Caucasian member in good standing brought plaintiff, a Negro, to the Lodge's dining room and bar as his guest and requested service of food and beverages. The Lodge through its employees refused service to plaintiff solely because he is a Negro." 318 F.Supp. 1246, 1247. It is undisputed that each local Moose Lodge is bound by the constitution and general bylaws of the Supreme Lodge, the latter of which contain a provision limiting membership in the lodges to white male Caucasians. The District Court in this connection found that "[t]he lodges accordingly maintain a policy and practice of restricting membership to the Caucasian race and permit-

ting members to bring only Caucasian guests on lodge premises, particularly to the dining room and bar." *Ibid.*

[The Court holds that Irvis, who had not applied for or been denied membership in the lodge, had no standing to contest the lodge's membership practices. He did, however, have standing to litigate the constitutional validity of the lodge's discriminatory policies toward members' guests.]

II

Moose Lodge is a private club in the ordinary meaning of that term. It is a local chapter of a national fraternal organization having well-defined requirements for membership. It conducts all of its activities in a building that is owned by it. It is not publicly funded. Only members and guests are permitted in any lodge of the order; one may become a guest only by invitation of a member or upon invitation of the house committee.

Appellee, while conceding the right of private clubs to choose members upon a discriminatory basis, asserts that the licensing of Moose Lodge to serve liquor by the Pennsylvania Liquor Control Board amounts to such state involvement with the club's activities as to make its discriminatory practices forbidden by the Equal Protection Clause of the Fourteenth Amendment. The relief sought and obtained by appellee in the District Court was an injunction forbidding the licensing by the liquor authority of Moose Lodge until it ceased its discriminatory practices. We conclude that Moose Lodge's refusal to serve food and beverages to a guest by reason of the fact that he was a Negro does not, under the circumstances here presented, violate the Fourteenth Amendment.

In 1883, this Court in *The Civil Rights Cases,* 109 U.S. 3, set forth the essential dichotomy between discriminatory action by the State, which is prohibited by the Equal Protection Clause, and private conduct, "however discriminatory or wrongful," against which that clause "erects no shield," *Shelley* v. *Kraemer,* 334 U.S. 1, 13 (1948). That dichotomy has been subsequently reaffirmed in *Shelley* v. *Kraemer, supra,* and in *Burton* v. *Wilmington Parking Authority,* 365 U.S. 715 (1961).

While the principle is easily stated, the question of whether particular discriminatory conduct is private, on the one hand, or amounts to "state action," on the other hand, frequently admits of no easy answer. "Only by sifting facts and weighing circumstances can the nonobvious involvement of the State in private conduct be attributed its true significance." *Burton* v. *Wilmington Parking Authority, supra,* at 722.

Our cases make clear that the impetus for the forbidden discrimination need not originate with the State if it is state action that enforces privately originated discrimination. *Shelley* v. *Kraemer, supra.* The Court held in *Burton* v. *Wilmington Parking Authority, supra,* that a private restaurant owner who refused service because of a customer's race violated the Fourteenth Amendment, where the restaurant was located in a building owned by a state-created parking authority and leased from the authority....

The Court has never held, of course, that discrimination by an otherwise private entity would be violative of the Equal Protection Clause if the private entity receives any sort of benefit or service at all from the State, or if it is subject to state regulation in any degree whatever. Since state-furnished services include such necessities of life as electricity, water, and police and fire protection, such a holding would utterly emasculate the distinction between private as distinguished from state conduct set forth in *The Civil Rights Cases, supra,* and adhered to in subsequent decisions. Our holdings indicate that where the impetus for the discrimination is private, the State must have "significantly involved itself with invidious discriminations," *Reitman* v. *Mulkey,* 387 U.S. 369, 380 (1967), in order for the discriminatory action to fall within the ambit of the constitutional prohibition.

. . .

Here there is nothing approaching the symbiotic relationship between lessor and lessee that was present in *Burton,* where the private lessee obtained the benefit of locating in a building owned by the state-created parking authority, and the parking authority was enabled to carry out its primary public purpose of furnishing parking space by advantageously leasing portions of the building constructed for that purpose to commercial lessees such as the owner of the Eagle Restaurant. Unlike *Burton,* the Moose Lodge building is located on land owned by it, not by any public authority. Far from apparently holding itself out as a place of public accommodation, Moose Lodge quite ostentatiously proclaims the fact that it is not open to the public at large. Nor is it located and operated in such surroundings that although private in name, it discharges a function or performs a service that would otherwise in all likelihood be performed by the State. In short, while Eagle was a public restaurant in a public building, Moose Lodge is a private social club in a private building.

. . .

Even though the Liquor Control Board regulation in question is neutral in its terms, the result of its application in a case where the constitution and bylaws of a club required racial discrimination would be to invoke the sanctions of the State to enforce a concededly discriminatory private rule. State action, for purposes of the Equal Protection Clause, may emanate from rulings of administrative and regulatory agencies as well as from legislative or judicial action. *Robinson* v. *Florida,* 378 U.S. 153, 156 (1964). *Shelley* v. *Kraemer,* 334 U.S. 1 (1948), makes it clear that the application of state sanctions to enforce such a rule would violate the Fourteenth Amendment. Although the record before us is not as clear as one would like, appellant has not persuaded us that the District Court should have denied any and all relief.

Appellee was entitled to a decree enjoining the enforcement of § 113.09 of the regulations promulgated by the Pennsylvania Liquor Control Board insofar as that regulation requires compliance by Moose Lodge with provisions of its constitution and bylaws containing racially discriminatory provisions. He was entitled to no more. The judgment of the District Court is reversed, and the cause remanded with instructions to enter a decree in conformity with this opinion.

Reversed and remanded.

MR. JUSTICE DOUGLAS, with whom MR. JUSTICE MARSHALL joins, dissenting.

My view of the First Amendment and the related guarantees of the Bill of Rights is that they create a zone of privacy which precludes government from interfering with private clubs or groups. The associational rights which our system honors permit all white, all black, all brown, and all yellow clubs to be formed. They also permit all Catholic, all Jewish, or all agnostic clubs to be established. Government may not tell a man or woman who his or her associates must be. The individual can be as selective as he desires. So the fact that the Moose Lodge allows only Caucasians to join or come as guests is constitutionally irrelevant, as is the decision of the Black Muslims to admit to their services only members of their race.

. . .

. . . [T]he fact that a private club gets some kind of permit from the State or municipality does not make it *ipso facto* a public enterprise or undertaking, any more than the grant to a householder of a permit to operate an incinerator puts the householder in the public domain. We must, therefore, examine whether there are special circumstances involved in the Pennsylvania scheme which differentiate the liquor license possessed by Moose Lodge from the incinerator permit.

Pennsylvania has a state store system of alcohol distribution. Resale is permitted by hotels, restaurants, and private clubs which all must obtain licenses from the Liquor Control Board.... Once a license is issued the licensee must comply with many detailed requirements or risk suspension or revocation of the license. Among these requirements is Regulation § 113.09 which says: "Every club licensee shall adhere to all of the provisions of its Constitution and By-laws." This regulation means, as applied to Moose Lodge, that it must adhere to the racially discriminatory provision of the Constitution of its Supreme Lodge....

. . . [W]e have held that "a State is responsible for the discriminatory act of a private party when the State, by its law, has compelled the act." *Adickes* v. *Kress & Co.,* 398 U.S. 144, 170.... The result, as I see it, is the same as though Pennsylvania had put into its liquor licenses a provision that the license may not be used to dispense liquor to blacks, browns, yellows—or atheists or agnostics. Regulation § 113.09 is thus an invidious form of state action.

Were this regulation the only infirmity in Pennsylvania's licensing scheme, I would perhaps agree with the majority that the appropriate relief would be a decree enjoining its enforcement. But there is another flaw in the scheme not so easily cured. Liquor licenses in Pennsylvania, unlike driver's licenses, or marriage licenses, are not freely available to those who meet racially neutral qualifications. There is a complex quota system, which the majority accurately describes.... What the majority neglects to say is that the quota for Harrisburg, where Moose Lodge No. 107 is located, has been full for many years. No more club licenses may be issued in that city.

This state-enforced scarcity of licenses restricts the ability of blacks to obtain liquor, for liquor is commercially available *only* at private clubs for a significant portion of each week. Access by blacks to places that serve liquor is further limited by the fact that the state quota is filled. A group desiring to form a nondiscriminatory club which would serve blacks must purchase a license held by an existing club, which can exact a monopoly price for the transfer. The availability of such a license is speculative at best, however, for, as Moose Lodge itself concedes, without a liquor license a fraternal organization would be hard pressed to survive.

Thus, the State of Pennsylvania is putting the weight of its liquor license, concededly a valued and important adjunct to a private club, behind racial discrimination.

. . .

MR. JUSTICE BRENNAN, with whom MR. JUSTICE MARSHALL joins, dissenting.

. . .

E. EMPLOYMENT AND AFFIRMATIVE ACTION

Racial segregation persists because of a number of interlocking cycles. Segregated housing contributes to segregated education; segregated education is a factor in segregated employment. One way to combat racial segregation is through job opportunities. Blacks and

Hispanics with stable jobs and higher incomes have greater choices in deciding where to live and where to send their children to school. To broaden these choices, the government has relied on the controversial tools of quotas and affirmative action ("reverse discrimination").

Executive Orders

From 1941 to 1958, Presidents Roosevelt, Truman, and Eisenhower issued a number of Executive Orders to improve employment opportunities for blacks. Under pressure from civil rights activists who protested discrimination in hiring, Roosevelt issued an Executive Order in 1941 to establish the Committee on Fair Employment Practices. The purpose was to increase black employment in the defense industry. Executive Order 8802 declared that "there shall be no discrimination in the employment of workers in defense industries or government because of race, creed, color, or national origin...." Outbreaks of racial violence after World War II prompted Truman, in 1946, to issue Executive Order 9808 to establish the President's Committee on Civil Rights. The Committee attacked segregation and the separate-but-equal doctrine as morally wrong and economically wasteful. In a major address to Congress on February 2, 1948, Truman set forth an agenda for civil rights. The goals he established, including a commission to prevent unfair discrimination in employment, had to await passage of the civil rights bills from 1957 to 1964.

In the meantime, President Kennedy issued Executive Order 10925 in 1961 to establish the President's Committee on Equal Employment Opportunity. There were two goals: equal access to employment within the government and equal opportunity for those who receive government contracts. As a condition for receiving federal contracts, private companies had to agree to nondiscriminatory policies. Executive Order 11114, issued in 1963, extended the Committee's authority to include federally assisted construction. President Johnson issued Executive Order 11246 in 1965, vesting in the Secretary of Labor the responsibility for ensuring nondiscrimination by government contractors.

Legislative Action

Title VII of the Civil Rights Act of 1964 prohibits employment practices based on race, color, religion, sex, or national origin. Congress created the Equal Employment Opportunity Commission (EEOC) to oversee this title but gave the Commission authority only to conciliate complaints of job bias. It had no power to issue cease-and-desist orders to employers or to file suit in court. Enforcement powers were strengthened in 1972 by authorizing the EEOC to take discrimination cases to federal court if conciliation efforts fail. 86 Stat. 103 (1972). The 1972 amendments also extended Title VII coverage to state and local government employees.

In 1971 a unanimous Court interpreted Title VII to prohibit the use of hiring practices that are not job-related and that operate to exclude blacks. In this case, a company required a high school diploma and the taking of an intelligence test. The Court said it was immaterial whether the employer had a discriminatory intent. Griggs v. Duke Power Co., 401 U.S. 424 (1971). The *Griggs* test appeared to require an employee to prove only disparate *results*, not the employer's *intent*.

Another case on employment tests was decided in 1976. Two blacks, after being rejected as police officers, claimed that the written personnel tests bore no relation to job performance and were racially discriminatory. Although the police department had made affirmative efforts to recruit black officers, the tests excluded a disproportionately high number of black applicants. The tests measured verbal ability, vocabulary, reading, and comprehension. The Court, by a 7–2 vote, held that the tests were not unconstitutional solely because they had a racially disproportionate impact. In an apparent conflict with *Griggs*, the Court said that there

Congressional Policy on "Affirmative Action"

Civil rights legislation appeared to prohibit racial discrimination in any form, For example, Section 703 of Title VII of the Civil Rights Act of 1964 makes it unlawful to "discriminate... because of... race" in hiring and in the selection of apprentices for training programs. Moreover, Section 703(j) states that nothing in Title VII shall be interpreted to require "preferential treatment" to any individual for reasons of race or color. On the other hand, Section 706(g) authorized a court to order "such affirmative action as may be appropriate, which may include reinstatement or hiring of employees, with or without backpay...." This authority was strengthened in 1972 to read: "such affirmative action as may be appropriate, which may include, but is not limited to, reinstatement or hiring of employees, with or without back pay... or any other equitable relief as the court deems appropriate." 86 Stat. 107. Senator Ervin in 1972 offered an amendment to prohibit any federal agency or office from requiring employees to practice "discrimination in reverse." His amendment was rejected by the decisive margin of 44 to 22, in part because it would deprive courts of their power to remedy cases of discrimination. 118 Cong. Rec. 1661–76 (1972).

must be a purpose to discriminate. The Court justified a different conclusion because this was not a Title VII case. The plaintiffs asserted that the tests violated their rights under the Due Process Clause of the Fifth Amendment, under 42 U.S.C. § 1981, and under the D.C. Code. Washington v. Davis, 426 U.S. 229 (1976).

Affirmative Action

A number of government and private programs give preferential treatment to certain races. Congressional attitudes and policy on "affirmative action" have been inconsistent and often contradictory (see box). Little opposition exists to programs that make special efforts to recruit minorities, assuring that a sufficient number will be in the pool of candidates. But should race be a factor in making the selections? Can employers prefer, for reasons of race, a minority over an equally qualified white? Does affirmative action allow the acceptance of a minority who is less qualified? Is racial discrimination an appropriate means to compensate for past injuries and injustices? Should quotas or "goals" be established to guarantee the acceptance of a specific number of blacks, Hispanics, and other minorities?

Initially, the judiciary interpreted congressional policy to require a standard of racial neutrality in hiring. Race was not to be a factor. In 1971 a unanimous Court stated that Congress did not, in Title VII of the Civil Rights Act of 1964, command "that the less qualified be preferred over the better qualified simply because of minority origins. Far from disparaging job qualifications as such, Congress has made such qualifications the controlling factor, so that race, religion, nationality, and sex become irrelevant." Griggs v. Duke Power Co., 401 U.S. at 436. Congress prohibited discriminatory preference "for any group, minority or majority." Id. at 431. A unanimous Court in 1976 held that Title VII prohibits racial discrimination whether the victim is black or white. Employers could not dismiss whites for an offense and retain a black who committed the same offense. McDonald v. Santa Fe Trail Transp. Co., 427 U.S. 273 (1976).

Yet various administrations used race as a criterion in overseeing the award of federal contracts. Under the Philadelphia Plan, developed by the Nixon administration, contractors had to set specific goals for hiring members of minority groups as a condition for working on federally assisted projects. Federal courts upheld the legality of the plan in 1970 and 1971, as well as the Executive Order that placed it in operation.[9]

The question of affirmative action confronted the Court in 1974. Marco DeFunis, Jr., a white applicant to the University of Washington Law School, was denied admission. He claimed that the school's policy discriminated against him. Out of 150 openings for first-year students, the school set aside a specific number of places for minority applicants (blacks, Chicanos, American Indians, and Filipinos). DeFunis scored higher than most of the minorities accepted. Had the minority applicants been considered under the same procedure applied to him, none of those eventually enrolled would have been admitted.

After DeFunis' claim of discrimination was upheld by a state trial court, he was admitted to the law school. The trial court was reversed by the Washington Supreme Court, but by that time DeFunis was in his second year. The U.S. Supreme Court, reviewing his appeal when he was in his final year, held the case moot. DeFunis v. Odegaard, 416 U.S. 312 (1974). Among the questions the Court was able to avoid: If positions are reserved for blacks, Chicanos, Native Americans, and Filipinos, why not Asians and other "minorities"? How are courts to draw and justify such lines? Excerpts of this decision are reprinted in Chapter 3.

The *Bakke* Case

Within a few years the issue of affirmative action returned to the Court, this time involving Allan Bakke's application to the medical school at the University of California at Davis. The school had two admissions programs: a regular admissions program (for Bakke and other nonminority candidates) and a special admissions program for "disadvantaged" minorities (blacks, Chicanos, Asians, and Native Americans). Disadvantaged whites were not admitted to the special program, although many applied. Out of 100 openings for entering students, 16 were reserved for special admissions. Bakke was rejected twice; minorities with significantly lower scores were admitted under the special program. The Supreme Court decided that Bakke should be admitted to the medical school and that the special admissions program was invalid. However, it reversed the judgment of lower courts that race could not be taken into account in an admissions program. Race would be a permissible factor in promoting diverse student bodies. The judgment of the Court, concurrences, and separate opinions filled 156 rambling pages. Eight Justices found fault with parts of the opinion of the Court written by Powell. REGENTS OF THE UNIVERSITY OF CALIFORNIA v. BAKKE, 438 U.S. 265 (1978).

The following year, a 5–2 Court supported the use of affirmative action for private employment. It had been the practice in some industries to hire as craftworkers only persons with prior craft experience; blacks were usually excluded from craft unions. To open up opportunities for the well-paying craft jobs, Kaiser Aluminum and the United Steelworkers union agreed upon an affirmative action plan. Fifty percent of craft-training openings were reserved for black employees until the percentage of black craftworkers equaled the percentage of blacks in the local labor force. The most senior black trainee had less seniority than several whites who were rejected. One of the whites, Brian Weber, filed a class action claiming that

9. Contractors Ass'n of Eastern Pa. v. Secretary of Labor, 442 F.2d 159 (3d Cir. 1971), cert. denied, 404 U.S. 854 (1971). See also Contractors Ass'n of Eastern Pa. v. Secretary of Labor, 311 F.Supp. 1002 (E.D. Pa. 1970); Robert P. Schuwerk, "The Philadelphia Plan: A Study in the Dynamics of Executive Power," 39 U. Chi. L. Rev. 723 (1972); and "Committee Analysis of Executive Order 11246 (The Affirmative Action Program)," prepared by the Senate Committee on Labor and Human Resources, 97th Cong., 2d Sess. (Comm. Print April 1982).

the plan violated Title VII by discriminating on the basis of race. The Court held that Title VII does not prohibit private, voluntary, race-conscious affirmative action programs to overcome past discrimination. Chief Justice Burger and Justice Rehnquist dissented, accusing the majority of rewriting Title VII. Justice Blackmun, in a concurrence, pointed out that if the Court "has misperceived the political will, it has the assurance that because the question is statutory Congress may set a different course if it so chooses." United Steelworkers v. Weber, 443 U.S. 193, 216 (1979).

Set-Asides

Although language in some of the civil rights acts appeared to announce a race-neutral policy, other statutes endorsed preferential treatment. Two years before *Weber,* Congress passed legislation to set aside 10 percent of public works funds for "minority business enterprises." The statute defined minority group members as U.S. citizens "who are Negroes, Spanish-speaking, Orientals, Indians, Eskimos, and Aleuts." 91 Stat. 117. Congressional action had been preceded by several Executive Orders during the Nixon administration directing federal agencies to increase the proportion of procurement contracts to minority business enterprises.[10]

A 6–3 Court found the set-aside an acceptable exercise of congressional authority under the spending power. The Court said the statute could also be justified on the basis of congressional power under the Commerce Clause or Section 5 of the Fourteenth Amendment. The use of racial and ethnic criteria as a condition attached to a federal grant did not violate the equal protection component of the Due Process Clause of the Fifth Amendment. FULLILOVE v. KLUTZNICK, 448 U.S. 448 (1980).

The decision in *Fullilove* did not necessarily support the use of set-asides by states and cities. In 1989 the Court, by a 6–3 vote, struck down a city of Richmond plan that required contractors receiving city construction contracts to subcontract at least 30 percent of the funds to "minority business enterprises" (blacks, Hispanics, Asians, Native Americans, Eskimos, and Aleuts). The Court rejected *Fullilove* as an acceptable precedent, pointing out that the Fourteenth Amendment authorizes Congress, not cities or states, to act against racial discrimination. Also, the plan was not narrowly tailored to accomplish a remedial purpose. With regard to the set-aside for such groups as the Aleuts, the Court remarked: "The gross overinclusiveness of Richmond's racial preference strongly impugns the city's claim of remedial motivation." RICHMOND v. CROSON CO., 488 U.S. 469, 506 (1989). The 22 states that set aside a specific percentage of funds for minority business enterprises had to reexamine them in light of *Croson's* demand for a detailed, documentary record of past discrimination and the selection of narrowly tailored remedies. They can also shift the emphasis from minority businesses to "disadvantaged businesses" in distressed communities, accomplishing much the same purpose.

The difference between the use of race-conscious remedies by Congress (as in *Fullilove*) and by the states (as in *Croson*) is highlighted by a 5–4 decision in 1990. The Federal Communications Commission (FCC) adopted two minority preference policies in awarding licenses and ownership of radio and television broadcast stations. These policies were part of FCC's effort to promote diversification of programming. After the filing of a lawsuit that challenged the FCC policy, Congress enacted legislation prohibiting the agency from spending any appropriated funds to examine or change its minority policies. The Supreme Court upheld the minority-preference policies because they bear the "imprimatur" of longstanding congressional support and direction and were substantially related to the achievement of the important government ob-

---

10. Executive Order 11458, 34 Fed. Reg. 4937 (1969); Executive Order 11518, 35 Fed. Reg. 4939 (1970); Executive Order 11625, 36 Fed. Reg. 19967 (1971); Public Papers of the Presidents, 1969, at 197–98; 994–95; Public Papers of the Presidents, 1970, at 284–88.

jective of broadcast diversity. Metro Broadcasting, Inc. v. FCC, 497 U.S. 547 (1990). This ruling would be reexamined and revised within a few years.

Title VII Disputes

After resolving the question of congressional power in *Fullilove,* the Court turned to a Title VII case. Two black members of a Memphis, Tennessee, fire department filed a complaint of racial discrimination. A district court issued a consent decree (incorporating the agreement of the two parties) to remedy the department's hiring and promotion practices. When budget deficits required the release of some city employees, the court enjoined the department from following its seniority system to decide layoffs. A modified layoff plan resulted in white employees, with more seniority than black employees, being laid off. A 6–3 Court held that the injunction exceeded the consent decree, which had made no mention of layoffs, demotions, or departures from the seniority system. Firefighters v. Stotts, 467 U.S. 561 (1984).

Two years later, in another Title VII case, the Court affirmed a lower court's judgment that established a 29 percent nonwhite membership goal in a union, based on the percentage of nonwhites in the local labor force. The decision is significant because the Court agreed that race-conscious relief can be granted to benefit individuals who are not identified victims of unlawful discrimination. The Justice Department, and the Justices who dissented, argued that the legislative history of Title VII indicates that Congress intended that affirmative relief could benefit only those who had been identified as victims of past discrimination. Sheet Metal Workers v. EEOC, 478 U.S. 421 (1986). In a second case issued that day, the Court decided that Title VII does not preclude consent decrees that benefit individuals who were not the actual victims of discriminatory practices. Firefighters v. Cleveland, 478 U.S. 501 (1986).

Although the Court has deferred to congressional actions that benefit minorities and has supported private efforts to hire minorities or admit them to universities, a more stringent review is applied to the use of racial classification for layoffs. Nonminority school teachers in Michigan challenged a provision in a collective bargaining agreement that allowed the school board to give preferential protection to minorities in case of layoffs. A 5–4 decision held that the agreement violated the Fourteenth Amendment. The Court reasoned that when affirmative action is used for hiring goals, the burden on innocent individuals is diffused among society generally, whereas layoffs represent a greater and more intrusive loss to specific employees. Wygant v. Jackson Bd. of Educ., 476 U.S. 267 (1986). Throughout recent decades the three branches have developed basic principles for affirmative action (see box on next page).

The general support for some form of affirmative action is underscored by a 1987 decision. For almost four decades, Alabama had excluded blacks as state troopers. In 1972 a district court ordered a hiring quota and directed the state to refrain from discrimination in hiring practices, including promotions. Other court actions were ineffective in producing promotions for blacks. Finally, under court order, the state promoted eight blacks and eight whites. A 5–4 Court affirmed this remedy, citing the long and systematic exclusion of blacks, the continuous practice of discrimination, and the state's record of delay and resistance. Even the four dissenters did not totally oppose affirmative action or quotas. They merely objected that the district court's particular remedy was not narrowly tailored to achieve the appropriate results. United States v. Paradise, 480 U.S. 149 (1987). Also in 1987, the Court approved affirmative action to increase promotional opportunities for women. Johnson v. Transportation Agency, 480 U.S. 616 (1987), discussed in Chapter 16.

The *Adarand* Decision

The holdings in *Fullilove* and *Metro Broadcasting* were revisited by the Court in 1995 when it decided a case involving federal agency contracts that give prime contractors a financial in-

Affirmative Action Principles

A series of Supreme Court decisions, congressional statutes, and presidential policies have established several general guidelines for permissible affirmative action:

1. Presidents used such policies as the Philadelphia Plan to require governmental contractors to set specific goals for hiring members of minority groups as a condition for receiving federal funds. Contractors Ass'n of Eastern Pa. v. Secretary of Labor, 442 F.2d 159 (3d Cir. 1971), cert. denied, 404 U.S. 854 (1971).

2. Affirmative action programs must be narrowly tailored to meet a legitimate governmental objective.

3. Race or gender may be included as one of several factors in determining admission to a university or for employment. Regents of the University of California v. Bakke, 438 U.S. 265 (1978) (race); Johnson v. Transportation Agency, 480 U.S. 616 (1987) (gender).

4. Voluntary initiatives by the private sector may be race-conscious for employment decisions. United Steelworkers v. Weber, 443 U.S. 193 (1979).

5. Congress supported preferential treatment for minorities, through set-asides and other programs, but states and localities must meet a higher standard. Fullilove v. Klutznick, 448 U.S. 448 (1980); Metro Broadcasting, Inc. v. FCC, 497 U.S. 547 (1990); Richmond v. Croson Co., 488 U.S. 506 (1989). In 1995, the Court adopted a high standard (strict scrutiny) for federal programs. Adarand Constructors, Inc. v. Pena, 515 U.S. 200 (1995).

6. It is more difficult to defend affirmative action in court when used for layoffs than for hiring. Firefighters v. Stotts, 467 U.S. 561 (1984); Wygant v. Jackson Bd. of Educ., 476 U.S. 267 (1986).

7. Quotas may be used when employers are intransigent and refuse to comply with repeated court orders. United States v. Paradise, 480 U.S. 149 (1987) (constitutional question); Sheet Metal Workers v. EEOC, 478 U.S. 421 (1986) (Title VII question).

8. Congress has remedied societal discrimination (Fullilove v. Klutznick) and promoted diversity (Metro Broadcasting, Inc. v. FCC). Those programs must now satisfy the strict-scrutiny standard of *Adarand*.

---

centive to hire subcontractors who are black, Hispanic, or belong to other minorities. Split 5 to 4, the Court ruled that federal race-based policies must now satisfy the same judicial standard — "strict scrutiny" — applied to state and local programs. Such programs must serve a compelling governmental interest and be narrowly tailored to address identifiable past discrimination. Writing for the Court, Justice O'Connor said that the Constitution protects "*persons, not groups.*" To the extent that *Fullilove* and *Metro Broadcasting* are inconsistent with the Court's new standard, they are overruled. The decision will require federal courts, Congress, and federal agencies to reassess affirmative action programs. ADARAND CONSTRUCTORS, INC. v. PENA, 515 U.S. 200 (1995).

On July 19, 1995, President Clinton delivered a major speech summarizing his administration's five-month review of federal affirmative action programs. Acknowledging problems in some programs, such as set-asides, he concluded: "We should reaffirm the principle of affirmative action and fix the practices. We should have a simple slogan: Mend it, but don't end it." Public Papers of the Presidents, 1995, II, at 1113. On the same day he issued a memorandum to departments and agencies, stating that policy principles must be eliminated or reformed if they (1) create a quota, (2) create preferences for unqualified individuals, (3) create reverse discrimination, or (4) continue even after its equal opportunity purposes have been achieved. Id. at 1114. In 1996, the Clinton administration announced a three-year moratorium on set-aside programs for minority and women-owned companies. Nevertheless, the administration said it would allow federal agencies, if they can justify it, to use other kinds of preferences, such as giving price breaks and extra points in evaluating contract bids by minority and woman-headed firms. The New York Times, March 8, 1996, at A1. The moratorium was later reduced to two years. Other affirmative action guidelines were released by the White House in 1998. The New York Times, June 25, 1998, at A1.

The impact of *Adarand* is still unclear. In deciding the case, the Court remanded it for further proceedings consistent with the Court's opinion. The matter ended up with a district court judge, who ruled in 1997 that the highway project at issue satisfied the compelling governmental interest test of strict scrutiny but was not narrowly tailored. Adarand Constructors, Inc. v. Pena, 965 F.Supp. 1556 (D. Colo. 1997). The Clinton administration appealed that decision to the Tenth Circuit, which ruled that Colorado's certification of Adarand as a DBE (disadvantaged business enterprise) mooted its constitutional challenge to federal subcontractor preferences. Rocked by the litigation, Colorado had modified its DBE regulations to eliminate the automatic presumption of social and economic disadvantage for racial and ethnic minorities. The sole inquiry would be whether the head of a company was *socially* disadvantaged. Adarand Constructors, Inc. v. Slater, 169 F.3d 1292 (10th Cir. 1999). Under this modified regulation, Adarand (headed by a white male) was certified as a DBE.

The story keeps going! The Supreme Court in 2000 held that Colorado's certification of Adarand as a DBE did *not* moot the case. The Tenth Circuit's decision was therefore reversed and remanded. Adarand Constructors, Inc. v. Slater, 120 S.Ct. 722 (2000). Not to be lost sight of in these multiple decisions is that Colorado was pressured to change its regulation to remove the preferences for racial and ethnic minorities.

Another potentially hot issue was headed to the Supreme Court in 1997, involving a white schoolteacher who was laid off by a Piscataway, N.J., school board that wanted to preserve the job of a black teacher. Had the Court decided the case, it would have likely overruled the decision as in violation of *Wygant* and might have announced other standards restrictive of affirmative action. Before the Court could decide, the parties settled out of court. A black civil rights group put up about 70 percent of the $433,500 needed to pay the white teacher's back salary and legal bills. She had already been rehired by the school.

State Initiatives

Affirmative action programs have been successfully attacked in court in a number of states, including California, Texas, and Michigan (see box on next page). Following California's lead, the state of Washington passed a referendum in 1998 banning preferential treatment on the basis of race, sex, color, ethnicity, or national origin. In Texas, after a federal appellate court had outlawed affirmative action at the University of Texas, the legislature adopted an alternative plan that granted automatic admission to the flagship public colleges to all state high school students who graduated in the top 10 percent of their classes. Although this plan does not mention race, it has increased the number of blacks, Hispanics, and other minorities who are now enrolled in the Texas university system. A similar plan has been adopted by Florida, which in 2000 abolished affirmative action in favor of guaranteeing a spot in one of ten state universities to Florida high school students who rank in the top 20 percent of their class and complete a college preparatory curriculum. California, moving in the same direction as Texas and Florida, plans to guarantee provisional admission to the top 12.5 percent of students at every high school (provided that they take a college preparatory curriculum) and provide financial aid to needy high school students with good grades.

In other state initiatives, California voters in 1998 supported Proposition 227 to end bilingual education. Immigrant students would receive one year of English immersion before moving into regular classes unless their parents obtained a waiver. Progress varies from one school district to the next. The transition to full English is now expected to take several years but still much quicker than critics of Proposition 227 anticipated.

Challenges from the States

At the state level, a number of governmental programs that give preferences to race and gender are being openly and often successfully challenged:

California. In 1996, the citizens of California passed a state constitutional amendment that banned affirmative action. Proposition 209 provides that the state "shall not discriminate against, or grant preferential treatment to, any individual or group on the basis of race, sex, color, ethnicity, or national origin in the operation of public employment, public education, or public contracting." Although this language incorporated concepts and language from the equal protection clause of the 14th Amendment and the Civil Rights Act of 1964, a federal district judge issued an injunction to prevent state officials from implementing the amendment. The judge concluded that the amendment might violate the equal protection clause by "clos[ing] the narrow but significant window" that permits governmental race- and gender-conscious affirmative action programs. Coalition for Economic Equity v. Wilson, 946 F.Supp. 1480, 1489 (N.D. Cal. 1996). That decision was reversed on appeal. In a bow to the force of public opinion, the Ninth Circuit remarked: "A system which permits one judge to block with the stroke of a pen what 4,736,180 state residents voted to enact as law tests the integrity of our constitutional democracy." Coalition for Economic Equity v. Wilson, 110 F.3d 1431, 1437 (9th Cir. 1997). After the 9th Circuit refused to rehear the case en banc, the Supreme Court denied cert. 122 F.3d 692 (9th Cir. 1997), cert. denied, 522 U.S. 963 (1997).

Texas. Cheryl J. Hopwood, a white female, along with three white males, sued the University of Texas School of Law for its affirmative action admissions program. They said the law school discriminated against them by using a system of "targets" to favor less qualified black and Mexican American applicants. A federal district court held that the program, though needed to achieve compelling governmental interests, was not narrowly tailored. Hopwood v. State of Tex., 861 F.Supp. 551 (W.D. Tex. 1994). On appeal, the Fifth Circuit agreed that the admissions program—by using racial preferences to discriminate in favor of minority applicants—violated the equal protection clause of the 14th Amendment. The appellate court concluded that the law school had presented no compelling justification for the program. Unlike the district court, which left the door open for some kind of affirmative action, the appellate court ruled that the law school "may not use race as a factor in law school admissions." Hopwood v. State of Tex., 78 F.3d 932, 935 (5th Cir. 1996), cert. denied, 518 U.S. 1033 (1996).

Michigan. Jennifer Gratz, a white applicant to the University of Michigan's undergraduate program, sued the school in 1997 to challenge its admission policy. Gratz graduated from high school with a 3.765 grade point average and was student council leader, a math tutor, an aide to senior citizens, and a homecoming queen. Yet she was denied entry while minorities with lower grades and fewer extracurricular activities were accepted. In response to her lawsuit the university eliminated a two-tiered admission procedure that operated as an impermissible quota system. However, relying on *Bakke*, the university adopted a new policy that gives minority applicants 20 points towards a 150-point maximum. The new system was upheld by a federal district court on December 13, 2000. Gratz v. Bollinger, 122 F. Supp. 2d 811 (E.D. Mich. 2000).

Civil Rights Act of 1991

After Anthony Kennedy replaced Lewis Powell in 1988, the Court began to backtrack from its previous positions on civil rights. This pattern became pronounced during the spring of 1989, when the Court issued a series of stunning rulings. One decision shifted the burden to employees to prove that racial disparities in the work force result from employment practices and are not justified by business needs. This new test conflicted with the *Griggs* ruling in 1971, which appeared to require an employee to demonstrate disparate results, not intent. Wards Cove Packing Co. v. Atonio, 490 U.S. 642 (1989). Since this decision was a statutory interpretation of Title VII, Congress could rewrite the statute and overturn the Court.

Another decision limited the reach of a civil rights statute passed in 1866, codified at 42 U.S.C. § 1981. The law gives blacks the same right to "make and enforce contracts" as whites. Brenda Patterson, a black woman, claimed that her employer had harassed her, withheld promotion, and discharged her for reasons of race. The Court decided that Section 1981 is limited to prohibiting discriminatory actions *before* someone is hired, not after, and advised Patterson that she should have acted under Title VII. Patterson v. McLean Credit Union, 491 U.S. 164 (1989). Although Title VII is not a full substitute for Section 1981, nothing prevented Congress from changing this statute to prohibit racial harassment on the job.

A third decision gave white men new authority to challenge consent decrees that embody court-approved affirmative action plans. To avoid future challenges, consent decrees had to reach out to all groups that might be affected. Martin v. Wilks, 490 U.S. 755 (1989). Since the Court decided the case by interpreting the Federal Rules of Civil Procedure, Congress could enter the fray and reverse the Court. Also during the spring of 1989 the Court handed down two other rulings restrictive of Title VII rights: Independent Fed. of Flight Attendants v. Zipes, 491 U.S. 754, and Lorance v. AT&T Technologies, Inc., 490 U.S. 900.

The Civil Rights Act of 1991 reversed or modified nine Court rulings dealing with employment discrimination: (1) *Wards Cove Packing Co. v. Atonio* (by returning to the employer the burden of proving that a discriminatory practice is a business necessity); (2) *Patterson v. McLean Credit Union* (by prohibiting discrimination on the job); (3) *Martin v. Wilks* (by providing notice to interested nonparties and giving them an opportunity to be heard when a consent decree is proposed); (4) *Lorance v. AT&T Technologies, Inc.* (by allowing challenges to a discriminatory action when a person is actually harmed); (5) *Price Waterhouse v. Hopkins* (once a plaintiff proves that race, color, religion, national origin, or sex was a "motivating factor" in an employer's decision, the employer is liable for a Title VII violation); (6) *EEOC v. Aramco* (by protecting from federal job discrimination U.S. citizens working for American companies abroad); (7) *West Virginia University Hospitals v. Casey* (by reversing this 1991 decision that denied successful civil rights plaintiffs the right to recover the costs of hiring expert witnesses); (8) *Crawford Fitting Co. v. J.T. Gibbons* (a 1987 case that also denied the costs of hiring expert witnesses); and (9) *Library of Congress v. Shaw* (by allowing parties in bias cases against the federal government to recover interest to compensate for delays in obtaining payment).

The most controversial change was the response to *Wards Cove*. Critics claimed that shifting the burden to employers would force them to adopt racial quotas, a charge that supporters of the bill denied. The administration endorsed portions of the bill (the response to *Patterson* and *Lorance*), but President Bush vetoed the bill in 1990, and Congress failed to override. Congress revised the bill slightly in 1991, and Bush, facing a probable override, signed it.

In passing the Civil Rights Act of 1991, Congress equivocated on whether it would be retroactive. Parts of the legislative history said yes; others said no. In two rulings decided in 1994, the Supreme Court held that the statute did not apply to complaints that were pending at the time the statute was enacted. Landgraf v. USI Film Products, 511 U.S. 244 (1994); Rivers v. Roadway Exp. Inc., 511 U.S. 298 (1994).

Regents of the University of California v. Bakke

438 U.S. 265 (1978)

Allan Bakke, a white applicant to the medical school at the University of California at Davis, was twice rejected by the regular admissions program. "Disadvantaged" applicants from minority groups (blacks, Chicanos, Asians, and American Indians) were screened by a special admissions program. Although these minorities had lower grade point averages from undergraduate school and scored lower on the medical admissions test, they were accepted to fill 16 out of 100 openings for first-year students. The California Supreme Court, while agreeing that increasing the number of minorities in the medical profession was a compelling state interest, concluded that the special admissions program was not the least intrusive means of achieving that goal. It held that the Equal Protection Clause of the Fourteenth Amendment required that "no applicant may be rejected because of his race, in favor of another who is less qualified, as measured by standards applied without regard to race." When the University conceded its inability to prove that Bakke would not have been admitted even in the absence of a special admissions program, the California court directed that Bakke be admitted. That order was stayed pending review by the Supreme Court. "Petitioner" in this case is the University of California; the "respondent" is Bakke.

MR. JUSTICE POWELL announced the judgment of the Court.

This case presents a challenge to the special admissions program of the petitioner, the Medical School of the University of California at Davis, which is designed to assure the admission of a specified number of students from certain minority groups. The Superior Court of California sustained respondent's challenge, holding that petitioner's program violated the California Constitution, Title VI of the Civil Rights Act of 1964, 42 U. S. C. § 2000d *et seq.*, and the Equal Protection Clause of the Fourteenth Amendment. The court enjoined petitioner from considering respondent's race or the race of any other applicant in making admissions decisions. It refused, however, to order respondent's admission to the Medical School, holding that he had not carried his burden of proving that he would have been admitted but for the constitutional and statutory violations. The Supreme Court of California affirmed those portions of the trial court's judgment declaring the special admissions program unlawful and enjoining petitioner from considering the race of any applicant. It modified that portion of the judgment denying respondent's requested injunction and directed the trial court to order his admission.

For the reasons stated in the following opinion, I believe that so much of the judgment of the California court as holds petitioner's special admissions program unlawful and directs that respondent be admitted to the Medical School must be affirmed. For the reasons expressed in a separate opinion, my Brothers THE CHIEF JUSTICE, MR. JUSTICE STEWART, MR. JUSTICE REHNQUIST, and MR. JUSTICE STEVENS concur in this judgment.

I also conclude for the reasons stated in the following opinion that the portion of the court's judgment enjoining petitioner from according any consideration to race in its admissions process

must be reversed. For reasons expressed in separate opinions, my Brothers MR. JUSTICE BRENNAN, MR. JUSTICE WHITE, MR. JUSTICE MARSHALL, and MR. JUSTICE BLACKMUN concur in this judgment.

Affirmed in part and reversed in part.

I

The Medical School of the University of California at Davis opened in 1968 with an entering class of 50 students. In 1971, the size of the entering class was increased to 100 students, a level at which it remains. No admissions program for disadvantaged or minority students existed when the school opened, and the first class contained three Asians but no blacks, no Mexican-Americans, and no American Indians. Over the next two years, the faculty devised a special admissions program to increase the representation of "disadvantaged" students in each Medical School class. The special program consisted of a separate admissions system operating in coordination with the regular admissions process.

Under the regular admissions procedure, a candidate could submit his application to the Medical School beginning in July of the year preceding the academic year for which admission was sought.... Because of the large number of applications, the admissions committee screened each one to select candidates for further consideration. Candidates whose overall undergraduate grade point averages fell below 2.5 on a scale of 4.0 were summarily rejected.... About one out of six applicants was invited for a personal interview.... Following the interviews, each candidate was rated on a scale of 1 to 100 by his interviewers and four other members of the admissions committee. The rating embraced the interviewers' summaries, the candidate's overall grade point average, grade point average in science courses, scores on the Medical College Admissions Test (MCAT), letters of recommendation, extracurricular activities, and other biographical data.... The ratings were added together to arrive at each candidate's "benchmark" score. Since five committee members rated each candidate in 1973, a perfect score was 500; in 1974, six members rated each candidate, so that a perfect score was 600. The full committee then reviewed the file and scores of each applicant and made offers of admission on a "rolling" basis. The chairman was responsible for placing names on the waiting list. They were not placed in strict numerical order; instead, the chairman had discretion to include persons with "special skills.".....

The special admissions program operated with a separate committee, a majority of whom were members of minority groups.... On the 1973 application form, candidates were asked to indicate whether they wished to be considered as "economically and/or educationally disadvantaged" applicants; on the 1974 form the question was whether they wished to be considered as members of a "minority group," which the Medical School apparently viewed as "Blacks," "Chicanos," "Asians," and "American Indians.".... If these questions were answered affirmatively, the application was forwarded to the special admissions committee. No formal definition of "disadvantaged" was ever produced, ... but the chairman of the special committee screened each application to see whether it reflected economic or educational deprivation. Having passed this initial hurdle, the applications then were rated by the special committee in a fashion similar to that used by the general admissions committee, except that special candidates did not have to meet the 2.5 grade point average cutoff applied to regular applicants. About one-fifth of the total number of special applicants were invited for interviews in 1973 and 1974. Following each interview, the special committee assigned each special applicant a benchmark score. The special committee then presented its top choices to the general admissions committee. The latter did not rate or compare the special candidates against the general applicants, ... but could reject recommended special candidates for failure to meet course requirements or other specific deficiencies.... The special committee continued to recommend special applicants until a number prescribed by faculty vote were admitted. While the overall class size was still 50, the prescribed number was 8; in 1973 and 1974, when the class size had doubled

to 100, the prescribed number of special admissions also doubled, to 16....

From the year of the increase in class size— 1971—through 1974, the special program resulted in the admission of 21 black students, 30 Mexican-Americans, and 12 Asians, for a total of 63 minority students. Over the same period, the regular admissions program produced 1 black, 6 Mexican-Americans, and 37 Asians, for a total of 44 minority students. Although disadvantaged whites applied to the special program in large numbers, ... none received an offer of admission through that process. Indeed, in 1974, at least, the special committee explicitly considered only "disadvantaged" special applicants who were members of one of the designated minority groups....

Allan Bakke is a white male who applied to the Davis Medical School in both 1973 and 1974. In both years Bakke's application was considered under the general admissions program, and he received an interview.... Despite a strong benchmark score of 468 out of 500, Bakke was rejected. His application had come late in the year, and no applicants in the general admissions process with scores below 470 were accepted after Bakke's application was completed.

[Bakke was also rejected in 1974, after scoring 549 out of 600. In both years, applicants were admitted under the special program with grade point averages, MCAT scores, and benchmark scores significantly lower than Bakke's.]

[After assuming that Bakke could sue under the Civil Rights Act of 1964, Justice Powell explored the meaning of Title VI, especially § 601: "No person in the United States shall, on the ground of race, color, or national origin, be excluded from participation in, be denied the benefits of, or be subjected to discrimination under any program or activity receiving Federal financial assistance." Powell concluded, from the legislative history, that Title VI proscribes only racial classifications that would violate the Equal Protection Clause of the Fourteenth Amendment.]

[III.B]

Petitioner urges us to adopt for the first time a more restrictive view of the Equal Protection Clause and hold that discrimination against members of the white "majority" cannot be suspect if its purpose can be characterized as "benign." The clock of our liberties, however, cannot be turned back to 1868. *Brown* v. *Board of*

Education, supra, at 492; accord, *Loving* v. *Virginia, supra,* at 9. It is far too late to argue that the guarantee of equal protection to *all* persons permits the recognition of special wards entitled to a degree of protection greater than that accorded others. "The Fourteenth Amendment is not directed solely against discrimination due to a 'two-class theory'—that is, based upon differences between 'white' and Negro." *Hernandez,* 347 U. S., at 478.

Once the artificial line of a "two-class theory" of the Fourteenth Amendment is put aside, the difficulties entailed in varying the level of judicial review according to a perceived "preferred" status of a particular racial or ethnic minority are intractable. The concepts of "majority" and "minority" necessarily reflect temporary arrangements and political judgments. As observed above, the white "majority" itself is composed of various minority groups, most of which can lay claim to a history of prior discrimination at the hands of the State and private individuals. Not all of these groups can receive preferential treatment and corresponding judicial tolerance of distinctions drawn in terms of race and nationality, for then the only "majority" left would be a new minority of white Anglo-Saxon Protestants. There is no principled basis for deciding which groups would merit "heightened judicial solicitude" and which would not. Courts would be asked to evaluate the extent of the prejudice and consequent harm suffered by various minority groups. Those whose societal injury is thought to exceed some arbitrary level of tolerability then would be entitled to preferential classifications at the expense of individuals belonging to other groups. Those classifications would be free from exacting judicial scrutiny. As these preferences began to have their desired effect, and the consequences of past discrimination were undone, new judicial rankings would be necessary. The kind of variable sociological and political analysis necessary to produce such rankings simply does not lie within the judicial competence—even if they otherwise were politically feasible and socially desirable.

· · ·

[V.A]

· · ·

It has been suggested that an admissions program which considers race only as one factor is simply a subtle and more sophisticated—but no less effective—means of according racial preference than the Davis program. A facial intent to discriminate, however, is evident in petitioner's preference program and not denied in this case. No such facial infirmity exists in an admissions program where race or ethnic background is simply one element—to be weighed fairly against other elements—in the selection process....

B

In summary, it is evident that the Davis special admissions program involves the use of an explicit racial classification never before countenanced by this Court. It tells applicants who are not Negro, Asian, or Chicano that they are totally excluded from a specific percentage of the seats in an entering class. No matter how strong their qualifications, quantitative and extracurricular, including their own potential for contribution to educational diversity, they are never afforded the chance to compete with applicants from the preferred groups for the special admissions seats. At the same time, the preferred applicants have the opportunity to compete for every seat in the class.

The fatal flaw in petitioner's preferential program is its disregard of individual rights as guaranteed by the Fourteenth Amendment. *Shelley* v. *Kraemer,* 334 U. S., at 22. Such rights are not absolute. But when a State's distribution of benefits or imposition of burdens hinges on ancestry or the color of a person's skin, that individual is entitled to a demonstration that the challenged classification is necessary to promote a substantial state interest. Petitioner has failed to carry this burden. For this reason, that portion of the California court's judgment holding petitioner's special admissions program invalid under the Fourteenth Amendment must be affirmed.

C

In enjoining petitioner from ever considering the race of any applicant, however, the courts below failed to recognize that the State has a substantial interest that legitimately may be served by a properly devised admissions program involving the competitive consideration of race and ethnic origin. For this reason, so much of the California court's judgment as enjoins petitioner from any consideration of the race of any applicant must be reversed.

VI

With respect to respondent's entitlement to an injunction directing his admission to the Medical School, petitioner has conceded that it could not carry its burden of proving that, but for the existence of its unlawful special admissions program, respondent still would not have been admitted. Hence, respondent is entitled to the injunction, and that portion of the judgment must be affirmed.

. . .

Opinion of MR. JUSTICE BRENNAN, MR. JUSTICE WHITE, MR. JUSTICE MARSHALL, and MR. JUSTICE BLACKMUN, concurring in the judgment in part and dissenting in part.

The Court today, in reversing in part the judgment of the Supreme Court of California, affirms the constitutional power of Federal and State Governments to act affirmatively to achieve equal opportunity for all. The difficulty of the issue presented—whether government may use race-conscious programs to redress the continuing effects of past discrimination—and the mature consideration which each of our Brethren has brought to it have resulted in many opinions, no single one speaking for the Court. But this should not and must not mask the central meaning of today's opinions: Government may take race into account when it acts not to demean or insult any racial group, but to remedy disadvantages cast on minorities by past racial prejudice, at least when appropriate findings have been made by judicial, legislative, or administrative bodies with competence to act in this area.

. . .

MR. JUSTICE WHITE. . . .

MR. JUSTICE MARSHALL.

I agree with the judgment of the Court only insofar as it permits a university to consider the race of an applicant in making admissions decisions. I do not agree that petitioner's admissions program violates the Constitution. For it must be remembered that, during most of the past 200 years, the Constitution as interpreted by this Court did not prohibit the most ingenious and pervasive forms of discrimination against the Negro. Now, when a State acts to remedy the effects of that legacy of discrimination, I cannot believe that this same Constitution stands as a barrier.

. . .

III

I do not believe that the Fourteenth Amendment requires us to accept that fate. Neither its history nor our past cases lend any support to the conclusion that a university may not remedy the cumulative effects of society's discrimination by giving consideration to race in an effort to increase the number and percentage of Negro doctors.

A

This Court long ago remarked that

"in any fair and just construction of any section or phrase of these [Civil War] amendments, it is necessary to look to the purpose which we have said was the pervading spirit of them all, the evil which they were designed to remedy. . . ." *Slaughter-House Cases,* 16 Wall., at 72.

It is plain that the Fourteenth Amendment was not intended to prohibit measures designed to remedy the effects of the Nation's past treatment of Negroes. The Congress that passed the Fourteenth Amendment is the same Congress that passed the 1866 Freedmen's Bureau Act, an Act that provided many of its benefits only to Negroes. . . .

. . .

MR. JUSTICE BLACKMUN.

I participate fully, of course, in the opinion . . . that bears the names of my Brothers BRENNAN, WHITE, MARSHALL, and myself. I add only some general observations that hold particular significance for me, and then a few comments on equal protection.

I

. . .

I yield to no one in my earnest hope that the time will come when an "affirmative action" program is unnecessary and is, in truth, only a relic of the past. I would hope that we could reach this stage within a decade at the most. But the story of *Brown* v. *Board of Education,* 347 U.S. 483 (1954), decided almost a quarter of a century ago, suggests that that hope is a slim one. At some time, however, beyond any period of what some would claim is only transitional inequality, the United States must and will reach a stage of maturity where action along this line is no longer necessary. Then persons will be regarded as persons, and discrimination of the type we address today will be an ugly feature of history that is instructive but that is behind us.

. . .

II

. . .

It is worth noting, perhaps, that governmental preference has not been a stranger to our legal life. We see it in veterans' preferences. We see it in the aid-to-the-handicapped programs. We see it in the progressive income tax. We see it in the Indian programs. We may excuse some of these on the ground that they have specific constitutional protection or, as with Indians, that those benefited are wards of the Government. Nevertheless, these preferences exist and may not be ignored. And in the admissions field, as I have indicated, educational institutions have always used geography, athletic ability, anticipated financial largess, alumni pressure, and other factors of that kind.

. . . In order to get beyond racism, we must first take account of race. There is no other way. And in order to treat some persons equally, we must treat them differently. . . .

MR. JUSTICE STEVENS, with whom THE CHIEF JUSTICE, MR. JUSTICE STEWART, and MR. JUSTICE REHNQUIST join, concurring in the judgment in part and dissenting in part.

. . .

III

Section 601 of the Civil Rights Act of 1964, 78 Stat. 252, 42 U.S.C. § 2000d, provides:

"No person in the United States shall, on the ground of race, color, or national origin, be excluded from participation in, be denied the benefits of, or be subjected to discrimination under any program or activity receiving Federal financial assistance."

The University, through its special admissions policy, excluded Bakke from participation in its program of medical education because of his race. The University also acknowledges that it was, and still is, receiving federal financial assistance. The plain language of the statute therefore requires affirmance of the judgment below. . . .

Fullilove v. Klutznick

448 U.S. 448 (1980)

Congress passed legislation in 1977 providing that at least 10 percent of federal funds granted for local public works projects must be used to obtain services or supplies from businesses owned by minority groups, defined as United States citizens "who are Negroes, Spanish-speaking, Orientals, Indians, Eskimos, and Aleuts." H. Earl Fullilove and several associations of construction contractors and subcontractors filed suit for declaratory and injunctive relief in federal district court, alleging that they had sustained economic injury due to enforcement of the statute. They claimed that the provision for minority businesses violated, on its face, the Equal Protection Clause of the Fourteenth Amendment and the equal protection component of the Due Process Clause of the Fifth Amendment. The district court upheld the statute; the Second Circuit affirmed. Defending the statute was Philip M. Klutznick, Secretary of Commerce.

MR. CHIEF JUSTICE BURGER announced the judgment of the Court and delivered an opinion, in which MR. JUSTICE WHITE and MR. JUSTICE POWELL joined.

We granted certiorari to consider a facial constitutional challenge to a requirement in a congressional spending program that, absent an administrative waiver, 10% of the federal funds granted for local public works projects must be used by the state or local grantee to procure services or supplies from businesses owned and con-

trolled by members of statutorily identified minority groups. 441 U. S. 960 (1979).

I

In May 1977, Congress enacted the Public Works Employment Act of 1977, . . . which amended the Local Public Works Capital Development and Investment Act of 1976, . . . The 1977 amendments authorized an additional $4 billion appropriation for federal grants to be made by the Secretary of Commerce, acting through the Economic Development Administration (EDA), to state and local governmental entities for use in local public works projects. Among the changes made was the addition of the provision that has become the focus of this litigation. Section 103 (f)(2) of the 1977 Act, referred to as the "minority business enterprise" or "MBE" provision, requires that:

"Except to the extent that the Secretary determines otherwise, no grant shall be made under this Act for any local public works project unless the applicant gives satisfactory assurance to the Secretary that at least 10 per centum of the amount of each grant shall be expended for minority business enterprises. For purposes of this paragraph, the term 'minority business enterprise' means a business at least 50 per centum of which is owned by minority group members or, in case of a publicly owned business, at least 51 per centum of the stock of which is owned by minority group members. For the purposes of the preceding sentence, minority group members are citizens of the United States who are Negroes, Spanish-speaking, Orientals, Indians, Eskimos, and Aleuts."

[The Secretary promulgated regulations to implement the grant program and the EDA issued supplementary guidelines. A district court and the Second Circuit upheld the statute against constitutional challenge on equal protection grounds.]

II

A

[The 10 percent provision for minorities originated as an amendment in the House of Representatives, where it was argued that in fiscal year 1976 less than 1 percent of all federal procurement was concluded with minority business enterprises, although minorities comprised 15 to 18 percent of the population. It was also stated that the concept of a set-aside for minorities had been used for ten years in the Small Business Administration. The Senate adopted the amendment, slightly modified, without debate.]

B

The legislative objectives of the MBE provision must be considered against the background of ongoing efforts directed toward deliverance of the century-old promise of equality of economic opportunity. The sponsors of the MBE provision in the House and the Senate expressly linked the provision to the existing administrative programs promoting minority opportunity in government procurement, particularly those related to § 8 (a) of the Small Business Act of 1953. [As Congress began consideration of the Public Works Employment Act of 1977, the House Committee on Small Business issued a lengthy report which included an evaluation of the Section 8 (a) program, pointing out discriminatory practices against minorities in the economy. Minorities had difficulties gaining access to government contracting opportunities at the federal, state, and local levels.]

. . .

III

When we are required to pass on the constitutionality of an Act of Congress, we assume "the gravest and most delicate duty that this Court is called on to perform." *Blodgett v. Holden*, 275 U.S. 142, 148 (1927) (opinion of Holmes, J.). A program that employs racial or ethnic criteria, even in a remedial context, calls for close examination; yet we are bound to approach our task with appropriate deference to the Congress, a co-equal branch charged by the Constitution with the power to "provide for the . . . general Welfare of the United States" and "to enforce, by appropriate legislation," the equal protection guarantees of the Fourteenth Amendment. . . .

A

(1)

In enacting the MBE provision, it is clear that Congress employed an amalgam of its specifically delegated powers. The Public Works Employment Act of 1977, by its very nature, is primarily an exercise of the Spending Power. U.S. Const., Art. I, § 8, cl. 1. This Court has recognized that the power to "provide for the . . . general Welfare" is an independent grant of legislative authority, distinct from other broad congressional powers. . . . Congress has frequently employed the Spending Power to further broad policy objectives by conditioning receipt of federal moneys upon compliance by the recipient with federal statutory and administrative directives. This Court has repeatedly upheld against constitutional challenge the use of this technique to induce governments and private parties to cooperate voluntarily with federal policy. . . .

Here we need not explore the outermost limitations on the objectives attainable through such an application of the Spending Power. The reach of the

Spending Power, within its sphere, is at least as broad as the regulatory powers of Congress. If, pursuant to its regulatory powers, Congress could have achieved the objectives of the MBE program, then it may do so under the Spending Power. And we have no difficulty perceiving a basis for accomplishing the objectives of the MBE program through the Commerce Power insofar as the program objectives pertain to the action of private contracting parties, and through the power to enforce the equal protection guarantees of the Fourteenth Amendment insofar as the program objectives pertain to the action of state and local grantees.

(2)

We turn first to the Commerce Power. U. S. Const., Art. I, § 8, cl. 3. Had Congress chosen to do so, it could have drawn on the Commerce Clause to regulate the practices of prime contractors on federally funded public works projects.... The legislative history of the MBE provision shows that there was a rational basis for Congress to conclude that the subcontracting practices of prime contractors could perpetuate the prevailing impaired access by minority businesses to public contracting opportunities, and that this inequity has an effect on interstate commerce. Thus Congress could take necessary and proper action to remedy the situation....

. . .

(3)

In certain contexts, there are limitations on the reach of the Commerce Power to regulate the actions of state and local governments. *National League of Cities* v. *Usery*, 426 U. S. 833 (1976). To avoid such complications, we look to § 5 of the Fourteenth Amendment for the power to regulate the procurement practices of state and local grantees of federal funds. *Fitzpatrick* v. *Bitzer*, 427 U.S. 445 (1976). A review of our cases persuades us that the objectives of the MBE program are within the power of Congress under § 5 "to enforce, by appropriate legislation," the equal protection guarantees of the Fourteenth Amendment.

...Congress had abundant evidence from which it could conclude that minority businesses have been denied effective participation in public contracting opportunities by procurement practices that perpetuated the effects of prior discrimination....

B

We now turn to the question whether, as a *means* to accomplish these plainly constitutional objectives, Congress may use racial and ethnic criteria, in this limited way, as a condition attached to a federal grant....

(1)

As a threshold matter, we reject the contention that in the remedial context the Congress must act in a wholly "color-blind" fashion. In *Swann* v. *Charlotte-Mecklenburg Board of Education*, 402 U. S. 1, 18–21 (1971), we rejected this argument in considering a court-formulated school desegregation remedy on the basis that examination of the racial composition of student bodies was an unavoidable starting point and that racially based attendance assignments were permissible so long as no absolute racial balance of each school was required....

Here we deal...not with the limited remedial powers of a federal court, for example, but with the broad remedial powers of Congress. It is fundamental that in no organ of government, state or federal, does there repose a more comprehensive remedial power than in the Congress, expressly charged by the Constitution with competence and authority to enforce equal protection guarantees. Congress not only may induce voluntary action to assure compliance with existing federal statutory or constitutional antidiscrimination provisions, but also, where Congress has authority to declare certain conduct unlawful, it may, as here, authorize and induce state action to avoid such conduct....

. . .

IV

Congress, after due consideration, perceived a pressing need to move forward with new approaches in the continuing effort to achieve the goal of equality of economic opportunity.... That the program may press the outer limits of congressional authority affords no basis for striking it down.

Petitioners have mounted a facial challenge to a program developed by the politically responsive branches of Government. For its part, the Congress must proceed only with programs narrowly tailored to achieve its objectives, subject to continuing evaluation and reassessment; administration of the programs must be vigilant and flexible; and, when such a program comes under judicial review, courts must be satisfied that the legislative objectives and projected administration give reasonable assurance that the program will function within constitutional limitations....

...The MBE provision of the Public Works Employment Act of 1977 does not violate the Constitution.

Affirmed.

MR. JUSTICE POWELL, concurring.

. . .

V

In the history of this Court and this country, few questions have been more divisive than those arising from governmental action taken on the basis of race.... The time cannot come too soon when no governmental decision will be based upon immutable characteristics of pigmentation or origin....

MR. JUSTICE MARSHALL, with whom MR. JUSTICE BRENNAN and MR. JUSTICE BLACKMUN join, concurring in the judgment.

. . .

MR. JUSTICE STEWART, with whom MR. JUSTICE REHNQUIST joins, dissenting.

"Our Constitution is color-blind, and neither knows nor tolerates classes among citizens.... The law regards man as man, and takes no account of his surroundings or of his color...." Those words were written by a Member of this Court 84 years ago. *Plessy* v. *Ferguson,* 163 U. S. 537, 559 (Harlan, J., dissenting). His colleagues disagreed with him, and held that a statute that required the separation of people on the basis of their race was constitutionally valid because it was a "reasonable" exercise of legislative power and had been "enacted in good faith for the promotion [of] the public good...." *Id., at* 550. Today, the Court upholds a statute that accords a preference to citizens who are "Negroes, Spanish-speaking, Orientals, Indians, Eskimos, and Aleuts," for much the same reasons. I think today's decision is wrong for the same reason that *Plessy* v. *Ferguson* was wrong, and I respectfully dissent.

A

The equal protection standard of the Constitution has one clear and central meaning—it absolutely prohibits invidious discrimination by government.... Under our Constitution, any official action that treats a person differently on account of his race or ethnic origin is inherently suspect and presumptively invalid....

. . .

B

On its face, the minority business enterprise (MBE) provision at issue in this case denies the equal protection of the law....

. . .

MR. JUSTICE STEVENS, dissenting.

. . .

I

. . .

Even if we assume that each of the six racial subclasses has suffered its own special injury at some time in our history, surely it does not necessarily follow that each of those subclasses suffered harm of identical magnitude. Although "the Negro was dragged to this country in chains to be sold in slavery," *Bakke, supra,* at 387 (opinion of MARSHALL, J.), the "Spanish-speaking" subclass came voluntarily, frequently without invitation, and the Indians, the Eskimos and the Aleuts had an opportunity to exploit America's resources before the ancestors of most American citizens arrived. There is no reason to assume, and nothing in the legislative history suggests, much less demonstrates, that each of the subclasses is equally entitled to reparations from the United States Government.

. . .

Richmond v. Croson Co.

488 U.S. 469 (1989)

Following the precedent established by Congress and upheld by the Court in *Fullilove*, the city of Richmond, Virginia, adopted a Minority Business Utilization Plan requiring prime contractors of city construction contracts to subcontract at least 30 percent of the

dollar amount of each contract to one or more "Minority Business Enterprises" (MBEs). The Plan defined an MBE as a business from anywhere in the country at least 51 percent of which is owned and controlled by black, Spanish-speaking, Oriental, Indian, Eskimo, or Aleut citizens. The issue here is whether the city could identify evidence and legal justification to refute the claim by a firm, J.A. Croson Company, that there had been discrimination in violation of the Equal Protection Clause.

JUSTICE O'CONNOR announced the judgment of the Court and delivered the opinion of the Court with respect to Parts I, III-B, and IV, an opinion with respect to Part II, in which THE CHIEF JUSTICE and JUSTICE WHITE join, and an opinion with respect to Parts III-A and V, in which THE CHIEF JUSTICE, JUSTICE WHITE, and JUSTICE KENNEDY join.

In this case, we confront once again the tension between the Fourteenth Amendment's guarantee of equal treatment to all citizens, and the use of race-based measures to ameliorate the effects of past discrimination on the opportunities enjoyed by members of minority groups in our society....

II

The parties and their supporting *amici* fight an initial battle over the scope of the city's power to adopt legislation designed to address the effects of past discrimination. Relying on our decision in *Wygant [v.* Jackson Bd. of Educ. *(1986)]*, appellee argues that the city must limit any race-based remedial efforts to eradicating the effects of its own prior discrimination. This is essentially the position taken by the Court of Appeals below. Appellant argues that our decision in *Fullilove* is controlling, and that as a result the city of Richmond enjoys sweeping legislative power to define and attack the effects of prior discrimination in its local construction industry. We find that neither of these two rather stark alternatives can withstand analysis.

. . .

What appellant ignores is that Congress, unlike any State or political subdivision, has a specific constitutional mandate to enforce the dictates of the Fourteenth Amendment. The power to "enforce" may at times also include the power to define situations which *Congress* determines threaten principles of equality and to adopt prophylactic rules to deal with those situations.... The Civil War Amendments themselves worked a dramatic change in the balance between congressional and state power over matters of race. Speaking of the Thirteenth and Fourteenth Amendments in *Ex parte Virginia*, 100 U. S. 339,

345 (1880), the Court stated: "They were intended to be, what they really are, limitations of the powers of the States and enlargements of the power of Congress."

That Congress may identify and redress the effects of society-wide discrimination does not mean that, *a fortiori,* the States and their political subdivisions are free to decide that such remedies are appropriate. Section 1 of the Fourteenth Amendment is an explicit *constraint* on state power, and the States must undertake any remedial efforts in accordance with that provision. To hold otherwise would be to cede control over the content of the Equal Protection Clause to the 50 state legislatures and their myriad political subdivisions....

It would seem equally clear, however, that a state or local subdivision (if delegated the authority from the State) has the authority to eradicate the effects of private discrimination within its own legislative jurisdiction. This authority must, of course, be exercised within the constraints of § 1 of the Fourteenth Amendment. Our decision in *Wygant* is not to the contrary. *Wygant* addressed the constitutionality of the use of racial quotas by local school authorities pursuant to an agreement reached with the local teachers' union. It was in the context of addressing the school board's power to adopt a race-based layoff program affecting its own work force that the *Wygant* plurality indicated that the Equal Protection Clause required "some showing of prior discrimination by the governmental unit involved." *Wygant*, 476 U.S., at 274. As a matter of state law, the city of Richmond has legislative authority over its procurement policies, and can use its spending powers to remedy private discrimination, if it identifies that discrimination with the particularity required by the Fourteenth Amendment. To this extent, on the question of the city's competence, the Court of Appeals erred in following *Wygant* by rote in a case involving a state entity which has state-law authority to address discriminatory practices within local commerce under its jurisdiction.

Thus, if the city could show that it had essentially become a "passive participant" in a system of racial exclusion practiced by elements of the local construction industry, we think it clear that the city could take affirmative steps to dismantle such a system. It is beyond dispute that any public entity, state or federal, has a compelling interest in assuring that public dollars, drawn from the tax contributions of all citizens, do not serve to finance the evil of private prejudice....

[III.B]

We think it clear that the factual predicate offered in support of the Richmond Plan suffers from the same two defects identified as fatal in *Wygant.* The District Court found the city council's "findings sufficient to ensure that, in adopting the Plan, it was remedying the present effects of past discrimination in the *construction industry.*"...Like the "role model" theory employed in *Wygant,* a generalized assertion that there has been past discrimination in an entire industry provides no guidance for a legislative body to determine the precise scope of the injury it seeks to remedy....

While there is no doubt that the sorry history of both private and public discrimination in this country has contributed to a lack of opportunities for black entrepreneurs, this observation, standing alone, cannot justify a rigid racial quota in the awarding of public contracts in Richmond, Virginia....

It is sheer speculation how many minority firms there would be in Richmond absent past societal discrimination,...

These defects are readily apparent in this case. The 30% quota cannot in any realistic sense be tied to any injury suffered by anyone....

...[N]one of the evidence presented by the city points to any identified discrimination in the Richmond construction industry. We, therefore, hold that the city has failed to demonstrate a compelling interest in apportioning public contracting opportunities on the basis of race. To accept Richmond's claim that past societal discrimination alone can serve as the basis for rigid racial preferences would be to open the door to competing claims for "remedial relief" for every disadvantaged group....

The foregoing analysis applies only to the inclusion of blacks within the Richmond set-aside program. There is *absolutely no evidence* of past discrimination against Spanish-speaking, Oriental, Indian, Eskimo, or Aleut persons in any aspect of the Richmond construction industry. The District Court took judicial notice of the fact that the vast majority of "minority" persons in Richmond were black....It may well be that Richmond has never

had an Aleut or Eskimo citizen. The random inclusion of racial groups that, as a practical matter, may never have suffered from discrimination in the construction industry in Richmond suggests that perhaps the city's purpose was not in fact to remedy past discrimination.

If a 30% set-aside was "narrowly tailored" to compensate black contractors for past discrimination, one may legitimately ask why they are forced to share this "remedial relief" with an Aleut citizen who moves to Richmond tomorrow? The gross overinclusiveness of Richmond's racial preference strongly impugns the city's claim of remedial motivation....

V

Nothing we say today precludes a state or local entity from taking action to rectify the effects of identified discrimination within its jurisdiction. If the city of Richmond had evidence before it that nonminority contractors were systematically excluding minority businesses from subcontracting opportunities, it could take action to end the discriminatory exclusion....

JUSTICE STEVENS, concurring in part and concurring in the judgment.

. . .

JUSTICE KENNEDY, concurring in part and concurring in the judgment.

. . .

JUSTICE SCALIA, concurring in the judgment.

I agree with much of the Court's opinion, and, in particular, with JUSTICE O'CONNOR's conclusion that strict scrutiny must be applied to all governmental classification by race, whether or not its asserted purpose is "remedial" or "benign."...I do not agree, however, with JUSTICE O'CONNOR's dictum suggesting that, despite the Fourteenth Amendment, state and local governments may in some circumstances discriminate on the basis of race in order (in a broad sense) "to ameliorate the effects of past discrimination."...The benign purpose of compensating for social disadvantages, whether they have been acquired by reason of prior discrimination or otherwise, can no more be pursued by the illegitimate means of racial discrimination than can other assertedly benign purposes we have repeatedly rejected....

JUSTICE MARSHALL, with whom JUSTICE BRENNAN and JUSTICE BLACKMUN join, dissenting.

It is a welcome symbol of racial progress when the former capital of the Confederacy acts forthrightly to confront the effects of racial discrimination in its midst. In my view, nothing in the Constitution can be construed to prevent Richmond, Virginia, from allocating a portion of its contracting dollars for businesses owned or controlled by members of minority groups....

JUSTICE BLACKMUN, with whom JUSTICE BRENNAN joins, dissenting.

I join JUSTICE MARSHALL's perceptive and incisive opinion revealing great sensitivity toward those who have suffered the pains of economic discrimination in the construction trades for so long.

I never thought that I would live to see the day when the city of Richmond, Virginia, the cradle of the Old Confederacy, sought on its own, within a narrow confine, to lessen the stark impact of persistent discrimination. But Richmond, to its great credit, acted. Yet this Court, the supposed bastion of equality, strikes down Richmond's efforts as though discrimination had never existed or was not demonstrated in this particular litigation....

Adarand Constructors, Inc. v. Pena,

515 U.S. 200 (1995)

Federal agency contracts contain a subcontractor compensation clause, giving a prime contractor a financial incentive to hire subcontractors certified as small businesses controlled by socially and economically disadvantaged individuals, and require the contractor to presume that such individuals include minorities or any other individuals found to be disadvantaged by the Small Business Administration. The prime contractor in this case awarded a subcontract to a company that was certified as a small disadvantaged business. Adarand Constructors, Inc., submitted the low bid on the subcontract but was not a certified business. It filed this suit against Federico Pena, the Secretary of Transportation, claiming that the race-based presumptions used in these subcontractor clauses violated the equal protection component of the Fifth Amendment's Due Process Clause. The Tenth Circuit upheld the federal contracts under the lenient standard of Fullilove v. Klutznick (1980) and Metro Broadcasting, Inc. v. FCC (1990).

JUSTICE O'CONNOR announced the judgment of the Court and delivered an opinion with respect to Parts I, II, III-A, III-B, III-D, and IV, which is for the Court except insofar as it might be inconsistent with the views expressed in JUSTICE SCALIA's concurrence, and an opinion with respect to Part III-C in which JUSTICE KENNEDY joins.

Petitioner Adarand Constructors, Inc., claims that the Federal Government's practice of giving general contractors on Government projects a financial incentive to hire subcontractors controlled by "socially and economically disadvantaged individuals," and in particular, the Government's use of race-based presumptions in identifying such individuals, violates the equal protection component of the Fifth Amendment's Due Process Clause. The Court of Appeals rejected Adarand's claim. We conclude, however, that courts should analyze cases of this kind under a different standard of review than the one the Court of Appeals applied.

We therefore vacate the Court of Appeals' judgment and remand the case for further proceedings.

I

In 1989, the Central Federal Lands Highway Division (CFLHD), which is part of the United States Department of Transportation (DOT), awarded the prime contract for a highway construction project in Colorado to Mountain Gravel & Construction Company. Mountain Gravel then solicited bids from subcontractors for the guardrail portion of the contract. Adarand, a Colorado-based highway construction company specializing in guardrail work, submitted the low bid. Gonzales Construction Company also submitted a bid.

The prime contract's terms provide that Mountain Gravel would receive additional compensation if it hired subcontractors certified as small businesses controlled by "socially and economically disadvantaged individuals," ... Gonzales is certified as such a business; Adarand is not. Mountain Gravel awarded the subcontract to Gonzales, despite Adarand's low bid, and Mountain Gravel's Chief Estimator has submitted an affidavit stating that Mountain Gravel would have accepted Adarand's bid, had it not been for the additional payment it received by hiring Gonzales instead.... Federal law requires that a subcontracting clause similar to the one used here must appear in most federal agency contracts, and it also requires the clause to state that "[t]he contractor shall presume that socially and economically disadvantaged individuals include Black Americans, Hispanic Americans, Native Americans, Asian Pacific Americans, and other minorities, or any other individual found to be disadvantaged by the [Small Business] Administration pursuant to section 8(a) of the Small Business Act." ... Adarand claims that the presumption set forth in that statute discriminates on the basis of race in violation of the Federal Government's Fifth Amendment obligation not to deny anyone equal protection of the laws.

[Here the Court reviews the federal statutes and regulations that guide federal agencies in awarding contracts to small business and economically disadvantaged individuals. The dispute in this case arose from the Surface Transportation and Uniform Relocation Assistance Act of 1987, which contained a provision that "not less than 10 percent" of the appropriated funds "shall be expended with small business concerns owned and controlled by socially and economically disadvantaged individuals." The record does not reveal how Gonzales obtained its certification as a small disadvantaged business. In Section II of this decision, the Court concludes that Adarand has standing to bring this suit.]

III

Respondents urge that "[t]he Subcontracting Compensation Clause program is...a program based on *disadvantage,* not on race," and thus that it is subject only to "the most relaxed judicial scrutiny." ... To the extent that the statutes and regulations involved in this case are race neutral, we agree. Respondents concede, however, that "the race-based rebuttable presumption used in some certification determinations under the Subcontracting Compensation Clause" is subject to some heightened level of scrutiny.... The parties disagree as to what that level should be. (We note, incidentally, that this case concerns only classifications

based explicitly on race, and presents none of the additional difficulties posed by laws that, although facially race neutral, result in racially disproportionate impact and are motivated by a racially discriminatory purpose. See generally *Arlington Heights v. Metropolitan Housing Development Corp.,* 429 U.S. 252 (1977); *Washington v. Davis,* 426 U.S. 229 (1976).)

Adarand's claim arises under the Fifth Amendment to the Constitution, which provides that "No person shall...be deprived of life, liberty, or property, without due process of law." Although this Court has always understood that Clause to provide some measure of protection against *arbitrary* treatment by the Federal Government, it is not as explicit a guarantee of *equal* treatment as the Fourteenth Amendment, which provides that "No *State* shall...deny to any person within its jurisdiction the equal protection of the laws" (emphasis added). Our cases have accorded varying degrees of significance to the difference in the language of those two Clauses. We think it necessary to revisit the issue here.

A

Through the 1940's, this Court had routinely taken the view in non-race-related cases that, "[u]nlike the Fourteenth Amendment, the Fifth contains no equal protection clause and it provides no guaranty against discriminatory legislation by Congress." *Detroit Bank v. United States,* 317 U.S. 329, 337 (1943); *[Here the Court summarizes the two Japanese-American cases that upheld a curfew and an exclusion order, even though in the latter* (Korematsu) *the Court announced a "most rigid scrutiny" standard. It also refers to* Bolling v. Sharpe *(1954), interpreting the due process clause of the Fifth Amendment to strike down segregated education in the District of Columbia.]*

Bolling's facts concerned school desegregation, but its reasoning was not so limited.... *Bolling...* reiterated " 'that the Constitution of the United States, in its present form, forbids, so far as civil and political rights are concerned, discrimination *by the General Government, or by the States,* against any citizen because of his race,' " *id.,* at 499 (quoting *Gibson v. Mississippi,* 162 U.S. 565, 591 (1896)) (emphasis added)....

Later cases in contexts other than school desegregation did not distinguish between the duties of the States and the Federal Government to avoid racial classifications. *[Here the Court summarizes McLaughlin v. Florida, 379 U.S. 184 (1964), Loving v. Virginia, 388 U.S. 1 (1967), Frontiero v.*

Richardson, 411 U.S. 677 (1973), Weinberger v. Wiesenfeld, 420 U.S. 636 (1975), and other cases.]

B

[This section reviews the inability of the Court, in decisions like Bakke, Fullilove, *and* Wygant, *to produce a majority opinion on the level of scrutiny required for racial classifications. Repeatedly, the Court issued plurality opinions in debating the choice between strict scrutiny and less stringent standards.]*

With *Croson*, the Court finally agreed that the Fourteenth Amendment requires strict scrutiny of all race-based action by state and local governments. But *Croson* of course had no occasion to declare what standard of review the Fifth Amendment requires for such action taken by the Federal Government.... Thus, some uncertainty persisted with respect to the standard of review for federal racial classifications...

Despite lingering uncertainty in the details, however, the Court's cases through *Croson* had established three general propositions with respect to governmental racial classifications. First, skepticism: " 'Any preference based on racial or ethnic criteria must necessarily receive a most searching examination,'" *Wygant*, 476 U.S., at 273 (plurality opinion of Powell, J.);.... Second, consistency: "[T]he standard of review under the Equal Protection Clause is not dependent on the race of those burdened or benefited by a particular classification," *Croson*, 488 U.S., at 494 (plurality opinion);...*i.e.*, all racial classifications reviewable under the Equal Protection Clause must be strictly scrutinized. And third, congruence: "Equal protection analysis in the Fifth Amendment area is the same as that under the Fourteenth Amendment," *Buckley* v. *Valeo, 424 U.S.*, at 93;.... Taken together, these three propositions lead to the conclusion that any person, of whatever race, has the right to demand that any governmental actor subject to the Constitution justify any racial classification subjecting that person to unequal treatment under the strictest judicial scrutiny....

[The Court acknowledges in this section that Metro Broadcasting *took "a surprising turn" by holding that "benign" federal racial classifications need only satisfy intermediate scrutiny, after Cro-son had decided that such classifications enacted by a state must satisfy strict scrutiny.* Metro Broadcasting, *said the Court, rejected the propo-*

sition of congruence and undermined the propositions of skepticism and consistency.]

The three propositions undermined by *Metro Broadcasting* all derive from the basic principle that the Fifth and Fourteenth Amendments to the Constitution protect *persons*, not *groups*, It follows from that principle that all governmental action based on race — a *group* classification long recognized as "in most circumstances irrelevant and therefore prohibited," *Hirabayashi, 320 U.S.*, at 100 — should be subjected to detailed judicial inquiry to ensure that the *personal* right to equal protection of the laws has not been infringed.... Accordingly, we hold today that all racial classifications, imposed by whatever federal, state, or local governmental actor, must be analyzed by a reviewing court under strict scrutiny. In other words, such classifications are constitutional only if they are narrowly tailored measures that further compelling governmental interests. To the extent that *Metro Broadcasting is* inconsistent with that holding, it is overruled.

In dissent, JUSTICE STEVENS criticizes us for "deliver[ing] a disconcerting lecture about the evils of governmental racial classifications,"... With respect, we believe his criticisms reflect a serious misunderstanding of our opinion.

. . .

JUSTICE STEVENS also claims that we have ignored any difference between federal and state legislatures. But requiring that Congress, like the States, enact racial classifications only when doing so is necessary to further a "compelling interest" does not contravene any principle of appropriate respect for a coequal branch of the Government. It is true that various Members of this Court have taken different views of the authority § 5 of the Fourteenth Amendment confers upon Congress to deal with the problem of racial discrimination, and the extent to which courts should defer to Congress' exercise of that authority.... We need not, and do not, address these differences today. For now, it is enough to observe that JUSTICE STEVENS' suggestion that any Member of this Court has repudiated in this case his or her previously expressed views on the subject,... is incorrect.

C

[This section responds to the issue of stare decisis, *because the Court here is rejecting the doctrine announced in* Metro Broadcasting. *It justifies the rejection by pointing out that* Metro Broadcasting *undermined important principles that the Court*

had been developing, and that Metro Broadcasting *was quite recent.].*

D

. . .

Finally, we wish to dispel the notion that strict scrutiny is "strict in theory, but fatal in fact." *Fullilove, supra,* at 519 (Marshall, J., concurring in judgment). The unhappy persistence of both the practice and the lingering effects of racial discrimination against minority groups in this country is an unfortunate reality, and government is not disqualified from acting in response to it.... When race-based action is necessary to further a compelling interest, such action is within constitutional constraints if it satisfies the "narrow tailoring" test this Court has set out in previous cases.

IV

Because our decision today alters the playing field in some important respects, we think it best to remand the case to the lower courts for further consideration in light of the principles we have announced. The Court of Appeals, following *Metro Broadcasting* and *Fullilove,* analyzed the case in terms of intermediate scrutiny....

Accordingly, the judgment of the Court of Appeals is vacated, and the case is remanded for further proceedings consistent with this opinion.

It is so ordered.

JUSTICE SCALIA, concurring in part and concurring in the judgment.

I join the opinion of the Court, except Part III-C, and except insofar as it may be inconsistent with the following: In my view, government can never have a "compelling interest" in discriminating on the basis of race in order to "make up" for past racial discrimination in the opposite direction.... Individuals who have been wronged by unlawful racial discrimination should be made whole; but under our Constitution there can be no such thing as either a creditor or a debtor race. That concept is alien to the Constitution's focus upon the individual, see Amdt. 14, § 1 ("[N]or shall any State...deny to *any person*" the equal protection of the laws) (emphasis added), and its rejection of dispositions based on race, see Amdt. 15, § 1 (prohibiting abridgment of the right to vote "on account of race"), or based on blood, see Art. III, § 3 ("[N]o Attainder of Treason shall

work Corruption of Blood"); Art. I, § 9, cl. 8 ("No Title of Nobility shall be granted by the United States"). To pursue the concept of racial entitlement—even for the most admirable and benign of purposes—is to reinforce and preserve for future mischief the way of thinking that produced race slavery, race privilege and race hatred. In the eyes of government, we are just one race here. It is American.

It is unlikely, if not impossible, that the challenged program would survive under this understanding of strict scrutiny, but I am content to leave that to be decided on remand.

JUSTICE THOMAS, concurring in part and concurring in the judgment.

...[U]nder our Constitution, the government may not make distinctions on the basis of race. As far as the Constitution is concerned, it is irrelevant whether a government's racial classifications are drawn by those who wish to oppress a race or by those who have a sincere desire to help those thought to be disadvantaged....

...So-called "benign" discrimination teaches many that because of chronic and apparently immutable handicaps, minorities cannot compete with them without their patronizing indulgence. Inevitably, such programs engender attitudes of superiority or, alternatively, provoke resentment among those who believe that they have been wronged by the government's use of race. These programs stamp minorities with a badge of inferiority and may cause them to develop dependencies or to adopt an attitude that they are "entitled" to preferences....

JUSTICE STEVENS, with whom JUSTICE GINSBURG joins, dissenting.

. . .

I

The Court's concept of skepticism is, at least in principle, a good statement of law and of common sense. Undoubtedly, a court should be wary of a governmental decision that relies upon a racial classification.... But, as the opinions in *Fullilove* demonstrate, substantial agreement on the standard to be applied in deciding difficult cases does not necessarily lead to agreement on how those cases actually should or will be resolved. In my judgment, because uniform standards are often anything but uniform, we should evaluate the Court's comments on "consistency," "congruence," and *stare decisis* with the same type of skepticism that the Court advocates for the underlying issue.

II

The Court's concept of "consistency" assumes that there is no significant difference between a decision by the majority to impose a special burden on the members of a minority race and a decision by the majority to provide a benefit to certain members of that minority notwithstanding its incidental burden on some members of the majority. In my opinion that assumption is untenable. There is no moral or constitutional equivalence between a policy that is designed to perpetuate a caste system and one that seeks to eradicate racial subordination....

III

The Court's concept of "congruence" assumes that there is no significant difference between a decision by the Congress of the United States to adopt an affirmative-action program and such a decision by a State or a municipality. In my opinion that assumption is untenable. It ignores important practical and legal differences between federal and state or local decisionmakers.

. . .

JUSTICE SOUTER, with whom JUSTICE GINSBURG and JUSTICE BREYER join, dissenting.

...I agree with JUSTICE STEVENS's conclusion that *stare decisis* compels the application of *Fullilove*. Although *Fullilove* did not reflect doctrinal consistency, its several opinions produced a result on shared grounds that petitioner does not attack: that discrimination in the construction industry had been subject to government acquiescence, with effects that remain and that may be addressed by some preferential treatment falling within the congressional power under § 5 of the Fourteenth Amendment.... Once *Fullilove* is applied, as JUSTICE STEVENS points out, it follows that the statutes in question here (which are substantially better tailored to the harm being remedied than the statute endorsed in *Fullilove...)* pass muster under Fifth Amendment

due process and Fourteenth Amendment equal protection.

JUSTICE GINSBURG, with whom JUSTICE BREYER joins, dissenting.

For the reasons stated by JUSTICE SOUTER, and in view of the attention the political branches are currently giving the matter of affirmative action, I see no compelling cause for the intervention the Court has made in this case. I further agree with JUSTICE STEVENS that, in this area, large deference is owed by the Judiciary to "Congress' institutional competence and constitutional authority to overcome historic racial subjugation."...I write separately to underscore not the differences the several opinions in this case display, but the considerable field of agreement— the common understandings and concerns—revealed in opinions that together speak for a majority of the Court.

I

. . .

The divisions in this difficult case should not obscure the Court's recognition of the persistence of racial inequality and a majority's acknowledgment of Congress' authority to act affirmatively, not only to end discrimination, but also to counteract discrimination's lingering effects.... Those effects, reflective of a system of racial caste only recently ended, are evident in our workplaces, markets, and neighborhoods. Job applicants with identical resumes, qualifications, and interview styles still experience different receptions, depending on their race. White and African-American consumers still encounter different deals. People of color looking for housing still face discriminatory treatment by landlords, real estate agents, and mortgage lenders....

Given this history and its practical consequences, Congress surely can conclude that a carefully designed affirmative action program may help to realize, finally, the "equal protection of the laws" the Fourteenth Amendment has promised since 1868.

. . .

CONCLUSIONS

The preoccupation with race in American constitutional law continues with little interruption. The first effort to reconcile the Declaration of Independence and the Constitution came from Congress, which passed the three Civil War amendments (the Thirteenth, Fourteenth, and Fifteenth) and the Civil Rights Acts of 1866 and 1875. The nation then turned its back on this commitment for decades. During the 1930s and 1940s, the courts and the President began to take some initiatives to eliminate discrimination against blacks. America's contribution in World War II to combat racism in Europe made it imperative, after the war, for America to honor its democratic ideals. That was important to prevent communist leaders from taunting the United States for its betrayal of democratic principles. All of those forces produced the political momentum for *Brown v. Board of Education.*

Since 1954 the effort to eradicate racism has collided with stubborn counterforces: state resistance, housing patterns, and job discrimination. Despite a series of court orders, beginning in 1954 and stretching over the next decade, little was accomplished toward desegregation until Congress and the President in the Civil Rights Act of 1964 confronted the injustices of racism. Judicial remedies in the form of school busing proved counterproductive and were abandoned. Although substantial progress has been achieved in recent decades, the policy of affirmative action has created major strains in a society that wants to eliminate racial discrimination without abandoning the merit principle or the principle that the Constitution protects individuals, not groups. Precisely how to implement affirmative action, and for how long, is a task that remains unsettled and unresolved. There seems to be a growing consensus that affirmative action is justified not on race or gender alone but on economic class. This policy would support preferential action for people, whether white or black, from poor families.

SELECTED READINGS

BICKEL, ALEXANDER M. "The Original Understanding and the Segregation Decision." 69 Harvard Law Review 1 (1955).

BLAUSTEIN, ALBERT P., AND CLARENCE CLYDE FERGUSON, JR. Desegregation and the Law. New York: Vintage, 1962.

BLAUSTEIN, ALBERT P., AND ROBERT L. ZANGRANDO, EDS. Civil Rights and the American Negro. New York: Washington Square Press, 1968.

CASPER, GERHARD. "Jones v. Mayer: Clio, Bemused and Confused Muse." 1968 Supreme Court Review 89.

DORSEN, NORMAN. Discrimination and Civil Rights. Boston: Little, Brown, 1969.

ELY, JOHN HART. "The Constitutionality of Reverse Racial Discrimination." 41 University of Chicago Law Review 723 (1974).

FALLON, RICHARD H., JR., AND PAUL C. WEILER. "Firefighters v. Stotts: Conflicting Models of Racial Justice." 1984 Supreme Court Review 1.

FINCH, MINNIE. The NAACP: Its Fight for Justice. Metuchen, N.J.: Scarecrow Press, 1981.

FRANKLIN, JOHN HOPE. From Slavery to Freedom: A History of Negro Americans. New York: Knopf, 1980.

FREED, MAYER G., AND DANIEL D. POLSBY. "Race, Religion, and Public Policy: Bob Jones University v. United States." 1983 Supreme Court Review 1.

GLAZER, NATHAN. Affirmative Discrimination. New York: Basic Books, 1975.

GRAGLIA, LINO A. Disaster by Decree: The Supreme Court's Decisions on Race and the Schools. Ithaca, N.Y.: Cornell University Press, 1976.

GRAHAM, HUGH DAVIS. The Civil Rights Era: Origins and Development of National Policy, 1960–1972. New York: Oxford University Press, 1990.

GREENAWALT, KENT. Discrimination and Reverse Discrimination. New York: Knopf, 1983.

GREENBERG, JACK. Crusaders in the Courts. How a Dedicated Band of Lawyers Fought for the Civil Rights Revolution. New York: Basic Books, 1994.

HAMILTON, CHARLES V. The Bench and the Ballot: Southern Federal Judges and Black Voters. New York: Oxford University Press, 1973.

HYMAN, HAROLD M., AND WILLIAM M. WEICEK. Equal Justice Under Law. New York: Harper & Row, 1982.

KITCH, EDMUND W. "The Return of Color-Consciousness to the Constitution: Weber, Dayton and Columbus." 1979 Supreme Court Review. 1.

KLUGER, RICHARD. Simple Justice. New York: Knopf, 1976.

LIVINGSTON, JOHN C. Fair Game? Inequality and Affirmative Action. San Francisco: W.H. Freeman, 1979.

MORGAN, RUTH. The President and Civil Rights: Policy-Making by Executive Order. New York: St. Martin's Press, 1970.

PELTASON, JACK. Fifty-Eight Lonely Men: Southern Federal Judges and School Desegregation. New York: Harcourt, Brace & World, 1961.

POSNER, RICHARD A. "The DeFunis Case and the Constitutionality of Preferential Treatment of Racial Minorities." 1974 Supreme Court Review 1.

SINDLER, ALLAN P. Bakke, DeFunis, and Minority Admissions. New York: Longman, 1978.

STRAUSS, DAVID A. "The Myth of Colorblindness." 1986 Supreme Court Review 99.

———. "Affirmative Action and the Public Interest," 1995 Supreme Court Review 1.

VOSE, CLEMENT E. Causasians Only: The Supreme Court, the NAACP, and the Restrictive Covenant Cases. Berkeley: University of California Press, 1959.

WILKINSON, J. HARVIE, III. From Brown to Bakke: The Supreme Court and School Integration. New York: Oxford University Press, 1979.

WILLIAMS, JUAN. Thurgood Marshall: American Revolutionary. New York: Times Books, 1998.

WOLK, ALLAN. The Presidency and Black Civil Rights: Eisenhower to Nixon. Cranbury, N.J.: Fairleigh Dickinson University Press, 1971.

16

Emerging Group Pressures

Building on the rights established for black Americans, women pressed for fundamental changes in their rights. Also from this period of "rights consciousness" emerged efforts to secure rights for other groups: Hispanics, Indians, aliens, the indigent, the aged, the handicapped, juveniles, illegitimate children, and institutionalized persons.[1] This extension of individual rights placed heavy demands on Congress and the judiciary as well as state and local governments.

Several groups are studied in this chapter. The trio of women, juveniles, and prisoners may seem an odd, even offensive, combination, but all three share certain characteristics. In each case they were initially denied constitutional rights available to the rest of the population. In each case they had to overcome entrenched ideas and customs. The chapter concludes by examining the constitutional rights of the poor. People within groups have constitutional rights as *individuals* and should not be deprived of rights simply because they happen to be women, juveniles, prisoners, or poor.

A. THE STRUGGLE FOR WOMEN'S RIGHTS

When the framers proclaimed in the Declaration of Independence that "all men are created equal," they meant men literally, and not even all men. Blacks were excluded from equal treatment, as were nonpropertied white males. Although the phrase "all men are created equal" did not protect women, blacks, or nonpropertied white males in 1776, it is best understood as a fundamental principle meant to apply to all human beings, even if the aspiration was unfulfilled at the time of the framers.

On March 31, 1776, Abigail Adams appealed to her husband, John Adams, who was busily engaged with the Continental Congress in Philadelphia. She urged that "in the new code of laws which I suppose it will be necessary for you to make, I desire you would remember the ladies and be more generous and favorable to them than your ancestors. Do not put such unlimited power into the hands of the husbands. Remember, all men would be tyrants if they could." His curt reply mirrored the attitude of the times: "As to your extraordinary code of laws, I cannot but laugh." C. F. Adams, ed., Familiar Letters of John Adams and His Wife Abigail Adams During the Revolution 149–50, 155 (1876).

The customs of 1776 included the ancient doctrine of *coverture,* which placed women in a subordinate position to men. Blackstone, the great English jurist, stated that marriage made husband and wife "one person in law: that is, the very being or legal existence of the woman is suspended during the marriage, or at least is incorporated and consolidated into that of the husband: under whose wing, protection, and *cover,* she performs every thing." 2 Commen-

---

1. In a major case in 1982, the Supreme Court struck down a Texas statute that withheld from local school districts any state funds for the education of children who were not "legally admitted" into the United States. The state authorized schools to deny enrollment to such children. The Court held that the statute violated the Equal Protection Clause of the Fourteenth Amendment, which protects *persons,* including illegal aliens. Plyler v. Doe, 457 U.S. 202 (1982).

taries *442. The legal status of women inspired a scene in Charles Dickens' *Oliver Twist*. Mr. Bumble, trying to dissociate himself from his wife's theft, is instructed that he is "the more guilty of the two, in the eye of the law; for the law supposes that your wife acts under your direction." Bumble explodes: "If the law supposes that, the law is a ass — a idiot. If that's the eye of the law, the law is a bachelor; and the worst I wish the law is, that his eye may be opened by experience — by experience."

The Right to Practice Law

Blackstone's philosophy animates the early Supreme Court rulings on women's rights. A prominent example is *Bradwell* v. *State* (1873). Myra Bradwell had a law degree but needed the approval of a panel of judges (all men, of course) to practice law in Illinois. They turned her down solely because she was a woman. The Supreme Court denied that her rejection violated the privileges and immunities of the Fourteenth Amendment. The Slaughter-House Cases, announced earlier that year, left those questions to the states, not the federal government. Eight Justices voted against Mrs. Bradwell; only Chief Justice Chase (without a written opinion) dissented.

Significantly, Mrs. Bradwell prevailed at the state level as a result of *legislative* action. The Supreme Court of Illinois rejected her application for a license to practice law partly on "the deference and delicacy with which it is the pride of our ruder sex to treat her," but largely because the state legislature had not explicitly authorized women to practice law. The state court clearly invited the legislature to act. In re Bradwell, 55 Ill. 535, 542 (1869). Three years later the state legislature passed a bill stating that no person "shall be precluded or debarred from any occupation, profession or employment (except military) on account of sex." Illinois Laws, 1871–72, p. 578. The issue before the U.S. Supreme Court in 1873 was, therefore, Bradwell's *national* right under the Privileges or Immunities Clause.

The concurrence by Justice Bradley in *Bradwell* claimed that the "natural and proper timidity and delicacy which belongs to the female sex evidently unfits it for many of the occupations of civil life." A woman's responsibility to domestic life and to the family institution made it "repugnant" for her to adopt a career independent from that of her husband. Bradley recognized that his argument was irrelevant for unmarried women, but they were exceptions to the general rule: "The paramount destiny and mission of woman are to fulfill the noble and benign offices of wife and mother. This is the law of the Creator. And the rules of civil society must be adapted to the general constitution of things, and cannot be based on exceptional cases." BRADWELL v. STATE, 83 U.S. (16 Wall.) 130 (1873). Similar stereotypes appear in an 1875 decision by the Supreme Court of Wisconsin (see box on next page).

After Myra Bradwell lost her case in the U.S. Supreme Court in 1873, congressional action was possible. A rule adopted by the Court prohibited women from practicing there. In 1878 Congress began consideration of a bill "to relieve certain legal disabilities of women." The bill provided that any woman who shall have been a member of the bar of the highest court of any state or territory or of the Supreme Court of the District of Columbia for three years, and who qualified on moral character, may be admitted to the Supreme Court of the United States. The bill passed the House of Representatives on February 21, 1878, by a vote of 169 to 87. 7 Cong. Rec. 1235 (1878). The Senate Judiciary Committee reported the bill adversely, concluding that such matters should be left to the Court through its own rules. Id. at 1821. During Senate debate, members recognized that women were entering a number of professions, including law and medicine, and appeared to take the *Bradwell* case of 1873 as an invitation to Congress to act. Id. at 2704.

When the bill was debated the following year, Senator Aaron Sargent argued: "No man has a right to put a limit to the exertions or the sphere of woman. That is a right which only can be possessed by that sex itself.... The enjoyment of liberty, the pursuit of happiness in her own

Prohibiting Women from Practicing Law

[R. Lavinia Goodell requested permission to practice law before the Wisconsin Supreme Court. Unlike Myra Bradwell, Goodell was not married. Nonetheless, the court denied her motion, arguing that the "law of nature" destines women to bear and nurture children, take care of the custody of homes, and love and honor their husbands. In re Goodell, 39 Wis. 232 (1875).]

RYAN, C.J.... we find no statutory authority for the admission of females to the bar of any court of this state. And, with all the respect and sympathy for this lady which all men owe to all good women, we cannot regret that we do not. We cannot but think the common law wise in excluding women from the profession of the law. The profession enters largely into the well being of society; and to be honorably filled and safely to society, exacts the devotion of life. The law of nature destines and qualifies the female sex for the bearing and nurture of the children of our race and for the custody of the homes of the world and their maintenance in love and honor. And all life-long callings of women, inconsistent with these radical and sacred duties of their sex, as is the profession of the law, are departures from the order of nature; and when voluntary, treason against it.... There are many employments in life not unfit for female character. The profession of the law is surely not one of these. The peculiar qualities of womanhood, its gentle graces, its quick sensibility, its tender susceptibility, its purity, its delicacy, its emotional impulses, its subordination of hard reason to sympathetic feeling, are surely not qualifications for forensic strife. Nature has tempered woman as little for the juridical conflicts of the court room, as for the physical conflicts of the battle field. Womanhood is moulded for gentler and better things. And it is not the saints of the world who chiefly give employment to our profession. It has essentially and habitually to do with all that is selfish and malicious, knavish and criminal, coarse and brutal, repulsive and obscene in human life. It would be revolting to all female sense of the innocence and sanctity of their sex, shocking to man's reverence for womanhood and faith in woman, on which hinge all the better affections and humanities of life, that woman should be permitted to mix professionally in all the nastiness of the world which finds its way into courts of justice; all the unclean issues, all the collateral questions of sodomy, incest, rape, seduction, fornication, adultery, pregnancy, bastardy, legitimacy, prostitution, lascivious cohabitation, abortion, infanticide, obscene publications, libel and slander of sex, impotence, divorce: all the nameless catalogue of indecencies, *la chronique scandaleuse* of all the vices and all the infirmities of all society, with which the profession has to deal, and which go towards filling judicial reports which must be read for accurate knowledge of the law. This is bad enough for men....

way, is as much the birthright of woman as of man. In this land man has ceased to dominate over his fellow — let him cease to dominate over his sister; for he has no higher right to do the latter than the former" (see reading). The bill passed the Senate, 39 to 20, and was enacted into law. 20 Stat. 292 (1879). Thus, an all-male legislative body provided impressive support for women's rights — rights unavailable from the Courts.

As a result of that statute, Belva Lockwood became the first woman admitted to practice before the U.S. Supreme Court. When she later appealed to the U.S. Supreme Court for the right to practice in Virginia, a unanimous Court deferred to the Supreme Court of Virginia in construing the statute that authorized persons to practice in the state. The interpretation of the Privileges or Immunities Clause was again at stake. In re Lockwood, 154 U.S. 116 (1894).

Within two years of *Bradwell*, the judiciary delivered another major blow against women's rights. A lawsuit by Mrs. Virginia Minor argued that she was a "citizen" within the meaning of the Constitution and therefore entitled to vote as one of the privileges and immunities protected by the Fourteenth Amendment. A unanimous Court agreed that women are citizens but denied that the Fourteenth Amendment added substantive rights to previous privileges and immunities. According to the Court, Section 2 of the Fourteenth Amendment limited suffrage to male inhabitants. Indeed, it took the Fifteenth Amendment to give blacks the right to vote. The Court ruled that women, like children, were "citizens" and "persons" in the constitutional sense, but that status did not automatically entitle either to vote. Minor v. Happersett, 88 U.S. (21 Wall.) 162 (1875). Women did not gain the right to vote until the Nineteenth Amendment was ratified in 1920. Although women, nationwide, had to await the Nineteenth Amendment to vote in federal elections, in a number of states they were already voting in both state and federal elections. M. Margaret Conway, et al., Women and Political Participation 8–9 (1997).

Protective Legislation

Although women later won important cases in the courts, the victories were often premised on their inferiority, not their equality. A decision in 1908, in which the Supreme Court unanimously upheld Oregon's ten-hour day for women, helped perpetuate the stereotype of women advanced in *Bradwell*. Speaking for the Court, Justice Brewer remarked: "Still again, history discloses the fact that woman has always been dependent upon man. He established his control at the outset by superior physical strength, and this control in various forms, with diminishing intensity, has continued to the present." Muller v. Oregon, 208 U.S. 412, 421 (1908). Despite new opportunities for women to acquire knowledge, "it is still true that in the struggle for subsistence she is not an equal competitor with her brother. Though limitations upon personal and contractual rights may be removed by legislation, there is that in her disposition and habits of life which will operate against a full assertion of those rights." Id. at 422. Acknowledging that individual exceptions existed, Brewer felt confident that even with the elimination of political and contractual restrictions "it would still be true that she is so constituted that she will rest upon and look to him for protection." Blackstone still reigned.

By 1923 the Court concluded that protective legislation for women was no longer necessary because of the Nineteenth Amendment and changes in statutory and contractual law. Adkins v. Children's Hospital, 261 U.S. 525, 553 (1923). Chief Justice Taft, in one of the dissents, wondered whether the majority believed that previous Court doctrines had been invalidated by the Nineteenth Amendment, which "did not change the physical strength or limitations of women upon which the decision in *Muller v. Oregon* rests." Id. at 567. A dissent by Justice Holmes wryly observed: "It will need more than the Nineteenth Amendment to convince me that there are no differences between men and women, or that legislation cannot take those differences into account." Id. at 569–70.

The Court continued to support certain types of protective legislation for women. In 1924 it upheld a New York law that prohibited women in large cities from working between 10 P.M. and 6 A.M. Radice v. New York, 264 U.S. 292 (1924). But the spirit of *Adkins* survived through 1936 when the Court (divided 5–4) struck down New York's minimum wage law for women and minors. The Court saw no justification for protective legislation for women when men "in need of work are as likely as women to accept the low wages offered by unscrupulous employers." Morehead v. N.Y. ex rel. Tipaldo, 298 U.S. 587, 616 (1936). *Adkins* was overturned the next year. A 5–4 majority accepted minimum wage legislation for women. States were entitled to consider "the fact that they are in the class receiving the least pay, that their bargaining power is relatively weak, and that they are the ready victims of those who would take advantage of their necessitous circumstances." West Coast Hotel Co. v. Parrish, 300 U.S. 379, 398 (1937). The Court also took "judicial notice" of the public relief needed during the Great Depression. Inadequate wages for women had placed demands on state agencies for public assistance: "The community is not bound to provide what is in effect a subsidy for unconscionable employers." Id. at 399.

Court doctrines had not advanced very far by 1948, when the Supreme Court upheld a Michigan law that prohibited female bartenders unless they were the wife or daughter of the male owner. Attitudes in state legislatures and the judiciary had not changed much since *Bradwell*. By a 6–3 vote, the Court decided that Michigan had not violated the Equal Protection Clause of the Fourteenth Amendment. Frankfurter's opinion for the majority has a smug quality: "Beguiling as the subject is, it need not detain us for long. To ask whether or not the Equal Protection of the Laws Clause of the Fourteenth Amendment barred Michigan from making the classification the State has made between wives and daughters of owners of liquor places and wives and daughters of non-owners, is one of those rare instances where to state the question is in effect to answer it." Goeseart v. Cleary, 335 U.S. 464, 465 (1948). Frankfurter concluded that Michigan could, "beyond question," forbid all women from working behind a bar. To the three dissenters, Michigan's statute arbitrarily discriminated between men and women.

In 1960 Frankfurter wrote an opinion rejecting the "medieval view" that husband and wife are one person with but a single will and, therefore, legally incapable of entering into a criminal conspiracy. To the extent that this outmoded doctrine of coverture rested on a legal fiction, three dissenters preferred that it be corrected by Congress, not the judiciary. United States v. Dege, 364 U.S. 51 (1960). Medieval thinking triumphed in 1961, when the Court agreed unanimously that women could be largely exempted from jury service because they are "still regarded as the center of home and family life." Hoyt v. Florida, 368 U.S. 57, 62 (1961). Remnants of the law of coverture persisted until 1966. United States v. Yazell, 382 U.S. 341 (1966).

Abolishing Sexual Stereotypes

Judicial attitudes on sex discrimination did not change until long after the desegregation case of 1954. Judges, at both the federal and state level, held fast to anachronous legal doctrines. Yet World War II had done much to change public attitudes about the kind of work that was suitable for women. During the war, women filled many jobs previously associated with "men's work": machine tools, aircraft production, shipbuilding, and munitions. The dainty image of women gave way to "Rosie the Riveter." Women began entering a number of professions that were new to them. An amusing case came out of Oregon, where the legislature had excluded women from wrestling exhibitions (see box).

Not until 1971 did the U.S. Supreme Court issue a decision striking down sex discrimina-

---

No Wrestling for Women

In 1956, the Supreme Court of Oregon upheld a state statute that prohibited women from participating in wrestling exhibitions. In sustaining the statute, the court poked some fun at the legislators. After taking judicial notice that the legislative assembly that enacted the statute was predominantly male, the court speculated on what might have driven the lawmakers:

It seems to us that its purpose, although somewhat selfish in nature, stands out in the statute like a sore thumb. Obviously it intended that there should be at least one island on the sea of life reserved for man that would be impregnable to the assault of woman.... She had already invaded practically every activity formerly considered suitable and appropriate for men only.... In these circumstances, is it any wonder that the legislative assembly took advantage of the police power of the state in its decision to halt this ever-increasing feminine encroachment upon what for ages had been considered strictly as manly arts and privileges? State v. Hunter, 300 P.2d 455, 458 (Ore. 1956).

These statutory efforts to halt the "assault of woman" gave way in time to female participation not only in wrestling but boxing as well.

tion. The judicial record before 1971 was deplorable. According to one study: "Our conclusion, independently reached, but completely shared, is that by and large the performance of American judges in the area of sex discrimination can be succinctly described as ranging from poor to abominable." Johnston & Knapp, "Sex Discrimination by Law: A Study in Judicial Perspective," 46 N.Y.U.L. Rev. 675, 676 (1971).

Progress came primarily from the legislative and executive branches, which showed a much greater capacity to recognize wrongs and to right them. Using its constitutional power to regulate commerce, Congress passed the Equal Pay Act in 1963 to prohibit employers in the private sector from discriminating on the basis of sex. 77 Stat. 56. The debate demonstrates how Congress can respond to constitutional inequities before they are addressed, or redressed, by the courts (see reading).

Title VII of the Civil Rights Act of 1964 made it illegal for any employer to discriminate against anyone with respect to "compensation, terms, conditions, or privileges of employment" because of the person's sex. 42 U.S.C. § 2000e-2(a)(1) (1994). It is sometimes claimed that the word "sex" was added to the bill to ridicule and perhaps sabotage the enactment of a civil rights bill. However, the debate suggests a different motivation. By prohibiting discrimination on the basis of race, members of Congress were concerned that a white woman applying for a job would be at a disadvantage, legally, to a black woman (see reading). No doubt the person who offered the amendment prohibiting gender discrimination, Congressman Howard Smith (D-Va.), was well-known for his opposition to civil rights. Yet he was also a supporter of the Equal Rights Amendment and had the backing of women's groups. The National Women's Party (NWP) objected to the civil rights bill because it only prohibited discrimination on the basis of race, color, religion, or national origin. The NWP said that the bill gave no protection "to a *White Woman*, a *Woman of the Christian Religion*, or a *Woman of United States origin.*" The NWP worked with Smith on his amendment to the Civil Rights Act. Cynthia Harrison, On Account of Sex 21, 176–77 (1988).

Congress established the Equal Employment Opportunity Commission (EEOC) to investigate claims of discrimination. Much of the agency's workload deals with cases of sex discrimination. Upholding congressional policy and EEOC regulations, the Court held that a company could not deny employment to a woman because she had preschool-aged children if the company agreed to hire men with preschool-aged children. Phillips v. Martin Marietta Corp., 400 U.S. 542 (1971). In another initiative, Congress passed Title IX of the Education Amendments of 1972 to withdraw federal financial assistance from any educational institution that practices sex discrimination. 86 Stat. 373 (1972).

Bradwell v. State

83 U.S. 130 (1873)

Myra Bradwell, a resident of Illinois, applied to the judges of the Illinois Supreme Court for a license to practice law. In addition to listing her qualifications, she asserted that she was entitled to the license by virtue of the privileges and immunities guaranteed to U.S. citizens under Section 2 of Article IV and under Section 1 of the Fourteenth Amendment. Her application was denied, with only one Justice dissenting. The concurrence by Justice Bradley is of special interest because of his instruction regarding the "mission of woman."

Mr. Justice MILLER delivered the opinion of the court.

The record in this case is not very perfect, but it may be fairly taken that the plaintiff asserted her right to a license on the grounds, among oth-

ers, that she was a citizen of the United States, and that having been a citizen of Vermont at one time, she was, in the State of Illinois, entitled to any right granted to citizens of the latter State.

The court having overruled these claims of

right founded on the clauses of the Federal Constitution before referred to, those propositions may be considered as properly before this court.

As regards the provision of the Constitution that citizens of each State shall be entitled to all the privileges and immunities of citizens in the several States, the plaintiff in her affidavit has stated very clearly a case to which it is inapplicable.

The protection designed by that clause, as has been repeatedly held, has no application to a citizen of the State whose laws are complained of. If the plaintiff was a citizen of the State of Illinois, that provision of the Constitution gave her no protection against its courts or its legislation.

The plaintiff seems to have seen this difficulty, and attempts to avoid it by stating that she was born in Vermont.

While she remained in Vermont that circumstance made her a citizen of that State. But she states, at the same time, that she is a citizen of the United States, and that she is now, and has been for many years past, a resident of Chicago, in the State of Illinois.

The fourteenth amendment declares that citizens of the United States are citizens of the State within which they reside; therefore the plaintiff was, at the time of making her application, a citizen of the United States and a citizen of the State of Illinois.

We do not here mean to say that there may not be a temporary residence in one State, with intent to return to another, which will not create citizenship in the former. But the plaintiff states nothing to take her case out of the definition of citizenship of a State as defined by the first section of the fourteenth amendment.

In regard to that amendment counsel for the plaintiff in this court truly says that there are certain privileges and immunities which belong to a citizen of the United States as such; otherwise it would be nonsense for the fourteenth amendment to prohibit a State from abridging them, and he proceeds to argue that admission to the bar of a State of a person who possesses the requisite learning and character is one of those which a State may not deny.

In this latter proposition we are not able to concur with counsel. We agree with him that there are privileges and immunities belonging to citizens of the United States, in that relation and character, and that it is these and these alone which a State is forbidden to abridge. But the right to admission to practice in the courts of a State is not one of them. This right in no sense depends on cit-

izenship of the United States. It has not, as far as we know, ever been made in any State, or in any case, to depend on citizenship at all. Certainly many prominent and distinguished lawyers have been admitted to practice, both in the State and Federal courts, who were not citizens of the United States or of any State. But, on whatever basis this right may be placed, so far as it can have any relation to citizenship at all, it would seem that, as to the courts of a State, it would relate to citizenship of the State, and as to Federal courts, it would relate to citizenship of the United States.

The opinion just delivered in the *Slaughter-House Cases* renders elaborate argument in the present case unnecessary; for, unless we are wholly and radically mistaken in the principles on which those cases are decided, the right to control and regulate the granting of license to practice law in the courts of a State is one of those powers which are not transferred for its protection to the Federal government, and its exercise is in no manner governed or controlled by citizenship of the United States in the party seeking such license.

It is unnecessary to repeat the argument on which the judgment in those cases is founded. It is sufficient to say they are conclusive of the present case.

JUDGMENT AFFIRMED.

Mr. Justice BRADLEY:

I concur in the judgment of the court in this case, by which the judgment of the Supreme Court of Illinois is affirmed, but not for the reasons specified in the opinion just read.

The claim of the plaintiff, who is a married woman, to be admitted to practice as an attorney and counsellor-at-law, is based upon the supposed right of every person, man or woman, to engage in any lawful employment for a livelihood. The Supreme Court of Illinois denied the application on the ground that, by the common law, which is the basis of the laws of Illinois, only men were admitted to the bar, and the legislature had not made any change in this respect, but had simply provided that no person should be admitted to practice as attorney or counsellor without having previously obtained a license for that purpose from two justices of the Supreme Court, and that no person should receive a license without first obtaining a certificate from the court of some county of his good moral character. In other respects it was left to the discretion of the court to establish the rules by which admission to the profession should be determined. The court, however, regarded itself as bound by at least two limitations. One was that it should establish such terms of admission as would promote the proper administration of justice, and the other that it should not admit any persons, or class of persons, not intended by the legislature to be admitted, even though not expressly excluded by statute. In view of this latter limitation the court felt compelled to deny the application of females to be admitted as members of the bar. Being contrary to the rules of the common law and the usages of Westminster Hall from time immemorial, it could not be supposed that the legislature had intended to adopt any different rule.

The claim that, under the fourteenth amendment of the Constitution, which declares that no State shall make or enforce any law which shall abridge the privileges and immunities of citizens of the United States, the statute law of Illinois, or the common law prevailing in that State, can no longer be set up as a barrier against the right of females to pursue any lawful employment for a livelihood (the practice of law included), assumes that it is one of the privileges and immunities of women as citizens to engage in any and every profession, occupation, or employment in civil life.

It certainly cannot be affirmed, as an historical fact, that this has ever been established as one of the fundamental privileges and immunities of the sex. On the contrary, the civil law, as well as nature herself, has always recognized a wide difference in the respective spheres and destinies of man and woman. Man is, or should be, woman's protector and defender. The natural and proper timidity and delicacy which belongs to the female sex evidently unfits it for many of the occupations of civil life. The constitution of the family organization, which is founded in the divine ordinance, as well as in the nature of things, indicates the domestic sphere as that which properly belongs to the domain and functions of womanhood. The harmony, not to say identity, of interests and views which belong, or should belong, to the family institution is repugnant to the idea of a woman adopting a distinct and independent career from that of her husband. So firmly fixed was this sentiment in the founders of the common law that it became a maxim of that system of jurisprudence that a woman had no legal existence separate from her husband, who was regarded as her head and representative in the social state; and, notwithstanding some recent modifications of this civil status, many of the special rules of law flowing from and dependent upon this cardinal prin-

ciple still exist in full force in most States. One of these is, that a married woman is incapable, without her husband's consent, of making contracts which shall be binding on her or him. This very incapacity was one circumstance which the Supreme Court of Illinois deemed important in rendering a married woman incompetent fully to perform the duties and trusts that belong to the office of an attorney and counsellor.

It is true that many women are unmarried and not affected by any of the duties, complications, and incapacities arising out of the married state, but these are exceptions to the general rule. The paramount destiny and mission of woman are to fulfil the noble and benign offices of wife and mother. This is the law of the Creator. And the rules of civil society must be adapted to the general constitution of things, and cannot be based upon exceptional cases.

The humane movements of modern society, which have for their object the multiplication of avenues for woman's advancement, and of occupations adapted to her condition and sex, have my heartiest concurrence. But I am not prepared to say that it is one of her fundamental rights and privileges to be admitted into every office and position, including those which require highly special qualifications and demanding special responsibilities. In the nature of things it is not every citizen of every age, sex, and condition that is qualified for every calling and position. It is the prerogative of the legislator to prescribe regulations founded on nature, reason, and experience for the due admission of qualified persons to professions and callings demanding special skill and confidence. This fairly belongs to the police power of the State; and, in my opinion, in view of the peculiar characteristics, destiny, and mission of woman, it is within the province of the legislature to ordain what offices, positions, and callings shall be filled and discharged by men, and shall receive the benefit of those energies and responsibilities, and that decision and firmness which are presumed to predominate in the sterner sex.

For these reasons I think that the laws of Illinois now complained of are not obnoxious to the charge of abridging any of the privileges and immunities of citizens of the United States.

Mr. Justice SWAYNE and Mr. Justice FIELD concurred in the foregoing opinion of Mr. Justice BRADLEY.

The CHIEF JUSTICE dissented from the judgment of the court, and from all the opinions.

Congress Responds to *Bradwell*

Congress passed legislation in 1879 to permit women to practice before the U.S. Supreme Court (20 Stat. 292), thus explicitly rejecting the principles and reasoning announced by the Court in *Bradwell* v. *State* (1873). Instead of following the contemporary attitude of courts, which concluded that women were temperamentally unfitted to practice law and engage in other professional activities, legislators at both the national and state level decided to remove legal impediments that interfered with the right of women to pursue a legal career. The following passages appear at 7 Cong. Rec. 2704 (1878) and 8 Cong. Rec. 1084 (1879).

[Senator Aaron] SARGENT [R-Cal.]. Mr. President, the best evidence that members of the legal profession have no jealousy against the admission of women to the bar who have the proper learning is shown by that document which I hold in my hand, signed by one hundred and fifty-five lawyers of the District of Columbia, embracing the most eminent men in the ranks of that profession, [exhibiting a petition.] That there is no jealousy or consideration of impropriety on its part in the various States is shown by the fact that the Legislatures of many of the States have recently admitted women to the bar; and my own State, California, has passed such a law within the last week or two. Illinois has done the same thing: so have Michigan, Minnesota, Missouri, and North Carolina; and Wyoming, Utah, and the District of Columbia among the Territories have also done it. There is no reason in principle why women should not be admitted to this profession or the profession of medicine, provided they have the learning to enable them to be useful in those professions, and useful to themselves. Where is the propriety in opening our colleges, our higher institutions of learning, or any institutions of learning to women, and then when they have acquired in the race with men the cultivation for higher employment to shut them out? There certainly is none.

... Some excellent lady lawyers in the United States are now practicing at the bar, behaving themselves with propriety, acceptably received before courts and juries; and when they have conducted their cases to a successful issue or an unsuccessful one in any court below, why should the United States courts to which an appeal may be taken and where their adversary of the male sex may follow the case up, why should they be debarred from appearing before those tribunals?

. . .

[Senator Augustus] GARLAND [D-Ark.]. I should like to ask the Senator from California if the courts of the United States cannot admit them upon their own motion anyhow?

Mr. SARGENT. I think there is nothing in the law prohibiting it, but the Supreme Court of the United States recently in passing upon the question of a certain lady said that until some legislation took place they did not like to depart from the precedent set in England, or until there was more general practice among the States.... I think the Supreme Court should not have required further legislation, but they seem to have done so, and that makes the necessity for this legislation which I have now offered.

. . .

Mr. SARGENT.... The medical universities of the world are receiving women and instructing them in medicine and surgery, and there are many women engaged in these studies and practicing this profession. In France the universities are open to them. The prejudice in England has been gradually overcome in this direction, and the London Medical College receives them. They are admitted into the Scotch schools and into some of the best medical schools of the United States, and they are making their way in them all. There are in the various States of the Union women lawyers; and women in literature have won a very high place. No man has a right to put a limit to the exertions of the sphere of woman. That is a right which only can be possessed by that sex itself.

I say again, men have not the right, in contradiction to the intentions, the wishes, the ambition, of women, to say that their sphere shall be circumscribed, that bounds shall be set which they cannot pass. The enjoyment of liberty, the pursuit of happiness in her own way, is as much the birthright of woman as of man. In this land man has ceased to dominate over his fellow — let him cease to dominate over his sister; for he has no higher right to do that latter than the former. It is mere oppression to say to the bread-seeking woman, you shall labor only in certain narrow ways for your living, we will hedge you out by law from profitable employments, and monopolize them for ourselves.

. . .

[Senator George] HOAR [R-Mass.]....Mr. President, I understand the brief statement which was made I think during the last session by the majority of the Judiciary Committee in support of their opposition to this bill, did not disclose that the majority of the committee were opposed to permitting women to engage in the practice of law or to be admitted to practice it in the Supreme Court of the United States, but the point they made was that the legislation of the United States left to the Supreme Court the power of determining by rule who should be admitted to practice before that tribunal, and that we ought not by legislation to undertake to interfere with their rules. Now, with the greatest respect for that tribunal, I conceive that the law-making and not the law-expounding power in this Government ought to determine the question what class of citizens shall be clothed with the office of the advocate....

Now, Mr. President, this bill is not a bill merely to admit women to the privilege of engaging in a particular profession; it is a bill to secure to the citizen of the United States the right to select his counsel, and that is all. At present a case is tried and decided in the State courts of any State of this Union which may be removed to the Supreme Court of the United States. In the courts of the State women are permitted to practice as advocates, and a woman has been the advocate under whose direction and care and advocacy the case has been won in the court below. Is it tolerable that the counsel who has attended the case from its commencement to its successful termination in the highest court of the State should not be permitted to attend upon and defend the rights of that client when the case is transferred to the Supreme Court of the United States? Everybody knows, at least every lawyer of experience knows the impossibility of transferring with justice to the interests of a client a cause from one counsel to another....

Equal Pay Act of 1963: Congressional Debate

The federal government had prohibited discrimination on the basis of sex for federal salaries, but the private sector was at liberty to pay women less than men for the same job. Congress passed legislation in 1963 to place restrictions on private employers. Although the bill permitted some exceptions, Congress used its power over commerce to bring a measure of fairness and justice to private wages. The debate below occurred in the House of Representatives on May 23, 1963.

Mrs. ST. GEORGE. Mr. Speaker,...this resolution, House Resolution 362, makes in order the consideration of H.R. 6060 to prohibit discrimination on account of sex in the payment of wages by employers engaged in commerce or in the production of goods for commerce....

For those who fear this legislation—and there are some—I would like to point out that all women are by no means covered in this act. As a matter of fact, we see, according to the supplemental views in the report, that the prohibition against discrimination because of sex is placed under the Fair Labor Standards Act, with the act's established coverage of employers and employees. All of the Fair Labor Standards exemptions apply; and, this is very noteworthy, agriculture, hotels, motels, restaurants, and laundries are excluded. Also all professional, managerial, and administrative personnel and outside salesmen are excluded. So, a very great quantity of women will not be covered in this act, especially because it considers hotels, motels, restaurants, and laundries, where women are by far the majority of the workers. They will not be included.

Mr. Speaker, I have always felt that these bills would come to us from now on, and I hope that they will, but in every instance it is only one bite of the cherry. In other words, we are just nibbling away at a thing that could have been completely covered by an amendment to the Constitution simply giving women equal rights and letting it go at that. That apparently has not been the will of the House so far. I hope someday that it will be. However, in the meantime, we are going to have to have these bills which will help, which will do a little, which will get a foot in the door, and they will have to continue to come to us.

Mr. COLMER. Mr. Speaker, . . . I recognize that this bill is going to pass. It is going to pass overwhelmingly, I suspect, because it has an appeal to a minority or special group. It deals with women. I recognize the seeming popular appeal and then, too, Mr. Speaker, I recognize in addition to the futility of my stating my position the politically unwise situation in which I find myself. I certainly do not want to be put in the position of opposing the women of this country, and I could dwell at some length on that subject. I am not so sure that the women want this bill. However, I am opposed to this proposal because I think it is basically unsound, just as I have opposed proposals here that were aimed at other minority or special groups.

I doubt seriously, Mr. Speaker, if this bill is constitutional. I do not like the idea of pointing out women here as if they are an inferior group and that the Federal Government with its strong arm must step in and try to protect them. I think they can stand on their own. They have been doing that for many, many generations.

Mr. Speaker, there are many instances where women are entitled to more pay than the opposite sex and why should we just put them on an equal basis? This strikes at the merit system.

Mr. Speaker, I am principally opposed to this legislation because it represents further regimentation of our people.

This sets up another army of Federal agents to go about snooping into every little, as well as every big business in the country to see whether the Federal law is being enforced.

. . .

Mrs. FRANCES P. BOLTON. Mr. Speaker, as a long-time advocate of the principle of equal pay for equal work, I am very glad to speak in favor of H.R. 6060. I am very much interested in the remarks of the previous speaker because it is some time since the women of this country have been in the minority. We are rather far ahead of you in that regard, my distinguished colleague. Of course, if you care to be the spokesman for the actual minority. Equal pay legislation has been in-

troduced in every Congress since 1945 by Members of both parties, a truly bipartisan effort.

. . .

It is a matter of simple justice to pay a woman the same rate as a man when she is performing the same duties. We have had equal pay in the Government for some years through the Federal classified civil service. Some 22 States have enacted equal-pay laws, but let me say right there that in many of these they do not work too well. However, a Federal law is needed to give complete and adequate coverage.

. . .

Mr. POWELL. . . .
The payment of wages on a basis other than that of the job performed is not only harmful to the individual worker and our economy, but also to our Nation's image abroad. The fact that employers still pay lower wage rates to women workers for the same or comparable work as that performed by men workers in the same place is contrary to every concept of equality and justice in which we so strongly believe.

This principle of equality has been endorsed by labor, by leaders in both political parties, and by numerous business organizations and spokesmen. The International Labor Organization — of which we are a member and which I shall attend next week — provides in its constitution that "men and women should receive equal remuneration for work of equal value." Thirty-eight countries have ratified an ILO Convention which sets up standards and procedures for establishing equal pay in fact as well as in principle. The European Common Market agreement, the Rome Treaty, also carries a specific provision for equal pay.

Thus we come to this legislation buttressed by support at home and abroad, from labor and management, from men and women, and from Democrats and Republicans.

. . .

Civil Rights Act of 1964: Congressional Debate

During debate on the Civil Rights Act of 1964, Congressman Howard Smith of Virginia offered an amendment to prohibit discrimination not only on the basis of race but also on "sex" as well. This amendment has been widely interpreted as an effort by a Southern opponent of civil rights to jeopardize the entire bill by weighing it down with a ludicrous amendment. But the concerns of Congressman Smith and his colleagues from the South were real. If Congress only prohibited discrimination on the basis of race, white women would consistently lose out to black women in the competition for jobs. Employers would tend to favor black women as a way of avoiding discrimination suits. An alternative motivation for the amendment — defending the interests of white women — comes out strongly in the debate, taken from 110 Cong. Rec. 2577–84 (1964).

Mr. SMITH of Virginia. Mr. Chairman, I offer an amendment.

The Clerk read as follows:

"Amendment offered by Mr. SMITH of Virginia: On page 68, line 23, after the word 'religion,' insert the word 'sex.'

"On page 69, line 10, after the word 'religion,' insert the word 'sex.'

"On page 69, line 17, after the word 'religion,' insert the word 'sex.'

"On page 70, line 1, after the word 'religion,' insert the word 'sex.'

"On page 71, line 5, after the word 'religion,' insert the word 'sex.' "

Mr. SMITH of Virginia. Mr. Chairman, this amendment is offered to the fair employment practices title of this bill to include within our desire to prevent discrimination against another minority group, the women, but a very essential minority group, in the absence of which the majority group would not be here today.

Now, I am very serious about this amendment. It has been offered several times before, but it was offered at inappropriate places in the bill. Now, this is the appropriate place for this amendment to come in. I do not think it can do any harm to this legislation; maybe it can do some good. I think it will do some good for the minority sex.

I think we all recognize and it is indisputable fact that all throughout industry women are discriminated against in that just generally speaking they do not get as high compensation for their work as do the majority sex. Now, if that is true, I hope that the committee chairman will accept this amendment.

. . .

Mrs. GRIFFITHS. Mr. Chairman, . . . I rise in support of the amendment primarily because I feel as a white woman when this bill has passed this House and the Senate and has been signed by the President that white women will be last at the hiring gate.

In his great work "The American Dilemma,"

the Swedish sociologist pointed out 20 years ago that white women and Negroes occupied relatively the same position in American society.

. . .

Mrs. GRIFFITHS. . . . I come from a city in which there is a university. It is my understanding that there has never been a woman political scientist employed at that university to teach political science. Suppose a colored woman political scientist applied for a job. Could she or could she not invoke the act?

Mr. CELLER. Of course, we are addressing ourselves to business activity. It is conceivable that colleges might be covered. There again, if there were discrimination then there would be a violation.

Mrs. GRIFFITHS. Could a white woman turned away from the college or from the restaurant where all the employees were white invoke the act? Would a white woman have any recourse under the act?

Mr. CELLER. I think we covered that in colloquies we had in the earlier part of the afternoon. There could be discrimination against white people and there could be against colored people.

Mrs. GRIFFITHS. Mr. Chairman, you know well and good if every employee of that restaurant were white, that that woman cannot go to the FEPC or to a district attorney and say, "I was turned away from there because I was white," because every employee is white there.

. . .

Now, Mr. Chairman, I would like to proceed to some of the arguments I have heard on this floor against adding the word "sex." In some of the arguments, I have heard the comment that the chairman is making, which is, that this makes it an equal rights bill. Of course it does not even approach making it an equal rights bill. This is equal employment rights. In one field only — employment. And if you do not add sex to this bill, I really do not believe there is a reasonable person sitting here who does not by now understand perfectly that you are going to have white men in one bracket, you are going to try to take colored men and colored women and give them equal employment rights, and down at the bottom of the list is going to be a white woman with no rights at all.

. . .

Mr. ANDREWS of Alabama...I rise in support of this amendment offered by the gentleman from Virginia [Mr. SMITH]. Unless this amendment is adopted, the white women of this country would be drastically discriminated against in favor of a Negro woman.

If a white woman and a Negro woman applied for the same job, and each woman had the identical qualifications, the chances are about 99 to 1 that the Negro woman would be given the job because if the employer did not give the job to the Negro woman he could be prosecuted under this bill. Failure to employ the white woman would not subject the employer to such action.

Commonsense tells us that the employer would hire the Negro woman to avoid prosecution. The white woman will be at a great disadvantage in the business world unless this amendment is adopted.

Mr. RIVERS of South Carolina. I rise in support of the amendment offered by the gentleman from Virginia [Mr. SMITH] making it possible for the white Christian woman to receive the same consideration for employment as the colored woman. It is incredible to me that the authors of this monstrosity — whomever they are — would deprive the white

woman of mostly Anglo-Saxon or Christian heritage equal opportunity before the employer. I know this Congress will not be a party to such an evil.

Mr. SMITH of Virginia....I put a question to you in behalf of the white women of the United States. Let us assume that two women apply for the same job and both of them are equally eligible, one a white woman and one a Negro woman. The first thing that employer will look at will be the provision with regard to the records he must keep. If he does not employ that colored woman and has to make that record, that employer will say, "Well, now, if I hire the colored woman I will not be in any trouble, but if I do not hire the colored woman and hire the white woman, then the Commission is going to be looking down my throat and will want to know why I did not. I may be in a lawsuit."

That will happen as surely as we are here this afternoon. You all know it.

. . .

The CHAIRMAN. The question is on the amendment offered by the gentleman from Virginia [Mr. SMITH].

Mrs. GRIFFITHS. Mr. Chairman, on that I demand tellers.

Tellers were ordered, and the Chairman appointed as tellers Mr. CELLER and Mrs. GRIFFITHS.

The Committee divided, and the tellers reported that there were — ayes 168, noes 133.

So the amendment was agreed to.

B. CONTEMPORARY GENDER ISSUES

Supreme Court doctrines began to shift after Warren Burger replaced Earl Warren as Chief Justice in 1969. A major pressure for this change came from Congress and the country during debate on the Equal Rights Amendment, which passed the House in 1970 by the top-heavy margin of 350–15. After Senate action, the language submitted to the states for ratification read: "Equality of rights under the law shall not be denied or abridged by the United States or by any State on account of sex." Members of the House argued strongly that a constitutional amendment was necessary because the Supreme Court had failed to protect the rights of women. Congressman Martha Griffiths, a leader behind the ERA, put the matter bluntly in October 1971: "Mr. Chairman, what the equal rights amendment seeks to do, and all it seeks to do, is to say to the Supreme Court of the United States, "Wake up! This is the 20th century. Before it is over, judge women as individual human beings.'" 117 Cong. Rec. 35323 (1971). (See box in Chapter 19, page 1169.)

A month later, a unanimous Supreme Court struck down an Idaho law that preferred men over women in administering estates. The statute, the Court held, arbitrarily discriminated on the basis of sex and violated the Equal Protection Clause of the Fourteenth Amendment. Reed

---

Standards of Review

The Supreme Court uses different standards when reviewing governmental actions. The three tests below are general guidelines. Actual application in a given case can vary widely from the theoretical model. For example, the intermediate standard applied to sex discrimination often approaches strict-scrutiny analysis.

Rational basis	Legislation is valid if the legislature's purpose is legitimate and the law is "rationally" related to that purpose. Following the post-1937 period, this standard governs review of economic regulation.
Intermediate	A position between the customary two-tiered analysis (rational basis and strict scrutiny). Governmental action is valid if it serves an "important" purpose and is "substantially related" to that purpose. Often applied in cases of sex discrimination and commercial speech.
Strict scrutiny	A heightened standard used to review legislation that discriminates against fundamental interests (examples: race, voting, marriage). This category is sometimes called a suspect classification. To satisfy this test, a legislative classification must be necessary to achieve a compelling governmental interest and be narrowly tailored to satisfy that interest.

---

v. Reed, 404 U.S. 71 (1971). Since that time, a flood of cases has gradually challenged and eliminated sexual stereotypes of an earlier age. In 1973 the Court said that sex discrimination had survived in America as "romantic paternalism," whereas the practical effect was to put women "not on a pedestal, but in a cage." Statutes were "laden with gross, stereotyped distinctions between the sexes." Frontiero v. Richardson, 411 U.S. 677, 684–85 (1973).[2] Customs of earlier times were "no longer tenable" to exclude women from juries. Taylor v. Louisiana, 419 U.S. 522, 537 (1975). The Court rejected "old notions" about a man's primary responsibility to provide a home. Stanton v. Stanton, 421 U.S. 7, 10 (1975). In 1994 the Court prohibited lawyers from using gender to exclude people from a jury. Stereotypes regarding sex (that men or women jurors are likely to vote a certain way) may not be used. J.E.B. v. Alabama ex rel T.B., 511 U.S. 127 (1994).

The Supreme Court had an opportunity in 1973 to declare sex a "suspect classification" as it had done with race and alienage. Under this classification, the strict-scrutiny test is applied to governmental actions that discriminate and the government must show a compelling interest to support its policy and be narrowly tailored. The more lenient standard permits a legislature to make classifications if the statute is rational and furthers an important governmental interest (see box).

The case before the Court in 1973 involved a congressional statute that permitted a serviceman to claim his wife as a "dependent" even if she was not dependent on him. In contrast, a female member of the armed forces could not claim her husband as a dependent (and therefore obtain increased housing allowances and medical and dental benefits) unless he relied on her for more than one-half of his support. An 8–1 majority found the statute unconstitutional. Justice Brennan was one of four members of the Court who urged that sex be made a suspect classification. Other Justices thought that the Court should defer to the workings of the con-

---

2. The clever pedestal-cage image was lifted from a 1971 decision by the Supreme Court of California: "The pedestal upon which women have been placed has all too often, upon closer examination, been revealed as a cage." Sail'er Inn, Inc. v. Kirby, 485 P.2d 529, 541 (Cal. 1971).

stitutional amendment process under way with the ERA. FRONTIERO v. RICHARDSON, 411 U.S. 677 (1973).[3]

In *Frontiero*, Justice Brennan took note of the fact that Congress had passed the ERA and submitted it to the states for ratification: "Thus, Congress itself has concluded that classifications based upon sex are inherently invidious, and this conclusion of a coequal branch of Government is not without significance to the question presently under consideration." Id. at 687–88.

When the ERA failed to be ratified by the end of the seven-year period specified in the amendment, Congress extended the deadline to June 30, 1982. Even with this extra time, the amendment fell short of the necessary states. The ERA failed for a number of reasons. Some women were concerned that they might lose traditional benefits from divorce settlements or be subject to the military draft. The major setback, however, was the Supreme Court's decision in *Roe v. Wade* (1973), upholding a woman's right to have an abortion in the first two trimesters of pregnancy (reprinted in Chapter 17). ERA proponents had tried to keep abortion as a separate issue. *Roe* seemed to link ERA with the pro-choice philosophy. Moreover, it appeared throughout the 1970s that many of the goals of the feminist movement could be accomplished by legislative action and judicial decisions rather than by constitutional amendment.

Statutory Standards

In 1966, EEOC permitted employers to place want ads that had "Male" or "Female" headings. 31 Fed. Reg. 6414 (1966). EEOC's decision ran counter to language in Section 704(b) of Title VII making it "an unlawful employment practice...to print or publish...any notice or advertisement relating to employment...indicating any preference, limitation, specification, or discrimination, based on race, color, religion, sex, or national origin," other than for bfoq's (bona fide occupational qualifications, such as male and female actors, male and female models, and so forth). Congresswoman Martha Griffiths assailed the EEOC both for its "Jane Crow" policy and its attitudes about women. 112 Cong. Rec. 13689, 13693 (1966). The next year the EEOC changed its policy to clearly oppose sex-based want ads. 32 Fed. Reg. 5999 (1967).

Not until six years later did the Supreme Court agree that a city could prohibit a newspaper from printing ads that listed job opportunities under "Male Interest" and "Female Interest" headings. Pittsburgh Press Co. v. Human Rel. Comm'n, 413 U.S. 376 (1973). Two years later the Court held that the systematic exclusion of women from jury panels violates the right to a jury trial in the Sixth Amendment. Taylor v. Louisiana, 419 U.S. 522 (1975), overruling Hoyt v. Florida, 368 U.S. 57 (1961).

Discrepancies in the age of majority (twenty-one for men and eighteen for women) were declared unconstitutional. Old notions of viewing men as the breadwinners, requiring additional years to obtain an education and training before assuming the position as head of the house, were rejected by the Court as justification for the difference between twenty-one and eighteen.

---

3. Two years later, the Court accepted a congressional decision to establish different periods of tenure for servicemen and servicewomen before forcing them out. Male officers were subject to mandatory discharge after nine years unless they were promoted; female officers faced that test after thirteen years. The Court decided that the legislative classification was rational because Congress had taken into account the restrictions placed upon women with regard to combat duty and sea service. Schlesinger v. Ballard, 419 U.S. 498 (1975). Another congressional decision was accepted in *Mathews* v. *De Castro,* 429 U.S. 181 (1976), which concluded that it was not irrational for Congress in the Social Security Act to grant monthly benefits to a married woman under 62 whose husband retires or becomes disabled and she has a minor or dependent child in her care, whereas a divorced woman under 62 whose ex-husband retires or becomes disabled receives no such benefits. Congress recognized that divorced couples typically live separate lives, giving the divorced woman greater financial independence.

The Court noted that women are increasingly involved in education, business, the professions, and government. Stanton v. Stanton, 421 U.S. 7, 15 (1975). State laws describing the husband as "head and master" and giving him unilateral power to sell jointly owned property were struck down as a violation of the Equal Protection Clause. Kirchberg v. Feenstra, 450 U.S. 455 (1981).

Increased professional activity by women produced other changes. Women lawyers denied partnership in their firm may take a sex discrimination claim to court. Hishon v. King & Spalding, 467 U.S. 69 (1984). It is still uncertain how much evidence is required to prove discrimination under Title VII. It is clear that employers may not rely on sex-based considerations in denying a woman a promotion. However, a 6–3 decision by the Supreme Court held that when a woman shows that gender played a motivating part in an unfavorable employment decision, the employer may avoid a finding of liability by proving that it would have made the same decision even if it had not allowed gender to play a role. The plurality of four, plus a concurrence by Justice O'Connor, agreed that employers have to prove their case by a preponderance of the evidence. Price Waterhouse v. Hopkins, 490 U.S. 228 (1989). As part of the Civil Rights Act of 1991 (see page 898), Congress gave this statutory response to *Price Waterhouse*: Once a plaintiff proves that race, color, religion, national origin, or sex was a motivating factor in an employer's decision, the employer would be liable for a Title VII violation.

Title VII is not limited to economic or "tangible" discrimination. A claim of "hostile environment" because of sexual harassment by a supervisor is a valid basis for a lawsuit. Meritor Savings Bank v. Vinson, 477 U.S. 57 (1986). A unanimous Court in 1993 ruled that a woman need not prove psychological injury to win money damages for a claim of sexual harassment. A hostile or abusive work environment is sufficient to sustain a claim. Harris v. Forklift Systems, Inc., 510 U.S. 17 (1993). Title VII was further addressed by two Court decisions in 1998. In one case, the Court ruled that sexual harassment can exist even when the employee—subject to unwelcome and threatening sexual advances by a supervisor—suffers no adverse, tangible job consequences. Burlington Industries, Inc. v. Ellerth, 524 U.S. 742 (1998). In the second case, the Court provided additional guidelines in determining employer liability for sexual discrimination by a supervisor. Faragher v. Boca Raton, 524 U.S. 775 (1998).

Private Clubs

Although some private clubs and organizations have the constitutional freedom of association to exclude women, organizations can be required to accept women when the organizational purpose concerns economic advancement of its members through the use of commercial programs and benefits. Roberts v. United States Jaycees, 468 U.S. 609, 626 (1984). Rotary Clubs, because of their assistance to businesses and professions, have been forced to admit women as members. Bd. of Dirs. of Rotary Int'l v. Rotary Club, 481 U.S. 537 (1987). Other organizations, including the Kiwanis International and the Lions Club International, now accept female members. In 1988 a unanimous court upheld a New York City law that prohibited discrimination based on sex in any private club with more than 400 members involved directly or indirectly in furthering trade or business. New York State Club Assn. v. New York City, 487 U.S. 1 (1988). As a result of the Court's decision in 1991 not to review a New Jersey holding, the last remaining all-male eating club at Princeton University was forced to admit women as members. Tiger Inn v. Frank, 498 U.S. 1073 (1991).

Discrimination against Men

Sex discrimination may injure men as well as women. In 1972 the Court struck down an Illinois law that took children from the custody of an unwed father without a hearing, although a hearing was required for an unwed mother. Under state law, his fitness as a father was irrelevant. This procedure violated the Equal Protection Clause of the Fourteenth Amendment.

Widowers, Alimony, and Nurses

A Missouri law was struck down because it denied a widower the benefits from his wife's work-related death unless he was mentally or physically incapacitated or could prove dependence on the wife's earnings. No such test was required for widows. Wengler v. Druggists Mutual Ins. Co., 446 U.S. 142 (1980). Alimony laws were successfully challenged. In 1979, the Court held that an Alabama statute violated the Equal Protection Clause by requiring husbands, but not wives, to pay alimony. Although assisting needy spouses is "a legitimate and important governmental objective," needy males along with needy females can be helped "with little if any additional burden on the States." Orr v. Orr, 440 U.S. 268, 280–81 (1979). In 1982, the Court held that a state-supported university could not limit its nursing school to women. The school attempted to justify its admission policy as compensation for past discrimination against women, but the Court concluded that the policy merely perpetuated the stereotype that nursing is exclusively a woman's job. The decision applied only to professional nursing school; other single-sex colleges were not affected by the ruling. Mississippi University for Women v. Hogan, 458 U.S. 718 (1982).

Stanley v. Illinois, 405 U.S. 645 (1972). In cases where an unwed father fails to legitimate a child or take responsibility for the child's care, states can use a "best interests of the child" standard in permitting only the mother's consent for the adoption of an illegitimate child. Quillion v. Walcott, 434 U.S. 246 (1978); Lehr v. Robertson, 463 U.S. 248 (1983). Variations on this issue can send the Court scattering in various directions. Compare Caban v. Mohammed, 441 U.S. 380 (1979) with Parham v. Hughes, 441 U.S. 347 (1979).[4]

Under a social security law struck down by a unanimous Court in 1975, a man's benefits went to both the widow and the children. If the wife died, the benefits went only to the children, not to the widower. This law violated the Equal Protection Clause by giving a female wage earner and the male survivor less protection. Weinberger v. Wiesenfeld, 420 U.S. 636 (1975). In another social security case, Congress provided benefits to the widow regardless of dependency. However, if the wife died, the widower received benefits only if he was receiving at least half of his support from her. The Court held this an invidious and unconstitutional discrimination. Califano v. Goldfarb, 430 U.S. 199 (1977). In that same year, however, the Court upheld a social security law in which Congress deliberately used classification by gender to compensate for previous economic discrimination against women. Califano v. Webster, 430 U.S. 313 (1977).

An Oklahoma law was invalidated in 1976 on equal-protection grounds. It prohibited the sale of 3.2 percent beer to males under twenty-one while allowing females at age eighteen to purchase the beer. The Court dismissed as inconsequential the slight percentage difference between females and males arrested for drunk driving. CRAIG v. BOREN, 429 U.S. 190 (1976). Other traditional laws—governing widowers, alimony, and nurses—were also struck down (see box).

Some sexual stereotypes persist. In 1974 the Court upheld a Florida statute that granted widows an annual $500 property tax exemption but denied widowers the same benefit. Ac-

---

4. In 1968 the Supreme Court ruled that an illegitimate child is a "person" under the Fourteenth Amendment and capable of challenging practices and laws as a denial of equal protection. Levy v. Louisiana, 391 U.S. 68 (1968). The rights of illegitimate children have been further explored and defined in Glona v. American Guarantee Co., 391 U.S. 73 (1968); Labine v. Vincent, 401 U.S. 532 (1971); Weber v. Aetna Casualty & Surety Co., 406 U.S. 164 (1972); Gomez v. Perez, 409 U.S. 535 (1973); New Jersey Welfare Rights Org. v. Cahill, 411 U.S. 619 (1973); Jimenez v. Weinberger, 417 U.S. 628 (1974); Mathews v. Lucas, 427 U.S. 495 (1976); Norton v. Mathews, 427 U.S. 524 (1976); Trimble v. Gordon, 430 U.S. 762 (1977); Mills v. Habluetzel, 456 U.S. 91 (1982); Pickett v. Brown, 462 U.S. 1 (1983).

cording to the Court, the law was reasonably designed to further the state's policy of cushioning the financial impact when a spouse dies. The Court accepted the generalization that widows are more needy than widowers, even if some heiresses and rich widows have no need for largesse from the state. Kahn v. Shevin, 416 U.S. 351 (1974).

State laws on "statutory rape"—sexual intercourse with a female under eighteen who is not the wife of the perpetrator—have been upheld even though they discriminate on the basis of gender. Men alone are criminally liable. These laws are based on the premise that young women (but not young men) are legally incapable of consenting to sex. MICHAEL M. v. SONOMA COUNTY SUPERIOR COURT, 450 U.S. 464 (1981).

In another decision in 1981, the Court again placed its imprimatur on discrimination between men and women. By a 6–3 majority it upheld the decision of Congress to require registration of males, but not females, for possible military service. The Court deferred to congressional judgment on this constitutional question, claiming unconvincingly that the exemption for women was not the "accidental byproduct of a traditional way of thinking about females." Rostker v. Goldberg, 453 U.S. 57, 74 (1981).[5] (The issue of women in the military is explored more fully in a subsequent section.)

In 1998, a unanimous Court held that Title VII's prohibition against sex discrimination on the job covers misconduct even when the victim and the harasser are of the same sex. In this case, a male worker was sexually harassed by other men. Oncale v. Sundowner Offshore Services, 523 U.S. 75 (1998). Another case in 1998, relying on a sexual stereotype to favor mothers over fathers in citizenship cases, split the Court 6 to 3. Federal law automatically grants citizenship to a child born out of wedlock in a foreign country if the mother is American, but adopts a higher standard if the father is the American. In upholding the law, the Court reasoned that there is a closer connection between a mother and her child than a father and his child. Actually, the six Justices in the majority could not agree on their reasoning. Stevens, joined by Rehnquist, wrote for the Court. O'Connor, joined by Kennedy, wrote one concurrence. Scalia, joined by Thomas, wrote another concurrence. The three dissenters (Ginsburg, Souter, and Breyer) accused the Court of needlessly perpetuating a stereotype, especially after the availability of DNA paternity tests. Miller v. Albright, 523 U.S. 420 (1998).

Preferential Hiring

Despite efforts to eliminate gender-based employment, a person's sex may still be a factor in hiring decisions. In 1979 the Court upheld a Massachusetts law that gave a lifetime preference to veterans for state jobs. Although a woman received higher test scores than her male competitors, they were entitled under state laws to be considered first if they were veterans. The Court rationalized that the law distinguished between veterans and nonveterans, not men and women. While necessarily admitting that the statute "today benefits an overwhelmingly male class," the Court announced that the law was "neutral on its face." PERSONNEL ADMINISTRATOR OF MASS. v. FEENEY, 442 U.S. 256, 269, 274 (1979).

In 1987 the Court issued a major decision that supported affirmative action programs to hire women. An agency in California had employed 238 workers in a skilled craft position; all had been men. The company took gender into account in selecting the first woman, even though a man had scored slightly higher during an interview. The Court allowed employers to consider as one factor the sex of a qualified applicant. JOHNSON v. TRANSPORTATION AGENCY, 480 U.S. 616 (1987).

---

5. On the question of granting wives a portion of their husbands' military retired pay (required by certain state laws), the Court has held that federal law preempts state action. McCarty v. McCarty, 453 U.S. 210 (1981).

Pregnancy

The rights of pregnant women have proved particularly troublesome for Congress and the courts. Total elimination of gender-based discrimination would make it impossible to address the special needs of pregnant workers. In 1974, by a 7–2 majority, the Court struck down the policy of requiring pregnant teachers to quit their jobs without pay several months before expecting a child. Some states forced teachers to quit as much as five months before the delivery date, all done on the quaint notion that schoolchildren should be spared the sight of a pregnant woman. Cleveland Board of Education v. LaFleur, 414 U.S. 632 (1974).

The question of paying benefits to pregnant women was more difficult to resolve. A California law paid benefits to persons temporarily disabled from working and not covered by workers' compensation. Payment was not made for certain disabilities attributable to pregnancy. The Court upheld the statute in Geduldig v. Aiello, 417 U.S. 484 (1974). Building on this precedent, two years later the Court supported a company's disability plan that gave benefits for nonoccupational sickness and accidents but not for disabilities arising from pregnancy. The Court decided that the plan did not violate Title VII of the Civil Rights Act of 1964. General Electric Co. v. Gilbert, 429 U.S. 125 (1976). This decision was "distinguished" a year later when the Court held that a company policy on leave of absence for pregnant workers violated Title VII. Nashville Gas Co. v. Satty, 434 U.S. 136 (1977).

Congress passed the Pregnancy Discrimination Act of 1978 to reverse Gilbert. The statute amended Title VII to prohibit employment discrimination on the basis of pregnancy and to require fringe benefit and insurance plans to cover pregnant workers. 92 Stat. 2076 (1978). When a company responded to this statute by amending its health insurance plan to provide female workers with hospitalization benefits for pregnancy-related conditions, it provided less extensive pregnancy benefits for the wives of male employees. The Court held that this plan discriminated against male employees in violation of Title VII of the Civil Rights Act of 1964. Newport News Shipbuilding & Dry Dock v. EEOC, 462 U.S. 669 (1983).

In 1987, the Court upheld state laws that require employers to give female workers an unpaid pregnancy disability leave and guarantee them their jobs when they return. The Court ruled that these laws, granting greater benefits to pregnant women than under the 1978 congressional statute, are not preempted by federal action. Moreover, the state laws necessarily discriminate on the basis of sex because pregnant women are given preferential treatment not available to other workers. California Federal S. & L. v. Guerra, 479 U.S. 272 (1987). See also Wimberly v. Labor & Industrial Rel. Comm'n, 479 U.S. 511 (1987). A decision by the Court in 1991 examined the policy of some companies to prohibit fertile women from working in certain hazardous jobs for the purpose of protecting a potential fetus. The Court held that such policies violate the Pregnancy Discrimination Act of 1978. AUTOMOBILE WORKERS v. JOHNSON CONTROLS, 499 U.S. 187 (1991).

In 1993, Congress passed the Family and Medical Leave Act, requiring employers with fifty or more employees to provide workers with up to twelve weeks of unpaid leave for the birth or adoption of a child or the illness of a close family member. The option is available to both fathers and mothers. In the findings section of the law, Congress noted the importance of "fathers and mothers" participating in early childrearing, although the primary responsibility for family caretaking "often falls on women." Yet the purpose of the statute was to promote "the goal of equal employment opportunity for women and men." 107 Stat. 7. If both spouses work for the same employer, the aggregate number of weeks is limited to twelve.

Title IX Actions

By enacting Title IX of the Education Amendments of 1972, Congress announced that it would withdraw federal financial assistance from any educational institution that practiced sex discrimination. The Court interprets Title IX broadly to apply not only to students but to employees as well. North Haven Board of Education v. Bell, 456 U.S. 512 (1982). Enforcement of Title IX depends largely on the executive branch, but private parties have a right of action to bring disputes to the courts. Cannon v. University of Chicago, 441 U.S. 677 (1979). In 1992, a unanimous Court expanded the rights of students who are victims of sexual harassment by giving them, for the first time, the right to win money damages in Title IX suits. Franklin v. Gwinnett County Public Schools, 503 U.S. 60 (1992). Legislation by Congress in 1986 helped push the Court in this direction. 100 Stat. 1845, § 1003 (1986). In 1998, the Court held that students may not be awarded money damages in a sexual harassment suit unless a district school official knows of the misconduct and does nothing about it. Gebser v. Lago Vista Independent School Dist., 524 U.S. 274 (1998).

In 1984 the Court construed Title IX narrowly. An educational institution, Grove City College, did not accept direct federal assistance, but some of its students received federal grants. The Court held that the student aid triggered Title IX. However, it declined to make the coverage institutionwide. Title IX therefore applied only to the financial aid program, not to other activities at the college. Grove City College v. Bell, 465 U.S. 555 (1984). This meant that Title IX could be used to withhold funds only from the particular program or activity that practiced sex discrimination; federal funds would continue to flow to other programs and activities at the school. Congress tried repeatedly to pass legislation to reverse the decision, but action was stalled by numerous complications, especially language dealing with abortion. In 1988 Congress managed to pass legislation overturning *Grove City,* thereby enacting broad coverage for civil rights. President Reagan vetoed the bill but was overridden. 102 Stat. 28 (1988).

The Court split 5 to 4 in 1999 in deciding that public schools receiving Title IX funds can be sued and forced to pay damages when they fail to stop sexual harassment by one student against another. Damages are not available for simple acts of teasing and name-calling, but only when schools act with "deliberate indifference" to severe acts of harassment that effectively bar a student's access to an educational opportunity or benefit. Davis v. Monroe County Bd. of Educ., 526 U.S. 629 (1999).

Women in the Military

The requirements of World War II pulled approximately 350,000 women into the armed forces. In 1948 Congress limited women to 2 percent of the total enlisted strength and prohibited women in the Navy and the Air Force from being involved in combat. In 1967 Congress removed the 2-percent limit and the statutory limits that restricted promotions for women. Both changes resulted from the need for women to serve in the Vietnam War. 81 Stat. 376 (1967). The decision in 1970 to end the draft (which actually terminated in 1973) created new demands for women in the military. The percentage of women in the armed forces eventually reached more than 10 percent. Congress passed legislation in 1975 to permit women to enter the service academies: the Military Academy at West Point, New York; the Naval Academy at Annapolis, Maryland; and the Air Force Academy at Colorado Springs, Colorado. 89 Stat. 537, § 803 (1975).

Job opportunities within the military also expanded for women. Before 1970 women could participate in about 35 percent of military jobs. By 1989 the proportion of jobs open to women in the military had grown substantially: Coast Guard (100 percent), Air Force (97 percent), Navy (59 percent), Army (52 percent), and Marine Corps (20 percent).

The issue of using women in combat has divided the nation in recent decades. During debate in 1972, Senator Marlow Cook (R-Ky.) denied that combat necessarily meant marching across the fields in France and Germany: "Combat today may be a lady sitting at a computer at a missile site in North Dakota." 118 Cong. Rec. 9349 (1972). Nurses served in combat zones during the Vietnam War and were paid combat pay. Women in the Navy brought suit in federal court to object to the statutory ban on assigning female personnel to duty on navy vessels other than hospital ships and transports. They claimed that this limited their opportunities for assignments and promotions. A federal district judge ruled that the restriction abridged the equal protection guarantee embodied in the Due Process Clause of the Fifth Amendment. Owens v. Brown, 455 F.Supp. 291 (D.D.C. 1978). In response to this decision, Congress gave some slight ground. 92 Stat. 1623, § 808 (1978); S. Rept. No. 826, 95th Cong., 2d Sess. 119–21 (1978).

The Soviet Union's invasion of Afghanistan in 1979 put pressure on the Carter administration to reconsider military registration as a supplement to the volunteer force. The male-only nature of this registration led to a challenge in court. A three-judge court concluded that the principal reason given by Congress for male-only registration was military flexibility, and yet flexibility was "in fact limited by the complete exclusion of women." Goldberg v. Rostker, 509 F.Supp. 586, 605 (E.D. Pa. 1980). This court held that male-only registration unconstitutionally discriminated between males and females, but the Supreme Court reversed and sustained the congressional policy. ROSTKER v. GOLDBERG, 453 U.S. 57 (1981).

By the late 1980s, the issue of women in the military returned, in part because the U.S. invasion of Panama in December 1989 included 800 Army women, some of whom saw combat. When U.S. forces were sent to the Persian Gulf in August 1990 to resist Iraq's invasion of Kuwait, approximately 26,000 women were in the deployment. More than 40,000 American female soldiers served in the Persian Gulf. They flew helicopters to transport personnel, directed artillery, drove trucks, and served with Patriot missile battalions in Saudi Arabia, Israel, and Turkey. Among the 123 U.S. troops killed in action, 5 were women. There were 8 other women killed in accidents.

In 1991 the House Armed Services Committee voted to repeal the statutory limitation on assigning women to combat aircraft. A floor amendment to retain the statutory prohibition on women in combat was rejected. The Senate Armed Services Committee opposed any change in the statutory prohibition, but the full Senate voted overwhelmingly to allow women to fly combat missions (see reading). In conference, the two Houses agreed to repeal the statutory limitations on the assignment of women to combat aircraft. The statute also established a commission to assess the laws and policies restricting the assignment of women to military duties. 105 Stat. 2365–70 (1991). The commission's report, released during the Bush administration, was generally critical of using women in combat, but the issue was explored anew during the Clinton administration. In 1993, Congress enacted legislation to repeal the statutory restriction on the assignment of women to combat in the Navy and Marine Corps. 107 Stat. 1659, § 541 (1993).

The constitutional issue of women in combat has been debated and resolved almost entirely outside the courts. Legislators and executive officials analyzed the constitutional options under heavy pressure from interest groups. The decisive factors were nonjudicial: the government's need for women to serve in the military, technological changes in the meaning of "combat," and a fundamental rethinking within American society of the opportunities that should be made available to women.

In a closely-watched case, in 1996 the Court held that the exclusion of women from the state-supported Virginia Military Institute (VMI) was unconstitutional. The state had offered a parallel program for women at Mary Baldwin College, but the Court ruled that this alternative did not provide equal tangible and intangible benefits. UNITED STATES v. VIRGINIA, 518 U.S. 515 (1996). Following the Court's decision, the Citadel (the only other all-male, public military college, located in South Carolina) announced that it would begin accepting women. VMI has also accepted women.

Frontiero v. Richardson

411 U.S. 677 (1973)

Sharron Frontiero, a lieutenant in the U.S. Air Force, sought increased quarters allowances and housing and medical benefits for her husband on the ground that he was her "dependent." The law provided that wives of servicemen automatically were treated as dependents, but husbands of servicewomen were not dependents unless they depended on their wives for more than one-half their support. Lt. Frontiero and her husband brought suit on the ground that the congressional statute deprived servicewomen of due process.

MR. JUSTICE BRENNAN announced the judgment of the Court and an opinion in which MR. JUSTICE DOUGLAS, MR. JUSTICE WHITE, and MR. JUSTICE MARSHALL join.

The question before us concerns the right of a female member of the uniformed services to claim her spouse as a "dependent" for the purposes of obtaining increased quarters allowances and medical and dental benefits under 37 U. S. C. §§ 401, 403, and 10 U. S. C. §§ 1072, 1076, on an equal footing with male members. Under these statutes, a serviceman may claim his wife as a "dependent" without regard to whether she is in fact dependent upon him for any part of her support. 37 U. S. C. § 401 (1); 10 U. S. C. § 1072 (2)(A). A servicewoman, on the other hand, may not claim her husband as a "dependent" under these programs unless he is in fact dependent upon her for over one-half of his support....

I

In an effort to attract career personnel through reenlistment, Congress established...a scheme for the provision of fringe benefits to members of the uniformed services on a competitive basis with business and industry. Thus,...a member of the uniformed services with dependents is entitled to an increased "basic allowance for quarters" and...a member's dependents are provided comprehensive medical and dental care.

Appellant Sharron Frontiero, a lieutenant in the United States Air Force, sought increased quarters allowances, and housing and medical benefits for her husband, appellant Joseph Frontiero, on the ground that he was her "dependent." Although such benefits would automatically have been granted with respect to the wife of a male member of the uniformed services, ap-

pellant's application was denied because she failed to demonstrate that her husband was dependent on her for more than one-half of his support.... In essence, appellants asserted that the discriminatory impact of the statutes is twofold: first, as a procedural matter, a female member is required to demonstrate her spouse's dependency, while no such burden is imposed upon male members; and, second, as a substantive matter, a male member who does not provide more than one-half of his wife's support receives benefits, while a similarly situated female member is denied such benefits. Appellants therefore sought a permanent injunction against the continued enforcement of these statutes and an order directing the appellees to provide Lieutenant Frontiero with the same housing and medical benefits that a similarly situated male member would receive.

Although the legislative history of these statutes sheds virtually no light on the purposes underlying the differential treatment accorded male and female members, a majority of the three-judge District Court surmised that Congress might reasonably have concluded that, since the husband in our society is generally the "breadwinner" in the family — and the wife typically the "dependent" partner — "it would be more economical to require married female members claiming husbands to prove actual dependency than to extend the presumption of dependency to such members." 341 F.Supp., at 207. Indeed, given the fact that approximately 99% of all members of the uniformed services are male, the District Court speculated that such differential treatment might conceivably lead to a "considerable saving of administrative expense and manpower." *Ibid.*

II

At the outset, appellants contend that classifications based upon sex, like classifications based upon race, alienage, and national origin, are inherently suspect and must therefore be subjected to close judicial scrutiny. We agree and, indeed, find at least implicit support for such an approach in our unanimous decision only last Term in *Reed* v. *Reed*, 404 U. S. 71 (1971).

In *Reed,* the Court considered the constitutionality of an Idaho statute providing that, when two individuals are otherwise equally entitled to appointment as administrator of an estate, the male applicant must be preferred to the female....

The Court noted that the Idaho statute "provides that different treatment be accorded to the applicants on the basis of their sex; it thus establishes a classification subject to scrutiny under the Equal Protection Clause." 404 U. S., at 75. Under "traditional" equal protection analysis, a legislative classification must be sustained unless it is "patently arbitrary" and bears no rational relationship to a legitimate governmental interest....

In an effort to meet this standard, appellee contended that the statutory scheme was a reasonable measure designed to reduce the workload on probate courts by eliminating one class of contests. Moreover, appellee argued that the mandatory preference for male applicants was in itself reasonable since "men [are] as a rule more conversant with business affairs than...women." Indeed, appellee maintained that "it is a matter of common knowledge, that women still are not engaged in politics, the professions, business or industry to the extent that men are." And the Idaho Supreme Court, in upholding the constitutionality of this statute, suggested that the Idaho Legislature might reasonably have "concluded that in general men are better qualified to act as an administrator than are women."

Despite these contentions, however, the Court held the statutory preference for male applicants unconstitutional. In reaching this result, the Court implicitly rejected appellee's apparently rational explanation of the statutory scheme, and concluded that, by ignoring the individual qualifications of particular applicants, the challenged statute provided "dissimilar treatment for men and women who are...similarly situated." 404 U. S., at 77. The Court therefore held that, even though the State's interest in achieving administrative efficiency "is not without some legitimacy," "[t]o give a mandatory preference to members of either sex over members of the other, merely to accomplish the elimination of hearings on the merits, is to make the very kind of arbitrary legislative choice forbidden by the [Constitution]...." *Id.,* at 76. This departure from "traditional" rational-basis analysis with respect to sex-based classifications is clearly justified.

There can be no doubt that our Nation has had a long and unfortunate history of sex discrimination. Traditionally, such discrimination was rationalized by an attitude of "romantic paternalism" which, in practical effect, put women, not on a pedestal, but in a cage....

...[O]ur statute books gradually became laden with gross, stereotyped distinctions between the sexes and, indeed, throughout much of the 19th century the position of women in our society was, in many respects, comparable to that of blacks under the pre-Civil War slave codes. Neither slaves nor women could hold office, serve on juries, or bring suit in their own names, and married women traditionally were denied the legal capacity to hold or convey property or to serve as legal guardians of their own children.... And although blacks were guaranteed the right to vote in 1870, women were denied even that right—which is itself "preservative of other basic civil and political rights"—until adoption of the Nineteenth Amendment half a century later.

. . .

...[S]ince sex, like race and national origin, is an immutable characteristic determined solely by the accident of birth, the imposition of special disabilities upon the members of a particular sex because of their sex would seem to violate "the basic concept of our system that legal burdens should bear some relationship to individual responsibility...." *Weber* v. *Aetna Casualty & Surety Co.,* 406 U. S. 164, 175 (1972). And what differentiates sex from such nonsuspect statuses as intelligence or physical disability, and aligns it with the recognized suspect criteria, is that the sex characteristic frequently bears no relation to ability to perform or contribute to society. As a result, statutory distinctions between the sexes often have the effect of invidiously relegating the entire class of females to inferior legal status without regard to the actual capabilities of its individual members.

We might also note that, over the past decade, Congress has itself manifested an increasing sensitivity to sex-based classifications. In Tit. VII of the Civil Rights Act of 1964, for example, Congress expressly declared that no employer, labor union, or other organization subject to the provisions of the Act shall discriminate against any individual on the basis of "race, color, religion, *sex,* or national origin." Similarly, the Equal Pay Act of 1963 provides that no employer covered by the Act "shall discriminate...between employees on the basis of *sex.*" And § 1 of the Equal Rights Amendment, passed by Congress on March 22, 1972, and submitted to the legislatures of the States for ratification, declares that "[e]quality of rights under the law shall not be denied or abridged by the United States or by any State on account of sex." Thus, Congress itself has concluded that classifications based upon sex are inherently invidious, and this conclusion of a coequal branch of Government is not without significance to the question presently under consideration....

With these considerations in mind, we can only conclude that classifications based upon sex, like classifications based upon race, alienage, or national origin, are inherently suspect, and must therefore be subjected to strict judicial scrutiny. Applying the analysis mandated by that stricter standard of review, it is clear that the statutory scheme now before us is constitutionally invalid.

. . .

III

...We therefore conclude that, by according differential treatment to male and female members of the uniformed services for the sole purpose of achieving administrative convenience, the challenged statutes violate the Due Process Clause of the Fifth Amendment insofar as they require a female member to prove the dependency of her husband.

Reversed.

MR. JUSTICE STEWART concurs in the judgment, agreeing that the statutes before us work an invidious discrimination in violation of the Constitution. *Reed* v. *Reed,* 404 U. S. 71.

MR. JUSTICE REHNQUIST dissents for the reasons stated by Judge Rives in his opinion for the District Court, *Frontiero* v. *Laird,* 341 F. Supp. 201 (1972).

MR. JUSTICE POWELL, with whom THE CHIEF JUSTICE and MR. JUSTICE BLACKMUN join, concurring in the judgment.

I agree that the challenged statutes constitute an unconstitutional discrimination against servicewomen in violation of the Due Process Clause of the Fifth Amendment, but I cannot join the opinion of MR. JUSTICE BRENNAN, which would hold that all classifications based upon sex, "like classifications based upon race, alienage, and national origin," are "inherently suspect and must therefore be subjected to close judicial scrutiny."...It is unnecessary for the Court in this case to characterize sex as a suspect classification, with all of the far-reaching implications of such a holding. *Reed* v. *Reed,* 404 U. S. 71 (1971), which abundantly supports our decision today, did not add sex to the narrowly limited group of classifications which are inherently suspect. In my view, we can and should decide this case on the authority of *Reed* and reserve for the future any expansion of its rationale.

There is another, and I find compelling, reason for deferring a general categorizing of sex classifications as invoking the strictest test of judicial scrutiny. The Equal Rights Amendment, which if adopted will resolve the substance of this precise question, has been approved by the Congress and submitted for ratification by the States. If this Amendment is duly adopted, it will represent the will of the people accomplished in the manner prescribed by the Constitution. By acting prematurely and unnecessarily, as I view it, the Court has assumed a decisional responsibility at the very time when state legislatures, functioning within the traditional democratic process, are debating the proposed Amendment. It seems to me that this reaching out to pre-empt by judicial action a major political decision which is currently in process of resolution does not reflect appropriate respect for duly prescribed legislative processes.

There are times when this Court, under our system, cannot avoid a constitutional decision on issues which normally should be resolved by the elected representatives of the people. But democratic institutions are weakened, and confidence in the restraint of the Court is impaired, when we appear unnecessarily to decide sensitive issues of broad social and political importance at the very time they are under consideration within the prescribed constitutional processes.

Craig v. Boren

429 U.S. 190 (1976)

Curtis Craig, a male then between eighteen and twenty-one years old, together with a licensed vendor of 3.2 percent beer, brought an action in federal court for declaratory and injunctive relief, claiming that an Oklahoma law constituted a gender-based discrimination in violation of the Equal Protection Clause. The law prohibited the sale of "nonintoxicating" 3.2 percent beer to males under the age of twenty-one and to females under the age of eighteen. A three-judge court held that the state's statistical evidence regarding young males' drunk-driving arrests and traffic injuries demonstrated that the gender-based discrimination was substantially related to the achievement of traffic safety on Oklahoma roads. David Boren was governor of Oklahoma.

MR. JUSTICE BRENNAN delivered the opinion of the Court.

The interaction of two sections of an Oklahoma statute...prohibits the sale of "nonintoxicating" 3.2% beer to males under the age of 21 and to females under the age of 18. The question to be decided is whether such a gender-based differential constitutes a denial to males 18–20 years of age of the equal protection of the laws in violation of the Fourteenth Amendment.

[In Section I, the Court addressed the preliminary question of standing. Craig had turned twenty-one by the time the Court noted probable jurisdiction. Since only declaratory and injunctive relief against enforcement of the gender-based differential had been sought, the controversy was moot as to Craig. However, the Court held that the licensed vendor (Whitener) who had joined the case with Craig, had standing to raise an equal protection challenge to the Oklahoma law.]

II

A

. . .

Analysis may appropriately begin with the reminder that Reed emphasized that statutory classifications that distinguish between males and females are "subject to scrutiny under the Equal Protection Clause." 404 U. S., at 75. To withstand constitutional challenge, previous cases establish that classifications by gender must serve important governmental objectives and must be substantially related to achievement of those objectives....

...We turn then to the question whether, under Reed, the difference between males and females with respect to the purchase of 3.2% beer warrants the differential in age drawn by the Oklahoma statute. We conclude that it does not.

. . .

C

. . .

The appellees introduced a variety of statistical surveys. First, an analysis of arrest statistics for 1973 demonstrated that 18–20-year-old male arrests for "driving under the influence" and "drunkenness" substantially exceeded female arrests for that same age period. Similarly, youths aged 17–21 were found to be overrepresented among those killed or injured in traffic accidents, with males again numerically exceeding females in this regard. [A footnote by the Court explains that this survey did not draw a correlation between the accident figures for any age group and levels of intoxication found in those killed or injured.] Third, a random roadside survey in Oklahoma City revealed that young males were more inclined to drive and drink beer than were their female counterparts. Fourth, Federal Bureau of Investigation nationwide statistics exhibited a notable increase in arrests for "driving under the influence." [The Court notes that the FBI did not attempt to relate the arrest figures either to beer drinking or to an eighteen–twenty-one age differential.] Finally, statistical evidence gathered in other jurisdictions, particularly Minnesota and Michigan, was offered to corroborate Oklahoma's experience by indicating the pervasiveness of youthful participation in motor vehicle accidents following the imbibing of alcohol. Conceding that "the case is not free from doubt," 399 F. Supp., at 1314, the District Court nonetheless concluded that this statistical showing substantiated "a rational basis for the legislative judgment underlying the challenged classification." Id., at 1307.

Even were this statistical evidence accepted as accurate, it nevertheless offers only a weak answer to the equal protection question presented here. The most focused and relevant of the statistical surveys, arrests of 18–20-year-olds for alcohol-related driving offenses, exemplifies the ultimate unpersuasiveness of this evidentiary record. Viewed in terms of the correlation between sex and the actual activity that Oklahoma seeks to regulate — driving while under the influence of alcohol — the statistics broadly establish that .18% of females and 2% of males in that age group were arrested for that offense. While such a disparity is not trivial in a statistical sense, it hardly can form the basis for employment of a gender line as a classifying device. Certainly if maleness is to serve as a proxy for drinking and driving, a correlation of 2% must be considered an unduly tenuous "fit." Indeed, prior cases have consistently rejected the use of sex as a decisionmaking factor even though the statutes in question certainly rested on far more predictive empirical relationships than this.

Moreover, the statistics exhibit a variety of other shortcomings that seriously impugn their value to equal protection analysis. Setting aside the obvious methodological problems, the surveys do not adequately justify the salient features of Oklahoma's gender-based traffic-safety law. None purports to measure the use and dangerousness of 3.2% beer as opposed to alcohol generally, a detail that is of particular importance since, in light of its low alcohol level, Oklahoma apparently considers the 3.2% beverage to be "nonintoxicating." ... Moreover, many of the studies, while graphically documenting the unfortunate increase in driving while under the influence of alcohol, make no effort to relate their findings to age-sex differentials as involved here. Indeed, the only survey that explicitly centered its attention upon young drivers and their use of beer — albeit apparently not of the diluted 3.2% variety — reached results that hardly can be viewed as impressive in justifying either a gender or age classification.

There is no reason to belabor this line of analysis. It is unrealistic to expect either members of the judiciary or state officials to be well versed in the rigors of experimental or statistical technique. But this merely illustrates that proving broad sociological propositions by statistics is a dubious business, and one that inevitably is in tension with the normative philosophy that underlies the Equal Protection Clause. Suffice to say that the showing offered by the appellees does not satisfy us that sex represents a legitimate, accurate proxy for the regulation of drinking and driving....

We hold, therefore, that under *Reed*, Okla-

homa's 3.2% beer statute invidiously discriminates against males 18–20 years of age.

D

[In this section, the Court considers Oklahoma's contention that Sections 241 and 245 enforce state policies concerning the sale and distribution of alcohol and by force of the Twenty-first Amendment should therefore be held to withstand the equal protection challenge. The Court holds that the Amendment does not save the invidious gender-based discrimination from invalidation.]

We conclude that the gender-based differential contained in Okla. Stat., Tit. 37, § 245 (1976 Supp.) constitutes a denial of the equal protection of the laws to males aged 18–20 and reverse the judgment of the District Court.

It is so ordered.

MR. JUSTICE POWELL, concurring.

[In a footnote, Powell refers to the dissatisfaction with the Court's "two-tier" analysis of the Equal Protection Clause, adopting a strict-scrutiny test for discrimination in cases of race and alienage and a more lenient test that permits a legislature to make classifications if the statute is rational and furthers an important governmental interest. He even suggests that the holding in the Oklahoma case implies a "middle-tiered" approach.]

MR. JUSTICE STEVENS, concurring.

There is only one Equal Protection Clause. It requires every State to govern impartially. It does not direct the courts to apply one standard of review in some cases and a different standard in other cases. Whatever criticism may be leveled at a judicial opinion implying that there are at least three such standards applies with the same force to a double standard.

I am inclined to believe that what has become known as the two-tiered analysis of equal protection claims does not describe a completely logical method of deciding cases, but rather is a method the Court has employed to explain decisions that actually apply a single standard in a reasonably consistent fashion. I also suspect that a careful explanation of the reasons motivating particular decisions may contribute more to an identification of that standard than an attempt to articulate it in all-encompassing terms. It may therefore be appropriate for me to state the principal reasons which persuaded me to join the Court's opinion.

In this case, the classification is not as obnoxious as some the Court has condemned, nor as inoffensive as some the Court has accepted. It is objectionable because it is based on an accident of birth, because it is a mere remnant of the now almost universally rejected tradition of discriminating against males in this age bracket, and because, to the extent it reflects any physical difference between males and females, it is actually perverse. *[Stevens points out in a footnote that because males are generally heavier than females, they have a greater capacity to consume alcohol without impairing their driving ability.]* ...

Mr. Justice Blackmun, concurring in part.

I join the Court's opinion except Part II-D thereof. I agree, however, that the Twenty-first Amendment does not save the challenged Oklahoma statute.

Mr. Justice Stewart, concurring in the judgment.

. . .

Mr. Chief Justice Burger, dissenting.

I am in general agreement with Mr. Justice Rehnquist's dissent, ...

Mr. Justice Rehnquist, dissenting.

The Court's disposition of this case is objectionable on two grounds. First is its conclusion that *men* challenging a gender-based statute which treats them less favorably than women may invoke a more stringent standard of judicial review than pertains to most other types of classifications. Second is the Court's enunciation of this standard, without citation to any source, as being that "classifications by gender must serve *important* governmental objectives and must be *substantially* related to achievement of those objectives." *Ante,* at 197 (emphasis added). The only redeeming feature of the Court's opinion, to my mind, is that it apparently signals a retreat by

those who joined the plurality opinion in *Frontiero* v. *Richardson,* 411 U. S. 677 (1973), from their view that sex is a "suspect" classification for purposes of equal protection analysis. I think the Oklahoma statute challenged here need pass only the "rational basis" equal protection analysis expounded in cases such as *McGowan* v. *Maryland,* 366 U. S. 420 (1961), and *Williamson* v. *Lee Optical Co.,* 348 U. S. 483 (1955), and I believe that it is constitutional under that analysis.

I

. . .

The Court's conclusion that a law which treats males less favorably than females "must serve important governmental objectives and must be substantially related to achievement of those objectives" apparently comes out of thin air. The Equal Protection Clause contains no such language, and none of our previous cases adopt that standard. I would think we have had enough difficulty with the two standards of review which our cases have recognized—the norm of "rational basis," and the "compelling state interest" required where a "suspect classification" is involved—so as to counsel weightily against the insertion of still another "standard" between those two. How is this Court to divine what objectives are important? How is it to determine whether a particular law is "substantially" related to the achievement of such objective, rather than related in some other way to its achievement? Both of the phrases used are so diaphanous and elastic as to invite subjective judicial preferences or prejudices relating to particular types of legislation, masquerading as judgments whether such legislation is directed at "important" objectives or, whether the relationship to those objectives is "substantial" enough.

. . .

Michael M. v. Sonoma County Superior Court

450 U.S. 464 (1981)

Michael M., a seventeen-and-one-half-year-old male, was charged with violating California's "statutory rape" law, which defines unlawful sexual intercourse as "an act of sexual intercourse accomplished with a female not the wife of the perpetrator, where the female is under the age of 18 years." He sued on the ground that the statute unlawfully discriminated on the basis of gender since men alone were criminally liable. The Supreme Court of California held that the classification, when subjected to "strict scrutiny," was justified

by the state's compelling interest to avoid the cost of illegitimate teenage pregnancies, abortions, and teenage childbearing.

JUSTICE REHNQUIST announced the judgment of the Court and delivered an opinion, in which THE CHIEF JUSTICE, JUSTICE STEWART, and JUSTICE POWELL joined.

The question presented in this case is whether California's "statutory rape" law, § 261.5 of the Cal. Penal Code Ann. (West Supp. 1981), violates the Equal Protection Clause of the Fourteenth Amendment. Section 261.5 defines unlawful sexual intercourse as "an act of sexual intercourse accomplished with a female not the wife of the perpetrator, where the female is under the age of 18 years." The statute thus makes men alone criminally liable for the act of sexual intercourse.

. . .

We are satisfied not only that the prevention of illegitimate pregnancy is at least one of the "purposes" of the statute, but also that the State has a strong interest in preventing such pregnancy. At the risk of stating the obvious, teenage pregnancies, which have increased dramatically over the last two decades, have significant social, medical, and economic consequences for both the mother and her child, and the State. Of particular concern to the State is that approximately half of all teenage pregnancies end in abortion. And of those children who are born, their illegitimacy makes them likely candidates to become wards of the State.

We need not be medical doctors to discern that young men and young women are not similarly situated with respect to the problems and the risks of sexual intercourse. Only women may become pregnant, and they suffer disproportionately the profound physical, emotional, and psychological consequences of sexual activity. The statute at issue here protects women from sexual intercourse at an age when those consequences are particularly severe.

The question thus boils down to whether a State may attack the problem of sexual intercourse and teenage pregnancy directly by prohibiting a male from having sexual intercourse with a minor female. We hold that such a statute is sufficiently related to the State's objectives to pass constitutional muster.

Because virtually all of the significant harmful and inescapably identifiable consequences of teenage pregnancy fall on the young female, a legislature acts well within its authority when it elects to punish only the participant who, by nature, suffers few of the consequences of his conduct. It is hardly unreasonable for a legislature acting to protect minor females to exclude them from punishment. Moreover, the risk of pregnancy itself constitutes a substantial deterrence to young females. No similar natural sanctions deter males. A criminal sanction imposed solely on males thus serves to roughly "equalize" the deterrents on the sexes.

. . .

There remains only petitioner's contention that the statute is unconstitutional as it is applied to him because he, like Sharon, was under 18 at the time of sexual intercourse. Petitioner argues that the statute is flawed because it presumes that as between two persons under 18, the male is the culpable aggressor. We find petitioner's contentions unpersuasive. Contrary to his assertions, the statute does not rest on the assumption that males are generally the aggressors. It is instead an attempt by a legislature to prevent illegitimate teenage pregnancy by providing an additional deterrent for men. The age of the man is irrelevant since young men are as capable as older men of inflicting the harm sought to be prevented.

In upholding the California statute we also recognize that this is not a case where a statute is being challenged on the grounds that it "invidiously discriminates" against females. To the contrary, the statute places a burden on males which is not shared by females. But we find nothing to suggest that men, because of past discrimination or peculiar disadvantages, are in need of the special solicitude of the courts. Nor is this a case where the gender classification is made "solely for . . . administrative convenience," as in *Frontiero* v. *Richardson,* 411 U. S. 677, 690 (1973) (emphasis omitted), or rests on "the baggage of sexual stereotypes" as in *Orr* v. *Orr,* 440 U. S., at 283. As we have held, the statute instead reasonably reflects the fact that the consequences of sexual intercourse and pregnancy fall more heavily on the female than on the male.

Accordingly the judgment of the California Supreme Court is

Affirmed.

JUSTICE STEWART, concurring.

. . .

JUSTICE BLACKMUN, concurring in the judgment. . . .

JUSTICE BRENNAN, with whom JUSTICES WHITE and MARSHALL join, dissenting.

I

It is disturbing to find the Court so splintered on a case that presents such a straightforward issue: Whether the admittedly gender-based classification in Cal. Penal Code Ann. § 261.5 (West Supp. 1981) bears a sufficient relationship to the State's asserted goal of preventing teenage pregnancies to survive the "mid-level" constitutional scrutiny mandated by *Craig* v. *Boren,* 429 U. S. 190 (1976). Applying the analytical framework provided by our precedents, I am convinced that there is only one proper resolution of this issue: the classification must be declared unconstitutional. I fear that the plurality opinion and JUSTICES STEWART and BLACKMUN reach the opposite result by placing too much emphasis on the desirability of achieving the State's asserted statutory goal — prevention of teenage pregnancy — and not enough emphasis on the fundamental question of whether the sex-based discrimination in the California statute is *substantially* related to the achievement of that goal.

. . .

. . . there are at least two serious flaws in the State's assertion that law enforcement problems created by a gender-neutral statutory rape law would make such a statute less effective than a gender-based statute in deterring sexual activity.

First, the experience of other jurisdictions, and California itself, belies the plurality's conclusion that a gender-neutral statutory rape law "may well be incapable of enforcement." There are now at least 37 States that have enacted gender-neutral statutory rape laws. Although most of these laws protect young persons (of either sex) from the sexual exploitation of older individuals, the laws of Arizona, Florida, and Illinois permit prosecution of both minor females and minor males for engaging in mutual sexual conduct. California has introduced no evidence that those States have been handicapped by the enforcement problems the plurality finds so persuasive. . . .

. . .

The second flaw in the State's assertion is that

even assuming that a gender-neutral statute would be more difficult to enforce, the State has still not shown that those enforcement problems would make such a statute less effective than a gender-based statute in deterring minor females from engaging in sexual intercourse. Common sense, however, suggests that a gender-neutral statutory rape law is potentially a *greater* deterrent of sexual activity than a gender-based law, for the simple reason that a gender-neutral law subjects both men and women to criminal sanctions and thus arguably has a deterrent effect on twice as many potential violators. Even if fewer persons were prosecuted under the gender-neutral law, as the State suggests, it would still be true that twice as many persons would be *subject* to arrest. . . .

III

Until very recently, no California court or commentator had suggested that the purpose of California's statutory rape law was to protect young women from the risk of pregnancy. Indeed, the historical development of § 261.5 demonstrates that the law was initially enacted on the premise that young women, in contrast to young men, were to be deemed legally incapable of consenting to an act of sexual intercourse. Because their chastity was considered particularly precious, those young women were felt to be uniquely in need of the State's protection. In contrast, young men were assumed to be capable of making such decisions for themselves; the law therefore did not offer them any special protection.

It is perhaps because the gender classification in California's statutory rape law was initially designed to further these outmoded sexual stereotypes, rather than to reduce the incidence of teenage pregnancies, that the State has been unable to demonstrate a substantial relationship between the classification and its newly asserted goal. . . .

. . .

JUSTICE STEVENS, dissenting.

. . .

In this case, the fact that a female confronts a greater risk of harm than a male is a reason for applying the prohibition to her — not a reason for granting her a license to use her own judgment on whether or not to assume the risk. Surely, if we examine the problem from the point of view of society's interest in preventing the risk-creating conduct from occurring at all, it is irrational to exempt 50% of the potential violators. . . .

Personnel Administrator of Mass. v. Feeney

442 U.S. 256 (1979)

Under a Massachusetts statute, all veterans who qualify for state civil service positions must be considered for appointment ahead of any qualifying nonveteran. The statute made the preference available to "any person, male or female, including a nurse," who was honorably discharged from the United States armed forces after at least ninety days of active service, at least one day of which was during "wartime." Helen B. Feeney, who was not a veteran, passed a number of open competitive civil service examinations but, because of the veterans' preference law, was ranked below male veterans who had lower test scores. A three-judge district court held that the veterans' preference statute violated the Equal Protection Clause.

MR. JUSTICE STEWART delivered the opinion of the Court.

This case presents a challenge to the constitutionality of the Massachusetts veterans' preference statute, Mass. Gen. Laws Ann., ch. 31, § 23, on the ground that it discriminates against women in violation of the Equal Protection Clause of the Fourteenth Amendment. Under ch. 31, § 23, all veterans who qualify for state civil service positions must be considered for appointment ahead of any qualifying nonveterans. The preference operates overwhelmingly to the advantage of males.

The appellee Helen B. Feeney is not a veteran. She brought this action pursuant to 42 U. S. C. § 1983, alleging that the absolute-preference formula established in ch. 31, § 23, inevitably operates to exclude women from consideration for the best Massachusetts civil service jobs and thus unconstitutionally denies them the equal protection of the laws....

. . .

I

A

The Federal Government and virtually all of the States grant some sort of hiring preference to veterans. The Massachusetts preference, which is loosely termed an "absolute lifetime" preference, is among the most generous. It applies to all positions in the State's classified civil service, which constitute approximately 60% of the public jobs in the State. It is available to "any person, male or female, including a nurse," who was honorably discharged from the United States Armed Forces after at least 90 days of active service, at least one day of which was during "wartime." Persons who are deemed veterans and who are otherwise qualified for a particular civil service job may exercise the preference at any time and as many times as they wish.

Civil service positions in Massachusetts fall into two general categories, labor and official. For jobs in the official service, with which the proofs in this action were concerned, the preference mechanics are uncomplicated. All applicants for employment must take competitive examinations. Grades are based on a formula that gives weight both to objective test results and to training and experience. Candidates who pass are then ranked in the order of their respective scores on an "eligible list." Chapter 31, § 23, requires, however, that disabled veterans, veterans, and surviving spouses and surviving parents of veterans be ranked—in the order of their respective scores—above all other candidates.

Rank on the eligible list and availability for employment are the sole factors that determine which candidates are considered for appointment to an official civil service position. When a public agency has a vacancy, it requisitions a list of "certified eligibles" from the state personnel division. Under formulas prescribed by civil service rules, a small number of candidates from the top of an appropriate list, three if there is only one vacancy, are certified. The appointing agency is then required to choose from among these candidates. Although the veterans' preference thus does not guarantee that a veteran will be appointed, it is obvious that the preference gives to veterans who achieve passing scores a well-nigh absolute advantage.

B

. . .

During her 12-year tenure as a public employee, Ms. Feeney took and passed a number of open competitive civil service examinations. On several she did quite well, receiving in 1971 the second highest score on an examination for a job with the Board of Dental Examiners, and in 1973 the third highest on a test for an Administrative Assistant position with a mental health center. Her high scores, however, did not win her a place on the certified eligible list. Because of the veterans' preference, she was ranked sixth behind five male veterans on the Dental Examiner list. She was not certified, and a lower scoring veteran was eventually appointed. On the 1973 examination, she was placed in a position on the list behind 12 male veterans, 11 of whom had lower scores. Following the other examinations that she took, her name was similarly ranked below those of veterans who had achieved passing grades.

. . .

C

The veterans' hiring preference in Massachusetts, as in other jurisdictions, has traditionally been justified as a measure designed to reward veterans for the sacrifice of military service, to ease the transition from military to civilian life, to encourage patriotic service, and to attract loyal and well-disciplined people to civil service occupations. . . .

D

The first Massachusetts veterans' preference statute defined the term "veterans" in gender-neutral language. See 1896 Mass. Acts, ch. 517 § 1 ("a person" who served in the United States Army or Navy), and subsequent amendments have followed this pattern, see, *e. g.*, 1919 Mass. Acts, ch. 150, § 1 ("any person who has served . . ."); 1954 Mass. Acts, ch. 627, § 1 ("any person, male or female, including a nurse") . . . .

Notwithstanding the apparent attempts by Massachusetts to include as many military women as possible within the scope of the preference, the statute today benefits an overwhelmingly male class. This is attributable in some measure to the variety of federal statutes, regulations, and policies that have restricted the number of women who could enlist in the United States Armed Forces, and largely to the simple fact that women have never been subjected to a military draft. . . .

II

The sole question for decision on this appeal is whether Massachusetts, in granting an absolute lifetime preference to veterans, has discriminated against women in violation of the Equal Protection Clause of the Fourteenth Amendment.

A

The equal protection guarantee of the Fourteenth Amendment does not take from the States all power of classification. *Massachusetts Bd. of Retirement* v. *Murgia,* 427 U. S. 307, 314. Most laws classify, and many affect certain groups unevenly, even though the law itself treats them no differently from all other members of the class described by the law. When the basic classification is rationally based, uneven effects upon particular groups within a class are ordinarily of no constitutional concern. . . .

Certain classifications, however, in themselves supply a reason to infer antipathy. Race is the paradigm. A racial classification, regardless of purported motivation, is presumptively invalid and can be upheld only upon an extraordinary justification. . . .

III

A

The question whether ch. 31, § 23, establishes a classification that is overtly or covertly based upon gender must first be considered. The appellee has conceded that ch. 31, § 23, is neutral on its face. She has also acknowledged that state hiring preferences for veterans are not *per se* invalid, for she has limited her challenge to the absolute lifetime preference that Massachusetts provides to veterans. The District Court made two central findings that are relevant here: first, that ch. 31, § 23, serves legitimate and worthy purposes; second, that the absolute preference was not established for the purpose of discriminating against women. The appellee has thus acknowledged and the District Court has thus found that the distinction between veterans and nonveterans drawn by ch. 31, § 23, is not a pretext for gender discrimination. The appellee's concession and the District Court's finding are clearly correct.

. . . Veteran status is not uniquely male. Although few women benefit from the preference, the nonveteran class is not substantially all female. To the contrary, significant numbers of nonveterans are men, and all nonveterans — male as well as female — are placed at a disadvantage. Too many men are affected by ch. 31, § 23, to permit the inference that the statute is but a pretext for preferring men over women.

. . . The distinction made by ch. 31, § 23, is, as it seems to be, quite simply between veterans and nonveterans, not between men and women.

B

The dispositive question, then, is whether the appellee has shown that a gender-based discriminatory purpose has, at least in some measure, shaped the Massachusetts veterans' preference legislation. As did the District Court, she points to two basic factors which in her view distinguish ch. 31, § 23, from the neutral rules at issue in the *Washington* v. *Davis* and *Arlington Heights* cases. The first is the nature of the preference, which is said to be demonstrably gender-biased in the sense that it favors a status reserved under federal military policy primarily to men. The second concerns the impact of the absolute lifetime preference upon the employment opportunities of women, an impact claimed to be too inevitable to have been unintended. The appellee contends that these factors, coupled with the fact that the preference itself has little if any relevance to actual job performance, more than suffice to prove the discriminatory intent required to establish a constitutional violation.

1

The contention that this veterans' preference is "inherently nonneutral" or "gender-biased" presumes that the State, by favoring veterans, intentionally incorporated into its public employment policies the panoply of sex-based and assertedly discriminatory federal laws that have prevented all but a handful of women from becoming veterans. There are two serious difficulties with this argument. First, it is wholly at odds with the District Court's central finding that Massachusetts has not offered a preference to veterans for the purpose of discriminating against women. Second, it cannot be reconciled with the assumption made by both the appellee and the District Court that a more limited hiring preference for veterans could be sustained. Taken together, these difficulties are fatal.

. . .

2

The appellee's ultimate argument rests upon the presumption, common to the criminal and civil law, that a person intends the natural and foreseeable consequences of his voluntary actions....
... The decision to grant a preference to veterans was of course "intentional." So, necessarily, did an adverse impact upon nonveterans follow from that decision. And it cannot seriously be argued that the Legislature of Massachusetts could have been unaware that most veterans are men. It would thus be disingenuous to say that the adverse consequences of this legislation for women were unintended, in the sense that they were not volitional or in the sense that they were not foreseeable.

"Discriminatory purpose," however, implies more than intent as volition or intent as awareness of consequences.... It implies that the decision-maker, in this case a state legislature, selected or

reaffirmed a particular course of action at least in part "because of," not merely "in spite of," its adverse effects upon an identifiable group. Yet nothing in the record demonstrates that this preference for veterans was originally devised or subsequently re-enacted because it would accomplish the collateral goal of keeping women in a stereotypic and predefined place in the Massachusetts Civil Service.

. . .

IV

Veterans' hiring preferences represent an awkward—and, many argue, unfair—exception to the widely shared view that merit and merit alone should prevail in the employment policies of government. After a war, such laws have been enacted virtually without opposition. During peacetime, they inevitably have come to be viewed in many quarters as undemocratic and unwise. Absolute and permanent preferences, as the troubled history of this law demonstrates, have always been subject to the objection that they give the veteran more than a square deal.... The substantial edge granted to veterans by ch. 31, § 23, may reflect unwise policy. The appellee, however, has simply failed to demonstrate that the law in any way reflects a purpose to discriminate on the basis of sex.

The judgment is reversed, and the case is remanded for further proceedings consistent with this opinion.

It is so ordered.

Mr. Justice Stevens, with whom Mr. Justice White joins, concurring....

Mr. Justice Marshall, with whom Mr. Justice Brennan joins, dissenting.

Although acknowledging that in some circumstances, discriminatory intent may be inferred from the inevitable or foreseeable impact of a statute... the Court concludes that no such intent has been established here. I cannot agree. In my judgment, Massachusetts' choice of an absolute veterans' preference system evinces purposeful gender-based discrimination. And because the statutory scheme bears no substantial relationship to a legitimate governmental objective, it cannot withstand scrutiny under the Equal Protection Clause.

. . .

II

... [T]here are a wide variety of less discriminatory means by which Massachusetts could effect its

compensatory purposes. For example, a point preference system, such as that maintained by many
States and the Federal Government,... or an absolute preference for a limited duration would reward veterans without excluding all qualified
women from upper level civil service positions....

Johnson v. Transportation Agency

480 U.S. 616 (1987)

Paul E. Johnson, a male employee, was passed over for promotion to the position of road
dispatcher. Instead, the Transportation Agency selected a female employee, Diane Joyce.
Both were rated as well qualified for the job, but Joyce was picked in part because the
Agency took into account her gender as a factor. Johnson filed suit, claiming that the
Agency had violated Title VII of the Civil Rights Act of 1964. The district court agreed;
the Ninth Circuit reversed.

JUSTICE BRENNAN delivered the opinion of the
Court.

. . .

I

A

In December 1978, the Santa Clara County
Transit District Board of Supervisors adopted an
Affirmative Action Plan (Plan) for the County
Transportation Agency. The Plan implemented a
County Affirmative Action Plan, which had been
adopted, declared the County, because "mere
prohibition of discriminatory practices is not
enough to remedy the effects of past practices
and to permit attainment of an equitable representation of minorities, women and handicapped
persons." App. 31. Relevant to this case, the
Agency Plan provides that, in making promotions to positions within a traditionally segregated job classification in which women have
been significantly underrepresented, the Agency
is authorized to consider as one factor the sex of
a qualified applicant.

In reviewing the composition of its work force,
the Agency noted in its Plan that women were
represented in numbers far less than their proportion of the county labor force in both the
Agency as a whole and in five of seven job categories. Specifically, while women constituted
36.4% of the area labor market, they composed
only 22.4% of Agency employees. Furthermore,
women working at the Agency were concentrated
largely in EEOC job categories traditionally held
by women: women made up 76% of Office and
Clerical Workers, but only 7.1% of Agency Officials and Administrators, 8.6% of Professionals,
9.7% of Technicians, and 22% of Service and
Maintenance workers. As for the job classification

relevant to this case, none of the 238 Skilled Craft
Worker positions was held by a woman....

B

On December 12, 1979, the Agency announced a vacancy for the promotional position
of road dispatcher in the Agency's Roads Division. Dispatchers assign road crews, equipment,
and materials, and maintain records pertaining
to road maintenance jobs.... The position requires at minimum four years of dispatch or road
maintenance work experience for Santa Clara
County. The EEOC job classification scheme designates a road dispatcher as a Skilled Craft
worker.

Twelve County employees applied for the promotion, including Joyce and Johnson. Joyce had
worked for the County since 1970, serving as an
account clerk until 1975. She had applied for a
road dispatcher position in 1974, but was deemed
ineligible because she had not served as a road
maintenance worker. In 1975, Joyce transferred
from a senior account clerk position to a road
maintenance worker position, becoming the first
woman to fill such a job.... During her four years
in that position, she occasionally worked out of
class as a road dispatcher.

Petitioner Johnson began with the county in
1967 as a road yard clerk, after private employment that included working as a supervisor and
dispatcher. He had also unsuccessfully applied for
the road dispatcher opening in 1974. In 1977, his
clerical position was downgraded, and he sought
and received a transfer to the position of road
maintenance worker.... He also occasionally
worked out of class as a dispatcher while performing that job.

Nine of the applicants, including Joyce and
Johnson, were deemed qualified for the job, and

were interviewed by a two-person board. Seven of the applicants scored above 70 on this interview, which meant that they were certified as eligible for selection by the appointing authority. The scores awarded ranged from 70 to 80. Johnson was tied for second with score of 75, while Joyce ranked next with a score of 73. A second interview was conducted by three Agency supervisors, who ultimately recommended that Johnson be promoted. Prior to the second interview, Joyce had contacted the County's Affirmative Action Office because she feared that her application might not receive disinterested review. The Office in turn contacted the Agency's Affirmative Action Coordinator, whom the Agency's Plan makes responsible for, *inter alia,* keeping the Director informed of opportunities for the Agency to accomplish its objectives under the Plan. At the time, the Agency employed no women in any Skilled Craft position, and had never employed a woman as a road dispatcher. The Coordinator recommended to the Director of the Agency, James Graebner, that Joyce be promoted.

Graebner, authorized to choose any of the seven persons deemed eligible, thus had the benefit of suggestions by the second interview panel and by the Agency Coordinator in arriving at his decision. After deliberation, Graebner concluded that the promotion should be given to Joyce. As he testified: "I tried to look at the whole picture, the combination of her qualifications and Mr. Johnson's qualifications, their test scores, their expertise, their background, affirmative action matters, things like that...I believe it was a combination of all those."...

The certification form naming Joyce as the person promoted to the dispatcher position stated that both she and Johnson were rated as well-qualified for the job. The evaluation of Joyce read: "Well qualified by virtue of 18 years of past clerical experience including 3½ years at West Yard plus almost 5 years as a [road maintenance worker]." App. 27. The evaluation of Johnson was as follows: "Well qualified applicant; two years of [road maintenance worker] experience plus 11 years of Road Yard Clerk. Has had previous outside Dispatch experience but was 13 years ago." *Ibid.* Graebner testified that he did not regard as significant the fact that Johnson scored 75 and Joyce 73 when interviewed by the two-person board....

. . .

II

. . .

As an initial matter, the Agency adopted as a benchmark for measuring progress in eliminating underrepresentation the long-term goal of a work force that mirrored in its major job classifications the percentage of women in the area labor market....

As the Agency Plan recognized, women were most egregiously underrepresented in the Skilled Craft job category, since *none* of the 238 positions was occupied by a woman....

...[I]t was plainly not unreasonable for the Agency to determine that it was appropriate to consider as one factor the sex of Ms. Joyce in making its decision. The promotion of Joyce thus satisfies the first requirement enunciated in *Weber* [Steelworkers v. Weber, 443 U.S. 193 (1979)], since it was undertaken to further an affirmative action plan designed to eliminate Agency work force imbalances in traditionally segregated job categories.

We next consider whether the Agency Plan unnecessarily trammeled the rights of male employees or created an absolute bar to their advancement. In contrast to the plan in *Weber,* which provided that 50% of the positions in the craft training program were exclusively for blacks, and to the consent decree upheld last term in *Firefighters* v. *Cleveland,* 478 U.S. 501 (1986), which required the promotion of specific numbers of minorities, the Plan sets aside no positions for women....As the Agency Director testified, the sex of Joyce was but one of numerous factors he took into account in arriving at his decision....

In addition, petitioner had no absolute entitlement to the road dispatcher position. Seven of the applicants were classified as qualified and eligible, and the Agency Director was authorized to promote any of the seven. Thus, denial of the promotion unsettled no legitimate firmly rooted expectation on the part of the petitioner. Furthermore, while the petitioner in this case was denied a promotion, he retained his employment with the Agency, at the same salary and with the same seniority, and remained eligible for other promotions.

. . .

III

. . .

We therefore hold that the Agency appropriately took into account as one factor the sex of Diane Joyce in determining that she should be promoted to the road dispatcher position. The decision to do so was made pursuant to an affirmative action plan that represents a moderate, flexible, case-by-case approach to effecting a gradual improvement in the representation of minorities and women in the Agency's work force. Such a plan is fully consistent with Title VII, for it embodies the contribution that voluntary employer action can make in eliminating the vestiges of discrimination in the workplace. Accordingly, the judgment of the Court of Appeals is

Affirmed.

JUSTICE STEVENS, concurring.

. . .

JUSTICE O'CONNOR, concurring in the judgment.

. . .

JUSTICE WHITE, dissenting.

I agree with Parts I and II of JUSTICE SCALIA's dissenting opinion. Although I do not join Part III, I also would overrule *Weber....*

JUSTICE SCALIA, with whom THE CHIEF JUSTICE joins, and with whom JUSTICE WHITE joins in Parts I and II, dissenting.

... Title VII of the Civil Rights Act of 1964 declares:

"It shall be an unlawful employment practice for an employer—

"(1) to fail or refuse to hire or to discharge any individual, or otherwise to discriminate against any individual with respect to his compensation,

terms, conditions, or privileges, of employment, because of such individual's race, color, religion, sex, or national origin; or

"(2) to limit, segregate, or classify his employees or applicants for employment in any way which would deprive or tend to deprive any individual of employment opportunities or otherwise adversely affect his status as an employee, because of such individual's race, color, religion, sex, or national origin." 42 U.S.C. § 2000e-2(a).

The Court today completes the process of converting this from a guarantee that race or sex will *not* be the basis for employment determinations, to a guarantee that it often *will....*

III

. . .

...It is well to keep in mind just how thoroughly *Weber* rewrote the statute it purported to construe.... In effect, *Weber* held that the legality of intentional discrimination by private employers against certain disfavored groups or individuals is to be judged not by Title VII but by a judicially crafted code of conduct, the contours of which are determined by no discernible standard, aside from (as the dissent convincingly demonstrated) the divination of congressional "purposes" belied by the face of the statute and by its legislative history. We have been recasting that self-promulgated code of conduct ever since—and what it has led us to today adds to the reasons for abandoning it.

. . .

Automobile Workers v. Johnson Controls

499 U.S. 187 (1991)

Johnson Controls, manufacturer of batteries, prohibited fertile women from working in jobs that would expose them to lead and possible health hazards to the fetus a woman might conceive. The question for the Court was whether the company's policy was barred by the Pregnancy Discrimination Act of 1978, which amended the sex discrimination provision in the Civil Rights Act of 1964. The Court was unanimous in deciding that Johnson Controls had discriminated against women, but the Justices who concurred disagreed with the majority's analysis of congressional policy.

JUSTICE BLACKMUN delivered the opinion of the Court.

In this case we are concerned with an employer's gender-based fetal-protection policy. May an employer exclude a fertile female employee

from certain jobs because of its concern for the health of the fetus the woman might conceive?

I

Respondent Johnson Controls, Inc., manufactures batteries. In the manufacturing process, the element lead is a primary ingredient. Occupational exposure to lead entails health risks, including the risk of harm to any fetus carried by a female employee.

Before the Civil Rights Act of 1964, 78 Stat. 241, became law, Johnson Controls did not employ any woman in a battery-manufacturing job. In June 1977, however, it announced its first official policy concerning its employment of women in lead-exposure work:

"[P]rotection of the health of the unborn child is the immediate and direct responsibility of the prospective parents. While the medical profession and the company can support them in the exercise of this responsibility, it cannot assume it for them without simultaneously infringing their rights as persons.

. . .

"...Since not all women who can become mothers wish to become mothers (or will become mothers), it would appear to be illegal discrimination to treat all who are capable of pregnancy as though they will become pregnant." App. 140.

Consistent with that view, Johnson Controls "stopped short of excluding women capable of bearing children from lead exposure," *id.,* at 138, but emphasized that a woman who expected to have a child should not choose a job in which she would have such exposure. The company also required a woman who wished to be considered for employment to sign a statement that she had been advised of the risk of having a child while she was exposed to lead....

Five years later, in 1982, Johnson Controls shifted from a policy of warning to a policy of exclusion *[of pregnant women or women capable of bearing children]....*

II

[Petitioners included a woman who had chosen to be sterilized in order to avoid losing her job, a woman who had suffered a loss in compensation when she was transferred out of a job where she was exposed to lead, and a man who had been denied a request for a leave of absence for the purpose of lowering his lead level because he intended to become a father.]

III

The bias in Johnson Controls' policy is obvious. Fertile men, but not fertile women, are given a choice as to whether they wish to risk their re-

productive health for a particular job. Section 703(a) of the Civil Rights Act of 1964, 78 Stat. 255, as amended, 42 U. S. C. § 2000e-2(a), prohibits sex-based classifications in terms and conditions of employment, in hiring and discharging decisions, and in other employment decisions that adversely affect an employee's status. Respondent's fetal-protection policy explicitly discriminates against women on the basis of their sex....

Nevertheless, the Court of Appeals assumed, as did the two appellate courts who already had confronted the issue, that sex-specific fetal-protection policies do not involve facial discrimination.... These courts analyzed the policies as though they were facially neutral, and had only a discriminatory effect upon the employment opportunities of women. Consequently, the courts looked to see if each employer in question had established that its policy was justified as a business necessity. The business necessity standard is more lenient for the employer than the statutory BFOQ *[bona fide occupational qualification]* defense. The Court of Appeals here went one step further and invoked the burden-shifting framework set forth in *Wards Cove Packing Co. v. Atonio,* 490 U. S. 642 (1989), thus requiring petitioners to bear the burden of persuasion on all questions.... The court assumed that because the asserted reason for the sex-based exclusion (protecting women's unconceived offspring) was ostensibly benign, the policy was not sex-based discrimination. That assumption, however, was incorrect.

First, Johnson Controls' policy classifies on the basis of gender and childbearing capacity, rather than fertility alone. Respondent does not seek to protect the unconceived children of all its employees. Despite evidence in the record about the debilitating effect of lead exposure on the male reproductive system, Johnson Controls is concerned only with the harms that may befall the unborn offspring of its female employees.... Johnson Controls' policy is facially discriminatory because it requires only a female employee to produce proof that she is not capable of reproducing.

Our conclusion is bolstered by the Pregnancy Discrimination Act of 1978 (PDA), 92 Stat. 2076, 42 U. S. C. § 2000e(k), in which Congress explicitly provided that, for purposes of Title VII, discrimination "on the basis of sex" includes discrimination "because of or on the basis of pregnancy, childbirth, or related medical conditions." "The Pregnancy Discrimination Act has now made clear that, for all Title VII purposes, discrimination based on a woman's pregnancy is, on its face, discrimination because of her sex." *Newport News Shipbuilding & Dry Dock Co. v. EEOC*, 462 U. S. 669, 684 (1983). In its use of the words "capable of bearing children" in the 1982 policy statement as the criterion for exclusion, Johnson Controls explicitly classifies on the basis of potential for pregnancy. Under the PDA, such a classification must be regarded, for Title VII purposes, in the same light as explicit sex discrimination. Respondent has chosen to treat all its female employees as potentially pregnant; that choice evinces discrimination on the basis of sex.

. . .

...We hold that Johnson Controls' fetal-protection policy is sex discrimination forbidden under Title VII unless respondent can establish that sex is a "bona fide occupational qualification."

IV

Under § 703(e)(1) of Title VII, an employer may discriminate on the basis of "religion, sex, or national origin in those certain instances where religion, sex, or national origin is a bona fide occupational qualification reasonably necessary to the normal operation of that particular business or enterprise." 42 U. S. C. § 2000e-2(e)(1). We therefore turn to the question whether Johnson Controls' fetal-protection policy is one of those "certain instances" that come within the BFOQ exception.

The BFOQ defense is written narrowly, and this Court has read it narrowly....

The wording of the BFOQ defense contains several terms of restriction that indicate that the exception reaches only special situations. The statute thus limits the situations in which discrimination is permissible to "certain instances" where sex discrimination is "reasonably necessary" to the "normal operation" of the "particular" business. Each one of these terms—certain, normal, particular—prevents the use of general subjective standards and favors an objective, verifiable requirement. But the most telling term is "occupational"; this indicates that these objective, verifiable requirements must concern job-related skills and aptitudes.

The concurrence defines "occupational" as meaning related to a job.... According to the concurrence, any discriminatory requirement imposed by an employer is "job-related" simply because the employer has chosen to make the requirement a condition of employment. In effect, the concurrence argues that sterility may be an occupational qualification for women because Johnson Controls has chosen to require it. This reading of "occupational" renders the word mere surplusage. "Qualification" by itself would encompass an employer's idiosyncratic requirements. By modifying "qualification" with "occupational," Congress narrowed the term to qualifications that affect an employee's ability to do the job.

. . .

We conclude that the language of both the BFOQ provision and the PDA which amended it, as well as the legislative history and the case law, prohibit an employer from discriminating against a woman because of her capacity to become pregnant unless her reproductive potential prevents her from performing the duties of her job....

V

We have no difficulty concluding that Johnson Controls cannot establish a BFOQ. Fertile women, as far as appears in the record, participate in the manufacture of batteries as efficiently as anyone else. Johnson Controls' professed moral and ethical concerns about the welfare of the next generation do not suffice to establish a BFOQ of female sterility. Decisions about the welfare of future children must be left to the parents who conceive, bear, support, and raise them rather than to the employers who hire those parents. Congress has mandated this choice through Title VII, as amended by the Pregnancy Discrimination Act....

VII

. . .

The judgment of the Court of Appeals is reversed and the case is remanded for further proceedings consistent with this opinion.

It is so ordered.

JUSTICE WHITE, with whom THE CHIEF JUSTICE and JUSTICE KENNEDY join, concurring in part and concurring in the judgment.

The Court properly holds that Johnson Controls' fetal protection policy overtly discriminates against women, and thus is prohibited by Title VII unless it falls within the bona fide occupational qualification (BFOQ) exception, set forth at 42 U. S. C. § 2000e-2(e). The Court erroneously holds, however, that the BFOQ defense is so narrow that it could never justify a sex-specific fetal protection policy. I nevertheless concur in the judgment of reversal because on the record before us summary judgment in favor of Johnson Controls was improperly entered by the District Court and affirmed by the Court of Appeals.

I

In evaluating the scope of the BFOQ defense, the proper starting point is the language of the statute.... [N]othing in the statute's language indicates that it could *never* support a sex-specific fetal protection policy.

On the contrary, a fetal protection policy would be justified under the terms of the statute if, for example, an employer could show that exclusion of women from certain jobs was reasonably necessary to avoid substantial tort liability. Common sense tells us that it is part of the normal operation of business concerns to avoid causing injury to third parties, as well as to employees, if for no other reason than to avoid tort liability and its substantial costs. This possibility of tort liability is not hypothetical; every State currently allows children born alive to recover in tort for prenatal injuries caused by third parties, ...

. . .

JUSTICE SCALIA, concurring in the judgment.

I generally agree with the Court's analysis, but have some reservations, several of which bear mention.

First, I think it irrelevant that there was "evidence in the record about the debilitating effect of lead exposure on the male reproductive system," ... Even without such evidence, treating women differently "on the basis of pregnancy"

constitutes discrimination "on the basis of sex," because Congress has unequivocally said so....

Second, the Court points out that "Johnson Controls has shown no factual basis for believing that all or substantially all women would be unable to perform safely... the duties of the job involved," ... (internal quotations omitted). In my view, this is not only "somewhat academic in light of our conclusion that the company may not exclude fertile women at all," ...; it is entirely irrelevant. By reason of the Pregnancy Discrimination Act, it would not matter if all pregnant women placed their children at risk in taking these jobs, just as it does not matter if no men do so....

Third, I am willing to assume, as the Court intimates,... that any action required by Title VII cannot give rise to liability under state tort law....

Last, the Court goes far afield, it seems to me, in suggesting that increased cost alone — short of "costs... so prohibitive as to threaten survival of the employer's business," ... cannot support a BFOQ defense.... I agree with JUSTICE WHITE's concurrence,... that nothing in our prior cases suggests this, and in my view it is wrong. I think, for example, that a shipping company may refuse to hire pregnant women as crew members on long voyages because the on-board facilities for foreseeable emergencies, though quite feasible, would be inordinately expensive. In the present case, however, Johnson has not asserted a cost-based BFOQ.

I concur in the judgment of the Court.

Rostker v. Goldberg

453 U.S. 57 (1981)

In 1980 Congress reactivated the registration process for military service but denied President Carter the authority he requested to permit the registration and conscription of women as well as men. After President Carter ordered the registration of specified groups of young men, several men, including Robert L. Goldberg, brought a lawsuit challenging the statute's constitutionality. A three-judge district court held that the statute's gender-based discrimination violated the Due Process Clause of the Fifth Amendment and enjoined registration under the statute. Bernard Rostker, Director of Selective Service, brought this appeal to the Supreme Court.

JUSTICE REHNQUIST delivered the opinion of the Court.

The question presented is whether the Military Selective Service Act, 50 U. S. C. App. § 451 *et*

seq. (1976 ed. and Supp. III), violates the Fifth Amendment to the United States Constitution in authorizing the President to require the registration of males and not females.

I

Congress is given the power under the Constitution "To raise and support Armies," "To provide and maintain a Navy," and "To make Rules for the Government and Regulation of the land and naval Forces." Art. I, § 8, cls. 12–14. Pursuant to this grant of authority Congress has enacted the Military Selective Service Act, 50 U. S. C. App. § 451 *et seq.* (1976 ed. and Supp. III) (the MSSA or the Act). Section 3 of the Act, 62 Stat. 605, as amended, 50 U. S. C. App. § 453, empowers the President, by proclamation, to require the registration of "every male citizen" and male resident aliens between the ages of 18 and 26. The purpose of this registration is to facilitate any eventual conscription....

. . .

...Although Congress considered the question at great length,...it declined to amend the MSSA to permit the registration of women.

. . .

II

Whenever called upon to judge the constitutionality of an Act of Congress—"the gravest and most delicate duty that this Court is called upon to perform."...the Court accords "great weight to the decisions of Congress."...The Congress is a coequal branch of government whose Members take the same oath we do to uphold the Constitution of the United States....

This is not, however, merely a case involving the customary deference accorded congressional decisions. The case arises in the context of Congress' authority over national defense and military affairs, and perhaps in no other area has the Court accorded Congress greater deference. In rejecting the registration of women, Congress explicitly relied upon its constitutional powers under Art. I, § 8, cls. 12–14. The "specific findings" section of the Report of the Senate Armed Services Committee, later adopted by both Houses of Congress, began by stating:

"Article I, section 8 of the Constitution commits exclusively to the Congress the powers to raise and support armies, provide and maintain a Navy, and make rules for Government and regulation of the land and naval forces, and pursuant to these powers it lies within the discretion of the Congress to determine the occasions for expansion of our Armed Forces, and the means best

suited to such expansion should it prove necessary." S. Rep. No. 96-826, *supra,* at 160.

. . .

Not only is the scope of Congress' constitutional power in this area broad, but the lack of competence on the part of the courts is marked. In *Gilligan* v. *Morgan,* 413 U. S. 1, 10 (1973), the Court noted:

"[I]t is difficult to conceive of an area of governmental activity in which the courts have less competence. The complex, subtle, and professional decisions as to the composition, training, equipping, and control of a military force are essentially professional military judgments, subject *always* to civilian control of the Legislative and Executive Branches."

. . .

None of this is to say that Congress is free to disregard the Constitution when it acts in the area of military affairs. In that area, as any other, Congress remains subject to the limitations of the Due Process Clause,...but the tests and limitations to be applied may differ because of the military context. We of course do not abdicate our ultimate responsibility to decide the constitutional question, but simply recognize that the Constitution itself requires such deference to congressional choice....

III

This case is quite different from several of the gender-based discrimination cases we have considered in that, despite appellees' assertions, Congress did not act "unthinkingly" or "reflexively and not for any considered reason."...The question of registering women for the draft not only received considerable national attention and was the subject of wide-ranging public debate, but also was extensively considered by Congress in hearings, floor debate, and in committee. Hearings held by both Houses of Congress in response to the President's request for authorization to register women adduced extensive testimony and evidence concerning the issue....

The MSSA established a plan for maintaining "adequate armed strength...to insure the security of [the] Nation." 50 U. S. C. App. § 451 (b). Registration is the first step "in a united and continuous process designed to raise an army speedily and efficiently,"..."A functioning registration system is a vital part of any mobilization plan."...

Women as a group, however, unlike men as a

group, are not eligible for combat. The restrictions on the participation of women in combat in the Navy and Air Force are statutory. Under 10 U. S. C. § 6015 (1976 ed., Supp. III), "women may not be assigned to duty on vessels or in aircraft that are engaged in combat missions," and under 10 U. S. C. § 8549 female members of the Air Force "may not be assigned to duty in aircraft engaged in combat missions." The Army and Marine Corps preclude the use of women in combat as a matter of established policy....

The existence of the combat restrictions clearly indicates the basis for Congress' decision to exempt women from registration. The purpose of registration was to prepare for a draft of combat troops. Since women are excluded from combat, Congress concluded that they would not be needed in the event of a draft, and therefore decided not to register them....

. . .

In light of the foregoing, we conclude that Congress acted well within its constitutional authority when it authorized the registration of men, and not women, under the Military Selective Service Act. The decision of the District Court holding otherwise is accordingly

Reversed.

JUSTICE WHITE, with whom JUSTICE BRENNAN joins, dissenting.

I assume what has not been challenged in this case — that excluding women from combat positions does not offend the Constitution. Granting that, it is self-evident that if during mobilization for war, all noncombat military positions must be filled by combat-qualified personnel available to be moved into combat positions, there would be no occasion whatsoever to have any women in the Army, whether as volunteers or inductees. The Court appears to say . . . that Congress concluded as much and that we should accept that judgment even though the serious view of the Executive

Branch, including the responsible military services, is to the contrary. The Court's position in this regard is most unpersuasive....

. . .

JUSTICE MARSHALL, with whom JUSTICE BRENNAN joins, dissenting.

The Court today places its imprimatur on one of the most potent remaining public expressions of "ancient canards about the proper role of women," *Phillips* v. *Martin Marietta Corp.,* 400 U. S. 542, 545 (1971) (MARSHALL, J., concurring). It upholds a statute that requires males but not females to register for the draft, and which thereby categorically excludes women from a fundamental civic obligation. Because I believe the Court's decision is inconsistent with the Constitution's guarantee of equal protection of the laws, I dissent.

. . .

VI

. . .

In concluding that the Government has carried its burden in this case, the Court adopts "an appropriately deferential examination of *Congress'* evaluation of [the] evidence," . . . The majority then proceeds to supplement Congress' actual findings with those the Court apparently believes Congress could (and should) have made. Beyond that, the Court substitutes hollow shibboleths about "deference to legislative decisions" for constitutional analysis. It is as if the majority has lost sight of the fact that "it is the responsibility of this Court to act as the ultimate interpreter of the Constitution." *Powell* v. *McCormack,* 395 U. S., at 549. See *Baker* v. *Carr,* 369 U. S., at 211. Congressional enactments in the area of military affairs must, like all other laws, be *judged* by the standards of the Constitution....

Senate Debates Women in Combat

During action on the defense authorization bill in 1991, the Senate considered an amendment to remove the statutory prohibition on using women in combat roles. The debate, reflecting the performance of women soldiers in the Persian Gulf War, shows how changing political attitudes affect constitutional discourse. Much of the support voiced by Senators for women in combat, especially as combat aviators, would have been inconceivable decades earlier.

Mr.[William V.] ROTH [R-Del.]. Mr. President, the amendment which Senator KENNEDY and I will propose later is not about gender, but about excellence. It is not about women pilots flying combat missions, but about the best pilots flying combat missions.

The readiness and preparedness of our military defense is a serious matter. When our Nation's future is at stake—and the future of free nations is at stake—we want the most skilled and seasoned men and women on the job.

Make no mistake—military excellence must be our first priority. Our Secretary of Defense must have the greatest flexibility and maneuverability to marshall the forces at his command. We want the best and brightest pilots in the air, not on the ground. We want the best person in the cockpit of a Stealth fighter or a B-1 bomber—not the second best.

Mr. President, America is with us on this issue. A Newsweek poll released just this week shows that 63 percent of Americans favor allowing women to fly combat aircraft. The American people know that what is good for our military defense is also good for the country. And what is good for the country is excellence, readiness, preparedness, strength, and flexibility.

Forty years ago Congress imposed a rule which now prevents women from serving as combat pilots. This congressional restriction is as old and outdated in today's military as a World War II propeller plane.

. . .

In removing the ban, we give women the opportunity to compete for these positions as DOD sees fit—nothing more and nothing less. And, we give the military the opportunity to make the best use of its talent.

The Senate Armed Services Committee—instead of adopting my proposal—has called for a study commission. We do not need a commission to study the issue. A commission will not tell us anything we do not already know about the performance of women pilots in battle.

Women have proven themselves—the documentation is clear and well-documented. The best arguments are performance, experience, and aptitude—and women military pilots have come through with flying colors on all three counts.

For anyone who thinks we need more studies,

SOURCE: 137 Cong. Rec. 20710–11, 20713, 20722 (1991).

more evidence, I say, look at the record. Women have been pulling G's in high performance aircraft for over 15 years now. Women aviators train our male combat pilots. They test the newest generation aircraft. They fly the space shuttle. Women pilots test FA-18's and C-27's, they fly transport planes and refueling planes, they fly AWACS and helicopters. In fact, women have flown just about every plane that the Pentagon has built in the past three decades. There is no question about their performance, or their experience, in this regard.

But women have proven themselves, not only in the instructor's seat and in the test pilot's seat, but in battle conditions and in the line of fire. Their aptitude and ability may have been proven here at home—but their courage and mettle were proven in the skies over Saudi Arabia, Kuwait, and Iraq.

. . .

Mr. [Edward] KENNEDY [D-Mass.]. Mr. President, I commend my friend and colleague, the Senator from Delaware [Mr. ROTH] for the leadership he has provided on this issue and I am delighted to have the chance to join with him, Senator McCONNELL, Senator LEAHY, and Senator BINGAMAN in support of our amendment to repeal the statutes that bar women from serving in combat aircraft. These exclusionary statutes are relics of the 1940's that Congress should have repealed long ago.

The Armed Forces claim that they are an equal opportunity employer, and they are, partly. They have made great strides in opening up all branches of the service to racial minorities.

But the same cannot be said with regard to sex discrimination, because archaic statutes still in the books deny equal opportunity to women.

Barriers based on sex discrimination are coming down in every part of our society. The Armed Forces should be no exception. Women should be allowed to play a full role in our national defense, free of any arbitrary and discriminatory restrictions. The only fair and proper test of a women's role is not gender but ability to do the job.

. . .

Mr. ROTH. . . .

What about women in ground combat? Some have raised that specter, that fear, that the Kennedy and Roth amendment will lead women down the slippery slope into the trenches of ground combat. That is an unfounded fear, and it is an unnecessary fear. Our amendment is surgical, precise, circumscribed, and only germane to the role of women combat aviators; nothing more, nothing less. We are not establishing a dangerous precedent here.

Legal experts agree that lifting the combat aircraft restriction will not mean a dramatic change in the woman's role in the military.

They raise a question about unit cohesion and bonding. Just let me point out that something like 35,000 women served in the Persian Gulf, and military leader after military leader including Mr. Cheney [Secretary of Defense], have said women pilots are successful members of aircraft crews. As one woman pilot said, "The old so-called male bonding of former days was replaced with unit bonding in the gulf." We have the testimony of male pilots who have verified the team spirit of their women colleagues. So, once again, we see [*stalking*] horses being raised just to be knocked down.

What about gender norming, lower standards for women pilots? Some say allowing women to fly as combat pilots will result in a double standard and will place less capable women in critical positions. If anyone reads the testimony of the Chiefs of Staff before the Armed Services Subcommittee a few short days ago, it will become very clear by what the Chief of Staff, for example, of the Air Force said:

"There would be no lowering of the standard. What we are really doing is permitting the military to do what is in the best interests of the national defense."

United States v. Virginia

518 U.S. 515 (1996)

Virginia Military Institute (VMI) operated as the sole single-sex school among Virginia's public institutions of higher learning. The distinctive mission of the school was to produce "citizen-soldiers," men prepared for leadership in civilian life and in military service. Only about 15% of VMI cadets entered career military service. The United States sued Virginia and VMI on the ground that the school's exclusively male admission policy violated the Fourteenth Amendment's Equal Protection Clause. The district court ruled in VMI's favor; the Fourth Circuit reversed. To remedy the constitutional problem, Virginia proposed a parallel program for women: Virginia Women's Institute for Leadership (VWIL), located at Mary Baldwin College, a private liberal arts school for women. The district court and the Fourth Circuit found that this proposal satisfied the equal protection requirement.

JUSTICE GINSBURG delivered the opinion of the Court.

Virginia's public institutions of higher learning include an incomparable military college, Virginia Military Institute (VMI). The United States maintains that the Constitution's equal protection guarantee precludes Virginia from reserving exclusively to men the unique educational opportunities VMI affords. We agree.

I

Founded in 1839, VMI is today the sole single-sex school among Virginia's 15 public institutions of higher learning. VMI's distinctive mission is to produce "citizen-soldiers," men prepared for leadership in civilian life and in military service. VMI pursues this mission through pervasive training of a kind not available anywhere else in Virginia. Assigning prime place to character development, VMI uses an "adversative method"

modeled on English public schools and once characteristic of military instruction. VMI constantly endeavors to instill physical and mental discipline in its cadets and impart to them a strong moral code....

Neither the goal of producing citizen-soldiers nor VMI's implementing methodology is inherently unsuitable to women. And the school's impressive record in producing leaders has made admission desirable to some women. Nevertheless, Virginia has elected to preserve exclusively for men the advantages and opportunities a VMI education affords.

II

A

From its establishment in 1839 as one of the Nation's first state military colleges,... VMI has remained financially supported by Virginia and "subject to the control of the [Virginia] General Assembly," . . .

VMI today enrolls about 1,300 men as cadets. Its academic offerings in the liberal arts, sciences, and engineering are also available at other public colleges and universities in Virginia. But VMI's mission is special. It is the mission of the school

" 'to produce educated and honorable men, prepared for the varied work of civil life, imbued with love of learning, confident in the functions and attitudes of leadership, possessing a high sense of public service, advocates of the American democracy and free enterprise system, and ready as citizen-soldiers to defend their country in time of national peril.' " 766 F. Supp. 1407, 1425 (WD Va. 1991) (quoting Mission Study Committee of the VMI Board of Visitors, Report, May 16, 1986).

In contrast to the federal service academies, institutions maintained "to prepare cadets for career service in the armed forces," VMI's program "is directed at preparation for both military and civilian life"; "[o]nly about 15% of VMI cadets enter career military service." . . .

VMI produces its "citizen-soldiers" through "an adversative, or doubting, model of education" which features "[p]hysical rigor, mental stress, absolute equality of treatment, absence of privacy, minute regulation of behavior, and indoctrination in desirable values." . . . As one Commandant of Cadets described it, the adversative method " 'dissects the young student,' " and makes him aware of his " 'limits and capabilities,' " so that he knows " 'how far he can go with his anger, . . . how much he can take under stress, . . . exactly what he can do when he is physically exhausted.' " . . .

VMI cadets live in spartan barracks where surveillance is constant and privacy nonexistent; they wear uniforms, eat together in the mess hall, and regularly participate in drills. . . . Entering students are incessantly exposed to the rat line, "an extreme form of the adversative model," comparable in intensity to Marine Corps boot camp. . . . Tormenting and punishing, the rat line bonds new cadets to their fellow sufferers and, when they have completed the 7-month experience, to their former tormentors. . . .

B

In 1990, prompted by a complaint filed with the Attorney General by a female high-school student seeking admission to VMI, the United States sued the Commonwealth of Virginia and VMI, alleging that VMI's exclusively male admission policy violated the Equal Protection Clause of the Fourteenth Amendment. . . .

In the two years preceding the lawsuit, the District Court noted, VMI had received inquiries from 347 women, but had responded to none of them. . . . [I]t was also established that "some women are capable of all of the individual activities required of VMI cadets." . . . In addition, experts agreed that if VMI admitted women, "the VMI ROTC experience would become a better training program from the perspective of the armed forces, because it would provide training in dealing with a mixed-gender army." . . .

"Women are [indeed] denied a unique educational opportunity that is available only at VMI," the District Court acknowledged. . . . But "[VMI's] single-sex status would be lost, and some aspects of the [school's] distinctive method would be altered" if women were admitted, . . . : "Allowance for personal privacy would have to be made" . . . ; "[p]hysical education requirements would have to be altered, at least for the women" . . . ; the adversative environment could not survive unmodified, . . . Thus, "sufficient constitutional justification" had been shown, the District Court held, "for continuing [VMI's] single-sex policy." . . .

The Court of Appeals for the Fourth Circuit disagreed and vacated the District Court's judgment. The appellate court held: "The Commonwealth of Virginia has not . . . advanced any state policy by which it can justify its determination, under an announced policy of diversity, to afford VMI's unique type of program to men and not to women." . . .

. . .

The parties agreed that "*some* women can meet the physical standards now imposed on men," . . . and the court was satisfied that "neither the goal of producing citizen soldiers nor VMI's implementing methodology is inherently unsuitable to women," . . . The Court of Appeals, however, accepted the District Court's finding that "at least these three aspects of VMI's program—physical training, the absence of privacy, and the adversative approach—would be materially affected by coeducation." . . . Remanding the case, the appeals court assigned to Virginia, in the first instance, responsibility for selecting a remedial course. The court suggested these options for the Commonwealth: Admit women to VMI; establish parallel institutions or programs; or abandon state support, leaving VMI free to pursue its policies as a private institution. . . .

C

In response to the Fourth Circuit's ruling, Virginia proposed a parallel program for women: Virginia Women's Institute for Leadership (VWIL). The 4-year, state-sponsored undergraduate program would be located at Mary Baldwin College, a private liberal arts school for women, and would be open, initially, to about 25 to 30 students. Although VWIL would share VMI's mission—to produce "citizen-soldiers"—the VWIL program would differ, as does Mary Baldwin College, from VMI in academic offerings, methods of education, and financial resources....

D

Virginia returned to the District Court seeking approval of its proposed remedial plan, and the court decided the plan met the requirements of the Equal Protection Clause....*[A divided Fourth Circuit Affirmed.]*

IV

...[W]e conclude that Virginia has shown no "exceedingly persuasive justification" for excluding all women from the citizen-soldier training afforded by VMI. We therefore affirm the Fourth Circuit's initial judgment, which held that Virginia had violated the Fourteenth Amendment's Equal Protection Clause. Because the remedy proffered by Virginia—the Mary Baldwin VWIL program—does not cure the constitutional violation, *i.e.,* it does not provide equal opportunity, we reverse the Fourth Circuit's final judgment in this case.

V

...Virginia...asserts two justifications in defense of VMI's exclusion of women. First, the Commonwealth contends, "single-sex education provides important educational benefits,"...and the option of single-sex education contributes to "diversity in educational approaches,"...Second, the Commonwealth argues, "the unique VMI method of character development and leadership training," the school's adversative approach, would have to be modified were VMI to admit women.... We consider these two justifications in turn.

A

Single-sex education affords pedagogical benefits to at least some students, Virginia emphasizes, and that reality is uncontested in this litigation. Similarly, it is not disputed that diversity among public educational institutions can serve the public good. But Virginia has not shown that VMI was established, or has been maintained, with a view to diversifying, by its categorical exclusion of women, educational opportunities within the Commonwealth....

Neither recent nor distant history bears out Virginia's alleged pursuit of diversity through single-sex educational options. In 1839, when the Commonwealth established VMI, a range of educational opportunities for men and women was scarcely contemplated. Higher education at the time was considered dangerous for women; reflecting widely held views about women's proper place, the Nation's first universities and colleges—for example, Harvard in Massachusetts, William and Mary in Virginia—admitted only men.... VMI was not at all novel in this respect: In admitting no women, VMI followed the lead of the Commonwealth's flagship school, the University of Virginia, founded in 1819.

[Excluded from universities in Virginia, women were admitted to a state seminary in 1884 and to women's colleges in 1908 and 1910. In 1972, women were admitted to the University of Virginia.]

B

Virginia next argues that VMI's adversative method of training provides educational benefits that cannot be made available, unmodified, to women. Alterations to accommodate women would necessarily be "radical," so "drastic," Virginia asserts, as to transform, indeed "destroy," VMI's program....

...[I]t is uncontested that women's admission would require accommodations, primarily in arranging housing assignments and physical training programs for female cadets....It is also undisputed, however, that "the VMI methodology could be used to educate women."...and "some women," the expert testimony established, "are capable of all of the individual activities required of VMI cadets,"...The parties, furthermore, agree that *some* women can meet the physical standards [VMI] now impose[s] on men."...In sum, as the Court of Appeals stated, "neither the goal of producing citizen soldiers," VMI's *raison d'être,* "nor VMI's implementing methodology is inherently unsuitable to women."...

Women's successful entry into the federal military academies, and their participation in the Nation's military forces, indicate that Virginia's fears for the future of VMI may not be solidly grounded. The Commonwealth's justification for excluding all women from "citizen-soldier" training for which some are qualified, in any event, cannot rank as "exceedingly persuasive," as we have explained and applied that standard.

. . .

VI

In the second phase of the litigation, Virginia presented its remedial plan—maintain VMI as a male-only college and create VWIL as a separate program for women....

A

. . .

VWIL affords women no opportunity to experience the rigorous military training for which VMI is famed.... Instead, the VWIL program "deemphasize[s]" military education ... and uses a "cooperative method" of education "which reinforces self-esteem," ...

VWIL students participate in ROTC and a "largely ceremonial" Virginia Corps of Cadets, ... but Virginia deliberately did not make VWIL a military institute. The VWIL House is not a military-style residence and VWIL students need not live together throughout the 4-year program, eat meals together, or wear uniforms during the school day..... VWIL students thus do not experience the "barracks" life "crucial to the VMI experience," the spartan living arrangements designed to foster an "egalitarian ethic." ...

VWIL students receive their "leadership training" in seminars, externships, and speaker series, ... episodes and encounters lacking the "[p]hysical rigor, mental stress, ... minute regulation of behavior, and indoctrination in desirable values" made hallmarks of VMI's citizen-soldier training, ...

Virginia maintains that these methodological differences are "justified pedagogically," based on "important differences between men and women in learning and developmental needs," "psychological and sociological differences" Virginia describes as "real" and "not stereotypes." ... The Task Force charged with developing the leadership program for women, drawn from the staff and faculty at Mary Baldwin College, "determined that a military model and, especially VMI's adversative method, would be wholly inappropriate for educating and training *most women*." ...

As earlier stated, ... generalizations about "the way women are," estimates of what is appropriate for *most women*, no longer justify denying opportunity to women whose talent and capacity place them outside the average description. No-

tably, Virginia never asserted that VMI's method of education suits *most men*....

B

In myriad respects other than military training, VWIL does not qualify as VMI's equal. VWIL's student body, faculty, course offerings, and facilities hardly match VMI's. Nor can the VWIL graduate anticipate the benefits associated with VMI's 157-year history, the school's prestige, and its influential alumni network.

Mary Baldwin College, whose degree VWIL students will gain, enrolls first-year women with an average combined SAT score about 100 points lower than the average score for VMI freshmen.... The Mary Baldwin faculty holds "significantly fewer Ph.D.'s" ... and receives substantially lower salaries....

Mary Baldwin does not offer a VWIL student the range of curricular choices available to a VMI cadet. VMI awards baccalaureate degrees in liberal arts, biology, chemistry, civil engineering, electrical and computer engineering, and mechanical engineering.... VWIL students attend a school that "does not have a math and science focus," ... they cannot take at Mary Baldwin any courses in engineering or the advanced math and physics courses VMI offers....

Although Virginia has represented that it will provide equal financial support for in-state VWIL students and VMI cadets, ... and the VMI Foundation has agreed to endow VWIL with $5.4625 million, ... the difference between the two schools' financial reserves is pronounced. Mary Baldwin's endowment, currently about $19 million, will gain an additional $35 million based on future commitments; VMI's current endowment, $131 million—the largest public college per-student endowment in the Nation—will gain $220 million....

The VWIL student does not graduate with the advantage of a VMI degree. Her diploma does not unite her with the legions of VMI "graduates [who] have distinguished themselves" in military and civilian life.... "[VMI] alumni are exceptionally close to the school," and that closeness accounts, in part, for VMI's success in attracting applicants.... A VWIL graduate cannot assume that the "network of business owners, corporations, VMI graduates and non-graduate employers ... interested in hiring VMI graduates" ... will be equally responsive to her search for employment, ...

C

[The Court describes the "deferential review"

used by the Fourth Circuit in accepting the VWIL plan as a remedy and regards it as inconsistent with "the more exacting standard our precedent requires." Contemporary gender-based classifications require "heightened scrutiny."] In sum, Virginia's remedy does not match the constitutional violation; the Commonwealth has shown no "exceedingly persuasive justification" for withholding from women qualified for the experience premier training of the kind VMI affords.

VII

. . .

For the reasons stated, the initial judgment of the Court of Appeals, 976 F. 2d 890 (CA4 1992), is affirmed, the final judgment of the Court of Appeals, 44 F. 3d 1229 (CA4 1995), is reversed, and the case is remanded for further proceedings consistent with this opinion.

It is so ordered.

Justice Thomas took no part in the consideration or decision of this case.

Chief Justice Rehnquist, concurring in the judgment.

[While agreeing with the Court's conclusions, he objects to the requirement that Virginia must demonstrate an "exceedingly persuasive justification" to support a gender-based classification. He would have adhered more closely to the traditional standard that a gender-based classification "must bear a close and substantial relationship to important governmental objectives." Although VMIL failed as a remedy because it was no match for VMI, Rehnquist states that Virginia could have remedied the problem by creating a single-sex institution for women had it offered the same quality of education and the same overall caliber.]

Justice Scalia, dissenting

Today the Court shuts down an institution that has served the people of the Commonwealth of Virginia with pride and distinction for over a century and a half. To achieve that desired result, it rejects (contrary to our established practice) the factual findings of two courts below, sweeps aside the precedents of this Court, and ignores the history of our people. As to facts: It explicitly rejects the finding that there exist "gender-based developmental differences" supporting Virginia's restriction of the "adversative" method to only a men's institution, and the finding that the all-male composition of the Virginia Military Institute (VMI) is essential to that institution's character. As to precedent: It drastically revises our established standards for reviewing sex-based classifications. And as to history: It counts for nothing the long tradition, enduring down to the present, of men's military colleges supported by both States and the Federal Government.

. . . The virtue of a democratic system with a First Amendment is that it readily enables the people, over time, to be persuaded that what they took for granted is not so, and to change their laws accordingly. That system is destroyed if the smug assurances of each age are removed from the democratic process and written into the Constitution. So to counterbalance the Court's criticism of our ancestors, let me say a word in their praise: They left us free to change. The same cannot be said of this most illiberal Court, which has embarked on a course of inscribing one after another of the current preferences of the society (and in some cases only the countermajoritarian preferences of the society's law-trained elite) into our Basic Law. Today it enshrines the notion that no substantial educational value is to be served by an all-men's military academy . . .

I

. . . [I]t is my view that "when a practice not expressly prohibited by the text of the Bill of Rights bears the endorsement of a long tradition of open, widespread, and unchallenged use that dates back to the beginning of the Republic, we have no proper basis for striking it down." *Rutan* v. *Republican Party of Ill.,* 497 U. S. 62, 95 (1990) (Scalia, J., dissenting). . . .

. . . [T]he tradition of having government-funded military schools for men is as well rooted in the traditions of this country as the tradition of sending only men into military combat. The people may decide to change the one tradition, like the other, through democratic processes; but the assertion that either tradition has been unconstitutional through the centuries is not law, but politics-smuggled-into-law.

. . .

III

With this explanation of how the Court has succeeded in making its analysis seem orthodox—and indeed, if intimations are to be believed, even overly generous to VMI—I now proceed to describe how the analysis should have been conducted. The question to be answered, I repeat, is whether the exclusion of women from VMI is "substantially related to an important governmental objective."

[Scalia concludes, after much analysis, that VMI

meets the traditional intermediate standard for gender-based classifications.]

. . .

C. JUSTICE FOR JUVENILES

Rights for juveniles date largely from the 1960s, although earlier cases recognized certain elementary rights. In 1943 the Supreme Court, after first upholding a compulsory flag salute in public schools, declared that it unconstitutionally infringed on a child's free exercise of religion. West Virginia Board of Education v. Barnette, 319 U.S. 624 (1943), overturning Minersville v. Gobitis, 310 U.S. 586 (1940). Youths charged with serious offenses were protected by basic rules against coerced confessions. Haley v. Ohio, 332 U.S. 596 (1948). Children in public schools had a right to be free of segregation. Brown v. Board of Education, 347 U.S. 483 (1954).

For most of our history, juvenile rights depended on a paternalistic system. Under the doctrine *parens patriae* (with the government taking the role as parent), juvenile courts served as guardians for youthful offenders. Procedural rights and protections were considered unnecessary because it was assumed that the judge would act in the best interest of the child. In many cases, however, judges acted arbitrarily and harshly toward juveniles, meting out periods of incarceration that exceeded the penalties imposed on adults for the same crime.

Congress passed several statutes during the 1960s to deal with the mounting problem of juvenile delinquency. 75 Stat. 572 (1961); 82 Stat. 462 (1968). Beginning in 1971, the Senate Judiciary Committee held a series of hearings on juvenile delinquency and the methods used for treatment and rehabilitation. The hearings revealed widespread inadequacies in correctional facilities. For example, eight-year-old youths were placed in these institutions for several years at a time. Initial efforts to protect the constitutional rights of juveniles centered on procedural safeguards but later spread to free speech, privacy, and other elements of due process.

Criminal Procedures

How many of the procedural safeguards available to adults should protect the rights of juveniles? A 1948 case involved a fifteen-year-old boy who was arrested about midnight on a charge of murder. He was questioned by relays of police from that point until about 5 A.M., without benefit of counsel or friends to advise him. After the police told him that his friends had confessed to the crime, he signed a confession and was later convicted. He was not taken before a magistrate and formally charged with a crime until three days after his confession. A lawyer tried to see him twice but the police refused. The Court held his confession inadmissible. Haley v. Ohio, 332 U.S. 596 (1948). Similar circumstances led the Court to declare inadmissible the confession of a fourteen-year-old boy held for five days without seeing a lawyer, parent, or other friendly adult, although his mother twice tried to see him. Gallegos v. Colorado, 370 U.S. 49 (1962).

After these cases, the Court began to challenge some conventional notions about the protections accorded by juvenile courts. In theory, juvenile courts acted toward a child in a "parental" relationship and not as adversary. Since the proceedings were civil in nature and not criminal, the youth had no opportunity to complain that basic rights of criminal law had been denied.

A major breakthrough occurred in 1966. A sixteen-year-old was accused of housebreaking, robbery, and rape. He was committed to the juvenile court unless it waived jurisdiction

Juvenile Rights after *Gault*

In 1967 the Supreme Court ruled that juveniles are entitled to such basic procedural rights as adequate notice, right to counsel, privilege against self-incrimination, and the rights of confrontation and sworn testimony. In re Gault, 387 U.S.1 (1967). As explained by Paul Marcotte in "Criminal Kids," 76 A.B.A.J. 60, 62–63 (1990), state procedures often fall short of these Supreme Court standards:

"Despite *In Re Gault*, kids often are not represented by lawyers. About half of the youths who appeared before juvenile courts in Minnesota, Nebraska and North Dakota were not represented by counsel, according to [research by Barry Feld, a University of Minnesota law professor.] In another study last year, he found that one-third of Minnesota juveniles removed from their homes and one-fourth incarcerated in training schools never saw a lawyer.

"The Arkansas Supreme Court's removal of exclusive jurisdiction over juveniles from the county courts in 1987 also illustrates this problem. *Walker v. Arkansas Department of Human Resources*, 722 S.W.2d 558. The *Gault* requirements were not being met. County courts did not have the 'same judicial safeguards as other state courts.... County courts, by their very nature, have been unable to ensure the proper disposition of juvenile delinquency cases,' the opinion states.

"... States were beginning the campaign to revise their juvenile codes. New laws required youths with a history of misbehavior to be tried as adults. Other laws excluded certain crimes from the authority of juvenile judges. Prosecutors also were given more authority to charge youths directly in adult court.

"For example, Delaware requires a mandatory waiver for juveniles charged with certain violent crimes. Florida requires a waiver hearing for youths charged with violent crimes who committed a prior crime against the person. California requires juveniles to show that they should be in juvenile court rather than adult court.

"Vermont permits juvenile judges to waive kids as young as 10 into criminal court. In Montana it's 12, and in Georgia, Illinois and Mississippi it's 13, according to a 1987 survey. Many laws set age limits by type of offense. In New York, 14-year-olds are regularly tried as adults."

after "full investigation" and assigned his case to a federal court. Jurisdiction was waived; he was indicted and convicted. The Supreme Court held that such waivers were invalid unless the juvenile received a hearing and his counsel had access to social records and probation reports. Moreover, the juvenile court had to give reasons for a waiver. Under the system existing at that time, a child received "the worst of both worlds: that he gets neither the protections accorded to adults nor the solicitous care and regenerative treatment postulated for children." Kent v. United States, 383 U.S. 541, 556 (1966).

After these ad hoc efforts to protect the rights of juveniles, the Court took a more comprehensive approach in 1967. Gerald Gault, a fifteen-year-old, was taken into custody for allegedly making obscene phone calls. No notice was left at his home for his parents. After hearings, a juvenile court committed him to the State Industrial School until he reached majority (a commitment of almost six years). No appeal was permitted by state law for juvenile cases. The Supreme Court held that minors are entitled to certain procedural rights: adequate notice, right to counsel, privilege against self-incrimination, and the rights of confrontation and sworn testimony. IN RE GAULT, 387 U.S. 1 (1967). Many of the requirements of *Gault* are not being met in contemporary juvenile courts (see box).

Closely resembling this case was the decision of a state family court to place a twelve-year-old boy in a "training school" for up to six years for stealing $112 from a woman's pocketbook. The Supreme Court held that when a juvenile is charged with an act that would constitute a crime if committed by an adult, due process requires proof beyond a reasonable doubt during the adjudicatory phase. The family court had relied on a preponderance of the evidence. In re Winship, 397 U.S. 358 (1970).

Other rights have been recognized for juveniles. A case in 1975 involved a youth who had been prosecuted as an adult following a finding in juvenile court that he violated a criminal law and was unfit for treatment as a juvenile. The Supreme Court held that the procedure violated the Double Jeopardy Clause. Breed v. Jones, 421 U.S. 519 (1975). Questions also concern the *Miranda* warning, Fare v. Michael C., 442 U.S. 707 (1979), and pretrial detention for juvenile delinquents, Schall v. Martin, 467 U.S. 253 (1984).

In extending these rights to juveniles, the Court decided that a jury trial is not constitutionally required for a state juvenile court delinquency proceeding. At least in this area, the Court was "reluctant to disallow the States to experiment further and to seek in new and different ways the elusive answers to the problems of the young...." McKeiver v. Pennsylvania, 403 U.S. 528, 547 (1971). In 1988 the Supreme Court vacated the death sentence of someone who had participated in a murder at age fifteen. However, a majority of the Court did not agree that the Constitution prohibits the execution of persons who were under sixteen at the time of the offense. Although there appears to be a national consensus against executing such minors, the Court allowed state legislatures leeway in determining standards and punishment. Thompson v. Oklahoma, 487 U.S. 815 (1988).

A year later, five Justices of the Supreme Court affirmed the death sentence for Kevin Stanford (seventeen at the time he committed murder) and Heath Wilkins (sixteen when he committed murder). In its search for objective criteria to decide the constitutional issue, the Court looked to statutes passed by state legislatures. As Justice Scalia noted with his usual crisp style: "The audience for these arguments, in other words, is not this Court but the citizenry of the United States. It is they, not we, who must be persuaded.... [O]ur job is to *identify* the 'evolving standards of decency'; to determine, not what they *should* be, but what they *are*." Justice O'Connor joined the majority but wrote a concurrence rejecting Scalia's deference to majority opinion. The Court, she said, has a constitutional obligation to determine that a punishment is proportional to the crime. Stanford v. Kentucky, 492 U.S. 361 (1989).

Students' Rights

School authorities and judges have wrestled with novel questions about a student's rights to free speech, due process, protection against cruel and unusual punishment (corporal punishment), and the scope of search and seizure on school premises.

In a leading First Amendment case, public school children were suspended from a junior high school for wearing black arm bands to protest the Vietnam War. The Court held that their conduct—quiet and not disruptive—was protected by the Free Speech Clause of the First Amendment and the Due Process Clause of the Fourteenth Amendment. TINKER v. DES MOINES SCHOOL DIST., 393 U.S. 503 (1969). In deciding which books to remove from school libraries, a board of education may not suppress ideas and impose an orthodoxy. Board of Education v. Pico, 457 U.S. 853 (1982). High school students have successfully resorted to lawsuits to gain the right to hold religious club meetings in school rooms. Bender v. Williamsport Area School Dist., 475 U.S. 534 (1986). Many other issues of religious activities in school, including prayers at football games and the Equal Access Act, are treated in Chapter 12.

Juveniles do not automatically gain access to First Amendment rights available to adults. States may restrict minors under seventeen from reading materials that are not obscene for adults. Ginsberg v. New York, 390 U.S. 629 (1968). Schools may discipline students for lewd and indecent speech that would be impermissible for adults. Bethel School Dist. No.

403 v. Fraser, 478 U.S. 675 (1986). School officials may delete from student newspapers articles or stories that might identify and embarrass certain students (such as pregnant students) or that are one-sided accounts critical of parents. Schools can exercise editorial control over the style and content of student speech in school-sponsored newspapers so long as the control is reasonably related to legitimate educational concerns. Hazelwood School District v. Kulhmeier, 484 U.S. 260 (1988). In response to this restrictive ruling on students' rights, some states have begun to pass legislation that permits greater freedom of speech by students.

Before students can be suspended from public school, they must be given an informal opportunity to be heard. On the basis of state law, students have legitimate claims of entitlement to a public education, and this entitlement is a property interest protected by the Due Process Clause. "Neither the property interest in educational benefits temporarily denied nor the liberty interest in reputation, which is also implicated, is so insubstantial that suspensions may constitutionally be imposed by any procedure the school chooses, no matter how arbitrary." Goss v. Lopez, 419 U.S. 565, 576 (1975).

The Court split 5–4 on this decision and divided by the same margin in holding that the Cruel and Unusual Punishment Clause does not apply to disciplinary corporal punishments in public schools. A state law authorized a wooden paddle applied against the buttocks. The evidence in this case showed that the paddling was exceptionally harsh, keeping the child out of school for several days. Nevertheless, the Court held that the Eighth Amendment deals only with criminal punishments. Ingraham v. Wright, 430 U.S. 651 (1977).

Another issue is search and seizure. In 1985 the Court decided that the Fourth Amendment applies to minors on public school property. Although teachers need not obtain a warrant or adhere to the probable-cause requirement, their actions must be reasonable under the circumstances in order to search students. NEW JERSEY v. T.L.O, 469 U.S. 325 (1985). For the use of German shepherds to perform "sniff tests" while searching students for drugs in junior and senior high schools, see Doe v. Renfrow, 451 U.S. 1022 (1981).

The T.L.O. decision was further developed in 1995 when the Court upheld an Oregon school district's policy that required junior high students interested in participating in sports to provide urine samples as a means of testing for drug use. Athletes are tested at the beginning of the season for their sport and thereafter on a random basis. No suspicion of drug use is necessary. Safeguards are taken to protect student privacy. The Court sustained the Oregon policy because (1) it applies to children and (2) the children are committed to the temporary custody of the State as schoolmaster. As the Court noted, Fourth Amendment rights, "no less than First and Fourteenth Amendment rights, are different in public schools than elsewhere." Vernonia School Dist. v. Acton, 515 U.S. 646 (1995). In 1997, the Court let stand an 11th Circuit ruling that second-graders may be strip-searched to investigate the theft of $7 from a classmate. Jenkins v. Herring, 522 U.S. 966 (1997).

Other decisions on the rights of juveniles, involving questions of abortion and privacy, are reserved for the next chapter.

In re Gault

387 U.S. 1 (1967)

Gerald Gault, fifteen years old, was taken into custody for allegedly making obscene phone calls to a woman. The police did not leave notice with his parents. After hearings before a juvenile court judge, he was ordered committed to the State Industrial School as a juvenile delinquent until he reached the age of majority (age twenty-one). His parents challenged the constitutionality of the Arizona Juvenile Code and the procedures used in Ger-

ald's case. The Supreme Court of Arizona concluded that the proceedings that led to Gault's commitment did not offend due process requirements.

MR. JUSTICE FORTAS delivered the opinion of the Court.

. . .

I.

On Monday, June 8, 1964, at about 10 A.M., Gerald Francis Gault and a friend, Ronald Lewis, were taken into custody by the Sheriff of Gila County. Gerald was then still subject to a six months' probation order which had been entered on February 25, 1964, as a result of his having been in the company of another boy who had stolen a wallet from a lady's purse. The police action on June 8 was taken as the result of a verbal complaint by a neighbor of the boys, Mrs. Cook, about a telephone call made to her in which the caller or callers made lewd or indecent remarks. It will suffice for purposes of this opinion to say that the remarks or questions put to her were of the irritatingly offensive, adolescent, sex variety.

At the time Gerald was picked up, his mother and father were both at work. No notice that Gerald was being taken into custody was left at the home. No other steps were taken to advise them that their son had, in effect, been arrested. Gerald was taken to the Children's Detention Home. When his mother arrived home at about 6 o'-clock, Gerald was not there. Gerald's older brother was sent to look for him at the trailer home of the Lewis family. He apparently learned then that Gerald was in custody. He so informed his mother. The two of them went to the Detention Home. The deputy probation officer, Flagg, who was also superintendent of the Detention Home, told Mrs. Gault "why Jerry was there" and said that a hearing would be held in Juvenile Court at 3 o'clock the following day, June 9.

Officer Flagg filed a petition with the court on the hearing day, June 9, 1964. It was not served on the Gaults. Indeed, none of them saw this petition until the habeas corpus hearing on August 17, 1964. The petition was entirely formal. It made no reference to any factual basis for the judicial action which it initiated. It recited only that "said minor is under the age of eighteen years, and is in need of the protection of this Honorable Court; [and that] said minor is a delinquent minor." It prayed for a hearing and an order regarding "the care and custody of said minor." Officer Flagg executed a formal affidavit in support of the petition.

On June 9, Gerald, his mother, his older brother, and Probation Officers Flagg and Henderson appeared before the Juvenile Judge in chambers. Gerald's father was not there. He was at work out of the city. Mrs. Cook, the complainant, was not there. No one was sworn at this hearing. No transcript or recording was made. No memorandum or record of the substance of the proceedings was prepared. Our information about the proceedings and the subsequent hearing on June 15, derives entirely from the testimony of the Juvenile Court Judge, Mr. and Mrs. Gault and Officer Flagg at the habeas corpus proceeding conducted two months later. From this, it appears that at the June 9 hearing Gerald was questioned by the judge about the telephone call. There was conflict as to what he said. His mother recalled that Gerald said he only dialed Mrs. Cook's number and handed the telephone to his friend, Ronald. Officer Flagg recalled that Gerald had admitted making the lewd remarks. Judge McGhee testified that Gerald "admitted making one of these [lewd] statements." At the conclusion of the hearing, the judge said he would "think about it." Gerald was taken back to the Detention Home. He was not sent to his own home with his parents. On June 11 or 12, after having been detained since June 8, Gerald was released and driven home. There is no explanation in the record as to why he was kept in the Detention Home or why he was released. At 5 P.M. on the day of Gerald's release, Mrs. Gault received a note signed by Officer Flagg. It was on plain paper, not letterhead. Its entire text was as follows:

"Mrs. Gault:

"Judge McGHEE has set Monday June 15, 1964 at 11:00 A.M. as the date and time for further Hearings on Gerald's delinquency

"/s/Flagg"

At the appointed time on Monday, June 15, Gerald, his father and mother, Ronald Lewis and his father, and Officers Flagg and Henderson were present before Judge McGhee. Witnesses at the habeas corpus proceeding differed in their recollections of Gerald's testimony at the June 15 hearing. Mr. and Mrs. Gault recalled that Gerald again testified that he had only dialed the number and that the other boy had made the remarks. Officer Flagg agreed that at this hearing Gerald did not admit making the lewd remarks. But Judge

McGhee recalled that "there was some admission again of some of the lewd statements. He—he didn't admit any of the more serious lewd statements." Again, the complainant, Mrs. Cook, was not present. Mrs. Gault asked that Mrs. Cook be present "so she could see which boy that done the talking, the dirty talking over the phone." The Juvenile Judge said "she didn't have to be present at that hearing." The judge did not speak to Mrs. Cook or communicate with her at any time. Probation Officer Flagg had talked to her once—over the telephone on June 9.

At this June 15 hearing a "referral report" made by the probation officers was filed with the court, although not disclosed to Gerald or his parents. This listed the charge as "Lewd Phone Calls." At the conclusion of the hearing, the judge committed Gerald as a juvenile delinquent to the State Industrial School "for the period of his minority [that is, until 21], unless sooner discharged by due process of law." ...

No appeal is permitted by Arizona law in juvenile cases....

II.

. . .

From the inception of the juvenile court system, wide differences have been tolerated—indeed insisted upon—between the procedural rights accorded to adults and those of juveniles. In practically all jurisdictions, there are rights granted to adults which are withheld from juveniles. In addition to the specific problems involved in the present case, for example, it has been held that the juvenile is not entitled to bail, to indictment by grand jury, to a public trial or to trial by jury. It is frequent practice that rules governing the arrest and interrogation of adults by the police are not observed in the case of juveniles.

The history and theory underlying this development are well-known, but a recapitulation is necessary for purposes of this opinion. The Juvenile Court movement began in this country at the end of the last century. From the juvenile court statute adopted in Illinois in 1899, the system has spread to every State in the Union, the District of Columbia, and Puerto Rico. The constitutionality of Juvenile Court laws has been sustained in over 40 jurisdictions against a variety of attacks.

The early reformers were appalled by adult procedures and penalties, and by the fact that children could be given long prison sentences and mixed in jails with hardened criminals. They were profoundly convinced that society's duty to the child could not be confined by the concept of justice alone. They believed that society's role was not to ascertain whether the child was "guilty" or "innocent," but "What is he, how has he become what he is, and what had best be done in his interest and in the interest of the state to save him from a downward career." The child—essentially good, as they saw it—was to be made "to feel that he is the object of [the state's] care and solicitude," not that he was under arrest or on trial. The rules of criminal procedure were therefore altogether inapplicable. The apparent rigidities, technicalities, and harshness which they observed in both substantive and procedural criminal law were therefore to be discarded. The idea of crime and punishment was to be abandoned. The child was to be "treated" and "rehabilitated" and the procedures, from apprehension through institutionalization, were to be "clinical" rather than punitive.

These results were to be achieved, without coming to conceptual and constitutional grief, by insisting that the proceedings were not adversary, but that the state was proceeding as *parens patriae*. The Latin phrase proved to be a great help to those who sought to rationalize the exclusion of juveniles from the constitutional scheme; but its meaning is murky and its historic credentials are of dubious relevance. The phrase was taken from chancery practice, where, however, it was used to describe the power of the state to act *in loco parentis* for the purpose of protecting the property interests and the person of the child. But there is no trace of the doctrine in the history of criminal jurisprudence. At common law, children under seven were considered incapable of possessing criminal intent. Beyond that age, they were subjected to arrest, trial, and in theory to punishment like adult offenders....

. . .

If Gerald had been over 18, he would not have been subject to Juvenile Court proceedings. For the particular offense immediately involved, the maximum punishment would have been a fine of $5 to $50, or imprisonment in jail for not more than two months. Instead, he was committed to custody for a maximum of six years. If he had been over 18 and had committed an offense to which such a sentence might apply, he would have been entitled to substantial rights under the Constitution of the United States as well as under Arizona's laws and constitution. The United States

Constitution would guarantee him rights and protections with respect to arrest, search and seizure, and pretrial interrogation. It would assure him of specific notice of the charges and adequate time to decide his course of action and to prepare his defense. He would be entitled to clear advice that he could be represented by counsel, and, at least if a felony were involved, the State would be required to provide counsel if his parents were unable to afford it. If the court acted on the basis of his confession, careful procedures would be required to assure its voluntariness. If the case went to trial, confrontation and opportunity for cross-examination would be guaranteed....

· · ·

III.

NOTICE OF CHARGES.

· · ·

We cannot agree with the...conclusion that adequate notice was given in this case. Notice, to comply with due process requirements, must be given sufficiently in advance of scheduled court proceedings so that reasonable opportunity to prepare will be afforded, and it must "set forth the alleged misconduct with particularity."...

IV.

RIGHT TO COUNSEL.

· · ·

We conclude that the Due Process Clause of the Fourteenth Amendment requires that in respect of proceedings to determine delinquency which may result in commitment to an institution in which the juvenile's freedom is curtailed, the child and his parents must be notified of the child's right to be represented by counsel retained by them, or if they are unable to afford counsel, that counsel will be appointed to represent the child.

· · ·

V.

CONFRONTATION, SELF-INCRIMINATION, CROSS-EXAMINATION.

· · ·

We conclude that the constitutional privilege against self-incrimination is applicable in the case of juveniles as it is with respect to adults. We appreciate that special problems may arise with respect to waiver of the privilege by or on behalf of children, and that there may well be some differences in technique — but not in principle — depending upon the age of the child and the presence and competence of parents. The participation of counsel will, of course, assist the police, Juvenile Courts and appellate tribunals in administering the privilege. If counsel was not present for some permissible reason when an admission was obtained, the greatest care must be taken to assure that the admission was voluntary, in the sense not only that it was not coerced or suggested, but also that it was not the product of ignorance of rights or of adolescent fantasy, fright or despair.

...Mrs. Cook, the complainant, was not present. The Arizona Supreme Court held that "sworn testimony must be required of all witnesses including police officers, probation officers and others who are part of or officially related to the juvenile court structure." We hold that this is not enough. No reason is suggested or appears for a different rule in respect of sworn testimony in juvenile courts than in adult tribunals. Absent a valid confession adequate to support the determination of the Juvenile Court, confrontation and sworn testimony by witnesses available for cross-examination were essential for a finding of "delinquency" and an order committing Gerald to a state institution for a maximum of six years.

· · ·

VI.

APPELLATE REVIEW AND TRANSCRIPT OF PROCEEDINGS.

· · ·

This Court has not held that a State is required by the Federal Constitution "to provide appellate courts or a right to appellate review at all." In view of the fact that we must reverse the Supreme Court of Arizona's affirmance of the dismissal of the writ of habeas corpus for other reasons, we need not rule on this question in the present case or upon the failure to provide a transcript or recording of the hearings — or, indeed, the failure of the Juvenile Judge to state the grounds for his conclusion....

For the reasons stated, the judgment of the Supreme Court of Arizona is reversed and the cause remanded for further proceedings not inconsistent with this opinion.

It is so ordered.

MR. JUSTICE BLACK, concurring.

. . .

MR. JUSTICE WHITE, concurring.

I join the Court's opinion except for Part V....

MR. JUSTICE HARLAN, concurring in part and dissenting in part.

[Justice Harlan agreed that juvenile courts must give timely notice, counsel must be present (appointed by the court, if necessary), and a written record must be maintained of the proceedings. He disagreed with the Court's analysis of self-incrimination, confrontation, and cross-examination.]

MR. JUSTICE STEWART, dissenting.

The Court today uses an obscure Arizona case as a vehicle to impose upon thousands of juvenile courts throughout the Nation restrictions that the Constitution made applicable to adversary criminal trials. I believe the Court's decision is wholly unsound as a matter of constitutional law, and sadly unwise as a matter of judicial policy.

Juvenile proceedings are not criminal trials. They are not civil trials. They are simply not adversary proceedings. Whether treating with a delinquent child, a neglected child, a defective child, or a dependent child, a juvenile proceeding's whole purpose and mission is the very opposite of the mission and purpose of a prosecution in a criminal court. The object of the one is correction of a condition. The object of the other is conviction and punishment for a criminal act.

. . .

Tinker v. Des Moines School Dist.

393 U.S. 503 (1969)

In the midst of the Vietnam War, three public school students were suspended from school for wearing black arm bands to protest U.S. involvement. They claimed that their protest, which was quiet and nondisruptive, was protected by the Free Speech Clause of the First Amendment. The school argued that school discipline and questions of suspension were within the power and jurisdiction of school authorities. A federal district court upheld the school's policy, and that ruling was affirmed by an equally divided Eighth Circuit.

MR. JUSTICE FORTAS delivered the opinion of the Court.

Petitioner John F. Tinker, 15 years old, and petitioner Christopher Eckhardt, 16 years old, attended high schools in Des Moines, Iowa. Petitioner Mary Beth Tinker, John's sister, was a 13-year-old student in junior high school.

In December 1965, a group of adults and students in Des Moines held a meeting at the Eckhardt home. The group determined to publicize their objections to the hostilities in Vietnam and their support for a truce by wearing black armbands during the holiday season and by fasting on December 16 and New Year's Eve. Petitioners and their parents had previously engaged in similar activities, and they decided to participate in the program.

The principals of the Des Moines schools became aware of the plan to wear armbands. On December 14, 1965, they met and adopted a policy that any student wearing an armband to school would be asked to remove it, and if he refused he would be suspended until he returned without the armband. Petitioners were aware of the regulation that the school authorities adopted.

On December 16, Mary Beth and Christopher wore black armbands to their schools. John Tinker wore his armband the next day. They were all sent home and suspended from school until they would come back without their armbands. They did not return to school until after the planned period for wearing armbands had expired—that is, until after New Year's Day.

. . .

I.

The District Court recognized that the wearing of an armband for the purpose of expressing certain views is the type of symbolic act that is within the Free Speech Clause of the First Amendment.... As we shall discuss, the wearing of armbands in the circumstances of this case was entirely divorced from actually or potentially disruptive conduct by those participating in it. It was closely akin to "pure speech" which, we have repeatedly held, is entitled to comprehensive protection under the First Amendment....

First Amendment rights, applied in light of the special characteristics of the school environment, are available to teachers and students. It can hardly be argued that either students or teachers shed their constitutional rights to freedom of speech or expression at the schoolhouse gate. This has been the unmistakable holding of this Court for almost 50 years....

. . .

...On the other hand, the Court has repeatedly emphasized the need for affirming the comprehensive authority of the States and of school officials, consistent with fundamental constitutional safeguards, to prescribe and control conduct in the schools.... Our problem lies in the area where students in the exercise of First Amendment rights collide with the rules of the school authorities.

II.

The problem posed by the present case does not relate to regulation of the length of skirts or the type of clothing, to hair style, or deportment.... It does not concern aggressive, disruptive action or even group demonstrations. Our problem involves direct, primary First Amendment rights akin to "pure speech."

...[T]he school authorities did not purport to prohibit the wearing of all symbols of political or controversial significance. The record shows that students in some of the schools wore buttons relating to national political campaigns, and some even wore the Iron Cross, traditionally a symbol of Nazism. The order prohibiting the wearing of armbands did not extend to these. Instead, a particular symbol — black armbands worn to exhibit opposition to this Nation's involvement in Vietnam — was singled out for prohibition. Clearly, the prohibition of expression of one particular opinion, at least without evidence that it is necessary to avoid material and substantial interference with schoolwork or discipline, is not constitutionally permissible.

In our system, state-operated schools may not be enclaves of totalitarianism. School officials do not possess absolute authority over their students. Students in school as well as out of school are "persons" under our Constitution. They are possessed of fundamental rights which the State must respect, just as they themselves must respect

their obligations to the State. In our system, students may not be regarded as closed-circuit recipients of only that which the State chooses to communicate. They may not be confined to the expression of those sentiments that are officially approved....

As we have discussed, the record does not demonstrate any facts which might reasonably have led school authorities to forecast substantial disruption of or material interference with school activities, and no disturbances or disorders on the school premises in fact occurred. These petitioners merely went about their ordained rounds in school. Their deviation consisted only in wearing on their sleeve a band of black cloth, not more than two inches wide. They wore it to exhibit their disapproval of the Vietnam hostilities and their advocacy of a truce, to make their views known, and, by their example, to influence others to adopt them. They neither interrupted school activities nor sought to intrude in the school affairs or the lives of others. They caused discussion outside of the classrooms, but no interference with work and no disorder. In the circumstances, our Constitution does not permit officials of the State to deny their form of expression.

We express no opinion as to the form of relief which should be granted, this being a matter for the lower courts to determine. We reverse and remand for further proceedings consistent with this opinion.

Reversed and remanded.

MR. JUSTICE STEWART, concurring.

. . .

MR. JUSTICE WHITE, concurring.

. . .

MR. JUSTICE BLACK, dissenting.

The Court's holding in this case ushers in what I deem to be an entirely new era in which the power to control pupils by the elected "officials of state supported public schools..." in the United States is in ultimate effect transferred to the Supreme Court....

While the record does not show that any of these armband students shouted, used profane language, or were violent in any manner, detailed testimony by some of them shows their armbands caused comments, warnings by other students, the poking of fun at them, and a warning by an older football player that other, nonprotesting students had better let them alone. There is also evidence that a teacher of mathematics had his lesson period practically "wrecked" chiefly by disputes with Mary Beth Tinker, who wore her armband for her "demonstration." Even a casual reading of the record shows that this armband did divert students' minds from their regular lessons, and that talk, comments, etc., made John Tinker "self-conscious" in attending school with his armband. While the absence of obscene remarks or boisterous and loud disorder perhaps justifies the Court's statement that the few armband students did not actually "disrupt" the classwork, I think the record overwhelmingly shows that the armbands did exactly what the elected school officials and principals foresaw they would, that is, took the students' minds off their classwork and diverted them to thoughts about the highly emotional subject of the Vietnam war. And I repeat that if the time has come when pupils of state-supported schools, kindergartens, grammar schools, or high schools, can defy and flout orders of school officials to keep their minds on their own schoolwork, it is the beginning of a new revolutionary era of permissiveness in this country fostered by the judiciary....

. . .

...This case, therefore, wholly without constitutional reasons in my judgment, subjects all the public schools in the country to the whims and caprices of their loudest-mouthed, but maybe not their brightest, students. I, for one, am not fully persuaded that school pupils are wise enough, even with this Court's expert help from Washington, to run the 23,390 public school systems in our 50 States. I wish, therefore, wholly to disclaim any purpose on my part to hold that the Federal Constitution compels the teachers, parents, and elected school officials to surrender control of the American public school system to public school students. I dissent.

MR. JUSTICE HARLAN, dissenting.

I certainly agree that state public school authorities in the discharge of their responsibilities are not wholly exempt from the requirements of the Fourteenth Amendment respecting the freedoms of expression and association. At the same time I am reluctant to believe that there is any disagreement between the majority and myself on the proposition that school officials should be accorded the widest authority in maintaining discipline and good order in their institutions. To translate that proposition into a workable constitutional rule, I would, in cases like this, cast upon those complaining the burden of showing that a particular school measure was motivated by other than legitimate school concerns—for example, a desire to prohibit the expression of an unpopular point of view, while permitting expression of the dominant opinion.

Finding nothing in this record which impugns the good faith of respondents in promulgating the armband regulation, I would affirm the judgment below.

New Jersey v. T.L.O.

469 U.S. 325 (1985)

T.L.O., a fourteen-year-old high school freshman, was caught smoking in the school bathroom. After being taken to the Principal's office, she denied that she had been smoking and claimed that she did not smoke at all. The Assistant Vice Principal opened her purse, found a pack of cigarettes, and also noticed a package of cigarette rolling papers that are commonly associated with the use of marijuana. A thorough search of the purse uncovered some marijuana, a pipe, plastic bags, a fairly substantial amount of money, an index card containing a list of students who owed her money, and two letters that implicated her in marijuana dealing. The state of New Jersey brought delinquency charges against her in Juvenile Court. After denying her motion to suppress the evidence found in her purse, the court held that the Fourth Amendment applied to searches by school officials but that the search in question was a reasonable one. The Appellate Division of the New Jersey Superior Court affirmed that there had been no Fourth Amendment violation. The New Jersey Supreme Court reversed and ordered the suppression of the evidence on the ground that the search of the purse was unreasonable.

JUSTICE WHITE delivered the opinion of the Court.

We granted certiorari in this case to examine the appropriateness of the exclusionary rule as a remedy for searches carried out in violation of the Fourth Amendment by public school authorities. Our consideration of the proper application of the Fourth Amendment to the public schools, however, has led us to conclude that the search that gave rise to the case now before us did not violate the Fourth Amendment. Accordingly, we here address only the questions of the proper standard for assessing the legality of searches conducted by public school officials and the application of that standard to the facts of this case.

I

On March 7, 1980, a teacher at Piscataway High School in Middlesex County, N.J., discovered two girls smoking in a lavatory. One of the two girls was the respondent T.L.O., who at that time was a 14-year-old high school freshman. Because smoking in the lavatory was a violation of a school rule, the teacher took the two girls to the Principal's office, where they met with Assistant Vice Principal Theodore Choplick. In response to questioning by Mr. Choplick, T. L. O.'s companion admitted that she had violated the rule. T. L. O., however, denied that she had been smoking in the lavatory and claimed that she did not smoke at all.

Mr. Choplick asked T. L. O. to come into his private office and demanded to see her purse. Opening the purse, he found a pack of cigarettes, which he removed from the purse and held before T. L. O. as he accused her of having lied to him. As he reached into the purse for the cigarettes, Mr. Choplick also noticed a package of cigarette rolling papers. In his experience, possession of rolling papers by high school students was closely associated with the use of marihuana. Suspecting that a closer examination of the purse might yield further evidence of drug use, Mr. Choplick proceeded to search the purse thoroughly. The search revealed a small amount of marihuana, a pipe, a number of empty plastic bags, a substantial quantity of money in one-dollar bills, an index card that appeared to be a list of students who owed T. L. O. money, and two letters that implicated T. L. O. in marihuana dealing.

Mr. Choplick notified T. L. O.'s mother and the police, and turned the evidence of drug dealing over to the police. At the request of the police, T. L. O.'s mother took her daughter to police headquarters, where T. L. O. confessed that she had been selling marihuana at the high school. On the basis of the confession and the evidence seized by Mr. Choplick, the State brought delinquency charges against T. L. O. in the Juvenile and Domestic Relations Court of Middlesex County. Contending that Mr. Choplick's search of her purse violated the Fourth Amendment, T. L. O. moved to suppress the evidence found in her purse as well as her confession, which, she argued, was tainted by the allegedly unlawful search.

. . .

Although we originally granted certiorari to decide the issue of the appropriate remedy in juvenile court proceedings for unlawful school searches, our doubts regarding the wisdom of deciding that question in isolation from the broader question of what limits, if any, the Fourth Amendment places on the activities of school authorities prompted us to order reargument on that question. Having heard argument on the legality of the search of T. L. O.'s purse, we are satisfied that the search did not violate the Fourth Amendment.

II

In determining whether the search at issue in this case violated the Fourth Amendment, we are faced initially with the question whether that Amendment's prohibition on unreasonable searches and seizures applies to searches conducted by public school officials. We hold that it does.

. . .

These two propositions—that the Fourth Amendment applies to the States through the Fourteenth Amendment, and that the actions of public school officials are subject to the limits placed on state action by the Fourteenth Amendment—might appear sufficient to answer the suggestion that the Fourth Amendment does not proscribe unreasonable searches by school officials. On reargument, however, the State of New Jersey has argued that the history of the Fourth Amendment indicates that the Amendment was intended to regulate only searches and seizures carried out by law enforcement officers; accordingly, although public school officials are concededly state agents for purposes of the Fourteenth Amendment, the Fourth Amendment creates no rights enforceable against them.

It may well be true that the evil toward which the Fourth Amendment was primarily directed was the resurrection of the pre-Revolutionary practice of using general warrants or "writs of assistance" to authorize searches for contraband by officers of the Crown.... But this Court has never limited the Amendment's prohibition on unreasonable searches and seizures to operations conducted by the police. Rather, the Court has long spoken of the Fourth Amendment's strictures as restraints imposed upon "governmental action" — that is, "upon the activities of sovereign authority." ...

III

To hold that the Fourth Amendment applies to searches conducted by school authorities is only to begin the inquiry into the standards governing such searches.... On one side of the balance are arrayed the individual's legitimate expectations of privacy and personal security; on the other, the government's need for effective methods to deal with breaches of public order.

. . .

Although this Court may take notice of the difficulty of maintaining discipline in the public schools today, the situation is not so dire that students in the schools may claim no legitimate expectations of privacy....

...Students at a minimum must bring to school not only the supplies needed for their studies, but also keys, money, and the necessaries of personal hygiene and grooming. In addition, students may carry on their persons or in purses or wallets such nondisruptive yet highly personal items as photographs, letters, and diaries. Finally, students may have perfectly legitimate reasons to carry with them articles of property needed in connection with extracurricular or recreational activities. In short, schoolchildren may find it necessary to carry with them a variety of legitimate, noncontraband items, and there is no reason to conclude that they have necessarily waived all rights to privacy in such items merely by bringing them onto school grounds.

Against the child's interest in privacy must be set the substantial interest of teachers and administrators in maintaining discipline in the classroom and on school grounds. Maintaining order in the classroom has never been easy, but in recent years, school disorder has often taken particularly ugly forms: drug use and violent crime in the schools have become major social problems....

How, then, should we strike the balance between the schoolchild's legitimate expectations of privacy and the school's equally legitimate need to maintain an environment in which learning can take place? It is evident that the school setting requires some easing of the restrictions to which searches by public authorities are ordinarily subject. The warrant requirement, in particular, is unsuited to the school environment: requiring a teacher to obtain a warrant before searching a child suspected of an infraction of school rules (or of the criminal law) would unduly interfere with the maintenance of the swift and informal disciplinary procedures needed in the schools....

The school setting also requires some modification of the level of suspicion of illicit activity needed to justify a search. Ordinarily, a search — even one that may permissibly be carried out without a warrant — must be based upon "probable cause" to believe that a violation of the law has occurred.... However, "probable cause" is not an irreducible requirement of a valid search. The fundamental command of the Fourth Amendment is that searches and seizures be reasonable....

...Determining the reasonableness of any search involves a twofold inquiry: first, one must consider "whether the...action was justified at its inception," *Terry* v. *Ohio,* 392 U. S., at 20; second, one must determine whether the search as actually conducted "was reasonably related in scope to the circumstances which justified the interference in the first place," *ibid.* Under ordinary circumstances, a search of a student by a teacher or other school official will be "justified at its inception" when there are reasonable grounds for suspecting that the search will turn up evidence that the student has violated or is violating either the law or the rules of the school. Such a search will be permissible in its scope when the measures adopted are reasonably related to the objectives of the search and not excessively intrusive in light of the age and sex of the student and the nature of the infraction.

. . .

IV

There remains the question of the legality of the search in this case....

...T. L. O. had been accused of smoking, and had denied the accusation in the strongest possible terms when she stated that she did not smoke at all. Surely it cannot be said that under these circumstances, T. L. O.'s possession of cigarettes would be irrelevant to the charges against her or to her response to those charges. T. L. O.'s possession of cigarettes, once it was discovered, would both corroborate the report that she had been smoking and undermine the credibility of her defense to the charge of smoking....

Our conclusion that Mr. Choplick's decision to open T. L. O.'s purse was reasonable brings us to the question of the further search for marihuana once the pack of cigarettes was located. The suspicion upon which the search for marihuana was founded was provided when Mr. Choplick observed a package of rolling papers in the purse as he removed the pack of cigarettes. Although T. L. O. does not dispute the reasonableness of Mr. Choplick's belief that the rolling papers indicated the presence of marihuana, she does contend that the scope of the search Mr. Choplick conducted exceeded permissible bounds when he seized and read certain letters that implicated T. L. O. in drug dealing. This argument, too, is unpersuasive. The discovery of the rolling papers concededly gave rise to a reasonable suspicion that T. L. O. was carrying marihuana as well as cigarettes in her purse. This suspicion justified further exploration of T. L. O.'s purse, which turned up more evidence of drug-related activities: a pipe, a number of plastic bags of the type commonly used to store marihuana, a small quantity of marihuana, and a fairly substantial amount of money. Under these circumstances, it was not unreasonable to extend the search to a separate zippered compartment of the purse; and when a search of that compartment revealed an index card containing a list of "people who owe me money" as well as two letters, the inference that T. L. O. was involved in marihuana trafficking was substantial enough to justify Mr. Choplick in examining the letters to determine whether they contained any further evidence. In short, we cannot conclude that the search for marihuana was unreasonable in any respect.

Because the search resulting in the discovery of the evidence of marijuana dealing by T. L. O. was reasonable, the New Jersey Supreme Court's decision to exclude that evidence from T. L. O.'s juvenile delinquency proceedings on Fourth Amendment grounds was erroneous. Accordingly, the judgment of the Supreme Court of New Jersey is

Reversed.

JUSTICE POWELL, with whom JUSTICE O'CONNOR joins, concurring.

. . .

JUSTICE BLACKMUN, concurring in the judgment.

. . .

JUSTICE BRENNAN, with whom JUSTICE MARSHALL joins, concurring in part and dissenting in part.

I fully agree with Part II of the Court's opinion. Teachers, like all other government officials, must conform their conduct to the Fourth Amendment's protections of personal privacy and personal security....

I do not, however, otherwise join the Court's opinion. Today's decision sanctions school officials to conduct full-scale searches on a "reasonableness" standard whose only definite content is that it is *not* the same test as the "probable cause" standard found in the text of the Fourth Amendment. In adopting this unclear, unprecedented, and unnecessary departure from generally applicable Fourth Amendment standards, the Court carves out a broad exception to standards that this Court has developed over years of considering Fourth Amendment problems. Its decision is supported neither by precedent nor even by a fair application of the "balancing test" it proclaims in this very opinion.

. . .

JUSTICE STEVENS, with whom JUSTICE MARSHALL joins, and with whom JUSTICE BRENNAN joins as to Part I, concurring in part and dissenting in part.

. . .

...The Court has...seized upon this "no smoking" case to announce "the proper standard" that should govern searches by school officials who are confronted with disciplinary problems far more severe than smoking in the restroom. Although I join Part II of the Court's opinion, I continue to believe that the Court has unnecessarily and inappropriately reached out to decide a constitutional question. See 468 U. S. 1214 (1984) (STEVENS, J., dissenting from reargument order). More importantly, I fear that the concerns that motivated the Court's activism have produced a holding that will permit school administrators to search students suspected of violating only the most trivial school regulations and guidelines for behavior.

. . .

D. PRISONERS' RIGHTS

Prisoners and inmates of mental institutions were long kept in a constitutional backwater. Legislators had little incentive to provide adequate funds for shelter, food, clothing, and medical care. Constituents were content, perhaps out of ignorance, to have public funds spent elsewhere.[6] Congressman Robert Kastenmeier reflected on his service as chairman of the Subcommittee on Corrections of the House Judiciary Committee: "[F]ew organizations have lobbied for prison reform. This apparent lack of interest creates little external pressure for action, while there is growing and vocal opposition to penal reform based on the widespread sentiment that high crime rates can only be reduced by long and harsh incarceration."[7] Because of the crimes they committed, prisoners were considered undeserving of even minimal care. At one time in our history, an inmate in a penitentiary was considered "the slave of the State." Ruffin v. Commonwealth, 62 Va. 790, 796 (1871).

Litigation has been the chief instrument for initiating prison reform. In the 1960s, professional journals began to focus on the primitive conditions in mental hospitals and prisons. Out of these studies came the concept of a right to treatment for institutionalized persons. U.S. Judge David Bazelon pioneered some of the reforms in mental hospitals, ruling in 1966 that a failure to provide suitable treatment would justify a patient's release. Rouse v. Cameron, 373 F.2d 451 (D.C. Cir. 1966). A few years later, U.S. Judge Frank Johnson held that inadequate treatment for institutionalized persons represented a violation of the basic fundamentals of due process. Wyatt v. Stickney, 325 F.Supp. 781 (M.D. Ala. 1971). It is difficult to criticize Johnson's efforts as an exercise in "judicial activism." The counsel for the state admitted in open court that the evidence conclusively established violations of the Eighth Amendment rights of prisoners. Pugh v. Locke, 406 F.Supp. 318, 322, 329 n.13 (M.D. Ala. 1976). (For additional material on Johnson's efforts, see p. 21.)

Even before the attention devoted to prisoner rights in recent years, certain rights were conceded. States cannot impair a prisoner's right to apply to the federal courts for a writ of habeas corpus.[8] Prisoners must be given a reasonable opportunity to pursue their religious faith, but prison officials are not expected to sacrifice their legitimate objectives in accommodating every religious need.[9] Prisoners may not be segregated by race. Lee v. Washington, 390 U.S. 333 (1968). A prisoner's desire to marry may not be prevented by prison regulations that rely on an exaggerated and unreasonable concern for security.[10]

---

6. For basic cases on the rights of inmates in mental institutions, see Foucha v. Louisiana, 504 U.S. 71 (1992); Youngberg v. Romeo, 457 U.S. 307 (1982); Mills v. Rogers, 457 U.S. 291 (1982); Vitek v. Jones, 445 U.S. 480 (1980); Secretary of Public Welfare v. Institutionalized Juveniles, 442 U.S. 640 (1979); Parham v. J.R., 442 U.S. 584 (1979); O'Connor v. Donaldson, 422 U.S. 563 (1975).

7. Robert W. Kastenmeier, "The Legislator and the Legislature: Their Roles in Prison Reform," in Michele G. Hermann and Marilyn G. Haft, eds., Prisoners' Rights Sourcebook 456 (1973).

8. Ex parte Hull, 312 U.S. 546 (1941); Johnson v. Avery, 393 U.S. 483 (1969). See also Procunier v. Martinez, 416 U.S. 396 (1974), in which the Court held that a ban on attorney-client interviews conducted by law students or paralegals constituted an unjustifiable restriction on the inmates' right of access to the courts. States must even assist inmates in preparing and filing legal papers by providing adequate law libraries and assistance from persons trained in the law. Bounds v. Smith, 430 U.S. 817 (1977). The Court restricted Bounds in 1996 by holding that prisoners who seek access to a law library or legal assistance must demonstrate that they are pursuing a nonfrivolous legal claim. Inmates do not have a right to file any and every type of legal claim. They need only the tools to attack their sentences and to challenge the conditions of their confinement. Lewis v. Casey, 518 U.S. 343 (1996).

9. O'Lone v. Estate of Shabazz, 482 U.S. 342 (1987); Cruz v. Beto, 405 U.S. 319 (1972); Cooper v. Pate, 378 U.S. 333 (1968).

10. Turner v. Safley, 482 U.S. 78 (1987); Butler v. Wilson, 415 U.S. 953 (1974), aff'g, Johnson v. Rockefeller, 365 F.Supp. 377 (S.D. N.Y. 1973).

Due Process Protections

Beginning in the early 1970s, the Supreme Court announced a series of new rights for prisoners and parolees. Authorities may no longer revoke paroles and return a person to prison without an informal hearing. The parolee must be given written notice of claimed violations, the evidence against him, an opportunity to be heard, to present witnesses and evidence, and to confront and cross-examine adverse witnesses. Morrissey v. Brewer, 408 U.S. 471 (1972). These procedural protections also apply to those under the status of "pre-parole" (persons released to reduce prison overcrowding). Young v. Harper, 520 U.S. 143 (1997). Parole *revocation* is a serious deprivation of liberty, requiring procedural protections, but the possible *granting* of parole does not create the same entitlement of due process. Greenholtz v. Nebraska Penal Inmates, 442 U.S. 1 (1979).

Due process does not require a state prisoner to be given a hearing simply because he is being transferred to a prison with less favorable conditions. Meachum v. Fano, 427 U.S. 215 (1976); Montanye v. Haymes, 427 U.S. 236 (1976); Olim v. Wakinekona, 461 U.S. 238 (1983). Only informal, nonadversary review is required before placing a prisoner in confinement, provided he receives notice of the charges and has an opportunity to present his views. Hewitt v. Helms, 459 U.S. 460 (1983).

If a state creates the right to "good time" credits (to reduce a sentence), a prisoner is entitled to minimal procedures to ensure that this right is not arbitrarily abrogated. The prisoner must be given advance written notice of the claimed violation, a statement of the evidence, and the reasons for the disciplinary action. The inmate has a right to call witnesses and to present evidence; there is no right of confrontation and cross-examination. Wolff v. McDonnell, 418 U.S. 539 (1974).[11] The *Wolff* standards divided the Court 5 to 4 in 1995 when it held that the Due Process Clause did not afford a prisoner a protected liberty interest to prevent prison officials from denying him the right to present witnesses during a disciplinary hearing that led to segregated confinement. Sandin v. Conner, 515 U.S. 472 (1995).

In 1990, the Court divided 6 to 3 in holding that mentally ill prisoners are not entitled to a judicial hearing before the state administers antipsychotic drugs against their will. These drugs can have serious, even fatal, side effects. Prisoners are entitled to certain rights from prison officials, such as the right to notice of a hearing on the decision to administer the drugs and the right to attend, present evidence, and cross-examine witnesses. Washington v. Harper, 494 U.S. 210 (1990). In 1992, a 7–2 Court held that a state judge erred in forcing a criminal defendant to take an antipsychotic drug during a trial, in which his insanity defense was unsuccessful. The error was a narrow one; the Court only insisted that the judge should have made a determination of the need for the medication and should have made findings about reasonable alternatives. Riggins v. Nevada, 504 U.S. 127 (1992).

Prison Conditions

Prisoners do not have the same rights as other citizens regarding privacy and First Amendment freedoms. Their letters may be turned over and given to government officials. Stroud v.

---

11. In 1973, the Court held that prisoners who lose "good time" credits because of disciplinary reasons must use the remedy of a writ of habeas corpus. They were not allowed to rely on 42 U.S.C. § 1983 suits in an effort to circumvent the state courts. Preiser v. Rodriguez, 411 U.S. 475 (1973). Prisoners have brought § 1983 suits since that time, but not with successful results. O'Lone v. Estate of Shabazz, 482 U.S. 342 (1987); Whitley v. Albers, 475 U.S. 312 (1986); Davidson v. Cannon, 474 U.S. 344 (1986); Daniels v. Williams, 474 U.S. 327 (1986); Hudson v. Palmer, 468 U.S. 517 (1984); Rhodes v. Chapman, 452 U.S. 337 (1981); Parratt v. Taylor, 451 U.S. 527 (1981). A successful § 1983 suit was brought in Hudson v. McMillian, 503 U.S. 1 (1992). For subsequent actions under § 1983, see Heck v. Humphrey, 512 U.S. 477 (1994) and Edwards v. Balisok, 520 U.S. 641 (1997).

United States, 251 U.S. 15 (1919). Prison officials may censor or restrict personal correspondence if necessary for security, order, and the rehabilitation of inmates. Turner v. Safley, 482 U.S. 78 (1987); Procunier v. Martinez, 416 U.S. 396 (1974). The Supreme Court defers considerably to prison officials who monitor and exclude incoming publications that they find detrimental to the "security, good order, or discipline" of the institution. Prisoners have greater First Amendment rights with regard to *outgoing* correspondence because it presents less of a risk to institutional security. Thornburgh v. Abbott, 490 U.S. 401 (1989). Prisoners have no right to "contact visits" (physical touching) with their spouses, relatives, children, or friends. This privilege may be denied by prison officials concerned about the introduction of drugs, weapons, and other contraband. Block v. Rutherford, 468 U.S. 576 (1984). In deciding which visitors to exclude, prison officials are not bound by the Due Process Clause (such as providing a hearing before the exclusion). Kentucky Dept. of Corrections v. Thompson, 490 U.S. 454 (1989).

Conversations may be monitored and intercepted through electronic listening devices. Lanza v. New York, 370 U.S. 139 (1962). Because the Court holds that prisoners have no reasonable expectation of privacy in their prison cells, they are not entitled to Fourth Amendment protections against unreasonable searches. HUDSON v. PALMER, 468 U.S. 517 (1984); Block v. Rutherford, 468 U.S. 576 (1984).

Although the press has an interest in reporting on prison conditions, the government may prohibit interviews between news reporters and inmates in medium-security and maximum-security prisoners.[12] States may prohibit prisoners from soliciting other inmates to join the prisoners' labor union, from holding union meetings, and from making and receiving bulk mailings concerning the union. Jones v. North Carolina Prisoners' Union, 433 U.S. 119 (1977).

In some cases, the judiciary intervenes to put pressure on states to upgrade their prison facilities. The Supreme Court upheld a court order placing a maximum limit of thirty days for Arkansas' isolation cells. Confinement beyond that period constituted cruel and unusual punishment. Conditions in the Arkansas prisons, with a history of overcrowding, physical violence, and malnutrition, were described as "a dark and evil world completely alien to the free world." Hutto v. Finney, 437 U.S. 678, 681 (1978). Conditions in the Attica, N.Y., prison led to riots in 1971. By the end of the five-day uprising, eleven guards and 32 prisoners had died. After decades of litigation, New York agreed in 2000 to set aside $12 million: $8 million for the former inmates and $4 million for lawyers' fees.

For the most part, the judiciary defers to prison officials on questions of "double-bunking," body-cavity searches, and restrictions on incoming packages. BELL v. WOLFISH, 441 U.S. 520 (1979). See also Rhodes v. Chapman, 452 U.S. 337 (1981). Prison rules and regulations are not subject to strict-scrutiny analysis. The Court applies a lesser and more lenient standard of scrutiny. Turner v. Safley, 482 U.S. 78 (1987). The Court recognizes that running a prison "is an inordinately difficult undertaking that requires expertise, planning, and the commitment of resources, all of which are peculiarly within the province of the legislative and executive branches of government." Id. at 84–85 (see box).

In 1991, a 5–4 Court ruled that prisoners who file lawsuits regarding conditions in prison must overcome two hurdles: that the conditions constitute cruel and unusual punishment in violation of the Eighth Amendment and that prison officials exhibited "deliberate indifference." As the dissenters pointed out, this two-part test may mean that inhumane prison con-

---

12. Houchins v. KQED, Inc., 438 U.S. 1 (1978); Saxbe v. Washington Post, 417 U.S. 843 (1974); Pell v. Procunier, 417 U.S. 817 (1974).

Prisoners' Rights

Through a series of rulings in recent decades, the Supreme Court has gradually outlined the basic rights that are available to prisoners and detainees. The table below identifies some of the fundamental issues.

Protected rights:	Permissible restrictions:
Prisoners may not be segregated by race. Lee v. Washington, 390 U.S. 333 (1968).	Double-bunking in detention centers. Bell v. Wolfish, 441 U.S. 520 (1979).
Procedural protections for parole *revocation*. Morrissey v. Brewer, 408 U.S. 471 (1972).	No procedural protections for *granting* parole. Greenholtz v. Nebraska Penal Inmates, 442 U.S. 1 (1979).
Detainees may not be punished prior to adjudication of guilt. Bell v. Wolfish, 441 U.S. 520 (1979).	Searches and seizures unrestricted by Fourth Amendment. Hudson v. Palmer, 468 U.S. 517 (1984).
Limits on time in isolation cells. Hutto v. Finney, 437 U.S. 678 (1978).	No right to contact visits. Block v. Rutherford, 468 U.S. 576 (1984).
Reasonable opportunity to pursue religious faith. O'Lone v. Estate of Shabazz, 482 U.S. 342 (1987).	Strip search, exposing body cavities, after contact visits. Bell v. Wolfish, 441 U.S. 520 (1979).
Freedom from excessive physical force even when there is no serious injury. Hudson v. McMillian, 503 U.S. 1 (1992).	Restrictions on incoming mail and packages. Thornburgh v. Abbott, 490 U.S. 401 (1989).

ditions cannot be effectively challenged if they are the result of insufficient funding by state legislators rather than deliberate indifference by prison officials. Wilson v. Seiter, 501 U.S. 294 (1991).

In 1992, the Court divided 7–2 in holding that excessive physical force against a prisoner may constitute cruel and unusual punishment even though the prisoner does not suffer serious injury. The prisoner, placed in handcuffs and shackles, was punched in the mouth, eyes, chest, and stomach by one guard while another guard kicked and punched him from behind. The prison supervisor watched the beating and told the guards "not to have too much fun." The prisoner suffered minor bruises and swelling of his face, mouth, and lip. The blows also loosened his teeth and cracked his partial dental plate. Hudson v. McMillian, 503 U.S. 1 (1992).

Also in 1992, the Court made it easier for state and local officials to modify court settlements that required them to improve conditions in prisons and other public institutions. For example, judicial requirements for single-cell occupancy in jails can be lifted if the state demonstrates that significant changes in circumstances (such as financial constraints) warrant revision of a consent decree. Rufo v. Inmates of Suffolk County Jail, 502 U.S. 367 (1992). A decision by the Court in 1993 allowed prisoners to sue prison officials on the ground that smoking by a cellmate posed health hazards and constituted cruel and unusual punishment under the Eighth Amendment. Helling v. McKinney, 509 U.S. 25 (1993). A year later a unanimous Court held that a prison official may be held liable for acting with "deliberate indifference" to inmate health or safety, but only if he knows that inmates face a substantial risk of serious harm and fails to take reasonable measures to abate the risk. In this case a transsexual prisoner was transferred from a correctional institution to a penitentiary, where he was beaten and raped. Farmer v. Brennan, 511 U.S. 825 (1994).

Congressional Legislation

In 1995, Congress passed legislation to restrict the ability of prisoners to sue over their living conditions and to limit the scope of court-ordered settlements in such lawsuits. In a case that reached the Supreme Court, inmates at a correctional facility brought a class action and a district court found that living conditions at the prison violated both state and federal law, including the Cruel and Unusual Punishment Clause. The Seventh Circuit issued a remedial order concerning overcrowding, quality of food, and other issues. The statute allowed a defendant (such as the state or prison official) to file for the immediate termination of any prospective relief and required the court to make certain findings to continue the relief. The Seventh Circuit ruled that the statutory procedure was unconstitutional because it allowed court orders to be set aside by legislative determination, violating the separation of powers. However, the Supreme Court interpreted the statute to avoid constitutional problems. Congress could set up a procedure triggering an automatic stay of a court order for prospective relief, and prohibit the continuation of the relief unless the court finds that the relief is narrowly drawn, extends no further than necessary to correct the violation of the federal right, and is the least intrusive means to correct the violation. Miller v. French, 120 S.Ct. 2246 (2000).

Hudson v. Palmer

468 U.S. 517 (1984)

Russell Palmer, a prisoner in a Virginia penal institution, filed an action in federal district court under 42 U. S. C. § 1983 against Ted Hudson, an officer at the institution. Palmer alleged that Hudson had conducted an unreasonable "shakedown" search of his prison locker and cell and had brought a false charge, under prison disciplinary procedures, of destroying state property solely to harass him. The district court granted summary judgment for Hudson. The Fourth Circuit held that a prisoner has a "limited privacy right" in his cell entitling him to protection against searches conducted solely to harass or to humiliate, and that a remand was necessary to determine the purpose of the search by Hudson.

CHIEF JUSTICE BURGER delivered the opinion of the Court.

We granted certiorari in No. 82-1630 to decide whether a prison inmate has a reasonable expectation of privacy in his prison cell entitling him to the protection of the Fourth Amendment against unreasonable searches and seizures....

I

The facts underlying this dispute are relatively simple. Respondent Palmer is an inmate at the Bland Correctional Center in Bland, Va., serving sentences for forgery, uttering, grand larceny, and bank robbery convictions. On September 16, 1981, petitioner Hudson, an officer at the Correctional Center, with a fellow officer, conducted a "shakedown" search of respondent's prison locker and cell for contraband. During the "shakedown," the officers discovered a ripped pillowcase in a trash can near respondent's cell bunk. Charges against Palmer were instituted under the prison

disciplinary procedures for destroying state property. After a hearing, Palmer was found guilty on the charge and was ordered to reimburse the State for the cost of the material destroyed; in addition, a reprimand was entered on his prison record.

. . .

II

A

The first question we address is whether respondent has a right of privacy in his prison cell entitling him to the protection of the Fourth Amendment against unreasonable searches....

We have repeatedly held that prisons are not beyond the reach of the Constitution. No "iron curtain" separates one from the other. *Wolff* v. *McDonnell,* 418 U. S. 539, 555 (1974). Indeed, we have insisted that prisoners be accorded those rights not fundamentally inconsistent with imprisonment itself or incompatible with the objectives of incarceration....

. . .

However, while persons imprisoned for crime enjoy many protections of the Constitution, it is also clear that imprisonment carries with it the circumscription or loss of many significant rights. See *Bell* v. *Wolfish,* 441 U. S., at 545. *[Next reading.]*

We have not before been called upon to decide the specific question whether the Fourth Amendment applies within a prison cell, but the nature of our inquiry is well defined. We must determine here, as in other Fourth Amendment contexts, if a "justifiable" expectation of privacy is at stake. *Katz* v. *United States,* 389 U. S. 347 (1967). The applicability of the Fourth Amendment turns on whether "the person invoking its protection can claim a 'justifiable,' a 'reasonable,' or a 'legitimate expectation of privacy' that has been invaded by government action." *Smith* v. *Maryland,* 442 U. S. 735, 740 (1979), and cases cited. We must decide, in Justice Harlan's words, whether a prisoner's expectation of privacy in his prison cell is the kind of expectation that "society is prepared to recognize as 'reasonable.' " *Katz, supra,* at 360, 361 (concurring opinion).

Notwithstanding our caution in approaching claims that the Fourth Amendment is inapplicable in a given context, we hold that society is not prepared to recognize as legitimate any subjective expectation of privacy that a prisoner might have in his prison cell and that, accordingly, the Fourth Amendment proscription against unreasonable searches does not apply within the confines of the prison cell. The recognition of privacy rights for prisoners in their individual cells simply cannot be reconciled with the concept of incarceration and the needs and objectives of penal institutions.

Prisons, by definition, are places of involuntary confinement of persons who have a demonstrated proclivity for anti-social criminal, and often violent, conduct. Inmates have necessarily shown a lapse in ability to control and conform their behavior to the legitimate standards of society by the normal impulses of self-restraint; they have shown an inability to regulate their conduct in a way that reflects either a respect for law or an appreciation of the rights of others. Even a partial survey of the statistics on violent crime in our Nation's prisons illustrates the magnitude of the problem. During 1981 and the first half of 1982, there were over 120 prisoners murdered by fellow inmates in state and federal prisons. A number of prison personnel were murdered by prisoners during this period. Over 29 riots or similar disturbances were reported in these facilities for the same time frame. And there were over 125 suicides in these institutions....

Within this volatile "community," prison administrators are to take all necessary steps to ensure the safety of not only the prison staffs and administrative personnel, but also visitors. They are under an obligation to take reasonable measures to guarantee the safety of the inmates themselves. They must be ever alert to attempts to introduce drugs and other contraband into the premises which, we can judicially notice, is one of the most perplexing problems of prisons today; they must prevent, so far as possible, the flow of illicit weapons into the prison; they must be vigilant to detect escape plots, in which drugs or weapons may be involved, before the schemes materialize. In addition to these monumental tasks, it is incumbent upon these officials at the same time to maintain as sanitary an environment for the inmates as feasible, given the difficulties of the circumstances.

The administration of a prison, we have said, is "at best an extraordinarily difficult undertaking." *Wolff* v. *McDonnell,* 418 U. S., at 566; *Hewitt* v. *Helms,* 459 U. S. 460, 467 (1983). But it would be literally impossible to accomplish the prison objectives identified above if inmates retained a right of privacy in their cells. Virtually the only place inmates can conceal weapons, drugs, and other contraband is in their cells. Unfettered access to these cells by prison officials, thus, is imperative if drugs and contraband are to be ferreted out and sanitary surroundings are to be maintained.

Determining whether an expectation of privacy is "legitimate" or "reasonable" necessarily entails a balancing of interests.... We strike the balance in favor of institutional security, which we have noted is "central to all other corrections goals," *Pell* v. *Procunier,* 417 U. S., at 823. A right of privacy in traditional Fourth Amendment terms is fundamentally incompatible with the close and continual surveillance of inmates and their cells required to ensure institutional security and internal order. We are satisfied that society would insist that the prisoner's expectation of privacy always yield to what must be considered the paramount interest in institutional security.

. . .

III

We hold that the Fourth Amendment has no applicability to a prison cell. We hold also that, even if [*officer Hudson*] intentionally destroyed [*Palmer's*] personal property during the challenged shakedown search, the destruction did not violate the Fourteenth Amendment since the Commonwealth of Virginia has provided respondent an adequate postdeprivation remedy.

Accordingly, the judgment of the Court of Appeals reversing and remanding the District Court's judgment on respondent's claim under the Fourth and Fourteenth Amendments is reversed. The judgment affirming the District Court's decision that respondent has not been denied due process under the Fourteenth Amendment is affirmed.

It is so ordered.

JUSTICE O'CONNOR, concurring.

. . .

JUSTICE STEVENS, with whom JUSTICE BRENNAN, JUSTICE MARSHALL, and JUSTICE BLACKMUN join, concurring in part and dissenting in part.

This case comes to us on the pleadings. We must take the allegations in Palmer's complaint as true. Liberally construing this *pro se* complaint as we must, it alleges that after examining it, prison guard Hudson maliciously took and destroyed a quantity of Palmer's property, including legal materials and letters, for no reason other than harassment.

For the reasons stated in Part II-B of the opinion of the Court, I agree that Palmer's complaint does not allege a violation of his constitutional right to procedural due process. The reasoning in Part II-A of the Court's opinion, however, is seriously flawed—indeed, internally inconsistent. The Court correctly concludes that the imperatives of prison administration require random searches of prison cells, and also correctly states that in the prison context "[o]f course, there is a risk of maliciously motivated searches, and of course, intentional harassment of even the most hardened criminals cannot be tolerated by a civilized society.". . . But the Court then holds that no matter how malicious, destructive, or arbitrary a cell search and seizure may be, it cannot constitute an unreasonable invasion of any privacy or possessory interest that society is prepared to recognize as reasonable. . . .

. . .

Personal letters, snapshots of family members, a souvenir, a deck of cards, a hobby kit, perhaps a diary or a training manual for an apprentice in a new trade, or even a Bible—a variety of inexpensive items may enable a prisoner to maintain contact with some part of his past and an eye to the possibility of a better future. Are all of these items subject to unrestrained perusal, confiscation, or mutilation at the hands of a possibly hostile guard? Is the Court correct in its perception that "society" is not prepared to recognize *any* privacy or possessory interest of the prison inmate—no matter how remote the threat to prison security may be?

. . .

Bell v. Wolfish

441 U.S. 520 (1979)

Louis Wolfish and other inmates brought a class action to challenge the conditions in the Metropolitan Correctional Center (MCC), a federal facility in New York City designed to hold pretrial detainees. The defendant in the suit was Griffin B. Bell, Attorney General of the United States. A federal district court enjoined certain practices as unconstitutional; the Second Circuit affirmed.

MR. JUSTICE REHNQUIST delivered the opinion of the Court.

Over the past five Terms, this Court has in several decisions considered constitutional challenges to prison conditions or practices by convicted prisoners. This case requires us to examine the constitutional rights of pretrial detainees—those persons who have been charged with a crime but who have not yet been tried on the charge. The parties concede that to ensure their presence at trial, these persons legitimately may be incarcerated by the Government prior to a determination of their guilt or innocence, . . . and it is the scope of their rights during this period of confinement prior to trial that is the primary focus of this case.

. . .

I

The MCC was constructed in 1975 to replace the converted waterfront garage on West Street that had served as New York City's federal jail since 1928. It is located adjacent to the Foley Square federal courthouse and has as its primary objective the housing of persons who are being detained in custody prior to trial for federal criminal offenses.... In addition to pretrial detainees, the MCC also houses some convicted inmates who are awaiting sentencing or transportation to federal prison or who are serving generally relatively short sentences in a service capacity at the MCC, convicted prisoners who have been lodged at the facility under writs of habeas corpus *ad prosequendum* or *ad testificandum* issued to ensure their presence at upcoming trials, witnesses in protective custody, and persons incarcerated for contempt.

The MCC differs markedly from the familiar image of a jail; there are no barred cells, dank, colorless corridors, or clanging steel gates. It was intended to include the most advanced and innovative features of modern design of detention facilities. As the Court of Appeals stated: "[I]t represented the architectural embodiment of the best and most progressive penological planning." 573 F. 2d, at 121. The key design element of the 12-story structure is the "modular" or "unit" concept, whereby each floor designed to house inmates has one or two largely self-contained residential units that replace the traditional cell-block jail construction. Each unit in turn has several clusters or corridors of private rooms or dormitories radiating from a central 2-story "multipurpose" or common room, to which each inmate has free access approximately 16 hours a day. Because our analysis does not turn on the particulars of the MCC concept or design, we need not discuss them further.

When the MCC opened in August 1975, the planned capacity was 449 inmates, an increase of 50% over the former West Street facility. *Id.*, at 122. Despite some dormitory accommodations, the MCC was designed primarily to house these inmates in 389 rooms, which originally were intended for single occupancy. While the MCC was under construction, however, the number of persons committed to pretrial detention began to rise at an "unprecedented" rate.... The Bureau of Prisons took several steps to accommodate this unexpected flow of persons assigned to the facility, but despite these efforts, the inmate population at the MCC rose above its planned capacity

within a short time after its opening. To provide sleeping space for this increased population, the MCC replaced the single bunks in many of the individual rooms and dormitories with double bunks. Also, each week some newly arrived inmates had to sleep on cots in the common areas until they could be transferred to residential rooms as space became available....

. . .

II

As a first step in our decision, we shall address "double-bunking" as it is referred to by the parties, since it is a condition of confinement that is alleged only to deprive pretrial detainees of their liberty without due process of law in contravention of the Fifth Amendment....

B

In evaluating the constitutionality of conditions or restrictions of pretrial detention that implicate only the protection against deprivation of liberty without due process of law, we think that the proper inquiry is whether those conditions amount to punishment of the detainee. For under the Due Process Clause, a detainee may not be punished prior to an adjudication of guilt in accordance with due process of law....

Not every disability imposed during pretrial detention amounts to "punishment" in the constitutional sense, however. Once the Government has exercised its conceded authority to detain a person pending trial, it obviously is entitled to employ devices that are calculated to effectuate this detention. Traditionally, this has meant confinement in a facility which, no matter how modern or how antiquated, results in restricting the movement of a detainee in a manner in which he would not be restricted if he simply were free to walk the streets pending trial....

...We need not here attempt to detail the precise extent of the legitimate governmental interests that may justify conditions or restrictions of pretrial detention. It is enough simply to recognize that in addition to ensuring the detainees' presence at trial, the effective management of the detention facility once the individual is confined is a valid objective that may justify imposition of conditions and restrictions of pretrial detention and dispel any inference that such restrictions are intended as punishment.

C

Judged by this analysis, respondents' claim

that "double-bunking" violated their due process rights fails. . . .

. . .

We disagree with both the District Court and the Court of Appeals that there is some sort of "one man, one cell" principle lurking in the Due Process Clause of the Fifth Amendment. While confining a given number of people in a given amount of space in such a manner as to cause them to endure genuine privations and hardship over an extended period of time might raise serious questions under the Due Process Clause as to whether those conditions amounted to punishment, nothing even approaching such hardship is shown by this record.

Detainees are required to spend only seven or eight hours each day in their rooms, during most or all of which they presumably are sleeping. The rooms provide more than adequate space for sleeping. During the remainder of the time, the detainees are free to move between their rooms and the common area. . . . Nearly all of the detainees are released within 60 days. . . . We simply do not believe that requiring a detainee to share toilet facilities and this admittedly rather small sleeping place with another person for generally a maximum period of 60 days violates the Constitution.

III

Respondents also challenged certain MCC restrictions and practices that were designed to promote security and order at the facility on the ground that these restrictions violated the Due Process Clause of the Fifth Amendment, and certain other constitutional guarantees, such as the First and Fourth Amendments. . . .

A

[The MCC permitted inmates to receive books and magazines from outside the institution only if the materials were mailed directly from the publisher or a book club. Other items might contain contraband. The policy was later amended to permit the receipt of books and magazines from bookstores as well as publishers and book clubs, and to allow receipt of paperback books, magazines, and other soft-covered materials from any source. The Court concluded that the prohibition against receipt of hardback books unless mailed directly from publishers, book clubs, or bookstores does not violate the First Amendment rights of MCC inmates.]

B

Inmates at the MCC were not permitted to receive packages from outside the facility containing items of food or personal property, except for one package of food at Christmas. This rule was justified by MCC officials on three grounds. First, officials testified to "serious" security problems that arise from the introduction of such packages into the institution, the "traditional file in the cake kind of situation" as well as the concealment of drugs "in heels of shoes [and] seams of clothing." . . . Second, officials were concerned that the introduction of personal property into the facility would increase the risk of thefts, gambling, and inmate conflicts, the "age-old problem of you have it and I don't." . . . Finally, they noted storage and sanitary problems that would result from inmates' receipt of food packages. . . . Inmates are permitted, however, to purchase certain items of food and personal property from the MCC commissary.

[The district court and the Second Circuit rejected MCC's justifications as "dire predictions," but the Supreme Court concluded that the policy was based on legitimate security concerns.] . . .

C

The MCC staff conducts unannounced searches of inmate living areas at irregular intervals. These searches generally are formal unit "shakedowns" during which all inmates are cleared of the residential units, and a team of guards searches each room. . . .

[The district court and the Second Circuit invalidated the room-search rule, the former stating that the rule infringed the detainee's interest in privacy founded on the Fourth Amendment.]

It is difficult to see how the detainee's interest in privacy is infringed by the room-search rule. No one can rationally doubt that room searches represent an appropriate security measure and neither the District Court nor the Court of Appeals prohibited such searches. . . . The room-search rule simply facilitates the safe and effective performance of the search which all concede may be conducted. The rule itself, then, does not render the searches "unreasonable" within the meaning of the Fourth Amendment.

D

Inmates at all Bureau of Prisons facilities, including the MCC, are required to expose their body cavities for visual inspection as a part of a strip search conducted after every contact visit with a person from outside the institution. *[If the inmate is a male, he must lift his genitals and bend over to spread his buttocks for visual inspection. The vaginal and anal cavities of female inmates also are visually inspected. The inmate is not touched by security personnel at any time during the visual search procedure.]* Corrections officials testified that visual cavity searches were necessary not only to discover but also to deter the smuggling of weapons, drugs, and other contraband into the institution....

Admittedly, this practice *[body-cavity search]* instinctively gives us the most pause. However, assuming for present purposes that inmates, both convicted prisoners and pretrial detainees, retain some Fourth Amendment rights upon commitment to a corrections facility, see *Lanza* v. *New York, supra; Stroud* v. *United States,* 251 U. S. 15, 21 (1919), we nonetheless conclude that these searches do not violate that Amendment. The Fourth Amendment prohibits only unreasonable searches, *Carroll* v. *United States,* 267 U. S. 132, 147 (1925), and under the circumstances, we do not believe that these searches are unreasonable.

. . .

MR. JUSTICE POWELL, concurring in part and dissenting in part.

I join the opinion of the Court except the discussion and holding with respect to body-cavity searches. In view of the serious intrusion on one's privacy occasioned by such a search, I think at least some level of cause, such as a reasonable suspicion, should be required to justify the anal and genital searches described in this case. I therefore dissent on this issue.

MR. JUSTICE MARSHALL, dissenting.

The Court holds that the Government may burden pretrial detainees with almost any restriction, provided detention officials do not proclaim a punitive intent or impose conditions that are "arbitrary or purposeless."...As if this standard were not sufficiently ineffectual, the Court dilutes

it further by according virtually unlimited deference to detention officials' justifications for particular impositions. Conspicuously lacking from this analysis is any meaningful consideration of the most relevant factor, the impact that restrictions may have on inmates. Such an approach is unsupportable, given that all of these detainees are presumptively innocent and many are confined solely because they cannot afford bail.

[Marshall believed that a remand was necessary on the issue of double-bunking to produce further evidence. He took the same position on the rule limiting the sources of hardbound books and concluded that the record did not establish that unobserved searches were substantially necessary to jail administration. Finally, Marshall said that body-cavity searches should be conducted only when there is probable cause to believe that an inmate is concealing contraband.]

MR. JUSTICE STEVENS, with whom MR. JUSTICE BRENNAN joins, dissenting.

. . .

I.

Some of the individuals housed in the Metropolitan Correction Center (MCC) are convicted criminals. As to them, detention may legitimately serve a punitive goal, and there is strong reason, even apart from the rules challenged here, to suggest that it does. But the same is not true of the detainees who are also housed there and whose rights we are called upon to address. Notwithstanding the impression created by the Court's opinion,...these people are not "prisoners": they have not been convicted of any crimes, and their detention may serve only a more limited, regulatory purpose....

In my judgment, each of the rules at issue here is unconstitutional. The four rules do indiscriminately inflict harm on all pretrial detainees in MCC. They are all either unnecessary or excessively harmful, particularly when judged against our historic respect for the dignity of the free citizen....

E. RIGHTS OF THE POOR

The Constitution extends rights to all persons. The full realization of those rights, however, often depends on one's income. The Sixth Amendment guarantees that the accused may have the assistance of counsel. It did not require the government to provide counsel to a defendant unable to afford an attorney. Not until 1963, in *Gideon* v. *Wainwright,* did the Supreme Court rule that the government must provide a lawyer if an indigent person is accused of a felony. As explained in Chapter 13, this right has been expanded by subsequent decisions. Similarly, in 1966, the Court struck down the poll tax, concluding that lines drawn on the basis of wealth or property, like those of race, "are traditionally disfavored." Harper v. Virginia Board of Elections, 383 U.S. 663 (1966).

The fact that these decisions did not come until the 1960s suggests a quite different conclusion: tradition has very much favored the distribution of justice on the basis of wealth. Anatole France made his famous remark about the law, "in all its majestic equality," prohibiting both rich and poor from sleeping under bridges, begging in the streets, and stealing bread. Even with a court-appointed attorney, an indigent defendant is unlikely to fare as well as the wealthy defendant who hires three or four attorneys from a major law firm. By creating the Legal Services Corporation in 1974, Congress attempted to provide financial support for legal assistance for low-income people, but this program is designed only for noncriminal proceedings and is funded at modest levels.

Welfare Benefits

There is no constitutional right to receive welfare payments or other forms of public assistance for the indigent. The extent of public funding for these purposes is determined by legislative action. Once granted, however, assistance may be terminated only by observing procedural safeguards. In 1970 the Supreme Court held that individuals receiving financial aid under the federally assisted Aid to Families with Dependent Children (AFDC) program or under New York's general home-relief program could not have their assistance terminated without prior notice and hearing. Goldberg v. Kelly, 397 U.S. 254 (1970). In the case of disability benefits, the Court has ruled that an evidentiary hearing is not required before the initial termination of benefits. The Court distinguished *Goldberg* on the ground that welfare recipients have greater financial need than the disabled. Mathews v. Eldridge, 424 U.S. 319 (1976).

The Court has reviewed state restrictions that make people ineligible for welfare benefits. One-year residency requirements were struck down as an unconstitutional interference with the right of interstate movement. SHAPIRO v. THOMPSON, 394 U.S. 618 (1969). Applying the same principle, states may not require a year's residence in a county as a condition for an indigent to receive nonemergency hospitalization or medical care at the county's expense. Memorial Hospital v. Maricopa County, 415 U.S. 250 (1974).

For the most part, judges confine their review of welfare rights to questions of statutory interpretation and congressional intent, not constitutional law. The Supreme Court decided that an Alabama regulation, denying AFDC payments to the children of a mother who kept "a man in the house," was inconsistent with federal law. King v. Smith, 392 U.S. 309 (1968). On the other hand, state efforts to impose a ceiling on AFDC payments, regardless of family size or need, have been sustained as not prohibited by federal law. Dandridge v. Williams, 397 U.S. 471 (1970). The "intractable economic, social, and even philosophical problems presented by public welfare assistance programs are not the business of this Court." Id. at 487.[13]

In 1971, the Court confronted the sensitive issue of caseworkers entering the home of a welfare recipient. New York required caseworkers to visit beneficiaries during working hours and prohibited forcible entry and snooping. A beneficiary under the AFDC program refused

13. For other statutory interpretations of the AFDC program, see Bowen v. Gilliard, 483 U.S. 587 (1987); Quern v. Mandley, 436 U.S. 725 (1978); Philbrook v. Glodgett, 421 U.S. 707 (1975); Burns v. Alcala, 420 U.S. 575 (1975); Jefferson v. Hackney, 406 U.S. 535 (1972); Townsend v. Swank, 404 U.S. 282 (1971); Rosado v. Wyman, 397 U.S. 397 (1970).

to admit caseworkers, contending that home visitation amounted to a search and required either consent or a warrant supported by probable cause. The Court, divided 6–3, decided that constitutional rights had not been violated. Home visitation is not a search within the traditional criminal law context of the Fourth Amendment. Wyman v. James, 400 U.S. 309 (1971).

In that same year the Court, with only Justice Black dissenting, ruled that due process is denied by refusing indigents (including welfare recipients) access to the courts to dissolve a marriage simply because of their inability to pay court fees and costs. Such a policy amounts to denying them an opportunity to be heard. Boddie v. Connecticut, 401 U.S. 371 (1971). On other matters the Court has upheld filing fees for indigents when the fee "does not rise to the same constitutional level" as in *Boddie,* especially where alternative procedures are available without payment of a fee. Ortwein v. Schwab, 410 U.S. 656 (1973); United States v. Kras, 409 U.S. 434 (1973). In 1995, the Court ruled that a state may not refuse to hear a mother's appeal of a court decision terminating her parental rights to her two minor children just because she cannot pay court fees. M.L.B. v. S.L.J., 519 U.S. 102 (1996).

In 1999, the Supreme Court ruled that state welfare programs may not restrict new residents to the welfare benefits they were entitled to receive in the state from which they moved. Instead of relying on the "right to travel" (language not found in the Constitution), the 7 to 2 decision exhumed the Fourteenth Amendment's Privileges or Immunities Clause, which provides: "No State shall make or enforce any law which shall abridge the privileges or immunities of citizens of the United States." The last time the Court relied on that clause was in 1935, but that ruling was overturned five years later. Colgate v. Harvey, 296 U.S. 404 (1935); Madden v. Kentucky, 309 U.S. 83, 90–93 (1940). To find full discussion of the clause one has to go back to the *Slaughter-House Cases* of 1873. In a dissent to the 1999 ruling, Rehnquist spoke of "unearthing from its tomb the right to become a state citizen and to be treated equally in the new State of residence." Saenz v. Roe, 526 U.S. 489, 516 (1999).

School Financing

The Supreme Court split 5–4 on a major case in 1973 involving the financing of public schools. In Texas, half of the revenues for public elementary and secondary schools came from a state-funded program. Each district then supplemented that amount through an ad valorem tax on property within its jurisdiction. The higher the value of the properties, the higher the supplement. Rich communities could therefore support better schools than poor neighborhoods. A class action brought by Mexican-American parents argued that the system violated the Equal Protection Clause by favoring students in more affluent districts. The Court held that the system did not disadvantage any suspect class. The fundamental right of education is not interfered with, said the Court, if state-supported revenues assure at least a minimum education. With respect to wealth, the Court announced that the Equal Protection Clause does not require absolute equality of precisely equal advantages. SAN ANTONIO SCHOOL DISTRICT v. RODRIGUEZ, 411 U.S. 1 (1973). Justice Marshall, penning one of the dissents, pointed to the inconsistency between this decision and the cases on desegregation that invalidated inequality in educational facilities. However, the Court may have concluded that it lacked the legitimacy or power to dictate funding levels in public schools throughout the states.

State courts have reached different results. The Supreme Court of New Jersey reviewed the state's system of financing public education, which relied heavily on local taxation to cover public school costs and created substantial variations in spending per pupil. The court held that the system violated the provision in the state constitution that requires the state to furnish "thorough and efficient" public schooling. The New Jersey court explained why it could be more demanding on the question of equal protection than the U.S. Supreme Court: "For one thing, there is absent the principle of federalism which cautions against too expansive a

State Litigation on School Financing

In *San Antonio School District* v. *Rodriguez* (1973), the Supreme Court held that school financing systems that provided greater funding for affluent districts did not violate the Equal Protection Clause. Since that time a number of state courts have upheld such systems. Other state courts have declared that disparate financing schemes are invalid under the state constitution, often because state charters contain explicit requirements and standards for public education. For example, Art X, § 1, of the Montana constitution provides: "Equality of educational opportunity is guaranteed to each person of the state." When state legislatures responded with inadequate funding and reforms, state courts issued additional rulings. The following state courts have invalidated school financing systems because they discriminate against poorer districts and deny equal education:

Arizona	Roosevelt Elem. Sch. Dist. v. Bishop, 877 P.2d 806 (1994); Hull v. Albrecht, 960 P.2d 634 (1998).
Arkansas	Dupree v. Alma School Dist. No. 30, 651 S.W.2d 90 (1983).
California	Serrano v. Priest, 557 P.2d 929 (1977).
Connecticut	Horton v. Meskill, 376 A.2d 359 (1977); Sheff v. O'Neill, 678 A.2d 1267 (1996). Sheff v. O'Neill, 733 A.2d 925 (1999), held that the state had complied with the 1996 decision.
Kentucky	Rose v. Council for Better Educ., Inc., 790 S.W.2d 186 (1989).
Massachusetts	McDuffy v. Sec'y of Exec. Off. of Educ., 615 N.E.2d 516 (1993).
Montana	Helena Elementary School Dist. v. State, 769 P.2d 684 (1989).
New Jersey	Robinson v. Cahill, 303 A.2d 273 (1973), cert. denied, sub nom. Dickey v. Robinson, 414 U.S. 976 (1973); Robinson v. Cahill, 355 A.2d 129 (1976); Abbott v. Burke, 575 A.2d 359 (1990); Abbott ex rel. Abbott v. Burke, 751 A.2d 1032 (2000).
Ohio	DeRolph v. State, 677 N.E.2d 733 (1997).
Tennessee	Tenn. Small School Systems v. McWherter, 851 S.W.2d 139 (1993), 894 S.W.2d 734 (1995).
Texas	Edgewood Indep. School Dist. v. Kirby, 777 S.W.2d 391 (1989); Edgewood Indep. Sch. Dist. v. Kirby, 804 S.W.2d 491 (1991).
Vermont	Brigham v. State, 692 A.2d 384 (1997).
Washington	Seattle Sch. Dist. No. 1 of King Cty. v. State, 585 P.2d 71 (1978).
West Virginia	Pauley v. Kelly, 255 S.E.2d 859 (1979).
Wyoming	Washakie Co. Sch. Dist. No. One v. Herschler, 606 P.2d 310 (1980), cert. denied, 449 U.S. 824 (1980).

view of a federal constitutional limitation upon the power and opportunity of the several States to cope with their own problems in the light of their own circumstances." Robinson v. Cahill, 303 A.2d 273, 282 (N.J. 1973), cert. denied, sub nom. Dickey v. Robinson, 414 U.S. 976 (1973). Other state courts have struck down systems of financing public schools because they violated equal protection (see box). State legislatures have restructured their financing systems to provide more equitable funding for schools in poorer communities, but litigation continues to test the constitutionality of school financing. Although suits of this nature are often brought by blacks and Mexican-Americans, plaintiffs can also be overwhelmingly white and rural.

Abortion

In 1980 the Supreme Court upheld the Hyde Amendment, passed by Congress to deny public funds for abortions except to save the mother's life or in cases of rape or incest. Harris v. McRae, 448 U.S. 297 (1980). As with the school financing cases, state courts reached different conclusions. In California, Connecticut, Massachusetts, Michigan, New Jersey, and Oregon, state courts struck down state versions of the Hyde Amendment. They held that states have no obligation to provide medical care to the poor, but that it is a violation of the state constitution to give money to indigent women wanting to bear a child and deny funds to those who seek an abortion. This issue is explored more fully in Chapter 17.

Shapiro v. Thompson

394 U.S. 618 (1969)

A number of states, citing budgetary reasons, established a one-year waiting period before residents could qualify for welfare assistance. In this case, Vivian Marie Thompson moved from Massachusetts to Connecticut and applied for welfare benefits under the Aid to Families with Dependent Children (AFDC) program. Denied assistance, she sued the Commissioner of Welfare, Bernard Shapiro. This case, implicating the constitutional right to travel, also involved residency requirements in Pennsylvania and the District of Columbia. A three-judge district court held that residency requirements violate the Equal Protection Clause of the Fourteenth Amendment (covering the states) and the Due Process Clause of the Fifth Amendment (covering D.C.).

Mr. Justice Brennan delivered the opinion of the Court.

. . .

I.

In No. 9, the Connecticut Welfare Department invoked § 17-2d of the Connecticut General Statutes to deny the application of appellee Vivian Marie Thompson for assistance under the program for Aid to Families with Dependent Children (AFDC). She was a 19-year-old unwed mother of one child and pregnant with her second child when she changed her residence in June 1966 from Dorchester, Massachusetts, to Hartford, Connecticut, to live with her mother, a Hartford resident. She moved to her own apartment in Hartford in August 1966, when her mother was no longer able to support her and her infant son. Because of her pregnancy, she was unable to work or enter a work training program. Her application for AFDC assistance, filed in August, was denied in November solely on the ground that, as required by § 17-2d, she had not lived in the State for a year before her application was filed....

II.

There is no dispute that the effect of the waiting-period requirement in each case is to create two classes of needy resident families indistinguishable from each other except that one is composed of residents who have resided a year or more, and the second of residents who have resided less than a year, in the jurisdiction. On the basis of this sole difference the first class is granted and the second class is denied welfare aid upon which may depend the ability of the families to obtain the very means to subsist — food, shelter, and other necessities of life. In each case, the District Court found that appellees met the test for residence in their jurisdictions, as well as all other eligibility requirements except the requirement of residence for a full year prior to their applications. On reargument, appellees' central contention is that the statutory prohibition of benefits to residents of less than a year creates a classification which constitutes an invidious discrimination denying them equal protection of the laws. We agree. The interests which appellants assert are promoted by the classification either may not constitutionally be promoted by government or are not compelling governmental interests.

III.

Primarily, appellants justify the waiting-period requirement as a protective device to preserve the fiscal integrity of state public assistance programs.

It is asserted that people who require welfare assistance during their first year of residence in a State are likely to become continuing burdens on state welfare programs....

We do not doubt that the one-year waiting-period device is well suited to discourage the influx of poor families in need of assistance. An indigent who desires to migrate, resettle, find a new job, and start a new life will doubtless hesitate if he knows that he must risk making the move without the possibility of falling back on state welfare assistance during his first year of residence, when his need may be most acute. But the purpose of inhibiting migration by needy persons into the State is constitutionally impermissible.

This Court long ago recognized that the nature of our Federal Union and our constitutional concepts of personal liberty unite to require that all citizens be free to travel throughout the length and breadth of our land uninhibited by statutes, rules, or regulations which unreasonably burden or restrict this movement. That proposition was early stated by Chief Justice Taney in the *Passenger Cases*, 7 How. 283, 492 (1849):

"For all the great purposes for which the Federal government was formed, we are one people, with one common country. We are all citizens of the United States; and, as members of the same community, must have the right to pass and repass through every part of it without interruption, as freely as in our own States."

We have no occasion to ascribe the source of this right to travel interstate to a particular constitutional provision. It suffices that, as Mr. Justice Stewart said for the Court in *United States v. Guest*, 383 U. S. 745, 757–758 (1966):

"The constitutional right to travel from one State to another...occupies a position fundamental to the concept of our Federal Union. It is a right that has been firmly established and repeatedly recognized.

"...[T]he right finds no explicit mention in the Constitution. The reason, it has been suggested, is that a right so elementary was conceived from the beginning to be a necessary concomitant of the stronger Union the Constitution created. In any event, freedom to travel throughout the United States has long been recognized as a basic right under the Constitution."

Thus, the purpose of deterring the in-migration of indigents cannot serve as justification for the classification created by the one-year waiting period, since that purpose is constitutionally impermissible....

. . .

We recognize that a State has a valid interest in preserving the fiscal integrity of its programs. It may legitimately attempt to limit its expenditures, whether for public assistance, public education, or any other program. But a State may not accomplish such a purpose by invidious distinctions between classes of its citizens. It could not, for example, reduce expenditures for education by barring indigent children from its schools. Similarly, in the cases before us, appellants must do more than show that denying welfare benefits to new residents saves money. The saving of welfare costs cannot justify an otherwise invidious classification.

In sum, neither deterrence of indigents from migrating to the State nor limitation of welfare benefits to those regarded as contributing to the State is a constitutionally permissible state objective.

[In Section IV, the Court rejects a number of administrative justifications for the waiting-period requirement: that it facilitates the planning of the welfare budget, provides an objective test of residency, minimizes the opportunity for recipients fraudulently to receive payments from more than one jurisdiction, and encourages early entry of new residents into the labor force. There was no evidence to support these justifications.]

...For the reasons we have stated in invalidating the Pennsylvania and Connecticut provisions, the District of Columbia provision is also invalid—the Due Process Clause of the Fifth Amendment prohibits Congress from denying public assistance to poor persons otherwise eligible solely on the ground that they have not been residents of the District of Columbia for one year at the time their applications are filed.

Accordingly, the judgments in Nos. 9, 33, and 34 are

Affirmed.

Mr. Justice Stewart, concurring.

. . .

Mr. Chief Justice Warren, with whom Mr. Justice Black joins, dissenting.

In my opinion the issue before us can be simply stated: May Congress, acting under one of its enumerated powers, impose minimal nationwide residence requirements or authorize the States to do so? Since I believe that Congress does have this power and has constitutionally exercised it in these cases, I must dissent.

I.

The Court insists that § 402 (b) of the Social Security Act "does not approve, much less prescribe, a one-year requirement." ... From its reading of the legislative history it concludes that Congress did not intend to authorize the States to impose residence requirements. An examination of the relevant legislative materials compels, in my view, the opposite conclusion, *i.e.*, Congress intended to authorize state residence requirements of up to one year.

. . .

II.

Congress has imposed a residence requirement in the District of Columbia and authorized the States to impose similar requirements. The issue before us must therefore be framed in terms of whether Congress may create minimal residence requirements, not whether the States, acting alone, may do so.... Appellees insist that a congressionally mandated residence requirement would violate their right to travel. The import of their contention is that Congress, even under its "plenary" power to control interstate commerce, is constitutionally prohibited from imposing residence requirements. I reach a contrary conclusion for I am convinced that the extent of the burden on interstate travel when compared with the justification for its imposition requires the Court to uphold this exertion of federal power.

. . .

Mr. Justice Harlan, dissenting.

. . .

II.

In upholding the equal protection argument, the Court has applied an equal protection doctrine of relatively recent vintage: the rule that statutory classifications which either are based upon certain "suspect" criteria or affect "fundamental rights" will be held to deny equal protection unless justified by a "compelling" governmental interest.

. . .

I think that this branch of the "compelling interest" doctrine is sound when applied to racial classifications, for historically the Equal Protection Clause was largely a product of the desire to eradicate legal distinctions founded upon race. However, I believe that the more recent extensions have been unwise. For the reasons stated in my dissenting opinion in *Harper* v. *Virginia Bd. of Elections, supra,* at 680, 683–686, I do not consider wealth a "suspect" statutory criterion....

. . .

For reasons hereafter set forth, ... a legislature might rationally find that the imposition of a welfare residence requirement would aid in the accomplishment of at least four valid governmental objectives. It might also find that residence requirements have advantages not shared by other methods of achieving the same goals. In light of this undeniable relation of residence requirements to valid legislative aims, it cannot be said that the requirements are "arbitrary" or "lacking in rational justification." Hence, I can find no objection to these residence requirements under the Equal Protection Clause of the Fourteenth Amendment or under the analogous standard embodied in the Due Process Clause of the Fifth Amendment.

III.

... Today's decision, it seems to me, reflects to an unusual degree the current notion that this Court possesses a peculiar wisdom all its own whose capacity to lead this Nation out of its present troubles is contained only by the limits of judicial ingenuity in contriving new constitutional principles to meet each problem as it arises....

San Antonio School Dist. v. Rodriguez

411 U.S. 1 (1973)

Elementary and secondary schools in Texas are financed by state and local contributions. In this case, almost half of the revenues came from the state in order to provide a basic minimum for schools. Supplemental funds were derived from a property tax

adopted by each school district. A class action was brought on behalf of schoolchildren from members of poor families, who claimed that the Texas system of relying on local property taxes favored the more affluent neighborhoods and violated the Equal Protection Clause. A federal district concluded that the system could be upheld only upon a showing, which the school district failed to make, that there was a compelling state interest for the system. Demetrio Rodriguez and other Mexican-American parents brought this suit.

MR. JUSTICE POWELL delivered the opinion of the Court.

. . .

I

. . .

Recognizing the need for increased state funding to help offset disparities in local spending and to meet Texas' changing educational requirements, the state legislature in the late 1940's undertook a thorough evaluation of public education with an eye toward major reform. In 1947, an 18-member committee, composed of educators and legislators, was appointed to explore alternative systems in other States and to propose a funding scheme that would guarantee a minimum or basic educational offering to each child and that would help overcome interdistrict disparities in taxable resources. The Committee's efforts led to the ... Texas Minimum Foundation School Program. Today, this Program accounts for approximately half of the total educational expenditures in Texas.

The Program calls for state and local contributions to a fund earmarked specifically for teacher salaries, operating expenses, and transportation costs. The State, supplying funds from its general revenues, finances approximately 80% of the Program, and the school districts are responsible—as a unit—for providing the remaining 20%. The districts' share, known as the Local Fund Assignment, is apportioned among the school districts under a formula designed to reflect each district's relative taxpaying ability. The Assignment is first divided among Texas' 254 counties pursuant to a complicated economic index that takes into account the relative value of each county's contribution to the State's total income from manufacturing, mining, and agricultural activities. It also considers each county's relative share of all payrolls paid within the State and, to a lesser extent, considers each county's share of all property in the State. Each county's assignment is then divided among its school districts on the basis of each district's share of assessable property within the county. The district, in turn, finances its share of the Assignment out of revenues from local property taxation.

. . .

The school district in which appellees reside, the Edgewood Independent School District, has been compared throughout this litigation with the Alamo Heights Independent School District. This comparison between the least and most affluent districts in the San Antonio area serves to illustrate the manner in which the dual system of finance operates and to indicate the extent to which substantial disparities exist despite the State's impressive progress in recent years. Edgewood is one of seven public school districts in the metropolitan area. Approximately 22,000 students are enrolled in its 25 elementary and secondary schools. The district is situated in the core-city sector of San Antonio in a residential neighborhood that has little commercial or industrial property. The residents are predominantly of Mexican-American descent: approximately 90% of the student population is Mexican-American and over 6% is Negro. The average assessed property value per pupil is $5,960—the lowest in the metropolitan area—and the median family income ($4,686) is also the lowest. At an equalized tax rate of $1.05 per $100 of assessed property—the highest in the metropolitan area—the district contributed $26 to the education of each child for the 1967–1968 school year above its Local Fund Assignment for the Minimum Foundation Program. The Foundation Program contributed $222 per pupil for a state-local total of $248. Federal funds added another $108 for a total of $356 per pupil.

Alamo Heights is the most affluent school district in San Antonio. Its six schools, housing approximately 5,000 students, are situated in a residential community quite unlike the Edgewood District. The school population is predominantly "Anglo," having only 18% Mexican-Americans and less than 1% Negroes. The assessed property value per pupil exceeds $49,000, and the median family income is $8,001. In 1967–1968 the local tax rate of $.85 per $100 of valuation yielded $333 per pupil over and above its contribution to the Foundation Program. Coupled with the $225 provided from that Program, the district was able to supply $558 per student. Supplemented by a $36 per-pupil grant from federal sources, Alamo Heights spent $594 per pupil.

Although the 1967–1968 school year figures provide the only complete statistical breakdown for each category of aid, more recent partial statistics indicate that the previously noted trend of increasing state aid has been significant. For the 1970–1971 school year, the Foundation School Program allotment for Edgewood was $356 per pupil, a 62% increase over the 1967–1968 school year. Indeed, state aid alone in 1970–1971 equaled Edgewood's entire 1967–1968 school budget from local, state, and federal sources. Alamo Heights enjoyed a similar increase under the Foundation Program, netting $491 per pupil in 1970–1971. These recent figures also reveal the extent to which these two districts' allotments were funded from their own required contributions to the Local Fund Assignment. Alamo Heights, because of its relative wealth, was required to contribute out of its local property tax collections approximately $100 per pupil, or about 20% of its Foundation grant. Edgewood, on the other hand, paid only $8.46 per pupil, which is about 2.4% of its grant. It appears then that, at least as to these two districts, the Local Fund Assignment does reflect a rough approximation of the relative taxpaying potential of each.

. . .

Texas virtually concedes that its historically rooted dual system of financing education could not withstand the strict judicial scrutiny that this Court has found appropriate in reviewing legislative judgments that interfere with fundamental constitutional rights or that involve suspect classifications. . . .

This, then, establishes the framework for our analysis. We must decide, first, whether the Texas system of financing public education operates to the disadvantage of some suspect class or impinges upon a fundamental right explicitly or implicitly protected by the Constitution, thereby requiring strict judicial scrutiny. If so, the judgment of the District Court should be affirmed. If not, the Texas scheme must still be examined to determine whether it rationally furthers some legitimate, articulated state purpose and therefore does not constitute an invidious discrimination in vio-

lation of the Equal Protection Clause of the Fourteenth Amendment.

II

The District Court's opinion does not reflect the novelty and complexity of the constitutional questions posed by appellees' challenge to Texas' system of school financing. In concluding that strict judicial scrutiny was required, that court relied on decisions dealing with the rights of indigents to equal treatment in the criminal trial and appellate processes, and on cases disapproving wealth restrictions on the right to vote. Those cases, the District Court concluded, established wealth as a suspect classification. Finding that the local property tax system discriminated on the basis of wealth, it regarded those precedents as controlling. It then reasoned, based on decisions of this Court affirming the undeniable importance of education, that there is a fundamental right to education and that, absent some compelling state justification, the Texas system could not stand.

We are unable to agree that this case, which in significant aspects is *sui generis,* may be so neatly fitted into the conventional mosaic of constitutional analysis under the Equal Protection Clause. Indeed, for the several reasons that follow, we find neither the suspect-classification nor the fundamental-interest analysis persuasive.

A

. . .Apart from the unsettled and disputed question whether the quality of education may be determined by the amount of money expended for it, a sufficient answer to appellees' argument is that, at least where wealth is involved, the Equal Protection Clause does not require absolute equality or precisely equal advantages. Nor, indeed, in view of the infinite variables affecting the educational process, can any system assure equal quality of education except in the most relative sense. . . .

B

In *Brown v. Board of Education,* 347 U. S. 483 (1954), a unanimous Court recognized that "education is perhaps the most important function of state and local governments." *Id.,* at 493. What was said there in the context of racial discrimination has lost none of its vitality with the passage of time. . . .

Nothing this Court holds today in any way detracts from our historic dedication to public education. We are in complete agreement with the conclusion of the three-judge panel below that "the grave significance of education both to the individual and to our society" cannot be doubted.

But the importance of a service performed by the State does not determine whether it must be regarded as fundamental for purposes of examination under the Equal Protection Clause....

Education, of course, is not among the rights afforded explicit protection under our Federal Constitution. Nor do we find any basis for saying it is implicitly so protected. As we have said, the undisputed importance of education will not alone cause this Court to depart from the usual standard for reviewing a State's social and economic legislation. It is appellees' contention, however, that education is distinguishable from other services and benefits provided by the State because it bears a peculiarly close relationship to other rights and liberties accorded protection under the Constitution. Specifically, they insist that education is itself a fundamental personal right because it is essential to the effective exercise of First Amendment freedoms and to intelligent utilization of the right to vote....

We need not dispute any of these propositions. The Court has long afforded zealous protection against unjustifiable governmental interference with the individual's rights to speak and to vote. Yet we have never presumed to possess either the ability or the authority to guarantee to the citizenry the most *effective* speech or the most *informed* electoral choice....

C

. . .

...This case represents far more than a challenge to the manner in which Texas provides for the education of its children. We have here nothing less than a direct attack on the way in which Texas has chosen to raise and disburse state and local tax revenues....

In addition to matters of fiscal policy, this case also involves the most persistent and difficult questions of educational policy, another area in which this Court's lack of specialized knowledge and experience counsels against premature interference with the informed judgments made at the state and local levels....

[In Section III, the Court holds that the Texas school finance system rationally furthers a legitimate state purpose or interest and therefore satisfies the Equal Protection Clause.]

IV

...The consideration and initiation of fundamental reforms with respect to state taxation and education are matters reserved for the legislative processes of the various States, and we do no violence to the values of federalism and separation of powers by staying our hand. We hardly need add that this Court's action today is not to be viewed as placing its judicial imprimatur on the status quo. The need is apparent for reform in tax systems which may well have relied too long and too heavily on the local property tax. And certainly innovative thinking as to public education, its methods, and its funding is necessary to assure both a higher level of quality and greater uniformity of opportunity. These matters merit the continued attention of the scholars who already have contributed much by their challenges. But the ultimate solutions must come from the lawmakers and from the democratic pressures of those who elect them.

Reversed.

MR. JUSTICE STEWART, concurring.

. . .

MR. JUSTICE BRENNAN, dissenting.

Although I agree with my Brother WHITE that the Texas statutory scheme is devoid of any rational basis, and for that reason is violative of the Equal Protection Clause, I also record my disagreement with the Court's rather distressing assertion that a right may be deemed "fundamental" for the purposes of equal protection analysis only if it is "explicitly or implicitly guaranteed by the Constitution."...

...[T]here can be no doubt that education is inextricably linked to the right to participate in the electoral process and to the rights of free speech and association guaranteed by the First Amendment.... This being so, any classification affecting education must be subjected to strict judicial scrutiny, and since even the State concedes that the statutory scheme now before us cannot pass constitutional muster under this stricter standard of review, I can only conclude that the Texas school-financing scheme is constitutionally invalid.

MR. JUSTICE WHITE, with whom MR. JUSTICE DOUGLAS and MR. JUSTICE BRENNAN join, dissenting.

. . .

There is no difficulty in identifying the class that is subject to the alleged discrimination and that is entitled to the benefits of the Equal Protection Clause. I need go no farther than the parents and children in the Edgewood district, who are plaintiffs here and who assert that they are entitled to the same choice as Alamo Heights to augment local expenditures for schools but are denied that choice by state law. This group constitutes a class sufficiently definite to invoke the protection of the Constitution....

MR. JUSTICE MARSHALL, with whom MR. JUSTICE DOUGLAS concurs, dissenting.

The Court today decides, in effect, that a State may constitutionally vary the quality of education which it offers its children in accordance with the amount of taxable wealth located in the school districts within which they reside. The majority's decision represents an abrupt departure from the mainstream of recent state and federal court decisions concerning the unconstitutionality of state educational financing schemes dependent upon taxable local wealth. More unfortunately, though, the majority's holding can only be seen as a retreat from our historic commitment to equality of educational opportunity and as unsupportable acquiescence in a system which deprives children in their earliest years of the chance to reach their full potential as citizens....

[II. B}

. . .

The special concern of this Court with the educational process of our country is a matter of common knowledge. Undoubtedly, this Court's most famous statement on the subject is that contained in *Brown* v. *Board of Education,* 347 U. S., at 493:

"Today, education is perhaps the most important function of state and local governments. Compulsory school attendance laws and the great expenditures for education both demonstrate our recognition of the importance of education to our democratic society. It is required in the performance of our most basic public responsibilities, even service in the armed forces. It is the very foundation of good citizenship. Today it is a principal instrument in awakening the child to cultural values, in preparing him for later professional training, and in helping him to adjust normally to his environment...."

...[T]he majority seeks refuge in the fact that the Court has "never presumed to possess either the ability or the authority to guarantee to the citizenry the most *effective* speech or the most *informed* electoral choice."...This serves only to blur what is in fact at stake. With due respect, the issue is neither provision of the most *effective* speech nor of the most *informed* vote. Appellees do not now seek the best education Texas might provide. They do seek, however, an end to state discrimination resulting from the unequal distribution of taxable district property wealth that directly impairs the ability of some districts to provide the same educational opportunity that other districts can provide with the same or even substantially less tax effort....

CONCLUSIONS

The group rights studied in this chapter illustrate the strong social forces and customs that help shape constitutional law. They also highlight the pressures applied to legislative and judicial bodies, with one branch or the other initiating action in response to changing conditions. Although the courts take the lead in some instances, the sections on women's rights show that Congress and the President were more important and took the initiative earlier. The sections on prisoner rights and school financing demonstrate that judges are cautious in ordering remedies that involve vast appropriations. Such allocations of state or federal funds are left generally to legislative action and the priorities established by the two political branches. State courts are demonstrating increasing independence in interpreting constitutional values through their own state charters.

SELECTED READINGS

ALPERT, GEOFFREY P., ed. Legal Rights of Prisoners. Beverly Hills, Calif.: Sage Publications, 1980.

BABCOCK, BARBARA A., et al. Sex Discrimination and the Law. Boston: Little, Brown, 1975.

BAER, JUDITH. "Sexual Equality and the Burger Court." 31 Western Political Quarterly 470 (1978).

BELAIR, ROBERT R., ed. Legal Rights of Children. Fair Lawn, N.J.: R. E. Burdick, 1973.

BENNETT, ROBERT W. "The Burger Court and the Poor," in Vincent Blasi, ed. The Burger Court: The Counter-Revolution That Wasn't. New Haven, Conn.: Yale University Press, 1983.

CLARK, HOMER H., JR. "Children and the Constitution." 1992 University of Illinois Law Review 1 (1992).

CLUTE, PENELOPE D. The Legal Aspects of Prisons and Jails. Springfield, Ill.: Charles C. Thomas, 1980.

FAIR, DARYL R. "Prison Reform by the Courts," in Richard A.L. Gambitta et al. Governing Through Courts. Beverly Hills, Calif.: Sage Publications, 1981.

FEELEY, MALCOLM M., AND EDWARD L. RUBIN. Judicial Policy Making and the Modern State: How the Courts Reformed America's Prisons. New York: Cambridge Uinversity Press, 1999.

FOX, SANFORD J. The Law of Juvenile Courts. St. Paul, Minn.: West, 1984.

GETMAN, JULIUS. "The Emerging Constitutional Principle of Sexual Equality." 1972 Supreme Court Review 157.

GINSBURG, RUTH BADER. "Gender in the Supreme Court: The 1973 and 1974 Terms." 1975 Supreme Court Review 1.

———. "The Burger Court's Grapplings with Sex Discrimination," in Vincent Blasi, ed. The Burger Court: The Counter-Revolution That Wasn't. New Haven, Conn.: Yale University Press, 1983.

GUGGENHEIM, MARTIN, AND ALAN SUSSMAN. The Rights of Young People. New York: Bantam Books, 1985.

HAPPERLE, WINIFRED, AND LAURA CRITES. Women in the Courts. Williamsburg, Va.: National Center for State Court, 1978.

JOHNSON, JOHN W. The Struggle for Student Rights. Lawrence, Kan.: University Press of Kansas, 1997.

KANOWITZ, LEO. Women and the Law. Albuquerque: University of New Mexico Press, 1969.

MANFREDI, CHRISTOPHER P. The Supreme Court and Juvenile Justice. Lawrence, Kan.: University Press of Kansas, 1998.

MANSBRIDGE, JANE J. Why We Lost the ERA. Chicago: University of Chicago Press, 1986.

NEIER, ARYEH. "Reforming Asylums: No Other Way," in Only Judgment. Middletown, Conn.: Wesleyan University Press, 1982.

O'CONNOR, KAREN. Women's Organizations' Use of the Courts. Lexington, Mass.: Lexington Books, 1980.

PAULSEN, MONRAD G. "Kent v. United States: The Constitutional Context of Juvenile Cases." 1966 Supreme Court Review 167.

———. "The Constitutional Domestication of the Juvenile Court." 1967 Supreme Court Review 233.

SCHEINGOLD, STUART. The Politics of Rights. New Haven, Conn.: Yale University Press, 1974.

STEINER, GILBERT Y. Constitutional Inequality: The Political Fortunes of the Equal Rights Amendment. Washington, D.C.: The Brookings Institution, 1985.

WILKINSON, J. HARVIE, III. "Goss v. Lopez: The Supreme Court as School Administrator." 1975 Supreme Court Review 25.

17

Rights of Privacy

The right to privacy is invoked repeatedly by Congress, the President, federal courts, and the states to uphold basic rights of individual conduct and choice. If privacy includes the right of a person to prevent intrusion into certain thoughts and activities, privacy is protected by the First Amendment (freedom of speech, religion, and association), the Third Amendment (quartering of troops in private homes), the Fourth Amendment (freedom from unreasonable searches and seizures), and the Fifth Amendment (freedom from self-incrimination). At times there is reliance on the Ninth Amendment, which states that the "enumeration in the Constitution, of certain rights, shall not be construed to deny or disparage others retained by the people." The Due Process and Equal Protection Clauses provide other shields for privacy interests, while a number of state constitutions include express rights of privacy.

A. DIMENSIONS OF PRIVACY

In contemporary times, privacy has a special urgency because of industrialization, urbanization, electronic surveillance methods, and computer data banks. The U.S. Constitution does not mention privacy, and yet a zone of autonomy is implicit in the framers' support for individual rights and limited government. The notion of privacy is part of our presocietal "natural rights." Areas of private conduct and thought have always been protected from state intrusion. James Madison felt strongly that people had a property interest in their opinions, the free communication of ideas, religious beliefs, and conscience (pages 433–34).

The Declaration of Independence attacked England's practice of "quartering large bodies of armed troops among us." In response, the Third Amendment provides that no soldier shall, "in time of peace be quartered in any house, without the consent of the owner, nor in time of war, but in a manner to be prescribed by law." The Fourth Amendment was adopted to prevent the hated general warrants and writs of assistance used by England to invade the homes and businesses of American colonists. In a famous dissent in 1928, Justice Brandeis interpreted the trilogy in the Declaration of Independence—life, liberty, and the pursuit of happiness—in these terms:

> The makers of our Constitution undertook to secure conditions favorable to the pursuit of happiness. They recognized the significance of man's spiritual nature, of his feelings and of his intellect. They knew that only a part of his pain, pleasure and satisfactions of life are to be found in material things. They sought to protect Americans in their beliefs, their thoughts, their emotions and their sensations. They conferred, as against the Government, the right to be let alone—the most comprehensive of rights and the right most valued by civilized men. Olmstead v. United States, 277 U.S. 438, 478 (1928).

The phrase "the right to be let alone" appeared earlier in an article published by Brandeis and Samuel D. Warren in 1890. Building on Judge Thomas Cooley's treatise on torts, they concluded that the right to privacy evolved from transformations that had occurred in property rights: from tangible to intangible interests; from actual bodily injury (battery) to the mere threat of injury (assault). Protections were extended to reputation (slander and libel) and to intellectual property (copyright, trademarks, and trade secrets). Brandeis and Warren were especially offended by reporters and photographers who invaded "the sacred precincts of private and domestic life." 4 Harv. L. Rev. 193, 195 (1890).

The right of citizens to conduct their own lives was recognized by the Supreme Court in 1923 when it struck down a Nebraska law prohibiting the teaching in any school of any modern language other than English to any child who had not passed the eighth grade. The statute, reflecting an anti-German mentality following World War I, interfered with the liberty of individuals to pursue their interests: "the right of the individual to contract, to engage in any of the common occupations of life, to acquire useful knowledge, to marry, to establish a home and bring up children, to worship God according to the dictates of his own conscience, and generally to enjoy those privileges long recognized at common law as essential to the orderly pursuit of happiness by free men." Meyer v. Nebraska, 262 U.S. 390, 399 (1923).

Two years later, the Court invalidated an Oregon law that required all children between the ages of eight and sixteen to attend public school. A Roman Catholic orphanage and a military academy brought suit to defend the rights of parents to send their children to private schools. Following the doctrine of *Meyer v. Nebraska,* the Court held that the Oregon statute unreasonably interfered with the liberty of parents and guardians to direct the upbringing and education of their children: "The child is not the mere creature of the State; those who nurture him and direct his destiny have the right, coupled with the high duty, to recognize and prepare him for additional obligations." Pierce v. Society of Sisters, 268 U.S. 510, 535 (1925).[1]

Sterilization

At the same time that the Supreme Court defended the right to teach foreign languages and operate private schools, it endorsed a major governmental intrusion into individual privacy: sterilization of the "unfit." Some of the early decisions by federal courts rejected state efforts to sterilize prisoners for eugenic reasons. In 1914 a federal district court struck down a law in Iowa that required a vasectomy for criminals convicted twice of a felony (even if "felonies" consisted of breaking an electric globe and unfastening a strap on a harness). The court regarded vasectomy as a cruel and unusual punishment that "belongs to the Dark Ages." Davis v. Berry, 216 Fed. 413, 416 (S.D. Iowa 1914). A Nevada law on sterilization was struck down in 1918 because it gave judges too much discretion. Mickle v. Henrichs, 262 Fed. 687 (D. Nev. 1918).

A Virginia court in 1925 upheld a sterilization law as a proper use of the police power to prevent the transmission of insanity, idiocy, imbecility, epilepsy, and crime. Buck v. Bell, 143 Va. 310 (1925). The case involved Carrie Buck, committed to a state institution at the age of eighteen. Her mother had been committed to the same institution, and Carrie had just given birth to an illegitimate child that the state claimed was of "defective mentality."

By an 8–1 majority, a three-page opinion by Justice Holmes affirmed the state law. The decision is marred by illogic, hasty assumptions of unproved assertions, and a judgment that is

---

1. For historical background and analysis of *Meyer* and *Pierce*, see William G. Ross, Forging New Freedoms: Nativism, Education, and the Constitution, 1917–1927 (1994).

Controlling Crime with Eugenics

An 1877 study by Richard Louis Dugdale, *The Jukes*, popularized the notion that crime was largely hereditary. Cesare Lombroso's *Criminal Man* (1896–97) identified anthropological features that marked the born criminal. A study published in 1893 claimed that "it is established beyond controversy that criminals and paupers, both, are degenerate; the imperfect, knotty, knurly, worm-eated, half-rotten fruit of the race" (Henry M. Boies, *Prisoners and Paupers*, p. 266). The eugenics movement had the answer: sterilization.

In the hands of reformers and progressives, eugenics became a respected argument for opposing mixed marriages and for excluding "lower stock" immigrants from the Mediterranean countries, Eastern Europe, and Russia. Experts proposed that sterilization be directed against such vague categories as the feeble-minded, the criminalistic (including the delinquent and the "wayward"), the epileptic, inebriates and drug users, the diseased (including tuberculosis, syphilis, and leprosy), the blind (including seriously impaired vision), the deaf (including seriously impaired hearing), the deformed (including the crippled), and dependents, "including orphans, ne'er-do-wells, the homeless, tramps, and paupers" (Harry Hamilton Laughlin, Eugenical Sterilization in the United States 446–47 (1922)).

The Supreme Court's decision in *Buck* v. *Bell* preceded by a few years Nazi Germany's biological experiments and its extermination of millions of Jews, Poles, gypsies, and other groups, all part of a plan to produce a "master race." Today, instead of sterilization's being forced on the "unfit," the operation is submitted to voluntarily each year by thousands of fit adults for the purpose of population control.

harsh if not cruel. Holmes dashed off one of his famous aphorisms: "Three generations of imbeciles are enough." BUCK v. BELL, 274 U.S. 200, 207 (1927). In fact, Carrie's child was not mentally impaired.[2] The Court handed down its decision in an environment that believed that crime and other social problems could be controlled by sterilization (see box).

Buck v. *Bell* has never been explicitly overruled. However, its tenets were challenged by the Supreme Court in 1942 when it struck down an Oklahoma law that provided for the sterilization of "habitual criminals." A unanimous opinion held that the state statute violated the Equal Protection Clause of the Fourteenth Amendment by making an invidious distinction. Under the statute, someone who stole more than $20 three times would be sterilized, whereas someone who embezzled that amount three times was exempt, even though both crimes were a felony under state law.

The Court did not comment on the scope of the police power to mandate sterilization. It did note that the case involved "one of the basic civil rights of man. Marriage and procreation are fundamental to the very existence and survival of the race." Skinner v. Oklahoma, 316 U.S. 535, 541 (1942). Chief Justice Stone, concurring, thought that a state could, after appropriate inquiry, sterilize someone "to prevent the transmission by inheritance of his socially injurious tendencies." Justice Jackson, also concurring, insisted that there are limits to the extent that legislatures "may conduct biological experiments at the expense of the dignity and personality and natural powers of a minority—even those who have been guilty of what the

---

2. For good critiques of *Buck* v. *Bell,* see J. David Smith and K. Ray Nelson, The Sterilization of Carrie Buck: Was She Feebleminded of Society's Pawn? (1989); Paul A. Lombardo, "Three Generations, No Imbeciles: New Light on *Buck* v. *Bell,*" 60 N.Y.U. L. Rev. 30 (1985); Clement E. Vose, Constitutional Change 5–20 (1972); James B. O'Hara and T. Howland Sanks, "Eugenic Sterilization," 45 Geo. L. J. 20 (1956); Walter Berns, "*Buck* v. *Bell*: Due Process of Law?," 6 West. Pol. Q. 762 (1953).

majority defines as crimes." Jackson's reservations have been underscored by more recent cases involving the rights of marriage, family, and privacy.

Privacy and Family

In 1967 the Supreme Court issued an important decision that recognized the essential value of privacy in the Fourth Amendment. After decades of tortured reasoning on what constitutes a "search," the Court finally came to terms with an individual's constitutional right to preserve certain activities as private, even in an area accessible to the public. Katz v. United States, 389 U.S. 347 (1967), reprinted in Chapter 14.

Two years later, a unanimous Supreme Court held that the private possession of obscene materials by an adult cannot constitutionally be made a crime. State claims that the materials are obscene cannot override an individual's liberty: "If the First Amendment means anything, it means that a State has no business telling a man, sitting alone in his own house, what books he may read or what films he may watch. Our whole constitutional heritage rebels at the thought of giving government the power to control men's minds." STANLEY v. GEORGIA, 394 U.S. 557, 565 (1969). *Stanley* was qualified by the Court in 1990 when it upheld state efforts to prohibit the possession or viewing of child pornography even in the privacy of one's home. Osborne v. Ohio, 495 U.S. 103 (1990).

The relationship between privacy and the choice of family and marriage has been explored in other decisions. A zoning case in 1977 involved a local ordinance that denied a woman the right to remain in her house because she lived with her son and two grandsons (who were first cousins). Because of the latter, she did not qualify under the definition of "family" included in the ordinance. The Court held that the ordinance arbitrarily interfered with the family unit. The Constitution "protects the sanctity of the family precisely because the institution of the family is deeply rooted in this Nation's history and tradition." Moore v. East Cleveland, 431 U.S. 494 (1977). In that same year, a unanimous Court upheld a New York law that provided for expedited procedures for removing a child from foster parents and placing the child with the natural parents. The liberty interest in family privacy "has its source, and its contours are ordinarily to be sought, not in state law, but in intrinsic human rights...." Smith v. Organization of Foster Families, 431 U.S. 816, 845 (1977).

In 2000, the Court ruled that a Washington state law providing for court-ordered visitation rights for grandparents and "any person" was constitutionally overbroad and violated the rights of parents to make fundamental decisions about their children. Writing for a 6 to 3 Court, Justice O'Connor held that a Washington state judge improperly granted visitation rights to grandparents of two young girls against the wishes of their mother. The Court decided that the statute violated the Due Process Clause of the Fourteenth Amendment. Troxel v. Granville, 120 S.Ct. 2054 (2000).

The right to marry is a decision that an individual is free to make without governmental interference. Loving v. Virginia, 388 U.S. 1, 12 (1967). A Wisconsin statute prohibited a certain class of state resident from marrying without first obtaining a court order granting permission. The class was anyone with a child not in his custody and whom he is obligated to support by court order or judgment. An 8–1 Court held that the statute violated the Due Process Clause by interfering with the fundamental right to marry. The decision to marry is "among the personal decisions protected by the right of privacy." Zablocki v. Redhail, 434 U.S. 374, 384 (1978).

Reputation

Part of our intangible property is reputation. The precious quality of this commodity is captured in Shakespeare's *Othello*: "Good name in man and woman, dear my lord, is the immediate jewel of their souls: who steals my purse steals trash; 'tis something, nothing; 'twas mine, 'tis his, and has been slave to thousands; but he that filches from me my good name robs me of that which not enriches him, but makes me poor indeed."

A case in 1971 involved the action of a Wisconsin police chief who posted a notice in all retail stores forbidding for one year the sale of liquor to a woman. State law required these postings—without notice or hearing—whenever a designated official decided that the sale of liquor to a particular person would endanger the community or place the individual or the individual's family in a state of want. The Supreme Court, by a 6–3 majority, held that notice and an opportunity to be heard are essential safeguards whenever a person's name, reputation, honor, or integrity is at stake. Wisconsin v. Constantineau, 400 U.S. 433, 437 (1971).

The Court decided a similar case in 1976, but this time left the individual's reputation unprotected. The police in Kentucky authorized the preparation and distribution of a flyer containing the names and mug shots of persons described as "subjects known to be active in this criminal field" of shoplifting. About 800 flyers were distributed to merchants and businesspeople in downtown Louisville. A newspaper photographer was arrested, but not convicted, of shoplifting. Although the charges against him were eventually dropped, his name and photograph appeared in the flyer. He filed suit, claiming injury to reputation and impairment of earning ability. The Sixth Circuit rejected the idea that police chiefs can determine the guilt or innocence of an accused. However, a 5–3 Court—distinguishing this case from *Constantineau*—reversed the Sixth Circuit by holding that distribution of the flyer did not deprive the plaintiff of any "liberty" or "property" rights secured against state deprivation by the Fourteenth Amendment. PAUL v. DAVIS, 424 U.S. 693 (1976).

Buck v. Bell

274 U.S. 200 (1927)

A Virginia statute provided for the sexual sterilization of inmates in state institutions who were found to be afflicted with a hereditary form of insanity or imbecility. The state intended to perform on Carrie Buck the operation of salpingectomy, which consists of opening the abdominal cavity and cutting the Fallopian tubes. The statute, upheld by the Virginia Supreme Court of Appeals, provided for a hearing before the operation could be performed. The defendant in this case was Dr. J. H. Bell, Superintendent of the Colony for Epileptics and Feeble Minded.

MR. JUSTICE HOLMES delivered the opinion of the Court.

. . .

Carrie Buck is a feeble minded white woman who was committed to the State Colony *[for Epileptics and Feeble Minded]* in due form. She is the daughter of a feeble minded mother in the same institution, and the mother of an illegitimate feeble minded child. She was eighteen years old at the time of the trial of her case in the Circuit Court, in the latter part of 1924. An Act of Virginia, approved March 20, 1924, recites that the health of the patient and the welfare of society may be promoted in certain cases by the sterilization of mental defectives, under careful safeguard, &c.; that the sterilization may be effected in males

by vasectomy and in females by salpingectomy, without serious pain or substantial danger to life; that the Commonwealth is supporting in various institutions many defective persons who if now discharged would become a menace but if incapable of procreating might be discharged with safety and become self-supporting with benefit to themselves and to society; and that experience has shown that heredity plays an important part in the transmission of insanity, imbecility, &c. The statute then enacts that whenever the superintendent of certain institutions including the above named State Colony shall be of opinion that it is for the best interests of the patients and of society that an inmate under his care should be sexually sterilized, he may have the operation performed upon any patient afflicted with hereditary forms of insanity, imbecility, &c., on complying with the very careful provisions by which the act protects the patients from possible abuse.

The superintendent first presents a petition to the special board of directors of his hospital or colony, stating the facts and the grounds for his opinion, verified by affidavit. Notice of the petition and of the time and place of the hearing in the institution is to be served upon the inmate, and also upon his guardian, and if there is no guardian the superintendent is to apply to the Circuit Court of the County to appoint one. If the inmate is a minor notice also is to be given to his parents if any with a copy of the petition. The board is to see to it that the inmate may attend the hearings if desired by him or his guardian. The evidence is all to be reduced to writing, and after the board has made its order for or against the operation, the superintendent, or the inmate, or his guardian, may appeal to the Circuit Court of the County. The Circuit Court may consider the record of the board and the evidence before it and such other admissible evidence as may be offered, and may affirm, revise, or reverse the order of the board and enter such order as it deems just. Finally any party may apply to the Supreme Court of Appeals, which, if it grants the appeal, is to hear the case upon the record of the trial in the Circuit Court and may enter such order as it thinks the Circuit Court should have entered. There can be no doubt that so far as procedure is concerned the rights of the patient are most carefully considered, and as every step in this case was taken in scrupulous compliance with the statute and after months of observation, there is no doubt that in that respect the plaintiff in error has had due process of law.

The attack is not upon the procedure but upon the substantive law. It seems to be contended that in no circumstances could such an order be justified. It certainly is contended that the order cannot be justified upon the existing grounds. The judgment finds the facts that have been recited and that Carrie Buck "is the probable potential parent of socially inadequate offspring, likewise afflicted, that she may be sexually sterilized without detriment to her general health and that her welfare and that of society will be promoted by her sterilization," and thereupon makes the order. In view of the general declarations of the legislature and the specific findings of the Court, obviously we cannot say as matter of law that the grounds do not exist, and if they exist they justify the result. We have seen more than once that the public welfare may call upon the best citizens for their lives. It would be strange if it could not call upon those who already sap the strength of the State for these lesser sacrifices, often not felt to be such by those concerned, in order to prevent our being swamped with incompetence. It is better for all the world, if instead of waiting to execute degenerate offspring for crime, or to let them starve for their imbecility, society can prevent those who are manifestly unfit from continuing their kind. The principle that sustains compulsory vaccination is broad enough to cover cutting the Fallopian tubes. *Jacobson v. Massachusetts*, 197 U.S. 11. Three generations of imbeciles are enough.

But, it is said, however it might be if this reasoning were applied generally, it fails when it is confined to the small number who are in the institutions named and is not applied to the multitudes outside. It is the usual last resort of constitutional arguments to point out shortcomings of this sort. But the answer is that the law does all that is needed when it does all that it can, indicates a policy, applies it to all within the lines, and seeks to bring within the lines all similarly situated so far and so fast as its means allow. Of course so far as the operations enable those who otherwise must be kept confined to be returned to the world, and thus open the asylum to others, the equality aimed at will be more nearly reached.

Judgment affirmed.

MR. JUSTICE BUTLER dissents.

Stanley v. Georgia

394 U.S. 557 (1969)

Law enforcement officers obtained a warrant to search Robert Eli Stanley's home for evidence of alleged bookmaking activities. While conducting this search, they found some films in his bedroom, used a projector to view the films, and judged them to be obscene. He was later convicted for violating a Georgia law that prohibits the possession of obscene matter. The conviction was confirmed by the Georgia Supreme Court.

MR. JUSTICE MARSHALL delivered the opinion of the Court.

. . .

Appellant raises several challenges to the validity of his conviction. We find it necessary to consider only one. Appellant argues here, and argued below, that the Georgia obscenity statute, insofar as it punishes mere private possession of obscene matter, violates the First Amendment, as made applicable to the States by the Fourteenth Amendment. For reasons set forth below, we agree that the mere private possession of obscene matter cannot constitutionally be made a crime.

...The State and appellant both agree that the question here before us is whether "a statute imposing criminal sanctions upon the mere [knowing] possession of obscene matter" is constitutional. In this context, Georgia concedes that the present case appears to be one of "first impression...on this exact point," but contends that since "obscenity is not within the area of constitutionally protected speech or press," *Roth* v. *United States,* 354 U. S. 476, 485 (1957), the States are free, subject to the limits of other provisions of the Constitution, see, *e.g., Ginsberg* v. *New York,* 390 U. S. 629, 637–645 (1968), to deal with it any way deemed necessary, just as they may deal with possession of other things thought to be detrimental to the welfare of their citizens. If the State can protect the body of a citizen, may it not, argues Georgia, protect his mind?

It is true that *Roth* does declare, seemingly without qualification, that obscenity is not protected by the First Amendment....However, neither *Roth* nor any subsequent decision of this Court dealt with the precise problem involved in the present case. Roth was convicted of mailing obscene circulars and advertising, and an obscene book, in violation of a federal obscenity statute. The defendant in a companion case, *Alberts* v. *California,* 354 U. S. 476 (1957), was convicted of "lewdly keeping for sale obscene and indecent books, and [of] writing, composing and publishing an obscene advertisement of them...." *Id.,* at 481. None of the statements cited by the Court in *Roth* for the proposition that "this Court has always assumed that obscenity is not protected by the freedoms of speech and press" were made in the context of a statute punishing mere private possession of obscene material; the cases cited deal for the most part with use of the mails to distribute objectionable material or with some form of public distribution or dissemination. Moreover,

none of this Court's decisions subsequent to *Roth* involved prosecution for private possession of obscene materials. Those cases dealt with the power of the State and Federal Governments to prohibit or regulate certain public actions taken or intended to be taken with respect to obscene matter. Indeed, with one exception, we have been unable to discover any case in which the issue in the present case has been fully considered.

. . .

It is now well established that the Constitution protects the right to receive information and ideas. "This freedom [of speech and press]...necessarily protects the right to receive...." *Martin* v. *City of Struthers,* 319 U. S. 141, 143 (1943);...[t]his right to receive information and ideas, regardless of their social worth, see *Winters* v. *New York,* 333 U. S. 507, 510 (1948), is fundamental to our free society. Moreover, in the context of this case—a prosecution for mere possession of printed or filmed matter in the privacy of a person's own home—that right takes on an added dimension. For also fundamental is the right to be free, except in very limited circumstances, from unwanted governmental intrusions into one's privacy.

"The makers of our Constitution undertook to secure conditions favorable to the pursuit of happiness. They recognized the significance of man's spiritual nature, of his feelings and of his intellect. They knew that only a part of the pain, pleasure and satisfactions of life are to be found in material things. They sought to protect Americans in their beliefs, their thoughts, their emotions and their sensations. They conferred, as against the Government, the right to be let alone—the most comprehensive of rights and the right most valued by civilized man." *Olmstead* v. *United States,* 277 U.S. 438, 478 (1928) (Brandeis, J., dissenting).

See *Griswold* v. *Connecticut, supra;* cf. *NAACP* v. *Alabama,* 357 U. S. 449, 462 (1958).

These are the rights that appellant is asserting in the case before us. He is asserting the right to read or observe what he pleases—the right to satisfy his intellectual and emotional needs in the privacy of his own home. He is asserting the right to be free from state inquiry into the contents of his library. Georgia contends that appellant does not have these rights, that there are certain types of materials that the individual may not read or even possess. Georgia justifies this assertion by arguing that the films in the present case are obscene. But we think that mere categorization of these films as "obscene" is insufficient justification for such a drastic invasion of personal liberties guaranteed by the First and Fourteenth Amendments. Whatever may be the justifications for other statutes regulating obscenity, we do not think they reach into the privacy of one's own home. If the First Amendment means anything, it means that a State has no business telling a man, sitting alone in his own house, what books he may read or what films he may watch. Our whole constitutional heritage rebels at the thought of giving government the power to control men's minds.

. . .

. . . Georgia asserts that exposure to obscene materials may lead to deviant sexual behavior or crimes of sexual violence. There appears to be little empirical basis for that assertion. But more important, if the State is only concerned about printed or filmed materials inducing antisocial conduct, we believe that in the context of private consumption of ideas and information we should adhere to the view that "[a]mong free men, the deterrents ordinarily to be applied to prevent crime are education and punishment for violations of the law. . . ." *Whitney* v. *California,* 274 U. S. 357, 378 (1927) (Brandeis, J., concurring). See Emerson, Toward a General Theory of the First Amendment, 72 Yale L. J. 877, 938 (1963). Given the present state of knowledge, the State may no more prohibit mere possession of obscene matter on the ground that it may lead to antisocial conduct than it may prohibit possession of chemistry books on the ground that they may lead to the manufacture of homemade spirits.

It is true that in *Roth* this Court rejected the necessity of proving that exposure to obscene material would create a clear and present danger of antisocial conduct or would probably induce its recipients to such conduct. 354 U. S., at 486–487. But that case dealt with public distribution of obscene materials and such distribution is subject to different objections. For example, there is always the danger that obscene material might fall into the hands of children, see *Ginsberg* v. *New York, supra,* or that it might intrude upon the sensibilities or privacy of the general public. See *Redrup*

v. *New York,* 386 U. S. 767, 769 (1967). No such dangers are present in this case.

Finally, we are faced with the argument that prohibition of possession of obscene materials is a necessary incident to statutory schemes prohibiting distribution. That argument is based on alleged difficulties of proving an intent to distribute or in producing evidence of actual distribution. We are not convinced that such difficulties exist, but even if they did we do not think that they would justify infringement of the individual's right to read or observe what he pleases. Because that right is so fundamental to our scheme of individual liberty, its restriction may not be justified by the need to ease the administration of otherwise valid criminal laws. See *Smith* v. *California,* 361 U. S. 147 (1959).

We hold that the First and Fourteenth Amendments prohibit making mere private possession of obscene material a crime. *Roth* and the cases following that decision are not impaired by today's holding. As we have said, the States retain broad power to regulate obscenity; that power simply does not extend to mere possession by the individual in the privacy of his own home. Accordingly, the judgment of the court below is reversed and the case is remanded for proceedings not inconsistent with this opinion.

It is so ordered.

Mr. Justice Black, concurring.

I agree with the Court that the mere possession of reading matter or movie films, whether labeled obscene or not, cannot be made a crime by a State without violating the First Amendment, made applicable to the States by the Fourteenth. My reasons for this belief have been set out in many of my prior opinions, as for example, *Smith* v. *California,* 361 U. S. 147, 155 (concurring opinion), and *Ginzburg* v. *United States,* 383 U. S. 463, 476 (dissenting opinion).

Mr. Justice Stewart, with whom Mr. Justice Brennan and Mr. Justice White join, concurring in the result.

. . .

Paul v. Davis

424 U.S. 693 (1976)

A photocopy of Edward Charles Davis III, bearing his name, was included in a "flyer" of "active shoplifters" and distributed to area merchants by the police department. Davis

had been arrested on a shoplifting charge. After circulation of the flyer, the charge was dismissed. He brought an action against Edgar Paul, Chief of Police of the Louisville, Kentucky, Division of Police, and Russell McDaniel, Chief of Police of the Jefferson County, Kentucky, Division of Police. Davis claimed that their defamation of him violated 42 U.S.C. § 1983 (official deprivation of rights, privileges, or immunities secured by the Constitution and laws) and the Fourteenth Amendment. His suit was dismissed by the district court, but the Sixth Circuit supported his Section 1983 complaint.

MR. JUSTICE REHNQUIST delivered the opinion of the Court.

We granted certiorari, 421 U. S. 909 (1975), in this case to consider whether respondent's charge that petitioners' defamation of him, standing alone and apart from any other governmental action with respect to him, stated a claim for relief under 42 U.S.C. § 1983 and the Fourteenth Amendment. For the reasons hereinafter stated, we conclude that it does not.

Petitioner Paul is the Chief of Police of the Louisville, Ky., Division of Police, while petitioner McDaniel occupies the same position in the Jefferson County, Ky., Division of Police. In late 1972 they agreed to combine their efforts for the purpose of alerting local area merchants to possible shoplifters who might be operating during the Christmas season. In early December petitioners distributed to approximately 800 merchants in the Louisville metropolitan area a "flyer," which began as follows:

"TO: BUSINESS MEN IN THE
METROPOLITAN AREA

"The Chiefs of The Jefferson County and City of Louisville Police Departments, in an effort to keep their officers advised on shoplifting activity, have approved the attached alphabetically arranged flyer of subjects known to be active in this criminal field.

"This flyer is being distributed to you, the business man, so that you may inform your security personnel to watch for these subjects. These persons have been arrested during 1971 and 1972 or have been active in various criminal fields in high density shopping areas.

"Only the photograph and name of the subject is shown on this flyer, if additional information is desired, please forward a request in writing...."

The flyer consisted of five pages of "mug shot" photos, arranged alphabetically. Each page was headed:

"NOVEMBER 1972
CITY OF LOUISVILLE
JEFFERSON COUNTY

POLICE DEPARTMENTS
ACTIVE SHOPLIFTERS"

In approximately the center of page 2 there appeared photos and the name of the respondent, Edward Charles Davis III.

Respondent appeared on the flyer because on June 14, 1971, he had been arrested in Louisville on a charge of shoplifting. He had been arraigned on this charge in September 1971, and, upon his plea of not guilty, the charge had been "filed away with leave [to reinstate]," a disposition which left the charge outstanding. Thus, at the time petitioners caused the flyer to be prepared and circulated respondent had been charged with shoplifting but his guilt or innocence of that offense had never been resolved. Shortly after circulation of the flyer the charge against respondent was finally dismissed by a judge of the Louisville Police Court.

At the time the flyer was circulated respondent was employed as a photographer by the Louisville Courier-Journal and Times. The flyer, and respondent's inclusion therein, soon came to the attention of respondent's supervisor, the executive director of photography for the two newspapers. This individual called respondent in to hear his version of the events leading to his appearing in the flyer. Following this discussion, the supervisor informed respondent that although he would not be fired, he "had best not find himself in a similar situation" in the future.

. . .

I

Respondent's due process claim is grounded upon his assertion that the flyer, and in particular the phrase "Active Shoplifters" appearing at the head of the page upon which his name and photograph appear, impermissibly deprived him of some "liberty" protected by the Fourteenth Amendment. His complaint asserted that the "active shoplifter" designation would inhibit him from entering business establishments for fear of being suspected of shoplifting and possibly apprehended, and would seriously impair his future employment opportunities. Accepting that such consequences may flow from the flyer in question, respondent's complaint would appear to state a classical claim for defamation actionable in the courts of virtually every State. Imputing criminal behavior to an individual is generally considered defamatory *per se,* and actionable without proof of special damages.

Respondent brought his action, however, not in the state courts of Kentucky, but in a United States District Court for that State. He asserted not a claim for defamation under the laws of Kentucky, but a claim that he had been deprived of rights secured to him by the Fourteenth Amendment of the United States Constitution. Concededly if the same allegations had been made about respondent by a private individual, he would have nothing more than a claim for defamation under state law. But, he contends, since petitioners are respectively an offical of city and of county government, his action is thereby transmuted into one for deprivation by the State of rights secured under the Fourteenth Amendment.

· · ·

If respondent's view is to prevail, a person arrested by law enforcement officers who announce that they believe such person to be responsible for a particular crime in order to calm the fears of an aroused populace, presumably obtains a claim against such officers under § 1983. And since it is surely far more clear from the language of the Fourteenth Amendment that "life" is protected against state deprivation than it is that reputation is protected against state injury, it would be difficult to see why the survivors of an innocent bystander mistakenly shot by a policeman or negligently killed by a sheriff driving a government vehicle, would not have claims equally cognizable under § 1983.

It is hard to perceive any logical stopping place to such a line of reasoning. Respondent's construction would seem almost necessarily to result in every legally cognizable injury which may have been inflicted by a state official acting under "color of law" establishing a violation of the Fourteenth Amendment. We think it would come as a great surprise to those who drafted and shepherded the adoption of that Amendment to learn that it worked such a result, and a study of our decisions convinces us they do not support the construction urged by respondent.

II

The result reached by the Court of Appeals, which respondent seeks to sustain here, must be bottomed on one of two premises. The first is that the Due Process Clause of the Fourteenth Amendment and § 1983 make actionable many wrongs inflicted by government employees which had heretofore been thought to give rise only to state-law tort claims. The second premise is that the infliction by state officials of a "stigma" to one's reputation is somehow different in kind from the infliction by the same official of harm or injury to other interests protected by state law, so that an injury to reputation is actionable under § 1983 and the Fourteenth Amendment even if other such harms are not. We examine each of these premises in turn.

A

The first premise would be contrary to pronouncements in our cases on more than one occasion with respect to the scope of § 1983 and of the Fourteenth Amendment. In the leading case of *Screws* v. *United States,* 325 U. S. 91 (1945), the Court considered the proper application of the criminal counterpart of § 1983, likewise intended by Congress to enforce the guarantees of the Fourteenth Amendment. In his opinion for the Court plurality in that case, Mr. Justice Douglas observed:

"Violation of local law does not necessarily mean that federal rights have been invaded. The fact that a prisoner is assaulted, injured, or even murdered by state officials does not necessarily mean that he is deprived of any right protected or secured by the Constitution or laws of the United States." 325 U.S., at 108–109.

· · ·

B

The second premise upon which the result reached by the Court of Appeals could be rested — that the infliction by state officials of a "stigma" to one's reputation is somehow different in kind from infliction by a state official of harm to other interests protected by state law — is equally untenable. The words "liberty" and "property" as used in the Fourteenth Amendment do not in terms single out reputation as a candidate for special protection over and above other interests that may be protected by state law. While we have in a number of our prior cases pointed out the frequently drastic effect of the "stigma" which may result from defamation by the government in a variety of contexts, this line of cases does not establish the proposition that reputation alone, apart from some more tangible interests such as employment, is either "liberty" or "property" by itself sufficient to invoke the procedural protection of the Due Process Clause....

. . .

There is undoubtedly language in *Constantineau,* which is sufficiently ambiguous to justify the reliance upon it by the Court of Appeals:

"Yet certainly where the state attaches 'a badge of infamy' to the citizen, due process comes into play. *Wieman* v. *Updegraff,* 344 U. S. 183, 191. '[T]he right to be heard before being condemned to suffer grievous loss of any kind, even though it may not involve the stigma and hardships of a criminal conviction, is a principle basic to our society.' *Anti-Fascist Committee* v. *McGrath,* 341 U. S. 123, 168 (Frankfurter, J., concurring).

"Where a person's good name, reputation, honor, or integrity is at stake *because of what the government is doing to him,* notice and an opportunity to be heard are essential." *Id., at 437* (emphasis supplied).

. . .

We think that the italicized language in the last sentence quoted, "because of what the government is doing to him," referred to the fact that the governmental action taken in that case deprived the individual of a right previously held under state law — the right to purchase or obtain liquor in common with the rest of the citizenry. "Posting," therefore, significantly altered her status as a matter of state law, and it was that alteration of legal status which, combined with the injury resulting from the defamation, justified the invocation of procedural safeguards. The "stigma" resulting from the defamatory character of the posting was doubtless an important factor in evaluating the extent of harm worked by that act, but we do not think that such defamation, standing alone, deprived Constantineau of any "liberty" protected by the procedural guarantees of the Fourteenth Amendment.

. . .

...[T]he interest in reputation alone which respondent seeks to vindicate in this action in federal court is quite different from the "liberty" or "property" recognized in those decisions. Kentucky law does not extend to respondent any legal guarantee of present enjoyment of reputation which has been altered as a result of petitioners' actions. Rather his interest in reputation is simply one of a number which the State may protect against injury by virtue of its tort law, providing a forum for vindication of those interests by means of damages actions. And any harm or injury to that interest, even where as here inflicted by an officer of the State, does not result in a deprivation of any "liberty" or "property" recognized by state or federal law, nor has it worked any change of respondent's status as theretofore recognized under the State's laws. For these reasons we hold that the interest in reputation asserted in this case is neither "liberty" nor "property" guaranteed against state deprivation without due process of law.

. . .

IV

Respondent's complaint also alleged a violation of a "right to privacy guaranteed by the First, Fourth, Fifth, Ninth, and Fourteenth Amendments." *[The Court finds that previous cases on privacy — relating to marriage, procreation, contraception, family relationships — do not apply to Davis's complaint.]*

. . .

MR. JUSTICE STEVENS took no part in the consideration or decision of this case.

MR. JUSTICE BRENNAN, with whom MR. JUSTICE MARSHALL concurs and MR. JUSTICE WHITE concurs in part, dissenting.

I dissent. The Court today holds that police officials, acting in their official capacities as law enforcers, may on their own initiative and without trial constitutionally condemn innocent individuals as criminals and thereby brand them with one of the most stigmatizing and debilitating labels in our society. If there are no constitutional restraints on such oppressive behavior, the safeguards constitutionally accorded an accused in a criminal trial are rendered a sham, and no individual can feel secure that he will not be arbitrarily singled out for similar *ex parte* punishment by those primarily charged with fair enforcement of the law. The Court accomplishes this result by excluding a person's interest in his good name and reputation from all constitutional protection, regardless of the character of or necessity for the government's actions....

B. USE OF CONTRACEPTIVES

Family and marriage cases rely heavily on a landmark case in 1965 regarding the right to privacy. A Connecticut law made it a crime for any person to use any drug or article to prevent conception. This type of statute can be traced to the Comstock Act of 1873, which Congress passed to suppress the circulation of obscene literature and "immoral" articles. The statute prohibited selling, giving away, exhibiting, possessing, or promoting "any drug or medicine, or any article whatever, for the prevention of conception" and prohibited the mailing of any article designed to prevent conception. 17 Stat. 598, §§ 1, 2 (1873).

The constitutional issue of using contraceptives did not reach the Supreme Court until 1943, when it dismissed a case on the ground that the physician bringing it lacked standing to challenge a Connecticut statute. Tileston v. Ullman, 318 U.S. 44 (1943). The Court avoided the issue again in 1961, arguing that the case lacked ripeness because the plaintiff had not been prosecuted. However, two of the four dissents argued that the statute invaded the right to privacy. To Justice Douglas, the Connecticut law "touches the relationship between man and wife [and] reaches into the intimacies of the marriage relationship." Poe v. Ullman, 367 U.S. 497, 519 (1961). Efforts to enforce the law would mark "an invasion of the privacy that is implicit in a free society." Id. at 521. Only in totalitarian regimes, he said, could the government seek to bring the married couple completely within the control of the state: "Can there be any doubt that a Bill of Rights that in time of peace bars soldiers from being quartered in a home 'without the consent of the Owner' should also bar the police from investigating the intimacies of the marriage relation?" Id. at 522.

Justice Harlan's dissent also invoked the right of privacy to condemn the Connecticut law: "I believe that a statute making it a criminal offense for *married couples* to use contraceptives is an intolerable and unjustifiable invasion of privacy in the conduct of the most intimate concerns of an individual's life." Id. at 539. The law was "grossly offensive to this privacy" and forced the machinery of criminal law "into the very heart of marital privacy." Id. at 549, 553. *Poe v. Ullman* is reprinted in Chapter 3.

By 1965 the Supreme Court was prepared to decide the constitutionality of the Connecticut statute. An administrator and physician had been convicted for giving married persons information and medical advice on how to prevent conception and prescribing a contraceptive device for the wife's use. Writing for the Court, Justice Douglas held that the law violated the Due Process Clause of the Fourteenth Amendment, "emanations" and "penumbras" from the First Amendment (including association and privacy), and other privacy values derived from the Third, Fourth, Fifth, and Ninth Amendments. Justice Goldberg, joined by Chief Justice Warren and Justice Brennan, relied primarily on the Ninth Amendment. GRISWOLD v. CONNECTICUT, 381 U.S. 479 (1965). Robert Bork's critique of *Griswold* was a major factor in the Senate's decision to reject him in 1987 as a nominee to the Supreme Court. Subsequent nominees to the Court recognized that there do exist unenumerated privacy rights (see box on next page).

The next question was whether contraceptives could be denied to single people. In 1972 the Court struck down a Massachusetts law that made it a felony to give away a drug, medicine, instrument, or article for the prevention of conception except when registered physicians or registered pharmacists gave them to married persons. A 6–1 Court held that the statute violated the rights of single persons. "If the right of privacy means anything, it is the right of the *individual,* married or single, to be free from unwarranted governmental intrusion into matters so fundamentally affecting a person as the decision whether to bear or beget a child." Eisenstadt v. Baird, 405 U.S. 438, 453 (1972).

Having sustained the use of contraceptives by adults, whether married or single, the next issue waiting to be resolved concerned the use of contraceptives by minors. New York argued

Unenumerated Privacy Rights

In a 1971 article, Robert Bork used *Griswold* v. *Connecticut* to illustrate the problems of judge-made law. He thought that *Griswold* embodied the Warren Court's tendency to make its own value choices supreme and thereby displace elected government. For Bork, *Griswold* was "an unprincipled decision" that "fails every test of neutrality." Robert H. Bork, "Neutral Principles and Some First Amendment Problems," 47 Ind. L. J. 1 (1971). The Senate's rejection of Bork as nominee to the Supreme Court relied heavily on his views on privacy and his objection to privacy rights that were not enumerated in the Constitution.

Bork's defeat made it unlikely that subsequent judicial nominees would challenge privacy and unenumerated rights. Anthony Kennedy, nominated to replace Bork, was quick to embrace privacy at his confirmation hearing. Kennedy noted that "the concept of liberty in the due process clause is quite expansive, quite sufficient, to protect the values of privacy that Americans legitimately think are part of their constitutional heritage." Kennedy was confirmed by a unanimous Senate.

The next nominee to the Supreme Court, David Souter, told the Senate Judiciary Committee that he believed that "the due process clause of the 14th amendment does recognize and does protect an unenumerated right of privacy." In his first day of hearings as nominee to the Court, Clarence Thomas said that it was his view "that there is a right to privacy in the Fourteenth Amendment." Clinton nominees Ruth Bader Ginsburg and Stephen Breyer also embraced privacy rights at their confirmation hearings.

---

that the cases striking down state prohibitions on the *use* of contraceptives did not prevent states from prohibiting the *sale* and *manufacture* of contraceptives. This fine distinction did not convince the Court, which held that the New York law prohibiting the selling or distribution of any contraceptive to a minor under the age of sixteen was unconstitutional as it applied to nonprescription contraceptives. Restrictions on the distribution of contraceptives necessarily interfered with their use. The Court also struck down New York's prohibition of any advertisement or display of contraceptive devices. The law was considered unreasonable in part because New York allowed girls to marry at the age of fourteen with parental consent. Carey v. Population Services International, 431 U.S. 678 (1977).

In 1983 the Supreme Court reviewed a law passed by Congress that prohibited the mailing of unsolicited advertisements for contraceptives. A unanimous decision held that the statute violated the First Amendment: "where — as in this case — a speaker desires to convey truthful information relevant to important social issues such as family planning and the prevention of venereal disease, we have previously found the First Amendment interest served by such speech paramount." Bolger v. Youngs Drug Products Corp., 463 U.S. 60, 69 (1983). The law was also defective because it denied parents information bearing on their ability to discuss birth control and make informed decisions. Id. at 74.

Griswold v. Connecticut

381 U.S. 479 (1965)

Estelle Griswold, the executive director of the Planned Parenthood League of Connecticut, was convicted for giving married persons information on how to prevent conception. C. Lee Buxton, medical director of the League, was convicted for giving medical advice on conception and for prescribing a contraceptive device for a married woman. A Connecticut statute made it a crime for any person to use any drug or article to prevent conception.

Mr. Justice Douglas delivered the opinion of the Court.

. . .

The statutes whose constitutionality is involved in this appeal are §§ 53-32 and 54-196 of the General Statutes of Connecticut (1958 rev.). The former provides:

"Any person who uses any drug, medicinal article or instrument for the purpose of preventing conception shall be fined not less than fifty dollars or imprisoned not less than sixty days nor more than one year or be both fined and imprisoned."

Section 54-196 provides:

"Any person who assists, abets, counsels, causes, hires or commands another to commit any offense may be prosecuted and punished as if he were the principal offender."

The appellants were found guilty as accessories and fined $100 each, against the claim that the accessory statute as so applied violated the Fourteenth Amendment. . . .

We think that appellants have standing to raise the constitutional rights of the married people with whom they had a professional relationship. *Tileston* v. *Ullman*, 318 U. S. 44, is different, for there the plaintiff seeking to represent others asked for a declaratory judgment. In that situation we thought that the requirements of standing should be strict, lest the standards of "case or controversy" in Article III of the Constitution become blurred. Here those doubts are removed by reason of a criminal conviction for serving married couples in violation of an aiding-and-abetting statute. Certainly the accessory should have standing to assert that the offense which he is charged with assisting is not, or cannot constitutionally be, a crime.

. . . The rights of husband and wife, pressed here, are likely to be diluted or adversely affected unless those rights are considered in a suit involving those who have this kind of confidential relation to them.

Coming to the merits, we are met with a wide range of questions that implicate the Due Process Clause of the Fourteenth Amendment. Overtones of some arguments suggest that *Lochner* v. *New York*, 198 U. S. 45, should be our guide. But we decline that invitation as we did in *West Coast Hotel Co.* v. *Parrish*, 300 U. S. 379; *Olsen* v. *Nebraska*, 313 U. S. 236; *Lincoln Union* v. *Northwestern Co.*, 335 U. S. 525; *Williamson* v. *Lee Optical Co.*, 348 U. S. 483; *Giboney* v. *Empire Storage Co.*, 336 U. S. 490. We do not sit as a super-legislature to determine the wisdom, need, and propriety of laws that touch economic problems, business affairs, or social conditions. This law, however, operates directly on an intimate relation of husband and wife and their physician's role in one aspect of that relation.

The association of people is not mentioned in the Constitution nor in the Bill of Rights. The right to educate a child in a school of the parents' choice—whether public or private or parochial—is also not mentioned. Nor is the right to study any particular subject or any foreign language. Yet the First Amendment has been construed to include certain of those rights.

. . .

The foregoing cases suggest that specific guarantees in the Bill of Rights have penumbras, formed by emanations from those guarantees that help give them life and substance. See *Poe* v. *Ullman*, 367 U. S. 497, 516–522 (dissenting opinion). Various guarantees create zones of privacy. The right of association contained in the penumbra of the First Amendment is one, as we have seen. The Third Amendment in its prohibition against the quartering of soldiers "in any house" in time of peace without the consent of the owner is another facet of that privacy. The Fourth Amendment explicitly affirms the "right of the people to be secure in their persons, houses, papers, and effects, against unreasonable searches and seizures." The Fifth Amendment in its Self-Incrimination Clause enables the citizen to create a zone of privacy which government may not force him to surrender to his detriment. The Ninth Amendment provides: "The enumeration in the Constitution, of certain rights, shall not be construed to deny or disparage others retained by the people."

The Fourth and Fifth Amendments were described in *Boyd* v. *United States*, 116 U. S. 616, 630, as protection against all governmental invasions "of the sanctity of a man's home and the privacies of life." We recently referred in *Mapp* v. *Ohio*, 367 U. S. 643, 656, to the Fourth Amendment as creating a "right to privacy, no less important than any other right carefully and particularly reserved to the people." . . .

The present case, then, concerns a relationship lying within the zone of privacy created by several fundamental constitutional guarantees. And it concerns a law which, in forbidding the *use* of contraceptives rather than regulating their manufacture or sale, seeks to achieve its goals by means having a maximum destructive impact upon that relationship. Such a law cannot stand in light of the familiar principle, so often applied by this Court, that a "governmental purpose to control or prevent activities constitutionally subject to state regulation may not be achieved by means which sweep unnecessarily broadly and thereby invade the area of protected freedoms." *NAACP v. Alabama*, 377 U. S. 288, 307. Would we allow the police to search the sacred precincts of marital bedrooms for telltale signs of the use of contraceptives? The very idea is repulsive to the notions of privacy surrounding the marriage relationship.

We deal with a right of privacy older than the Bill of Rights — older than our political parties, older than our school system. Marriage is a coming together for better or for worse, hopefully enduring, and intimate to the degree of being sacred. It is an association that promotes a way of life, not causes; a harmony in living, not political faiths; a bilateral loyalty, not commercial or social projects. Yet it is an association for as noble a purpose as any involved in our prior decisions.

Reversed.

Mr. Justice Goldberg, whom The Chief Justice and Mr. Justice Brennan join, concurring.

I agree with the Court that Connecticut's birth-control law unconstitutionally intrudes upon the right of marital privacy, and I join in its opinion and judgment. Although I have not accepted the view that "due process" as used in the Fourteenth Amendment incorporates all of the first eight Amendments (see my concurring opinion in *Pointer v. Texas*, 380 U. S. 400, 410, and the dissenting opinion of Mr. Justice Brennan in *Cohen v. Hurley*, 366 U. S. 117, 154), I do agree that the concept of liberty protects those personal rights that are fundamental, and is not confined to the specific terms of the Bill of Rights. My conclusion that the concept of liberty is not so restricted and that it embraces the right of marital privacy though that right is not mentioned explicitly in the Constitution is supported both by numerous decisions of this Court, referred to in the Court's opinion, and by the language and history of the Ninth Amendment. In reaching the conclusion that the right of marital privacy is protected, as being within the protected penumbra of specific guarantees of the Bill of Rights, the Court

refers to the Ninth Amendment, *ante*, at 484. I add these words to emphasize the relevance of that Amendment to the Court's holding.

. . .

The Ninth Amendment reads, "The enumeration in the Constitution, of certain rights, shall not be construed to deny or disparage others retained by the people." The Amendment is almost entirely the work of James Madison. It was introduced in Congress by him and passed the House and Senate with little or no debate and virtually no change in language. It was proffered to quiet expressed fears that a bill of specifically enumerated rights could not be sufficiently broad to cover all essential rights and that the specific mention of certain rights would be interpreted as a denial that others were protected.

In presenting the proposed Amendment, Madison said:

"It has been objected also against a bill of rights, that, by enumerating particular exceptions to the grant of power, it would disparage those rights which were not placed in that enumeration; and it might follow by implication, that those rights which were not singled out, were intended to be assigned into the hands of the General Government, and were consequently insecure. This is one of the most plausible arguments I have ever heard urged against the admission of a bill of rights into this system; but, I conceive, that it may be guarded against. I have attempted it, as gentlemen may see by turning to the last clause of the fourth resolution [the Ninth Amendment]." I Annals of Congress 439 (Gales and Seaton ed. 1834).

. . .

...To hold that a right so basic and fundamental and so deep-rooted in our society as the right of privacy in marriage may be infringed because that right is not guaranteed in so many words by the first eight amendments to the Constitution is to ignore the Ninth Amendment and to give it no effect whatsoever....

Mr. Justice Harlan, concurring in the judgment.

I fully agree with the judgment of reversal, but find myself unable to join the Court's opinion. The reason is that it seems to me to evince an approach to this case very much like that taken by my Brothers Black and Stewart in dissent, namely: the Due Process Clause of the Fourteenth Amendment does not touch this Connecticut statute unless the enactment is found to violate some right assured by the letter or penumbra of the Bill of Rights.

In other words, what I find implicit in the Court's opinion is that the "incorporation" doctrine may be used to *restrict* the reach of Fourteenth Amendment Due Process. For me this is just as unacceptable constitutional doctrine as is the use of the "incorporation" approach to *impose* upon the States all the requirements of the Bill of Rights as found in the provisions of the first eight amendments and in the decisions of this Court interpreting them....

In my view, the proper constitutional inquiry in this case is whether this Connecticut statute infringes the Due Process Clause of the Fourteenth Amendment because the enactment violates basic values "implicit in the concept of ordered liberty," *Palko v. Connecticut*, 302 U. S. 319, 325. For reasons stated at length in my dissenting opinion in *Poe v. Ullman, supra,* I believe that it does. While the relevant inquiry may be aided by resort to one or more of the provisions of the Bill of Rights, it is not dependent on them or any of their radiations. The Due Process Clause of the Fourteenth Amendment stands, in my opinion, on its own bottom.

. . .

MR. JUSTICE WHITE, concurring in the judgment.

In my view this Connecticut law as applied to married couples deprives them of "liberty" without due process of law, as that concept is used in the Fourteenth Amendment. I therefore concur in the judgment of the Court reversing these convictions under Connecticut's aiding and abetting statute.

. . .

MR. JUSTICE BLACK, with whom MR. JUSTICE STEWART joins, dissenting.

I agree with my Brother STEWART's dissenting opinion. And like him I do not to any extent whatever base my view that this Connecticut law is constitutional on a belief that the law is wise or that its policy is a good one. In order that there may be no room at all to doubt why I vote as I do, I feel constrained to add that the law is every bit as offensive to me as it is to my Brethren of the majority and my Brothers HARLAN, WHITE and GOLDBERG who, reciting reasons why it is offensive to them, hold it unconstitutional. There is no single one of the graphic and eloquent strictures and criticisms fired at the policy of this Connecticut law either by the Court's opinion or by those of my concurring Brethren to which I cannot subscribe—except their conclusion that the evil qualities they see in the law make it unconstitutional.

. . .

...I get nowhere in this case by talk about a constitutional "right of privacy" as an emanation from one or more constitutional provisions. I like my privacy as well as the next one, but I am nevertheless compelled to admit that government has a right to invade it unless prohibited by some specific constitutional provision. For these reasons I cannot agree with the Court's judgment and the reasons it gives for holding this Connecticut law unconstitutional.

. . .

I realize that many good and able men have eloquently spoken and written, sometimes in rhapsodical strains, about the duty of this Court to keep the Constitution in tune with the times. The idea is that the Constitution must be changed from time to time and that this Court is charged with a duty to make those changes. For myself, I must with all deference reject that philosophy. The Constitution makers knew the need for change and provided for it. Amendments suggested by the people's elected representatives can be submitted to the people or their selected agents for ratification. That method of change was good for our Fathers, and being somewhat old-fashioned I must add it is good enough for me. And so, I cannot rely on the Due Process Clause or the Ninth Amendment or any mysterious and uncertain natural law concept as a reason for striking down this state law....

MR. JUSTICE STEWART, whom MR. JUSTICE BLACK joins, dissenting.

Since 1879 Connecticut has had on its books a law which forbids the use of contraceptives by anyone. I think this is an uncommonly silly law. As a practical matter, the law is obviously unenforceable, except in the oblique context of the present case. As a philosophical matter, I believe the use of contraceptives in the relationship of marriage should be left to personal and private choice, based upon each individual's moral, ethical, and religious beliefs. As a matter of social policy, I think professional counsel about methods of birth control should be available to all, so that each individual's choice can be meaningfully made. But we are not asked in this case to say whether we think this law is unwise, or even asinine. We are asked to hold that it violates the United States Constitution. And that I cannot do.

In the course of its opinion the Court refers to no less than six Amendments to the Constitution: the First, the Third, the Fourth, the Fifth, the Ninth, and the Fourteenth. But the Court does not say which of these Amendments, if any, it thinks is infringed by this Connecticut law.

. . .

The Court also quotes the Ninth Amendment, and my Brother GOLDBERG' s concurring opinion relies heavily upon it. But to say that the Ninth Amendment has anything to do with this case is to turn somersaults with history. The Ninth Amendment, like its companion the Tenth, which this Court held "states but a truism that all is retained which has not been surrendered," *United States* v. *Darby*, 312 U. S. 100, 124, was framed by James Madison and adopted by the States simply to make clear that the adoption of the Bill of Rights did not alter the plan that the *Federal* Government was to be a government of express and limited powers, and that all rights and powers not delegated to it were retained by the people and the individual States. Until today no member of this Court has ever suggested that the Ninth Amendment meant anything else, and the idea that a federal court could ever use the Ninth Amendment to annul a law passed by the elected representatives of the people of the State of Connecticut would have caused James Madison no little wonder.

What provision of the Constitution, then, does make this state law invalid? The Court says it is the right of privacy "created by several fundamental constitutional guarantees." With all deference, I can find no such general right of privacy in the Bill of Rights, in any other part of the Constitution, or in any case ever before decided by this Court.

At the oral argument in this case we were told that the Connecticut law does not "conform to current community standards." But it is not the function of this Court to decide cases on the basis of community standards. We are here to decide cases "agreeably to the Constitution and laws of the United States." It is the essence of judicial duty to subordinate our own personal views, our own ideas of what legislation is wise and what is not. If, as I should surely hope, the law before us does not reflect the standards of the people of Connecticut, the people of Connecticut can freely exercise their true Ninth and Tenth Amendment rights to persuade their elected representatives to repeal it. That is the constitutional way to take this law off the books.

C. ABORTION RIGHTS

No contemporary issue has inflamed the country, Congress, and the courts more than the right of a woman to abort her pregnancy. What balance should be struck between a woman's interest in deciding to have an abortion and the state's interest in protecting the health and life of the mother and child? If a wife decides to abort, must the husband first consent? Does government have an obligation to fund abortions? Do abortion rights extend to minors? Is a fetus a "person" entitled to constitutional protection under the Fourteenth Amendment? Other emotional issues bombard the courts, executive agencies, and legislatures.

The question that reached the Supreme Court in 1973 was not the abstract issue of whether abortions should be performed. The record was abundantly clear that they would take place, with or without the law. In states that had prohibited or severely restricted abortion, some women attempted self-abortion by using coat hangers and other life-threatening instruments. Others placed their life and health in the hands of whoever was willing, with or without medical training, to do the job. Women with higher incomes were more fortunate. They could travel to another state or country for the operation. The issue before the Court in 1973 was exceedingly complex: How could abortions be performed within a legal structure that satisfied the conflicting values of those who wanted abortion on demand and those who believed equally strongly in the right to life?

In *Roe* v. *Wade* (1973), the Supreme Court attempted to steer a middle course by rejecting both abortion on demand and the absolute right to life. The Court held that state laws permitting abortions only to save the mother's life violated due process, which the Court said protects the right to privacy and a woman's *qualified* right to terminate her pregnancy. The state has legitimate interests in protecting both the pregnant woman's health and the potential life of the fetus. Each of those interests grows and reaches a "compelling" point at later stages of the woman's pregnancy. Over the first three months (the first trimester), the decision to abort is left to the woman and her physician. After the first trimester, states may regulate the abortion procedure in ways that are reasonably related to the health of the mother. After the fetus becomes viable (about seven months), the state may prohibit abortion except where necessary to preserve the life or health of the mother. ROE v. WADE, 410 U.S. 113 (1973).

This decision was widely condemned as the work of an activist Court behaving like a legislature, even to the extent of identifying the stages of pregnancy where the state's interest prevails over the woman's. The decision was also vulnerable to criticism because of the difficulty the Court had in identifying its source of authority. In discussing the right of privacy, the Court pointed to the First, Fourth, Fifth, and Ninth Amendments; "the penumbras of the Bill of Rights;" and the "concept of liberty guaranteed by the first section of the Fourteenth Amendment." Precisely where to anchor the decision did not seem to matter: "This right of privacy, whether it be founded in the Fourteenth Amendment's concept of personal liberty and restrictions upon state action, as we feel it is, or, as the District Court determined, in the Ninth Amendment's reservation of rights to the people, is broad enough to encompass a woman's decision whether or not to terminate her pregnancy." Id. at 153.

The Court specifically rejected the argument that a fetus is a "person" within the language and meaning of the Fourteenth Amendment. After examining the various instances in the Constitution where the word *person* is used, the Court concluded that they apply only postnatally. The constitutional meaning of person "does not include the unborn." Id. at 157–58.

The constitutional issue was mixed with factual questions. The ruling depended on "the light of present medical knowledge." Id. at 163. The "compelling" point for state intervention, said the Court, is viability, a condition that is not fixed but varies with medical competence and techniques. As the Court noted in a subsequent case, viability is "a matter of medical judgment, skill, and technical ability, and we preserved the flexibility of the term." Planned Parenthood of Missouri v. Danforth, 428 U.S. 52, 64 (1976). As medical knowledge advanced, the Court's identification of trimester stages would provide less guidance. In fact, the Court later struck down a Pennsylvania statute that required doctors to determine first the viability of a fetus. If the fetus was viable, the statute mandated that the doctor exercise the same care to preserve the fetus' life and health as would be necessary for a regular birth. The Court held the statute void for vagueness. Colautti v. Franklin, 439 U.S. 379 (1979).

The companion case to *Roe* v. *Wade* reviewed the requirement in Georgia's law that abortion be performed in a hospital accredited by a joint commission. The Court determined that the statute was unconstitutional because it unduly restricted a woman's rights, particularly the indigent married woman who brought the case. The state law also required that the abortion procedure be approved by a hospital committee, a condition the Court again found too restrictive on a woman's rights. Finally, by requiring that her doctor's judgment be confirmed by two other licensed physicians, the state law infringed impermissibly on a doctor's right to practice. Doe v. Bolton, 410 U.S. 179 (1973).

Although the Court had announced its constitutional decision, full compliance with the ruling was not forthcoming. Dr. Kenneth Edelin, a physician in Boston, was indicted in 1974 for performing an abortion and subsequently found guilty of manslaughter. His conviction was later overturned, but the opposition to *Roe* v. *Wade* intensified. Over the following years, right-to-lifers would bomb abortion clinics, send letter bombs through the mails, and use other tactics to intimidate and harass women and physicians.

The Court addressed new legal issues in 1976. It upheld Missouri's requirement that a woman consent to an abortion in writing and certify that her consent is freely given. However, the state's requirement for a written consent from the woman's spouse (unless the physician certified that an abortion was necessary to save her life) was struck down. Also, a blanket requirement for parental consent for minors was declared unconstitutional. Planned Parenthood of Missouri v. Danforth, 428 U.S. 52 (1976). See also Bellotti v. Baird, 443 U.S. 622 (1979).

Public Funding

A series of cases involved the issue of providing public funds for abortion. Acting under its interpretation of federal law, Pennsylvania denied women medical assistance for nontherapeutic abortions. State regulations limited assistance to abortion certified by physicians as medically necessary. The Court, split 6–3, held that federal law did not require the funding of nontherapeutic abortions as a condition for states to participate in the federal Medicaid program. This decision turned on statutory construction, not constitutional interpretation. Beal v. Doe, 432 U.S. 438 (1977). Evidently the Court regarded these issues as moral questions to be resolved by legislatures, not the judiciary. It recognized the risk of trying to direct legislatures how to spend public funds, at least in this area. On the same day, the Court held that the Constitution does not obligate states to pay the pregnancy-related medical expenses of indigent women. Maher v. Roe, 432 U.S. 464 (1977). See also Poelker v. Doe, 432 U.S. 519 (1977).

The major challenge came from the Hyde Amendment, first passed by Congress in 1976 (see reading). In the version that eventually came to the Supreme Court, the language provided that

> ... none of the funds provided by this joint resolution shall be used to perform abortions except where the life of the mother would be endangered if the fetus were carried to term; or except for such medical procedures necessary for the victims of rape or incest when such rape or incest has been reported promptly to a law enforcement agency or public health service. 93 Stat. 926, § 109 (1979).

A federal district court, without deciding the constitutional issue, enjoined the Secretary of Health, Education, and Welfare from enforcing the Hyde Amendment. The court order required the Secretary to continue providing federal reimbursement for abortions. McRae v. Mathews, 421 F.Supp. 533 (E.D. N.Y. 1976). The Supreme Court vacated the injunction and remanded the case for reconsideration in light of its holdings. In 1980 the district court held that the Hyde Amendment impermissibly used appropriation language to change substantive (legislative) language in federal law, violated an individual's liberty to terminate pregnancy for medical reasons, and unreasonably denied funds for medically necessary abortions. McRae v. Califano, 491 F.Supp. 630 (E.D. N.Y. 1980).

Clearly a major collision loomed between Congress and the judiciary. In 1980, by a 5–4 vote, the Supreme Court upheld the Hyde Amendment. According to the Court, government may not place obstacles in the path of a woman's decision to choose abortion, but neither has it an obligation to remove obstacles it did not create (including a woman's indigency). Poverty, standing alone, was not considered a suspect classification. The Court concluded that the Hyde Amendment, by encouraging childbirth except in the most urgent circumstances, was rationally related to legitimate governmental objectives of protecting potential life. HARRIS v. McRAE, 448 U.S. 297 (1980). In a companion decision, the Court (again split 5–4) upheld the right of state legislatures to limit public funds for abortions. Williams v. Zbaraz, 448 U.S.

Independent State Action

Although Congress (with the Hyde Amendment) withheld federal funds for abortion and the Supreme Court sustained this legislation, some of the states followed a different course in interpreting their constitutions. California restricted the circumstances under which public funds would be authorized to pay for abortions for Medi-Cal recipients. The California courts struck down these statutes as unconstitutional, holding that the state has no constitutional obligation to provide medical care to the poor, but that once it does it bears the heavy burden of justifying a provision that withholds benefits from otherwise qualified individuals solely because they chose to exercise their constitutional right to have an abortion. Committee to Defend Reprod. Rights v. Myers, 625 P.2d 779 (Cal. 1981). Similar decisions were issued by the New Jersey and Massachusetts courts, overturning state laws that restricted public funding for abortions. Right to Choose v. Byrne, 450

A.2d 925 (N.J. 1982); Moe v. Secretary of Administration, 417 N.E.2d 387 (Mass. 1981).

State regulations denying funds for abortion were also declared invalid under other state constitutions. An agency regulation in Oregon, restricting funds to indigent women seeking abortions, was struck down by a state court as a violation of the state constitution's privileges and immunities clause. Planned Parenthood Ass'n v. Dept. of Human Res., 663 P.2d 1247 (Or. App. 1983). A Connecticut court invalidated a state agency's rule that restricted funding of abortion for indigent women unless to save their lives. The regulation exceeded the statutory authority of the agency and violated various provisions of the state constitution. Dating back to 1650, Connecticut had compiled a record of almost 350 years of paying for all necessary expenses for the poor. Doe v. Maher, 515 A.2d 134, 143 (Conn. Super. 1986).

358 (1980). When the issue of public funding is framed entirely as a state matter to be decided under the state constitution, the results can differ from *Harris* v. *McRae* (see box).

Chronic Challenges

Roe v. *Wade* was not accepted as the last word on the rights of abortion. Legislative efforts by state and local bodies put constant pressure on the Court to clarify and modify the boundaries of its 1973 ruling. A 1981 case involved Utah's statute requiring a physician to notify, if possible, the parents or guardian of a minor facing an abortion. Concluding that the statute did not amount to a parental veto, the Court upheld the law as a legitimate opportunity for parents to supply essential medical and other information to the physician. Three members of the *Roe* majority (Marshall, Brennan, and Blackmun) dissented. H.L. v. Matheson, 450 U.S. 398 (1981).

A cluster of three cases in 1983 raised a multitude of new issues. An Akron, Ohio, ordinance set forth five requirements: (1) abortions after the first trimester had to be performed in a hospital, (2) abortions were prohibited for unmarried minors under the age of fifteen without parental consent or court order, (3) the physician had to inform the woman of various facts concerning the operation, (4) abortions were delayed for at least twenty-four hours after the woman's consent, and (5) the physician had to ensure that fetal remains were disposed of in a "humane and sanitary manner." The Court found each provision unconstitutional. Justices White and Rehnquist continued to dissent from the *Roe* doctrine, but Justice O'Connor, added to the Court in 1981, now joined them by penning a major critique of the premises supporting *Roe*. AKRON v. AKRON CENTER FOR REPRODUCTIVE HEALTH, 462 U.S. 416 (1983).

Two other decisions handed down on the same day as *Akron* explored additional restrictions on abortion rights. A Missouri statute required that abortions, after twelve weeks of pregnancy, be performed in a hospital. Consistent with previous rulings, the Court struck down the hospital requirement, but it sustained three other requirements in the Missouri law: a pathology report for each abortion, the presence of a second physician for abortions performed after viability, and either parental or court consent for minors. The latter marked a major departure from past rulings. Planned Parenthood Ass'n v. Ashcroft, 462 U.S. 476 (1983). The 7–2 majority from *Roe* had clearly evaporated. Four Justices (Blackmun, Brennan, Marshall, and Stevens) dissented from the Court's support for pathology reports, second physicians, and parental or court consent.

In the second case, the Court upheld Virginia's law that second trimester abortions be performed either in hospitals or licensed outpatient clinics. The requirement furthered the state's interest in protecting the health of a woman after the end of the first trimester. Justice Stevens was the sole dissenter. Simopoulos v. Virginia, 462 U.S. 506 (1983).

Reexamining *Roe*

In 1986 the Supreme Court faced another major case on the right to abort. A Pennsylvania statute required that the woman be informed of the following: the physician who would perform the abortion; the "particular medical risks" of the abortion procedure, including physical and psychological effects; the medical assistance benefits available for prenatal care, childbirth, and care immediately after birth; the father's liability to provide financial support for the child; and printed materials that describe fetal characteristics at two-week intervals and that list agencies offering alternatives to abortion. The state also required other procedures, such as the presence of a second physician during an abortion performed when viability is possible. The responsibility of the second physician was to take all reasonable steps to preserve the child's life and health.

With a 5–4 majority, the Court invalidated the statute. It held that states are not free, under the guise of protecting maternal health or potential life, to intimidate women into continuing their pregnancies. The statute impermissibly intruded upon a decision to be made by the woman and her physician. The dissent by Chief Justice Burger was significant, since he formed part of the 7–2 majority in *Roe v. Wade*. He agreed with the dissenters that "we should reexamine *Roe*." The three other dissenters (White, Rehnquist, and O'Connor) were much more emphatic in rejecting the premises of *Roe*. Thornburgh v. American Coll. of Obst. & Gyn., 476 U.S. 747 (1986).

Support for *Roe v. Wade* continued to erode. With Antonin Scalia replacing Burger in 1986 and Anthony Kennedy taking Powell's seat in 1988, the Court was positioned to overhaul and possibly overrule *Roe*. The opportunity came in 1989, when the Court reviewed a Missouri statute that imposed a number of severe restrictions on a woman's decision to have an abortion. Without overruling *Roe*, four Justices rejected the trimester framework (Justice O'Connor, who declined to join that part of the Court's decision, had criticized the trimester concept in previous opinions). The 5–4 decision upheld key portions of the Missouri statute and allowed governmental regulation that would have been prohibited under earlier decisions. WEBSTER v. REPRODUCTIVE HEALTH SERVICES, 492 U.S. 490 (1989). *Webster* triggered a flurry of legislative activity by the states (see box on next page).

In 1992 the Court decided the constitutionality of a Pennsylvania statute that restricted abortions. With David Souter succeeding William Brennan, Jr., and Clarence Thomas replacing Thurgood Marshall, it was thought that the Court might overturn *Roe v. Wade*. However, the Court managed to hold on to what it called the "central holding" of *Roe*: the constitutional liberty of women to have some freedom to terminate pregnancies. In so deciding, the Court rejected *Roe*'s trimester framework and announced an "undue burden" standard that would hold a law invalid if its purpose or effect is to place substantial obstacles in the path of

The States Respond to *Webster*

Pennsylvania enacted new restrictions on abortion, leading immediately to challenges in the courts. Idaho and Louisiana passed restrictive statutes in 1990, but the governors vetoed them. In 1991, the governor of Louisiana again vetoed a restrictive abortion statute, but this time the legislature overrode him. An antiabortion law enacted by Guam was regarded as unconstitutional by the territory's attorney general, a federal district judge, and the Ninth Circuit. Connecticut in 1990 became the first state to give women the legal right to abortion, even if *Roe v. Wade* were overturned. Maryland passed a similar law in 1991; that law survived a statewide referendum vote in November 1992. In 1991, the governor of North Dakota vetoed what would have been the strictest antiabortion bill in the nation. Utah passed a stringent antiabortion law. A Michigan appeals court invalidated a voter-approved ban on state-paid abortions for poor women.

In 1990, a 5–4 Court struck down as unconstitutional a Minnesota law that prohibited an abortion performed on a woman under eighteen years of age until at least 48 hours after notifying *both* of her parents. The Court found the provision too restrictive in part because nine percent of the minors in Minnesota lived with neither parent, 33 percent lived with only one parent, and only 50 percent resided with both biological parents. Justice O'Connor supplied the fifth vote, casting her first vote to strike down an antiabortion restriction. Dissenters were Scalia, Kennedy, Rehnquist, and White. O'Connor voted with those four in holding that it would be constitutional if minors had the option of asking a judge to waive the notification requirement. Hodgson v. Minnesota, 497 U.S. 417 (1990). In a second ruling, the Court voted 6 to 3 to uphold an Ohio law requiring a physician to notify one parent of a pregnant minor's intent to have an abortion. Ohio provided for a judicial bypass but required the minor to prove by "clear and convincing" evidence that she should not be forced to notify a parent. Ohio v. Akron Center for Reproductive Health, 497 U.S. 502 (1990).

a woman seeking an abortion before the fetus attains viability. That standard was accepted by only a three-Justice plurality: O'Connor, Kennedy, and Souter. Using this standard, most of the Pennsylvania statute was held constitutional. A provision requiring a woman to notify her husband was struck down. PLANNED PARENTHOOD v. CASEY, 505 U.S. 833 (1992).

Following this decision, Congress began work on the Freedom of Choice Act (FOCA) to codify many of the protections originally announced in *Roe*. Pro-choice groups, previously dependent on the courts to advance their agenda, now turned to Congress for the protection of rights. NARAL (National Abortion Rights Action League) sent a "Supreme Court Alert" to its membership on June 27, 1991, stating a new outlook: "Clearly Congress is our Court of Last Resort. All hope of protecting our constitutional rights to choose depends upon our elected representatives in Congress responding to the will of the American people." In urging support for FOCA, the Religious Coalition for Abortion Rights also called Congress "our court of last resort."

FOCA was never enacted, but it represented the efforts of political groups — both liberal and conservative — to seek legislative solutions. In an address delivered in 1993, Judge (now Justice) Ruth Bader Ginsburg argued that *Roe v. Wade* failed to recognize that judicial decisions must work in concert with the coequal executive and legislative branches at the national level and with state authorities (see box on next page).

Access to Abortion Clinics

Pro-life groups have been active in trying to block access to abortion clinics. In 1993, the Supreme Court held that abortion clinics and abortion rights organizations could not use a

Ruth Bader Ginsburg on *Roe* v. *Wade*

[In an address in 1993, Judge (now Justice) Ruth Bader Ginsburg said that the Supreme Court's ruling in *Roe* v. *Wade* (1973) was too broadly decided and failed to take proper account of other political institutions involved in shaping constitutional law.]

In *The Federalist* No. 78, Alexander Hamilton said that federal judges, in order to preserve the people's rights and privileges, must have authority to check legislation and acts of the executive for constitutionality. But he qualified his recognition of that awesome authority. The judiciary, Hamilton wrote, from the very nature of its functions, will always be "the least dangerous" branch of government, for judges hold neither the sword nor the purse of the community; ultimately, they must depend upon the political branches to effectuate their judgments....

... [J]udges play an interdependent part in our democracy. They do not alone shape legal doctrine but, as I suggested at the outset, they participate in a dialogue with other organs of government, and with the people as well....

The seven to two judgment in *Roe* v. *Wade* declared "violative of the Due Process Clause of the Fourteenth Amendment" a Texas criminal abortion statute that intolerably shackled a woman's autonomy; the Texas law "except[ed] from criminality only a *life-saving* procedure on behalf of the [pregnant] woman." Suppose the Court had stopped there, rightly declaring unconstitutional the most extreme brand of law in the nation, and had not gone on, as the Court

did in *Roe,* to fashion a regime blanketing the subject, a set of rules that displaced virtually every state law then in force. Would there have been the twenty-year controversy we have witnessed, reflected most recently in the Supreme Court's splintered decision in *Planned Parenthood* v. *Casey?* A less encompassing *Roe,* one that merely struck down the extreme Texas law and went no further ... might have served to reduce rather than to fuel controversy.

[In a series of cases involving gender discrimination, the Court] opened a dialogue with the political branches of government. In essence, the Court instructed Congress and state legislatures: rethink ancient positions on these questions....

The ball, one might say, was tossed by the Justices back into the legislators' court, where the political forces of the day could operate. The Supreme Court wrote modestly, it put forward no grand philosophy; but by requiring legislative reexamination of once customary sex-based classifications, the Court helped to ensure that laws and regulations would "catch up with a changed world."

Roe v. *Wade,* in contrast, invited no dialogue with legislators. Instead, it seemed to remove the ball from the legisators' court. In 1973, when *Roe* was issued, abortion law was in a state of change across the nation. As the Supreme Court itself noted, there was a marked trend in state legislatures "toward liberalization of abortion statutes." ...

SOURCE: Ruth Bader Ginsburg, "Speaking in a Judicial Voice," 67 N.Y.U. L. Rev. 1185 (1992) (footnotes omitted).

civil rights statute (passed in 1871 to curb the Ku Klux Klan) to find a private conspiracy against the members of Operation Rescue, which organized demonstrations to block access to abortion clinics. Bray v. Alexandria Women's Health Clinic, 506 U.S. 263 (1993). Congress responded by passing legislation to make it a federal crime to obstruct the entrance to an abortion clinic. 108 Stat. 694 (1994). The Fourth Circuit upheld the constitutionality of this statute (against a First Amendment challenge) and the Supreme Court denied cert. Woodall v. Reno, 515 U.S. 1141 (1995).

In 1994, a unanimous Court held that abortion clinics may use a federal racketeering law (RICO) to sue protesters who conspire to shut them down. No proof is needed that the racketeering enterprise is motivated by an economic purpose. National Organization for Women, Inc. v. Scheidler, 510 U.S. 249 (1994). Also in 1994, the Court ruled that judges may prevent demonstrators from coming within 36 feet of abortion clinics. The purpose of this buffer zone is to prevent intimidation and to ensure clinic access. Madsen v. Women's Health Center, Inc., 512

U.S. 753 (1994). In 1997, the Court refined its position on buffer zones by holding that it was permissible to place a 15-foot buffer around clinic entrances but that a "floating buffer zone" (a 15-foot shield around patients and clinic staff) interfered with the free speech rights of abortion opponents. Schenck v. Pro-Choice Network of Western New York, 519 U.S. 357 (1997). In 2000, the Court upheld a Colorado law that requires opponents of abortion to stay at least eight feet away from people entering health care facilities. Hill v. Colorado, 120 S.Ct. 2480 (2000).

Late-Term Abortions

In 1996, President Clinton vetoed a bill that would have prohibited late-term abortions except to save the life of a woman. He said he opposed late-term abortions but insisted on another exception to cover adverse health consequences. The bill would have made it a federal crime for a doctor to perform the procedure, also known as "partial birth" abortion. Although the House overrode the veto, the Senate was nine votes short. In 1997, Clinton vetoed a similar bill. The Senate delayed the override effort until 1998 to attract additional votes, but it fell three votes short. Lower courts struck down Ohio's ban on late-term abortions. When the dispute was appealed to the Supreme Court, it denied cert. Voinovich v. Women's Medical Professional Corporation, 523 U.S. 1036 (1998).

About thirty states passed legislation to prohibit late-term abortions, with a number of the statutes struck down by federal courts on the grounds that they were vague and placed an undue burden on a woman's right to decide on an abortion. Nebraska's law, banning "partial birth abortions," was struck down by the Supreme Court in 2000. Divided 5 to 4, the Court split in many directions: an opinion written by Justice Breyer, separate concurrences by Stevens, O'Connor, and Ginsburg, and dissenting opinions by Rehnquist, Scalia, Kennedy, and Thomas. STENBERG v. CARHART, 120 S.Ct. 2597 (2000). States are now redrafting these bills to place prohibitions on partial-birth abortion in a manner designed to withstand constitutional scrutiny.

Post-*Casey* Record

Other than *Stenberg*, the pattern since *Casey* has been for the Supreme Court to decline to hear major abortion cases. In 1993 it let stand a Mississippi law that required women under 18 to obtain *both* parents' permission before having an abortion. The state law allows the permission of only one parent in case of divorce, separation, and other factors. Barnes v. Mississippi, 510 U.S. 976 (1993). In 1996, the Court refused to review a South Dakota law that had been invalidated by the Eighth Circuit. The federal appeals court struck down a parental notice statute that required teen-agers seeking abortions to notify a parent 48 hours in advance. Janklow v. Planned Parenthood, 517 U.S. 1174 (1996). Also in 1996, the Court relied on a procedural dispute to revive a Utah law that prohibits abortion after the twentieth week of pregnancy. The Tenth Circuit had declared that prohibition invalid because it was not severable from another provision struck down, but the Court ruled that the Utah Code required courts to analyze statutory provisions independently. Under this severability analysis, the prohibition on abortion after the twentieth week survived. Four Justices dissented. Leavitt v. Jane L., 518 U.S. 137 (1996). The judicial record from 1973 to the present consists of a number of rulings that sustain some regulations on abortion while disallowing others (see box on next page).

The Gag Rule

The Reagan administration took steps to limit the use of federal funds for family-planning activities and for abortion counseling. Congress had passed legislation in 1970 to provide

Abortion Regulations

Ever since the Supreme Court issued *Roe* v. *Wade* (1973), it has ruled on the permissibility of state regulations that affect a woman's decision to have an abortion.

Permissible regulations

Assuring that woman's consent is freely given. Planned Parenthood of Mo. v. Danforth (1976).

A pathology report prepared for each abortion. Planned Parenthood Ass'n v. Ashcroft (1983).

Presence of a second physician for abortions after viability. Planned Parenthood Ass'n v. Ashcroft (1983).

Performance of second-trimester abortions either in hospitals or in licensed outpatient clinics. Simopoulos v. Virginia (1983).

Viability test at twenty weeks or more. Webster v. Reproductive Health Services (1989).

"Informed consent" requirements to advise a woman about fetal developments and alternatives to abortion, including adoption. Planned Parenthood v. Casey (1992).

Twenty-four-hour wait between informed consent and the procedure for abortion. Planned Parenthood v. Casey (1992).

Prohibiting use of public facilities or public employees to perform abortion. Webster v. Reproductive Health Services (1989).

Impermissible regulations

Consent from a woman's spouse. Planned Parenthood of Mo. v. Danforth (1976).

Parental consent for minors; must provide option for consent by a judge. Planned Parenthood of Mo. v. Danforth (1976).

Performance of abortion after first trimester in a hospital. Akron v. Akron Center for Reproductive Health (1983).

Performance of abortion after twelve weeks in a hospital. Planned Parenthood Ass'n v. Ashcroft (1983).

Notification of both parents by women under the age of eighteen. Hodgson v. Minnesota (1990).

[Informed-consent requirements had been invalidated earlier. Akron v. Akron Center (1983); Thornburgh v. American Coll. of Obst. & Gyn. (1986).]

[Twenty-four-hour delays had been held invalid in earlier cases, such as Akron v. Akron Center for Reproductive Health (1983).]

Requiring women under the age of eighteen to notify both parents. Hodgson v. Minnesota (1990).

Requiring women to notify their spouses. Planned Parenthood v. Casey (1992).

Prohibitions on "partial birth abortion." Stenberg v. Carhart (2000).

funds for family planning, specifying that none of the funds "shall be used in programs where abortion is a method of family planning." 84 Stat. 1508, § 1008. On September 1, 1987, the Department of Health and Human Services issued a proposed rule prohibiting family-planning clinics from using federal funds to counsel women on abortions or referring them to a doctor for abortion, even if women requested the information. Congress placed language in a conference report stating that changes in existing law must be achieved through the regular legislative process and not through executive regulations. H. Rept. No. 100-498, at 943. Nevertheless, the Reagan administration made the regulations final in 1988.

In 1991, a 5–4 decision by the Supreme Court upheld the regulations, which had been challenged as a violation of congressional intent and of constitutional rights available under the First and Fifth Amendments. Rust v. Sullivan, 500 U.S. 173 (1991). Both Houses of Congress began drafting legislation to reverse *Rust*. Language in an appropriation bill prohibited the use of funds to enforce the rule that barred abortion counseling, but President Bush vetoed the bill on November 19, 1991. Shortly before his veto, Bush prepared a memorandum stating that there was no Gag Rule to interfere with the doctor-patient relationship. In implementing the regulation, nothing should prevent a woman from receiving complete medical information about her condition from a physician. However, since abortion counseling in family-planning clinics is done largely by nurses and other nonphysician health-care personnel, the Gag Rule still retained its restrictive force. Late in 1992, the D.C. Circuit nullified the Gag Rule because when the administration modified it (to permit physicians to counsel patients on abortion), it had failed to submit the regulation for public notice and comment. *National Family Planning and Reproductive Health Ass'n, Inc. v. Sullivan*, 979 F.2d 227 (D.C. Cir. 1992).

During the 1992 presidential campaign, Bill Clinton promised to cancel the Gag Rule if elected. On January 22, 1993, he lifted the restriction on abortion counseling. At the same time, he reversed the Reagan-Bush restrictions on federally sponsored research on medical use of fetal tissue. Such research has been used to discover cures for victims of Alzheimer's disease, juvenile diabetes, and Parkinson's disease.

Roe v. Wade

410 U. S. 113 (1973)

Using the pseudonym "Jane Roe," a pregnant single woman brought a class action challenging the constitutionality of a Texas law that made it a criminal offense to attempt an abortion except for the purpose of saving the mother's life. Other parties were allowed to intervene in this case. A three-judge district court declared the Texas law void as vague and infringing the rights under the Ninth and Fourteenth Amendments. Henry Wade, the District Attorney of Dallas County, cross-appealed on the district court's grant of declaratory relief to Roe and to a physician who intervened, while Roe appealed on the district court's ruling to bar injunctive relief.

MR. JUSTICE BLACKMUN delivered the opinion of the Court.

. . .

We forthwith acknowledge our awareness of the sensitive and emotional nature of the abortion controversy, of the vigorous opposing views, even among physicians, and of the deep and seemingly absolute convictions that the subject inspires. One's philosophy, one's experiences, one's exposure to the raw edges of human existence, one's religious training, one's attitudes toward life and family and their values, and the moral standards one establishes and seeks to observe, are all likely to influence and to color one's thinking and conclusions about abortion.

In addition, population growth, pollution, poverty, and racial overtones tend to complicate and not to simplify the problem.

Our task, of course, is to resolve the issue by constitutional measurement, free of emotion and of predilection....

I

The Texas statutes that concern us here are

Arts. 1191–1194 and 1196 of the State's Penal Code. These make it a crime to "procure an abortion," as therein defined, or to attempt one, except with respect to "an abortion procured or attempted by medical advice for the purpose of saving the life of the mother." Similar statutes are in existence in a majority of the States.

. . .

II

Jane Roe, a single woman who was residing in Dallas County, Texas, instituted this federal action in March 1970 against the District Attorney of the county....

. . .

James Hubert Hallford, a licensed physician, sought and was granted leave to intervene in Roe's action. In his complaint he alleged that he had been arrested previously for violations of the Texas abortion statutes and that two such prosecutions were pending against him.

. . .

John and Mary Doe *[pseudonyms]*, a married couple, filed a companion complaint to that of Roe.... The Does alleged that they were a childless couple; that Mrs. Doe was suffering from a "neural-chemical" disorder; that her physician had "advised her to avoid pregnancy until such time as her condition has materially improved" (although a pregnancy at the present time would not present "a serious risk" to her life); that, pursuant to medical advice, she had discontinued use of birth control pills; and that if she should become pregnant, she would want to terminate the pregnancy by an abortion performed by a competent, licensed physician under safe, clinical conditions....

[After deciding that Jane Roe had standing to sue, that she presented a justiciable controversy, that the termination of her 1970 pregnancy did not render the case moot, and that neither Hallford nor the Does had standing, the Court moves to the merits and substance of the case.]

V

The principal thrust of appellant's attack on the Texas statutes is that they improperly invade a right, said to be possessed by the pregnant woman, to choose to terminate her pregnancy.... Before addressing this claim, we feel it desirable briefly to survey, in several aspects, the history of abortion, for such insight as that history may afford us, and then to examine the state purposes and interests behind the criminal abortion laws.

VI

It perhaps is not generally appreciated that the restrictive criminal abortion laws in effect in a majority of States today are of relatively recent vintage. Those laws, generally proscribing abortion or its attempt at any time during pregnancy except when necessary to preserve the pregnant woman's life, are not of ancient or even of common-law origin. Instead, they derive from statutory changes effected, for the most part, in the latter half of the 19th century.

[The Court devotes seventeen pages to ancient attitudes toward abortion, the Hippocratic oath, the common law, the English statutory law, the American law, and the positions of the American Medical Association, the American Public Health Association, and the American Bar Association.]

VII

Three reasons have been advanced to explain historically the enactment of criminal abortion laws in the 19th century and to justify their continued existence.

It has been argued occasionally that these laws were the product of a Victorian social concern to discourage illicit sexual conduct. Texas, however, does not advance this justification in the present case, and it appears that no court or commentator has taken the argument seriously....

A second reason is concerned with abortion as a medical procedure. When most criminal abortion laws were first enacted, the procedure was a hazardous one for the woman....

Modern medical techniques have altered this situation. Appellants and various *amici* refer to medical data indicating that abortion in early pregnancy, that is, prior to the end of the first trimester, although not without its risk, is now relatively safe. Mortality rates for women undergoing early abortions, where the procedure is legal, appear to be as low as or lower than the rates for normal childbirth....

The third reason is the State's interest—some phrase it in terms of duty—in protecting prenatal life. Some of the argument for this justification rests on the theory that a new human life is present from the moment of conception. The State's interest and general obligation to protect life then extends, it is argued, to prenatal life. Only when the life of the pregnant mother herself is at stake, balanced against the life she carries within her, should the interest of the embryo or fetus not prevail. Logically, of course, a legitimate state interest in this area need not stand or fall on acceptance of the belief that life begins at conception or at some other point prior to live birth. In assessing the State's interest, recognition may be given to the less rigid claim that as long as at least *potential* life is involved, the State may assert interests beyond the protection of the pregnant woman alone.

· · ·

VIII

The Constitution does not explicitly mention any right of privacy. In a line of decisions, however, going back perhaps as far as *Union Pacific R. Co. v. Botsford*, 141 U. S. 250, 251 (1891), the Court has recognized that a right of personal privacy, or a guarantee of certain areas or zones of privacy, does exist under the Constitution...

This right of privacy, whether it be founded in the Fourteenth Amendment's concept of personal liberty and restrictions upon state action, as we feel it is, or, as the District Court determined, in the Ninth Amendment's reservation of rights to the people, is broad enough to encompass a woman's decision whether or not to terminate her pregnancy. The detriment that the State would impose upon the pregnant woman by denying this choice altogether is apparent. Specific and direct harm medically diagnosable even in early pregnancy may be involved. Maternity, or additional offspring, may force upon the woman a distressful life and future. Psychological harm may be imminent. Mental and physical health may be taxed by child care. There is also the distress, for all concerned, associated with the unwanted child, and there is the problem of bringing a child into a family already unable, psychologically and otherwise, to care for it. In other cases, as in this one, the additional difficulties and continuing stigma of unwed motherhood may be involved. All these are factors the woman and her responsible physician necessarily will consider in consultation.

On the basis of elements such as these, appellant and some *amici* argue that the woman's right is absolute and that she is entitled to terminate her pregnancy at whatever time, in whatever way, and for whatever reason she alone chooses. With this we do not agree.... The Court's decisions recognizing a right of privacy also acknowledge that some state regulation in areas protected by that right is appropriate. As noted above, a State may properly assert important interests in safeguarding health, in maintaining medical standards, and in protecting potential life....

We, therefore, conclude that the right of personal privacy includes the abortion decision, but that this right is not unqualified and must be considered against important state interests in regulation.

. . .

IX

. . .

A. The appellee and certain *amici* argue that the fetus is a "person" within the language and meaning of the Fourteenth Amendment. In support of this, they outline at length and in detail the well-known facts of fetal development. If this suggestion of personhood is established, the appellant's case, of course, collapses, for the fetus' right to life would then be guaranteed specifically by the Amendment....

The Constitution does not define "person" in so many words. Section 1 of the Fourteenth Amendment contains three references to "person." The first, in defining "citizens," speaks of "persons born or naturalized in the United States." The word also appears both in the Due Process Clause and in the Equal Protection Clause. "Person" is used in other places in the Constitution: in the listing of qualifications for Representatives and Senators, ...; in the Apportionment Clause, ...; in the Migration and Importation provision, ...; in the Emolument Clause, ...; in the Electors provisions, ...; in the provision outlining qualifications for the office of President, ...; in the Extradition provisions, ...; and the superseded Fugitive Slave Clause 3; and in the Fifth, Twelfth, and Twenty-second Amendments, as well as in §§ 2 and 3 of the Fourteenth Amendment. But in nearly all these instances, the use of the word is such that it has application only postnatally. None indicates, with any assurance, that it has any possible pre-natal application.

. . .

B.... Texas urges that, apart from the Fourteenth Amendment, life begins at conception and is present throughout pregnancy, and that, therefore, the State has a compelling interest in protecting that life from and after conception. We need not resolve the difficult question of when life begins. When those trained in the respective disciplines of medicine, philosophy, and theology are unable to arrive at any consensus, the judiciary, at this point in the development of man's knowledge, is not in a position to speculate as to the answer.

. . .

X

In view of all this, we do not agree that, by adopting one theory of life, Texas may override the rights of the pregnant woman that are at stake. We repeat, however, that the State does have an important and legitimate interest in preserving and protecting the health of the pregnant woman, ... These interests are separate and distinct. Each grows in substantiality as the woman approaches term and, at a point during pregnancy, each becomes "compelling."

With respect to the State's important and legitimate interest in the health of the mother, the "compelling" point, in the light of present medical knowledge, is at approximately the end of the first trimester. This is so because of the now-established medical fact...that until the end of the first trimester mortality in abortion may be less than mortality in normal childbirth. It follows that, from and after this point, a State may regulate the abortion procedure to the extent that the regulation reasonably relates to the preservation and protection of maternal health. Examples of permissible state regulation in this area are requirements as to the qualifications of the person who is to perform the abortion; as to the licensure of that person; as to the facility in which the procedure is to be performed, that is, whether it must be a hospital or may be a clinic or some other place of less-than-hospital status; as to the licensing of the facility; and the like.

This means, on the other hand, that, for the period of pregnancy prior to this "compelling" point, the attending physician, in consultation with his patient, is free to determine, without regulation by the State, that, in his medical judgment, the patient's pregnancy should be terminated. If that decision is reached, the judgment may be effectuated by an abortion free of interference by the State.

With respect to the State's important and legitimate interest in potential life, the "compelling" point is at viability. This is so because the fetus then presumably has the capability of meaningful life outside the mother's womb. State regulation protective of fetal life after viability thus has both logical and biological justifications. If the State is interested in protecting fetal life after viability, it may go so far as to proscribe abortion during that period, except when it is necessary to preserve the life or health of the mother.

Measured against these standards, Art. 1196 of the Texas Penal Code, in restricting legal abortions to those "procured or attempted by medical advice for the purpose of saving the life of the mother," sweeps too broadly. The statute makes no distinction between abortions performed early in pregnancy and those performed later, and it limits to a single reason, "saving" the mother's life, the legal justification for the procedure. The statute, therefore, cannot survive the constitutional attack made upon it here.

. . .

XI

To summarize and to repeat:

. . .

(a) For the stage prior to approximately the end of the first trimester, the abortion decision and its effectuation must be left to the medical judgment of the pregnant woman's attending physician.

(b) For the stage subsequent to approximately the end of the first trimester, the State, in promoting its interest in the health of the mother, may, if it chooses, regulate the abortion procedure in ways that are reasonably related to maternal health.

(c) For the stage subsequent to viability, the State in promoting its interest in the potentiality of human life may, if it chooses, regulate, and even proscribe, abortion except where it is necessary, in appropriate medical judgment, for the preservation of the life or health of the mother.

. . .

[Chief Justice Burger and Justices Douglas and Stewart wrote separate concurring opinions.]

MR. JUSTICE REHNQUIST, dissenting.

. . .

II

. . . I have difficulty in concluding, as the Court does, that the right of "privacy" is involved in this case. Texas, by the statute here challenged, bars the performance of a medical abortion by a licensed physician on a plaintiff such as Roe. A transaction resulting in an operation such as this is not "private" in the ordinary usage of that word. Nor is the "privacy" that the Court finds here even a distant relative of the freedom from searches and seizures protected by the Fourth Amendment to the Constitution, which the Court has referred to as embodying a right to privacy. *Katz* v. *United States,* 389 U. S. 347 (1967).

If the Court means by the term "privacy" no more than that the claim of a person to be free from unwanted state regulation of consensual transactions may be a form of "liberty" protected by the Fourteenth Amendment, there is no doubt that similar claims have been upheld in our earlier decisions on the basis of that liberty. I agree with the statement of MR. JUSTICE STEWART in his concurring opinion that the "liberty," against deprivation of which without due process the Fourteenth Amendment protects, embraces more than the rights found in the Bill of Rights. But that liberty is not guaranteed absolutely against deprivation, only against deprivation without due process of law. The test traditionally applied in the area of social and economic legislation is whether or not a law such as that challenged has a rational relation to a valid state objective. . . . If the Texas statute were to prohibit an abortion even where the mother's life is in jeopardy, I have little doubt that such a statute would lack a rational relation to a valid state objective.... But the Court's sweeping invalidation of any restrictions on abortion during the first trimester is impossible to justify under that standard, and the conscious weighing of competing factors that the Court's opinion apparently substitutes for the established test is far more appropriate to a legislative judgment than to a judicial one.

. . .

While the Court's opinion quotes from the dissent of Mr. Justice Holmes in *Lochner v. New York,* 198 U. S. 45, 74 (1905), the result it reaches is more closely attuned to the majority opinion of Mr. Justice Peckham in that case. As in *Lochner* and similar cases applying substantive due process standards to economic and social welfare legislation, the adoption of the compelling state interest standard will inevitably require this Court to examine the legislative policies and pass on the wisdom of these policies in the very process of deciding whether a particular state interest put forward may or may not be "compelling." The decision here to break pregnancy into three distinct terms and to outline the permissible restrictions the State may impose in each one, for example, partakes more of judicial legislation than it does of a determination of the intent of the drafters of the Fourteenth Amendment.

. . .

MR. JUSTICE WHITE, with whom MR. JUSTICE REHNQUIST joins, dissenting.

. . .

...I find nothing in the language or history of the Constitution to support the Court's judgment. The Court simply fashions and announces a new constitutional right for pregnant mothers and, with scarcely any reason or authority for its action, invests that right with sufficient substance to override most existing state abortion statutes. The upshot is that the people and the legislatures of the 50 States are constitutionally disentitled to weigh the relative importance of the continued existence and development of the fetus, on the one hand, against a spectrum of possible impacts on the mother, on the other hand. As an exercise of raw judicial power, the Court perhaps has authority to do what it does today; but in my view its judgment is an improvident and extravagant exercise of the power of judicial review that the Constitution extends to this Court.

The Court apparently values the convenience of the pregnant mother more than the continued existence and development of the life or potential life that she carries. Whether or not I might agree with that marshaling of values, I can in no event join the Court's judgment because I find no constitutional warrant for imposing such an order of priorities on the people and legislatures of the States....

Hyde Amendment of 1976: Congressional Debate

As an amendment to the Labor-HEW appropriations bill for fiscal 1977, Cong. Henry J. Hyde (R-Ill.) offered language to prohibit any of the funds appropriated in the bill "to pay for abortions or to promote or encourage abortions." His amendment passed in the Committee of the Whole, 207–167, and again by the full House, 199–165. After action by the Senate and conference committee, the enacted language read: "None of the funds contained in this Act shall be used to perform abortions except where the life of the mother would be endangered if the fetus were carried to term." 90 Stat. 1434, § 209 (1976).

Mr. HYDE. Mr. Chairman, I offer an amendment.

The Clerk read as follows:

"Amendment offered by Mr. HYDE: On page 36, after line 9, add the following new section:

'SEC. 209. None of the funds appropriated under this Act shall be used to pay for abortions or to promote or encourage abortions.' "

Mr. HYDE. Mr. Chairman, this amendment may stimulate a lot of debate—but it need not—

because I believe most Members know how they will vote on this issue.

Nevertheless, there are those of us who believe it is to the everlasting shame of this country that in 1973 approximately 800,000 legal abortions were performed in this country—and so it is fair to assume that this year over a million human lives will be destroyed because they are inconvenient to someone.

The unborn child facing an abortion can best

be classified as a member of the innocently inconvenient and since the pernicious doctrine that some lives are more important than others seems to be persuasive with the pro-abortion forces, we who seek to protect that most defenseless and innocent of human lives, the unborn — seek to inhibit the use of Federal funds to pay for and thus encourage abortion as an answer to the human and compelling problem of an unwanted child.

We are all exercised at the wanton killing of the porpoise, the baby seal. We urge big game hunters to save the tiger, but we somehow turn away at the specter of a million human beings being violently destroyed because this great, society does not want them.

And make no mistake, an abortion is violent.

I think in the final analysis, you must determine whether or not the unborn person is human. If you think it is animal or vegetable then, of course, it is disposable like an empty beer can to be crushed and thrown out with the rest of the trash.

But medicine, biology, embryology, say that growing living organism is not animal or vegetable or mineral — but it is a human life.

And if you believe that human life is deserving of due process of law — of equal protection of the laws, then you cannot in logic and conscience help fund the execution of these innocent defenseless human lives.

If we are to order our lives by the precepts of animal husbandry, then I guess abortion is an acceptable answer. If we human beings are not of a higher order than animals then let us save our pretentious aspirations for a better and more just world and recognize this is an anthill we inhabit and there are no such things as ideals or justice or morality.

Once conception has occurred a new and unique genetic package has been created, not a potential human being, but a human being with potential. For 9 months the mother provides nourishment and shelter, and birth is no substantial change, it is merely a change of address.

We are told that bringing an unwanted child into the world is an obscene act. Unwanted by whom? Is it too subtle a notion to understand it is more important to be a loving person than to be one who is loved. We need more people who are capable of projecting love.

We hear the claim that the poor are denied a right available to other women if we do not use tax money to fund abortions.

Well, make a list of all the things society denies poor women and let them make the choice of what we will give them.

Don't say "poor women, go destroy your young, and we will pay for it."

An innocent, defenseless human life, in a caring and humane society deserves better than to be flushed down a toilet or burned in an incinerator.

The promise of America is that life is not just for the privileged, the planned, or the perfect.

. . .

Mr. FLOOD. Mr. Chairman, I rise in opposition to the amendment.

Mr. Chairman, I would like the attention of the Members on this. I will tell them why. Nobody, but nobody in this room, has a better right to be standing here this minute on this subject, and everybody knows this, than the gentleman from Pennsylvania that is talking to the House now.

Mr. Chairman, everybody knows my position for many years with respect to abortion. I believe it is wrong, with a capital "W". It violates the most basic rights, the right of the unborn child, the right to life.

It is for that reason that I have supported for many, many years constitutional amendments which would address this very serious matter, and the Members know it. So, what am I doing down here now? Well, I will tell you. I oppose this amendment, and I will tell you why. Listen. This is blatantly discriminatory; that is why.

The Members do not like that? Of course they do not. It does not prohibit abortion. No, it does not prohibit abortion. It prohibits abortion for poor people. That is what it does.... It does not require any change in the practice of the middle-income and the upper-income people. Oh, no. They are able to go to their private practitioners and get the service done for a fee. But, it does take away the option from those of our citizens who must rely on medicaid — and other public programs for medical care.

Now abortion, Mr. Chairman, abortion is not an economic issue; not at all. The morality — all right, the morality of abortion is no different for a poor family — the morality of abortion is no different for a poor family than it is for a rich family. Is that right? Of course: a standard of morality is a standard.

To accept — now, this is coming from me — to accept this amendment, the right of this country to impose on its poor citizens, impose on them a morality which it is not willing to impose on the rich as well, we would not dare do that. That is what this amendment does....

This is not the place, on an appropriation bill,

to address that kind of issue. This is not. Mr. Chairman, this is an appropriation bill. This is not a constitutional amendment.

I urge my colleagues to reject this amendment.

Mr. GUYER....

Mr. Chairman, this issue has all but become threadbare, largely due to the fact that we cannot get action from the proper committee to really correct the wrong by a constitutional amendment that would solve the problem totally and properly.... What a woman does with her body is her own business.

What she does with the body of someone else is not her business.

I think that we here should go on record as safeguarding that most precious commodity, the gift of little children from God, who have a right to live.

Mr. BAUMAN....

The gentleman from Pennsylvania objects to using an appropriation bill for the purpose of making public policy, but no question was raised against the form of this amendment, and none could be, because it is a legitimate limit on the expenditure of Federal funds.

The gentleman raises an interesting, but I think answerable, point on the grounds that this would discriminate against poor people. The answer is that we have not been able to pass a constitutional amendment that would permit the right to life, regardless of poverty or wealth. But I do not understand that the child of a poor parent has any less right to live than the child of a rich parent. If we could protect the right to life for all children, we would do it. But the fact of the matter is, under medicaid and other programs that are financed in this bill, the Federal Government has been paying for more than 300,000 abortions annually at a cost of $40 to $50 million.

I think the unborn children whose lives are being snuffed out, even though they may not be adults have a right to live, too, regardless of the mistaken and immoral Supreme Court decision. I do not think the taxpayers of the United States have any obligation to permit their money to be used in this manner for federally financed abortions. That is the only issue here today.

. . .

Ms. ABZUG. Mr. Chairman,... the issue confronting this body is whether it will conduct itself with respect for the normal processes in which we engage and for which we were sent here. The issue being discussed here today is irrelevant, nongermane, and inappropriate as it relates to this measure, because the relief that is being sought by those who have a very particular point of view cannot be accomplished by this amendment.

This amendment is a cruel amendment, as was very ably pointed out by the chairman of the subcommittee presenting this appropriations bill. The passage of this amendment will not overcome the fact that every survey and every poll in this country show that a majority of people support the Supreme Court decision.

This is not to say that I and others who support the Supreme Court decision and the right to privacy that is protected therein do not respect the right of others to differ with us. We do respect the right of those who take an opposite point of view to differ with us on this subject. As a matter of fact, people like myself probably have more contact with those who differ on this subject than those who claim to represent them in the House. They understand our differences, and they and we understand that there is a right to differ with a decision. Still, there must be an understanding that those who differ as a matter of conscience or religious belief have no right to impose their views on others who also wish to exercise their rights in their own way.

The implementation of this amendment or an amendment like this, if agreed to in this House, will mean only one thing, and that will be, as was pointed out by the subcommittee chairman, to deny to some people the rights the majority have in this country.

Harris v. McRae

448 U.S. 297 (1980)

Since 1976, versions of the Hyde Amendment passed by Congress severely limited the use of any federal funds to reimburse the cost of abortions under the Medicaid program. Cora McRae brought an action in federal court, challenging the Hyde Amendment on the ground that it violated the Due Process Clause of the Fifth Amendment and the Religion

Clauses of the First Amendment. The defendant was Patricia R. Harris, Secretary of Health and Human Services. The district court held that the Amendment violated the equal protection component of the Fifth Amendment's Due Process Clause and the Free Exercise Clause of the First Amendment.

MR. JUSTICE STEWART delivered the opinion of the Court.

This case presents statutory and constitutional questions concerning the public funding of abortions under Title XIX of the Social Security Act, commonly known as the "Medicaid" Act, and recent annual Appropriations Acts containing the so-called "Hyde Amendment." The statutory question is whether Title XIX requires a State that participates in the Medicaid program to fund the cost of medically necessary abortions for which federal reimbursement is unavailable under the Hyde Amendment. The constitutional question, which arises only if Title XIX imposes no such requirement, is whether the Hyde Amendment, by denying public funding for certain medically necessary abortions, contravenes the liberty or equal protection guarantees of the Due Process Clause of the Fifth Amendment, or either of the Religion Clauses of the First Amendment.

I

The Medicaid program was created in 1965, when Congress added Title XIX to the Social Security Act ... for the purpose of providing federal financial assistance to States that choose to reimburse certain costs of medical treatment for needy persons. Although participation in the Medicaid program is entirely optional, once a State elects to participate, it must comply with the requirements of Title XIX.

One such requirement is that a participating State agree to provide financial assistance to the "categorically needy" with respect to five general areas of medical treatment....

Since September 1976, Congress has prohibited — either by an amendment to the annual appropriations bill for the Department of Health, Education, and Welfare or by a joint resolution — the use of any federal funds to reimburse the cost of abortions under the Medicaid program except under certain specified circumstances. This funding restriction is commonly known as the "Hyde Amendment," after its original congressional sponsor, Representative Hyde. The current version of the Hyde Amendment, applicable for fiscal year 1980, provides:

"[N]one of the funds provided by this joint resolution shall be used to perform abortions ex-

cept where the life of the mother would be endangered if the fetus were carried to term; or except for such medical procedures necessary for the victims of rape or incest when such rape or incest has been reported promptly to a law enforcement agency or public health service." Pub. L. 96-123, § 109, 93 Stat. 926.

See also Pub. L. 96-86, § 118, 93 Stat. 662. This version of the Hyde Amendment is broader than that applicable for fiscal year 1977, which did not include the "rape or incest" exception, Pub. L. 94-439, § 209, 90 Stat. 1434, but narrower than that applicable for most of fiscal year 1978, and all of fiscal year 1979, which had an additional exception for "instances where severe and long-lasting physical health damage to the mother would result if the pregnancy were carried to term when so determined by two physicians," Pub. L. 95-205, § 101, 91 Stat. 1460; Pub. L. 95-480, § 210, 92 Stat. 1586.

. . .

II

It is well settled that if a case may be decided on either statutory or constitutional grounds, this Court, for sound jurisprudential reasons, will inquire first into the statutory question.... Accordingly, we turn first to the question whether Title XIX requires a State that participates in the Medicaid program to continue to fund those medically necessary abortions for which federal reimbursement is unavailable under the Hyde Amendment. If a participating State is under such an obligation, the constitutionality of the Hyde Amendment need not be drawn into question in the present case, for the availability of medically necessary abortions under Medicaid would continue, with the participating State shouldering the total cost of funding such abortions.

[The Court interprets Title XIX as part of "cooperative federalism" in which the federal government contributes to participating states. It concludes that Title XIX does not require a participating state to include in its plan any service for which Congress has withheld federal funding.]

III

Having determined that Title XIX does not obligate a participating State to pay for those medically necessary abortions for which Congress has withheld federal funding, we must consider the constitutional validity of the Hyde Amendment....

. . .

A

We address first the appellees' argument that the Hyde Amendment, by restricting the availability of certain medically necessary abortions under Medicaid, impinges on the "liberty" protected by the Due Process Clause as recognized in *Roe* v. *Wade,* 410 U.S. 113, and its progeny.

[Roe *v.* Wade *recognized a woman's freedom to decide whether to terminate a pregnancy in the early stages, but the interests of a state grew substantially as the woman approached term. In* Maher *v.* Roe, *432 U.S. 464, the Court held that the constitutional freedom recognized in* Roe *v.* Wade *did not prevent a state from making a value judgment by providing funds to favor childbirth over abortion. A state has no constitutional obligation to subsidize abortions.]*

The Hyde Amendment, like the Connecticut welfare regulation at issue in *Maher,* places no governmental obstacle in the path of a woman who chooses to terminate her pregnancy, but rather, by means of unequal subsidization of abortion and other medical services, encourages alternative activity deemed in the public interest. The present case does differ factually from *Maher* insofar as that case involved a failure to fund nontherapeutic abortions, whereas the Hyde Amendment withholds funding of certain medically necessary abortions. Accordingly, the appellees argue that because the Hyde Amendment affects a significant interest not present or asserted in *Maher*—the interest of a woman in protecting her health during pregnancy—and because that interest lies at the core of the personal constitutional freedom recognized in *Wade,* the present case is constitutionally different from *Maher.* It is the appellees' view that to the extent that the Hyde Amendment withholds funding for certain medically necessary abortions, it clearly impinges on the constitutional principle recognized in *Wade.*

...[R]egardless of whether the freedom of a woman to choose to terminate her pregnancy for health reasons lies at the core or the periphery of the due process liberty recognized in *Wade,* it simply does not follow that a woman's freedom of choice carries with it a constitutional entitlement to the financial resources to avail herself of the full range of protected choices. The reason why was explained in *Maher:* although government may not place obstacles in the path of a woman's exercise of her freedom of choice, it need not remove those not of its own creation. Indigency falls in the latter category. The financial constraints that restrict an indigent woman's ability to enjoy the full range of constitutionally protected freedom of choice are the product not of governmental restrictions on access to abortions, but rather of her indigency....

...Whether freedom of choice that is constitutionally protected warrants federal subsidization is a question for Congress to answer, not a matter of constitutional entitlement. Accordingly, we conclude that the Hyde Amendment does not impinge on the due process liberty recognized in *Wade.*

B

The appellees also argue that the Hyde Amendment contravenes rights secured by the Religion Clauses of the First Amendment. It is the appellees' view that the Hyde Amendment violates the Establishment Clause because it incorporates into law the doctrines of the Roman Catholic Church concerning the sinfulness of abortion and the time at which life commences. Moreover, insofar as a woman's decision to seek a medically necessary abortion may be a product of her religious beliefs under certain Protestant and Jewish tenets, the appellees assert that the funding limitations of the Hyde Amendment impinge on the freedom of religion guaranteed by the Free Exercise Clause.

1

...[I]t does not follow that a statute violates the Establishment Clause because it "happens to coincide or harmonize with the tenets of some or all religions." *McGowan* v. *Maryland,* 366 U.S. 420, 442. That the Judaeo-Christian religions oppose stealing does not mean that a State or the Federal Government may not, consistent with the Establishment Clause, enact laws prohibiting larceny....

C

It remains to be determined whether the Hyde Amendment violates the equal protection component of the Fifth Amendment. This challenge is premised on the fact that, although federal reimbursement is available under Medicaid for medically necessary services generally, the Hyde Amendment does not permit federal reimbursement of all medically necessary abortions. The

District Court held, and the appellees argue here, that this selective subsidization violates the constitutional guarantee of equal protection.

The guarantee of equal protection under the Fifth Amendment is not a source of substantive rights or liberties....

1

For the reasons stated above, we have already concluded that the Hyde Amendment violates no constitutionally protected substantive rights. We now conclude as well that it is not predicated on a constitutionally suspect classification. In reaching this conclusion, we again draw guidance from the Court's decision in *Maher* v. *Roe*....

It is our view that the present case is indistinguishable from *Maher* in this respect. Here, as in *Maher*, the principal impact of the Hyde Amendment falls on the indigent. But that fact does not itself render the funding restriction constitutionally invalid, for this Court has held repeatedly that poverty, standing alone, is not a suspect classification....

2

The remaining question then is whether the Hyde Amendment is rationally related to a legitimate governmental objective. It is the Government's position that the Hyde Amendment bears a rational relationship to its legitimate interest in protecting the potential life of the fetus. We agree.

In *Wade*, the Court recognized that the State has an "important and legitimate interest in protecting the potentiality of human life." 410 U.S., at 162. That interest was found to exist throughout a pregnancy, "grow[ing] in substantiality as the woman approaches term."...Moreover, in *Maher*, the Court held that Connecticut's decision to fund the costs associated with childbirth but not those associated with nontherapeutic abortions was a rational means of advancing the legitimate state interest in protecting potential life by encouraging childbirth....

It follows that the Hyde Amendment, by encouraging childbirth except in the most urgent circumstances, is rationally related to the legitimate governmental objective of protecting potential life. By subsidizing the medical expenses of indigent women who carry their pregnancies to term while not subsidizing the comparable expenses of women who undergo abortions (except those whose lives are threatened), Congress has established incentives that make childbirth a more attractive alternative than abortion for persons eligible for Medicaid. These incentives bear a direct relationship to the legitimate congressional interest in protecting potential life....

. . .

IV

For the reasons stated in this opinion, we hold that a State that participates in the Medicaid program is not obligated under Title XIX to continue to fund those medically necessary abortions for which federal reimbursement is unavailable under the Hyde Amendment. We further hold that the funding restrictions of the Hyde Amendment violate neither the Fifth Amendment nor the Establishment Clause of the First Amendment. It is also our view that the appellees lack standing to raise a challenge to the Hyde Amendment under the Free Exercise Clause of the First Amendment. Accordingly, the judgment of the District Court is reversed, and the case is remanded to that court for further proceedings consistent with this opinion.

It is so ordered.

MR. JUSTICE WHITE, concurring.

. . .

MR. JUSTICE BRENNAN, with whom MR. JUSTICE MARSHALL and MR. JUSTICE BLACKMUN join, dissenting.

...*Roe* and its progeny established that the pregnant woman has a right to be free from state interference with her choice to have an abortion—a right which, at least prior to the end of the first trimester, absolutely prohibits any governmental regulation of that highly personal decision. The proposition for which these cases stand thus is not that the State is under an affirmative obligation to ensure access to abortions for all who may desire them; it is that the State must refrain from wielding its enormous power and influence in a manner that might burden the pregnant woman's freedom to choose whether to have an abortion. The Hyde Amendment's denial of public funds for medically necessary abortions plainly intrudes upon this constitutionally protected decision, for both by design and in effect it serves to coerce indigent pregnant women to bear children that they would otherwise elect not to have.

. . .

MR. JUSTICE MARSHALL, dissenting.

. . .

III

The consequences of today's opinion — consequences to which the Court seems oblivious — are not difficult to predict. Pregnant women denied the funding necessary to procure abortions will be restricted to two alternatives. First, they can carry the fetus to term — even though that route may result in severe injury or death to the mother, the fetus, or both. If that course appears intolerable, they can resort to self-induced abortions or attempt to obtain illegal abortions — not because bearing a child would be inconvenient, but because it is necessary in order to protect their health. The result will not be to protect what the Court describes as "the legitimate governmental objective of protecting potential life," *ante,* at 325, but to ensure the destruction of both fetal and maternal life....

. . .

MR. JUSTICE BLACKMUN, dissenting.

I join the dissent of MR. JUSTICE BRENNAN and agree wholeheartedly with his and MR. JUSTICE STEVENS' respective observations and descriptions of what the Court is doing in this latest round of "abortion cases."...

MR. JUSTICE STEVENS, dissenting.

. . .

Having decided to alleviate some of the hardships of poverty by providing necessary medical care, the government must use neutral criteria in distributing benefits. It may not deny benefits to a financially and medically needy person simply because he is a Republican, a Catholic, or an Oriental — or because he has spoken against a program the government has a legitimate interest in furthering. In sum, it may not create exceptions for the sole purpose of furthering a governmental interest that is constitutionally subordinate to the individual interest that the entire program was designed to protect. The Hyde Amendments not only exclude financially and medically needy persons from the pool of benefits for a constitutionally insufficient reason; they also require the expenditure of millions and millions of dollars in order to thwart the exercise of a constitutional right, thereby effectively inflicting serious and long-lasting harm on impoverished women who want and need abortions for valid medical reasons. In my judgment, these Amendments constitute an unjustifiable, and indeed blatant, violation of the sovereign's duty to govern impartially.

I respectfully dissent.

Akron v. Akron Center for Reproductive Health

462 U.S. 416 (1983)

An Akron, Ohio, ordinance required all abortions after the first trimester of pregnancy to be performed in a hospital. The ordinance also established other requirements, including regulations for abortion on an unmarried minor, counseling of the patient by the physician, a twenty-four-hour delay in performing an abortion after a pregnant woman signed a consent form, and procedures for disposing of the fetal remains. A federal district court invalidated some of the requirements and upheld others. The Sixth Circuit sustained some of the lower court's rulings but reversed others.

JUSTICE POWELL delivered the opinion of the Court.

In this litigation we must decide the constitutionality of several provisions of an ordinance enacted by the city of Akron, Ohio, to regulate the performance of abortions....

. . .

I

In February 1978 the City Council of Akron enacted Ordinance No. 160-1978, entitled "Reg-

ulation of Abortions." The ordinance sets forth 17 provisions that regulate the performance of abortions, see Akron Codified Ordinances, ch. 1870, 5 of which are at issue in this case:

(i) Section 1870.03 requires that all abortions performed after the first trimester of pregnancy be performed in a hospital.

(ii) Section 1870.05 sets forth requirements for notification of and consent by parents before abortions may be performed on unmarried minors.

(iii) Section 1870.06 requires that the attending physician make certain specified statements to the patient "to insure that the consent for an abortion is truly informed consent."

(iv) Section 1870.07 requires a 24-hour waiting period between the time the woman signs a consent form and the time the abortion is performed.

(v) Section 1870.16 requires that fetal remains be "disposed of in a humane and sanitary manner."

A violation of any section of the ordinance is punishable as a criminal misdemeanor. § 1870.18. If any provision is invalidated, it is to be severed from the remainder of the ordinance. The ordinance became effective on May 1, 1978.

. . .

III

Section 1870.03 of the Akron ordinance requires that any abortion performed "upon a pregnant woman subsequent to the end of the first trimester of her pregnancy" must be "performed in a hospital."...

...[W]e now hold that § 1870.03 is unconstitutional.

. . .

B

There can be no doubt that § 1870.03's second-trimester hospitalization requirement places a significant obstacle in the path of women seeking an abortion. A primary burden created by the requirement is additional cost to the woman. The Court of Appeals noted that there was testimony that a second-trimester abortion costs more than twice as much in a hospital as in a clinic....Moreover, the court indicated that second-trimester abortions were rarely performed in Akron hospitals....Thus, a second-trimester hospitalization requirement may force women to travel to find available facilities, resulting in both financial expense and additional health risk. It therefore is apparent that a second-trimester hospitalization requirement may significantly limit a woman's ability to obtain an abortion.

Akron does not contend that § 1870.03 imposes only an insignificant burden on women's access to abortion, but rather defends it as a reasonable health regulation. This position had strong support at the time of *Roe* v. *Wade*, as hospitalization for second-trimester abortions was recommended by the American Public Health Association (APHA)...and the American College of Obstetricians and Gynecologists (ACOG)....Since then, however, the safety of second-trimester abortions has increased dramatically.

...The evidence is strong enough to have con-

vinced the APHA to abandon its prior recommendation of hospitalization for all second-trimester abortions....

. . .

Similarly, the ACOG no longer suggests that all second-trimester abortions be performed in a hospital....

IV

We turn next to § 1870.05(B), the provision prohibiting a physician from performing an abortion on a minor pregnant woman under the age of 15 unless he obtains "the informed written consent of one of her parents or her legal guardian" or unless the minor obtains "an order from a court having jurisdiction over her that the abortion be performed or induced."...

The relevant legal standards are not in dispute. The Court has held that "the State may not impose a blanket provision...requiring the consent of a parent or person *in loco parentis* as a condition for abortion of an unmarried minor." *Danforth, supra*, at 74. In *Bellotti* v. *Baird*, 443 U.S. 622 (1979) *(Bellotti II)*, a majority of the Court indicated that a State's interest in protecting immature minors will sustain a requirement of a consent substitute, either parental or judicial.... The *Bellotti II* plurality cautioned, however, that the State must provide an alternative procedure whereby a pregnant minor may demonstrate that she is sufficiently mature to make the abortion decision herself or that, despite her immaturity, an abortion would be in her best interests. 443 U.S., at 643–644. Under these decisions, it is clear that Akron may not make a blanket determination that *all* minors under the age of 15 are too immature to make this decision or that an abortion never may be in the minor's best interests without parental approval.

...[W]e do not think that the Akron ordinance, as applied in Ohio juvenile proceedings, is reasonably susceptible of being construed to create an "opportunity for case-by-case evaluations of the maturity of pregnant minors." *Bellotti II, supra*, at 643, n. 23 (plurality opinion). We therefore affirm the Court of Appeals' judgment that § 1870.05(B) is unconstitutional.

V

The Akron ordinance provides that no abortion shall be performed except "with the informed written consent of the pregnant woman,...given freely and without coercion." § 1870.06(A). Furthermore, "in order to insure that the consent for an abortion is truly informed consent," the woman must be "orally informed by her attending physician" of the status of her pregnancy, the development of her fetus, the date of possible viability, the physical and emotional complications that may result from an abortion, and the availability of agencies to provide her with assistance and information with respect to birth control, adoption, and childbirth. § 1870.06(B). In addition, the attending physician must inform her "of the particular risks associated with her own pregnancy and the abortion technique to be employed ... [and] other information which in his own medical judgment is relevant to her decision as to whether to have an abortion or carry her pregnancy to term." § 1870.06(C).

. . .

B

... [W]e believe that § 1870.06(B) attempts to extend the State's interest in ensuring "informed consent" beyond permissible limits. First, it is fair to say that much of the information required is designed not to inform the woman's consent but rather to persuade her to withhold it altogether. Subsection (3) requires the physician to inform his patient that "the unborn child is a human life from the moment of conception," a requirement inconsistent with the Court's holding in *Roe* v. *Wade* that a State may not adopt one theory of when life begins to justify its regulation of abortions.... subsection (5), that begins with the dubious statement that "abortion is a major surgical procedure" and proceeds to describe numerous possible physical and psychological complications of abortion, is a "parade of horribles" intended to suggest that abortion is a particularly dangerous procedure.

. . .

C

Section 1870.06(C) presents a different question. Under this provision, the "attending physician" must inform the woman

"of the particular risks associated with her own pregnancy and the abortion technique to be employed including providing her with at least a general description of the medical instructions to be followed subsequent to the abortion in order to insure her safe recovery, and shall in addition provide her with such other information which in his own medical judgment is relevant to her deci-

sion as to whether to have an abortion or carry her pregnancy to term."

The information required clearly is related to maternal health and to the State's legitimate purpose in requiring informed consent. Nonetheless, the Court of Appeals determined that it interfered with the physician's medical judgment "in exactly the same way as section 1870.06(B). It requires the doctor to make certain disclosures in all cases, regardless of his own professional judgment as to the desirability of doing so." 651 F. 2d, at 1207....

... [W]e believe that it is unreasonable for a State to insist that only a physician is competent to provide the information and counseling relevant to informed consent. We affirm the judgment of the Court of Appeals that § 1870.06(C) is invalid.

VI

The Akron ordinance prohibits a physician from performing an abortion until 24 hours after the pregnant woman signs a consent form. § 1870.07.... The Court of Appeals reversed, finding that the inflexible waiting period had "no medical basis," and that careful consideration of the abortion decision by the woman "is beyond the state's power to require." 651 F. 2d, at 1208. We affirm the Court of Appeals' judgment.

The District Court found that the mandatory 24-hour waiting period increases the cost of obtaining an abortion by requiring the woman to make two separate trips to the abortion facility. See 479 F. Supp., at 1204. Plaintiffs also contend that because of scheduling difficulties the effective delay may be longer than 24 hours, and that such a delay in some cases could increase the risk of an abortion....

VII

Section § 1870.16 of the Akron ordinance requires physicians performing abortions to "insure that the remains of the unborn child are disposed of in a humane and sanitary manner." The Court of Appeals found that the word "humane" was impermissibly vague as a definition of conduct subject to criminal prosecution. The court invalidated the entire provision, declining to sever the word "humane" in order to uphold the requirement that disposal be "sanitary." See 651 F. 2d, at 1211. We affirm this judgment.

. . .

VIII

We affirm the judgment of the Court of Appeals invalidating those sections of Akron's "Regulations of Abortions" ordinance that deal with parental consent, informed consent, a 24-hour waiting period, and the disposal of fetal remains. The remaining portion of the judgment, sustaining Akron's requirement that all second-trimester abortions be performed in a hospital, is reversed.

It is so ordered.

JUSTICE O'CONNOR, with whom JUSTICE WHITE and JUSTICE REHNQUIST join, dissenting.

. . .

I

The trimester or "three-stage" approach adopted by the Court in *Roe,* and, in a modified form, employed by the Court to analyze the regulations in these cases, cannot be supported as a legitimate or useful framework for accommodating the woman's right and the State's interests. The decision of the Court today graphically illustrates why the trimester approach is a completely unworkable method of accommodating the conflicting personal rights and compelling state interests that are involved in the abortion context.

As the Court indicates today, the State's compelling interest in maternal health changes as medical technology changes, and any health regulation must not "depart from accepted medical practice." ... In applying this standard, the Court holds that "the safety of second-trimester abortions has increased dramatically" since 1973, when *Roe* was decided.... Although a regulation such as one requiring that all second-trimester abortions be performed in hospitals "had strong support" in 1973 "as a reasonable health regulation," ... this regulation can no longer stand because, according to the Court's diligent research into medical and scientific literature, the dilation

and evacuation (D&E) procedure, used in 1973 only for first-trimester abortions, "is now widely and successfully used for second-trimester abortions." ... Further, the medical literature relied on by the Court indicates that the D&E procedure may be performed in an appropriate nonhospital setting for "at least ... the early weeks of the second trimester...." ... The Court then chooses the period of 16 weeks of gestation as that point at which D&E procedures may be performed safely in a nonhospital setting, and thereby invalidates the Akron hospitalization regulation.

It is not difficult to see that despite the Court's purported adherence to the trimester approach adopted in *Roe,* the lines drawn in that decision have now been "blurred" because of what the Court accepts as technological advancement in the safety of abortion procedure....

Just as improvements in medical technology inevitably will move *forward* the point at which the State may regulate for reasons of maternal health, different technological improvements will move *backward* the point of viability at which the State may proscribe abortions except when necessary to preserve the life and health of the mother.

In 1973, viability before 28 weeks was considered unusual.... However, recent studies have demonstrated increasingly earlier fetal viability. It is certainly reasonable to believe that fetal viability in the first trimester of pregnancy may be possible in the not too distant future....

The *Roe* framework, then, is clearly on a collision course with itself. As the medical risks of various abortion procedures decrease, the point at which the State may regulate for reasons of maternal health is moved further forward to actual childbirth. As medical science becomes better able to provide for the separate existence of the fetus, the point of viability is moved further back toward conception....

Webster v. Reproductive Health Services

492 U.S. 490 (1989)

A Missouri statute, based on the premise that the "life of each human being begins at conception," placed a number of restrictions on abortions: prohibiting public employees and facilities from performing or assisting in abortions not necessary to save the mother's life; prohibiting any encouragement or counseling to have an abortion; and requiring physicians to perform a viability test at twenty weeks or more. A federal district court struck down each restriction and enjoined their enforcement. The Eighth Circuit affirmed, ruling that the Missouri law violated the decisions in *Roe* v. *Wade* and subsequent cases. This lawsuit was brought against William L. Webster, Attorney General of Missouri.

CHIEF JUSTICE REHNQUIST announced the judgment of the Court and delivered the opinion of the Court with respect to Parts I, II-A, II-B, and II-C, and an opinion with respect to Parts II-D and III, in which JUSTICE WHITE and JUSTICE KENNEDY join.

. . .

II

Decision of this case requires us to address four sections of the Missouri Act: (a) the preamble; (b) the prohibition on the use of public facilities or employees to perform abortions; (c) the prohibition on public funding of abortion counseling; and (d) the requirement that physicians conduct viability tests prior to performing abortions. We address these *seriatim.*

A

The Act's preamble, as noted, sets forth "findings" by the Missouri legislature that "[t]he life of each human being begins at conception," and that "[u]nborn children have protectable interests in life, health, and well-being."... The Act then mandates that state laws be interpreted to provide unborn children with "all the rights, privileges, and immunities available to other persons, citizens, and residents of this state," subject to the Constitution and this Court's precedents....

The State contends that the preamble itself is precatory and imposes no substantive restrictions on abortions, and that appellees therefore do not have standing to challenge it....

In our view, the Court of Appeals misconceived the meaning of the *Akron* dictum,...The Court has emphasized that *Roe* v. *Wade* "implies no limitation on the authority of a State to make a value judgment favoring childbirth over abortion." *Maher* v. *Roe,* 432 U. S., at 474. The preamble can be read simply to express that sort of value judgment.

We think the extent to which the preamble's language might be used to interpret other state statutes or regulations is something that only the courts of Missouri can definitively decide.... It will be time enough for federal courts to address the meaning of the preamble should it be applied to restrict the activities of appellees in some concrete way.... We therefore need not pass on the constitutionality of the Act's preamble.

B

Section 188.210 provides that "[i]t shall be unlawful for any public employee within the scope of his employment to perform or assist an abortion, not necessary to save the life of the mother," while § 188.215 makes it "unlawful for any public facility to be used for the purpose of performing or assisting an abortion not necessary to save the life of the mother."...

. . .

...Nothing in the Constitution requires States to enter or remain in the business of performing abortions. Nor, as appellees suggest, do private physicians and their patients have some kind of constitutional right of access to public facilities for the performance of abortions.... Indeed, if the State does recoup all of its costs in performing abortions, and no state subsidy, direct or indirect, is available, it is difficult to see how any procreational choice is burdened by the State's ban on the use of its facilities or employees for performing abortions.

Maher, Poelker, and *McRae* all support the view that the State need not commit any resources to facilitating abortions, even if it can turn a profit by doing so.... Thus we uphold the Act's restrictions on the use of public employees and facilities for the performance or assistance of nontherapeutic abortions.

C

The Missouri Act contains three provisions relating to "encouraging or counseling a woman to have an abortion not necessary to save her life." Section 188.205 states that no public funds can be used for this purpose; § 188.210 states that public employees cannot, within the scope of their employment, engage in such speech; and § 188.215 forbids such speech in public facilities....

Missouri has chosen only to appeal the Court of Appeals' invalidation of the public funding provision, § 188.205....

...A majority of the Court agrees with appellees that the controversy over § 188.205 is now moot, because appellees' argument amounts to a decision to no longer seek a declaratory judgment that § 188.205 is unconstitutional and accompanying declarative relief....

D

Section 188.029 of the Missouri Act provides: "Before a physician performs an abortion on a woman he has reason to believe is carrying an unborn child of twenty or more weeks gestational age, the physician shall first determine if the unborn child is viable by using and exercising that degree of care, skill, and proficiency commonly exercised by the ordinarily skillful, careful, and prudent physician engaged in similar practice under the same or similar conditions. In making this determination of viability, the physician shall perform or cause to be performed such medical examinations and tests as are necessary to make a finding of the gestational age, weight, and lung maturity of the unborn child and shall enter such findings and determination of viability in the medical record of the mother."

. . .

We think the viability-testing provision makes sense only if the second sentence is read to require only those tests that are useful to making subsidiary findings as to viability. If we construe this provision to require a physician to perform those tests needed to make the three specified findings *in all circumstances,* including when the physician's reasonable professional judgment indicates that the tests would be irrelevant to determining viability or even dangerous to the mother and the fetus, the second sentence of § 188.029 would conflict with the first sentence's *requirement* that a physician apply his reasonable professional skill and judgment. It would also be incongruous to read this provision, especially the word "necessary," to require the performance of tests irrelevant to the expressed statutory purpose of determining viability....

We think that the doubt cast upon the Missouri statute by these cases is not so much a flaw in the statute as it is a reflection of the fact that the rigid trimester analysis of the course of a pregnancy enunciated in *Roe* has resulted in subsequent cases like *Colautti* and *Akron* making constitutional law in this area a virtual Procrustean bed....

. . .

In the first place, the rigid *Roe* framework is hardly consistent with the notion of a Constitution cast in general terms, as ours is, and usually speaking in general principles, as ours does. The key elements of the *Roe* framework — trimesters and viability — are not found in the text of the Constitution or in any place else one would expect to find a constitutional principle. Since the bounds of the inquiry are essentially indeterminate, the result has been a web of legal rules that have become increasingly intricate, resembling a code of regulations rather than a body of constitutional doctrine....

In the second place, we do not see why the State's interest in protecting potential human life

should come into existence only at the point of viability, and that there should therefore be a rigid line allowing state regulation after viability but prohibiting it before viability....

The dissent takes us to task for our failure to join in a "great issues" debate as to whether the Constitution includes an "unenumerated" general right to privacy as recognized in cases such as *Griswold* v. *Connecticut,* 381 U. S. 479 (1965), and *Roe.* But *Griswold* v. *Connecticut,* unlike *Roe,* did not purport to adopt a whole framework, complete with detailed rules and distinctions, to govern the cases in which the asserted liberty interest would apply. As such, it was far different from the opinion, if not the holding, of *Roe* v. *Wade,* which sought to establish a constitutional framework for judging state regulation of abortion during the entire term of pregnancy....

. . .

III

Both appellants and the United States as *Amicus Curiae* have urged that we overrule our decision in *Roe* v. *Wade....* The facts of the present case, however, differ from those at issue in *Roe.* Here, Missouri has determined that viability is the point at which its interest in potential human life must be safeguarded. In *Roe,* on the other hand, the Texas statute criminalized the performance of *all* abortions, except when the mother's life was at stake.... This case therefore affords us no occasion to revisit the holding of *Roe,...*

Because none of the challenged provisions of the Missouri Act properly before us conflict with the Constitution, the judgment of the Court of Appeals is

Reversed.

Justice O'Connor, concurring in part and concurring in the judgment.

I concur in Parts I, II-A, II-B, and II-C of the Court's opinion.

I

[O'Connor agrees with the Court's analysis of the provisions of the Missouri statute dealing with the use of public facilities, the preamble, and the lack of a case or controversy regarding Section 188.205.]

II

. . .

It is clear to me that requiring the performance

of examinations and tests useful to determining whether a fetus is viable, when viability is possible, and when it would not be medically imprudent to do so, does not impose an undue burden on a woman's abortion decision. On this ground alone I would reject the suggestion that § 188.029 as interpreted is unconstitutional.…

JUSTICE SCALIA, concurring in part and concurring in the judgment.

I join Parts I, II-A, II-B, and II-C of the opinion of THE CHIEF JUSTICE. As to Part II-D, I share JUSTICE BLACKMUN's view…that it effectively would overrule Roe v. Wade, 410 U. S. 113 (1973). I think that should be done, but would do it more explicitly. Since today we contrive to avoid doing it, and indeed to avoid almost any decision of national import, I need not set forth my reasons, some of which have been well recited in dissents of my colleagues in other cases.…

The outcome of today's case will doubtless be heralded as a triumph of judicial statesmanship. It is not that, unless it is statesmanlike needlessly to prolong this Court's self-awarded sovereignty over a field where it has little proper business since the answers to most of the cruel questions posed are political and not juridicial—a sovereignty which therefore quite properly, but to the great damage of the Court, makes it the object of the sort of organized public pressure that political institutions in a democracy ought to receive.

JUSTICE O'CONNOR's assertion…that a "'fundamental rule of judicial restraint'" requires us to avoid reconsidering Roe, cannot be taken seriously. By finessing Roe we do not, as she suggests…adhere to the strict and venerable rule that we should avoid "'decid[ing] questions of a constitutional nature.'" We have not disposed of this case on some statutory or procedural ground, but have decided, and could not avoid deciding, whether the Missouri statute meets the requirements of the United States Constitution. The only choice available is whether, in deciding that constitutional question, we should use Roe v. Wade as the benchmark, or something else.…

The real question, then, is whether there are valid reasons to go beyond the most stingy possible holding today.… It thus appears that the mansion of constitutionalized abortion-law, constructed overnight in Roe v. Wade, must be disassembled door-jamb by door-jamb, and never entirely brought down, no matter how wrong it may be.

Of the four courses we might have chosen today—to reaffirm Roe, to overrule it explicitly, to overrule it *sub silentio,* or to avoid the question—the last is the least responsible. On the question of the constitutionality of § 188.029, I concur in the judgment of the Court and strongly dissent from the manner in which it has been reached.

JUSTICE BLACKMUN, with whom JUSTICE BRENNAN and JUSTICE MARSHALL join, concurring in part and dissenting in part.

Today, Roe v. Wade, 410 U. S. 113 (1973), and the fundamental constitutional right of women to decide whether to terminate a pregnancy, survive but are not secure. Although the Court extricates itself from this case without making a single, even incremental, change in the law of abortion, the plurality and JUSTICE SCALIA would overrule Roe (the first silently, the other explicitly) and would return to the States virtually unfettered authority to control the quintessentially intimate, personal, and life-directing decision whether to carry a fetus to term.…

Nor in my memory has a plurality gone about its business in such a deceptive fashion. At every level of its review, from its effort to read the real meaning out of the Missouri statute, to its intended evisceration of precedents and its deafening silence about the constitutional protections that it would jettison, the plurality obscures the portent of its analysis. With feigned restraint, the plurality announces that its analysis leaves Roe "undisturbed," albeit "modif[ied]" and narrow[ed]."… But this disclaimer is totally meaningless. The plurality opinion is filled with winks, and nods, and knowing glances to those who would do away with Roe explicitly, but turns a stone face to anyone in search of what the plurality conceives as the scope of a woman's right under the Due Process Clause to terminate a pregnancy free from the coercive and brooding influence of the State. The simple truth is that Roe would not survive the plurality's analysis, and that the plurality provides no substitute for Roe's protective umbrella.

I fear for the future. I fear for the liberty and equality of the millions of women who have lived and come of age in the 16 years since Roe was decided. I fear for the integrity of, and public esteem for, this Court.

. . .

[I.B.1]

. . .

But rather than arguing that the text of the Constitution makes no mention of the right to privacy, the plurality complains that the critical elements of the *Roe* framework — trimesters and viability — do not appear in the Constitution and are, therefore, somehow inconsistent with a Constitution cast in general terms. . . . Were this a true concern, we would have to abandon most of our constitutional jurisprudence. As the plurality well knows, or should know, the "critical elements" of countless constitutional doctrines nowhere appear in the Constitution's text. The Constitution makes no mention, for example, of the First Amendment's "actual malice" standard for proving certain libels, see *New York Times* v. *Sullivan,* 376 U. S. 254 (1964), or of the standard for determining when speech is obscene. See *Miller* v. *California,* 413 U. S. 15 (1973). . . .

. . .

II

For today, at least, the law of abortion stands undisturbed. For today, the women of this Nation still retain the liberty to control their destinies. But the signs are evident and very ominous, and a chill wind blows.

I dissent.

JUSTICE STEVENS, concurring in part and dissenting in part.

. . .

Planned Parenthood v. Casey

505 U.S. 833 (1992)

Five provisions of the Pennsylvania Abortion Control Act required that a woman seeking an abortion give her informed consent prior to the procedure, be provided with certain information at least twenty-four hours before the abortion is performed, required the informed consent of one parent for a minor to obtain an abortion (subject to a judicial bypass procedure), provided that women first notify their husband (with some exceptions), and imposed certain reporting requirements on facilities providing abortion services. A three-Justice plurality (O'Connor, Kennedy, and Souter) joined with Justices Stevens and Blackmun to preserve a central principle of *Roe* v. *Wade* and to strike down the provision for spousal notification.

JUSTICE O'CONNOR, JUSTICE KENNEDY, and JUSTICE SOUTER announced the judgment of the Court and delivered the opinion of the Court with respect to Parts I, II, III, V-A, V-C, and VI, an opinion with respect to Part V-E, in which JUSTICE STEVENS joins, and an opinion with respect to Parts IV, V-B, and V-D.

I

Liberty finds no refuge in a jurisprudence of doubt. Yet 19 years after our holding that the Constitution protects a woman's right to terminate her pregnancy in its early stages, *Roe* v. *Wade,* 410 U.S. 113 (1973), that definition of liberty is still questioned. Joining the respondents as *amicus curiae,* the United States, as it has done in five other cases in the last decade, again asks us to overrule *Roe.* . . .

At issue in these cases are five provisions of the Pennsylvania Abortion Control Act of 1982 as amended in 1988 and 1989. . . . The Act requires that a woman seeking an abortion give her informed consent prior to the abortion procedure, and specifies that she be provided with certain information at least 24 hours before the abortion is performed. § 3205. For a minor to obtain an abortion, the Act requires the informed consent of one of her parents, but provides for a judicial bypass option if the minor does not wish to or cannot obtain a parent's consent. § 3206. Another provision of the Act requires that, unless certain exceptions apply, a married woman seeking an abortion must sign a statement indicating that she has notified her husband of her intended abortion. § 3209. The Act exempts compliance with these three requirements in the event of a "medical emergency," which is defined in § 3203 of the Act. See §§ 3202, 3205(a), 3206(a), 3209(c). In addition to the above provisions regulating the performance of abortions, the Act imposes certain reporting requirements on facilities that provide abortion services. §§ 3207(b), 3214(a), 3214(f).

. . .

After considering the fundamental constitutional questions resolved by *Roe,* principles of institutional integrity, and the rule of *stare decisis,* we are led to conclude this: the essential holding of *Roe* v. *Wade* should be retained and once again reaffirmed.

It must be stated at the outset and with clarity that *Roe*'s essential holding, the holding we reaffirm, has three parts. First is a recognition of the right of the woman to choose to have an abortion before viability and to obtain it without undue interference from the State. Before viability, the State's interests are not strong enough to support a prohibition of abortion or the imposition of a substantial obstacle to the woman's effective right to elect the procedure. Second is a confirmation of the State's power to restrict abortions after fetal viability, if the law contains exceptions for pregnancies which endanger a woman's life or health. And third is the principle that the State has legitimate interests from the outset of the pregnancy in protecting the health of the woman and the life of the fetus that may become a child. These principles do not contradict one another; and we adhere to each.

. . .

III

A

The obligation to follow precedent begins with necessity, and a contrary necessity marks its outer limit. With Cardozo, we recognize that no judicial system could do society's work if it eyed each issue afresh in every case that raised it. See B. Cardozo, The Nature of the Judicial Process 149 (1921). Indeed, the very concept of the rule of law underlying our own Constitution requires such continuity over time that a respect for precedent is, by definition, indispensable....

So in this case we may inquire whether *Roe*'s central rule has been found unworkable; whether the rule's limitation on state power could be removed without serious inequity to those who have relied upon it or significant damage to the stability of the society governed by the rule in question; whether the law's growth in the intervening years has left *Roe*'s central rule a doctrinal anachronism discounted by society; and whether *Roe*'s premises of fact have so far changed in the

ensuing two decades as to render its central holding somehow irrelevant or unjustifiable in dealing with the issue it addressed.

1

Although *Roe* has engendered opposition, it has in no sense proven "unworkable," see *Garcia* v. *San Antonio Metropolitan Transit Authority,* 469 U.S. 528, 546 (1985), representing as it does a simple limitation beyond which a state law is unenforceable....

2

The inquiry into reliance counts the cost of a rule's repudiation as it would fall on those who have relied reasonably on the rule's continued application....

...[F]or two decades of economic and social developments, people have organized intimate relationships and made choices that define their views of themselves and their places in society, in reliance on the availability of abortion in the event that contraception should fail. The ability of women to participate equally in the economic and social life of the Nation has been facilitated by their ability to control their reproductive lives....

3

No evolution of legal principle has left *Roe*'s doctrinal footings weaker than they were in 1973. No development of constitutional law since the case was decided has implicitly or explicitly left *Roe* behind as a mere survivor of obsolete constitutional thinking.

. . .

4

We have seen how time has overtaken some of *Roe*'s factual assumptions: advances in maternal health care allow for abortions safe to the mother later in pregnancy than was true in 1973,... and advances in neonatal care have advanced viability to a point somewhat earlier.... But these facts go only to the scheme of time limits on the realization of competing interests, and the divergences from the factual premises of 1973 have no bearing on the validity of *Roe*'s central holding, that viability marks the earliest point at which the State's interest in fetal life is constitutionally adequate to justify a legislative ban on nontherapeutic abortions. The soundness or unsoundness of that constitutional judgment in no sense turns on whether viability occurs at approximately 28 weeks, as was usual at the time of *Roe,* at 23 to 24 weeks, as it sometimes does today, or at some moment even slightly earlier in pregnancy, as it may if fetal respiratory capacity can somehow be enhanced in the future....

5

The sum of the precedential inquiry to this point shows *Roe*'s underpinnings unweakened in any way affecting its central holding.... Within the bounds of normal *stare decisis* analysis, then, and subject to the considerations on which it customarily turns, the stronger argument is for affirming *Roe*'s central holding, with whatever degree of personal reluctance any of us may have, not for overruling it.

B

[In this section O'Connor contrasts Roe *with two earlier decisions eventually overruled in full by the Court:* Lochner v. New York *(1905), which limited the authority of government to regulate health and welfare; and* Plessy v. Ferguson *(1896), which upheld legislatively mandated racial segregation in public transportation.* Lochner *was overruled by* West Coast Hotel Co. v. Parrish *(1937), and* Plessy *was repudiated by* Brown v. Board of Education *(1954). O'Connor concluded that* Lochner *represented a "fundamentally false factual assumption" about the capacity of an unregulated market to satisfy minimal levels of human welfare, while it was clear at least by 1954 that legally sanctioned segregation stigmatized blacks with a "badge of inferiority" (an assertion denied by the* Plessy *Court). She also stated that* Plessy *"was wrong the day it was decided." In contrast to those decisions, O'Connor said that "neither the factual underpinning of* Roe*'s central holding nor our understanding of it has changed...."]*

C

The examination of the conditions justifying the repudiation of *Adkins* by *West Coast Hotel* and *Plessy* by *Brown* is enough to suggest the terrible price that would have been paid if the Court had not overruled as it did. In the present case, however, as our analysis to this point makes clear, the terrible price would be paid for overruling....

. . .

In two circumstances...the Court would almost certainly fail to receive the benefit of the doubt in overruling prior cases. There is, first, a point beyond which frequent overruling would overtax the country's belief in the Court's good faith. Despite the variety of reasons that may inform and justify a decision to overrule, we cannot forget that such a decision is usually perceived (and perceived correctly) as, at the least, a statement that a prior decision was wrong. There is a limit to the amount of error that can plausibly be imputed to prior courts....

...only the most convincing justification under accepted standards of precedent could suffice to demonstrate that a later decision overruling the first was anything but a surrender to political pressure, and an unjustified repudiation of the principle on which the Court stakes its authority in the first instance. So to overrule under fire in the absence of the most compelling reason to reexamine a watershed decision would subvert the Court's legitimacy beyond any serious question....

...A decision to overrule *Roe*'s essential holding under the existing circumstances would address error, if error there was, at the cost of both profound and unnecessary damage to the Court's legitimacy, and to the Nation's commitment to the rule of law. It is therefore imperative to adhere to the essence of *Roe*'s original decision, and we do so today.

IV

[O'Connor states that it is the duty of the Court to draw a line to determine a woman's right to terminate her pregnancy.]

We conclude the line should be drawn at viability, so that before that time the woman has a right to choose to terminate her pregnancy. We adhere to this principle for two reasons. First, as we have said, is the doctrine of *stare decisis*....

The second reason is that the concept of viability, as we noted in *Roe,* is the time at which there is a realistic possibility of maintaining and nourishing a life outside the womb, so that the independent existence of the second life can in reason and all fairness be the object of state protection that now overrides the rights of the woman.... The viability line also has, as a practical matter, an element of fairness. In some broad sense it might be said that a woman who fails to act before viability has consented to the State's intervention on behalf of the developing child.

. . .

Though the woman has a right to choose to terminate or continue her pregnancy before viability, it does not at all follow that the State is prohibited from taking steps to ensure that this choice is thoughtful and informed. Even in the earliest stages of pregnancy, the State may enact rules and regulations designed to encourage her to know that there are philosophic and social arguments of great weight that can be brought to bear in favor of continuing the pregnancy to full term and that there are procedures and institutions to allow adoption of unwanted children as well as a certain degree of state assistance if the mother chooses to raise the child herself....

We reject the trimester framework, which we do not consider to be part of the essential holding of *Roe*.... The trimester framework suffers from these basic flaws: in its formulation it misconceives the nature of the pregnant woman's interest; and in practice it undervalues the State's interest in potential life, as recognized in *Roe*.

. . .

A finding of an undue burden is a shorthand for the conclusion that a state regulation has the purpose or effect of placing a substantial obstacle in the path of a woman seeking an abortion of a nonviable fetus. A statute with this purpose is invalid because the means chosen by the State to further the interest in potential life must be calculated to inform the woman's free choice, not hinder it.

...In our considered judgment, an undue burden is an unconstitutional burden....

. . .

V

The Court of Appeals applied what it believed to be the undue burden standard and upheld each of the provisions except for the husband notification requirement. We agree generally with this conclusion, but refine the undue burden analysis in accordance with the principles articulated above. We now consider the separate statutory sections at issue.

A

Because it is central to the operation of various other requirements, we begin with the statute's definition of medical emergency. Under the statute, a medical emergency is

"[t]hat condition which, on the basis of the physician's good faith clinical judgment, so complicates the medical condition of a pregnant woman as to necessitate the immediate abortion of her pregnancy to avert her death or for which a delay will create serious risk of substantial and irreversible impairment of a major bodily function." 18 Pa. Cons. Stat. (1990). § 3203.

[O'Connor accepted this interpretation of "serious risk" by the Court of Appeals: "we read the medical emergency exception as intended by the Pennsylvania legislature to assure that compliance with its abortion regulations would not in any way pose a significant threat to the life or health of a woman." Under that interpretation, the medical emergency definition "imposes no undue burden on a woman's abortion right."]

B

We next consider the informed consent requirement.... Except in a medical emergency, the statute requires that at least 24 hours before performing an abortion a physician inform the woman of the nature of the procedure, the health risks of the abortion and of childbirth, and the "probable gestational age of the unborn child." The physician or a qualified nonphysician must inform the woman of the availability of printed materials published by the State describing the fetus and providing information about medical assistance for childbirth, information about child support from the father, and a list of agencies which provide adoption and other services as alternatives to abortion. An abortion may not be performed unless the woman certifies in writing that she has been informed of the availability of these printed materials and has been provided them if she chooses to view them.

. . .

To the extent *Akron I* and *Thornburgh* find a constitutional violation when the government requires, as it does here, the giving of truthful, nonmisleading information about the nature of the procedure, the attendant health risks and those of childbirth, and the "probable gestational age" of the fetus, those cases go too far, and inconsistent with *Roe*'s acknowledgement of an important interest in potential life, and are overruled....

. . .

C

Section 3209 of Pennsylvania's abortion law provides, except in cases of medical emergency, that no physician shall perform an abortion on a married woman without receiving a signed statement from the woman that she has notified her spouse that she is about to undergo an abortion. The woman has the option of providing an alternative signed statement certifying that her husband is not the man who impregnated her; that her husband could not be located; that the pregnancy is the result of spousal sexual assault which she has reported; or that the woman believes that notifying her husband will cause him or someone else to inflict bodily injury upon her. A physician who performs an abortion on a married woman without receiving the appropriate signed statement will have his or her license revoked, and is liable to the husband for damages.

[O'Connor reviews professional studies that suggest that from one-fifth to one-third of all women are physically assaulted by a partner or ex-partner during their lifetime, and notes that many victims of domestic violence remain with their abusers, because they see no alternative. She concluded that the spousal notification requirement is invalid because it imposes a substantial obstacle for many women.]

D

We next consider the parental consent provision. Except in a medical emergency, an unemancipated young woman under 18 may not obtain an abortion unless she and one of her parents (or guardian) provides informed consent as defined above. If neither a parent nor guardian provides consent, a court may authorize the performance of an abortion upon a determination that the young woman is mature and capable of giving informed consent and has in fact given her informed consent, or that an abortion would be in her best interests.

We have been over most of this ground before. Our cases establish, and we reaffirm today, that a State may require a minor seeking an abortion to obtain the consent of a parent or guardian, provided that there is an adequate judicial bypass procedure....

E

[She now turns to the recordkeeping and reporting requirements.]

In *Danforth,* 428 U.S., at 80, we held that recordkeeping and reporting provisions "that are reasonably directed to the preservation of maternal health and that properly respect a patient's confidentiality and privacy are permissible." We think that under this standard, all the provisions at issue here except that relating to spousal notice are constitutional....

Subsection (12) of the reporting provision requires the reporting of, among other things, a married woman's "reason for failure to provide notice" to her husband. § 3214(a)(12). This provision in effect requires women, as a condition of obtaining an abortion, to provide the Commonwealth with the precise information we have already recognized that many women have pressing reasons not to reveal. Like the spousal notice requirement itself, this provision places an undue burden on a woman's choice, and must be invalidated for that reason.

VI

Our Constitution is a covenant running from the first generation of Americans to us and then to future generations. It is a coherent succession. Each generation must learn anew that the Constitution's written terms embody ideas and aspirations that must survive more ages than one. We accept our responsibility not to retreat from interpreting the full meaning of the covenant in light of all of our precedents. We invoke it once again to define the freedom guaranteed by the Constitution's own promise, the promise of liberty.

. . .

JUSTICE STEVENS, concurring in part and dissenting in part.

[Stevens agreed with the three-judge plurality with two exceptions. He regarded the provision for informed consent and the twenty-four-hour waiting period as invalid. Although he agreed that the parental-consent requirement was valid, he did not join that part of the plurality's opinion.]

JUSTICE BLACKMUN, concurring in part, concurring in the judgment in part, and dissenting in part.

I join parts I, II, III, V-A, V-C, and VI of the joint opinion of JUSTICES O'CONNOR, KENNEDY, and SOUTER, *ante.*

[While agreeing with those parts of the plurality opinion, Blackmun held that the statute was invalid with regard to recordkeeping, informed consent, the twenty-four waiting period, and parental consent. He also disagreed with much of the analysis in Part IV regarding viability, the trimester approach, and the undue burden test.]

CHIEF JUSTICE REHNQUIST, with whom JUSTICE WHITE, JUSTICE SCALIA, and JUSTICE THOMAS join, concurring in the judgment in part and dissenting in part.

The joint opinion, following its newly-minted

variation on *stare decisis,* retains the outer shell of *Roe* v. *Wade,* 410 U.S. 113 (1973), but beats a wholesale retreat from the substance of that case. We believe that *Roe* was wrongly decided, and that it can and should be overruled consistently with our traditional approach of the plurality in *Webster* v. *Reproductive Health Services,* 492 U.S. 490 (1989), and uphold the challenged provisions of the Pennsylvania statute in their entirety.

. . .

II

. . .

The end result of the joint opinion's paeans of praise for legitimacy is the enunciation of a brand new standard for evaluating state regulation of a woman's right to abortion—the "undue burden" standard.

In evaluating abortion regulations under that standard, judges will have to decide whether they place a "substantial obstacle" in the path of a woman seeking an abortion.... In that this standard is based even more on a judge's subjective determinations than was the trimester framework, the standard will do nothing to prevent "judges from roaming at large in the constitutional field" guided only by their personal views. *Griswold* v. *Connecticut,* 381 U.S., at 502 (Harlan, J., concurring in judgment). Because the undue burden standard is plucked from nowhere, the question

of what is a "substantial obstacle" to abortion will undoubtedly engender a variety of conflicting views....

. . .

JUSTICE SCALIA, with whom THE CHIEF JUSTICE, JUSTICE WHITE, and JUSTICE THOMAS join, concurring in the judgment in part and dissenting in part.

. . .

It is no more realistic for us in this case, than it was for [CHIEF JUSTICE TANEY in *Dred Scott*], to think that an issue of the sort they both involved—an issue involving life and death, freedom and subjugation—can be "speedily and finally settled" by the Supreme Court, as President James Buchanan in his inaugural address said the issue of slavery in the territories would be.... Quite to the contrary, by foreclosing all democratic outlet for the deep passions this issue arouses, by banishing the issue from the political forum that gives all participants, even the losers, the satisfaction of a fair hearing and an honest fight, by continuing the imposition of a rigid national rule instead of allowing for regional differences, the Court merely prolongs and intensifies the anguish.

We should get out of this area, where we have no right to be, and where we do neither ourselves nor the country any good by remaining.

Stenberg v. Carhart

120 S.Ct. 2597 (2000)

Dr. Leroy Carhart, a physician, brought this lawsuit against Attorney General Don Stenberg of Nebraska, charging that Nebraska's law banning "partial birth abortion" violated the Federal Constitution. The District Court held the statute unconstitutional, the Eighth Circuit affirmed, and the Supreme Court granted cert to decide whether the statute, under the guidelines of *Planned Parenthood* v. *Casey* (1992), constituted an "undue burden" on a woman's right to choose to have an abortion.

JUSTICE BREYER delivered the opinion of the Court.

We again consider the right to an abortion. We understand the controversial nature of the problem. Millions of Americans believe that life begins at conception and consequently that an abortion

is akin to causing the death of an innocent child; they recoil at the thought of a law that would permit it. Other millions fear that a law that forbids abortion would condemn many American women to lives that lack dignity, depriving them of equal liberty and leading those with least resources to undergo illegal abortions with the attendant risks of death and suffering. Taking account of these virtually irreconcilable points of view, aware that constitutional law must govern a society whose different members sincerely hold directly opposing views, and considering the matter in light of the Constitution's guarantees of fundamental individual liberty, this Court, in the course of a generation, has determined and then redetermined that the Constitution offers basic protection to the woman's right to choose. *Roe v. Wade*, 410 U.S. 113 (1973); *Planned Parenthood of Southeastern Pa. v. Casey*, 505 U.S. 833 (1992)....

Three established principles determine the issue before us. We shall set them forth in the language of the joint opinion in *Casey*. First, before "viability...the woman has a right to choose to terminate her pregnancy." *Id.*, at 870 (joint opinion of O'CONNOR, KENNEDY, and SOUTER, JJ.).

Second, "a law designed to further the State's interest in fetal life which imposes an undue burden on the woman's decision before fetal viability" is unconstitutional. *Id.*, at 877. An "undue burden is...shorthand for the conclusion that a state regulation has the purpose or effect of placing a substantial obstacle in the path of a woman seeking an abortion of a nonviable fetus." *Ibid.*

Third, " 'subsequent to viability, the State in promoting its interest in the potentiality of human life may, if it chooses, regulate, and even proscribe, abortion except where it is necessary, in appropriate medical judgment, for the preservation of the life or health of the mother.' " *Id.*, at 879 (quoting *Roe v. Wade, supra*, at 164–165).

We apply these principles to a Nebraska law banning "partial birth abortion." The statute reads as follows:

"No partial birth abortion shall be performed in this state, unless such procedure is necessary to save the life of the mother whose life is endangered by a physical disorder, physical illness, or physical injury, including a life-endangering physical condition caused by or arising from the pregnancy itself." ... [*The statute defines "partial birth abortion" as "an abortion procedure in which the person performing the abortion partially delivers vaginally a living unborn child before killing the unborn child and completing the delivery." ... It defines "partially delivers vaginally a living unborn child before killing the unborn child" to mean "deliberately and intentionally delivering into the vagina a living unborn child, or a substantial portion thereof, for the purpose of performing a procedure that the person performing*

such procedure knows will kill the unborn child and does kill the unborn child."]

The law classifies violation of the statute as a "Class III felony" carrying a prison term of up to 20 years, and a fine of up to $25,000.... It also provides for the automatic revocation of a doctor's license to practice medicine in Nebraska....

We hold that this statute violates the Constitution.

[I.B]

Because Nebraska law seeks to ban one method of aborting a pregnancy, we must describe and then discuss several different abortion procedures. Considering the fact that those procedures seek to terminate a potential human life, our discussion may seem clinically cold or callous to some, perhaps horrifying to others. There is no alternative way, however, to acquaint the reader with the technical distinctions among different abortion methods and related factual matters, upon which the outcome of this case depends....

The evidence before the trial court, as supported or supplemented in the literature, indicates the following:

1. About 90% of all abortions performed in the United States take place during the first trimester of pregnancy, before 12 weeks of gestational age.... During the first trimester, the predominant abortion method is "vacuum aspiration," which involves insertion of a vacuum tube (cannula) into the uterus to evacuate the contents....

2. Approximately 10% of all abortions are performed during the second trimester of pregnancy (12 to 24 weeks).... The most commonly used procedure is called "dilation and evacuation" (D&E). That procedure (together with a modified form of vacuum aspiration used in the early second trimester) accounts for about 95% of all abortions performed from 12 to 20 weeks of gestational age....

3. D&E "refers generically to transcervical procedures performed at 13 weeks gestation or later." [*Between 13 and 15 weeks of gestation, D&E is similar to vacuum aspiration except that the cervix is dilated more widely to remove larger pieces of tissue. Because fetal tissue is easily broken, the fetus may not be removed intact. After 15 weeks, the fetus is larger (particularly the head) and bones are more rigid. Dismemberment or other destructive procedures are therefore more likely to be required. After 20 weeks, some physicians use potassium chloride or digoxin to kill the fetus to facilitate evacuation. D&E carries certain*

risks. The use of instruments within the uterus may cause accidental perforation and damage neighboring organs. Sharp fetal bone fragments create dangers. Fetal tissue accidentally left behind may cause infection and other complications.]

[A variation of D&E, referred to as an "intact D&E," begins with induced dilation of the cervix and removal of the fetus from the uterus through the cervix "intact" (in one pass rather than in several passes). It is used after 16 weeks at the earliest. Vacuum aspiration becomes ineffective because the fetal skull is too large to pass through the cervix. If the fetus comes head first, the doctor collapses the skull and extracts the entire fetus through the cervix. If the fetus comes feet first (a breech presentation), the doctor pulls the fetal body through the cervix, collapses the skull, and extracts the fetus through the cervix. The breech extraction version of the intact D&E is also known as "dilation and extraction" (D&X). "Despite the technical differences we have just described, intact D&E and D&X are sufficiently similar for us to use the terms interchangeably."]

II

The question before us is whether Nebraska's statute, making criminal the performance of a "partial birth abortion," violates the Federal Constitution, as interpreted in *Planned Parenthood of Southeastern Pa. v. Casey...and Roe v. Wade....* We conclude that it does for at least two independent reasons. First, the law lacks any exception " 'for the preservation of the...health of the mother.' " *Casey*, 505 U.S., at 879 (joint opinion of O'CONNOR, KENNEDY, and SOUTER, JJ.). Second, it "imposes an undue burden on a woman's ability" to choose a D&E abortion, thereby unduly burdening the right to choose abortion itself....

A

The *Casey* joint opinion reiterated what the Court held in *Roe*; that " 'subsequent to viability, the State in promoting its interest in the potentiality of human life may, if it chooses, regulate, and even proscribe, abortion *except where it is necessary, in appropriate medical judgment, for the preservation of the life or health of the mother.*' " 505 U.S., at 879 (quoting *Roe, supra*, at 164–165) (emphasis added).

The fact that Nebraska's law applies both pre- and postviability aggravates the constitutional problem presented. The State's interest in regulat-

ing abortion previability is considerably weaker than postviability.... Since the law requires a health exception in order to validate even a postviability abortion regulation, it at a minimum requires the same in respect to previability regulation....

...[T]his Court has made clear that a State may promote but not endanger a woman's health when it regulates the methods of abortion....

1

Nebraska responds that the law does not require a health exception unless there is a need for such an exception. And here there is no such need, it says. It argues that "safe alternatives remain available" and "a ban on partial-birth abortion/D&X would create no risk to the health of women."...The problem for Nebraska is that the parties strongly contested this factual question in the trial court below; and the findings and evidence support Dr. Carhart. The State fails to demonstrate that banning D&X without a health exception may not create significant health risks for women, because the record shows that significant medical authority supports the proposition that in some circumstances, D&X would be the safest procedure.

. . .

[2-3]

[Nebraska, along with supporting amici, says that the D&X procedure is "little-used" and only by "a handful of doctors." Breyer agrees that D&E is infrequently used, "but the health exception question is whether protecting women's health requires an exception for those infrequent occasions." Nebraska argues that D&E and labor induction are at all times "safe alternative procedures." The District Court agreed that alternatives, such as D&E and induced labor, are "safe" but found that D&X was significantly safer in certain circumstances. Nebraska emphasizes that there are no medical studies "establishing the safety of the partial-birth abortion/D&X procedure" and "no medical studies comparing the safety of partial-birth abortion/D&X to other abortion procedures." Breyer agrees that there "are no general medical studies documenting comparative safety."]

4

...[T]he division of medical opinion about the matter at most means uncertainty, a factor that signals the presence of risk, not its absence. That division here involves highly qualified knowledgeable experts on both sides of the issue. Where a significant body of medical opinion believes a procedure may bring with it greater safety for some patients and explains the medical reasons supporting that view, we cannot say that the presence of a different view by itself proves the contrary. Rather, the uncertainty means a significant likelihood that those who believe that D&X is a safer abortion method in certain circumstances may turn out to be right. If so, then the absence of a health exception will place women at an unnecessary risk of tragic health consequences. If they are wrong, the exception will simply turn out to have been unnecessary.

In sum, Nebraska has not convinced us that a health exception is "never necessary to preserve the health of women." ... Rather, a statute that altogether forbids D&X creates a significant health risk. The statute consequently must contain a health exception. This is not to say, as JUSTICE THOMAS and JUSTICE KENNEDY claim, that a State is prohibited from proscribing an abortion procedure whenever a particular physician deems the procedure preferable. By no means must a State grant physicians "unfettered discretion" in their selection of abortion methods....

B

The Eighth Circuit found the Nebraska statute unconstitutional because, in *Casey*'s words, it has the "effect of placing a substantial obstacle in the path of a woman seeking an abortion of a nonviable fetus." ... It thereby places an "undue burden" upon a woman's right to terminate her pregnancy before viability.... Nebraska does not deny that the statute imposes an "undue burden" if it applies to the more commonly used D&E procedure as well as to D&X. And we agree with the Eighth Circuit that it does so apply.

Our earlier discussion of the D&E procedure ... shows that it falls within the statutory prohibition. The statute forbids "deliberately and intentionally delivering into the vagina a living unborn child, or a substantial portion thereof, for the purpose of performing a procedure that the person performing such procedure knows will kill the unborn child." ... We do not understand how one could distinguish, using this language, between D&E (where a foot or arm is drawn through the cervix) and D&X (where the body up to the head is drawn through the cervix)....

Even if the statute's basic aim is to ban D&X, its language makes clear that it also covers a much broader category of procedures. The language does not track the medical differences between D&E and D&X—though it would have been a simple matter, for example, to provide an exception for the performance of D&E and other abortion procedures....

[Breyer does not accept Stenberg's argument that the statute differentiates between the two procedures and that the statutory words "substantial portion" mean "the child up to the head." The two lower courts rejected Stenberg's narrowing interpretation and so does Breyer. Stenberg points to the legislature's debates, but Breyer finds that the debates "hurt his argument more than they help it," because some lawmakers understood "substantial" to mean as small a portion of the fetus as a foot.]

In sum, using this law some present prosecutors and future Attorneys General may choose to pursue physicians who use D&E procedures, the most commonly used method for performing previability second trimester abortions. All those who perform abortion procedures using that method must fear prosecution, conviction, and imprisonment. The result is an undue burden upon a woman's right to make an abortion decision. We must consequently find the statute unconstitutional.

The judgment of the Court of Appeals is

Affirmed.

JUSTICE STEVENS, with whom JUSTICE GINSBURG joins, concurring.

Although much ink is spilled today describing the gruesome nature of late-term abortion procedures, that rhetoric does not provide me a reason to believe that the procedure Nebraska here claims it seeks to ban is more brutal, more gruesome, or less respectful of "potential life" than the equally gruesome procedure Nebraska claims it still allows....

[Justice O'Connor wrote a separate concurrence, as did Justice Ginsburg (joined by Justice Stevens.)]

CHIEF JUSTICE REHNQUIST, dissenting.

I did not join the joint opinion in *Planned Parenthood of Southeastern Pa. v. Casey* ... and continue to believe that case is wrongly decided. Despite my disagreement with the opinion, ... the *Casey* joint opinion represents the holding of the Court in that case. I believe JUSTICE KENNEDY and JUSTICE THOMAS have correctly applied *Casey*'s principles and join their dissenting opinions.

JUSTICE SCALIA, dissenting.

. . .

. . . [*The issue depends*] upon how much one respects (or believes society ought to respect) the life of a partially delivered fetus, and how much one respects (or believes society ought to respect) the freedom of the woman who gave it life to kill it. Evidently, the five Justices in today's majority value the former less, or the latter more, (or both), than the four of us in dissent. Case closed. There is no cause for anyone who believes in *Casey* to feel betrayed by this outcome. It has been arrived at by precisely the process *Casey* promised—a democratic vote by nine lawyers, not on the question whether the text of the Constitution has anything to say about this subject (it obviously does not); nor even on the question (also appropriate for lawyers) whether the legal traditions of the American people would have sustained such a limitation upon abortion (they obviously would); but upon the pure policy question whether this limitation upon abortion is "undue"—*i.e.*, goes too far.

. . . [T]hose who believe that a 5-to-4 vote on a policy matter by unelected lawyers should not overcome the judgment of 30 state legislatures have a problem, not with the application of *Casey*, but with its existence. *Casey* must be overruled.

. . . If only for the sake of its own preservation, the Court should return this matter to the people—where the Constitution, by its silence on the subject, left it—and let them decide, State by State, whether this practice should be allowed. *Casey* must be overruled.

JUSTICE KENNEDY, with whom THE CHIEF JUSTICE joins, dissenting.

. . . When the Court reaffirmed the essential holding of *Roe*, a central premise was that the States retain a critical and legitimate role in legislating on the subject of abortion, as limited by the woman's right the Court restated and again guaranteed. *Planned Parenthood of Southeastern Pa. v. Casey*, 505 U.S. 833 (1992). The political processes of the State are not to be foreclosed from enacting laws to promote the life of the unborn and to ensure respect for all human life and its potential. *Id.*, at 871 (joint opinion of O'CONNOR, KENNEDY, and SOUTER, JJ.). The State's constitutional authority is a vital means for citizens to address these grave and serious issues, as they must if we are to progress in knowledge and understanding and in the attainment of some degree of consensus.

The Court's decision today, in my submission, repudiates this understanding by invalidating a statute advancing critical state interests, even though the law denies no woman the right to choose an abortion and places no undue burden upon the right. . . .

. . .

II

Demonstrating a further and basic misunderstanding of *Casey*, the Court holds the ban on the D&X procedure fails because it does not include an exception permitting an abortionist to perform a D&X whenever he believes it will best preserve the health of the woman. Casting aside the views of distinguished physicians and the statements of leading medical organizations, the Court awards each physician a veto power over the State's judgment that the procedures should not be performed. . . . [I]t is now Dr. Leroy Carhart who sets abortion policy for the State of Nebraska, not the legislature or the people. . . .

. . .

Courts are ill-equipped to evaluate the relative worth of particular surgical procedures. The legislatures of the several States have superior factfinding capabilities in this regard. . . .

JUSTICE THOMAS, with whom THE CHIEF JUSTICE and JUSTICE SCALIA join, dissenting.

. . . Nothing in our Federal Constitution deprives the people of this country of the right to determine whether the consequences of abortion to the fetus and to society outweigh the burden of an unwanted pregnancy on the mother. Although a State may permit abortion, nothing in the Constitution dictates that a State must do so.

In the years following Roe, this Court applied, and, worse, extended, that decision to strike down numerous state statutes that purportedly threatened a woman's ability to obtain an abortion. . . .

. . . Today, the Court inexplicably holds that the States cannot constitutionally prohibit a method of abortion that millions find hard to distinguish from infanticide and that the Court hesitates even to describe. . . .

II

Nebraska, along with 29 other States, has attempted to ban the partial birth abortion procedure. Although the Nebraska statute purports to prohibit only "partial birth abortion," a phrase which is commonly used, as I mentioned, to refer to the breech extraction version of intact D&E, the majority concludes that this statute could also be read in some future case to prohibit ordinary D&E, . . . The majority errs with its very first step. I think it is clear that the Nebraska statute does not prohibit the D&E procedure. . . .

[In analyzing the statutory language, Thomas concludes that it is "highly doubtful that the statute could be applied to ordinary D&E," and that if there is any ambiguity in the meaning of the statute the ambiguity would be "conclusively resolved" by the fact that the Nebraska statute, by its own terms, applies only to "partial birth abortion." Moreover, if there were any doubt remaining whether the statute could apply to D&E, "we are bound to first consider whether a construction of the statute is fairly possible that would avoid the constitutional question." Thomas says that "there is no doubt that the Nebraska statute is susceptible of a narrowing construction by Nebraska courts that would preserve a physician's ability to perform D&E."]

[IV.D.1]

The majority justifies its result by asserting that a "significant body of medical opinion" supports the view that partial birth abortion may be a safer abortion procedure. . . . I find this assertion puzzling. If there is a "significant body of medical opinion" supporting this procedure, no one in the majority has identified it. In fact, it is uncontested that although this procedure has been used since at least 1992, no formal studies have compared partial birth abortion with other procedures. . . . The majority's conclusion makes sense only if the undue-burden standard is not whether a "significant body of medical opinion," supports the result, but rather, as JUSTICE GINSBURG candidly admits, whether any doctor could reasonably believe that the partial birth abortion procedure would best protect the woman. . . .

Moreover, even if I were to assume credible evidence on both sides of the debate, that fact should resolve the undue-burden question in favor of allowing Nebraska to legislate. Where no one knows whether a regulation of abortion poses any burden at all, the burden surely does not amount to a "substantial obstacle." Under *Casey*, in such a case we should defer to the legislative judgment.

. . .

D. THE RIGHT TO DIE

Questions of privacy include the right to die for the elderly and for patients who survive solely because of life-support systems with no hope of recovery. An especially tragic case concerned Karen Ann Quinlan, who at 22 years of age, lay in a New Jersey hospital in what the state court called a "vegetative existence." Her parents wanted to withdraw the life-sustaining mechanism and allow her to die naturally. After lengthy and anguished litigation, they gained that right. Matter of Quinlan, 355 A.2d 647 (N.J. 1976) (see box on next page).

The issue in the Quinlan case reached the U.S. Supreme Court in 1990. The Court divided 5–4 in deciding that the federal constitution does not forbid Missouri to require "clear and convincing" evidence that an incompetent, permanently unconscious person wishes the withdrawal of life-support systems. The Court also held that a competent person has a constitutional right to refuse such systems. Other states may adopt more liberal laws than Missouri's, and individuals may protect their privacy rights to some extent by signing "living wills" that express their desire to reject life-support systems. CRUZAN v. DIRECTOR, MISSOURI DEPT. OF HEALTH, 497 U.S. 261 (1990). Six months after the Court's ruling, a Missouri court ruled that clear and convincing evidence justified the withdrawal of food and water from Nancy Cruzan. She died on December 26, 1990.

In response to *Cruzan*, Congress passed the Patient Self-Determination Act to require health-care providers in Medicare and Medicaid programs to give patients information about living wills and to educate staff about rights and procedures under state law. For example, patients must be informed about their right to grant power of attorney to someone else to make such a decision. 104 Stat. 1388–117, § 4027 (1990).

The Karen Ann Quinlan Case

[The father of Karen Ann Quinlan, a 22-year-old in a persistent vegetative state, asked the state to discontinue all extraordinary procedures for sustaining her life. The Supreme Court of New Jersey, concluding that "she can *never* be restored to cognitive or sapient life," granted his request. Excerpts from the court's decision appear below. Matter of Quinlan, 355 A.2d 647, 662–64 (N.J. 1976).]

HUGHES, C.J....

It is the issue of the constitutional right of privacy that has given us most concern, in the exceptional circumstances of this case....

The claimed interests of the State in this case are essentially the preservation and sanctity of human life and defense of the right of the physician to administer medical treatment according to his best judgment. In this case the doctors say that removing Karen from the respirator will conflict with their professional judgment. The plaintiff answers that Karen's present treatment serves only a maintenance function; that the respirator cannot cure or improve her condition but at best can only prolong her inevitable slow deterioration and death; and that the interests of the patient, as seen by her surrogate, the guardian, must be evaluated by the court as predominant, even in the face of an opinion *contra* by the present attending physicians. Plaintiff's distinction is significant. The nature of Karen's care and the realistic changes of her recovery are quite unlike those of the patients discussed in many of the cases where treatments were ordered. In many of those cases the medical procedure required (usually a transfusion) constituted a minimal body invasion and the chances of recovery and return to functioning life were very good. We think that the State's interest *contra* weakens and the individual's right to privacy grows as the degree of bodily invasion increases and the prognosis dims. Ultimately there comes a point at which the individual's rights overcome the State interest. It is for that reason that we believe Karen's choice, if she were competent to make it, would be vindicated by the law....

Our affirmation of Karen's independent right of choice, however, would ordinarily be based upon her competency to assert it. The sad truth, however, is that she is grossly incompetent and we cannot discern her supposed choice based on the testimony of her previous conversations with friends, where such testimony is without sufficient probative weight.... Nevertheless, we have concluded that Karen's right of privacy may be asserted on her behalf by her guardian under the peculiar circumstances here present.

Assisted Suicide

At the state level, legal questions were raised about individuals who assisted others to commit suicide. Jack Kevorkian, a retired pathologist, used a machine that allowed terminally ill patients to inhale carbon monoxide. By 1993 he had assisted nineteen people with such procedures. Murder charges brought by Michigan prosecutors were dropped because the state had no law against assisted suicide. Although Michigan passed legislation in 1992 to make assisted suicide a felony, Kevorkian continued to defy the law. In several subsequent prosecutions, Kevorkian was acquitted, but he was sentenced to prison in 1999. In 1996, the Second Circuit struck down New York's law making it a crime for a physician to assist in a suicide. The Court reasoned that if patients have a right to have physicians withdraw life support systems, they also have a right for physicians to prescribe drugs to hasten death. Quill v. Vacco, 80 F.3d 716 (2d Cir. 1996). The Second Circuit's ruling was similar to an earlier decision by the Ninth Circuit. Compassion in Dying v. State of Wash., 79 F.3d 790 (9th Cir. 1996).

A year later those issues reached the Supreme Court, which overturned the Second and Ninth Circuits by holding that there was no right, under the U.S. Constitution, to assisted suicide. The effect was to reinstate the New York and Washington laws that made it a crime for doctors to give lethal drugs to dying patients who wanted to end their lives. But the Court's ruling also allowed other states to permit physician-assisted suicide, shifting the matter from courts to state legislatures. The Court found a fundamental difference between patients refusing life-support systems (at issue in *Cruzan*) and doctors intervening with lethal medications. Although all of the Justices agreed to uphold the New York and Washington statutes, a number of concurring opinions offered a wide variety of views and recognized that some patients, in extreme cases, might seek assisted suicide. Washington v. Glucksberg, 521 U.S. 702 (1997); VACCO v. QUILL, 521 U.S. 793 (1997).

The scope for variety among the states was made evident later in the year when the Supreme Court denied cert on a case out of Oregon that had upheld a law allowing physician-assisted suicide. Oregon voters adopted the Death With Dignity Act in 1994 in a statewide referendum. Under the Oregon law, a mentally competent adult suffering from a terminal illness may receive a lethal dose of medication after consulting with two physicians and waiting fifteen days. Lee v. Harcleroad, 522 U.S. 927 (1997). To assure that federal taxpayer dollars will not be used to subsidize or promote assisted suicide, Congress passed legislation in 1997 to ban federal funding for assisted suicide. 111 Stat. 23 (1997). Any risk that doctors who used the Oregon law to prescribe lethal drugs to terminally ill patients would be prosecuted or sanctioned by the federal government was removed in 1998 when Attorney General Janet Reno ruled that states may enact and implement such laws without federal interference.

Cruzan v. Director, Missouri Dept. of Health

497 U.S. 261 (1990)

The parents of Nancy Cruzan, a thirty-two-year-old woman in a "persistent vegetative state," wanted to remove her life-support systems against the wishes of the state of Missouri. This case explores complex moral and ethical questions. Is there a "right to die"? Who decides that question for someone legally incompetent and therefore unable to express a preference? What criteria guide that choice? What of infants in a vegetative state, never able to express a preference?

CHIEF JUSTICE REHNQUIST delivered the opinion of the Court.

Petitioner Nancy Beth Cruzan was rendered incompetent as a result of severe injuries sustained during an automobile accident. Co-petitioners Lester and Joyce Cruzan, Nancy's parents and co-guardians, sought a court order directing the withdrawal of their daughter's artificial feeding and hydration equipment after it became apparent that she had virtually no chance of recovering her cognitive faculties. The Supreme Court of Missouri held that because there was no clear and convincing evidence of Nancy's desire to have life-sustaining treatment withdrawn under such circumstances, her parent lacked authority to effectuate such a request....

...The Missouri trial court in this case found that permanent brain damage generally results after 6 minutes in an anoxic state; it was estimated that Cruzan was deprived of oxygen from 12 to 14 minutes. She remained in a coma for approximately three weeks and then progressed to an unconscious state in which she was able to orally ingest some

nutrition. In order to ease feeding and further the recovery, surgeons implanted a gastrostomy feeding and hydration tube in Cruzan with the consent of her then husband. Subsequent rehabilitative efforts proved unavailing. She now lies in a Missouri state hospital in what is commonly referred to as a persistent vegetative state: generally, a condition in which a person exhibits motor reflexes but evinces no indications of significant cognitive function. The State of Missouri is bearing the cost of her care.

[The state trial court found that a person in Nancy's condition had a fundamental right under the state and federal constitutions to refuse or direct the withdrawal of "death prolonging procedures," and that her conversation at age twenty-five with a housemate friend indicated she would not wish to live unless she could live at least halfway normally. The Supreme Court of Missouri reversed, rejecting the trial court's constitutional analysis and deciding that the Missouri Living Will statute embodied a state policy strongly favoring the preservation of life. Nancy's state-

ment to her roommate was considered unreliable. Chief Justice Rehnquist reviews right-to-die holdings in New Jersey, Massachusetts, New York, California, Minnesota, and Illinois.]

As these cases demonstrate, the common-law doctrine of informed consent is viewed as generally encompassing the right of a competent individual to refuse medical treatment. Beyond that, these decisions demonstrate both similarity and diversity in their approach to what all agree is a perplexing question with unusually strong moral and ethical overtones. State courts have available to them for decision a number of sources—state constitutions, statutes, and common law—which are not available to us. In this Court, the question is simply and starkly whether the United States Constitution prohibits Missouri from choosing the rule of decision which it did. . . .

The Fourteenth Amendment provides that no State shall "deprive any person of life, liberty, or property, without due process of law." The principle that a competent person has a constitutionally protected liberty interest in refusing unwanted medical treatment may be inferred from our prior decisions. . . .

But determining that a person has a "liberty interest" under the Due Process Clause does not end the inquiry; "whether respondent's constitutional rights have been violated must be determined by balancing his liberty interests against the relevant state interests." *Youngberg* v. *Romeo,* 457 U.S. 307, 321 (1982). See also *Mills* v. *Rogers,* 457 U.S. 291, 299 (1982).

Petitioners insist that under the general holdings of our cases, the forced administration of life-sustaining medical treatment, and even of artificially-delivered food and water essential to life, would implicate a competent person's liberty interest. Although we think the logic of the cases discussed above would embrace such a liberty interest, the dramatic consequences involved in refusal of such treatment would inform the inquiry as to whether the deprivation of that interest is constitutionally permissible. But for purposes of this case, we assume that the United States Constitution would grant a competent person a constitutionally protected right to refuse lifesaving hydration and nutrition.

Petitioners go on to assert that an incompetent person should possess the same right in this respect as is possessed by a competent person. . . .

The difficulty with petitioners' claim is that in a sense it begs the question: an incompetent person is not able to make an informed and voluntary choice to exercise a hypothetical right to refuse treatment or any other right. Such a "right" must be exercised for her, if at all, by some sort of surrogate. Here, Missouri has in effect recognized that under certain circumstances a surrogate may act for the patient in electing to have hydration and nutrition withdrawn in such a way as to cause death, but it has established a procedural safeguard to assure that the action of the surrogate conforms as best it may to the wishes expressed by the patient while competent. Missouri requires that evidence of the incompetent's wishes as to the withdrawal of treatment be proved by clear and convincing evidence. The question, then, is whether the United States Constitution forbids the establishment of this procedural requirement by the State. We hold that it does not.

Whether or not Missouri's clear and convincing evidence requirement comports with the United States Constitution depends in part on what interests the State may properly seek to protect in this situation. Missouri relies on its interest in the protection and preservation of human life, and there can be no gainsaying this interest. As a general matter, the States—indeed, all civilized nations—demonstrate their commitment to life by treating homicide as serious crime. Moreover, the majority of States in this country have laws imposing criminal penalties on one who assists another to commit suicide. We do not think a State is required to remain neutral in the face of an informed and voluntary decision by a physically-able adult to starve to death.

But in the context presented here, a State has more particular interests at stake. The choice between life and death is a deeply personal decision of obvious and overwhelming finality. We believe Missouri may legitimately seek to safeguard the personal element of this choice through the imposition of heightened evidentiary requirements. It cannot be disputed that the Due Process Clause protects an interest in life as well as an interest in refusing life-sustaining medical treatment. Not all incompetent patients will have loved ones available to serve as surrogate decisionmakers. And even where family members are present, "[t]here will, of course, be some unfortunate situations in which family members will not act to protect a patient." *In re Jobes,* 108 N.J. 394, 419, 529 A.2d 434, 477 (1987). A State is entitled to guard against potential abuses in such situations. . . .

In our view, Missouri has permissibly sought to advance these interests through the adoption of a "clear and convincing" standard of proof to govern such proceedings....

...We believe that Missouri may permissibly place an increased risk of an erroneous decision on those seeking to terminate an incompetent individual's life-sustaining treatment. An erroneous decision not to terminate results in a maintenance of the status quo; the possibility of subsequent developments such as advancements in medical science, the discovery of new evidence regarding the patient's intent, changes in the law, or simply the unexpected death of the patient despite the administration of life-sustaining treatment, at least create the potential that a wrong decision will eventually be corrected or its impact mitigated. An erroneous decision to withdraw life-sustaining treatment, however, is not susceptible of correction....

[Rehnquist points out that most states, if not all, forbid oral testimony in determining the wishes of parties in such transactions as contracts and the making of wills. Nancy Cruzan's statements to her housemate about a year before her accident were not, to the Court, clear and convincing evidence.]

Petitioners alternatively contend that Missouri must accept the "substituted judgment" of close family members even in the absence of substantial proof that their views reflect the views of the patient....

No doubt is engendered by anything in this record but that Nancy Cruzan's mother and father are loving and caring parents. If the State were required by the United States Constitution to repose a right of "substituted judgment" with anyone, the Cruzans would certainly qualify. But we do not think the Due Process Clause requires the State to repose judgment on these matters with anyone but the patient herself. Close family members may have a strong feeling—a feeling not at all ignoble or unworthy, but not entirely disinterested, either—that they do not wish to witness the continuation of the life of a loved one which they regard as hopeless, meaningless, and even degrading. But there is no automatic assurance that the view of close family members will necessarily be the same as the patient's would have been had she been confronted with the prospect of her situation while competent. All of the reasons previously discussed for allowing Missouri to require clear and convincing evidence of the patient's wishes lead us to conclude that the State may choose to defer only to those wishes, rather than confide the decision to close family members.

The judgment of the Supreme Court of Missouri is

Affirmed.

JUSTICE O'CONNOR, concurring.

[O'Connor provides separate reasons why a protected liberty interest in refusing unwanted medical treatment, including artificially delivered food and water, may be inferred from prior decisions.]

JUSTICE SCALIA, concurring.

[Scalia expresses concern that the Court might confuse the "right to die" issue "as we have confused the enterprise of legislating concerning abortion—requiring it to be conducted against a background of federal constitutional imperatives that are unknown because they are being newly crafted from Term to Term. That would be a great misfortune." He would have preferred that the Court announce "that the federal courts have no business in this field." The point at which life becomes "worthless" and the point at which efforts to preserve life are "inappropriate," Scalia says, "are neither set forth in the Constitution nor known to the nine Justices of this Court any better than they are known to nine people picked at random from the Kansas City telephone directory." He would have left the issue to the citizens of Missouri to decide through their elected representatives.]

JUSTICE BRENNAN, with whom JUSTICE MARSHALL and JUSTICE BLACKMUN join dissenting.

...Because I believe that Nancy Cruzan has a fundamental right to be free of unwanted artificial nutrition and hydration, which right is not outweighed by any interests of the State, and because I find that the improperly biased procedural obstacles imposed by the Missouri Supreme Court impermissibly burden that right, I respectfully dissent. Nancy Cruzan is entitled to choose to die with dignity.

[Brennan argues that the right to die is a fundamental right and therefore can be set aside only if Missouri identifies sufficiently important state interests and closely tailors its remedies to effectuate those interests.]

JUSTICE STEVENS, dissenting.

. . .

II

...[I]f Nancy Cruzan has no interest in continued treatment, and if she has a liberty interest in being free from unwanted treatment, and if the cessation of treatment would have no adverse impact on third parties, and if no reason exists to doubt the good faith of Nancy's parents, then what possible basis could the State have for insisting upon continued medical treatment? Yet, instead of questioning or endorsing the trial court's conclusions about Nancy Cruzan's interests, the State Supreme Court largely ignored them.

. . .

Vacco v. Quill

521 U.S. 793 (1997)

Physicians brought this action challenging the constitutionality of a New York statute making it a crime to aid persons in committing suicide or attempting to commit suicide. Timothy E. Quill was one of the physicians bringing this case against Dennis C. Vacco, Attorney General of New York.

CHIEF JUSTICE REHNQUIST delivered the opinion of Court.

In New York, as in most States, it is a crime to aid another to commit or attempt suicide, but patients may refuse even lifesaving medical treatment. The question presented by this case is whether New York's prohibition on assisting suicide therefore violates the Equal Protection Clause of the Fourteenth Amendment. We hold that it does not.

Petitioners are various New York public officials. Respondents Timothy E. Quill, Samuel C. Klagsbrun, and Howard A. Grossman are physicians who practice in New York. They assert that although it would be "consistent with the standards of [their] medical practice[s]" to prescribe lethal medication for "mentally competent, terminally ill patients" who are suffering great pain and desire a doctor's help in taking their own lives, they are deterred from doing so by New York's ban on assisting suicide.... Respondents, and three gravely ill patients who have since died, sued the State's Attorney General in the United States District Court. They urged that because New York permits a competent person to refuse life-sustaining medical treatment, and because the refusal of such treatment is "essentially the same thing" as physician-assisted suicide, New York's assisted-suicide ban violates the Equal Protection Clause. *Quill v. Koppell*, 870 F.Supp. 78, 84–85 (S.D.N.Y. 1994).

The District Court disagreed: "[I]t is hardly unreasonable or irrational for the State to recognize a difference between allowing nature to take its course, even in the most severe situations, and intentionally using an artificial death-producing device." *Id*, at 84. The court noted New York's "obvious legitimate interests in preserving life, and in protecting vulnerable persons," and concluded that "[u]nder the United States Constitution and the federal system it establishes, the resolution of this issue is left to the normal democratic processes within the State." *Id.*, at 84–85.

The Court of Appeals for the Second Circuit reversed. 80 F.3d 716 (1996). The court determined that, despite the assisted-suicide ban's apparent general applicability, "New York law does not treat equally all competent persons who are in the final stages of fatal illness and wish to hasten their deaths," because "those in the final stages of terminal illness who are on life-support systems are allowed to hasten their deaths by directing the removal of such systems; but those who are similarly situated, except for the previous attachment of life-sustaining equipment, are not allowed to hasten death by self-administering prescribed drugs." *Id.*, at 727, 729. In the court's view, "[t]he ending of life by [the withdrawal of life-support systems] is *nothing more nor less than assisted suicide.*" *Id.*, at 729 (emphasis added) (citation omitted). The Court of Appeals then examined whether this supposed unequal treatment was rationally related to any legitimate state interests, and concluded that "to the extent that [New York's statutes] prohibit a physician from prescribing medications to be self-administered by a mentally competent, terminally-ill person in the final stages of his terminal illness, they are not rationally related to any legitimate state interest." *Id.*, at 731. We granted certiorari, 518 U.S. 1055 (1996), and now reverse.

The Equal Protection Clause commands that no State shall "deny to any person within its jurisdiction the equal protection of the laws." This provision creates no substantive rights. *San Antonio Independent School Dist. v. Rodriguez*, 411 U.S. 1, 33 (1973); *id.*, at 59 (Stewart, J., concurring). Instead, it embodies a general rule that States must treat like cases alike but may treat unlike cases accordingly. *Plyler v. Doe*, 457 U.S. 202, 216 (1982). ("'[T]he Constitution does not require things which are different in fact or opinion to be treated in law as though they were the same'") (quoting *Tigner v. Texas*, 310 U.S. 141, 147 (1940)). If a legislative classification or distinction "neither burdens a fundamental right nor targets a suspect class, we will uphold [it] so long as it bears a rational relation to some legitimate end." *Romer v. Evans*, 517 U.S. 620, 631 (1996).

New York's statutes outlawing assisting suicide affect and address matters of profound significance to all New Yorkers alike. They neither infringe fundamental rights nor involve suspect classifications.... These laws are therefore entitled to a "strong presumption of validity." *Heller v. Doe*, 509 U.S. 312, 319 (1993).

On their faces, neither New York's ban on assisting suicide nor its statutes permitting patients to refuse medical treatment treat anyone differently than anyone else or draw any distinctions between persons. *Everyone*, regardless of physical condition, is entitled, if competent, to refuse unwanted lifesaving medical treatment; *no one* is permitted to assist a suicide. Generally speaking, laws that apply evenhandedly to all "unquestionably comply" with the Equal Protection Clause....

The Court of Appeals, however, concluded that some terminally ill people—those who are on life-support systems—are treated differently than those who are not, in that the former may "hasten death" by ending treatment, but the latter may not "hasten death" through physician-assisted suicide. 80 F.3d, at 729. This conclusion depends on the submission that ending or refusing lifesaving medical treatment "is nothing more nor less than assisted suicide." *Ibid*. Unlike the Court of Appeals, we think the distinction between assisting suicide and withdrawing life-sustaining treatment, a distinction widely recognized and endorsed in the medical profession and in our legal traditions, is both important and logical; it is certainly rational....

The distinction comports with fundamental legal principles of causation and intent. First, when a patient refuses life-sustaining medical treatment, he dies from an underlying fatal disease or pathology; but if a patient ingests lethal medication prescribed by a physician, he is killed by that medication....

Given these general principles, it is not surprising that many courts, including New York courts, have carefully distinguished refusing life-sustaining treatment from suicide.... In fact, the first state-

court decision explicitly to authorize withdrawing lifesaving treatment noted the "real distinction between the self-infliction of deadly harm and a self-determination against artificial life support" *In re Quinlan*, 70 N.J. 10, 43, 52, and n. 9, 355 A.2d 647, 665, 670, and n. 9, cert. denied *sub nom. Garger v. New Jersey*, 429 U.S. 922 (1976)....

Similarly, the overwhelming majority of state legislatures have drawn a clear line between assisting suicide and withdrawing or permitting the refusal of unwanted lifesaving medical treatment by prohibiting the former and permitting the latter.... And "nearly all states expressly disapprove of suicide and assisted suicide either in statutes dealing with durable powers of attorney in health-care situations, or in 'living will' statutes." *Kevorkian*, 447 Mich., at 478–479, and nn. 53–54, 627 N.W.2d, at 731–732, and nn. 53–54. Thus, even as the States move to protect and promote patients' dignity at the end of life, they remain opposed to physician-assisted suicide.

New York is a case in point. The State enacted its current assisted-suicide statutes in 1965. Since then, New York has acted several times to protect patients' common-law right to refuse treatment.... In so doing, however, the State has neither endorsed a general right to "hasten death" nor approved physician-assisted suicide. Quite the opposite: The State has reaffirmed the line between "killing" and "letting die."...

This Court has also recognized, at least implicitly, the distinction between letting a patient die and making that patient die. In *Cruzan v. Director, Mo. Dept. of Health*, 497 U.S. 261, 278 (1990), we concluded that "[t]he principle that a competent person has a constitutionally protected liberty interest in refusing unwanted medical treatment may be inferred from our prior decisions," and we assumed the existence of such a right for purposes of that case, *id.*, at 279. But our assumption of a right to refuse treatment was grounded not, as the Court of Appeals supposed, on the proposition that patients have a general and abstract "right to hasten death," 80 F.3d, at 727–728, but on well established, traditional rights to bodily integrity and freedom from unwanted touching, *Cruzan*, 497 U.S., at 278–279; *id.*, at 287–288 (O'CONNOR, J., concurring). In fact, we observed that "the majority of States in this country have laws imposing criminal penalties on one wbo assists another to commit suicide." *Id.*, at 280. *Cruzan* therefore provides no support for the notion that refusing life-sustaining medical treatment is "nothing more nor less than suicide."

For all these reasons, we disagree with respondents' claim that the distinction between refusing lifesaving medical treatment and assisted suicide is "arbitrary" and "irrational." . . . By permitting everyone to refuse unwanted medical treatment while prohibiting anyone from assisting a suicide, New York law follows a longstanding and rational distinction.

New York's reasons for recognizing and acting on this distinction—including prohibiting intentional killing and preserving life; preventing suicide; maintaining physicians' role as their patients' healers; protecting vulnerable people from indifference, prejudice, and psychological and financial pressure to end their lives; and avoiding a possible slide towards euthanasia—are discussed in greater detail in our opinion in *Glucksberg, ante*. These valid and important public interests easily satisfy the constitutional requirement that a legislative classification bear a rational relation to some legitimate end.

The judgment of the Court of Appeals is reversed.

It is so ordered.

. . .

E. GAY RIGHTS

States have attempted to criminalize homosexuality by passing laws that prohibit "crimes against nature," "buggery," "deviancy," and sodomy. States sometimes borrowed from English common law to define the offense as "the abominable and detestable crime against nature, either with mankind or with beast." Frequently these laws are challenged for being vague, unenforceable, and an invasion of privacy. It is often unclear whether the laws apply only to homosexuals or to married couples as well.

Opponents of these laws generally limit their attack to governmental efforts to control private, consensual sex acts between adults. For cases in which the activity concerns married couples and there is no issue of force or coercion, legal action has been successful in striking down the statute or reversing a conviction. Buchanan v. Batchelor, 308 F.Supp. 729 (N.D. Tex. 1970); Cotner v. Henry, 394 F.2d 873 (7th Cir. 1968). A state sodomy statute proscribing "the abominable and detestable crime against nature, either with mankind or with beast," was held to be not unconstitutionally vague when applied against two adult males. Wainwright v. Stone, 414 U.S. 21 (1973).

Opponents of sodomy statutes acknowledge that states have certain legitimate interests if the activity involves minors, unwilling participants, or actions that occur in public.[3] If the activity involves two males, one of them a minor, a conviction is likely to stand. State v. Crawford, 478 S.W.2d 314 (Mo. 1972), appeal dismissed for want of substantial federal question, 409 U.S. 811 (1972). Similarly, if consenting adults commit sodomy in private and allow their activity to become known to a minor, the state can convict them on that ground. Lovisi v. Slayton, 363 F.Supp. 620 (E.D. Va. 1973).

A major case involving adults was decided by a federal court in 1975. An action was brought claiming that a Virginia statute deprived adult males, engaging in homosexual relations consensually and in private, of their constitutional rights to due process, freedom of expression, and privacy. The court upheld the statute by distinguishing between the right of privacy in *Griswold* (the use of contraceptives by married couples in private) and the practices of adultery, homosexuality, and other sexual intimacies, which the state may forbid. Interestingly, the court relied on the *dissenting* opinion of Justice Harlan in *Poe v. Ullman* in making this distinction. Doe v. Commonwealth, 403 F.Supp. 1199, 1201 (E.D. Va. 1975), aff'd, 425 U.S. 901 (1976). In a dissent, Judge Merhige read *Griswold* and the abortion cases to stand

---

3. "Statement as to Jurisdiction," Buchanan v. Wade, U.S. Supreme Court, October Term, 1969, at 8.

for the principle that "every individual has a right to be free from unwarranted governmental intrusion into one's decisions on private matters of individual concern." More particularly, he said: "A mature individual's choice of an adult sexual partner, in the privacy of his or her own home, would appear to me to be a decision of the utmost private and intimate concern. Private consensual sex acts between adults are matters, absent evidence that they are harmful, in which the state has no legitimate interest."

In 1986 the Supreme Court narrowly sustained—by a 5–4 vote—the constitutionality of a Georgia statute that criminalized sodomy. Michael Hardwick, a homosexual, was arrested for committing sodomy with another adult in the bedroom of his home. After the district attorney decided not to present the matter to the grand jury, Hardwick challenged the statute as it applied to private, consensual sodomy. The majority held that the Constitution does not confer a fundamental right upon homosexuals to engage in sodomy. BOWERS v. HARDWICK, 478 U.S. 186 (1986). Justice Powell, concurring in the opinion, suggested that had Hardwick been "tried, much less convicted and sentenced" and had he raised the Eighth Amendment, he might have decided differently. Powell later admitted that he switched his vote to create the majority upholding Georgia's statute. Washington Post, August 13, 1986, at A4; see also Washington Post, July 13, 1986, at A1.

The Court did not pretend to have the last word on consensual sodomy. It emphasized that its decision "raises no question about the right or propriety of state legislative decisions to repeal their laws that criminalize homosexual sodomy, or of state-court decisions invalidating those laws on state constitutional grounds." 478 U.S. at 190. A number of state courts have invalidated state statutes that criminalize consensual sodomy. People v. Onofre, 415 N.E.2d 936 (N.Y. 1980); Commonwealth v. Bonadio, 415 A.2d 47 (Pa. 1980); Commonwealth v. Wasson, 842 S.W.2d 487 (Ky. 1992). State v. Morales, 826 S.W.2d 201 (Tex. App. 1992); City of Dallas v. England, 846 S.W.2d 957 (Tex. App. 1993); Campbell v. Sundquist, 926 S.W.2d 250 (Tenn. App. 1996) [the state supreme court denied appeal without an opinion]; Gryczan v. State, 942 P.2d 112 (Mont. 1997); Powell v. State, 510 S.E.2d. 18 (Ga. 1998). (For excerpts from Kentucky decision, see box on next page.) In recent years, 25 states have repealed their sodomy laws, as has the District of Columbia.

Civil Rights Protections

In 1996, the Supreme Court struck down a provision of the Colorado Constitution that nullified existing civil rights protections for homosexuals in the state. The constitutional language prohibited all legislative, executive, or judicial action at any level of state or local government designed to protect the status of persons based on their "homosexual, lesbian or bisexual orientation, conduct, practices or relationships." Several cities in the state had adopted ordinances to prohibit discrimination against gays. The 6 to 3 decision stated that the constitutional provision, by placing the state's homosexuals "in a solitary class" and singling them out, had violated the U.S. Constitution's equal protection guarantee. The Colorado provision, said the Court, failed to show a rational relationship to a legitimate governmental purpose. The Court rejected the argument that the provision merely took away "special rights," not equal rights. The Court made no mention of Bowers v. Hardwick (1986). Romer v. Evans, 517 U.S. 620 (1996). [In 1995, the Court decided a case involving the exclusion of gay marchers in a parade; see entry on page 510 of Chapter 10.]

Two years after the Court's decision in Romer v. Evans, the Court denied cert on a Sixth Circuit ruling that upheld a Cincinnati anti-gay initiative that was quite similar to Colorado's provision. Cincinnati's city charter amendment removed gays, lesbians, and bisexuals from protections of municipal antidiscrimination ordinances. The Sixth Circuit held that the charter amendment was rationally related to the city's valid interest in conserving public costs that

Kentucky Court Invalidates Sodomy Law

[In 1992 the Supreme Court of Kentucky held that the state's criminal statute prohibiting consensual homosexual sodomy violates the privacy and equal protection guarantees of the Kentucky Constitution. *Commonwealth v. Wasson*, 842 S.W.2d 487 (Ky. 1992). Below are excerpts from the decision by Justice Leibson.]

Appellee, Jeffrey Wasson, is charged with having solicited an undercover Lexington policeman to engage in deviate sexual intercourse. KRS 510.100 punishes "deviate sexual intercourse with another person of the same sex" as a criminal offense, and specifies "consent of the other person shall not be a defense." Nor does it matter that the act is private and involves a caring relationship rather than a commercial one. *[The sexual activity was intended to have taken place in Wasson's home by consenting adults; no money was offered or solicited.]*
... [W]e hold the guarantees of individual liberty provided in our 1891 Kentucky Constitution offer greater protection of the right of privacy than provided by the Federal Constitution as interpreted by the United States Supreme Court, and that the statute in question is a violation of such rights; and, further, we hold that the statute in question violates rights of equal protection as guaranteed by our Kentucky Constitution.

I. RIGHTS OF PRIVACY

No language specifying "rights or privacy," *as such,* appears in either the Federal or State Constitution. The Commonwealth recognizes such rights exist, but takes the position that, since they are implicit rather than explicit, our Court should march in lock step with the United States Supreme Court in declaring when such rights exist. Such is not the formulation of federalism. On the contrary, under our system of dual sovereignty, it is our responsibility to interpret and apply our state constitution independently. We are not bound by decisions of the United States Supreme Court when deciding whether a state statute impermissibly infringes upon individual rights guaranteed in the State Constitution so long as state constitutional protection does not fall below the federal *floor.* ...
The clear implication is that immorality in private which does "not operate to the detriment of others," is placed beyond the reach of state action by the guarantees of liberty in the Kentucky Constitution.

· · ·

... The statute before us is in violation of Kentucky constitutional protection in Section Three that "all men (persons), when they form a social compact, are equal," and in Section Two that "absolute and arbitrary power over the lives, liberty and property of free men (persons) exist nowhere in a republic, not even in the largest majority." We have concluded that it is "arbitrary" for the majority to criminalize sexual activity solely on the basis of majoritarian sexual preference, and that it denied "equal" treatment under the law when there is no rational basis, as this term is used and applied in our Kentucky cases.

accrue from investigating and adjudicating sexual orientation discrimination complaints. *Equality Foundation v. City of Cincinnati*, 128 F.3d 289 (6th Cir. 1997), cert. denied, 525 U.S. 943 (1998). Justices Stevens, Souter and Ginsburg played down the cert denial, explaining that the Court may simply have concluded that the Cincinnati case did "not constitute an appropriate forum in which to decide a significant case."

In 2000, the Court ruled that the Boy Scouts of America had a right to expel an adult Scout leader after he announced he was gay. Although he sued under a New Jersey law that prohibits discrimination in public places based on sexual orientation, the Court held that the Boy Scouts have a First Amendment right of "expressive association" to control the message and values it directs to the public. *Boy Scouts of America v. Dale*, 120 S.Ct. 2446 (2000). For further discussion of the First Amendment issue, see p. 510.

Gay Marriages

Litigation in Hawaii challenged a state marriage law that prohibited same-sex couples from obtaining marriage licenses. Under pressure from this lawsuit, Congress passed the Defense of Marriage Act (DOMA) which allowed states to refuse to recognize such marriages performed in other states and also prohibited federal recognition of same-sex marriages. The latter provision prevents gay couples from filing joint tax returns or gaining access to spousal benefits under Social Security and other federal programs. President Clinton signed the legislation without comment. 110 Stat. 2419 (1996). Congress acted under Section 1 of Article IV: "Full Faith and Credit shall be given in each State to the public Acts, Records, and judicial Proceedings of every other State; And the Congress may by general Laws prescribe the Manner in which such Acts, Records and Proceedings shall be proved, and the Effect thereof."

After the enactment of DOMA, gay rights interests sought to convince state courts and state legislatures to legalize same-sex unions. In Vermont, a 1997 lawsuit challenging the state's prohibition of same-sex marriages led to legislation in 2000 that allowed gays to form a "civil union," giving them the same benefits, protections, and responsibilities granted to spouses in a marriage. Baker v. State, 744 A.2d 864 (Vt. 1999). Other states have adopted explicit prohibitions on same-sex marriages.

Gays in the Military

President Clinton inherited an issue that had been simmering for decades: the rights of homosexual soldiers. In an early case, a Navy officer, discharged for homosexual conduct, brought an action seeking to be reinstated in the service. He acknowledged engaging in homosexual acts in a Navy barracks. In 1984 a federal appellate court held that the Navy's policy of mandatory discharge for homosexual conduct did not violate constitutional rights to privacy or equal protection. If government may proscribe homosexual conduct in a civilian context, as in *Doe* v. *Commonwealth,* "then such a regulation is certainly sustainable in a military context" where discipline and good order justify restrictions "that go beyond the needs of civilian society." Dronenberg v. Zech, 741 F.2d 1388, 1392 (D.C. Cir. 1984).

In 1990 the Supreme Court refused to consider constitutional challenges to the military's policy of excluding persons who acknowledge they are homosexual, even if there is no evidence of actual homosexual conduct. One case involved a woman who had been discharged from the Army because of homosexual tendencies but was reinstated under court order. After her enlistment terminated, she sought reenlistment, admitting that she is a lesbian, but the Army opposed her entry. Ben-Shalom v. Stone, 494 U.S. 1004 (1990); Ben-Shalom v. Marsh, 881 F.2d 454 (7th Cir. 1989). The other case involved a man who was accepted into Navy flight school after acknowledging that he had homosexual tendencies. He was released from active duty when he visited the officer's club in the company of an enlisted man who was awaiting discharge because of homosexuality. Woodward v. United States, 494 U.S. 1003 (1990); Woodward v. United States, 871 F.2d 1068 (Fed. Cir. 1989).

During the 1992 presidential campaign, Bill Clinton promised to end the U.S. prohibition on gay people in the armed services. Throughout the 1980s, an average of 1,500 men and women were discharged from the military because of their homosexuality. After Clinton's election, the Supreme Court let stand a lower court ruling that gay status, by itself, is insufficient justification to exclude homosexuals from the military. The burden is on the military to show that discrimination against homosexuals is rationally related to a permissible governmental purpose. Cheney v. Pruitt, 506 U.S. 1020 (1993); Pruitt v. Cheney, 963 F.2d 1160 (9th Cir. 1991).

"Don't Ask/Don't Tell"

President Clinton ordered the Defense Department to draft an executive order and departmental directives by July 15, 1993. The resulting policy was characterized as "don't ask/don't tell." The Pentagon would no longer ask volunteers whether they are gay or bisexual. Military personnel would not be asked to disclose their sexual orientation when they apply for security clearances. However, they can be discharged for homosexual conduct. A lower court ruling prohibited the Pentagon from discriminating against gays, but the Supreme Court lifted that court order. The Courts's action permitted full implementation of the Clinton policy, including discharge for homosexual conduct. U.S. Department of Defense v. Meinhold, 510 U.S. 939 (1993). In the meantime, Congress legislated on the issue, establishing conditions for gays in the military that are more stringent than the policy envisioned in the Clinton administration regulations. 107 Stat. 1670, § 571 (1993).

In 1996, the Fourth Circuit upheld the Clinton administration's "don't ask/don't tell" policy. A Navy lieutenant was dismissed after giving a letter to his commanding officer stating "I am gay." The court held that the statute does not target speech declaring homosexuality; it targets homosexual acts and the propensity or intent to engage in homosexual acts, and permissibly uses speech as evidence. Thomasson v. Perry, 80 F.3d 915 (4th Cir. 1996), cert. denied, 519 U.S. 948 (1996). Other federal appellate court decisions also upheld the "don't ask, don't tell" policy.[4]

Although the Clinton policy was adopted to make it easier for homosexuals to serve in the military, more gay service members are being discharged than before it took effect. In a number of cases military officials directly asked members about their sexual orientation. The Defense Department states that the discharges are due to an increasing number of voluntary statements to commanders by homosexuals who want to leave the military.[5] In 1999, Clinton concluded that his policy on gays in the military is "out of whack now" and that it wasn't being implemented "as it was announced and as it was intended." 35 Weekly Comp. Pres. Doc. 2612 (1999). In 2000, the Pentagon issued new guidelines to enforce Clinton's policy.

Bowers v. Hardwick

478 U.S. 186 (1986)

Michael Hardwick was charged with violating Georgia law by committing sodomy with another adult male in the bedroom of his home. After the district attorney decided not to present the matter to the grand jury, Hardwick brought suit in federal court to have the statute declared unconstitutional because it criminalized consensual sodomy. A district court granted the state's motion to dismiss; the Eleventh Circuit reversed, holding that the statute violated Hardwick's fundamental rights. The defendant in this case is Michael J. Bowers, Attorney General of Georgia. John and Mary Doe joined Hardwick as plaintiffs in the action, claiming that they wished to engage in sexual activity proscribed by the statute. The Court examined only Hardwick's challenge and expressed no opinion on the constitutionality of the Georgia statute as applied to other acts of sodomy.

---

4. E.g., Richenberg v. Perry, 97 F.3d 256 (8th Cir. 1996), cert. denied, 522 U.S. 807 (1997); Philips v. Perry, 106 F.3d 1420 (9th Cir. 1997); Holmes v. California Army National Guard, 124 F.3d 1126 (9th Cir. 1997).

5. "Number of Recruits Discharged for Being Gay Increase for Fifth Year," Washington Post, January 23, 1999, at A5; "Military Discharges of Homosexuals Soar," The New York Times, April 7, 1998, at A24; "Military, Despite Policy Shift, Discharged More Gays in '95," Washington Post, February 28, 1996, at A2.

JUSTICE WHITE delivered the opinion of the Court.

. . .

Because other Courts of Appeals have arrived at judgments contrary to that of the Eleventh Circuit in this case, we granted the State's petition for certiorari questioning the holding that its sodomy statute violates the fundamental rights of homosexuals. We agree with the State that the Court of Appeals erred, and hence reverse its judgment.

This case does not require a judgment on whether laws against sodomy between consenting adults in general, or between homosexuals in particular, are wise or desirable. It raises no question about the right or propriety of state legislative decisions to repeal their laws that criminalize homosexual sodomy, or of state court decisions invalidating those laws on state constitutional grounds. The issue presented is whether the Federal Constitution confers a fundamental right upon homosexuals to engage in sodomy and hence invalidates the laws of the many States that still make such conduct illegal and have done so for a very long time. The case also calls for some judgment about the limits of the Court's role in carrying out its constitutional mandate.

We first register our disagreement with the Court of Appeals and with respondent that the Court's prior cases have construed the Constitution to confer a right of privacy that extends to homosexual sodomy and for all intents and purposes have decided this case. The reach of this line of cases was sketched in *Carey v. Population Services International,* 431 U.S. 678, 685 (1977). *Pierce v. Society of Sisters,* 268 U.S. 510 (1925), and *Meyer v. Nebraska,* 262 U.S. 390 (1923), were described as dealing with child rearing and education; *Prince v. Massachusetts,* 321 U.S. 158 (1944), with family relationships; *Skinner v. Oklahoma ex rel. Williamson,* 316 U.S. 535 (1942), with procreation; *Loving v. Virginia,* 388 U.S. 1 (1967), with marriage; *Griswold v. Connecticut, supra,* and *Eisenstadt v. Baird, supra,* with contraception; and *Roe v. Wade,* 410 U.S. 113 (1973), with abortion. The latter three cases were interpreted as construing the Due Process Clause of the Fourteenth Amendment to confer a fundamental individual right to decide whether or not to beget or bear a child. *Carey v. Population Services International, supra,* 431 U.S., at 688–689.

Accepting the decisions in these cases and the above description of them, we think it evident that none of the rights announced in those cases bears any resemblance to the claimed constitutional right of homosexuals to engage in acts of sodomy that is asserted in this case. No connection between family, marriage, or procreation on the one hand and homosexual activity on the other has been demonstrated, either by the Court of Appeals or by respondent. Moreover, any claim that these cases nevertheless stand for the proposition that any kind of private sexual conduct between consenting adults is constitutionally insulated from state proscription is unsupportable. Indeed, the Court's opinion in *Carey* twice asserted that the privacy right, which the *Griswold* line of cases found to be one of the protections provided by the Due Process Clause, did not reach so far. 431 U.S., at 688, n. 5, 694, n. 17.

Precedent aside, however, respondent would have us announce, as the Court of Appeals did, a fundamental right to engage in homosexual sodomy. This we are quite unwilling to do. It is true that despite the language of the Due Process Clauses of the Fifth and Fourteenth Amendments, which appears to focus only on the processes by which life, liberty, or property is taken, the cases are legion in which those Clauses have been interpreted to have substantive content, subsuming rights that to a great extent are immune from federal or state regulation or proscription. Among such cases are those recognizing rights that have little or no textual support in the constitutional language. *Meyer, Prince,* and *Pierce* fall in this category, as do the privacy cases from *Griswold* to *Carey.*

Striving to assure itself and the public that announcing rights not readily identifiable in the Constitution's text involves much more than the imposition of the Justices' own choice of values on the States and the Federal Government, the Court has sought to identify the nature of the rights qualifying for heightened judicial protection. In *Palko v. Connecticut,* 302 U.S. 319, 325, 326, (1937), it was said that this category includes those fundamental liberties that are "implicit in the concept of ordered liberty," such that "neither liberty nor justice would exist if [they] were sacrificed." A different description of fundamental liberties appeared in *Moore v. East Cleveland,* 431 U.S. 494, 503, (1977) (opinion of POWELL, J.), where they are characterized as those liberties that are "deeply rooted in this Nation's history and tradition." *Id.,* at 503, (POWELL, J.). See also *Griswold v. Connecticut,* 381 U.S., at 506.

It is obvious to us that neither of these formulations would extend a fundamental right to homosexuals to engage in acts of consensual sodomy. Proscriptions against that conduct have ancient roots. See generally, Survey on the Constitutional Right to Privacy in the Context of Homosexual Activity, 40 U. Miami L. Rev. 521, 525 (1986). Sodomy was a criminal offense at common law and was forbidden by the laws of the original thirteen States when they ratified the Bill of Rights. In 1868, when the Fourteenth Amendment was ratified, all but 5 of the 37 States in the Union had criminal sodomy laws. In fact, until 1961, all 50 States outlawed sodomy, and today, 24 States and the District of Columbia continue to provide criminal penalties for sodomy performed in private and between consenting adults. Survey, U. Miami L. Rev., *supra*, at 524, n. 9. Against this background, to claim that a right to engage in such conduct is "deeply rooted in this Nation's history and tradition" or "implicit in the concept of ordered liberty" is, at best, facetious.

Nor are we inclined to take a more expansive view of our authority to discover new fundamental rights imbedded in the Due Process Clause. The Court is most vulnerable and comes nearest to illegitimacy when it deals with judge-made constitutional law having little or no cognizable roots in the language or design of the Constitution. That this is so was painfully demonstrated by the face-off between the Executive and the Court in the 1930's, which resulted in the repudiation of much of the substantive gloss that the Court had placed on the Due Process Clause of the Fifth and Fourteenth Amendments. There should be, therefore, great resistance to expand the substantive reach of those Clauses, particularly if it requires redefining the category of rights deemed to be fundamental. Otherwise, the Judiciary necessarily takes to itself further authority to govern the country without express constitutional authority. The claimed right pressed on us today falls far short of overcoming this resistance.

· · ·

Even if the conduct at issue here is not a fundamental right, respondent asserts that there must be a rational basis for the law and that there is none in this case other than the presumed belief of a majority of the electorate in Georgia that homosexual sodomy is immoral and unacceptable. This is said to be an inadequate rationale to support the law. The law, however, is constantly based on notions of morality, and if all laws representing essentially moral choices are to be invalidated under the Due Process Clause, the courts will be very busy indeed. Even respondent makes no such claim, but insists that majority sentiments about the morality of homosexuality should be declared inadequate. We do not agree, and are unpersuaded that the sodomy laws of some 25 States should be invalidated on this basis.

Accordingly, the judgment of the Court of Appeals is

Reversed.

CHIEF JUSTICE BURGER, concurring.

· · ·

JUSTICE POWELL, concurring.

I join the opinion of the Court. I agree with the Court that there is no fundamental right — *i.e.,* no substantive right under the Due Process Clause — such as that claimed by respondent, and found to exist by the Court of Appeals. This is not to suggest, however, that respondent may not be protected by the Eighth Amendment of the Constitution. The Georgia statute at issue in this case, Ga.Code Ann. § 16-6-2, authorizes a court to imprison a person for up to 20 years for a single private, consensual act of sodomy. In my view, a prison sentence for such conduct — certainly a sentence of long duration — would create a serious Eighth Amendment issue. Under the Georgia statute a single act of sodomy, even in the private setting of a home, is a felony comparable in terms of the possible sentence imposed to serious felonies such as aggravated battery, § 16-5-24, first degree arson, § 16-7-60 and robbery, § 16-8-40.

In this case, however, respondent has not been tried, much less convicted and sentenced. Moreover, respondent has not raised the Eighth Amendment issue below. For these reasons this constitutional argument is not before us.

JUSTICE BLACKMUN, with whom JUSTICE BRENNAN, JUSTICE MARSHALL, and JUSTICE STEVENS join, dissenting.

This case is no more about "a fundamental right to engage in homosexual sodomy," as the Court purports to declare, *ante,* at 191, than *Stanley v. Georgia,* 394 U.S. 557 (1969), was about a fundamental right to watch obscene movies, or *Katz v. United States,* 389 U.S. 347 (1967), was about a fundamental right to place interstate bets from a telephone booth. Rather, this case is about "the most comprehensive of rights and the right most valued by civilized men," namely, "the right to be let alone." *Olmstead v. United States,* 277 U.S. 438, 478 (1928) (Brandeis, J., dissenting).

The statute at issue, Ga.Code Ann. § 16-6-2, denies individuals the right to decide for themselves whether to engage in particular forms of private, consensual sexual activity. The Court concludes that § 16-6-2 is valid essentially because "the laws of...many States...still make such conduct illegal and have done so for a very long time." *Ante,* at 190. But the fact that the moral judgments expressed by statutes like § 16-6-2 may be "natural and familiar...ought not to conclude our judgment upon the question whether statutes embodying them conflict with the Constitution of the United States." *Roe v. Wade,* 410 U.S. 113, 117 (1973), quoting *Lochner v. New York,* 198 U.S. 45, 76 (1905) (Holmes J., dissenting). Like Justice Holmes, I believe that "[i]t is revolting to have no better reason for a rule of law than that so it was laid down in the time of Henry IV. It is still more revolting if the grounds upon which it was laid down have vanished long since, and the rule simply persists from blind imitation of the past." Holmes, The Path of the Law, 10 Harv.L.Rev. 457, 469 (1897). I believe we must analyze respondent's claim in the light of the values that underlie the constitutional right to privacy. If that right means anything, it means that, before Georgia can prosecute its citizens for making choices about the most intimate aspects of their lives, it must do more than assert that the choice they have made is an " 'abominable crime not fit to be named among Christians.' " *Herring v. State,* 119 Ga. 709, 721, 46 S.E. 876, 882 (1904).

I

...[T]he Court's almost obsessive focus on homosexual activity is particularly hard to justify in light of the broad language Georgia has used.... Georgia has provided that "[a] person commits the offense of sodomy when he performs or submits to any sexual act involving the sex organs of one person and the mouth or anus of another." Ga.Code Ann. § 16-6-2(a). The sex or status of the persons who engage in the act is irrelevant as a matter of state law. In fact, to the extent I can discern a legislative purpose for Georgia's 1968

enactment of § 16-6-2, that purpose seems to have been to broaden the coverage of the law to reach heterosexual as well as homosexual activity....

JUSTICE STEVENS, with whom JUSTICE BRENNAN and JUSTICE MARSHALL join, dissenting.

Like the statute that is challenged in this case, the rationale of the Court's opinion applies equally to the prohibited conduct regardless of whether the parties who engage in it are married or unmarried, or are of the same or different sexes....

I

Our prior cases make two propositions abundantly clear. First, the fact that the governing majority in a State has traditionally viewed a particular practice as immoral is not a sufficient reason for upholding a law prohibiting the practice; neither history nor tradition could save a law prohibiting miscegenation from constitutional attack. Second, individual decisions by married persons, concerning the intimacies of their physical relationship, even when not intended to produce offspring, are a form of "liberty" protected by the Due Process Clause of the Fourteenth Amendment. *Griswold v. Connecticut,* 381 U.S. 479 (1965). Moreover, this protection extends to intimate choices by unmarried as well as married persons. *Carey v. Population Services International,* 431 U.S. 678 (1977); *Eisenstadt v. Baird,* 405 U.S. 438 (1972).

. . .

II

If the Georgia statute cannot be enforced as it is written—if the conduct it seeks to prohibit is a protected form of liberty for the vast majority of Georgia's citizens—the State must assume the burden of justifying a selective application of its law....

...A policy of selective application must be supported by a neutral and legitimate interest—something more substantial than a habitual dislike for, or ignorance about, the disfavored group. Neither the State nor the Court has identified any such interest in this case....

F. DEFINING THE LIMITS OF PRIVACY

Privacy has a multitude of meanings. In part, it preserves an individual's interest in seclusion or solitude. At other times, it protects against the public disclosure of embarrassing private facts or avoids placing someone in a "false light" in the public eye. On other occasions, it prevents the appropriation of one's name or likeness. Prosser, 48 Cal. L. Rev. 383, 389 (1960).

Alan Westin, in *Privacy and Freedom* (1967), recommended that personal information (the right of decision over one's private personality) be defined as a property right. A citizen would be entitled to have due process of law before his "property" could be taken and misused, including access to information in the person's file and a right to challenge its accuracy. By passing the Fair Credit Reporting Act of 1970, Congress supplied that type of protection. Credit agencies are required to disclose to a consumer information about that person in their files, including the sources of the information. If a consumer successfully challenges the completeness or accuracy of any item in the file, the information must be promptly deleted. 84 Stat. 1127 (1970).

Congress intervened to protect the privacy interests of bank depositors. In 1976 the Supreme Court held that a Fourth Amendment interest could not be vindicated in court by challenging a government subpoena for microfilms of checks, deposit slips, and other records in a bank. The Court treated the materials as business records of a bank, not private papers of a person. Justice Brennan noted in a dissent that a depositor "reveals many aspects of his personal affairs, opinions, habits and associations. Indeed, the totality of bank records provides a virtual current biography." United States v. Miller, 425 U.S. 435, 451 (1976). Two years later Congress passed the Right to Financial Privacy Act, giving depositors certain procedural rights and protections that were unavailable from the Court. 92 Stat. 3697 (1978). The legislative debate illustrates that privacy interests left unprotected by the judiciary can be secured by congressional action (see reading).

In 1978 the Supreme Court upheld the right of law enforcement officers to use warrants to come onto the premises of a newspaper. Zurcher v. Stanford Daily, 436 U.S. 547 (1978). In quick response, Congress passed the Privacy Protection Act of 1980. With certain exceptions, the statute requires the use of a subpoena instead of a search warrant to obtain documentary materials from those who disseminate newspapers, books, broadcasts, or other similar forms of public communication. 94 Stat. 1879 (1980). The effect is to protect the privacy rights of those engaged in First Amendment activities. Here, too, the congressional debate is instructive (pages 771, 772–73).

During hearings in 1987 on the nomination of Judge Robert H. Bork to be Associate Justice of the Supreme Court, a reporter obtained from a local video store a list of the movies that Bork and his family had rented. After the list was published in a newspaper, this invasion of Bork's privacy was roundly condemned. Congress responded by enacting the Video Privacy Protection Act of 1988, which makes video stores liable for actions forbidden by the statute. With certain exceptions, stores may be sued for disclosing the videotapes rented by customers. 102 Stat. 3195 (1988).

The Right to Publish

The right to privacy does not carry with it a comprehensive right to be "let alone." Legitimate actions by private agencies and government may intrude upon the individual. Carried to its extreme, the right to privacy would practically extinguish the freedom of the press. No one would dare publish or broadcast anything for fear of a lawsuit from an aggrieved citizen or public official. Even when state law prohibits the broadcasting of a rape victim's name, this right to privacy yields to the freedom of the press to publish accurately names obtained from judicial records that are open to public inspection. Cox Broadcasting v. Cohn, 420 U.S. 469 (1975). Newspapers may not be punished for publishing the name of a rape victim if the woman's full name appeared in a police report available to the press. The Florida Star v. B.J.F., 491 U.S. 524 (1989).

There are many anomalies to the right of privacy. Entertainers demand both the right to privacy and the right to publicity. In the same year that Congress substantially strengthened the Freedom of Information Act of 1974, which gave the public access to federal agency

---

Anthony Kennedy on Privacy

[During his confirmation hearings in 1987 to become Associate Justice of the Supreme Court, Anthony M. Kennedy testified that he believed that a right of privacy is implicit in the U.S. Constitution.]

Now, how far can you continue that inquiry away from the words of the text? Your question is whether or not there are unenumerated rights. To begin with, most of the inquiries that the Supreme Court has conducted in cases of this type have centered around the word "liberty." Now, the framers had that, what I call "spacious phrase," both in the fifth amendment, almost contemporaneous with the Constitution, and again in the 14th amendment they reiterated it.

The framers had an idea which is central to Western thought.

...It is central to our American tradition. It is central to the idea of the rule of law. That is there is a zone of liberty, a zone of protection, a line that is drawn where the individual can tell the Government: Beyond this line you may not go.

...It seems to me that most Americans, most lawyers, most judges, believe that liberty includes protection of a value that we call privacy....

Source: "Nomination of Anthony M. Kennedy to be Associate Justice of the Supreme Court of the United States," hearings before the Senate Committee on the Judiciary, 100th Cong., 1st Sess. 86, 88 (1987).

---

records, it also passed the Privacy Act. This statute prohibits access by the public to certain materials in agency records. It also provides U.S. citizens the right to examine their own federal agency files and correct erroneous entries.

Governmental Powers

Although one may object to vaccination and regard it as a deprivation of personal liberty, states may invoke their police power to make it compulsory in order to prevent the spread of contagious diseases, such as smallpox. Jacobson v. Massachusetts, 197 U.S. 11 (1905). Playing radio programs on bus and streetcar systems may seem an invasion of privacy to some passengers, but the practice does not offend the Constitution. Public Utilities Comm'n v. Pollak, 343 U.S. 451 (1952). However, the state does have a right to protect citizens from assault from raucous loudspeakers. Kovacs v. Cooper, 336 U.S. 77 (1949).

In criminal law, a defendant can expect no success when invoking the right of privacy for certain activities, such as incest. Criminal procedures often affect sensitive areas of privacy, particularly those involving the body. Suspects accused of drunk driving can be subjected to compulsory blood tests and breath tests. Breithaupt v. Abram, 352 U.S. 432 (1957); Schmerber v. California, 384 U.S. 757 (1966). The Court has held that no one has an expectation of privacy if law enforcement officers decide to fly over their backyard and take photographs of marijuana plants. California v. Ciraolo, 476 U.S. 207 (1986); Florida v. Riley, 488 U.S. 445 (1989).

There are, of course, limits on the search for evidence. The police cannot use stomach pumps on a narcotics suspect to recover forbidden substances. Rochin v. California, 342 U.S. 165 (1952). States have been prohibited from compelling an armed robbery suspect to undergo surgery to remove a bullet lodged in his chest. Winston v. Lee, 470 U.S. 753 (1985). Individuals arrested and booked for misdemeanors may not be subjected to the indignity of strip searches and body-cavity searches, regardless of whether they are reasonably suspected of concealing contraband. Weber v. Dell, 804 F.2d 796 (2nd Cir. 1986), cert. denied, 483 U.S. 1020 (1987).

Justice Douglas' decision in *Griswold* v. *Connecticut,* discovering a right of privacy in various "emanations" and "penumbras" in the Constitution, has been the target of harsh critiques and ridicule. However, the nation's commitment to privacy is not grounded in ephemeral judicial doctrine. Citizens harbor a natural resistance to government intrusions. The Senate 1987 hearings on the ill-fated nomination of Robert Bork to the Supreme Court underscore the deep roots of privacy in America (see reading).[6] After Bork was rejected by the Senate, the next nominee, Anthony M. Kennedy, was forthright in recognizing an implicit right of privacy in the Constitution (see box on previous page).

Financial Privacy Act of 1978: Congressional Debate

In *United States* v. *Miller,* 425 U.S. 435 (1976), the Supreme Court held that bank depositors were not protected by the Fourth Amendment when the government wanted to gain access to microfilms of checks, deposit slips, or other bank records. These materials were regarded as business records of a bank, not the private papers of a person. Congress responded by passing legislation — the Right to Financial Privacy Act — that gave depositors certain procedural rights and protections. The debate in the House of Representatives illustrates how members of Congress are involved in deciding questions of Fourth Amendment rights and privacy interests. The excerpts below come from 124 Cong. Rec. 33310–11, 33818–19, 33835 (1978).

Mr. WHALEN. Mr. Chairman, the legislation now before us, the Financial Institution's Regulatory Act, is a complex bill, for the most part dealing with relatively esoteric questions of banking regulation. One title, however, is of direct and immediate concern to every American and is one with which I have been involved personally.

I am referring, of course, to title XI, the Right to Financial Privacy Act of 1968.

Title XI represents an enormous step forward in the protection of the rights to privacy of American citizens. I am delighted to see this legislation come to the floor of the House.

During the 93rd Congress, Senator CHARLES MATHIAS of Maryland first proposed the Bill of Rights Procedures Act. Its primary purpose was to prevent warrantless Government searches of bank, credit, medical, telephone toll billing, and other records that reveal the nature of one's private affairs. This was the first legislative proposal ever to address the problem of access to third party records.

At the start of the 94th Congress, Senator MATHIAS reintroduced the Bill of Rights Procedures Act with our former colleague, the Honorable Charles A. Mosher, serving as the chief House sponsor. I was pleased to join as a cosponsor of that measure (H.R. 214). The bill under-

went more than 40 days of hearings and markup in the House Judiciary Subcommittee on Courts, Civil Liberties and the Administration of Justice, but was reported out of subcommittee too late to reach the floor in 1976.

. . .

. . . [T]he new legislation preserves our basic principle that third party records of a personal nature, in this case bank and credit records, should not be accessed by Government agents except with the knowledge of the subject individual or else with the supervision of the courts.

This is a crucial concept. It returns to the individual some measure of control over dissemination of records that contain very detailed information about one's daily life. And it puts the courts into a proper role of resolving conflicts between a citizen's rights to privacy and society's needs for information.

Moreover, it also restores the record holders, the banks, and credit card companies to their proper role as impartial custodians of records. I know that the financial community welcomes this opportunity to get out of the middle of disputes between customers and Government. And they surely will welcome being able once again to as-

---

6. Another aspect of privacy is associational rights. The compelled disclosure of membership lists can seriously infringe on privacy of association and belief. Brown v. Socialist Workers '74 Campaign Comm., 459 U.S. 87 (1982); Buckley v. Valeo, 424 U.S. 1, 64 (1976); Gibson v. Florida Legislative Comm., 372 U.S. 539 (1963); NAACP v. Button, 371 U.S. 415 (1963).

sure their clients that they can have a reasonable expectation that the confidentiality of their records will be maintained. Surely, everyone will benefit from the establishment of a clear set of rules and procedures.

. . .

Mr. LA FALCE. Mr. Chairman, . . . I rise in support of this bill.

. . .

The overriding purpose of this title is to let an individual know when the Federal Government is seeking access to his financial records and what use is made of those records after the Government acquires them. The individual is given an opportunity to challenge the access to his records if he thinks that there is no legitimate reason for the Government to be seeking them. The first step is that the Government informs the individual that it wishes to review his records for a given purpose. The individual is also given a form to fill out which will enable him to challenge the Government's access to the records.

It is then up to the Government to show that the records are relevant to the investigation and that the investigation itself is a legitimate one, and not being conducted to harass an individual for political reasons, to intimidate a witness, or for other bad faith motives. The important point to remember is that we are dealing here with the preliminary stages of an investigation and, especially in cases of white collar crime, financial records are the best, if not the only evidence of the crime. At the beginning of investigations into alleged embezzlement, bribery, public corruption, extortion, drug trafficking and the like, financial records provide the information needed to begin or continue the investigation, and it is not the intent of the framers of this title to inhibit these legitimate activities of Government law enforcement authorities. To require excessively detailed demonstrations of the basis for the investigation at this point in the process would lead to the courts making preliminary decisions on investigations rather than prosecutors, and would be a violation of the separation of powers doctrine.

Some very limited exceptions are included in the title to allow for situations in which prior notice to the individual would cause serious harm to that individual, another person, or to the investigation. In these cases, the Government is required to demonstrate the potential harm to a court, and the individual is notified after the fact that the records have been obtained, and may challenge the access if it was improper. Notice is also given to the individual of transfers of his records between Government agencies, so that at all times, unless there is a compelling reason not to disclose the transfer, he or she will know which agencies in the Federal Government have reviewed the bank records.

. . .

Mr. PATTISON of New York. . . .

Many of us on both sides of the aisle strongly believe that individual bank records must be afforded basic privacy rights. Furthermore, it is our belief that the framers of the Constitution intended to provide protection for all individual records. At the time the fourth amendment to the Constitution was drafted, however, almost all personal records were kept at home. Protecting those records actually in the possession of the individual citizen was an adequate safeguard. In this century, however, increasingly financial records have been held by banks and other financial institutions. Furthermore, advances in communications and recordkeeping technology now allow financial institutions to store and quickly retrieve vast amounts of information.

These records can tell a complete story about the customer's life and lifestyle: His religious and political affiliations, what medical services he requires, how much he drinks, and a vast array of his personal habits.

Despite their personal nature, these records are not afforded privacy protections. In its 1976 Miller decision, the Supreme Court ruled that, under current law, records held by a financial institution are the property of the institution, rather than the customer's. These records are therefore not entitled to safeguards from unwarranted government access. Therefore, under Miller, a citizen does not have "standing" to sue to prevent unreasonable access to those records.

Clearly, it is an empty gesture to protect individual records held in the home when a much richer store of information is readily available at the individual's bank. This inconsistency led the Privacy Protection Study Commission, in its 1977 report entitled "Personal Privacy in an Information Society," to call for the creation of "a legitimate, enforceable expectation of confidentiality."

The legislation before us today is based on the premise that bank customers have a right to reasonable expectation of privacy. . . .

The Right to Privacy: The Bork Hearings

During the hearings in 1987 on the nomination of Robert H. Bork to be Associate Justice of the U.S. Supreme Court, questions zeroed in on Bork's position on privacy. The questioning below is directed by the Chairman of the Senate Judiciary Committee, Joseph R. Biden, Jr., followed by questions from Senators Edward M. Kennedy and Alan K. Simpson. These passages come from "Nomination of Robert H. Bork to be Associate Justice of the Supreme Court of the United States," hearings before the Senate Committee on the Judiciary, 100th Cong., 1st Sess. 114–21, 240–42 (Part 1 of 5 Parts) (1987).

The CHAIRMAN. Well, let's talk about another case. Let's talk about the *Griswold* case. Now, while you were living in Connecticut, that State had a law—I know you know this, but for the record—that it made it a crime for anyone, even a married couple, to use birth control. You indicated that you thought that law was "nutty," to use your words and I quite agree. Nevertheless, Connecticut, under that "nutty" law, prosecuted and convicted a doctor and the case finally reached the Supreme Court.

The Court said that the law violated a married couple's constitutional right to privacy. You criticized this opinion in numerous articles and speeches, beginning in 1971 and as recently as July 26th of this year. In your 1971 article, "Neutral Principles and Some First Amendment Problems," you said that the right of married couples to have sexual relations without fear of unwanted children is no more worthy of constitutional protection by the courts than the right of public utilities to be free of pollution control laws.

You argued that the utility company's right or gratification, I think you referred to it, to make money and the married couple's right or gratification to have sexual relations without fear of unwanted children, as "the cases are identical." Now, I am trying to understand this. It appears to me that you are saying that the government has as much right to control a married couple's decision about choosing to have a child or not, as that government has a right to control the public utility's right to pollute the air. Am I misstating your rationale here?

Judge BORK. With due respect, Mr. Chairman, I think you are. I was making the point that where the Constitution does not speak—there is no provision in the Constitution that applies to the case—then a judge may not say, I place a higher value upon a marital relationship than I do upon an economic freedom. Only if the Constitution gives him some reasoning. Once the judge begins to say economic rights are more important than marital rights or vice versa, and if there is nothing

in the Constitution, the judge is enforcing his own moral values, which I have objected to. Now, on the *Griswold* case itself—

The CHAIRMAN. Can we stick with that point a minute to make sure I understand it?

Judge BORK. Sure.

The CHAIRMAN. So that you suggest that unless the Constitution, I believe in the past you used the phrase, textually identifies, a value that is worthy of being protected, then competing values in society, the competing value of a public utility, in the example you used, to go out and make money—that economic right has no more or less constitutional protection than the right of a married couple to use or not use birth control in their bedroom. Is that what you are saying?

Judge BORK. No, I am not entirely, but I will straighten it out. I was objecting to the way Justice Douglas, in that opinion, *Griswold* v. *Connecticut,* derived this right. It may be possible to derive an objection to an anti-contraceptive statute in some other way. I do not know.

But starting from the assumption, which is an assumption for purposes of my argument, not a proven fact, starting from the assumption that there is nothing in the Constitution, in any legitimate method of constitutional reasoning about either subject, all I am saying is that the judge has no way to prefer one to the other and the matter should be left to the legislatures who will then decide which competing gratification, or freedom, should be placed higher.

The CHAIRMAN. Then I think I do understand it, that is, that the economic gratification of a utility company is as worthy of as much protection as the sexual gratification of a married couple, because neither is mentioned in the Constitution.

Judge BORK. All that means is that the judge may not choose.

The CHAIRMAN. Who does?

Judge BORK. The legislature.

The CHAIRMAN. Well, that is my point, so it is not a constitutional right. I am not trying to be picky here. Clearly, I do not want to get into a debate with a professor, but it seems to me that what you are saying is what I said and that is, that the Constitution—if it were a constitutional right, if the Constitution said anywhere in it, in your view, that a married couple's right to engage in the decision of having a child or not having a child was a constitutionally-protected right of privacy, then you would rule that that right exists. You would not leave it to a legislative body no matter what they did.

Judge BORK. That is right.

The CHAIRMAN. But you argue, as I understand it, that no such right exists.

Judge BORK. No, Senator, that is what I tried to clarify. I argued that the way in which this unstructured, undefined right of privacy that Justice Douglas elaborated, that the way he did it did not prove its existence.

The CHAIRMAN. You have been a professor now for years and years, everybody has pointed out and I have observed, you are one of the most well-read and scholarly people to come before this committee. In all your short life, have you come up with any other way to protect a married couple, under the Constitution, against an action by a government telling them what they can or cannot do about birth control in their bedroom? Is there any constitutional right, anywhere in the Constitution?

Judge BORK. I have never engaged in that exercise....

The CHAIRMAN.

...Does a State legislative body, or any legislative body, have a right to pass a law telling a married couple, or anyone else, that behind—let's stick with the married couple for a minute—behind their bedroom door, telling them they can or cannot use birth control? Does the majority have the right to tell a couple that they cannot use birth control?

Judge BORK. There is always a rationality standard in the law, Senator. I do not know what rationale the State would offer or what challenge the married couple would make. I have never decided that case. If it ever comes before me, I will have to decide it. All I have done was point out that the right of privacy, as defined or undefined by Justice Douglas, was a free-floating right that was not derived in a principled fashion from constitutional materials. That is all I have done.

The CHAIRMAN. Judge, I agree with the rationale offered in the case. Let me just read it to you and it went like this. I happen to agree with it. It said, in part, "would we allow the police to search the sacred precincts of marital bedrooms for tell-tale signs of contraceptives? The very idea is repulsive to the notions of privacy surrounding the marriage relationship. We deal with the right of privacy older than the Bill of Rights. Marriage is a coming together for better or worse, hopefully enduring, and intimate to the degree of being sacred. The association promotes a way of life, not causes. A harmony of living, not political *[faiths]*. A bilateral loyalty, not a commercial or social projects."

Obviously, that Justice believes that the Constitution protects married couples, anyone.

Judge BORK. I could agree with almost every—I think I could agree with every word you read but that is not, with respect, Mr. Chairman, the rationale of the case. That is the rhetoric at the end of the case. What I objected to was the way in which this right of privacy was created and that was simply this. Justice Douglas observed, quite correctly, that a number of provisions of the Bill of Rights protect aspects of privacy and indeed they do and indeed they should.

But he went on from there to say that since a number of the provisions did that and since they had emanations, by which I think he meant buffer zones to protect the basic right, he would find a penumbra which created a new right of privacy that existed where no provision of the Constitution applied, so that he—

The CHAIRMAN. What about the ninth amendment?

Judge BORK. Wait, let me finish with Justice Douglas.

The CHAIRMAN. All right.

Judge BORK. He did not rest on the ninth amendment. That was Justice Goldberg.

The CHAIRMAN. Right. That is what I was talking about.

Judge BORK. Yes. And I want to discuss first Justice Douglas and then I would be glad to discuss Justice Goldberg.

The CHAIRMAN. OK.

Judge BORK. Now you see, in that way, he could have observed, equally well, the various provisions of the Constitution protect individual freedom and therefore, generalized a general right of freedom that would apply where no provision of the Constitution did. That is exactly what Justice Hugo Black criticized in dissent in that case, in some heated terms—and Justice Potter Stewart also dissented in that case.

So, in observing that *Griswold* v. *Connecticut* does not sustain its burden, the judge's burden of showing that the right comes from constitutional materials, I am by no means alone. A lot of people, including Justices, have criticized that decision.

The CHAIRMAN. I am not suggesting whether you are alone or in the majority. I am just trying to find out where you are. As I hear you, you do not believe that there is a general right of privacy that is in the Constitution.

Judge BORK. Not one derived in *that* fashion. There may be other arguments and I do not want to pass upon those.

. . .

Senator SIMPSON . . .

I want to ask you if it is fair to say that you believe that privacy is protected under the Constitution, but that you just do not believe that there is a general and unspecified right that protects everything including homosexual conduct, incest, whatever—and you mentioned that yesterday. Is that correct?

Judge BORK. That is correct, Senator. I think the fact that I did not get everything I wanted to say out was my fault because I was trying to discuss with Senator Biden and others the constitutional problem. But I think it requires a fuller answer than that and that is this: No civilized person wants to live in a society without a lot of privacy in it. And the framers, in fact, of the Constitution protected privacy in a variety of ways.

The first amendment protects free exercise of religion. The free speech provision of the first amendment has been held to protect the privacy of membership lists and a person's associations in order to make the free speech right effective. The fourth amendment protects the individual's home and office from unreasonable searches and seizures, and usually requires a warrant. The Fifth amendment has a right against self-incrimination.

There is much more. There is a lot of privacy in the Constitution. *Griswold,* in which we were talking about a Connecticut statute which was unenforced against any individual except the birth control clinic, *Griswold* involved a Connecticut statute which banned the use of contraceptives. And Justice Douglas entered that opinion with a rather eloquent statement of how awful it would be to have the police pounding into the marital bedroom. And it would be awful, and it would never happen because there is the fourth amendment.

Nobody ever tried to enforce that statute, but the police simply could not get into the bedroom without a warrant, and what magistrate is going to give the police a warrant to go in to search for signs of the use of contraceptives? I mean it is a wholly bizarre and imaginary case.

. . . [T]he only reason that Connecticut statute stayed on the statute book—it was an old, old statute, dating back from the days when Connecticut was entirely a Yankee State—the only reason it stayed on the statute book was that it was not enforced. If anybody had tried to enforce that against a married couple, he would have been out of office instantly and the law would have been repealed. . . .

CONCLUSIONS

Although not expressly mentioned in the U.S. Constitution, the right of privacy is strongly defended by all sectors of society, liberal and conservative, even though their notions of privacy may differ. The framers cherished privacy as an essential condition for the development of the mind and the foundation for religious liberty. Precisely where the right of privacy ends and the power of government begins is a complex process in which all three branches of government are engaged with the general public.

In its decisions on privacy, the Court initially adopted sweeping and ambitious theories of fundamental rights (*Griswold* and *Roe*). Under heavy criticism from the public—raising core questions of illegitimate judicial power—the Court was forced to carve out a more modest role for itself while recognizing a larger function for elected branches and the states. Having overstepped in *Roe*, the Court was not about to recognize a fundamental constitutional right to sodomy (*Bowers*) or to a right to die (*Glucksberg* and *Vacco*). In many ways, it was a costly lesson in humility.

Some of the privacy issues are perennial topics of debate, such as reputation and the scope of the Fourth Amendment. Other issues, including the quartering of troops proscribed by the Third Amendment, seem archaic. A number of the privacy issues of recent decades are controversies brought about by technology, ranging from electronic surveillance to medical advances that affect the right of abortion and the right to die. On all these issues the announcement of what constitutes privacy may originate at first as an agency regulation, congressional statute, or court decision, with no branch having the final say. Increasingly, state legislatures, governors, and state courts are pursuing their own concepts of privacy, as seen under state constitutions. A number of state constitutions expressly provide for the right of privacy. The driving force behind these governmental actions, whether at the national or state level, are the individuals and the groups pressing their particular principles of privacy.

SELECTED READINGS

BERGER, RAOUL. "The Ninth Amendment." 66 Cornell Law Review 1 (1980).

BLOUSTEIN, EDWARD J. "Privacy as an Aspect of Human Dignity: An Answer to Dean Prosser." 39 New York University Law Review 962 (1964).

BRECKINRIDGE, ADAM CARLYLE. The Right to Privacy. Lincoln: University of Nebraska Press, 1970.

CAPLAN, RUSSELL L. "The History and Meaning of the Ninth Amendment." 69 Virginia Law Review 223 (1983).

CRAVEN, J. BRAXTON, JR. "Personhood: The Right to Be Let Alone," 1976 Duke Law Journal 699.

DEVINS, NEAL. Shaping Constitutional Values: Elected Government, the Supreme Court, and the Abortion Debate. Baltimore, Md.: Johns Hopkins University Press, 1996.

ELY, JOHN HART. "The Wages of Crying Wolf: A Comment on Roe v. Wade." 82 Yale Law Journal 920 (1973).

EPSTEIN, LEE AND JOSEPH F. KOBYLKA. The Supreme Court and Legal Change: Abortion and the Death Penalty. Chapel Hill: University of North Carolina Press, 1992.

EPSTEIN, RICHARD A. "Substantive Due Process by Any Other Name: The Abortion Cases." 1973 Supreme Court Review 159.

FRIED, CHARLES. "Privacy." 77 Yale Law Journal 475 (1968).

GARROW, DAVID J. Liberty and Sexuality: The Right to Privacy and the Making of Roe v. Wade. New York: Macmillan, 1994.

HENKIN, LOUIS. "Privacy and Autonomy." 74 Columbia Law Review 1410 (1974).

LUKER, KRISTIN. Abortion and the Politics of Motherhood. Berkeley: University of California Press, 1984.

MAYER, MICHAEL. Rights of Privacy. New York: Law-Arts Publishers, 1972.

McCLELLAN, GRANT S., ed. The Right to Privacy. New York: H.W. Wilson, 1976.

MILLER, ARTHUR R. The Assault on Privacy. Ann Arbor: University of Michigan Press, 1971.

O'BRIEN, DAVID M. Privacy, Law, and Public Policy. New York: Praeger, 1979.

PEMBER, DON R. Privacy and the Press. Seattle: University of Washington Press, 1972.

PENNOCK, J. ROLAND, AND JOHN W. CHAPMAN, eds. Privacy. New York: Atherton, 1971.

PROSSER, WILLIAM L. "Privacy." 48 California Law Review 383 (1960).

REHNQUIST, WILLIAM H. "Is an Expanded Right of Privacy Consistent with Fair and Effective Law Enforcement? Or, Privacy, You've Come a Long Way, Baby." 23 University of Kansas Law Review 1 (1974).

RUBIN, EVA R. Abortion, Politics, and the Courts: Roe v. Wade and Its Aftermath. New York: Greenwood Press, 1987.

SHATTUCK, JOHN H. F. Rights of Privacy. Skokie, Ill.: National Textbook Co., 1977.

STEINER, GILBERT Y., ed. The Abortion Dispute and the American System. Washington, D.C.: The Brookings Institution, 1983.

WARREN, SAMUEL D., AND LOUIS D. BRANDEIS. "The Right to Privacy." 4 Harvard Law Review 193 (1890).

WESTIN, ALAN F. Privacy and Freedom. New York: Atheneum, 1967.

18

Political Participation

Constitutional interpretations by all three branches have helped shape the rights and privileges of the political process. Previous chapters discussed political participation in terms of free speech, free press, the right of petition, and freedom of assembly. This chapter focuses on voting rights, the conduct of primaries and general elections, reapportionment, campaign financing, and lobbying. An important subtheme running throughout this history is the systematic effort to disenfranchise black citizens, either by depriving them of the right to vote or by diluting their vote through districting schemes.

A. PRESIDENTIAL ELECTIONS

The framers decided against a direct election for the President. Instead, they chose an indirect method that depends on a body of electors equal to the "whole Number of Senators and Representatives to which the State may be entitled in the Congress" (Art. II, § 1). This system is not "anti-democratic" or opposed to the popular will. Citizens still vote for the President, but their choices are state by state rather than expressed though a national referendum. Second, the formula offers an advantage to small states. No matter how small in population, each state has at least three electors. Third, in addition to this initial advantage to small states, the Electoral College offers benefits to populous states and to concentrations of voters within states because electoral votes are awarded on a winner-take-all basis. Fourth, since all but two states follow the winner-take-all principle, the existing system favors the two principal political parties over the interests of minor parties.

In the early years state legislatures generally chose the electors, but all states now provide for popular election of the electors. Voters actually choose a slate of electors for a particular candidate, even though the names of the electors usually do not appear on the ballot. Congress passed legislation to require electors to meet in their state capitals on the first Monday after the second Wednesday in December to cast their votes for President and Vice President. In 2000, that date came on December 18. A successful presidential candidate must garner a majority of the Electoral College (270 out of 538 votes).

Twelfth Amendment. If no presidential candidate wins a majority of electoral votes, the selection goes to the House of Representatives, with each state delegation given a single vote. That process was followed in 1800 when a defect in the Constitution led to a tie vote. The Constitution provided that the electors "vote by Ballot for two Persons." If a political party voted in a disciplined way for President and Vice President, each person would receive the identical number of electoral votes. That happened in 1800 when every Democratic-Republican (the current Democratic Party) elector cast their votes for the two party nominees: Thomas Jefferson and Aaron Burr. The intent was to elect Jefferson as President and Burr as Vice President, but each ended up with 73 electoral votes. After 36 ballots over a six-day period, the House selected Jefferson as President. The Twelfth Amendment, adopted in1804, fixed this problem by requiring electors to vote not for "two persons" but to vote "by ballot for President and Vice President." However, another problem arose in 1824 when electoral votes were split among four candidates: Andrew Jackson, William Crawford, John Quincy Adams, and Henry Clay, throwing the matter into the House again, which elected Adams on the first ballot.

Statutory Action. A candidate who wins a majority of electoral votes may fail to win a majority of the popular vote and may even receive a smaller popular vote than the losing candidate. In 1876, Democrat Samuel J. Tilden polled 4,287,670 votes against 4,035,924 for Republican Rutherford B. Hayes. A majority of the Electoral College at that time was 185. Tilden had 184 to Hayes's 165. After an Electoral Commission created by Congress gave Hayes twenty disputed votes, he was declared President. In 1887, Congress passed legislation in an effort to prevent a repetition of what happened a decade earlier. Congress set up a system that encouraged states to pass legislation for the appointment of electors. If the states followed specified procedures, their decisions would be treated as "conclusive" on Congress when it met to receive electoral votes. 24 Stat. 373, sec. 2 (1887). That provision is now codified at 3 U.S.C. § 5 (analyzed later).

The 2000 Election. Presidential elections worked fairly smoothly until 2000. For thirty-five excruciating days—from election day November 7 to December 12—the contest between Al Gore and George W. Bush kept a dizzying pace. At issue were 25 crucial electoral votes in Florida. One could scarcely leave the house for three hours without discovering, upon one's return, that the legal landscape had (once again) been dramatically altered. At various times rulings were handed down by lower courts in Florida, federal district courts, the 11th Circuit, the Florida Supreme Court (four times), and the U.S. Supreme Court (twice). Sitting in the wings were other political institutions waiting to exercise their constitutional duties: the Florida Legislature and the U.S. Congress. On December 12, the U.S. Supreme Court ruled against a recount requested by Gore and the following day he gave his concession speech. On January 6, 2001, a joint session of Congress officially tallied the electoral votes that made Bush the next President.

This extraordinary election raised many questions. Why did the U.S. Supreme Court take the case? Was its decision persuasive? Who might have won had the recount been allowed to go forward? Were voters (as some claimed) "disenfranchised"? Should the Electoral College be abolished? The controversy provided an educational primer on the election process and the intricacies of voting machines and ballots. Everyone added a word to their vocabulary: *chad* (the piece of paper punched out of a ballot). The election also revealed serious deficiencies in Florida's voting machines, with similar deficiencies no doubt existing in other states. Nevertheless, amidst feverish legal maneuvering by both sides, the political and legal process was followed and delivered a winner.

What Happened in 2000

On the evening of election day, November 7, television networks first projected Gore as the winner in Florida (and therefore President). By early morning, the networks switched to announce Bush as the winner. Gore called Bush to concede defeat but then called back with a retraction. Bush's lead on November 8 stood at 1,784 votes. Because that margin was less than one-half of one percent of the total votes cast, state law mandated an automatic machine recount in all 67 counties. The recount cut Bush's lead to 327.

Florida law offers candidates two ways to challenge election results. One occurs before certification of the election results, the other after. Under Section 102.166, candidates may file a "protest" with the canvassing board, which has authority to call for a manual recount. An initial test recount is conducted in at least three precincts. Under Section 102.168, covering the period after certification, unsuccessful candidates may "contest" an election by filing a lawsuit in circuit court. The complaint must establish grounds to show that the result of the election can be changed or "place[d] in doubt." (See box for details of these two procedures.)

Protest and Contest Procedures

102.166. Protest of election returns

Any candidate for nomination or election has the right to protest election returns "as being erroneous" by filing with the appropriate canvassing board a sworn, written protest. The protest must be filed prior to the time the canvassing board certifies the results for the office being protested or within 5 days after midnight of the date the election is held, whichever occurs later. Requests for a manual recount may also be made by political committees and political parties.

The county canvassing board "may authorize a manual recount," which must include at least three precincts and at least one percent of the total votes cast for such candidate or issue. If the manual recount indicates an error in the vote tabulation "which could affect the outcome of the election," the county canvassing board shall (a) correct the error and recount the remaining precincts with the vote tabulation system; (b) request the Department of State to verify the tabulation software; or (c) manually recount all ballots. If a counting team "is unable to determine *a voter's intent* in casting a ballot, the ballot shall be presented to the county canvassing board for it to determine *the voter's intent*" (emphasis supplied).

102.168. Contest of election

The certification of election, nomination, or the result of any referendum question "may be contested in the circuit court by any unsuccessful candidate for such office or nomination thereto or by any elector qualified to vote in the election related to such candidacy, or by any taxpayer, respectively." A contestant shall file a complaint with the clerk of the circuit court within 10 days after midnight of the date the last county canvassing board certifies the results of the election being contested, or within 5 days after midnight of the date the last county canvassing board certifies the results of that particular election following a protest pursuant to 102.166, whichever occurs later.

The grounds for contesting an election include (a) misconduct, fraud, or corruption on the part of any election official or any member of the canvassing board "sufficient to change or *place in doubt* the result of the election" (emphasis supplied); (b) ineligibility of the successful candidate for the nomination or office in dispute; (c) receipt of a number of illegal votes or rejection of a number of legal votes "sufficient to change or *place in doubt* the result of the election" (emphasis supplied). The circuit judge handling the contest "may fashion such orders as he or she deems necessary to ensure that each allegation in the complaint is investigated, examined, or checked, to prevent or correct any alleged wrong, and to provide any relief appropriate under such circumstances."

On November 9, the Florida Democratic Executive Committee exercised the protest option by requesting manual recounts in four counties: Miami-Dade, Broward, Palm Beach, and Volusia. Bush went to federal district court to bar the manual recount, but the court on November 13 denied his request. Siegel v. Lepore, Case No. 00-9009-Civ (Nov. 13, 2000). Legal action was also started by Democrats to challenge the counting of absentee ballots in Seminole County. With the manual and machine recounts underway, Florida law required that all county returns be certified by 5 p.m. on the seventh day after an election, unless the Secretary of State exercised statutory discretion to accept ballots (such as overseas ballots) counted after the deadline. On November 13, Florida Secretary of State Katherine Harris announced that she would ignore returns of manual recounts received after the statutory deadline of November 14 at 5 p.m.

Conflicts existed between federal and state law regarding absentee ballots received from members of the armed services. Florida law required that the envelopes containing the ballots be postmarked. Federal law (controlling) provided that balloting materials by the armed services be carried "free of postage." 39 U.S.C. § 3406 (1994).

The Volusia County Canvassing Board filed suit in Florida court, claiming that it was not bound by her decision; the Palm Beach County Canvassing Board and the Florida Democratic Party joined as intervenors. On November 14, Judge Terry Lewis ruled that the deadline was mandatory and that he had no authority to "rewrite the Statute" creating another deadline. However, he said that the Volusia Board could amend its returns at a later date and that Harris could exercise her discretion (but "not do so arbitrarily") in determining whether to ignore the amended returns. McDermott v. Harris, Case No. 00-2700 (Nov. 14, 2000). Subsequent to his order, Harris instructed Florida's Supervisors of Elections to submit to her by 2 p.m. on November 15 why they should be allowed to amend certified returns previously filed. After considering their reasons in light of specific criteria, Harris announced on November 15 that the amended returns would not be accepted and that she would certify the results of the presidential election on November 18.

Florida Supreme Court (I). After Judge Lewis denied Gore relief, the Florida Supreme Court on November 21 issued a unanimous ruling in favor of Gore. Guided in part by "the will of the people" as the "guiding principle in election cases," the Court looked to language in the Florida Constitution providing that "[a]ll political power is inherent in the people." It called the right to vote "the pre-eminent right"in the Declaration of Rights of the Florida Constitution. The Court also examined two conflicting sections of Florida law (analyzed later in "Why Did the U.S. Supreme Court Intervene?"). From these provisions, the Court concluded that the Secretary was required to accept returns after the seven-day deadline set forth in Florida law. It moved the November 14 certification deadline to 5 p.m. on November 26. Palm Beach County Canvassing Board v. Harris, Nos. SC00-2346, SC00-2348 & SC00-2349 (Nov. 21, 2000).

U.S. Supreme Court (I). To the surprise of many court watchers, the U.S. Supreme Court on November 24 granted Bush's motion for expedited consideration of a cert petition to consider two questions: (1) whether the Florida Supreme Court, by effectively changing elector appointment procedures after the election day, violated the Due Process Clause or 3 U.S.C. § 5, and (2) whether the Florida Supreme Court changed the manner in which the state's electors are to be selected, in violation of the state legislature's power under the U.S. Constitution, Art. II, § 1, cl. 2:

> Each State shall appoint, in such Manner as the Legislature thereof may direct, a Number of Electors, equal to the whole Number of Senators and Representatives to which the State may be entitled in the Congress:...

In addition, the Court added another question: (3) what would be the consequences of finding that Florida Supreme Court's decision does not comply with 3 U.S.C. § 5? That provision of federal law offers a "safe harbor" for electors appointed in accordance with state law enacted prior to the election day by making their appointment, completed six days before the time fixed for the meeting of the electors, "conclusive" on Congress. In 2000, that meant that states should appoint electors by December 12 (six days before the electors met on December 18). 3 U.S.C. § 5 provides:

> If any State shall have provided, by laws enacted prior to the day fixed for the appointment of the electors, for its final determination of any controversy or contest concerning the appointment of all or any of the electors of such State, by judicial or other methods or procedures, and such determination shall have been made at least six days before the time fixed for the meeting of the electors, such determination made pursuant to such law so existing on said day, and made at least six days prior to said time of meeting of the electors, shall be conclusive, and shall govern in the counting of the electoral votes as provided in the Constitution, and as hereinafter regulated, so far as the ascertainment of the electors appointed by such State is concerned.

During oral argument on December 1, several Justices sharply questioned the ruling of the Florida Supreme Court (see box on next page).

Justices Uneasy About Florida Ruling

Responding to the Florida Supreme Court's use of equitable power to extend a statutory deadline, Kennedy asked: "Isn't that such an amorphous, general, abstract standard that it can't possibly be said to be law that was enacted and in place at the time of the election?" Also on altering the deadline, O'Connor remarked: "Well, but certainly the date changed. That is a dramatic change. The date for certification. Right?" She later asked: "who would have thought that the [Florida] Legislature was leaving open the date for change by the court? Who would have thought that?" Gore's attorney, Laurence Tribe, appeared to make light of the change in deadlines, saying that "it is part of the popular culture to talk about how unfair it is to change the rules of the game." He dismissed the change in deadlines as "nothing extraordinary. It's not like suddenly moving Heartbreak Hill or adding a mile or subtracting a mile from a marathon." Kennedy jumped in with some sarcasm: "In fact, we can change the rules after the game; it's not important. Popular culture."

The Deputy Attorney General of Florida noted that 102.166 authorizes manual re-counts, but Scalia corrected him: "That's different from requires." On a different point, Scalia asked Tribe: "Can I ask you why you think the Florida Legislature delegated to the Florida Supreme Court the authority to interpose the Florida Constitution?" Rehnquist made the same point: "It seems to me a federal question arises if the Florida Supreme Court, in its opinion, rather clearly says that we're using the Florida Constitution to reach the result we reach in construing the statute," referring to *McPherson v. Blacker*, 146 U.S. 1 (1892) for the proposition that Art. II, § 1, cl. 2, gives plenary power to the state legislature to appoint electors.

Some Justices were inclined to leave the matter to other political institutions. Ginsburg argued that the Court has generally deferred to state courts when they interpret to state law: "I mean, in case after case, we have said we owe the highest respect to what the State Supreme Court says is the state's law." Souter suggested it might be better to let Congress resolve the dispute under 5 U.S.C. § 15. Breyer wondered whether the issue was too speculative to warrant intervention by the Court.

SOURCE: Oral argument of December 1, 2000.

The Decision. With a per curiam order on December 4, the Supreme Court vacated the judgment of the Florida Supreme Court. Acknowledging that the U.S. Supreme Court generally defers to a state court's interpretation of a state statute, the per curiam noted that in the selection of presidential electors the Florida legislature was not acting solely under state authority but also by virtue of authority granted under Art. II, § 2, cl. 2, of the U.S. Constitution. The per curiam found considerable uncertainty as to the grounds used by the Florida Supreme Court, particularly the extent to which it saw the Florida Constitution as circumscribing the authority of the Florida legislature under Article. II. The Court was also unclear how much consideration the Florida Supreme Court gave to 3 U.S.C. § 5. Bush v. Palm Beach County Canvassing Board, 121 S.Ct. 471 (2000). The underlying message: Try again, but this time be more careful. Interestingly, nothing in the grant of cert on November 24 or in the per curiam of December 4 mentioned what would later be the key issue: the Equal Protection Clause.

Judge Sauls' Ruling. While the U.S. Supreme Court was considering its case, Judge N. Sanders Sauls of Leon County Circuit Court presided over a case brought by Gore, who contested the state certification of Bush as erroneous. Gore claimed that the vote totals wrongly included illegal votes and failed to include legal votes that were improperly rejected. Much of the two-day trial focused on the legitimacy of counting indented ("dimpled") ballots—where the voter had not punched through the ballot. Were these votes being discovered or manufactured?

On December 4, Sauls announced that he found "no credible statistical evidence, and no other competent substantial evidence to establish by a preponderance of a reasonable probability that the results of the statewide election in the State of Florida would be different from the result which had been certified by the State Elections Canvassing Commission." He found no evidence of illegality, dishonesty, gross negligence, improper influence, coercion, or fraud in the balloting and counting procedures. He also concluded that Gore's request for a partial recount would create "a two-tier situation within one county, as well as with respect to other counties." A two-tier system, he said, would treat voters differently depending upon the county they voted in. Voters in a county with a manual count would have a better chance of having their votes counted. Any remedy requested by a plaintiff would require "a review and recount of all ballots, and all of the counties in this state." Gore v. Harris, Case No. CV 00-2808 (Dec. 4, 2000).

Florida Supreme Court (II). In reviewing Sauls' ruling, the Florida Supreme Court agreed that any recount would have to be done statewide, not just the counties selected by Gore. However, a 4 to 3 Court on December 8 reversed Sauls by granting Gore a manual recount in all Florida counties. The Court held that Sauls had failed to apply the proper standard in determining Gore's burden under the contest statute. Sauls required a "preponderance of a reasonable probability," but under 102.168 it was enough for Gore to show that the results of the election had been "placed in doubt." Chief Justice Charles T. Wells and two other Justices issued strong dissents. Wells flagged a serious problem with the majority's opinion: By failing to provide a meaningful standard for counting ballots, the majority created equal protection problems. Gore v. Harris, No. SC00-2431 (Dec. 8, 2000). On the evening of December 8, Judge Terry Lewis ordered the counting of ballots to begin at 8 a.m. the following day (Saturday) and be concluded by 2 p.m. on Sunday, December 10. He left it up to the canvassing boards to determine the standards for judging the "clear indication of the intent of the voter." Any disagreements would be returned to him for final determination. Gore v. Harris, Case No. 00-2808 (Dec. 9, 2000). In this manner, Judge Lewis promised to supply a single, impartial standard to review these contested ballots. The uniform standard would be imposed afterwards, not before.

Back to the U.S. Supreme Court

Early on the afternoon of December 9, while ballots were being segregated into different categories in Florida and some votes counted, the U.S. Supreme Court ordered a stay to the recount process. In a concurrence, Scalia highlighted the issue that troubled a number of his colleagues: "the propriety, indeed the constitutionality, of letting the standard for determination of voters' intent—dimpled chads, hanging chads, etc.—vary from county to county, as the Florida Supreme Court opinion, as interpreted by the Circuit Court, permits." He also expressed concern that "each manual recount produces a degradation of the ballots, which renders a subsequent recount inaccurate." Bush v. Gore, 121 S.Ct. 512, 512 (2000). Stevens, joined by Souter, Ginsburg, and Breyer, dissented. The case was set for oral argument on Monday, December 11, at 11 a.m.

Florida Supreme Court (III). During oral argument on Monday, O'Connor said she found it "troublesome" that the Florida Supreme Court had not responded to the remand by the U.S. Supreme Court on December 4: "It just seemed to kind of bypass it and assume that all those changes and deadlines were just fine and they'd go ahead and adhere to them." Later that day, the Florida Supreme Court released its opinion in response to the remand. It reviewed its arguments on the "shall" versus "may" statutory conflict and maintained that the November 26 deadline it established on November 11 "was not a new 'deadline' and has no effect in future elections." Footnote 17 indicated that manual recounts were circumscribed by 3 U.S.C. § 5, "which sets December 12, 2000 as the date for final determination to be given conclusive effect in Congress." Palm Beach County Canvassing Board v. Harris, Nos. SC00-2346, SC00-2348 & SC00-2349 (Dec. 11, 2000). If December 12 was indeed the deadline, how could the

Florida Supreme Court on December 8 have set in motion a recount procedure that was almost certainly impossible (given inevitable appeals) to complete by December 12?

U.S. Supreme Court (II). In oral argument, six Justices expressed concern about the inadequate standards for recounting votes in Florida: Breyer, Kennedy, O'Connor, Rehnquist, Scalia, and Souter. Because Thomas had joined the stay order, he was likely the seventh Justice troubled by the lack of standards. When Kennedy asked whether the "intent of the voter" standard could vary from county to county, Gore attorney David Boies said it "can vary from individual to individual."

At about 10 p.m. on December 12, the Court released its opinion reversing the Florida Supreme Court. The per curiam opinion, finding a violation of the Equal Protection Clause because of the standardless manual recounts, said a state "may not, by later arbitrary and disparate treatment, value one person's vote over that of another." The Court held that no recount procedure in place under the Florida Supreme Court's order would both comply with minimal constitutional standards and meet the December 12 date. Seven Justices found constitutional problems with the recount ordered by the Florida Supreme Court, but Souter and Breyer would have returned the matter to Florida with instructions to establish uniform acceptable standards. Rehnquist wrote a concurrence, joined by Scalia and Thomas. Stevens, Souter, Ginsburg, and Breyer issued separate dissenting opinions. BUSH v. GORE, 121 S.Ct. 525 (2000).

Deadlines and Standards. The per curiam suggests that the December 12 deadline came from *the Florida Supreme Court*: "The Supreme Court of Florida has said that the legislature intended the State's electors to 'participat[e] fully in the federal electoral process,' as provided in 3 U.S.C. § 5." The per curiam contains conflicting statements about whether the Florida Supreme Court, or a Florida trial judge, could have issued uniform standards. At one place the per curiam states that for purposes of resolving the equal protection challenge "it is not necessary to decide whether the Florida Supreme Court had the authority under the legislative scheme for resolving whether disputes to define what a legal vote is and to mandate a manual recount implementing that decision." A few pages later, however, the per curiam remarks: "we are presented with a situation where a state court with the power to assure uniformity has ordered a statewide recount with minimal procedural safeguards. When a court orders a statewide remedy, there must be at least some assurance that the rudimentary requirements of equal treatment and fundamental fairness are satisfied." This seems like a pretty clear rebuke to the Florida judiciary, and yet, given the remand of December 4 by the U.S. Supreme Court, Florida courts were no doubt leery of crafting standards that might be taken as the creation of "new law" and thus invite further reversals.

Why Did the U.S. Supreme Court Intervene? Serious issues were created by the Florida Supreme Court when it (1) established a new deadline for issuing the certification, (2) performed a strained statutory interpretation of the conflict between "shall" and "may," and (3) called for a statewide manual recount without uniform standards. Changing the statutory deadline from November 14 to November 26 looked too much like the creation of new law. On statutory interpretation, it is true that there was a conflict between two statutory provisions. 102.111 directed that the Secretary of State "shall" ignore county returns not received by 5 p.m. of the seventh day following an election; 102.112 said that late returns "may" be ignored. It was proper for the Court to treat 102.112 as controlling, because it was added in 1989 while 102.111 went back to 1951. However, the Court created a third category: the Secretary "must" accept late returns up to the Court's November 26 deadline. It transformed statutory discretion ("may") to a mandate. Regarding the lack of uniform standards, the Florida Supreme Court may have been gun-shy about "creating new law" and running afoul of 3 U.S.C. § 5.

In reversing the Florida Supreme Court, the U.S. Supreme Court relied heavily on the December 12 deadline. For several reasons, this analysis was artificial and unconvincing. First, states can forgo the "safe harbor" of 3 U.S.C. § 5 and submit their results on December 18 and even later. Second, the ballots probably could have been counted by December 12 had the Court not issued its stay. Of course, any result of the manual recount announced by December 12 would have been subject to legal challenges, with the case going back to the Florida Supreme Court and probably to the U.S. Supreme Court.

It might have been more presuasive if the Court had issued this ruling: "The standardless manual recount provisions in place in Florida for the presidential election violate fundamental principles of equal protection. We have no authority to create new standards in the middle of the game. Neither does the Florida Supreme Court, a Florida trial judge, or the Florida Legislature. The Florida Legislature has authority to create uniform standards that will satisfy equal protection guarantees, but those standards would necessarily govern future elections, not this one." Instead of relying on the December 12 deadline, the Court could have emphasized the inability of any political institution (judicial, executive, or legislative) to change the rules in the middle of an election contest. Moreover, by stating that it had no authority to issue such standards, it would have looked less "activist" and less intent on arrogating power that belongs in the hands of other political bodies.

Other options were available. The U.S. Supreme Court, by a 7–2 margin, could have given Florida until December 18 to develop acceptable standards for the recount. Florida courts would have had to hear testimony in creating those standards, let the recount go forward, permit Gore and Bush to object to particular ballots, and then allow judicial review by the Florida Supreme Court and the U.S. Supreme Court. This process could not have been completed by December 18, but the spotlight would have been taken off the U.S. Supreme Court and redirected to the impossibility of correcting inadequacies in the Florida system.

Florida Supreme Court (IV). On December 22, the Florida Supreme Court responded to the remand of December 12. It explained that the "intent of the voter" standard it ordered on December 8 was the legislative standard in place as of November 7, 2000, and that "a more expansive ruling would have raised an issue as to whether this Court would be substantially rewriting the Code after the election, in violation of article II, section 1, clause 2 of the United States Constitution and 3 U.S.C. § 5 (1994)." It explained in detail the technical and legal problems of conducting a manual recount. First, it would be necessary to adopt (after opportunity for argument) adequate statewide standards for determining a "legal vote." Judicial review must be available to decide objections raised by the candidates. Moreover, the Secretary of State advised that the recount of only a portion of the ballots required that "undervotes" (when voters did not register a choice for President) be screened out. However, the voting machines were not designed for that function. If a recount of "overvotes" (when voters registered a choice for both presidential candidates) were required, a second screening would be necessary. In creating equipment and developing new software, Florida law requires that the Secretary of State evaluate such changes for accuracy. Finally, the Florida Supreme Court concluded that the development of uniform standards belonged to a different political body: the Florida Legislature. Gore v. Harris, No. SC00-2431 (Dec. 22, 2000).

Some Mopping Up. On January 5, 2001, the U.S. Supreme Court denied cert on several issues that had been decided by lower courts. One involved an 11th Circuit decision rejecting a challenge to absentee ballots cast by overseas voters. The other concerned a suit arguing that George W. Bush and Richard B. Cheney were both "inhabitants" of Texas and thus in violation of the Twelfth Amendment, which prohibits the President and Vice President from being inhabitants of the same state. The Fifth Circuit had ruled that Cheney, who had a home in Dallas, Texas, was a resident of Wyoming. Harris v. Florida Elections Canvassing Commission, 121 S.Ct. 749 (2001); Jones v. Bush, 121 S.Ct. 749 (2001).

Issues Along the Way

1. The Political Context. Complaints about the Florida election were inflamed by some extraordinary factors. The governor of Florida, Jeb Bush, was the brother of George W. Bush. The Florida Secretary of State, Katherine Harris, had co-chaired the Bush campaign committee in Florida. The Florida legislature threatened to appoint its own electors (for Bush) if Gore won a recount. Divisions were rampant on all sides. The national vote for Bush and Gore was close to 50:50. The U.S. Senate was evenly divided, 50 Democrats and 50 Republicans, while the Republicans held a narrow margin in the House of Representatives. The Florida Supreme Court consisted of six Democratic Justices plus a seventh jointly appointed by Democratic Governor Lawton Chiles and the incoming governor, Jeb Bush. The court delivered a unanimous opinion on November 21, favoring Gore, but split 4 to 3 on December 8. The U.S. Supreme Court divided 5 to 4 with its December 12 ruling. Everyone was aware that if neither Gore nor Bush gained 270 electoral votes, the issue would go to the U.S. House of Representatives. Under the Constitution, each state would cast a single vote. Because of the makeup of state delegations, the House would select Bush.

2. Opening Pandora's Box? Critics argued that the U.S. Supreme Court, by speaking broadly about equal protection, invited thousands of lawsuits raising questions about disparate treatment of voters. Some of the language in the per curiam on December 12 was indeed broad: "Having once granted the right to vote on equal terms, the State may not, by later arbitrary and disparate treatment, value one person's vote over that of another." However, the per curiam also noted that "[o]ur consideration is limited to the present circumstances." At a minimum, the decision should stimulate states to adopt clearer standards for determining the meaning of a "legal vote."

3. Did the U.S. Supreme Court "Elect" Bush? The front page story in the *New York Times* on December 13 said that the Court "effectively handed the presidential election to George W. Bush tonight." A more balanced lead might have read: "The Supreme Court sustained the election of George W. Bush by turning back, on equal protection grounds, an effort by Al Gore to manually recount ballots in Florida without an adequate standard." Bush won because he was able, through the popular vote, to gain the necessary 270 electoral votes. He won in Florida, won after the automatic machine recount, and was still winning after manual recounts in heavily Democratic districts. Had Gore been elected on the basis of a Florida recount, it would have been just as inaccurate to say that the Florida Supreme Court "effectively handed him the election."

4. Gore's Popular Vote. Gore and his supporters made much of the fact that he won the popular vote by over 300,000 votes (eventually reaching over 500,000). An interesting statistic, but it has no bearing on the presidential contest. Both Gore and Bush knew what mattered and organized their campaigns accordingly to deliver the only constitutional result that matters: 270 electoral votes. Had the popular vote mattered, Bush would have milked his own state of Texas for the maximum margin and pumped Republican districts elsewhere (such as upstate New York) for additional votes.

5. Did Bush Run Out the Clock? Democrats accused the Republicans of delaying judicial proceedings to prevent a full manual recount. Most of the time, however, was consumed by two decisions of the Gore legal team. First, they tried to prevent the Secretary of State from certifying Bush on November 14 or shortly thereafter. By taking the case to the Florida Supreme Court, Gore successfully moved the deadline to November 26, but that strategy (under the protest phase) ate into the time he needed for the contest phase. Under Florida law, contests begin after certification. Secondly, Gore's request for manual recounts in several districts that were Democratic strongholds looked untenable from the start. Could a losing candidate, say someone running for sheriff in a county, ask that votes be recounted in precincts that went heavily for him? Eventually, the Florida Supreme Court and the U.S. Supreme Court agreed that selective recounts ("cherry picking") were inherently unfair and that only statewide recounts would satisfy constitutional requirements. In public statements, Gore invited Bush to request a statewide recount, but that remedy was never pursued in court by the Gore legal team.

6. Who Won? Bush won at least three times. The manual recount stopped by the U.S. Supreme Court would have produced new votes: some for Bush, some for Gore. Organizations may be able to examine the ballots to see what the final tally might have been, but the results most likely will be inconclusive. First, ballots are damaged after multiple handling by humans and machines. Second, there will be sharp (and insoluble) disagreements on other controversies, such as how to count "dimpled" ballots.

7. Were Voters "Disenfranchised"? The Florida Supreme Court, in the concluding section of its December 8 ruling, referred three times to "uncounted votes." That careless phrase revealed poor judgment, if not demagoguery. All votes *were* counted: at least two times by machines. Many were counted a third time by hand. Justice Stevens' dissent on December 12 accused the majority of "effectively order[ing] the disenfranchisement of an unknown number of voters whose ballots reveal their intent—and are therefore legal under state law—but were for some reason rejected by ballot-counting machines." That argument is disingenuous. To determine whether ballots reveal "intent" raises the question of a lack of standards that troubled seven of Stevens'colleagues.

The issue was not *uncounted votes*. It was "undervotes" and "overvotes." An undervote occurs when a voter registers decisions on a number of issues on the ballot, but does not record (at least to the machine) a vote for President. That is not unusual. Approximately two percent of the voters in America do not indicate a preference for President. They vote on other races and issues. An overvote happens when someone votes for both presidential candidates. The machine does not count such votes (nor should it).

Many voters (white, black, and Hispanic) complained that they were unable to vote, but it was never demonstrated in court that election officials committed fraud or took any other illegal act to invalidate a vote. The Justice Department collected the various charges of voter intimidation and disenfranchisement and had all the political incentive to take legal action but never did, presumably because the evidence was insufficient or unpersuasive. The quality and reliability of voting machines did vary from county to county. Investigations by Florida, the U.S. Civil Rights Commission, and other organizations will highlight the difficulties experienced by voters and suggest ways of alleviating those problems in the future.

8. Illegal Voting. More tangible than the "disenfranchisement" issue were the 2,000 or so votes that were illegal and never should have been counted. These votes came from unregistered voters, ineligible felons, and some citizens who voted absentee first and then voted again at the local precinct after claiming that they had not voted. Some people voted in one county but lived in another. "Fla. Officials Urge Uniform Voting Technology," Wash. Post, Jan. 24, 2001, p. A5.

9. Butterfly Ballot. Objections were raised to the form of the "butterfly" ballot used in Palm Beach County. Appellants claimed that the ballot was defective on its face, confusing to voters, and may have forced citizens to cast a vote for a candidate other than the one they intended to support. As a remedy, they wanted a re-vote, a new election, or a statistical reallocation of the election totals in that county. The trial court denied relief, as did a unanimous Florida Supreme Court, which ruled that the ballot did not constitute substantial noncompliance with Florida election law. Fladell v. Palm Beach County Canvassing Board, Nos. SC00-2373 and SC00-2376 (Dec. 1, 2000). Even if the butterfly ballot survived legal challenges, officials in Florida (and other states using it) should revisit the design to assure that it does not mislead the voter.

10. Absentee Ballots. Democratic voters filed suit to throw out nearly 25,000 absentee ballots in Martin and Seminole counties. They argued that the ballots, which favored Bush over

Gore by about 2 to 1, should be discarded because election officials allowed Republican workers to fix Republican ballot applications by adding voter identification numbers. Judges Terry Lewis and Nikki Clark agreed that the changes to the ballot applications violated state law, but found no evidence of fraud, gross negligence, intentional wrongdoing, or partisan misconduct. Election officials treated Republicans and Democrats differently, but that was because a number of Republican request forms had missing or incorrect voter identification number on them, while there were no similar problems with the Democratic request forms. Although there was not strict compliance with the election law, Florida caselaw only requires "substantial compliance." The two judges decided that the voters were qualified, registered, and had cast valid absentee ballots that should be counted. Taylor v. Martin County Canvassing Board, Case No. 00-2850 (Dec. 8, 2000); Jacobs v. Seminole County Canvassing Board, Case No. CV-00-2816 (Dec. 8, 2000). Their rulings were affirmed by the Florida Supreme Court. Taylor v. Martin County Canvassing Board, No. SC00-2448 (Dec. 12, 2000); Jacobs v. Seminole County Canvassing Board, No. SC00-2447 (Dec. 12, 2000).

Some Lessons Learned

1. Are Courts Political? Many experts and citizens expressed dismay that the Florida courts and the U.S. Supreme Court had become involved in "politics." Writing for the *Washington Post* on December 14 (A25), Robert Kaiser remarked: "Observers on all sides agreed that *Bush* v. *Gore* represented a departure from past Supreme Courts' great reluctance to interfere in purely political issues." In the *New York Times* on December 11 (A22), Linda Greenhouse warned that the Court could lose credibility by "stepping over the fine but nonetheless distinct line that separates law and politics." Why these concerns? The courts are a part of government and regularly decide political matters, including abortion, affirmative action, federalism, public funding of sectarian schools, race-based districting, and reapportionment.

2. Why Let Courts Decide? Courts have a legitimate right to participate in election contests to review accusations of misconduct, fraud, and other charges. The Florida trial courts did an excellent job of airing complaints and educating citizens. Each side brought in experts and statisticians, trying to prove a case. Judges Lewis and Clark ventilated the dispute over absentee ballots, showing convincingly that the irregularities committed by elected officials did not invalidate the votes. Although Judge Sauls was reversed by the Florida Supreme Court, his position that manual recounts had to be done on a statewide basis — and not by selected counties — was accepted both by the Florida Supreme Court and the U.S. Supreme Court. Much of the work by the judiciary was constructive and beneficial.

3. Democracy Under the Microscope. Because of Florida's "sunshine laws," people around the world watched state officials squint at ballots, peer through magnifying glasses to divine voter intent, and hold ballots aloft searching for telltale signs of light showing through. Protesters in Florida gathered around courthouses and the buildings where canvassing board members did their work. They showed up in large numbers outside the U.S. Supreme Court. In none of these spirited demonstrations was there violence or bloodshed. Political and legal channels were available and they played themselves out, peacefully. Quite impressive.

4. Antiquated Voting Machines. Hand counts and litigation spotlighted the variations in voting machine quality from county to county. Across the country, voting systems varied from punch cards to optical scanners to lever machines. Other counties used electronic machines that rely on keyboards or touch-screens to record votes, or paper ballots marked with pen or pencil. States and the federal government will be under pressure to provide the funds necessary to update the voting machines. Punch card machines, discredited because of the chad problem, are likely to be eliminated.

5. Accuracy of Election Results. Just as Gore supporters objected to the accuracy of the results because they failed to include undervotes, so did Bush supporters warn about inaccuracies produced by standardless manual recounts. What we all learned from the 2000 presidential election is that voting results are *approximate*. Machine and human errors make it impossible to produce a totally accurate result.

6. **Abolish the Electoral College?** Because Gore won the popular vote and lost the election, many people want to abolish the Electoral College and elect Presidents directly by popular vote. Adopting that reform may create worse problems. In a close presidential contest with a popular vote system, it would be necessary to do a hand count not only in one state, like Florida, but for the entire country. Not an appealing prospect. Also, depending on the system used for a direct election, the nation is likely to move from a two-party system to a multi-party system. Some people may want that, but they have to think it through. A two-party system tends to push both parties toward the center and counsel moderation. A multi-party system may invite more extreme positions. Finally, the present system of the Electoral College offers benefits to small states and to some interests (labor unions, ethnic groups, etc.) that have leverage in key states. Why would they support a constitutional amendment to eliminate that advantage? Congressional hearings will once again evaluate the practicality of various options.

Bush v. Gore,

121 S.Ct. 525 (2000)

The Florida Supreme Court, divided 4 to 3, ordered an immediate manual recount of all ballots where no vote for Al Gore or George W. Bush for President had been recorded by machines. On the following day, the U.S. Supreme Court issued a stay on the manual recount. Lawyers for Bush claimed that the manual recount violated the constitutional guarantee for equal protection. The Gore legal team argued the importance of counting every legal vote.

PER CURIAM.

. . .

I

. . .

The petition presents the following questions: whether the Florida Supreme Court established new standards for resolving Presidential election contests, thereby violating Art. II, §1, cl. 2, of the United States Constitution and failing to comply with 3 U. S. C. §5, and whether the use of standardless manual recounts violates the Equal Protection and Due Process Clauses. With respect to the equal protection question, we find a violation of the Equal Protection Clause.

[II.B]

The individual citizen has no constitutional right to vote for electors for the President of the United States unless and until the state legislature chooses a statewide election as the means to implement its power to appoint members of the Electoral College....

The right to vote is protected in more than the initial allocation of the franchise. Equal protection applies as well to the manner of its exercise. Having once granted the right to vote on equal terms, the State may not, by later arbitrary and disparate treatment, value one person's vote over that of another....

Much of the controversy seems to revolve around ballot cards designed to be perforated by a stylus but which, either through error or deliberate omission, have not been perforated with sufficient precision for a machine to count them. In some cases a piece of the card—a chad—is hanging, say by two corners. In other cases there is no separation at all, just an indentation [a *"dimpled" ballot*].

The Florida Supreme Court has ordered that the intent of the voter be discerned from such ballots. For purposes of resolving the equal protection challenge, it is not necessary to decide whether the Florida Supreme Court had the authority under the legislative scheme for resolving election disputes to define what a legal vote is and to mandate a manual recount implementing that definition. The recount mechanisms implemented in response to the decisions of the Florida Supreme Court do not satisfy the minimum requirement for non-arbitrary treatment of voters necessary to secure the fundamental right. Florida's basic command for the count of legally cast votes is to consider the "intent of the voter."....This is unobjectionable as an abstract proposition and a starting principle. The problem inheres in the absence of specific standards to ensure its equal application. The formulation of uniform rules to determine intent based on these recurring circumstances is practicable and, we conclude, necessary.

...[T]he recounts in [*Miami-Dade, Palm Beach, and Broward*] were not limited to so-called undervotes but extended to all of the ballots. The distinction has real consequences. A manual recount of all ballots identifies not only those ballots which show no vote but also those which contain more than one, the so-called overvotes. Neither category will be counted by the machine. This is not a trivial concern. At oral argument, respondents estimated there are as many as 110,000 overvotes statewide. As a result, the citizen whose ballot was not read by a machine because he failed to vote for a candidate in a way readable by a machine may still have his vote counted in a manual recount; on the other hand, the citizen who marks two candidates in a way discernable by the machine will not have the same opportunity to have his vote count, even if a manual examination of the ballot would reveal the requisite indicia of intent. Furthermore, the citizen who marks two candidates, only one of which is discernable by the machine, will have his vote counted even though it should have been read as an invalid ballot....

In addition to these difficulties the actual process by which the votes were to be counted under the Florida Supreme Court's decision raises further concerns. That order did not specify who would recount the ballots. The county canvassing boards were forced to pull together ad hoc teams comprised of judges from various Circuits who had no previous training in handling and interpreting ballots. Furthermore, while others were permitted to observe, they were prohibited from objecting during the recount.

...Our consideration is limited to the present circumstances, for the problem of equal protection in election processes generally presents many complexities.

The question before the Court is not whether local entities, in the exercise of their expertise, may develop different systems for implementing elections. Instead, we are presented with a situation where a state court with the power to assure uniformity has ordered a statewide recount with minimal procedural safeguards. When a court orders a statewide remedy, there must be at least some assurance that the rudimentary requirements of equal treatment and fundamental fairness are satisfied.

...[I]t is obvious that the recount cannot be conducted in compliance with the requirements of equal protection and due process without substantial additional work. It would require not only the adoption (after opportunity for argument) of adequate statewide standards for determining what is a legal vote, and practicable procedures to implement them, but also orderly judicial review of any disputed matters that might arise....

The Supreme Court of Florida has said that the legislature intended the State's electors to "participat[e] fully in the federal electoral process," as provided in 3 U. S. C. §5....That statute, in turn, requires that any controversy or contest that is designed to lead to a conclusive selection of electors be completed by December 12. That date is upon us, and there is no recount procedure in place under the State Supreme Court's order that comports with minimal constitutional standards. Because it is evident that any recount seeking to meet the December 12 date will be unconstitutional for the reasons we have discussed, we reverse the judgment of the Supreme Court of Florida ordering a recount to proceed.

Seven Justices of the Court agree that there are constitutional problems with the recount ordered by the Florida Supreme Court that demand a remedy [*referring to dissenting opinions by Souter and Breyer*]....The only disagreement is as to the remedy. Because the Florida Supreme Court has said that the Florida Legislature intended to obtain the safe-harbor benefits of 3 U. S. C. §5, JUSTICE BREYER's proposed remedy — remanding to the Florida Supreme Court for its ordering of a constitutionally proper contest until December 18 — contemplates action in violation of the Florida election code, and hence could not be part of an "appropriate" order authorized by Fla. Stat. §102.168(8) (2000).

. . .

None are more conscious of the vital limits on

judicial authority than are the members of this Court, and none stand more in admiration of the Constitution's design to leave the selection of the President to the people, through their legislatures, and to the political sphere. When contending parties invoke the process of the courts, however, it becomes our unsought responsibility to resolve the federal and constitutional issues the judicial system has been forced to confront.

The judgment of the Supreme Court of Florida is reversed, and the case is remanded for further proceedings not inconsistent with this opinion.

. . .

It is so ordered.

CHIEF JUSTICE REHNQUIST, with whom JUSTICE SCALIA and JUSTICE THOMAS join, concurring.

. . .

I

. . .

In most cases, comity and respect for federalism compel us to defer to the decisions of state courts on issues of state law. That practice reflects our understanding that the decisions of state courts are definitive pronouncements of the will of the States as sovereigns.... But there are a few exceptional cases in which the Constitution imposes a duty or confers a power on a particular branch of a State's government. This is one of them....

.... Isolated sections of the [*state*] code may well admit of more than one interpretation, but the general coherence of the legislative scheme may not be altered by judicial interpretation so as to wholly change the statutorily provided apportionment of responsibility among these various bodies. In any election but a Presidential election, the Florida Supreme Court can give as little or as much deference to Florida's executives as it chooses, so far as Article II is concerned, and this Court will have no cause to question the court's actions. But, with respect to a Presidential election, the court must be both mindful of the legislature's role under Article II in choosing the manner of appointing electors and deferential to those bodies expressly empowered by the legislature to carry out its constitutional mandate.

. . .

This inquiry does not imply a disrespect for state *courts* but rather a respect for the constitutionally prescribed role of state *legislatures.* To attach definitive weight to the pronouncement of a state court, when the very question at issue is whether the court has actually departed from the statutory meaning, would be to abdicate our responsibility to enforce the explicit requirements of Article II.

II

. . .

[*The first decision by the Florida Supreme Court on November 21, 2000*] extended the 7-day statutory certification deadline established by the legislature. This modification of the code, by lengthening the protest period, necessarily shortened the contest period for Presidential elections. Underlying the extension of the certification deadline and the shortchanging of the contest period was, presumably, the clear implication that certification was a matter of significance: The certified winner would enjoy presumptive validity, making a contest proceeding by the losing candidate an uphill battle. In its latest opinion, however, the court empties certification of virtually all legal consequence during the contest, and in doing so departs from the provisions enacted by the Florida Legislature.

... [T]he court's interpretation of "legal vote," and hence its decision to order a contest-period recount, plainly departed from the legislative scheme. Florida statutory law cannot reasonably be thought to require the counting of improperly marked ballots....

...No reasonable person would call it "an error in the vote tabulation," FLA. STAT. §102.166(5), or a "rejection of legal votes," FLA. STAT. §102.168(3)(c), when electronic or electro-mechanical equipment performs precisely in the manner designed, and fails to count those ballots that are not marked in the manner that these voting instructions explicitly and prominently specify. The scheme that the Florida Supreme Court's opinion attributes to the legislature is one in which machines are *required* to be "capable of correctly counting votes," §101.5606(4), but which nonetheless regularly produces elections in which legal votes are predictably not tabulated, so that in close elections manual recounts are regularly required. This is of course absurd. The Secretary of State, who is authorized by law to issue binding interpretations of the election code, §§97.012, 106.23, rejected this peculiar reading of the statutes....

III

The scope and nature of the remedy ordered by the Florida Supreme Court jeopardizes the "legislative wish" to take advantage of the safe harbor provided by 3 U. S. C. §5.... December 12, 2000, is the last date for a final determination of the Florida electors that will satisfy §5. Yet in the late afternoon of December 8th—four days before this deadline—the Supreme Court of Florida ordered recounts of tens of thousands of so-called "undervotes" spread through 64 of the State's 67 counties. This was done in a search for elusive—perhaps delusive—certainty as to the exact count of 6 million votes. But no one claims that these ballots have not previously been tabulated; they were initially read by voting machines at the time of the election, and thereafter reread by virtue of Florida's automatic recount provision. No one claims there was any fraud in the election. The Supreme Court of Florida ordered this additional recount under the provision of the election code giving the circuit judge the authority to provide relief that is "appropriate under such circumstances." Fla. Stat. §102.168(8) (2000).

Surely when the Florida Legislature empowered the courts of the State to grant "appropriate" relief, it must have meant relief that would have become final by the cutoff date of 3 U. S. C. §5. In light of the inevitable legal challenges and ensuing appeals to the Supreme Court of Florida and petitions for certiorari to this Court, the entire recounting process could not possibly be completed by that date....

...[T]he remedy prescribed by the Supreme Court of Florida cannot be deemed an "appropriate" one as of December 8. It significantly departed from the statutory framework in place on November 7, and authorized open-ended further proceedings which could not be completed by December 12, thereby preventing a final determination by that date.

For these reasons, in addition to those given in the *per curiam*, we would reverse.

JUSTICE STEVENS, with whom JUSTICE GINSBURG and JUSTICE BREYER join, dissenting.

. . .

The federal questions that ultimately emerged in this case are not substantial.... The legislative power in Florida is subject to judicial review pursuant to Article V of the Florida Constitution, and nothing in Article II of the Federal Constitution frees the state legislature from the constraints in the state constitution that created it. Moreover, the Florida Legislature's own decision to employ a unitary code for all elections indicates that it intended the Florida Supreme Court to play the same role in Presidential elections that it has historically played in resolving electoral disputes. The Florida Supreme Court's exercise of appellate jurisdiction therefore was wholly consistent with, and indeed contemplated by, the grant of authority in Article II.

...Neither §5 nor Article II grants federal judges any special authority to substitute their views for those of the state judiciary on matters of state law.

Nor are petitioners correct in asserting that the failure of the Florida Supreme Court to specify in detail the precise manner in which the "intent of the voter," Fla. Stat. §101.5614(5) (Supp. 2001), is to be determined rises to the level of a constitutional violation.... [T]here is no reason to think that the guidance provided to the factfinders, specifically the various canvassing boards, by the "intent of the voter" standard is any less sufficient—or will lead to results any less uniform—than, for example, the "beyond a reasonable doubt" standard employed everyday by ordinary citizens in courtrooms across this country.

Admittedly, the use of differing substandards for determining voter intent in different counties employing similar voting systems may raise serious concerns. Those concerns are alleviated—if not eliminated—by the fact that a single impartial magistrate [*Judge Terry Lewis*] will ultimately adjudicate all objections arising from the recount process....

Even assuming that aspects of the remedial scheme might ultimately be found to violate the Equal Protection Clause, I could not subscribe to the majority's disposition of the case.... [T]he appropriate course of action would be to remand to allow more specific procedures for implementing the legislature's uniform general standard to be established.

In the interest of finality, however, the majority effectively orders the disenfranchisement of an unknown number of voters whose ballots reveal their intent—and are therefore legal votes under state law—but were for some reason rejected by ballot-counting machines. It does so on the basis of the deadlines set forth in Title 3 of the United States Code.... But, as I have already noted, those provisions merely provide rules of decision for Congress to follow when selecting among conflicting slates of electors.... They do not prohibit a State from counting what the majority concedes to be legal votes until a bona fide winner is determined. Indeed, in 1960, Hawaii appointed two slates of electors and Congress chose to count the one appointed on January 4, 1961, well after the Title 3 deadlines....

What must underlie petitioners' entire federal assault on the Florida election procedures is an unstated lack of confidence in the impartiality and capacity of the state judges who would make the critical decisions if the vote count were to proceed. Otherwise, their position is wholly without merit. The endorsement of that position by the majority of this Court can only lend credence to the most cynical appraisal of the work of judges throughout the land.... Although we may never know with complete certainty the identity of the winner of this year's Presidential election, the identity of the loser is perfectly clear. It is the Nation's confidence in the judge as an impartial guardian of the rule of law.

I respectfully dissent.

JUSTICE SOUTER, with whom JUSTICE BREYER joins and with whom JUSTICE STEVENS and JUSTICE GINSBURG join with regard to all but Part C, dissenting.

. . .

C

It is only on the third issue before us [*equal protection or due process*] that there is a meritorious argument for relief, as this Court's *Per Curiam* opinion recognizes. It is an issue that might well have been dealt with adequately by the Florida courts if the state proceedings had not been interrupted, and if not disposed of at the state level it could have been considered by the Congress in any electoral vote dispute....

Petitioners have raised an equal protection claim (or, alternatively, a due process claim,...) in the charge that unjustifiably disparate standards are applied in different electoral jurisdictions to otherwise identical facts. It is true that the Equal Protection Clause does not forbid the use of a variety of voting mechanisms within a jurisdiction, even though different mechanisms will have different levels of effectiveness in recording voters' intentions; local variety can be justified by concerns about cost, the potential value of innovation, and so on. But evidence in the record here suggests that a different order of disparity obtains

under rules for determining a voter's intent that have been applied (and could continue to be applied) to identical types of ballots used in identical brands of machines and exhibiting identical physical characteristics (such as "hanging" or "dimpled" chads)....I can conceive of no legitimate state interest served by these differing treatments of the expressions of voters' fundamental rights. The differences appear wholly arbitrary.

In deciding what to do about this, we should take account of the fact that electoral votes are due to be cast in six days. I would therefore remand the case to the courts of Florida with instructions to establish uniform standards for evaluating the several types of ballots that have prompted differing treatments, to be applied within and among counties when passing on such identical ballots in any further recounting (or successive recounting) that the courts might order.

Unlike the majority, I see no warrant for this Court to assume that Florida could not possibly comply with this requirement before the date set for the meeting of electors, December 18....

I respectfully dissent.

JUSTICE GINSBURG, with whom JUSTICE STEVENS joins, and with whom JUSTICE SOUTER and JUSTICE BREYER join as to Part I, dissenting.

I

. . .

No doubt there are cases in which the proper application of federal law may hinge on interpretations of state law. Unavoidably, this Court must sometimes examine state law in order to protect federal rights....

The extraordinary setting of this case has obscured the ordinary principle that dictates its proper resolution: Federal courts defer to state high courts' interpretations of their state's own law. This principle reflects the core of federalism, on which all agree.... Were the other members of this Court as mindful as they generally are of our system of dual sovereignty, they would affirm the judgment of the Florida Supreme Court.

II

...[T]he December 12 "deadline" for bringing Florida's electoral votes into 3 U. S. C. §5's safe harbor lacks the significance the Court assigns it. Were that date to pass, Florida would still be entitled to deliver electoral votes Congress must count unless both Houses find that the votes "ha[d] not been...regularly given." 3 U. S. C. §15. The statute identifies other significant dates. See, e.g., §7 (specifying December 18 as the date electors "shall meet and give their votes"); §12 (specifying "the fourth Wednesday in December" — this year, December 27 — as the date on which Congress, if it has not received a State's electoral votes, shall request the state secretary of state to send a certified return immediately). But none of these dates has ultimate significance in light of Congress' detailed provisions for determining, on "the sixth day of January," the validity of electoral votes. §15.

. . .

I dissent.

JUSTICE BREYER, with whom JUSTICE STEVENS and JUSTICE GINSBURG join except as to Part I-A-1, and with whom JUSTICE SOUTER joins as to Part I, dissenting.

The Court was wrong to take this case. It was wrong to grant a stay. It should now vacate that stay and permit the Florida Supreme Court to decide whether the recount should resume.

I

The political implications of this case for the country are momentous. But the federal legal questions presented, with one exception, are insubstantial.

A

1

The majority's third concern does implicate principles of fundamental fairness. The majority concludes that the Equal Protection Clause requires that a manual recount be governed not only by the uniform general standard of the "clear intent of the voter," but also by uniform subsidiary standards (for example, a uniform determination whether indented, but not perforated, "undervotes" should count). The opinion points out that the Florida Supreme Court ordered the inclusion of Broward County's undercounted "legal votes" even though those votes included ballots that were not perforated but simply "dimpled," while newly recounted ballots from other counties will likely include only votes determined to be "legal" on the basis of a stricter standard. In light of our previous remand, the Florida Supreme Court may have been reluctant to adopt a more

specific standard than that provided for by the legislature for fear of exceeding its authority under Article II. However, since the use of different standards could favor one or the other of the candidates,...I agree that, in these very special circumstances, basic principles of fairness may well have counseled the adoption of a uniform standard to address the problem....

2

Nonetheless, there is no justification for the majority's remedy, which is simply to reverse the lower court and halt the recount entirely. An appropriate remedy would be, instead, to remand this case with instructions that, even at this late date, would permit the Florida Supreme Court to require recounting *all* undercounted votes in Florida, including those from Broward, Volusia, Palm Beach, and Miami-Dade Counties, whether or not previously recounted prior to the end of the protest period, and to do so in accordance with a single-uniform substandard.

. . .

II

...[T]he selection of the President is of fundamental national importance. But that importance is political, not legal. And this Court should resist the temptation unnecessarily to resolve tangential legal disputes, where doing so threatens to determine the outcome of the election.

The Constitution and federal statutes themselves make clear that restraint is appropriate. They set forth a road map of how to resolve disputes about electors, even after an election as close as this one. That road map foresees resolution of electoral disputes by *state* courts. See 3 U. S. C. §5 (providing that, where a "State shall have provided, by laws enacted prior to [election day], for its final determination of any controversy or contest concerning the appointment of...electors...by *judicial* or other methods," the subsequently chosen electors enter a safe harbor free from congressional challenge). But it nowhere provides for involvement by the United States Supreme Court.

To the contrary, the Twelfth Amendment commits to Congress the authority and responsibility to count electoral votes. A federal statute, the Electoral Count Act, enacted after the close 1876 Hayes-Tilden Presidential election, specifies that, after States have tried to resolve disputes (through "judicial" or other means), Congress is the body primarily authorized to resolve remaining disputes. See Electoral Count Act of 1887, 24 Stat. 373, 3 U. S. C. §§5, 6, and 15.

...Justice Brandeis once said of the Court, "The most important thing we do is not doing."...What it does today, the Court should have left undone. I would repair the damage done as best we now can, by permitting the Florida recount to continue under uniform standards.

I respectfully dissent.

B. VOTING RIGHTS

The right to vote would seem inherent in the republican form of government envisaged in the Constitution. "The United States shall guarantee to every State in this Union a Republican Form of Government." Art. IV, § 4. Nevertheless, it took the Fifteenth Amendment, ratified in 1870, to establish the right of blacks to vote. A unanimous Supreme Court in 1875, announcing that the Constitution "does not confer the right of suffrage upon any one," denied that women were entitled to vote as a privilege and immunity protected by the Constitution. Minor v. Happersett, 88 U.S. 162, 178 (1875). Yet in 1886 a unanimous opinion of the Court could refer to voting as "a fundamental political right, because preservative of all rights." Yick Wo v. Hopkins, 118 U.S. 356, 370 (1886). Not until 1920, with the Nineteenth Amendment, did women gain the *general* right to vote. (They had voted in some states.)

Voting rights in America have been hammered out by state action, judicial decisions, congressional initiatives, and constitutional amendment. Members of the House of Representatives are chosen directly by the people. Senators were originally selected by state legislatures but have been elected directly by the people after ratification of the Seventeenth Amendment in 1913. The time, place, and manner of elections of Representatives and Senators are left to the states; Congress may alter state regulations except as to the place of choosing Senators. Art. I, § 4, Cl. 1; Amend. XVII.

Fifteenth Amendment

Congress passed the Enforcement Act of 1870 to guarantee blacks the right to vote in state elections. 16 Stat. 140. Using a strict dual-federalism model, the Supreme Court eviscerated the statute by holding that it was not "appropriate legislation" under Section 2 of the Fifteenth Amendment. It said that the Amendment "does not confer the right of suffrage upon any one." United States v. Reese, 92 U.S. 214, 217 (1876). Another decision further undermined the Enforcement Act by holding that jurisdiction and sovereignty to bring indictments under the statute rested solely with the states. United States v. Cruikshank, 92 U.S. 542 (1876). The Court did sustain the power of Congress, in elections for U.S. Representatives, to enact penalties for those who stuff the ballot box. Ex parte Siebold, 100 U.S. 371 (1880).

A few years later, a unanimous Court upheld a congressional statute that prohibited two or more persons from conspiring to threaten or intimidate any citizen (in this case a black) from exercising the right to vote for national office. The Court stated that the Fifteenth Amendment conferred upon blacks the right to vote "and Congress has the power to protect and enforce that right." Ex parte Yarbrough, 110 U.S. 651, 665 (1884). See also United States v. Mosley, 238 U.S. 383 (1915); Swafford v. Templeton, 185 U.S. 487 (1902); Wiley v. Sinkler, 179 U.S. 58 (1900).

States tried to nullify the Fifteenth Amendment by adopting a "Grandfather Clause," extending voting rights only to those who were entitled to vote before the Amendment. These tactics were overturned by the Court in 1915. Guinn v. United States, 238 U.S. 347; Myers v.

Anderson, 238 U.S. 368. Oklahoma then changed its law to provide that those who had voted in 1914 automatically remained qualified voters. This requirement affected only blacks, forcing them to apply between April 30 and May 11, 1916, or risk permanent disfranchisement. The Court held the statute unconstitutional, remarking that the Fifteenth Amendment "nullifies sophisticated as well as simple-minded modes of discrimination." Lane v. Wilson, 307 U.S. 268, 275 (1939).

In 2000, the Court relied on the Fifteenth Amendment to strike down a Hawaiian voting restriction designed to benefit persons whose ancestry qualified them as either a "Hawaiian" or "native Hawaiian." Using ancestry as a proxy for race represented a prohibited race-based voting qualification. In this case the Fifteenth Amendment was used to safeguard the rights of a white man. Rice v. Cayetano, 120 S.Ct. 1044 (2000).

Primaries

In some states, a primary election victory is tantamount to winning the general election. Although the Fifteenth Amendment protected the right of blacks to vote, some states restricted that right to the general election and used different strategems to bar blacks from participating in primary elections. In the "white primary" cases, the Supreme Court reviewed a Texas statute that barred blacks from voting in the Democratic party primary for U.S. Senator and Representatives. A unanimous Court held that this violated the Fourteenth Amendment. Texas claimed that the suit was political and hence inappropriate for the courts, an objection Justice Holmes called "little more than a play upon words." Nixon v. Herndon, 273 U.S. 536, 540 (1927).

Texas tried to achieve the same result through a different method. It gave state political parties the power to prescribe qualifications for party membership, including the right to vote. The Democratic party then adopted a resolution that only white Democrats could participate in primaries. By a 5–4 vote, the Court held the statute in violation of the Fourteenth Amendment. It rejected the argument that the Amendment operates against the states, not private parties (in this case, officials of the Democratic party). The Court pointed out that the statute lodged the power to determine voter qualification in the executive committee of each party; to that extent the parties were organs of the state. Nixon v. Condon, 286 U.S. 73 (1932).

Three years later, however, a unanimous Court agreed that a county clerk in Texas could refuse to give a ballot to a black who wanted to vote in the Democratic party primary. The party convention, acting on its own without state legislation, had voted to restrict party membership to whites. The Court decided that the clerk was not a state officer, there was no "state action," and the conduct did not violate the federal Constitution. Grovey v. Townsend, 295 U.S. 45 (1935). In 1941 the Court backed away from *Grovey* by holding that election officials in a Louisiana primary (conducted at public expense) acted "under color of" state law in altering and falsely counting ballots. Voters had a right under the U.S. Constitution to cast their ballots and have them counted. United States v. Classic, 313 U.S. 299 (1941). *Grovey* was finally overruled by the Court in 1944, when it declared (8 to 1) that Texas could not exclude blacks by limiting participation in state conventions to white citizens. This was held to be state action in violation of the Fifteenth Amendment. SMITH v. ALLWRIGHT, 321 U.S. 649 (1944).

This ruling did not exhaust the bag of tricks. Texas excluded blacks from participating in elections conducted by the Jaybird Democratic Association, which selected candidates for county offices. These candidates were invariably the ones nominated to run in the Democratic primary and elected to office. The Jaybirds claimed that their association was not a political party but a self-governing voluntary club. Although the elections for candidates were not governed by state laws and did not use state machinery or state funds, an 8–1 Court held that the process violated the Fifteenth Amendment. The Democratic primary and the general election became "no more than the perfunctory ratifiers of the choice that has already been made in Jaybird elections from which Negroes have been excluded." Terry v. Adams, 345 U.S. 461, 469 (1953).

Poll Taxes

Another technique for restricting or discouraging the black vote was to require payment of a poll tax before a person could register to vote. This type of tax was upheld by the Court in Breedlove v. Suttles, 302 U.S. 277 (1937). A later case involved the Virginia Constitution, which required a poll tax to vote. Although some members of the state constitutional convention expressed a desire to eliminate the black vote in Virginia, a three-judge federal court in 1951 found insufficient evidence that the state requirement discriminated against blacks. Butler v. Thompson, 97 F.Supp. 17, 21 (E.D. Va. 1951). A per curiam ruling by the Supreme Court affirmed this judgment. Only Justice Douglas dissented. Butler v. Thompson, 341 U.S. 937 (1951).

Congress took steps to eliminate the poll tax in federal elections. By 1962, when both the House and the Senate passed the Twenty-fourth Amendment, only five states used the tax: Alabama, Arkansas, Mississippi, Texas, and Virginia. The Amendment, ratified in 1964, provides that the right of the U.S. citizens to vote in any primary or other election for federal office "shall not be denied or abridged by the United States or any State by reason of failure to pay any poll tax or other tax."

States were still permitted to use poll taxes for state and local elections. In the Voting Rights Act of 1965, Congress declared that the poll tax placed an unreasonable hardship on voter rights and did not bear a reasonable relationship to any legitimate state interest. It also authorized the Attorney General to institute actions against state poll taxes and gave federal courts jurisdiction to decide these cases. Attorney General Katzenbach supported a challenge to the poll tax brought by Annie E. Harper. With this case as the vehicle, the Supreme Court declared Virginia's poll tax for its elections a violation of the Equal Protection Clause of the Fourteenth Amendment. Writing for the Court, Justice Douglas said that voter qualifications "have no relation to wealth nor to paying or not paying this or any other tax." HARPER v. VIRGINIA BOARD OF ELECTIONS, 383 U.S. 663, 666 (1966).

In 1996, the Court held that the Voting Rights Act gives the Justice Department authority to review changes in the rules that state parties adopt for nominating conventions. The change at issue in this case was the imposition of a $35 or $45 registration fee to attend the Republican party convention in Virginia that selected the 1994 Senate nominee, Oliver L. North. The fee, which had not been previously charged, was challenged by three law students as equivalent to a poll tax. A three-judge federal court ruled that the preclearance requirement of Section 5 of the Voting Rights Act did not apply to party conventions, and that the challenge to the poll-tax provisions could be brought only by the government, not by individuals. The Court, split 5 to 4, overturned both of those conclusions. Morse v. Republican Party of Virginia, 517 U.S. 186 (1996).

Literacy Tests

Still another contrivance to limit the black vote was the literacy test. A unanimous Court in 1959 held that states may apply a literacy test to all voters irrespective of race or color. The particular statute at issue, a North Carolina law, required that the prospective voter "be able to read and write any section of the Constitution of North Carolina in the English language." The Court concluded that the law did not, on its face, violate the Fifteenth Amendment. Lassiter v. Northampton Election Bd., 360 U.S. 45 (1959).

The Voting Rights Act of 1965 placed temporary suspensions on the use of literacy tests. This provision was upheld in South Carolina v. Katzenbach, 383 U.S. 301 (1966). In 1965 a unanimous Court held that election commissioners and voting registrars in Mississippi could be sued for using literacy tests and other devices to disfranchise blacks. State techniques had reduced the percentage of black "qualified" voters from over 50 percent to about 5 percent. To register for voting, a citizen of Mississippi had to read and copy any section of the state constitution, *and* give a reasonable interpretation of that section to the county registrar, *and* demonstrate to the registrar "a reasonable understanding of the duties and obligations of citizenship under a constitutional form of government." The opportunities for racial discrimination and abuse were immense. United States v. Mississippi, 380 U.S. 128 (1965). The use of these "interpretation tests" gave the state unbridled discretion to keep blacks from voting. Blacks, even those "with the most advanced education and scholarship, were declared by voting registrars with less education to have an unsatisfactory understanding of the Constitution of Louisiana or of the United States. This is not a test but a trap, sufficient to stop even the most brilliant man on his way to the voting booth." Louisiana v. United States, 380 U.S. 145, 153 (1965).

In the Voting Rights Act Amendments of 1970, Congress enacted a five-year ban on literacy tests for the entire nation. These tests had been used to restrict the registration of blacks, Spanish-Americans, and Indians. The ban was upheld by every member of the Supreme Court. Oregon v. Mitchell, 400 U.S. 112, 131–34, 144–47, 216–17, 231–36, 282–84 (1970).

Residency Requirements

In other cases, the Court ruled that states may not discriminate against members of the armed forces by denying them the right to vote if they moved their home to another state. Carrington v. Rush, 380 U.S. 89 (1965). Residency requirements were also subject to congressional restrictions. In 1970 Congress abolished residency requirements as a precondition to vote for President and Vice President. Such restrictions, it said, bore no "reasonable relationship to any compelling State interest." 84 Stat. 316. This provision was upheld by eight Justices in Oregon v. Mitchell, 400 U.S. 112, 134, 147–50, 236–39, 285–87 (1970). In 1972 the Court struck down residency requirements in excess of 30 days as a prerequisite to register for voting. Such provisions violated the Equal Protection Clause and were not necessary to further a compelling state interest. Dunn v. Blumstein, 405 U.S. 330 (1972). A year later the Court upheld a fifty-day residency requirement. Marston v. Lewis, 410 U.S. 679 (1973); Burns v. Fortson, 410 U.S. 686 (1973).

Civil Rights Statutes

Congress passed the Civil Rights Act of 1957 to protect the voting rights of blacks. If someone was about to engage in any practice to deprive a person of the right to vote, the U.S. Attorney General could seek an injunction. 71 Stat. 637, § 131. This provision was upheld by a unanimous Court. United States v. Raines, 362 U.S. 17 (1960). The Civil Rights Act of 1960 adopted additional measures, including the appointment of "voting referees" by federal judges to protect the right of blacks to register and vote. 74 Stat. 86. The voting-rights provision was strengthened again in Title I of the Civil Rights Act of 1964. 78 Stat. 241.

The Voting Rights Act of 1965 represents the most comprehensive measure since 1870 to protect the voting rights of blacks. The statute suspended literacy tests, authorized the appointment of federal voting examiners, and created federal machinery to supervise voter registration. These statutes, in combination with other political forces, have led to a dramatic increase in the election of black officials (see Table 18.1). To increase the number of Puerto Rican voters in New York, Congress prohibited a state from conditioning the right to vote on the ability to read, write, understand, or interpret any matter in the English language. The statute waived English language literacy requirements for persons who had completed the sixth grade

TABLE 18.1   Growth in the Number of Elected Black Officials

Year	Number	Federal	State	County	Municipal	Judicial/Law Enforcement	Education
1970	1,469	10	169	92	623	213	362
1971	1,860	14	202	120	785	274	465
1972	2,264	14	210	176	932	263	669
1973	2,621	16	240	211	1,053	334	767
1974	2,991	17	239	242	1,360	340	793
1975	3,503	18	281	305	1,573	387	939
1980	4,912	17	323	451	2,356	526	1,214
1985	6,056	20	396	611	2,898	661	1,438
1990	7,370	24	423	810	3,671	769	1,655
1998	8,868	40	587	930	4,277	998	2,017

SOURCE: Joint Center for Political and Economic Studies, Black Elected Officials: A National Roster, 1993, xxii (1994). Updated with information supplied by the Joint Center.

in a school under the American flag (including the Commonwealth of Puerto Rico) where the language of instruction was other than English.

South Carolina filed an original suit to test the validity of the Voting Rights Act. The state claimed that Congress exceeded its constitutional powers and invaded states' rights. Twenty-one states filed amici briefs supporting the statute; five Southern states joined with South Carolina in opposition. With Justice Black dissenting in part, an 8–1 Court upheld all challenged provisions of the Act. The decision gives broad recognition to the power of Congress to enforce the Fifteenth Amendment. SOUTH CAROLINA v. KATZENBACH, 383 U.S. 301 (1966).

Another case challenged a provision that waived the English language requirement for Puerto Ricans. A three-judge court found the provision unconstitutional. Judge McGowan, dissenting, said that Congress had power under Article IV, Section 3, of the Constitution, which gives Congress authority to "make all needful rules and regulations" for American territories. Because Congress had sanctioned schools teaching only Spanish in Puerto Rico, McGowan concluded that Congress could protect the voting rights of Puerto Ricans once they moved to the mainland. Morgan v. Katzenbach, 247 F.Supp. 196 (D.D.C. 1965).

A 7–2 Supreme Court held that the waiver was "a proper exercise of the powers granted to Congress by § 5 of the Fourteenth Amendment." Fact-finding was a legislative, not a judicial, responsibility. "It was for Congress, as the branch that made this judgment, to assess and weigh the various conflicting considerations.... It is not for us to review the congressional resolution of these factors. It is enough that we be able to perceive a basis upon which the Congress might resolve the conflict as it did." Morgan v. Katzenbach, 384 U.S. 641, 653 (1966).

In 1970 Congress extended the Voting Rights Act and lowered the voting age to eighteen for federal, state, and local elections. In signing the bill, President Nixon said that this provision for an eighteen-year-old vote was unconstitutional because Congress lacked authority to extend the suffrage by statute. The issue was taken directly to the Supreme Court, as a case of original jurisdiction, where a 5–4 decision held that the voting age provision was constitutional as applied to national elections but invalid for state and local contests. Oregon v. Mitchell, 400 U.S. 112 (1970). The cost and confusion of dual voting rolls (one established for the federal government and another for state and local elections) created sufficient incentive to override the Court. The Twenty-sixth Amendment quickly passed the House and the Senate and was ratified on July 1, 1971, imposing the eighteen-year-old vote for all national, state, and local elections.

Although Section 2 of the Voting Rights Act provides that voting qualifications or practices may not deny or abridge the voting rights of any U.S. citizen on account of race or color, is discriminatory impact alone sufficient to find a violation of the statute? In 1980 a plurality of the Court held that states are prohibited only from *purposefully* discriminating against the voting rights of blacks. Abridgement of voting rights had to be intentional, not incidental. To be held invalid, the voting plan had to be conceived for the purpose of furthering racial discrimination. MOBILE v. BOLDEN, 446 U.S. 55 (1980).

Nevertheless, on the same day, the Court upheld the power of Congress to go beyond discriminatory purpose to include discriminatory effect. At issue was Section 5 of the Voting Rights Act, which requires that changes in state voting practices be submitted for preclearance to the U.S. Attorney General or a federal judge. Section 5 provides that the Attorney General may clear a voting practice only if it "does not have the purpose and will not have the effect of denying or abridging the right to vote on account of race or color." A 6–3 Court held that Congress had deliberately used the conjunctive (purpose *and* effect) and that this objective was within its power to enact "appropriate legislation" to enforce the Fifteenth Amendment. City of Rome v. United States, 446 U.S. 156 (1980).

Congress responded to *Mobile* v. *Bolden* by amending the Voting Rights Act to allow plaintiffs to show discrimination solely on the *effects* of a voting plan (see reading). The statute borrowed language from an earlier opinion by the Court in *White* v. *Regester*, 412 U.S. 755 (1973). 96 Stat. 134, § 3 (1982). The Court accepted the statute's "results test" to invalidate districting plans that have the effect of diluting the black vote, whether intended by the state or not. Thornburgh v. Gingles, 478 U.S. 30 (1986).[1] Sections 2 and 5 of the Voting Rights Act are litigated with great frequency (see box on next page).

Recent Cases

In three decisions in 1991 the Court broadened the Voting Rights Act to cover judicial elections. In the first, a unanimous Court ruled that Section 5 of the Act requires states to seek approval from the U.S. Attorney General before they proceed with elections for state judges. The case was brought by black voters in Louisiana who claimed that the state's electoral scheme diluted minority voting strength. Clark v. Roemer, 500 U.S. 646 (1991). Earlier, in a summary affirmance of a district court decision, the Court had indicated that Section 5 applied to judges. Martin v. Haith, 477 U.S. 901 (1986), aff'g; Haith v. Martin, 618 F.Supp. 410 (E.D. N.C. 1985).

The other two decisions involved Section 2 of the Voting Rights Act. As amended in 1982, the statute refers to the ability of minority voters to elect "representatives" of their choice. Divided 6 to 3, the Court held that judicial elections are covered by Section 2, as amended. The word "representatives" describes the winners of representative, popular elections, including elected judges. Chisom v. Roemer, 501 U.S. 380 (1991). A companion case also concerned a challenge to the election of state judges. Houston Lawyers' Assn. v. Texas Attorney Gen., 501 U.S. 419 (1991). Both decisions are expected to increase the number of black and Hispanic state judges.

In 1992 the Court split 6 to 3 in deciding that Section 5 of the Voting Rights Act did not apply to an Alabama system that relied on county commissioners to supervise and control the

---

1. For other cases on preclearance under Section 5, see Lopez v. Monterey County, 525 U.S. 266 (1999); McCain v. Lybrand, 465 U.S. 236 (1984); Lockhart v. United States, 460 U.S. 125 (1983); Port Arthur v. United States, 459 U.S. 159 (1982); McDaniel v. Sanchez, 452 U.S. 130 (1981).

Voting Rights Act of 1965

The Voting Rights Act of 1965 suspended the use of literacy tests and authorized the appointment of federal voting examiners to order the registration of blacks in certain states and counties. The Supreme Court upheld the constitutionality of the Act in such cases as South Carolina v. Katzenbach, 383 U.S. 301 (1966) and Morgan v. Katzenbach, 384 U.S. 641 (1966). The two sections of the statute most litigated are Section 2 and Section 5:

Section 2. Provides that voting qualifications or practices may not deny or abridge the voting rights of any U.S. citizen on account of race or color. In Mobile v. Bolden, 446 U.S. 55 (1980), the Court held that abridgement of voting rights had to be *intentional,* not incidental. In response to that decision, Congress amended the Voting Rights Act in 1982 to allow plaintiffs to show that discrimination exists solely on the *effects* (not intent) of a voting plan. The Court accepted this "results test" in Thornburgh v. Gingles, 478 U.S. 30 (1986).

Section 5. Requires that changes in voting practices in certain states be first submitted to the U.S. Attorney General or to a federal district judge in the District of Columbia Circuit. By declaratory judgment a court may approve the change in voting practice. As an alternative, a state may submit the change to the Attorney General, who has sixty days to review it. The Attorney General may clear a voting practice only if it "does not have the purpose and will not have the effect of denying or abridging the right to vote on account of race or color...." In City of Rome v. United States, 446 U.S. 156 (1980), the Court reasoned that Congress had used the conjunctive (purpose *and* effect) to prohibit voting plans that have the *effect* of discrimination.

SOURCE: 42 U.S.C. §§ 1973(a), 1973c (1994).

maintenance, repair, and construction of county roads. In 1986, for the first time in modern history, three blacks were elected as county commissioners, but resolutions were subsequently adopted that prevented the three blacks from exercising the decision-making authority traditionally associated with their offices. The Court denied that the changes brought about by the resolutions were "with respect to voting" within the meaning of Section 5. The resolutions concerned only the internal operations of an elected body and did not have a direct relation to voting. Thus, the changes were not subject to judicial or administrative preclearance. Presley v. Etowah County Com'n, 502 U.S. 491 (1992).

The Court decided in 1994 that a Florida reapportionment plan, which created single-member districts in the two houses of the state legislature, did not violate Section 2 of the Voting Rights Act. "One may suspect vote dilution from political famine, but one is not entitled to suspect (must less infer) dilution from mere failure to guarantee a political feast." Johnson v. DeGrandy, 512 U.S. 997, 1017 (1994). On the same day, the Court held that a single-commissioner form of government in Georgia did not dilute the influence of blacks. The size of a governing authority, said the Court, is not subject to a vote-dilution challenge under Section 2 of the Voting Rights Act. Holder v. Hall, 512 U.S. 874 (1994).

Ballot Initiatives

Unrelated to race is the voting right of citizens to participate in the initiative and referendum petition process. A number of states allow citizens to make laws directly through initiatives placed on election ballots. These initiatives often express positions on constitutional values. In 1999, the Court reviewed three conditions that Colorado placed on the ballot-initiative process: (1) initiative-petition circulators had to be registered voters, (2) they had to wear an identification badge showing their name; and (3) proponents of an initiative had to report the names and the addresses of all paid circulators and the amount paid to each circulator. The Court struck down the conditions on the ground that they significantly inhibited communication with voters about proposed political change and were not warranted by the state's interests. Buckley v. American Constitutional Law Foundation, 525 U.S. 182 (1999).

(The Supreme Court's 1995 decision regarding term limits is treated in Chapter 6. A number of voting rights issues are covered in the next section on reapportionment.)

Smith v. Allwright

321 U.S. 649 (1944)

The statutes of Texas provided for primary elections for U.S. Senators, U.S. Representatives, and state officers. The Democratic party of Texas, which the Texas Supreme Court called a "voluntary association," adopted in a state convention a resolution permitting only white citizens of the state to participate in the Democratic primary. The issue in this case was whether the resolution constituted "state action" in violation of the Fifteenth Amendment. Lonnie Smith, a black, sued an election judge, S.E. Allwright.

MR. JUSTICE REED delivered the opinion of the Court.

This writ of certiorari brings here for review a claim for damages in the sum of $5,000 on the part of petitioner, a Negro citizen of the 48th precinct of Harris County, Texas, for the refusal of respondents, election and associate election judges respectively of that precinct, to give petitioner a ballot or to permit him to cast a ballot in the primary election of July 27, 1940, for the nomination of Democratic candidates for the United States Senate and House of Representatives, and Governor and other state officers. The refusal is alleged to have been solely because of the race and color of the proposed voter.

The actions of respondents are said to violate §§ 31 and 43 of Title 8 of the United States Code in that petitioner was deprived of rights secured by §§ 2 and 4 of Article I and the Fourteenth, Fifteenth and Seventeenth Amendments to the United States Constitution. The suit was filed in the District Court of the United States for the Southern District of Texas, which had jurisdiction under Judicial Code § 24, subsection 14.

The District Court denied the relief sought and the Circuit Court of Appeals quite properly affirmed its action on the authority of *Grovey* v. *Townsend,* 295 U.S. 45. We granted the petition for certiorari to resolve a claimed inconsistency between the decision in the *Grovey* case and that of *United States* v. *Classic,* 313 U. S. 299. 319 U.S. 738.

The State of Texas by its Constitution and statutes provides that every person, if certain other requirements are met which are not here in issue, qualified by residence in the district or county "shall be deemed a qualified elector." Con-

stitution of Texas, Article VI, § 2; Vernon's Civil Statutes (1939 ed.), Article 2955. Primary elections for United States Senators, Congressmen and state officers are provided for by Chapters Twelve and Thirteen of the statutes. Under these chapters, the Democratic party was required to hold the primary which was the occasion of the alleged wrong to petitioner....

The Democratic party of Texas is held by the Supreme Court of that State to be a "voluntary association,"... protected by § 27 of the Bill of Rights, Art. 1, Constitution of Texas, from interference by the State except that:

"In the interest of fair methods and a fair expression by their members of their preferences in the selection of their nominees, the State may regulate such elections by proper laws."...

That court stated further:

"Since the right to organize and maintain a political party is one guaranteed by the Bill of Rights of this State, it necessarily follows that every privilege essential or reasonably appropriate to the exercise of that right is likewise guaranteed, — including, of course, the privilege of determining the policies of the party and its membership. Without the privilege of determining the policy of a political association and its membership, the right to organize such an association would be a mere mockery. We think these rights, — that is, the right to determine the membership of a political party and to determine its policies, of necessity are to be exercised by the state convention of such party, and cannot, under any circumstances, be conferred upon a state or governmental agency."...

The Democratic party on May 24, 1932, in a state convention adopted the following resolution, which has not since been "amended, abrogated, annulled or avoided":

"Be it resolved that all white citizens of the State of Texas who are qualified to vote under the Constitution and laws of the State shall be eligible to membership in the Democratic party and, as such, entitled to participate in its deliberations."

It was by virtue of this resolution that the respondents refused to permit the petitioner to vote.

Texas is free to conduct her elections and limit her electorate as she may deem wise, save only as her action may be affected by the prohibitions of the United States Constitution or in conflict with powers delegated to and exercised by the National Government. The Fourteenth Amendment forbids a State from making or enforcing any law which abridges the privileges or immunities of citizens of the United States and the Fifteenth Amendment specifically interdicts any denial or abridgement by a State of the right of citizens to vote on account of color. Respondents appeared in the District Court and the Circuit Court of Appeals and defended on the ground that the Democratic party of Texas is a voluntary organization with members banded together for the purpose of selecting individuals of the group representing the common political beliefs as candidates in the general election. As such a voluntary organization, it was claimed, the Democratic party is free to select its own membership and limit to whites participation in the party primary. Such action, the answer asserted, does not violate the Fourteenth, Fifteenth or Seventeenth Amendment as officers of government cannot be chosen at primaries and the Amendments are applicable only to general elections where governmental officers are actually elected. Primaries, it is said, are political party affairs, handled by party, not governmental, officers....

The right of a Negro to vote in the Texas primary has been considered heretofore by this Court. The first case was *Nixon v. Herndon*, 273 U.S. 536. At that time, 1924, the Texas statute...declared "in no event shall a Negro be eligible to participate in a Democratic Party primary election in the State of Texas." [*The Court held that the statute violated the Equal Protection Clause of the Fourteenth Amendment, after which the legislature of Texas gave the State Executive Committee of a party the power to prescribe the voting qualifications of its members. In* Nixon v. Condon, *286*

U.S. 73 (1932), the Court held that the Committee action was state action and invalid as discriminatory under the Fourteenth Amendment. In Grovey v. Townsend, *295 U.S. 45 (1935), the Court decided that the refusal of a county clerk in Texas to give a black an absentee ballot, for reasons only of race, was permissible because the clerk was not a state officer and there was no "state action." After* Grovey, *the Court held in* United States v. Classic, *313 U.S. 299 (1941), that Section 4 of Article I of the Constitution authorized Congress to regulate primary as well as general elections.]*

...The fusing by the *Classic* case of the primary and general elections into a single instrumentality for choice of officers has a definite bearing on the permissibility under the Constitution of excluding Negroes from primaries. This is not to say that the *Classic* case cuts directly into the rationale of *Grovey v. Townsend*. This latter case was not mentioned in the opinion. *Classic* bears upon *Grovey v. Townsend* not because exclusion of Negroes from primaries is any more or less state action by reason of the unitary character of the electoral process but because the recognition of the place of the primary in the electoral scheme makes clear that state delegation to a party of the power to fix the qualifications of primary elections is delegation of a state function that may make the party's action the action of the State. When *Grovey v. Townsend* was written, the Court looked upon the denial of a vote in a primary as a mere refusal by a party of party membership. 295 U.S. at 55. As the Louisiana statutes for holding primaries are similar to those of Texas, our ruling in *Classic* as to the unitary character of the electoral process calls for a reexamination as to whether or not the exclusion of Negroes from a Texas party primary was state action.

The statutes of Texas relating to primaries and the resolution of the Democratic party of Texas extending the privileges of membership to white citizens only are the same in substance and effect today as they were when *Grovey v. Townsend* was decided by a unanimous Court. The question as to whether the exclusionary action of the party was the action of the State persists as the determinative factor. In again entering upon consideration of the inference to be drawn as to state action from a substantially similar factual situation, it should be noted that *Grovey v. Townsend* upheld exclusion of Negroes from primaries through the denial of party membership by a party convention. A few years before, this Court refused approval of exclusion by the State Executive Committee of the party. A different result was reached on the theory that the Committee action was state authorized and the Convention action was unfettered by statutory control. Such a variation in the result from so slight a change in form influences us to consider anew the legal validity of the distinction which has resulted in barring Negroes from participating in the nominations of candidates of the Democratic party in Texas....

It may now be taken as a postulate that the right to vote in such a primary for the nomination of candidates without discrimination by the State, like the right to vote in a general election, is a right secured by the Constitution.... By the terms of the Fifteenth Amendment that right may not be abridged by any State on account of race. Under our Constitution the great privilege of the ballot may not be denied a man by the State because of his color.

We are thus brought to an examination of the qualifications for Democratic primary electors in Texas, to determine whether state action or private action has excluded Negroes from participation.... Texas requires electors in a primary to pay a poll tax. Every person who does so pay and who has the qualifications of age and residence is an acceptable voter for the primary. Art. 2955. As appears above in the summary of the statutory provisions set out in note 6, Texas requires by the law the election of the county officers of a party. These compose the county executive committee. The county chairmen so selected are members of the district executive committee and choose the chairman for the district. Precinct primary election officers are named by the county executive committee. Statutes provide for the election by the voters of precinct delegates to the county convention of a party and the selection of delegates to the district and state conventions by the county convention. The state convention selects the state executive committee. No convention may place in platform or resolution any demand for specific legislation without endorsement of such legislation by the voters in a primary. Texas thus directs the selection of all party officers.

Primary elections are conducted by the party under state statutory authority. The county executive committee selects precinct election officials and the county, district or state executive committees, respectively, canvass the returns. These party committees or the state convention certify the party's candidates to the appropriate officers for inclusion on the official ballot for the general election. No name which has not been so certified may appear upon the ballot for the general election as a candidate of a political party. No other name may be printed on the ballot which has not been placed in nomination by qualified voters who must take oath that they did not participate in a primary for the selection of a candidate for the office for which the nomination is made.

The state courts are given exclusive original jurisdiction of contested elections and of mandamus proceedings to compel party officers to perform their statutory duties.

We think that this statutory system for the selection of party nominees for inclusion on the general election ballot makes the party which is required to follow these legislative directions an agency of the State in so far as it determines the participants in a primary election. The party takes its character as a state agency from the duties imposed upon it by state statutes; the duties do not become matters of private law because they are performed by a political party.... This is state action within the meaning of the Fifteenth Amendment. *Guinn* v. *United States,* 238 U.S. 347, 362.

The United States is a constitutional democracy. Its organic law grants to all citizens a right to participate in the choice of elected officials without restriction by any State because of race. This grant to the people of the opportunity for choice is not to be nullified by a State through casting its electoral process in a form which permits a private organization to practice racial discrimination in the election. Constitutional rights would be of little value if they could be thus indirectly denied. *Lane* v. *Wilson,* 307 U.S. 268, 275.

. . .

...In reaching this conclusion we are not unmindful of the desirability of continuity of decision in constitutional questions. However, when convinced of former error, this Court has never felt constrained to follow precedent. In constitutional questions, where correction depends upon amendment and not upon legislative action this Court throughout its history has freely exercised its power to reexamine the basis of its constitutional decisions. This has long been accepted practice, and this practice has continued to this day. This is particularly true when the decision believed erroneous is the application of a constitutional principle rather than an interpretation of the Constitution to extract the principle itself. Here we are applying, contrary to the recent decision in *Grovey* v. *Townsend,* the well-established principle of the Fifteenth Amendment, forbidding the abridgment by a State of a citizen's right to vote. *Grovey* v. *Townsend* is overruled.

Judgment reversed.

MR. JUSTICE FRANKFURTER concurs in the result.

MR. JUSTICE ROBERTS:

. . .

...[T]he instant decision, overruling that announced about nine years ago, tends to bring adjudications of this tribunal into the same class as a restricted railroad ticket, good for this day and train only. I have no assurance, in view of current decisions, that the opinion announced today may not shortly be repudiated and overruled by justices who deem they have new light on the subject. In the present term the court has overruled three cases.

. . .

Harper v. Virginia Board of Elections

383 U.S. 663 (1966)

Annie E. Harper and other residents of Virginia brought this action to have Virginia's poll tax declared unconstitutional. A three-judge district court dismissed the complaint. The Supreme Court decided whether the poll tax violated the Equal Protection Clause of the Fourteenth Amendment. The three dissenters (Douglas, Harlan and Stewart) believed that the decision to invalidate the poll tax at the state level should have been left to Congress or to the states, not to the courts.

MR. JUSTICE DOUGLAS delivered the opinion of the Court.

These are suits by Virginia residents to have declared unconstitutional Virginia's poll tax. The three-judge District Court, feeling bound by our decision in *Breedlove* v. *Suttles,* 302 U.S. 277, dismissed the complaint....

While the right to vote in federal elections is conferred by Art. I, § 2, of the Constitution (*United States* v. *Classic,* 313 U.S. 299, 314–315), the right to vote in state elections is nowhere expressly mentioned. It is argued that the right to vote in state elections is implicit, particularly by reason of the First Amendment and that it may not constitutionally be conditioned upon the payment of a tax or fee. Cf. *Murdock* v. *Pennsylvania,* 319 U.S. 105, 113. We do not stop to canvass the relation between voting and political expression. For it is enough to say that once the franchise is granted to the electorate, lines may not be drawn which are inconsistent with the Equal Protection Clause of the Fourteenth Amendment. That is to say, the right of suffrage "is subject to the imposition of state standards which are not discriminatory and which do not contravene any restriction that Congress, acting pursuant to its constitutional powers, has imposed." *Lassiter* v. *Northampton*

Election Board, 360 U.S. 45, 51. We were speaking there of a state literacy test which we sustained, warning that the result would be different if a literacy test, fair on its face, were used to discriminate against a class. *Id.,* at 53. But the *Lassiter* case does not govern the result here, because, unlike a poll tax, the "ability to read and write... has some relation to standards designed to promote intelligent use of the ballot." *Id.,* at 51.

We conclude that a State violates the Equal Protection Clause of the Fourteenth Amendment whenever it makes the affluence of the voter or payment of any fee an electoral standard. Voter qualifications have no relation to wealth nor to paying or not paying this or any other tax. Our cases demonstrate that the Equal Protection Clause of the Fourteenth Amendment restrains the States from fixing voter qualifications which invidiously discriminate. Thus without questioning the power of a State to impose reasonable residence restrictions on the availability of the ballot (see *Pope* v. *Williams,* 193 U.S. 621), we held in *Carrington* v. *Rash,* 380 U.S. 89, that a State may not deny the opportunity to vote to a bona fide resident merely because he is a member of the armed services. "By forbidding a soldier ever to controvert the presumption of non-residence, the

Texas Constitution imposes an invidious discrimination in violation of the Fourteenth Amendment."...

We say the same whether the citizen, otherwise qualified to vote, has $1.50 in his pocket or nothing at all, pays the fee or fails to pay it. The principle that denies the State the right to dilute a citizen's vote on account of his economic status or other such factors by analogy bars a system which excludes those unable to pay a fee to vote or who fail to pay.

It is argued that a State may exact fees from citizens for many different kinds of licenses; that if it can demand from all an equal fee for a driver's license, it can demand from all an equal poll tax for voting. But we must remember that the interest of the State, when it comes to voting, is limited to the power to fix qualifications. Wealth, like race, creed, or color, is not germane to one's ability to participate intelligently in the electoral process. Lines drawn on the basis of wealth or property, like those of race (*Korematsu* v. *United States,* 323 U.S. 214, 216), are traditionally disfavored.... To introduce wealth or payment of a fee as a measure of a voter's qualifications is to introduce a capricious or irrelevant factor....

We have long been mindful that where fundamental rights and liberties are asserted under the Equal Protection Clause, classifications which might invade or restrain them must be closely scrutinized and carefully confined....

Those principles apply here. For to repeat, wealth or fee paying has, in our view, no relation to voting qualifications; the right to vote is too precious, too fundamental to be so burdened or conditioned.

Reversed.

MR. JUSTICE BLACK, dissenting.

[Black points out that the Court in Breedlove v. Suttles, *302 U.S. 277 (1937), and* Butler v. Thompson, *341 U.S. 937 (1951), upheld poll taxes.]*

Since the *Breedlove* and *Butler* cases were decided the Federal Constitution has not been amended in the only way it could constitutionally have been, that is, as provided in Article V of the Constitution. I would adhere to the holding of those cases. The Court, however, overrules *Breedlove* in part, but its opinion reveals that it does so not by using its limited power to interpret the original meaning of the Equal Protection Clause, but by giving that clause a new meaning which it believes represents a better governmental policy. From this action I dissent.

...All voting laws treat some persons differently from others in some respects. Some bar a person from voting who is under 21 years of age; others bar those under 18. Some bar convicted felons or the insane, and some have attached a freehold or other property qualification for voting. The *Breedlove* case upheld a poll tax which was imposed on men but was not equally imposed on women and minors, and the Court today does not overrule that part of *Breedlove* which approved those discriminatory provisions. And in *Lassiter* v. *Northampton Election Board,* 360 U.S. 45, this Court held that state laws which disqualified the illiterate from voting did not violate the Equal Protection Clause. From these cases and all the others decided by this Court interpreting the Equal Protection Clause it is clear that some discriminatory voting qualifications can be imposed without violating the Equal Protection Clause.

...The equal protection cases carefully analyzed boil down to the principle that distinctions drawn and even discriminations imposed by state laws do not violate the Equal Protection Clause so long as these distinctions and discriminations are not "irrational," "irrelevant," "unreasonable," "arbitrary," or "invidious."... [I]t would be difficult to say that the poll tax requirement is "irrational" or "arbitrary" or works "invidious discriminations." State poll tax legislation can "reasonably," "rationally" and without an "invidious" or evil purpose to injure anyone be found to rest on a number of state policies including (1) the State's desire to collect its revenue, and (2) its belief that voters who pay a poll tax will be interested in furthering the State's welfare when they vote. Certainly it is rational to believe that people may be more likely to pay taxes if payment is a prerequisite to voting.

. . .

MR. JUSTICE HARLAN, whom MR. JUSTICE STEWART joins, dissenting.

. . .

...In substance the Court's analysis of the equal protection issue goes no further than to say that the electoral franchise is "precious" and "fundamental," *ante,* p. 670, and to conclude that "[t]o introduce wealth or payment of a fee as a measure of a voter's qualifications is to introduce a capricious or irrelevant factor," *ante,* p. 668. These are of course captivating phrases, but they are wholly inadequate to satisfy the standard governing adjudication of the equal protection issue: Is there a rational basis for Virginia's poll tax as a voting qualification? I think the answer to that question is undoubtedly "yes."

Property qualifications and poll taxes have been a traditional part of our political structure. In the Colonies the franchise was generally a restricted one....

. . .

Property and poll-tax qualifications...are not

in accord with current egalitarian notions of how a modern democracy should be organized. It is of course entirely fitting that legislatures should modify the law to reflect such changes in popular attitudes. However, it is all wrong, in my view, for the Court to adopt the political doctrines popularly accepted at a particular moment of our history and to declare all others to be irrational and invidious, barring them from the range of choice by reasonably minded people acting through the political process....

South Carolina v. Katzenbach
383 U.S. 301 (1966)

By passing the Voting Rights Act of 1965, Congress acted against states that used various tests and devices to prevent blacks from registering and voting. The statute authorized federal examiners to qualify applicants for registration, entitling them to vote in elections. South Carolina filed suit to have the Act declared unconstitutional as an encroachment on states' rights and a violation of due process protections. The case was one of original jurisdiction, with South Carolina supported by Alabama, Georgia, Louisiana, Mississippi, and Virginia, while the states supporting Attorney General Katzenbach included California, Illinois, and Massachusetts, joined by Hawaii, Indiana, Iowa, Kansas, Maine, Maryland, Michigan, Montana, New Hampshire, New Jersey, New York, Oklahoma, Oregon, Pennsylvania, Rhode Island, Vermont, West Virginia, and Wisconsin.

MR. CHIEF JUSTICE WARREN delivered the opinion of the Court.

By leave of the Court, 382 U.S. 898, South Carolina has filed a bill of complaint, seeking a declaration that selected provisions of the Voting Rights Act of 1965 violate the Federal Constitution, and asking for an injunction against enforcement of these provisions by the Attorney General. Original jurisdiction is founded on the presence of a controversy between a State and a citizen of another State under Art. III, § 2, of the Constitution. See *Georgia v. Pennsylvania R. Co.,* 324 U.S. 439. Because no issues of fact were raised in the complaint, and because of South Carolina's desire to obtain a ruling prior to its primary elections in June 1966, we dispensed with appointment of a special master and expedited our hearing of the case.

Recognizing that the questions presented were of urgent concern to the entire country, we invited all of the States to participate in this proceeding as friends of the Court. A majority responded by submitting or joining in briefs on the merits, some

supporting South Carolina and others the Attorney General....

The Voting Rights Act was designed by Congress to banish the blight of racial discrimination in voting, which has infected the electoral process in parts of our country for nearly a century. The Act creates stringent new remedies for voting discrimination where it persists on a pervasive scale, and in addition the statute strengthens existing remedies for pockets of voting discrimination elsewhere in the country. Congress assumed the power to prescribe these remedies from § 2 of the Fifteenth Amendment, which authorizes the National Legislature to effectuate by "appropriate" measures the constitutional prohibition against racial discrimination in voting. We hold that the sections of the Act which are properly before us are an appropriate means for carrying out Congress' constitutional responsibilities and are consonant with all other provisions of the Constitution. We therefore deny South Carolina's request that enforcement of these sections of the Act be enjoined.

I.

The constitutional propriety of the Voting Rights Act of 1965 must be judged with reference to the historical experience which it reflects. Before enacting the measure, Congress explored with great care the problem of racial discrimination in voting. The House and Senate Committees on the Judiciary each held hearings for nine days and received testimony from a total of 67 witnesses. More than three full days were consumed discussing the bill on the floor of the House, while the debate in the Senate covered 26 days in all. At the close of these deliberations, the verdict of both chambers was overwhelming. The House approved the bill by a vote of 328–74, and the measure passed the Senate by a margin of 79–18.

Two points emerge vividly from the voluminous legislative history of the Act contained in the committee hearings and floor debates. First: Congress felt itself confronted by an insidious and pervasive evil which had been perpetuated in certain parts of our country through unremitting and ingenious defiance of the Constitution. Second: Congress concluded that the unsuccessful remedies which it had prescribed in the past would have to be replaced by sterner and more elaborate measures in order to satisfy the clear commands of the Fifteenth Amendment....

The Fifteenth Amendment to the Constitution was ratified in 1870. Promptly thereafter Congress passed the Enforcement Act of 1870, which made it a crime for public officers and private persons to obstruct exercise of the right to vote. The statute was amended in the following year to provide for detailed federal supervision of the electoral process, from registration to the certification of returns. As the years passed and fervor for racial equality waned, enforcement of the laws became spotty and ineffective, and most of their provisions were repealed in 1894. The remnants have had little significance in the recently renewed battle against voting discrimination.

Meanwhile, beginning in 1890, the States of Alabama, Georgia, Louisiana, Mississippi, North Carolina, South Carolina, and Virginia enacted tests still in use which were specifically designed to prevent Negroes from voting. Typically, they made the ability to read and write a registration qualification and also required completion of a registration form. These laws were based on the fact that as of 1890 in each of the named States, more than two-thirds of the adult Negroes were illiterate while less than one-quarter of the adult whites were unable to read or write. At the same time, alternate tests were prescribed in all of the named States to assure that white illiterates would not be deprived of the franchise. These included grandfather clauses, property qualifications, "good character" tests, and the requirement that registrants "understand" or "interpret" certain matter.

The course of subsequent Fifteenth Amendment litigation in this Court demonstrates the variety and persistence of these and similar institutions designed to deprive Negroes of the right to vote. Grandfather clauses were invalidated in *Guinn* v. *United States,* 238 U.S. 347, and *Myers* v. *Anderson,* 238 U.S. 368. Procedural hurdles were struck down in *Lane* v. *Wilson,* 307 U.S. 268. The white primary was outlawed in *Smith* v. *Allwright,* 321 U.S. 649, and *Terry* v. *Adams,* 345 U.S. 461. Improper challenges were nullified in *United States* v. *Thomas,* 362 U.S. 58. Racial gerrymandering was forbidden by *Gomillion* v. *Lightfoot,* 364 U.S. 339. Finally, discriminatory application of voting tests was condemned in *Schnell* v. *Davis,* 336 U.S. 933; *Alabama* v. *United States,* 371 U.S. 37; and *Louisiana* v. *United States,* 380 U.S. 145.

According to the evidence in recent Justice Department voting suits, the latter stratagem is now the principal method used to bar Negroes from the polls. Discriminatory administration of voting qualifications has been found in all eight Alabama cases, in all nine Louisiana cases, and in all nine Mississippi cases which have gone to final judgment. Moreover, in almost all of these cases, the courts have held that the discrimination was pursuant to a widespread "pattern or practice." White applicants for registration have often been excused altogether from the literacy and understanding tests or have been given easy versions, have received extensive help from voting officials, and have been registered despite serious errors in their answers. [*A footnote observes:* "A white applicant in Louisiana satisfied the registrar of his ability to interpret the state constitution by writing, "FRDUM FOOF SPETGH.' *United States* v. *Louisiana,* 225 F. Supp. 353, 384. A white applicant in Alabama who had never completed the first grade of school was enrolled after the registrar filled out the entire form for him. *United States* v. *Penton,* 212 F. Supp. 193, 210–211."] Negroes, on the other hand, have typically been required to pass difficult versions of all the tests, without any outside assistance and without the slightest error. The good-morals requirement is so vague and subjective that it has constituted an open invitation to abuse at the hands of voting officials. Negroes obliged to obtain vouchers from registered voters have found it virtually impossible to comply in areas where almost no Negroes are on the rolls.

In recent years, Congress has repeatedly tried to cope with the problem by facilitating case-by-case litigation against voting discrimination. The Civil Rights Act of 1957 authorized the Attorney General to seek injunctions against public and private interference with the right to vote on racial grounds. Perfecting amendments in the Civil Rights Act of 1960 permitted the joinder of States as parties defendant, gave the Attorney General access to local voting records, and authorized courts to register voters in areas of systematic discrimination. Title I of the Civil Rights Act of 1964 expedited the hearing of voting cases before three-judge courts and outlawed some of the tactics used to disqualify Negroes from voting in federal elections.

Despite the earnest efforts of the Justice Department and of many federal judges, these new laws have done little to cure the problem of voting discrimination. According to estimates by the Attorney General during hearings on the Act, registration of voting-age Negroes in Alabama rose only from 14.2% to 19.4% between 1958 and 1964; in Louisiana it barely inched ahead from 31.7% to 31.8% between 1956 and 1965; and in Mississippi it increased only from 4.4% to 6.4% between 1954 and 1964. In each instance, registration of voting-age whites ran roughly 50 percentage points or more ahead of Negro registration.

· · ·

II.

The Voting Rights Act of 1965 reflects Congress' firm intention to rid the country of racial discrimination in voting. The heart of the Act is a complex scheme of stringent remedies aimed at areas where voting discrimination has been most flagrant. Section 4(a)–(d) lays down a formula defining the States and political subdivisions to which these new remedies apply. The first of the remedies, contained in § 4(a), is the suspension of literacy tests and similar voting qualifications for a period of five years from the last occurrence of substantial voting discrimination. Section 5 prescribes a second remedy, the suspension of all new voting regulations pending review by federal authorities to determine whether their use would perpetuate voting discrimination. The third remedy, covered in §§ 6(b), 7, 9, and 13(a), is the assignment of federal examiners on certification by the Attorney General to list qualified applicants who are thereafter entitled to vote in all elections.

Other provisions of the Act prescribe subsidiary cures for persistent voting discrimination. Section 8 authorizes the appointment of federal poll-watchers in places to which federal examiners have already been assigned. Section 10(d) excuses those made eligible to vote in sections of the country covered by § 4(b) of the Act from paying accumulated past poll taxes for state and local elections. Section 12(e) provides for balloting by persons denied access to the polls in areas where federal examiners have been appointed.

The remaining remedial portions of the Act are aimed at voting discrimination in any area of the country where it may occur. Section 2 broadly prohibits the use of voting rules to abridge exercise of the franchise on racial grounds. Sections 3, 6(a), and 13(b) strengthen existing procedures for attacking voting discrimination by means of litigation. Section 4(c) excuses citizens educated in American schools conducted in a foreign language from passing English-language literacy tests. Section 10(a)–(c) facilitates constitutional litigation challenging the imposition of all poll taxes for state and local elections. Sections 11 and 12(a)–(d) authorize civil and criminal sanctions against interference with the exercise of rights guaranteed by the Act.

At the outset, we emphasize that only some of the many portions of the Act are properly before us. . . . the only sections of the Act to be reviewed at this time are §§ 4(a)–(d), 5, 6(b), 7, 9, 13(a), and certain procedural portions of § 14, all of which are presently in actual operation in South Carolina. We turn now to a detailed description of these provisions and their present status.

Coverage Formula.

The remedial sections of the Act assailed by South Carolina automatically apply to any State, or to any separate political subdivision such as a county or parish, for which two findings have been made: (1) the Attorney General has determined that on November 1, 1964, it maintained a "test or device," and (2) the Director of the Census has determined that less than 50% of its voting-age residents were registered on November 1, 1964, or voted in the presidential election of November 1964. [*Under this Section 4(b) procedure, coverage was extended to Alabama, Alaska, Georgia, Louisiana, Mississippi, South Carolina, Virginia, twenty-six counties in North Carolina, three counties in Arizona, one county in Hawaii, and one county in Idaho.*]

· · ·

Suspension of Tests.

In a State or political subdivision covered by § 4(b) of the Act, no person may be denied the right to vote in any election because of his failure to comply with a "test or device." § 4(a).

. . .

Review of New Rules.

In a State or political subdivision covered by § 4(b) of the Act, no person may be denied the right to vote in any election because of his failure to comply with a voting qualification or procedure different from those in force on November 1, 1964. This suspension of new rules is terminated, however, under either of the following circumstances: (1) if the area has submitted the rules to the Attorney General, and he has not interposed an objection within 60 days, or (2) if the area has obtained a declaratory judgment from the District Court for the District of Columbia, determining that the rules will not abridge the franchise on racial grounds. These declaratory judgment actions are to be heard by a three-judge panel, with direct appeal to this Court. § 5.

. . .

Federal Examiners.

In any political subdivision covered by § 4(b) of the Act, the Civil Service Commission shall appoint voting examiners whenever the Attorney General certifies either of the following facts: (1) that he has received meritorious written complaints from at least 20 residents alleging that they have been disenfranchised under color of law because of their race, or (2) that the appointment of examiners is otherwise necessary to effectuate the guarantees of the Fifteenth Amendment. § 6(b)

. . .

III.

These provisions of the Voting Rights Act of 1965 are challenged on the fundamental ground that they exceed the powers of Congress and encroach on an area reserved to the States by the Constitution. South Carolina and certain of the *amici curiae* also attack specific sections of the Act for more particular reasons. They argue that the coverage formula prescribed in § 4(a) – (d) violates the principle of the equality of States, denies due process by employing an invalid presumption and

by barring judicial review of administrative findings, constitutes a forbidden bill of attainder, and impairs the separation of powers by adjudicating guilt through legislation. They claim that the review of new voting rules required in § 5 infringes Article III by directing the District Court to issue advisory opinions. They contend that the assignment of federal examiners authorized in § 6(b) abridges due process by precluding judicial review of administrative findings and impairs the separation of powers by giving the Attorney General judicial functions; also that the challenge procedure prescribed in § 9 denies due process on account of its speed. Finally, South Carolina and certain of the *amici curiae* maintain that §§ 4(a) and 5, buttressed by § 14(b) of the Act, abridge due process by limiting litigation to a distant forum.

Some of these contentions may be dismissed at the outset. The word "person" in the context of the Due Process Clause of the Fifth Amendment cannot, by any reasonable mode of interpretation, be expanded to encompass the States of the Union, and to our knowledge this has never been done by any court. . . . Likewise, courts have consistently regarded the Bill of Attainder Clause of Article I and the principle of the separation of powers only as protections for individual persons and private groups, those who are peculiarly vulnerable to nonjudicial determinations of guilt. . . . Nor does a State have standing as the parent of its citizens to invoke these constitutional provisions against the Federal Government, the ultimate *parens patriae* of every American citizen. . . . The objections to the Act which are raised under these provisions may therefore be considered only as additional aspects of the basic question presented by the case: Has Congress exercised its powers under the Fifteenth Amendment in an appropriate manner with relation to the States?

. . .

. . . § 2 of the Fifteenth Amendment expressly declares that "Congress shall have power to enforce this article by appropriate legislation." By adding this authorization, the Framers indicated that Congress was to be chiefly responsible for implementing the rights created in § 1. "It is the power of Congress which has been enlarged. Congress is authorized to *enforce* the prohibitions by appropriate legislation. Some legislation is contemplated to make the [Civil War] amendments fully effective." *Ex parte Virginia*, 100 U.S. 339, 345. Accordingly, in addition to the courts, Congress has full remedial powers to effectuate the constitutional prohibition against racial discrimination in voting.

. . .

We . . . reject South Carolina's argument that Congress may appropriately do no more than to forbid violations of the Fifteenth Amendment in general terms—that the task of fashioning specific remedies or of applying them to particular localities must necessarily be left entirely to the courts. Congress is not circumscribed by any such artificial rules under § 2 of the Fifteenth Amendment. In the oft-repeated words of Chief Justice Marshall, referring to another specific legislative authorization in the Constitution, "This power, like all others vested in Congress, is complete in itself, may be exercised to its utmost extent, and acknowledges no limitations, other than are prescribed in the constitution." *Gibbons* v. *Ogden,* 9 Wheat. 1, 196.

IV.

Congress exercised its authority under the Fifteenth Amendment in an inventive manner when it enacted the Voting Rights Act of 1965. First: The measure prescribes remedies for voting discrimination which go into effect without any need for prior adjudication. This was clearly a legitimate response to the problem, for which there is ample precedent under other constitutional provisions. See *Katzenbach* v. *McClung,* 379 U. S. 294, 302–304; *United States* v. *Darby,* 312 U.S. 100, 120–121. Congress had found that case-by-case litigation was inadequate to combat widespread and persistent discrimination in voting, because of the inordinate amount of time and energy required to overcome the obstructionist tactics invariably encountered in these lawsuits. After enduring nearly a century of systematic resistance to the Fifteenth Amendment, Congress might well decide to shift the advantage of time and inertia from the perpetrators of the evil to its victims. . . .

[The Court upholds the sections on coverage formula, suspension of tests, review of new rules, and federal examiners.]

. . . We may finally look forward to the day when truly "[t]he right of citizens of the United States to vote shall not be denied or abridged by the United States or by any State on account of race, color, or previous condition of servitude."

The bill of complaint is

Dismissed.

Mr. Justice Black, concurring and dissenting.

I agree with substantially all of the Court's opinion sustaining the power of Congress under § 2 of the Fifteenth Amendment to suspend state literacy tests and similar voting qualifications and to authorize the Attorney General to secure the appointment of federal examiners to register qualified voters in various sections of the country. . . . I also agree with the judgment of the Court upholding § 4 (b) of the Act which sets out a formula for determining when and where the major remedial sections of the Act take effect. I reach this conclusion, however, for a somewhat different reason. . . .

Though, as I have said, I agree with most of the Court's conclusions, I dissent from its holding that every part of § 5 of the Act is constitutional. Section 4(a), to which § 5 is linked, suspends for five years all literacy tests and similar devices in those States coming within the formula of § 4(b). Section 5 goes on to provide that a State covered by § 4(b) can in no way amend its constitution or laws relating to voting without first trying to persuade the Attorney General of the United States or the Federal District Court for the District of Columbia that the new proposed laws do not have the purpose and will not have the effect of denying the right to vote to citizens on account of their race or color. I think this section is unconstitutional on at least two grounds.

(a) The Constitution gives federal courts jurisdiction over cases and controversies only. If it can be said that any case or controversy arises under this section which gives the District Court for the District of Columbia jurisdiction to approve or reject state laws or constitutional amendments, then the case or controversy must be between a State and the United States Government. But it is hard for me to believe that a justiciable controversy can arise in the constitutional sense from a desire by the United States Government or some of its officials to determine in advance what legislative provisions a State may enact or what constitutional amendments it may adopt. . . .

The form of words and the manipulation of presumptions used in § 5 to create the illusion of a case or controversy should not be allowed to cloud the effect of that section. By requiring a State to ask a federal court to approve the validity of a proposed law which has in no way become operative, Congress has asked the State to secure precisely the type of advisory opinion our Constitution forbids....

(b) My second and more basic objection to § 5 is that Congress has here exercised its power under § 2 of the Fifteenth Amendment through the adoption of means that conflict with the most basic principles of the Constitution.... Section 5, by providing that some of the States cannot pass state laws or adopt state constitutional amendments without first being compelled to beg federal authorities to approve their policies, so distorts our constitutional structure of government as to render any distinction drawn in the Constitution between state and federal power almost meaningless.... Certainly if all the provisions of our Constitution which limit the power of the Federal Government and reserve other power to the States are to mean anything, they mean at least that the States have power to pass laws and amend their constitutions without first sending their officials hundreds of miles away to beg federal authorities to approve them....

Mobile v. Bolden

446 U.S. 55 (1980)

In this case the Court decides whether voting practices must discriminate purposefully or only in effect. Wiley L. Bolden and other residents of Mobile, Alabama, brought a class action in federal court against the city on behalf of all black citizens in the city. They alleged that the practice of electing city commissioners at-large unfairly diluted the voting strength of blacks in violation of the Fourteenth and Fifteenth Amendments and Section 2 of the Voting Rights Act of 1965. Although finding that blacks registered and voted "without hindrance," the district court held that the at-large electoral system violated the Fifteenth Amendment and invidiously discriminated against blacks in violation of the Equal Protection Clause of the Fourteenth Amendment. The Fifth Circuit affirmed.

MR. JUSTICE STEWART announced the judgment of the Court and delivered an opinion, in which THE CHIEF JUSTICE, MR. JUSTICE POWELL, and MR. JUSTICE REHNQUIST joined.

The city of Mobile, Ala., has since 1911 been governed by a City Commission consisting of three members elected by the voters of the city at large. The question in this case is whether this at-large system of municipal elections violates the rights of Mobile's Negro voters in contravention of federal statutory or constitutional law.

. . .

I

In Alabama, the form of municipal government a city may adopt is governed by state law. Until 1911, cities not covered by specific legislation were limited to governing themselves through a mayor and city council. In that year, the Alabama Legislature authorized every large municipality to adopt a commission form of government. Mobile established its City Commission in the same year, and has maintained that basic system of municipal government ever since.

The three Commissioners jointly exercise all legislative, executive, and administrative power in the municipality. They are required after election to designate one of their number as Mayor, a largely ceremonial office, but no formal provision is made for allocating specific executive or administrative duties among the three. As required by the state law enacted in 1911, each candidate for the Mobile City Commission runs for election in the city at large for a term of four years in one of three numbered posts, and may be elected only by a majority of the total vote. This is the same basic electoral system that is followed by literally thousands of municipalities and other local governmental units throughout the Nation.

II

Although required by general principles of judicial administration to do so, ... neither the District Court nor the Court of Appeals addressed the complaint's statutory claim—that the Mobile electoral system violates § 2 of the Voting Rights Act of 1965. Even a cursory examination of that claim, however, clearly discloses that it adds nothing to the appellees' complaint.

Section 2 of the Voting Rights Act provides:

"No voting qualification or prerequisite to voting, or standard, practice, or procedure shall be imposed or applied by any State or political subdivision to deny or abridge the right of any citizen of the United States to vote on account of race or color." 79 Stat. 437, as amended, 42 U.S.C. § 1973.

Assuming, for present purposes, that there exists a private right of action to enforce this statutory provision, it is apparent that the language of § 2 no more than elaborates upon that of the Fifteenth Amendment, and the sparse legislative history of § 2 makes clear that it was intended to have an effect no different from that of the Fifteenth Amendment itself.

Section 2 was an uncontroversial provision in proposed legislation whose other provisions engendered protracted dispute. The House Report on the bill simply recited that § 2 "grants...a right to be free from enactment or enforcement of voting qualifications...or practices which deny or abridge the right to vote on account of race or color." H. R. Rep. No. 439, 89th Cong., 1st Sess., 23 (1965). See also S. Rep. No. 162, 89th Cong., 1st Sess., pt. 3, pp. 19–20 (1965). The view that this section simply restated the prohibitions already contained in the Fifteenth Amendment was expressed without contradiction during the Senate hearings. Senator Dirksen indicated at one point that all States, whether or not covered by the preclearance provisions of § 5 of the proposed legislation, were prohibited from discriminating against Negro voters by § 2, which he termed "almost a rephrasing of the 15th [A]mendment." Attorney General Katzenbach agreed....

In view of the section's language and its sparse but clear legislative history, it is evident that this statutory provision adds nothing to the appellees' Fifteenth Amendment claim. We turn, therefore, to a consideration of the validity of the judgment of the Court of Appeals with respect to the Fifteenth Amendment.

III

The Court's early decisions under the Fifteenth Amendment established that it imposes but one limitation on the powers of the States. It forbids them to discriminate against Negroes in matters having to do with voting....

Our decisions, moreover, have made clear that action by a State that is racially neutral on its face violates the Fifteenth Amendment only if motivated by a discriminatory purpose. [Guinn v. United States, 238 U. S. 347 (1915)]...

The Court's more recent decisions confirm the principle that racially discriminatory motivation

is a necessary ingredient of a Fifteenth Amendment violation. [Gomillion v. Lightfoot, 364 U. S. 339 (1960)]...

While other of the Court's Fifteenth Amendment decisions have dealt with different issues, none has questioned the necessity of showing purposeful discrimination in order to show a Fifteenth Amendment violation....

[Bolden argued that the at-large system was unconstitutional because the effect of racially polarized voting in Mobile was the same as that of a racially exclusionary primary.]

The answer to the appellees' argument is that, as the District Court expressly found, their freedom to vote has not been denied or abridged by anyone. The Fifteenth Amendment does not entail the right to have Negro candidates elected, and neither *Smith v. Allwright* nor *Terry v. Adams* contains any implication to the contrary. That Amendment prohibits only purposefully discriminatory denial or abridgment by government of the freedom to vote "on account of race, color, or previous condition of servitude." Having found that Negroes in Mobile "register and vote without hindrance," the District Court and Court of Appeals were in error in believing that the appellants invaded the protection of that Amendment in the present case.

IV

The Court of Appeals also agreed with the District Court that Mobile's at-large electoral system violates the Equal Protection Clause of the Fourteenth Amendment. There remains for consideration, therefore, the validity of its judgment on that score.

A

The claim that at-large electoral schemes unconstitutionally deny to some persons the equal protection of the laws has been advanced in numerous cases before this Court. That contention has been raised most often with regard to multimember constituencies within a state legislative apportionment system. The constitutional objection to multimember districts is not and cannot be that, as such, they depart from apportionment on a population basis in violation of *Reynolds v. Sims*, 377 U. S. 533, and its progeny. Rather the focus in such cases has been on the lack of representation multimember districts afford various elements of the voting population in a system of representative legislative democracy. "Criticism [of multimember districts] is rooted in their winner-take-all aspects, their tendency to submerge minorities ..., a general preference for legislatures reflecting community interests as closely as possible and disenchantment with political parties and elections as devices to settle policy differences between contending interests." *Whitcomb* v. *Chavis,* 403 U. S. 124, 158–159.

Despite repeated constitutional attacks upon multimember legislative districts, the Court has consistently held that they are not unconstitutional *per se,* ... We have recognized, however, that such legislative apportionments could violate the Fourteenth Amendment if their purpose were invidiously to minimize or cancel out the voting potential of racial or ethnic minorities.... To prove such a purpose it is not enough to show that the group allegedly discriminated against has not elected representatives in proportion to its numbers.... A plaintiff must prove that the disputed plan was "conceived or operated as [a] purposeful devic[e] to further racial ... discrimination," *id.,* at 149.

. . .

[The Court noted that no black had been elected to the Mobile City Commission. However, blacks had the only active "slating" organization in the city. "It may be that Negro candidates have been defeated, but that fact alone does not work a constitutional deprivation."]

V

The judgment is reversed, and the case is remanded to the Court of Appeals for further proceedings.

It is so ordered.

MR. JUSTICE BLACKMUN, concurring in the result.

Assuming that proof of intent is a prerequisite to appellees' prevailing on their constitutional claim of vote dilution, I am inclined to agree with MR. JUSTICE WHITE that, in this case, "the findings of the District Court amply support an inference of purposeful discrimination," *post,* at 103. I concur in the Court's judgment of reversal, however, because I believe that the relief afforded appellees by the District Court was not commensurate with the sound exercise of judicial discretion.

It seems to me that the city of Mobile, and its citizenry, have a substantial interest in maintaining the commission form of government that has been in effect there for nearly 70 years. The District Court recognized that its remedial order,

changing the form of the city's government to a mayor-council system, "raised serious constitutional issues." 423 F. Supp. 384, 404 (SD Ala. 1976). Nonetheless, the court was "unable to see how the impermissibly unconstitutional dilution can be effectively corrected by any other approach." *Id.,* at 403.

. . .

MR. JUSTICE STEVENS, concurring in the judgment.

. . .

As MR. JUSTICE STEWART points out, Mobile's basic election system is the same as that followed by literally thousands of municipalities and other governmental units throughout the Nation. *Ante,* at 60. The fact that these at-large systems characteristically place one or more minority groups at a significant disadvantage in the struggle for political power cannot invalidate all such systems....

MR. JUSTICE BRENNAN, dissenting.

I dissent because I agree with MR. JUSTICE MARSHALL that proof of discriminatory impact is sufficient in these cases. I also dissent because, even accepting the plurality's premise that discriminatory purpose must be shown, I agree with MR. JUSTICE MARSHALL and MR. JUSTICE WHITE that the appellees have clearly met that burden.

MR. JUSTICE WHITE, dissenting.

In *White* v. *Regester,* 412 U. S. 755 (1973), this Court unanimously held the use of multimember districts for the election of state legislators in two counties in Texas violated the Equal Protection Clause of the Fourteenth Amendment because, based on a careful assessment of the totality of the circumstances, they were found to exclude Negroes and Mexican-Americans from effective participation in the political processes in the counties. Without questioning the vitality of *White* v. *Regester* and our other decisions dealing with challenges to multimember districts by racial or ethnic groups, the Court today inexplicably rejects a similar holding based on meticulous factual findings and scrupulous application of the principles of these cases by both the District Court and the Court of Appeals. The Court's decision is flatly inconsistent with *White* v. *Regester* and it cannot be understood to flow from our recognition in *Washington* v. *Davis,* 426 U. S. 229 (1976), that the Equal Protection Clause forbids only purposeful discrimination. Both the District Court and the Court of Appeals properly found that an invidious discriminatory purpose could be inferred from the totality of facts in this case. The Court's cryptic rejection of their conclusions ignores the principles that an invidious discriminatory purpose can be inferred from objective factors of the kind relied on in *White* v. *Regester* and that the trial courts are in a special position to make such intensely local appraisals.

. . .

Because I believe that the findings of the District Court amply support an inference of purposeful discrimination in violation of the Fourteenth and Fifteenth Amendments, I respectfully dissent.

MR. JUSTICE MARSHALL, dissenting.

. . .

[II.B]

The plurality concludes that our prior decisions establish the principle that proof of discriminatory intent is a necessary element of a Fifteenth Amendment claim. In contrast, I continue to adhere to my conclusion in *Beer* v. *United States*, 425 U. S., at 148, n. 4 (dissenting opinion), that "[t]he Court's decisions relating to the relevance of purpose-and/or-effect analysis in testing the constitutionality of legislative enactments are somewhat less than a seamless web." As I there explained, at various times the Court's decisions have seemed to adopt three inconsistent approaches: (1) that purpose alone is the test for unconstitutionality; (2) that effect alone is the test; and (3) that purpose or effect, either alone or in

combination, is sufficient to show unconstitutionality. *Ibid.* In my view, our Fifteenth Amendment jurisprudence on the necessity of proof of discriminatory purpose is no less unsettled than was our approach to the importance of such proof in Fourteenth Amendment racial discrimination cases prior to *Washington* v. *Davis*, 426 U. S. 229 (1976). What is called for in the present cases is a fresh consideration—similar to our inquiry in *Washington* v. *Davis, supra,* with regard to Fourteenth Amendment discrimination claims—of whether proof of discriminatory purpose is necessary to establish a claim under the Fifteenth Amendment....

... [I]t is beyond dispute that a standard based solely upon the motives of official decisionmakers creates significant problems of proof for plaintiffs and forces the inquiring court to undertake an unguided, tortuous look into the minds of officials in the hope of guessing why certain policies were adopted and others rejected.... An approach based on motivation creates the risk that officials will be able to adopt policies that are the products of discriminatory intent so long as they sufficiently mask their motives through the use of subtlety and illusion....

I continue to believe, then, that under the Fifteenth Amendment an "[e]valuation of the purpose of a legislative enactment is just too ambiguous a task to be the sole tool of constitutional analysis.... [A] demonstration of effect ordinarily should suffice. If, of course, purpose may conclusively be shown, it too should be sufficient to demonstrate a statute's unconstitutionality." *Beer* v. *United States*, 425 U. S., at 149–150, n. 5 (MARSHALL, J., dissenting).

. . .

Congress Reverses *Mobile* v. *Bolden*

In *Mobile* v. *Bolden,* 446 U. S. 55 (1980), the Supreme Court held that the Voting Rights Act of 1965 only prohibits states from purposefully discriminating against the voting rights of blacks. There had to be an *intent* on the part of states to abridge voting rights. In 1982 Congress amended the Act to allow plaintiffs to show discrimination solely on the *effects* of a voting plan. As explained in the congressional debate, members of Congress borrowed language that had appeared in an earlier decision by the Supreme Court, in *White* v. *Regester,* 412 U. S. 755 (1973). The selections below come from 128 Cong. Rec. 14100, 14111, 14113–15, 14936 (1982).

Mr. DeCONCINI. Mr. President, for the past several months the attention of the Nation's civil

rights community, this Congress, and of the Nation itself has been focused upon the extension of the Voting Rights Act of 1965. I join in this concern, for as the Supreme Court noted almost a century ago,

"the political franchise of voting is...a fundamental political right, because preservative of all rights."

. . .

In the years since the passage of the Voting Rights Act, many subtle and complex means have been developed to avoid inclusion of minority persons in the political process. With the recent Supreme Court decision of *Mobile* v. *Bolden,* 446 U.S. 55 (1980), which requires a finding of discriminatory intent to establish a violation of the 15th amendment, a new statutory tool became necessary to avoid the consequences of such subtle discriminatory mechanisms. S. 1992 would establish a "results" test in section 2 of the act, and thus provide the necessary tool.

. . .

In the course of the debate over a "results" versus an "intent" test for section 2 of the act, opponents of "results" have asserted that intent to discriminate is, and always has been, the standard of proof in civil rights law. This assertion involves a number of misunderstandings of the history of civil rights law.

First, while intentional discrimination has always been clearly prohibited by the 14th and 15th amendments to the Constitution, it has not always been understood to be the sole standard by which discrimination could be attacked under those provisions. Indeed, it was entirely consistent for Attorney General Katzenbach to state in 1965 that section 2 would reach any practice or procedure "if its purpose or effect was to deny or abridge the right to vote on account of race or color," and to agree with Senator Dirksen's assertion that section 2 was "a restatement, in effect, of the 15th amendment." That same year, the Supreme Court had held that multimember district systems would be unconstitutional if it were shown that—

"designedly or otherwise, a multi-member constituency scheme...would operate to minimize or cancel out the voting strength of racial... elements of the voting population." *Fortson* v. *Dorsey,* 379 U. S. 433 at 439 (1965). (Emphasis added.)

Intent has been expressly required by the Supreme Court as a necessary element of a 14th amendment equal protection case only since 1976. It has been expressly required in 15th amendment cases only since the Mobile against Bolden decision in 1980.

Second, "effect" standards have been used, and are being used today, in civil rights law. Both title VII of the Civil Rights Act of 1964 and section 5 of the Voting Rights Act employ effects-based standards. It is true that the proposed "results" standards of S. 1992 would not be identical to these standards, however. S. 1992 employs language designed to assure that the mere numbers of minorities elected to office would not, by themselves, provide a basis for alleging a violation of section 2 nor provide a standard for remedies of adjudicated violations of section 2. In other words, the section 2 "results" test would be a more difficult test under which to establish a violation than either the section 5 or title VII "effects" tests.

A "results" test would be superior to the present "intent" test for a variety of reasons. First and most fundamentally, "results" language in section 2 of the act would reimpose the standard which most Federal courts used in vote dilution cases prior to the Bolden decision in 1980. This standard was arrived at through interpretation of a number of landmark Supreme Court decisions over the past two decades. Most important among these decisions are Fortson against Dorsey, Burns against Richardson, Whitcomb against Chavis, and White against Regester. These Supreme Court decisions did not create a standard of proof which required discriminatory intent; rather, they outlined objective factors which could be analyzed to determine whether or not minority voting strength had been unconstitutionally diluted by the existing electoral system.

As a result of these decisions, some 23 cases were litigated in the lower Federal courts between 1972 and 1979....

These 23 cases are extremely important in the evaluation of a "results" test which would incorporate their standards into statutory law. It is important to note, for instance, that in these 23 cases, the defendants prevailed 13 times. Thus, a "results" test would not mean automatic victory for plaintiffs in vote dilution cases....

. . .

Mr. MATHIAS. [*This bill would amend the Voting Rights Act*] to prohibit any voting practice or procedure which results in voting discrimination. This amendment is designed to make clear that proof of discriminatory intent is not required to establish a violation of section 2....

. . .

...In Bolden, a plurality of the Supreme Court broke with precedent and substantially increased the burden on plaintiffs by requiring proof of discriminatory intent. As noted in the committee report, the Bolden intent test is unacceptable for a number of reasons.

First, the intent test asks the wrong question. Rather than focusing on the crucial question of whether or not minority voters now have a fair chance to participate in the electoral process, the intent test diverts the inquiry to an analysis of the subjective motives of public officials. Thus the intent test requires Federal judges to engage in protracted, burdensome inquiries into the motives of lawmakers, which often have little or no bearing on the ability of minority voters to participate in their electoral process. For example, on remand, following the Supreme Court's decision in Bolden, the district court was required to make an inquiry into the motives of legislators to determine if the system was devised or maintained for a discriminatory purpose. In order to comply with Bolden, the district court was forced to recreate events shedding light on the motivation of politicians who held office during the several crucial periods under investigation between 1814 and the present.

Second, as Arthur Flemming, former Chairman of the U.S. Commission on Civil Rights, told the Subcommittee on the Constitution that inquiries under the intent test "can only be divisive, threatening to destroy any existing racial progress in a community."

Third, the intent test places an unacceptable burden on plaintiffs in voting discrimination cases. It creates the risk that electoral systems will be free from challenge even where there is overwhelming evidence of unequal access to the political process....

. . .

[Debate in the House of Representatives produced this colloquy:]

Mr. HYDE...I would like to ask the gentle-

man from California about the test which the Senate incorporated in the proposed section 2 of the act. I have read the language, and I believe it comes virtually word for word from page 766 of the Supreme Court's 1973 decision in White against Regester, and I would like to ask the gentleman whether I am correct.

Mr. EDWARDS of California. If the gentleman will yield, the gentleman from Illinois is correct. It comes right out of the Supreme Court's decision in White against Regester.

Mr. HYDE. I thank the gentleman.... Under the Senate amendments, the "results" test remains in the statute but, since it has no precursor in the law, it is explained by the adoption of clarifying language. Specifically, the amendments provide that a violation of the results test can be shown by an examination of the totality of the circumstances surrounding the alleged discrimination, and the determination that "the political processes leading to nomination or election in the State or political subdivision are not equally open to participation by members of the class of citizens protected" by the Voting Rights Act. While this language may give the appearance to some of being an "effects" test, and indeed has been marketed as such in some quarters, it has been taken, virtually word for word, from the Supreme Court's 1973 holding in *White v. Regester*, 412 U. S. 755, 766, a case which, according to its author, Justice Byron White, underscored the requirement that an "invidious discriminatory purpose [must] be inferred from the totality of facts" to constitute a violation. *Mobile v. Bolden*, 466 U. S. 55, 95 (1980).

It is also worth noting that the language adopted in the Senate was suggested during the House debate by the minority (see House hearings, page 2053) but was rejected and, during negotiations for a compromise in which I was intimately involved, no one would consider it. Therefore, it is clear, and I suspect will be clear by a reviewing court, that the language adopted through the Senate compromise is language which was rejected in the House and which, therefore, represents the intent standard articulated by White, not an effects standard as some would suggest.

C. REAPPORTIONMENT

The activism of the Warren Court revolutionized many areas of constitutional law: criminal rights, desegregation, reapportionment, church and state, and other sensitive issues. Of all these initiatives and innovations, it is widely assumed that the desegregation case of *Brown* v. *Board of Education* (1954) was the most important decision. Chief Justice Warren, author of the 1954 ruling, disagreed. The "accolade," he said, should go to *Baker* v. *Carr* (1962), which opened the door to the "one person, one vote" rule for reapportionment. This decision helped return power to the people, giving them a direct means of protecting their rights and responsibilities through representative government. The Memoirs of Earl Warren 306–08 (1977).

Taking the Census

The Constitution requires that every ten years there be a national counting of the people. On the basis of those counts the Census Bureau reports the state populations and they are used to reapportion the seats in the House of Representatives. Because of substantial errors and undercounts in the 1990 census, the Census Bureau planned to use statistical sampling for the 2000 census. However, in 1999 the Supreme Court ruled that the Census Act prohibits the use of statistical sampling for the apportionment of House seats. The Court did not foreclose statistical sampling for other purposes, such as drawing political boundaries or allocating federal funds to the states. Dept. of Commerce v. U.S. House of Representatives, 525 U.S. 316 (1999).

Apportioning Legislative Seats

The first major reapportionment case appeared in 1946, involving congressional districts in Illinois. Because of changes in population and the state's failure to reapportion districts for forty years, the districts ranged from a low of 112,116 to a high of 914,053. Voters in the most populous district therefore had one-ninth the voting power of those in the smallest district. A 4–3 decision by the Supreme Court dismissed the complaint. Justice Frankfurter said it was "hostile to a democratic system to involve the judiciary in the politics of the people." COLE-GROVE v. GREEN, 328 U.S. 549, 554 (1946). Although nothing in previous decisions suggested that reapportionment was outside the jurisdiction of the courts,[2] Frankfurter warned that courts "ought not to enter this political thicket" and counseled that the ultimate remedy lay with the people to insist on fair apportionment. How citizens could protect their interests when disfranchised by malapportioned districts he never explained.

In a concurrence that supplied the fourth vote, Rutledge rejected Frankfurter's position that reapportionment was nonjusticiable. Rutledge believed that the Court had jurisdiction to decide the case, but that the shortness of time remaining before the election (a few months off) prevented judicial action. Thus, a majority of Justices (4–3) agreed that the Court could take jurisdiction in reapportionment cases. Because of Rutledge's position, Frankfurter had actually written a *minority* opinion on the question of jurisdiction. However, the circumstances of the Illinois case did not allow sufficient time to draw new district lines. Declaring them invalid would have forced candidates to run at-large on a statewide ticket. The pressure of an impending election also dictated the Court's decision two years later to refuse jurisdiction. MacDougall v. Green, 335 U.S. 281 (1948).

In a 1950 case, Georgia's apportionment law was considered a political matter unfit for judicial review. South v. Peters, 339 U.S. 276 (1950). Georgia allotted each county a number of unit votes, giving residents of the less populous rural counties an advantage over the more populous counties in the cities. The vote in the least populous county was worth more than 120 times the vote of residents in the most populous county (Fulton County). The system did more than disfranchise urban voters. The large cities had a heavy black population. In their

---

2. See Wood v. Broom, 287 U.S. 1 (1932); Smiley v. Holm, 285 U.S. 355 (1932); Koenig v. Flynn, 285 U.S. 375 (1932); Carroll v. Becker, 285 U.S. 380 (1932).

Frankfurter's Dissent in *Baker*

Having argued in *Colegrove* that courts should not take jurisdiction in reapportionment cases, Frankfurter insisted in *Baker* v. *Carr* that the remedy for malapportionment should be left not to the courts but to the political process, "to an informed, civically militant electorate. In a democratic society like ours, relief must come through an aroused popular conscience that sears the conscience of the people's representatives." 369 U.S. at 270. However, a concurrence by Justice Clark pointed out that there were no practical means by which voters could correct malapportionment. Tennessee had no initiative or referendum. Constitutional con-

ventions could be called only by the legislature. Appeal to the state courts had been futile. Clark concluded that the majority of voters "have been caught up in a legislative strait jacket." Id. at 259. When the Court, during oral argument, asked whether there was any remedy in the courts of Tennessee for the citizens of that state, the response from state's counsel was refreshingly candid: "[O]n the present status of the case law in Tennessee and of the views held as to the constitutional law in Tennessee, . . . this right, this alleged right, is not enforceable in any of the courts of Tennessee to any degree whatsoever." 56 Landmark Briefs 54 (1975).

---

dissent, Justices Douglas and Black pointed out that the County Unit System "has indeed been called the 'last loophole' around our decisions holding that there must be no discrimination because of race in primary as well as in general elections." Id. at 278. With regard to the issue of nonjusticiability, Douglas and Black assumed that the Court would strike down state efforts to reduce the votes of blacks, Catholics, or Jews "so that each got only one-tenth of a vote." Id. at 277.

In 1960 a unanimous Court agreed to strike down the political boundaries drawn by the Alabama legislature for the city of Tuskegee. Black citizens challenged the legislature's decision to change the boundaries from a square to an irregular twenty-eight-sided figure. Through this process of gerrymandering, the state eliminated all but four or five of the city's 400 black voters without eliminating a single white voter. The Court invalidated the redistricting, but not on the general ground of the Equal Protection Clause. It disposed of the case on the specific commands of the Fifteenth Amendment, which forbids a state to deprive any citizen of the right to vote because of race. Justice Whittaker, concurring, would have decided the case on equal protection grounds. Gomillion v. Lightfoot, 364 U.S. 339 (1960).

Baker v. Carr

With *Gomillion* the Court stepped into the "political thicket" of redistricting. Two years later it completed the journey. Tennessee had failed to reapportion its state legislature since 1900, despite massive population shifts over the course of six census takings. A single vote in Moore County was worth nineteen votes in Hamilton County. Basing its decision on the Equal Protection Clause, a 6–2 Court held that (1) it possessed jurisdiction over reapportionment; (2) plaintiffs could obtain appropriate relief in the courts; and (3) plaintiffs had standing to challenge the Tennessee apportionment statutes. The particular remedy was left to the district court. BAKER v. CARR, 369 U.S. 186 (1962). Justice Frankfurter wrote an impassioned dissent (see box).

The Court explained that the question in the Tennessee case was "the consistency of state action with the Federal Constitution. We have no question decided, or to be decided, by a political branch of government coequal with this Court." 369 U.S. at 226. That calculus changed in 1964 when the Court accepted a case involving *congressional* districts and held that it had jurisdiction, plaintiffs had standing, and relief could be granted by the courts. Drawing upon constitutional history and the framers' intent, the Court concluded that the U.S. House of Representatives was bound by the principle of equal representation for equal numbers of people. Although it might not be possible to draw congressional districts with "mathematical precision," the principle of "one person, one vote" applied to the House. WESBERRY v. SANDERS, 376 U.S. 1 (1964). In a dissent, Justice Harlan calculated that the decision impugned the validity of 398 Representatives, leaving a "constitutional" House of thirty-seven members.

In 1968 the Court extended the one-person, one-vote principle to any legislative or administrative body in the state subject to popular election, including units of local government with general governmental powers over the entire geographical area served by the body. Avery v. Midland County, 390 U.S. 474. The Court rejected the idea of limiting equal apportionment to "important" elections. "In some instances the election of a local sheriff may be far more important than the election of a United States Senator." Hadley v. Junior College District, 397 U.S. 50, 55 (1970). On the other hand, nonlegislative state or local officials need not be chosen by election. Their selection is not governed by the one-person, one-vote requirement. Sailors v. Board of Education, 387 U.S. 105 (1967). The Court also refused to extend the one-person, one-vote principle to specialized state agencies that govern limited jurisdictions.[3]

New York City's Board of Estimate was struck down by a unanimous Court in 1989. The Board consists of the Mayor, the comptroller, and the president of the City Council (all elected citywide and each with two votes on the Board), plus the elected presidents of the city's five boroughs (each casting one vote). This arrangement gave Brooklyn's 2.2 million people, about half of them minorities, the same voting strength on the Board as the 400,000 residents of Staten Island, which is mostly white. The Board exercises major powers with respect to zoning, franchises, sewer and water rates, and city contracts. Although the city offered various arguments to justify the composition of the Board, including efforts to accommodate natural and political boundaries, the Court found that the Board violated the Equal Protection Clause. Board of Estimate of City of New York v. Morris, 489 U.S. 688 (1989).

Federal and state courts often exercise concurrent jurisdiction over redistricting disputes. When this occurs, federal judges are expected to defer consideration whenever a state (through either its legislative or judicial branch) has begun to address the controversy. Growe v. Emison, 507 U.S. 25 (1993).

Single-Member Districts

In requiring a population-based formula for redistricting, the Supreme Court allows state legislatures to experiment with other variations. For example, the Court does not insist that state legislators be selected from single-member districts. Some districts can be multimember.[4] However, when federal courts are forced to fashion an apportionment plan, single-member districts are generally preferred.[5] Under certain conditions, multimember districts are declared unconstitutional if they discriminate against minorities and ethnic groups. The capacity of these groups to elect one of their own is diluted when their votes are cast in a large, multimember district controlled by whites. White v. Regester, 412 U.S. 755 (1973).

---

3. Ball v. James, 451 U.S. 355 (1982); Salyer Land Co. v. Tulare Lake Basin Water Storage Dist., 410 U.S. 719 (1973); Associated Enterprises, Inc. v. Toltec District, 410 U.S. 743 (1973).

4. Reynolds v. Sims, 377 U.S. 533, 577 (1964). See also Fortson v. Dorsey, 379 U.S. 433 (1965) and Burns v. Richardson, 384 U.S. 73, 88–89 (1966). The merits and demerits of multimember voting were explored more fully in Whitcomb v. Chavis, 403 U.S. 124 (1971).

5. Growe v. Emison, 507 U.S. 25, 40 (1993); Connor v. Finch, 431 U.S. 407, 415 (1977); East Carroll Parish School Bd. v. Marshall, 424 U.S. 636 (1976); Chapman v. Meier, 420 U.S. 1 (1975); Connor v. Johnson, 402 U.S. 690 (1971).

The problem is similar with an at-large electoral system, where voters of an entire county elect a multimember governing board. If at-large voting discriminates against blacks or other groups, the county may have to be divided into districts to avoid vote dilution. Rogers v. Lodge, 458 U.S. 613 (1982). These cases generally required plaintiffs to prove that an at-large system was designed with the *intent* to further racial discrimination. There had to be not only a discriminatory effect but also a discriminatory purpose. Mobile v. Bolden, 446 U.S. 55 (1980). The distinction between effect and purpose was also explored in City of Rome v. United States, 446 U.S. 156 (1980).

In response to *Bolden,* Congress amended the Voting Rights Act in 1982 to provide that a violation could be proved by showing discriminatory effect alone. The new language adopted the "results test." 96 Stat. 134, § 3. This amendment has been used to challenge and overturn multimember districting that impairs black voting, but blacks are not automatically guaranteed seats in the legislature because of their percentage of the population. Thornburgh v. Gingles, 478 U.S. 30 (1986). Congress specifically provided that there is no right "to have members of a protected class elected in numbers equal to their proportion of the population." 96 Stat. 134, § 3.

Equality in Population

Over the years, Congress has adopted different policies on the question of making election districts equal in population. The text of the Constitution contradicted the principle of equality of representation. In counting the "whole Number of free Persons," certain Indians were excluded and only "three-fifths of all other Persons" (blacks) were added to the total. Art. I, § 2. The Civil War Amendments eliminated these constitutional supports for racism. In 1872 Congress required Representatives to be elected from districts "containing as nearly as practicable an equal number of inhabitants." 17 Stat. 28, § 2. That standard was continued in 1882, 1891, 1901, and 1911, dropped in 1929, and not revived by subsequent statutes.[6]

In 1963 the Supreme Court held that the concept of political equality could mean only one thing with regard to apportionment systems: "one person, one vote." Gray v. Sanders, 372 U.S. 368, 381. A year later it announced a softer standard. The constitutional command of Article I, Section 2, that members of the U.S. House of Representatives be chosen "by the People of the several States," means that "as nearly as is practicable one man's vote in a congressional election is to be worth as much as another's." Wesberry v. Sanders, 376 U.S. at 8. In 1964 the Court said that "mathematical nicety is not a constitutional requisite." Reynolds v. Sims, 377 U.S. 533, 568 (1964).

Although states are not compelled to achieve mathematical exactness in population among districts, a failure to articulate acceptable reasons for variations can result in the invalidation of a reapportionment plan. In cases involving *congressional* districts, population variations, no matter how small, have to be justified by the state.[7] Even variations of less than one percent from the ideal must be justified by good-faith efforts to achieve population equality. Karcher v. Daggett, 462 U.S. 725 (1983). Efforts to preserve intact whole regions of less populous counties are unacceptable justifications for population variations. Wells v. Rockefeller, 394 U.S. 542 (1969). Yet the Court recognizes some flexibility (see box on next page).

In a 1992 case, Montana wanted the minimum population variations of *Wesberry* v. *Sanders* (1964) applied to congressional districts after the most recent census. The 1990 census revealed

---

6. 22 Stat. 6, § 3 (1882); 26 Stat. 735, § 3 (1891); 31 Stat. 734, § 3 (1901); 37 Stat. 14, § 3 (1911); 46 Stat. 26, § 22 (1929).

7. Kirkpatrick v. Preisler, 394 U.S. 526 (1969); White v. Weiser, 412 U.S. 783 (1973). Population variations in state legislatures also had to be explained: Swann v. Adams, 385 U.S. 440 (1967); Kilgarin v. Hill, 386 U.S. 120 (1967).

Deviations from Mathematical Exactness

With regard to apportioning seats in a state legislature, the Court permits some population variations in an effort to preserve the integrity of political subdivision lines. Mahan v. Howell, 410 U.S. 315 (1973); Gaffney v. Cummings, 412 U.S. 735 (1973). When state constitutions ensure that each county (no matter how small its population) will have one representative in the state legislature, the Court has upheld population deviations as large as 16 percent as necessary to maintain political subdivisions. Brown v. Thomson, 462 U.S. 835 (1983). The Court tolerates "slightly greater percentage deviations" for local government apportionment schemes than for state and national counterparts. Abate v. Mundt, 403 U.S. 182, 185 (1971). When courts devise a reapportionment plan, they are held to a higher standard than legislatures in making districts as nearly of equal populations as is practicable. Connor v. Finch, 431 U.S. 407 (1997).

a population of 803,655 for Montana and an average size of 572,466 for the 435 congressional districts. A single district would have put Montana 231,189 above the average size, while an allotment of two seats would have placed Montana 170,638 below the average size. Montana was awarded one seat. A three-judge district court held that this allocation violated *Wesberry*, but a unanimous Supreme Court ruled that the quest for mathematical equality can run into insuperable hurdles at the federal level. U.S. Dept. of Commerce v. Montana, 503 U.S. 442 (1992).[8]

Bicameralism

The federal Constitution provides for a House of Representatives based on population and a Senate that gives two Senators to each state regardless of population. In the states, this "federal analogy" was invoked to argue for a population-based lower house, while allowing for factors other than population to determine seats in the other house.

In 1964 the Supreme Court extended the principle of equal representation to both houses of a state legislature. Relying on the Equal Protection Clause, the Court held that seats in both houses of a bicameral state legislature must be apportioned substantially on a population basis. The Court found the federal analogy irrelevant. Whereas the original states surrendered some of their sovereignty to form the Union and insisted on equal representation in the Senate as part of the Grand Compromise, counties did not form the states. They are creatures of the state and were never sovereign entities. REYNOLDS v. SIMS, 377 U.S. 533 (1964).[9] It mattered not to the Court whether the voters of a state specifically supported a constitutional

---

8. In 1992, the Court accepted as constitutional the decision of the Secretary of Commerce to allocate the Defense Department's overseas employees to particular states for reapportionment purposes in the 1990 decision. The result was to shift a Representative from Massachusetts to Washington State. Franklin v. Massachusetts, 505 U.S. 788 (1992). In 1996, a unanimous Court rejected a challenge to the Secretary of Commerce's decision not to statistically adjust the 1990 census for differential underaccounting. The Court held that the Secretary's decisions were not subject to heightened scrutiny and were well within constitutional bounds of discretion over the conduct of the federal census. Wisconsin v. City of New York, 517 U.S. 1 (1996).

9. The Court also struck down New York's apportionment law, which gave greater representation to the less populous counties for both houses of the state legislature. WMCA, Inc. v. Lomenzo, 377 U.S. 633 (1964). The Court held that both houses of Maryland's legislature must be apportioned substantially on a population basis. Maryland Committee v. Tawes, 377 U.S. 656 (1964). The same standard was applied to the two houses of the legislatures in Virginia and in Delaware. Davis v. Mann, 377 U.S. 678 (1964); Roman v. Sincock, 377 U.S. 695 (1964).

amendment to allow one house of a state legislature to be apportioned on a basis other than population. The constitutional meaning of the Equal Protection Clause does not depend on majority vote. Lucas v. Colorado Gen. Assembly, 377 U.S. 713, 736–37 (1964).

Senator Everett Dirksen, Republican from Illinois, took the lead in trying to reverse the Court's ruling that both houses of a state legislature had to be based on population. The Republican National Convention adopted a platform plank in 1964 in support of a constitutional amendment to allow one house to be based on other than population. Congressman William Tuck, Democrat of Virginia, introduced a bill to strip the federal courts of jurisdiction to hear apportionment cases. After a pitched battle, these and other court-curbing efforts were defeated.[10]

Compactness and Gerrymandering

The term *gerrymander* originates from an election district in Massachusetts so tortured in shape that it resembled a salamander. The district lines were drawn by Governor Elbridge Gerry, a member of the Jeffersonian party. The Federalist party complained that the district was configured in this odd way intentionally to disadvantage them. Congress passed legislation to limit gerrymandering. In 1842 it provided that members of the House of Representatives be elected from districts of "contiguous territory." 5 Stat. 491. Over the years, this requirement was periodically dropped and reinstated.[11]

In *Gomillion* (1960), the Supreme Court struck down a gerrymandered district because it deprived blacks of their voting rights. In 1964, however, the Court decided a case in which gerrymandering was used in New York City to *promote* the interests of black voters. The evidence strongly suggests that district lines had been drawn to segregate white voters from black and Puerto Rican voters. The result was a white congressional district and a nonwhite congressional district, giving black voters control of the Representative from the latter. A 7–2 Court decided that a district court's ruling—that plaintiffs had failed to show that the apportionment was motivated by racial considerations—"was not clearly erroneous." The dissent by Douglas and Goldberg claimed that New York supported segregation not on the "separate but equal" theory of *Plessy* v. *Ferguson* but on the theory of "separate but better off." Wright v. Rockefeller, 376 U.S. 52, 62 (1964).

With the Court applying constant pressure on state legislatures to attain mathematical equivalence in the population among districts, states were tempted to create strange configurations through gerrymandering. As Justice Harlan noted in one dissent: "The fact of the matter is that the rule of absolute equality is perfectly compatible with 'gerrymandering' of the worst sort." Wells v. Rockefeller, 394 U.S. at 542, 551 (1969). Justice Stevens remarked in 1983 that advances in computer technology since the time Harlan wrote "have made the task of the gerrymander even easier." Karcher v. Daggett, 462 U.S. 725, 752 (1983).

In the Voting Rights Act of 1965, Congress directed that states were not to adopt practices or procedures that have the purpose or effect "of denying or abridging the right to vote on account of race or color." 79 Stat. 439, § 5 (1965); 42 U.S.C. § 1973c (1988). These practices and procedures include redistricting that discriminates against blacks. Allen v. State Board of

---

10. Richard C. Cortner, The Apportionment Cases 236–46 (1970); Robert G. Dixon, Jr., Democratic Representation 385–435 (1968); Royce Hanson, The Political Thicket 82–101 (1966).

11. The requirement of "contiguous territory" was dropped in 1850, 9 Stat. 432, § 25, and reinstated in 1862, 1872, 1882, and 1891. 12 Stat. 572 (1862); 17 Stat. 28, § 2 (1872); 22 Stat. 6, § 3 (1882); 26 Stat. 735, § 3 (1891). The language in 1901 and 1911 became "contiguous and compact territory." 31 Stat. 734, § 3 (1901); 37 Stat. 14, § 3 (1911). This requirement was dropped in 1929. 46 Stat. 26, § 22 (1929).

Support for Racial Gerrymandering

In 1964, the Supreme Court supported racial gerrymandering in New York City, which divided citizens in such a way as to create a white congressional district and a nonwhite congressional district. Wright v. Rockefeller, 376 U.S. 52 (1964). Race was also used in Brooklyn to divide the Hasidic Jewish community in order to maintain certain percentages in the white and nonwhite districts. In upholding this reapportionment, the Second Circuit reasoned that the Voting Rights Act contemplated that the Attorney General and the state legislature would have "to think in racial terms" to satisfy the Act, which "necessarily deals with race or color." The Supreme Court affirmed this judgment. United Jewish Organizations v. Carey, 430 U.S. 144, 154–55 (1977). Compliance with the Act in apportionment cases "would often necessitate the use of racial considerations in drawing district lines." Id. at 159. The Court recognized that New York "deliberately increased the nonwhite majorities in certain districts in order to enhance the opportunity for election of nonwhite representatives from those districts." Id. at 165. In the 1990s, the Court would begin to place curbs on racial gerrymandering.

Elections, 393 U.S. 544, 569–70 (1969). Although race may not be used to deny or abridge voting rights, it may be used to enhance voting power (see box).[12]

In addition to gerrymanders along racial lines, the Court has reviewed gerrymanders that favor one political party over another. In 1983 it sidestepped a New Jersey political gerrymandering case by deciding it on grounds of equal population. Karcher v. Daggett, 462 U.S. 725 (1983). A political gerrymandering case decided by the Court in 1986 involved the Indiana legislature, which consists of a 100-member House of Representatives and a 50-member Senate. Following the 1980 census, the legislature (controlled by Republicans) reapportioned the districts. The Democrats claimed that the reapportionment plan constituted a political gerrymander that violated their right to equal protection. In a decision marked by confusion of gigantic proportions (see political cartoon on next page), a badly fractured Court agreed that it had jurisdiction over political gerrymandering. The standards it established, however, were quite vague. DAVIS v. BANDEMER, 478 U.S. 109 (1986).

Rethinking in the 1990s

Two Supreme Court decisions in 1993 gave further thought to race-conscious redistricting. In one case, an Ohio apportionment board adopted a plan to create several districts in which racial minorities would predominate. A unanimous Court held that the plan did not violate Section 2 of the Voting Rights Act. Opponents of the plan argued that packing black voters in a few districts diluted their voting power elsewhere. The Court concluded that the plaintiffs had failed to satisfy one prong of the vote-dilution test: they did not demonstrate that the white majority voted in such a bloc to frustrate the election of a minority group's candidate. There was no proof of racially polarized voting. Voinovich v. Quilter, 507 U.S. 146 (1993).

---

12. Race is also a factor when cities annex nearby counties to reduce the percentage of the black population. Part of the compromise may be the creation of wards with substantial black populations. City of Richmond v. United States, 422 U.S. 358 (1975); Georgia v. United States, 411 U.S. 526 (1973); Perkins v. Matthews, 400 U.S. 379 (1971). See also Beer v. United States, 425 U.S. 130 (1976). When cities try to annex only white areas, they may be unable to obtain either the approval of the Attorney General or a federal judge. City of Pleasant Grove v. United States, 479 U.S. 462 (1987).

The second case concerned a North Carolina congressional district that snaked 160 miles through the state in search of a black majority (see next page). For much of its length it followed Interstate 85 and was no wider than the highway's corridor. One state legislator remarked that "[i]f you drove down the interstate with both car doors open, you'd kill most of the people in the district." Divided 5–4, the Court held that white voters may challenge the constitutionality of "bizarre" restricting plans that are designed to separate voters by race. In returning the case to the district court for further proceedings, the Court said that state officials must demonstrate a "compelling" reason in order to meet the constitutionality of equal protection of the laws. Writing for the majority, Justice O'Connor said that racial gerrymandering may "balkanize" the United States into competing racial factions, reinforce racial stereotypes, and undermine representative democracy by signaling to elected officials that they represent only a particular racial group rather than the constituency as a whole. SHAW v. RENO, 509 U.S. 630 (1993).

The decision threw into question the constitutionality of a number of other odd-looking congressional districts that were drawn after the 1990 census. Other than a plea that districts be made more compact in shape, the ruling gives little guidance on what states must do to avoid invalid "bizarre" shapes. Politicians are torn on the value of race-based districting. Packing blacks into particular districts may increase their chance of winning those seats, but it also dilutes their strength in other districts and gives Republicans a better chance of prevailing in districts formerly held by Democrats.

NORTH CAROLINA'S 12TH CONGRESSIONAL DISTRICT

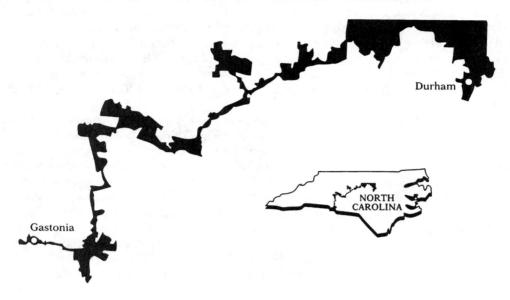

The Court gave further definition to *Shaw v. Reno* in 1995 when it rejected a race-based redistricting plan in Georgia. The initial plan by the state legislature provided for two congressional districts drawn in a way to elect two blacks. The Justice Department denied clearance on that plan, and the legislature redrew the lines to provide for three blacks (out of a total of eleven congressional seats). Divided 5 to 4, the Court held that a congressional district, regardless of its shape, could be unconstitutional if race was the prominent factor in drawing its lines. By subjecting redistricting plans to strict scrutiny, the Court requires states to show that it had a compelling governmental interest in adopting the plan, and that the plan was narrowly tailored to meet that interest. It is clear from this decision that complying with preclearance mandates from the Justice Department does not constitute a compelling interest, but the Court's decision (including the concurrence by Justice O'Connor) permits race to continue to be a factor in redistricting. MILLER v. JOHNSON, 515 U.S. 900 (1995). On the same day as the Georgia case, a unanimous Court held that voters in Louisiana lacked standing to challenge a redistricting plan as a racial gerrymander because they lived in a different district. United States v. Hays, 515 U.S. 737 (1995). In summary action the Court affirmed a California redistricting plan for state legislators and members of Congress that considered race but also other factors, including population equality, geographic compactness, contiguity, political boundaries, and the presence or absence of a sense of community. DeWitt v. Wilson, 515 U.S. 1170 (1995); 856 F.Supp. 1409 (D. Cal. 1994).

Continued Tinkering

In 1996, the Supreme Court issued two more decisions on race-based districting, invalidating one congressional district in North Carolina and three in Texas but failed again to provide clear guidelines for the acceptable use of race in drawing district lines. The decisions are becoming as twisted and disjointed as the districts the Court reviews. There was no majority opinion in the Texas case. O'Connor wrote a plurality opinion for herself, Rehnquist, and Kennedy. Thomas and Scalia agreed that the Texas districts were unconstitutional but refused to sign her opinion because it suggested that race could be legitimately used as one factor in deciding the boundaries of a district. O'Connor recognized that race was not the only factor for the Texas districts, but rejected the state's explanation that old-fashioned partisan politics and the traditional goal of protecting incumbents were the overriding objectives. Pointing out that Texas used a computer program that provided racial data on a block-by-block basis while other data such as party registration and past voting records were available only at the precinct-by-precinct level, she concluded that race was the dominant motivation. Bush v. Vera, 517 U.S. 952 (1996).

The North Carolina case, also splitting the Justices 5 to 4, allowed the Court to revisit the district it had called "bizarre" in *Shaw v. Reno* (1993). The Court decided that the contours of the skinny, 160-mile district were still not "narrowly tailored" to achieve the state's goal. Shaw v. Hunt, 517 U.S. 899 (1996). The 12th congressional district, redrawn to make it more compact, returned to the Court in 1999. The Court was persuaded by an expert's analysis that the state was motivated primarily by political, not racial, considerations in drawing the district lines. The state could engage in constitutional political gerrymandering even when it is conscious that most loyal Democrats happen to be black Democrats. The Court reversed a summary judgment by a three-judge district court that the district was an unconstitutional racial gerrymander. Hunt v. Cromartie, 526 U.S. 541 (1999). In other words, there is often substantial overlap between acceptable political gerrymandering and unacceptable racial gerrymandering.

When the case went back to the district court, that court declared the 12th district an unconstitutional racial gerrymander. However, the Supreme Court set aside that ruling to allow the congressional primaries to take place as scheduled with the redrawn district. Hunt v. Cromartie, 120 S.Ct. 1415 (2000).

Racial districting has been challenged elsewhere. In 1996, a three-judge court ruled unconstitutional a horseshoe-shaped congressional district in Florida that had been drawn to assure the election of a black. The district was redrawn. In 1997, federal judges invalidated an Hispanic-majority congressional district in New York City (represented by Democratic Rep. Nydia M. Velazquez), prompting a redrawing of the district.

On a separate issue, the Supreme Court made it easier for the Justice Department to approve state redistricting as part of the preclearance procedure without insisting on extreme measures to maximize the representation of minorities. Reno v. Bossier Parish School Bd., 520 U.S. 471 (1997). That decision was reinforced in 2000 when the Court held that the Voting Rights Act prevents nothing but "backsliding" (putting minority voters in a worse position than before), and preclearance affirms nothing but the absence of backsliding. Reno v. Bossier Parish School Bd., 120 S.Ct. 866 (2000).

By a vote of 5 to 4, the Court upheld a redrawn Georgia district map that contained only one majority-black district. The districting plan that had been struck down by the Court two years earlier, in *Miller v. Johnson*, had provided for three black-minority districts. Abrams v. Johnson, 521 U.S. 74 (1997). In another 1997 development, a three-judge court in Virginia held that the 3rd congressional district had been racially gerrymandered in violation of equal protection and the Supreme Court affirmed that judgment. Moon v. Meadows, 952 F.Supp. 1141 (D. Va. 1997) (three-judge court), aff'd sub nom. Harris v. Moon, 521 U.S. 1113 (1997).

Colegrove v. Green

328 U.S. 549 (1946)

Congressional districts in Illinois varied widely in population, ranging from 112,116 to 914,000. Kenneth W. Colegrove and two other citizens of Illinois qualified to vote in the

upcoming congressional elections brought suit in federal court under the Declaratory Judgments Act to restrain state officers from arranging for an election. They alleged that the congressional districts lacked compactness of territory and approximate equality of population, violating various provisions of the federal Constitution and the Reapportionment Act of 1911. The district court dismissed the complaint. The defendant was Dwight H. Green, an Illinois election official.

MR. JUSTICE FRANKFURTER announced the judgment of the Court and an opinion in which MR. JUSTICE REED and MR. JUSTICE BURTON concur.

... The District Court, feeling bound by this Court's opinion in *Wood v. Broom,* 287 U.S. 1, dismissed the complaint. 64 F. Supp. 632.

The District Court was clearly right in deeming itself bound by *Wood v. Broom, supra,* and we could also dispose of this case on the authority of *Wood v. Broom.* The legal merits of this controversy were settled in that case, inasmuch as it held that the Reapportionment Act of June 18, 1929, 46 Stat. 21, as amended, 2 U.S.C. § 2 (a), has no requirements "as to the compactness, contiguity and equality in population of districts." 287 U.S. at 8. The Act of 1929 still governs the districting for the election of Representatives. It must be remembered that not only was the legislative history of the matter fully considered in *Wood v. Broom,* but the question had been elaborately before the Court in *Smiley v. Holm,* 285 U.S. 355, *Koenig v. Flynn,* 285 U.S. 375, and *Carroll v. Becker,* 285 U.S. 380, argued a few months before *Wood v. Broom* was decided. Nothing has now been adduced to lead us to overrule what this Court found to be the requirements under the Act of 1929, the more so since seven Congressional elections have been held under the Act of 1929 as construed by this Court. No manifestation has been shown by Congress even to question the correctness of that which seemed compelling to this Court in enforcing the will of Congress in *Wood v. Broom.*

But we also agree with the four Justices (Brandeis, Stone, Roberts, and Cardozo, JJ.) who were of opinion that the bill in *Wood v. Broom, supra,* should be "dismissed for want of equity." ...

We are of opinion that the appellants ask of this Court what is beyond its competence to grant. This is one of those demands on judicial power which cannot be met by verbal fencing about "jurisdiction." It must be resolved by considerations on the basis of which this Court, from time to time, has refused to intervene in controversies. It has refused to do so because due regard for the effective working of our Government revealed this issue to be of a peculiarly political nature and therefore not meet for judicial determination.

This is not an action to recover for damage because of the discriminatory exclusion of a plaintiff from rights enjoyed by other citizens. The basis for the suit is not a private wrong, but a wrong suffered by Illinois as a polity. ... In effect this is an appeal to the federal courts to reconstruct the electoral process of Illinois in order that it may be adequately represented in the councils of the Nation. Because the Illinois legislature has failed to revise its Congressional Representative districts in order to reflect great changes, during more than a generation, in the distribution of its population, we are asked to do this, as it were, for Illinois.

Of course no court can affirmatively re-map the Illinois districts so as to bring them more in conformity with the standards of fairness for a representative system. At best we could only declare the existing electoral system invalid. The result would be to leave Illinois undistricted and to bring into operation, if the Illinois legislature chose not to act, the choice of members for the House of Representatives on a state-wide ticket. The last stage may be worse than the first. The upshot of judicial action may defeat the vital political principle which led Congress, more than a hundred years ago, to require districting. This requirement, in the language of Chancellor Kent, "was recommended by the wisdom and justice of giving, as far as possible, to the local subdivisions of the people of each state, a due influence in the choice of representatives, so as not to leave the aggregate minority of the people in a state, though approaching perhaps to a majority, to be wholly overpowered by the combined action of the numerical majority, without any voice whatever in the national councils." 1 Kent, *Commentaries* (12th ed., 1873) *230–31, n. (c). Assuming acquiescence on the part of the authorities of Illinois in the selection of its Representatives by a mode that defies the direction of Congress for selection by districts, the House of Representatives may not acquiesce. In the exercise of its power to judge the qualifications of its own members, the House may reject a delegation of Representatives-at-large. Article I, § 5, Cl. 1.... Nothing is clearer than that this controversy concerns matters that bring courts into immediate and active relations with party contests. From the determination of such issues this Court has traditionally held aloof. It is hostile to a democratic system to involve the judiciary in the politics of the people. And it is not less pernicious if such judicial intervention in an essentially political contest be dressed up in the abstract phrases of the law.

The appellants urge with great zeal that the conditions of which they complain are grave evils and offend public morality. The Constitution of the United States gives ample power to provide against these evils. But due regard for the Constitution as a viable system precludes judicial correction. Authority for dealing with such problems resides elsewhere. Article I, § 4 of the Constitution provides that "The Times, Places and Manner of holding Elections for ... Representatives, shall be prescribed in each State by the Legislature thereof; but the Congress may at any time by Law make or alter such Regulations, ..." The short of it is that the Constitution has conferred upon Congress exclusive authority to secure fair representation by the States in the popular House and left to that House determination whether States have fulfilled their responsibility. If Congress failed in exercising its powers, whereby standards of fairness are offended, the remedy ultimately lies with the people. Whether Congress faithfully discharges its duty or not, the subject has been committed to the exclusive control of Congress. An aspect of government from which the judiciary, in view of what is involved, has been excluded by the clear intention of the Constitution cannot be entered by the federal courts because Congress may have been in default in exacting from States obedience to its mandate.

. . .

To sustain this action would cut very deep into the very being of Congress. Courts ought not to enter this political thicket. The remedy for unfairness in districting is to secure State legislatures that will apportion properly, or to invoke the ample powers of Congress. The Constitution has many commands that are not enforceable by courts because they clearly fall outside the conditions and purposes that circumscribe judicial action. Thus, "on Demand of the executive Authority," Art. IV, § 2, of a State it is the duty of a sister State to deliver up a fugitive from justice. But the fulfilment of this duty cannot be judicially en-

forced. *Kentucky v. Dennison,* 24 How. 66. The duty to see to it that the laws are faithfully executed cannot be brought under legal compulsion, *Mississippi v. Johnson,* 4 Wall. 475. Violation of the great guaranty of a republican form of government in States cannot be challenged in the courts. *Pacific Telephone Co.* v. *Oregon,* 223 U.S. 118. The Constitution has left the performance of many duties in our governmental scheme to depend on the fidelity of the executive and legislative action and, ultimately, on the vigilance of the people in exercising their political rights.

Dismissal of the complaint is affirmed.

MR. JUSTICE JACKSON took no part in the consideration or decision of this case.

MR. JUSTICE RUTLEDGE.

I concur in the result. But for the ruling in *Smiley* v. *Holm,* 285 U.S. 355, I should have supposed that the provisions of the Constitution, Art. I, § 4, that "The Times, Places and Manner of holding Elections for ... Representatives, shall be prescribed in each State by the Legislature thereof; but the Congress may at any time by Law make or alter such Regulations ...": Art. I, § 2, vesting in Congress the duty of apportionment of representatives among the several states "according to their respective Numbers"; and Art. I, § 5, making each House the sole judge of the qualifications of its own members, would remove the issues in this case from justiciable cognizance. But, in my judgment, the *Smiley* case rules squarely to the contrary, save only in the matter of degree.

Moreover, we have but recently been admonished again that it is the very essence of our duty to avoid decision upon grave constitutional questions, especially when this may bring our function into clash with the political departments of the Government, if any tenable alternative ground for disposition of the controversy is presented.

I was unable to find such an alternative in that instance. There is one, however, in this case. And I think the gravity of the constitutional questions raised so great, together with the possibilities for collision above mentioned, that the admonition is appropriate to be followed here. Other reasons support this view, including the fact that, in my opinion, the basic ruling and less important ones in *Smiley* v. *Holm, supra,* would otherwise be brought into question.

Assuming that that decision is to stand, I think, with Mr. Justice Black, that its effect is to rule that this Court has power to afford relief in a case of this type as against the objection that the issues are not justiciable.

. . .

The shortness of the time remaining makes it doubtful whether action could, or would, be taken in time to secure for petitioners the effective relief they seek. To force them to share in an election at large might bring greater equality of voting right. It would also deprive them and all other Illinois citizens of representation by districts which the prevailing policy of Congress commands. 46 Stat. 26, as amended; 2 U.S.C. § 2a.

If the constitutional provisions on which appellants rely give them the substantive rights they urge, other provisions qualify those rights in important ways by vesting large measures of control in the political subdivisions of the Government and the state....

The right here is not absolute. And the cure sought may be worse than the disease.

I think, therefore, the case is one in which the Court may properly, and should, decline to exercise its jurisdiction. Accordingly, the judgment should be affirmed and I join in that disposition of the cause.

MR. JUSTICE BLACK, dissenting.

. . .

...It is my judgment that the District Court had jurisdiction; that the complaint presented a justiciable case and controversy; and that appellants had standing to sue, since the facts alleged show that they have been injured as individuals....

...It is true that declaration of invalidity of the State Act and the enjoining of state officials would result in prohibiting the State from electing Congressmen under the system of the old congressional districts. But it would leave the State free to elect them from the State at large, which, as we held in the *Smiley* case, is a manner authorized by the Constitution. It is said that it would be inconvenient for the State to conduct the election in this manner. But it has an element of virtue that the more convenient method does not have—namely, it does not discriminate against some groups to favor others, it gives all the people an equally effective voice in electing their representatives as is essential under a free government, and it is constitutional.

MR. JUSTICE DOUGLAS and MR. JUSTICE MURPHY join in this dissent.

Baker v. Carr

369 U.S. 186 (1962)

Charles W. Baker and other residents of Tennessee brought this suit against Joe C. Carr, the Secretary of State of Tennessee. They alleged that a state statute passed in 1901 arbitrarily and capriciously apportioned the seats in the General Assembly among the state's ninety-five counties and the state failed to reapportion the seats notwithstanding substantial growth and redistribution of the state's population. Through this "debasement of their votes" they claimed they were denied the equal protection of the laws guaranteed by the Fourteenth Amendment. After dismissing the argument that the matter constituted a "political question" (see the portion of the decision reprinted on pages 110–12), the Court decided whether the issue was justiciable.

MR. JUSTICE BRENNAN delivered the opinion of the Court.

. . .

The General Assembly of Tennessee consists of the Senate with 33 members and the House of Representatives with 99 members. The Tennessee Constitution provides in Art. II as follows:

"Sec. 3. Legislative authority—Term of office.—The Legislative authority of this State shall be vested in a General Assembly, which shall consist of a Senate and House of Representatives, both dependent on the people; who shall hold their offices for two years from the day of the general election.

"Sec. 4. Census.—An enumeration of the qualified voters, and an apportionment of the Representatives in the General Assembly, shall be made in the year one thousand eight hundred and seventy-one, and within every subsequent term of ten years.

"Sec. 5. Apportionment of representatives.— The number of Representatives shall, at the several periods of making the enumeration, be apportioned among the several counties or districts, according to the number of qualified voters in each; and shall not exceed seventy-five, until the population of the State shall be one million and a half, and shall never exceed ninety-nine; Provided, that any county having two-thirds of the ratio shall be entitled to one member.

"Sec. 6. Apportionment of senators. — The number of Senators shall, at the several periods of making the enumeration, be apportioned among the several counties or districts according to the number of qualified electors in each, and shall not exceed one-third the number of representatives. In apportioning the Senators among the different counties, the fraction that may be lost by any county or counties, in the apportionment of members to the House of Representatives, shall be made up to such county or counties in the Senate, as near as may be practicable. When a district is composed of two or more counties, they shall be adjoining; and no county shall be divided in forming a district."

Thus, Tennessee's standard for allocating legislative representation among her counties is the total number of qualified voters resident in the respective counties, subject only to minor qualifications. Decennial reapportionment in compliance with the constitutional scheme was effected by the General Assembly each decade from 1871 to 1901. The 1871 apportionment was preceded by an 1870 statute requiring an enumeration. The 1881 apportionment involved three statutes, the first authorizing an enumeration, the second enlarging the Senate from 25 to 33 members and the House from 75 to 99 members, and the third apportioning the membership of both Houses. In 1891 there were both an enumeration and an apportionment. In 1901 the General Assembly abandoned separate enumeration in favor of reliance upon the Federal Census and passed the Apportionment Act here in controversy. In the more than 60 years since that action, all proposals in both Houses of the General Assembly for reapportionment have failed to pass.

. . .

We come, finally, to the ultimate inquiry whether our precedents as to what constitutes a nonjusticiable "political question" bring the case before us under the umbrella of that doctrine. A natural beginning is to note whether any of the common characteristics which we have been able to identify and label descriptively are present. We find none: The question here is the consistency of state action with the Federal Constitution. We have no question decided, or to be decided, by a political branch of government coequal with this Court. Nor do we risk embarrassment of our government abroad, or grave disturbance at home if we take issue with Tennessee as to the constitutionality of her action here challenged. Nor need the appellants, in order to succeed in this action, ask the Court to enter upon policy determinations for which judicially manageable standards are lacking. Judicial standards under the Equal Protection Clause are well developed and familiar, and it has been open to courts since the enactment of the Fourteenth Amendment to determine, if on the particular facts they must, that a discrimination reflects *no* policy, but simply arbitrary and capricious action.

This case does, in one sense, involve the allocation of political power within a State, and the appellants might conceivably have added a claim under the Guaranty Clause. Of course, as we have seen, any reliance on that clause would be futile. But because any reliance on the Guaranty Clause could not have succeeded it does not follow that appellants may not be heard on the equal protection claim which in fact they tender. True, it must be clear that the Fourteenth Amendment claim is not so enmeshed with those political question elements which render Guaranty Clause claims nonjusticiable as actually to present a political question itself. But we have found that not to be the case here.

. . .

When challenges to state action respecting matters of "the administration of the affairs of the State and the officers through whom they are conducted" have rested on claims of constitutional deprivation which are amenable to judicial correction, this Court has acted upon its view of the merits of the claim. For example, . . . [O]nly last Term, in *Gomillion* v. *Lightfoot*, 364 U.S. 339, we applied the Fifteenth Amendment to strike down a redrafting of municipal boundaries which effected a discriminatory impairment of voting rights, in the face of what a majority of the Court of Appeals thought to be a sweeping commitment to state legislatures of the power to draw and redraw such boundaries.

. . .

We conclude that the complaint's allegations of a denial of equal protection present a justiciable constitutional cause of action upon which appellants are entitled to a trial and a decision. The right asserted is within the reach of judicial protection under the Fourteenth Amendment.

The judgment of the District Court is reversed and the cause is remanded for further proceedings consistent with this opinion.

Reversed and remanded.

MR. JUSTICE WHITTAKER did not participate in the decision of this case.

. . .

MR. JUSTICE DOUGLAS, concurring.

. . .

I agree with my Brother CLARK that if the allegations in the complaint can be sustained a case for relief is established. We are told that a single vote in Moore County, Tennessee, is worth 19 votes in Hamilton County, that one vote in Stewart or in Chester County is worth nearly eight times a single vote in Shelby or Knox County. The opportunity to prove that an "invidious discrimination" exists should therefore be given the appellants.

. . .

MR. JUSTICE CLARK, concurring.

One emerging from the rash of opinions with their accompanying clashing of views may well find himself suffering a mental blindness. The Court holds that the appellants have alleged a cause of action. However, it refuses to award relief here — although the facts are undisputed — and fails to give the District Court any guidance whatever. One dissenting opinion, bursting with words that go through so much and conclude with so little, contemns the majority action as "a massive repudiation of the experience of our whole past." Another describes the complaint as merely asserting conclusory allegations that Tennessee's apportionment is "incorrect," "arbitrary," "obsolete," and "unconstitutional." I believe it can be shown that this case is distinguishable from earlier cases dealing with the distribution of political power by a State, that a patent violation of the Equal Protection Clause of the United States Constitution has been shown, and that an appropriate remedy may be formulated.

. . .

III.

Although I find the Tennessee apportionment

statute offends the Equal Protection Clause, I would not consider intervention by this Court into so delicate a field if there were any other relief available to the people of Tennessee. But the majority of the people of Tennessee have no "practical opportunities for exerting their political weight at the polls" to correct the existing "invidious discrimination." Tennessee has no initiative and referendum. I have searched diligently for other "practical opportunities" present under the law. I find none other than through the federal courts. The majority of the voters have been caught up in a legislative strait jacket. Tennessee has an "informed, civically militant electorate" and "an aroused popular conscience," but it does not sear "the conscience of the people's representatives." This is because the legislative policy has riveted the present seats in the Assembly to their respective constituencies, and by the votes of their incumbents a reapportionment of any kind is prevented. The people have been rebuffed at the hands of the Assembly; they have tried the constitutional convention route, but since the call must originate in the Assembly it, too, has been fruitless. They have tried Tennessee courts with the same result, and Governors have fought the tide only to flounder. It is said that there is recourse in Congress and perhaps that may be, but from a practical standpoint this is without substance. To date Congress has never undertaken such a task in any State. We therefore must conclude that the people of Tennessee are stymied and without judicial intervention will be saddled with the present discrimination in the affairs of their state government.

. . .

MR. JUSTICE STEWART, concurring.

The separate writings of my dissenting and concurring Brothers stray so far from the subject of today's decision as to convey, I think, a distressingly inaccurate impression of what the Court decides. For that reason, I think it appropriate, in joining the opinion of the Court, to emphasize in a few words what the opinion does and does not say.

The Court today decides three things and no more: "(a) that the court possessed jurisdiction of the subject matter; (b) that a justiciable cause of action is stated upon which appellants would be entitled to appropriate relief; and (c) . . . that the appellants have standing to challenge the Tennessee apportionment statutes." *Ante,* pp. 197–198.

The complaint in this case asserts that Tennessee's system of apportionment is utterly arbitrary—without any possible justification in rationality. The District Court did not reach the merits of that claim, and this Court quite properly expresses no view on the subject. Contrary to the suggestion of my Brother HARLAN, the Court does not say or imply that "state legislatures must be so structured as to reflect with approximate equality the voice of every voter." *Post,* p. 332. The Court does not say or imply that there is anything in the Federal Constitution "to prevent a State, acting not irrationally, from choosing any electoral legislative structure it thinks best suited to the interests, temper, and customs of its people." *Post,* p. 334. And contrary to the suggestion of my Brother DOUGLAS, the Court most assuredly does not decide the question, "may a State weight the vote of one county or one district more heavily than it weights the vote in another?" *Ante,* p. 244.

. . .

MR. JUSTICE FRANKFURTER, whom MR. JUSTICE HARLAN joins, dissenting.

The Court today reverses a uniform course of decision established by a dozen cases, including one by which the very claim now sustained was unanimously rejected only five years ago. The impressive body of rulings thus cast aside reflected the equally uniform course of our political history regarding the relationship between population and legislative representation—a wholly different matter from denial of the franchise to individuals because of race, color, religion or sex. Such a massive repudiation of the experience of our whole past in asserting destructively novel judicial power demands a detailed analysis of the role of this Court in our constitutional scheme. Disregard of inherent limits in the effective exercise of the Court's "judicial Power" not only presages the futility of judicial intervention in the essentially political conflict of forces by which the relation between population and representation has time out of mind been and now is determined. It may well impair the Court's position as the ultimate organ of "the supreme Law of the Land" in that vast range of legal problems, often strongly entangled in popular feeling, on which this Court must pronounce. The Court's authority—possessed of neither the purse nor the sword—ultimately rests on sustained public confidence in its moral sanction. Such feeling must be nourished by the Court's complete detachment, in fact and in appearance, from political entanglements and by abstention

from injecting itself into the clash of political forces in political settlements.

. . .

...The Framers carefully and with deliberate forethought refused so to enthrone the judiciary. In this situation, as in others of like nature, appeal for relief does not belong here. Appeal must be to an informed, civically militant electorate. In a democratic society like ours, relief must come through an aroused popular conscience that sears the conscience of the people's representatives. In any event there is nothing judicially more unseemly nor more self-defeating than for this Court to make *in terrorem* pronouncements, to indulge in merely empty rhetoric, sounding a word of promise to the ear, sure to be disappointing to the hope.

. . .

Dissenting opinion of MR. JUSTICE HARLAN, whom MR. JUSTICE FRANKFURTER joins.

. . .

Once one cuts through the thicket of discussion devoted to "jurisdiction," "standing," "justiciability," and "political question," there emerges a straightforward issue which, in my view, is determinative of this case. Does the complaint disclose a violation of a federal constitutional right, in other words, a claim over which a United States District Court would have jurisdiction under 28 U.S.C. § 1343 (3) and 42 U.S.C. § 1983? The majority opinion does not actually discuss this basic question, but, as one concurring Justice observes, seems to decide it *"sub silentio."* *Ante,* p. 261. However, in my opinion, appellants' allegations, accepting all of them as true, do not, parsed down or as a whole, show an infringement by Tennessee of any rights assured by the Fourteenth Amendment. Accordingly, I believe the complaint should have been dismissed for "failure to state a claim upon which relief can be granted." Fed. Rules Civ. Proc., Rule 12(b)(6).

. . .

I.

I can find nothing in the Equal Protection Clause or elsewhere in the Federal Constitution which expressly or impliedly supports the view that state legislatures must be so structured as to reflect with approximate equality the voice of every voter. Not only is that proposition refuted by history, as shown by my Brother FRANKFURTER, but it strikes deep into the heart of our federal system. Its acceptance would require us to turn our backs on the regard which this Court has always shown for the judgment of state legislatures and courts on matters of basically local concern.

In the last analysis, what lies at the core of this controversy is a difference of opinion as to the function of representative government. It is surely beyond argument that those who have the responsibility for devising a system of representation may permissibly consider that factors other than bare numbers should be taken into account. The existence of the United States Senate is proof enough of that....

Wesberry v. Sanders

376 U.S. 1 (1964)

After the Court decided in *Baker* v. *Carr* (1962) to accept jurisdiction in reapportionment cases, it had to determine whether judicial scrutiny would cover only malapportionment in state legislatures or in Congress as well. This case involved Georgia's Fifth Congressional District, which had a population two to three times greater than some other congressional districts in the state. A three-judge district court dismissed the complaint filed by James P. Wesberry, Jr., a citizen of Fulton County, for "want of equity." The defendant was Carl E. Sanders, Governor of Georgia.

MR. JUSTICE BLACK delivered the opinion of the Court.

Appellants are citizens and qualified voters of Fulton County, Georgia, and as such are entitled to vote in congressional elections in Georgia's Fifth Congressional District. That district, one of ten created by a 1931 Georgia statute, includes Fulton, DeKalb, and Rockdale Counties and has a population according to the 1960 census of 823,680. The average population of the ten districts is 394,312, less than half that of the Fifth. One district, the Ninth, has only 272,154 people, less than one-third as many as the Fifth. Since there is only one Congressman for each district, this inequality of population means that the Fifth District's Congressman has to represent from two to three times as many people as do Congressmen from some of the other Georgia districts.

Claiming that these population disparities deprived them and voters similarly situated of a right under the Federal Constitution to have their votes for Congressmen given the same weight as the votes of other Georgians, the appellants brought this action under 42 U.S.C. §§ 1983 and 1988 and 28 U.S.C. § 1343 (3) asking that the Georgia statute be declared invalid and that the appellees, the Governor and Secretary of State of Georgia, be enjoined from conducting elections under it. The complaint alleged that appellants were deprived of the full benefit of their right to vote, in violation of (1) Art. I, § 2, of the Constitution of the United States, which provides that "The House of Representatives shall be composed of Members chosen every second Year by the People of the several States..."; (2) the Due Process, Equal Protection, and Privileges and Immunities Clauses of the Fourteenth Amendment; and (3) that part of Section 2 of the Fourteenth Amendment which provides that "Representatives shall be apportioned among the several States according to their respective numbers...."

. . .

I.

[The Court summarizes its holding in Baker v. Carr *(1962), concluding that the district court erred in dismissing the complaint.]*

II.

This brings us to the merits. We agree with the District Court that the 1931 Georgia apportionment grossly discriminates against voters in the Fifth Congressional District. A single Congressman represents from two to three times as many Fifth District voters as are represented by each of the Congressmen from the other Georgia congressional districts. The apportionment statute thus contracts the value of some votes and expands that of others. If the Federal Constitution intends that when qualified voters elect members of Congress each vote be given as much weight as any other vote, then this statute cannot stand.

We hold that, construed in its historical context, the command of Art. I, § 2, that Representatives be chosen "by the People of the several States" means that as nearly as is practicable one man's vote in a congressional election is to be worth as much as another's. This rule is followed automatically, of course, when Representatives are chosen as a group on a statewide basis, as was a widespread practice in the first 50 years of our Nation's history. It would be extraordinary to suggest that in such statewide elections the votes of inhabitants of some parts of a State, for example, Georgia's thinly populated Ninth District, could be weighted at two or three times the value of the votes of people living in more populous parts of the State, for example, the Fifth District around Atlanta. Cf. *Gray v. Sanders*, 372 U.S. 368. We do not believe that the Framers of the Constitution intended to permit the same vote-diluting discrimination to be accomplished through the device of districts containing widely varied numbers of inhabitants. To say that a vote is worth more in one district than in another would not only run counter to our fundamental ideas of democratic government, it would cast aside the principle of a House of Representatives elected "by the People," a principle tenaciously fought for and established at the Constitutional Convention. The history of the Constitution, particularly that part of it relating to the adoption of Art. I, § 2, reveals that those who framed the Constitution meant that, no matter what the mechanics of an election, whether statewide or by districts, it was population which was to be the basis of the House of Representatives.

. . .

The question of how the legislature should be constituted precipitated the most bitter controversy of the Convention. One principle was uppermost in the minds of many delegates: that, no matter where he lived, each voter should have a voice equal to that of every other in electing members of Congress. In support of this principle, George Mason of Virginia

"argued strongly for an election of the larger branch by the people. It was to be the grand depository of the democratic principle of the Govt."

James Madison agreed, saying "If the power is not immediately derived from the people, in proportion to their numbers, we may make a paper confederacy, but that will be all." Repeatedly, delegates rose to make the same point: that it would be unfair, unjust, and contrary to common sense to give a small number of people as many Senators or Representatives as were allowed to much larger groups—in short, as James Wilson of Pennsylvania put it, "equal numbers of people ought to have an equal no. of representatives..." and representatives "of different districts ought clearly to hold the same proportion to each other, as their respective constituents hold to each other."

[*The Court describes the fear of small states that they would be overwhelmed in a legislature based only on population. As part of the Grand Compromise, each state would have two Senators, elected by the state legislatures, while members of the House of Representatives would be chosen directly by the people and "apportioned among the several States . . . according to their respective Numbers."*]

It would defeat the principle solemnly embodied in the Great Compromise—equal representation in the House for equal numbers of people—for us to hold that, within the States, legislatures may draw the lines of congressional districts in such a way as to give some voters a greater voice in choosing a Congressman than others. The House of Representatives, the Convention agreed, was to represent the people as individuals, and on a basis of complete equality for each voter. The delegates were quite aware of what Madison called the "vicious representation" in Great Britain whereby "rotten boroughs" with few inhabitants were represented in Parliament on or almost on a par with cities of greater population. Wilson urged that people must be represented as individuals, so that America would escape the evils of the English system under which one man could send two members to Parliament to represent the borough of Old Sarum while London's million people sent but four. The delegates referred to rotten borough apportionments in some of the state legislatures as the kind of objectionable governmental action that the Constitution should not tolerate in the election of congressional representatives.

. . .

Soon after the Constitution was adopted, James Wilson of Pennsylvania, by then an Associate Justice of this Court, gave a series of lectures at Philadelphia in which, drawing on his experience as one of the most active members of the Constitutional Convention, he said:

"[A]ll elections ought to be equal. Elections are

equal, when a given number of citizens, in one part of the state, choose as many representatives, as are chosen by the same number of citizens, in any other part of the state. In this manner, the proportion of the representatives and of the constituents will remain invariably the same."

It is in the light of such history that we must construe Art. I, § 2, of the Constitution, which, carrying out the ideas of Madison and those of like views, provides that Representatives shall be chosen "by the People of the several States" and shall be "apportioned among the several States... according to their respective Numbers."... No right is more precious in a free country than that of having a voice in the election of those who make the laws under which, as good citizens, we must live. Other rights, even the most basic, are illusory if the right to vote is undermined. Our Constitution leaves no room for classification of people in a way that unnecessarily abridges this right. In urging the people to adopt the Constitution, Madison said in No. 57 of *The Federalist*:

"Who are to be the electors of the Fœderal Representatives? Not the rich more than the poor; not the learned more than the ignorant; not the haughty heirs of distinguished names, more than the humble sons of obscure and unpropitious fortune. The electors are to be the great body of the people of the United States...."

Readers surely could have fairly taken this to mean, "one person, one vote." Cf. *Gray v. Sanders*, 372 U.S. 368, 381.

While it may not be possible to draw congressional districts with mathematical precision, that is no excuse for ignoring our Constitution's plain objective of making equal representation for equal numbers of people the fundamental goal for the House of Representatives. That is the high standard of justice and common sense which the Founders set for us.

Reversed and remanded.

MR. JUSTICE CLARK, concurring in part and dissenting in part.

Unfortunately I can join neither the opinion of the Court nor the dissent of my Brother HARLAN. It is true that the opening sentence of Art. I, § 2, of the Constitution provides that Representatives are to be chosen "by the People of the several States...." However, in my view, Brother HARLAN

has clearly demonstrated that both the historical background and language preclude a finding that Art. I, § 2, lays down the *ipse dixit* "one person, one vote" in congressional elections.

On the other hand, I agree with the majority that congressional districting is subject to judicial scrutiny.... I therefore cannot agree with Brother HARLAN that the supervisory power granted to Congress under Art. I, § 4, is the exclusive remedy.

. . .

MR. JUSTICE HARLAN, dissenting.

I had not expected to witness the day when the Supreme Court of the United States would render a decision which casts grave doubt on the constitutionality of the composition of the House of Representatives. It is not an exaggeration to say that such is the effect of today's decision. The Court's holding that the Constitution requires States to select Representatives either by elections at large or by elections in districts composed "as nearly as is practicable" of equal population places in jeopardy the seats of almost all the members of the present House of Representatives.

In the last congressional election, in 1962, Representatives from 42 States were elected from congressional districts. *[Representatives were elected at large in Alabama, Alaska, Delaware, Hawaii, Nevada, New Mexico, Vermont, and Wyoming, accounting for seventeen Representatives. In addition, Connecticut, Maryland, Michigan, Ohio, and Texas each elected one of their Representatives at large.]*In all but five of those States, the difference between the populations of the largest and smallest districts exceeded 100,000 persons. A difference of this magnitude in the size of districts the average population of which in each State is less than 500,000 is presumably not equality among districts "as nearly as is practicable," although the Court does not reveal its definition of that phrase. Thus, today's decision impugns the validity of the election of 398 Representatives from 37 States, leaving a "constitutional" House of 37 members now sitting.

Only a demonstration which could not be avoided would justify this Court in rendering a decision the effect of which, inescapably as I see it, is to declare constitutionally defective the very composition of a coordinate branch of the Federal Government. The Court's opinion not only fails to make such a demonstration, it is unsound logically on its face and demonstrably unsound historically.

I.

Before coming to grips with the reasoning that carries such extraordinary consequences, it is important to have firmly in mind the provisions of Article I of the Constitution which control this case:

"Section 2. The House of Representatives shall be composed of Members chosen every second Year by the People of the several States, and the Electors in each State shall have the Qualifications requisite for Electors of the most numerous Branch of the State Legislature.

· · ·

"Representatives and direct Taxes shall be apportioned among the several States which may be included within this Union, according to their respective Numbers, which shall be determined by adding to the whole Number of free Persons, including those bound to Service for a Term of Years, and excluding Indians not taxed, three fifths of all other Persons. The actual Enumeration shall be made within three Years after the first Meeting of the Congress of the United States, and within every subsequent Term of ten Years, in such Manner as they shall by Law direct. The Number of Representatives shall not exceed one for every thirty Thousand, but each State shall have at Least one Representative....

"Section 4. The Times, Places and Manner of holding Elections for Senators and Representatives, shall be prescribed in each State by the Legislature thereof; but the Congress may at any time by Law make or alter such Regulations, except as to the Places of chusing Senators.

· · ·

"Section 5. Each House shall be the Judge of the Elections, Returns and Qualifications of its own Members...."

As will be shown, these constitutional provisions and their "historical context," *ante,* p. 7, establish:

1. that congressional Representatives are to be apportioned among the several States largely, but not entirely, according to population;
2. that the States have plenary power to select their allotted Representatives in accordance with

any method of popular election they please, subject only to the supervisory power of Congress; and
3. that the supervisory power of Congress is exclusive.

· · ·

II.

...The fact is, however, that Georgia's 10 Representatives *are* elected "by the People" of Georgia, just as Representatives from other States are elected "by the People of the several States." This is all that the Constitution requires.

Although the Court finds necessity for its artificial construction of Article I in the undoubted importance of the right to vote, that right is not involved in this case. All of the appellants do vote. The Court's talk about "debasement" and "dilution" of the vote is a model of circular reasoning, in which the premises of the argument feed on the conclusion....

[In the remainder of this lengthy dissent, Harlan states that it is unlikely that "most or many" delegates to the Constitutional Convention would have subscribed to the one-person, one-vote principle; that state legislatures had plenary power to district, subject only to the supervisory power of Congress; and that the Court is not simply undertaking to exercise a power which the Constitution reserves to Congress but is also overruling congressional judgment expressed in previous statutes and legislative history. Harlan warns that the "promise of judicial intervention in matters of this sort cannot but encourage popular inertia in efforts for political reform through the political process, with the inevitable result that the process is itself weakened."]

Mr. Justice Stewart.

I think it is established that "this Court has power to afford relief in a case of this type as against the objection that the issues are not justiciable," and I cannot subscribe to any possible implication to the contrary which may lurk in Mr. Justice Harlan's dissenting opinion. With this single qualification I join the dissent because I think Mr. Justice Harlan has unanswerably demonstrated that Art. I, § 2, of the Constitution gives no mandate to this Court or to any court to ordain that congressional districts within each State must be equal in population.

Reynolds v. Sims

377 U.S. 533 (1964)

In this case the Court faces the question of whether the principle of equal representation applies to both houses of a state legislature, or whether one house, following the federal model (the U.S. Senate), may be apportioned on a basis other than population. M.O. Sims and other voters from Alabama brought suit to challenge the apportionment of the state legislature as a violation of the Equal Protection Clause of the Fourteenth Amendment and the Alabama Constitution. They sued B. A. Reynolds, judge of probate of Dallas County, Alabama. Under the state constitution, each county was entitled to at least one state representative, no matter how small the population. A three-judge federal court refused to order the May 1962 primary election to be held at large, stating that it should not act until the legislature had an opportunity to take corrective action before the general election. After the legislature acted, the district court held that neither of the two apportionment plans fashioned by the legislature would cure the violation of the Equal Protection Clause and proceeded to combine features of the two plans to produce a more equitable apportionment. The state appealed, claiming that a federal court lacks power to apportion a legislature.

MR. CHIEF JUSTICE WARREN delivered the opinion of the Court.

. . .

I.

. . .

The complaint stated that the Alabama Legislature was composed of a Senate of 35 members and a House of Representatives of 106 members. It set out relevant portions of the 1901 Alabama Constitution, which prescribed the number of members of the two bodies of the State Legislature and the method of apportioning the seats among the State's 67 counties, and provide as follows:

[Each county was entitled to at least one representative. The state was to be divided into as many senatorial districts as there were senators, with each district as "nearly equal" to each other in population. Representation in the legislature "shall be based upon population." Although the state constitution required that the legislature be apportioned every ten years, the last apportionment was based on the 1900 census. Population-variance ratios of up to about 41-to-1 existed in the Senate and up to about 16-to-1 in the House.]

II.

Undeniably the Constitution of the United States protects the right of all qualified citizens to vote, in state as well as in federal elections. A consistent line of decisions by this Court in cases involving attempts to deny or restrict the right of suffrage has made this indelibly clear.... The right to

vote freely for the candidate of one's choice is of the essence of a democratic society, and any restrictions on that right strike at the heart of representative government. And the right of suffrage can be denied by a debasement or dilution of the weight of a citizen's vote just as effectively as by wholly prohibiting the free exercise of the franchise.

[The Court reviews the holdings in Baker v. Carr (1962), Gray v. Sanders (1963), and Wesberry v. Sanders (1964).]

III.

A predominant consideration in determining whether a State's legislative apportionment scheme constitutes an invidious discrimination violative of rights asserted under the Equal Protection Clause is that the rights allegedly impaired are individual and personal in nature....

Legislators represent people, not trees or acres. Legislators are elected by voters, not farms or cities or economic interests. As long as ours is a representative form of government, and our legislatures are those instruments of government elected directly by and directly representative of the people, the right to elect legislators in a free and unimpaired fashion is a bedrock of our political system. It could hardly be gainsaid that a constitutional claim had been asserted by an allegation that certain otherwise qualified voters had been entirely prohibited from voting for members of their state legislature. And, if a State should provide that the votes of citizens in one part of the State should be given two times, or five times, or

10 times the weight of votes of citizens in another part of the State, it could hardly be contended that the right to vote of those residing in the disfavored areas had not been effectively diluted. It would appear extraordinary to suggest that a State could be constitutionally permitted to enact a law providing that certain of the State's voters could vote two, five, or 10 times for their legislative representatives, while voters living elsewhere could vote only once. And it is inconceivable that a state law to the effect that, in counting votes for legislators, the votes of citizens in one part of the State would be multiplied by two, five, or 10, while the votes of persons in another area would be counted only at face value, could be constitutionally sustainable. Of course, the effect of state legislative districting schemes which give the same number of representatives to unequal numbers of constituents is identical....

...[T]he concept of equal protection has been traditionally viewed as requiring the uniform treatment of persons standing in the same relation to the governmental action questioned or challenged.... Since the achieving of fair and effective representation for all citizens is concededly the basic aim of legislative apportionment, we conclude that the Equal Protection Clause guarantees the opportunity for equal participation by all voters in the election of state legislators....

· · ·

...A citizen, a qualified voter, is no more nor no less so because he lives in the city or on the farm. This is the clear and strong command of our Constitution's Equal Protection Clause. This is an essential part of the concept of a government of laws and not men. This is at the heart of Lincoln's vision of "government of the people, by the people, [and] for the people." The Equal Protection Clause demands no less than substantially equal state legislative representation for all citizens, of all places as well as of all races.

IV.

We hold that, as a basic constitutional standard, the Equal Protection Clause requires that the seats in both houses of a bicameral state legislature must be apportioned on a population basis. Simply stated, an individual's right to vote for state legislators is unconstitutionally impaired when its weight is in a substantial fashion diluted when compared with votes of citizens living in other parts of the State. Since, under neither the existing apportionment provisions nor either of the pro-

posed plans was either of the houses of the Alabama Legislature apportioned on a population basis, the District Court correctly held that all three of these schemes were constitutionally invalid....

V.

Since neither of the houses of the Alabama Legislature, under any of the three plans considered by the District Court, was apportioned on a population basis, we would be justified in proceeding no further. However, one of the proposed plans, that contained in the so-called 67-Senator Amendment, at least superficially resembles the scheme of legislative representation followed in the Federal Congress. Under this plan, each of Alabama's 67 counties is allotted one senator, and no counties are given more than one Senate seat. Arguably, this is analogous to the allocation of two Senate seats, in the Federal Congress, to each of the 50 States, regardless of population. Seats in the Alabama House, under the proposed constitutional amendment, are distributed by giving each of the 67 counties at least one, with the remaining 39 seats being allotted among the more populous counties on a population basis. This scheme, at least at first glance, appears to resemble that prescribed for the Federal House of Representatives, where the 435 seats are distributed among the States on a population basis, although each State, regardless of its population, is given at least one Congressman. Thus, although there are substantial differences in underlying rationale and result, the 67-Senator Amendment, as proposed by the Alabama Legislature, at least arguably presents for consideration a scheme analogous to that used for apportioning seats in Congress.

Much has been written since our decision in *Baker* v. *Carr* about the applicability of the so-called federal analogy to state legislative apportionment arrangements. After considering the matter, the court below concluded that no conceivable analogy could be drawn between the federal scheme and the apportionment of seats in the Alabama Legislature under the proposed constitutional amendment. We agree with the District Court, and find the federal analogy inapposite and irrelevant to state legislative districting schemes....

· · ·

The system of representation in the two Houses of the Federal Congress is one ingrained in our Constitution, as part of the law of the land. It is one conceived out of compromise and concession indispensable to the establishment of our federal republic. Arising from unique historical circumstances, it is based on the consideration that in establishing our type of federalism a group of formerly independent States bound themselves together under one national government. Admittedly, the original 13 States surrendered some of their sovereignty in agreeing to join together "to form a more perfect Union." But at the heart of our constitutional system remains the concept of separate and distinct governmental entities which have delegated some, but not all, of their formerly held powers to the single national government....

Political subdivisions of States—counties, cities, or whatever—never were and never have been considered as sovereign entities. Rather, they have been traditionally regarded as subordinate governmental instrumentalities created by the State to assist in the carrying out of state governmental functions....The relationship of the States to the Federal Government could hardly be less analogous.

. . .

VI.

By holding that as a federal constitutional requisite both houses of a state legislature must be apportioned on a population basis, we mean that the Equal Protection Clause requires that a State make an honest and good faith effort to construct districts, in both houses of its legislature, as nearly of equal population as is practicable. We realize that it is a practical impossibility to arrange legislative districts so that each one has an identical number of residents, or citizens, or voters. Mathematical exactness or precision is hardly a workable constitutional requirement.

. . .

...[W]e affirm the judgment below and remand the cases for further proceedings consistent with the views stated in this opinion.

It is so ordered.

MR. JUSTICE CLARK, concurring in the affirmance.

The Court goes much beyond the necessities of this case in laying down a new "equal population" principle for state legislative apportionment. This principle seems to be an offshoot of *Gray v. Sanders*, 372 U.S. 368, 381 (1963), *i. e.,* "one person, one vote," modified by the "nearly as is practicable" admonition of *Wesberry v. Sanders*, 376 U.S. 1, 8 (1964). Whether "nearly as is practicable" means "one person, one vote" qualified by

"approximately equal" or "some deviations" or by the impossibility of "mathematical nicety" is not clear from the majority's use of these vague and meaningless phrases. But whatever the standard, the Court applies it to each house of the State Legislature.

It seems to me that all that the Court need say in this case is that each plan considered by the trial court is "a crazy quilt," clearly revealing invidious discrimination in each house of the Legislature and therefore violative of the Equal Protection Clause. See my concurring opinion in *Baker v. Carr*, 369 U.S. 186, 253–258 (1962).

I, therefore, do not reach the question of the so-called "federal analogy." But in my view, if one house of the State Legislature meets the population standard, representation in the other house might include some departure from it so as to take into account, on a rational basis, other factors in order to afford some representation to the various elements of the State. See my dissenting opinion in *Lucas v. Forty-Fourth General Assembly of Colorado, post,* p. 741, decided this date.

MR. JUSTICE STEWART.

All of the parties have agreed with the District Court's finding that legislative inaction for some 60 years in the face of growth and shifts in population has converted Alabama's legislative apportionment plan enacted in 1901 into one completely lacking in rationality. Accordingly, for the reasons stated in my dissenting opinion in *Lucas v. Forty-Fourth General Assembly of Colorado, post,* p. 744, I would affirm the judgment of the District Court holding that this apportionment violated the Equal Protection Clause.

I also agree with the Court that it was proper for the District Court, in framing a remedy, to adhere as closely as practicable to the apportionments approved by the representatives of the people of Alabama, and to afford the State of Alabama full opportunity, consistent with the requirements of the Federal Constitution, to devise its own system of legislative apportionment.

MR. JUSTICE HARLAN, dissenting.

In these cases the Court holds that seats in the legislatures of six States are apportioned in ways that violate the Federal Constitution. Under the Court's ruling it is bound to follow that the legislatures in all but a few of the other 44 States will meet the same fate. These decisions, with *Wesberry v. Sanders*, 376 U.S. 1, involving congressional districting by the States, and *Gray v.*

Sanders, 372 U.S. 368, relating to elections for statewide office, have the effect of placing basic aspects of state political systems under the pervasive overlordship of the federal judiciary. Once again, I must register my protest.

[Harlan proceeds to set forth a detailed account

of the proposal and ratification of the Fourteenth Amendment, concluding that Congress deliberately excluded from the Amendment any restriction on the states' power "to control voting rights because it believed that if such restrictions were included," the Amendment would not have been adopted.]

Davis v. Bandemer

478 U.S. 109 (1986)

A suit was brought by Indiana Democrats challenging the constitutionality of Indiana's 1981 state apportionment. They claimed that the apportionment, drawn up by Republicans, unconstitutionally diluted the votes of Democrats. A three-judge court sustained the equal protection challenge. The Supreme Court faced the question of whether political gerrymandering cases are properly justiciable under the Equal Protection Clause. State officials, defending the apportionment, are represented here by Susan J. Davis. The position of Indiana Democrats is represented by Irwin C. Bandemer. In an interesting twist, the state Democrats were joined by the Republican National Committee, which hoped to use the case to challenge the reapportionment of other state legislatures, most of which are controlled by Democrats.

JUSTICE WHITE announced the judgment of the Court and delivered the opinion of the Court as to Part II and an opinion as to Parts I, III, and IV, in which JUSTICE BRENNAN, JUSTICE MARSHALL, and JUSTICE BLACKMUN join.

In this case, we review a judgment from a three-judge District Court, which sustained an equal protection challenge to Indiana's 1981 state apportionment on the basis that the law unconstitutionally diluted the votes of Indiana Democrats. 603 F.Supp. 1479 (1984). Although we find such political gerrymandering to be justiciable, we conclude that the District Court applied an insufficiently demanding standard in finding unconstitutional vote dilution. Consequently, we reverse.

I

The Indiana Legislature, also known as the "General Assembly," consists of a House of Representatives and a Senate. There are 100 members of the House of Representatives, and 50 members of the Senate. The members of the House serve two-year terms, with elections held for all seats every 2 years. The members of the Senate serve 4-year terms, and Senate elections are staggered so that half of the seats are up for election every two years. The members of both Houses are elected from legislative districts; but, while all Senate members are elected from single-member districts, House members are elected from a mixture of sin-

gle-member and multi-member districts. The division of the State into districts is accomplished by legislative enactment, which is signed by the Governor into law. Reapportionment is required every 10 years and is based on the federal decennial census. There is no prohibition against more frequent reapportionments.

In early 1981, the General Assembly initiated the process of reapportioning the State's legislative districts pursuant to the 1980 census. At this time, there were Republican majorities in both the House and the Senate, and the Governor was Republican. Bills were introduced in both Houses, and a reapportionment plan was duly passed and approved by the Governor. This plan provided 50 single-member districts for the Senate; for the House, it provided 7 triple-member, 9 double-member, and 61 single-member districts. In the Senate plan, the population deviation between districts was 1.15%; in the House plan, the deviation was 1.05%. The multi-member districts generally included the more metropolitan areas of the State, although not every metropolitan area was in a multi-member district. Marion County, which includes Indianapolis, was combined with portions of its neighboring counties to form five triple-member districts. Fort Wayne was divided into two parts, and each part was combined with portions of the surrounding county or counties to make two double-member districts. On the other hand, South Bend was divided and put partly into a double-member district and partly into a single-member district (each part combined with part of the surrounding county or counties). Although county and city lines were not consistently followed, township lines generally were. The two plans, the Senate and the House, were not nested; that is, each Senate district was not divided exactly into two House districts. There appears to have been little relation between the lines drawn in the two plans.

In early 1982, this suit was filed by several Indiana Democrats (here the appellees) against various state officials (here the appellants), alleging that the 1981 reapportionment plans constituted a political gerrymander intended to disadvantage Democrats....

In November 1982, before the case went to trial, elections were held under the new districting plan. All of the House seats and half of the Senate seats were up for election. Over all the House races statewide, Democratic candidates received 51.9% of the vote. Only 43 Democrats, however, were elected to the House. Over all the Senate races statewide, Democratic candidates received 53.1% of the vote. Thirteen (of 25) Democrats were elected. In Marion and Allen Counties, both divided into multi-member House districts, Democratic candidates drew 46.6% of the vote, but only 3 of the 21 House seats were filled by Democrats.

On December 13, 1984, a divided District Court issued a decision declaring the reapportionment to be unconstitutional, enjoining the appellants from holding elections pursuant to the 1981 redistricting, ordering the General Assembly to prepare a new plan, and retaining jurisdiction over the case. See 603 F.Supp. 1479 (1984).

To the District Court majority, the results of the 1982 elections seemed "to support an argument that there is a built-in bias favoring the majority party, the Republicans, which instituted the reapportionment plan."... In the course of this further examination, the court noted the irregular shape of some district lines, the peculiar mix of single- and multi-member districts, and the failure of the district lines to adhere consistently to political subdivision boundaries to define communities of interest. The court also found inadequate the other explanations given for the configuration of the districts, such as adherence to the one-person, one-vote imperative and the Voting Right Act's no retrogression requirement. These factors, concluded the court, evidenced an intentional effort to favor Republican incumbents and candidates and to dis-

advantage Democratic voters. This was achieved by "stacking" Democrats into districts with large Democratic majorities and "splitting" them in other districts so as to give Republicans safe but not excessive majorities in those districts....

II

We address first the question whether this case presents a justiciable controversy or a nonjusticiable political question....

A

[The Court reviews its principal holdings, including the principle "one person, one vote"; actions against racial gerrymandering; and decisions that struck down multimember districts that operated to minimize the voting strength of racial or political elements. Although the Court had summarily affirmed some lower-court decisions that rejected the justiciability of purely political gerrymandering, it stated that it was not bound by those affirmances. In addressing the issue of justiciability, the Court restates the political question doctrine announced in Baker v. Carr.*]*

This analysis applies equally to the question now before us. Disposition of this question does not involve us in a matter more properly decided by a coequal branch of our Government. There is no risk of foreign or domestic disturbance, and in light of our cases since *Baker* we are not persuaded that there are no judicially discernible and manageable standards by which political gerrymander cases are to be decided. *[The Court later adds that the fact that the claim "is submitted by a political group, rather than a racial group, does not distinguish it in terms of justiciability."]*

III

Having determined that the political gerrymandering claim in this case is justiciable, we turn to the question whether the District Court erred in holding that appellees had alleged and proved a violation of the Equal Protection Clause.

A

Preliminarily, we agree with the District Court that the claim made by the appellees in this case is a claim that the 1981 apportionment discriminates against Democrats on a statewide basis....

We also agree with the District Court that in order to succeed the Bandemer plaintiffs were required to prove both intentional discrimination against an identifiable political group and an actual discriminatory effect on that group. See, *e.g., Mobile v. Bolden,* 446 U.S., at 67–68. Further, we are confident that if the law challenged here had discriminatory effects on Democrats, this record would support a finding that the discrimination was intentional. Thus, we decline to overturn the District Court's finding of discriminatory intent as clearly erroneous.

Indeed, quite aside from the anecdotal evidence, the shape of the House and Senate Districts, and the alleged disregard for political boundaries, we think it most likely that whenever a legislature redistricts, those responsible for the legislation will know the likely political composition of the new districts and will have a prediction as to whether a particular district is a safe one for a Democratic or Republican candidate or is a competitive district that either candidate might win....

[From Gaffney v. Cummings, *412 U.S., at 752–753 (1973), the Court states that the consideration of political factors in a reapportionment plan is not sufficient to invalidate it. "Politics and political considerations are inseparable from districting and apportionment."]*

B

We do not accept, however, the District Court's legal and factual bases for concluding that the 1981 Act visited a sufficiently adverse effect on the appellees' constitutionally protected rights to make out a violation of the Equal Protection Clause. The District Court held that because any apportionment scheme that purposely prevents proportional representation is unconstitutional, Democratic voters need only show that their proportionate voting influence has been adversely affected. 603 F.Supp., at 1492. Our cases, however, clearly foreclose any claim that the Constitution requires proportional representation or that legislatures in reapportioning must draw district lines to come as near as possible to allocating seats to the contending parties in proportion to what their anticipated statewide vote will be....

In cases involving individual multi-member districts, we have required a substantially greater showing of adverse effects than a mere lack of proportional representation to support a finding of unconstitutional vote dilution. Only where there is evidence that excluded groups have "less opportunity to participate in the political processes and to elect candidates of their choice"

have we refused to approve the use of multimember districts. *Rogers v. Lodge,* 458 U.S., at 624....

*[Our]*holdings rest on a conviction that the mere fact that a particular apportionment scheme makes it more difficult for a particular group in a particular district to elect the representatives of its choice does not render that scheme constitutionally infirm. This conviction, in turn, stems from a perception that the power to influence the political process is not limited to winning elections. An individual or a group of individuals who votes for a losing candidate is usually deemed to be adequately represented by the winning candidate and to have as much opportunity to influence that candidate as other voters in the district. We cannot presume in such a situation, without actual proof to the contrary, that the candidate elected will entirely ignore the interests of those voters. This is true even in a safe district where the losing group loses election after election....

... [U]nconstitutional discrimination occurs only when the electoral system is arranged in a manner that will consistently degrade a voter's or a group of voters' influence on the political process as a whole.

. . .

Based on these views, we would reject the District Court's apparent holding that *any* interference with an opportunity to elect a representative of one's choice would be sufficient to allege or make out an equal protection violation, unless justified by some acceptable state interest that the State would be required to demonstrate. In addition to being contrary to the above-described conception of an unconstitutional political gerrymander, such a low threshold for legal action would invite attack on all or almost all reapportionment statutes. District-based elections hardly ever produce a perfect fit between votes and representation. The one-person, one-vote imperative often mandates departure from this result as does the no-retrogression rule required by § 5 of the Voting Rights Act. Inviting attack on minor departures from some supposed norm would too much embroil the judiciary in second-guessing what has consistently been referred to as a political task for the legislature, a task that should not be monitored too closely unless the express or tacit goal is to effect its removal from legislative halls. We decline to take a major step toward that end, which would be so much at odds with our history and experience.

. . .

D

[In his concluding section, White rejects an alternative method proposed by Powell, who suggested a number of factors to consider in judging equal protection claims of political gerrymandering. White disagreed that the intentional drawing of district boundaries for partisan ends and for no other reason violates the Equal Protection Clause in and of itself.]

IV

In sum, we hold that political gerrymandering cases are properly justiciable under the Equal Protection Clause. We also conclude, however, that a threshold showing of discriminatory vote dilution is required for a prima facie case of an equal protection violation. In this case, the findings made by the District Court of an adverse effect on the appellees do not surmount the threshold requirement. Consequently, the judgment of the District Court is

Reversed.

CHIEF JUSTICE BURGER, concurring in the judgment.

I join JUSTICE O'CONNOR's opinion.

. . .

JUSTICE O'CONNOR, with whom THE CHIEF JUSTICE and JUSTICE REHNQUIST join, concurring in the judgment.

Today the Court holds that claims of political gerrymandering lodged by members of one of the political parties that make up our two-party system are justiciable under the Equal Protection Clause of the Fourteenth Amendment. Nothing in our precedents compels us to take this step, and there is every reason not to do so. I would hold that the partisan gerrymandering claims of major political parties raise a nonjusticiable political question that the judiciary should leave to the legislative branch as the Framers of the Constitution unquestionably intended. Accordingly, I would reverse the District Court's judgment on the grounds that appellees' claim is nonjusticiable.

. . .

To turn these matters over to the federal judiciary is to inject the courts into the most heated partisan issues. It is predictable that the courts will respond by moving away from the nebulous standard a plurality of the Court fashions today and toward some form of rough proportional representation for all political groups. The consequences of this shift will be as immense as they are unfortunate. I do not believe, and the Court offers not a shred of evidence to suggest, that the Framers of the Constitution intended the judicial power to encompass the making of such fundamental choices about how this Nation is to be governed. Nor do I believe that the proportional representation towards which the Court's expansion of equal protection doctrine will lead is consistent with our history, our traditions, or our political institutions.

. . .

JUSTICE POWELL, with whom JUSTICE STEVENS joins, concurring in Part II, and dissenting.

...[T]he plurality expresses the view, with which I agree, that a partisan political gerrymander violates the Equal Protection Clause only on proof of "both intentional discrimination against an identifiable political group and an actual discriminatory effect on that group." *Ante,* at 127. The plurality acknowledges that the record in this case supports a finding that the challenged redistricting plan was adopted for the purpose of discriminating against Democratic voters. *Ibid.* The plurality argues, however, that appellees failed to establish that their voting strength was diluted statewide despite uncontradicted proof that certain key districts were grotesquely gerrymandered to enhance the election prospects of Republican candidates. This argument appears to rest solely on the ground that the legislature accomplished its gerrymander consistent with "one person, one vote," in the sense that the legislature designed voting districts of approximately equal population and erected no direct barriers to Democratic voters' exercise of the franchise. Since the essence of a gerrymandering claim is that the members of a political party as a group have been denied their right to "fair and effective representation," *Reynolds* v. *Sims,* 377 U.S. 533, 565 (1964), I believe that the claim cannot be tested solely by reference to "one person, one vote." Rather, a number of other relevant neutral factors must be considered. Because the plurality ignores such factors and fails to enunciate standards by which to determine whether a legislature has enacted an unconstitutional gerrymander, I dissent.

. . .

Shaw v. Reno

509 U.S. 630 (1993)

As a result of the 1990 census, North Carolina increased its number of seats in Congress from eleven to twelve. The Justice Department rejected an initial state plan that provided for only one majority black congressional district (the state is about 20 percent black). The Justice Department approved a subsequent plan that provided for two majority black districts. Five white voters sued North Carolina lawmakers and the Justice Department, claiming that the state's racial separation of voters violated their constitutional right to participate in "colorblind" elections. Ruth O. Shaw, one of the plaintiffs, sued Attorney General Janet Reno and state officials.

JUSTICE O'CONNOR delivered the opinion of the Court.

This case involves two of the most complex and sensitive issues this Court has faced in recent years: the meaning of the constitutional "right" to vote, and the propriety of race-based state legislation designed to benefit members of historically disadvantaged racial minority groups. As a result of the 1990 census, North Carolina became entitled to a twelfth seat in the United States House of Representatives. The General Assembly enacted a reapportionment plan that included one majority-black congressional district. After the Attorney General of the United States objected to the plan pursuant to § 5 of the Voting Rights Act of 1965, 79 Stat. 439, as amended, 42 U.S.C. § 1973c, the General Assembly passed new legislation creating a second majority-black district. Appellants allege that the revised plan, which contains district boundary lines of dramatically irregular shape, constitutes an unconstitutional racial gerrymander. The question before us is whether appellants have stated a cognizable claim.

I

The voting age population of North Carolina is approximately 78% white, 20% black, and 1% Native American; the remaining 1% is predominantly Asian.... The black population is relatively dispersed; blacks constitute a majority of the general population in only 5 of the State's 100 counties....

[The General Assembly's first redistricting plan contained one majority-black district centered in the eastern coastal plain. After the Attorney General objected, the General Assembly revised the plan to create a second majority-black district.]

The second majority-black district, District 12, is even more unusually shaped. It is approximately 160 miles long and, for much of its length, no wider than the I-85 corridor. It winds in snake-like fashion through tobacco country, financial centers, and manufacturing areas "until it gobbles in enough enclaves of black neighborhoods." 808 F.Supp., at 476–477 (Voorhees, C.J., concurring in part and dissenting in part). Northbound and southbound drivers on I-85 sometimes find themselves in separate districts in one county, only to "trade" districts when they enter the next county. Of the 10 counties through which District 12 passes, five are cut into three different districts; even towns are divided. At one point the district remains contiguous only because it intersects at a single point with two other districts before crossing over them....

The Attorney General did not object to the General Assembly's revised plan. But numerous North Carolinians did. The North Carolina Republican Party and individual voters brought suit in Federal District Court alleging that the plan constituted an unconstitutional political gerrymander under *Davis* v. *Bandemer,* 478 U.S. 109 (1986). That claim was dismissed, see *Pope* v. *Blue,* 809 F. Supp. 392 (WDNC 1992), and this Court summarily affirmed, 506 U.S. 801 (1992).

Shortly after the complaint in *Pope* v. *Blue* was filed, appellants instituted the present action in the United States District Court for the Eastern District of North Carolina. Appellants alleged not that the revised plan constituted a political gerrymander, nor that it violated the "one person, one vote" principle, see *Reynolds* v. *Sims,* 377 U.S. 533, 558 (1964), but that the State had created an unconstitutional *racial* gerrymander....

Appellants contended that the General Assembly's revised reapportionment plan violated several provisions of the United States Constitution, including the Fourteenth Amendment. They alleged that the General Assembly deliberately "create[d] two Congressional Districts in which a majority of black voters was concentrated arbitrarily — without regard to any other considerations, such as compactness, contiguousness, geographical boundaries, or political subdivisions" with the purpose "to create Congressional Districts along racial lines" and to assure the election of two black representatives to Congress....

[A three-judge district court dismissed the case, agreeing unanimously that it lacked subject matter jurisdiction because the Voting Rights Act vests exclusive jurisdiction in the district court for the District of Columbia. By a 2-to-1 vote it found no support for the contention that race-based districting is prohibited by the Constitution.]

II

A

[In this section O'Connor reviews how the essential right to vote had been denied to blacks in the past — despite the Fifteenth Amendment — through a variety of tactics including literacy tests, Grandfather Clauses, "good character" provisos, and racial gerrymandering. One result was the Voting Rights Act of 1965.]

B

It is against this background that we confront the questions presented here. In our view, the District Court properly dismissed appellants' claims against the federal appellees. Our focus is on appellants' claim that the State engaged in unconstitutional racial gerrymandering. That argument strikes a powerful historical chord: It is unsettling how closely the North Carolina plan resembles the most egregious racial gerrymanders of the past.

An understanding of the nature of appellants' claim is critical to our resolution of the case. In their complaint, appellants did not claim that the General Assembly's reapportionment plan unconstitutionally "diluted" white voting strength. They did not even claim to be white. Rather, appellants' complaint alleged that the deliberate segregation of voters into separate districts on the basis of race violated their constitutional right to participate in a "color-blind" electoral process....

Despite their invocation of the ideal of a "color-blind" Constitution, see *Plessy* v. *Ferguson*, 163 U.S. 537, 559 (1896) (Harlan, J., dissenting), appellants appear to concede that race-conscious redistricting is not always unconstitutional.... That concession is wise: This Court never has held that race-conscious state decisionmaking is impermissible in *all* circumstances. What appellants

object to is redistricting legislation that is so extremely irregular on its face that it rationally can be viewed only as an effort to segregate the races for purposes of voting, without regard for traditional districting principles and without sufficiently compelling justification. For the reasons that follow, we conclude that appellants have stated a claim upon which relief can be granted under the Equal Protection Clause. See Fed. Rule Civ. Proc. 12(b)(6).

III

A

The Equal Protection Clause provides that "[n]o State shall...deny to any person within its jurisdiction the equal protection of the laws." U.S. Const., Amdt. 14, § 1. Its central purpose is to prevent the States from purposefully discriminating between individuals on the basis of race....

Classifications of citizens solely on the basis of race "are by their very nature odious to a free people whose institutions are founded upon the doctrine of equality." *Hirabayashi* v. *United States*, 320 U.S. 81, 100 (1943). Accord, *Loving* v. *Virginia*, 388 U.S. 1, 11 (1967). They threaten to stigmatize individuals by reason of their membership in a racial group and to incite racial hostility.... Accordingly, we have held that the Fourteenth Amendment requires state legislation that expressly distinguishes among citizens because of their race to be narrowly tailored to further a compelling governmental interest....

B

Appellants contend that redistricting legislation that is so bizarre on its face that it is "unexplainable on grounds other than race," *Arlington Heights, supra,* at 266, demands the same close scrutiny that we give other state laws that classify citizens by race. Our voting rights precedents support that conclusion.

[O'Connor reviews the Court's holdings in previous racial gerrymandering cases, including Gomillion v. Lightfoot *(1960) and* Wright v. Rockefeller *(1964), and explains the burden of proof needed by plaintiffs to successfully challenge a redistricting plan.]*

The difficulty of proof, of course, does not mean that a racial gerrymander, once established, should receive less scrutiny under the Equal Protection Clause than other state legislation classifying citizens by race. Moreover, it seems clear to us that proof sometimes will not be difficult at all. In some exceptional cases, a reapportionment plan may be so highly irregular that, on its face, it rationally cannot be understood as anything other than an effort to "segregat[e] ... voters" on the basis of race. *Gomillion, supra,* at 341. *Gomillion,* in which a tortured municipal boundary line was drawn to exclude black voters, was such a case. So, too, would be a case in which a State concentrated a dispersed minority population in a single district by disregarding traditional districting principles such as compactness, contiguity, and respect for political subdivisions. We emphasize that these criteria are important not because they are constitutionally required—they are not, cf. *Gaffney* v. *Cummings,* 412 U.S. 735, 752, n. 18 (1973)—but because they are objective factors that may serve to defeat a claim that a district has been gerrymandered on racial lines....

Put differently, we believe that reapportionment is one area in which appearances do matter. A reapportionment plan that includes in one district individuals who belong to the same race, but who are otherwise widely separated by geographical and political boundaries, and who may have little in common with one another but the color of their skin, bears an uncomfortable resemblance to political apartheid. It reinforces the perception that members of the same racial group—regardless of their age, education, economic status, or the community in which they live—think alike, share the same political interests, and will prefer the same candidates at the polls. We have rejected such perceptions elsewhere as impermissible racial stereotypes....

The message that such districting sends to elected representatives is equally pernicious. When a district obviously is created solely to effectuate the perceived common interests of one racial group, elected officials are more likely to believe that their primary obligation is to represent only the members of that group, rather than their constituency as a whole. This is altogether antithetical to our system of representative democracy....

For these reasons, we conclude that a plaintiff challenging a reapportionment statute under the Equal Protection Clause may state a claim by alleging that the legislation, though race-neutral on its face, rationally cannot be understood as anything other than an effort to separate voters into different districts on the basis of race, and that the separation lacks sufficient justification. It is unnecessary for us to decide whether or how a reapportionment plan that, on its face, can be explained in nonracial terms successfully could be challenged. Thus, we express no view as to whether "the intentional creation of majority-minority districts, without more" always gives rise to an equal protection claim. *Post,* at 668 (WHITE, J., dissenting). We hold only that, on the facts of this case, plaintiffs have stated a claim sufficient to defeat the state appellees' motion to dismiss.

C

[In this section O'Connor states that (1) nothing in case law compels the conclusion that racial and political gerrymanders are subject to precisely the same constitutional scrutiny, (2) racial gerrymandering is not automatically acceptable simply because it favors the minority, and (3) nothing in United Jewish Organizations *dictates the results in the North Carolina case. For example, the districts in* UJO *were basically compact, unlike the district challenged here.]*

. . .

V

Racial classifications of any sort pose the risk of lasting harm to our society. They reinforce the belief, held by too many for too much of our history, that individuals should be judged by the color of their skin. Racial classifications with respect to voting carry particular dangers. Racial gerrymandering, even for remedial purposes, may balkanize us into competing racial factions; it threatens to carry us further from the goal of a political system in which race no longer matters—a goal that the Fourteenth and Fifteenth Amendments embody, and to which the Nation continues to aspire. It is for these reasons that race-based districting by our state legislatures demands close judicial scrutiny.

In this case, the Attorney General suggested that North Carolina could have created a reasonably compact second majority-minority district in the south-central to southeastern part of the State. We express no view as to whether appellants successfully could have challenged such a district under the Fourteenth Amendment. We also do not decide whether appellants' complaint stated a claim under constitutional provisions other than the Fourteenth Amendment. Today we hold only that appellants have stated a claim under the Equal Protection Clause by alleging that the North Carolina General Assembly adopted a reapportionment scheme so irrational on its face that it can be understood only as an effort to segregate voters into separate voting districts because of their race, and that the separation lacks sufficient justification. If the allegation of racial gerrymandering remains uncontradicted, the District Court further must determine whether the North Carolina plan is narrowly tailored to further a compelling governmental interest. Accordingly, we reverse the judgment of the District Court and remand the case for further proceedings consistent with this opinion.

It is so ordered.

JUSTICE WHITE, with whom JUSTICE BLACKMUN and JUSTICE STEVENS join, dissenting.

[They argue that the facts in the North Carolina case "mirror" those presented in UJO. With regard to the compelling-interest standard, they conclude that the North Carolina plan was narrowly tailored to meet that test. Finally, they raise a number of questions about the manner in which states will engage in "narrow tailoring" in response to this decision: "Is it more 'narrowly tailored' to create an irregular majority-minority district as opposed to one that is compact but harms other State interests such as incumbency protection or the representation of rural interests?"]

[Justices Blackmun, Stevens, and Souter wrote separate dissenting opinions.]

Miller v. Johnson

515 U.S. 900 (1995)

After the 1990 census increased the number of congressional seats in Georgia from ten to eleven, the state legislature prepared a districting plan that provided for two majority-black districts. The Justice Department refused to clear this plan, and the legislature eventually redrew the lines to provide for three black seats. Here the Court applies the general principles from *Shaw v. Reno* to determine whether the Georgia redistricting plan is valid under the Equal Protection Clause.

JUSTICE KENNEDY delivered the opinion of the Court.

The constitutionality of Georgia's congressional redistricting plan is at issue here. In *Shaw v. Reno, 509 U.S. 630 (1993)*, we held that a plaintiff states a claim under the Equal Protection Clause by alleging that a state redistricting plan, on its face, has no rational explanation save as an effort to separate voters on the basis of race. The question we now decide is whether Georgia's new Eleventh District gives rise to a valid equal protection claim under the principles announced in *Shaw*, and, if so, whether it can be sustained nonetheless as narrowly tailored to serve a compelling governmental interest.

I

A

The Equal Protection Clause of the Fourteenth Amendment provides that no State shall "deny to any person within its jurisdiction the equal protection of the laws." U.S. Const., Amdt. 14, § 1. Its central mandate is racial neutrality in governmental decisionmaking.... Laws classifying citizens on the basis of race cannot be upheld unless they are narrowly tailored to achieving a compelling state interest....

In *Shaw v. Reno, supra*, we recognized that these equal protection principles govern a State's drawing of congressional districts, though, as our cautious approach there discloses, application of these principles to electoral districting is a most delicate task...

B

[In 1965, the Attorney General designated Georgia a covered jurisdiction under the Voting Rights Act, requiring Georgia to obtain either administrative preclearance from the Attorney General or approval by the U.S. District Court for the District of Columbia of any change in "standard, practice, or procedure with respect to voting." Between 1980 and 1990, one of Georgia's ten congressional districts was a majority-black district (where a majority of the district's voters were black). The 1990 census entitled Georgia to an additional eleventh congressional seat. 27% of the population in Georgia is black.]

[Georgia's legislature submitted a congressional redistricting plan to the Attorney General for preclearance. The plan contained two majority-black districts, the Fifth and Eleventh, and an additional district, the Second, in which blacks comprised just over 35% of the voting age population. Despite the plan's increase in the number of majority-black districts from one to two, the Justice De-

partment refused preclearance, noting that Georgia had created only two majority-black districts. A new plan, increasing the black populations in the Second, Fifth, and Eleventh Districts, was also rejected by the Justice Department, which relied on an alternative plan proposing three majority-black districts. As the trial court noted, the third plan from the legislature used the alternative plan as a benchmark, bearing "all the signs [of the Justice Department's] involvement." The populations of the Eleventh "are centered around four discrete, widely spaced urban centers that have absolutely nothing to do with each other, and stretch the district hundreds of miles across rural counties and narrow swamp corridors." In the 1992 elections, black candidates were elected to Congress from all three majority-black districts. Five white voters from the Eleventh filed an action against various state officials, alleging that Georgia's Eleventh District was a racial gerrymander and violated the Equal Protection Clause. A three-judge court ruled that the Eleventh was invalid under Shaw, with one judge dissenting.]

II

A

Finding that the "evidence of the General Assembly's intent to racially gerrymander the Eleventh District is overwhelming, and practically stipulated by the parties involved," the District Court held that race was the predominant, overriding factor in drawing the Eleventh District. 864 F. Supp., at 1374; see *id.*, at 1374–1378. Appellants do not take issue with the court's factual finding of this racial motivation. Rather, they contend that evidence of a legislature's deliberate classification of voters on the basis of race cannot alone suffice to state a claim under *Shaw*. They argue that, regardless of the legislature's purposes, a plaintiff must demonstrate that a district's shape is so bizarre that it is unexplainable other than on the basis of race, and that appellees failed to make that showing here. Appellants' conception of the constitutional violation misapprehends our holding in *Shaw* and the Equal Protection precedent upon which *Shaw* relied.

Shaw recognized a claim "analytically distinct" from a vote dilution claim. 509 U.S., at 652; see *id.*, at 649–650. Whereas a vote dilution claim alleges that the State has enacted a particular voting scheme as a purposeful device "to minimize or

cancel out the voting potential of racial or ethnic minorities," *Mobile v. Bolden*, 446 U.S. 55, 56 (1980) (citing cases) an action disadvantaging voters of a particular race, the essence of the equal protection claim recognized in *Shaw is* that the State has used race as a basis for separating voters into districts. Just as the State may not, absent extraordinary justification, segregate citizens on the basis of race in its public parks, . . . buses, . . . golf courses, . . . beaches, . . . and schools, . . . so did we recognize in *Shaw* that it may not separate its citizens into different voting districts on the basis of race. . . .

Our observation in *Shaw* of the consequences of racial stereotyping was not meant to suggest that a district must be bizarre on its face before there is a constitutional violation. Nor was our conclusion in *Shaw* that in certain instances a district's appearance (or, to be more precise, its appearance in combination with certain demographic evidence) can give rise to an equal protection claim, 509 U.S., at 649, a holding that bizarreness was a threshold showing, as appellants believe it to be. Our circumspect approach and narrow holding in *Shaw* did not erect an artificial rule barring accepted equal protection analysis in other redistricting cases. Shape is relevant not because bizarreness is a necessary element of the constitutional wrong or a threshold requirement of proof, but because it may be persuasive circumstantial evidence that race for its own sake, and not other districting principles, was the legislature's dominant and controlling rationale in drawing its district lines. The logical implication, as courts applying *Shaw* have recognized, is that parties may rely on evidence other than bizarreness to establish race-based districting. . . .

Appellants and some of their *amici* argue that the Equal Protection Clause's general proscription on race-based decisionmaking does not obtain in the districting context because redistricting by definition involves racial considerations. Underlying their argument are the very stereotypical assumptions the Equal Protection Clause forbids. It is true that redistricting in most cases will implicate a political calculus in which various interests compete for recognition, but it does not follow from this that individuals of the same race share a single political interest. The view that they do is "based on the demeaning notion that members of the defined racial groups ascribe to certain 'minority views' that must be different from those of other citizens," *Metro Broadcasting*, 497 U.S., at 636 (KENNEDY, J., dissenting), the precise use of race as a proxy the Constitution prohibits. . . .

In sum, we make clear that parties alleging that a State has assigned voters on the basis of race are neither confined in their proof to evidence regarding the district's geometry and makeup nor required to make a threshold showing of bizarreness. Today's case requires us further to consider the requirements of the proof necessary to sustain this equal protection challenge.

B

Federal court review of districting legislation represents a serious intrusion on the most vital of local functions. It is well settled that "reapportionment is primarily the duty and responsibility of the State." *Chapman v. Meier,* 420 U.S. 1, 27 (1975); . . . Electoral districting is a most difficult subject for legislatures, and so the States must have discretion to exercise the political judgment necessary to balance competing interests. . . . Redistricting legislatures will, for example, almost always be aware of racial demographics; but it does not follow that race predominates in the redistricting process. . . . The plaintiff's burden is to show, either through circumstantial evidence of a district's shape and demographics or more direct evidence going to legislative purpose, that race was the predominant factor motivating the legislature's decision to place a significant number of voters within or without a particular district. To make this showing, a plaintiff must prove that the legislature subordinated traditional race-neutral districting principles, including but not limited to compactness, contiguity, and respect for political subdivisions or communities defined by actual shared interests, to racial considerations. Where these or other race-neutral considerations are the basis for redistricting legislation, and are not subordinated to race, a state can "defeat a claim that a district has been gerrymandered on racial lines." *Shaw, supra* at 647. These principles inform the plaintiff's burden of proof at trial. . . .

In our view, the District Court applied the correct analysis, and its finding that race was the predominant factor motivating the drawing of the Eleventh District was not clearly erroneous. . . . Although by comparison with other districts the geometric shape of the Eleventh District may not seem bizarre on its face, when its shape is considered in conjunction with its racial and population densities, the story of racial gerrymandering seen by the District Court becomes much clearer. . . . Although this evidence is quite compelling, we need not determine whether it was, standing alone, suf-

ficient to establish a *Shaw* claim that the Eleventh District is unexplainable other than by race. The District Court had before it considerable additional evidence showing that the General Assembly was motivated by a predominant, overriding desire to assign black populations to the Eleventh District and thereby permit the creation of a third majority-black district in the Second. 864 F. Supp., at 1372, 1378.

The court found that "it became obvious," both from the Justice Department's objection letters and the three preclearance rounds in general, "that [the Justice Department] would accept nothing less than abject surrender to its maximization agenda." . . . It further found that the General Assembly acquiesced and as a consequence was driven by its overriding desire to comply with the Department's maximization demands. . . . Hence the trial court had little difficulty concluding that the Justice Department "spent months demanding purely race-based revisions to Georgia's redistricting plans, and that Georgia spent months attempting to comply." 864 F. Supp., at 1377. On this record, we fail to see how the District Court could have reached any conclusion other than that race was the predominant factor in drawing Georgia's Eleventh District; and in any event we conclude the court's finding is not clearly erroneous. . . .

. . . Georgia's Attorney General objected to the Justice Department's demand for three majority-black districts on the ground that to do so the State would have to "violate all reasonable standards of compactness and contiguity." . . .

. . . A State is free to recognize communities that have a particular racial makeup, provided its action is directed toward some common thread of relevant interests. "[W]hen members of a racial group live together in one community, a reapportionment plan that concentrates members of the group in one district and excludes them from others may reflect wholly legitimate purposes." *Shaw,* 509 U.S. at 646. But where the State assumes from a group of voters' race that they "think alike, share the same political interests, and will prefer the same candidates at the polls," it engages in racial stereotyping at odds with equal protection mandates. . . .

Race was, as the District Court found, the predominant, overriding factor explaining the General Assembly's decision to attach to the Eleventh District various appendages containing dense majority-black populations. 864 F.Supp., at 1372, 1378. As a result, Georgia's congressional redistricting plan cannot be upheld unless it satisfied strict scrutiny, our most rigorous and exacting standard of constitutional review.

III

To satisfy strict scrutiny, the State must demonstrate that its districting legislation is narrowly tailored to achieve a compelling interest.... There is a "significant state interest in eradicating the effects of past racial discrimination." *Shaw, supra,* at 656. The State does not argue, however, that it created the Eleventh District to remedy past discrimination, and with good reason: There is little doubt that the State's true interest in designing the Eleventh District was creating a third majority-black district to satisfy the Justice Department's preclearance demands....

We do not accept the contention that the State has a compelling interest in complying with whatever preclearance mandates the Justice Department issues.... Were we to accept the Justice Department's objection itself as a compelling interest adequate to insulate racial districting from constitutional review, we would be surrendering to the Executive Branch our role in enforcing the constitutional limits on race-based official action. We may not do so....

... One of the two Department of Justice line attorneys overseeing the Georgia preclearance process himself disclosed that " 'what we did and what I did specifically was to take a ... map of the State of Georgia shaded for race, shaded by minority concentration, and overlay the districts that were drawn by the State of Georgia and see how well those lines adequately reflected black voting strength.' " 864 F. Supp., at 1362, n. 4. In utilizing § 5 to require States to create majority-minority districts wherever possible, the Department of Justice expanded its authority under the statute beyond what Congress intended and we have upheld.

* * *

IV

The Voting Rights Act, and its grant of authority to the federal courts to uncover official efforts to abridge minorities' right to vote, has been of vital importance in eradicating invidious discrimination from the electoral process and enhancing the legitimacy of our political institutions. Only if our political system and our society cleanse themselves of that discrimination will all members of the polity share an equal opportunity to gain public office regardless of race. As a Nation we share both the obligation and the aspiration of working toward this end. The end is neither assured nor well served, however, by carving electorates into racial blocs....

* * *

The judgment of the District Court is affirmed, and the case is remanded for further proceedings consistent with this decision.

It is so ordered.

* * *

JUSTICE O'CONNOR, concurring.

* * *

Application of the Court's standard does not throw into doubt the vast majority of the Nation's 435 congressional districts, where presumably the States have drawn the boundaries in accordance with their customary districting principles. That is so even though race may well have been considered in the redistricting process. See *Shaw v. Reno,* 509 U.S. 630, 646 (1993); ... But application of the Court's standard helps achieve *Shaw's* basic objective of making extreme instances of gerrymandering subject to meaningful judicial review. I therefore join the Court's opinion.

JUSTICE STEVENS, dissenting.

... Neither in *Shaw* itself nor in the cases decided today has the Court coherently articulated what injury this cause of action is designed to redress. Because respondents have alleged no legally cognizable injury, they lack standing, and these cases should be dismissed....

* * *

JUSTICE GINSBURG, with whom JUSTICE STEVENS and JUSTICE BREYER join, and with whom JUSTICE SOUTER joins except as to Part III-B, dissenting.

Legislative districting is highly political business. This Court has generally respected the competence of state legislatures to attend to the task. When race is the issue, however, we have recognized the need for judicial intervention to prevent dilution of minority voting strength. Generations of rank discrimination against African-Americans, as citizens and voters, account for that surveillance.

Two Terms ago, in *Shaw v. Reno,* 509 U.S. 630 (1993), this Court took up a claim "analytically distinct" from a vote dilution claim. *Id.,* at 652. *Shaw* authorized judicial intervention in "extremely irregular" apportionments, *id.,* at 642, in which the legislature cast aside traditional districting practices to consider race alone—in the *Shaw* case, to create a district in North Carolina in which African-Americans would compose a majority of the voters.

Today the Court expands the judicial role, announcing that federal courts are to undertake searching review of any district with contours "predominant[ly] motivat[ed]" by race: "[S]trict scrutiny" will be triggered not only when traditional districting practices are abandoned, but also when those practices are "subordinated to"—given less weight than—race. See *ante,* at 916. Applying this new "race-as-predominant-factor" standard, the Court invalidates Georgia's districting plan even though Georgia's Eleventh District, the focus of today's dispute, bears the imprint of familiar districting practices. Because I do not endorse the Court's new standard and would not upset Georgia's plan, I dissent.

I

At the outset, it may be useful to note points on which the Court does not divide. First, we agree that federalism and the slim judicial competence to draw district lines weigh heavily against judicial intervention in apportionment decisions; as a rule, the task should remain within the domain of state legislatures.... Second, for most of our Nation's history, the franchise has not been enjoyed equally by black citizens and white voters. To redress past wrongs and to avert any recurrence of exclusion of blacks from political processes, federal courts now respond to Equal Protection Clause and Voting Rights Act complaints of state action that dilutes minority voting strength. See, *e.g., Thornburg v. Gingles,* 478 U.S. 30 (1986); *White v. Regester,* 412 U.S. 755 (1973). Third, to meet statutory requirements, state legislatures must sometimes consider race as a factor highly relevant to the drawing of district lines.... Finally, state legislatures may recognize communities that have a particular racial or ethnic makeup, even in the absence of any compulsion to do so, in order to account for interests common to or shared by the persons grouped together....

A

...District lines are drawn to accommodate a myriad of factors—geographic, economic, historical, and political—and state legislatures, as arenas of compromise and electoral accountability, are best positioned to mediate competing claims; courts, with a mandate to adjudicate, are ill equipped for the task.

B

Federal courts have ventured into the political thicket of apportionment when necessary to secure to members of racial minorities equal voting rights—rights denied to many States, including Georgia, until not long ago.

The Fifteenth Amendment, ratified in 1870, declares that the right to vote "shall be denied... by any State on account of race." That declaration, for generations, was often honored in the breach;...*[Ginsburg reviews obstacles placed in the path of black voting, including poll taxes, "white primaries," property and literacy requirements, and grandfather clauses.]*

It was against this backdrop that the Court, construing the Equal Protection Clause, undertook to ensure that apportionment plans do not dilute minority voting strength.... By enacting the Voting Rights Act of 1965, Congress heightened federal judicial involvement in apportionment,...

[II.B]

The record before us does not show that race...overwhelmed traditional districting practices in Georgia. Although the Georgia General Assembly prominently considered race in shaping the Eleventh District, race did not crowd out all other factors, as the Court found it did in North Carolina's delineation of the *Shaw* district.

In contrast to the snake-like North Carolina district inspected in *Shaw,* Georgia's Eleventh District is hardly "bizarre," "extremely irregular," or "irrational on its face."...

C

The Court suggests that it was not Georgia's legislature, but the U.S. Department of Justice, that effectively drew the lines, and that Department officers did so with nothing but race in mind. Yet the "Max-Black" plan advanced by the Attorney General was not the plan passed by the Georgia General Assembly....

And although the Attorney General refused preclearance to the first two plans approved by Georgia's legislature, the State was not thereby disarmed; Georgia could have demanded relief from the Department's objections by instituting a civil action in the United States District Court for the District of Columbia, with ultimate review in this Court. Instead of pursuing that avenue, the State chose to adopt the plan here in controversy—a plan the State forcefully defends before us. We should respect Georgia's choice by taking its position on brief as genuine.

D

Along with attention to size, shape, and political subdivisions, the Court recognizes as a appropriate districting principle, "respect for... communities defined by actual shared interests." *Ante,* at 916. The Court finds no community here, however, because a report in the record showed "fractured political, social, and economic interests within the Eleventh District's black population." *Ante,* at 919.

But ethnicity itself can tie people together, as volumes of social science literature have documented — even people with divergent economic interests. For this reason, ethnicity is a significant force in political life...

To accommodate the reality of ethnic bonds, legislatures have long drawn voting districts along ethnic lines. Our Nation's cities are full of districts identified by their ethnic character—Chinese, Irish, Italian, Jewish, Polish, Russian, for example....

[III.A]

...If Chinese-Americans and Russian-Americans may seek and secure group recognition in the delineation of voting districts, then African-Americans should not be dissimilarly treated. Otherwise, in the name of equal protection, we would shut out "the very minority group whose history in the United States gave birth to the Equal Protection Clause." See *Shaw,* 509 U.S., at 679 (STEVENS, J., dissenting).

· · ·

D. CAMPAIGN FINANCING

As a result of court rulings, elections now operate under the broad slogan of "one person, one vote." This superficial equality, giving equal weight to each voter, is seriously skewed by large campaign contributions from individuals, corporations, and political action committees (PACs). Congress has attempted to regulate campaign spending to remove the most serious abuses, but these efforts have been circumscribed and limited by court rulings. The one-person, one-vote principle collides with the reality of wealthy and powerful financial contributors. Moreover, the Democratic and Republican parties have been creative in locating major loopholes in statutory constraints.

Legislation on Corrupt Practices

Congress has to juggle two conflicting interests: (1) the right of private citizens to make financial contributions to elections, and (2) the need to protect campaigns from corrupting influences. One of the first efforts to reconcile this conflict came in 1907, when Congress responded to large corporate contributions to political candidates. Legislation in 1907 prohibited any national bank or any corporation created by Congress from contributing money for political elections. 34 Stat. 864. The Federal Corrupt Practices Act of 1910 limited the amount of money that congressional candidates could contribute to their own nomination or election. Political committees had to record their contributions and make regular reports to Congress. 36 Stat. 822 (1910); 37 Stat. 25 (1911).

The Supreme Court held that this statute, to the extent that it covered primaries, was unconstitutional. Although Article I, Section 4, empowers Congress to alter state regulations concerning the "Manner of holding Elections" for U.S. Senators and Representatives, four members of the Court ruled that elections in the constitutional sense meant "the final choice of an officer." Pushing original intent and strict construction to the limit, the Court said that primaries "were then unknown" at the time of the Constitution. Primaries were "in no sense elections for an office." Newberry v. United States, 256 U.S. 232, 250 (1921). As applied to primaries and nominating conventions, therefore, the statute usurped state power. Justice McKenna joined the four Justices in setting aside the conviction but offered no opinion on the constitutional issue.

In one of the dissents, Chief Justice White denounced the appeal to original intent as "suicidal." Id. at 262. To underscore his point, he reviewed the expectation of the framers that members of the electoral college would be free agents, capable of exercising discretion when choosing the President. In 1876, however, when James Russell Lowell was urged to exercise independence and vote for Tilden, he refused on the ground that "whatever the first intent of the Constitution was, usage had made the presidential electors strictly the instruments of the party which chose them." Id. at 266. White concluded that whatever case could have been made for state autonomy in matters of national elections had evaporated in 1913 with the Seventeenth Amendment, which provided for the election of U.S. Senators by the people rather than by state legislatures. Justice Pitney, joined by Justices Brandeis and Clarke, also repudiated the Court's foray into strict construction. Pitney wrote: "It is said primaries were unknown when the Constitution was adopted. So were the steam railway and the electric telegraph. But the authority of Congress to regulate commerce among the several States extended over these instrumentalities...." Id. at 282.

Congress rewrote the Federal Corrupt Practices Act to conform to the Court's ruling but also strengthened several provisions in the statute. 43 Stat. 1070 (1925). The Court upheld the power of Congress to require political committees to keep detailed accounts of all financial contributions and to file with Congress a statement containing the name and address of each contributor to a federal election. The Court denied that the statute invaded state power. The operation of the statute was confined to situations which, "if not beyond the power of the state to deal with at all, are beyond its power to deal with adequately." The authority of Congress to safeguard federal elections comes from "the power of self protection." Burroughs v. United States, 290 U.S. 534, 544–45 (1934). In the Hatch Act, Congress enacted additional legislation in 1939 and 1940 to protect campaigns from corruption and "pernicious political activities." 53 Stat. 1147; 54 Stat. 767. The Hatch Act was liberalized in 1993 to permit federal employees to participate in a greater range of political activities, including managing campaigns, raising funds, and holding positions within political parties. Some restrictions on political activities remain. 107 Stat. 1001 (1993).

Newberry Reversed

Although the Court in *Newberry* had denied Congress the power to regulate primary elections, the Justice Department challenged the Court's decision by returning to first principles. In a subsequent case, the government argued that the right of voters in congressional primaries is secured by Article I, Section 2, calling for the choice of Representatives "by the People," as well as the Times, Places, and Manner Clause of Section 4. Richard Claude, The Supreme Court and the Electoral Process 33 (1970). Under these pressures and with a reconstituted membership, the Court reversed *Newberry* and held that congressional power embraced not merely the final election but primaries as well. Even the three dissenters, Justices Douglas, Black, and Murphy, rejected *Newberry*'s conclusion that Congress had no power to control primary elections. United States v. Classic, 313 U.S. 299, 329–30 (1941).

The prohibition that Congress had placed on corporate and national bank campaign contributions was later extended to cover labor organizations. 57 Stat. 167, § 9 (1943); 61 Stat. 159, § 304 (1947). Labor unions responded by setting up PACs to pursue campaign goals. Initially, union members were required to contribute to these political funds, which were used to support the campaigns of candidates friendly to the labor cause. These political funds were later replaced by a "voluntary" organization, with funds segregated from union dues. Congress authorized this type of fund in 1972 by stating that the prohibition on labor contributions did not include "the establishment, administration, and solicitation of contributions to a separate segregated fund to be utilized for political purposes by a corporation or labor organization." 86 Stat. 10, § 205 (1972). Partly on the basis of this law, the Supreme Court upheld political funds operated by labor unions. Pipefitters v. United States, 407 U.S. 385 (1972).

The high cost of federal campaigns, especially for TV ads, led to the Federal Election Campaign Act of 1971. New limits were placed on campaign contributions and expenditures. 86 Stat. 3. Congress created the Presidential Election Campaign Fund in 1971 to provide public subsidies for presidential candidates in the general election. 85 Stat. 562–74. On the heels of the Watergate scandal, which exposed widespread corruption during the presidential campaign of 1972, Congress enacted new legislation. The Federal Election Campaign Act Amendments of 1974 placed limits on contributions and expenditures, created the Federal Election Commission (FEC) to enforce the law, and provided optional public funding for presidential elections. 88 Stat. 1263.

The *Buckley* Case

A strange alliance challenged the constitutionality of the 1974 amendments. Opponents of the legislation included conservative Senator James L. Buckley, liberal Senator Eugene J. McCarthy, the Conservative party of New York State, the Libertarian party, the New York Civil Liberties Union, and *Human Events,* a conservative publication. They argued that the limits on campaign contributions and expenditures represented a violation of the First Amendment right of expression, both by contributors and candidates.

In *Buckley* v. *Valeo* (1976), the Court upheld limits on how much individuals and political action committees may contribute to candidates. These limits serve the important governmental interest of preventing corruption of the political process. The contribution limits on a candidate's personal funds (or family funds) were declared invalid constraints on the ability of persons to become engaged in protected First Amendment expression. The Court upheld the Federal Election Campaign Act's disclosure-recordkeeping provisions and the public financing of presidential campaigns. If presidential candidates accept public funds, expenditure limits are imposed on campaign costs. The Court upheld those limits. Other limits on campaign expenditures were struck down as a violation of the freedoms of speech and association protected by the First Amendment. The Court made a key distinction between contributions and expenditures, concluding that the risk of corruption is greater in *giving,* rather than *spending,* money. Quid pro quos, said the Court, pose a more serious threat with contributions than with expenditures. Finally, the Court found the composition of the FEC to be unconstitutional (an issue addressed in Chapter 6). BUCKLEY v. VALEO, 424 U.S. 1 (1976).

Congress corrected the defect in the FEC (p. 199) and adopted other reforms, but years of effort have been unsuccessful in providing public funding for congressional campaigns or limiting the amount spent by PACs. Members of Congress and committees are directly influenced by PAC spending. Dairy PACs give money to members of the agriculture committees, corporate PACs contribute to members of the tax committees, and other PACs donate funds to committee members that have jurisdiction over their activities. These issues of *influence* are not covered by the Court's preoccupation with *corruption.* In other cases the Court has expressed concern not only about electoral corruption but the *integrity* of the electoral process.[13]

The cost of running for Congress continues to spiral upward. The average expenditure by the winning House candidate rose from an estimated $87,000 in 1976 to $666,000 in 1998. Comparable figures for the winning Senate candidate were $609,000 and $4.5 million. As the cost of campaigns goes up, qualified candidates are less able to enter the race. Instead of the "robust debate" promised by the Supreme Court in *Buckley,* including enhanced protection to

---

13. For example, Storer v. Brown, 415 U.S. 724 (1974); Kusper v. Pontikes, 414 U.S. 51 (1973); Rosario v. Rockefeller, 410 U.S. 752 (1973); Bullock v. Carter, 405 U.S. 134 (1972); Williams v. Rhodes, 393 U.S. 23 (1968).

First Amendment values, the high cost of campaigning may reduce the field of candidates to an ever-narrowing band of wealthy politicians or those skilled in raising large sums of money.

Adjudication After *Buckley*

The basic thrust of *Buckley* has been sustained in subsequent decisions. Congress may set limits on how much presidential candidates spend as a condition on their receiving public funds. Republican National Committee v. FEC, 445 U.S. 955 (1980), aff'g summarily, 487 F.Supp. 280 (S.D.N.Y. 1980) (three-judge court) and 616 F.2d 1 (2d Cir. 1980) (en banc). Congress can place limits on some contributions. California Medical Assn. v. FEC, 453 U.S. 182 (1982). However, the Court has held that other restrictions on contributions run afoul of First Amendment freedoms. In 1978 a 5–4 Court held that Massachusetts violated the First Amendment by prohibiting business corporations from contributing funds to influence a referendum. The "speech" protected, of course, was not by natural persons but by artificial entities created in the form of corporations. In a dissent, Justice White warned that in the area of campaign financing "the expertise of legislators is at its peak and that of judges is at its very lowest." First National Bank of Boston v. Bellotti, 435 U.S. 765, 804 (1978). Members of the Court have increasing difficulty in understanding the contribution/expenditure distinction in *Buckley*. See the dissents in FEC v. National Conservative PAC, 470 U.S. 480 (1985). A critical issue of campaign financing is the control of "independent expenditures" (see box on next page).[14]

In addition to the loophole for independent expenditures, other techniques have been devised to circumvent restrictions in federal law. One method is "soft money": contributions to political parties for administrative costs and party-building activities (such as voter registration drives). These contributions from individuals and corporations may far exceed the statutory limits of $1,000 for individual contributions to a candidate per election and $20,000 a year from individuals to a national party committee. Using soft money, contributions in excess of $100,000 are not unusual.

In 1991 the Court grappled with a sensitive issue: When does a politician's plea for campaign contributions become extortion punishable by federal law? Simply receiving money and providing assistance is insufficient grounds for proving extortion. "Serving constituents and supporting legislation that will benefit the district and individuals and groups therein is the everyday business of a legislator." McCormick v. United States, 500 U.S. 257, 272 (1991). Candidates are constantly soliciting funds and making promises in return. Criminal conduct occurs only when contributions are accepted with an explicit promise to perform an official act.

Rethinking *Buckley*

Over the years, in a series of rulings, the Supreme Court has gradually set forth criteria on limitations established on campaign funding, upholding some while invalidating others (see box). In 1995, the Court decided whether Ohio's election law could prohibit the distribution of anonymous campaign literature. The Court held that Ohio had failed to justify the ban as necessary to prevent fraudulent and libelous statements. McIntyre v. Ohio Elections Comm'n, 514 U.S. 334 (1995). A year later, the Court ruled that the First Amendment prohibits the Federal Government from placing limits on the amounts that political parties can spend by assuming that those expenditures are always "coordinated" with the campaign of a candidate.

---

14. Government cannot compel minor political parties, such as the Socialist Workers party, to report the names and addresses of campaign contributors and recipients of campaign disbursements if disclosure is likely to result in harassment and reprisals. Brown v. Socialists Workers '74 Campaign Comm., 459 U.S. 87 (1982); Buckley v. Valeo, 424 U.S. at 64–74. Other questions of campaign financing are explored in FEC v. National Right to Work Committee, 459 U.S. 197 (1982) and Citizens Against Rent Control v. Berkeley, 454 U.S. 290 (1981).

Controls on Independent Expenditures

"Independent expenditures" consist of the expenses of a person or political committee free of any coordination with a candidate's official campaign committee. The Federal Election Campaign Act amendments of 1974 imposed a $1,000 limit on independent expenditures, but the Court struck down that limit in *Buckley*. As a result, while federal law limits contributions made directly to political candidates, no such restraints operate on independent expenditures. A three-judge court in 1980 ruled that the $1,000 limit on independent expenditures of political committees was facially unconstitutional under the First Amendment. Common Cause v. Schmitt, 512 F.Supp. 489 (D.D.C. 1980). This ruling was affirmed by an equally divided (4–4) Supreme Court in a per curiam decision. 455 U.S. 129 (1982). In 1986 a 5–4 Court struck down as unconstitutional FEC's regulation that prohibited political expenditures by nonprofit advocacy groups that take positions on abortion, busing, gun control, and other issues. Under the Court's reading of the First Amendment, those groups may take out advertisements urging voters to support or oppose specific candidates. These independent expenditures are not subject to federal limits. FEC v. Massachusetts Citizens for Life, Inc., 479 U.S. 238 (1986).

Massachusetts Citizens invalidated a federal restriction on independent expenditures by nonprofit, advocacy groups such as an antiabortion organization. In 1990 the Court refused to extend that protection to business-oriented organizations. At issue was a Michigan law that prohibited corporations (other than media corporations, such as newspapers and broadcasting stations) from using general treasury funds to make independent expenditures in connection with candidates in state elections. Corporations had to establish segregated funds or political action committees to support these political purposes. The Court, divided 6 to 3, held that although the requirement burdened a corporation's freedom of expression, it was justified by a compelling state interest: preventing corruption—or the appearance of corruption—in the political arena by reducing the threat of huge corporate treasuries. The Court pointed out that these treasuries are amassed with the aid of favorable state law. Austin v. Michigan Chamber of Commerce, 494 U.S. 652 (1990).

In their dissents, Justices Scalia, Kennedy, and O'Connor issued vigorous objections to the Court's validation of "censorship" of speech. Scalia said that if there was a compelling state need to prevent corporate wealth from skewing the political debate, media corporations should be included, not excluded. Kennedy and O'Connor also criticized the exception for media corporations: "The web of corporate ownership that links media and nonmedia corporations is difficult to untangle for the purpose of any meaningful distinction. Newspapers, television networks, and other media may be owned by parent corporations with multiple business interests."

The FEC had concluded that party expenditures can never be "independent," a position the Court rejected. In disposing of this narrow question, the multiple opinions of the Justices raised the question whether the Court would reexamine the soundness of *Buckley* v. *Valeo*. Colorado Republican Campaign Comm. v. FEC, 518 U.S. 604 (1996).

The nature of the 1996 election campaigns—the most expensive in history, and one raising the issue of illegal foreign campaign contributions from China—intensified the pressure for legislative action. Some of the proposals considered by Congress would eliminate "soft money," while others would place limits on independent, issue-oriented television advertisements that implicitly promote the campaigns of particular individuals. Progress on this legislation stalled in 1998 and again in 2000.

At the state level, a Cincinnati ordinance enacted in 1995 posed a direct challenge to *Buckley* by imposing a $140,000 political spending cap on candidates for city council. The restriction was overturned by a federal judge and later by the Sixth Circuit in 1998 as an unconstitutional restriction on free speech. Kruse v. City of Cincinnati, 142 F.3d 907 (6th Cir. 1998), cert. denied, 525 U.S. 1001 (1998). Thirty-three states had filed briefs supporting Cincinnati's position.

Federal and State Controls on Campaign Funding

Limits	Court Response
$1,000 limit on contributions by individuals and groups to candidates and authorized campaign committees	Upheld in Buckley v. Valeo (1976)
$5,000 limit on contributions to a candidate by political committees	Upheld in Buckley
$25,000 limit on total contributions by an individual during any calendar year	Upheld in Buckley
Expenditure ceilings on candidates, their campaigns, and political parties in connection with election campaigns	Held invalid in Buckley
Limits on independent expenditures	Held invalid in Buckley
Public financing of presidential election campaigns	Upheld in Buckley
Limits on expenditures by candidates from personal or family resources	Held invalid in Buckley
Prohibition by Massachusetts of business corporations from contributing funds to influence a referendum	Held invalid in First National Bank of Boston v. Bellotti (1978)
Prohibition by FEC regulation of political expenditures by nonprofit advocacy groups that take positions on public issues	Held invalid in FEC v. Massachusetts Citizens for Life, Inc. (1986)
Prohibition by Michigan of corporations (other than media corporations) from using general treasury funds to assist candidates in state elections	Upheld in Austin v. Michigan Chamber of Commerce (1990)

Challenges continue to come from other states. In 2000, the Court upheld Missouri's ceiling of $1,000 on political contributions, rejecting the argument that the $1,000 limit upheld in *Buckley* was now too low because of inflation. Nixon v. Shrink Missouri Government PAC, 120 S.Ct. 897 (2000). Several opinions for the 6 to 3 majority indicate that a number of Justices are troubled by *Buckley* and are ready to reexamine and possibly reject it. In a concurrence, Justice Stevens said that "Money is property; it is not speech." A concurrence by Breyer, with Ginsburg joining, remarked that the decision to make a campaign contribution is a First Amendment concern "not because money *is* speech (it is not); but because it *enables* speech." He also thought that campaign finance was "a difficult question best left, in the main, to the political branches," and recognized that if *Buckley* denied the political branches sufficient leeway to enact comprehensive solutions, the Court should reconsider *Buckley*. In a dissent, Kennedy accused the Court in *Buckley* of creating "covert speech" that "mocks the First Amendment," said that *Buckley* "has not worked," and urged that it be overruled to free Congress and state legislatures to attempt new solutions. A dissent by Thomas, joined by Scalia, spoke of the "analytic fallacies of our flawed decision" in *Buckley* and recommended that it be overruled.

Buckley v. Valeo

424 U.S. 1 (1976)

In response to the scandals uncovered by the Watergate affair, Congress rewrote campaign finance laws to impose stricter limits on contributions and expenditures. The Federal Elec-

tion Campaign Act amendments of 1974 also created a Federal Election Commission (FEC) to enforce the statute. The Supreme Court considered the objectives of Congress in light of First Amendment freedoms of speech and association. It concluded that the restrictions on contributions were legitimate means to accomplish the purpose of combating campaign corruption but held that the limits on expenditures violated the First Amendment. James L. Buckley, U.S. Senator, was the lead plaintiff in filing this case against Francis R. Valeo, Secretary of the Senate.

PER CURIAM.

These appeals present constitutional challenges to the key provisions of the Federal Election Campaign Act of 1971 (Act), and related provisions of the Internal Revenue Code of 1954, all as amended in 1974.

[After determining that the lawsuit constituted a "case or controversy" within the meaning of Article III of the Constitution, the Court turned to the merits. The Court examined limits on individual poitical contributions and expenditures, reporting and disclosure requirements, public funding of presidential campaigns, and the establishment of a Federal Election Commission (an issue dealt with in Chapter 6).]

I. CONTRIBUTION AND EXPENDITURE LIMITATIONS

The intricate statutory scheme adopted by Congress to regulate federal election campaigns includes restrictions on political contributions and expenditures that apply broadly to all phases of and all participants in the election process. The major contribution and expenditure limitations in the Act prohibit individuals from contributing more than $25,000 in a single year or more than $1,000 to any single candidate for an election campaign and from spending more than $1,000 a year "relative to a clearly identified candidate." Other provisions restrict a candidate's use of personal and family resources in his campaign and limit the overall amount that can be spent by a candidate in campaigning for federal office.

The constitutional power of Congress to regulate federal elections is well established and is not questioned by any of the parties in this case. Thus, the critical constitutional questions presented here go not to the basic power of Congress to legislate in this area, but to whether the specific legislation that Congress has enacted interferes with First Amendment freedoms or invidiously discriminates against nonincumbent candidates and minor parties in contravention of the Fifth Amendment.

A. General Principles

The Act's contribution and expenditure limitations operate in an area of the most fundamental First Amendment activities. Discussion of public issues and debate on the qualifications of candidates are integral to the operation of the system of government established by our Constitution. The First Amendment affords the broadest protection to such political expression in order "to assure [the] unfettered interchange of ideas for the bringing about of political and social changes desired by the people." *Roth v. United States,* 354 U.S. 476, 484 (1957)....

The First Amendment protects political association as well as political expression. The constitutional right of association explicated in *NAACP v. Alabama,* 357 U.S. 449, 460 (1958), stemmed from the Court's recognition that "[e]ffective advocacy of both public and private points of view, particularly controversial ones, is undeniably enhanced by group association."...

It is with these principles in mind that we consider the primary contentions of the parties with respect to the Act's limitations upon the giving and spending of money in political campaigns. Those conflicting contentions could not more sharply define the basic issues before us. Appellees contend that what the Act regulates is conduct, and that its effect on speech and association is incidental at most. Appellants respond that contributions and expenditures are at the very core of political speech, and that the Act's limitations thus constitute restraints on First Amendment liberty that are both gross and direct.

. . .

A restriction on the amount of money a person or group can spend on political communication during a campaign necessarily reduces the quantity of expression by restricting the number of issues discussed, the depth of their exploration, and the size of the audience reached. This is because virtually every means of communicating ideas in today's mass society requires the expenditure of money. The distribution of the humblest handbill or leaflet entails printing, paper, and circulation costs. Speeches and rallies generally necessitate hiring a hall and publicizing the event. The electorate's increasing dependence on television, radio, and other mass media for news and information has made these expensive modes of communication indispensable instruments of effective political speech.

The expenditure limitations contained in the Act represent substantial rather than merely theoretical restraints on the quantity and diversity of political speech.

. . .

By contrast with a limitation upon expenditures for political expression, a limitation upon the amount that any one person or group may contribute to a candidate or political committee entails only a marginal restriction upon the contributor's ability to engage in free communication. A contribution serves as a general expression of support for the candidate and his views, but does not communicate the underlying basis for the support.

. . .

In sum, although the Act's contribution and expenditure limitations both implicate fundamental First Amendment interests, its expenditure ceilings impose significantly more severe restrictions on protected freedoms of political expression and association than do its limitations on financial contributions.

B. Contribution Limitations

1. The $1,000 Limitation on Contributions by Individuals and Groups to Candidates and Authorized Campaign Committees

Section 608(b) provides, with certain limited exceptions, that "no person shall make contributions to any candidate with respect to any election for Federal office which, in the aggregate, exceed $1,000." . . .

It is unnecessary to look beyond the Act's primary purpose — to limit the actuality and appearance of corruption resulting from large individual financial contributions — in order to find a constitutionally sufficient justification for the $1,000 contribution limitation. . . . To the extent that large contributions are given to secure a political *quid pro quo* from current and potential office holders, the integrity of our system of representative democracy is undermined. . . .

. . .

We find that, under the rigorous standard of review established by our prior decisions, the weighty interests served by restricting the size of financial contributions to political candidates are sufficient to justify the limited effect upon First Amendment freedoms caused by the $1,000 contribution ceiling.

. . .

2. The $5,000 Limitation on Contributions by Political Committees

Section 608 (b)(2) permits certain committees, designated as "political committees," to contribute up to $5,000 to any candidate with respect to any election for federal office. . . . Appellants argue that these qualifications unconstitutionally discriminate against *ad hoc* organizations in favor of established interest groups and impermissibly burden free association. The argument is without merit. Rather than undermining freedom of association, the basic provision enhances the opportunity of bona fide groups to participate in the election process, and the registration, contribution, and candidate conditions serve the permissible purpose of preventing individuals from evading the applicable contribution limitations by labeling themselves committees.

3. Limitations on Volunteers' Incidental Expenses

The Act excludes from the definition of contribution "the value of services provided without compensation by individuals who volunteer a portion or all of their time on behalf of a candidate or political committee." § 591(e)(5)(A). Certain expenses incurred by persons in providing volunteer services to a candidate are exempt from the $1,000 ceiling only to the extent that they do not exceed $500. . . .

If, as we have held, the basic contribution limitations are constitutionally valid, then surely these provisions are a constitutionally acceptable accommodation of Congress' valid interest in encouraging citizen participation in political campaigns while continuing to guard against the corrupting potential of large financial contributions to candidates.

. . .

4. The $25,000 Limitation on Total Contributions During any Calendar Year

In addition to the $1,000 limitation on the nonexempt contributions that an individual may make to a particular candidate for any single election, the Act contains an overall $25,000 limitation on total contributions by an individual during any calendar year.... The overall $25,000 ceiling does impose an ultimate restriction upon the number of candidates and committees with which an individual may associate himself by means of financial support. But this quite modest restraint upon protected political activity serves to prevent evasion of the $1,000 contribution limitation by a person who might otherwise contribute massive amounts of money to a particular candidate through the use of unearmarked contributions to political committees likely to contribute to that candidate, or huge contributions to the candidate's political party. The limited, additional restriction on associational freedom imposed by the overall ceiling is thus no more than a corollary of the basic individual contribution limitation that we have found to be constitutionally valid.

C. Expenditure Limitations

The Act's expenditure ceilings impose direct and substantial restraints on the quantity of political speech. The most drastic of the limitations restricts individuals and groups, including political parties that fail to place a candidate on the ballot, to an expenditure of $1,000 "relative to a clearly identified candidate during a calendar year." § 608(e)(1). Other expenditure ceilings limit spending by candidates, § 608(a), their campaigns, § 608(c), and political parties in connection with election campaigns, § 608(f). It is clear that a primary effect of these expenditure limitations is to restrict the quantity of campaign speech by individuals, groups, and candidates....

1. The $1,000 Limitation on Expenditures "Relative to a Clearly Identified Candidate"

. . .

We find that the governmental interest in preventing corruption and the appearance of corruption is inadequate to justify § 608(e)(1)'s ceiling on independent expenditures. First, assuming, *arguendo,* that large independent expenditures pose the same dangers of actual or apparent *quid pro quo* arrangements as do large contributions, § 608(e)(1) does not provide an answer that sufficiently relates to the elimination of those dangers. Unlike the contribution limitations' total ban on the giving of large amounts of money to candidates, § 608(e)(1) prevents only some large expenditures. So long as persons and groups eschew expenditures that in express terms advocate the election or defeat of a clearly identified candidate,

they are free to spend as much as they want to promote the candidate and his views....

For the reasons stated, we conclude that § 608(e)(1)'s independent expenditure limitation is unconstitutional under the First Amendment.

2. Limitation on Expenditures by Candidates from Personal or Family Resources

The Act also sets limits on expenditures by a candidate "from his personal funds, or the personal funds of his immediate family, in connection with his campaigns during any calendar year." § 608(a)(1). These ceilings vary from $50,000 for Presidential or Vice Presidential candidates to $35,000 for senatorial candidates, and $25,000 for most candidates for the House of Representatives.

The ceiling on personal expenditures by candidates on their own behalf, like the limitations on independent expenditures contained in § 608(e)(1), imposes a substantial restraint on the ability of persons to engage in protected First Amendment expression. The candidate, no less than any other person, has a First Amendment right to engage in the discussion of public issues and vigorously and tirelessly to advocate his own election and the election of other candidates....

The primary governmental interest served by the Act—the prevention of actual and apparent corruption of the political process—does not support the limitation on the candidate's expenditure of his own personal funds.... Indeed, the use of personal funds reduces the candidate's dependence on outside contributions and thereby counteracts the coercive pressures and attendant risks of abuse to which the Act's contribution limitations are directed.

. . .

3. Limitations on Campaign Expenditures

Section 608(c) places limitations on overall campaign expenditures by candidates seeking nomination for election and election to federal office....

No governmental interest that has been suggested is sufficient to justify the restriction on the quantity of political expression imposed by § 608(c)'s campaign expenditure limitations. The major evil associated with rapidly increasing campaign expenditures is the danger of candidate dependence on large contributions. The interest in alleviating the corrupting influence of large contributions is served by the Act's contribution limitations and disclosure provisions rather than by § 608(c)'s campaign expenditure ceilings. The

Court of Appeals' assertion that the expenditure restrictions are necessary to reduce the incentive to circumvent direct contribution limits is not persuasive....

II. REPORTING AND DISCLOSURE REQUIREMENTS

...the disclosure requirements of the Act...are not challenged by appellants as *per se* unconstitutional restrictions on the exercise of First Amendment freedoms of speech and association....

. . .

Each political committee is required to register with the Commission, § 433, and to keep detailed records of both contributions and expenditures, §§ 432(c), (d). These records must include the name and address of everyone making a contribution in excess of $10, along with the date and amount of the contribution. If a person's contributions aggregate more than $100, his occupation and principal place of business are also to be included. § 432(c)(2). These files are subject to periodic audits and field investigations by the Commission. § 438(a)(8).

. . .

In summary, we find no constitutional infirmities in the recordkeeping, reporting, and disclosure provisions of the Act.

III. PUBLIC FINANCING OF PRESIDENTIAL ELECTION CAMPAIGNS

A series of statutes for the public financing of Presidential election campaigns produced the scheme now found in § 6096 and Subtitle H of the Internal Revenue Code of 1954.... Both the District Court... and the Court of Appeals... sustained Subtitle H against a constitutional attack. Appellants renew their challenge here, contending that the legislation violates the First and Fifth Amendments. We find no merit in their claims and affirm.

A. Summary of Subtitle H

Section 9006 establishes a Presidential Election Campaign Fund (Fund), financed from general revenues in the aggregate amount designated by individual taxpayers, under § 6096, who on their income tax returns may authorize payment to the Fund of one dollar of their tax liability in the case of an individual return or two dollars in the case of a joint return. The Fund consists of three separate accounts to finance (1) party nominating conventions, § 9008(a), (2) general election campaigns, § 9006(a), and (3) primary campaigns, § 9037(a).

. . .

For expenses in the general election campaign, § 9004(a)(1) entitles each major-party candidate to $20,000,000. This amount is also adjusted for inflation.... To be eligible for funds the candidate must pledge not to incur expenses in excess of the entitlement under § 9004(a)(1) and not to accept private contributions except to the extent that the fund is insufficient to provide the full entitlement. § 9003(b)....

B. Constitutionality of Subtitle H

Appellants argue that Subtitle H is invalid (1) as "contrary to the 'general welfare,'" Art. I, § 8, (2) because any scheme of public financing of election campaigns is inconsistent with the First Amendment, and (3) because Subtitle H invidiously discriminates against certain interests in violation of the Due Process Clause of the Fifth Amendment. We find no merit in these contentions.

Appellants' "general welfare" contention erroneously treats the General Welfare Clause as a limitation upon congressional power. It is rather a grant of power, the scope of which is quite expansive, particularly in view of the enlargement of power by the Necessary and Proper Clause. *M'Culloch* v. *Maryland,* 4 Wheat. 316, 420 (1819). Congress has power to regulate Presidential elections and primaries, *United States* v. *Classic,* 313 U.S. 299 (1941); *Burroughs* v. *United States,* 290 U.S. 534 (1934); and public financing of Presidential elections as a means to reform the electoral process was clearly a choice within the granted power.... In this case, Congress was legislating for the "general welfare" — to reduce the deleterious influence of large contributions on our political process, to facilitate communication by candidates with the electorate, and to free candidates from the rigors of fundraising. See S. Rep. No. 93-689, pp. 1–10 (1974). Whether the chosen means appear "bad," "unwise," or "unworkable" to us is irrelevant; Congress has concluded that the means are "necessary and proper" to promote the general welfare, and we thus decline to find this legislation without the grant of power in Art. I, § 8.

. . .

Mr. Justice Stevens took no part in the consideration or decision of these cases.

. . .

MR. CHIEF JUSTICE BURGER, concurring in part and dissenting in part.

For reasons set forth more fully later, I dissent from those parts of the Court's holding sustaining the statutory provisions (a) for disclosure of small contributions, (b) for limitations on contributions, and (c) for public financing of Presidential campaigns. In my view, the Act's disclosure scheme is impermissibly broad and violative of the First Amendment as it relates to reporting contributions in excess of $10 and $100. The contribution limitations infringe on First Amendment liberties and suffer from the same infirmities that the Court correctly sees in the expenditure ceilings. The system for public financing of Presidential campaigns is, in my judgment, an impermissible intrusion by the Government into the traditionally private political process.

... [I]t seems to me that the threshold limits fixed at $10 and $100 for anonymous contributions are constitutionally impermissible on their face. As the Court's opinion notes, *ante,* at 83, Congress gave little or no thought, one way or the other, to these limits, but rather lifted figures out of a 65-year-old statute. As we are all painfully aware, the 1976 dollar is not what it used to be and is surely not the dollar of 1910. Ten dollars in 1976 will, for example, purchase only what $1.68 would buy in 1910.... To argue that a 1976 contribution of $10 or $100 entails a risk of corruption or its appearance is simply too extravagant to be maintained....

. . .

MR. JUSTICE WHITE, concurring in part and dissenting in part.

[He dissents from the Court's view that the expenditure limits violate the First Amendment.]

It would make little sense to me, and apparently made none to Congress, to limit the amounts an individual may give to a candidate or spend with his approval but fail to limit the amounts that could be spent on his behalf. Yet the Court permits the former while striking down the latter limitation. No more than $1,000 may be given to a candidate or spent at his request or with his approval or cooperation; but otherwise, apparently, a contributor is to be constitutionally protected in spending unlimited amounts of money in support of his chosen candidate or candidates.

Let us suppose that each of two brothers spends $1 million on TV spot announcements that he has individually prepared and in which he appears, urging the election of the same named candidate in identical words. One brother has sought and obtained the approval of the candidate; the other has not. The former may validly be prosecuted under § 608(e); under the Court's view, the latter may not, even though the candidate could scarcely help knowing about and appreciating the expensive favor. For constitutional purposes it is difficult to see the difference between the two situations. I would take the word of those who know—that limiting independent expenditures is essential to prevent transparent and widespread evasion of the contribution limits.

. . .

I also disagree with the Court's judgment that § 608(a), which limits the amount of money that a candidate or his family may spend on his campaign, violates the Constitution. Although it is true that this provision does not promote any interest in preventing the corruption of candidates, the provision does, nevertheless, serve salutary purposes related to the integrity of federal campaigns. By limiting the importance of personal wealth, § 608(a) helps to assure that only individuals with a modicum of support from others will be viable candidates. This in turn would tend to discourage any notion that the outcome of elections is primarily a function of money. Similarly, § 608(a) tends to equalize access to the political arena, encouraging the less wealthy, unable to bankroll their own campaigns, to run for political office.

As with the campaign expenditure limits, Congress was entitled to determine that personal wealth ought to play a less important role in political campaigns than it has in the past. Nothing in the First Amendment stands in the way of that determination.

. . .

MR. JUSTICE MARSHALL, concurring in part and dissenting in part.

I join in all of the Court's opinion except Part I-C-2, which deals with 18 U.S.C. § 608(a) (1970 ed., Supp. IV). That section limits the amount a candidate may spend from his personal funds, or family funds under his control, in connection with his campaigns during any calendar year.... The Court invalidates § 608(a) as violative of the candidate's First Amendment rights. "[T]he First Amendment," the Court explains, "simply cannot tolerate § 608(a)'s restriction upon the freedom of a candidate to speak without legislative limit on behalf of his own candidacy."... I disagree.

. . .

MR. JUSTICE BLACKMUN, concurring in part and dissenting in part.

I am not persuaded that the Court makes, or indeed is able to make, a principled constitutional distinction between the contribution limitations, on the one hand, and the expenditure limitations, on the other, that are involved here. I therefore do not join Part I-B of the Court's opinion or those portions of Part I-A that are consistent with Part I-B. As to those, I dissent. *[Blackmun also dissented from the Court's responses to limits on contributions, limits on incidental expenditures by volunteers, and the definition of "political committee."]*

MR. JUSTICE REHNQUIST, concurring in part and dissenting in part. *[Rehnquist dissented from the Court's opinion that certain aspects of the statutory treatment of minor parties and independent candidates are constitutionally valid.]*

... Congress in this legislation has ... enshrined the Republican and Democratic Parties in a permanently preferred position, and has established requirements for funding minor-party and independent candidates to which the two major parties are not subject. Congress would undoubtedly be justified in treating the Presidential candidates of the two major parties differently from minor-party or independent Presidential candidates, in view of the long demonstrated public support of the former. But because of the First Amendment overtones of the appellants' Fifth Amendment equal protection claim, something more than a merely rational basis for the difference in treatment must be shown, as the Court apparently recognizes. I find it impossible to subscribe to the Court's reasoning that because no third party has posed a credible threat to the two major parties in Presidential elections since 1860, Congress may by law attempt to assure that this pattern will endure forever.

I would hold that, as to general election financing, Congress has not merely treated the two major parties differently from minor parties and independents, but has discriminated in favor of the former in such a way as to run afoul of the Fifth and First Amendments to the United States Constitution.

E. LOBBYING

A variety of interest groups maintain regular contacts with members of Congress, congressional committees, and executive agencies, supplying advice and information they hope will influence government policy. The pejorative term *lobbying* is often applied to these activities, but it is healthy and appropriate in a democracy for private groups to intervene in the process of government. As the Supreme Court remarked in 1961, "the whole concept of representation depends upon the ability of the people to make their wishes known to their representatives." Eastern Railroad Presidents Conference v. Noerr Motors, Inc., 365 U.S. 127, 137 (1961). The First Amendment recognizes the right of citizens to petition their government for a redress of grievances. How can this activity be regulated through constitutional means?

It is difficult to conceive of a democratic government operating in a sterile environment never contaminated by private lobbyists. However, the activity of interest groups has been cast in negative terms from the start. In Federalist No. 10, Madison defined *faction* as a number of citizens "united and actuated by some common impulse of passion, or of interest, adverse to the rights of other citizens, or to the permanent and aggregate interests of the community." Under his definition, almost every interest group in America is rendered suspect. Although Madison disapproved of factions, he did not urge that they be abolished. The answer was not in removing the cause of faction but in "controlling its effects" (see reading).

Regulatory Efforts

In 1919, Congress passed legislation to prevent executive officials from using appropriated funds to stimulate grass roots lobbying against Congress. Officials had used telephones, telegrams, letters, and other forms of communication to drum up pressure against Congress from the private sector. Legislation prohibited this practice and the restriction remains part of current law. 41 Stat. 68, § 6 (1919); 18 U.S.C. § 1913 (1994). In 1934 Congress amended the tax code to restrict expenditures by charitable organizations for lobbying. The amendment applied to organizations covered by Section 501(c)(3) of the Internal Revenue Code, which gives tax-exempt status to various groups. As a condition attached to this tax benefit, Congress required that "no substantial part" of the activities of tax-exempt groups should consist of "carrying on propaganda, or otherwise attempting, to influence legislation." 48 Stat. 690 (1934); 26 U.S.C. § 501(c)(3) (1994).

A year later, Congress required representatives of public utility holding companies to file a report with the Securities and Exchange Commission (SEC) before attempting to influence Congress, the SEC, or the Federal Power Commission. 49 Stat. 825 (1935). Similar requirements were applied in 1936 to lobbyists for the merchant marine and in 1938 to agents of foreign governments. 49 Stat. 2014, § 807 (1936); 52 Stat. 631 (1938).

The most extensive effort to control lobbying is the Federal Regulation of Lobbying Act of 1946, which required lobbyists to register with Congress and file quarterly reports of their activities. 60 Stat. 839 (1946); 2 U.S.C. §§ 261–70 (1994). The statute was criticized for using vague language to cover activities that carried criminal penalties for violations. The statute has limited reach. It applies only to lobbyists whose "principal purpose" is to influence Congress. A more general critique is that the Act interferes with the First Amendment freedom to petition government. National Ass'n of Mfrs. v. McGrath, 103 F.Supp. 510 (D.D.C. 1952), vacated as moot, 344 U.S. 804 (1952). Moreover, a large number of lobbyists, consultants, and trade associations never register, even though they meet regularly with members of Congress and seek to influence legislation. For years Congress tried to revise and strengthen the lobbying act (see box on next page).

Section 307 of the Lobbying Act covered persons who, "directly or indirectly," solicit, collect, or receive money to influence Congress. In 1953 the Supreme Court restricted the reach of the lobbying statute to "direct" appeals to members of Congress, rather than the more general definition of influencing the thinking of the community. United States v. Rumely, 345 U.S. 41, 47 (1953). That restricted interpretation was followed a year later in a case that dealt more specifically with the Act. The Court dismissed the charge of vagueness leveled against the statute but agreed with *Rumely* that the statute covered only direct communications with members of Congress. As to the First Amendment challenge, the Court held that Congress is not forbidden to require the disclosure of lobbying activities. United States v. Harriss, 347 U.S. 612 (1954).

The Lobbying Disclosure Act of 1995 — the first general lobbying statute since 1946 — tightens registration requriements for those who lobby members of Congress and their staff, the White House, and federal agencies. Lobbyists will have to disclose the issue they lobbied on, the specific legislative or executive agency they contacted, and the amount of money they spent on the effort. 109 Stat. 691 (1995). The previous law covered only those who lobbied members of Congress.

The Internal Revenue Code, as interpreted by Treasury Department regulations, forbids the deduction of sums expended for "the promotion or defeat of legislation." In upholding these regulations, a unanimous Court held that they apply to expenditures made in connection with efforts to promote or defeat legislation by persuasion of the general public (as in initiative measures and referenda) as well as efforts to influence legislative bodies directly through "lobbying." Cammarano v. United States, 358 U.S. 498 (1959). In granting tax exemptions to certain nonprofit organizations on the condition that "no substantial part" of their activities involve propaganda or attempts to influence legislation, Congress does not violate the First Amendment. Members of Congress may legitimately choose not to subsidize lobbying activities. Regan v. Taxation With Representation of Wash., 461 U.S. 540 (1983).

Federal Lobbying

By virtually all indications, the activities of lobbyists and pressure groups have increased significantly in the last two decades. This increase is reflected in many areas: the numbers of corporations that have opened offices in Washington, the numbers of trade and other non-profit associations that have either made Washington their headquarters or opened offices here, the numbers of out-of-town law firms that have opened offices in Washington, and the numbers of public relations firms new to Washington.

Where once most Washington lobbying centered around economic interests, the last twenty years have witnessed the development of an array of groups representing social, environmental, philosophical and ideological interests.

While there is no single theory to account for this activity, a number of factors are clearly involved: growth of the Federal Government and the expansion of its influence—often as manager and provider; increased levels of relative affluence and education; advances in communications technology; and changes in Congress and in the elections process. These factors create a fertile environment for pressure group politics.

Not surprisingly, as Congress delegated decision-making authority to the executive agencies, so the agencies became the focus of increasing pressure group activity. At the same time that groups made heightened efforts to influence agency policies, the agencies themselves were making efforts to open up their decision-making processes to public scrutiny and involvement.

Although Congress periodically sought to control pressure group activities, mostly through registration and reporting requirements, none of its actions was particularly effective. In the past twenty years, the growth in numbers and diversity of pressure groups saw a similar rise in allegations of abuse of the lobbying process, claims that "secrecy" in the lobbying process was inimical to democratic government, and the belief of many that certain lobbying activities should be restricted or at least disclosed....

SOURCE: "Congress and Pressure Groups: Lobbying in a Modern Democracy," S. Prt. 99–161, 99th Cong., 2d Sess. 39 (1986).

The Supreme Court has recognized a broad right of citizens to demonstrate against governmental policies, including those of the Court itself and also foreign governments. Congress had passed legislation to prohibit the display of any flag, banner, or device in the Supreme Court or on its grounds "to bring into public notice any party, organization, or movement." The statute was meant to insulate the Court from direct lobbying, but in 1983 the Court held that the acts of distributing leaflets and carrying picket signs on the public sidewalk around the building were protected by the First Amendment. United States v. Grace, 461 U.S. 171 (1983).

Five years later, in a case involving demonstrations against foreign governments, the Court issued a decision that illustrates the dialogue between Congress and the judiciary on constitutional questions. The D.C. government made it unlawful for individuals, within 500 feet of a foreign embassy, to display any sign that tended to bring the foreign government into "public odium" or "public disrepute." Congress had also passed an antipicketing provision to protect foreign officials but repealed it in 1976 because of First Amendment concerns. In 1986 Congress passed legislation to suggest that the D.C. law on demonstrations near foreign missions may be inconsistent with First Amendment rights. The D.C. government repealed the law, contingent on Congress's extending to the District the federal law on foreign embassies. Against this background, the Court held that the D.C. law violated the First Amendment because it represented a content-based restriction on political speech in a public forum. Boos v. Barry, 485 U.S. 312 (1988).

Madison's Views on Factions

In Federalist No. 10, James Madison defined *faction* as citizens "united and actuated by some common impulse of passion, or of interest, adverse to the rights of other citizens, or to the permanent and aggregate interests of the community." As a very rough and often unfair characterization, the definition could apply to interest groups or the even more pejorative "lobbyists." In a careful and insightful analysis, Madison reconciles the activity of factions to democratic government.

Among the numerous advantages promised by a well-constructed Union, none deserves to be more accurately developed than its tendency to break and control the violence of faction. The friend of popular governments never finds himself so much alarmed for their character and fate, as when he contemplates their propensity to this dangerous vice. He will not fail, therefore, to set a due value on any plan which, without violating the principles to which he is attached, provides a proper cure for it. The instability, injustice, and confusion introduced into the public councils, have, in truth, been the mortal diseases under which popular governments have everywhere perished; ...

By a faction, I understand a number of citizens, whether amounting to a majority or minority of the whole, who are united and actuated by some common impulse of passion, or of interest, adverse to the rights of other citizens, or to the permanent and aggregate interests of the community.

There are two methods of curing the mischiefs of faction: the one, by removing its causes; the other, by controlling its effects.

There are again two methods of removing the causes of faction: the one, by destroying the liberty which is essential to its existence; the other, by giving to every citizen the same opinions, the same passions, and the same interests.

It could never be more truly said than of the first remedy, that it was worse than the disease. Liberty is to faction what air is to fire, an aliment without which it instantly expires. But it could not be less folly to abolish liberty, which is essential to political life, because it nourishes faction, than it would be to wish the annihilation of air, which is essential to animal life, because it imparts to fire its destructive agency.

The second expedient is as impracticable as the first would be unwise. As long as the reason of man continues fallible, and he is at liberty to exercise it, different opinions will be formed. As long as the connection subsists between his reason and his self-love, his opinions and his passions will have a reciprocal influence on each other: and

the former will be objects to which the latter will attach themselves. The diversity in the faculties of men, from which the rights of property originate, is not less an insuperable obstacle to a uniformity of interests. The protection of these faculties is the first object of government. From the protection of different and unequal faculties of acquiring property, the possession of different degrees and kinds of property immediately results; and from the influence of these on the sentiments and views of the respective proprietors, ensues a division of the society into different interests and parties.

The latent causes of faction are thus sown in the nature of man; and we see them everywhere brought into different degrees of activity, according to the different circumstances of civil society. A zeal for different opinions concerning religion, concerning government, and many other points, as well of speculation as of practice; an attachment to different leaders ambitiously contending for pre-eminence and power; or to persons of other descriptions whose fortunes have been interesting to the human passions, have, in turn, divided mankind into parties, inflamed them with mutual animosity, and rendered them much more disposed to vex and oppress each other than to co-operate for their common good. So strong is this propensity of mankind to fall into mutual animosities, that where no substantial occasion presents itself, the most frivolous and fanciful distinctions have been sufficient to kindle their unfriendly passions and excite their most violent conflicts. But the most common and durable source of factions has been the various and unequal distribution of property. Those who hold and those who are without property have ever formed distinct interests in society. Those who are creditors, and those who are debtors, fall under a like discrimination. A landed interest, a manufacturing interest, a mercantile interest, a moneyed interest, with many lesser interests, grow up of necessity in civilized nations, and divide them into different classes, actuated by different sentiments and views. The regulation of these various and interfering interests forms the principal task of modern legislation, and involves the spirit of party and faction in the necessary and ordinary operations of the government.

No man is allowed to be a judge in his own cause, because his interest would certainly bias his judgment, and, not improbably, corrupt his integrity. With equal, nay with greater reason, a body of men are unfit to be both judges and parties at the same time; yet what are many of the most important acts of legislation, but so many judicial determinations, not indeed concerning the rights of single persons, but concerning the rights of large bodies of citizens? And what are the different classes of legislators but advocates and parties to the causes which they determine? Is a law proposed concerning private debts? It is a question to which the creditors are parties on one side and the debtors on the other. Justice ought to hold the balance between them. Yet the parties are, and must be, themselves the judges; and the most numerous party, or, in other words, the most powerful faction must be expected to prevail....

It is in vain to say that enlightened statesmen will be able to adjust these clashing interests, and render them all subservient to the public good. Enlightened statesmen will not always be at the helm. Nor, in many cases, can such an adjustment be made at all without taking into view indirect and remote considerations, which will rarely prevail over the immediate interest which one party may find in disregarding the rights of another or the good of the whole.

The inference to which we are brought is, that the *causes* of faction cannot be removed, and that relief is only to be sought in the means of controlling its *effects*.

If a faction consists of less than a majority, relief is supplied by the republican principle, which enables the majority to defeat its sinister views by regular vote. It may clog the administration, it may convulse the society; but it will be unable to execute and mask its violence under the forms of the Constitution. When a majority is included in a faction, the form of popular government, on the other hand, enables it to sacrifice to its ruling passion or interest both the public good and the rights of other citizens. To secure the public good and private rights against the danger of such a faction, and at the same time to preserve the spirit and the form of popular government, is then the great object to which our inquiries are directed. Let me add that it is the great desideratum by which this form of government can be rescued from the opprobrium under which it has so long

labored, and be recommended to the esteem and adoption of mankind.

By what means is this object attainable? Evidently by one of two only. Either the existence of the same passion or interest in a majority at the same time must be prevented, or the majority, having such coexistent passion or interest, must be rendered, by their number and local situation, unable to concert and carry into effect schemes of oppression. If the impulse and the opportunity be suffered to coincide, we well know that neither moral nor religious motives can be relied on as an adequate control. They are not found to be such on the injustice and violence of individuals, and lose their efficacy in proportion to the number combined together, that is, in proportion as their efficacy becomes needful.

From this view of the subject it may be concluded that a pure democracy, by which I mean a society consisting of a small number of citizens, who assemble and administer the government in person, can admit of no cure for the mischiefs of faction. A common passion or interest will, in almost every case, be felt by a majority of the whole; a communication and concert result from the form of government itself; and there is nothing to check the inducements to sacrifice the weaker party or an obnoxious individual. Hence it is that such democracies have ever been spectacles of turbulence and contention....

A republic, by which I mean a government in which the scheme of representation takes place, opens a different prospect, and promises the cure for which we are seeking. Let us examine the points in which it varies from pure democracy, and we shall comprehend both the nature of the cure and the efficacy which it must derive from the Union.

The two great points of difference between a democracy and a republic are: first, the delegation of the government, in the latter, to a small number of citizens elected by the rest; secondly, the greater number of citizens, and greater sphere of country, over which the latter may be extended.

The effect of the first difference is, on the one hand, to refine and enlarge the public views, by passing them through the medium of a chosen body of citizens, whose wisdom may best discern the true interest of their country, and whose patriotism and love of justice will be least likely to sacrifice it to temporary or partial considerations. Under such a regulation, it may well happen that the public voice, pronounced by the representatives of the people, will be more consonant to the public good than if pronounced by the people themselves, convened for the purpose. On the other hand, the effect may be inverted. Men of factious tempers, of local prejudices, or of sinister designs, may, by intrigue, by corruption, or by other means, first obtain the suffrages, and then betray the interests, of the people. The question resulting is, whether small or extensive republics are more favorable to the election of proper guardians of the public weal; and it is clearly decided in favor of the latter by two obvious considerations:

In the first place, it is to be remarked that, however small the republic may be, the representatives must be raised to a certain number, in order to guard against the cabals of a few; and that, however large it may be, they must be limited to a certain number, in order to guard against the confusion of a multitude. Hence, the number of representatives in the two cases not being in proportion to that of the two constituents, and being proportionally greater in the small republic, it follows that, if the proportion of fit characters be not less in the large than in the small republic, the former will present a greater option, and consequently a greater probability of a fit choice.

In the next place, as each representative will be chosen by a greater number of citizens in the large than in the small republic, it will be more difficult for unworthy candidates to practise with success the vicious arts by which elections are too often carried; and the suffrages of the people being more free, will be more likely to centre in men who possess the most attractive merit and the most diffusive and established characters.

It must be confessed that in this, as in most other cases, there is a mean, on both sides of which inconveniences will be found to lie. By enlarging too much the number of electors, you render the representative too little acquainted with all their local circumstances and lesser interests; as by reducing it too much, you render him unduly attached to these, and too little fit to comprehend and pursue great and national objects. The federal Constitution forms a happy combination in this respect; the great and aggregate interests being referred to the national, the local and particular to the State legislatures.

The other point of difference is, the greater number of citizens and extent of territory which may be brought within the compass of republican than of democratic government; and it is this circumstance principally which renders factious combinations less to be dreaded in the former than in the latter. The smaller the society, the fewer probably will be the distinct parties and interests composing it; the fewer the distinct parties and interests, the more frequently will a majority be found of the same party; and the smaller the number of individuals composing a majority, and the smaller the compass within which they are placed, the most easily will they concert and execute their plans of oppression. Extend the sphere, and you take in a greater variety of parties and interests; you make it less probable that a majority of the whole will have a common motive to invade the rights of other citizens; or if such a common motive exists, it will be more difficult for all who feel it to discover their own strength, and to act in unison with each other. Besides other impediments, it may be remarked that, where there is a consciousness of unjust or dishonorable purposes, communication is always checked by distrust in proportion to the number whose concurrence is necessary.

Hence, it clearly appears, that the same advantage which a republic has over a democracy, in controlling the effects of faction, is enjoyed by a large over a small republic, — is enjoyed by the Union over the States composing it. Does the advantage consist in the substitution of representatives whose enlightened views and virtuous sentiments render them superior to local prejudices and to schemes of injustice? It will not be denied that the representation of the Union will be most likely to possess these requisite endowments. Does it consist in the greater security afforded by a greater variety of parties, against the event of any one party being able to outnumber and oppress the rest? In an equal degree does the increased variety of parties comprised within the Union, increase this security. Does it, in fine, consist in the greater obstacles opposed to the concert and accomplishment of the secret wishes of an unjust and interested majority? Here, again, the extent of the Union gives it the most palpable advantage.

The influence of factious leaders may kindle a flame within their particular States, but will be unable to spread a general conflagration through the other States. A religious sect may degenerate into a political faction in a part of the Confederacy; but the variety of sects dispersed over the entire face of it must secure the national councils against any danger from that source. A rage for paper money, for an abolition of debts, for an equal division of property, or for any other improper or wicked project, will be less apt to pervade the whole body of the Union than a particular member of it; in the same proportion as such a malady is more likely to taint a particular county or district, than an entire State.

In the extent and proper structure of the Union, therefore, we behold a republican remedy for the diseases most incident to republican government. And according to the degree of pleasure and pride we feel in being republicans, ought to be our zeal in cherishing the spirit and supporting the character of Federalists.

PUBLIUS

CONCLUSIONS

The sections in this chapter provide further evidence of the essentially shared nature of constitutional interpretation involving the combined efforts of legislators, executive officials, and judges. The responsibility for keeping the political process free and open is not entrusted to a single branch. Members of the judiciary must exercise careful judgment in deciding which cases to accept and resolve. Harold Leventhal, for many years a distinguished federal judge on the D.C. Circuit, recognized that the "political thicket" did not constitute a flat ban on judicial involvement: "For me the 'thicket' sign does not mean out of bounds, but a caution to walk carefully in the work of interpreting and determining the validity of the legislature's efforts to structure the political process." 77 Colum. L. Rev. 345, 346 (1977). The Court in *Buckley* waded deep into the political thicket and is now in the process of deciding whether it overstepped and should allow the elected branches more leeway in fashioning a solution to the problem of campaign finance. Other constraints on judicial activism are addressed in the next chapter.

SELECTED READINGS

ALEXANDER, HERBERT E. Financing Politics: Money, Elections, and Political Reform. Washington, D.C.: Congressional Quarterly, 1992.

ALFANGE, DEAN, JR. "Gerrymandering and the Constitution: Into the Thorns of the Thicket at Last." 1986 Supreme Court Review 175.

AUERBACH, CARL A. "The Reapportionment Cases: One Person, One Vote—One Vote, One Value." 1964 Supreme Court Review 1.

BAKER, GORDON E. The Reapportionment Revolution. New York: Random House, 1966.

BALL, HOWARD. The Warren Court's Conceptions of Democracy: An Evaluation of the Supreme Court's Apportionment Cases. Rutherford, N.J.: Fairleigh Dickinson University Press, 1971.

BICKEL, ALEXANDER. "The Voting Rights Cases." 1966 Supreme Court Review 79.

CAIN, BRUCE E. The Reapportionment Puzzle. Berkeley: University of California Press, 1984.

CLAUDE, RICHARD. The Supreme Court and the Electoral Process. Baltimore, Md.: Johns Hopkins University Press, 1970.

CORRADO, ANTHONY., et al., eds., Campaign Finance Reform: A Sourcebook. Washington, D.C.: Brookings Institution Press, 1997.

CORTNER, RICHARD C. The Apportionment Cases. Knoxville: University of Tennessee Press, 1970.

DIXON, ROBERT G., JR. Democratic Representation: Reapportionment in Law and Politics. New York: Oxford University Press, 1968.

———. "The Warren Court Crusade for the Holy Grail of 'One Man-One Vote.'" 1969 Supreme Court Review 219.

ELLIOTT, WARD. "Prometheus, Proteus, Pandora, and Procrustes Unbound: The Political Consequences of Reapportionment." 37 University of Chicago Law Review 474 (1970).

HAMILTON, HOWARD D., ed. Legislative Reapportionment: Key to Power. New York: Harper & Row, 1964.

HANSON, ROYCE. The Political Thicket: Reapportionment and Constitutional Democracy. Englewood Cliffs, N.J.: Prentice-Hall, 1966.

LEVENTHAL, HAROLD. "Courts and Political Thickets." 77 Columbia Law Review 345 (1977).

LEWIS, ANTHONY. "Legislative Apportionment and the Federal Courts." 71 Harvard Law Review 1057 (1958).

NEAL, PHIL C. "Baker v. Carr: Politics in Search of Law." 1962 Supreme Court Review 252.

PENNOCK, J. ROLAND, AND JOHN W. CHAPMAN, eds. Representation. New York: Atherton Press, 1968.

POLSBY, DANIEL D. "Buckley v. Valeo: The Special Nature of Political Speech." 1976 Supreme Court Review 1.

POLSBY, NELSON W., ed. Reapportionment in the 1970s. Berkeley: University of California Press, 1971.

SCHER, RICHARD K., et al. Voting Rights and Democracy: The Law and Politics of Districting. Chicago: Nelson-Hall Publishers, 1997.

SCHRAM, MARTIN. Speaking Freely: Former Members of Congress Talk About Money in Politics. Washington, D.C.: Center for Responsive Politics, 1995.

SORAUF, FRANK J. "Caught in a Political Thicket: The Supreme Court and Campaign Finance." 3 Constitutional Commentary 97 (1986).

———. Inside Campaign Finance: Myths and Realities. New Haven, Conn.: Yale University Press, 1992.

TAPER, BERNARD. Gomillion versus Lightfoot: Apartheid in Alabama. New York: McGraw-Hill, 1967.

WRIGHT, J. SKELLY. "Money and the Pollution of Politics: Is the First Amendment an Obstacle to Political Equality?" 82 Columbia Law Review 609 (1982).

19

Efforts to Curb the Court

Justice Stone once chided his brethren: "the only check upon our own exercise of power is our own sense of self-restraint." United States v. Butler, 297 U.S. 1, 79 (1936). While that is an important check, it is by no means the only one. Judges act within an environment that constantly tests the reasonableness and acceptability of their rulings. Courts issue the "last word" only for an instant, for after the release of an opinion the process of interaction begins: with Congress, the President, executive agencies, states, professional associations, law journals, and the public at large.

Earlier chapters identified some of the constraints that operate on the judiciary: the President's power to appoint; the Senate's power to confirm; congressional powers over the purse, impeachment, and court jurisdiction; the force of public opinion, the press, and scholarly studies. Other restraints, covered in this chapter, include constitutional amendments, statutory reversals, changing the number of Justices (court packing), withdrawing jurisdiction, and noncompliance with court rulings.

Court-curbing periods often emerge when the judiciary acts by nullifying statutes, particularly those passed by Congress. But the judiciary can also create enemies by *upholding* legislation, such as the broad nationalist rulings issued by Chief Justice John Marshall. To restrain the courts, members of Congress introduce a variety of legislative bills and constitutional amendments. Hearings are held to explore ways to curb the judiciary. State legislatures prepare petitions of protest; state judges pass resolutions of "concern," if not condemnation. Citizens pass initiatives, propositions, and take other positions on constitutional issues. To reduce the tension, the federal judiciary may decide to conduct a partial and possibly graceful retreat.

Judicial-congressional confrontations were especially sharp between 1858 and 1869 (reflecting the *Dred Scott* case and congressional efforts to protect Reconstruction legislation), 1935 and 1937 (reacting to the Court's nullification of New Deal legislation), and 1955 and 1959 (triggered by decisions involving desegregation, congressional investigations, and national security).[1] A new round of court-curbing efforts began in the late 1970s to challenge judicial rulings on school prayer, school busing, abortion, and affirmative action.

The judiciary is most likely to be out of step with Congress or the President during periods of electoral and partisan realignment, when the country is undergoing sharp shifts in political directions while the courts retain the orientation of an age gone by.[2] During earlier periods, attacks on the judiciary generally came from liberal groups: Jeffersonians, Jacksonians, Radical Republicans, LaFollette Republicans, and New Deal Democrats. However, conservatives dominated the 1955–59 confrontation and have inspired most of the court-curbing efforts since then.

---

1. See Stuart S. Nagel, "Court-Curbing Periods in American History," 18 Vand. L. Rev. 925 (1965). For a review of proposals to remedy judicial activism, see Charles Grove Haines, The American Doctrine of Judicial Supremacy 467–99 (1932).

2. Richard Funston, "The Supreme Court and Critical Elections," 69 Am. Pol. Sci. Rev. 795 (1975); David Adamany, "Legitimacy, Realigning Elections, and the Supreme Court," 1973 Wisc. L. Rev. 790.

A. CONSTITUTIONAL AMENDMENTS

Whenever two-thirds of both Houses of Congress deem it necessary, they may propose amendments to the Constitution. Ratification requires three-fourths of the states. Alternatively, two-thirds of the states may call a convention for constitutional amendment, but thus far all successful amendments have been initiated by Congress. The process of amending the Constitution is extraordinarily difficult and time-consuming. On only four occasions has Congress successfully used constitutional amendments to reverse Supreme Court decisions.

The Eleventh Amendment responded to *Chisholm* v. *Georgia,* 2 U.S. (2 Dall.) 419 (1793), which decided that a state could be sued in federal court by a plaintiff from another state. The lower house of the Georgia legislature adopted the modest proposal that any federal marshal attempting to enforce that ruling would be guilty of a felony and hanged until death "without the benefit of the clergy." To protect states from a flood of costly citizen suits, Congress quickly passed a constitutional amendment. Although a sufficient number of states ratified it by 1795, not until 1798 did President John Adams notify Congress that the amendment was effective. The Eleventh Amendment reads: "The Judicial power of the United States shall not be construed to extend to any suit in law or equity, commenced or prosecuted against one of the United States by Citizens of another State, or by Citizens or Subjects of any Foreign States."

The Fourteenth Amendment nullified the Supreme Court's decision in *Dred Scott* v. *Sandford,* 60 U.S. (19 How.) 393 (1857), which held that blacks as a class were not citizens protected under the Constitution. After the nation had fought a bloody civil war, North against South, the Fourteenth Amendment was ratified in 1868. Section 1 provides: "All persons born or naturalized in the United States and subject to the jurisdiction thereof, are citizens of the United States and of the State wherein they reside." *Dred Scott* had been partially reversed by statute in 1862 when Congress passed legislation to prohibit slavery in the territories. 12 Stat. 432.

The Sixteenth Amendment overruled *Pollock* v. *Farmers' Loan and Trust Co.,* 158 U.S. 601 (1895), which struck down a federal income tax. The need to finance national expansion and new international responsibilities, combined with a desire to reduce the dependence on high tariffs as the main source of revenue, triggered the drive for a constitutional amendment. Ratified in 1913, the Sixteenth Amendment gave Congress the power "to lay and collect taxes on incomes, from whatever source derived, without apportionment among the several States, and without regard to any census or enumeration."

The Twenty-sixth Amendment was ratified in 1971 to overturn *Oregon* v. *Mitchell,* 400 U.S. 112 (1970), a Supreme Court decision of the previous year that had voided a congressional effort to lower the minimum voting age in state elections to eighteen. Proponents of lowering the voting age argued that if eighteen-year-olds could be drafted to fight in wars, they were old enough to vote in elections. As a way to encourage youths to participate constructively in the political process and to avoid the cost and confusion of a dual registration system of eighteen years for national elections and twenty-one years for state and local elections, Congress sent a constitutional amendment to the states. In record time, three months later, a sufficient number of states ratified this language: "The right of citizens of the United States, who are eighteen years of age or older, to vote shall not be denied or abridged by the United States or any State on account of age."

Other Amendment Efforts

Other constitutional amendments, driven by seemingly irresistible political forces, have fallen by the wayside. A successful amendment process requires an extraordinary combination of social, economic, and political forces. If any one of these factors is absent, an amendment may fail. For example, Congress made a concerted effort in 1964 to amend the Constitution to

Debate on Equal Rights Amendment

[During House debate in 1970 and 1971, Congresswoman Martha Griffiths used the proposed Equal Rights Amendment as a vehicle for attacking the Supreme Court for its failure to address laws and practices that discriminated against women. These debates helped provoke the Court to act in Reed v. Reed, 404 U.S. 71 (1971).*]*

Mrs. GRIFFITHS. . . . We will show you that the Supreme Court which has readily moved to change the boundaries of your District and the boundaries of your school district has on not one single occasion granted to women the basic protection of the fifth or 14th amendment. The only right guaranteed to women today by the Constitution of the United States is the right to vote and to hold public office.

It is time, Mr. Speaker, that in this battle with the Supreme Court, that this body and the legislatures of the States come to the aid of women by passing this amendment. . . .

Mr. Speaker, this is not a battle between the sexes — nor a battle between this body and women. This body and State legislatures have supported women. This is a battle with the Supreme Court of the United States.

. . . Let me repeat again and again that the States, their legislatures and frequently their courts or Federal district courts have shown more sense than the Supreme Court ever has. . . .

Mr. Chairman, what the equal rights amendment seeks to do, and all it seeks to do, is to say to the Supreme Court of the United States, "Wake up! This is the 20th century. Before it is over, judge women as individual human beings. They, too, are entitled to the protection of the Constitution, the basic fundamental law of this country."

SOURCE: 116 Cong. Rec. 28000, 28004, 28005 (1970); 117 Cong. Rec. 35323 (1971).

overturn the Supreme Court's decisions in the reapportionment and school prayer cases. Because of delays by House committees and filibusters on the Senate side, these efforts proved fruitless.

Even when Congress reacts against a Court decision by clearing an amendment for ratification by the states, the hurdles are immense. After the Supreme Court in 1918 and 1922 denied Congress the right to regulate child labor conditions, opponents of the Court rulings tried unsuccessfully to reverse them by constitutional amendment. Hammer v. Dagenhart, 247 U.S. 251 (1918); Bailey v. Drexel Furniture Co., 259 U.S. 20 (1922). In 1924 both Houses of Congress passed a constitutional amendment to give Congress the power to "limit, regulate and prohibit the labor of persons under 18 years of age." By 1937 only twenty-eight of the necessary thirty-six states had ratified the amendment. The issue became moot after Congress regulated child labor through the Fair Labor Standards Act of 1938 and the Supreme Court upheld the statute three years later. United States v. Darby, 312 U.S. 100 (1941).

Unsuccessful constitutional amendments can sometimes prod the Court to address neglected issues. In 1970 the House of Representatives passed the Equal Rights Amendment. After Senate action, the language sent to the states for ratification read: "Equality of rights under the law shall not be denied or abridged by the United States or by any State on account of sex." The ERA was never ratified, even with an extension by Congress to June 30, 1982, but the debate on the amendment had an obvious impact on the Court. Congresswoman Martha Griffiths, during debate in October 1971, said that the whole purpose of the ERA was to tell the Supreme Court "Wake up! This is the 20th century." 117 Cong. Rec. 35323 (1971). A month later the Court invalidated an Idaho law that preferred men over women in administering estates, the first time in its history that the Court had struck down sex discrimination on constitutional grounds (see box).

Once the Constitution is successfully amended to overturn a Court decision, there is no guarantee that the judiciary will interpret the amendment consistent with the intent of the framers and ratifiers. Although the Thirteenth, Fourteenth, and Fifteenth Amendments were meant to overturn *Dred Scott* and protect the rights of blacks, such decisions as *The Civil Rights Cases,* 109 U.S. 3 (1883) and *Plessy* v. *Ferguson,* 163 U.S. 537 (1896), were more in line with racial attitudes that flourished before the Civil War.

In addition to constitutional amendments aimed at particular decisions, there have been other proposals aimed at curbing the Court's strength by imposing certain procedural requirements. These amendments have in every instance been unsuccessful. Of recurring interest are the following: requiring more than a majority of Justices to strike down a statute; subjecting the Court's decisions to another tribunal, such as the Senate or a judicial body consisting of a judge from each state; submitting the Court's decisions to popular referenda; allowing Congress by two-thirds vote to override a Court decision just as it does a presidential veto; and making laws held unconstitutional by the Court valid if reenacted by Congress.

Other amendments are directed at the Court's tenure and qualifications: allowing the removal of Supreme Court Justices and other federal judges by majority vote of each House of Congress; restricting the term of a Justice to a set number of years; having Justices retire at the age of seventy-five years; requiring direct election from the judicial districts; itemizing the qualifications for Justices, such as requiring prior judicial service in the highest court of a state or excluding anyone who has, within the preceding five years, served in the executive or legislative branch; and vesting the appointment of Justices in judges from the highest state courts.[3] Although unsuccessful in every case, these amendments serve the purpose of venting popular and professional resentment toward Court decisions and may even temper future rulings.

The Court held in 1921 that constitutional amendments must be ratified within some reasonable time after their submission to the states. Ratification "must be sufficiently contemporaneous in that number of States to reflect the will of the people in all sections at relatively the same period...." Dillon v. Gloss, 256 U.S. 368, 375 (1921). However, in 1939 the Court declined to be the judge of what constituted a reasonable period for ratification. Coleman v. Miller, 307 U.S. 433, 452 (1939). In 1992 Congress agreed that 202 years were not too long to ratify a constitutional amendment proposed in 1789. That language, now the Twenty-seventh Amendment, reads: "No law, varying the compensation for the services of the Senators and Representatives, shall take effect, until an election of Representatives shall have intervened."

B. STATUTORY REVERSALS

When decisions turn on the interpretation of federal statutes, Congress may overturn a ruling simply by passing a new statute to clarify legislative intent. The private sector often uses Congress as an "appellate court" to reverse judicial interpretations of a statute. At a congressional hearing in 1959, Congressman Wilbur Mills leaned across the witness table and told a company president: "It seems that it is becoming more and more almost a full-time job of the Congress to correct the Supreme Court's desire to legislate." The company president, seeking to have a major Supreme Court decision modified to his advantage, nodded his approval. Emmette S. Redford, et al., Politics and Government in the United States 518 (1965).

In 1969 the Supreme Court struck down a joint operating agreement by two newspapers on the ground that it violated the Antitrust Act. Citizen Publishing Co. v. United States, 394 U.S. 131 (1969). Congress responded within a year with the Newspaper Preservation Act, specifically exempting from the Act any authorizing agreement needed to prevent newspapers from going out of business. 84 Stat. 466 (1970).

---

3. Maurice S. Culp, "A Survey of the Proposals to Limit or Deny the Power of Judicial Review by the Supreme Court of the United States," 4 Ind. L. J. 386 (1929); Shelden D. Elliott, "Court-Curbing Proposals in Congress," 33 Notre Dame Lawyer 597, 606 (1958).

Judicial-legislative conversations helped shape the meaning of the Freedom of Information Act (FOIA). In one case, 33 members of the House of Representatives went to court to obtain documents prepared for President Nixon concerning an underground nuclear test. In 1973 the Supreme Court decided that it had no authority to examine the documents *in camera* to sift out "non-secret components" for their release. EPA v. Mink, 410 U.S. 73 (1973). Congress passed legislation a year later to override the decision, clearly authorizing federal courts to examine sensitive records in judges' chambers. 88 Stat. 1562, § 4(B) (1974).

A later example of statutory reversal involved *Smith* v. *Robinson,* 468 U.S. 992 (1984), which held that parents who brought legal action to obtain schooling for their handicapped child were not entitled to attorney's fees if they prevailed in the litigation. Justice Brennan, writing a dissent joined by Justices Marshall and Stevens, said that "with today's decision...Congress will now have to take the time to revisit the matter" of attorney's fees. Legislation two years later authorized the award of attorney's fees to prevailing parties. 100 Stat. 796 (1986).

The *Grove City* Confrontation

Another successful congressional effort concerned the case of *Grove City College* v. *Bell,* 465 U.S. 555 (1984). Title IX of the Education Amendments of 1972 prohibited sex discrimination in any education program or activity that received federal financial assistance. After the Reagan administration had issued statements indicating that its interpretation of Title IX was not as broad as rulings from previous administrations, the House of Representatives on November 16, 1983, passed a resolution by a vote of 414–8 opposing the administration's position. The resolution stated the sense of the House that Title IX and regulations issued pursuant to the title "should not be amended or altered in any manner which will lessen the comprehensive coverage of such statute in eliminating gender discrimination throughout the American educational system." The resolution, of course, was not legally binding, but it was passed because the Supreme Court was about to hear oral argument on the *Grove City* case. As Congressman Paul Simon noted: "Passing this resolution the House can send the Court a signal that we believe that no institution should be allowed to discriminate on the basis of sex if it receives Federal funds." 129 Cong. Rec. 33105 (1983).

The issue before the Court was whether Title IX required federal funds to be terminated only for specific programs in which discrimination occurs or for the entire educational institution. The Supreme Court adopted the narrow interpretation. Justices Brennan and Marshall dissented in part, stating that the Court was ignoring congressional intent for institution-wide coverage. Within four months the House of Representatives, by a vote of 375–32, passed legislation to amend not only Title IX but also three other statutes to adopt broad coverage of the antidiscrimination provisions. 130 Cong. Rec. 18880 (1984). (See reading.) The Senate resisted action that year, and subsequent efforts were complicated by questions of church-state and abortion. Finally, in 1988, Congress was able to forge a compromise. President Reagan vetoed the measure, but both Houses overrode the veto to enact the broader coverage for civil rights that had been rejected in *Grove City.*

Continued Challenges

In 1988, Congress passed two other statutes to reverse the Supreme Court. In one decision, the Court ruled that federal employees could be sued for common law torts committed on the job. They were not entitled to absolute immunity from lawsuit. However, the Court remarked: "Congress is in the best position to provide guidance for the complex and often highly empirical inquiry into whether absolute immunity is warranted in a particular context." Westfall v. Erwin, 484 U.S. 292, 300 (1988). Congress passed legislation to overturn this decision by protecting federal employees from personal liability for common law torts committed within the scope of their employment. The statute provides the injured person with a remedy against the United States government. Thus, compensation would come from the U.S. Treasury, not the employee's pocketbook. 102 Stat. 4563 (1988).

The other statutory reversal in 1988 concerned a Supreme Court decision that accepted the definition of the Veterans Administration that alcoholism results from "willful misconduct" rather than from a disease. For those who regarded the Court's position as erroneous, they were advised that their arguments would be "better presented to Congress than to the courts." Traynor v. Turnage, 485 U.S. 535 (1988). Legislation enacted by Congress recognized that veterans seeking education or rehabilitation would not be denied those benefits under the willful-misconduct standard. 102 Stat. 4170, § 109 (1988).

The Jencks Bill

These cases involve matters of statutory interpretation, an area in which Congress can ultimately prevail. However, even in cases where constitutional rights are present, Congress may pass legislation to modify a Court ruling. A 1957 case involved access by defendants to government files bearing on their trial. On the basis of statements by two informers for the FBI, the government prosecuted Clifford Jencks for failing to state that he was a member of the Communist party. He asked that the FBI reports be turned over to the trial judge for examination to determine whether they had value in impeaching the statements of the two informers. The Supreme Court went beyond Jencks' request by ordering the government to produce for *his* inspection all FBI reports "touching the events and activities" at issue in the trial. Jencks v. United States, 353 U.S. 657, 668 (1957). The Court specifically rejected the option of producing government documents to the trial judge for his determination of relevancy and materiality. Id. at 669.

In their concurrence, Justices Burton and Harlan believed that Jencks was only entitled to have the records submitted to the trial judge. A dissent by Justice Clark agreed that the documents should be delivered only to the trial judge. In a remarkable statement he incited Congress to act: "Unless the Congress changes the rule announced by the Court today, those intelligence agencies of our Government engaged in law enforcement may as well close up shop, for the Court has opened their files to the criminal and thus afforded him a Roman holiday for rummaging through confidential information as well as vital national secrets."

The Court announced its decision on June 3, 1957. Both Houses of Congress quickly held hearings and reported remedial legislation. The Jencks Bill (after much redrafting) passed the Senate by voice vote on August 26 and passed the House on August 27 by a vote of 351 to 17. The conference report was adopted with huge majorities: 74–2 in the Senate and 315–0 in the House. The bill became law on September 2, 1957. The statute provides that in any federal criminal prosecution, no statement or report in the possession of the government "which was made by a Government witness or prospective Government witness (other than the defendant) to an agent of the Government shall be the subject of subpena, discovery, or inspection unless said witness has testified on direct examination in the trial of the case." If a witness testifies, statements may be delivered to the defendant for examination and use unless the United States claims that the statement contains irrelevant matter, in which case the statement shall be inspected by the court *in camera*. The judge may excise irrelevant portions of the statement before submitting it to the defendant. 71 Stat. 595 (1957); 18 U.S.C. § 3500 (1994).

The Record in the 1990s

Congress has resorted to statutory reversals with greater frequency in recent years. A single statute — the Civil Rights Act of 1991 — overturned or modified nine Supreme Court decisions (see page 898). By increasing its staff, Congress can monitor judicial rulings more closely. Interest groups are now better organized to follow court decisions and bring them to the attention of Congress. Finally, the judicial appointments by Republican Presidents Reagan and Bush gave the courts a decidedly conservative cast, putting pressure on the more liberal Congress to respond with statutory reversals.

With President Clinton in the White House and Republicans controlling Congress, the pattern of statutory reversals continues. In 1995, Congress passed legislation to overturn the Supreme Court's opinion in *Dole* v. *United Steelworkers of America*, 494 U.S. 26 (1990), which had restricted OMB's authority to review and countermand agency regulations. The new legislation (P.L. 104-13) makes all paperwork requirements subject to OMB review. Also in 1995, Congress passed legislation to reverse a Court decision regarding workers' compensation benefits. Adams Fruit Co., Inc. v. Barrett, 494 U.S. 638 (1990), reversed on November 15, 1995. 109 Stat. 432. See 141 Cong. Rec. 28125–29 (1995). Legislation in 1996 reversed a Court decision of the previous year concerning false statements to Congress (p. 240).

On February 25, 1998, the Supreme Court held that the National Credit Union Administration had improperly interpreted its statutory authority by allowing mergers to take place between credit unions that had a different common bond of occupation. Nat. Cred. Union Admin. v. First Nat. Bank & Trust, 522 U.S. 479 (1998). Within two weeks the House Committee on Banking and Financial Services held a comprehensive hearing and two weeks after that marked up a bill to reverse the Court's decision. The bill passed the House in April and the Senate in July. P.L. 105-219 (1998).

Statutory Reversal: *Grove City*

After the Supreme Court announced *Grove City College* v. *Bell* on February 28, 1984, which restricted the reach of congressional prohibitions on sex discrimination, the House quickly passed legislation that year to overturn the Court's statutory interpretation. Senate action was delayed and complicated by questions of church-state and abortion. Finally, in 1988 the Senate acted, and the legislation was sent to President Reagan. Both Houses had the votes to override his veto and enact this statutory reversal. The Senate debate below is taken from 134 Cong. Rec. 97 (1988).

Mr. KENNEDY. Mr. President, today the Senate begins consideration of the Civil Rights Restoration Act, one of the most important civil rights measures in recent years. A broad, bipartisan coalition of 56 Senators is sponsoring the bill. Our goal is to reverse the 1984 Supreme Court decision in Grove City College versus Bell, which permits tax dollars to be spent in support of discrimination.

The moment is ripe for Congress to renew its commitment to civil rights. The historic struggle to secure these rights for all Americans has known both triumph and tragedy.

Over the past 200 years, the American people have worked hard to make the promises of the Constitution a reality for all of our citizens. The harsh fact remains, however, that discrimination still prevents too many of our citizens from enjoying the American dream.

Despite the 1954 Supreme Court decision in Brown versus Board of Education, subsequent predictions about the demise of racial segregation proved grossly premature. Faith in what the

Brown case would accomplish swiftly turned to frustration and then cynicism. It took inspiration and leadership from Presidents Eisenhower and Kennedy, Martin Luther King Jr., and other great leaders to advance the legislation that has achieved so much in the past two decades.

Twenty-four summers ago, Congress distinguished itself by passing the landmark Civil Rights Act of 1964. In enacting this monumental measure, we initiated a new assault against the injustices which pervaded America's social fabric and political order. One of the most significant components of the 1964 legislation is title VI, which prohibits discrimination based on race, color, or national origin in any "program or activity" which receives Federal aid.

In terms of eradicating racial injustice, the success of title VI surpassed our expectations. Under its impact, many engines of discrimination began grinding to a halt. Faced with the prospect of losing Federal aid, schools, hospitals, and State and local governments had no choice but to dismantle their discriminatory practices. For example, black enrollment in colleges increased by 92 percent in the decade of the 1970's.

Influenced by a new national awareness, Congress in the 1970's grew sensitive to additional groups which suffer from the effects of prejudice and discrimination. In this climate, title VI emerged as a prime model for new initiatives. In 1972, Congress enacted title IX, which prohibits sex discrimination in educational programs or activities receiving Federal aid. In 1973, Congress adopted section 504 of the Rehabilitation Act, which prevents the recipients of Federal funds from discriminating against the disabled. And the Age Discrimination Act of 1975 was written into law to guarantee the same protection for the elderly.

Each of these statutes achieved remarkable results. Under title IX, the participation of women in high school and college athletic activities has soared. And their achievements have soared, too, including the extraordinary successes of American women in the summer and winter Olympic games. Equally impressive is the record for section 504, which has brought disabled citizens into the mainstream of American life by dismantling the barriers to education and employment of the handicapped.

But suddenly, in 1984, much of the progress against discrimination in each of these areas was placed at risk by the decision of the Supreme Court in the Grove City College case. In that case, a divided court interpreted the antidiscrimination language in title IX extremely narrowly. Since the only Federal money reaching the college was in the form of student aid, the Court concluded that only the financial aid office was covered by the law. The rest of the college was left free to deny equal opportunities to women.

The decision affects all of the civil rights statutes which prohibit discrimination in federally funded programs or activities, since each of these statutes is identical to the phrasing which the Supreme Court interpreted in the Grove City case. If this decision is permitted to stand, millions of female, minority, disabled, and senior citizens will be denied simple, basic protections.

Repercussions from the decision proved to be swift and substantial. Within a matter of weeks, the Department of Education's Office of Civil Rights dropped 18 antidiscrimination cases in higher education and 4 cases in elementary and secondary education. To date, 674 pending cases have been closed or suspended by the Department of Education.

Regrettably, our Nation has yet to achieve the goal of full justice for disabled persons. Society is often hostile to those who appear different; therefore, progress is particularly slow in breaking down the prejudices which prevent disabled citizens from enjoying full integration. Section 504 is the only Federal statute which prohibits discrimination against disabled persons in employment. In the aftermath of the Grove City College case, numerous section 504 complaints have been dismissed.

The dramatic progress of the past two decades in desegregating our society would never have been possible if the narrow interpretation of the Supreme Court in the Grove City case had been in effect for the first 20 years after title VI was enacted.

From the beginning, the sponsors of this legislation have stated and restated our intention to do nothing more than restore the status quo which existed before the Supreme Court decision in the Grove City College case. The legislative history of the civil rights laws shows that broad coverage is consistent with the original intent of Congress. That construction has been followed by past Democratic and Republican administrations alike, and it deserves to be restored so that we can keep the faith of the four great statutes that protect the basic rights of millions of Americans to be free from federally subsidized discrimination.

Our goal is clear and our legislation is straightforward. The bill adds no new operative language to the four civil rights laws. It merely adds a definition of "program or activity" which restores the meaning that these terms had prior to the Grove City College decision.

. . .

C. COURT PACKING

Congress has altered the number of Justices on the Supreme Court throughout its history. Congress authorized six Justices in 1789, lowered that to five in the ill-fated Judiciary Act of 1801, returned to six a year later, and increased the number in subsequent years to keep pace with the creation of new circuits. Since 1869 the number of Justices has remained fixed at nine. Appointments to the Court have often produced marked changes in judicial policy, as witnessed by the abrupt shift in the Legal Tender Cases (pp. 129–30). In none of these earlier examples was the alteration of court size linked so blatantly to changing judicial policy as in FDR's court-packing plan.

In his inaugural address in 1933, Franklin D. Roosevelt struck a confident note for presidential-judicial relations. He said that the Constitution "is so simple and practical that it is possible always to meet extraordinary needs by changes in emphasis and arrangement without loss of essential form." Privately, he tempered that public optimism with the knowledge that members of the Supreme Court were essentially conservative and business-oriented.

Black Monday

Presidential hopes were routed on "Black Monday," May 27, 1935, when the Supreme Court unanimously struck down the National Industrial Recovery Act (NIRA). Schechter Corp. v. United States, 295 U.S. 495 (1935). On that same day it ruled that Presidents could remove members of independent regulatory commissions only by following the statutory reasons for removal, and it held unconstitutional a statute for the relief of farm mortgagors. Humphrey's Executor v. United States, 295 U.S. 602 (1935); Louisville Bank v. Radford, 295 U.S. 555 (1935). Feeling betrayed by the liberal members on the Court, Roosevelt asked plaintively: "Well, where was Ben Cardozo? And what about old Isaiah [Brandeis]?"[4] Direct attacks on the Court were shelved after the public reacted unfavorably to Roosevelt's sneering accusation at a press conference that the Justices had adopted a "horse-and-buggy definition of interstate commerce." At a cabinet meeting in December 1935, Roosevelt reviewed several methods of restraining the Court. Packing the Court, Interior Secretary Harold Ickes recorded in his diary, "was a distasteful idea." 1 The Secret Diary of Harold L. Ickes 495 (1953).

Roosevelt's patience was tested again on January 6, 1936, when the Court struck down the processing tax in the Agricultural Adjustment Act. The ruling divided the Court, 6 to 3, with Justice Stone penning a stinging dissent. He reminded the other Justices that they were not the only branch of government assumed to have the capacity to govern. United States v. Butler, 297 U.S. at 87. This time there appeared to be a ground swell of public support for adding younger Justices more attuned to the temper of the times. Yet Roosevelt bided his time, not wanting to give his opponents in an election year the opportunity to rally behind the Constitution and the Court. Other decisions in 1936, striking down federal and state laws, provided extra incentives to curb the Court. Some of those decisions attracted three or four dissents.[5] The climate for curbing the Court was further encouraged by the national popularity of The Nine Old Men (1936), a caustic portrait of the Justices written by Drew Pearson and Robert Allen. Peppered by such chapters as "The Lord High Executioners," the book charged that "justice has no relation whatsoever to popular will. Administrations may come and go, the temper of the people may reverse itself, economic conditions may be revolutionalized, the Nine Old Men sit on."

Roosevelt's landslide victory in 1936, capturing all but two states, paved the way for a direct assault on the Court. Constitutional amendments seemed to him wholly impracticable. They were difficult to frame and nearly impossible to pass. Statutory remedies, such as requiring a unanimous or 8-to-1 decision in the Supreme Court to invalidate a law, were of

---

4. William E. Leuchtenburg, "The Origins of Franklin D. Roosevelt's "Court-Packing' Plan," 1966 Sup. Ct. Rev. 347, 357.

5. Jones v. SEC, 298 U.S. 1 (1936) (Cardozo, Brandeis, and Stone dissenting); St. Joseph Stock Yards Co. v. United States, 298 U.S. 38 (1936) (Cardozo, Brandeis, and Stone dissenting in part); Carter v. Carter Coal Co., 298 U.S. 238 (1936); Morehead v. New York ex rel. Tipaldo, 298 U.S. 587 (1936) (Hughes, Brandeis, Stone, and Cardozo dissenting).

doubtful constitutionality. After rejecting a number of alternatives, he considered court packing the only feasible solution.

Roosevelt Shows His Hand

Working closely with his Attorney General and Solicitor General, but without the advice of congressional leaders, Roosevelt ordered the preparation of a draft bill. The President would be authorized to nominate Justices to the Supreme Court whenever an incumbent over the age of seventy declined to resign or retire. He proposed the same procedure for the lower courts, limiting the number of additional appointments to fifty and setting the maximum size of the Supreme Court at fifteen. Under this scenario, Roosevelt could name as many as six new Justices to the Supreme Court. When he submitted his proposal to Congress on February 5, 1937, he attempted to disguise it primarily as an economy and efficiency measure. Additional Justices would help relieve the delay and congestion he claimed resulted from aged or infirm judges. FDR's "indirection" (a euphemism for his deception and deviousness) offended some potential supporters. Robert H. Jackson, who served as Solicitor General and Attorney General under Roosevelt before being appointed to the Supreme Court in 1941, admitted that the plan "lacked the simplicity and clarity which was the President's genius and, to men not learned in the procedures of the Court, much of it seemed technical and confusing." Robert H. Jackson, The Struggle for Judicial Supremacy 189 (1941).

Roosevelt soon revealed his real purpose: to pack the Supreme Court with liberal Justices. In a "fireside chat" on March 9, 1937, he told the country that he wanted a Supreme Court that "will enforce the Constitution as written." But a mechanical application of that document by six additional Justices would not alleviate the problem Roosevelt faced. Later in that address he called for judges "who will bring to the Courts a present-day sense of the Constitution." He wanted "younger men who have had personal experience and contact with modern facts and circumstances." More concretely, he promised to appoint Justices "who will not undertake to override the judgment of the Congress on legislative policy." The result of this reform, he said, would be a "reinvigorated, liberal-minded Judiciary."

Repudiation by the Senate

The Senate Judiciary Committee denounced Roosevelt's bill. Its report methodically and mercilessly shreds the bill's premises, structure, content, and motivation. This searing indictment constituted an extraordinary determination on the part of the committee to pulverize Roosevelt's creation and bury it forever. The first of six reasons for rejecting the plan bluntly noted: "the bill does not accomplish any one of the objectives for which it was originally offered." S. Rept. No. 711, 75th Cong., 1st Sess., 3 (1937). Among other points in this scathing attack, the committee said that the courts "with the oldest judges have the best records in the disposition of business." The bill called for retirement only for judges who had served for ten years (penalizing not age itself but age combined with experience). Nothing in the bill prevented Roosevelt from nominating someone sixty-nine years and eleven months of age without prior judicial service. The result could be a Court of fifteen members, all of them older than seventy, and with no means of altering its composition. To the committee, the bill had one purpose and one purpose only: to apply force to the judiciary.

The committee condemned the bill as a "needless, futile, and utterly dangerous abandonment of constitutional principle." The report's harsh language (see reading) was designed to repudiate the bill so emphatically "that its parallel will never again be presented to the free representatives of the free people of America." The committee's position was reinforced by a letter from Chief Justice Hughes stating that the Court was "fully abreast of its work" and there was "no congestion of cases upon our calendar" (see box on next page).

Chief Justice Hughes Writes to Congress

March 21, 1937

Hon. Burton K. Wheeler
United States Senate
Washington, D.C.

My Dear Senator Wheeler: In response to your inquiries, I have the honor to present the following statement with respect to the work of the Supreme Court:

1. The Supreme Court is fully abreast of its work. When we rose on March 15 (for the present recess) we had heard argument in cases in which certiorari had been granted only 4 weeks before — February 15.

During the current term, which began last October and which we call "October term, 1936", we have heard argument on the merits in 150 cases (180 numbers) and we have 28 cases (30 numbers) awaiting argument. We shall be able to hear all these cases, and such others as may come up for argument, before our adjournment for the term. There is no congestion of cases upon our calendar.

This gratifying condition has been obtained for several years. We have been able for several terms to adjourn after disposing of all cases which are ready to be heard.

[*At this point Chief Justice Hughes supplies statistics for six years on total cases on docket (original and appellate), cases disposed of during term and cases remaining on dockets. He also explains internal Court procedures in handling cert petitions.*]

7. An increase in the number of Justices of the Supreme Court, apart from any question of policy, which I do not discuss, would not pro-mote the efficiency of the Court. It is believed that it would impair that efficiency so long as the Court acts as a unit. There would be more judges to hear, more judges to confer, more judges to discuss, more judges to be convinced and to decide....

I understand that it has been suggested that with more Justices the Court could hear cases in divisions. It is believed that such a plan would be impracticable. A large proportion of the cases we hear are important and a decision by a part of the Court would be unsatisfactory.

I may also call attention to the provisions of article III, section 1, of the Constitution that the judicial power of the United States shall be vested "in one Supreme Court" and in such inferior courts as the Congress may from time to time ordain and establish. The Constitution does not appear to authorize two or more Supreme Courts or two or more parts of a supreme court functioning in effect as separate courts.

On account of the shortness of time I have not been able to consult with the members of the Court generally with respect to the foregoing statement, but I am confident that it is in accord with the views of the Justices. I should say, however, that I have been able to consult with Mr. Justice Van Devanter and Mr. Justice Brandeis, and I am at liberty to say that the statement is approved by them.

I have the honor to remain,
Respectfully yours,

Charles E. Hughes
Chief Justice of the Supreme Court

SOURCE: S. Rept. No. 711, 75th Cong., 1st Sess. 38–40 (1937).

A number of unexpected developments sealed the fate of the court-packing bill. Senate Majority Leader Joe Robinson, who Roosevelt hoped would steer the bill through the Senate, died on July 14 after a week of debate in the sweltering capital. By that time the Court had already begun to modify some of its earlier rulings. On March 29, 1937, it upheld a state law establishing a minimum wage law for women, basically reversing a decision handed down ten months earlier.[6] This reversal occurred because of a change in position by Justice Roberts, or what has

---

6. West Coast Hotel Co. v. Parrish, 300 U.S. 379 (1937), overturning Adkins v. Children's Hospital, 261 U.S. 525 (1923) and "distinguishing" (in fact reversing) Morehead v. New York ex rel. Tipaldo, 298 U.S. 587 (1936).

been called the "switch in time that saved nine." However, before FDR submitted his court-packing plan Roberts had already broken with his doctrinaire laissez-faire colleagues. He wrote the opinion for a 5–4 Court in *Nebbia v. New York*, 291 U.S. 502 (1934), upholding a New York price-setting statute. With his support, the Court was prepared to sustain minimum-wage legislation in the fall of 1936 but had delayed its ruling because of Justice Stone's illness. Late in 1936, Roberts had voted with the liberals to affirm a state unemployment insurance law.[7]

Other decisions in 1937 confirmed that the Court had become more accepting of New Deal programs. Roosevelt remarked with obvious relish: "The old minority of 1935 and 1936 had become the majority of 1937—without a single new appointment of a justice!"[8] Because Congress finally passed legislation early in 1937 to provide full judicial pay during retirement, Justice Van Devanter stepped down on June 2, 1937, giving Roosevelt his first chance in more than four years to nominate a Justice to the Supreme Court. Other retirements were imminent. Within a matter of months, the need for the court-packing plan had evaporated. President Roosevelt would be able to "reorganize" the Court through the regular constitutional process.

FDR's Court-Packing Plan: Senate Report

President Franklin D. Roosevelt submitted to Congress on February 5, 1937, a proposal for "judicial reorganization." In actual fact, it was a plan that would have allowed him to pack the Supreme Court and lower federal courts with liberal judges. With top-heavy majorities in both Houses, he hoped for quick passage. His hopes were permanently dashed on June 7, when the Senate Judiciary Committee reported the bill adversely and so excoriated the President's idea that any parallels to it would "never again be presented to the free representatives of the free people of America." S. Rept. No. 711, 75th Cong., 1st Sess. (1937).

The Committee on the Judiciary, to whom was referred the bill (S. 1392) to reorganize the judicial branch of the Government, after full consideration, having unanimously amended the measure, hereby report the bill adversely with the recommendation that it do not pass....

THE ARGUMENT

The committee recommends that the measure be rejected for the following primary reasons:

I. The bill does not accomplish any one of the objectives for which it was originally offered.

II. It applies force to the judiciary and in its initial and ultimate effect would undermine the independence of the courts.

III. It violates all precedents in the history of our Government and would in itself be a dangerous precedent for the future.

IV. The theory of the bill is in direct violation of the spirit of the American Constitution and its employment would permit alteration of the Constitution without the people's consent or approval; it undermines the protection our constitutional system gives to minorities and is subversive of the rights of individuals.

V. It tends to centralize the Federal district judiciary by the power of assigning judges from one district to another at will.

VI. It tends to expand political control over the judicial department by adding to the powers of the legislative and executive departments respecting the judiciary.

---

7. W. H. H. Chamberlin, Inc. v. Andrews, 299 U.S. 515, decided November 23, 1936. The Court was equally divided. For Roberts' vote, see John W. Chambers, "The Big Switch: Justice Roberts and the Minimum-Wage Cases," 10 Labor Hist. 44, 57 (1969). See also Felix Frankfurter, "Mr. Justice Roberts," 104 U. Pa. L. Rev. 311 (1955); 2 Merlo J. Pusey, Charles Evans Hughes 757 (1963). For a challenge to Roberts' recollection of key events in 1936, see Clement E. Vose, Constitutional Change: Amendment Politics and Supreme Court Litigation Since 1900, 228–34 (1972).

8. 6 Public Papers and Addresses of Franklin D. Roosevelt lxviii (1941). See also Virginian Ry. v. Federation, 300 U.S. 515 (1937); Wright v. Vinton Branch, 300 U.S. 440 (1937); NLRB v. Jones & Laughlin, 301 U.S. 1 (1937); NLRB v. Fruehauf Co., 301 U.S. 49 (1937); NLRB v. Clothing Co., 301 U.S. 58 (1937); Steward Machine Co. v. Davis, 301 U.S. 548 (1937); Helvering v. Davis, 301 U.S. 619 (1937).

. . .

BILL FAILS OF ITS PURPOSE

In the first place, as already pointed out, the bill does not provide for any increase of personnel unless judges of retirement age fail to resign or retire. Whether or not there is to be an increase of the number of judges, and the extent of the increase if there is to be one, is dependent wholly upon the judges themselves and not at all upon the accumulation of litigation in any court. To state it another way the increase of the number of judges is to be provided, not in relation to the increase of work in any district or circuit, but in relation to the age of the judges and their unwillingness to retire.

In the second place, as pointed out in the President's message, only 25 of the 237 judges serving in the Federal courts on February 5, 1937, were over 70 years of age. Six of these were members of the Supreme Court at the time the bill was introduced.... Moreover, the facts indicate that the courts with the oldest judges have the best records in the disposition of business. It follows, therefore, that since there are comparatively few aged justices in service and these are among the most efficient on the bench, the age of sitting judges does not make necessary an increase of personnel to handle the business of the courts.

. . .

QUESTION OF AGE NOT SOLVED

The next question is to determine to what extent "the persistent infusion of new blood" may be expected from this bill.

It will be observed that the bill before us does not and cannot compel the retirement of any judge, whether on the Supreme Court or any other court, when he becomes 70 years of age. It will be remembered that the mere attainment of three score and ten by a particular judge does not, under this bill, require the appointment of another. The man on the bench may be 80 years of age, but this bill will not authorize the President to appoint a new judge to sit beside him unless he has served as a judge for 10 years. In other words, age itself is not penalized; the penalty falls only when age is attended with experience.

No one should overlook the fact that under this bill the President, whoever he may be and whether or not he believes in the constant infusion of young blood in the courts, may nominate a man 69 years and 11 months of age to the Supreme Court, or to any court, and, if confirmed, such nominee, if he never had served as a judge, would continue to sit upon the bench unmolested by this law until he had attained the ripe age of 79 years and 11 months.

We are told that "modern complexities call also for a constant infusion of new blood in the courts, just as it is needed in executive functions of the Government and in private business." Does this bill provide for such? The answer is obviously no....

It thus appears that the bill before us does not with certainty provide for increasing the personnel of the Federal judiciary, does not remedy the law's delay, does not serve the interest of the "poorer litigant" and does not provide for the "constant" or "persistent infusion of new blood" into the judiciary. What, then, does it do?

THE BILL APPLIES FORCE TO THE JUDICIARY

The answer is clear. It applies force to the judiciary. It is an attempt to impose upon the courts a course of action, a line of decision which, without that force, without that imposition, the judiciary might not adopt.

Can there be any doubt that this is the purpose of the bill? Increasing the personnel is not the object of this measure; infusing young blood is not the object; for if either one of these purposes had been in the minds of the proponents, the drafters would not have written the following clause to be found on page 2, lines 1 to 4, inclusive:

"Provided, That no additional judge shall be appointed hereunder if the judge who is of retirement age dies, resigns, or retires prior to the nomination of such additional judge."

Let it also be borne in mind that the President's message submitting this measure contains the following sentence:

"If, on the other hand, any judge eligible for retirement should feel that his Court would suffer because of an increase of its membership, he may retire or resign under already existing provisions of law if he wishes to do so."

Moreover, the Attorney General in testifying before the committee (hearings, pt. 1, p. 33) said:

"If the Supreme Court feels that the addition of six judges would be harmful to that Court, it can avoid that result by resigning."

Three invitations to the members of the Supreme Court over 70 years of age to get out despite all the talk about increasing personnel to expedite the disposition of cases and remedy the law's delay. One by the bill. One by the President's message. One by the Attorney General.

Can reasonable men by any possibility differ about the constitutional impropriety of such a course?

... For the protection of the people, for the preservation of the rights of the individual, for the maintenance of the liberties of minorities, for maintaining the checks and balances of our dual system, the three branches of the Government were so constituted that the independent expression of honest difference of opinion could never be restrained in the people's servants and no one branch could overawe or subjugate the others. That is the American system. It is immeasurably more important, immeasurably more sacred to the people of America, indeed, to the people of all the world than the immediate adoption of any legislation however beneficial. ...

A PRECEDENT OF LOYALTY TO THE CONSTITUTION

Shall we now, after 150 years of loyalty to the constitutional ideal of an untrammeled judiciary, duty bound to protect the constitutional rights of the humblest citizen even against the Government itself, create the vicious precedent which must necessarily undermine our system? The only argument for the increase which survives analysis is that Congress should enlarge the Court so as to make the policies of this administration effective.

. . .

This is the first time in the history of our country that a proposal to alter the decisions of the court by enlarging its personnel has been so boldly made. Let us meet it. Let us now set a salutary precedent that will never be violated. Let us, of the Seventy-fifth Congress, in words that will never be disregarded by any succeeding Congress, declare that we would rather have an independent Court, a fearless Court, a Court that will dare to announce its honest opinions in what it believes to be the defense of the liberties of the people, than a Court that, out of fear or sense of obligation to the appointing power, or factional passion, approves any measure we may enact. We are not the judges of the judges. We are not above the Constitution.

Even if every charge brought against the so-called "reactionary" members of this Court be true, it is far better that we await orderly but inevitable change of personnel than that we impa-

tiently overwhelm them with new members. Exhibiting this restraint, thus demonstrating our faith in the American system, we shall set an example that will protect the independent American judiciary from attack as long as this Government stands. ...

SUMMARY

We recommend the rejection of this bill as a needless, futile, and utterly dangerous abandonment of constitutional principle.

It was presented to the Congress in a most intricate form and for reasons that obscured its real purpose.

It would not banish age from the bench nor abolish divided decisions.

It would not affect the power of any court to hold laws unconstitutional nor withdraw from any judge the authority to issue injunctions.

It would not reduce the expense of litigation nor speed the decision of cases.

It is a proposal without precedent and without justification.

It would subjugate the courts to the will of Congress and the President and thereby destroy the independence of the judiciary, the only certain shield of individual rights.

It contains the germ of a system of centralized administration of law that would enable an executive so minded to send his judges into every judicial district in the land to sit in judgment on controversies between the Government and the citizen.

It points the way to the evasion of the Constitution and establishes the method whereby the people may be deprived of their right to pass upon all amendments of the fundamental law.

It stands now before the country, acknowledged by its proponents as a plan to force judicial interpretation of the Constitution, a proposal that violates every sacred tradition of American democracy.

Under the form of the Constitution it seeks to do that which is unconstitutional.

Its ultimate operation would be to make this Government one of men rather than one of law, and its practical operation would be to make the Constitution what the executive or legislative branches of the Government choose to say it is — an interpretation to be changed with each change of administration.

It is a measure which should be so emphatically rejected that its parallel will never again be presented to the free representatives of the free people of America.

D. WITHDRAWING JURISDICTION

During the past several decades, Congress has been under strong pressure to withdraw the Supreme Court's jurisdiction to hear appeals in cases of abortion, school busing, school prayer, and other issues on the conservatives' "social agenda." This strategy is based on language in Article III of the Constitution: "The Supreme Court shall have appellate jurisdiction, both as to law and fact, with such exceptions, and under such regulations, as the Congress shall make." The Exceptions Clause, it is argued, gives Congress plenary power to determine the Court's appellate jurisdiction.

Although this approach appears to be grounded on constitutional language, the Exceptions Clause must be read in concert with other provisions in the Constitution. An aggressive use of the Exceptions Clause by Congress would make an exception the rule and deny citizens access to the Supreme Court to vindicate constitutional rights. Stripping the Supreme Court of jurisdiction to hear certain issues would vest ultimate judicial authority in the lower federal and state courts, producing contradictory and conflicting legal doctrines.

A more radical proposal would prevent even the lower federal courts from ruling on specific social issues. Under Article III, the judicial power is vested in a Supreme Court "and in such inferior Courts as the Congress may from time to time ordain and establish." Because Congress creates the lower courts, it may by statute confer, define, and withdraw jurisdiction. Sheldon v. Sill, 49 U.S. (8 How.) 441, 449 (1850). Although Congress has withdrawn jurisdiction to adjudicate certain issues, the exercise of that power "is subject to compliance with at least the requirements of the Fifth Amendment. That is to say, while Congress has the undoubted power to give, withhold, and restrict the jurisdiction of courts other than the Supreme Court, it must not so exercise that power as to deprive any person of life, liberty, or property without due process of law or to take private property without just compensation." Battaglia v. General Motors Corp., 169 F.2d 254, 257 (2d Cir. 1948), cert. denied, 335 U.S. 887 (1948). To deny the lower federal courts jurisdiction to hear claims arising under the Constitution would upset the system of checks and balances, alter the balance of power between the national government and the states, and strengthen the force of majority rule over individual rights (see reading on ABA report).

Withdrawing appellate jurisdiction from the Supreme Court and withdrawing jurisdiction from the lower federal courts would also undercut the Supremacy Clause in Article VI, which states that the Constitution and federal laws "made in Pursuance thereof...shall be the supreme Law of the Land; and the Judges in every State shall be bound thereby, any Thing in the Constitution or Laws of any State to the contrary notwithstanding." In 1982 the chief justices of the highest state courts issued a unanimous resolution expressing "serious concerns" about bills introduced in Congress to give the states sole authority to decide certain social issues. Among other objections, the chief justices pointed out that the result of such legislation would be contrary to what conservatives professed to be their goal. Instead of overturning Supreme Court decisions, they would be "cast in stone" when state judges continued to honor their oaths to obey the federal Constitution and to give full force (pursuant to the Supremacy Clause) to Supreme Court precedents. The practical effect, therefore, would be to place a body of legal doctrine outside the reach of federal courts or state courts either to alter or overrule. 128 Cong. Rec. 689–90 (1982).

Members of Congress have also attempted to use their power to enforce the Fourteenth Amendment as a lever to alter the jurisdiction of the federal courts. Section 5 of the Fourteenth Amendment gives Congress the power "to enforce, by appropriate legislation," the provisions of that Amendment. In 1981 the Senate Judiciary Committee held hearings on a bill that looked to Section 5 as the vehicle for overturning the Supreme Court's 1973 abortion decision. The hearings covered the scope of Section 5, the issue of whether Congress would be exercising judgments over "facts" or "law," and a possible shift of balance of power between the national government and the states (see reading).

The *McCardle* Case

In a number of early decisions, the Supreme Court recognized the power of Congress to make exceptions and to regulate the Court's appellate jurisdiction.[9] For example, in 1847 the Court stated that it possessed "no appellate power in any case, unless conferred upon it by act of Congress; nor can it, when conferred be exercised in any other form, or by any other mode of proceeding than that which the law prescribes." Barry v. Mercein, 5 How. 103, 119 (1847). These early decisions defined the congressional power too broadly, as will be shown.

The leading case for empowering Congress to withdraw appellate jurisdiction from the Supreme Court is *Ex parte McCardle* (1869). In 1868 Congress withdrew the Court's jurisdiction to review circuit court judgments on habeas corpus actions. The clear purpose was to prevent the Court from deciding a case on the constitutionality of the Reconstruction military government in the South, even though the Court had already heard oral argument in the case of William McCardle. He had been held in custody awaiting trial by military commission, charged with publishing articles that incited "insurrection, disorder, and violence." Under an act of February 5, 1867, he petitioned a federal circuit court for the writ of habeas corpus. The writ was issued, directing the military commander to deliver McCardle to a federal marshal. After the commander complied with the writ (denying that the restraint was unlawful), the circuit court rejected McCardle's petition.

At that point McCardle appealed to the Supreme Court. On February 17, 1868, the Court dismissed the government's argument that the Court lacked jurisdiction to hear the case. 73 U.S. (6 Wall.) 318 (1868). The case was argued March 2, 3, 4, and 9. Before the Court could meet in conference to decide the case, Congress passed legislation to nullify McCardle's relief under the act of February 5, 1867. The new legislation provided that the portion of the 1867 statute that authorized an appeal from the judgment of the circuit court to the Supreme Court, "or the exercise of any such jurisdiction by said Supreme Court on appeals which have been or may hereafter be taken, be, and the same is, hereby repealed." 15 Stat. 44 (1868). Congress wanted to sweep McCardle's case from the docket, fearing that the Court might use it to invalidate the Reconstruction laws.

In a unanimous opinion upholding the repeal statute, Chief Justice Chase stated that the Court was "not at liberty to inquire into the motives of the legislature. We can only examine into its power under the Constitution; and the power to make exceptions to the appellate jurisdiction of this court is given by express words." EX PARTE MCCARDLE, 74 U.S. (7 Wall.) 506, 514 (1869). The Court dismissed the case for want of jurisdiction. The Court might have used Section 14 of the Judiciary Act of 1789 to review habeas corpus actions. 1 Stat. 81-82, § 14. However, to do that in the face of the repeal statute, with the prospect of overturning Reconstruction legislation, risked a major collision with Congress. The House of Representatives had already passed legislation to require a two-thirds majority of the Court to invalidate a federal statute, and some of the more rambunctious Radicals wanted to abolish the Supreme Court.

There is some question whether Congress acted under the Exceptions Clause, even though it forms the basis for the Court's decision. Congress may have merely repealed a special statutory

---

9. Wiscart v. Dauchy, 3 Dall. 321 (1796); Durousseau v. United States, 10 U.S. (6 Cr.) 306 (1810); Daniels v. Railroad Co., 70 U.S. (3 Wall.) 250, 254 (1866).

Congress Responds to *Milligan*

[James Falconer Wilson, floor manager of this bill for the House Judiciary Committee, explains why Congress had not only the authority but also the obligation to respond to the Court's decision in Ex parte Milligan*]:*

Mr. WILSON, of Iowa....

The object of this part of the bill cannot be mistaken. It is alleged that the President of the United States, in regard to the various matters here enumerated, has acted without authority of law, and that all who have been in any manner associated with him, as instruments in rendering effective his acts, proclamations, and orders, are guilty of infractions of the law, for which they may be indicted, convicted, punished, and subjected to civil actions for the recovery of damages. Many officers and soldiers of the United States have already been made defendants in civil and criminal actions for acts which it is proposed to cover by the broad mantle of this bill....

[He reviews congressional and judicial precedents that support the pending bill.] The legislative and judicial action of the Government presents no difficulty in this regard until we reach the recent decision of the Supreme Court in the Milligan case, and even that case interposes no real and valid objection to the passage of this bill. It is true that a majority of the court, in the opinion announced by Mr. Justice Davis, declares that Congress could grant no power to try, in the State of Indiana, a citizen in civil life, in nowise connected with the military service, by a court-martial or military commission, and in so far as this goes the court stands in opposition to this bill. But this is a piece of judicial impertinence which we are not bound to respect. No such question was before the court in the Milligan case, and that tribunal wandered beyond the record in treating of it. Its discussion by the court was out of place, uncalled for, and wholly unjustifiable....

The purpose of the bill is very plainly indicated in its terms, and that is to deprive the civil courts of the United States of all jurisdiction in relation to the acts of military commissions and courts-martial.

SOURCE: Congressional Globe, 39th Cong., 2d Sess. 1484, 1487 (1867).

right of access that it had previously granted. As the Court noted a year later, Congress did not repeal alternative rights of access, such as under the Judiciary Act of 1789 and later statutes that expanded the writ of habeas corpus. Ex parte Yerger, 75 U.S. (8 Wall.) 85, 101–02 (1869).

During this same period, Congress passed legislation to remove from federal and state courts their jurisdiction to hear other cases arising from the Civil War. The legislation responded to the Supreme Court's decision in *Ex parte Milligan* (1866), holding that military courts could not function in states where federal courts had been open and operating. Although cases were already pending with regard to the conduct of U.S. officials during and immediately after the war, Congress gave indemnity to all officials who implemented presidential proclamations from March 4, 1861, to June 30, 1866, with respect to martial law and military trials. The statute adds: "And no civil court of the United States, or of any State, or of the District of Columbia, or of any district or territory of the United States, shall have or take jurisdiction of, or in any manner reverse any of the proceedings had or acts done as aforesaid...." 14 Stat. 432, 433 (1867). Legislative debate underscored the determination of Congress to limit the jurisdiction of the courts (see box).

Refinements to *McCardle*

McCardle remains in a shadowy realm, surrounded on both sides by conflicting cases that both limit and legitimate congressional power under the Exceptions Clause. Shortly after *McCardle,* the Supreme Court decided *United States* v. *Klein* (1872), which involved a congressional attempt to use the appropriations power to nullify the President's power to pardon. The Court said that Congress had exceeded its authority, first by trying to limit a presidential power granted by the Constitution, and second by preventing a presidential pardon or amnesty from being admitted as evidence in court. The statute was meant to strip the Supreme Court of its jurisdiction over such cases. The Court agreed that the Exceptions Clause gave Congress the power to deny the right of appeal in a particular class of cases, but it could not withhold appellate jurisdiction "as a means to an end" if the end was forbidden under the Constitution. In this case, the effect of withholding appellate jurisdiction was to prescribe impermissible rules of decision for the judiciary in a pending case. 80 U.S. (13 Wall.) 128, 146 (1872).

Other restrictions limit the power of Congress under the Exceptions Clause. For example, Congress could not extend certain rights and then attempt, through the Exceptions Clause, to exclude a particular race or religious group. Such actions would violate the Due Process Clause and the First Amendment. As noted by Laurence H. Tribe, Congress could not deny access to federal courts "to all but white Anglo-Saxon Protestants, or to all who voted in the latest election for a losing candidate." 127 Cong. Rec. 13360 (1981).

The Supreme Court has announced since *McCardle* and *Klein* that its appellate jurisdiction "is confined within such limits as Congress sees fit to prescribe." The "Francis Wright," 105 U.S. 381, 385 (1881). However, the establishment of exceptions and regulations must give "due regard to all the provisions of the Constitution." United States v. Bitty, 208 U.S. 393, 399–400 (1908). For district and appellate courts, Congress "may give, withhold or restrict such jurisdiction at its discretion, provided it be not extended beyond the boundaries fixed by the Constitution." Kline v. Burke Const. Co., 260 U.S. 226, 234 (1922). Precisely what those boundaries are is never said, which is probably prudent. The Court has allowed Congress to limit the availability of certain judicial remedies, such as prohibiting district courts from issuing injunctions to control labor disputes or the enforcement of price regulations. Lauf v. E.G. Shinner & Co., 303 U.S. 323 (1938); Lockerty v. Phillips, 319 U.S. 182 (1942).

Contemporary Issues

An appropriations bill enacted in 1989 raised a possible violation of *Klein*. The bill stated that Congress determined and directed that the management of forests covered by previous legislation was "adequate consideration for the purpose of meeting the statutory requirements" that were the basis for two pending lawsuits. The Ninth Circuit held that the language in the appropriations bill was unconstitutional under *Klein* because it attempted to direct courts to reach a particular decision. A unanimous Supreme Court disagreed, concluding that the language in the appropriations bill merely changed the law underlying the litigation. Robertson v. Seattle Audubon Soc., 503 U.S. 429 (1992).

Although not technically an issue of withdrawing jurisdiction, in 1995 the Supreme Court referred to the *Klein* and *Seattle Audubon* cases in determining that Congress cannot pass legislation that has the effect of reopening cases that had been dismissed in response to a Supreme Court ruling. The congressional statute was considered a violation of separation of powers. Plaut v. Spendthrift Farm, Inc., 514 U.S. 211 (1995). This case is described in greater detail in Chapter 5, page 159.

A 1996 decision by the Supreme court directly concerned a possible challenge to the Exceptions Clause. In a unanimous opinion, the Court upheld a congressional statute that placed limits on prisoners who seek to make successive habeas petitions to the Court. Such petitions must first be approved by a three-judge panel. Felker v. Turpin, 518 U.S. 651 (1996). Further details appear on page 754.

These precedents cannot be read to justify the exclusion of whole areas of constitutional law from the Supreme Court.[10] The mere existence of a power does not mean that it may be used without limit. Such a construction runs counter to basic principles of constitutionalism, separation of powers, and checks and balances. Congress has the "power" to determine the size of the Supreme Court, but the availability of that power did not support Roosevelt's effort to pack the Court. Indeed, the Senate Judiciary Committee rejected the proposal with such force that it hoped no President would ever dare repeat the suggestion. The President has the "power" to withhold documents and appropriations, but we live under a system that recognizes limits on executive privilege and impoundment. The Court has the "power" to declare presidential and congressional acts unconstitutional, but it can exercise that power effectively only by acknowledging the limits imposed on it by the political system. The use of the Exceptions Clause must take due regard of an independent judiciary, the Supremacy Clause, and the constitutional rights available to citizens.

Jurisdiction-Stripping Proposals: ABA Report

Congress has authority under Article III of the Constitution to regulate the jurisdiction of federal district and appellate courts and to make "exceptions" to the appellate jurisdiction of the Supreme Court. That authority, however, must be placed in the context of other constitutional principles and restrictions, an issue discussed below by the Association of the Bar of the City of New York, "Jurisdiction-Stripping Proposals in Congress: The Threat to Judicial Constitutional Review," December 1981. Footnotes omitted.

... There are pending in both houses of Congress at least 25 bills that, if enacted and upheld as constitutional, would have the effect of scrapping the federal courts' historical role in the system of checks and balances. These bills, listed in the Appendix to this Report, would divest the federal courts of all original and appellate jurisdiction to hear cases relating to (1) the constitutionality of programs of "voluntary" prayer in the public schools or other public places, (2) the constitutionality of laws or regulations affecting abortions, (3) busing as a remedy for school segregation, and (4) the constitutionality of treating men and women differently in connection with the armed forces or the draft. One bill, H.R. 114, may be read to go even further—to eliminate all federal judicial review of state court decisions.

In this Report, we do not address the merits of the various federal court decisions on these subjects that have prompted the proposed legislation, nor do we analyze the individual bills in detail. Rather, we address a question that is raised by all such proposals: Is the elimination of federal court jurisdiction to hear constitutional claims a lawful and appropriate response to judicial decisions of which a current majority in Congress disapproves? That question is fundamental to the structure of our government because, if Congress can legitimately curtail the federal courts' jurisdiction to hear constitutional claims concerning such specific issues as school prayer, abortion, and desegregation, then there is no principled limitation on Congress' power effectively to eliminate the judicial branch as a check on the other branches of the federal government or the states. By enacting any of the present bills, Congress would necessarily be claiming the power, should it so choose, to forbid the federal courts to hear *any* claim asserted under the Bill of Rights or under any other provision of the Constitution.

Although most of the proponents of these bills generally style themselves as "conservatives," our review of the historical record reveals that their proposals are *radical* in the most extreme sense of that word. They would not only cast doubt upon the abortion, school prayer, and busing decisions of the past few years, but two centuries of historical development and constitutional doctrine. For the reasons set forth below, we conclude that this radical departure from the system of checks and

10. For studies cautioning unbounded use of the Exceptions Clause, see Lawrence Gene Sager, "The Supreme Court, 1980 Term—Foreword: Constitutional Limitations on Congress' Authority to Regulate the Jurisdiction of the Federal Courts," 95 Harv. L. Rev. 17 (1981); Leonard G. Ratner, "Congressional Power over the Appellate Jurisdiction of the Supreme Court," 109 U. Pa. L. Rev. 157 (1960); and Henry M. Hart, Jr., "The Power of Congress to Limit the Jurisdiction of Federal Courts: An Exercise in Dialectic," 66 Harv. L. Rev. 1362 (1953).

balances that has served our nation well for the past two centuries is unwise and probably unconstitutional. There is no precedent of enacted legislation eliminating all federal court jurisdiction to hear claims of deprivation of constitutional rights. To find any precedent for the present bills, one must look to many bills that have been proposed over the years but *not* enacted. Congress wisely declined these previous invitations to tamper with our constitutional structure of government, and should decline the same invitation presented by the current bills.

Article III of the Constitution does grant Congress power to regulate the jurisdiction of the federal courts.... But, as the following analysis shows, this power cannot fairly be construed to permit Congress to deprive the courts of jurisdiction to hear claims arising under the Constitution itself, particularly on an issue-by-issue basis. If Congress' power were so extensive, it would undo the elaborate system of checks and balances that the Framers of the Constitution so carefully crafted. First, it would upset the checks and balances among the three coordinate branches of the federal government, eliminating the judiciary as a check upon unconstitutional actions of the political branches by the simple expedient of removing

their jurisdiction to consider challenges to such actions. Second, it would disrupt the allocation of power between the federal government and the states, by eliminating the power of the federal judiciary to restrain acts of the states that violate the Constitution. Third, and perhaps most significant, it would alter the constitutional balance between individual rights and majority will, since the judiciary is the only organ of government that is institutionally suited to protect the rights that our Constitution guarantees to individuals against the wishes of a strong-willed majority.

Another serious objection to legislation of the sort currently proposed is that it is undesirable to deal with complex and controversial social issues, particularly those of constitutional dimension, by eliminating the opportunity for full airing and debate in the federal judiciary. Indeed, one of the ironies of the present bills is that the constitutional interpretations with which the bills' sponsors differ would remain frozen as the supreme law of the land forever, binding upon the state courts under the Supremacy Clause and the doctrine of *stare decisis,* without any possibility of change through the evolution of legal thought or a change in judicial (particularly Supreme Court) personnel....

Human Life Bill: Senate Hearings

In response to the Supreme Court's decision in *Roe v. Wade,* 410 U.S. 113 (1973), which upheld a woman's right to an abortion at least in the first trimester of pregnancy, members of Congress looked for ways to overturn the Court's ruling. One approach was to define *person* in the Fourteenth Amendment to include life beginning at conception, to allow states to enact antiabortion laws, and to prevent lower federal courts from striking down those state laws. Members argued that a statutory route was available pursuant to the power of Congress under Section 5 of the Fourteenth Amendment "to enforce, by appropriate legislation, the provisions of this article." In the selections below, this approach is defended by Stephen H. Galebach, attorney for Covington & Burling, and is opposed by Professor Laurence H. Tribe of Harvard Law School. The selections are taken from "The Human Life Bill," hearings before the Senate Committee on the Judiciary, 97th Cong., 1st Sess. (1981).

STEPHEN H. GALEBACH:

. . .

In its 1973 abortion decision, the Supreme Court declared that it was unable to determine whether unborn children were human beings. The Court also held that unborn children were not persons within the meaning of the 14th amendment and that a woman's right to privacy took

precedence over the State's right to protect potential life until a fetus had become viable.

The Supreme Court thus left unresolved the fundamental question of whether unborn children are human beings. The answer to this question necessarily influences the proper resolution of the abortion issue. However, if the Supreme Court is unable to decide when human life begins, who can make that decision? I submit that under the Constitution, Congress can make that decision.

The 5th and 14th amendments to the Constitution provide that no person may be deprived of life without due process of law. The 14th amendment expressly authorizes Congress to enforce its protections by appropriate legislation.

If Congress examines the question the Supreme Court was unable to answer and concludes that unborn children are human beings, then the Court's conclusion that they are not persons would be subject to change, and Congress would have the power to enforce the 14th amendment by declaring that unborn children are persons within the meaning of that amendment.

In my law review, I explained the constitutional justification of the human life bill in terms of two leading theories advanced by Supreme Court Justices concerning the power of Congress to enforce 14th amendment rights.

The first theory is found in Justice Brennan's majority opinion in the landmark case of *Katzenbach* v. *Morgan*. Under this theory, Congress has broad power to define the scope and meaning of the 14th amendment rights so long as it acts to expand those rights.

The second theory is found in Justice Harlan's dissenting opinion in *Katzenbach* v. *Morgan*. Justice Harlan took a narrower view of Congress power, allowing Congress to make legislative findings that influence constitutional determinations, but reserving to the Court the authority to make the ultimate constitutional decision.

The majority opinion in *Katzenbach* v. *Morgan* is controversial because it confers on Congress such broad power to redefine the 14th amendment rights and to force its view on the Supreme Court. There is serious question whether the Court would or should reaffirm such a broad precedent today.

However, the constitutionality of the human life bill does not depend on the validity of such a broad theory of Congress power. The narrow enforcement power described by Justice Harlan is sufficient to justify the human life bill.

For that reason, I would like to focus today on the applicability of Justice Harlan's theory to the human life bill. The key sentence in Justice Harlan's opinion in *Katzenbach* v. *Morgan* is as follows:

"To the extent 'legislative facts' are relevant to a judicial determination, Congress is well equipped to investigate them, and such determinations are of course entitled to due respect."

According to this theory, congressional findings influence the Supreme Court, but do not necessarily control the Court's decisions. For example, in the 1965 and 1970 Voting Rights Acts, Congress influenced the Supreme Court to conclude that literacy tests for voting were racially discriminatory, even though in 1959 the Court held them not to be discriminatory. The Supreme Court was not persuaded, on the other hand, by Congress finding that equal protection requires the extension of voting rights to 18-year-olds in State elections.

. . .

...[T]he Supreme Court will have to reevaluate the proper balance between the privacy right and the right to life of unborn children. The Supreme Court will still have the final say. The human life bill does not dictate what the result must be. All the bill does is ask the Court to look at the issue again in light of Congress' answer to the question that the Court said it could not resolve, namely, when does human life begin.

The Court's role as the final interpreter of the Constitution is not threatened by this approach. Congress is merely exercising its prerogative to inform the Court of its views in accordance with Justice Harlan's understanding of the appropriate role of Congress and the Court....

If these decisions are left to the private consciences of individuals, if individuals are free to choose whether someone else shall live or die, then life ultimately has no protection.

However, our Constitution does not take such an irresponsible path. The Constitution protects life, and gives Congress power to enforce that protection. That is why the human life bill is in no sense a circumvention of the Constitution, but rather a fulfillment of it.

LAURENCE H. TRIBE:

. . .

The Court, it is true, expressed its inability to give a definitive answer to what it took to be an unanswerable question: When does human life begin?

Mr. Galebach says that some branch of Government must be able to decide this intimate moral question; but I have thought if we have learned anything in the modern era, it is that sometimes Government does not have an answer and cannot have an answer.

The fact that a question is profound and important does not mean that Government must tell us how to answer it. The whole point of the Supreme Court's decision in 1973 was not simply one of judicial incapacity, for right after the Court said that it was unable to answer the question of when human life begins, the Court explained that what it really meant was that no State, by adopting its own answer to that question—choosing one theory of life rather than another—could be permitted to override the fundamental right of the pregnant woman to give an answer for herself.

One may disagree with that view. One may disagree with the view that this fundamental question must be left to the woman. However, if one disagrees with that view, one is not disagreeing on a question of fact—What is the fetus? What is a human being?—but on a basic proposition of constitutional law.

The only way to undo a proposition of constitutional law announced by the Court is by constitutional amendment, not by legislative redefinition of constitutional language and not by waving the magic wand of section 5 of the 14th amendment and saying, "We will now inform the Court as to what the fertilized ovum is."

. . .

Let me close with a concern that I have that would persist even if this law were to be upheld, even if it were deemed to be constitutional.

I believe that S. 158 is inherently and unavoidably defective as measured by its own aims. I think the chairman stated the reasonable aims in a way that I found almost compelling when he said that we are simply trying to return to the States a matter that perhaps ought never to have been taken over by the Federal Government in the first place. If these matters are divisive, if they are unclear, why try to resolve them nationally? Why not decentralize?

However, observe that that is not, despite its intentions, what this law does. To begin with, on the matter of State and local funding for abortions, the law leaves States no choice. In Massachusetts and in California, the State constitutions require public funds to be expended without discrimination against abortion. Under this law, spending on abortion would be forbidden because that would, if this law were upheld, amount to State action which destroys the lives of persons.

To that degree at least, the matter is suddenly nationalized and not restored to its condition as it was in 1973.

. . .

It seems to me this measure is clearly unconstitutional. That it would be so held by the Supreme Court is not a matter of guesswork. It is not a responsible thing, however well-intentioned, for this Congress to do. I would regard it as a very sad day were this very serious, difficult issue to become the occasion for futile confrontation between the Congress and the Supreme Court, with a predictable outcome—one that would not enhance respect for either body, and one that would not advance the cause either of women or of unborn life.

Ex Parte McCardle

74 U.S. (7 Wall.) 506 (1869)

William H. McCardle, a Southern editor, had been arrested under the Reconstruction Acts and tried before a military commission for publishing articles considered incendiary and libelous. After his petition for a writ of habeas corpus was denied by a federal circuit court in Mississippi, the Supreme Court accepted jurisdiction and held oral argument. It was widely speculated that the Court might hold the Reconstruction Acts unconstitutional. Congress had begun the impeachment of President Andrew Johnson, partly for his opposition to the Reconstruction Acts. To prevent a decision on the constitutionality of the Reconstruction Acts, Congress passed legislation to withdraw the appellate jurisdiction of the Supreme Court in McCardle's case.

The CHIEF JUSTICE delivered the opinion of the court.

The first question necessarily is that of jurisdiction; for, if the act of March, 1868, takes away the jurisdiction defined by the act of February, 1867, it is useless, if not improper, to enter into any discussion of other questions.

It is quite true, as was argued by the counsel

for the petitioner, that the appellate jurisdiction of this court is not derived from acts of Congress. It is, strictly speaking, conferred by the Constitution. But it is conferred "with such exceptions and under such regulations as Congress shall make."

It is unnecessary to consider whether, if Congress had made no exceptions and no regulations, this court might not have exercised general appellate jurisdiction under rules prescribed by itself. For among the earliest acts of the first Congress, at its first session, was the act of September 24th, 1789, to establish the judicial courts of the United States. That act provided for the organization of this court; and prescribed regulations for the exercise of its jurisdiction.

The source of that jurisdiction, and the limitations of it by the Constitution and by statute, have been on several occasions subjects of consideration here. In the case of *Durousseau* v. *The United States,* particularly, the whole matter was carefully examined, and the court held, that while "the appellate powers of this court are not given by the judicial act, but are given by the Constitution," they are, nevertheless, "limited and regulated by that act, and by such other acts as have been passed on the subject." The court said, further, that the judicial act was an exercise of the power given by the Constitution to Congress "of making exceptions to the appellate jurisdiction of the Supreme Court." "They have described affirmatively," said the court, "its jurisdiction, and this affirmative description has been understood to imply a negation of the exercise of such appellate power as is not comprehended within it."

The principle that the affirmation of appellate jurisdiction implies the negation of all such jurisdiction not affirmed having been thus established, it was an almost necessary consequence that acts of Congress, providing for the exercise of jurisdiction, should come to be spoken of as acts granting jurisdiction, and not as acts making exceptions to the constitutional grant of it.

The exception to appellate jurisdiction in the case before us, however, is not an inference from the affirmation of other appellate jurisdiction. It is made in terms. The provision of the act of 1867, affirming the appellate jurisdiction of this court in cases of *habeas corpus* is expressly repealed. It is hardly possible to imagine a plainer instance of positive exception.

We are not at liberty to inquire into the mo-

tives of the legislature. We can only examine into its power under the Constitution; and the power to make exceptions to the appellate jurisdiction of this court is given by express words.

What, then, is the effect of the repealing act upon the case before us? We cannot doubt as to this. Without jurisdiction the court cannot proceed at all in any cause. Jurisdiction is power to declare the law, and when it ceases to exist, the only function remaining to the court is that of announcing the fact and dismissing the cause. And this is not less clear upon authority than upon principle.

Several cases were cited by the counsel for the petitioner in support of the position that jurisdiction of this case is not affected by the repealing act. But none of them, in our judgment, afford any support to it. They are all cases of the exercise of judicial power by the legislature, or of legislative interference with courts in the exercising of continuing jurisdiction.

On the other hand, the general rule, supported by the best elementary writers, is, that "when an act of the legislature is repealed, it must be considered, except as to transactions past and closed, as if it never existed." And the effect of repealing acts upon suits under acts repealed, has been determined by the adjudications of this court. The subject was fully considered in *Norris* v. *Crocker,* and more recently in *Insurance Company* v. *Ritchie.* In both of these cases it was held that no judgment could be rendered in a suit after the repeal of the act under which it was brought and prosecuted.

It is quite clear, therefore, that this court cannot proceed to pronounce judgment in this case, for it has no longer jurisdiction of the appeal; and judicial duty is not less fitly performed by declining ungranted jurisdiction than in exercising firmly that which the Constitution and the laws confer.

Counsel seemed to have supposed, if effect be given to the repealing act in question, that the whole appellate power of the court, in cases of *habeas corpus,* is denied. But this is an error. The act of 1868 does not except from that jurisdiction any cases but appeals from Circuit Courts under the act of 1867. It does not affect the jurisdiction which was previously exercised.

The appeal of the petitioner in this case must be

Dismissed for want of jurisdiction.

E. NONCOMPLIANCE

In a masterful phrase, rendered almost hypnotic by its elegance, Justice Jackson said: "We are not final because we are infallible, but we are infallible only because we are final." Brown v. Allen, 344 U.S. 443, 540 (1953). The historical record demonstrates convincingly that the Supreme Court is neither infallible nor final. The lack of finality is evident in the fluid quality of its decisions, reshaped over the years by all three branches. Furthermore, the Court often experiences substantial difficulty in obtaining full compliance with decisions when they are handed down. Noncompliance is a direct threat to the Court's dignity, authority, legitimacy, and reputation (see reading "Sustaining Public Confidence").

In theory, judicial opinions are binding on the public and the other branches of government. In practice, judicial opinions are implemented with varying degrees of fidelity by local and federal officials. Noncompliance sometimes results from deliberate evasion, as in the South's "massive resistance" to the desegregation cases. Unintentional violations may also occur, but they can be relieved by adequate education and clear judicial rulings. In between these two positions are various shades of avoidance and evasion.

In 1983 the Supreme Court held that the "legislative veto," used by Congress for fifty years to control executive actions, was unconstitutional. INS v. Chadha, 462 U.S. 919 (1983). Over the following years, however, Congress passed more than four hundred additional legislative vetoes, all signed into law by Presidents Reagan, Bush, and Clinton. Moreover, Congress continued to exercise other instruments of control that are the functional equivalent of the legislative veto. Although the Court had announced one of the most important separation of powers cases of all time, the practical effect was not nearly as sweeping as the Court's decision (pp. 235–37).

One source of noncompliance is poor communication of judicial opinions. Scholars have found that most people do not know or understand decisions rendered by the courts. Instead, the public receives abbreviated interpretations, often erroneous, from the media and local officials. For a variety of reasons, the media have difficulty providing adequate coverage of the courts.

Second, the sheer force of inertia limits compliance. Court decisions must pass through the perceptual screens of citizens who believe that current practices can persist with only slight modifications. Four decades after *Engel* v. *Vitale* (1962), which struck down state-sponsored prayers in public schools, school authorities continue to set aside time during the day for students to say prayers (see reading). Local officials may prefer to reinterpret judicial decisions on church-state separation to minimize the level of conflict and dissension within their communities.[11]

Lower-Court Implementation

Finally, decisions by the Supreme Court and federal appellate courts are filtered through U.S. district courts and state courts. Lower courts, legislatures, and administrators have a number of ways to avoid full compliance. Lower courts can reinterpret rulings. Parties can relitigate to delay implementation or appeal to legislators to reverse a ruling that turns on statutory interpretation. When the Supreme Court reverses a lower court decision, it may remand the case for disposition "not inconsistent with this opinion." In this new round, the litigant who found success at the Supreme Court level may lose out in the lower courts. 67 Harv. L. Rev. 1251 (1954).

---

11. Kenneth M. Dolbeare and Phillip E. Hammond, The School Prayer Decisions: From Court Policy to Local Practice (1971); Frank J. Sorauf, "*Zorach* v. *Clauson*: The Impact of a Supreme Court Decision," 53 Am. Pol. Sci. Rev. 777 (1959); Gordon Patric, "The Impact of a Court Decision: Aftermath of the McCollum Case," 6 J. Pub. L. 455 (1957).

Justice Thurgood Marshall Encourages Lower Courts to Protect Rights More Expansively than Supreme Court

Dissenting in *Bell* v. *Wolfish* (1979), a case involving the rights of prisoners, Justice Marshall argued that the lower courts were correct the first time when they concluded that pretrial detainees should not be subjected to certain procedures (such as body-cavity searches) while in jail awaiting trial. As part of his responsibilities for supervising the Second Circuit (which had been reversed in this case), Marshall gave an address before the judges of that circuit and said that he "can only hope that district and appellate judges will read the [Court's] decision narrowly." His conclusion produced gasps from the audience: "Ill-conceived reversals should be considered as no more than temporary interruptions." The New York Times, May 28, 1979, at A1, A11.

As noted by political scientist Sotirios Barber: "Justice Marshall's remarks attracted an unusual amount of public attention, for this was not the kind of talk one usually hears from members of the Supreme Court.... Surely, a measure of shock was understandable; here was a top judicial official appearing to exhort the judges of his circuit to take advantage of whatever opportunities they might have to undermine the will of the Supreme Court. Justice Marshall knew that his advice could have an effect on the course of decision in the lower courts." Sotirios A. Barber, On What the Constitution Means 3 (1984).

If the Court's opinion is a patchwork quilt, stitched together from disparate strands of conflicting views in the majority, the leeway for lower courts will be substantial. Ambiguities can result from "inadvertence, or because of a deliberate fudging or vagueness built into the opinion to secure the support of a wavering colleague." Davis & Reynolds, 1974 Duke L. J. 59, 71. When the Supreme Court is unable to muster a majority of Justices behind a decision and instead merely releases a plurality opinion, a confused message is sent to lower courts (state and federal) and to the legislative and executive branches.

Judges in the lower courts have substantial latitude in applying Supreme Court doctrines. Justice Thurgood Marshall, after dissenting in a case that reversed the Second Circuit, later met with the judges from that circuit and urged them to read the Court's decision narrowly (see box). In 1985 Justice Brennan said that the Court's rulings on *Miranda*-type cases "have led nearly every lower court to reject its simplistic reasoning." Oregon v. Elstad, 470 U.S. 298, 320 (1985) (dissenting opinion). He pointed out that the Court's reasoning "is sufficiently obscured and qualified as to leave state and federal courts with continued authority to combat obvious flouting by the authorities of the privilege against self-incrimination. I am confident that lower courts will exercise this authority responsibly, as they have for the most part prior to this Court's intervention." Id. at 346.

After the Supreme Court handed down its Desegregation Decision in 1954, lower court judges followed different paths in implementing the ruling. Some were faithful; others were defiant or evasive. Many federal judges were torn between the edict of the High Court and the sentiments and customs of their local communities. It has been said that the Constitution is what the Supreme Court says it is, but Supreme Court decisions often mean what district courts say they mean. Jack W. Peltason, Federal Courts in the Political Process 14 (1955).

Sustaining Public Confidence

In *Baker* v. *Carr,* 369 U.S. 186 (1962), the Supreme Court accepted jurisdiction to decide the politically volatile issue of legislative reapportionment. Justice Frankfurter, who had written the Court's opinion in *Colegrove* v. *Green,* 328 U.S. 549 (1946), describing reapportionment as "of a peculiarly political nature and therefore not meet for judicial determination," dissented in *Baker.* Although he proved to be a false prophet by overstating the difficulties of judicial remedies to malapportionment, his dissent explains that the Court's ultimate authority is not its status as the "court of last resort" but rather its ability to sustain public confidence in the moral force of its opinions. There was "nothing judicially more unseemly nor more self-defeating than for this Court to make *in terrorem* pronouncements, to indulge in merely empty rhetoric, sounding a word of promise to the ear, sure to be disappointing to the hope."

MR. JUSTICE FRANKFURTER, whom MR. JUSTICE HARLAN joins, dissenting.

The Court today reverses a uniform course of decision established by a dozen cases, including one by which the very claim now sustained was unanimously rejected only five years ago. The impressive body of rulings thus cast aside reflected the equally uniform course of our political history regarding the relationship between population and legislative representation—a wholly different matter from denial of the franchise to individuals because of race, color, religion or sex. Such a massive repudiation of the experience of our whole past in asserting destructively novel judicial power demands a detailed analysis of the role of this Court in our constitutional scheme. Disregard of inherent limits in the effective exercise of the Court's "judicial Power" not only presages the futility of judicial intervention in the essentially political conflict of forces by which the relation between population and representation has time out of mind been and now is determined. It may well impair the Court's position as the ultimate organ of "the supreme Law of the Land" in that vast range of legal problems, often strongly entangled in popular feeling, on which this Court must pronounce. The Court's authority—possessed of neither the purse nor the sword—ultimately rests on sustained public confidence in its moral sanction. Such feeling must be nourished by the Court's complete detachment, in fact and in appearance, from political entanglements and by abstention from injecting itself into the clash of political forces in political settlements.

A hypothetical claim resting on abstract assumptions is now for the first time made the basis for affording illusory relief for a particular evil even though it foreshadows deeper and more pervasive difficulties in consequence. The claim is hypothetical and the assumptions are abstract because the Court does not vouchsafe the lower courts—state and federal—guidelines for formulating specific, definite, wholly unprecedented remedies for the inevitable litigations that today's

umbrageous disposition is bound to stimulate in connection with politically motivated reapportionments in so many States. In such a setting, to promulgate jurisdiction in the abstract is meaningless. It is as devoid of reality as "a brooding omnipresence in the sky," for it conveys no intimation what relief, if any, a District Court is capable of affording that would not invite legislatures to play ducks and drakes with the judiciary. For this Court to direct the District Court to enforce a claim to which the Court has over the years consistently found itself required to deny legal enforcement and at the same time to find it necessary to withhold any guidance to the lower court how to enforce this turnabout, new legal claim, manifests an odd—indeed an esoteric—conception of judicial propriety. One of the Court's supporting opinions, as elucidated by commentary, unwittingly affords a disheartening preview of the mathematical quagmire (apart from divers judicially inappropriate and elusive determinants) into which this Court today catapults the lower courts of the country without so much as adumbrating the basis for a legal calculus as a means of extrication. Even assuming the indispensable intellectual disinterestedness on the part of judges in such matters, they do not have accepted legal standards or criteria or even reliable analogies to draw upon for making judicial judgments. To charge courts with the task of accommodating the incommensurable factors of policy that underlie these mathematical puzzles is to attribute, however flatteringly, omnicompetence to judges. The Framers of the Constitution persistently rejected a proposal that embodied this assumption and Thomas Jefferson never entertained it.

...there is not under our Constitution a judicial remedy for every political mischief, for every undesirable exercise of legislative power. The Framers carefully and with deliberate forethought refused so to enthrone the judiciary. In this situation, as in others of like nature, appeal for relief does not belong here. Appeal must be to an informed, civically militant electorate. In a democratic society like ours, relief must come through an aroused popular conscience that sears the conscience of the people's representatives. In any event there is nothing judicially more un-seemly nor more self-defeating than for this Court to make *in terrorem* pronouncements, to indulge in merely empty rhetoric, sounding a word of promise to the ear, sure to be disappointing to the hope.

Prayers in Public Schools

In *Engel v. Vitale,* 370 U.S. 421 (1962), the Supreme Court struck down state-sponsored prayers in public schools. Nevertheless, school authorities across the nation permitted prayers to continue, sometimes by acquiescing to the initiatives of individual teachers, sometimes by directly intervening to assure a daily prayer. The following extracts are from an article by David E. Rosenbaum, "Prayer in Many Schoolrooms Continues Despite '62 Ruling," *The New York Times,* March 11, 1984, Section 1, pp. 1, 32.

The 31 children in Alvenia P. Hunter's second-grade class at the Pratt Elementary School in Birmingham, Ala., began the school day Thursday as they do every day, by bowing their heads for prayer.

In unison, they recited: "O, help me please each day to find new ways of just being kind. At home, at work, at school and play, please help me now and every day. Amen."

Mrs. Hunter's class is one of many across the nation where, despite the Supreme Court's prohibition of organized prayer in the schools more than 20 years ago, students continue to recite prayers, sing hymns or read the Bible aloud.

Many more students observe a period of silence in which they can pray if they want, a practice the Supreme Court has neither upheld nor rejected.

There is no organized worship in most of the country's public schools. In the main, educators have accepted the Supreme Court's doctrine that prayer prescribed by government or led by a teacher, a government employee, violates the First Amendment sanction against "establishment of religion." ...

A spot check of schools in communities from coast to coast last week revealed practices ranging from that in Iowa, where few schools had organized prayers even before the Supreme Court outlawed them in 1962, a practice that continues, to that in North Carolina, where a survey found regular prayer recitation and Bible readings in 39 of the state's 100 counties.

Mrs. Hunter, who has been a teacher for 18 years, said she had never heard an objection to her classroom prayer from a parent or a principal. "I believe in doing things right," she said. "I have been given the strength to come here and the abil-ity to teach. This way I am thanking my God for enabling me to come here to work."

Louis Dale, president of the Birmingham School Board, said that the board had an official policy against organized prayer in the schools but that the policy was not enforced. He said he was personally of two minds about the matter.

SILENT PERIODS IN DISPUTE

Jean Lancaster, who teaches the second grade at Fulwiler Elementary School in Greenville, Miss., also chooses to lead her pupils in prayer. Every day before lunch, they bow heads and recite: "God is great. God is good. Let us thank him for our food. Amen."

"If I forget to lead it, they remind me," Mrs. Lancaster said. She also said no one had ever objected to her prayer.

Much more common than organized worship in the schools are periods of silence set aside to allow children time to pray or meditate.

Nearly half the states, including New York and Connecticut, have laws that require or permit periods of silent prayer or meditation in the school day. The Federal courts have struck down such statutes as an unconstitutional subterfuge for mandating prayer in some states, including New Jersey, and have upheld them in others, where the courts said there was a difference between periods of silence and organized prayer. The issue is now before the Supreme Court.

Few if any schools in New York City observe periods of silence, but they are part of the regular curriculum in many places. Two weeks ago the school board in Hicksville, L.I., decided to end a 30-second silent period after several residents threatened to sue.

PARENTS OFFER VIEWS

Cheryl Sweet, who has a daughter in the first grade in Shelton, Conn., said of the silent period in that community, "The teacher explains to them they are to think good thoughts. It puts no pressure on them. I don't think parents can find a way to object to it."

Vicky Rohr, a Buddhist who lives in Evanston, Ill., where her daughter is in a public school, said, "Silent prayer wouldn't bother me, but a God-oriented prayer would offend me."

Other parents and teachers, however, do find regular periods of silence objectionable.

"I have no problem with the kids praying individually at any time or place," said Joan Marie Shelley, a French teacher at Lowell High School in San Francisco, "but to create a time for a group activity is absolutely inappropriate."

Proponents of prayer in the schools say that students who do not wish to participate are always free to leave the room.

But Melanie Wolf, a New Haven schoolteacher and mother of two small children, said, "It's not fair to ostracize people like that."

STUDENTS' VIEWS DIFFER

Students also have varied views about silent periods. Jody Kunkel, a ninth grader at Hillcrest Junior High School in Trumbull, Conn., said: "You just stand there. There's a little fooling around, but they're basically quiet."

Isabel Copa, a Roman Catholic eighth-grader at the Pompano Beach Middle School in Florida, said that even a period of silence would be "unfair to some students who don't believe in God."

"I go to church school and we pray over there," she said. "I have friends that are all dif-ferent kinds of religions. If they want to pray, they can do it at home or at church." ...

SOME ARE OSTRACIZED

In some places, parents who complained about prayers in the schools have been ostracized, or worse.

Three years ago, two mothers sued to stop organized prayers in the schools in Little Axe, Okla., a rural community southeast of Oklahoma City. One of the women, JoAnn Bell, a member of the Church of the Nazarene, argued that other people should not tell her children how to pray. She said last week that after she won her suit in Federal court, she was beaten by a school worker and her home was set afire, so she moved.

In some places, the public schools have made accommodations to specific religious groups that dominate the communities.

In Utah, Mormon seminary buildings are situated near every high school in the state, and the schools make time available for students to attend the seminaries for religious education.

At the Swan Meadow School in Gortner, a small community in western Maryland, nearly all the students are Amish or Mennonites, and the morning routine includes the recital of prayers and the singing of such hymns as "His Yoke Is Easy" and "God Put the Rainbow in His Clouds."

County officials allow the prayers and the hymns because they feel it is the only way to keep the Amish and Mennonite children in the public schools. In other communities, the officials said, the religious groups had started their own schools with inferior curriculums. ...

F. CONSTITUTIONAL DIALOGUES

"Judicial sacrosanctity" can be a useful rallying cry to protect the independence of the courts from external attacks. The concept is a powerful talisman for warding off major court-curbing efforts, such as court packing or the withdrawal of appellate jurisdiction. However, it is ineffective in preventing Congress from passing laws to reverse statutory interpretations by the courts. No one doubts the right of Congress to pass legislation that overturns what it considers to be judicial misinterpretations of statutes. But even when the courts render a constitutional interpretation, it is usually only a matter of time before Congress prevails. Through changes in the composition of courts or adjustments in the attitudes of judges who continue to sit, a determined majority in Congress is likely to have its way. At some point a similar statute, struck down in the past as unconstitutional, will find acceptance in the courts. That pattern has been evident in such areas as commerce, federalism, and civil rights.

Do these congressional challenges to the Court threaten to usurp judicial responsibilities? If the Constitution could be interpreted in mechanical fashion, left unchanged over the years and with few dissenting or even concurring opinions, and if the record were barren of instances in which the judiciary had reversed itself, this argument might have merit. But if the function of the Supreme Court is to apply the general language of the Constitution to changing needs, and if the Constitution is developmental rather than static in meaning, there can be no doubt about the propriety of legislation that prompts the Court to reconsider its decisions.

When the Supreme Court struck down the first effort by Congress to regulate child labor, Congress shifted the basis for this federal regulation from the commerce power to the taxing power. That effort was also invalidated by the Supreme Court. By 1938 Congress had returned to the commerce power, and this time the legislation was upheld by a unanimous court. United States v. Darby, 312 U.S. 100 (1941). Similar examples can be cited. Congress decided to pass the Civil Rights Act of 1964, despite its apparent collision with the *Civil Rights Cases* of 1883. This conflict between judicial doctrine and legislative aspirations did not prevent Congress from acting. It avoided a direct confrontation with the judiciary by basing the statute not only on the Fourteenth Amendment but also on the Commerce Clause. The Supreme Court promptly upheld the Act as a valid exercise of congressional power. Heart of Atlanta Motel, Inc. v. United States, 379 U.S. 241 (1964); Katzenbach v. McClung, 379 U.S. 294 (1964).

The "Continuing Colloquy"

Through what Alexander Bickel once called the Court's "continuing colloquy" with the political branches and society at large, the judiciary's search for constitutional principles can be reconciled with democratic values. Bickel, The Least Dangerous Branch 240 (1962). An open dialogue between Congress and the courts is a more fruitful avenue for constitutional interpretation than simply believing that the judiciary possesses certain superior skills.

No one doubts that Congress, like the Court, can reach unconstitutional results. As Justice Brennan said in a 1983 dissent: "Legislators, influenced by the passions and exigencies of the moment, the pressure of constituents and colleagues, and the press of business, do not always pass sober constitutional judgment on every piece of legislation they enact...." Marsh v. Chambers, 463 U.S. 783, 814 (1983). Yet if we count the times that Congress has been "wrong" about the Constitution and compare those lapses with the occasions when the Court has been "wrong" by its own later admissions, the results make a compelling case for legislative confidence and judicial modesty. George Anastaplo has noted that "in the great crises over the past two hundred years, when Congress and the Supreme Court have differed on major issues, Congress has been correct." Center Magazine, November/December 1986, at 15.

There is no justification for deferring automatically to the judiciary because of its technical skills and political independence. Each decision by a court is subject to scrutiny and rejection by private citizens and public officials. What is "final" at one stage of our political development may be reopened at some later date, leading to revisions, fresh interpretations, and reversals of Court doctrines. Through this process of interaction among the branches, all three institutions are able to expose weaknesses, hold excesses in check, and gradually forge a consensus on constitutional issues. Also through that process, the public has an opportunity to add a legitimacy and a meaning to what might otherwise be an alien and short-lived document.

Arguments for Judicial Finality

At certain moments in our constitutional history, there is a compelling need for an authoritative and binding decision by the Supreme Court. The unanimous ruling in 1958, signed by each Justice, was essential in dealing with the Little Rock crisis. Cooper v. Aaron, 358 U.S. 1 (1958). Another unanimous decision in 1974 disposed of the confrontation between President

Nixon and the judiciary regarding the Watergate tapes. *United States v. Nixon*, 418 U.S. 683 (1974). These moments are rare. Usually the Court makes a series of exploratory movements followed by backing and filling—a necessary and sensible tactic for resolving constitutional issues that have profound political, social, and economic ramifications.

For the most part, Court decisions are tentative and reversible like other political events. The Court is not the Constitution. To accept the two as equivalent is to relinquish individual responsibility and the capacity for self-government. Constitutional determinations are not matters that can be left exclusively to the judiciary. Individuals outside the courts have their own judgments to make. Even with our own consent, we cannot abdicate the duty to think for ourselves. What is constitutional or unconstitutional must be left for us to explore, ponder, and come to terms with. Attorney General Edwin Meese III presented a controversial speech in 1986, in which he challenged the belief that the Constitution is equivalent to Supreme Court decisions (see reading). The "finality" of Supreme Court decisions was examined during Senate hearings in 1986 on William Rehnquist's nomination as Chief Justice and again in 1987 on Anthony Kennedy's nomination as Associate Justice. The attitudes of Rehnquist and Kennedy are fundamentally different on this issue (see reading).

An "activist" member of the judiciary, Earl Warren, explained the limits of the courts. In times of political stress, the courts may acquiesce to actions that we later deplore. Commenting on the Court's role in upholding the treatment of Japanese-Americans during World War II, he said: "the fact that the Court rules in a case like *Hirabayashi* that a given program is constitutional, does not necessarily answer the question whether, in a broader sense, it actually is." That the courts fail to strike down a governmental action does not mean that constitutional standards have been followed. The habit of looking automatically to the courts to protect constitutional liberties is ill-advised. Warren concluded that under our political system the judiciary must play a limited role: "In our democracy it is still the Legislature and the elected Executive who have the primary responsibility for fashioning and executing policy consistent with the Constitution" (see box on next page).

The belief in judicial supremacy imposes a burden that the Court cannot carry. It sets up expectations that invite disappointment if not disaster. A President once reassured his country in an inaugural address that an issue over which the nation was seriously divided "legitimately belongs to the Supreme Court of the United States, before whom it is now pending, and will, it is understood, be speedily and finally settled." The President was James Buchanan. The case about to be decided: *Dred Scott v. Sandford.*[12]

The Last-Word Doctrine

Although constitutional law and constitutional values have never been monopolized by the courts over the past two centuries, scholars, judges, reporters and other observers continue to say that the Supreme Court has the final word on constitutional disputes. Such statements fail to address the following realities.

1. The fact that the Supreme Court upholds the constitutionality of a measure, as when it sustained the U.S. Bank in *McCulloch,* places no obligation on executive and legislative branches to adopt that measure in the future. Congress was free to discontinue the Bank. If it passed legislation to renew it, President Jackson was within his rights to veto the bill. A decision by the Supreme Court did not relieve the other branches of their duty or freedom to reach independent interpretations.

2. A decision by the Supreme Court that a certain practice is not prohibited by the Consti-

---

12. Judicial supremacy on constitutional issues was recently endorsed by Larry Alexander and Frederick Schauer, "On Extrajudicial Constitutional Interpretation," 110 Harv. L. Rev. 1359 (1997). For a rebuttal, see Neal Devins and Louis Fisher, "Judicial Exclusivity and Political Instability," 84 Va. L. Rev. 83 (1998).

Chief Justice Warren Disputes Judicial Supremacy

Whatever may be the correct view of the specific holding of these cases [regarding the rights of Japanese-Americans during World War II], their importance for present purposes lies in a more general consideration. These decisions demonstrate dramatically that there are some circumstances in which the Court will, in effect, conclude that it is simply not in a position to reject descriptions by the Executive of the degree of military necessity. Thus, in a case like *Hirabayashi*, only the Executive is qualified to determine whether, for example, an invasion is imminent....

The consequence of the limitations under which the Court must sometimes operate in this area is that other agencies of government must bear the primary responsibility for determining whether specific actions they are taking are consonant with our Constitution. To put it another way, the fact that the Court rules in a case like *Hirabayashi* that a given program is constitutional, does not necessarily answer the question whether, in a broader sense, it actually is....

In concluding, I must say that I have, of course, not touched upon every type of situation having some relation to our military establishment which the Court considers. Those to which I have pointed might suggest to some that the Court has at times exceeded its role in this area. My view of the matter is the opposite. I see how limited is the role that the courts can truly play in protecting the heritage of our people against military supremacy. In our democracy it is still the Legislature and the elected Executive who have the primary responsibility for fashioning and executing policy consistent with the Constitution. Only an occasional aberration from norms of operation is brought before the Court by some zealous litigant. Thus we are sometimes provided with opportunities for reiterating the fundamental principles on which our country was founded and has grown mighty. But the day-to-day job of upholding the Constitution really lies elsewhere. It rests, realistically, on the shoulders of every citizen.

SOURCE: Earl Warren, "The Bill of Rights and the Military," 37 N.Y.U. L. Rev. 181, 192–93, 202 (1962).

tution, such as the use of search warrants in *Zurcher* v. *Stanford Daily* (1978) or access to bank records in *United States* v. *Miller* (1976), does not prevent the other branches from passing legislation to prohibit or restrict these practices. Rights unprotected by the courts may be secured by Congress and the President.

3. When the Supreme Court concludes that an action has no constitutional protection in the federal courts — for example, distributing petitions in a shopping center, as in *PruneYard Shopping Center* v. *Robins* (1980) — the states are not inhibited in any way from protecting these actions through their own constitutional interpretations. Decisions by the Supreme Court set a floor, or minimum, for constitutional rights. States may exceed those rights through independent interpretations of their own constitutions and unique cultures.

4. Many constitutional issues are resolved through rules of evidence, statutes, customs, and accommodations — a common-law method of settling disputes. Through these techniques, institutions outside the courts play a decisive role in shaping not only constitutional values but also constitutional doctrines.

5. There are occasions when Supreme Court rulings strike such a discordant note in the body politic that they will be tested again and again with new variations on the same theme. Court decisions are entitled to respect, not adoration. When the Court issues its judgment, we should not suspend ours. These challenges and collisions help keep the constitutional dialogue open and vigorous. In the search for a harmony between constitutional law and self-government, we all participate.

6. It is unrealistic to expect the Court to "settle" an important issue at a single stroke. Typ-

ically, the Court tackles one slice of an issue, leaving the rest for subsequent court decisions and nonjudicial actions. Justice Ginsburg put it this way: "In our system of adjudication, matters seldom can be fully settled 'on the basis of one or two cases'; they generally 'require a closer working out,' often involving responses by, or a continuing dialogue with, other branches of government, the States, or the private sector." Ginsburg, 83 Geo. L. J. 2119, 2125 (1995), citing language from Roscoe Pound.

7. The Court generally announces broad guidelines: "undue burden," "compelling governmental interest," "narrowly tailored," "all deliberate speed," and "prurient" material. It is up to elected officials (and juries) to translate those principles and rules and apply them to particular cases. The Court defines the edges; nonjudicial actors fill in the important middle.

8. In many cases the Court does have finality, of a sort. When it decides that the *New York Times* is not subject to a libel suit from L. B. Sullivan, or that the *Hustler* magazine is not subject to a libel suit from Jerry Falwell, that is the end of it. In the summer of 1998, when Chief Justice Rehnquist turned down a White House effort to prevent the Office of Independent Counsel from questioning Secret Service agents about Monica Lewinsky's visits to President Clinton, within two hours the agents were called to testify in the grand jury room. However, Congress may reopen the issue by enacting legislation that gives Secret Service agents greater privilege not to testify about presidential activities. Thus, there are interim points of finality. On complex and overarching issues, like abortion, affirmative action, religious freedom, and the death penalty, there is no finality until a consensus is reached by all of the branches and society at large.

Is the Supreme Court the Constitution?

On October 21, 1986, Attorney General Edwin Meese III presented an address at Tulane University called "The Law of the Constitution." He referred to the Constitution as fundamental law, capable of change only by constitutional amendment, and contrasted that "higher law" to the body of law developed by the Supreme Court. He quoted from constitutional historian Charles Warren that "however the Court may interpret the provisions of the Constitution, it is still the Constitution which is the law, not the decisions of the Court." Meese's address sent shock waves across the country. Some columnists called the speech a "stink bomb" that showed disrespect for the Court. One newspaper column claimed that the speech invited anarchy. Other commentators predicted "enormous chaos" if Meese's view ever prevailed. His speech provides an important backdrop for the next reading, which is a colloquy between Senator Arlen Specter and Judge Anthony Kennedy on the Court's authority and power to issue the "final word" in constitutional law.

· · ·

Since becoming Attorney General, I have had the pleasure to speak about the Constitution on several occasions. I have tried to examine it from many angles. I have discussed its moral foundations. I have also addressed on separate occasions its great structural principles—federalism and separation of powers. Tonight I would like to look at it from yet another perspective and try to develop further some of the views that I have already expressed. Specifically, I would like to consider a distinction that is essential to maintaining our limited form of government. That is the nec-

essary distinction between the Constitution and constitutional law. The two are not synonymous.

What, then, is this distinction?

The Constitution is—to put it simply but, one hopes, not simplistically—the Constitution. It is a document of our most fundamental law. It begins "We the People of the United States, in Order to form a more perfect Union..." and ends up, some 6,000 words later, with the 26th Amendment. It creates the institutions of our government, it enumerates the powers those institutions may wield, and it cordons off certain areas into which government may not enter. It prohibits the national authority, for example, from passing *ex post facto* laws while it prohibits the states from violating the obligations of contracts.

The Constitution is, in brief, the instrument by which the consent of the governed—the fundamental requirement of any legitimate government—is transformed into a government complete with "the powers to act and a structure designed to make it act wisely or responsibly." Among its various "internal contrivances" (as James Madison called them) we find federalism, separation of powers, bicameralism, representation, an extended commercial republic, an energetic executive, and an independent judiciary. Together, these devices form the machinery of our popular form of government and secure the rights of the people. The Constitution, then, is the Constitution, and as such it is, in its own words, "the supreme Law of the Land."

Constitutional law, on the other hand, is that body of law which has resulted from the Supreme Court's adjudications involving disputes over constitutional provisions or doctrines. To put it a bit more simply, constitutional law is what the Supreme Court says about the Constitution in its decisions resolving the cases and controversies that come before it.

And in its limited role of offering judgment, the Court has had a great deal to say. In almost two hundred years, it has produced nearly 500 volumes of *Reports* of cases. While not all these opinions deal with constitutional questions, of course, a good many do. This stands in marked contrast to the few, slim paragraphs that have been added to the original Constitution as amendments. So, in terms of sheer bulk, constitutional law greatly overwhelms the Constitution. But in substance, it is meant to support and not overwhelm the Constitution whence it is derived.

And this body of law, this judicial handiwork, is, in a fundamental way, unique in our scheme. For the Court is the only branch of our government that routinely, day in and day out, is charged with the awesome task of addressing the most basic, the most enduring political questions: What *is* due process of law? How *does* the idea of separation of powers affect the Congress in certain circumstances? And so forth. The answers the Court gives are very important to the stability of the law so necessary for good government. But as constitutional historian Charles Warren once noted, what's most important to remember is that "however the Court may interpret the provisions of the Constitution, it is still the Constitution which is the law, not the decisions of the Court."

By this, of course, Charles Warren did not mean that a constitutional decision by the Supreme Court lacks the character of law. Obviously it does have binding quality: It binds the parties in a case and also the executive branch for whatever enforcement is necessary. But such a decision does not establish a "supreme Law of the Land" that is binding on all persons and parts of government, henceforth and forevermore.

This point should seem so obvious as not to need elaboration. Consider its necessity in particular reference to the Court's own work. The Supreme Court would face quite a dilemma if its own constitutional decisions really were "the supreme Law of the Land" binding on all persons and governmental entities, including the Court itself, for then the Court would not be able to change its mind. It could not overrule itself in a constitutional case. Yet we know that the Court has done so on numerous occasions. I do not have to remind a New Orleans audience of the fate of *Plessy* v. *Ferguson,* the infamous case involving a Louisiana railcar law, which in 1896 established the legal doctrine of "separate but equal." It finally and fortunately was struck down in 1954, in *Brown* v. *Board of Education.* Just this past term, the Court overruled itself in *Batson* v. *Kentucky* by reversing a 1965 decision that had made preemptory challenges to persons on the basis of race virtually unreviewable under the Constitution.

...If a constitutional decision is not the same as the Constitution itself, if it is not binding in the same way that the Constitution is, we as citizens may respond to a decision we disagree with. As Lincoln in effect pointed out, we can make our responses through the presidents, the senators, and the representatives we elect at the national level. We can also make them through those we elect at the state and local levels.

Thus, not only can the Supreme Court respond to its previous constitutional decisions and change them, as it did in *Brown* and has done on many other occasions. So can the other branches of government, and, through them, the American people.

As we know, Lincoln himself worked to overturn *Dred Scott* through the executive branch. The Congress joined him in this effort. Fortunately, *Dred Scott*—the case—lived a very short life.

Once we understand the distinction between constitutional law and the Constitution, once we see that constitutional decisions need not be seen as the last words in constitutional construction, once we comprehend that these decisions do not necessarily determine future public policy—once we see all of this, we can grasp a correlative point: that constitutional interpretation is not the business of the Court only, but also, and properly, the business of all branches of government.

The Supreme Court, then, is not the only interpreter of the Constitution. Each of the three coordinate branches of government created and empowered by the Constitution—the executive and legislative no less than the judicial—has a duty to interpret the Constitution in the performance of its official functions. In fact, every official takes an oath precisely to that effect.

For the same reason that the Constitution cannot be reduced to constitutional law, the Constitution cannot simply be reduced to what Congress or the President say it is either. Quite the contrary. The Constitution, the original document of 1787 plus its amendments, is and must be understood to be the standard against which all laws, policies and interpretations must be measured. It is the consent of the governed with which the actions of the governors must be squared.

And this also applies to the power of judicial review. For as Justice Felix Frankfurter once said, "The ultimate touchstone of constitutionality is the Constitution itself and not what we have said about it."

. . .

The "Finality" of Supreme Court Decisions: Senate Hearings

During the hearings in 1986 on the nomination of William Hubbs Rehnquist as Chief Justice of the U.S. Supreme Court, Senator Arlen Specter referred to the "binding precedent" of *Marbury* v. *Madison* (1803). Specter claimed that the Supreme Court "is the final arbiter, the final decisionmaker of what the Constitution means." Asked whether he agreed with that assessment, Rehnquist responded: "Unquestionably" (p. 187 of Rehnquist's 1986 hearings). A year later, when Senator Specter put that same question to Anthony M. Kennedy during his confirmation hearings for appointment as Associate Justice of the U.S. Supreme Court, Kennedy did not agree that the Court is the final arbiter of all constitutional issues. Instead, Kennedy develops an interesting picture of the constant interaction between the Court and the political branches (pp. 221–225 of Kennedy's 1987 hearings).

Senator SPECTER. There was a comment in a speech you made before the Los Angeles Patent Lawyers Association back in February of 1982, which I would like to call to your attention and ask you about.

Quote: As I have pointed out, the Constitution, in some of its most critical aspects, is what the political branches of the government have made it, whether the judiciary approves or not.

By making that statement, you didn't intend to undercut, to any extent at all, your conviction that the Supreme Court of the United States has the final word on the interpretation of the Constitution?

Judge KENNEDY. That is my conviction. And I think that the Court has an important role to play in umpiring disputes between the political branches.

Senator SPECTER. What did you mean by that, that in most critical aspects, it is what the political branches of the government have made it, whether the judiciary approves or not?

Judge KENNEDY. I was thinking in two different areas. One in this area of separation of powers and the growth of the office of the presidency. The courts just have had nothing to do with that.

Second, and even more importantly, is the shape of federalism. It seems to me that the independence of the States, or their nonindependence, as the case may be, is really largely now committed to the Congress of the United States, in the enactment of its grants-in-aid programs, and in the determination whether or not to impose conditions that the States must comply with in order to receive federal monies; that kind of thing.

Senator SPECTER. Well, this is a very important subject. And I want to refer you to a comment which was made by Attorney General Meese in a speech last year at Tulane, and ask for your reaction to it.

He said this:

"But as constitutional historian Charles Warren once noted, what is most important to remember is that, quote, however the Court may interpret the provisions of the Constitution, it is still the Constitution which is the law, not the decisions of the Court.

"By this, of course, Charles Warren did not mean that a constitutional decision by the Supreme Court lacks the character of law. Obviously it does have binding quality. It binds the parties in a case, and also the executive branch for whatever enforcement is necessary.

"But such a decision does not establish a supreme law of the land that is binding on all persons and parts of government henceforth and evermore."

Do you agree with that?

Judge KENNEDY. Well, I am not sure—I am not sure I read that entire speech. But if we can just take it as a question, whether or not I agree that the decisions of the Supreme Court are or are not the law of the land. They are the law of the land, and they must be obeyed.

I am somewhat reluctant to say that in all circumstances each legislator is immediately bound by the full consequences of a Supreme Court decree.

Senator SPECTER. Why not?

Judge KENNEDY. Well, as I have indicated before, the Constitution doesn't work very well if there is not a high degree of voluntary compliance, and, in the school desegregation cases, I think, it was not permissible for any school board to refuse to implement *Brown* v. *Board of Education* immediately.

On the other hand, without specifying what the situations are, I can think of instances, or I can accept the proposition that a chief executive or a Congress might not accept as doctrine the law of the Supreme Court.

Senator SPECTER. Well, how can that be if the Supreme Court is to have the final word?

Judge KENNEDY. Well, suppose that the Supreme Court of the United States tomorrow morning in a sudden, unexpected development were to overrule in *New York Times* v. *Sullivan*. Newspapers no longer have protection under the libel laws. Could you, as a legislator, say I think that decision is constitutionally wrong and I want to have legislation to change it? I think you could. And I think you should.

Senator SPECTER. Well, there could be legislation—

Judge KENNEDY. And I think you could make that judgment as a constitutional matter.

Senator SPECTER. Well, there could be legislation in the hypothetical you suggest which would give the newspapers immunity for certain categories of writings.

Judge KENNEDY. But I think you could stand up on the floor of the U.S. Senate and say I am introducing this legislation because in my view the Supreme Court of the United States is 180 degrees wrong under the Constitution. And I think you would be fulfilling your duty if you said that.

Senator SPECTER. Well, you can always say it, but the issue is whether or not I would comply with it.

Judge KENNEDY. Well, I am just indicating that it doesn't seem to me that just because the Supreme Court has said it legislators cannot attempt to affect its decision in legitimate ways.

Senator SPECTER. Well, but the critical aspect about the final word that the Supreme Court has is that there is a significant school of thought in this country that the Supreme Court does not have the final word. That the President has the authority to interpret the Constitution as the President chooses and the Congress has the authority to interpret the Constitution as the Congress chooses, and there is separate but equal and the Supreme Court does not have the final word.

And, if *Marbury* v. *Madison* is to have any substance, then it seems to me that we do have to recognize the Supreme Court as the final arbiter of the Constitution, just as rockbed.

Judge KENNEDY. Well, as I have indicated earlier in my testimony, I think it was a landmark in constitutional responsibility for the Presidents in the *Youngstown* case and the *Nixon* case to instantly comply with the Court's decisions. I think that was an exercise of the constitutional obligation on their part. I have no problem with that at all.

Senator SPECTER. Well, there has been compliance because it has been accepted that the Supreme Court is the final arbiter. I just want to be sure that you agree with that proposition.

Judge KENNEDY. Yes, but there just may be instances in which I think it is consistent with constitutional morality to challenge those views. And I am not saying to avoid those views or to refuse to obey a mandate.

Senator SPECTER. Well, I think it is fine to challenge them. You can challenge them by constitutional amendment, you can challenge by taking another case to the Supreme Court. But, as long as the Court has said what the Court concludes the Constitution means, then I think it is critical that there be an acceptance that that is the final word.

Judge KENNEDY. I would agree with that as a general proposition. I am not sure there are not exceptions.

Senator SPECTER. But you can't think of any at the moment?

Judge KENNEDY. Not at the moment.

Senator SPECTER. Okay. If you do think of any between now and the time we vote, would you let me know?

Judge KENNEDY. I will let you know, Senator.

Senator SPECTER. Let me pick up some specific issues on executive power and refer to a speech that you presented in Salzburg, Austria, back in November of 1980, where you talk about the extensive discretion saying, "The blunt fact is that American Presidents have in the past had a significant degree of discretion in defining their constitutional powers."

Then you refer to, "The President in the international sphere can commit us to a course of conduct that is all but irrevocable despite the authority of Congress to issue corrective instructions in appropriate cases." Then you refer to President Truman, saying he committed thousands of troops to Korea without a congressional declaration. And then you say, "My position has always been that as to some fundamental constitutional questions it is best not to insist on definitive answers."

And you say further, "I am not one who believes that all of the important constitutional declarations of most important constitutional evolutions come from pronouncements of the courts."

And, without asking you for a specific statement on the War Powers Act, that is a matter of enormous concern that engulfs us with frequency. Major questions arise under the authority of the Congress to require notice from the President on covert operations coming out of the Iran-contra hearings. What is the appropriate range of redress for the Congress? Do we cut off funding for military action in the Persian Gulf? Do we cut off funding for covert operations? Are these justiciable issues which we can expect the Supreme Court of the United States to decide?

Judge KENNEDY. Well, whether or not they are justiciable issues, of course, depends on the peculiar facts of the case, and I would not like to commit myself on that. But the very examples you gave indicate to me that there are within the political powers of the Congress, within its great arsenal of powers under article I of the Constitution, very strong remedies that it can take to bring a chief executive into compliance with its will, and this is the way the political system was designed to work.

The framers knew about fighting for turf. I don't think they knew that term, but they deliberately set up a system wherein each branch would compete somewhat with the other in an orderly constitutional fashion for control over key policy areas. And these are the kinds of things where the political branches of the government may have a judgment that is much better than that of the courts.

Senator SPECTER. But isn't it unrealistic, Judge Kennedy, to expect the Congress to respond by cutting off funds for U.S. forces in the Persian Gulf? If you accept the proposition that the President can act to involve us in war without a formal declaration, and the President and the Congress ought to decide those questions for themselves, isn't that pretty much an abdication of the Supreme Court's responsibility to be the arbiter and the interpreter of the Constitution?

Judge KENNEDY. Well, I don't know if it is an abdication of responsibility for a nominee not to say that under all circumstances he thinks the Court can decide that broad of an issue. If the issue is presented in a manageable judicial form, in a manageable form, I have no objection to the Court being the umpire between the branches.

On the other hand, I point out that having to rely on the courts may infer, or may imply an institutional weakness on the part of the Congress that is ultimately debilitating. It seems to me that in some instances Congress is better off standing on its own feet and making its position known and then its strength in the federal system will be greater than if it had relied on the assistance of the courts.

CONCLUSIONS

Judicial review fits our constitutional system because we like to fragment power. We feel safer with checks and balances, even when an unelected Court tells an elected legislature or elected President that they have overstepped. This very preference for fragmented power denies the Supreme Court an authoritative and final voice for deciding constitutional questions. We do not accept the concentration of legislative power in Congress or executive power in the President. For the same reason, we cannot permit constitutional interpretation to reside only in the courts. We reject supremacy in all three branches because of the value placed upon freedom, discourse, democracy, and limited government. The dialogue that takes place between the Court, elected government, and the American people is not merely inevitable and a conspicuous part of our history. It is also constructive and stabilizing because this dynamic adds to public understanding and public support of constitutional values.

We all have a need to respect procedure and our institutions. Nevertheless, respect for the judiciary does not mean blind deference and an unwillingness by other actors to think independently and critically. Congress can respect the President's duties in foreign affairs without abdicating its own constitutionally assigned powers. The history of American law provides convincing evidence that national policies hammered out jointly by two or more branches is superior to singlehanded efforts by one branch, especially when that branch is isolated and vulnerable to penetrating critiques by the other two. From such scrutiny no branch is immune.

SELECTED READINGS

ALEXANDER, LARRY, AND FREDERICK SCHAUER. "On Extrajudicial Constitutional Interpretation." 110 Harvard Law Review 1359 (1997).

BECKER, THEODORE L., AND MALCOLM M. FEELEY, eds. The Impact of Supreme Court Decisions. New York: Oxford University Press, 1973.

BRECKENRIDGE, ADAM CARLYLE. Congress Against the Court. Lincoln: University of Nebraska Press, 1970.

CULP, MAURICE S. "A Survey of the Proposals to Limit or Deny the Power of Judicial Review by the Supreme Court of the United States." 4 Indiana Law Journal 386, 474 (1929).

DEVINS, NEAL, AND LOUIS FISHER. "Judicial Exclusivity and Political Instability." 84 Virginia Law Review 83 (1998).

"Efforts in the Congress to Curtail the Federal Courts: Pro & Con." Congressional Digest, May 1982.

ELLIOTT, SHELDEN D. "Court-Curbing Proposals in Congress." 33 Notre Dame Lawyer 597 (1958).

ESKRIDGE, WILLIAM N, JR. "Overriding Supreme Court Statutory Interpretation Decisions." 101 Yale Law Journal 331 (1991).

FISHER, LOUIS. "One of the Guardians Some of the Time," in Is the Supreme Court the Guardian of the Constitution? (Robert A. Licht, ed. Washington, D.C.: American Enterprise Institute, 1993).

HALPER, THOMAS. "Supreme Court Responses to Congressional Threats: Strategy and Tactics." 19 Drake Law Review 292 (1970).

HANDBERG, ROGER, AND HAROLD F. HILL, JR. "Court Curbing, Court Reversals, and Judi-

cial Review: The Supreme Court Versus Congress." 14 Law & Society Review 309 (1980).

HENSCHEN, BETH. "Statutory Interpretations of the Supreme Court: Congressional Responses." 11 American Politics Quarterly 441 (1983).

IGNAGNI, JOSEPH AND JAMES MEERNIK. "Explaining Congressional Attempts to Reverse Supreme Court Decisions." 47 Political Research Quarterly 353 (1994).

JACKSON, ROBERT H. The Struggle for Judicial Supremacy. New York: Knopf, 1941.

KYVIG, DAVID E. Explicit and Authentic Acts: Amending the U.S. Constitution, 1776–1995. Lawrence, Kansas: University Press of Kansas, 1996.

LEUCHTENBURG, WILLIAM E. "The Origins of Franklin D. Roosevelt's 'Court-Packing' Plan." 1966 Supreme Court Review 347.

LICHT, ROBERT A. Is the Supreme Court the Guardian of the Constitution? Washington, D.C.: American Enterprise Institute, 1993.

LYTLE, CLIFFORD M. "Congressional Response to Supreme Court Decisions in the Aftermath of the School Desegregation Cases." 12 Journal of Public Law 290 (1963).

McDOWELL, GARY L. Curbing the Courts: The Constitution and the Limits of Judicial Power. Baton Rouge: Louisiana State University Press, 1988.

MIKVA, ABNER J., AND JEFF BLEICH. "When Congress Overrules the Court." 79 California Law Review 729 (1991).

MURPHY, WALTER F. Congress and the Court. Chicago: University of Chicago Press, 1962.

———. "Lower Court Checks on Supreme Court Power." 53 American Political Science Review 1017 (1959).

NAGEL, STUART S. "Court-Curbing Periods in American History." 18 Vanderbilt Law Review 925 (1965).

NICHOLS, EGBERT RAY, ed. Congress or the Supreme Court: Which Shall Rule America? New York: Noble and Noble, 1935.

NOTE. "Congressional Reversal of Supreme Court Decisions: 1945–1957." 71 Harvard Law Review 1324 (1958).

———. "Tension Between Judicial and Legislative Powers as Reflected in Confrontations Between Congress and the Courts." 13 Georgia Law Review 1513 (1979).

PASCHAL, RICHARD A. "The Continuing Colloquy: Congress and the Finality of the Supreme Court." 8 Journal of Law & Politics 143 (1991).

PRITCHETT, C. HERMAN. Congress Versus the Supreme Court: 1957–1960. Minneapolis: University of Minnesota Press, 1961.

ROSS, WILLIAM G. A Muted Fury: Populists, Progressives, and Labor Unions Confront the Courts, 1890–1937. Princeton, N.J.: Princeton University Press, 1994.

SCHMIDHAUSER, JOHN R., AND LARRY L. BERG. The Supreme Court and Congress: Conflict and Interaction, 1945–1968. New York: The Free Press, 1972.

SOLIMINE, MICHAEL E. AND JAMES L. WALKER. "The Next Word: Congressional Response to Supreme Court Statutory Decisions." 65 Temple Law Review 425 (1992).

STEAMER, ROBERT J. The Supreme Court in Crisis. Amherst: University of Massachusetts Press, 1971.

STUMPF, HARRY P. "Congressional Response to Supreme Court Rulings: The Interaction of Law and Politics." 14 Journal of Public Law 377 (1965).

TUSHNET, MARK. Taking the Constitution Away from the Courts. Princeton, N.J.: Princeton University Press, 1999.

VOSE, CLEMENT E. Constitutional Change: Amendment Politics and Supreme Court Litigation Since 1900. Lexington, Mass.: D.C. Heath, 1972.

WARREN, CHARLES. "Legislative and Judicial Attacks on the Supreme Court of the United States—A History of the Twenty-Fifth Section of the Judiciary Act." 47 American Law Review 1, 161 (1913).

Appendix 1

The Constitution of the United States

We the People of the United States, in Order to form a more perfect Union, establish Justice, insure domestic Tranquility, provide for the common defence, promote the general Welfare, and secure the Blessings of Liberty to ourselves and our Posterity, do ordain and establish this Constitution for the United States of America.

ARTICLE 1

Section 1. All legislative Powers herein granted shall be vested in a Congress of the United States, which shall consist of a Senate and House of Representatives.

Section 2. The House of Representatives shall be composed of Members chosen every second Year by the People of the several States, and the Electors in each State shall have the Qualifications requisite for Electors of the most numerous Branch of the State Legislature.

No Person shall be a Representative who shall not have attained to the Age of twenty five Years, and been seven Years a Citizen of the United States, and who shall not, when elected, be an Inhabitant of that State in which he shall be chosen.

[Representatives and direct Taxes shall be apportioned among the several States which may be included within this Union, according to their respective Numbers, which shall be determined by adding to the whole Number of free Persons, including those bound to Service for a Term of Years, and excluding Indians not taxed, three fifths of all other Persons.][1] The actual Enumeration shall be made within three Years after the first Meeting of the Congress of the United States, and within every subsequent Term of ten Years, in such Manner as they shall by Law direct. The Number of Representatives shall not exceed one for every thirty Thousand, but each State shall have at Least one Representative; and until such enumerations shall be made, the State of New Hampshire shall be entitled to chuse three, Massachusetts eight, Rhode-Island and Providence Plantations one, Connecticut five, New-York six, New Jersey four, Pennsylvania eight, Delaware one, Maryland six, Virginia ten, North Carolina five, South Carolina five, and Georgia three.

When vacancies happen in the Representation from any State, the Executive Authority thereof shall issue Writs of Election to fill such Vacancies.

The House of Representatives shall chuse their speaker and other Officers; and shall have the sole Power of Impeachment.

Section 3. The Senate of the United States shall be composed of two Senators from each State, [chosen by the Legislature thereof,][2] for six Years; and each Senator shall have one Vote.

Immediately after they shall be assembled in Consequence of the first Election, they shall

---

1. Changed by Section 2 of the Fourteenth Amendment.
2. Changed by the Seventeenth Amendment.

be divided as equally as may be into three Classes. The Seats of the Senators of the first Class shall be vacated at the Expiration of the second Year, of the second Class at the Expiration of the fourth Year, and of the third Class at the Expiration of the sixth Year, so that one third may be chosen every second Year; [and if Vacancies happen by Resignation, or otherwise, during the Recess of the Legislature of any State, the Executive thereof may make temporary Appointments until the next Meeting of the Legislature, which shall then fill such Vacancies.][3]

No Person shall be a Senator who shall not have attained to the Age of thirty Years, and been nine Years a Citizen of the United States, and who shall not, when elected, be an Inhabitant of that State for which he shall be chosen.

The Vice President of the United States shall be President of the Senate, but shall have no Vote, unless they be equally divided.

The Senate shall chuse their other Officers, and also a President pro tempore, in the Absence of the Vice President, or when he shall exercise the Office of President of the United States.

The Senate shall have the sole Power to try all Impeachments. When sitting for that Purpose, they shall be on Oath or Affirmation. When the President of the United States is tried, the Chief Justice shall preside: And no Person shall be convicted without the concurrence of two thirds of the Members present. Judgment in Cases of Impeachment shall not extend further than to removal from Office, and disqualification to hold and enjoy any Office of honor, Trust or Profit under the United States: but the Party convicted shall nevertheless be liable and subject to Indictment, Trial, Judgment and Punishment, according to law.

Section 4. The Times, Places and Manner of holding Elections for Senators and Representatives, shall be prescribed in each State by the Legislature thereof; but the Congress may at any time by Law make or alter such Regulations, except as to the Places of chusing Senators.

The Congress shall assemble at least once in every Year, and such Meeting shall be [on the first Monday in December,][4] unless they shall by Law appoint a different Day.

Section 5. Each House shall be the Judge of the Elections, Returns and Qualifications of its own Members, and a Majority of each shall constitute a Quorum to do business; but a smaller Number may adjourn from day to day, and may be authorized to compel the Attendance of absent Members, in such Manner, and under such Penalties as each House may provide.

Each House may determine the Rules of its Proceedings, punish its Members for disorderly Behaviour, and, with the Concurrence of two thirds, expel a Member.

Each House shall keep a Journal of its Proceedings, and from time to time publish the same, excepting such Parts as may in their Judgment require Secrecy; and the yeas and Nays of the Members of either House on any question shall, at the Desire of one fifth of those Present, be entered on the Journal.

Neither House, during the Session of Congress, shall, without the Consent of the other, adjourn for more than three days, nor to any other place than that in which the two Houses shall be sitting.

Section 6. The Senators and Representatives shall receive a Compensation for their Services, to be ascertained by Law, and paid out of the Treasury of the United States. They shall in all Cases, except Treason, Felony and Breach of the Peace, be privileged from Arrest during their Attendance at the Session of their respective Houses, and in going to and returning from the same; and for any Speech or Debate in either House, they shall not be questioned in any other Place.

No Senator or Representative shall, during the Time for which he was elected, be appointed

---

3. Changed by the Seventeenth Amendment.
4. Changed by Section 2 of the Twentieth Amendment.

to any civil Office under the Authority of the United States, which shall have been created, or the Emoluments whereof shall have been encreased during such time; and no Person holding any Office under the United States, shall be a Member of either House during his Continuance in Office.

Section 7. All Bills for raising Revenue shall originate in the House of Representatives; but the Senate may propose or concur with Amendments as on other Bills.

Every Bill which shall have passed the House of Representatives and the Senate, shall, before it become a Law, be presented to the President of the United States; If he approve he shall sign it, but if not he shall return it, with his Objections to that House in which it shall have originated, who shall enter the Objections at large on their Journal, and proceed to reconsider it. If after such Reconsideration two thirds of that House shall agree to pass the Bill, it shall be sent, together with the Objections, to the other House, by which it shall likewise be reconsidered, and if approved by two thirds of that House, it shall become a Law. But in all such Cases the Votes of both Houses shall be determined by yeas and Nays, and the Names of the Persons voting for and against the Bill shall be entered on the Journal of each House respectively. If any Bill shall not be returned by the President within ten Days (Sundays excepted) after it shall have been presented to him, the Same shall be a Law, in like Manner as if he had signed it, unless the Congress by their Adjournment prevent its Return, in which Case it shall not be a Law.

Every Order, Resolution, or Vote to which the Concurrence of the Senate and House of Representatives may be necessary (except on a question of Adjournment) shall be presented to the President of the United States; and before the Same shall take Effect, shall be approved by him, or being disapproved by him, shall be repassed by two thirds of the Senate and House of Representatives, according to the Rules and Limitations prescribed in the Case of a Bill.

Section 8. The Congress shall have Power To lay and collect Taxes, Duties, Imposts and Excises, to pay the Debts and provide for the common Defence and general Welfare of the United States; but all duties, Imposts and Excises shall be uniform throughout the United States;

To borrow Money on the Credit of the United States;

To regulate Commerce with foreign Nations, and among the several States, and with the Indian Tribes;

To establish an uniform Rule of Naturalization, and uniform Laws on the subject of Bankruptcies throughout the United States;

To coin Money, regulate the Value thereof, and of foreign Coin, and fix the Standard of Weights and Measures;

To provide for the Punishment of counterfeiting the Securities and current Coin of the United States;

To establish Post Offices and post Roads;

To promote the Progress of Science and useful Arts, by securing for limited Times to Authors and Inventors exclusive Right to their respective Writings and Discoveries;

To constitute Tribunals inferior to the supreme Court;

To define and punish Piracies and Felonies committed on the high Seas, and Offences against the Law of Nations;

To declare War, grant Letters of Marque and Reprisal, and make rules concerning Captures on Land and Water;

To raise and support Armies, but no Appropriation of Money to that Use shall be for a longer Term than two Years;

To provide and maintain a Navy;

To make rules for the Government and Regulation of the land and naval Forces;

To provide for calling forth the Militia to execute the Laws of the Union, suppress Insurrections and repel Invasions;

To provide for organizing, arming, and disciplining, the Militia, and for governing such Part of them as may be employed in the Service of the United States, reserving to the States respectively, the Appointment of the Officers, and the Authority of training the Militia according to the discipline prescribed by Congress;

To exercise exclusive Legislation in all Cases whatsoever, over such District (not exceeding ten Miles square), as may, by Cession of particular States, and the Acceptance of Congress, become the Seat of the Government of the United States, and to exercise like Authority over all Places purchased by the Consent of the Legislature of the State in which the Same shall be for the Erection of Forts, Magazines, Arsenals, dock-Yards, and other needful Buildings;—And

To make all Laws which shall be necessary and proper for carrying into Execution the foregoing Powers, and all other Powers vested by this Constitution in the Government of the United States, or in any Department or Officer thereof.

Section 9.   The Migration or Importation of such Persons as any of the States now existing shall think proper to admit, shall not be prohibited by the Congress prior to the Year one thousand eight hundred and eight, but a Tax or duty may be imposed on such Importation, not exceeding ten dollars for each Person.

The Privilege of the Writ of Habeas Corpus shall not be suspended, unless when in Cases of Rebellion or Invasion the public Safety may require it.

No Bill of Attainder or ex post facto Law shall be passed.

[No Capitation, or other direct, Tax shall be laid, unless in Proportion to the Census or Enumeration herein before directed to be taken.][5]

No Tax or Duty shall be laid on Articles exported from any State.

No Preference shall be given by any Regulation of Commerce or Revenue to the Ports of one State over those of another: nor shall Vessels bound to, or from, one State, be obliged to enter, clear, or pay Duties in another.

No money shall be drawn from the Treasury, but in Consequence of Appropriations made by Law; and a regular Statement and Account of the Receipts and Expenditures of all public Money shall be published from time to time.

No Title of Nobility shall be granted by the United States: And no Person holding any Office of Profit or Trust under them, shall, without the Consent of the Congress, accept of any present, Emolument, Office, or Title, of any kind whatever, from any King, Prince, or foreign State.

Section 10.   No State shall enter into any Treaty, Alliance, or Confederation; grant Letters of Marque and Reprisal; coin Money; emit Bills of Credit; make any Thing but gold and silver Coin a Tender in Payment of Debts; pass any Bill of Attainder, ex post facto Law, or Law impairing the Obligation of Contracts, or grant any Title of Nobility.

No State shall, without the Consent of the Congress, lay any Imposts or Duties on Imports or Exports, except what may be absolutely necessary for executing it's inspection Laws: and the net Produce of all Duties and Imposts, laid by any State on Imports or Exports, shall be for the Use of the Treasury of the United States; and all such Laws shall be subject to the Revision and Controul of the Congress.

No State shall, without the Consent of Congress, lay any Duty of Tonnage, keep Troops, or Ships of War in time of Peace, enter into any Agreement or Compact with another State, or with a foreign Power, or engage in War, unless actually invaded, or in such imminent Danger as will not admit of delay.

---

5. Changed by the Sixteenth Amendment.

ARTICLE II

Section 1.   The executive Power shall be vested in a President of the United States of America. He shall hold his Office during the Term of four Years, and, together with the Vice President, chosen for the same term, be elected, as follows

Each State shall appoint, in such Manner as the Legislature thereof may direct, a Number of Electors, equal to the whole Number of Senators and Representatives to which the State may be entitled in the Congress: but no Senator or Representative, or Person holding an Office of Trust or Profit under the United States, shall be appointed an Elector.

[The Electors shall meet in their respective States, and vote by Ballot for two Persons, of whom one at least shall not be an Inhabitant of the same State with themselves. And they shall make a List of all the Persons voted for, and of the Number of Votes for each; which List they shall sign and certify, and transmit sealed to the Seat of the Government of the United States, directed to the President of the Senate. The President of the Senate shall, in the Presence of the Senate and House of Representatives, open all the Certificates, and the Votes shall then be counted. The Person having the greatest Number of Votes shall be the President, if such Number be a Majority of the whole Number of Electors appointed; and if there be more than one who have such Majority, and have an equal Number of Votes, then the House of Representatives shall immediately chuse by Ballot one of them for President: and if no Person have a Majority, then from the five highest on the List the said House shall in like Manner chuse the President. But in chusing the President, the Votes shall be taken by States, the Representation from each State having one Vote; A quorum for this Purpose shall consist of a Member or Members from two thirds of the States, and a Majority of all the States shall be necessary to a Choice. In every Case, after the Choice of the President, the Person having the greatest Number of Votes of the Electors shall be the Vice President. But if there should remain two or more who have equal Votes, the Senate shall chuse from them by Ballot the Vice President.][6]

The Congress may determine the Time of chusing the Electors, and the Day on which they shall give their Votes; which Day shall be the same throughout the United States.

No Person except a natural born Citizen, or a Citizen of the United States, at the time of the Adoption of this Constitution, shall be eligible to the Office of President; neither shall any Person be eligible to that Office who shall not have attained to the Age of thirty five Years, and been fourteen Years a Resident within the United States.

[In Case of the Removal of the President from Office, or of his Death, Resignation, or Inability to discharge the Powers and Duties of the said Office, the Same shall devolve on the Vice President, and the Congress may by Law provide for the Case of Removal, Death, Resignation or Inability, both of the President and Vice President, declaring what Officer shall then act as President, and such Officer shall act accordingly, until the Disability be removed, or a President shall be elected.][7]

The President shall, at stated Times, receive for his Services, a Compensation, which shall neither be increased nor diminished during the Period for which he shall have been elected, and he shall not receive within that Period any other Emolument from the United States, or any of them.

Before he enter on the Execution of his Office, he shall take the following Oath or Affirmation: — "I do solemnly swear (or affirm) that I will faithfully execute the Office of President of the United States, and will to the best of my Ability, preserve, protect and defend the Constitution of the United States."

---

6. Changed by the Twelfth Amendment.
7. Changed by the Twenty-Fifth Amendment.

Section 2. The President shall be Commander in Chief of the Army and Navy of the United States, and of the Militia of the several States, when called into the actual Service of the United States; he may require the Opinion, in writing, of the principal Officer in each of the executive Departments, upon any Subject relating to the Duties of their respective Offices, and he shall have Power to grant Reprieves and Pardons for Offences against the United States, except in Cases of Impeachment.

He shall have Power, by and with the Advice and Consent of the Senate, to make Treaties, provided two thirds of the Senators present concur; and he shall nominate, and by and with the Advice and Consent of the Senate, shall appoint Ambassadors, other public Ministers and Consuls, Judges of the supreme Court, and all other Officers of the United States, whose Appointments are not herein otherwise provided for, and which shall be established by Law; but the Congress may by Law vest the Appointment of such inferior Officers, as they think proper, in the President alone, in the Courts of Law, or in the Heads of Departments.

The President shall have Power to fill up all Vacancies that may happen during the Recess of the Senate, by granting Commissions which shall expire at the End of their next Session.

Section 3. He shall from time to time give to the Congress Information of the State of the Union, and recommend to their Consideration such Measures as he shall judge necessary and expedient; he may, on extraordinary Occasions, convene both Houses, or either of them, and in Case of Disagreement between them, with Respect to the Time of Adjournment, he may adjourn them to such Time as he shall think proper; he shall receive Ambassadors and other public Ministers; he shall take Care that the Laws be faithfully executed, and shall Commission all the Officers of the United States.

Section 4. The President, Vice President and all civil Officers of the United States, shall be removed from Office on Impeachment for, and Conviction of, Treason, Bribery, or other High Crimes and Misdemeanors.

ARTICLE III

Section 1. The judicial Power of the United States, shall be vested in one supreme Court, and in such inferior Courts as the Congress may from time to time ordain and establish. The Judges, both of the supreme and inferior Courts, shall hold their Offices during good Behaviour, and shall, at stated Times, receive for their Services, a Compensation, which shall not be diminished during their Continuance in Office.

Section 2. The judicial Power shall extend to all Cases, in Law and Equity, arising under this Constitution, the Laws of the United States, and Treaties made, or which shall be made, under their Authority;—to all Cases affecting Ambassadors, other public Ministers and Consuls;—to all Cases of admiralty and maritime Jurisdiction;—to Controversies to which the United States shall be a Party;—to Controversies between two or more States; [between a State and Citizens of another State;]⁸—between Citizens of different States;—between Citizens of the same State claiming Lands under Grants of different States, [and between a State, or the Citizens thereof, and foreign States, Citizens or Subjects.]⁹

In all Cases affecting Ambassadors, other public Ministers and Consuls, and those in which a State shall be Party, the supreme Court shall have original Jurisdiction. In all the other Cases before mentioned, the supreme Court shall have appellate Jurisdiction, both as to Law and Fact, with such Exceptions, and under such Regulations as the Congress shall make.

---

8. Changed by the Eleventh Amendment.
9. Changed by the Eleventh Amendment.

The Trial of all Crimes, except in Cases of Impeachment, shall be by Jury; and such Trial shall be held in the State where the said Crimes shall have been committed; but when not committed within any State, the Trial shall be at such Place or Places as the Congress may by Law have directed.

Section 3. Treason against the United States, shall consist only in levying War against them, or in adhering to their Enemies, giving them Aid and Comfort. No Person shall be convicted of Treason unless on the Testimony of two Witnesses to the same overt Act, or on Confession in open Court.

The Congress shall have Power to declare the Punishment of Treason, but no Attainder of Treason shall work Corruption of Blood, or Forfeiture except during the Life of the Person attainted.

ARTICLE IV

Section 1. Full Faith and Credit shall be given in each State to the public Acts, Records, and judicial Proceedings of every other State. And the Congress may by general Laws prescribe the Manner in which such Acts, Records and Proceedings shall be proved, and the Effect thereof.

Section 2. The Citizens of each State shall be entitled to all Privileges and Immunities of Citizens in the several States.

A Person charged in any State with Treason, Felony, or other Crime, who shall flee from Justice, and be found in another State, shall on Demand of the executive Authority of the State from which he fled, be delivered up, to be removed to the State having Jurisdiction of the Crime.

[No person held to Service or Labour in one State, under the Laws thereof, escaping into another, shall, in Consequence of any Law or Regulation therein, be discharged from such Service or Labour, but shall be delivered up on Claim of the Party to whom such Service or Labour may be due.][10]

Section 3. New States may be admitted by the Congress into this Union; but no new State shall be formed or erected within the Jurisdiction of any other State; nor any State be formed by the Junction of two or more States, or Parts of States, without the Consent of the Legislatures of the States concerned as well as of the Congress.

The Congress shall have Power to dispose of and make all needful Rules and Regulations respecting the Territory or other Property belonging to the United States; and nothing in this Constitution shall be so construed as to Prejudice any Claims of the United States, or of any particular State.

Section 4. The United States shall guarantee to every State in this Union a Republican Form of Government, and shall protect each of them against Invasion; and on Application of the Legislature, or of the Executive (when the Legislature cannot be convened) against domestic Violence.

ARTICLE V

The Congress, whenever two thirds of both Houses shall deem it necessary, shall propose Amendments to this Constitution, or, on the Application of the Legislatures of two thirds of the several States, shall call a Convention for proposing Amendments, which, in either Case, shall be valid to all Intents and Purposes, as Part of this Constitution, when ratified by the

---

10. Changed by the Thirteenth Amendment.

Legislatures of three fourths of the several States, or by Conventions in three fourths thereof, as the one or the other Mode of Ratification may be proposed by the Congress; Provided that no Amendment which may be made prior to the Year One thousand eight hundred and eight shall in any Manner affect the first and fourth Clauses in the Ninth Section of the first Article; and that no State, without its Consent, shall be deprived of its equal Suffrage in the Senate.

ARTICLE VI

All Debts contracted and Engagements entered into, before the Adoption of this Constitution, shall be as valid against the United States under this Constitution, as under the Confederation.

This Constitution, and the Laws of the United States which shall be made in Pursuance thereof; and all Treaties made, or which shall be made, under the Authority of the United States, shall be the supreme Law of the Land; and the Judges in every State shall be bound thereby, any Thing in the Constitution or Laws of any State to the Contrary notwithstanding.

The Senators and Representatives before mentioned, and the Members of the several State Legislatures, and all executive and judicial Officers, both of the United States and of the several States, shall be bound by Oath or Affirmation, to support this Constitution; but no religious Test shall ever be required as a Qualification to any Office or public Trust under the United States.

ARTICLE VII

The Ratification of the Conventions of nine States, shall be sufficient for the Establishment of this Constitution between the States so ratifying the Same.

AMENDMENTS

(The first 10 Amendments were ratified December 15, 1791, and form what is known as the "Bill of Rights")

AMENDMENT 1

Congress shall make no law respecting an establishment of religion, or prohibiting the free exercise thereof; or abridging the freedom of speech, or of the press; or the right of the people peaceably to assemble, and to petition the Government for a redress of grievances.

AMENDMENT 2

A well regulated Militia, being necessary to the security of a free State, the right of the people to keep and bear Arms, shall not be infringed.

AMENDMENT 3

No Soldier shall, in time of peace be quartered in any house, without the consent of the Owner, nor in time of war, but in a manner to be prescribed by law.

AMENDMENT 4

The right of the people to be secure in their persons, houses, papers, and effects, against unreasonable searches and seizures, shall not be violated, and no Warrants shall issue, but upon probable cause, supported by Oath or affirmation, and particularly describing the place to be searched, and the persons or things to be seized.

AMENDMENT 5

No person shall be held to answer for a capital, or otherwise infamous crime, unless on a presentment or indictment of a Grand Jury, except in cases arising in the land or naval forces, or in the Militia, when in actual service in time of War or public danger; nor shall any person be subject for the same offence to be twice put in jeopardy of life or limb; nor shall be compelled in any criminal case to be a witness against himself, nor be deprived of life, liberty, or property, without due process of law; nor shall private property be taken for public use, without just compensation.

AMENDMENT 6

In all criminal prosecutions, the accused shall enjoy the right to a speedy and public trial, by an impartial jury of the State and district wherein the crime shall have been committed, which district shall have been previously ascertained by law, and to be informed of the nature and cause of the accusation; to be confronted with the witnesses against him; to have compulsory process for obtaining witnesses in his favor, and to have the Assistance of Counsel for his defence.

AMENDMENT 7

In Suits at common law, where the value in controversy shall exceed twenty dollars, the right of trial by jury shall be preserved, and no fact tried by a jury, shall be otherwise re-examined in any Court of the United States, than according to the rules of the common law.

AMENDMENT 8

Excessive bail shall not be required, nor excessive fines imposed, nor cruel and unusual punishments inflicted.

AMENDMENT 9

The enumeration in the Constitution, of certain rights, shall not be construed to deny or disparage others retained by the people.

AMENDMENT 10

The powers not delegated to the United States by the Constitution, nor prohibited by it to the States, are reserved to the States respectively, or to the people.

AMENDMENT 11
(Ratified February 7, 1795)

The Judicial power of the United States shall not be construed to extend to any suit in law or equity, commenced or prosecuted against one of the United States by Citizens of another State, or by Citizens or Subjects of any Foreign State.

AMENDMENT 12
(Ratified July 27, 1804)

The Electors shall meet in their respective states and vote by ballot for President and Vice-President, one of whom, at least, shall not be an inhabitant of the same state with themselves;

they shall name in their ballots the person voted for as President, and in distinct ballots the person voted for as Vice-President, and they shall make distinct lists of all persons voted for as President, and of all persons voted for as Vice-President, and of the number of votes for each, which lists they shall sign and certify, and transmit sealed to the seat of the government of the United States, directed to the President of the Senate;—The President of the Senate shall, in the presence of the Senate and House of Representatives, open all the certificates and the votes shall then be counted;—The person having the greatest number of votes for President, shall be the President, if such number be a majority of the whole number of Electors appointed; and if no person have such majority, then from the persons having the highest numbers not exceeding three on the list of those voted for as President, the House of Representatives shall choose immediately, by ballot, the President. But in choosing the President, the votes shall be taken by states, the representation from each state having one vote; a quorum for this purpose shall consist of a member or members from two-thirds of the states, and a majority of all the states shall be necessary to a choice. [And if the House of Representatives shall not choose a President whenever the right of choice shall devolve upon them, before the fourth day of March next following, then the Vice-President shall act as President, as in the case of the death or other constitutional disability of the President.—]* The person having the greatest number of votes as Vice-President, shall be the Vice-President, if such number be a majority of the whole number of Electors appointed, and if no person have a majority, then from the two highest numbers on the list, the Senate shall choose the Vice-President; a quorum for the purpose shall consist of two-thirds of the whole number of Senators, and a majority of the whole number shall be necessary to a choice. But no person constitutionally ineligible to the office of President shall be eligible to that of Vice-President of the United States.

AMENDMENT 13
(Ratified December 6, 1865)

Section 1.   Neither slavery nor involuntary servitude, except as a punishment for crime whereof the party shall have been duly convicted, shall exist within the United States, or any place subject to their jurisdiction.

Section 2.   Congress shall have power to enforce this article by appropriate legislation.

AMENDMENT 14
(Ratified July 9, 1868)

Section 1.   All persons born or naturalized in the United States, and subject to the jurisdiction thereof, are citizens of the United States and of the State wherein they reside. No State shall make or enforce any law which shall abridge the privileges or immunities of citizens of the United States; nor shall any State deprive any person of life, liberty, or property, without due process of law; nor deny to any person within its jurisdiction the equal protection of the laws.

Section 2.   Representatives shall be apportioned among the several States according to their respective numbers, counting the whole number of persons in each State, excluding Indians not taxed. But when the right to vote at any election for the choice of electors for President and Vice President of the United States, Representatives in Congress, the Executive and Judicial officers of a State, or the members of the Legislature thereof, is denied to any of the male inhabitants of such State, being twenty-one years of age, and citizens of the

---

* Superseded by Section 3 of the Twentieth Amendment.

United States, or in any way abridged, except for participation in rebellion, or other crime, the basis of representation therein shall be reduced in the proportion which the number of such male citizens shall bear to the whole number of male citizens twenty-one years of age in such State.

Section 3.   No person shall be a Senator or Representative in Congress, or elector of President and Vice President, or hold any office, civil or military, under the United States, or under any State, who, having previously taken an oath, as a member of Congress, or as an officer of the United States, or as a member of any State legislature, or as an executive or judicial officer of any State, to support the Constitution of the United States, shall have engaged in insurrection or rebellion against the same, or given aid or comfort to the enemies thereof. But Congress may by a vote of two-thirds of each House, remove such disability.

Section 4.   The validity of the public debt of the United States, authorized by law, including debts incurred for payment of pensions and bounties for services in suppressing insurrection or rebellion, shall not be questioned. But neither the United States nor any State shall assume or pay any debt or obligation incurred in aid of insurrection or rebellion against the United States, or any claim for the loss or emancipation of any slave; but all such debts, obligations and claims shall be held illegal and void.

Section 5.   The Congress shall have power to enforce, by appropriate legislation, the provisions of this article.

AMENDMENT 15
(Ratified February 3, 1870)

Section 1.   The right of citizens of the United States to vote shall not be denied or abridged by the United States or by any State on account of race, color, or previous condition of servitude.

Section 2.   The Congress shall have power to enforce this article by appropriate legislation.

AMENDMENT 16
(Ratified February 3, 1913)

The Congress shall have power to lay and collect taxes on incomes, from whatever source derived, without apportionment among the several States, and without regard to any census or enumeration.

AMENDMENT 17
(Ratified April 8, 1913)

The Senate of the United States shall be composed of two Senators from each State, elected by the people thereof for six years; and each Senator shall have one vote. The electors in each State shall have the qualifications requisite for electors of the most numerous branch of the State legislatures.

When vacancies happen in the representation of any State in the Senate, the executive authority of such State shall issue writs of election to fill such vacancies: *Provided,* That the legislature of any State may empower the executive thereof to make temporary appointments until the people fill the vacancies by election as the legislature may direct.

This amendment shall not be so construed as to affect the election or term of any Senator chosen before it becomes valid as part of the Constitution.

AMENDMENT 18
(Ratified January 16, 1919. Repealed December 5, 1933 by Amendment 21)

Section 1.   After one year from the ratification of this article the manufacture, sale, or transportation of intoxicating liquors within, the importation thereof into, or the exportation thereof from the United States and all territory subject to the jurisdiction thereof for beverage purposes is hereby prohibited.

Section 2.   The Congress and the several States shall have concurrent power to enforce this article by appropriate legislation.

Section 3.   This article shall be inoperative unless it shall have been ratified as an amendment to the Constitution by the legislatures of the several States as provided in the Constitution, within seven years from the date of the submission hereof to the States by the Congress.

AMENDMENT 19
(Ratified August 18, 1920)

The right of citizens of the United States to vote shall not be denied or abridged by the United States or by any State on account of sex.

Congress shall have power to enforce this article by appropriate legislation.

AMENDMENT 20
(Ratified January 23, 1933)

Section 1.   The terms of the President and Vice President shall end at noon on the 20th day of January, and the terms of Senators and Representatives at noon on the 3d day of January, of the years in which such terms would have ended if this article had not been ratified; and the terms of their successors shall then begin.

Section 2.   The Congress shall assemble at least once in every year, and such meeting shall begin at noon on the 3d day of January, unless they shall by law appoint a different day.

Section 3.   If, at the time fixed for the beginning of the term of the President, the President elect shall have died, the Vice President elect shall become President. If a President shall not have been chosen before the time fixed for the beginning of his term, or if the President elect shall have failed to qualify, then the Vice President elect shall act as President until a President shall have qualified; and the Congress may by law provide for the case wherein neither a President elect nor a Vice President elect shall have qualified, declaring who shall then act as President, or the manner in which one who is to act shall be selected, and such person shall act accordingly until a President or Vice President shall have qualified.

Section 4.   The Congress may by law provide for the case of the death of any of the persons from whom the House of Representatives may choose a President whenever the right of choice shall have devolved upon them, and for the case of the death of any of the persons from whom the Senate may choose a Vice President whenever the right of choice shall have devolved upon them.

Section 5.   Sections 1 and 2 shall take effect on the 15th day of October following the ratification of this article.

Section 6.   This article shall be inoperative unless it shall have been ratified as an amendment to the Constitution by the legislatures of three-fourths of the several States within seven years from the date of its submission.

AMENDMENT 21
(Ratified December 5, 1933)

Section 1. The eighteenth article of amendment to the Constitution of the United States is hereby repealed.

Section 2. The transportation or importation into any State, Territory, or possession of the United States for delivery or use therein of intoxicating liquors, in violation of the laws thereof, is hereby prohibited.

Section 3. This article shall be inoperative unless it shall have been ratified as an amendment to the Constitution by conventions in the several States, as provided in the Constitution, within seven years from the date of the submission hereof to the States by the Congress.

AMENDMENT 22
(Ratified February 27, 1951)

Section 1. No person shall be elected to the office of the President more than twice, and no person who has held the office of President, or acted as President, for more than two years of a term to which some other person was elected President shall be elected to the office of the President more than once. But this Article shall not apply to any person holding the office of President when this Article was proposed by the Congress, and shall not prevent any person who may be holding the office of President, or acting as President, during the term within which this Article becomes operative from holding the office of President or acting as President during the remainder of such term.

Section 2. This article shall be inoperative unless it shall have been ratified as an amendment to the Constitution by the legislatures of three-fourths of the several States within seven years from the date of its submission to the States by the Congress.

AMENDMENT 23
(Ratified March 29, 1961)

Section 1. The District constituting the seat of Government of the United States shall appoint in such manner as the Congress may direct:

A number of electors of President and Vice President equal to the whole number of Senators and Representatives in Congress to which the District would be entitled if it were a State, but in no event more than the least populous State; they shall be in addition to those appointed by the States, but they shall be considered, for the purposes of the election of President and Vice President, to be electors appointed by a State; and they shall meet in the District and perform such duties as provided by the twelfth article of amendment.

Section 2. The Congress shall have power to enforce this article by appropriate legislation.

AMENDMENT 24
(Ratified January 23, 1964)

Section 1. The right of citizens of the United States to vote in any primary or other election for President or Vice President, for electors for President or Vice President, or for Senator or Representative in Congress, shall not be denied or abridged by the United States or any State by reason of failure to pay any poll tax or other tax.

Section 2. The Congress shall have power to enforce this article by appropriate legislation.

AMENDMENT 25
(Ratified February 10, 1967)

Section 1.   In case of the removal of the President from office or of his death or resignation, the Vice President shall become President.

Section 2.   Whenever there is a vacancy in the office of the Vice President, the President shall nominate a Vice President who shall take office upon confirmation by a majority vote of both Houses of Congress.

Section 3.   Whenever the President transmits to the President pro tempore of the Senate and the Speaker of the House of Representatives his written declaration that he is unable to discharge the powers and duties of his office, and until he transmits to them a written declaration to the contrary, such powers and duties shall be discharged by the Vice President as Acting President.

Section 4.   Whenever the Vice President and a majority of either the principal officers of the executive departments or of such other body as Congress may by law provide, transmit to the President pro tempore of the Senate and the Speaker of the House of Representatives their written declaration that the President is unable to discharge the powers and duties of his office, the Vice President shall immediately assume the powers and duties of the office as Acting President.

Thereafter, when the President transmits to the President pro tempore of the Senate and the Speaker of the House of Representatives his written declaration that no inability exists, he shall resume the powers and duties of his office unless the Vice President and a majority of either the principal officers of the executive department or of such other body as Congress may by law provide, transmit within four days to the President pro tempore of the Senate and the Speaker of the House of Representatives their written declaration that the President is unable to discharge the powers and duties of his office. Thereupon Congress shall decide the issue, assembling within forty-eight hours for that purpose if not in session. If the Congress, within twenty-one days after receipt of the latter written declaration, or, if Congress is not in session, within twenty-one days after Congress is required to assemble, determines by two-thirds vote of both Houses that the President is unable to discharge the powers and duties of his office, the Vice President shall continue to discharge the same as Acting President; otherwise, the President shall resume the powers and duties of his office.

AMENDMENT 26
(Ratified July 1, 1971)

Section 1.   The right of citizens of the United States, who are eighteen years of age or older, to vote shall not be denied or abridged by the United States or by any State on account of age.

Section 2.   The Congress shall have the power to enforce this article by appropriate legislation.

AMENDMENT 27
(Ratified May 7, 1992)

No law, varying the compensation for the services of the Senators and Representatives, shall take effect, until an election of Representatives shall have intervened.

Appendix 2

Justices of the Supreme Court (1789–2000)

Year	Chief Justice	Associate Justices							
1789	Jay	Rutledge	Cushing	Wilson	Blair				
1790	Jay	Rutledge	Cushing	Wilson	Blair	Iredell			
1791	Jay	Johnson	Cushing	Wilson	Blair	Iredell			
1793	Jay	Paterson	Cushing	Wilson	Blair	Iredell			
1795	Rutledge	Paterson	Cushing	Wilson	Blair	Iredell			
1796	Ellsworth	Paterson	Cushing	Wilson	Chase	Iredell			
1798	Ellsworth	Paterson	Cushing	Washington	Chase	Iredell			
1799	Ellsworth	Paterson	Cushing	Washington	Chase	Moore			
1801	Marshall	Paterson	Cushing	Washington	Chase	Moore			
1804	Marshall	Paterson	Cushing	Washington	Chase	Johnson			
1806	Marshall	Livingston	Cushing	Washington	Chase	Johnson			
1807	Marshall	Livingston	Cushing	Washington	Chase	Johnson	Todd		
1811	Marshall	Livingston	Story	Washington	Duvall	Johnson	Todd		
1823	Marshall	Thompson	Story	Washington	Duvall	Johnson	Todd		
1826	Marshall	Thompson	Story	Washington	Duvall	Johnson	Trimble		
1829	Marshall	Thompson	Story	Washington	Duvall	Johnson	McLean		
1830	Marshall	Thompson	Story	Baldwin	Duvall	Johnson	McLean		
1835	Marshall	Thompson	Story	Baldwin	Duvall	Wayne	McLean		
1836	Taney	Thompson	Story	Baldwin	Barbour	Wayne	McLean		
1837	Taney	Thompson	Story	Baldwin	Barbour	Wayne	McLean	McKinley		Catron
1841	Taney	Thompson	Story	Baldwin	Daniel	Wayne	McLean	McKinley		Catron
1845	Taney	Nelson	Woodbury	Baldwin	Daniel	Wayne	McLean	McKinley		Catron
1846	Taney	Nelson	Woodbury	Grier	Daniel	Wayne	McLean	McKinley		Catron
1851	Taney	Nelson	Curtis	Grier	Daniel	Wayne	McLean	McKinley		Catron
1853	Taney	Nelson	Curtis	Grier	Daniel	Wayne	McLean	Campbell		Catron
1858	Taney	Nelson	Clifford	Grier	Daniel	Wayne	McLean	Campbell		Catron
1862	Taney	Nelson	Clifford	Grier	Miller	Wayne	Swayne	Davis		Catron
1863	Taney	Nelson	Clifford	Grier	Miller	Wayne	Swayne	Davis	Field	Catron
1864	Chase	Nelson	Clifford	Grier	Miller	Wayne	Swayne	Davis	Field	Catron
1865	Chase	Nelson	Clifford	Grier	Miller	—	Swayne	Davis	Field	Catron
1867	Chase	Nelson	Clifford	Grier	Miller	—	Swayne	Davis	Field	—
1870	Chase	Nelson	Clifford	Strong	Miller	Bradley	Swayne	Davis	Field	
1872	Chase	Hunt	Clifford	Strong	Miller	Bradley	Swayne	Davis	Field	
1874	Waite	Hunt	Clifford	Strong	Miller	Bradley	Swayne	Davis	Field	
1877	Waite	Hunt	Clifford	Strong	Miller	Bradley	Swayne	Harlan	Field	
1880	Waite	Hunt	Clifford	Woods	Miller	Bradley	Swayne	Harlan	Field	
1881	Waite	Hunt	Gray	Woods	Miller	Bradley	Matthews	Harlan	Field	
1882	Waite	Blatchford	Gray	Woods	Miller	Bradley	Matthews	Harlan	Field	
1888	Fuller	Blatchford	Gray	Lamar	Miller	Bradley	Matthews	Harlan	Field	
1889	Fuller	Blatchford	Gray	Lamar	Miller	Bradley	Brewer	Harlan	Field	
1890	Fuller	Blatchford	Gray	Lamar	Brown	Bradley	Brewer	Harlan	Field	
1892	Fuller	Blatchford	Gray	Lamar	Brown	Shiras	Brewer	Harlan	Field	
1893	Fuller	Blatchford	Gray	Jackson	Brown	Shiras	Brewer	Harlan	Field	
1894	Fuller	White	Gray	Jackson	Brown	Shiras	Brewer	Harlan	Field	
1895	Fuller	White	Gray	Peckham	Brown	Shiras	Brewer	Harlan	Field	
1898	Fuller	White	Gray	Peckham	Brown	Shiras	Brewer	Harlan	McKenna	
1902	Fuller	White	Holmes	Peckham	Brown	Shiras	Brewer	Harlan	McKenna	
1903	Fuller	White	Holmes	Peckham	Brown	Day	Brewer	Harlan	McKenna	
1906	Fuller	White	Holmes	Peckham	Moody	Day	Brewer	Harlan	McKenna	
1909	Fuller	White	Holmes	Lurton	Moody	Day	Brewer	Harlan	McKenna	

1910	White	Van Devanter	Holmes	Lurton	Lamar	Day	Hughes	Harlan	McKenna
1912	White	Van Devanter	Holmes	Lurton	Lamar	Day	Hughes	Pitney	McKenna
1914	White	Van Devanter	Holmes	McReynolds	Lamar	Day	Hughes	Pitney	McKenna
1916	White	Van Devanter	Holmes	McReynolds	Brandeis	Day	Clarke	Pitney	McKenna
1921	Taft	Van Devanter	Holmes	McReynolds	Brandeis	Day	Clarke	Pitney	McKenna
1922	Taft	Van Devanter	Holmes	McReynolds	Brandeis	Butler	Sutherland	Pitney	McKenna
1923	Taft	Van Devanter	Holmes	McReynolds	Brandeis	Butler	Sutherland	Sanford	McKenna
1925	Taft	Van Devanter	Holmes	McReynolds	Brandeis	Butler	Sutherland	Sanford	Stone
1930	Hughes	Van Devanter	Holmes	McReynolds	Brandeis	Butler	Sutherland	Roberts	Stone
1932	Hughes	Van Devanter	Cardozo	McReynolds	Brandeis	Butler	Sutherland	Roberts	Stone
1937	Hughes	Black	Cardozo	McReynolds	Brandeis	Butler	Sutherland	Roberts	Stone
1938	Hughes	Black	Cardozo	McReynolds	Brandeis	Butler	Reed	Roberts	Stone
1939	Hughes	Black	Frankfurter	McReynolds	Douglas	Butler	Reed	Roberts	Stone
1940	Hughes	Black	Frankfurter	McReynolds	Douglas	Murphy	Reed	Roberts	Stone
1941	Stone	Black	Frankfurter	Byrnes	Douglas	Murphy	Reed	Roberts	Jackson
1943	Stone	Black	Frankfurter	Rutledge	Douglas	Murphy	Reed	Roberts	Jackson
1945	Stone	Black	Frankfurter	Rutledge	Douglas	Murphy	Reed	Burton	Jackson
1946	Vinson	Black	Frankfurter	Rutledge	Douglas	Murphy	Reed	Burton	Jackson
1949	Vinson	Black	Frankfurter	Minton	Douglas	Clark	Reed	Burton	Jackson
1953	Warren	Black	Frankfurter	Minton	Douglas	Clark	Reed	Burton	Jackson
1955	Warren	Black	Frankfurter	Minton	Douglas	Clark	Reed	Burton	Harlan
1956	Warren	Black	Frankfurter	Brennan	Douglas	Clark	Reed	Burton	Harlan
1957	Warren	Black	Frankfurter	Brennan	Douglas	Clark	Whittaker	Burton	Harlan
1958	Warren	Black	Frankfurter	Brennan	Douglas	Clark	Whittaker	Stewart	Harlan
1962	Warren	Black	Goldberg	Brennan	Douglas	Clark	White	Stewart	Harlan
1965	Warren	Black	Fortas	Brennan	Douglas	Clark	White	Stewart	Harlan
1967	Warren	Black	Fortas	Brennan	Douglas	Marshall	White	Stewart	Harlan
1969	Burger	Black	Fortas	Brennan	Douglas	Marshall	White	Stewart	Harlan
1970	Burger	Black	Blackmun	Brennan	Douglas	Marshall	White	Stewart	Harlan
1972	Burger	Powell	Blackmun	Brennan	Douglas	Marshall	White	Stewart	Rehnquist
1975	Burger	Powell	Blackmun	Brennan	Stevens	Marshall	White	Stewart	Rehnquist
1981	Burger	Powell	Blackmun	Brennan	Stevens	Marshall	White	O'Connor	Rehnquist
1986	Rehnquist	Powell	Blackmun	Brennan	Stevens	Marshall	White	O'Connor	Scalia
1988	Rehnquist	Kennedy	Blackmun	Brennan	Stevens	Marshall	White	O'Connor	Scalia
1990	Rehnquist	Kennedy	Blackmun	Souter	Stevens	Marshall	White	O'Connor	Scalia
1991	Rehnquist	Kennedy	Blackmun	Souter	Stevens	Thomas	White	O'Connor	Scalia
1993	Rehnquist	Kennedy	Blackmun	Souter	Stevens	Thomas	Ginsburg	O'Connor	Scalia
1994	Rehnquist	Kennedy	Breyer	Souter	Stevens	Thomas	Ginsburg	O'Connor	Scalia

Appendix 3

Glossary of Legal Terms

Abstention doctrine Permits a federal court to relinquish jurisdiction where necessary to avoid needless friction with the state's administration of its own affairs.

Acquittal Certifying the innocence of a person charged with a crime.

Advisory opinion An opinion rendered by a court indicating how the court would rule on a matter; an interpretation of a law without binding effect. Federal courts do not issue advisory opinions.

Affidavit A written statement of facts, made voluntarily and confirmed by oath or affirmation before a judge or magistrate.

Affirm To declare that a lower court's judgment is valid and right. This is done by an appellate court.

Amicus curiae "Friend of the court." A person or group, not a party to a case, that submits a brief detailing its views on a case.

Ante "Before."

Appeal A review by a superior court of an inferior court's decision. There may also be levels of appeal within an administrative agency.

Appellant The party appealing a case.

Appellate jurisdiction The power of an appellate court to review and revise the judicial action of an inferior court; distinguished from *original jurisdiction.*

Appellee The party responding to a case brought by an appellant; sometimes called "respondent."

Arraignment Bringing an accused before a court, stating the criminal charge against him or her and calling on him or her to enter a plea.

Article I court See *legislative court.*

Article III court See *constitutional court.*

Aver In a pleading, to declare, assert, or allege.

Balancing test A constitutional doctrine in which a court weighs an individual's rights with the rights or powers of the state.

Battery The unlawful use of force, either bodily injury or offensive touching, against another person.

Bill of attainder A legislative act that inflicts punishment without judicial proceeding.

Brandeis brief A brief that includes, along with legal citations and principles, references to economic and social surveys. It takes its name from Louis D. Brandeis, who used such practices before joining the Supreme Court.

Brief A written statement prepared by the counsel arguing a case in court.

Case A general term for an action, cause, suit, or controversy, at law or in equity.

Case law The aggregate of reported cases that forms a body of jurisdiction; distinguished from statutory law.

Case or controversy A constitutional prerequisite, from Article III, that determines the justiciability of a question before a federal court.

Cause of action The facts that give a person a right of judicial relief.

Certification, writ of A method of taking a case from a federal appellate court to the Supreme Court. The appellate court may certify any question of law on which it requests instruction from the Court.

Certiorari, writ of An order by the Supreme Court when it exercises discretion to hear an appeal. It may grant or deny "cert."

Circuit courts Federal appellate courts with jurisdiction over several states.

Civil law The body of law that is concerned with private rights and remedies; distinguished from *criminal law.*

Class action A suit brought by a person or group of persons to represent the interests of a class.

Collateral estoppel The doctrine that prevents relitigation of the same issue in a suit upon a different claim or cause of action.

Common law The body of law that derives its authority from usages and customs or from court decrees regarding these usages and customs; distinguished from law created by legislative enactments (statutory law).

Compelling state interest The term used to uphold state action in the area of Equal Protection or First Amendment rights because of an overriding need for state action.

Concurrent powers   Powers that may be exercised independently by Congress and state legislatures on the same subject matter.

Concurring opinion   An opinion that agrees with the decision of the majority but offers separate reasons for reaching that decision.

Consent decree   A decree entered by a judge expressing the consent of both parties in resolving their dispute; a contract by the parties made under the sanction of the court.

Constitutional court   A court protected by Article III rights (life tenure and no diminution of salary). See *legislative court.*

Criminal law   The body of law created to prevent harm to society; distinguished from *civil law.*

Curtilage   The land and buildings immediately adjacent to a home.

Declaratory judgment   A binding adjudication of the legal rights of litigants but with no award of relief.

De facto   "In fact"; in reality; distinguished from *de jure.*

Defendant   The party against whom relief is sought in an action or suit; the accused in a criminal case.

De jure   "By law"; the result of official action; distinguished from *de facto.* For example, de jure segregation is mandated by law; de facto segregation exists but is not officially sanctioned.

Demurrer   A defendant admits the facts of a complaint but states that they are insufficient to proceed upon or to oblige the defendant to answer.

De novo   "From the beginning."

Dicta   Expressions in a court opinion that go beyond the necessities of the case and are not binding. Singular is *dictum.* See *obiter dictum.*

Dissenting opinion   A disagreement with the majority opinion. A dissent may or may not be accompanied by an opinion.

Distinguish   A court's explanation of why a previous decision does not apply.

District courts   Trial courts. Each state has one or more federal judicial districts.

Diversity jurisdiction   The jurisdiction of federal courts over cases between citizens of different states.

Docket   The list of cases set to be tried at a specified term.

Eo nomine   "Under that name."

Eleemosynary   Devoted to charity.

En banc   The full bench of an appellate court, as distinguished from a panel of three judges.

Enjoin   To require or command; specifically, to require a person to perform or desist from some act. See *injunction.*

Equity   Justice administered according to fairness rather than the stricter rules of common law.

Estop   To stop, bar, or prevent.

Exclusionary rule   A rule that prohibits the introduction in a criminal trial of evidence obtained by illegal means, such as from a search or seizure that violates the Fourth Amendment.

Ex parte   "On one side only"; by or for one party.

Ex post facto   "After the fact."

Ex post facto law   A law that inflicts punishment on a person for an act done which, at the time committed, was not illegal. This is forbidden by the U.S. Constitution.

Express   Clear; definite; explicit; set forth in words; distinguished from *implied.*

Ex proprio vigore   "By their own force."

Federal question   A case arising under the U.S. Constitution, federal statutes, or treaties. It generally involves a significant or major issue.

Grand jury   A jury of inquiry to hear accusations in criminal cases and find bills of indictment when it is satisfied that the accused should be tried. See *petit jury.*

Habeas corpus   "You have the body." A writ commanding a law officer to bring a party before a court or judge. The purpose is to release someone from unlawful imprisonment.

Harmless error   An error that is not prejudicial to the substantial rights of a person convicted. It does not provide grounds for granting a new trial.

Implied   Not manifested by explicit and direct words. The meaning is gathered by necessary deduction; distinguished from *express.*

Inalienable rights   Rights that are not capable of being surrendered without the consent of the person possessing such rights.

In camera   "In chambers"; in private. In camera hearings occur in the judge's private chambers or when all spectators are excluded from the courtroom.

Indictment   An accusation in writing presented by a grand jury. It charges the person named with an act that is a public offense.

In forma pauperis (I.F.P.)   "In the character or manner of a pauper." Permission is given to a poor person to proceed without liability for court fees or costs.

Information An accusation against a person for some criminal offense. It differs from indictment in that it is presented by a public officer instead of by a grand jury.

Infra "Below."

Injunction A prohibitive remedy issued by a court that forbids the defendant to do some act.

In re "In the matter of."

Ipse dixit "He himself said it." A bare assertion resting on an individual's authority.

Judicial Conference The policy-making organization of the federal judiciary. Annual meetings consist of the Chief Justice of the United States, the chief judge of each judicial circuit, and a district judge from each judicial circuit.

Judicial council The meeting of judges of each circuit to assure expeditious and effective administration of the business of the courts.

Judicial review A court's authority to review the constitutionality of legislative and executive acts.

Jure belli "By the law of war."

Jurisdiction The authority, the right, or the power by which courts take cognizance of and decide cases. This term embraces every kind of judicial action.

Jurisprudence The philosophy of law; the science that treats the principles of law.

Jury A body of persons sworn to inquire into matters of fact and to declare the truth upon evidence laid before them.

Jus belli "The law of war."

Justiciable A matter appropriate for court review.

Legislative court Courts created by Congress (Article I courts) in contrast to those created by the Constitution (Article III courts). See *constitutional court*.

Litigant A party to a lawsuit.

Magistrate A person, such as a public civil officer, invested with executive or judicial power.

Mandamus "We command." The name of a writ issued from a court and commanding the performance of a particular act.

Mandatory jurisdiction The jurisdiction that a court must accept.

Moot A question is moot when it presents no actual controversy or where the issues have ceased to exist or have become academic or dead.

Motion An application made to a court or judge for the purpose of obtaining a rule or order.

Natural law A universal system of rules and principles that guide human conduct. It applies to all nations and people; distinguished from *positive law*. Also called *"jus naturale."*

Natural rights Rights that grow out of the nature of human beings; distinguished from rights created by *positive law*.

Obiter dictum "A remark by the way." A statement in an opinion that is not essential to the case at hand. Plural is *dicta*.

Order A direction of a court or judge made in writing but not included in the judgment.

Original jurisdiction The jurisdiction in the first instance; distinguished from *appellate jurisdiction*.

Overbreadth doctrine The requirement that a statute be aimed specifically at evils within the allowable area of governmental control. A statute cannot reach conduct that is constitutionally protected.

Per curiam "By the court." An unsigned opinion reflecting a majority of the court.

Perjury False, material statement under oath or equivalent affirmation.

Petitioner The party filing a petition seeking action or relief from a court.

Petit jury Trial jury; the ordinary jury to try civil or criminal action.

Plaintiff The party bringing an action to obtain relief for a claimed injury.

Plurality opinion An opinion of an appellate court that has the support of less than a majority of judges.

Police power The power of government to protect the health, safety, welfare, and morals of its citizens.

Political question An issue that must be resolved by the nonjudicial branches.

Positive law A law enacted by a governmental body; distinguished from *natural law*.

Post "After."

Preemption The doctrine adopted by the U.S. Supreme Court holding that certain matters are of such a national character that federal laws take precedence over state laws.

Prima facie "At first sight." A fact presumed to be true unless disproved by contrary evidence.

Pro se "For himself." One who appears in court without legal representation.

Quash To overthrow, vacate, annul; to make void.

Recuse For a judge to disqualify himself or herself from hearing a case because of interest or prejudice.

Remand To send a case back to a lower court with instructions to correct specified irregularities. This is done by an appellate court.

Respondent One who answers. When the Supreme Court grants a writ of certiorari, the party seeking review is the petitioner and the party responding is the respondent.

Reverse To overthrow or set aside. An appellate court may send a case back to a lower court with instructions to change the result reached.

Ripeness The doctrine that requires a court to consider whether a case has matured or developed into a controversy worthy of adjudication.

Saving clause The clause that returns to the states the power to enforce state laws not preempted by federal law. It is often used in federal statutes that preempt state action. Also refers to an exception for a particular provision in a statute that distinguishes it from the rest of the statute (see *severability clause*, which is a specific form of a saving clause).

Scienter "Knowingly." Used to signify the defendant's guilty knowledge.

Seriatim "One after another." Initially, each Justice of the Supreme Court prepared a separate opinion rather than have one Justice write for the majority.

Severability clause Language in a statute providing that in the event one or more provisions are declared unconstitutional, the balance of the statute remains valid. Also called *separability clause*.

Standing A position from which one may assert legal rights. To have standing to sue, a person must have a sufficient stake in a controversy to merit judicial resolution.

Stare decisis "Stand by things decided." To abide by, or adhere to, decided cases.

State action A term used to determine whether an action complained of has its source in state authority or policy.

Statutory law Law created by legislative enactments.

Stay To stop, arrest, or hold in abeyance.

Strict constructionism A close or rigid reading and interpretation of a law or constitutional provision.

Sua sponte "On its own initiative."

Sub nomine "Under the name of."

Suborn To procure or persuade another person to commit perjury.

Subpoena "Under pain." A command to appear at a certain time and place. A *subpoena duces tecum* requires the production of books, papers, or objects. A *subpoena ad testificandum* requires testimony.

Sub silentio "Under silence"; without notice taken.

Summary judgment A short opinion written by the Court without receiving briefs or oral argument.

Supra "Above."

Temporary restraining order (TRO) An emergency remedy issued by a court until it can hear arguments or evidence on a controversy.

Three-judge court A panel that combines federal district and appellate judges to expedite the review of a challenged action.

Trial court The first court to consider litigation.

Trover A remedy for any wrongful interference with or detention of the goods of another.

Ultra vires "Beyond powers." Acts in excess of powers granted.

Underinclusiveness The challenge that a statute is invalid because it limits benefits to a specified group rather than making them available to all groups.

Vacate To annul; to set aside.

Vel non "Or not." For example, the Court might say, "We now judge the merits vel non of this claim."

Venire "To come." This is used in summoning a jury.

Vested rights Rights so settled in a person that they cannot be taken or diminished without the person's consent.

Vicinage Neighborhood; vicinity.

Voir dire "To speak the truth." Preliminary examination by a court to determine competency and impartiality of a witness or juror.

Warrant A writ issued by a judge or magistrate authorizing a law officer to make an arrest, a search, or a seizure or to perform other acts in the administration of justice. An *arrest warrant*, made on behalf of the state, commands a law enforcement officer to arrest a person and bring him before a magistrate. A *search warrant*, issued in writing by a judge or magistrate, directs a law enforcement officer to search for and seize specified property.

Writ An order issued from a court requiring the performance of a specified act.

Appendix 4

How to Research the Law

When a bill passes Congress and is signed by the President, or is vetoed by the President and Congress overrides the veto, the bill is printed either as a public law or a private law. The latter series is reserved for legislation intended for the relief of private parties, especially bills dealing with claims against the United States, the waiver of claims by the government against individuals, and exceptions for individuals subject to certain immigration and naturalization requirements.

The enacted bill first appears as a "slip law." The heading indicates the public law number, date of approval, and bill number. For example, the Civil Rights Restoration Act of 1987, which originated as S. 557, was enacted on March 22, 1988, and designated Public Law 100-259 (the 259th public law of the One Hundredth Congress). The heading also indicates the volume and page in the *U.S. Statutes at Large,* where the public law will appear. For the Civil Rights Restoration Act of 1987, the citation is 102 Stat. 28 (Volume 102, page 28). At the end of the slip law is a convenient legislative history that refers to the House and Senate reports and floor debates that preceded the bill's enactment. Private laws are numbered by a separate series, also prefixed by the Congress. Thus, a bill for the relief of Miriama Jones, enacted October 28, 1978, was called Private Law 95-110.

Bound volumes, called the *U.S. Statutes at Large,* contain public laws, private laws, reorganization plans, joint resolutions, concurrent resolutions, and proclamations issued by the President. There is little practical difference between a bill and a joint resolution. Both forms of legislation must be presented to the President for his signature; both are legally binding. Concurrent resolutions, adopted by the House and the Senate, are not presented to the President and do not have the force of law. Nor are simple resolutions, adopted either by the House or the Senate.

Beginning with Volume 52 (1938), each volume of the *Statutes at Large* contains the laws enacted during a calendar year. After Volume 64, treaties and other international agreements were no longer printed in the *Statutes.* They are printed in a new series of volumes, published by the State Department, called *United States Treaties and Other International Agreements.* The documents first appear in pamphlet form numbered in the "Treaties and Other International Acts Series" (TIAS). Citations are usually given to both the TIAS number and the volume of *United States Treaties and Other International Agreements,* as in 30 UST 617, TIAS 9207 (1978).

Treaties may supersede prior conflicting statutes.[1] By virtue of Article VI, Section 2, the Constitution, statutes, and treaties are collectively called "the supreme Law of the Land." On the other hand, executive agreements cannot be "inconsistent with legislation enacted by Congress in the exercise of its constitutional authority."[2] In cases where executive agreements violate rights secured by the Constitution, they have been struck down by the courts.[3]

---

1. United States v. Schooner Peggy, 5 U.S. (1 Cr.) 103 (1801).
2. 11 Foreign Affairs Manual [FAM] 721.2(b)(3) (1974); United States v. Guy W. Capps, Inc., 204 F.2d 655, 660 (4th Cir. 1953), aff'd on other grounds, 348 U.S. 296 (1955).
3. Seery v. United States, 127 F.Supp. 601, 606 (Ct. Cl. 1955); Reid v. Covert, 354 U.S. 1, 16 (1956).

As laws are modified or repealed by subsequent enactments of Congress, the need arises for a publication that consolidates the permanent body of law. The first codification of U.S. laws, enacted June 22, 1874, appeared in the *Revised Statutes*. A second edition was published in 1878, followed by supplements. In 1926 Congress passed a law to provide for a code intended to embrace the laws of the United States that are general and permanent in their character. The first volume, reflecting the laws in force as of December 7, 1925, was printed as Volume 44, Part I, of the *Statutes at Large*. This series is now known as the *United States Code*. New editions of the code appeared in 1934, 1940, 1946, 1952, 1958, 1964, 1970, 1976, 1982, 1988, and 1994. Supplements to the code are issued after each session of Congress. The code consists of fifty titles organized by subject matter (Agriculture, Highways, Money and Finance, and so forth). Index references are to title, section, and year, as in 7 U.S.C. 443 (1982) and 10 U.S.C. 1437 (Supp. IV, 1986).

Administrative Legislation

Unless superseded by federal statute or invalidated by the courts, presidential proclamations, executive orders, and regulations are other sources of law. Not until 1935 did Congress pass legislation to provide for the custody and publication of these administrative rules and pronouncements. This publication, the *Federal Register,* includes all presidential proclamations and executive orders that have general applicability and legal effect, as well as agency regulations and orders that prescribe a penalty. Based partly on the statutory authority vested in him by the Federal Register Act, President Franklin D. Roosevelt issued an executive order in 1936 that vested in the Bureau of the Budget (now Office of Management and Budget) the responsibility for reviewing all proposed executive orders and proclamations.[4]

The *Federal Register* is published daily, Monday through Friday, except for official holidays. A typical citation is 46 Fed. Reg. 36707 (1981). The rules, regulations, and orders that constitute the current body of administrative regulations are arranged under fifty titles (generally parallel to those of the *United States Code*) and printed as the *Code of Federal Regulations*. Citations are by title and section, as in 50 C.F.R. 17.13 (1980).

There is continuing controversy over the range and legal effect of executive orders and proclamations. Executive orders cannot supersede a statute or override contradictory congressional expressions,[5] but the latitude for presidential lawmaking is still substantial and a source of concern.[6] Proclamations also operate in a twilight zone of legality. When a statute prescribes a specific procedure and the President elects to follow a different course, a proclamation by him is illegal and void.[7] Proclamations have been upheld, however, with only tenuous ties to statutory authority.[8]

---

4. 49 Stat. 500, § 5 (1935). Roosevelt's Executive Order 7298, February 18, 1936, appeared too early for the first volume of the Federal Register. It is reprinted in James Hart, "The Exercise of Rule-Making Power," the President's Committee on Administrative Management 355 (1937).

5. Marks v. CIA, 590 F.2d 997, 1003 (D.C. Cir. 1978); Weber v. Kaiser Aluminum & Chemical Corp., 563 F.2d 216, 227 (5th Cir. 1977), rev'd on other grounds, Steelworkers v. Weber, 443 U.S. 193 (1979). The judiciary has struck down executive orders that exceed presidential authority; for example, Youngstown Co. v. Sawyer, 343 U.S. 579 (1952) and Panama Refining Co. v. Ryan, 293 U.S. 388, 433 (1935). See Louis Fisher, "Laws Congress Never Made," Constitution, Fall 1993, pp. 59–66.

6. Note, "Judicial Review of Executive Action in Domestic Affairs," 80 Colum. L. Rev. 1535 (1980); "Presidential Control of Agency Rulemaking: An Analysis of Constitutional Issues That May be Raised by Executive Order 12291," a Report Prepared for the Use of the House Committee on Energy and Commerce, 97th Cong., 1st Sess. (Comm. Print, June 15, 1981).

7. Schmidt Pritchard & Co. v. United States, 167 F.Supp. 272 (Cust. Ct. 1958); Carl Zeiss, Inc. v. United States, 76 F.2d 412 (Ct. Cust. & Pa. App. 1935).

8. United States v. Yoshida Intern., Inc., 526 F.2d 560 (Ct. Cust. & Pat. App. 1975); Louis Fisher, Constitutional Conflicts between Congress and the President 106–18 (1997).

Constitutional Interpretation

As a general guide to constitutional powers, students can consult what has become known as the "Annotated Constitution." The actual title is *The Constitution of the United States of America: Analysis and Interpretation,* prepared periodically by the Congressional Research Service of the Library of Congress and printed as a Senate document. Edward S. Corwin wrote the 1952 edition, which is revised every ten years. Other basic sources include *The Records of the Federal Convention of 1787,* a four-volume work edited by Max Farrand and published by Yale University Press in 1937, and the *Federalist Papers* of Hamilton, Jay, and Madison, a prominent edition of which was published by Harvard University Press in 1966 under the guidance of Benjamin Fletcher Wright.

Other than brief accounts that appear in daily newspapers announcing major decisions by the Supreme Court, a researcher must rely on more specialized sources to keep track of legal interpretations—especially lower-court decisions. Decisions by federal district and appellate courts are fascinating for two reasons: (1) they are the first step in shaping constitutional and statutory law and (2) often they are the last step, for few of their rulings are reviewed by the Supreme Court.

This huge body of material is conveniently organized by the *United States Law Week,* which consists of four major sections: (1) a summary and analysis of major decisions, with page references to more extended treatment in the *Law Week;* (2) congressional and agency actions; (3) Supreme Court proceedings, including oral arguments before the Court, reviews granted, summary actions, reviews denied, cases recently filed, and special articles summarizing and analyzing the most significant Supreme Court opinions rendered for each term; and (4) Supreme Court opinions. The *Law Week* is published by the Bureau of National Affairs. Citations are by volume, page, and year, as in *Maher v. Roe,* 45 U.S.L.W. [or L.W.] 4787 (1977).

Two weekly newspapers, catering to the legal profession, are especially valuable. Both newspapers contain stories on appointments to the federal agencies, personnel actions, departmental politics, budget cutbacks, executive-legislative clashes, regulatory policy, and administrative law. They also regularly review the literature. *The National Law Journal* is published weekly by the New York Law Publishing Company. The *Legal Times of Washington* is published weekly by Legal Times of Washington. These periodicals contain incisive, sophisticated, and well-written accounts on current developments.

Supreme Court decisions are printed first in the form of "slip opinions." They may be purchased from the Government Printing Office and are usually available from libraries that serve as depositories for government documents. The full decisions are republished in paperbacks called "preliminary prints" and finally in bound volumes of the *United States Reports.* Citations take this form: *Ohio v. Roberts,* 448 U.S. 56 (1980), which indicates that the decision may be found in Volume 448, beginning on page 56.

The first ninety volumes of the *Reports* were named after court reporters. Volumes 1 through 4 (1790–1800) were named after Dallas. Later volumes, 5 through 90, carry the names of Cranch, Wheaton, Peters, Howard, Black, and Wallace. Volumes 91–107 (1875–1882) are designated "1 to 17 Otto" as well as "United States Reports 91–107." Reprints of Volumes 1 through 90 generally have a dual numbering system to the *Reports* and to court reporters, requiring such citations as *Marbury v. Madison,* 5 U.S. (1 Cr.) 137 (1803).

The full text of each Supreme Court decision also appears in the *Supreme Court Reporter,* issued by West Publishing Company. The citations for these decisions are in the form *Maryland v. Louisiana,* 101 S.Ct. 2114 (1981).

Another source of Supreme Court decisions is *United States Supreme Court Reports, Lawyers' Edition,* published by the Lawyers Co-Operative Publishing Company. A unique feature of the *Lawyers' Edition* is a summary of the arguments in each case for the majority of the Court and for justices who concur and dissent. The first series of the *Lawyers' Edition,* consisting of 100 volumes, covers the period from 1790 to 1956. There is now a second series. A typical citation is *Steagald v. United States,* 68 L.Ed. 2d 38 (1981).

Briefs and oral arguments to the Supreme Court, for major cases, are published in *Landmark Briefs and Arguments of the Supreme Court of the United States: Constitutional Law,* edited by Gerald Gunther and Gerhard Casper and published by University Publications of America.

Significant decisions by federal district courts are printed in the *Federal Supplement,* issued first in a paper edition and later in bound volumes. The citation shows the volume, page, state, and year, as in *United States v. Mandel,* 505 F.Supp. 189 (D. Md. 1981). The "D" in parentheses indicates that the decision occurred at the district court level. For decisions that are not reported in the *Federal Supplement,* or in situations where immediate access to a decision is needed, a researcher may call the judge's chamber and receive a copy of the memorandum decision from a law clerk or filing clerk.

To follow appeals of district court decisions, the source is the *Federal Reporter,* consisting of two series. The first series (F. or Fed.) stopped with Volume 300; the second series (F.2d) ended with Volume 999. The *Federal Reporter* is now in its third series (F.3d). Typical citations are *Rowe v. Drohen,* 262 F. 15 (2d Cir. 1919) and *Romeo v. Youngberg,* 644 F.2d 147 (3d Cir. 1980). These decisions are initially available as slip opinions and in memorandum form either from the court or libraries.

Finding Citations

Various databases, including LEXIS and WESTLAW, are used to find citations to statutes, administrative legislation, and court decisions. *U.S. Code Congressional and Administrative News,* published by West, reprints the full text of public laws and selected House and Senate documents, as well as presidential proclamations, executive orders, presidential messages, and federal regulations. The *CIS/Index* provides citations to all congressional publications, including reports, hearings, and other legislative documents.

The "citator" or citation book tells the student whether a decision is still valid and authoritative. A decision by a lower court may be affirmed, reversed, or modified. *Shepard's Citations,* a widely used sourcebook, has spawned such words as *Shepardize* and *Shepardizing* to describe the process of determining the current state of the law. *Shepard's United States Citations* includes citations to Supreme Court decisions, U.S. statutes, treaties, and court rules for federal courts. *Shepard's Federal Citations,* covering decisions by federal courts below the Supreme Court, is issued in two series. One series covers the *Federal Supplement,* and the other the *Federal Reporter.*

DOJ and GAO

Many of the issues that come before the courts have been first explored by the Justice Department and the General Accounting Office. These analyses are published in *Official Opinions of the Attorneys General* and *Decisions of the Comptroller General.* Among his other duties, the Attorney General renders important opinions on legal issues presented to him by Presidents and departmental heads. Citations to these opinions are by volume, page, and year, as in 40 Ops. Att'y Gen. [or Op. A.G.] 469 (1946). A new series, called *Opinions of the Office of Legal Counsel,* is now available to record the memorandum opinions from the Office of Legal Counsel, which advises the President, the Attorney General, and other executive officers.

The Comptroller General determines the legality of payments of appropriated funds by federal officials. This function was vested in the Treasury Department from 1817 to 1921 but passed thereafter to the Comptroller General as the head of the newly created General Accounting Office. The decisions are cited as 49 Comp. Gen. 59 (1969). In 1969 the Comptroller General and the Attorney General disagreed completely about the legality of the Nixon administration's "Philadelphia Plan," designed to increase the number of minority workers in federally assisted contracts.[9] In this dispute the courts sided with the Attorney General's interpretation.[10]

General Literature

An indispensable guide to the literature is the *Index to Legal Periodicals,* published by the H.W. Wilson Company. Currently covering more than 400 legal periodicals, it indexes the articles under subject and author. Entries of special interest include administrative agencies, administrative law, administrative procedure, delegation of powers, discrimination, executive agreements, executive power, federalism, freedom of information, freedom of religion, freedom of speech, freedom of the press, government, judicial review, legislation, political science, politics, public finance, separation of powers, United States: Congress, United States: President, and United States: Supreme Court. Legal periodicals can also be accessed through *Current Law Index,* published by Information Access Company, and InfoTrac/LegalTrac Database, a computerized system offered by Information Access Company.

State Decisions

Decisions by state courts are reported in volumes published by each state. They are also published in seven regional reporters. For example, decisions by Connecticut, Delaware, the District of Columbia, Maine, Maryland, New Hampshire, New Jersey, Pennsylvania, Rhode Island, and Vermont appear in the *Atlantic Reporter.* The citation for the second series is A.2d. Other state court decisions appear in the following reporters, with citations given to the second series: *North Eastern Reporter* (N.E.2d; Illinois, Indiana, Massachusetts, New York, Ohio); *North Western Reporter* (N.W.2d; Iowa, Michigan, Minnesota, Nebraska, North Dakota, South Dakota, Wisconsin); *Pacific Reporter* (P.2d; Alaska, Arizona, California, Colorado, Hawaii, Idaho, Kansas, Montana, Nevada, New Mexico, Oklahoma, Oregon, Utah, Washington, Wyoming); *South Eastern Reporter* (S.E.2d; Georgia, North Carolina, South Carolina, Virginia, West Virginia); *Southern Reporter* (So.2d; Alabama, Florida, Louisiana, Mississippi); and *South Western Reporter* (S.W.2d; Arkansas, Kentucky, Missouri, Tennessee, Texas).

---

9. 49 Comp. Gen. (1969); 42 Ops. Att'y Gen. 405 (1969).
10. Contractors Ass'n of Eastern Pa. v. Secretary of Labor, 442 F.2d 159 (3d Cir. 1971), cert. denied, 404 U.S. 854 (1971).

Table of Cases

This table includes cases discussed in chapter essays and cases excerpted for readings (shown in **bold** for case names and page references). Cases cited in readings are not included in this table.

Index